American Casebook Series, and the West Group symbol
are registered trademarks used herein under license.

 TEXT IS PRINTED ON 10% POST CONSUMER RECYCLED PAPER

1st Reprint — 2004

CASES AND MATERIALS ON

EUROPEAN UNION LAW

Second Edition

By

George A. Bermann
Beekman Professor of Law,
Jean Monnet Professor of European Union Law, and
Director, European Legal Studies Center,
Columbia University School of Law

Roger J. Goebel
Professor of Law and Director,
Fordham Center on European Union Law,
Fordham University School of Law

William J. Davey
Edwin M. Adams Professor of Law,
University of Illinois College of Law

Eleanor M. Fox
Walter J. Derenberg Professor of Trade Regulation,
New York University School of Law

AMERICAN CASEBOOK SERIES®

WEST
GROUP

A THOMSON COMPANY

ST. PAUL, MINN., 2002

West's Law School
Advisory Board

To my wife, Sandra, and to my children,
Sloan, Suzanne and Grant

G.A.B.

To the memory of my father, Frank L. Goebel,
and to the memory of my mother,
Anne M. Goebel

R.J.G.

To my mother, Jean M. Davey,
and to my father, Norman B. Davey

W.J.D.

To my children, Douglas, Margot and Randy,
to my mother, Elizabeth S. Cohen,
and to the memory of my father,
Herman Cohen

E.M.F.

*

Preface

The study of European Community law, always of interest since the Community's creation, has taken on special importance in recent years. As the Community perfects its goal of a true internal market and monetary union, while contemplating an unprecedented enlargement to the east and profound constitutional reform, American lawyers and law students naturally seek to learn more about the Community and its law. With the advent of the European Union in 1993, following the Maastricht Treaty, the European-level legal framework has become still more complex. Each of the Union's three "pillars" (Community law, common foreign and security policy, and police and judicial cooperation in criminal matters) has generated its own "law." We may truly speak today about both European Community law and European Union law, though the former predominates in this casebook and in the legal literature more generally.

This casebook is intended to provide a basic understanding of the Community and Union, their structures, goals, fields of action, achievements and aspirations, as well as to lay a foundation for further research, analysis and legal writing.

There are many valid reasons to study Community and Union law. We present here three of the most important ones. The most pragmatic of them is that the Community has become the largest trading partner of the US, constitutes the largest overseas single market in the world, and represents a major site of investment for US firms. US lawyers, both international house counsel and outside counsel, can no longer afford to possess only a limited knowledge of Community structure, law-making processes and substantive law. Community competition and trade law have long been staples of international practice. Today, the European Community's harmonization of health, safety and technical standards, banking, securities and company law, environmental and consumer protection measures, and actions in the field of agricultural and social policy (to name just a sampling of sectors) represent matters of practical concern to US interests and their lawyers. The Community's achievement of an economic and monetary union, with a single currency and a single monetary policy, is also of evident importance to the international business and legal world.

Second, Community and Union law are rewarding fields for comparative law study. This has long been true in competition and trade law, where academics and practitioners have found provocative points of comparison and contrast. Today a rich source of comparative study is to be found in the Community programs for harmonization of laws. In some fields, as in environmental and securities law, the Community has been significantly influenced by US models, but still strikes certain different notes. In other fields, such as banking, company law, consumer protection and social policy, the Community has taken quite a different path from the US, and its law has had its echoes in American law. Constitutional comparisons and contrasts between the US and EU have acquired unprecedented interest among comparatists. The divergences between US and Community law have provoked thoughtful reflection on the context and underlying values of each system. They should continue to do so.

Third, Community law provides a laboratory for study of law formation: the development of an entire legal system in modern times. The study includes the Community's constitutional framework, its institutions, substantive legislation and judicial law, and the constant interplay of policy and politics in an evolving federal-type system, one comprised of fifteen (and soon more) nations having many commonalities but also divergent systems, demographics and interests.

The casebook rewards the student who has come to the course for any or all of these reasons. The book covers virtually all major fields of Community law. (We regret that, despite the book's increase in size over the first edition, space considerations prevented coverage of certain important topics, such as public procurement, transport, agriculture and telecommunications law.) The notes and questions have been crafted to facilitate reflection on how and why the Community and Union institutions, and especially the Court of Justice and Court of First Instance, have reached their legal and policy conclusions. The text and notes make frequent comparisons with US law. The authors hope that the reader will thereby achieve not only a good comprehension of Community and Union law, but also a critical one.

The casebook is intended for use in US law schools, but it may also be suitable for faculties in Europe and elsewhere. Our casebook follows traditional US teaching methods which give central attention to primary materials, such as legislation and court judgments, inviting students to examine these materials critically through focused questions. Accordingly, Court of Justice and Court of First Instance judgments and Community legislation are subjected to the same kind of analytic review as US laws and Supreme Court opinions would be in a standard constitutional law casebook. We hope that European professors and students will find that the process of analytic examination of judgments and legislation through questions will assist in a more reflective comprehension of Community rules and judicial doctrines.

The preparation of this edition and the teaching of the subject in general has been complicated by the decision implemented in the 1998 Treaty of Amsterdam (effective 1999) to renumber the articles of the treaties establishing both the European Community (EC Treaty) and the European Union (TEU). For instance, generations of Community law scholars have written and discussed the impact of Article 30's ban on quantitative restrictions and measures with equivalent effect and the exceptions thereto in Article 36, only now to be faced with a numbering system that has the exception in Article 30 and the ban in Article 28. Likewise, probably the most familiar EC Treaty articles to American lawyers—the competition provisions in Articles 85 and 86—have become Articles 81 and 82. We have, of course, used the new numbering system in our text, with indications in parentheses of the old numbers. Similarly, in cases where we have kept the old article numbers, we have indicated the new numbers in brackets.

While this new edition was in preparation, new amendments to both the EC Treaty and the TEU were agreed to in the Treaty of Nice, signed in December 2000. (The proposed amendments will already undermine the purity of the new numbering system by adding, for example, new Articles 11a and 181a.) Where significant, we have indicated in the text and notes the changes that will be made if and when the Treaty of Nice is ratified. As of November 2001, only Denmark, France and Luxembourg had deposited their ratifications, although the process of ratification was at an advanced stage in several other Member States. Unfortunately, in June 2001, Irish voters rejected the Treaty, reflecting the now longstanding complaints that there is too great a distance between the leadership and the people and, notwithstanding impressive institutional reform in recent years, still something of a "democratic deficit."

The Selected Documents, which accompanies the casebook, contains the EC Treaty (as last amended by the Treaty of Amsterdam in 1999), the TEU (likewise as amended at Amsterdam), followed by (a) a conversion table of article numbers for both treaties showing the pre- and post-Amsterdam numbering, and (b) the 2000 Treaty of Nice which, as of this writing, remains to be ratified. The Nice Treaty consists primarily of amendments to the EC Treaty and TEU, and users are strongly encouraged when considering any treaty article to turn to the Nice Treaty (Document 4) for an indication of how, if at all, that particular provision would be altered upon the Nice Treaty's entry into force. (Where highly significant, the projected changes will in any event be brought to the reader's attention in text and notes throughout the book.) Because the treaties constitute the foundation of the Community legal system, they should in any case be read in tandem with the casebook as and when reference to treaty articles is made. Editors' note in the Selected Documents try to make the interplay between these texts as clear as possible.

The Selected Documents volume also contains a large sample of important secondary legislation, excerpted lightly and with care. Students will profit from working with these complex legislative texts. The accessibility of these important Community law documents should also be helpful in research.

* * *

Users of the book commonly wonder how best to use its voluminous materials. Clearly there is more material (and more subjects) than can be responsibly covered in a single semester course. Those using the book for such a course have a range of possibilities at their disposal. Teachers who wish especially to emphasize constitutional and institutional issues will find that Parts I and II of the book provide a comprehensive picture of the legal and institutional framework of the European Community and European Union, furnishing material for up to at least a full half-semester of teaching, thereby allowing constitutional and institutional themes to become the course's leitmotif. They may then assign substantive law chapters that best match their and their students' interests. We recommend that any such substantive law selection include a very healthy dose of the material in Part III on the Internal Market, one or two basic chapters on competition policy (from Part IV), and one or two basic chapters on external relations and trade (from Part V) or economic and monetary union and free movement of capital (from Part VI).

Many other teachers will wish to leave considerably more room for inquiry into substantive aspects of Community and Union law. For them it will be necessary to select among the materials in Part I and Part II chapters, either deleting certain chapters (such as the chapters on preliminary references or infringement actions, or the lengthy chapter on the reception of Community law in the Member State legal systems) or assigning only portions of them. That will leave them far the greater portion of the semester for the study of substantive European law. We facilitate this by placing in Part II, rather than Part I, all the chapters that focus on the reception, implementation and enforcement of Community law in the Member States.

As implied above, in the authors' judgment, no course in Community law is complete without extended reference to the fascinating range of issues surrounding the Internal Market. Those materials therefore receive privileged attention in Part III of the book. (The free movement of capital and the economic and monetary union have been placed in their own part—Part VI—but should be considered features of the internal market as well.) Part III chapters deserve a conspicuous place in any basic Community law course, however much attention may be given to constitutional and institutional issues in Parts I and II. Even so, Part III is structured to enable teachers to dispense with certain aspects of the internal market by simply deleting one or more chapters or portions thereof, if they wish to make more room for substantive law chapters in the remaining parts of the book.

Competition law (and related subjects) and external relations (including trade) comprise their own Parts of the book, Parts IV and V, respectively. Teachers clearly will differ on the extent to which they devote class hours to these materials. As noted, we believe that any introductory course should include at least some materials from both of these parts. But those who place emphasis on these matters will find that each Part thoroughly covers its domain and can sustain classroom study for over a third of a semester.

Without pretending to be exhaustive, Part VII presents assorted substantive law topics not falling within the domains of Parts III, IV, V or VI. They are a varied lot—from consumer protection to social policy to equal rights to jurisdiction and the enforcement of foreign country judgments. Should teachers find that they wish to address a particular policy area that is not covered in this Part, they will find that outside materials are readily available. (See the Note on Legal Sources following this Preface.) The authors invite suggestions from users as to policy areas that they recommend be included in subsequent editions of this book.

Ideally, Community law will be studied over the course of two semesters. The casebook is of a length and organization to facilitate such usage. It is recommended that, in that event, the first semester of the course emphasize Parts I through III and the second semester the remainder.

It is also possible to teach a variety of advanced semester-long courses making use of parts of the casebook. As noted above (in the context of a second-semester offering in a year-long curriculum), a course could concentrate entirely on Community competition and trade law, Parts IV and V. In the alternative, one could construct a comparative competition law or trade law course, using the relevant part of the casebook together with materials on US or other nations' antitrust or trade law, coupled with the emerging body of international law materials on these subjects. An advanced course might also center on the Community's integrated internal market, including the chapters on harmonization of laws, services, establishment (from Part III) and capital and economic and monetary union (from Part VI), again possibly supplemented by market integration materials from other countries (such as the US) or the world trading system. Even Parts I and II lend themselves to use in a comparative federalism course.

We hope that the casebook will prove easy to use while also highly instructive, and that it will stimulate further study and scholarship in the ever-widening and seemingly always rich arenas of European Community and European Union.

*

Foreword

I said in the Foreword to the first edition "From any standpoint this is a remarkable work". I remain of that opinion, indeed even more strongly since the first edition, already widely used, has been admirably brought up to date to include many recent cases (Keck is a good example) and the changes proposed in the Nice Agreement. The revision was an enormous and an important task, even increasing the wealth of detail to be found in the first edition.

The book deals with really three parts. First the institutions and the jurisdiction of the Court, its scope, its remedies, its attitudes. It deals secondly with the relationship between national law and domestic law and it analyses how far national courts have accepted the transplant or transfusion in a union of states which is far from being a federation. Thirdly it deals with many aspects of the substantive law—the freedom of movement of persons, goods and services, competition policy, external relations, the free movement of capital and monetary union and specific Community policies such as environment protection and consumer rights. Needless to say the problems arising from the creation of an internal market are dealt with in considerable detail.

I have found in using this book, both for my own benefit and in an occasional class, that the system adopted has been very valuable. There is a concise introduction of the particular subject followed by the reference to the cases. For each case there is a summary of the issues or facts followed by extracts from the judgment and then questions, comments and cross references including comparative law comments. The analysis by the authors of the judgment and their selection of paragraphs gives the student a very clear idea of what is to be got from the case without in any way discouraging him or her from going to the actual reports. Since students do not always have ready access to full reports this is a very useful technique to enable the student to see the cases in their context and to understand them. Many of the questions which are raised are far from superficial and require considerable thought and discussion by the student and the professor. Thus some of the questions require not only a detailed study of the facts of a case but more important a real attempt to understand what is the principle and how it may apply to other factual situations.

I am convinced that the teaching of European Union law outside the Community and especially in the English speaking world will be greatly enhanced by this new edition. I think also that the book is a very good working book for classes in other countries where students' knowledge of English may be not so complete. The style is concise and clear and forceful. I repeat what I said in the first Foreword "Any student who masters this book, or specific sections of it, will have a profound and detailed knowledge of what European law is all about."

SLYNN OF HADLEY

*

Acknowledgments to the First Edition

The authors of every project of this scope owe a multitude of debts to those who have inspired and assisted them along the way. While it is not possible to acknowledge all those who have helped us, a number of contributions deserve special mention.

We jointly give our thanks to those who have made suggestions that have helped to shape the coverage or text of this casebook. Preeminent among them are Bernhard Schloh of the Council Legal Service, Peter Oliver of the Commission Legal Service, and Professor Valentine Korah of University College, London.

George Bermann wishes to thank especially Professor Henry G. Schermers and Bernhard Schloh for their profound guidance in Community law over the years, as well as Judges Koen Lenaerts, Pierre Pescatore and Lord Gordon Slynn and Professor Meinhard Hilf for their helpful comments on his text. Mary Dominick, Lee Neuman, Carlin Stratton, April Tash and Sally Zelikovsky afforded essential research assistance. The secretarial help of Susan Martin and Kam Metcalf is also warmly appreciated.

Roger Goebel thanks the many members of the Court of Justice, the Council and the Commission who have enriched his knowledge of Community law, in particular Judge David Edward and former Judges Pierre Pescatore and Lord Gordon Slynn, Rafaello Fornasier, Hans-Joachim Glaesner and Bernhard Schloh of the Council Legal Service, Karen Banks, Daniel Calleja, Bernd Langeheine, Jörn Pipkorn, Rolf Wägenbaur and Richard Wainwright of the Commission Legal Service, Auke Haagsma, Helmut Schröder and John Temple Lang of DG IV, Christopher Cruickshank and Severine Israel of DG IV, and George Zavvos, Member of the European Parliament. Thanks are also due to Jacques Buhart, Stephen Spinks and Paulette Vander Schueren, his former colleagues at Coudert Brothers. He is most appreciative of the aid provided by his research assistants, Diane Duszak, Stephen Jones and Stewart Muglich, and the faculty secretaries, Carol DeVito and Mary Whelan.

William Davey would like to thank Professor Eric Stein for kindling his interest in EC law many years ago, as well as Judge Pierre Pescatore, Jacques Bourgeoise, Edwin Vermulst and his former colleagues at Cleary, Gottlieb, Steen and Hamilton in Brussels, Donald L. Holley, Dirk Vandermeersch and Marc Hansen, for comments on various draft chapters and for assisting in obtaining materials. He would also like to acknowledge the invaluable help of his research assistant, Gordon Wagner, and his secretary, Terri Macfarland.

Eleanor Fox would like to thank Professor Valentine Korah for her extraordinarily helpful comments on various drafts, and Professor Korah, Professor Barry Hawk, Donald L. Holley, and the dedicated staff and officials of the EC Competition Directorate for innumerable insightful conversations. Also she wishes to acknowledge the valuable research assistance of James R. Farnsworth, Randall M. Fox, Robert Grundstein and Lene Skou and the dedicated assistance of her secretary, Linda Smalls.

We further wish to pay tribute to Professors Eric Stein, Peter Hay, Michel Waelbroeck and Joseph Weiler, whose earlier casebook representing a pioneering text from which we all profited when first teaching in this field.

Finally, we acknowledge the permission given by Sweet & Maxwell Ltd. for the use of excerpts from a number of national court judgments reported in the Common Market Law Reports, and thank the staff of the Court of Justice and of the information services of the EC Delegations in New York City and Washington, D.C., for their assistance in obtaining current materials.

Acknowledgments to the Second Edition

Professor Bermann acknowledges with special gratitude the research and editorial assistance of Richard H. Langan II and the research and secretarial assistance of Karina Rodriguez. Professor Bermann expresses thanks as well for the exceptionally valuable suggestions of Judge Koen Lenaerts of the Court of First Instance and Kurt Riechenberg, chef de cabinet of the President of the European Court of Justice.

Professor Goebel would like to thank his research assistant, Thomas Maeglin, together with Mary Whelan, Judy Haskell and Christian Steriti, members of the faculty secretariat, for their invaluable assistance.

Professor Davey would like to thank his research assistant, Valerie Demaret, and his administrative assistant, Ruth Manint.

Professor Fox expresses her appreciation for the research assistance of Krzysztof Kuik, David P. Herlihy, James Harvey and John Marco.

The authors wish to thank Duncan E. Alford, reference librarian at Columbia Law School, for his assistance in preparing the revised note on "Legal Sources and Citation Forms" (p. xvii).

*

Legal Sources and Citation Forms

American students, academicians and lawyers encountering European Community and European Union law for the first time may find it difficult to deal with the source material, which is quite different in character and style from US legislation, case law and legal commentary. The purpose of this note is to explain briefly how to access European Community documents and secondary research materials, as well as to indicate the mode of citation used in this casebook.

1. The Constitutive Treaties

The basic treaties—the Treaty Establishing the European Community (EC Treaty) and the Treaty on European Union (TEU)—are published by the European Office for Publications or EOP (previously EC Office for Official Publications), Luxembourg, in both a complete and an abridged edition. They reflect the changes introduced by the Single European Act, the Treaty of Maastricht and the Treaty of Amsterdam. The Selected Documents volume published in conjunction with this casebook also sets out the constitutive treaties as amended to date.

The Treaty of Nice, agreed to in December 2000 and signed on February 26, 2001, but still in the process of ratification, appears in the Official Journal at O.J. C 80/1 (Oct. 3, 2001). The complete text has also been published by the European Office for Publications, and likewise appears in the Selected Documents volume published in conjunction with this casebook.

Major compilations of Community law, such as the Commerce Clearing House (CCH), European Union Law Reporter, and the Encyclopedia of European Union Law (K. Simmonds ed., Sweet & Maxwell looseleaf) also contain all of the treaties. The treaties are also available in electronic form from several sources. EurLex, the free legal database maintained by EUR-OP on the Internet, contains recent consolidated versions of the treaties (http://europa.eu.int/eur-lex). Copies of the treaties, along with their declarations, can be accessed for a fee on WESTLAW in the EU-TREATIES database, on LEXIS in the EC Treaties database (provided by CELEX) and in CELEX, the fee-based database of legal documents maintained by the European Union.

2. Secondary Legislation

Community legislation consists of regulations and directives. These, together with legally binding decisions and proposals for legislation, are published in a journal in each of the eleven working languages of the Community and Union (Danish, Dutch, English, Finnish, French, German, Greek, Italian, Portuguese, Spanish and Swedish). The English language version is called the Official Journal of the European Union (previously Official Journal of the European Communities), typically abbreviated O.J. The French version is the Journal Officiel, or J.O. The Journal is published daily, except for holidays. (Occasionally more than one number is printed on the same date.)

There are two different series in the Journal. Council regulations and directives, Commission decisions in competition and antidumping cases, and similar items, are found in the "L" (for "Legislation") series. Proposed legislation, proceedings of the Parliament, recommendations of the Economic and Social Committee and various notices are published in the "C" (for "Communications") series.

Each issue of the official Journal is separately paged. The Journal is commonly cited by series, issue number, page and date, for example: O.J. L 44/33 (Feb. 1, 1999). The Journal was not published in English prior to the accession of the United Kingdom and Ireland in 1973. Legislation prior to that date was translated and published in a special edition, cited, for example, as O.J. English Spec. Ed. 1968, at (page) 12.

A piece of legislation is typically cited by its number, its date of adoption and its title, followed by the journal reference. Thus, a complete citation would read as follows: Council Directive 85/374 of July 25, 1985, on the approximation of the laws, regulations and administrative provisions of the Member States concerning liability for defective products, O.J. L 210/29 (Aug. 7, 1985). Secondary sources, including this casebook, frequently shorten long titles of legislative acts or refer to them only by number and date, or only the number. Example: Council Directive 85/374 of July 25, 1985 on product liability, or simply Council Directive 85/374.

The Community publishes twice a year, as part of the Official Journal, a list of legislation in force (showing all amendments), on a topical and chronological basis. See, e.g., Official Journal of the European Union, Directory of Community Legislation In Force and Other Acts of the Community Institutions, the latest being from July 1, 2001 (37th ed.). The Official Journal publishes monthly and annual alphabetical and methodological indices. The latest version of the Directory of Community Legislation in Force is also available on EurLex (http://europa.eu.int/eur-lex/en/lif/index.html).

EurLex provides free access to the Official Journal since January 1, 1998 (in all the official languages of the EU), which can be searched full-text. Both WESTLAW and LEXIS publish databases of European Union legislation that allow searching full text. WESTLAW provides coverage beginning in 1952 in its European Union Legislation (EU-LEG) database. LEXIS provides coverage beginning in 1980 in its EC Legislation (EURCOM; LEGIS) database. CELEX provides access to all issues of the Official Journal with enhanced search capability compared to that provided by EurLex. The CCH European Union Law Reporter and the Encyclopedia of European Union Law mentioned above each publish a substantial quantity of secondary legislation.

3.   Judgments of the Court of Justice and Court of First Instance

All judgments and important interlocutory orders of the Court of Justice and the Court of First Instance, as well as all opinions of the Advocates-General, are printed in the official Court reports, officially entitled Reports of Cases before the Court of Justice and the Court of First Instance (and often catalogued under that name), but more commonly called the European Court Reports (ECR). These are issued in all of eleven working languages of the Community. Since 1989, the volumes have been divided between the Court of Justice and the Court of First Instance, with separate pagination for each court.

The pages for the Court of Justice decisions are preceded by "I–"; the pages for the Court of First Instance decisions by "II–".

Due to the delay in translation, the English series of these reports appears about fifteen to eighteen months after judgments are rendered. The Court of Justice publishes Weekly Proceedings containing summaries of the judgments and opinions, appearing about two months after they are rendered. The Court also makes issues of the Proceedings since 1998 available on its web site, http://curia.eu.int/en/act/index.htm. Moreover, the French text the (working language of the Court), as well as the text of the language initially used in each case, are both available on request from the Court's information office, usually within a few weeks after the date of the judgment or opinion. Incidentally, it is often useful to consult the French text of judgments because it represents the initial formulation of the Court's thinking, and the English translations may sometimes be imprecise or awkward.

CELEX contains all judgments and opinions after their publication in the ECR and is searchable full-text. WESTLAW in its database EU-CS similarly contains all judgments and opinions as provided in CELEX. WESTLAW's EU-CS-ALL database contains judgments and opinions published in the ECR and selected commercial law reporters, including the Common Market Law Reports, mentioned below. LEXIS likewise provides full-text access to the contents of the ECR in its European Court of Justice Cases (EURCOM; ECJ) database.

The European Court of Justice publishes its opinions and judgments on its official web site, http://curia.eu.int. Full-text search capability is available for opinions and judgments since 1997. Access to opinions and judgments by case number is available from 1953 for the Court of Justice and since its inception in 1989 for the Court of First Instance.

Many, but not all, Court of Justice judgments and opinions are also published unofficially. The two primary English language sources are the CCH European Union Law Reporter and the Common Market Law Reports (Sweet & Maxwell), or CMLR. Both often publish judgments before the ECR does so. In addition, the Common Market Law Reports publishes selected judgments from the UK and other Member State courts dealing with Community law issues. CCH publishes recent cases in its current binders, which are then periodically transferred to permanent volumes, cited since 1989 as the CEC.

It is customary to cite Court of Justice decisions by name, case number, year and page and to abbreviate the title of the reports as ECR. Where the name of the case is common (e.g., Commission v. Belgium or Commission v. Council), we have devised (or borrowed from other sources) descriptive names as means of identification and put them into parentheses following the official name in the ECR. These descriptive names are not part of the official name of the case.

Thus, we use the following citation forms: Commission v. Council (ERTA), Case 22/70, [1971] ECR 263; In re Kramer, Cases 3, 4 & 6/76, [1976] ECR 1279; GB–INNO–BM v. Confederation de Commerce Luxembourgeois, Case C–362/88, [1990] ECR I683. If a judgment excerpted or cited in the casebook has not yet been published in the ECR, we indicate the ECR year, leave the page blank, and provide a parenthetical reference to the date.

We deliberately do not follow the "bluebook" citation forms, either for judgments, legislation or other materials. Our citation forms are adapted from those commonly used by European writers and are designed to provide maximum clarity in use.

In our excerpting of cases, we denote omissions of whole paragraphs by three asterisks and omissions of words or sentences within a paragraph simply by three dots. For simplicity and conciseness, we have commonly omitted the Court's own citations without indicating the omission.

4. Community Reports and Bulletins

The Community publishes as substantial volume of reports and studies each year, many of which are available on the EU's official web site, Europa. The most important is the Commission's Annual General Report on the Activities of the European Union (addressed to the Parliament) which contains a valuable summary of the activities of each of the EU Community institutions in all of the important fields of Community and Union operations. This report is usually published in March. It should be cited both by reference to the year being reviewed and the year of publication. Example: Twenty-fifth General Report 1991, at 25 (1992). The full text of recent Annual Reports are available on the Europa web site by clicking on the Official Documents link or using the following link: http://europa.eu.int/abc/doc/off/rg/en/rgset.htm.

The Commission publishes a number of annual special reports, e.g., on agricultural policy, antidumping, competition policy, the environment, social policy, etc., which are useful research tools in those fields. The Commission also publishes a Bulletin of the European Union, usually on a monthly basis, but combining July and August. This Bulletin summarizes important developments, sector by sector, each month. Due to translation delays, the Bulletin usually appears several months late. We use the Annual General Report form of citing the Bulletin: Bull. EU 1990–3, at 17. The full text of recent Monthly Bulletins are available on the Europa web site by clicking on the Official Documents link or using the following link: http://europa.eu.int/abc/doc/off/bull/en/welcome.htm.

The Commission and the other EU institutions or agencies publish a great variety of special studies and reports. These are available, either for a charge or free, from the Office of Official Publications in Luxembourg. There are several US distributors including Bernan Associates, 4611–F Assembly Drive, Lanham, MD 20706–4391, Telephone: 800–274–4447, Fax 800–865–3450, email query@bernan.com; URL: http://www.bernan.com

5. Secondary Source Material

We have previously mentioned the CCH European Union Law Reporter and the Encyclopedia of European Union Law (K. Simmonds, ed. Sweet & Maxwell) as valuable sources of general information. Smit & Herzog, Law of the European Economic Community (Matthew Bender looseleaf), is a loose-leaf service analyzing the EC Treaty, article by article. In addition to its annual updates, it is being updated at the present time to reflect the amendments brought by the Treaty of Amsterdam.

Eurowatch is a semimonthly newsletter containing valuable information on current developments in the EU. A number of law firms, accounting firms and information offices in Brussels publish newsletters, often quite useful. The Economist and the Financial Times probably provide the best English-language news coverage.

There are many valuable books on the structure and institutions of the Community and Union or on specific substantive law aspects. Reference to some of these is made at various points in the casebook. The following three treatises merit particular attention as good, comprehensive introductions to European Union law and institutions: (1) Trevor C. Hartley, Foundations of European Community Law (4th ed. 1998), (2) P.S.R.F. Mathijsen, A Guide to European Community Law (7th ed. 1999), and (3) P.J.G. Kapteyn, Introduction to the Law of the European Communities: From Maastricht to Amsterdam (3rd ed. 1998).

Law review commentary has become abundant in recent years. Three leading European reviews in English which specialize in Community law are the Common Market Law Review (Kluwer), the European Law Review (Sweet & Maxwell), and the European Law Journal (Sweet & Maxwell). Other reviews concentrate on Community competition or trade law, or on economic aspects of Community law. There are counterpart specialized Community journals in most of the Member States, such as Europarecht in Germany, and Revue de Marché Commun and Revue Trimestrielle de Droit Européen in France.

In the US, the Columbia Journal of European Law, which appears three times a year, is devoted entirely to European law, primarily at the EC and EU level, with articles, case notes, legislative notes and book reviews. Boston College International Law Journal and the Fordham International Law Journal devote one issue each year to Community law. The Fordham Corporate Law Institute (Transnational Juris) publishes each year a volume devoted to Community and international antitrust law.

In addition to the Index for Foreign Legal Periodicals published by the University of California Press, which is useful in finding law review articles on any international law topic, there are two useful indexes focused on European legal topics, including European Union law. European Legal Journals Index, published by Sweet & Maxwell, indexes articles from European law reviews and journals published in English from 1993 onward. This index is published monthly, with quarterly and annual cumulative issues. The last print edition was published in 1999, but current issues are available on WESTLAW as part of Legal Journals Index (LJI). European Current Law, also published by Sweet & Maxwell, contains a monthly index of articles from law reviews and journals. In addition, this monthly publication contains digests of important case law and statutes of the European Union and of member states of the EU.

The European Commission maintains the European Commission Library Catalogue (ECLAS), a bibliographic database on the Internet at http://europa.eu.int/eclas/. Developed from the SCAD database (which is no longer being updated), ECLAS organizes selected articles and documents on EU affairs by subject and nearly 7,000 items are added to the catalog annually. In addition to print materials, ECLAS catalogs Internet resources on EU affairs.

6. EC Information Service

The EU's Delegation to the United States includes an information service and library. The information service not only permits academic use of the library, but can provide assistance, within reasonable limits, in research on current topics. The EU Delegation maintains a very useful website on EU matters (http://www.eurunion.org). Its A–Z Index of EU Websites is organized alphabetically by subject for quick access to EU information. The Delegation's address is 2300 M St., N.W., Washington DC 20038, tel: (202) 862–9500, fax: (202) 429–1766.

7. Electronic Information

Over the past ten years, European Union ("EU") legal information has increasingly become available in electronic format. The European Union has developed Europa, a comprehensive web site that has become the principal portal to all official European Union information, including legal documents and information (http://www.europa.eu.int).

Through EurLex (http://www.europa.eu.int/eur-lex/en/index.html), many official EU documents are available over the Internet, including the text of EU treaties, legislation, and parliamentary questions. EurLex significantly expanded its content in early January 2002. For instance, EurLex provides access to issues of the Official Journal since January 1, 1998 (previously, only issues published during the most recent 45 days were available on EurLex). Many documents are available online without charge. In addition, EurLex provides links to the other primary legal databases maintained by the principal institutions of the EU including:

_ Curia (http://curia.eu.int), the official web site of the European Court of Justice, which contains copies of judgments, opinions and orders of the Court of Justice since 1953 and the Court of First Instance since 1989.

_ Oeil, the Legislative Observatory (http://wwwdb.europarl.eu.int/ dors/oeil/en/default.htm), is the official legal database of the European Parliament and contains full-text copies of many official parliamentary documents, including parliamentary reports.

_ Prelex, available through the EurLex web site, is a database used to track EU legislation. Using this database, researchers can follow all Commission proposals (e.g., legislative and budgetary dossiers, conclusions of international agreements) and communications from their transmission to the Council or the European Parliament right through to their adoption or rejection by the Council, their adoption by Parliament or their withdrawal by the Commission.

_ RAPID is a searchable database of European Commission press releases, which are frequently useful in finding recently issued legal documents and information (http://europa.eu.int/rapid/start/cgi/ guesten.ksh).

_ IDEA is the Electronic Directory of the European Institutions managed by EUR-OP (http://europa.eu.int/idea/en/index.htm). The directory may be searched by an individual's name or by the hierarchy of EU institutions.

The documentation available on Europa is improving constantly and the Commission plans for EurLex to become the comprehensive portal for all EU legal information, including legislation, court decisions, Commission documents and various reports. In its 2001 Work Programme, the European Commission stated that that the opening of a "single portal for accessing legislative and legal texts" was an important step in improving "the links between the Union and its citizens" and improving trust in EU institutions.

The fee-based commercial databases WESTLAW and LEXIS provide access to much of EU law. Attorneys and researchers can search databases on EU law using the same commands as in other WESTLAW and LEXIS databases. Each company has greatly improved its respective EU databases over the past few years and researchers will find that their research needs are well-served by the databases on EU legal materials made available through both services.

*

Summary of Contents

PART V. EXTERNAL RELATIONS AND COMMERCIAL POLICY

*

Table of Contents

Table of Community Cases in the European Court of Justice

The principal cases are in bold type. Cases cited or discussed in the text are roman type. References are to pages. Cases cited in principal cases and within other quoted materials are not included.

*

Table of Community Cases in the Court of First Instance

The principal cases are in bold type. Cases cited or discussed in the text are roman type. References are to pages. Cases cited in principal cases and within other quoted materials are not included.

Table of National Court Cases
(and Cases in the European Court of Human Rights)

The principal cases are in bold type. Cases cited or discussed in the text are roman type. References are to pages. Cases cited in principal cases and within other quoted materials are not included.

*

Table of European Commission Decisions

The principal cases are in bold type. Cases cited or discussed in the text are roman type. References are to pages. Cases cited in principal cases and within other quoted materials are not included.

*

CASES AND MATERIALS ON
EUROPEAN UNION LAW

Second Edition

*

Part I

THE EUROPEAN COMMUNITY AND EUROPEAN UNION: LEGAL AND INSTITUTIONAL FRAMEWORK

The European Community, like the European Union of which it forms a part, performs a wide variety of functions across a vast regulatory domain. The chapters that constitute Parts III through VII of this book will find the institutions of the Community and the Union addressing concerns ranging from market integration, to competition policy, to international trade (and external relations generally), to an ever-wider range of sectoral (e.g. labor, telecommunications) and non-sectoral (e.g. consumer and environmental protection) "policies." The Community's 1993 change of name from "European Economic Community" to "European Community," like its recognition of distinct rights of "European citizenship," captures this remarkable evolution.

To accomplish its wide-ranging and important purposes, the European Community and European Union have need of viable legal and political systems which can organize their activities, while at the same time giving these European entities a continuity and stability that match the challenges they face. Part I of this book explores this stable, though not unchanging, legal and political framework.

After an historical introduction identifying the roots of European integration and the broad outlines of its institutional evolution (Chapter 1), Chapter 2 examines successively the basic treaty foundations of the European "project" and the political and judicial institutions that manage it. Because so much of this book deals with legal measures of various sorts, Chapter 3 describes the nature of those measures and analyzes the legislative and administrative processes from which they emerge.

Community law's sphere of concern is not, however, unlimited. Chapter 4 examines the various bounds on Community law's "reach," including such aspects of the problem as implied powers, "internal affairs," preemption and subsidiarity. The Community courts play the central role not only in defining these limits, but more generally in determining the scope and meaning of Community law. Issues of interpretation and validity abound, and the Community's courts—the Court of Justice and Court of First Instance—are equipped with a jurisdiction and a set of remedies designed to address them. Chapter 5 explores the role and function of these courts, while Chapter 6 traces the "fundamental rights" and "human rights" norms that increasingly inform their jurisprudence.

Pervading the book is an ongoing discussion of the Community/Member State relationship. Since the efficacy of European Community law depends so heavily on its taking precedence over national law and policy that might weaken or defeat it, the Court of Justice devoted its early decades to securing the "primacy" of Community law norms. That jurisprudential process continues to this day, and is the subject of Chapter 7.

Chapter 1

THE HISTORY OF THE EUROPEAN COMMUNITY AND THE EUROPEAN UNION

In a period of little over four decades, the European Community (originally the European Economic Community) has achieved extraordinary results in economic and legal integration. The Community's architects sought to create on the historically fragmented continent of Europe an integrated economic market that would afford enterprise the benefits of harmonization and economies of scale, while bringing to the population as a whole a higher standard of living. Although principally designed to serve economic ends, the Community also acquired political, social and cultural dimensions, with active programs in fields such as environmental, consumer and investor protection, occupational safety, cultural and linguistic identity, research and development, health and education. By the time the nations of Central and Eastern Europe threw off Soviet hegemony in the late 1980s, Western Europe had become an arena of concerted social and economic action whose scale and dynamism were remarkable by any standard.

European integration also had a more purely political dimension. The notion of a political union of sorts was present in the minds of many of the Community's founders. The Preamble to the 1957 Treaty Establishing the European Economic Community set as one of its goals the achievement of "an ever closer Union among the peoples of Europe." Although this goal has not always been aggressively pursued over the Community's forty-plus years, it has never been abandoned. With the Treaty of Maastricht Treaty (signed in February 1992, effective November 1993), the Community was placed within the framework of a broader European Union, which encompassed the full range of European integration initiatives while at the same time presenting the world a unified European political face.

Given the Member States' traditional commitment to the rule of law, it is not surprising that the European Community has also evolved into a highly structured and principled legal environment. Community law is the product of political institutions operating through regular instruments and means. It is also subject to conventional Member State political controls and to review by an independent Community judiciary. As those engaged in international transactions take increasing interest in the development of Europe-wide

3

policies, so the international legal community has taken a parallel interest in the workings of the relatively young but sophisticated Community law system.

A. THE POSTWAR MOVEMENT TOWARD EUROPEAN UNIFICATION

The vast destruction of life and property brought about by the Second World War, coupled with accompanying political instability, provided the immediate background for a series of important steps toward European integration. The war had left a power vacuum in a Europe suffering from severe economic disarray. The Soviet presence in Eastern Europe had led in the meantime to a coup d'etat in the former Czechoslovakia (1948) and a blockade of Berlin (1948–49). Military and political tensions between the two superpowers escalated in 1949, with the Soviet Union's development of the A-bomb and the victory of the Communists in China. At the same time, the United States was making its influence felt in Western Europe both through conduct of the war and through a variety of postwar political arrangements.

In order to confront the Soviet threat, while at the same time reducing their dependence on the US, the nations of Western Europe launched a number of economic and political initiatives. A customs union among Belgium, the Netherlands and Luxembourg was planned by the leaders of those countries in exile in London in 1944. Their efforts yielded the Benelux Customs Convention (effective in 1948) and led ten years later to the creation of a common trading area.[1] As early as September 1946, in a speech at Zurich University, Winston Churchill spoke in terms of a closer political union, calling for the construction of "a kind of United States of Europe," based on "a partnership between France and Germany." He made it clear that, although European leaders had geopolitical considerations in mind in developing their postwar arrangements, they were determined to follow different paths than those that Charlemagne, Napoleon or the German empire-builders had followed; they were committed to economic integration under law and, above all, to the use of peaceful means and to the principle of popular consent.

A general interest in European unity led to the calling of a Congress of Europe at the Hague in May 1948. This was followed a year later by the adoption of a Statute of the Council of Europe, which was signed by ten Western European nations. Although it never acquired legislative power, the Council of Europe has issued important political recommendations to the member governments. Its major achievement is probably the European Convention for the Protection of Human Rights and Fundamental Freedoms, signed in November 1950.[2] The European Court of Human Rights (like its predecessor institutions at Strasbourg) plays an increasingly important role in human rights protection, and the Convention, as we shall see, has become an important source of European Community law.

US foreign policy in the postwar period encouraged political cooperation and the development of new structures in Western Europe. To help coordinate the administration of Marshall Plan aid, the US urged the sixteen recipient nations to create a new intergovernmental body, the Organization for Europe-

---

1. Treaty Instituting the Benelux Union, Feb. 3, 1958, 381 UNTS 260 (eff. Nov. 1, 1960).   **2.** Europ. T.S. 5.

an Economic Cooperation (OEEC), set up in 1948. Soon enough, however, the OEEC was engaged in broader policy aspects of the postwar European economy. In 1960, Canada and the US joined the OEEC, which was then renamed the Organization for Economic Cooperation and Development (OECD). Like the Council of Europe, the OECD lacks formal lawmaking powers, but its reports, analyses and recommendations have importantly developed the study of the "European economy" and influenced national economic policies.

Different postwar organizations were created to promote cooperation in other spheres of shared interest. In 1949, Canada, the US and a majority of Western European states set up NATO as a defensive military alliance, featuring an integrated military command structure and a collective decision-making mechanism. As tensions in Europe have abated with the dramatic collapse of Communist regimes in the Soviet Union and Eastern Europe, NATO has understandably come in for reexamination.

B.   THE EUROPEAN COAL AND STEEL COMMUNITY AND LATER COMMUNITY EFFORTS

The first major European Community, the European Coal and Steel Community (ECSC), developed out of a focused concern over the peaceful and efficient use of Europe's coal and steel resources. In the wake of World War II, France above all was seeking effective guarantees against a revival of German military power, while the US and the UK viewed a strong, rearmed Germany as an important defense against Soviet expansionism. The French found a common answer to these needs in a Franco–German partnership for regulating the production of coal and steel, two important sectors for the redevelopment of national power, economic and military alike.

On May 9, 1950, the French government formally proposed the Schuman Plan, inspired by Jean Monnet (the great French proponent of European integration), but named after France's foreign minister Robert Schuman. Under the plan, the whole of Franco–German coal and steel production was to be placed under a common High Authority composed of independent persons named by the participating national governments, but acting within an organization open to participation by other European countries. The High Authority would make decisions binding on the states without further national consent. The Treaty of Paris of April 18, 1951, establishing the European Coal and Steel Community, was eventually signed by the three Benelux countries, France, Germany and Italy, and it entered into force on July 25, 1952.[3] Jean Monnet fittingly became the High Authority's first President.

Significantly, the ECSC Treaty sought not only to rationalize coal and steel production, but also to promote free trade in these sectors by prohibiting government subsidies, quantitative restrictions, and duties on imports and exports or charges having equivalent effect, measures that discriminated

---

3. Treaty Establishing the European Coal and Steel Community (ECSC), April 18, 1951, 261 UNTS 140, as amended. The ECSC will be allowed to lapse in 2002, at the expiry of its 50–year term, with its achievements and programs incorporated into the Treaty Establishing the European Community (EC Treaty, previously EEC Treaty), discussed below.

between producers, purchasers or consumers, and restrictive practices tending toward the division or exploitation of markets. The Treaty also created several new institutions, in addition to the High Authority, for administering the ECSC. These were a Special Council of Ministers set up mainly to advise the High Authority by unanimous or qualified majority opinion on pending decisions, a Common Assembly originally composed of members of the national parliaments and empowered to dismiss the High Authority and, finally, a Court of Justice to ensure implementation of the Treaty and of the secondary legislation expected to follow. The institutional shape of this Community and its concept of economic integration was to influence powerfully the outlines of the further communities to come. In the Paris Declaration of May 9, 1950, Foreign Minister Schuman described the Coal and Steel Community as "the first stage of the European Federation."

The next efforts at community-building occurred in quite different sectors. The early 1950s witnessed a continuing rise in European military tensions. In this cold war environment, the United States urged German rearmament, which France continued to oppose. Meanwhile Churchill, though no longer in power, called in the Council of Europe for the creation of a European Army. In due course, France proposed a plan for such an army (the Pleven Plan, named after the French Minister of Defense) to be organized under a European Ministry of Defense and structured in a fashion parallel to the ECSC. On May 27, 1952, a European Defense Community (EDC) Treaty was signed by all six ECSC countries. The Treaty was immediately criticized on the ground that it had gone forward without an adequate basis in European foreign policy or general military strategy. Moreover, it was evidently lacking in democratic safeguards.

The political deficiencies of the proposed EDC in turn prompted a call by ministers of the ECSC countries in late 1952 for the creation of a European Political Community, or EPC. Early the next year, a leading Europeanist, Belgium's foreign minister Paul–Henri Spaak, prepared a statute for such a community along the general lines of the ECSC and the EDC. However, France meanwhile had reconsidered its position even on the EDC, ultimately withdrawing its support for fear that in the absence of the UK, the EDC would leave a rearmed Germany dangerously free of foreign political control. The French government also had strong reservations about relinquishing full control over its own armed forces. With the thaw in East–West relations in 1953 after the Korean armistice and the death of Stalin, the EDC and the EPC ideas finally collapsed.

C. THE EUROPEAN ECONOMIC COMMUNITY AND EURATOM

The advocates of European integration eventually rallied to the view that any political union had to be preceded by one form or another of economic union. Early in 1955, a memorandum from the Benelux countries proposed paving the way to political integration through economic integration, and thus called at an early stage for a common transportation infrastructure, coordination of atomic and other energy resources and the creation of a common market. The Benelux memorandum was endorsed by the foreign ministers of

France, Italy and Germany in June 1955 at a meeting in Messina, Italy, and they in turn asked Paul–Henri Spaak to coordinate a series of conferences to develop a design and strategy for European integration. Although the UK was invited to participate, it did so only briefly. It continued to favor an approach based on intergovernmental cooperation within the OEEC and the establishment of a free trade area rather than a customs union. The UK also sought to maintain its traditionally privileged relationship with the US.

The Spaak Report, which strongly supported the idea of a common market and a common atomic energy policy, was adopted by the foreign ministers of the six participating states formally adopted the Spaak Report in May 1956. Then, working with extraordinary speed, an intergovernmental conference chaired by Spaak drafted within a few months the text of two complex community treaties. The Treaty Establishing the European Economic Community (EEC) was signed in Rome on March 25, 1957.[4] (As of the entry into force of the Maastricht Treaty in 1993, the EEC Treaty is known as the Treaty Establishing the European Community (EC), or EC Treaty.) Due to fears that the French might reject the EEC at the last moment, a separate European Atomic Energy Community (EAEC or Euratom) was established through a separate treaty, also signed in Rome on that date.[5] The six signatory states readily ratified the two treaties, and both came into effect on January 1, 1958. (The EC Treaty, as it stands today, is found in Part I of the Selected Documents, document 1.)

The creation of the Community prompted the remaining members of the OEEC, under the UK's leadership, to establish a free trade area in the form of the European Free Trade Association (EFTA). EFTA, linking Austria, Denmark, Norway, Portugal, Sweden, Switzerland and the UK (the "outer seven" as opposed to the EC's "inner six"), was agreed to on January 4, 1960.[6] Unlike the EC, which is committed to common external trade policies and a common internal market, EFTA was only a free trade area marked by certain loose forms of economic cooperation. Although the EC and EFTA were popularly seen as rivals ("Europe at sixes and sevens"), in fact the two blocs enjoyed close and harmonious trade relations which culminated in 1992 in an agreement to create a European Economic Area (EEA). (See Chapter 28).

D. THE EUROPEAN ECONOMIC COMMUNITY PROGRAM: 1958–1985

The Preamble to the EC Treaty calls for "common action to eliminate the barriers which divide Europe." Article 2, in its 1958 version, mandated the creation of a "common market" with a view to the harmonious development of economic activities, a continuous and balanced expansion, increased economic stability, a rise in the standard of living in Europe and closer relations among Member States. Article 3 prescribed as means to these ends the establishment of a common external tariff and commercial policy, the progres-

---

4. Treaty Establishing the European Economic Community (EEC), March 25, 1957, 298 UNTS 11, 4 Eur.Y.B. 412, as amended.

5. Treaty Establishing the European Atomic Energy Community (Euratom), March 25, 1957, 298 UNTS 167, 5 Eur.Y.B. 454, as amended.

6. Convention Establishing the European Free Trade Association, Jan. 4, 1960, 370 UNTS 3, 7 Eur.Y.B. 662, 15 Eur.Y.B. 733.

sive elimination of barriers to the free movement of the principal factors of production (goods, persons, services and capital), the creation of a common Community policy in certain key sectors (notably agriculture, transport and competition), the coordination of economic and monetary policy, and the progressive harmonization of Member State laws in other areas to the extent that this would contribute to the proper functioning of the common market.

The story of the Community's gradual success and occasional setbacks in achieving the objectives of the EC Treaty is, of course, too long and detailed for summary in this historical introduction. To a large extent, that story is told in the various chapters of this book. An initial overview should, however, be useful.

The EC Treaty provided a phased transitional period finally set at twelve years, ending in 1969, for introducing the common external tariff and more generally the common market. The 1960s were a period of energetic effort, unfortunately not always successful, to achieve these goals. Strong leadership was provided by the first President of the Commission, Walter Hallstein, a former German Secretary of State for Foreign Affairs and ally of Chancellor Konrad Adenauer. He was assisted by other prominent Commissioners, several of whom went on themselves to become Commission Presidents.

The removal of internal tariffs and the creation of a common external tariff were accomplished ahead of schedule on July 1, 1968, rather than December 31, 1969 as envisaged. The Community also established a common commercial policy toward third countries, entering into trade and foreign aid agreements with many of them, in the form notably of commercial or association treaties with adjacent states (e.g., Greece, Turkey, the former Yugoslavia) and with former colonies. The Community also began representing the Member States in GATT, participating in the Kennedy Round of negotiations which successfully reduced tariff and other trade barriers in 1967.

Substantial progress was also made in attaining the common market. Legislation in the form of framework action programs was adopted between 1960 and 1962 to organize the free movement of goods, workers, services and capital and the right of commercial establishment. The principle of national treatment, or non-discrimination, was firmly established, and many significant barriers were legislatively removed. For example, the first and second capital directives, adopted in 1961 and 1962, provided for the free movement of capital in most commercial and personal transactions, and established the principle of freedom of investment.

While some sectors were marked by progress, others lagged behind. Directives harmonizing safety and technical standards began in 1962 with the foodstuffs sector, and continued during the 1960s and 1970s in fields like pharmaceuticals, cosmetics and dangerous products. A 1968 regulation legislated the virtually free movement of workers and their families, covering not only blue-collar and agricultural workers, but also skilled labor and management personnel. On the other hand, little was done in the 1960s and early 1970s to remove state licensing barriers to the mobility of professionals or the regulatory barriers to trans-border banking, insurance or securities operations. Likewise little was achieved by way of a common transport policy.

Agriculture undoubtedly proved the most difficult sector. Nevertheless, the basic market organizations that still characterize the common agricultural policy were put in place in the 1960s. The model was the market organization for cereals in 1962, followed some years later by market organizations for dairy products, wine and other commodities. Integrated European markets were created and farm income protected. Production was fostered to such an extent that by the 1970s the Community became a substantial net exporter of agricultural products and troublesome surpluses of certain commodities accumulated.

By the 1960s, the Community had also launched a competition policy to implement EC Treaty Articles 85 and 86 (renumbered as Articles 81 and 82 by the 1999 Treaty of Amsterdam). The Council enacted basic secondary legislation giving the Commission power to issue regulations, to investigate and punish anti-competitive conduct, and to authorize such conduct when justified by certain economic benefits. The Commission began to enforce the Treaty and secondary legislation in major cases against cartels and market-partitioning license and distribution networks. The Commission's energetic pursuit of Community competition policy was largely endorsed by Court of Justice decisions starting in 1965 and has continued with undiminished vigor, albeit with increasing complexity, to the present day.

The 1970s also saw both successes and setbacks, some of them major. New progress was marked in the fields of establishment and services, with important legislation harmonizing company and securities law and, to a lesser extent, banking and insurance. Some harmonization of rules governing the liberal professions, notably medicine and architecture, was also achieved.

Social policy, which had been a stated Community concern from the outset, began to develop with the Social Action Program of 1974. That program yielded several significant measures in the field of employee protection and equal rights for women, as well as legislation to protect on-the-job health and safety. Supplemented by case law of the Court of Justice, and given new impetus by the Social Charter of 1989, social policy is now one of the Community's more active though still controversial domains.

Two other fields of activity, environmental and consumer protection, were launched with action programs in 1974. Although neither sector was specifically addressed in the original EC Treaty, both had come to be considered integral parts of a common market. Since the mid–1970s, the Community has adopted minimum standards for water and air quality, for limiting pollution and waste, and for protecting wildlife, and it has entered into many international agreements on these subjects. As for consumer rights, over a dozen harmonization directives have been enacted on consumer information, labeling and advertising, and the elimination of unfair business practices in various fields. Among the earliest and most famous is the 1985 directive on products liability which fixed strict liability as the general rule in this field. (See Chapter 35.)

Despite this progress, the late 1970s and early 1980s ushered in a sense of "Europessimism." Since adoption of most Community legislation required unanimity, measures were often slow to pass and in some cases watered down or totally blocked. The enormous complexity and expense of the common agricultural policy caused deep dissatisfaction, but political pressures from farming interests prevented reform. Meanwhile, the Community experienced chronic and severe budgetary problems, with member state wrangling over the Community budget becoming an annual affair. Business had the impression, founded or not, that non-tariff barriers to trade and other forms of protectionism had increased markedly in the late 1970s and were not effectively being addressed.

In 1985, under its new French Socialist President, Jacques Delors, and with the aid of the British Tory Commissioner, Lord Cockfield, the Commission developed a plan of action to overcome these problems. The solution was largely embodied in a White Paper of June 1985 on Completing the Internal Market. The White Paper called for adoption before the end of 1992 of 279 pieces of legislation covering every major element of a proposed more fully integrated market. Thus came into being the famous "1992" or "single market" program, enthusiastically endorsed by the European Parliament, business and industry leaders and the media.

With this impetus, and with a view to enabling Europe to compete more vigorously with the US and Japan, the Member States made the internal market goal the centerpiece of a new treaty known as the Single European Act (SEA). The SEA, which consists mainly of amendments to the EC Treaty, also introduced important procedural changes that built upon various political developments that had been occurring since the Community's founding. We turn now to these developments.

E.   THE EVOLUTION OF COMMUNITY STRUCTURE: 1958–1985

While the institutions were pursuing the original Treaty objectives, important transformations were taking place within the Community. Some of these changes were territorial, some institutional, and still others programmatic.

1.   THE ACCESSION OF NEW STATES

An obvious respect in which the Community had evolved since 1957 is, of course, territorial. The Preamble to the EC Treaty had foreseen that "other peoples of Europe" might join the Community, and Article 237 (replaced in 1993 by Article 49, formerly Article O, of the Treaty on European Union) laid down an accession procedure.

As early as 1961, British Prime Minister Macmillan initiated negotiations with a view to UK membership, but these ended, chiefly on account of French objections. President de Gaulle, who had come to power in France in 1958, was uncomfortable with the UK's close military ties with the US and distrusted its commitment to Europe. In 1967, the UK again sought admission, along with Denmark, Ireland and Norway. Once again President de Gaulle vetoed their accession. But eventually, at a December 1969 summit meeting in the Hague, French President Pompidou and the other heads of government agreed to favor accession of the applicants. After nearly two years of negotiation, all four prospective members signed at Brussels a Treaty of Accession. Denmark, Ireland and the UK ratified the Treaty and entered the Communities on January 1, 1973. However, a referendum in Norway produced a narrow majority against its joining; although the referendum was not constitutionally required, the government chose not to proceed with accession.

What is often called the "second enlargement" of the Community began when Greece, Spain and Portugal, all freed from right-wing dictatorships, applied for membership. Greece joined, effective January 1, 1981, followed five years later by Spain and Portugal, thus bringing membership to a total of twelve. Because Community structures and policies had by then become so complex, enlargement required extended negotiations and elaborate transitional provisions. Transitional periods for phasing in various aspects of Community policy were as long as ten years in particularly sensitive areas like fishing rights.

The unification of Germany in 1990 did not necessitate any formal accession of East Germany or its constituent states. However, complex transitional provisions needed to be established in very short order. Community legislation, adopted at the end of 1990, set out the detailed adjustments, notably with respect to East European trade and the environment.

2. INSTITUTIONAL CHANGE

The 1960s and 1970s saw a number of important institutional changes apart from new memberships. An April 1965 "Merger Treaty," effective July 1, 1967, simplified the structure of the three Communities by providing for a shared Council and Commission (the latter thereby replacing the ECSC's High Authority), alongside the single Court and Assembly that were already in place.[7] An important structural improvement came in 1971, when the existing system of financial contributions from Member States was replaced by the Community's so-called "own resources" system, which automatically assigned to the Community all customs duties and agricultural levies as well as a share of each State's value added tax revenues, thus rendering the Community more fiscally independent and less vulnerable to national political pressures.

The European Parliament also underwent important structural change. Although EC Treaty Article 138 (renumbered as Article 190 by the Treaty of Amsterdam) contemplated from the start that Parliament would be directly elected, for twenty years it was composed of representatives from national parliaments. After years of urging by Parliament, the heads of government decided at the Paris summit of December 1974 to move to a system of direct elections, and the necessary legal action was taken by an act of the Council in 1976. The first popular election of Members of Parliament occurred in June 1979. The change has given Parliament greater moral and political authority and enhanced the Community's democratic character. In addition, in 1975 the Treaties were amended to give Parliament as of 1977 a role (albeit still a junior one) alongside that of the Council in adopting the Community budget.

3. THE EUROPEAN COUNCIL AND EUROPEAN POLITICAL CO-OPERATION

In December 1969, the heads of state or government convened at the Hague to discuss major policy issues affecting the Community, and it was

7. Treaty Establishing a Single Council and a Single Commission of the European Communities, April 8, 1965, J.O. 152/1 (July 13, 1967), Treaties Establishing the European Communities (EC Off'l Pub. Office, 1987).

there that agreement was reached to open negotiations with the four states that had applied for membership, to embark on an economic and monetary union, and to provide the Community with its own resources. The format proved useful for dealing with large issues of common concern and so-called summit meetings among the heads of state or government became frequent. The Member States thereafter agreed that such intergovernmental meetings would be held on a regular basis, and they became commonly (and rather confusingly) known as meetings of the "European Council." Since 1974, the heads of state or government (accompanied by their foreign ministers) have met two to four times a year as the European Council, presided over by the Member State that at the time holds the Presidency of the Council of Ministers.

The European Council, which has become the forum for airing sensitive political matters and for considering structural changes to the Community, was formally recognized in the Single European Act, effective 1987. It is treated more fully in Chapter 2 *infra.*

Following the 1969 summit, the European Council initiated a program of cooperation among the Member States in foreign policy that became known as European Political Cooperation (EPC). Later summit meetings of the 1970s and 1980s substantially reinforced EPC, which was further institutionalized in 1987 in the Single European Act. Joint actions and declarations in foreign affairs on the part of the Member States have now become so commonplace that it is easy to assume, erroneously, that these were a Community feature from the very beginning. The 1992 Treaty on European Union expanded the EPC field of action (notably to include security) and integrated it more fully into a larger entity, the European Union. A fuller discussion of EPC is deferred until Part V of the book.

4. TOWARD A MORE COMPLETE UNION

The 1970s and 1980s were also a period of intense self-examination on the part of the Community. With the expiry of the transitional period and the Community's considerable success in establishing the common market, the time seemed ripe for addressing certain institutional questions and possibly for charting new courses, including closer political union.

Political integration first received conspicuous attention at the 1974 Paris summit, at which the European Council commissioned a report on the possibility of a form of European Union. The 1975 Tindemans Report (named after the Belgian foreign minister) generated considerable discussion. By this time, the economic "crisis" of the mid–1970s was fully affecting Western Europe and, like the economy itself, the momentum associated with the Community appeared to have stalled. Political and institutional reform accordingly took on a new sense of urgency. There followed a number of further proposals, including a noted 1979 Report to the European Council by "Three Wise Men" (Messrs. Biesheuvel, Dell and Marjolin) on the subject of institutional and procedural reform, and a proposal for union jointly developed by the German and Italian foreign ministers, Genscher and Colombo.

However, the early 1980s was also a period of serious internal political differences, notably over reform of the common agricultural policy, Community financial difficulties and the UK's demand for a reduction in its budgetary contribution. Parliament meanwhile was demanding greater institutional power for itself. The 1983 European Council meeting in Stuttgart addressed some of these issues and produced a Solemn Declaration on European Union, affirming the Member States' aspirations "to achieve a comprehensive and coherent common political approach" and to build a European Union.[8]

Sentiment in favor of fundamentally reforming the Community was strong in certain Member States, notably Italy and Germany, and enjoyed particular resonance in the European Parliament. An Italian parliamentarian, Alfiero Spinelli, headed an effort by the Parliament to produce a blueprint for far-reaching constitutional change. In February 1984, a large parliamentary majority voted to support the resulting Draft Treaty Establishing the European Union,[9] prepared by Parliament's own Spinelli Committee. The Draft Treaty meant to replace the three basic Community treaties with a single constitutional document establishing a kind of European federal government. It would also have substantially increased the legislative and budgetary powers of Parliament and given it a power of appointment over the Commission and, to a lesser extent, the Court of Justice. These enhancements in parliamentary authority would have come largely at the expense of the Council, where the Member States find their most direct representation.

The European Council, now under pressure for reform, decided in June 1984 to establish a committee of its own to develop proposals for closer European integration. By the time the resulting Dooge Committee report (named after the Irish senator who chaired the committee) was presented to the Milan European Council in June 1985, the European Council had also received from the Commission its White Paper on Completing the Internal Market, with its ambitious set of legislative proposals for enactment before the end of 1992. At Milan the European Council approved both the Dooge Report and the White Paper, and created a pair of committees which in turn formulated more concrete constitutional proposals for completing the internal market, as well as for reforming the institutions, enlarging the Community's fields of action and heightening a sense of European identity.

5. THE SINGLE EUROPEAN ACT

Article 236 of the EC Treaty (replaced in 1999 by Article 48, formerly Article N, of the TEU) requires the convening of an intergovernmental conference for amendments to the Treaty. Such a conference was held in Luxembourg in the fall of 1985 to consider all the different proposals then before the European Council. The conference took place even though Denmark, Greece and the UK voted against holding it, and fortunately all twelve Member States chose to participate actively in the proceedings. Due to the substantial differences of views among the participants, the amendments to the EC and other treaties that were agreed upon at the conference reflect a number of compromises and "a careful tempering of integrationist impulses with preoccupations of national sovereignty."[10]

The resulting Single European Act, which entered into force on July 1, 1987, consists mostly of additions and modifications to the Community

---

8. Solemn Declaration on European Union, Bull. EC 1983/6, pp. 18–29, at 24.

9. O.J. C 77/33 (Feb. 14, 1984).

10. G. Bermann, The Single European Act: A New Constitution for the Community?, 27 Colum. J.Transnat'l L. 529 (1989).

treaties. Some of these changes are of a basically substantive character. The SEA's central focus was on completing the single internal market by the end of 1992, and it specifically promised in Article 8a of the EC Treaty (subsequently renumbered as Article 7a and then again renumbered by the 1999 Amsterdam Treaty as Article 14) that all technical, legal and fiscal barriers to trade between Member States would be eliminated by that date. The SEA also formally authorized legislative action in the areas of environmental protection, occupational safety and health, research and technological development and regional development, and it foresaw in a new Article 102a (replaced by Article 98) the creation of an Economic and Monetary Union.

Some of the SEA's most important changes were institutional in character. These included the introduction of a new legislative procedure giving Parliament some share in the legislative process, a broad increase in the number of fields where legislation could be adopted by a qualified majority vote of the Council instead of unanimity, and more extensive delegations of authority from the Council to the Commission. Reforms like expanded use of qualified majority voting were undertaken largely to facilitate political and legislative aspects of completing the internal market by the 1992 deadline, particularly with the Community then having twelve members in its Council. The extent to which the SEA advanced economic and political integration within the Community, as opposed to merely codifying practices which had developed over time, was initially the subject of lively debate.[11] It soon came to be recognized that the SEA brought significant change, but was also likely to be overtaken even in the short run by still further reform.

The structural changes introduced by the SEA proved highly effective in practice. Virtually all of the legislation proposed in the 1985 White Paper came to be adopted, even in fields (like banking, insurance and securities regulation, transport, intellectual property, telecommunications, taxation and public procurement) where progress had been limited or blocked for years. By the end of 1992, over 500 internal market measures had been adopted, promoting the harmonization and liberalization of rules and indeed revolutionizing commercial and financial law. In 1996, the Commission estimated that the internal market program had increased intra-Community trade by 20–30% and added measurably to the growth of GDP and levels of employment.

Meanwhile, enthusiasm for the internal market program, coupled with an awareness that the SEA was not in any event to be a final architectural blueprint, fueled still further efforts at institutional reform.

F.   THE MAASTRICHT TREATY AND THE EUROPEAN UNION

If 1992 represented the culmination of the Single Act's ambitious single market program, it also opened up still more significant vistas of reform. These included prospects both of a further "deepening" of the Community through a new TEU and a "widening" through enlarged membership.

---

11. See, e.g., H.–J. Glaesner, The Single European Act: An Attempt at an Appraisal, 10 Fordham Int'l L.J. 446 (1987); P. Pescatore, Some Critical Remarks on the Single European Act, 24 Common Mkt. L. Rev. 9 (1987).

Incited by proposals from the Commission, the Parliament and certain Member States (notably Germany under Chancellor Kohl and France under President Mitterand), the European Council at its meeting in Dublin in June 1990 agreed to open, not one, but two intergovernmental conferences in Rome the following December. The first conference dealt with the idea of a European Monetary Union and the second with various proposals for political union promising an extension of Community competences and further institutional and procedural reform. The conferences proved contentious, owing in part to British opposition to many of the proposals, but also to certain divisions even among States largely in favor of them. The conferences reported on the key issues to the Maastricht European Council in December 1991, where a compromise agreement was reached on a Treaty of Maastricht, which was formally signed on February 7, 1992, and became effective in November 1993. Like the intergovernmental conferences themselves, the provisions of the Maastricht Treaty fall into two main categories, one of them economic and monetary union, and the other political union.

1. ECONOMIC AND MONETARY UNION

The EC Treaty originally contained two chapters on economic and monetary coordination, with Article 2 citing the progressive approximation of Member State economic policies as a principal goal. Nonetheless, little had been achieved in this sector in the 1960s and the global monetary crises of the 1970s, if anything, led to greater nationalism in economic and monetary policy.

At a meeting in Bremen in 1978, the European Council finally agreed to create a European Monetary System (EMS). As set up the following year, the EMS provided for joint support among Member States in case of serious monetary instability in any one of them and more generally for increased cooperation among central banks. However, the EMS system is best known for its system of controlled exchange parities between national currencies and for its creation of an artificial currency unit, the ECU. Although the UK would not agree to participate in the EMS until over ten years had passed, the system largely achieved its goal of bringing about monetary stability within the Community.

The Single European Act added to the EC Treaty a new Article 102a which contemplated still further Treaty amendments with a view to creating an Economic and Monetary Union (EMU). At the invitation of the European Council meeting in Hanover, Germany in 1988, a committee of central bank directors and monetary experts convened by Commission President Delors produced in April 1989 a report to the next European Council meeting in Madrid outlining the essential features of an EMU. The European Council approved the "Delors Report" at Madrid and it was finally decided in 1990 at Dublin that the task of drafting appropriate Treaty language should be committed to an intergovernmental conference to be opened in Rome in December of that year.

In December 1991 at Maastricht, the European Council reached final agreement on the EMU. The Maastricht Treaty and related protocols (signed in February 1992, effective November 1993) committed the Member States over the course of the 1990s to bring about a convergence of their economic and monetary policies and to eliminate deficit spending while reducing inflation. In 1994, a European Monetary Institute (EMI) was created to coordinate the activities of the various central banks and to make recommendations on general monetary policy. 1994 also began a second stage in monetary coordination in which Member States without independent central banks were required to create one and States with excessive deficits had to eliminate them. There eventually followed the creation in May 1998 (effective January 1999) of a European System of Central Banks (ESCB), analogous to the US Federal Reserve System, with a European Central Bank (ECB) at its core. The Maastricht Treaty's amendments to the EC Treaty envisaged a final EMU stage in which the national currencies would be replaced by a single currency. Due to concerns expressed by the UK, the Maastricht European Council decided that the UK could opt out of the monetary control exercised by the European Central Bank and out of the single currency system for as long as it wished, but without prejudice to its joining at a later date.

2. POLITICAL UNION

As far as political union is concerned, the Maastricht Treaty pursued the same basic strategies that shaped the Single European Act: extending the Community's sphere of activity, streamlining the institutions' decisional procedures and improving the framework for a common foreign and security policy. It expanded the Community sphere to include formally such matters as health, education, tourism, culture and consumer protection, thus endorsing the Community's longstanding involvement in certain of these fields while of course promising more. Finally, the Maastricht Treaty expanded European Political Cooperation and brought it more closely into the Community framework.

Successful experience under the SEA led the drafters at Maastricht to extend the fields in which qualified majority voting obtained. However, the UK's strong opposition to such voting on social (mostly labor-related) legislation resulted in a compromise solution, a new Protocol on Social Policy. The Protocol, attached to the EC Treaty, enabled the other eleven Member States to adopt social legislation by a qualified majority vote, without that legislation applying to Britain. The Community thus to some extent adopted what is known as a "two-tiered Europe" approach as the price for extending its competence in the social domain.

Inevitable also was some further enhancement in the powers of the European Parliament. Under the Maastricht Treaty, Parliament won the right to approve the appointment of the Commission, and to request the Commission to initiate legislative proposals. Parliament's legislative role under the SEA's "parliamentary cooperation procedure" was extended to new areas, while, more importantly, in other areas (notably completion of the internal market) a new "parliamentary codecision procedure" was introduced. The latter gave Parliament an effective veto over new legislation.

Besides amending the three "Community" treaties (notably the EC Treaty), the Treaty of Maastricht brought with it a new "constitutive" treaty, namely the Treaty on European Union ("TEU"). As evidenced by its name, the TEU was meant to represent a decisive step in political integration. Although the UK prevented use of the term "federal," the Member States accepted the concept of a "European Union," whose core was now to be termed the "European Community" ("EC") rather than the "European Economic Community" (EEC), underscoring the centrality of the Community's non-economic goals. Through amendments to the EC Treaty, the Maastricht Treaty introduced provisions on European citizenship and the civil rights of European Union citizens, including the right to vote in and stand for local elections in one's place of residence, the right to travel freely within the territory of the Union, and the right to petition the European Parliament.

Most notably, the TEU established a new political entity, the "European Union" (or "EU"). The Union has been described as comprised of three "pillars": a "first pillar" consisting of the three existing European Communities (ECSC, EC and Euratom), a "second pillar" comprising the EU's system of a common foreign and security policy (CFSP), and a "third pillar" denoting a new sphere referred to obliquely as "cooperation in justice and home affairs." (The second and third pillars are commonly called "intergovernmental" to emphasize their separateness from the special legal structures and processes that characterize the European Community.) The EU is accordingly sometimes depicted as a "roof" connecting these three "pillars."

While Title I of the TEU established the EU as such, Titles II, II and IV brought amendments to the treaties that constituted the three communities. The most important of the amendments to the EC Treaty were mentioned earlier in this section. In establishing the second pillar, Title V repealed the provisions on cooperation in foreign and security policy that the SEA had introduced. Under the pillar structure, such cooperation still took place outside of the Community law framework—meaning outside the principles of Community law primacy and direct effect, outside the legal forms of Community law (regulations, directives, decisions), outside the scope of the Commission's enforcement powers as such, and outside the ambit of judicial review by the European Court of Justice and Court of First Instance.

Title VI of the TEU inaugurated the "third pillar" on cooperation in the fields of justice and home affairs—fields declared by the TEU to be "matters of common interest." Though the TEU left the term "justice and home affairs" undefined, it included within it asylum policy, immigration policy, combat against drug addiction and international fraud, judicial cooperation in civil and criminal matters, cooperation in customs affairs, and police cooperation in regard to terrorism, drug trafficking and other serious international crimes. Like the second pillar, this pillar operates outside the framework of Community law as such, and action under it remains basically intergovernmental. The emphasis is on Member State consultation and cooperation, and in the drafting of conventions for adoption by the States.

Despite the differences among the pillars, all three are served, according to TEU Article C (now TEU Article 3), by "a single institutional framework," consisting of the European Council and the principal "Community" institutions: the Council, Commission, Parliament, Court of Justice (and Court of First Instance), and Court of Auditors. However, within the second pillar, the Commission does not have its customary power of initiative; rather, it merely assists the Member States in their pillar two activities. For its part, the Parliament performs basically consultative functions. Within pillar three, the Commission shares a power of initiative with the Member States, while the

Parliament's functions are once again purely consultative. On the other hand, although the Council does not "legislate" as such under pillars two and three, it does exercise specific decisional authority. Article L of the TEU initially provided that the Court of Justice was without jurisdiction over the institutions in their actions within these spheres, but that was subsequently changed by the Treaty of Amsterdam (see TEU Article 46).

3.   RATIFICATION OF THE TEU

National processes for ratification of the TEU brought severe stresses to the surface. The June 1992 Danish referendum rejecting the TEU gave voice to misgivings over the scale and pace of political integration and the dangers of excessive centralization. However, the Irish electorate soon thereafter gave its support to the Treaty and the French did likewise, albeit by a very slim majority. After winning certain concessions from its partners and exercising its option not to participate in the third stage of EMU, the Danish government achieved a successful result in a second referendum held in May 1993.

Other States encountered difficulties too. For its part, the UK, after bruising parliamentary debates, eventually ratified the TEU, though opting out of the Social Protocol. The key event in German ratification was the Constitutional Court's so-called *Maastricht* ruling (see page 308 *infra*). That ruling—ultimately favorable to German ratification—enabled the European Council, at a special meeting in Brussels on October 29, 1993, to announce that the TEU would come into effect on November 1. But the TEU had plainly exposed popular sensitivities on the subject of European federalism.

The TEU, as it stands today, is found in Part I of the Selected Documents, document 2.

4.   POST–TEU ACCESSIONS

Having decided to "deepen" the Community before "widening" it, the Member States agreed to postpone acting on any new membership applications until the TEU had been ratified. But with its entry into force, the way to new accessions seemed clear. On January 1, 1995, Austria, Finland and Sweden became EU Members, bringing membership to fifteen. Their accession increased the population of the Union from 348.7 to 370.4 million, making it 40% more populous than the US. The Treaty of Accession of these states (and of Norway) was signed at the Corfu Summit of June 1994, a summit in which the heads of state or government of those four countries participated.[12] With Norway's subsequent decision not to accede (following a November 1994 referendum), the Act of Accession was itself amended in pertinent respects.[13] See generally R. Goebel, The European Union Grows: The Constitutional Impact of the Accession of Austria, Finland and Sweden, 18 Fordham Int'l L. J. 1092 (1995).

Even before the 1995 enlargement, EC–EFTA relations had been undergoing profound change. Following several years of negotiations, the two trading blocs had agreed in October 1991 to form on January 1, 1993 a new

12.   Treaty of Accession and Act Concerning the Conditions of Accession of the Kingdom of Norway, the Republic of Austria, the Republic of Finland, and the Kingdom of Sweden, and the Adjustments to the Treaties on which the European Union is Founded, O.J. C 241/21 (Aug. 29, 1994).

13.   Council Decision 95/1 of January 1, 1995, O.J. L 1/1 (Jan. 1, 1995).

entity known as the European Economic Area (EEA). Under the EEA Agreement, goods, persons, services and capital would flow freely among the participating states, on condition that the non-EU states accept virtually all Community harmonizing legislation, not only on trade, but also on a wider range of subjects including environmental and consumer protection, competition policy, company, securities, banking and insurance law and social policy. The prospect of being bound by EU rules without having participated in their making doubtless contributed to the readiness of certain EFTA states to join the EU. With the 1995 EU enlargement, the only EEA members that remain outside the EU are Iceland, Liechtenstein and Norway. (Switzerland is neither an EU nor an EEA member.)

While the accession of Austria, Finland and Sweden was achieved rather smoothly, and visibly augmented the Community's economic power by creating a still larger internal market, it also showed that enlargement stood to make decisional processes more difficult, both by increasing the size of the institutions and by making the achievement of consensus among the Member States more problematic.

5.   POST–TEU DEVELOPMENTS: INTERNAL AND EXTERNAL

Although 1992 brought the Maastricht Treaty, it did not bring an end to consolidation of the internal market program associated with that year. Each year since 1992, supplemental legislation has been adopted in various internal market fields, yielding progress, for example, in the recognition of professional diplomas and the right of residence for students and other non-workers. Since 1996, the Commission has also undertaken to simplify and codify the existing complex corpus of legislation through the "Simpler Legislation in the Internal Market" (or "SLIM") project.

In tandem with progress toward achieving an integrated economic market, the Community in the 1990s initiated important developments in employee rights and employment policy. Building on the 1989 Social Charter of the Rights of Workers (signed by all the Member States except the UK), the Commission inaugurated a new Social Action Program. Whether using the authority to legislate over worker health and safety, or exercising the Maastricht Treaty's Social Protocol (which again excepted the UK), the Parliament and Council enacted a series of important new social policy directives, such as those mandating protection of adolescent workers and pregnant workers, limiting working time, and requiring consultation with workers on matters relating to employment conditions. With the election of Prime Minister Blair's Labor government in 1997, the way was cleared for the UK to accept an end to the Social Protocol and to embrace the legislation that had been adopted under that Protocol.

At the same time, the persistence of high unemployment levels through the 1990s, and prompting from successive European Councils following the 1994 Essen Council, led the Commission to propose a series of action plans to create new jobs, retrain workers, and better exploit information technology. Anxiety over employment would subsist, however, and eventually culminate in the 1999 Treaty of Amsterdam's inclusion in the EC Treaty of the latest new policy chapter, on employment.

The 1990's also witnessed external relations developments crucial to the EU, including the GATT negotiations which ultimately led to the creation of the World Trade Organization. The negotiations, conducted by the EU as part of the Community's Common Commercial Policy, necessitated major reforms of the Common Agricultural Policy. At the same time, they raised serious institutional issues due to the fact that the WTO Agreement dealt with intellectual property and external trade in services—areas (unlike external trade in goods) in which the Community did not have exclusive power. An important opinion by the Court of Justice on WTO accession (discussed in Part V of this book) left a significant role for the Member States in the external aspect of these matters. That opinion in turn led to significant revisions of the EC Treaty provisions on the Common Commercial Policy.

Clearly the WTO dispute settlement system, in effect since 1997, has exerted a major impact on Community policy. To mention highlights only, the system has upheld other countries' WTO challenges to the Community's regulation of banana imports and ban on the importation of hormone-treated beef. (The system has, of course, also afforded occasional victories to the EU in its complaints against foreign government practices and policies.) The WTO became in these years a vital—though of course not the only—forum for sorting out EU–US economic relations.

G. ENLARGEMENT PROSPECTS AND THE TREATIES OF AMSTERDAM AND NICE

By the mid–1990s it was clear that the real enlargement stakes lay further to the East. In the aftermath of the fall of communist and socialist regimes in Central and Eastern Europe between 1989 and 1991, the EU entered into a series of association agreements with those countries, commonly called "Europe Agreements." The first two—with Poland and Hungary—entered into force in February 1994, with eight others following. These agreements created an association between the EU and the individual countries, entailing political dialogue, expansion of trade and economic relations, a phased adoption of competition rules and many internal market measures, financial and technical assistance, and eventual integration into the EU. The European Council decided in Copenhagen in June 1993 that, assuming they created and maintained democratic regimes, free markets, and adequate administrative infrastructure, the associated countries of central and eastern Europe should in time become EU members. The December 1994 European Council meeting in Essen outlined a "pre-accession strategy" and charged the Commission with producing a White Paper detailing it.

1. THE NEW APPLICANT STATES

By 1996, formal applications for membership had been filed by Hungary, Poland, Romania, Slovakia, Latvia, Estonia, Lithuania, Bulgaria, the Czech Republic and Slovenia. They joined the already pending applications of Turkey, Cyprus and Malta. The Commission charted the course of enlargement in a White Paper on Preparation of the Associated Countries of Central and Eastern Europe for Integration into the Internal Market of the Union.[14]

---

14. COM(95)163, EU Bull. 5–1995, point 1.4.63.

Following a detailed review of each applicant's situation, the Commission in July 1997 issued its recommendation on the opening of accession negotiations. Believing that six of the applicant countries (Hungary, Poland, Estonia, the Czech Republic, Slovenia and Cyprus) were likely to satisfy the conditions of membership in the medium term, the Commission recommended that negotiations be opened in 1998 with them alone. Later that year the European Council agreed, though it included all the applicant states in its "pre-accession strategy." As part of that strategy, the heads of state or government of the EU Member States have met periodically since March 1998 in a "European Conference" with their counterparts from the applicant states (except Turkey, which declined to participate) focusing on such issues as foreign and security policy cooperation, environmental protection and combat against organized crime.

Accession negotiations with the six began in March 1998 in a process that entailed reviewing 31 chapters covering all aspects of membership obligations and the applicant states' readiness to assume them. With the review process completed in fall 1999, the negotiations currently continue in earnest, with a focus on the issues that had emerged as most problematic, including agriculture, the environment, free movement of persons and the security of external frontiers. The Commission has subsequently produced annual country-by-country progress reports.

In October 1999, the Commission proposed that accession negotiations be opened with the additional applicant states of Latvia, Lithuania, Slovakia, Romania, and Bulgaria. (Malta, which had withdrawn but later reactivated its application, was added shortly thereafter.) In December, at Helsinki, the European Council agreed. At the same time, the Council advised Turkey that, while it was ultimately capable of membership, and that negotiations accordingly would at one point start, current democratic and economic considerations required their postponement.

The Commission has consistently placed its views on enlargement in a notably wide context. Its basic strategy, captured in a document entitled Agenda 2000: For a Stronger and Wider Europe, DOC/97/6 (July 15, 1997), was that enlargement could not satisfactorily proceed without a strengthening of Community policies, continued economic growth, modernization of employment systems, enhanced environmental protection, reform of the various EU Funds and of agricultural policy, and augmented financial resources. In the event, new regulations governing the Cohesion, Structural, Regional Development and European Social Funds were all adopted in June 1999.[15] In the case of no country have specific dates for accession been set. However, accession by at least some of the applicant states is foreseen as early as 2003 or 2004.

2. THE 1996–97 INTERGOVERNMENTAL CONFERENCE

The TEU (Article N) had mandated the holding of a new intergovernmental conference in 1996. But the prospects of enlarged Community membership and the continued unfolding of dramatic changes in Eastern Europe and the former Soviet Union—coupled with the unique challenges of constructing an economic and monetary union—confirmed its necessity. In March 1996, an Intergovernmental Conference was formally opened in Turin, Italy. It formal-

---

15. Bull. EU 6/99, at 38–40.

ly ended in June 1997, with political agreement on a Draft Treaty of
Amsterdam.

3. BACKGROUND DEVELOPMENTS

IGCs do not, of course, take place in a political vacuum, and the 1996 IGC
was no exception. Just as the IGC was opening, a serious dispute erupted over
the Community's response to the incidence of BSE (bovine spongiform encephalopathy or "mad cow disease") traceable to UK beef. When the Community imposed and maintained a series of bans on the marketing of beef and beef
products from the UK, the latter criticized the Community position as unduly
severe. Unsuccessful in its protests and efforts at persuasion, the UK announced in May 1996 a campaign of so-called "non-cooperation," under which
the UK government refused to participate in the decisions then before various
of the EU's political institutions, notably the Council. For a period, this policy
did in fact prevent the institutions from taking action requiring a unanimous
vote, although on a few occasions (e.g. votes on a trade agreement with
Algeria, on financial aid for the holding of Bosnian elections, and on the
association agreement with Slovenia), the UK relented and, as a good will
gesture, consented to vote.

By the time of the June 1996 summit in Florence, the Council was able to
agree on a conditional lifting of the ban and Britain terminated its formal
"non-cooperation." But that did not bring an end either to concern over mad
cow disease or to recriminations among the Member States over their handling of the danger.

While developments such as this heightened tensions within the EU,
other developments in this period strengthened EU cohesion. Probably none
was more important than the successful launch of the Economic and Monetary Union along the lines that had been sketched at Maastricht.

Recent developments in the Economic and Monetary Union are reserved
for a later chapter. Suffice it to say here that the second stage of evolution
toward EMU began on January 1, 1994, marked particularly by creation in
Frankfurt of the transition European Monetary Institute (EMI), composed of
a President and representatives of all States' central banks. Together with the
Commission, the EMI helped coordinate Member State monetary policies and
develop the legal framework necessary for the launch of the third stage of
EMU. During these years, every Member State made substantial (and in some
cases quite surprising) progress toward achieving most of the "convergence
criteria"—inflation rate, long-term interest rate, currency stability and deficit
spending—established at Maastricht for entry into the third stage.

Although persistently high unemployment rates led to levels of spending
that diminished certain governments' chances of satisfying the deficit spending criterion, the Council (in its extraordinary composition of Heads of State
or Government under what was then Article 109j and is now Article 121 of
the EC Treaty) was able to decide in May 1998, based on reports by the
Commission and the EMI, that all States other than Greece wishing to join
the third stage of EMU were qualified to do so as of January 1, 1999. (The
Council was subsequently able, in June 2000, to endorse Greece's entry.) Only
Denmark and the UK (both of which invoked the protocol permitting them to

"opt out") and Sweden (which deliberately persisted in a policy of not making its central bank independent) have remained outside.

In 1997 and 1998, essential regulations were adopted on the introduction of the Euro (whose value in relation to the participating national currencies was to be fixed as of January 1, 1999), as was a Stability and Growth Pact designed to ensure that States adopting the Euro maintain strict monetary policies and budgetary discipline and that non-adopting States make progress toward convergence. The European System of Central Banks (ESCB) came into being, with a European Central Bank (ECB) replacing the EMI and taking control of monetary policy for the States that had entered the third stage of EMU.

4. THE TREATY OF AMSTERDAM

Signed in October 1997, the Treaty of Amsterdam overcame the inevitable national referenda and court challenges more readily than the Maastricht Treaty had done. Nevertheless 18 months were required before the treaty received the necessary ratifications and could enter into force on May 1, 1999. Like the Maastricht Treaty, the Treaty of Amsterdam contains titles that amend the treaties establishing the three basic European Communities. But rather than constitute a new EU Treaty, it contents itself with amending the TEU. Thus, even after Amsterdam, the EC Treaty and the TEU, as amended, remain the fundamental constitutive texts.

A conspicuous feature of the Amsterdam Treaty is its wholesale renumbering of virtually all provisions in both the EC Treaty and the TEU. For persons accustomed to using "shorthand" numbered references to treaty articles, the changeover is bothersome; but the treaty organization is probably improved. At a minimum, users of this book will quickly have to become accustomed to the juxtaposition of the old and new numbers of treaty articles. (A convenient "conversion table" of article numbers of the EC Treaty and the TEU is found in Part I of the Selected Documents, document 3.)

Considering the effort expended on the preparatory IGC, the Treaty of Amsterdam is widely considered as disappointing in results and, in certain crucial respect, entirely inconclusive. This is not to say, however, that the Treaty is without innovation or complexity.

Among other things, the Amsterdam Treaty inserted into the TEU a new provision (now Article 7) setting out procedures for dealing with "serious and persistent" breaches by Member States of principles of democracy, human rights and the rule of law. These are dealt with in Chapter 6C *infra*. Also deserving special mention are new provisions of both the EC Treaty (Article 11) and the TEU (Articles 43–45, confined in their application to pillar three issues) entitled "Closer Cooperation: Flexibility." These provisions allow Member States "which intend to establish closer cooperation between themselves" to use the European Union's procedures and mechanisms for doing so. See Chapter 4F *infra*.

Another complexity of the Amsterdam Treaty is its provision for the progressive legislative establishment of an "area of freedom, security and justice," covering many issues (such as immigration from third countries, visas and asylum) that, since the TEU, had been subject to governance under the "third pillar" on justice and home affairs. To this extent, many "third pillar" items were effectively transferred to pillar one, including the essential provisions of the 1990 Schengen Convention (see *infra* Chapter 16). Heightening the complexity are the opportunities for derogation in the "area of freedom, security and justice" in favor of the UK, Ireland and, to a lesser extent, Denmark.

By contrast to pillar three, the TEU provisions on a common foreign and security policy were not radically altered at Amsterdam. Still, development of the CFSP is facilitated in several ways (e.g. provision for unanimous Council authorization of international agreements in the CFSP sphere, introduction of "constructive abstention" to relax the strait-jacket of unanimous voting, occasional qualified majority voting, and creation of a new office—the "High Representative" for CFSP)—dealt with in a later chapter of this book.

The Treaty of Amsterdam specifically addressed two policy areas. First, acting on a growing concern over persistently high unemployment levels, the Member States expressly made maintenance of a high level of employment an objective of the Union, thus adding a new EC Treaty title (VIII) on employment. The Community could encourage and complement Member State action (for example, through incentive measures), as well as issue recommendations to the Member States. Second, the Treaty integrated into the social policy chapter of the EC Treaty all of the topics previously covered by the Social Protocol and the Social Agreement (see *infra* Chapter 36). The Social Protocol, which had been necessitated by the UK's non-participation, was repealed, while the Social Agreement was essentially incorporated into the EC Treaty's Social Policy chapter, with legislative action generally speaking to be taken through the codecision rather than the cooperation procedure. At the same time, the Amsterdam Treaty extended the codecision procedure (EC Treaty Article 251, as renumbered) to new and important areas, while discarding the parliamentary cooperation procedure in all but one area of Community action (viz. certain decisions under EMU). Meanwhile, the codecision procedure was itself further simplified and unanimous voting sharply curtailed.

The Treaty of Amsterdam contained its share of special protocols. It notably added to the EC Treaty a protocol on the application of the principles of subsidiarity and proportionality, and a protocol on the role of the national parliaments within the EU.

For all its complexity, the Treaty of Amsterdam failed to resolve certain basic institutional questions, most urgently (in light of prospective enlargement) the number and allocation of Commissioners and the weighting of votes in the Council for "qualified majority" voting purposes. A "Protocol on the Institutions with the Prospect of Enlargement" (or "Enlargement Protocol") mandated that a further IGC be held at least one year before the EU membership exceeded twenty so as to tie up these technical, but contentious, "leftover" issues.

5. THE TREATY OF NICE

At meetings in Cologne and Helsinki in 1999, the European Council determined that the envisioned IGC should be convened in February 2000 and should conclude by the end of the year. On the table were not only the core institutional questions, but also such issues as extension of qualified majority voting and parliamentary co-decision, judicial reform, electoral reform for the

European Parliament, amendment of the treaties' "closer cooperation" provisions, revision of the treaties to render them more readable, and eventual adoption of a Charter of Fundamental Rights (whose drafting the European Council had entrusted to a special working group the previous year and which the Council eventually endorsed in September 2000 at Biarritz). In May 2000, the German Foreign Minister Joschka Fischer advanced ambitious plans for a stronger EU federation. But, while President Chirac gave them his support in principle, they were not in the end endorsed by the French Presidency or placed on the IGC agenda.

Like its predecessors, the Nice IGC took place in a somewhat politically charged atmosphere. Just prior to its opening, the EU experienced a major—fortunately not very protracted—crisis of confidence surrounding the Commission. As a result of investigations by committees of the European Parliament into the Commission's mismanagement and toleration of fraud in Community programs, Parliament considered but narrowly rejected two motions of censure. On March 15, 1999, however, a Committee of Independent Experts presented a report to the Commission and the President of the Parliament which severely criticized two particular Commissioners for certain acts and omissions and condemned President Santer and the Commission as a whole for failing to exercise proper supervision. On the same night as the report was issued, the Commission resigned as a whole, functioning thereafter only on an interim basis until a successor Commission was approved the following September. The episode and its political aftermath are more fully explored in this casebook's discussion of the Commission as an institution (*infra* Chapter 2).

The Council did not escape controversy in this period either. Surprising electoral gains by the right-wing Peoples' Party in Austria, headed by party leader Jorg Haider, caused the party to be included in the Austrian coalition government as a junior partner of the Conservatives under Prime Minister Schlüssel. Following a critical reaction throughout the European Union, the Portuguese presidency in February 2000 (pressured by Belgium, France and Germany, all keenly aware of their own sizeable extreme right-wing parties) urged the Member States to follow a policy of isolation of Austria. Although Austria continued to participate in Council meetings, its partners reduced bilateral contacts to an essential minimum and systematically gave other signals of official disapproval. The Austrian government bitterly protested, but the policy remained in effect until mid-September of 2000 when a committee of three "wise men" (former Finnish President Ahtisari, former Commissioner from Spain Oreja, and Jochem Frowein, director of the Max Planck Institute in Heidelberg) reviewed the Austrian situation and issued a report citing serious Austrian government efforts to combat racism and xenophobia. The Member States promptly ended their policy of modified ostracism.

In spite of—perhaps even because of—these difficulties, the Member States at the Nice IGC showed their determination to dispose of the institutional questions remaining from Amsterdam. The Enlargement Protocol to the Treaty of Nice, which remains to be ratified, addresses with specificity the composition of the Council, Commission and Parliament once all applicant states have acceded to the EU. Those details are reserved for a later chapter.

A special achievement loosely linked to the Nice Treaty is the Charter of Fundamental Rights, which had been endorsed by the European Council at Biarritz in October 2000 and then "proclaimed" at Nice, with the understanding that it might later actually be incorporated into the Treaties. Adoption of such a Charter had been decided upon by the Cologne European Council in June 1999, with its drafting entrusted by the European Council meeting at Tampere, Finland, the following October, to a special working group. As described in much greater detail in Chapter 6D, the Charter represents the first complete statement of rights pertaining to EU citizenship.

In other respects the Treaty of Nice pursues familiar strategies. It would extend qualified majority voting still further, to the point that only a handful of matters deemed most sensitive by one or more Member States would remain under the regime of unanimity. The Nice Treaty authorizes a further unburdening of the Court of Justice, necessitating the possibility of attaching specialized "judicial panels" to the Court of First Instance. In addition, it would relax the ground rules for the "closer cooperation," or flexibility, that the Treaty of Amsterdam had introduced. These matters are taken up in the relevant chapters of this book.

For the text of the Nice Treaty, including its prospective amendments to the EC Treaty and the TEU, see Part I of the Selected Documents, document 4.

Considering that the institutional issues were the focus of the Nice IGC and that a failure to dispose of them in anticipation of an unprecedentedly large wave of accessions would have been considered disastrous, the Treaty of Nice must be counted a success. As of this writing, however, the defeat of ratification of the Nice Treaty in a national referendum required by the Irish Constitution has put the timetable for the Treaty's entry into force into doubt and raised the prospect of substantive adjustments having to be made.

Like its predecessors, the Nice IGC acknowledged the need for a sequel intergovernmental conference in the not-too-distant future. A declaration identifies as among the ongoing issues: a more precise delineation of EU and Member State competences, the status of the Charter of Fundamental Rights, the role of national parliaments, further simplification of the Treaties, and the democratic legitimacy and transparency of the Union more generally. A next IGC—in which candidate States are invited as participants or observers, depending on whether or not their accession negotiations have been successfully concluded—is scheduled for 2004. In preparation, the Commission produced a White Paper on European Governance setting out its preliminary thoughts on these "governance" issues and inviting public comment. COM(2001) 428 (July 25, 2001). At its December 2001 Laeken Summit, the European Council decided to establish a hundred-member Convention, chaired by former French President Valery Giscard d'Estaing (and co-vice-chaired by former prime ministers Amato of Italy and Dehaene of Belgium) to draw up one or more blueprints for a European Constitution—this too in advance of the 2004 IGC.

6. ONGOING POLICY DEVELOPMENTS

During the pendency of this, as any, IGC, important policy developments continue to occur. In no area was this demonstrated more clearly than in competition policy. The globalization of markets, the recognized imperative of linking a free flow of goods and services with freedom of competition and market access, the increased visibility of cross-border mergers and cross-border cartels, and a growing cross-fertilization of ideas all combined to make competition policy in the EU a bourgeoning field of theory and practice. As later chapters will detail, one result has been a recent radical liberalization in the analysis of restraints in the course of distribution of products (vertical restraints) as well as in the procedures for analyzing them. Thus, the requirement of notification of agreements to the Commission has been curtailed while opportunities for group exemptions have been widened. Even more far-reaching plans for modernizing the process of dealing with agreements in restraint of trade are currently underway, permitting more regulatory activity to be performed at the Member State as compared to the Community level.

No less dramatic are developments on the merger front, such as the advent of "one-stop shopping" for large mergers of Community dimension, permitting the Commission to vet more mergers that would otherwise be reportable in three or more Member States. At the same time, some of the mergers having the greatest Community impact are increasingly international and global mergers, raising—as in the case of the Community's prohibition of the GE–Honeywell merger—the real prospect of international regulatory conflict. In parallel fashion, the firms whose behavior is most apt to be considered as a possible abuse of a dominant position under EC Treaty Article 82 (formerly 86) are firms operating in world markets. Once again, opportunities for conflict with overseas regulators abound. Thus, the Commission is investigating bundling behavior on the part of the Microsoft Corporation, just as US authorities are dropping their own bundling allegations against Microsoft. European authorities are among those most warm to the idea of placing competition regulation on a world level, possibly in the context of the WTO.

Notes and Questions

1. The European Community represents the most ambitious example of deliberate political and economic integration in recent times, possibly ever. Unlike the United States, whose federalism has evolved over a period of more than two centuries, the Community sought to create a fully-developed form of federation in a matter of three or four decades. What effect would you expect this concentration of effort to have on the priorities and means favored by the architects of European integration?

2. Despite repeated "reforms," the Community and Union frameworks continue to be criticized as unduly complicated, even obscure. Do you agree?

3. With the collapse of communism in Eastern Europe and the subsequent need to develop new political and economic policies toward that part of the world, the Community has had to reexamine its own priorities. What effect would you expect those developments to have on the nature and pace of European integration?

4. Note that major policy decisions within the EU are taken both through negotiation in intergovernmental conferences and through legislation and administration by the Community's political institutions. What do you suppose are the essential differences between these two modes of decisionmaking, and what difficulties might their coexistence present?

Chapter 2

THE TREATIES AND THE INSTITUTIONS

In this chapter, we examine the essential treaty framework on the basis of which the law and policy of the EC and the EU are framed. As the history related in Chapter 1 suggests, this framework is not a simple one. We necessarily also look at the institutions that have been put in place on the European level to make and administer that law and policy pursuant to the treaties. As later chapters will make clear, Member State authorities have a major, indeed daily, role to play in the implementation of this law and policy, but our institutional focus in the present chapter is on the European-level institutions.

A. THE TREATY FRAMEWORK OF THE EUROPEAN COMMUNITY AND THE EUROPEAN UNION

1. THE CONSTITUTIVE TREATIES

Each of the two entities with which this book is chiefly concerned—the European Community (EC) and the European Union (EU)—has its own constitutive treaty entered into by the Member States. (So too do the other two original and sector-specific Communities—the European Coal and Steel Community and Euratom—about which we shall have a good deal less to say. As noted in Chapter 1, the ECSC Treaty is being allowed to lapse in 2002 at the expiry of its 50–year term.[1])

The EC Treaty (formally the Treaty Establishing the European Community) and the TEU (Treaty on European Union) are commonly characterized as "constitutive" because they have given rise to institutions and processes of law independent of the Member States. The fact remains, however, that the law and policies thereby generated are still a product of international agreements. In signing and ratifying the treaties, the national authorities were thus obliged to follow their own domestic constitutional procedures for treaty-

---

1. Upon lapse of the ECSC in 2002, its assets and programs will be absorbed into the EC. O.J. C 190/1 (July 7, 1999).

making. In countries whose constitutions or legislation did not allow the transfer of competences contemplated by the treaties, appropriate constitutional or legislative adaptations had to be made.

With the passage of time, the EC Treaty has been importantly amended, notably by the Single European Act and by the Treaties of Maastricht, Amsterdam and (subject to ratification) Nice. It was in fact the Maastricht Treaty which also, through the TEU, brought a European Union into existence. The TEU was likewise to be importantly amended by the Treaties of Amsterdam and Nice. (The Amsterdam Treaty also thoroughly renumbered the articles of both the EC Treaty and the TEU.)

Distinguishing precisely between the nature and ambit of the EC and EU has not been altogether easy. In the vast majority of circumstances encountered in this book, the European institutions will have taken the actions in question in pursuit of an objective set out in the EC Treaty and will accordingly have invoked authority derived from a particular article of that treaty. To that extent we can properly speak of "a Community measure" or of "Community action."

The European Union denotes a functionally broader entity.[2] Indeed all that is accomplished pursuant to the EC Treaty (as well as the ECSC and Euratom Treaties) is said to have taken place under the Europe Union's "first pillar." The EU also consists of two other "pillars," known today as the TEU's "pillar two" ("Provisions on a Common Foreign and Security Policy," found in TEU, title V) and "pillar three" ("Provisions on Police and Judicial Cooperation in Criminal Matters," found in TEU, title VI). The activities in which the institutions engage by virtue of the second and third pillars are commonly referred to as "intergovernmental" in nature or as constituting "forms of cooperation," so as to differentiate them from the lawmaking *strictu senso* that is contemplated by the EC Treaty.

Some confusion in this regard arises from the fact that the same major European institutions which we explore below in this chapter—the Council, Commission, Parliament and the courts—derive authority both from the EC Treaty (and the other two Community treaties), on the one hand, and from the TEU, on the other. The fact remains that, since each of the three Communities as well as the EU springs from a different constitutive treaty, each is a distinct legal entity with a separate legal existence. While they may share common institutions, these institutions may only act pursuant to the powers and procedures set out in the treaty establishing the entity under whose authority they are at any given point acting.

Notes and Questions

1. In principle, the EC Treaty governs *all* economic sectors within the territory of the Member States. Accordingly, even today, to the extent the ECSC or Euratom Treaties do not provide a rule on a particular matter within the coal, steel or atomic energy sectors, the provisions of the EC Treaty apply. The ECSC and Euratom Treaties are therefore not, in any strong sense, "preemptive." On the other hand, where specific provisions of the ECSC or Euratom Treaties do apply, EC Treaty Article 305 (ex 232) specifies that they take precedence over any

---

2. The TEU (art. 1) describes the Union as "founded on the European Communities, sup- plemented by the policies and forms of cooperation established by this Treaty."

contrary provisions of the EC Treaty. Despite the separateness of the three Community treaties, the Court of Justice has on occasion consulted one of them in interpreting or filling gaps in another. See, e.g., Geitling v. High Authority, Case 13/60, [1962] ECR 83, 102; Meroni v. High Authority, Case 9/56, [1957–1958] ECR 133, 139–41.

2.   Precisely because they are "constitutive," the treaties may receive a broader construction than international agreements typically receive. For an early illustration, consider the case of Fédération Charbonnière de Belgique v. High Authority (Fédéchar), Case 8/55, [1954–1956] ECR 245 (see page 107 *infra*), where the Court of Justice had to decide whether the High Authority enjoyed price-fixing powers in circumstances other than those expressly set out in the ECSC Treaty. Addressing the Court, Advocate–General Lagrange acknowledged that international treaties traditionally receive a narrow interpretation. He remarked, however, that "although the [ECSC] Treaty ... was concluded in the form of an international treaty and although it unquestionably is one, it is nevertheless, from a material point of view, the charter of the Community, since the rules of law which derive from it constitute the internal law of that Community." [1954–1956] ECR at 277. Partly on this basis, the Advocate–General concluded that the High Authority's duty to "ensure that the objectives set out in this Treaty are attained" (ECSC Treaty, art. 8) permitted it to fix prices even in the absence of explicit authorization by the Treaty to do so. The Court reached that result.

3.   As we shall see in later chapters, the Court of Justice treats the constitutive treaties as creating a "new legal order" which is governed by its own rules, rather than as ordinary international agreements construed according to conventional international law principles. In its 1986 *Les Verts* judgment, discussed at page 130 *infra*, the Court described the EC Treaty as the Community's "basic constitutional charter." [1986] ECR 1339, 1365.

2.   OTHER BASIC COMMUNITY TREATIES

Besides the treaties establishing the three original Communities and the European Union, the Member States have entered into a number of other agreements relating to the organization and functioning of the Community. Some of these have resulted in amendments to the constitutive treaties, while others have not.

A first set of treaties worth mentioning in this regard are purely institutional. Even though the drafters had as of 1957 created three separate Communities, they could not justify maintaining a complete separation of institutions. The Member States accordingly entered at that same time into a convention establishing a single Assembly (later the Parliament) and a single Court of Justice for all three Communities.[3] Eventually a 1965 Merger Treaty was adopted, combining the ECSC High Authority and the Commissions of the EC and Euratom into a single Commission of the European Communities, and merging the Councils of the three communities into a single Council.[4]

Basic budgetary reforms likewise have been introduced through treaties among the Member States. A First Budgetary Treaty of 1970 was based on a Council decision of that year replacing the system of Member State contribu-

---

3. Convention on Certain Institutions Common to the European Communities, March 25, 1957, Treaties Establishing the European Communities (EC Off'l Pub. Office, 1987).

4. See Chapter 1, note 7 *supra*.

tions to the Community with one giving the latter its own resources. It also conferred on the Parliament limited budgetary powers that were later enhanced by a Second Budgetary Treaty of 1975. With the Treaty of Maastricht, the budgetary provisions were formally integrated into the EC Treaty.

A third category of fundamental treaties are those by which new Member States have acceded to the European Union. To each of these treaties was annexed an Act of Accession setting out in considerable detail the terms and conditions of accession. Under Article 49 (ex O) of the TEU, applications for admission may be approved by the Council acting unanimously, after obtaining the opinion of the Commission and the assent of an absolute majority of Parliament. Accession treaties are entered into between the applicant state and the existing Member States (rather than the EU as such), and require ratification by each State in accordance with its own constitutional procedures.

3. AMENDMENTS TO THE EC AND EU TREATIES

Like other international instruments, the European treaties are subject to amendment. The amendment process, set out for all the treaties in TEU Article 48 (ex N), is particularly important in view of the Community's anticipated longevity. (The EC and EU Treaties are, by their terms, of unlimited duration.)

As TEU Article 48 states, proposals for treaty amendments may be made either by Member States or by the Commission. If the Council so decides, after consulting Parliament (and where appropriate the Commission and European Central Bank), it may convene a conference of Member State representatives for the purpose of considering such proposals. Article 48 does not require unanimous Council support for holding an intergovernmental conference,[5] and the 1985 Luxembourg conference that produced the SEA was in fact convened over the objections of Denmark, Greece and the UK.

On the other hand, Article 48 requires intergovernmental conferences, once convened, to act by common accord. In addition, amendments to the constitutive treaties have to be ratified by all Member States. Intergovernmental conferences accordingly operate in a climate of consensus decision-making and tend to produce compromise solutions.

Notes and Questions

1. Note that although the Council does not have authority to propose treaty amendments, it alone may convene an intergovernmental conference to prepare amendments. The European Parliament likewise lacks authority to initiate proposed amendments, although it needs to be consulted. Do these ground rules make sense?

2. Do you attach any significance to the fact that accession agreements are entered into among the Member States, new and old, rather than between the new member or members and the Community (or Union) itself?

NOTE ON THE SOURCES OF COMMUNITY LAW

In the continental European tradition it is customary to identify the authoritative "sources" of law for any given legal system. Within the EU, the

---

5. EC Treaty Article 205(1) (ex 148) provides that, unless otherwise specified, the Council acts by a majority of its members.

constitutive treaties, along with the other basic treaties we have identified, clearly constitute the primary sources of law. Secondary sources consist chiefly of the legally binding acts adopted by the European institutions. As Chapter 3 explains, these acts include the voluminous regulations, directives and decisions issued from time to time by the Council or the Commission. Secondary sources also include the treaties to which the EU or EC itself is a party, including trade and association agreements with third countries entered into under EC Treaty Articles 133 (ex 113) and 310 (ex 238), respectively.[6] Both of these types of agreements are dealt with in Part V of this book, as are certain "mixed" agreements with third countries entered into by *both* the Community *and* the Member States because their subject matter is considered to fall only partly within the Community law sphere.

We also defer until Part V of the book the further question of the place that international treaties to which the European Community is a party occupy within the hierarchy of European Community law. Likewise deferred is the broader question of the relationship between European Community law and customary international law. We note only that this question has arisen, with indications from the Court of Justice that both Community treaties and rules of customary international law take precedence over Community legislation. See A. Racke GmbH & Co. v. Hauptzollamt Mainz, Case C–162/96, [1998] ECR I–3655.

To what extent decisions of the Court of Justice and Court of First Instance constitute formal sources of Community law is a matter best left to Chapters 5 and 6, which discuss the courts and the legal effect of their judgments. Suffice it here to mention that the Court of Justice considers the institutions and the Member States alike to be bound by the Court's interpretations of Community law and also by certain "general principles of law," such as the principles of proportionality and legitimate expectations (see Chapter 5 *infra*) and various fundamental rights which the Court has recognized in its case law (see Chapter 6 *infra*). These general principles not only constitute sources of Community law, but sources superior in rank to the Community's secondary legislation.

Does a convention among the Member States (and to which the EC as such is not a party) have a Community law character merely because it deals with a subject related to the purposes of the Community? The answer is probably no, with the result that such treaties do not share the special legal force and effect of Community law within the Member States. By the same token, the Commission presumably has no enforcement powers with respect to them and the Court of Justice presumptively lacks authority to interpret their terms in the way that it interprets Community law proper.

A good example of a non-Union treaty closely linked to Community objectives was the Schengen Convention of June 19, 1990, eliminating controls at the common borders of seven participating states. (Other Member

---

6. See Demirel v. Stadt Schwäbisch Gmünd, Case 12/86, [1987] ECR 3719; Hauptzollamt Mainz v. C.A. Kupferberg & Cie, Case 104/81, [1982] ECR 3641; Haegeman v. Belgium, Case 181/73, [1974] ECR 449.

States, but not all, subsequently joined, as did two non-EU States, viz. Norway and Iceland.) As noted in Chapter 1, the Amsterdam Treaty formally brought the Schengen arrangement into the Community law framework ("pillar one"), while still maintaining the special position of Denmark and the exclusion of the UK and Ireland. In order to facilitate the transfer, the Council issued Decision 1999/436/EC assigning a specific legal basis in the EC Treaty to each provision of the Schengen agreement. For a fuller discussion, see Chapter 16 of the casebook.

Is the situation any different when the EC Treaty expressly contemplates the establishment of a given convention. Article 293 (ex 220) calls on the Member States "so far as is necessary" to negotiate reciprocal agreements on nondiscrimination against nationals of other EC States, avoidance of double taxation, mutual recognition of companies and the merger of companies of different nationality, and finally "the simplification of formalities governing the reciprocal recognition and enforcement of judgments of courts or tribunals and of arbitration awards." Pursuant to this provision, the Member States in 1968 concluded a Convention on Jurisdiction and Enforcement of Judgments in Civil and Commercial Matters, otherwise commonly known as the Brussels Convention. The Convention governs jurisdiction and the enforcement of foreign judgments in Member State courts.

Shortly after signature of the Brussels Convention, the Member States entered into a Protocol conferring jurisdiction on the Court of Justice to render preliminary rulings on the interpretation of the Brussels Convention,[7] in effect conceding that the Convention does not by itself constitute Community law. Moreover, the Acts of Accession to the Community have uniformly obligated new Member States "to accede to the conventions provided for in Article [293] ... and to the protocols on the interpretation of those conventions by the Court of Justice" and "to enter into negotiations with the original Member States in order to make the necessary adjustments." This further suggests that such conventions, as distinct from the obligation to accede to them, do not themselves form part of Community law.

The Brussels Convention, amplified by a subsequent Lugano Convention on the same subject, has in fact subsequently been converted from an international agreement into Community legislation, by way of Council Regulation (EC) No. 44/2001, of December 22, 2000, on Jurisdiction and the Recognition of Enforcement of Judgments in Civil and Commercial Matters, (O.J. L012, 12/01/2001 P.0001–0023). We deal with the Conventions, the Regulation and related matters in Chapter 38.

B. THE INSTITUTIONS

Considering their scale of governance and range of concerns, the European Community and European Union enjoy a relatively simple institutional structure. This is to some extent due to the fact that enforcement of European law and policy is heavily entrusted to Member State administrative authorities, and that courts of the Member States rather than the Community bear primary responsibility for securing their observance.

---

7. Protocol Concerning the Interpretation by the Court of Justice of the Convention of 27 Sept. 1968 on Jurisdiction and Enforcement of Judgments in Civil and Commercial Matters, 75/464, O.J. L 204/28 (Aug. 2, 1975).

Focusing on the European Community, we can identify four major institutions.[8] Three of them—the Council, the Commission and the European Parliament—share the political tasks of making and administering Community law at the European level. The fourth is the Court of Justice which, aided by a more recently created Court of First Instance, represents the Community's judicial arm. All four institutions date back to the ECSC Treaty, but since the 1965 Merger Treaty have served the three European Communities in common. TEU Article 5 (ex E) refers to the same institutions as serving the European Union.

Although the institutions still bear a striking resemblance to those of the 1950s, they have undergone a distinct evolution in their respective powers and functions. Much of this evolution—e.g., the steady increase in the administrative power of the Commission and in the doctrinal authority of the Court of Justice—has been gradual. Other aspects stem from structural and procedural reforms brought about by the Single European Act and the Treaties of Maastricht, Amsterdam and Nice, all of which have notably increased the legislative power of the Parliament. This evolution is of course ongoing, and the years ahead will doubtless see further intergovernmental conferences bringing further institutional change.

During this period, a good deal of activity also occurred outside the institutional framework of the European Community. Much of it took place in the hands of the heads of state or government of the EC Member States assembled in an intergovernmental formation that came to be known as the European Council. (The European Council's functions are dealt with in a later section of this chapter.) When the Maastricht Treaty came into effect in 1993, the new European Union, although intergovernmental in nature and lacking legal personality, required some institutional structure in order to operate in pillars two and three. Under both pillars, the Council serves as the decision-making organ, which helps explain why the Council formally changed its name to the Council of the European Union (or EU Council).[9] The Commission (whose official name remains the Commission of the European Communities) shares with the Member States the power of initiative in proposing pillar three actions and may be called upon by the Council to assist in matters under pillar two. The Parliament is to be kept informed of developments under the second pillar and on specified issues must be consulted. (The Court of Justice has no role in pillar two and a very limited one—discussed below in this chapter—in pillar three.)

1. THE COUNCIL

The Council (or the Council of Ministers, as it is sometimes called to distinguish it from other "Councils") does not have a perfect analogue among conventional government structures at the nation-state level.

Within the framework of the European Community, the Council functions as a kind of collective head of state of the European Community, deciding external trade policies and concluding international agreements. The Council also exercises primary legislative power within the Community, although it

---

8. EC Treaty Article 7 (ex 4) identifies the Community institutions, including among them the Court of Auditors.

9. Council Decision 93/591, O.J. L 281/18 (Nov. 16, 1993).

now shares that power with the European Parliament through the introduction into the EC Treaty of legislative procedures requiring the participation of both bodies. By virtue of some of this legislation, the Council's legislative authority has been delegated to the Commission. Viewed structurally, the Council consists of representatives of the governments of the Member States, voting in the name of their State and (to the extent qualified majority voting obtains) with a voting strength crudely weighted according to the State's relative population size. The Council thus resembles in some degree a head of state in status, a legislature in function and an assembly of constituent states in structure.

The Council also has significant decisional (though technically not "legislative") authority under the TEU's pillars two and three. The circumstances are discussed in the relevant chapters of this book.

Article 203 (ex 146) of the EC Treaty states that the Council is to be composed of a representative of each Member State "at ministerial level" authorized to commit that member State's government. (Originally, Member States could be represented in the Council only by government ministers, but the term "representative . . . at ministerial level" was introduced by the Maastricht Treaty so as to permit representatives of the German *Länder* to act in the name of Germany in the Council as appropriate.) It is commonly the Ministers of Foreign Affairs who come together as the Council. When they meet as the Council on institutional or internal affairs, they are known as the "General Affairs Council," as distinct from the "Foreign Affairs Council," the name used when they meet for purposes of action under the Common Commercial Policy (i.e. external economic relations) or under pillar two (the Common Foreign and Security Policy). When a meeting concerns a specialized subject, such as transport, agriculture or finance, the Council may consist of the relevant ministers (or pairs of ministers, when two distinct matters— foreign affairs and agriculture, for example—are involved). With the advent of EMU, Council meetings of the economic and finance ministers (known for short as the Ecofin Council) are increasingly common. In April 2000, the Council set at 16 its maximum number of different "compositions."

The Presidency of the Council is held for a six-month term, typically rotating among the Member States in a substantially modified alphabetical order. Article 203 empowers the Council to decide upon the order by unanimous decision Recently, the order has been drawn up to ensure that a large state—France, Germany, Italy, Spain or the UK—holds the Presidency at least once in every third six-month period. Besides increasing the frequency of Presidencies by large states (as was its purpose), the pattern ensures that at least one large state will at all times participate in the Council's "troika" system, described just below. Sweden and Belgium held the Presidency in 2001, and Spain and Denmark will do so in 2002. On the presidency, see B. Schloh, The Presidency of the Council, 25 Syr. J. Int'l L. 93 (1998).

The Council meets when convened by its President, whether on the latter's own initiative or at the request of a Member State or the Commission. It meets frequently, over 80 times a year on the average, usually in Brussels. In recent years, the Presidency has assumed increased importance as each Member State in succession uses its term to advance certain agenda items. In the interest of continuity, a "troika" staff has been established, consisting in part of representatives of the immediate past and future Presidents.

As a legislator, the Council operates under special constraints. In the first place, the Commission has exclusive authority to initiate legislation. Thus, a Commission proposal is required before the Council may consider and adopt virtually any legislative measure. Article 208 (ex 152) allows the Council to instruct the Commission to undertake studies and submit proposals, but this rarely occurs. Further, the Single European Act and the Maastricht, Amsterdam and (prospectively) Nice Treaties have brought the European Parliament into the legislative process in decisive ways taken up in Chapter 3. Finally, as we know, the Council does not enjoy plenary legislative power, the scope of its legislative authority being specified in various articles of the EC Treaty.

In international affairs, the Council plays a leading role. As amended, Article 300 (ex 228) authorizes the Council to approve most international agreements between the Community and other states or international organizations. Such agreements may be entered into by the Council by qualified majority vote, except in the case of association agreements under Article 310 (ex 238) or when the agreement covers a field on which the Council can legislate internally only if it acts unanimously. The Council is required to consult the European Parliament before concluding any international agreement, with the exception of commercial agreements under Article 133 (ex 113); in some instances (e.g. agreements by the Community establishing an association involving reciprocal rights and obligations, common actions or special procedures, or agreements having important budgetary implications for the Community), the Parliament must not only be consulted but its assent must be had. Agreements for the accession of new Member States are separately addressed by TEU Article 49 (ex O): both unanimity in the Council and parliamentary assent are required. The legal aspects of the EU's external relations are covered in a subsequent chapter.

Article 202 (ex 145) describes the Council's internal functions in general terms as "ensur[ing] that the objectives set out in [the] Treaty are attained." More specifically, it calls upon the Council to "ensure coordination of the general economic policies of the Member States," to "take decisions," and to "confer on the Commission, in the acts which the Council adopts, powers for the implementation of the rules which the Council lays down"—all of this, however, to be accomplished "in accordance with the provisions of [the] Treaty." Of course, particular articles of the EC Treaty assign the Council still more precise tasks. Every measure is required to be taken in the manner set out in the Treaty articles governing the matter in question, be it agriculture, commercial policy, competition law or the free movement of goods, persons, services or capital. Finally, although the Parliament and the Commission are also importantly involved, the Council has the chief role in the budgetary process described in Chapter 3C.

The EC Treaty specifies the manner of Council voting. On certain matters, such as the procedure for accession of new states or the harmonization of tax legislation, unanimity is still required. In rare non-legislative instances (notably in adopting internal rules of procedure), a simple majority vote suffices. Today, by far the most widespread manner of voting is by qualified majority. Qualified majority voting (QMV) originally applied in a relatively small number of sectors, such as agriculture, transport, competition law and commercial policy. However, every major Treaty amendment starting with the Single European Act (in the area of harmonizing national laws in aid of the internal market) has expanded the scope of application of QMV to the point that it is now the decidedly preponderant voting formula in the Council.

Qualified majority voting is outlined in Article 205 (ex 148) as follows:

1. Save as otherwise provided in this Treaty, the Council shall act by a majority of its members.

2. Where the Council is required to act by a qualified majority, the votes of its members shall be weighted as follows:

Belgium	5
Denmark	3
Germany	10
Greece	5
Spain	8
France	10
Ireland	3
Italy	10
Luxembourg	2
Netherlands	5
Austria	4
Portugal	5
Finland	3
Sweden	4
United Kingdom	10

For their adoption, acts of the Council shall require at least:

—62 votes in favour where this Treaty requires them to be adopted on a proposal from the Commission,

—62 votes in favour, cast by at least 10 members, in other cases.

Under qualified majority voting all of a Member State's votes must be cast as a bloc. Since the total number of votes in the Council under qualified majority voting is now 87, the "blocking minority" is set at 26. The formula is designed in part to secure the interests of the larger states. Simple calculation shows that the opposition of three large states will defeat a proposal in a qualified majority vote, but that the opposition of the five smallest ones will not. On the other hand, the support of the five largest states is not sufficient for the passage of legislation; at least three of the smaller states must also support it. Significantly, each time the Community's membership has grown, the numbers in the qualified majority formula have been changed to produce a similar sort of equilibrium. What are the logical premises of the qualified majority voting system? Are they sound? How does the system compare with state representation rules in the US Congress?

Among the Member States' main objectives at the Nice Intergovernmental Conference was to decide upon the future re-weighting of votes in the Council in anticipation of expanded EU membership. The Treaty of Nice provides that, as of January 1, 2005, the weighting of votes among the current Member States should be as follows:

Belgium	12
Denmark	7
Germany	29
Greece	12
Spain	27
France	29
Ireland	7
Italy	29
Luxembourg	4
Netherlands	13
Austria	10
Portugal	12
Finland	7
Sweden	10
United Kingdom	29

Of this total of 237 votes, at least 170 would be required for the passage of legislation by qualified majority. In addition, where the EC Treaty requires measures to be adopted upon proposal by the Commission, a majority of Member States would have to have cast their votes in favor of the measure. (In the case of all other measures, the fraction rises to 2/3 of the Member States.) Finally, any State could demand verification that the total population among the States supporting the measure constitutes 62% of the total EU population; if verification is demanded and cannot be shown, the measure could not be enacted. In short, adoption would require a *triple* majority: a qualified majority of total Member State votes, a majority (or in some cases a qualified majority) of Member States, and a qualified majority of the EU population.

By increasing the vote allocation of each current Member State, the IGC cleared the way for assigning smaller vote allocations to new Member States having small populations. A Declaration on Enlargement, while keeping vote numbers for the current Member States at the levels prescribed for January 1, 2005, assigns Council votes to the applicant States as follows:

Poland	27
Romania	14
Czech Republic	12
Hungary	12
Bulgaria	10
Slovakia	7
Lithuania	7
Latvia	4
Slovenia	4
Estonia	4
Cyprus	4
Malta	3

Upon the accession of all twelve, the combined total of Council votes would be 345. Passage of legislation by qualified majority would require at least 258 votes, cast by either a majority of Member States (for measures requiring a proposal from the Commission) or 2/3 of the Member States (for all other measures). The requirement that it be shown, upon demand by a Member State, that the supporting States account for 62% of the total EU population, would continue to apply. Obviously, if the twelve applicant States do not all accede at the same moment in time, temporary adjustments in the qualified majority threshold of weighted votes will have to be made.[10]

The Council does not consist merely of government ministers (one per State) convening as the occasion requires. The Council is assisted by a large technical and administrative staff of several, based in Brussels. (The Council also has its own Legal Service of over 30 lawyers functioning entirely independently of the Commission Legal Service. Its Director–General Jean–Claude Piris served as general counsel for both the Amsterdam and Nice IGCs.) The Council's highest staff level is known as COREPER, an acronym for the French term for "Committee of Permanent Representatives." As its name suggests, COREPER, whose existence is recognized in EC Treaty Article 207 (ex 151), consists of permanent representatives of the Member States. These representatives conduct a preliminary review of all legislative measures before they go to the Council. COREPER in turn is assisted by both standing and ad hoc working groups of a technical and/or policy character. The advice of these national officials, as well as of ministry staff in the home capitals, informs the permanent representatives and, through them, the ministers who on any given occasion constitute the Council. In many instances, COREPER is able to work out an agreement and forward a proposal for routine approval by the Council; in other cases, COREPER isolates the major unsettled issues and sends them to the Council for their specific resolution if possible. Through their expertise, COREPER and the Council staff enable the Council to scrutinize the technical and policy proposals of the Commission, and their input understandably strengthens the Council in its dealings with the Commission.

As one might expect with such an institution, all Council meetings require simultaneous translation into all official languages, and are canceled or postponed if that is not possible. All draft texts must be presented in all languages.

NOTE ON THE LUXEMBOURG ACCORD

The "Luxembourg Accord," at one time prominent and controversial, has become mostly a historical footnote, albeit a quite interesting one. In 1965, the Commission under President Walter Hallstein proposed that the Community have its own source of revenues and that the Parliament share in the budgetary process, proposals that were ultimately to be adopted in the 1970s. Irritated by these proposals, President de Gaulle ordered an end to French participation in Community meetings for a six-month period. Through this "empty chair" policy, de Gaulle managed not only to block Commission proposals for the period, but also to prevent Hallstein's renewal as Commission President. At a special session in Luxembourg in January 1966, the Member State Governments defused the crisis by issuing a statement com-

---

10. See the Declaration on the Qualified Majority Threshold and the Number of Votes for a Blocking Minority, agreed upon at Nice in December 2000. The Declaration recognizes that when some but not all of the applicant States accede to the EU, the percentage of votes constituting a qualified majority will be lower than the percentage required as of January 1, 2005. It provides for the applicable percentage to progressively increase until it reaches 73.4%.

monly but misleadingly known as the Luxembourg Accord (occasionally also as the Luxembourg Compromise). The statement provided that where decisions could be taken in the Council by majority vote, but one or more States raises objections on the basis of very important interests, the Council "will endeavor, within a reasonable time, to reach solutions which can be adopted by all the Members of the Council while respecting their mutual interests and those of the Community." In a separate article, the Accord recited the French position that where such issues are at stake, "the discussion must continue until unanimous agreement is reached." Finally, it recorded a divergence of views among the then six Member States as to what should be done in the event of a failure to reach complete agreement, while adding the cryptic observation that "[t]he six delegations nevertheless consider that this divergence does not prevent the Community's work being resumed in accordance with the normal procedure."

Clearly, the Luxembourg Accord did not reflect much of an agreement. Beyond that, it had no solid constitutional footing for, in effect, it sought to modify the Treaty provisions on majority voting without following the Treaty's amendment procedures (then EC Treaty Article 236, now TEU art. 48). On the other hand, the Luxembourg Accord did reflect the customary practice of the Council until the 1980s. Decisions deemed politically sensitive by one or more Member States would in fact not be taken by qualified majority vote even though the terms of the Treaty permitted that. Decision-making by consensus—admittedly easier in a Community of six—became the rule.

Virtually every significant reform proposal of the 1970s and 1980s condemned the Luxembourg Accord as a return to intergovernmentalism and called for the restoration of true majority voting. Even after States later began failing in their attempts to invoke the Accord (as when, in 1981, the UK failed to block an increase in agricultural support until the other States agreed to reduce the UK's budgetary contribution), the Accord was not formally repudiated.

With the progressive displacement of unanimity by qualified majority voting under the Single European Act and the Treaties of Maastricht, Amsterdam and Nice, the Luxembourg Accord became less tenable than ever. Since the entry into force of the SEA, even the larger Member States have allowed themselves to be outvoted on measures they strongly opposed. (Germany and Denmark, for example, did not attempt to block the adoption of automobile emission standards they considered much too weak, and the UK accepted securities law measures that it feared would adversely affect the London financial center.)

NOTE ON THE EUROPEAN COUNCIL

As mentioned in Chapter 1, the heads of state or government of the Member States began as early as the 1960s the custom of holding summit meetings to discuss Community policy issues. This body, supplemented by the President of the Commission, has come to be known as the European Council. Since 1974, European Council meetings have been held regularly—at least twice or three times a year—in the State then holding the six-month Presidency of the Council of the European Union. A declaration adopted by the

Member States at Nice stipulates that, starting in 2002, half the annual meetings of the European Council (and a minimum of one meeting a year) will be held in Brussels. Upon the EU's reaching a membership of 18, all European Council meetings will take place there.

The European Council is not properly speaking an "institution." TEU Article 4 (ex D) merely identifies it as "bring[ing] together the Heads of State or Government of the Member States and the President of the Commission," and it does not figure among the institutions authorized by TEU Article 5 (ex E) to exercise powers under the TEU. While it sets policies and guidelines—notably under the EC Treaty provisions on EMU and under pillars two and three—the European Council does not take legally binding decisions; such legally binding decisions as are taken will be taken by the Council. The European Council is nevertheless politically vital.

Among the European Council's most prominent functions has been coordinating Member State foreign policy, a process that evolved into the European Political Cooperation (EPC) system (see page 12 *supra*) and thereafter the CFSP (see page 17 *supra*). The Single European Act gave this activity a firm—if intergovernmental—treaty foundation, and the Treaties of Maastricht, Amsterdam and Nice expanded and strengthened it. (For example, the European Council may now unanimously establish guidelines which enable the Council of Ministers itself to take foreign policy decisions on a qualified majority basis.) Closely linked to the Community's external affairs, this sphere of European Council activity is covered in detail in Part V.

Over the years, the European Council has resolved difficult political issues that the Council lacked authority under the Treaties or lacked the political ability to resolve. The European Council, for example, has set long-term policy guidelines for the Community, agreed on the accession of new Member States, endorsed institutional reforms, embraced the idea of an Economic and Monetary Union (EMU), supported German reunification within the Community, set the criteria for accession of central and eastern European states, scheduled successive intergovernmental conferences in contemplation of treaty amendments, and commissioned and eventually endorsed the EU's Charter of Fundamental Rights. Of course the European Council has also provided a convenient forum for discussing non-Community matters of interest to the Member States.

Given the European Council's importance, the absence of any treaty reference to it came to seem highly anomalous. Belatedly, the Single European Act recognized the European Council as a body composed of the heads of state or government together with the President of the Commission. The SEA required the European Council to meet biannually, but still assigned it no specific role. Understandably, it was the Maastricht Treaty, establishing the European Union as such, that finally consolidated the European Council's position.[11] TEU Article 4 (ex D) calls on the European Council to "provide the Union with the necessary impetus for its development and [to] define the general political guidelines thereof." It requires the European Council to meet

---

11. TEU Article 4 (ex D) describes the European Council as "bring[ing] together the Heads of State or Government of the Member States and the President of the Commission," and provides for assistance to be given them "by the Ministers for Foreign Affairs of the Member States and by a Member of the Commission."

at least twice a year (with, as chair, the head of state or government of the Member State then holding the Presidency of the Council) and to submit to Parliament annual progress reports on the Union and reports after each of its meetings.

As noted, the European Council has never legally supplanted the Council; the latter continues to take all the action necessary to carry out policy decisions of the European Council falling within the Community sphere. But some confusion between the two has arisen. For example, EC Treaty Article 99 (ex 103) authorizes the European Council to set "broad guidelines" on the economic policies of Member States and the Community, guidelines that the Council of Ministers might then act to implement. Still more significantly, EC Treaty Article 121 (ex 109j) empowered the Council of Ministers, meeting as "Heads of State or of Government," to take the decision whether and when to enter the third stage of Monetary Union, creating a European Central Bank and a single European currency.

Occasionally, the treaties elsewhere prescribe that the Council shall act in the composition of heads of government. Examples include TEU Article 7 (ex F.1), authorizing the Council to determine Member State breaches of democratic principles, and EC Treaty Article 11 (ex 5a), authorizing the Council to decide whether "closer cooperation" may be engaged in over a Member State's opposition on important national policy grounds.

Notes and Questions

1. In Commission v. Council (FAO fisheries agreement), Case C–25/94, [1996] ECR I–1469, the Commission brought suit against the Council over the terms on which the Council had voted in favor of the Community's participation in an FAO fisheries convention. (Those terms reserved to the Member States the right, alongside the Community, to cast votes in FAO meetings.) The Council (supported by the UK) argued that the Council's decision was not a justiciable "act" within the meaning of the EC Treaty's basic judicial review provision, Article 230 (ex 173); it claimed that the decision had for all practical purposes been taken by the Member States in COREPER and that the Council had merely "ratified" it.

The Court observed that COREPER is not a Community institution with powers of its own under the Treaty, but merely an auxiliary to the Council. Accordingly, "COREPER could not adopt ... a decision on the [matter] and ... the Council's vote ... cannot therefore be regarded as confirming a previous COREPER decision" (para. 28).

2. As noted, it is foreseen, notwithstanding the scale of the enlargements to come, that each Member State will continue to have its own representation in the Council (albeit with weighted voice in matters governed by qualified majority). As we shall see below, that is not the case with the Commission. Can you explain this?

2. THE COMMISSION

The European Commission bears a striking but imperfect resemblance to a Government in the usual European sense of the term. Often referred to as the Community's executive organ, the Commission in fact performs tasks commonly identified with the executive: formulating a general legislative program, initiating the legislative process by drafting specific pieces of legislation, exercising the powers delegated to it by the Council, making the decisions and carrying out the administrative tasks assigned to it, and overseeing (and if need be enforcing) compliance with the law. Much of this is captured in the language of Article 211 (ex 155) of the EC Treaty. The breadth of functions performed by the Commission will become even more apparent as the reader moves through the various substantive law chapters of this book.

Despite its close affinity to a modern Government in the European sense, the Commission has certain structural features that set it apart. The term and mode of appointment of the Commission has changed over time. Under the amended EC Treaty Article 214 (ex 158), the Commission is appointed for a five-year renewable term. The Member State governments nominate by common accord a Commission President, whose appointment is subject to Parliamentary assent. In concert with the nominee, the Member States then nominate the other members of the Commission. (As amended at Nice, the Treaty would place in the Council, acting by qualified majority, the power to nominate both the Commission President and the body of Commissioners. In nominating the President, the Council would sit in the composition of heads of state or government.) The Commission's total membership is fixed at present by Article 213 (ex 157) of the EC Treaty at 20, with the understanding that each smaller State may nominate one member apiece, while the five larger States nominate two. (As indicated below, the Nice Treaty would bring a change.)

Before assuming office, the Commission must, as a body, receive a "vote of approval" by the Parliament.[12] In January 1995, the Parliament made conspicuous use of this then-new power, by expressing reservations about certain individual Commission nominees before approving the Commission as a whole. (At the Maastricht IGC, Parliament had unsuccessfully sought the right to approve or disapprove the appointment of individual commissioners.)

Over the years, starting with the first President, Walter Hallstein, Commission Presidents have shaped the Commission's agenda and often exerted great influence over Commission policy. This was decidedly the case with Jacques Delors, the former French Socialist Minister of Finance and President of the Commission between 1985 and 1994, who strongly promoted the Community's 1992 "internal market" program, the EMU, and further steps toward political union.

The President's authority within the Commission has been progressively strengthened. As noted, he or she participates in the designation of the other Commissioners. Under the EC Treaty, as amended by the Treaty of Nice, the President appoints from among the Commissioners, with the Commission's collective approval, an unstated number of Vice–Presidents.[13] By virtue of the same amendment, the President is given the power to allocate and reallocate portfolios among the Commission's members, to dismiss a Commissioner (with the Commission's collective approval), to determine the Commission's

12. EC Treaty art. 214 (ex 158). Following Parliament's approval, the Council, acting by qualified majority, formally appoints the Commission and its President.

13. EC Treaty art. 217 (ex 161). Prior to the amendment at Nice, the Commission ap- pointed the Vice–President whose number the Treaty fixed at either one or two. (Previously the Member States named the Vice–Presidents, of whom there were required to be six.)

internal organization, and more generally to give the Commission its "political guidance."[14] The current Commission President is Romano Prodi.

As its functions suggest, the Commission may be considered the Community's primary engine of integration. Although its members are effectively selected by nationality, the Commission is expected to act so as to promote the Community's interests and development rather than those of any of its Member States. The Commission's record of performance largely bears out this expectation. The independence of the Commission from the Member States is forcefully guaranteed: Commissioners are required to be "completely independent in the performance of their duties," to "neither seek nor take instructions from any Government or from any other body" and to "refrain from any action incompatible with their duties."[15] The Commission acts by a simple majority of its members and its deliberations are secret.

The Treaty says little about the Commission's relationship to the Council.[16] The Commission's relationship to the Parliament, which is treated, does not fully correspond to what an analogy to parliamentary models of government might lead one to expect. Commissioners neither come from Parliament nor necessarily reflect the political sentiments dominant in that body, though Parliament is entitled to ask questions of the Commission, to receive from it an annual report on Community activities, and to censure the Commission as a body and thus force its resignation. However, the rules of the Parliament provide for "confirmation hearings" on each individual Commissioner, a practice in which the Prodi Commission acquiesced. Moreover, the change of the Commission's term of office from four to five years permitted the Commission's appointment to become congruent with Parliamentary elections. Along with other changes recently made (such as the requirement that Parliament approve the Commission as a whole before it takes office), this is meant to increase the "parliamentary" character of the government while strengthening the Commission's political and popular accountability.

As described in Chapter 1, Commission accountability came conspicuously to the fore in 1998–99 during the Presidency of Jacques Santer, former Luxembourg Prime Minister. Following a period of growing parliamentary disenchantment with the Santer Commission, a report specially prepared for the Parliament concluded that certain Commissioners had behaved improperly (notably through a pattern of favoritism in decisionmaking) and that the Commission as a whole had failed to exercise sufficient collective responsibility or oversight. As noted, the Commission resigned in the immediate wake of the report, thereby preempting a highly likely vote of censure.

In late March 1999, the European Council in Berlin accepted the Commission's resignation and selected Romano Prodi, former Italian Prime Minister, as the next Commission President, both to complete the 1995–99 term and for the new 2000–04 term. However, it decided that designation of the full Commission should await the June 1999 parliamentary elections on the understanding that Parliament would then promptly consider the nomina-

---

14. Article 217, as amended at Nice, further requires the Commissioners to "carry out the duties devolved upon them by the President under his authority."

15. EC Treaty art. 213 (ex 157). Article 213 also deals specifically with the limitations on

Commissioners' freedom of action during and after office, and their removal from office.

16. "The Council and Commission shall consult each other and shall settle by common accord their methods of cooperation." EC Treaty art. 218 (ex 162).

tions. (Meanwhile, Parliament resolved that the naming of the new Commission should be subject to parliamentary approval in accordance with the amendment to EC Treaty Article 214 (ex 158) introduced by the Amsterdam Treaty.) In May, Parliament approved Mr. Prodi's nomination as President-designate and the Member States' nomination of new Commissioners followed. Parliament conducted its hearings on the proposed Commissioners following the June 1999 elections, and in September the Commissioners were confirmed as a body by a large parliamentary majority both to complete the remainder of the 1995–99 term and to constitute the new 2000–04 Commission.

At its Berlin meeting, the European Council urged that the new Commission reform its organization, management and control, and the new Commission wasted no time. Commissioner *cabinets* were made smaller (but with requirements of nationality and gender balance), and shifts made in the top positions in the Directorates–General. A task force on Commission administrative reform was set up under the direction of Commission Vice–President Neil Kinnock, who was one of only four Commissioners reappointed to the new Commission. The result was a March 2000 White Paper on Reforming the Commission (COM (2000) 200), a plan which has since been acted upon in various respects, including recruitment and promotion (once again to promote nationality and gender diversity, as well as access from persons outside the Commission) and improved financial management for each Directorate–General. Under a new system inaugurated in December 2000, Directors–General and directors of units are evaluated every two years and ordinarily expected to serve in their posts no more than five years prior to reassignment.

With prospects of further EU enlargement, the growing size of the Commission has also become a serious preoccupation. The Amsterdam IGC failed to resolve the "numbers" issue. Only at Nice in December 2000 did the Member States agree on changes in the composition of the Commission, to be reflected in EC Treaty Article 213 (ex 157) as of January 1, 2005. From that date, every State—large and small—would name only a single Commissioner. Then, at the point when the EU has 27 Member States, the number of Commissioners would be set by the Council, acting unanimously, at a number less than the number of States. From then, Commissioners would be chosen according to a rotation system likewise to be decided upon by the Council acting unanimously. While based on the principle of equality,[17] the rotation system would also be required "to reflect satisfactorily the demographic and geographical range" of Member States.

The Commission in 1993 published detailed procedural rules for use at its meetings, in its written procedures, and in decisionmaking by delegation. O.J. L 230/17 (Sept. 11, 1993). The latter two procedures refer to decisionmaking in the absence of a meeting and to authorization of a single Commissioner to take definitive action in the name of the full Commission. The rules were revised in 1999,[18] so as to incorporate certain reforms provided for by the Amsterdam Treaty, such as the President's power to allocate portfolios and

---

17. Protocol on the Enlargement of the European Union, agreed upon at Nice in December 2000, art. 4. The Protocol, in art. 4(3)(a), specifies by way of equality that the difference between the total number of terms of office held by any pair of Member States may never be more than one.

18. O.J. L 252/41 (Sept. 18, 1999).

other responsibilities among Commissioners. Also, by a decision of the European Council of December 23, 1992, reiterated in an Amsterdam Treaty Protocol on the Location of the Seats of the Institutions, Brussels has been confirmed as the Commission's permanent seat.

In terms of functions, the Commission is in part a legislative and in part a regulatory body. In a few areas, the EC Treaty gives the Commission certain powers of "primary" or "original" legislative authority. A current example is Article 86 (ex 90), authorizing the Commission to issue directives or decisions to Member States on the application of competition rules to public undertakings or undertakings to which the States may have granted special rights. Indeed, in the case of Spain, Belgium and Italy v. Commission (Competition in the market for telecommunications services), Joined Cases C–271, 281 & 289/90, [1992] ECR I–5833, the Court held that the Commission's issuance of directives setting out the Member States' obligations in relation to their public undertakings does not impinge upon the general legislative powers given to the Council by Articles 83 (ex 87) and 94 (ex 100) of the Treaty. More generally, though, the Commission enjoys the very significant monopoly on the proposal of legislation to the Council, which means that it essentially sets the Community's legislative agenda and initially drafts its legal texts.

In addition to exercising original legislative authority under the EC Treaty, the Commission has been delegated extensive rulemaking powers by the Council. Agriculture is a sector in which such delegation occurs with particular regularity. Under the Common Agricultural Policy (CAP), the Community comprehensively regulates product standards, prices and marketing for a great number of different commodities, and these regulations must be adapted at short intervals in response to changed economic circumstances. Lodging rulemaking powers in the Commission allows detailed production, pricing and marketing standards for goods as diverse as cereals, pork and preserves to be devised and regularly modified. Other sectors in which the Council has delegated rulemaking authority to the Commission include competition policy and the harmonization of technical and safety standards.

The Commission's other institutional tasks include drafting the initial annual budget for review and adoption by the Council and Parliament, and administering the Community's finances. (See Chapter 3C below.) The Commission also brings enforcement actions against Member States under Article 226 (ex 169) for their violations of Community law, such as maintaining barriers to trade or failing to adopt the legislation or regulations that Community directives require. Enforcement actions against Member States, which constitute a significant part of the Commission's business, are discussed in Chapter 11.

Certainly not to be overlooked are the myriad specific administrative decisions (typified by rulings on competition law violations or violation of the prohibition on state aids) that the Commission, as the Community's chief executive arm, is called upon to make on a daily basis Such decisions will appear throughout the substantive chapters of this book. Another prime area of Commission activity is, of course, external relations and trade. Under Article 300 (ex 228), the Commission, upon authorization by the Council, opens and conducts negotiations over international agreements for eventual conclusion by the Council. The Commission also represents the Community in the WTO and other international organizations and enforces the Community's protective trade legislation. See Part V *infra*.

In aid of these many functions, but also independent of them, the Commission performs the vital role of gathering and providing information. The general report on Community activities that the Commission submits to Parliament each year provides a wealth of information and guidance. The Commission also publishes specialized annual reports (e.g., on competition, the environment and social affairs) and numerous economic and social studies and statistics.[19]

To help discharge its far-ranging responsibilities, the Commission has, as of the year 2000, a permanent staff of over 16,400, divided into 24 large sections known as Directorates General (or "DGs"), as well as a number of other services and offices. As recently re-titled, the DGs are named by subject (e.g. competition, agriculture, internal market, enlargement) rather than number I, II, etc. Each DG is further subdivided into subdirectorates and the latter into divisions along policy lines. Most Community activities fall within the portfolio of one of the Directorates General, whether the matter is agriculture, external relations, the internal market, competition, or budget and finance. Each DG is headed by a Director General who in turn reports to one of the Commissioners. Since each Commissioner supervises one or two DGs, he or she has authority over a broad field of action. Each Commissioner also has a personal cabinet headed by a "chef de cabinet". The chefs de cabinet not only perform administrative duties, including liaison with the other Commissioners, but attempt through their weekly meetings to resolve among themselves matters not requiring the Commissioners' personal involvement.

The Commission Legal Service, consisting of some 125 lawyers, reviews the texts of all draft legislation and decisions, renders legal advice, and represents the Commission in litigation before the Court of Justice. Translation of documents and interpretation at meetings alone require a Commission staff of over 1900 in the Translation Service. All measures (including drafts), as well as major reports and studies, must be translated into all eleven official Community languages,[20] and all official meetings require simultaneous translation. These are daunting tasks for the Commission no less than for the other institutions, and they have noticeably slowed the legislative and decisionmaking processes.

Under Article 290 (ex 217), the Council determines unanimously "the rules governing the languages of the institutions." In practice, not only the Official Journal (and all its contents), but also (1) Court judgments and orders, (2) resolutions and proceedings of Parliament and the Communities' advisory bodies, and (3) informational sources like the Commission's annual

---

19. The Court of Justice has ruled that the Commission must make Community documents (including ones that are ordinarily confidential) available to national judges investigating infringements of Community law, and allow its officials to appear and testify before those judges as necessary. The Court based this conclusion on EC Treaty Article 10 (ex 5), which imposes an obligation of "sincere cooperation" between the Member States and the Community. Zwartveld, Case C–2/88 Imm., [1990] ECR I–3365. The Commission may only avoid the obligation by demonstrating "imperative reasons" for doing so.

20. Danish, Dutch, English, Finnish, French, German, Greek, Italian, Portuguese, Spanish and Swedish. (Irish is technically also an official language, but Ireland does not require that it be used for translation purposes.)

general and sectoral reports, the Bulletin of the Union, and reports and studies by the Commission, Council and Parliament, appear in all the official languages (with the exception of Irish). Notwithstanding the burdens, no serious consideration has been given up to now to the idea of withholding official status from the languages of the new Member States. In 1995, Parliament adopted a resolution strongly opposing any reduction in the number of official languages.[21] Even with the prospective enlargements and growing linguistic complexity, the situation is unlikely to change.

NOTE ON DELEGATIONS OF POWER
TO THE COMMISSION

As noted, and as is hardly surprising, the Commission commonly exercises rulemaking authority delegated to it by the Council. EC Treaty Articles 202 (ex 145) and 211 (ex 155) expressly call upon the Council to delegate power to the Commission and direct the Commission to use that power. The advantages of executive legislation—speed, flexibility and expertise—are especially pronounced in the Community, where legislative authority vests chiefly in a Council that sits only intermittently and in different compositions, and where most legislative action now requires a complex and protracted interplay between the Council and Parliament.

The Council often delegates rulemaking powers to the Commission only on condition that the latter first submit its draft rules for an opinion from, and in some cases actual approval by, specialized committees representing the Member States. The most common structure is the so-called "management committee," chaired by a non-voting Commission official, but composed of Member State representatives whose votes are weighted by State in the fashion of the Council itself. Under this system, the Commission's draft legislation is reviewed by the relevant management committee, and if the committee by qualified majority gives a favorable opinion of the legislation or expresses no opinion at all, the draft automatically becomes law. If, on the other hand, the committee by qualified majority disapproves the proposal, its effectiveness is postponed for one month, during which time the Council itself may act to reject it. However, only a vote of disapproval by the Council will prevent the measure from coming into effect; the management committee's disapproval alone is not sufficient.

Variations on the management committee system are the so-called "advisory committees" and "regulatory committees." The former committees, as their name suggests, exercise purely consultative functions in that the Commission is bound to solicit and presumably consider their advice before finally adopting a measure pursuant to delegation. Neither approval by the advisory committee nor by the Council itself is necessary in order for the delegated legislation to become effective. "Regulatory committees" resemble the management committees, but actually go further in restricting the Commission's freedom of action. Under this system, formal committee opposition to a Commission proposal is not needed in order for implementation to be delayed. The measure may not legally come into force until it receives a favorable

---

21. O.J. C 43/91 (Feb. 20, 1995).

opinion from the regulatory committee (or the Council itself) acting by a qualified majority vote.

The Court of Justice considered the legality of the management committee system in the case of Einfuhr- und Vorratsstelle für Getreide und Futtermittel v. Köster, Berodt & Co., Case 25/70, [1970] ECR 1161, where it ruled:

> ... The function of the Management Committee is to ensure permanent consultation in order to guide the Commission in the exercise of the powers conferred on it by the Council and to enable the latter to substitute its own action for that of the Commission. The Management Committee does not therefore have the power to take a decision in place of the Commission or the Council. ...[The] machinery enables the Council to delegate to the Commission an implementing power of appreciable scope, subject to its power to take the decision itself if necessary.

[1970] ECR at 1171. Does the Court's reasoning also support the validity of the regulatory committee system? The Court subsequently rejected the claim that such a system "[has] the effect of paralyzing the Commission" or has any other feature that would "affect [its] validity." Tedeschi v. Denkavit, Case 5/77, [1977] ECR 1555, 1579–80.

As amended, Article 202 (ex 145) now expressly permits the Council to impose conditions on the Commission's use of delegated powers in accordance with "principles and rules" established by the Council upon proposal by the Commission and advice by Parliament. The Council eventually adopted a so-called Comitology Decision,[22] which established three committee models (plus certain variants) for reviewing the Commission's exercise of delegated powers. That decision has been updated[23] and supplemented by an agreement between the Parliament and Commission which guarantees that the Parliament will receive essential documents (e.g. draft agendas, draft measures) from the Commission at the same time as committee members do. The committee models mirror the advisory, management and regulatory models and operate as a menu from which the Council on any given occasion may freely select a preestablished mode of committee review. The decision thus regularizes the committee system and tends to limit political debate over details of the review procedure to be incorporated by the Council in any given delegation of power.[24]

Questions occasionally arise over the scope of delegations to the Commission. A notable example is ACF Chemiefarma NV v. Commission, Case 41/69, [1970] ECR 661. Acting under EC Article 83 (ex 87), which authorizes it to enact legislation for the implementation of Community competition rules, the Council adopted Regulation 17, which in turn empowered the Commission to

---

22. Council Decision 87/373, O.J. L 197/33 (July 18, 1987).

23. Council Decision 1999/468, O.J. L 184 (June 28, 1999).

24. The Comitology Decision was challenged by Parliament in the Court of Justice, but the suit was dismissed for lack of standing. See page 131 *infra*. The committee system nevertheless continues to come under criticism from the European Parliament. The latter complains that it is denied information about how the committees arrive at their recommen- dations on how legislation approved by the Council and Parliament should be implemented. This sentiment has spawned proposals for legislation modeled on the U.S. Federal Advisory Committee Act, which requires like committees in the U.S. to announce agendas in advance, to hold public meetings, to publish their minutes, and to disclose their members' financial interests. Among other means invoked in this effort, Parliament blocked the appropriation of the $28 million earmarked in 1996 for the committees' administrative budgets.

issue procedural rules for investigating suspected violations, holding hearings and fining violators. (Regulation 17 is examined in Chapter 20.) A party that had been fined by the Commission under these rules challenged the action on the ground that Regulation 17 delegated powers to the Commission going beyond the "implementation" of Council rules, within the meaning of Article 211 (ex 155). The Court rejected the argument that the Council was required by itself to exercise all the rulemaking authority that Article 83 confers on it. "[T]he rules laying down the procedure to be followed ..., however important they may be, constitute implementing provisions within the meaning of [former] Article 155." [1970] ECR at 668.

Notes and Questions

1.   Although the management committee procedure presents some difficulties in principle, its use has occasioned very little conflict. A committee referral to the Council tends to occur no more than once or twice in an entire year, if at all, even though hundreds of measures may be adopted under the management committee system during that time period.

2.   What about delegations of regulatory authority to outside bodies? In Meroni v. High Authority, Case 9/56, [1957–1958] ECR 133, the ECSC High Authority set up two agencies under Belgian law to manage an "equalization fund" used to subsidize the import of scrap iron, which was then costly and scarce. The fund was financed by a levy on users of scrap according to their usage. When an Italian steel producer refused to report its scrap consumption, the agencies estimated its usage and the High Authority imposed a levy on that basis. The Court of Justice annulled that decision, citing several factors, including the fact that the agencies were not directly established by the Treaty, that they had not been required to follow certain procedures that the High Authority itself would have had to follow if it had administered the system, and that the delegation did not expressly authorize the agencies to estimate iron consumption. The Court also found that the delegation simply left the agencies too much discretion in setting objectives and in making "difficult choices."

The Court has taken a similarly dim view of delegations of power to the Member States. In the leading case, the Council delegated authority to the Commission to take the measures needed to stabilize the sugar market, and the Commission in turn delegated that authority to Italy insofar as certain problems peculiar to the Italian market were concerned. The Italian government used this authority to impose a levy on stockholders of sugar. Upon challenge, the Court upheld the delegation to the Commission, but invalidated the subdelegation to Italy. Rey Soda v. Cassa Conguaglio Zucchero, Case 23/75, [1975] ECR 1279.

3.   For a political science view on comitology, see Egan & Wolf, Regulation and Comitology: The EC Committee System in Regulatory Perspective, 4 Colum. J. Eur. L. 499 (1998).

4.   The committee systems evoke in some respects the US "legislative veto," whereby Congress reserves the right to repudiate a federal agency rule promulgated under a prior delegation of authority to the agency. The legislative veto has been found unconstitutional to the extent that it allows Congress (or a house of Congress) to circumvent the usual constitutional ground rules for the enactment of legislation. See Immigration and Naturalization Service v. Chadha, 462 U.S. 919, 103 S.Ct. 2764, 77 L.Ed.2d 317 (1983).

3. THE EUROPEAN PARLIAMENT

While the Commission functions as the principal engine of integration, and the Council as a kind of intergovernmental legislature, the Parliament is designed to express the political sentiments of the Member State populations. The EC Treaty describes the Parliament in Article 189 (ex 137) as composed of "representatives of the peoples of the States brought together in the Community." Contrary to what one might expect from its name, however, the Parliament received from the drafters of the original treaties scant legislative power. (The drafters actually used the term "Assembly," but that body began calling itself the European Parliament in 1962, and the other institutions eventually accepted the term. The Single European Act formalized the name change as of 1987.)

In its original wording, Article 189 (ex 187) specifically referred to Parliament's powers as "advisory and supervisory." Indeed Parliament initially had no decisional role in either the legislative or budgetary process. However, Parliament has continually demanded increased authority and, as Chapter 3 will show, the Single European Act and the Treaties of Maastricht, Amsterdam and Nice have all granted it. For its part, the Maastricht Treaty deleted the terms "advisory and supervisory."

Although Article 190 (ex 138) foresaw from the start the direct election of Members of Parliament (or MEPs) by universal suffrage, until 1979 MEPs were drawn from the membership of the national legislatures. Belatedly, at a December 1974 summit meeting in Paris, the heads of state and government endorsed the idea of direct elections. A 1976 Council decision (with its annexed "Act") set out the terms, and direct elections were held for the first time in 1979. While Article 190 called for a uniform electoral procedure throughout the Member States, none was forthcoming. In 1982 Parliament proposed a proportional representation system, but the UK, which uses a district constituency system, blocked this at the Council of Ministers level. Electoral methods thus have accordingly varied among the Member States, though with all except the UK using proportional representation in some form.

The Amsterdam Treaty finally amended Article 190 to provide, as an alternative to a uniform electoral procedure, that elections might be conducted "in accordance with principles common to all Member States." By a 1998 resolution,[25] Parliament formally endorsed the use of multi-member constituencies for which MEPs would be elected by proportional representation, and the UK adopted this method. (The resolution also forbid common mandates as MEPs and members of national parliaments.) The June 1999 parliamentary elections followed this common system.

The number and allocation of seats in the Parliament has changed with the Union's progressive enlargement. With the accession of Spain and Portugal, the Parliament grew to a size of 518. German unification later prompted still a further enlargement, as did the accessions of Austria, Finland and Sweden, which brought the seat total to 626.

The current allocation of seats is as follows:

25. O.J. C 292 (Sept. 21, 1998).

Belgium	25
Denmark	16
Germany	99
Greece	25
Spain	64
France	87
Ireland	15
Italy	87
Luxembourg	6
Netherlands	31
Austria	21
Portugal	25
Finland	16
Sweden	22
United Kingdom	87

The table shows that seats are allocated among the Member States in crude proportion to their populations. Obviously, on a per capita basis, Luxembourg is highly overrepresented and the larger states—Germany, in particular—are underrepresented.

Foreseeing that similar increases in size with the accessions to come would render Parliament impossibly large, the Amsterdam Treaty fixed a maximum of 700 for the number of seats. (See EC Treaty art. 189, ex 137). The Treaty of Nice would change that number to 732. Meanwhile, a Protocol adopted at Nice provides for the allocation of seats among the current Member States to be adjusted effective January 1, 2004—the idea being to decrease the number of seats of every State (apart from Germany at the top end and Luxembourg at the bottom), thereby enabling the anticipated accession States to pick up seats without Parliament exceeding the 732–member ceiling. In January 2004 the allocation of the then-total 535 seats will be as follows:

Belgium	22
Denmark	13
Germany	99
Greece	22
Spain	50
France	72
Ireland	12
Italy	72
Luxembourg	6
Netherlands	25
Austria	17
Portugal	22
Finland	13
Sweden	18
United Kingdom	72

The Protocol provides that during the 2004–2009 term, the 535 seats with which that term starts will be increased to reflect the accession of new Member States, in accordance with a table of seat allocations agreed upon at Nice for each of the twelve candidate countries. (According to that table, when all twelve accede, Parliament will have reached its 732–seat ceiling.) The number of seats ranges from 5 for Malta to 50 for Poland. For the complete allocation, see the Selected Documents, Part I, document 4, protocols. Recognizing that not all candidate States may accede at the same moment (or indeed at all), the IGC further directed the Council, until such time as the figure of 732 is reached, to make a "pro rata correction" upwards to each Member State's allocation for 2004–2009, so as to bring the total number of seats as close as possible to 732—without, however, allowing the number of seats of any State to exceed the number held by that State during the 1999–2004 parliamentary term. (Since it could easily happen that additional candidate States will join the EU after the Council has made an upward correction, the Protocol permits the number of MEPs "temporarily" to exceed 732.)

MEPs, elected for five-year terms, are supposed to represent the European people rather than a Member State government as such. Consistent with this view, they are elected on the basis of political party affiliation, and sit together in Parliament according to that affiliation rather than nationality.[26] Recognized groups span the political spectrum, from parties at the extreme left to the European Right Group. The largest bloc in the Parliament elected in 1999 is (for the first time) the European People's Party (or EPP), largely Christian Democrats, numbering 233. The next largest group is the Socialists, occupying 180 seats, followed at some distance by the Liberals with 51. Some MEPs are unaffiliated. The MEPs elect their own President and twelve vice-presidents for 2½ year terms. (Nicole Fontaine, a French EPP member, is President for 1999–2001, and Patrick Cox, an Irish Liberal, for 2002–04.) These officers comprise the Bureau, responsible for the organization of parliamentary business, including the appointment of committee chairs and members.

In addition to holding an annual session, the European Parliament meets at the request of a majority of its members or at the request of the Council or Commission. Unless otherwise provided, it votes by an absolute majority of votes cast.

The European Parliament has multiple seats. Pursuant to a 1965 decision of the representatives of the Member State Governments, Parliament holds its plenary sessions in Strasbourg and its committee meetings in Brussels, while its Secretariat is based in Luxembourg. A Court of Justice decision confirms that Parliament has a right to meet in either Luxembourg or Strasbourg, until such time as the Member States definitively fix its seat under Article 289 (ex 216) or otherwise reached a common accord on the matter.[27] In the 1980s, the Parliament built a large facilities complex in Brussels (ultimately costing $1.2 billion), but at its 1992 Edinburgh summit, the European Council nevertheless decided that Parliament would have its seat and continue to hold its twelve monthly plenary sessions in Strasbourg.

26. Article 191 (ex 138a) acknowledges the importance of political parties in "forming a European awareness and ... expressing the political will of the citizens of the Union." As amended at Nice, Article 191 authorizes the Council to enact through co-decision (art. 251) regulations concerning political parties at the European level, including their funding.

27. Luxembourg v. Parliament, Case 230/81, [1983] ECR 255. In the same judgment,

the Court interpreted the 1965 Council decision as requiring that the Secretariat be in Luxembourg. However, the Court subsequently ruled that Parliament's expanded presence in Brussels did not jeopardize Luxembourg's status as site of Parliament's Secretariat. Luxembourg v. Parliament, Cases C–213/88 & C–39/89, [1991] ECR I–5643.

(Brussels is the site of committee meetings and any extraordinary plenary sessions, while the Parliament's general secretariat remains in Luxembourg.) These arrangements are confirmed in a special protocol to the Amsterdam Treaty. A new Parliament building has now also been constructed in Strasbourg. The current arrangements are undoubtedly inefficient and are estimated to entail over 100 million dollars in travel expenses.

The European Parliament has proven quite difficult to describe from a functional point of view. Its name notwithstanding, the Parliament enjoys only limited legislative power. It is the Commission, not the Parliament, that proposes legislation, though, by amendment at Maastricht, the EC Treaty (Article 192, ex 138b) now expressly invites Parliament to request that the Commission submit legislative proposals.

More significantly, Parliament originally had at best the right to be consulted, i.e., to give its opinion, before the Council took legislative action, and even then only where expressly provided for in the treaties. (As a matter of practice, the Council, since the 1970s, tended to seek Parliament's advice even when not required to do so.) Particularly since becoming directly elected in 1979, Parliament pressed vigorously for a greater voice in the legislative process, most notably in its own 1984 Draft Treaty Establishing the European Union, which would have required parliamentary assent for the passage of virtually all Community legislation. Instead, the Single European Act devised a new legislative process, called the "parliamentary cooperation procedure," which created a complicated multi-stage process through which Parliament won a substantial legislative voice but still not a legislative veto. The Maastricht Treaty created an additional legislative procedure known as "parliamentary codecision," which made Parliament more of a legislative co-equal. As a result of further EC Treaty amendments at Amsterdam and Nice described in Chapter 3B, codecision has steadily gained ground.

Parliamentary review of proposed legislation is still largely carried out at the committee level, but as noted in EC Treaty Article 198 (ex 141), formal parliamentary action is taken in plenary session by an absolute majority of votes cast. Supported by an impressive role in budgetary matters (see below), Parliament is enjoying an ever-increasing role in the legislative processes of the Community. By virtue of a July 2000 Framework Agreement with the Commission designed to enhance Parliament's legislative involvement,[28] Parliament has won the right to a prompt response to its requests for legislation under Article 192 (ex 138b) and to close attention to amendments that the European Parliament proposes during the "second reading" phase of the legislative process (see Chapter 3B). In the same vein, the Commission undertook to keep Parliament informed, on a par with the Council, at every stage of any legislative or budgetary procedure.

Regarding certain international agreements, Parliament has won the right of assent. The Single European Act gave that right to Parliament with respect to the accession of new Member States (see TEU Article 49) and to association agreements with third countries (EC Treaty Articles 300 (ex 228) and 310 (ex 238)). Parliament subsequently also won a veto power over any international agreements by the Community that entail new institutional frameworks, "important budgetary implications," or the amendment of an

28. EU Bull. 7/8–00.

Community act adopted under the legislative co-decision procedure. All other international agreements merely require parliamentary consultation; tariff and trade agreements under Article 133(3) (ex 113(3)) do not even require that.

The European Parliament still serves as a general forum for discussing and debating topics of interest to the peoples of the Member States, and for supervising the activities of the other institutions. Nevertheless, Parliament still does not have the relationship to the Commission that one might expect in a parliamentary system. Though, as a result of the Maastricht Treaty, Parliament must approve the nomination of Commission President and the appointment of the Commission as a body, Commissioners are still not chosen from among the members of Parliament, nor even in consideration of relative political party strengths in Parliament.

Parliament has other means of supervising the Commission. As noted, the Parliament has undertaken by internal rules to conduct "confirmation hearings" on individual Commissioners, warning by resolution that it would not approve the full Commission until satisfied with the entire membership. (The July 2000 framework agreement between the Commission and Parliament, referred to earlier, confirmed this understanding.) Moreover, EC Treaty Article 197 (ex 140) specifically calls upon the Commission to reply orally or in writing to questions put to it by Parliament or its members (while allowing Commissioners to attend and be heard at parliamentary meetings). "Question time," modeled after British parliamentary practice, offers Parliament a regular opportunity to question the Commission or its members and to debate publicly the answers given. These can be spirited occasions, with both questions and answers recorded in the Official Journal. Parliamentary questions, asked in plenary session or committee, currently run into the thousands annually. The 2000 General Report shows Parliament addressing 3678 written, 89 oral and 650 "question time" questions to the Commission. Through this "gadfly" function, MEPs may incite the Commission to act or at least to air information. Written questions may also be addressed to the Commissioners and their somewhat more formal answers are likewise recorded in the Official Journal.

Article 200 (ex 143) further calls upon the Parliament to discuss in open session the annual general report submitted to it by the Commission. This report's valuable summary of Community activities always provokes lively parliamentary discussion. Moreover, although the Treaty does not so require, every January the Commission President presents Parliament with the Commission's proposed program for that year.

Since the European Council meeting at Stuttgart in June 1983, the Council of Ministers has also voluntarily submitted to parliamentary questioning, answering hundreds of questions annually. It also reports periodically to the Parliament on its own program of activities. Each Council President, at the outset of the six-month presidency, presents the Council's program for the term, and also presents conclusions at the term's end. Parliament is also entitled to periodic reports by the European Council on progress toward European Union (see TEU art. 4).

The Parliament may now also assemble a "Committee of Inquiry" to address emerging problems at the Community level. Borrowing a device that some Member States had found useful for reviewing government misconduct, the drafters of the Maastricht Treaty introduced Article 193 (ex 138c) of the EC Treaty, allowing one-quarter of the MEPs to require the constitution of a committee to investigate "alleged contraventions or maladministration" by the Community.[29] Among its most high-profile uses was Parliament's inquiry into the Commission's handling of the "mad cow disease" crisis (see *supra* page 22.

EC Treaty Article 201 (ex 144) provides for a censure procedure under which Parliament may compel the Commission to resign as a body by adopting a motion of censure by a two-thirds majority of votes cast representing a majority of the membership. In the wake of certain fundamental policy differences with the Commission, motions of censure have on several occasions been tabled, but none has ever carried. As part of the July 2000 Commission–EP Framework Agreement referred to earlier, President Prodi agreed to consider requesting the resignation of an individual Commissioner if the Parliament expressed a lack of confidence in him or her.

Parliament came close to censuring the Commission in 1997 in the wake of the "mad cow disease" episode. Parliament took the Commission, and particularly President Santer, to task for what it considered to be a severe mishandling of that entire problem. Following a harsh set of hearings, President Santer narrowly escaped censure of the Commission by admitting error, reshuffling certain portfolios and promising prompt remedial action. Censure prospects resurfaced in 1998–99 and were headed off only by the Commission's March 1999 resignation, described above.

Once directly elected, the European Parliament became in a sense the most democratic arm of Community government. With its steadily augmented role in the legislative and budgetary processes, Parliament has begun to exhibit the indicia that a body of that name and character ordinarily enjoys in a modern democracy. In particular, the Maastricht, Amsterdam and Nice Treaties launched and extended a parliamentary codecision procedure which now ensures that by far most legislation requires Parliament's consent for adoption. While Parliament continues to urge ways in which EU governance may be made more democratic and transparent, it complains less now than it used to about the Community's "democratic deficit." A conspicuous remaining gap is in the EMU area; but even here Parliament managed to conduct confirmation hearings for members of the ECB Executive Board and has been receiving quarterly reports from the ECB.

NOTE ON THE OMBUDSMAN

Another innovation of Maastricht, reflected in EC Treaty Article 195 (ex 138e), was the office of Ombudsman based on the Scandinavian model. Like its namesakes elsewhere, the Ombudsman reviews complaints of maladministration brought to it by MEPs or by any Community national or resident. It may compel the cooperation of any institution (except the Court of Justice) in its investigations, and ultimately make findings and recommendations, supported by reports to the Parliament. Each new Parliament names an Ombudsman for the parliamentary term of office.

29.   See also O.J. L 113/2 (May 19, 1995).

In 1994, Parliament issued a decision governing the performance of duties by the Ombudsman.[30] While Article 195 merely requires that the Ombudsman be completely independent (neither seeking nor taking instructions from any body, and engaging in no other occupation while in office),[31] the decision adopted by Parliament imposes as an eligibility requirement that the Ombudsman have the qualifications for exercising the highest judicial office in his or her country and possess "the acknowledged competence and experience to undertake the duties" of the office. The term of office is coterminous with the appointing Parliament, unless there are grounds for earlier termination. The term is renewable.

Any EU citizen or person resident or established in an EU Member State may complain to the Ombudsman, either directly or through an MEP, about maladministration on the part of the Community institutions (other than the Court of Justice and the Court of First Instance acting in their judicial role). Any such complaint must be filed within two years of the underlying act and must show that efforts were made to remedy the problem through direct contact with the institution or body responsible. (Staff complaints may not be heard until all administrative remedies have been exhausted.) The filing of an application with the Ombudsman does not affect the time limits for bringing administrative or judicial challenges against the measure in question. On the other hand, if a legal challenge is brought, the Ombudsman must immediately suspend proceedings on the complaint in deference to the litigation. Even without having received a complaint, the Ombudsman is free to conduct all the inquiries he or she deems necessary to "clarify" a possible instance of maladministration. The institution complained about is entitled to be informed immediately of the complaint; on the other hand, it is required to cooperate fully in furnishing information and files (except where needs of secrecy dictate otherwise) and in making officials available to testify. The Ombudsman has no means of enforcing its investigative powers, though Parliament may make representations on the Ombudsman's behalf. All information supplied to the Ombudsman is deemed confidential. If, however, it relates to possible criminal violations, it must be reported to the competent authorities.

Once addressed, the Ombudsman may require that the institution produce all documents or other information that is relevant to the complaint, and may have direct access to the files, subject to substantiated claims of secrecy by the institution. All the institutions have a duty of cooperation with the Ombudsman, as indeed do the Member States (subject, once again, to legal rules governing secrecy), although the Ombudsman has no available sanctions in the event of non-cooperation or non-reply. On the other hand, the rules make it clear that the Ombudsman may only examine acts of the Community institutions, and not of national institutions, even when the latter act in implementation of Community law.

If the Ombudsman finds there to be a prima facie case of maladministration, he or she must inform the institution or body and give it an opportunity of three months in which to respond. Eventually, the Ombudsman issues a

---

30. O.J. L 113/15 (May 4, 1994).

31. The Ombudsman may be dismissed by the Court of Justice at the request of the European Parliament if he or she no longer fulfills the conditions required for the performance of duties or is guilty of serious misconduct. EC Treaty art. 195 (ex 138c), para. 2.

report to the Parliament (and to the institution in question, with notice to the complainant) as appropriate. The Ombudsman may propose (though not impose) corrective action. On the Ombudsman's significance in the development of legal norms, see Bonnor, The European Ombudsman: A Novel Source of Soft Law in the European Union, 25 Eur. L. Rev. 39 (2000).

In 1995, the Parliament chose as first Ombudsman Jacob Söderman, Finland's national ombudsman and former social affairs and health minister. He was reappointed in 2000.

Notes and Questions

1.   Unlike some national legislatures, the European Parliament has no power under the relevant treaty articles to censure an individual commissioner, but only the Commission as a whole. Why do you suppose such a power was omitted, and what do you suppose are the consequences of the omission? Is it obvious why Parliament has no right of censure with respect to the Council?

2.   What room do you see for further curtailing the Community's "democratic deficit"?

One much-discussed strategy is to enhance the role of the national parliaments in supervising Community policy and practices. A Declaration annexed to the Maastricht Treaty proposes a "greater involvement" of national parliaments in Community affairs. A Protocol to the Amsterdam Treaty takes things a step further. The Commission must promptly forward all consultation documents (both "green" and "white" papers) to the national parliaments, and it must also make its legislative proposals available in sufficient time to enable each Member State in turn to furnish them to its national parliament. To reinforce these requirements, the Protocol provides, subject to a showing of urgency, for a minimum of six weeks between the time a proposal is advanced by the Commission and the time it is placed on the Council's agenda for action.

The Protocol also acknowledges the Conference of European Affairs Committees (COSAC), a body that the European Council had established in 1989 to coordinate oversight activity among national parliaments of the Member States. Besides generally inviting COSAC to communicate to the institutions its views on policy issues and proposals, the Protocol specifically solicits COSAC's contributions on any legislative proposals relating to the establishment of "an area of freedom, security and justice," the principle of subsidiarity, and fundamental rights.[32]

3.   In 1996, in the wake of ever more intensive lobbying of MEPs, the Parliament adopted regulations governing that activity. In addition to requiring that ministerial staff members, private business and business association interests register before contacting members of Parliament and adhere to a code of conduct, the regulations require MEPs to make public an account of their financial interests and financial support provided by third parties.

4.   THE COURT OF JUSTICE

The Court of Justice of the European Communities, whose seat is in Luxembourg, is dealt with extensively in the constitutive treaties. Article 220 (ex 164) of the EC Treaty gives the Court responsibility for "ensur[ing] that

---

32.   "Contributions made by COSAC shall in no way bind national parliaments or pre-   judge their position" Protocol, para. 3.

in the interpretation and application of this Treaty the law is observed." The Court's various judicial functions are examined closely in later chapters. Suffice it here to say that the Court entertains legal actions against both the institutions and the Member States for their alleged nonobservance of Community law. These are all in the nature of original actions. More significant, in numbers and arguably also in function, is the Court's jurisdiction to render "preliminary rulings" under EC Treaty Article 234 (ex 177) on the interpretation and validity of Community acts at the request of Member State courts.[33]

Through all these forms of action, the Court plays a vital role in securing a Community legal order that is both effective and respectful of the rule of law and of individual rights. The Court's doctrinal contributions include the fundamental concepts of direct effect and supremacy, taken up in Chapter 7. More generally, it has sought through its jurisprudence to clarify the Member States' responsibilities under Community law. At the same time, the Court is continually defining the freedom of action of the Community institutions themselves. On all such issues, the Court's understanding of the relevant Community norms is considered authoritative. This is why Court of Justice judgments figure so prominently throughout the substantive no less than the institutional chapters of this book.

As amended, EC Treaty Article 221 (ex 165) provides for one judge per Member State.[34] (When the EU had an even number of Member States, an additional judge, selected from one of the larger States on a rotating basis, was provided for as an eventual tie-breaker.) The Treaty is likewise silent on the manner of judicial selection, but in practice each Member State effectively names its own judge after consultation with the other Member States. Appointments can thus fairly be said to be "by common accord."

Judges of the Court serve for six years. An important measure of continuity is provided by their staggered system of appointment. The Treaty at present provides for partial replacements every three years, with eight and seven judges, alternately, being replaced. On each such occasion four advocates-general (about whom more below) are also replaced.[35] Moreover, judges can and very commonly do serve more than one term. Given the judges' manner of appointment and the kinds of issues they are likely to decide, judicial independence is obviously a matter of first importance. Article 223 (ex 167) leaves no doubt that complete independence of judgment is expected, particularly in regard to pressures coming from the Member States. It provides that judges, besides being qualified for appointment to their nation's highest court or being "jurisconsults of recognized competence," should "be chosen from persons whose independence is beyond doubt." It is established that judges may not be dismissed by Member States during their terms, and that they may not hold any political or administrative office during their

---

33. Under EC Treaty Article 300 (ex 228), the Court also has jurisdiction to give an opinion on the compatibility with the Treaty of any proposed international agreement of the Community. The Council, the Commission, a Member State, and (as of the Treaty of Nice) the Parliament have standing to request such an opinion. See Part IV *infra* for examples of such opinions.

34. Historically, the Treaty fixed the number of seats at the then current membership. As amended at Nice, the Treaty simply adopts a one-judge-per-Member–State formula.

35. Adapting the Treaty to a future enlargement in unknown numbers, Article 223 simply leaves details of the partial replacements of Judges and Advocates–General to the Statute of the Court of Justice.

service on the Court. In practice, most judges have previously served on a national supreme or appellate court, or been a university law professor or high government official.

Judicial neutrality is aided by certain practices not mandated by the Treaty, but nevertheless uniformly respected and in some respects required by the Statute of the Court. Thus, deliberations are held in private and the Court's decisions are signed by all judges sitting and deliberating in the relevant formation (plenary session or chamber), whatever their personal viewpoints may have been. Even after the accession of the UK and Ireland, concurring or dissenting opinions remain unknown. The position of the individual judge on a specific issue or case is accordingly not made public. On the other hand, some judges have done important and extensive academic writing while on the Court, and thus had unusual personal influence both on and off the Court.

Recent intergovernmental conferences have occasioned discussions over the possibility of changing the mode of appointment of judges to the Court of Justice. For example, the European Parliament has proposed that they be elected jointly by the Parliament and the Council, with members restricted to a single term of office (possibly extended to nine years). It has also urged that nominees to the Court appear for hearings before the Parliament's Committee on Legal Affairs and Citizens' Rights. No such reform proposal has been adopted. Indeed, in its report to the 1996 IGC, the Court of Justice described as indispensable to the rule of law in the EU the requirement that "the [Community] courts remain independent and their judgments binding."

The President of the Court is elected by its members every three years, rather than by the Member States, and may be renewed in office (Article 223, ex 167). It is the President who assigns cases, deals with urgent requests for interim relief, and presides in deliberations. The Court's current president is Gil Carlos Rodriguez Iglesias, of Spain.

Article 245 (ex 188) provides for a separate Statute of the Court of Justice, in the form of a protocol to the EC Treaty. The Council, acting unanimously at the Court's request and after consulting the Commission and Parliament, may amend the statute.[36] On the other hand, the Court's Rules of Procedure of the Court need the Council's unanimous approval.[37] Selected provisions of both the Statute and the Rules may be found in the Selected Documents. (See Part I, documents 5 and 6, respectively.)

When the Court had fewer members and a lighter case load, it favored sitting in plenary sessions. Now it sits more frequently in chambers. Currently, the Court has 4 chambers of three judges and 2 chambers of five judges. (Nine judges now constitute a quorum for action by the full Court.) Article 221 (ex 165) requires the Court to sit in plenary session in all suits brought by a Member State or Community institution as a party if it so requests.[38] As amended at Nice in December 2000, Article 221 would leave it to the Statute

36. As amended by the Treaty of Nice, Article 245 also permits the Council to amend the Statute at the request of the Commission, upon consulting Parliament and the Court of Justice.

37. As amended by the Treaty of Nice, the Court's Rules of Procedure only need approval

by a qualified majority of the Council. EC Treaty, art. 223.

38. Prior to the Maastricht Treaty, the Court was also required to sit in plenary session in all preliminary references under Article 234 (ex 177) of the EC Treaty.

of the Court of Justice to determine when the Court shall sit in chambers of 3 or 5 judges, in a Grand Chamber (of 11 judges), or in true plenary session. (As of Nice, the Statute (art. 16) would also require the Court to sit in plenary session in actions brought under certain Treaty articles.[39] Moreover, where it considers the case to have exceptional importance, the Court could decide, after hearing the Advocate-General, to refer the case to plenary session.[40])

By tradition, when the Court sits in plenary session, it deliberates and initially drafts its judgments in French, which makes some facility with that language a virtual prerequisite to membership on the Court. All judgments must be translated into all of the Community's other languages. The "official" language of a case (that is, the language used in the pleadings, documents and oral hearings) is in principle the language of the claimant, except that in preliminary references (art. 234, ex 177) and enforcement actions against a Member State (art. 226, ex 169), it is the language of the referring court or the defendant state, respectively (including Irish, which is not otherwise a working language). In all cases for which French is not the official language, the pleadings and documents will be translated into that language. Simultaneous translation is used at the oral hearings, though not in the Court's deliberations.

Whether a case is heard in plenary session or in chamber, it is assigned to one judge, the *juge rapporteur* (reporting judge), who bears special responsibility for preparing the case. The *juge rapporteur* studies the file and presents a preliminary report to the Court on the issues of fact and/or law that appear to be in dispute. This will determine whether a preparatory inquiry into the facts is required. Prior to the oral proceeding, the *juge rapporteur* drafts a statement of the facts and of the parties' submissions. Upon completion of the oral hearing and after receiving the opinion of the Advocate–General (see below), the *juge rapporteur* prepares a draft judgment, which will serve as the point of departure for the Court's deliberations. Depending on the outcome and reasoning adopted, the *juge rapporteur* in the end may have to rewrite the opinion so as to reflect the prevailing view. The use of largely written procedures, the "inquisitorial" style, the reliance on a *juge rapporteur* and the Court's collective decisionmaking will all be entirely familiar to students of French administrative law, which has in many ways served as the Court's procedural model.

The Advocate–General, provided for in Article 222 (ex 166), plays an especially important role in the Court's work. It is the Advocate–General's duty, "acting with complete impartiality and independence, to make, in open court, reasoned submissions on cases brought before the Court of Justice, in order to assist the Court in the performance of [its] task[s]."[41] In this, the Advocate-General is highly reminiscent of the *commissaire du gouvernement* before the French Conseil d'Etat (see Chapter 8A *infra*). At present there are eight Advocates–General,[42] who have the same rank as judges and are subject

39. These Treaty articles are 195(2) (dismissal of Ombudsman), 213 and 216 (discipline of a Commissioner), and 247(7) (discipline of a member of the Court of Auditors).

40. Treaty of Nice, Protocol on the Statute of the Court of Justice, art. 16.

41. Under Article 222, as amended at Nice, the Statute of the Court of Justice determines the classes of cases in which the Advocate–General participates.

42. As amended at Nice, Article 222 allows the Council, acting unanimously at the Court to the same rules with respect to appointment, qualification, term of office and removal. Every three years, four Advocates–General are replaced (subject to reappointment). By decision of the Member States, at present each of the five largest Member States appoints an Advocate–General, while the other three are named by the remaining States in rotation.[43] Cases are distributed among the Advocates–General by the first Advocate–General, who is appointed by his or her colleagues for the same period of time as the chamber presidents, namely one year.

The function of the Advocate–General is to examine the case independently on the basis of the file and the *juge rapporteur's* report. After the close of the pleadings and hearings, the Advocate–General presents an analysis of the case and an indication of how it should be decided. In keeping with the French administrative law model, the parties do not comment on the Advocate–General's opinion and the Court is in no respect bound to follow it. Traditionally, however, the opinion carries great weight in the Court's deliberations and often the Court will reach the same conclusion, though perhaps on different grounds. The opinion of the Advocate–General is published in the official and unofficial reports of the Court's decisions along with the judgment of the Court, is cited by academic writers, and is likely to influence the later evolution of the case law. See N. Fennelly, Reflections of an Irish Advocate General, 5 Irish J. Eur. L. 5 (1996).

The office of Advocate–General in the Community law system has only recently given rise to "constitutional" doubt as a result of case law of the European Court of Human Rights. In Vermeulen v. Belgium,[44] that Court ruled, 15–4, that participation by the *procureur-général* of the Belgian Court of Cassation in the adjudication of a civil case infringes Article 6(1) of the European Human Rights Convention due to the fact that the *procureur-général* takes part in the court's deliberations (albeit without a vote) and that the private litigant has no right of reply to the *procureur-général*'s submissions.[45] Note that, while private litigants in the Community courts have no right of reply to the opinion of the Advocate-General, the latter does not participate in the Court's deliberations as such. Should this make a difference? The situations have been further distinguished on the ground that the Belgian *procureur-général* intervenes in litigation before the Court of Cassation in the name of the Belgian public authorities, while the Advocate–General represents in all respects an integral part of the Community judiciary and is correspondingly independent. See Tridimas, The Advocate–General, 34 Comm. Mkt. L. Rev. 1349,1380–82 (1997).

Since the European Union is not a party to the European Human Rights Convention (see Chapter 6B *infra*), its institutions are not directly bound, as

of Justice's request, to increase the number of Advocates–General.

43. Joint Declaration of January 1, 1995 on Article 31 of the Decision Adjusting the Instruments Concerning the Accession of the New Member States to the European Union, O.J. L 1/221 (Jan. 1, 1995). The Declaration designates the order of rotation up to 2003.

44. Case 58/1994/505/587.

45. More recently, the Human Rights Court ruled, 10–7, that Article 6(1) is likewise violated by the fact that the *commissaire du gouvernment* in the French Conseil d'Etat, having publicly indicated how he or she thinks the court should decide a case, then personally attends the deliberations at which the Conseil reaches its judgment. Kress v. France, no. 39594/98 (June 7, 2001). Note that the *commissaire du gouvernment*, unlike the *procureur-général* in *Vermeulen*, does not represent the government.

such, by the Convention or by its interpretation by the Human Rights Court. Nevertheless, the Court of Justice took an early opportunity to distinguish its Advocates–General from the Belgian *procureur-général*, holding in Emesa Sugar (Free Zone) NV v. Aruba, Case C–17/98, [2000] ECR I–675, that since the opinion of the Advocate–General "does not form part of the proceedings between the parties, but rather opens the stage of deliberation by the Court [and] is not therefore an opinion addressed to the judges or to the parties which stems from an authority outside the Court," the parties to a preliminary reference proceeding have no right (as both parties in the *Emesa Sugar* case had asserted) to submit written observations on the Advocate–General's opinion.

Each Judge and Advocate–General has at least three *Référendaires,* or legal secretaries, who perform duties similar to those of a judicial clerk in the US, but usually have had experience in government, academia or the judiciary. Besides a Registrar, the Court also has an extensive library of Community law, international law, comparative law and of course also Member State law. Among the staff is at least one person from each Member State equipped to assist the Judges and their legal secretaries in the research of national law.

The Court receives submissions and hears oral argument from a wide variety of counsel. Counsel represent parties from both the public and the private sector. Lawyers in the service of both the Community institutions and the Member States (and their subdivisions and agencies) regularly participate and appear. Counsel speak different languages and are trained, and practice, in a range of different legal cultures. (These include American lawyers who are admitted to a Member State bar.) With this in mind, the Court has produced a comprehensive Note for Guidance of Counsel,[46] covering matters ranging from pleadings and the availability of interim relief to the use of language and lawyerly dress.

Judgments of the Court, together with the corresponding Advocate–General opinion, are published in the official court reports, though they are available much sooner in advance sheet form and, now, on the Internet. Until 1994, the Court of Justice also published contemporaneously (and in all official languages) a "Report of the Hearing." Now that Report is available only in the official language of the case.

The drafters of the treaties did not see fit to provide the Court of Justice with enforcement machinery of its own. According to EC Treaty Articles 244 and 256 (ex 187 and 192), enforcement of a Court judgment "shall be governed by the rules of civil procedure in force in the State in the territory of which it is carried out." Enforcement may be suspended only by a decision of the Court itself, except to the extent that there is a complaint about the irregularity of the method of enforcement.

NOTE ON THE COURT'S JURISDICTION OVER HUMAN RIGHTS, "CLOSER COOPERATION" AND "PILLAR THREE"

The Court presumably has jurisdiction to determine the meaning and validity of all Community law norms, wherever they may be found in the

---

46. Note for Guidance of Counsel in Written and Oral Proceedings before the Court of Justice of the European Communities, [1999] All ER (EC) 545 (Jan. 2, 1998). An amended version was published by the Court in February 2001.

Community treaties or in the Community's secondary legislation or international agreements. TEU Article 46 (ex L) expressly so provides. In fact, until recent treaty amendments, the Court's jurisdiction was in principle coextensive with the treaties. The Single European Act initiated a change, by excluding the Court of Justice from matters of cooperation in the sphere of foreign policy. When the TEU introduced a "third pillar" for justice and home affairs, it removed action under that pillar from the Court's jurisdiction as well. TEU Article 46 (ex L) thus excluded the Court's involvement in matters falling within pillars two (common foreign and security policy) and three (cooperation in justice and home affairs), as well as most of the TEU's common provisions, including the then important TEU Article F (now TEU Article 6), which required the European Union to respect the national identities of the Member States as well as fundamental rights (as guaranteed by the 1950 European Human Rights Convention and the constitutional traditions common to the Member States).

The exclusion of judicial recourse in these domains occasioned misgivings. To a very limited extent, the Court of Justice has been able to construe it narrowly. For example, in Commission v. Council (Airport transit arrangements), Case C–170/96, [1998] ECR I–2763, the Court essentially ruled that, while decisions taken under pillar three were generally not reviewable, they could be reviewed insofar as they were claimed to have been wrongly based on that pillar instead of on a provision of the EC Treaty (i.e. pillar one). (In the event, the Court ruled that a "joint action" on airport transit arrangements that the Council had adopted under the third pillar could not in fact have been adopted under the provision of the EC Treaty advanced by the Commission; it accordingly denied the Commission's claim for annulment.)

Certain of the exclusions of the Court's jurisdiction were eventually eliminated through amendments to TEU Article 47 introduced by the Treaty of Amsterdam. Accordingly, today, the Court has jurisdiction to interpret and determine the validity of measures taken within the TEU's third pillar (renamed as title VI, "police and judicial cooperation in criminal matters"), the provisions in the TEU's title VII on "closer cooperation" (see casebook page 125 *infra*), and the TEU's guarantee in Article 6 (ex F) of respect of fundamental rights by the institutions.[47] These were considered to be the least defensible gaps in judicial protection. However, the scope of judicial activity in these areas is in various ways attenuated,[48] thus introducing variations in the

47. TEU Article 46 also subjects the TEU's "final provisions" (arts. 47–53, ex L through S) to the Court's jurisdiction.

48. For example, in ruling on matters within the third pillar, the Court may not review the validity of operations carried out by Member State law enforcement officers or of decisions regarding the maintenance of law and order or the safeguard of internal security. Also, the ground rules for direct actions, preliminary references, and the resolution of disputes between Member States or between Member States and the Commission differ sig-

nificantly from those that generally obtain in the Community law system. TEU art. 35 (ex K.7). On these differences, see Chapters 5, 7 and 9 *infra*.

The Court's jurisdiction to rule on the application of the flexibility ("closer cooperation") clauses of the Treaties is somewhat limited. Its review of flexibility under the EC Treaty is not unusual; Article 11 gives the Court the same jurisdiction that it enjoys under the EC Treaty generally both as to the decision to launch closer cooperation and as to the legislation adopted pursuant to that cooperation. But the scope of jurisdiction according to subject matter and, as a result, unprecedented complexity. Moreover, when the Amsterdam Treaty moved visa, asylum and immigration policies from pillar three to pillar one, it subjected the Court's role in those areas to significant limitations,[49] with the result that the judicial function is now not uniform even within the first pillar.

The Treaty of Nice would give the Court a further specific role in connection with the TEU's provisions for sanctioning Member States for violations of fundamental rights. As amended, TEU Article 46 (ex L) would give the Court jurisdiction, at the request of the Member State concerned, to enforce "the purely procedural stipulations" of TEU Article 7 (ex F.1) whereby the Council may determine that there is a clear risk of a serious breach of fundamental rights by a State and may suspend certain rights of that State upon finding that it has committed a serious and persistent breach in that regard.

NOTE ON THE COURT OF FIRST INSTANCE

Like many other jurisdictions around the world, the Court of Justice found itself increasingly burdened with a large docket of cases and subject to delays in their dispatch. After years of urging by the Court, the EC Treaty was finally amended by the Single European Act to permit the creation by a unanimous vote of the Council of a lower Community court under the name of a Court of First Instance (CFI). In October 1988, the Council established the CFI, basing it in Luxembourg. (The Treaty of Nice would eliminate the CFI's description as "attached" to the Court of Justice.[50])

EC Treaty Article 225 (ex 168a), has been several times amended not only to recognize the CFI,[51] but also to permit enlargement of its jurisdiction. (Note

situation is different regarding the judicial role in the operation of flexibility under pillar three. TEU Article 40(4) states that only disputes relating to the launch of closer cooperation (essentially paragraphs one to three of Article 40 TEU) are governed by the usual jurisdictional rules; other aspects of flexibility (notably review of the legislation adopted pursuant to the cooperation mechanism) are governed by the more restrictive jurisdictional rules applicable to the Court's role in pillar three (see earlier this note).

Finally, concerning fundamental rights, TEU Article 46(1)(d) only authorizes the Court to rule on the conformity with those human rights as described in TEU Article 6(2) in those areas in which the Court enjoys jurisdiction under the Treaties. As a result, the Court does not play such a role at all concerning legislation enacted under pillar two; as for legislation enacted under pillar three, the Court's review operates under the same limitations as its review of pillar three issues generally (see above).

49. EC Treaty Article 68 (ex 73p). Of course, the opt-outs by the UK, Ireland and Denmark from this title complicate matters

further. Protocols to the Amsterdam Treaty expressly stipulate that Court decisions interpreting the provisions of Title IV (as well as measures implementing those provisions) are not binding on those States. By the same token, while the Schengen Protocol to the Amsterdam Treaty provides that each element of the Schengen *acquis*, once having been assigned an EC Treaty legal basis by the Council, is fully subject to ECJ jurisdiction, the fact remains that the UK and Ireland have not acceded to Schengen and that Denmark, while acceding to Schengen, does not participate in the Schengen *acquis'* incorporation into pillar one.

50. Decision 88/591, O.J. C 215/1 (Aug. 21, 1989). On the new court, see T. Kennedy, The Essential Minimum: The Establishment of the Court of First Instance, 14 Eur. L.Rev. 7 (1989); H. Schermers, The European Court of First Instance, 25 Common Mkt. L.Rev. 541 (1988).

51. The Treaty of Nice also expands Article 220 (ex 164) to state that the CFI, like the Court of Justice, "shall ensure that in the interpretation and application of [the EC] Treaty the law is observed."

that, as of ratification of the Treaty of Nice, most of what Article 225 contains would become part of Article 224.) Each time, Article 225 left it to the Council to fix the CFI's jurisdiction, within certain stated limitations. Initially, it permitted only actions brought by natural or legal persons to be brought in the CFI, and expressly excluded actions brought by Member States and by the institutions of the Community, as well as preliminary rulings under Article 234 (ex 177). Article 225 was subsequently amended at Maastricht to permit the CFI to hear all cases other than preliminary references.

The Council has never conferred on the CFI the full measure of jurisdiction that the Treaty permitted. Initially, the CFI won jurisdiction only over staff and competition cases, as well as coal and steel cases arising from application of ECSC Treaty. (These were cases whose fact-specificity and potential technicality tended to occasion substantial delays. They were also numerous; the transfer relieved the Court of Justice of about one-quarter of its caseload.) Upon urging by the Court of Justice, the Council has since gone further. In 1993, the Council extended the CFI's jurisdiction to *all* direct actions brought by natural or legal persons, whether for annulment or damages, except for anti-dumping and anti-subsidy cases and actions to which a Member State government is a party. Jurisdiction over anti-dumping and anti-subsidy cases soon followed. (With each extension, the cases within that category then pending before the Court of Justice, and for which a Preliminary Report had not been prepared, have been transferred to the CFI.) As of this writing, the Council still has not acted on the Court's suggestion in 1998 that the CFI be given jurisdiction over actions brought by the institutions or the Member States, including enforcement actions under Article 226 (ex 169).

The Treaty of Nice would change the CFI into a true court of "general jurisdiction by giving the CFI original jurisdiction over virtually all cases except those specifically reserved to the Court of Justice or assigned to a newly-created "judicial panel" (see below). The only classes of cases that the Treaty would leave outside this grant of general jurisdiction are enforcement actions by the Commission against a Member State (arts. 226–29, ex 169–72) and certain cases against Member State central banks or against or otherwise involving the European Investment Bank (art. 237, ex 180). As far as preliminary references to the CFI are concerned, the Treaty of Nice would finally lift the prohibition contained in the EC Treaty. However, under the amended Article 225, the CFI could entertain preliminary references only in the specific areas provided for in the Statute of the Court of Justice.[52] With the eventual creation of judicial panels "attached" to the Court of First Instance, the CFI would acquire appellate jurisdiction of its own.

Except to the extent the Council decides otherwise, all provisions of the treaties relating to the Court of Justice apply to the CFI as well. CFI judges are named by the Member State governments acting by common accord; they must possess the same qualifications as required for appointment to judicial office in their own states,[53] and they must be completely independent. They

---

52. By way of exception (viz. in cases where the reference raises a question of principle likely to affect the unity or consistency of Community law), the CFI may refer the preliminary reference to the Court of Justice or the CFI's preliminary rulings may be reviewed by the Court of Justice. EC Treaty art. 225, as amended by the Treaty of Nice.

53. The Treaty of Nice, amending EC Treaty Article 224, provides that nominees to the CFI, like nominees to the Court of Justice, serve for six-year terms, staggered at three-year intervals, but renewable. While the Court of First Instance currently consists of fifteen judges (by custom one per Member State[54]), it ordinarily sits in chambers of three or five judges. As a result of the obvious docket pressure, even this is changing. In 1999, the Council amended the decision establishing the CFI so as to permit that court to sit as a single judge,[55] and the CFI amended its rules of procedure accordingly.[56] In certain categories of actions,[57] a single *juge-rapporteur* ("*juge unique*") may now hear and decide the case provided it does not raise difficult questions of law or fact, is not especially important, and does not present other special circumstances. Within less than six months of the change of rules, the first judgment was rendered by a single CFI judge.[58]

EC Treaty Article 224, as amended at Nice, would provide for the judges of the CFI to elect a President for a three-year renewable term from among their members. Up to now, the CFI has had no separately designated Advocates–General; instead judges of the CFI perform that function on an ad hoc basis.[59] In agreement with the Court of Justice and with the approval of the Council, the CFI has established its own rules of procedure.[60] (See Part I of the Selected Documents, document 7.)

The CFI's decisions are made "subject to a right of appeal to the Court of Justice on points of law only," so as to enable the Court of Justice to ensure the correct interpretation of Community law. Article 51 of the Statute of the Court of Justice is still more explicit: appeals from the Court of First Instance are limited to issues of law, and more particularly to claims that the CFI lacked competence, committed a procedural violation or infringed a rule of Community law.

This formulation sounds deceptively simple. Does a party raise an issue of law, for these purposes, when it claims that the CFI made an improper assessment of the evidence? When it claims that the CFI made an improper legal characterization of the facts?

The answer to the first of these questions is quite clear:

must be qualified for appointment "to *high* judicial office" (emphasis added).

54. The Treaty of Nice, amending EC Treaty Article 224, provides for "*at least* one judge from each Member State" (emphasis added), with the number fixed by the Statute of the Court of Justice.

55. Council Decision 99/291, O.J. 1999 L 114/52 (May 1, 1999).

56. 1999 O.J. L 135/92 (May 29, 1999). The decision to refer a case to a single judge requires that the parties first be heard on the question and that the CFI chamber before which the case is pending unanimously agree. If a Member State or Community institution objects, the case may not be referred.

57. The actions covered are (a) cases concerning Community officials, (b) direct challenges by natural or legal persons to decisions of the Community institutions that are addressed to them or are of direct and individual

concern to them, (c) actions based on the non-contractual liability of the Community, and (d) cases in which the CFI's jurisdiction arises from an arbitration clause in a contract to which the Community is a party. On the other hand, single-judge jurisdiction is excluded for a number of categories of disputes, including (but not limited to) competition cases, state aid cases, cases relating to trade protection measures and certain cases relating to the common agricultural policy.

58. Cotrim v. CEDEFOP, Case T–180/98, [1999] ECR II–1077.

59. As amended at Nice, Article 224 permits the position of Advocate–General on the CFI to be established by the Statute of the Court of Justice.

60. Article 224, as amended at Nice, authorizes the CFI, in agreement with the Court of Justice, to establish its Rules of Procedure, subject to Council approval by qualified majority.

¹³   [A]n appeal may rely only on grounds relating to the infringement of rules of law, to the exclusion of any appraisal of the facts, and is therefore admissible only in so far as it is claimed that the decision of the Court of First Instance is incompatible with the rules of law the application of which it had to ensure.

¹⁴   The Court of Justice is no more competent, in principle, to examine the evidence accepted by the Court of First Instance in support of those facts than it is to find the facts themselves. In so far as the evidence was duly obtained and the rules and general principles of law relating to the burden of proof were observed, as well as the procedural rules in relation to the taking of evidence, it is for the Court of First Instance alone to assess the value which should be attached to the items of evidence produced to it.

¹⁵   Since the Court has no jurisdiction to review the assessment of the Court of First Instance, the appellant's arguments on that aspect . . . must be rejected as manifestly inadmissible.

D v. Commission, Case C–89/95P, [1996] ECR I–53.

    The answer to the second question is less clear. On the one hand, the Court has reiterated that "[once] the CFI has established or assessed the facts, the Court of Justice has jurisdiction . . . to review the legal characterization of those facts by the Court of First Instance and the legal conclusions it has drawn from them."[61] But, as to the standard by which the Court of Justice conducts this review, the Court seems prepared, on most issues of importance, to accept the CFI's conclusions unless it finds them to be "manifestly erroneous." What is the difference between the CFI's "appraisal" of the facts (as to which there is in principle no review by the Court of Justice) and its "legal characterization of the facts" (as to which such review, albeit under a relaxed standard, is still available)? For a review of the Court's record as a court of appeals, see Sonelli, Appeals on Points of Law in the Community System: A Review, 35 Comm. Mkt. L. Rev. 871 (1998).

    As we have seen, appeals from the CFI to the Court of Justice invite the Court to review the CFI's rulings on issues of Community law. Occasionally, though, the legal issue raised concerns the legality, not of acts of the political institutions, but of acts of the Court of First Instance itself. For a good example, see Ismeri Europa Srl v. Court of Auditors, Case C–315/99P, [2001] ECR I-____ (July 10, 2001). The Court of First Instance had dismissed a management company's claim for damages against the Court of Auditors for losses resulting from criticism of it contained in a report made public by the Court of Auditors. On appeal, the company claimed that the CFI erred in refusing to hear certain witnesses, to which the Court of Justice replied (paras. 19–20):

    [T]he Court of First Instance is the sole judge of any need for the information available to it concerning the cases before it to be supplemented. Whether or not the evidence before it is convincing is a matter to be appraised by it alone and is not subject to review by the Court of Justice on appeal, except where the clear sense of that evidence has been

---

61. San Marco Impex Italiana Srl, Case C–19/95P, [1996] ECR I–4435 (para. 39). See also Commission v. Brazzelli Lualdi, Case 136/92P, [1994] ECR I–1981 (paras. 48–49).

distorted or the substantive inaccuracy of the Court of First Instance's findings is apparent from the documents in the case-file.

No matter has been adverted to in the course of this appeal to lead the Court to believe that anything of that kind occurred in the present case.

Consider also the case of Baustahlgewerbe GmbH v. Commission, Case C–185/95P, [1998] ECR I–8417. The underlying question in that appeal was whether the CFI had erred in sustaining most portions of a Commission decision that certain agreements among producers in the welded steel mesh sector violated European competition law. However, the claimants also challenged the legality of the Court of First Instance's *own* procedures at first instance, asserting that the duration of the proceedings in the CFI and the length of time before the CFI issued its ruling violated the right to a hearing within a reasonable time under the European Human Rights Convention as well as a general Community law principle of "promptitude," that the CFI's refusal to consider certain evidence or to order access to certain Commission documents infringed procedural due process, and that the CFI failed to issue a reasoned judgment. The Court rejected most of those contentions, but did find that the CFI proceedings had taken an unreasonably long period of time. It accordingly reduced the 3 million ecu fine by 50,000 ecus, the latter sum to be viewed as compensation for the unreasonable delay.

While disappointed parties before the Court of First Instance have an appeal as of right to the Court of Justice, the ECJ's Rules of Procedure (art. 119) allow the Court to dismiss the appeal, even prior to opening the oral procedure, where the appeal is "clearly inadmissible or clearly unfounded." On appeal, the appellant will not be permitted to introduce for the first time "new pleas in law" or, evidently, even new legal arguments.[62]

An appeal from the CFI to the Court of Justice must be filed within two months of notification of the lower court decision. If an appeal succeeds, the Court of Justice quashes the decision; it may then either give final judgment itself or remand the case to the CFI for judgment. The appeal does not as a general rule have suspensive effect. See Statute of the Court of Justice (EC), art. 53. However, pursuant to EC Treaty Articles 242 and 243 (ex 185 and 186), the Court of Justice may suspend the effectiveness of a Court of First Instance judgment pending appeal (or prescribe other interim measures), if the circumstances so require. As with grants of interim relief generally, the Court will consider whether there is urgency and whether the elements of law and fact establish a prima facie case for suspension. See Rules of Procedure of the Court of Justice, art. 83(2).

Now it is the Court of First Instance that is experiencing substantial overload, due both to the volume and complexity of the cases before it. Trademark cases challenging decisions of the Office for Harmonisation in the Internal Market (OHIM) are an excellent and recent example. See, for example, Procter & Gamble Co. v. OHIM ("Baby–Dry"), Case T–163/98, [1999] ECR II–2383, a judgment which was in turn reversed by the Court of Justice. Procter & Gamble Co. v. OHIM, Case C–383/99P, [2001] ECR I-___ (Sept. 20, 2001).

62. See San Marco Impex Italiana Srl, *supra* note 61, paras. 47–49.

Recent IGC's have all considered reform measures, including increasing the number of CFI judges. At the Nice IGC, the Member States finally agreed to amend the EC Treaty (through a new Article 225a) to authorize the Council to create, and "attach" to the CFI, certain specialized "judicial panels."[63] Panel members, to be appointed by the Council acting unanimously, would have to meet the usual standards—independence and eligibility for national judicial office. Each judicial panel would establish its own Rules of Procedure, subject to approval by the Court of Justice and the Council, the latter acting by qualified majority. Except where otherwise provided, decisions by judicial panels may only be appealed to the CFI on points of law. In a special declaration at Nice, the IGC specifically urged that a panel "swiftly" be set up to deal with staff cases.

If the growth of the CFI has now rendered the Court of Justice's original jurisdiction reasonably manageable, the latter's appellate jurisdiction has become burdensome. Reform measures under consideration include giving the Court discretion to decide not to hear cases on appeal, and to so decide without the necessity of first holding oral procedures or making a formal explanatory statement.

Notes and Questions

1. A very large percentage of cases before the Court of Justice has always come to it by way of preliminary reference from Member State courts under Article 234 (ex 177), seeking interpretations of Community law as needed for disposing of those cases. If the need for a Court of First Instance was in fact prompted by the existing overload on Court of Justice resources, why has CFI jurisdiction to issue preliminary rulings been so long in coming?

2. A more radical solution would be to create below the Court of Justice a system of regional Community courts or a series of specialized Community courts. On these and other strategies, see J.–P. Jacqué & J. Weiler, On the Road to European Union—A New Judicial Architecture: An Agenda for the Intergovernmental Conference, 27 Common Mkt. L. Rev. 185 (1990); Editorial, The Future Development of the Community's Judicial System, 28 Common Mkt. L. REV. 5 (1991).

3. For an insider's account of the workings of the Court of Justice, see David Edward, How the Court of Justice Works, 20 Eur. L. REV. 539 (1995).

4. Based simply on this chapter's institutional description of the Community, how would you describe the separation of powers among its institutions? See generally K. Lenaerts, Some Reflections on the Separation of Powers in the European Community, 28 Common Mkt. L. REV. 11 (1991).

5. OTHER INSTITUTIONS

With time, certain existing institutions have received formal recognition in the constitutive treaties and, in some cases, status as a Community institution.

As amended at Maastricht, Article 7 (ex 4) of the EC Treaty ordains the Court of Auditors (located in Luxembourg) as a Community institution

---

63. In doing so, the Council acts unanimously, either (a) on a proposal from the Commission, after consulting the Parliament and the Court of Justice, or (b) at the request of the Court, after consulting the Parliament and Commission. EC Treaty art. 225a, added by the Treaty of Nice.

empowered to examine the accounts of all revenue and expenditure of the Community and of the bodies set up by the Community. Its structure and functions are set out in Articles 246–48 (ex 188a–188c).[64]

The Economic and Social Committee (ECOSOC), located in Brussels, is described in Article 257 (ex 193) of the EC Treaty as having "advisory status." The Council and Commission (as well as Parliament) may consult ECOSOC whenever they choose, but they must do so whenever the Treaty so requires. ECOSOC may also issue an opinion on its own initiative. Article 257 provides that it shall consist of persons representing those who are engaged in different kinds of economic and social activity, such as manufacturing, agriculture, artisanry and the professions, as well as various representatives of the public. (The Treaty of Nice refers generally to "economic and social components of organised civil society," while specifically adding consumers to the list of groups to be represented.)

Each Member State is allocated a certain number of seats on the Committee[65] and permitted to advance lists of nominees. After consulting the Commission, the Council votes unanimously (and, after ratification of the Nice Treaty, by qualified majority) to appoint Committee members from among the nominees. Members serve four-year renewable terms, during which they "may not be bound by any mandatory instructions." Article 261 (ex 197) contemplates the creation of specialized sections for agriculture, transport and possibly other sectors, but requires that the Committee be consulted only as a whole. (The Treaty of Nice imposes a ceiling on ECOSOC membership of 350.)

The European Investment Bank is dealt with in Articles 266–67 (ex 198d–198e).

The 1990s brought to the Community newer bodies worthy of mention. Chief among these are (a) the Committee of the Regions and (b) a host of so-called "specialized agencies."

(a) The Committee of the Regions

The Maastricht Treaty created a new institution, the Committee of the Regions. Mirroring in some measure the Economic and Social Committee, this body performs essentially advisory functions, including the issuance of non-binding opinions to other EC institutions. The Council, Commission and Parliament may consult the Committee of the Regions as they deem appropriate. (Occasionally, the EC Treaty requires that it be consulted.) The Committee may also issue opinions on its own initiative. The Member States have a weighted number of seats on the Committee.[66]

The Committee of the Regions is composed of representatives of regional and local entities within the Member States, who are not also members of the European Parliament. (The Treaty of Nice would amend Article 263 (ex 198a) of the EC Treaty to require members either to hold a regional or local

64. The Nice Treaty provides for members of the Court of Auditors to be named by the Council (after consulting Parliament) by qualified majority rather than unanimity.

65. A Declaration on Enlargement adopted at Nice reassigns seats among the Member States in anticipation of accession by the twelve applicant States.

66. A Declaration on Enlargement adopted at Nice reassigns seats among the Member States in anticipation of accession by the twelve applicant States.

electoral mandate or to be politically accountable to an elected assembly; it also sets a ceiling of 350 members.) Committee members are appointed for four-year renewable terms by the Council,[67] acting unanimously on proposal from the Member States. (The Nice Treaty, however, would substitute qualified majority voting for unanimity in the Council.) Although enjoined under Article 263 to be independent and to act in accordance with the general Community interest, Committee members almost certainly function in part as representatives of their regions and thus promote more or less particular interests. Currently, the Committee has 222 members, allocated among Member States as provided in Article 263.

At recent IGC's, the Committee unsuccessfully sought greater recognition and influence. It failed to win wider powers of consultation in Community decision-making or standing to bring annulment actions against Community measures in the Court of Justice. (In the latter quest, it had been supported by regional interests such as the German *Länder*.) It even failed to win formal designation under Article 7 (ex 4) of the EC Treaty as a Community "institution."

(b) The Specialized Agencies

During the 1990s, with the completion of the internal market, a number of decentralized European "agencies" were created to carry out particular tasks in more or less specialized policy fields within the Community sphere. A Community agency is a public authority set up pursuant to secondary legislation, separate from the Community institutions proper and enjoying legal personality. The agencies generally fulfil tasks that are scientific, technical or managerial in nature.

As of 2001, there were twelve agencies, based at locations assigned to them by the European Council as follows:

Office for Harmonization in the Internal Market (Trademark and Designs) (Alicante)

European Agency for the Evaluation of Medicinal Products (London)

The Community Plant Variety Office (Angers)

European Environment Agency (Copenhagen)

European Monitoring Centre for Drugs and Drug Addiction (Lisbon)

European Monitoring Centre on Racism and Xenophobia (Vienna)

European Center for Development of Vocational Training (Thessaloniki)

European Foundation for the Improvement of Living and Working Conditions (Dublin)

European Agency for Health and Safety at Work (Bilbao)

European Training Foundation (Turin)

Translation Center for the Bodies of the European Union (Luxembourg)

European Agency for Reconstruction (Thessaloniki)

---

67. Since the Treaty of Nice would require Committee members to hold a regional or local electoral mandate (or to be politically accountable to an elected assembly), a term of office terminates automatically, even midstream, if and when the political mandate comes to an end. See Article 263, as amended at Nice.

While each agency has its own structure and functions,[68] generally speaking they perform purely information-gathering, information processing, research and general administrative tasks in aid of the institutions, most notably the Commission. The European Environment Agency (EEA) may be taken as an example. The EEA is a monitoring center funded by the general Community budget, which began its operations in 1995. Its mission is to "collect and disseminate objective, reliable and comparable information at the European level enabling EU Member States to take measures to protect the environment, to assess the results of such measures and to ensure that the public is properly informed about the state of the environment and offer technical support."

The EEA is governed by a management board consisting of one representative per Member State, two Commission representatives, two representatives of the European Parliament and, in addition, one representative from each of the non-EU countries that participates in the agency pursuant to the agreements referred to above. On a proposal by the Commission, the board elects an Executive Director who serves for a renewable five-year term of office and is accountable to the board. The Director is assisted by a scientific committee which delivers opinions and publishes reports. The management board has broad discretion in further organizing the EEA, adopts the agency's annual and multi-annual work programs, and transmits the EEA's annual report to the Commission, Council and Parliament. Discussions on restructuring the work of the EEA and the management Board so as to accommodate the enlargement process started in 2000.[69]

The intervening years have seen other specialized agencies of the Community put firmly in place. Thus, for example, in January 1996, the EU's Office for Harmonisation in the Internal Market (Trademark and Design) in Alicante, Spain, began accepting applications for a single Community trademark for products and services marketed within the Union. Businesses no longer have to file separate applications for trademark protection in the different Member States. An application may be made to the Office (also known by the acronym OHIM) in any of the EC's eleven official languages, and a trademark, once duly registered at the Office, is subject to uniform rules for the entire EU. A similar scheme, vesting non-exclusive licensing authority in an EC-level agency, operating parallel to its separate national agency counterparts, has been introduced in the pharmaceutical sector, through the European Agency for the Evaluation of Medicinal Products (London). Prescription drug manufacturers have the option of applying either to this agency for Community-wide marketing approval or to a national agency whose determinations are entitled, under established conditions, to mutual recognition by the agencies of the other Member States. These procedures have become known, respectively, as "centralized" and "decentralized."

Among the proposed new agencies is a European Food Authority to be established to facilitate the harmonization of food law within the Member

---

68. For an overview, see the Commission's Background Report on New Community Institutions (Doc. ISEC/B7/94).

69. On the EEA's organization, see Council Regulation 90/1210 of May 7, 1990, O.J. L

120/1 (May 11, 1990), as amended by Council Regulation 933/1999 of April 29, 1999, O.J. L 117/1 (May 5, 1999).

States and promote a high level of health and safety protection within the context of the internal market.[70] The initiative, prompted by recent "mad cow" and "foot-and-mouth" disease scares, has led to lobbying by Member States and candidate countries to have the new agency established on their soil. As of this writing, the matter is unresolved.

Largely due to their institutional separation from the Council, Commission and Parliament (as well as from the Member States), these agencies are commonly characterized as "independent." Unlike their US namesakes, however, they are not generally envisaged as exercising regulatory power. Nevertheless, an important and controversial issue is the extent to which regulatory powers may eventually be delegated to them to the possible detriment of the Commission. See K. Lenaerts, Regulating the Regulatory Process: "Delegation of Powers" in the European Community, 18 Eur. L. Rev. 23 (1993); Editorial, 33 Common Mkt. L. Rev. 623 (1996).

70. Commission Proposal for a Regulation of the European Parliament and Council laying down the general principles and requirements of food law, establishing the European Food Authority, and laying down procedures in matters of food. COM (2000) 716 final (Nov. 8, 2000).

Chapter 3

COMMUNITY LEGISLATION AND THE LEGISLATIVE PROCESS

The Treaties examined in the previous chapter authorize the institutions to adopt policies and take actions across an extraordinarily wide field. Not all of that policy and action takes the form of legally binding measures, but a great deal does. Foreseeing that, the treaty drafters provided that the institutions might adopt certain species of "legal acts" and do so through a number of different preestablished "legislative procedures."

This chapter explores the nature of these acts and procedures not only as abstract notions, but also by way of concrete example. The chapter closes with a look at the budgetary system—the system by which the European institutions can "afford" their activities, legislative and non-legislative alike.

A. FORMS OF COMMUNITY ACTION

The EC Treaty defines the kinds of legal acts that the political institutions of the Community may take and the legal effects those acts shall have. Article 249 (ex 189) states that the Council, the Parliament (acting jointly with the Council), and the Commission may, "in accordance with the provisions of this Treaty," issue regulations, directives, decisions, recommendations or opinions. The article goes on to describe these instruments as follows:

A regulation shall have general application. It shall be binding in its entirety and directly applicable in all Member States.

A directive shall be binding, as to the result to be achieved, upon each Member State to which it is addressed, but shall leave to the national authorities the choice of form and methods.

A decision shall be binding in its entirety upon those to whom it is addressed.

Recommendations and opinions shall have no binding force.

Article 253 (ex 190) requires that regulations, directives and decisions state the reasons on which they are based and refer to whatever proposal or opinion the Treaty may have required the institutions to obtain before adopting them.

The terms "regulation" and "decision" are not in principle difficult to grasp. A regulation is a general rule of conduct applicable to all persons falling within its scope, while a decision relates only to the one or more persons specifically addressed in it. There is less certainty over precisely what the descriptions "binding" and "directly applicable" were meant to convey. At a minimum, however, a "binding" norm (in contrast to a mere recommendation or opinion) may be regarded as one that has the force of law, and a "directly applicable" norm as one that, once enacted at the Community level, becomes an effective part of the national legal order as well.

The directive is a more distinctive measure, defined as "binding" only as to result but not as to "the choice of form and methods." When directives are addressed to Member States (as they usually are), the latter are called upon to take the legislative and/or administrative action needed to implement the purposes set out in the directive. Although a directive does not have to be very detailed, in practice directives are often quite specific as to how they are to be implemented. The language of Article 249 (ex 189) implies that directives, though "binding" on Member States, may not be "directly applicable." (This matter is taken up in Chapter 7A).

As Article 249 implies, legally binding acts—regulations, directives and decisions—may be taken either by the Council alone, by the Council together with the Parliament, or by the Commission. Which body (or bodies) is competent to adopt a measure in any given circumstance, and what form that action must take, can only be determined by reference to the specific article of the treaty involved. This is yet another way of underscoring the point that the constitutive treaties confer only limited decisional powers upon the institutions. These powers are limited not only because the relevant treaty articles designate the institution that may act in any given case and the instruments it may employ in doing so, but also because—as this and later chapters will show—they prescribe, sometimes with remarkable specificity, various other procedural requirements as well as substantive conditions for action.

Article 254 (ex 191) provides that regulations, directives and decisions that are adopted under the now-dominant "codecision" procedure (see page 97 *infra*) are to be signed by the Presidents of the Parliament and Council and published in the Community's *Official Journal*,[1] entering into force on the date they specify (or, absent a date, twenty days following their publication). Other regulations of the Council and Commission, as well as directives issued by them to all the Member States, are likewise required to be published in the *Official Journal*, with the same rules on entry into force. Other directives and decisions take effect upon notification to the persons addressed.

As noted, a measure's classification may determine whether and to what extent it has binding force. It also may have implications for judicial review, and in particular for deciding who may bring a legal challenge and indeed whether a legal challenge may be brought at all (questions largely taken up in Chapter 5A on judicial review).

NOTE ON THE *ERTA* CASE

The case of Commission v. Council (ERTA), Case 22/70, [1971] ECR 263, gave the Court of Justice an early opportunity to expand the notion of a

---

1. The Treaty of Nice renames the Official Journal of the European Communities as the Official Journal of the European Union. EC Treaty, art. 254, as amended.

Community "act," at least for judicial review purposes. In 1962, five of the then six Member States entered into a European Road Transport Agreement (ERTA) with certain European states outside the Community. The agreement, which meant to harmonize certain labor regulations in road transport, never came into effect, and in 1967 negotiations were reopened with all six Member States participating. In 1969, during the pendency of these negotiations, the Council adopted a related Regulation 543/69 governing labor aspects of internal Community road transport.

In March 1970, the Council took up the question of the position that the Member States should take in the reopened ERTA negotiations. It resolved that while the Member States would continue negotiating on their own behalf and become individual parties to ERTA, they were nevertheless to coordinate their positions and speak in the negotiations through the Member State holding the Presidency of the Council.

The Commission then brought an action in the Court of Justice challenging the legality of this action by the Council. It claimed that since the Community (through Regulation 543/69) had already legislated on the subject matter, the negotiations could no longer be left to the Member States. It contended that the matter should be dealt with either through further Community legislation or though an international treaty to which the Community would be a party. In either event the Commission would have a role to play.

The Court dealt initially with the threshold question of whether its March 1970 determination was a justiciable act, the Council having argued that it represented merely a coordination of Member State policies without any Community law implications. The Court reasoned that since EC Treaty Article 173 (now 230) authorized the Court to review the legality of acts of the Council other than recommendations or opinions (which lack binding force), it should be interpreted as subjecting to judicial review all measures adopted by the institutions which are intended to have legal force and effect. Invoking Article 164 (now 220) of the Treaty, which gives the Court responsibility for ensuring that the law is observed in the interpretation and application of the Treaty, the Court concluded that it would be wrong to limit the availability of review to the categories of measures referred to in Article 189 (now 249).

The Court then considered whether the Council's March 1970 determination was an act intended to have legal effect.

48   As regards negotiating, the Council decided ... that the negotiations should be carried on and concluded by the six Member States, which would become contracting parties to [ERTA].

49   Throughout the negotiations and at the conclusion of the agreement, the States would act in common and would constantly coordinate their positions according to the usual procedure in close association with the Community institutions, the delegation of the Member State currently occupying the Presidency of the Council acting as spokesman.

* * *

53   It thus seems that in so far as they concerned the objective of the negotiations as defined by the Council, the proceedings of 20 March 1970 could not have been simply the expression or the recognition of a volun-

tary coordination, but were designed to lay down a course of action binding on both the institutions and the Member States, and destined ultimately to be reflected in the tenor of the regulation.

[54] In the part of its conclusions relating to the negotiating procedure, the Council adopted provisions which were capable of derogating in certain circumstances from the procedure laid down by the Treaty regarding negotiations with third countries and the conclusion of agreements.

[55] Hence, the proceedings of 20 March 1970 had definite legal effects both on relations between the Community and the Member States and on the relationship between [the] institutions.

THE REQUIREMENT OF REASONS

EC Treaty Article 253 (ex 190) requires that regulations, directives and decisions state the "reasons" on which they are based. The Court of Justice has many times reaffirmed that the required statement must disclose in a clear and unequivocal fashion the reasoning that the institution or institutions followed, so that the persons concerned are aware of the reasons for the measure and may defend their rights, and so that the Court may exercise its supervisory jurisdiction.

GERMANY v. COMMISSION

(Brennwein)
Case 24/62, [1963] ECR 63.

[The introduction of the common external tariff caused a sudden and significant increase in the import duties on the wine used to produce Brennwein (a low-priced wine-based alcoholic drink). The government of Germany, where Brennwein was chiefly produced, asked the Commission for approval to import 450,000 hectoliters of the wine at a lower rate of duty. The Commission allowed only 100,000 hectoliters to be imported at that rate, stating:

> On the basis of the existing information it has been possible to ascertain that the production of the wines in question within the Community is amply sufficient. The grant of a tariff quota of the volume requested might therefore lead to serious disturbances of the market in the products in question.

The Commission never specified the "existing information" on which it relied. Germany sued to have the decision set aside, in part on account of the insufficiency of the Commission's statement of reasons.]

[The then] Article 25 [of the EC Treaty] contains derogations from the common external tariff, which constitutes one of the "foundations" of the Community. . . .

. . . [Article 25] provides an exception to this common tariff with a view to remedying difficulties which may result from the alignment of national duties with those of the Common Customs Tariff in supplying the demands of a Member State.

* * *

Taken as a whole, [Article 25] implies that the Commission has a duty to evaluate the state of the market for the products concerned and the difficulties encountered in connection with supplying the demands of the Member State which has made the request for Article 25(3) to be applied. It must ... consider the nature of any disturbance, its seriousness and its likelihood. Finally, having found that the said Article 25(3) is applicable, the Commission ... "may" still evaluate the expediency and amount of any quota.

It follows, therefore, from the wording and the general scheme of Article 25, that the Commission's discretionary power, which it exercises independently within the limits laid down by the Treaty and subject to review by the Court, is in no way fettered.

[T]he applicant on the other hand rightly submits that the statement of reasons for the Decision is deficient and that therefore Article 190 [now 253] is contravened.

In imposing upon the Commission the obligation to state reasons for its decisions, Article 190 is not taking mere formal considerations into account but seeks to give an opportunity to the parties of defending their rights, to the Court of exercising its supervisory functions and to Member States and to all interested nationals of ascertaining the circumstances in which the Commission has applied the Treaty. To attain these objectives, it is sufficient for the Decision to set out, in a concise but clear and relevant manner, the principal issues of law and of fact upon which it is based and which are necessary in order that the reasoning which has led the Commission to its Decision may be understood. Apart from general considerations, which apply without distinction to other cases, or which are confined to repeating the wording of the Treaty, the Commission has been content to rely upon "the information collected", without specifying any of it, in order to reach a conclusion "that the production of the wines in question is amply sufficient".

This elliptical reasoning is all the more objectionable because the Commission gave no indication, as it did belatedly before the Court, of the evolution and size of the surpluses, but only repeated, without expanding the reasons for it, the same statement "that there was no indication that the existing market situation within the Community did not allow these branches of the industry in the German Federal Republic a supply which is adequate in quantity and in quality". On the other hand, although it maintained that the production of the Community was sufficient, the Commission restricted itself to "deducing from this" that "the grant of a tariff quota of the volume requested might therefore lead to serious disturbances of the market in the products in question", but these disturbances were not specified. Thus it neither described the risk involved in this case, nor did it disclose what it considered to be the necessary and sufficient connection in the present case between the two concepts which it links one with the other by a simple deduction. However, by granting a restricted quota notwithstanding its description of production as "amply sufficient", and thereby admitting that Article 25(3) applied, the Commission thus conceded that this factor was not enough to make it possible "to deduce from it" the risk of serious disturbance.

Thus the statement of reasons expressed appears on this point to be contradictory, since in spite of its statement with regard to an adequate supply and of the automatic conclusion to be drawn therefrom the Commission grants a quota and thereby implies that it would not cause any serious disturbance. Moreover, several of the recitals in the German text, which is authentic, lack the necessary clarity.

It follows from these factors that the inadequacy, the vagueness and the inconsistency of the statement of reasons for the Decision, both in respect of the refusal of the quota requested and of the concession of the quota granted, do not satisfy the requirements of Article 190.

Those parts of the Decision which have been submitted to the Court must therefore be annulled.

Notes and Questions

1. If, as the Court stated, the Treaty gives the Commission unfettered discretion, what purpose is served by a requirement of reasons justifying its use? In the *Noordwijks cement accord* case, *infra* page 135, the Court annulled for insufficient reasoning the Commission's decision that the conditions for competition law liability under Article 81(1) (ex 85(1)) were "met" and that the grant of an Article 81(3) (ex 85(3)) exemption "was not justified." The Court said that the decision failed "to allow the Court and all concerned to determine whether the provisions have been applied correctly." [1967] ECR at 94. For a more recent example, see Compagnia Italiana Alcool SaS di Mario Mariano & Co. v. Commission, Case C–358/90, [1992] ECR I–2457.

2. In Groupement des Fabricants de Papiers Peints de Belgique v. Commission, Case 73/74, [1975] ECR 1491, the Commission imposed fines on several companies for price-fixing in the wholesale wallpaper market. The Court annulled the decision for insufficient reasoning because the Commission, in finding that the companies' conduct affected trade between Member States, had significantly extended the principles of earlier decisions and thus should have given a more detailed statement of the grounds for its finding. The Court allowed that rulings fitting into "a well-established line of decisions" may be reasoned in a summary manner, "for example by a reference to those decisions." [1975] ECR at 1514. Had the decision merely followed established policy, reliance on previous decisions evidently would have passed muster.

3. Note that Article 253 (ex 190) applies to regulations and directives as well as decisions. Is this surprising? The requirement of reasons may account for the practice of introducing regulations and directives with a long series of recitals ("whereas ..."). On the degree of specificity required for the reasons underlying general regulations, see Beus GmbH & Co. v. Hauptzollamt München, Case 5/67, [1968] ECR 83. On the acceptability of incorporating by reference the reasons stated in prior measures of the same kind (as for example in the short-term fixing of prices, duties and refund levels), see Schwarze v. Einfuhr– und Vorratsstelle für Getreide und Futtermittel, Case 16/65, [1965] ECR 877.

4. The requirement of reasons has particular significance when the Treaty expressly makes Community action conditional on a more or less specific finding. Perhaps the best example is Article 95(4) (ex 100a(4)), which authorizes the Commission to excuse a State from complying with a directive adopted by

qualified majority voting on account of certain "major needs." In France v. Commission (PCP prohibition), Case C–41/93, [1994] ECR I–1829, the Court annulled the Commission's first grant of such a derogation for the inadequacy of its statement of reasons. For that judgment, see page 548 *infra*.

5. A group of French companies challenged a decision by the Commission that a benefit that the French government had granted to their competitor did not constitute a forbidden state aid. The Court of First Instance, in annulling the decision, remarked:

[78]   The Court considers, moreover, that the Commission's obligation to state reasons for its decisions may in certain circumstances require an exchange of views and arguments with the complainant, since, in order to justify to the requisite legal standard its assessment of the nature of a measure characterized by the complainant as State aid, the Commission needs to ascertain what view the complainant takes of the information gathered by it in the course of its inquiry. In those circumstances, that obligation constitutes a necessary extension of the Commission's obligation to deal diligently and impartially with its inquiry into the matter by eliciting all such views as may be necessary.

[79]   [I]t is not open to the Commission to claim ... that to undertake such an exchange of views and arguments in relation to the contents of the complaint and its own investigation would in fact result in its being required to initiate the procedure provided for by Article 93(2) [now 88(2)] of the Treaty, and thus suspend the implementation of the measure in question, even though that measure might ultimately prove not to constitute State aid within the meaning of Article 92 [now 87] of the Treaty.... The Commission ... has at its disposal, during the preliminary stage of the procedure, adequate means to carry out a diligent and impartial examination of the complaint and to comply with its obligation to give reasons for its decision to reject a complaint on the ground that the measure complained of does not constitute State aid within the meaning of Article 92 of the Treaty....

Chambre Syndicale Nationale des Entreprises de Transport de Fonds et Valeurs (Sytraval) v. Commission, Case T–95/94, [1995] ECR II–2651. Is this result predicated on an insufficiency of the statement of reasons or on an insufficiency of reasoning? Is there any significance to this distinction? The Commission's appeal from the CFI's judgment was unsuccessful. Commission v. Chambre Syndicale Nationale des Entreprises de Transport de Fonds et Valeurs (Sytraval), Case C–367/95P, [1998] ECR I–1719.

THE INTERPRETATION OF COMMUNITY LAW

On many occasions, the Court of Justice has emphasized that Community legislation merits a broad and purposive interpretation, by which is meant an interpretation that will generously serve the legislation's underlying objectives. See, e.g., von Colson and Kamann v. Land Nordrhein–Westfalen, Case 14/83, [1984] ECR 1891, 1909. This mode of interpretation is not unlike the so-called teleological interpretation that continental courts commonly profess to give to their codes and to certain of their more basic statutes. At the same time, the Court has said that legislation should be interpreted, whenever possible, so as to conform with higher Community law. "It is settled law that where the wording of secondary Community law is open to more than one interpretation, preference should be given to the interpretation which renders the provision consistent with the Treaty rather than the interpretation which leads to its being incompatible with the Treaty." Spain v. Commission (Motor vehicle aid), Case C–135/93, [1995] ECR I–1651 (para. 37).

The Court has suggested that national authorities are under a similar obligation to give Community legislation a broad and purposive construction, and thus to extend that construction to national legislation enacted to implement Community law. See *von Colson and Kamann, supra*. Although this was thought at one time to create special difficulties for the English judiciary, accustomed to narrower and more circumscribed methods of statutory construction, most English judges (including members of the House of Lords) now have embraced the methodology for these purposes. See Litster v. Forth Dry Dock & Engineering Co. Ltd., [1990] 4 A.C. 546, [1989] 2 WLR 634, [1989] 1 All ER 1134, [1989] 2 CMLR 194, 201 (H.L., March 16, 1989) (per Lord Templeman). Lord Oliver, writing in the *Litster* case, was explicit:

> [If] legislation enacted to give effect to the United Kingdom's obligations under the EEC Treaty ... can reasonably be construed so as to conform with those obligations—obligations which are to be ascertained not only from the wording of the relevant directive but from the interpretation placed upon it by the European Court of Justice at Luxembourg—such a purposive construction will be applied even though, perhaps, it may involve some departure from the strict and literal application of the words the legislature has elected to use.

[1989] 2 CMLR at 202–03. See also Foster v. British Gas plc, [1991] 2 WLR 1075, [1991] 2 CMLR 217, 224 (H.L., April 18, 1991) (per Lord Templeman); J. Rothschild Holdings plc v. Commissioners of Inland Revenue, [1989] 2 CMLR 621, 639 (C.A., March 10, 1989). For earlier and somewhat different views from the UK courts, see Chapter 8G *infra*.

Indeed, Community legislation, once adopted, does commonly require interpretation. A principal purpose of the preliminary reference mechanism (see Chapter 9) is precisely to enable the Court of Justice to guide national courts in the proper interpretation of the EC law that is potentially applicable in cases before them. A good example of an interpretive question is whether a harmonization measure should be read as merely establishing *minimum* Community standards (thus enabling Member States to impose more exacting standards) or rather *uniform* standards that the Member States may not then vary, even in the direction of greater stringency. This question will be addressed in Chapter 4C *infra*.

B. THE LEGISLATIVE PROCESS OF THE COMMUNITY

One of the institutional features of the Community that has been modified most significantly in recent years is the legislative process. Although that process has always in some way involved the Council, Commission and Parliament, their modes of involvement have changed. The legislative process was originally quite simple. Certain legislative acts could only be adopted by the Council after receiving a non-binding opinion ("consultation") of the Parliament, while others could be adopted without any parliamentary input at all. The Single European Act and the Maastricht Treaty introduced two new and complicated procedures, the "cooperation" and "codecision" procedures, respectively, both of which significantly increased Parliament's legislative role.

1. THE PARLIAMENTARY CONSULTATION PROCEDURE

Until 1987, the European Parliament did not figure into Article 250 (ex 189a), the EC Treaty's general provision on legislative process. Only where some particular article stated that the Council had to consult Parliament before acting, e.g., in agriculture, competition policy or freedom of establishment, was a parliamentary opinion required. Such instances were common. Nothing of course prevented the Council from soliciting Parliament's opinion voluntarily, and the Council frequently would do so.

With the advent of newer procedures giving Parliament a good deal more than the right to be consulted, parliamentary consultation has lost ground in the treaty as a mode of legislation. Nevertheless, it continues to apply, to varying degrees, to measures in the fields of agriculture, competition, freedom of services, harmonization of internal taxation, state aids, and visa policy.

Consultation is also the extent of Parliament's involvement in most measures taken under the Economic and Monetary Union and under the "third pillar." In fact, in the case of many measures in these fields, even consultation is not required.

Under the consultation procedure, the Commission initially delivers to the Council a proposal, which is published in the Official Journal. The proposal is sent for review to Parliament, which considers it first at the committee level, and then expresses its opinion by a vote in plenary session. Parliament often suggests amendments, which will be weighed seriously by the Commission. Indeed, the Commission commonly publishes a revised proposal in the Official Journal incorporating various parliamentary amendments. (Some proposals must also be reviewed at this stage by the Economic and Social Committee, and its suggestions too may be incorporated in the Commission revision.) This legislative phase may take many months and often a year or two. Since the initial and all revised proposals are made public, private interests have substantial opportunities during this period to lobby both the Commission and Parliament.

Even while Parliament is being consulted, the Council begins taking up the Commission proposal. The proposal is first dealt with by a Council working group, in contact with Member State experts, and then by COREPER. If COREPER approves a text unanimously, the Council often adopts it without further debate. If COREPER cannot reach agreement, the Council will try to do so. Council review, from initial working group to final adoption, usually takes months or even years, and lobbyists will once again be active, seeking to influence both the Member States and Council staff. Of course, sometimes the Council cannot reach agreement and draft proposals are then effectively tabled for years, and occasionally formally rejected. In addition, before acting the Council may have to await opinions not only of the Parliament but of other bodies required to have been consulted, such as the Economic and Social Committee. What is more, the Commission, as we shall see below, has the right to amend its proposal any time prior to adoption. If such amendment occurs, it may occasion further delay.

If the Council votes, it does so either unanimously or by qualified majority, depending on the particular Treaty article under which the measure is being adopted. However, Article 250 (ex 189a) contains the important general rule that if the Council wishes to adopt a measure whose terms deviate from the terms of the Commission's proposed text as it then stands (the Commission possibly having revised it), then it must do so by unanimous vote, even if action on the matter ordinarily requires only a qualified majority vote in the Council. This rule greatly strengthens the Commission's hand because, while its own proposal may be adopted over the objection of a certain number of Member States, an amended version can be defeated by any one of them. Moreover, Article 250 gives the Commission the continuing prerogative power to amend its legislative proposals at any time prior to adoption. This enables the Commission to change at any time the terms of the text that may be adopted by qualified majority vote, subjecting all variations on it to a regime of unanimity.

Despite its relative simplicity, the consultation procedure has occasionally given rise to difficulties. Consider the case of Roquette Frères v. Council (Isoglucose), Case 138/79, [1980] ECR 3333. There, the Council, as required by Article 37 (ex 43), had asked Parliament for its advice on a proposed regulation setting production quotas for isoglucose, a starch-based sweetener made from maize or corn (and known in the US as high fructose corn syrup). However, Parliament ended its final session without acting on the proposal, which was recommitted to its agriculture committee. Finally, some three and a half months after making its request to the Parliament, the Council adopted the regulation. (The Council considered it vital to do so, since it considered a system of quotas to be essential and its predecessor regulation had been invalidated by the Court of Justice.) The preamble to the regulation recited that Parliament had been consulted.

Roquette Frères was found to have standing to sue in the Court of Justice to have the regulation annulled for violating an essential procedural requirement, and Parliament intervened in its support. The Court invalidated the regulation.

33 The consultation provided for in the third subparagraph of Article 43(2), as in other similar provisions of the Treaty, is the means which allows the Parliament to play an actual part in the legislative process of the Community. Such power represents an essential factor in the institutional balance intended by the Treaty. Although limited, it reflects at [the] Community level the fundamental democratic principle that the peoples should take part in the exercise of power through the intermediary of a representative assembly. Due consultation of the Parliament in the cases provided for by the Treaty therefore constitutes an essential formality disregard of which means that the measure concerned is void.

34 In that respect it is pertinent to point out that observance of that requirement implies that the Parliament has expressed its opinion. It is impossible to take the view that the requirement is satisfied by the Council's simply asking for the opinion. . . .

35 The Council . . . maintains . . . that in the circumstances of the present case the Parliament, by its own conduct, made observance of that requirement impossible and that it is therefore not proper to rely on the infringement thereof.

36 Without prejudice to the questions of principle raised by that argument of the Council, it suffices to observe that in the present case . . . , when the Council adopted [the regulation] without the opinion of the Assembly, the

Council had not exhausted all the possibilities of obtaining the preliminary opinion of the Parliament. In the first place the Council did not request the application of the emergency procedure provided for by the internal regulation of the Parliament although in other sectors and as regards other draft regulations it availed itself of that power at the same time. Further the Council could have made use of the possibility it had under Article 139 [now 196] of the Treaty to ask for an extraordinary session of the Assembly. . . .

Notes and Questions

1. While Parliament prevailed in the *Isoglucose* case, the question nevertheless arises whether limits should be placed on the duration of Parliament's opportunity for review. (Note that Parliament's rules of procedure allow for repeated references between committee and plenary session on any given piece of legislation.) For a case in which the Court excused the Council's failure to await a parliamentary opinion before adopting a regulation requiring consultation—and in which the Court actually blamed Parliament for causing that failure—see Parliament v. Council (Consultation of Parliament) Case C–65/93, [1995] ECR I–643. The Court spoke there, and has frequently spoken since, of the institutions' "duty of sincere cooperation."

2. A more interesting question under parliamentary consultation is whether the right to be consulted on a proposal implies a right to be re-consulted if and when the proposal undergoes change prior to adoption.

In Parliament v. Council (Passenger transport), Case C–388/92, [1994] ECR I–2067, the Court annulled a Council regulation allowing non-resident road transport firms to operate passenger service within a Member State, citing the fact that the Council failed to re-consult the Parliament after making major changes to the regulation as reviewed by the Parliament. The Council had modified the scope of the regulation from the broad category of all regular, chartered or shuttle services to the narrower category of non-regular services and regular services for the transport of workers and students in border areas. The Court ruled that this constituted a major change and that the Council had failed to show that the change was actually an accommodation of the views that Parliament had expressed.

See also Parliament v. Council (Carriage of heavy goods), Case C–21/94, [1995] ECR I–1827, where the Court ruled that the Council had so significantly altered a draft directive (93/89) on Member State taxation of vehicles for the carriage of heavy goods (notably by broadening the bases for exemption from the tax to such an extent that exemption could no longer be regarded as "exceptional" and by dropping language requiring the Council to adopt a harmonized system by a given date) that Parliament had a right to be re-consulted before the measure was adopted. The Parliament was once again broadly successful in Parliament v. Council (Visas for third country nationals), Case C–392/95, [1997] ECR I–3213.

For a case in which the amendments adopted by the Council were found by the Court *not* to be "substantial" for these purposes, see Parliament v. Council (Technical assistance to former Soviet States), Case C–417/93, [1995] ECR I–1185.

NOTE ON THE PARLIAMENTARY COOPERATION PROCEDURE AND THE EMERGENCE OF "CORRECT LEGAL BASIS" DISPUTES

When adopting the Single European Act, the Member States responded to the Parliament's demand for a stronger legislative voice. They introduced into the Treaty a so-called "parliamentary cooperation procedure" whose objective was to cause the Commission and Council to take Parliament's views more seriously into consideration. The procedure is detailed in EC Treaty Article 252 (ex 189c).

Suffice it to say that the parliamentary cooperation procedure enabled Parliament not merely to be consulted, but also to "reject" or seek to "amend" a Commission proposal that the Council had "provisionally" adopted in the from of a so-called "common position." By "rejecting" the common position, Parliament could not prevent the Council from enacting it into law, but could require that the Council enact it, if at all, by unanimity rather than by the usual qualified majority. Moreover, by seeking to "amend" the common position, Parliament in effect invited the Commission to revise its proposal in line with Parliament's thinking. (The procedure specifically gave the Commission the opportunity to do so.) If the Commission were persuaded to embrace Parliament's amendments, then of course only that "reexamined" version of the proposal could be adopted by the Council by qualified majority; if by contrast the Council chose to adopt its own prior "common position," it would have to do so unanimously. The procedure clearly enhanced Parliament's legislative power, but at whose expense? Specifically, what effect did it have on the power of the Commission? See generally R. Bieber, Legislative Procedure for the Establishment of the Single Market, 25 Comm. Mkt. L. Rev. 711 (1988).

The Single European Act made parliamentary cooperation immediately applicable in certain key Treaty articles, such as Article 95 (ex 100a), providing for harmonization of Member State law in furtherance of the internal market. Also subject to the procedure was legislation on the free movement of workers, the right of establishment, health and safety at work and the promotion of research and technological development.

While the Maastricht Treaty was later to transfer several of these matters (including Article 95 harmonization) to a still newer "parliamentary codecision procedure," it also moved certain matters into parliamentary cooperation that had previously only been subject to parliamentary consultation, such as environmental protection, vocational training and social policy. However, the Amsterdam Treaty subsequently reduced the scope of application of parliamentary cooperation still further—indeed practically to the vanishing point— once again in favor of codecision. Parliamentary cooperation has today thus been virtually completely overtaken by codecision. It is at present still in use only in connection with certain measures under EMU.

In any event, the introduction of parliamentary cooperation alongside parliamentary consultation gave rise to a continuing problem of deciding which is the procedurally correct legal basis for the enactment of legislation when there are two or more plausible bases involving different legislative procedures. Given the differences between the consultation and cooperation procedures (as well as between Council unanimity, on the one hand, and the qualified majority voting entailed in parliamentary cooperation, on the other), the institutions had divergent procedural interests.

A noted instance in which the Parliament successfully challenged the Council's choice of legal basis is Parliament v. Council (Government procurement), Case C–360/93, [1996] ECR I–1195. There the Court invalidated a 1993 Council decision approving the conclusion of a Memorandum of Understanding with the US on government procurement. The Council adopted that decision on the basis of EC Treaty Article 133 (ex 113) on external trade, entailing qualified majority voting upon a Commission proposal but without consultation of Parliament. Upon suit by Parliament, the Court ruled that, to the extent that the agreement dealt with the provision of services that are not supplied across frontiers, the Council decision approving the agreement could not be based on Article 133 of the Treaty alone. Unable to craft a partial annulment, the Court annulled the Council decision approving the agreement in its entirety. (For a fuller explanation as to why the Court considers Article 133 incapable of supporting an EU trade agreement pertaining to non-frontier-crossing services, see Opinion 1/94 of the Court of Justice, treated at page 1084 *infra*.)

The Commission has likewise on occasion challenged the Council's choice of legal basis, though not so much because the competing treaty articles differed in the parliamentary prerogatives that they entail as because they differed in the voting rules within the Council. Consider Commission v. Council (Erasmus), Case 242/87, [1989] ECR 1425. The Commission contested the Council's use of Article 308 (ex 235)—the "implied powers" provision, which is discussed in Chapter 4A *infra* and which required Council unanimity—in adopting the "Erasmus" program for promoting the mobility of university students within the Community, arguing that Article 150 (ex 127) on vocational training, which entailed qualified majority voting, was available. The Court found that most of the program could indeed have been adopted under Article 150, but that programs of scientific research (as opposed to university education) fell outside the scope of vocational training. To that extent, resort to implied powers was proper.

A leading legal basis case is Commission v. Council (Titanium dioxide), Case C–300/89, [1991] ECR I–2867. In 1989, the Council by unanimous vote enacted a directive harmonizing rules on the reduction of pollution caused by titanium dioxide waste. In doing so, it used the then Article 130s (now 175) governing environmental legislation. The Commission, supported by Parliament, challenged the legality of the directive on the ground that the Council should have acted under Article 100a (now 95) instead. Although the Treaty provisions have since changed, at that time Article 130s required unanimity in the Council and parliamentary consultation, while Article 100a called for parliamentary cooperation and qualified majority voting.

The Commission and Parliament maintained that the directive, though contributing to environmental protection, was mainly concerned with improving competitive conditions in the titanium dioxide industry and was therefore an internal market measure within the meaning of Article 100a. The Council, on the other hand, insisted that the "center of gravity" of the measure was reducing pollution caused by titanium dioxide production, hence environmental.

The Court disposed of the "legal basis question" as follows:

[10] It must first be observed that in the context of the organization of the powers of the Community, the choice of the legal basis for a measure may not depend simply on an institution's conviction as to the objective pursued but must be based on objective factors which are amenable to judicial review. Those factors include in particular the aim and content of the measure.

[11] As regards the aim pursued, Article 1 of [the directive] indicates that it is intended, on the one hand, to harmonize the programmes for the reduction and ultimate elimination of pollution caused by waste from existing establishments in the titanium dioxide industry and, on the other, to improve the conditions of competition in that industry. It thus pursues the twofold aim of environmental protection and improvement of the conditions of competition.

[12] As regards its content, [the directive] prohibits, or, according to strict standards, requires reduction of the discharge of waste from existing establishments in the titanium dioxide industry and lays down time-limits [for doing so. Thus it] conduces, at the same time, to the reduction of pollution and to the establishment of greater uniformity of production conditions and therefore of conditions of competition, since the national rules on the treatment of waste which the directive seeks to harmonize have an impact on production costs in the titanium dioxide industry.

[13] It follows that according to its aim and content ... the directive is concerned, indissociably, with both the protection of the environment and the elimination of disparities in conditions of competition.

* * *

[16] [T]he directive at issue displays the features both of action relating to the environment with which Article 130s of the Treaty is concerned and of a harmonizing measure which has as its object the establishment and functioning of the internal market, within the meaning of Article 100a of the Treaty.

[17] As the Court [has previously] held, ... where an institution's power is based on two provisions of the Treaty, it is bound to adopt the relevant measures on the basis of the two relevant provisions. However, that ruling is not applicable to the present case.

[18] ... In a case like this [in which one provision provides for parliamentary cooperation and the other for unanimous voting upon the mere consultation of Parliament], combining the two legal bases would tend to render the parliamentary cooperation procedure devoid of any substance.

* * *

[20] The very purpose of the cooperation procedure, which is to increase the involvement of the European Parliament in the legislative process of the Community, would thus be jeopardized. As the Court stated in its judg-

ments [in the *Roquette Frères* case, *supra* page 84], that participation reflects a fundamental democratic principle that the peoples should take part in the exercise of power through the intermediary of a representative assembly.

21 It follows that in the present case recourse to the dual legal basis of Articles 100a and 130s is excluded and that it is necessary to determine which of those two provisions is the appropriate legal basis.

22 It must be observed in the first place that, pursuant to the second sentence of Article 130r(2) of the Treaty, "environmental protection requirements shall be a component of the Community's other policies." That principle implies that a Community measure cannot be covered by Article 130s merely because it also pursues objectives of environmental protection.

23 Secondly, as the Court [has previously] held, provisions which are made necessary by considerations relating to the environment and health may be a burden upon the undertakings to which they apply and, if there is no harmonization of national provisions on the matter, competition may be appreciably distorted. It follows that action intended to approximate national rules concerning production conditions in a given industrial sector with the aim of eliminating distortions of competition in that sector is conducive to the attainment of the internal market and thus falls within the scope of Article 100a. . . .

24 Finally, it must be observed that Article 100a(3) requires the Commission, in its proposals for measures for the approximation of the laws of the Member States which have as their object the establishment and functioning of the internal market, to take as a base a high level of protection in matters of environmental protection. That provision thus expressly indicates that the objectives of environmental protection referred to in Article 130r may be effectively pursued by means of harmonizing measures adopted on the basis of Article 100a. . . .

25 In view of all the foregoing considerations, the contested measure should have been based on Article 100a . . . and must therefore be annulled.

The Court revisited the question several years later in another environmental case, Commission v. Council (Waste directive), Case C–155/91, [1993] ECR I–939. In 1991, due in part to the *Titanium dioxide* judgment, the Commission felt confident in relying on Article 100a (now 95) on internal market harmonization as the basis for amending a longstanding directive (75/442) on waste disposal. (Directive 75/442 had originally been adopted under a rule of unanimity, as required under the only then-available treaty bases: Articles 100 (now 94) on harmonization for the common market and 235 (now 308), the implied powers provision.) When finally adopting the amendment (in the form of Directive 91/156), the Council, rather than citing Article 100a, relied on Article 130s (now 175) which at the time still required unanimity. The Commission challenged the measure as having been adopted on the wrong legal basis. The Court ruled as follows:

8 As for the aim pursued by Directive 91/156, the . . . preamble state[s] that, in order to achieve a high level of environmental protection, the Member States must take measures to restrict the production of waste

and to encourage the recycling of waste and its re-use as raw materials, and they must become self-sufficient in waste disposal and reduce movements of waste.

9 As for the content of the directive, it requires the Member States, in particular, to encourage the prevention or reduction of waste production and waste recovery and disposal without endangering human health and without harming the environment, and to prohibit the abandonment, dumping and uncontrolled disposal of waste (Articles 3 and 4). Accordingly, the directive requires the Member States to establish an integrated and adequate network of disposal installations which will enable the Community as a whole and the Member States individually to become self-sufficient in waste disposal, with the waste being disposed of in one of the nearest installations (Article 5). In order to attain those objectives, the Member States are to draw up waste management plans and may prevent movements of waste which are not in accordance with those plans (Article 7). Lastly, the directive requires the Member States to subject disposal undertakings and establishments to rules providing for permits, registration and inspections (Articles 9 to 14) and confirms, in the field of waste disposal, the 'polluter pays' principle enshrined in Article 130r(2) of the Treaty (Article 15).

10 It appears from the above particulars that, according to its aim and content, the directive at issue has the object of ensuring the management of waste, whether it is of industrial or domestic origin, in accordance with the requirements of environmental protection.

* * *

16 The Commission ... argues that the directive leads to the approximation of legislation inasmuch as Article 1 introduces a single, common definition of waste and related activities. ... [The Commission] refers in particular to the ... preamble to the directive, according to which any disparity between Member States' laws on waste disposal and recovery can affect the quality of the environment and interfere with the functioning of the internal market.

17 Lastly, the Commission refers to the fact that the directive also contributes to harmonization of the conditions of competition, at the level of both industrial production and waste disposal. In that connection, it argues that to some extent the directive brings to an end the advantages enjoyed by industries in certain Member States in terms of production costs owing to the fact that their legislation on the treatment of waste is less strict than that of other Member States. ...

18 Admittedly, it must be acknowledged that some provisions of the directive, in particular the definitions set out in Article 1, affect the functioning of the internal market.

19 However ... the mere fact that the establishment or functioning of the internal market is affected is not sufficient for Article 100a of the Treaty to apply. It appears from the Court's case-law that recourse to Article 100a is not justified where the measure to be adopted has only the incidental effect of harmonizing market conditions within the Community.

[20] That is the case here. The harmonization provided for in Article 1 of the directive has as its main object to ensure, with a view to protecting the environment, the effective management of waste in the Community, regardless of its origin, and has only ancillary effects on the conditions of competition and trade. As a result, it differs from [the directive at issue in the *Titanium dioxide* case], which . . . is intended to approximate national rules concerning production conditions in a given industrial sector with the aim of eliminating distortions of competition in that sector.

[21] Accordingly, the contested directive must be deemed to have been validly adopted on the sole basis of Article 130s of the Treaty.

The Court did not acknowledge any inconsistency between the two judgments. Are they consistent? At a minimum, the Court appears to have abandoned its suggestion in earlier cases—repeated in *Titanium dioxide*—that where an institution's power is based on two Treaty provisions, it ordinarily must adopt the relevant measures in compliance with both of them (the "double legal basis" theory). The approach adopted by the Court in the *Waste directive* case is commonly likened to a "center of gravity" test.[2] Is this an apt description? Do you see why the Commission would generally favor qualified majority over unanimous voting? Might the Commission also favor parliamentary cooperation (or codecision) over consultation?

The choice of legal basis is of course not only of concern to the institutions. Member States may likewise have an interest in having one legislative procedure followed rather than the other. This again has mostly to do with differences in Council voting requirements. The phenomenon arose at an early point in regard to several agricultural measures whose adoption had been prompted in part by non-agricultural considerations. At that time, most agricultural measures could be taken by qualified majority voting under Article 37 (then 43), whereas other policies—such as consumer protection, for example—could only be pursued through treaty articles requiring unanimity in the Council. The latter included implied powers under Article 308 (then 235) or pre-SEA harmonization under Article 94 (then 100).

For example, in United Kingdom v. Council (Agricultural hormones), Case 68/86, [1988] ECR 855, the UK and Denmark objected to the fact that the Council used Article 43 rather than Article 100 in adopting its ban on the use of hormones for fattening livestock. They claimed the ban was a consumer protection rather than an agricultural policy measure. The Court sustained the measure, finding that qualified majority voting was the appropriate procedural course. For a similar situation and result, see United Kingdom v. Council (Laying hens), Case 131/86, [1988] ECR 905. Sometimes in "legal basis" litigation between the institutions, the Member States line up behind one or the other institution, and vice versa, as their interest dictates. In Commission v. Council (Trade in animal glands), Case C–131/87, [1989] ECR 3743, the Commission was supported by the Netherlands in its claim that the Council in adopting a certain directive should have used the then Article 43 (hence qualified majority voting) instead of the then Article 100 (hence

---

2. For still more recent applications of the Court's approach in an environmental case, see Spain v. Council (Danube Convention), Case C–36/98, [2001] ECR I–779; Parliament v. Council (Waste movement), Case C–187/93, [1994] ECR I–2857.

unanimity). The UK and Denmark came unsuccessfully to the Council's defense.

On the legal basis problem, see A. Bradley, The European Court and the Legal Basis of Community Legislation, 13 Eur. L Rev. 379 (1988); N. Emiliou, Opening Pandora's Box: The Legal Basis of Community Measures before the Court of Justice, 19 Eur. L. Rev. 488 (1994).

The following high-profile case had a strong, but not exclusive, "legal basis" dimension.

UNITED KINGDOM v. COUNCIL

(Working time directive)
Case C–84/94, [1996] ECR I–5755.

[In this action for annulment, the UK challenged the legality of Council Directive 93/104, commonly known as the "working time directive." The directive, which the Council had adopted on the basis of the then Article 118a of the EC Treaty (an article whose provisions, as amended, are now chiefly found in Article 137), lays down certain minimum standards of working time in both the public and private sectors, including periods of daily and weekly rest on the job, annual leave, maximum work week, and special protection for night workers and shift workers. Article 15 of the directive allows States to establish and apply more protective standards than those laid down.

The UK claimed, among other things, that the Council wrongly relied on Article 118a (entailing qualified majority and parliamentary cooperation), when it should have used either the then Article 100 (now 94) on harmonization of the common market or the then Article 235 (now 308), the implied powers provision—both of which required unanimity in the Council.]

The scope of Article 118a

11   The applicant observes in the first place that, because Article 118a of the Treaty must be regarded as an exception to Article 100—which, pursuant to Article 100a(2), is the article that covers provisions "relating to the rights and interests of employed persons"—it must be strictly interpreted.

12   ... Article 118a confers upon the Community internal legislative competence in the area of social policy. The existence of other provisions in the Treaty does not have the effect of restricting the scope of Article 118a. Appearing as it does in the chapter of the Treaty which deals with "Social Provisions", Article 118a relates only to measures concerning the protection of the health and safety of workers. It therefore constitutes a more specific rule than Articles 100 and 100a. That interpretation is confirmed by the actual wording of Article 100a(1) itself, which states that its provisions are to apply "save where otherwise provided in this Treaty".....

13   Second, ... the applicant argues ... that [Article 118a] permits the adoption only of directives which have a genuine and objective link to the "health and safety" of workers. That does not apply to measures concerning, in particular, weekly working time, paid annual leave and rest periods, whose connection with the health and safety of workers is too tenuous.

That interpretation is borne out by the expression "working environment" used in Article 118a, which implies that directives based on that provision must be concerned only with physical conditions and risks at the workplace.

* * *

15 There is nothing in the wording of Article 118a to indicate that the concepts of "working environment", "safety" and "health" as used in that provision should, in the absence of other indications, be interpreted restrictively, and not as embracing all factors, physical or otherwise, capable of affecting the health and safety of the worker in his working environment, including in particular certain aspects of the organization of working time. On the contrary, the words "especially in the working environment" militate in favour of a broad interpretation of the powers which Article 118a confers upon the Council for the protection of the health and safety of workers. . . .

* * *

18 [Further], the applicant argues that, in the light of previous directives based on Article 118a, that provision does not authorize the Council to adopt directives, such as that in dispute here, which deal with the question of health and safety in a generalized, unspecific and unscientific manner. [The Court then cited several Council directives that clearly focus upon a specific health or safety problem in a specific situation.]

* * *

20 [In fact], there is no support in the wording of Article 118a for the argument that Community action should be restricted to specific measures applicable to given groups of workers in particular situations, whilst measures for wider purposes should be adopted on the basis of Article 100 of the Treaty. Article 118a refers to "workers" generally and states that the objective which it pursues is to be achieved by the harmonization of "conditions" in general existing in the area of the health and safety of those workers.

21 In addition, the delimitation of the respective fields of application of Articles 100 and 100a, on the one hand, and Article 118a, on the other, rests not upon a distinction between the possibility of adopting general measures in the former case and particular measures in the latter, but upon the principal aim of the measure envisaged.

22 It follows that, where the principal aim of the measure in question is the protection of the health and safety of workers, Article 118a must be used, albeit such a measure may have ancillary effects on the establishment and functioning of the internal market.

. . .

The choice of legal basis for the directive

. . .

26 As regards the aim of the directive, the applicant argues that it represents a continuation . . . of a series of earlier initiatives at Community level

concerned with the organization of working time in the interests of job creation and reduced unemployment. It is in reality a measure concerned with the overall improvement of the living and working conditions of employees and with their general protection, and is so broad in its scope and coverage as to be capable of classification as a social policy measure, for the adoption of which other legal bases exist.

27   It is to be noted in that respect that, according to [the] preamble, the directive constitutes a practical contribution towards creating the social dimension of the internal market. However, it does not follow from the fact that the directive falls within the scope of Community social policy that it cannot properly be based on Article 118a, so long as it contributes to encouraging improvements as regards the health and safety of workers. . . .

        . . .

29   The approach taken by the directive, viewing the organization of working time essentially in terms of the favourable impact it may have on the health and safety of workers, is apparent from several recitals in its preamble. Thus, for example, the eighth recital states that, in order to ensure the safety and health of Community workers, they must be granted minimum rest periods and adequate breaks and that it is also necessary in that context to place a maximum limit on weekly working hours. In addition, the eleventh recital states that "research has shown that . . . long periods of night work can be detrimental to the health of workers and can endanger safety at the workplace", while the fifteenth recital states that specific working conditions may have detrimental effects on the safety and health of workers and that the organization of working according to a certain pattern must take account of the general principle of adapting work to the worker.

30   While, in the light of those considerations, it cannot be excluded that the directive may affect employment, that is clearly not its essential objective.

31   As regards the content of the directive, the applicant argues that the connection between the measures it lays down, on the one hand, and health and safety, on the other, is too tenuous for the directive to be based on Article 118a of the Treaty.

32   In that respect, it argues that no adequate scientific evidence exists to justify the imposition of a general requirement to provide for breaks where the working day is longer than six hours (Article 4), a general requirement to provide for a minimum uninterrupted weekly rest period of twenty-four hours in addition to the usual eleven hours' daily rest (Article 5, first sentence), a requirement that the minimum rest period must, in principle, include Sunday (Article 5, second sentence), a general requirement to ensure that the average working time for each seven-day period, including overtime, does not exceed forty-eight hours (Article 6(2)), and a general requirement that every worker is to have a minimum of four weeks' paid annual leave (Article 7).

[At this point, the Court focused on the specific requirement in the directive that the mandatory weekly rest period is normally to comprise a Sunday. Finding that the Council had failed to explain why Sunday, as a weekly rest day, was more closely connected with the health and safety of workers than any other day of the week, and finding this requirement to be severable from the rest of the directive, the Court annulled this particular provision.]

[38] The other measures laid down by the directive, which refer to minimum rest periods, length of work, night work, shift work and the pattern of work, relate to the "working environment" and reflect concern for the protection of "the health and safety of workers"....

* * *

[45] Since it is clear from the above considerations that, in terms of its aim and content, the directive has as its principal objective the protection of the health and safety of workers by the imposition of minimum requirements for gradual implementation, neither Article 100 nor Article 100a could have constituted the appropriate legal basis for its adoption.

* * *

[48] Finally, as regards Article 235 of the Treaty, it is sufficient to point to the Court's case-law, which holds that that article may be used as the legal basis for a measure only where no other Treaty provision confers on the Community institutions the necessary power to adopt it.

[49] It must therefore be held that the directive was properly adopted on the basis of Article 118a, save for the [Sunday weekly rest requirement,] which must accordingly be annulled.

Notes and Questions

1. Did the Court here confine itself to discussing the correct legal basis of the working time directive or did it venture into other issues? What, for example, does the adequacy of the available scientific evidence (para. 32) have to do with the correctness of the legal basis used?

2. The Court also alluded in its judgment to the principle of subsidiarity. For that discussion, see Chapter 4D *infra*.

3. See also Germany v. Council (General product safety), Case C–359/92, [1994] ECR I–3681. Here, Germany sought the annulment of one provision (Article 9) of Council Directive 92/59 harmonizing Member State laws on general product safety, which the Council had adopted as an internal market measure under Article 100a (now 95) of the EC Treaty. Article 9 authorized the Commission, upon learning that a product raises a serious and immediate risk to consumer health, to require the Member States to impose temporary measures with respect to that product. Germany maintained that Article 9 of the Directive lacked any legal basis in the EC Treaty, while the Council and Commission insisted that Article 100a furnished an adequate basis.

[30] Under the scheme established by the directive, it is possible, even likely, that differences may exist between the measures taken by Member States. As the preamble states, such differences may "entail unacceptable disparities in consumer protection and constitute a barrier to intra-Community trade".

* * *

³² The Community legislature therefore considered it necessary, in order to cope with a serious and immediate risk to the health and safety of consumers, to provide for an adequate mechanism allowing, in the last resort, for the adoption of measures applicable throughout the Community, in the form of decisions addressed to the Member States. . . .

* * *

³⁴ As is apparent from the ... preamble to the directive and from the structure of Article 9, [Article 9's] purpose ... is to enable the Commission to adopt, as promptly as possible, temporary measures applicable throughout the Community with respect to a product which presents a serious and immediate risk to the health and safety of consumers, so as to ensure compliance with the objectives of the directive. The free movement of goods can be secured only if product safety requirements do not differ significantly from one Member State to another. A high level of protection can be achieved only if dangerous products are subject to appropriate measures in all the Member States.

* * *

³⁷ Such action is not contrary to Article 100a(1) of the Treaty. The measures which the Council is empowered to take under that provision are aimed at "the establishment and functioning of the internal market". In certain fields, and particularly in that of product safety, the approximation of general laws alone may not be sufficient to ensure a unified market. Consequently, the concept of "measures for the approximation" of provisions must be interpreted as encompassing the Council's power to lay down measures relating to a specific product or class of products and, if necessary, individual measures concerning those products.

Is the Court's position convincing? What limits do you discern on the Council's right to adopt a directive harmonizing Member State laws?

For the Court's rejection of Germany's further claim that Article 9 of the Directive violated the Community law principle of "proportionality," see page 178 *infra*. Germany also advanced the argument that, by regulating a matter within the constitutional competence of the German *Länder,* rather than the German federal government, Article 9 impermissibly interfered with principles of German federalism. The response of the Court of Justice to this argument (in para. 38 of the judgment) was simple:

> [I]t must be borne in mind that the rules governing the relationship between the Community and its Member States are not the same as those which link the *Bund* with the *Länder.* Furthermore, the measures taken for the implementation of Article 100a of the Treaty are addressed to Member States and not to their constituent entities. Nor do the powers conferred on the Commission by Article 9 of the directive have any bearing upon the division of powers within the Federal Republic of Germany.

4. The Court of Justice does not invariably favor qualified majority voting and/or the cooperation procedure. See Parliament v. Council (Post–Chernobyl), Case C–70/88, [1991] ECR I–4529. In 1987, the Commission proposed and the Council adopted a so-called "Post–Chernobyl" regulation on maximum radiation levels, acting unanimously under the Euratom Treaty rather than by parliamentary cooperation and qualified majority voting under EC Treaty 95 (ex 100a). Parliament sued, claiming that Euratom should not have been used since it applied only to protection against direct injury from the use of nuclear energy and

not against "secondary radiation" and that parliamentary cooperation had been improperly circumvented. Parliament lost its suit (on the ground that the Post–Chernobyl regulation had only an "incidental" effect on the free movement of goods and did not constitute an internal market measure within the meaning of Article 95), but won a landmark ruling to the effect that Parliament enjoyed standing to sue. (On parliamentary standing, see Chapter 5A *infra*).

　　5. For a case in which the Council, Commission and Parliament all asserted that a different treaty article was the one and only proper legal basis for a measure, see Parliament v. Council (Telematic networks), Case C–271/94, [1996] ECR 1689. Do you see how this could happen?

2. THE PARLIAMENTARY CODECISION PROCEDURE

　　While greatly preferring the cooperation procedure to the consultation procedure, Parliament was far from satisfied. Even before the Single European Act entered into force, Parliament made clear its intent to place further reform of the legislative process on the agenda of the next IGC. In point of fact, the subsequent Maastricht Treaty created yet a third general legislative process more to Parliament's liking. This was the "codecision procedure," currently codified at EC Treaty Article 251 (ex 189b).

　　The Maastricht Treaty prescribed codecision very widely, including for the adoption of harmonization directives under Article 100a (now 95) of the EC Treaty, measures promoting the free movement of workers and the right of establishment, and measures in the newer fields of education, culture, public health and consumer protection. Thus certain measures that prior to the SEA might have required no more than consultation now, after Maastricht, actually required codecision.

　　Parliamentary codecision (like parliamentary cooperation) is a "staged" legislative process. In its first phase, it actually mirrors the consultation procedure. The Commission drafts a proposed text which is published in the Official Journal; the Parliament in a "first reading" may suggest amendments; the proposal, possibly amended by the Commission as Parliament will have suggested and published in the Official Journal, then receives a "first reading" by the Council, making use of its working groups and COREPER. This may take a year or longer.

　　Instead of finally approving the text (as in the consultation process), the Council merely adopts a "common position" or tentative approval. If the text being considered mirrors the Commission proposal as it then stands, it may then be adopted as a common position by a qualified majority of the Council. However, adoption of an amended version will require Council unanimity. The common position, once adopted, is sent to the Parliament, along with a statement of reasons, thus starting a second legislative phase.

　　At this stage, Parliament has three months to conduct its "second reading." It has the choice, voting by absolute majority, among accepting the common position, rejecting it, or proposing amendments. If Parliament affirmatively accepts the text (or fails to take any action at all within the three months), the Council "shall" then definitively adopt the measure by qualified majority in its then current form. (To this extent, the codecision procedure is identical to the cooperation procedure.)

If, on the other hand, Parliament votes to reject the common position, the Council, under the codecision procedure, may no longer adopt it. (Here, codecision brought a change. Under parliamentary cooperation, the Council could still enact its common position at this stage, even after parliamentary rejection, though it could only do so unanimously.)

Typically, Parliament neither simply accepts nor rejects the common position, but proposes amendments to it. In this event, the text as the Parliament proposes amending it returns to the Commission, which will then likely seek a solution satisfactory to both the Council and Parliament. Within one month, the Commission must send the Council a "reexamined" proposal. This text may now reflect Parliament's amendments, or some portion or version of them, but it need not do so. (To the extent that it fails to incorporate Parliament's proposed amendments, the Commission must specifically inform the Council of those amendments and of its own opinion of them.)

The Council now has three months in which to act. One thing the Council may do is adopt Parliament's amendments by qualified majority vote—that is, unless the Commission issues an opinion opposing them, in which case the Council may only adopt Parliament's amendments by a unanimous vote. The Council may of course not adopt Parliament's amendments. It may adopt instead a text lacking those amendments—either the Commission's "reexamined" proposal (which the Council may adopt by QMV) or some variation on that proposal (which it may adopt unanimously). To this extent, parliamentary codecision still strongly resembles parliamentary cooperation. (Also as in cooperation, unless the Council adopts some text on the matter within three months, the entire Commission proposal lapses.)

It is at this point that the real innovation of codecision appears. Under cooperation, the Council could hold its ground and definitively adopt a text that lacked Parliament's amendments and that Parliament had not otherwise approved. (The required voting margin—QMV or unanimity—depended on where the Commission then stood.) Such a text became law.

Under codecision, by contrast, a text cannot become law unless it is approved in the same terms by both the Council and Parliament. To this end, if the Council does not approve all of Parliament's amendments, the matter goes to a Conciliation Committee, consisting of representatives of all the Council members and an equal number of MEPs, assisted by Commission representatives. The Committee has six weeks in which to try to find an acceptable compromise. Ideally, it will produce a compromise text supported both by a qualified majority of the Council representatives on the Committee and by a majority of the MEPs on it. Such a text may be enacted into law if and only if, within the next six weeks, both the Council (by a qualified majority) and the Parliament (by an absolute majority of votes cast) approve it. If either fails for any reason to do so—or if the Conciliation Committee never produces a compromise text in the first place—the draft measure once again lapses.

Actually, when first introduced at Maastricht, the codecision procedure offered yet a further possible scenario. Following an unsuccessful conciliation process, the Council still had the possibility of voting to "reaffirm" its prior common position, and if Parliament failed at that stage to take the actual step of voting by absolute majority to reject it, the measure would pass on the Council's terms. In this initial version, Parliament enjoyed a legislative veto, but the Council still had a practical and psychological advantage. The Council's position could be enacted over Parliament's failure to act, but not vice versa. Also Parliament might face the awkward choice between making the passage of legislation possible (by acquiescing in the Council's reaffirmed position) and preventing passage of any legislation altogether.

The Amsterdam Treaty removed this vestige of Council primacy, by eliminating any possibility of a legislative measure being enacted, upon completion of the Conciliation Committee's work, with only the Council's affirmative support. With the removal of this residual asymmetry, the codecision procedure finally placed the Council and Parliament on a fundamentally equal footing in a more or less "bicameral" legislative process.

With the Amsterdam Treaty also came a significant expansion in the the codecision procedure's field of application. Codecision thereafter obtained in virtually all legislative areas of the Treaty that previously were subject to parliamentary consultation or cooperation (e.g., rules prohibiting nationality discrimination, measures on the right of establishment, transport policy, vocational training, environmental protection). It also applied in new Community law areas (e.g. employment incentive measures, certain social policy and public health measures, prevention of fraud, customs cooperation, and general principles on transparency).

When the parliamentary cooperation procedure was first introduced by the SEA, it gave rise to fears of legislative delay and paralysis. Those fears on the whole did not materialize. (The 1992 internal market program after all was chiefly legislated in this fashion.) By the time that parliamentary codecision arrived on the scene, those fears had abated. In any event, giving Parliament a co-equal legislative voice had by then come widely to be seen as a democratic imperative.

Despite its complexity, the codecision procedure appears to work reasonably well in practice, with the Council frequently accepting Parliament's proposed amendments and the Conciliation Committee achieving a breakthrough. There are casualties, of course. In July 1994, the Parliament for the first time exercised its power to reject outright a common position adopted by the Council in the first phase of the co-decision procedure. The occasion was a vote on a new text liberalizing the European voice telecommunications market; Parliament found the proposal insufficiently protective of consumers. In March 1995, Parliament formally rejected a compromise text on protection of biotechnological inventions arrived at by a Conciliation Committee because a majority of MEPs found the text lacking in safeguards of animal welfare and limitations on the use of human genes and organs. More recently, in July 2001, the Parliament voted, by a margin of one vote, to reject the Conciliation Committee's compromise text on the draft Thirteenth Company Law Directive on takeovers.

Notes and Questions

1.   The codecision procedure diminishes the power of the Commission in at least one respect. Throughout the evolution of the EC legislative process, the Commission has enjoyed the privilege of requiring the Council to vote by unanimi-

ty whenever it sought to adopt a text in a form other than the one favored at that time by the Commission, even if the Council would normally have been able to adopt the Commission's proposal by qualified majority. Once a Conciliation Committee is convened under the codecision procedure, however, this rule is suspended. A joint text adopted by the Conciliation Committee may be adopted by the Council by qualified majority even over the Commission's objection. If Parliament also approves the measure in that form, it becomes law.

The Commission is nevertheless intimately involved in the conciliation process. According to Article 251 (ex 189b), the Commission takes part in the proceedings and "shall take all the necessary initiatives with a view to reconciling the positions of the European Parliament and the Council." See generally, N. Foster, The New Conciliation Committee under Article 189b EC, 19 Eur. L. Rev. 185 (1994).

2.   With codecision, Parliament of course has an even greater incentive to examine the "legal basis" question and possibly assert that an incorrect legal basis was used. Parliament has succeeded in mounting such a challenge. See, e.g., Parliament v. Council (Trans–European telematic networks), Case C–22/96, [1998] ECR I–3231.

3.   With a view to perfecting the codecision procedure, the Parliament, Council and Commission in May 1999 adopted a joint declaration on "practical arrangements" for its conduct. Bull. EU 5–1999. The declaration requires the institutions to endeavor to reconcile their positions on draft legislation as far as possible during the legislation's first reading. It calls on the Commission in particular to promote agreement between the Council and Parliament in a second reading, as well as in Conciliation Committee should the latter need to be convened. It prescribes various conciliation procedures (e.g. alternate hosting of meetings by the Council and Parliament and alternate hosting by their Presidents) in order to facilitate agreement in Committee.

4.   Linked to pressures for greater transparency (see Chapter 6E *infra*) and respect for subsidiarity (see Chapter 4D *infra*) in the adoption of Community legislation has been a drive toward improving the quality of Community legislation. (The Commission has spoken of "legislating less, but legislating better.") The Commission has accordingly undertaken periodically to simplify and consolidate existing legislation in the interest of greater clarity and consistency. See Timmermans, How Can One Improve the Quality of Community Legislation?, 34 Comm. Mkt. L. Rev. 1229 (1997). For further discussion, see Chapter 14 *infra*.

5.   As mentioned in Chapter 1, the Amsterdam Treaty added a new "wrinkle" to the legislative process by introducing the possibility of legislation by and for less than the full complement of Member States. We refer here to that Treaty's introduction of a "closer cooperation" (or "flexibility") regime for the enactment of legislation that, while constituting Community law in all essential respects, constitutes the law in some but not all the Member States. The details of this regime are reserved for Chapter 4E, where we examine other doctrines and mechanisms that have the potential for reducing the "reach" of Community law.

C.   COMMUNITY FINANCES AND THE BUDGET

No picture of the Community institutions and activities would be complete without some understanding of the Community's financial and budgetary system. This system has changed over time with a view both to enhancing the Community's financial independence and strengthening the role of the Parliament in budgetary matters.

Initially, the Community derived its revenue from Member State contributions. At a 1969 meeting of the heads of state and government at the Hague, the Member States agreed to place Community finances on a more secure and independent footing. The following year, the Council brought into being a system of so-called "own resources" for the Community.[3] However, not all the machinery of that system was put in place until the end of that decade.

Under its "own resources" system, the Community receives all revenues from customs duties and levies on imported agricultural products. These are collected by the Member States, which keep a percentage of the proceeds to cover their collection costs, remitting the balance to the Community. By a Council Decision on "Own Resources" of October 2000 (see below), the figure has now been substantially increased, from 10% to 25%. The third and largest source of Community revenue is a share of each Member State's collection of value added tax, a share currently set at 1.4% of the value of the products subject to the tax. Severe and chronic budgetary problems of the 1980s, accompanied by actual talk of Community bankruptcy, finally led in 1988 to the addition of a new and important revenue source, namely a direct levy on the Member States calculated in proportion to their GNPs.

The creation of this additional own resource for the Community ("the 4th resource"), based on the GNP of the Member States, was necessary to ensure adequate funding for the Community and its activities. Having a GNP-based component of the budget made it necessary to reinforce the comparability and reliability of GNP aggregates by harmonizing the definition of GNP and the method of its calculation. This was effectuated by Council Directive, 89/130/EC on the harmonization of the compilation of gross national product at market prices, O.J. L 49 (Feb. 21, 1989).

In 1991, the Community's revenues totaled about 56.2 billion euros. By 1996 this figure had become 81.3 billion and, by 2001, 93.9 billion.

In October 1998, the Commission submitted a report evaluating the "own resources" system. (Commission report COM (1998) 560 final). The report reviewed possibilities for improving the operation of the own resources system and tackled the question of budgetary balances. On the basis of the report, the Berlin European Council of March 1999 decided that a new own resources system should come into force from 2002. The Berlin European Council requested the Commission to draw up such a decision, taking into account the following factors: the need for the Union to have adequate resources to finance its policies, while maintaining strict budgetary discipline; the need for a system of own resources that is equitable, transparent and cost-effective; and, finally, the Member States' abilities to pay.

A new Council Decision on "Own Resources" was adopted in October 2000.[4] The main features are that the own resources ceiling will remain at 1.27% of the Union's GNP; the allowance for the collection cost of own resources will rise from 10% to 25%; the maximum call-in rate of VAT will be reduced to 0.75% in 2002 and 2003, and to 0.50% from 2004; and the costs of the longstanding budgetary rebate to the UK are shifted as among the other Member States.

3. Decision 70/243, O.J. English Spec. Ed.1970, vol. 1, at 224, subsequently revised.   **4.** Decision 2000/597, O.J. L 253/42 (Oct. 7, 2000).

The greatest part of Community revenue by far is spent to support the common agricultural policy. In 1991, this expenditure came to over 30 billion ECUs, or about 55% of the total budget. By 1999, appropriations for agricultural expenditure totaled euro 40.4 billion. In the Commission's proposed budget for 2002, agricultural expenditure represents the biggest share (46%) of the proposed budget and shows the highest increase (+5.0% in relation to 2001 spending). The agriculture budget currently faces a particular challenge, namely meeting the financial burden of combating "mad cow" and "foot-and-mouth" disease. The budget shows an increase in spite of the fact that the budget voted for 2001 was already increased by almost 1 billion euro to cover BSE-related costs.

Assistance to central and eastern European countries is another major expenditure factor. The majority of candidate countries for EU accession will remain far behind the current Community average in terms of economic structures and levels of income for many years to come. The Community institutions decided, therefore, to introduce pre-accession aid for applicant countries to support the adjustment programs they will have to implement in order to adopt the *aquis communautaire*. This is all set out in the EU's program for financing enlargement, commonly known as Agenda 2000.

Since 1988, decisions on budgetary discipline, together with inter-institutional agreements on budgetary discipline, have brought about a stable relationship between the European Union's commitments and its own resources. In 1999, the Council, the European Parliament and the Commission reached agreement on a new financial framework for 2000–06 to implement on a multi-annual basis budgetary discipline at the Community level.[5] The agreement stresses that budgetary discipline covers all expenditures and is binding on all the institutions involved in its implementation. Likewise, the Council issued a regulation on September 26, 2000 on budgetary discipline (O.J. L 244, Sept. 29, 2000), containing provisions on monetary reserve, the reserve relating to Community loans and loan guarantees to non-member countries, and the reserve for emergency aid, as well as specifications on the method of calculation of the agricultural guidelines. It also provides for additional measures to strengthen and simplify the rules on the application of budgetary discipline.

The Community's budget planning and approval process is complex, in part because of the institutions' shared involvement. The Commission drafts a preliminary budget, submitting it to the Council no later than September 1 (EC Treaty art. 272, ex 203), and in practice during the month of July. The draft budget is reviewed and adopted by the Council and then by the Parliament, followed by a second examination by both institutions. By December 31, the President of the Parliament must declare the budget adopted. Article 272 gives the Council the final decision on expenditures required by the Treaty, notably the agricultural policy. The Parliament has the final voice (within a fixed "maximum rate of increase") on so-called discretionary expenditures such as certain administrative expenses. Since most expenditures are

---

5. Inter-institutional Agreements of May 6, 1999 between the European Parliament, the Council and the Commission on budgetary discipline and improvements of the budgetary procedure, O.J. C 172 (June 18, 1999).

deemed to be compulsory for these purposes, the Council has the larger share of power in budgetary decisionmaking.

The Community's awkward budgetary process both reflects and contributes to contention between the Council and the Parliament over their respective shares of power in the process and over substantive budgetary issues. As early as 1980 (its first year as a directly elected body), the Parliament sought to reject the draft budget in its entirety, and twice in the early 1980s and once again in the early 1990s the two institutions went before the Court of Justice to resolve their differences. One of the Parliament's principal substantive claims of recent years is that agricultural spending should be reduced and amounts spent on regional development and research and development funding increased.

Budgetary politics also produce divisions along Member State lines. In the early 1980s, the UK, under the leadership of Prime Minister Thatcher, strongly contended that the budget should be adjusted to reflect the fact that Britain (not being a major agricultural producer) paid much more into Community revenues than it received. The European Council finally agreed at its 1984 Fontainebleau meeting to give the UK a rebate, referred to earlier, of a portion of the amount by which its contribution to Community revenue exceeded its receipts. Since that time, the UK has in fact become a major recipient of EC regional development aid, especially for Scotland and Wales. The budgetary breakthrough was a factor in the Community's emergence from the period of "Europessimism" referred to in Chapter 1.

Once the budget is adopted, the Commission has responsibility under Article 274 (ex 205) for administering the receipt of revenues, the control of cash flow and the disbursement of expenditures. Its administration of Community finances is reviewed by the Court of Auditors, whose composition and role are described in Articles 246–48 (ex 188a–188c). The Court of Auditors in effect carries out an annual audit and reports to the Council and the Parliament.

In United Kingdom v. Commission (Payments to combat social exclusion), Case C–106/96, [1998] ECR I–2729, the Court of Justice ruled that Community implementation of the budget requires not only the entry of the relevant appropriation in the budget, but (except in the case of "non-significant" Community action) also the previous enactment of basic secondary legislation authorizing the expenditure. (The Court relied on a 1982 joint declaration of the Parliament, Council and Commission on improvements in the budgetary procedure which stated that "[t]he implementation of appropriations entered for significant new Community action shall require a basic regulation.")

Fraud, especially in payments under the Common Agricultural Policy, has become a serious problem and EC Treaty Article 280 (ex 209a) enjoins the Member States and the Community to make serious efforts to combat it. For its part, the Commission has launched its own program of investigation, chiefly through its anti-fraud unit known as OLAF. The Commission's annual reports count many thousands of incidents entailing hundred of millions of euros implicated, mostly in connection with agricultural supports under the Common Agricultural Policy and in regional aid. As noted, the Santer Commission's failure to act energetically to combat fraud in these areas helped fuel the critique that eventually led to the Commission's forced resignation. A significant portion of the EU budget is now devoted to detecting and preventing fraud.

Chapter 4

THE SPHERE OF COMMUNITY LAW AND POLICY

As we have seen, the EC Treaty does not confine itself to any determined economic sector, and indeed is no longer confined to matters that are strictly economic in nature. The scope of Community law as such is defined in EC Treaty Articles 2 and 3. As amended, Article 2's purposes are far-ranging; they include, in addition to more narrowly economic objectives "social protection," "equality between men and women," and "improvement of the quality of the environment." Article 2 foresees as means to these ends the establishment both of a common market and an economic and monetary union, as well as the development of certain "common policies."

Article 3, as amended, specifies the activities that the Community may pursue in furtherance of Article 2's objectives. These activities are quite varied. Some specifically target the elimination of barriers to the free movement of goods, persons, services and capital (¶¶ a, c), as through the harmonization of Member State laws in non-designated fields (¶ h). Some contemplate the adoption of "common policies" in designated areas: external trade (known as "commercial policy") (¶ b), agriculture and fisheries (¶ e), and transport (¶ f). Some merely contemplate "policies": competition (¶ g), the environment (¶ l), and international development and aid (¶¶ r, s). Some contemplate categories of "measures": visa, asylum and immigration measures (¶ d) and measures in the field of energy, civil protection and tourism (¶ u). Some simply identify particular objectives: employment (¶ i), "economic and social cohesion"(¶ k), industrial policy (¶ m), research and development (¶ n), creation of trans-European networks (¶ o), health protection (¶ p), education and culture (¶ q), and consumer protection (¶ t). Finally, at least one paragraph points to the creation of a specific accessory body, the European Social Fund (¶ j). Much of this enumeration—particularly policy areas, measures and objectives—was added by the Single European Act and by the Treaties of Maastricht and Amsterdam. Set apart as a sphere of activity in Article 4 is economic and monetary union, with a special emphasis on the goals of price stability, sound public finances, and an open competitive market, and on the instruments of a single currency, an exchange rate policy, and a monetary policy.

These recitations must be read in the context of Article 5 (ex 3b) of the EC Treaty: "The Community shall act within the limits of the powers conferred upon it by this Treaty and of the objectives assigned to it therein." This means, as commentators and political figures alike are quick to point out, that the Community is subject to the principle of enumerated powers, and that its powers are in that sense "limited."

It is the case of course that, despite the lengthy enumeration, the Community's objectives and fields of action are expressed in very general terms. It might appear that virtually any measure likely to advance the common market, promote the convergence of Member State economic policies or simply enhance economic performance within the Community would respond to a legitimate Community purpose. It is difficult to imagine that the institutions would choose to engage in very many activities or adopt very many measures that lie outside the scope of Community purpose as so defined. As we will see in Chapter 5 on judicial review, there have been surprisingly few cases before the Court of Justice challenging a Community measure as lying wholly outside the subject matter scope of the EC Treaty. (But see the *Tobacco advertising* judgment, *infra* page 156.)

On the other hand, the EC Treaty is quite particular about the means the institutions may employ in pursuit of the objectives and activities set out in Articles 2 and 3. The Treaty deals in separate chapters with each component of the Community's subject matter jurisdiction, providing as to each more extensive substantive and procedural detail than is commonly found in national constitutions. Thus, when a Community institution acts within a given sphere, it must observe all the substantive and procedural limitations provided in the relevant Treaty article. To the extent it does not, it in a sense acts *ultra vires*.

The EC Treaty's quantity of substantive and procedural detail naturally makes it an important source of limitations on the institutions' freedom to act within their admittedly broad sphere of action. Its provisions confine the institutions much as enabling legislation in the US confines the administrative agencies, and in this sense the Treaty more closely resembles a legislative than a constitutional document. What does this suggest about the nature of the EC Treaty? Would it be fair to conclude that the EC Treaty takes the *form* of an international agreement, enjoys the *status* of a constitution, and performs the *function* of legislation?

We have referred up to now in this chapter only to the EC Treaty, primarily because it is under that treaty that "European law" as such is made and enforced. But the TEU has its own sphere, which should be noted. TEU Article 2 (ex B) sets out the objectives of the Union as distinct from the Community. In addition to echoing the basically economic objectives of the EC Treaty, Article 2 introduces a concept of EU citizenship, promises to implement a common foreign and security policy (CFSP), and promotes development of "an area of freedom, security and justice." As under the EC Treaty, these general objectives are given sharper substantive and procedural focus through the articles set out in subsequent treaty titles, in particular title V on the CFSP ("the second pillar") and title VI on police and judicial cooperation in criminal matters ("the third pillar").

The TEU says relatively little about the political dimension of the Union. It mentions in Articles 4 (ex D) and 5 (ex E) the principal bodies: the European Council, the European Parliament, the Council, the Commission, the Court of Justice and the Court of Auditors. (Chapter 3 introduced these institutions.) Article 6 (ex F), however, deserves particular attention:

1. The Union is founded on the principles of liberty, democracy, respect for human rights and fundamental freedoms, and the rule of law, principles which are common to the Member States.

2. The Union shall respect fundamental rights, as guaranteed by the European Convention for the Protection of Human Rights and Fundamental Freedoms signed in Rome on 4 November 1950 and as they result from the constitutional traditions common to the Member States, as general principles of Community law.

3. The Union shall respect the national identities of its Member States.

4. The Union shall provide itself with the means necessary to attain its objectives and carry through its policies.

Interestingly, European Union citizenship as such is dealt with not in the TEU but rather in the EC Treaty (Articles 17–22, ex 8–8e), presumably because only the EC Treaty provides the mechanisms necessary for lawmaking in these respects. Persons holding the nationality of a Member State immediately acquire EU citizenship, which "shall contemplate and not replace national citizenship" (Article 17, ex 8). EU citizenship entails the right to move and reside freely within the territory of the Member States, to vote and stand as a candidate (where resident) in their municipal elections and in their elections to the European Parliament, to invoke the diplomatic and consular protection of the other Member States, to petition the European Parliament for redress and to apply to the Community's Ombudsman (using any official language and expecting an answer in the same language). For a more probing discussion of what EU citizenship entails, see Chapter 16 *infra*.

To understand what the Community law sphere is, however, it is not sufficient simply to enumerate "competences." There are other factors that help determine the "reach" of Community law. Though they differ substantially from one another, each of the topics covered in this chapter—implied powers, preemption, subsidiarity, and flexibility and "closer cooperation"— represents a defining aspect of the Community law sphere. We deal with each in turn.

A. IMPLIED POWERS

Although committed to a fairly particularized program of action, the drafters of the EC Treaty also included the following provision:

Article 308 (ex 235)

If action by the Community should prove necessary to attain, in the course of the operation of the common market, one of the objectives of the Community and this Treaty has not provided the necessary powers, the Council shall, acting unanimously on a proposal from the Commission and after consulting the European Parliament, take the appropriate measures.

Commonly called an "implied powers," an "elastic" or a "necessary and proper" clause, Article 308 enables the institutions to employ means not specifically provided for in the Treaty, when doing so is desirable for accomplishing a stated Treaty objective and when adequate means are not otherwise provided. Article 308 thus compensates in part for the drafters' inability to foresee all the instruments that the institutions would need to carry out the Community's purposes. It has been used to adopt legislation in a number of fields (e.g., environmental policy prior to the SEA's inclusion of an environmental chapter in the Treaty) that at the time no Treaty article specifically addressed. While expansion of treaty subjects under the SEA and the Maastricht and Amsterdam Treaties lessened the need for resort to implied powers, they did not obviate it altogether.

In fact, the Court of Justice has upheld expansive interpretations of Community competence on an "implied power" theory even without invoking Article 308. The *Fédéchar* case, *supra* page 30, is an early example arising out of the ECSC. When Belgium signed the ECSC Treaty in 1951, the costs of Belgian coal production were substantially higher than in Germany or the Netherlands, and Belgian producers were temporarily to receive so-called equalization payments (a form of subsidy) to help offset production costs, thus enabling them to reduce prices to consumers and make Belgian coal more competitive. To ensure that the Belgian producers would in fact reduce their prices, the High Authority decided in 1955 actually to fix reduced prices for Belgian coal. A federation of Belgian coal producers (Fédéchar) challenged this action on the ground that the Treaty did not authorize the fixing of prices. To the claim that the High Authority could only exercise powers expressly granted it by the ECSC Treaty, the Court replied:

> [T]he rules laid down by an international treaty or a law presuppose the rules without which that treaty or law would have no meaning or could not be reasonably and usefully applied. Furthermore, under the terms of Article 8 of the Treaty, it shall be the duty of the High Authority to ensure that the objectives set out in that Treaty are attained in accordance with the provisions thereof. It must be concluded ... that [the High Authority] enjoys a certain independence in determining the implementing measures necessary for the attainment of the objectives referred to in the Treaty. ... As, in this instance, it is necessary to achieve the aim of Article 26 ..., the High Authority has the power, if not the duty, to adopt—within the limits laid down by that provision—measures to reduce the prices of Belgian coal.

> The result is that the accomplishment of its task in this instance assumes a power [on its part] to fix prices.

Fédération Charbonnière de Belgique v. High Authority (Fédéchar), Case 8/55, [1954–1956] ECR 245, 292, 299–300.

Note that the Court in *Fédéchar* did not actually invoke the ECSC Treaty's implied powers language (then Article 95), which was identical to EC Treaty Article 308 (ex 235).[1] Thus, the Court in effect acknowledged the existence of an "inherent" implied powers. For a more recent example, see

---

1. The Euratom Treaty also contains an implied powers provision, Article 203.

Germany v. Commission (Immigration of non-Community workers), Cases 281, 283–85, 287/85, [1987] ECR 3203.

Since Article 308 requires unanimity in the Council, while other treaty articles increasingly permit qualified majority voting, the Council's resort (or non-resort) to implied powers may raise the now-familiar question of the "correct legal basis," discussed in Chapter 3B. The following case explores this prospect.

SPAIN v. COUNCIL
(Medicinal product certificates)
Case C–350/92, [1995] ECR I–1985.

[In 1992, in order to compensate pharmaceutical manufacturers for delays in the marketing of patented drugs occasioned by lengthy pharmaceutical review process, the Council adopted a Regulation (1768/92) creating a supplementary protection certificate for medicinal products. The regulation, which extended the same rights as the basic patent for a period of time partially reflecting the period of delay, up to an absolute maximum of five years, was adopted under Article 95 (ex 100a), which contemplated internal market harmonization and at the time entailed parliamentary cooperation and qualified majority voting in the Council.

Spain, supported by Greece, challenged the regulation as "a grave infringement of the sovereignty of Member States," because the EC Treaty did not give the Community legislative power to create patent rights, or indeed any other form of intellectual property rights, citing various Treaty provisions (notably Articles 30 and 295, ex 36 and 222) and cases. As a fallback position, Spain claimed that if legislative competence existed at all, it could only be by virtue of Article 308 (ex 235) and not 95 (ex 100a), entailing unanimous voting. The Council, supported by France, argued that it could legislate in the field of intellectual property under Article 95 where necessary to achieve the internal market.]

26   It is settled case-law [citing Commission v. Council (Generalized tariff preferences), Case 45/86, [1987] ECR 1493] that Article 235 may be used as the legal basis for a measure only where no other provision of the Treaty gives the Community institutions the necessary power to adopt it.

* * *

30   Spain argues that the regulation does not pursue the objectives set out in Article 8a [later 7a and, after Amsterdam, 14] of the ... Treaty, to which Article 100a [now 95] refers. . . .

* * *

32   In its judgment in [the *Titanium dioxide* case (Commission v. Council, Case C–300/89, discussed at page 87 *supra*)], the Court held that, in order to give effect to the fundamental freedoms mentioned in Article 8a [now 14], harmonizing measures are necessary to deal with disparities between the laws of the Member States in areas where such disparities are liable to create or maintain distorted conditions of competition. For that reason,

Article 100a empowers the Community to adopt measures for the approximation of the provisions laid down by law, regulation or administrative action in Member States and lays down the procedure to be followed for that purpose.

[33] In the same way, harmonizing measures are necessary to deal with disparities between the laws of the Member States in so far as such disparities are liable to hinder the free movement of goods within the Community.

[34] In this case, the Council has pointed out that, at the time the contested regulation was adopted, provisions concerning the creation of a supplementary protection certificate for medicinal products existed in two Member States and were at the draft stage in another State. The contested regulation is intended precisely to establish a uniform Community approach by creating a supplementary certificate which may be obtained by the holder of a national or European patent under the same conditions in each Member State, and by providing, in particular, for a uniform duration of protection.

[35] The regulation thus aims to prevent the heterogeneous development of national laws leading to further disparities which would be likely to create obstacles to the free movement of medicinal products within the Community and thus directly affect the establishment and the functioning of the internal market.

[36] The Council rightly emphasizes that differences in the protection given in the Community to one and the same medicine would give rise to a fragmentation of the market, whereby the medicine would still be protected in some national markets but no longer protected in others. Such differences in protection would mean that the marketing conditions for the medicines would themselves be different in each of the Member States.

* * *

[40] It follows from the above that the regulation was validly adopted on the basis of Article 100a of the Treaty, and did not therefore have to be adopted on the basis of . . . Article 235.

Notes and Questions

1. Note that while the EC Treaty was amended by the SEA and the Maastricht Treaty to provide legislative competence (in some instances quite limited) in fields like the environment, consumer protection, culture, education and health, this was not the case for intellectual property. Even today, intellectual property legislation must be rationalized in terms of the internal market and typically based on Article 95 (ex 100a).

Do you find the Court's reliance on Article 100a persuasive? Should it had to have relied on Article 235 instead?

2. The *Generalized tariff preferences* case referred to in paragraph 26 is interesting. The Council, acting upon proposal of the Commission, issued regulations implementing a system of preferential tariffs in favor of developing countries, described in Chapter 28 *infra*. Because the Commission and Council were unable to agree on the treaty article to be recited as the legal basis for these regulations, the Council eventually employed instead in their preamble merely the

words "having regard to the Treaty ..." The Commission brought an action in the Court of Justice to have the regulations annulled on the ground that they failed to "state the reasons on which they are based," in violation of Article 190 (now 253) of the EC Treaty. Admitting the indication was not precise, the Council contended that the recitals in the regulations' preambles gave sufficient information as to their aims, which were two-fold: common commercial policy and development aid.

The Court agreed that failure to cite a precise treaty article could be overlooked when the legal basis may fairly be determined from other parts of the measure. But it held the recitals here to be inadequate; indeed the vague formula "having regard to the Treaty" was adopted precisely because of differences of opinion over the choice of legal basis.

[10] The Council has stated that when it adopted the contested regulations it intended to base them on both Articles 113 [now 133] and 235 [now 308] of the EEC [now EC] Treaty. It has explained that it departed from the Commission's proposal to base the regulations on Article 113 alone because it was convinced that the contested regulations had not only commercial-policy aims, but also major development-policy aims. [According to the Council, the] implementation of development policy goes beyond the scope of Article 113 of the Treaty and necessitates recourse to Article 235.

* * *

[13] It follows from the very wording of Article 235 that its use as the legal basis for a measure is justified only where no other provision of the Treaty gives the Community institutions the necessary power to adopt the measure in question.

[14] It must therefore be considered whether in this case the Council had the power to adopt the contested regulations pursuant to Article 113 of the Treaty alone, as the Commission maintains.

[The Court concluded, in light of its opinion in *International Agreement on Natural Rubber,* discussed at page 1036 *infra,* that tariff preferences did fall within the sphere of commercial policy provided for in Article 113.]

[21] It follows that the contested regulations are measures falling within the sphere of the common commercial policy and that since the Council had the power to adopt them pursuant to Article 113 of the Treaty, it was not justified in taking as its basis Article 235.

We know from the "legal basis" cases, *supra,* why, as a general matter, the Commission might challenge the legality of a measure that it itself had originally proposed. Can you also speculate as to why, from a development aid policy point of view, the Commission objected to the Council's use of Article 235, requiring unanimity, rather than exclusively the then Article 113, permitting qualified majority voting?

The Commission's reliance on Article 190 is curious. Like the current Article 253, Article 190 did not state that reference to a particular treaty provision was required for all regulations, directives and decisions. It stated a requirement of "reasons." Why did the Court apparently believe that a requirement of reasons necessarily entails mentioning one or more treaty articles? For further discussion of the reasons requirement, see Chapter 3A *supra.*

3.   Given the specificity with which the EC Treaty defines the Community's legislative powers, how readily should the Council use Article 308 as the basis for action not expressly authorized by the Treaty? Is there any practical difference between relying on Article 308 or simply giving a particular Treaty provision an expansive interpretation, as occurred in *Immigration of non-Community workers, supra* page 107?

4.   As noted, before the Single European Act expressly made environmental protection a matter of Community concern, the Council based much of its environmental legislation on the implied powers provision (then Article 235). Was that legitimate? See the discussion of this issue in Chapter 34 *infra*. For a particularly good example of the difficulties in giving environmental initiatives a "common market" rationale, consider Directive 79/409 on the conservation of migratory birds. O.J. L 103/1 (April 25, 1979).

5.   The use of implied powers was an important aspect of the Court of Justice's Opinion 1/94 on the validity of the EC's accession, independent of the Member States, to the WTO. For that judgment, see page 1084 *infra*.

B. INTERNAL AFFAIRS
KNOORS v. SECRETARY OF STATE FOR ECONOMIC AFFAIRS
Case 115/78, [1979] ECR 399.

[Knoors, a Dutch national, who resided and conducted a heating and plumbing business in Belgium, sought to operate regularly in the Netherlands as well. Though Dutch law ordinarily forbade conduct of such a business in the Netherlands without a local license, it expressly waived that rule to the extent any EC directive required. The Dutch authorities denied Knoors an exemption on the ground that, as a Dutch national, he could not invoke the relevant directive (64/427 on the freedom of establishment and freedom of services in respect of self-employed persons), which had been adopted pursuant to Articles 43 and 44 (ex 52 and 54) on the right of establishment. The denial was affirmed on administrative appeal. The administrative court in which Knoors then sought judicial review referred a question to the Court of Justice under EC Treaty Article 234 (ex 177).]

[9]   Directive No. 64/427 is intended to facilitate the realization of freedom of establishment and of freedom to provide services in a large group of trade activities relating to industry and small craft industries, pending harmonization of the conditions for access to the trades in question in the various Member States, which is an indispensable precondition for complete freedom in this sphere.

* * *

[11]   With a view to resolving the problems created by this disparity, Article 3 of the directive provides that, where, in a Member State, the taking up or pursuit of any activity referred to in the directive is dependent on the possession of certain qualifications, "that Member State shall accept as sufficient evidence of such knowledge and ability the fact that the activity in question has been pursued in another Member State".

* * *

17　It may therefore be stated that Directive No. 64/427 is based on a broad definition of the "beneficiaries" of its provisions, in the sense that the nationals of all Member States must be able to avail themselves of the liberalizing measures which it lays down, provided that they come objectively within one of the situations provided for by the directive, and no differentiation of treatment on the basis of their residence or nationality is permitted.

18　Thus the provisions of the directive may be relied upon by the nationals of all the Member States who are in the situations which the directive defines for its application, even in respect of the State whose nationality they possess.

19　This interpretation is justified by the requirements flowing from freedom of movement for persons, freedom of establishment and freedom to provide services, which are guaranteed by Articles 3(c), 48, 52 and 59 [now 3(c), 39, 43 and 49] of the Treaty.

20　In fact, these liberties, which are fundamental in the Community system, could not be fully realized if the Member States were in a position to refuse to grant the benefit of the provisions of Community law to those of their nationals who have taken advantage of the facilities existing in the matter of freedom of movement and establishment and who have acquired, by virtue of such facilities, the trade qualifications referred to by the directive in a Member State other than that whose nationality they possess.

21　In contesting this solution, the Netherlands Government states, first, that the first paragraph of Article 52 [now 43] provides for the abolition of "restrictions on the freedom of establishment of nationals of a Member State in the territory of another Member State" and, secondly, that according to the second paragraph of the same article, freedom of establishment is to include the right to take up activities as self-employed persons under the conditions laid down by the law of the country where such establishment is effected "for its own nationals".

22　It is claimed that those provisions of the Treaty show that the nationals of the host State are not regarded by the Treaty as being beneficiaries of the liberalization measures for which provision is made and that they therefore remain entirely subject to the provisions of their national legislation.

23　Moreover, the Netherlands Government draws attention to the risk that the nationals of a Member State might evade the application of their national provisions in the matter of training for a trade if they were authorized to avail themselves, as against their own national authorities, of the facilities created by the directive.

24　Although it is true that the provisions of the Treaty relating to establishment and the provision of services cannot be applied to situations which are purely internal to a Member State, the position nevertheless remains that the reference in Article 52 to "nationals of a Member State" who wish to establish themselves "in the territory of another Member State" cannot be interpreted in such a way as to exclude from the benefit of Community law a given Member State's own nationals when the latter, owing to the fact that they have lawfully resided on the territory of another Member State and have there acquired a trade qualification which is recognized by the provisions of Community law, are, with regard to their State of origin, in a situation which may be assimilated to that of any other persons enjoying the rights and liberties guaranteed by the Treaty.

25 However, it is not possible to disregard the legitimate interest which a Member State may have in preventing certain of its nationals, by means of facilities created under the Treaty, from attempting wrongly to evade the application of their national legislation as regards training for a trade.

26 In this case, however, it should be borne in mind that, having regard to the nature of the trades in question, the precise conditions set out in Article 3 of Directive No. 64/427, as regards the length of periods during which the activity in question must have been pursued, have the effect of excluding, in the fields in question, the risk of abuse referred to by the Netherlands Government.

* * *

28 The answer to be given to the question referred to the Court should therefore be that Council Directive No. 64/427 ... must be understood to mean that persons who possess the nationality of the host Member State are also "beneficiaries" within the meaning of Article 1(1) of the directive.

Notes and Questions

1. Is *Knoors* merely a case of statutory interpretation or does it imply the exclusion of Community competence over matters "internal" to a Member State? In Criminal proceedings against Bekaert, Case 204/87, [1988] ECR 2029, a French national and resident operating a supermarket in France was prosecuted for giving false information in his application for a permit to enlarge his business premises. He claimed that the French permit requirement violated Community legislation on freedom of trade, competition and establishment. The Court of Justice gave the French criminal court the following preliminary ruling under Article 234 (then 177):

> The absence of any element going beyond a purely national setting in a given case therefore means, in matters of freedom of establishment, that the provisions of Community law are not applicable to such a situation.

> ... Article 52 [now 43] of the EEC [now EC] Treaty and [the directives] implementing Article 52 ... do not apply to situations which are purely internal to a Member State, such as that of a national of a Member State who has never resided or worked in any other Member State.

[1988] ECR at 2039. For comparable problems in the area of free movement of workers, see Moser v. Land Baden–Württemberg, Case 180/83, [1984] ECR 2539, excerpted at page 627 *infra*, and Steen v. Deutsche Bundespost (*Steen II*), Case C–132/93, [1994] ECR I–2715, discussed at page 628 *infra*.

2. The problem raised by *Knoors* is commonly described as one of discrimination by a Member State against its own nationals, or "reverse discrimination." Is that a useful way of characterizing the problem?

3. In Ministère Public v. Aubertin, Joined Cases C–29–35/94, [1995] ECR I–301, French hairdressers (none of whom claimed to have obtained any professional qualifications in another Member State) were charged with operating hair salons without being in possession of the necessary French professional diploma. They

claimed "reverse discrimination" on the ground that French law (implementing an EC directive) permitted nationals of other Member States to operate hair salons in France without any diploma, provided they had lawfully operated a salon in another Member State for a specified length of time. The Court could not find a "connecting factor between [their] situations and ... those contemplated by Community law, so that the Treaty rules on freedom of establishment are inapplicable." The Court noted that the directive in question did not aim to harmonize the conditions laid down by national law for pursuit of the hairdressing profession. If the directive had had such an aim, would that have changed the result or would the cases still be purely "internal"?

4. EC Treaty Article 12 (ex 6) prohibits nationality-based discrimination "[w]ithin the scope of application of [the] Treaty." In Hayes v. Kronenberger GmbH, Case C–323/95, [1997] ECR I–1711, a British couple claimed that German law unlawfully discriminated against them by requiring non-German plaintiffs to post security for costs in the German courts, while not requiring German plaintiffs to do so. The Court had no difficulty concluding that the alleged discrimination fell within the scope of application of the Treaty:

[14]   It must be held that a national procedural rule, such as the one described above, is liable to affect the economic activity of traders from other Member States on the market of the State in question. Although it is, as such, not intended to regulate an activity of a commercial nature, it has the effect of placing such traders in a less advantageous position than nationals of that State as regards access to its courts. Since Community law guarantees such traders free movement of goods and services in the common market, it is a corollary of those freedoms that they must be able, in order to resolve any disputes arising from their economic activities, to bring actions in the courts of a Member State in the same way as nationals of that State.

       . . .

[17]   [T]herefore ... a rule of domestic civil procedure, such as the one at issue in the main proceedings, falls within the scope of the Treaty within the meaning of the first paragraph of Article 6 and is subject to the general principle of non-discrimination laid down by that article in so far as it has an effect, even though indirect, on trade in goods and services between Member States. ...

On the merits, the Court found the German provision to be discriminatory, and thus forbidden.

5. Italian legislation gave German-speaking citizens of the province of Bolzano the right to have criminal proceedings against them conducted in the German rather than the Italian language. An Austrian truck driver and a German tourist, having been separately charged with criminal offenses while in the province, and having no facility in the Italian language, requested that the proceedings against them be conducted in German. In response to a preliminary reference from the Italian magistrate, Italy argued that since only Italians resident in the province were entitled to demand the use of German, national treatment required that nationals of other Member States be given that right only if they too were resident in the province. Does the discrimination complained of here arise within the scope of the Treaty? The Court found that it did, and that German-speaking nationals of other Member States had to be given the same right as German-speaking residents of Bolzano. Re Criminal Proceedings against Bickel and Franz, Case C–274/96, [1998] ECR I–7637.

Does this also mean that German-speaking residents of other regions of Italy have the same entitlement when prosecuted in Bolzano? Do French nationals who speak neither German nor Italian have a right to have criminal proceedings against them in Bolzano conducted in French? *Bickel and Franz* is treated more fully in Chapter 17 *infra*. For other recent judgments broadly construing the "scope" of Community law for these purposes, see Ferlini v. Centre hospitalier de Luxembourg, Case C–411/98, [2000] ECR I–8081; Angonese v. Cassa di Risparmio di Bolzano SpA, Case C–281/98, [2000] ECR I–4139.

On the sphere of application of Community human rights law, see page 217 *infra*.

C. PREEMPTION OF MEMBER STATE LAW

In a federal-type system, it is necessary not only to establish areas of federal competence, but also to determine whether, and to what extent, conferral of legislative authority on the federal government precludes the states from acting on the subjects in question. Analogous preemption problems arise in EC law, particularly in the agricultural and competition law fields and in the area of harmonization of Member State laws. Consider the following landmark competition law judgment.

WILHELM v. BUNDESKARTELLAMT

(Walt Wilhelm)
Case 14/68, [1969] ECR 1.

[In 1967, the Commission began proceedings under Regulation 17 against several dyestuffs manufacturers (including four German companies) for allegedly engaging in concerted activity in the pricing of aniline in violation of EC Treaty Article 81 (ex 85). Later that year, the German Bundeskartellamt (Federal Cartel Office) imposed fines on these German companies, among others, under the 1957 German law against restraints of competition. The companies challenged the Cartel Office decision before a Berlin court, which sought a preliminary ruling from the Court of Justice on the question whether the Bundeskartellamt could take action against conduct that at the time was the subject of proceedings before the Commission.]

[2]   In the first question the national court asks whether, when a procedure has already been initiated by the Commission under ... Regulation No. 17 ... it is compatible with the Treaty for the national authorities to apply to the same facts the prohibitions laid down by the national law on cartels. This request is elaborated in particular in the third question, relating to the risk of a different legal assessment of the same facts and to the possibility of distortions of competition in the common market to the detriment of those subject to the said national law. ...

[3]   ... Community and national law on cartels consider cartels from different points of view. Whereas Article 85 [now 81] regards them in the light of the obstacles which may result for trade between Member States, each body of national legislation proceeds on the basis of the considerations peculiar to it and considers cartels only in that context. It is true that as the economic phenomena and legal situations under consideration may in

individual cases be interdependent, the distinction between Community and national aspects could not serve in all cases as the decisive criterion for the delimitation of jurisdiction. However, it implies that one and the same agreement may, in principle, be the object of two sets of parallel proceedings, one before the Community authorities under Article 85 of the EEC [now EC] Treaty, the other before the national authorities under national law.

⁴ Moreover this interpretation is confirmed by the provision in Article 87(2)(e) [now 83(2)(e)], which authorizes the Council to determine the relationship between national laws and the Community rules on competition; it follows that in principle the national cartel authorities may take proceedings also with regard to situations likely to be the subject of a decision by the Commission. However, if the ultimate general aim of the Treaty is to be respected, this parallel application of the national system can only be allowed in so far as it does not prejudice the uniform application throughout the Common Market of the Community rules on cartels and the full effect of the measures adopted in implementation of those rules.

⁵ Any other solution would be incompatible with the objectives of the Treaty and the character of its rules on competition. Article 85 of the EEC Treaty applies to all the undertakings in the Community whose conduct it governs either by prohibitions or by means of exemptions, granted— subject to conditions which it specifies—in favour of agreements which contribute to improving the production or distribution of goods or to promoting technical or economic progress. While the Treaty's primary object is to eliminate by this means the obstacles to the free movement of goods within the common market and to confirm and safeguard the unity of that market, it also permits the Community authorities to carry out certain positive, though indirect, action with a view to promoting a harmonious development of economic activities within the whole Community, in accordance with Article 2 of the Treaty. Article 87(2)(e), in conferring on a Community institution the power to determine the relationship between national laws and the Community rules on competition, confirms the supremacy of Community law.

* * *

⁷ It follows from the foregoing that should it prove that a decision of a national authority regarding an agreement would be incompatible with a decision adopted by the Commission at the culmination of the procedure initiated by it, the national authority is required to take proper account of the effects of the latter decision.

* * *

⁹ Consequently, and so long as a regulation adopted pursuant to Article 87(2)(e) of the Treaty has not provided otherwise, national authorities may take action against an agreement in accordance with their national law, even when an examination of the agreement from the point of view of its compatibility with Community law is pending before the Commission, subject however to the condition that the application of national law may

not prejudice the full and uniform application of Community law or the effects of measures taken or to be taken to implement it.

[The German court's second question to the Court was whether any general Community law principle prohibits exposing enterprises to the risk of a "double sanction." The Court answered in the negative, but suggested that principles of "natural justice" might prevent the imposition of consecutive sanctions or at least require that a previous sanction be taken into account in fixing a second sanction for the same conduct.]

Notes and Questions

1. *Walt Wilhelm* establishes that the Community and the Member States share, albeit unequally, prescriptive and adjudicatory authority over competition law matters. The relationship between national and Community competition law is taken up in greater detail in Chapter 20 *infra*.

2. Note the Court's qualification in paragraph 9 of the judgment to the effect that national law may not be permitted to "prejudice the full and uniform application of Community law or the effects of measures taken or to be taken to implement it." The Court brought the point forcefully home in Masterfoods Ltd. v. HB Ice Cream Ltd., Case C–344/98, [2000] ECR I–6659. HB, a leading Irish ice cream producer, sued in Irish court to prevent Masterfoods (a subsidiary of Mars Inc.) from inducing retailers to breach their contractual undertaking not to display non-HB products in the freezer cabinets supplied to them by HP. In the same court, Masterfoods sought a declaration that the exclusivity clause was null and void under both Irish and Community competition law. The Irish court found in favor of HP, and issued the requested injunction. Masterfoods appealed to the Irish Supreme Court and at the same time lodged a competition law complaint with the Commission. When the Commission eventually found HP's policy to infringe Community law and not deserve an exemption, HP sought review in the Court of First Instance. At this point, the Irish Supreme Court asked the Court of Justice whether it was required to stay Masterfoods' appeal, pending the result of Masterfoods' action. The Court replied:

49   It is ... clear from the case-law of the Court that the Member States' duty [of sincere cooperation] under Article 5 [now 10] of the EC Treaty to take all appropriate measures, whether general or particular, to ensure fulfilment of the obligations arising from Community law and to abstain from any measure which could jeopardise the attainment of the objectives of the Treaty is binding on all the authorities of Member States including, for matters within their jurisdiction, the courts.

* * *

56   [A]pplication of the Community competition rules is based on an obligation of sincere cooperation between the national courts, on the one hand, and the Commission and the Community Courts, on the other. . . .

57   When the outcome of the dispute before the national court depends on the validity of the Commission decision, it follows ... that the national court should, in order to avoid reaching a decision that runs counter to that of the Commission, stay its proceedings pending final judgment in the action for annulment by the Community Courts, unless it considers that, in the circumstances of the case, a reference to the Court of Justice for a preliminary ruling on the validity of the Commission decision is warranted.

3. The Court has not been as tolerant of concurrent competences in all fields of Community law governance. The following agricultural policy case illustrates the point, but the reader should also be sensitive to the preemption question in cases throughout the substantive law chapters of this book. For a general discussion, see Soares, Pre-emption, Conflicts of Powers and Subsidiarity, 23 Eur. L. Rev. 132 (1998).

PIGS MARKETING BOARD v. REDMOND

Case 83/78, [1978] ECR 2347.

[Legislation in Northern Ireland required producers to sell certain categories of pigs through a Pigs Marketing Board which was empowered to regulate price and other conditions of sale. Under the law, transporting pigs without authorization by the Board subjected a producer to criminal sanctions and forfeiture of the livestock. Redmond was charged with transporting pigs without Board authorization.]

11 The defendant argued in his defence [in national court] that the provisions of the Pigs Marketing Scheme and the Movement of Pigs Regulations under which he was charged were incompatible with the provisions of Community law, in particular with the regulations on the common organization of the market in pigmeat . . .

* * *

51 [T]he decisive questions for the solution of the case before the [national court] concern the compatibility with the provisions relating to the free movement of goods and the common organization of the market in pigmeat of a market system laid down by the legislation of a Member State and managed by a body which has power . . . to control the sector of the market in question by measures such as [those taken in the present case].

* * *

56 As the Court has stated in . . . Case 111/76, Officier van Justitie v. van den Hazel ([1977] ECR at p. 909), once the Community has, pursuant to Article 40 [now 34] of the Treaty, legislated for the establishment of the common organization of the market in a given sector, Member States are under an obligation to refrain from taking any measure which might undermine or create exceptions to it.

57 With a view to applying that statement in the case of the Pigs Marketing Scheme it should be borne in mind that the common organization of the market in pigmeat, like the other common organizations, is based on the concept of an open market to which every producer has free access and the functioning of which is regulated solely by the instruments provided for by that organization.

58 Hence any provisions or national practices which might alter the pattern of imports or exports or influence the formation of market prices by preventing producers from buying and selling freely within the State in which they are established, or in any other Member State, [on] conditions laid down by Community rules and from taking advantage directly of intervention measures or any other measures for regulating the market

laid down by the common organization are incompatible with the principles of such organization of the market.

59 Any action of this type, which is brought to bear upon the market by a body set up by a Member State and which does not come within the arrangements made by Community rules cannot be justified by the pursuit of special objectives of economic policy, national or regional; the common organization of the market ... is intended precisely to attain such objectives on the Community scale [on] conditions acceptable for the whole of the Community and taking account of the needs of all its regions.

60 Any intervention by a Member State or by its regional or subordinate authorities in the market machinery apart from such intervention as may be specifically laid down by the Community regulation runs the risk of obstructing the functioning of the common organization of the market and of creating unjustified advantages for certain groups of producers or consumers to the prejudice of the economy of other Member States or of other economic groups within the Community.

* * *

65 [A] marketing system [of the sort presented here is] to be considered as incompatible with the requirements of Articles 30 and 34 [now 28 and 29] of the EEC [now EC] Treaty and [the regulation] on the common organization of the market in pigmeat.

Notes and Questions

1. *Pigs Marketing Board* is only one of many cases holding that Member States may not establish national systems restricting business in a sector specifically covered by a common market organization adopted by the Community. According to these cases, once the Community exercises its legislative power to install such an organization, national power to regulate various stages of production and distribution within that market is preempted.

Even in the agricultural area, where the preemption principle is clearly accepted, application of the principle may not be obvious. Consider the case of Bussone v. Italian Ministry for Agriculture and Forestry, Case 31/78, [1978] ECR 2429. Community regulation of the egg market required that egg packages bear a non-reusable labeling band containing certain consumer information. The Italian law implementing the regulation provided for a labeling band fee to be fixed by decree. An eggpacker sought recovery of moneys paid on the ground that the fee charged was unreasonably high. Does the regulation, which says nothing about fees, bar Italy from imposing them? Assuming the regulation bars only "exorbitant" fees, how should "exorbitant" be defined and who should decide whether a given fee is exorbitant?

2. The fact that a matter is not preempted by Community legislation does not of course mean that the national measure in question necessarily comports with Community law. For example, Germany was able to show that the Community's common organization of the dairy market did not preempt national regulation of imitation milk products, but it nevertheless failed to show that the regulation in question was a justifiable restriction on the free movement of goods under EC Treaty Articles 28 and 30 [ex 30 and 36]. Commission v. Germany (Milk substitutes), Case 76/86, [1989] ECR 1021.

3.   In enacting legislation, the Council and Parliament can of course address the preemption question directly and clearly. See, for example, Republic v. Di Pinto, Case C–361/89, [1991] ECR I–1189, where a national court asked the ECJ whether Council Directive 85/577, protecting consumers from contracts "negotiated away from business premises," precluded States from extending its protection of consumers to traders seeking to sell an ongoing business, a category of persons evidently not reached by the directive. The Court relied on Article 8 of the directive which stated that the directive "shall not prevent Member States from adopting or maintaining more favourable provisions to protect consumers in the field which it covers."

On the other hand, Directive 65/65 on the marketing of proprietary medicines expressly provides that "authorization ... shall not be refused, suspended or revoked except on the grounds set out in this Directive." Such language may be regarded as conclusive evidence of preemption. See, for example, Pierrel SpA v. Ministero della Sanità, Case C–83/92, [1993] ECR I–6419.

4.   Even if a Member State is not precluded by a harmonizing directive from applying higher standards, it may be barred from applying such standards to goods that have been produced in another Member State in conformity with the directive. For a good example, see Queen v. Secretary of State for Health (ex parte Gallaher Ltd.), Case C–11/92, [1993] ECR I–3545, excerpted at page 565 *infra*.

5.   When the Single European Act and the TEU amended the EC Treaty to enlarge the Community's legislative jurisdiction, it included in certain sections language bearing on the preemption question. Thus Article 137 [ex 118], on the harmonization of worker health and safety standards, provides that provisions adopted by the Council "shall not prevent any Member State from maintaining or introducing more stringent protective measures compatible with this Treaty." New provisions on the environment (EC Treaty Article 176 [ex 130t]) and consumer protection (EC Treaty Article 153 [ex. 129a]) contain comparable language.

Such express non-preemption language makes it clear that Community standards in these areas constitute a floor on Member State regulation and not a ceiling. Does its selective inclusion in the EC Treaty imply that in other areas of Community action harmonization directives *are* ordinarily preemptive? Note in any event that the articles cited contain a condition that the Member States' "more stringent measures" still must be "compatible with this Treaty."

D.   THE SUBSIDIARITY PRINCIPLE

As noted in section A of this chapter, the Community institutions enjoy powers of attribution only; the Member States are presumed to have reserved all legislative powers not delegated. On the other hand, once a measure is found to fall within the Community sphere, then the institutions have generally been thought free to legislate as broadly or narrowly as they see fit, provided they respect all the substantive and procedural conditions in the pertinent treaty provisions.

The Maastricht Treaty introduced into the EC Treaty a rather different notion, namely that even when exercising the powers conferred on them, the institutions may do so only to the extent that Community governance of an issue presents demonstrable advantages over Member State governance. The treaty language, as now found in Article 5 (ex 3b), reads as follows:

In areas which do not fall within its exclusive competence, the Community shall take action, in accordance with the principle of subsidiarity, only if and insofar as the objectives of the proposed action cannot be sufficiently achieved by the Member States and can therefore, by reason of the scale or effects of proposed action, be better achieved by the Community.

Article 5 adds that Community action "shall not go beyond what is necessary to achieve the objectives of this Treaty."

According to this principle, known as the principle of "subsidiarity," the Member States retain their legislative prerogatives, even on matters falling within the Community sphere, if they can achieve regulatory objectives as efficiently and effectively as the Community itself can. Community competence is in this sense "subsidiary." At the same time that it was added to the EC Treaty, the principle of subsidiarity found its way into Article 2 (ex art. B) of the Treaty of European Union.

When first injected into Community law, the notion of subsidiarity was confined to the sphere of environmental policy; the Single European Act introduced an article into the EC Treaty (ex art. 130r4) to the effect that Community action in the field of environmental protection should be taken only when environmental objectives "can be attained better at [the] Community level" than at the level of the Member States. It was introduced at the urging of Denmark and Germany, which feared that Community governance of environmental policy might have the effect of lowering their national environmental standards. With the Maastricht Treaty, however, subsidiarity became a Community law principle applicable to all matters within the concurrent competence of the Community and the Member States.

Subsidiarity took on heightened resonance in the wake of the June 1992 Danish referendum rejecting the Maastricht agreement and the close French vote in its favor (see page 18 *supra*). At its December 1992 Edinburgh Summit, the European Council announced a set of "guidelines" to help ensure that the Community institutions observe the subsidiarity principle in their daily operations.[2] At Edinburgh, the European Council resolved, among other things, that the Commission should include in the explanatory memorandum to the Council accompanying any proposed legislation a statement "justif[ying] the initiative with regard to the principle of subsidiarity." The required inquiry has been likened to a "subsidiarity impact statement." G. Bermann, Taking Subsidiarity Seriously: Federalism in the European Community and the United States, 94 Colum. L. Rev. 331, 379 (1994). The following year, the Parliament, Council and Commission adopted two subsidiarity-related instruments: an Interinstitutional Declaration on Democracy, Transparency and Subsidiarity and an Interinstitutional Agreement on Procedures for Implementing the Principle of Subsidiarity (Selected Documents, Part I, documents 8 and 9, respectively).

Although Article 5 of the EC Treaty targets "proposed action" (and therefore conceivably required that subsidiarity be given prospective application only), the Commission promised to review existing legislation from that viewpoint as well. Accordingly, in November 1993, the Commission issued a report on the adaptation of existing legislation to the principle of subsidiarity,

---

2. Bull. EC 12/92, point 1.4.

a report specially commissioned by the European Council. In this "Adaptation Report," the Commission announced that it was withdrawing nine legislative proposals, while simplifying and consolidating a great many others.[3] In December 1993, the European Council at Brussels requested that the Commission report back to it regularly on the application of the principle of subsidiarity. The Commission's first annual report, detailing progress and proposals, appeared in November 1994.[4] Since then, the Commission has filed annual reports on the same subject.

At the 1996–97 IGC, the Member States adopted and attached to the TEU a special "Subsidiarity Protocol." Although a number of Member States—notably France, Germany, and the UK—had advanced quite different formulations, the IGC, ultimately adopted a protocol that tracks the Edinburgh guidelines very closely. Besides requiring the Commission to state its reasons for believing that proposed legislation comports with the subsidiarity principle, the Protocol's states:

5. For Community action to be justified, both aspects of the subsidiarity principle shall be met: the objectives of the proposed action cannot be sufficiently achieved by Member States' action in the framework of their national constitutional system and can therefore be better achieved by action on the part of the Community.

    The following guidelines should be used in examining whether the above-mentioned condition is fulfilled:

    —the issue under consideration has transnational aspects which cannot be satisfactorily regulated by action by Member States;

    —actions by Member States alone or lack of Community action would conflict with requirements of the Treaty ... or would otherwise significantly damage Member States' interests;

    —action at Community level would produce clear benefits by reason of its scale or effects compared with action at the level of the Member States.

For the Protocol's complete text, see Selected Documents, Part I, document 1, protocols.

Notes and Questions

1. Why did the drafters of the TEU introduce the subsidiarity principle across the board (except, that is, in areas within the Community's exclusive jurisdiction) if they were only concerned about Community intrusiveness in certain traditionally domestic law spheres?

2. While dismissed by many commentators as essentially meaningless, the subsidiarity principle has excited political tensions. For example, when former Commission President Santer, invoking subsidiarity, announced to the European Parliament in February 1995 that "[w]e have to legislate less in order to legislate better," the Parliament quickly responded that it would be alert to the danger of subsidiarity's being used as a pretext for reversing important and valuable Community legislation and threatened to sue the Commission in the Court of

---

3. Report to the European Council on the Adaptation of Community Legislation to the Subsidiarity Principle, COM(93) 545 final (Nov. 24, 1993).

4. Report to the European Council on the Application of the Subsidiarity Principle— 1994. COM (94) 533, Bull. EU 11/94, point 1.1.1.

Justice if it attempted to withdraw certain existing environmental directives in the name of subsidiarity, as jointly urged by France and Britain, without first consulting the Parliament. According to the Parliament, the withdrawal of directives had to follow exactly the same procedures used in their enactment. For an expression of Parliament's concern over the possible misuse or overuse of the subsidiarity principle, see Resolution on the Commission's Report to the European Council on "Better Lawmaking," 1999 O.J. C 98 (Dec. 18, 1998).

3.   Member States can and do invoke the subsidiarity principle in their political opposition to various legislative proposals at the European level. But will the Community courts entertain challenges to Community legislation brought by Member States on the ground that the legislation seeks to advance objectives that could just as well be attained at or below the national level? In other words, is the subsidiarity principle justiciable. The following case considers that question.

GERMANY v. PARLIAMENT AND COUNCIL

(Deposit-guarantee schemes)
Case C–233/94, [1997] ECR I–2405.

[Germany challenged a Community directive which required the Member States to set up a "deposit guarantee system" and to ensure that all credit institutions established on their territory participate in it. The Council, acting on the basis of EC Treaty Article 57, para. 2 (now 47, para. 2), had adopted the measure over Germany's opposition. Germany claimed, among other things, that the Council and Parliament had failed to comply with the requirement of a statement of reasons under Article 190 (now 253) of the Treaty. Germany reasoned that an adequate statement must necessarily address the principle of subsidiarity. More specifically, it maintained that the institutions had to "indicate in a detailed way why the Community may be considered as alone capable of taking action on the matter in question [or why] the objectives [of the measure] could not sufficiently be achieved through action taken at the level of the Member States."]

26   In the present case, the Parliament and the Council stated in the ... preamble to the Directive that "consideration should be given to the situation which might arise if deposits in a credit institution that has branches in other Member States became unavailable" and that it was "indispensable to ensure a harmonized minimum level of deposit protection wherever deposits are located in the Community". This shows that, in the Community legislature's view, the aim of its action could, because of the dimensions of the intended action, be best achieved at Community level. The same reasoning appears [elsewhere in the preamble], from which it is clear that the decision regarding the guarantee scheme which is competent in the event of the insolvency of a branch situated in a Member State other than that in which the credit institution has its head office has repercussions which are felt outside the borders of each Member State.

27   Furthermore, in the [preamble] the Parliament and the Council stated that the action taken by the Member States in response to the Commission's Recommendation has not fully achieved the desired result. The Community legislature therefore found that the objective of its action could not be achieved sufficiently by the Member States.

[28]   Consequently, it is apparent that, on any view, the Parliament and the Council did explain why they considered that their action was in conformity with the principle of subsidiarity and, accordingly, that they complied with the obligation to give reasons as required under Article 190 of the Treaty. An express reference to that principle cannot be required.

Notes and Questions

1.   Rather than charge the institutions with violating the principle of subsidiarity, Germany charged them with failing to state reasons that demonstrated their compliance with the principle. Can you explain this?

By contrast, in United Kingdom v. Council (Working time directive), Case C–84/94, [1996] ECR I–5755, excerpted at page 92 *supra*, the UK charged that the Council, in enacting a directive setting minimum standards of worker protection with respect to time on the job, failed to respect the subsidiarity principle itself. Here is what the Court had to say:

[46]   The applicant further maintains that the Community legislature neither fully considered nor adequately demonstrated whether there were transnational aspects which could not be satisfactorily regulated by national measures, whether such measures would conflict with the requirements of the EC Treaty or significantly damage the interests of Member States or, finally, whether action at Community level would provide clear benefits compared with action at national level. In its submission, Article 118a [now Article 137] should be interpreted in the light of the principle of subsidiarity, which does not allow adoption of a directive in such wide and prescriptive terms as the contested directive, given that the extent and the nature of legislative regulation of working time vary very widely between Member States. The applicant explains in this context, however, that it does not rely upon infringement of the principle of subsidiarity as a separate plea.

[47]   In that respect, it should be noted that it is the responsibility of the Council, under Article 118a, to adopt minimum requirements so as to contribute, through harmonization, to achieving the objective of raising the level of health and safety protection of workers which, in terms of Article 118a(1), is primarily the responsibility of the Member States. Once the Council has found that it is necessary to improve the existing level of protection as regards the health and safety of workers and to harmonize the conditions in this area while maintaining the improvements made, achievement of that objective through the imposition of minimum requirements necessarily presupposes Community-wide action, which otherwise, as in this case, leaves the enactment of the detailed implementing provisions required largely to the Member States. ...

Did the Court sidestep the subsidiarity issue? For the Court's judgment on the UK's other challenges to the working time directive, see pages 92 *supra* and 175, *infra*.

2.   "What is to prevent the institutions from satisfying the requirement of reasons through conclusory statements about the need for Community-wide action? Consider that, in its most recent reference to subsidiarity, the Court held that the institutions' compliance with the principle "is necessarily implicit" in recitals in the preamble to the challenged directive to the effect that "in the absence of action at Community level, the development of the laws and practices of the different Member States impedes the proper functioning of the internal market." Netherlands v. Parliament and Council (Biotechnological inventions), Case C–377/98, [2001] ECR I-___ (Oct. 9, 2001).

3.   Related to subsidiarity is the question of strengthening the representation of sub-Community interests in EC decisionmaking. See pages 305–08 *infra.*

4.   What are the understandings about subsidiarity in the US, which, like the Community, is a divided-power system in which federal jurisdiction depends heavily on the notion of interstate commerce, and in which maintaining the proper balance of power between the states and the federal government is considered to be of utmost importance? For a comparative discussion of EC subsidiarity and US federalism, see G. Bermann, Taking Subsidiarity Seriously: Federalism in the European Community and the United States, 94 Colum. L. Rev. 331 (1994).

E.   FLEXIBILITY AND "CLOSER COOPERATION"

The sphere of Community law has yet a further aspect that is in a very real sense spatial, the question being whether Community law must apply throughout the entire territory of the EU. It appears to have been at one time assumed that if EC law were enacted, it necessarily applied, according to its terms, in all of the Member States. Academic and political commentators referred to the alternatives under various labels: "a two-speed Europe," "a multi-speed Europe," and a Europe "of variable geometry," but Community law reflected very little if any of it.

The Maastricht Treaty saliently changed expectations in this respect. As noted in an earlier chapter, the UK and Denmark demanded the right to opt out of the final stage of economic and monetary union—an option that both States have exercised. (Though Sweden did not receive an "opt-out," it is effectively not participating either.) Denmark also preserved a right of derogation under pillar two in respect of defense. In addition, the UK declined at Maastricht to participate in action taken by the Community under the Agreement on Social Policy, thus necessitating a Social Protocol providing for the enactment of Community law without participation by, or binding effect on, the UK. (The Amsterdam Treaty brought this particular exercise in "variable geometry" to an end. See page 24 *supra.*). Unlike other obligations undertaken by subsets of the Member States (—historically, the Schengen Convention, *supra* page 32, was an outstanding example—), measures taken in the third stage of EMU and under the Social Protocol, though not applicable in certain parts of the EU, otherwise enjoyed the full force and effect of Community law.

At the Amsterdam IGC, this development expanded. Denmark, Ireland and the UK demanded and received derogations from certain obligations regarding the provisions on visas, asylum and immigration newly transferred from the EU's pillar three to pillar one. (See page ___ *supra.*)

More importantly, the Member States introduced into both the EC and EU Treaties what can only be called a general regime for the differential application of Community law and policy, under the somewhat euphemistic name of "closer cooperation." TEU Article 43 authorized "Member States which intend to establish closer cooperation between themselves [to] make use of the institutions, procedures and mechanisms laid down by the Treaties" when doing so within the spheres of pillars one and three. The innovation was undoubtedly prompted by the prospect of substantial enlargement, with the attendant risk that some States, for economic or political reasons, might prevent the others from taking further important integration steps. The "closer cooperation" provisions give very concrete meaning to the various notions of "multi-speed Europe" that had long been circulating.

TEU Articles 43 to 45 (ex K.15–.17) are the umbrella provisions on closer cooperation within the EU. They lay down the conditions on which such cooperation may take place. Thus, closer cooperation must (i) be aimed at furthering Union objectives and interests, (ii) respect existing Treaty principles and institutions, as well as the *acquis communautaire,* (iii) involve the participation of at least a majority of States, (iv) avoid prejudice to the competences, rights and interests of non-participating States, while remaining open to their joining at any time (assuming they are ready to comply with all measures and decisions previously taken under it), and (v) be used as "a last resort," that is, only when the normal decisionmaking procedures are unavailing.

TEU Article 44 provides that when legislative measures are finally adopted pursuant to closer cooperation, they shall adopted in accordance with the procedures laid down in the ordinarily applicable provision of the EC Treaty or TEU, as the case may be, with the understanding that while non-participating States may take part in the deliberations over the proposed implementation, they do not have a vote. (Their assent is accordingly unnecessary in decisionmaking by unanimity; in qualified majority voting, the qualified majority required for passage of legislation is recomputed so as to ensure support by the same proportion of weighted votes as usual.) Any costs imposed by the implementing measures are in principle required to be borne solely by the participating member States, unless the Council unanimously decides otherwise.

Depending on whether closer cooperation is carried on within the Community law sphere or in pillar three, further provisions of the EC Treaty or the TEU, respectively, are also applicable. The relevant provision of the EC Treaty, Article 11 (ex 5a), makes closer cooperation broadly available throughout pillar one, but it does impose additional restrictions on its use. Closer cooperation may take place only within the limits of the powers conferred upon the Community under the Treaty, but at the same time is forbidden in areas where Community competence is exclusive of the Member States. In addition, closer cooperation must not (i) affect existing Community policies, actions or programs, (ii) affect EU citizenship or discriminate between nationals of Member States, or (iii) restrict trade between Member States or distort the conditions of competition.

Member States intending to launch closer cooperation among themselves within pillar one may submit a request to the Commission, which may then in turn propose to the Council that such cooperation be authorized. (A Commission decision not to do so requires a statement of reasons.) If a proposal is made, the Council may, after consulting the European Parliament, decide by qualified majority vote to grant the authorization. (Article 11 of the EC Treaty makes Council authorization a precondition to closer cooperation.) However, any single Member State may block such authorization "for important and stated reasons of national policy." In that circumstance, the Council may, by qualified majority vote, refer the matter to the Heads of State or

Government, where the authorization may only be granted on the basis of unanimity.

Article 11 also sets out the procedures whereby a non-participating State may join in cooperation that is already underway. If a State wishes to join an existing exercise in closer cooperation, it notifies the Council and the Commission, the latter having three months within which to issue an opinion on the application and an additional month in which to make a decision.

As far as the TEU is concerned, closer cooperation is specifically authorized under the third pillar, but not under the second; its sphere of application is therefore confined to action under TEU title VI, on police and judicial cooperation in criminal matters. TEU Article 40 (ex K.12) adds very little to the general conditions for closer cooperation laid out in the umbrella provisions, Articles 43–45. Closer cooperation must respect the powers of the European Community, support the objectives of pillar three, and facilitate the EU in becoming "an area of freedom, security and justice." A proposal for closer cooperation in pillar three must emanate from a Member State; the Commission may merely give its opinion and Parliament need only be informed. The Council may then, by qualified majority vote, give its authorization, subject to the same Member State veto possibility ("for important and stated reasons of national policy") mentioned above. However, at least ten Member States must support the authorization and they must comprise at least 62 votes in the Council.

Once again, a State may apply to join cooperation that is already underway, but that application is acted upon by the Council rather than the Commission, which may nevertheless offer its opinion. Interestingly, Council approval of the application under pillar three does not require a qualified majority vote in support; rather, authorization is deemed to be given four months after the application is made, unless the Council, by qualified majority vote, affirmatively decides to hold it in abeyance for future consideration. Upon an application to join, only the then participating States vote in the Council, with the qualified majority threshold of weighted votes adjusted as provided for in TEU Article 44.

The role of the Court of Justice in policing the exercise of closer cooperation under the EC Treaty and the TEU is reserved for Chapter 5 (see page 191 *infra*).

The Amsterdam Treaty's flexibility provisions occasioned a good deal of political and academic commentary. The stringency of the conditions for its use have led to widespread doubts that closer cooperation would ever be employed. Yet, with the impending enlargement, a workable closer cooperation system looked more and more like a necessity. Within a year and a half of their entry into force, the Member States agreed at the Nice IGC to a relaxation of the ground rules.

The amended TEU Article 43—the umbrella provision—would not only consolidate and rephrase certain of the existing conditions for closer cooperation, but add several more. Most significantly—and evidently with enlargement in mind—the requirement of participation by a majority of States becomes a requirement of participation by a minimum of eight States. (While eight States at present constitute a majority, they would cease to do so with the very first accession.) The revision also confirms that non-participating

States must not impede the cooperation engaged in by others and that late-joining States must comply with the basic decisions previously taken under the cooperation and with any further implementing decisions taken. It confirms that acts and decisions taken pursuant to closer cooperation do not form part of the European Union *acquis* and clarifies that, as for financing closer cooperation, all implementation costs (other than administrative costs for the EU institutions) are to be borne by the participating States, unless the full Council unanimously decides otherwise. Finally, the Council and Commission are enjoined to ensure consistency between closer cooperation activities and the policies of the EC and EU.

The Nice Treaty would also alter the specific provisions on closer cooperation found in the EC Treaty (for pillar one) and TEU title VI (for pillar three). In an important gesture to the European Parliament, a Council decision authorizing closer cooperation under the EC Treaty would require parliamentary assent whenever the cooperation relates to a matter on which legislation is ordinarily subject to the parliamentary co-decision procedure. Perhaps most significant, the amendment eliminates the Member States' right to cast a veto "for important and stated reasons of national policy." If a proposal musters a qualified majority in the Council, all that an objecting State could do is refer the matter to the European Council, following which the Council would once again decide by qualified majority. The Nice Treaty would also bring changes to closer cooperation under pillar three by, among other things, eliminating the Member State veto and allowing eight Members States to seek authorization from the Council even if the Commission declines to do so.

Finally, the Nice Treaty would introduce a version of closer cooperation into the TEU's pillar two on common foreign and security policy (CFSP), an area from which the Amsterdam Treaty had excluded such cooperation. Only matters having military or defense implications would be off limits to closer cooperation. Nor is there any provision for judicial review by the Court of Justice.

Clearly, closer cooperation raises more basic questions than the emphasis on procedure thus far in this discussion would suggest. Does closer cooperation represent a dangerous breach in the notion of unity and solidarity that up to now has largely informed European Community law? Is the price— whether in principle or in sheer complexity—too high for the differentiation among Member States that closer cooperation will allow? What will be the cost in economic and legal integration? Are the substantive restrictions that the Treaties impose on recourse to closer cooperation sufficient to address the danger, or are they so strict as to ensure that no effective closer cooperation ever takes place? Would it not be possible to provide sufficiently diverse options within the framework of legislation that is adopted by and applicable to all Member States, so that flexibility is achieved without leaving one or more States wholly "outside" the scope of application of that legislation?

Chapter 5

JUDICIAL REVIEW OF COMMUNITY ACTS

This chapter takes up the subject of judicial review of Community acts, both legislative and administrative. The focus will be upon EC Treaty Articles 230–233 (ex 173–176), which expressly deal with the subject. The validity of Community acts, however, can also be challenged indirectly in national court proceedings, giving rise where appropriate to preliminary rulings by the Court under the preliminary reference procedure of Article 234 (ex 177). Preliminary references are taken up separately in Chapter 9.

That the drafters of the EC Treaty would give the Court of Justice express authority to review legislative acts of the institutions was not to be lightly assumed. The US Constitution contains no such grant of authority and an important chapter of early US constitutional history concerns the Supreme Court's efforts to develop this implied power. Moreover, in several Member States, judicial power to review legislative acts is either limited or non-existent. On the other hand, direct review of Community acts in the Court of Justice was viewed as an important protection against abuses of authority by the Community institutions and was provided for in all three Treaties.

This chapter deals mostly with procedural issues: who may seek judicial review, by what means and on what grounds. However, since a principal ground for review is the violation of Community rules of law, this chapter will also deal with the Court's concept of legality. One aspect of legality is, of course, respect for fundamental rights, including human rights. The rapidly expanding developments in that area are the subject of a separate chapter, Chapter 6.

A. THE ACTION FOR ANNULMENT (ARTICLES 230 AND 231)

Articles 230 (ex 173) and 231 (ex 174) provide that certain qualified persons may challenge the validity of Community acts directly in the Court of Justice and, if successful, have those acts declared void. This remedy is derived from the *action en recours pour excès de pouvoir,* central to the French and other continental systems of administrative law. As Article 231 suggests, judgments of the Court in actions for annulment are essentially declaratory.

However, Article 233 specifically provides that when an act of a Community institution is declared void, that institution must also "take the necessary measures to comply with the judgment of the Court."

While the EC Treaty originally provided for review only of acts of the Council and Commission, later amendments also made reviewable joint acts of the Parliament and Council, acts of the European Central Bank, and acts of the Parliament that are intended to produce legal effects vis-à-vis third parties. The term "acts adopted jointly by the European Council and the Parliament" now found in Article 230 obviously refers to measures that may be adopted pursuant to the "co-decision" procedure introduced by the Maastricht Treaty (see Chapter 3B *supra*.) The reason for originally omitting acts of Parliament from the category of reviewable acts is less clear. It was most likely assumed that since Parliament had advisory functions only, its actions did not warrant review.

That assumption was reexamined by the Court in the case of Parti écologiste "Les Verts" v. Parliament, Case 294/83, [1986] ECR 1339, in which the French ecologist party complained that Parliament, in excluding "les Verts" from the political parties eligible to receive a subsidy for expenses relating to EP elections, wrongly discriminated against parties seeking representation in Parliament for the first time. The Court allowed the action to proceed even though Article 230 at that time mentioned only the Council and Commission as possible defendants. Observing that the Community is one "based on the rule of law," the Court concluded that, in principle, a direct action should be available against "all measures adopted by the institutions ... which are intended to have legal effects" (citing the *ERTA* case, discussed at page 76 *supra*.) To immunize parliamentary decisions from judicial review "would lead to a result contrary to the spirit of the Treaty ... and to its system" and "therefore ... an action for annulment [must] lie against measures adopted by the European Parliament intended to have legal effects vis-à-vis third parties." [1986] ECR at 1366.

As for possible plaintiffs, the Treaty originally conferred institutional standing under Article 230 only on the Council, Commission or a Member State. These institutions could challenge a reviewable act without demonstrating any particular "interest" in doing so. The Court brought the point forcefully home in Italy v. Council (Premium for potato starch), Case 166/78, [1979] ECR 2575, where it ruled that a Member State is free to challenge the validity of a measure that it unreservedly supported when the Council voted to adopt it.

Shortly after becoming directly elected, Parliament began militating in favor of institutional standing—alongside the Council and Commission—to challenge reviewable acts taken by the other institutions. The issue became especially live when the Single European Act introduced the parliamentary cooperation procedure and Parliament had reason to insist that the Commission and Council follow the procedure whenever applicable. Finally, in Parliament v. Council (Post–Chernobyl), Case C–70/88, [1990] ECR I–2041, the Court permitted Parliament to challenge a Council regulation fixing maximum permissible levels of radioactivity in foodstuffs polluted by fallout from Chernobyl nuclear accident, on the ground that the Council had not used Article 95 (ex 100a) and the parliamentary cooperation procedure in its adoption. While conceding that Parliament was not among the institutions given standing by the language of the Treaty as it then stood, the Court nevertheless recognized parliamentary standing in this case:

[21]   [Parliament's legislative] prerogatives are one of the elements of the institutional balance created by the treaties. The treaties set up a system for distributing powers among the different Community institutions, assigning to each institution its own role in the institutional structure of the Community and the accomplishment of the tasks entrusted to the Community.

[22]   Observance of the institutional balance means that each of the institutions must exercise its powers with due regard for the powers of the other institutions. It also requires that it should be possible to penalize any breach of that rule which may occur.

[23]   The Court, which under the treaties has the task of ensuring that in the interpretation and application of the treaties the law is observed, must therefore be able to maintain the institutional balance and, consequently, review the observance of the Parliament's prerogatives when called upon to do so by the Parliament, by means of a legal remedy which is suited to the purpose which the Parliament seeks to achieve.

[24]   In carrying out that task the Court cannot, of course, include the Parliament among the institutions which may bring an action ... without being required to demonstrate an interest in [doing so].

[25]   However, it is the Court's duty to ensure that the provisions of the treaties concerning the institutional balance are fully applied and to see to it that the Parliament's prerogatives, like those of the other institutions, cannot be breached without it having available a legal remedy, among those laid down in the treaties, which may be exercised in a certain and effective manner.

The Court relied in *Post-Chernobyl* on EC Treaty Article 220 (ex 164). Does that provision adequately justify giving Parliament standing to sue when the Treaty specifically mentioned only the Council and Commission as institutional plaintiffs?

Note also that only a few years earlier the Court had ruled in Parliament v. Council (Comitology), Case 302/87, [1988] ECR 5615, 5641, that standing to sue was not essential to Parliament's defense of its institutional prerogatives. The Court in *Post-Chernobyl* did not acknowledge overruling *Comitology*, although for all practical purposes it did. In fact the Court of Justice rarely announces that it is overruling a prior decision, even when it is in effect doing so. Why would that be? (Incidentally, despite all this, in *Post-Chernobyl*, Parliament ended up losing the suit on the merits).[1]

A subsequent treaty amendment to Article 230, adopted by the Maastricht Treaty, effective 1993, codified the *Post-Chernobyl* approach to parliamentary standing and likewise gave the European Central Bank and the Court of Auditors standing to sue "for the purpose of protecting their

---

1. The Court declined to address Parliament's other grievances (viz. that the Council could only adopt directives and not regulations, and that the Council failed to delegate suffi-cient implementing authority to the Commission) because they did not implicate parliamentary prerogatives.

prerogatives." Predictably, there has been dispute over whether an alleged treaty violation does or does not implicate Parliament's prerogatives. (For example, in Parliament v. Council (Plant protection products), Case C–303/94, [1996] ECR I–2943, the Court ruled that a failure by the Council to give a statement of reasons for adopting a directive does not impair those prerogatives.[2]) As a result of a treaty amendment agreed upon at Nice, that inquiry would no longer need to be made in the case of parliamentary standing, since Parliament's standing under Article 230 would become as general as the Council's and Commission's. On the other hand, the ECB and Court of Auditors would still enjoy standing only to the extent of "protecting their prerogatives."

In keeping with the French administrative law model, an Article 230 action must be brought within a very short time period, in principle two months from publication or notification of the challenged measure. This requirement is justified on grounds of judicial orderliness and legal security. A Community act that has not been challenged within this short time period may not thereafter be directly challenged in the Court of Justice. (However, as we shall see, the validity of a Community act may possibly be called into question as an incidental issue in litigation before Member State courts. The preliminary reference device under Article 234 (ex 177) allows and, under certain circumstances, requires a national court to put the issue before the Court of Justice as the occasion arises, and long after the Article 230 limitations period has passed.)

The effect of the two-month statute of limitations is illustrated by the case of Commission v. AssiDoman Kraft Products AB, Case C–310/97, [1999] ECR I–5363. Twenty-six woodpulp producers were partially successful in their challenge to the Commission's decision fining the producers for their anti-competitive behavior, and received a refund of fines. A number of Swedish producers which had not participated in that challenge then asked the Commission to reconsider their fines in light of that ruling, notwithstanding the fact that more than two months had passed since the Commission had fined them. When the Commission refused, the Swedish producers appealed successfully to the Court of First Instance, which ruled that Article 233 (ex 176) of the EC Treaty (which requires the institutions to take the measures necessary to comply with judgments of the Court declaring their legal acts void) placed the Commission under a duty to reconsider. The Court of Justice reversed. Essentially, since the Commission had fined the enterprises on an individual basis, each one had to challenge the decision as addressed to it, and to do so in a timely fashion. Which court has taken the sounder view?

Students of American administrative law will be familiar with the threshold problems of defining an "act" whose legality may be challenged and of determining whether a particular party has standing to bring such a challenge.

1.   WHAT ACTS MAY BE CHALLENGED UNDER ARTICLE 230?

We first encountered the problem of defining an act within the meaning of Article 230 in the *ERTA* case, discussed at page 76 *supra*, where the

---

2. To a broadly similar effect regarding Parliament's role in approving certain international agreements, see Parliament v. Council (Mauritania fisheries agreement), Case C–189/97, [1999] ECR I–4741, excerpted at page 132, *infra*.

Commission sought to contest action taken by the Council. The problem arises with some frequency.

IBM v. COMMISSION

Case 60/81, [1981] ECR 2639.

[After several years' investigations, the Commission initiated proceedings against IBM for abuse of a dominant position in violation of EC Treaty Article 86 (now renumbered as Article 82). Pursuant to the Commission's procedural rules, notably Regulation 17, the Director General for Competition notified IBM in writing of the basis of the claims against it. The letter invited IBM to reply in writing, assuring IBM that it also had the right at a later stage to an oral hearing. IBM immediately challenged the proceedings, raising numerous procedural and substantive objections (including the inadequacy of the Commission's complaint and of the time given IBM to reply, the impropriety of delegating the decision to prosecute to a single official and the allegedly extraterritorial application of Community competition law). When the Commission declined to terminate the proceedings, IBM brought suit under Article 173 (now Article 230).]

8   According to Article 173 of the Treaty proceedings may be brought for a declaration that acts of the Council and the Commission other than recommendations or opinions are void. That remedy is available in order to ensure, as required by Article 164 [now 220], that in the interpretation and application of the Treaty the law is observed, and it would be inconsistent with that objective to interpret restrictively the conditions under which the action is admissible by limiting its scope merely to the categories of measures referred to in Article 189 [now 249].

9   In order to ascertain whether the measures in question are acts within the meaning of Article 173 it is necessary, therefore, to look to their substance. According to the consistent case-law of the Court any measure the legal effects of which are binding on, and capable of affecting the interests of, the applicant by bringing about a distinct change in his legal position is an act or decision which may be the subject of an action under Article 173 for a declaration that it is void. However, the form in which such acts or decisions are cast is, in principle, immaterial as regards the question whether they are open to challenge under that article.

10   In the case of acts or decisions adopted by a procedure involving several stages, in particular where they are the culmination of an internal procedure, it is clear from the case-law that in principle an act is open to review only if it is a measure definitively laying down the position of the Commission or the Council on the conclusion of that procedure, and not a provisional measure intended to pave the way for the final decision.

11   It would be otherwise only if acts or decisions adopted in the course of the preparatory proceedings not only bore all the legal characteristics referred to above but in addition were themselves the culmination of a special procedure distinct from that intended to permit the Commission or the Council to take a decision on the substance of the case.

* * *

[14]   The [Regulation 17] procedure was designed to enable the undertakings concerned to communicate their views and to provide the Commission with the fullest information possible before it adopted a decision affecting the interests of an undertaking. Its purpose is to create procedural guarantees for the benefit of the latter and, as may be seen in the eleventh recital in the preamble . . ., to ensure that the undertakings have the right to be heard by the Commission.

* * *

[16]   In support of its submission that the application is admissible IBM relies on a number of effects arising from the initiation of a procedure and from communication of the statement of objections.

* * *

[18]   [The] effects relied on by IBM do not adversely affect the interests of the undertaking concerned. One . . . such effect is the fact that communication of the statement of objections is recognized as crystallizing the Commission's position, which means in effect that the Commission is prevented from relying in its decision, in the absence of a fresh statement of objections, on the existence of any objections other than those on which the undertaking has been given an opportunity to make known its views, though it does not prevent the Commission from withdrawing its objections and thereby altering its standpoint in favour of the undertaking.

[19]   A statement of objections does not compel the undertaking concerned to alter or reconsider its marketing practices and it does not have the effect of depriving it of the protection hitherto available to it against the application of a fine. . . . Whilst a statement of objections may have the effect of showing the undertaking in question [that] it is incurring a real risk of being fined by the Commission, that is merely a consequence of fact, and not a legal consequence which the statement of objections is intended to produce.

[20]   An application for a declaration that the initiation of a procedure and a statement of objections are void might make it necessary for the Court to arrive at a decision on questions on which the Commission has not yet had an opportunity to state its position and would as a result anticipate the arguments on the substance of the case, confusing different procedural stages, both administrative and judicial. It would thus be incompatible with the system of the division of powers between the Commission and the Court and of the remedies laid down by the Treaty, as well as the requirements of the sound administration of justice and the proper course of the administrative procedure to be followed in the Commission.

[21]   It follows from the foregoing that neither the initiation of a procedure nor a statement of objections may be considered, on the basis of their nature and the legal effects they produce, as being decisions within the meaning of Article 173 of the EEC [now EC] Treaty which may be challenged in an action for a declaration that they are void. . . .

* * *

[24]   [I]n this instance adequate legal protection for IBM does not require that the measures in question be subject to immediate review. If, on the

conclusion of the administrative procedure and after any observations which IBM may submit in the course of it have been examined, the Commission were to adopt a decision which affects IBM's interests, that decision will, in accordance with Article 173 of the EEC Treaty, be subject to judicial review in the course of which it will be permissible for IBM to advance all the appropriate arguments. It will then be for the Court to decide whether anything unlawful has been done in the course of the administrative procedure and if so whether it is such as to affect the legality of the decision taken by the Commission on the conclusion of the administrative procedure.

25   The application must therefore be dismissed as inadmissible.

Notes and Questions

1.   The *IBM* case raises questions that are commonly associated with the problems of ripeness and finality in US administrative law, that is questions of timing. The Court held that all of IBM's complaints were properly raised, but not at the proper moment. Do you agree that all the complaints were premature? Is the Court's unwillingness to entertain the action at this stage consistent with its previous ruling in the *ERTA* case?

2.   Can you imagine any challenges to Commission antitrust proceedings that would be considered "ripe" at the stage at which IBM brought suit? In AKZO Chemie BV v. Commission, Case 53/85, [1986] ECR 1965, a company against which the Commission had brought competition law charges objected to the disclosure of certain confidential business documents to the party that had complained to the Commission. Although the Commission proceedings were still in progress, the Court considered that the decision to disclose confidential information was ripe for review. It held that AKZO's grievance was independent of the competition law charge and, if founded, would not adequately be redressed through review of the final Commission decision. Do you agree? On this rationale, should any of IBM's claims have been heard at the time IBM raised them?

3.   The same Regulation 17 at issue in the *IBM* case allows enterprises to notify restrictive agreements to the Commission for a ruling on whether they infringe Article 81(1) (ex 85(1)) of the EC Treaty and, if so, whether they are eligible for exemption under Article 81(3) (ex 85(3)). Article 15(5) of the Regulation immunizes enterprises from fines with respect to acts taking place after notification to the Commission and before a Commission decision under Articles 81(1) and (3). However, article 15(6) of Regulation 17 provides that this immunity ends once the Commission informs the undertakings of its view, upon preliminary examination, that Article 81(1) applies and that no exemption under Article 81(3) is justified. (See the Selected Documents for the text of Regulation 17.)

A group of cement companies notified the Commission of a marketing agreement among them and sought an exemption. The Commission responded that the agreement appeared both to run afoul of Article 81 and not to be exempt, and that the companies therefore had no further immunity from fines. The companies brought suit under Article 230 and the Commission objected on the ground that it had issued a mere opinion and not a decision. The Court ruled as follows:

> The effect of the [challenged measure] was that the undertakings ceased to be protected ... from fines, and came under the contrary rules ... which thenceforth exposed them to the risk of fines. This measure deprived them of

the advantages of a legal situation which [Regulation 17] attached to the notification of the agreement, and exposed them to a grave financial risk. Thus the said measure affected the interests of the undertakings by bringing about a distinct change in their legal position. It is unequivocally a measure which produces legal effects touching the interests of the undertakings concerned and which is binding on them. It thus constitutes not a mere opinion but a decision.

SA Cimenteries CBR Cementbedrijven NV v. Commission (Noordwijks cement accord), Cases 8–11/66, [1967] ECR 75, 91. The Court explained that the Commission could not conclude that a notified agreement falls within the terms of Article 81(1), and is ineligible for exemption under Article 81(3), without in effect making a "decision" on the facts and the law about the agreement. It continued:

> Neither the fact that the word "decision" is not used ... nor the fact that the procedure ... is of a preliminary nature justifies the conclusion that the Commission is empowered to proceed by a mere opinion. ... The silence of the text in a matter which affects the protection of the rights of individuals cannot be construed in the manner most unfavourable to them. Notwithstanding its preliminary nature, the measure by which the Commission takes a decision in such a case constitutes the culmination of a special procedure which is distinct from the procedure under which ... a decision on the substance of the case can be taken.

Id. at 92. Finally, the Court rejected the Commission's claim that allowing review at this stage would be "excessively cumbersome." It ruled that such a claim "cannot prevail against the guarantees for the protection of individuals [which are] laid down by the Treaty and which take precedence over all regulations." Id. at 93.

Why wasn't it sufficient for the companies to have their claim heard by the Court at the end of the entire procedure? Are the judgments consistent? Note that since IBM was charged with abuse of a dominant position under Article 82 (ex 86), rather than restrictive agreements under Article 85 (ex 81), it had no opportunity to seek an exemption and thus no opportunity to have the assessment of fines tolled. (US law does not provide an opportunity to seek a tolling of the assessment of fines in either situation.)

4.   When, if ever, may internal administrative instructions be deemed to have binding legal effects on third parties and therefore to constitute challengeable acts under Article 230? In France v. Commission (FEOGA inspections), Case C–366/88, [1990] ECR I–3571, the Court found that "the circumstances in which it was adopted and ... the conditions under which it was prepared, drawn up and published" suggested, by way of exception, that the procedural instruction issued to Commission inspectors for use in sampling and analyzing agricultural products to check their eligibility for agricultural aid was justiciable. The Court found the instruction invalid and annulled it.

5.   The Court of Justice has decided a series of cases involving challenges by France to various "soft" Commission instruments. In each case, the Court had to decide whether the "soft" legal instrument in question was an act subject to review under Article 230. See France v. Commission (State aid communication), Case C–325/91, [1993] ECR I–3283 ("Communication" to the Member States on application of state aid policy to public undertakings in the manufacturing sector held reviewable because it creates additional obligations); France v. Commission (Code of conduct), Case C–303/90, [1991] ECR I–5315 ("Code of conduct" only

establishes a "partnership" relation with the States and is not reviewable); France v. Commission (Pension funds), Case C–57/95, [1997] ECR I–1627. (Commission communication on an internal market for pension funds lays down specific obligations going beyond the Treaty's free movement provisions and is a reviewable act).

6.   Does it matter, for reviewability purposes, whether a measure is taken by the Council or by representatives of the Member States meeting as such? In Parliament v. Council and Commission (Aid to Bangladesh), Joined Cases C–181/91 & C–248/91, [1993] ECR I–3685, the Parliament attacked decisions both by the Council granting special aid to Bangladesh and by the Commission implementing that aid. The Court ruled that, though announced in a press release entitled "Conclusions of the Council," the aid decision was not an act of the Council but rather of the Member States (albeit collectively), and furthermore that the Commission implementation was a task delegated to it by the Member States and not by the Council. The action was thus ruled inadmissible in its entirety.

See also Roujansky v. Council, Case T–584/93, [1994] ECR II–585, in which the Court of First Instance deemed inadmissible an Article 230 action against the Council attacking both the European Council's proclamation of the TEU's entry into force on November 1, 1993 and the TEU itself. The Court ruled that acts of the European Council are not "acts" within the meaning of Article 173, and that the TEU is not itself the act of a Community institution. Its judgment was affirmed by the Court of Justice, Case C–253/94P, [1995] ECR I–7.

2.   PRIVATE PARTY STANDING TO SEEK JUDICIAL REVIEW

Article 230, paragraph 4 (ex 173, para. 2) reads as follows:

> Any natural or legal person may, under the same conditions [as set out in connection with institutional standing], institute proceedings against a decision addressed to that person or against a decision which, although in the form of a regulation or a decision addressed to another person, is of direct and individual concern to the former.

The main purpose of this paragraph is to enable private parties to challenge action taken against them in the form of a decision. A clear example would be an appeal from the imposition of a fine in a Commission competition decision. The quoted language, however, also allows judicial review in some cases by a party who is *not* the addressee of the decision in question, though only if the decision is "of direct and individual concern" to that party. Article 230 goes even a step further, allowing a private party to challenge a regulation, provided it too is "of direct and individual concern" to the party or, as the matter is sometimes put, represents for the party "a disguised decision." Thus, unless a person is the addressee of the challenged decision, that person must in effect demonstrate standing. Article 230, as we have seen, does not require any such showing on the part of institutional plaintiffs, such as the Commission or a Member State.

This section takes up the problem of determining when a private party may challenge measures that take the form either of a regulation or of a decision addressed to another. The focus tends to be on whether a given measure is "of individual concern" to the plaintiff. See generally A. Arnull, Private Applicants and the Action for Annulment under Article 173 of the EC Treaty, 32 Comm. Mkt. L. Rev. 7 (1995).

(a) Private Party Standing to Challenge a Regulation

FRANCE v. COMAFRICA SpA AND DOLE FRESH FRUIT EUROPE LTD. & CO.

Case C–73/97P, [1999] ECR I–185.

[Two banana producers brought suit in the Court of First Instance for annulment of Commission Regulation 3190/93 fixing a uniform "reduction coefficient" for determining the quantities of bananas to be allocated to each operator for the following year. The CFI rejected the Commission's claim that the producers lacked standing, finding that the regulation applied only to those firms that had applied for and obtained reference quantities for imports, that it "informs each operator concerned that the quantity of bananas it was entitled to import under the tariff quota for the year 1994 may be determined by applying the stated uniform reduction coefficient to its reference quantity," and that this "enable[s] each operator to ascertain his own precise entitlement by applying that coefficient to the reference quantity already allocated to him." The CFI described the measure, though denominated a regulation, as "properly construed as a collection of individual decisions addressed to each operator." The Court of First Instance then ruled in favor of the Commission on the merits.

The French government, supported by the Commission, appealed from the CFI's judgment, and the Court of Justice reversed, declaring the producers' claim inadmissible.

The Court observed that the establishment of reference quantities is a multi-step affair, with the operators first supplying prior years' marketing information to the national authorities and the authorities then verifying the accuracy of the information supplied (using expert studies and audit reports), applying a weighted coefficient to the reported quantities, and sending all this information to the Commission (but not necessarily to the operators). At that point, the Commission fixes a single reduction coefficient for each category of operator to be applied to the operators' final reference quantities. The Court continued:]

29   It is apparent from the [preamble] to Regulation 3190/93 that the notifications made by the Member States ... reveal that the same quantities in respect of the same activity were counted twice for different operators in several Member States and that the reduction coefficient was determined on the basis of the notifications from the Member States after the quantities counted twice had been estimated by the Commission and the figures corrected accordingly.

30   It follows that the figures notified by the operators ... may be altered several times in the course of the procedure before the reduction coefficient is fixed, without the alterations made by the competent authorities or the Commission being brought to the attention of the operators concerned.

31   Consequently, an operator is not able to ascertain, on the basis of either the figures notified by it to the national competent authority or the provisions of Regulation 3190/93 the reference quantity to which the reduction coefficient is to be applied.

[At this point, the Court distinguished the instant case from an earlier case in which reference quantities of beef and veal had been based on the exact quantities shown on the operators' quota applications, without adjustment, so that the operators themselves could multiply a quantity known to them by a reduction coefficient laid down in the relevant regulation.]

37   By contrast . . . the operators [here] did not obtain a reference quantity before the adoption of Regulation 3190/93, nor were they able to ascertain the definitive quantity they would be entitled to import in 1994 by carrying out a simple multiplication of a quantity known to them by the reduction coefficient determined by the regulation.

38   The Court of Instance was therefore wrong to conclude . . . that Regulation 3190/93, properly construed, was a collection of individual decisions addresses to each operator effectively informing him of the precise quantities which he would be entitled to import in 1994.

Notes and Questions

1.   *Comafrica* proceeds on the premise that regulations are presumptively not directly challengeable by individuals in the Community courts. That presumption was spelled out early on by the Court in the case of Confédération Nationale des Producteurs de Fruits et Légumes v. Council, Cases 16, 17/62, [1962] ECR 471.

There, an association of French fruit and vegetable producers sought annulment of a Council regulation establishing a common market organization in that sector. The regulation, adopted on the basis of EC Treaty Articles 36 and 37 (ex 42 and 43), contained an article 9 prescribing a specific timetable for the progressive elimination of quantitative restrictions on imports. The Court underscored that "a regulation, being essentially of a legislative nature, is applicable not to a limited number of persons, defined or identifiable, but to categories of persons viewed abstractly and in their entirety." On the other hand, the Court allowed that "if a measure entitled by its author a regulation contains provisions which are capable of being not only of direct but also of individual concern to certain natural or legal persons, it must be admitted that . . . those provisions do not have the character of a regulation and may therefore be [challenged] by those persons." Finding that the regulation addressed "objectively determined situations" and applied to "categories of persons viewed in a general and abstract manner," the Court concluded that the claimant was not individually concerned. "[M]embers [of the association] are concerned by the said provision in the same way as all other agricultural producers of the Community."

The case was important not only because of its treatment of the notion of a disguised decision, but also because of its practical impact. The Common Agricultural Policy entails literally thousands of Council and Commission regulations on the market organization for different products, regulations that are very detailed, often affect private interests quite specifically and are frequently amended. If they were easily challenged by private parties, the administration of the CAP would be gravely impaired and the Community courts would be seriously burdened.

2.   One field in which the Court of Justice has found regulations to be disguised decisions is antidumping or protective trade measures. For discussion of cases in which the Court recognized the standing of private persons who are affected by antidumping regulations to challenge them under Article 230, see Chapter 31 *infra*.

3. In Zunis Holding SA v. Commission, Case T–83/92, [1993] ECR II–1169, appeal denied, Case C–480/93P, [1996] ECR I–1, the Court of First Instance held that a group of minority shareholders in an Italian insurance company lacked standing to challenge the Commission's approval of the acquisition of additional shares in the company by an Italian bank. The minority shareholders were deemed not directly and individually affected by the decision. Their shareholdings represented less than 0.5 percent of the company's shares and they failed to show that the Commission's decision placed them in a position different from any other shareholder. (This was the first case in which an EC court ruled on a legal challenge to a Commission decision taken under the Community's 1989 Merger Regulation.)

4. Codorniu SA v. Council, Case C–309/89, [1994] ECR I–1853, is the rare case in which a regulation was not a "disguised decision," but was nevertheless found to be challengeable by an individual. There, Codorniu, a Spanish producer of sparkling wine, was allowed to challenge a 1989 regulation organizing the market in wine, which provided that the term "crémant" could only be used for certain quality sparkling wines made in France and Luxembourg. Codorniu had been using the term "Gran Cremant" since 1924, under a Spanish trademark, to designate a part of its production. The Court found that the regulation affected Codorniu by reason of attributes peculiar to it and circumstances differentiating it from all other persons.

For a similar reasoning and result, see Exporteurs in Levende Varkens v. Commission, Case T–481 & 484/93, [1995] ECR II–2941.

5. Might a private party ever have standing to challenge the validity of a *directive* addressed to the Member States? Might there, in other words, be such a thing as a "disguised decision in the form of a directive," or a directive that sufficiently "differentiates" one private party from all others to justify standing? The Court of First Instance has refused to exclude the possibility that a private party might be "affected by [a directive] by reason of certain attributes which are peculiar to it or by reason of a factual situation which differentiates it from all other persons." Union Européenne de l'artisanat et des petites et moyennes entreprises (UEAPME) v. Council, [1998] ECR II–2335. But, as in *UEAPME*, the Court has yet to find that to be the case.

(b) Private Party Standing to Challenge Decisions Addressed to Member States

ALFRED TÖPFER AND GETREIDE–IMPORT GESELLSCHAFT v. COMMISSION

Cases 106–107/63, [1965] ECR 405.

[On October 1, 1963, two German grain dealers filed applications with the German authorities to import maize (or corn) from France. Because the import levy at that time happened to be zero, the dealers stood to realize exorbitant profits, and the German authorities therefore chose to reject the applications until the rates could be increased. The authorities invoked certain "safeguard" measures that Germany had previously adopted to guard against grave market disturbances caused by low-priced imports. The Commission, however, still had to confirm the rejection. Upon notification to it, the Commission immediately raised the rate of levy (effective October 2). Then, on October 3, the Commission issued a decision to the German government authorizing it to reject all applications filed from October 1 through 4 inclusive. The dealers sued the Commission in the Court of Justice for the annulment of that decision.]

It is clear from the fact that on 1 October 1963 the Commission took a decision fixing new free-at-frontier prices for maize imported into the Federal Republic as from 2 October that ... the only persons concerned by the said measures were importers who had applied for an import licence during the course of the day of 1 October 1963. The number and identity of these importers had already become fixed and ascertainable before 4 October, when the contested decision was made. The Commission was in a position to know that its decision affected the interests and the position of the said importers alone.

The factual situation thus created differentiates the said importers, including the applicants, from all other persons and distinguishes them individually just as in the case of the person addressed.

Therefore the objection of inadmissibility which has been raised is unfounded and the applications are admissible.

[The Court concluded on the merits that the Commission was wrong in finding that the maize imports in question were capable of causing grave market disturbances, as required to justify use of a safeguard measure.]

Notes and Questions

1.   Why didn't the plaintiffs in *Töpfer* bring their action in national court against the German agency? Bear in mind that the Commission decision merely authorized the action of the national authorities. It did not direct it.

2.   One class of decisions addressed to Member States that private parties have a definite interest in challenging is Commission action on state aids. Philip Morris Holland v. Commission, Case 730/79, [1980] ECR 2671, is a good example. The Dutch government, intending to grant financial assistance to Philip Morris to expand its cigarette production facilities, notified the aid to the Commission as required under Articles 87 and 88 (ex 92 and 93) governing state aids. The Commission wrote to the Dutch government denying permission to grant the aid, and Philip Morris (not the Dutch government) brought suit in the Court of Justice. The Commission conceded that Philip Morris, as the prospective recipient of the aid, had standing to sue. (The suit failed on the merits.)

This principle has been extended to competitors of the recipients of state aid. Competitors have been held to be entitled to challenge decisions addressed to Member States authorizing them to grant aid. See COFAZ v. Commission, Case 169/84, [1986] ECR 391; William Cook plc v. Commission, Case C–198/91, [1993] ECR I–2487; Association of Sorbitol Producers within the EC (ASPEC) v. Commission, Case T–435/93, [1995] ECR II–1281. Is the extension justified? Should standing be limited to rivals who participated in the procedures leading up to the grant of aid? In any case, demonstrating that a firm constitutes a competitor of the aid recipient for these purposes, and is thus individually and directly concerned by a decision to approve the aid, may not be a simple matter. The Court was left unpersuaded of this in Società Eridania Zuccherifici Nazionali v. Commission, Cases 10, 18/68, [1969] ECR 459.

The Court of First Instance has ruled that, under Article 93(2) (ex 88(2)) of the EC Treaty, the Commission must actually open its administrative proceedings to objectors before making a decision on a grant of aid in the first place. Société

Internationale de Diffusion et d'Edition (SIDE) v. Commission, Case T–49/93, [1995] ECR II–2501. (There, the court annulled the Commission's approval of a French grant of aid on the ground that the Commission had considered only the arguments and evidence advanced by the French government.) What bearing does the procedural ruling in *SIDE* have on the standing of competitors to bring judicial challenges to state aids?

3.   Despite the clarity of the rule that Community decisions may ordinarily be challenged in the Community courts only by those persons to whom those decisions are addressed, the rule continues to be challenged. Stichting Greenpeace Council (Greenpeace International) and others v. Commission, Case C–321/95 P, [1998] ECR I–1651, is a good example.

The Commission decided to finance the construction of two fossil-fueled power stations on the Canary Islands. Sixteen local residents and two environmental interest groups (including Greenpeace) complained that since the Spanish authorities had failed to conduct a timely and adequate environmental impact assessment of the project, as required by Community legislation, the Commission's financing decision was illegal and should be annulled. (The plaintiffs concurrently sued the Spanish authorities in national court.)

The action having been declared inadmissible by the Court of First Instance for want of standing, the claimants appealed to the Court of Justice stressing the importance of private party standing in a case involving a "common" value such as environmental quality. The Court declined to modify the rules on standing and denied that a legal vacuum existed, due to the fact that the authorization to build the plants was presumably challengeable in a national court which was in a position to ensure compliance with the environmental impact assessment directive.

4.   The *Greenpeace* case, *supra* note 3, also gave the Court a chance to revisit its case law on associational standing. The Court basically reaffirmed case law to the effect that an association has standing in the Community courts only under three special circumstances: (a) when a Community law provision expressly grants associations procedural rights, (b) when the association actually represents persons who themselves have individualized standing,[3] or (c) when the association's own interests qua association (e.g. its position as negotiator) are directly affected.[4] The Court also reaffirmed that an association's mere participation in the Commission's decisionmaking (and even its consultation by the Commission) is not in itself enough to "individualize" the decision; the Commission must have initiated or otherwise privileged that participation.

Regarding associational standing, could the Court reasonably take the position that, while associations generally lack standing to bring direct challenges in the Community courts, the effectiveness of Community law in the Member States requires that national courts recognize associational standing to enforce the States' EC law obligations, at least where diffuse interests are concerned? See Afilalo, Towards a "Common Law" of Europe: Effective Judicial protection, National Procedural Autonomy, and Standing to Litigate Diffuse Interests in the European Union, 22 Suffolk Transnat'l L. Rev. 349 (1999). You may want to revisit this question after reading the materials in Chapter 10 *infra*.

---

3.   See UFADE v. Council and Commission, Case C–117/86, [1986] ECR 3255; AITEC v. Commission, Case T–447–49/93, [1995] ECR II–1971.

4.   See van der Kooy, Joined Cases 67, 68 & 70/85, [1988] ECR 219; CIRFS, Case C–313/90, [1993] ECR I–1125.

(c) Private Party Standing to Challenge Decisions Addressed to Other Parties

METRO–SB–GROSSMÄRKTE GMBH & CO. KG v. COMMISSION

(Metro I)

Case 26/76, [1977] ECR 1875.

[SABA, a German electronics manufacturer, notified the Commission of its complicated selective distribution system as required under Community competition rules. After several years of careful review, the Commission issued a decision of December 15, 1975, addressed to SABA, approving the distribution system. Metro, a discount wholesaler that had complained to the Commission about SABA's refusal to allow Metro to participate in the system, had provided the Commission with material adverse to SABA for use in its review. The Commission ultimately wrote to Metro on January 14, 1976, notifying it of the December 15 decision favorable to SABA. Metro then challenged the decision in the Court of Justice.]

6   Since the contested decision was not addressed to Metro it is necessary to consider whether it is of direct and individual concern to it.

7   Metro is a so-called self-service wholesale trading undertaking....

***

This form of marketing is ... characterized both by special sales methods and by the nature of the customers sought by the wholesaler.

8   When the applicant applied to SABA for recognition as a wholesaler ... SABA refused because the applicant would not agree to a number of conditions to which SABA subjects the grant of the status of a SABA wholesaler and which, the applicant maintains, are not compatible with the structure of the self-service wholesale trade as Metro engages in it.

[The Court then outlined the Commission's proceedings with respect to SABA, describing certain changes in the distribution system agreed to by SABA at the Commission's request.]

12   Since Metro considered that the distribution system thereby approved retained features unlawfully preventing its appointment as a SABA wholesaler it lodged this application.

13   The abovementioned facts establish that the contested decision was adopted in particular as the result of a complaint submitted by Metro and that it relates to the provisions of SABA's distribution system, on which SABA relied and continues to rely as against Metro in order to justify its refusal to sell to the latter or to appoint it as a wholesaler, and which the applicant had for this reason impugned in its complaint.

It is in the interests of a satisfactory administration of justice and of the proper application of Articles 85 and 86 [now 81 and 82] that natural or legal persons who are entitled to request the Commission to find an infringement of Articles 85 and 86 should be able, if their request is not complied with either wholly or in part, to institute proceedings in order to protect their legitimate interests.

In those circumstances the applicant must be considered to be directly and individually concerned ... by the contested decision and the application is accordingly admissible.

[On the merits, the Court sustained the Commission decision. For that ruling, see page 924 *infra*.]

Notes and Questions

1. The implications of *Metro I* are unclear. Metro was adversely affected by the Commission's approval of the SABA network. Is that in itself sufficient to allow Metro to appeal the SABA decision? Or is appeal only allowed when the appellant a) formally complained to the Commission prior to the decision, and/or b) provided relevant information and participated in the proceeding? Does *Metro* suggest that all persons who unsuccessfully petition the Commission for action will have standing in the Court of Justice to challenge the Commission decision denying that action?

2. There are numerous variations on the *Metro I* scenario, with possibly different results. Consider the case of Kruidvat BVBA v. Commission, Case C–70/97 P, [1998] ECR I–7183.

Givenchy, the perfume manufacturer, notified the Commission of a network of selective distribution contracts for marketing its products, seeking a negative clearance from the application of EC Treaty Article 81 (ex 85). In response to a Commission notice of a proposed grant of the clearance, and invitation for comments from interested parties, the Raad FGB (an association of Dutch department stores) replied, urging that the clearance not be granted. Meanwhile, Givenchy's exclusive Belgian agent brought suit in Belgian court against Kruidvat, the Belgian subsidiary of a Dutch chain of health and beauty shops (also a Raad FGB member store) which carried Givenchy perfumes obtained on the parallel market, for an order under Belgium's unfair business practice laws to stop selling Givenchy products in Belgium. The Commission granted the clearance.

Does Kruidvat have standing in the Court of First Instance to challenge the Commission's grant of clearance? The Court of First Instance and Court of Justice both ruled that Kruidvat does not have standing merely by virtue of the fact that the Raad FGB (of which it was a member) had participated in the Commission proceeding; association members must "establish a link between their individual situation and the action of the association." (How might Kruidvat have established such a "link"?) Also unavailing was Kruidvat's argument that the pendency of the lawsuit against it in Belgium by Givenchy's agent (in which the legality of Givenchy's selective distribution contracts was an incidental issue) rendered Kruidvat "individually" concerned.

3. In Timex Corporation v. Council and Commission, Case 264/82, [1985] ECR 849, the Community imposed an antidumping duty on exporters of watches at the request of the European industry association. Timex, the largest UK watch producer and member of the association, provided the Commission with a good deal of information in its investigation. Timex considered the antidumping duty to be too low and was found to have standing to sue to press that claim. Would Timex have had standing to challenge a decision by the Commission not to impose any antidumping duties at all? See Chapter 31 *infra*.

NOTE ON "OF DIRECT CONCERN"

Although the emphasis in the cases seems to be on the question whether a regulation or a decision addressed to another person is "of individual concern" to the plaintiff, Article 230 requires that it also be of "direct" concern to the plaintiff. Sometimes the Court of Justice fails to distinguish clearly between these two aspects of standing. In the *Philip Morris* case, discussed in note 3 on page 141 *supra,* the Court decided that Philip Morris was individually concerned by the Commission's refusal to permit the Dutch government to favor the company with a state aid, but did not separately consider whether the refusal affected Philip Morris directly. The Court may have thought that to be self-evident.

In other cases, the Court squarely requires the plaintiff to demonstrate that the challenged measure affected it directly as well as individually. In *Töpfer, supra* page 140, the Court concluded that the Commission decision confirming the German ban on maize imports concerned the plaintiff importers individually. However, the Court also considered whether the Commission decision affected them directly. The Court concluded that the decision was of direct concern because it rendered the German ban "valid."

An interesting pair of cases in this connection is Comité Central d'Entreprise de la Société Générale des Grandes Sources et Comité d'Etablissement de la Source Perrier v. Commission, Case T–96/92, [1995] ECR II–1213, and Comité Central d'Entreprise de la Société Anonyme Vittel v. Commission, Case T–12/93, [1995] ECR II–1247. There, the recognized representatives of the employees of Perrier and Vittel (the works councils) challenged a decision by the Commission conditionally approving the takeover of Source Perrier by Nestlé SA (a Swiss company). The Commission contested their standing to do so.

The Court found that the decision affected the claimants *individually,* noting that the applicable regulations required the Commission in making its decision to take into account the collective interests of employees, and that the claimants were in fact the employees' recognized representatives.

On the other hand, the Court found that the claimants were not *directly* affected by the takeover approval. It first found that the takeover could not possibly be considered as prejudicing the works councils' *own* rights. As for the alleged prejudice to the employees (in the form of lost jobs and benefits), the Court found that it had not been established, since other Community legislation safeguards the interests of employees in these circumstances and since therefore "job losses and changes in social benefits ... are not inevitable following a concentration."

The Court continued:

45   It follows that in the present case the acquisition of Perrier by Nestlé ... does not in itself entail any direct consequences for the rights which the Perrier employees derive from their contracts or employment relationship. In the absence of any direct causal link between the alleged attack on those rights and the Commission's decision ..., the persons concerned must have an appropriate legal remedy available for the defence of their legitimate interests not at the stage of the review of the lawfulness of the

said decision, but at the stage of the measures which are the immediate origin of the adverse effects thus alleged, and which may be adopted by the undertakings ... without any intervention by the Commission. It is at the stage of the adoption of such measures, review of which is within the jurisdiction of the national courts, that the safeguards intervene which are given to employees by the provisions of national law and of Community law.

Thus, the claimants were found not to be directly concerned by the Commission's decision refusing to find the takeover to be anti-competitive.

Yet despite this lack of standing, the Court agreed to hear the works councils' claim that the Commission had followed improper procedures in reaching its decision. As to this claim, the works councils were deemed to have standing, since any violation of their procedural rights necessarily prejudiced them. However, they ultimately lost on the procedural merits because, according to the Court, they had a right to be heard only if they so requested, which they had not done. If the works councils had requested to be heard, and that request had been improperly denied, what claims would they be permitted to advance?

NOTE ON INTERIM RELIEF

Actions before the Court of Justice do not normally have suspensive effect. However, according to Articles 242 and 243 (ex 185 and 186) of the Treaty, the Court may, "if it considers that circumstances so require," suspend application of the challenged act or order other necessary interim measures. The Court is commonly called upon by applicants to order interim relief, and its Statute and Rules of Procedure lay down some simple guidelines for this purpose. Thus Article 83(2) of the Court Rules requires applicants for interim relief to state the subject matter of the proceedings, the reasons for the urgency of relief (typically a risk of serious and irreparable damage), and the elements of law and fact that create a prima facie case for such relief.

Decisions on interim relief applications are made by the President of each court, with several being made each year. Appeals from interim relief decisions by the President of the CFI are taken directly to the President of the ECJ.

Under the case law of the Court, applicants for interim relief must show not only that the relief sought is prima facie justified in law and in fact, but also that it must be ordered and produce its effects before a decision is reached in the main action so as to avoid serious and irreparable damage to the applicant's interests. At the same time, the Court considers that it must take into account the prejudice that the interim relief sought would cause to the public interest and other private interests. Commission v. Atlantic Container Line, Case C–149/95P(R), [1995] ECR I–2165 (para. 22).

Article 86(4) of the Rules (reiterating Article 36 of the Statute) confirms that the issuance of an order of interim relief is without prejudice to the ultimate decision of the Court. As a corollary, the Court seeks to avoid issuing any order that may "prejudge the points of law or fact in issue or neutralize in advance the effects of the decision subsequently to be given in the main action." (id., para. 23).

The request for interim relief is vividly illustrated by the case of United Kingdom v. Commission (Mad cow disease), Case C–180/96R, [1996] ECR I–3903, arising out of the Commission's ban on the export of British beef due to evidence that it transmitted to humans BSE, or "mad cow disease," discussed in Chapter 1. Imposition of the ban prompted the UK to bring this action before the Court of Justice and to seek the ban's interim suspension. Although the Commission subsequently relaxed the ban in certain particulars, the UK maintained both the suit and the application for interim relief.

The UK's claims were comprehensive: that the ban was not justified by any serious hazard to human or animal health, that it infringed the principles of proportionality, non-discrimination and legal certainty (discussed later in this chapter), that it unlawfully impeded the free movement of goods within the internal market, that it conflicted with the objectives of the common agricultural policy as set out in the Treaty, that it was inadequately reasoned, and that it represented a misuse of power since it was adopted for economic rather than public health reasons.

The Court canvassed all the factors bearing upon the justification or non-justification of the ban, including particulars about the disease and its incidence and about the possible effectiveness of lesser measures. It nevertheless focused primarily on the question "whether it is necessary to make a provisional ruling in order to avoid the occurrence of serious and irreparable harm as a result of [the immediate] application of the measure." Although the Court did not doubt the severity of the economic impact on British beef producers, it expressed doubt that the ban (rather than the disease) was the principal cause, and it pointed to various measures the Community institutions had adopted to compensate those producers, at least in part. Above all, the Court concluded, in light of the magnitude of the risk to human health (and, in particular, the difficulty of reversing the effects on human health if the ban were temporarily lifted but later determined by the Court to have been justified), that "a balancing of interests would, on any view, favour maintaining the Commission's decision, inasmuch as the interest in having the contested decision maintained is not really comparable to the applicant's interest in having its operation suspended." Even admitting that much of the damage suffered by the UK interests would be irreparable, were the UK ultimately to prevail in the action, the Court found that "[t]hat damage cannot ... outweigh the serious harm to public health which is liable to be caused by suspension of the contested decision, and which could not be remedied if the main action were subsequently dismissed."

Did the Court determine whether the UK had established a case, prima facie, in law and in fact for relief? Did the Court avoid prejudging the merits? (In the end, the Court sustained the ban.[5])

For a striking example of an order of the President suspending application of a Council regulation (albeit only in part), see Austria v. Council (Ecopoints), Case C–445/00R, [2001] ECR I–__ (Feb. 23, 2001).

The question has arisen whether interim relief may take the form of a provisional award of damages or whether, on the contrary, such an award

---

5. United Kingdom v. Commission (Mad cow disease), Case C–180/96, [1998] ECR I– 2265.

necessarily impermissibly prejudges the merits of a case. According to the President of the Court of Justice, "an absolute prohibition on obtaining a measure of that kind, irrespective of the circumstances of the case, would not be compatible with the right of individuals to complete and effective judicial protection under Community law." Antonissen v. Council and Commission, Case C–393/96 P(R), [1997] ECR I–441 (paras. 36, 37).

B. COMPLAINT FOR FAILURE TO ACT (ARTICLE 232)

Article 232 (ex 175) of the EC Treaty deals with what French administrative law knows as an *action en carence,* that is, a complaint for failure to act. All Community institutions and the Member States are entitled to bring an action against the Council or the Commission should either of them, by an omission to act, violate an EC Treaty obligation. In theory, the failure to fulfil a duty can be as harmful as a malperformance of the duty. In practice, however, courts tend to defer to exercises of administrative discretion as to when and how a duty should be performed. Not surprisingly, complaints of failure to act rarely meet with success.

Probably the best known Article 232 case is Parliament v. Council (Transport policy), Case 13/83, [1985] ECR 1513. One of the Community's most conspicuous failures in the early 1980s was the absence of a Common Transport Policy, the adoption of which was under Article 70 (ex 74) an original Community goal. In 1983, Parliament brought an action against the Council for its failure to act on long-pending Commission proposals for a transport policy or to take action to secure freedom to provide transport services under Articles 49–51 (ex 59–61) and Article 71 (ex 75). A threshold question was whether Parliament is privileged under the language of then Article 175 to bring such a suit. The Court found Parliament to be an "institution of the Community" within the meaning of the article. (On the merits, the Court held that Article 70 did not impose a sufficiently precise obligation on the Council with respect to adoption of a common transport policy to justify a ruling in Parliament's favor. On the other hand, the Court condemned the Council's failure to take action to secure freedom to provide transport services, action that the Court found to be sufficiently well-defined in Articles 49 through 51 and Article 75 of the Treaty, and clearly overdue). Although Parliament technically did not prevail on the transport policy claim, the case doubtless added to the pressure to develop transport policy measures and may help account for the Council's adoption in the late 1980s of some key transport legislation.

Article 232 originally named only the Council and Commission as institutions whose failure to act would be actionable. As in the case of Article 230, the drafters doubtless viewed Parliament's functions as advisory only and thus its failure to act as essentially harmless. Of course, Parliament's legislative and budgetary functions have developed significantly since then, and the Maastricht Treaty, effective November 1, 1993, accordingly amended Article 232 to permit actions for failure to act against Parliament, and indeed also against the European Central Bank.

The complaint for failure to act is subject to a kind of exhaustion of remedies requirement. The complainant must first call upon the defendant institution to act, giving it two months in which to "define its position." If at the end of that period the complainant is dissatisfied, it has a further two months within which to sue for inaction. If successful, the suit results in a declaration that the institution's failure to act is contrary to the Treaty. Curiously, although an Article 232 suit must be brought within two months after the failure to act is established, the prior request itself is not apparently subject to a time limitation. For an indication that the request nevertheless must be made within a "reasonable time" following the circumstances giving rise to the infringement, see Netherlands v. Commission (Aids to iron and steel industry), Case 59/70, [1971] ECR 639.

Any institution of the Community may bring an Article 232 suit. So too may private parties, but they must be able to show not only that the institution failed to act, but also that the institution's duty to act was a duty owed to them. As the following case shows, this may be difficult.

LORD BETHELL v. COMMISSION

Case 246/81, [1982] ECR 2277.

[Lord Bethell was a member of the European Parliament and of the House of Lords, a regular user of scheduled air passenger services within the Community and an advocate of greater airline competition. After a lengthy correspondence, he formally asked the Commission to take action against certain airlines for price fixing and other concerted practices in violation of Articles 81 and 82 (ex 85 and 86). The Commission wrote to Lord Bethell stating that fares were fixed among the Member States rather than the airlines, but promising to study the matter further and to take action if justified. The Commission also stated that it would notify the Member States that even government-fixed fares must not be so excessive as to constitute an abuse of dominant position. It also stated that it was drafting a directive to the Member States on criteria for airfare approvals and intended to investigate other non-fare-related restrictive practices. Dissatisfied with this response, Lord Bethell brought suit under both Articles 230 and 232 (ex 173 and 175).]

13 It appears from [the then Articles 173 and 175] that the applicant, for his application to be admissible, must be in a position to establish either that he is the addressee of a measure of the Commission having specific legal effects with regard to him, which is, as such, capable of being declared void, or that the Commission, having been duly called upon to act in pursuance of the second paragraph of Article 175, has failed to adopt in relation to him a measure which he was legally entitled to claim by virtue of the rules of Community law.

* * *

15 The principal question to be resolved in this case is whether the Commission had, under the rules of Community law, the right and the duty to adopt in respect of the applicant a decision in the sense of the request made by the applicant to the Commission in his letter of 13 May 1981. It is apparent from the content of that letter and from the explanations given

during the proceedings that the applicant is asking the Commission to undertake an investigation with regard to the airlines in the matter of the fixing of air fares with a view to a possible application to them of the provisions of the Treaty with regard to competition.

[16] It is clear therefore that the applicant is asking the Commission, not to take a decision in respect of him, but to open an inquiry with regard to third parties and to take decisions in respect of them. No doubt the applicant, in his double capacity as a user of the airlines and a leading member of an organization of users of air passenger services, has an indirect interest ... in such proceedings and their possible outcome, but he is nevertheless not in the precise legal position of the actual addressee of a decision, which may be declared void under the second paragraph of Article 173, or in [the precise legal position] of the potential addressee of a legal measure which the Commission has a duty to adopt with regard to him, as is [the] position under the third paragraph of Article 175.

[17] It follows that the application is inadmissible from the point of view of both Article 175 and Article 173.

Notes and Questions

1. *Lord Bethell* suggests that whether a party has standing to challenge a failure to act may depend upon whether that party would have had standing to challenge the act if it had been taken. See also the *Società Eridania* case, *supra* page 141, where the Court held that if the Commission's approval of a state aid is not of sufficient individual and direct concern to a competitor of the recipient to give the competitor standing to challenge the approval, then the competitor also lacks standing to challenge the Commission's failure to revoke the approval. Thus, too, if a private person asks that a regulation be adopted, and the request is not acted upon, the failure to act will be treated for standing purposes as if it were a regulation, and will therefore normally not be subject to review under Article 232 (ex 175).

Does this make sense to you? Would you expect a US court to make the same analysis in an analogous case?

2. Under the analysis in *Lord Bethell,* would the plaintiff in *Metro–SB–Grossmärkte, supra* page 143, have had standing to bring an action for failure to act against the Commission if the latter had declined to investigate SABA?

3. The materials thus far suggest the prospect of using Article 232 in order to avoid the standing limitations that govern Article 230 actions. A parallel problem arises in attempts to bring an action under Article 232 against the Council's or Commission's failure to repeal an act whose direct challenge under Article 230 is time-barred. Under what circumstances should the Court entertain such an action?

4. Article 226 (ex 169) of the EC Treaty, treated in Chapter 11, requires the Commission, when it considers a Member State to be in violation of its duties under the Treaty, to issue "a reasoned opinion on the matter." It further authorizes the Commission, if dissatisfied with the State's response, to bring the matter before the Court of Justice. Should the Commission be subject to an Article 230 or 232 action by a complainant who is unhappy with the Commission's failure to "prosecute" a Member State? See Alfons Lütticke GmbH v. Commission, Case 48/65, [1966] ECR 19; Star Fruit v. Commission, Case 247/87, [1989] ECR 291. (Both cases are discussed at page 427 *infra.*)

NOTE ON COMMISSION "INACTION" ON
COMPETITION LAW COMPLAINTS

Given the multitude of complaints that the Commission receives about private anti-competitive conduct, it is small wonder that the Commission's response, or alleged non-response, has given rise to "failure to act" claims and to "failure to act" case law. An important threshold question in this respect is whether the Commission is accused of refusing to act on a complaint or, rather, of ignoring a complaint altogether. Presumably the Commission is not permitted to ignore a complaint altogether, and if it were to do so, an action for failure to act under Article 232 would lie. Such was the case in United Parcel Service Europe SA v. Commission, Case T–127/98, [1999] ECR II–2633, where the Court of First Instance ruled that the Commission failed in its duties to UPS by not taking a position on UPS' four-year old complaint that Germany's subsidization of Deutsche Post AG violated Articles 82, 86 and 88 (ex 86, 90 and 93) of the EC Treaty.

More commonly the Commission more or less expressly declines to act, in which case the complainant's remedy is presumably a suit to annul a "negative" act. In Schmidt v. Commission, Case 210/81, [1983] ECR 3045, Schmidt, a retailer, complained that his exclusion from the Revox selective distribution network amounted to anticompetitive conduct by Revox in violation of Article 81 (ex 85). After reviewing the matter, the Commission decided not to take action against Revox and so notified Schmidt. Upon suit by Schmidt, the Court ruled that the Commission had made a negative decision which was reviewable under Article 230 (ex 173), rather than merely failed to act under Article 232 (ex 175). (Schmidt lost on the merits.)

Where the Commission positively declines to act (rather than ignores a request to do so), the principal question becomes the scope of judicial review of such a decision. The Court of First Instance established its framework of analysis in the case of Automec Srl. v. Commission, Case T–24/90, [1992] ECR II–2223. In *Automec*, an Italian car dealer complained to the Commission about BMW's termination of its distributorship contract. The Commission declined to investigate whether BMW had committed a competition law violation and the dealer brought suit. The Court of First Instance held that "the Commission cannot be required to give a ruling [on a competition law infringement] unless the subject-matter of the complaint is within its exclusive remit," which it was not. Moreover, since the Commission is not obligated to issue a ruling, "it [also] cannot be compelled to conduct an investigation, because this could have no purpose other than to seek evidence of the existence or otherwise of an infringement, the existence of which it is not required to establish." The Court emphasized the Commission's prerogative to decide for itself how best to spend its time and resources. "[F]or an institution performing a public-interest task, the power to ... settl[e] priorities in the framework laid down by law, where those priorities have not been settled by the legislature, is an inherent part of the work of administration."

The Court in *Automec* did not, however, treat the Commission's exercise of investigatorial discretion as wholly unreviewable. If challenged, the decision to close the files on a complaint without further investigation is subject to judicial review on the question whether the Commission "evaluat[ed] with all the requisite care the [complaint's] factual and legal aspects," whether the Commission gave proper reasons (duly allowing for its right to set priorities), and whether the Commission committed "a mistake in law or a manifest error of assessment or ... a misuse of powers." (On the meaning of the latter terms, see Section D of this Chapter *infra*.)

For an application of these standards, see Bureau Européen des Unions des Consommateurs (BEUC) and National Consumer Council v. Commission, Case T–37/92, [1994] ECR II–285, where the Court of First Instance annulled the Commission's decision not to investigate under Article 81 (ex 85) the agreement between the UK and Japanese automobile manufacturers associations limiting Japanese car imports to the UK. Based on its own ten-page critique of the Commission's reasoning, the Court found all three grounds that the Commission gave for not investigating the matter further to be defective, either as insufficiently reasoned or as containing errors of law or "a manifest error of assessment." For a still more recent annulment, albeit partial, of a Commission decision not to investigate an Article 81 complaint, see Tremblay v. Commission, Case T–5/93, [1995] ECR II–185, affirmed by a judgment of the same name in Case C–91/95P, [1996] ECR I–5547. (Following the annulment, the Commission reexamined Tremblay's complaint and again chose not to pursue it. Once more, Tremblay sued in the Court of First Instance, again alleging, among other things, an inadequate statement of reasons. This time it failed completely. Case T–224/95, [1997] ECR II–2215.

A requirement that the Commission explain and justify its enforcement priorities is not without significance. Consider Syndicat de l'Express Internationale (SFEI) v. Commission, Case C–119/97P, [1999] ECR I–1341. There, an association of international express mail services complained to the Commission that the French post office infringed EC Treaty Article 82 (ex 86) by giving logistical and commercial assistance to its subsidiary which operated in that sector. The Commission rejected the complaint, and the association unsuccessfully appealed to the Court of First Instance. The Court of Justice reversed on the ground that, while the Commission has discretion in reviewing complaints, it must set out the facts and legal considerations leading to its decision not to pursue a claim. In doing so, the Commission had to consider the duration and extent of the alleged infringements and their effect on competition. Moreover, the Commission could not, in deciding to go no further, rely solely on the fact that the alleged practices had ceased; it had to be certain that their anti-competitive effects no longer continued and that in other respects the complaint no longer had a Community interest. Is the Court too demanding?

Our assumption up to now may have been that the Commission declined to pursue a competition law complaint as a result of an exercise in investigative and prosecutorial discretion, i.e. as a decision on investigative and prosecutorial priorities. But it may equally be that the Commission *has* investigated and concluded that no competition law violation occurred. Should this make any difference either in terms of scope of review?

The Court of First Instance addressed this precise question in Asia Motor France SA v. Commission (Asia Motor France III), Case T–387/94, [1996] ECR II–961. The Court reiterated that the Commission is normally not obligated to rule on whether a private party's competition law complaints are well-founded (citing, among other judgments, *Automec*). However, it went on to hold that "where the Commission rejects a complaint on the ground that there has been no infringement of the competition rules of the Treaty, it is under a duty to set out in its decision the facts and considerations on which that conclusion is based" (para. 46). As for the reviewing court's role, its review of any such rejection by the Commission of a complaint "should involve verifying whether the facts have been accurately stated and whether there has been any manifest error in assessing the facts or a misuse of powers or any errors of law." The Court in *Asia Motor France III* ruled that the Commission made a manifest error in assessing the facts. (By way of sequel, the Commission made further investigations and then once again declined to pursue the competition law complaint. This time, the complainant's suit in the CFI alleging manifest error was unsuccessful. Asia Motor France SA v. Commission (Asia Motor France IV), Case T–154/98, [2000] ECR II–3453).

Is this a sensible approach? Does it give the Commission an incentive, in rejecting private competition law complaints, to present that rejection merely as a decision not to investigate rather than as a decision on the merits?

C. THE PLEA OF ILLEGALITY (ARTICLE 241)

Article 241 (ex 184) of the EC Treaty permits a challenge to a regulation adopted by the Council (acting alone or jointly with Parliament), the Commission or the European Central Bank as an incidental issue in the course of some other proceeding brought on a proper and timely basis in a Community court. Article 241's significance lies in the fact that, by its terms, it allows a regulation to be challenged indirectly even after the time for bringing a direct challenge under Article 230 (ex 173) has expired. This so-called "plea of illegality" derives from French administrative law, more particularly the *exception d'illégalité*. The usual scenario is one in which a party seeks the annulment of an individual decision addressed to it, in whole or in part because the decision in turn is based on an illegal regulation. If two months have passed since the regulation's effective date, the regulation itself may no longer be challenged directly, even by a party that otherwise would have had standing under Article 230. However, an action to annul the individual decision implementing the regulation may still be timely, and Article 241 expressly allows the regulation to be collaterally attacked in that proceeding.

If the Article 241 claim in our example is successful, the regulation will not be formally annulled. However, since it cannot serve as the legal basis for the challenged decision, the decision itself will be annulled. Although the institutions could conceivably continue in the future to take action on the basis of the regulation (precisely because it has not been annulled), they are unlikely to do so. The Court of Justice itself maintains that a ruling on the legality of a Community measure made under Article 241 in a preliminary reference from a national court, though addressed only to that court, constitutes "sufficient reason for any other national court to regard that [measure] as void." SpA International Chemical Corporation v. Amministrazione delle Finanze dello Stato, Case 66/80, [1981] ECR 1191.

Simmenthal v. Commission (Simmenthal III), Case 92/78, [1979] ECR 777, is a well-known Article 241 case. The Italian intervention authorities solicited bids for the purchase of some of their stock of frozen beef, and the Simmenthal firm submitted one. Before action on the bid could be taken, the Commission addressed a decision to the Member States fixing maximum quantities and minimum prices for beef sales by national intervention agencies. The Italian authorities accordingly rejected Simmenthal's tender as falling outside the allowable limits. Simmenthal brought a direct action for annulment of the Commission decision. (Simmenthal was found to have standing because the decision, though addressed to the Member States, was of direct and individual concern to it.) Simmenthal invoked Article 241 (then 184), arguing that the Commission guidelines which formed the basis of the decision limiting Member States beef sales were themselves invalid. The guidelines were found both in prior Commission regulations and in certain "notices of invitation to tender." The Court entertained the claim, not only against the regulations but also against the "notices of invitation," finding that the latter, "although ... not in the form of a regulation, nevertheless produce similar effects." (The Court found the regulations and notices to be invalid, annulled the limitation on beef sales that was based on them, and remanded the matter to the Commission and the Italian authorities.)

According to the Court in *Simmenthal III,* Article 241 permits the collateral attack of prior measures only if the party bringing the attack "was not entitled under Article 173 [now 230] ... to bring a direct action challenging those measures." The Court cited a "need to provide those persons who are precluded by ... Article 173 from instituting proceedings directly in respect of general acts with the benefit of a judicial review of [those acts] at the time when they are affected by ... decisions [implementing those acts.]" [1979] ECR at 800. This comment may help explain why the Article 241 remedy is limited to the indirect challenge of *regulations* (and the like) and does not extend to the indirect challenge of *individual decisions.*

The Court's comment may also help explain why, despite the term "any party" in Article 241, a Member State may not invoke the remedy. In Commission v. Belgium (Aid to railways), Case 156/77, [1978] ECR 1881, the Belgian Government sought to defend enforcement proceeding brought against it under Article 226 (ex 169) for granting a state aid previously disapproved by the Commission. Belgium did not at the time challenge the decision disallowing the proposed aid, and the Court thought Belgium should not be permitted to challenge it for the first time at the enforcement stage via Article 241.

Notes and Questions

1.   Upon the accession to the EU of Austria, Finland and Sweden, the Commission proposed a regulation authorizing all the institutions to give early retirement to staff so as to make room in employment for nationals of the new States. In enacting the measure, the Council limited the regulation to European Parliament staff. Chvatal and Losch, officials of the Court of Justice, nevertheless applied to the Registrar of the Court for early retirement under the regulation. Their requests having been denied, the two brought suit in the Court of First Instance challenging the legality of the Registrar's denial. The CFI considered the suit to be a proper vehicle under Article 241 for indirectly challenging the validity of the regulation and, proceeding to the merits, held the regulation to be invalid as

contrary, among other things, to the fundamental Community law principle of equality.

The Court of Justice reversed. Since by its own terms the regulation covered only persons in the employ of the Parliament, and not of the Court of Justice, it could not constitute the legal basis for the decision of the Registrar whose annulment Chvatal and Losch were seeking. Chvatal and Losch, Case C–432/98, [2000] ECR I–8535.

Which court has taken the sounder view?

2.   There is every reason to suppose that national courts likewise will permit the indirect challenge of a Community measure. The preliminary reference mechanism plainly contemplates that in the course of litigation before them, national courts may encounter questions about the validity of Community acts, and may (and in some cases must) refer those questions to the Court of Justice.

In Universität Hamburg v. Hauptzollamt Hamburg–Kehrwieder, Case 216/82, [1983] ECR 2771, a German university applied for an exemption from customs duties on the import of a US-manufactured instrument needed for scientific research. The Commission instructed the German authorities not to permit import of the instrument duty-free because a substantially similar instrument of Community origin was available. The university sued the German agency in national court, claiming that both the agency's denial of the request and the Commission's decision instructing the agency to issue the denial were wrongful. The national court sought a preliminary ruling from the Court of Justice on the validity of the Commission decision. The Court accepted the reference, confirming that Member State courts may in principle entertain indirect challenges to individual Community acts.

On the other hand, as we shall see in Chapter 7 (and more particularly in the *Foto–Frost* case, *infra* page 276), national courts may not themselves invalidate a Community act. If they question the validity of such an act, they must (as the German court did in the *Universität Hamburg* case, *supra*) ask for an authoritative preliminary ruling.

D.   THE SCOPE OF JUDICIAL REVIEW

Article 230 sets out four distinct grounds for invalidating Community measures. These grounds, which are recognized in most continental administrative law systems, are lack of competence, infringement of an essential procedural requirement, infringement of the Treaty or implementing law, and misuse of powers. (When the Court reviews the validity of a Community act under Article 241 or by way of preliminary reference from a national court under Article 234, it may do so on the same four grounds.) Although these grounds for review bear an affinity to the principles governing judicial review of administrative action in the US, they also present certain distinctive features that warrant a closer look.

1.   LACK OF COMPETENCE

Claims of lack of competence (or jurisdiction) may raise either or both of two related questions.

The first question is whether the Community, as an entity, has authority to take the measure or action being challenged. This question was foreshadowed in Chapter 4, *supra*, on the "sphere" of Community law. A good example of a broad *ultra vires* claim of this sort is a challenge by foreign producers to the Commission's alleged attempt to apply competition rules extraterritorially, as in the *IBM* case, *supra* page 133, or the *Wood pulp* case, *infra* pages 815 and 826. A second competence question is whether the particular institution that took the challenged measure or action was the competent authority to do so. A leading decision of this kind is France v. Commission (Antitrust agreement with the US), Case C–327/91, [1994] ECR I–3641. Here, the Commission was found lacking in competence to enter into a binding agreement with the United States for mutual cooperation and assistance in matters of antitrust enforcement. The Court held that any such agreement required action by the Council, upon consultation of Parliament. The Commission subsequently laid the agreement before both institutions, resulting in Parliament's approval and the Council's adoption. See Chapter 20, *infra*.

GERMANY v. PARLIAMENT AND COUNCIL

(Tobacco advertising)
Case C–376/98, [2000] ECR I–8419.

[Germany sought to annul Directive 98/43/EC of the Council and Parliament on "the approximation of the laws, regulations and administrative provisions of the member States relating to the advertising and sponsorship of tobacco products." Adopted on the basis of Articles 47(2) (ex 57(2)) on freedom of establishment, 55 (ex 66) on freedom of services, and 95 (ex 100a) on harmonization, the directive basically banned all advertising and sponsorship of tobacco products in the Community. ("Sponsorship" was defined as "any public or private contribution to an event or activity with the aim or the direct or indirect effect of promoting a tobacco product.")

The Court noted that EC Treaty Article 152(4) (ex 129(4)) on public health specifically excluded the harmonization of Member State laws designed to protect and improve human health, and that the national measures to be harmonized by the directive did in fact chiefly pursue public health objectives. On the other hand, according to the Court, this does not mean that harmonization measures cannot have any impact on the protection of human health; indeed Article 152(1) (ex 129(1)) provides that health needs should be a component of the Community's other policies—provided, the Court stressed, that "[o]ther articles of the Treaty ... not ... be used as a legal basis in order to circumvent [Article 152(4)'s] express exclusion of harmonisation" of public health law. Against this background, the Court turned to the institutions' choice of legal basis:]

The choice of Articles 100a, 57(2) and 66 of the Treaty as a legal basis and judicial review thereof

* * *

[80]   In this case, the approximation of national laws on the advertising and sponsorship of tobacco products provided for by the Directive was based on Articles 100a, 57(2) and 66 [now 95, 47(2) and 55] of the Treaty.

[The Court quoted Article 95 (ex 100a) as well as the definition of the "internal market" in Article 3 and in Article 14 (ex 7a).]

83   Those provisions, read together, make it clear that the measures referred to in Article 100a(1) of the Treaty are intended to improve the conditions for the establishment and functioning of the internal market. To construe that article as meaning that it vests in the Community legislature a general power to regulate the internal market would not only be contrary to the express wording of the provisions cited above but would also be incompatible with the principle embodied in Article 3b [now 5] of the EC Treaty that the powers of the Community are limited to those specifically conferred on it.

84   Moreover, a measure adopted on the basis of Article 100a of the Treaty must genuinely have as its object the improvement of the conditions for the establishment and functioning of the internal market. If a mere finding of disparities between national rules and of the abstract risk of obstacles to the exercise of fundamental freedoms or of distortions of competition liable to result therefrom were sufficient to justify the choice of Article 100a as a legal basis, judicial review of compliance with the proper legal basis might be rendered nugatory. The Court would then be prevented from discharging the function entrusted to it by Article 164 [now 220] of the EC Treaty of ensuring that the law is observed in the interpretation and application of the Treaty.

85   So, in considering whether Article 100a was the proper legal basis, the Court must verify whether the measure whose validity is at issue in fact pursues the objectives stated by the Community legislature.

86   It is true ... that recourse to Article 100a as a legal basis is possible if the aim is to prevent the emergence of future obstacles to trade resulting from multifarious development of national laws. However, the emergence of such obstacles must be likely and the measure in question must be designed to prevent them.

* * *

88   [P]rovided that the conditions for recourse to Articles 100a, 57(2) and 66 as a legal basis are fulfilled, the Community legislature cannot be prevented from relying on that legal basis on the ground that public health protection is a decisive factor in the choices to be made. On the contrary, the third paragraph of Article 129(1) [now the first paragraph of article 152(1)] provides that health requirements are to form a constituent part of the Community's other policies and Article 100a(3) [now 95(3)] expressly requires that, in the process of harmonisation, a high level of human health protection is to be ensured.

89   It is therefore necessary to verify whether, in the light of the foregoing, it was permissible for the Directive to be adopted on the basis of Articles 100a, 57(2) and 66 of the Treaty.

The Directive

90   In the ... preamble to the Directive, the Community legislature notes that differences exist between national laws on the advertising and sponsorship of tobacco products and observes that, as a result of such advertising and sponsorship transcending the borders of the Member States, the differences in question are likely to give rise to barriers to the movement of the products which serve as the media for such activities and the exercise of

freedom to provide services in that area, as well as to distortions of competition, thereby impeding the functioning of the internal market.

91   According to the [preamble], it is [also] necessary to eliminate such barriers, and, to that end, approximate the rules relating to the advertising and sponsorship of tobacco products, whilst leaving Member States the possibility of introducing, under certain conditions, such requirements as they consider necessary in order to guarantee protection of the health of individuals.

* * *

95   It therefore is necessary to verify whether the Directive actually contributes to eliminating obstacles to the free movement of goods and to the freedom to provide services, and to removing distortions of competition.

Elimination of obstacles to the free movement of goods and the freedom to provide services

96   It is clear that, as a result of disparities between national laws on the advertising of tobacco products, obstacles to the free movement of goods or the freedom to provide services exist or may well arise.

97   In the case, for example, of periodicals, magazines and newspapers which contain advertising for tobacco products, it is true, as the applicant has demonstrated, that no obstacle exists at present to their importation into Member States which prohibit such advertising. However, in view of the trend in national legislation towards ever greater restrictions on advertising of tobacco products, reflecting the belief that such advertising gives rise to an appreciable increase in tobacco consumption, it is probable that obstacles to the free movement of press products will arise in the future.

98   In principle, therefore, a Directive prohibiting the advertising of tobacco products in periodicals, magazines and newspapers could be adopted on the basis of Article 100a of the Treaty with a view to ensuring the free movement of press products . . .

99   However, for numerous types of advertising of tobacco products, the prohibition under Article 3(1) of the Directive cannot be justified by the need to eliminate obstacles to the free movement of advertising media or the freedom to provide services in the field of advertising. That applies, in particular, to the prohibition of advertising on posters, parasols, ashtrays and other articles used in hotels, restaurants and cafés, and the prohibition of advertising spots in cinemas, prohibitions which in no way help to facilitate trade in the products concerned.

* * *

103   Under Article 5 of the Directive, Member States retain the right to lay down, in accordance with the Treaty, such stricter requirements concerning the advertising or sponsorship of tobacco products as they deem necessary to guarantee the health protection of individuals.

104   Furthermore, the Directive contains no provision ensuring the free movement of products which conform to its provisions, in contrast to other directives allowing Member States to adopt stricter measures for the protection of a general interest.

105 In those circumstances, it must be held that the Community legislature cannot rely on the need to eliminate obstacles to the free movement of advertising media and the freedom to provide services in order to adopt the Directive on the basis of Articles 100a, 57(2) and 66 of Treaty.

Elimination of distortion of competition

106 In examining the lawfulness of a directive adopted on the basis of Article 100a of the Treaty, the Court is required to verify whether the distortion of competition which the measure purports to eliminate is appreciable.

107 In the absence of such a requirement, the powers of the Community legislature would be practically unlimited. National laws often differ regarding the conditions under which the activities they regulate may be carried on, and this impacts directly or indirectly on the conditions of competition for the undertakings concerned. It follows that to interpret Articles 100a, 57(2) and 66 of the Treaty as meaning that the Community legislature may rely on those articles with a view to eliminating the smallest distortions of competition would be incompatible with the principle ... that the powers of the Community are those specifically conferred on it.

108 It is therefore necessary to verify whether the Directive actually contributes to eliminating appreciable distortions of competition.

109 First, as regards advertising agencies and producers of advertising media, undertakings established in Member States which impose fewer restrictions on tobacco advertising are unquestionably at an advantage in terms of economies of scale and increase in profits. The effects of such advantages on competition are, however, remote and indirect and do not constitute distortions which could be described as appreciable. They are not comparable to the distortions of competition caused by differences in production costs, such as those which, in particular, prompted the Community legislature to adopt [the titanium dioxide waste directive, see page 87 *supra*].

110 It is true that the differences between certain regulations on tobacco advertising may give rise to appreciable distortions of competition.... [T]he fact that sponsorship is prohibited in some Member States and authorised in others gives rise, in particular, to certain sports events being relocated, with considerable repercussions on the conditions of competition for undertakings associated with such events.

111 However, such distortions, which could be a basis for recourse to Article 100a of the Treaty in order to prohibit certain forms of sponsorship, are not such as to justify the use of that legal basis for an outright prohibition of advertising of the kind imposed by the Directive.

112 Second, as regards distortions of competition in the market for tobacco products, irrespective of the applicant's contention that such distortions are not covered by the Directive, it is clear that, in that sector, the Directive is likewise not apt to eliminate appreciable distortions of competition.

113 Admittedly, as the Commission has stated, producers and sellers of tobacco products are obliged to resort to price competition to influence their market share in Member States which have restrictive legislation.

However, that does not constitute a distortion of competition but rather a restriction of forms of competition which applies to all economic operators in those Member States. By imposing a wide-ranging prohibition on the advertising of tobacco products, the Directive would in the future generalise that restriction of forms of competition by limiting, in all the Member States, the means available for economic operators to enter or remain in the market.

[114] In those circumstances, it must be held that the Community legislature cannot rely on the need to eliminate distortions of competition, either in the advertising sector or in the tobacco products sector, in order to adopt the Directive on the basis of Articles 100a, 57(2) and 66 of the Treaty.

[115] In view of all the foregoing considerations, a measure such as the directive cannot be adopted on the basis of Articles 100a, 57(2) and 66 of the Treaty.

[While acknowledging that a directive prohibiting certain forms of advertising and sponsorship of tobacco products could have been validly adopted under Article 100a, the Court thought that, given the deliberate generality of the prohibition, partial annulling the directive would amount to amending it, which is the province of the Community's political branches.]

[118] .... The Directive must [accordingly] be annulled in its entirety.

Notes and Questions

1. *Tobacco advertising* is the first instance in which the Court of Justice has ruled that provisions of a directive adopted under Article 95 (ex 100a) could not validly be regarded as an internal market harmonization measure within the meaning of that Article. To what extent does the language of EC Treaty Article 152(4) (ex 129(4)) on public health protection account for that result? Is the Court giving a long-overdue definition to "measures ... which have as their object the establishment and functioning of the internal market"? Or is it impermissibly "second-guessing" the policy judgment of the institutions?

2. Note the Court's reliance once again (in para. 84) on Article 220 (ex 164) of the EC Treaty. Does Article 220 support the Court's reasoning or result?

3. What implications does *Tobacco advertising* have for the Court's manifold "choice of legal basis" cases, discussed in Chapter 3B? What implications does it have for the institutions' use of "implied powers," discussed in Chapter 4A?

4. The Commission has since introduced a proposal for a new directive on tobacco advertising and sponsorship that excludes provisions that the *Tobacco advertising* judgment suggested could not be predicated on promotion of internal market trade. European Union Law Reporter, European Union Update, para. 1756 (May 2001).

5. The Netherlands recently mounted a similar challenge to Directive 98/44, which requires Member States to afford patent protection to biotechnological inventions and, among other things, determines which inventions involving plants, animals or the human body may and may not be patented. The Court cited *Tobacco advertising*, but rejected the charge that the measure fell outside the definition of internal market measures under Article 95 (ex 100a). It thought that differences in national laws on the patentability of such inventions could damage the unity of the internal market. Netherlands v. Parliament and Council (Biotechnological inventions), Case C–377/98, [2001] ECR I-___ (Oct. 9, 2001).

6. Interestingly, US courts have recently shown a reawakened interest in setting constitutional limits on federal legislative jurisdiction. In addition to its rulings in New York v. United States, 505 U.S. 144, 112 S.Ct. 2408, 120 L.Ed.2d 120 (1992), and in Printz v. United States, 521 U.S. 898, 117 S.Ct. 2365, 138 L.Ed.2d 914 (1997), declaring it unconstitutional for federal authorities (including Congress) to "commandeer" state legislative or administrative powers, the Supreme Court ruled 5–4, in the case of United States v. Lopez, 514 U.S. 549, 115 S.Ct. 1624, 131 L.Ed.2d 626 (1995), that the Federal Gun–Free School Zones Act (making it a federal offense to possess a firearm on school grounds or within 1000 feet of them) is unconstitutional as in excess of Congress' power to legislate under the Interstate Commerce Clause. See, more recently, United States v. Morrison, 529 U.S. 598, 120 S.Ct. 1740, 146 L.Ed.2d 658 (2000).

The Court has also severely curtailed Congress' use of its legislative powers under the 14th Amendment. See United States v. Morrison, *supra*; City of Boerne v. Flores, 521 U.S. 507, 117 S.Ct. 2157, 138 L.Ed.2d 624 (1997).

2. INFRINGEMENT OF AN ESSENTIAL PROCEDURAL SAFE-GUARD

The EC Treaty and secondary legislation are fairly specific about the procedures that the institutions are to follow in taking the various measures that they are authorized to take. Whether a measure's validity depends on observance of those procedures is a somewhat different question. Echoing Article 230 (ex 173), the Court of Justice has ruled that the violation of a procedural requirement justifies setting aside the resulting measure only if the requirement in question is an "essential" one.

An example of a procedural norm generally held to be essential is the requirement of prior consultation of a designated advisory body, including of course the requirement to consult the Parliament, as in Roquette Frères v. Council (Isoglucose), *supra* page 84. We have already seen that the Treaty is replete with consultation requirements and typically failure to perform a required consultation will be regarded as reason enough for a measure's annulment. Determining whether consultation is mandatory or merely optional may not, however, be as simple as it may seem. See Angelopharm GmbH v. Freie und Hansestadt Hamburg, Case C–212/91, [1994] ECR I–171. One might also regard the requirement of reasons, as set forth in EC Treaty Article 253 (ex 190), as procedural in nature; in any event, it too is considered to be by definition essential.

Procedural norms are not only to be found in the Treaties, but in secondary legislation as well. Indeed, in one case, Germany won the annulment of a Commission decision establishing procedures for testing the conformity of construction products to specifications because the Commission, upon consulting the Standing Committee on Construction prior to adopting the decision, failed to send the Member States a notice and agenda of the Committee meeting, the draft decision and the relevant working papers in German (rather than merely in English), as required by the Committee's rules of procedure. Germany v. Commission (Construction products), Case C–263/95, [1998] ECR I–441.

Claims of procedural irregularity should be framed specifically and convincingly. In one case, a Community steel producer objected to its production quota under a quota system that the Commission introduced to deal with a "manifest crisis" in the steel industry under the then Article 58 of the Coal and Steel Community Treaty. Among the producer's claims was that the Council did not truly give its assent to the quota system, as required by Article 58. It claimed that although the Council formally approved the measure, it had only casually considered the problems of the steel industry and had failed to examine a draft of the measures the Commission intended to take under the system. The producer also sought access to Council documents that would indicate how and why the Council gave its approval. The Court dismissed the suit as based on "vague allegations." Klöckner–Werke v. Commission, Case 119/81, [1982] ECR 2627.

TRANSOCEAN MARINE PAINT ASSOCIATION v. COMMISSION

Case 17/74, [1974] ECR 1063.

[The plaintiff, an association of medium-sized maritime paint producers, applied for renewal of a competition law exemption that the Commission had granted under Article 81(3) (ex 85(3)) for the producers' agreement to coordinate manufacturing and marketing practices. In July 1973, the Commission notified the Association of certain new conditions that the producers would have to satisfy in order to have the exemption renewed, and it gave the Association an opportunity to comment and (in September 1973) a hearing. When, in December, the Commission finally renewed the exemption, it did so subject to an additional condition (on the reporting of interlocking directorates with non-Community paint manufacturers) of which the Association had not had prior notice and on which it had not commented. The Association objected to the new condition strictly on substantive grounds, and asked the Court to annul the decision granting the exemption to the extent that it carried this condition. The Advocate–General discerned a procedural due process issue in the case, and the court addressed it.]

4   The applicants firstly state that the obligation in issue was mentioned neither in the "notice of objections" ... nor at the time of the hearing ... and that furthermore it was not mentioned in any letter or memorandum from the Commission, prior to the Decision, so that they were never given the opportunity to make their views known on this subject.

* * *

6   In [its] notice of objections the Commission stated that a simple renewal of the exemption could not be envisaged, since the position of the members of the Association on the marine paints market had changed as a result of the increase in the number of undertakings composing the Association, the increased size of certain of them and the links which two of the members ... had forged with large industrial chemical concerns.

7   The Commission added that it was nevertheless willing to renew the exemption for a period of five years, but at the same time making it subject to fresh conditions and obligations, one of which was formulated so as to involve, for the members of the Association ..., the further obligation to notify to the Commission without delay ... any change in the participatory relationships of the members.

8   The applicants claim that at no time could they infer from this statement that the Commission intended to impose on them a condition such as that contained in the provision in issue, and one to which they would not be able, by reasons of its breadth, to adhere and which, without good reason, would harm their interests. If they had been in a position to realize the Commission's intentions they would not have failed to make known their objections on this matter so as to draw the Commission's attention to the inconvenience which would result from the obligation in issue and to the illegality by which it is vitiated. Since they were not given this opportunity, they allege that the Decision, insofar as the obligation in issue is concerned, must be annulled since it is vitiated by a procedural defect.

* * *

11   [According to Council Regulation 17] the Commission, before taking decisions . . ., shall give the undertakings or associations of undertakings concerned the opportunity of being heard on the matters to which the Commission has taken objection. . . .

* * *

14   On the other hand, the Commission cannot be expected to anticipate the conditions and obligations to which it is entitled to subject the exemption laid down in Article 85(3) [now 81(3)]. In fact, the investigation of a request for exemption may bring to light various ways in which the operation of an agreement or the control of that operation may be undertaken, thus prompting the Commission to withdraw the objections which it had raised against the request and justifying the grant, possibly subject to certain conditions, of the benefit of Article 85(3).

15   It is clear, however, both from the nature and objective of the procedure for hearings, and from [the applicable regulation] that this regulation . . . applies the general rule that a person whose interests are perceptibly affected by a decision taken by a public authority must be given the opportunity to make his point of view known. This rule requires that an undertaking be clearly informed, in good time, of the essence of conditions to which the Commission intends to subject an exemption and it must have the opportunity to submit its observations to the Commission. This is especially so in the case of conditions which, as in this case, impose considerable obligations having far-reaching effects.

16   Since Article 85(3) constitutes, for the benefit of undertakings, an exception to the general prohibition contained in Article 85(1), the Commission must be in a position at any moment to check whether the conditions justifying the exemption are still present. Accordingly, in relation to the detailed rules to which it may subject the exemption, the Commission enjoys a large measure of discretion, while at the same time having to act within the limits imposed upon its competence by Article 85. On the other hand, the exercise of this discretionary power is linked to a preliminary canvassing of objections which may be raised by the undertakings.

17   It is clear from the file that this requirement was not fulfilled in respect of the obligation in issue.

18 The statement contained in the [notice of objections] could be interpreted in widely differing ways....

19 [T]he minutes of the hearing ... show that at no time was the general condition later contained in the Decision the subject of an exchange of points of view. This fact confirms the applicants' assertion that they were convinced that the obligation as stated in the "notice of objections" concerned only the mutual relations between members of the Association and not such links as might exist with outside undertakings, including those operating outside the Common Market and concerned with the manufacture of paints other than marine paints.

20 Accordingly, the [added] condition ... was imposed in breach of procedural requirements and the Commission must be given the opportunity to reach a fresh decision on this point after hearing the observations or suggestions of the members of the Association.

Notes and Questions

1. *Transocean Marine Paint* is one of the first judgments in which the Court seems to have drawn upon English law principles in developing its jurisprudence. Discussion of British "natural justice" figured prominently in the conclusions of Advocate–General Warner, though not to the exclusion of analogous doctrines in the other Member States. [1974] ECR at 1082, 1088.

2. The Court has ruled that a consumer protection group does not have a procedural due process right to inspect documents in an anti-dumping proceeding to which it is not a party and which does not entail allegations against it. Bureau Européen des Unions de Consommateurs (BEUC) v. Commission, Case C–170/89, [1991] ECR I–5709. The case stands for the important proposition that the fact that a party may be granted leave to intervene in ECJ (or CFI) proceedings for judicial review of a Commission measure (and as an intervenor have a right of access to non-confidential documents in the Commission file) does not mean that that party necessarily enjoys that same right during the administrative proceedings leading up to the measure eventually adopted.

NOTE ON "ADMINISTRATIVE DUE PROCESS"

The *Transocean* judgment (¶ 15) guarantees a certain measure of what might be called procedural due process to "a person whose interests are perceptibly affected by a decision taken by a public authority." This language leaves open several questions. Is the procedural guarantee limited to competition cases? How important must an individual's interests be, and how specifically and dramatically must they be affected, in order to trigger the due process requirement? Assuming due process is triggered, what precise procedural safeguards might due process entail?

While the Treaties[6] and secondary legislation[7] commonly impose procedural requirements on the Community decisionmaking process, the European

6. The EC Treaty itself does not by its terms expressly require fair hearings; the closest it comes to doing so is in Article 88(2) (ex 93(2)) which requires the Commission to give "notice to the parties concerned to submit their comments" before declaring a state aid incompatible with the common market.

7. A field in which secondary legislation established significant procedural protections for private parties is trademarks, notably for

Community has no general code of administrative procedure. Whether more is required by way of procedural protection of private parties than the Treaties and secondary legislation expressly provide is thus largely a matter for determination by the Court of Justice, and more lately the Court of First Instance, through the notion of unwritten general principles of law. This case law has arisen from disputes in which the Community courts have been called upon to review the legality of the measures that ultimately emerge across a broad range of fields—e.g. competition law, anti-dumping law, state aids, trademarks, anti-fraud activities, financial assistance programs—in which the Community institutions rather than the Member States are the primary decisionmakers. The ultimate question, commonly, is whether complaining parties enjoyed a "fair hearing." See Lenaerts & Vanhamme, Procedural Rights of Private Parties in the Community Administrative Process, 34 Comm. Mkt. L. Rev. 531 (1997).

Under the case law of the Court, a fair hearing (or, as it is sometimes called, the "right of defense") is in principle required for proceedings which are initiated against a person and are liable to culminate in a measure adversely affecting that person. Commission v. Lisrestal, Case C–32/95P, [1996] ECR I–5373. Under some circumstances it may be required even when the private party, rather than the Community institution, initiated the proceedings, and nothing even approaching a "sanction" is concerned. In Technische Universität München v. Hauptzollamt München–Mitte, Case C–269/90, [1991] ECR I–5469, the German Supreme Tax Court asked the Court of Justice to reconsider its approval of the adequacy of the Commission's procedures for allowing (or disallowing) the duty-free import of scientific instruments from outside the Community. The Commission had denied a university's request to import a certain electron microscope duty-free from Japan on the statutory ground that an apparatus of equivalent scientific value, capable of serving the same purpose, was available on the Community market. The university challenged the German authorities' implementation of that refusal. In its reference, the German court questioned the adequacy of the judicial review that the Court of Justice ordinarily gives to Commission decisions of this sort. In its view, the high degree of deference that the Court of Justice shows on these occasions (annulling Commission decisions only if "a manifest error of appraisal" or "a misuse of power" is proven) rendered the available judicial review inadequate. The German court inquired whether this inadequacy in turn rendered the Commission's decision invalid.

The Court of Justice acknowledged that the complex and technical nature of the issues required that the Commission have "a power of appraisal." The Court went on:

> However, where the Community institutions have such a power of appraisal, respect for the rights guaranteed by the Community legal order in administrative procedures is of even more fundamental importance. Those guarantees include, in particular, the duty of the competent institution to examine carefully and impartially all the relevant aspects of the individual case [and] the right of the person concerned to make his views known and to have an adequately reasoned decision. Only in this

persons seeking to obtain or enforce a trademark. Regulation 40/94.

way can the Court verify whether the factual and legal elements upon which the exercise of the power of appraisal depends were present.

The Court then examined the Commission's usual procedures, in particular its reliance on the opinions of the Member States and, where necessary, a group of experts. It continued:

> The Commission has admitted that it has always followed the opinions of the group of experts because it has no other sources of information concerning the apparatus being considered.

> In those circumstances, the group of experts cannot possibly carry out its task unless it is composed of persons possessing the necessary technical knowledge of the various fields in which the scientific instruments concerned are used or the members of that group are advised by experts having that knowledge. Neither the minutes of the meeting of the group of experts nor the oral proceedings before the Court have shown that the members of the group themselves possessed the necessary knowledge in the fields of chemistry, biology and geographical science, or that they sought advice from experts in those fields in order to be able to address the technical problems raised by the examination of the equivalence of the scientific instruments in question. Consequently, the Commission has infringed its obligation to examine carefully and impartially all the relevant aspects of the case in point.

> Secondly, [the relevant procedural regulation] does not provide any opportunity for the person concerned, the importer of scientific apparatus, to explain his position to the group of experts or to comment on the information before the group or to take a position on the group's recommendation.

> However, it is the importing institution which is best aware of the technical characteristics which the scientific instrument must have in view of the work for which it is intended. The comparison between the imported apparatus and the instruments originating in the Community must, consequently, be made according to the information about the intended research projects and the actual intended use of the apparatus provided by the persons concerned.

> The right to be heard in such an administrative procedure requires that the person concerned should be able, during the actual procedure before the Commission, to put his own case and properly make his views known on the relevant circumstances and, where necessary, on the documents taken into account by the Community institution. This requirement was not met when the disputed decision was adopted.

The Court found, in addition, that the Commission had failed to provide a sufficiently clear and precise indication of the scientific reasons for its conclusion that an equivalent domestic instrument was available, and had thus violated Article 253 (ex 190). Ultimately the Court annulled the Commission decision.

What exactly does a fair hearing entail? An important incident of fair procedure is access to (and the opportunity to comment upon) essential documents, particularly documents upon which the institutions intend to rely in reaching their adverse decision. The right of access to documents is discussed more generally in Chapter 6E *infra*, but that right clearly takes on procedural due process dimensions when the requesting party is the one against whom the authorities intend to make an adverse decision. See Solvay v. Commission, Case T–30/91, [1995] ECR II–1775, a competition case in which the Court of First Instance invoked "the general principle of equality of arms [which] presupposes that in a competition case the knowledge which the undertaking concerned has of the file used in the proceeding is the same as that of the Commission." To the Commission's argument that the documents withheld would not have been exculpatory, the Court replied that "where ... difficult and complex economic appraisals are to be made, the Commission must give the advisers of the undertaking concerned the opportunity to examine documents which may be relevant so that their probative value for the defence can be assessed."

Due process also entails the availability of an independent and impartial tribunal.[8] While it is sometimes complained that the Commission combines rulemaking, prosecutorial and quasi-adjudicatory functions, the Court of Justice has found no constitutional infirmity in that situation. Crucial to this conclusion is, of course, the availability to legitimately aggrieved persons of an independent and impartial tribunal (in the form of the Court of First Instance and the Court of Justice). Naturally, the efficacy of such review in the courts depends in turn on its scope and on the courts' degree of scrutiny of administrative decisions, as well as the stringency with which the courts enforce the requirement of reasons set out in Article 253 (ex 190) of the EC Treaty.

The Commission's investigative and enforcement activities in the competition law area have understandably given rise to a large number of procedural due process issues. For example, in SA Musique Diffusion Francaise v. Commission (Pioneer), Cases 100–103/80, [1983] ECR 1825, European distributors and their Japanese supplier complained about a great variety of irregularities in the Commission's decisional process that culminated in fines for their anticompetitive behavior, including (in addition to the Commission's combination of the functions of judge and prosecutor) (a) insufficiency of the statement of objections, (b) failure to notify the full extent of the period of violation claimed, (c) failure to state the basis for the proposed fine, (d) failure to disclose certain documents on which the Commission would rely, and (e) failure to disclose the opinion of the relevant advisory committee. In the end, the Court found two procedural violations: failure to disclose certain documents (as a result of which the Court ruled that those documents could not be relied upon) and failure to notify the full extent of the period of violation claimed (as a result of which the Commission's fine had to be reduced by more than 50%).

In BASF et al. v. Commission (Low-density polyethylene), Joined Cases T–80–112/89, [1995] ECR II–729, the Court of First Instance was called upon to review the Commission's imposition of fines in excess of $49 million for fixing prices in, and partitioning the market for, low-density polyethylene used in the production of film and plastic packaging. The Court annulled the

---

8. See Article 6(1) of the European Human Rights Convention, which provides that "[i]n the determination of his civil rights and obligations or any criminal charge against him, everyone is entitled to a fair and public hearing within a reasonable time by an independent and impartial tribunal established by law."

decisions due to the Commission's alteration of those decisions after their adoption, excessive delegation of authority to an individual commissioner, and failure to authenticate the measures in the other necessary languages on a timely basis. The Commission subsequently amended its rules in 1999 to make its delegation procedures more precise. For an earlier ruling by the Court of Justice on these issues, see BASF AG v. Commission (PVC cases), Case C–137/92P, [1994] ECR I–2555.

Among the most notable procedural cases in the competition law field are National Panasonic (UK) Ltd. v. Commission, Case 136/79, [1980] ECR 2033, and Hoechst AG v. Commission, Case 46/87 & 227/88, [1989] ECR 2859 (both concerning companies' privacy and related rights in Commission investigations), and AM & S Europe Ltd. v. Commission, Case 155/79, [1982] ECR 1575, and Orkem SA v. Commission, Case 74/87, [1989] ECR 3283 (on privileges in competition law enforcement).

In *National Panasonic*, the company contested the Commission's failure to give advance notice of an on-site search and seizure of company files (or an opportunity to be heard before the decision to conduct such a search and seizure was taken). While conceding that fundamental rights limit the Commission's procedural freedom, the Court did not consider surprise raids disproportionate to the Commission's aim to determine whether a competition law infringement had occurred or otherwise violative of the right to privacy under Article 8 of the European Human Rights Convention. In *Hoechst*, the Court further clarified the Commission's right of investigation by holding that, subject to compliance with the requirements of Regulation 17, and absent manifest unconstitutionality, the Commission could conduct a search, seek documents without specifically identifying them, enlist the assistance of national law enforcement officers in accordance with national law, and fine a company for refusing to submit to the investigation.

In *AM & S*, the company refused to tender certain documents to the Commission on account of attorney-client privilege, though it agreed to disclose enough of the documents to satisfy the inspectors that they were indeed privileged. The Commission demanded the documents in full so as to be able to determine itself the applicability of the privilege. The Court found that all Member States accord an attorney-client privilege, though of differing scope. It accordingly concluded that the Commission had to respect the confidentiality of written communications between lawyer and client, where the communications were made in the interest of the client's defense and where the lawyer enjoyed independence from the client. The Court further held that a firm does not need to reveal the contents of the communications in question in order to assert their confidentiality; it need only provide material sufficient to demonstrate the applicability of the privilege. If the Commission is not persuaded, and continues to contest the applicability of the privilege, it may order production and fine subsequent non-production, though the issue of the validity of such an order and fine could presumably be brought before the Community courts for an independent determination. As to the case at hand, the Court concluded that most of the documents in question met the conditions for application of the attorney-client privilege.

Faced with a claim of privilege against self-incrimination in *Orkem*, the Court could not find such a privilege in the constitutional traditions of the

Member States, as it had with the attorney-client privilege. (The States generally limited the privilege to natural persons charged with committing a criminal offense.) Moreover, the Court could not find any broader privilege under either the European Human Rights Convention or the 1966 International Covenant on Civil and Political Rights. The Court nevertheless found the right against self-incrimination to be necessary to safeguard the "rights of the defence" fundamental to the Community legal order (para. 32). Thus, "the Commission may not compel an undertaking to provide it with answers which might involve an admission on its part of the existence of an infringement which it is incumbent on the Commission to prove" (para. 35). In the event, the Court found that some of the Commission's informational demands were subject to the privilege and others were not. (For a recent application by the Court of First Instance of the *Orkem* rule, see Mannesmannrohren–Werke AG v. Commission, Case T–112/98, [2001] ECR II–729.)

Future competition law cases may be expected to raise still other aspects of the right to be heard and procedural due process more generally.

Notes and Questions

1.   In Imperial Chemical Industries plc v. Commission, Case T–36/91, [1995] ECR II–1847, ICI (a major producer of synthetic soda ash, used in the manufacture of glass) challenged the Commission's decision to impose a 7 million ECU fine on ICI for illegally partitioning the market with Solvay, the other main Community producer, in violation of Article 81 (ex 85) of the EC Treaty. ICI objected to the Commission's refusal, on grounds of business confidentiality, to disclose documents that ICI maintained would have aided its defense. Focusing its attention on whether "the non-disclosure of the documents in question might have influenced the course of the procedure and the content of the decision to the applicant's detriment," the Court went very deeply into the charges against ICI, the tenor of the other available evidence, the applicable competition law rules (and related burdens of proof), the extent to which the documents withheld were genuinely confidential or could have been sanitized, and of course the extent to which they were capable of substantiating significant elements of a defense.

2.   In many situations, the Court of Justice applies a kind of "harmless error" rule, to the effect that a procedural irregularity will only cause a measure to be set aside if, but for the defect, the outcome would (or would likely) have been different. The complainant may bear the burden of establishing that the error was harmful. Distillers Company Ltd. v. Commission, Case 30/78, [1980] ECR 2229.

In the *ICI* case, *supra* note 1, the Commission maintained that, even if the procedural errors had been avoided, the outcome would have been the same. The Court, however, was reluctant to exclude the possibility of the procedural error being outcome-determinative:

[108]   [A]ny infringement of the rights of the defence which occurred during the administrative procedure cannot be regularized during the proceedings before the Court of First Instance, which carries out a review solely in relation to the pleas raised and which cannot therefore be a substitute for a thorough investigation of the case in the course of the administrative procedure. If during the administrative procedure the applicant had been able to rely on documents which might exculpate it, it might have been able to influence the assessment of the college of Commissioners, at least with regard to the conclusiveness of the evidence of its alleged passive and parallel conduct as

regards the beginning and therefore the duration of the infringement. The Court cannot therefore rule out the possibility that the Commission would have found the infringement to be shorter and less serious and would, consequently, have fixed the fine at a lower amount.

However, in a closely related case (in which ICI challenged the Commission's decision to fine it 10 million ECU for abuse of a dominant position under Article 82 (ex 86)), ICI failed to convince the Court that the Commission's refusal to disclose certain documents had "hindered [it] in exercising its rights of defence." Imperial Chemical Industries plc v. Commission, Case T–37/91, [1995] ECR II–1901, appeal denied, Case C–200/92P, [1999] ECR I–4399.

3. INFRINGEMENT OF THE TREATY OR ANY RULE OF LAW RE-LATING TO ITS APPLICATION

While the first two grounds for judicial review set out in Article 230 (ex 173) cover most defects of a jurisdictional or procedural kind, the third ground for review—"infringement of [the] Treaty or of any rule of law relating to its application"—commonly covers claims of a substantive character. Most such claims assert that a Community act violates a Treaty article, a provision of secondary legislation or an international agreement entered into by the Community. A smaller number of cases—and they are among the most interesting—involve claims that a Community act violates some "general principle of law" or some basic right recognized by the Court's own case law.

In urging that the Council or Commission has acted in violation of law, a claimant typically means to say that the institution failed to satisfy the substantive conditions set out in the Treaty or legislative provisions governing such action. For the Court to determine whether the applicable legal conditions for action are met may be a simple matter of verification. If, however, it is not (as is often the case with the application of legal norms to social, economic or political factors), the Court will have to decide how closely to review the Council's or Commission's exercise of discretion. Specifically, when should the Court substitute its independent judgment for that of the Council or Commission in taking the action in question? When instead should the Court show deference to the judgment that the Council or Commission has brought to the matter, and how should such deference be expressed? Article 33 of the ECSC Treaty had sought to address these questions as follows:

> The Court may not ... examine the evaluation of the situation, resulting from economic facts or circumstances, in the light of which the High Authority took its decisions or made its recommendations, save where the High Authority is alleged to have misused its powers or to have manifestly failed to observe the provisions of this Treaty or any rule of law relating to its application.

This provision appears to embody a distinction between more or less purely factual questions of an economic or other nature, on which the Court of Justice owes no particular deference to Community decisionmakers, and questions entailing the characterization or evaluation of those facts, on which deference may be due. The distinction between mistakes in the "material existence" of the facts, on the one hand, and in their "legal characterization," on the other, is recognized in French and other European systems of administrative law, and has roughly the same significance. See G. Bermann, The Scope of Judicial Review in French Administrative Law, 16 Colum. J. Transnat'l L. 195 (1977). For an interesting discussion of whether US law recognizes the distinction, see Hospital Corporation of America v. Federal Trade Commission, 807 F.2d 1381 (7th Cir.1986), cert. denied, 481 U.S. 1038, 107 S.Ct. 1975, 95 L.Ed.2d 815 (1987).

Although the EC Treaty contains no analogous provision, the Court's attitude toward the standard of judicial review under that treaty seems to be much the same. The Court frequently remarks that the Commission enjoys a wide discretion in evaluating complex economic situations and that its exercise of discretion should not be set aside unless clearly erroneous or otherwise manifestly abusive. See SMW Winzersekt GmbH v. Land Rheinland–Pfalz, Case C–306/93, [1994] ECR I–5555; EEC Seed Crushers' and Oil Processors' Federation (FEDIOL) v. Commission, Case 187/85, [1988] ECR 4155; Philip Morris Holland v. Commission, Case 730/79, [1980] ECR 2671.

Thus far the approach taken by the Court of Justice as a reviewing court is not especially remarkable. However, the Court also has developed some more far-reaching doctrines that allow it greater scope in securing the rule of law within the Community. These doctrines include a number of unwritten "general principles of law" of sweeping application, mostly derived from norms of continental administrative law.

a. The Principle of Proportionality

INTERNATIONALE HANDELSGESELLSCHAFT MBH v. EINFUHR- UND VORRATSSTELLE FÜR GETREIDE UND FUTTERMITTEL

Case 11/70, [1970] ECR 1125.

[A 1967 Council regulation made the grant of export licenses for certain agricultural products conditional on the prior payment of a deposit which was to be forfeited if the export was not made. A German exporter challenged enforcement of the regulation on the ground that it violated the principle of "proportionality" (*Verhältnismässigkeit*) recognized in German public law. (According to that principle, a governmental measure must be reasonably related, and not "out of proportion," to the public good sought to be achieved.) The German administrative court referred the matter of the regulation's proportionality to the Court of Justice.]

[2]   ... According to the evaluation of the [administrative court], the system of deposits is contrary to certain structural principles of national constitutional law which must be protected within the framework of Community law, with the result that the primacy of supranational law must yield before the principles of the German [Constitution, or Basic Law]. More particularly, the system of deposits runs counter to the principles of freedom of action and of disposition, of economic liberty and of proportionality arising in particular from Articles 2(1) and 14 of the Basic Law. The obligation to import or export resulting from the issue of the licences, together with the deposit attaching thereto, constitutes an excessive intervention in the freedom of disposition in trade, as the objective of the regulations could have been attained by methods of intervention having less serious consequences.

The Protection of Fundamental Rights in the Community Legal System

3   Recourse to the legal rules or concepts of national law in order to judge the validity of measures adopted by the institutions of the Community would have an adverse effect on the uniformity and efficacy of Community law. The validity of such measures can only be judged in the light of Community law. In fact, the law stemming from the Treaty, an independent source of law, cannot because of its very nature be overridden by rules of national law, however framed, without being deprived of its character as Community law and without the legal basis of the Community itself being called in question. Therefore the validity of a Community measure or its effect within a Member State cannot be affected by allegations that it runs counter to either fundamental rights as formulated by the constitution of that State or the principles of a national constitutional structure.

4   However, an examination should be made as to whether or not any analogous guarantee inherent in Community law has been disregarded. In fact, respect for fundamental rights forms an integral part of the general principles of law protected by the Court of Justice. The protection of such rights, whilst inspired by the constitutional traditions common to the Member States, must be ensured within the framework of the structure and objectives of the Community. It must therefore be ascertained, in the light of the doubts expressed by the [administrative court], whether the system of deposits has infringed rights of a fundamental nature, respect for which must be ensured in the Community legal system.

* * *

6   According to the ... preamble to [the challenged regulation], "the competent authorities must be in a position constantly to follow trade movements in order to assess market trends and to apply the measures ... as necessary" and "to that end, provision should be made for the issue of import and export licenses accompanied by the lodging of a deposit guaranteeing that the transactions for which such licences are requested are effected". It follows from these considerations and from the general scheme of the regulation that the system of deposits is intended to guarantee that the imports and exports for which the licences are requested are actually effected in order to ensure both for the Community and for the Member States precise knowledge of the intended transactions.

7   This knowledge, together with other available information on the state of the market, is essential to enable the competent authorities to make judicious use of the instruments of intervention, both ordinary and exceptional, which are at their disposal for guaranteeing the functioning of the system of prices instituted by the regulation, such as purchasing, storing and distributing, fixing denaturing premiums and export refunds, applying protective measures and choosing measures intended to avoid deflections of trade. This is all the more imperative in that the implementation of the common agricultural policy involves heavy financial responsibilities for the Community and the Member States.

8   It is necessary, therefore, for the competent authorities to have available not only statistical information on the state of the market but also precise

forecasts on future imports and exports. Since the Member States are obliged by [the challenged regulation] to issue import and export licences to any applicant, a forecast would lose all significance if the licences did not involve the recipients in an undertaking to act on them. And the undertaking would be ineffectual if observance of it were not ensured by appropriate means.

9   The choice for that purpose by the Community legislature of the deposit cannot be criticized in view of the fact that that machinery is adapted to the voluntary nature of requests for licences and that it has the dual advantage over other possible systems of simplicity and efficacy.

10   A system of mere declaration of exports effected and of unused licences, as proposed by the plaintiff in the main action, would, by reason of its retrospective nature and lack of any guarantee of application, be incapable of providing the competent authorities with sure data on trends in the movement of goods.

11   Likewise, a system of fines imposed *a posteriori* would involve considerable administrative and legal complications at the stage of decision and of execution, aggravated by the fact that the traders concerned may be beyond the reach of the intervention agencies by reason of their residence in another Member State, since the regulation imposes on Member States the obligation to issue the licences to any applicant "irrespective of the place of his establishment in the Community."

12   It therefore appears that the requirement of import and export licences involving for the licensees an undertaking to effect the proposed transactions under the guarantee of a deposit constitutes a method which is both necessary and appropriate to enable the competent authorities to determine in the most effective manner their interventions on the market in cereals.

13   The principle of the system of deposits cannot therefore be disputed.

14   However, examination should be made as to whether or not certain detailed rules of the system of deposits might be contested [as imposing [a] burden [that] is excessive for trade, to the extent of violating fundamental rights.

15   In order to assess the real burden of the deposit on trade, account should be taken not so much of the amount of the deposit which is repayable— namely 0.5 unit of account per 1000 kg—as of the costs and charges involved in lodging it. . . .

16   The costs involved in the deposit do not constitute an amount disproportionate to the total value of the goods in question and of the other trading costs. It appears therefore that the burdens resulting from the system of deposits are not excessive and are the normal consequence of a system of organization of the markets conceived to meet the requirements of the general interest. . . .

17   The plaintiff in the main action also points out that forfeiture of the deposit in the event of the undertaking to import or export not being fulfilled really constitutes a fine or a penalty which the Treaty has not authorized the Council and the Commission to institute.

[18] This argument is based on a false analysis of the system of deposits which cannot be equated with a penal sanction, since it is merely the guarantee that an undertaking voluntarily assumed will be carried out.

* * *

[20] It follows from all these considerations that the system of licenses ... does not violate any right of a fundamental nature. The machinery of deposits constitutes an appropriate method for carrying out the common organization of the agricultural markets. ...

[The German court's second question was whether the regulation's exemption from forfeiture for cases of *force majeure* was too narrow because it did not excuse certain commercially justifiable failures to export. The Court determined that *force majeure* should not be limited to situations of absolute impossibility but understood more flexibly to cover "unusual circumstances, outside the control of the importer or exporter, the consequences of which, in spite of the exercise of all due care, could not have been avoided except at the cost of excessive sacrifice." The Court found that, so construed, the *force majeure* exception was appropriately defined for ensuring the proper functioning of the cereal market organization.]

Notes and Questions

1. Does the Court reach a desirable result? Why should an exporter be expected to export what it is no longer sound to export? Does inducing the exporter to do so help "assess market trends" (¶ 6)? On the other hand, what fundamental right of the exporter is at stake? Is there a fundamental right to freedom of trade, or to freedom from restrictions on trade that are not justified by the public good? Are you satisfied with the Court's reasoning?

The Court has on several occasions held "that there is no such thing as a general principle of objective unfairness under Community law [or any] legal basis ... for exemption [from Community law obligations] on grounds of natural justice." Nor is there a general principle "that a Community provision ... may not be applied by a national authority if it causes the person concerned hardship which the Community legislature would clearly have sought to avoid if it had envisaged [it]." Hoche v. Bundesanstalt für landwirtschaftliche Marktordnung, Case C–174/89, [1990] ECR I–2681, 2711. Does this still leave room for an inquiry into the proportionality of Community measures?

2. Did the Court adequately explain why the forfeiture regulation should not be examined under fundamental German constitutional principles? Although it upheld the regulation's validity, the Court was eager to demonstrate its willingness to subject Community legislation to "constitutional" review. However, the ruling did not prevent the German Constitutional Court from later conducting a similar review of the regulation under German constitutional law principles. For the result of that inquiry, see the German court's own *Internationale Handelsgesellschaft* ruling, *infra* page 298.

3. On what authority does the Court of Justice invoke and apply general principles of law? It has been suggested that warrant may be found in Articles 220 (ex 164), 230 (ex 173) and 288(2) (ex 215(2)) of the EC Treaty. Do you agree? Does the Court indicate the source of the particular principle relied on here? Does the proportionality principle have a counterpart in US constitutional or administrative law?

4. A proportionality claim succeeded in the later case of Buitoni v. Fonds d'orientation et de régularisation des marchés agricoles, Case 122/78, [1979] ECR 677. When Buitoni sought to recover from the French authorities the security it had deposited upon applying for a license to import tomato concentrate, it learned that while the imports were timely, its application to recover the security was not. A Commission regulation required the importer, within six months following expiry of the license, to submit proof to the authorities that all import formalities had been completed. Because it failed to apply in time, Buitoni was denied its security and it brought suit in French court. On preliminary reference, the Court of Justice held the forfeiture penalty to be "excessively severe in relation to the objectives of administrative efficiency." It objected to the fact that the failure to apply promptly for the refund was essentially punished as heavily as the failure to import, and ruled that only a "considerably less onerous" penalty than forfeiture of the whole security would be commensurate with the administrative inconvenience caused. Do you agree? What would be a "proportionate" penalty?

For recent decisions invalidating an EC regulation and an EC decision, respectively, on proportionality grounds, see Molkereignossenschaft Wiedergeltingen eG v. Hauptzollamt Lindau, Case C–356/97, [2000] ECR I–5461, and Ampafrance SA v. Directeur des Services Fiscaux de Maine–et–Loire, Joined Cases C–177, 181/99, [2000] ECR I–7013.

5. In Germany v. Council (Bananas), Case C–280/93, [1994] ECR I–4973, the Court sustained a 1993 Council regulation on the common organization of the banana market in the face of an unusually comprehensive attack (claiming violation, among other things, of the principle of non-discrimination, the rights of property and freedom of trade, the protection of vested interests, the principle of proportionality, the Lomé Convention and the GATT rules). On the proportionality claim, the Court stressed that its review had to be "limited" because the Council has "a broad discretion" and must "reconcile divergent interests and thus select options within the context of the policy choices which are its own responsibility." It then added (para. 94):

> While other means for achieving the desired result were indeed conceivable, the Court cannot substitute its assessment for that of the Council as to the appropriateness or otherwise of the measures adopted by the Community legislature if those measures have not been proved to be manifestly inappropriate for achieving the objective pursued.

For a fuller treatment of the *Bananas* case and sequels, see page 318 *infra*.

UNITED KINGDOM v. COUNCIL

(Working time directive)
Case C–84/94, [1996] ECR I–5755.

[For the facts of the case, see page 92 *supra*. As noted there, the Court first disposed of the UK's arguments based on the correctness of the directive's legal basis, while briefly taking into account the principle of subsidiarity. The Court then turned to the principle of proportionality and, in that connection, once again to the principle of subsidiarity.]

The plea of breach of the principle of proportionality

50   The applicant points out that the Council may adopt on the basis of Article 118a [now 137] of the Treaty only "minimum requirements for gradual implementation, having regard to the conditions and technical rules ob-

taining in each of the Member States", and that those requirements must avoid "imposing administrative, financial and legal constraints in a way which would hold back the creation and development of small and medium-sized undertakings". In its submission, four broad principles are relevant in assessing whether or not the requirements imposed by the contested directive are minimum requirements within the meaning of Article 118a.

51   First, it argues, not all measures which may "improve" the level of health and safety protection of workers constitute minimum requirements. In particular, those consisting in global reductions in working time or global increases in rest periods, whilst having a certain beneficial effect on the health or safety or workers, do not constitute "minimum requirements" within the meaning of Article 118a.

52   Second, a provision cannot be regarded as a "minimum requirement" if the level of health and safety protection of workers which it establishes can be attained by measures that are less restrictive and involve fewer obstacles to the competitiveness of industry and the earning capacity of individuals. In the applicant's submission, neither the Commission's proposals nor the directive provide any explanation as to why the desired level of protection could not have been achieved by less restrictive measures, such as, for example, the use of risk assessments if working hours exceeded particular norms.

53   Third, the conclusion that the measures envisaged will in fact improve the level of health or safety protection of workers must be based on reasonable grounds. In its view, the present state of scientific research in the area concerned falls far short of justifying the contested measures.

54   Fourth, a measure will be proportionate only if it is consistent with the principle of subsidiarity. The applicant argues that it is for the Community institutions to demonstrate that the aims of the directive could better be achieved at Community level than by action on the part of the Member States. There has been no such demonstration in this case.

[The Court rejected the subsidiarity argument straightaway, referring to its conclusions in paragraph 47 of this judgment (see page 124 *supra*). The Court also rejected the notion that the reference to "minimum requirements" under Article 118a means that the Community is limited to "the lowest common denominator" of protection among the Member States. Rather, "minimum requirements" simply means that Member States may establish a higher level of protection than that prescribed by Community law.]

57   As regards the principle of proportionality, the Court has held that, in order to establish whether a provision of Community law complies with that principle, it must be ascertained whether the means which it employs are suitable for the purpose of achieving the desired objective and whether they do not go beyond what is necessary to achieve it.

58   As to judicial review of those conditions, however, the Council must be allowed a wide discretion in an area which, as here, involves the legislature in making social policy choices and requires it to carry out complex assessments. Judicial review of the exercise of that discretion must therefore be limited to examining whether it has been vitiated by manifest error

or misuse of powers, or whether the institution concerned has manifestly exceeded the limits of its discretion.

59   So far as concerns the first condition, it is sufficient that ... the measures on the organization of working time [with the exception of the designation of Sunday as the mandatory weekly day of rest, *supra* page 94], contribute directly to the improvement of health and safety protection for workers within the meaning of Article 118a, and cannot therefore be regarded as unsuited to the purpose of achieving the objective pursued.

60   The second condition is also fulfilled. Contrary to the view taken by the applicant, the Council did not commit any manifest error in concluding that the contested measures were necessary to achieve the objective of protecting the health and safety of workers.

61   In the first place, Article 4, which concerns the mandatory rest break, applies only if the working day is longer than six hours. Moreover, the relevant details, particularly the duration of the break and the terms on which it is granted, are to be laid down in collective agreements or agreements between the two sides of industry or, failing that, by national legislation. Finally, that provision may be the subject of several derogations, relating either to the status of the worker (Article 17(1)) or to the nature or characteristics of the activity pursued (Article 17(2), points 2.1 and 2.2), to be implemented by means of collective agreements or agreements concluded between the two sides of industry at national or regional level (Article 17(3)).

62   Second, the minimum uninterrupted weekly rest period of twenty-four hours provided for by the first sentence of Article 5, plus the eleven hours' daily rest referred to in Article 3, may be the subject of the same derogations as those authorized in relation to Article 4, referred to above. Further derogations relate to shift work activities and activities involving periods of work split up over the day (Article 17(2), point 2.3). In addition, the reference period of seven days may be extended to fourteen days (Article 16(1)).

63   Third, as regards Article 6(2), which provides that the average working time for each seven-day period is not to exceed forty-eight hours, Member States may lay down a reference period not exceeding four months (Article 16(2)), which may in certain cases be extended to six months for the application of Article 17(2), points 2.1 and 2.2, and 17(3) (Article 17(4), first sentence), or even to twelve months (Article 17(4), second sentence). Article 18(1)(b)(i) even authorizes Member States, under certain conditions, not to apply Article 6.

64   Fourth, in relation to Article 7 concerning paid annual leave of four weeks, Article 18(1)(b)(ii) authorizes Member States to allow a transitional period of three years, during which workers must be entitled to three weeks' paid annual leave.

65   Finally, as to the applicant's argument that adoption of the contested directive was unnecessary since [an existing directive] already applies to the areas covered by the contested directive, it is sufficient to note that [that directive] merely lays down, in order to encourage improvements in the health and safety of workers at work, general principles, as well as

general guidelines for their implementation, concerning the prevention of occupational risks, the protection of health and safety, the elimination of risk and accident factors, and the provision of information to, consultation, participation and training of workers and their representatives. It is not therefore apt to achieve the objective of harmonizing minimum rest periods, rest breaks and a maximum limit to weekly working time, which form the subject-matter of the contested directive.

[66] It follows that, in taking the view that the objective of harmonizing national legislation on the health and safety of workers, while maintaining the improvements made, could not be achieved by measures less restrictive than those that are the subject-matter of the directive, the Council did not commit any manifest error.

[67] In the light of all the foregoing considerations, the plea of breach of the principle of proportionality must also be rejected.

Notes and Questions

1. Do you find the Court's proportionality analysis convincing? The Court's *Working time directive* ruling—coming on the heels of the "mad cow disease" imbroglio (see Chapter 1 *supra*)—created a major stir in the UK. Prime Minister Major denounced the ruling as, among other things, an attempt to restrain Britain's free-market economy, and threatened renewed "non-cooperation" in the Council unless the UK were exempted from it. (The UK clearly could not be exempted from the ruling as such, though it could of course seek, by legislative amendment, to be exempted from the directive.)

The Blair government, elected in 1997, soon after the judgment, strongly endorsed the working time directive.

2. Issues of proportionality and subsidiarity likewise arose in Germany's challenge to the General Product Safety Directive, discussed in note 3 on page 96 *supra*. Regarding proportionality, Germany argued that "the adoption of a decision at Community level is no guarantee that the measures taken will be the most suitable." It also argued that the Commission could adequately attain its objectives by pursuing infringement proceedings against a Member State under Article 226 (ex 169) for its failure adequately to protect public health. The Court had this to say:

[47] In the first place, no obligation can be placed on Member States by means of the infringement procedure to take a specified measure from among those listed in . . . the directive.

[48] Secondly, . . . even if Member States are required to adopt certain specified measures under the directive, the Commission would be obliged to bring proceedings for failure to fulfil its obligations against every Member State that had not adopted such measures, inevitably rendering the procedure more cumbersome.

[49] Lastly, even if such proceedings were initiated and held by the Court to be well founded, it is not certain that a declaration by the Court to that effect would enable the objectives set out in the directive to be achieved as effectively as would be the case by a Community harmonization measure.

[50] In particular, the infringement procedure would not enable consumer protection to be secured in the shortest possible time. . . . Furthermore, a declaration that a Member State has failed to fulfil its obligations would, in the circum-

stances envisaged, presuppose a cautious appraisal, scarcely compatible with urgency of the need to adopt a particular measure....

Germany v. Council (General product safety), Case C–359/92, [1994] ECR I–3681.

3.   In Queen v. Secretary of State for the Environment, ex parte Standley, Case C–293/97, [1999] ECR I–2603, UK farmers complained in the High Court that by fixing a ceiling of 50 mg per liter on nitrate concentrations in waters found to be "nitrate vulnerable," Council Directive 91/676 on water pollution by nitrates from agricultural sources offended the principle of proportionality, the right of property, and the "rectification at source" and "polluter pays" principles set out in EC Treaty Article 174(2) (ex 130r(2)). The farmers essentially argued that while agricultural producers were not solely responsible for the nitrate concentration in those waters, they were nevertheless being made solely responsible for ensuring that the nitrate ceiling was not exceeded. On preliminary reference, the Court of Justice found that the directive was sufficiently flexible so as to allow Member States to take account of other sources of pollution when implementing its provisions and to avoid imposing disproportionate costs on farmers or any other single pollution source. In conclusion, "[w]hile ... the Member States are bound by the principle of proportionality [and the principles invoked] when [giving effect to the directive], the Directive does not ... offend against that principle."

Is the Court in effect shifting the burden of ensuring respect for the principle of proportionality under Community law from the Community institutions that enacted that law to the national legislatures, administrations and courts that are compelled to implement it?

b.   The Principles of Equal Treatment and Non–Discrimination

BELA-MUHLE JOSEF BERGMANN KG v. GROWS–FARM GMBH

(Skimmed-milk powder)
Case 114/76, [1977] ECR 1211.

[In an effort to reduce the accumulated surplus of skimmed-milk powder in the Community, the Council adopted Regulation 563/76 requiring animal feed producers to use skimmed-milk powder (held in stock by the Member State intervention agencies) as the protein ingredient in their product. A purchaser of feed refused to pay its supplier for the resulting increase in the price of raw materials (as required by their contract) on the ground that Regulation 563/76, which had occasioned the increase, was invalid. It maintained that the regulation required use of a form of protein several times more expensive than the protein element that producers customarily used (soya), and was therefore unreasonably burdensome. The case reached the Court of Justice on preliminary reference from the German civil court hearing the main contract action.]

[5]   The validity of these arrangements has been contested on grounds of conflict in particular with the objectives of the common agricultural policy as defined in Article 39 [now 33] of the Treaty, the prohibition of discrimination laid down in the second subparagraph of Article 40(3) [now 34(2)] and the principle of proportionality between the means employed

and the end in view. Because of the close connection between these grounds of complaint, it will be appropriate to consider them together.

[6] Under Article 39, the objectives of the common agricultural policy are to be the rational development of agricultural production, the assurance of a fair standard of living for the whole of the agricultural community, the stabilization of markets and the availability of supplies to consumers at reasonable prices. ... Furthermore, [Article 40(3)] lays down that the common organization of the markets "shall exclude any discrimination between producers or consumers within the Community." Thus the statement of the objectives contained in Article 39, taken together with the rules in the second subparagraph of Article 40(3), supplies both positive and negative criteria by which the legality of the measures adopted in this matter may be appraised.

[7] The arrangements made by Regulation (EEC) No. 563/76 constituted a temporary measure intended to counteract the consequences of a chronic imbalance in the common organization of the market in milk and milk products. A feature of these arrangements was the imposition not only on producers of milk and milk products but also, and more especially, on producers in other agricultural sectors of a financial burden which took the form, first, of the compulsory purchase of certain quantities of an animal feed product and, secondly, of the fixing of a purchase price for that product at a level three times higher than that of the substances which it replaced. The obligation to purchase at such a disproportionate price constituted a discriminatory distribution of the burden of costs between the various agricultural sectors. Nor, moreover, was such an obligation necessary in order to attain the objective in view, namely, the disposal of stocks of skimmed-milk powder. It could not therefore be justified for the purposes of attaining the objectives of the common agricultural policy.

[8] In consequence, the answer must be that Council Regulation No. 563/76 is null and void.

Notes and Questions

1. As the first occasion on which the Court invalidated a significant agricultural regulation, the *Skimmed-milk powder* case generated some controversy. Note that the Court relied substantially on the prohibition in Article 34 [ex 40] against discrimination in agricultural policy. What made the discrimination between dairy farmers, on the one hand, and animal feed producers (or rather the chicken and hog farmers required to bear the higher animal feed costs), on the other, an unjustified one? Did the regulation also impermissibly discriminate against soy bean producers?

2. The judgment also invokes the principle of proportionality. To the extent that it relies on that principle, does the Court find that the regulation (a) fails to pursue a legitimate agricultural policy objective, (b) is not a rational means of achieving a legitimate objective, (c) does not serve a compelling public interest, (d) is a manifestly less advantageous (or more drastic) means of achieving its objective than others that were available, or (e) entails costs outweighing (or greatly outweighing) the regulation's benefits?

3. For an interesting equality case, see Kik v. Office for Harmonisation in the Internal Market (OHIM), Case T–120/99, [2001] ECR II-___ (July 12, 2001), where the Court of First Instance examined the requirement that would-be registrants of a Community trademark indicate a "second language" for possible use in certain "opposition" or "invalidity" proceedings (depending on the languages of opposing parties), and that that language necessarily be either English, French, German, Italian or Spanish. (The applicant had deliberately listed Dutch as both the "first" and "second" language. She claimed that having to use a foreign language in the applications that she, as a Dutch trademark lawyer, filed created competitive disadvantages for her, such as the need to retain translators). The Court found the limitation to be an appropriate and defensible one in light of the purpose of the requirement of designating a second language.

4. The principle of equal treatment binds not only the Community institutions, but also the Member States, insofar as discrimination based on nationality is concerned. Article 12 (formerly 6) of the EC Treaty speaks categorically to the issue: "Within the scope of application of this Treaty ... any discrimination on grounds of nationality shall be prohibited." The Court of Justice understandably takes a very dim view of any form of discrimination in Member State law against nationals of other Member States, and its enforcement of Article 12 is correspondingly strict.

Article 12, however, applies only to nationality-based discrimination "[w]ithin the scope of application of [the EC] Treaty." Whether this "scope of Treaty application" requirement is met will not always be clear. Consider the case of Mund & Fester, Case C–398/92, [1994] ECR I–467. The issue there was whether a German court, in an action by a German company against a Dutch company, properly ordered the preliminary attachment of property belonging to the defendant in Germany under Section 917 of the German Civil Procedure Code, which allows attachment when enforcement of a judgment would otherwise be made "impossible or substantially more difficult," and which specifically declares that the fact that a judgment will be enforced abroad constitutes sufficient grounds for an attachment.

The German court wondered whether it would violate Article 12 (ex 6) of the EC Treaty to treat the prospective enforcement of a judgment in the Netherlands as *per se* justification for an attachment, while authorizing attachment in the case of a judgment to be enforced in Germany only upon a showing that enforcement would otherwise be "impossible or substantially more difficult."

The Court of Justice first considered whether the alleged discrimination in question arose within the EC Treaty's scope of application. The Court concluded that it did. In the first place, it found that, since the Brussels Convention on recognition and enforcement of Member State judgments was specifically contemplated by Article 293 (ex 220) of the EC Treaty (see page 33 *supra*) as an aid to the workings of the common market, that Convention was sufficiently linked to the EC Treaty. Only then did the Court decide whether the German provision, as applied to the prospective enforcement of a German judgment in the Netherlands, entailed a nationality-based discrimination. The Court concluded that it did, for the reason that "the great majority of enforcements abroad [are] against persons who are not of German nationality or against legal persons not established in the Federal Republic of Germany." This fact rendered the German provision discriminatory, if only "covert[ly]" so.

Finally, the Court inquired whether, though discriminatory, the German provision could nevertheless "be justified by objective circumstances." It found—

precisely because of the guarantees offered by the Brussels Convention on Recognition and Enforcement of Judgments—that it could not be justified. Suppose there were no Brussels Convention. Could the discrimination in question still be said to arise within the EC Treaty's scope of application? Could it still be considered as not justified by "objective circumstances"?

c. Legal Certainty, Non-retroactivity and Legitimate Expectations

A general principle of law that has found fertile ground in the Community sphere is that of "legal certainty," derived from general principles of French and German public law, *sécurité juridique* and *Rechtssicherheit,* respectively. This principle posits, within limits of course, that the political institutions may not act unilaterally to disturb settled legal relationships.

The principle of "non-retroactivity" is an important manifestation of the notion of legal certainty. The Court has ruled that the Community institutions may not in principle apply regulations retroactively, if doing so would cause private parties serious economic loss that they cannot avoid by adjusting their conduct. A proper analysis of non-retroactivity cases, however, may be more difficult than at first appears.

Take the case of Amylum v. Council, Case 108/81, [1982] ECR 3107, for example. That case grew out of tensions between isoglucose and sugar producers. In 1979, the Council adopted a regulation imposing a system of temporary production quotas and levies to promote economic equality between producers of isoglucose and sugar. It was that regulation that the Court of Justice later annulled in the *Roquette Frères* case (*supra* page 84), due to the Council's failure to consult the European Parliament. By the time *Roquette Frères* was decided, however, the Council had extended the production quota and levy system for an additional year, and several isoglucose producers (including Roquette Frères) immediately challenged the extension on the same grounds. Before judgment could be had, the Council (this time taking care fully to consult the Parliament) adopted regulations reinstating the system for the first year with retroactive effect and extending the system the additional year. Amylum, another isoglucose producer, sued to have the regulation annulled on account of its retroactivity.

The Court upheld the regulation because it merely replicated the system in force prior to the *Roquette Frères* ruling and because reinstatement of the system with retroactive effect following that ruling was not unforeseeable. It noted that the isoglucose producers were "reasonably well aware of the interdependence of the markets in ... sugar and isoglucose [and] of the situation of the Community market in sweeteners," and could not reasonably expect to remain exempt from the kind of constraints under which sugar producers operated. [1982] ECR at 3123–33. It also thought the Council's previous decision to extend the system for another year had been an early and clear indication of its intentions. The Court may well have believed that under the circumstances the Council action was more supportive of legal certainty than harmful to it.

The regulation in *Amylum* expressly stated that it was to apply retroactively. In other cases, the temporal effect of a measure is not specified. When that is the case, the retroactivity or non-retroactivity of a measure becomes a matter of interpretation. Based on considerations of legal certainty and reliance, Community regulations are commonly interpreted "as applying to situations existing before their entry into force only in so far as [that] clearly follows from their terms, objectives or general scheme." Openbaar Ministerie v. Bout, Case 21/81, [1982] ECR 381, 390.

Another aspect of the principle of legal certainty is the protection of legitimate expectations (*Vertrauensschutz* or *la protection de la confiance légitime,* as it is known in German and French law, respectively). The idea is to protect a private party's reliance on current Community rules when that party could reasonably have expected those rules to remain in force. The very nature of the Council's and Commission's regulatory tasks suggests that traders will commonly claim loss due to unexpected changes in Community rules.

The Court's protection of legitimate expectations is well illustrated by the case of Mulder v. Minister van Landbouw en Visserij, Case 120/86, [1988] ECR 2321. In return for a non-marketing premium made available pursuant to a 1977 Council regulation, a Dutch farmer agreed not to market milk for five years (1979 to 1984). When he decided in 1984 to re-enter the dairy business, he applied for a milk production quota, but was denied any on the ground that such quotas were, according to a 1984 regulation, to be issued on the basis of 1983 production of which he had none. The Dutch court in which the farmer sued made a preliminary reference. The Court squarely addressed the question of the farmer's legitimate expectations:

[23] It must be conceded ... that a producer who has voluntarily ceased production for a certain period cannot legitimately expect to be able to resume production under the same conditions as those which previously applied and not to be subject to any rules of market or structural policy adopted in the meantime.

[24] The fact remains that where such a producer ... has been encouraged by a Community measure to suspend marketing for a limited period in the general interest and against payment of a premium he may legitimately expect not to be subject, upon the expiry of his undertaking, to restrictions which specifically affect him precisely because he availed himself of the possibilities offered by the Community provisions.

* * *

[26] [T]otal and continuous exclusion ... for the entire period of application of the regulations ..., preventing the producers concerned from resuming the marketing of milk at the end of the five-year period, was not an occurrence which those producers could have foreseen when they entered into an undertaking, for a limited time, not to deliver milk. ... Such an effect therefore frustrates those producers' legitimate expectations that the effects of the system to which they had rendered themselves subject would be limited.

* * *

[28] [T]he [1984 regulation] is invalid in so far as it does not provide for the allocation of a reference quantity for producers who, pursuant to an

undertaking entered into under [the 1977 regulation], did not deliver milk during the reference year. . . .

Note that the Court invalidated neither the 1977 nor the 1984 regulation, but merely held that the latter could not validly be applied by its terms under the circumstances of a case like this. Incidentally, how should the reference quantity for such a farmer be calculated?

Besides laying the basis for a suit to annul (and possibly for damages), the principle of protection of legitimate expectations may also operate as a rule of interpretation. Thus, when the French authorities and the Commission sought to interpret a tariff exemption narrowly, contrary to its normal reading, the Court disagreed:

> The principle of legal certainty requires that rules imposing charges on the taxpayer must be clear and precise so that he may know without ambiguity what are his rights and obligations and may take steps accordingly.

Administration des Douanes v. SA Gondrand Frères, Case 169/80, [1981] ECR 1931, 1942. See also Deuka v. Einfuhr-und Vorratsstelle für Getreide und Futtermittel, Case 78/74, [1975] ECR 421.

The principle of legitimate expectations protects only justifiable expectations and reasonable reliance, presumably measured by the objective standard of an ordinarily prudent person in the plaintiff's situation. However, these notions necessarily have a subjective component. In Einfuhr- und Vorratsstelle für Getreide und Futtermittel v. Mackprang, Case 2/75, [1975] ECR 607, a German grain dealer bought wheat in France at a time when the price had fallen sharply in anticipation of a devaluation of the franc. The dealer then sold the wheat at a very large profit to the German agency (the EVGF) that is obligated by law to "intervene" by buying grain at a fixed price whenever the grain's market price falls below a certain level. The quantities of wheat that the EVGF was thus compelled to buy were so great that the agency's storage facilities were exhausted. At this juncture, the Commission authorized the EVGF to refuse any further interventions for the purchase of non-German products, specifying that the ban could be applied even to wheat that had been made available to the agency prior to that time. The EVGF accordingly refused to buy large quantities of grain belonging to the dealer although the grain was already en route from France. The dealer sued the German agency, claiming that the principle of legitimate expectations obligated it to purchase the wheat. How should the case be decided?

For a particularly interesting judgment invalidating a Council regulation outside the agricultural field on the basis of the principle of legal certainty, see Opel Austria GmbH v. Council, Case T–115/94, [1997] ECR II–39, discussed at page 1041 *infra*.

NOTE ON THE RETROACTIVE EFFECT
OF COURT OF JUSTICE RULINGS

Discussion of legal certainty is a suitable context in which to consider the retroactive effect of the Court of Justice's own rulings on Community law. The Court's general view is that such rulings merely clarify what was always the proper interpretation of a rule of law, and thus date back to the coming into effect of the rule of the law in question. Amministrazione delle Finanze dello Stato v. Denkavit Italiana, Case 61/79, [1980] ECR 1205. In Procureur de la République v. Waterkeyn, Cases 314–16/81 & 83/82, [1982] ECR 4337, a French court inquired about the temporal effect of a recent Court of Justice judgment striking down aspects of French legislation on the advertising of alcohol as in violation of the free movement of goods principle in Article 28 (ex 30). Pending before the French court were several prosecutions for violation of the same French law. The Court of Justice reasoned that the invalidity of the French legislation flowed from Article 28 of the Treaty, and not from the Court's decision, and that the French courts could therefore not entertain prosecutions under the French law even if the conduct in question occurred prior to the Court's decision.

By the same general reasoning, the Court has required States to make back benefit payments available to claimants where the regulations on the basis of which such payments had been refused were invalidated by the Court, and to give refunds to parties who had made payments pursuant to regulations later declared invalid.

In exceptional circumstances, the Court has decided that its judgments should not have retroactive effect, invoking precisely the notion of legal certainty. The most famous example is Defrenne v. Société Anonyme Belge de Navigation Aérienne Sabena, Case 43/75, [1976] ECR 455. As we shall see (page 248 *infra*), the Court there discarded a widely-held assumption that the principle of equal pay for women in Article 141 (ex 119) was not legally effective until implemented by Member State legislation, and it therefore allowed discrimination victims to claim damages directly on the basis of Article 141, even if unimplemented. Fearing that claims for back pay dating to as early as 1962 (when Article 119 became effective for the original Member States) or 1973 (for the then new Member States) might be so substantial as to create a risk of bankruptcy for some employers, the Court held that while plaintiffs who by then had filed claims might recover under the *Defrenne* ruling, the ruling would not otherwise have retroactive effect:

> [I]t is appropriate to take exceptionally into account the fact that, over a prolonged period, the parties concerned have been led to continue with practices which were contrary to Article 119, although not yet prohibited under their national law.

* * *

> In these circumstances ... important considerations of legal certainty affecting all the interests involved, both public and private, make it impossible in principle to reopen the question as regards the past.

The Court concluded that, except for claims already then filed, "the direct effect of Article 119 cannot be relied on in order to support claims concerning pay periods prior to the date of this judgment." [1976] ECR at 480–81.

The Court again invoked the principle of non-retroactivity to deny claims for pension benefits earned prior to the Court's 1990 *Barber* ruling (Barber v. Guardian Royal Exchange Assurance Group, page ___ *infra*) that the ban on gender discrimination in pay applies to pension benefits. The Court limited the retroactive effect of the ruling to persons who had initiated legal proceedings or their equivalent under national law prior to the time of the 1990 ruling. Ten Oever v. Stichting Bedrijfspensioenfonds voor het Glazenwassers en Schoonmaakbedrijf, Case C–109/91, [1993] ECR I–4879. The result was to spare European employers hundreds of billions of dollars in potential liability. Although several different "limited retroactivity" formulas were possible (such as limiting the ruling to new pension schemes set up the date of the ruling, or to employees who joined pension schemes after that date, or to pension payments made after that date), the Court chose to limit the ruling to periods of employment prior to that date.[9]

Deciding when to suspend the retroactivity of ECJ judgments may itself be a difficult judgment call. In Blaizot v. University of Liège, Case 24/86, [1988] ECR 379, the Court decided that a discriminatorily higher Belgian university fee (the *minerval*) for students from Member States other than Belgium violated the treaty article on equal access to vocational training, but only allowed those students who by then had already filed claims for reimbursement to avail themselves of the ruling. Is this a sound result? Significantly, in a related case, the Court held that a Member State may not itself enact a law restricting the retroactive effect of a Court of Justice ruling unless that ruling expressly so provides. Barra v. Belgium and City of Liège, Case 309/85, [1988] ECR 355. "The fundamental need for a general and uniform application of Community law implies that it is for the Court of Justice alone to decide upon the temporal restrictions to be placed on [its judgments]." Id. at 375.

The issue of fairness in the retroactive application of new legal principles has also vexed the US Supreme Court. A divided Court has insisted on the requirement that newly-announced principles, particularly constitutional ones, receive retroactive application even if they result in very heavy new liabilities. Harper v. Virginia Department of Taxation, 509 U.S. 86, 113 S.Ct. 2510, 125 L.Ed.2d 74 (1993).

d. Basic Rights

In further application of general principles of law, the Court of Justice has identified certain other "basic rights" which the Community institutions are similarly required to respect. While the basic rights first recognized by the Court were substantive "economic" rights in nature (such as the right not to be unreasonably deprived of the enjoyment of private property), their scope has steadily broadened over the years to the point that they now embrace the protection of what might be considered—and in the European Union are now denominated—as fundamental freedoms and human rights. This evolution is traced separately in Chapter 6 *infra*.

4. MISUSE OF POWERS

Misuse of powers—the fourth general ground for annulment—is an English rendition of a traditional concept of French administrative law known as *détournement de pouvoir*. A misuse of power in this sense occurs when authority is exercised for purposes other than those for which it was con-

---

9. The Court opted for the precise formula that the Member States had specifically agreed upon for this purpose in a special protocol attached to the 1992 Maastricht Treaty.

ferred. In Community law, as in French administrative law, misuse of power is said to denote a "subjective" wrong, in contrast with the other grounds for review which are intrinsically "objective". More specifically, it entails an inquiry into the motives or purposes behind an act rather than the act itself or, as the matter is sometimes put, into the act's "internal" as opposed to "external" aspects. See F. Schockweiler, La notion de détournement de pouvoir en droit communautaire, [1990] Actualité Juridique, Droit Administratif 435.

The following case illustrates the misuse of power concept.

GIUFFRIDA v. COUNCIL
Case 105/75, [1976] ECR 1395.

[Giuffrida was an unsuccessful applicant for a high administrative post in the Directorate–General for regional policy. When the appointment was given to someone else, Giuffrida brought suit alleging that the competition was not genuine. He contended that the post had been reserved in advance for his competitor, one Emilio Martino, basing that claim largely on the fact that the Council had established as a condition for the post unusual qualifications almost uniquely held by Martino, namely four years' or more experience as secretary for meetings of the working parties or committees of the Council.]

5   Under the terms of the first paragraph of Article 27 of the Staff Regulations "Recruitment shall be directed to securing for the institution the services of officials of the highest standard of ability, efficiency and integrity...."

6   In addition, Article 29 of the Staff Regulations lays down the necessary recruitment procedures—which, in paragraph 1(b), include the internal competition—so that vacant posts may be filled by officials chosen on the basis of objective criteria and only in the interests of the service.

* * *

10   It is clear from the [admissions made by the Council's Secretary General] that [the competition] was organized by the appointing authority for the sole purpose of remedying the anomalous administrative status of a specific official and of appointing that same official to the post declared vacant.

11   The pursuit of such a specific objective is contrary to the aims of any recruitment procedure, including the internal competition procedure, and thus constitutes a misuse of powers.

12   The existence of [a] misuse of powers in this instance is moreover confirmed by the fact that one of the conditions for admission to the competition was that the successful candidate must have held the secretariat for meetings of Council working parties or committees on regional policy for at least four years.

13   It is not disputed that such a restrictive condition corresponds exactly to the duties performed by Emilio Martino in his previous post.

14   Furthermore, none of the information provided by the defendant shows why it was necessary in the interests of the service to lay down such a specific condition as regards the duration of the duties referred to.

15/16   Furthermore ... a memorandum [from] the Secretary–General ... provided, in particular, that "in order to ensure the equal treatment of all officials internal competitions will take place on the basis of qualifications and tests offering the same guarantees of selection as open competitions although adapted to the internal nature of the competition and the types of post to be filled".

17   Whether or not the memorandum in question was at that time in the nature of a decision, the fact remains that ... the appointing authority should have regarded itself as under a moral obligation to comply with it and, therefore, to organize the competition in question on the basis not only of qualifications but of tests also.

18   On these grounds it must be concluded that the decision to make the appointment in question involves a misuse of powers and must therefore be annulled.

Notes and Questions

1.   Would there have been anything wrong with requiring experience as a working group secretary if two or more candidates possessed that credential? In other words, was fixing this qualification for the post "objectively" wrong or only "subjectively" wrong? Do you find it helpful to draw such lines? Is this a familiar distinction in the US law of judicial review?

2.   Suppose the actual purpose behind an act is not a wholly improper one (as it arguably was in *Giuffrida*), but a proper one that simply does not correspond with the precise purpose for which authority was granted. It is well established in French law that the *détournement de pouvoir* doctrine condemns this as well. But if a permissible interest is being pursued, what harm is there in the fact that this interest does not correspond precisely to the one that was meant to be pursued? If the action cannot be objectively justified in terms of the relevant Treaty provision or secondary legislation, then shouldn't it be invalidated on that "objective" ground alone. See Bock v. Commission, Case 62/70, [1971] ECR 897.

In Gutmann v. Commission, Cases 18, 35/65, [1966] ECR 103, a Euratom official objected to being transferred from one installation to another, ostensibly "in the interests of the service" (as was ordinarily permissible), when he was actually being transferred as a disciplinary measure. Assuming the official is correct in his allegations (as the Court found him to be), what harm is he likely to have suffered?

3.   Consider the case of Booss and Fischer v. Commission, Case T–58/91, [1993] ECR II–147. Booss (a German) and Fischer (a Dutchman) were legal advisers attached since 1984 to the agriculture and fisheries team of the Commission Legal Service. In 1990, the Commission reorganized the Directorate General for Fisheries (then DG XIV), publishing three vacancy notices for a post as director in DG XIV. In a first round limited to applicants seeking promotion from within the Commission, none of the candidates (including Booss and Fischer) was found to be qualified, although Booss had been President of the International Convention for the North Atlantic Fisheries. The Commission proceeded to a second "outside" round at the end of which, by a decision of July 11, 1990, Arnal Monreal (a Spanish national) and Mastracchio (an Italian national) were selected for posts in Directorates B and D, respectively. Booss and Fischer complained that the results of the competition had been prearranged in violation of staff regulations and in an abuse of procedure. (They also claimed that neither of the

successful candidates possessed the required knowledge of the fisheries policy called for in the vacancy notices.) Unsuccessful, they sued. In their suit, they raised for the first time the claim that the posts had been reserved for candidates on the basis of nationality. In fact, Article 27 of the Staff Regulations forbade reserving posts for nationals of any specific Member State, unless required for the proper functioning of the service. (See Schloh v. Council, Case 85/82, [1983] ECR 2105.)

The Court found that neither Arnal Monreal nor Mastracchio had the thorough knowledge of Community fisheries policy called for by the vacancy notice. Regarding Arnal Monreal, the Court also noted that in the hearing before the Court, the Commission's representative stated that the Spanish Government had urged, with obvious reference to its great interest in fisheries policy, that the Court "not be oblivious to certain political realities." The Court concluded:

95   ... It is apparent [that] the Spanish Government ... considered, in the light of the vacancies which had arisen in 1990, that, politically speaking, it was "owed" a director's post. It is apparent that, by accepting the "Spanish" application presented to it, the Commission accepted, at least by implication, the "political reality" to which its representative referred at the hearing. ... It is also apparent that, without any need to await the results of the consideration of the internal applications, the Commission already knew, at least in June 1990, that the Spanish Government's candidate would in any event be appointed.

96   Consequently, ... the post in question had been reserved, within the Commission and on the basis of at least an implied agreement, for the only candidate of Spanish nationality, and ... it had been so reserved before the decisions rejecting the applicants' candidatures had been adopted. The Commission agreed to accept a "less ideal" candidate for the purpose of assigning the post to the only candidate of Spanish nationality. That decision was motivated by the "political reality" pleaded before the Court, whilst considerations concerning the proper functioning of the service ... within the meaning of ... Article 27 of the Staff Regulations played no part.

The Court reached essentially the same conclusion about the naming of Mastracchio to the Directorate D post:

100   [T]he circumstances indicate that the post in question was regarded as an "Italian post", even though no contacts with the Italian Government were established. ... [T]he Court finds that ... the post [in Directorate D also] was reserved within the Commission for a candidate of a predetermined nationality. Once again, without its being necessary to await the results of the consideration of the internal applications, the Commission and Mr. Mastracchio already knew in June 1990 that only an "Italian" application had any prospect of being accepted. ... Considerations regarding the proper functioning of the service ... once again played no part.

Note that, while Booss and Fischer alleged an "abuse of procedure" as such, the Court decided the case on grounds of violation of Staff Regulations. This may illustrate an aversion to deciding cases on "misuse" or "abuse" of power grounds, when violation of an applicable rule of law will do. Is it not obvious, though, that the Court thought that an abuse of procedure had occurred?

We learn that positions cannot be reserved in advance for particular nationalities. Does this mean that nationality is an altogether impermissible consideration in the filling of positions? Should it be an impermissible consideration in a political entity such as the European Union? In fact there is no question that a fair representation of different nationalities in positions within the institutions is in fact sought, even in bodies like the Commission which are sworn to independence from the Member States. Where and how would you draw the line between fair representation and nationality favoritism?

4.   Claims of misuse of powers rarely result in the annulment of Community measures. (Advocate–General Warner began his opinion in *Giuffrida* with the words, "Misuse of power [is] often pleaded but seldom proved. ... [I]n this case, it has been proved." [1976] ECR at 1405.) One of the reasons for this rarity was alluded to in the previous note. Consider the problem also from a remedial angle. What should the Court of Justice do if it concludes that a Community official has made a decision based on his or her private interest, or on an "incorrect" public interest, but that the same decision could have been justified in terms of the "correct" public interest? The Court has held, much as the French administrative courts have done, that an "error" in motive should be deemed harmless unless the mistaken purpose was in fact the dominant one or otherwise substantially affected the outcome.

NOTE ON THE SCOPE OF REVIEW UNDER "PILLAR THREE", UNDER EC TREATY TITLE IV, AND UNDER "CLOSER COOPERATION"

It will be recalled that the Amsterdam Treaty made a number of changes in structure to the EC Treaty and the TEU. In varying ways, these changes have extended the Court's jurisdiction, but they have also complicated it. These variations from the usual judicial review regime that we have examined in this chapter are taken up briefly in this Note.

Pillar Three

The Amsterdam Treaty broadly introduced judicial review under pillar three, from where it had largely been absent since the Maastricht Treaty first brought us the "pillar" structure. (Pillar two still remains largely outside the Court's purview.) However, this new jurisdiction is not without limits. In terms of subject matter, TEU Article 35(5) (ex K.7) excludes the Court from reviewing the validity of operations carried out by law enforcement officers or of decisions relating to the maintenance of law and order and the safeguard of internal security. Article 35 confines the Court's direct action jurisdiction functionally as well. Only certain kinds of annulment actions are permitted. First, Article 35(6) makes the action to annul available only insofar as it targets pillar three "decisions" (including "framework decisions"), and it makes them available only to the Commission and the Member States (and neither to Parliament nor to private parties).[10] Second, while Article 35(7) also specifically empowers the Court to rule on certain disputes between Member

---

10.   Decisions (including framework decisions) under pillar three are explicitly described by TEU Article 34(2) as lacking direct effect. Note that the rules on timing of review and the grounds of illegality remain the same as under conventional suits to annul.

States[11] and between Member States and the Commission,[12] all other types of direct actions that are ordinarily available, and that we have either already studied (viz. actions for failure to act) or will study (viz. damage actions against the Community, as described immediately below, and infringement actions by the Commission against Member States, as described in Chapter 11 *infra*), are excluded.[13]

"Freedom, Security and Justice"

At the same time that it introduced some judicial review into pillar three, the Amsterdam Treaty, it will be recalled, also transferred legislative competence over visas, asylum and immigration from pillar three to pillar one, in the form of a new EC Treaty Title IV on "freedom, security and justice." However, the judicial review that is available respecting measures in these fields is not as complete as the usual system of review of Community law. EC Treaty Article 68 (ex 73p) once again excludes from the Court's review measures relating to the maintenance of law and order and the safeguard of internal security. (The same article also imposes restrictions on the availability of preliminary references from national courts to the Court of Justice, as compared to the usual preliminary reference ground rules. See Chapter 9 *infra* for an account of the differences.)

"Closer Cooperation"

Finally, variations in judicial review accompanied the general flexibility provisions introduced by the Treaty of Amsterdam. (See Chapter 4E *supra*.) Those provisions, it will be recalled, permit some Member States, if they so wish, to use the institutions and mechanisms of the EU and EC to integrate more closely than the other Member States in certain fields. A new Title VII TEU, comprising Articles 43 to 45 (ex K.15–.17) lays out the general flexibility regime, which is then supplemented by provisions of the EC Treaty (art. 11) and the TEU (art. 40) when this regime is employed under pillar one and pillar three, respectively.

Article 46 of the TEU gives the Court of Justice jurisdiction to rule on disputes arising out of the Member States' resort to closer cooperation under this regime. When closer cooperation takes place within the realm of pillar one, the Court will presumably enjoy its usual jurisdiction and scope of review under the Community law system, as described in this chapter. Thus, the Court will review both the decision to launch closer cooperation (examining whether the conditions and criteria for its use are met) and the legality of the measure ultimately adopted. The situation is otherwise when closer cooperation takes place under pillar three. TEU Article 40(4) expressly provides that the Court will enjoy its usual jurisdiction and scope of review only as to disputes relating to the decision to launch closer cooperation; review of the measures ultimately adopted is governed by the judicial review established in TEU Title VI for the review of third pillar action.[14]

11. Under TEU Article 35(7), the Court's jurisdiction extends to disputes between Member States on the interpretation or application of decisions (including framework decisions) under pillar three, provided such disputes cannot be settled by the Council within six months. (As noted above, TEU Article 34(2) provides that such measures lack direct effect.)

12. The Court's jurisdiction under TEU Article 35(7) also extends to disputes between Member States and the Commission concerning the interpretation or application of conventions under pillar three.

13. However, a restricted form of preliminary reference (the subject of Chapter 11 *infra*) is available under pillar three. It is described in that chapter.

14. The scope of judicial review established in TEU Title VI for review of third pillar action is discussed earlier in this Note.

Of course, the decision to engage in closer cooperation (and hence the determination that the criteria and conditions for the exercise of flexibility are met) is a highly political matter, as may well be determining the contours of the legislation ultimately to be adopted under closer cooperation. Thus, whether the Court conducts its review according to the judicial review ground rules of pillar one or pillar three, it is likely to approach the matter at hand with prudence and to refrain from the exercise of strict scrutiny. The Court's cautious attitude thus far to review of the Community institutions' respect for the principle of subsidiarity (see Chapter 4D *supra*) may give us a good indication of its likely response to any legal challenges that might be brought to decisions and measures taken under the flexibility regime.

E.   DAMAGE ACTIONS AGAINST THE COMMUNITY

This chapter has thus far dealt with various ways of contesting Community acts directly in the Community courts. Parties, however, are not always content with rulings that merely "declare" Community measures invalid or "call upon" the offending institution to set matters right. They may seek more tangible and immediate benefits in the form of monetary relief against the institutions.

Article 235 (ex 178) of the EC Treaty vests the Court of Justice with jurisdiction over damage actions against the Community, taking the scope of liability from Article 288(2) (ex 215(2)) of the Treaty, which reads as follows:

> In the case of non-contractual liability, the Community shall, in accordance with the general principles common to the laws of the Member States, make good any damage caused by its institutions or by its servants in the performance of their duties.[15]

This section deals with the scope of Article 288(2), first as a basis for the Community's tort liability and then as a basis of liability for the legal actions of the institutions.

1.   THE COMMUNITY'S LIABILITY IN TORT

The language of Article 288(2) (ex 215(2)) suggests that the Community is liable in tort, and that this liability will be at least in part vicarious in nature. Interestingly, very few tort actions have been brought against the Community on account of the acts of its "servants." That damage suits are more commonly brought on account of the Community's institutional acts is due to the fact that the Community normally acts through legal measures rather than through physical conduct on the part of specifically identifiable persons.

Another reason for the paucity of cases is the Court's own initial response to the central question in vicarious liability, namely the employee's "scope" of office or employment. In the early case of Sayag v. Leduc, Case 9/69, [1969] ECR 329, a businessman sued a Euratom engineer in Belgian court for injuries suffered in an automobile accident during a visit to certain Euratom

---

15. As amended at Maastricht, Article 288 (ex 215) permits damage actions for non-contractual liability also to be brought against the European Central Bank, which is still not formally listed as a Community institution in Article 7 (ex 4) of the EC Treaty.

installations. The engineer had been instructed to conduct the visit and was specifically given a travel order to use his own car. On preliminary reference from the highest Belgian court, the Court of Justice gave an exceedingly restrictive definition of the term "in the performance of their duties" in the provision of the Euratom Treaty which parallels EC Treaty Article 288(2):

> By referring at one and the same time to damage caused by the institutions and to that caused by the servants of the Community, [the Treaty] indicates that the Community is only liable for those acts of its servants which, by virtue of an internal and direct relationship, are the necessary extension of the tasks entrusted to the institutions.

* * *

> A reference to a servant's private car in a travel order does not bring the driving of such car within the performance of his duties, but is basically intended to enable any necessary reimbursement of the travel expenses involved in the use of this means of transport to be made in accordance with the standards laid down for this purpose.

> Only in the case of *force majeure* or in exceptional circumstances of such overriding importance that without the servant's using private means of transport the Community would have been unable to carry out the tasks entrusted to it, could such use be considered to form part of the servant's performance of his duties, within the meaning of the ... Treaty.

[1969] ECR at 335–36. The plaintiff's only option was thus the suit he had also brought against the engineer in Belgium.[16] Is this a sound result?

Adams v. Commission, Case 145/83, [1985] ECR 3539, is the rare case in which the Court awarded damages on account of the personal conduct of Community officials, rather than the institutions' legal acts. Stanley Adams, an employee of the Swiss pharmaceutical firm Hoffmann–LaRoche, reported to the Commission certain corporate activities he thought to be in violation of Community competition law, and the Commission eventually issued a decision unfavorable to the company. Although the Commission at Adams' request did not disclose his identity as informant, documents that the Commission supplied to Hoffmann–LaRoche enabled the company to identify Adams as the whistle-blower and have him arrested and prosecuted under Swiss law for betraying his former employer's economic secrets. Following a period of solitary confinement and news of his wife's suicide in the wake of the police investigation, Adams confessed to having been the informant, a fact that the Commission then confirmed. After receiving a one-year suspended sentence, Adams sued the Commission for failing to protect his identity. The Court held the Commission liable in tort for breach of its duty to protect Adams' identity, though it reduced Adams' recovery by half by reason of his own negligence in allowing his identity to become known and exposing himself to arrest.

---

16. Ordinarily, Community officials are immune from suit in national court for liability arising out of "acts performed in their official capacity." Protocol on the Privileges and Immunities of the European Communities, art. 12(a). But such immunity would not obtain here, once the Court of Justice had held the engineer's conduct not to be within the performance of his duties. In fact, the Court of Justice had held in a previous preliminary ruling arising out of the same incident that the engineer was not entitled to immunity under the Protocol. Sayag v. Leduc, Case 5/68, [1968] ECR 395.

Article 288(2) fixes the Community's vicarious liability by reference to "the general principles common to the laws of the Member States." The branch of Member State law relevant to this quest for general principles is governmental rather than private tort law where, as in France, there is a difference in substance between the two.

In practice, French administrative tort law appears to have had singular influence over this aspect of Community law. Under that law, the Community basically may be held liable for its officers' fault committed within the scope of office, including negligence or bad faith or conduct contrary to instructions or law. Besides vicarious liability for acts of Community employees, Community tort law also recognizes a concept of service-related fault, likewise borrowed from French administrative law. This idea is less familiar to us. A *faute de service,* as it is known in French, occurs whenever the government fails to function in the manner to be expected of a reasonably efficient and well-ordered service. The lapse does not have to be specifically traceable to negligent or wrongful conduct by identifiable officials. A *faute de service* may take many forms, including excessive delay, inadequate surveillance or unexcused misinformation (or non-information) of the public.[17] In situations like these, the element of vicarious liability for personal misconduct is obviously attenuated.

General principles of law are also consulted on narrower issues of substance in the field of tort. In Grifoni v. Euratom, Case C–308/87, [1990] ECR I–1203, for example, a contracting party was awarded damages for Euratom's failure to maintain safe physical conditions at a meteorological installation at which the claimant was making improvements. The Court found Euratom at fault for failing to comply with the local Italian legislation governing the prevention of industrial accidents. The Court rejected the Commission's defense that Grifoni's injury was entirely his own fault, thus destroying the "causal link" required for recovery, but it recognized and applied a principle of comparative negligence, ruling that under the circumstances "responsibility must be shared equally between the parties" (para. 17).

The Court of Justice does not require a principle to be expressly recognized in all Member States in order to qualify under this heading, and Community tort law is therefore not necessarily a lowest common denominator. Moreover, the Court tends to conceive of principles at a general level of expression and not in the form of specific rules. On the Court's methodology in identifying general principles of law, see the conclusions of the Advocate General in Aktien–Zuckerfabrik Schöppenstedt v. Council, Case 5/71, [1971] ECR 975, 989.

Articles 235 and 288(2) provide no guidance at all on matters of procedure. Standing to sue in tort is not mentioned and presumably not specifically required. Neither is a limitations period stated, though the Statute of the Court of Justice (art. 43) prescribes a five-year period. If a monetary judgment is recovered against the Community, Articles 244 (ex 187) and 256 (ex 192),

---

17. See, e.g., Compagnie Continentale
France v. Council, Case 169/73, [1975] ECR   117.

taken together, suggest that the judgment will be enforceable under the procedures of the state where enforcement is sought.

2.   LIABILITY FOR THE COMMUNITY'S LEGAL ACTS

Considering the functions they characteristically perform, the Community institutions are not often charged with the kind of "garden variety" torts—negligent driving, poor maintenance of premises, police misconduct and the like—commonly associated with government tort liability. More usual are claims for economic relief from Community measures shown to be illegal on one or more of the grounds for review discussed in Section D of this chapter. This kind of claim may not be a very promising one in the US, due to the statutory exemptions for policy or discretionary decisions typically found in American government tort claim statutes. In the Community, however, damage actions for economic injury are increasingly common, though, for reasons to be explored in the cases that follow, not very often successful.

Damage actions of this sort raise an important threshold question, namely whether a party that lacks standing to challenge a Community measure in the Court of Justice under Article 230 (ex 173) is nevertheless entitled to seek damages for losses resulting from that measure. Initially the Court ruled in Plaumann & Co. v. Commission, Case 25/62, [1963] ECR 95, that such an action could not proceed because allowing it would effectively defeat the strict standing limitations that govern annulment actions. Eight years later, however, in Alfons Lütticke GmbH v. Commission, Case 4/69, [1971] ECR 325, the Court essentially reversed itself.

In *Lütticke*, which is a sequel to the case of the same name discussed at page 426 *infra*, the plaintiff sought damages from the Commission on account of its failure to prosecute Germany under Article 226 (ex 169) for noncompliance with EC Treaty Article 90 (ex 95) barring discriminatory taxation. (In the earlier case, the Court ruled that Lütticke lacked standing to challenge the Commission's refusal to prosecute Germany.) The Commission contested the damage action's admissibility on the ground that "although introduced on the basis of Article 178 [now 235] and ... Article 215 [now 288], it seeks in reality to establish a failure to act on the part of the Commission and to constrain it indirectly to initiate [action] against Germany" and thus "has the effect of distorting the conditions to which Article 232 (ex 175) has subjected actions for failure to act." The Court squarely ruled the claim admissible:

> The action for damages provided for by Article 178 and ... Article 215 was established by the Treaty as an independent form of action with a particular purpose to fulfil within the system of actions and subject to conditions for its use, conceived with a view to its specific purpose. It would be contrary to the independent nature of this action as well as to the efficacy of the general system of forms of action created by the Treaty to regard as a ground of inadmissibility the fact that, in certain circumstances, an action for damages might lead to a result similar to that of an action for failure to act under Article 175.

Do you agree? [1971] ECR at 336. On the merits, the Court denied damages, as it consistently has in suits against the Commission for its allegedly inadequate enforcement efforts against Member States under Article 226. See, e.g., Denkavit v. Commission, Case 14/78, [1978] ECR 2497; Société Commerciale Antoine Vloeberghs SA v. High Authority, Cases 9, 12/60, [1961] ECR 197. In fact, the Court has rarely imposed tort liability on the Community under any circumstance, mostly to avoid unduly hampering the administrative process or imposing an excessive burden on the public purse.

The Court continues to treat annulment and damages actions as mutually independent, with the inadmissibility of the former not necessarily implying the inadmissibility of the latter. It reaffirmed the "autonomy" of liability actions during the complex litigation over the EC's regulation of trade in bananas with non-EC states (see generally page 318 *infra*), when it dismissed an annulment action by a group of banana producers for lack of standing, but nevertheless allowed their damage actions against the Community to proceed. Pacific Fruit Company NV and others v. Commission, Joined Cases C–256, 257, 262, 276, 282, 283, 286–88/93, [1993] ECR I–3345.

The Court has drawn the line, however, at suits for damages when the relief sought is practically indistinguishable from the relief that a successful annulment action would have afforded. For a recent application of this exception, see Cobrecaf SA v. Commission, Case T–514/93, [1995] ECR II–621, where the Court of First Instance considered the claimant's suit for damages as, at least in part, aimed at securing payment of the sum of money (a financial aid) that the Commission had refused to pay to the claimant in a decision that was no longer open to direct challenge. Is the distinction that the Court has drawn a logical one? a workable one?

Turning to the more substantive dimension, when is it proper for the Court to award damages against the Community? The Court sought to address that question in principle in a judgment rendered shortly after *Lütticke*. In Aktien–Zuckerfabrik Schöppenstedt v. Council, Case 5/71, [1971] ECR 975, a German sugar producer objected to a Council regulation that compensated sugar producers who were adversely affected by price changes under a new common market organization in that commodity, but that expressly excluded German firms producing white or raw sugar (of which the plaintiff was one). The Council considered such firms to be only "marginally" affected by the changes. The plaintiff argued that the excluded producers were affected more than marginally and claimed damages on account of the discrimination.

Closely tracking its ruling in *Lütticke,* the Court held the damages action to be admissible even though in some sense it resembled an annulment action, which the plaintiff would not have had standing to bring. On the merits, the Court laid down the following rule:

> Where legislative action involving measures of economic policy is concerned, the Community does not incur noncontractual liability for damage suffered by individuals as a consequence of that action [under] Article 215 [now 288] ... of the Treaty, unless a sufficiently flagrant violation of a superior rule of law for the protection of the individual has occurred.

[1971] ECR at 984. The quoted language has become known as the "*Schöppenstedt* formula". The Court concluded in the case that under the circumstances the exclusion was not discriminatory and thus no violation of a "superior rule of law" had occurred.

Among the best-known judgments in this area is the following:

BAYERISCHE HNL VERMEHRUNGSBETRIEBE GMBH v. COUNCIL AND COMMISSION

(second Skimmed-milk powder case)

Cases 83, 94/76 & 4, 15, 40/77, [1978] ECR 1209.

[It will be recalled that in the *Bela–Mühle Josef Bergmann* case, *supra* page 179, the Court struck down as discriminatory and "disproportionate" a regulation requiring animal feed producers to use skimmed-milk powder as the protein ingredient in their product and thus forcing poultry farmers to buy more expensive feed. In the present cases, Bayerische HNL Vermehrungsbetriebe and other producers of poultry and eggs sought damages from the Council and Commission for losses due to the higher feed prices they had to pay until the regulation was invalidated. The Court first recalled the grounds on which it had invalidated the regulation in *Bela–Mühle* and then turned to the damages question.]

4   The finding that a legislative measure ... is null and void is ... insufficient by itself for the Community to incur non-contractual liability for damage caused to individuals. . . .

5   In the present case there is no doubt that the prohibition on discrimination ... is in fact designed for the protection of the individual, and that it is impossible to disregard the importance of this prohibition in the system of the Treaty. . . . Although [the principles in the legal systems of the Member States governing the liability of public authorities for damage caused to individuals by legislative measures] vary considerably from one Member State to another, it is however possible to state that the public authorities can only exceptionally and in special circumstances incur liability for legislative measures which are the result of choices of economic policy. This restrictive view is explained by the consideration that the legislative authority ... cannot always be hindered in making its decisions by the prospect of applications for damages whenever it has occasion to adopt legislative measures in the public interest which may adversely affect the interests of individuals.

6   It follows from these considerations that individuals may be required ... to accept within reasonable limits certain harmful effects on their economic interests as a result of a legislative measure without being able to obtain compensation from public funds even if that measure has been declared null and void. In a legislative field such as the one in question, in which one of the chief features is the exercise of a wide discretion essential for the implementation of the Common Agricultural Policy, the Community does not therefore incur liability unless the institution concerned has manifestly and gravely disregarded the limits on the exercise of its powers.

7   This is not so in the case of a measure of economic policy such as that in the present case. ... [T]his measure affected ... all buyers of compound feeding-stuffs containing protein, so that its effects on individual undertakings were considerably lessened. Moreover, the effects of the regulation on the price of feeding-stuffs as a factor in the production costs of those buyers were only limited since that price rose by little more than 2%. This

price increase was particularly small in comparison with the price increases resulting, during the period of application of the regulation, from the variations in the world market prices of feeding-stuffs containing protein, which were three or four times higher than the increase resulting from the obligation to purchase skimmed-milk powder introduced by the regulation. The effects of the regulation on the profit-earning capacity of the undertakings did not ultimately exceed the bounds of the economic risks inherent in the activities of the agricultural sectors concerned.

[8] In these circumstances the fact that the regulation is null and void is insufficient for the Community to incur liability under ... Article 215 [now 288] of the Treaty.

Notes and Questions

1. If the regulation in the *second Skimmed-milk powder* case was so indefensible as to violate both the principles of equality and proportionality, how could the Court conclude that the breach was not "sufficiently serious?"

2. A broadly similar result occurred in the damage actions arising out of the Court's isoglucose cases. After the Court invalidated a tax on isoglucose producers as in violation of the principle of equal treatment, three isoglucose manufacturers brought separate actions for many millions of dollars in damages, due largely to massive lost investments in isoglucose production. The three were the Community's only significant producers and each had allegedly suffered grievously, one of them going into bankruptcy as a result. Recovery was nevertheless denied. The Court did not dispute the seriousness of the plaintiffs' loss, but found that the Commission's error in adopting the illegal measure was not a grave one. The Court underscored that the Community sugar surplus was an "emergency," that the Commission had reasonably decided that some restriction on isoglucose production was needed, and also that maize was not in great supply. It thus found that the Commission had not erred in conceiving of the levy, but only in fixing its scope and amount. In sum, although the Commission had imposed "manifestly unequal" burdens and thus acted illegally, it did not "manifestly or gravely disregard the limits on its discretion." Koninklijke Scholten–Honig NV v. Council and Commission, Case 143/77, [1979] ECR 3583; G.R. Amylum NV and Tunnel Refineries Ltd. v. Council and Commission, Cases 116, 124/77, [1979] ECR 3497. Does this make sense to you?

3. Does it follow from the *Schöppenstedt* formula that a party may not invoke a superior rule of law for the protection of individuals unless that party falls within the class of individuals intended to be protected by the rule? See Société Commerciale Antoine Vloeberghs SA v. High Authority, Cases 9, 12/60, [1961] ECR 197.

The Court has held that, although a Community measure may have violated the separation of powers (or, as the Court calls it, the "division" of powers) among the institutions, and therefore be subject to annulment, it cannot for that reason alone be said to have violated a superior rule of law for the protection of the individual, for Community liability purposes. Industrie-en Handelsonderneming Vreugdenhil BV v. Commission, Case C–282/90, [1992] ECR I–1937. As a general matter, would you agree? The Court has taken a similar view of an institution's violation of the requirement in Article 253 (ex 190) of a statement of reasons. Compagnia Italiana Alcool SaS di Mario Mariano & Co. v. Commission, Case C–358/90, [1992] ECR I–2457.

SOFRIMPORT S.A.R.L. v. COMMISSION

Case C–152/88, [1990] ECR I–2477.

[In April 1988, the Commission adopted regulations suspending the issuance of import licenses for dessert apples from Chile. By this time Sofrimport, a French importer of fresh fruit, had already shipped a cargo of Chilean apples to France, the ship reaching Marseille one week after the suspension of licenses took effect. The French authorities refused to issue the necessary papers and Sofrimport brought an action for annulment of the regulations as applied and for damages.

The Court ruled that the regulations were of both direct and individual concern to Sofrimport. On the merits, it found that if the regulations were applied to apples already in transit, they would impermissibly disappoint an importer's legitimate expectations, particularly since the Council regulation that initially set up the market organization in fruits and vegetables required that the Commission "take account of the special position of products in transit" (art. 3(3)). The Court then turned to Sofrimport's claim for damages due to its inability to market the apples until June 1988 when the suspension was lifted.]

25   ... According to [our previous rulings] the Community does not incur liability on account of a legislative measure which involves choices of economic policy unless a sufficiently serious breach of a superior rule of law for the protection of the individual has occurred.

26   [T]he purpose of ... Article 3(3) of [the Council regulation] is to protect traders who import goods covered by that regulation into the Community from the unfavourable consequences of protective measures which might be adopted by the Community institutions. That provision thus gives rise to a legitimate expectation the disregard of which constitutes a breach of that superior rule of law.

27   Secondly, it must be held that by failing completely to take account of the position of traders such as Sofrimport, without invoking any overriding public interest, the Commission committed a sufficiently serious breach of Article 3(3).

28   Thirdly, the damage alleged by Sofrimport goes beyond the limits of the economic risks inherent in the business in issue inasmuch as the purpose of that provision is precisely to limit those risks with regard to goods in transit.

29   Consequently, the Community must make good the damage caused to Sofrimport by the adoption of the contested regulations.

Notes and Questions

1.   Were the regulations in *Sofrimport* "legislative measures which involve choices of economic policy?" What "superior rule of law for the protection of the individual" did they violate?

2.   Does Sofrimport produce a good result? Is the Community's exposure to liability too great? In January 2001, Chiquita Bananas sued the Commission in the Court of First Instance for $525 million in damages allegedly caused by the

EU's banana quota system previously condemned by a decision of a WTO dispute resolution panel (the latter decision having been upheld by the WTO Appeals Body). According to Chiquita, this sum only represents lost profits from January 1, 1999, when the latest quota system was put in place. Chiquita claims the Community quota system drove it to the brink of bankruptcy.

3. The Court did not dwell in *Sofrimport* on questions of causation and compensable loss. But these can be significant issues. (Do you expect them to surface in the *Chiquita Banana* litigation, *supra* note 2?) In P. Dumortier Frères SA v. Council, Cases 64, 113/76, 167, 239/78 & 27, 28, 45/79, [1979] ECR 3091, the Court barred the recovery of otherwise provable economic losses that could have been passed on to others through higher prices without an unreasonable risk of market loss.

The case of Firma E. Kampffmeyer v. Commission, Cases 5, 7, 13–24/66, [1967] ECR 245, raised more complicated issues of causation and loss. There, the Court awarded damages to a group of German grain dealers whose applications for licenses to import maize were wrongfully denied through action of the German authorities and the Commission. But the damages were limited. The dealers were allowed to recover the duties they had been required to pay when they were belatedly able to import the grain, but only if they showed that at the outset they had reasonably relied on not having to pay duty. Furthermore, dealers who repudiated purchase contracts after the import licenses were denied were allowed to recover their contract penalties. However, the Court allowed them only a fraction of the profit lost on the postponed import transactions, mostly because it thought that they had tried, through "the hasty lodging of an abnormally large number of applications for import licenses," to take advantage of an obvious Commission error in the setting of free-at-frontier prices. It regarded the dealers' behavior, to that extent, as "abnormally speculative" and not fully worthy of protection. Finally, anticipated profits on grain sales for which the disappointed license applicants never made any substitute purchases were entirely disallowed. What might explain these various results?

4. Another issue in cases of liability in tort for the Community's legal acts is the *extent* of liability. In Mulder and Heinemann v. Council and Commission, Joined Cases C–104/89 & C–37/90, [1992] ECR I–3061, the Court ruled that recoverable damages should include all relevant forms of lost income. At the same time, the Court inferred from the general principles common to the laws of the Member States a requirement that the injured party make all reasonable efforts to mitigate its damages, and bear its own losses to the extent that it fails to do so.

3. THE RELATIONSHIP BETWEEN COMMUNITY AND MEMBER STATE LIABILITY

HAEGEMAN v. COMMISSION
Case 96/71, [1972] ECR 1005.

[Haegeman was a Belgian importer of Greek wine at a time when Greece was not yet an EU Member State but party to a 1961 association agreement with the Community. Over Haegeman's protest, the German authorities collected a countervailing duty on imports of Greek wine and Haegeman sought a refund from the Commission on the ground that the Greek association agreement forbade such duties. He also sought damages. When the Commission refused, Haegeman sued to have the refusal annulled and to recover his losses.]

[5] Under the Council Decision of 21 April 1970 on the replacement of financial contributions from Member States by the Communities' own resources, the Community's own resources shall be collected by Member States on behalf of the Community "in accordance with national provisions imposed by law, regulation or administrative action" and made available to the Commission.

[6] Under [the applicable regulations] the establishment of these resources and the control of their collection is primarily the responsibility of the competent departments or agencies of the Member States.

[7] Disputes concerning the levying on individuals of the charges and levies referred to by this provision must be resolved, applying Community law, by the national authorities and following the practices laid down by the law of the Member States.

[8] Issues ... which are raised during such a procedure as to the interpretation and validity of regulations ... must be brought before the national courts which have at their disposal the procedure under Article 177 [now 234] of the Treaty in order to ensure the uniform application of Community law.

[9] The countervailing charge in question is part of the "own resources" referred to in the Council Decision of 21 April 1970.

[10] It is therefore for the competent national authorities to rule on claims for the refund of that charge.

[11] The applicant's claim for a refund should therefore have been made to those authorities.

[12] In these circumstances the Commission's refusal of the applicant's request is not an act capable of being the subject of an application for annulment within the meaning of Article 173 [now 230] of the Treaty.

[13] The application for annulment is therefore inadmissible.

[14] The applicant maintains further that by reason of the defendant's behaviour it has suffered exceptional damage as a result of loss of profit, unforeseen financial outlay and losses on existing contracts.

[15] The question of the possible liability of the Community is in the first place linked with that of the legality of the levying of the charge in question.

[16] It has just been found that, in the context of the relationship between individuals and the taxation authority which has levied the charge in dispute, the latter question comes under the jurisdiction of the national courts.

[17] Accordingly, at the present stage the claim for compensation for possible damage must be dismissed.

Notes and Questions

1. *Haegeman* is only one of many cases disallowing direct damage actions against the Commission in the Court of Justice, and requiring resort to national remedies against the Member States.

Presumably tort actions in national court will proceed under national law. (But see Chapter 10B *infra* on the ECJ's recent case law on Member State liability for Community law violations.) Note that Member State courts have refused to impose liability on the States for implementing measures for whose wrongfulness the Community legislature is responsible. A judgment by the Landgericht Bonn illustrates the point. The plaintiff sued the German Government for losses flowing from the issuance of a German decree prohibiting exports to Iraq, the decree having been mandated by a Council regulation. At the time of the decree, the plaintiff had delivered, and received payment for, only a portion of the goods sold. The Landgericht ruled that where national legislation implementing a Community regulation merely repeats the prohibition contained in the regulation, and adds penalties, any injury caused to a private party derives from the Community measure, and not the national measure. Any action in damages would thus have to be brought against the Community. Judgment of February 26, 1992, Case 10–446/90 (Re Trade with Iraq), [1993] 1 CMLR 66 (Landgericht Bonn).

2. Suppose Haegeman's suit in German court fails. May Haegeman later bring an action in the Community courts?

3. How would you like the following possible approach? All claims for sums unlawfully collected or withheld by Member State agencies pursuant to Community law must be brought in national court rather than the Court of Justice, even if the unlawfulness flows from Community law or action rather than national law or action, and even if the sums in question are in the ordinary course retained by or turned over to the Community. However, all claims for consequential economic loss resulting from the unlawfulness or unlawful application of Community policy (including consequential economic loss due to the unlawful withholding of sums due or collection of sums not due) must be brought in the court of the jurisdiction (Member State or Community) to whose action the element of unlawfulness is traceable.

Would you favor such a rule? It could explain the result in Krohn & Co. Import–Export GmbH & Co. v. Commission, Case 175/84, [1986] ECR 753. There, the German authorities, acting on the instructions of the Commission, refused Krohn's application for import licenses. Krohn concurrently sued the German agency in German court (for what amounted to declaratory and injunctive relief) and the Commission in the Court of Justice (for damages caused by the refusal). The Court of Justice held that this was jurisdictionally proper.

Chapter 6

FUNDAMENTAL RIGHTS, HUMAN RIGHTS AND TRANSPARENCY

The previous chapter explored the role of certain general principles (notably proportionality, equality, legal certainty and the protection of legitimate expectations) in assessing the legality of Community law measures. There has arisen alongside these principles the recognition of certain "basic" or "fundamental" rights whose growing importance justifies a separate chapter in this book. Those terms are now commonly used to designate a set of rights pertaining to the political, social and personal interests of those who are subject to Community law.

The drafters of the constitutive treaties did not include in them any comprehensive, much less entrenched, statement of basic or fundamental rights, even though by then a number of post-war European national constitutions (notably the German and Italian) contained statements of that kind. This may have been due to the fact that Community law was expected to be implemented in the main by Member State officials, who were themselves subject to national and international human rights constraints. Note that a Universal Declaration of Human Rights had been adopted by the United Nations General Assembly in 1948, and that a European Convention on Human Rights, drafted two years later under the auspices of the Council of Europe, was eventually signed and ratified by all the Member States.

The EC Treaty did of course contain certain express prohibitions reflecting basic rights. Thus, it established the principle of non-discrimination based on nationality and a prohibition of gender discrimination in pay. The Treaty's provisions on the free movement and residence rights of workers may also be regarded not only as aspects of the internal market but also as aspects of basic rights. Clearly, though, these rights were limited in scope. As we shall see in this chapter, however, the Court of Justice has been led to give human rights broader recognition in its case law, placing particular reliance on Article 220 (ex 164) according to which the Court's responsibility is to ensure, in the interpretation and application of the Treaty, "that ... the law is observed." By giving "law" an especially deep meaning, the Court managed to bring unwritten fundamental rights into the corpus of Community law.

The assumption that the Community law had no reason for a human rights dimension as such was, for several reasons, misplaced. First, important areas of Community law governance (competition law being the prime example) were and still are very largely administered by officials of the Community rather than the Member States. Moreover, a proper understanding of Community measures, whether on the part of Community or national officials, requires an appreciation of the extent to which those measures are to be interpreted in keeping with and under the influence of emerging human rights norms. The possibility also has to be reckoned with that national courts, enforcing either domestic or international protections of human rights, might regard Community law measures as deficient in that respect and refuse on that account to give them the primacy intended at the Community level. (Chapter 8 tells in part the story of how certain national courts, notably German and Italian, served notice that the supremacy and direct effect of Community law over national law in their legal orders would depend on the Community's respect for fundamental rights and on the Court of Justice's readiness to ensure such respect.)

More generally, as the Community evolved in the direction of a true political entity, it seemed increasingly anomalous that its "constitution" contained no bill of rights comparable to those found in the constitutions of the Member States. A first response was the Court's recognition in its case law of the 1970s of certain fundamental rights inspired by international human rights agreements and Member State constitutional traditions. In a 1977 Joint Declaration, the political institutions of the Community endorsed this jurisprudential development. (See Selected Documents, Part I, document 11.) Eventually, the Court of Justice and the institutions felt called upon to give content to the notion of European citizenship that the Maastricht Treaty prominently introduced, for it is impossible to imagine articulating a notion of "citizenship" without addressing the "civil" rights that citizenship entails.

For all these reasons, fundamental rights protection came to occupy center stage in Community law.

Inevitably, the political, and occasionally the judicial, institutions of the Community faced more pointed questions such as whether the EU could and should subscribe to the European Human Rights Convention and submit to its enforcement machinery, or whether and how (and with what judicial enforceability) the EU should embrace a human rights protection regime of its own. While deciding in 1994 that the EU could not, in the present state of the Treaty, become a member of the Human Rights Convention system, the Court of Justice has repeatedly borrowed from the Convention, as well as from the constitutions of the Member States, in elaborating fundamental rights doctrine. The Maastricht and Amsterdam Treaties made significant advances in committing the Community to fundamental rights protection. At Nice in December 2000, the Presidents of the Parliament, Council and Commission "proclaimed" a new Charter of Fundamental Rights (which the European Council had two months earlier endorsed at its Biarritz meeting). However, the European Council at Nice deliberately stopped short of inscribing the Charter directly in either the EC Treaty or the TEU, or of making its protections directly enforceable judicially.

The EU, like the US, has also introduced a human rights dimension into its overall and rapidly emerging foreign policy. It is obvious that the EU can not credibly play a human rights "card" in its dealings with foreign nations—

not to mention with candidates for EU accession—without guaranteeing, and being seen to guarantee, an adequate protection of those rights in the Community itself.

The present chapters attempts to follow all of these strands in the evolution of fundamental rights at the EU Level.

A. THE EUROPEAN COURT OF JUSTICE: ORIGINS OF THE HUMAN RIGHTS DISCUSSION

STAUDER v. CITY OF ULM, SOZIALAMT

Case 29/69, [1969] ECR 419.

[In an attempt to reduce the Community's stock of surplus butter, a 1969 Commission decision authorized the Member States to make butter available to certain categories of social assistance recipients at prices below the market and at a par with the price of margarine. The decision required persons seeking to benefit from the program to present certain coupons to retailers. The German text of the decision provided for the coupon to identify the recipient. Stauder, a war victim who was entitled to participate in the program, objected to having to disclose his identity, characterizing the requirement as discriminatory and violative of his right to privacy guaranteed by the German Constitution. His suit in a German administrative court gave rise to the following preliminary ruling.]

2　The [Commission] decision is addressed to all the Member States and authorizes them, with a view to stimulating the sale of surplus quantities of butter on the Common Market, to make butter available at a lower price than normal to certain categories of consumers who are in receipt of certain social assistance. This authorization is subject to certain conditions designed, *inter alia,* to ensure that the product, when marketed in this way, is not prevented from reaching its proper destination. To that end [the decision] stipulates in two of its versions, one being the German version, that the States must take all necessary measures to ensure that beneficiaries can only purchase the product in question on presentation of a "coupon indicating their names", whilst in the other versions, however, it is only stated that a "coupon referring to the person concerned" must be shown, thus making it possible to employ other methods of checking in addition to naming the beneficiary. It is therefore necessary in the first place to ascertain exactly what methods the provision at issue prescribes.

3　When a single decision is addressed to all the Member States, the necessity for uniform application and accordingly for uniform interpretation makes it impossible to consider one version of the text in isolation, but requires that it be interpreted on the basis of both the real intention of its author and the aim he seeks to achieve, in the light in particular of the versions in all four languages.

4　In a case like the present one, the most liberal interpretation must prevail, provided that it is sufficient to achieve the objectives pursued by the decision in question. It cannot, moreover, be accepted that the authors of the decision intended to impose stricter obligations in some Member States than in others.

* * *

[6] It follows that the provision in question must be interpreted as not requiring—although it does not prohibit—the identification of beneficiaries by name. The Commission was thus able to publish on 29 July 1969 an amending decision to this effect. Each of the Member States is accordingly now able to choose from a number of methods by which the coupons may refer to the person concerned.

[7] Interpreted in this way the provision at issue contains nothing capable of prejudicing the fundamental human rights enshrined in the general principles of Community law and protected by the Court.

Notes and Questions

1.   *Stauder* was the first judgment of the Court to state that Community law includes the protection of "fundamental human rights" (¶ 7) and to imply that Community measures will be set aside if they fall short in this respect. What human rights principle did the German government violate? On what theory was the Court able to avoid annulling the Council decision that the German government was implementing?

More generally where, or more precisely how, are fundamental rights "enshrined" in Community law? Could the Court draw support from Article 220 (ex 164)?

2.   As the *Stauder* case illustrates, fundamental rights may operate not only to determine the validity of Community legislation, but also to determine its scope and meaning. See, for example, the Court's decisions in Kalanke v. Freie Hansestadt Bremen, Case C–450/93, 1995 ECR I–3051, and Marschall v. Land Nordrhin–Westfalen, Case C–409/95, [1997] ECR I–6363, on the meaning of Directive 76/207 on sex discrimination in employment, and whether and to what extent it permits "affirmative action" mandates. See also P v. S and Cornwall County Council, Case C–13/94, [1996] ECR I–2143, where the Court extended the protections of Directive 76/207 to transsexuals, reasoning in part that "the directive is simply the expression, in the relevant field, of the principle of equality which is one of the fundamental principles of Community law" (para. 18), and that "the right not to be discriminated against on grounds of sex is one of the fundamental human rights whose observance the Court has a duty to ensure" (para. 19).

3.   *Stauder* illustrates the influence of fundamental rights on statutory interpretation. But do fundamental rights go further and actually limit legislative freedom? That is, are they in a sense "constitutional"?

Recall in this regard the 1970 *Internationale Handelsgesellschaft* judgment, *supra* page 171, where the Court effectively treated the principle of proportionality as expressing a fundamental right that Community law measures had to respect. In paragraph 4 of that judgment, the Court stated broadly that "respect for fundamental rights forms an integral part of the general principles of law protected by the Court of Justice."

Shortly thereafter, in the case of Nold v. Commission, Case 4/73, [1974] ECR 491, the Court revisited the question whether a Community measure might so severely impair an operator's economic interests that it offends a "basic" or "fundamental" right to freedom of commerce and industry and is therefore illegal.

The measure in *Nold* was a requirement, in the interest of efficiency in the production and distribution of coal, that the German national coal producer (Ruhrkohle) sell only to wholesalers able to enter into large two-year supply contracts. Nold, a small wholesaler, unable to buy in such quantities, claimed that the measure constituted a deprivation of its right to property and to the free pursuit of economic activity. (Ruhrkohle sold coal on favorable price terms.) The Court concluded that the measure was justified by the recession in the coal industry and was applied in a nondiscriminatory fashion. It then considered the measure in terms of basic rights:

> [F]undamental rights form an integral part of the general principles of law . . . .

> In safeguarding these rights, the Court is bound to draw inspiration from constitutional traditions common to the Member States, and it cannot therefore uphold measures which are incompatible with fundamental rights recognized and protected by the Constitutions of those States.

> Similarly, international treaties for the protection of human rights on which the Member States have collaborated, or of which they are signatories, can supply guidelines which should be followed within the framework of Community law.

[1974] ECR at 507. However, the Court underscored that the rights asserted by Nold were less than absolute:

> If rights of ownership are protected by the constitutional laws of all the Member States and similar guarantees are given in respect of their right freely to choose and practice their trade or profession, the rights thereby guaranteed, far from constituting unfettered prerogatives, must be viewed in the light of the social function of the property and activities protected thereunder.

> For this reason, rights of this nature are protected by law, subject always to limitations laid down in accordance with the public interest.

> Within the Community legal order it likewise seems legitimate that these rights should, if necessary, be subject to certain limits justified by the overall objectives pursued by the Community, on condition that the substance of these rights is left untouched.

Id. at 508. More specifically, the Court considered that Nold was asserting "mere commercial interests or opportunities, the uncertainties of which are part of the very essence of economic activity," and that he bore responsibility for adapting to adverse economic circumstances. Are you satisfied with the reasoning and result? Should a party that is driven out of business in order to rationalize an industry have some remedy at law? Would the result in *Nold* have been different if the Court had employed a proportionality analysis? Was the Court in *Nold* less protective because a somewhat outmoded "economic freedom" argument was being advanced? If so, why did the Court decide the *Skimmed-milk powder* case, *supra* page 179, as it did?

4. In Prais v. Council, Case 130/75, [1976] ECR 1589, the Council had declined to reschedule an examination for a Community post, even after it learned that an applicant was unable to sit for the examination because the date set was a Jewish holiday. The applicant brought an action to annul both the decision to hold the examination on that day and the results of the competition, relying on the non-discrimination provisions of the Staff Regulations and a general Community law principle of equal treatment. The Court ruled that while the institutions are

in principle required to avoid such conflicts with religious observances to the fullest extent practicable, they must reschedule an examination only if notified of the conflict by an applicant a reasonable time before the examination. What do you think of the result?

5.   Staff cases have generated recognition of several other basic rights. See Maurissen v. Court of Auditors, Cases C–193, 194/87, [1990] ECR I–95, where the Court ruled that the Community institutions may not prohibit their officials from joining a trade union or participating in trade union activities. The Court found that freedom of union activity guarantees the right to time off from work to help the Commission prepare employment-related proposals to be submitted to the Council. The Court found that it also guarantees the right to disseminate union literature at work, but that it does not require the institutions to make their own messenger services available for this purpose. See also Oyowe and Traore v. Commission, Case C–100/88, [1989] ECR 4285.

B.   THE EUROPEAN CONVENTION FOR THE PROTECTION OF HUMAN RIGHTS AND FUNDAMENTAL FREEDOMS

Among the most prominent of the international human rights treaties referred to in the previous cases is the Council of Europe's 1950 Convention for the Protection of Human Rights and Fundamental Freedoms (effective 1953), of which all the EU Member States are signatories. For the text of the Convention, to which all 41 members of the Council of Europe have subscribed, see Part I of the Selected Documents, document 10.

The Convention both lays down important human rights principles and establishes a serious enforcement regime. Until 1998, a European Commission of Human Rights operated as a sort of gatekeeper, screening individual petitions to the Court of Human Rights in Strasbourg. Only if the Commission determined that a claimant had exhausted all available domestic remedies would he or she be permitted to proceed further. Moreover, a Committee of Ministers had the final authority to determine whether or not a case had sufficient merit to proceed before the Court. With the ratification of Protocol No. 11 to the Convention, effective November 1, 1998, the Commission is abolished and the Committee of Ministers confined to monitoring compliance with Court judgments, thus fully leaving substantive responsibility to a new, single permanent European Court of Human Rights, likewise in Strasbourg.

Parties to the Convention agree to accept and be bound by the judgments of the Court. In fact most members of the Council of Europe, including all EU member states, have incorporated the Convention into their domestic legal systems. As a result of the UK Human Rights Act of 1998 (discussed in Chapter 8G *infra*), this is now true even of the UK, which until then had resisted incorporation, due to the time-honored doctrine of parliamentary sovereignty according to which no Parliament could bind its successors.

Although the Community was not a party to the Convention, and the constitutive treaties did not expressly incorporate the Convention into Community law, as early as 1977 the Parliament, Council and Commission issued a Joint Declaration on the European Human Rights Convention proclaiming their attachment to "the protection of fundamental rights, as derived in particular from the constitutions of the Member States and the European [Human Rights] Convention," as well as their intention to respect those rights.[1] Moreover, as noted especially in the *Nold* case, *supra* page 206, the Court of Justice acknowledged drawing partial inspiration for its fundamental rights case law from the European Human Rights Convention, including presumably the case law of the European Human Rights Court. Shortly after *Nold*, the Court reinforced the point in the *Rutili* case, excerpted at page 603 *infra*, where it invoked several Convention articles so as to interpret the "public policy" exception to the free movement of workers as justifying Member States in restricting individual freedoms only to the extent absolutely necessary for the protection of national security or public safety "in a democratic society."

The Court was at its most explicit in Hauer v. Land Rheinland–Pfalz, Case 44/79, [1979] ECR 3727. Liselotte Hauer wanted to plant a vineyard on a parcel of land that she claimed was suitable for that purpose. The German authorities denied her permission to do so, eventually citing a Council regulation that sought to deal with the Community's wine surplus by prohibiting for three years all new cultivation of vines.

Hauer brought suit in German court, and the Court of Justice was asked whether the regulation violated her fundamental rights to property and the free pursuit of commerce. Recalling its position in *Internationale Handelsgesellschaft*, *supra* page 171, that a possible infringement of fundamental rights by the EC institutions may only be judged by the Court itself in the light of Community law criteria, the Court reaffirmed its view that fundamental rights form an "integral" part of Community law and that the Court itself was committed to protecting them. The Court continued:

> The right to property is guaranteed in the Community legal order in accordance with the ideas common to the constitutions of the Member States, which are also reflected in the first Protocol to the European Convention for the Protection of Human Rights.

[1979] ECR at 3745. Noting the institutions' 1977 Joint Declaration and quoting language on the right to property found in the Convention's first Protocol, the Court held that a State may only restrict the use of property where necessary for protection of the general interest. Conceding the vagueness of this principle, the Court then turned to the relevant Member State sources:

> ... One of the first points to emerge in this regard is that those [Member State] rules and practices permit the legislature to control the use of private property in accordance with the general interest. Thus, some constitutions refer to the obligations arising out of the ownership of property, to its social function, to the subordination of its use to the requirements of the common good, or of social justice [citing specific articles of the German, Irish and Italian Constitutions]. In all the Member States, numerous legislative measures have given concrete expression to that social function of the right to property. Thus in all the Member States there is legislation on agriculture and forestry, the water supply, the protection of the environment and town and country plan-

1. 1 O.J. C 103/1 (April 27, 1997). See Selected Documents, Part I, document 11.

ning, which imposes restrictions, sometimes appreciable, on the use of real property.

Id. at 3746–47. The Court found that all the wine-producing countries of the Community regulate the planting of vines and related matters, and that none considers those restrictions to be incompatible with the constitutional right to property. The Court went on:

> However, that finding does not deal completely with the problem raised by the [national court]. Even if it is not possible to dispute in principle the Community's ability to restrict the exercise of the right to property in [this] context ... it is still necessary to examine whether the restrictions ... in fact correspond to objectives of general interest pursued by the Community or whether, with regard to the aim pursued, they constitute a disproportionate and intolerable interference with the rights of the owner, impinging upon the very substance of the right to property. ... It is therefore necessary to identify the aim pursued by the disputed regulation and to determine whether there exists a reasonable relationship between the measures provided for in the regulation and the aim pursued by the Community in this case.

Id. at 3747. The Court closely examined the regulation's background and identified its objectives as achieving a balanced and fairly priced production of wine and improving wine quality. It emphasized the need, for these purposes, to halt the increase in surplus production and to gain time to develop permanent structural measures on land selection, choice of grape varieties, production methods and the like. It further emphasized the nondiscriminatory and temporary character of the ban.

> Seen in this light, the measure criticized does not entail any undue limitation upon the exercise of the right to property. Indeed, the cultivation of new vineyards in a situation of continuous over-production would not have any effect, from an economic point of view, apart from increasing the volume of the surpluses; further [it] would entail the risk of making more difficult the implementation of a structural policy at the Community level in the event of such a policy [employing] criteria more stringent than the current provisions of national legislation concerning the selection of land accepted for wine growing.

> Therefore it is necessary to conclude that the restriction imposed upon the use of property by the prohibition on the new planting of vines ... is justified by the objectives of general interest pursued by the Community and does not infringe the substance of the right to property. ...

Id. at 3749. The Court then briefly disposed of Hauer's claim that the ban on new plantings violated her freedom to pursue trade or professional activities. It found the restriction on this freedom to be "justified by the same reasons which justify the restriction placed upon the use of property." Id. at 3750.

The Court's reliance on the Convention, alongside the constitutional traditions of the Member States, has become commonplace. For example, the Court held that the right to respect for private life, embodied in Article 8 of the Convention (and supported by the Members States' common constitutional traditions) is a fundamental right protected by the Community legal order, although it is susceptible of being restricted in the general public interest, provided the restriction is not "disproportionate" and does not constitute "intolerable interference ... infring[ing] upon the very substance of the right protected." Commission v. Germany (Private imports of medicine), Case C–62/90, [1992] ECR I–2575.

The Court later applied this principle in the context of testing for the AIDS virus. Reversing a judgment of the Court of First Instance, it held that the Commission violated a candidate's right to privacy by relying on a dissimulated AIDS test after the candidate had declined to be tested directly for AIDS, in order to conclude that he was not physically fit for employment. X v. Commission, Case C–404/92P, [1994] ECR I–4737. According to the Court, however, if a person, after being properly informed, withholds consent to a test which a medical officer deems necessary in order to evaluate the candidate's suitability for the post, "the institutions cannot be obliged to take the risk of recruiting him." Since this means that X may still be denied employment on medical grounds, is the Court adequately protecting the right to privacy?

Throughout the 1970s and 1980s, certain voices—including the Commission[2] and European Parliament[3]—urged that the Community formally accede to the Convention, thus rendering the Convention's catalogue of basic rights directly binding on the institutions. The Maastricht Treaty, while not taking this step, placed in the new TEU an Article F (now Article 6) requiring the newly-formed European Union to respect fundamental rights as guaranteed by the European Human Rights Convention and as recognized in the Member States' common constitutional traditions.[4] The Maastricht Treaty also made respect for human rights and fundamental freedoms an objective both of the common foreign and security policy (pillar two)[5] and of the provisions on justice and home affairs, notably immigration and anti-crime activities (pillar three).[6] Maastricht also added Article 177(2) (ex 130u(2)) to the EC Treaty requiring Community policy in the sphere of development cooperation to "contribute to the general objective of developing and consolidating democracy and the rule of law, and ... of respecting human rights and fundamental freedoms." On the other hand, the TEU's Article L (now Article 46) on the role of the Court of Justice under the TEU failed to include Article F among the provisions of the TEU subject to the powers of the Court. (This omission was to be corrected by the Treaty of Amsterdam, as noted below).

In April 1994, the Commission decided to obtain an opinion of the Court of Justice on whether the Community could legally accede to the Convention. In Opinion 2/94, [1996] ECR I–1759, the Court acknowledged that, since respect for human rights is in any event a condition of the lawfulness of all

---

2. Commission Report on Accession to the European Convention (Feb. 1979), Bull. EC Supp. 2/79.

3. Bull. EC 3/93, point 1.2.155.

4. At the same time, the TEU amended the EC Treaty to confer "citizenship of the Union" on all Member State nationals (EC Treaty art. 17, ex 8) and to establish certain "civil rights" accompanying citizenship. These include the right to move and reside freely within the Community (art. 18, ex 8a), the right of citizens residing in another Member State to vote in and stand for local elections (including elections to the European Parliament) (art. 19, ex. 8b), the right of a citizen to diplomatic protection by other Member States while present in third countries where the citizen's own state is not represented (art. 21, ex 8c) and the right to petition Parliament and a new Community Ombudsman (art. 21, ex 8d).

5. TEU Article 11 (ex J.1).

6. TEU Article 29 (ex K.1).

Community acts, accession to an international human rights regime could not be considered as going beyond the scope of Community powers. However, it found that formal accession "would entail the entry of the Community into a distinct international institutional system as well as integration of all the provisions of the Convention into the Community legal order." Consequently,

35 [s]uch a modification of the system for the protection of human rights in the Community, with equally fundamental institutional implications for the Community and the Member States, would be of constitutional significance and would therefore be such as to go beyond the scope of Article 235 [now 308]. It could be brought about only by way of Treaty amendment.

36 [T]herefore ..., as Community law now stands, the Community has no competence to accede to the Convention.

Do you find the Opinion convincing?

CONNOLLY v. COMMISSION
Case C–274/99P, [2001] ECR I-1611.

[During a leave of absence granted for personal reasons, Connolly, a senior Commission in the Directorate of Monetary Affairs, published a book entitled "The Rotten Heart of Europe: The Dirty War for Europe's Money." Upon being dismissed following a disciplinary proceeding for undermining the dignity of his post and the interests of the institution (as well as for failing to obtain the prior authorization required for a publication related to his Commission activities), Connolly brought suit in the Court of First Instance. The Court recognized the principle of freedom of expression, as guaranteed by the European Human Rights Convention, but found that Connolly's punishment did not run afoul of it. Connolly appealed.

The Court of Justice quoted TEU Article 6(2) (ex F), introduced by the Maastricht Treaty, and continued.]

39 As the Court of Human Rights has held, "Freedom of expression constitutes one of the essential foundations of [a democratic society], one of the basic conditions for its progress and for the development of every man. Subject to paragraph 2 of Article 10 [of the ECHR], it is applicable not only to "information" or "ideas" that are favourably received or regarded as inoffensive or as a matter of indifference, but also to those that offend, shock or disturb; such are the demands of that pluralism, tolerance and broadmindedness without which there is no 'democratic society'" [citing H. R. Handyside v. United Kingdom, Series A no. 24, §§ 49 (Dec. 7, 1976); Müller and Others, Series A no. 133, §§ 33 (May 24, 1988); and Vogt v. Germany, Series A no. 323, §§ 52 (Sept. 26, 1995)].

40 Freedom of expression may be subject to the limitations set out in Article 10(2) of the ECHR. [The Court quoted here Article 10 (see Selected Documents, Part I, document 10).]

41 Those limitations must, however, be interpreted restrictively. According to the Court of Human Rights, the adjective "necessary" involves, for the purposes of Article 10(2), a "pressing social need" and, although "[t]he

contracting States have a certain margin of appreciation in assessing whether such a need exists," the interference must be "proportionate to the legitimate aim pursued" and "the reasons adduced by the national authorities to justify it" must be "relevant and sufficient" [citing the *Vogt* judgment, *supra*, §§ 52; and Wille v. Liechtenstein, no 28396/95, §§ 61–63 (Oct. 28, 1999)]. Furthermore, any prior restriction requires particular consideration [citing Wingrove v. United Kingdom, Reports of Judgments and Decisions 1996–V, p. 1957, §§ 58 and §§ 60 (Nov. 25, 1996)].

42   Furthermore, the restrictions must be prescribed by legislative provisions which are worded with sufficient precision to enable interested parties to regulate their conduct, taking, if need be, appropriate advice [citing Sunday Times v. United Kingdom, Series A no. 30, §§ 49 (Apr. 26, 1979)].

43   As the Court has ruled, officials and other employees of the European Communities enjoy the right of freedom of expression, even in areas falling within the scope of the activities of the Community institutions. That freedom extends to the expression, orally or in writing, of opinions that dissent from or conflict with those held by the employing institution.

44   However, it is also legitimate in a democratic society to subject public servants, on account of their status, to obligations such as those contained in Articles 11 and 12 of the Staff Regulations. Such obligations are intended primarily to preserve the relationship of trust which must exist between the institution and its officials or other employees.

45   It is settled that the scope of those obligations must vary according to the nature of the duties performed by the person concerned or his place in the hierarchy.

46   In terms of Article 10(2) of the ECHR, specific restrictions on the exercise of the right of freedom of expression can, in principle, be justified by the legitimate aim of protecting the rights of others. The rights at issue here are those of the institutions that are charged with the responsibility of carrying out tasks in the public interest. Citizens must be able to rely on their doing so effectively.

47   That is the aim of the regulations setting out the duties and responsibilities of the European public service. So an official may not, by oral or written expression, act in breach of his obligations under the regulations, particularly Articles 11, 12 and 17, towards the institution that he is supposed to serve. That would destroy the relationship of trust between himself and that institution and make it thereafter more difficult, if not impossible, for the work of the institution to be carried out in cooperation with that official.

48   In exercising their power of review, the Community courts must decide, having regard to all the circumstances of the case, whether a fair balance has been struck between the individual's fundamental right to freedom of expression and the legitimate concern of the institution to ensure that its officials and agents observe the duties and responsibilities implicit in the performance of their tasks.

[The Court observed that Connolly had violated the Staff Regulations by publishing material dealing with the work of the Community without permission, thus preventing the Commission from determining whether publication would "prejudice the interests of the Communities" and should, exceptionally, be prohibited. The Court also noted that the regulations provide a means of challenging refusals of permission to publish. The Court found nothing procedurally or substantively objectionable in principle to this regime.

The Court reported the CFI's conclusions to the effect that Connolly should have known that he would have been denied permission to publish had he asked for it and that the publication, in any event, "contain[ed] numerous aggressive, derogatory and frequently insulting statements, which are detrimental to the honour of the persons and institutions to which they refer and which have been extremely well publicised, particularly in the press."]

62   The foregoing observations of the Court of First Instance ... make it clear that Mr. Connolly was dismissed not merely because he had failed to apply for prior permission, contrary to the requirements of ... the Staff Regulations, or because he had expressed a dissentient opinion, but because he had published, without permission, material in which he had severely criticised, and even insulted, members of the Commission and other superiors and had challenged fundamental aspects of Community policies which had been written into the Treaty by the Member States and to whose implementation the Commission had specifically assigned him the responsibility of contributing in good faith. In those circumstances, he committed " 'an irremediable breach of the trust which the Commission is entitled to expect from its officials' " and, as a result, made "it impossible for any employment relationship to be maintained with the institution" [quoting the decision removing Connolly from service].

63   As to the measures intended to prevent distribution of the book, which, the appellant claims, the Commission should have adopted in order to protect its interests effectively, suffice it to say that the adoption of such measures would not have restored the relationship of trust between the appellant and the institution and would have made no difference to the fact that it had become impossible for him to continue to have any sort of employment relationship with the institution.

* * *

65   [This] ground of appeal must therefore be rejected.

Notes and Questions

1. Do you find the Court's result and reasoning persuasive? Did the Court strike the right balance between competing interests? Did it satisfactorily explore the availability of less drastic means of vindicating the Community interest?

2. Note especially the Court's citation in *Connolly* of numerous specific European Human Rights Court rulings, not only for purposes of interpreting the Convention, but also for defining fundamental rights and their limitations under Community law.

3. The Human Rights Convention surfaces with regularity in sex discrimination cases, often in conjunction with the Community law principle of equal pay for equal work. See D. and Sweden v. Council, Joined Cases C–122, 125/99, [2001] ECR II-___ (May 31, 2001), where the Court ruled that a refusal to recognize homosexual partnerships as equivalent to marriage for purposes of household

allowances offends neither the equal pay for equal work principle in the Treaty, nor a more general fundamental principle of equal treatment, nor the right to respect for privacy and family life under Article 8 of the European Human Rights Convention.

NOTE ON THE INTERPLAY BETWEEN COMMUNITY AND CONVENTION HUMAN RIGHTS CONVENTION LAW

Unless and until EU accession occurs, the Community institutions may not be called directly to account before the Court of Human Rights. The situation for the Member States is of course different. Where Member States are implementing Community law, or acting under Community authority, are they not subject to both the strictures of the Convention and Community law, as construed by the Strasbourg and Luxembourg courts, respectively? In the perhaps unlikely event of a head-on conflict, which takes priority? To be more precise, suppose the Convention, as interpreted, would forbid Member State authorities from acting in the fashion that Community law, as construed by the Court of Justice, requires?

The question became very real with the decision of the European Court of Human Rights in Matthews v. United Kingdom, 28 E.H.R.R. 461 (Feb. 18, 1999). Matthews, a UK citizen resident in Gibraltar, was not allowed to vote for elections to the European Parliament, since the 1976 Act providing for direct elections excluded residents of Gibraltar from the franchise. (In fact, the treaty of accession of the UK to the Community had excluded Gibraltar from various parts of the EC Treaty, including the free movement of goods.) She appealed to the Court of Human Rights on the basis of Article 3 of Protocol no. 1 to the Convention guaranteeing free parliamentary elections.

Prior to *Matthews*, the Strasbourg court had refrained from questioning not only Community law, but also national law enacted pursuant to Community law. (In most cases the then European Human Rights Commission had simply treated such complaints as inadmissible.[7]) Indeed, in a complaint that a Greek court had taken an unreasonably long period of time to decide a case, in violation of the Convention's Article 6, the Strasbourg court actually refused to take into consideration the over two-and-a-half years required for a preliminary reference from the Greek court to the European Court of Justice.[8]

The Human Rights Court declared the absence of elections to the European Parliament in Gibraltar to be contrary to the Convention, laying emphasis on the fact that the 1976 Act concerning direct elections was not subject to judicial review by the European Court of Justice. (Not being a piece of Community legislation enacted by the Community institutions, the Act in effect constituted primary Community law whose validity, like that of the EC Treaty itself, was unreviewable by the ECJ.) In reaching its result on the merits, the Strasbourg court held that, notwithstanding its supranational character, the European Parliament was a "legislature" within the meaning of protocol no. 1, due in part to its various increases in power under the Maastricht Treaty.

---

7. See, e.g. M & Co. v. Germany, 64 D.R. 138 (Feb. 9, 1990).

8. Pafitis and others v. Greece, 1998–1 E.H.R.R. 458, para. 96 (Feb. 26, 1998).

The *Matthews* case raises many questions, not the least of which is whether the unavailability of judicial review of in the Community courts will continue to be the critical factor in determining the Human Rights Court's willingness to review national measures implementing Community law. See the case note by Schermers in 36 Comm. Mkt. L. Rev. 673 (1999). See also Canor, *Primus inter pares:* Who is the Ultimate Guardian of Fundamental Rights in Europe?, 25 Eur. L. Rev. 3 (2000).

That question is already upon us, due to the pendency in the European Human Rights Court of the DSR–Senator Lines GmbH case. The Commission had fined DSR heavily (close to 14 million euros, payable within three months, representing 11.53% of its worldwide annual turnover) for abuse of a dominant position under EC Treaty Article 82 (ex 86). As is its usual practice, the Commission did not seek to collect the fine pending DSR's challenge to the Commission decision in the Court of First Instance, on condition that DSR provided an adequate bank guarantee. Claiming to be on the brink of bankruptcy and unable to secure financial assistance from its shareholders, DSR asked to be relieved of the requirement of a guarantee. The Commission refused and the Court of First Instance and Court of Justice both denied provisional relief, evidently because they considered that the shareholders' mere unwillingness (as opposed to inability) to help did not constitute an adequate basis for being excused from the requirement. The Commission then asked the German Ministry of Justice to provide it with the "execution clause" that would be necessary to start enforcement.

At this point, DSR turned to the Human Rights Court alleging that the Commission's position (and the CFI's and ECJ's denial of interim relief) deprived DSR of its fundamental right to judicial recourse under Article 6 of the Human Rights Convention, as well as the benefit of a presumption of innocence. Since the Community is not a member of the Convention system, neither it nor its institutions were sued. However, all 15 Member States (including Germany which actually supported DSR in its petitions to the Commission and courts) were named as respondents. According to the complaint they are individually and collectively responsible for the acts of the Community institutions, and the Human Rights Court is competent to rule on the compatibility of those acts with the Convention.

Do you agree that Community measures may be challenged under the Convention even if the Community institutions as such cannot be sued? Do you agree that the Member States should be responsible under the Convention system for the invalidity of measures taken by the Community institutions? Or is it necessary that one or more Member States first have taken action to implement those measures? If so, at what point in this scenario could a Member State (presumably Germany) be said to have taken such action? Suppose the Human Rights Court eventually declares the Community acts to be in violation of DSR's rights under Article 6 of the Convention (and one or Member States to be responsible for those acts). What if anything is the Commission to do? What are the German authorities to do?

NOTE ON THE APPLICATION OF FUNDAMENTAL COMMUNITY RIGHTS TO MEMBER STATE MEASURES

A premise of the immediately preceding note is that Member States are expected to respect fundamental rights, as understood in the Community legal order, whenever there is a sufficient "nexus" between the Member State measure and Community law itself. (Where there is not a sufficient nexus, then the fundamental rights protections that are applicable will presumably emanate exclusively from domestic constitutional law and from international law as received by the national courts.)

But under what circumstances in a sufficient nexus present? The issue has presented itself to the Court from time to time, but has come up more frequently with the increasing prominence of fundamental rights as an aspect of Community law. A few examples will illustrate the problem.

Consider the case of Vereinigte Familiapress Zeitungsverlags- und Vertriebs GmbH v. Heinrich Bauer Verlag, Case C–368/95, [1997] ECR I–3689. Familiapress, an Austrian newspaper publisher, asked a Vienna commercial court for an order requiring a German newspaper publisher (Bauer) to cease marketing publications in Austria that offered readers the chance to play games for prizes, in violation of the Austrian Law on Unfair Competition (the UWG), which bars offering consumers free gifts linked to the sale of goods or the supply of services. Since German competition law imposes no such prohibition, the Vienna court inquired whether the Austrian prohibition constituted a barrier to the free movement of goods within the meaning of Article 28 [ex 30].

The Court readily found that the ban fell within the scope of Article 28 and turned to Austria's argument that it could be justified in the overriding public interest in maintaining press diversity. Austria cited fierce competition among publishers to offer games and drawings for ever larger prizes, with small publishers unable to compete in this marketing practice. It claimed that (a) the low selling price of periodicals caused consumers to attach undue importance to the chance of winning and too little importance to the quality of the publication, and (b) the Austrian press is highly concentrated, the largest press group accounting for 54.5% of the market, as compared with only 34.7% in the UK and 23.9% in Germany.

The Court ruled (para. 18) that because press diversity helps to safeguard freedom of expression, as protected by Article 10 of the European Human Rights Convention, and because freedom of expression is among the fundamental rights guaranteed by the Community legal order, a State may invoke it as an overriding requirement justifying a restriction on the free movement of goods. On the other hand, in keeping with settled ECJ case law, any such restriction "must be proportionate to the objective pursued and that objective must not be capable of being achieved by measures which are less restrictive of intra-Community trade" (para. 19). This is especially so when a restriction justified in terms of freedom of expression itself curtails freedom of expression, as did the Austrian measure:

26   A prohibition on selling publications which offer the chance to take part in prize games competitions may detract from freedom of expression. Article 10 of the [Convention] does, however, permit derogations from that freedom for the purposes of maintaining press diversity, in so far as they are prescribed by law and are necessary in a democratic society [citing the European Court of Human Rights judgment in Informationsverein Lentia and Others v. Austria, 17 E.H.R.R. 93 (Nov. 24, 1993)].

27   [I]t must therefore be determined whether a national prohibition such as that in issue in the main proceedings is proportionate to the aim of maintaining press diversity and whether the objective might not be attained by measures less restrictive of both intra-Community trade and freedom of expression.

28   To that end, it should be determined, first, whether newspapers which offer the chance of winning a prize in games, puzzles or competitions are in competition with those small press publishers who are deemed to be unable to offer comparable prizes and whom the contested legislation is intended to protect and, second, whether such a prospect of winning constitutes an incentive to purchase capable of bringing about a shift in demand.

29   It is for the national court to determine whether those conditions are satisfied on the basis of a study of the Austrian press market.

30   In carrying out that study, it will have to define the market for the product in question and to have regard to the market shares of individual publishers or press groups and the trend thereof.

31   Moreover, the national court will also have to assess the extent to which, from the consumer's standpoint, the product concerned can be replaced by papers which do not offer prizes, taking into account all the circumstances which may influence the decision to purchase, such as the presence of advertising on the title page referring to the chance of winning a prize, the likelihood of winning, the value of the prize or the extent to which winning depends on a test calling for a measure of ingenuity, skill or knowledge.

Finally, the Court required that consideration be given to the availability and efficacy of less restrictive means of achieving Austria's objective, such as removing the relevant newspaper page in copies intended for Austria or including a notice that readers in Austria are ineligible to win a prize.

How would you characterize the "nexus" between national law and Community law that justified the Court in subjecting the former to Community law-based human rights principles? See Elliniki Radiophonia Tileorassi v. Dimotiki Etairia Plioforisses (the ERT case), Case C–260/89, [1991] ECR I–2925, where the Court stated in general terms that where a Member State relies on an express derogation provided for by the Treaty to justify national legislation that would otherwise violate the Treaty's free movement principles, it effectively acts "within the scope" of Community law and its fundamental rights. Having found the required nexus, did the Court provide sound and useful guidance to the national court? (On the free movement of goods aspect of the *Familiapress* case and similar cases, see Chapter 14 *infra*.)

Konstantinidis v. Stadt Altensteig–Standesamt, Case C–168/91, [1993] ECR I–1191, is an intriguing case in this regard. A Greek national established in Germany complained about the transliteration of his name into Latin characters by the German authorities. The Court, viewing the complaint in strictly economic terms, held that the German policy of transliterating foreign names did not implicate freedom of establishment under the Treaty unless it could be shown to favor German nationals over non-nationals in law or in fact. Absent that, there was presumably no sufficient nexus. Advocate–General Jacobs saw the matter differently. In his view, there is a fundamental right (*ius nominis*) to be called by one's own proper name, and any Member State national exercising free movement rights within the EU is entitled to assert that right. Which is the better view?

Clearly, there are limits to the applicability of Community law notions of fundamental rights to measures taken under national law. The case of Kremzow v. Austria, Case C–299/95, [1997] ECR I–2629, nicely illustrates the point. In December 1982, Kremzow, a retired Austrian judge, confessed to the murder of an Austrian lawyer, but subsequently retracted his confession. In 1984, the Court of Assizes found Kremzow guilty of murder and unlawful possession of a firearm, sentencing him to a term of 20 years' imprisonment and committing him to a mental institution for convicted criminals. After a hearing held in the absence of the accused (who had not sought to attend and whose presence had not been ordered by the court on its own motion), the appeals court in July 1986 affirmed the conviction, extending Kremzow's punishment to life imprisonment, while annulling the decision to commit him to a psychiatric hospital.

Kremzow filed a complaint with the European Court of Human Rights, which ruled in September 1993 that Article 6(3)(c) of the Human Rights Convention required, in view of the stakes, that Kremzow be allowed to defend himself in person on the appeal, notwithstanding his failure to make a request to that effect, and that his sentencing therefore violated the Convention (Kremzow v Austria, Series A, No 268–B, Sept. 21, 1993). The Human Rights Court awarded Kremzow 230,000 shillings in respect of fees and expenses.

Kremzow thereafter brought an action in the Austrian courts seeking a reduction in sentence and close to 4 million shillings in damages for his unlawful detention between July 1986 and September 1993. The lower courts denied relief in both respects. On further appeal, Kremzow specifically advanced a Community law claim, namely that his unlawful imprisonment infringed his right as a citizen of the EU under Article 18 (ex 8a) of the EC Treaty to move freely throughout the Community. (He did not claim worker status so as to invoke the free movement of workers.) The national court, observing that "the fundamental right of freedom of the person and the civil sanctions for infringement of that right ... constitute the basis and precondition for the undisturbed exercise of all other freedoms, especially free movement of persons and freedom to carry on one's trade or profession," asked the Court of Justice for an interpretation of Articles 5, 6 and 53 of the Convention.

The Court denied that it had jurisdiction to rule.

15   [W]here national legislation falls within the field of application of Community law, the Court, in a reference for a preliminary ruling, must give the national court all the guidance as to interpretation necessary to enable it to assess the compatibility of that legislation with the fundamental rights as laid down in particular in the Convention.... However, the Court has no such jurisdiction with regard to national legislation lying outside the scope of Community law.

16   The appellant in the main proceedings is an Austrian national whose situation is not connected in any way with any of the situations contemplated by the Treaty provisions on freedom of movement for persons. Whilst any deprivation of liberty may impede the person concerned from exercising his right to free movement, the Court has held that a purely hypothetical prospect of exercising that right does not establish a sufficient connection with Community law to justify the application of Community provisions.

17   Moreover, Mr. Kremzow was sentenced for murder and for illegal possession of a firearm under provisions of national law which were not designed to secure compliance with rules of Community law.

18   It follows that the national legislation applicable in the main proceedings relates to a situation which does not fall within the field of application of Community law.

The question of the applicability of federal constitutional rights to actions taken by state officials, or persons acting under color of state law, has received a rather different answer in the U.S. Surely the Fourteenth Amendment to the US Constitution has a great deal to do with that. Under what circumstances do you think the EU might move in that direction?

C.   FUNDAMENTAL RIGHTS AND THE AMSTERDAM TREATY

Opinion 2/94 of the Court of Justice plainly left it open to subsequent intergovernmental conferences to amend the Treaties to permit accession to the Human Rights Convention. The intergovernmental conference that prepared the Amsterdam Treaty did not do so. It took various other steps, however.

First, the Amsterdam Treaty amended TEU Article 6 (ex F) to declare that "[t]he Union is founded on the principles of liberty, democracy, respect for human rights and fundamental freedoms, and the rule of law," while adding Article 6 to the provisions of the TEU that are subject to the powers of the Court of Justice under TEU Article 46 (ex art. L) and thus judicially enforceable at the EU level. While this guaranteed judicial protection of human rights against the acts of the institutions taken within the Community law sphere, it did so only to a limited extent with respect to legislation enacted under the third pillar (see TEU art. 35) and not at all with respect to pillar two.

Second, and more adventurously, the Amsterdam Treaty added a new Article 13 (ex 6a) to the EC Treaty, as follows:

Without prejudice to the other provisions of this Treaty and within the limits of the powers conferred by it upon the Community, the Council, acting unanimously on a proposal from the Commission and after consulting the European Parliament, may take appropriate action to combat discrimination based on sex, racial or ethnic origin, religion or belief, disability, age or sexual orientation.

The Nice Treaty would amend Article 13 to permit the Council to use the parliamentary codecision procedure (hence QMV) to adopt incentive measures to promote the Member States' contribution to these objectives. Measures harmonizing Member State laws are, however, expressly excluded.

Note that Article 13 operates, by its terms, only "within the limits of the powers conferred by [the EC Treaty] upon the Community." How do you expect this limitation to be interpreted? For a discussion of the possible reach of Article 13, see Bell, The New Article 13 EC Treaty: A Sound Basis for European Anti–Discrimination Law?, 6 M.J. 1 (1999).

Third, personal privacy received special recognition as a fundamental right. A new provision of the EC Treaty, Article 286 (ex 213b), requires the institutions to comply, effective January 1, 1999, with all Community measures for the protection of individuals regarding the processing and free movement of personal data. It directed the Council, by means of the legislative codecision procedure, to establish an independent supervisory body to monitor the institutions' compliance with such data protection measures, and authorized it to adopt other relevant legislation. The principal Community measure that Article 286 makes applicable to the European institutions is Directive 95/46/EC on the Protection of Individuals with Regard to the Processing of Personal Data and on the Free Movement of Such Data, adopted under Article 95 (ex 100a) of the EC Treaty, which imposes significant limitations on business processing and use of personal data and which authorizes the Community to prohibit data transfer to any third country that fails to ensure "an adequate level of protection" of data privacy rights. See Shaffer, Globalization and Social Protection: The Impact of EU and International Rules in the Ratcheting Up of U.S. Privacy Standards, 25 Yale J. Int'l Law, 1 (2000). (The Data Privacy Directive is discussed in Chapter 34 *infra*.)

Fourth, the Amsterdam Treaty amended TEU Article 49 (ex art. O) to make respect for the principles of Article 6(1) of the TEU a condition for accession of new Member States. In so doing, the Treaty confirms in part what the European Council had decided at Copenhagen in 1993, namely that "membership requires that the candidate country has achieved stability of institutions guaranteeing democracy, the rule of law, human rights and respect for and protection of minorities." In fact, the Commission's periodic reports on progress among the candidate states and Turkey have given attention to the state of democracy, the rule of law, protection of civil and political rights and the rights of minorities in those States. (Enlargement is discussed more generally in Part V *infra*.)

Finally, the Amsterdam Treaty introduced the possibility of sanctions against a Member State that is guilty of "a serious and persistent breach" of the principles set out in Article 6(1), namely "liberty, democracy, respect for human rights and fundamental freedoms, and the rule of law." Under TEU Article 7, the Council (meeting as the heads of state or government) may only find such a breach if it acts unanimously upon a proposal to that effect by the Commission or by one-third of the Member States, upon approval by the Parliament acting by a two-thirds majority of EP members and after giving the State in question an opportunity to be heard.[9] If a serious and persistent breach is determined, the Council may, but need not, suspend some of the Member State's rights under the Treaty, including its voting rights; at this stage, the Council acts by qualified majority.[10] The State in question, however, remains bound by its obligations under Community law. If there is a subsequent change in the situation that led to imposition of the sanction, the Council may decide to vary or revoke the measures taken.

The Nice Treaty would supplement the sanctions regime with provisions for situations short of a serious and persistent breach of fundamental rights. Upon a proposal by one third of the Member States, the Parliament or the Commission, the Council may—this time acting by a majority of four-fifths of its members and with the assent of Parliament—determine that there is "a clear risk of a serious breach" by a Member State of the principles in question, and issue appropriate recommendations. Sanctions as such are not contemplated. The change was undoubtedly prompted by the controversy surrounding Jorg Haider's Freedom Party joining the Austrian coalition government, as described in Chapter 1 (page 25 *supra*). So too is the new provision for "independent persons" to submit a report on the situation in the Member State in question, a procedure that was eventually used before sanctions against Austria were lifted. (Query whether the "clear risk" language would in fact have permitted resort to Article 7 against Austria.) Note that the Community institutions themselves took no direct measures against Austria; the Member States did. Should the amendments adopted at Nice, which authorize Council action, be construed as preempting Member State action, either individual or collective? Are there circumstances under which the Community could be held responsible for such Member State action?

The Nice Treaty, by an amendment to TEU Article 46, would also permit the Court of Justice to enforce "the purely procedural stipulations" of the Article 7 regime (though only at the request of the Member State concerned and only within one month of the Council's determination).

See generally Duvigneau, From Advisory Opinion 2/94 to the Amsterdam Treaty: Human Rights Protection in the European Union, 25 Legal Issues of European Integration 61 (1998); Toth, The European Union and Human Rights: The Way Forward, 34 Comm. Mkt. L. Rev. 491 (1997).

D.   THE CHARTER OF FUNDAMENTAL RIGHTS: A NEW HUMAN RIGHTS REGIME?

In the year 2000, the heads of state and government endorsed a new Charter of Fundamental Rights, "proclaiming" it at a meeting of the Europe-

---

9.   When the Council acts under Article 7, it sits in the form of heads of state or government, with the exclusion of the representative of the State in question. Article 7 expressly provides that Member State abstentions will not prevent the adoption of an otherwise unanimous determination. Under Article 7 as amended by the Treaty of Nice, the Council would be required to act by a four-fifths majority of its members.

10.   Qualified majority voting for this purpose excludes participation by the Member State in question. It requires the same proportion of weighted votes in the Council as is ordinarily required under article 205 (ex 148).

an Council in Biarritz. The Nice intergovernmental conference in December of that year was an opportunity for the Presidents of the Council, Commission and Parliament to adopt it as a policy statement. In so doing, they brought to the EU the closest thing to a catalogue of human rights of its own.

The Charter is the culmination of several developments. In 1998, an Expert Group on Fundamental Rights issued a report entitled, "Affirming Fundamental Rights in The European Union: Time to Act," deploring the confusing situation of human rights protection at the EU level, including the unevenness of protection across the three pillars, the absence of any mention of the Human Rights Convention in the EC Treaty as distinct from the TEU, and the obscurity surrounding the role of the Court of Justice. This sentiment was echoed in a study by a special committee entitled "Leading by Example: A Human Rights Agenda for the European Union for the Year 2000." The Committee made numerous recommendations—for the appointment within the Commission of a Commissioner for Human Rights, the creation within the Council of a Human Rights Office to assist the High Representative for the Common Foreign and Security Policy (CFSP), the establishment of an EU Human Rights Monitoring Agency, and the insertion of human rights clauses in Community agreements with third countries. It was also urged, once again, that the Community itself accede to the European Human Rights Convention.

With the vigorous support of the German Presidency, the European Council decided at Cologne in 1999 in favor of consolidating the fundamental rights applicable at the Union level into a new, separate and highly visible instrument. At its Tampere meeting the following October, it resolved to empanel a committee to prepare a draft Charter of Fundamental Rights of the European Union, consisting of fifteen representatives of the Member States, one representative of the President of the Commission, sixteen MEPs, and two national parliamentarians per Member State, and chaired by Roman Herzog, the former President of Germany. The committee began meeting in Brussels in December 1999, working, in keeping with the transparency movement, as a "Convention" in full public view, and independently of the intergovernmental conference that was at the same time preparing the Treaty of Nice. Considering the sensitivity of some of the issues (such as asylum and immigration), extraordinary progress was made, with a complete first draft available by July 2000.

The first draft came in for heavy criticism from Parliament, the Commission, organized labor and non-governmental organizations. Parliament in particular found the draft insufficiently sensitive to threats to fundamental rights emanating from information technology, biotechnological innovation, and environmental degradation, while objecting to the Charter's lack of binding legal status. Labor found the draft unresponsive to workers rights. A second draft Charter, of September 2000, responded to some of the critiques, introducing the right to unionize and strike and strengthening employees' right to information, while acknowledging environmental protection and still other "social" rights.

As revised, the Charter was quickly endorsed by the Commission and shortly thereafter unanimously endorsed by the European Council at Biarritz. It was signed by the presidents of the major European institutions in December 2000 in a short separate ceremony at the opening of the Nice intergovernmental conference. The Charter, along with a "Communication from the Commission on the Legal Nature of the Charter of Fundamental Rights of the European Union" prepared for the Biarritz European Council, may be found in Part I of the Selected Documents, documents 12 and 13, respectively.

The Charter sets out a concise, yet comprehensive statement of fundamental rights, divided among six chapters corresponding to six fundamental values: dignity, freedoms, equality, solidarity, citizens' rights and justice. The chapter on dignity, among other things, declares the inviolability of human dignity, forecloses the death penalty and outlaws trafficking in human beings. It establishes innovative, if vague, guarantees against the abuse of information technology, genetic engineering and biotechnology, for example expressly prohibiting "the reproductive cloning of human beings." The chapter on freedoms consecrates, among other things, the right of privacy (including data privacy protection), freedom of expression and information, pluralism of the media, and numerous social rights such as the right to education and the right to work. Conspicuous in the chapter on equality are prohibitions on discrimination on the basis of "sex, race, colour, ethnic or social origin, genetic features, language, religion or belief, political or other opinion, membership of a national minority, property, birth, disability, age or sexual orientation," as well as the inclusion of additional social rights: the rights of children and the elderly, and the right to cultural diversity The chapter on solidarity, for example, provides for various workers' rights, the right to health care, and rights to environmental and consumer protection. Citizens' rights (chapter five) include the right of access to documents and the right of petition. Chapter six on justice promises, among other things, the right to a fair trial and an effective remedy, as well as certain rights for criminal defendants. The Charter also sets out a general prohibition on "abuse of rights."[11]

The Charter is specifically addressed to the institutions and bodies of the EU and, when implementing EU law, also the Member States. To underscore that the Charter does not make human rights protection as such a Community competence, the Charter disclaims "establish[ing] any new power or task for the Community or the Union, or modify[ing] powers and tasks defined by the Treaties."

As regards its relationship to the European Human Rights Convention, the Charter specifies (art. 52) that it is to be interpreted, insofar as it corresponds to rights guaranteed by the Convention, in a way that is consistent with the Convention, while allowing for the possibility of a still higher level of protection. More generally, the Charter claims not to restrict any human rights or fundamental freedoms otherwise recognized by EU law, international law, domestic constitutional law, or international agreements to which the EC, EU or the Member States are party (art. 53).

Although certain guarantees in the Charter have come in for criticism as contradictory, vague or insufficiently protective, by all accounts the Charter's

---

11. "Nothing in this Charter shall be interpreted as implying any right to engage in any activity or to perform any act aimed at the destruction of any of the rights and freedoms recognised in this Charter or at their limitation to a greater extent than is provided for herein." Art. 54.

principal weakness (apart from its not having been made part of the TEU or EC Treaty) is that it is declared by the Protocol annexing it to the Nice Treaty to be judicially unenforceable. In applauding the Charter, both President Romano Prodi of the Commission and President Nicole Fontaine of the Parliament cited this as a serious shortcoming. On the other hand, it is certainly possible that the Court of Justice and Court of First Instance will draw upon the Charter as a source of fundamental rights principles.

Notes and Questions

1. Reading through the Charter of Fundamental Rights, what do you regard as its major advances over the European Human Rights Convention? Is it just another catalogue of rights, or a substantially improved one? How would you revise it to make it a more perfect document? Was its adoption preferable to accession to the European Human Rights Convention? See Apt, On the Right of Freedom of Expression in the European Union, 4 Colum. J. Eur. L. 69 (1998).

2. Does the Charter significantly move the EU closer toward having a Constitution and constituting a true political union? Assuming it does, does it imply any particular form of government? Does it in any event strike the proper balance between economic efficiency and individual rights? See Lenaerts and de Smijter, A 'Bill of Rights' for the European Union, 38 Comm. Mkt. L. Rev. 273 (2000); de Búrca, The Drafting of the European Union Charter of Fundamental Rights, 26 Eur. L. Rev. 126 (2001).

3. Does the advent of the Charter affect the problem of reconciling divergent conceptions of rights by the Court of Justice and the European Court of Human Rights?

4. In October 1999, the European Council issued its first ever EU Annual Report on Human Rights (covering the time period June 1, 1998 to June 30, 1999). The report cited Member States for human rights shortcomings. Belgium and France, for example, were cited for inadequate protection of national minorities, Greece for its refusal to recognize the right to conscientious objection, Ireland for its failure to ratify the UN Convention against Torture, and Italy for excessive use of pre-trial detention. Also cited were candidate states, for example, Romania for neglect of the country's tens of thousands of orphans. (Turkey was reminded of its need to meet the Copenhagen criteria on protection of minorities in order to embark on accession negotiations.)

Partly as a result of concern over human rights protection in the accession states, the EU has become increasingly vocal on the subject internationally. Note, however, that the EU's international human rights activities are customarily conducted by the European Council. In United Kingdom v. Commission (Payments to combat social exclusion), Case C–106/96, [1998] ECR I–2729, the Court confirmed that the Commission lacked competence to commit expenditure for projects that the Council had not approved. In doing so, the Commission acted in breach of the principle of enumerated powers in Article 5 (ex 3b). As a result of the judgment, funding of a large number of EU programs in third countries has been suspended. More generally, the judgment effectively casts doubt on the competence of the Community as such to promote human rights and democratic principles abroad. See "Just How Effective is EU Promotion of Human Rights in Third Countries?," EU Focus, Feb. 17, 2000.

NOTE ON THE RIGHTS OF EUROPEAN UNION CITIZENSHIP

Any discussion of fundamental rights would be incomplete without reference to the evolving concept of European citizenship. It will be recalled that the Maastricht Treaty introduced the citizenship concept, specifically attaching to it the right to move freely and reside in another Member State (EC Treaty art. 18, ex 8a), the right to vote and stand for election in municipal and European Parliament elections in one's place of residence (EC Treaty art. 19, ex 8b), the right to diplomatic protection while abroad (EC Treaty art. 20, ex 8c), and the right of petition to the Ombudsman and the European Parliament (EC Treaty art. 21, ex 8d). The drafters of the Maastricht Treaty saw this as only a beginning. Articles 22 (ex 8e) specifically provided that the Council, acting alone and unanimously, may add to the enumeration of rights.

Although the Council has not as yet acted pursuant to Article 22 to expand the specific attributes of EU citizenship, the Court of Justice has underlined citizenship's dynamic character. In a series of recent rulings, the Court has directly linked EU citizenship status as such with the enjoyment by Member State nationals of various rights on the territory of other Member States. For discussion of these case law developments, see Chapter 16 *infra* on citizenship rights.

E. TRANSPARENCY AS A FUNDAMENTAL RIGHT: THE COMMUNITY'S "ACCESS TO DOCUMENTS" POLICY

An important and rapidly developing aspect of fundamental rights protection in the EU is access to official documents (commonly known as "information policy"). Such access may in turn be seen as part of a larger movement in favor of "transparency," a basic principle of democracy enabling citizens to see how the powers they have attributed to public institutions are being exercised. The demand for transparency was doubtless fueled by the perception of excessive secrecy and bureaucracy on the part of the institutions that surfaced around the time of ratification of the Maastricht Treaty. Significantly, Declaration no. 17 to the Maastricht Treaty called specifically for a right of access to Community information.

The first formal step in establishing a progressive information policy was the adoption by the Commission and Council in December 1993 of a "Code of Conduct" on public access to Community documents,[12] promising "the widest possible access to documents held by the Commission and the Council," whether through on-site inspection or through delivery of photocopies. Code of Conduct Relating to Access to Documents Within the Community, O.J. L 340/41 (Dec. 31, 1993).[13] The notion of "document" was sweeping, covering in principle even internal preparatory documents and notes.

The Code stipulated a strong presumption of openness, permitting access to documents to be refused only to the extent required in the interest of one

---

12. "Document" is defined by the Code as "any written text, whatever its medium, which contains existing data and is held by Commission or the Council."

13. The Code grew out of two reports produced by the Commission at the European Council's request. Public Access to the Institu-

or more of the following interests: individual privacy, commercial secrecy, the Community's financial interest, confidentiality of the institutions' proceedings, the confidentiality interest of the supplier of the information, or other stated interests (public security, international relations, monetary stability, or the integrity of judicial proceedings, inspections or investigations).

Procedurally, the Code of Conduct distinguished between "initial" and "confirmatory" applications. Upon an initial application, which must be in writing and "sufficiently precise," the competent department of the relevant institution has one month in which to inform the applicant either that the request is approved or that the department intends to recommend that the institution deny it. In the latter case, the department must so inform the applicant, advising of the right within one month to file a confirmatory application with the institution seeking reconsideration. The institution likewise has one month in which to decide. Should it deny access, it must state its reasons and notify the applicant of the availability of recourse to the Ombudsman and of judicial review under Article 230 (ex 173) of the EC Treaty.

Both the Council (in Decision 93/731)[14] and the Commission (in Decision 94/90)[15] formally adopted the Code, together with implementing provisions, as internal decisions. The Commission decision provides that requests may be made to the relevant department at the Commission's central offices, its offices in the Member States, or its delegations in third countries. (If the document originated outside the Commission, the applicant is asked to redirect the application to that source.) It specifies that failure by the department (at the initial stage) or the Secretary–General (at the "confirmatory" stage) to reply to an application within one month shall be deemed to constitute a refusal. It also sets a copying fee for documents in excess of 30 pages of 10 ECU, plus an additional .036 ECU per page.

Understandably, it was the Council whose disclosure habits were most subject to change under the new information policy. While the Council continued mostly to meet strictly behind closed doors, it began maintaining a public register of the vote of Member State representatives in the Council, with explanation of votes and publication of statements in the minutes, when acting in a legislative capacity.[16] The Amsterdam Treaty made these practices mandatory.[17]

Council Decision 93/731 was challenged by the Netherlands on the ground that adoption of the Code required a legislative act and not a mere internal regulation. Parliament joined in the action, complaining that parliamentary consultation had been bypassed. The Court rejected both claims, holding that until such time as general legislation on access to documents is enacted for all the Community institutions, each institution may adopt suitable policies for responding to requests by using their respective powers of internal organization. Netherlands v. Council (Access to documents), Case C–58/94, [1996] ECR I–2169. (Interestingly, neither the Netherlands nor Parlia-

tions' Documents, O.J. 1993 C 156/5; Openness in the Community, O.J. 1993 C 166/4.

14. Council Decision 93/731, O.J. L 340/43 (Dec. 31, 1993).

15. Commission Decision 94/90, O.J. L 45/68 (Feb. 18, 1994).

16. Bull. EC 10/93, point 1.6.8; Bull. EC 12/93, point 1.7.10.

17. TEU, arts. 28, 41 (ex J.18, K.13); EC Treaty art. 207(3) (ex 151).

ment attacked the substance of the Council's information policy and the Court had no comment on that aspect of Decision 93/731.)

Somewhat belatedly, in July 1997, the Parliament adopted an access to documents decision of its own,[18] citing Article 199 (ex 142) of the EC Treaty and the Maastricht Treaty's declaration on the right of access to information. The decision governs only documents "drawn up" by Parliament, and does not reach documents merely "held" by it. It provides for access to documents "on the spot or in Parliament's information offices, or alternatively the delivery of a copy of the document at the applicant's expense," setting a time limit for reply of 45 days following receipt of the application. The decision provides that access to an EP document "may not be granted" where disclosure would undermine public safety, the Community's financial interests, the integrity of court proceedings or investigations at the EU level, protection of private commercial and industrial secrecy, individual privacy, confidentiality, privileges provided for by legislation of the Member State that supplied an item of information, and the confidentiality of deliberations of political groups and parliamentary bodies meeting *in camera*. Again, a denial requires both a statement of reasons and an indication of the available means of redress.

Soon after the Codes were adopted, the Commission published in all official languages a Users' Guide, giving practical advice on securing Community documents, explaining the procedures and exceptions, and reproducing the relevant texts. Private interests and NGOs were quick to invoke the Code and to sue when dissatisfied with the results. For example, when the Council refused a request by The Guardian for copies of minutes of Council meetings on immigration, police cooperation and social policy, the newspaper (supported by Parliament and two Member States, Denmark and the Netherlands) brought suit. The Court of First Instance annulled the refusal on the basis of Council Decision 93/731. The Court held that the Decision required the Council, in exercising its discretion to allow or disallow access to documents pertaining to the Council's deliberations, to genuinely balance the interest of citizens in having access to the documents against the Council's own interest in maintaining such confidentiality. It therefore rejected the Council's "blanket" refusal to give access to whole categories of documents. Carvel and Guardian Newspapers Ltd. v. Council, Case T–194/94, [1995] ECR II–2765.

Shortly thereafter, the World Wide Fund for Nature (WWF) took the Commission to court for an alleged breach of Decision 94/90. WWF had sought information on the use of structural funds for construction of the Mullaghmore tourist site in Ireland, but was refused access by Commission's Secretary–General under the Code's exception for "protection of the public interest." The Court first concluded that, while the Commission had adopted Decision 94/90 as a voluntary measure of internal organization, the measure was capable of conferring rights on third parties that the Commission was required to respect. The Court then distinguished between the two broad categories of exceptions to the right of access contained in the Decision. Based on the language of the text, it considered the first exception—where disclosure would undermine the public interest—to be mandatory, and the second one— where nondisclosure is required in the confidentiality of Commission proceed-

---

18.   O.J. No. L 263 (Sept. 25, 1997).

ings—to be discretionary. Accordingly, if the Commission invokes the confidentiality ground, it must make a genuine exercise of discretion, by balancing the individual's interest in access against its own interest in confidentiality. Moreover, although the Commission may conceivably proceed both under the first and the second exception to bar access to documents relating to its investigation of a possible breach of Community law, in either case it must indicate specifically why it considers that the particular documents requested are related to the possible opening of an infringement proceeding. The inadequacy of explanation also meant that the Commission's refusal violated the requirement of reasons in EC Treaty Article 253 (ex 190). World Wide Fund for Nature (WWF UK) v. Commission, Case T–105/95, [1997] ECR II–313.

Requests for access to documents have markedly increased; the Commission alone, which received 180 requests in 1994, now receives well over a thousand a year. (Close to a quarter of them emanate from academics.). Statistics suggest that ninety percent are answered favorably. The Council receives somewhat fewer requests and grants a somewhat smaller percentage of them. In the case of both institutions, both the public interest exceptions and the exception for the confidentiality of proceedings are commonly invoked. For a discussion of the cases that have gone to court, and the problems they raise, see Dyrberg, Current Issues in the Debate on Public Access to Documents, 24 Eur. L. Rev. 157 (1999).

INTERPORC IM- UND EXPORT GMBH v. COMMISSION

(Interporc I)
Case T–124/96 [1998] ECR II–231.

[Interporc, a German importer of high-grade Argentine beef, was subjected by German authorities to a post-clearance recovery of import duties upon a finding that it had falsified the certificates of authenticity, despite its claims that it had presented the certificates in good faith. Thereafter, the Commission addressed a decision to Germany determining that remission of duties was not justified.

At this point, Interporc sought access to certain Commission documents which it claimed to need in order to avoid liability for duty. The Commission invoked various of the Code's exceptions: protection of the public interest in international relations and in the conduct of inspections and investigations, protection of privacy, and protection of the institution's interest in the confidentiality of its proceedings, While a confirmatory application was pending with the Secretary–General of the Commission, Interporc and two other German firms brought an action in the Court of First Instance to annul the Commission's decision that a remission of duty was unjustified (Primex and Others v. Commission, Case T–50/96).

The Secretary–General then confirmed the denial of access to the documents sought, invoking (without prejudice to the exceptions that had already been invoked) the exception for protection of the public interest in court proceedings, due to the pendency of the *Primex* case. Interporc again brought suit, arguing that the Commission had failed to justify its refusal in terms of the individual documents and the likelihood that their disclosure would specifically harm the public interest.]

[48] From its overall scheme, it is clear that Decision 94/90 is intended to apply generally to requests for access to documents. By virtue of that decision, any person may request access to any unpublished Commission document, and is not required to give a reason for the request.

[49] In accordance with the Code of Conduct, however, the right of access to documents is subject to certain exceptions. Those exceptions must be interpreted strictly, in order not to frustrate the application of the general principle of giving the public "the widest possible access to documents held by the Commission" [citing *WWF UK*].

[The Court then recalled *WWF UK*'s two categories of exceptions, placing the exception invoked in the present case in the first category: "where disclosure could undermine ... the protection of the public interest (public security, international relations, monetary stability, court proceedings, inspections and investigations)."]

[52] The use of the form "could" means that before deciding on a request for access to documents the Commission must consider, for each document requested, whether in the light of the information in its possession disclosure is in fact likely to undermine one of the interests protected under the first category of exceptions. If so, the Commission is bound to refuse access to the document in question, that being a case in which the Code of Conduct provides that the institutions "will refuse" access.

[53] Such a decision on the part of the institution must state the reasons on which it is based, in accordance with Article 190 [now 253] of the Treaty. . . .

[54] The statement of the reasons for a decision refusing access to documents must ... contain—at least for each category of documents concerned—the specific reasons for which the Commission considers that disclosure of the documents requested is precluded by one of the exceptions provided for in the first category of exceptions, in order to enable the person to whom the decision is addressed to satisfy himself that the Commission did in fact consider the documents in the manner described in paragraph 52 above and to assess whether the grounds for refusal are justified.

[55] In the present case, however, the contested decision contains only the conclusion that the exception for protection of the public interest (court proceedings) is applicable. It provides no explanation, even for categories of documents, from which it might be ascertained whether all the documents requested, some of which are several years old, do indeed fall within the scope of the exception relied upon because they bear a relation to the decision whose annulment is sought in the *Primex* case, referred to above.

[56] The statement of reasons in the contested decision is therefore inadequate.

[57] It follows that the contested decision must be annulled. . . .

Notes and Questions

1. Note the *Interporc I* Court's remark (para. 48) that persons requesting documents do not need to give a reason for their requests. If reasons are not

given, how can the court properly apply a balancing test? Following *Interporc I*, what must the Commission do to ensure that its decision refusing access to documents withstands review?

2. In Interporc Im- und Export GmbH v. Commission (*Interporc II*), Case T–92/98, [1999] ECR II–3521, the claimant sought access to a different set of documents. Its success was partial. On the one hand, the Court ruled that the exception based on the protection of the public interest in court proceedings does not entitle the Commission to withhold documents "drawn up in connection with a purely administrative matter," and that this was so "even if the disclosure of such documents . . . might be prejudicial to the Commission."

On the other hand, the Court applied a so-called "authorship rule," shielding from disclosure documents in the Commission's file that individual Member States or Argentine authorities, rather than the Commission, had authored. (It derived the rule from the Code of Conduct's provision that "[w]here the document held by an institution was written by a natural or legal person, a Member State, another Community institution or body or any other national or international body, the application must be sent direct to the author.")

3. The "authorship rule," cited in the previous note, gives rise to interesting questions of identity. In Rothmans International BV v. Commission, Case T–188/97, [1999] ECR II–2463, Rothmans, a manufacturer and distributor of tobacco products, asked the Commission for access to the minutes of the Customs Code Committee, a "comitology" committee composed of representatives of the Member States and presided over by a Commission representative, as described at page 48 *supra*. The Commission invoked the authorship rule to refuse access, and Rothmans sued.

Noting that all exceptions to the general principle of transparency are to be strictly construed, the Court concluded that the comitology committees are not sufficiently distinct from and independent of the Commission to render their documents "non-Commission" for purposes of the authorship rule. The Court emphasized that the committees assist the Commission in the performance of its tasks, borrow the Commission's secretarial services, and lack an administration, budget, archives or premises of their own. "[T]he Committee cannot be regarded as being 'another Community institution or body' within the meaning of the Code of Conduct." Clearly the Court considered the committees too central to the work of the Community to be sheltered from disclosure under the Community's information policy. (Upon questioning by the Court, the Council denied that the "comitology" committees could be considered working groups of the Council, and the Court evidently agreed.)

The *Rothmans* rule was in effect codified by the new "Comitology Decision" (Council Decision 1999/468, O.J. 1999 L184/23), which repealed the comitology decision, *supra* page 49, in light of which *Rothmans* was decided. The new Decision expressly makes the Commission's Code of Conduct applicable to requests for documents produced by the committees. See Comitology Procedures More Transparent and Democratically Accountable?, EU Focus, Nov. 14, 2000, pp. 2–5.

4. van der Wal, in his capacity as competition lawyer, requested copies of replies by the Commission to certain questions it reported (in its 1994 annual report on competition policy) having received from national courts. The Director–General of the then DG IV (competition law), refused, citing the protection of the public interest in court proceedings. He wrote: "When the Commission replies to questions submitted to it by national courts . . . the Commission intervenes as an

amicus curiae. It is expected to show a certain reserve not only as regards acceptance of the manner in which the questions are submitted to it but also as regards the use which it makes of the replies to those questions. I consider that, once the replies have been sent, they form an integral part of the [national] proceedings and are in the hands of the court which raised the question." When the Secretary–General confirmed the refusal, van der Wal, supported by the Netherlands, sued.

The Court of First Instance upheld the refusal, basing its decision on the European Human Rights Convention's guarantee, in Article 6, of a fair hearing by an independent tribunal, reasoning that an independent tribunal requires procedural autonomy on issues such as the confidentiality of documents produced for the sole purposes of a particular court proceeding (as opposed to documents which exist independently of those proceedings). Consequently, only the court hearing a case could grant access to documents prepared for the case.

The Court of Justice reversed:

[20] In order to determine under what conditions, in the context of its cooperation with national courts with a view to the application by them of Articles 85 and 86 [now 81 and 82] of the Treaty, the Commission must refuse access to documents which it holds, on the ground that the protection of the public interest ... may be undermined, it is necessary to consider the manner in which such cooperation works in practice.

[21] As [Commission Notice 93/C 39/05 on cooperation between national courts and the Commission in applying Articles 85 and 86 of the EC Treaty, O.J. 1993 C 93/6] shows, [national] courts may need information of a procedural nature "to enable them to discover whether a certain case is pending before the Commission, whether a case has been the subject of a notification, whether the Commission has officially initiated a procedure or whether it has already taken a position through an official decision or through a comfort letter sent by its services. If necessary, national courts may also ask the Commission to give an opinion as to how much time is likely to be required for granting or refusing individual exemption for notified agreements or practices, so as to be able to determine the conditions for any decision to suspend proceedings or whether interim measures need to be adopted."

[22] According to ... the Notice, national courts may also consult the Commission on points of law where the application of Articles 85 and 86 causes them particular difficulties. [For example,] ... where national courts have doubts as to whether an agreement, decision or concerted practice in issue before them is eligible for an individual exemption, they may ask the Commission to provide them with an interim opinion.

[23] Lastly, ... national courts can obtain information from the Commission regarding factual data: statistics, market studies and economic analyses.

[24] It follows ... that documents supplied by the Commission to national courts are often documents which it already possesses or which, although drafted with a view to particular proceedings, merely refer to the earlier documents, or in which the Commission merely expresses an opinion of a general nature, independent of the data relating to the case pending before the national court. In relation to those documents, the Commission must assess in each individual case whether they fall within the exceptions listed in the code of conduct....

25   Documents supplied by the Commission may also contain legal or economic analyses, drafted on the basis of data supplied by the national court. In those cases, the Commission acts as a legal or economic adviser to the national court and documents drafted in the exercise of that function must be subject to national procedural rules in the same way as any other expert report, in particular as regards disclosure.

26   In those cases, national law may preclude the disclosure of those documents and compliance with that law may be regarded as a public interest worthy of protection under the exceptions provided for by Decision 94/90.

27   That is, however, not enough to exonerate the Commission entirely from its obligation to disclose those documents. In so far as they are held by the Commission, such documents fall within the scope of Decision 94/90, which provides for the widest public access possible. Any exception to that right of access must therefore be interpreted and applied strictly.

28   Consequently, the Commission does not discharge its duty merely by refusing any request for access to the documents in question. Compliance with national procedural rules is sufficiently safeguarded if the Commission ensures that disclosure of the documents does not constitute an infringement of national law. In the event of doubt, it must consult the national court and refuse access only if that court objects to disclosure of the documents.

Netherlands and van der Wal v. Commission, Joined Cases C–174/98P & C–189/98P, [2000] ECR I–1.

5.   In Hanne–Norup Carlsen v. Council, Case T–610/97R, [1998] ECR II–485, ten Danish citizens brought a suit in Danish court challenging the Prime Minister's right to ratify the Maastricht Treaty on the ground that accession was contrary to the Danish Constitution. During the proceedings, the plaintiffs sought access to certain documents in the Council's possession. The Council eventually transmitted the documents, with the exception of those expressing the views of the Legal Services of the Council and the Commission. It justified withholding those opinions on the ground that their disclosure would be detrimental to the public interest, and notably to the institutions' ability to obtain independent legal advice. The plaintiffs, maintaining that the refusal was "generic," sued and asked for interim relief.

The President of the Court of First Instance dismissed the application for interim relief, finding the Council's reasons sufficiently specific and the grounds justified. As to the latter, he held that the categories of public interest recited in the Code were illustrative only and that, moreover, disclosure would be an inappropriate form of interim relief since, by definition, its effects would continue even after final judgment in the annulment action.

Was the Court backtracking from *WWF UK* and *Interporc I*, or are the judgments consistent?

On the Danish court action itself, see Chapter 8E *infra*.

6.   The Court of First Instance has upheld the Commission's refusal, on public interest grounds, to disclose a draft reasoned opinion in an enforcement proceeding against UK. Bavarian Lager, a UK importer of German beer, found itself stymied by the fact that many British pubs were bound under UK regulations by exclusive purchasing agreements with particular breweries. Bavarian Lager lodged a complaint with the Commission, which opened infringement proceedings against the UK. The Commission drafted a reasoned opinion, but decided not to issue it once the UK had suitably amended its regulations. Bavarian

Lager then asked for a copy of the draft opinion, and the Commission refused on the basis of the need for confidentiality, emphasizing the provisional and internal character of the document. Bavarian Lager brought suit. Finding that the document was indeed preparatory only, the Court of First Instance upheld the refusal on the ground that disclosure would violate the Members State's right to confidentiality and undermine the proper conduct of the infringement procedure. Bavarian Lager Company, Ltd. v. Commission, Case T–309/97, [1999] ECR II–3217.

Do you agree with the reasoning and result?

NOTE ON ACCESS TO DOCUMENTS UNDER PILLARS TWO AND THREE

It would not be long before private parties sought access to documents relating to matters falling within pillars two and three—domains to which the Code of Conduct might conceivably not apply. The requests were bound to be controversial, given the sensitive nature of pillar two and three matters— common foreign and security policy and judicial cooperation in criminal matters, respectively. Even if the Codes did apply, there was question as to whether the Community courts had jurisdiction to review the legality of a refusal of access. The case of Svenska Journalistforbundet v. Council, Case T–174/95, [1998] ECR II–2289, raised these issues.

Upon Swedish accession to the EU, the Swedish Journalists' Union decided to test its right of access to information relating to EU activities. It asked 46 Swedish authorities, including the Ministry of Justice and the National Police Authority for access to 20 Council documents relating to the creation of Europol, the European Police Office. Access to 18 of the 20 documents was granted, with some deletions. The Union also asked the Council for access to the same documents, only two of which the Council disclosed. Upon confirmatory application, the Council disclosed just two more documents, withholding the others on the ground that their release could be harmful to public security and would reveal the political positions of the Member States in the Council. The Union sued.

The Council challenged the suit's admissibility, winning the support of several governments. (France argued that Decision 93/731, having been adopted on the basis of the EC Treaty, had no application to documents falling under the third pillar; the UK argued that, even if the decision did apply to third pillar documents, judicial review does not extend to denials of access to them.) Sweden, Denmark and the Netherlands, on the other hand, argued that Decision 93/731 was fully applicable.

Taking the language of the Decision ("all Council documents") at face value, the Court ruled that pillar three documents were covered.[19] As to judicial review, the Court drew a distinction between reviewing the legality of pillar three measures, on the one hand, and reviewing the denial of access to those measures, on the other. "The fact that the documents relate to Title VI only is relevant ... to the examination of the substantive lawfulness of the decision taken by the Council and not to the admissibility of the application as

---

19. The Court also cited TEU Article 28 (ex J.18), which provides that measures adopted under EC Treaty Article 207(3) (ex 151(3)), as Decision 93/731 had been, have application to third pillar measures.

such" (para. 86). On the merits, the Court annulled the Council's refusal as containing an inadequate statement of reasons. The Court found that the Council had failed to furnish, at least for each category of documents concerned, the particular reasons why they should be shielded from disclosure (citing *WWF UK* and *Interporc I*). The Council also had not specified whether, for any given document, the mandatory or the discretionary exception applied, which made it impossible to know "whether the Council has complied with its duty to carry out a genuine balancing of the interests concerned as the application of [the discretionary exception in] Article 4(2) of Decision 93/731 requires" (para. 125).

On the other hand, the Court found that the Union had committed an abuse of procedure by unilaterally publishing an edited version of the Council's defense in the case on the Internet, together with a request to the public to send comments to the Council's agents in the case, whose names and contact information it supplied. In doing so, the Union had violated CFI rules of procedure requiring parties to obtain court permission before making procedural documents available to third parties, rules that were designed to protect the parties from undue external influences. The Court accordingly ordered the Council to pay only two-thirds, rather than all, of the Union's court costs.

What about access to documents relating to the Title V of the TEU (Common Foreign and Security Policy)? Heidi Hautala, a member of the European Parliament, put a written question to the Council seeking clarification of the eight criteria for arms exports that the European Council had laid down in its summit meetings of 1991 and 1992. The Council answered, referring to a report from its Working Group on Conventional Arms Exports. When Hautala then requested a copy of that report, the Council refused, asserting the public interest in the conduct of international relations.

Relying on *Swedish Journalists' Union*, the Court of First Instance asserted jurisdiction, notwithstanding the fact that the contested report dealt exclusively with CFSP matters falling under pillar two of the TEU. On the merits, it upheld the Council's refusal to disclose the report, citing the Council's wide latitude in the exercise of political responsibilities in foreign relations. However, the Court accepted Hautala's contention (supported by Sweden) that the Council had infringed Decision 93/731 by refusing access to the entire Report when only parts of it were covered by the public interest exception. While Decision 93/731 did not expressly require the Council to consider the possibility of partial access to documents, neither did the Decision forbid it. On the other hand, the Court held that partial access was subject to the principle of proportionality, so that it would not be required if the administrative burden entailed in removing confidential matter outweighed the value of disclosing a redacted and possibly fragmentary document. Hautala v. Council, Case T–14/98, [1999] ECR II–2489.

More recently, the Court has held that the Council was justified not only in invoking the international relations arm of the public interest exception to withhold documents relating to the EU's relations with Russia and Ukraine and to the EU's negotiations with the US on the subject of those relations, but also in declining to provide partial access as the latter would be unworkable. Mattila v. Council, Case T–204/99, [2001] ECR II–___ (July 12, 2001).

However, for a judgment that the Commission's failure to analyze each requested document individually and its refusal to partially disclose a CFSP document ran afoul of the principle of proportionality, see Kuijer v. Council, Case T–188/98, [2000] ECR II–1959.

NOTE ON THE NEW ACCESS TO DOCUMENTS REGULATION

The Amsterdam Treaty finally placed information access on a firm treaty basis.[20] A new EC Treaty Article 255 grants EU citizens and residents (including businesses having their registered office in a Member State) a right of access to documents of all three institutions, while at the same time inviting the Commission to propose legislation (to be adopted prior to May 1, 2001 by the codecision procedure) setting out the general principles governing this right. Such legislation, based on a comparative look at the legislation of the Member States and other countries with a tradition of openness, has been adopted. Regulation 1049/2001, O.J. L 145/43 (May 31, 2001).

The new regulation, set out in the Selected Documents (Part I, document 14), applies to all documents relating to the policies, activities and decisions of the three institutions within their sphere of responsibility, whatever their form (paper, electronic, recordings). Under pressure from Parliament, a categorical exclusion in the Commission draft for internal memoranda, discussion documents, and informal messages was eliminated during the legislative process. Disclosure is subject to a "harm test," meaning that access must be granted unless disclosure would seriously harm one of a series of specified interests. In advancing the proposed legislation, the Commission maintained that the grounds for non-disclosure in Article 4 were more clearly spelled out and narrowly drawn than in the Code of Conduct. Looking at the regulation in the Selected Documents, would you agree? To what extent does the regulation incorporate the case law of the Court of First Instance and Court of Justice under the Code?

Article 7 of the regulation provides, in accordance with TEU Articles 28(1) and 41(1) (ex J.18(1) and K.13(1)), that the right of access applies equally to documents relating to pillars two and three, respectively.

An important innovation of the new access regulation is its application to all documents "held" by the institutions, thereby bringing within the scope of the right of access documents not actually drawn up by the institutions, but emanating from third parties and merely found in the institutions' files.[21] This extension, urged by both the Parliament and the Ombudsman, actually aligns the EU's documents policy with existing access to documents legislation in most Member States. The regulation's grounds for refusal of access apply equally to documents drawn up by third parties, though where there is doubt

---

20. Article 42 of the EU's Charter on Fundamental Rights similarly declares that EU citizens and residents have a right of access to documents of the Parliament, Council and Commission. Attached to the Nice Treaty is a declaration on Article 21 of the EC Treaty on "Replying Within a Reasonable Period to Written Requests Made to the Institutions and Bodies of the Union," requiring in general terms that the institutions respond within a reasonable time period to any written request by an EU citizen.

21. Access to documents from third parties is limited to documents delivered to the institution after the date of entry into force of the regulation.

about the applicability of an exception, the institution must first consult the document's author. (If the author fails to reply, the institution may proceed to disclose.)

As far as procedures and remedies are concerned, the regulation differs in only modest ways from the preexisting regime. For example, the time limit for reply may now be extended by one month, provided the applicant is notified in advance and given detailed reasons. Codifying the Court of First Instance judgment in *Hautala, supra* page 235, the regulation also imposes a "redaction" requirement, i.e. where only certain passages of a document fall within an exception to the right of access, those passages are to be deleted and the balance of the document disclosed (art. 4(6)). Silence in response to a confirmatory request is deemed to constitute a refusal and entitle the applicant to institute court proceedings against the institution or file a complaint with the Ombudsman (art. 8(3)).

Chapter 7

THE RELATIONSHIP BETWEEN COMMUNITY AND MEMBER STATE LAW

The materials thus far suggest that the activities of the European Community are heavily legislative and regulatory in nature. The fact that so much implementation of Community policy remains in Member State hands makes the legal relationship between Community and national law a matter of the utmost importance. Not surprisingly, the fundamentals of this relationship received early attention from the Court of Justice. This chapter deals chiefly with direct effect and supremacy, the two main features of the relationship between Community and Member State law from the Court's point of view.

At the same time, the courts of the Member States have understandably claimed a voice in determining the force and effect of Community law in their own domestic legal orders, and precisely because the Community relies pervasively on national authorities to effectuate Community policy, their attitudes cannot be ignored. Developments on this front, which of course differ from state to state, are presented in Chapter 8.

A. THE DIRECT EFFECTS DOCTRINE IN COMMUNITY LAW

We know that Article 249 (ex 189) declares a regulation to be "binding in its entirety and directly applicable in all Member States." But what precisely does this language mean? At a minimum, it means that Member State institutions are bound to act in conformity with the rules and principles laid down by Community law. But there are further and in some sense more searching questions to ask. For example, does Community law need transposition of any sort into national law? Does it give rise to rights in favor of private parties that Member State institutions (including the courts) are legally bound to enforce against the Member States themselves and possibly against other private persons? Does Community law also impose obligations on private persons that the Member States are bound to enforce, if need be judicially? If so, to what extent must the Member State use all the coercive

238

means normally at their disposal to give effect to these rights and duties? Is more than that ever required of the Member States? Finally, who determines, and by what criteria and with what effect, whether Member State authorities are in fact adequately enforcing the Community-based rights and obligations that they are in principle bound to enforce? The term "direct effect," though not found in the Treaty, is often used to denote this whole range of questions.

Matters are complicated by the fact that Article 249 does not describe directives as directly applicable, much less directly effective. Because directives only bind the Member States as to the result to be achieved, expressly leaving them free to choose the form and method, they would seem by their nature not to be directly effective. Decisions are also described in Article 249 as "binding," but they too are not necessarily directly applicable or directly effective in the Member States. The fact remains, however, that directives and decisions are crucial to the Community legal system, and so too therefore is their effectiveness. Recall, for example, that until the Single European Act, directives were the only available instrument in the field of harmonization of national laws.

Due to the intrinsic interest of these questions from both a legal and political point of view, they attracted an enormous amount of attention in early scholarship on Community law. At the same time, enterprising lawyers began asserting Community law-based claims in litigation before national courts, which in turn were prompted to refer questions to the Court under Article 234 (ex 177). These questions pertained not only to the meaning of a particular Treaty article or piece of secondary legislation, but also to the fundamentals of the relationship between Community and Member State law. As shown by the cases that follow, the Court indeed seized its early opportunities to establish basic and novel principles for defining that relationship. The principles are ones that distinctly tend, as the Court put it, to promote *l'effet utile* of Community law, that is to say, the effectiveness of Community law in the national legal orders.

1. THE DIRECT EFFECT OF THE EC TREATY AND EC REGULATIONS

VAN GEND EN LOOS v. NEDERLANDSE ADMINISTRATIE DER BELASTINGEN

Case 26/62, [1963] ECR 1.

[van Gend en Loos, a Dutch importer of ureaformaldehyde, objected to the imposition by Dutch customs authorities of an 8% tariff on a quantity of the product imported from Germany. It claimed that when Dutch law reclassified ureaformaldehyde under a new tariff category, resulting in an increase in the applicable rate of duty, it violated Article 25 (ex 12) of the EC Treaty, as it then stood. The then Article 12 required Member States to "refrain from ... increasing [the customs duties on imports] which they already apply in their trade with each other."

The Dutch Tariff Commission (Tariefcommissie) referred two questions to the Court of Justice. It asked whether an individual may invoke Article 12 before a national court or tribunal, and whether reclassifying ureaformaldehyde as the Netherlands had done constituted a violation of Article 12.]

THE FIRST QUESTION

A. *Jurisdiction of the Court*

The Government of the Netherlands and the Belgian Government challenge the jurisdiction of the Court on the ground that the reference relates not to the interpretation but to the application of the Treaty in the context of the constitutional law of the Netherlands, and that in particular the Court has no jurisdiction to decide ... whether the provisions of the EEC [now EC] Treaty prevail over Netherlands legislation ... The solution of such a problem, it is claimed, falls within the exclusive jurisdiction of the national courts, subject to an application in accordance with the provisions laid down by Articles 169 [now 226] and 170 [now 227] of the Treaty.

However in this case the Court is not asked to adjudicate upon the application of the Treaty according to the principles of the national law of the Netherlands, which remains the concern of the national courts, but is asked, in conformity with ... Article 177 [now 234] of the Treaty, only to interpret the scope of Article 12 of the said Treaty within the context of Community law and with reference to its effect on individuals. This argument has therefore no legal foundation.

* * *

B. *On the Substance of the Case*

The first question of the Tariefcommissie is whether Article 12 of the Treaty has direct application in national law in the sense that nationals of Member States may on the basis of this Article lay claim to rights which the national court must protect.

To ascertain whether the provisions of an international treaty extend so far in their effects it is necessary to consider the spirit, the general scheme and the wording of those provisions.

The objective of the EEC Treaty, which is to establish a Common Market, the functioning of which is of direct concern to interested parties in the Community, implies that this Treaty is more than an agreement which merely creates mutual obligations between the contracting states. This view is confirmed by the preamble to the Treaty which refers not only to governments but to peoples. It is also confirmed more specifically by the establishment of institutions endowed with sovereign rights, the exercise of which affects Member States and also their citizens.

In addition the task assigned to the Court of Justice under Article 177, the object of which is to secure uniform interpretation of the Treaty by national courts and tribunals, confirms that the states have acknowledged that Community law has an authority which can be invoked by their nationals before those courts and tribunals.

The conclusion to be drawn from this is that the Community constitutes a new legal order of international law for the benefit of which the states have limited their sovereign rights, albeit within limited fields, and the subject of which comprise not only Member States but also their nationals. Independently of the legislation of Member States, Community law therefore not only imposes obligations on individuals but is also intended to confer upon them rights which become part of their legal heritage. These rights arise not only where they are expressly granted by the Treaty, but also by reason of obligations which the Treaty imposes in a clearly defined way upon individuals as well as upon the Member States and upon the institutions of the Community.

With regard to the general scheme of the Treaty as it relates to customs duties and charges having equivalent effect, it must be emphasized that Article 9 [now 23], which bases the Community upon a customs union, includes as an essential provision the prohibition of these customs duties and charges. This provision is found at the beginning of the part of the Treaty which defines the "Foundations of the Community". It is applied and explained by Article 12.

The wording of Article 12 contains a clear and unconditional prohibition which is not a positive but a negative obligation. This obligation, moreover, is not qualified by any reservation on the part of states which would make its implementation conditional upon a positive legislative measure enacted under national law. The very nature of this prohibition makes it ideally adapted to produce direct effects in the legal relationship between Member States and their subjects.

The implementation of Article 12 does not require any legislative intervention on the part of the states. The fact that under this Article it is the Member States who are made the subject of the negative obligation does not imply that their nationals cannot benefit from this obligation.

In addition the argument based on Articles 169 and 170 [now 226 and 227] of the Treaty put forward by the three Governments which have submitted observations to the Court ... is misconceived. The fact that these Articles of the Treaty enable the Commission and the Member States to bring before the Court a State which has not fulfilled its obligations does not mean that individuals cannot plead these obligations, should the occasion arise, before a national court, any more than the fact that the Treaty places at the disposal of the Commission ways of ensuring that obligations imposed upon those subject to the Treaty are observed, precludes the possibility, in actions between individuals before a national court, of pleading infringements of these obligations.

A restriction of the guarantees against an infringement of Article 12 by Member States to the procedures under Article 169 and 170 would remove all direct legal protection of the individual rights of their nationals. There is the risk that recourse to the procedure under these Articles would be ineffective if it were to occur after the implementation of a national decision taken contrary to the provisions of the Treaty.

The vigilance of individuals concerned to protect their rights amounts to an effective supervision in addition to the supervision entrusted by Articles 169 and 170 to the diligence of the Commission and of the Member States.

It follows from the foregoing considerations that, according to the spirit, the general scheme and the wording of the Treaty, Article 12 must be interpreted as producing direct effects and creating individual rights which national courts must protect.

THE SECOND QUESTION

A. The Jurisdiction of the Court

According to the observations of the Belgian and Netherlands Governments, the wording of this question appears to require, before it can be answered, an examination by the Court of the tariff classification of ureaformaldehyde imported into the Netherlands, a ... question [that] clearly does not call for an interpretation of the Treaty but concerns the application of Netherlands customs legislation to the classification of [products], which is outside the jurisdiction conferred upon the Court of Justice [by the preliminary reference procedure].

The Court [under this view] has therefore no jurisdiction to consider the reference made by the Tariefcommissie.

However, the real meaning of the question put by the Tariefcommissie is whether, in law, an effective increase in customs duties charged on a given product as a result not of an increase in the rate but of a new classification of the product arising from a change of its tariff description contravenes the prohibition in Article 12 of the Treaty.

Viewed in this way the question put is concerned with an interpretation of this provision of the Treaty and more particularly of the meaning which should be given to the concept of duties applied before the Treaty entered into force.

Therefore the Court has jurisdiction to give a ruling on this question.

B. On the Substance

[On the merits of the second question, the Court ruled that Article 12 is violated by product reclassifications that result in an increase in the applicable rate of customs duty.]

The application of Article 12, in accordance with the interpretation given above, comes within the jurisdiction of the national court which must enquire whether the dutiable product, in this case ureaformaldehyde originating in the Federal Republic of Germany, is charged ... with an import duty higher than that with which it was charged on 1 January 1958.

The Court has no jurisdiction to check the validity of the conflicting views on this subject ... but must leave them to be determined by the national courts.

Notes and Questions

1. *van Gend en Loos* is a landmark decision of the Court of Justice. Although 40 years old, it remains one of the Court's most forceful statements of view on the legal nature of the Community. The Court's reference to "a new legal order" in which "the states have limited their sovereign rights" has become the Court's classic legal conception of the Community. Note the words, "of international law," following the "new legal order" language. Those words do not appear in later Court references to the new legal order concept. See, e.g., *Costa v. ENEL, infra* page ___ (second excerpted paragraph). Is that significant?

Like the Treaty itself, the Court in *van Gend en Loos* refrains from using the terms federation or confederation to describe the Community. Why? (In 1991, the UK prevented the Treaty of European Union drawn up at Maastricht from being called the Treaty of European Federal Union, or even from using the term "federal," even though use of the term was strongly urged by Germany, France and other states.) What, incidentally, does it mean to say (in the fifth paragraph of the excerpted opinion) that the Community institutions are "endowed with sovereign rights?"

2.　*van Gend en Loos* is also one of the Court's first customs cases. It appears that the Netherlands did not mean to defy the Article 12 prohibition against higher tariffs, but was merely engaged in tariff reform under Benelux auspices. The Dutch had adopted the so-called Brussels Nomenclature, which substantially reduced the number of tariff classifications of goods. This entailed giving some goods a lower tariff (which posed no EC problem) and others, like ureaformaldehyde, a higher one. The Community itself has subsequently adopted a simplified uniform customs classification for the Community's external tariff. See Chapter 30 *infra*.

3.　Do you agree with the Court (in the second excerpted paragraph) that the preliminary reference only called for a ruling on the interpretation of the Treaty and not on its application? Did the Court in fact confine its ruling to the interpretation of Article 12?

4.　Under *van Gend en Loos,* whether a Treaty provision has direct effect turns on whether it is "clear and unconditional" or instead "require[s] legislative intervention by the States." What is the logical basis for such a test? Does Article 12 in your judgment satisfy it? Why did the Court not merely establish the test for direct effectiveness and then allow the Dutch court to decide whether Article 12 satisfied it?

5.　Note the Court's rejection of the argument that the availability of enforcement actions under Articles 226 and 227 (ex 169 and 170) rendered direct effect unnecessary. Do you agree with the Court?

6.　In what respect does *van Gend en Loos* remind you of early constitutional law decisions of the US Supreme Court? Note the reference (in the fifth paragraph) to the Preamble of the Treaty and the admonition (in the fourth paragraph) "to consider the spirit [and] the general scheme" as well as the "wording" of the Treaty. In what respect is the Court's emphasis on securing enforcement of Community law through "[t]he vigilance of individuals" (13th paragraph) as well as through the Commission also reminiscent of US law?

COSTA v. ENTE NAZIONALE PER L'ENERGIA ELETTRICA (ENEL)

Case 6/64, [1964] ECR 585.

[Italy nationalized its electricity production and distribution industries in 1962, transferring their property to a new organization, ENEL. Costa, in a dispute arising out of his failure to pay a roughly $3 electric bill, challenged the act of nationalization which created ENEL. Besides being a consumer, Costa was a shareholder of the nationalized company and an Italian taxpayer and lawyer.

Costa argued that the nationalization act violated the Italian Constitution and Articles 31 (ex 37), 53 (since repealed), 88 (ex 93) and 97 (ex 102) of the

EC Treaty. The Milan court sought preliminary rulings both from the Italian Constitutional Court on the relevant questions of Italian constitutional law and from the Court of Justice on the proper interpretation of the Treaty articles. The Italian Government maintained that only the Italian Constitutional Court could set aside a national statute, and even then only by reference to the Italian Constitution, and that a preliminary reference accordingly should have been made to it alone.

The Court dealt first with the claim that by finding that a Treaty provision has direct effect in national law, and then interpreting the provision, the Court might in effect declare a national law invalid, which is not its province. The Court insisted that it could determine the direct effectiveness and meaning of a Treaty provision, and still not "apply the Treaty to a specific case or ... decide upon the validity of a provision of domestic law in relation to the Treaty."

The Court also rejected the notion that a Member State court is bound to apply national law even if it violates the Treaty. For this discussion, see page 269 *infra*. The Court then turned to the direct effect and meaning of the relevant Treaty articles.]

ON THE INTERPRETATION OF ARTICLE 102 [NOW 97]

Article 102 [now 97] provides that, where "there is reason to fear" that a provision laid down by law may cause "distortion", the Member State desiring to proceed therewith shall "consult the Commission"; the Commission has power to recommend to the Member States the adoption of suitable measures to avoid the distortion feared.

This Article, placed in the chapter devoted to the "Approximation of Laws", is designed to prevent the differences between the legislation of the different nations with regard to the objectives of the Treaty from becoming more pronounced. By virtue of this provision, Member States have limited their freedom of initiative by agreeing to submit to an appropriate procedure of consultation. By binding themselves unambiguously to prior consultation with the Commission in all those cases where their projected legislation might create a risk, however slight, of a possible distortion, the States have undertaken an obligation to the Community which binds them as States, but which does not create individual rights which national courts must protect. ...

ON THE INTERPRETATION OF ARTICLE 93 [NOW 88]

Under Article 93(1) and (2) [now 88(1) and (2)], the Commission, in cooperation with Member States, is to "keep under constant review all systems of aid existing in those States" with a view to the adoption of appropriate measures required by the functioning of the Common Market.

By virtue of Article 93(3) [now 88(3)], the Commission is to be informed, in sufficient time, of any plans to grant or alter aid, the Member State concerned not being entitled to put its proposed measures into effect until the Community procedure, and, if necessary, any proceedings before the Court of Justice, have been completed.

These provisions ... are designed, on the one hand, to eliminate progressively existing aids and, on the other hand, to prevent the individual States in the conduct of their internal affairs from introducing new aids "in any form whatsoever" which are likely directly or indirectly to favour certain undertakings or products in an appreciable way, and which threaten, even potentially, to distort competition. By virtue of Article 92 [now 87], the Member States have acknowledged that such aids are incompatible with the Common Market and have thus implicitly undertaken not to create any more, save as otherwise provided in the Treaty; in Article 93 [now 88], on the other hand, they have merely agreed to submit themselves to appropriate procedures for the abolition of existing aids and the introduction of new ones.

By so expressly undertaking to inform the Commission "in sufficient time" of any plans for aid, and by accepting the procedures laid down in Article 93, the States have entered into an obligation with the Community, which binds them as States but creates no individual rights except in the case of the final provision of Article 93(3) [now 88(3)], which is not in question in the present case.

* * *

ON THE INTERPRETATION OF ARTICLE 53 [SINCE REPEALED]

By Article 53 [since repealed] the Member States undertake not to introduce any new restrictions on the right of establishment in their territories of nationals of other Member States, save as otherwise provided in the Treaty. The obligation thus entered into by the States simply amounts legally to a duty not to act, which is neither subject to any conditions, nor, as regards its execution or effect, to the adoption of any measure either by the States or by the Commission. It is therefore legally complete in itself and is consequently capable of producing direct effects on the relations between Member States and individuals. Such an express prohibition which came into force with the Treaty throughout the Community, and thus became an integral part of the legal system of the Member States, forms part of the law of those States and directly concerns their nationals, in whose favour it has created individual rights which national courts must protect.

[The Court proceeded to interpret Article 53 as barring a Member State from introducing measures subjecting the establishment of nationals of other Member States to more severe rules than those that the State prescribes for its own nationals. (Freedom of establishment is dealt with in Chapter 17 *infra*.)]

ON THE INTERPRETATION OF ARTICLE 37 [NOW 31]

Article 37(1) [now 31(1)] provides that Member States shall progressively adjust any "State monopolies of a commercial character" so as to ensure that no discrimination regarding the conditions under which goods are procured and marketed exists between nationals of Member States. By Article 37(2) [now 31(2)], the Member States are under an obligation to refrain from introducing any new measure which is contrary to the principles laid down in Article 37(1).

Thus, Member States have undertaken a dual obligation: in the first place, an active one to adjust State monopolies, in the second place, a passive one to avoid any new measures. The interpretation requested is of the second obligation together with any aspects of the first necessary for this interpretation.

Article 37(2) contains an absolute prohibition: not an obligation to do something but an obligation to refrain from doing something. This obligation is not accompanied by any reservation which might make its implementation subject to any positive act of national law. This prohibition is essentially one which is capable of producing direct effects on the legal relations between Member States and their nationals.

Such a clearly expressed prohibition which came into force with the Treaty throughout the Community, and so became an integral part of the legal system of the Member States, forms part of the law of those States and directly concerns their nationals, in whose favour it creates individual rights which national courts must protect.

[The Court then interpreted Article 37 as prohibiting any new commercial monopolies giving rise to national discrimination in the procurement or marketing of goods, and left it to the national court to decide whether these conditions were satisfied in the given case.]

Notes and Questions

1. Do you agree with the Court that it was able to determine the direct effectiveness and meaning of the Treaty provisions in question without presuming to apply those provisions to the specific case or passing on the validity of national law?

2. Why did the Court conclude that Articles 37 and 53 were directly effective, but that Articles 93 and 102 were not? What criteria did it consult? Are they the same as the criteria identified in *van Gend en Loos* and were they properly applied here?

3. Unsurprisingly, the Court has ruled that the statement of Community objectives in Article 2 of the EC Treaty does not create privately enforceable obligations for the Member States. Alsthom Atlantique v. Sulzer, Case 339/89, [1991] ECR I–107.

VAN DUYN v. HOME OFFICE

Case 41/74, [1974] ECR 1337.

[The British government, considering the Church of Scientology to be socially harmful and a threat to public welfare, instituted a policy of denying admission into the UK of any foreign national seeking to study or work at the Church's UK headquarters. There were no restrictions on British nationals seeking to practice scientology.

van Duyn, a Dutch national, was refused entry into Britain because she intended to work as a secretary at a college of the Scientology Church. She brought an action against the Home Office claiming a violation, among other things, of Article 48 [now 39] of the EC Treaty guaranteeing the free movement of workers.

The High Court asked the Court of Justice whether Article 48 was directly effective.]

[5]   It is provided, in Article 48(1) and (2) [now 39(1) and (2)], that freedom of movement for workers shall be secured by the end of the transitional

period and that such freedom shall entail "the abolition of any discrimination based on nationality between workers of Member States as regards employment, remuneration and other conditions of work and employment."

[6] These provisions impose on Member States a precise obligation which does not require the adoption of any further measure on the part either of the Community institutions or of the Member States and which leaves them, in relation to its implementation, no discretionary power.

[7] Paragraph 3 [of the then Article 48], which defines the rights implied by the principle of freedom of movement for workers, subjects them to limitations justified on grounds of public policy, public security or public health. The application of these limitations is, however, subject to judicial control, so that a Member State's right to invoke the limitations does not prevent the provisions of Article 48, which enshrine the principle of freedom of movement for workers, from conferring on individuals rights which are enforceable by them and which the national courts must protect.

Notes and Questions

1.   Compare the language of Article 48 [now 39] with that of the since-amended language of Article 12 at issue in *van Gend en Loos*. Do you agree with the Court's remark (¶ 6) that Articles 48(1) and (2) impose a "precise" obligation and leave Community and Member State authorities "no discretionary power" as to its implementation? Do you agree with its remark (¶ 7) that because a Member State's resort to the "public policy, public security or public health" exception in Article 48(3) is subject to judicial review, the exception does not deprive Article 48 of direct effect?

2.   Since the 1970s, the Court has had occasion to decide whether many EC Treaty articles have direct effect, in whole or in part. Some of these cases will appear in later chapters of this book. Notable among other provisions held to have direct effect are Articles 23 (ex 9) and 28 (ex 30) (on free movement of goods), 39 (ex 48) (on free movement of workers), 43 (ex 52) (on the right of establishment), 49 (ex 59) (on the right to perform services) and 81 and 82 (ex 85 and 86) (on competition law).

3.   Hurd was headmaster of the European School at Culham, Oxfordshire, UK. Although the Board of Governors of the European Schools had decided that a portion of the teachers' salaries (namely the "European supplement," or amount needed to bring the Member State's national teacher salary up to a standard salary level fixed by the Board) was not to be taxed under national law, the British tax authorities indeed sought to tax that portion of Hurd's salary (as well as a so-called "differential allowance" which the Board paid to teachers to make up the differences in after-tax salaries caused by differences in national tax rates, and which the Board likewise declared to be nontaxable.) The British Income Tax Commissioners, hearing Hurd's objections, asked the Court of Justice for a preliminary ruling. The Court held that the UK's taxation of these two amounts constituted a drain on Community resources and thus jeopardized the attainment of Community objectives in violation of Article 10 (ex 5) of the EC Treaty, which imposes on the Member States a "duty of genuine cooperation and assistance" toward the Community.

Hurd was nevertheless found not to be entitled under Community law to avoid payment of the disputed tax in the British courts. Why? See Hurd v. Jones,

Case 44/84, [1986] ECR 29. Do you agree with that result on legal and policy grounds?

DEFRENNE v. SOCIETE ANONYME BELGE DE NAVIGATION AERIENNE SABENA

Case 43/75, [1976] ECR 455.

[Defrenne, a flight attendant with Sabena Airlines since 1951, was required by her contract to cease employment as a crew member on account of her age. She brought several actions against Sabena in a Belgian labor court for losses resulting from alleged gender discrimination in salary, severance pay and pension rights, invoking the right to equal pay for equal work under Article 141 (ex 119) of the EC Treaty. On appeal from a dismissal of certain of her claims, a preliminary reference was made to the Court of Justice regarding the effect of the then Article 119 in the Belgian courts.]

[7] The question of the direct effect of Article 119 [now 141] must be considered in the light of the nature of the principle of equal pay, the aim of this provision and its place in the scheme of the Treaty.

[8] Article 119 pursues a double aim.

[9] First, in the light of the different stages of the development of social legislation in the various Member States, the aim of Article 119 is to avoid a situation in which undertakings established in States which have actually implemented the principle of equal pay suffer a competitive disadvantage in intra-Community competition as compared with undertakings established in States which have not yet eliminated discrimination against women workers as regards pay.

[10] Secondly, this provision forms part of the social objectives of the Community, which is not merely an economic union, but is at the same time intended, by common action, to ensure social progress and seek the constant improvement of the living and working conditions of their peoples. . . .

* * *

[12] This double aim, which is at once economic and social, shows that the principle of equal pay forms part of the foundations of the Community.

* * *

[18] [A] distinction must be drawn within the whole area of application of Article 119 between, first, direct and overt discrimination which may be identified solely with the aid of the criteria based on equal work and equal pay referred to by the article in question and, secondly, indirect and disguised discrimination which can only be identified by reference to more explicit implementing provisions of a Community or national character.

[19] It is impossible not to recognize that the complete implementation of the aim pursued by Article 119, by means of the elimination of all discrimination, direct or indirect, between men and women workers . . . may in certain cases involve the elaboration of criteria whose implementation

necessitates the taking of appropriate measures at [the] Community and national level.

* * *

21   Among the forms of direct discrimination which may be identified solely by reference to the criteria laid down by Article 119 must be included in particular those which have their origin in legislative provisions or in collective labour agreements and which may be detected on the basis of a purely legal analysis of the situation.

22   This applies even more in cases where men and women receive unequal pay for equal work carried out in the same establishment or service, whether public or private.

23   As is shown by the very findings of the judgment making the reference, in such a situation the court is in a position to establish all the facts which enable it to decide whether a woman worker is receiving lower pay than a male worker performing the same tasks.

24   In such [a] situation, at least, Article 119 is directly applicable and may thus give rise to individual rights which the courts must protect.

[The Court then rejected the argument that use of the term "principle" in Article 119 shows that the Article was not meant to have direct effect or was otherwise to be considered only "a vague declaration." It held that, on the contrary, the term showed the "fundamental nature" of the provision.]

30   It is also impossible to put forward arguments based on the fact that Article 119 only refers expressly to "Member States".

31   Indeed, as the Court has already found in other contexts, the fact that certain provisions of the Treaty are formally addressed to the Member States does not prevent rights from being conferred at the same time on any individual who has an interest in the performance of the duties thus laid down.

32   The very wording of Article 119 shows that it imposes on States a duty to bring about a specific result to be mandatorily achieved within a fixed period.

33   The effectiveness of this provision cannot be affected by the fact that the duty imposed by the Treaty has not been discharged by certain Member States and that the joint institutions have not reacted sufficiently energetically against this failure to act.

34   To accept the contrary view would be to risk raising the violation of the right to the status of a principle of interpretation, a position the adoption of which would not be consistent with the task assigned to the Court by Article 164 [ex 220] of the Treaty.

35   Finally, in its reference to "Member States", Article 119 is alluding to those States in the exercise of all those of their functions which may usefully contribute to the implementation of the principle of equal pay.

* * *

[37]   Therefore, the reference to "Member States" in Article 119 cannot be interpreted as excluding the intervention of the courts in direct application of the Treaty.

* * *

[39]   [S]ince Article 119 is mandatory in nature, the prohibition on discrimination between men and women applies not only to the action of public authorities, but also extends to all agreements which are intended to regulate paid labour collectively, as well as to contracts between individuals.

[40]   The reply to the first question must therefore be that the principle of equal pay contained in Article 119 may be relied upon before the national courts and that these courts have a duty to ensure the protection of the rights which this provision vests in individuals, in particular ... in cases in which men and women receive unequal pay for equal work which is carried out in the same establishment or service, whether private or public.

[However, "considerations of legal certainty affecting all the interests involved" caused the Court to hold that Article 119 should not be given direct effect in support of claims for periods of work prior to the date of the Court's judgment (except for claims that by then had already been filed).]

Notes and Questions

1.   In light of its requirement that Member States "ensure and subsequently maintain" the principle of equal pay for men and women, how could Article 119 (now 141) be said to be unconditional or not to require implementing legislation? Compare Article 119 in this respect with the then Articles 12 and 48 in the *van Gend en Loos* and *van Duyn* cases. In Chapter 32, we will see that Article 67 on the free movement of capital (since repealed), containing language similar to that of Article 119, was held not to have direct effect.

2.   The Court in *Defrenne* (¶¶ 18–24) confined the direct effect of Article 119 to cases of "direct" as opposed to "indirect" discrimination or, to be more precise, discrimination "which may be identified solely by reference to the criteria laid down by Article 119." Does this make sense to you?

3.   In another portion of the judgment, the Court ruled that the fact that certain Member States had failed to implement Article 119 according to schedule (by 1962 or, in the case of the new Member States, 1973), and that the Council had to issue a 1975 directive (75/117) to promote compliance and improve remedies for noncompliance, did not detract from the Article's direct effect. In other words, the fact that the Council felt it needed to adopt legislation in the area of Article 119 did not lessen Article 119's direct effect. Is this a sound position?

4.   As noted at the end of the judgment, the Court in *Defrenne* went on to rule that Article 119 should not be given "retroactive" direct effect, that is, be directly applied to claims for pay periods prior to the date of judgment (except for claims that by then had already been filed). On this issue, see page 185 *supra*. Is this consistent with the very principle of direct effect? Does saying (as *Defrenne* does in ¶ 75) that "the direct effect of Article 119 cannot be relied on to support claims concerning pay periods prior to the date of this judgment" mean that Member State agencies and courts are actually *barred* in such cases from basing

pay discrimination relief on Article 119, or does it merely mean that Community law *does not require* them to give Article 119 direct effect to that extent?

5. Since most EC Treaty provisions impose obligations on the Member States rather than on private parties, direct effect was initially conceived of as pertaining to legal claims directed against Member State authorities. *van Gend en Loos, Costa v. ENEL* and *van Duyn* typify such claims. Defrenne, however, invoked Article 119 in support of a claim against her employer for damages due to discrimination in a private law employment relationship. Note that the Court in *Defrenne* deliberately extended the direct effect of Article 119 to all establishments or services "whether public or private" (¶ 40). As Chapter 37 *infra* relates, since *Defrenne,* Article 119 has regularly been applied horizontally to purely private sector employment relationships.

Few other provisions of the EC Treaty have been found by the Court to give rise to direct horizontal effect. Among the most prominent are the competition law Articles 81 and 82 (ex 85 and 86), forbidding private commercial agreements in restraint of trade and abuses by enterprises of a dominant position. In an important development, however, the Court has now affirmed that the prohibition of nationality discrimination contained in Article 39 (ex 48) of the EC Treaty on the free movement of workers applies to discrimination by private parties as well. See Angonese v. Cassa di Risparmio di Bolzano SpA, Case C–281/98, [2000] ECR I–4139, excerpted in Chapter 15 *infra.*

We will return to the question of "horizontal" direct effect later in this chapter in connection with the question whether directives should be given direct effect between private parties when those directives are based upon treaty articles which, unlike Article 141, do not specifically target private legal relationships.

6. The question whether international treaties entered into by the EU are capable of having direct effect, as understood in Community law, is best deferred to Part V. Suffice it here to say that the Court of Justice has reaffirmed that the provisions of the GATT, by virtue of the GATT's "spirit, general scheme and terms," are not capable of having direct effect, see Amministrazione delle Finanze dello Stato v. Chiquita Italia SpA, Case C–469/93, [1995] ECR I–4533. (On the other hand, the Court found in that case that certain pertinent provisions of the Lomé Convention did have direct effect.)

NOTE ON DIRECT APPLICABILITY AND DIRECT EFFECT

The Court of Justice in *van Gend en Loos* did not employ the term "directly applicable," which is the term that Article 249 (ex 189) uses to describe the status of regulations. Instead it described Article 12 as producing "direct effects," a term not found in the Treaty. The discrepancy in usage has given rise to much discussion in academic and non-academic literature alike. The Court itself sometimes appears to use the terms interchangeably and at other times not.

In this book, as in much of the literature, the terms direct applicability and direct effect carry different meanings. A provision of Community law will be considered directly applicable within the domestic legal order if it becomes an element of that order without need of any formal "incorporation" into Member State law. This is certainly the case for legislation taking the form of regulations under Article 249. The term directly applicable, as used in this sense, has an obvious affinity with the more conventional international law term "self-executing."

The Court of Justice has always maintained that directly applicable Community law does not need to be incorporated into domestic legislation before becoming an element of the national legal orders. (In fact, the Court considers it wrong and dangerous for Member States to incorporate regulations into domestic law in ways that might obscure their Community law status.) In the Court's view, binding Community law rules directly engage the Member States as, when and to the extent those rules themselves provide. However, some Member States, as we shall see, considered it necessary upon joining the Community to adopt a constitutional or legislative text doing away with the need for the separate incorporation of the Treaties or secondary legislation into the domestic legal order. The implication is that in these States, absent the constitutional or legislative language adopted, each Community law instrument would have had to be separately transposed by some national enactment in order to become directly applicable domestically.

What does the notion of "direct effect," as employed in *van Gend en Loos* and elsewhere, add to "direct applicability?" As that case suggests, a Community law rule has direct effect if it creates rights for private parties, and not merely obligations for the Member States. The practical consequence is that private parties can then enforce these rights against the Member States in national courts, the latter guided as necessary by the Court of Justice through preliminary rulings. To say further that certain Community law provisions have horizontal direct effect, as we now know, is to say that they create rights and obligations as between private parties and not merely against Member States. Once again, the practical consequence is that national courts are bound to provide a suitable remedy for the enforcement of such private rights and obligations.

Does it follow from the fact that regulations are directly applicable under Article 249 that they necessarily also have direct effect? Some of the Court's language suggests that this may be the case. In Variola SpA v. Amministrazione Italiana delle Finanze, Case 34/73, [1973] ECR 981, a Trieste court sought to know whether certain "administrative" and "statistical" duties imposed by Italian customs officials were charges equivalent to customs duties in violation of Council regulations purporting to abolish such duties. It asked the Court of Justice both to interpret the regulations and to decide if they have direct effect. The Court's ruling and reasoning are strikingly simple:

> Article 189 [now 249] of the Treaty [provides that] a Regulation "shall have general application" and "shall be directly applicable in all Member States."

> Accordingly, owing to its very nature and its place in the system of sources of Community law, a Regulation has immediate effect and, consequently, operates to confer rights on private parties which the national courts have a duty to protect.

[1973] ECR at 990. On the other hand, although regulations would seem necessarily to invite direct effect, that may not be the case if their language is not "clear and capable of direct application without difficulty." See De Sociale Voorzorg Mutual Insurance Fund v. Bertholet, Case 31/64, [1965] ECR 81, 86.

A lingering question is whether and how a Community law norm can possibly have direct effect as defined above without also being directly applicable. The question arises most urgently, of course, with directives. Article 249 does not describe directives as directly applicable in the Member States and yet, as we shall see, the Court of Justice often attributes direct effect to them, in whole or in part. One possibility is that the drafters of the Treaty confused direct applicability with direct effect, and meant by the language of Article 249 merely to suggest that regulations are presumptively directly effective, but directives not. Another possibility is that the drafters used direct applicability and direct effect in the distinctive ways we have used those terms in this book, and merely meant by Article 249 to suggest that regulations are *always* directly applicable, while directives are only *sometimes* so. Under this view, only directly applicable directives would be capable of having direct effect, and in fact any directly effective directive would automatically be deemed directly applicable as well. Under either theory, it is easy to see how the Court of Justice might end up using the terms directly applicable and directly effective interchangeably.

In any case, it is direct effect that above all determines the real effectiveness of Community law. Unless private parties have access to Community law in the only legal channels that are normally open to them (namely national administrations and national courts), and unless those fora make appropriate remedies available, the purposes of Community law may well be frustrated.

2. THE DIRECT EFFECT OF EC DIRECTIVES AND DECISIONS

As just implied, the question whether directives are capable of having direct effect in the national legal orders was a problematic one. If Article 249 means to deny the direct applicability of directives, then directives can scarcely be thought to have direct effect. But even if Article 249 allows at least some directives to be directly applicable, there still remains other troubling language in Article 249, namely that directives "leave to the national authorities the choice of form and methods" by which directives are implemented. Still, there is no doubt that attributing direct effect to directives would enhance Community law's overall effectiveness, especially as the Council and Commission frequently use directives as the vehicle for harmonizing national laws. The question is whether directives can properly be given that effect and whether such effect, if given, may run horizontally as well as vertically.

The following cases laid the foundations, notwithstanding the problematic language of Article 249, for treating directives as capable of having direct effect—vertical and horizontal—in the national legal orders.

(a) Vertical Direct Effect

VAN DUYN v. HOME OFFICE
Case 41/74, [1974] ECR 1337.

[For the facts of the case and part of the Court's judgment, see page 246 *supra*. The English High Court also asked the Court of Justice whether Directive 64/221, which sets limits on the public policy exception to the free movement of workers under Article 39 [ex 48] (see Chapter 15 *infra*), was directly effective.]

9　The second question asks the Court to say whether Council Directive No. 64/221 ... is directly applicable so as to confer on individuals rights enforceable by them in the courts of a Member State.

10　[T]he only provision of the Directive which is relevant is ... Article 3(1) which provides that "measures taken on grounds of public policy or public security shall be based exclusively on the personal conduct of the individual concerned."

11　The United Kingdom observes that, since Article 189 [now 249] of the Treaty distinguishes between the effects ascribed to regulations, directives and decisions, it must therefore be presumed that the Council, in issuing a directive rather than making a regulation, must have intended that the directive should have an effect other than that of a regulation and accordingly that the former should not be directly applicable.

12　If, however, by virtue of the provisions of Article 189 regulations are directly applicable and, consequently, may by their very nature have direct effects, it does not follow from this that other categories of acts mentioned in that Article can never have similar effects. It would be incompatible with the binding effect attributed to a directive by Article 189 to exclude, in principle, the possibility that the obligation which it imposes may be invoked by those concerned. In particular, where the Community authorities have, by directive, imposed on Member States the obligation to pursue a particular course of conduct, the useful effect [*l'effet utile*] of such an act would be weakened if individuals were prevented from relying on it before their national courts and if the latter were prevented from taking it into consideration as an element of Community law. Article 177 [now 234], which empowers national courts to refer to the Court questions concerning the validity and interpretation of all acts of the Community institutions, without distinction, implies furthermore that these acts may be invoked by individuals in the national courts. It is necessary to examine, in every case, whether the nature, general scheme and wording of the provision in question are capable of having direct effects on the relations between Member States and individuals.

13　By providing that measures taken on grounds of public policy shall be based exclusively on the personal conduct of the individual concerned, Article 3(1) of Directive No. 64/221 is intended to limit the discretionary power which national laws generally confer on the authorities responsible for the entry and expulsion of foreign nationals. First, the provision lays down an obligation which is not subject to any exception or condition and which, by its very nature, does not require the intervention of any act on the part either of the institutions of the Community or of Member States. Secondly, because Member States are thereby obliged, in implementing a clause which derogates from one of the fundamental principles of the Treaty in favour of individuals, not to take account of factors extraneous to personal conduct, legal certainty for the persons concerned requires that they should be able to rely on this obligation even though it has been laid down in a legislative act which has no automatic direct effect in its entirety.

14   If the meaning and exact scope of the provision raise questions of interpretation, these questions can be resolved by the courts, taking into account also the procedure under Article 177 of the Treaty.

[On the merits, the court gave an interpretation of Article 39 (ex 48) and Directive 64/221 that allowed the UK to exclude van Duyn from entry on public policy grounds. See Chapter 15 *infra*.]

Notes and Questions

1.   How can the Court find that Directive 64/221 is precise enough to have direct effect if it believes (¶ 14) that Member State courts may have such doubts about the directive's meaning as to need preliminary rulings from the Court of Justice?

2.   The Court strongly reaffirmed its position on the direct effect of directives in Becker v. Finanzamt Münster–Innenstadt, Case 8/81, [1982] ECR 53. Becker, a self-employed credit negotiator, claimed an exemption from certain "turnover" taxes on income she received from March to June 1979 in the form of commissions, basing the exemption on a May 1977 Council directive (the Sixth VAT Directive) which required the Member States by January 1, 1979 to exempt from turnover taxation all income earned from credit negotiation. However, since Germany had not yet implemented the directive (and in fact did not do so until January 1, 1980), the German tax law contained no exemption on which Becker could rely, and the authorities accordingly assessed a turnover tax on her commission income for the period in question. The German tax court to which Becker appealed asked the Court of Justice whether the directive was "directly applicable" in Germany. Echoing *van Duyn,* the Court of Justice held:

> [W]herever the provisions of a directive appear ... to be unconditional and sufficiently precise, those provisions may, in the absence of implementing measures adopted within the prescribed period, be relied upon as against any national provision which is incompatible with the directive....

[1982] ECR at 71.

In a similar case several years later, the Supreme Tax Court of Germany refused to follow the *Becker* decision and continued to deny direct effect to the Sixth VAT Directive. For discussion of that judgment (*Kloppenburg*) and the German Constitutional Court's disapproval of it, see page 304 *infra*.

3.   In Comitato di Coordinamento per la Difesa della Cava & Others v. Regione Lombardia & Others, Case C–236/92, [1994] ECR I–483, the Court held that Council Directive 75/442 on the prevention, recycling and processing of waste lacks direct effect, and that individuals may not therefore rely on it to challenge the region's approval of a solid urban waste facility as abridging their rights to protection of the environment. It interpreted the directive as establishing a framework for action to be taken by the Member States on waste treatment, and not as in itself requiring the adoption of specific measures or the adoption of a particular waste disposal method. Many recent internal market directives take the form of "framework" directives and, by this reasoning, also ordinarily lack direct effect.

Compare World Wildlife Fund v. Autonome Provinz Bozen, Case C–435/97, [1999] ECR I–5613. Two neighbors of a Bolzano airport and two environmental associations sought in an Italian court to have set aside the decision approving a project to convert a previously military and private airport into a commercial one, on the ground that an environmental impact assessment, required by Directive

85/337, had not been performed. On preliminary reference, the Court of Justice ruled that individuals may rely on the directive and obtain the setting aside of national measures taken in violation of it. Do you agree?

4. Are Commission and Council *decisions* addressed to Member States also capable of having direct effect so as to give rise to privately enforceable rights? The question arose in the case of Grad v. Finanzamt Traunstein, Case 9/70, [1970] ECR 825. Grad, a long-distance hauler based in Austria, refused to pay a German tax for long distance travel on German roads, claiming that the tax violated a 1965 Council decision requiring the Member States to introduce a statutory value added tax by January 1, 1972, and barring them after that point from collecting turnover taxes on imports or exports between Member States. Germany enacted its value added tax on January 1, 1968, but the next year introduced the long-distance-travel tax contested by Grad. The Court ruled as follows:

> ... It would be incompatible with the binding effect attributed to decisions by Article 189 to exclude in principle the possibility that persons [not as such addressed by a decision but nevertheless] affected may invoke the obligation imposed by [the] decision. ... [T]he effectiveness (*"l'effet utile"*) of [a Community decision imposing an obligation on a Member State] would be weakened if the nationals of that State could not invoke it in the courts and the national courts could not take it into consideration as part of Community law.
> * * *
>
> [I]n each particular case, it must be ascertained whether the nature, background and wording of the provision in question are capable of producing direct effects in the legal relationships between the addressee of the act and third parties.

[1970] ECR at 837. In *Grad,* the decision was not only addressed to Member States, but also bore some resemblance to a regulation. Suppose a decision is instead addressed to a private party, as in the Commission's grant or denial to an enterprise of an exemption from Community competition rules. Might that decision give rise to claims by or against the enterprise that national courts, under the notion of direct effect, would then be bound to enforce? Remember that Article 81 (ex 85), under which the Commission may take such action, has horizontal direct effect.

PUBBLICO MINISTERO v. RATTI
Case 148/78, [1979] ECR 1629.

[The board of directors of an Italian solvent and varnish manufacturer, represented by Ratti, decided to package and label its products in accordance with two Community directives, 73/173 (on solvents) and 77/728 (on varnishes), even though the directives had not yet been implemented in Italy. Ratti was prosecuted for not including labeling information that was required by the Italian law then in force, but not required under the directives. At the time the goods were marketed, Italy's deadline for implementing Directive 73/173 on solvents had passed, but the deadline for implementing Directive 77/728 on varnishes had not. Ratti raised the directives in his defense, and the Criminal Court of Milan asked the Court of Justice several questions about the enforceability of the penalties prescribed by Italian law.]

A. The Interpretation of Directive No. 73/173

[The Court repeated its language in *van Duyn, Becker* and *Grad* on the capacity of directives and decisions to have direct effect.]

22   Consequently a Member State which has not adopted the implementing measures required by the directive in the prescribed periods may not rely, as against individuals, on its own failure to perform the obligations which the directive entails.

23   It follows that a national court, requested by a person who has complied with the provisions of a directive not to apply a national provision incompatible with the directive not incorporated into the internal legal order of a defaulting Member State, must uphold that request if the obligation in question is unconditional and sufficiently precise.

24   Therefore the answer to the first question must be that after the expiration of the period fixed for the implementation of a directive, a Member State may not apply its internal law—even if it is provided with penal sanctions—which has not yet been adapted in compliance with the directive, to a person who has complied with the requirements of the directive.

[The Court then found that the 1973 solvents directive preempted the different Italian law. This aspect of the case is treated at page 557 *infra*.]

B. THE INTERPRETATION OF DIRECTIVE NO. 77/728

39   [T]he national court asks whether Council Directive No. 77/728 ... is immediately and directly applicable with regard to the obligations imposed on Member States to refrain from action as from the date of notification of that directive in a case where a person, acting upon a legitimate expectation, has complied with the provisions of that directive before the expiry of the period within which the Member State must comply with the said directive.

* * *

41   Article 12 of that directive provides that Member States must implement it within 24 months of its notification, which took place on 9 November 1977.

42   That period has not yet expired and the States to which the directive was addressed have until 9 November 1979 to incorporate the provisions of Directive No. 77/728 into their internal legal orders.

43   It follows that, for the reasons expounded in the grounds of the answer to the national court's first question, it is only at the end of the prescribed period and in the event of the Member State's default that the directive ... will be able to have the effects described in the answer to the first question.

44   Until that date is reached the Member States remain free in that field.

* * *

46   In conclusion, since a directive by its nature imposes obligations only on Member States, it is not possible for an individual to plead the principle of "legitimate expectation" before the expiry of the period prescribed for its implementation.

[47] Therefore the answer to the [present] question must be that Directive No. 77/728 ... cannot bring about with respect to any individual who has complied with the provisions of the said directive before the expiration of the adaptation period prescribed for the Member State any effect capable of being taken into consideration by national courts.

Notes and Questions

1. The Court in *Ratti* (¶ 46) concluded that it was "not possible" for a person to avoid criminal liability under Member State law by invoking the Community directive on varnishes, since Italy still had time to implement it. Does this mean that Italy was actually *barred* from exempting Ratti from liability in this case, or was simply *not required* to exempt him from such liability? Which would be the better rule?

The Dutch courts have allowed a criminal defendant to invoke a Community directive as a defense even when the alleged offense predated the directive. Division of the Hof, the Hague, no. 541, [1989] NJ 1990, 17 Eur.L.Dig. 462 (Feb. 3, 1989). Should a directive be given such "retroactive" direct effect only in cases where the directive is raised as a criminal defense, or also where the directive serves as the basis of an affirmative claim?

2. Criminal charges were brought against a restaurant in Arnhem, the Netherlands, for offering for sale a beverage that it called mineral water but that was in fact only carbonated tap water. The charges were brought under a municipal ordinance that prohibited marketing for human consumption goods of unsound composition. The prosecution cited a Council directive requiring the Member States to take the measures necessary to ensure that only certified natural mineral waters were marketed as such, but that the Dutch government at the time of the events in question was overdue in implementing. May a criminal charge be based on the Council directive on the theory of direct effect? The Court has said that it may not. See Criminal Proceedings against Kolpinghuis Nijmegen BV, Case 80/86, [1987] ECR 3969. To the same effect, see Procura della Repubblica v. X, Joined Cases C–74 & 129/95, [1996] ECR I–6609; Criminal Proceedings against Arcaro, Case C–168/95, [1996] ECR I–4705. Do you see the logic and policy behind this rule? Would you extend the rule to non-criminal (i.e. civil) suits by the government against private parties?

3. In light of the *Ratti* case, what counsel would you give to enterprises doing business in the Community to help protect them from committing violations of national law through their good faith reliance on Community law?

4. As we shall see, EC Treaty Article 95(4) (ex 100a(4)) permits Member States to seek a derogation from most harmonization directives adopted to promote the functioning of the internal market. The Swedish authorities charged a confectioner under Swedish law for selling sweets from Germany containing a red colorant, despite the fact that the colorant was specifically approved by the relevant EC directive, on the ground that Sweden had applied for a derogation under Article 95(4). The Court ruled that neither the possibility that a Member State could apply for a derogation, nor even the fact that a Member State had applied for one, lessens a directive's direct effect after the transposition period has ended. Criminal Proceedings against Kortas, Case C–319/97, [1999] ECR I–3143.

5. *Ratti* makes the direct effect of a directive against the State conditional upon the directive's transposition period having fully elapsed; until such time, the State evidently may continue to apply non-conforming Member State law. Is the

Court making too much turn on the distinction between fully elapsed and partially elapsed transposition periods?

In fact the Court has subsequently softened the line somewhat. In Inter–Environnement Wallonie ASBL v. Région Wallonne, Case C–129/96, [1997] ECR I–7411, the Walloon regional executive issued an order on hazardous waste that allegedly violated an unimplemented directive whose period for transposition had not fully elapsed at the time the Walloon order was issued. In answer to a question put by the Belgian Conseil d'Etat, which was hearing a legal challenge to the order, the Court of Justice ruled that, as of the time a directive is adopted—and throughout its transposition period—Member States are precluded from adopting any national measures contrary to that directive. According to the Court, a directive has legal effect vis-à-vis the Member States from the moment it is addressed to them, and that effect entails for the States the obligation during the transition period to take the measures necessary to ensure that the prescribed result is achieved by the end of that period. (The Court derived this conclusion from Articles 249 and 251 (ex 189 and 191), in conjunction with Article 10 (ex 5) of the EC Treaty.) The adoption during that period of measures that seriously compromise a State's ability to achieve the intended result is itself inconsistent with that obligation.

While stating that national courts were to determine whether a measure adopted in that period seriously compromises achievement of the intended result, the Court gave some indications as to how that determination might be made:

[47] In making that assessment, the national court must consider, in particular, whether the provisions in issue purport to constitute full transposition of the directive, as well as the effects in practice of applying those incompatible and of their duration in time.

[48] For example, if the provisions in issue are intended to constitute full and definitive transposition of the directive, their incompatibility with the directive might give rise to the presumption that the result prescribed by the directive will not be achieved within the period prescribed if it is impossible to amend them in time.

[49] Conversely, the national court could take into account the right of a Member State to adopt transitional measures or to implement the directive in stages. In such cases, the incompatibility of the transitional national measures with the directive, or the non-transposition of certain of its provisions, would not necessarily compromise the result prescribed.

Would it not have been simpler, and just as effective, if the Court had taken the position that national implementing legislation at variance with a directive is valid as long as it is adopted during (and not after) the transposition period, but that the legislation cannot, to the extent of the inconsistency, be applied in favor of the State, and to the detriment of a private party, once the implementation period has passed?

The national measure in *Walloon waste* was an enactment of *general* application. Suppose the Walloon region had instead merely issued an *individual* administrative act inconsistent with the unimplemented directive. Would that have changed the outcome? If not, how can the case be distinguished from *Ratti*, which permitted a prosecution within that interval?

(b) Horizontal Direct Effect

MARSHALL v. SOUTHAMPTON AND SOUTH–WEST HAMPSHIRE AREA HEALTH AUTHORITY

Case 152/84, [1986] ECR 723.

[Marshall was employed by the Southampton and South–West Hampshire Area Health Authority from June 1966 until March 1980, when she was dismissed solely because she had passed the retirement age (60) that the Health Authority applied to women. Because the Authority's retirement age for men was 65, Marshall claimed that she was the victim of sex discrimination in violation of Directive 76/207 on equal work conditions for men and women, and the industrial tribunal agreed. The Employment Appeal Tribunal reversed this decision on the ground that the directive had not been adequately implemented by UK legislation, and that individuals may not invoke Community directives directly in proceedings before a UK court.

The Court of Appeal, noting that the Health Authority was an emanation of the British state, referred two questions to the Court of Justice: whether the dismissal violated Directive 76/207, and whether a directive may be directly relied upon by an individual in national court if the directive is not adequately implemented by national law. The first question is taken up in Chapter 37 *infra*. On the second question, the Court began by recalling its position in *van Duyn* and *Becker* on the vertical direct effect of directives. The Court then turned to the possibility that directives addressed to the States might confer on private parties rights enforceable against other private parties.]

48   With regard to the argument that a directive may not be relied upon against an individual, it must be emphasized that according to Article 189 [now 249] of the EEC [now EC] Treaty the binding nature of a directive, which constitutes the basis for the possibility of relying on the directive before a national court, exists only in relation to "each Member State to which it is addressed". It follows that a directive may not of itself impose obligations on an individual and that a provision of a directive may not be relied upon as such against such a person. It must therefore be examined whether, in this case, the respondent must be regarded as having acted as an individual.

49   In that respect it must be pointed out that where a person involved in legal proceedings is able to rely on a directive as against the State he may do so regardless of the capacity in which the latter is acting, whether employer or public authority. In either case it is necessary to prevent the State from taking advantage of its own failure to comply with Community law.

* * *

51   The argument submitted by the United Kingdom that the possibility of relying on provisions of the directive against the respondent *qua* organ of the State would give rise to an arbitrary and unfair distinction between the rights of State employees and those of private employees does not

justify any other conclusion. Such a distinction may easily be avoided if the Member State concerned has correctly implemented the directive in national law.

[The Court then examined the language of Article 5(1) of the directive according to which "[a]pplication of the principle of equal treatment with regard to working conditions, including the conditions governing dismissal, means that men and women shall be guaranteed the same conditions without discrimination on grounds of sex." It concluded that Article 5(1) spoke "in a general manner and in unequivocal terms [and] is therefore sufficiently precise to be relied on by an individual and to be applied by the national courts." The Court then turned to the question whether the directive's prohibition of discrimination was sufficiently unconditional, noting that (1) Article 2 of the directive contained certain exceptions, (2) Article 5(2) called on the Member States to take the measures necessary "to ensure the application of the principle of equality of treatment in the context of national law," and (3) Article 1(2) required the Council to adopt legislation for "the progressive implementation of the principle of equal treatment in matters of social security."]

54   With regard ... to the reservation contained in Article 1(2) ... concerning the application of the principle of equality of treatment in matters of social security, it must be observed that, although the reservation limits the scope of the directive, ... it does not lay down any condition on the application of that principle in its field of operation. ... Similarly, the exceptions to Directive No. 76/207 provided for in Article 2 thereof are not relevant to this case.

55   It follows that Article 5 of Directive No. 76/207 does not confer on the Member States the right to limit the application of the principle of equality of treatment in its field of operation or to subject it to conditions and that that provision is sufficiently precise and unconditional to be capable of being relied upon by an individual before a national court in order to avoid the application of any national provision which does not conform to Article 5(1).

Notes and Questions

1.   What is the Court's stated reason for denying directives horizontal direct effect? Are you persuaded by it? What other reasons might the Court have had for doing so?

2.   Is the question whether an entity is an instrumentality of the State or other public authority to be determined by reference to Community or national law rules? Given the great disparity between the classification of state-owned enterprises in Member States, this is an important issue. See the Court's attempt at a definition in Foster v. British Gas plc, Case C–188/89, [1990] ECR I–3313, discussed at page 1347 *infra*, and the House of Lords' attempt to apply it in that case. [1991] 2 WLR 1075, [1991] 2 CMLR 217 (H.L., April 18, 1991).

MARLEASING SA v. LA COMERCIAL INTERNACIONAL DE ALIMENTACION SA

Case C–106/89, [1990] ECR I–4135.

[Marleasing sued La Comercial in a Spanish court to have declared null and void the contract of incorporation of La Comercial on the ground that the contract lacked "cause" (a requirement of a contract's validity under the Spanish Civil Code) and also had been procured through misrepresentation and fraud. More specifically, Marleasing claimed that La Comercial had been formed by a third company, Barviesa, for the sole purpose of placing Barviesa's assets beyond the reach of its creditors, one of whom was Marleasing. (All three companies were of Spanish nationality.) Under Spanish law, misrepresentation or fraud ordinarily would justify a court in declaring such a contract null, but La Comercial claimed that the availability of relief was governed by the company law principles set out in Council Directive 68/151 (the First Company Law Directive).

Article 11 of Directive 68/151 provided that companies could be declared null and void for the specific reasons set out in that article, and only for those reasons. Several reasons (such as the unlawfulness of the corporate purposes or their violation of public policy) were included, but not fraud or misrepresentation toward the creditors of the founding shareholders. However, at the time in question, implementation of the directive in Spain had yet to occur and was in fact overdue.

The Spanish court asked the Court of Justice whether it could nullify La Comercial's incorporation for reasons other than those mentioned in article 11 of the directive.]

6   With regard to the question whether an individual may rely on the directive against a national law, it should be observed that, as the Court has consistently held, a directive may not of itself impose obligations on an individual and, consequently, a provision of a directive may not be relied upon as such against such a person [citing the *Marshall* case, *supra* page 260].

7   However, it is apparent ... that the national court seeks in substance to ascertain whether a national court hearing a case which falls within the scope of Directive 68/151 is required to interpret its national law in the light of the wording and the purpose of that directive in order to preclude a declaration of nullity of a public limited company on a ground other than those listed in Article 11 of the directive.

8   In order to reply to that question, it should be observed that the Member States' obligation arising from a directive to achieve the result envisaged by the directive and their duty under Article 5 [now 10] of the Treaty to take all appropriate measures, whether general or particular, to ensure the fulfilment of that obligation, is binding on all the authorities of Member States including, for matters within their jurisdiction, the courts. It follows that, in applying national law, whether the provisions in question were adopted before or after the directive, the national court called upon to

interpret it is required to do so, as far as possible, in the light of the wording and the purpose of the directive in order to achieve the result pursued by the latter and thereby comply with the third paragraph of Article 189 [now 249] of the Treaty.

9   It follows that the requirement that national law must be interpreted in conformity with Article 11 of Directive 68/151 precludes the interpretation of provisions of national law relating to public limited companies in such a manner that the nullity of a public limited company may be ordered on grounds other than those exhaustively listed in Article 11 of the directive in question.

10 With regard to the interpretation to be given to Article 11 of the directive, in particular Article 11(2)(b), it should be observed that that provision prohibits the laws of the Member States from providing for a judicial declaration of nullity on grounds other than those exhaustively listed in the directive, amongst which is the ground that the objects of the company are unlawful or contrary to public policy.

11 According to the Commission, the expression "objects of the company" must be interpreted as referring exclusively to the objects of the company as described in the instrument of incorporation or the articles of association. It follows, in the Commission's view, that a declaration of nullity of a company cannot be made on the basis of the activity actually pursued by it, for instance defrauding the founders' creditors.

12 That argument must be upheld. As is clear from the preamble to Directive 65/151, its purpose was to limit the cases in which nullity can arise and the retroactive effect of a declaration of nullity in order to ensure "certainty in the law as regards relations between the company and third parties, and also between members" (sixth recital). Furthermore, the protection of third parties "must be ensured by provisions which restrict to the greatest possible extent the grounds on which obligations entered into in the name of the company are not valid". It follows, therefore, that each ground of nullity provided for in Article 11 of the directive must be interpreted strictly. In those circumstances the words "objects of the company" must be understood as referring to the objects of the company as described in the instrument of incorporation or the articles of association.

13 The answer to the question submitted must therefore be that a national court hearing a case which falls within the scope of Directive 68/151 is required to interpret its national law in the light of the wording and the purpose of that directive in order to preclude a declaration of nullity of a public limited company on a ground other than those listed in Article 11 of the directive.

Notes and Questions

1.   Does *Marleasing* require Member State courts in all events to interpret national legislation in a way that renders it consistent with Community directives even if those directives have not been implemented? If so, can *Marleasing* be squared with *Marshall*? If not, when are Member State courts permitted to avoid such an interpretation? Professor Paul Craig calls what the Court requires in *Marleasing* "indirect effect." Craig, Directives: Direct Effect, Indirect Effect, 22 Eur. L. Rev. 519 (1997).

2.   Notice that the Spanish law that was the subject of interpretation in *Marleasing* was the Spanish Civil Code, the fundamental private law text in Spain, dating to 1889. Does it surprise you that the interpretation of such a text should be so heavily influenced by Community legislation?

3.   Member State courts vary in their willingness to interpret national law in conformity with an unimplemented directive, particularly when the law predates that directive. For example, the English Court of Appeal ruled in a December 1991 employment discrimination case that, while a national court faced with a directive that lacks direct effect must interpret its national law in such a way as to give effect to the directive, it should not do so where the result would be to distort the meaning of the national law being interpreted. Webb v. EMO Air Cargo (UK) Ltd., [1992] 2 All ER 43, [1992] 1 CMLR 793 (Dec. 20, 1991). On appeal, the House of Lords ruled that the national legislation had to be open to an interpretation consistent with the prior directive. The Lords accordingly referred a series of substantive law questions to the Court of Justice on the meaning of the directive. Webb v. EMO Air Cargo (UK) Ltd., [1992] 4 All ER 929, [1993] 1 CMLR 259 (Nov. 26, 1992). (The Court of Justice's preliminary ruling on those questions is Webb v. EMO Air Cargo (UK) Ltd., Case C–32/93, [1994] ECR I–3567.)

4.   In *Marleasing*, the time period for implementation had fully lapsed. Suppose it had not yet fully lapsed. Should national courts in that period likewise be bound by *Marleasing*'s interpretive obligations? The Court has ruled that it is bound. Criminal Proceedings against Kolpinghuis Nijmegen BV, Case 80/86, [1987] ECR 3969, discussed at page 258 *supra*, note 2.

FACCINI DORI v. RECREB SRL

Case C–91/92, [1994] ECR I–3325.

[While at the Milan railroad station, Faccini Dori signed a contract with Interdiffusion Srl for an English-language correspondence course. Four days later she wrote to the company, attempting to cancel the contract. Interdiffusion replied that it had assigned its claim to another company, Recreb Srl, which in turn rejected her cancellation. Litigation ensued, at the end of which Faccini Dori was found liable for the sum due under the contract.

Directive 85/577, concerning protection of consumers in respect of contracts negotiated away from business premises—which was due to be implemented by the end of 1987—required that consumers be given the right to cancel a contract, be informed of that right, and have seven days thereafter in which to give notice of cancellation. Italy did not implement the directive until 1992; if it had implemented it on time, Faccini Dori would presumably not have been held liable.

When Faccini Dori asked the Italian court to vacate its order, the court made a preliminary reference to the Court of Justice. The Court first concluded that the directive's provisions on the right of cancellation were sufficiently precise and unconditional to have direct effect.]

[19]   The second issue raised by the national court relates ... to the question whether, in the absence of measures transposing the directive within the prescribed time-limit, consumers may derive from the directive itself a

right of cancellation against traders with whom they have concluded contracts and enforce that right before a national court.

* * *

[22] [A]s is clear from the judgment in *Marshall*, the case-law on the possibility of relying on directives against State entities is based on the fact that under Article 189 [now 249] a directive is binding only in relation to "each Member State to which it is addressed." That case-law seeks to prevent "the State from taking advantage of its own failure to comply with Community law."

[23] It would be unacceptable if a State, when required by the Community legislature to adopt certain rules intended to govern the State's relations— or those of State entities—with individuals and to confer certain rights on individuals, were able to rely on its own failure to discharge its obligations so as to deprive individuals of the benefits of those rights. . . .

[24] The effect of extending the case-law to the sphere of relations between individuals would be to recognize a power in the Community to enact obligations for individuals with immediate effect, whereas it has competence to do so only where it is empowered to adopt regulations.

[25] It follows that, in the absence of measures transposing the directive within the prescribed time-limit, consumers cannot derive from the directive a right of cancellation as against traders with whom they have concluded a contract or enforce such a right in a national court.

[26] [A]s the Court has consistently held since [*von Colson and Kamann*, excerpted at page 390 *infra*], the Member States' obligation arising from a directive to achieve the result envisaged by the directive and their duty under Article 5 [now 10] of the Treaty to take all appropriate measures, whether general or particular, is binding on all the authorities of Member States, including, for matters within their jurisdiction, the courts. The judgments of the Court in [*Marleasing*] and [*Miret*, see page 409, note 1, *infra*], make it clear that, when applying national law, whether adopted before or after the directive, the national court that has to interpret that law must do so, as far as possible, in the light of the wording and the purpose of the directive so as to achieve the result it has in view and thereby comply with the third paragraph of Article 189 [now 249] of the Treaty.

[The Court then dealt with the possibility that "the result prescribed by the directive cannot be achieved by way of interpretation." For the Court's suggested solution, see page 410, note 5, *infra*.]

Notes and Questions

1. In what respects, if any, does the Court's rationale in *Faccini Dori* for denying horizontal direct effect to directives differ from the rationale given in *Marshall*? Does its "rule of interpretation" differ in any way from the one set out in *Marleasing*? Do any of the differences you discern bear a relationship to the principle of subsidiarity?

2. In Oceano Grupo Editorial SA v. Rocio Murciano Quintero, Joined Cases C–240–44/98. [2000] ECR–I 4941, several individuals entered into contracts with Oceano Grupo for the installment purchase of an encyclopedia; each of the

contracts contained a choice-of-forum clause vesting exclusive jurisdiction over disputes arising under the contract in the courts in Barcelona, where Oceano Grupo had its principal place of business but none of the purchasers had their domicile. Upon nonpayment, Oceano Grupo sued. None of the purchasers objected to the Barcelona court's jurisdiction, but the court itself questioned whether, assuming the choice-of-forum clause violated Council Directive 93/13/EEC on unfair terms in consumer contracts (which Spain was overdue in implementing), it should raise that point *sua sponte*, since the purchasers had not.

Invoking *Marleasing* and *Faccini Dori* for the proposition that national courts must, so far as possible, interpret national law so as to achieve the directive's intended result, the Court of Justice concluded that "[t]he requirement for an interpretation in conformity with the Directive requires the national court, in particular, to favour the interpretation that would allow it to decline of its own motion the jurisdiction conferred on it by virtue of an unfair term." Was this specific inference justified? Was the inference for the Court of Justice or for the national court to draw?

3. *Faccini Dori* shows the importance of horizontal direct effect (or its denial) to directives in the consumer protection field, where most such measures by their nature target private legal relationships. The case of El Corte Inglés SA v. Blázquez Rivero, Case C–192/94, [1996] ECR I–1281, is another fine example. Claiming that the travel arrangements made by the travel agency, Viajes El Corte Inglés, were substandard, a Spanish tourist refused to repay in full a loan that she had taken out to finance the holiday travel abroad. The finance company that had financed the trip (El Corte Inglés) was a close corporate affiliate of the travel agency and had the exclusive contractual right to extend credit to the agency's customers. The finance company brought suit in a Seville trial court for the outstanding loan balance.

The court concluded that Council Directive 87/102, harmonizing Member State laws on consumer credit should be interpreted to permit the tourist under such circumstances to assert remedies directly against the finance company. However, Directive 87/102 had not been transposed into Spanish law, even though the period for doing so had expired. Moreover, the Spanish court felt unable to interpret the existing Spanish law in such a way as to attain the directive's objectives. Acknowledging that directives lack horizontal direct effect, the Spanish court nevertheless wondered whether the intervening entry into force of Article 153 (ex 129a) of the EC Treaty, requiring the Community to pursue "a high level of consumer protection," justified reaching a different result. The Court of Justice thought not:

18   Article 129a [now 153] of the Treaty cannot alter that case-law, even if only in relation to directives on consumer protection.

19   Suffice it to say in this connection that the scope of Article 129a is limited. On the one hand, it provides that the Community is under a duty to contribute to the attainment of a high level of consumer protection. On the other, it creates Community competence with a view to specific action relating to consumer protection policy apart from measures taken in connection with the internal market.

20   In so far as it merely assigns an objective to the Community and confers powers on it to that end without also laying down any obligation on Member States or individuals, Article 129a cannot justify the possibility of clear, precise

and unconditional provisions of directives on consumer protection which have not been transposed into Community law within the prescribed period being directly relied on as between individuals.

NOTE ON DIRECT EFFECT IN "TRIANGULAR" SITUATIONS

The Court's refusal to extend horizontal direct effect to directives has not gone unchallenged in the literature. Nor is it unchallenged within the Court. Advocate–General Jacobs, for one, has specifically called upon the Court to abandon its position, remarking in part:

> There are sound reasons of principle for assigning direct effect to directives without any distinction based on the status of the defendant. It would be consistent with the need to ensure the effectiveness of Community law and its uniform application in all the Member States. It would be consistent, in particular, with the recent emphasis in the Court's case-law on the overriding duty of national courts to provide effective remedies for the protection of Community rights. ... Distortions will obviously result, both between and within Member States, if directives are enforceable, for example, against employers or suppliers of goods or services in the public sector but not in the private sector. It is no answer to suggest that such distortions will be removed if the directive is properly implemented; the situation which has to be envisaged is one in which the directive has not been properly implemented.

Vaneetveld v. Le Foyer SA, Case C–316/93, [1994] ECR I–763, opinion of the Advocate–General, para. 29. The Court ultimately avoided the question. For an even more detailed analysis, proposing that the Court change its case law to give directives horizontal effect "as far as the future is concerned," see Advocate–General Lenz's opinion in the *Faccini Dori* case itself.

In fact, some inroads have been made in the principle that unimplemented directives are undeserving of horizontal direct effect, though the scope and significance of the re-thinking are not yet clear.

Consider the case of Pafitis v. Trapeza Kentrikis Ellados AE, Case 441/93, [1996] ECR I–1347. There, the original shareholders of a Greek bank brought suit against the bank and its new shareholders, contending that the decision by the Greek authorities under Greek law to increase the bank's capital violated Directive 77/91, according to which any such increase required approval at a general meeting of shareholders. In a preliminary ruling, the Court of Justice held that Article 25 of the directive precluded the capital increase. In other words, absent an appropriate shareholder resolution, the national court was to deny legal effect to national law permitting an increase in capital. While it is true that the target of the challenge was an act of the public authorities, the fact remains that the challenge directly affected the parties' private legal relationship and, more particularly, disappointed the new shareholders' reliance on the validity of the capital increase. Is the result consistent with the principle that directives lack direct horizontal effect?

Cases like *Pafitis* are sometimes described as entailing "triangular" relationships to distinguish them from the bilateral relationships said to be involved in most of the horizontal direct effect cases discussed thus far. In what sense is *Pafitis* a triangular scenario? Is this distinction defensible? helpful? workable?

In the view of some,[1] there are three types of "triangular" relationships. First, a directive may grant a private party the right to demand action (or inaction) from a public authority act, which action (or inaction) necessarily imposes a burden on another private party. In this scenario, the horizontal direct effect may be described as "incidental." Second, national authorities may have failed to comply with a directive which required them to impose a certain burden on a private party, and a third (private) party may bring an action against the authorities to compel them to do so. In the third type of situation, the directive calls upon the State to confer a particular right or benefit on a private party. If, by conferring some right or benefit on a third (private) party, the State denies the first party the right or benefit conferred by the directive, that party may bring an action the effect of which would be to adversely affect the third party. In all these cases, a private party's claim against the State has a necessarily adverse effect on another private party— hence "triangular".

Does the "triangular" relationship exception help explain the following outcomes?

(a) A Spanish insurance company refused to indemnify losses caused by an insured driver who was intoxicated at the time of the accident. Both Spanish law and the insurance policy provided for that exclusion. On preliminary reference, the Court of Justice ruled that neither the Spanish law nor the contractual provision could be given effect, in light of Directive 72/166 whose purpose was to ensure third party recovery (up to an amount determined by the directive) under compulsory insurance contracts for all personal and property damage caused by motor vehicles. Ruiz Bernáldez, Case C–129/94, [1996] ECR I–1829.

(b) A German company that was passed over for a public contract for architectural and engineering services sought to prevent the contract from being awarded, citing a violation in the awarding process of Directive 92/50, which was overdue for transposition in German law. On preliminary reference, the Court of Justice went no further than to hold that the German court had to interpret national law if at all possible as giving the complaining company the right to block the award. Dorsch Consult Ingenieursgesellschaft mbH v. Bundesbaugesellschaft Berlin, Case C–54/96, [1997] ECR I–4961.

(c) As we will have occasion to see (Chapter 14 *infra*), Council Directive 83/189 of March 28, 1983 (as amended in 1988), requires Member States to notify the Commission before enacting new technical standards and regulations. In parallel civil actions among competing Belgian security alarm companies, a Belgian commercial court was called upon to recognize and enforce certain national rules governing technical aspects of security systems—rules that had not been notified to the Commission. (In one of the actions, a party asked the court to order the others to cease certain trade practices alleged to be unfair under the Belgian rules; the others counterclaimed for an order enjoining the plaintiff company from conducting business, on the ground that

---

1. See Lackhoff & Nyssens, Direct Effect of Directives in Triangular Situations, 23 Eur. L. Rev. 397 (1998).

it was not authorized under Belgian law to do so and was, in any event, marketing a alarm system that had not been approved under that law.) The Belgian court asked whether the Belgian regulations could be enforced against individual companies, even though Belgium had adopted them in violation of Directive 83/189's notification requirement. The Court ruled that the regulations were unenforceable. CIA Security International SA v. Signalson SA and Securitel SPRL, Case C–194/94, [1996] ECR I–2201, excerpted at page 568 *infra*.[2]

B. THE DOCTRINE OF SUPREMACY OF COMMUNITY LAW

Distinct from the question of the direct applicability and direct effect of Community law in the national legal orders is the question of priority between Community and national law in the event of conflict. In keeping with its view that the treaties created "a new legal order," the Court of Justice has not felt constrained to apply traditional national rules, or even prevailing public international law rules, on the question whether Community or national law should prevail in the case of conflict.

The Community treaties do not themselves provide a particularly firm textual foundation for the supremacy of Community law. Unlike the US Constitution, which contains an express Supremacy Clause in favor of federal over state law, the Treaties do not expressly address the issue. The closest approximation is EC Treaty Article 10 (ex 5), which imposes on the Member States a general obligation of loyalty to Community law:

> Member States shall take all appropriate measures, whether general or particular, to ensure fulfillment of the obligations arising out of this Treaty or resulting from action taken by the institutions of the Community. They shall facilitate the achievement of the Community's tasks.

> They shall abstain from any measure which could jeopardize the attainment of the objectives of this Treaty.

Ultimately, the question whether and to what extent Community law prevails over conflicting Member State law was left to the case law of the Court of Justice and to the reception of that case law by Member State courts. The former is taken up here and the latter in the next chapter.

COSTA v. ENTE NAZIONALE PER l'ENERGIA ELETTRICA (ENEL)
Case 6/64, [1964] ECR 585.

[For the facts of the case and part of the Court's judgment, see page 243 *supra*. As noted there, the Milan court had also referred the nationalization law to the Italian Constitutional Court for a ruling on its validity under the Italian Constitution. (Under Italian procedure, a court having doubts about the constitutionality of an Italian statute must refer the question to the

---

2. For a similar result, see Unilever Italia SpA v. Central Food SpA, Case C–443/98, [2000] ECR I–7535, holding that a national court must decline to give effect in contract litigation between private parties to a technical regulation whose application was required by Directive 83/189 to be postponed pending the Commission's post-notification review.

Constitutional Court for an authoritative ruling. An ordinary court may not itself declare an Italian statute invalid.) The Italian Constitutional Court ruled that the EC Treaty ranked as a law in the Italian legal order because Italy had ratified it by a simple statute, and that the Treaty was therefore subordinate to any subsequent Italian legislation.

The Court of Justice was well aware of the Italian Constitutional Court ruling when it decided *Costa v. ENEL.* Advocate–General Lagrange sharply criticized it as having "disastrous consequences [for] the very future of the Common Market" and as threatening to "undermine the very foundations of the Treaty." [1964] ECR at 605–06. He suggested that a State whose Constitution prevents national courts from giving immediate application to Community law over a conflicting domestic statute has "only two courses of action . . .: either to amend its Constitution . . . or to renounce the Treaty itself." Id. at 606. The opinion of the Court of Justice on the supremacy question follows.]

The Italian Government submits that the request of the [Milan court] is "absolutely inadmissible", inasmuch as a national court which is obliged to apply a national law cannot avail itself of Article 177 [now 234].

By contrast with ordinary international treaties, the EEC [now EC] Treaty has created its own legal system which, on the entry into force of the Treaty, became an integral part of the legal systems of the Member States and which their courts are bound to apply.

By creating a Community of unlimited duration, having its own institutions, its own personality, its own legal capacity and capacity of representation on the international plane and, more particularly, real powers stemming from a limitation of sovereignty or a transfer of powers from the States to the Community, the Member States have limited their sovereign rights, albeit within limited fields, and have thus created a body of law which binds both their nationals and themselves.

The integration into the laws of each Member State of provisions which derive from the Community, and more generally the terms and the spirit of the Treaty, make it impossible for the States, as a corollary, to accord precedence to a unilateral and subsequent measure over a legal system accepted by them on a basis of reciprocity. Such a measure cannot therefore be inconsistent with that legal system. The executive force of Community law cannot vary from one State to another in deference to subsequent domestic laws, without jeopardizing the attainment of the objectives of the Treaty set out in Article 5(2) [now 10(2)] and giving rise to the discrimination prohibited by Article 7 [now 12].

The obligations undertaken under the Treaty establishing the Community would not be unconditional, but merely contingent, if they could be called in question by subsequent legislative acts of the signatories. Wherever the Treaty grants the States the right to act unilaterally, it does this by clear and precise provisions (for example Articles 15 [since repealed], 93(3) [now 88(3)], 223 [now 296], 224 [now 297] and 225 [now 298]). Applications by Member States for authority to derogate from the Treaty are subject to a special authorization procedure (for example Articles 8(4), 17(4), 25, 26, 73 [all of which have since been repealed], the third subparagraph of Article 93(2) [now

88(3)], and 226 [since repealed], which would lose its purpose if the Member States could renounce their obligations by means of an ordinary law.

The precedence of Community law is confirmed by Article 189 [now 249], whereby a regulation "shall be binding" and "directly applicable in all Member States". This provision, which is subject to no reservation, would be quite meaningless if a State could unilaterally nullify its effects by means of a legislative measure which could prevail over Community law.

It follows from all these observations that the law stemming from the Treaty, an independent source of law, could not, because of its special and original nature, be overridden by domestic legal provisions, however framed, without being deprived of its character as Community law and without the legal basis of the Community itself being called into question.

The transfer by the States from their domestic legal system to the Community legal system of the rights and obligations arising under the Treaty carries with it a permanent limitation of their sovereign rights, against which a subsequent unilateral act incompatible with the concept of the Community cannot prevail. Consequently Article 177 [now 234] is to be applied regardless of any domestic law, whenever questions relating to the interpretation of the Treaty arise.

[Having decided that Community law has primacy over conflicting Member State law, the Court turned to the question whether the relevant EC Treaty articles had direct effect in the national legal orders. For that discussion, see page 243 *supra*.]

Notes and Questions

1.   The Italian Government initially urged the Court of Justice not to answer the questions put by the Milan judge, because it considered them to be improperly motivated by opposition to the nationalization. The Court categorically refused to examine the judge's motives in making the reference, and its willingness to answer substantially all questions that national courts refer to it is now a firm rule in preliminary reference proceedings. See Chapter 9.

2.   Do you consider this portion of *Costa v. ENEL* to be justified in terms of "original intent" or is it an example of judicial activism comparable to early US Supreme Court assertions of federal power? In any event, do you agree with the Court as a matter of interpretation and policy?

3.   Recall the judgment in Masterfoods Ltd. v. HB Ice Cream Ltd, discussed in note 2 page 117 *supra*. The Court there held that, once the Commission had issued a decision condemning HB for a competition law violation in the form of a contractual restraint of trade, the Irish Supreme Court could not exercise its appellate jurisdiction to sustain a lower court judgment awarding HB contract damages for violation of the offending agreement. Should this be regarded as a simple application of the supremacy principle?

4.   Upon receiving the Court's ruling in *Costa*, the Milan judge found the Italian nationalization to violate Articles 31 (ex 37) and 53 [a standstill provision on the right of establishment, since repealed] of the EC Treaty. This decision was ultimately appealed to the Italian Supreme Court which held that Costa lacked standing to challenge the nationalization through an action contesting his electric bill! Thus the litigation ended without a result on the merits.

5. The Italian Constitutional Court's views on the relationship between the EC Treaty and Italian legislation have evolved very significantly since the early 1960s. For a discussion, see Chapter 8D *infra*.

6. *Costa* involved the relationship between Community and national *legislation*. Recall that in 1970, in the case of *Internationale Handelsgesellschaft, supra* page 171, the Court directly addressed the question whether Community legislation also enjoys primacy over national *constitutional* norms, and held in effect that it does. This was a momentous step, which is echoed in the judgment that follows.

AMMINISTRAZIONE DELLE FINANZE DELLO STATO v. SIMMENTHAL SpA

(Simmenthal II)
Case 106/77, [1978] ECR 629.

[Simmenthal, an Italian importer of beef from France, disputed charges imposed by the local authorities for veterinary and public health inspection of such beef. The local court asked the Court of Justice to decide whether the charges were equivalent in effect to quantitative restrictions within the meaning of Article 28 (ex 30) and as such violated the principle of the free movement of goods. The Court ruled in Simmenthal SpA v. Italian Minister for Finance, Case 35/76, [1976] ECR 1871, that the charges indeed amounted to quantitative restrictions and were invalid.

When the national court ordered the Italian Finance Ministry to repay the charges with interest, the Ministry appealed, arguing that an Italian statute had authorized the charges and that a national court could not, under Italian constitutional procedure, treat an Italian statute as invalid on account of its conflict with a higher norm, but instead had to refer the matter to the Italian Constitutional Court. (As noted earlier, under Italian law, only the Constitutional Court may invalidate an Italian statute.) The Italian judge then sought a further ruling from the Court of Justice on the proper course to follow.]

14   Direct applicability ... means that rules of Community law must be fully and uniformly applied in all the Member States from the date of their entry into force and for so long as they continue in force.

15   These provisions are therefore a direct source of rights and duties for all those affected thereby, whether Member States or individuals, who are parties to legal relationships under Community law.

16   This consequence also concerns any national court whose task it is as an organ of a Member State to protect, in a case within its jurisdiction, the rights conferred upon individuals by Community law.

[The Court then clearly reiterated the principle of Community law primacy.]

18   [A]ny recognition that national legislative measures which encroach upon the field within which the Community exercises its legislative power or which are otherwise incompatible with the provisions of Community law had any legal effect would amount to a corresponding denial of the effectiveness of obligations undertaken unconditionally and irrevocably by

Member States pursuant to the Treaty and would thus imperil the very foundations of the Community.

19   The same conclusion emerges from the structure of Article 177 [now 234] of the Treaty which provides that any court or tribunal of a Member State is entitled to make a reference to the Court whenever it considers that a preliminary ruling on a question of interpretation or validity relating to Community law is necessary to enable it to give judgment.

20   The effectiveness of that provision would be impaired if the national court were prevented from forthwith applying Community law in accordance with the decision or the case-law of the Court.

21   It follows from the foregoing that every national court must, in a case within its jurisdiction, apply Community law in its entirety and protect rights which the latter confers on individuals and must accordingly set aside any provision of national law which may conflict with it, whether prior or subsequent to the Community rule.

22   Accordingly any provision of a national legal system and any legislative, administrative or judicial practice which might impair the effectiveness of Community law by withholding from the national court having jurisdiction to apply such law the power to do everything necessary at the moment of its application to set aside national legislative provisions which might prevent Community rules from having full force and effect are incompatible with those requirements which are the very essence of Community law.

* * *

24   [Thus] a national court which is called upon, within the limits of its jurisdiction, to apply provisions of Community law is under a duty to give full effect to those provisions, if necessary refusing of its own motion to apply any conflicting provision of national legislation ... and it is not necessary for the court to request or await the prior setting aside of such provision by legislative or other constitutional means.

Notes and Questions

1.   Note that the Ministry of Finance did not question the primacy of Community law as such, but only the procedural implications of that principle within Italy. Does Member State procedure properly fall within the province of the Court of Justice? Is it appropriate for the Court to insist that a Member State trial court apply Community law at once in preference to national law, without first seeking the judgment of the national Constitutional Court on whether the two are indeed in conflict? What factors may explain the Court of Justice's strictness? Concern over procedural delay? Concern over disparate treatment of litigation in the courts of different States? Concern that supreme or constitutional courts of a Member State might be less willing than lower courts to make preliminary references?

The Italian Constitutional Court ultimately accepted the position of the Court of Justice on the procedural question at issue in *Simmenthal II*. See the *Granital* decision, discussed *infra* page 325.

2.   *Simmenthal II* raises a more general question of the minimum procedural instruments that Member State courts must make available to litigants who assert

Community law-based claims. To what extent does the notion of Community law primacy dictate that Member State courts provide remedies suitable to such claims? That question is taken up in Chapter 10A, but is an inseparable art of the following landmark ruling of the Court on supremacy.

THE QUEEN v. SECRETARY OF STATE FOR TRANSPORT, EX PARTE FACTORTAME LTD.

(Factortame I)

Case C–213/89, [1990] ECR I–2433.

[In 1988, the UK amended its Merchant Shipping Act quite deliberately to prevent Spanish fishing interests from taking a share of the fishing quota allotted to the UK under the Common Fisheries Policy. The amendment effectively prevented Spanish-owned fishing vessels from being registered as UK vessels. (In order to prevent so-called "quota-hopping," even vessels owned by a UK company were to be deemed non-British if less than 75% of the company's shares were owned by persons resident and domiciled in the UK or if less than 75% of its directors were persons of that description.) A group of UK companies and their directors and shareholders brought suit challenging the 1988 amendment. All of the companies had a majority of Spanish directors and shareholders and the 95 UK-registered vessels they owned were therefore ineligible under the amendment to fish against the UK quota.

The UK trial court thought it probable that the plaintiffs would prevail on the merits and issued an interim order suspending application of the 1988 Act as to the plaintiffs. The Court of Appeal reversed, holding that under UK constitutional tradition, a court may never enjoin an Act of Parliament. The House of Lords found that the plaintiffs would suffer irreparable damage if interim relief were denied and they were ultimately to win the case, but it agreed that British law barred the relief sought. Because they thought that Community law might require a different result, the Law Lords referred questions to the Court of Justice asking whether national courts had the power or the obligation to grant interim relief against an Act of Parliament that might violate Community law.]

[17]   It is clear from the information before the Court ... that the preliminary question raised by the House of Lords seeks essentially to ascertain whether a national court which, in a case before it concerning Community law, considers that the sole obstacle which precludes it from granting interim relief is a rule of national law, must disapply that rule.

[18]   [In the *Simmenthal II* case, *supra* page 272,] the Court held that directly applicable rules of Community law "must be fully and uniformly applied in all the Member States from the date of their entry into force and for so long as they continue in force" and that ... "provisions of the Treaty and directly applicable measures of the institutions ... render automatically inapplicable any conflicting provision of ... national law."

[19]   In accordance with [this] case law of the Court, it is for the national courts, in application of the principle of co-operation laid down in Article 5

[now 10] of the EEC [now EC] Treaty, to ensure the legal protection which persons derive from the direct effect of provisions of Community law.

20   The Court has also held that any provision of a national legal system and any legislative, administrative or judicial practice which might impair the effectiveness of Community law by withholding from the national court having jurisdiction to apply such law the power to do everything necessary at the moment of its application to set aside national legislative provisions which might prevent, even temporarily, Community rules from having full force and effect are incompatible with those requirements, which are the very essence of Community law.

21   It must be added that the full effectiveness of Community law would be just as much impaired if a rule of national law could prevent a court seised of a dispute governed by Community law from granting interim relief in order to ensure the full effectiveness of the judgment to be given on the existence of the rights claimed under Community law. It follows that a court which in those circumstances would grant interim relief, if it were not for a rule of national law, is obliged to set aside that rule.

22   That interpretation is reinforced by the system established by Article 177 [now 234] of the EEC Treaty whose effectiveness would be impaired if a national court, having stayed proceedings pending the reply by the Court of Justice to the question referred to it for a preliminary ruling, were not able to grant interim relief until it delivered its judgment following the reply given by the Court of Justice.

23   Consequently ... Community law must be interpreted as meaning that a national court which, in a case before it concerning Community law, considers that the sole obstacle which precludes it from granting interim relief is a rule of national law must set aside that rule.

Notes and Questions

1.   Do you think the Court gave sufficient consideration to the weight of the British constitutional tradition at stake?

2.   The House of Lords accepted the Court's answer and granted the interim injunction. Regina v. Secretary of State for Transport ex parte Factortame, [1991] 1 All ER 70, [1990] 3 CMLR 375 (Oct. 11, 1990). For Lord Bridge's forceful acceptance of the primacy doctrine, see page 342 *infra*.

3.   The trial court in *Factortame* had also referred questions to the Court of Justice, but they were on the merits. The Court of Justice gave its answers to those questions a year after issuing the ruling reprinted above. The Court held that the 1988 amendment violated EC Article 43 (ex 52) in so far as it required direct or indirect owners of British-registered fishing vessels to be either UK citizens or resident in the UK. The Queen v. Secretary of State for Transport, ex parte Factortame (Factortame II), Case C–221/89, [1991] ECR I–3905, excerpted at page 694 *infra*. (In October 1991, the Court also gave judgment for the Commission in its Article 226 (ex 169) enforcement action against the UK arising out of this episode. Commission v. United Kingdom (Nationality of fishermen), Case C–246/89, [1991] ECR I–4585.) The Spanish fishing vessel owners subsequently sought damages from the UK. See page 411 *infra*.

4.   Like direct applicability and direct effect, the supremacy principle is addressed not only to national courts, but also to the legislative and executive

arms of the Member States. The emphasis on judicial enforcement of the principle simply reflects the fact that Member State courts are the legal arenas in which battles of this sort are authoritatively resolved.

The obligation to give precedence to Community law is sweeping. It does not matter whether a national law precedes or follows the Community law with which it conflicts. It does not matter where in their respective legal hierarchies the national and Community law provisions are situated; in the event of conflict the latter always prevail.[3] As we shall see in Chapter 11, the primacy of Community law in the national courts does not depend on whether a State's legislative or executive branches, or local governments, have taken the steps necessary to bring domestic law into line with it.

The Court of Justice's uncompromising attitude toward Community law supremacy can only be fully understood in light of its attachment to legal uniformity. In the Court's view, unless Community law at all times prevails throughout the Member States, the Community's effectiveness and integrity would be at risk. This belief has led the Court of Justice to perhaps a still more fundamental claim, namely that the Court itself determines the legal relationship between Community and national law, and draws the specific procedural and substantive consequences. Decisions of the Court from *van Gend en Loos* and *Costa v. ENEL* down through *Simmenthal II* and *Factortame* amply illustrate this. Evidently, even longstanding constitutional traditions in the Member States will not be allowed to stand in the way.

5. The only basis, consistent with this view, upon which a Member State court might plausibly claim the right to withhold application of a Community law instrument is that the latter itself violates a higher Community law norm. One might argue that the very logic that mandates giving direct effect and primacy to Community law within the national legal orders also dictates that Member State courts prefer higher over lower Community law norms where the two are themselves in conflict. In the case of Granaria BV v. Hoofdproduktschap voor Akkerbouwprodukten, Case 101/78, [1979] ECR 623, the Court of Justice ruled that Community regulations adopted pursuant to the EC Treaty must be presumed to be valid as long as a competent court has not declared them to be invalid, but it did not clearly specify the competent court. The following decision by the Court of Justice addresses that issue.

FIRMA FOTO–FROST v. HAUPTZOLLAMT LÜBECK–OST

Case 314/85, [1987] ECR 4199.

[Foto–Frost raised a challenge in German court to a Commission decision denying it a "post-clearance recovery of duties" under Regulation 1697/79. Foto–Frost maintained that it satisfied all the conditions that the regulation laid down for the recovery of duty and that the Commission should have granted the request. The German court asked the Court of Justice whether it had competence to declare the Commission decision invalid as contrary to the regulation.]

[14] [National] courts may consider the validity of a Community act and, if they consider that the grounds put forward before them by the parties in

---

3. Rewe v. Hauptzollamt Kiel, Case 158/80, [1981] ECR 1805.

support of invalidity are unfounded, they may reject them, concluding that the measure is completely valid. By taking that action they are not calling into question the existence of the Community measure.

15 On the other hand, those courts do not have the power to declare acts of the Community institutions invalid. ... [T]he main purpose of the powers accorded to the Court by Article 177 [now 234] is to ensure that Community law is applied uniformly by national courts. That requirement of uniformity is particularly imperative when the validity of a Community act is in question. Divergences between courts in the Member States as to the validity of Community acts would be liable to place in jeopardy the very unity of the Community legal order and detract from the fundamental requirement of legal certainty.

16 The same conclusion is dictated by consideration of the necessary coherence of the system of judicial protection established by the Treaty. In that regard it must be observed that requests for preliminary rulings, like actions for annulment, constitute means for reviewing the legality of acts of the Community institutions. ...

17 Since Article 173 [now 230] gives the Court exclusive jurisdiction to declare void an act of a Community institution, the coherence of the system requires that where the validity of a Community act is challenged before a national court the power to declare the act invalid must also be reserved to the Court of Justice.

18 It must also be emphasized that the Court of Justice is in the best position to decide on the validity of Community acts. Under Article 20 of the Protocol on the Statute of the Court of Justice,[4] Community institutions whose acts are challenged are entitled to participate in the proceedings in order to defend the validity of the acts in question. Furthermore, under the second paragraph of Article 21 of that Protocol,[5] the Court may require the Member States and institutions which are not participating in the proceedings to supply all information which it considers necessary for the purposes of the case before it.

19 It should be added that the rule that national courts may not themselves declare Community acts invalid may have to be qualified in certain circumstances in the case of proceedings relating to an application for interim measures; however, that case is not referred to in the national court's question.

20 The answer to the ... question must therefore be that the national courts have no jurisdiction themselves to declare that acts of Community institutions are invalid.

Notes and Questions

1. *Foto–Frost* holds that national courts may not purport to invalidate Community measures even on account of their conflict with higher Community law. Does it follow that they also may not withhold application of such measures on account of their invalidity? May a national court, in referring a question of

---

4. This article would become Article 23 of the Protocol on the Statute of the Court of Justice annexed to the Treaty of Nice.

5. This article would become Article 24 of the Protocol on the Statute of the Court of Justice annexed to the Treaty of Nice.

validity to the Court of Justice at least state its view that a particular Community measure is invalid?

2. The Court in *Foto–Frost* expressly observed that a national court may reject a party's challenge to the validity of a Community measure and declare the measure valid, because in so doing it is "not calling the existence of the Community measure into question" (¶ 14). Do you find this convincing? Do you believe it to be sound policy?

3. As we shall see in Chapter 8, winning assent to the proposition that only the Court of Justice may invalidate a Community law measure required a belief on the part of the Member States (and particularly their constitutional courts) that the Court of Justice would in fact enforce certain fundamental "constitutional" claims against the institutions. The Court went a long way toward securing that belief through its case law on the general principles of law and on basic rights (including the *Internationale Handelsgesellschaft, Stauder, Nold* and *Hauer* decisions) treated in Chapter 6 *supra*.

4. Suppose, following *Foto–Frost*, a national court refers a question to the Court of Justice on the validity of a Community measure, but is asked to award interim relief suspending the measure's application (or, more specifically, suspending application of the national law implementing the measure). Is a national court free to do so? For discussion of what has become a complex area of Community law, see Section 9G *infra*.

NOTE ON SUPREMACY AND THE "ABUSE OF RIGHTS" DOCTRINE

Most civil law jurisdictions recognize a general "abuse of rights" principle, whereby the exercise of a right (even a clearly recognized legal right) is not legally protected when it is exercised under circumstances that render it "abusive," as that term is defined in the relevant jurisdiction. Article 281 of the Greek Civil Code, for example, declares that "the exercise of a right is prohibited where it manifestly exceeds the bounds of good faith or morality or the economic or social purpose of that right." In the *Pafitis* case, discussed in another context at page 267 *supra*, a Greek court wondered whether the exercise of a right conferred by Community law—in that case, the right of shareholders under a Community law directive to vote an increase in company capital—could be limited by Article 281.

What do you think the Court's response should and would be? In fact, the Court avoided deciding the question because it found that the exercise of the right in question could not, in any event, be considered abusive. The Court was nevertheless quite dubious about the application of national "abuse of rights" principles:

68   [A]s to whether it is permissible, under the Community legal order, to apply a national rule in determining whether a right conferred by the provisions of Community law at issue is being exercised abusively, the fact remains that, in any event, the application of such a rule must not detract from the full effect and uniform application of Community law in the Member States.

69   It must be borne in mind ... that it is for the Court of Justice, in relation to rights relied on by an individual on the basis of Community provisions,

to verify whether the judicial protection available under national law is appropriate.

Pafitis v. Trapeza Kentrikis Ellados AE, Case C–441/93, [1996] ECR I–1347. (The company law aspects of this case are discussed at page 708 *infra*.)

This is not to say that the Court is insensitive to allegations of the abuse of Community law rights. The case of Brennet AG v. Paletta (Paletta II), Case C–206/94, [1996] ECR I–2357, is instructive. An Italian family of four, living and working in Germany, sought disability payments from their German employer (Brennet) on account of their incapacity to work. Brennet, suspicious of the Italian certificates of disability furnished by the Palettas, refused to pay.

When a German labor court ordered Brennet to pay, the latter appealed. The case reached the German Supreme Labor Court, which sought guidance on what national authorities are permitted to do in the event of a suspected abuse of Community law rights. The Court of Justice had this to say:

24 As to whether the national courts may, where there has been an abuse by the worker concerned, query the certification of incapacity for work . . ., the Court has consistently held that Community law cannot be relied on for the purposes of abuse or fraud [citing various judgments of the Court limiting assertions of the free movement of goods, persons and services].

25 Although the national courts may, therefore, take account—on the basis of objective evidence—of abuse or fraudulent conduct on the part of the worker concerned in order, where appropriate, to deny him the benefit of the provisions of Community law on which he seeks to rely, they must nevertheless assess such conduct in the light of the objectives pursued by those provisions.

26 However, the [German] case-law referred to by the Supreme Labor Court, according to which the worker must produce additional evidence that the medically certified incapacity for work is genuine, in cases where the employer argues on the basis of adequate supporting evidence that there are serious grounds for doubting the existence of the alleged incapacity, is not compatible with the objectives pursued by [Community legislation]. A worker whose incapacity for work arises in a Member State other than the competent Member State would, as a result, be confronted with difficulties involved in obtaining evidence which the Community rules in fact seek to eliminate.

27 On the other hand, that provision does not preclude employers from adducing evidence to support, where appropriate, a finding by the national court of abuse or fraudulent conduct on the part of the worker concerned, in that, although he may claim to have become incapacitated for work, such incapacity having been certified in accordance with the Community legislation, he was not sick at all.

Does this mean that there is a European Community law "abuse of rights" doctrine? If so, how would you formulate it?

Even in the absence of a Community law abuse of rights doctrine as such, the rule that national law must not impair the full effect and uniform application of Community law gives the Court of Justice an opportunity to police the application of the abuse of rights notion by national courts. A good example is Kefalas v. Greece, Case C–367/96, [1998] ECR I–2843, where a Greek court wondered whether a shareholder "abuses" the same capital increase directive at issue in the *Pafitis* case, *supra*, by contesting an increase that had actually improved the company's economic situation while at the same time foregoing the exercise of a preferential right to acquire new shares. The Court on preliminary reference took the occasion to interpret the purposes of the directive so as to preclude the national court from treating the shareholder's claim as abusive. It held squarely that "a shareholder cannot be deemed to be abusing the right ... merely because the increase in capital contested by him has resolved the financial difficulties threatening the existence of the company concerned and has clearly enured to his economic benefit or because he has not exercised his preferential right ... to acquire new shares issued [up]on the increase in capital." It explained that the "very nature" of a capital increase is precisely to improve a company's situation and the non-exercise of preferential rights merely reflected the original shareholder's disagreement with the increase.

Should the Court not just go ahead and declare that Community law-based are claims are subject exclusively to a Community law abuse of rights analysis?

Part II

THE RECEPTION AND ENFORCE-
MENT OF EUROPEAN LAW IN
THE MEMBER STATES

In exploring the framework of European Community and Union law, Part I of this book–and particularly Chapters 6 and 7–drew heavily on the perspective of the European Court of Justice. In doing so, it necessarily overlooked the question of whether and to what extent national authorities share that perspective. The fact remains, however, that national authorities enjoy considerable opportunity to determine how completely and how well Community law is integrated into and implemented at the Member State level and below, where most administration of Community law in fact occurs. Chapter 8 in a sense presents the corresponding "view from the States," focusing on those States whose courts have given these issues the most sustained attention.

This is by no means to suggest that the European authorities are prepared to leave the determinations of the correctness of Member State understandings of EU law, or the adequacy of its implementation by the States, up to the Member States themselves–far from it. The very existence of the preliminary reference mechanism, and the obligations for Member State courts that it entails, demonstrates this fact. Given the importance of preliminary references on Community law issues, both of interpretation and invalidity, we devote a separate chapter–Chapter 9–to this mechanism.

Precisely because Member States participate so intensively in the implementation of Community law, their administrative and judicial remedies go a long way in determining the effectiveness of Community law in the national legal orders. The matter is complicated by the fact that the administrative and judicial systems in each Member State present their own peculiarities. Consequently, questions about the adequacy of those remedies arise with great frequency, making their way to the Court of Justice both by preliminary reference and through direct actions. The extremely interesting "remedies" case law that has resulted is the subject of Chapter 10.

Finally, we consider in Chapter 11 the direct enforcement mechanisms with which the EC Treaty has equipped the Community. Their role in essence is to permit the Community institutions–notably the Commission and the Court of Justice–to ascertain whether Member States have failed in their obligations under Community law and, if so, to determine whether sanctions are appropriate.

Chapter 8

THE RECEPTION OF COMMUNITY LAW IN THE MEMBER STATES

The previous chapter explored the notions of direct effect and supremacy as the doctrinal pillars of Community law. As we have seen, these are largely creations of the Court of Justice. However, because the architects of the Community chose to leave basic responsibility for implementing Community law in the hands of the Member States, the attitudes and practices of national institutions also require consideration. These are the subject of the present chapter.

The subject is a rich one because the Member States have expressed diverse views on the place of Community law in their legal orders. Even within a single nation, the views of the Court of Justice on direct effect and supremacy have sometimes evoked different responses. Moreover, national attitudes have evolved significantly over time. Although limitations of space prevent a full canvassing of the situation in all Member States, this chapter will treat the most important tensions and, where relevant, describe their apparent resolution.

The starting point for discussing the national reception of Community law is a reminder that each of the three Communities grows out of an international treaty and not in a vacuum. Not surprisingly, Member State attitudes toward the integration of Community norms into the domestic legal order have therefore been influenced by more general understandings about the effect of treaty law in the national legal systems.

A distinction is commonly drawn between what have been called monist and dualist attitudes toward international law. Under a monist view, domestic and international (including treaty) law constitute a single integrated legal system. Although treaties initially become effective in a given state only when entered into under domestic constitutional procedures, once they are effective they become a source of law within that state. Under a monist view, therefore, treaties are normally directly applicable in the national legal orders. Treaties also have direct effect (as that term was used in Chapter 7A) to the extent that they are intended to have that effect. For neither purpose is a national act of incorporation necessary. Moreover, while monism does not logically imply the superiority of international over national law in the event of conflict, it is commonly associated with that principle.

The monist perspective has obvious appeal to the Court of Justice, since it obviates the question of direct applicability and leaves the direct effect of Community law norms to be determined largely by the Court itself. As noted, monism also creates a doctrinal setting that is hospitable to the supremacy of Community over national law. If direct applicability, direct effect and supremacy attach not only to the Community Treaties, but also to the secondary legislation adopted by the institutions that those Treaties create, then monism indeed goes a long way toward giving Community law the full supranationalist effect championed by the Court of Justice.

By contrast, a dualist approach to international law is said to view domestic and international law as separate and distinct spheres, with different purposes and different constituencies. Under this view, a treaty may engage a state in its international relations, but does not of its own force affect internal legal relationships except to the extent that appropriate national enactments so provide. What legislative or administrative form these measures take does not matter, provided the one selected is constitutionally adequate.

Dualism presents certain obvious disadvantages from the Community point of view. First, it would seem by definition to deny Community law's direct applicability, as that term is used in this book. To require that each Community law instrument be separately incorporated in national law before it acquires domestic binding force is essentially to foreclose direct applicability. Moreover, if Community law is not of its own force directly applicable within the Member States, it can hardly exert direct effect within them, much less claim legal supremacy over domestic law norms.

A Member State that subscribes to the dualist view may still, of course, confer a privileged status on Community law within the national legal order. Thus, primary and secondary Community law alike may be entrenched in national law through an express constitutional amendment or other special enactment to that effect. Depending on the instrument and language used, Community law may accordingly enjoy direct applicability, direct effect and even supremacy within the domestic legal order.

A common though somewhat confusing way of describing these arrangements is to say that the relevant constitutional or legislative texts have effected a limited "transfer" of Member State sovereignty to the Community institutions. Sometimes reference is made to a partial "delegation" of legislative authority to those institutions. In either event, the extent to which these processes secure direct applicability, direct effect or supremacy for Community law depends on the language of the transfer or delegation, and of course also on the extent to which the transfer or delegation is constitutionally entrenched. Unfortunately, Member States sometimes employ language that is quite ambiguous as to the conditions on which they have made a transfer or delegation of power. This ambiguity has contributed to doubts over the willingness of certain Member States to accept fully the Court's supranationalist tenets.

Whether and to what extent a Member State satisfies the supranationalist claims of Community law ultimately depends on the practices of countless national and local administrative officers—tax, customs, immigration and a host of different regulatory and enforcement officials—throughout the national territory. However, the attitudes of these officers are in turn likely to be shaped by the legal principles that the national judiciaries adopt. Although, as we have seen, the Court of Justice has constructed a powerful set of doctrinal tools for ensuring the primacy and immediacy of Community law, the Member State judiciaries also have well-developed constitutional procedures and modes of constitutional analysis. These are the courts that determine the legal framework within which the conflicting demands of domestic and Community law are resolved on a daily basis. This chapter highlights the accommodations that the courts of various Member States—often their highest courts—have had to make to reconcile their practices, and sometimes their long- and deeply-held legal traditions, with Community law's weighty imperatives.[1]

A.   COMMUNITY LAW IN FRANCE

At the time of French entry into the European Communities, the then-new French Constitution provided as follows:

CONSTITUTION OF THE FRENCH REPUBLIC (1958)

Article 54

If the Constitutional Council, when consulted by the President of the Republic, the Prime Minister, or the president of one of the houses of Parliament, declares that an international treaty or agreement contains a clause contrary to the Constitution, the Constitution must be revised before the treaty or agreement can be ratified or approved.

Article 55

Once published, properly ratified or approved treaties or agreements have priority over municipal law, provided that the other contracting parties fully apply them.

Although Article 55 apparently privileged treaties in the French legal order, the supremacy of Community law had to be worked out by the courts. The process was complicated by the division of the French judiciary into two families of courts functioning independently of one other and according to their own legal traditions. While a system of ordinary, or judicial, courts deals primarily with civil, commercial and criminal matters, most disputes over the exercise of public authority in France are decided in separate administrative courts. The latter, though formally part of the administrative rather than judicial branch of government, operate in practice as courts completely independent of the executive. Each of the two systems has its own court of last resort, the Cour de Cassation for the judicial courts and the Conseil d'Etat for the administrative courts. A further complication stems from the creation in 1958 of a separate Conseil Constitutionnel (Constitutional Coun-

---

1. For a general review by the Court of Justice of the Member State judiciaries' compliance with Community law obligations, see the report, "Apercu sur l'application du droit communautaire par les juridictions nationales" (Direction Bibliothèque, Recherche et Documentation, report 01/008, Feb. 2001).

cil) whose functions include deciding the constitutionality of treaties and new legislation when challenged.

ADMINISTRATION DES DOUANES v. SOCIETE CAFES JACQUES VABRE & J. WEIGEL ET CIE SARL

French Cour de Cassation (combined chambers)
[1974] cass. ch. mix. 6, [1975] 2 CMLR 336
May 24, 1975.

[Jacques Vabre, a coffee importer, claimed that a French consumption tax levied on Dutch coffee imported for resale in France violated Article 90 (ex 95) of the EC Treaty prohibiting discriminatory taxation. The tax was levied under the 1966 French Customs Code. Vabre sued for a refund, plus damages.

The lower courts ruled in favor of Vabre, observing that, under Article 55 of the French Constitution, Article 90 of the Treaty takes precedence over a contrary French statute, even one of a later date. The customs authorities, ordered to pay the refund plus damages, appealed to the Cour de Cassation.

The Procureur Général (an officer who performs a function in the Cour de Cassation broadly analogous to that of the Advocate–General in the Court of Justice) presented his views to the Court. He first referred to the views of the Conseil d'Etat, which in its 1968 *Semoules de France* ruling (Syndicat général de fabricants de semoules de France, [1968] Recueil Lebon 149, [1970] CMLR 395) (March 1, 1968)), had held that the administrative courts could not review the conformity of a French statute to a prior treaty. The Conseil d'Etat had come to that conclusion, notwithstanding Article 55 of the Constitution, because it thought that to engage in such review would be to "criticize" a statute, which is forbidden to the courts under French concepts of legislative supremacy and the separation of powers.

The Procureur Général then cited Articles 10 (ex 5) and 249 (189) of the Treaty and observed that the Community institutions have authority to "produce sources of law and procedures which ... limit the powers of the Member States." He also referred to "the preeminence of Community law over internal law," quoting extensively from the *Costa v. ENEL* case, *supra* page 269. The Procureur Général continued:

> The force of Community law cannot in fact vary from one State to another in favor of subsequent internal laws without imperiling the realization of the aims of the Treaty.

* * *

> It would be possible for you to give precedence to the application of Article 95 [now 90] of the Treaty over the subsequent statute by relying on Article 55 of our Constitution, but personally I would ask you not to mention it and instead base your reasoning on the very nature of the legal order instituted by the Treaty.

> [If] you restricted yourselves to deriving from Article 55 of our Constitution the primacy in the French internal system of Community law over national law, you would be explaining and justifying that action as regards our country, but such reasoning would suggest that it is on our

Constitution and on it alone that the ranking of Community law in our internal legal system depends. . . .

* * *

This is . . . why I ask you not to base your reasoning on Article 55 of our Constitution. [If you do as I propose] you will recognize that the transfer made by the States from their internal legal order to the Community legal order . . . involves a definitive limitation of their sovereign rights against which a subsequent unilateral act which is incompatible with the notion of Community cannot prevail.

The Procureur Général finally surveyed how the other Member States had received Community law in their national legal orders, discerning from the survey "a European legal consciousness within all the national courts . . . [of] the primacy of Community law without which there could not be created that unity of the market which is desired."

The judgment of the Cour de Cassation itself follows.]

It is . . . complained that the judgment below invalidated the internal consumption tax established by . . . the Customs Code as a consequence of its incompatibility with the provisions of Article 95 [now 90] of the [Treaty] on the ground that by virtue of Article 55 of the Constitution the latter has an authority higher than that of internal statute, even if the statute be later in time. According to the appeal, a court may judge the legality of regulations laying down a tax which is challenged, but cannot without exceeding its powers discard the application of an internal statute on the pretext that it is unconstitutional. [According to the appeal], the provisions of the Customs Code . . . were enacted by [an] Act of 14 December 1966 which conferred on them the absolute authority which belongs to legislative provisions and which are binding on all French courts.

But the [Treaty], which by virtue of [Article 55] of the Constitution has an authority greater than that of statutes, institutes a separate legal order integrated with that of the Member States. Because of that separateness, the legal order which it has created is directly applicable to the nationals of those States and is binding on their courts. Therefore the [lower court] was correct and did not exceed its powers in deciding that Article 95 of the Treaty was to be applied in the instant case, and not the Customs Code, even though the latter was later in date. It follows that the [claim] must be dismissed.

It is also complained that the judgment applied Article 95 of the [Treaty] when, according to the appeal, Article 55 of the Constitution expressly subjects the authority which it gives to treaties ratified by France to the condition that they should be applied by the other party. The judge at first instance was not therefore able validly to apply this constitutional provision without investigating whether the State (Holland) from which the product in question was imported has met this condition of reciprocity.

But in the Community legal order the failings of a Member State . . . to comply with the obligations falling on it by virtue of the [Treaty] are subject to the [Member State enforcement] procedure laid down by Article 170 [now

227] of that Treaty and so the plea of lack of reciprocity cannot be made before the national courts. It follows that this ground must be dismissed.

[The Court also rejected all of the appellant's other grounds for appeal.]

Notes and Questions

1. On what theory did the Cour de Cassation ultimately enforce Community law over a later conflicting provision of national law?

2. Even before *Jacques Vabre*, the French civil courts were willing to disregard a French statute if it conflicted with Community measures of a *later* rather than *earlier* date. In one such case, a German national (von Kempis) owning farmland in France gave his tenants notice under the French Agricultural Tenancies Act to quit the property so that he could take over its cultivation. The tenants resisted, citing a 1954 French decree that required aliens to obtain the approval of the Ministry of Agriculture before engaging in farming, which von Kempis had not done. von Kempis argued that the 1954 decree had been implicitly repealed as between EC nationals by a 1969 French ordinance giving farmers from other EC Member States the same rights as French farmers under the Agricultural Tenancies Act. The Cour de Cassation agreed, stating:

> Since the end of the transitional period on January 1, 1970, Article 52 [now 43] of the [EC] Treaty, which is directly applicable to the nationals of the Member States ... and is enforceable by their courts, prohibits any restriction of the freedom of establishment of such nationals in France. The provisions of French internal law which imposed the requirement of an administrative permit on those who wanted to farm an agricultural holding in France therefore have ceased to be applicable to them. . . .

von Kempis v. Geldof, [1975] cass. civ. 3e 282 (no. 373), [1976] 2 CMLR 152, 176–77 (Dec. 15, 1975).

3. A significant factor in the Cour de Cassation's reasoning was a then-fresh decision of the French Conseil Constitutionnel, in which the Conseil upheld a new statute liberalizing abortion against various principles of domestic law, but refused to address the question whether the law violated the European Convention on Human Rights, as alleged. Décision No. 75–54, Jan. 15 1975, Rev. Droit Pub. 1975.165. Emphasizing that its jurisdiction is limited to determining the constitutionality of statutes, the Conseil maintained that the Convention-based claim was not a "constitutional" one, Article 55 notwithstanding, a statute's incompatibility with a treaty does not in itself render the statute unconstitutional. According to the Conseil, the principle of supremacy of treaties is vindicated in French law by another method, namely by the ordinary courts (civil, criminal and administrative) giving preference to treaties over legislation whenever a conflict between them should arise in the course of litigation. (Under this theory, a statute is not declared unconstitutional, or even invalid; it is merely "disapplied" on a case-by-case basis to the extent of the conflict.) Do you see how this reasoning facilitated the outcome in *Jacques Vabre*?

4. The 1968 *Semoules de France* ruling of the Conseil d'Etat, referred to by the Procureur–General, was controversial because it effectively prevented the administrative courts (and indirectly the French administration) from ensuring the primacy of EC law over subsequent national legislation.

However, the Conseil d'Etat later rallied to the position of the Cour de Cassation in *Jacques Vabre*. The occasion was the *Boisdet* case, 1990 Recueil Lebon 250, 1991 1 CMLR 3 (Sept. 24, 1990). Under a 1962 French statute, as amended in 1980, a regional agricultural committee could have its rules extended by ministerial order to regional producers who were not members of the committee. Boisdet, a French apple grower, brought suit challenging the application to him under this procedure of rules on the grading and pricing of apples that had been adopted by a regional committee of which he was not a member. As it happens, the Court of Justice had previously ruled in the 1986 *Le Campion* judgment (Association comité économique agricole régional fruits et légumes de Bretagne v. Le Campion, Case 218/85, [1986] ECR 3513) that the Community's 1972 apple market regulation preempted all national rules of the sort adopted by the regional committee. The Conseil d'Etat held in *Boisdet* that in view of its preemptive effect, the 1972 Community regulation prevented the Minister from extending the regional agricultural committee's rules to non-members even though the subsequent French legislation of 1980 specifically permitted it.

Boisdet was the first occasion on which the Conseil d'Etat denied effect to a French statute on account of its conflict with an earlier Community instrument. However, in a noted decision rendered one year earlier, Nicolo, [1989] Recueil Lebon 190, [1989] Actualité Juridique, Droit Administratif 788, [1990] 1 CMLR 173 (Oct. 20, 1989), it had clearly signaled its readiness to do so.

What significance, if any, should be attached to the fact that the Conseil d'Etat in *Boisdet* mentioned neither Article 55 of the French Constitution nor any provision of the EC Treaty, but merely the *Le Campion* ruling and the 1972 Community apple market regulation.

5.   The Conseil d'Etat's acceptance of the supremacy principle was confirmed in SA Rothmans International France and SA Philip Morris France, Rec. Leb. 1992.81, [1993] 1 CMLR 253, 255 (C.E., Feb. 28, 1992). There, two French tobacco companies brought an action to annul ministerial decisions denying them permission to raise their resale prices for imported tobacco products. (The ministerial decisions were issued on the basis of a 1976 French law granting the French Government the power to fix the sale price of manufactured tobacco products imported from other Member States.) The companies claimed that those decisions violated a 1972 directive entitling manufacturers and importers to set their own retail price ceilings. The Conseil d'Etat ruled that the 1976 law was incompatible with the earlier directive, and that the ministerial decisions thus "had no legal basis." In so ruling, the Conseil d'Etat also aligned its interpretation of the directive with the interpretation twice given to it by the Court of Justice (in 1983 and 1988) in Article 226 (ex 169) rulings condemning France for failing to comply with EC rules on the retail prices of tobacco products. Commission v. France (Tobacco prices I), Case 90/82, [1983] ECR 2011; Commission v. France (Tobacco prices II), Case 169/87, [1988] ECR 4093.

In related cases, the Conseil d'Etat further ruled that the tobacco companies were entitled to damages from the French State reflecting "the difference between the earnings they received on the basis of the retail selling prices fixed pursuant to the decisions which have been declared illegal above and the earnings they would have received on the basis of legally fixed prices," specifically 230,000 French francs, plus interest from May 1984. SA Arizona Tobacco Products and SA Philip Morris France, Rec. Leb. 1992.78, [1993] 1 CMLR 253, 256 (C.E., Feb. 28, 1992). (Shortly thereafter, in another case, the Administrative Court of Appeal of Paris awarded damages against France to an insurance broker for the French Parliament's failure to implement the exemption for insurance operations contained in the Sixth Community Directive on the common system of VAT. Dangeville, Rec. 1992.558 (Ct.App. Paris, Ass. Plen., July 1, 1992).) See the comment on

Rothmans and *Philip Morris* by Dutheil de la Rochère, 30 Comm. Mkt. L. Rev. 187 (1993).

MINISTRE DE L'INTERIEUR v. COHN–BENDIT

French Conseil d'Etat (Assemblée)
[1978] Recueil Lebon 524, [1979] Recueil Dalloz 155, [1980] 1 CMLR 543
Dec. 22, 1978.

[Daniel Cohn–Bendit, a German citizen born in France, was one of the leaders of the French student revolt of May 1968. In the wake of that event, he was deported by the Minister of the Interior as a threat to public order. In 1975, Cohn–Bendit sought to re-enter France to take up an offer of employment. The Minister denied the request without any statement of reasons, and Cohn–Bendit challenged that action in the administrative tribunal of Paris as infringing EC Article 39 (ex 48) and article 6 of Council Directive 64/221, both of which figured in the *van Duyn* case, *supra* pages 246 and 253. Article 39 provides for the free movement of workers, subject to limitations based on public policy, public security or public health, and article 6 of Directive 64/221 requires national authorities to give their reasons for denying entry on grounds of public policy, unless doing so would threaten national security.

The administrative tribunal stayed proceedings and referred certain questions to the Court of Justice for a preliminary ruling. The Minister appealed the order of reference to the Conseil d'Etat. In a matter of days, the Conseil d'Etat reversed the order of reference. Its opinion, based largely on its view of the legal effect of Community directives in France, follows:]

According to Article 56 [now 46] of the [EC] Treaty, which does not authorize any European Community body to issue regulations on the subject of public order that would be directly applicable in the Member States, the coordination of legislative and regulatory provisions "creating special rules for foreign nationals in the interest of public order, public safety and public health" is to be accomplished by Council directives adopted on Commission proposal and after consultation of the European Parliament. It appears clearly from Article 189 [now 249] of the Treaty that, while these directives bind the Member States "as to the result to be achieved," ... national authorities alone have the authority to choose how to execute the directives and to establish for themselves, under national judicial control, the proper means of giving them effect in domestic law. Therefore, irrespective of the provisions that they may address to the Member States, directives may not be invoked by nationals of these States in support of legal claims directed against an individual administrative act. It thus follows that M. Cohn–Bendit cannot effectively call upon the administrative tribunal of Paris to annul the decision of the Minister of the Interior on the ground that it violates the provisions of the Council directive. ... Accordingly, absent any challenge to the regulations adopted by the French Government to implement the Council's directive, the answer to M. Cohn–Bendit's lawsuit cannot in any event depend upon an interpretation of the directive. ... The Minister of the Interior is therefore correct in claiming that the administrative tribunal of Paris improperly referred questions to the Court of Justice on the interpretation of this directive and improperly stayed proceedings pending the decision of that Court. ...

The decision of the administrative tribunal of Paris is reversed.

Notes and Questions

1.   Is the decision in *Cohn–Bendit* compatible with the Court of Justice's direct effects doctrine, a doctrine with which the Conseil d'Etat was of course familiar? What recourse did Cohn–Bendit have in the wake of the decision? The Commission protested to the French Government, but did not bring an enforcement action against France under Article 226 (ex 169). Is *Cohn–Bendit* still good law after *Boisdet*?

2.   The Conseil d'Etat remarked that the *Cohn–Bendit* case was not a "challenge to the regulations adopted by the French Government to implement the Council's directive," but merely a challenge to an individual decision as in direct violation of the directive. Is there a significant difference between the two situations? The Conseil d'Etat evidently believes so. In Fédération française des sociétés de protection de la nature, [1984] Recueil Lebon 410, [1985] Revue trimestrielle de droit européen 187 (C.E., Dec. 7, 1984), environmental groups sued to annul a general measure permitting the hunting of turtle doves—a measure that allegedly violated a 1979 Council directive on the protection of birds. The Conseil d'Etat annulled the measure. "While national authorities ... alone have the authority to choose how to execute the directives [addressed to them], ... [they] cannot legally issue administrative regulations which would be contrary to the objectives defined in the directives in question."

3.   In Alitalia, Rec. Leb. 1989.44 (C.E., Feb. 3, 1989), the Conseil d'Etat ruled in effect that a public authority may not legally enforce a French regulation that is inconsistent with a Community directive whose deadline for implementation has passed. There, the Conseil d'Etat declared invalid the Prime Minister's tacit refusal to repeal administrative provisions in conflict with Sixth VAT Directive. Then in 1995, the Conseil d'Etat barred the State from invoking a directive for its own benefit when it had failed properly to transpose the directive into French law. SA Lilly France, Rev. Fr. Droit Adm. 1995.1037 (C.E., June 23, 1995). On the other hand, in a later ruling, it held that a French national may not invoke the unimplemented Directive 90/531 on the conclusion of water supply contracts in an action challenging the decision by a city council to enter into a new water supply contract. Compagnie Générale des Eaux, Rec. Leb. 1993.225 (C.E., July 23, 1993). How might these decisions be reconciled? See generally P. Roseren, The Application of Community Law by French Courts from 1982 to 1993, 31 Common Mkt. L. Rev. 315 (1994).

CONSTITUTION OF THE FRENCH REPUBLIC (1958)

Article 88–1

The French Republic participates in the European Communities and in the European Union, which are composed of States that have chosen freely, pursuant to the treaties that have constituted these entities, to exercise certain of their competences in common.

Article 88–4

The Government shall submit all proposed Community measures containing provisions of a legislative character to the National Assembly and to the Senate at the same time that those proposed measures are transmitted for action to the Council of the Communities.

During legislative sessions as well as outside of them, resolutions within the scope of this article may be adopted according to procedures determined by the rules of each assembly.

Notes and Questions

1. Articles 88–1 and 88–4 were added to the French Constitution in June 1992 following negotiation of the Maastricht Treaty. Constitutional Law No. 92–554 of June 25, 1992, adding to the Constitution a new title, "On the European Communities and the European Union." The French Conseil Constitutionnel had previously ruled that ratification of the TEU necessitated these amendments. Decision No. 92–554 of April 9, 1992, JCP 1992. J. 162, Rev. gen. dr. int'l pub. 1992.507, [1993] 3 CMLR 345, paras. 21852–54. Why do you suppose these amendments were deemed necessary to permit French ratification?

At the same time, the French Constitution was also amended to permit non-French EU nationals to vote and hold office at both the municipal and the European Parliament levels (new art. 88–3 of the Constitution), and to allow France to participate fully in the EMU and in an EU-wide visa policy for non-EU nationals (new art. 88–2 of the Constitution).

2. Notwithstanding the fact that the Constitution was amended in order to obviate challenges to ratification, the bill of ratification of the Maastricht Treaty was nevertheless challenged in the Conseil Constitutionnnel, which ultimately dismissed all the claims on the ground that decisions by the "constituent authorities" themselves are not constitutionally reviewable. Decision No. 92–312 of Sept. 2, 1992, [1992] 3 J.O. 8406, JCP 1992. J. 382, para. 21943, 8 Rev. Fr. Droit Adm. 937 (1992). It was shortly thereafter that the French people by referendum narrowly authorized the President of the Republic to ratify the Maastricht Treaty. (There followed yet another challenge in the Conseil Constitutionnel, this time to the law of ratification as authorized by the referendum. Not surprisingly, the Conseil Constitutionnel ruled that it lacked jurisdiction to question the constitutionality of a law that had been adopted pursuant to a referendum.) The next day, the President promulgated Law No. 92–1017 of September 24, 1992, authorizing ratification.

3. The Conseil Constitutionnel has been asked on occasion to determine whether the passage of legislation required by EC law necessitated an amendment to the French Constitution. One such case was a challenge to a French law allowing non-French EU nationals to enter the French civil service. (The Conseil Constitutionnel declined to decide the case on the ground that it lacks jurisdiction to decide the compatibility of a French statute with a treaty. Decision No. 91–293 of July 23, 1991.) Another was a challenge to the French law authorizing ratification of the convention, pursuant to the 1985 Schengen Agreement (*supra* page 32) abolishing frontier checks as between the signatory states. (On this claim, the Conseil Constitutionnel reached the merits, concluding that the convention violated nothing in the French Constitution. Decision No. 91–294 of July 25, 1991.)

A third example was the constitutional challenge to a French law implementing the Schengen Agreement which made individual asylum decisions by other Contracting States binding on France. The Constitutional Council declared the French law incompatible with the French constitutional right of asylum. Decision No. 93–325 of August 13, 1993. The result was thus yet another constitutional amendment, of November 1993, adding a new Article 53–1 to the Constitution. Article 53–1 allows France to contract with other European states that are "bound in the same way that France is on issues of asylum and of the protection of human rights and fundamental freedoms" on rules of jurisdiction in asylum cases. However, it reserves France's right in all cases to "give asylum to any foreign national who is persecuted by reason of his or her conduct in support of freedom or who seeks protection from France for any other reason." Do you suppose that this proviso is consistent with France's obligations under the Schengen Agreement?

4. Ratification of the Amsterdam Treaty presented a new set of constitutional issues. Upon application by the President and the Prime Minister, the Conseil Constitutionnel decided that provisions in the new Title IV of the EC Treaty relating to visas, immigration and border control and the free movement of persons, amounted to a new transfer of competence from France to the European Union that affected the conditions for the exercise of national sovereignty. Decision No. 97–394 of December 31, 1997. The Constitution was accordingly further amended so that Article 88–2 now reads as follows:

Article 88–2

Subject to reciprocity and in accordance with the terms of the [TEU], France agrees to the transfer of powers necessary for the establishment of European economic and monetary union.

Subject to the same reservation and in accordance with the terms of the [EC Treaty], as amended by the [Maastricht Treaty], the transfer of powers necessary for the determination of rules concerning freedom of movement for persons and related matters may be agreed upon.

On the Decision, see S. Millns, The Treaty of Amsterdam and Constitutional Revision in France, 5 Eur. Pub. L. 61 (1999); S. Mouthaan, Amending the Amended Constitution, 23 Eur. L. Rev. 592 (1998).

What does the manner of reviewing the constitutionality of proposed treaties in France, and remedying constitutional difficulties, tell you about the relationship between treaties and the Constitution?

5. In Sarran et Lavacher, [1998] Rev. Fr. dr. adm. 1081 (1998), [1998] A.J.D.A. 1039 (1998) (Oct. 30, 1998), the Conseil d'Etat in plenary session ruled that international treaties do not enjoy a status superior to that of the French Constitution within the national legal order. The case did not involve the EC Treaty or the TEU; rather it concerned the compatibility between the Constitution's provisions on voting rights in New Caledonia, on the one hand, and the European Human Rights Convention and the International Covenant on Civil and Political Rights, on the other. But does the decision have implications for the supremacy of Community law in France?

B.   COMMUNITY LAW IN THE NETHERLANDS, BELGIUM AND LUXEMBOURG

1. NETHERLANDS

Several provisions of the 1983 Dutch Constitution bear importantly upon the status of Community law in the Netherlands. Article 92 permits the transfer by treaty of legislative, executive and judicial powers to international institutions. Article 93 provides that treaties and "resolutions" of international institutions, if by their terms capable of binding effect, shall become binding upon publication. Finally, Article 94 renders Dutch statutes unenforceable in the Netherlands to the extent that they conflict with binding treaties or "resolutions" of international institutions. Articles 93 and 94, which largely replicate provisions of the previous (1953) Constitution designed to accommodate Dutch membership in the Benelux Union, are all the more significant because Dutch courts in principle lack authority to examine the constitutionality of national laws. Though not perfectly explicit,[2] these three constitutional provisions have enabled the courts to give a preeminent place to Community law in the Dutch legal order, thus enhancing the Netherlands' generally excellent reputation for supporting the Community.

After having apparently closely considered the matter, the Dutch Government decided that, given the breadth of language of Article 92 of the Constitution, ratification of the TEU required no further constitutional changes. Although the Council of State rendered a non-binding opinion on the TEU, disapproving its wide use of intergovernmental decisionmaking, its "confusion" between the European Community and the European Union, and the "political" character of the subsidiarity principle, the basic constitutional principles of the EU, as elaborated by the Court of Justice, have not been challenged by the Dutch judiciary.

2. BELGIUM

The Belgian Constitution is less explicitly supportive of Community law. The 1831 Constitution was amended in 1970 to provide that "exercise of given powers may be conferred by a treaty or by a law on institutions created under public international law" (art. 34). But even today, the Constitution does not speak to Community law's direct applicability or direct effect, much less its supremacy in the Belgian legal order.[3]

Under these circumstances, acceptance of Community supranationalism by the Belgian courts could not have been taken for granted. The 1971 *Fromagerie "Le Ski"* decision of the Belgian Cour de Cassation, the highest civil court in Belgium, is therefore especially striking. After the Court of Justice ruled in 1964 that Belgian decrees of 1958 violated the then Article 12 by introducing import duties on dairy products, Belgium eliminated the duties. However, a 1968 Belgian statute declared that the imposition of duties under the decrees was not subject to judicial review of any kind, and that duties once paid could not be recovered. Fromagerie "Le Ski" nevertheless sued to recover duties it had paid. Before the Cour de Cassation, the Belgian Government argued that since the EC Treaty had been ratified by statute, it took effect in Belgium as a statute and could be superseded by later national legislation such as the 1968 statute. (Note that the *Costa v. ENEL* judgment of the Court of Justice, *supra* page 269, had by then squarely rejected this argument.) Second, Belgium argued that the courts could not in any event

---

2. Articles 93 and 94 require for the direct applicability of treaty provisions that they be "binding upon all persons."

3. Article 77 gives the Parliament competence to enact laws referred to in Article 34, as well as laws enacted to guarantee Belgium's international obligations. Article 168 provides that the chambers of Parliament are to be informed when negotiations are opened with a view to any revision of the treaties establishing the Communities or the EU or any acts that would modify or complete them. Finally, Article 8 extends the right of non-Belgian EU nationals to vote in Belgium as required by Community law.

annul a Belgian statute because Article 97 of the Constitution vested that authority exclusively in the Belgian Parliament.

The Belgian Procureur Général, obviously influenced by *Costa v. ENEL,* argued as follows:

> The [Community] Treaties ... have in relation to conventional international treaties special features [making] the relationship between Community law and national legislation ... a special one.

> * * *

> First, by their agreement on the transfer of their rights and obligations under the Treaty to the Community legal system, the States definitively limited "their sovereign rights", or to put it more accurately, "the exercise of their sovereign powers." ...

> * * *

> Secondly, Community law is a specific and autonomous law which is binding on the courts of Member States and makes it impossible to set against it any domestic law whatsoever. The very nature of the legal system instituted by the Treaties of Rome confers on that primacy its own foundation, independently of the constitutional provisions in States. This specific character of Community law stems from the objectives of the Treaty which are the establishment of a new legal system to which are subject not only States but also the nationals of those States. It also stems from the fact that the Treaty has set up institutions having their own powers and especially that of creating new sources of law.

[1972] CMLR at 352, 355–56.

The Belgian Cour de Cassation found preliminarily that the 1968 statute violated EC Treaty Article 12. It also held that when a domestic statute conflicts with a Treaty introduced into national law by statute, it is to be regarded as conflicting with a Treaty. Then, echoing the Procureur Général, it concluded:

> The rule that a statute repeals a previous statute in so far as there is a conflict between the two does not apply in the case of a conflict between a treaty and a statute.

> In the event of a conflict between a norm of domestic law and a norm of international law which produces direct effects in the internal legal system, the rule established by the treaty shall prevail. The primacy of the treaty results from the very nature of international treaty law.

> This is *a fortiori* the case when a conflict exists, as in the present case, between a norm of internal law and a norm of Community law.

> The reason is that the treaties which have created Community law have instituted a new legal system in whose favor the Member States have restricted the exercise of their sovereign powers in the areas determined by those treaties.

Etat Belge, Ministre des Affaires Economiques v. SA Fromagerie Franco–Suisse "Le Ski," [1971] Pasicrisie Belge 886, [1972] CMLR 330, 373 (Belgian Cour de Cassation, first chamber, May 21, 1971). Observing that the then Article 12 was directly effective and conferred rights on individuals that national courts must uphold, the Cour de Cassation held that the Belgian courts were permitted and indeed required not to enforce the 1968 Belgian statute. The court maintained that refusing to enforce a national statute (that is, "finding that its effects are stopped") does not amount to declaring the statute null and void. Although *Le Ski* entailed conflict between a Belgian statute and the EC Treaty, the result would apparently have been no different if the conflict had been with a piece of secondary Community legislation instead.

The Belgian Conseil d'Etat (the Supreme Administrative Court) has had no difficulty following the Cour de Cassation's line of reasoning. Even before the *Le Ski* case, the Conseil d'Etat had ruled that directly applicable treaties are a source of administrative law and a basis upon which to review not only the validity of administrative regulations and decisions, but also the enforceability of national legislation, even if enacted subsequently.[4] In a later case, however, the Conseil d'Etat was asked to go a step further.

ORFINGER v. BELGIUM

Belgian Conseil d'Etat
Case no. 62.9222, A.61.059/VI–12.193, 2000 Comm. Mkt. L. Rep. 612 (2000)
Nov. 5, 1996

[*Orfinger* involved a challenge to a 1994 royal decree on recruitment criteria for the Belgian civil service. Article 1(3) of the decree required applicants to be Belgian nationals or nationals of an EU Member State. Orfinger invoked Article 10(2) of the Constitution which provides that "Belgians ... are the only ones eligible for civil and military service, but for the exceptions provided for by law." More generally, he argued that the notion of pre-eminence of international law over the Constitution had no basis in the text of the Constitution and that rules of international law derived mandatory force in Belgium only upon their reception into domestic law pursuant to the rules laid down by the Constitution. Orfinger maintained that international law does not authorize States to make treaties contrary to their own Constitution and that a constitutional amendment is needed before Belgium can ratify a treaty contrary to the Constitution. Finally, he argued that for the Community judiciary to dictate the eligibility of candidates for the civil service would violate the principle of subsidiarity.]

* * *

5. The point raised in the applicant's argument is not that of the contradiction between the Constitution and the directly applicable rule of a treaty. The applicant does not dispute the fact that when Belgium ratified the EC Treaty, there was no apparent incompatibility between the Constitution and Article 48 [now 39] of the Treaty. The situation considered under this argument only arose in 1980, when the European Court of Justice gave an interpretation of Article 48 ... which made it mandatory to open to all nationals of the European Union public administrative positions which did not involve direct or indirect participation in the exercise of public authority

---

4. A recent example is Decision no. 32026 (Feb. 17, 1989), where the Conseil d'Etat upheld the legality of municipal elections, notwithstanding their violation of a 1985 statute on opinion polls, because it found that the statute itself infringed the guarantee of freedom of expression in Article 10 of the European Human Rights Convention.

and positions which were not concerned with the safeguard of the general interests of the State or other public authorities. The problem therefore is that of compatibility between the Constitution and the interpretation of one of the provisions of the Treaty, long after its ratification, by the authorities established under this Treaty for the purpose of ensuring a uniform interpretation of its own provisions valid in all the Member States of the Union.

6.   Article 34 of the Constitution allows the exercise of specific powers to be conferred through a treaty or a statute to public international law bodies. Although [Article 34] is posterior to the ratification of the EC Treaty, ... it provides a constitutional basis for the institutional mechanisms which the Treaty established with a particular view to guaranteeing its uniform interpretation in all Member States of the European Union. [Article 34] in no way determines the powers that can be attributed, and therefore puts no limit on them.

* * *

8.   In case of conflict between a rule of national law and a rule of international law of direct effect in the national legal order, the rule established by the Treaty must prevail. According to the established case law of the European Court of Justice, relying on provisions of national law with a view to limiting the effect of the Community law would result in undermining the unity and efficiency of Community law and therefore cannot be accepted, even where the provisions of national law are those of the Constitution. Under Belgian constitutional law, the authority conferred upon the Court of Justice's interpretation of the Treaty of Rome is based on Article 34 of the Constitution, even where such interpretation would result in blocking the effects of certain parts of Articles 8 and 10 of the Constitution.

9.   This conclusion is not in contradiction with any of the principles on which the applicant has based his action. The application of all the provisions of the EC Treaty, and their interpretation by the European Court of Justice, is the result of Belgium's membership of the European Union and this application could possibly be set aside following an initiative by the Belgian authorities to either denounce their membership or renegotiate the conditions thereof. As long as such an initiative has not taken place, the principle of the rule of law requires that the Community law be fully applied. Although it may be recommended, as did the Conseil d'Etat's Legislation Division, that the text of the Constitution should be amended to meet the requirements of European law, the application of that law cannot be subject to an amendment of the Constitution to meet the requirements of European law which is mandatory even in the absence of such an amendment.

Notes and Questions

1.   How would you compare the Belgian Conseil d'Etat's views on the relation between EC law and the national Constitution with those of the French Cour de Cassation and Conseil d'Etat? Do you find the *Orfinger* judgment convincing?

2.   On the reception of Community law in Belgium, see K. Lenaerts & P. Foubert, Belgian Law and the European Community: 1993–1996, 22 Eur. L. Rev. 599 (1997); K. Lenaerts & K. Coppenholle, The Application of Community Law in

Belgium: 1989–1992, 17 Eur. L. Rev. 447 (1992); P. Wytinck, The Application of Community Law in Belgium: 1986–1992, 30 Common Mkt. L. Rev. 981 (1993).

3.   Effective February 1994, Belgium became a federal state, consisting of three Communities (Flemish, French and German-speaking) and three Regions (Flemish, Walloon and Brussels–Capital). These units have congruent territorial competences, but different subject matter competences. The Communities regulate cultural matters, education and personal status, while the Regions regulate land use planning, environmental and energy policy, housing, economic affairs, public works, and water, transport and employment policy.

Interestingly, Article 167 of the newly amended Constitution (Consolidated Constitution of Belgium of February 17, 1994) reserves to the Communities and Regions the right to conclude treaties on matters falling within their competence under the Constitution. But even prior to the amendment, the three Belgian Communities had participated in the approval process of the Maastricht Treaty, pursuant to Article 16 of the Special Act of August 8, 1980, requiring separate approvals by the Councils of the Communities insofar as the Treaty dealt with cultural, educational and personal status matters. Each Community conducted debates on the Treaty within its respective Council during the course of 1992, and each Council eventually approved it by a large majority.

With the 1994 amendments to the Constitution also came a new Article 169 permitting national authorities to substitute themselves temporarily for the Communities and Regions where necessary "[i]n order to guarantee respect for [Belgium's] international and supranational obligations." For an excellent account of the provisions and practices whereby the Communities and Regions are specifically represented in decisionmaking in the EU institutions (including the Parliament and Council) and before the Court of Justice, see K. Lenaerts & P. Foubert, Belgian Law and the European Community: 1993–1996, 22 Eur. L. Rev. 599 (1997).

3.   LUXEMBOURG

For its part, the Luxembourg Supreme Court ruled in 1954 that international treaties take precedence over national legislation, even when the latter comes later in time. Chambre des Métiers–Pagani v. Ministère Public, 16 Pas.Lux. 150, 152 (July 14, 1954). Two years later, the Luxembourg Constitution was amended to allow governmental authority to be "temporarily delegated by treaty to international institutions set up by international law." Although the status of Community law in Luxembourg has not been finally determined in the courts, neither has it been sharply questioned.

C. COMMUNITY LAW IN GERMANY

BASIC LAW OF THE FEDERAL REPUBLIC OF GERMANY (1949)

Upon Germany's entry into the European Communities in 1957, the seemingly relevant provisions of the Constitution were as follows:

Article 24

(Entry into a collective security system)

(1) The Federation may by legislation transfer sovereign powers to intergovernmental institutions. . . .

Article 25

(International law integral part of federal law)

The general rules of public international law shall be an integral part of federal law. They shall take precedence over the laws and shall directly create rights and duties for the inhabitants of the federal territory.

From rather early on, the German courts expressed reservations about the categorical supremacy of Community law claimed by the Court of Justice. The first major pronouncement occurred in the case of Internationale Handelsgesellschaft mbH v. Einfuhr- und Vorratsstelle für Getreide und Futtermittel (*Solange I*), Case 2 BvL 52/71, 37 BVerfGE 271, [1974] 2 CMLR 540 (Fed. Const'l Court, second senate, May 29, 1974). This case arose out of the same circumstances as the 1970 Court of Justice judgment of the same name, *supra* page 171. After that judgment, which upheld the forfeiture feature of the Community's export license regulation, the German administrative court turned to the German Federal Constitutional Court (the *Bundesverfassungsgericht*) for a preliminary ruling on whether the Community regulation violated fundamental human rights provisions of the German Constitution.

The majority opinion of the Court first laid down the premise that "Community law is neither a component part of the national legal system nor international law, but forms an independent system of law flowing from an autonomous legal source." From that it deduced that while the competent Community organs (notably the European Court of Justice) rules on the construction and binding force of Community law, the competent national organs (notably the Constitutional Court itself) rules on the construction and binding force of German constitutional law. This, the Court asserted, "does not lead to any difficulties as long as the two systems of law do not come into conflict with one another in their substance...."

Referring to Article 24 of the Constitution, the majority insisted that this provision not be taken literally, but rather understood and construed in the overall context of the Constitution. As a result, it can not be relied upon to justify "amending the basic structure of the Constitution, which forms the basis of [the Federal Republic of Germany's] identity, without a formal amendment to the Constitution," whether by treaty or by the rules of secondary Community law.

The majority then turned specifically to the "basic rights" set out in the German Constitution:

4. The part of the Constitution dealing with fundamental rights is an inalienable essential feature of the valid Constitution of the Federal Republic of Germany and one which forms part of the constitutional structure of the Constitution. Article 24 of the Constitution does not without reservation allow it to be subjected to qualifications. In this, the present state of integration of the Community is of crucial importance. The Community still lacks a democratically legitimated parliament directly elected by general suffrage which possesses legislative powers and to which the Community organs empowered to legislate are fully responsible on a political level; it still lacks in particular a codified catalogue of fundamental rights, the substance of which is reliably and unambiguously fixed for the future in the same way as the substance of the Constitution.

... As long as this legal certainty, which is not guaranteed merely by the decisions of the European Court of Justice, favourable though these have been to fundamental rights, is not achieved in the course of the further integration of the Community, the reservation derived from Article 24 of the Constitution applies. What is involved is, therefore, a legal difficulty arising exclusively from the Community's continuing integration process, which is still in flux....

Provisionally, therefore, in the hypothetical case of a conflict between Community law and ... the guarantees of fundamental rights in the Constitution, ... the guarantee of fundamental rights in the Constitution prevails as long as the competent organs of the Community have not removed the conflict of norms in accordance with the Treaty mechanism.

5. ... [While] the European Court of Justice has jurisdiction to rule on the legal validity of the norms of Community law (including the unwritten norms of Community law which it considers exist) and on their construction, it does not decide incidental questions of national law of the Federal Republic of Germany (or of any other Member State) with binding force for this State. Statements in the reasoning of its judgments that a particular aspect of a Community norm accords or is compatible in its substance with a constitutional rule of national law—here, with a guarantee of fundamental rights in the Constitution—constitute non-binding *obiter dicta*.

* * *

[Conversely, the German Constitutional Court] never rules on the validity or invalidity of a rule of Community law. At most, it can come to the conclusion that such a rule cannot be applied by the authorities or courts of the Federal Republic of Germany in so far as it conflicts with a rule of the Constitution relating to fundamental rights. ...

The majority's much-quoted conclusion was:

7. ... As long as the integration process has not progressed so far that Community law also receives a catalogue of fundamental rights decided on by a parliament and of settled validity, which is adequate in comparison with the catalogue of fundamental rights contained in the Constitution, a reference by a court in the Federal Republic of Germany to the [German Constitutional Court] following the obtaining of a ruling of the European Court under Article 177 [now 234] of the Treaty, is admissible and necessary if the German court regards the rule of Community law which is relevant to its decision as inapplicable in the interpretation given by the European Court, because and in so far as it conflicts with one of the fundamental rights in the Constitution.

Turning to the merits, the court ruled that the Council regulation, as interpreted by the European Court of Justice, did not conflict with the principle of proportionality or any other guarantee of fundamental rights in the German Constitution.

Three members of the court dissented, finding the reference to the court inadmissible. According to them, the autonomy of Community law dictated a different result. For them, the German Constitution is not the only guarantor of fundamental rights within Germany. The Court of Justice, acting on the recognition in EC Article 288(2) (ex 215(2)) of the general legal principles common to the Member States, had amply recognized fundamental rights (including the principle of proportionality that was relevant to the case at hand), and the Treaty's system of remedies adequately protected those rights. While individual standing in the Court of Justice was very limited, the preliminary reference mechanism enabled national courts to obtain a ruling from the Court of Justice on the conformity of Community law to fundamental rights whenever that law furnishes the basis of a national implementation measure. The minority concluded:

> ... The rules of law issued by [the Community organs] cannot therefore be dependent in their validity and applicability on whether they match the criteria of national law. In content, Community law takes precedence over divergent provisions of national law. This applies not only in relation to norms of simple national law, but also *vis-à-vis* norms of the national constitution dealing with fundamental rights.

> The "basic structure of the Constitution, on which its identity rests" is not at stake in this process. ... It is ... mistaken from the start for the majority of the Court to believe that it has to ward off some "encroachment" on the structures which go to make up the Constitution, and in particular its section dealing with fundamental rights, by binding Community law to the fundamental rights norms of the national Constitution. Nor can such an assumption be founded by reference to the fact that the European Communities do not yet possess any codified catalogue of fundamental rights. In this context, the mode of guaranteeing the fundamental rights is irrelevant, and the assertion that only a codification offers adequate certainty of law does not bear examination. ... The argument that the fundamental rights of the Constitution must also prevail over secondary Community law because the Community still lacks a directly legitimated parliament is not in itself conclusive. The protection of fundamental rights and the democratic principle are not interchangeable inside a democratically constituted Community based on the idea of freedom; they complement one another. While the achievement of the democratic principle in the EEC [now EC] would cause the legislator and the executive to be more deeply concerned with fundamental rights, this would not make the judicial protection of fundamental rights superfluous.

The minority thought the position taken by the majority would fundamentally undermine Community law:

> The [majority's] view leads, moreover, to unacceptable results. If the applicability of secondary Community law were dependent on its satisfying the fundamental rights norms of a national Constitution, then—since the Member States guarantee fundamental rights to differing extents— the situation could arise where legal rules of the Communities are applicable in some Member States, but not in others. This would result precisely ... in a fragmentation of law. To open up this possibility means exposing a part of European legal unity, endangering the existence of the Community, and negating the basic idea of European unification.

The conclusion for the dissenters: "The [German Constitutional Court] possesses no jurisdiction to examine rules of Community law against the criteria of the Constitution, in particular of its section on fundamental rights."

The decision is known as *Solange I* (*solange* meaning "as long as") because of its conditional nature. Note that neither the majority nor minority considered as alternatives: (a) permitting national courts to review the conformity of Community action with basic rights, on condition that the latter are defined by reference to Community rather than national constitutional norms, or (b) permitting review by the Court of Justice under *both* Community and national constitutional norms.

In the years following *Solange I*, the Constitutional Court never found a Community measure violative of fundamental rights under German law.

Twelve years later, in an otherwise unremarkable opinion, the German court revisited the question of principle it had addressed in *Solange I*. The case was In re Application of Wünsche Handelsgesellschaft (Solange II), Case 2 BvR 197/83, 73 BVerfGE 339, [1987] 3 CMLR 225 (Fed. Const'l Court, second senate, Oct. 22, 1986). Wünsche, a German importer, was denied a license to import mushrooms from Taiwan under an import license system dating back to 1974. Wünsche claimed that the market disturbances that originally prompted the adoption of that system no longer existed, and that there was in fact a shortage of mushrooms, both domestic and imported. At Wünsche's request, Germany's supreme administrative court (the *Bundesverwaltungsgericht*) referred the question of the system's legality to the European Court of Justice, which upheld the system as a reasonable exercise of the Commission's discretion. The German court refused, however, to refer Wünsche's further constitutional claims (including the right to a fair hearing) either to the Court of Justice or to the German Constitutional Court. Maintaining that this refusal in itself was a deprivation of its constitutional rights, Wünsche then brought a constitutional complaint directly to the German Constitutional Court.

The Court issued a unanimous judgment. It first confirmed its position in *Solange I* that Article 24(1) of the Constitution does not allow Germany "to surrender ... the identity of the prevailing constitutional order [or] undermine essential structural parts of the Constitution [such as] fundamental rights," and then reexamined the question of how those fundamental rights are to be protected:

> (d) In the judgment of this Chamber, a measure of protection of fundamental rights has been established [since 1974] within the sovereign jurisdiction of the European Communities which in its conception, substance and manner of implementation is essentially comparable with the standards of fundamental rights provided for in the Constitution. All the main institutions of the Community have since acknowledged in a legally significant manner that in the exercise of their powers and the pursuit of the objectives of the Community they will be guided as a legal duty by respect for fundamental rights, in particular as established by the constitutions of Member States and by the European Convention on Human Rights. There are no decisive factors to lead one to conclude that the standard of fundamental rights which has been achieved under Community law is not adequately consolidated. . . .

(aa) This standard of fundamental rights has in the meantime, particularly through the decisions of the European Court, been formulated in content, consolidated and adequately guaranteed. [The court here made reference to several Court of Justice rulings on fundamental rights discussed in Chapters 5 and 6 *supra*.]

For the purposes of defining under Community law the content and extent of fundamental rights, the Court has also referred to the European Human Rights Convention. . . .

(bb) The European Parliament, the Council and the Commission of the Community adopted the . . . joint declaration on 5 April 1977 [to the effect that] "in the exercise of their powers and in pursuance of the aims of the European Communities they respect and will continue to respect these rights."

(e) Compared with the standard of fundamental rights under the Constitution, it may be that the guarantees for the protection of such rights established thus far by the decisions of the European Court, since they have naturally been developed case by case, still contain gaps in so far as specific legal principles recognised by the Constitution or the nature, content or extent of a fundamental right have not individually been the object of a judgment delivered by the Court. What is decisive nevertheless is the attitude of principle which the Court maintains at this stage towards . . . the incorporation of fundamental rights in Community law under legal rules and the legal connection of that law (to that extent) with the constitutions of Member States and with the European Human Rights Convention. [What] is also [decisive is] the practical significance which has been achieved by the protection of fundamental rights in the meantime in the Court's application of Community law. . . . [The Court of Justice's] rules of procedure, in relation to access to the Court, the given types of procedures, the powers of the Court to review and make decisions, the procedural principles and the effect of its decisions, are organised in a way which in general guarantees an effective protection of fundamental rights which is to be regarded as substantially similar to the unconditional protection of fundamental rights under the Constitution.

[The Court noted that circumstances had changed since *Solange I* found the Community to lack a directly elected parliament that possessed legislative powers and to which the legislative institutions were politically responsible. The Court returned to the question of fundamental rights:]

Nor is it to be expected in view of the state of the case law of the European Court . . . that a decline in the standards of fundamental rights under Community law will result [from the Court's reliance on] the constitutions of Member States . . . In the first place, the Court is not obliged to determine the general principles of Community law according to the lowest common denominator derived from a comparison of the constitutions of Member States, even if such deep differences between their Constitutions exist at all or do arise in the future. It is to be expected rather that the European Court will strive to ensure the best possible development of any particular principle of fundamental rights in Community law. In the second place, [reference to] the European Human Rights Convention, together with the now extensive case law of the

European Court in favour of human rights, guarantees a minimum standard of substantive protection of fundamental rights which in principle satisfies the legal requirements of the Constitution as such. That position is not altered by the fact that the Community as such is not a party to the European Human Rights Convention.

The Court's conclusion followed:

(f) In view of those developments, it must be held that, so long as the European Communities, and in particular ... the case law of the European Court, generally ensure an effective protection of fundamental rights as against the sovereign powers of the Communities which is to be regarded as substantially similar to the protection of fundamental rights required unconditionally by the Constitution, and in so far as they generally safeguard the essential content of fundamental rights, the Federal Constitutional Court will no longer exercise its jurisdiction to decide on the applicability of secondary Community legislation cited as the legal basis for any acts of German courts or authorities within the sovereign jurisdiction of the Federal Republic of Germany, and it will no longer review such legislation by the standard of the fundamental rights contained in the Constitution....

(g) The question [referred to the Court] must therefore remain unanswered....

Notes and Questions

1. Note the Court's reference to the difference between adopting the highest level of rights protection among the Member States and adopting the lowest common denominator. Based on your reading thus far, what level of protection has the Court of Justice actually adopted? Do you see why this judgment is referred to as *Solange II*?

2. Might a party seek to enjoin the German government on constitutional grounds from participating in the adoption of Community legislation in the Council? In M GmbH v. Bundesregierung, Case 2 BvQ 3/89, [1990] 1 CMLR 570 (Federal Constitutional Court, May 12, 1989), such an effort was rebuffed on the ground that the plaintiffs, a group of German tobacco companies opposed to a draft Council directive on tobacco product labeling, lacked standing to press a claim in the Constitutional Court that the directive would infringe their fundamental rights of free expression, property and freedom of commerce. The Court also suggested that the claim was unripe and should in no event be heard until the directive is adopted and implemented: "The Federal Government's participation ... is only a contribution to the creation of a directive, which does not adversely affect the applicants until it has come into force and is implemented into national law." [1990] 1 CMLR at 574.

Suppose the tobacco companies eventually challenge the German implementing statute. To what extent and by what means may the statute's validity be questioned? In *M GmbH* the German Constitutional Court stated:

... The question whether the applicants' constitutional ... rights are infringed in the implementation of the directive ... is one which is open to constitutional judicial review in all respects.

In so far as the directive may infringe the basic constitutional standards of Community law, the European Court of Justice ensures legal protection of rights. If the constitutional standards laid down as unconditional by the German Constitution should not be satisfied by this route, recourse can be had to the Federal Constitutional Court.

Id. Is the Court's position in *M GmbH* consistent with its position in *Wünsche Handelsgesellschaft?*

3.   In *Solange II,* the Constitutional Court confined itself to the question of the supremacy of Community over national law. Does the opinion also imply that the German courts will regard themselves as bound to give an EC directive direct effect once the Court of Justice interprets that directive as having direct effect?

The Bundesfinanzhof, the highest German tax court, did not take that view. In 1985, it ruled that a German taxpayer could not claim a tax exemption for 1978 income from certain credit transactions by invoking a 1977 Council Directive (the Sixth VAT Directive) that required the Member States to provide such an exemption by January 1, 1978. Its reason was that the Sixth VAT Directive had not been implemented in Germany by 1978. (The directive was in fact not implemented until 1980). The Bundesfinanzhof so held (citing the French Conseil d'Etat decision in *Cohn–Bendit, supra* page 289), even though the Court of Justice had already twice ruled in 1981 and 1982 (Becker v. Finanzamt Münster–Innenstadt, *supra* page 255; R.A. Grendel GmbH v. Finanzamt für Körperschaften in Hamburg, Case 255/81, [1982] ECR 2301) that the directive had direct effect. In fact, the lower court had earlier requested a preliminary ruling from the Court of Justice on the same question, and the Court of Justice had reaffirmed its 1981 rulings. Kloppenburg v. Finanzamt Leer, Case 70/83, [1984] ECR 1075, 1087. The Bundesfinanzhof's decision was thus all the more striking, and it produced a constitutional complaint by the taxpayer to the German Constitutional Court.

The Constitutional Court held that the Bundesfinanzhof indeed violated the taxpayer's constitutional rights. According to the Court, her constitutional right to her "lawful judge" (under Article 101(1) of the German Constitution) was infringed when the tax court knowingly disregarded the Court of Justice's rulings on the direct effect of the Sixth VAT Directive instead of asking the Court of Justice to reconsider its position.

> ... If the Bundesfinanzhof did not wish to accept that the preliminary ruling by the Court of Justice on the same question in the same main action had binding effect and did not wish to follow the latter's view of the law, it had an obligation to resubmit the question to the Court of Justice under Article 177 [now 234]. It acted in an objectively arbitrary way in not complying with this obligation.

* * *

> ... It is not an unjustifiable conclusion for the Court to infer, from the provision in Article 189 [now 249] that a regulation shall be directly applicable, that this does not rule out the possibility that other legal acts (decisions, directives) also have direct effect. Furthermore, it is logically justifiable for the Court ... to arrive at the conclusion that in certain limited cases the Community citizen can "invoke" the directive against the Member State in legal proceedings and the State concerned cannot plead that it has not implemented the directive. ...
>
>   [R]eaching this conclusion ... does not involve an extension of the Community's legislative power. The actual purpose of enabling an individual to invoke a directive is not to extend the Community's legislative power, but

to sanction effectively ... the Member State's obligation created by the directive....

* * *

In the present case it is unnecessary to decide where the general limits to the scope of the Community's authority run in this connection. The existing case law of the Court of Justice concerning the possibility open to the Community citizen to invoke directives of a certain kind directly is far from overstepping those limits. ... In view of the considerable differences between Member States in implementing directives, this serves to create equality in application of the law among Community nationals. ...

* * *

Therefore the Bundesfinanzhof was bound by the preliminary ruling which the [lower tax court] obtained from the Court of Justice. ...

* * *

If the Bundesfinanzhof had not wished to follow the view of the law stated by the Court of Justice, it ought to have requested another preliminary ruling from the Court of Justice. ...

* * *

[Not doing so] constitutes a violation of Article 101(1) of the Constitution.

In re Application of Frau Kloppenburg, Case 2 BvR 687/85, 75 BVerfGE 223, [1987] EurR 333, [1988] 3 CMLR 1 (Federal Constitutional Court, second senate, April 8, 1987). For a recent reaffirmation, see In re Application of Frau R, Case 1 BvR 1036/99 (Jan. 9, 2001).

4. The German Constitutional Court's preoccupation with fundamental rights is a consequence of the special prominence of entrenched human rights provisions in Germany's postwar constitution. Another striking feature of German constitutionalism is its federalism. In the Federal Republic of Germany, federal and state (or *Länder*) governments have constitutionally separate and limited spheres of authority. The *Länder* governments have repeatedly complained that Germany's transfer of legislative powers to the Community is unconstitutional to the extent that it purports to transfer authority reserved to the states. See Beyerlin, German Federalism: A Dynamic Process (Report to 13th International Congress of Comparative Law, Montreal, August 1990) at 21.

In one noted instance, Bayerische Staatsregierung v. Bundesregierung, Case 2 BvG 1/89, 80 BVerfGE 68, [1989] EuGRZ 337, [1990] 1 CMLR 649 (Federal Constitutional Court, second senate, April 11, 1989), the state of Bavaria tried to enjoin the Federal Government from voting in the Council in favor of a directive harmonizing rules on television broadcasting, a matter reserved under the German Constitution to the *Länder* and on which the *Länder* were divided. The Court denied an interim injunction, stating:

> [If the claim is well-founded], the Federal Government would have encroached on an area constitutionally reserved to the [Bavarian government]. ... But in the Federal Government's view the content [of the Community legislation eventually adopted] could be shaped in a way which takes more account of the jurisdiction of the *Länder* if the Government can use the room to manoeuvre available to it [by participating in the legislation]....

[1990] 1 CMLR at 654–55. As it did in *M GmbH, supra* page 303, the Constitutional Court said that the federalism issue could be raised after the directive was implemented.

After the broadcasting directive was adopted by the Council, the Bavarian government renewed its complaint before the Constitutional Court, seeking a declaration that the Federal Government's consent to the directive violated Bavaria's rights under the German Constitution. The Court ruled (1) that the Federal Government's assent in the Council was a justiciable act and (2) that the Federal Government had indeed violated Bavaria's rights by assenting to the directive without consulting the Bundesrat further about the results of its negotiations within the Council. The Court considered such consultation to be required under the constitutional principle of "loyal cooperation" between the Federation and the *Länder*. Although mostly procedural in nature, the obligation of "loyalty" has, in the Court's view, a substantive dimension, viz. preventing the erosion in the Council of the competence of the Member States and of the *Länder:*

> . . . the federal principle of federal loyalty obliges the organs to resist a long-term development which damages the remaining regulatory powers of the Member States and consequently of *Länder* rights by a gradual stretching of Community competences.

Judgment of March 22, 1995, 2 BvG 1/89, [1995] EuGRZ 125, [1995] EuR 104, [1995] EuZW 77, [1995] JZ 669. To what relief is Bavaria entitled? Is the directive unenforceable in Germany? For a discussion and partial translation, see M. Herdegen, After the TV Judgment of the German Constitutional Court: Decision–Making within the EU Council and the German Lander, 32 Comm. Mkt. L. Rev. 1369 (1995).

The adequacy of *Länder* representation in the EU Council of Ministers became a very live issue in 1992 in the context of Germany's decision on ratifying the Maastricht Treaty. A special joint committee of the Bundestag and Bundesrat, which had been formed in the context of the German reunification process, assumed the task of drafting needed amendments to the German Constitution. This culminated in the inclusion in the German Constitution of a new Article 23, the so-called *Europa-Artikel*:

Article 23

(European Union)

(1) For the realization of a united Europe, the Federal Republic of Germany may participate in the development of a European Union which is bound by the principles of democracy, the rule of law, social responsibility and federalism, and by the principle of subsidiarity, and which guarantees a protection of fundamental rights that is essentially comparable to this Basic Law. The Federation may for this purpose transfer sovereign rights through legislation enacted with the approval of the Bundesrat. Articles 79, section 2 and 3 [of the Basic Law], shall apply to the establishment of the European Union as well as to any amendments of its treaty bases or comparable enactments by which this Basic Law is amended or supplemented in its content or by which any such amendment or supplementing is made possible.

(2) The Bundestag and, through the Bundesrat, the States shall participate in matters of the European Union. The Federal Government must inform the Bundestag and the Bundesrat fully and at the earliest possible point in time.

(3) Before participating in legislative acts of the European Union, the Federal Government shall give the Bundestag an opportunity to take a position. The Federal Government shall take account of the position of the Bundestag in its deliberations. The details shall be governed by a statute.

(4) The Bundesrat shall be given a part in the formation of the political will of the Federation, to the extent that it would be entitled to participate in a corresponding domestic law measure or to the extent that the States enjoy internal competence.

(5) Insofar as a matter of exclusive federal jurisdiction may affect the interests of the States, or insofar as the Federation otherwise has legislative competence, the Federal Government shall take account of the positions of the Bundesrat. When, essentially, the legislative competences of the States, the organization of their agencies, or State administrative procedures are affected, the point of view of the Bundesrat shall to that extent be given dominant consideration in the formation of the political will of the Federation. The national political responsibility of the Federation must at the same time be safeguarded. In matters that may lead to increases in expenditures or diminutions in revenue for the Federation, the approval of the Federal Government shall be necessary.

(6) Whenever the exclusive legislative competences of the States are essentially affected, the exercise of the rights which the Federal Republic enjoys as a Member State of the European Union shall be entrusted by the Federation to a representative of the States designated by the Bundesrat. These rights shall be exercised with the participation of and in agreement with the Federal Government. The national political responsibility of the Federation shall thereby be safeguarded.

(7) The details concerning sections 4 through 6 shall be governed by a statute which requires the approval of the Bundesrat.

Article 23 plainly addresses the problems raised by Germany's federal character and by the necessity of preserving the voice of the *Länder* and the Bundesrat, the parliamentary chamber in which they are represented. The cooperation required by Article 23 between the Federal Government, on the one hand, and the Bundestag and Bundesrat, on the other, has since been more fully spelled out in legislation.[5] (In preparation for ratifying the Maastricht Treaty, Articles 28 and 88 of the Constitution were also amended so as to permit other EC nationals to enjoy voting rights and to permit the transfer of powers to the European Central Bank called for by the TEU.) For an analysis of the adaptations in Germany's representation in the EU to accommodate German federalism, see M. Rogoff, The European Union, Germany, and the *Länder*: Patterns of Political Relations in Europe, 5 Colum. J. Eur. L. 415 (1999).

Germany is by no means the only Member State keen on strengthening the role of the national parliaments in decisionmaking at the European level. The British and Danish Parliaments have insisted through specialized oversight committees on reviewing European-level decisionmaking, and more particularly the conduct of their own Member State governments in decisionmaking in the Council. Recall that the French Constitution was also amended in this regard. (See page 290 *supra*.)

5. Statutes of March 11, 1993, 1993 Bundesgesetzblatt 1993.I.310–11. On the new Article 23, see R. Hrbek, The German *Länder* and EC Integration, 15 J. Eur. Integr. 173 (1992).

Tensions over the impact of Community law on the domestic federalism of the Member States have not subsided. Much discussion of the issue occurred at the 1996 IGC, reflected in a Protocol to the Amsterdam Treaty on the role of the national parliaments, specifically requiring that all Commission communications (including green and white papers) be promptly forwarded to the national parliaments and that all Commission proposals for legislation be made available in good time so that national parliaments may review them and effectively make their views known to their respective Member State governments. The Protocol declares that the Conference of European Affairs Committees (COSAC)—a body established in 1989 to assemble the Member State parliamentary committees that specializing in Community affairs—should be heard on any legislative proposal in the justice and home affairs area that might have a direct bearing on individual rights or on respect for the principle of subsidiarity.

As shown by the following judgment, rendered on the eve of Germany's ratification of the Maastricht Treaty, the then-recent amendments to the German Constitution were insufficient to forestall constitutional challenges.

BRUNNER AND OTHERS v. THE EUROPEAN UNION TREATY

(The Maastricht Judgment) German Constitutional Court, second senate
Case 2 BvR 2134/92 & 2159/92, [1994] 1 CMLR 57, 1993 WL 965303 Oct. 12, 1993.

[Following Germany's signature of the Maastricht Treaty, twenty separate lawsuits were filed against the bill of ratification, one of them by Manfred Brunner, the former chief of staff to EC Commissioner Martin Bangemann. The essence of the complaints was that approval of the TEU would violate the principle that all state power emanates from the people—a principle implicit in the requirement of Article 38 of the German Basic Law that members of the Bundestag (the principal legislative chamber, which elects the Federal Chancellor and exercises political control over the Government) be elected through "general, direct, free, equal, and secret elections" and function as "representatives of the whole people." Other claims were that ratification of the TEU would infringe the basic rights enshrined in the German Constitution (notably Articles 1(1), 2(1), 5(1), 9(1) in conjunction with 21(1), 12(1), 14(1), and 20(4)), as well as principles of German federalism.]

B.

1.

* * *

(a) Article 38(1) and (2) of the Constitution guarantees to Germans entitled to vote the individually assertable right to participate in the election of deputies to the German Bundestag. In the act of voting the power of the state proceeds from the people. The Bundestag then exercises state power as a legislative body, which also chooses the Federal Chancellor and controls the government (Article 20(2), first and second sentences).[6] Article 38 not only contains a safeguard to ensure that the citizen is accorded the right to elect the German Bundestag and that in the election the constitutional principles

---

6. "All state authority emanates from the people. It is ... exercised by the people through elections and voting and by specific organs of the legislature, the executive power and the judiciary."

of electoral law will be upheld; the safeguard also extends to the fundamental democratic content of that right: what is guaranteed to Germans entitled to vote is the individually assertable right to participate in the election of the Bundestag and thereby to co-operate in the legitimation of state power by the people at federal level and to have an influence over its exercise. ...

* * *

The complainant's right arising from Article 38 of the Constitution can ... be infringed if the exercise of the powers within the competence of the Bundestag is transferred to an institution of the European Union or European Communities formed by the member-States' governments to such an extent that the minimum requirements, which under Article 20(1) and (2) in conjunction with Article 79(3)[7] may not be dispensed with, for the democratic legitimation of the sovereign power exercised in respect of citizens are no longer satisfied.

(b) The complainant ... submits that at present already nearly 80 per cent of regulations in the economic sphere are determined by Community law and nearly 50 per cent of all German legislation is occasioned by Community law. He says that the [TEU] will now substantially extend these areas of competence of the Council as an executive organ with legislative power, and will deprive the Bundestag of decision-making competence over a wide range.... For these purposes the Treaty establishes the majority principle in the Council for a range of competences, and thus allows legislation by the executive as regards Germany even against the will of the German organs concerned. In the monetary union, monetary policy will be withdrawn from any parliamentary influence and other democratic legitimation. The powers and competences of the Bundestag will finally become devoid of all substance as a result of Article F(3) [now 6(4)] of the Union Treaty, which gives the Union a power to extend its own powers, since it enables it to provide itself with any necessary powers and competences.

* * *

(c) In the event, it appears possible on the arguments set out above that the Act of Accession to the [TEU] is an infringement of the complainant's rights under Article 38 of the Constitution.

[In Parts 2 through 5, the Court ruled the complaint for a variety of reasons inadmissible insofar as it asserted an infringement of basic rights under Articles 1(1), 2(1), 5(1), 12(1), 14(1) and 20(4) of the Constitution or an infringement of Articles 23 and 28. In the course of doing so, the Court reaffirmed *Solange II*.]

C.

In so far as the first complainant's constitutional complaint is admissible it is unfounded. ... The content of [Article 38] is not infringed by the Act of Accession, as appears from the content of the Treaty: the Treaty establishes a European federation of states, which is based on the member-States and respects their identities; it concerns Germany's membership of supra-national

---

7. Article 79(3) excludes any amendment to the Constitution that would affect the basic rights in Articles 1 and 20 of the Constitu- tion, or the division of the German state into *Länder* or the participation of the *Länder* in legislation.

organisations, not its belonging to a European state. The functions of the European Union and the powers granted for their implementation are regulated in a sufficiently foreseeable manner, because the principle of limited individual powers is adhered to, no power to extend its powers is conferred on the European Union, and the claiming of further functions and powers by the European Union and the Communities is made dependent on supplementation and amendment of the Treaty, and is therefore subject to the affirmative decision of the national parliaments. The scope of the functions and powers granted to the European Union and to the institutions of the European Communities and the means of formation of political intentions laid down by the Treaty do not at present have the effect of reducing the content of the decision-making and supervisory powers of the Bundestag to an extent which infringes the democratic principle in so far as it is declared by Article 79(3) of the Constitution to be unassailable.

I.

1.

The right guaranteed by Article 38 of the Constitution to participate in the legitimation of state power and to acquire influence on its exercise through the electoral process excludes the possibility, within the sphere of application of Article 23, of its being made so devoid of content through the transfer of the functions and powers of the Bundestag that there is a breach of the democratic principle in so far as it is declared by Article 79(3), in conjunction with Article 20(1) and (2), to be unassailable.

2.

It is part of the unassailable content of the democratic principle under Article 79(3) of the Constitution that the carrying-out of state functions and the exercise of state powers is derived from the people of the state and the persons doing so are fundamentally answerable to the people.... What is decisive is that a sufficiently effective content of democratic legitimation, that is, a specific level of legitimation, should be achieved.

(a) If the Federal Republic of Germany becomes a member of a community of states that is entitled to act on its own in sovereign matters, and if that community is given the right to exercise independent sovereign powers—both of which are expressly allowed by the Constitution for the purposes of achieving a united Europe (Article 23(1))—then democratic legitimation for these purposes cannot be produced in the same way as it is within a national order governed uniformly and conclusively by a state constitution. If sovereign rights are granted to international institutions, then the representative body elected by the people—the German Bundestag—and along with it the citizens entitled to vote, necessarily lose some influence on the processes of political will-formation and decision-making....

... The conferring of sovereign powers has the consequence that their exercise no longer depends solely on the will of one member-State all the time. [But] to see that as a breach of the constitutional principle of democracy would not only contradict the openness of the Constitution to integration, which was intended, and stated expressly, by the makers of the Constitution in 1949; it would also entail a conception of democracy that would make every democratic state incapable of any integration going beyond the principle of unanimity.... The conferring of sovereign powers which ... Articles [23 and 24] authorise, requires a prior legislative resolution. The requirement of a statute gives the political responsibility for conferring sovereign rights to the Bundestag (together with the Bundesrat) as the national representative body; it has to debate the wide-ranging consequences (not least for the competences of the Bundestag itself) bound up with the assent to such a course, and has to reach a decision on them. In the statute assenting to accession to a community of States is found the democratic legitimation both of the existence of the community of States itself and of its powers to take majority decisions which are binding on the member-States ...

(b) The democratic principle thus does not prevent the Federal Republic of Germany from becoming a member of a community of States (organised on a supra-national basis). ...

(b.1) ...

At the same time, with the building-up of the functions and powers of the Community, it becomes increasingly necessary to allow the democratic legitimation and influence provided by way of the national parliaments to be accompanied by a representation of the peoples of the member-States through a European Parliament as the source of a supplementary democratic support for the policies of the European Union....

Democracy, if it is not to remain a merely formal principle of accountability, is dependent on the presence of certain pre-legal conditions, such as a continuous free debate between opposing social forces, interests and ideas, in which political goals also become clarified and change course and out of which comes a public opinion which forms the beginnings of political intentions. That also entails that the decision-making processes of the organs exercising sovereign powers and the various political objectives pursued can be generally perceived and understood, and therefore that the citizen entitled to vote can communicate in his own language with the sovereign authority to which he is subject.

Such factual conditions, in so far as they do not yet exist, can develop in the course of time within the institutional framework of the European Union. ...

(b.2) In the federation of States formed by the European Union, therefore, democratic legitimation necessarily comes about through the feed-back of the actions of the European institutions into the parliaments of the member-States; and within the institutional structure of the Union there is the additional factor ... of the provision of democratic legitimation by way of the European Parliament elected by the citizens of the States. Already at the present stage of development the legitimation provided by the European Parliament has a supporting function, which could become stronger if it were to be elected by equivalent electoral rules in all the member-States in accordance with Article 138(3) [now 190(4)] of the EC Treaty and if its influence on the policies and legislation of the European Community were to increase. What is decisive is that the democratic bases of the European Union are built-up in step with integration, and that as integration proceeds a thriving democracy is also maintained in the member-States. ...

If the peoples of the individual States provide democratic legitimation through the agency of their national parliaments (as at present) limits are then set by virtue of the democratic principle to the extension of the European Communities' functions and powers. Each of the peoples of the individual States is the starting point for a state power relating to that people. The States need sufficiently important spheres of activity of their own in which the people of each can develop and articulate itself in a process of political will-formation. . . .

From all that it follows that functions and powers of substantial importance must remain for the German Bundestag.

(c) The exercise of sovereign power through a federation of States like the European Union is based on authorisations from States which remain sovereign and which in international matters generally act through their governments and control the integration process thereby. It is therefore primarily determined governmentally. If such a community power is to rest on the political will-formation which is supplied by the people of each individual State, and is to that extent democratic, that presupposes that the power is exercised by a body made up of representatives sent by the member-States' governments, which in their turn are subject to democratic control. The passing of European legal regulations, too, may (without prejudice to the consequent need for a democratic control of the governments) lie with an institution composed of representatives of the member-States' governments, that is to say, on an executive basis, to a greater extent than would be constitutionally acceptable at national level.

3.

* * *

There is . . . a breach of Article 38 of the Constitution if an Act that opens up the German legal system to the direct validity and application of the law of the (supra-national) European Communities does not establish with sufficient certainty the powers that are transferred and the intended programme of integration. If it is not clear to what extent and degree the German legislature has assented to the transfer of the exercise of sovereign powers, then it will be possible for the European Communities to claim functions and powers that were not specified. That would be equivalent to a general enablement and would therefore be a surrender of powers, something against which Article 38 of the Constitution provides protection.

. . . What is decisive is that Germany's membership and the rights and duties that follow therefrom . . . have been defined in the Treaty so as to be predictable for the legislature and are enacted by it in the Act of Accession with sufficient certainty. That also means that subsequent important alterations to the integration programme set up in the [TEU] and to the Union's powers of action are no longer covered by the Act of Accession to the present Treaty. Thus, if European institutions or agencies were to treat or develop the [TEU] in a way that was no longer covered by the Treaty in the form that is the basis for the Act of Accession, the resultant legislative instruments would not be legally binding within the sphere of German sovereignty. The German state organs would be prevented for constitutional reasons from applying them in Germany. Accordingly the Federal Constitutional Court will review legal instruments of European institutions and agencies to see whether they remain within the limits of the sovereign rights conferred on them or transgress them.

II.

The [TEU] satisfies the above-stated requirements . . .

* * *

1.

[The Court here noted that the Maastricht Treaty obliges the EU to respect the national identities of the Member States (TEU Article 6, ex F) and that both the EC Treaty and TEU embrace the principles of enumeration of competences and subsidiarity.]

As to the question of where a process of European integration will eventually lead after further amendments to the Treaties, the term "European Union" may indicate a concern for further integration, but as regards the intended objective the question is ultimately open. In any event the establishment of a "United States of Europe," in a way comparable to that in which the United States of America became a state, is not at present intended. . . .

The competences and powers which are granted to the European Union and the Communities belonging to it remain essentially the activities of an economic union in so far as they are exercised through the implementation of sovereign rights. The central areas of activity of the European Community in this respect are the customs union and the free movement of goods, the internal market, the [harmonization] of laws to ensure the proper functioning of the common market, co-ordination of the member-States' economic policies, and the development of a monetary union. Outside the European Communities, co-operation stays on an inter-governmental basis; that applies particularly in the case of foreign and security policy and the fields of justice and home affairs.

The Federal Republic of Germany, therefore, even after the [TEU] comes into force, will remain a member of a federation of States, the common authority of which is derived from the member-States and can only have binding effects within the German sovereign sphere by virtue of the German instruction that its law be applied. Germany is one of the "Masters of the Treaties," which have established their adherence to the [TEU] concluded "for an unlimited period' " with the intention of long-term membership, but could also ultimately revoke that adherence by a contrary act. . . .

(b) The necessary influence of the Bundestag is guaranteed in the first place because, under Article 23(1) of the Constitution, German membership of the European Union, and the further development of the Union through a change in its treaty bases or an extension of its powers, all require legislation, which under the conditions of the third sentence of that Article require . . . qualified majorities [under] the Constitution. . . .

Finally, the Bundestag also influences the European policy of the Federal Government through the latter's responsibility to Parliament. This function of initiation and control, which it basically exercises in public proceedings, causes the general public and the political parties to take positions on the government's European policy and thus becomes a factor in the citizen's voting decisions.

The governments of the member-States also stressed, in connection with the signing of the [TEU], the great significance attributed to the parliaments of the individual States in the Union: their Declaration on the role of the parliaments of individual States in the European Union stresses the necessity for a greater involvement by the parliaments in the activities of the European Union, and requires the governments to provide the parliaments with information in good time about the Commission's proposals in order to enable them to be examined.

2.

The [TEU] satisfies the requirements of certainty because it lays down the future course of implementation, that is to say, the possible uses to be made of the sovereign powers granted, in a manner which is sufficiently predictable: that establishes that the Act of Accession adheres to the requirements of parliamentary responsibility. There are no grounds for the complainant's concern that the European Community will be able, because of its widely set objectives, to develop into a political union having unspecified sovereign rights without a renewed parliamentary instruction for its laws to apply. The [TEU] adopts the principle of limited individual empowerment, which already applied to the European Communities, and strengthens it....

[Here the Court once again cited the principles of enumerated powers and subsidiarity, as well as the principle of proportionality. "The requirement of an attribution of powers under the Treaties had always been a basic feature of the Community legal order; the powers of the individual States have always been the rule, those of the Community, the exception." While the Maastricht Treaty introduces binding rules on EMU, it nevertheless restricts the Community on matters of general economic policy to a "coordinating" function ("encouragement" and "contribution"), and the same applies to the new provisions of Articles 126–129 [now 149–152] on vocational training, youth, culture, and public health, with the harmonization of laws expressly excluded.]

(b) This system of rules is not penetrated or unhinged by Article F(3) [now 6(4)] of the Union Treaty. The requirement of an adequate level of legal certainty for the sovereign rights conferred, and therefore of the existence of parliamentary responsibility as regards the conferring of such rights, would no doubt be breached if Article F(3) established a power to extend its powers in favour of the European Union as a Community of sovereign States. But Article F(3) does not empower the Union to provide itself by its own authority with the financial means and other resources it considers necessary for the fulfilment of its objectives; rather, Article F(3) merely makes a statement of intent in the context of policies and programmes to the effect that the member-States (which form the Union) wish to provide it with adequate resources under whichever particular procedure is necessary for that purpose. If European institutions were to interpret, and act under, Article F(3) in a sense contrary to the content of this Treaty provision as accepted by the German Act of Accession, such action would not be covered by the Act and would therefore not be legally binding within the German member-State. The organs of the German state would have to refuse to supply the personnel to implement any legal instruments based on such a treatment of Article F(3).

* * *

(b.3–6) An interpretation of Article F(3) which would give the Union a power to extend its powers would also contradict the consistently expressed intention of the Contracting Parties to define by Treaty provisions the principle of restricted specific empowerment and to set clear limits to individual rules conferring powers. . . .

* * *

The Federal Government has made it clear, and informed this Court, that its view of the interpretation of Article F(3) of the Union Treaty is shared by the other member-States.

* * *

(c) The member-States have given the European Union objectives in Article B [now 2] of the Union Treaty, and laid down that these may only be achieved as provided in the Treaty. In addition they have defined the tasks and powers of the three European Communities in detail and confined the European institutions and agencies to carrying them out. Any alterations and extensions of those definitions of tasks and powers are subject to their prior formal agreement, which restricts the possibilities for further legal developments on the basis of the existing Treaty. . . . But any such alterations or extensions of the Treaty presuppose that the member-States give their consent in accordance with their rules of constitutional law. . . .

[The Court dwelled at length on the Maastricht Treaty's provisions on EMU, emphasizing its incorporation of specific mandatory "convergence criteria" and the fact that "the time for the commencement of the third stage of economic and monetary union must also be understood as a target rather than as a legally enforceable date." According to the Court, retention of unanimous voting preserves the Bundestag's right to make its own examination on the transition to the third stage of EMU and on the desirability (or not) of relaxing its stability criteria: ". . . Germany is not subjecting itself to an 'automatic' progress to a monetary union, which is unsupervisable and the momentum of which puts it beyond control. . . ."]

This does not raise a question of constitutional law, however, but of politics. The decision to agree on a monetary union and put it into operation without a simultaneous or immediately subsequent political union is a political one, for which the institutions with competence on the matter must take political responsibility. If it emerges that the desired monetary union cannot in reality be achieved without a (not yet desired) political union, a fresh political decision will be required as to how to proceed further. . . .

3.

The granting of functions and powers to the European institutions provided for in the Union Treaty still leaves sufficient functions and powers of substantial political weight to the German Bundestag. The Treaty also imposes a sufficiently reliable limit on the dynamic towards further integration which it engenders, and that preserves a balance between the structure of governmental decision-making in the European federation of states and the matters reserved to the decision of the German Bundestag together with its rights of co-decision.

(a) The possibilities for influence by the Bundestag, and therefore by the electorate, on the exercise of sovereign powers by European institutions have no doubt been taken away almost completely in so far as the European Central Bank has been made independent as regards the European Community and the member-States (Article 108 [now 109] of the EC Treaty).... Placing most of the tasks of monetary policy on an autonomous basis in the hands of an independent central bank releases the exercise of sovereign powers of the state from direct national or supra-national control in order to withdraw monetary matters from the reach of interest groups and holders of political office concerned about re-election.

This restriction of the democratic legitimation which proceeds from the voters in the member-States affects the principle of democracy, but, as a modification of that principle provided for in Article 88, second sentence, of the Constitution,[8] is compatible with Article 79(3). ... This modification of the democratic principle for the purpose of protecting the confidence placed in the redemption value of a currency is acceptable because it takes account of the special characteristic ... that an independent central bank is a better guarantee of the value of the currency, and thus of a generally sound economic basis for the state's budgetary policies and for private planning and transactions in the exercise of rights of economic freedom, than state bodies, which as regards their opportunities and means for action are essentially dependent on the supply and value of the currency, and rely on the short-term consent of political forces. To that extent the placing of monetary policy on an independent footing within the sovereign jurisdiction of an independent European Central Bank (a jurisdiction not transferable to other political areas) satisfies the constitutional requirements under which a modification may be made to the principle of democracy.

(b) In other respects, too, the functions and powers of the European Union and the Communities belonging to it, as already explained, are defined in terms of restricted factual circumstances, so that the wide-ranging statement of objectives in the Preamble to, and Article B [now 2] of, the [TEU] do not sanction the exercise of sovereign powers, but only emphasise the political intention to realise an ever closer union of the peoples of Europe. The [TEU] therefore satisfies the requirement ... that possibilities for action by the European institutions not only should be defined in relation to their objectives, but should also be framed ... so as to set objective limits to their functions and powers.

* * *

(c) The way in which this principle of limited individual empowerment is to be treated is then clarified and further restricted by the subsidiarity principle.... In addition, individual powers, such as those conferred by Articles 126 to 129b, 130 and 130g [now 149 to 154, 157 and 164] of the EC

---

8. Section 88 provides for a federal bank (*Bundesbank*) to issue notes and currency, and specifically authorizes the bank to transfer its tasks and powers to an independent European Central Bank which is committed to a policy of price stability.

Treaty, restrict Community activity to the supplementation of the policies of the member-States, which in principle have precedence.

The subsidiarity principle therefore does not establish any powers in favour of the European Community, but sets limits on the exercise of powers already given elsewhere. . . .

Through this principle of subsidiarity, adherence to which is a matter for the European Court to scrutinise, the national identities of the member-States are to be preserved and their powers to be retained. How far the subsidiarity principle will counteract an erosion of the jurisdictions of the member-States, and therefore an exhaustion of the functions and powers of the Bundestag, depends to an important extent (apart from the case law of the European Court relating to the subsidiarity principle) on the practice of the Council as the Community's real legislative body. It is there that the Federal Government has to assert its influence in favour of a strict treatment of Article 3b(2) [now 5(2)] of the EC Treaty and so fulfil the constitutional duty imposed on it by Article 23(1), first sentence, of the Constitution. The Bundestag for its part has the opportunity . . . to have an effect on the Council's practice's and to exercise an influence on them within the terms of the subsidiarity principle. . . . In addition, it is to be expected that the Bundesrat, too, will pay particular attention to the subsidiarity principle.

[The Court turned here to the principle of proportionality as "the third fundamental principle of the Community constitution."]

4.

In the result, the [TEU] makes provisions for limited powers of action by the agencies and institutions of the three Communities, the exercise of the powers being graduated as regards the means of implementation and the intensity of regulation. The Treaty confers sovereign rights of which the scope is legally ascertainable; that could be done within the sphere of parliamentary responsibilities, and is therefore democratically legitimated. . . .

D.

The Maastricht Treaty . . . sets up a new stage of European unification, which . . . is to enhance further the democratic and efficient functioning of the institutions. For these purposes democracy and efficiency are not to be separated. . . . At the same time the Union . . . will respect the national identities of its member-States, the governmental systems of which are based on democratic principles. To that extent the Union preserves the democratic bases already existing in the member-States and builds on them.

Any further development of the European Union cannot escape from the conceptual framework set out above. The legislature in amending the Constitution took that into account in connection with this Treaty by the insertion of Article 23 into the Constitution, since express mention is made there of the development of the European Union, which is subject to the principles of democracy and the rule of law, social and federal principles, and the subsidiarity principle. What is decisive, therefore, from the viewpoint both of the Treaties and of constitutional law, is that the democratic bases of the Union will be built up in step with the integration process, and a living democracy will also be maintained in the member-States as integration progresses.

Notes and Questions

1.   The *Maastricht* judgment essentially sustained the German law of ratification of the TEU as constitutional, thus empowering the Federal President to sign it. However, the Court's reasoning has led commentators to view it as giving to the TEU not a simple "yes," but rather a "yes but."[9] Would you agree? For an excellent analysis, see M. Herdegen, Maastricht and the German Constitutional Court: Constitutional Restraints for an "Even Closer Union," 31 Comm. Mkt. L. Rev. 235 (1994).

2.   In a portion of the judgment not reproduced, the Court pointed out that, insofar as the Court of Justice does not exercise powers of judicial review on matters falling within the Maastricht Treaty's second and third pillars, such measures, as applied in Germany, would be subject to the Constitutional Court's scrutiny for protection of fundamental rights.

3.   The Court's *Maastricht* ruling is especially interesting for its assumptions about the nature of the European Union. It specifically characterizes the European Union as an association or union of European states (*Staatenverbund*), which retain their separate national identities, rather than as a Federal State (*Bundesstaat*), having its own national identity.

4.   To what extent does the *Maastricht* ruling distance the German Constitutional Court's views on the primacy of Community law over national constitutional law and on the exclusive role of the Court of Justice in determining the validity and effectiveness of Community law from those espoused in ECJ case law. The ruling has spawned a rich literature on democracy and representation in the EU, on the existence of a European *demos*, and on the relationship between the European Court of Justice and the Member States' domestic guardians of fundamental rights. See, for example, M. Kumm, Who is the Final Arbiter of Constitutionality in Europe?: The German Federal Constitutional Court and the European Court of Justice, 36 Comm. Mkt. L. Rev. 351 (1999). That the issues remain sharply contested, at least in Germany, is shown by the following Note.

NOTE ON THE GERMAN "BANANAS" LITIGATION

German opposition to the Community's common organization of the banana market, particularly the regime governing the import of third-country bananas, has provided an extended opportunity to test the force and effect of the Constitutional Court's *Maastricht* ruling. As noted earlier (page 175 *supra*), Germany (supported by Belgium and the Netherlands) challenged the Council Regulation 404/93's phasing out of a longstanding special arrangement ("the Banana Protocol") whereby Germany had been permitted to import an annual quota of third-country bananas free of customs duty. (The Commission and other Member States—France, Greece, Italy, Portugal, Spain and the UK—supported the Council.)

Germany's claims were manifold: (a) that the regulation was adopted in breach of essential procedural requirements (chiefly because the Commission's initial proposal had been modified by action of a single commissioner rather than by the Commission as a whole and without re-consultation of Parliament), (b) that the regulation violated the Treaty rules on the common agricultural policy, (c) that it infringed the objective of undistorted competi-

---

9.   See H. G. Crossland, Three Major Decisions Given by the Bundesverfassungsgericht   (Federal Constitutional Court), 19 Eur. L. Rev. 202, 212 (1994).

tion, (d) that it breached traders' fundamental right of property and freedom of commerce, as well as the Community law principles of non-discrimination and proportionality, and (e) that it violated the Lomé Convention, the Banana Protocol and, above all, the GATT.

The Court rejected all these claims. Germany v. Council (Common organization of the banana market), Case C–280/93, [1994] ECR I–4973. Particularly noteworthy was the Court's finding that the GATT, by its nature, is incapable within the Community law system of legally binding the Community institutions or having direct effect in Member State courts.

The German challenge was not the only piece of litigation over the banana regulation. Other Member States brought annulment actions against the Commission and/or Council concerning various acts taken in connection with the new import regime. Numerous Community importers (German and other) also challenged the banana regulation directly in the Court of Justice, but they were found to lack standing. See, e.g., van Parijs v. Council and Commission, Case C–257/93, [1993] ECR I–3335, 3353.

Certain Latin American states that traditionally exported bananas to the Community brought their own objections to a GATT panel, which upheld them. The EU eventually reached an arrangement with several of the complaining Latin American states in the form of a "framework agreement on bananas" fixing a global tariff quota for 1994 and subsequent years and allocating that quota among the exporting countries. The agreement was incorporated into a schedule to the GATT 1994 agreed upon in the Uruguay Round,[10] and when the Council adopted a decision (94/800) approving the GATT 1994, Germany sued to have the decision annulled insofar as it incorporated the framework agreement. Germany v. Council, Case C–122/95. It would be nearly three years before the Court would render that ruling (see below).

Meanwhile, application of the new banana import regime in Germany sparked numerous challenges to the regime's legality. In one instance, an importer of third-country bananas (T. Port) claimed that it risked bankruptcy on account of the insufficiency of its quota. When the administrative court in Kassel in which T. Port had brought suit over its future years' quota declined to afford relief, T. Port filed a constitutional complaint in the German Constitutional Court. In its ruling, the Constitutional Court declared that Article 19(4) of the German Constitution demands effective judicial protection (including provisional remedies) where a claimant faces the risk of bankruptcy, and on that basis annulled the decision of the Kassel court for failing to conduct a sufficiently careful balance between the claimant's interest and the general interest, especially in light of the possibilities that the banana regulation itself afforded for a possible increase in quotas. Judgment of January 25, 1995, [1995] EuZW 126, [1995] EuR 91 (Const. Ct.). The Constitutional Court did not address the question whether the Kassel court could or should treat the regulation as inapplicable within Germany under the *Maastricht* ruling.

---

10. Germany sought an opinion from the Court to the effect that the framework agreement was invalid, but the Court declined to render one because it considered that 1994 GATT Agreement rendered the question moot.

On remand, the Kassel administrative court referred a number of questions to the Court of Justice (mostly concerning the scope of the banana regulation's hardship provisions), while at the same time ordering limited interim relief. Impatient with this result, T. Port applied directly to the German customs authorities for permission to import third-country bananas without licenses and duty free. Upon refusal, the importer returned to the German Constitutional Court, again invoking Article 19(4) of the German Constitution, but the Court ruled that T. Port had failed to exhaust its administrative remedies. Judgment of April 26, 1995, [1995] EuZW 222 (Const. Ct.).

T. Port then had recourse to the Hamburg Tax Court which, in view of the urgency of the situation, provisionally granted the plaintiff permission to import additional quantities of bananas from Ecuador without a license and at a lower rate of duty. In doing so, the tax court expressed its view that the banana regulation violated the GATT rules and that those rules take precedence over Community law. The German customs authority appealed the tax court's order of interim relief to the German Supreme Tax Court, which reversed it on substantive grounds (namely, that provisional relief in customs matters may only take the form of a suspension of duties). Meanwhile, the customs authority issued an order to T. Port to pay post-clearance duties on the imported bananas, an order that the Hamburg tax court provisionally suspended pending a preliminary ruling from the ECJ in T. Port GmbH & Co. KG v. Hauptzollamt Hamburg–Jonas, Joined Cases C–364 & 365/95. While the German Supreme Tax Court affirmed the suspension order on appeal, it too expressed doubts as to the banana regulation's compatibility with the GATT and opined that the GATT rules take priority over Community law. The Supreme Tax Court specifically contemplated that, even if the Court of Justice were fully to uphold the validity of the banana regulation, the German courts might nevertheless regard it as in excess of Community competence and, under the *Maastricht* ruling, inapplicable in Germany. Judgment of January 9, 1996, [1996] EuZW 126 (Ger. Sup. Tax Ct.).

By this time, the Court of Justice had rendered its ruling on the preliminary questions on hardship that the administrative court in Kassel had referred. T. Port GmbH & Co. KG v. Bundesanstalt für Landwirtschaft und Ernährung, Case C–68/95, [1996] ECR I–6065. According to the Court's ruling in *T. Port,* the banana regulation did not permit the Commission to lay down hardship rules for the benefit of importers of third-country bananas who happen to receive exceptionally (and even ruinously) low quota allocations under the new regime. On the other hand, the Court ruled that the regulation allowed, and under some circumstances even required, the Commission to lay down hardship rules for those traders "where [the] difficulties [those traders experience] are inherent in the transition from the [previous] national arrangements . . . to the [new] common organization of the market and are not caused by a lack of care on the part of the traders concerned."

The Court then turned to the more specific question whether national courts may grant provisional relief to such traders before the Commission has adopted the kind of hardship rules contemplated by the regulation. Citing its decisions in *Zuckerfabrik Süderdithmarschen* (page 382 *infra*), *Atlanta Fruchthandelsgesellschaft* (page 383 *infra*), and *Factortame* (page 274 *supra*), the Court confirmed the circumstances under which national courts may grant interim relief against the national implementation of a Community regulation. However, the Court considered the present case to be fundamentally different precisely because the Commission had had the authority (indeed, the obligation) to enact hardship rules but had not yet done so. In this circumstance, a trader's only recourse would be an Article 232 (ex 175) action against the Commission for failure to act. This did not bring T. Port's efforts to an end. Within weeks, it applied to the Commission for licenses under the regulation's hardship provision; when the Commission denied the application, T. Port unsuccessfully sued in the Court of First Instance to annul the refusal. T. Port GmbH & Co. v. Commission, Case T–251/97, [2000] ECR–II–1775.

In March 1998, the Court of Justice finally issued two rulings partially invalidating the framework agreement on bananas that had been entered into between the EU and the Latin American exporting countries. Both in Germany v. Council (Banana framework agreement), Case C–122/95, [1998] ECR I–973, and in T. Port GmbH & Co. KG v. Hauptzollamt Hamburg–Jonas, Joined Cases C–364 & 365/95, [1998] ECR I–1023, the Court ruled that the agreement's disparate treatment of three categories of banana importers (categories A, B and C) violated a fundamental EU law principle of non-discrimination.

T. Port was not the only operator to contest the banana market regulation and its implementation in German court. A preliminary reference from the administrative court of Frankfurt in an action by the Atlanta group of importers gave the German Constitutional Court an opportunity to determine the conformity of Council Regulation 404/93 with the German Basic Law. The Court's widely anticipated and unanimous decision follows:

ORDER OF THE SECOND SENATE OF THE CONSTITUTIONAL COURT ON THE CONSTITUTIONALITY OF THE APPLICATION OF THE EUROPEAN UNION'S COMMON MARKET FOR BANANAS IN GERMANY

(Banana ruling)
German Constitutional Court, second senate
2 BvL 1/97
June 7, 2000.

[Nineteen companies of the so-called Atlanta group of banana importers were classified as Category A operators and allotted a provisional quota of imports for the third quarter of 1993. Objecting to the limitation on imports, they brought an action in the Frankfurt administrative court for a declaration that Regulation 404/93 infringed Community law. (They subsequently also challenged Regulation 478/95 setting their quota for 1995.) References to the ECJ resulted in a preliminary ruling on the availability of interim relief in national court against Community measures (see page 383 *infra*), as well as a preliminary ruling reaffirming the validity of Regulations 404/93. Atlanta Fruchthandelsgesellschaft mbH v. Bundesamt für Ernährung und Forstwirtschaft, Cases C–465 & 466/93, [1995] ECR I–3761.

The Frankfurt court subsequently turned to the question whether enforcing Regulation 404/93 in Germany would infringe Articles 3(1), 12(1), 14(1) or 23(1), sentence 1, of the Grundgesetz (GG or Basic Law).]

B.

The submission is inadmissible.

I.

Submissions of cases to the Federal Constitutional Court for constitutional review under Article 100(1) GG [Basic Law or Constitution] which refer to rules that are part of secondary European Community law are only admissible if their grounds show in detail that the present evolution of law concerning the protection of fundamental rights in European Community law, especially in European Court of Justice case law, does not generally ensure the protection of fundamental rights required unconditionally in the respective case.

Certainly the submitting Court has [satisfactorily explained why it believes that] the application of the submitted legal rules would be unconstitutional.... However, the court cannot be followed in holding that ... Regulation 404/93 ... may be submitted to the Federal Constitutional Court for constitutional review under Article 100(1)GG.

II.

[The Court recalled its *Solange I*, *Solange II* and *Maastricht* rulings, as well as the substance of Article 23 of the Basic Law.]

c) ... Pursuant to [Article 23], the Federal Republic of Germany shall participate, with a view to establishing a united Europe, in the development of the European Union ... that guarantees a level of protection of fundamental rights essentially comparable to that afforded by the Basic Law. An identical protection in the different areas of fundamental rights afforded by European Community law and by the rulings of the Court of Justice, which are based on Community law, is not called for. The constitutional requirements are satisfied ... if the rulings of the European Court of Justice generally ensure effective protection of fundamental rights as against the sovereign powers of the Communities which is to be regarded as substantially similar to the protection of fundamental rights required unconditionally by the Basic Law, and in so far as they generally safeguard the essential content of fundamental rights.

d) Thus, constitutional complaints and references by courts [to this Court] are ... inadmissible from the outset if their grounds do not state that the European evolution of law, including the rulings of the European Court of Justice, has resulted in a decline below the required standard of fundamental rights.... Therefore the grounds for a reference by a national court or a constitutional complaint claiming an infringement by secondary European Community Law of the fundamental rights guaranteed in the Basic Law must state in detail that the protection of fundamental rights required unconditionally in the respective case is not generally ensured. This requires a comparison of the protection of fundamental rights on the national and on the Community level similar to the one made by the Federal Constitutional Court in [*Solange II*.]

III.

Such a statement is lacking in this case.

1. The grounds of this reference fail from the outset to satisfy the special requirement for admissibility, as they are based on a misunderstanding of the *Maastricht* decision. The submitting court is of the opinion that the Federal Constitutional Court, pursuant to the *Maastricht* decision, contrary to the *Solange II* decision, explicitly exercises its review authority again, albeit in co-operation with the European Court of Justice.

This conclusion cannot be drawn from the *Maastricht* decision. In the passage that the administrative court refers to, the Constitutional Court explicitly quotes the statements of its *Solange II* decision which show that it exercises its jurisdiction to a limited extent. The fact that the Senate in its *Maastricht* decision has neither in this passage nor elsewhere given up its opinion laid down in *Solange II* on the delimitation of the authority for jurisdiction of the European Court of Justice vis-à-vis the Federal Constitutional Court and vice versa is ... evident from the *Maastricht* decision.... [Thus,] the assumption of a contradiction between the *Solange II* and the *Maastricht* decisions lacks a sound basis.

2. In the present case, there was, beyond these requirements, a special cause for detailed statements concerning a negative evolution of the standard of fundamental rights in the jurisdiction of the European Court of Justice, as the European Court of Justice had, in [*T. Port, supra* page 320], which had been decided after this submission was made, required the Commission pursuant to Article 30 of Regulation No. 404/93 to take any transitional measures it judges necessary. Such transitional measures must serve, according to this judgment, to overcome the difficulties which occurred after the coming into force of the common organization of the market but which originated in the state of the national markets before the enactment of the Regulation....

At this point in time at the latest, the referring court should have recognized the insufficiency of its submission and should have remedied it. ... It [was not] possible for the administrative court to infer a general decline of the standard of fundamental rights in the jurisdiction of the European Court of Justice against the background of this European Court of Justice decision.

[The Court pointed out that the ruling of the European Court of Justice required as much protection against hardship as the German court had previously held to be required in its ruling in Cases 2 BvR 2689/94 and 2 BvR 52/95, 1995 EuZW 126 (Jan. 25, 1995). "Thus, both decisions illustrate that the judicial protection of fundamental rights by national courts of justice and Community courts of justice interlock at the European level."]

Notes and Questions

1. The *Bananas* saga had generated extensive academic commentary even before the Court's 2000 *Banana* judgment. See, for example, Everling, Will Europe Slip on Bananas? The *Bananas* Judgment of the Court of Justice and National Courts, 33 Comm. Mkt. L. Rev. 401 (1996); Everling, The Maastricht Judgment of the German Federal Constitutional Court and its Significance for the Development of the European Union, 14 Ybk. of Eur. L. 1 (1994).

2. For commentary on the *Banana* judgment, see U. Elbers & N. Urban, The Order of the German Federal Constitutional Court of 7 June 2000 and *Kompetenz-Kompetenz* in the European Judicial System, 7 Eur. Pub. L. 21 (2001).

D. COMMUNITY LAW IN ITALY

Italian courts also have had difficulty unreservedly accepting the supremacy of Community law, particularly when fundamental individual rights may be in the balance. Both the German and Italian reactions reflect the prominence in those countries' postwar constitutions of a catalogue of individual rights supported by a highly respected constitutional court.

Article 11 of the 1948 Italian Constitution, designed to permit Italy's membership in the United Nations, allows (on condition of reciprocity) such limitations of national sovereignty "as may be necessary ... to ensure peace and justice between Nations." Given its date, the Constitution does not specifically contemplate the legal effects of Italy's membership in the Community.

The initial view of the Italian Constitutional Court, reflected in *Costa v. ENEL*, page 269 *supra*, was that in the event of conflict a later Italian statute takes precedence even over the EC Treaty itself. The strongly negative reaction of the Court of Justice in the *Costa* case, among other factors, prompted a change of views on the Constitutional Court's part, culminating in the landmark ruling in Frontini v. Ministero delle Finanze, Case 183, [1974] Il Foro It. 314, [1974] 2 CMLR 372 (Dec. 27, 1973). Frontini, an importer, challenged an increase in Italian customs duties on dairy products brought about by a 1967 Council regulation. He argued that, absent a specific Italian statute authorizing the measure, the increase in duties violated Article 23 of the Italian Constitution according to which "[n]o personal service or payment may be forced on anyone, save according to law." The issue ultimately reached the Italian Constitutional Court.

Citing Article 11 of the Constitution, the Court confirmed the constitutionality of the 1957 statute by which Italy had ratified the EC Treaty. It then turned to the nature of Community law and the effect of EC Article 249 (ex 189):

> ... The regulations issuing from the organs of the EEC [now EC] [under] Article 249 (ex 189) belong to the Community's own order: its laws and the internal law of the individual Member States can be described as autonomous and distinct legal systems, albeit coordinated in accordance with the division of power laid down and guaranteed by the Treaty. Fundamental requirements of equality and legal certainty demand that the Community norms ... have full compulsory efficacy and direct application in all the Member States, without the necessity of reception and implementation statutes, as acts having the force and value of statute in every country of the Community, to the extent of entering into force everywhere simultaneously and receiving equal and uniform application to all their addressees.

[1974] 2 CMLR at 386–87. The Court concluded that this duality rendered inapplicable to Community legislation the various procedural guarantees under the Italian Constitution, such as publication of statutes and judicial review. Having thus largely accepted the Court of Justice's "new legal order" doctrine, the Constitutional Court remarked, perhaps naively, that since the Treaty confined the institutions "to matter[s] concerning economic relations," and itself contained "precise and exact provisions," Community measures were unlikely ever to violate the Italian Constitution. The Court also voiced doubt that any violation that might occur would fail to be remedied through one of the forms of judicial review available in the Court of Justice. It added, however, the reassurance that if in an "aberrant" case a Community measure should violate "the fundamental principles of our constitutional order or the inalienable rights of man," and still survive Court of Justice review, then the Constitutional Court "would control the continuing compatibility of the Treaty with the above-mentioned fundamental principles." Id. at 389.

Following the Court of Justice ruling in *Simmenthal II, supra* page 272, the Italian Constitutional Court for all practical purposes conceded the primacy of Community law in SpA Granital v. Amministrazione delle Finanze dello Stato, Case 170/84, [1984] Il Foro It. 2062, 29 Giur.Cost. I 1098, no. 170, 21 Comm. Mkt. L. Rev. 756 (June 8, 1984). The substantive issue there was whether importers could claim a tariff adjustment under a 1978 Italian decree when EC regulations already in place before 1978 disallowed any such adjustment.

The Court first stated that Italian courts should wherever possible interpret national law to conform to Community norms but, in the event of "an unavoidable conflict," should give precedence to Community law. Where the Community norm comes later in time, it automatically overrides the national law, rendering it "inoperative." But even where the Community norm comes earlier in time (as in *Granital*), the courts should apply the Community norm in preference to the later national law, without first seeking a Constitutional Court ruling on the law's validity. This represented a change in the Court's case law. (For the prior view, see Società industrie chimiche Italia centrale v. Ministero del Commercio con l'estero, no. 232, 20 Giur.Cost. I 2211 (Oct. 30, 1975)). The Court thus in effect reached the result required by the Court of Justice in *Simmenthal II,* though it based that result on a different ground, namely that Community norms lie outside the system of domestic law and are not subject to the rules governing conflicts between domestic law norms.

The *Granital* decision also clearly endorsed the primacy of Community law:

> Directly applicable EEC [now EC] legal provisions enter and stay in force in Italy ... without their direct effect being impaired by any municipal statute. It is irrelevant, for this purpose, whether a statute was previously or subsequently enacted. A Community regulation is in any event paramount with regard to the matters it covers.[11]

21 Comm. Mkt. L. Rev. at 761–62. The constitutional complaint in *Granital* was accordingly dismissed. At the same time, however, the Court reasserted the reservation stated in *Frontini* that the fundamental rights guaranteed by

---

11. See also Società B.e.c.a. SpA v. Amministrazione delle Finanze, [1985] Il Foro It. 1600 (Constitutional Court, April 23, 1985), where the Italian Court acknowledged that the Court of Justice is the authoritative interpreter of Community law, and that its decisions are entitled to respect within the Italian legal system.

the Italian Constitution may require protection, if need be even against Community legislation. Id. at 763–64.

Germany is not the only Member State whose highest court has called into question the primacy of Community law over individual rights enshrined in the national constitution. See the broad language of the Italian Constitutional Court in SpA Fragd v. Amministrazione delle Finanze, decision no. 232 of April 13, 1989, 34 Giur. Cost. I 1001, 1990 Il Foro It. 1855, 72 Rivista di Diritto Internazionale 103 (1989), discussed in G. Gaja, New Developments in a Continuing Story: The Relationship between EEC Law and Italian Law, 27 Common Mkt. L. Rev. 83 (1990); M. Cartabia, The Italian Constitutional Court and the Relationship between the Italian Legal System and the European Community, 12 Mich. J. Int'l L. 173 (1990); H. Schermers, The Scales in Balance: National Constitutional Court v. Court of Justice, 27 Comm. Mkt. L. Rev. 97 (1990).

E. COMMUNITY LAW IN DENMARK

Community law's reception in Denmark more closely resembles its reception in the Benelux countries than in either France, Germany or Italy. Well before Danish accession to the Community, the 1953 Constitution (art. 20) authorized the government to delegate its powers by statute to international bodies set up to "promot[e] . . . international rules of law and cooperation." A Danish national's constitutional challenge to Denmark's accession to the Community was dismissed due to the plaintiff's lack of standing,[12] and the matter was never again raised.

On no occasion since have the Danish courts questioned the direct applicability, direct effect or supremacy of Community law as understood by the Court of Justice. Moreover, Denmark appears to have an excellent record in implementing Community law and in addressing Community law issues in cases before the courts, while at the same time exercising national parliamentary oversight of the Community institutions.

Nevertheless, Denmark's rejection of the Maastricht agreements in the referendum of June 1992 reflected popular misgivings over the pace and scale of centralization of EC governance in Brussels. It is perhaps not surprising that a state having as exemplary a record of Community law compliance as Denmark's would view the TEU's legal steps toward closer EC integration with particular seriousness and concern.

As a result of the negative vote in the 1992 Danish referendum on the Maastricht Treaty, certain adjustments in the Treaty were negotiated in Denmark's favor and agreed to by the heads of state or government at the Edinburgh Summit of December 1992. Notable among these were: (a) recognition of Denmark's decision to opt out of the third stage of Economic and Monetary Union (an option Denmark had originally reserved in the form of a TEU Protocol), without prejudice to Denmark's continued participation in the European Monetary System exchange-rate mechanism, and (b) recognition of

---

12. Tegen v. Prime Minister, [1973] CMLR 1 (Eastern Court of Appeal, Dec. 4, 1972). Tegen argued that the Community's "economic" ends were unrelated to those for which Article 20 of the Constitution allows the delegation of power to international bodies. He also claimed that the Danish government failed adequately to examine "the emotional consequences of Danish membership [in] the Common Market [for] Danish citizens."

Denmark's unwillingness to join the Western European Union or to participate in EU actions having defense implications. On the other hand, Denmark reserved the right at any time to decide not to avail itself of these privileges, on condition that it apply in full all relevant measures then in force. The European Council also confirmed, at Denmark's request, that EU citizenship does not replace national citizenship, and that whether an individual possesses a Member State's nationality would continue to be determined solely by the domestic law of that State.

The European Council declared these agreements to be compatible with the TEU and to apply exclusively to Denmark (and not to any other Member State, present or future). The second Danish referendum, in which 57% of the electorate approved ratification, followed on May 18, 1993.

With a new set of EU treaty revisions on the horizon, Denmark once again presented a political and legal challenge. Twelve Danish citizens brought suit challenging the prime minister's signing of the Maastricht Treaty on account of the Treaty's having retained EC Article 308 (ex 235) on implied powers. According to the complaint, the provision violated Article 20 of the Danish Constitution which permits the parliament to delegate sovereignty to international organizations only "to an extent which is more closely defined." In August 1996, the Danish Supreme Court (the *Hjesteret*) overturned a lower court ruling that had declared the suit inadmissible, and remanded the case for trial.

By 1997, the case, Carlsen et. al. v. Rasmussen, reached the *Hjesteret,* yielding the "Danish *Maastricht* Judgment."

CARLSEN ET AL. v. RASMUSSEN

(Danish Maastricht judgment)
Danish Supreme Court
Case I 361/1997 (1988), UfR 1998, p. 800, para. 9.6, [1999] 3 CMLR 854 (1999)
April 6, 1998.

[7] ... What the Supreme court is considering in this case is whether the implementation in Denmark of the [EC Treaty] as framed in [the TEU] was lawfully made in pursuance of section 20 of the Danish Constitution or, alternatively, such implementation required an amendment of the Constitution....

[8] Primarily, the appellants have pleaded that section 20(1) of the Danish Constitution grants authority for the transfer of sovereignty only "to an extent specified by statute", and that this condition has not been met. In this connection they have referred, in particular, to the powers vested in the Council under Article 235 [now 308] of the EC Treaty, and to the lawmaking activities of the European Court of Justice. Secondly, the appellants have pleaded that the delegation of sovereignty is on such a scale and of such a nature that it is inconsistent with the Constitution's premise of a democratic form of government.

* * *

[10] Section 20 of the Danish Constitution is framed as follows:

(1) Powers vested in the authorities of the realm under this Constitutional Act may, to an extent specified by statute, be delegated to international

authorities set up by mutual agreement with other states for the promotion of international rules of law and co-operation. (2) For the enactment of a bill dealing with the above, a majority of five-sixths of the
members of the Parliament [*Folketing*] shall be required. If this majority
is not obtained, whereas the majority required for the passing of ordinary
bills is obtained, and if the Government maintains it, the bill shall be
submitted to the electorate for approval or rejection in accordance with
the rules for referenda laid down in section 42.

[11] Section 20 was included in the 1953 Constitutional Act to enable Denmark
to participate without amending the Constitution ... in international cooperation, [entrusting] the exercise of legislative, administrative or judicial
authority ... to an international organisation with direct effect in [Den-
mark]. ... However, it was emphasised in the provision that the delegation of powers can occur only "to an extent specified by statute"....

* * *

[14] The term "to an extent specified by statute" must be interpreted to the
effect that a positive delimitation must be made of the powers delegated,
partly as regards the fields of responsibility and partly as regards the
nature of the powers. The delimitation must enable an assessment to be
made of the extent of the delegation of sovereignty. The fields of responsibility may be described in broad categories and there is no requirement for
the extent of the delegation of sovereignty to be stated so precisely that
there is no room left for discretion or interpretation. The powers delegated
may be indicated by means of reference to a treaty.

[15] The demand for specification in section 20(1) precludes [leaving it] to the
international organisation to make its own specification of its powers.

[16] [On the other hand,] the term "to an extent specified by statute" cannot
be interpreted to the effect that powers which are vested in the authorities
of [Denmark] can be entrusted to an international organisation only to a
limited—i.e. minor—extent.

* * *

[18] The EC Treaty is based on the principle of conferred powers. The institutions of the Community may act only within such limits ... as appear
from the provisions of the Treaty, and within these limits the institutions
may only exercise such powers as have been conferred upon them by or
pursuant to the Treaty.

[19] The principle of conferred powers thus implies a restriction on the powers
of the institutions which is in keeping with the demand for specification in
section 20 of the Constitution. The Supreme Court finds that the specific
rules of authority in the EC Treaty meet this demand.

[20] [T]he appellants specifically claimed that the general provision of authority in Article 235 [now 308] EC enables the incorporation of new areas of
responsibility under the powers of the EC to an extent which implies that
the demand for specification in section 20 of the Danish Constitution has
not been observed. ...

* * *

24　It appears from the wording of Article 235 that the fact that action by the Community is considered necessary in order to attain one of the objectives of the Community does not in itself constitute [a] sufficient [basis] for applying the provision. It is a further condition that the intended action is "in the course of the operation of the common market." ...

25　The stated interpretation of Article 235 must be taken as the basis, even though prior to the amendment of the Treaty the provision may have been applied on the basis of a wider interpretation.

26　A legislative act, which does not go any further than to confer powers to issue legislative acts or decide upon other measures in accordance with the interpretation of Article 235 stated above, does not constitute a violation of the demand for specification in section 20 of the Constitution.

27　[The adoption of any measure] pursuant to Article 235 must be unanimous. Therefore the Government may prevent the provision from being applied to any adoption which is beyond the stated scope of Denmark's delegation of powers to the EC.... [Given the purpose of Article 235], it is unavoidable that the precise delimitation of the scope of application of the provision may give rise to doubts. [This means] that the Act of Accession grants the Government a not insignificant margin [of judgment].

[Here the court noted that, in view of Article 220 (ex 164), any use of then Article 235 would be subject to judicial review by the European Court of Justice through judgments on the interpretation and validity of Community law.]

30　The fact that the detailed determination of the powers vested in the institutions of the Community may give rise to doubts, and that the jurisdiction to give rulings [on such questions] is transferred to the European Court of Justice, cannot in itself be regarded as incompatible with the requirement of specification in section 20 of the Constitution.

* * *

32　The appellants have pleaded that the jurisdiction of the European Court of Justice under the Treaty [in light of the principle of supremacy of EC law] implies that Danish courts of law are prevented from enforcing the limits for the surrender of sovereignty [made] by the Act of Accession....

33　By adopting the Act of Accession, it has been recognised that the power to test the validity and legality of EC acts lies with the European Court of Justice. This implies that Danish courts of law cannot hold that an EC act is inapplicable in Denmark, without the question of its compatibility with the Treaty having been tried by the European Court of Justice.... However, the Supreme Court finds that the demand for specification in section 20(1) of the Constitution ... [implies] that the [Danish] courts of law cannot be deprived of their right to try questions as to whether an EC [legal] act exceeds the limits for the surrender of sovereignty made by the Act of Accession. Therefore, Danish courts must rule that an EC act is inapplicable in Denmark if the extraordinary situation should arise that with the required certainty it can be established that an EC act [whose validity] has been upheld by the European Court of Justice is based on an application of the Treaty which lies beyond the surrender of sovereignty [made by] the Act of Accession. ...

34　[Against this background], the Supreme Court finds that neither the additional powers that have been delegated to the Council in pursuance of Article 235, nor the law-making activities of the Court of Justice, can be regarded as incompatible with the demand for specification in section 20(1) of the Constitution.

35　... It must be ... assumed in the Constitution that no transfer of powers can take place to such an extent that Denmark can no longer be considered an independent state. ... The Supreme Court finds it beyond any doubt that by the Act of Accession no sovereignty has been transferred to the Community to such an extent [as to violate this assumption].

Notes and Questions

1. On the decision, see K. Heogh, The Danish Maastricht Judgment, 24 Eur. L. Rev. 80 (1999).

2. Denmark gave concrete expression to its reservations over the use of Article 308 (ex 235) at the time the Council adopted "blocking legislation" in response to Congress' enactment of the Helms–Burton legislation asserting extraterritorial jurisdiction over parties owning property confiscated by the Castro regime in Cuba. While fully supportive of the legislation, Denmark refused to endorse it if it were based on Article 235. In the end, the Council cited as an additional basis the 1968 Brussels Convention on the enforcement of judgments in civil and commercial matters (see Chapter 38 *infra*).

3. It has been suggested that the Danish *Maastricht* ruling "may be evidence of a horizontal dynamic whereby the highest courts in member states will be influenced by each other in the warnings issued to the European Court and the reasoning adopted in doing so [and that] such concerted action will increase the pressure on the European Court to act within its competence." S. Weatherill and P. Beaumont, EU Law 451 (3d ed. 1999). Do you agree?

4. Danish ratification of the Amsterdam Treaty required a further referendum due to the fact that the Treaty would again transfer sovereignty, notably in the areas of non-discrimination (EC Art. 13 (ex 6a)), consumer protection (EC Art. 153 (ex 129(a)), and sanctions for human rights violations (EC Art. 309 (ex 236)). On May 28, 1998, a majority of the Danish population voted in favor of ratification of the Amsterdam Treaty; this result was certainly facilitated by the inclusion of a number of opt-outs and special protocols favored by Denmark. Denmark also specifically insisted on the inclusion of a new third sentence of EC Article 17(1) (ex 8(1)) to the effect that EU citizenship "complements" rather than "replaces" national citizenship. See generally, P. Biering, The Application of EU Law in Denmark: 1986 to 2000, 37 Comm. Mkt. L. Rev. 925 (2000). (Biering reports that the Denmark's practice of "opting-out" is now being called into question even in Denmark as creating the risk of marginalizing the country.)

5. A Danish referendum on participating in the third stage of EMU was held on September 28, 2000. Participation was defeated 53.2% to 46.8%.

F.　COMMUNITY LAW IN IRELAND

Article 29(4)(3) of the 1937 Irish Constitution, added in 1972, provides a basis for Irish membership in the Community:

The State may become a member of the [ECSC, EEC and Euratom]. No provision of this Constitution invalidates laws enacted, acts done or measures adopted by the State necessitated by the obligations of membership of the Communities or prevents laws enacted, acts done or measures adopted by the Communities, or institutions thereof, from having the force of law in the State.

The 1972 European Communities Act (no. 27, Dec. 6, 1972) followed. In December 1986, the Irish Parliament amended the 1972 Act to bring certain provisions of the Single European Act into Irish law. European Communities (Amendment) Act of 1986, no. 37, Dec. 23, 1986. Before Ireland could ratify the Single Act, one Crotty brought a suit challenging the constitutionality of the 1986 statute. The Irish Supreme Court ruled that Article 29(4)(3) of the Constitution was broad enough to authorize Irish ratification of the Single Act's provisions on qualified majority voting, on the new Court of First Instance and on the introduction of new Community competences. However, it found that Title III (art. 30) of the Single Act, on European Political Cooperation (EPC), was not covered by Article 29(4)(3) since it altered "the essential scope and objectives of the Communities," chiefly by envisioning "a form of European political union between the Member States ... as an addition to the existing economic union between them." [1987] 2 CMLR at 729–30. The Irish Supreme Court accordingly ruled that the government needed the fresh assent of the Irish people in order to curtail Ireland's freedom of action in foreign policy, and the SEA's entry into force was in fact postponed from January 1, 1987 to July 1, 1987 to permit a referendum and a constitutional amendment to that effect. Crotty v. An Taoiseach, [1987] ILRM 400, [1987] 2 CMLR 666 (April 9, 1987). On the other hand, Chief Justice Finlay chose to affirm in *Crotty* that decisions of the Council have "primacy" over domestic law and that decisions of the Court of Justice "take precedence" both over domestic law and over national court rulings on the meaning of the Community Treaties.

Although the *Crotty* opinion contains this reassuring language, Article 6 of the Irish Constitution provides that all governmental powers "derive, under God, from the people [who] ... decide all questions of national policy, according to the requirements of the common good." Moreover, Irish courts have claimed authority to test the constitutionality of Irish legislation against fundamental human rights. Under these circumstances, the reception of Community law in Ireland could not be considered a foregone conclusion.

Consider in this connection the decision of the Irish High Court in Murphy v. Bord Telecom Eireann, [1989] ILRM 53, [1988] 2 CMLR 753 (April 11, 1988). This opinion followed a preliminary ruling from the Court of Justice (Murphy v. Bord Telecom Eireann, Case 157/86, [1988] ECR 673, excerpted at page 1342 *infra*, to the effect that the principle of equal pay under EC Article 141 (ex 119) applies not only to cases in which women are paid less than men for equal work, but also to cases in which they are paid less than men for work of higher value. This ruling led the Irish High Court to remand the case to the Labor Court, which had previously held that in such cases men and women are not engaged in "like work." In the remand, the High Court remarked as follows:

> 1. Article 119 [now 141] of the EEC [now EC] Treaty is part of the domestic law of the State by virtue of ... the European Communities Act 1972. So too is Article 177 [now 234], which enables a judge of a national

court to obtain a ruling on the interpretation of any Article of the Treaty, which ruling once obtained is binding on the national court.

* * *

4. The interpretation of the relevant sections of the [1974 Irish statute implementing the Community's equal employment rules] is exclusively a matter for the Irish courts.

5. The interpretation of those sections, in accordance with the canons of construction normally applied in Irish courts, has in the present case yielded a result which is in conflict with Article 119 of the Treaty as interpreted by the Court of Justice....

6. Where such a conflict exists, national law must yield primacy to Community law....

7. Where such a conflict arises, the national law is, accordingly, inapplicable.

[1988] 2 CMLR at 755. The High Court accordingly instructed the Labor Court to give the 1974 Irish statute implementing the Community's equal employment rules the same meaning the Court of Justice had given to Article 119 and to disregard its own narrower interpretation. More specifically, it instructed the Labor Court to discard the previous literal construction of the 1974 Act dictated by "[Irish] principles of statutory construction." The Court considered itself bound "if possible to adopt a teleological construction ... i.e. one which looks to the effect of the legislation rather than the actual words used by the legislature." Although this "necessarily involves a departure from the ordinary and natural meaning of the words 'equal in value,' ... it is this approach ... which must be adopted." Id. at 756–57. The Irish courts continue to maintain that a teleological approach is appropriate for the interpretation of Community law and national measures implementing Community law. See, e.g., Lawlor v. Minister for Agriculture, [1988] ILRM 400, [1988] 3 CMLR 22 (High Court, Oct. 2, 1987).

A further constitutional question has belatedly arisen in the Irish courts. In July 1993, the High Court ruled that the practice under Ireland's European Communities Act of 1972 of delegating power to ministries to act by regulation to alter Irish statutory law, when "necessary" to bring it into conformity with as yet unimplemented EC directives, was unconstitutional under the principle that national legislative authority is vested exclusively in the Irish Parliament. Pending an appeal of that decision, the Government felt obliged to introduce legislation retroactively validating many such ministerial rules, a solution that itself stirred some controversy, particularly insofar as criminal law measures were concerned. However, the High Court's ruling was reversed on appeal. The Irish Supreme Court held that the 1972 European Communities Act did not violate the constitutional principle of parliamentary supremacy, and that the particular rule at issue in that case—a rule extending the limitations period for administrative searches and seizures in connection with policing the Community's beef hormone ban beyond the period laid down by Irish statute for searches and seizures generally—could reasonably be said to be "necessary" for implementing the EC hormone directive. Meagher v. Minister for Agriculture and Food, [1994] ILRM 1, [1994] 2 CMLR 654 (Nov. 18, 1993).

The language in the *Crotty*, *Murphy* and *Meagher* judgments would suggest that Community law is securely anchored in the Irish legal order. Commentators largely agree. See N. Travers, Community Directives: Effects, Efficiency, Justiciability, 1998 Irish J. Eur. L. 165. But neither of those cases pitted Community law against claims based on fundamental individual rights guaranteed by the Irish Constitution. The following case, however, did.

SOCIETY FOR THE PROTECTION OF UNBORN CHILDREN (IRELAND) LTD. v. GROGAN

Irish Supreme Court
[1989] IR 753, [1990] 1 CMLR 689
Dec. 19, 1989.

[Article 40.3.3 of the Irish Constitution protects the right to life of unborn children and prohibits abortions. The plaintiff organization sought an interlocutory and permanent injunction prohibiting certain student unions and their officers from publishing student handbooks with the names and addresses of abortion clinics in the UK, where abortions were legal. The defendants argued that Community law, notably the principle of free movement of services, protected their right to publish such information. When the Irish High Court asked the Court of Justice for a preliminary ruling on the issue, the plaintiff immediately appealed to the Irish Supreme Court. It claimed that the lower court's failure to award interim relief pending the Court of Justice's ruling amounted to unconstitutionally enjoining enforcement of the right to life.

The Irish Supreme Court agreed that the High Court had effectively denied the plaintiff interim relief. After dealing with certain other threshold questions, the Court turned to the merits. It began by citing its own prior decision that assisting pregnant women in Ireland to travel abroad to obtain abortions violated Article 40.3.3 of the Constitution and could be enjoined.]

Finlay, C.J.:

This application for an interlocutory injunction . . . consists of an application to restrain an activity which has been clearly declared by this Court to be unconstitutional and therefore unlawful and which could assist, and is intended to assist, in the destruction of the right to life of an unborn child, a right acknowledged and protected under the Constitution.

That constitutionally guaranteed right must be fully and effectively protected by the Courts.

If and when a decision of the European Court of Justice rules that some aspect of European Community law affects the activities of the defendants impugned in this case, the consequence of that decision on these constitutionally guaranteed rights and their protection by the Courts will then fall to be considered by these Courts.

Having regard to that duty of the Court, it is clearly quite inappropriate to approach the exercise of the discretion to grant or refuse an interlocutory injunction upon the basis of a supposed *status quo ante* consisting of activities which are constitutionally forbidden acts.

* * *

With regard to the issue of the balance of convenience, I am satisfied that where an injunction is sought to protect a constitutional right, the only matter which could properly be capable of being weighed in a balance against the granting of such protection would be another competing constitutional right.

I am quite satisfied that in the instant case where the right sought to be protected is that of a life, there can be no question of a possible or putative right which might exist in European law as a corollary to a right to travel so as to avail of services, counterbalancing as a matter of convenience the necessity for an interlocutory injunction.

[The Chief Justice also rejected the defendants' claim that, before granting an interlocutory injunction, the court was required to refer to the Court of Justice under Article 234 (ex 177) the question whether granting such a remedy was possible and appropriate under Community law. The separate opinions of the other justices, all concurring in the result, are omitted.]

Notes and Questions

1.   Do you think the Irish Supreme Court properly reconciled protection of fundamental constitutional values with the principle of supremacy of Community law?

2.   In the awaited ruling, the Court of Justice held that medical termination of pregnancy that is lawful where performed is a service within the meaning of Article 50 (ex 60) of the EC Treaty, but that the link between the students' activities in *Grogan* and the availability of UK abortion services was "too tenuous" to render interference with those activities a restriction on freedom of services within the meaning of Article 49 (ex 59). For the Court's opinion, see Society for the Protection of Unborn Children Ireland Ltd. v. Grogan, Case C–159/90, [1991] ECR I–4685, *infra* page 682.

Following receipt of the ECJ's preliminary ruling in *Grogan*, the Irish High Court (per Judge Morris) issued a permanent injunction forbidding the student leaders from distributing the abortion information in question. Society for the Protection of Unborn Children Ireland Limited (SPUC) v. Grogan, [1994] 1 IR 46, [1993] 1 CMLR 197 (Aug. 7, 1992). However, the Court evidently also referred the students' alleged breaches of the prior interlocutory injunction to the Director of Public Prosecutions. See The Irish Times, Aug. 8, 1992, pp. 1, 4.

The European Court of Human Rights meanwhile passed judgment on certain aspects of Ireland's anti-abortion policies. The Irish Supreme Court had upheld a High Court decision granting an injunction against Open Door Counselling Ltd. and the Dublin Well Women Centre Ltd., which forbade them under Article 40.3.3 of the Irish Constitution to provide information or non-directive counseling on the availability of abortion. Complainants to the European Human Rights Commission argued that the restraint violated the right both to impart and receive such information under Article 10 of the Convention on freedom of expression. Eventually, on October 29, 1992, the Human Rights Court in Strasbourg ruled, by a majority of 15 to eight, that the restriction was disproportionate to the aim pursued and thus violated Article 10. By a majority of 17 to six, it awarded compensation. Eur. Court H.R., 1992, Series A, No. 246. See Note, 18 Eur. L. Rev. 253 (1993). (The counselling organizations then asked the Irish Supreme Court to discharge the injunction. The Court declined to do so on the ground that, barring exceptional circumstances, the petition first had to be brought before the lower courts.) The sole dissenter, Justice Denham, a woman, found such exceptional circumstances to be present. Attorney General v. Well Women Centre Ltd., The Irish Times, July 21, 22, 1993.

3. Note Justice Finlay's remark (¶ 3) that, depending on the Court of Justice's ruling on the merits in *Grogan,* the Irish courts may have to rule on "the consequence [on] constitutionally guaranteed rights and their protection." This suggests that the Irish Supreme Court may be reserving the right to give certain Irish constitutional principles priority over the EC Treaty as interpreted by the Court of Justice.

The Supreme Court had another opportunity to address the question in February 1992, when the Irish Attorney General barred a 14–year–old pregnant girl, who claimed to have been raped and impregnated by the father of a friend, from traveling to Britain for an abortion. A lower court affirmed the order, but the Supreme Court set it aside. Justice Finlay justified the decision on the ground that the Constitution allowed abortion in the case of a real and substantial risk to the mother's life that could only be avoided by terminating pregnancy, and that there was reason to believe the girl would kill herself if prevented from having an abortion. Justice Finlay did not decide whether the Attorney General's ban also violated the girl's Community law right to travel to receive services, but he said (in what must be regarded as dictum) that the right to travel is secondary to the fetus' right to life. Attorney General v. X, [1992] 2 CMLR 277 (March 5, 1992). The UK abortion was performed shortly thereafter.

Should the Irish Supreme Court have asked the Court of Justice for a ruling on the scope of the free movement of services before deciding this case, or was a ruling from the Court unnecessary? (See Chapter 9(E) *infra*). If a referral had been made, how would the Court of Justice likely have ruled in the light of its judgment in *Grogan*?

4. The case of Attorney General v. X, discussed in note 3, brought the abortion issue to political center stage in Ireland, just as the Maastricht ratification process was taking place. Anticipating that the abortion question would affect Irish ratification, Ireland obtained at Maastricht a protocol to the TEU to the effect that nothing in that Treaty "shall affect the application in Ireland of Article 40.3.3 of the Constitution." In a June 1992 national referendum, the Irish people voiced substantial support for the TEU. Three separate Irish referenda on the abortion issue were then held in November 1992. A first proposal would have restricted the grounds for abortion in Ireland to circumstances in which it is necessary to save the life, as distinct from the health, of the mother; a second protected the right to travel outside Ireland for abortion purposes; and a third guaranteed the right to supply and receive information on abortion services lawfully available in other states. The results were striking: the first proposal was defeated two to one, while the second and third both passed by that same margin. Article 40.3.3. of the Irish Constitution was then amended accordingly. On the prominence of the abortion issue in Irish debates over the ratification of the TEU, see F. Murphy, Maastricht: Implementation in Ireland, 19 Eur. L. Rev. 94 (1994).

5. The impact of EU law on Ireland's policy-making freedom has also been brought home in the budgetary arena. In January 2001, the Commission rebuked Ireland for its deviation from the broad economic guidelines adopted by the European Council under the EMU system. The Commission, disapproving of Ireland's plans for tax cuts and increased government spending due to fears an "overheating" of the Irish economy (i.e. inflation), for the first time proposed that the Council issue a formal censure of Ireland under EC Treaty Article 99(4) (ex

103(4)), which the Council did, albeit using "recommendation" language. The move was widely viewed as a warning to new entrants applying for membership in the euro-zone.

G.　COMMUNITY LAW IN THE UNITED KINGDOM

The United Kingdom has no written constitution. It was therefore not possible to base Community membership on a constitutional provision or amendment as in the other Member States. Moreover, the UK maintains a dualist approach to international law, which prevents treaties from taking effect in domestic law unless implemented by national legislation. The English Court of Appeal remarked in a decision rendered just after British accession: "Even though the Treaty of Rome has been signed, it has no effect, so far as these Courts are concerned, until it is made an Act of Parliament. Once it is implemented by an Act of Parliament, these Courts must go by the Act of Parliament. Until that day comes, we take no notice of it." McWhirter v. Attorney General, [1972] CMLR 882 (C.A., June 30, 1972). A related problem is the traditional notion of parliamentary sovereignty, according to which the British Parliament enjoys final authority to establish the legal norms effective in the UK. It is against this background that Parliament upon accession enacted the European Communities Act of 1972.

EUROPEAN COMMUNITIES ACT OF 1972

(1972 ch. 68).

2.　General implementation of Treaties.

(1) All such rights, powers, liabilities, obligations and restrictions from time to time created or arising by or under the Treaties, and all such remedies and procedures from time to time provided for by or under the Treaties, as in accordance with the Treaties are without further enactment to be given legal effect or used in the United Kingdom, shall be recognised and available in law, and be enforced, allowed and followed accordingly; and the expression "enforceable Community right" and similar expressions shall be read as referring to one to which this subsection applies.

(2) Subject to schedule 2 to the Act,[13] at any time after its passing Her Majesty may by Order in Council, and any designated Minister or department may by regulations, make provision—

(a) for the purpose of implementing any Community obligation of the United Kingdom, or enabling any such obligation to be implemented, or of enabling any rights enjoyed or to be enjoyed by the United Kingdom under or by virtue of the Treaties to be exercised; or

(b) for the purpose of dealing with matters arising out of or related to any such obligation or rights or the coming into force, or the operation from time to time, of subsection (1) above;

---

13. Schedule 2 excludes the use of subordinate legislation, among other things, to impose or increase taxes, to prescribe rules of law with retroactive application or to create significant new criminal offenses.

and in the exercise of any statutory power or duty, including any power to give directions or to legislate by means of orders, rules, regulations or other subordinate instrument, the person entrusted with the power or duty may have regard to the objects of the Communities and to any such obligation or rights as aforesaid.

* * *

(4) [A]ny enactment passed or to be passed, other than one contained in this Part of this Act, shall be construed and have effect subject to the foregoing provisions of this section, but except as may be provided by any Act passed after this Act.

* * *

3.   Decisions on, and proof of, Treaties and Community instruments, etc.

(1) For the purposes of all legal proceedings any question as to the meaning or effect of any of the Treaties, or as to the validity, meaning or effect of any Community instrument, shall be treated as a question of law (and, if not referred to the European Court, be for determination as such in accordance with the principles laid down by any relevant decision of the European Court).

(2) Judicial notice shall be taken of the Treaties, of the Official Journal of the Communities and of any decision of, or expression of opinion by, the European Court on any such question as aforesaid. . . .

The parliamentary debates leading up to ratification of the Maastricht Treaty in the UK were difficult and protracted. Prime Minister Major faced a rebellion within his own party over ratification, with debate in the House of Commons alone lasting nearly a year before passage of the ratification bill on May 20, 1993. Debates in the House of Lords, featuring Lady Thatcher, resulted in Section 7 of the eventual European Communities (Amendment) Act 1993, which permitted that Act to come into force only after both Houses of Parliament had passed a resolution on the question of adopting the Social Protocol. A tie vote in the Commons on a Labor Party proposal to adopt the Social Policy Protocol led Prime Minister Major to seek a vote of confidence on ratification of the TEU without adherence to the Social Protocol, which he won by a vote of 339 to 301.

In a last-minute challenge to ratification, Lord Rees–Mogg, a Conservative peer and former editor of The Times of London, sought a declaration that the UK could not lawfully ratify the TEU (notably its title on the common foreign and security policy). The High Court rejected all of his arguments and there was no appeal. Regina v. Secretary of State for Foreign Affairs, ex parte Lord Rees–Mogg, [1994] 1 All ER 457, [1993] 3 CMLR 101 (July 30, 1993). The UK government finally ratified the TEU on August 2, 1993.

The European Communities (Amendment) Act 1993 formally adds to Section 1(2) of the European Communities Act 1972 a new paragraph (k) embracing Titles II, III and IV TEU, "together with the other provisions of the Treaty so far as they relate to those Titles, and the Protocols adopted at Maastricht . . . with the exception of the Protocol on Social Policy." The Act specifically provides (sec. 2) that the UK may not participate in the third stage of economic and monetary union without the prior approval of the British Parliament based on reports submitted to it by the British Government. See generally C. Barnard & R. Greaves, The Application of Community Law in the United Kingdom, 1986–1993, 31 Comm. Mkt. L. Rev. 1055 (1994).

Notes and Questions

1.   Does Section 2(1) of the European Communities Act establish the direct effectiveness of Community law in the UK? Does it at least provide a standard for determining whether a particular Community measure is to have direct effect? Does Section 3 help?

2.   Parliamentary sovereignty is said to mean that Parliament has perfect freedom to legislate except that it cannot limit its future legislative freedom. If that is so, how could the European Communities Act possibly establish the supremacy of Community law? Note that Section 2(4) of the Act states that any act "passed or to be passed . . . shall be construed and have effect subject to the foregoing provisions," which include Section 2(1), acknowledging the legal effect of Community law in the UK. The key words are "be construed," which amount to an instruction to UK courts to interpret acts of Parliament to the maximum extent possible as in conformity with existing Community law. While this does not in itself ensure Community law primacy, it should reduce the likelihood of conflict. Notice, on the other hand, the saving clause in Section 2(4) ("except as may be provided by any Act passed after this Act").

Mr. Albert Blackburn thought that any British statute effective to implement the Community Treaties in the UK would necessarily surrender British sovereignty, and on that account he had sued to prevent Britain from acceding to the Communities. The Court of Appeal dismissed the suit as premature. On the question whether the courts would refuse to enforce a British statute that was squarely in conflict with existing Community legislation, Lord Denning, in his opinion, remarked that "we will wait till that day comes." Blackburn v. Attorney General, [1971] 2 All ER 1380, [1971] CMLR 784, 790 (C.A., civ. div., Feb. 27 & May 10, 1971). As shown by the House of Lords' ruling in the *Factortame* case, *infra* page 342, that day has come.

MACARTHYS LTD. v. SMITH

English Court of Appeal (civil division)
[1979] 3 All ER 325, [1979] 3 CMLR 44
May 23–25, July 25, 1979.

[Smith successfully sued Macarthys under UK sex discrimination legislation intended to implement EC Article 141 (ex 119) on the ground that Macarthys paid her only £50 a week, while it had paid £60 a week to the male employee she was hired to replace. Macarthys argued on appeal that Smith's recovery contravened the plain meaning of the British statute which by its terms only covered discrimination between persons employed by the same employer for the same work at the same time. The Court of Appeal referred several questions to the Court of Justice on the proper interpretation of Article 119. The Court of Appeal judges had this to say before making the reference.]

Lord Denning, M.R.:

* * *

[T]he United Kingdom has passed legislation with the intention of giving effect to the principle of equal pay [under EC Article 141 (ex 119)]. It has done it by the Sex Discrimination Act [of] 1975. . . .

* * *

. . . In construing our statute, we are entitled to look to the Treaty as an aid to its construction; but not only as an aid but as an overriding force. If on close investigation it should appear that our legislation is deficient or is inconsistent with Community law by some oversight of our draftsmen then it is our bounden duty to give priority to Community law. Such is the result of § 2(1) and (4) of the European Communities Act [of] 1972.

I pause here, however, to make one observation on a constitutional point. Thus far I have assumed that our Parliament, whenever it passes legislation, intends to fulfil its obligations under the Treaty. If the time should come when our Parliament deliberately passes an Act with the intention of repudiating the Treaty or any provision in it or intentionally of acting inconsistently with it and says so in express terms, then I should have thought that it would be the duty of our courts to follow the statute of our Parliament. I do not however envisage any such situation. . . . In the present case I assume that the United Kingdom intended to fulfil its obligations under Art. 119 [now 141]. Has it done so?

[Lord Denning found that Article 119 clearly applied "not only to cases where the woman is employed on like work at the same time with a man in the same employment, but also when she is employed on like work in succession to a man." He conceded that the UK's 1970 equal pay legislation (adopted prior to EC membership) required employment "at the same time." However, he thought that the 1975 amendment, enacted to implement the then Article 119, did not impose that condition and, in light of Article 119, should not be interpreted as imposing it. Lord Denning thus reached "this very desirable result . . . that there is no conflict between Article 119 of the Treaty and [the UK legislation]." He continued.]

Now my colleagues take a different view. They are of [the] opinion that [the UK legislation] should be given its natural and ordinary meaning, and that is, they think, that it is confined to cases where the woman is employed *at the same time* as a man.

* * *

[A]s my colleagues think that Article 119 is not clear on the point, I agree that reference should be made to the European Court at Luxembourg to resolve the uncertainty in that article.

Lawton, L.J.:

In my judgment the grammatical construction of [the UK statute] is consistent only with a comparison between a woman and a man in the same employment at the same time. The words, by the tenses used, look to the present and the future but not to the past. They are inconsistent with a comparison between a woman and a man, no longer in the same employment, who was doing her job before she got it.

* * *

As the meaning of the words ... is clear, ... under our rules for the construction of Acts of Parliament the statutory intention must be found within those words. It is not permissible to read into the statute words which are not there....

* * *

We cannot [however] ignore Article 119 and apply what I consider to be the plain meaning of the Act.

* * *

Being in doubt as to the ambit of Article 119 and being under an obligation ... to apply that article in our courts, ... a decision is necessary as to the construction of Article 119.

... I consider myself under a judicial duty not to guess how [the Court of Justice] would construe it but to find out how it does.

[The opinion of Cumming–Bruce L.J., agreeing substantially with that of Lawton L.J., is omitted.]

Notes and Questions

1. Does *Macarthys* base the primacy of Community law on the European Communities Act of 1972 or treat it as an imperative of Community law itself? Does it matter?

2. Although Lord Denning did not succeed in persuading his colleagues in *Macarthys,* his approach to the interpretation of UK legislation is widely accepted. Lord Templeman described British courts as "willing and anxious" to find UK legislation to be consistent with Community law. Duke v. GEC Reliance Ltd., [1988] A.C. 618, 638 [1988] 2 WLR 359, [1988] 1 All ER 626 (H.L., Feb. 11, 1988). Particularly when a statute is passed to implement a Community directive, Parliament will be presumed to have meant to satisfy its obligations, and the statute will if possible be interpreted accordingly. See, e.g., Customs and Excise Commissioners v. Bell Concord Educational Trust Ltd., [1989] 2 All ER 217, [1989] 1 CMLR 845 (C.A., Feb. 3, 1989).

Lord Denning has also endorsed a teleological interpretation of Community law. That approach, he has written, "is not really so alarming as it sounds." Under it, judges go "not ... by the literal meaning of the words or by the grammatical structure of the sentence, [but] by the design or purpose which lies behind it. When they come upon a situation which is to their minds within the spirit—but not the letter—of the legislation, ... they interpret the legislation so as to produce the desired effect. This means that they fill in gaps, quite unashamedly...." James Buchanan & Co., Ltd. v. Babco Forwarding & Shipping (U.K.) Ltd., [1977] Q.B. 208, 213, [1977] 2 CMLR 455, 458–59 (Dec. 2, 1976). On the other hand, the House of Lords, on appeal from Lord Denning's opinion, suggested that British courts are not bound to follow a teleological approach to interpreting national statutes that implement Community law. Buchanan v. Babco, [1978] A.C. 141, [1978] 1 CMLR 156 (H.L., Nov. 9, 1977). Similarly, in the *Duke* case, supra, Lord Templeman emphasized that the proper interpretation of a British statute, even one passed to implement Community law, "is a matter of judgment to be determined by British courts and to be derived from the language of the legislation in the light of the circumstances prevailing at the date of enactment." [1988] A.C. at 638. However, more recent comments from the House of Lords (see note 4 below) suggest that Lord Denning's attitude may now be winning favor.

3. In the *Duke* case cited in the preceding note, Duke brought suit under the 1975 UK Sex Discrimination Act, claiming that she was forced to retire at age 60, while her male colleagues were allowed to work until 65. The lower British courts found for her employer on the basis of the Act's exception for cases of "retirement." Duke appealed to the House of Lords, arguing that the 1975 Act should be construed so as to implement Council Directive 76/207 (the Equal Treatment Directive), which would have covered her case.

The Lords ruled unanimously that the 1975 Act was not enacted to implement the 1976 directive. (The Act clearly preceded the directive.) The Lords further ruled that since directives lack horizontal direct effect, Duke could not rely directly on the equal treatment directive as the basis of her claim.

Is *Duke* consistent with the European Communities Act of 1972 and with *Macarthys?* (Note that article 9 of the Equal Treatment Directive required the Member States to implement the directive within 30 months of its adoption, but only in 1986 did the Court of Justice actually rule that the directive had direct effect.)

4. The House of Lords had a further opportunity to attempt reconciling UK legislation with an EC directive in Webb v. EMO Air Cargo (UK) Ltd., [1992] 4 All ER 929, [1993] 1 WLR 49 (Nov. 26, 1992). In *Webb,* the House of Lords acknowledged that UK courts have the responsibility to "construe domestic legislation in any field covered by a Community directive so as to accord with the interpretation of the directive as laid down by the European Court, if that can be done without distorting the meaning of domestic legislation," and that this is so whether the domestic legislation predates or postdates the directive. Lord Keith of Kinkel, delivering the judgment on behalf of the court, underscored that national courts only need to construe domestic legislation in conformity with a directive insofar as the law is open to an interpretation consistent with it. The Lords subsequently asked the Court of Justice whether, on the facts of the case, there was discrimination in violation of the directive. The Court of Justice held that there plainly was. Webb v. EMO Air Cargo (UK) Ltd., Case C–32/93, [1994] ECR I–3567.

In Webb v. EMO Air Cargo (UK) Ltd. *(Webb 2),* [1995] 4 All ER 577, [1995] 1 WLR 1454 (Oct. 19, 1995), the House of Lords concluded that the UK legislation at issue (section 1(1)(a) of the Sex Discrimination Act 1975) could be interpreted in conformity with the ECJ's ruling on the directive in *Webb.* Specifically, the Lords held that there is discrimination in violation of the 1975 Act where a woman is dismissed from work due to her temporary unavailability as a result of pregnancy—a holding contrary to the House of Lords' earlier interpretation of the Act.

5. The question of the primacy of Community law over a subsequent act of Parliament finally arose sharply in connection with the Court of Justice's preliminary ruling in the *Factortame* case, discussed at page 274 *supra*. The House of Lords had implicitly accepted the primacy doctrine by asking the Court of Justice whether a UK court should temporarily enjoin enforcement of an act of Parliament as in probable violation of earlier Community law. The issue would have been irrelevant if a subsequent British statute necessarily prevailed over Community law.

Still more telling was the House of Lords' reaction upon receiving the Court's ruling in *Factortame*.

REGINA v. SECRETARY OF STATE FOR TRANSPORT EX PARTE FACTORTAME LTD.

House of Lords
[1991] 1 All ER 70, [1990] 3 CMLR 375
Oct. 11, 1990.

LORD BRIDGE OF HARWICH:

Some public comments on the [Court of Justice's] decision [in *Factortame*] ... have suggested that this was a novel and dangerous invasion by a Community institution of the sovereignty of the United Kingdom Parliament. But such comments are based on a misconception. If the supremacy ... of Community law over the national law of Member States was not always inherent in the EEC [now EC] Treaty it was certainly well established in the jurisprudence of the European Court of Justice long before the United Kingdom joined the Community. ... Under the terms of the [European Communities] Act of 1972 it has always been clear that it was the duty of a United Kingdom court, when delivering final judgment, to override any rule of national law found to be in conflict with any directly enforceable rule of Community law. ... Thus there is nothing in any way novel in according supremacy to rules of Community law in those areas to which they apply and to insist that, in the protection of rights under Community law, national courts must not be inhibited by rules of national law from granting interim relief in appropriate cases is no more than a logical recognition of that supremacy.

[Lord Bridge then concluded that under English principles an interim injunction should be ordered. All of the Lords reached the same conclusion, though the opinion of Lord Goff ([1990] 3 CMLR at 382) provides the fullest analysis.]

Notes and Questions

1. Immediately after making the excerpted remarks, Lord Bridge added that "the judgment of the ... Court of Justice does not fetter our discretion to determine whether an appropriate case for the grant of interim relief has been made out." [1991] 1 All ER at 108, [1990] 3 CMLR at 380. Do you agree?

A subsequent judgment by the House of Lords suggests that such discretion will be far from complete. According to Lord Goff, "the question of the terms upon which an injunction may be granted to enforce, or to restrain the enforcement of, a law which is under challenge on Community law grounds, cannot ... necessarily be regarded as a matter of procedure for the national law where the imposition of the term under consideration is directed towards preserving rights which may arise under Community law." Kirklees Borough Council v. Wickes Building Supplies Ltd., [1992] 3 All ER 717, [1992] WLR 170, [1992] 2 CMLR 765 (H.L., June 25, 1992). For further discussion of the circumstances under which national courts provide injunctive relief in aid of Community law, see Chapter 10A *infra*.

2. As we have seen (page 694 *supra*), the Court of Justice subsequently ruled that the 1988 amendments to the UK Merchant Shipping Act at issue in *Factortame* violated EC Treaty Article 43 (ex 52) prohibiting national discrimina-

tion in the freedom of establishment. This was the first time the Court of Justice had found an Act of the British Parliament to be contrary to Community law. Does it necessarily follow from Lord Bridge's opinion excerpted above that the UK courts will refuse to enforce the 1988 amendments?

NOTE ON THE UK HUMAN RIGHTS ACT

Acceptance of Community law's primacy in the UK has had wider implications. In light of the ECJ's rulings on the role of the European Human Rights Convention in Community jurisprudence, the UK revisited the place of the Convention itself, and international human rights more generally, in the UK's unwritten constitution.

On November 9, 1998, in a momentous step, the UK enacted the Human Rights Act, effective October 2, 2000. The Act deepens the protection afforded by the European Human Rights Convention in the UK by rendering sixteen basic substantive rights in the Convention directly enforceable by British courts. These include the rights set out in Articles 2–12 and 14 of the Convention,[14] Articles 1–3 of the Convention's First Protocol, and Articles 1 and 2 of the Sixth Protocol, read in conjunction with Articles 16 to 18 of the Convention. (The Act authorizes the Secretary of State to amend the Act as necessary to give effect to any future protocols accepted by the UK.)

The Act's section 6 makes it unlawful for "public authorities," as defined in section 10,[15] to "act in a way which is incompatible with a Convention right," including a failure to act other than a failure to introduce legislation in Parliament or to make remedial orders. Claimants may either bring a direct action against the relevant authority or invoke the Act in the context of other ongoing proceedings (section 7). An action brought directly under the Human Rights Act must be brought within one year from the date on which the act complained of took place, or within such longer period as the court considers to be equitable under the circumstances. In order to bring suit or otherwise invoke the Convention, a claimant must be deemed capable of qualifying as a "victim of an unlawful act," for purposes of instituting an action in the European Court of Human Rights under Article 34 of the Convention, as amended by protocol no. 11.

Section 3 of the Act provides that primary and subordinate legislation must be read and given effect, if at all possible, in a way that is compatible with the Convention. In ensuring this, the Act requires UK courts and tribunals to take into account any prior judgment, declaration or advisory opinion of the European Court of Human Rights. The Act provides that if a court is satisfied that a provision of primary legislation is incompatible with a Convention right, it still must give effect to that legislation; a court must do the same with subordinate legislation even if, despite all attempts to construe it to the contrary, the court finds the legislation to be in breach of Convention rights (notwithstanding the fact that it is *intra vires* its enabling legislation,

14. Article 1 of the Convention was excluded as hortatory in nature. Article 13, guaranteeing an effective judicial remedy for human rights violations, was deemed superfluous in view of the enactment of the Human Rights Act itself.

15. The term expressly includes courts and tribunals and "any person certain of whose functions are functions of a public nature," but not including the private acts of public authorities.

the latter being construed as fully as possible as consistent with the Convention). However, in these situations, the higher UK courts—and they alone—may make a "declaration of incompatibility." Such a declaration has no effect on the enforceability of the provision, but it sets in motion a "fast track" mechanism for parliamentary amendment of the offending legislation. Section 10 permits the amendment of primary legislation by subordinate legislation where there are "compelling reasons" for not seeking the full consent of Parliament.

Where a public authority has breached a Convention right, the court may make any order or grant any relief or remedy within its powers that it considers just and appropriate. The Act distinctly favors equitable remedies over damages. An award of damages is prohibited unless the court is satisfied that such an award is necessary to afford "just satisfaction" to the victim. The Act calls for the court to award such relief or remedy, within its powers, as it considers "just and appropriate." If it does award damages, a court is to take into account the principles that the European Court of Human Rights applies in awarding compensation under Article 41 of the Convention, subject to special rules for judicial acts taken in good faith.

For more on the UK act, see Oliver, The Human Rights Act and Public Law/Private Law Divides, 2000 Eur. Human Rts. L. Rev. 343 (2000); Greer, A Guide to the Human Rights Act 1998, 24 Eur. L. Rev. 3 (1999); Supperstone & Coppel, Judicial Review after the Human Rights Act, 1999 Eur. Human Rts. L. Rev. 301 (1999); Demetriou, Using Human Rights Through European Community Law, 1999 Eur. Human Rts. L. Rev. 484 (1999).

H.   COMMUNITY LAW IN GREECE, SPAIN AND PORTUGAL

By the time of Greek, Spanish and Portuguese accession, the Court of Justice's supranationalist view of Community law was well known. This view, as we have just seen, had also largely been accepted by the Member State judiciaries. Direct applicability, direct effect and supremacy figured prominently in the *acquis communautaire,* the French term commonly used to denote the fundamental legal understandings or "givens" that new Member States were expected to respect upon assuming Community membership.

Although only the Greek and Portuguese Constitutions were expressly modified to accommodate Community membership,[16] the courts of all three Member States appear to accept the Court of Justice's basic supranationalist tenets. On the other hand, the high authority of the Constitution in these nations, their commitment to constitutional review in support of fundamental

---

16. The Constitution of Greece (1975), art. 28 (international treaties form "an integral part of Greek domestic law" and "prevail over any contrary provision of the law;" Parliament may implement treaties transferring constitutional powers to international organizations).

The Constitution of Portugal (1976), art. 8 (as amended 1982) (international conventions "shall apply domestically;" "standards" of certain international organizations to which Por-

tugal belongs are directly enforceable in Portugal if the organizations' charters so provide).

The Constitution of Spain (1978), arts. 93 (constitutional powers may be transferred by treaty to international organizations and Government must comply with such a treaty and measures adopted under it), 96(1) (treaties once published form part of the internal legal order).

rights and, in the case of Greece, express language of reservation in the Constitution, all suggest that the primacy question may not be so easily settled. In particular, the close patterning of Portuguese and Spanish institutions after those of Germany and Italy creates some likelihood that their courts will question the unreserved primacy of Community law in the event of conflict with fundamental rights and freedoms guaranteed by the national Constitution.

1. GREECE

Full acceptance of the ECJ's views on the relation between Community and national law was not in all respects immediate. While the Greek courts early on embraced the principle of direct effect, some courts in the early 1980s were reluctant to accept the direct effect of unimplemented directives. The issue arose in connection with a 1983 statute (Law 1386/1983 on the Organization of Economic Reconstruction of Enterprises) which authorized the government to increase the capital and regulate the debts of companies that were highly indebted to public banks, in evident violation of Directive 77/91 on coordination of capital requirements for companies. After a number of preliminary references to the Court of Justice,[17] the Greek courts finally gave unconditional effect to the directive. See K. Ioannou & D. Anagnostopoulou, The Application of Community Law in Greece, 19 Eur. L. Rev. 412, 420 (1994).

The Greek Supreme Court (the *Areios Pagos*) affirmed the supremacy principle in Case 1008/1993, 35 Helliniki Dikaiosyni 355 (1994), ruling that, notwithstanding a Presidential Decree of 1927 barring the acquisition of property by non-Greeks in border areas, an Italian national was entitled to acquire such property on the same terms as a Greek national. See Bull. Leg. Dev., Aug. 15, 1994, p. 190.

Still, the Community law's supremacy over the Constitution continues to occasion doubts. Article 28 of Greece's 1975 Constitution provides that international treaties form "an integral part of Greek domestic law" and "prevail over any contrary provision of the law," and specifically authorizes Parliament to implement treaties that transfer constitutional powers to international organizations. On the other hand, Article 28(3) creates an exception for laws that "infringe upon human rights and the foundations of democratic government." This has produced ambiguous and sometimes inconsistent results in the courts.

A lower Greek court—the Athens Justice of the Peace—recognized the supremacy of EC Treaty Article 39 (ex 48) even as against a provision of the Greek Constitution laying down a requirement of Greek nationality for employment in the public service. Case 66/1990.[18] The Athens Court of First Instance reached the same conclusion by invoking the jurisprudence of the European Court of Justice. Case 2228/1992. Dictum from the Athens Court of

---

17. See Karellas v. Minister of Industry, Cases C–19 & 20/90, [1991] ECR I–2691; Association of Members of the Evangelic Church v. Greece, Case C–381/89, [1992] ECR I–2111; Kerafina Keramische und Finanz Holding Actiengesellschaft v. Greece, Cases C–134–35/91, [1992] ECR I–5699.

18. See also Cases 2152/1986 and 3312/1989 of the Greek Conseil d'Etat; Cases 657 & 658/1992, 1360/1992, and 79/1993 of the Greek Supreme Court (*Areios Pagos*); Cases 2343/1987 and 1443/1993 of the Athens Administrative Court of Appeals.

Appeals in Case 9162/1992, "disapplying" certain provisions of Law 1386/1983 on the Organization of Economic Reconstruction of Enterprises' as contrary to EC Directive 77/91, supports the supremacy of Community law over the Greek Constitution.

However, recent decisions of the Greek Council of State tell a somewhat different story. In Decision 3502/1994, a panel of the Council of State described national legislation which prohibited a Greek citizen from leaving the country on account of being a debtor of the Greek State as "in conflict with the superior-to-the-Constitution Community legal order," and more particularly the free movement of persons. Nevertheless, a majority of the plenary session of the Council of State, to which the panel referred the case due to its importance, reversed, finding no inconsistency between the Greek law and Community law. Decision 1545/1995.

The Council of State's views became clearer in the case of Katsarou v. DI.KATSA, decision 3458/1998 (Sept. 25, 1998). Article 16 of the Greek Constitution reserves the provision of university education exclusively to recognized national institutions that are established, financed and regulated by the Greek State, and the establishment of private universities is expressly prohibited. Katsarou obtained a postgraduate degree from the University of Lille in France, based in part on a two-year course of study at a private Greek institution lacking university status. When she sought recognition of that degree as equivalent to a Greek degree for purposes of admission to an advanced degree program in Greece, the Greek authorities refused. She was only allowed to enter directly into the third year of a Greek law school program leading to a basic law degree. Katsarou argued that the refusal was in breach of the Community law principles of free movement of persons and freedom of establishment, as well as Directive 89/48 on the mutual recognition of qualifications regarding the legal profession.

After determining that Article 16 of the Constitution and European law were incompatible, six out of seven judges of the panel ruled that the Greek Constitution was hierarchically superior to Community law and therefore prevailed. However, they considered the question sufficiently important to refer it to the plenary session of the Council of State. A majority of the Council (seventeen judges) treated as of paramount importance Article 149 (ex 126) of the EC Treaty, according to which the Community fully respects "the responsibility of the Member States for the content of teaching and the organization of education systems and their cultural and linguistic diversity." The article specifically provides that the Council "shall adopt incentive measures, excluding any harmonization of the laws and regulations of the Member States." As a result, the organization of the educational systems of the Member States (higher education included), the recognition of foreign degrees as equivalent, and the content of teaching all fall outside the sphere of Community regulation and remain within the exclusive control of the Member States. The Council of State also cited Article 128's reference to the Community's contributing to "the flowering of the cultures of the Member States, while respecting their national and regional diversity." The judges dismissed the application of Directive 89/48 as irrelevant to the issues of higher education referred to by Article 126 EC Treaty and as, in any event, subordinate to Article 126. Finally, as the issue was one of national jurisdiction, outside the scope of Community law, no preliminary reference to the Court of Justice was necessary.

Twelve judges dissented, insisting that Community law was implicated and that a reference should be made to the Court of Justice. The dissenters took the view that higher education, in a sense, falls within the sphere of vocational training, which is critical for the promotion of the freedom of movement of persons and the right of establishment within the Community. These rights and freedoms would be hampered if Member States could deny recognition to the qualifications earned in other Member States by Greek nationals who had availed themselves of such rights and freedoms.

Note that the Council of State did not align itself with the panel, which had directly challenged the principle of supremacy of Community law. Rather, it managed, by virtue of its interpretation of Community law, to skirt that issue for the time being, albeit by means of a questionable refusal to refer the relevant questions to the Court of Justice.[19] Not that the Council of State's position was completely untenable. Article 149 (ex 126) does make an attempt at a clear demarcation of competences between the Member States and the Community in the educational domain. Educational "franchising" is in fact a very sensitive issue in Greece.

For critical commentary on the *Katsarou* case, see E. Maganaris, The Principle of Supremacy of Community Law in Greece: From Direct Challenge to Non–Application, 24 Eur. L. Rev. 426 (1999). More generally, academic views on the relation between the Constitution and Community law are divided. For some, the very nature and functionality of Community law exclude national constitutional review. But the prevailing academic view holds that the Greek Constitution establishes a nucleus of rights that are inalienable and thus untouchable even by Community law. See generally T. Stragas, Greek Constitutional Law and European Integration 62–83, 102–08 (1996); N. Skandamis, European Law and Elements of Greek Adjustment Law 171–176 (1994); K. Ioannou, Recent Applications of Community Law in Greece, 14 Eur. L. Rev. 461 ff. (1989).

Consider, finally, the case of Diamatopoulos v. IKA, Decision no. 4674/1998 (Nov. 27, 1998), in which the Council of State ruled in plenary session that an administrative order prohibiting a Greek citizen from leaving the country on account of being a debtor of the Greek State, represents a wholly internal matter, despite his contention that the order prevented him from traveling to the UK to receive medical services or traveling to France or Germany on business, and violated his right of free movement as a European Union citizen (under Article 18 (ex 8a)) and as a worker (under Article 39 (ex 48)). For a critical assessment of the judgment see E. Maganaris, The Greek Council of State: Europhobic or Simply Overprotective?, 25 Eur. L. Rev. 200 (2000).

2. SPAIN

Article 93 of the Spanish Constitution, adopted in contemplation of Spain's accession to the Community, reads as follows:

---

19. Case law of the Court of Justice (see the Court's judgments in *Blaizot*, Case 24/86, [1998] ECR 379; *Gravier*, Case 293/83, [1985] ECR 593, and *Kraus*, Case C–19/92, [1993] ECR I–1663) suggested that the Court might indeed have taken a different view on the critical issues.

By means of an organic law, authorization may be granted for concluding treaties by which the exercise of powers derived from the Constitution shall be vested in an international organization or institution.

This does not mean that the Community treaties have constitutional status. The Spanish Constitutional Court specifically ruled that, before Spain could ratify the Maastricht Treaty, the Constitution (art. 13.2) had to be amended so as to permit non-Spanish EU nationals to stand for office in local elections. Case 1236/1992 (re Municipal Electoral Rights), [1994] 3 CMLR 101, 19 Rev. Inst. Eur. 633 (1991) (July 1, 1992). (This was the first time that the Court exercised *a priori* review of the constitutionality of treaties.)

On the other hand, nothing in Spanish constitutional doctrine interferes with the supremacy, direct applicability or direct effect of Community law vis-à-vis national legislation. In Judgment 28/1991, 18 Rev. Inst. Eur. 237 (1991) (Feb. 14, 1991), the Constitutional Court took the view (similar to that of the French *Conseil Constitutionnel*, *supra* page 287, note 3) that, notwithstanding Article 93 of the Constitution, the fact that a Spanish statute violates Community law does not for that reason alone render the statute "unconstitutional." According to the Constitutional Court, such a conflict is "constitutionally irrelevant," even where fundamental rights are concerned. It also described Community law in this connection as "infra-constitutional," a term that unfortunately can easily be misunderstood. At the same time, however, the court effectively adopted the reasoning of the Court of Justice in the *Simmenthal II* case (page 272 *supra*) that, in the event of conflict, national judges must directly apply Community law measures in preference to national legislation, without first seeking a ruling from the Constitutional Court. Commentators report generally wide acceptance of the principles of supremacy, direct applicability and direct effect at all levels of the Spanish judiciary. See D. Linan Nogueras & J. Roldan Barbero, The Judicial Application of Community Law in Spain, 30 Comm. Mkt. L. Rev. 1135, 1145 (1993).

The situation is apparently otherwise as concerns the direct effect of directives, as understood by the Court of Justice. In a series of decisions, the Supreme Court of Spain has decided that directives can be given direct effect after the period for transposition has passed only in the case of absolute non-transposition, but not in the case of erroneous transposition. The stated reason is that the judiciary lacks competence to compare the Community directive with the national implementing legislation. See, for example, Judgment of November 30, 1990, Rep. 5371, 83 Noticias C.E.E. 121 (1991). These judgments have been described as "defiant" of Community law principles clearly established by the Court of Justice. D. Linan Nogueras & J. Roldan Barbero, *supra*, at 1148.

Interestingly, Article 10(2) of the Constitution provides that Community legislation may be referred to for the purpose of defining the scope of human rights and public freedoms in Spain.[20] But it is not regarded as conclusive by the Spanish Constitutional Court. Indeed that court, like its German and Italian counterparts, appears to be troubled by the notion that national

---

20. Article 10(2) of the Spanish Constitution provides: "The norms relative to fundamental rights and freedoms recognized by the Constitution will be interpreted in compliance with the Universal Declaration of Human Rights and the international treaties and agreements on the same matter ratified by Spain."

authorities might be bound to enforce Community law domestically even when it violates fundamental rights and freedoms guaranteed by the national Constitution. In Judgment 64/1991, 18 Rev. Inst. Eur. 674 (1991) (March 22, 1991), the Constitutional Court implied that national measures implementing Community law in Spain would indeed be subject to Spanish constitutional review for the protection of fundamental rights. In Case 1236/1992 (re Municipal Electoral Rights), referred to above, the Court underscored that, even when applying Community law, Spanish authorities are "national" authorities and presumably remain subject to national constitutional constraints.

3. PORTUGAL

The Portuguese Constitution was amended not only to permit Portugal's participation in the common foreign and security policy, to extend voting and office-holding rights to other EC nationals, and to adjust the legal status of the Central Bank (arts. 7, 15.4, 105), as required by the TEU, but also to promote democratic accountability. Article 166 was thus amended to ensure that the Parliament would have an opportunity to review and evaluate Portuguese participation in the further development of the European Union. Article 200.1 was amended as well to require the Government to submit all necessary information on European affairs to the Parliament on a timely basis. See A. Alves Vieira, Portugal: Ratifying the Treaty on European Union, 18 Eur. L. Rev. 448 (1993).

I. COMMUNITY LAW IN AUSTRIA, FINLAND AND SWEDEN

None of the three newest Member States has faced significant problems in accepting the Court of Justice's tenets on the relationship between Community law and national law. This is not to say, however, that legal scholars within each of these countries are in complete agreement as to the extent to which EU law should prevail over domestic constitutional law, especially where fundamental and human rights are concerned.

1. AUSTRIA

The Austrian Constitution merely provides, in Article 9(2), that "the specific sovereign powers of the federal government may be transferred by statute or duly ratified treaty to international organizations and their organs." However, due to the prevailing monist tradition in Austria, Austria's accession to the EU is widely viewed as entailing a recognition of the supremacy (*Anwendungsvorrang*) of Community law. In fact, Austria's accession was approved by way of a referendum pursuant to Article 43 of the Constitution and implemented by an Act on Accession.

In its judgment of April 30, 1998, 8ObA224/97t, the Austrian Supreme Court expressly accorded primacy to EU law as against national legislation, and lower courts have followed suit. See, for example, Judgment 97/16/0304 of the Austrian Administrative Court (Aug. 19, 1997), denying application to a provision of the Austrian Tax Code as contrary to the EU Common Customs Tariff. However, the position taken by the German Constitutional Court in *Solange II*—that the supremacy of EC law is conditional on its affording nationals a level of human rights protection comparable to that guaranteed by the national Constitution—is widely endorsed by academic commentary. Indications are that the Austrian Constitutional Court (*Verfassungsgerichtshof*) is intent on upholding its own benchmark of human rights, which may set the stage for tensions between it, too, and the European Court of Justice at some future point in time.[21]

2. FINLAND

Finland has traditionally followed the dualist approach to international law and treaties, requiring formal incorporation of international law rules through national legislation. Accordingly, the 1994 Treaty of Accession was considered to require the adoption of implementing legislation in the form of the Finnish EU Act (Act. 1540/94, Statutes of Finland), an act that is understood as effectively precluding claims that the application of secondary Community law in Finland would be contrary to the Finnish Constitution. The Act was adopted as a so-called "Exception Act," a statute whose effect is to vary the Constitution without formally amending it. (Exception Acts require approval by a qualified majority—specifically, two-thirds—of Parliament.) See N. Jaaskinen, The Application of Community Law in Finland: 1995–1998, 36 Comm. Mkt. L. Rev. 407–09 (1999); Lenaerts, Nuffel & Bray, Constitutional Law of the European Union 526 (1999). When an international agreement is incorporated into law by an Exception Act, it takes precedence over domestic law, including provisions of the Constitution itself. Jaaskinen, *supra*, at 409.

The new 1999 Finnish Constitution (chapter 8, Sections 93 and 94), effective March 1, 2000, speaks directly to the status of international agreements within the Finnish legal system. It requires that the acceptance or denunciation of international obligations be made upon the approval of a majority of the Parliament, while preserving the use of Exception Acts (requiring approval by at least two thirds of the votes cast in Parliament). Significant, however, is Section 93's last paragraph, which states that "[a]n international obligation shall not endanger the democratic foundations of the Constitution." Exactly what rights make up the "democratic foundations" of the Constitution, and whether the Finnish courts will regard the European Court of Justice as capable of guaranteeing them, remains to be seen. Historically, there has been no constitutional review of legislation in Finland, the assessment of the constitutionality of a statute being considered to be part of the legislative process. It is unclear whether this will change.

Otherwise the situation of Community law in Finland is unproblematic. In several judgments to date, the Finnish Supreme Administrative Court has required that national legislation be interpreted as consistent with Community law. The leading example is Case KHO 1996 B 577 (Dec. 31, 1996), in which the court barred the government from granting a Finnish company VAT tax deductions provided for by national law where such deductions ran afoul of a Community law directive, even one that had not yet been implemented in Finland. EuroWatch, vol. 8, no. 20, p. 8 (Jan. 24, 1997). Lower

---

21. The Austrian Constitutional Court is accordingly making significant preliminary references to the Court of Justice. See, e.g., Oest- erreichische Rundfunk, Case C–465/00; Adria–Wien Pipeline and Wietersdorfer & Peggauer, Case C–143/99.

courts have routinely enforced the doctrine of supremacy of EC law. See generally, Jaaskinen, *supra*, at 417–20.

3. SWEDEN

Chapter 10, article 5, of the Swedish Constitution purports to guarantee the supremacy of Community law in Sweden through proviso language that is explicitly reminiscent of the German *Solange II* decision:

> (1) Decision-making pursuant to the present Instrument of Government ... may be entrusted, to a limited extent, to an international organization for peaceful cooperation of which Sweden is, or is to become, a member or to an international court of law. No right of decision-making relating to matters concerning the enactment, amendment, or repeal of a fundamental law ... or regarding a limitation of any of the rights and freedoms referred to in Chapter 2 [of this Instrument] may be thus delegated.

The Swedish Parliament accordingly passed an Act affirming the validity of Community law and its effects in Sweden, thus presumably incorporating the doctrine of supremacy of Community law over national law. See Lenaerts, Nuffel & Bray, Constitutional Law of the European Union 526 (1999). In its *Laasagard* judgment, Case 219/97 (Nov. 25, 1997), the Swedish Supreme Administrative Court expressly enforced the doctrine.

Chapter 9

THE PRELIMINARY REFERENCE

Article 234 (ex 177) provides for the Court of Justice to issue rulings on the interpretation of the EC Treaty or on the validity or meaning of acts of the institutions of the Community,[1] when a Member State court or tribunal "considers that a decision on the question is necessary to enable it to give judgment" in a pending case. Requests to the Court under Article 234 are commonly known as "preliminary references" or "referrals" and the judgments the Court renders as "preliminary rulings." By the terms of Article 234, a reference is mandatory when the Member State court is one against whose decisions national law affords no judicial remedy; otherwise it is discretionary. The idea of preliminary references comes from Germany and Italy, whose courts are required to refer certain constitutional questions to a separate Constitutional Court when an answer to those questions is necessary for the decision of a pending case.

The preliminary reference is the critical link between the Member State judiciaries and the Court of Justice. In the first place, it enables national courts to secure an authoritative ruling from the Court of Justice on the interpretation and validity of Community law whenever the proper solution of a case before them so requires. Referrals are in fact the most common kind of case on the Court's docket, constituting about one-half. This is not surprising. Since Community law in most sectors is enforced chiefly by Member State rather than Community bodies, disputes over the meaning of Community law normally surface in national litigation.

Second, referrals provide the Court with a continuous opportunity to develop substantive Community law, whether by clarifying the meaning of Community instruments or by formulating and applying general principles of law. Former Judge Pescatore of the Court of Justice has written: "The decisions of the Court which have made the most conspicuous contribution to the development of Community law have been delivered [by preliminary ruling] ... : the direct effect of Community law, its primacy over national law, the protection of fundamental rights, the principles relating to the common market and the law of competition [and] the social dimension of the Commu-

---

1. The Maastricht Treaty amended former Article 177 to include the European Central Bank among the bodies whose acts may be the subject of preliminary references. Since the Court of Auditors is now under Article 7 (ex 4) formally a Community institution, its acts are a proper subject of preliminary rulings.

nity." P. Pescatore, References for Preliminary Rulings Under Article 177 (EC Off'l Pub. Office, 1986) at 11.

Because preliminary references thus serve the needs both of the Member State courts and the Court of Justice, the procedure is widely viewed (and has been described by the Court of Justice) as an important form of "cooperation" between the Community and national judiciaries.

Third, preliminary references must be seen as an important, albeit indirect, way for individuals to bring their Community law assertions to the Court of Justice. Enterprising lawyers before the national courts increasingly raise claims that are based on Community law rights and obligations. Although these claims have to be adjudicated in a national forum, rulings under Article 234 enable the Court of Justice to supply the forum with the applicable Community law principles.

Finally, it should by now be clear that the concept of direct effect, which in a sense is the cornerstone of supranationalism, depends utterly on the preliminary reference mechanism. When national courts refer Community law questions to the Court of Justice, secure guidance through the Court's preliminary rulings, and then follow those rulings, they engage in a vital form of Community law enforcement.

A.   THE REFERENCE PROCEDURE

The national court itself, not the parties before it, has the authority to decide that a preliminary ruling will be sought. Although courts usually refer questions raised by a party, sometimes they decide to refer a question entirely on their own. Thus a preliminary reference differs fundamentally from an appeal. The extent to which a judge relies on counsel to help formulate the questions for referral depends almost entirely on that judge's inclination and on judicial traditions in his or her state. (Reliance on counsel is common in the UK, much less so on the Continent.) But in any event, the national courts are the ones to decide whether, when and what to refer.

There are wide discrepancies in the incidence of preliminary references from national courts. According to one report,[2] Germany leads by far in absolute terms, with some 60 references a year (many on VAT and social security issues); Italy, France, the Netherlands and the UK follow. References from Greece, Ireland, Luxembourg and Portugal are reportedly rare.

In a preliminary reference, the referring court sends the Court of Justice the file of the case, including the facts to the extent then ascertained. It also provides a summary of the procedure to that point, the parties' claims, the relevant national law, the court's reasons for making the reference and the specific questions of Community law presented. The Registrar of the Court of Justice then notifies the Member States, the Commission and the Council, each of which may submit written observations and appear at an oral hearing. (The Commission invariably does so, and its views are treated rather like those of the US Justice Department acting through the Solicitor General as *amicus curiae*. The Council, on the other hand, normally participates only if the validity, and not merely the interpretation, of one of its own acts is called

---

2.   O.J. C 354/182 (Dec. 7, 1999).

into question.) Otherwise, only parties to the national court proceeding (or persons who have been granted to leave by the national court to intervene in those proceedings) may participate in the preliminary reference procedure in Luxembourg. Others may not do so, even if they have an "interest" in the question being referred. Biogen Inc. v. Smithkline Beecham Biological S.A., Case C–181/95, [1996] ECR I–717.

Following presentation of the Advocate–General's opinion, the Court renders judgment in the usual way. Its judgment will discuss the questions presented and give reasoned rulings on them. In theory, the Court does not decide questions of fact, but its answers often indicate quite clearly how the national court should approach and possibly even decide them.

Although Article 234 enables the Court of Justice to clarify Community law for the benefit of national courts, the latter are ultimately responsible for applying Community law to the cases out of which preliminary references grow. Because, in principle, the Court of Justice simply rules on the questions of Community law submitted to it, without itself applying that law or otherwise deciding the case, it neither overrules decisions of the national courts nor invalidates national legislation. It does not even pass explicitly on the compatibility of national law with Community law, though it often makes its views on this matter so clear that the question is all but answered. Needless to say, the Court does not in any event rule on the meaning of national law as such.

The logic of Article 234 would suggest that referring courts are bound to follow preliminary rulings of the Court in the cases that occasion them, and the Court has so held. Benedetti v. Munari, Case 52/76, [1977] ECR 163; Milch-, Fett- und Eierkontor GmbH v. Hauptzollamt Saarbrücken, Case 29/68, [1969] ECR 165. Moreover, though preliminary rulings only answer the questions put by a national court in a particular case, they are cast in general terms and have been held by the Court also to apply to future cases. Thus, despite the absence of a formal rule of *stare decisis* binding the Court of Justice itself, Article 234 rulings constitute binding precedents for national courts in later cases. Like other Court of Justice rulings, they allow Community law to acquire a determined meaning throughout the territory of the Community, and thus promote legal certainty and unity.

If a national court disagrees with a Court of Justice ruling on the meaning of Community law, or otherwise would like the Court to reconsider the ruling in a subsequent case, the most it may do is resubmit the question in the expectation or simple chance that the Court will change its mind. The national court is not at liberty simply to apply a different rule. Recall that in the *Kloppenburg* case, discussed at page 304 *supra*, the Supreme Tax Court of Germany declined to follow the ruling that the Court of Justice gave to the lower court in that very case, and it did so without resubmitting the question to the Court of Justice. Recall further that the German Constitutional Court in *Kloppenburg* found that the Supreme Tax Court's decision thereby violated the taxpayer's constitutional right to her "lawful judge," and invalidated it.

The same principle applies *a fortiori* to preliminary rulings on the *validity* of Community law:

> [A]lthough a judgment of the Court ... under Article 177 [now 234] ... declaring an act of an institution ... to be void is directly addressed only

to the national court which brought the matter before the Court, it is sufficient reason for any other national court to regard that act as void for the purposes of [any] judgment which it has to give.

* * *

There may [of course] be ... a need [for a further reference] if questions arise as to the grounds, the scope and possibly the consequences of the invalidity established earlier.

SpA International Chemical Corporation v. Amministrazione delle Finanze dello Stato, Case 66/80, [1981] ECR 1191, 1215.

Do referring courts follow the answers provided by the Court of Justice? While there is no assurance that they will apply a preliminary ruling properly in the pending case, there is every indication that they try to do so. Judge Pescatore has stated: "Only in wholly exceptional cases have national courts misunderstood the rulings or showed reluctance to implement them." P. Pescatore, op. cit., page 352 *supra* at 23. One of these rare cases is *Foglia v. Novello II*, discussed at page 363 *infra*.

Even though it appears to work rather well, the preliminary reference mechanism entails a price. That price is delay in awaiting the Court's response. As a result of its heavy caseload and exacting procedures, the Court of Justice averages 18 months, and this must be added to delays already present in the national court system. Worse yet, national courts sometimes suspect that a litigant may be raising an EC law issue "mischievously, not in the bona fide hope of success but in order to obstruct or delay an almost inevitable adverse judgment, denying the other party his remedy meanwhile." Commissioners of Customs and Excise v. Samex ApS, [1983] 1 All ER 1042, [1983] 3 CMLR 194, 211 (High Court, Dec. 14, 1982) (per Bingham, J.). The Maastricht Treaty acknowledged the problem by amending Article 221 (ex 165) to excuse the Court of Justice from having to sit in plenary session in preliminary reference proceedings. Panel rulings naturally accelerate the handling of more routine preliminary questions, with more difficult and weighty ones still going to the full Court.

A possible reform strategy would be to restrict the level of national courts from which preliminary references may be made. Proposals to this effect have been made at recent IGCs; Germany, for one, proposed that only national appellate courts—and possibly only national supreme courts—be permitted to refer questions. Although this would greatly reduce the flow of preliminary reference, it would also severely limit the Court's opportunity to issue preliminary rulings, and it could of course leave lower national courts with unresolved uncertainties about the meaning of Community law measures. What, for example, should a lower court do if convinced that an EC law measure, applicable to the case before it, is actually invalid under the EC Treaty? The Court of Justice has expressed dismay at the prospect of such a curtailment of the Court's reference authority (most recently in its reflection papers in preparation for the Amsterdam and Nice IGCs), citing jeopardy to the uniform interpretation of Community law and erosion of effective judicial protection of individuals in national court. What is your view?

Another possibility would, of course, be for the Court to refrain more often than it has from answering requests for a preliminary ruling. It could do so by reinforcing various existing means that we shall explore, such as requiring a fuller national record or demanding a higher showing by the referring court of the relevance of the question asked. A purely discretionary *certiorari*-type system is also imaginable. Advocate–General Jacobs has urged a variant on that, according to which the Court should agree to render rulings only in cases raising important problems of interpretation or implying serious risks of non-uniformity in the application of Community law. Opinion of the Advocate–General in Wiener, Case C–338/95, [1997] ECR I–6495. In a 1999 joint report on "The Future of the Judicial System of the European Union," the ECJ and CFI advanced a number of other ideas, including not only a *certiorari*-type (i.e. filtering) procedure, but also an "accelerated" procedure for urgent references and a "simplified" procedure for routine ones. An accelerated procedure is now already in use. In Jippes v. Minister van Landbouw, Natuurbeheer en Visserij, Case C–189/01, [2001] ECR I–___ (July 12, 2001), the President of the Court acceded to the referring court's plea, under the urgent circumstances of "foot-and-mouth" disease outbreaks in the Netherlands, that its reference be handled under the accelerated procedure provided for by Article 104a of the Court's Rules of Procedure. Yet another proposed remedy for delay is that referring courts be required to propose answers to their own questions.

The intergovernmental conference at Nice finally addressed the question in its own way. The Nice Treaty would amend Article 225 (ex 168a) of the EC Treaty to empower the Court of First Instance to entertain preliminary references to the extent the Statute of the Court of Justice specifically permits. The Statute that was appended to the Nice Treaty does not provide specifically for Article 234 jurisdiction by the CFI. Thus, a further amendment would be needed before any Article 234 cases could actually go to the CFI. (Article 62 of the Statute which makes reference to CFI jurisdiction in cases under Art 225(3) simply underscores this lacuna). Pursuant to the Nice amendments, preliminary rulings by the CFI would be appealable to the Court of Justice only exceptionally, as where there is "a serious risk of the unity or consistency of Community law being affected." On the other hand, if the CFI received a reference that "requires a decision of principle likely to affect the unity or consistency of Community law," it could forward the reference directly to the Court of Justice rather than issue a ruling itself.

Notes and Questions

1. Why did the drafters of the Community treaties adopt a reference mechanism rather than a Community trial court system? Why has a system of appeals from national courts to the Court of Justice, an idea that has frequently been urged and that has a US analogue, never been adopted? An analogy to Article 234 may be found in the US system, but in reverse direction. A majority of states now allow federal courts, when dealing with state law, to refer questions on that law to the highest state court, but that opportunity is not widely used. Can you explain this?

2. Why do you suppose the Community has been so slow to confer preliminary reference jurisdiction on the Court of First instance?

NOTE ON THE "REFERABILITY" OF QUESTIONS

The discussion above implies that parties in national court litigation are free to ask the national court to refer any questions of Community law that are relevant to the pending action. However, there are circumstances when referral of an otherwise relevant question of Community law might be disallowed.

One important exception relates to questions of the validity of Community acts. Suppose a party had standing to bring a direct challenge in the Community courts to a decision addressed to it (or, exceptionally, to a regulation or a decision addressed to another party), but failed to do so at all, or within the time limit allowed. May that party later on raise the validity question in a national court proceeding and in that context secure a preliminary ruling from the Court of Justice on the question?

In Nachi Europe GmbH v. Hauptzollamt Krefeld, Case C–239/99, [2001] ECR I–1197, the Council by regulation imposed anti-dumping duties on ball bearings produced by three named Japanese manufacturers. Two of the three manufacturers (NTN and Koyo Seiko) sued to annul the regulation insofar as it imposed duties on their products. They were successful in the CFI and, on appeal, in the ECJ, at which point the Commission published a notice entitling importers of those products to refunds from national customs authorities. Nachi Europe, an importer of Japanese ball bearings, then sought reimbursement from the German authorities of duties it had paid on the import of ball bearings produced by the third Japanese manufacturer, which happened to be Nachi Europe's Japanese parent company (Nachi Fujikoshi). Upon refusal, Nachi Europe brought a refund suit in a German tax court, which wondered whether it could entertain the action and award the refund sought.

On preliminary reference, the Court of Justice ruled that, since only NTN and Koyo Seiko had brought the annulment action, the annulment affected the anti-dumping regulation only insofar as NTN and Koyo Seiko products were concerned, leaving intact the duty applicable to Nachi Fujikoshi ball bearings. The question then arose whether Nachi (and its parent), having failed to challenge the regulation in the CFI as concerned them, could now question the regulation's validity in a refund action in national court, thus prompting a preliminary reference on the validity question.

The Court held the national court action—and thus the preliminary reference as well—to be barred. Since, according to the Court, Nachi Europe "undoubtedly" could have sought annulment of the regulation in a direct action in the CFI insofar as it imposed duties on Nachi Fujikoshi products, but had failed to do so, it could not subsequently plead the invalidity of the duty in national court. "In such a case, the national court is bound by the definitive nature of the anti-dumping duty applicable ... to ball bearings manufactured by Nachi Fujikoshi and imported by Nachi Europe." A preliminary reference could not be entertained.

Is this a sound result, considering that there is no reason to doubt the invalidity of the Nachi anti-dumping duties? Is the Court of Justice in effect deciding who has standing to sue in a *national* court? If so, is that appropriate? If Nachi Europe is at this point estopped from obtaining a preliminary ruling from the CFI, is the German court likewise barred from doing so *sua sponte*?

The Court expressly predicated its decision on a finding that Nachi Europe "undoubtedly" had enjoyed standing to seek the anti-dumping duty's annulment in the Court of First Instance. Reviewing the material in Chapter 5A on private party standing to sue, do you agree? The Court analogized to its judgment in TWD Textilwerke Deggendorf v. Germany, Case C–188/92, [1994] ECR I–833, in which it held that where the Commission has denied a Member State's bid to make a state aid available to an enterprise, and the enterprise fails to challenge that denial in the Community courts, the enterprise cannot thereafter indirectly challenge the denial in national court and thereby obtain a preliminary ruling on its validity. Were the *locus standi* of Nachi and of TWD Textilwerke Deggendorf equally "undoubted"?

There may be a second quite different category of Community law questions that, though relevant, are "off-limits" to the preliminary reference process. Consider Proceedings against Déménagements–Manutention Transport SA, Case C–256/97, [1999] ECR I–3913. Belgian law allowed the State, through the Social Security Office, to grant a grace period to financially troubled employers for collecting social security contributions. The Tribunal de Commerce, which had to approve the grant, asked the Court of Justice (a) whether such a grant constituted a state aid and (b) if so, whether it was compatible with the common market. The Court answered the first question (basically in the affirmative), but refused to answer the second:

[14] Article 88 EC (ex Article 93) provides for a special procedure by which the Commission is to keep State aid under constant review. As regards proposed new grants of aid by the Member States, it establishes a procedure which must be followed before any aid can be regarded as lawfully granted . . .

* * *

[16] . . . . [T]he intention of the Treaty is that the finding that an aid may be incompatible with the common market is to be made, subject to review by the Court, by means of an appropriate procedure which it is the Commission's responsibility to set in motion. It follows that the Court has no jurisdiction to reply to the second question. . . .

What is the Belgian Tribunal de Commerce now to do?

A third and still different situation arises when a court asks for a preliminary ruling on the meaning of national legislation which, while modeled upon a Community directive, has been extended by the national legislature to reach cases not covered by the directive. The case of Leur–Bloem v. Inspecteur der Belastingdienst/Ondernemingen Amsterdam 2, Case C–28/95, [1997] ECR I–4161, is illustrative. Leur–Bloem, the sole shareholder and director of two Dutch companies, sought to exchange her shares for shares in a third company, which was a holding company for the other two, thereby becoming in effect the sole shareholder of all three. She claimed that this constituted a merger by exchange of shares which was exempt under Dutch law from taxation of gains. The tax authorities disagreed and she sued in Dutch court.

The applicable Dutch legislation had been enacted to implement a Community law directive which only applied to mergers and exchanges of shares between companies of different Member States (and whose purpose was to make such mergers and exchanges as fiscally attractive as comparable transactions involving companies within a single Member State). Thus, while the directive did not cover Leur–Bloem's transaction, the Dutch implementing legislation did.

The Dutch court thought that a preliminary ruling on the meaning of the directive would be helpful to it and asked whether it could be had. The Commission, joined by the Dutch and German governments, objected on the ground that the Court lacks jurisdiction to reply to questions concerning situations not governed by the directive, but the Court disagreed. The Court first referred to prior case law according to which it could render a preliminary ruling on the meaning of a Community measure, even though the case at hand lay outside the measure's scope, provided the domestic law or contract that was applicable had incorporated the Community law measure by reference.[3] On the other hand, it also cited case law in which the Court refused to construe a Community law measure where the applicable national law had simply been modeled upon it, with divergences.[4]

The Court continued:

[32]   ... [W]here in regulating internal situations, domestic legislation adopts the same solutions as those adopted in Community law in order, in particular, to avoid discrimination against foreign nationals or, as in [this] case ..., any distortion of competition, it is clearly in the Community interest that, in order to forestall future differences of interpretation, provisions or concepts taken from Community law should be interpreted uniformly, irrespective of the circumstances in which they are to apply.

* * *

[34]   [Therefore] the Court of Justice has jurisdiction under Article 177 [now 234] to interpret Community law where the situation in question is not governed directly by Community law but the national legislature, in transposing the provisions of a directive into domestic law, has chosen to apply the same treatment to purely internal situations and to those governed by the directive, so that it has aligned its domestic legislation to Community law.

In your judgment, is this a good move?

B. FRAMING THE REFERENCE AND THE RULING

National courts, especially trial courts, are not expert in Community law and may not know exactly how to formulate their questions under Article 234. References may be imprecise or verbose; they may address the wrong parts of the Treaty or secondary legislation; they may confuse Community law con-

3. See Dzodzi, Joined Cases C–297/88 & 197/89, [1990] ECR I–3763; Gmurzynska–Bscher, Case C–231/89, [1990] ECR I–4003.

4. See Kleinwort Benson Ltd. v. City of Glasgow District Council, Case C–346/93, [1995] ECR I–615.

cepts. Moreover, a referring court may be mistaken in its belief that an answer to a Community law question is really necessary for resolving the case before it.

The Court of Justice understands these difficulties. From its earliest judgments, the Court has followed a policy of answering questions whether or not the answers are truly essential to the national litigation, while at the same time reformulating the questions if they are imprecise or confused. Moreover, since its *Costa v. ENEL* ruling, *supra* page 271, note 1, the Court has in principle declined to examine the motives that may have caused a national court to make a reference. For an affirmation of that view, see Tedeschi v. Denkavit, Case 5/77, [1977] ECR 1555, 1574. The cases that follow, however, illustrate certain limitations on the Court's willingness to answer all questions asked of it.

PRETORE DI SALO v. PERSONS UNKNOWN

Case 14/86, [1987] ECR 2545.

[An Italian magistrate was investigating possible criminal liability for water pollution under the Italian law that implemented a 1978 Council directive on the protection of fresh water quality and fish life. He first asked the Court of Justice whether Italian water pollution rules were "consistent with the principles and quality objectives" set out in the 1978 directive. His second question was extremely obscure, asking whether the directive called for "rules ... capable of ensuring a constant flow [of water and thus] preserving the minimum volume ... essential for the development of fish species." Italy argued that the questions were premature, since no criminal proceeding had as yet begun. The Commission also considered the questions inappropriate.]

10   [I]f the interpretation of Community law is to be of use to the national court, it is essential to define the legal context in which the interpretation requested should be placed. In that perspective, it might be convenient in certain circumstances for the facts of the case to be established and for questions of purely national law to be settled at the time when the reference is made to the Court of Justice so as to enable the latter to take cognizance of all the matters of fact and law which may be relevant to the interpretation of Community law which it is called upon to give.

11   However, as the Court has already held ... in Case 72/83, Campus Oil v. Minister for Industry and Energy, [1984] ECR 2727, those considerations do not in any way restrict the discretion of the national court, which alone has a direct knowledge of the facts of the case and of the arguments of the parties, which will have to take responsibility for giving judgment in the case and which is therefore in the best position to appreciate at what stage of the proceedings it requires a preliminary ruling from the Court of Justice. The decision at what stage in proceedings a question should be referred to the Court of Justice for a preliminary ruling is therefore dictated by considerations of procedural economy and efficiency to be weighed only by the national court and not by the Court of Justice.

* * *

[16] [Furthermore, t]he Court may ... extract from the wording of the questions formulated by the national court, and having regard to the facts stated by the latter, those elements which concern the interpretation of Community law for the purpose of enabling that court to resolve the legal problems before it. In this case, however, in view of the generality of the question and the absence of any specific elements which would make it possible to identify the doubts entertained by the national court, it is not possible for the Court to reply to the question referred to it.

Notes and Questions

1. The Court of Justice in *Pretore di Salò* (¶ 11) emphasized its duty to respect the views of national courts on the appropriateness of a preliminary reference. It acts on the assumption that Member State judges have a greater knowledge of the facts, the issues and the posture of a case, and ultimately are the ones responsible for delivering a judgment. See also Campus Oil v. Minister for Industry and Energy, Case 72/83, [1984] ECR 2727. Is this a sound attitude? Note that the Court nevertheless declined to answer the Pretore's question. Can you square this refusal with the Court's stated deference to national court requests for preliminary rulings?

2. The Court of Justice has also stated that it will reject a reference "if it is quite obvious that the interpretation of Community law ... sought by [a national] court bears no relation to the actual nature of the case or to the subject matter of the main action." Salonia v. Poidomani, Case 126/80, [1981] ECR 1563, 1576–77. See also Crispoltoni v. Fattoria Autonoma Tabacchi di Città di Castello, Case C–368/89, [1991] ECR I–3695. Is this policy of reviewing a reference's "relevance" consistent with the Court's remarks in *Pretore di Salò?*

Since determining whether Community law is obviously not relevant to a case for Article 234 purposes naturally presupposes some understanding of the scope of Community law, the Court may find itself anticipating to some extent the merits of the case. A striking example is Grado and Bashir, Case C–291/96, [1997] ECR I–5531. When applying to a local court for a summary punishment order against an Italian national for committing a traffic offense in Germany, the local prosecutor deliberately omitted from his petition the courtesy title, "Herr," which he ordinarily would have used in charging a German male. The German court itself asked the Court of Justice for a ruling on the compatibility of this manner of proceeding with Community law. The Court refused, regarding such a discrimination in the context of prosecuting traffic offenses as falling outside the scope of Community law. Do you agree?

3. Recent rulings suggest that the Court is prepared to take an even "harder look" at the admissibility of preliminary references, focusing on the adequacy of the material provided by the referring court by way of context. The Court in plenary session has announced that a valid preliminary reference requires the national court to define the factual and legislative background to the case (or at least the factual hypotheses on the basis of which the reference was made) and that in the absence of such information, the reference will be deemed inadmissible. Telemarsicabruzzo SpA v. Circostel, Joined Cases C–320–22/90, [1993] ECR I–393. The Court has since regularly delivered on that threat. See, for example, Banco de Fomento e Exterior SA v. Martins Pechim, Case C–326/95, [1996] ECR I–1385.

In a non-binding "Note" addressed to national courts and tribunals,[5] the Court admonishes that preliminary references should state succinctly but completely the reasons, so as to give the Court of Justice, the Member States, the Community institutions, and interested parties "a clear understanding of the factual and legal context of the main proceedings" and enable the Court to give an answer that will be of assistance to the national court. An amendment to the Court's Rules of Procedure of May 2000 permits the Court to "request clarification from the national court,"[6] and it has subsequently done so.

In fact, Member States themselves not infrequently object to the admissibility of a preliminary reference on the ground that the referring court failed to define adequately the factual or legal context of the questions submitted. Sometimes, the objecting state is the state whose court made the reference to begin with. (See, for example, Saddik, Case C–458/93, [1995] ECR I–511, and Job Centre, Case C–111/94, [1995] ECR I–3361, where Italy objected to references from Italian courts.) Do you see why the government in whose courts the main action is proceeding might have a special reason for complaining?

The trend may reflect the Court's desire to protect itself, and its limited resources, from references that it may find unreasonably difficult to answer, thus significantly reducing its preliminary ruling workload. On the other hand, raising the threshold requirements for a reference—even to the modest extent that this new case law does—may have the effect of deterring national courts from making references when it would be useful and appropriate for them to do so.

For critical commentary on the trend, see Barnard & Sharpston, The Changing Face of Article 177 References, 34 Comm. Mkt. L. Rev. 1113 (1997); O'Keeffe, Is the Spirit of Article 177 under Attack? Preliminary References and Admissibility, 23 Eur. L. Rev. 509 (1998).

4. Not surprisingly, parties and intervenors sometimes object to an Article 234 reference on the ground that the referring court lacks jurisdiction under national law to entertain the action that gave rise to the reference. The Court of Justice consistently ignores such complaints on the ground that the competence of the referring court is entirely a matter of national law, and that the referring court's determination of its own jurisdiction can be overturned only on appeal under national law. Syndicat Français de l'Express International (SFEI) v. La Poste, Case C–39/94, [1996] ECR I–3547.

5. A noted instance in which the Court reformulated questions put to it under Article 234 is Pigs Marketing Board v. Redmond, Case 83/78, *supra* page 118. The Northern Ireland magistrate before whom a prosecution was pending for the unlicensed sale of hogs referred pages of questions on the nature of the Pigs Marketing Board and its regulatory powers in the light of virtually all the Treaty provisions on agriculture. Perhaps embarrassed by the questions' volume and hopeless mixing of facts and law, the UK urged the Court not to answer them. However, the Court ruled that it could still extract the critical Community law issues in the "improperly formulated" questions.

6. French broadcasters refused to air an advertisement for fuel sold by a French importer in its chain of supermarkets, citing a French law that prohibited televised advertising by the distribution sector. The importer sued, alleging that the French law violated both the EC Treaty and the 1989 television broadcasting

---

5. Note for Guidance on References by National Courts for Preliminary Rulings (Proceedings of the Court, no. 34/96, Dec. 9, 1996, para. 6), [1997] 1 CMLR 78), 22 Eur. L. Rev. 55 (1997).

6. O.J. L 122/43 (May 24, 2000).

directive. Plaintiff and defendants alike supported the French commercial court in referring this question to the Court of Justice. In fact, they prevailed on the French court to phrase the reference, not simply in terms of the French law ban on televised advertising in the distribution sector, but in all the sectors to which the French ban applied (viz. alcoholic beverages, literary publications, cinema and the press).

The Court answered the question insofar as the ban on televised advertising in the distribution sector was concerned. (On the merits, it ruled that the ban violated neither Article 30, 85 nor 86, nor the television broadcasting directive.) However, the Court positively refused to answer the question in terms of any of the other sectors because, to that extent, "the interpretation of Community law has no connection whatever with the circumstances or purpose of the main proceedings." Société d'Importation Edouard Leclerc–Siplec v. TF1 Publicité SA and M6 Publicité SA, Case C–412/93, [1995] ECR I–179. (The substantive law issues in this case are discussed at page 363 *infra*).

7. The Court maintains that, in rendering a preliminary ruling, it does no more than clarify the scope and meaning of the Community law provision in question, and refrains from deciding whether or how that provision applies to the facts of the case at hand:

> The Court has no power in the context of [preliminary reference] proceedings ... either to interpret provisions of national law or to rule on their possible incompatibility with Community law. However, in the context of the interpretation of Community law, it may provide the national court with the criteria enabling it to deal with the action before it. ...

Enka v. Inspecteur der Invoerrechten en Accijnzen, Case 38/77, [1977] ECR 2203, 2213; Rustica Semences SA v. Finanzamt Kehl, Case C–438/92, [1994] ECR I–3519. Judging by the opinions you have read, to what extent does the Court in fact follow this policy?

8. Common law commentators sometimes complain that the Court's preliminary rulings are too abstract, too devoid of factual references and too literal in responding to the questions presented. As you read the many Article 234 cases in this book, reflect on whether you agree, or whether you think the critics are simply accustomed to the lengthy, detailed and fact-oriented style of common law judgments, which civil law lawyers sometimes find confusing.

NOTE ON "PUT UP" QUESTIONS

The Court of Justice has on rare occasion faced the question whether to entertain preliminary references arising out of disputes that the parties in national court appear to have contrived (or "put up") for no reason other than to secure a preliminary ruling. It might be said in such a case that the parties do not have a "real" case or controversy (i.e. are not really "opposed.").

This scenario is closely associated with the case of Foglia v. Novello (II), Case 244/80, [1981] ECR 3045. Two Italian wine dealers included in their contract for the sale of Italian wine a provision barring any charge to the buyer (Novello) for French or Italian taxes or duties that were contrary to the EC Treaty provisions on the free movement of goods. The seller (Foglia) in turn put a disclaimer of liability for such taxes or duties in his contract with the French firm that was chosen to receive the shipment and transport it to

Novello. The obvious purpose of these contract provisions was to make it possible for the French excise tax to be challenged in an Italian court. When the transporter paid a French excise tax and included that amount in its bill to Foglia, Foglia unsuccessfully sought reimbursement from Novello. Foglia then sued Novello in an Italian court. Both parties urged the court to ask the Court of Justice certain questions about the legality of the French tax under EC Articles 87 and 90 (ex 92 and 95). The Italian court referred those questions, but the Court of Justice declined to rule on them, maintaining that the dispute was not a genuine one. Foglia v. Novello (I), Case 104/79, [1980] ECR 745.

Back again in the Italian court, Novello argued that the Court of Justice's refusal to issue a ruling violated its duty of deference to the national court's determination that a Community law question needed to be answered, and prevented the national court from deciding the case before it. The Italian court, obviously sympathetic to this view, submitted a new round of questions to the Court of Justice on the division of authority between referring courts and the Court of Justice. The Court stated as follows:

18   [T]he duty assigned to the Court by Article 177 is not that of delivering advisory opinions on general or hypothetical questions but of assisting in the administration of justice in the Member States. It accordingly does not have jurisdiction to reply to questions of interpretation which are submitted to it within the framework of procedural devices arranged by the parties in order to induce the Court to give its views on certain problems of Community law which do not correspond to an objective requirement inherent in the resolution of a dispute. A declaration by the Court that it has no jurisdiction in such circumstances does not in any way trespass upon the prerogatives of the national court but makes it possible to prevent the application of the procedure under Article 177 for purposes other than those appropriate for it.

* * *

21   [W]hilst ... an assessment of the need to obtain an answer to the questions of interpretation raised ... is a matter for the national court, it is nevertheless for the Court of Justice, in order to confirm its own jurisdiction, to examine, where necessary, the conditions in which the case has been referred to it by the national court.

The Court seemed most disturbed by the prospect of private parties "putting up" a question in a court of one Member State calling into question the validity of the law of another Member State, as in the situation at hand:

29   ... [T]he possibility arises that the conduct of the parties may ... make it impossible for the State concerned to arrange for an appropriate defence of its interests by causing the question of the invalidity of its legislation to be decided by a court of another Member State. Accordingly, in such procedural situations, it is impossible to exclude the risk that the procedure under Article 177 may be diverted by the parties from the purposes for which it was laid down by the Treaty.

30   The foregoing considerations as a whole show that the Court of Justice for its part must display special vigilance when, in the course of proceedings between individuals, a question is referred to it with a view to permitting

the national court to decide whether the legislation of another Member State is in accordance with Community law.

Do you agree with the Court that it was inappropriate for the French tax law to be challenged in an Italian court? What difference does it make whether the question reaches the Court from an Italian or a French court? In any case, all that the Italian court can do is obtain a Court of Justice ruling that the transporter might later rely on in a French court to recover the French tax paid. If Novello's manner of challenging the French tax was improper, what was the proper manner of challenging it? How should the Italian court go about interpreting the relevant Community law if the Court of Justice refuses to provide a ruling? Should it decline to decide the case at all, since deprived of the benefit of a preliminary ruling?

Foglia was not an entirely isolated case. For a similar scenario, see Union Laitière Normande v. French Dairy Farmers Ltd., Case 244/78, [1979] ECR 2663. There, the Court declined to pass on the validity under EC law of UK rules governing the sale of milk. The reference had come from a French court hearing a challenge brought by French farmers.

Note the contradiction between the result (and reasoning) in *Foglia* with the Court's often-repeated claim that it does not inquire into a national court's reasons for referring a question. (The-then Advocate–General Sir Gordon Slynn, now a member of the House of Lords, thought the Court should have answered the questions put to it in *Foglia*.) By the test that it used in *Foglia*, should the Court have answered the questions put to it in *Costa v. ENEL, supra* page 243? Recall that Costa challenged Italy's nationalization of certain electric utilities by contesting a roughly $3.00 electric bill before an Italian small claims court, and the Court of Justice accepted the referral. See also Firma Anton Dürbeck v. Hauptzollamt Frankfurt am Main–Flughafen, Case 112/80, [1981] ECR 1095, where the Court agreed to rule on the validity of Community quotas on apples in an obvious test case involving the importation from Chile of only two boxes of apples.

Actually *Foglia* is very much the exception that proves the rule that the Court of Justice almost invariably answers questions that are put to it under Article 234. It has been suggested that a factor contributing to the result in *Foglia* may have been the inadequate preparation of the record in the case. Even the rule stated in *Foglia*, which was heavily criticized at the time, is now very much in doubt. In Kommanditgesellschaft in Firma Eau de Cologne & Parfümerie–Fabrik Glockengasse No. 4711 v. Provide SRL, Case C–150/88, [1989] ECR 3891, Italy objected to a German court's referral of questions about the conformity of Italian legislation to Council directives on the labeling of cosmetic products. (The questions arose in a contract dispute over an Italian distributor's refusal to accept delivery from a German manufacturer of a product that did not meet the requirements of the Italian legislation.) Italy cited *Foglia* in its objection, but the Court of Justice gave a ruling on the merits anyway. The Court said that there is no problem in a court of one Member State examining the conformity to EC law of another State's legislation, provided the underlying dispute is genuine. To the same effect, see Walter Rau Lebensmittelwerke v. De Smedt PvbA, Case 261/81, [1982] ECR 3961, 3971. In Société d'Importation Edouard Leclerc–Siplec v. TFI Publicité SA, Case C–412/93, [1995] ECR I–179, *supra* page 363, note 6, the Court issued a ruling on the merits in a major free movement of goods case in a situation no less "put up" than Foglia, albeit a case where the national court, the parties and the national law in question were all French.

C. WHAT IS AN ARTICLE 234 "COURT OR TRIBUNAL"?

Only a "court or tribunal" of a Member State may make a preliminary reference to the Court of Justice under Article 234. Whether a referring body is a "court or tribunal" for these purposes is normally not an issue, but occasionally it is. Each Member State has not only a variety of courts, some of which (like certain commercial and labor courts) consist of both judges and lay persons, but also administrative and quasi-judicial tribunal whose members rarely are judges. Which of these bodies may refer questions to the Court?

The Court of Justice has given a generally expansive definition of "court or tribunal," with a view to enabling a broad range of official bodies to avail themselves of Article 234. It has not required that a court be composed entirely of judges, provided its members in fact adjudicate disputes. Even the latter condition is broadly construed. The Italian Pretore di Salò (see page 360 *supra*), who only conducted preliminary investigations before criminal trial, was allowed to make a reference. The Court of Justice considered the *pretore* to be a judge for these purposes because he was in the business of "judging, independently and in accordance with the law, cases coming within the jurisdiction conferred on [him] by law." [1987] ECR at 2567. On the other hand, an Italian public prosecutor (*Procura della Repubblica*) is not empowered to make preliminary references, since the role of that officer is "not to rule on an issue in complete independence but, acting as prosecutor in the proceedings, to submit that issue, if appropriate, for consideration by the competent judicial body." See Procura della Repubblica v. X, Joined Cases C–74 & 129/95, [1996] ECR I–6609.

It appears that the Court, in determining whether a national body is a court or tribunal for these purposes, considers both the body's status (is it a public authority or at least a delegee acting on behalf of a public authority?) and its functions (does it perform judicial or quasi-judicial tasks?) The Court has accordingly treated as "tribunals" a number of different tariff and customs, social security, immigration and tax appeal boards. On the other hand, administrative agencies performing ordinary executive functions do not qualify under Article 234 even though they obviously have occasion to apply Community law, possibly on a daily basis. Thus, in Corbiau v. Administration des Contributions, Case C–24/92, [1993] ECR I–1277, the Court held that the Director of Taxation of Luxembourg could not be considered a court or tribunal when conducting a proceeding to determine whether a taxpayer was entitled to obtain repayment of an over-withholding of income tax. The Court ruled that a court or tribunal for preliminary reference purposes must stand in a third party relationship with the body that took the decision being challenged. Since the Director headed the tax administration and was organizationally linked to the department that made the contested calculation, he did not meet that requirement.

More recently, the Court has identified the following as the catalogue of factors relevant to deciding the "court or tribunal" question: whether the referring body is established by law, whether it is permanent, whether its jurisdiction is compulsory, whether its procedures are *inter partes*, whether it applies rules of law, and whether it is independent of the administration. In recent judgments applying these criteria (some of them quite detailed on the issue), the Catalonian Regional Economic–Administrative Tribunal[7] and the German federal public procurement awards supervisory board[8] were found to meet the test. However, the Swedish Revenue Board (the Skatterattsnamnden) was not,[9] even though it was independent, had full-time judicially-trained presidents for each of its two divisions (for direct and indirect taxation), and had permanent members, and even though its rulings were binding on the State. Decisive was the fact that the board rendered initial decisions on the tax treatment of specific transactions, rather than review the legality of such decisions. In sum, the board made administrative decisions rather than adjudicate disputes. Were the stated criteria properly applied to this case?

The standing of self-governing professional bodies to refer questions under Article 234 has been particularly problematic. The Court has accepted referrals from bodies of that kind when they exercise quasi-judicial authority (as in professional licensing or discipline), but it has refused referrals arising out of those bodies' more purely administrative tasks. Broekmeulen v. Huisarts Registratie Commissie, Case 246/80, [1981] ECR 2311, is a leading case. There the Court faced a reference from the appeals committee of the Royal Netherlands Society for the Promotion of Medicine. The Society had the authority under Dutch law to certify licensed doctors for the treatment of patients covered by national health insurance. Evidently even doctors not serving national health insurance patients had difficulty obtaining professional insurance if not registered by the Society. The appeals committee, hearing an appeal from the Society's decision not to certify a licensed doctor, asked the Court of Justice certain questions about a Council directive on the mutual recognition of Member State diplomas.

The Court held that the appeals committee was an Article 234 court or tribunal. It was influenced by the fact that, practically-speaking, registration with the Society was "essential" to becoming established as a doctor in the Netherlands, that the appeals committee operated with the consent of the public authorities, that no case could be found in which an adverse decision by the committee had been challenged in the ordinary courts, and that the committee itself followed adversarial procedures in reaching decisions. The Court thought it "imperative" that it be in a position to guide such a body in its application of Community law. [1981] ECR at 2328.

More dubious is the status under Article 234 of arbitral bodies, often called tribunals. If such bodies are accessory to the state judicial system, as in compulsory commercial or labor arbitration, they may well qualify as courts or tribunals. The following case involves the more usual situation.

---

7. Gabalfrisa SL v. Agencia Estatal de Administracion Regional de Cataluna, Joined Cases C–110–147/98, [2000] ECR I–1577.

8. Dorsch Consult Ingenieurgesellschaft mbH v. Bundesbaugesellschaft Berlin mbH, Case C–54/96, [1997] ECR I–4961.

9. Victoria Film A/S v. Riksskatteverket, Case C–134/97, [1998] ECR I–7023.

NORDSEE DEUTSCHE HOCHSEEFISCHEREI GMBH v. REEDEREI MOND HOCHSEEFISCHEREI NORDSTERN AG

Case 102/81, [1982] ECR 1095.

[Three German shipping groups contracted for the joint construction of freezer ships and sought financial aid for the project from the EC's European Agricultural Guidance and Guarantee Fund (EAGGF). Learning that funds would be available for some but not all the ships they planned to build, the companies entered into a secret "pooling" agreement to share the available financial aid equally among themselves, in proportion to the number of ships each actually built and irrespective of which ships the EAGGF saw fit to fund. One of the groups (Nordsee) later sought payment under the pooling agreement from another of them (Nordstern) because it had built six ships while the other had only built three. Nordstern refused payment, alleging that the agreement was in violation of Community law. The Commission, viewing pooling contracts as a fraudulent diversion of EAGGF aid, had received advance assurances from all three groups that they had no intention of pooling any aid awarded to them.

The pooling agreement contained an arbitration clause excluding recourse to the ordinary courts, and an arbitrator (the president of the highest state court in the city and state of Bremen) eventually heard the case. The German Civil Procedure Code requires private arbitrators to apply German civil procedure, makes arbitral awards definitive and provides for judicial enforcement of awards, subject to certain challenges. The arbitrator decided that the validity of the agreement under German law depended on whether or not pooling was permissible under Community law, and he sought a preliminary ruling from the Court of Justice on that question.]

7   Since the arbitration tribunal ... was established pursuant to a contract between private individuals the question arises whether it may be considered as a court or tribunal of one of the Member States within the meaning of Article 177 [now 234].

* * *

10   It is true ... that there are certain similarities between the activities of the arbitration tribunal in question and those of an ordinary court or tribunal inasmuch as the arbitration is provided for within the framework of the law, the arbitrator must decide according to law and his award has, as between the parties, the force of *res judicata,* and may be enforceable if leave to issue execution is obtained. However, those characteristics are not sufficient to give the arbitrator the status of a "court or tribunal of a Member State"....

11   The first important point to note is that when the contract was entered into in 1973 the parties were free to leave their disputes to be resolved by the ordinary courts or to opt for arbitration by inserting a clause to that effect in the contract. From the facts of the case it appears that the parties were under no obligation, whether in law or in fact, to refer their disputes to arbitration.

¹² The second point to be noted is that the German public authorities are not involved in the decision to opt for arbitration, nor are they called upon to intervene automatically in the proceedings before the arbitrator. The Federal Republic of Germany, as a Member State of the Community responsible for the performance of obligations arising from Community law within its territory . . ., has not entrusted or left to private individuals the duty of ensuring that such obligations are complied with in the sphere in question in this case.

¹³ It follows from these considerations that the link between the arbitration procedure in this instance and the organization of legal remedies through the courts in the Member State in question is not sufficiently close for the arbitrator to be considered as a "court or tribunal of a Member State" . . . .

¹⁴ As the Court has confirmed in its [*Broekmeulen* judgment, *supra* page 367], Community law must be observed in its entirety throughout the territory of all the Member States. . . . [I]f questions of Community law are raised in an arbitration resorted to by agreement, the ordinary courts may be called upon to examine them either in the context of their collaboration with arbitration tribunals, in particular in order to assist them in certain procedural matters or to interpret the law [that is] applicable, or in the course of a review of an arbitration award . . . which they may be required to effect in case of an appeal or objection, in proceedings for leave to issue execution or by any other method of recourse available under the relevant national legislation.

¹⁵ It is for those national courts and tribunals to ascertain whether it is necessary for them to make a reference . . . in order to obtain the interpretation or assessment of the validity of provisions of Community law which they may need to apply when exercising such auxiliary or supervisory functions.

¹⁶ It follows that in this instance the Court has no jurisdiction to give a ruling.

Notes and Questions

1. The Commission in *Nordsee* argued that German procedural law sufficiently governed the arbitration to justify allowing a preliminary reference. The UK and Italy argued the contrary. What do you think? Would it have made any difference to the Court if the contract had stipulated that Community law as well as German law governed any dispute arising under it?

2. Why do you think the Court declined the opportunity to enlarge the circle of institutions authorized to seek rulings on Community law? Consider that private arbitrations are increasingly favored in Europe. The Commission has voiced particular concern that arbitrators deciding competition law claims (which they often do) may misconstrue EC competition law principles, and possibly disregard them entirely. Does this concern justify amending Article 234 to allow private arbitrators to refer questions to the Court of Justice?

3. What do you think of the Court's suggestion (¶ 14) that Community law issues can still be raised in national court proceedings ancillary to the arbitration? The Court has accepted preliminary references from national courts hearing an appeal against an arbitral award. In Gemeente Almelo v. Energiebedrijf Ijsselmij NV, Case C–393/92, [1994] ECR I–1477, the Court did so even though the

arbitration agreement provided for the arbitrator to decide the case not according to a national body of law, but rather according to what is "fair and reasonable."

4. In May 1994, Parliament adopted a resolution calling for greater use of arbitration—and for the enactment of a uniform set of arbitral procedures—for the resolution of disputes arising out of transactions within the Community, O.J. C 205/457 (July 25, 1994). Under Article 238 (ex 181) the Court can be given jurisdiction under an arbitration clause in a contract concluded by the Community. Does this suggest to you that Article 234 reference jurisdiction should be extended to arbitral bodies after all?

D. DISCRETIONARY AND MANDATORY REFERENCES

Article 234 draws a distinction between courts that may refer questions to the Court of Justice and courts that must do so. The basic notion is that the highest national courts are bound to make preliminary references whenever a preliminary ruling would be appropriate, but that lower courts should have discretion in the matter. If a lower court decides against seeking a preliminary ruling, it is still possible that an appellate may do so, if the case has been appealed and the Community law issue remains live. On the other hand, the lower court may seek a ruling straightaway if it so chooses.

Article 234 specifically defines the national courts for which preliminary references are mandatory as ones "against whose decisions there is no judicial remedy under national law." This formula is ambiguous. Under one interpretation, only courts that are hierarchically designated as of last resort, or supreme, must refer matters to the Court when the conditions for a reference are met; under the second, the last available court of appeal in any given case, irrespective of its general place in the judicial hierarchy, has that obligation.

Although the Court of Justice has ruled that the purpose behind making references mandatory is to prevent there from developing a body of national case law that is contrary to the principles of Community law (Morson and Jhanjan v. Netherlands, Cases 35, 36/82, [1982] ECR 3723, 3734), it has not had occasion to decide this precise question. In most Member States the question lacks practical importance. In systems where appeal to the highest national court is of right, the question simply does not arise. The question has, however, arisen in the UK. Under British procedure, leave of either the Court of Appeal or the House of Lords is required for appeal to the latter court. Suppose the Court of Appeal refuses to refer a question and at the same time denies leave to appeal its judgment in the case. Unless the House of Lords grants leave to appeal and then finds the conditions for a preliminary ruling to be met (as for example happened in Regina v. Henn and Darby, [1981] A.C. 850, [1980] 2 WLR 597, [1980] 2 All ER 166, [1980] 2 CMLR 229 (H.L., Jan. 29, 1979, Feb. 21 & March 27, 1980)), no English court will have been bound to refer. The Court of Appeal has ruled that it will only consider itself to be a court of last resort for Article 234 purposes when "there is no possibility of any further appeal from it." Regina v. Statutory Committee of the Pharmaceutical Society of Great Britain, [1987] 3 CMLR 951, 969, The Times (Sept. 15, 1987) (C.A., July 30, 1987). Might it be argued that the House of Lords is bound under Community law to grant leave to appeal (and eventually make a preliminary reference) whenever the Court of Appeal has neither granted leave to appeal nor agreed to make a preliminary reference on a pertinent question of Community law? See F. Jacobs, Which Courts and Tribunals Are Bound to Refer to the European Court?, 2 Eur. L. Rev. 119 (1977).

The Court has, however, answered the related question whether a preliminary reference is mandatory in an action in Member State court for provisional relief (such as a preliminary injunction) when the grant or denial of such relief is not subject to appeal. A reference might be thought to be mandatory because the question of provisional relief may not as such be appealed. However, the Court of Justice has ruled that, when the merits of the application for provisional relief are essentially the same as the merits of the main action for permanent relief, and when such a subsequent proceeding will be available, the court deciding on provisional relief is not a court of last resort within the meaning of Article 234, and is not bound to make a preliminary reference. Hoffmann–La Roche AG v. Centrafarm, Case 107/76, [1977] ECR 957.

E. WHEN SHOULD A COURT REFER A QUESTION?

Article 234 states that the test for deciding when a preliminary reference (discretionary or mandatory) is appropriate is whether a decision on the question is "necessary" to enable the national court to give judgment. While seemingly simple, this requirement has given rise to disparate Member State practices. In practice, some state courts—notably those of Belgium, Germany and the Netherlands—seem much more inclined than others to refer questions to the Court.

At a minimum, the Community law issue must be relevant to the disposition of the case at hand. Absent relevance, a decision on the issue can scarcely be said to be necessary. But how much more than bare relevance might have to be shown? The only Member State for which attempts have been made to set precise guidelines for deciding when a reference is "necessary" is the UK.

Much of the discussion in the UK was prompted by the celebrated opinion by Lord Denning, in the case of H.P. Bulmer Ltd. v. J. Bollinger S.A., [1974] 2 Ch. 401, [1974] 3 WLR 202, [1974] 2 All ER 1226, [1974] 2 CMLR 91 (Ct. of Appeal, civ. div., May 22, 1974). Bollinger and other French champagne producers sought in 1970 to enjoin Bulmer and others from marketing English cider under the names "champagne cider" and "champagne perry," claiming that "champagne" was a protected designation of origin. Upon UK accession to the Community in 1973, the French producers amended their complaint to include claims based on the protection of designations of origin under Community agricultural regulations. (The British companies meanwhile sought a declaratory judgment recognizing their right to continue using the term "champagne.") The French producers asked the trial court to refer to the Court of Justice not only the substantive question, but also the question whether such a question should even be referred. When the trial court refused to make a reference, the French producers appealed.

Before addressing the referral issue, Lord Denning made the often-quoted remark that "when we come to matters with a European element, the Treaty is like an incoming tide. It flows into the estuaries and up the rivers. It cannot be held back." Noting that under the European Communities Act of 1972, *supra* page 336, British courts must "without more ado" give Community law effect in the UK, Lord Denning conceded that the Court of Justice is the supreme authority on the meaning of that law. However, he proceeded to lay down guidelines for lower courts to follow in deciding whether to seek rulings from the Court:

The Discretion to Refer or Not to Refer

[S]hort of the House of Lords, no other English court is bound to refer a question to the European Court at Luxembourg. In England the trial judge has complete *discretion*. If a question arises on the interpretation of the Treaty, an English judge can decide it for himself. He need not refer it to the Court at Luxembourg unless he wishes. He can say: "It will be too costly", or "It will take too long to get an answer", or "I am well able to decide it myself." If he does decide it himself, the European Court cannot interfere. None of the parties can go off to the European Court and complain. The European Court would not listen to any party who went moaning to them. . . . If a party wishes to challenge the decision of the trial judge . . . to refer or not to refer, he must appeal to the Court of Appeal.

* * *

The judges of the Court of Appeal, in their turn, have complete discretion. They can interpret the Treaty themselves if they think fit. If the Court of Appeal do interpret it themselves, the European Court will not rebuke them for doing so. If a party wishes to challenge the decision of the Court of Appeal—to refer or not to refer—he must get leave to go to the House of Lords and go there. It is only in that august place that there is no discretion. If the point of interpretation is one [for] which [it] is "necessary" to give a ruling, the House *must* refer it to the European Court at Luxembourg.

* * *

The Condition Precedent to a Reference. It Must Be "Necessary."

* * *

An English court can only refer [a] matter to the European Court "*if it considers* that a decision on the question is necessary to enable it to give judgment". Note the words "if *it* considers". That is, "if the *English court* considers". On this point again the opinion of the English courts is final, just as it is on the matter of discretion. An English judge can say either "I consider it necessary", or "I do not consider it necessary". His discretion in that respect is final. . . . If the English judge considers it *necessary* to refer the matter, no one can gainsay it save the Court of Appeal. The European Court will accept his opinion. . . . If the English judge considers it "*not necessary*" to refer a question of interpretation to the European Court—but instead decides it himself—that is the end of the matter. It is no good a party going off to the European Court. They would not listen to him.

The Guide Lines

(1) Guide Lines as to Whether a Decision is Necessary

    (i) The Point Must Be Conclusive.

The English court has to consider whether "a decision of the question is *necessary* to enable it to give *judgment*" ... in the very case which is before the court. The judge must have got to the stage when he says to himself: "This clause of the Treaty is capable of two or more meanings. If it means *this,* I give judgment for the plaintiff. If it means *that,* I give judgment for the defendant". In short, the point must be ... conclusive of the case.

* * *

    (ii) Previous Ruling.

In some cases, however, it may be found that the same point—or substantially the same point—has already been decided by the European Court in a previous case. In that event it is not necessary for the English court to decide it. It can follow the previous decision without troubling the European Court. But, as I have said, the European Court is *not* bound by its previous decisions. So if the English court thinks that a previous decision of the European Court may have been wrong—or if there are new factors which ought to be brought to the notice of the European Court—the English court may consider it *necessary* to re-submit the point to the European Court.

* * *

    (iii) Acte Clair.

In other cases the English court may consider [that] the point is reasonably clear and free from doubt. In that event there is no need to interpret the Treaty but only to apply it: and that is the task of the English court.

    (iv) Decide the Facts First.

[T]he word ... "necessary" ... is much stronger than "desirable" or "convenient". There are some cases where the point, if decided one way, would shorten the trial greatly. But, if decided the other way, it would mean that the trial would have to go its full length. In such a case it might be "convenient" or "desirable" to take it as a preliminary point because it might save much time and expense. But it would not be "necessary" at that stage. When the facts were investigated, it might turn out to have been quite unnecessary. The case would be determined on another ground altogether. As a rule you cannot tell whether it is necessary to decide a point until all the facts are ascertained. So in general it is best to decide the facts first.

(2) Guide Lines as to the Exercise of Discretion

Assuming that the condition about "necessary" is fulfilled, there remains the matter of discretion. ... The national courts of the various member countries have had to consider how to exercise this discretion. The cases show that they have taken into account such matters as the following:

(i) The Time to Get a Ruling.

The length of time which may elapse before a ruling can be obtained from the European Court. This may take months and months. The lawyers have to prepare their briefs; the Advocate-General has to prepare his submissions; the case has to be argued; the Court has to give its decision. The average length of time at present seems to be between six and nine months. Meanwhile, the whole action in the English court is stayed until the ruling is obtained. This may be very unfortunate, especially in a case where an injunction is sought or there are other reasons for expedition.

* * *

(ii) Do Not Overload the Court.

The importance of not overwhelming the European Court by references to it. If it were overloaded, it could not get through its work.

* * *

(iii) Formulate the Question Clearly.

The need to formulate the question clearly. It must be a question of *interpretation only* of the Treaty. It must not be mixed up with the facts. It is the task of the national courts to find the facts and apply the Treaty. The European Court must not take that task on themselves. ... In any case, the task of interpretation is better done with the facts in mind rather than in ignorance of them.

(iv) Difficulty and importance.

The difficulty and importance of the point. Unless the point is really difficult and important, it would seem better for the English judge to decide it himself. For in so doing, much delay and expense will be saved. So far the English judges have not shirked their responsibilities. They have decided several points of interpretation on the Treaty to the satisfaction, I hope, of the parties. At any rate, there has been no appeal from them.

(v) Expense.

The expense to the parties of getting a ruling from the European Court. ... On a request for interpretation, the European Court ... only gives advice on the meaning of the Treaty. If either party wishes to get the costs of the reference, he must get it from the English court when it eventually decides the case.

(vi) Wishes of the Parties.

The wishes of the parties. If both parties want the point to be referred to the European Court, the English court should have regard to their wishes, but it should not give them undue weight. The English court should hesitate before making a reference against the wishes of one of the parties, seeing the expense and delay which it involves.

Applying his guidelines to the case before him, Lord Denning agreed with the trial court that referral of the question whether use of the word "Champagne" in connection with a beverage other than Champagne is a violation of Community law was not "necessary":

> ... If the French growers succeeded in [their] claim [under] English law for an injunction and damages, it would not be necessary to decide the point under the regulations. So the facts must be found before it can be said that a reference is "necessary".

> [As for] the claim of the French growers for a declaration that the use of the expression "Champagne cider" and "Champagne perry" was contrary to European Community law ... [i]t is always a matter for the discretion of the judge whether to grant a declaration or not. He could very properly say in the present case: Whatever the true interpretation of the regulations, it is not a case in which I would make any declaration on the point.

> Even if it could be said to be necessary to decide the point, I think that an English court ... should not, as matter of discretion, refer it to the European Court. It should decide the point itself. It would take much time and money to get a ruling from the European Court. Meanwhile, the whole action would be held up. It is, no doubt, an important point, but not a difficult one to decide. I think it would be better to deal with it as part of the whole case. . . .

Lord Denning turned finally to whether the question he had just answered should itself be referred to the Court of Justice, and decided that it should not: "It is not the province of the European Court to give any guidance or advice to the national court as to when it should, or should not, refer a question. That is a matter for the national court itself. It is no concern of the European Court."

An important development since 1974 when *Bulmer* was decided is a sharp increase in Community harmonization of national laws. (See Chapter 1E *supra.*) What bearing might this have on the utility of Lord Denning's guidelines? For a ruling in general keeping with Lord Denning's approach, see Regina v. Secretary of State for Social Services ex parte Wellcome Foundation Ltd., [1988] 1 WLR 635, [1988] 2 All ER 684, [1988] 3 CMLR 95 (H.L., May 19, 1988).

The acceptability of Lord Denning's guidelines to the Court of Justice is questionable. In Irish Creamery Milk Suppliers Association v. Ireland, Cases 36, 71/80, [1981] ECR 735, the Court conceded that national courts might find it convenient to establish both the facts and the applicable national law before referring a question to it, but it emphasized that the trial judge is in the best position to decide at what stage a preliminary ruling should be had.

Whatever the weight Lord Denning's guidelines in *Bulmer* might have carried at the time, they are no longer authoritative or reliable. To begin with, a judge on the High Court described them as "no more than a general rule, to which exceptions might have to be made." Regina v. Minister for Agriculture, Fisheries and Food ex parte Fédération Européenne de la Santé Animale (FEDESA), [1988] 3 CMLR 661, 683 (Q.B., Sept. 20, 1988) (per Henry, J.). In fact they have not been regularly followed. See, for example, Regina v. Inland

Revenue Commissioners ex parte Commerzbank AG, [1991] T.C. Leaflet No. 3270, [1991] 3 CMLR 633, 645–46 (High Court, April 12, 1991) (per Nolan, L.J.). Even when they are applied, the *Bulmer* guidelines do not invariably lead to refusals to refer. See, e.g., Commissioners of Customs and Excise v. Samex ApS, [1983] 1 All ER 1042, [1983] 3 CMLR 194 (High Court, Dec. 14, 1982), especially the opinion of Judge Bingham, pointing out the many advantages of preliminary rulings.

A good illustration of the differences of view even on the Court of Appeal is Polydor Ltd. v. Harlequin Record Shops Ltd., [1980] FSR 362, [1980] 2 CMLR 413, 426 (May 15, 1980), in which the Court (per Templeman, L.J.), in full knowledge of the *Bulmer* guidelines, referred a question to the Court of Justice at an interlocutory stage of a case and well before the facts had been found. Concurring in the result, Ormond, L.J. pointedly interpreted the term "necessary" in Article 234 to mean "reasonably necessary" rather than "unavoidable," remarking that "[i]f ever a situation called for the decision at the earliest possible moment [by] the one Court that is in a position to finally decide it, it is this case." [1980] 2 CMLR at 428.

The Court of Appeal eventually took a fresh look at the *Bulmer v. Bollinger* guidelines in the case of Regina v. International Stock Exchange of the United Kingdom and the Republic of Ireland, ex parte Else, [1993] 1 All ER 420, [1993] 2 CMLR 677 (Oct. 16, 1992). There, three shareholders of a company sought judicial review of the Stock Exchange's decision to cancel the company's listing. The relevant directive (Council Directive 79/279, art. 15(1)) was unclear as to whether the shareholders had standing for these purposes. When the High Court referred the question to the Court of Justice, the Stock Exchange appealed. The Court of Appeal overturned the decision to make the reference. Speaking through Bingham, M.R., the Court stated that, once the facts have been clarified, the decision to refer or not should depend on whether the Community law provision in question is critical to the outcome of the case and whether the national court can resolve the question of its interpretation with complete confidence. If the answer to the first question is yes, and the answer to the second question is no, then, according to Bingham, M.R., the national court should "ordinarily" make the reference. In other words, while discretion still plays a role, references are under those circumstance to be preferred. According to a leading comment on the case, "the discretion is subject to a presumption in favour of referral at the outset. The court will be under an obligation to refer unless there are some exceptional circumstances sufficient for it to decide otherwise." D. Walsh, The Appeal of an Article 177 EEC Referral, 56 Mod. L. Rev. 881 (1993).

The *International Stock Exchange* guidelines were cited and followed by the High Court in Regina v. Secretary of State for the National Heritage, ex parte Continental Television BV, [1993] 2 CMLR 333 (Apr. 30, 1993). The case arose out of an order prohibiting the transmission to the UK by a Dutch television company of pornographic programs from the Netherlands and Denmark. The television company challenged the order as in violation of Council Directive 89/552 (see Selected Documents). The High Court entertained doubts about the interpretation of the directive in two respects and issued preliminary references accordingly. First, it wondered whether the transmissions in question might constitute a "re-transmission," which Member States were permitted under the directive to block. Second, it questioned the proper interpretation of the article of the directive requiring Member States to ensure that television broadcasts do not include programs that could seriously impair the physical, mental or moral development of minors; more specifically, it sought to know whether the company's timing of the broadcasts (midnight to 4 A.M.), and the fact that the broadcasts could not be received by a subscriber without having a special decoder, satisfied this requirement. (In the end, the national court's questions were never answered because the references were withdrawn.) An official "Practice Direction on References to the European Court of Justice by the Court of Appeal and the High Court" issued in 2000 does not echo any of the *Bulmer* restrictions.

Note Lord Denning's reference in *Bulmer* to the notion of *acte clair*. The *acte clair* doctrine, derived from French law, holds in this context that a national court need not refer a Community law question to the Court of Justice if the answer to that question is clear. The doctrine, which courts sometimes invoke to avoid otherwise proper references, makes considerable sense, but also is subject to abuse, particularly by courts of last resort. It was inevitable that the Court of Justice would eventually address the limits on national court use of the *acte clair* doctrine.

SRL CILFIT v. MINISTRY OF HEALTH (I)
Case 283/81, [1982] ECR 3415.

[Several Italian textile firms claimed that an Italian health inspection levy on the import of wool violated a 1968 Community agricultural regulation. The firms lost in the lower courts, which felt that the levy so clearly conformed to Community rules that a preliminary reference was unnecessary. On appeal to the Italian Supreme Court (Corte di Cassazione), the firms argued that the absence of any further judicial remedy under national law rendered a preliminary reference obligatory. The Supreme Court evidently doubted this, since, rather than make a reference on the merits, it made one on the question of its duty to make references at all when Community law seems to be clear beyond "a reasonable interpretative doubt."]

13   [T]he Court ruled [in Da Costa v. Nederlandse Belastingadministratie, Cases 28–30/62, [1963] ECR 31] that: "Although the third paragraph of Article 177 unreservedly requires courts or tribunals of a Member State against whose decisions there is no judicial remedy under national law ... to refer to the Court every question of interpretation raised before them, the authority of an interpretation under Article 177 already given by the Court may deprive the obligation of its purpose and thus empty it of its substance. Such is the case especially when the question raised is materially identical with a question which has already been the subject of a preliminary ruling in a similar case."

14   The same effect ... may be produced where previous decisions of the Court have already dealt with the point of law in question, irrespective of the nature of the proceedings which led to those decisions, even though the questions at issue are not strictly identical.

15   However, it must not be forgotten that in all such circumstances national courts and tribunals remain entirely at liberty to bring a matter before the Court of Justice if they consider it appropriate to do so.

[16]   Finally, the correct application of Community law may be so obvious as to leave no scope for any reasonable doubt as to the manner in which the question raised is to be resolved. Before it comes to the conclusion that such is the case, the national court or tribunal must be convinced that the matter is equally obvious to the courts of the other Member States and to the Court of Justice. Only if those conditions are satisfied may the national court or tribunal refrain from submitting the question to the Court of Justice and take upon itself the responsibility for resolving it.

[17]   However, the existence of such a possibility must be assessed on the basis of the characteristic features of Community law and the particular difficulties to which its interpretation gives rise.

[18]   To begin with, it must be borne in mind that Community legislation is drafted in several languages and that the different language versions are all equally authentic. An interpretation of a provision of Community law thus involves a comparison of the different language versions.

[19]   It must also be borne in mind, even where the different language versions are entirely in accord with one another, that Community law uses terminology which is peculiar to it. Furthermore, it must be emphasized that legal concepts do not necessarily have the same meaning in Community law and in the law of the various Member States.

[20]   Finally, every provision of Community law must be placed in its context and interpreted in the light of the provisions of Community law as a whole, regard being had to the objectives thereof and to its state of evolution at the date on which the provision in question is to be applied.

Notes and Questions

1.   As *CILFIT* makes plain in ¶ 13, as early as 1963 (in the *Da Costa* case cited there), the Court held that national courts prepared to follow Court of Justice precedents are free to avoid a reference on the same issue. (The Court of Justice precedent in *Da Costa* was in fact the *van Gend en Loos* decision, *supra* page 239). However, a number of national courts, including the French Conseil d'Etat (as illustrated in the *Cohn–Bendit* case, *supra* page 289) have considered themselves free not to make a referral whenever *they* feel that Community law is clear. Sometimes they then proceed to misconstrue or misapply Community law. Advocate–General Capotorti in his opinion in *CILFIT* sharply criticized this practice and urged that the Italian Supreme Court be told to refer otherwise necessary questions except when a *Court of Justice* precedent makes a reference unnecessary. Did the Court of Justice follow his view? If not, should it have?

2.   The Court's approval of the *acte clair* doctrine in *CILFIT* is obviously highly conditional. Look especially at paragraphs 16–20. Do the conditions imposed adequately address the risks that the doctrine poses? For the view that the Court actually went too far in constraining Member State courts in their use of *acte clair*, see H. Rasmussen, The European Court's Acte Clair Strategy in CILFIT, 9 Eur. L. Rev. 242 (1984).

3.   After *CILFIT*, the Supreme Court of Italy decided to refer its questions about the 1968 regulation to the Court of Justice for a ruling on the merits. See Srl CILFIT v. Ministry of Health (II), Case 77/83, [1984] ECR 1257, where the Court issued a long ruling on the merits. What does that tell you about the risks of the *acte clair* doctrine?

4. In 1987, Lord Justice Kerr of the English Court of Appeal remarked as follows:

> [The *CILFIT* case] makes it clear that the principle of "acte clair" is ... applicable ... where there can be no doubt about the correct answer. However ... our courts should hesitate long before reaching such a conclusion....

* * *

> [I]n Polydor Ltd. v. Harlequin Record Shops Ltd. [cited *supra* page 376], Ormrod and Templeman L.JJ. expressed strong views in this Court about the apparently clearly correct answer to a question of Community law which had been raised before them. But they nevertheless referred the case to the Court of Justice, and we were told that the ultimate decision was in fact the other way.

Regina v. Statutory Committee of the Pharmaceutical Society of Great Britain, [1987] 3 CMLR 951, 969, 971, The Times (Sept. 15, 1987) (C.A., July 30, 1987). Lord Justice Kerr concluded that the answer to the question before him "is miles away from being '*acte clair*.'" "On the view which I take," he continued, "I would respectfully expect the House of Lords to feel bound to make a reference ... in any event. On that basis an immediate reference by this Court will obviously save considerable time and costs." [1987] 3 CMLR at 969–70, 972.

5. The German Constitutional Court (in some cases sitting as a chamber, or panel, of three judges) has placed its own limits on the *acte clair* doctrine. In Re Value Added Tax Exemption, Case 2 BvR 876/85, [1988] NJW 2173, [1989] 1 CMLR 113 (second senate, first chamber, Nov. 4, 1987), it held that the Supreme Tax Court's intentional departure from Court of Justice case law and its use of the *acte clair* doctrine to avoid a reference to the Court was a violation of its duty to follow Community law where applicable. (Recall too the Constitutional Court's then recent *Kloppenburg* ruling, *supra* page 304.) In the case of Re Patented Feedingstuffs, Case 2 BvR 808/82, [1988] NJW 1456, [1989] 2 CMLR 902 (second senate, first chamber, Nov. 9, 1987), the Constitutional Court went further, squarely holding it to be a violation of due process under the German Constitution for a court of last resort to "give no consideration at all" to referring a question that the court itself considers relevant to the case at hand and on which it "entertains doubts as to the correct answer." The Constitutional Court stated in *Feedingstuffs* that a court of last resort acts unconstitutionally when, in a case where Court of Justice precedent is not decisive or lends itself to different future developments, it refuses to make a reference, if in so doing it "exceed[s] to an indefensible extent the scope ... of discretion which it must necessarily have in such cases." [1989] 2 CMLR at 909.

Certain civil law systems recognize the right of lower courts to "resist" a ruling of a higher court, not only in analogous cases but possibly even in the case that generated the ruling. Such resistance may be viewed as a form of judicial dissent that might cause the higher court to reconsider and modify its views. Is there any room under Community law for national courts to adopt a similar attitude of "resistance" to preliminary rulings of the Court of Justice?

6. Suppose after *CILFIT* a national court declines to refer a question on *acte clair* grounds and proceeds to misconstrue Community law in the case before it. Judge Pescatore considers that this may sometimes be "merely a cloak for the resistance of certain highly placed courts to the authority of Community law, or for their desire not to give the Court an opportunity to clarify certain problems."

P. Pescatore, References for Preliminary Rulings under Article 177 (EC Off'l Pub. Office, 1986) at 28, citing *Cohn–Bendit* (*supra* page 289) and the ruling of the Supreme German Tax Court in *Kloppenburg* (*supra* page 304). What should be done in such cases?

To a 1983 parliamentary question on the Commission's readiness to bring Article 226 (ex 169) enforcement proceedings against a Member State for its courts' abuse of the *acte clair* doctrine, the Commission replied:

> [T]he Commission does not in principle exclude the possibility of initiating an infringement procedure where a national court has ignored the scope and conditions of Article 177 [now 234].... However ... this procedure does not provide the most effective basis for cooperation between national courts and the European Court of Justice.
>
> ... Article 169 [now 226] of the EEC [now EC] Treaty was not conceived as a means of reviewing judgments of national supreme courts. For this reason ... infringement proceedings in respect of such judgments can only be considered when a judgment by a court of last instance shows clearly that the court is systematically and deliberately unprepared to comply with Article 177.

Answer to Written Question 526/83 by Mr. Alan Tyrell, O.J. C 268/25 (Oct. 6, 1983).

F.   THE APPEALABILITY OF PRELIMINARY REFERENCES AND REFUSALS TO REFER

It may be unrealistic to assume that the national litigation from which a preliminary reference arises will be "frozen" until the Court's ruling is received, and only resume thereafter. After all, a trial court's decision to refer may be subject to interlocutory appeal. (The successful appeal to the Conseil d'Etat in *Cohn–Bendit*, *supra* page 289, from the lower court's decision to refer illustrates this possibility.) A trial court's decision *not* to refer likewise may be appealed (as occurred in *Bulmer v. Bollinger, supra* page 371). These scenarios raise questions about the legal status and effect of a national court's decision to issue, or not issue, a preliminary reference.

The first question is whether and to what extent a decision to refer a question to the Court of Justice may be appealed. In Rheinmühlen–Düsseldorf v. Einfuhr- und Vorratsstelle für Getreide und Futtermittel, Cases 146, 166/73, [1974] ECR 33, 139, Advocate–General Warner argued that allowing an order for a preliminary reference to be appealed would violate the treaty, which grants lower courts complete discretion to seek a preliminary ruling when they find that it is necessary and appropriate to do so. [1974] ECR at 43, 47. The Court, however, disagreed, holding that an order for a preliminary reference is subject to appeal to the same extent as similar interlocutory orders under national law. The Court of Justice has not as yet decided whether Community law places any limits on a national court's right to set aside a lower court's decision to refer.

What effect should the pendency of an appeal have on the Court of Justice's jurisdiction to render a preliminary ruling? The appellant's hope in *Rheinmühlen, supra*, doubtless was that the Court would refrain from issuing a ruling until the appeal was decided. However, the Court held in that case that the lodging of an appeal does not deprive it of jurisdiction to decide the question referred or otherwise require it to suspend proceedings. As early as 1962, in de Geus v. Robert Bosch GmbH, Case 13/61, [1962] ECR 45, the Court recognized that the importance of a ruling by the Court might transcend the specific national litigation out of which the issue arose. An important exception is when an appeal from an order of reference has the effect *under national law* of suspending the effectiveness of the order. SA Chanel v. Cepeha Handelsmaatschappij NV, Case 31/68, [1970] ECR 404. At the same time, the Court of Justice has asserted the right in its discretion to suspend proceedings pending the national appeal. If the prospect that the referral order will be reversed is sufficiently promising, or if a decision on the question is otherwise best postponed, the Court may well exercise its discretion not to proceed.

The net effect is that the national appeal of a preliminary reference order and the Court of Justice's own preliminary reference proceedings may go on simultaneously. Though this may seem to be wasteful of resources, it does protect the autonomy of both the national and Community judicial systems. What should the Court of Justice do in the rare event that a preliminary reference order is reversed on appeal? In the *Rheinmühlen* case, the Court held that in those circumstances it will proceed no further and will refrain from issuing a ruling even if otherwise prepared to issue one. [1974] ECR at 47. See also Amministrazione delle Finanze dello Stato v. Simmenthal SpA (II), Case 106/77, [1978] ECR 629, *supra* page 272. In other words, the existence of a valid preliminary reference order is a continuing condition of the Court's Article 234 jurisdiction.

Now suppose the national court refuses to refer a question to the Court of Justice and that decision is appealed. This scenario is a simpler one. The availability of an appeal and the standard of appellate review are once again presumably matters of national law. Whether Community law itself requires that Member States provide some sort of appellate remedy from a lower court's refusal to refer has never had to be decided. As for the Court of Justice's own freedom of action, the situation is clear: the Court cannot exercise jurisdiction under Article 234 unless and until it has received a valid preliminary reference from a national court.

Notes and Questions

1. Based on an independent interpretation of Article 234, which it considers to be part of Irish law, the Irish Supreme Court has ruled that reference orders by the Irish courts are not subject to appeal. Campus Oil v. Minister for Industry and Energy, [1983] IR 82, [1984] 1 CMLR 479 (June 17, 1983). The Supreme Court thus sided with the Advocate–General's opinion in *Rheinmühlen* rather than with the Court of Justice. Is the Irish Supreme Court free to disagree with the Court of Justice on the appealability in national court of preliminary reference orders? See D. O'Keefe, Appeals against an Order to Refer under Article 177 of the EEC Treaty, 9 Eur. L. Rev. 87 (1984).

2. UK law tries to forestall unnecessary preliminary rulings by postponing the transmission of a preliminary reference to the Court of Justice until the time limit for appeal has expired or, if an appeal is filed within that period, until after the appeal has been decided. R.S.C. Ord. 114, r. 5. Is this legitimate under Community law principles?

NOTE ON NATIONAL PROVISIONAL RELIEF
PENDING A PRELIMINARY RULING

Appeals are not the only national court prospect following a reference to the Court of Justice. The referring court may well consider it appropriate to award some from of interim relief pending receipt of the ruling from Luxembourg. (This is what the Irish Supreme Court chose to do in the *Grogan* case, *supra* page 333.) One circumstance in which interim relief may suggest itself is where a court suspects that a litigant has raised a Community law issue solely for delay or tactical advantage. See Portsmouth City Council v. Richards and Quietlynn Ltd., [1989] 1 CMLR 673 (C.A., Nov. 16, 1988).

The availability of provisional relief is presumptively a matter of domestic procedural law. However, we have already seen in the *Factortame* case, *supra* page 274, that the Court of Justice may regard a form of provisional relief as indispensable, at least in some circumstances, where the litigant is challenging a national measure as violative of EC law.

Consider a different preliminary reference scenario, one in which the referring court questions the validity of secondary EC legislation, rather than a national law measure, under the Treaty or some other superior principle of Community law, such as fundamental rights. We know from the *Foto-Frost* case, *supra* page 276, that a national court may not treat the EC measure as invalid, but must put the question to the Court of Justice. Thus has arisen the question whether, pending the Court's ruling, the national court may issue interim relief, for example, provisionally suspending enforcement of the national implementing measure.

Only recently have the Court's views on this emerged. Rather than categorically preclude provisional relief in these circumstances, the Court has offered up a more nuanced solution. Its first expression of views came in Zuckerfabrik Süderdithmarschen AG v. Hauptzollamt Itzehoe, Cases C–143/88 & C–92/89, [1991] ECR I–415. There the Court laid down a first requirement: an injunction is only proper if issued in connection with a "challenge that is based on *Community* law itself" (emphasis added). Does this mean that national courts may never enjoin the enforcement of a national measure implementing Community law on the ground that it violates *Member State* law? If so, is that a sound rule? Suppose a State, in implementing a Community directive, adopts a statute or rule in a manner contrary to basic national law principles, substantive or procedural, when the directive itself does not require implementation in that fashion?

The Court in *Süderdithmarschen* did not give national courts *carte blanche* to suspend the enforcement of national law implementing a Community measure. An interim injunction may be issued only if (a) the measure's validity is seriously in doubt, (b) there is urgent need for relief to prevent serious and irreparable harm (which, according to the Court, is unlikely when the alleged harm is purely economic), and (c) the national judge immediately refers the question of the measure's validity to the Court of Justice if that has not already been done. Finally, the Court admonished national courts to take fully into account the Community's interest in not having a measure lightly set aside pending a ruling on its validity. According to the Court, this not only means that national courts should consider whether the Community measure will lose all value if not given immediate effect, but also that they should where appropriate require the applicant for relief to post security in the event suspension of the measure subjects the Community to financial loss.

The Court revisited this range of questions in Atlanta Fruchthandelsgesellschaft mbH v. Bundesamt für Ernährung und Forstwirtschaft, Cases C–465 & 466/93, [1995] ECR I–3761. Atlanta was one in a succession of "bananas" cases on the legality of the EC's banana market regulation. (See page 318 *supra*.) Dissatisfied with the quotas that the German authorities (the "Bundesamt") had allocated to them for the import of bananas from third countries, the Atlanta group of German companies lodged an administrative complaint and eventually a lawsuit in a Frankfurt administrative court (the *Verwaltungsgericht*).

When the *Verwaltungsgericht*, sharing the Atlanta companies' doubts about the regulation, made a preliminary reference to the Court of Justice on this question, the Atlanta companies asked the national court also for an interim order requiring the Bundesamt to grant them additional import licenses. At this point, the *Verwaltungsgericht* asked the Court of Justice about the propriety of ordering interim relief. The Court replied:

41　[T]he damage relied on by the applicant must be such as to materialize before the Court of Justice has been able to rule on the validity of the contested Community act. As to the nature of the damage, purely financial damage cannot ... be regarded in principle as irreparable. However, it is for the national court hearing the application for interim relief to examine the circumstances particular to the case before it. ...

42　Furthermore, a national court ... is under an obligation to ensure that full effect is given to Community law and, consequently, where there is doubt as to the validity of Community regulations, to take account of the interest of the Community, namely that such regulations should not be set aside without proper guarantees.

43　In order to comply with that obligation, the national court to which an application for interim relief has been made must first examine whether the Community act in question would be deprived of all effectiveness if not immediately implemented.

44　In that respect the national court must take account of the damage which the interim measure may cause the legal regime established by that regulation for the Community as a whole. It must consider, on the one hand, the cumulative effect which would arise if a large number of courts were also to adopt interim measures for similar reasons and, on the other, those special features of the applicant's situation which distinguish him from the other operators concerned.

45　If the grant of interim relief represents a financial risk for the Community, the national court must also be in a position to require the applicant to provide adequate guarantees, such as the deposit of money or other security.

* * *

48　The national court, when called upon to protect the rights of individuals, may ... assess the extent to which refusal to order an interim measure may be liable to have a serious and irreparable effect on important individual interests.

49　However, if an applicant is unable to show a specific situation which distinguishes him from other operators in the relevant sector, the national court must accept any findings already made by the Court of Justice concerning the serious and irreparable nature of the damage.

Has the Court found the right balance among the competing interests?

In another twist, a different banana importer (T. Port) was unable to get provisional relief in the form of enlarged import quotas, pending a ruling by the Court of Justice on the availability of a "hardship" exception. Interpreting the regulation as permitting, and indeed requiring, the Commission to adopt hardship rules, the Court required T. Port (or Germany) to petition the Commission for relief, and, if need be, bring an action in the Community courts for the Commission's failure to act under Article 232 (ex 175). An award of interim relief directly by a national court would be off-limits. T. Port Gmbh & Co. KG v. Bundesanstalt fur Landwirtschaft und Ernährung, Case C–68/95, [1996] ECR I–6065. For more on the T. Port litigation, see pages 319–21 *supra*.

Chapter 10

NATIONAL REMEDIES FOR THE ENFORCEMENT OF COMMUNITY LAW CLAIMS

Any overview of Community law enforcement must forcefully convey the point that responsibility for this function is shared, though by no means equally, between Community and Member State institutions.

Before turning in this chapter to the enforcement role of Member States, we need to recognize the range and importance of the Commission's functions as Community law enforcer. Among the most prominent aspects of Commission law enforcement activity is the investigation and eventual "prosecution" Member State violations of their various Community law obligations under EC Treaty Article 226 (ex 169) and related articles. In the US, the federal government also undertakes some "policing" of state and local government action, as in the civil rights or environmental protection areas, but the Commission's enforcement role is far more general and pervasive. Chapter 11 *infra* is devoted to this kind of enforcement.

The Commission also enforces Community law in the sense of implementing Community policy, often enough on a daily basis. Competition law is a prime example. The Commission investigates allegedly anti-competitive behavior, decides whether or not to prosecute competition law violations and, eventually, whether to impose sanctions (and if so at what level). It also grants or denies exemptions. Implementation of Community competition law under Articles 81 and 82 (ex 85 and 86), as well as secondary legislation in that field, probably engages the Commission in its fullest range of administrative conduct, beginning as early as the gathering of information on possible breaches of competition policy. The procedural rules governing Commission activity in this area—as well as the review of state aids under Article 88 (ex 93) of the EC Treaty—are discussed in Part IV of this book.

The Commission has still more general administrative powers. EC Treaty Article 211 (ex 155) provides that the Commission, besides exercising authority delegated by the Council, enjoys "its own power of decision," that is, the power to take action of one kind or another specifically contemplated by the Treaty. For example, EC Treaty Article 86 (ex 90) empowers it to address directives or decisions to the Member States on the application of competition rules to "public undertakings and undertakings to which Member States grant special or exclusive rights." The Commission also has the specific power to approve or disapprove the use that Member States make of the "safeguard clauses" that are found in certain Treaty articles and that permit them to avoid a specific obligation when highly exceptional circumstances spelled out in those articles are present. An example is Article 95 (ex 100a). The Commission's task in such cases is to determine whether a Member State's reliance on a safeguard clause is justified.

More significant than the Commission's relatively few Treaty-based powers of decision are the extensive decisional powers delegated to it by the Council (or the Council and Parliament) through secondary legislation. The Common Agricultural Policy (CAP) is an arena in which the Commission regularly makes important decisions by delegation. Agricultural regulations not only confer certain normative powers on the Commission, but specifically empower it to allow particular enterprises or Member States dispensation from the usual rules, provided a serious market disturbance or other threat to the CAP objectives has arisen.

There is in fact virtually no sphere of Community law in which the Commission does not exercise at least some type and measure of administrative function. The many decisions that the Treaty and secondary legislation call upon the Commission to make closely resemble action taken daily by US administrative agencies under the procedures of administrative law. Precisely because this kind of decisionmaking is best appreciated in context, it is taken up as appropriate in the various substantive law chapters that follow in this book.

The fact remains that the vast bulk of day-to-day enforcement of EC law and policy rests in the hands of Member State officials. Community rules on agriculture, customs, tariffs, tax, and cross-border inspections and formalities, for example, are virtually all entrusted to the same national bureaucracies that otherwise execute these bodies of law. This may seem obvious enough on core common market matters. But it is equally so in the many regulatory spheres, such as industrial standards, the environment, pharmaceutical licensing and occupational health, which have been harmonized by Community legislation. Where Community law takes the form of directives, the law that Member State officials administer, though shaped by Community standards, remains in all respects national law. In fact, those officials may not always realize that in administering *national law* they are actually implementing *Community policy*.

Primary enforcement of Community policy in the Member States takes place not only in national administrative agencies, but in some cases also directly in national courts. This will of course normally be the case for problems over which a Member State's courts, rather than its agencies, have primary enforcement responsibility. A good example is products liability. In 1985, a Council directive harmonized Member State law on products liability (see Chapter 35). Each Member State was then to adopt products liability legislation conforming to that directive, either through amendment of its Civil Code (if it had one) or through special enactment. Products liability actions are thus still brought directly through private litigation in Member State courts, but effectively governed by Community law principles. In this way, national judges too can be primary Community law enforcers.

To the extent that Community policy is carried out through national decisionmakers using domestic law means, its administration naturally takes on the institutional and procedural coloration of the various Member States. Each of the fifteen has its distinctive administrative institutions, as well as its characteristic processes for functions as diverse as inspection, licensing and taxation, not to mention adjudication. This book cannot, of course, enter into the details of national administrative law and procedure.

The essential point is that the Community has a significant interest in the adequacy of Member State enforcement, both administrative and judicial. Questions of procedural adequacy surfaced earlier in Chapter 7 in connection with certain implications of the direct effect and supremacy doctrines. However, these questions have gained attention in their own right and they are taken up more systematically in the present chapter. Following that discussion (Part A), we turn to the question of the Member States' liability for their Community law failures, remedial or otherwise (Part B).

A. THE ADEQUACY OF NATIONAL REMEDIES

If private parties are to enforce their Community law rights directly in Member States courts, then those courts must have and make available the appropriate remedies. For national judges this means, first of all, identifying the domestic forms of relief that are suitable for the claims brought under the Community law banner. Second, it raises the question whether national remedies ever need to be adapted to suit the requirements of Community law, and what is to be done in the event the available remedies cannot be so adapted. Obviously, the Community itself (particularly the Court of Justice) has a definite stake in ensuring the availability and adequacy of Member State remedies for enforcing Community law claims.

This issue plainly raises lots of opportunities for dialogue between the national courts and the Court of Justice.

REWE–ZENTRALFINANZ EG v. LANDWIRTSCHAFTS-KAMMER FÜR DAS SAARLAND
Case 33/76, [1976] ECR 1989.

[In 1968, two German companies paid charges for the phyto-sanitary inspection of apples imported from France. Some years later, in a 1973 judgment (Rewe–Zentralfinanz eGmbH v. Direktor der Landwirtschaftskammer Westfalen–Lippe, Case 39/73, [1973] ECR 1039), the Court of Justice held such charges to be illegal under EC law. When the companies sought a refund with interest from the German authorities, they discovered that under German procedure their claim was time-barred. The case worked its way up to Germany's highest administrative court, which made a preliminary reference to the Court of Justice.]

[5]   The prohibitions laid down in [the Treaty and the regulation] have a direct effect and confer on citizens rights which the national courts are required to protect.

Applying the principle of cooperation laid down in Article 5 [now 10] of the Treaty, it is the national courts which are entrusted with ensuring the legal protection which citizens derive from the direct effect of the provisions of Community law.

Accordingly, in the absence of Community rules on this subject, it is for the domestic legal system of each Member State to designate the courts having jurisdiction and to determine the procedural conditions governing actions at law intended to ensure the protection of the rights which citizens have from the direct effect of Community law, it being understood that such conditions cannot be less favourable than those relating to similar actions of a domestic nature.

Where necessary, Articles 100 to 102 [now 94 to 97] and 235 [now 308] of the Treaty enable appropriate measures to be taken to remedy differences between the provisions laid down by law, regulation or administrative action in Member States if they are likely to distort or harm the functioning of the Common Market.

In the absence of such measures of harmonization the right conferred by Community law must be exercised before the national courts in accordance with the conditions laid down by national rules.

The position would be different only if the conditions and time-limits made it impossible in practice to exercise the rights which the national courts are obliged to protect.

This is not the case where reasonable periods of limitation of actions are fixed.

The laying down of such time-limits with regard to actions of a fiscal nature is an application of the fundamental principle of legal certainty protecting both the taxpayer and the administration concerned.

6   The answer to be given to the first question is therefore that in the present state of Community law, there is nothing to prevent a citizen who contests before a national court a decision of a national authority on the ground that it is incompatible with Community law from being confronted with the defence that limitation periods laid down by national law have expired, it being understood that the procedural conditions governing the action may not be less favourable than those relating to similar actions of a domestic nature.

Notes and Questions

1.   Do you consider the Court's approach in *Rewe-Zentralfinanz* to be sound and adequate?

Not surprisingly, the Court has also held that the Member States are free to decide which court has jurisdiction to hear disputes involving individual rights derived from Community law, provided they ensure that those rights are in any event effectively protected. Bozzetti v. Invernizzi SpA and Ministero del Tesoro, Case 179/84, [1985] ECR 2301.

2.   With respect to the precise problem in *Rewe-Zentralfinanz*—national statutes of limitations—the "national treatment" (or "equivalence" or "non-discrimination") branch of the inquiry is rarely problematic. (For one case in which it arose, see Edilizia Industriale Siderurgica Srl v. Ministero delle Finanze, Case C–231/96, [1998] ECR I–4951.) But when is a limitations period so short as to make it impossible or excessively difficult to assert Community law rights?

And how about the tolling of statutes of limitations? In Fantask A/S v. Industriministeriet, Case C–188/95, [1997] ECR I–6783, the Court ruled, in a case in which a Danish taxpayer sought recovery of charges imposed as a result of the improper implementation of a Community law directive, that national courts may not "dismiss claims for the recovery of charges levied over a long period in breach of Community law without either the authorities of that State or the persons liable to pay the charges having been aware that they were unlawful." Doing so "would make it excessively difficult to obtain recovery of charges which are contrary to Community law [and] would, moreover, have the effect of encouraging infringements of Community law which have been committed over a long period." (However, the Court found the Danish five-year limitations period reasonable as such. It also ruled that the fact that Denmark had not properly implemented the relevant directive did not bar Denmark from invoking the time bar against the claimant.)

2. Hans Just, a Danish importer of spirits, sued in national court to recover the amount by which the Danish levy on imports exceeded the levy on domestic products, in violation of EC Article 90 (ex 95). The authorities invoked a Danish rule, inspired by the principle of unjust enrichment, that sums unlawfully levied may not be recovered if they can be presumed to have been passed along to the consumer. May the national court apply such a principle in this case? Hans Just v. Danish Ministry for Fiscal Affairs, Case 68/79, [1980] ECR 501. In the case of Amministrazione delle Finanze dello Stato v. SpA San Giorgio, Case 199/82, [1983] ECR 3595, the question was whether a Member State may make recovery of charges levied in breach of Community law conditional on the claimant's proving that the charges had not been passed on to third parties. The Court approved the rule, provided it was applied equally to claims for the recovery of improper charges under national law, and provided the requirements of proof were not such as to make recovery "virtually impossible or excessively difficult to secure."

In Société Comateb v. Directeur Général des Douanes et Droits Indirects, Joined Cases C–192–218/95, [1997] ECR I–165, the Court took a rather close look at national practices in the recovery of illegally levied charges. It not only ruled that repayment may be withheld from a trader only where it is proven that the illegal charge was borne entirely by someone else and that recovery by the trader would amount to unjust enrichment; it also ruled that the fact that a trader has a legal obligation (possibly with penalty) to build the charge into the cost price does not entitle a national court to assume that the entire charge has been passed on. On the other hand, the Court ruled that even if a charge is fully passed on, the trader might still have a claim for provable market losses in sales (and profits) on account of the increased price.

3. Does the Court's conditional tolerance of remedial differences among Member States raise the spectre of forum-shopping and, if so, how serious is the problem? Would you favor the enactment of Community legislation prescribing the national law remedies that Member States must make available for vindicating Community law claims? If so, would you urge that the legislation also lay down uniform procedural rules (e.g., on standing, statutes of limitations, forms of relief, measurement of damages) governing these remedies, or would you prefer that national law determine them, either by express provision or through application of the procedural rules governing the most closely analogous domestic cause of action?

4. Must a Member State court give retroactive effect to a Court of Justice ruling even if a comparable ruling under national law would not be applied retroactively? See Carberry v. Minister for Social Welfare, [1990] 1 CMLR 29 (Irish High Court, April 28, 1989), giving retroactive effect to McDermott and Cotter v. Minister for Social Welfare (I), Case 286/85, [1987] ECR 1453. (In *McDermott I*, the Court ruled that after the implementation deadline for the EC directive on nondiscrimination in social security had passed, women could automatically claim the same advantages to which men in the same situation were entitled.)

5. Suppose that instead of levying a charge that is forbidden under Community law principles (as in *Rewe–Zentralfinanz*), the Member State authorities refused to furnish plaintiff a remedy on the ground that the State had never implemented the Council directive mandating the remedy. Suppose also that the deadline for implementation has passed, but so has the ordinarily applicable domestic statute of limitations for challenging the refusal. Assuming the limitations period meets the two-part test set out in *Rewe–Zentralfinanz*, must the suit be dismissed? In one case, the Court of Justice has said no. "[U]ntil such time as a directive has been properly transposed, a defaulting Member State may not rely on an individual's delay in initiating proceedings against it in order to protect rights conferred ... by the provisions of the directive and [the usual domestic limitations period] cannot begin to run before that time." Emmott v. Minister for Social Welfare, Case C–208/90, [1991] ECR I–4269. By what reasoning do you suppose the Court reached that result?

However, the Court subsequently refused to extend the *Emmott* rule to the question of the length of time prior to the bringing of an employment discrimination action for which arrears of benefits are payable. In other words, the UK's failure to implement the directive did not prevent it, in entertaining the claim recognized by the directive, from applying the UK rule that back payment may be ordered only for the period of one year prior to the filing of a claim. Johnson v. Chief Adjudication Officer, Case C–410/92, [1994] ECR I–5483. Can *Emmott* and *Johnson* be reconciled? To the same effect as *Johnson,* see Steenhorst–Neerings v. Bestuur van de Bedrijfsvereniging voor Detailhandel, Case C–338/91, [1993] ECR I–5475.

VON COLSON AND KAMANN v. LAND NORDRHEIN–WESTFALEN

Case 14/83, [1984] ECR 1891.

[Two female social workers, von Colson and Kamann, complained to a local labor court that the German state of North Rhine–Westphalia refused to hire them for work in an all-male prison, hiring less well-qualified male candidates instead. They claimed that the state thereby violated their rights under Council Directive 76/207 on equal treatment in access to employment.

The labor court found that there had indeed been discrimination, but also found that the German Civil Code amendment implementing Directive 76/207 limited damages in employment discrimination cases to losses resulting from the victim's reliance on there being no discrimination in hiring (in German, *Vertrauensschaden*). The court concluded that under that rule it could award Kamann nothing and von Colson only her 7.20 DM (i.e. $4–$5) job application fee. However, it referred several questions to the Court of Justice concerning Directive 76/207.

On preliminary reference, the Court of Justice ruled that an employer who is guilty of discrimination is not necessarily required under the directive to conclude a contract of employment with the victim. But though the directive did not prescribe that, or any other, specific sanction, it did require Member States "to adopt measures which are sufficiently effective to achieve the objective of the directive and to ensure that those measures may in fact be relied on before the national courts by the persons concerned" (¶ 18). The Court continued.]

22   It is impossible to establish real equality of opportunity without an appropriate system of sanctions. That follows not only from the actual purpose of the directive but more specifically from Article 6 thereof which, by granting applicants for a post who have been discriminated against recourse to the courts, acknowledges that those candidates have rights of which they may avail themselves before the courts.

23   Although ... full implementation of the directive does not require any specific form of sanction for unlawful discrimination, it does entail that that sanction be such as to guarantee real and effective judicial protection. Moreover it must also have a real deterrent effect on the employer. It follows that where a Member State chooses to penalize the breach of the prohibition of discrimination by the award of compensation, that compensation must in any event be adequate in relation to the damage sustained.

24   In consequence it appears that national provisions limiting the right to compensation of persons who have been discriminated against as regards access to employment to a purely nominal amount, such as, for example, the reimbursement of expenses incurred by them in submitting their application, would not satisfy the requirements of an effective transposition of the directive.

[The Court recalled that the Member States have a duty under EC Article 10 (ex 5) to achieve the results envisaged by the directive and that this duty also binds the national courts. In language repeated in the *Marleasing* case, *supra* page 262, the Court held that national courts must interpret national law enacted to implement a directive "in the light of the wording and the purpose of the directive."

On the other hand, the Court found Directive 76/207 not to be sufficiently precise and unconditional so as to have direct effect, that is, to create by itself (and apart from national implementing legislation) a right to specific compensation that individuals could assert in Member State court. The Court proceeded as follows.]

28   [But] although Directive [76/207] ... leaves the Member States free to choose between the different solutions suitable for achieving its objective, it nevertheless requires that if a Member State chooses to penalize breaches of that prohibition by the award of compensation, then in order to ensure that it is effective and that it has a deterrent effect, that compensation must in any event be adequate in relation to the damage sustained and must therefore amount to more than purely nominal compensation such as, for example, the reimbursement only of the expenses incurred in connection with the application. It is for the national court to interpret and apply the legislation adopted for the implementation

of the directive in conformity with the requirements of Community law, in so far as it is given discretion to do so under national law.

Notes and Questions

1.   *von Colson and Kamann* (¶ 28) expressly left it to the national court to decide whether the German implementing legislation could be construed to meet the Member States' obligations under Directive 76/207. Suppose the legislation could not be so construed. Considering that the Court found Directive 76/207 to lack direct effect, what is going to be the result in German court for persons like von Colson and Kamann? full damages? nominal damages? no damages at all?

2.   In Johnston v. Chief Constable of the Royal Ulster Constabulary, Case 222/84, [1986] ECR 1651, excerpted at page 1352 *infra*, a member of the constabulary challenged in UK court a police force policy of denying arms to female officers. She invoked the same directive (76/207) at issue in *von Colson and Kamann*. The Court of Justice ruled on preliminary reference that article 6 of the directive, which required Member States to introduce the measures needed to enable discrimination victims "to pursue their claims by judicial process," had direct effect in the national courts. It also ruled that the British implementing legislation, which exempted from judicial review any act taken to safeguard national security or public order, and which provided that the Secretary of State's certificate stating that a measure was taken for those purposes "shall be conclusive," ran afoul of the directive, and more specifically article 6. The case shows how Community law may restrict a Member State's freedom to preclude judicial review of administrative action or to create irrebuttable legal presumptions.

By the same token, the Court has more recently held that the principle of free movement of workers requires that a decision by the French authorities refusing to recognize a Belgian football-coaching diploma as equivalent to a French one must state its reasons and be subject to judicial review. Union nationale des entraineurs et cadres techniques professionnels du football v. Heylens, Case 222/86, [1987] ECR 4097.

3.   When the Court condemned the UK under Article 226 (ex 169) for failing adequately to implement certain social policy directives, it did so partly on account of certain remedial deficiencies in the UK implementing legislation. For example, the Court rejected the UK's implementation of the collective redundancies directive (75/129), in part because the UK measure permitted an employer to "set off" any amounts owed to a dismissed employee for failure to consult the latter's representatives, as required, against any sums payable to the employee under the employee's contract of employment or on account of its breach. The Court found that this mechanism largely deprived the UK sanction of its deterrent value. Commission v. United Kingdom (Collective redundancies), Case C–383/92, [1994] ECR I–2479. See also Commission v. United Kingdom (Transfer of undertakings), Case C–382/92, [1994] ECR I–2435, where the Court also rejected a feature of the UK legislation on employee rights in the event of transfers of undertakings, whereby an employer who failed to consult employee representatives, as required by Directive 77/187, could "set off" any amounts paid as a penalty against any amounts it was also required to pay for noncompliance with the consultation requirement in Directive 75/129 (see above) in the event of collective employee dismissals for redundancy. Was the UK rightly condemned in both cases? (Both cases are dealt with more fully in Chapter 36 on Social Policy.)

4.   A recurring question in EU law has been whether Community legislation ever requires Member States to criminalize private conduct. In Belgium v.

Vandevenne, Case C–7/90, [1991] ECR I–4371, the Court (citing a prior case, *Hansen*, Case C–326/88, [1990] ECR I–2911), ruled that when a Community regulation does not specify a penalty in case of breach, but refers to national provisions, Member States are free to refrain from imposing criminal penalties, provided they treat the Community law infringement in a procedural and substantive fashion comparable to similar infringements of national law, and provided that the treatment is in any event "effective, proportionate and dissuasive." See also Gallotti and Others, Joined Cases C–58, 75, 112, 119, 123, 135, 140, 141, 154 & 157/95, [1996] ECR I–4345.

MARSHALL v. SOUTHAMPTON AND SOUTH–WEST HAMPSHIRE AREA HEALTH AUTHORITY

(Marshall II)

Case C–271/91, [1993] ECR I–4367.

[This case is a sequel to the *Marshall* judgment at page 260 of the casebook. The industrial tribunal awarded Marshall £ 10,695 for financial losses, £ 1000 for injury to her feelings and £ 7710 in interest, in spite of the fact that the UK law implementing the equal treatment directive set a ceiling on recovery of £ 6250 and disallowed the payment of interest. On appeal, the House of Lords inquired of the Court of Justice whether Community law permitted UK courts to enforce the damages limitations set out in UK law.]

22 Article 6 of the directive puts Member States under a duty to take the necessary measures to enable all persons who consider themselves wronged by discrimination to pursue their claims by judicial process. Such obligation implies that the measures in question should be sufficiently effective to achieve the objective of the directive and should be capable of being effectively relied upon by the persons concerned before national courts.

23 As the Court held in [*von Colson and Kamann*], Article 6 does not prescribe a specific measure to be taken in the event of a breach of the prohibition of discrimination, but leaves Member States free to choose between the different solutions suitable for achieving the objective of the directive, depending on the different situations which may arise.

24 However, the objective is to arrive at real equality of opportunity and cannot therefore be attained in the absence of measures appropriate to restore such equality when it has not been observed. As the Court stated in paragraph 23 in *von Colson and Kamann* ... those measures must be such as to guarantee real and effective judicial protection and have a real deterrent effect on the employer.

25 ... In the event of discriminatory dismissal contrary to Article 5(1) of the directive, a situation of equality could not be restored without either reinstating the victim of discrimination or, in the alternative, granting financial compensation for the loss and damage sustained.

26 Where financial compensation is the measure adopted in order to achieve the objective indicated above, it must be adequate, in that it must enable the loss and damage actually sustained as a result of the discriminatory dismissal to be made good in full in accordance with the applicable national rules.

* * *

29   The Court's interpretation of Article 6 as set out above provides a direct reply to the ... question relating to the level of compensation required by that provision.

30   It ... follows ... that the fixing of an upper limit of the kind at issue in the main proceedings cannot, by definition, constitute proper implementation of Article 6 of the directive, since it limits the amount of compensation *a priori* to a level which is not necessarily consistent with the requirement of ensuring real equality of opportunity through adequate reparation for the loss and damage sustained as a result of discriminatory dismissal.

31   With regard to the ... question relating to the award of interest, suffice it to say that full compensation for the loss and damage sustained as a result of discriminatory dismissal cannot leave out of account factors, such as the effluxion of time, which may in fact reduce its value. The award of interest, in accordance with the applicable national rules, must therefore be regarded as an essential component of compensation for the purposes of restoring real equality of treatment.

32   Accordingly, the reply to be given ... [is] that reparation of the loss and damage sustained by a person injured as a result of discriminatory dismissal may not be limited to an upper limit fixed *a priori* or by excluding an award of interest to compensate for the loss sustained by the recipient of the compensation as a result of the effluxion of time until the capital sum awarded is actually paid.

[The Court then concluded that the pertinent provisions of the directive have direct effect:]

35   Accordingly, the combined provisions of Article 6 and Article 5 of the directive give rise, on the part of a person who has been injured as a result of discriminatory dismissal, to rights which that person must be able to rely upon before the national courts as against the State and authorities which are an emanation of the State.

* * *

37   It should be pointed out in that connection that ... the right of a State to choose among several possible means of achieving the objectives of a directive does not exclude the possibility for individuals of enforcing before national courts rights whose content can be determined sufficiently precisely on the basis of the provisions of the directive alone.

Notes and Questions

1.   Does *Marshall II* in any sense overrule *von Colson and Kamann*? Would you answer the questions in note 1 following *von Colson and Kamann* any differently after *Marshall II*?

2.   Does *Marshall II* go too far? Does it implicate the principle of subsidiarity? Note that Advocate–General van Gerven opined in the case that the UK ceiling on damages could be accepted even if it meant "less than ... full" compensation, provided it permitted "adequate" compensation (adequacy to be determined in light of the most important components of damages traditionally taken into account in liability rules). He thought the comparability requirement would in any event have to be satisfied.

van SCHIJNDEL AND van VEEN v. SPF

Joined Cases C–430, 431/93, [1995] ECR I–4705.

[van Schijndel and van Veen, Dutch physiotherapists, applied for exemption from compulsory membership in the Dutch "Pension Fund Foundation for Physiotherapists" [the "Fund"]. According to the applicable rules, membership was not mandatory in cases where a physiotherapist practices the profession under a contract of employment and the employer makes pension insurance coverage available to all members of the profession whom it employs.

The Fund refused to exempt van Schijndel and van Veen on the ground that their company did not in fact make pension arrangements applicable to all members of the profession whom the company employed. The Fund thus ordered van Schijndel and van Veen to continue to make contributions, whereupon the two physiotherapists brought suit. Unsuccessful in court, they appealed to the Dutch Hoge Raad. For the first time at this point, van Schijndel and van Veen argued that the lower court should have considered, "if necessary of its own motion," the compatibility of compulsory Fund membership with Articles 3(f), 10 (para. 2) (ex 5 (para. 2)), 43–48 (ex 52–58), 49–55 (ex 59–66), 82 (ex 86) and 86 (ex 90) of the EC Treaty.

The Hoge Raad asked the Court of Justice whether a national court could or indeed must apply these treaty articles even when the party having an interest in their application has failed to invoke them. Not surprisingly, the Court ruled that national courts have an obligation to apply these articles if domestic law permits national courts to do so under those circumstances.

The Court then considered whether the same result obtains when, in order to apply EC rules on its own initiative, "the court would have to abandon the passive role assigned to it by going beyond the ambit of the dispute defined by the parties themselves and/or by relying on facts and circumstances other than those on which the party to the proceedings with an interest in application of the provisions of the Treaty bases his claim." After reiterating its prior case law on the problem of remedial adequacy, the Court continued:]

19 For the purposes of applying those principles, each case which raises the question whether a national procedural provision renders application of Community law impossible or excessively difficult must be analysed by reference to the role of that provision in the procedure, its progress and its special features, viewed as a whole, before the various national instances. In the light of that analysis the basic principles of the domestic judicial system, such as protection of the rights of the defence, the principle of legal certainty and the proper conduct of procedure, must, where appropriate, be taken into consideration.

20 In the present case, the domestic law principle that in civil proceedings a court must or may raise points of its own motion is limited by its obligation to keep to the subject-matter of the dispute and to base its decision on the facts put before it.

21 That limitation is justified by the principle that, in a civil suit, it is for the parties to take the initiative, the court being able to act of its own motion

only in exceptional cases where the public interest requires its intervention. That principle reflects conceptions prevailing in most of the Member States as to the relations between the State and the individual; it safeguards the rights of the defence; and it ensures proper conduct of proceedings by, in particular, protecting them from the delays inherent in examination of new pleas.

22 In those circumstances, the answer to the second question must be that Community law does not require national courts to raise of their own motion an issue concerning the breach of provisions of Community law where examination of that issue would oblige them to abandon the passive role assigned to them by going beyond the ambit of the dispute defined by the parties themselves and relying on facts and circumstances other than those on which the party with an interest in application of those provisions bases his claim.

Notes and Questions

1. Does *van Schijndel* represent a sound application of established legal principles? What was objectionable anyway about applying the usual Dutch rules to these two parties?

2. On the same day that it decided *van Schijndel,* the Court handed down judgment in Peterbroeck, van Campenhout & Cie., Case C–312/93, [1995] ECR I–4599. Peterbroeck, a Belgian limited liability partnership, filed a complaint with the Belgian regional tax authorities on behalf of the Dutch company (CBT) that held an interest in the partnership. Specifically, Peterbroeck argued that the Belgian government erred in taxing CBT at the non-resident rate (44.9%), rather than the resident rate (at most 42%), on the income that CBT had withdrawn from the partnership. Unsuccessful in its complaint, Peterbroeck appealed to the Court of Appeals of Brussels, raising for the first time the argument that application of a higher tax rate to a Dutch company than a Belgian company was an infringement of Article 43 (ex 52), guaranteeing freedom of establishment.

The Belgian government considered the argument inadmissible because it was raised beyond the time limit laid down in the Belgian Tax Code: under the code, "new" pleas, not raised in the initial complaint or considered by the authorities on their own motion, could only be raised within 60 days of the filing of the tax ruling. The Belgian court asked the Court of Justice whether the time bar could validly be applied in this case:

15 In the present case, according to domestic law, a litigant may no longer raise before the Cour d'Appel a new plea based on Community law once the 60–day period with effect from the lodging by the Director of a certified true copy of the contested decision has elapsed.

16 Whilst a period of 60 days so imposed on a litigant is not objectionable *per se,* the special features of the procedure in question must be emphasized.

17 First of all, the Cour d'Appel is the first court which can make a reference to the Court of Justice since the Director before whom the first-instance proceedings are conducted is a member of the fiscal authorities and, consequently, is not a court or tribunal within the meaning of Article 177 [now 234] of the Treaty.

18 Secondly, the limitation period whose expiry prevented the Cour d'Appel from examining of its own motion the compatibility of a measure of domestic law with Community law started to run from the time when the Director lodged a

certified true copy of the contested decision. That meant, in this case, that the period during which new pleas could be raised by the appellant had expired by the time the Cour d'Appel held its hearing so that the Cour d'Appel was denied the possibility of considering the question of compatibility.

19 Thirdly, it seems that no other national court or tribunal in subsequent proceedings may of its own motion consider the question of the compatibility of a national measure with Community law.

20 Finally, the impossibility for national courts or tribunals to raise points of Community law of their own motion does not appear to be reasonably justifiable by principles such as the requirement of legal certainty or the proper conduct of procedure.

21 The answer to be given to the question submitted by the Cour d'Appel, Brussels, must therefore be that Community law precludes application of a domestic procedural rule whose effect, in procedural circumstances such as those in question in the main proceedings, is to prevent the national court, seised of a matter falling within its jurisdiction, from considering of its own motion whether a measure of domestic law is compatible with a provision of Community law when the latter provision has not been invoked by the litigant within a certain period.

Is the distinction between the facts of *van Schijndel* and *Peterbroeck* significant enough to justify the difference in result?

3. In a legal challenge in Dutch court against the government's approval of a "dyke reinforcement" project, the plaintiff neglected to raise the question whether the government should have prepared an environmental impact assessment, as required for certain public projects by an EC directive of 1985. The Dutch court accordingly included among its preliminary references to the Court of Justice the question whether, assuming an impact assessment for the project was required, the Dutch court should enforce that requirement even though the plaintiff had failed to raise the issue.

The Court of Justice (citing the *Marleasing* case, page 262 *supra*), recalled that it is incumbent on all Member State authorities—including the courts—to take the measures necessary to achieve the results prescribed by a directive. The Court took this to mean, first, that national law can not *prevent* national courts from raising a Community law violation on their own motion. The Court also took it to mean that, if the courts are *required* by national law to raise points of domestic law, then they are likewise *required* to raise points of Community law. That left only the situation in which national law neither requires nor forbids courts to raise points of domestic law, but merely *permits* them to do so. As to this situation, the Court ruled:

58 The position is the same if national law confers on courts and tribunals a discretion to apply of their own motion binding rules of law. Indeed, pursuant to the principle of cooperation laid down in Article 5 [now 10] of the Treaty, it is for national courts to ensure the legal protection which persons derive from the direct effect of provisions of Community law.

59 The fact that in this case the Member States have a discretion under ... the directive does not preclude judicial review of the question whether the national authorities exceeded their discretion.

60 Consequently where, pursuant to national law, a court must or may raise of its own motion pleas in law based on a binding national rule which were not put forward by the parties, it must, for matters within its jurisdiction, examine of

its own motion whether the legislative or administrative authorities of the Member State remained within the limits of their discretion under ... the directive, and take account thereof when examining the action for annulment.

[61] If that discretion has been exceeded and consequently the national provisions must be set aside in that respect, it is for the authorities of the Member State, according to their respective powers, to take all the general or particular measures necessary to ensure that projects are examined in order to determine whether they are likely to have significant effects on the environment and, if so, to ensure that they are subject to an impact assessment.

Aannemersbedrijf P.K. Kraaijeveld BV v. Gedeputeerde Staten van Zuid–Holland, Case C–72/95, [1996] ECR I–687.

ECO SWISS CHINA TIME LTD. v. BENETTON INTERNATIONAL NV

Case C–126/97, [1999] ECR I–4493.

[Benetton entered into an eight-year licensing agreement with Eco Swiss and Bulova Watch, giving Eco Swiss the right to manufacture watches and clocks bearing the words "Benetton by Bulova" to be sold by Eco Swiss and Bulova. Under the agreement, Eco Swiss could not sell watches and clocks in Italy and Bulova could not sell them elsewhere in the EU. The contract contained a disputes clause providing for arbitration in the Netherlands. Five years into the agreement, Benetton terminated it, and arbitration proceedings were launched. The arbitrators ruled in favor of Eco Swiss and Bulova in an interim award on liability and fixed damages in a subsequent final award.

Benetton sued in Dutch court to have the award set aside on the ground that it violated public policy because the underlying licensing agreement was null and void as anti-competitive under Article 81 (ex 85) of the EC Treaty, invoking the Dutch Civil Procedure Code providing for vacatur of an arbitration award that is contrary to public policy. At the time Benetton brought suit, the three-month limitations period prescribed by Dutch law for challenging the interim award had lapsed. Moreover, neither the parties nor the arbitrators had raised the Article 81 issue during the arbitration.

The district court dismissed the action and Benetton appealed. Finding that enforcing a contract contrary to Article 81 would indeed violate Dutch public policy and justify setting aside the award, the appellate court issued a stay of enforcement of the award, and Eco Swiss appealed. The Dutch Supreme Court observed that Dutch law would not consider it contrary to public policy to enforce an arbitral award based upon a contract in violation of *Dutch* competition law. The Court also noted Benetton's twin failures to raise the competition law claim during the arbitration and to seek vacatur of the interim award of liability on a timely basis. (On the other hand, the Court called attention to the *Nordsee* case, page 368 *supra*, holding that arbitral tribunals constituted pursuant to private contract cannot make preliminary references to the Court of Justice even when Community law issues arise in an arbitration.) A preliminary reference ensued.

The Court of Justice recalled *Nordsee* and, in particular, paragraph 15 of the judgment which emphasized that national courts may make preliminary references on the meaning of Community competition law when relevant to their review of the validity or enforceability of the award. It continued.]

* * *

The second question

35 [I]t is in the interest of efficient arbitration proceedings that review of arbitration awards should be limited in scope and that annulment of or refusal to recognise an award should be possible only in exceptional circumstances.

36 However, according to Article 3(g) (now ... Article 3(1)(g) EC), Article 81 EC (ex Article 85) constitutes a fundamental provision which is essential for the accomplishment of the tasks entrusted to the Community and, in particular, for the functioning of the internal market. The importance of such a provision led the framers of the Treaty to provide expressly, in Article 81(2) EC (ex Article 85(2)), that any agreements or decisions prohibited pursuant to that article are to be automatically void.

37 It follows that where its domestic rules of procedure require a national court to grant an application for annulment of an arbitration award where such an application is founded on failure to observe national rules of public policy, it must also grant such an application where it is founded on failure to comply with the prohibition laid down in Article 81(1) EC (ex Article 85(1)).

* * *

39 For the reasons stated in paragraph 36 above, the provisions of Article 81 EC (ex Article 85) may be regarded as a matter of public policy....

40 Lastly ... arbitrators, unlike national courts and tribunals, are not in a position to request this Court to give a preliminary ruling on questions of interpretation of Community law. However, it is manifestly in the interest of the Community legal order that, in order to forestall differences of interpretation, every Community provision should be given a uniform interpretation, irrespective of the circumstances in which it is to be applied. It follows that, in the circumstances of the present case, unlike *van Schijndel and van Veen*, Community law requires that questions concerning the interpretation of the prohibition laid down in Article 81(1) EC (ex Article 85(1)) should be open to examination by national courts when asked to determine the validity of an arbitration award and that it should be possible for those questions to be referred, if necessary, to the Court of Justice for a preliminary ruling.

41 [T]herefore ... a national court to which application is made for annulment of an arbitration award must grant that application if it considers that the award in question is in fact contrary to Article 81 EC (ex Article 85), where its domestic rules of procedure require it to grant an application for annulment founded on failure to observe national rules of public policy

* * *

The fourth and fifth questions

⁴³ [T]he referring court is asking essentially whether Community law requires a national court to refrain from applying domestic rules of procedure according to which an interim arbitration award which is in the nature of a final award and in respect of which no application for annulment has been made within the prescribed time-limit acquires the force of *res judicata* and may no longer be called in question by a subsequent arbitration award, even if this is necessary in order to examine, in proceedings for annulment of the subsequent award, whether an agreement which the interim award held to be valid in law is nevertheless void under Article 81 EC (ex Article 85).

* * *

⁴⁵ [The three-month period for annulling an interim arbitration award which is in the nature of a final award], which does not seem excessively short compared with those prescribed in the legal systems of the other Member States, does not render excessively difficult or virtually impossible the exercise of rights conferred by Community law.

⁴⁶ Moreover, domestic procedural rules which, upon expiry of that period, restrict the possibility of applying for annulment of a subsequent arbitration award proceeding upon an interim arbitration award which is in the nature of a final award, because it has become *res judicata*, are justified by the basic principles of the national judicial system, such as the principle of legal certainty. . . .

⁴⁷ In those circumstances, Community law does not require a national court to refrain from applying such rules, even if this is necessary in order to examine, in proceedings for annulment of a subsequent arbitration award, whether an agreement which the interim award held to be valid in law is nevertheless void under Article 81 EC (ex Article 85).

Notes and Questions

1. Having ruled that the Dutch court could enforce the national limitations period and the principle of *res judicata*, the Court of Justice found it unnecessary to answer the other principal question referred, namely whether (assuming the action to set aside the award was timely) Benetton's failure to raise the Article 81 claim during the arbitration could operate to estop it from invoking the violation of Article 81 as a public policy ground for having the award vacated.

How do you suppose the Court would have answered that question? Might the Court, for example, have ruled that, while the Dutch court *could* enforce the Dutch limitations period on the action to vacate the award, notwithstanding the public policy character of Article 81, it *could not* treat Benetton as having waived the claim by not raising it before the arbitrators?

2. Recall the case of Pafitis v. Trapeza Kentrikis Ellados AE, discussed at page 278 *supra*, regarding application of national "abuse of rights" doctrine as a limitation on Community law-based claims.

3. For a thoughtful discussion of these issues, see John Temple Lang, The Duties of National Authorities under Community Constitutional law, 23 Eur. L. Rev. 109 (1998).

THE QUEEN v. SECRETARY OF STATE
FOR TRANSPORT ex parte
FACTORTAME LTD.

Case C–213/89, [1990] ECR I–2433.

[For the facts of the case and judgment of the Court, see page 274 *supra.*]

Notes and Questions

1. As noted (*supra* page 342), the House of Lords later granted an interim injunction, and the Court of Justice eventually held the UK Merchant Shipping Act amendments to be in violation of Article 43 (ex 52) of the EC Treaty.

2. Why was it not sufficient for the UK to show that interim injunctive relief is not available in comparable domestic law cases against the Crown, and that Community law claims are therefore not treated disadvantageously? Suppose interim relief was *never* available in British court, in any class of cases. Might EC law still require that it be available in Community law cases? If so, do you think the Court of Justice has become too demanding about the availability and adequacy of national remedies for vindicating Community law claims?

3. Do the same considerations that require national courts to entertain petitions for interim injunctive relief in aid of EC law claims also limit their freedom in setting the standards for such relief or in deciding whether or not to grant it in any given case?

4. Most of the cases in this section involve private party claims against a Member State. Suppose, however, Community law gives Member States a claim against a private party and requires them to enforce that claim. Does Community law demand a minimally effective judicial remedy in this situation as well? The question has arisen concretely in connection with the requirement that Member States recover moneys improperly granted to private parties. See Lippische Hauptgenossenschaft v. Bundesanstalt für landwirtschaftliche Marktordnung, Cases 119, 126/79, [1980] ECR 1863; Ferwerda BV v. Produktschap voor Vee en Vlees, Case 265/78, [1980] ECR 617.

The case of Deutsche Milchkontor GmbH v. Germany, Cases 205–15/82, [1983] ECR 2633, arose out of the German authorities' discovery that they had paid sums in aid to processors of foods that contained ingredients disqualifying them from aid under the applicable Community regulations. Council Regulation 729/70, the basic regulation on financing the Common Agricultural Policy, requires Member States to recover all funds erroneously disbursed, and the authorities accordingly demanded repayment. The recipient firms challenged the order in German court on various equitable grounds, and preliminary references to the Court of Justice ensued.

The Court took the general view that, absent uniform Community rules, national authorities should apply their own procedural and substantive rules of law (for example, on burden of proof). However, it also reaffirmed the two conditions set out in the *Rewe–Zentralfinanz* case (*supra* page 387).

The German court further asked whether Community law permitted it to take the legitimate expectations of the recipients into account in fixing the amounts to be repaid. (Under German law, the government may not recover money unlawfully paid to a private party to the extent that the recipient relied upon the grant "and [that its] expectation, weighed against the public interest in revoking the decision, merits protection," or to the extent that the authorities knew or should have known that they had made the grant unlawfully. In any event, the government must act within a year of learning of its error.) The Court of Justice, noting that protection of legitimate expectations and legal certainty are part of Community law as well, suggested that such national rules may be applied as long as in each case the Community's interest in revoking an illegal aid is also taken into account. As to whether recipients of aid may rely on the authorities' failure adequately to supervise the grant of aid as a defense to an action for recovery (a point the German firms obviously had pressed in the case), the Court merely observed that "in the present state of development of Community law those consequences are determined by national law and not by Community law." [1983] ECR at 2672. What do you think of these guidelines? Do you expect that they will put matters to rest?

5. Issues surrounding the recovery of illegally paid funds commonly arise in the state aid arena, treated in Chapter 26 *infra*.

The Court has ruled that where a Member State grants a state aid without notifying the Commission in advance, as required under EC Article 88(3) (ex 93(3)), it may not invoke the legitimate expectations of the recipient as an excuse for not complying with a Commission order to recover the aid. Commission v. Germany (State aid to BUG–Alutechnik), Case C–5/89, [1990] ECR I–3437. However, the Court has recognized an exception for circumstances where, "by reason of exceptional circumstances, repayment is inappropriate." Syndicat Français de l'Express International (SFEI) v. La Poste, Case C–39/34, [1996] ECR Is–3547 (paras. 69–71).

Recipients of allegedly illegal state aids will of course want to contest the finding of illegality, and Community law principles guarantee them the right to do so. In British Aerospace plc & Rover Group Holdings plc v. Commission, Case C–294/90, [1992] ECR I–493, the Commission directed the UK to recover £44.4 million in state aid granted to British Aerospace. British Aerospace successfully challenged the order on the ground that the Commission had failed to give it (or the UK) an opportunity to challenge the finding of illegality under Article 88(2) (ex 93(2)) prior to ordering recovery. If given that opportunity, a recipient of the allegedly illegal state aid had better use it, since if it waits until the State takes action to recover the aid, it may be too late. This happened in TWD Textilwerke Deggendorf GmbH v. Germany, Case C–188/92, [1994] ECR I–833. Neither TWD nor Germany challenged the Commission decision declaring illegal aids given to TWD by Germany and demanding its recovery. Only when the German authorities actually sought to revoke the aids, did TWD react by bringing suit in a German administrative court. On preliminary reference, the ECJ ruled that the legality of the Commission decision was no longer challengeable and that a preliminary reference on its legality was out of order. TWD had had, and had missed, the opportunity to attack the Commission decision at the time it was made.

Are you comfortable with this holding? Recall that the Commission decision would have been addressed to Germany alone.

6. Recipients of illegal state aids have sought to resist recovery by invoking various national constitutional protections. Consider the case of Land Rheinland–Pfalz v. Alcan Deutschland GmbH, Case C–24/95, [1997] ECR I–1591. Following Germany's condemnation by the Court for failing to comply with a Commission order that it recover a state aid that it had illegally paid to Alcan to keep open its aluminum plant, the state government of Rheinland–Pfalz revoked the aid and

demanded that Alcan repay the 8 million DMs it had received. Alcan successfully challenged the order in German court on the ground that it violated a state administrative procedure act provision barring the revocation of administrative acts after one year from the time the government becomes aware of the facts justifying the revocation.

When the case reached the highest German administrative court, that court asked the Court of Justice whether Community law requires that the aid be revoked, notwithstanding the violation of state administrative law. Indeed, the referring court thought that revocation might violate still other rules of German law: (a) the principle of good faith, which arguably bars the government from suing to recover an aid for whose illegality it was itself primarily responsible and whose legality it had failed to bring in a timely way to the recipient's attention, and (b) the principle of the German Civil Code (sec. 818(3)) which precludes recovery where the gain arising from an unlawful administrative measure has ceased to exist. (Alcan argued that this provision applied because Alcan had in the intervening period closed the plant in question after incurring further losses.)

The Court squarely rejected the notion that the recipient of an unlawful aid should be able to resist repayment on the ground that the State failed to act to recover the payment within the time limits laid down by national law. The Court then turned to the claim based on the recipient's good faith, rejecting that claim as well on the ground that permitting a recipient to retain an aid that (as in this case) had not been notified to the Commission as required by the Treaty "would seriously and adversely affect the Community interest and render practically impossible the recovery required by Community law" (para. 41). The Court finally turned to Alcan's claim that any gain accruing to it from the unlawful aid had ceased to exist, and under such circumstances German law precludes recovery. Here is how it ruled:

49 It has already been pointed out that undertakings receiving aid cannot have a legitimate expectation as to the lawfulness of the aid unless it has been granted in compliance with the procedure laid down in Article 93 [now 88] of the Treaty.

50 The same conclusion therefore applies to the plea that the gain has ceased to exist, which would in this case render the recovery required by Community law practically impossible.

51 Contrary to Alcan's claims, the fact that the gain has ceased to exist is not unusual from an accounting point of view; it is in fact the rule in the case of State aid, which is generally granted to undertakings in difficulty, whose balance sheet, when aid is recovered, no longer reveals the added value indisputably resulting from the aid.

52 Moreover, an undertaking which incurs losses after the grant of aid may nevertheless obtain ongoing benefits from its temporary survival in terms of retention of its place on the market, reputation and goodwill. Accordingly, it cannot be maintained that the gain no longer exists simply because the benefit resulting from the grant of State aid no longer appears on the recipient undertaking's balance sheet.

* * *

54 Accordingly, Community law requires the competent authority to revoke a decision granting unlawful aid, in accordance with a final decision of the Commission declaring the aid incompatible with the common market and

ordering recovery, even where such recovery is excluded by national law because the gain no longer exists....

Are you persuaded that Alcan should have to repay the aid? Does the Court's ruling still leave open any possibility for the aid recipient to prove that the aid no longer exists and should not therefore have to be repaid?

7.   For an interesting comparative survey of Member State remedies for restitution of sums levied by national authorities in violation of Community law (as required by the *San Giorgio* case, discussed *supra* page 389, note 2), see A. Tatham, Restitution of Charges and Duties Levied by the Public Administration in Breach of European Community Law: A Comparative Analysis, 19 Eur. L. Rev. 146 (1994). See also L. Papadias, Interim Protection under Community Law before the National Courts: The Right to a Judge with Jurisdiction to Grant Interim Relief, 1994/2 Legal Issues of Eur. Integration 153; Note, Remedies for European Community Law Claims in Member States Courts: Toward a European Standard, 31 Colum. J. Transnat'l L. 377 (1993).

8.   The US Supreme Court has ruled that a state must provide an adequate remedy to taxpayers against whom unconstitutional taxes have been levied. While stopping short of requiring that the state necessarily issue a refund of the money, and while allowing that the states have flexibility in fashioning a remedy, the Court insisted that if the state had not provided a full "pre-deprivation hearing," then it would have to provide "meaningful backward-looking relief to rectify any unconstitutional deprivation" or otherwise "create in hindsight a nondiscriminatory scheme." Harper v. Virginia Department of Taxation, 509 U.S. 86, 113 S.Ct. 2510, 2519–20, 125 L.Ed.2d 74 (1993).

B.   DAMAGES FOR MEMBER STATE VIOLATIONS OF EC LAW

GARDEN COTTAGE FOODS LTD. v. MILK MARKETING BOARD

House of Lords [1984] A.C. 130, [1983] 3 CMLR 43
June 23, 1983.

[The plaintiff company sued the Milk Marketing Board (MMB) for an interim order enjoining it from refusing to supply the company with bulk butter, an action it considered to be an abuse of a dominant market position. The lower court refused the injunction on the ground that damages would be an adequate remedy for any losses during the period before trial, citing also the risk of disrupting the Board's business. The Court of Appeal granted the relief, though on different terms than requested, and the case reached the House of Lords. Lord Diplock expressed the views of the majority.]

LORD DIPLOCK:

[T]he only issue which falls for determination by your Lordships at the present stage is whether the Court of Appeal [was] justified in interfering with the [lower court's] refusal ... in the exercise of [its] discretion to grant to the plaintiff in the action ("the company") an interlocutory injunction against the Milk Marketing Board ("MMB") in either of the alternative terms in which an injunction was sought.

[Lord Diplock turned to the facts of the case and then to EC Treaty Article 82 (ex 86).]

This Article of the Treaty of Rome was held by the European Court of Justice in [the *SABAM* case] to produce direct effects in relations between individuals and to create direct rights in respect of the individuals concerned which the national courts must protect. This decision of the European Court of Justice ... is one which ... the European Communities Act 1972 requires your Lordships to follow. The rights which [Article 86 (now 82)] confers upon citizens in the United Kingdom ... are without further enactment to be given legal effect in the United Kingdom and enforced accordingly.

A breach of the duty imposed by Article 86 not to abuse a dominant position in the Common Market or in a substantial part of it, can thus be categorised in English law as a breach of a statutory duty that is imposed not only for the purpose of promoting the general economic prosperity of the Common Market but also for the benefit of private individuals to whom loss or damage is caused by a breach of that duty.

If this categorisation be correct, and I can see none other that would be capable of giving rise to a civil cause of action in English private law on the part of a private individual who sustained loss or damage by reason of a breach of a directly applicable provision of the Treaty of Rome, the nature of the cause of action cannot, in my view, be affected by the fact that the legislative provision by which the duty is imposed takes the negative form of a prohibition of particular kinds of conduct rather than the positive form of an obligation to do particular acts.

[Lord Diplock found that the trial judge had reasonably concluded that an eventual award of damages to the plaintiff would provide adequate compensation for any violation of Article 86 that MMB might be found to have committed.]

The only reason why the Court of Appeal held that the judge was wrong in his view that damages would provide an adequate remedy to the company for any interference with its bulk butter business pending the trial of the action, appears to have been ... doubt ... as to whether the company's cause of action sounded in damages at all.

[Lord Diplock, citing the *SABAM* case and *Rewe–Zentralfinanz, supra* page 387, thought it likely that a violation of Article 86 causing injury to a person would give rise to a cause of action for damages in English law for breach of a statutory duty.]

It is private law, not public law, to which the company has had recourse. ... No reasons are to be found in any of the judgments of the Court of Appeal and none has been advanced at the hearing before your Lordships, why in law, in logic or in justice, if contravention of Article 86 of the Treaty of Rome is capable of giving rise to a cause of action in English private law at all, there is any need to invent a cause of action ... in order to deal with breaches of Articles of the Treaty of Rome which have in the United Kingdom the same effect as statutes.

* * *

[T]he Court of Appeal was in my view wrong in suggesting that if it were established at the trial (a) that MMB had contravened Article 86, and (b) that such contravention had (i) caused the company pecuniary loss, and (ii) thereby given rise to a cause of action in English law on the part of the company against MMB, it was a seriously arguable proposition that such cause of action did not entitle the company to a remedy in damages although it did entitle the company to a remedy by injunction. [The trial judge] did not misunderstand the law in this respect. He was entitled to take the view that a remedy in damages would be available and, for the reasons I have stated earlier, that such remedy would be adequate.

[There is] no ground which would justify an appellate court in interfering with the way in which [the trial judge] exercised his discretion [to refuse an injunction and] the only ground upon which the Court of Appeal appears to have relied for doing so is bad in law.

I would accordingly . . . discharge the order of the Court of Appeal.

[A long dissent by Lord Wilberforce, along with statements of concurrence by Lords Keith, Bridge and Brandon, is omitted.]

Notes and Questions

1.   The Commission has long urged more frequent use of private civil enforcement actions in the competition law field, but they have remained relatively uncommon. A Commission notice and proposals for "modernization" of competition law enforcement would encourage the bringing of actions in Member State courts. See Part IV of this book for full treatment.

2.   Two years after the House of Lords decided *Garden Cottage Foods,* the English Court of Appeal had to decide whether UK law also provides a cause of action in damages for violation of Article 28 (ex 30) on the free movement of goods. The plaintiffs were French turkey producers who complained that the UK's restriction of turkey imports on public health grounds constituted disguised protectionism in violation of that article. Their complaint caused the Commission to bring an Article 226 (ex 169) enforcement action against the UK in the Court of Justice, in which the Commission prevailed. The French turkey producers then sued the competent UK ministry for consequential damages. The Court of Appeal concluded that the plaintiffs had no cause of action. Bourgoin SA v. Ministry of Agriculture, Fisheries and Food, [1986] Q.B. 716, [1986] 1 CMLR 267 (C.A., July 29, 1985).

Parker, L.J., writing for the majority in *Bourgoin,* thought that the Court of Justice's case law on direct effect (notably *van Gend en Loos*) "goes no further than establishing that where an Article has direct effect . . . [the] individual rights . . . thereby created . . . must be protected by national courts," but does not define either "[t]he precise nature of the right [or] the remedy to be afforded." He also thought it odd for a Member State to be held liable in damages for breach of a Treaty article conferring individual rights, when the Community itself would only be liable in damages for such a breach in the rare circumstances described in the Court of Justice's *Schöppenstedt* formula, *supra* page 196. Parker, L.J. continued:

> . . . I would have no hesitation in holding that a breach of Article 30 [now 28] . . . affords in English law a right to judicial review by anyone with sufficient interest, a declaration as to the invalidity of the measure constituting the breach and *possibly* a mandamus to the relevant officials to permit the landing of the goods concerned. . . . [This is because] such rights and

remedies would be available for a similar domestic wrong. . . . [But] for a mere breach of the Article, not amounting to an abuse, damages are not available. . . .

[1986] 1 CMLR at 301 (emphasis in original). Can this result be squared with the House of Lords' *Garden Cottage Foods* case? Note in *Garden Cottage* that, although the Marketing Board represented the State, it was sued as an "undertaking" that was bound by Article 86 (now 82). Justice Parker reasoned that the plaintiffs in *Garden Cottage,* in suing for breach of Article 86 (now 82), "were resorting purely to private law," but that the French Turkey producers in *Bourgoin* were not:

> I can find nothing in Lord Diplock's speech [in *Garden Cottage*] to suggest that he had in mind for one moment that breach by a Member State of a negative obligation in relation to measures could be categorized as . . . a breach of statutory duty giving rise to a civil cause of action in private law. . . . The reference to individual rights is in my judgment without significance. . . . A breach [of Article 30, now 28, cannot] be categorized as . . . a breach of statutory duty in any sense known to English law.

Id. at 311.

The following landmark ruling by the Court of Justice may be considered a response to the views that Parker, L.J. had expressed for the English Court of Appeal in *Bourgoin.*

FRANCOVICH v. ITALY

Cases C–6/90, 9/90, [1991] ECR I–5357.

[Two Italian workers found themselves unable to collect salary owed to them by their bankrupt employers. They eventually sought recovery from the Italian Government for its failure to implement Council Directive 80/987, which had required the Member States to set up a system of salary protection for workers of bankrupt enterprises, a failure that the Court of Justice had previously condemned in Commission v. Italy (Worker protection directive), Case 22/87, [1989] ECR 143. A preliminary reference to the Court of Justice followed.

The Court first held that the unimplemented directive could not fairly be read to have direct effect in the sense of giving the plaintiffs a salary claim directly against Italy. It turned to the question of Italy's possible liability in damages to the workers for its failure to implement Directive 80/987.]

30 [This] issue must be considered in the light of the general system of the Treaty and its fundamental principles.

[The Court recalled its landmark decisions on supremacy and direct effect, including *van Gend en Loos, Costa v. ENEL, Simmenthal* and *Factortame*].

33 The full effectiveness of Community rules would be impaired and the protection of the rights which they grant would be weakened if individuals were unable to obtain redress when their rights are infringed by a breach of Community law for which a Member State can be held responsible.

34 The possibility of obtaining redress from the Member State is particularly indispensable where, as in this case, the full effectiveness of Community

rules is subject to prior action on the part of the State and where, consequently, in the absence of such action, individuals cannot enforce before the national courts the rights conferred upon them by Community law.

35 It follows that the principle whereby a State must be liable for loss and damage caused to individuals as a result of breaches of Community law for which the State can be held responsible is inherent in the system of the Treaty.

36 A further basis for the obligation of Member States to make good such loss and damage is to be found in Article 5 of the Treaty, under which the Member States are required to take all appropriate measures, whether general or particular, to ensure fulfilment of their obligations under Community law. Among these is the obligation to nullify the unlawful consequences of a breach of Community law.

37 It follows from all the foregoing that it is a principle of Community law that the Member States are obliged to make good loss and damage caused to individuals by breaches of Community law for which they can be held responsible.

[The Court then identified the three conditions under which a State would be liable in damages for failing to carry out its duties under a directive.]

40 The first of those conditions is that the result prescribed by the directive should entail the grant of rights to individuals. The second condition is that it should be possible to identify the content of those rights on the basis of the provisions of the directive. Finally, the third condition is the existence of a causal link between the breach of the State's obligation and the loss and damage suffered by the injured parties.

41 Those conditions are sufficient to give rise to a right on the part of individuals to obtain reparation, a right founded directly on Community law.

42 Subject to that reservation, it is on the basis of the rules of national law on liability that the State must make reparation for the consequences of the loss and damage caused. In the absence of Community legislation, it is for the internal legal order of each Member State to designate the competent courts and lay down the detailed procedural rules for legal proceedings intended fully to safeguard the rights which individuals derive from Community law.

43 Further, the substantive and procedural conditions for reparation of loss and damage laid down by the national law of the Member States must not be less favourable than those relating to similar domestic claims and must not be so framed as to make it virtually impossible or excessively difficult to obtain reparation.

44 In this case, the breach of Community law by a Member State by virtue of its failure to transpose Directive 80/987 within the prescribed period has been confirmed by a judgment of the Court. The result required by that directive entails the grant to employees of a right to a guarantee of payment of their unpaid wage claims. As is clear from the examination of

the first part of the first question, the content of that right can be identified on the basis of the provisions of the directive.

45   Consequently, the national court must, in accordance with the national rules on liability, uphold the right of employees to obtain reparation of loss and damage caused to them as a result of failure to transpose the directive.

Notes and Questions

1.   Do you agree that Member State liability to private parties for Community law violations is "inherent" in the Community law system (¶ 35)? What is the scope of this "inherent" liability? When they commit Community law violations, do the Member States lose all the sovereign immunity in tort they otherwise enjoy? If so, is this a sound result?

In a case arising out of facts similar to *Francovich*, the Court ruled that Directive 80/987 was intended to benefit members of the management of an undertaking with respect to salary arrears and that a Member State's exclusion of them from the benefit of the directive gave rise to a claim for compensation against the State for the damage suffered as a result. Miret v. Fondo de Garantía Salarial, Case C–334/92, [1993] ECR I–6911.

2.   The Court in *Francovich* decided that the first two conditions of Member State liability were met. However, the Court effectively left it to the Italian courts to decide whether the third condition was met. Why? How free are national courts to fix the rules on "the existence of a link of causality" (¶ 40) between the Community law violation and the injury suffered?

The UK Court of Appeal decision in Regina v. Secretary of State for the Home Department ex parte Gallagher, [1996] 2 CMLR 951 (June 10, 1996), shows that reserving issues of causation to Member State law can have an important effect on outcomes.

John Gallagher, an Irish national, was arrested in the UK and subjected to an exclusion order, under the 1989 Prevention of Terrorism Act. The UK court in which Gallagher challenged that order made a preliminary reference to the Court of Justice, which ruled that EC Directive 64/221 prohibited the government from issuing an exclusion order until after the subject of that order has been interviewed by an independent authority and the report of that interview has been received. (See Queen v. Secretary of State for the Home Department ex parte Gallagher, Case C–175/94, [1995] ECR I–4253.) Parliament shortly thereafter amended the 1989 Act to bring it into conformity with the directive; meanwhile Gallagher, alleging that the government had failed to follow the procedures required by the directive, amended his complaint to seek damages.

The Court of Appeal was unpersuaded that Gallagher had shown a sufficiently serious violation of Community law to justify the imposition of liability, in part because the violation involved merely the mis-implementation, rather than non-implementation, of a directive. However, where the Court of Appeal chiefly parted ways with Gallagher was over the causation issue. It was unpersuaded "that the Home Secretary's decision would have been any different had he awaited receipt of Mr. Gallagher's representations and the report of the nominated person before making an exclusion order;" in fact, it considered it "probable that [had the proper procedures been followed] Mr. Gallagher would have been detained longer." [1996] 2 CMLR at 964–65.

3. *Francovich* has its sequel. After the ruling, the Italian government issued a decree transposing the insolvency directive into Italian law. The decree prescribed the terms of the salary guarantee to be paid to employees of insolvent employers and extended those terms to the calculation of damages to be paid by Italy to employees as a result of the belated transposition. Several Italian courts wondered about the compatibility of those terms with the directive as well as about the propriety of applying them retroactively to the calculation of *Francovich* damages. The Court ruled that the terms could be applied retroactively provided the directive has finally been properly transposed and provided those terms ensure adequate reparation for the loss suffered. Bonifaci and Berto v. Istituto Nazionale della Previdenza Sociale, Joined Cases C–94 & 95/95, [1997] ECR I–4006. In a companion case,[1] it disapproved of the Italian legislation's prohibition on the employee's aggregating the reparation due under the directive with the job seeker's allowance (the latter being a general entitlement aimed at supporting an employee for three months following termination of employment).

4. Did the Court satisfactorily address Justice Parker's objections in *Bourgoin* (*supra* page 406, note 2) to the idea of imposing damages liability on Member States for violating Community law when the Community (under the *Schöppenstedt* formula) is only liable for such breaches in highly exceptional circumstances?

5. For a resounding affirmation of the *Francovich* principle, see Faccini Dori v. Recreb Srl, excerpted at page 264 *supra*. After determining that the "cooling-off period" provision of the consumer protection directive did not have direct horizontal effect, the Court instructed the Italian court to interpret national law "as far as possible" in its light. The Court continued as follows:

27 If the result prescribed by the directive cannot be achieved by way of interpretation, ... Community law [nevertheless] requires the Member States to make good damage caused to individuals through failure to transpose a directive [citing *Francovich* and restating its three conditions for liability].

28 The directive on contracts negotiated away from business premises is undeniably intended to confer rights on individuals and it is equally certain that the minimum content of those rights can be identified by reference to the provisions of the directive alone.

29 Where damage has been suffered and that damage is due to a breach by the State of its obligation, it is for the national court to uphold the right of aggrieved consumers to obtain reparation in accordance with national law on liability.

Did the Court's answer exceed the scope of the question referred to it?

6. In *Francovich*, Italy had failed to transpose the directive altogether. The Court evidently regarded such a total failure as a serious breach of Community law *per se*, and it has subsequently confirmed that view. See Dillenkofer v. Germany, Joined Cases C–178–79, 188, 190/94, [1996] ECR I–4845, a damage action against Germany by purchasers of package holidays and tours for Germany's failure to transpose into law an EC directive that required the Member States to enact legislation ensuring that package holiday and tour companies refund moneys and repatriate travelers in the event of insolvency.

---

1. Maso and Gazzetta v. Istituto Nazionale della Previdenza Sociale, Case C–373/95, [1997] ECR I–4062. In another companion case, Palmisani v. Istituto Nazionale della Previdenza Sociale, Case C–261/95, [1997] ECR I–4037, the Court sustained as reasonable and non-discriminatory the decree's requirement that damage claims arising out of Italy's belated transposition of the insolvency directive be brought within one year of the decree's entry into force.

Suppose a Member State, instead of failing altogether to implement a directive, simply implements it incorrectly. Under what circumstances is the State then liable to a private party that suffers economic loss as a result? We will revisit this question in the notes following the next case.

BRASSERIE DU PÊCHEUR SA v. GERMANY
AND
THE QUEEN V. SECRETARY OF STATE FOR
TRANSPORT, EX PARTE FACTORTAME LTD.

(Brasserie du Pêcheur) and (Factortame III)
Joined Cases C–46, 48/93, [1996] ECR I–1029.

[Following the judgments of the Court in the *German beer* case (excerpted at pages 499 and 516 *infra*) and in *Factortame II* (excerpted at page 694 *infra*), the successful parties brought damage actions against Germany and Britain, respectively, in those countries' courts. Both actions provoked preliminary references to the Court of Justice on the scope of Member State liability under the *Francovich* judgment. The Court jointed the two references.]

[18] The German, Irish and Netherlands Governments contend that Member States are required to make good loss or damage caused to individuals only where the provisions breached are not directly effective: in *Francovich*, the Court simply sought to fill a lacuna in the system for safeguarding rights of individuals. . . .

[19] That argument cannot be accepted.

[20] The Court has consistently held that the right of individuals to rely on the directly effective provisions of the Treaty before national courts is only a minimum guarantee and is not sufficient in itself to ensure the full and complete implementation of the Treaty. The purpose of that right is to ensure that provisions of Community law prevail over national provisions. It cannot, in every case, . . . avoid [individuals] sustaining damage as a result of a breach of Community law attributable to a Member State. As appears from paragraph 33 of the judgment in *Francovich*, the full effectiveness of Community law would be impaired if individuals were unable to obtain redress when their rights were infringed by a breach of Community law.

* * *

[22] It is all the more so in the event of infringement of a right directly conferred by a Community provision upon which individuals are entitled to rely before the national courts. In that event, the right to reparation is the necessary corollary of the direct effect of the Community provision whose breach caused the damage sustained.

[23] In this case, it is undisputed that the Community provisions at issue, namely Article 30 [now 28] of the Treaty in [*Brasserie de Pêcheur*] and Article 52 [now 43] [in *Factortame*], have direct effect in the sense that they confer on individuals rights upon which they are entitled to rely directly before the national courts. Breach of such provisions may give rise to reparation.

24 The German Government further submits that a general right to reparation for individuals could be created only by legislation and that for such a
right to be recognized by judicial decision would be incompatible with the
allocation of powers as between the Community institutions and the
Member States and with the institutional balance established by the
Treaty.

25 It must, however, be stressed that the existence and extent of State
liability for damage ensuing as a result of a breach of obligations incumbent on the State by virtue of Community law are questions of Treaty
interpretation which fall within the jurisdiction of the Court.

* * *

27 Since the Treaty contains no provision expressly and specifically governing
the consequences of breaches of Community law by Member States, it is
for the Court, in pursuance of the task conferred on it by Article 164 [now
220] of the Treaty of ensuring that in the interpretation and application of
the Treaty the law is observed, to rule on such a question in accordance
with generally accepted methods of interpretation, in particular by reference to the fundamental principles of the Community legal system and,
where necessary, general principles common to the legal systems of the
Member States.

* * *

29 The principle of the non-contractual liability of the Community expressly
laid down in Article 215 [now 288] of the Treaty is simply an expression of
the general principle familiar to the legal systems of the Member States
that an unlawful act or omission gives rise to an obligation to make good
the damage caused. That provision also reflects the obligation on public
authorities to make good damage caused in the performance of their
duties.

* * *

32 [T]hat principle holds good for any case in which a Member State breaches
Community law, whatever be the organ of the State whose act or omission
was responsible for the breach.

* * *

35 The fact that, according to national rules, the breach complained of is
attributable to the legislature cannot affect the requirements inherent in
the protection of the rights of individuals who rely on Community law. . . .

* * *

*Conditions under which the State may incur liability for acts and omissions of
the national legislature contrary to Community law (second question in [Bras-
serie du Pêcheur] and first question in [Factortame])*

37 By these questions, the national courts ask the Court to specify the
conditions under which a right to reparation of loss or damage caused to

individuals by breaches of Community law attributable to a Member State is, in the particular circumstances, guaranteed by Community law.

* * *

39   In order to determine those conditions, account should first be taken of the principles inherent in the Community legal order which form the basis for State liability, namely, first, the full effectiveness of Community rules and the effective protection of the rights which they confer and, second, the obligation to cooperate imposed on Member States by Article 5 [now 10] of the Treaty.

40   In addition, as the Commission and the several governments which submitted observations have emphasized, it is pertinent to refer to the Court's case-law on non-contractual liability on the part of the Community.

41   First, the second paragraph of Article 215 [now 288] of the Treaty refers, as regards the non-contractual liability of the Community, to the general principles common to the laws of the Member States, from which, in the absence of written rules, the Court also draws inspiration in other areas of Community law.

42   Second, the conditions under which the State may incur liability for damage caused to individuals by a breach of Community law cannot, in the absence of particular justification, differ from those governing the liability of the Community in like circumstances. . . .

43   The system of rules which the Court has worked out with regard to Article 215 of the Treaty, particularly in relation to liability for legislative measures, takes into account, *inter alia,* the complexity of the situations to be regulated, difficulties in the application or interpretation of the texts and, more particularly, the margin of discretion available to the author of the act in question.

44   Thus, in developing its case-law on the non-contractual liability of the Community, in particular as regards legislative measures involving choices of economic policy, the Court has had regard to the wide discretion available to the institutions in implementing Community policies.

45   The strict approach taken towards the liability of the Community in the exercise of its legislative activities is due to two considerations. First, even where the legality of measures is subject to judicial review, exercise of the legislative function must not be hindered by the prospect of actions for damages whenever the general interest of the Community requires legislative measures to be adopted which may adversely affect individual interests. Second, in a legislative context characterized by the exercise of a wide discretion, which is essential for implementing a Community policy, the Community cannot incur liability unless the institution concerned has manifestly and gravely disregarded the limits on the exercise of its powers.

46   That said, the national legislature—like the Community institutions—does not systematically have a wide discretion when it acts in a field governed by Community law. Community law may impose upon it obligations to achieve a particular result or obligations to act or refrain from acting which reduce its margin of discretion, sometimes to a considerable degree. This is so, for instance, where, as in the circumstances to which the

judgment in *Francovich* relates, Article 189 [now 249] of the Treaty places the Member State under an obligation to take, within a given period, all the measures needed in order to achieve the result required by a directive. In such a case, the fact that it is for the national legislature to take the necessary measures has no bearing on the Member State's liability for failing to transpose the directive.

47 In contrast, where a Member State acts in a field where it has a wide discretion, comparable to that of the Community institutions in implementing Community policies, the conditions under which it may incur liability must, in principle, be the same as those under which the Community institutions incur liability in a comparable situation.

48 In the case which gave rise to the reference in [*Brasserie du Pêcheur*], the German legislature had legislated in the field of foodstuffs, specifically beer. In the absence of Community harmonization, the national legislature had a wide discretion in that sphere in laying down rules on the quality of beer put on the market.

49 As regards the facts of [*Factortame*], the United Kingdom legislature also had a wide discretion. The legislation at issue was concerned, first, with the registration of vessels, a field which, in view of the state of development of Community law, falls within the jurisdiction of the Member States and, secondly, with regulating fishing, a sector in which implementation of the common fisheries policy leaves a margin of discretion to the Member States.

50 Consequently, in each case the German and United Kingdom legislatures were faced with situations involving choices comparable to those made by the Community institutions when they adopt legislative measures pursuant to a Community policy.

51 In such circumstances, Community law confers a right to reparation where three conditions are met: the rule of law infringed must be intended to confer rights on individuals; the breach must be sufficiently serious; and there must be a direct causal link between the breach of the obligation resting on the State and the damage sustained by the injured parties.

* * *

54 The first condition is manifestly satisfied in the case of Article 30 [now 28] of the Treaty, the relevant provision in [*Brasserie du Pêcheur*], and in the case of Article 52 [now 43], the relevant provision in Case [*Factortame*]. Whilst Article 30 imposes a prohibition on Member States, it nevertheless gives rise to rights for individuals which the national courts must protect. Likewise, the essence of Article 52 is to confer rights on individuals.

55 As to the second condition, as regards both Community liability under Article 215 and Member State liability for breaches of Community law, the decisive test for finding that a breach of Community law is sufficiently serious is whether the Member State or the Community institution concerned manifestly and gravely disregarded the limits on its discretion.

56 The factors which the competent court may take into consideration include the clarity and precision of the rule breached, the measure of discretion left by that rule to the national or Community authorities,

whether the infringement and the damage caused was intentional or involuntary, whether any error of law was excusable or inexcusable, the fact that the position taken by a Community institution may have contributed towards the omission, and the adoption or retention of national measures or practices contrary to Community law.

57 On any view, a breach of Community law will clearly be sufficiently serious if it has persisted despite a judgment finding the infringement in question to be established, or a preliminary ruling or settled case-law of the Court on the matter, from which it is clear that the conduct in question constituted an infringement.

58 While, in the present cases, the Court cannot substitute its assessment for that of the national courts, which have sole jurisdiction to find the facts in the main proceedings and decide how to characterize the breaches of Community law at issue, it will be helpful to indicate a number of circumstances which the national courts might take into account.

59 In [*Brasserie du Pêcheur*] a distinction should be drawn between the question of the German legislature's having maintained in force provisions of the *Biersteuergesetz* concerning the purity of beer prohibiting the marketing under the designation "Bier" of beers imported from other Member States which were lawfully produced in conformity with different rules, and the question of the retention of the provisions of that same law prohibiting the import of beers containing additives. As regards the provisions of the German legislation relating to the designation of the product marketed, it would be difficult to regard the breach of Article 30 [now 28] by that legislation as an excusable error, since the incompatibility of such rules with Article 30 was manifest in the light of earlier decisions of the Court, in particular [*Cassis de Dijon,* page 508 *infra*, and Commission v. Italy (Vinegar), Case 193/80, [1981] ECR 3019]. In contrast, having regard to the relevant case-law, the criteria available to the national legislature to determine whether the prohibition of the use of additives was contrary to Community law were significantly less conclusive until the Court's judgment in [the *German beer* case], in which the Court held that prohibition to be incompatible with Article 30.

60 A number of observations may likewise be made about the national legislation at issue in [*Factortame*].

61 The decision of the United Kingdom legislature to introduce in the Merchant Shipping Act 1988 provisions relating to the conditions for the registration of fishing vessels has to be assessed differently in the case of the provisions making registration subject to a nationality condition, which constitute direct discrimination manifestly contrary to Community law, and in the case of the provisions laying down residence and domicile conditions for vessel owners and operators.

62 The latter conditions are prima facie incompatible with Article 52 [now 43] of the Treaty in particular, but the United Kingdom sought to justify them in terms of the objectives of the common fisheries policy. In the judgment in *Factortame II,* cited above, the Court rejected that justification.

63 In order to determine whether the breach of Article 52 thus committed by the United Kingdom was sufficiently serious, the national court might

take into account, *inter alia,* the legal disputes relating to particular features of the common fisheries policy, the attitude of the Commission, which made its position known to the United Kingdom in good time, and the assessments as to the state of certainty of Community law made by the national courts in the interim proceedings brought by individuals affected by the Merchant Shipping Act.

64   Lastly, consideration should be given to the assertion made by [one of the claimants] in [*Factortame*] that the United Kingdom failed to adopt immediately [the provisional measure that the President of the Court of Justice had ordered in connection with the Commission's enforcement action against the UK arising out of the UK's fishing quotas], and that this needlessly increased the loss it sustained. If this allegation . . . should prove correct, it should be regarded by the national court as constituting in itself a manifest and, therefore, sufficiently serious breach of Community law.

65   As for the third condition, it is for the national courts to determine whether there is a direct causal link between the breach of the obligation borne by the State and the damage sustained by the injured parties.

66   The aforementioned three conditions are necessary and sufficient to found a right in individuals to obtain redress, although this does not mean that the State cannot incur liability under less strict conditions on the basis of national law.

67   [T]he State must make reparation for the consequences of the loss and damage caused in accordance with the domestic rules on liability, provided that the conditions for reparation of loss and damage laid down by national law must not be less favourable than those relating to similar domestic claims and must not be such as in practice to make it impossible or excessively difficult to obtain reparation.

68   In that regard, restrictions that exist in domestic legal systems as to the noncontractual liability of the State in the exercise of its legislative function may be such as to make it impossible in practice or excessively difficult for individuals to exercise their right to reparation, as guaranteed by Community law, of loss or damage resulting from the breach of Community law.

69   In [*Brasserie du Pêcheur*] the national court asks in particular whether national law may subject any right to compensation to the same restrictions as apply where a law is in breach of higher-ranking national provisions, for instance, where an ordinary Federal law infringes the *Grundgesetz* [Constitution] of the Federal Republic of Germany.

* * *

71   The condition imposed by German law . . . , which makes reparation dependent upon the legislature's act or omission being referable to an individual situation, would in practice make it impossible or extremely difficult to obtain effective reparation for loss or damage resulting from a breach of Community law, since the tasks falling to the national legislature relate, in principle, to the public at large and not to identifiable persons or classes of person.

72   Since such a condition stands in the way of the obligation on national courts to ensure the full effectiveness of Community law by guaranteeing effective protection for the rights of individuals, it must be set aside where an infringement of Community law is attributable to the national legislature.

73   Likewise, any condition that may be imposed by English law on State liability requiring proof of misfeasance in public office, such an abuse of power being inconceivable in the case of the legislature, is also such as in practice to make it impossible or extremely difficult to obtain effective reparation for loss or damage resulting from a breach of Community law where the breach is attributable to the national legislature.

* * *

The possibility of making reparation conditional upon the existence of fault (third question in [Brasserie du Pêcheur])

75   By its third question, the *Bundesgerichtshof* [German Constitutional Court] essentially seeks to establish whether, pursuant to the national legislation which it applies, the national court is entitled to make reparation conditional upon the existence of fault (whether intentional or negligent) on the part of the organ of the State to which the infringement is attributable.

* * *

79   The obligation to make reparation for loss or damage caused to individuals cannot ... depend upon a condition based on any concept of fault going beyond that of a sufficiently serious breach of Community law. Imposition of such a supplementary condition would be tantamount to calling in question the right to reparation founded on the Community legal order.

* * *

The actual extent of the reparation (question 4(a) in [Brasserie du Pêcheur] and the second question in [Factortame])

81   By these questions, the national courts essentially ask the Court to identify the criteria for determination of the extent of the reparation due by the Member State responsible for the breach.

82   Reparation for loss or damage caused to individuals as a result of breaches of Community law must be commensurate with the loss or damage sustained so as to ensure the effective protection for their rights.

83   In the absence of relevant Community provisions, it is for the domestic legal system of each Member State to set the criteria for determining the extent of reparation. However, those criteria must not be less favourable than those applying to similar claims based on domestic law and must not be such as in practice to make it impossible or excessively difficult to obtain reparation.

84   In particular, in order to determine the loss or damage for which reparation may be granted, the national court may inquire whether the injured person showed reasonable diligence in order to avoid the loss or damage or limit its extent and whether, in particular, he availed himself in time of all the legal remedies available to him.

[85] Indeed, it is a general principle common to the legal systems of the Member States that the injured party must show reasonable diligence in limiting the extent of the loss or damage, or risk having to bear the damage himself.

[86] The *Bundesgerichtshof* asks whether national legislation may generally limit the liability to make reparation to damage done to certain, specifically protected individual interests, for example property, or whether it should also cover loss of profit by the claimants. It states that the opportunity to market products from other Member States is not regarded in German law as forming part of the protected assets of the undertaking.

[87] Total exclusion of loss of profit as a head of damage for which reparation may be awarded in the case of a breach of Community law cannot be accepted. Especially in the context of economic or commercial litigation, such a total exclusion of loss of profit would be such as to make reparation of damage practically impossible.

* * *

[89] As regards in particular [in the UK] the award of exemplary damages, such damages are based under domestic law ... on the finding that the public authorities concerned acted oppressively, arbitrarily or unconstitutionally. In so far as such conduct may constitute or aggravate a breach of Community law, an award of exemplary damages pursuant to a claim or an action founded on Community law cannot be ruled out if such damages could be awarded pursuant to a similar claim or action founded on domestic law.

[In the final paragraphs of the judgment, the Court ruled that national courts are not permitted to limit a Member State's liability for an infringement of Community law to the damage sustained after the delivery of a judgment of the Court finding the infringement in question. The Court also denied the German government's request that its liability, if any, be limited to loss sustained after the date of judgment, except where the victim had brought legal proceedings, or made an equivalent claim, before that date.]

Notes and Questions

1.   The Court concludes that a Member State bears liability for non-compliance with Community law even in cases in which the Community law measure in question has direct effect and may therefore be invoked directly in national court. Does this mean that, in such a case, the claimant may demand of the national court *both* that it give the measure direct effect *and* that it award damages against the state. What should the measure of damages be in such a case?

2.   Suppose that a national court systematically finds that the Member State's breaches of Community law are not "sufficiently serious." What recourse, if any, do the Community institutions have?

3.   When the *Factortame* case came back to it, the English High Court decided that the UK had committed a sufficiently serious breach of Community law intended to confer rights on individuals. It also decided that punitive damages could be withheld without violating the principle of equivalence between remedies for breaches of national law and breaches of Community law. The Court of Appeal affirmed. The House of Lords took a more nuanced view. In the principal opinion,

Lord Slynn of Hadley (former Advocate–General Slynn), distinguished among the nationality, domicile and residence requirements. He found the UK's imposition of the first two requirements to have been at the time a manifest breach of fundamental Treaty obligations. The residence requirement gave him greater pause, but he came to the same conclusion about it. Regina v. Secretary of State for Transport *ex parte* Factortame Ltd, [1999] 4 All ER 906, [1999] 3 CMLR 597, [1999] 3 WLR 1062 (H.L., July 13–15, Oct. 28, 1999).

4. Predictably, the question of the seriousness of breaches of Community law has occasioned numerous preliminary references to the Court. Although the Court has said that it is for national courts to decide whether a breach is or is not sufficiently serious for liability purposes, it requires them to take into account the following factors: "the clarity and precision of the rule infringed, whether the infringement and the damage caused was intentional or involuntary, whether any error of law was excusable or inexcusable, and the fact that the position taken by a Community institution may have contributed towards the adoption or maintenance of national measures contrary to Community law." Haim v. Kassenzahnärztliche Vereinigung Nordrhein, Case C–424/97, [2000] ECR I–5123.

Moreover, the Court will frequently give its own view of the direction in which certain of these factors point. In *Haim*, for example, a German professional licensing agency was found to have infringed an Italian dentist's rights under the Treaty by not taking account, in applying the dentistry directive, of his prior experience in practice in another Member State. On preliminary reference arising out of a subsequent damages claim, the Court noted that, while the rule of law violated in this case (freedom of establishment) was a directly applicable and longstanding Treaty provision, the facts of the case predated the judgment (*Vlassopoulou, infra* page 721) in which the Court first announced a rule requiring States to give full faith and credit to other Member States' equivalent tests and certifications.

On other occasions, the Court squarely decides by itself whether or not a breach is sufficiently serious. It did so in Rechberger, Greindl, Hofmeister and others v. Austria, Case C–140/97, 1999 ECR I–3499, where the question concerned Austria's implementation of the directive on package travel, holidays and tours. Article 7 of the directive required that tour organizers provide "sufficient evidence of security for the refund of money paid over and for the repatriation of the consumer in the event of insolvency." In transposing the directive, Austria limited the security guarantee to trips booked after January 1, 1995 (the effective date of Austria's accession) and having a departure date of May 1, 1995 or later. It also fixed the required security at a given percentage of the organizer's business turnover in the corresponding quarter of the previous calendar year. As a result, when a certain organizer went bankrupt, some disappointed travelers received no refund and others only a pro rata refund.

On preliminary reference, the Court ruled:

> The Member State ... enjoyed no margin of discretion as to the entry into force, in its own law, of the provisions of Article 7. That being so, the limitation of the protection ... to trips with a departure date of 1 May 1995 or later is manifestly incompatible with the obligations under the Directive and thus constitutes a sufficiently serious breach of Community law.

> The fact that the Member State has implemented all the other provisions of the Directive does not alter that finding.

The Court also ruled that since the directive imposes a guarantee of result (viz. full indemnification of the consumer), Austria's requirement of insurance only up to a fixed percentage of the prior year's turnover was "structurally incapable" of coping with certain eventualities, such as sharp increases in bookings from one year to the next. (Because the directive intended to guarantee a result, the Court also ruled that Austria could invoke neither the negligence of the tour organizer nor the unforeseeability of the circumstances to reduce its liability.)

The Court was not asked, and did not answer, the question whether this particular defect in implementation constituted a sufficiently serious breach to generate liability on Austria's part. How would you decide that question? (If you decide in the negative, then purchasers who were denied recovery because their departure date preceded May 1, 1995 would presumably collect full damages from Austria, while those who received a pro rata refund, due to the inadequacy of the organizer's security, would presumably have to settle for that.)

5. The German court's question (para. 86) whether a Member State's liability could be limited in scope to "certain, specifically protected individual interests," or had to include compensation for "loss of profit" was prompted by the fact that the German Civil Code limits tort liability, in the ordinary tort situation, to certain named categories of loss, which do not include economic expectancies. However, lost profit is a category of loss that claimants are very likely to raise in actions against Member States for violations of their Community law obligations. It is therefore not surprising that the Court rejected a "[t]otal exclusion of loss of profit as a head of damage" (para. 87). Do you suppose that the Court would accept a rule of national law that provides for a *partial* exclusion of lost profits as a head of damage?

6. The question of liability for mis-implementation, as opposed to non-implementation, arose in The Queen v. H.M. Treasury ex parte British Telecommunications plc, Case C–392/93, [1996] ECR I–1631. Council Directive 90/531, laying down procurement procedures (including reporting and disclosure requirements) for, *inter alia*, the telecommunications sector, applied to all private firms that "operate on the basis of special or exclusive rights granted by a competent authority of a Member State," notably the right to expropriate private property for telecommunication network purposes.

According to Article 8(1) of the directive, these procedures do not apply to "contracts which contracting entities ... award for purchases intended exclusively to enable them to provide one or more telecommunications services where other entities are free to offer the same services in the same geographical area and under substantially the same conditions." Article 8(2) required firms to notify the Commission of any services they regarded as covered by this exemption.

The 1992 regulations that transposed the directive in the UK specified that British Telecom (BT) did not satisfy the directive's criteria for exemption from the procurement rules, and BT challenged those regulations as having "incorrectly" transposed the directive. BT maintained that, in transposing the directive, the Member States were supposed to transpose the criteria quoted above rather than "apply" them to specific enterprises. BT claimed that this error imposed undue compliance costs on it and placed it at a competitive disadvantage vis-à-vis competitors. The UK court issued a preliminary reference to the Court of Justice, asking not only for the correct interpretation of the directive, but also for guidance on the damages that the UK might possibly owe BT in the event that it had in fact transposed the directive incorrectly.

The Court of Justice agreed with BT that, under a proper interpretation of the directive, the UK's transposition was faulty. The Court then turned to the damages issue, recalling the three conditions for liability laid down in the *Francovich* and the *Brasserie du Pêcheur and Factortame* judgments:

40   Those same conditions must be applicable to the situation ... in which a Member State incorrectly transposes a Community directive into national law. A restrictive approach to State liability is justified in such a situation, for the reasons already given by the Court to justify the strict approach to non-contractual liability of Community institutions or Member States when exercising legislative functions in areas covered by Community law where the institution or State has a wide discretion, in particular, the concern to ensure that the exercise of legislative functions is not hindered by the prospect of actions for damages whenever the general interest requires the institutions or Member States to adopt measures which may adversely affect individual interests.

* * *

43   In the present case, Article 8(1) is imprecisely worded and was reasonably capable of bearing, as well as the construction applied to it by the Court in this judgment, the interpretation given to it by the United Kingdom in good faith and on the basis of arguments which are not entirely devoid of substance. That interpretation, which was also shared by other Member States, was not manifestly contrary to the wording of the directive or to the objective pursued by it.

44   Moreover, no guidance was available to the United Kingdom from case-law of the Court as to the interpretation of the provision at issue, nor did the Commission raise the matter when the 1992 Regulations were adopted.

45   In those circumstances, the fact that a Member State, when transposing the directive into national law, thought it necessary itself to determine which services were to be excluded from its scope in implementation of Article 8, albeit in breach of that provision, cannot be regarded as a sufficiently serious breach of Community law of the kind intended by the Court in its judgment in *Brasserie du Pêcheur* and *Factortame*.

Is the Court in *British Telecom* correct in distinguishing between the faulty implementation and the non-implementation of a directive and suggesting that it would take a more indulgent look at the former than the latter?

7. The UK government denied Hedley Lomas authorization to export live sheep to Spain on the ground that Spain had failed to implement properly a Community directive governing the treatment of livestock in slaughterhouses. (In fact, for this reason, the UK had imposed a general ban on the export of livestock to Spain.) The UK also notified the Commission of its suspicions about the standards of Spanish slaughterhouses. When the Commission later decided, based on Spanish government assurances, not to pursue Spain under Article 226 (ex 169), it also advised the UK that any continuation of the export ban would violate Article 29 (ex 34) of the Treaty. The UK then lifted the ban.

At that point, Hedley Lomas sued the UK government for damages. On preliminary reference, the Court of Justice ruled that, in unilaterally determining that Spain was in breach of its duties of implementation, and in acting on that belief by barring exports to Spain, the UK had engaged in impermissible self-help and thus interfered with the free movement of goods:

A Member State may not unilaterally adopt, on its own authority, corrective or protective measures designed to obviate any breach by another Member State of rules of Community law [citing Commission v. Luxembourg and Belgium, Joined Cases 90 & 91/63, [1964] ECR 625, and Commission v. France (Mutton and lamb), Case 232/78, [1979] ECR 2729, excerpted at page 432 *infra*].

As to damages, the Court once again quoted the three conditions of liability reaffirmed in *Brasserie du Pêcheur* and *Factortame*. It found the first two conditions of liability to be satisfied (the latter because the UK "was not called upon to make any legislative choices and had only considerably reduced, or even no, discretion"). The question whether the third condition was satisfied was once again left to the national court. The Queen v. Ministry of Agriculture, Fisheries and Food ex parte Hedley Lomas (Ireland) Ltd., Case C–5/94, [1996] ECR I–2553. Is this the preliminary ruling that you would have recommended that the Court issue in this case?

8. Let us return to the bovine spongiform encephalopathy (BSE), or "mad cow disease," episode mentioned at several points in this book. After the Commission eventually decided in 1999, based on scientific committee advice, to lift its 1996 ban on the export of British beef, the French food safety agency announced that it regarded that step as premature, and in December 1999 the French government declared the embargo still in effect. Within one month, the Commission had issued a reasoned opinion and filed suit in the Court of Justice. The Commission prevailed. Commission v. France, (Ban on import of British beef), Case C–1/00, [2001] ECR I–___ (Dec. 13, 2001). How likely is it that France has subjected itself to *Francovich* liability? To whom?

Chapter 11

ENFORCEMENT PROCEEDINGS AGAINST THE MEMBER STATES

As we have seen, the Community has a very real interest in ensuring that Member States properly carry out the Community law tasks entrusted to them. To this end, Article 10 (ex 5) lays down a so-called "duty of loyalty," enjoining Member States to "take all appropriate measures ... to ensure fulfillment of [their] obligations" under Community law, to "facilitate the achievement of the Community's tasks" and to "abstain from any measure which could jeopardise the attainment of [Treaty] objectives." However, negligence or inefficiency sometimes keeps a Member State from implementing Community policy in a timely and proper way. Not often does a State deliberately fail to comply with Community law, but that too has occurred.

Article 226 (ex 169) of the EC Treaty accordingly empowers the Commission to "police" Member State compliance by drawing a State's attention to alleged defaults and, if necessary, bringing an action in the Court of Justice. Article 226 provides:

> If the Commission considers that a Member State has failed to fulfil an obligation under this Treaty, it shall deliver a reasoned opinion on the matter after giving the State concerned the opportunity to submit its observations.

> If the State concerned does not comply with the opinion within the period laid down by the Commission, the latter may bring the matter before the Court of Justice.

Should the Court find a Member State to be in default of its Treaty obligations, the Member State is required under Article 228 (ex 171) "to take the necessary measures to comply with the [Court's] judgment." As a result of an amendment to Article 228 introduced by the Treaty of Maastricht, and discussed more fully below, the Commission may seek, and the Court may impose, a pecuniary fine where a Member State is found not to have complied with a previous Court of Justice judgment condemning it for the same violation.

Until the late 1970s, the then Article 169 received relatively little use. In 1977, however, Commission President Roy Jenkins made the decision to prosecute Member State infringements more vigorously, and Article 169 became an important Community law weapon. Today, enforcement actions are common, roughly matching in number the judicial review cases brought under Article 230 (ex 173); their number is exceeded only by that of preliminary references. Since the Statute of the Court of Justice requires Article 226 cases to be heard in plenary session if a Member State party so requests, and since States usually do, the burden on the Court is considerable. The Protocol on the Statute of the Court of Justice (art. 16) agreed upon at Nice in December 2000 requires the Court to sit not as a full court but as a "Grand Chamber" of eleven judges whenever a Member State (or a Community institution) is a party to the proceeding and so requests.

At one time, the largest number of enforcement actions by far (around 30% of the total) had involved Italy. This was largely due not to any hostility toward Community policy, but rather to institutional difficulties and conceded inefficiencies in Italy's processes for implementing Community directives. Italy repeatedly tried to remedy the situation, for example by adopting legislation in 1982 (law no. 42) and 1987 (law no. 183) requiring the Government to implement a large number of specified directives whose implementation deadlines had passed. In 1989, Italy put in place a new system (law no. 86) providing for improved parliamentary review of implementation and the enactment of an annual "Community Act" (proposed by the Minister for Coordination of Community Policies) containing, rather than merely mentioning, the measures needed to implement Community directives since the previous year's act. See R. Pettricione, A New Mechanism for the Implementation of Community Law, 14 Eur. L. Rev. 456 (1989). This reform reportedly substantially reduced the incidence of noncompliance. While enforcement proceedings have by no means abated, no single Member State stands out any longer as an Article 226 target.

Article 227 (ex 170) provides a second enforcement device, permitting one Member State to sue another for the latter's alleged violation of Community law obligations. Member States, however, rarely invoke Article 227, preferring instead to notify the Commission of the alleged delinquency and allow the Commission to proceed under Article 226. Article 227 is accordingly dealt with only briefly at the end of this chapter (section D).

A.   THE ARTICLE 226 PROCEDURE

The various stages of the Article 226 enforcement procedure are clearly designed to encourage Member State compliance and to obviate the need for judicial recourse. If it considers a Member State to be in default of its Treaty obligations, the Commission will first give the State informal notice of that fact and allow it a right of reply. The time for reply must be one that is reasonable under the circumstances. Commission v. Belgium (University fees), Case 293/85, [1988] ECR 305. The Commission may find itself satisfied that a violation did not occur or has been ended, but it also may maintain its initial view. If the latter is the case, it may next issue a "reasoned opinion" which spells out the basis for its views and calls on the Member State to take remedial action within a specified period. Should timely and sufficient action not be taken, the Commission may then bring the State before the Court of Justice.

Member States have occasionally challenged the Commission's reasoned opinion as unclear or insufficiently detailed. Usually the Court of Justice is not impressed with that complaint and proceeds to the merits. Rarely, the Court finds that the Commission was not precise enough as to what the Member State should or should not have done, and the Court will then decide in the State's favor because it views the Commission's failure as an essential procedural defect.[1] In no event may the Commission raise issues before the Court that were not fairly covered in the reasoned opinion.[2]

In Article 226 actions, as in any other, the Court will entertain applications for interim relief. A notable example is Commission v. Germany (Charges for road use by heavy vehicles), Case C–195/90R, [1990] ECR I–3351. There, the Commission asked the Court to enjoin the German authorities temporarily from collecting a road tax on heavy vehicles that was then the subject of a Commission challenge before the Court. The Court ordered collection of the tax provisionally suspended on the ground that the tax was prima facie invalid and that its collection would cause serious and irreparable harm to the affected parties. In doing so, the Court rejected Germany's demand that the Commission put up some 500 million DM as security to cover the taxes that Germany might not later be able to recover if it won the action. (The Court thought there was no reason to believe the Community could not pay any damages that might be awarded against it.)

The principal issue in an Article 226 case is typically the scope of a Member State's obligations under Community law. To this extent, Article 226 proceedings are not unlike other actions before the Court, notably preliminary references. However, the Court will also decide whether the defendant State failed to fulfil those obligations.[3] Thus, unlike in preliminary references, the Court actually decides the case before it, with the Commission bearing the burden of proof.[4] Article 226 is the only vehicle by which the Court may rule directly on the compatibility of a provision of national law with Community law;[5] in all other cases, the power to rule on the compatibility of national law with Community law belongs to the national courts, aided where appropriate by preliminary rulings from the Court of Justice.

The Court has also remarked that it considers an Article 226 action to be less a form of judicial review of the Commission's reasoned opinion than an adjudication of the Member State's alleged infringement.[6] What significance is there to this distinction?

The conduct of a Member State during enforcement proceedings may itself become a compliance issue. For example, the Court has sharply condemned Member States for refusing or failing to provide information to the Commission during the investigative stage of an Article 226 action. Thus, in Commission v. Greece (Olive oil trade restriction), Case 272/86, [1988] ECR 4875, the Court considered the Greek Government's refusal to supply requested documents to the Commission to be a violation of Article 10 (ex 5), since it

1. See, for example, Commission v. Denmark (Taxation of imported motor vehicles), Case C–52/90, [1992] ECR I–2187.

2. Commission v. Italy (Transit of live animals), Case 121/84, [1986] ECR 107.

3. Commission v. France (Redfish quotas), Case C–62/89, [1990] ECR 925.

4. Commission v. Belgium (Pharmaceutical prices), Case C–249/88, [1991] ECR I–1275.

5. Triveneta Zuccheri SpA v. Commission, Case C–347/87, [1990] ECR I–1083.

6. Commission v. Italy (Road haulage directive), Case 28/81, [1981] ECR 2577.

hampered both the Commission in its duty to enforce the Treaty under Article 226 and the Court in its duty to enforce the law under Article 220 (ex 164). The Court called the refusal "a serious impediment to the administration of justice." See also Commission v. Belgium (Prices of crude oil and petroleum products), Case C–374/89, [1991] ECR I–367; Commission v. Greece (Obstacles to cereal imports), Case 240/86, [1988] ECR 1835.

The Commission prevails in the vast majority, almost 90%, of Article 226 proceedings that reach the Court of Justice. The figure, however, is deceptive, since the Commission takes cases that far only very selectively. Moreover, a Member State government may mount only a pro forma defense if the reason for noncompliance, for example, is the national parliament's failure to implement a directive properly or on time, or inefficiency at some level of the administration. The Member State government may actually welcome the pressure for action coming from an adverse Court of Justice ruling.

In any case, the utility of Article 226 cannot be measured simply by the number of judgments rendered. Article 226 gives the Commission an administrative as well as a judicial remedy, and Commission success at the earlier stage is certainly no less welcome than at the later stage. In fact, only about 20% of all cases in which the Commission formally complains about a Member State's conduct (and about 40% of those that produce reasoned opinions) ultimately reach the Court of Justice. The remainder are settled, often with full compliance by the State.

Since 1983, the Commission has issued annual reports on its monitoring of the application of Community law. Initially prompted by a parliamentary resolution to that effect (O.J. C 68 (March 14, 1983)), such reports were again called for by the Heads of State or Government at the Maastricht Summit in December 1991 (Declaration 19, annexed to the TEU). The reports recite the major Member State infringements of the Treaties and regulations, and record the States' progress in implementing directives. They also contain various statistical analyses of the infringements noted. The annual report for 2000 states that the Commission that year initiated 1317 infringement proceedings, issued 460 reasoned opinions, and filed 172 court cases.

Notes and Questions

1. Note that Article 226 allows the Commission to set a deadline for Member State compliance with a reasoned opinion. What limits if any would you expect the Court to place on the Commission's discretion in fixing that deadline? See Commission v. Ireland (Poultry import control), Case 74/82, [1984] ECR 317; Commission v. Italy (Road haulage directive), Case 28/81, [1981] ECR 2577.

2. In Alfons Lütticke GmbH v. Commission, Case 48/65, [1966] ECR 19, the Court decided that a private party has no cause of action for the Commission's express refusal to bring enforcement proceedings against a delinquent State. The Court ruled out an Article 230 (ex 173) annulment action because a reasoned opinion (or lack thereof) under Article 226 is without binding force and therefore not challengeable; it ruled out an Article 232 (ex 175) action (for failure to act) because the Commission's refusal to proceed under Article 226 constitutes "defin[ing] its position" for Article 232 purposes. See also Nordgetreide GmbH v. Commission, Case 42/71, [1972] ECR 105.

Should the result under Article 232 be different if the Commission simply fails rather than expressly declines to proceed against a Member State under Article 226? Although it would appear in this situation that the Commission has not "defined its position" and that an Article 232 claim might be admissible, the Court decided otherwise in Star Fruit v. Commission, Case 247/87, [1989] ECR 291. It held that Article 226 gives the Commission "discretion" in deciding whether to act, and that this discretion "excludes the right for individuals to require that institution to adopt a specific position." The Commission issues a reasoned opinion only if it "*considers*" a Member State to be in default; as for bringing the Member State to court, that (under the "may" language of Article 226) is "in any event the [Commission's] right, but not [its] duty." [1989] ECR at 301. See also Ladbroke Racing Ltd. v. Commission, Case T–32/93, [1994] ECR II–1015, involving the Commission's alleged failure to take action against a Member State monopoly under Article 86(3) (ex 90(3)) .

Thus, whether a private party has standing under Article 232 to require the Commission to "define its position" on a request that the Commission prosecute a violation of Community law will depend on the Treaty provision under which (and perhaps the kind of party against which) the Commission was requested to take action. In *Star Fruit* and *Ladbroke Racing, supra*, the Commission had been asked to prosecute a Member State (under Articles 226 and 86(3), respectively) for violating its Community law obligations. Will this explain why, in a separate action, Ladbroke Racing (Deutschland) was permitted to require the Commission to "define its position" on Ladbroke's complaints that DSV, a German owner of broadcasting right, had abused its dominant position under Article 82 (ex 86) of the Treaty by refusing to permit Ladbroke to broadcast French horse races in Germany? See Ladbroke Racing (Deutschland) GmbH v. Commission, Case T–74/92, [1995] ECR II–115.

If a private party cannot compel the Commission to take action under Article 226, what remedy does it have? See the sequel to the *Lütticke* case in Alfons Lütticke GmbH v. Hauptzollamt Saarlouis, Case 57/65, [1966] ECR 205.

It is also conceivable that a private party might want to challenge a decision by the Commission to take action under Article 226. (The party might be benefitting from the alleged infringement and want it to continue, or it might have complained to the Commission about the infringement and believe that the reasoned opinion does not go far enough in condemning it.) If, as seems clear, the private party has no direct remedy in the Court of Justice, what remedy might it have in Member State court? See Amministrazione delle Finanze dello Stato v. Essevi SpA and Carlo Salengo, Cases 142, 143/80, [1981] ECR 1413.

3. Infringement actions occasionally result in judgments that importantly expand our understanding of the scope of Member State obligations. An excellent example is Commission v. France (Produce imports), Case C–265/95, [1997] ECR I–6959, excerpted at page 485 *infra,* where the Court condemned France for "manifestly and persistently" failing to put an end to acts of violence by French farmers designed to prevent the import of less expensive produce from other Member States. The Court effectively held that a Member State breaches its obligations under Article 10 (ex 5) of the EC Treaty when it fails adequately to address certain patterns of private conduct engaged in by its nationals or residents to the detriment of fundamental Community policies. Has the Court gone too far? Or is the judgment a proportionate response by the Court to an exceptionally urgent and intolerable situation? Query, how far does U.S. law go in imposing a duty on governments to prevent private conduct that impairs other persons'

fundamental rights? See DeShaney v. Winnebago County Department of Social Services, 489 U.S. 189, 195, 109 S.Ct. 998, 1003, 103 L.Ed.2d 249, 258 (1989), where a majority of the Court stated that "nothing in the language of the Due Process Clause itself requires the State to protect the life, liberty, and property of its citizens against invasion by private actors."

B. EXCUSES FOR MEMBER STATE NONCOMPLIANCE

The discussion thus far suggests that the crucial issues in Article 226 proceedings will likely concern the scope of a Member State's Community law obligations and the question of what constitutes a violation of those obligations. It is also possible that the existence of both the obligation and the violation will be essentially conceded, and a State will in a sense seek only to "excuse" the violation. Often enough, States will plead in the alternative: they have not violated EC law, but if they have, the violation is excused.

As to available defenses as such, Article 226 simply does not address the question. One plausible defense is that the Community measure a State is accused of breaching is itself illegal because in violation of a higher Community law principle. This is a species of the plea of illegality (art. 241 (ex 184)) discussed in Chapter 5C *supra*. As might be expected from the *Foto–Frost* judgment, *supra* page 276, the Court of Justice does not look favorably on such a defense. The Court regards the Member States as bound to comply with all Community measures unless and until annulled by the Court or suspended pending final judgment. Granaria BV v. Hoofdproduktschap voor Akkerbouwprodukten, Case 101/78, [1979] ECR 623, 636. Only in the rare case where a measure "contain[s] such particularly serious and manifest defects that it could be deemed non-existent" will the Court consider the measure's invalidity to be a defense to an Article 226 action. Commission v. Greece (Public sector insurance), Case 226/87, [1988] ECR 3611.

A Member State may find itself unwittingly precluded from raising as a defense that the Community measure it is charged with infringing is itself illegal. Greece was charged under Article 226 with failing to comply with a Commission decision requiring it to recover a state aid that it had illegally paid to certain Greek export companies. The Court held that Greece could not contest the validity of the prior Commission determination that the state aid was illegal since it had failed to contest that determination at the time the Commission made it. According to the Court, the only defense still available to Greece at the Article 226 stage would be that Greece did not have any possibility of carrying out the Commission's decision. Commission v. Greece (Aid and tax exemptions), Case C–183/91, [1993] ECR I–3131.

States may, of course, by way of defense also object to procedural aspects of the prosecution. Commission v. Germany (First Company Directive penalties), Case C–191/95, [1998] ECR I–5449, offers an important example. The Commission brought infringement proceedings against Germany for failing to provide adequate penalties in the implementing legislation for Community directives requiring corporate disclosure of accounts. Germany maintained that the action was inadmissible because the Commission had effectively delegated to a single Commissioner the decision to issue a reasoned opinion and, subsequently, to go to court, and that this violated the "principle of collegiality." The Court ruled that, while these decisions must be the subject of collective deliberation by the college of Commissioners (with the information on which they are based available to all members), it is not necessary that the full Commission formally adopt the decisions. The Court held:

39   According to settled case-law, the principle of collegiality is based on the equal participation of the Commissioners in the adoption of decisions, from which it follows ... that decisions should be the subject of collective deliberation and that all members of the college of Commissioners should bear collective responsibility at political level for all decisions adopted.

40   The Court has also held that compliance with that principle is of concern to individuals affected by the legal consequences of a Commission decision.

41   Nevertheless, the formal requirements for effective compliance with the principle of collegiality vary according to the nature and legal effects of the acts adopted by that institution.

Looking at a reasoned opinion's "nature and legal effects," the Court emphasized that issuance of such an opinion, however essential a step it may be in the enforcement process, is still only a "preliminary" procedure lacking in binding legal effect. As to the Commission's decision to bring a Member State to court, the Court found that that act too "does not *per se* alter the legal position in question."

48   It follows ... that [while] the Commission's decision to issue a reasoned opinion and its decision to bring an [Article 226] action ... must be the subject of collective deliberation by the college of Commissioners [and] the information on which those decisions are based must therefore be available to the members of the college, [i]t is not ... necessary for the college itself formally to decide on the wording of the acts which give effect to those decisions and put them in final form.

The Court found that these requirements were satisfied. (For discussion of the company law issues in the case, see page 428 *infra*.)

The Member States have urged the Court to recognize a variety of other, more substantive, excuses for noncompliance. The cases that follow take up the more prominent among these.

COMMISSION v. LUXEMBOURG AND BELGIUM

(Milk products)
Cases 90, 91/63, [1964] ECR 625.

[In 1958, Belgium and Luxembourg introduced a new tax on the import of certain milk products. After several years of complaint, the Commission finally brought an Article 226 (ex 169) action challenging the tax as a violation of then Article 12 of the EC Treaty, the subsequently-repealed "standstill" provision barring the introduction of new customs duties on intra-Community trade. (See the *van Gend en Loos* case, *supra* page 239.) Belgium and Luxembourg conceded their violation of Article 12, but argued that the tax was necessary to protect their markets, since the Community itself had failed to create in due time a market organization under the Common Agricultural Policy for the dairy products in question.]

Admissibility

The defendants ... complain that the Community failed to comply with the obligations falling on it ... and was thus responsible for the continuance of the alleged infringement of the Treaty. ... In their view, since international law allows a party, injured by the failure of another party to perform its obligations, to withhold performance of its own, the Commission has lost the right to plead infringement of the Treaty. However this relationship between the obligations of parties cannot be recognized under Community law.

In fact the Treaty is not limited to creating reciprocal obligations between the different natural and legal persons to whom it is applicable, but establishes a new legal order which governs the powers, rights and obligations of the said persons, as well as the necessary procedures for taking cognizance of and penalizing any breach of it. Therefore, except where otherwise expressly provided, the basic concept of the Treaty requires that the Member States shall not take the law into their own hands. Therefore the fact that the Council failed to carry out its obligations cannot relieve the defendants from carrying out theirs.

* * *

The application is therefore admissible.

The Substance

It is not disputed that the contested measures are customs duties on imports or charges having equivalent effect within the meaning of Article 12 of the Treaty. . . .

* * *

Article 12 prohibits the introduction of new customs barriers, so as to facilitate the integration of national markets and the establishment of a common market. Without constituting of itself a measure removing economic protection, this prohibition of any new form of protection by way of customs duties constitutes an essential requirement both for the substitution of a common market for the different national markets and for the substitution of a common agricultural organization for the national organizations. Thus Article 12 constitutes a fundamental rule and any possible exception, which in any event must be strictly construed, must be clearly laid down.

* * *

... The Treaty expressly provides means and special procedures for remedying ... difficulties in [market effectiveness] under the supervision of the Community authorities or with their approval.

* * *

Therefore the applications are well founded.

Notes and Questions

1. Note how the Court in *Milk products* employed the "new legal order" language it had then only recently used in *van Gend en Loos, supra* page 239.

2. In *Milk products,* Belgium and Luxembourg invoked the *tu quoque* or "you too" principle of public international law: if one party to a treaty violates it, the other party is justified in taking defensive measures. If this principle offers no

defense, what recourse do Belgium and Luxembourg have to protect their dairy industry within the "new legal order?" One way is of course through adoption of a Community market organization for dairy products. Creation of such agricultural product organizations was among the most difficult political decisions of the Community in the 1960s.

COMMISSION v. ITALY
(Pork import ban)
Case 7/61, [1961] ECR 317.

[In June 1960, Italy instituted a ban on the import of certain pork products, a ban that it periodically renewed. The Commission objected, citing the standstill provision on new quantitative restrictions contained in the then Article 31 (since repealed). In January 1961, the Italian government responded to the Commission's reasoned opinion by asking the Commission to approve the ban as a safeguard measure under the then Article 226. (Article 22, which has subsequently been repealed, allowed Member States to seek Commission approval of safeguard measures that a Member State might need in the face of serious economic difficulties during the transitional period.) This action by the Commission in the Court of Justice followed.

Italy argued that the Commission should have treated the import ban from as early as June 1960 as an application for a safeguard measure under Article 226, and that such an application was sufficient compliance with the reasoned opinion. The Court disagreed, stressing that a safeguard measure requires an "unequivocal, formal application by the government concerned," which Italy had not made until January 1961. Italy also argued that the import ban should be allowed because it was only "provisional" in nature. The Court again disagreed, emphasizing that the standstill obligation was "absolute."

Italy raised a further argument based on necessity.]

The defendant maintains, thirdly, that it had no other means than the provisional suspension of imports at its disposal to remedy the artificially low prices prevailing in the pigmeat sector. Moreover, the general principles of public law authorize every State, in an emergency, to take such provisional measures as are necessary to remedy serious occurrences.

Article 226 contains a formal provision laying down an emergency procedure which allows a remedy to be brought to the most serious situations in the shortest time.

The very fact that an emergency procedure has been provided excludes any unilateral action by Member States, which may not therefore rely on either the urgency or the seriousness of the situation to evade the procedure of Article 226.

In the present case such a procedure was not begun until several months after the start of the administrative stage of the dispute.

The arguments based on necessity and urgency must be rejected.

Notes and Questions

1. A defense related to those raised in both the *Milk products* and *Pork import ban* cases is in the nature of laches or estoppel on the Commission's part.

Suppose the Commission tolerates a Member State's unlawful practices or otherwise waits a very long time before challenging them. Is an infringement action under Article 226 action barred? See Commission v. France (Euratom supply agency), Case 7/71, [1971] ECR 1003. Suppose the Commission previously tolerated similar practices by another Member State? See Germany v. Commission (Import duties on mutton), Cases 52, 55/65, [1966] ECR 159.

2.   Compare with *Pork import ban* the case of Commission v. Italy (Lead and zinc), Case 38/69, [1970] ECR 47. During the Community's transitional period for eliminating customs duties, the Commission allowed Italy to retain duties on lead and zinc through the end of 1967 in order to protect its mining interests in Sardinia, a depressed region. Italy maintained these duties after 1968, and the Commission brought an Article 226 proceeding. Italy claimed that when the Council took its second so-called "Acceleration Decision" in July 1966 (ending the initial transitional period for some purposes on June 30, 1968, rather than December 31, 1969, as scheduled), Italy reserved the right to maintain the lead and zinc duties in question. Unfortunately the minutes of the 1966 meeting were unclear on the extent, if at all, to which this reservation was accepted by the Council.

The Court noted that the Acceleration Decision was taken under Article 308 (ex 235), the implied powers provision (see Chapter 4A *supra*), and therefore constituted a Community law measure. It concluded that, whatever weight might be given to Member State reservations in the interpretation of conventional international law agreements, duly adopted Community law was not subject to any such reservations. Italy, it said, "cannot refer to the circumstances in which the Acceleration Decision was adopted in order to justify the protective measures which it maintained beyond the entry into force of that decision...." [1970] ECR at 57. Italy also argued that accelerating the expiry of the transitional period fixed in the Treaty should have been done by Treaty amendment, and that if it had been done that way, Italy would have been entitled to make a binding unilateral reservation. By rejecting that claim too, the Court also gave support to the Council's use of the implied powers provision in lieu of a Treaty amendment.

COMMISSION v. FRANCE
(Mutton and lamb)
Case 232/78, [1979] ECR 2729.

[In the absence at the time of a common organization of the market in mutton and lamb, that market was still regulated nationally. France sought to stabilize domestic prices by restricting the import of these products not only from non-member countries but also from new Member States including the UK. Following complaints from British trade and diplomatic circles, the Commission initiated infringement proceedings.]

[6]   The French Government does not dispute the fact that this system is incompatible with the Treaty provisions relating to ... the free movement of goods within the Community. However ... it puts forward in substance three arguments. First, it emphasizes the serious social and economic effects on the economy of certain economically less-favoured areas for which sheep-rearing is an important source of wealth, of discontinuing the national organization of the market. Secondly, it draws attention to the progress made in ... setting up a common organization of the market in mutton and lamb and stresses the harmful effects of interposing a phase of

free trade between the discontinuance of the national organization and replacing it by a common organization. Finally it points to the inequality in the field of competition deriving from the fact that it would have to abolish its own organization of the market even though in the United Kingdom a national organization of the market, ... result[ing] in subsidizing exports of mutton and lamb to France, would remain intact in the sector under consideration.

7   Although the Court is aware of the genuine problems which the French authorities have to solve in the sector under consideration and of the desirability of achieving the establishment, in the shortest possible time, of a common organization of the market in mutton and lamb, it must again draw attention to the fact that ... after the expiration of the transitional period ... a national organization of the market must no longer operate in such a way as to prevent the Treaty provisions relating to the elimination of restrictions on intra-Community trade from having full force and effect. ... [A] decision to adopt [special measures] can no longer be made unilaterally by the Member States concerned; they must be adopted within the Community system which is designed to guarantee that the general public interest of the Community is protected.

8   Consequently it is for the competent institutions and for them alone to adopt within the appropriate periods ... [and] in a Community context ... a comprehensive solution of the problem of the market in mutton and lamb and of the special difficulties which arise in this connection.... [T]he fact that this work has not yet been successful is not a sufficient justification for the maintenance by a Member State of a national organization of the market which includes features which are incompatible with the requirements of the Treaty relating to the free movement of goods....

9   The French Republic cannot justify the existence of such a system with the argument that the United Kingdom, for its part, has maintained a national organization of the market in the same sector. If the French Republic is of the opinion that that system contains features which are incompatible with Community law it has the opportunity to take action, either within the Council, or through the Commission, or finally by recourse to judicial remedies with a view to achieving the elimination of such incompatible features. A Member State cannot under any circumstances unilaterally adopt, on its own authority, corrective measures or measures to protect trade designed to prevent any failure on the part of another Member State to comply with the rules laid down by the Treaty.

10   The Court must therefore conclude that the national organization of the market in mutton and lamb maintained by the French authorities is incompatible with the Treaty ....

Notes and Questions

1.   Reciprocity has never been successfully invoked as an Article 226 defense, though the attempt has repeatedly been made. See, e.g., Steinike and Weinlig v. Germany, Case 78/76, [1977] ECR 595.

2.   Note that some Member State constitutions excuse the nonperformance of an international treaty obligation if the other state parties to the treaty are themselves in breach. See, e.g., Article 55 of the French Constitution, *supra* page

284. It seems clear that such provisions may not be invoked to justify a Member State's nonperformance of its Community law obligations.

3.   In every Article 226 case examined thus far, the defendant State sought to justify its noncompliance on some claim of necessity. The following case is the rare one in which a national parliament indicated that it took exception to Community law as a matter of policy. The Court reacted with unusually vigorous language.

COMMISSION v. ITALY

(Slaughtered cows II)
Case 39/72, [1973] ECR 101.

[Council Regulation 1975/69, together with implementing Commission Regulation 2195/69, attempted to deal with chronic surpluses of dairy products by 1) authorizing premiums to be paid to dairy farmers who slaughtered a portion of their dairy herd, and 2) creating a system of payments to farmers ("non-marketing premiums") for withholding dairy products from the market. The Member States were to set up the systems, notify farmers, verify that slaughter took place between February and May 1970, and pay the premiums. Italy failed to take any action in time, partly because "doubts appeared during the Parliamentary debates as to the expediency" of the non-marketing premiums. Italy finally acted on the slaughtering premium system in October 1971. When the Commission brought an infringement proceeding, Italy argued that the issue was essentially moot, since the Council had terminated both programs in 1971.]

8   The defendant ... claims that the pursuit of the action commenced by the Commission is no longer warranted because of the circumstances.

The difficulties which had originally delayed the payment of the premiums for slaughtering having been overcome, the payment of these premiums is in process and therefore the *raison d'être* of the proceedings instituted by the Commission has disappeared.

As for the omission to pay the premium for non-marketing, the situation has become in the meantime irremediable, because it would no longer be possible physically to comply retroactively with the obligations which should have been performed during the period provided by the Community provisions in question.

In these circumstances, the action brought by the Commission has lost its purpose. . . .

9   The object of an action under Article 169 [now 226] is established by the Commission's reasoned opinion, and even when the default has been remedied subsequent to the time limit prescribed by paragraph 2 of the same Article, pursuit of the action still has an object.

***

11   Moreover, in the face of both a delay in the performance of an obligation and a definite refusal, a judgment by the Court under Articles 169 and 171 [now 226 and 228] of the Treaty may be of substantive interest as establishing the basis of a responsibility that a Member State can incur as a result of its default, as regards other Member States, the Community or private parties.

¹²   The preliminary objection raised by the defendant must therefore be rejected.

* * *

1.   With Regard to the Premiums for Slaughtering

¹⁴   The Regulations of the Council and of the Commission have provided precise time limits for the carrying into effect of the system of premiums for slaughtering.

The efficacy of the agreed measures depended upon the observation of these time limits, since the measures could only attain their object completely if they were carried out simultaneously in all the Member States. . . .

Over and above this ... Regulations Nos. 1975/69 and 2195/69 conferred on farmers a right to payment of the premium as from the time when all the conditions provided by the Regulations were fulfilled.

It consequently appears that the delay on the part of the Italian Republic in performing the obligations imposed on it by the introduction of the system of premiums for slaughtering constitutes by itself a default in its obligations.

* * *

2.   As to the Premiums for Non-marketing

¹⁹   The default in putting into operation the provisions of Regulations Nos. 1975/69 and 2195/69 with regard to premiums for non-marketing is due to a deliberate refusal by the Italian authorities.

***

[A]ccording to the Italian Government, measures intended to restrict the production of milk were inappropriate to the needs of the Italian economy, which is characterized by insufficient food production.

During the debate stages of Regulation No. 1975/69 of the Council the Italian delegation made these difficulties known and expressed clear reservations at that time with regard to the carrying out of the Regulation.

In these circumstances, [Italy claims that] complaint ought not to be made against [it] for having refused to put into effect on its national territory provisions passed in spite of the opposition which it has manifested.

[The Court observed that under Articles 37(2) and 249 (ex 43(2) and 189) of the EC Treaty, Regulation 1975/69 was validly enacted and binding on the Member States.]

²⁰   [I]t cannot be accepted that a Member State should apply in an incomplete or selective manner provisions of a Community Regulation so as to render abortive certain aspects of Community legislation which it has opposed or which it considers contrary to its national interests.

²¹   In particular ... the Member State which omits to take, within the requisite time limits and simultaneously with the other Member States, the measures which it ought to take, undermines the efficacy

of the provision decided upon in common, while at the same time taking an undue advantage to the detriment of its partners in view of the free circulation of goods.

***

24   In permitting Member States to profit from the advantages of the Community, the Treaty imposes on them also the obligation to respect its rules.

For a State unilaterally to break, according to its own conception of national interest, the equilibrium between advantages and obligations flowing from its adherence to the Community brings into question the equality of Member States before Community law and creates discriminations at the expense of their nationals, and above all of the nationals of the State itself which places itself outside the Community rules.

25   This failure in the duty of solidarity accepted by Member States by the fact of their adherence to the Community strikes at the fundamental basis of the Community legal order.

It appears therefore that, in deliberately refusing to give effect on its territory to one of the systems provided for by Regulations Nos. 1975/69 and 2195/69, the Italian Republic has failed in a conspicuous manner to fulfil the obligations which it has assumed by virtue of its adherence to the European Economic Community [now European Community].

Notes and Questions

1.   Normally the Commission will not bring suit if a Member State actually ends an infringement during Article 226's preliminary phase. Commission v. Italy (Public supply contracts), Case C–362/90, [1992] ECR I–2353.) However, the fact that a case has lost practical importance will not necessarily cause the Court to consider the case moot, particularly if the case provides an opportunity to state an important principle for the future. *Slaughtered cows II* is a good example.

Note also the Court's suggestion that a ruling of this kind might provide the basis for liability of a Member State to private parties injured by the infringement. Is that so? See the *Francovich* judgment, *supra* page 407.

2.   In *Slaughtered cows I* (Leonesio v. Ministry for Agriculture, Case 93/71, [1972] ECR 287), the Court had held that principles of supremacy and direct effect required Italy to pay premiums to farmers who slaughtered cows between February and May 1970 in reliance on the regulations, even though Italy had made no allocation in its annual budget for the premiums.

3.   Clearly, local opposition to a national measure implementing a Community law directive—however strenuous—will not justify a Member State's failing to adopt such a measure. See Commission v. Greece (Kouroupitos rubbish tip I), Case C–45/91, [1992] ECR I–2525. (The sequel to this case is discussed below, in section C of this chapter.)

COMMISSION v. FRANCE

(French merchant seamen)
Case 167/73, [1974] ECR 359.

[Article 3(2) of the French Maritime Code of 1926, as implemented by a ministerial decree, required that at least 75% of the crew of certain French vessels be composed of French nationals. The Commission complained that the French law violated EC Article 39 (ex 48) and Regulation 1612/68 issued under it, and it eventually invoked Article 226. The French government assured the Court that the Maritime Code provision was not and would not be applied to discriminate against other Member State nationals, and cited verbal instructions to the maritime authorities to treat nationals of all other Member States as if they were "French nationals." For its part, the Commission cited no instance in which the authorities had in fact treated EC nationals as "foreign" for these purposes.]

34 [T]he [French] Government ... has sought to deny that a default exists in the case in question solely as a result of the maintenance in the national legal system of the law in dispute without taking into consideration the application which is made of it in practice.

35 [According to it], a correct assessment of the legal position should have led the French authorities to find that since the provisions of Article 48 [now 39] and of Regulation 1612/68 are directly applicable in the legal system of every Member State and Community law has priority over national law, these provisions give rise, on the part of those concerned, to rights which the national authorities must respect and safeguard and as a result of which all contrary provisions of internal law are rendered inapplicable to them.

* * *

40 It appears ... that freedom of movement for workers in the sector in question continues to be considered by the French authorities not as a matter of right but as dependent on their unilateral will.

41 It follows that although ... Article 48 and Regulation 1612/68 are directly applicable in the territory of the French Republic, nevertheless the maintenance in these circumstances of the wording of the Code ... gives rise to an ambiguous state of affairs by maintaining, as regards those subject to the law who are concerned, a state of uncertainty as to the possibilities available to them of relying on Community law.

42 This uncertainty can only be reinforced by the internal and verbal character of the purely administrative directions to waive the application of the national law.

43 The free movement of persons, and in particular workers, constitutes ... one of the foundations of the Community.

* * *

46 It thus follows from the general character of the prohibition on discrimination in Article 48 and the objective pursued by the abolition of discrimination that discrimination is prohibited even if it constitutes only an obstacle of secondary importance as regards the equality of access to employment and other conditions of work and employment.

47 The uncertainty created by the maintenance unamended of the [Code's] wording ... constitutes such an obstacle.

[48] It follows that in maintaining [the Code provisions] unamended ... as regards the nationals of other Member States, the French Republic has failed to fulfil its obligations under Article 39 (ex 48) of the Treaty.

Notes and Questions

1. Do you regard the Court's position in the principal case as formalistic? The case is not an isolated one. In Commission v. France (Waste oil directive), Case 173/83, [1985] ECR 491, the Court held that an administrative circular was insufficient to correct ambiguous legislation because the affected private interests were unlikely to know of the circular.

Are there any circumstances under which the French argument should prevail? In a more recent decision, the Court of Justice suggested that a Member State might successfully defend itself on this ground if it could demonstrate not only that Community law principles are unfailingly applied, but also that all persons concerned are fully and clearly aware of their rights. Commission v. Germany (Recognition and coordination directives), Case 29/84, [1985] ECR 1661. How likely is it that such a showing can be made? See Commission v. Italy (Freedom of establishment), Case 168/85, [1986] ECR 2945.

Why did France not simply amend the code provision in question rather than defend the action all the way to the Court of Justice? In March 1996, the Court condemned France for still—22 years later—not having complied with the Court's judgment in the principal case! Commission v. France (Registration of vessels), Case C–334/94, [1996] ECR I–1307.

2. Note that France argued in the *French merchant seamen* case that, since the prohibition of nationality discrimination in EC Treaty Article 12 (ex 6) has direct effect and prevails over national law, the French authorities could not in any event legally apply the code provision to discriminate against other Member State nationals, and the provision did not therefore need to be changed. The Court categorically rejected this argument, as it has elsewhere.[7] (The Court has rejected the converse argument as well, namely that a State that has failed to implement a directive has not breached an obligation within the meaning of Article 226 unless the provisions of the directive that are invoked have direct effect.[8])

3. Yet another unavailing claim raised in *French merchant seamen* was that the Commission lacked "a legal interest" in bringing the action in the first place. The Court held that, since enforcement is one of the Commission's general institutional functions, the Commission does not have to show a legal interest in order to bring an infringement action.

4. Enforcement actions have begun to venture into the adequacy of Member State remedies for Community law claims, a question taken up in Chapter 10. See Commission v. United Kingdom, Cases C–382/92 and 383/92, [1994] ECR I–2435 & 2479, discussed *supra* page 392, at note 3, and more fully in Chapter 36 on Social Policy.

COMMISSION v. ITALY

(Road haulage directive)
Case 28/81, [1981] ECR 2577.

[Council Directive 74/561, adopted in November 1974, established requirements for engaging in the occupation of road haulage operator. These

---

7. E.g., Commission v. Belgium (Type approval directives), Case 102/79, [1980] ECR 1473.

8. Commission v. Germany (Environmental impact assessment), Case C–431/91, [1995] ECR I–2189.

requirements were "good repute," "appropriate financial standing" and "professional competence," the latter specifically defined in the directive. Italy did not implement the directive by the due date of January 1, 1977, and the Commission brought suit.]

3   The Italian Government ... explains that the directive in question has been included for implementation in a draft law which is now under consideration by the Chamber of Deputies. The draft was not tabled until 12 December 1980 owing to the detailed scrutiny to which it was first subjected by all the administrative authorities concerned. The Italian Government states that it has asked the authorities concerned to expedite the procedure for approving the draft law and hopes to obtain approval within the shortest possible time. The Italian Government claims that in the circumstances it may be considered that the object of the action has been eliminated in substance so that this application has become devoid of purpose.

4   Those circumstances do not expunge the failure of the Italian Republic to fulfil its obligations. According to well-established case law, a Member State may not plead provisions, practices or circumstances in its internal legal system in order to justify a failure to comply with obligations under Community directives.

5   [T]he Italian Government requested the Court to grant it an extension of the period allowed by the Commission pursuant to Article 169 [now 226] of the Treaty for fulfilling the obligations under the directive in question.

6   The powers conferred on the Court ... under Article 169 of the Treaty do not include the power to substitute a different period for that laid down by the Commission ... in its reasoned opinion, although the legality of that opinion is subject to review by the Court. Subject to the same reservation, it is for the Commission to decide whether such a request from a Member State is to be granted.

7   [T]he Italian Republic has failed to fulfil one of its obligations under the Treaty.

Notes and Questions

1. The Court has consistently rejected the claim that constitutional or institutional difficulties within a Member State excuse its noncompliance with a Community law obligation.[9] In many of these cases, a Member State government denies responsibility for the legislature's failure to act, a failure that may be attributed to parliamentary delay or inefficiency, or to political conflict (including possibly the fall of a government). Do you understand why the Court refuses to entertain such a defense? Suppose a Member State government fails to act as required by Community law because its courts have, for reasons of domestic (possibly domestic *constitutional*) law, enjoined it from doing so. Would, or should, that make any difference?

9. See, e.g., Commission v. Italy (Quality control of fruits and vegetables II), Case 69/86, [1987] ECR 773; Commission v. Belgium (Type approval directives), Case 102/79, [1980] ECR 1473; Commission v. Italy (Administrative levy), Case 8/70, [1970] ECR 961; Commission v. Belgium (Stamp tax on timber), Case 77/69, [1970] ECR 237.

2. Compare to the "horizontal" (or "separation of powers") problem the "vertical" (or "division of powers") situation in which a Member State claims to be powerless to remedy a violation for which a constituent state or local unit of government is exclusively responsible under the national constitution. Should such a case be treated differently? The Court evidently thinks not. See, for example, Germany v. Commission (Suckler cows), Case C–8/88, [1990] ECR I–2321, in which Germany unsuccessfully challenged its loss of certain agricultural funds on the ground that the German *Länder,* not the federal government, were responsible for the administrative lapses that caused the Commission to act. Similarly, in Commission v. Italy (Toxic waste in Campania), Case C–33/90, [1991] ECR I–5987, the Court was wholly unsympathetic to Italy's claim that responsibility for noncompliance lay with "autonomous" regional authorities.[10]

Slaughtered cows II (*supra* page 434) presents a variation on this theme. Italy also sought in that case to justify its failure to implement a system of "non-marketing premiums" on account of "the difficulty of providing an effective and serious inspection and control of the quantities of milk which are not marketed but destined for other use." It cited a "lack of adequate administration at a lower level." The Court emphatically rejected the defense:

> [P]ractical difficulties which appear at the stage when a Community measure has to be put into effect cannot permit a Member State unilaterally to opt out of observing its obligations.

> The Community institutional system provides the Member State ... with the necessary means to secure that its difficulties should be reasonably considered within the framework and principles of the Common Market and the legitimate interests of other Member States.

[1973] ECR at 115. Should it make any difference whether an offending State merely claims that a Community law requirement is too burdensome (as when Germany argued that the costs of enforcing penalties against companies that fail to publish their accounts as required by a Community directive were excessive and disproportionate to the directive's aims)[11], or that it simply cannot afford the implementation costs (as when Ireland argued that it lacked the personnel and other resources to comply with a periodic reporting requirement on wholesale fish prices imposed by the Council)?[12] The Court dismissed both defenses as legally insufficient.

3. Previous cases (such as *Pork import ban, supra* page 431) show the Court's general lack of sympathy toward the defense of "economic emergency" under Article 226. The Court has similarly rejected as a defense that a new Member State's accession treaty gave it too short a time period within which to implement an existing directive. Commission v. Spain (Midwives), Case C–313/89, [1991] ECR I–5231.

Consider in this light an enforcement action in which Italy claimed that the terrorist bombing of a data processing center had unavoidably prevented it from implementing a Community law directive on a timely basis. Should the Court entertain a necessity defense of this sort? Are there additional facts you would

---

10. See also Commission v. Belgium (Synthetic fibres), Case C–74/89, [1990] ECR I–491; Commission v. Italy (Measuring instruments), Case 100/77, [1978] ECR 879; Casagrande v. Landeshauptstadt München, Case 9/74, [1974] ECR 773.

11. Commission v. Germany (First Company Directive penalties), Case C–191/95, [1998] ECR I–5449.

12. Commission v. Ireland (Fishery price information), Case C–39/88, [1990] ECR I–4271.

want to have before deciding? Commission v. Italy (Transport statistics), Case 101/84, [1985] ECR 2629.

The Court has adopted the following formula for expressing, on the one hand, the narrowness of the "impossibility" defense and, on the other, the Commission's and Member States' duties of good faith in overcoming unforeseen difficulties in compliance:

> The only defence available to a Member State in opposing an application by the Commission ... for a declaration that it has failed to fulfil its Treaty obligations is to plead that it was absolutely impossible for it to implement the decision properly.

> However, a Member State which, in giving effect to a Commission decision ..., encounters unforeseen and unforeseeable difficulties or becomes aware of consequences overlooked by the Commission, must submit those problems to the Commission for consideration, together with proposals for suitable amendments to the decision in question. In such cases, the Commission and the Member State must, by virtue of the rule imposing on the Member States and the Community institutions a duty of genuine cooperation which underlies, in particular, Article 5 [now 10] of the Treaty, work together in good faith with a view to overcoming the difficulties whilst fully observing the Treaty provisions....

See, e.g., Commission v. Italy (Aid to Aluminia), Case C–349/93, [1995] ECR I–343. The Court has not been quick to find that Member State compliance would be impossible. See, e.g., Commission v. Greece (Interest rebates on exports), Case 63/87, [1988] ECR 2875; Commission v. Netherlands (Preferential tariff for natural gas), Case 213/85, [1988] ECR 281; Commission v. Belgium (State equity holding), Case 52/84, [1986] ECR 89.

4. The Commission has not to date brought an Article 226 action against a Member State for the judiciary's failure to fulfil an obligation under the Treaties (as in the case of the French Conseil d'Etat's *Cohn–Bendit* decision, *supra* page 289). Why has the Commission not formally called the Member States to account for these failures? Is the tradition of judicial independence a sufficient reason? Why don't the Commission and Court simply require the State to take legislative action to establish a rule that would then bind the national courts in future cases?

C. ARTICLE 226 RULINGS AND THEIR EFFECT

Judgments against a Member State in Article 226 actions take the form of a simple declaration that the State has failed to fulfil an EC Treaty obligation. By the terms of Article 228 (ex 171), however, the State is required to take the necessary measures to comply with the judgment. The Court has held that the process of compliance must begin at once and be completed in the shortest time possible.[13] The Court has not, however, traditionally asserted the power to impose sanctions on a Member State on account of its default, or even to order the State to take specific action to eliminate the infringement.

The state aid cases appear to allow the Court to go a bit further, however. In Commission v. Germany (Investment grants for mining), Case 70/72, [1973] ECR 813, the Commission sued Germany for continuing to make

---

13. Commission v. France (Tobacco prices II), Case 169/87, [1988] ECR 4093; Commission v. Italy (Quality control of fruits and vegetables II), Case 69/86, [1987] ECR 773.

payments under a state aid scheme that the Commission had previously found to be improper under Article 88 (ex 93). The Commission asked the Court not only to declare that the payments were illegal, but also that Germany had to recover from the recipients all grants of aid made in disregard of the Commission's ruling. Germany argued that Article 228 (ex 171) does not permit the Court to order a State to take any specific remedial steps. The Court disagreed, holding that, in order to be effective, the Commission's disapproval of a state aid may have to be coupled with an order to recover aid impermissibly granted. For another more recent example, see Commission v. Belgium (State equity holding), Case 52/84, [1986] ECR 89.

The Member States have a generally very good record of complying with Court rulings in enforcement actions, though compliance is sometimes delayed. There have been cases, however, where the Commission felt it had to return to the Court of Justice:

COMMISSION v. ITALY

(second Art treasures)
Case 48/71, [1972] ECR 529.

[In 1968, in the *first Art treasures* case (Commission v. Italy, Case 7/68, [1968] ECR 423), the Court held that export charges imposed by Italy on parties removing art and archaeological works from Italy constituted a charge equivalent to an export duty in violation of then Article 16, subsequently repealed. Italy's failure to implement the judgment led the Commission to bring a new infringement action, this time charging Italy with violating its obligations under Article 228 (ex 171). Italy pleaded in defense "difficulties . . . in regard to parliamentary procedure aimed at abolishing the [art export] tax and reforming the system of protection of the national artistic treasures." It claimed that repeal of the tax entailed delays "due to circumstances outside the control of the competent authorities."]

[5] Without having to examine the validity of such arguments, it suffices for the Court to observe that [in the *first Art treasures* judgment] it answered in the affirmative the question in dispute between the Italian Government and the Commission . . . .

[6] Since it is a question of a directly applicable Community rule, the argument that the infringement can be terminated only by the adoption of measures constitutionally appropriate to repeal the provision establishing the tax would amount to saying that the application of the Community rule is subject to the law of each Member State and more precisely that this application is impossible where it is contrary to a national law.

[7] In the present case the effect of Community law, declared as *res judicata* in respect of the Italian Republic, is a prohibition having the full force of law on the competent national authorities against applying a national rule recognized as incompatible with the Treaty and, if the circumstances so require, an obligation on them to take all appropriate measures to enable Community law to be fully applied.

* * *

[10]   It is therefore necessary to find that in not complying with the judgment of the Court [in the *first Art treasures* judgment] the Italian Republic has failed to fulfil the obligations imposed on it by Article 171 [now 228] of the Treaty.

Notes and Questions

1.   *Second Art treasures* is also a significant decision on the supremacy of Community law. In language that it was later to echo in the *Simmenthal II* case on Community law primacy, *supra* page 272, the Court said:

> The attainment of the objectives of the Community requires that the rules of Community law ... are fully applicable at the same time and with identical effects over the whole territory of the Community without the Member States being able to place any obstacles in the way.

> The grant made by Member States to the Community of rights and powers [under] the Treaty involves a definitive limitation on their sovereign rights and no provisions whatsoever of national law may be invoked to override this limitation.

[1972] ECR at 532.

2.   The *Mutton and lamb* case, discussed at page 432 *supra*, proved to be an even more serious challenge to the Court's authority. France openly refused to follow the judgment of the Court striking down the French quotas and charges on British lamb imports, thus creating a political crisis which received great publicity and contributed to some degree to the "Europessimism" of the early 1980s. The French government took the position that it would maintain its restrictions until the Council voted an agricultural support program favorable to French farmers and opposed at the time by the UK. A new round of enforcement proceedings by the Commission ensued and, following the Commission's unsuccessful bid to the Court for an interim order against France (Cases 24, 97/80R, [1980] ECR 1319), yielded an essentially political solution. After nearly a year of bitter dispute, the European Council resolved the crisis through a policy compromise of the agricultural and budgetary issues involved.

3.   Member State defiance of a Court of Justice ruling is fortunately rare. One example is Commission v. Italy (Collective redundancies II), Case 131/84, [1985] ECR 3531, in which Italy was held in violation of Article 228 (ex 171) for deliberately failing to adopt a social policy directive even after a prior ruling requiring it to do so. See H. Schermers, Note, 23 Common Mkt. L. Rev. 441 (1986).

NOTE ON SANCTIONS FOR VIOLATING JUDGMENTS OF THE COURT IN INFRINGEMENT CASES

As noted above, an initial judgment by the Court of Justice that a Member State has failed to comply with its Community law obligations is basically declaratory only and unaccompanied by formal sanctions. The Court has not assumed a general power to "punish" Member States for their Community law violations, however egregious. Indeed, even after a State was condemned a second time for the same violation, the Court did not do so.

The Maastricht Treaty, effective 1993, partially altered the situation by amending Article 228 (ex 171) to allow the Commission, when suing a

Member State for noncompliance with a prior judgment, to request the Court to impose on the delinquent State a "lump sum or penalty payment." Note that pecuniary sanctions are expressly reserved for post-judgment infringements; the Commission is not authorized to seek, nor the Court authorized to impose, such sanctions in the initial judgment of condemnation.

Article 228 makes it plain that the Commission's decision whether to seek a pecuniary sanction is discretionary, as is the Court's decision whether (and if so in what amount) to impose one. In view of its wide discretion, the Commission has adopted guidelines for determining whether in any given case the imposition of sanctions is appropriate and, if so, what their level should be. Those guidelines are referred to, and actually play a prominent role, in the Court of Justice judgment which follows:

COMMISSION v. GREECE

(Kouroupitos rubbish tip II)
Case C–387/97, [2000] ECR I–5047.

[In 1987, the Commission received a complaint about uncontrolled waste disposal in the Kouroupitos River by several towns in the Chania area of Crete. (The waste came from military, and industrial installations, as well as hospitals and households.) An infringement action by the Commission culminated in a 1992 Court of Justice judgment, condemning Greece for its violation of environmental directives of 1975 and 1978, which Greece was bound to apply as from 1981. Commission v. Greece (Kouroupitos rubbish tip I), Case C–45/91, [1992] ECR I–2509. In 1993, having not been notified of any compliance measures, the Commission reminded Greece of its obligations under the judgment. At the end of 1995, convinced that Greece had not drawn up, much less implemented, the necessary plans, the Commission launched a fresh infringement proceeding and issued a reasoned opinion. Unpersuaded by Greece's claims that it had made suitable progress in compliance, the Commission filed an Article 228 (ex 171) action, seeking a penalty payment of 24,600 ecu from the date of judgment in that action for each further day of noncompliance with the Court's initial 1992 judgment. (The UK intervened in the Commission's support.)

Greece argued that the claim was both inadmissible (because the Commission's launch of the pre-litigation phase of the Article 228 action predated the Maastricht Treaty amendment introducing the possibility of fines) and non-meritorious. It argued, in the alternative, that the Commission sought too high a penalty.

The Court disposed of the retroactivity point on the ground that all the important stages of the pre-litigation procedure occurred after the Maastricht Treaty had come into effect. It then satisfied itself that the obligations that Greece had been found in the initial enforcement action to have breached were still in effect and binding on it. The Court turned to Greece's record of compliance.]

Compliance with the obligations flowing from Article 171(1) [now 228] of the Treaty

* * *

[Turning first to Directive 75/442, which required that waste be disposed of in ways that do not endanger human health or the environment, the Court noted the Greek Government's admissions that (a) solid waste was still being deposited into the Kouroupitos River in breach of the directive, (b) only installation of a completely new system would meet the directive's requirements and (c) notwithstanding promises made by Greece in 1998, no such installation had been built. The Court then rejected Greece's excuse based on public opposition to the project and the pendency of administrative and judicial challenges, citing settled case law that a Member State may not plead internal difficulties to justify a failure to comply with its Community law obligations. Greece was accordingly found to have failed to comply with the Court's judgment in *Kouroupitos rubbish tip I.*

Regarding next the prohibition in Directive 78/319 against disposing toxic and other dangerous waste, the Court found that the Commission had failed to carry its burden of proof that disposal of such wastes was still occurring. (Greece asserted that all such disposal had ceased in 1996.)

Finally, regarding the obligations to draw up plans for general waste disposal plans and for the disposal of toxic and dangerous waste, imposed by Directives 75/442 and 78/319, respectively, the Court ruled that the incomplete and fragmentary steps taken by Greece did not satisfy the obligation of Member States under the directive to draw up "an organised and coordinated system." Greece had therefore failed to comply with the judgment in *Kouroupitos rubbish tip I* in that regard as well. The Court turned to the question of sanctions.]

Setting of the penalty payment

79   ... [T]he Commission has proposed that the Court should, in respect of failure to comply with the judgment in [*Kouroupitos rubbish tip I*], impose a penalty payment of ecu 24,600 for each day of delay from the date of notification of the present judgment until the breach of obligations has been remedied. The Commission contends that a financial penalty in the form of a periodic penalty payment is the most appropriate means of achieving the objective of compliance with the judgment as soon as possible.

80   The Greek Government claims that the Court should set the penalty payment on the basis of [calculations] which are more favourable to [Greece].... It contends that the coefficient relating to the duration of the infringement, determined unilaterally by the Commission without considering the extent to which the judgment has been complied with, does not reflect the existing situation and would be unfair to [Greece]. ...

* * *

84   In the absence of provisions in the Treaty, the Commission may adopt guidelines for determining how the lump sums or penalty payments which it intends to propose to the Court are calculated, so as, in particular, to ensure equal treatment between the Member States.

85   [Commission] Memorandum 96/C 242/07[14] states that decisions as to the amount of a fine or penalty payment must be taken with an eye to their

---

14. Memorandum on applying Article 171 [now 228] of the EC Treaty, O.J. 1996 C 242, p. 6 (Aug. 21, 1996).

purpose, namely the effective enforcement of Community law. The Commission therefore considers that the amount must be calculated on the basis of three fundamental criteria: the seriousness of the infringement, its duration and the need to ensure that the penalty itself is a deterrent to continuation of the infringement and to further infringements.

86   [Commission] Communication 97/C 63/02[15] identifies the mathematical variables used to calculate the amount of penalty payments, that is to say a uniform flat-rate amount, a coefficient of seriousness, a coefficient of duration, and a factor intended to reflect the Member State's ability to pay while ensuring that the penalty payment is proportionate and has a deterrent effect, calculated on the basis of the gross domestic product of the Member States and the weighting of their votes in the Council.

87   Those guidelines ... help to ensure that [the Commission] acts in a manner which is transparent, foreseeable and consistent with legal certainty, and are designed to achieve proportionality in the amounts of the penalty payments to be proposed by it.

* * *

89   It should be stressed that [the] suggestions of the Commission cannot bind the Court. However, [they] are a useful point of reference.

90   First, since the principal aim of penalty payments is that the Member State should remedy the breach of obligations as soon as possible, a penalty payment must be set that will be appropriate to the circumstances and proportionate both to the breach which has been found and to the ability to pay of the Member State concerned.

91   Second, the degree of urgency that the Member State concerned should fulfil its obligations may vary in accordance with the breach.

92   In that light, and as the Commission has suggested, the basic criteria which must be taken into account in order to ensure that penalty payments have coercive force and Community law is applied uniformly and effectively are, in principle, the duration of the infringement, its degree of seriousness and the ability of the Member State to pay. In applying those criteria, regard should be had in particular to the effects of failure to comply on private and public interests and to the urgency of getting the Member State concerned to fulfil its obligations.

93   In the present case, having regard to the nature of the breaches of obligations, which continue to this day, a penalty payment is the means best suited to the circumstances.

94   As regards the seriousness of the infringements and in particular the effects of failure to comply on private and public interests, the obligation to dispose of waste without endangering human health and without harming the environment forms part of the very objectives of Community environmental policy as set out in Article 130r [now 174] of the EC Treaty. The failure to comply with the obligation resulting from ... Directive 75/442 could, by the very nature of that obligation, endanger

15. Communication on the method of calculating penalty payments, O.J. 1997 C 63, p. 2 (Jan. 8, 1997).

human health directly and harm the environment and must, in the light of the other obligations, be regarded as particularly serious.

[95] The failure to fulfil the more specific obligations of drawing up a waste disposal plan and drawing up, and keeping up to date, plans for the disposal of toxic and dangerous waste ... must be regarded as serious in that compliance with those specific obligations was necessary in order for the objectives set out in [Directives 75/442 and 78/319] to be fully achieved.

[96] Thus, contrary to the Commission's submissions, the fact that specific measures have been taken ... to reduce the quantities of toxic and dangerous waste cannot have a bearing on the seriousness of the failure to comply with the obligation ... to draw up, and keep up to date, plans for the disposal of toxic and dangerous waste.

* * *

[98] As regards the duration of the infringement, suffice it to state that it is considerable, even if the starting date be that on which the Treaty on European Union entered into force and not the date on which the judgment in [*Kouroupitos rubbish tip I*] was delivered.

[99] Having regard to all the foregoing considerations, [Greece] should be ordered to pay to the Commission, into the account "EC own resources", a penalty payment of 20,000 euros for each day of delay in implementing the measures necessary to comply with the judgment in [*Kouroupitos rubbish tip I*], from delivery of the present judgment until the judgment in Case C–45/91 has been complied with.

Notes and Questions

1. *Kouroupitos rubbish tip II* was the first occasion for the imposition of a fine under Article 228. The Commission made two other applications to the Court for fines (Commission v. France (Nightwork by women), Case C–224/99, and Commission v. Greece (Diploma recognition), Case C–197/98), but both cases were subsequently dropped.

2. Are you surprised at the Member States' willingness to grant the Commission such wide discretion in deciding whether to apply for a penalty, whether to seek a lump sum or a periodic payment, and in what amount? For discussion of that discretion, see A. Bonnie, Commission Discretion under Article 171(2) EC, 23 Eur. L. Rev. 537 (1998). Clearly the Court need not impose a pecuniary sanction under Article 228 merely because the Commission asks it to do so. But may the Court impose such a sanction when the Commission has not asked it to do so (i.e. *sua sponte*)?

3. In Commission v. France (Product liability directive), Case C–293/91, [1993] ECR I–1, the Court condemned France for failing to implement the 1985 product liability directive, discussed in Chapter 35 *infra*. In fact, France did not actually implement the directive until 1998, five years following the Court's judgment. Would this have been a good case for a fine under Article 228?

4. If a penalty is imposed, how will it be enforced? See Commission Memorandum on applying Article 171 [now 228] of the EC Treaty, O.J. C242/6 (Aug. 21, 1996); Commission Communication on the method of calculating penalty payments, O.J. C63/2 (Jan. 8, 1997).

5. Do you think that Article 228 will operate as an effective deterrent to Member State infringements of Community law? (Would it have been a sufficient deterrent to Italy in the *second Art treasures* case or to France in the *Mutton and lamb* case?) Do not lose sight of the *Francovich* judgment, *supra* page 407, which holds that Member States must subject themselves to damage actions in national courts for their infringements of Community law. Will the prospect of tort liability to private parties give States a significant incentive to comply with Court of Justice rulings?

6. EC Treaty Article 228 is not the only Treaty provision authorizing sanctions against Member States. Under the EMU, a State may be sanctioned for impermissible deviations from the rules of budgetary discipline. Moreover, as noted in Chapter 6C on human rights, the Amsterdam Treaty introduced a procedure for suspending certain rights of a Member State found to have committed a "serious and persistent breach" of the principles of "liberty, democracy, respect for human rights and fundamental freedoms, and the rule of law." See TEU Articles 6 and 7 (ex F and F.1) and EC Treaty Article 309 (ex 236).

D. MEMBER STATE ENFORCEMENT ACTIONS AGAINST OTHER MEMBER STATES

As noted earlier, Article 227 (ex 170) also gives Member States the right to initiate enforcement proceedings against another Member State. Article 226 and 227 proceedings are not however entirely parallel. A complaining State may not proceed formally in the Court of Justice without first "bring[ing] the matter before the Commission," and giving the latter three months in which to solicit the oral and written views of all States concerned and to issue a reasoned opinion. All interested States may present their own views to the Commission and comment on the views of the others. If the Commission adopts the complaining State's position, or otherwise finds that a violation has occurred, it may proceed to the Court of Justice just as if it had initiated the matter itself. On the other hand, if the Commission fails to issue a reasoned opinion within the prescribed time, concludes that no violation occurred or otherwise fails to act, the complainant State is then free itself to go before the Court.

Thus far very few actions has been brought under Article 227. In one case, France v. United Kingdom, Case 141/78, [1979] ECR 2923, France complained that the UK had failed to enforce against British fishing interests a Community enactment regulating the dimensions of fishing net mesh. (The Commission had previously initiated an infringement proceeding in the case and had issued a reasoned opinion largely favorable to France, but it never went to the Court.) France, on whose side the Commission intervened, ultimately prevailed in its action against the UK. More recently, Belgium (supported by Denmark, Finland, Netherlands and the UK) sued Spain (supported by Italy and Portugal) for violating Article 29 (ex 34) of the Treaty by granting wine produced in Spain's La Rioja region a "controlled designation of origin," limiting use of that name to wine bottled in registered regional cellars. Belgium lost. Belgium v. Spain, Case C–388/95, [2000] ECR I–3123. (On the merits of the case, see page 750 *infra*.)

The relative paucity of Member-State-to-Member-State confrontations in the Court of Justice is understandable. Even without the required referral of

Member State complaints to the Commission under Article 227 (ex 170), it is all but certain that the Commission will become involved in controversies that pit Member States directly against one another on account of alleged Community law infringements. The Commission is very likely to respond favorably to Member State complaints that have substantial merit; perhaps more important, it has proved exceptionally adept at bringing about the amicable settlement of interstate disputes. An aggrieved Member State may of course actively support the Commission prosecution as, for example, the UK did in the Commission's Article 226 action against France (*supra* page 422) for its continued ban on the import of British beef.

*

Part III

THE COMMON MARKET, THE INTERNAL MARKET AND THE FOUR FREEDOMS

Part II presents the heart of the substantive law of the European Community, namely, the rules relating to the EC Treaty's initial goal of a common market, whose achievement would promote "a harmonious development of economic activities, a continuous and balanced expansion, an increase in stability, an accelerated raising of the standard of living and closer relations between the States belonging to it."

The common market is essentially based upon the well-known "four freedoms" (sometimes called the "pillars of the Community"): free movement of goods; free movement of persons (especially workers); freedom to provide commercial and professional services, together with the right of establishment; and free movement of capital. Each of the first three of the four freedoms is the subject of a chapter in Part II which sets out the relevant Treaty provisions, the influential Court of Justice doctrines, and key legislative measures. Later, in Part V, a chapter on free movement of capital is presented in tandem with one on the Economic and Monetary Union (EMU), added as a Community goal by the Treaty of Maastricht in November 1993.

One of the most important chapters in Part II is that on the internal market and its harmonization of laws program. The Community made a great deal of progress toward attaining the common market in the 1960s and 70s, adopting important legislative measures and benefitting from expansive Court interpretations of the scope of the four freedoms. Unfortunately, the early 1980s were marked by diminished progress during the period of "Europessimism" described in Chapter I. Dynamic leadership, both by the Commission under the Presidency of Jacques Delors and by the European Council, led to renewed legislative efforts in the internal market program from 1985 to 1992. The remarkable success of that program led in turn to the adoption of the Maastricht Treaty, which not only provided for EMU but also enunciated the concept of citizenship of the Union. Chapter 17 describes the background of this concept, notably the Peoples' Europe program, the scope and consequences of citizenship of the Union, and the current EC Treaty provisions on the achievement of an area of freedom, security and justice, added by the Treaty of Amsterdam in May 1999.

Chapter 12

FREE MOVEMENT OF GOODS: DUTIES, CHARGES, INTERNAL TAXES

Within the "four freedoms," the free movement of goods is undoubtedly the key concept. Not only is the free flow of commercial and industrial products throughout the Community the most tangible illustration of an integrated market, but the principles that have been elaborated in this field have significantly shaped those applicable to the free movement of persons, services and capital.

Free movement of goods itself can be analytically divided into three parts. This chapter deals with the elimination of Member State customs duties and analogous charges, along with discriminatory or protectionist internal taxes. Chapter 13 covers the elimination of non-tariff quantitative restrictions and analogous barriers to the free flow of goods, while Chapter 19 deals with the interplay between industrial and commercial property rights and free movement of goods.

In the US Constitution, the Interstate Commerce Clause serves a function analogous to that of the free movement of goods principle—analogous, but by no means precisely parallel. In the US constitutional framework, Congress has among its enumerated powers the ability "to regulate * * * commerce * * * among the several States." The US Constitution does not expressly set as a goal the free flow of goods between the states, but the power to regulate includes the power to facilitate interstate trade by limiting state restrictions upon it, and the Commerce Clause has historically served that purpose.

The central issue in Community law is whether a Member State regulation or practice constitutes an impermissible restriction of free movement of goods. The analogous issue in the US, commonly referred to as that of the dormant or negative Commerce Clause, is whether restrictions on trade resulting from state regulation should be struck down because they impede free interstate commerce in a particular sector. Another major issue in US federal/state relations is the preemptive effect of federal legislation upon state legislation in the same area. This is also an important concern of European Community law, and is analyzed in Chapter 15.

A. CUSTOMS DUTIES AND CHARGES HAVING EQUIVALENT EFFECT

Part 3, Title I of the Treaty, "Free Movement of Goods," begins with Article 23(1) (Article 9(1) in the initial EEC Treaty):

> The Community shall be based upon a customs union which shall cover all trade in goods and which shall involve the prohibition between Member States of customs duties on imports and exports and of all charges having equivalent effect, and the adoption of a common customs tariff in their relations with third countries.

Note at the outset that Article 23 (formerly Article 9) regulates both external and internal trade. It mandates a "common customs tariff" for products coming from countries outside the Community. Chapter 29 surveys this fundamental part of Community trade law. With regard to internal trade, Article 23 prohibits import and export duties between Member States. Article 23 is supplemented by Article 24 (ex Article 10), which provides that products imported into the Community "shall be considered to be in free circulation" as soon as import formalities are completed and customs duties paid. In articles now deleted, the Treaty initially set a transitional period of twelve years for the removal of customs duties between States. Whenever new Member States joined the Community later, similar transitional periods were set for certain products by each Treaty of Accession, but all such periods have now expired.

The removal of customs duties between Member States is inherent in the concept of a customs union. Less obvious is Article 23's prohibition of "all charges having equivalent effect." This may well have been intended only to cover disguised duties, but, as will be seen, the Court of Justice has broadly construed this concept to eliminate virtually all charges, fees or costs imposed by Member States on goods in trade between the States.

1. WHAT IS A CHARGE EQUIVALENT TO A DUTY?

SOCIAAL FONDS v. SA CH. BRACHFELD

Cases 2 & 3/69, [1969] ECR 211.

[In 1962, Belgium required all importers of uncut diamonds to contribute to the diamond workers' social benefit fund, with the contribution calculated as 0.33% of the value of the uncut diamonds. When the fund took action against 200 importers to collect unpaid contributions, they challenged the 1962 law. The trial court in an Article 234 proceeding asked the Court of Justice whether the 1962 Belgian law constituted a charge equivalent to a duty in violation of Article 23 (ex Article 9).]

7/10   The position of [Article 23] at the beginning of that Part of the Treaty reserved for the "Foundations of the Community" * * * is sufficient to show the fundamental role of the prohibitions laid down therein.

11/14   In prohibiting the imposition of customs duties, the Treaty does not distinguish between goods according to whether or not they enter into competition with the products of the importing country. Thus, the purpose of the abolition of customs barriers is not merely to eliminate their protective nature, [but] to ensure the free movement of goods. It follows from the system as a whole and from the general and absolute nature of the prohibition of any customs duty applicable to goods moving between Member States that customs duties are prohibited independently of any consideration of the purpose for which they were introduced and the destination of the revenue obtained therefrom. The justification for this prohibition is based on the fact that any pecuniary charge—however small—imposed on goods by reason of the fact that they cross a frontier constitutes an obstacle to the movement of such goods.

15/18   The extension of the prohibition of customs duties to charges having equivalent effect is intended to supplement the prohibition against obstacles to trade created by such duties by increasing its efficiency. The use of these two complementary concepts thus tends, in trade between Member States, to avoid the imposition of any pecuniary charge on goods circulating within the Community by virtue of the fact that they cross a national frontier. * * * Consequently, any pecuniary charge, however small and whatever its designation and mode of application, which is imposed unilaterally on domestic or foreign goods by reason of the fact that they cross a frontier, and which is not a customs duty in the strict sense, constitutes a charge having equivalent effect within the meaning of Articles [23 and 25] of the Treaty, even if it is not imposed for the benefit of the State, is not discriminatory or protective in effect or if the product on which the charge is imposed is not in competition with any domestic product.

19/21   It follows * * * that the prohibition of new customs duties or charges having equivalent effect, linked to the principle of the free movement of goods, constitutes a fundamental rule which, without prejudice to the other provisions of the Treaty, does not permit of any exceptions. * * *

22/23   The provisions of the Treaty laying down the abovementioned prohibitions impose precise and clearly-defined obligations on Member States which do not require any subsequent intervention by Community or national authorities for their implementation. For this reason, these provisions directly confer rights on individuals concerned.

24/26   [The prohibition] of any new pecuniary charge to goods circulating within the Community when they cross a frontier [applies] irrespective of the nationality of the traders who might be placed at a disadvantage by such measures. Thus,* * * there is no justification for a distinction to be made according to whether the measures in question adversely affect certain Member States and their nationals, or all the citizens of the Community, or only the nationals of the Member State which was responsible for the measures in question.

Notes and Questions

1.   How broad is the definition of a "charge equivalent to a duty"? Wouldn't one normally think a charge to benefit retired or injured diamond cutters has nothing to do with a duty? Why did the Court consider it immaterial that this charge did not bring in revenues to Belgium or protect a Belgian industry, the two usual motives for adopting a customs duty?

2. Belgium does not have diamond mines. If Belgium produced a significant quantity of diamonds, and the benefit fund contribution was imposed both on imported and domestic uncut diamonds, should it be evaluated under Article 23? After reading section B, consider whether the contribution might violate Article 90.

3. Another leading judgment is Commission v. Italy (First art treasures), Case 7/68, [1968] ECR 423, which involved a charge equivalent to an export duty, forbidden by the then Treaty Article 16. Since 1939, Italy had imposed a substantial charge upon the export of works of art and archaeological treasures, as a means of encouraging their retention in Italy. The Court of Justice held that Italy's motive and the absence of a revenue-raising intent were both irrelevant, since the charge operated as a restriction on exports.

The judgment also defined the term "goods" upon which duties fall. Italy had argued that this meant consumer or commercial goods, and therefore wouldn't cover works of art. The Court held that "goods" meant any "products which can be valued in money and which are capable, as such, of forming the subject of commercial transactions." [1968] ECR at 428.

4. Undoubtedly the most important type of "charge equivalent to a duty" is the fee charged for the health inspection of imports of slaughtered meat, fruits and vegetables, or living animals and plants. Assuming for the moment that such an inspection itself does not violate the Treaty (an issue covered on page 482), the question is whether a fee charged for the inspection violates Article 23.

This has given rise to a complex body of case law. In 1972, the Court held that health inspection fees levied only on imported products constituted a charge in violation of Article 23, even though some other inspection fee was levied on similar domestic products. SpA Marimex v. Italian Finance Administration, Case 29/72, [1972] ECR 1309. Later, the Court held that a State could not justify the fee on the ground that the inspection is necessary to protect general health, stating that the public should bear the cost and not the importer. Bresciani v. Amministrazione Italiana delle Finanze, Case 87/75, [1976] ECR 129. However, the Court added that if the same fee is charged for the inspection of imported products and of domestic products, "applied according to the same criteria and at the same stage of production," then the fee is not a charge equivalent to a duty, but rather a systematically applied internal tax, which is to be analyzed under Article 90. [1976] ECR at 139. These are certainly not easy criteria to apply. See Commission v. Belgium (Poultry inspection fees), Case 314/82, [1984] ECR 1543, holding that inspection fees for imported poultry meat could not be considered to be part of an internal tax system because they were different in character from fees charged for inspection of domestic products.

In many sectors, the Community has set up a system of Community-wide health and safety inspections for animals, plants and meat or plant products. In Bauhuis v. Netherlands, Case 46/76, [1977] ECR 5, the Court held that a fee for the health inspection of bovine animals, required by a Community agricultural regulation before export to another State, did not constitute an illegal charge equivalent to an export duty, provided the fee covered only the actual cost of the inspection.

2. ARE EMERGENCY DUTIES PERMISSIBLE?

How absolute is Article 23's ban on intra-community tariffs? Can Article 23 be construed to allow an exception when a Member State, allegedly on an emergency basis, temporarily imposes a customs duty on goods from other Member States?

SOCIÉTÉ LES COMMISSIONAIRES RÉUNIS
v. RECEVEUR DES DOUANES

Cases 80 & 81/77, [1978] ECR 927.

[In 1975, France imposed an emergency duty on Italian wine. France claimed it had the power to do so under the Community agricultural policy Regulation 816/70 governing the market in wine. That regulation contained a national safeguard clause which authorized Member States, in order to "avoid disturbances on their markets, to take measures that may limit imports from another Member State."

Following a Commission complaint, France repealed its decree. Plaintiffs had paid the duty on Italian wine while the decree was in force and sued for a refund. The trial court asked the Court of Justice, in an Article 234 proceeding, whether the safeguard clause of Regulation 816/70 was "contrary to the rules of the Treaty on the free movement of goods."]

14   The first question asks in substance whether Article 31(2) of Regulation No. 816/70 is valid in so far as it authorizes producer Member States to prescribe and to levy * * * charges having an effect equivalent to customs duties in intra-Community trade on a product * * *, in the present case table wine.

15   The answer to this question requires the interpretation of Article [32(2)] of the EEC Treaty which reads: "Save as otherwise provided in Articles [33 to 40], the rules laid down for the establishment of the Common Market shall apply to agricultural products."

* * *

17   [I]n the view of the Government of the French Republic, having regard to the place of agriculture in the Common Market, its characteristics and the specific objectives of the Common Agricultural Policy, this provision allows the Council to derogate from the rules of the Treaty in general and those on the free movement of goods in particular when such derogations are based on Articles [33 to 40] of the Treaty.

* * *

22   Article 2 of the EEC Treaty provides that it is by establishing a common market and progressively approximating the economic policies of Member States that the Community must promote throughout the Community development of economic activities, the raising of the standard of living and closer relations between the Member States.

23   As is stressed by Article [32(1)] of the Treaty, placed at the head of the title devoted to the Common Agricultural Policy, the Common Market shall extend to agriculture and trade in agricultural products.

24   The abolition between Member States of customs duties and charges having equivalent effect constitutes a fundamental principle of the Common Market applicable to all products and goods with the result that

[citing prior cases] "any possible exception, which in any event must be strictly construed, must be clearly laid down". * * *

26　Therefore in order that the exception provided for in Article 32(2) should apply to the introduction of charges having an effect equivalent to customs duties in intra-Community trade at the end of the transitional period, it is necessary to find in Articles [33 to 40] a provision which either expressly or by necessary implication provides for or authorizes the introduction of such charges.

27　Articles [33 to 40] contain no provision of this nature.

* * *

29　Under Article [37(3)(b)] each common organization of the market "ensures conditions for trade within the Community similar to those existing in a national market".

* * *

35　It is clear * * * that the extensive powers, in particular of a sectorial and regional nature, granted to the Community institutions in the conduct of the Common Agricultural Policy must be exercised from the perspective of the unity of the market to the exclusion of any measure compromising the abolition between Member States of customs duties and quantitative restrictions or charges or measures having equivalent effect.

* * *

38　Therefore, Article 31(2) of Regulation No. 816/70 in so far as it authorizes producer Member States to prescribe and levy, in intra-Community trade in [wine], charges having an effect equivalent to customs duties, is incompatible with Article [25] * * * and is consequently invalid.

Notes and Questions

1.　The Common Agricultural Policy (CAP), is certainly an important sphere of Community action. Does this case show that free movement of goods is more important than the CAP, or is the Court merely trying to interpret two Treaty chapters in a harmonious fashion? Can there ever be any basis for an emergency duty?

2.　This is a "Treaty supremacy" judgment in its important holding that the Council of Ministers cannot adopt legislation contrary to a Treaty provision. This "Treaty supremacy" doctrine parallels the US Supreme Court's constitutional interpretation which invalidates laws of Congress when they violate the Constitution. Note that this aspect of "Treaty supremacy" is not a self-evident principle. In fact, Advocate General Warner took the contrary view that the Council had the power to adopt the safeguard clause. This judgment complements those on Treaty supremacy over Member State legislation in Chapter 7.

3.　In striking contrast is Prudential Ins. Co. v. Benjamin, 328 U.S. 408, 66 S.Ct. 1142, 90 L.Ed. 1342 (1946), in which the Supreme Court held that Congress had the power to authorize a discriminatory state tax on insurance which was levied only upon out-of-state insurers, and not domestic insurers. The opinion held that the McCarren Act implicitly permitted state taxes on insurance operations to be discriminatory, and specifically stated that the Commerce Clause "enables Congress not only to promote but also to prohibit interstate commerce." Id. at

434, 66 S.Ct. at 1157. In accord, as to a "retaliatory" California tax levied upon out-of-state insurers, is Western & Southern Life Ins. Co. v. State Board, 451 U.S. 648, 101 S.Ct. 2070, 68 L.Ed.2d 514 (1981). Does the difference in language ("regulate commerce" versus ensuring "free movement of goods") account for the difference in attitude between the Court of Justice and the Supreme Court? Or do you suspect that the two courts are also influenced by their impression of how far market integration has been achieved in the US as compared to the Community?

B. DISCRIMINATORY OR PROTECTIVE INTERNAL TAXATION

Although Article 90 (ex Article 95) is located in a later chapter of the Treaty entitled "Tax Provisions," its obvious role is to further free movement of goods. In fact, Article 90, which was inspired by corresponding GATT provisions (see Chapter 28), was intended to prevent Member States from replacing customs duties with protectionist indirect taxes. Article 90 states that:

> No Member State shall impose, directly or indirectly, on the products of other Member States any internal taxation of any kind in excess of that imposed directly or indirectly on similar domestic products.

> Furthermore, no Member State shall impose on the products of other Member States any internal taxation of such a nature as to afford indirect protection to other products.

Thus, the first paragraph prohibits discriminatory internal taxation and the second forbids protectionist internal taxation.

Like Articles 23 and 25, Article 90 has been held to have direct effect. In Alfons Lütticke GmbH v. Hauptzollamt Saarlouis, Case 57/65, [1966] ECR 205 at 210, the Court said that the prohibition in paragraph one of Article 90 is "complete, legally perfect and consequently capable of producing direct effects on the legal relationships between the Member States and persons within their jurisdiction." The Court subsequently held in Firma Fink–Frucht GmbH v. Hauptzollamt Munchen, Case 27/67, [1968] ECR 223, that the second paragraph of Article 90 likewise had direct effect. This means that private parties can invoke both parts of Article 90 in national litigation to challenge a State's internal tax system.

1. BASIC APPLICATION OF ARTICLE 90

The most common types of internal taxes relating to goods and services are value added taxes levied at stages in the production and sale of most consumer products (analogous to sales taxes levied by U.S. states), and excise taxes on alcohol, tobacco, jewelry, cars and other products.

It occasionally happens that an internal tax is clearly discriminatory. Thus, in Bobie Getränkevertrieb GmbH v. Hauptzollamt Aachen, Case 127/75, [1976] ECR 1079, the German excise tax on beer was levied at a flat rate per hectolitre for imported beer, but at a progressively increasing rate for domestic beer. Since this meant that producers of small quantities of German beer were taxed at a lower rate than importers of identical quantities of foreign beer, the tax system obviously violated Article 90.

A more difficult issue is raised when the taxing state argues that there is no domestic production of the goods subject to the tax.

HUMBLOT v. DIRECTEUR DES SERVICES FISCAUX

Case 112/84, [1985] ECR 1367.

[France imposed a tax on the purchase of all new cars. For low-and medium-level horsepower cars, the tax was levied at a progressively increasing rate depending on the horsepower level, up to a ceiling of F1100. For the most powerful cars, at or above 16 CV (horsepower rating), a special flat-rate tax of F5000 was imposed. All cars at or above 16 CV were imported, chiefly from Germany and the UK. Humblot, purchaser of a 16 CV car, claimed that the special tax violated Article 90. The issue was referred by the French court under Article 234.]

7   [T]he essence of the question is whether Article [90] prohibits the charging on cars exceeding a given power rating for tax purposes of a special fixed tax the amount of which is several times the highest amount of the progressive tax payable on cars of less than the said power rating for tax purposes, where the only cars subject to the special tax are imported, in particular from other Member States.

8   Mr. Humblot argues that * * * vehicles of 16 CV or less and vehicles exceeding 16 CV are completely comparable as regards their performance, price and fuel consumption. As a result, he contends that the French State, by subjecting imported vehicles alone to a special tax much greater in amount than the differential tax, has created discrimination contrary to Article [90] of the Treaty.

9   [T]he French Government * * * argues that the special tax is charged solely on luxury vehicles, which are not similar, within the meaning of the first paragraph of Article [90], to cars liable to the differential tax. Moreover, whilst the French Government concedes that some vehicles rated at 16 CV or less and others rated at more than 16 CV are in competition and so subject to the second paragraph of Article [90], it maintains that the special tax is not contrary to that provision, since it has not been shown that the tax has the effect of protecting domestic products. It argues that there is no evidence that a consumer who may have been dissuaded from buying a vehicle of more than 16 CV will purchase a car of French manufacture of 16 CV or less.

10   The Commission considers that the special tax is contrary to the first paragraph of Article [90] of the Treaty. It argues that all cars, irrespective of their power rating for tax purposes, are similar within the meaning of the case-law of the Court. That being so, it is no longer possible for a Member State to create discrimination between imported and domestically-produced vehicles. The only exception is where a Member State taxes products differently—even identical products—on the basis of neutral criteria consistent with objectives of economic policy which are compatible with the Treaty. * * * The Commission contends, however, that [France's] power rating for tax purposes, is not geared to an economic policy objective, such as heavier taxation of luxury products or vehicles with high fuel consumption. Accordingly, the Commission considers that

the special tax, which is almost five times the highest rate of differential tax and affects imported vehicles only * * * is contrary to the first paragraph of Article [90] of the Treaty.

* * *

[12] It is appropriate in the first place to stress that as Community law stands at present the Member States are at liberty to subject products such as cars to a system of road tax which increases progressively in amount depending on an objective criterion, such as the power rating for tax purposes * * *.

[13] Such a system of domestic taxation is, however, compatible with Article [90] only in so far as it is free from any discriminatory or protective effect.

[14] That is not true of a system like the one at issue in the main proceedings. Under that system there are two distinct taxes: a differential tax which increases progressively and is charged on cars not exceeding a given power rating for tax purposes and a fixed tax on cars exceeding that rating which is almost five times as high as the highest rate of the differential tax. Although the system embodies no formal distinction based on the origin of products it manifestly exhibits discriminatory or protective features contrary to Article [90], since the power rating determining liability to the special tax has been fixed at a level such that only imported cars, in particular from other Member States, are subject to the special tax whereas all cars of domestic manufacture are liable to the distinctly more advantageous differential tax.

[15] In the absence of considerations relating to the amount of the special tax, consumers seeking comparable cars as regards such matters as size, comfort, actual power, maintenance costs, durability, fuel consumption and price would naturally choose from among cars above and below the critical power rating laid down by French law. However, liability to the special tax entails a much larger increase in taxation than passing from one category of car to another in a system of progressive taxation embodying balanced differentials * * * . The resultant additional taxation is liable to cancel out the advantages which certain cars imported from other Member States might have in consumers' eyes over comparable cars of domestic manufacture, particularly since the special tax continues to be payable for several years. In that respect the special tax reduces the amount of competition to which cars of domestic manufacture are subject and hence is contrary to the principle of neutrality with which domestic taxation must comply.

Notes and Questions

1. Was the high horsepower car tax discriminatory or protectionist or both? What is meant by the "principle of neutrality," cited by the Court in ¶ 15, and frequently applied as a guiding principle in later cases?

2. In contrast to *Humblot* is Commission v. Greece (Car tax), Case C–132/88, [1990] ECR I–1567. Greece's consumption tax on cars was substantially higher for high horsepower cars than for intermediate or low horsepower cars. Greece manufactured only low horsepower cars. The Court held that the tax appeared to be motivated by social policy considerations (presumably meaning that it consti-

tuted an indirect tax on wealth). The Court further held that the Commission had not proved that the Greek tax incited consumers to buy domestic cars rather than intermediate or low horsepower imports. Is this result compatible with *Humblot?*

3. In Commission v. Denmark (Car tax), Case C–47/88, [1990] ECR 4509, the Commission contended that a Danish car registration tax on new cars, imposed at rates of 105–180% of the purchase price, violated Article 90. Denmark maintained that the tax could not violate Article 90 because no cars are produced in Denmark. The Commission argued that the rate was so high that it substantially impeded car sales and hence the importation of cars. What result? Can cars be considered to be in competition with bicycles or other modes of transport? Denmark also imposed a 90% registration tax on the sale of imported used cars, but not on the sale of used cars already in Denmark. What result?

4. After *Humblot*, France modified its horsepower rate tax system, creating ten bands ranging from under 4 CV cars to those with 23 CV and over, with each band subject to a progressively higher tax. Only imported cars fall in the higher taxed bands above 18 CV. In Jacquier v. Directeur Generale des Imports, Case C–113/94, [1995] ECR I–4203, the Court held that the revised fiscal system's more gradual increase in tax for each horsepower range would not violate Article 90, provided that the trial court found that the system did not lead consumers to favor the purchase of domestically produced cars.

Subsequently in Tarantik v. Direction des Services Fiscaux, Case C–421/97, [1999] ECR I–3633, an owner of a Jaguar refused to pay his annual tax (approximately equal to $1000) based on its 24 CV capacity, claiming that the tax rate was excessively high in comparison to that imposed on French produced cars in the 15–16 CV range. The Court observed that only some car models in the 15–16 CV range could be considered to be in competition to a Jaguar in the 24 CV category. Whether car models are in competition depends on an assessment of consumer views concerning "price, size, comfort, performance, fuel consumption, durability, reliability and other matters" (¶ 28). Accordingly, the higher French tax on car models above 18 CV (all imported) would violate Article 90 only if the trial court found that this tax level, when compared with the tax on those French produced car models in the 15–16 CV range which are found to be in competition with the imported cars, would be sufficient to "favour the sale of vehicles of domestic manufacture" (¶ 32). Do you think the trial court will find it easy to apply this more nuanced approach?

5. The line between a charge equivalent to a duty and an internal tax is not always easy to draw, but the difference is critical, because a State cannot impose a charge equivalent to an import duty under Article 23, while many internal taxes pass muster under Article 90. In Commission v. France (Reprographic machines), Case 90/79, [1981] ECR 283, a French law imposed a 3% levy on the sale price of reprographic (photocopy) machines. This levy was intended to supplement a levy on the sale of books. The proceeds went to the Centre National des Lettres to pay for subsidies for "quality" literature and French translations of foreign works. The Commission brought an Article 226 proceeding against France, claiming that the levy constituted a charge equivalent to a duty under Article 23, because only about 1% of all reprographic machines sold in France were of domestic origin.

The Court declined to find that 1% domestic production was *de minimis*. Moreover, the Court held that even if there were no domestic production, the levy should be categorized as an internal tax because it supplemented the more general levy on the sale of books and formed part of a system to compensate copyright holders indirectly for unauthorized reproduction of their works. It defined an internal tax as one "applied systematically to categories of products in accordance with objective criteria irrespective of the origin of the products." Id. at 301. The Court concluded by finding that the levy did not violate Article 90. Consider again *Sociaal Fonds*: why is it that a nondiscriminatory economic policy can justify a tax or charge under Article 90, but not Article 23?

WEST LYNN CREAMERY, INC. v. HEALY

512 U.S. 186, 114 S.Ct. 2205, 129 L.Ed.2d 157 (1994).

[Massachusetts levied a 'premium payment' on milk sold by distributors, with the proceeds used for a subsidy for Massachusetts dairy farmers. Most of the milk subject to the "premium payment" came from other states. The Massachusetts Supreme Judicial Court held that the charge was not discriminatory and that the incidental burden on interstate commerce was outweighed by the benefit to the local dairy industry. The Supreme Court reversed, 7–2, with Justice Stevens writing for five justices.]

The 'negative' aspect of the Commerce Clause prohibits economic protectionism–that is, regulatory measures designed to benefit in-state economic interests by burdening out-of-state competitors * * * unless the discrimination is demonstrably justified by a valid factor unrelated to economic protectionism.

* * *

The "premium payments" are effectively a tax which makes milk produced out of State more expensive. Although the tax also applies to milk produced in Massachusetts, its effect on Massachusetts producers is entirely (indeed more than) offset by the subsidy provided exclusively to Massachusetts dairy farmers. Like an ordinary tariff, the tax is thus effectively imposed only on out-of-state products.

* * *

A pure subsidy funded out of general revenue ordinarily imposes no burden on interstate commerce, but merely assists local business. The pricing order in this case, however, is funded principally from taxes on the sale of milk produced in other States. By so funding the subsidy, [Massachusetts] not only assists local farmers, but burdens interstate commerce.

* * *

Finally, Massachusetts argues that any incidental burden on interstate commerce "is outweighed by the 'local benefits' of preserving the Massachusetts dairy industry. [Massachusetts contends that] to save an industry from collapse, is not protectionist." If we were to accept these arguments, we would make a virtue of the vice that the rule against discrimination prohibits. Preservation of local industry by protecting it from the rigors of interstate competition is the hallmark of the economic protectionism that the Commerce Clause prohibits.

Notes and Questions

1. *West Lynn Creamery* is a good example of US cases in which state taxes or charges have been invalidated as providing a commercial advantage to local

business at the expense of out-of-state competitors. Another leading case is New Energy Co. of Indiana v. Limbach, 486 U.S. 269, 108 S.Ct. 1803, 100 L.Ed.2d 302 (1988), invalidating as discriminatory under the Commerce Clause an Ohio statute that granted a tax credit to fuel dealers for the sale of ethanol produced in Ohio, but not generally for ethanol produced out-of-state.

2. Would the Court of Justice reach a similar conclusion in a parallel case? See Commission v. Italy (Sugar subsidy), Case 73/79, [1980] ECR 1533, in which Italy used revenue from a surcharge on both domestic and imported white sugar for a fund to subsidize the domestic sugar industry.

2. ALCOHOL EXCISE AND CONSUMPTION TAXES

A series of cases significantly increased the use of Article 90 as a weapon to foster free movement of goods. In the late 1970s, the Commission brought several Article 226 proceedings against Member States challenging their alcohol excise tax systems. The Commission urged the Court of Justice to broaden the concept of the relevant product market within which the domestic and imported alcohols could be said to be competing.

COMMISSION v. FRANCE

(Alcohol excise tax)
Case 168/78, [1980] ECR 347.

[France had a substantially higher excise tax on strong alcohol derived from grain (whisky, rum, gin, vodka) than on those derived from wine or fruit (cognac, armagnac, calvados). France produced negligible quantities of grain-based alcohol, but substantial quantities of wine or fruit-based alcohol. The Commission challenged this tax structure in an Article 226 proceeding as a violation of Article 90.]

4   As the Commission has correctly stated, Article [90] must guarantee the complete neutrality of internal taxation as regards competition between domestic products and imported products.

5   The first paragraph of Article [90], which is based on a comparison of the tax burdens imposed on domestic products and on imported products which may be classified as "similar", is the basic rule in this respect. This provision * * * must be interpreted widely so as to cover all taxation procedures which conflict with the principle of the equality of treatment of domestic products and imported products; it is therefore necessary to interpret the concept of "similar products" with sufficient flexibility. * * * [I]t is necessary to consider as similar products which "have similar characteristics and meet the same needs from the point of view of consumers". It is therefore necessary to determine the scope of the first paragraph of Article [90] on the basis not of the criterion of the strictly identical nature of the products but on that of their similar and comparable use.

6   The function of the second paragraph of Article [90] is to cover * * * indirect tax protection in the case of products which, without being similar within the meaning of the first paragraph, are nevertheless in competition, even partial, indirect or potential, with certain products of the importing country. * * * [I]t is sufficient for the imported product to be in competition with the protected domestic production by reason of one or several economic uses to which it may be put, even though the condition of

similarity for the purposes of the first paragraph of Article [90] is not fulfilled.

[The Commission argued that all spirits constituted a single product market, meeting essentially the same needs of consumers. France contended that spirits broke down into a variety of product markets, depending on their raw material source, physical characteristics or consumer usages. The Court reviewed the characteristics of spirits and considered that they had "common generic features" since they were all produced by distillation and all had high alcohol content. On the other hand, spirits did come from a variety of raw materials (wine, fruit or cereals), had different odors and tastes, and were consumed in different modes (neat, diluted, or with mixes).]

12   Two conclusions follow from this analysis of the market in spirits. First, there is * * * an indeterminate number of beverages which must be classified as "similar products" within the meaning of the first paragraph of Article [90], although it may be difficult to decide this in specific cases, in view of the nature of the factors implied by distinguishing criteria such as flavour and consumer habits. Secondly, even in cases in which it is impossible to recognize a sufficient degree of similarity between the products concerned, there are nevertheless, in the case of all spirits, common characteristics which are sufficiently pronounced to accept that in all cases there is at least partial or potential competition. It follows that the application of the second paragraph of Article [90] may come into consideration in cases in which the relationship of similarity between the specific varieties of spirits remains doubtful or contested.

13   It appears from the foregoing that Article [90], taken as a whole, may apply without distinction to all the products concerned.

* * *

The Application of the Contested Tax System

* * *

29   [T]he Commission observes that the French tax system is adjusted so as to place at a disadvantage spirits obtained from cereals which are almost exclusively imported from other Member States, whereas domestic production of those products is insignificant. * * * It thus seems that this tax system, even if it were necessary to state that spirits obtained from wine and fruit on the one hand and spirits obtained from cereals on the other are not similar, is of such a nature as to afford an indirect competitive advantage to national production.

* * *

32   As regards the criteria which may be used for the classification of the products, the French Government considers that it is the "flavour" of the distillate, in other words, a number of organoleptic properties combining taste, aroma and smell, which, from the point of view of satisfying the needs of the consumer, forms the basis of the classification of products which are neither similar nor even interchangeable or competing within Article [90].

33   [France further argues that its] tax legislation is based on the distinction between "digestives" on the one hand, in other words beverages consumed at the end of the meal including in particular spirits obtained from the distillation of wine and fruit, such as cognac, armagnac and calvados, and "aperitifs" on the other, which are beverages drunk before meals including above all grain-based spirits, most frequently consumed diluted with water, such as whisky [and] gin. * * *

* * *

36   [T]he Court [does not] think it is possible to adopt as a relevant classification the distinction advocated by the French Government between "aperitifs" and "digestives". * * * [T]he distinction between aperitifs and digestives does not take into account many circumstances in which the products in question may be consumed before, during or after meals or even completely unrelated to such meals; * * * according to consumer preferences the same beverage may be used indiscriminately as an "aperitif" or "digestive". Therefore it is impossible to recognize * * * the distinction upon which French tax practice is based.

37   The same observation applies to the criterion for distinction based on the flavour of the various spirits for the purpose of * * * the application of tax legislation. There is no question of denying the reality of and the shades of difference in the flavour of the various alcoholic products; it is necessary however to bear in mind that this criterion is too variable in time and space to supply by itself a sufficiently sound basis for distinction * * *. The same applies to consumer habits which also differ from region to region and even according to social environment, so that they cannot supply appropriate differentiating criteria for the purpose of Article [90].

38   Classifications based on the flavour of the products and consumer habits are all the more difficult to lay down since the products in question, such as whisky and genevas, may be consumed in very varied circumstances, either neat or diluted or in the form of mixtures. Owing in particular to this flexibility of use, those drinks may be considered as similar to a particularly large number of other alcoholic beverages or as in at least partial competition which those beverages.

39   After considering all these factors the Court deems it unnecessary for the purposes of solving this dispute to give a ruling on the question whether or not the spirituous beverages concerned are wholly or partly similar products within the meaning of the first paragraph of Article [90] when it is impossible reasonably to contest that without exception they are in at least partial competition with the domestic products * * * and that it is impossible to deny the protective nature of the French tax system within the second paragraph of Article [90].

* * *

41   As the competitive and substitution relationships between the beverages in question are such, the protective nature of the tax system criticized by the Commission is clear. * * * As for the fact that the market share of whisky has increased in spite of the tax disadvantage which it suffers, this fact does not prove that there is no protective effect.

BACCHUS IMPORTS, LTD. v. DIAS

468 U.S. 263, 104 S.Ct. 3049, 82 L.Ed.2d 200 (1984).

[Hawaii imposed a 20% excise tax on sales of liquor, but exempted Okolehao (brandy made from a Hawaiian shrub) and pineapple wine from the tax. When challenged as a violation of the dormant Commerce Clause, the Hawaiian Supreme Court held the tax exemptions "rationally related to the State's legitimate interest in promoting domestic industry." The U.S. Supreme Court reversed.]

A cardinal rule of Commerce Clause jurisprudence is that "[n]o State, consistent with the Commerce Clause, may impose a tax which discriminates against interstate commerce ... by providing a direct commercial advantage to local business." Boston Stock Exchange v. State Tax Comm'n, 429 U.S. 318, 329 (1977).

* * *

The State relies in part on statistics showing that for the years in question sales of Okolehao and pineapple wine constituted well under one percent of the total liquor sales in Hawaii. It also relies on the statement by the Hawaii Supreme Court that "[w]e believe we can safely assume these products pose no competitive threat to other liquors produced elsewhere and consumed in Hawaii." * * * However, neither the small volume of sales of exempted liquor nor the fact that the exempted liquors do not constitute a present "competitive threat" to other liquors is dispositive of the question whether competition exists between the locally produced beverages and foreign beverages; instead, they go only to the extent of such competition. It is well settled that "[w]e need not know how unequal the Tax is before concluding that it unconstitutionally discriminates."

* * *

No one disputes that a State may enact laws pursuant to its police powers that have the purpose and effect of encouraging domestic industry. However, the Commerce Clause stands as a limitation on the means by which a State can constitutionally seek to achieve that goal. One of the fundamental purposes of the Clause "was to insure ... against discriminating State legislation." Welton v. Missouri, 91 U.S. 275, 280 (1876).

* * *

[Hawaii contends that its law was intended] "to subsidize nonexistent (pineapple wine) and financially troubled (okolehao) liquor industries peculiar to Hawaii." However, we perceive no principle of Commerce Clause jurisprudence supporting a distinction between thriving and struggling enterprises under these circumstances, and the State cites no authority for its proposed distinction. In either event, the legislation constitutes "economic protectionism" in every sense of the phrase.

Notes and Questions

1. What is the Court of Justice's test for determining "similar products" in the *French alcohol excise tax* case? What did you think of the French argument

that these products aren't similar because cereal-based alcohol tends to be consumed as an aperitif while wine or fruit-based alcohol tends to be consumed as a digestif? Why isn't the distinction between aperitifs and digestives a valid indication of consumer views in France?

2.   Omitted from the judgment is France's argument that the Community's own Common Customs Tariff classifies gin and whisky in one subheading and wine-based alcohol in another. The Court did not find this a persuasive analogy. Do you agree? The Court's disregard of the customs classification represented a disavowal of language in an earlier judgment, Firma Fink–Frucht GmbH v. Hauptzollamt München, Case 27/67, [1968] ECR 223, where it stated: "Similarity between products * * * exists when the products in question are normally to be considered as coming within the same fiscal, customs or statistical classification." Id. at 232. A later judgment made quite clear that customs tariff categories are not relevant in Article 90 cases. Cogis v. Amministrazione delle Finanze, Case 216/81, [1982] ECR 2701.

3.   Although most of the *French alcohol excise tax* judgment is devoted to the "similar products" issue, at the end the Court switches to Article 90 paragraph 2. Why? Were you convinced by the Court's analysis? How can dissimilar products still be competitive? What is meant by saying imported and domestic spirits are in "partial competition"? When later you have read Part III of this casebook on Competition Policy, consider whether this judgment accords with the product market analysis made there.

4.   In *Bacchus* the tax discrimination is evident. However, as we shall see in *Maine v. Taylor*, infra page 494, in rare cases the Supreme Court has held that a state's discrimination against interstate commerce can be justified. Do you agree that neither of Hawaii's arguments for its discriminatory tax exemption are justified? Would the Court of Justice rule the same way on analogous facts? Would the Supreme Court find that a state's excise tax discrimination between types of alcohol in circumstances parallel to those in the *Alcohol excise tax* case violate the dormant Commerce Clause?

5.   Although in the *French Alcohol excise tax* case, the Court concentrated its analysis of "similar products" on the consumer's views, in other cases another criterion, that of objective physical characteristics, has been decisive. Thus, in Commission v. Denmark (Wine tax), Case 106/84, [1986] ECR 833, the Court considered the beverage's production process, taste and alcohol content, as well as consumer preferences, in finding that normal grape wine and other fruit-based wines constituted similar products. The Court then found that a tax rate on imported grape wine that was 50% higher than that on domestic fruit-based wines constituted discriminatory treatment under Article 90 paragraph 1. However, in John Walker & Sons Ltd. v. Ministeriet for Skatter, Case 243/84, [1986] ECR 875, the Court held that distillation, the production process for Scotch whiskey, as well as its stronger alcohol content and taste, made Scotch whiskey an intrinsically different product from Danish fruit liqueurs under Article 90 paragraph 1. Do you agree with the result in these cases? In any event, do you think that physical characteristics should be considered in determining whether products are similar for Article 90 purposes, except insofar as physical considerations may be a factor in showing the basis for consumer preferences?

6.   In F.G. Roders BV v. Inspecteur der Invoerrechten, Cases C–367 to 377/93, [1995] I–2229, eleven Dutch sellers of wine made from grapes challenged under Article 90 the Dutch excise tax levied from 1976 to 1992 on such wine, because no excise tax was levied on wine made from fruit other than grapes. The

Court held that ordinary grape table wine was "similar" to wine made from other fruit, applying the criteria used in the *Danish Wine Tax* case, supra. It further held that sherry, madeira, vermouth and champagne were not "similar," but that the national court should review whether they might still be in competition with other fruit-based wine under the second paragraph of Article 90. In the final issue, the Netherlands contended that giving refunds to sellers over a sixteen year period would represent a heavy fiscal burden, and therefore argued that the ruling should not be retroactive. Refer to the note on retroactive effect, page 184 *supra*. How should the Court resolve this issue?

COMMISSION v. UNITED KINGDOM

(Wine and beer taxes)
Case 170/78, [1983] ECR 2265.

[The United Kingdom excise tax on light wine was about five times that levied on beer, calculated per gallon, and represented about 38% of the consumer sale price for light wine, versus 25% for beer. The UK produces almost no wine, but substantial amounts of beer. The Commission challenged the UK's wine tax as a violation of Article 90. The Court first reiterated its findings in a prior interlocutory judgment in the case.]

Competitive Relationship Between Wine and Beer

8   As regards the question of competition between wine and beer, the Court considered that, to a certain extent at least, the two beverages in question were capable of meeting identical needs, so that it had to be acknowledged that there was a degree of substitution for one another. * * * [F]or the purpose of measuring the possible degree of substitution, attention should not be confined to consumer habits in a Member State or in a given region. Those habits, which were essentially variable in time and space, could not be considered to be immutable; the tax policy of a Member State must not therefore crystallize given consumer habits so as to consolidate an advantage acquired by national industries concerned to respond to them.

9   The Court nonetheless recognized that, in view of the substantial differences between wine and beer, it was difficult to compare the manufacturing processes and the natural properties of those beverages * * *. For that reason, the Court requested the parties to provide additional information with a view to dispelling the doubts which existed concerning the nature of the competitive relationship between the two products.

10   The Government of the United Kingdom did not give any opinion on that question in its subsequent statements. * * *

11   The Italian Government contended * * * that it was inappropriate to compare beer with wines of average alcoholic strength or, *a fortiori,* with wines of greater alcoholic strength. In its opinion, it was the lightest wines with [low alcoholic content], that is to say the most popular and cheapest wines, which were genuinely in competition with beer. * * * [T]hose wines should be chosen for purposes of comparison where it was a question of measuring the incidence of taxation on the basis of either alcoholic strength or the price of the products.

12   The Court considers that observation by the Italian Government to be pertinent. In view of the substantial differences in the quality and,

therefore, in the price of wines, the decisive competitive relationship between beer, a popular and widely consumed beverage, and wine must be established by reference to those wines which are the most accessible to the public at large, that is to say, generally speaking, the lightest and cheapest varieties.

* * *

Determination of an Appropriate Tax Ratio

[19] It is not disputed that comparison of the taxation of beer and wine by reference to the volume of the two beverages reveals that wine is taxed more heavily than beer in both relative and absolute terms. Not only was the taxation of wine increased substantially in relation to the taxation of beer when the United Kingdom replaced customs duty with excise duty * * *, but it is also clear that during the years to which these proceedings relate, namely 1976 and 1977, the taxation of wine was, on average, five times higher, by reference to volume, than the taxation of beer; in other words, wine was subject to an additional tax burden of 400% in round figures.

[Applying the criteria for comparison based upon the relative alcoholic strength of beer and wine and upon the price of beer and cheaper types of wine, the Court concluded that in each case imported cheap wine was taxed more heavily than beer to a substantial degree.]

[27] It is clear, therefore, following the detailed inquiry conducted by the Court—whatever criterion for comparison is used, there being no need to express a preference for one or the other—that the United Kingdom's tax system has the effect of subjecting wine imported from other Member States to an additional tax burden so as to afford protection to domestic beer production. * * * Since such protection is most marked in the case of the most popular wines, the effect of the United Kingdom tax system is to stamp wine with the hallmarks of a luxury product which, in view of the tax burden which it bears, can scarcely constitute in the eyes of the consumer a genuine alternative to the typical domestically produced beverage.

[28] It follows from the foregoing considerations that, by levying excise duty on still light wines made from fresh grapes at a higher rate, in relative terms, than on beer, the United Kingdom has failed to fulfill its obligations under the second paragraph of Article [90] of the EEC Treaty.

Notes and Questions

1. Did the UK tax violate Article 90 paragraph 1 or paragraph 2? Should attention be paid to UK consumer habits or Community-wide consumer habits? Why was the Italian intervention helpful to the Court's conclusion?

2. The cumulative effect of these Article 226 proceedings against Member State alcohol excise tax systems has been quite substantial, since States have had to re-examine their excise tax systems to see whether they constitute indirect barriers to Community trade, and in some cases have decided to modify the systems.

3. How sizable must a tax differential be in order to be considered protectionist? In Commission v. Belgium (Wine vs. beer), Case 356/85, [1987] ECR 3299, the Commission argued that Belgium's 25% value added tax rate on wine (largely imported) versus the 19% rate on beer (substantial domestic production) violated Article 90. The Court held that the 6% difference was not sufficient to have a protectionist effect, even though the consumer price of wine in Belgium is on average four times that of beer. Contrast Commission v. Greece (Alcohol excise tax), Case C–230/89, [1991] ECR I–1909 where the Court found a 36% value added tax on whisky, gin, rum, etc. (largely imported) to have a protectionist effect, since only a 16% rate was imposed on ouzo and brandy (largely domestic). Where should the line be drawn?

4. On several occasions, the WTO Appellate Body has confirmed panel findings that Japan, Korea and Chile have violated GATT rules by imposing higher excise taxes on imported alcoholic beverages than on domestically produced beverages. See Chapter 28. Thus, in March 2001 the Community agreed not to contest Chile's reduction of excise taxes on imported whisky, gin and cognac to levels closer too the excise tax on Chile's own pisco (a type of hard alcohol). Chile acted to comply with a December 1999 WTO ruling.

COMMISSION v. ITALY

(Banana tax)
Case 184/85, [1987] ECR 2013.

[In 1985, Italy imported 357,500 tons of bananas, largely from French overseas departments, while producing only 120 tons in Sicily. Italy produces large quantities of other table fruit, notably apples, pears, peaches, plums, apricots, cherries and oranges. Italy imposes a consumption tax on a variety of products, among which are bananas, but not other fruit. In 1985, the consumption tax amounted to almost half the import price for bananas. The Commission brought an Article 226 proceeding against Italy, contending that the consumption tax violated the second paragraph of Article 90.]

8   Italian banana production is completely negligible and must therefore be left out of account. Consequently, the criterion of similarity on which the prohibition set out in the first paragraph of Article [90] is based must be assessed in relation to table fruit typically produced in Italy.

9   It must therefore be considered * * * whether bananas and other table fruit typically produced in Italy have similar characteristics and meet the same consumer needs. Consequently, in order to assess similarity, account must be taken, on the one hand, of a set of objective characteristics of the two categories of product in question, such as their organoleptic characteristics and their water content, and, on the other hand, whether or not the two categories of fruit can satisfy the same consumer needs.

10   [T]he two categories of fruit in question, that is to say, on the one hand, bananas, and, on the other, table fruit typically produced in Italy have different characteristics. As the Commission has conceded, the organoleptic characteristics and the water content of the two categories of product differ. By way of example, the higher water content of pears and other fruit typically grown in Italy give them thirst-quenching properties which bananas do not possess. Moreover, the observation of the Italian Government that the banana is regarded, at least on the Italian market, as a

foodstuff which is particularly nutritious, of a high energy content and well-suited for infants must be accepted. It must therefore be held that those two categories of fruit are not similar within the meaning of the first paragraph of Article [90].

11 [T]he function of [the second paragraph of Article 90 is to cover all forms of indirect tax protection in the case of products which, without being similar * * * are nevertheless in competition, even partial, indirect or potential competition, with each other.

12 Although bananas and table fruit typically produced in Italy are not similar products * * * bananas do afford an alternative choice to consumers of fruit. As a result, bananas must be regarded as being in partial competition with such fruit. Therefore the taxation of bananas must not have the effect of affording indirect protection to table fruit typically produced in Italy.

13 [T]he relevant consumer tax [assessed on bananas] does not apply to the most typical Italian–produced table fruit. That the tax is protective is underscored by its rate * * * which is almost half the 1985 import price. Hence, that difference in taxation influences the market in the products in question by reducing the potential consumption of the imported products. That being so, the protective nature of the tax system criticized by the Commission clearly emerges.

Notes and Questions

1. Since Sicilian bananas also bear the consumption tax, how did the Court find a violation of Article 90? Note that the Court held that bananas are not similar to other fruit in terms of Article 90 paragraph 1 because, among other things, bananas are not thirst-quenching, unlike other fruit. Are apples thirst-quenching? Do consumers usually buy fruit to quench their thirst? Shouldn't the Court have advised the referring national court to determine consumer buying habits more scientifically instead of deciding the issue on the basis of such generalizations?

2. The Court found that bananas do compete with Italian fruit for purposes of Article 90 paragraph 2. Do you agree? Is this a case where the unusually high level of tax could "freeze" an Italian consumer habit of preferring cheaper Italian fruit?

3. It is interesting to compare the judgment's conclusion that bananas are in competition with other fruit with the Court's famous judgment ten years earlier in United Brands v. Commission, Case 27/76, [1978] ECR 207, where the Court held that bananas were to be considered as a separate product market from other fruit for purposes of competition law analysis under Article 82 (ex Article 86). *United Brands* is a leading Article 82 case excerpted at page 843. When reviewing *United Brands,* consider whether additional facts or the different Treaty context justified the different result, or whether the judgments are inconsistent to some degree.

3. HARMONIZATION OF INTERNAL TAXES

EC Treaty Article 93 (ex Article 99) authorizes the Council to "adopt provisions for the harmonization of legislation concerning turnover [i.e., value added] taxes, excise duties and other forms of indirect taxation." There are, however, two significant limitations on the exercise of this legislative grant.

First, the Council must act unanimously, which gives every State veto power over a proposal. Moreover, the Council may only adopt legislation "necessary to ensure the establishment and functioning of the internal market," a limitation which enables States hostile to a proposal to launch a policy debate as to the proposal's necessity.

The Council has made use of Article 93 principally to harmonize the substantive coverage and the procedural operation of national value added tax systems. (Value added taxes are imposed on most products at every stage of production and distribution, and are ultimately paid by consumers when buying the products.) The Council deemed this harmonization indispensable, because the Community takes a percentage share of the value added tax collected by each State. This share of national value added tax represents a large part of Community revenues, so naturally the base and mode of collection must be essentially the same in each State. Building upon several earlier measures, the Sixth Value Added Tax Directive 77/388 on a uniform basis of assessment, O.J. L 145/1 (June 13, 1977), sets out the harmonized provisions in elaborate detail. Nonetheless, the application of the Sixth Directive requires interpretation. Each year the Court of Justice decides ten to fifteen cases interpreting its provisions.

Since the late 1980s, the Commission has frequently urged proposals to harmonize the rates at which both value added taxes and excise taxes are levied on specific fields of products. The obvious goal is to achieve a more nearly level impact of taxation on commercial transactions throughout the Community. These efforts have largely failed, because indirect taxation constitutes a sensitive political sector, representing a large part of the global revenues of many States. In 1992, the Council was able to achieve a modest degree of success by adopting several directives to require Member States to set minimum (but not maximum) rates for tobacco, petroleum and alcoholic beverages. Directives 92/83, O.J. L 316/21 (Oct. 19, 1992) and 92/84, O.J. L 316/29 (Oct. 19, 1992), setting minimum rates for wine and beer, were subsequently challenged in an interesting Court proceeding.

SOCRIDIS v. RECEVEUR PRINCIPAL des DOUANES

Case C–166/98, [1999] ECR I–3791.

[Council Directives 92/83 and 92/84 require Member States to set a minimum tax rate of ECU 1.87 per degree per hectolitre for beer, but permit States to set a zero minimum rate for wine. France, which formerly had relatively parallel tax rates for beer and wine, implemented the directives by adopting significantly higher rates for beer than for wine. Moreover, Austria, Germany, Greece, Italy, Luxembourg and Spain imposed no tax on wine. A French distributor challenged the directives on the grounds that they violated the neutrality principles of Article 90 and that they permitted an increase in the disparities in national tax rates, instead of harmonizing them pursuant to Article 93. The French Tribunal referred questions concerning these issues to the Court of Justice.]

16   The first point to note is that the general purpose of Article [90] of the Treaty is to guarantee the free movement of goods between the Member States under normal conditions of competition by eliminating all forms of

protection which may result in the application of internal taxation which discriminates against products from other Member States and to guarantee that internal taxation is wholly neutral for the purposes of competition between domestic and imported products.

* * *

[18] In that connection, only commonly consumed wines, which in general are cheap wines, have enough characteristics in common with beer to constitute an alternative choice for consumers and may therefore be regarded as being in competition with beer for the purposes of the second paragraph of Article [90].... Consequently, the ground of invalidity based on that provision relied on by Socridis to challenge the minimum excise duty fixed by Directive 92/84 arises only to the extent that it applies to commonly consumed wines.

[19] Next, the Court has consistently held that directives do not infringe the Treaty if they leave the Member States a sufficiently wide margin of appreciation to enable them to transpose them into national law in a manner consistent with the requirements of the Treaty.

[20] It is common ground that Directives 92/83 and 92/84 merely require Member States to apply a minimum excise duty on beer. Consequently, the Member States retain a sufficiently wide margin of discretion to ensure that the relationship of the taxes on wine and beer excludes any protection for domestic production within the meaning of Article [90] of the Treaty.

[21] The plea that Directives 92/83 and 92/84 are invalid because they are incompatible with the second paragraph of Article [90] of the Treaty must therefore be rejected.

Breach of Article [93] of the Treaty

[22] Socridis contends that any action by the Council under Article [93] must seek not only to reduce disparities in taxation, including those between competing products, but also to avoid sanctioning the introduction or retention of tax ratios which do not, or may not, comply with the second paragraph of Article [90] of the Treaty.

[23] Socridis maintains that Directives 92/83 and 92/84 fall far short of what is necessary to bring about a minimum harmonisation of the taxes on wine and beer, with the result that the Council is in breach of Article [93] of the Treaty.

[24] That argument cannot be upheld.

[25] As the Advocate General rightly observed, the intention of the Community legislature in adopting Directives 92/83 and 92/84 was not to harmonise taxation as between wine and beer * * *. [T]he Council was seeking to harmonise, first, national legislation on excise duty applicable to wine and, secondly, that relating to excise duty on beer.

[26] Furthermore, the Court has consistently held that the Community institutions are free to introduce harmonisation gradually or in stages. It is generally difficult to implement such measures because they require the competent Community institutions to draw up, on the basis of diverse and complex national provisions, common rules in harmony with the aims laid

down by the Treaty and approved by a qualified majority of the Members of the Council, or even, as is the case in fiscal matters, the unanimous agreement of the latter.

Notes and Questions

1. Like *Commissionaires Reunis*, *Socridis* poses an issue of Treaty supremacy. Could the Council validly adopt legislation that permitted States to use tax rates to protect their domestic wine production against foreign beer imports? Do you agree with the Court's disposition of this issue? Does the language in ¶ 20 constitute a warning to States that do not tax wine but import substantial quantities of beer?

2. As a matter of policy, do you think it is desirable, or not, to retain the unanimous voting requirement for Council action to harmonize indirect taxation? Also, is it desirable, or not, to augment Parliament's present advisory role in the legislative process? Compare with the US–would Congress ever seriously undertake to harmonize the rates of state sales taxes or excise taxes?

Chapter 13

FREE MOVEMENT OF GOODS: QUANTITATIVE RESTRICTIONS

This chapter continues the topic of free movement of goods, but deals with a different sort of barrier: quantitative restrictions and measures equivalent to them. The Court's interpretation of what constitute "measures equivalent" has evolved considerably over time. Moreover, the case law on the extent to which certain State measures restricting free movement of goods are permitted is both voluminous and complex. The doctrines developed by the Court of Justice are among the core principles of Community law today.

The Treaty articles involved here are contained in Title I on "Free Movement of Goods." Article 28 (initially Article 30 in the EEC Treaty) prohibits "quantitative restrictions on imports and all measures having equivalent effect." Article 29 (ex Article 34), which prohibits "quantitative restrictions on exports, and all measures having equivalent effect," parallels Article 28. However, restrictions on exports are far less common than those on imports, so that Article 29 has been infrequently applied. The EEC Treaty initially contained supplementary provisions: Article 31 forbid the creation of new quantitative restrictions or measures equivalent thereto, and Article 32 required States to abolish existing ones by 1970, the end of the initial Treaty transitional period. The Treaty of Amsterdam deleted these two articles as now superfluous.

What is the meaning of a "quantitative restriction"? The obvious sense is a quota, a numerical limitation on products in inter-state trade. In fact, the initial EEC Treaty Article 32 used the word "quota" as though it were synonymous with quantitative restriction, and the initial Article 33 contained a lengthy description of how intra-Community quotas should be progressively eliminated. The term "quantitative restriction" comes from GATT Article XI, which generally prohibits "quotas, import or export licenses or other measures," subject however to various exceptions.

Given this rather clear sense of quantitative restrictions, one might think that "measures having equivalent effect" (not a GATT term) would have a fairly narrow meaning, referring to some form of state licensing or other express limit on trade. Instead, as we will see, the Court of Justice has given this innocuous-seeming phrase an extraordinarily expansive interpretation, and it has become a powerful weapon in the efforts to achieve market integration within the common market.

The Commission's role in expanding the meaning of "measures having equivalent effect" has also been significant. The initial EEC Treaty Article 33(7) gave the Commission the power to issue directives as to the "procedure and timetable" for the abolition of measures equivalent to quotas. This is one of the rare instances in which the Treaty granted legislative power to the Commission, rather than the Council of Ministers. More importantly, since 1970 the Commission has made aggressive use of Article 226 (ex Article 169) to challenge a variety of Member States measures having equivalent effect.

The Treaty contains an express exception to the general abolition of quantitative restrictions and measures equivalent thereto. Article 30 (initially Article 36) allows States to maintain such restrictions for a number of specifically enumerated policy reasons, which will be considered in detail later in this chapter. Many of the cases brought before the Court involve the proper demarcation of the Article 30 exceptions.

Attacking the many varied barriers to Community trade through Court proceedings alone would be a laborious and piecemeal method of achieving free movement of goods. The Commission and the Council accordingly commenced a program of legislative action in the 1960s to harmonize national rules which could adversely affect intra-Community trade. This program of harmonizing national legislation under Article 94 (ex Article 100) was steadily expanded in scope in the 1970s and 1980s. It received substantial new impetus through the Single European Act's commitment to the goal of completing the internal market by 1992.

We will postpone to Chapter 14 the description of harmonization of law and the internal market program. However, it should be emphasized that the Court of Justice case law described in this chapter evolved in tandem with the legislative program discussed in Chapter 14 and that the two reciprocally influenced one another.

Finally, mention should be made of Article 31 (ex Article 37), which deals with "State monopolies of a commercial character," i.e., state-owned or controlled agencies, bodies or enterprises. Since the end of the transitional period in 1969, Article 31 has forbidden state monopolies to discriminate in any way against any Community persons or entities in the procurement or supply of goods. Public procurement as an economic sector has become increasingly important in Community law. It was identified as a sector requiring priority action in the 1985 Commission White Paper on Completing the Internal Market. Since the late 1980s, a series of legislative measures have been adopted for the purpose of removing barriers to Community trade in public procurement, but unfortunately space constraints prevent coverage of this topic. For a helpful review, see J. Winter, Public Procurement in the EEC, 28 Common Mkt.L.Rev. 741 (1991).

A. ARTICLE 28: QUANTITATIVE RESTRICTIONS AND MEASURES HAVING EQUIVALENT EFFECT

Article 28 (ex Article 30) prohibits "quantitative restrictions on imports and all measures having equivalent effect." Because the prohibition in Article 28 is clear and unconditional, Article 28 is an obvious candidate for treatment as a Treaty article which has direct effect. The Court of Justice so held in Ianelli & Volpi SpA. v. Meroni, Case 74/76, [1977] ECR 557, 575, referring to the prohibition as "mandatory and explicit," and therefore creating "individual rights which national courts must protect." Because Article 28's prohibition came into force only after the transitional period, the direct effect of Article 28 started on January 1, 1970.

A quantitative restriction's usual sense is that of a quota, a numerical limitation on imported products in some form. But suppose a State totally bans the import of products for some policy reason. This occurred in *Regina v. Henn & Darby, infra*, where the United Kingdom totally banned the importation of indecent or obscene literature. The UK Court of Appeal considered that a total ban does not violate Article 28 because, in literal terms, a ban does not limit imports to a certain quantity. The Court of Justice took the more common sense view that the prohibition of quantitative restrictions also covers a total ban of products. The Court has taken the same position on bans on imports for health and safety reasons, e.g., the Dutch prohibition of the sale of Italian apples with a residue of a specific pesticide, the issue in *Prosecutor v. Heijn, infra*.

1. WHAT ARE "MEASURES HAVING EQUIVALENT EFFECT"?

The concept of "measures having equivalent effect" to quantitative restrictions is obviously a highly indefinite term. In an effort to provide guidance as to its meaning, the Commission used its legislative power under Article 33(7) to issue Directive 70/50 of December 22, 1969, on the abolition of measures which have an effect equivalent to quantitative restrictions on imports. At this point, read carefully its text in the Selected Documents.

Notes and Questions

1. Observe the Commission's attempt to define generically "measures having equivalent effect" to quantitative restrictions in article 2(1) and (2). Is a protectionist intent necessary? What is the Commission trying to achieve by adopting such an expansive definition?

2. Note that in article 2(1), the Commission does not forbid State measures that are "applicable equally to domestic or imported products," i.e., that do not discriminate against imported products. As we shall see in analyzing the *Cassis de Dijon* judgment in section C, the Court of Justice has rejected the Commission's view on this point.

3. When reading the illustrative list in Directive 70/50, try to think of concrete examples. Even though non-exhaustive, this list indicates the great variety of measures affecting Community trade forbidden by Article 28. Since 1969, the Court of Justice has delivered judgments covering fact situations

comparable to virtually every item on this list. The directive accordingly represents a useful summary of prohibited measures.

More authoritative than the Commission's view is the Court of Justice's definition of "measures having equivalent effect." We turn to the leading cases on this subject.

PROCUREUR DU ROI v. DASSONVILLE
Case 8/74, [1974] ECR 837.

[A 1934 Belgian law not only required importers to furnish a certificate of origin for certain types of hard liquor, but further stipulated that the certificate must come from the country of origin. A Belgian firm was prosecuted for importing Scotch whisky bought in France, providing evidence of its Scotch origin derived from a French register instead of the required certificate of origin from Scotland. The trial court made an Article 234 reference as to whether the Belgian law violated Article 28.]

4   [A] trader, wishing to import into Belgium Scotch whisky which is already in free circulation in France, can obtain such a certificate only with great difficulty, unlike the importer who imports directly from the producer country.

5   All trading rules enacted by Member States which are capable of hindering, directly or indirectly, actually or potentially, intra-Community trade are to be considered as measures having an effect equivalent to quantitative restrictions.

6   In the absence of a Community system guaranteeing for consumers the authenticity of a product's designation of origin, if a Member State takes measures to prevent unfair practices in this connexion, it is however subject to the condition that these measures should be reasonable and that the means of proof required should not act as a hinderance to trade between Member States and should, in consequence, be accessible to all Community nationals.

* * *

9   Consequently, the requirement by a Member State of a certificate of authenticity which is less easily obtainable by importers of an authentic product which has been put into free circulation in a regular manner in another Member State than by importers of the same product coming directly from the country of origin constitutes a measure having an effect equivalent to a quantitative restriction as prohibited by the Treaty.

Notes and Questions

1.   Compare the Court's definition of "measures having equivalent effect" with that of the Commission in Directive 70/50. Which is broader? The Court's expansive definition of what could have been treated as a narrow, quota-related term is a clear illustration of the Court's "activist" interpretation of the Treaty, applauded by most commentators but sharply criticized by some. What do you suppose motivated the Court of Justice in its approach? Is it a justifiable instance of judicial rulemaking?

2. If the Court had concluded with ¶5, a State could never have "trading rules" which hinder Community trade, except when allowed to do so by Article 30. Can one draw from ¶6 the inference that ¶5 is subject to a "reasonableness" test? We will return to this point when discussing *Cassis de Dijon* in section C.

3. In 1993, the *Keck* judgment, excerpted at page 522, significantly limited *Dassonville's* broad definition of "measures equivalent" to measures relating to products, excluding measures relating to the merchandising of products. For clarity, *Keck* and the case law immediately prior thereto will be postponed to section C.

COMMISSION v. GERMANY

(Pharmaceutical representatives)
Case 247/81, [1984] ECR 1111.

[The Commission brought an action under Article 226 of the Treaty for a declaration that by reserving the placing of medicinal preparations on the market to pharmaceutical undertakings having their headquarters, or a branch or agent in Germany, Germany failed to fulfil its obligations under Article 28. The Court agreed.]

2 * * * By so limiting the opportunities for marketing medicinal preparations, that condition is undeniably, according to the Commission, a restriction on imports which entails for foreign undertakings an increase in their costs and which constitutes a serious interference with their freedom of action. According to Directive 70/50 of 22 December 1969, measures which make access of imported products to the domestic market conditional upon having an agent or representative in the territory of the importing Member State are to be considered as having an effect equivalent to a quantitative restriction (Article 2(3)(g)).

3 According to the German Government, the provisions in question do not constitute an obstacle to imports, since in practice all pharmaceutical undertakings established in another Member State and wishing to export to the Federal Republic of Germany will have recourse to a subsidiary, a branch or a representative body already established in the territory of the Federal Republic. The obligation to have a representative resident in Germany corresponds therefore to a choice which the undertakings would in any event have to make for commercial reasons.

4 That argument cannot be accepted. According to the consistent case-law of the Court all commercial rules of Member States likely to hinder directly or indirectly, actually or potentially, trade within the Community are to be considered as measures having an effect equivalent to a quantitative restriction. The Court considers in this respect that the disputed provision is likely to involve additional costs for undertakings which find no good reason for having a representative of their own established in the Federal Republic of Germany for the purpose of promoting their exports to that Member State, and which sell directly to several customers. The disputed provision is therefore likely to hinder trade within the Community and in particular parallel imports, and must be regarded as a measure having an effect equivalent to a quantitative restriction.

COMMISSION v. GERMANY

(Sekt and Weinbrand)
Case 12/74, [1975] ECR 181.

[A 1971 German law permitted the use of the word "Sekt" only for German sparkling wine and "Weinbrand" only for German brandy distilled from wine, while imported sparkling wine had to be called "Schaumwein" and imported wine-brandy "Branntwein aus Wein". The apparent purpose was to create consumer recognition of the German products in a fashion analogous to that for the French products "champagne" and "cognac," which are protected appellations of origin. The Commission brought an Article 226 proceeding to challenge the law, arguing that "Sekt" and "Weinbrand" should not qualify as appellations of origin, and that the German law adversely affected intra-Community trade in violation of Article 28.]

5   The Common Market is based upon the free circulation of goods within the Community.

* * *

6   Directive No 70/50/EEC * * * states in Article 1 that its purpose is to abolish measures which have an effect equivalent to quantitative restrictions on imports operative at the date of entry into force of the Treaty and sets out in Article 2(3) the measures which must be regarded as prohibited * * *; it refers under Article 2(3)(s) to measures which "confine names which are not indicative of origin or source to domestic products only".

7   Whatever the factors which may distinguish them, registered designations of origin and indirect indications of origin * * * always describe at the least a product coming from a specific geographical area.

   To the extent to which these appellations are protected by law they must satisfy the objectives of such protection, in particular the need to ensure not only that the interests of the producers concerned are safeguarded against unfair competition, but also that consumers are protected against information which may mislead them.

   These appellations only fulfil their specific purpose if the product which they describe does in fact possess qualities and characteristics which are due to the fact that it originated in a specific geographical area.

   As regards indications of origin in particular, the geographical area of origin of a product must confer on it a specific quality and specific characteristics of such a nature as to distinguish it from all other products.

8   The German legislation on vine products provides that the appellations "Sekt" and "Weinbrand" shall describe products originating in the Federal Republic of Germany or [Austria].

   An area of origin which is defined on the basis either of the extent of national territory or a linguistic criterion cannot constitute a geographical area * * * capable of justifying an indication of origin, particularly as the products in question may be produced from grapes of indeterminate origin.

In this instance, it is not disputed that the area of origin referred to by the legislation on vine products does not show homogeneous natural features which distinguish it in contrast to adjacent areas * * *.

The German Government maintains, however, that the products covered by the appellations "Sekt" and "Weinbrand" are clearly distinguished from all other products as a result of the particular method of manufacture used in Germany which confers on them a typical flavour * * *.

9   In the case of vine products, the natural features of the area of origin, such as the grape from which these products are obtained, play an important role in determining their quality and their characteristics.

Although the method of production used for such products may play some part in determining their characteristics, it is not alone decisive, independently of the quality of the grape used, in determining its origin.

* * *

14   * * * Under the terms of Article 2(3)(s) of Directive No 70/50/EEC of the Commission, measures which "confine names which are not indicative of origin or source to domestic products only" are to be regarded as prohibited * * *.

By reserving these appellations to domestic production and by compelling the products of the other Member States to employ appellations which are unknown or less esteemed by the consumer, the legislation on vine products is calculated to favour the disposal of the domestic product on the German market to the detriment of the products of other Member States.

Thus, this legislation on vine products involves measures having an effect equivalent to quantitative restrictions on imports * * *.

For the purposes of this prohibition it is not necessary to show that such measures actually restrict imports of the products concerned but, in accordance with Article 2(1) of the abovementioned Directive, that they may merely hinder "imports which could otherwise take place".

Notes and Questions

1. On their face, do the German laws in these two cases appear to be protectionist, or rather designed to achieve a consumer interest goal? Does the German motivation matter? Note also the Court's conclusion in ¶ *14* that the German law violated Article 28 even if it could not be proved that it actually reduced imports. Why?

2. In Commission v. France (Alcohol advertising), Case 152/78, [1980] ECR 2299, the Commission challenged a French law regulating alcohol advertising. Wine and beer (produced domestically and imported, both in substantial volumes) could be freely advertised; advertising of brandy, calvados and other fruit-based liquors (largely domestic products) was partially restricted, while no advertising at all was allowed for whisky, gin and vodka (imported products). France defended its law as intended to combat alcoholism. Is the law a measure equivalent to a quantitative restriction? If it is, can the French categories of restrictions on advertising be justified?

3.   In the preceding chapter, we discussed the status under Article 23 of fees for health inspections of slaughtered meat, fruits and vegetables, live animals and plants. Are such inspections themselves a measure equivalent to a quantitative restriction? See Rewe–Zentralfinanz v. Landwirtschaftskammer, Case 4/75, [1975] ECR 843, which held that a health inspection of apples imported into Germany constituted a measure equivalent to a quantitative restriction, but was justified as a health protection measure under Article 30 (ex Article 36), because the inspection sought to prevent the spread of insect pests not present in Germany.

4.   Luxembourg's health insurance system reimbursed in part the cost of eyeglasses with corrective lenses when purchased in Luxembourg, but not when purchased elsewhere, absent prior authorization of the purchase. Does this non-reimbursement policy constitute a measure equivalent to a quantitative restriction? See *Decker, infra*.

2.   WHAT ARE "MEASURES"?

Thus far, we have assumed that we know the meaning of the word "measure." But do we? Clearly, a measure means at least any state law, regulation or administrative practice. Does it have a wider sense?

COMMISSION v. IRELAND

(Buy Irish)
Case 249/81, [1982] ECR 4005.

[Troubled by an unfavorable balance of trade, in 1978 Ireland launched a program to promote Irish products. The Irish Goods Council organized a major publicity campaign to urge consumers to buy domestic products and encouraged the use of a "Guaranteed Irish" symbol for Irish products. The Irish Goods Council was a private company, but its Management Committee was appointed by Ireland's Minister for Industry and Commerce. Moreover, Ireland provided a subsidy to finance most of the Irish Goods Council's activities. In an Article 226 proceeding, the Commission claimed that Ireland had violated Article 28.]

[5]   The Irish Government admits that there was a three-year programme in favour of buying Irish products in Ireland * * * [consisting] of an advertising campaign, by means of the press and television, the publication of posters and pamphlets and the use of the "Guaranteed Irish" symbol, designed to make Irish consumers better acquainted with products made in Ireland and to stimulate awareness in the Irish public of the link between the marketing of such products in Ireland and the unemployment problem in that country.

[6]As far as the advertising campaign is concerned, the Irish Government confirms that it forms part of the activities of the Irish Goods Council [but contends that the] activities of the Irish Goods Council are not based on any official enactment and the involvement of the Government consists exclusively of financial aid and moral support.

* * *

[After reviewing the facts, the Court concluded:]

[15]   It is thus apparent that the Irish Government appoints the members of the Management Committee of the Irish Goods Council, grants it public

subsidies which cover the greater part of its expenses and, finally, defines the aims and the broad outline of the campaign conducted by that institution to promote the sale and purchase of Irish products. In the circumstances the Irish Government cannot rely on the fact that the campaign was conducted by a private company in order to escape any liability it may have under the provisions of the Treaty.

* * *

The Application of Article [28] of the Treaty

20   The Commission maintains that the "Buy Irish" campaign and the measures taken to prosecute the campaign must be regarded, as a whole, as measures encouraging the purchase of domestic products only. * * * The Commission refers to Article 2(3)(k) of Commission Directive No 70/50/EEC stating that measures which encourage the purchase of domestic products only must be regarded as contrary to the prohibitions contained in the Treaty.

21   The Irish Government maintains that the prohibition against measures having an effect equivalent to quantitative restrictions in Article 28 is concerned only with * * * binding provisions emanating from a public authority. * * *

22   The Irish Government goes on to emphasize that the campaign has had no restrictive effect on imports since the proportion of Irish goods to all goods sold on the Irish market fell from 49.2% in 1977 to 43.4% in 1980.

23   The first observation to be made is that the campaign cannot be likened to advertising by private or public undertakings, * * * to encourage people to buy goods produced by those undertakings.

* * *

25   Whilst it may be true that the two elements of the programme which have continued in effect, namely the advertising campaign and the use of the "Guaranteed Irish" symbol, have not had any significant success in winning over the Irish market to domestic products, it is not possible to overlook the fact that, regardless of their efficacity, those two activities form part of a government programme which is designed to achieve the substitution of domestic products for imported products and is liable to affect the volume of trade between Member States.

* * *

27   In the circumstances the two activities in question amount to the establishment of a national practice * * * the potential effect of which on imports from other Member States is comparable to that resulting from government measures of a binding nature.

28   Such a practice cannot escape the prohibition laid down by Article [28] of the Treaty solely because it is not based on decisions which are binding upon undertakings. Even measures adopted by the government of a Member State which do not have binding effect may be capable of

influencing the conduct of traders and consumers in that State and thus of frustrating the aims of the Community * * *.

* * *

[30] Ireland has therefore failed to fulfil its obligations under the Treaty by organizing a campaign to promote the sale and purchase of Irish goods within its territory.

Notes and Questions

1. Is this a natural or an excessively elastic interpretation of "measure"? Do you agree with the Court? Is a State responsible in this context for the acts of every private firm which receives substantial state subsidies? Or for the acts of firms or associations whose management the State designates? Where should the line be drawn?

2. Cf. Apple & Pear Development Council v. K.J. Lewis Ltd., Case 222/82, [1983] ECR 4083, where the Court of Justice held that a UK body's advertising campaign to encourage British consumers to buy British apples and pears constituted a measure having equivalent effect to a quantitative restriction. Suppose the state of Washington financed a Washington Apple Growers Association, whose board is also named by the Governor. Suppose then that the Association launched a publicity campaign to urge Washington residents to consume domestic apples, rather than apples grown elsewhere in the US. Would this violate the dormant Commerce Clause?

3. Building upon the Court's doctrine in leading cases, the Commission frequently issues policy guidelines intended to assist courts, lawyers and business managers to comply with Community rules. Thus, the Commission Guidelines for Member States' Involvement in Promotion of Agricultural and Fisheries Products, O.J. C 272/3 (Oct. 28, 1986), gave examples both of promotional actions which are permissible (e.g., advertising products in a generic manner without reference to national origin), as well as promotional actions which violate Article 28 (ex Article 30) (e.g., campaigns intended to disparage the quality or discourage the purchase of products from other States).

4. In The Queen v. Royal Pharmaceutical Society, Cases 266 & 267/87, [1989] ECR 1295, a national professional body, the Royal Pharmaceutical Society, included in its Code of Ethics a provision forbidding pharmacists to substitute another product for that named in the prescription. The Association of Pharmaceutical Importers challenged this provision as a violation of Article 28, claiming that it prevented the substitution of an identical imported drug sold under a generic or a different brand name. UK legislation endorses the Royal Pharmaceutical Society as the sole professional body in which pharmacists must be enrolled in order to handle prescriptions under the National Health Service, which accounts for 95% of all prescriptions in the UK. Appeals from the Society's ethical proceedings can be taken to UK appellate courts. In an Article 234 referral, the Court of Justice had to decide whether the Code of Ethics constituted a UK "measure." How should the Court respond?

COMMISSION v. FRANCE

(Produce imports)

Case C–265/95, [1997] ECR I–6959.

[For over a decade and especially in 1993–95, French farmers engaged in an organized campaign to reduce the importation of vegetables and fruits, notably strawberries, from Spain. In addition to threats against retailers marketing these products, on repeated occasions some farmers blocked the movement of trucks carrying Spanish produce, destroyed the truck cargos, and committed acts of violence against the truck drivers. The French police rarely took any action to prevent these incidents, even though often present at the scene. Public prosecutors investigated, but rarely prosecuted anyone. After Commission protests proved unavailing, the Commission launched an Article 226 proceeding against France. In its defense, France claimed that it had a public policy discretion in executing police action in the face of serious public unrest and that the "commando-type" operations of the farmers were difficult to combat. France also contended that it had paid FF 17,000,000 in compensation to victims of the offences.]

30   As an indispensable instrument for the realization of a market without internal frontiers, Article [28] does not prohibit solely measures emanating from the State which, in themselves, create restrictions on trade between Member States. It also applies where a Member State abstains from adopting the measures required in order to deal with obstacles to the free movement of goods which are not caused by the State.

31   The fact that a Member State abstains from taking action or * * * fails to adopt adequate measures to prevent obstacles to the free movement of goods that are created by actions by private individuals on its territory aimed at products originating in other Member States is just as likely to obstruct intra-Community trade as is a positive act.

32   Article [28] therefore requires the Member States not merely themselves to abstain from adopting measures or engaging in conduct liable to constitute an obstacle to trade but also, when read with Article [10] of the Treaty, to take all necessary and appropriate measures to ensure that the fundamental freedom is respected on their territory.

33   [T]he Member States, which retain exclusive competence as regards the maintenance of public order and the safeguarding of internal security, unquestionably enjoy a margin of discretion in determining what measures are most appropriate to eliminate barriers to the importation of products in a given situation.

34   It is therefore not for the Community institutions to act in place of the Member States and to prescribe for them the measures which they must adopt and effectively apply in order to safeguard the free movement of goods on their territories.

35   However, it falls to the Court, taking due account of the discretion referred to above, to verify, in cases brought before it, whether the Member State concerned has adopted appropriate measures for ensuring the free movement of goods.

* * *

[38] The acts of violence committed in France and directed against agricultural products originating in other Member States, such as the interception of lorries transporting those products, the destruction of their loads and violence towards drivers, as well as threats to wholesalers and retailers and the damaging of goods on display, unquestionably create obstacles to intra-Community trade in those products.

[39] It is therefore necessary to consider whether in the present case the French Government complied with its obligations under Article [28], in conjunction with Article [10], of the Treaty, by adopting adequate and appropriate measures to deal with actions by private individuals which create obstacles to the free movement of certain agricultural products.

[40] [T]he Commission's written pleadings show that the incidents to which it objects in the present proceedings have taken place regularly for more than 10 years.

* * *

[43] [T]he French authorities had ample time to adopt the measures necessary to ensure compliance with their obligations under Community law.

[44] Moreover, notwithstanding the explanations given by the French Government, which claims that all possible measures were adopted in order to prevent the continuation of the violence and to prosecute and punish those responsible, it is a fact that, year after year, serious incidents have gravely jeopardized trade in agricultural products in France.

* * *

[48] Moreover, it is not denied that when such incidents occurred the French police were either not present on the spot, despite the fact that in certain cases the competent authorities had been warned of the imminence of demonstrations by farmers, or did not intervene, even where they far outnumbered the perpetrators of the disturbances. Furthermore, the actions in question were not always rapid, surprise actions by demonstrators who then immediately took flight, since in certain cases the disruption continued for several hours.

[49] Furthermore, it is undisputed that a number of acts of vandalism were filmed by television cameras, that the demonstrators' faces were often not covered and that the groups of farmers responsible for the violent demonstrations are known to the police.

[50] Notwithstanding this, only a very small number of the persons who participated in those serious breaches of public order has been identified and prosecuted.

* * *

[52] In the light of all the foregoing factors, the Court, while not discounting the difficulties faced by the competent authorities in dealing with situations of the type in question in this case, cannot but find that, having regard to the frequency and seriousness of the incidents cited by the Commission, the measures adopted by the French Government were manifestly inadequate to ensure freedom of intra-Community trade in agricultural products on its territory by preventing and effectively dissuad-

ing the perpetrators of the offences in question from committing and repeating them.

* * *

[54] The above finding is in no way affected by the French Government's argument that the situation of French farmers was so difficult that there were reasonable grounds for fearing that more determined action by the competent authorities might provoke violent reactions by those concerned, which would lead to still more serous breaches of public order or even to social conflict.

* * *

[56] [T]he Member State concerned, unless it can show that action on its part would have consequences for public order with which it could not cope by using the means at its disposal, [must] adopt all appropriate measures to guarantee the full scope and effect of Community law so as to ensure its proper implementation in the interests of all economic operators.

* * *

[59] As regards the fact that the French Republic has assumed responsibility for the losses caused to the victims, this cannot be put forward as an argument by the French Government in order to escape its obligations under Community law.

[60] Even though compensation can provide reparation for at least part of the loss or damage sustained by the economic operators concerned, the provision of such compensation does not mean that the Member State has fulfilled its obligations.

[61] Nor is it possible to accept the arguments based on the very difficult socio-economic context of the French market in fruit and vegetables after the accession of the Kingdom of Spain.

[62] It is settled case-law that economic grounds can never serve as justification for barriers prohibited by Article [28] of the Treaty.

* * *

[66] Consequently, it must be held that, by failing to adopt all necessary and proportionate measures in order to prevent the free movement of fruit and vegetables from being obstructed by actions by private individuals, the French Government has failed to fulfil its obligations under Article [28], in conjunction with Article [10], of the Treaty.

Notes and Questions

1. In Commission v. France (Postal franking machines), Case 21/84, [1985] ECR 1356, the Court concluded that a repeated refusal of the French Post Office to buy postal franking machines from a British manufacturer could constitute an administrative practice that in turn constituted a measure equivalent to a quantitative restriction. In ¶ 13, the Court held that it was however necessary that the administrative practice manifest "a certain degree of consistency and generality." Do you consider that the conduct of the French police and prosecutors can be said to constitute an "administrative practice?" A governmental measure akin to that

in the *Buy Irish* case? Can repeated or systemic inaction be deemed to be a governmental policy? Do you agree with the Court's ¶ 31?

2. Advocate General Lenz in a carefully reasoned opinion concluded that Article 28 could only be violated by a governmental measure, while in the *Produce imports* case only private individuals engaged in conduct obstructing the free movement of goods. He contended, however, that France had violated a duty of "due diligence" under Article 10 (ex Article 5) to carry out a policy protecting free movement of goods. Article 10 is frequently called the "duty of loyalty." Do you think the Court's reference to Article 10 in ¶ 32 is essential to its holding? Or is the reference merely intended to add greater weight to a finding that French inaction violated Article 28?

3. Catalyzed by this judgment, the Council rapidly adopted Council Regulation 2679/98 on the functioning of the internal market in relation to the free movement of goods, O.J. L 337/8 (Dec. 12, 1998) (see the Selected Documents). The Regulation requires States to remove any obstacle to the free movement of goods, including action by private individuals to obstruct free movement, and forbids State inaction, defined as the failure to "take all necessary and proportionate measures" to remove the obstacle (article 1(2)).

B. ARTICLE 30: TREATY–BASED LIMITATIONS ON ARTICLE 28

The Treaty itself creates an exception to the principle of free movement of goods. This is Article 30 (initially Article 36):

> The provisions of Articles [28 and 29] shall not preclude prohibitions or restrictions on imports, exports or goods in transit justified on grounds of public morality, public policy or public security; the protection of health and life of humans, animals or plants; the protection of national treasures possessing artistic, historic or archaeological value; or the protection of industrial and commercial property. Such prohibitions or restrictions shall not, however, constitute a means of arbitrary discrimination or a disguised restriction on trade between Member States.

Article 30 thus specifies several categories of interests which a Member State may protect even at the expense of free movement of goods. This section presents cases illustrating the scope of the exceptions for health and safety, public morality, public security and public policy. The exception for the protection of industrial and commercial property has given rise to an extensive and complex body of case law, treated in Chapter 19. In contrast, no case has raised issues concerning the protection of national treasures.

Note that Article 30 contains an exception to the exception. Generally speaking, Member States are sincerely motivated in adopting a measure to attain one of the Article 30 interests. Occasionally, however, a State is wholly or partially motivated by the desire to protect its own products and tries to use an Article 30 exception to mask its protectionism. This is forbidden by the last sentence of Article 30.

A major incentive for the harmonization of laws programs in the 1970s and 1980s has been the desire to reduce the impact of Article 30 exceptions by the creation of Community-wide health and safety or other standards. See Chapter 14A. If the Community standards completely cover the field, then

Member State rules and regulations are preempted. Article 30 then no longer justifies the State rules, which cease to be a barrier to trade. See Chapter 14C.

1. HEALTH AND SAFETY CASES

In the European Community, the Court of Justice frequently must decide whether a Member State rule can be deemed "justified [by] the protection of health and life of humans, animals or plants." The word, "justified," enables the Court to consider not only whether the rule is indeed intended to achieve a health and safety goal, as opposed to serving a disguised protectionist end, but also whether the rule is proportionate and narrowly tailored to its goal. Similar issues arise in the US when the Supreme Court or other courts must determine whether state health and safety rules are appropriate and do not violate the dormant Commerce Clause.

COMMISSION v. UNITED KINGDOM
(UHT milk)
Case 124/81, [1983] ECR 203.

[The Commission brought an action under Article 226 for a declaration that the United Kingdom failed to fulfill its obligations under Article 28 [initially Article 30] by placing restrictions on the importation of milk and cream treated by the Ultra Heat Treated (UHT) process and on the sale of those products in its territory. By use of the UHT process, which heats the product to over 100 degrees centigrade for a short time, milk and cream can be aseptically packed and kept in hermetically sealed containers for several months at room temperature. The Court summarized the UK rules as requiring: 1) all imported milk and cream to be authorized by an import license; and 2) UHT milk (whether domestic or imported) to be marketed in England, Wales and Scotland only by approved dairies or distributors holding a dealer's licence, certifying that the operator must pack the milk in a dairy approved by the competent local authority.]

The Requirement of a Specific Import Licence

9 The Court has already held that Article [28, ex Article 30] precludes the application to intra-Community trade of national provisions which require, even as a pure formality, import licences or any other similar procedure.

* * *

12 However, those provisions, whilst constituting measures having an effect equivalent to quantitative restrictions, must be examined to see whether they are permissible under Article [30, ex Article 36] of the Treaty * * *.

13 That article constitutes a derogation from the fundamental principle of the free movement of goods and must therefore be interpreted in such a way as not to extend its effects further than is necessary for the protection of the interests which it seeks to safeguard.

* * *

15 [T]he United Kingdom states, first, that the system of specific import licences which it operates enables it to impose conditions as to the heat treatment of imported milk varying according to the disease status of the

exporting country * * *. The United Kingdom also stresses that cattle infected with foot-and-mouth disease may yield infected milk before the outward symptoms of the disease become evident and before the outbreak is discovered by the health authorities. In such a case the import licences would be granted in the normal way and the milk, having undergone a treatment insufficient to inactivate the virus, might already be in transit or actually imported into the United Kingdom before the disease had been identified. It is therefore necessary, in the United Kingdom's view, that its authorities should be able, as soon as they are informed of the situation by the exporting country, to trace the infected consignments and to destroy them before they reach the market. According to the United Kingdom, only a system of specific licences enabling consignments of imported milk to be identified and traced meets that requirement.

16 Whilst the protection of the health of animals is one of the matters justifying the application of Article [30], it must none the less be ascertained whether the machinery employed in the present case by the United Kingdom constitutes a measure which is disproportionate in relation to the objective pursued, on the ground that the same result may be achieved by means of less restrictive measures * * *.

* * *

18 Even though * * * licences [may] be issued promptly and automatically, a system requiring the issue of an administrative authorization necessarily involves the exercise of a certain degree of discretion and creates legal uncertainty for traders. It results in an impediment to intra-Community trade which, in the present case, could be eliminated without prejudice to the effectiveness of the protection of animal health and without increasing the administrative or financial burden imposed by the pursuit of that objective. That result could be achieved if the United Kingdom authorities abandoned the practice of issuing licences and confined themselves to obtaining the information which is of use to them, for example, by means of declarations signed by the importers * * *.

19 It follows from the foregoing considerations that the requirement of import licences, which is incompatible with Article [28] of the Treaty, is not saved by the exception contained in Article [30].

The System of Dealers' Licences and the Requirement That Imported UHT Milk Be Packed on Premises Within the United Kingdom

20 [The UK regulations] which require [imported] UHT milk to be packed on premises within the United Kingdom, make it necessary to treat that milk again, since it is technically impossible to open the packs and then repack the milk without causing it to lose the characteristics of "Ultra Heat Treated" milk.

21 Therefore, the need to subject that product to a second heat treatment causes delays in the marketing cycle, involves the importer in considerable expense and, moreover, is likely to lower the organoleptic qualities of the milk. In fact, the requirement of re-treatment and repacking constitutes, owing to its economic effects, the equivalent of a total prohibition on imports * * *. The United Kingdom is therefore wrong in its submission

that the contested provisions, supposedly applying without distinction to domestic and imported products, have no discriminatory effect and, for that reason, escape the application of Article [28] of the Treaty.

* * *

23 The United Kingdom claims however, that in the present state of Community law such a prohibition is the only effective means of protecting the health of consumers and is therefore justified under Article [30].

24 The United Kingdom bases its view essentially on the disparities in the laws of the Member States relating to the production and treatment of UHT milk, on the varying degree of application of those different laws and on the impossibility of its exercising control over the production cycle of UHT milk in the other Member States from collection at the farm to packing and distribution. However, it asserts that such control is indispensable for ensuring that the milk obtained is free of any bacterial or virus infection.

25 Those arguments cannot be upheld. In the first place, it is clear from the evidence before the Court * * * that the alleged disparities in the laws of the Member States are in truth limited. In fact * * * the production of UHT milk is carried on in the different Member States in accordance with very similar rules * * *.

26 Secondly, an analysis of the scientific and technical documents submitted by the parties for the Court's examination demonstrates that UHT milk is produced in the different Member States with machines manufactured by a very small number of firms in accordance with comparable technical characteristics and that the milk, having undergone identical controls, is of similar quality from the point of view of health.

* * *

28 Under those circumstances, the United Kingdom * * * could ensure safeguards equivalent to those which it has prescribed for its domestic production of UHT milk, without having recourse to the measures adopted, which amount to a total prohibition on imports.

29 To that end, the United Kingdom would be entitled to lay down the objective conditions which it considers ought to be observed as regards the quality of the milk before treatment and as regards the methods of treating and packing UHT milk of whatever origin offered for sale on its territory. The United Kingdom could also stipulate that imported UHT milk must satisfy the requirements thus laid down, whilst however taking care not to go beyond that which is strictly necessary for the protection of the health of the consumer. It would be able to ensure that such requirements are satisfied by requesting importers to produce certificates issued for the purpose by the competent authorities of the exporting Member States.

31 [In addition,] the United Kingdom authorities [could carry] out controls by means of samples to ensure observance of the standards which it has laid

down, or from preventing the entry of consignments found not to conform with those standards.

* * *

[33] It follows from the foregoing considerations that the system of dealers' licences constitutes an impediment to the free movement of dairy produce which is disproportionate in relation to the objective pursued and is not therefore justified under Article [30] of the Treaty.

DEAN MILK CO. v. CITY OF MADISON

340 U.S. 349, 71 S.Ct. 295, 95 L.Ed. 329 (1951).

[A Madison ordinance forbid the sale of milk in the city unless it had been pasteurized and bottled at an authorized pasteurization plant within five miles of the city. Dean Milk, a distributor obtaining milk from dairy farms in northern Illinois, challenged the ordinance on Dormant Commerce Clause grounds. The Wisconsin Supreme Court upheld the ordinance as valid to achieve public health protection. Justice Clark spoke for six Justices in reversing.]

[W]e agree with appellant that the ordinance imposes an undue burden on interstate commerce.

* * *

[T]his regulation * * * in practical effect excludes from distribution in Madison wholesome milk produced and pasteurized in Illinois * * *. In thus erecting an economic barrier protecting a major local industry against competition from without the State, Madison plainly discriminates against interstate commerce. This it cannot do, even in the exercise of its unquestioned power to protect the health and safety of its people, if reasonable nondiscriminatory alternatives, adequate to conserve legitimate local interests, are available.

* * *

It appears that reasonable and adequate alternatives are available. If the City of Madison prefers to rely upon its own officials for inspection of distant milk sources, such inspection is readily open to it without hardship for it could charge the actual and reasonable cost of such inspection to the importing producers and processors.

* * *

[Alternatively, Madison could] determine the extent of enforcement of sanitary standards in the exporting area by verifying the accuracy of safety ratings of specific plants or of the milkshed in the distant jurisdiction through the United States Public Health Service, which routinely and on request spot checks the local ratings.

* * *

To permit Madison to adopt a regulation not essential for the protection of local health interests and placing a discriminatory burden on interstate commerce would invite a multiplication of preferential trade areas destructive of the very purpose of the Commerce Clause.

[Dissent by Justice Black, speaking for two other Justices.]

This health regulation should not be invalidated merely because the Court believes that alternative milk-inspection methods might insure the cleanliness and healthfulness of Dean's Illinois milk.

* * *

No case is cited, and I have found none, in which a bona fide health law was struck down on the ground that some other method of safeguarding health would be as good as, or better than, the one the Court was called on to review. In my view, to use this ground now elevates the right to traffic in commerce for profit above the power of the people to guard the purity of their daily diet of milk.

If, however, the principle announced today is to be followed, the Court should not strike down local health regulations unless satisfied beyond a reasonable doubt that the substitutes it proposes would not lower health standards. I do not think that the Court can so satisfy itself on the basis of its judicial knowledge.

Notes and Questions

1. Do you think that the UK's rules in *UHT milk* were protectionist or motivated by a sincere desire to protect the health of humans and animals? Does the UK's motivation really matter? Why is the Court so rigorous in its appraisal of import licenses? How does the Court apply the principle of proportionality, expressed in ¶ 16? What health protection measures can the UK still take as to imported UHT milk?

2. Do you agree with Justice Clark or with Justice Black in *Dean Milk*? How would each have dealt with the issues presented in *UHT Milk*? Note that the Supreme Court frequently applies a principle of proportionality in evaluating state rules in dormant Commerce Clause cases, although it does not use that terminology.

3. Compare the *UHT milk* case with Criminal proceedings against Melkunie BV, Case 97/83, [1984] ECR 2367, where a Dutch law on pasteurized dairy products prohibited the sale of products containing active coliform bacteria or any active micro-organisms in excess of a stated minimum per milliliter. Melkunie imported from Germany milk products which satisfied German health rules, but not the Dutch ones. In an Article 234 referral, the Court held that Article 30 entitled the Netherlands to bar imports which did not meet its standards because "the data available at the present stage of scientific research do not make it possible to determine with certainty the precise number of non-pathogenic microorganisms above which a pasteurized milk product becomes a source of danger to human health." Id. at 2386. If the Commission does not want to see Community trade impeded by such a barrier, allowed by Article 30, what measure could it take?

4. In Commission v. United Kingdom (Pasteurized milk), Case 261/85, [1988] ECR 547, the UK had barred the import of pasteurized milk, considering it less safe than UHT-treated milk. The Court held that even though UHT-treated milk was safer than pasteurized milk, the ban went too far. The UK should have adopted safety standards for imported pasteurized milk and a system for recognizing health certificates for pasteurized milk issued by authorities in other States. Is

this judgment consistent with that in *Melkunie*? Do you expect that UK milk consumers will either understand or welcome the Court's judgment?

COMMISSION v. GERMANY

(Crayfish import ban).
Case C–131/93, [1994] ECR I–3303.

[Fearful of the spread of crayfish plague, now widespread in the Community, Germany adopted a regulation in 1989 prohibiting the import of live crayfish for commercial purposes, whether for immediate consumption or for stocking fish farms. The regulation permitted the Food and Forestry Office (the 'Bundesamt') to grant derogations to prevent "excessive hardships." Complaints from importers led the Commission to bring an Article 226 procedure.]

18   [R]ules restricting intra-Community trade are compatible with the Treaty only in so far as they are indispensable for the purposes of providing effective protection for the health and life of animals. They cannot therefore be covered by the derogation provided for in Article [30] if that aim may be achieved just as effectively by measures having less restrictive effects on intra-Community trade.

* * *

25   [I]nstead of simply prohibiting imports of all species of live freshwater crayfish, Germany could have confined itself to making consignments of crayfish from other Member States * * * subject to health checks and only carrying out checks by sample if such consignments were accompanied by a health certificate issued by the competent authorities of the dispatching Member State certifying that the product in question presented no risk to health, or instead confined itself to regulating the marketing of crayfish in its territory, in particular by subjecting to authorization only the restocking of national waters with species likely to be carrying the disease and restricting release of animals into the wild and restocking in areas in which native species are to be found.

* * *

27   Moreover, the conditions which importers are required to observe under the authorization system applied by the German authorities so as to mitigate the harshness of the import ban laid down by the Federal legislation, which require the traders concerned to comply with all health measures, to use imported crayfish in a way which prevents them from being released into the environment and to ensure that the water in which they are kept is disinfected, show that the defendant Government itself considers that those means, less restrictive of intra-Community trade than a total import ban, are sufficient for achieving the objective of protecting native crayfish against crayfish plague and faunal distortion.

28   It follows that the Commission's complaint is well founded.

Notes and Questions

1.   The US Supreme Court in *Maine v. Taylor*, 477 U.S. 131, 106 S.Ct. 2440, 91 L.Ed.2d 110 (1986), came to the opposite conclusion in reviewing a Maine law

which prohibited the import of live bait fish based on a fear that imported fish might contain parasites that could spread to local wild fish. Justice Blackmun's majority opinion held that "Maine's unique and fragile fisheries * * * would be placed at risk by three types of parasites prevalent in out-of-state baitfish, but not common to wild fish in Maine." The Supreme Court upheld Maine's total interdiction of baitfish imports in a rare example of its acceptance of a compelling state interest as a justification for a discriminatory statute. Has the Court of Justice given sufficient importance to the wildlife health interest Germany tried to protect? Will the more proportionate measures the Court suggested adequately protect this interest? Is the judgment consistent with *Melkunie*?

2.　National animal health safeguard measures can result in the partitioning of the Community market. To reduce this risk, Council Directive 91/67, O.J. L 46/1 (Feb. 19, 1991), set in place a Community-wide system to regulate the production and marketing of fish that can be raised by aquaculture, including administrative supervision, health precautions, and on-site checks.

CRIMINAL PROCEEDINGS AGAINST ALBERT HEIJN

Case 94/83, [1984] ECR 3263.

3　Article 16 of the Netherlands Law on Pesticides * * * provides that foodstuffs or beverages containing a quantity of one or more pesticides * * * in excess of the level fixed by a public administrative regulation [may not] be marketed.

* * *

5　With regard to vinchlozoline, the level of residues generally allowed under the Order in question is zero. Exceptionally, a precisely defined level of residues is tolerated in the case of certain fruits and vegetables designated by name, but apples are not among them.

6　Before the national court, Albert Heijn BV contended that the apples found in its stock with residues of vinchlozoline had come from Italy, where they had been legally placed on the market, and that consequently the prohibition on their being marketed in the Netherlands was contrary to the provisions of the EEC Treaty on the free movement of goods.

* * *

9　Before replying to the questions raised, it should be noted * * * that the use of the pesticide in question is not regulated by Council Directive No 76/895 relating to the fixing of maximum levels of pesticide residues in and on fruit and vegetables * * *.

10　* * * [T]he German and Netherlands Governments contend that the prohibition in question is justified in the interests of the protection of public health, because pesticides are very dangerous substances *per se,* and that it is not necessary, before taking protective measures, to establish whether vinchlozoline on apples is dangerous.

11　Albert Heijn BV contends that such a prohibition is disproportionate in relation to the objective of protecting public health, since the pesticide in question is known to the national authorities and is tolerated on certain fruits and vegetables.

12   In the Commission's view, it is necessary to reconcile the requirements of fruit and vegetable growing with the need to protect human and animal health, whilst taking account of the progress of scientific knowledge regarding pesticides and of the dietary habits of the population. * * *

[The Court then stated its conclusions.]

13   It is not disputed that pesticides constitute a major risk to human and animal health and to the environment * * *.

* * *

15   Member States must take account of the fact that pesticides are substances which are both necessary to agriculture and dangerous to human and animal health. The fact that the quantities absorbed by the consumer, in particular in the form of residues on foodstuffs, can neither be predicted nor controlled justifies strict measures intended to reduce the risks faced by the consumer.

16   In so far as the relevant Community rules do not cover certain pesticides, Member States may regulate the presence of residues of those pesticides on foodstuffs in a way which may vary from one country to another according to the climatic conditions, the normal diet of the population and their state of health. In that context, they may permit different levels of the same pesticide in respect of different foodstuffs.

17   National rules of that nature may thus form part of a general policy designed to prevent the presence of pesticide residues on foodstuffs.

18   The authorities of the importing Member State are however obliged to review the prescribed maximum level if it appears to them that the reasons which led to its being fixed have changed, for example, as a result of the discovery of a new use for such and such a pesticide.

19   The reply to the questions raised by the national court must therefore be that Articles [28 and 30] of the EEC Treaty do not prevent a Member State from prohibiting the importation of apples from another Member State on account of the presence in or on those apples of a quantity of vinchlozoline greater than that authorized by the legislation of the first Member State, even though the maximum permitted vinchlozoline content * * * differs from that laid down for other kinds of food and drink.

Notes and Questions

1.   The presence of pesticide residue on fruits and vegetables certainly worries many health authorities and consumers, but in the absence of precise knowledge, how little is too much? It is obvious that strict standards can be a serious bar to imports, since States vary radically in their regulatory attitudes toward pesticides. Note that the Netherlands allowed the pesticide in question in minor quantities on lettuce and endives, but not on apples. Shouldn't that have troubled the Court? In Ministère public v. Mirepoix, Case 54/85, [1986] ECR 1067, the Court upheld a French ban on imported onions with a residue of a certain pesticide, but added a requirement that the ban be reviewed if scientific research produces further information. Is this useful? Who should have the burden of proof as to a pesticide residue's safety?

2.   In Criminal Proceedings against Brandsma, Case C–293/94, [1996] ECR I–3159, a Dutch supermarket chain was subject to penal charges in Belgium when

its Belgian branch sold a tile cleanser intended to eliminate algae from walls and tiles. The cleanser contained a biocide authorized by the Dutch authorities, but the defendant had never requested an authorization from the Belgian authorities. The defendant argued that the Dutch approval should be recognized on mutual trust principles and that the Belgian government should have the burden of proof to show that the cleanser was dangerous to health under Article 30. Belgium contended that in the absence of harmonized rules, it was free to use its discretion in determining what biocides must be subject to the Belgian authorization process. What should the Court decide?

CRIMINAL PROCEEDINGS AGAINST SANDOZ

Case 174/82, [1983] ECR 2445.

[A 1949 Dutch law prohibited the addition of vitamins to food without a Government authorization. Sandoz sought to import "muesli" bars and beverages, health foods containing Vitamins A and D, from Germany and Belgium, where they were lawfully marketed. When an authorization was rejected, Sandoz sued, and the trial court referred Article 234 questions. After finding that the Dutch law violated Article 28, the Court turned to Article 30.]

9   * * * [I]n the opinion of Sandoz and the Commission, it is only in the event of excessive consumption, which is excluded however in the case of products of the kind in question, that vitamins and in particular vitamins soluble in fat, such as Vitamins A and D, may have harmful effects. * * *

10   On the other hand the Netherlands and Danish Governments contend that [the Dutch] rules are necessary owing to the very nature of the substances added since the absorption of any vitamins in high doses or for a prolonged period may entail risks to health or at least undesirable side-effects such as malnutrition. In view on the one hand of scientific uncertainties and on the other of the fact that the harmfulness of vitamins depends on the quantity absorbed with the whole nutrition of a person it is not possible to say with certainty whether any food to which vitamins have been added is harmful or not.

11   [V]itamins are not in themselves harmful substances but on the contrary are recognized by modern science as necessary for the human organism. Nevertheless excessive consumption of them over a prolonged period may have harmful effects, the extent of which varies according to the type of vitamin: there is generally a greater risk with vitamins soluble in fat than with those soluble in water. According to the observations submitted to the Court, however, scientific research does not appear to be sufficiently advanced to be able to determine with certainty the critical quantities and the precise effects.

12   It is not disputed that the concentration of vitamins contained in the foodstuffs of the kind in issue is far from attaining the critical threshold of harmfulness so that even excessive consumption thereof cannot in itself involve a risk to public health. Nevertheless such a risk cannot be excluded in so far as the consumer absorbs with other foods further quantities of vitamins which it is impossible to monitor or foresee.

* * *

16   As the Court found in * * * (Frans–Nederlandse Maatschappij voor Biologische Producten, [1981] ECR 3277), in so far as there are uncertainties at the present state of scientific research it is for the Member States, in the absence of harmonization, to decide what degree of protection of the health and life of humans they intend to assure, having regard however for the requirements of the free movement of goods within the Community.

17   Those principles also apply to substances such as vitamins which are not as a general rule harmful in themselves but may have special harmful effects solely if taken to excess as part of the general nutrition, the composition of which is unforeseeable and cannot be monitored. In view of the uncertainties inherent in the scientific assessment, national rules prohibiting, without prior authorization, the marketing of foodstuffs to which vitamins have been added are justified on principle within the meaning of Article [30] of the Treaty on grounds of the protection of human health.

18   Nevertheless the principle of proportionality which underlies the last sentence of Article [30] of the Treaty requires that the power of the Member States to prohibit imports of the products in question from other Member States should be restricted to what is necessary to attain the legitimate aim of protecting health. Accordingly, national rules providing for such a prohibition are justified only if authorizations to market are granted when they are compatible with the need to protect health.

* * *

20   [Accordingly,] Community law permits national rules prohibiting without prior authorization the marketing of foodstuffs lawfully marketed in another Member State to which vitamins have been added, provided that the marketing is authorized when the addition of vitamins meets a real need, especially a technical or nutritional one.

21   In the second question the national court asks in essence whether Community law precludes national rules [which make] the authorization to market a subject to proof by the importer that the product in question is not harmful to health.

22   * * * Article [30] of the Treaty creates an exception, which must be strictly interpreted, to the rule of free movement of goods * * *. [Therefore], the national authorities who rely on that provision in order to adopt a measure restricting intra-Community trade [must] check in each instance that the measure contemplated satisfies the criteria of that provision.

23   Accordingly, although the national authorities may * * * ask the importer to produce the information in his possession relating to the composition of the product and the technical or nutritional reasons for adding vitamins, they must themselves assess, in the light of all the relevant information, whether authorization must be granted pursuant to Community law.

Notes and Questions

1. Why did the Court reject the Commission's view in this case? Did the Court go too far in giving a State absolute discretion to ban vitamin-enriched food

in the absence of serious evidence of risk? On the other hand, observe that the Court states that a State must grant a product authorization when "compatible with the need to protect health" (¶ 18), and that the burden of proof as to safety cannot be placed on the importer. Why is that important?

2.　A German law prohibited the import of medicinal preparations except to a pharmaceutical wholesaler or a pharmacy. A German resident ordered by mail an extract of artichoke, used to treat dyspepsia, from a Strasbourg pharmacy. He could have bought the extract in a German pharmacy without a prescription, but it was cheaper in France. The Commission and France argued that the German law was disproportionate to the need to protect health, while Germany and Denmark argued that restricting the sale of non-prescription medication to pharmacies helped ensure that consumers would receive instructions on use and advice on quality of such products. What result? See Schumacher v. Hauptzollamt Frankfurt, Case 215/87, [1989] ECR 617.

COMMISSION v. GERMANY

(German beer)
Case 178/84, [1987] ECR 1227.

[A German law, dating back to the Reinheitsgebot (purity law) of 1516, requires that beer be manufactured only from malted barley, hops, yeast and water. The word "Bier" can only be used for beer produced in this manner. In other Member States, beer is also produced from rice and other cereals, with extensive use of additives. When the Commission challenged the German rules as violating Article 28, Germany argued health grounds: some additives are dangerous, particularly since Germans consume far more beer per capita than other people do. The Court did not agree.]

The Absolute Ban on the Marketing of Beers Containing Additives

[38]　In the Commission's opinion the absolute ban on the marketing of beers containing additives cannot be justified on public-health grounds. It maintains that the other Member States control very strictly the utilization of additives in foodstuffs and do not authorize the use of any given additive until thorough tests have established that it is harmless. In the Commission's view, there should be a presumption that beers manufactured in other Member States which contain additives authorized there represent no danger to public health. The Commission argues that if the Federal Republic of Germany wishes to oppose the importation of such beers then it bears the onus of proving that such beers are a danger to public health. * * * In any event, the rules on additives applying to beer in the Federal Republic of Germany are disproportionate in so far as they completely preclude the use of additives whereas the rules for other beverages, such as soft drinks, are much more flexible.

[39]　For its part, the German Government considers that in view of the dangers resulting from the utilization of additives whose long-term effects are not yet known and in particular of the risks resulting from the accumulation of additives in the organism and their interaction with other substances, such as alcohol, it is necessary to minimize the quantity of additives ingested. Since beer is a foodstuff of which large quantities are consumed in Germany, the German Government considers that it is

particularly desirable to prohibit the use of any additive in its manufacture, especially in so far as the use of additives is not technologically necessary and can be avoided if only the ingredients laid down in the Biersteuergesetz are used. In those circumstances, the German rules on additives in beer are fully justified by the need to safeguard public health and do not infringe the principle of proportionality.

[The Court then stated its conclusions.]

40   [T]he prohibition on the marketing of beers containing additives constitutes a barrier to the importation from other Member States of beers containing additives authorized in those States, and is to that extent covered by Article [28] of the EEC Treaty. However, it must be ascertained whether it is possible to justify that prohibition * * * on grounds of the protection of human health.

41   The Court has consistently held that "in so far as there are uncertainties at the present state of scientific research it is for the Member States, in the absence of harmonization, to decide what degree of protection of the health and life of humans they intend to assure, having regard however to the requirements of the free movement of goods within the Community" [citing *Sandoz*].

42   * * * Community law does not preclude the adoption by the Member States of legislation whereby the use of additives is subjected to prior authorization granted by a measure of general application for specific additives, in respect of all products, for certain products only or for certain uses. Such legislation meets a genuine need of health policy, namely that of restricting the uncontrolled consumption of food additives.

* * *

44   [However, in *Sandoz* and other prior judgments,] the Court inferred from the principle of proportionality underlying the last sentence of Article [30] of the Treaty that prohibitions on the marketing of products containing additives authorized in the Member State of production but prohibited in the Member State of importation must be restricted to what is actually necessary to secure the protection of public health. The Court also concluded that the use of a specific additive which is authorized in another Member State must be authorized in the case of a product imported from that Member State where, in view, on the one hand, of the findings of international scientific research, and in particular of the work of the Community's Scientific Committee for Food, the Codex Alimentarius Committee of the Food and Agriculture Organization of the United Nations (FAO) and the World Health Organization, and, on the other hand, of the eating habits prevailing in the importing Member State, the additive in question does not present a risk to public health and meets a real need, especially a technical one.

45   Secondly, * * * by virtue of the principle of proportionality, traders must also be able to apply, under a procedure which is easily accessible to them and can be concluded within a reasonable time, for the use of specific additives to be authorized by a measure of general application.

46   [Furthermore,] it must be open to traders to challenge before the courts an unjustified failure to grant authorization. Without prejudice to the

right of the competent national authorities of the importing Member State to ask traders to produce the information in their possession which may be useful for the purpose of assessing the facts, it is for those authorities to demonstrate * * * that the prohibition is justified on grounds relating to the protection of the health of its population.

47   It must be observed that the German rules on additives applicable to beer result in the exclusion of all the additives authorized in the other Member States and not the exclusion of just some of them for which there is concrete justification by reason of the risks which they involve in view of the eating habits of the German population; moreover those rules do not lay down any procedure whereby traders can obtain authorization for the use of a specific additive in the manufacture of beer by means of a measure of general application.

48   As regards more specifically the harmfulness of additives, the German Government, citing experts' reports, has referred to the risks inherent in the ingestion of additives in general. It maintains that it is important, for reasons of general preventive health protection, to minimize the quantity of additives ingested, and that it is particularly advisable to prohibit altogether their use in the manufacture of beer, a foodstuff consumed in considerable quantities by the German population.

49   However, it appears from the tables of additives authorized for use in the various foodstuffs submitted by the German Government itself that some of the additives authorized in other Member States for use in the manufacture of beer are also authorized under the German rules * * * for use in the manufacture of all, or virtually all, beverages. Mere reference to the potential risks of the ingestion of additives in general and to the fact that beer is a foodstuff consumed in large quantities does not suffice to justify the imposition of stricter rules in the case of beer.

* * *

53   Consequently, in so far as the German rules on additives in beer entail a general ban on additives, their application to beers imported from other Member States is contrary to the requirements of Community law as laid down in the case-law of the Court, since that prohibition is contrary to the principle of proportionality and is therefore not covered by the exception provided for in Article [30] of the EEC Treaty.

Notes and Questions

1.   Recall that the Court held in *Sandoz* that the burden of proof as to safety could not be placed on the importer. In *German beer,* where did the Court place the burden of proof as to whether certain additives constitute a health hazard? Why is an allocation of burden of proof so important? Note also the specific further procedural safeguards for importers required by the Court. Why are they important? In recent Article 30 cases, the Court has often expressly placed the burden of proof on the importing State and expressly required procedural safeguards for importers. A leading authority, Peter Oliver, believes that the *Heijn* and *Mirepoix* pesticide judgments, which did not contain such limitations on Member States, "have been superseded, at least in part" by the *German beer* procedural safeguards language. Do you agree, or do you consider pesticides to be

in a different product category from food additives? See P. Oliver, Free Movement of Goods in the European Community ¶ 8.55 (3d ed. Sweet & Maxwell 1996).

2. In Debus, Cases C–13 & 113/91, [1992] ECR I–3617, the Court held that Italy's ban on imported French beer containing sulphur dioxide in excess of a stated percentage could not be justified on health grounds. The Court observed that Italy's approval of alternative preservatives did not warrant its ban of beer containing sulphur dioxide levels that France permitted as a preservative. Even consumption of large quantities of beer containing sulphur dioxide as a preservative would not create a serious risk of exceeding the maximum daily dose of sulphur dioxide set by the FAO and the WHO.

DECKER v. CAISSE DE MALADIE DES EMPLOYES PRIVES

Case C–120/95, [1998] ECR I–1831.

[The Luxembourg health insurance program in its social security system provides a flat-rate sum reimbursement of spectacles (eyeglasses) with corrective lenses. The reimbursement is automatic for spectacles purchased from Luxembourg opticians, but is conditioned upon prior authorization for spectacles bought outside Luxembourg. When Decker used an ophthalmologist's prescription to buy spectacles in Belgium without a prior authorization, he was denied reimbursement. A Luxembourg social security tribunal referred several questions to the Court. The Court initially held that social security system rules must comply with Article 28 (ex Article 30).]

[33] The Member States which have submitted observations argue essentially that rules such as those at issue do not have the purpose or effect of restricting trade flows, but merely lay down the conditions for the reimbursement of medical expenses. Such rules do not have the effect of prohibiting the import of spectacles, nor do they have any direct influence on the possibility of purchasing them outside the national territory. They do not prohibit Luxembourg opticians from importing spectacles and corrective lenses from other Member States, processing them and selling them.

[34] It must be observed that the rules at issue encourage persons insured under the Luxembourg social security scheme to purchase their spectacles from, and have them assembled by, opticians established in Luxembourg rather than in other Member States.

[35] While the national rules at issue in the main proceedings do not deprive insured persons of the possibility of purchasing medical products in another Member State, they do nevertheless make reimbursement of the costs incurred in that Member State subject to prior authorisation, and deny such reimbursement to insured persons who have not obtained that authorisation. Costs incurred in the State of insurance are not, however, subject to that authorisation.

[36] Such rules must be categorised as a barrier to the free movement of goods, since they encourage insured persons to purchase those products in Luxembourg rather than in other Member States, and are thus liable to curb the import of spectacles assembled in those States.

37   The Luxembourg Government submits, however, that the free movement of goods is not absolute and that the rules at issue * * * are justified [by the need to control health expenses].

38   Mr. Decker * * * claims that if his purchase were reimbursed, the financial burden on the Fund's budget would be the same, as it reimburses only a flat-rate sum for both frames and corrective lenses sold by an optician. [Thus,] there is no objective reason why the Fund should refuse reimbursement if the purchase is made from an optician established in another Member State.

39   * * * [A]ims of a purely economic nature cannot justify a barrier to the fundamental principle of the free movement of goods. However, it cannot be excluded that the risk of seriously undermining the financial balance of the social security system may constitute an overriding reason in the general interest capable of justifying a barrier of that kind.

40   But, as the Luxembourg Government acknowledged in reply to a question from the Court, it is clear that reimbursement at a flat rate of the cost of spectacles and corrective lenses purchased in other Member States has no effect on the financing or balance of the social security system.

41   The Belgian, German and Netherlands Governments have also submitted that the right of insured persons to have access to quality treatment constitutes a justification for the rules at issue, on the ground of the protection of public health * * *. The Belgian Government adds that spectacles must be supplied by persons authorized by law to pursue the profession. If they are supplied in another Member State, supervision to ensure that this has been carried out properly is seriously called into question, or even impossible.

42   It must be observed that the conditions for taking up and pursuing regulated professions have been the subject of Council Directive 92/51/EEC of 18 June 1992 on a second general system for the recognition of professional education and training [described in Chapter 18A].

43   This means that the purchase of a pair of spectacles from an optician established in another Member State provides guarantees equivalent to those afforded on the sale of a pair of spectacles by an optician established in the national territory [citing *Schumacher, supra*].

44   Furthermore, in the present case the spectacles were purchased on a prescription from an ophthalmologist, which guarantees the protection of public health.

45   It follows that [the Luxembourg] rules are not justified on grounds of public health in order to ensure the quality of medical products supplied in other Member States.

Notes and Questions

1.   Seven Member States provided their observations on the issues raised in *Decker*, together with those in the companion *Kohll* case involving the Luxembourg health insurance system's failure to reimburse an orthodontist's services provided outside Luxembourg (see page 681 infra). Most expressed concern that permitting persons to obtain medical goods (or services) outside their State of residence while obtaining health insurance reimbursement from that State would

jeopardize the financial integrity of the health insurance system. What was the Court's response to that concern? The Court has frequently declared that a State's economic concerns cannot justify a limitation on the free movement of goods (or the free movement of persons or services), but in ¶ 39 it indicates a certain nuance to this position. Why? Given the facts in this case (see ¶ 40), the Court's dictum did not matter, but it might have an impact in the future.

2.   How did the Court resolve the second public health issue, namely the concern about the qualifications of the Belgian optician who provided the spectacles? The Court's conclusion points up the utility of the harmonization of professional training and standards surveyed in Chapter 18A.

2. PUBLIC MORALITY, PUBLIC POLICY AND PUBLIC SECURITY CASES

The Court of Justice has only infrequently had to interpret the scope of the public morality, public policy or public security exceptions in Article 30 (ex Article 36). Overall, it would appear that the Court is rather deferential to State rules based upon public morality or public security, but quite skeptical of a State claim that its rules are justified by public policy, probably because the latter concept can be so amorphous.

REGINA v. HENN & DARBY
Case 34/79, [1979] ECR 3795.

[An 1876 UK customs law forbid the import of "indecent or obscene articles." Henn and Darby were convicted for importing Danish sex films and magazines. They argued on appeal that the statutory and/or common law rules in the constituent territories of the UK differed significantly in defining what constituted "indecent or obscene" materials and on the extent to which the sale of such materials was restricted or totally prohibited. The defendants therefore contended that the customs law violated the second sentence of Article 30, since it was more severe than some of the constituent territories' rules governing similar domestic materials. The House of Lords referred questions concerning the application of the public morality exception. As we noted earlier, the Court first held that a total ban on imported goods constituted a quantitative restriction.]

[15]   Under the terms of Article [30, ex Article 36] of the Treaty the provisions relating to the free movement of goods within the Community are not to preclude prohibitions on imports which are justified *inter alia* "on grounds of public morality". In principle, it is for each Member State to determine in accordance with its own scale of values and in the form selected by it the requirements of public morality in its territory. * * *

[16]   Each Member State is entitled to impose prohibitions on imports justified on grounds of public morality for the whole of its territory * * * whatever the structure of its constitution may be and however the powers of legislating in regard to the subject in question may be distributed. The fact that certain differences exist between the laws enforced in the different constituent parts of a Member State does not thereby prevent that State from applying a unitary concept in regard to prohibitions on imports imposed, on grounds of public morality, on trade with other Member States.

* * *

¹⁹ In [its final] questions the House of Lords takes account of the appellants' submissions based upon certain differences between, on the one hand, the prohibition on importing the goods in question, which is absolute, and, on the other, the laws in force in the various constituent parts of the United Kingdom, which appear to be less strict in the sense that the mere possession of obscene articles for non-commercial purposes does not constitute a criminal offence anywhere in the United Kingdom and that, even if it is generally forbidden, trade in such articles is subject to certain exceptions, notably those in favour of articles having scientific, literary, artistic or educational interest.

* * *

²¹ [The second sentence of Article 30] is designed to prevent restrictions on trade based on the grounds mentioned in the first sentence of Article [30] from being diverted from their proper purpose and used in such a way as either to create discrimination in respect of goods originating in other Member States or indirectly to protect certain national products. That is not the purport of a prohibition, such as that in force in the United Kingdom, on the importation of articles which are of an indecent or obscene character. Whatever may be the differences between the laws on this subject in force in the different constituent parts of the United Kingdom * * * these laws, taken as a whole, have as their purpose the prohibition, or at least, the restraining, of the manufacture and marketing of publications or articles of an indecent or obscene character. In these circumstances it is permissible to conclude, on a comprehensive view, that there is no lawful trade in such goods in the United Kingdom. A prohibition on imports which may in certain respects be more strict than some of the laws applied within the United Kingdom cannot therefore be regarded as amounting to a measure designed to give indirect protection to some national product or aimed at creating arbitrary discrimination between goods of this type depending on whether they are produced within the national territory or another Member State.

Notes and Questions

1. This judgment received considerable attention in 1979, because it was the first time the Court of Justice examined a public morality issue, and the first time the House of Lords made an Article 234 referral. Did the Court go too far in ¶ 15 when it deferred to the discretion of a Member State in setting up "its own scale of values"? Shouldn't the Court have engaged in some form of review of the appropriate level of protection of public morality, based on Community concepts, just as the Court does when health or consumer protection interests are advanced by Member States? The problem of the variation in the standards for what is "indecent or obscene" within different parts of the UK is even more troublesome. Are you satisfied with the Court's resolution of this issue? See the sharply critical discussion in L. Gormley, Prohibiting Restrictions on Trade Within the EEC 126–28 (North Holland 1985).

2. In Conegate Limited v. H.M. Customs, Case 121/85, [1986] ECR 1007, UK Customs seized a shipment of inflatable erotic dolls from Germany on the grounds that they were "indecent or obscene" articles. In an Article 234 referral, the importer, Conegate, argued that no specific UK law prohibited the manufacture of erotic articles (as distinguished from books or magazines) and that only England

and Wales limited the sale of erotic articles, by permitting local authorities to restrict such sale to licensed sex shops. The Court held that the prohibition on import of such articles constituted arbitrary discrimination or protectionism in violation of the second sentence of Article 30, in view of the absence of comparably strict rules against similar domestic erotic articles. Is *Conegate* consistent with *Henn* or has *Conegate* tacitly overruled the latter part of the *Henn* judgment?

3. In Queen v. Minister of Agriculture, Case C–1/96, [1998] ECR I–1251, the Royal Society for the Prevention of Cruelty to Animals, together with Compassion in World Farming, sued the United Kingdom to try to bar the export of calves to Member States which employ the "veal crate" system (use of a relatively small box enclosure for each calf) to raise calves for slaughter. The Court of Justice in a reference procedure held that an EC directive on the raising of calves set minimum protection standards which did not bar States from permitting the veal crate system. Accordingly, although the UK could adopt rules for its own farmers providing greater protection to calves than the directive did, the UK could not bar the export of calves to States that used the "veal crate" system. The animal rights groups had argued that public morality could justify the export ban. The Court held in ¶ 67 that the UK could not "rely on the views or the behavior of a sector of national public opinion" to justify a public morality exception to Article 30. Do you agree? Would it make a difference if Parliament had adopted a law to enforce such an export ban in reliance on the public morality exception?

CAMPUS OIL v. MINISTER FOR INDUSTRY AND ENERGY

Case 72/83, [1984] ECR 2727.

[Ireland has no domestic supply of crude oil. An Irish state-owned oil company owns the only oil refinery in Ireland. In 1982, an Irish Order required all oil importers to buy a certain percentage of their needs from this refinery, instead of from direct imports. Campus Oil challenged the law, which Ireland defended under the public policy and public security exceptions. The Court of Justice initially found the compulsory purchase obligation to constitute a quantitative restriction. Turning to Article 30 (ex Article 36), the Court considered whether Ireland could continue to rely upon the public security exception after the Community had taken measures under the Common Energy Policy to protect Community interests in an energy crisis.]

The Justification of the Measures at Issue in the Light of Community Rules on the Matter

28   Certain precautionary measures have indeed been taken at Community level to deal with difficulties in supplies of crude oil and petroleum products. Council Directives 68/414/EEC and 73/238/EEC require Member States to maintain minimum stocks and to coordinate to a certain extent the national measures adopted for the purpose of drawing on those stocks, of imposing specific restrictions on consumption and of regulating prices. Council Decision 77/706/EEC provides for the setting of a Community target for a reduction in consumption in the event of difficulties in supply and for the sharing out between the Member States of the quantities saved.

* * *

[30] Even though those precautions against a shortage of petroleum products reduce the risk of Member States being left without essential supplies, there would none the less still be real danger in the event of a crisis * * *.

[31] Consequently, the existing Community rules give a Member State whose supplies of petroleum products depend totally or almost totally on deliveries from other countries certain guarantees that deliveries from other Member States will be maintained in the event of a serious shortfall in proportions which match those of supplies to the market of the supplying State. However, this does not mean that the Member State concerned has an unconditional assurance that supplies will in any event be maintained at least at a level sufficient to meet its minimum needs. In those circumstances, the possibility for a Member State to rely on Article [30] to justify appropriate complementary measures at national level cannot be excluded, even where there exist Community rules on the matter.

The Scope of the Public Policy and Public Security Exceptions

* * *

[33] [T]he concept of public security * * * is the only one relevant in this case, since the concept of public policy is not pertinent * * *.

[34] * * * [P]etroleum products, because of their exceptional importance as an energy source in the modern economy, are of fundamental importance for a country's existence since not only its economy but above all its institutions, its essential public services and even the survival of its inhabitants depend upon them. An interruption of supplies of petroleum products, with the resultant dangers for the country's existence, could therefore seriously affect the public security that Article [30] allows States to protect.

[35] It is true that, as the Court has held on a number of occasions, * * * Article [30] refers to matters of a non-economic nature. A Member State cannot be allowed to avoid the effects of measures provided for in the Treaty by pleading the economic difficulties caused by the elimination of barriers to intra-Community trade. However, in the light of the seriousness of the consequences that an interruption in supplies of petroleum products may have for a country's existence, the aim of ensuring a minimum supply of petroleum products at all times is to be regarded as transcending purely economic considerations and thus as capable of constituting an objective covered by the concept of public security.

Notes and Questions

1. The Court of Justice justified the Irish legislation on public security grounds rather than public policy grounds, without giving any explanation for doing so. Perhaps the Court considers public policy to be a broader catch-all concept whose use should be avoided when a narrower ground can be applied. But is the public security rationale convincing? It seems strange that the Court of Justice, which usually presses so strongly for Community integration, should have allowed Ireland to adopt a unilateral energy protection policy, instead of relying on Community energy policy protection for all States in time of crisis. The judgment was sharply criticized for these reasons in L. Gormley, Prohibiting Restrictions on Trade Within the EEC 134–138 (North Holland 1985).

2. In contrast to *Campus Oil,* in Commission v. Greece (Oil monopoly), Case C–347/89, [1990] ECR I–4747, the Court held that Greece's state monopoly over the importation and marketing of finished petroleum products could not be justified on public security grounds under Article 30. The Court found that Greece had not proved the monopoly was necessary to ensure that state-owned refineries could market their finished products.

3. In Criminal proceedings against Richardt, Case C–367/89, [1991] ECR I–4621, a French exporter of scientific goods sold to a Soviet trade agency a device used in the production of bubble memory circuits. When the French exporter sent the device to Luxembourg for shipment by air freight to the Soviet Union, Luxembourg customs seized the device on the ground that its export violated Luxembourg rules prohibiting the export of strategic goods to Communist states. The Court of Justice first held that the device was in free circulation within the Community and that the Luxembourg measure violated Article 28, but it finally concluded that Luxembourg's limitation on the free transit and export of strategic goods was justified under the public security exception.

C. THE COURT'S ELABORATION OF FREE MOVEMENT OF GOODS PRINCIPLES

1. THE CASSIS DE DIJON DOCTRINE

Thus far, we have dealt only with the interpretation and direct application of Articles 28 and 30 (ex Articles 30 and 36). The Court of Justice has however significantly elaborated on the Treaty text, making a major contribution to the achievement of the common market in this sphere. Going beyond the precise wording of Article 28, the Court has enunciated the doctrine that national rules that are not discriminatory (somewhat awkwardly called "indistinctly applicable" rules) may nonetheless violate the basic principle of free movement of goods. Perceiving the functional utility of this approach, the Commission has both publicized the Court doctrine and relied upon it in developing the internal market program, as we shall see in Chapter 14B.

REWE–ZENTRAL v. BUNDESMONOPOLVERWALTUNG FÜR BRANNTWEIN

(Cassis de Dijon)
Case 120/78, [1979] ECR 649.

[When Rewe–Zentral applied for a license to import French-produced "Cassis de Dijon," a popular fruit liqueur, for sale in Germany, the Federal Monopoly Administration for Spirits refused the license on the grounds that the fruit liqueur had too low an alcohol content to be lawfully sold in Germany. On appeal, the Hesse tax court referred questions concerning the application of Articles 28 and 30 [ex 30 and 36] to the German rules.]

3 [German law requires] that the marketing of fruit liqueurs, such as "Cassis de Dijon", is conditional upon a minimum alcohol content of 25%, whereas the alcohol content of the product in question, which is freely marketed as such in France, is between 15 and 20%.

* * *

6 The national court is asking for assistance in the matter of interpretation in order to enable it to assess whether the requirement of a minimum

alcohol content may be covered * * * by the prohibition on all measures having an effect equivalent to quantitative restrictions in trade between Member States contained in Article [28] of the Treaty * * *.

* * *

8 In the absence of common rules relating to the production and marketing of alcohol * * * it is for the Member States to regulate all matters relating to the production and marketing of alcohol and alcoholic beverages on their own territory.

9 Obstacles to movement within the Community resulting from disparities between the national laws relating to the marketing of the products in question must be accepted in so far as those provisions may be recognized as being necessary in order to satisfy mandatory requirements relating in particular to the effectiveness of fiscal supervision, the protection of public health, the fairness of commercial transactions and the defense of the consumer.

* * *

10 As regards the protection of public health the German Government states that the purpose of the fixing of minimum alcohol contents by national legislation is to avoid the proliferation of alcoholic beverages on the national market, in particular alcoholic beverages with a low alcohol content, since, in its view, such products may more easily induce a tolerance towards alcohol than more highly alcoholic beverages.

11 Such considerations are not decisive since the consumer can obtain on the market an extremely wide range of weakly or moderately alcoholic products and furthermore a large proportion of alcoholic beverages with a high alcohol content freely sold on the German market is generally consumed in a diluted form.

12 The German Government also claims that the fixing of a lower limit for the alcohol content of certain liqueurs is designed to protect the consumer against unfair practices on the part of producers and distributors of alcoholic beverages.

This argument is based on the consideration that the lowering of the alcohol content secures a competitive advantage in relation to beverages with a higher alcohol content, since alcohol constitutes by far the most expensive constituent of beverages by reason of the high rate of tax to which it is subject.

13 However, this line of argument cannot be taken so far as to regard the mandatory fixing of minimum alcohol contents as being an essential guarantee of the fairness of commercial transactions, since it is a simple matter to ensure that suitable information is conveyed to the purchaser by requiring the display of an indication of origin and of the alcohol content on the packaging of products.

14 It is clear from the foregoing that the requirements relating to the minimum alcohol content of alcoholic beverages do not serve a purpose which is in the general interest and such as to take precedence over the requirements of the free movement of goods, which constitutes one of the fundamental rules of the Community.

In practice, the principal effect of requirements of this nature is to promote alcoholic beverages having a high alcohol content by excluding from the national market products of other Member States which do not answer that description.

It therefore appears that the unilateral requirement imposed by the rules of a Member State of a minimum alcohol content for the purposes of the sale of alcoholic beverages constitutes an obstacle to trade which is incompatible with the provisions of Article [28] of the Treaty.

There is therefore no valid reason why, provided that they have been lawfully produced and marketed in one of the Member States, alcoholic beverages should not be introduced into any other Member State; the sale of such products may not be subject to a legal prohibition on the marketing of beverages with an alcohol content lower than the limit set by the national rules.

[15] Consequently, * * * the concept of "measures having an effect equivalent to quantitative restrictions on imports" contained in Article [28] of the Treaty is to be understood to mean that the fixing of a minimum alcohol content for alcoholic beverages intended for human consumption by the legislation of a Member State also falls within the prohibition laid down in that provision where the importation of alcoholic beverages lawfully produced and marketed in another Member State is concerned.

Notes and Questions

1. Where in the judgment does the Court of Justice recognize consumer protection as a state interest which can limit the free movement of goods? What is the basis for this? Is the Court in effect adding consumer rights and other major state interests to the exceptions listed in Article 30? While that might seem plausible, the Court rejected such an interpretation in Commission v. Ireland (Irish souvenirs), Case 113/80, [1981] ECR 1625. A 1971 Irish law prohibited the sale of imported artifacts and jewelry representing motifs symbolic of Ireland (e.g., a shamrock or a wolfhound) unless the imported product indicated it was "foreign" or showed the country of origin. Ireland claimed this law protected consumer interests, and therefore fell under the public policy exception in Article 30. The Court said that this was "mistaken" and the exceptions in Article 30 must be "interpreted strictly." Rather, the Court said, its established caselaw permitted consumer rights to be recognized as an interest which constituted an exception to Article 28 itself. Is this a distinction without a real difference? The Court's approach is often referred to as a "rule of reason" interpretation of Article 28. See L. Gormley, Prohibiting Restrictions on Trade Within the EEC 51–57 (North–Holland 1985).

2. In *Cassis,* the Court allowed "the defense of the consumer" and other "mandatory requirements" to restrict intra-Community trade. ("Mandatory requirements" is an awkward translation of the French "exigences imperatives," which has been better translated in later judgments as imperative state or public interests.) It is sometimes said that such a "rule of reason" gloss on Article 28 constitutes a step back from *Dassonville's* expansive definition of measures equivalent to quantitative restrictions forbidden by Article 28. Do you think *Dassonville* and *Cassis de Dijon* are consistent or not?

3. The German minimum alcohol content law applied both to domestic and imported products. Would it have violated the guidelines of Commission Directive

70/50 discussed above? No, because that Directive says that national rules which are non-discriminatory are not measures having equivalent effect. Yet in *Cassis de Dijon* the Court found the German law to be a measure equivalent to a quantitative restriction in violation of Article 28. After reviewing *Cassis,* the Commission and most (but not all) commentators have concluded that Directive 70/50 was flawed when it made an exception for non-discriminatory state measures. This is one of the instances where reading the Advocate General's opinion is helpful, since Advocate General Capotorti cited Directive 70/50 and concluded that the Commission was excessively prudent (a polite way of saying the Commission was wrong) in believing Member State measures did not violate Article 28 if they did not discriminate, but rather applied equally to domestic and imported goods (sometimes referred to as "indistinctly applicable" measures). [1979] ECR at 669–70. For a full discussion of the conflicting views of commentators and the case law on this important issue before and after *Cassis de Dijon,* see P. Oliver, Free Movement of Goods in the EC ¶¶ 6.35–6.48 (3d ed. Sweet & Maxwell 1996).

NOTE ON THE COMMISSION 1980 COMMUNICATION ON CASSIS DE DIJON

The Commission has certainly read *Cassis de Dijon* as a landmark decision promoting the free movement of goods, rather than the reverse. On October 3, 1980, the Commission issued a policy Communication on the consequences to be drawn from *Cassis de Dijon*. This is contained in the Selected Documents and merits careful reading.

The Commission sees the main principle of *Cassis de Dijon* to be: "Any product lawfully produced and marketed in one Member State must, in principle, be admitted to the market of any other Member State." A corollary is that a State's commercial or technical rules may not take "an exclusively national viewpoint." This has been called the "mutual trust" principle: if one State's rules allow a product to be marketed, all other States should have confidence in the first State's judgment and likewise allow the product to be marketed. In later chapters, we will see how this concept is key to attaining an integrated internal market.

In its 1980 Communication, the Commission endorsed the Court of Justice's declaration that a State's protection of various "mandatory requirements (public health, protection of consumers or the environment, the fairness of commercial transactions, etc.)" constitutes a justifiable exception to Article 28. This list is non-exhaustive; as we shall see, other imperative state interests are possible. Note that the Commission lists environmental protection as a state interest, although it was not mentioned by the Court in *Cassis*. Do you think it qualifies? See Chapter 34.

The Commission limits a State's protection of interests to measures which are "the most appropriate and at the same time least hinder trade." Does this accurately reflect the Court's view? Consider the following cases:

In Criminal proceedings against Gilli, Case 788/79, [1980] ECR 2071, the defendant was prosecuted for importing apple vinegar from Germany in violation of an Italian law forbidding the marketing of vinegar made from anything other than wine, allegedly to protect consumers. The Court held that the ban on non-wine based vinegar was excessive, since a product labeling requirement would have been sufficient to protect consumer interests.

Criminal proceedings against Kelderman BV, Case 130/80, [1981] ECR 527, tested the validity of a Dutch law forbidding the sale of bread or pastry with less than a minimum dry matter content. Kelderman was prosecuted for importing from France brioche, a type of puffed-up rolls, which didn't have enough dry matter. What result?

In Walter Rau Lebensmittelwerke v. De Smedt, Case 261/81, [1982] ECR 3961, a German producer of margarine packaged in a long rectangular shape challenged a Belgian law forbidding the sale of margarine in any form other than cubes, allegedly in order to prevent Belgian consumers from confusing butter with margarine. What result?

Finally, in the 1980 Communication, the Commission stated its future policy in the promotion of free movement of goods. The Commission stated that it would monitor state rules for compliance with the Court's strict criteria. On the other hand, its future harmonization of law efforts would be directed at those sectors where state barriers to trade would not violate Article 28 under the Court's criteria, but would nonetheless economically impede the "creation of a single internal market." This language is seminal for the "new approach to technical harmonization" to be discussed in Chapter 14D.

Before turning to later case law under *Cassis de Dijon,* a word on the US constitutional analogue, the dormant Commerce Clause. Because the US case law is so voluminous and the governing Supreme Court doctrines have evolved significantly in American constitutional history, it is quite difficult to draw many parallels with the Community rules. As noted in the previous chapter, American courts certainly strike down state laws found to be discriminatory or protectionist in effect, which does parallel Community doctrine. See, e.g., H.P. Hood & Sons v. Du Mond, 336 U.S. 525, 69 S.Ct. 657, 93 L.Ed. 865 (1949) (New York milk dealer licensing system found to protect New York producers at expense of exporter of milk to Massachusetts).

In most US cases, however, the state regulation is not clearly discriminatory or protectionist. The Supreme Court's modern "balancing" approach consists in analyzing whether there exists a "legitimate local public interest" which the state regulation seeks to protect, and then whether the burden on interstate commerce imposed by the local rule is "excessive in relation to the putative local benefits." Pike v. Bruce Church, Inc., noted at page 752 *infra.*

There is a certain resemblance between the *Pike* test and that of *Cassis de Dijon.* The analysis of whether there exists a "legitimate local public interest" corresponds to some degree with that of whether there exists a "mandatory requirement" or imperative state interest. Likewise, the Supreme Court's balancing analysis has some similarity to the proportionality examination made by the Court of Justice in reviewing whether the state rules are narrowly tailored and not excessive in relation to the end sought. However, the analytic approaches and the goals sought in the two systems are sufficiently different to make comparisons decidedly difficult. For an interesting attempt at comparison, see D. Kommers & M. Waelbroeck, Legal Integration and the Free Movement of Goods: The American and European Experience, in Integration Through Law I/3 165 (M. Cappelletti, M. Seccombe & J. Weiler, eds. De Gruyter 1986).

While reading the Community cases which follow, consider whether the US Supreme Court would have reached the same result under a dormant Commerce Clause analysis.

2. CONSUMER PROTECTION CASES

Without any doubt, consumer protection is the state interest which has most often generated issues in the application of the *Cassis de Dijon* doctrine. Just as in the United States, Member States enacted a flood of legislative and regulatory measures to protect consumer interests from the 1960s onward. Although usually non-discriminatory on their face, these consumer protection rules often could adversely affect intra-Community trade. Thus, the Court has frequently had to determine the importance of the consumer interest concerned, the proportionality of the measure taken, and the degree of adverse impact on intra-Community imports or exports. Not surprisingly, consumer protection has also become one of the most important fields of Community legislation since the mid–1970s—see Chapter 35.

COMMISSION v. UNITED KINGDOM

(Marks of origin)
Case 207/83, [1985] ECR 1201.

[A UK regulation, the 1981 Trade Descriptions Order, required that retailers ensure that certain types of products (clothing and textile goods, household electrical appliances, footwear and cutlery) have a "clear and legible" indication of their national origin. The Commission brought an Article 226 proceeding to challenge the Order.]

13   [The United Kingdom] contends that the Order is a national measure which applies to imported and national products alike [whose] effect * * * on trade between Member States is uncertain, if not non-existent. Secondly, it maintains that, in the case of the goods to which the Order applies, the requirements relating to indications of origin meet the requirements of consumer protection since consumers regard the origin of the goods which they buy as an indicator of their quality or true value.

* * *

15   As regards the possible effect of the contested Order on trade, the United Kingdom points out that the requirements laid down in Article 2 of the Order concern the retail sale of all the goods covered by the Order, whether imported or not. Some of those goods, for example woolen knitwear and cutlery, are produced in the United Kingdom in substantial quantities.

16   It should first be observed, with regard to that argument, that in order to escape the obligations imposed on him by the legislation in question the retailer will tend * * * to ask his wholesalers to supply him with goods which are already origin-marked. That tendency has been confirmed by complaints received by the Commission. Thus, the * * * [French Domestic Appliance Manufacturers' Association] informed the Commission that French manufacturers of domestic appliances who wish to sell their products on the United Kingdom market have had to mark such products systematically in response to pressure brought to bear on them by their

distributors. The effects of the contested provisions are therefore liable to spread to the wholesale trade and even to manufacturers.

[17]   Secondly, * * * the purpose of indications of origin or origin-marking is to enable consumers to distinguish between domestic and imported products and this enables them to assert any prejudices which they may have against foreign products. As the Court has had occasion to emphasize in various contexts, the Treaty, by establishing a common market and progressively approximating the economic policies of the Member States seeks to unite national markets in a single market having the characteristics of a domestic market. Within such a market, the origin-marking requirement not only makes the marketing in a Member State of goods produced in other Member States in the sectors in question more difficult; it also has the effect of slowing down economic interpenetration in the Community by handicapping the sale of goods produced as the result of a division of labour between Member States.

[18]   It follows from those considerations that the United Kingdom provisions in question are liable to have the effect of increasing the production costs of imported goods and making it more difficult to sell them on the United Kingdom market.

[19]   The second argument advanced by the United Kingdom is in effect that the contested legislation, applicable without distinction to domestic and imported products, is necessary in order to satisfy imperative requirements relating to consumer protection. It states that a survey carried out amongst United Kingdom consumers has shown that they associate the quality of certain goods with the countries in which they are made. They like to know, for example, whether leather shoes have been made in Italy, woolen knitwear in the United Kingdom, fashionwear in France and domestic electrical appliances in Germany.

[20]   That argument must be rejected. The requirements relating to the indication of origin of goods are applicable without distinction to domestic and imported products only in form because, by their very nature, they are intended to enable the consumer to distinguish between those two categories of products, which may thus prompt him to give his preference to national products.

[21]   [I]f the national origin of goods brings certain qualities to the minds of consumers, it is in manufacturers' interests to indicate it themselves on the goods or on their packaging and it is not necessary to compel them to do so. In that case, the protection of consumers is sufficiently guaranteed by rules which enable the use of false indications of origin to be prohibited. Such rules are not called in question by the EEC Treaty.

Notes and Questions

1.   Is it clear that identifying the foreign country of origin would help UK producers? Are UK consumers likely to prefer UK household electrical goods over similar German products? Do American consumers prefer American cars over Japanese cars? A more obvious case of protectionist intent is Commission v. Ireland (Irish souvenirs), *supra* page 510 where the law required souvenirs of Ireland (e.g., showing shamrocks, wolfhounds or Irish scenes) to be clearly marked with the foreign origin, if not made in Ireland. The Court held that consumer

protection did not justify the law, as purchasers do not necessarily expect souvenirs to be locally manufactured. How happy is an American tourist of Irish origin who buys a souvenir mug at Blarney, only to discover later that it was made in Spain?

2. A Luxembourg law, allegedly based on consumer protection grounds, provides that advertisements for sales at reduced prices may not mention previous prices or the duration of the offer. A Belgian supermarket chain distributed sale leaflets in Luxembourg border areas near to its Belgian stores. When sued in Luxembourg, the chain argued that the Luxembourg law did not really serve consumer protection. What result? See GB–INNO–BM v. Confédération du Commerce Luxembourgeois, Case 362/88, [1990] ECR I–667.

3. In Commission v. Ireland (Hallmarking of precious metals), Case C–30/99, [2001] ECR ___ (June 21, 2001), the Commission contended that Irish rules on the hallmarking of articles made from gold, silver and platinum to indicate their precious metal content violated Article 28. Ireland required domestic and imported articles to bear marks set by the Assay Office in Ireland or the UK, or a hallmark set by an approved office under an international convention. The Commission contended that the Irish rules required a second hallmarking for articles produced in some Member States that did not satisfy these rules. The Court held that Ireland could rely on consumer protection to justify hallmarking of such articles, but that the principle of proportionality required Ireland to accept hallmarked products from other States where the marks are "intelligible to consumers." In ¶ 32, the Court applied its current standard: "the presumed expectations of an average consumer who is reasonably well informed and reasonably observant and circumspect."

HUNT v. WASHINGTON STATE APPLE ADVERTISING COMMISSION

432 U.S. 333, 97 S.Ct. 2434, 53 L.Ed.2d 383 (1977).

[A North Carolina regulation required all closed containers of apples shipped into or sold in the state to display only the U.S. Department of Agriculture (USDA) grade, but not state grades. Because 13 apple producing states had their own grading system, the ostensible purpose of the regulation was to eliminate deception and confusion. North Carolina did not have any state grades for its apples. The Washington State Apple Advertising Commission challenged the rule, observing that its apples are shipped in containers marked with its grades, which are equivalent to or superior to the USDA grades. Identifying and repacking or relabeling containers shipped to North Carolina would impose a substantial cost. The Supreme Court unanimously struck down the North Carolina regulation in an opinion by Chief Justice Burger.]

[A] finding that state legislation furthers matters of legitimate local concern, even in the health and consumer protection areas, does not end the inquiry.

* * *

Rather, when such state legislation comes into conflict with the Commerce Clause's overriding requirement of a national "common market," we are confronted with the task of effecting an accommodation of the competing national and local interests [citing *Pike v. Bruce Church*].

* * *

[T]he challenged statute has the practical effect of not only burdening interstate sales of Washington apples, but also discriminating against them.

* * *

[The discrimination] results from the fact that North Carolina apple producers, unlike their Washington competitors, were not forced to alter their marketing practices in order to comply with the statute. They were still free to market their wares under the USDA Grade or none at all as they had done prior to the statute's enactment. Obviously, the increased costs imposed by the statute would tend to shield the local apple industry from the competition of Washington apple growers and dealers who are already at a competitive disadvantage because of their great distance from the North Carolina market.

Second, the statute has the effect of stripping away from the Washington apple industry the competitive and economic advantages it has earned for itself through its expensive inspection and grading system.

Notes and Questions

1.   The Supreme Court early recognized that consumer protection rules represented a valid exercise of state police powers. In Plumley v. Massachusetts, 155 U.S. 461, 15 S.Ct. 154, 39 L.Ed. 223 (1894), the Court upheld a Massachusetts statute prohibiting the sale of oleomargarine colored yellow because the statute sought to "suppress false pretenses and to promote fair dealings." In *Hunt*, Chief Justice Burger accepted that states have "a substantial interest in protecting their citizens from confusion and deception in the marketing of foodstuffs," but considered that labelling rules on closed containers of apples did not really protect consumers, who buy apples which are removed from the containers at the retail level. Do you agree? How would the Court of Justice deal with a case parallel to *Hunt*?

COMMISSION v. GERMANY

(German beer).

[The excerpt of this judgment at page 499 considered whether Germany's prohibition of additives in the production of beer could be justified on public health grounds. The German law also had a consumer protection feature: it forbid imported beer to be labeled as "Bier," because consumers might be deceived into thinking that the imported product satisfied the German beer purity rules, when it did not.]

29   It is not contested that the [German law prohibiting the use of the word "Bier" for] beers from other Member States in whose manufacture raw materials other than malted barley have been lawfully used, in particular rice and maize, is liable to constitute an obstacle to their importation into the Federal Republic of Germany.

30   Accordingly, it must be established whether the application of that provision may be justified by imperative requirements relating to consumer protection.

31   The German Government's argument that [this provision of the beer law] is essential in order to protect German consumers because, in their minds, the designation "Bier" is inseparably linked to the beverage manufactured solely from the ingredients laid down in [the beer law] must be rejected.

32   Firstly, consumers' conceptions which vary from one Member State to the other are also likely to evolve in the course of time within a Member State. The establishment of the common market is, it should be added, one of the factors that may play a major contributory role in that development. Whereas rules protecting consumers against misleading practices enable such a development to be taken into account, legislation of the kind contained in [the beer law] prevents it from taking place. As the Court has already held in another context [in *the UK Wine and Beer case, supra* page 468], the legislation of a Member State must not "crystallize given consumer habits so as to consolidate an advantage acquired by national industries concerned to comply with them."

33   Secondly, in the other Member States of the Community the designations corresponding to the German designation "Bier" are generic designations for a fermented beverage manufactured from malted barley, whether malted barley on its own or with the addition of rice or maize. The same approach is taken in Community law as can be seen from heading No 22.03 of the Common Customs Tariff. * * *

34   The German designation 'Bier' and its equivalents in the languages of the other Member States of the Community may therefore not be restricted to beers manufactured in accordance with the rules in force in the Federal Republic of Germany.

35   It is admittedly legitimate to seek to enable consumers who attribute specific qualities to beers manufactured from particular raw materials to make their choice in the light of that consideration. However, * * * that possibility may be ensured by means which do not prevent the importation of products which have been lawfully manufactured and marketed in other Member States and, in particular, by the compulsory affixing of suitable labels giving the nature of the product sold. By indicating the raw materials utilized in the manufacture of beer "such a course would enable the consumer to make his choice in full knowledge of the facts and would guarantee transparency in trading and in offers to the public". It must be added that such a system of mandatory consumer information must not entail negative assessments for beers not complying with the requirements of [the beer law].

36   Contrary to the German Government's view, such a system of consumer information may operate perfectly well even in the case of a product which, like beer, is not necessarily supplied to consumers in bottles or in cans capable of bearing the appropriate details. That is borne out, once again, by the German legislation itself [which] provides for a system of consumer information in respect of certain beers, even where those beers are sold on draught, when the requisite information must appear on the casks or the beer taps.

37   It follows from the foregoing that by [forbidding the use of the word "Bier" for] beers imported from other Member States which were manufactured and marketed lawfully in those States the Federal Republic of

Germany has failed to fulfil its obligations under Article [28] of the EEC Treaty.

Notes and Questions

1.   Although this case did not raise any particularly novel issues, its resolution caused a popular outcry in Germany. The outcry was largely occasioned by the belief that the rigorous application of free movement of goods principles would lead to a lowering of quality standards on a domestic market which traditionally only has high quality products. Do you think that a genuine risk or only an imaginary one? Cf. 3 Glocken GmbH v. USL Centro–Sud, Case 407/85, [1988] ECR 4233, in which the Court struck down an Italian law requiring pasta to be made exclusively from durum wheat, because the Court found no health hazard in pasta made from common wheat, while consumer protection could be achieved by labeling.

Do most consumers pay much attention to ingredients listed on labels? Do you think the goal of Community market integration is sufficiently important to outweigh whatever risk there may be that free movement of goods might lower product quality in certain States? Or do you think the issue of concern for allegedly high quality domestic products is largely a red herring, and the real issue is whether national rules should be allowed to "crystallize" domestic tastes or customs? For a critical view, see H.–C. von Heydebrand, Free Movement of Foodstuffs, Consumer Protection and Food Standards in the European Community, 16 Eur.L.Rev. 391 (1991).

2.   Some observers thought that the German beer rules were protectionist, and therefore deserved to be struck down. Since Germany does not produce vermouth, there could be no protectionist motive behind a German law requiring vermouth to have the 16% minimum alcohol content fixed by Italian law for Italian domestic vermouth. Unfortunately for German consumers, Italian law allowed vermouth destined for export to be made with a lower alcohol content than domestic vermouth. In Schutzverband v. Weinvertriebs–GmbH, Case 59/82, [1983] ECR 1217, the Court held that the German law could not bar the weaker Italian vermouth made for export, because it had been lawfully produced in Italy. Germany had argued that consumers of the imported weak vermouth would be deceived into thinking it identical with the better quality domestic Italian vermouth. The Court found that adequate labeling could protect the consumer. One wonders how a label indicating only alcohol content could protect the average German consumer, who would really need a label stating that the imported vermouth was weaker than Italian domestic vermouth.

3.   Consumers in Germany appreciate tasty bearnaise and hollandaise sauces which are traditionally made with butter and eggs. The 1974 German food labelling law prohibits the sale of foodstuffs whose label does not precisely inform the public when they do not "correspond to commercial practice" because their ingredients do not provide the usual "level of customer satisfaction." May Germany require both domestic producers and the importers of bearnaise and hollandaise sauces made with vegetable fats to place on their labels a statement that only vegetable fats are used? Directive 79/112 on foodstuff labelling requires that the vegetable fats be included with other ingredients on the list of ingredients, but does not otherwise address the isssue. In Commission v. Germany (Bearnaise and hollandaise), Case C–51/94, [1995] ECR I–3599, the Court accordingly had to decide whether the consumer interest exception permitted the German rule. How would you decide the case?

3. THE EVOLUTION FROM CASSIS TO KECK

The *Cassis de Dijon* doctrine that products legally produced and marketed in their State of origin should enjoy a presumption in favor of being marketed in other States has served the Community very well in its efforts to achieve true market integration. Not only has the Court of Justice used it in its case law to further free movement of goods, but, even more important, the approach became the basis for the "mutual recognition" principle that is at the heart of the internal market legislative program for both goods and services, described in later chapters.

In contrast, the *Cassis de Dijon* doctrine that Member State rules limiting free movement of goods must be justified by an imperative state interest, recognized as such by the Court of Justice, and then subject to the principle of proportionality, has turned out to be difficult to apply in many contexts. The approach worked rather well in the fields of consumer protection and environmental protection, both easily accepted and fairly well defined state interests. However, the Court found it increasingly hard to deal with State rules adopted to serve less precise social, cultural and economic interests. Ultimately the Court found it prudent in *Keck* to reduce the ambit of the *Dassonville* doctrine and thus the field of review of state interests under *Cassis de Dijon*. To appreciate the Court's concerns, we turn first to the Sunday trading cases, which arose in several Member States.

TORFAEN BOROUGH COUNCIL v. B & Q PLC

Case C–145/88, [1989] ECR 3851.

[The 1950 UK Shops Act (which applies to England and Wales, but not Scotland), forbids retail sales on Sunday in general, but allows local authorities, on a local option basis, to permit certain retail outlets to sell on Sunday a number of products, e.g., newspapers and periodicals, certain foodstuffs, tobacco, alcoholic beverages. The Torfaen Borough Council prosecuted B & Q, a retailer of do-it-yourself goods and garden tools, for Sunday sales. The trial court specifically observed that the law restricting retail sales on Sunday did reduce "the volume of imports of goods from other Member States" when it asked the Court of Justice whether the law violated Article 28. The trial court also asked whether the law could be justified under Article 30 "or any other exception recognized in Community law."]

7 The national court found that the ban on Sunday trading had the effect of reducing B & Q's total sales, that approximately 10% of the goods sold by B & Q came from other Member States and that a corresponding reduction of imports from other Member States would therefore ensue.

* * *

10 [T]he national court seeks to establish whether the concept of measures having an effect equivalent to quantitative restrictions within the meaning of Article [28] of the Treaty also covers provisions prohibiting retailers from opening their premises on Sunday if the effect of the prohibition is to reduce in absolute terms the sales of goods * * * including goods imported from other Member States.

[11] The first point which must be made is that national rules prohibiting retailers from opening their premises on Sunday apply to imported and domestic products alike. In principle, the marketing of products imported from other Member States is not therefore made more difficult than the marketing of domestic products.

* * *

[13] * * * [I]t is therefore necessary in a case such as this to consider first of all whether rules such as those at issue pursue an aim which is justified with regard to Community law. As far as that question is concerned, the Court has already stated in its judgment in *Oebel* [see note 3, *infra*] that national rules governing the hours of work, delivery and sale in the bread and confectionery industry constitute a legitimate part of economic and social policy, consistent with the objectives of public interest pursued by the Treaty.

[14] The same consideration must apply as regards national rules governing the opening hours of retail premises. Such rules reflect certain political and economic choices in so far as their purpose is to ensure that working and non-working hours are so arranged as to accord with national or regional socio-cultural characteristics, and that, in the present state of Community law, is a matter for the Member States. Furthermore, such rules are not designed to govern the patterns of trade between Member States.

[15] Secondly, it is necessary to ascertain whether the effects of such national rules exceed what is necessary to achieve the aim in view. * * *

[16] The question whether the effects of specific national rules do in fact remain within that limit is a question of fact to be determined by the national court.

[17] The reply to the first question must therefore be that * * * the prohibition which [Article 28] lays down does not apply to national rules prohibiting retailers from opening their premises on Sunday where the restrictive effects on Community trade which may result therefrom do not exceed the effects intrinsic to rules of that kind.

Notes and Questions

1. Observe that the trial court in *Torfaen* prevented the Court of Justice from finding that the Sunday retail sales laws had no effect on Community trade by stating in the question referred that the laws reduced in absolute terms the sale of imported goods. Both the Commission and the UK wanted the Court to conclude that there was no effect on trade, despite the wording of the trial court's question. Advocate General van Gerven urged the Court to accept the question as worded, but went on to argue that the Sunday trading rules should be deemed to violate Article 28 (ex Article 30) only if they contributed to market partition within the Community. The Court's judgment declined to follow the approaches suggested by the Advocate General and the Commission. For a careful analysis, see K. Mortelmans, Article 30 of the EEC Treaty and Legislation Relating to Market Circumstances, 28 Common Mkt.L.Rev. 115 (1991).

2. What is the imperative interest the Court recognizes here? Economic? Social? Socio-cultural? The judgment is rather vague as to just what interest is

being protected. The original motivation for Sunday retail sales restrictions was the preservation of the sabbath as a day of rest (they are popularly called Sunday "blue laws"). In a modern pluralist society, that justification is hard to defend. Advocate General van Gerven argued, at ¶ 29 of his opinion, that such a "prevention of offence to religious convictions" could not fall within the Article 30 public morality exception.

3. One justification advanced for Sunday retail sales restrictions is that they protect retail workers' health and welfare. Presumably this influenced the Court, which cited Summary proceedings against Oebel, Case 155/80, [1981] ECR 1993, in which German legislation restricting the night working and delivery hours of bakeries was challenged as reducing export sales. The Court in *Oebel* held that a legitimate state interest in protecting the health of workers justified the German legislation. The Treaty's own employee health and safety protection provisions would seem to warrant that result. (See Chapter 36 on social policy.) Moreover, in UDS v. Sidef Conforama, Case C–312/89, [1991] ECR 997, the Court held unequivocally that French labor law which guarantees Sunday as a day of rest for employees did not violate Article 28, and in Criminal Proceedings against Marchandise, Case C–332/89, [1991] ECR 1027, it similarly held that a Belgian law forbidding the employment of retail workers on Sundays after noon did not violate Article 28. But are employees being protected in *Torfaen*? After all, the Shop Act deals with retail sales, not employee work conditions. Moreover, the Commission argued that less restrictive means could be found to protect workers, e.g., by permitting workers freely to choose their day or days off. Do you agree?

4. Another justification could be that States may legitimately encourage "non-working activities and social contacts on a specified day which is already devoted to those purposes by a large part of the population." Advocate General van Gerven espoused this position (at ¶ 34), but acknowledged that it was difficult to assess the proper weight to be given such an interest. Do you think this would represent a sufficiently imperative interest?

5. The most serious problem with the UK rules is that they were riddled with exceptions, and haphazardly enforced or not enforced at all by local authorities. A 1984 Home Office Report, discussed by the Advocate General at ¶ 28, showed this. Commentators have found it ironic that the public can buy alcoholic beverages, tobacco and pornographic articles on Sunday, but not the garden equipment and do-it-yourself tools sold by B & Q. Shouldn't the Court of Justice ensure, as a matter of Community law, that rules which limit imports in pursuit of an imperative interest are rationally and uniformly applied? Professor Gormley in a critical review of both the Court's judgment and the Advocate General's opinion suggests that the Court should have found the list of products whose sale is restricted on Sunday to be "so arbitrary as to deprive the policy of Sunday closing of any objective justification on socio-economic grounds." L. Gormley, Torfaen Borough Council, 27 Common Mkt.L.Rev. 141, 148 (1990).

6. In the next two years, English and Welsh courts reached quite different conclusions in applying the Court's reply. When on appeal the parties in *Torfaen* reached the House of Lords, it asked the Court of Justice for further guidance on how to evaluate the UK rules in terms of Article 28. In Council of the City of Stoke-on-Trent v. B & Q PLC, Case C–169/91, [1992] ECR–I–6635, the Court responded initially by essentially repeating ¶¶ 11–14 in Torfaen. The Court then declared that "in order to verify that the restrictive effects on intra-Community trade of the rules at issue do not exceed what is necessary to achieve the aim in view, it must be considered whether those effects are direct, indirect or purely

speculative and whether those effects do not impede the marketing of imported products more than the marketing of national products." (¶ 15.) Without any further analysis of the proportionality of the UK Sunday trading rules to their "socio-cultural" goals, the Court then ruled that they "were not excessive to the aim pursued" (¶ 16), and did not violate Article 28.

Advocate General van Gerven had thought that further examination of proportionality was necessary. He suggested that national courts must more precisely identify the "policy of objectives pursued" and then assess whether the national rules are objectively necessary and narrowly tailored to the objectives. The Court of Justice clearly did not want to go down that road. Some commentators have suggested that the Court thus ignored the proper division of functions between national courts and the Court of Justice in an Article 234 proceeding. Do you agree, or do you think the Court acted properly in providing clarity in appraising Sunday trading rules? For a further analysis, see A. Arnull, Anyone for Tripe?, 18 Eur. L. Rev. 314 (1993). The difficulties the Court encountered in trying to resolve the Sunday trading law cases undoubtedly weighed heavily in its decision to shift its doctrinal course in *Keck*.

KECK AND MITHOUARD

Cases C–267 & 268/91, [1993] ECR I–6097.

[Two supermarkets in Alsace, managed by Keck and Mithouard, sold French brands of beer and coffee at retail prices lower than their own purchase price. When prosecuted for violation of a 1963 French law which forbids merchants from selling products at prices lower than the acquisition cost, Keck and Mithouard contended that the French law violated Article 28. The Strasbourg trial court asked the Court whether the French rule violated "the principles of the free movement of goods" and "free competition," particularly because it might distort "competition * * * in frontier zones."]

[11] By virtue of Article [28], quantitative restrictions and all measures having equivalent effect are prohibited between Member States. The Court has consistently held that any measure which is capable of directly or indirectly, actually or potentially, hindering intra-Community trade constitutes a measure having equivalent effect to a quantitative restriction.

[12] It is not the purpose of national legislation imposing a general prohibition on resale at a loss to regulate trade in goods between Member States.

[13] Such legislation may, admittedly, restrict the volume of sales, and hence the volume of sales of products from other Member States, in so far as it deprives traders of a method of sales promotion. But the question remains whether such a possibility is sufficient to characterize the legislation in question as a measure having equivalent effect to a quantitative restriction on imports.

[14] In view of the increasing tendency of traders to invoke Article [28] of the Treaty as a means of challenging any rules whose effect is to limit their commercial freedom even where such rules are not aimed at products from other Member States, the Court considers it necessary to re-examine and clarify its case-law on this matter.

[15] In *"Cassis de Dijon"* it was held that, in the absence of harmonization of legislation, measures of equivalent effect prohibited by Article [28] include

obstacles to the free movement of goods where they are the consequence of applying rules that lay down requirements to be met by such goods (such as requirements as to designation, form, size, weight, composition, presentation, labelling, packaging) to goods from other Member States where they are lawfully manufactured and marketed, even if those rules apply without distinction to all products unless their application can be justified by a public-interest objective taking precedence over the free movement of goods.

16 However, contrary to what has previously been decided, the application to products from other Member States of national provisions restricting or prohibiting certain selling arrangements is not such as to hinder directly or indirectly, actually or potentially, trade between Member States within the meaning of the *Dassonville* judgment, provided that those provisions apply to all affected traders operating within the national territory and provided that they affect in the same manner, in law and in fact, the marketing of domestic products and of those from other Member States.

17 Where those conditions are fulfilled, the application of such rules to the sale of products from another Member State meeting the requirements laid down by that State is not by nature such as to prevent their access to the market or to impede access any more than it impedes the access of domestic products. Such rules therefore fall outside the scope of Article [28] of the Treaty.

18 Accordingly, the reply to be given to the national court is that Article [28] of the EEC Treaty is to be interpreted as not applying to legislation of a Member State imposing a general prohibition on resale at a loss.

Notes and Questions

1.   In ¶ 15 the translation of this judgment has replaced the awkward term, "mandatory requirements," used in *Cassis de Dijon*, with the more understandable term, "public-interest objective." Unfortunately, ¶ 16 introduces another awkward translation, "selling arrangements," quite difficult to understand in English. The sense of the French original "modalites de vente," although not free from ambiguity either, would come across better if translated as "modes of marketing" or "merchandising methods," or simply "modalities of sale of products."

2.   The Court certainly intended its judgment to be a major precedent: the case was transferred from a chamber to a plenary proceeding, and the Court expressly stated that it is partially overruling *Dassonville*, one of its landmark judgments. Why do you think the Court felt the application of the *Dassonville* rule had gone too far? Is this judgment in effect a response to the controversy over its Sunday trading judgments? Is this a "political" judgment, reacting in some measure to media criticism of "activist" Court judgments during the ratification of the Maastricht Treaty? Some commentators think that the Court's approach in *Keck* represents an analogue to the subsidiarity principle of Article 5 (ex Article 3b) introduced by the Maastricht Treaty. Would you agree?

3.   Try to interpret ¶ 16. Do you find the new rule clear-cut and easy to apply? Even if you find it to be ambiguous, do you agree with the basic policy thrust or do you think *Dassonville* represents a better rule? Put another way, is it desirable for many national rules to be examined by the Court under the *Cassis de Dijon* public-interest analysis, requiring perhaps further multiplication of justifi-

able imperative interests, or is it preferable that many national rules should be treated as raising no free movement of goods issue at all?

4.   Some commentators have suggested that the Court could have dealt with the case quite simply by applying its internal affairs doctrine, discussed at page 111, and stating that French merchants selling French products have no basis to claim that a Community law context exists. Advocate General Van Gerven suggested that the *Dassonville* rule could be modified so that only a national law which affects appreciably the volume of intra-Community trade by a partitioning of a national market from other markets should violate Article 28. Do you think either of these approaches is preferable to that chosen by the Court?

5.   In perhaps the final Sunday trading case, a Rome court referred questions in Semeraro Casa Uno Srl v. Sindaco del Commune di Erbusco, Cases C–418 to 421/93, [1996] ECR I–2975. In these questions the Rome court stated categorically that the Italian Sunday trading restrictions substantially and adversely reduced the potential sales of large-scale distributors which "on average sell a greater quantity of products imported from other Member States," to the advantage of smaller local retailers that "in general obtain their supplies only from domestic producers."

The Court of Justice applied the *Keck* doctrine, declaring that the Italian law only regulated a mode of sales promotion. Even though the law might reduce the total volume of sales, and hence of imports, its nature was not such as to impede the access of imported products to the Italian market. Advocate General Cosmas contended in ¶ 17 of his opinion that the Rome trial court had "no statistics or other evidence" to justify the conclusions expressed in its questions.

The Court was perhaps motivated in its strong statements by a concern that the trial court was attempting to strike down an Italian law by using unsupported factual conclusions in order to create an Article 28 issue, instead of permitting the political processes to decide on the merits of Sunday trading restrictions (which, incidentally, have recently been reduced in scale by German and UK legislation). Critics might however be concerned because the Court customarily leaves issues of fact to be resolved by trial courts, subject to appellate review. Should not the Court have accepted the factual evaluation made by the trial court, which obviously believed that the Italian rules have a disproportionate adverse impact in fact on imported products, even though that is not their intent? Note that the *Keck* doctrine requires that the national selling rules affect domestic products and imports in the same manner "in law and *in fact*."

6.   Some US judges and commentators have recently contended that in applying the dormant Commerce Clause, the "balancing" approach of Pike v. Bruce Church, discussed above, is too broad and requires review of too many state rules, and urged that only state rules that might be discriminatory or protectionist need review. This was the view of Justice Scalia in his dissenting opinion in Tyler Pipe Industries, Inc. v. Washington State Dept. of Revenue, 483 U.S. 232, 107 S.Ct. 2810, 97 L.Ed.2d 199 (1987). See Regan, The Supreme Court and State Protectionism: Making Sense of the Dormant Commerce Clause, 84 Mich. L. Rev. 1091 (1986). Although the Supreme Court recently has more often found a state statute to violate the dormant Commerce Clause because it is discriminatory, the majority opinions continue to cite *Pike* with favor. See West Lynn Creamery Inc. v. Healy, *supra* page 462, and Oregon Waste Systems, Inc. v. Department of Environmental Quality, 511 U.S. 93, 114 S.Ct. 1345, 128 L.Ed.2d 13 (1994).

8.   An article which may have influenced the Court's analysis in *Keck* is E. White, In Search of the Limits to Article 30, 26 Common Mkt. L. Rev. 235 (1989).

Among the many useful commentaries on *Keck* are: D. Chalmers, Repackaging the Internal Market—the Ramifications of the Keck Judgment, 19 Eur. L. Rev. 385 (1994); L. Gormley, Reasoning Renounced? The Remarkable Judgment in Keck & Mithouard, Eur. Bus. L. Rev. 63 (March 1994); N. Reich, The "November Revolution" of the European Court of Justice: Keck, Meng and Audi Revisited, 31 Common Mkt. L. Rev. 459 (1994); W.-H. Roth, Note on Keck & Mithouard and Huhnermund, 31 Common Mkt. L. Rev. 845 (1994); and W. Wils, The Search for the Rule in Article 30 EEC: Much Ado About Nothing?, 19 Eur. L. Rev. 475 (1994). The late Judge Rene Joliet advocated the *Keck* approach in the Free Circulation of Goods: The Keck and Mithouard Decision, 1 Colum. J. Eur. L. 436 (1995).

4. POST–KECK: DISTINGUISHING REGULATION OF PRODUCTS FROM REGULATION OF SELLING ARRANGEMENTS

Although controversial from the outset, and seriously questioned by Advocates General van Gerven, Jacobs and Lenz, the *Keck* doctrine appears now well-established. Its proper application, however, has not always been easy. The chief difficulty lies in properly demarcating the line between State rules regulating the sale, merchandising or promotion of products, which the Court will no longer examine (provided they are non-discriminatory in fact as well as in law), and State rules regulating products (together with their labels and packages), which the Court still must examine under the *Cassis de Dijon* imperative state interest analysis. Some of the more challenging cases follow.

VEREIN GEGEN UNWESEN IN HANDEL UND GEWERBE KOLN v. MARS

Case C–470/93, [1995] ECR I–1923.

[The French subsidiary of Mars, Inc. produces ice cream bars under the Mars, Snickers and Milky Way trademarks. The Mars group decided to launch a marketing campaign throughout Europe, increasing the size of the ice cream bars by 10% and inserting them in wrappers marked clearly with "+10%". A German consumer interest organization sued to prohibit the sale of these bars on the grounds of consumer deception. Its principal contention was that consumers would assume that the bars would be sold without any retail price increase, when in fact Mars could not legally guarantee that its retailers would not increase the price. (Any attempt by Mars to control retail prices would violate Community and German competition rules.)

In referring the question whether the consumer interest exception to Article 28 justified the German position, the trial court also asked whether the German rule should be examined at all under the *Keck* doctrine. The Court began by quoting the *Dassonville* and *Keck* doctrines, and then continued:]

Applicability of Article [28] of the Treaty

[13] Although it applies to all products without distinction, a prohibition * * * which relates to the marketing in a Member State of products bearing the same publicity markings as those lawfully used in other Member States, is by nature such to hinder intra-Community trade. It may compel the importer to adjust the presentation of his products according to the place

where they are to be marketed and consequently to incur additional packaging and advertising costs.

14   Such a prohibition therefore falls within the scope of Article [28] of the Treaty.

    The grounds of justification relied on

15   It is settled law that obstacles to intra-Community trade resulting from disparities between provisions of national law must be accepted in so far as such provisions may be justified as being necessary in order to satisfy overriding requirements relating, *inter alia,* to consumer protection and fair trading. However, in order to be permissible, such provisions must be proportionate to the objective pursued and that objective must be incapable of being achieved by measures which are less restrictive of intra-Community trade.

* * *

    The consumer's expectation that the price previously charged is being maintained

17   It is argued that the "+10%" marking may lead the consumer to think that the "new" product is being offered at a price identical to that at which the "old" product was sold.

18   [O]n the assumption that the consumer expects the price to remain the same, the referring court considers that the consumer could be the victim of deception within the meaning of [the German Unfair Competition Law] and that if the price did not increase the offer would meet the consumer's expectation but then a question would arise concerning the application of [the German competition law], which prohibits manufacturers from imposing prices on retailers.

19   As regards the first possibility, * * * Mars has not actually profited from the promotional campaign in order to increase its sale prices and there is no evidence that retailers have themselves increased their prices. In any case, the mere possibility that importers and retailers might increase the price of the goods and that consequently consumers may be deceived is not sufficient to justify a general prohibition which may hinder intra-Community trade. That fact does not prevent the Member States from taking action, by appropriate measures, against duly proved actions which have the effect of misleading consumers.

20   As regards the second possibility, the principle of freedom of retail trade in the matter of the fixing of prices, provided for by a system of national law, and intended in particular to guarantee the consumer genuine price competition, may not justify an obstacle to intra-Community trade such as that in question * * *. The constraint imposed on the retailer not to increase his prices is in fact favourable to the consumer. It does not arise from any contractual stipulation and has the effect of protecting the consumer from being misled in any way. It does not prevent retailers from continuing to charge different prices and applies only during the short duration of the publicity campaign in question.

VERBAND SOZIALER WETTBEWERB
v. CLINIQUE LABORATORIES

Case C–315/92, [1994] ECR I–317.

[Since the 1970s, Estée Lauder has sold cosmetics in Europe under the brand-name "Clinique," but substituted "Linique" in Germany because of a concern that use of the name, "Clinique," might raise an issue of non-compliance with the German Unfair Competition Law. In 1991, to save advertising and packaging costs, Estée Lauder decided to adopt "Clinique" for cosmetics in Germany. A German association created to help enforce the German Unfair Competition Law sued to enjoin sales under the name "Clinique" as deceptive of consumers. The Berlin trial court feared that some consumers might "attribute prophylactic or curative medical effects" to a cosmetic called "Clinique," but asked the Court of Justice whether such a concern was sufficient under Articles 28 or 30 to bar a product "lawfully marketed under that name" elsewhere in the Community. The Court initially stated that neither Directive 76/768 on the packaging and labelling of cosmetic products, nor Directive 84/450 on the prevention of misleading advertising, contained a provision which precisely decided the issue.]

13 [T]he Court has recently ruled that Article [28] of the Treaty prohibits obstacles to the free movement of goods resulting from rules that lay down requirements to be met by such goods (such as requirements as to designation, form, size, weight, composition, presentation, labelling, packaging), even if those rules apply without distinction to all products, unless their application can be justified by a public-interest objective taking precedence over the free movement of goods (*Keck and Mithouard*).

14 The rules contained in Directive 76/768 include the obligation [on] Member States to take "all measures necessary to ensure that in the labelling, presentation for sale and advertising of cosmetic products, the wording, use of names, trade marks, images or other signs, figurative or otherwise, suggesting a characteristic which the products in question do not possess, shall be prohibited."

15 [This text] defines the measures to be taken in the interests of consumer protection and fairness of commercial transactions, which are included among the imperative requirements specified in the case-law of the Court in the context of the application of Article [28] of the Treaty. It also pursues the objective of protecting the health of humans, within the meaning of Article [30] of the Treaty, in so far as misleading information as to the characteristics of such products may have an affect on public health.

* * *

19 The prohibition [under the German Unfair Competition Law] of the distribution within Germany of cosmetic products under the same name as that under which they are marketed in the other Member States constitutes in principle * * * an obstacle to intra-Community trade. The fact that by reason of that prohibition the undertaking in question is obliged in that Member State alone to market its products under a different name

and to bear additional packaging and advertising costs demonstrates that this measure does affect free trade.

20 In order to determine whether, in preventing a product being attributed with characteristics which it does not have, the prohibition of the use of the name "Clinique" for the marketing of cosmetic products in Germany can be justified by the objective of protecting consumers or the health of humans, it is necessary to take into account the information set out in the order of reference.

21 [I]t is apparent from that information that the range of cosmetic products manufactured by the Estée Lauder company is sold in Germany exclusively in perfumeries and cosmetic departments of large stores, and therefore none of those products is available in pharmacies. It is not disputed that those products are presented as cosmetic products and not as medicinal products. It is not suggested that, apart from the name of the products, this presentation does not comply with the rules applicable to cosmetic products. Finally, according to the very wording of the question referred, those products are ordinarily marketed in other countries under the name "Clinique" and the use of that name apparently does not mislead consumers.

22 In the light of these facts, the prohibition of the use of that name in Germany does not appear necessary to satisfy the requirements of consumer protection and the health of humans.

23 The clinical or medical connotations of the word "Clinique" are not sufficient to make that word so misleading as to justify the prohibition of its use on products marketed in the aforesaid circumstances.

Notes and Questions

1. *Mars* and *Clinique* illustrate product-related rules which continue to be analyzed under the *Cassis de Dijon* doctrine, rather than rules governing modes of marketing, which now escape Article 28 altogether under the *Keck* doctrine. Do you find the distinction between product-related and marketing rules functionally useful and easy to apply, or relatively arbitrary and difficult to apply?

2. In ¶ 25 of his opinion in *Clinique*, Advocate General Gulmann concluded that "there may be specific differences in linguistic, social and cultural conditions which have the result that something which does not mislead consumers in one country may do so in another." He thought the Berlin court might properly take a market research survey to test the risk that German consumers could be misled. Do you agree with his view, or that of the Court?

3. In Estee Lauder Cosmetics v. Lancaster Group, Case C–220/98, [2000] ECR I–117, a German court referred questions inquiring essentially how it should determine whether the name of a UK producer's face cream, "Monteil Firming Action Lifting Extreme Creme," should be held in violation of the Cosmetic Products Directive's article 6(2) (quoted in ¶ 14 of *Clinique*), prohibiting product names that mislead consumers. Estee Lauder had sued to enjoin the face cream name as one deceiving consumers into believing that it had health promotion characteristics which it lacked. The trial court's reference noted that a 1996 German Supreme Court ruling had held that trade names could be prohibited if surveys indicated that 10–15% of consumers could be deceived. Advocate General Fennelly followed Advocate General Gulman (coincidentally now a judge in the

chamber deciding the case) in urging the Court to give guidance to the trial court on the proper test for consumer deception, rather than resolving the issue itself.

The Court's formulation of the test was as follows: "in order to determine whether a particular description, trade mark or promotional description or statement is misleading, it is necessary to take into account the presumed expectations of an average consumer who is reasonably well informed and reasonably observant and circumspect" (¶ 27). The Court went on to observe that it was possible that a German consumer, unlike consumers elsewhere in the Community, might have a different understanding of the word "lifting," due to "social, cultural or linguistic factors" (¶ 29). Although the Court made clear that an average consumer was unlikely to believe that the word "lifting" suggested that the face cream could produce permanent health benefits, it left to the national court the final word on this issue, employing if necessary, "an expert opinion or a survey of public opinion," and deciding upon the appropriate percentage of consumers who might be deceived (¶ 31).

What is your reaction to the Court's test for determining whether consumers might be deceived? Note that this "reasonably well informed and reasonably observant" consumer test was also used in the *Irish Hallmarking of precious metals* case, supra, and is used in the recent trademark confusion opinions discussed in Chapter 19E. Do you consider the Court's deference to fact-finding by the trial court to represent a better indication of the respective roles of the Court of Justice and national courts in an Article 234 reference proceeding than, e.g., *B & Q*, supra page 521, and *Semeraro*, supra page 524?

4. Another recent judgment has important basic right overtones. In Vereinigte Familiapresse Zeitungsverlag v. Heinrich Bauer Verlag, Case C–368/95, [1997] ECR I–3689 an Austrian magazine publisher sought to enjoin the sale in Austria of a German magazine because it contained games of chance whose successful solution would entitle certain readers to prizes worth up to DM 5000. A 1993 Austrian law forbids magazines to contain games of chance. The Court of Justice initially concluded that the pages with the games formed a part of the magazine, so that the Austrian law affected the product and not a merchandising modality, even though the manifest intent of the games was to increase the magazine's circulation.

Applying the *Cassis de Dijon* doctrine, the Court recognized the need to ensure a diversity of publications ("pluralisme de la presse") as an imperative public interest, because it promotes a free press. However, when applying the principle of proportionality, the Court concluded that the Austrian law's absolute ban on the inclusion in magazines of games of chance affording minor prizes might limit too severely the freedom of the press.

As indicated in the excerpt in Chapter 6, *supra*, the Court left to the trial court the task of determining whether the fact that Austria had an unusually small number of publishers could justify the Austrian law as a reasonable protection against the risk that rich foreign publishers might successfully use games of chance as a marketing device to gain a substantial competitive advantage. The trial court also had the duty to determine whether some measure less than a total ban on the sale of imported magazines containing games of chance could adequately protect the public interest. (Note that in the US, magazines containing similar games of chance customarily add notices indicating that residents of certain states may not participate in the games, due to legal restrictions in those states.)

COMMISSION v. GREECE

(Processed milk for infants)
Case C–391/92, [1995] ECR I–1621.

[A 1988 Greek law required processed milk for infants up to the age of five months to be sold only in pharmacies. No Greek manufacturer produces such infant formula; it is all imported. Following complaints, the Commission brought an Article 226 procedure, contending that the law reduced imports, was discriminatory because only importers were affected, and served no serious public health interest. Greece claimed that processed milk sales had not declined and also contended that mothers of new-borns needed the advice of pharmacists before using processed milk, that label information was insufficient because so many Greek women were illiterate, and that Greece had an unusually high infant mortality rate, necessitating drastic measures.

Advocate General Lenz concluded that the Greek law did not fall within the *Keck* doctrine because it was not neutral "in law and in fact," since there existed no domestic production. He also considered that the volume of sales would be lower in pharmacies than in retail outlets so that there would be an adverse effect on imports, and that the Greek health concerns were exaggerated and did not justify the application of Article 30.

The Court of Justice began by restating both the *Dassonville* and *Keck* doctrines, and by finding that the Greek law was "not designed to regulate trade in goods between Member States" even though it may "restrict the volume of sales" and hence of imports. (¶ ¶ 11–12.) The Court continued:]

15   [The Greek] legislation, the effect of which is to limit the commercial freedom of traders irrespective of the actual characteristics of the product referred to, concerns the selling arrangements of certain goods, inasmuch as it prohibits the sale, other than exclusively by pharmacies, of processed milk for infants and thus generally determines the points of sale where they may be distributed.

16   [T]he legislation * * * applies, without distinction according to the origin of the products in question, to all of the traders operating within the national territory, [and] does not affect the sale of products originating in other Member States any differently from that of domestic products.

17   The fact, invoked by the Commission, that the Hellenic Republic does not itself produce processed milk for infants does not undermine those findings. The applicability of Article [28] of the Treaty to a national measure for the general regulation of commerce, which concerns all the products concerned without distinction according to their origin, cannot depend on such a purely fortuitous factual circumstance, which may, moreover, change with the passage of time. If it did, this would have the illogical consequence that the same legislation would fall under Article [28] in certain Member States but fall outside the scope of that provision in other Member States.

18   The situation would be different only if it was apparent that the legislation at issue protected domestic products which were similar to processed milk for infants from other Member States or which were in competition with milk of that type.

[19]   [T]he Commission has not shown that that was the case.

[20]   It follows * * * that the Greek legislation * * * is confined to limiting the places where the product concerned may be distributed by regulating the marketing of that product, without thereby preventing access to the market of products from other Member States or specifically placing them at a disadvantage.

[21]   That being so, the Greek legislation reserving the sale of processed milk for infants in principle exclusively to pharmacies falls outside the scope of Article [28] of the Treaty.

SOCIETE D'IMPORTATION EDOUARD LECLERC– SIPLEC v. TFI PUBLICITE

Case C–412/93, [1995] ECR I–179.

[A 1992 French law prohibits advertising on television for alcoholic beverages with a high alcohol content, literary works, cinema films, the press, and any distribution form. Leclerc–Siplec, a gas station operator within a supermarket chain, sought to engage TFI, a French TV advertising company, to broadcast advertisements for its imported gasoline products. When TFI stated that the law prohibited this, Leclerc–Siplec sued TFI. Both parties asked the trial court to raise questions concerning the law's compatibility with Article 28, which the court did. In the proceeding, France admitted that a major motive for the television advertising ban was to protect the advertising revenues of newspapers and magazines.

The Court initially held the questions referred to be admissible, even though both parties to the suit desired the same response. See the discussion of this issue in Chapter 9 *supra*. With regard to Article 28, the Court held:]

[19]   A law or regulation such as that at issue in the main proceedings, which prohibits televised advertising in the distribution sector, is not designed to regulate trade in goods between member states. Moreover, such a prohibition does not prevent distributors from using other forms of advertising.

[20]   Such a prohibition may, admittedly, restrict the volume of sales, and hence the volume of sales of products from other member states, in so far as it deprives distributors of a particular form of advertising their goods....

[The Court then quoted the *Keck* doctrine.]

[22]   A provision such as that at issue in the main proceedings concerns selling arrangements since it prohibits a particular form of promotion (televised advertising) of a particular method of marketing products (distribution).

[23]   Furthermore, those provisions, which apply regardless of the type of product to all traders in the distribution sector, even if they are both producers and distributors, affect the marketing of products from other member states and that of domestic products in the same manner.

[24]   The reply should accordingly be that on a proper construction art [28] of the Treaty does not apply where a member state, by statute or by regulation, prohibits the broadcasting of televised advertisements for the distribution sector.

[The trial court also raised questions on the application of Directive 89/522 on television broadcasting, which are dealt with at page 691, infra.]

Notes and Questions

1.   Whether one agrees with the Court or with the Commission and Advocate General Lenz in the *Greek processed milk* case depends largely on whether one views the Greek law as affecting "*in fact*" only imports, and hence outside of the *Keck* exception. What is your view—specifically, is the absence of Greek production of processed milk important or not? If the circumstances are seen as outside of the *Keck* exception, the principal issue then becomes whether the Greek law can be justified by a public health exception. What do you think? Is it significant, or not, that only Spain had similar rules?

2.   In *Leclerc-Siplec*, Advocate General Jacobs' able and detailed opinion continued to query the advisability of the *Keck* doctrine, but admitted that if it were applicable, the French prohibition of television advertising of distribution would fall outside of Article 28. He emphasized, however, the capital importance of television advertising for a foreign producer seeking to become a new market entrant. Advocate General Jacobs specifically suggested in ¶ 51 that if a German beer producer should seek to use television advertising to launch the sale of beer not previously marketed in France, the *Keck* rules should not apply. Do you agree? L. Idot's casenote on *Leclerc*, 33 Common Mkt. L. Rev. 113 (1996) generally endorses Advocate General Jacobs' views and criticizes the Court's approach.

Indeed, suppose that a challenge to the French law is raised not by a German beer producer, but rather by a Community advertising agency seeking to carry out a Community-wide television advertising campaign for a new brand of beer. Can the French law be used to restrict such trans-border providing of advertising services? See the discussion of the non-applicability of the *Keck* doctrine to rules restricting trans-border services following the *Schindler* and related cases in Chapter 17B.

KONSUMENTOMBUSMANNEN v. GOURMET INTERNATIONAL PRODUCTS

Case C–405/98, [2001] ECR __ (March 8, 2001).

[Swedish law provides that "in view of the health risks involved in alcohol consumption, alcoholic beverages should be marketed with particular moderation." It provides specifically that advertisements must not encourage alcohol consumption and totally prohibits advertising of alcoholic beverages on radio or television and in magazines and other periodicals. After Gourmet magazine published an issue for its subscribers (of whom 90% are retailers or merchants, but 10% are private individuals) containing three pages of advertisements for wine and whisky, the Swedish Consumer Ombudsman sued it, requesting a fine and an injunction. The trial court inquired whether the Swedish law violated Article 28 and could be justified on public health grounds. The key issue presented was whether the law might discriminate "in fact" against imports.]

[14]   The Consumer Ombudsman [accepts] that the prohibition on advertising in Sweden affects sales of alcoholic beverages there, including those imported from other Member States, since the specific purpose of the Swedish legislation is to reduce the consumption of alcohol.

[15] However, * * * the Consumer Ombudsman [contends] that the prohibition on advertising in issue in the main proceeding does not constitute an obstacle to trade between Member States, since it satisfies the criteria laid down by the Court in [*Keck*].

[16] GIP contends that an outright prohibition [on alcohol advertising in magazines] does not satisfy those criteria. It argues that such a prohibition is, in particular, liable to have a greater effect on imported goods than on those produced in the Member State concerned.

* * *

[18] [A]ccording to paragraph 17 in *Keck* and *Mithouard*, if national provisions restricting or prohibiting certain selling arrangements are to avoid being caught by Article [28] of the Treaty, they must not be of such a kind as to prevent access to the market by products from another Member State or to impede access any more than they impede the access of domestic products.

[19] The Court has also held, [in the *Swedish Consumer Ombudsman* case, *infra* page 688] that it cannot be excluded that an outright prohibition, applying in one Member State, of a type of promotion for a product which is lawfully sold there might have a greater impact on products from other Member States.

[20] It is apparent that a prohibition on advertising such as that at issue in the main proceedings not only prohibits a form of marketing a product but in reality prohibits producers and importers from directing any advertising messages at consumers, with a few insignificant exceptions.

[21] Even without its being necessary to carry out a precise analysis of the facts characteristic of the Swedish situation, which it is for the national court to do, the Court is able to conclude that, in the case of products like alcoholic beverages, the consumption of which is linked to traditional social practices and to local habits and customs, a prohibition of all advertising directed at consumers in the form of advertisements in the press, on the radio and on television, the direct mailing of unsolicited material or the placing of posters on the public highway is liable to impede access to the market by products from other Member States more than it impedes access by domestic products, with which consumers are instantly more familiar.

[22] The information provided by the Consumer Ombudsman and the Swedish Government concerning the relative increase in Sweden in the consumption of wine and whisky, which are mainly imported, in comparison with other products such as vodka, which is mainly of Swedish origin, does not alter that conclusion. First, it can not be precluded that, in the absence of the legislation at issue in the main proceedings, the change indicated would have been greater; second, that information takes into account only some alcoholic beverages and ignores, in particular, beer consumption.

* * *

[25] A prohibition on advertising such as that at issue in the main proceedings must therefore be regarded as affecting the marketing or products from other Member States more heavily than the marketing of domestic prod-

ucts and as therefore constituting an obstacle to trade between Member States caught by Article [28] of the Treaty.

[26] However, such an obstacle may be justified by the protection of public health, a general interest ground recognised by Article [30] of the Treaty.

[27] In that regard, it is accepted that rules restricting the advertising of alcoholic beverages in order to combat alcohol abuse reflect public health concerns.

[The Court concluded that the trial court must evaluate the "circumstances of law and of fact" in order to determine whether the Swedish limits on alcohol advertising were proportionate to the public health goal. The Court noted that the Commission in its intervention had expressed doubt on the proportionality of an absolute ban on alcohol advertising, suggesting that advertising restrictions should only require the exercise of moderation in consumption.

Notes and Questions

1. Advocate General Jacobs repeated in *Gourmet* his view that advertising restrictions may impact imports far more seriously than domestic products, noting that wine is essentially imported while there is a strong domestic beer production. His conclusion that the Swedish advertising limits accordingly "must have a greater adverse effect on [imported] new products" than on domestic products clearly influenced the Court's view in *Gourmet*. Do you agree that a total ban on certain fields of advertising is apt to discriminate "in fact" against imports, and hence falls outside of *Keck?*

2. How would you decide whether the alcohol advertising limits are proportionate to the public health goal? Is it relevant that Sweden has one of the highest alcoholism rates in the Community? Advocate General Jacobs noted that all Member States restrict alcohol advertising to some degree, but only Finland matches Sweden in the severity of its restrictions. He expressed concern that the Swedish restrictions might discourage switching of brands (e.g., from beer to wine), rather than reducing alcohol consumption. Would you accept the Swedish rules, or prefer restrictions that limit the nature of advertising (e.g., forbidding advertising directed at young people, or advertising that associates alcohol with sophistication or sexual attraction)?

3. In Schutzverband gegen unlauteren Wettbewerb v. TK–Heimdienst Sass, Case C–254/98, [2000] ECR I–151, an Austrian law forbid bakers, butchers and grocers to make "sales on rounds" (sales by travelling salesmen using trucks) unless they had a permanent establishment in the administrative region where the sales were made. The Commission agreed with Austria that the rule constituted one on selling arrangements under *Keck*. The Court concluded to the contrary that the rule would oblige a baker, butcher or grocer whose main business establishment existed outside Austria to incur added costs in order to set up a permanent establishment in Austria, which meant that the Austrian rule would discriminate "in fact" against non-Austrian traders, making the *Keck* selling arrangement exception inapplicable. The Court concluded further that this violation of Article 28 could not be justified on health grounds since Austria could require the sales to be made from refrigerated trucks, protecting health in a more proportionate manner .

4. The latest edition of Peter Oliver's Free Movement of Goods in the European Community (3d. ed. Sweet & Maxwell 1996), provides a detailed survey of all the topics treated in this chapter, as well as Chapters 12 and 19. Also valuable are two thoughtful articles analyzing the post-*Keck* case law, L. Gormley, Two Years After Keck, 19 Fordham Int'l L.J. 866 (1996), and S. Weatherill, After Keck: Some Thoughts on How to Clarify the Clarification, 33 Common Mkt. L. Rev. 879 (1996).

Further Reading

Useful books containing material relevant to this chapter (and often relevant to Chapters 12 and 14) are:

L. Gormley, Prohibiting Restrictions on Trade Within the EEC (North–Holland 1985)

N. Green, T. Hartley & J. Usher, The Legal Foundation of the Single European Market (Oxford Univ. Press 1991)

M. Horspool, European Union Law (2d ed. Butterworth 2000)

P. Kapteyn & P. Verloren Van Themaat, Introduction to the Law of the European Communities (L. Gormley, English ed.) (3d ed. Kluwer 1998)

P. Oliver, Free Movement of Goods in the European Community (3d ed. Sweet & Maxwell 1996)

S. Weatherill & P. Beaumont, European Community Law (2d ed. Penguin 1995)

D.Wyatt & A. Dashwood, Substantive Law of the EEC (3d ed. Sweet & Maxwell 1992)

Chapter 14

THE COMMON MARKET, THE INTERNAL MARKET AND HARMONIZATION OF LAWS

A. THE COMMON MARKET AND HARMONIZATION OF LAWS

1. INITIAL HARMONIZATION OF LAWS

The 1957 European Economic Community Treaty declared in Article 2 that one of its prime goals was to establish a common market in order to achieve a variety of benefits, notably "a harmonious development of economic activities [and] an accelerated raising of the standard of living." A common market by its nature represents a high level of economic integration, far more than a free trade zone or a common customs area. The scope of activities of the Community listed in Article 3 of the initial EEC Treaty suggest the principal dimensions of the common market: the elimination of obstacles to the free movement of goods, persons, services and capital (the "four freedoms"); common policies in the fields of agriculture, transport and competition; coordination of economic policies; and the approximation (or harmonization) of laws "for the proper functioning of the common market."

Chapters 12 and 13 have surveyed the vital role of the Court of Justice in removing barriers to the free movement of goods, and later chapters will describe the Court's important contributions to the achievement of the free movement of persons, services and capital. Indeed, the Court's role has always been crucial in stressing the fundamental nature of the four freedoms and articulating doctrines that have enabled both the Commission and private parties to sweep away many national barriers within the common market. Nonetheless the Court can only go so far towards achieving the common market goal, because it is always limited to enunciating doctrines based upon the particular circumstances that happen to be brought before the Court.

In contrast, Community legislation enables the adoption of rules, more precise and uniform in character, throughout an entire field within the common market. As we shall see in later chapters, the Treaty makes specific grants of legislative power in many sectors of the common market, e.g., in Article 40 for free movement of workers, Article 44 for the right of establishment, and Article 52 for the free movement of services.

By far the most sweeping legislative grant, however, was the generic one for the harmonization of laws contained in the initial Treaty Article 100 (now slightly reworded and renumbered as EC Treaty Article 94). The original text of the first paragraph in Article 100 was:

> The Council shall, acting unanimously on a proposal from the Commission, issue directives for the approximation of such provisions laid down by law, regulation or administrative action in Member States as directly affect the establishment or functioning of the common market.

The success of the Community depends in large measure on its ability to harmonize Member State laws. National health, safety and technical quality regulations, as well as rules to promote consumer interests or protect the environment, are the natural result of each state's independent effort to provide benefits to its citizens. Unfortunately, these Member State regulations become effective barriers to the free movement of goods when they impose specific technical product requirements and prevent the sale of imported products which do not conform to these requirements.

Such barriers make it difficult or more expensive for manufacturers to market throughout the Community, thus promoting the partition of national markets. Technical barriers also retard technological advance, since they divert capital from basic research to secondary development costs incurred to meet local market specifications. The benefits of free competition are diminished and consumers may be restricted in their freedom of choice. The creation of Community-wide rules and standards through harmonization therefore seeks to promote a Community market for products and services, while protecting the legitimate interests of consumers and the general public in a more uniform manner.

For the first thirty years of the Community, Article 100 (now Article 94) served as the chief legislative mode in adopting directives to remove barriers of trade in specific sectors in order to promote the common market. As we shall see in section B, the Single European Act introduced in 1987 an easier mode of legislation for this purpose, Article 100 a (now Article 95). A good understanding of Article 100 is, however, essential to appreciating the initial success, and limits, of harmonization prior to 1987.

Although some harmonization directives were adopted under Article 100 during the 1960s, widespread application started after the adoption of the General Program of May 28, 1969 for the elimination of technical barriers to trade, O.J. English Spec.Ed.2d Ser. 1974, at 25. By the mid–1980s, nearly 200 directives had been adopted pursuant to the technical barriers and related programs. The largest single sector was motor vehicles, where over 60 directives set technical regulations and standards for vehicle parts and equipment (e.g., brakes, doors, headlights, steering wheels, safety belts). Other important directives harmonized rules on the composition, labeling, packaging and review for safety of foodstuffs, cosmetics and pharmaceuticals, dangerous products of various kinds, electrical consumer goods, mechanical products and weighing equipment.

The adoption of the first environmental protection program in 1973 gave rise to an important new field of legislative harmonization. Because environmental protection was not one of the fields of the common market listed at that time in Article 3, the Council felt it necessary to employ the implied powers or "elastic clause," Article 308 (ex Article 235), as a supplement to Article 100. Article 308 permits legislative action by unanimous vote in the Council whenever necessary to achieve a Community objective in a field where the Treaty does not provide for a specific legislative power. Initial environmental protection measures included directives to harmonize clean drinking and bathing water standards, automobile emission rules, clean air standards and wild bird protection. Chapter 34 describes the initial and on-going legislative programs for environmental protection.

2. OPERATION OF ARTICLE 100

Article 100 (renumbered as Article 94)requires the Council to act unanimously, creating the risk of delay or even veto by any Member State. Moreover, Article 100 paragraph 2 gives the Parliament only a consultative, or advisory role, with no power of amendment. (Note that Article 100a, introduced by the Single European Act, discussed in section B, avoids both of these defects.)

Article 100 authorizes directives "for the approximation" of Member State laws or administrative acts. "Approximation" is a poor English translation of the terms used in the original Treaty languages, e.g. "rapprochement" in French, "Angleichung" in German. The Dutch version, the most precise, is "nader tot elkaar brengen," which translates into English as "to bring closer together." The English word "harmonization" conveys this better than "approximation" and is therefore customarily used by the Commission and commentators. Moreover, "harmonization" is the term used in some other initial Treaty articles, such as Articles 99 and 117 (renumbered as Articles 93 and 136), as a synonym for "approximation."

Harmonization of laws does not require that Member State rules be made absolutely uniform. It merely requires that the rules be made similar. Harmonization directives accordingly set up a basic structure, with more or less detailed provisions, to which Member States must conform. Some directives make the Community rules the exclusive standard for all products, while others allow States to apply stricter standards. Some directives even allow States to apply lower standards for domestic products which are sold domestically, as a way of reducing the burden on small manufacturers who concentrate on the local market (this approach is often called "optional harmonization").

There was some debate, especially during the 1960s, over whether a harmonization directive's provisions had to be modeled on specific rules in one or more Member States. One could argue that, in strict logic, harmonization requires the alignment of some pre-existing set of national rules. However, policy considerations have prevailed over logic. It is now generally accepted that a harmonization directive may contain provisions that are innovations, not represented in any state's legal system, so long as the field is one appropriate for Community action. This sort of innovation is especially likely to occur in environmental protection legislation.

Article 100 authorizes directives, not regulations. Hence a harmonization measure adopted under Article 100 cannot be passed as a regulation, with immediate force of law throughout the Community.

Directives require implementing Member State laws or regulations within the time period specified (usually two years). Since the mid–1970s, the Commission has frequently resorted to Article 226 proceedings against States that inadequately implemented harmonization directives, or failed to adopt them on time. Moreover, applying the "direct effect" doctrine (see Chapter 7), the Court of Justice has held some harmonization directives, or provisions thereof, to be clear, precise and unconditional, so that individuals may rely upon them even when a State has failed to implement them, or implemented them improperly.

3. A TYPICAL HARMONIZATION DIRECTIVE: DANGEROUS SUBSTANCES

At this point, it is helpful to analyze the structure and approach of a typical harmonization directive. The Selected Documents contains Directive 92/32 on the approximation of laws relating to the classification, packaging and labeling of dangerous substances, initially adopted in 1967, with substantial amendments in 1979 and 1992.

This directive has five principal aspects. First, it defines a dangerous substance as one dangerous to man or the environment. Article 2 gives illustrations of "dangerous": explosive, flammable, toxic, carcinogenic, etc. Second, Member States must ensure that no dangerous substances are placed on the Community market until they have been reviewed and properly packaged and labeled. The directive does not, however, restrict or regulate the export of dangerous substances outside the Community.

Third, the directive in Article 6 requires a review process before marketing. The producer or importer must carefully investigate all relevant aspects of the substance, using laboratory tests "in compliance with the principles of good laboratory practice." Then, under Article 7, the producer or importer must provide a technical file which evaluates the "foreseeable risks" and "unfavorable effects" of the product. Pursuant to articles 16–18, the competent national authority reviews this file in coordination with the Commission and comparable authorities in other States. Article 19 protects the producer's "commercially sensitive" information in this process.

Next, the national authority must approve an appropriate "strong and solid" package, so that the contents cannot escape. Since the 1979 amendment, the authority may require that the package be child-resistant or have a safety seal. Finally, the product must be "clearly and indelibly" labeled with a danger symbol, an indication of "special risks" and any "safety advice." Note that the danger symbol must be chosen from those in Annex II so as to be clearly recognizable throughout the Community, and must always be black on an orange-yellow background. (This approach of requiring that a single list of danger symbols be used in every state, so that the symbols will be recognizable to those who don't speak the local language, is also used for road safety and worksite safety signs.)

Notes and Questions

1. Read carefully the directive's article 30. The directive is intended not only to set acceptable minimum standards for the Community, but also to ensure that dangerous products, once reviewed by a national authority, may circulate freely

throughout the Community. It illustrates the basic "mutual trust" principle, because importing States must rely on the exporting State's competent authority to perform its duties adequately. Only "in the light of new information" may a State temporarily prohibit an approved dangerous substance, subject to review by the Commission (article 31). For a good review of harmonization, see P. Slot, Harmonization, 21 Eur. L. Rev. 378 (1996), and D. Vignes, The Harmonization of National Legislation and the EEC, 15 Eur.L.Rev. 358 (1990).

2. Article 24(5) allows Member States to require that imported products have labels in the importing state's official language or languages. This obviously represents an added expense and therefore a burden on trade. Do you think it is justified?

3. The dangerous substances directive was supplemented by Regulation 793/93 on the evaluation of risks of substances, O.J.L. 84/1 (Apr. 5, 1993), which requires the Commission and Member States to carry out an evaluation of the risks to workers, consumers and the environment of all dangerous substances being marketed. The dangerous substances directive has been the model for several others, e.g., the directive on dangerous solvents, O.J. L 189/7 (June 4, 1973); on paints, varnishes, printing inks, etc., O.J. L 303/23 (Nov. 7, 1977); and on pesticides, O.J. L 206/13 (June 26, 1978). Analogous principles of prior review of a technical dossier, proper packaging and labeling (but without danger symbols) are found in the directive on cosmetic products, O.J. L 262/69 (July 27, 1976). For a recent directive with parallel provisions, see Directive 98/8 on biocidal products, O.J.L. 123/1, (Apr. 24, 1998).

B. COMPLETION OF THE INTERNAL MARKET

1. THE WHITE PAPER OF JUNE 1985

As discussed in Chapter 1, in the early 1980s, the Community entered a period of "Europessimism" and "Eurostagnation." The process of harmonization of laws had appreciably slackened and there was widespread criticism, both within the Commission and the Member States, of the slow pace of Community action. In part this situation was due to the energy recession of the 1970s, but it also reflected a weakness in leadership within the Community and the difficulty in adopting legislation due to Article 100's requirement of unanimity.

The European Council, obviously disturbed by this state of affairs, discussed ways to reenergize the Community in several meetings during 1982–85. Notably, at its December 1984 meeting in Dublin, the European Council agreed that the Council "should take steps to complete the Internal Market." At its subsequent meeting in Brussels on March 29–30, 1985, the European Council "called upon the Commission to draw up a detailed program with a specific timetable" in order to "achieve a single large market by 1992."

A new Commission had taken office in January 1985, headed by President Jacques Delors, a leading French Socialist and former Minister of Finance. Much of the credit for the more dynamic Commission leadership since 1985 must be given to the vision and energy of President Delors. In response to the European Council's request, the Commission rapidly produced a White Paper. The principal author of this study was Lord Cockfield, a former Tory UK cabinet minister and adroit political leader, who was the Commissioner responsible for the internal market directorate-general.

THE WHITE PAPER COMPLETING THE INTERNAL MARKET
COM (85) 310 (June 1985)

3　[T]he Commission, which wholeheartedly shares the [European] Council's commitment [to the completion of the common market], sets out here the essential and logical consequences of accepting that commitment, together with an action program * * *.

* * *

5　[After initial Community achievements, in recent times] momentum was lost partly through the onset of the recession, partly through a lack of confidence and vision * * *.

6　[D]uring the recession, [non-tariff barriers] multiplied as each Member State endeavored to protect what it thought was its short term interests— not only against third countries but against fellow Member States as well. * * *

7　But the mood has begun to change, and the commitment to be rediscovered: gradually at first, but now with increasing tempo. * * * The time for talk has now passed. The time for action has come. That is what this White Paper is about.

* * *

8　[T]he objective of completing the internal market has three aspects:

— First, the welding together of the * * * individual markets of the Member States into one single market of 320 million people;

— Second, ensuring that this single market is also an expanding market—not static but growing;

— Third, to this end, ensuring that the market is flexible so that resources, both of people and materials, and of capital and investment, flow into the areas of greatest economic advantage.

* * *

10　For convenience the measures that need to be taken have been classified in this Paper under three headings:

— Part one: the removal of physical barriers

— Part two: the removal of technical barriers

— Part three: the removal of fiscal barriers.

11　The most obvious example of the first category are customs posts at frontiers. Indeed most of our citizens would regard the frontier posts as the most visible example of the continued division of the Community and their removal as the clearest sign of the integration of the Community into a single market. * * * Once we have removed [technical and fiscal] barriers, and found alternative ways of dealing with other relevant problems such as public security, immigration and drug controls, the reasons for the existence of the physical barriers will have been eliminated.

¹² The reason for getting rid entirely of physical and other controls between Member States is not one of theology or appearance, but the hard practical fact that the maintenance of any internal frontier controls will perpetuate the costs and disadvantages of a divided market * * *.

¹³ * * * [T]he elimination of technical barriers * * * will give the large market its economic and industrial dimension by enabling industries to make economies of scale and therefore to become more competitive. An example of this second category—technical barriers—are the different standards for individual products adopted in different Member States for health or safety reasons, or for environmental or consumer protection. * * * Technical barriers are technical barriers whether they apply to goods or services. * * * The general thrust of the Commission's approach in this area will be to move away from the concept of harmonisation towards that of mutual recognition and equivalence. But there will be a continuing role for the approximation of Member States' laws and regulations, as laid down in Article 100 of the Treaty. * * *

¹⁴ The removal of fiscal barriers may well be contentious and this despite the fact that the goals laid down in the Treaty are quite explicit and that important steps have already been taken along the road of approximation. * * *

¹⁵ * * *. The benefits to an integrated Community economy of the large, expanding and flexible market are so great that they should not be denied to its citizens because of difficulties faced by individual Member States. These difficulties must be recognised, to some degree they must be accommodated, but they should not be allowed permanently to frustrate the achievement of the greater progress, the greater prosperity and the higher level of employment that economic integration can bring to the Community.

* * *

¹⁷ This White Paper is not intended to cover every possible issue which affects the integration of the economies of the Member States of the community. It focuses on the Internal Market and the measures which are directly necessary to achieve a single integrated market embracing the 320m people of the enlarged Community.

* * *

¹⁹ * * * [A] strong and coherent competition policy must ensure that the partitioning of the internal market is not permitted to occur as a result of protectionist state aids or restrictive practices by firms. Moreover the commercial identity of the Community must be consolidated so that our trading partners will not be given the benefit of a wider market without themselves making similar concessions.

²⁰ There are many other areas of Community policy that interact with the Internal market * * * and will benefit from the stimulus that will be provided by its completion. This is particularly true of transport, social, environment and consumer protection policy.

The White Paper went on to review the current problems and the proposed legislative remedies to achieve the free movement of goods, persons, services and capital and accordingly to remove the frontier checks and other physical and technical barriers to trade. The Paper urged new efforts in a number of sectors where progress had long been stalemated, such as the banking and insurance industries, value added and other internal tax harmonization, industrial and commercial property rights, and the free movement of professionals.

The White Paper's Annex listed a total of 282 legislative measures in all of the sectors reviewed in the text, with a timetable for the drafting and adoption of each measure. The entire legislative process was to be completed by December 31, 1992.

What in retrospect is so astonishing is that the White Paper did not remain just another interesting Commission study, but became in fact the blueprint for the tremendously successful program for achieving the "Europe of 1992." The European Council decisively endorsed the White Paper's program in Milan on June 28–29, 1985. The Commission's energetic development of proposed legislation and its continuous exertions for passage of the proposals certainly played a key role. The Parliament also gave its enthusiastic support. But perhaps equally important was the recognition and endorsement of the "Europe of 1992" goal by the media, leading industry and commercial groups, and by the general public, which stimulated the political will necessary in the difficult decision-making process.

This endorsement of the "Europe of 1992" goal was reinforced by economic studies, notably the famous 1988 Cecchini report, made at the request of the Commission. This report consisted of 24 separate studies, including a survey of 11,000 business firms. The report estimated that the completed internal market would produce hundreds of billions of dollars in savings, substantially increase investment and production, and raise employment levels by over two million jobs. See P. Cecchini, The European Challenge (Gower 1988).

2. THE SINGLE EUROPEAN ACT'S INTRODUCTION OF ARTICLE 8a

Although the White Paper set the program for completing the internal market, this might well have been largely frustrated if the Single European Act had not introduced several structural Treaty improvements. The origins and critical importance of the SEA have been described in Chapter 1, but several points should be underlined here.

The SEA's insertion of Article 8a (presently renumbered as Article 14) into the EEC Treaty gave Treaty force to the policy goal of completing the internal market:

> The Community shall adopt measures with the aim of progressively establishing the internal market over a period expiring on 31 December 1992. * * *

> The internal market shall comprise an area without internal frontiers in which the free movement of goods, persons, services and capital is ensured in accordance with the provisions of this Treaty.

The definition of the internal market as "an area without internal frontiers" adds significantly to the attainment of the "four freedoms." Article

8a's goal is to achieve a global market area in which the legal boundaries of Member States do not constitute functional limits on any of the "four freedoms." As we shall see, this goal has been substantially attained, except with regard to the free movement of persons across frontiers (see Chapter 16D). Moreover, Article 8a set a time frame with treaty force: the internal market legislative program is meant to be completed by Dec. 31, 1992.

Is Article 8a one of those Treaty articles that can be given direct effect, and thus give rights to individuals, even in the absence of specified legislative measures? The Commission initially proposed to the Luxembourg Conference, which prepared the SEA, that Article 8a expressly be given direct effect. The Conference declined to do so. Instead, the Conference adopted a "Declaration on Article 8a" which was annexed to the SEA. Although this Declaration stated positively the "firm political will to take before 1 January 1993 the decisions necessary to complete the internal market," it ended with this sentence: "Setting the date of 31 December 1992 does not create an automatic legal effect."

Although some academic commentators contended that the Declaration on Article 8a had no binding legal force under public international law principles, it was always unlikely that the Court of Justice would ascribe direct effect to Article 8a. The Court has now definitely held that Article 8a does not have direct effect in *Wijsenbeek*, *infra* page , which permits States to retain border controls on persons.

Some initial commentators were also concerned that the White Paper's emphasis on legislation to achieve the internal market might lead to relegation of other Community programs and policies to a position of secondary importance. Former Judge Pierre Pescatore, a leading constitutional authority while serving on the Court of Justice, raised this concern in P. Pescatore, Some Critical Remarks on the Single European Act, 24 Common Mkt. L. Rev. 9 (1987). However, the White Paper itself had referred to the anticipated "stimulation" of social, environmental protection and consumer protection policies as an accessory to the internal market. As the legislation described in Chapters 34, 35 and 36 demonstrate, this has proved to be an accurate prediction.

Probably the best over-all analysis of the SEA is that by Claus–Dieter Ehlermann, the then-Director General of the Commission Legal Service, in The Internal Market Following the Single European Act, 24 Common Mkt. L.Rev. 361 (1987). Ehlermann contended that Article 8a's concept of the internal market as "an area without internal frontiers" represents a new substantive legal concept, in some respects more precise than Court of Justice case law. For the views of Hans–Joachim Glaesner, the then-Director General of the Council Legal Service, see H.J. Glaesner, The Single European Act: Attempt at An Appraisal, 10 Fordham Int'l L.J. 446 (1987).

3. THE SUCCESS OF THE INTERNAL MARKET PROGRAM

In any event, the White Paper has had a dramatic success. Its legislative agenda proved largely capable of attainment. In December 1992, the Edinburgh European Council "noted with particular satisfaction" the program's success, with the adoption of over 500 internal market measures, representing 95% of the White Paper list. Naturally, the internal market program did not end on Dec. 31, 1992. The Community continues to adopt important legislation in virtually all sectors to supplement the initial measures.

Perhaps the most significant internal market attainments have been in the achievement of the free movement of capital, the harmonization of the essential rules in banking, insurance and securities law, the harmonization of traditional intellectual property rights, together with the creation of some new ones, the liberalization of public procurement and telecommunications, and further technical harmonization. Some of the more important legislative measures are described in later chapters. Although highly useful measures to achieve recognition of professional rights and to enable rights of residence for students and other persons have been adopted, it has not proved possible to dismantle all frontier barriers to the free movement of persons. Also, to date little progress has been made upon initiatives to harmonize direct and indirect taxation.

About 75% of the measures adopted have been in the form of directives which require Member State implementation. For years some States lagged significantly behind in the implementation process, but the passage of time has alleviated this problem to some degree, even though the Commission regularly urges more rapid implementation of current measures. Not surprisingly in view of the technical complexity of many directives, the Commission considers that many States have improperly implemented some directives, leading to large numbers of new Article 226 proceedings, but, as usual, most of these are resolved satisfactorily before any Court action is required. However, many recent Article 234 questions concern the interpretation of internal market directives.

The Commission issued a report on the economic impact and effectiveness of the single market on Oct. 30, 1996, COM (96) 520. The report concluded that the internal market program had increased intra-Community trade by 20–30%, created over 1% in added GDP growth annually, and stimulated the creation of 900,000 jobs.

The Commission's new emphasis on transparency, clarity and coherence in internal market measures, in part prompted by criticism of allegedly excessively detailed and abstruse Community legislation during the period of ratification of the Maastricht Treaty, has led it to improve its internal procedures. When the Commission joined the Council and the Parliament in the Interinstitutional Declaration on Democracy, Transparency and Subsidiarity on October 25, 1993 (reproduced in the Selected Documents), the Commission committed itself to "wider consultations before presenting proposals, . . . publication of work programmes—and faster publication of Commission documents."

The 1993 Interinstitutional Declaration also stated that "[i]n expressing its rights of initiative, the Commission shall take into account the principle of subsidiarity." The Commission now expressly covers this in the explanatory memorandum for each new proposal. In the mid–1990's the Commission withdrew some proposals, e.g., the draft directives on the liability of providers of services and on the treatment of animals in zoos, while it reexamined many other proposals and amended them to reduce their scope, e.g., those on comparative advertising and on takeover bids. Protests from Parliament induced the Commission to retain some proposals that Member States wanted withdrawn.

In May 1996 the Commission launched the SLIM program for "Simpler Legislation in the Internal Market," pressing for transparent and codified texts. The December 1996 Dublin European Council endorsed the SLIM project. The Commission has since made some progress in codifying legislation in some fields (e.g., professional rights and banking law) but the process is slow and arduous.

In June 1997, the Commission adopted an Action Plan for the Single Market, ESC (97) 1, endorsed by the Amsterdam European Council. The Action Plan urged efforts to make existing rules more effective, to cope with tax and other market distortions, to remove sectoral obstacles, especially in financial services, and to provide further benefits for citizens, notably in eliminating border controls and improving rights of residence. Since 1998, the Commission publishes every six months a Single Market Scoreboard, registering legislative progress, implementation by Member States, and problems encountered. The initial Scoreboard indicated that 1339 single market directives had been adopted up to that time, with around 25% still not fully implemented. The Action Plan was succeeded in October 1999 by the Commission's Strategy for the Internal Market, endorsed by the December 1999 Helsinki European Council. The Commission's latest report, "Working Together to Maintain Momentum," issued in April 2001, lists 80 legislative measures and other 'target actions' for future adoption.

The steady progress of the Community toward an integrated internal market initially gave rise to considerable concern in the US, Japan and in EFTA and Eastern European states which feared that the Community might become a "fortress Europe," whose new rules would directly or indirectly impede imports of goods and services. In 1993, the EFTA countries, apart from Switzerland, entered into the European Economic Area Agreement with the European Community, which has provided them with most of the benefits of the internal market, although it obliged them to adopt rules to implement an estimated total of 1700 directives. Similarly, most of the Central European countries have entered into Europe Agreements which require them to adopt most of the internal market legislation as a prelude to ultimate membership in the European Union. See Chapter 28.

As far as the US is concerned, the Department of Commerce and the Office of the US Trade Representative have carefully followed the evolution of the Community legislative program and have energetically urged the Commission and Council to modify proposals they consider to be harmful to US trade or investment. American industry groups have also organized lobbying efforts to attempt to influence Community decisionmakers. During this dialogue, the Commission and other institutions have been attentive to US views and in many cases have modified proposals so as to reduce any adverse impact on the trade and investment interests of the US and the Community's other major trading partners. A good example is the change made to the reciprocity provision of the Second Banking Directive 89/646, discussed at page ___, after well-publicized protests by the US Government and banking community.

What was inevitable, however, was that the Community's economic power would substantially increase with the success of the internal market. The

Community has now almost attained a position of economic parity with the US, which was reflected in their relatively equal bargaining strength in the Uruguay Round GATT negotiations.

4. THE SINGLE EUROPEAN ACT'S INTRODUCTION OF ARTICLE 100a

One of the principal reasons for the level of success in completing the internal market was the modification of the legislative process introduced by the SEA as Article 100a(1) of the EEC Treaty (now reworded and renumbered as EC Treaty Article 95):

> By way of derogation from Article 100 and save where otherwise provided in this Treaty, the following provisions shall apply for the achievement of the objectives set out in Article 8a. The Council shall, acting by a qualified majority on a proposal from the Commission in co-operation with the European Parliament and after consulting the Economic and Social Committee, adopt the measures for the approximation of the provisions laid down by law, regulation or administrative action in Member States which have as their object the establishment and functioning of the internal market.

Article 100a avoided the principal defects of Article 100. First, Article 100a permitted the adoption of measures by a qualified majority vote of the Council, instead of unanimity. Second, Article 100a gave the Parliament a substantial role in the legislative process, thus making the process more democratic. Article 100a introduced the use of the parliamentary cooperation procedure described in Chapter 3. Subsequently, the Treaty of Maastricht replaced the cooperation procedure with the legislative co-decision procedure for legislation adopted by use of Article 100a (see the current text in Article 95). Thus Parliament has exercised essentially a veto power over internal market legislation since Nov. 1, 1993. Finally, Article 100a also authorized legislation in the form of regulations in addition to directives, but in fact only rarely have regulations been used for internal market measures.

Article 100a (now Article 95) has proved a decisive success. The psychology of Council operations significantly changed. Member States opposed to all or part of a proposal no longer remained inflexible in opposition, but tried to seek a compromise solution rather than see themselves outvoted. The process of deliberation thus accelerated. As for the Parliament, the Commission has observed in its annual General Reports that the Parliament's participation in the process has not significantly slowed the adoption of legislation and that about half of the Parliament's amendments are accepted by the Council.

Article 100a did not totally replace Article 100. Article 100a(2) (now Article 95(2)) excluded from the new legislative process measures relating to "fiscal provisions, * * * the free movement of persons [and] * * * the rights and interests of employed persons." These continue to be governed by Article 100 or more specific articles, such as Article 40 (ex Article 49), authorizing legislation to achieve the free movement of workers.

In an unusual action, the European Council itself insisted on Article 100a(4), commonly called an "opt-out" provision. This enables a Member State to decline to adopt all or part of a harmonized measure if the State feels such an action justified by an Article 30 interest or by a need to protect the environment or the working environment. However, the State must follow a complicated procedure to avail itself of this derogation and the Commission may request an accelerated review by the Court of Justice of the legitimacy of the State's action.

In practice, however, Member States have almost never made use of the Article 100a(4) opt-out procedure. One instance occasioned a helpful Court of Justice analysis. In France v. Commission (PCP Standards), Case C–41/93 [1994] ECR I–1829, France challenged a Commission decision under Article 100a(4) authorizing Germany to maintain higher standards for PCP, a dangerous chemical agent, than those set by a 1991 harmonization directive. The Court annulled the Commission decision, finding that it was based only on a reiteration of Germany's reasons, without any independent analysis. The Court stressed the need for the Commission to follow the general obligation pursuant to Article 253 (ex Article 190) to "state the reasons" justifying the decision. The Court underlined the importance of harmonization measures designed to merge "national markets into a single market" (¶ 19).

Article 100a (renumbered as Article 95) has been the legal basis for the adoption of a wide variety of legislation, using a broad interpretation of its purpose, to assist in "the establishment and functioning of the internal market." Thus, the Court of Justice has upheld the propriety of recourse to Article 100a in order to create an extension of the term of pharmaceutical patents, even though the Treaty contains no express power to legislate in the field of intellectual property. See Spain v. Council (Medicinal Products Certificates), excepted at page 108 *supra,* and discussed in Chapter 19E. However, in a well publicized recent judgment, the Court set limits on the use of Article 100a.

GERMANY v. PARLIAMENT AND COUNCIL

(Tobacco advertising)
[Read the excerpt at page 156, *supra,* especially ¶¶ 83–84.]

Notes and Questions

1. If Article 100a (now Article 95) can properly be employed to adopt a ban on the advertising of tobacco products by television in the Television Broadcasting Directive, and a ban on advertising of medicinal products for human use, in Directive 92/28, O.J.L. 113/13 (Apr. 30, 1992), why can't it be used to adopt a general ban on tobacco advertising? Do you agree with the Court that to do so would effectively circumvent the limited legislative powers concerning public health in Article 152 (ex Article 129)? Look at Article 153(3) concerning consumer protection measures—how does the text differ from Article 152(4)? Note that Article 149(4) on education and Article 151(5) on culture also expressly limit Community legislative competence to incentive measures.

2. On May 30, 2001 the Commission announced its intention to propose a revised directive to ban most tobacco advertising, with exceptions for the types of advertising which the Court considered could not be adopted by use of Article 95 (ex 100a) because of their negligible impact on the internal market, e.g., poster advertising and indirect advertising in hotels, restaurants and cafes. As a policy matter, do you think that such a directive would be desirable?

C. APPLICATION OF HARMONIZATION DIRECTIVES: ISSUES OF INTERPRETATION AND PREEMPTION

1. HOW SHOULD DIRECTIVES BE INTERPRETED

No matter how comprehensive and detailed harmonization directives may be, the Court of Justice is frequently called upon to interpret their provisions. This is inevitable for a variety of reasons. Thus, specific directive provisions may be imprecise, ambiguous text may have been inserted as a compromise during the drafting stage, issues may arise that were not envisaged during the legislative process, different language versions may not perfectly coincide, two different directives' provisions may overlap, etc. Does the Court of Justice have any guiding principle or principles in dealing with issues of interpretation?

In Stauder v. City of Ulm, previously discussed as a seminal judgment in basic rights protection (*supra* page 205), the Court had to reconcile substantially different official language versions of a Commission decision. The Court did not give priority to any language version, not even that used as a working draft during the legislative process. Rather, the Court held that the text should be "interpreted on the basis of both the real intention of its author and the aim he seeks to achieve, in the light [of all the language versions.]" The Court's approach is commonly described as teleological, interpreting a measure based upon the fundamental purpose it seeks to achieve.

The Court's teleological approach is somewhat analogous to the US Supreme Court's frequent resort to its perception of congressional intent in its interpretation of imprecise or ambiguous statutes. There is, however, a major difference. The Supreme Court often carefully examines the legislative history of a statute in its effort to ascertain Congress' legislative intent. Although Advocates General often discuss the legislative history of a Community measure in their opinions, the Court almost never makes reference to a draft text or a Commission, Council or Parliament document, but rather interprets the language of the final version.

In examining harmonization directives or regulations, the Court frequently interprets them liberally in order to better achieve the fundamental treaty goal in the sector concerned. In later chapters, we will see this clearly exemplified in the Court's broad interpretation of legislative measures to attain the free movement of workers or the free providing of services or the right of establishment. The following case illustrates this approach.

VEREIN GEGEN UNWESEN IN HANDEL KÖLN v. ADOLF DARBO

Case C–465/98, [2000] ECR (Apr. 4, 2000).

[Darbo manufactures strawberry jam in Austria in accordance with Austrian law. Its label calls the jam "naturrein" (naturally pure). A private consumer protection group sued to prevent the jam's sale in Germany, contending that the label reference was deceptive under the German foodstuff labeling law, which is intended to implement Directive 79/112 on the labeling, presentation and advertising of foodstuffs, O.J.L. 33/1 (Feb. 8, 1979). The directive's article 2(1) forbids labels that "could mislead the consumer to a material degree." The consumer group argued in particular that the jam contained traces of lead, cadmium and pesticides, so that the jam could not properly be called "naturally pure." When the Court of Justice was asked by the trial court to give guidance on the application of article 2(1), the Court began by indicating the proper standard to assess when consumers might be materially misled.]

20   As the Court has held on several occasions in relation to provisions similar to Article 2(1)(a) of the Directive, designed to prevent any deception of consumers and contained in a number of secondary legislative measures that are either of general application or are sectoral in scope, it is for the national court to assess whether an appellation, brand name or advertising statement may be misleading, taking into account the presumed expectations of an average consumer who is reasonably well informed and reasonably observant and circumspect.

* * *

26   According to the Verein and the Finnish Government, use of the term 'naturally pure' is likely to create in the consumer's mind the impression the d'arbo jam is a pure and natural product, free of any impurity or extraneous substance. However, the mere presence of residues of lead, cadmium and pesticides, whatever their respective amounts in the foodstuff, detracts from that description, which is therefore liable to mislead consumers as to the characteristics of the jam.

27   That argument cannot be upheld. It is common ground that lead and cadmium are present in the natural environment as a result, in particular, of air pollution and pollution of the aquatic environment* * *. Since garden fruit is grown in an environment of that kind, it is inevitably exposed to the pollutants present in it.

28   In those circumstances, even if it is assumed that, in certain cases, consumers might be unaware of that fact and thereby be misled, that risk remains minimal and cannot therefore justify a barrier to the free movement of goods [citing *Mars, supra* page 525].

29   The same conclusion is called for in relation to the presence of traces or residues of pesticides in d'arbo jam. As observed by the Advocate General * * *, the use of pesticides, even by private individuals, is one of the most usual means of combating the presence of harmful organisms on vegetables and agricultural products. Thus, the fact that garden strawberries are grown 'naturally' does not in any event mean that they are free of pesticide residues.

30   Lastly, it is necessary to verify whether the amounts of residues of lead, cadmium and pesticide measured in d'arbo jam render the presence of those substances incompatible with the description 'naturally pure' appearing on the label. Such a description might indeed be liable to mislead consumers if the foodstuff contained a high level of residues of toxic or polluting substances, even if they presented no risk to consumers' health.

[The Court concluded by noting that the traces of lead, cadmium and pesticides were well below the maximum levels permitted under either Community or national legislation, so that the "naturally pure" description did not violate Article 2(1) of the directive.]

Notes and Questions

1. In order to interpret the somewhat general language of the Foodstuffs Directive's Article 2(1), the Court resorts to the "reasonably well informed and reasonably observant" consumer standard, which we saw previously applied in the consumer protection cases in Chapter 13C. Do you agree with its application in the present case?

2. A Dutch producer sold ham in Germany under labels which the German authorities considered to be so defective as to constitute fraudulent representation under the German foodstuffs labeling rules. Again interpreting article 2(1) of the Foodstuffs Directive, the Court had to decide whether the failure to list water as an ingredient on the label, when water exceeded 5% of the product's weight, constituted a materially misleading omission. What do you think? See Criminal Proceedings against van der Laan, Case C–383/97, [1999] ECR I—731.

3. In Travel Vac v. Sanchis, Case C–423/97, [1999] ECR I—2195, Sanchis entered into a one week time-share agreement for a holiday apartment, but renounced the agreement three days later. The agreement contained a 25% liquidated damages clause if the time-share purchaser cancelled. Such a clause is not invalid under Directive 94/47 on time-share contracts for immovable properties. However, Directive 85/577 on contracts negotiated away from business premises (reproduced in the Selected Documents) grants a consumer an unconditional right to rescind within seven days a contract entered into while on an excursion organized by the trader. In this instance of overlapping directives, the Court held that Directive 85/577 did apply because Sanchis had signed the time-share agreement while on an excursion to the holiday apartment complex organized by the time-share operator. For another instance of the Court's reconciliation of overlapping directives, see *Swedish Consumer Ombudsman, infra* page 688.

2. THE ISSUE OF LOCAL LANGUAGE REQUIREMENTS

In reviewing the Dangerous Substances Directive, we noted that article 24(5) permits Member States to require that imported dangerous substances be labeled in the official national language(s). Such a provision is patently justified to ensure safe use of any product which is inherently dangerous. It is not surprising that article 20(6) of the recent Directive 98/8 on biocidal products, O.J.L. 123/1 (Apr. 24, 1998), makes the use of the national language(s) compulsory, and not merely optional, for labels.

In contrast, Directive 79/112 on the labeling, presentation and advertising of foodstuffs (reproduced in the Selected Documents) contained the following provision in the initial version of article 14 ¶ 2.

> The Member States shall, however, ensure that the sale of foodstuffs within their own territories is prohibited if the particulars [required on the labels] provided in Article 3 and Article 4(2) do not appear in a language easily understood by purchasers, unless other measures have been taken to ensure that the purchaser is informed. This provision shall not prevent such particulars from being indicated in various languages.

Although certain foodstuffs may contain ingredients which are dangerous to consumers with allergies or other health problems, foodstuffs are not dangerous for the average consumer. The harmonization of labeling requirements in articles 3 and 4 of the directive is intended both to achieve "free circulation of these products" (first recital) and "to inform and protect the consumer" (sixth recital). Whether either goal has priority over the other has posed a difficult issue for the Court of Justice.

PIAGEME & ORRS v. PEETERS (PIAGEME I)

Case C–369/89, [1991] ECR I—2971.

[A 1986 Belgian decree intended to implement the Foodstuffs Directive required that labels "must at least appear in the language or languages of the linguistic region where the foodstuffs are offered for sale." Peeters sold in Flanders bottles of mineral water labeled in French and German, but not in Dutch. Piageme, an organization of French mineral water producers and their authorized Belgian distributors, sued to enjoin future sales by Peeters (presumably a parallel importer) on the basis of the Belgian decree. When asked to provide guidance on the application of Treaty Article 28 and the directive, the Court of Justice first quoted article 14 ¶ 2 and then analyzed it.]

[13] The only obligation [of Article 14 ¶ 2] is therefore to prohibit the sale of products whose labeling is not easily understood by the purchaser rather than to require the use of a particular language.

[14] It is true that, according to a literal interpretation, art. 14 does not preclude a national law which allows, for the information of the consumer, only the use of the language or languages of the region where the products are sold, in so far as such a law would allow purchasers to understand easily the particulars appearing on the products. The language of the linguistic region is the language which seems to be the most "easily understood."

[15] Such an interpretation of art. 14 fails, however, to take account of the aims of the directive. It follows from the first three recitals in the preamble that Directive 79/112 seeks in particular to eliminate the differences which exist between national provisions and which hinder the free movement of goods. It is because of that aim that art. 14 is limited to the requirement of a language easily understood by the purchaser and authorized where the relevant particulars do not appear in a language easily understood if "other measures have been taken to ensure that the purchaser is informed."

[16] It follows from the foregoing that, on the one hand, imposing a stricter obligation than the use of a language easily understood, that is to say, for example, the exclusive use of the language of a linguistic region and, on the other hand, failing to acknowledge the possibility of ensuring that the purchaser is informed by other measures, goes beyond the requirements of the directive. The obligation exclusively to use the language of the linguistic region constitutes a measure having equivalent effect to a quantitative restriction on imports, prohibited by art. [28] of the Treaty.

Notes and Questions

1. The Court in ¶ 15 emphasizes the first goal of the directive, namely to promote the free movement of foodstuffs. What other measures could ensure that the "purchaser is informed?" Would a sign in Dutch adjacent to the products

suffice? Widespread advertising? Note that the product here is mineral water, singularly unlikely to occasion health risks for any consumer. However, Belgium has strongly emphasized the status of the customary language in each of its regions in an effort to reduce social tensions. Is the Court's approach apt to be favorably received in Flanders? Should the cultural implications of the case influence the Court?

2. A language labeling issue next arose in Meyhui v. Schott Zwiesel Glaswerke, Case C–51/93, [1994] ECR I–3879, concerning the proper construction of Directive 69/493 on crystal glass, which harmonized rules on the standards for the manufacture and labeling of crystal glass products. An Annex divided crystal glass into four quality categories. The Annex specified that the label description for a lower quality product, crystalline, must be in the "languages of the country in which the goods are marketed." When a German producer refused to affix labels in French and Dutch for crystalline intended for sale in Belgium, a Belgian importer sued the producer.

Advocate General Gulman thought that ¶ 16 in *Piageme I* meant that a labeling rule could never mandate only the local language without violating Article 28, and accordingly considered the Annex provision could not be binding. (Remember that a directive's provisions cannot restrict the free movement of goods—see *Commissionaires Reunis, supra* page 456.) The Court agreed that a local language labeling obligation caused additional costs to a producer, thus representing "a barrier to intra-Community trade" (¶ 13). Nonetheless the Court found the local language provision justified to prevent consumer deception, particularly for the average consumer. The Court therefore concluded:

19   The fact that consumers in a Member State in which the products are marketed are to be informed in the language or languages of that country is therefore an appropriate means of protection. In this regard it should be held that the hypothesis referred to by the national court that another language may be easily comprehensible to the purchaser is of only marginal importance.

PIAGEME v. PEETERS NV (PIAGEME II)

Case C–85/94, [1995] ECR I–2955.

[The trial court obviously had difficulty in applying the Court's answers in *Piageme I* and referred further questions. The Court initially reiterated its position that the Belgian requirement to use "the official language" of a region could not automatically be substituted for the directive's requirement to use "a language easily understood by purchasers," because the latter phrase was "designed to ensure that the consumer is provided with information rather than to impose the use of a specific language." (¶ 15.) The Court then went on to give guidance on how the directive's customer information requirements should be satisfied:]

23   The aim of Article 14 [of the Directive] is to ensure that the consumer is given easy access to the compulsory particulars specified in the Directive.

24   In order to satisfy the need to inform and protect consumers, it is necessary for them always to have access to the compulsory particulars specified in the Directive, not only at the time of purchase, but also at that of consumption. That is particularly true as regards the date of minimum durability and any special storage conditions or conditions of use of the product.

25   It should also be borne in mind that the ultimate consumer is not necessarily the person who purchased the foodstuffs.

26   It follows that consumer protection is not ensured by measures other than labeling such as, for example, information supplied at the sales point or as part of wide-ranging advertising campaigns.

27   All the compulsory particulars specified in the Directive must appear on the labeling in a language easily understood by purchasers or by means of other measures such as designs, symbols or pictograms.

28   It is for the national court to determine in each individual case whether what appears on the labeling is such as to give consumers full information as to the compulsory particulars specified in the Directive.

29   It is also for the national court to determine in each individual case whether the compulsory particulars given in a language other than the language mainly used in the Member State or region concerned can be easily understood by consumers in that State or region.

30   As to that, various factors may be relevant, though not decisive in themselves; for example, the possible similarity of words in different languages, the widespread knowledge amongst the population concerned of more than one language, or the existence of special circumstances such as a wide-ranging advertising campaign or widespread distribution of the product, provided that it can be established that the consumer is given sufficient information.

31   The reply to the second and third questions must therefore be that all the compulsory particulars specified in Directive 79/112 must appear on the labeling in a language easily understood by consumers in the State or region concerned or by means of other measures such as designs, symbols or pictograms. The ease with which the information supplied can be understood must be assessed in the light of all the circumstances in each individual case.

Notes and Questions

1.   Do you think the Belgian court can now forbid the sale in Flanders of French and German mineral water that is not labeled in Dutch, based on a finding that this is necessary for consumer protection, rather than to protect its "official language"? Or is there enough leeway for alternative modes of informing the consumer in the Court's guidance that a trial court could hardly make such a finding? For a useful appraisal of the Court's approach, see the casenote by M. Verbruggen, 2 Colum. J. Eur. L. 164 (1995–96).

2.   In *Geffroy*, Case C–366/98, [2000] ECR ___ (Sept. 12, 2000), Geffroy was subjected to substantial fines for offering for sale Coca Cola, Red Raw ginger ale and Merry Down cider labeled in English, in violation of a 1984 French decree that required all foodstuff labels to be in French. The court of appeals referred several questions on the application of Community law. Drawing upon *Piageme II*, the Court unequivocally declared that Article 28 and the directive's article 14 precluded "a national rule ... requiring the use of a specific language for the labeling of foodstuffs, without allowing for the possibility of using another language easily understood by purchasers or of ensuring that the purchaser is informed by other means." (¶ 28). Do you think Coca–Cola is so well known that it

need not be labeled in French? Would you consider English labels for the other beverages to be easily understood in France? In Germany? In the Netherlands?

3. When the Commission proposed several technical amendments to the Foodstuffs Directive, Parliament insisted upon an amendment inserting a new Article 16. The first paragraph replicated the text of Article 14 ¶ 2, except that "consumer" replaced "purchaser"—a sensible change in view of *Piageme II.* Article 16 (2) states:

> 2. Within its own territory, the Member State in which the product is marketed may, in accordance with the rules of the Treaty, stipulate that those labeling particulars shall be given in one or more languages which it shall determine from among the official languages of the Community.

The amended text gives a Member State the option to require that the label be in one or more of its official language(s). Does this represent sound policy? Would it change the result in *Piageme II* or in *Geffroy?* Is it consonant with the Court's reading of Article 28? The Foodstuffs Directive was reissued in a codified version, incorporating all amendments to date, in O.J.L 109/29 (May 6, 2000).

COLIM v. BIGG'S CONTINENT NOORD

Case C–33/97, [1999] ECR I—3175.

[Bigg's department store in the Netherlands sold foodstuffs, cosmetics, detergents and pet food labeled in languages other than Dutch. The 1991 Dutch Consumer Information and Protection Law requires labels and instructions for use to be in the language of the region of marketing, i.e., Dutch in this case. In an action to enjoin Bigg's from further marketing of products not in compliance with the law, the court referred questions to the Court of Justice.]

33   A point to be noted at the outset is that, for certain categories of product, Community directives require the national language or languages to be used in order to enhance consumer or public health protection.

34   When those directives fully harmonize the language requirements applicable for a given product, the Member States cannot impose additional language requirements.

35   By contrast, where there is only partial Community harmonization or none at all, the Member States in principle retain the power to impose additional language requirements.

36   However, while language requirements of the kind laid down by the national legislation at issue in the main proceedings are not technical regulations within the meaning of Directive 83/189, [discussed in section D, *infra*], they do constitute a barrier to intra-Community trade in so far as products coming from other Member states have to be given different labeling involving additional packaging costs [citing *Meyhui*].

[The Court then discussed whether the local language labeling rules could be considered to be "justified by a public-interest objective taking precedence over the free movement of goods" (¶ 38).]

39   [I]nformation addressed to the purchaser or end-user which can be communicated only by words is of no practical use unless it is given in a language which he can understand.

[40]   However, a national measure imposing such language requirements must, in any event, be proportionate to the aim pursued (see *Meyhui*).

[41]   It follows, first, that a measure requiring the use of a language which consumers can readily understand must not exclude the possible use of other means of informing them, such as designs, symbols or pictograms. It is for the national court to determine in each case whether what appears on the labeling is such as to give consumers full information [citing *Piageme II*].

[42]   Second, a measure of that kind must be restricted to the information made mandatory by the Member State concerned. Decisions as to the availability, in the language of the consumer, of information which, in the view of that State, need not be made mandatory must be left to the trader responsible for marketing the product, who may have it translated if he wishes.

Notes and Questions

1.   In *Colim,* the Court shifted from interpretation of directives to a direct application of free movement of goods principles. Can the judgment be construed as endorsing the approach of the new article 16 in the Foodstuffs Directive? Has the Court effectively transformed its gloss upon article 14 ¶ 1 in *Piageme II* into rules with Treaty force? In any event, do you consider that the Court has, or has not, struck the right balance between the goal of market integration and that of consumer protection?

3.   PREEMPTION OF NATIONAL RULES BY COMPREHENSIVE HARMONIZATION

The most important legal issue raised by harmonization is the extent to which a harmonizing directive prevents a Member State from supplementary regulation, whether stricter or simply different, in the field covered by the directive. (See the general review of preemption in Chapter 4.) The issue is particularly apt to arise when a Member State has prior legislation which the State does not repeal when it adopts the directive, or when a State subsequently passes new and stricter regulations to achieve a higher level of consumer protection or technical quality or safety.

In the US, the same issue has frequently arisen in application of the Interstate Commerce Clause and is characterized as one of possible preemption of state rules by a federal law. The test for determining when a federal law preempts state rules has evolved considerably in the last century. While formerly the Supreme Court was more inclined to develop various legal doctrines which justified preemption, its more modern view is that federal and state regulation can readily coexist and preemption occurs only when there is "evidence of a congressional intent to preempt the specific field covered by the state law." Wardair Canada, Inc. v. Florida Dept. of Revenue, 477 U.S. 1, 6, 106 S.Ct. 2369, 2372, 91 L.Ed.2d 1 (1986).

Given the volume of harmonization directives now in force, it is not surprising that the Court of Justice has frequent occasion to rule on the validity of national regulations that differ somehow from a directive's terms. One of the most common issues is whether the harmonization directive can be said to have fully harmonized the rules in a given sector, leaving accordingly no room for supplementary national rules. Whether federal rules are so comprehensive as to leave no room for state rules is a parallel issue in the U.S. Consider the following cases.

PUBBLICO MINISTERO v. RATTI

Case 148/78, [1979] ECR 1629

[For the facts of this case, see the excerpt at page 256. After deciding that the 1973 directive on dangerous solvents had direct effect, the Court went on to consider whether the directive preempted the 1963 Italian law.]

A. THE INTERPRETATION OF DIRECTIVE NO 73/173

10 That directive proved necessary because dangerous substances and preparations were subject to rules in the Member States which displayed considerable differences, particularly as regards labeling, packaging and classification according to the degree of risk presented by the said products.

11 Those differences constituted a barrier to trade and to the free movement of goods and directly affected the establishment and functioning of the market in dangerous preparations such as solvents used regularly in industrial, farming and craft activities, as well as for domestic purposes.

12 In order to eliminate those differences the directive made a number of express provisions concerning the classification, packaging and labeling of the products in question.

* * *

25 In the second question the national court asks, essentially, whether, in incorporating the provisions of the directive on solvents into its internal legal order, the State to which it is addressed may prescribe "obligations and limitations which are more precise and detailed than, or at all events different from, those set out in the directive", requiring in particular information not required by the directive to be affixed to the containers.

26 The combined effect of Articles 3 to 8 of Directive No 73/173 is that only solvents which "comply with the provisions of this directive and the annex thereto" may be placed on the market and that Member States are not entitled to maintain, parallel with the rules laid down by the said directive for imports, different rules for the domestic market.

27 Thus it is a consequence of the system introduced by Directive No 73/173 that a Member State may not introduce into its national legislation conditions which are more restrictive than those laid down in the directive in question, or which are even more detailed or in any event different, as regards the classification, packaging and labeling of solvents and that this prohibition on the imposition of restrictions not provided for applies both to the direct marketing of the products on the home market and to imported products.

* * *

33 Thus the answer to the national court must be that Directive No 73/173 must be interpreted as meaning that it is not permissible for national

provisions to prescribe that containers shall bear a statement of the presence of ingredients of the products in question in terms going beyond those laid down by the said directive.

[The Italian court's final question was whether the supplemental labeling requirements could be justified in terms of the protection of health exception to free movement of goods under Treaty Article 30. The Court responded:]

36   When, pursuant to Article [94, ex 100] of the Treaty, Community directives provide for the harmonization of measures necessary to ensure the protection of the health of humans and animals and establish Community procedures to supervise compliance therewith, recourse to Article [30] ceases to be justified and the appropriate controls must henceforth be carried out and the protective measures taken in accordance with the scheme laid down by the harmonizing directive.

37   Directive No 73/173 provides that where a Member State established that a dangerous preparation, although satisfying the requirements of that directive, presents a health or safety risk, it may have recourse, temporarily and subject to the supervision of the Commission, to a protective measure provided for in Article 9 of the directive in accordance with the procedure laid down in that article.

38   It follows that national provisions going beyond those laid down in Directive No 73/173 are compatible with Community law, only if they have been adopted in accordance with the procedures and formalities prescribed in Article 9 of the said directive.

Notes and Questions

1.   The hard issue presented in *Ratti* is whether Italy may enforce stricter health or consumer protection standards than those set down in a harmonizing directive. What has happened to Italy's powers under Article 30? *Ratti* demonstrates a very important principle: when a harmonization directive is intended to deal completely with a health or safety issue, States can no longer rely on Article 30. Do you think that this represents a sound Community policy? What is the trade-off for Italy's inability to protect its consumers at the higher level that it desires?

2.   In KG in Firma Eau de Cologne * * * No. 4711 v. Provide SRL, Case C–150/88, [1989] ECR 3891, the Court held that the provisions of the 1976 cosmetic products directive completely covered the labeling obligations of producers. Italy therefore could not enforce its law, which required that a label indicate the quantity and quality of vitamins contained in a cosmetic product, as well as the name of the Italian importer or distributor.

3.   In Commission v. Germany (Pharmaceutical expiration dates), Case C–317/92, [1994] ECR I–2039, the Court held that when Directive 65/65 required all pharmaceutical product containers to indicate the "expiry date in plain language," Germany could not require the use of either June 30 or December 31 as the sole expiration dates. Although the German approach facilitated pharmacy staff checks of shelf life of products, this did not constitute a sufficiently high interest to justify the restriction on imports, which would have to be specially labeled for Germany.

4.   A 1992 Belgian decree required anyone marketing a foodstuff to which nutrients have been added to make a prior notification to the Ministry of Public

Health. The notification is used to provide essential information about the product and the added nutrients. The decree further required the label for such foodstuffs with added nutrients to indicate the notification number. When this label requirement was challenged by the Commission, the Court considered the Belgian rule to be product-related, since it would cause an importer to incur added packaging and labeling costs. The Court further held that including the notification reference on the label did not provide the consumer with any helpful information that might protect the consumer's health. See Commission v. Belgium (Nutrient notification on labels), Case C–217–99, [2000] ECR ___ (Nov. 16, 2000).

5. The Supreme Court has held that the principal test for preemption is whether "Congress has legislated comprehensively, thus occupying an entire field of regulation and leaving no room for the States to supplement federal law * * *" Louisiana Public Service Com'n v. FCC, 476 U.S. 355, 368, 106 S.Ct. 1890, 1896, 90 L.Ed.2d 369 (1986). Rice v. Santa Fe Elevator Corp., 331 U.S. 218, 67 S.Ct. 1146, 91 L.Ed. 1447 (1947), is a good example of the Supreme Court's review of federal legislation before concluding that it was "so pervasive as to make reasonable the inference that Congress left no room for the states to supplement it." Id. at 230, 67 S.Ct. at 1152, 91 L.Ed. at 1459. That the issue can be difficult is shown by the 5–3 division of the Court in Morales v. Trans World Airlines, Inc., 504 U.S. 374, 112 S.Ct. 2031, 119 L.Ed.2d 157 (1992) (state guidelines to prevent deceptive air fare advertising held to be preempted by the Airline Deregulation Act.).

KEMIKALIENINSPEKTIONEN v. TOOLEX ALPHA

Case C—473/98, [2000] ECR ___ (July 11, 2000).

[A 1991 Swedish regulation forbid the use of trichloroethylene for industrial purposes. A 1997 amendment permitted the Chemicals Inspectorate to grant individual exemptions where an enterprise can show that it has no practicable alternative and that there is not an unacceptable exposure through the use of trichlorethylene. When Toolex was refused an exemption, it challenged the general ban itself under Community law. The Commission agreed with Toolex that the Community legislation described earlier in this chapter—the dangerous substance directive (see the Selected Documents), together with the substance risk evaluation regulation—constituted a comprehensive regulation that prevented Sweden from prescribing a general prohibition of trichlorethylene. When the trial court referred questions on the application of the Community rules, the Court rejected the Commission view.]

29   The classification directive covers a very clearly defined field, namely the notification, classification, packaging and labeling of dangerous substances. As regards the use of such substances, the classification directive merely requires that their packaging bear safety recommendations designed to inform the general public of the particular care that should be taken when handling the substance in question. It does not harmonize the conditions under which dangerous substances may be marketed or used, which are the very matters that fall within the purview of national legislation such as that in issue in the main proceedings.

* * *

31   Nor, finally, does the risks evaluation regulation, in itself, preclude the Member States from exercising such a power. Its objective is to establish a procedure for evaluating the risks associated with existing substances and

identifying priority substances which, because of their potential effects on man and the environment, require immediate attention at Community level. Although it is intended to assist in the management of such risks at Community level, the risks evaluation regulation neither imposes obligations nor harmonizes rules on the use of substances in general or trichlorethylene in particular.

[The Court thus interpreted the Community legislation concerning dangerous substances as not being so comprehensive that they prevented State regulation of the industrial use of trichloroethylene. The Court then easily concluded that the Swedish ban on trichloroethylene constituted a measure equivalent to a quantitative restriction. Next, the Court turned to the ban's possible justification under Article 30.]

41 The Swedish Government submits that trichlorethylene affects the central nervous system, the liver and kidneys. The fact that it is highly volatile increases the chances of exposure in circumstances that might result in damage to health. Inhaling the substance can cause fatigue, headaches, and difficulties with memory and concentration.

* * *

45 Taking account of the latest medical research on the subject, and also the difficulty of establishing the threshold above which exposure to trichlorethylene poses a serious health risk to humans, given the present state of the research, there is no evidence in this case to justify a conclusion by the Court that national legislation such as that at issue in the case in the main proceedings goes beyond what is necessary to achieve the objective in view.

46 In particular, the system of individual exemptions, granted subject to conditions, established by the Swedish regulation appears to be appropriate and proportionate in that it offers increased protection for workers, whilst at the same time taking account of the undertakings' requirements in the matter of continuity.

49 In light of the foregoing considerations, national legislation which lays down a general prohibition on the use of trichlorethylene for industrial purposes and establishes a system of individual exemptions, granted subject to conditions, is justified under Article [30] of the Treaty on grounds of the protection of health of humans.

Notes and Questions

1. The Commission certainly was not unreasonable in believing that the combination of the dangerous substances directive and the risk evaluation regulation amounted to comprehensive regulation. Why did the Court disagree? Note that the Swedish ban on industrial use of trichloroethylene was intended to protect industrial workers from health risk, not consumers of a product, so labeling or use instructions were not at issue.

2. In Commission v. Italy (Heater harmonization), Case C—112/97, [1999] ECR I—1821, the Court held that Directive 90/396 on appliances burning gaseous fuels constituted an exhaustive regulation of the field, replacing any national safety or health provisions, so that Italy's ban of a certain type of heater for alleged safety reasons was preempted. The Court noted that Italy had not made use of a directive provision that enabled a State to remove an appliance from the

market temporarily for safety reasons, but required immediate notification of such an emergency safeguard to the Commission, which could then review the matter. Article 31 of the dangerous substances directive sets forth a parallel procedure. Why shouldn't Sweden have been obliged to follow article 31 when it prohibited the industrial use of trichloroethylene?

COMMISSION v. UNITED KINGDOM

(Dim-dip lighting)
Case 60/86, 1988 ECR 3921.

[Directive 70/156, O.J.–English Spec.Ed. 1970–I, 96, set up a system of type approval for parts of motor vehicles. This was supplemented by Directive 76/756 on lighting and light-signalling devices on motor vehicles, which harmonized national rules as to these vehicle parts. In 1984, the UK adopted a regulation requiring all vehicles manufactured after October 1, 1986 to have "dim-dip" headlights. The UK believed that requiring this device would significantly improve road safety.

In an Article 226 proceeding, the Commission argued that the directive does not permit Member States to require any lighting devices for vehicles except those authorized in its annex. The UK argued that the directive's language was ambiguous and permitted States to require lighting devices in addition to those authorized in the annex. The Court analyzed the 1976 directive's language and concluded that the list of authorized lighting devices in the annex was exhaustive and did not permit later additions by Member States. The Court then continued:]

10   It is clear from the documents before the Court that the reason for which dim-dip devices were not included in the provisions, even as optional devices, is that the technical committee of national experts did not consider them acceptable given the state of technical progress at the time.
   * * *

11   Such an interpretation of the exhaustive nature of the list of lighting and light-signaling devices set out in Annex I to the directive is consistent with the purpose of Directive 70/156/EEC which is to reduce, and even eliminate, hindrances to trade within the Community resulting from the fact that mandatory technical requirements differ from one Member State to another * * *.

12   It follows that the Member States cannot unilaterally require manufacturers who have complied with the harmonized technical requirements set out in Directive 76/756/EEC to comply with a requirement which is not imposed by that directive, since motor vehicles complying with the technical requirements laid down therein must be able to move freely within the common market.

13   It must therefore be declared that, by prohibiting, in breach of Council Directive 76/756/EEC the use of motor vehicles * * * which are not equipped with a dim-dip device, the United Kingdom has failed to fulfil its obligations under Community law.

Notes and Questions

1.   Note that the judgment not only prevents the UK from requiring "dim-dip" headlights on vehicles imported into the UK, but also from requiring them

for UK-manufactured vehicles. This is obviously because a substantial number of UK-produced cars are exported to other States which do not allow "dim-dip" lights. But why shouldn't the UK be allowed to require "dim-dip" lights on UK-manufactured cars which are intended to be sold in the UK?

2. Let us assume that "dim-dip" headlights are a desirable innovation which improves road safety (although Advocate General Mancini said that this UK view was "disputed in numerous quarters"). Obviously a 1976 harmonization directive with an exhaustive list of authorized devices freezes the technological state of the art. How can a Member State improve consumer protection when a superior device is invented? Since amending an existing directive is a slow and laborious process, it would be unfortunate if this were the only solution.

Council harmonization directives are indeed frequently amended. However, the slowness of the Council amendment process has prompted a different approach: some directives delegate to the Commission the power to amend the lists of devices or products contained in the annexes in order to adapt the directive to technical progress. The Commission obviously can act faster than the Council. This is one of the most important examples of the delegation of rule-making authority to the Commission.

4. EXPRESS OR IMPLIED AUTHORIZATION FOR SUPPLEMENTARY STATE RULES

Many harmonization directives, particularly in the fields of environmental protection, consumer protection, and employee rights, contain express provisions authorizing Member States to have stricter rules in order to achieve the directive's goal. Only occasionally do these require any Court interpretation. (The US Congress sometimes adopts similar provisions or even expressly authorizes supplemental state regulation, e.g., in antitrust and securities law.) In addition, some harmonization directives expressly declare that they represent only initial, or first stage, harmonization, which implicitly authorizes supplemental (but not contradictory) State rules. Finally, the language of particular clauses in some directives that would generally be considered to represent fairly exhaustive coverage of a field may implicitly permit State rules to go further in regulating to achieve the goal of the directive. The following cases illustrate each of these possibilities.

BUET v. MINISTÈRE PUBLIC

Case 382/87, [1989] ECR 1235.

[Directive 85/577 on contracts negotiated away from business premiums (see the Selected Documents) contains various consumer protection provisions, notably the consumer's right to cancel the contract within seven days in article 5. A 1972 French law forbids canvassing at home for the signature of contracts for a course of instruction. When the UK company, Encyclopedia Britannica, marketed a course of English language tapes at prospective buyers' homes, its French manager was fined and sentenced to a jail term. On appeal, the Paris Court of Appeal raised Article 234 questions as to the compatibility of the French law with the directive and Article 28. The Court dealt summarily with the harmonization preemption issue.]

16 [W]hile the Council Directive requires Member States to ensure that consumers have the right to cancel a contract of sale concluded at their

home, Article 8 allows the State to adopt or maintain more favourable provisions to protect consumers. In the last recital in the preamble to the directive the Council expressly recognized that Member States might introduce or maintain a total or partial prohibition on the conclusion of contracts away from business premises.

[The Court devoted most of the judgment to analyzing whether the total ban on the conclusion of contracts for instruction courses at a consumer's home was compatible with Article 28.]

(A) The Existence of an Obstacle to the Free Movement of Goods

7   [T]o compel a trader either to adopt advertising or sales promotion schemes which differ from one Member State to another may constitute an obstacle to imports even if the legislation in question applies to domestic and imported products without distinction.

8   That finding applies *a fortiori* when the rules in question deprive the trader concerned of the possibility of using not a means of advertising but a method of marketing whereby he realizes almost all his sales.

9   Application of a prohibition on canvassing in order to sell foreign-language teaching material from another Member State must therefore be regarded as constituting an obstacle to imports.

(B) The Possibility of Justifying the Obstacle in Question by the Need to Protect Consumers

10   The Court has consistently held [citing *Cassis de Dijon*] that in the absence of common rules, obstacles to movement within the Community resulting from disparities between the national rules must be accepted, provided the rules are applied without distinction to domestic and imported products, as being necessary in order to satisfy mandatory requirements such as the protection of consumers and fair trading.

11   It is common ground that the French legislature adopted the prohibition of canvassing in question out of concern to protect consumers against the risk of ill-considered purchases. However, * * * such rules must be proportionate to the goals pursued, and if a Member State has at its disposal less restrictive means of obtaining the same goals, it is under an obligation to make use of them.

12   * * * To guard against [the risk of ill-considered purchases] it is normally sufficient to ensure that purchasers have the right to cancel a contract concluded in their home.

13   [However,] there is greater risk of an ill-considered purchase when the canvassing is for enrollment for a course of instruction or the sale of educational material. The potential purchaser often belongs to a category of people who, for one reason or another, are behind with their education and are seeking to catch up. That makes them particularly vulnerable when faced with salesmen of educational material who attempt to persuade them that if they use that material they will have better employment prospects. Moreover, as is apparent from the documents, it is as a result of numerous complaints caused by such abuses, such as the sale of

out-of-date courses, that the legislature enacted the ban on canvassing at issue.

* * *

[15] In those circumstances it is permissible for the national legislature of the Member State to consider that giving consumers a right of cancellation is not sufficient protection and that it is necessary to ban canvassing at private dwellings.

Notes and Questions

1. This 1985 "door-to-door" sales directive is a harmonization measure in the Community's consumer protection program (see Chapter 35). As Advocate General Tesauro observed, in this home sales technique "the consumer is exposed to a serious risk of fraud * * * especially if he is one of those who * * * may be more open to influence, such as the elderly, housewives or immigrant workers." [1989] ECR at 1240.

2. Note that the French law is stricter than the directive, because it totally prohibits a type of home sales, namely, courses of instruction. However, the 1985 directive's preamble specifically indicates an intent to permit Member States to adopt a total or partial prohibition of home sales. The directive is thus an example of the type that allows States to go beyond the level of harmonization for the purpose of greater consumer protection.

3. Now for some review of Chapter 13 D. If *Buet* had been decided after the *Keck* judgment, *supra* page 522, would the Court still reach the conclusion it did in ¶¶ 7–9? The judgment's consumer interest analysis in ¶¶ 10–15 is still valid— *Buet* continues to be cited approvingly on this aspect.

4. Directive 64/54 on preservatives for use in foodstuffs is an example of one whose recitals expressly state that it represents only the "first stage" in harmonization, setting out in an annex a list of all preservatives whose use is authorized throughout the Community. The directive envisages a second stage in which the foodstuffs will be specified to which identified preservatives may be added. In Ministère Public v. Grunert, Case 88/79, [1980] ECR 1827, Grunert was prosecuted for using lactic acid and citric acid as preservatives for pork. French law did not permit the use of lactic acid or citric acid as preservatives. In responding to referred questions, the Court of Justice held that in applying a first stage directive "Member States have retained a certain discretion to determine their own rules concerning the addition of preservatives" to various foodstuffs (¶ 8). However, the Court added that a State cannot totally forbid the use of a preservative authorized by the directive, which means that France must permit the use of lactic acid and citric acid for some type of foodstuffs.

In subsequent cases, the Court set limits on a State's discretion in supplementing such a first stage harmonization directive. Thus, in Ministère Public v. Muller, Case 304/84, [1986] ECR 1511, the Court permitted France to supplement the 1974 directive on emulsifiers in foodstuffs with legislation forbidding the use of any emulsifier until after its approval as a harmless agent in an administrative review process. However, the Court placed upon France the burden of proof that an emulsifier which was not approved presented a health danger:

[T]he marketing of such foodstuffs must be authorized, under a procedure easily accessible to manufacturers and traders, if the addition of the substance in question meets a genuine need and presents no danger to public health. It is for the competent national authorities to show in each case, in light of national eating habits and with due regard to the results of international scientific research, that the rules are necessary to give effective protection to the interests referred to in Article [28] of the Treaty. (*Id.* at 1530.)

THE QUEEN v. SECRETARY OF STATE FOR HEALTH EX PARTE GALLAHER

Case C–11/92, [1993] ECR I–3545.

[Directive 89/622 on the labeling of tobacco products provides that cigarette packages must display the warning, "Tobacco seriously damages health," on one large surface and a second specific health warning on the other large surface. One package side must display, in legible print in the language(s) of the country of sale, a precise indication of tar and nicotine yields. The warnings and the yield indication must cover "at least 4%" of the surface. The UK implementing regulation set the warnings and yield indication size at 6%, instead of 4%, for domestic cigarettes. Imported cigarettes were permitted if they satisfied the 4% requirement. When several UK tobacco producers challenged the UK regulation as implicitly forbidden by the Directive, the trial court referred the issue.]

10   [Directive 89/622] is designed to eliminate barriers to trade which might arise as a result of differences in national provisions on the labeling of tobacco products and thereby impede the establishment and operation of the internal market. With that end in view, the directive contains common rules concerning the health warnings to appear on the unit packet of tobacco products and the indications of the tar and nicotine yields to appear on cigarette packets.

11   These common rules are not always identical in nature.

12   Some of them give Member States no discretion to impose requirements stricter than those provided for in the directive, or even to impose more detailed or at any rate different requirements, with regard to the labeling of tobacco products.

13   Under Article 8(2), Member States still have the right to lay down * * * requirements concerning the import, sale and consumption of tobacco products which they deem necessary in order to protect public health, but only in so far as such requirements do not imply any changes to labeling as laid down in the directive.

14   Other provisions of the directive allow the Member States a degree of discretion to adapt the labeling of tobacco products to the requirements of public health protection. One such provision is Article 4(2), which allows the Member States to select the specific warnings which must appear on cigarette packets by choosing them from those listed in the annex to the directive. * * *

15   [The directive is in furtherance of] the Resolution of the Council * * * of 7 July 1986 on a programme of action of the European Communities against cancer to which the fifth recital in the preamble to the directive refers. Under that programme, the measures to be adopted by the Community with a view to limiting and reducing the consumption of tobacco were to be based on the practical experience gained in the various Member States

and were to contribute to increasing the effectiveness of national programmes and actions.

16 Member States which have made use of the powers conferred by the provisions containing minimum requirements cannot, according to Article 8 of the directive, prohibit or restrict the sale within their territory of products imported from other Member States which comply with the directive.

17 In order to reply to the question referred by the national court, it is therefore necessary to determine whether Articles 3(3) and 4(4) of the directive still allow the Member States a degree of latitude to require, with regard to domestic production, that the indications and warnings in question cover in each case more than 4% of the relevant surface area.

18 The applicants * * * consider that the rules in the directive requiring the indications and warnings to cover at least 4% of the relevant surface area must be incorporated as such by the Member States into their national law because the provisions in question confer on them no discretion. They argue that it is for manufacturers of tobacco products to decide whether the indications and warnings should cover a larger surface area. * * *

19 Those arguments cannot be accepted.

20 Articles 3(3) and 4(4) of the directive contain provisions directed to the Member States, to whom the directive is addressed, and not to the manufacturers of tobacco products, who have no interest in using a greater surface area for the indications and warnings in question. The expression 'at least' contained in both articles must be interpreted as meaning that, if they consider it necessary, Member States are at liberty to decide that the indications and warnings are to cover a greater surface area in view of the level of public awareness of the health risks associated with tobacco consumption.

21 The case-law on labeling cited by the applicants * * * concerns directives whose scope differs from that of Directive 89/622. So far as the decision in *Ratti* is concerned, the Court there ruled not on the interpretation of Article 6(1) of Directive 73/173, which also contains the expression 'at least', but on other provisions of that directive and on the nature of its provisions in general.

22 Admittedly, as the applicants * * * have pointed out, this interpretation of the provisions may imply less favourable treatment for national products in comparison with imported products and leaves in existence some inequalities in conditions of competition. However, those consequences are attributable to the degree of harmonization sought by the provisions in question, which lay down minimum requirements.

Notes and Questions

1. Unlike the directive examined in *Buet*, the tobacco labelling directive did not expressly state that it permitted stricter Member State regulation. Do you agree with the Court that the rather ambiguous words, "at least," implicitly permit States to go further? In a perceptive case note, 19 Eur. L. Rev. 55 (1994), Professor Weatherill views the Court's approach as a sharp shift from the classic preemption theory in *Ratti*. He wonders whether the judgment reflects a greater

respect for the principle of subsidiarity, allowing Member States to experiment with innovative regulations, or whether it constitutes a "political" judgment, taken to avoid further UK criticism of Court doctrines. In any event, do you believe the Court's result represents good policy? Also note ¶¶ 16 and 22. Might the UK regulation indirectly promote cigarette imports? Why does the Court accept this potential competitive inequality?

2. In contrast to *Gallaher*, in Ministero delle Finanze v. Phillip Morris Belgium SA, Case 222/91, [1993] ECR I–3469, the Court held that Italy could not require tobacco producers to affix two specific health warnings on cigarette packages. The Court interpreted the language used in the relevant articles of Directive 89/622 as implicitly forbidding more than one warning, in part because of the Court's concern that two warnings in smaller print might not sufficiently attract the attention of smokers.

3. Suppose that the UK forbid outdoor advertising (e.g., billboards or signs) of cigarettes within a 1000 foot radius of a school or playground. Would such a rule be implicitly preempted by the tobacco labeling directive? In Lorillard Tobacco Co. v. Reilly, 533 U.S. 525, 121 S.Ct. 2404, 150 L.Ed.2d 532 (2001), Massachusetts had adopted such an outdoor advertising ban. Reversing the First Circuit, the Supreme Court held that the ban (and other restrictions on cigarette advertising) was preempted by the Federal Cigarette Labeling and Advertising Act, which mandates health warnings on cigarette packages and in advertising for cigarettes. The Supreme Court relied heavily on the Act's provision forbidding any state "prohibition based on smoking and health ... with respect to the advertising or promotion of cigarettes."

4. Valuable analyses of the Court doctrines on preemption in contrast with US views are provided by E. Cross, Preemption of Member State Law in the EEC, 29 Common Mkt. L. Rev. 447 (1992), and A. Goucha Soares, Preemption, Conflicts of Power and Subsidiarity, 23 Eur. L. Rev. 132 (1998) . .

D. THE "NEW APPROACH" TO TECHNICAL HARMONIZATION

1. PRIOR NOTIFICATION OF NEW STATE RULES

Despite the substantial number of technical rules and standards directives adopted in the 1970s, the Community found in the early 1980s that the volume of Member State technical barriers to trade was inexorably increasing. This was due principally to the rapid rate of technological advances and to the demand for consumer and environmental protection legislation.

The initial step taken to alleviate this situation was the adoption of Directive 83/89 on the provision of information on technical standards and regulations (reproduced in the Selected Documents). The purpose of this directive, sometimes called the "transparency" or "slow-down" directive, was to ensure a certain level of coordination between Member States and the Commission before a State adopted a new technical rule or standard.

The directive obligates a State to notify the Commission in advance of the adoption of any legally binding regulation which sets a "technical specification," defined as any product requirement as to quality, performance, safety, testing, packaging or labelling. The Commission must immediately notify all other states. The Commission or any other State may demand a six-month delay in the adoption of the proposed State regulation in order to consider possible amendments. The Commission may demand a year's delay if it decides to propose a harmonization directive in the sector involved.

The directive also covers technical specification standards produced by public or private standards bodies or industry groups, as well as codes of practice or professional codes, because, although they are not usually legally binding, they significantly influence product quality and consumer preferences. Periodic reports of such proposed standards must be provided by each Member State to the Commission and to a new technical consulting committee representing all Member States. This committee may recommend changes in the proposed standard, or request a delay in adoption of the standard pending the consideration of a Community standard instead.

The Commission believes that the notification system of this "transparency" directive is operating satisfactorily. In its General Report—2000, ¶ 144 (2001), the Commission reported that Member States had notified 751 proposed technical regulations in 2000, and a total of 7527 since the directive went into force. After receiving comments from the Commission or other States, the notifying State frequently makes beneficial amendments when adopting the regulations. Nonetheless, obviously, the directive merely reduces the number of State technical barriers; it does not ensure Community-wide rules or standards.

The directive requiring notification of new State technical rules has given rise to a number of cases. Naturally, the Commission has on occasion sued Member States under Article 226 (ex Article 169) for failure to notify technical standards, e.g., in Commission v. Germany (Pharmaceutical expiration dates), Case C–317/92, [1994] ECR I—2039. The Court has also had occasion to decide what constitutes a "technical specification" that ought to have been notified. See Bic Benelux v. Belgium, Case C–13/96, [1997] ECR I—1753, which held that a Belgian rule requiring signs to be placed upon products to indicate the payment of an environmental damage tax constituted a technical specification. In contrast, the Court held that a prohibition of commercial advertising for radio transmission equipment that had not been authorized by the Netherlands did not constitute a technical specification, in Criminal proceedings against van der Burg, Case 278/99, [2001] ECR ___ (Mar. 8, 2001). A much more difficult issue is what should be the legal effect of a non-notified technical regulation.

CIA SECURITY INTERNATIONAL v. SIGNALSON

Case C–194/94, [1996] ECR I–2201.

[In 1991, Belgium adopted a decree which forbid the marketing of alarm systems intended to protect persons or property against crimes until the systems were authorized. Belgium never notified the decree pursuant to Directive 83/189. After CIA Security began marketing a burglar alarm system in Belgium without seeking authorization under the Belgian decree's procedures, a competitor, Signalson, sued under the Belgian unfair competition rules, requesting that CIA Security be enjoined from further sales. CIA Security questioned whether the decree was effective, since it had not been notified to the Commission.

After the trial court referred questions under Article 234, the Court of Justice initially decided, rather easily, that the 1991 decree's standards and laboratory testing provisions constituted a technical regulation that Belgium ought to have notified pursuant to Directive 83/629. The Court then turned to the harder question: do the directive's articles 8 and 9 (see the Selected Documents), which require States to send draft technical regulations to the Commission and other States for review during a standstill period of six to twelve months, have direct effect.]

40　Directive 83/189 is designed to protect, by means of preventive control, freedom of movement for goods, which is one of the foundations of the Community. This control serves a useful purpose in that technical regulations covered by the directive may constitute obstacles to trade in goods between Member States, such obstacles being permissible only if they are necessary to satisfy compelling public interest requirements. * * *

41　The notification and the period of suspension therefore afford the Commission and the other Member States an opportunity to examine whether the draft regulations in question create obstacles to trade contrary to the EC Treaty or obstacles which are to be avoided through the adoption of common or harmonized measures and also to propose amendments to the national measures envisaged. This procedure also enables the Commission to propose or adopt Community rules regulating the matter dealt with by the envisaged measure.

* * *

44　Articles 8 and 9 of Directive 83/189 lay down a precise obligation on Member States to notify draft technical regulations to the Commission before they are adopted. Being, accordingly, unconditional and sufficiently precise in terms of their content, those articles may be relied on by individuals before national courts.

45　It remains to examine the legal consequences to be drawn from a breach by Member States of their obligation to notify * * *.

46　The German and Netherlands Governments and the United Kingdom consider that Directive 83/189 is solely concerned with relations between the Member States and the Commission, that it merely creates procedural obligations which the Member States must observe when adopting technical regulations, their competence to adopt the regulations in question after expiry of the suspension period being, however, unaffected, and, finally, that it contains no express provision relating to any effects attaching to non-compliance with those procedural obligations.

47　The Court observes first of all in this context that none of those factors prevents non-compliance with Directive 83/189 from rendering the technical regulations in question inapplicable.

48　* * * [I]t is undisputed that the aim of the directive is to protect freedom of movement for goods by means of preventive control and that the obligation to notify is essential for achieving such Community control. The effectiveness of Community control will be that much greater if the directive is interpreted as meaning that breach of the obligation to notify constitutes a substantial procedural defect such as to render the technical regulations in question inapplicable to individuals.

Notes and Questions

1. In imposing this sanction to non-notified technical regulations, the Court has powerfully reinforced Directive 83/129's role in promoting the internal market. The directive itself imposed no specific penalty for non-compliance, and one may wonder whether the Member States would have adopted so strict a sanction in 1983. The Court has converted a procedural obligation, notification, into a substantive limitation, unenforceability unless notified.

Since the large majority of notified draft technical regulations are not amended due to Commission suggestions in this procedure, presumably most non-notified regulations do not violate internal market principles. The Court's judgment has accordingly been criticized as creating a serious state of uncertainty concerning the legal force of many non-notified regulations. (A review in the Netherlands in early 1997 turned up over 400 non-notified regulations that might be considered to be "technical.") What do you suppose are the policy factors that lay behind the Commission's and the Court's views? Advocate General Elmer suggested that States might deliberately fail to notify draft rules that they suspect "might not stand up to scrutiny in the light of day." Do you think this is plausible? For a strong endorsement of the Court's views, see the casenote by P. Slot, 33 Common Mkt. L. Rev. 1035 (1996).

2. Since the underlying lawsuit is between private parties, and the Court has firmly rejected the doctrine of horizontal direct effect of directives (see *Faccini Dori* and *El Corte Ingles*, *supra* pages 264–67), how could CIA Security rely on Directive 83/129 here? Advocate General Elmer explains that it is because the penalties requested under Belgian unfair competition law are created by the State. Do you find this a persuasive reason for the Court's use of the direct effect doctrine to protect CIA Security?

3. In Unilever Italia v. Central Food, Case C–443/98, [2000] ECR ___ (Sept. 26, 2000), Unilever had sold in September 1998 a type of olive oil to Central Food without a label of origin required by an August 1998 Italian law. Central Food rejected the olive oil for want of the label and Unilever sued for payment. The Commission had notified Italy that it should not adopt its draft law for a 12–month period until May 4, 1999, because the Commission intended to adopt a regulation on marketing standards for olive oil (which in fact it did). May Unilever obtain payment for the olive oil which was not labeled in accordance with the Italian law?

2. THE NEW APPROACH TO TECHNICAL HARMONIZATION

In Chapter 13 C, we reviewed the Commission's 1980 Communication on Cassis de Dijon (reproduced in the Selected Documents), noting that the Commission declared that it intended to apply the Court's principle of mutual recognition of State standards as a means of reducing the future volume of harmonization directives. In January 1985, the new Commission under President Jacques Delors issued a major policy statement on this subject (Com (85) 19).

TECHNICAL HARMONIZATION AND STANDARDS:
A NEW APPROACH

Bull. EC 1–1985.

EIGHTEEN YEARS' WORK ASSESSED

1.3.2. It has to be acknowledged that:

● given the multiplicity of technical regulations and standards in all the Member States, the results in certain industrial fields are still almost negligible;

● technology is now developing too fast for there to be any hope that the harmonization procedures and the decision-making process in the Council will ever manage to bring us within reach of the "European continuum" * * *.

THE COMMISSION'S NEW APPROACH

1.3.3. The new formula proposed by the Commission is based on [the following] fundamental principles;

(i) harmonization of laws will be restricted to the adoption of the essential safety requirements (or other requirements in the public interest) to which all products must conform if they are to be allowed to circulate freely within the Community;

(ii) the relevant industrial standardization bodies will be responsible for drawing up, with due regard to technological developments, the technical specifications that industry needs in order to produce and market products conforming to the essential requirements laid down by directive;

(iii) these technical specifications will not be mandatory: they will remain voluntary standards; * * *

1.3.4. * * * [When] a standard is approved by the Commission and published in the Official Journal, all Member States must accept goods which conform to it. Where a Member State disputes the conformity of a standard to the safety objectives set out in the Directive, it falls to that Member State to substantiate its contention. This reversal of the burden of proof means abandoning the rule of unanimity, which has been such a hindrance to the adoption of harmonization directives with extremely voluminous and detailed technical annexes.

Where European standards already exist, they will have absolute priority; in other cases, reference to standards which have undergone the Commission's acceptance procedure will be sufficient. The standards (national, European or international) are drawn up by bodies comprising representatives of industry, government, consumers and trade unions. In contrast to Council procedure, they are approved by a majority, which considerably accelerates and facilitates their preparation. Finally, they are essentially voluntary and have the same status as the already existing European standards. A manufacturer who wishes to market a new product without referring to an approved standard will remain free to do so; but he will bear the burden of proving that his product meets the safety requirements set out in the Directive covering the relevant sector.

Notes and Questions

1. Why did the Commission favor adoption of Community standards by Community-wide private standardization bodies, rather than through harmonization directives? Note the reference to majority voting in those bodies and remember that in 1985 Article 100 (now Article 94) provided the only legislative basis for harmonization directives. Are there further advantages in transferring the harmonization process from the political level of the Council to a body of technical experts? On the other hand, are there possible disadvantages? For example, might technical experts pay more attention to industry desires than consumer interests?

2. To what extent does the "new approach" follow the *Cassis de Dijon* doctrine? What happens if a State tries to prevent the sale of an imported Community product allegedly made in accordance with a Community standard? What happens if a manufacturer decides not to produce a product in accordance with the standard?

3. The Council approved the new approach by its Resolution of May 7, 1985, O.J. C 136/1 (June 4, 1985). The principal Community standardization bodies now being used in the new approach are the European Committee for Standardization (CEN) and the European Committee for Electrotechnical Standardization (CENELEC). Other specialized bodies exist for particular industries, e.g., the European Telecommunications Standards Institute (ETSI).

3. THE "NEW APPROACH" IN OPERATION

Although the "new approach" reduces the need for harmonization directives, it does not eliminate them. A smaller number of directives continue to be adopted, essentially as "frameworks" setting critical minimum health, safety and technical requirements, with details to be supplied by the Community standards bodies. Leading examples are Directive 88/378 of May 3, 1988 on the safety of toys, O.J. L 187/1 (July 16, 1988), and Directive 89/392 of June 14, 1989 on safety of machinery, O.J. L 183/9 (June 29, 1989), as amended, O.J.L. 207/1 (June 22, 1998). Other recent directives deal with active implantable medical devices, electrically operated elevators, non-automatic weighing instruments and simple pressure vessels.

Products certified by Community bodies as made in compliance with these directives may be identified by an EC mark, "CE," which indicates a presumption in favor of their right to be marketed throughout the Community. A Member State may challenge the safety of an imported product bearing the mark, but must then justify its position to the Commission and a coordinating committee representing all the states.

The Commission has indicated general satisfaction with the new approach to technical harmonization in its annual General Reports and in the progress reports on the implementation of the White Paper. However, two problems arose in the operating machinery for the "new approach." First, in 1985 Community standards bodies did not exist in all industrial sectors. Also, CEN, CENELEC and other bodies did not have sufficiently large or representative technical staff. Both of these deficiencies were eventually remedied. Moreover, a Commission Green Paper on European Standardization of January 28, 1991 proposed more efficient structures and decision-making procedures for both Community and national standard bodies. The second operational problem concerned certification: there did not exist a sufficient number of testing and product certification laboratories in 1985, nor universal standards for adequacy in testing. Accordingly, on July 24, 1989 the Commission proposed a "Global Approach to Certification and Testing," which the Council adopted by a Resolution of December 21, 1989, O.J. C 10 (Jan. 16, 1990). This mandates the creation of a Community system for authorizing certification laboratories and for establishing standards for testing, inspection procedures and the issue of certificates.

From the point of view of US industry groups and the US Government, the Community's progress in applying the "new approach" to facilitate technical harmonization of product standards throughout the Community market represented both an opportunity and a threat. It was an opportunity, because by adhering to the new standards, US producers could market on a Community-wide basis. On the other hand, the new approach was perceived as a threat to US interests to the extent that: 1) US producers do not participate in the European process of setting standards; 2) the new Community standards are different from those prevailing in the US. In May 1989, the Commission and the Department of Commerce agreed that US-manufactured products would be afforded equal access to Community certification procedures, and that ongoing negotiations should strive to achieve mutual recognition of standards between the US and the EEC. In June 1991, a further agreement permitted specified US certification laboratories to test the conformity of US products to Community standards. The US is, however, encountering considerable difficulty in implementing these accords, because it does not have many nationally recognized standards or standard setting bodies and US certification laboratories do not necessarily follow the same procedures as European ones.

One aspect of the TransAtlantic Economic Partnership (*infra* page 1095), agreed between the U.S. and the Community in London in May 1998, is further cooperation in science and technology. Pursuant to this, in November 1998, the Council authorized the Commission to negotiate with the US on the elimination of technical barriers to trade in industrial products. An earlier June 1997 mutual recognition agreement provided for the general mutual acceptance of standards and testing for telecommunication equipment, medical devices and most pharmaceutical products.

No sector of Community technical regulations is more sensitive than pharmaceuticals, due to the manifest health and safety concerns and the traditional autonomy of State administrative agencies in the approval process. Community rules commenced with Directive 65/65, O.J. 1965–1966, Eng. Spec. Ed., p. 20, which required States to have agencies for the review of all pharmaceutical products, forbid marketing without authorization, and set initial standards for authorization. Although frequently amended, notably in 1975 and 1987, Directive 65/65 continues to supply the basic structure. State agency autonomy in deciding whether a drug is safe for marketing within that State remains the rule, although Directive 87/21, O.J. L 15/36 (Jan. 17, 1987), requires an "abridged" review procedure for a drug that has already been authorized in another State, permitting in particular reliance upon pharmacological, toxicological and clinical tests carried out in the State of first approval.

The merit of a single Community-wide authorization process, saving costs and time in a "one-step" approach, long advocated by the pharmaceutical industry, finally reached fruition in 1993. Council Regulation 2309/93, O.J. L

214/1 (Aug. 24, 1993) created the European Agency for the Evaluation of Medicinal Products and gave it the power to review and authorize proposed medications for marketing throughout the Community. The Brussels European Council in October 1993 gave the Agency a site in London. The Agency commenced operation in 1995 and is considered to be functioning satisfactorily. Cooperative arrangements for the exchange of information and test results exist between the Agency and the US Food and Drug Administration.

Chapter 15

FREE MOVEMENT OF WORKERS

The second of the fundamental "four freedoms" to be attained by the EC Treaty of is the "free movement of persons," Article 3(c). In this chapter, we will deal with the principal rules concerning the free movement of workers.

In the post-World War II period, serious unemployment in most European countries led to the adoption of highly restrictive national employment policies. Foreign workers, commonly called migrant workers, were subject to restrictions in immigration and hiring, as well as discriminatory treatment once employed, in the state of employment (often called the host State). Articles 48 and 49 of the EEC Treaty (renumbered as Articles 39 and 40 of the EC treaty) required the dismantling of this protectionist structure by the end of the transitional period in 1969. The basic legislation to this effect was in fact adopted by the end of 1968.

Achieving the free movement of workers is one of the Community's most striking successes. The economic importance of unfettered mobility of labor should not be underestimated, since it enables employers to engage the most qualified personnel, regardless of nationality. Correlatively, it enables employees to seek better job opportunities or social advantages in other countries. States that have an insufficient work force for intensive physical labor or lower pay-scale employment (e.g., in construction, heavy industry, hotels, restaurants or household help) can draw thousands of migrant workers from States with a surplus of labor. Moreover, the right of free movement covers not only blue collar workers, but also senior management and technically-skilled labor. The ability of multinational enterprises centered in the Community to develop a European-wide commercial outlook is substantially due to the mobility of senior and middle management, as well as technical staff, to or from headquarters, or from one part of the Community to another.

The free movement of workers also has major political, social and cultural dimensions. When people are employed and reside for long periods of time in other countries, they usually develop a broader social and intellectual outlook. As they attain levels of authority and influence in society, they tend to promote a European consciousness, with impact on both political affairs and the world of ideas.

Finally, if the children of migrant workers reside in the host State, they are usually educated in the host State school system, and when they become adults, often choose to work and reside in the host State. Moreover, labor mobility increases the number of marriages between people of different nationalities. Over the last twenty years, the Community has moved significantly toward becoming a European "melting pot" of different cultures, largely because of the free movement of workers and their families.

The Court of Justice has also recognized a social or "human" dimension in the concept of free movement of workers. The Court has treated this freedom as one of the fundamental rights of human beings and has expansively developed the social consequences of the right.

A. THE TREATY AND BASIC LEGISLATION

The EC Treaty deals with this topic in Articles 39 and 40 (ex Articles 48 and 49). Article 39 reads as follows:

1. Freedom of movement for workers shall be secured within the Community.

2. Such freedom of movement shall entail the abolition of any discrimination based on nationality between workers of the Member States as regards employment, remuneration and other conditions of work and employment.

3. It shall entail the right, subject to limitations justified on grounds of public policy, public security or public health:

(a) to accept offers of employment actually made;

(b) to move freely within the territory of Member States for this purpose;

(c) to stay in a Member State for the purpose of employment in accordance with the provisions governing the employment of nationals of that State laid down by law, regulation or administrative action;

(d) to remain in the territory of a Member State after having been employed in that State, subject to conditions which shall be embodied in implementing regulations to be drawn up by the Commission.

4. The provisions of this Article shall not apply to employment in the public service.

Although Article 39 initially appears rather detailed, a closer look reveals that the term "worker" is not defined, nor is the full scope of free movement of workers indicated in subsections (2) and (3). As we shall see, the Court of Justice has defined the term "worker", and has expanded the scope of the rights of free movement and non-discrimination in employment. The exceptions to the right of free movement listed in (3) and (4) are important, but have been interpreted narrowly by the Court of Justice.

Article 40 (ex 49) contains a grant of legislative power. Prior to the Single European Act, Article 40 permitted the Council to enact either regulations or directives to implement Article 39 by a simple majority vote—one of the few instances of such voting in the Treaty. After the Single European Act, Article 40 required a qualified majority vote in the Council, acting in cooperation with the Parliament. After becoming effective in 1993, the Maastricht Treaty changed the mode of legislation to the co-decision procedure. (The cooperation and co-decision procedures are described in Chapter 3.)

Although earlier legislation adopted in 1961 and 1964 marked some progress toward free movement, decisive action came with Regulation 1612/68 of Oct. 15, 1968 on freedom of movement for workers, which is in the Selected Documents.

Title I covers the basic right of free movement. Article 1 defines it as the "right to take up an activity as an employed person" in any Community State. Article 2 describes the concomitant right to an employment contract under national law, without discrimination on grounds of nationality. Later articles seek to eliminate national legislation or administrative procedures which set quotas or other limits on foreigners, grant priority for nationals or discriminate against other Community nationals.

Although Article 39 does not expressly limit the concept of "workers" to citizens of a Community State, article 1 of Regulation 1612/68 does so by limiting its grant of rights to nationals of Member States. Non–EC nationals accordingly have no right of free movement as workers. In 1994, the European Economic Area agreement created a right of free movement of workers between the Community and Iceland, Norway and Liechtenstein. Although Swiss voters in a 1992 referendum rejected the EEA Agreement in part because of their concern about an influx of workers from adjacent Member States, Switzerland accepted an obligation to ensure free movement of persons in a series of treaties with the Community in June 1999. Also, some association treaties with adjacent States (e.g., Turkey and Morocco) grant their migrant workers some limited rights within the Community. But no such treaty exists with the US, and US citizens must therefore obtain permission to work on a country-by-country basis within the EC. While, generally speaking, Americans in senior management positions or with technical skills can obtain national work permits in Community countries, other personnel (e.g., actors or secretaries) often cannot.

Title II of Regulation 1612/68 amplifies the principle of non-discrimination in Article 39(2). Article 7 forbids discrimination in dismissal or re-hiring, as well as discrimination in conditions of employment. Article 7(2) adds the right to "enjoy the same social and tax advantages as national workers," a clause which the Court of Justice has interpreted broadly. Article 9 adds a right of equal treatment as to housing, including the right to own housing.

Article 8 deals with trade unions and workers' representatives. Article 8 originally granted only the right to vote for employee representatives and union delegates, but it was amended in 1976 to enable migrant workers also to serve in such posts.

Finally, Title III accords rights to family members of the migrant worker. Although rights of family members are not mentioned in Article 39, a worker's ability to have his or her family live with the worker is manifestly a crucial element in promoting the mobility of labor. Title III creates a decidedly liberal framework of accessory rights for the worker's immediate family, defined as the spouse, children under 21 or otherwise dependent, and dependent parents or grandparents of the worker or spouse.

The rights granted to family members include notably the right to live with the worker (art. 10); the right of the spouse or children under 21, or otherwise dependent, to be employed in the same State, even if they are not nationals of any Member State (art. 11); and the right of children to admission on a nondiscriminatory basis to "general educational, apprenticeship and vocational training courses" (art. 12). Article 12 is supplemented by Directive 77/486 on the education of migrant workers' children, O.J. L 199/32 (Aug. 6, 1977), which requires special efforts to integrate such children into the host State's educational system, for example, through the teaching of the national language (art. 2), and of their "mother tongue and culture of the country of origin" (art. 3).

Directive 68/360, describing rights of workers and their families to long-term residence permits, was adopted simultaneously with Regulation 1612/68. See section B(6) hereafter.

Commission Regulation 1251/70 of June 29, 1970 further supplements Article 39(3) by granting workers the right to remain in the territory of a Member State after having been employed in that State. O.J. English Spec.Ed. 1970–II, 402. This enables a migrant worker to retire in a host State, provided he or she has resided there continuously for more than three years and was continuously employed for the last year before reaching the host State's pensionable age (art. 2). The regulation also generally permits the worker's family or surviving spouse to reside permanently in the host State after the worker's death (art. 3).

Over the years, Regulation 1612/68 has strongly promoted the mobility of Community workers, in part because of its comprehensive coverage, but also due to its expansive interpretation by the Court of Justice. The Commission's 1985 White Paper on Completing the Internal Market cited free movement of workers as a sector already virtually complete.

In November 1998, the Commission proposed extensive amendments to Regulation 1612/68, O.J. C 344/9 (Nov. 12, 1998), both to take account of the Court's interpretative case law and also to liberalize key provisions. The most innovative change would be to introduce an article 1a which would forbid discrimination against migrant workers and their families based upon their sex, racial or ethnic origin, religion, belief, disability, age or sexual orientation. Other proposed amendments will be noted later in connection with the Court judgements that prompted them.

When Greece, Spain and Portugal joined the Community, free movement of workers proved a difficult issue in the accession negotiations. These States had substantial unemployment and large numbers of their nationals were employed as migrant labor in the Community. (For example, Portuguese nationals comprise 10% of the population of Luxembourg.) Each accession treaty accordingly provided a long transitional period (six or seven years) before full free movement was achieved. Somewhat surprisingly, the other Member States have experienced a net reduction in migrant workers from Greece, Portugal and Spain, rather than the reverse. The free movement of workers was never an issue in the accession negotiations for Austria, Finland and Sweden. In contrast, it is one of the most sensitive topics in the current accession negotiations with the Central European states, most of which have significant levels of unemployment. In particular, Austria and Germany are concerned about a substantial influx of migrant workers from the East. The accession treaties may well provide for long transition periods before full free movement of workers is attained.

The right of free movement of persons, commonly called the right to travel, is recognized by US law, although there is no express coverage of the topic in the Constitution. The Articles of Confederation contained a clause stating that "the people of each State shall have free ingress and egress to and from any other State, and shall enjoy therein all the privileges of trade and commerce * * * as the inhabitants thereof," but the Constitution is silent on the matter. The Supreme Court has concluded that the framers of the Constitution took the right for granted. The Fourteenth Amendment indirectly promotes the right by making any native born or naturalized citizens of the US likewise citizens "of the State wherein they reside."

Citizens residing in one US state are, generally speaking, free to travel to another state, take up employment and reside there. However, during the Depression many states adopted legislative or administrative measures to restrict the entry of persons without work or otherwise indigent. In Edwards v. California, 314 U.S. 160, 62 S.Ct. 164, 86 L.Ed. 119 (1941), the Supreme Court unanimously struck down a California law forbidding private parties to provide assistance to indigent persons to come to California. The Court could not agree on a rationale however: five Justices found a violation of the dormant Commerce Clause, while four considered the right to travel to be an inherent privilege of citizens.

Later Supreme Court and lower federal court opinions have invalidated state laws restricting rights or benefits to persons who have resided in the state for a period of time (usually a year). Thus, in Shapiro v. Thompson, 394 U.S. 618, 89 S.Ct. 1322, 22 L.Ed.2d 600 (1969), the Supreme Court struck down a state law that granted social welfare benefits only to persons who had resided one year within the state. Justice Brennan's majority opinion did not specify whether the right to travel was founded on the Privileges and Immunities Clause, or the Commerce Clause, or both. Recently, in Saenz v. Roe, 526 U.S. 489 , 119 S.Ct. 1518, 143 L.Ed.2d 689 (1999), Justice Stevens' majority opinion reaffirmed *Shapiro* in striking down a California law restricting welfare assistance to new residents during their first year of residence to the lower level of the assistance benefits of the state from which they had moved. The Court held that equal treatment of new residents is required by the Fourteenth Amendment's Privileges and Immunities clause.

For an excellent survey of US law, see J. Nowak & R. Rotunda Constitutional Law 8.10 & 14.38 (6th ed. West 2000); see also G. Rosberg, Free Movement of Persons in the United States, in 2 Courts and Free Markets: Perspectives from the United States and Europe 275 (T. Sandalow & E. Stein, eds., Clarendon Press 1982). As we analyze issues in cases in this chapter under Community law, consider also how they might be resolved under US principles.

B. RIGHTS OF THE MIGRANT WORKER, SPOUSE AND FAMILY

1. PROTECTION OF THE WORKER AGAINST DISCRIMINATORY TREATMENT

In Commission v. France (Merchant seamen) (discussed at page 436), the Court of Justice held that Article 39 (ex Article 48) has vertical direct effect. However, this has not proved very significant, because Regulation 1612/68 binds both States and private employers, and its terms are generally more detailed and far-reaching than Article 39 itself. Most of the case law involves interpretation of Regulation 1612/68. The issue that arises most frequently is whether States may deny to migrant workers benefits which are extended to host State nationals. The same issue has on occasion arisen in the United States.

WÜRTTEMBERGISCHE MILCHVERWERTUNG–SÜDMILCH v. UGLIOLA

Case 15/69, [1969] ECR 363.

[German law required employers to treat the period which an employee must spend in compulsory military service as though it were employment for purposes of seniority and pension benefits. Ugliola, an Italian, worked in a German dairy for several years before being required to perform his compulsory Italian military service obligation. When his employer refused to treat the period of Italian military service as it would that of German military service, Ugliola sued. The Supreme German Labor Court made an Article 234 reference.]

4 The fulfilment by migrant workers of an obligation for military service owed to their own State is liable to affect their conditions of work and employment in another Member State. * * *

5 A national law which is intended to protect a worker who resumes his employment with his former employer from any disadvantages occasioned by his absence on military service, by providing in particular that the period spent in the armed forces must be taken into account in calculating the period of his service with that employer falls within the context of conditions of work and employment. Such a law cannot therefore, on the basis of its indirect connexion with national defense, be excluded from the ambit of * * * Article 7 of EEC Regulation No 1612/68 on equality of treatment and protection for migrant workers "in respect of any conditions of employment and work".

6 Apart from the cases expressly referred to in paragraph (3), Article [39] of the Treaty does not allow Member States to make any exceptions to the equality of treatment and protection required by the Treaty for all workers within the Community by indirectly introducing discrimination in favor of their own nationals alone based upon obligations for military service. * * *

7 Therefore, the abovementioned provisions entitle a migrant worker who is a national of a Member State and who has had to interrupt his employment

with an undertaking in another Member State in order to fulfil his obligations for military service in the country of which he is a national, to have the period of his military service taken into account in the calculation of his seniority in that undertaking, to the extent to which the periods of military service in the country of employment are also taken into account for the benefit of national workers.

HICKLIN v. ORBECK

437 U.S. 518, 98 S.Ct. 2482, 57 L.Ed.2d 397 (1978).

[In 1972, concerned over a high level of unemployment, Alaska adopted the Local Hire under State Leases Act, which required all parties operating under Alaskan oil and gas leases or under Alaskan permits for oil and gas pipelines to give a hiring preference to Alaskan residents. The act set up a system of state issuance of "resident cards" to persons who had resided more than one year in Alaska. During the construction of the Trans–Alaska Pipeline in 1975, qualified non-resident job applicants challenged the Local Hire Act. The Alaskan Supreme Court sustained the Act's preference for hiring residents, but struck down the one year residence requirement as excessively long. On appeal, the US Supreme Court unanimously found the Local Hire Act unconstitutional in an opinion by Justice Brennan.]

Alaska Hire's discrimination against nonresidents cannot withstand scrutiny under the Privileges and Immunities Clause. For although the statute may not violate the Clause if the State shows "something to indicate that noncitizens constitute a peculiar source of evil at which the statute is aimed" [citing *Toomer v. Witsell*, infra page 666], certainly no showing was made on this record that nonresidents were "a peculiar source of the evil" Alaska Hire was enacted to remedy, namely, Alaska's "uniquely high unemployment." Alaska Stat. Ann. 38.40.020 (1977). What evidence the record does contain indicates that the major cause of Alaska's high unemployment was not the influx of nonresidents seeking employment, but rather the fact that a substantial number of Alaska's jobless residents—especially the unemployed Eskimo and Indian residents—were unable to secure employment either because of their lack of education and job training or because of their geographical remoteness from job opportunities * * *.

Moreover * * * the discrimination the Act works against nonresidents does not bear a substantial relationship to the particular "evil" they are said to present. Alaska Hire simply grants all Alaskans, regardless of their employment status, education, or training, a flat employment preference for all jobs covered by the Act. A highly skilled and educated resident who has never been unemployed is entitled to precisely the same preferential treatment as the unskilled, habitually unemployed Arctic Eskimo enrolled in a job-training program. If Alaska is to attempt to ease its unemployment problem by forcing employers within the State to discriminate against nonresidents—again, a policy which may present serious constitutional questions—the means by which it does so must be more closely tailored to aid the unemployed the Act is intended to benefit. Even if a statute granting an employment preference to unemployed residents or to residents enrolled in job-training programs might be permissible, Alaska Hire's across-the-board grant of a job preference to all Alaskan residents clearly is not.

Notes and Questions

1.   Germany clearly has an interest in promoting its citizens' willingness to perform their military service duty. Why didn't this national defense argument prevail in *Ugliola*? Would the result be the same under Article 39 alone, without Regulation 1612/68?

2.   Certainly a Member State could never adopt a local hire law granting an automatic employment preference to its residents. In *Hicklin*, the Supreme Court suggests that a hiring preference to unemployed residents enrolled in job—training programs might perhaps be permissible. Would that be possible under the terms of Regulation 1612/68? For a U.S. case with analogies to *Ugliola*, see Attorney General of New York v. Soto–Lopez, 476 U.S. 898, 106 S.Ct. 2317, 90 L.Ed.2d 899 (1986), where Justice Brennan's plurality opinion struck down a New York law giving a civil service employment preference to veterans who had been residents of New York before their military service, on the basis that the preference given to New York residents violated the Equal Protection Clause and the right to travel.

3.   In accord with *Ugliola* are Marsman v. Rosskamp, Case 44/72, [1972] ECR 1243 (Dutch worker in Germany, partly disabled in industrial accident, has the same procedural right to review of the level of incapacity before being dismissed as does a German worker) and Sotgiu v. Deutsche Bundespost, Case 152/73, [1974] ECR 153 (Italian worker is entitled to the same *per diem* allowance for work away from home as German workers).

4.   In Commission v. Greece (Ownership of housing), Case 305/87, [1989] ECR 1461, the Commission challenged a 1938 Greek law prohibiting foreigners from owning property in border areas and the islands, which amount to over 50% of Greek territory. It argued that the law constituted an indirect bar to free movement of workers, in violation of both Article 39 and Regulation 1612/68. How should the Court decide the case?

5.   The remedy for discrimination against migrant workers may be quite costly. In Commission v. France (Frontier worker pensions), Case C–35/97, [1998] ECR I–5325, the Court held that a complex French scheme of supplemental pension benefit to steel workers obliged to take early retirement discriminated against Belgian frontier workers, who resided in Belgium but worked in France. Because the discriminatory treatment dated back to 1979, France claimed that the liability might amount to around F175,000,000. The Court nonetheless denied France's request to limit the retroactive application of the judgement.

Although section D is devoted to border-line cases on the definition of a worker, it is useful at the outset to have some Court guidelines on when a person is to be considered a worker for free movement purposes, and on whether an employer can raise issues concerning violations of Article 39.

LAWRIE–BLUM v. LAND BADEN–WÜRTTEMBERG
Case 66/85, [1986] ECR 2121.

[Lawrie–Blum, a British national, obtained a teaching degree from a German university and applied to the Stuttgart teacher-training program. Teacher-training in Germany takes two years, consisting of further education and practice teaching in a high school for eleven hours a week, with a low salary in compensation for the teaching. Successful completion of this program is a prerequisite to becoming a German high school teacher. Lawrie–Blum was denied admission to the program because German law made high school teachers public officials and required German nationality. The Supreme German Administrative Court inquired under Article 234 whether a teacher-trainee should be considered a worker under Article 39 (ex article 48).]

16   Since freedom of movement for workers constitutes one of the fundamental principles of the Community, the term "worker" in Article [39] may not be interpreted differently according to the law of each Member State but has a Community meaning. Since it defines the scope of that fundamental freedom, the Community concept of a "worker" must be interpreted broadly.

17   That concept must be defined in accordance with objective criteria which distinguish the employment relationship by reference to the rights and duties of the persons concerned. The essential feature of an employment relationship, however, is that for a certain period of time a person performs services for and under the direction of another person in return for which he receives remuneration.

18   In the present case, * * * during the entire period of preparatory service the trainee teacher is under the direction and supervision of the school to which he is assigned. It is the school that determines the services to be performed by him and his working hours and it is the school's instructions that he must carry out and its rules that he must observe. During a substantial part of the preparatory service he is required to give lessons to the school's pupils and thus provides a service of some economic value to the school. The amounts which he receives may be regarded as remuneration for the services provided and for the duties involved in completing the period of preparatory service. Consequently, the three criteria for the existence of an employment relationship are fulfilled in this case.

19   The fact that teachers' preparatory service, like apprenticeships in other occupations, may be regarded as practical preparation * * * is not a bar to the application of Article [39] if the service is performed under the conditions of an activity as an employed person.

20   Nor may it be objected that services performed in education do not fall within the scope of the EEC Treaty because they are not of an economic nature. All that is required for the application of Article [39] is that the activity should be in the nature of work performed for remuneration, irrespective of the sphere in which it is carried out. Nor may the economic nature of those activities be denied on the ground that they are performed by persons whose status is governed by public law since the nature of the legal relationship between employee and employer, whether involving public law status or a private law contract, is immaterial as regards the application of Article [39].

21   The fact that trainee teachers give lessons for only a few hours a week and are paid remuneration below the starting salary of a qualified teacher does not prevent them from being regarded as workers [citing *Levin*, infra page 615].

CLEAN CAR AUTO SERVICE v. LANDESHAUPTMANN VON WIEN

Case C–350/96, [1998] ECR I–2521.

[The 1994 Austrian Trade Code requires legal entities to have a manager resident in Austria. When the Clean Car company applied to be registered as a service station business, the Vienna authorities rejected the application because the proposed manager was then resident in Berlin, although seeking living accommodations in Vienna. On appeal, Clean Car contended that the residence requirement for a company manager violated Article 39. The Supreme Administrative Court referred the issue to the Court of Justice, which first considered whether an employer, rather than the worker, could invoke Article 39.]

17 It should be borne in mind, first of all, that Articles 1 to 3 of Regulation No 1612/68 merely clarify and give effect to the rights already conferred by Article [39] of the Treaty.

* * *

19 While those rights are undoubtedly enjoyed by those directly referred to— namely, workers—there is nothing in the wording of Article [39] to indicate that they may not be relied upon by others, in particular employers.

20 It must further be noted that, in order to be truly effective, the right of workers to be engaged and employed without discrimination necessarily entails as a corollary the employer's entitlement to engage them in accordance with the rules governing freedom of movement of workers.

21 Those rules could easily be rendered nugatory if Member States could circumvent the prohibitions which they contain merely by imposing on employers requirements to be met by any worker whom they wish to employ which, if imposed directly on the worker, would constitute restrictions on the exercise of the right to freedom of movement to which that worker is entitled under Article [39] of the Treaty.

22 Finally, the above interpretation is corroborated * * * by Article 2 of Regulation No 1612/68 * * *.

23 It is made explicitly clear in Article 2 of Regulation No 1612/68 that any employer pursuing an activity in the territory of a Member State and any national of a Member State must be able to conclude and perform contracts of employment in accordance with the provisions in force laid down by law, regulation or administrative action, without any discrimination resulting therefrom.

* * *

25 [Therefore,] the rule of equal treatment in the context of freedom of movement for workers, enshrined in Article [39] of the Treaty, may also be relied upon by an employer in order to employ, in the Member State in which he is established, workers who are nationals of another Member State.

[The Court then considered whether the residence requirement for company managers constituted indirect discrimination under Article 39.]

27   The Court has consistently held that the rules of equal treatment prohibit not only overt discrimination based on nationality but also all covert forms of discrimination which, by applying other distinguishing criteria, achieve in practice the same result.

28   It is true that [the Austrian law in question] applies without regard to the nationality of the person to be appointed as manager.

29   However, as the Court has already held [citing *Schumacker, infra* page 595], national rules under which a distinction is drawn on the basis of residence are liable to operate mainly to the detriment of nationals of other Member States, as non-residents are in the majority of cases foreigners.

30   A requirement that nationals of other Member States must reside in the State concerned in order to be appointed managers of undertakings exercising a trade is therefore such as to constitute indirect discrimination based on nationality, contrary to Article [39(2)] of the Treaty.

31   It would be otherwise only if the imposition of such a residence requirement were based on objective considerations independent of the nationality of the employees concerned and proportionate to a legitimate aim pursued by the national law.

* * *

[Austria argued that the residence requirement was justified objectively by the need to ensure that the manager could "act effectively." The Court disagreed.]

35   [T]he fact that the manager resides in the Member State in which the undertaking is established and exercises its trade does not itself necessarily ensure that he will be in a position to act effectively as manager in the business. A manager residing in the State but at a considerable distance from the place at which the undertaking exercises its trade should normally find it more difficult to act effectively in the business than a person whose place of residence, even if in another Member State, is at no great distance from that at which the undertaking exercises its trade.

Notes and Questions

1.   In *Lawrie-Blum*, what are the three criteria in ¶ 17 that determine whether an employment relationship exists? How did the Court apply them to the status of a trainee-teacher? Do you find the Court's criteria helpful in analyzing border-line situations?

2.   In *Clean Car*, do you agree with the Court's conclusion that employers can rely on Article 39 in a proceeding against a State? Does it represent sound policy? Note that a prospective employee might not have the financial resources to seek administrative recourse in a case like *Clean Car*.

3.   The doctrine that a residence requirement, applied both to nationals and non-nationals, can constitute covert or indirect discrimination against non-national migrant workers was first enunciated by the Court in *Shumacker, infra* page 595, a seminal judgement in the field of discriminatory taxation of frontier

workers. Do you agree with the Court's application of the approach with regard to managers? Is it any more operationally difficult for a manager of a Vienna business to be resident in Berlin than to be resident in Lindau, an Austrian town near Switzerland?

4. Another doctrine frequently applied in the fields of the freedom to provide services and the right of establishment is that a national rule that does not discriminate on grounds of nationality must nonetheless be justified by a serious public interest if the rule limits or restricts the Treaty-based right. This doctrine has now also been recognized as applicable to the free movement of workers.

In Graf v. Filzmoser Maschinenbau, Case C–190/98, [2000] ECR I–493, Graf challenged an Austrian law which eliminates an employer's obligation to pay an employee an indemnity at the end of employment for more than three years, whenever the employee resigns voluntarily. Graf resigned to seek employment in Germany and contended that the law, although non-discriminatory, constituted a disincentive to his exercise of the right of free movement. The Court held that Article 39 "prohibits not only all discrimination, direct or indirect, based on nationality, but also national rules which are applicable irrespective of the nationality of the workers but impede their freedom of movement" (¶ 18) (citing *Bosman, infra* page 623). However, the Court then concluded that the Austrian rule could not be said to be a genuine deterrent to free movement. Although the latter conclusion may be debatable, the judgement's ¶ 18 is apt to prove an important precedent.

The final case in this section raises an intriguing issue: to what degree can a Member State require migrant workers in certain sectors to speak an official language of the State?

GROENER v. MINISTER FOR EDUCATION

Case C–379/87, [1989] ECR 3967.

[The Irish Constitution declares Irish to be the first official language. In 1979, the Ministry of Education issued a regulation requiring all lecturers in vocational education institutions to have a certificate of proficiency in the Irish language. Groener, a Dutch national, was employed in 1982 as a part-time art teacher in the Dublin College of Marketing and Design. She applied in 1984 for a permanent post, which the College wanted to grant, but she failed the Irish proficiency exam. When she sued the Ministry, the High Court asked the Court of Justice to interpret article 3(1) of Regulation 1612/68, which permits States to allow employment conditions "relating to linguistic knowledge required by reason of the nature of the post to be filled."]

13   It is apparent from the documents before the Court that the obligation to prove a knowledge of the Irish language imposed by the national provisions in question applies without distinction to Irish and other Community nationals * * *.

14   [I]t is appropriate to consider first * * * whether the nature of a permanent full-time post of lecturer in art in public vocational education institutions is such as to justify the requirement of a knowledge of the Irish language.

15   According to the documents before the Court, the teaching of art, like that of most other subjects taught in public vocational education schools, is conducted essentially or indeed exclusively in the English language. It

follows that * * * knowledge of the Irish language is not required for the performance of the duties which teaching of the kind at issue specifically entails.

16   However, that finding is not in itself sufficient to enable the national court to decide whether the linguistic requirement in question is justified "by reason of the nature of the post to be filled" * * *.

17   To apprehend the full scope of the second question, regard must be had to the special linguistic situation in Ireland, as it appears from the documents before the Court. By virtue of Article 8 of the "Bunreacht na hEireann" (Irish Constitution):

"(1) The Irish language as the national language is the first official language.

(2) The English language is recognized as a second official language.

(3) Provision may, however, be made by law for the exclusive use of either of the said languages for any one or more official purposes, either throughout the State or in any part thereof."

18   As is apparent from the documents before the Court, although Irish is not spoken by the whole Irish population, the policy followed by Irish governments for many years has been designed not only to maintain but also to promote the use of Irish as a means of expressing national identity and culture. It is for that reason that Irish courses are compulsory for children receiving primary education and optional for those receiving secondary education. The obligation imposed on lecturers in public vocational education schools to have a certain knowledge of the Irish language is one of the measures adopted by the Irish Government in furtherance of that policy.

19   The EEC Treaty does not prohibit the adoption of a policy for the protection and promotion of a language of a Member State which is both the national language and the first official language. However, the implementation of such a policy must not encroach upon a fundamental freedom such as that of the free movement of workers. Therefore, the requirements deriving from measures intended to implement such a policy must not in any circumstances be disproportionate in relation to the aim pursued and the manner in which they are applied must not bring about discrimination against nationals of other Member States.

20   The importance of education for the implementation of such a policy must be recognized. Teachers have an essential role to play, not only through the teaching which they provide but also by their participation in the daily life of the school and the privileged relationship which they have with their pupils. In those circumstances, it is not unreasonable to require them to have some knowledge of the first national language.

21   It follows that the requirement imposed on teachers to have an adequate knowledge of such a language must, provided that the level of knowledge required is not disproportionate in relation to the objective pursued, be regarded as a condition corresponding to the knowledge required by

reason of the nature of the post to be filled within the meaning of the last subparagraph of Article 3(1) of Regulation No 1612/68.

* * *

23   Moreover the principle of non-discrimination precludes the imposition of any requirement that the linguistic knowledge in question must have been acquired within the national territory. It also implies that the nationals of other Member States should have an opportunity to retake the oral examination, in the event of their having previously failed it, when they again apply for a post of assistant lecturer or lecturer.

24   Accordingly, the reply to the second question must be that a permanent full-time post of lecturer in public vocational education institutions is a post of such a nature as to justify the requirement of linguistic knowledge * * * provided that the linguistic requirement in question is imposed as part of a policy for the promotion of the national language which is, at the same time, the first official language and provided that that requirement is applied in a proportionate and non-discriminatory manner.

Notes and Questions

1.   Advocate General Darmon informs us that only one-third of the Irish population claim fluency in Irish, that most of the teachers and students at the Dublin College of Marketing and Design habitually use English, and that Groener's proposed full-time duties would not significantly differ from the temporary duties which she successfully performed without any knowledge of Irish. [1989] ECR at 3981. In view of these factors, do you agree with the Court that Irish is "required by reason of the nature of the post to be filled"?

2.   Advocate General Darmon later declares that: "The preservation of languages is one of those questions of principle which one cannot dismiss without striking at the very heart of cultural identity." "[E]very State has the right to determine the importance it wishes to attribute to its cultural heritage." Id. at 3982. The Court seems to have agreed when it concluded that Ireland could require teachers to be able to speak Irish as a part of their qualifications for teaching.

In an approving case comment, Professor McMahon of University College, Galway, concluded: "Cynics might say that the Court recognized the political necessity for such a decision and realised the cultural backlash which would have been inevitable if it had refused to recognise the legality of the Irish measures. * * * A more gracious and generous view, however, might be that we are here witnessing a real recognition of the legitimacy of national concerns in relation to national cultural heritage * * *." B. McMahon, Groener, 27 Common Mkt.L.Rev. 129, 139 (1990). Do you agree with the "cynics" or take the "more generous view"?

3.   Suppose the regional authorities in Wales or in Brittany or in Catalonia required a Dutch teacher of art in a college to speak, respectively, Welsh or Breton or Catalan. Would the result be the same? Why is the reference to the Irish language in the Irish Constitution so important?

4.   The final issue in *Groener* is proportionality. Even if it is appropriate for Ireland to require primary school teachers to speak Irish, is it necessary for the preservation of the Irish language that an art teacher in a vocational training school be able to speak Irish? Do you agree with the Court on this? (Note that

Irish law does not require teachers at the university level to be able to speak Irish.) Notice the procedural limits required of Ireland in ¶ 23. How helpful are they? Advocate General Darmon observed that Groener was the only one of six non-Irish candidates who failed the language exam when it was given. Is that significant or irrelevant?

2. HORIZONTAL DIRECT EFFECT

As already noted, the Court of Justice early concluded that Article 39 (ex Article 48) had vertical direct effect, enabling workers to challenge state measures that discriminated the basis of nationality. After *Defrenne* accorded horizontal direct effect to then EEC Treaty Article 119, enabling individuals to challenge gender-based discrimination in pay committed by private sector employees, the question naturally arose whether Article 39 might also have horizontal direct effect. Such a holding manifestly would have great impact, because it would enable workers to challenge discrimination based on nationality when committed by private sector employers. An indication that Article 39 could be considered to have horizontal direct effect came in *Walrave* and *Bosman*, discussed in section F infra, when the Court held that private sports associations could not discriminate on the basis of nationality in their rules on members of sports teams. The issue has recently been definitively resolved.

ANGONESE v. CASSA DI RISPARMIO DI BOLZANO

Case C–281/98, [2000] ECR (June 6, 2000).

[In Bolzano, a north Italian region where German is commonly spoken, a bank required its employees to be equally proficient in German and Italian. For this reason, it required applicants to obtain a certificate after passing a bilingual proficiency examination administered four times a year by the Bolzano authorities (who also used it for applications for public service employment). Angonese, an Italian citizen and resident of Bolzano, contested the bank's refusal to consider his application without having taken the examination, contending that his studies in the University of Vienna ought to be considered to prove his German proficiency. However, he had received no diploma from the University, and his formal studies there were in English, Polish, and Slovene.

When Angonese sued the bank, the trial court referred questions to the Court of Justice asking whether the requirement of the Bolzano examination constituted indirect discrimination on the basis of nationality. The Court first concluded that the fact that Angonese was an Italian citizen and resident did not mean that Community law was irrelevant to his suit, and left the trial court to decide the degree to which its responses to the questions referred were relevant. The Court then concluded that no provision of Regulation 1612/68 applied, so the issues were to be examined purely in terms of Article 39.]

[30]   It should be noted at the outset that the principle of non-discrimination set out in Article [39] is drafted in general terms and is not specifically addressed to the Member States.

[31]   Thus, the Court has held that the prohibition of discrimination based on nationality applies not only to the actions of public authorities but also to

rules of any other nature aimed at regulating in a collective manner gainful employment and the provision of services (citing *Walrave*).

[32]   The Court has held that the abolition, as between Member States, of obstacles to freedom of movement for persons would be compromised if the abolition of State barriers could be neutralized by obstacles resulting from the exercise of their legal autonomy by associations or organisations not governed by public law (citing *Walrave* and *Bosman*).

[33]   Since working conditions in the different Member States are governed sometimes by provisions laid down by law or regulation and sometimes by agreements and other acts concluded or adopted by private persons, limiting application of the prohibition of discrimination based on nationality to acts of public authority risks creating inequality in its application.

[34]   The Court has also ruled that the fact that certain provisions of the Treaty are formally addressed to the Member States does not prevent rights from being conferred at the same time on any individual who has an interest in compliance with the obligations thus laid down (see *Defrenne v Sabena* [supra page 248]). The Court accordingly held, in relation to a provision of the Treaty which was mandatory in nature, that the prohibition of discrimination applied equally to all agreements intended to regulate paid labour collectively, as well as to contracts between individuals (see *Defrenne*, paragraph 39).

[35]   Such considerations must, *a fortiori*, be applicable to Article [39] of the Treaty, which lays down a fundamental freedom and which constitutes a specific application of the general prohibition of discrimination contained in Article [12] of the EC Treaty. In that respect, like Article 119 [now, as revised, 141] of the EC Treaty [held to have horizontal direct effect in *Defrenne*], it is designed to ensure that there is no discrimination on the labour market.

[36]   Consequently, the prohibition of discrimination on grounds of nationality laid down in Article [39] of the Treaty must be regarded as applying to private persons as well.

[37]   The next matter to be considered is whether a requirement imposed by an employer, such as the Cassa di Risparmio, which makes admission to a recruitment competition conditional on possession of one particular diploma, such as the Certificate, constitutes discrimination contrary to Article [39] of the Treaty.

[38]   According to the order for reference, the Cassa di Risparmio accepts only the Certificate as evidence of the requisite linguistic knowledge and the Certificate can be obtained only in one province of the Member State concerned.

[39]   Persons not resident in that province therefore have little chance of acquiring the Certificate and it will be difficult, or even impossible, for them to gain access to the employment in question.

[40]   Since the majority of residents of the province of Bolzano are Italian nationals, the obligation to obtain the requisite Certificate puts nationals of other Member States at a disadvantage by comparison with residents of the province.

41   That is so notwithstanding that the requirement in question affects Italian nationals resident in other parts of Italy as well as nationals of other Member States. In order for a measure to be treated as being discriminatory on grounds of nationality under the rules of relating to the free movement of workers, it is not necessary for the measure to have the effect of putting at an advantage all the workers of one nationality or of putting at a disadvantage only workers who are nationals of other Member States, but not workers of the nationality in question.

42   A requirement, such as the one at issue in the main proceedings, making the right to take part in a recruitment competition conditional upon possession of a language diploma that may be obtained in only one province of a Member State and not allowing any other equivalent evidence could be justified only if it were based on objective factors unrelated to the nationality of the persons concerned and if it were in proportion to the aim legitimately pursued.

43   The Court has ruled that the principle of non-discrimination precludes any requirement that the linguistic knowledge in question must have been acquired within the national territory (see *Groener* paragraph 23).

44   So, even though requiring an applicant for a post to have a certain level of linguistic knowledge may be legitimate and possession of a diploma such as the Certificate may constitute a criterion for assessing that knowledge, the fact that it is impossible to submit proof of the required linguistic knowledge by any other means, in particular by equivalent qualifications obtained in other Member States, must be considered disproportionate in relation to the aim in view.

45   It follows that, where an employer makes a person's admission to a recruitment competition subject to a requirement to provide evidence of his linguistic knowledge exclusively by means of one particular diploma, such as the Certificate, issued only in one particular province of a Member State, that requirement constitutes discrimination on grounds of nationality contrary to Article [39] of the EC Treaty.

Notes and Questions

1.   Advocate General Fennelly had recommended that the case be considered not to raise a question of Community law, applying the internal affairs doctrine (see section G infra), because Angonese was an Italian citizen and resident of Bolzano and had not exercised any right of free movement to obtain a diploma in German studies at a foreign school or university. The Court's willingness to answer the referred question despite serious doubts that Angonese had standing to claim any Community rights may have been prompted in part by a desire to bring legal certainty to the resolution of the underlying issue of horizontal direct effect. Do you find the Court's reasoning in ¶¶ 30–36 persuasive? Do you agree with its view in ¶¶ 37–45 that the employer's requirement of the Bolzano bilingual proficiency examination constituted indirect discrimination on the basis of nationality?

2.   The practical implications of *Angonese* are considerable. Could a small retail store owner be sued for violation of Article 39 if he/she is proved to have dismissed an employee and expressed a clear bias against persons of the dismissed employee's nationality at the time of the firing? Could a factory in a region of high

unemployment give a hiring preference to residents of that city or region? Could a retail store owner in a rural region hire exclusively salespersons who are nationals from that region in the belief that his/her rural customers are uncomfortable with salespersons from outside that region?

3. NON–DISCRIMINATION IN "SOCIAL ADVANTAGES"

MINISTÈRE PUBLIC v. MUTSCH

Case 137/84, [1985] ECR 2681.

[Mutsch, a Luxembourg national whose native language was German, resided and worked in a German-speaking community in Belgium. Belgian law permits Belgian nationals speaking German in certain designated German language regions to demand that any criminal proceedings against them be conducted in German. When accused of a crime, Mutsch claimed the benefit of this law. He was convicted *in absentia* and appealed. An appellate court referred the question raised by Mutsch's claim to the Court of Justice.]

12 Article [12] of the Treaty provides that "within the scope of application of this Treaty and without prejudice to any special provisions contained therein, any discrimination on grounds of nationality shall be prohibited". That provision must be applied in every respect and in all circumstances governed by Community law to any person established in a Member State. Similarly, * * * Article [39], on the status of workers, is likewise based on the principle that nationals of any Member State lawfully established in another Member State for the purpose of employment must be treated in the same way as nationals of that State.

13 It is therefore necessary to determine whether the right to require that legal proceedings take place in a specific language falls within the scope of the Treaty and must therefore be assessed in the light of the prohibition of discrimination set out in the provisions referred to above.

14 Since it appears from the documents before the Court that the accused is a worker (in his application to set aside the judgment of 2 November 1982 he describes himself as a roofer working in his father's firm), that question must be examined more particularly in the light of [Article 39] of the Treaty and of the provisions of * * * Regulation No 1612/68 of the Council.

15 As is stated in the fifth recital in the preamble to Regulation No 1612/68, "the right of freedom of movement, in order that it may be exercised, by objective standards, in freedom and dignity, requires that equality of treatment shall be ensured in fact and in law in respect of all matters relating to the actual pursuit of activities as employed persons and to eligibility for housing, and also that obstacles to the mobility of workers shall be eliminated, in particular as regards the worker's right to be joined by his family and the conditions for the integration of that family into the host country".

16 The right to use his own language in proceedings before the courts of the Member State in which he resides, under the same conditions as national workers, plays an important role in the integration of a migrant worker

and his family into the host country, and thus in achieving the objective of free movement for workers.

[17] In those circumstances that right must be held to fall within the meaning of the term "social advantage" as used in Article 7(2) of Regulation No 1612/68, according to which a worker who is a national of another Member State is entitled, in the host Member State, to "the same social and tax advantages as national workers". * * * [T]hat term covers all advantages "which, whether or not linked to a contract of employment, are generally granted to national workers primarily because of their objective status as workers or by virtue of the mere fact of their residence on the national territory" [citing *Even*, infra].

[18] [Therefore,] the principle of free movement of workers, as laid down in Article [39] of the Treaty and more particularly in Regulation No 1612/68 of the Council, requires that a worker who is a national of one Member State and habitually resides in another Member State be entitled to require that criminal proceedings against him take place in a language other than the language normally used in proceedings before the court which tries him if workers who are nationals of the host Member State have that right in the same circumstances.

REINA v. LANDESKREDITBANK BADEN–WÜRTTEMBERG

Case 65/81, [1982] ECR 33.

[The German state of Baden–Württemberg had a system of interest-free loans provided by the Landeskreditbank, a state bank, to parents to cover childbirth expenses. Only couples with at least one German spouse were eligible. The avowed policy was to promote German population growth and to reduce voluntary abortions. After having twins, an Italian migrant worker and his wife sued to obtain a loan. An Article 234 reference was made.]

[9] In its first question, the national court asks in substance whether Article 7(2) of Regulation No 1612/68 * * * must be construed as meaning that the concept of "social advantage" referred to in that provision encompasses interest-free loans granted on childbirth by a credit institution incorporated under public law, on the basis of guidelines and with financial assistance from the State, to families with a low income with a view to stimulating the birth rate.

[10] The Landeskreditbank contends in the first place that Article 7(2) may not be applied to the loans in question in view of the absence of any connection between the grant of the loan and the recipient's status as a worker and on the ground that the refusal to grant the loan in no way hinders the mobility of workers within the Community.

* * *

[12] * * * [T]he advantages which [Article 7(2) of Regulation 1612/68] extends to workers who are nationals of other Member States are all those which, whether or not linked to a contract of employment, are generally granted to national workers primarily because of their objective status as workers or by virtue of the mere fact of their residence on the national territory

and the extension of which to workers who are nationals of other Member States therefore seems suitable to facilitate their mobility within the Community.

13   Consequently, childbirth loans such as those referred to by the national court satisfy in principle the criteria enabling them to be classified as social advantages to be granted to workers of all the Member States without any discrimination whatever on grounds of nationality, in particular in view of their aim which is to alleviate, in the case of families with a low income, the financial burden resulting from the birth of a child.

14   The Landeskreditbank disputes that conclusion by maintaining that childbirth loans, such as those at issue, fall outside the scope of the concept of "social advantage" within the meaning of Article 7(2) of Regulation No 1612/68 since they are granted principally for reasons of demographic policy in order to counteract the decline in the birth rate of the German population. It is therefore a measure adopted in the area of political rights, necessarily linked to nationality, and which as a result falls outside the ambit of Article [39] of the Treaty and of the rules adopted to implement those provisions.

15   [S]ince the Community has no powers in the field of demographic policy as such, the Member States are permitted, in principle, to pursue the achievement of the objectives of such a policy, even by means of social measures. This does not mean, however, that the Community exceeds the limits of its jurisdiction solely because the exercise of its jurisdiction affects measures adopted in pursuance of that policy. Accordingly, childbirth loans of that kind may not be considered as falling outside the scope of the rules of Community law relating to the free movement of persons and, more specifically, of Article 7(2) of Regulation No 1612/68, solely because they are granted for reasons of demographic policy.

Notes and Questions

1.   Does the result in *Mutsch* surprise you? Why do you think that the Court so expansively interpreted the term "social advantage"? Would an Italian worker in Belgium who spoke only Italian have the right to have criminal proceedings against him or her conducted in Italian? If not, could the worker claim the right to have an Italian interpreter? Is any provision of the European Convention on Human Rights helpful? Look at Article 6.

2.   In *Reina,* does the link between the status of a migrant worker and the childbirth loans stretch too far the concept of equal social advantages? What is the policy rationale for the Court's decision? In accord with *Reina* is Commission v. Greece (Family subsidies), Case C-185/96, [1998] I–6601 (Greece cannot refuse large family subsidies, granted on demographic policy reasons, to families of migrant workers from other Member States).

3.   In the United Kingdom, a regulation adopted within the social security system required the payment of funeral and burial expenses up to specified limits for any person of modest means. A retired Irish migrant worker residing in the UK applied for payment of the funeral expense for his deceased son, which was granted, but his request for payment of the cost of the burial in Ireland was refused, because the rules covered only burials in the UK. When he appealed, the social security authority asked the Court whether reimbursement of the burial

costs constituted a "social advantage." What result? See O'Flynn v. Adjudication Officer, Case C–237/94, [1996] ECR I–2617.

4.   In Lair v. Universitat Hanover, infra page 618, Lair, a French national, worked in Germany as a bank clerk for two years. Subsequently she commenced studies in German and Romance languages at the University of Hanover. When she sued to obtain state financial aid to cover tuition and living expenses, the national court asked the Court of Justice whether these constituted a "social advantage" under Regulation 1612/68. The Court responded that a migrant worker had a non-discriminatory right "to all the advantages available to [national] workers for improving their professional qualifications and promoting their social advancements" (¶ 22). Accordingly, the Court concluded that financial aid to facilitate vocational training at the university level is a "social advantage."

5.   In Ministère Public v. Even, Case 207/78, [1979] ECR 2019 (cited both in *Mutsch* and *Reina*), Even, a retired French migrant worker residing in Belgium, claimed the right to a special old age pension benefit granted only to Belgian soldiers wounded in World War II. Even had been wounded as a French soldier. In an Article 234 ruling, the Court held that Even was not entitled to this benefit, because it was not a "social advantage" granted in relation to a status as worker, but rather a benefit accorded for wartime service to the country. Can *Even* be reconciled with *Ugliola* and *Reina*? If not, which is right?

4.   DISCRIMINATION IN TAXATION

Article 7(2) of Regulation 1612/68 forbids discrimination with regard to "tax advantages." In 1994, the Commission issued a Recommendation concerning the tax treatment of non-resident workers, O.J. L 39/22 (Feb. 10, 1994). A typical example is a "frontier worker," living in one Member State, but crossing a border regularly, often daily, in order to work in another State. The Recommendation covers any worker earning more than 75% of his/her income in another State, including professionals, performing artists, and sports players as well as more typical employees. The State taxing the income of such non-resident workers is urged to provide any deductions, credits or benefits that would be accorded to its residents.

Presumably the Commission issued a recommendation instead of proposing a directive because any direct tax proposal would fall under Article 95(2) (ex Article 100a(2)) which requires a unanimous Council vote. The Commission's views have been reinforced by a series of Court judgements.

FINANZAMT KÖLN–ALTSTADT v. SCHUMACKER
Case C–279/93, [1995] ECR I–225.

[Schumacker, a Belgian national residing in Belgium with his wife and children, worked across the border in Germany in 1988–89. This employment provided his sole income and his wife was unemployed. German law taxes non-resident workers on their German income without giving them certain deductions and tax advantages granted to resident taxpayers. When Schumacker requested a more beneficial tax calculation mode granted only to married resident taxpayers, the tax court asked the Court of Justice whether Article 39 forbids discrimination in taxing non-residents.]

21   Although, as Community law stands at present, direct taxation does not as such fall within the purview of the Community, the powers retained by the

Member States must nevertheless be exercised consistently with Community law.

22 * * * Article [39(2)] of the Treaty requires the abolition of any discrimination based on nationality between workers of the Member States as regards, *inter alia*, remuneration.

23 [T]he principle of equal treatment with regard to remuneration would be rendered ineffective if it could be undermined by discriminatory national provisions on income tax. That is why the Council laid down the requirement in Article 7 of Regulation (EEC) No 1612/68 that workers who are nationals of a Member State are to enjoy, in the territory of another Member State, the same tax benefits as nationals working there.

24 In view of the foregoing, * * * Article [39] of the Treaty must be interpreted as being capable of limiting the right of a Member State to lay down conditions concerning the liability to taxation of a national of another Member State and the manner in which tax is to be levied on the income received by him within its territory, since that article does not allow a Member State, as regards the collection of direct taxes, to treat a national of another Member State employed in the territory of the first State in the exercise of his right of freedom of movement less favorably than one of its own nationals in the same situation.

[The Court then considered whether denial of tax advantages to non-resident migrant workers might constitute indirect discrimination.]

26 The Court has consistently held that the rules regarding equal treatment forbid not only overt discrimination by reason of nationality but also all covert forms of discrimination.

27 It is true that the rules at issue in the main proceedings apply irrespective of the nationality of the taxpayer concerned.

28 However, national rules of that kind, under which a distinction is drawn on the basis of residence in that non-residents are denied certain benefits which are, conversely, granted to persons residing within national territory, are liable to operate mainly to the detriment of nationals of other Member States. Non-residents are in the majority of cases foreigners.

29 In those circumstances, tax benefits granted only to residents of a Member State may constitute indirect discrimination by reason of nationality.

* * *

38 In the case of a non-resident who receives the major part of his income and almost all his family income in a Member State other than that of his residence, discrimination arises from the fact that his personal and family circumstances are taken into account neither in the State of residence nor in the State of employment.

Notes and Questions

1. That Article 39 forbids discriminatory tax treatment of resident migrant workers is not surprising, but that it also requires equal treatment of many, perhaps most, non-resident workers is less evident. Do you agree with the Court, or do you think it should have deferred to Member State discretion in the sensitive field of direct taxation in the absence of harmonization? Note that the

Commission's 1998 proposal to amend Regulation 1612/68 includes a new article 7a, which would expressly grant to frontier workers the social and tax benefits given to a host State's resident workers.

2. For many years, New York City imposed an income tax on nonresident commuters employed in the city. When in 1999, the New York State legislature eliminated the tax on commuters resident in New York, it continued to authorize New York City to tax out-of-state commuters. Recalling *Hicklin,* supra page 581, do you think the income tax imposed only on out-of-state commuters violates the dormant Commerce Clause? See City of New York v. State of New York, 94 N.Y.2d 577, 709 N.Y.S.2d 122, 730 N.E.2d 920 (2000). Could the Belgian city of Antwerp impose an income tax on Dutch frontier workers employed in Antwerp: 1) if it imposed the tax only on Dutch frontier workers; or 2) if it imposed the same tax on commuters residing outside Antwerp, but within Belgium?

5. PROTECTION OF THE SPOUSE OR FAMILY AGAINST DISCRIMINATORY TREATMENT

As there is no mention of the worker's spouse or family in Article 39, any grant of rights to them must either be based on Title III of Regulation 1612/68, or on the claim that rights given to the spouse or family further the migrant worker's ability to exercise his or her own rights. Both of these approaches figure in the case law.

CASAGRANDE v. LANDESHAUPTSTADT MÜNCHEN

Case 9/74, [1974] ECR 773.

[Bavaria gave a monthly grant to assist students from low income families, but restricted the grant to German nationals. Casagrande, an Italian secondary school student whose deceased father was an Italian migrant worker, resided in Munich and sued for the grant. Using Article 234, the national court inquired whether Regulation 1612/68, article 12, required Bavaria to grant the student aid to children of migrant workers.]

5   Under Article 12 "the children of a national of a Member State who is or has been employed in the territory of another Member State shall be admitted to that State's general educational, apprenticeship and vocational training courses under the same conditions as the nationals of that State, if such children are residing in its territory", and Member States are required to encourage "all efforts to enable such children to attend these courses under the best possible conditions".

6   According to the fifth recital of the Regulation, the latter was issued, *inter alia,* for the reason that "the right of freedom of movement, in order that it may be exercised, by objective standards, in freedom and dignity, requires * * * that obstacles to the mobility of workers shall be eliminated, in particular as regards the worker's right to be joined by his family and the conditions for the integration of that family into the host country".

7   Such integration presupposes that, in the case of the child of a foreign worker who wishes to have secondary education, this child can take advantage of benefits provided by the laws of the host country relating to educational grants, under the same conditions as nationals who are in a similar position.

8   It follows from the provision in the second paragraph of Article 12, according to which Member States are to encourage all efforts to enable such children to attend the courses under the best possible conditions, that the Article is intended to encourage special efforts, to ensure that the children may take advantage on an equal footing of the education and training facilities available.

9   It must be concluded that in providing that the children in question shall be admitted to educational courses "under the same conditions as the nationals" of the host State, Article 12 refers not only to rules relating to admission, but also to general measures intended to facilitate educational attendance.

* * *

11   In the Federal Republic of Germany [educational] policy is largely within the competence of the [German states], and therefore it must be asked whether Article 12 applies not only to the conditions laid down by laws emanating from the central power but also to those arising from measures taken by the authorities of a country which forms part of a Federal State, or of other territorial entities.

12   Although educational and training policy is not as such included in the spheres which the Treaty has entrusted to the Community institutions, it does not follow that the exercise of powers transferred to the Community is in some way limited if it is of such a nature as to affect the measures taken in the execution of a policy such as that of education and training.

* * *

14   As regards Article 12 of Regulation 1612/68, although the determination of the conditions referred to there is a matter for the authorities competent under national law, they must however be applied without discrimination between the children of national workers and those of workers who are nationals of another Member State who reside in the territory.

15   Further, since Regulations, under Article [249] of the Treaty, have general application and are binding in their entirety and directly applicable in all Member States, it is irrelevant that the conditions in question are laid down by rules issued by the central power, by the authorities of a country forming part of a Federal State or of other territorial entities, or even by authorities which the national law equates with them.

Notes and Questions

1.   Does any part of article 12 expressly or implicitly give any right to financial aid related to studies? Do you agree with the Court's approach? Why is the Court taking an expansive view of the rights of children of migrant workers?

2.   In accord are Michel S. v. Fonds national, Case 76/72, [1973] ECR 457 (mentally handicapped son of deceased Italian migrant worker, residing in Belgium, has right to benefits from Belgian fund to assist the mentally handicapped to obtain work); Alaimo v. Préfet du Rhône, Case 68/74, [1975] ECR 109 (daughter of Italian worker, residing in France, has right to financial aid granted by a French department to French students in a technical training school).

3. *Casagrande* poses an interesting constitutional issue. Under the German constitution, education is exclusively a domain for the *Länder,* or states. Moreover, the EEC Treaty did not then include education as a specific field of Community action. How does the Court conclude that the Community can legislate with regard to education? Since the *Länder* did not sign the EEC Treaty, how are they bound to observe it? If Bavaria declined to follow the Court's opinion, could the Commission bring an Article 226 proceeding against Germany? Remember that in the dialogue between the Court of Justice and the German Constitutional Court described in Chapter 8, the Constitutional Court has always said it would, if necessary, safeguard the organic structure of the Federal Republic.

4. Germany offers training grants for certain higher education studies in other Community States. Di Leo, an Italian and the daughter of Italian migrant workers in Germany, was denied such a grant when she proposed to study medicine in Italy. Should children of migrant workers be entitled to receive foreign training grants for studies in medicine under article 12 of Regulation 1612/68? If so, does it matter whether the child wants to study in the State of which she is a national? See Di Leo v. Land Berlin, Case C–308/89, [1990] ECR I–4185.

5. The Court of Justice has interpreted article 7 of Regulation 1612/68 expansively to grant equal social advantages not only to the migrant worker, but also to the worker's spouse and family. Cristini v. SNCF français, Case 32/75, [1975] ECR 1085, is the leading case. A French regulation granted special railroad fare reductions to families with three or more children under 18, but restricted this to French nationals. The Italian widow of a deceased Italian migrant worker, mother of four children under 18, was held to have the right to the reduced fare. The Court first concluded that the reduced fare would be a social advantage if the worker himself were claiming it. The Court then held that Commission Regulation 1251/70 gave the widow and dependent children of a deceased migrant worker the right to continued residence in the host State and a right to equal treatment, which would entitle the widow to the benefit of equal social advantages. In accord is Castelli v. Office National des Pensions, Case 261/83, [1984] ECR 3199 (aged Italian mother residing with her son, an Italian migrant worker in Belgium, is entitled to a minimum old age pension granted to persons never employed, because this is a social advantage).

6. RIGHT OF FREE ENTRY AND RESIDENCE

A right to work in other Community States must imply a right of free entry and residence. Although some frontier workers reside in their home State and commute to the State of employment, most migrant workers need to reside in the host State and wish to have their family live with them.

Article 39(3) only specifies certain "bare bones": the right of entry to accept employment and the right "to stay in a Member State for the purpose of employment." Council Directive 68/360 on the abolition of restrictions on movement and residence within the Community for workers of Member States and their families, spells out the basic applicable rules. The directive, reproduced in the Selected Documents, merits careful reading.

Directive 68/360 requires the host State to permit the entry of workers and their family members with either an identity card or a passport (art. 3). Normally, the host State must issue the worker or family member an EC residence permit (art. 6). How does this differ from residence permits for non-

Community nationals? What sort of documents must the worker or family member supply in order to obtain this EC residence permit? May the host State require the worker to obtain a labor permit? The residence permit may not be withdrawn when a worker is temporarily incapacitated or is dismissed by the employer (art. 7). Do you think that this implies that a residence permit can be withdrawn if the worker voluntarily resigns? Commentators often draw this inference, but it is by no means certain that the Court of Justice would do so. Under article 8, residence permits cannot be required for frontier workers, for seasonal workers (e.g., migrant workers harvesting crops), or temporary stay workers expected to remain no more than three months.

Some situations are not covered expressly by either Article 39 or Directive 68/30. Can implied rights be construed from either? For example, does a Community national have a temporary right of residence in a host State while looking for work and, if so, for how long? The issue is important, because looking for employment on the spot is generally more likely to prove successful than applying by mail or dealing through a distant employment agency. Member States have customarily allowed persons to reside temporarily for up to three months while ostensibly looking for work, in accord with a Council recommendation adopted along with Directive 68/360.

Another important question is how severe are the administrative penalties that a host State may impose on migrant workers lacking the necessary residence permit. In Royer, Case 48/75, [1976] ECR 497, the Court held that the host State may not expel a worker who did not obtain a residence permit, as that sanction is too severe.

WATSON AND BELMANN

Case 118/75, [1976] ECR 1185.

[Belmann, an Italian residing in Milan, hired Watson, a UK citizen, as an *au pair*. When she disappeared, he notified the police, only to learn that he had violated the Italian law by failing to notify the authorities of the employment. He was subject to a possible six-month jail term and a substantial fine. For failure to register as a resident, Watson faced a possible three-month jail sentence or deportation. The trial court made an Article 234 reference on whether these penalties were appropriate.]

[17] By creating the principle of freedom of movement for persons and by conferring on any person falling within its ambit the right of access to the territory of the Member States, for the purposes intended by the Treaty, Community law has not excluded the power of Member States to adopt measures enabling the national authorities to have an exact knowledge of population movements affecting their territory.

[18] Under the terms of Article 8(2) of Directive No 68/360 * * * the competent authorities in the Member States may require nationals of the other Member States to report their presence to the authorities of the State concerned.

Such an obligation could not in itself be regarded as an infringement of the rules concerning freedom of movement for persons.

However, such an infringement might result from the legal formalities in question if the control procedures to which they refer were such as to restrict the freedom of movement required by the Treaty or to limit the right conferred by the Treaty on nationals of the Member States to enter and reside in the territory of any other Member State for the purposes intended by Community law.

[19] In particular as regards the period within which the arrival of foreign nationals must be reported, the provisions of the Treaty are only infringed if the period fixed is unreasonable.

[20] Among the penalties attaching to a failure to comply with the prescribed declaration and registration formalities, deportation, in relation to persons protected by Community law, is certainly incompatible with the provisions of the Treaty since, as the Court has already confirmed in other cases, such a measure negates the very right conferred and guaranteed by the Treaty.

[21] As regards other penalties, such as fines and detention, whilst the national authorities are entitled to impose penalties in respect of a failure to comply with the terms of provisions requiring foreign nationals to notify their presence which are comparable to those attaching to infringements of provisions of equal importance by nationals, they are not justified in imposing a penalty so disproportionate to the gravity of the infringement that it becomes an obstacle to the free movement of persons.

COMMISSION v. BELGIUM

(Temporary residence limits)
Case C–344/95, [1997] ECR I–1035.

[Belgium permits nationals of other Member States to stay no longer than three months while looking for employment. Belgium also requires short term or seasonal workers to obtain a residence certificate. The Commission used Article 226 to challenge both rules. The Court began by stating that Article 39, as "one of the foundations of the Community * * * must be given a broad interpretation" (¶ 14). It then continued:]

[15] [F]reedom of movement for workers entails the right for nationals of Member States to move freely within the territory of other Member States and to stay there for the purposes of seeking employment.

* * *

[17] In the absence of Community provisions prescribing a period during which Community nationals who are seeking employment may stay in their territory, the Member States are entitled to lay down a reasonable period for this purpose. However, if after expiry of that period, the person concerned provides evidence that he is continuing to seek employment and that he has genuine chances of being engaged, he cannot be required to leave the territory of the host Member State.

[18] In view of the foregoing, it is sufficient to state that the Belgian legislation infringes Community law in automatically requiring nationals of other Member States who are looking for employment to leave Belgium after expiry of the period laid down.

[With regard to the residence certificates required for short term or seasonal workers, the Court declared that:]

[31] Although Article 8(2) of the Directive provides that the competent authorities of the host Member State may require the worker to report his presence, * * * anything going beyond having to report one's presence and having the character of an authorization or a residence permit is not compatible with the Directive.

[32] Furthermore, requiring a person to pay a charge when he reports his presence constitutes a financial obstacle to the movement of workers, which is also contrary to the Community rules.

Notes and Questions

1. In *Watson*, the Court states the basic principle of proportionality and lets the trial court apply it to the facts. Does the Court supply any measuring standard? Would a three-month jail sentence be appropriate? Indeed, would any jail sentence ever be appropriate for failure to obtain a residence permit? See Regina v. Pieck, Case 157/79, [1980] ECR 2171, which held that a jail sentence is never an appropriate penalty. Recently, the Court held that Germany could not impose a maximum fine of DM 5000 upon nationals of other Member States for failure to hold a valid EC residence permit when the maximum fine on German nationals for failure to hold an identity card was only DM 1000. Commission v. Germany (Residence permit penalties), Case C–24/97, [1998] ECR I–2133.

2. The Italian law in *Watson* required migrant workers to notify their place of residence to the authorities within three days after entering Italy. This time period was held to be too short in In re Messner, Case C–265/88, [1989] ECR 4209.

3. The Court's conclusion in the *Belgian Temporary residence limits* case that a right to look for work in another State is implied in Article 39 is not only plausible as an interpretation, but unquestionable on policy grounds. Why do you suppose the Court would not accept the three month period which the Council had initially recommended as a reasonable limit on a period of seeking employment? Will it be easy for a trial court to apply ¶ 17's approach? Note that the Commission has proposed to amend Directive 68/360's article 8 to give a Member State national six months to look for work in another State, and even longer if "he is actively looking for work and * * * has a reasonable chance of being offered employment." O.J.C. 344/12 (Nov. 12, 1998).

4. In Martinez Sala v. Freistaat Bayern, Case C–85/96, [1998] ECR I–2691, Martinez Sala, a Spanish national, had lived in Germany since she was twelve, initially as the child of a migrant worker. Since 1984, she has not held a German residence permit, but she did have various jobs until 1989, when she commenced receiving German social assistance. When in 1993, Martinez Sala had a baby, she applied for a child-raising allowance which the German authorities refused because she did not have a valid residence permit, an administrative prerequisite for the allowance. When she sued, the administrative tribunal referred several questions.

The Court of Justice easily concluded that the child-raising allowance constituted a "social advantage" in terms of article 7 of Regulation 1612/68. With regard to whether Martinez Sala could qualify as a migrant worker, the Court noted that a migrant worker's status "may produce certain effects after the [work] relationship has ended and a person who is genuinely seeking work must also be classified as a worker" (¶ 32), indicating that the referring tribunal must investigate the relevant facts further to determine whether Martinez Sala should be deemed a worker, and thus entitled to the child-raising allowance. The Court further invalidated the German requirement for a residence permit as a precondition for the allowance, declaring that "a residence permit can only have declaratory and probative force" (¶ 53). Failure to grant Martinez Sala the allowance when she is in fact a resident constitutes discriminatory treatment under Treaty Article 12 (ex Article 7). (Note that whether Martinez Sala enjoys any rights as a 'citizen of the Union' is discussed in the next chapter.)

C. ARTICLE 39's EXCEPTIONS TO FREE MOVEMENT

1. THE PUBLIC POLICY EXCEPTION

Article 39(3) (ex Article 48(3)) allows Member States to limit the right of free movement on grounds of public policy, public security or public health. In order to give substantive content to these terms, as well as to set procedural safeguards, in 1964 the Council adopted Directive 64/221 (reproduced in the Selected Documents), which merits careful reading.

Directive 64/221 applies both to self-employed persons and to workers, as well as their family members. It covers situations where a State invokes public policy, public security or public health either to deny entry, to deny the issuance or renewal of a residence permit, or to expel a person (art. 2).

Important substantive limits placed upon a State's recourse to Article 39(3) include requiring a State to take action on public policy or public security "exclusively on the personal conduct of the individual concerned," and forbidding action based exclusively on past criminal convictions (art. 3). As for public health, a State may not refuse entry or a residence permit except for a disability or disease listed on an annex, and a State may never expel a person for a disability or disease occurring after he or she has received a residence permit (art. 4).

Procedural rights granted by Directive 64/221 include notice to the person concerned of the grounds for the adverse decision "unless this is contrary to the interests or the security of the State involved" (art. 6); a right of administrative recourse (art. 8); and some form of judicial or administrative appeal (art. 9).

There have been a surprising number of cases interpreting the concept of public policy and the procedural rights outlined in Directive 64/221. States have a natural tendency to invoke the rather vague concept of public policy in order to expel or otherwise restrict individuals whose views or conduct are considered inimical to the public interest. The Court of Justice has been steadily limiting the use of public policy for this purpose and protecting the rights of migrant workers and their families. The Court's respect for basic human rights figures strongly in its judgments, especially in the following landmark case.

RUTILI v. MINISTER FOR THE INTERIOR
Case 36/75, [1975] ECR 1219.

[Rutili, an Italian national, resident in France since his birth, had his residence permit revoked in 1968 because of his alleged leftist trade union activities and participation in the May 1968 riots. French authorities granted him an EEC residence permit in 1970, but with a restriction preventing him from living in Alsace–Lorraine, his customary residence. French law permits barring French nationals from residing in certain regions after conviction of serious crimes or during a state of emergency. Rutili sued to challenge the restriction placed on his residence permit and the administrative court made an Article 234 reference.]

[8] The first question asks whether the expression "subject to limitations justified on grounds of public policy" in Article [39] of the Treaty concerns only the legislative decisions which each Member State has decided to take in order to limit within its territory the freedom of movement and residence for nationals of other Member States or whether it also concerns individual decisions taken in application of such legislative provisions.

* * *

[16] * * * [T]he courts [must] give the rules of Community law * * * precedence over the provisions of national law * * *.

[17] Inasmuch as the object of the provisions of the Treaty and of secondary legislation is to regulate the situation of individuals and to ensure their protection, it is also for the national courts to examine whether individual decisions are compatible with the relevant provisions of Community law.

* * *

[19] This conclusion is based in equal measure on due respect for the rights of the nationals of Member States, which are directly conferred by the Treaty and by Regulation No 1612/68, and the express provision in Article 3 of Directive No 64/221 which requires that measures taken on grounds of public policy or of public security "shall be based exclusively on the personal conduct of the individual concerned".

[20] It is all the more necessary to adopt this view of the matter inasmuch as national legislation concerned with the protection of public policy and security usually reserves to the national authorities discretionary powers which might well escape all judicial review if the courts were unable to extend their consideration to individual decisions taken pursuant to the reservation contained in Article [39(3)] of the Treaty.

* * *

[22] The second question asks what is the precise meaning to be attributed to the word "justified" in the phrase "subject to limitations justified on grounds of public policy" in Article [39(3)] of the Treaty.

[23] In that provision, the words "limitations justified" mean that only limitations which fulfil the requirements of the law, including those contained in Community law, are permissible with regard, in particular, to the right of nationals of Member States to freedom of movement and residence.

[24] In this context, regard must be had both to the rules of substantive law and to the formal or procedural rules subject to which Member States exercise the powers reserved under Article [39(3)].

* * *

*Justification of Measures Adopted on Grounds of Public
Policy From the Point of View of Substantive Law*

26   By virtue of the reservation contained in Article [39(3)], Member States continue to be, in principle, free to determine the requirements of public policy in the light of their national needs.

27   Nevertheless, the concept of public policy must, in the Community context * * *, be interpreted strictly, so that its scope cannot be determined unilaterally by each Member State without being subject to control by the institutions of the Community.

28   Accordingly, restrictions cannot be imposed on the right of a national of any Member State to enter the territory of another Member State, to stay there and to move within it unless his presence or conduct constitutes a genuine and sufficiently serious threat to public policy.

29   In this connexion Article 3 of Directive No 64/221 imposes on Member States the duty to base their decision on the individual circumstances of any person under the protection of Community law and not on general considerations.

30   Moreover, Article 2 of the same directive provides that grounds of public policy shall not be put to improper use by being "invoked to service economic ends".

31   Nor, under Article 8 of Regulation No 1612/68, which ensures equality of treatment as regards membership of trade unions and the exercise of rights attaching thereto, may the reservation relating to public policy be invoked on grounds arising from the exercise of those rights.

32   Taken as a whole, these limitations placed on the powers of Member States in respect of control of aliens are a specific manifestation of the more general principle, enshrined in Articles 8, 9, 10 and 11 of the Convention for the Protection of Human Rights and Fundamental Freedoms, signed in Rome on 4 November 1950 and ratified by all the Member States, and in Article 2 of Protocol No 4 of the same Convention, signed in Strasbourg on 16 September 1963, which provide, in identical terms, that no restrictions in the interests of national security or public safety shall be placed on the rights secured by the above-quoted articles other than such as are necessary for the protection of those interests "in a democratic society."

*Measures Adopted on Grounds of Public Policy: Justification
From the Procedural Point of View*

33   According to the third recital of the preamble to Directive No 64/221, one of the aims which it pursues is that "in each Member State, nationals of other Member States should have adequate legal remedies available to them in respect of the decisions of the administration" in respect of measures based on the protection of public policy.

[The Court then cited the procedural safeguards detailed in articles 6, 8 and 9 of the directive.]

37   [A]ny person enjoying the protection of the provisions quoted must be entitled to a double safeguard comprising notification to him of the

grounds on which any restrictive measure has been adopted in his case and the availability of a right of appeal.

38 It is appropriate to state also that all steps must be taken by the Member States to ensure that this double safeguard is in fact available to anyone against whom a restrictive measure has been adopted.

39 In particular, this requirement means that the State concerned must, when notifying an individual of a restrictive measure adopted in his case, give him a precise and comprehensive statement of the grounds for the decision, to enable him to take effective steps to prepare his defense.

The Justification for, in Particular, a Prohibition on Residence in Part of the National Territory

40 The questions put by the [administrative court] were raised in connection with a measure prohibiting residence in a limited part of the national territory.

41 In reply to a question from the Court, the Government of the French Republic stated that such measures may be taken in the case of its own nationals either, in the case of certain criminal convictions, as an additional penalty, or following the declaration of a state of emergency.

* * *

46 Right of entry into the territory of Member States and the right to stay there and to move freely within it is defined in the Treaty by reference to the whole territory of these States and not by reference to its internal subdivisions.

* * *

48 It follows that prohibitions on residence under the reservation inserted to this effect in Article [39(3)] may be imposed only in respect of the whole of the national territory.

49 On the other hand, in the case of partial prohibitions on residence, limited to certain areas of the territory, persons covered by Community law must, under Article [12] of the Treaty and within the field of application of that provision, be treated on a footing of equality with the nationals of the Member State concerned.

50 It follows that a Member State cannot, in the case of a national of another Member State covered by the provisions of the Treaty, impose prohibitions on residence which are territorially limited except in circumstances where such prohibitions may be imposed on its own nationals.

Notes and Questions

1. *Rutili* is a leading precedent on the direct effect of Article 39, Directive 68/360 and Directive 64/221. *Rutili* is also a leading basic rights case in its application of the 1950 European Human Rights Convention, and is frequently cited for its emphasis on protecting human rights in a democratic society. For discussion of Community basic rights protection, see Chapter 6.

2. Why is it important that the Court held "public policy" to have a Community law content rather than one based on national law concepts? Note the Court's emphasis on the procedural rights granted by Directive 64/221. In view of

the Court's "equal treatment" analysis, may France bar Rutili from living in Alsace–Lorraine?

3. What is the meaning of the "personal conduct" requirement in article 3 of Directive 64/221? In Bonsignore v. Oberstadtsdirektor Köln, Case 67/74, [1975] ECR 297, Bonsignore, an Italian worker, accidentally killed his brother with a pistol for which he had no permit. Although he was found guilty of negligent homicide, no penalty was imposed. The German authorities apparently sought to deport Bonsignore as a warning to others, even though there appeared to be no risk that he would repeat his conduct. When Bonsignore appealed the deportation order, an Article 234 reference was made. The Court held that "a deportation order may only be made for breaches of the peace and public security which might be committed by the individual affected." Id. at 307. The Court rejected any deportation "for the purpose of deterring other aliens." Ibid.

However, in Regina v. Bouchereau, Case 30/77, [1977] ECR 1999, Bouchereau, a French auto mechanic residing in London, was convicted twice for possessing small quantities of illegal drugs (marijuana and "pep" pills) for personal use. A deportation proceeding gave rise to an Article 234 reference. Although the Court cited Directive 64/221's language that "previous criminal convictions" are not as such sufficient to warrant deportation, the Court stated that the convictions could be considered as evidence of personal conduct which might constitute a "propensity to act in the same way in the future." Id. at 2013. The Court even added that "past conduct alone may constitute * * * a threat to the requirements of public policy." Ibid. The Court was perhaps influenced by Advocate General Warner's argument that an alien's conduct can cause "such deep public revulsion" that he can be deported, just as a houseguest may be thrown out for offensive behavior. Id. at 2022.

Are *Bonsignore* and *Bouchereau* consistent? Do you agree that past conduct should be used to predict future conduct? Should past conduct alone be enough to justify deportation? If so, what sort of conduct—soft drug use, hard drug use, or drug-dealing?

ADOUI v. BELGIUM

Cases 115 & 116/81, [1982] ECR 1665.

[Adoui and Cornuaille, French citizens, were refused residence permits in Liège, Belgium on public policy grounds. They worked as bar waitresses, allegedly scantily dressed, and on occasion would entertain customers privately. A 1948 Belgian law prohibited brothels, pimping and public solicitation, but not prostitution itself. The city of Liège prohibited streetwalking and public displays by prostitutes, but not prostitution. Adoui and Cornuaille appealed the refusal of residence permits and the national court made an Article 234 reference.]

5 [The initial question is] whether a Member State may, by virtue of the reservations contained in [Article 39], expel from its territory a national of another Member State or deny him access to that territory by reason of activities which, when attributable to the former State's own nationals, do not give rise to repressive measures.

6 [P]rostitution as such is not prohibited by Belgian legislation, although the Law does prohibit certain incidental activities, which are particularly

harmful from the social point of view, such as the exploitation of prostitution by third parties and various forms of incitement to debauchery.

7 The reservations contained in [Article 39] permit Member States to adopt,
with respect to the nationals of other Member States * * *, measures
which they cannot apply to their own nationals, inasmuch as they have no
authority to expel the latter from the national territory or to deny them
access thereto. Although that difference of treatment * * * must therefore
be allowed, it must nevertheless be stressed that, in a Member State, the
authority empowered to adopt such measures must not base the exercise of
its powers on assessments of certain conduct which would have the effect
of applying an arbitrary distinction to the detriment of nationals of other
Member States.

8 It should be noted in that regard that reliance by a national authority upon
the concept of public policy presupposes the existence of * * * "a genuine
and sufficiently serious threat affecting one of the fundamental interests of
society". Although Community law does not impose upon the Member
States a uniform scale of values as regards the assessment of conduct
which may be considered as contrary to public policy, it should nevertheless be stated that conduct may not be considered as being of a sufficiently
serious nature to justify restrictions on the admission to or residence
within the territory of a Member State of a national of another Member
State in a case where the former Member State does not adopt, with
respect to the same conduct on the part of its own nationals, repressive
measures or other genuine and effective measures intended to combat such
conduct.

* * *

10 In the tenth question, the national court asks whether the action taken by
a Member State which, "anxious to remove from its territory prostitutes
from a given country because they could promote criminal activities, does
so systematically, declaring that their business of prostitution endangers
the requirements of public policy and not taking the trouble to consider
whether the persons concerned may or may not be suspected of contact
with the 'underworld' ", constitutes a measure of a general preventive
nature within the meaning of Article 3 of Directive No 64/221.

11 It should be noted that Article 3(1) of the directive provides that measures
taken on grounds of public policy or of public security are to be based
exclusively on the personal conduct of the individual concerned. In that
regard it is sufficient to refer to the judgment [in *Bonsignore, supra*], in
which the Court held that "measures adopted on grounds of public policy
and for the maintenance of public security against the nationals of
Member States of the Community cannot be justified on grounds extraneous to the individual case" * * *.

Notes and Questions

1. What does the Court mean when it speaks of the need for a State to
"adopt, with respect to the same conduct on the part of its nationals, repressive
measures or other genuine and effective measures intended to combat such
conduct"? May deportation be ordered for conduct that a State deems socially
undesirable, or must the conduct be illegal? Must the State actively enforce the

law against the illegal conduct? Concretely, may Belgium expel Adoui? May a State deport a migrant worker who is gay or lesbian if homosexual relations are not illegal? May a State that makes the use of marijuana illegal, but does not systematically enforce the law, deport a migrant worker who habitually uses marijuana?

2. Review again the facts in *van Duyn,* excerpted at page 246 supra. The Court held that if a State finds an activity to be "socially harmful" and takes "administrative measures to counteract" the activity, this is a sufficient expression of public policy, and the activity need not be unlawful in order to justify the State's refusal of entry to a person involved in the activity. [1974] ECR at 1350. Has *van Duyn* been tacitly overruled by *Adoui?* Note that in *van Duyn* the only UK "administrative measures" appeared to be those directed against aliens.

3. In Commission v. Spain (Private security firms), Case C–114/97, [1998] I–6717, the issue was whether Spain could justifiably require that all managers and staff of private security firms (i.e., enterprises engaged in the protection of persons or property, or the installation and maintenance of surveillance and alarm systems) must be Spanish nationals. The Court held that private security firms were not engaged in ensuring public security and that Article 39(3) could not be used to exclude a private economic sector from the duty of non-discrimination on the basis of nationality. Subsequently, in Commission v. Belgium (Private security firm personnel), Case C–355/98, [2000] ERC ___ (March 9, 2000), the issue was whether Belgium could require the managers and most personnel of private security firms to be Belgian residents. How would you decide the issue?

4. The Queen v. Secretary of State for the Home Department ex parte Gallagher, Case C–175/94, [1995] ECR I–4253, attracted considerable media attention in the UK. Gallagher, an Irish migrant worker in the UK, is allegedly a prominent Irish terrorist leader. Under the 1989 Prevention of Terrorism Act, the UK Home Secretary held expedited hearings, concluded that he was "concerned in the commission, preparation or instigation of acts of terrorism," and deported him to Ireland. Pursuant to the 1989 Act, Gallagher was allowed to "make representations" challenging the order before "a person nominated" by the Home Secretary at the British Embassy in Dublin, but the exclusion order was subsequently confirmed. On appeal, the Court of Appeal asked the Court to interpret the procedural rights in article 9 of Directive 64/221.

The principal issue was whether the Home Secretary could appoint both the person deciding on expulsion and the "competent authority" conducting the review. The Court did not preclude this possibility, but indicated that the Court of Appeal must consider the following criteria in deciding whether or not this was proper procedure:

[24] The directive does not specify how the competent authority referred to in Article 9 is appointed. It does not require that that authority be a court or be composed of members of the judiciary. Nor does it require the members of the competent authority to be appointed for a specific period. The essential requirements are, first, that it be clearly established that the authority is to perform its duties in absolute independence and is not to be directly or indirectly subject, in the exercise of its duties, to any control by the authority empowered to take the measures provided for in the directive and, second, that the authority follow a procedure enabling the person concerned, on the terms laid down by the directive, effectively to present his defense [citing *Adoui*]. It is for the national court to determine in each case whether those requirements have been met.

An interesting final point is that the person conducting the review in Dublin declined to disclose his identity to Gallagher, and the Court of Justice found that such disclosure was not required, so long as the Court of Appeal knew the identity. Although the UK Parliament amended the 1989 Act to conform to the *Gallagher* judgment, Gallagher himself did not obtain any relief from the Court of Appeal. For a view that the Court should have set more precise procedural protections for the defendant in such a proceeding, see the casenote by S. O'Leary, 33 Common Mkt. L. Rev. 777 (1996). For a further Court elaboration upon the procedural safeguards set out in Directive 64/221, see Queen v. Secretary of State for the Home Department ex parte Shingara, Cases C–69/95 and 111/95, [1997] ECR I–3343.

2. THE EXCEPTION FOR PUBLIC SERVICE

The term "public service" is unfortunately an ambiguous one, differing significantly in scope among the various Member States. Should it be given a Community sense? Should it be interpreted broadly or restrictively? Should it cover only employees of the national government, or also employees of regional and local government? What about employees of State-owned post offices, utilities, railroads, or commercial enterprises?

The Court first interpreted Article 39(4) (ex article 48(4)) in Sotgiu v. Deutsche Bundespost, Case 152/73, [1974] ECR 153, when an Italian employee of the German post office, traditionally a State administration, claimed equal treatment with German workers as to benefits paid when working away from home. The Court stated that because of the "fundamental nature" of the free movement of workers and the principle of nondiscrimination, Article 39(4) should be construed narrowly to permit restrictions only at the time of the initial employment of foreign nationals. Once a migrant worker is actually employed in public service, Article 39(4) does not allow discrimination with regard to "remuneration or other conditions of employment." Id. at 162.

Moreover, the Court insisted that Article 39(4) must have a Community law meaning. Distinctions based upon national rules concerning whether an employee is to be considered a "public official" or not, or is subject to the rules of administrative law as opposed to civil law, or as to the legal nature of the employment relationship, should not determine whether a worker is employed in the "public service." The Court in *Sotgiu* did not, however, define "public service." That remained for a later case.

COMMISSION v. BELGIUM

(Public service I)

Case 149/79, [1980] ECR 3881.

[The Commission brought an Article 226 action against Belgium because it required Belgian citizenship for employment in certain posts with the city of Brussels and other local governments, and with the Belgian national railways. Belgium argued that its Constitution allowed only Belgian nationals to be admitted to State civil and military posts.]

10   Article [39(4)] removes from the ambit of Article [39(1) to (3)] a series of posts which involve direct or indirect participation in the exercise of powers conferred by public law and duties designed to safeguard the general interests of the State or of other public authorities. Such posts in

fact presume on the part of those occupying them the existence of a special relationship of allegiance to the State and reciprocity of rights and duties which form the foundation of the bond of nationality.

11   * * * [D]etermining the sphere of application of Article [39(4)] raises special difficulties since in the various Member States authorities acting under powers conferred by public law have assumed responsibilities of an economic and social nature or are involved in activities which are not identifiable with the functions which are typical of the public service yet which by their nature still come under the sphere of application of the Treaty. In these circumstances the effect of extending the exception contained in Article [39(4)] to posts * * * which do not involve any association with tasks belonging to the public service properly so called, would be to remove a considerable number of posts from the ambit of the principles set out in the Treaty and to create inequalities between Member States according to the different ways in which the State and certain sectors of economic life are organized.

12   * * * [There are] problems of appraisal and demarcation in specific cases. [The proper] classification depends on whether or not the posts in question are typical of the specific activities of the public service in so far as the exercise of powers conferred by public law and responsibility for safeguarding the general interests of the State are vested in it.

13   Where, in the case of posts which, although offered by public authorities, are not within the sphere to which Article [39(4)] applies, a worker from another Member State is, like a national worker, required to satisfy all other conditions of recruitment, in particular concerning the competence and vocational training required, * * * Article [39] and Regulation No 1612/68 do not allow him to be debarred from those posts simply on the grounds of his nationality.

* * *

16   The Belgian Government further mentions that the constitutional laws of certain Member States refer expressly to * * * the principle [of] the exclusion of non-nationals [from the public service], save for any possible derogations. Such is also, it claims, the effect of Article 6 of the Belgian Constitution by which "Belgians * * * only shall be admitted to civil and military posts save in special cases for which exception may be made". The Belgian Government has itself stated that it does not deny that "Community rules override national rules" but it believes that the similarity between the constitutional laws of those Member States should be used as an aid to interpretation to cast light on the meaning of Article [39(4)] and to reject the interpretation given to that provision by the Commission, which would have the effect of creating conflict with the constitutional provisions referred to.

* * *

18   * * * [T]he demarcation of the concept of "public service" within the meaning of Article [39(4)] cannot be left to the total discretion of the Member States.

[19]   [R]ecourse to provisions of the domestic legal systems to restrict the scope of the provisions of Community law would have the effect of impairing the unity and efficacy of that law and consequently cannot be accepted. That rule, which is fundamental to the existence of the Community, must also apply in determining the scope and bounds of Article [39(4)] of the Treaty. Whilst it is true that that provision takes account of the legitimate interest which the Member States have in reserving to their own nationals a range of posts connected with the exercise of powers conferred by public law and with the protection of general interests, at the same time it is necessary to ensure that the effectiveness and scope of the provisions of the Treaty on freedom of movement of workers and equality of treatment of nationals of all Member States shall not be restricted by interpretations of the concept of public service which are based on domestic law alone and which would obstruct the application of Community rules.

Notes and Questions

1.   Note that Belgium did not challenge the primacy of Community law over its Constitution. This is consistent with Belgium's judicial attitude toward the primacy of the Treaty described in Chapter 8 supra. Belgium argued instead that common constitutional traditions in several States should help in the interpretation of "public service." Why isn't it appropriate to look to common constitutional traditions for this purpose, even though the Court does look to such traditions in developing a Community doctrine of fundamental rights?

2.   Is the Court's test in ¶¶ 10–12 for deciding when employment falls in the public service too broad or too narrow or about right? Does it open many posts in State employment to migrant workers? The Court instructed the Commission and Belgium to apply its test to the contested posts, but they were unable to agree, so the issue returned to the Court in Commission v. Belgium (Public service II), Case 149/79, [1982] ECR 1845. After reviewing factual material provided with regard to the nature of the posts, the Court held that nurses, electricians, plumbers and gardeners employed by local governments, and drivers, signalmen, cleaners, painters, canteen staff, workshop hands and nightwatchmen employed by the State railway, were not engaged in public service employment. On the other hand, architects, supervisors and stock controllers employed by local governments were to be considered as employed in the public service.

Where does the Court seem to be drawing the line? Obviously, the majority of clerical and "blue collar" jobs with the State or its agencies are now open to migrant workers, which considerably reduces the potential scope of Article 39(4). However, the Commission accepted that certain nightwatchmen employed by local governments could be considered to be in the public service, because their positions gave them easy access to government secrets. The Court did not deal with this issue. Do you agree with the Commission?

3.   In Commission v. France (Status of nurses), Case 307/84, [1986] ECR 1725, France permitted foreign nationals to take temporary employment as nurses in public hospitals, but denied them permanent employment. The Commission contended that Community nationals should be allowed such permanent employment. At the time, 89,000 nurses were employed in French public hospitals, of whom about 150 were foreigners. Should public hospital nurses be considered to be employed in the public service? Similarly, in Commission v. Italy (Status of researchers), Case 225/85, [1987] ECR 2625, Italy allowed foreign nationals to have temporary employment with the Italian National Council for Research, but

denied them permanent posts. What result? Should it make a difference if the permanent post entails managerial responsibility, or involves research on defense matters, as opposed to consumer product safety studies?

4.   In a March 1988 statement, the Commission urged Member States to remove nationality restrictions for posts for which they are generally inappropriate. In the Commission's view, employment in State-owned airlines, public transport, utilities, post and telecommunications, and public health services should not be restricted to nationals. The Commission considered that nationality requirements were appropriate for high State offices, the judiciary, the armed forces, the police and tax authorities. In other sectors, such as regional and local governments and lower national government posts, an examination of the functions required for the post must be made to decide whether a nationality requirement is permissible. Obviously, drawing the line is not an easy task. Do you think the Commission's approach reasonably follows the Court's guidelines, or is it too broadly or narrowly conceived? For a careful analysis, see J. Handoll, Article 48(4) EEC and Non–National Access to Public Employment, 13 Eur.L.Rev. 223 (1988).

5.   In McCarthy v. Philadelphia Civil Service Commission, 424 U.S. 645, 96 S.Ct. 1154, 47 L.Ed.2d 366 (1976), a per curiam opinion of the Supreme Court upheld Philadelphia's requirement that city workers must be residents of the city, holding that the Equal Protection Clause was not applicable to such a rule. Many US cities have such residence requirements for particular categories of employees, notably policemen, firemen and administrative staff. Would similar city residence requirements be permitted by the Court of Justice, or would it consider them to constitute indirect discrimination based on nationality?

One of the largest categories of state employees is that of teachers, from the primary school through the university level. Most Member States have traditionally treated all teachers in public schools as state officials and reserved the position to their own nationals. Whether this was permissible after *Commission v. Belgium* soon became a major issue. In *Lawrie–Blum,* supra page 582, the Court held that trainee-teachers were not to be considered as "public service" employees. A few years later, the Court confronted the issue of the status of teachers.

ALLUÉ v. UNIVERSITÀ DI VENEZIA

Case 33/88, [1989] ECR 1591.

[In 1986, the University of Venice, a public university, refused to extend Allué's employment contract as a Spanish language lecturer. She had been employed since 1980, but an Italian decree set six years as the maximum period for the employment of a foreign language instructor. Allué sued to obtain permanent employment, and the national court asked whether the post of foreign language instructor at the university level should be considered to be one in "public service."]

7   [A]s the Court held in [*Lawrie–Blum,* supra page 582], a teaching post does not involve direct or indirect participation in the exercise of powers conferred by public law and in the discharge of functions whose purpose is to safeguard the general interests of the State or of other public authorities and which therefore require a special relationship of allegiance to the State on the part of persons occupying them and reciprocity of rights and duties which form the foundation of the bond of nationality.

* * *

9 [T]herefore * * * employment as a foreign-language assistant at a university is not employment in the public service within the meaning of Article [39(4)] of the EEC Treaty.

10 [In] the second question the national court seeks essentially to establish whether Article [39(2)] of the EEC Treaty precludes the application of a provision of national law which imposes a limit on the duration of the employment relationship between universities and foreign-language assistants where there is in principle no such limit for other workers.

11 [T]he principle of equal treatment of which Article [39(2)] is one embodiment prohibits not only overt discrimination based on nationality but all covert forms of discrimination which, by applying other distinguishing criteria, in fact achieve the same result * * *.

12 [A]lthough it applies regardless of the nationality of the worker concerned, the time-limit imposed by the legislation in question on working as a foreign-language assistant in a university essentially concerns workers who are nationals of other Member States. According to the statistics supplied by the Italian Government, only 25% of foreign-language assistants are Italian nationals.

13 In order to justify the legislation at issue in the main proceedings, the Italian Government claims that it is the only means of ensuring that universities have foreign-language assistants with an up-to-date knowledge and experience of the mother tongue which they teach.

14 [T]he danger of their losing contact with their mother tongue is slight, in the light of the increase in cultural exchanges and improved communications, and in addition it is open to the universities in any event to check the level of assistants' knowledge. Furthermore, it should be noted that under the legislation in question an assistant may be engaged by a university after working for six years in another university in the same Member State; the time-limit on the work in question therefore cannot be justified on the ground referred to by the Italian Government.

Notes and Questions

1. The Commission had argued in *Lawrie–Blum* that teachers as a class should not be deemed to be in the public service, but the Court carefully limited its holding to "preparatory service for the teaching profession." [1986] ECR 2121 at 2147. In *Allué,* the Court cites *Lawrie–Blum* as holding that a "teaching post" is not to be considered as in the public service and provides no further analysis of the issue. This illustrates that the Court is sometimes rather imprecise in dealing with its own precedents. In any event, do you consider that excluding foreign language lecturers at the university level from the public service category represents an appropriate application of the Court's guidelines in the two *Public service* cases? What about university professors?

2. In Bleis v. Ministère de l'Education Nationale, Case C–4/91, [1991] ECR I–5627, the Court held that secondary school teachers in the French educational system did not constitute a post in "public service." *Allué* and *Bleis* have a far-reaching impact, since States employ hundreds of thousands of teachers in primary, secondary and university level education. Migrant workers may readily qualify not only as foreign language instructors, but in virtually any educational

field. May, however, a State reserve administrative or supervisory posts in education, such as principals or deans, to its own nationals?

3.   In Commission v. Luxembourg (Public service employment), Case C–473/93, [1996] ECR I–3207, Luxembourg argued that all posts in public health, the railroad and urban transport, posts and telecommunication, and water, gas and electricity supply required Luxembourg nationality as a rule, while exceptions might be made on a case-by-case basis. The Court rejected this approach, holding that most posts in all these sectors could be deemed to be "remote from the specific activities of the public service" in the light of its prior case law. (¶ 31.) Luxembourg made a specific defense of its nationality requirement for teachers, contending that "in order to transmit traditional values," especially in view of Luxembourg's size and "specific demographic situation, the nationality require-ment is therefore an essential condition for preserving Luxembourg's national identity." (¶ 32.) How should the Court react to this argument? Is Luxembourg's policy of hiring only nationals as teachers as justifiable as Ireland's policy of requiring its teachers to speak Irish, discussed in *Groener*, supra?

D.   WHO IS A WORKER, SPOUSE OR FAMILY MEMBER?

Thus far we have assumed that we knew what is meant by a worker, a spouse, or a dependent family member. Border-line cases have, however, arisen, occasioning some difficulty in defining these terms, and therefore in determining the persons who are entitled to the rights described in Article 39 and Regulation 1612/68.

1.   DEFINITION OF A WORKER

LEVIN v. STAATSSECRETARIS VAN JUSTITIE
Case 53/81, [1982] ECR 1035.

[Levin, a UK national and the wife of a non-Community national, applied in 1978 for a Dutch residence permit. When her application was denied because she was not a "worker," Levin then took a low-paying but regular part-time job and reapplied. The Dutch authorities again refused her a residence permit, maintaining that her part-time employment earnings were insufficient for self-support and that her true motive was improper, since it was really to enable her husband to live in the Netherlands. On appeal, an Article 234 reference was made.]

6   In its first and second questions, * * * the national court is essentially asking whether the provisions of Community law relating to freedom of movement for workers also cover a national of a Member State whose activity as an employed person in the territory of another Member State provides him with an income less than the minimum required for subsis-tence within the meaning of the legislation of the second Member State. In particular the court asks whether those provisions cover such a person where he either supplements his income from his activity as an employed person with other income so as to arrive at that minimum or is content with means of support which fall below it.

* * *

9   [T]he terms "worker" and "activity as an employed person" are not expressly defined [in the Treaty or any legislation]. It is appropriate, therefore, in order to determine their meaning, to have recourse to the generally recognized principles of interpretation, beginning with the ordinary meaning to be attributed to those terms in their context and in the light of the objectives of the Treaty.

10   The Netherlands and Danish Governments have maintained that the provisions of Article [39] may only be relied upon by persons who receive a wage at least commensurate with the means of subsistence considered as necessary by the legislation of the Member State in which they work, or who work at least for the number of hours considered as usual in respect of full-time employment in the sector in question. * * *

11   That argument cannot, however, be accepted. As the Court has already stated in Case 75/63 *Hoekstra,* [1964] ECR 1977, the terms "worker" and "activity as an employed person" may not be defined by reference to the national laws of the Member States but have a Community meaning. If that were not the case, the Community rules on freedom of movement for workers would be frustrated, as the meaning of those terms could be fixed and modified unilaterally, without any control by the Community institutions, by national laws which would thus be able to exclude at will certain categories of persons from the benefit of the Treaty.

12   Such would, in particular, be the case if the enjoyment of the rights conferred by the principle of freedom of movement for workers could be made subject to the criterion of what the legislation of the host State declares to be a minimum wage, so that the field of application *ratione personae* of the Community rules on this subject might vary from one Member State to another. The meaning and the scope of the terms "worker" and "activity as an employed person" should thus be clarified in the light of the principles of the legal order of the Community.

13   In this respect it must be stressed that these concepts define the field of application of one of the fundamental freedoms guaranteed by the Treaty and, as such, may not be interpreted restrictively.

* * *

15   * * * Since part-time employment, although it may provide an income lower than what is considered to be the minimum required for subsistence, constitutes for a large number of persons an effective means of improving their living conditions, the effectiveness of Community law would be impaired and the achievement of the objectives of the Treaty would be jeopardized if the enjoyment of rights conferred by the principle of freedom of movement for workers were reserved solely to persons engaged in full-time employment * * *.

16   It follows that the concepts of "worker" and "activity as an employed person" must be interpreted as meaning that the rules relating to freedom of movement for workers also concern persons who pursue or wish to pursue an activity as an employed person on a part-time basis only and who, by virtue of that fact obtain or would obtain only remuneration lower than the minimum guaranteed remuneration in the sector under consideration. In this regard no distinction may be made between those who wish

to make do with their income from such an activity and those who supplement that income with other income, whether the latter is derived from property or from the employment of a member of their family who accompanies them.

[17] It should however be stated that whilst part-time employment is not excluded from the field of application of the rules on freedom of movement for workers, those rules cover only the pursuit of effective and genuine activities, [but not] activities on such a small scale as to be regarded as purely marginal and ancillary.

* * *

[19] The third question essentially seeks to ascertain whether the right to enter and reside in the territory of a Member State may be denied to a worker whose main objectives * * * are different from that of the pursuit of an activity as an employed person * * *.

[20] Under Article [39(3)] of the Treaty the right to move freely within the territory of the Member States is conferred upon workers for the "purpose" of accepting offers of employment actually made. By virtue of the same provision workers enjoy the right to stay in one of the Member States "for the purpose" of employment there.

* * *

[21] However, these formulations merely [indicate] that the advantages which Community law confers in the name of that freedom may be relied upon only by persons who actually pursue or seriously wish to pursue activities as employed persons * * *.

[22] Once this condition is satisfied, the motives which may have prompted the worker to seek employment in the Member State concerned are of no account and must not be taken into consideration.

Notes and Questions

1. Why is it important that "worker" have a Community law sense rather than a meaning based on national law concepts? Note the Court's emphasis in *Levin* on giving the term a broad meaning because freedom of movement of workers is a fundamental freedom. In this context, do you agree that a person's motive in taking employment is unimportant? Concretely, assume that Levin moved to the Netherlands and took a trivial part-time job only to enable her husband, who is not a Community national, to obtain an EEC residence permit there, when the UK would not have granted him a residence permit. Do you agree with the Court that both Levin and her husband should obtain rights of residence under Article 39?

2. Observe the social and economic importance of *Levin.* Any person who works part-time in "effective and genuine activities" has a right to residence in the host State. The Netherlands, supported by Denmark, had argued that only persons who earned a minimum wage for subsistence should qualify as workers. These two States were probably concerned that their reputation for being agreeable places to live might attract persons who lack substantial means of support and who choose to earn little in order to enjoy maximum leisure. States may fear that such persons pay low taxes and are not likely to be very productive economic participants in society, yet may become a substantial burden on the public health

and social security systems. If this concern is a valid one (which is a debatable proposition), do you consider the right of free movement important enough to outweigh it? Note in the next chapter that the 1990 directives on rights of residence for students, retired persons and the unemployed require that such persons have sufficient resources to avoid becoming a burden on the host State.

3. *Levin* creates a *de minimis* rule for part-time workers, excluding "marginal and ancillary" activities. Presumably babysitting for two hours a week would not qualify one for worker status. There are, however, several interesting cases on the borderline.

In Kempf v. Staatssecretaris van Justitie, Case 139/85, [1986] ECR 1741, a German musician resided in the Netherlands for a year. He worked initially as a part-time music teacher, giving twelve lessons a week, and earning less than $500 per month. Because of low earnings, he received public assistance benefits. He later became ill and unable to work, receiving health, unemployment and public assistance benefits. At this point, his application for an EEC residence permit was refused. On appeal, the court asked the Court of Justice whether a person whose part-time earnings have to be supplemented by public assistance funds can be considered a worker. What would you answer?

In Steymann v. Staatssecretaris van Justitie, Case 196/87, [1988] ECR 6159, a German member of the Bhagwan sect lived in the sect's community center in the Netherlands. The sect provided him with food, clothing and housing. He engaged in cleaning, plumbing and other household tasks, as well as working in the sect's disco-lounge, but received only pocket-money for minor personal expenses. His application for a residence permit was refused. On appeal, the court wanted to know whether Steymann's activities in this religious community entitled him to a residence permit. What do you think?

LAIR v. UNIVERSITAT HANOVER

Case 39/86, [1988] ECR 3161.

[Lair, a French national, became a student in 1984 at the University of Hanover, studying German and Romance languages and literature. Her request for state financial aid to cover tuition and living expenses was denied because Germany provides such aid only to German nationals, the children of migrant workers, and to migrant workers who have been regularly employed in Germany for the previous five years. Lair had worked in Germany as a bank clerk for two years. After her dismissal, she had only brief periods of employment for the next three years. When she sued to obtain the aid, an appellate court inquired whether Lair qualified as a "worker."]

The concept of worker

[31] Although [Article 39 and Regulation 1612/68 do] not provide an express answer to [the] question, there is nevertheless a basis in Community law for the view that the rights guaranteed to migrant workers do not necessarily depend on the actual or continuing existence of an employment relationship.

* * *

[33] Persons who have previously pursued in the host Member State an effective and genuine activity as an employed person as defined by the

Court [citing *Levin*] but who are no longer employed are nevertheless considered to be workers under certain provisions of Community law.

[The Court cited Directive 68/360, supra page 599, and Commission Regulation 1251/70, supra page 578, each of which grant workers certain rights to continued residence in the host State after ceasing employment.]

35   Furthermore, Article 7(3) of Regulation No 1612/68 guarantees migrant workers access, by virtue of the same right and under the same conditions as national workers, to training in vocational schools and retraining centres. That right to specific training, guaranteed by Community legislation, does not depend on the continued existence of an employment relationship.

36   It is therefore clear that migrant workers are guaranteed certain rights linked to the status of worker even when they are no longer in an employment relationship.

37   In the field of grants for university education, such a link between the status of worker and a grant awarded for maintenance and training with a view to the pursuit of university studies does, however, presuppose some continuity between the previous occupational activity and the course of study; there must be a relationship between the purpose of the studies and the previous occupational activity. Such continuity may not, however, be required where a migrant has involuntarily become unemployed and is obliged by conditions on the job market to undertake occupational retraining in another field of activity.

38   Such a conception of freedom of movement for migrant workers corresponds, moreover, to current developments in careers. Continuous careers are less common than was formerly the case. Occupational activities are therefore occasionally interrupted by periods of training or retaining.

39   The answer to the [referred] question should therefore be that a national of another Member State who has undertaken university studies in the host State leading to a professional qualification, after having engaged in occupational activity in that State, must be regarded as having retained his status as a worker and is entitled as such to the benefit of Article 7(2) of Regulation No 1612/68, provided that there is a link between the previous occupational activity and the studies in question.

[The Court concluded by rejecting an argument that the prior employment in Germany must have been pursued for some minimum period of time, effectively striking down Germany's condition of five years' employment.]

Notes and Questions

1.   Do you agree that a migrant worker who voluntarily gives up employment in order to pursue higher education should still be considered a worker for the purpose of securing equal treatment in the receipt of financial aid for the studies? How will studying German and Romance languages and literature enhance Lair's credentials for future employment?

2.   In Brown v. Secretary of State for Scotland, Case 197/86, [1988] ECR 3205, Brown, a French national, claimed the status of migrant worker in order to qualify for maintenance grants as an electrical engineering student at Cambridge. He had received eight months of "pre-university industrial training" at an

Edinburgh company which employed him temporarily solely because he had been accepted as an engineering student by Cambridge. Should Brown be considered a worker? Should electrical engineering studies be considered a type of vocational training?

2. DEFINITION OF "SPOUSE" AND "DEPENDENT"

Issues have also arisen as to the ability of a person to claim the status of a spouse or dependent under Regulation 1612/68. To resolve these issues, the Court of Justice has had, to some extent, to concern itself with family law.

THE NETHERLANDS v. REED

Case 59/85, [1986] ECR 1283.

[Ms. Reed, a UK national, lived since 1981 with Mr. W, an unmarried UK national, who worked and resided in the Netherlands. Although not herself a worker, she obtained a residence permit in 1982. Her application for a renewal was denied, because she was neither a worker nor the spouse of a worker. When she sued, the court held that an unmarried companion should be treated as a spouse under Regulation 1612/68. The appellate court affirmed, but on the principle of nondiscrimination, since under Dutch administrative rules the unmarried companion of a Dutch national would receive a residence permit, provided the two persons live together as one household and possess adequate housing and means of support. The Supreme Court referred questions under Article 234.]

9   Miss Reed argues that, in the light of legal and social developments, in applying Article 10 of Regulation No 1612/68, and in particular the word "spouse" in that article, * * * unmarried companions must in so far as is possible be treated as spouses.

10   The Netherlands Government points out that [Article 10 must] be interpreted in the Community context. The Community legislature used the word "spouse" in the sense given to that word in family law. When, in support of a dynamic interpretation, reference is made to developments in social and legal conceptions, those developments must be visible in the whole of the Community; such an argument cannot be based on social and legal developments in only one or a few Member States. There is no reason, therefore, to give the term "spouse" an interpretation which goes beyond the legal implications of that term, which embrace rights and obligations which do not exist between unmarried companions.

11   The Commission points out that there is no provision of Community law which defines the terms "spouse" and "marital relations". In the Community as it now stands it is impossible to speak of any consensus that unmarried companions should be treated as spouses.

* * *

12   According to Article [249] of the EEC Treaty, Regulation No 1612/68 has general application, is binding in its entirety and is directly applicable in all Member States.

13   It follows that an interpretation given by the Court to a provision of that regulation has effects in all of the Member States, and that any interpreta-

tion of a legal term on the basis of social developments must take into account the situation in the whole Community, not merely in one Member State.

* * *

[15] In the absence of any indication of a general social development which would justify a broad construction, * * * it must be held that the term "spouse" in Article 10 of the Regulation refers to a marital relationship only.

* * *

[18] [Miss Reed further argues] that Netherlands policy with regard to the unmarried companions of workers who are nationals of another Member State * * * results in discrimination in relation to Regulation No 1612/68, inasmuch as it authorizes a Netherlands national to bring to the Netherlands a companion of foreign nationality whereas that possibility is not open to a national of another Member State.

* * *

[22] It must therefore be ascertained whether the right to be accompanied by an unmarried companion falls within the scope of the Treaty and is thus governed by the principle of non-discrimination * * *.

* * *

[24] Article 7(2) of Regulation No 1612/68 provides that in the host State a worker who is a national of another Member State must "enjoy the same social and tax advantages as national workers".

* * *

[28] [T]he possibility for a migrant worker of obtaining permission for his unmarried companion to reside with him, where that companion is not a national of the host Member State, can assist his integration in the host State and thus contribute to the achievement of freedom of movement for workers. Consequently, that possibility must also be regarded as falling within the concept of a social advantage for the purposes of Article 7(2) of Regulation No 1612/68.

Notes and Questions

1. While declining to treat Reed as a sort of common-law spouse, the Court of Justice granted her a derivative right of residence through another expansive interpretation of the term "social advantages" in Regulation 1612/68. Do you agree with the Court? Suppose Reed receives her residence permit, but thereafter she and W quarrel and she ceases to be his companion. May the Netherlands then deport Reed? Suppose Reed is the companion of a migrant worker who is a woman? Do the answers to both questions turn on the nondiscrimination principle only?

2. In Diatta v. Land Berlin, Case 267/83, [1985] ECR 567, Diatta, a Senegalese national, married a French national who resided and worked in Berlin. She resided with him from February to August 1978, and then separated from him allegedly with the intention of securing a divorce, but never obtained one. Diatta's application to renew her residence permit was denied because she did not live

"with the worker" within the meaning of article 10 of Regulation 1612/68. In an Article 234 ruling, the Court of Justice held that Regulation 1612/68 did not require the spouse of a migrant worker to live with the worker. The Court added that "the marital relationship cannot be regarded as dissolved so long as it has not been terminated by the competent authority." Id. at 590. Do you agree? Suppose the "spouse" enters into a marriage with a migrant worker only for the purpose of securing a residence permit, but never intends to live with the migrant worker. May the national authorities deny a residence permit based on appropriate evidence that the parties never intended a true marriage?

3. The Commission's 1998 draft amendment to Regulation 1612/68 would add after "spouse" in article 10: "or any person corresponding to a spouse under the legislation of the host Member State." It would also grant to a third country national, who is the divorced spouse of a migrant worker, the right to continue in residence in a host State, provided the spouse has already resided there for three consecutive years. Do you agree with the policy view behind each amendment?

4. When is a migrant worker's child over 21 still to be considered a dependent with a right of residence under Regulation 1612/68, article 10? In Centre public d'aide sociale v. Lebon, Case 316/85, [1987] ECR 2811, the 25-year-old daughter of a French migrant worker residing in Belgium applied for social welfare assistance. The Court held that a child over 21, not herself a worker, generally is not entitled to rights accorded under Regulation 1612/68. However, a dependent child over 21 would still have the right to social welfare assistance, since this would constitute a "social advantage" for the migrant worker. The Court further held that the test for determining whether a child over 21 is dependent is whether the worker in fact provides the child with basic support, regardless of the motive for the support or whether the child is disabled or otherwise incapable of self-support. Do you agree with the Court?

3. PLAYERS ON PROFESSIONAL SPORTS TEAMS

Many European sports teams (e.g., soccer, football, basketball, hockey) represent cities or countries in various leagues or national or international competitive events. Understandably, the people of Liverpool tend to expect that their soccer team will be made up of British nationals, as the people of Milan expect their team to consist of Italians, and so on. The rules of many national or international sports federations require teams to be exclusively composed of a state's nationals, or limit the number of non-nationals.

Should Article 39 be applied to set aside these rules and prevent sports team owners from discriminating in hiring any Community nationals? Are professional sports team players to be considered "workers" in terms of Article 39? Moreover, how can a sports federation or a specific sports team be considered to be bound by Article 39 when they are part of the private sector and the discriminatory rules are not set by State law? All these issues had to be confronted.

Initially, in Walrave v. Union Cycliste Internationale, Case 36/64, [1974] ECR 1405, the Court of Justice held that Article 39 applied to limit not only public authorities, but also any national or international body's rules "aimed at collectively regulating gainful employment and services." Id. at 1421. The Court went on to hold that the rules of an international bicycle riding sports federation could not discriminate against Community nationals in the hiring of employees of bicycle riders. The Court did allow a federation to have rules which allow only nationals as competitors for "sports teams, in particular national teams, the formation of which is a question of purely sporting interest," but did not define "purely sporting interest."

The Court applied the same principle in Donà v. Mantero, Case 13/76, [1976] ECR 1333, invalidating Italian football federation rules forbidding Italian teams from having non-Italian players. Advocate General Trabucchi observed that this should not prevent a State from restricting participation in amateur competitions of an international character (e.g., the Olympics) to team members who are nationals of that State.

Not surprisingly, sports federations resisted compliance with this case law. The Commission attempted for years to enforce the nondiscrimination principle in direct discussions with certain federations, but with little success. Then came a 1995 judgement that attracted more media attention than any other that year.

UNION ROYALE BELGE DES SOCIETES DE FOOTBALL v. BOSMAN

Case C–415/93, [1995] ECR I–4921.

[Bosman, a Belgian football player, wanted to sign a contract with a French football club at the end of his two-year contract with the Belgian Liege club. However, the Belgian Football Association rules required his prospective French club employer to pay a substantial transfer fee to the Belgian club. The fee is calculated in function of a player's prior annual salary and may attain 14 times the annual salary. If agreement cannot be reached on paying the transfer fee, a player must enter into a new contract with his prior club; if not, he is suspended from professional play. In Bosman's case, the proposed transfer fee was 4.8 million Belgian francs (ca.$150,000), and the Liege club declined agreement out of concern that the French club's economic condition didn't assure payment. Bosman refused a new contract for lower pay with the Liege club, was suspended, and sued for damages and to enjoin interference with his transfer.

The Liege tribunal asked the Court of Justice not only whether the transfer fee system violated Article 39, but also whether the national and international sport federation rules limiting the number of non-national players violated it as well. The Belgian federation belongs to both the European football association (UEFA), and the international football association (FIFA), and the Belgian rules in question were set in accordance with UEFA and FIFA rules. The 1991 UEFA rules, set after discussion with the Commission, essentially limited the number of non-national active professional players to five per club.

The first important issue was whether Article 39 governed rules of private federations in the field of sports. The sports federations, supported by Germany, argued for "the autonomy of sport," claiming that Liege and most clubs "carry on an economic activity only to a negligible extent," so that Article 39 should not apply, or only apply with "a degree of flexibility." Germany also argued that sport formed a part of national culture which should be respected. The Court rejected this view.]

73   In response to those arguments, it is to be remembered that, having regard to the objectives of the Community, sport is subject to Community law only in so far as it constitutes an economic activity within the meaning of Article 2 of the Treaty.

* * *

75   Application of Article [39] of the Treaty is not precluded by the fact that the transfer rules govern the business relationships between clubs rather than the employment relationships between clubs and players. The fact that the employing clubs must pay fees on recruiting a player from another club affects the players' opportunities for finding employment and the terms under which such employment is offered.

76   As regards the difficulty of severing the economic aspects from the sporting aspects of football, the Court has held (in *Dona*) that the provisions of Community law concerning freedom of movement of persons and of provision of services do not preclude rules or practices justified on non-economic grounds which relate to the particular nature and context of certain matches. It stressed, however, that such a restriction on the scope of the provisions in question must remain limited to its proper objective. It cannot, therefore, be relied upon to exclude the whole of a sporting activity from the scope of the Treaty.

77   With regard to the possible consequences of this judgment on the organization of football as a whole, it has consistently been held that, although the practical consequences of any judicial decision must be weighed carefully, this cannot go so far as to diminish the objective character of the law and compromise its application on the ground of the possible repercussions of a judicial decision.

* * *

82   Once the objections concerning the application of Article [39] of the Treaty to sporting activities such as those of professional footballers are out of the way, it is to be remembered that, as the Court held in *Walrave,* cited above, Article [39] not only applies to the action of public authorities but extends also to rules of any other nature aimed at regulating gainful employment in a collective manner.

83   The Court has held that the abolition as between Member States of obstacles to freedom of movement for persons and to freedom to provide services would be compromised if the abolition of State barriers could be neutralized by obstacles resulting from the exercise of their legal autonomy by associations or organizations not governed by public law (see *Walrave,* cited above).

84   [W]orking conditions in the different Member States are governed sometimes by provisions laid down by law or regulation and sometimes by agreements and other acts concluded or adopted by private persons. Accordingly, if the scope of Article [39] of the Treaty were confined to acts of a public authority there would be a risk of creating inequality in its application (see *Walrave*). That risk is all the more obvious in a case such as that in the main proceedings in this case in that * * * the transfer

rules have been laid down by different bodies or in different ways in each Member State.

* * *

[87] Article [39] of the Treaty therefore applies to rules laid down by sporting associations such as URBSFA, FIFA or UEFA, which determine the terms on which professional sportsmen can engage in gainful employment.

[The Court then concluded that the transfer fee system constituted an indirect restriction of free movement.]

[96] Provisions which preclude or deter a national of a Member State from leaving his country of origin in order to exercise his right to freedom of movement therefore constitute an obstacle to that freedom even if they apply without regard to the nationality of the workers concerned.

* * *

[100] Since [the transfer rules] provide that a professional footballer may not pursue his activity with a new club established in another Member State unless it has paid his former club a transfer fee agreed upon between the two clubs or determined in accordance with the regulations of the sporting associations, the said rules constitute an obstacle to freedom of movement for workers.

[In ¶¶ 105–113, the Court rejected the arguments made to justify the transfer rules. The Court then turned to the non-national players restriction, noting first that article 4 of Regulation 1612/68 forbids any national rules which set quotas on employment by migrant workers.]

[119] The same principle applies to clauses contained in the regulations of sporting associations which restrict the right of nationals of other Member States to take part, as professional players, in football matches [citing *Dona,* supra].

[120] The fact that those clauses concern not the employment of such players, on which there is no restriction, but the extent to which their clubs may field them in official matches is irrelevant. In so far as participation in such matches is the essential purpose of a professional player's activity, a rule which restricts that participation obviously also restricts the chances of employment of the player concerned.

[The Court then rejected the justifications for the nationality clauses advanced by the sports federations.]

[123] [The sports federations and several governments argued that the] clauses serve to maintain the traditional link between each club and its country, a factor of great importance in enabling the public to identify with its favourite team and ensuring that clubs taking part in international competitions effectively represent their countries.

* * *

[129] [T]he nationality clauses cannot be deemed to be in accordance with Article [39] of the Treaty, otherwise that article would be deprived of its practical effect and the fundamental right of free access to employment

which the Treaty confers individually on each worker in the Community rendered nugatory * * *.

131 [A] football club's links with the Member State in which it is established cannot be regarded as any more inherent in its sporting activity than its links with its locality, town, region or, in the case of the United Kingdom, the territory covered by each of the four associations.

Notes and Questions

1. Advocate General Lenz's remarkably detailed and analytical opinion undoubtedly greatly influenced the Court. In particular, he urged that the Court answer the question on the nationality clause, although the issue arguably had little relevance to Bosman's lawsuit, because of the importance of the issue and the limited likelihood that it would be raised again.

2. Do you sympathize with the German government's view that sports teams ought to be able to restrict the number of non-nationals as an aspect of the "cultural" tradition of States? (Advocate General Lenz noted that foreign players were often among the most popular ones on specific teams, citing examples.)

Would you support Community legislation to exempt sports federations rules from the ambit of Article 39 (rather like the Congressional exemption of baseball from US antitrust rules)? Could the Council and Parliament validly adopt such legislation? *Bosman* is a good example of the type of case that popular opinion finds hard to understand, and that can accordingly lead to hostility toward the Court and Treaty rules. For a strong endorsement of the Court's view (and admiration for Advocate General Lenz's opinion), noting its revolutionary consequences for the sport, see the casenote by S. Weatherill, 33 Common Mkt. L. Rev. 991 (1996). Lobbying to try to obtain a treaty amendment to exclude sport from Treaty rules failed, but the Amsterdam Treaty does annex a Declaration on Sports urging that the views of sports federations be seriously considered.

3. The Liege club and the sports federations are private undertakings. Did the Court in *Bosman* hold that Article 39 has horizontal direct effect? The Court's language in ¶ ¶ 82–84 treats the sport federation rules rather like collective bargaining agreements, having an inherent trans-national character. In any event, *Bosman* certainly influenced *Angonese*, supra page 589.

E. THE ISSUE OF REVERSE DISCRIMINATION

In Chapter 4, we discussed the Court of Justice's internal affairs doctrine, which holds that Community law does not apply to factual situations which are considered to involve only internal state affairs. On occasion, when personal rights of free movement and residence are involved, parties claim that failure to apply Community law gives rise to reverse discrimination. Thus, when a particular right has been recognized for migrant workers in applying Article 39, Regulation 1612/68 or some relevant directive, may a national of a Member State residing within that State claim the same right, on the basis of the principle of nondiscrimination stated in Article 12 of the Treaty?

MOSER v. LAND BADEN–WÜRTTEMBERG

Case 180/83, [1984] ECR 2539.

[Moser, a German national, applied for admission to a teacher-training program in Baden–Württemberg, but was refused because he was a member of the Communist party. When he appealed, the national court asked the Court of Justice whether Moser should be considered a worker and therefore protected by the nondiscrimination provision in Article 39(2).]

12 [The German labor court] asks essentially whether [Moser] may rely on Article [39] to prevent the application to him of legislation, such as that in force in the *Land,* by virtue of which persons as regards whose loyalty to the Basic Law there is insufficient certainty are denied access to the vocational training necessary to enable them to become teachers in primary and secondary education.

* * *

15 [T]he provisions of the Treaty concerning the free movement of workers and particularly Article [39] cannot be applied to situations which are wholly internal to a Member State, in other words where there is no factor connecting them to any of the situations envisaged by Community law.

16 The case described by the national court concerns * * * a German national who has always lived and maintained his residence in the Federal Republic of Germany and who contests the refusal by the German authorities to allow him access, under the legislation of that State, to a particular kind of vocational training.

17 In order to establish a connection with the Community provisions, Mr. Moser claimed * * * that the application to him of the German legislation in question, by making it impossible for him to complete his training as a teacher, entails the result that he is precluded from applying for teaching posts in schools in the other Member States.

18 That argument cannot be upheld. A purely hypothetical prospect of employment in another Member State does not establish a sufficient connection with Community law to justify the application of Article [39] of the Treaty.

Notes and Questions

1. For other cases applying the internal affairs doctrine despite claims of reverse discrimination, see Regina v. Saunders, Case 175/78, [1979] ECR 1129 (UK national confined by court order to residence in Northern Ireland after committing a penal offense in England cannot claim nondiscrimination rights under Article 7 because she is not a migrant worker under Article 39); Morson v. The Netherlands, Cases 35 & 36/82 [1982] ECR 3723 (Surinamese nationals, parents of Dutch nationals, cannot claim rights under Regulation 1612/68 as family members because their children are not migrant workers, so no Community law issue is involved); and Land Nordrhein–Westfalen v. Uecker, Case C–64/96, [1997] ECR I–3171 (Norwegian spouse of a German national, who has never exercised the right of free movement, cannot challenge under Article 39 the terms

of her contract as a Norwegian language instructor at the University of Munster, because there is no factor linking her complaint to Community law).

2. Does the internal affairs doctrine as applied in *Moser* and similar cases represent sound policy? Since the Court has stressed repeatedly its respect for basic rights, among which the principle of non-discriminatory treatment clearly figures, why doesn't the Court consider that nationals (or their family members) should receive as favorable treatment by a Member State as a migrant worker would in similar circumstances? What about the argument that if there is no real Community law issue, the Court of Justice has no jurisdiction to provide any relief? The issue is certainly troublesome, because in the absence of Community law recourse, some national courts may be able to apply national constitutional principles to avoid reverse discrimination in these cases, but others will be unable to do so.

In Steen v. Deutsche Bundespost II, Case C–132/93, [1994] ECR I–2715, when a German trial court was told by the Court of Justice that a German national's claim against the German post office raised no Community law issue, the trial court referred a second question, namely, what relief might be given if a German national cannot claim rights in Germany that another Member State migrant worker would enjoy? The Court repled: "Community law does not preclude a national court from examining the compatibility with its constitution of a national rule which, in a situation unconnected with * * * Community law, treats national workers less favorably than nationals from other Member States." Presumably the Court's answer represents a helpful endorsement of a national court's use of its own constitutional equal treatment principles.

SCHOLZ v. OPERA UNIVERSITARIA DI CAGLIARI

Case C–419/92, [1994] ECR I–505.

[Scholz, a German citizen who acquired Italian citizenship by marriage, applied in 1984 for a canteen post at the University of Cagliari. In a competitive review, she lost, but she would have been one of the successful applicants if her prior work experience for the German post office had been taken into consideration. Work experience in the Italian public service would have been considered. When she sued, the trial court inquired whether this constituted indirect discrimination under Article 39.]

7 * * * Article [39] of the Treaty prohibits not only overt discrimination by reason of nationality but also all covert forms of discrimination which, by the application of other distinguishing criteria, lead in fact to the same result.

8 [I]t should be noted first of all that the fact that the plaintiff * * * has acquired Italian nationality has no bearing on the application of the principle of non-discrimination.

9 Any Community national who, irrespective of his place of residence and his nationality, has exercised the right to freedom of movement for workers and who has been employed in another Member State, falls within the scope of the aforesaid provisions.

* * *

11 [Accordingly,] the refusal to take into consideration the plaintiff's employment in the public service of another Member State, for the purposes of

the [competitive review of applicants' credentials] constitutes unjustified indirect discrimination.

[12]　[T]herefore * * * Article [39] must be interpreted as meaning that, where a public body of a Member State, in recruiting staff for posts which do not fall within the scope of Article [39(4)], provides for account to be taken of candidates' previous employment in the public service, that body may not, in relation to Community nationals, make a distinction according to whether such employment was in the public service of that particular State or in the public service of another Member State.

Notes and Questions

1.　The judgment demonstrates that the Court applies the internal affairs doctrine as narrowly as possible. Advocate General Jacobs remarks, "it may at first sight seem strange" that an Italian national seeking employment in Italy can claim rights under Article 39, but "it would be illogical" to say that she has such rights as a German citizen but loses them when she also becomes an Italian citizen by marriage (¶¶ 20–21). In fact, the Court's language goes even further. Look at ¶ 9. Suppose an Italian citizen without dual nationality claimed credit for work experience in Germany when the Cagliari University rules granted credit only for work in Italy. The plaintiff would still win. Does that seem "strange" to you, but still "logical"? For a perceptive comment, see the casenote by Robin White, 19 Eur. L. Rev. 308 (1994).

Chapter 16

EUROPEAN CITIZENSHIP AND THE FREE MOVEMENT OF PERSONS

_____

The political leadership of the European Community has long sought to provide to Member State citizens greater personal benefits from Community membership and simultaneously to make individuals more aware of the economic, social and cultural contributions provided by the Community, particularly in their daily lives. For this reason, in 1984 the European Council endorsed the People's Europe Program, with a legislative agenda continuing to the present, and a particular stress on efforts to achieve total free movement of persons.

In addition to legislation in the People's Europe program, striking judgments of the Court in the mid-1980's enabled students in higher education to pursue their studies throughout the Community without discrimination on the basis of nationality with regard to admission, tuition, fees or financial aid. In 1987, the Community launched the famous Erasmus program to encourage students to take courses and carry out research in other Member States. By the Treaty of Maastricht, the Member States amended the EC Treaty in 1993 to introduce the concept of European Citizenship, and to add education and culture as Community fields of action. Since May 1999, the Treaty of Amsterdam mandates Council efforts to achieve an "area of freedom, security, and justice," including the removal of frontier controls on persons between States and the harmonization and liberalization of rules governing the entry and status of persons from third countries.

This chapter can deal only summarily with these developments despite their intrinsic importance, because most of the legislation and other measures are highly technical in character and the scope of the action programs is very broad. At least this chapter, like those on free movement of workers, social policy and equal rights, can provide some sense of the human dimension of the European Union.

A. THE PEOPLE'S EUROPE

In June 1984, the European Council meeting at Fontainebleau decided that it was "essential that the Community should respond to the expectations of the people of Europe by adopting measures to strengthen and promote its identity and its image both for its citizens and for the rest of the world." Bull. EC 1985–7 Supp. 5. The European Council created an ad hoc committee to report on measures appropriate to this goal, in particular measures for "the abolition of all police and customs formalities for people crossing intra-Community frontiers," and for creating symbols for the Community. The ad hoc committee presented its report, called "A People's Europe," and the European Council endorsed its proposals at its Brussels meeting in March 1985.

The People's Europe program became a component of the June 1985 White Paper on Completing the Internal Market, described in Chapter 14B, which stressed the need to remove all controls of persons crossing intra-Community frontiers, "which to the ordinary citizen are the obvious manifestation of the continued division of the Community." The Commission proposed measures to grant rights of residence throughout the Community to persons who are neither employed nor self-employed, to recognize the equivalence of higher education diplomas, and to further student interchange and cooperation between educational institutions. All these initiatives have now borne fruit. We will discuss the student exchange and educational cooperation measures in section C and the diploma recognition directive in Chapter 18A.

The Council's adoption of three directives on rights of residence in 1990 represents one of the principal successes of the People's Europe program. The directives were all adopted through use of Article 308 (ex Article 235) because the Council considered that no specific Treaty grant of legislative power authorized the directives. The first, Directive 90/365,O.J. L 180/28 (July 13, 1990), grants a right of residence to all "persons who have ceased their occupational activity," which essentially means formerly employed or self-employed persons who have retired or become disabled. The second, Directive 90/364 O.J. L 180/26 (July 13, 1990), grants a right of residence in any Member State to nationals of other States who do not enjoy a right of residence under any other provision of Community law. This essentially means all those who are not workers, self-employed, retired, or students. The third directive covers students in a vocational training course (which the Court of Justice interprets as including most university studies), but allows the residence permit to be limited in time to the duration of studies. The student residence directive was readopted in 1993, O.J.L 317/59 (Dec. 18, 1993), using Article 12 (then Article 7) as its legal basis, after the initial 1990 student residence directive was annulled by the Court of Justice because it was invalidly based upon Article 308. The three directives are reproduced in the Selected Documents.

All three directives grant an accessory right of residence to the spouse of the person covered by the directive, and any dependent descendants or ancestors of either spouse, even if the person involved is not a Community national (art. 2). They thus parallel the right of residence granted to family members of workers by Regulation 1612/68, supra page 577.

On the other hand, article 1 of each directive sets an important condition on the residence right. In the first directive, the retired or disabled person must be a recipient of either a retirement or old age pension or an invalidity pension in an amount "sufficient to avoid becoming a burden on the social security system of the host Member State," and also be covered by all-risk health insurance. Those who seek to claim the right under the second directive must "have sufficient resources to avoid becoming a burden on the social assistance system of the host Member State during their period of residence" and must be covered by all-risk health insurance. The student residence directive has a parallel condition. "Sufficient resources" is defined in the directives as an amount higher than the level at which host State nationals may obtain state social assistance.

The three directives certainly enhance the mobility of persons who are neither employed nor self-employed. However, because they are limited to persons possessing sufficient resources, the directives do not achieve in the Community as broad a right of residence as the Supreme Court rulings discussed in Chapter 15A have produced in the US.

Several People's Europe measures produce considerable benefits in daily life. The Community introduced a Community passport in 1985, which has now replaced all national passports. Postal rates for mail within the Community are now charged on the same basis as domestic mail. A 1992 Council decision introduced 00 as the standard telephone access code for international calls, replacing a variety of international access numbers. Periodically, a directive sets common summertime (daylight savings time) standards for all the Member States which are effective for several years (except that the United Kingdom and Ireland are one hour earlier). Largely for its symbolic effect, in 1986, the Council authorized a Community flag (a circle of twelve gold stars on a blue background), which is flown in front of the buildings housing Community institutions and at conferences and meetings.

Of considerable practical importance are the two Council directives on driving licenses. The first, Directive 80/1263, O.J. L 375/1 (Dec. 31, 1980), introduced a Community model form for such licenses and set minimum levels for both drivers' tests and medical standards. The second, Directive 91/439, 1991 O.J. L 237/1 (Aug. 24, 1991), requires that any license issued by one State be recognized in all others. When a person changes residence to a new State, the initial license remains valid, although the license holder may have to pay a local license tax and is subject to the new State's rules on medical checks and on the duration of the license.

Without fanfare, in 1991 the Council adopted Directive 91/477 on control of the acquisition and possession of weapons, O.J.L 256/51 (Sept. 13, 1991). The directive harmonizes national rules on licenses for dealers in weapons, and requires that dealers keep registers which identify both the person buying the weapon and the weapon itself. Member States are to forbid persons from acquiring or possessing weapons without authorization, which is to be given only "for good cause" to persons "not likely to be a danger to themselves * * * or to public safety." The directive also sets conditions for all intra-Community trade in weapons, and requires controls on the importation of weapons from States outside the community. One of the motives for the directive was to reduce the need for border controls on persons. In addition, the directive manifestly contributes substantially to public and personal safety.

The most important recent directive intended to provide concrete benefits in daily life is Directive 95/46 on the protection of individuals with regard to the processing of personal data, O.J. L 281/31 (Nov. 23, 1995), commonly called the data privacy directive. The stated goal of the directive is to "protect the fundamental rights and freedoms of natural persons, and in particular their right of privacy with respect to the processing of personal data (art. 1).

The data privacy directive contains detailed provisions on the circumstances under which personal data can be processed (usually only when the subject "has unambiguously given his consent" or is under a legal obligation to provide the data) (art. 7) and generally prohibits the processing of sensitive data, e.g., "revealing racial or ethnic origin, * * * religious or philosophical beliefs," or "data concerning health or sex life" (art. 8). Further provisions govern the data subject's right of access to data concerning him or her (art. 12), and a right to object to use of the data, particularly for "direct marketing" (art. 14). Member States must provide judicial remedies and suitable sanctions for the breach of rights (arts. 22–24).

The data privacy directive also prohibits the transfer of personal data to a third country unless the country "ensures an adequate level of protection" (art. 25). This article provoked difficult negotiations with the United States, where there are few regulatory modes of protection of personal data and where the collection and use of such data, especially for direct marketing, has become a substantial business. In July 2000, the Commission and the Commerce Department reached a "safe harbor" arrangement under which US entities that desire to receive personal data from the Community should undertake to obtain the consent of the data subject and otherwise essentially follow the directive's requirement.

Since Jan. 1, 2002, Euro bills and Euro coins have supplanted the national currency and coins in the twelve States participating in the final stage of Monetary Union (see Chapter 33F). Most Member State nationals thus now experience the most far-reaching impact of the Community on their daily lives. Euro bills and coins represent a far more vivid symbol of European citizenship than the European passport or flag.

B. EUROPEAN CITIZENSHIP

A vital symbol with practical impact: that was undoubtedly the motivation for the Maastricht Treaty's introduction of Citizenship of the Union in a series of articles immediately following the EC Treaty's Principles. Article 17 (ex Article 8) makes every national of a Member State a "citizen of the Union."

The most important identified right of a citizen of the Union is set out in Article 18 (ex Article 8a—not to be confused with the earlier Article 8a on the internal market goal, which was renumbered as Article 7a by the Maastricht Treaty). Article 18 guarantees "the right to move and reside freely within the territory of the Member States," subject to any conditions set elsewhere in the Treaty or implementing legislation. This reference to conditions preserves the public policy, public security and public health limitations on free movement of workers in Article 39(3) and the parallel limitations on free movement of the self-employed in Articles 46 and 55. Article 18 authorizes the Parliament and Council to act by means of the co-decision procedure in order to facilitate the rights of movement and residence, but the Council must act unanimously in the procedure (an unusual provision presumably inserted to provide each State with a veto of, for example, measures to eliminate border controls). When it becomes effective, the Nice Treaty will delete this unusual unanimity requirement.

Article 19 permits every Union citizen resident in another State to "vote and to stand as a candidate at municipal elections," as well as in elections for the European Parliament in that State. Citizens of the Union also have the right to petition Parliament and to bring complaints to the new Community Ombudsman (Article 21) (discussed at page 56, *supra*), and to receive diplomatic and consular protection from any Member State in any third state in which their home Member State is not represented (Article 20).

The two directives intended to spell out the rights of Union citizens to vote in other Member States under Article 19 have been adopted. Directive 93/109, O.J. L 329/34 (Dec. 30, 1993), set out the conditions for voting or standing as a candidate for the European Parliament, just in time for use in the June 1994 elections. Parallel in approach, but somewhat more detailed, is Directive 94/80, O.J. L 368/38 (Dec. 31, 1994), effective January 1, 1996, stating the rights of citizens of the Union to vote or run for office in municipal elections in the State in which they reside.

Although the two directives grant voting and candidacy rights which had existed previously in only a few States, the rights are still rather limited in nature. Directive 94/80 covers only municipal elections, not national or even regional ones, and article 5(3) permits States to continue to reserve the chief executive office (or collegial executive board) of a municipality to its own nationals. Both directives also grant a derogation to a State if the total number of voting age nationals of other Union States exceeds 20% of the total voting age population. This was intended for Luxembourg, where almost 30% of the voting age population is comprised of nationals of other States, in part because so many Union institutions are located there. Most of the Member States had to amend their Constitutions in order to comply with the directive.

Although the right to vote in local elections is certainly of some value, a far greater contribution to Member State nationals residing long-term or even permanently in other States would be to permit them to vote in national elections. This, however, is not yet on the horizon. Moreover, since some States do not permit absentee voting in national elections, one may wonder why there has been no proposal to legislate to require this for migrant workers who often do not have the time or means to return to their home State to vote.

What functional impact might the concept of citizenship of the Union have with regard to free movement and residence? As a practical matter, the three directives on rights of residence for students, retired persons and other non-workers accorded a right of entry and residence throughout the Community. Naturally, Article 18 has constitutional force, so that future legislation cannot revoke or limit the three directives. Remember, however, that the directives grant no right of residence to those who cannot meet the standard of sufficient economic resources to avoid becoming a burden on the host State's social assistance. Is this limitation compatible with Article 18?

MARTINEZ SALA v. FREISTAAT BAYERN

[See the summary of facts at page 602. The Commission suggested to the Court that Martinez Sala, as a citizen of the Union, had a right to reside in Germany and hence automatically had a right to claim the child-raising allowance. The Court declined to take a position on whether she had a right to residence arising under Article 18, because "it is common ground" that Germany had in fact permitted her to reside there. (¶ 60). The Court did, however, declare that Article 18 carried over the right to non-discrimination based on nationality from Article 12.]

63   It follows that a citizen of the European Union, such as the appellant in the main proceedings, lawfully resident in the territory of the host Member State, can rely on Article [12, ex Article 7] of the Treaty in all situations which fall within the scope *ratione materiae* of Community law, including the situation where that Member state delays or refuses to grant to that claimant a benefit that is provided to all persons lawfully resident in the territory of that State on the ground that the claimant is not in possession of a document which nationals of that same State are not required to have and the issue of which may be delayed or refused by the authorities of that State.

Notes and Questions

1.   Does the right of non-discrimination based on nationality applied by the Court in *Martinez Sala* mean that, for example, a Member State national who retires with sufficient economic resources to enable his/her residence in a host State, but who later loses those resources, has a right to continue to reside there with the host State social assistance? Or, to the contrary, may the host State then expel the person? Does the judgment imply that the sufficient economic resources condition inserted in the three directives on residence of non-workers is no longer valid, even at the point in time at which a Member State national seeks to take up residence in a host State? Do you think the Court of Justice should adopt a policy stance parallel to that of the US Supreme Court in *Shapiro* and *Saenz, supra* page 579?

2.   Who are "nationals" of Member States who then become citizens of the Union? Declaration 2 to the Treaty on European Union states that that question is to be "settled solely by reference to the national law of the Member State concerned." The Court of Justice declined to set any Community law constraints on such a Member State determination of its own nationality in the Queen v. Secretary of State for the Home Department ex parte Kaur, Case C–192/99, [2001] ECR ___ (Feb. 20, 2001), permitting the United Kingdom to refuse residence rights to British Overseas Citizens (certain persons from former UK colonies who were granted UK citizenship in 1948, but without a right to reside in the UK).

3.   In Micheletti v. Delegacion del Gobierno, Case C–369/90, [1992] ECR 1–4239, the Court held that the Spanish authorities must deliver a Community residence permit to Micheletti, an Argentine–Italian dual national, even though he had apparently spent most of his life in Argentina and resided there immediately before coming to Spain. Spain could not apply its law treating dual nationals as essentially having only the nationality of the country of principal or most recent

residence. US citizens who enjoy also the citizenship of a Member State may find Micheletti a useful precedent.

4. On May 23, 2001, the Commission announced its intention to propose a directive that would facilitate the rights of free movement and residence for all citizens of the Union, notably to enable a right of residence for six months without any formalities, and to create a right of permanent residence after four years of actual residence in a host State.

CRIMINAL PROCEEDINGS AGAINST BICKEL AND FRANZ

Case C–274/96, [1998] ECR I–7637.

[Under Italian law, German speaking citizens of the Province of Bolzano (where most of the German speaking minority in Italy live) are entitled to have judicial proceedings involving them conducted in German. Bickel, an Austrian national and resident was arrested for driving his truck in Bonzano under the influence of alcohol. Franz, a German national and resident, was arrested while he was a tourist in Bolzano for possession of a knife prohibited by law. Each stated that he spoke no Italian and requested that the criminal proceedings be conducted in German. The trial court asked the Court of Justice whether either should be accorded that right pursuant to Articles 12 and 18 (ex Articles 7 and 8a). (In Chapter 17B, the Court's opinion is presented on whether Bickel and Franz have rights based upon their status as the providers or receivers of services.)

20 In the submission of Mr. Bickel and Mr. Franz, if any discrimination contrary to Article [12] of the Treaty is to be avoided, the right to have proceedings conducted in German must be extended to all citizens of the Union, since it is already available to nationals of one of the Member States.

21 The Italian Government contends that the only nationals upon whom the right in question is conferred are those who are both residents of the Province of Bolzano and members of its German-speaking community, the aim of the rules in issue being to recognize the ethnic and cultural identity of persons belonging to the protected minority.

* * *

25 Even on the assumption that, as the Italian Government maintains, German speaking nationals of other Member States who are resident in the Province of Bolzano may rely on the rules in issue and submit their pleadings in German—so that there is no discrimination on grounds of nationality as between residents of the region—Italian nationals are at an advantage by comparison with nationals of other Member States. The majority of Italian nationals whose language is German are in a position to demand that German be used throughout the proceedings in the Province of Bolzano, because they meet the residence requirement laid down by the rules in issue; the majority of German-speaking nationals of other Member States, on the other hand, cannot avail themselves of that right because they do not satisfy that requirement.

26   Consequently, rules such as those in issue in the main proceedings, which make the right, in a defined area, to have criminal proceedings conducted in the language of the person being resident in that area, favour nationals of the host State by comparison with nationals of other Member States exercising their right to freedom of movement and therefore run counter to the principle of non-discrimination laid down in Article [12] of the Treaty.

* * *

29   The Italian Government's contention that the aim of those rules is to protect the ethno-cultural minority residing in the province in question does not constitute a valid justification in this context. Of course, the protection of such a minority may constitute a legitimate aim. It does not appear, however, from the documents before the Court that that aim would be undermined if the rules in issue were extended to cover German-speaking nationals of other Member States exercising their right to freedom of movement.

30   Furthermore, it should be recalled that Mr. Bickel and Mr. Franz pointed out at the hearing, without being contradicted, that the courts concerned are in a position to conduct proceedings in German without additional complications or costs.

31   Consequently, the answer to the second part of the question referred for a preliminary ruling must be that Article [12] of the Treaty precludes national rules which in respect of a particular language other than the principal language of the Member State concerned, confer on citizens whose language is that particular language and who are resident in a defined area the right to inquire that criminal proceedings be conducted in that language, without conferring the same right on nationals of other Member States traveling or staying in that area, whose language is the same.

Notes and Questions

1.   *Bickel and Franz* is an important precedent because it indicates that the Court is willing to imply a right of nondiscrimination based on nationality to any citizen of the Union who moves for any reason into the territory of a host State. Advocate General Jacob suggested that non-discrimination on the basis of nationality in criminal proceedings flowed directly from Article 18, without any need to find a link to a specific treaty right (e.g. here, to the right to provide or receive services). Paragraphs 23–26 of the Court's judgement appear to reach that conclusion, although they are less clear cut.

2.   For a probing analysis of what citizenship of the union might, or should, come to mean, see S. O'Leary, The Evolving Concept of Community Citizenship (Kluwer, 1996); C. Closa, The Concept of Citizenship in the Treaty on European Union, 29 Com. Mkt. L. Rev. 1137 (1992); and J. Shaw, The Many Pasts and Futures of Citizenship in the European Union, 60 Mod. L. Rev. 554 (1997).

C. STUDENTS, EDUCATION AND CULTURE

The initial Treaty of Rome contained no provision on education as such, but Article 128, within the Title on Social Policy, authorized the Council to "lay down general principles for implementing a common vocational training policy" for the benefit of the common market. Presumably the intent was to facilitate skilled employment. The Court of Justice, however, expansively applied this text, in conjunction with the principle of non-discrimination on the basis of nationality, to develop a right of free movement for students in higher education. The Council subsequently employed Article 128 to justify the adoption of programs to promote inter-state student movement. Ultimately the political leadership concluded that it was time to bring education and culture at least partially within the scope of the EC Treaty by amendments in the Treaty of Maastricht. Article 128 was then revised and renumbered as Article 150. We briefly survey these developments, commencing with the Court case law on students' rights.

1. STUDENT ACCESS TO HIGHER EDUCATION

May Community nationals claim the right of equal treatment with host State nationals in access to higher education? With regard to financial assistance for tuition and fees? With regard to social assistance during studies? How does the Court's doctrine on the rights of students to access to higher education differ from that of the US Supreme Court?

GRAVIER v. CITY OF LIÈGE

Case 293/83, [1985] ECR 593.

[A 1983 regulation of the Belgian Ministry of Education required all state schools, from the elementary to the university level, to charge enrollment fees to foreign students whose parents are not resident in Belgium. Students of Belgian nationality were not charged any comparable fee. Gravier, a French student whose parents resided in France, sued to demand enrollment in the Liège fine arts academy without payment of a BF 24622 (ca. $600) annual enrollment fee. Gravier intended to study strip cartoon art. The trial court asked the Court of Justice whether Article 12 (ex Article 7) granted the right of non-discrimination based on nationality to students following vocational training courses and whether strip cartoon art study could be considered vocational training.]

12   The Belgian State * * * argued before the Court that the reason why foreign students in Belgium are required to contribute to the financing of education is the imbalance which has existed since 1976 between the number of foreign students studying in Belgium and the number of Belgian students living abroad. Since that imbalance had serious consequences for the national education budget the Belgian Government was compelled to ask students who are nationals of other Member States and who normally do not pay taxes in Belgium to make a proportional contribution to the cost of education. Far from being discriminatory, such a contribution puts foreign students on the same footing as Belgian nationals.

13   The Commission provided the Court with figures showing that the mobility of students within the Community is limited in scope but that Belgium is the Member State in which the percentage of students who are nationals of other Member States, in relation to the total number of students, is the highest. The information provided also shows that Belgium is the only

Member State which requires foreign students to pay an enrolment fee * * *.

[14] [I]t is clear from the content of the Belgian legislation and from the practice followed in relation to the fee, as summarized above, that the cost of higher art education is not borne by students of Belgian nationality, whereas foreign students must bear part of that cost. The inequality of treatment is therefore based on nationality * * *.

[15] Such unequal treatment based on nationality must be regarded as discrimination prohibited by Article [12, ex Article 7] of the Treaty if it falls within the scope of the Treaty.

[16] The Danish Government and the United Kingdom * * * argue that Article [12] of the Treaty does not prevent a Member State from treating its own nationals more favourably in the area of education, particularly as regards access to education, scholarships and grants, other social facilities provided for students and the contribution by students to the cost of education. On those points each Member State has special responsibilities toward its own nationals.

* * *

[18] [I]t is first necessary to define precisely the nature of the problem. In the first place, the questions referred concern neither the organization of education nor even its financing, but rather the establishment of a financial barrier to access to education for foreign students only. * * *

[19] [A]lthough educational organization and policy are not as such included in the spheres which the Treaty has entrusted to the Community institutions, access to and participation in courses of instruction and apprenticeship, in particular vocational training, are not unconnected with Community law.

* * *

[21] Article 128 [now revised as Article 150] of the Treaty provides that the Council is to lay down general principles for implementing a common vocational training policy capable of contributing to the harmonious development both of the national economies and of the common market. * * * Council Decision No 63/266/EEC of 2 April 1963 laying down those general principles (Official Journal, English Special Edition 1963–1964, p. 25) states that "the general principles must enable every person to receive adequate training, with due regard for freedom of choice of occupation, place of training and place of work."

[The Court then noted that the Council had adopted guidelines for vocational training policy in 1971 and later resolutions on the same subject.]

[23] The common vocational training policy referred to in Article 128 of the Treaty is thus gradually being established. It constitutes, moreover, an indispensable element of the activities of the Community * * *.

[24] Access to vocational training is in particular likely to promote free movement of persons throughout the Community, by enabling them to obtain a qualification in the Member State where they intend to work and by

enabling them to complete their training and develop their particular talents in the Member State whose vocational training programmes include the special subject desired.

25   It follows from all the foregoing that the conditions of access to vocational training fall within the scope of the Treaty.

26   The answer to the first question must therefore be that the imposition on students who are nationals of other Member States, of a charge [or] a registration fee * * * as a condition of access to vocational training, where the same fee is not imposed on students who are nationals of the host Member State, constitutes discrimination on grounds of nationality contrary to Article [12] of the Treaty.

27   In its second question the national court wishes to know what criteria must be used in deciding whether courses in strip cartoon art constitute vocational training.

* * *

29   The general guidelines laid down by the Council in 1971 state that "in view of the constantly changing needs of the economy the aim" of vocational training "should be to offer everyone the opportunity of basic and advanced training and a continuity of in-service training designed, from a general and vocational point of view, to enable the individual to develop his personality and to take up a career".

30   It follows from those statements that any form of education which prepares for a qualification for a particular profession, trade or employment or which provides the necessary training and skills for such a profession, trade or employment is vocational training, whatever the age and the level of training of the pupils or students, and even if the training programme includes an element of general education.

BLAIZOT v. UNIVERSITY OF LIÈGE

Case 24/86, [1988] ECR 379.

[Blaizot and other plaintiffs, students at several Belgian universities, sued for reimbursement of the enrollment fees they had paid prior to the date of judgment of *Gravier*. The plaintiffs were all French nationals studying veterinary medicine. The trial court asked the Court of Justice whether university studies leading to a doctorate in veterinary medicine were to be considered vocational training and whether the *Gravier* ruling should have retroactive effect to permit recovery of enrollment fees paid from 1979–85. The latter question is treated at page 186. Belgium argued that vocational training should be defined in its traditional sense of apprenticeship and technical training for certain trades and professions.]

16   [A] distinction must be drawn between the issue whether university studies can, by their nature, constitute vocational training for the purposes of Community law and the issue of the circumstances in which such studies may be said to prepare for a qualification for a particular profession, trade or employment or provide the necessary training and skills for such a profession, trade or employment.

[17] With regard to the first issue, neither the provisions of the Treaty, in particular Article 128 nor the objectives which these provisions seek to achieve, in particular those relating to freedom of movement for persons, give any indication that the concept of vocational training is to be restricted so as to exclude all university education. It is accepted in all the Member States that some university studies are indeed intended to provide students, at the academic level, with certain knowledge, training and skills as preparation for specific occupations. It should be added that Article 10 of the European Social Charter, to which most of the Member States are contracting parties, treats university education as a type of vocational training.

* * *

[19] With regard to the issue whether university studies prepare for a qualification for a particular profession, trade or employment * * *, that is the case not only where the final academic examination directly provides the required qualification for a particular profession, trade or employment but also in so far as the studies in question provide specific training and skills, that is to say where a student needs the knowledge so acquired for the pursuit of a profession, trade or employment, even if no legislative or administrative provisions make the acquisition of that knowledge a prerequisite for that purpose.

[20] In general, university studies fulfil these criteria. The only exceptions are certain courses of study which, because of their particular nature, are intended for persons wishing to improve their general knowledge rather than prepare themselves for an occupation.

* * *

[23] [T]he answer to the question referred by the national court must therefore be that university studies in veterinary medicine fall within the meaning of the term "vocational training", and consequently a supplementary enrolment fee charged to students who are nationals of other Member States and wish to enrol for such studies constitutes discrimination on grounds of nationality contrary to Article [12, ex Article 7] of the EEC Treaty.

VLANDIS v. KLINE

412 U.S. 441, 93 S.Ct. 2230, 37 L.Ed.2d 63 (1973).

[Connecticut required non-resident students to pay substantially higher state university tuition than that paid by state residents. Connecticut defined a non-resident as anyone whose "legal address" was outside Connecticut at any time within one year prior to admission. A non-resident could not acquire the status of a resident for tuition purposes during the period of university studies. Plaintiff Kline was a California resident when she was accepted as a student by the University of Connecticut, but subsequently married a Connecticut resident. The Klines had a home in Connecticut and the plaintiff obtained a Connecticut driver's license and registered as a Connecticut voter. Plaintiff Catapano moved from Ohio to Connecticut after being admitted as a student, and then resided there, with a Connecticut driver's license and voting registration. Justice Stevens, speaking for a majority of five, struck down the Connecticut statute.]

Statutes creating permanent irrebuttable presumptions have long been disfavored under the Due Process Clauses of the Fifth and Fourteenth Amendments.

* * *

It may be that most applicants to Connecticut's university system who apply from outside the State or within a year of living out of State have no real intention of becoming Connecticut residents and will never do so. But it is clear that not all of the applicants from out of State inevitably fall in this category. Indeed, in the present case, both appellees possess many of the indicia of Connecticut residency, such as year-round Connecticut homes, Connecticut drivers' licenses, car registrations, voter registrations, etc.; and both were found by the District Court to have become bona fide residents of Connecticut before the 1972 spring semester. Yet, under the State's statutory scheme, neither was permitted any opportunity to demonstrate the bona fides of her Connecticut residency for tuition purposes, and neither will ever have such an opportunity in the future so long as she remains a student.

[Justice Stevens rejected Connecticut's arguments that higher fees on initial non-residents were justified in order to equalize public education costs between residents and non-residents, to reward past taxpayers and to achieve administrative certainty.]

Our holding today should in no wise be taken to mean that Connecticut must classify the students in its university system as residents for purposes of tuition and fees, just because they go to school there. Nor should our decision be construed to deny a State the right to impose on a student, as one element in demonstrating bona fide residence, a reasonable durational residency requirement, which can be met while in student status. We fully recognize that a State has a legitimate interest in protecting and preserving the quality of its colleges and universities and the right of its own bona fide residents to attend such institutions on a preferential tuition basis.

We hold only that a permanent irrebuttable presumption of nonresidence—the means adopted by Connecticut to preserve that legitimate interest—is violative of the Due Process Clause, because it provides no opportunity for students who applied from out of State to demonstrate that they have become bona fide Connecticut residents.

[Justices Marshall and Brennan noted in a concurring opinion that they questioned the majority's view that a state could "impose a one-year residency requirement as a prerequisite to qualifying for in-state tuition benefits."]

[Chief Justice Burger dissented, together with Justice Rehnquist.]

A state university today is an establishment with capital costs of many millions of dollars of investment. Its annual operating costs likewise may run into the millions. Parents and other taxpayers willingly carry this heavy burden because they believe in the values of higher education. It is not narrow provincialism for the State to think that each

State should carry its own educational burdens. Until we redefine our system of government—as we are free to do by constitutionally prescribed means—the States may restrict subsidized education to their own residents.

Notes and Questions

1. *Gravier* is another judgment demonstrating the Court of Justice's tendency to construe broadly Treaty articles and secondary legislation. The Court's interpretation of Article 12 owes a great deal to its emphasis on basic rights protection. Are you persuaded by the Court's analysis or do you consider such an "activist" approach to be excessive in this case? Note that, at the time, Belgium was the only Member State which experienced a serious budgetary problem due to the large number of foreign students. Why should Belgian taxpayers bear the burden of educating Community nationals from other States? Suppose class size is limited, so that the more foreign students, the fewer Belgian students? For a critical policy assessment of the case law, see N. Green, T. Hartley & J. Usher, The Legal Foundations of the Single European Market 190–93 (Oxford University Press 1991). Most commentary on the Court rulings in this area is favorable. See J. Lonbay, Education and Law: The Community Context, 14 Eur.L.Rev. 363 (1989).

2. *Blaizot* effectively expands the scope of Article 12 protection to most forms of higher education. What fields of study would not qualify as vocational training, using the Court's analysis? Do you agree with the Court's broad conception of vocational training? Obviously, university studies in architecture, engineering or law would qualify, but what about traditional liberal arts studies in history, literature or philosophy?

3. In *Lair, supra* page 618, the national court inquired whether a French university student at a German university could claim a right to German financial aid for fees and for living expenses, when the German rules restricted such aid to German nationals and long-term residents. The Court replied that Article 12 forbid discrimination based on nationality in a grant of financial aid to cover university fees, in view of *Blaizot's* conclusion that vocational training in universities was within the scope of the EC Treaty (a conclusion rather parallel to *Casagrande, supra* page 597). In contrast, the Court held that German aid for living expenses fell within general social assistance and hence remained within the competence of the Member States, which could restrict such aid to their own nationals.

4. In *Vlandis*, although the Supreme Court required states to treat former non-resident students as residents for university tuition purposes once they have provided sufficient evidence of a change of residence, the Court majority did not question the ability of a state to charge non-resident students higher tuition (although Justices Marshall and Brennan queried this). Indeed, the Court previously affirmed without opinion a district court decision allowing Minnesota to charge university students from other states higher tuition until they had completed one year's residence in Minnesota. Starns v. Malkerson, 401 U.S. 985, 91 S.Ct. 1231, 28 L.Ed.2d 527 (1971), affirming 326 F.Supp. 234 (D.Minn.1970). The district court had stressed that access to higher education was not one of the "basic necessities of life," unlike social welfare assistance. The prevailing view today is that US states may charge out-of-state university students higher fees than residents, provided they apply reasonable standards in defining when residence is attained. See J. Nowak & R. Rotunda, Constitutional Law § 14.38 (6th

ed. West 2000). The Court of Justice and the Supreme Court obviously hold sharply contrasting views on the right of access by non-residents to higher education. As a matter of policy, with which court do you agree?

2. EDUCATION, VOCATIONAL TRAINING AND CULTURE

The promotion of the mobility of university students and cooperation between higher education institutions were two of the goals of the People's Europe program. After its endorsement by the European Council, in 1987 the Council adopted Erasmus, the well-known acronym for the European Action Scheme for the Mobility of University Students, Council Decision 87/327, O.J.L 166/20 (June 25, 1987).

Erasmus encouraged cooperation between academic institutions on courses of study and research and provided direct financial aid to students who engaged in studies in other States for up to one year. Although the financial aid grants were moderate in amount, Erasmus encouraged the home State institution to give full academic credit for the foreign studies and also required that students studying abroad continue to receive any grants to which they were entitled from their home institution.

Erasmus proved an immediate success. The Commission's 25th General Report 1991, §§ 475–76 (1992), indicated that 1200 institutions engaged in academic cooperation and 59,000 students received financial assistance in the academic year 1990–91. In 1990, Erasmus was supplemented by Tempus, a program to facilitate academic and student exchanges between the Community and Central European states. The Lingua program, adopted by the Council to encourage foreign language competence, O.J. L 239/24 (Aug. 16, 1989), also supplemented the Erasmus program. In 1994, the Council also adopted the Leonardo da Vinci program to assist inter-state cooperative programs in vocational training in 1995–99, and the program was renewed in 2000 for 2000–06, with a budget of over one billion Euros. A Commission study in January 2000 showed that four-fifths of the Erasmus exchange students were the first members of their family to study abroad. Stimulated by Erasmus, some universities created new masters degree and summer study programs designed principally for foreign students. In fact, some Belgian, Dutch and German universities decided to offer certain courses for all students in English in order to facilitate studies by Erasmus exchange students.

Probably no other Community program has enjoyed greater popularity and appreciation than Erasmus. The Member States presumably intended to build upon its success in inserting Article 149 (ex Article 126) into the EC Treaty as one of the Maastricht amendments. Article 149 expressly gives the Community competence to act for "the development of quality education," but, in accord with the principle of subsidiarity, the article guarantees that the Member States' principal role in determining "the content of teaching and the organization of educational systems and their cultural and linguistic diversity" should be respected.

The Community role in education is essentially to encourage cooperation among Member States and to adopt "incentive measures, excluding any harmonization of the laws," which can be enacted by use of the co-decision legislative procedure. Article 149 (2) lists the spheres of possible action, of which the most important are the first three: "developing the European dimension in education, particularly through the teaching and dissemination of the languages of the Member States; encouraging mobility of students and teachers, inter alia by encouraging the academic recognition of diplomas and periods of study; and promoting cooperation between educational establishments." For an analytical study of the education competence of the Community, see K. Lenaerts, Education in European Community Law after Maastricht, 31 Common Mkt. L. Rev. 7 (1994).

Since Article 149 (ex 126) became effective in 1993, the Community has steadily expanded the scope and diversity of its educational programs. Article 149 is not limited to higher education, although the principal emphasis in Community action has been at that level. Measures are also now in place to encourage cooperation among primary and secondary schools, especially in partnership programs, including exchanges of teaching staff and pupils.

In 1995, Erasmus and other programs were consolidated within the new Socrates program, whose initial five year action program was extended for 2000–06 by Parliament and Council Decision 253/2000, O.J. L 28/1 (Feb. 3, 2000), with a budget of 1.85 billion Euros. All of the Central European and Mediterranean countries currently negotiating for membership are entitled to participate in Socrates programs. In 2000, the Erasmus part of the Socrates program enabled 229,000 students and 45,000 teachers to study or do research in another Member State, provided financial aid to nearly 2000 universities and other higher education institutions, and funded several hundred curricular development projects. There are now nearly 500 Jean Monnet Chairs for university professors specializing in Community law, political science, economics and other disciplines. At the primary and secondary school level, Comenius, a program within Socrates, financed nearly 3000 school partnerships and enabled over 10,000 teachers to study and do research in other States.

The Nice European Council in December 2000 endorsed an Action Plan for Mobility, declaring that increasing the mobility of "all those being educated and their teachers in Europe is a major political goal" and that "it is through education that Europeans will acquire the shared cultural references that are the basis of European citizenship and of a political Europe." E.U. Bull. 12/2000, at 28–29. For a further description of the many Community initiatives in education, see the Commission General Report—2000, ¶¶ 493–513 (2001).

Fostering European cultural initiatives was also an aspect of the People's Europe program. We will note in the next chapter how the Television Without Frontiers Directive has as one of its goals the promotion of the production of television programs in Europe. The Maastricht Treaty amendments to the EC Treaty in 1993 included a new Article 151 (ex Article 128) which declares that the Community shall "contribute to the flowering of the cultures of the Member States." Just as for education, Community action is limited to promoting cooperation among Member States and adopting incentive measures, acting through the codecision legislative procedure, but requiring Council unanimity in this sensitive sector. Moreover, Article 151 (4) requires the Community to "take cultural aspects into account in its actions" in other fields.

The most significant legislation in the cultural field to date is undoubtedly Directive 93/7 on the return of cultural objects unlawfully removed from the territory of another Member State, O. J. L. 74/74 (Mar. 27, 1993), supplemented by Council Regulation 3911/92, O.J. L 395/1 (Dec. 9, 1992), which requires licenses for the export of cultural goods to third countries. The increasingly grave problem of the theft of art and archaeological treasures prompted the directive, whose scope covers "cultural objects classified as national treasures." The directive creates a right to obtain the return of the unlawfully removed cultural object and contains a long annex intended to indicate the variety of cultural objects concerned. For further discussion, see P. Oliver, Free Movement of Goods in the European Community 8.75–8.79 (3d ed. Sweet & Maxwell 1996), and V. Vitrano, Protecting Cultural Objects in an Internal Border–Free EC, 17 Fordham Int'l L.J. 1164 (1994).

Cultural interests certainly intersect with copyright and other intellectual property rights . Commission studies and directives adopted to harmonize such rights frequently refer to their cultural impact. A prime example is a draft directive that would create a resale right for the benefit of the author of an original work of art, originally proposed in 1996, with an amended text in O.J. C 125/ 8 (Apr. 23, 1998). The draft would provide painters, sculptors and other artists with a share of the proceeds of resale of their works, an idea analogous to that of copyright royalties.

On Feb. 14, 2000, the Parliament and Council adopted Decision 508/2000 setting out the Culture 2000 program for the period 2000–04, with a budget of 167 million Euros. For a description of current Community action, see the Commission General Report—2000, ¶¶ 514–34 (2001).

D. FREE MOVEMENT AND BORDER CONTROLS

Ever since the 1985 White Paper on Completing the Internal Market described border controls as "the obvious manifestation of the continued division of the Community," the Commission and a growing number of Member States have pressed for their abolition. However, the United Kingdom, under both Conservative and Labor governments, is convinced that the elimination of border controls poses too great a risk that terrorists, illegal immigrants and asylum seekers, and drug traffickers would move freely over its borders. Because legislation to remove border controls requires Council unanimity, the UK exercises an effective veto power.

After the Single European Act introduced Article 8a (renumbered as 7a by the Maastricht Treaty and now renumbered as Article 14) with its call to establish the internal market "area without internal frontiers" by December 31, 1992, the Commission came under pressure from the Parliament to propose legislation to remove frontier controls. The Commission eventually initiated a draft directive to end all air, sea and land border controls on persons, whatever their nationality, crossing internal frontiers within the Union, O.J.C. 289 /16 (Oct. 31, 1995). Although the proposal permitted spot checks and a safeguard exception in the event of serious threats to public security, the United Kingdom has adamantly opposed it and the draft is stalemated.

The Court of Justice has, however, set standards for the manner in which border controls can be carried out. In Commission v. Belgium (Border controls), Case 321/87, [1989] ECR 997, the Court held that Directive 68/360 on the abolition of restrictions on movement and residence for workers barred any systematic border check other than to establish that a person held a Member State passport or identity card, but allowed sporadic verification at the border of the residence papers of Belgian residents. In Commission v. The Netherlands (Border controls), Case 68/89, [1991] ECR 2637, the Court held that the Netherlands could not question Community nationals crossing the frontier about the purpose and duration of their journey and the financial means at their disposal.

In 1999, a frontal attack on the legitimacy of internal border controls came to the Court.

CRIMINAL PROCEEDINGS AGAINST WIJSENBEEK

Case C–378/97, [1999] ECR I—6207.

[On arriving at Rotterdam airport, which receives flights only from sites within the Community, Wijsenbeek, a Dutch national, refused to show a Dutch passport or identity card to the police officer at the border control post. Wijsenbeek claimed that Treaty Articles 14 and 18 conferred on citizens of Member States the right to move freely in the interior of the European Union without presenting a passport. In criminal proceedings to penalize Wijsenbeek for his conduct, the trial court requested the Court of Justice to interpret the two articles. Finland, Ireland, Spain and the UK intervened in support of the Netherlands.]

40 Article 14 cannot be interpreted as meaning that, in the absence of measures adopted by the Council before 31 December 1992 requiring the Member States to abolish controls of persons at the internal frontiers of the Community, that obligation automatically arises from expiry of that period. * * * As the Advocate General points out * * *, such an obligation presupposes harmonization of the laws of the Member States governing the crossing of the external borders of the Community, immigration, the grant of visas, asylum and the exchange of information on those questions.

41 Moreover, Article [18(1), ex 8a, introduced by the Maastricht Treaty] confers the right to move and reside freely in the territory of the Member States on citizens of the Union, subject to the limitations and conditions laid down in the Treaty and by the measures adopted to give it effect. According to Article [18(2)] of the Treaty, the Council may adopt provisions with a view to facilitating the exercise of those rights.

42 However, as the Commission has rightly pointed out, as long as Community provisions on controls at the external borders of the Community, which also imply common or harmonized rules on, in particular, conditions of access, visas and asylum, have not been adopted, the exercise of those rights presupposes that the person concerned is able to establish that he or she has the nationality of a Member State.

43 At the time of the events in question in the main proceedings, there were no common rules or harmonized laws of the Member States on, in particular, controls at external frontiers and immigration, visa and asylum policy. Consequently, even if, under Article [14] or Article [18] of the Treaty, nationals of the Member States did have an unconditional right to

move freely within the territory of the Member States, the Member States retained the right to carry out identity checks at the internal frontiers of the Community, requiring persons to present a valid identity card or passport * * * in order to be able to establish whether the person concerned is a national of a Member State, thus having the right to move freely within the territory of the Member States, or a national of a non-member country, not having that right.

44   In the absence of Community rules governing the matter, the Member States remain competent to impose penalties for breach of such an obligation, provided that the penalties applicable are comparable to those which apply to similar national infringements. However, Member States may not lay down a penalty so disproportionate as to create an obstacle to the free movement of persons, such as a term of imprisonment [citing *Messner, supra* page 602]. The same considerations apply as regards breach of the obligation to present an identity card or a passport upon entry into the territory of a Member State.

Notes and Questions

1.   *Wijsenbeek* answers the question, long debated in academic circles, whether Article 14 could be said to have direct effect when it required the completion of the internal market, "an area without internal frontiers," by December 31, 1992, at least with regard to the elimination of border controls on persons. The Commission and all the intervening States had argued that Article 14 did not have direct effect, and Advocate General Cosmos also supported this view.

2.   The Court's application of Article 18's guarantee of free movement to citizens of the Union is more nuanced. Might Article 18 have direct effect once the Community has in the future set common rules on controls at external frontiers and on immigration, visa and asylum policy? The United States, of course, has no border controls at state lines, although it has massive numbers of illegal immigrants who move rather easily throughout the country. From a policy point of view, do you think the benefits in ending internal border controls in the Community outweigh the risks, or not? For a thoughtful analysis of *Wijsenbeek* and later developments, see H. Toner, Passport Controls at Borders Between Member States, 25 Eur. L. Rev. 415 (2000).

3.   In fact, border controls have largely been ended among the States that comprise what is popularly called Schengenland. In 1985, the Benelux States, France, Germany and Italy signed the Schengen Accord to enable the elimination of frontier controls by first harmonizing key aspects of their immigration and visa policies, as well as coordinating their combat of illegal traffic in drugs and weapons. Implementing provisions followed in 1990. Over time, all of the Member States except the United Kingdom and Ireland have joined in the Schengen Accord, as have Iceland and Norway by a 1996 agreement. The implementation procedure has been complicated, requiring long transitional periods, but the accord is largely operational in most States. Accordingly, persons traveling across frontiers within "Schengenland" by car, rail, plane or boat are no longer stopped for passport or other frontier checks, except occasionally for spot checks. The Schengen Accord States have also instituted a central computer system in Strasbourg to aid in the identification of suspected drug dealers, terrorists and other criminals. As indicated in Section E, the Amsterdam Treaty's Schengen Protocol incorporates legal measures adopted under the Schengen Accord into the Community legal system in a rather complicated manner.

E.　TOWARD AN AREA OF "FREEDOM, SECURITY AND JUSTICE"

1.　COMMON VISA POLICIES

The Treaty of Maastricht inserted Article 100c into the EC Treaty, authorizing the Council to "determine the third countries whose national must be in possession of a visa when crossing the external borders of the Member States." Article 100c was intended to be the first step in harmonizing Member State rules on external border controls. A common visa policy ensures mutual trust among the States concerning the status of the large majority of non-Community nationals moving into the Union on a short term basis. With a common visa policy in place, the Community can turn to measures concerning rights of free movement and residence of legal immigrants.

Fulfilling its obligations under Article 100c, the Council adopted Regulation 1683/95 on the introduction of a common format for visas, O.J.L. 164/1 (July 14, 1995), which not only governs the visa format, but also requires that visas contain secret specifications set by the Commission to reduce the risk of counterfeit visas. Article 5 prescribes that the usual maximum term for a visa is three months. The Council also adopted Regulation 2317/95 on the third countries whose nationals must possess a visa, O.J.L. 234/1 (Oct. 3, 1995). Because the prior Member State lists varied radically, particularly in function of traditional ties to former colonies, agreement on this regulation was hard to reach. Thus, prior to the regulation, 93 countries' nationals required a visa in some Member States, but not others, while nationals from 73 countries required a visa in all States. As adopted, Regulation 2371/95 contained an Annex listing 98 countries whose nationals required a visa everywhere in the Community, but article 2(1) permitted States to continue to require visas for nationals from other States.

The Court of Justice annulled the regulation in Parliament v. Council (Third state visa list), Case C–392/95, [1997] ECR I–3213, on the ground that the Council failed to reconsult the Parliament when it made substantial amendments following Parliament's consultation. As it usually does, the Court exercised its discretion to retain the effects of Regulation 2317/95 in place until the Council should "within a reasonable period" properly adopt a new regulation. Regulation 574/1999, O.J.L 72/2 (Mar. 12, 1999) replaced the prior one, providing for an Annex listing 100 countries whose nationals required a visa, and retaining article 2(1). This text was updated and slightly revised in Regulation 539/2001, O.J.L 81/1 (Apr. 10, 2001).

The Treaty of Amsterdam, effective since May 1, 1999, introduced a new Title IV on Visas, Asylum, Immigration and Other Policies Related to Free Movement of Persons. Article 61 sets as a goal the progressive establishment of "an area of freedom, security and justice."

Article 62 mandates the Council, acting by unanimity after consulting Parliament, to adopt common rules on visas before May 1, 2004, including a list of countries whose nationals are exempt from visas, the procedures and conditions for issuing visas and rules on uniform visas. The Commission accordingly proposed an amendment to Regulation 574/1999, which is now well advanced in Council review. Article 62 also requires measures to enable third country nationals to move throughout the Community for up to three months.

More dramatically, Article 62 requires the adoption by May 1, 2004 of measures to set the standards and procedures to be followed by Member States in carrying out checks at external borders and "the absence of any controls on persons, be they citizens of the Union or nationals of third countries, when crossing internal borders." Thus, the long-sought goal of ending internal frontier controls may be in sight.

Ultimately, the Community will move on to common rules governing the right of residence, study and work for third country nationals—an approach long advocated by successive social affairs commissioners. About 3% of the Community workforce comes from third states, notably Algeria, Morocco, Poland and Turkey. Article 63, also introduced by the Amsterdam Treaty, mandates the Council to adopt before May 1, 2004 measures setting "standards on procedures for the issue by Member States of long term visas and residence permits, including those for the purpose of family reunion," and measures that would enable third state nationals legally resident in one Member State to take up residence in another State.

The first Commission initiative in this context is a draft directive on family reunification, proposed on December 1, 1999, which would enable third country nationals holding long-term residence permits, usually for employment or studies, to obtain the right to bring in a spouse, dependent children and parents for the length of the residence permit. A second Commission proposal on March 13, 2001 is for a directive that would give third country nationals who have resided legally in a Member State for five years a Community-wide residence permit valid for ten years, renewable, with rights of free movement to other States and access to employment and education comparable to those of citizens of the Union. A Council Resolution on long-term residents requested States to issue ten year residence permits, renewable, for all persons who had already resided for ten years in a State, and to grant them national treatment in a variety of social contexts (e.g., access to schooling, housing, social security, etc). O.J. C 80/2 (Mar. 18, 1996). The Council also adopted Joint Action 97/11/JHA on a uniform format for residence permits, O.J. L 7/1 (Jan. 10, 1997), to be used for all permits to stay for more than six months. Finally, the Commission has proposed a directive that would enable third-country nationals who have long-term residence permits to perform services throughout the Community. The amended proposal is at O.J.C 311/197 (Oct. 31, 2000).

2. OTHER MEASURES TO ACHIEVE AN AREA OF FREEDOM, SECURITY AND JUSTICE

The Maastricht Treaty created the "third pillar" of the European Union, Cooperation in Justice and Home Affairs (CJHA), set out in then Article K of the Treaty on European Union. When the pre-Maastricht Intergovernmental Conference was unable to reach agreement on adding this sector to the EC Treaty, a compromise enabled action to be taken at the inter-governmental level. See Chapter 1, *supra*. Article K.1. identified a number of areas of "common interest," notably immigration and asylum policies, control of frontiers with third countries, police cooperation and judicial cooperation. Under Article K.2, the Council might propose Conventions, adopt joint actions or propose cooperative measures to the Member States. Both the Commission and Member States might propose initiatives, and the Council usually had to act unanimously. Parliament was only to be kept informed.

Although such an intergovernmental approach is inherently slow-moving and cumbersome, CJHA proved reasonably successful in launching some important initiatives. Priority attention was given to the creation of a European Police Office (Europol), headquartered in the Hague. The Council proposed the Europol Convention to the Member States in 1995, O.J. C 316/1 (Nov. 27, 1995), and, after long debate, a Protocol permitting States to refer questions interpreting or applying the Protocol to the Court of Justice, O.J. C 299/1 (Oct. 9, 1996). The Hague Europol office began operations in 1995 as a center of information and intelligence, assisting national police efforts to combat drug traffic, money laundering, illegal immigration networks and trade in stolen vehicles. In March 2000, the Council adopted an Action Plan on Organized Crime, with a variety of proposals to boost the role of Europol and enhance inter-state cooperation. One result was Council Decision 2000/799/ JHA creating a Judicial Cooperation Unit (Eurojust), O.J.L 324/1 (Dec. 12, 2000).

The Council also proposed a Convention on simplified extradition procedure, O.J. C 78/1 (March 30, 1995), and an even more important one on general principles for extradition, O.J.C 313/11 (Oct. 23, 1996), which considerably reduces the grounds upon which a State can refuse extradition to another Member State.

By the time of the 1996 Intergovernmental Conference, most Member States were prepared to move beyond the inter-governmental cooperation in CJHA. Considerable credit goes to the Irish and Dutch presidencies, which made this a priority matter. As noted above, the Treaty of Amsterdam added a new title on visas, asylum, immigration and other policies and in Article 61 set the goal of "an area of freedom, security and justice."

In addition to the provisions on visas and immigration already described, Article 63 mandates the Council to adopt harmonization measures on asylum and refugees before May 1, 2004 and Article 65 authorizes action in the field of "judicial co-operation in civil matters having cross-border implications." The legislative procedure provisions are complex. Generally speaking, the Council must act unanimously after consulting Parliament, but in a few instances the Council may act by qualified majority vote. In an unusual reference procedure, Article 68 enables the Court of Justice to answer questions posed by courts or tribunals "against whose decisions there is no judicial remedy." P.J. Kuijper, Some Legal Problems Associated With the Communitarization of Policy on Visas, Asylum and Immigration Under the Amsterdam Treaty, 37 Common Mkt. L. Rev. 345 (2000), provides an expert analysis of the new provisions.

By three Protocols, Denmark, Ireland and the United Kingdom do not participate in the legislative process and have no obligation to comply with measures adopted under the new Title. The Protocols are to some degree modeled on the Maastricht Treaty's Social Protocol. However, the Protocols enable each State to "opt in" with regard to stated measures, in whole or in part. A "two-tier" Union thus exists in this sphere.

Another Protocol provides in a complex manner for the integration into the Community legal order of all measures adopted under the Schengen Accord (the "Schengen acquis") prior to the entry into force of the Treaty of Amsterdam.

The Treaty on European Union's third pillar, Title VI (ex Article K) survives to cover police and judicial cooperation in criminal matters, notably the combatting of "racism and xenophobia," terrorism, offenses against children, illegal drug and arms traffic, corruption and fraud (Article 29). Cooperation in Europol is described in Article 30. There are complex provisions on the types of measures and decisions, as well as on conventions, and the process for taking action, which is essentially that of the former Article K.

Shortly after the Treaty of Amsterdam became effective, the October 1999 European Council meeting in Tampere under the Finnish presidency devoted its attention primarily to a review of action necessary to attain the "area of freedom, security and justice." The meeting conclusions incited the Commission to make a number of legislative proposals, notably a draft directive on procedures for the granting and withdrawal of refugee status, COM (2000) 578 (Sept. 20, 2000). On April 3, 2001, the Commission proposed a draft directive that would set minimum standards for Member State procedures in reviewing requests for asylum.

In the field of judicial cooperation in civil matters, proposals initiated in 1999 were adopted with remarkable speed, producing Regulation 1347/2000 on jurisdiction and the recognition and enforcement of judgments in matrimonial matters, O.J. L 160/19 (June 30, 2000), and Regulation 1348/2000 on the service of judicial and extra-judicial documents in civil or commercial matters, O.J. L 160/37 (June 30, 2000). Most important of all is Regulation 44/2001 on jurisdiction and the recognition of judgments in civil and commercial matters, O.J.L 12/1 (Jan. 16, 2001), intended to replace the Brussels Convention discussed in Chapter 38. For a further review of action in this field, see the Commission General Report—2000, ¶¶ 442–87 (2001).

After the tragic destruction of the World Trade Center and the attack upon the Pentagon on Sept. 11, 2001, the European Council held an emergency session in Brussels on Sept. 21 to declare the Union's solidarity with the US in the combat of terrorism. The European Council instructed the Council of Justice Ministers to act expeditiously on concrete measures by the time of the December European Council meeting. The Council on Sept. 20, 2001 gave a political endorsement to a framework decision on combating terrorism, COM (2001) 521 final, and upon a far-reaching Commission proposal to create a European arrest warrant, issued by any State's competent authorities and valid for arrest throughout the Union, COM (2001) 522 final. Both proposals pose complex political, legal and judicial issues that must be resolved before final enactment.

Chapter 17

RIGHT OF ESTABLISHMENT AND RIGHT TO PROVIDE SERVICES

Although it would be difficult to decide which of the basic four freedoms of the EEC Treaty makes the greatest economic contribution to the achievement of the common market, a strong claim can be made for the right of establishment and the related right to provide services. These two rights facilitate the optimal allocation of factors of production and the efficient operation of commercial and financial entities throughout the Community.

An integrated internal market is impossible unless commercial and financial enterprises can conduct their business freely, either through cross-border services or through the operation of firms, subsidiaries and branches anywhere in the Community. This enables enterprises to exploit production capacity in regions where the costs of production are low, to market their products or services from regional or local centers, and to adapt their operations readily to the needs of a local market. Naturally, Community-wide commercial and financial operations also lead to substantial economies of scale and promote the development of larger, more sophisticated enterprises better able to compete in the global marketplace.

The two rights are also essential to the free exercise of professions and crafts by individuals and firms throughout the Community. For individuals engaged as entrepreneurs in business or exercising a profession, the two rights allow personal mobility and free choice of a site from which to conduct business or practice a profession. Accessory rights of personal residence, access to housing and eligibility for social benefits become important insofar as they facilitate personal mobility.

This chapter initially reviews the nature of the Treaty rights and the dimensions of the legislative program intended to enforce them. Because the Commercial Agents Directive is an excellent example of harmonization in this sector, we will then analyze its text and recent interpretative case law. The Court of Justice has liberally interpreted the Treaty rights in their application to commercial and financial enterprises. We will accordingly analyze in some detail the Court's doctrines on the right to provide and receive services, with particular attention devoted to the well-known Television Without Frontiers

Directive. The chapter concludes with a description of the right of establishment and a key harmonization of laws program, that for companies.

A. TREATY PROVISIONS AND LEGISLATIVE PROGRAMS

1. THE NATURE OF THE TREATY RIGHTS

Title III of the EC Treaty includes chapter 2 on the right of establishment, followed by chapter 3 on services. Commentators frequently consider these to be two aspects of the same right, namely, the right to conduct freely commercial, financial or professional activities throughout the Community, and find the line of demarcation between the two difficult to discern. There is a great deal of truth to this observation. Implementing legislation and interpretative case law often apply to the exercise of both rights, without any distinction drawn between them. However, in some instances, a particular aspect of the exercise of a right, or a particular limit on a right, is specific either to the provision of services or to establishment. Accordingly, one should try to keep the two Treaty rights distinct.

The chapter on establishment begins with Article 43 (ex Article 52):

[R]estrictions on the freedom of establishment of nationals of a Member State in the territory of another Member State shall be prohibited. Such prohibition shall also apply to restrictions on the setting up of agencies, branches or subsidiaries by nationals of any Member State established in the territory of any Member State.

Freedom of establishment shall include the right to take up and pursue activities as self-employed persons, and to set up and manage undertakings, in particular companies or firms * * * under the conditions laid down for its own nationals by the law of the country where such establishment is effected * * *.

Article 43 thus identifies three aspects of the right of establishment, namely 1) to set up agencies, branches and subsidiaries, 2) to conduct activities as a self-employed person, and 3) to set up and manage companies and firms.

However, the right of establishment is not unlimited. It essentially guarantees other Community nationals only national treatment, i.e., the same treatment that nationals enjoy. Because some conditions imposed by a state on the conduct of a business or profession can, for various reasons, be more easily satisfied by a national than a non-national, Article 43 may still permit an indirect impairment of the right of establishment. To minimize this, the Community has adopted measures in many fields to harmonize the standards and conditions for the conduct of business. Moreover, the Court of Justice has recently held that Member State rules that restrict the conduct of a business or profession must be justified by a serious public interest.

The initial EEC Treaty Article 52 provided for the abolition of restrictions on the right of establishment during the transitional period which ended on Dec. 31, 1969. Accordingly, in a now deleted provision, the Council was mandated to adopt before 1962 a general program to abolish restrictions on establishment. This general program is described in section 2.

Article 44 (ex Article 54) currently indicates that the codecision procedure of Article 251 shall be used to adopt legislation to achieve the right of establishment. Under the initial EEC Treaty, the Council needed only to consult Parliament. In provisions that have never been amended, Article 44(2) lists certain areas of concentration for the legislative program. Noteworthy is paragraph (e) which directs that Member State nationals be entitled to own land and buildings in any other State. Important for the harmonization of company law and rules regulating securities and the financial industries is paragraph (g), which calls for the coordination of Member State rules intended to protect members (usually partners or shareholders) of companies and firms.

Article 47 (ex Article 57) supplements Article 43 by authorizing legislation for the mutual recognition of diplomas and for the harmonization of the conditions that Member States may impose on the exercise of business or professional activities by self-employed persons. Article 48 (ex Article 58) stipulates that companies or firms are to be treated as having the same rights of establishment as natural persons. Article 48 further defines companies or firms to include entities created under civil as well as commercial law, thereby making it clear that partnerships of professionals are also covered. Finally, Article 294, in the final provisions of the Treaty, is also relevant: it grants national treatment in any Member State to Community nationals who participate in "the capital of companies and firms."

The Treaty places only two express limits on the right of establishment. Article 45 (ex Article 55) permits Member States to restrict establishment rights with regard to activities "connected, even occasionally, with the exercise of official authority", and Article 46 (ex Article 56) allows them to restrict the right on grounds of public policy, public security or public health. Article 46 parallels Articles 30 and 39(3) which permit similar limits on the free movement of goods and workers, respectively. As we shall see, the Court of Justice has interpreted narrowly the scope of both Articles 45 and 46.

Turning now to chapter 3 on services, Article 49(ex Article 59) states:

> [R]estrictions on freedom to provide services within the Community shall be prohibited in respect of nationals of Member States who are established in a State of the Community other than that of the person for whom the services are intended.

> The Council may, acting by a qualified majority on a proposal from the Commission, extend the provisions of the Chapter to nationals of a third country who provide services and who are established within the Community.

Article 50 (ex Article 60) defines services to include industrial, commercial and professional services and the activities of artisans, to the extent that they are "normally provided for remuneration." The remuneration need not, however, be provided by the recipient of the service. For example, a TV station broadcast constitutes a service to all persons who receive the program even though the station's remuneration comes from advertisers or public subsidies. Article 50 also enables the person providing a service to "temporarily pursue his activity" within another State. This is one of the instances in which the line between providing services and establishment can become blurred. It is not clear how long one can reside in a host State to provide services without being deemed to have become established there.

The initial EEC Treaty Article 63 required the Council, acting unanimously, to adopt before 1962 a general program to abolish restrictions on providing services. The current Article 52, a revised version of the initial Article 63, enables the Council to adopt directives to achieve liberalization of services, acting by qualified majority vote. Somewhat unusually, even today the Parliament need only be consulted. Note finally that Article 55 (ex Article 66) carries over to the field of services the "official authority" exception of Article 45 and the public policy, security and health limitations of Article 46.

At this point, a comparative note with the United States is of interest. Neither a right of establishment nor a right to provide services freely in other states is expressly mentioned in the Constitution, but both are treated as implicit in the Privileges and Immunities Clause and the Interstate Commerce Clause. There is abundant case law striking down state laws that discriminate against persons or entities from other states when providing services or seeking to create or operate branches or subsidiaries. Non-discriminatory state laws have also been examined under the balancing of interests approach of the dormant Commerce Clause. See generally J. Nowak & R. Rotunda, Constitutional Law Ch. 8 (6th ed. West 2000).

Nonetheless, the states regulate many spheres of corporate, commercial, financial and professional activity, with only limited intervention by the federal government. They have thus adopted the licensing rules for lawyers, accountants, architects, and other professionals, laws creating and governing corporations and partnerships, and regulations of state banking and insurance. Except for national banking and the securities sector, there has been little attempt to "federalize" these fields or to harmonize the diverse state systems. In contrast, the European Community has extensively harmonized Member State legislation in these areas.

2. LEGISLATION TO IMPLEMENT ARTICLES 43 AND 49

A moment's reflection reveals that the removal of Member State barriers to the right of establishment and the right to provide cross-border services is a tall order. Although some Member States had protectionist regulations designed to restrict foreign persons or enterprises from activities on their market, most barriers resulted from State regulation of particular business or professional sectors to achieve goals perceived as advancing legitimate local interests. The difficulty and added cost involved in complying with such local regulations inevitably reduced foreign participation in each national market. Opening each sector of the Community market accordingly required Community legislation not only to end express discrimination, but also to coordinate or harmonize the national rules regulating that sector.

Community action began when the Council adopted the General Program for the abolition of restrictions on freedom of establishment, and the General Program for the abolition of restrictions on freedom to provide services, O.J. English Spec.Ed. 1974, IX, at 3. These programs did not themselves have the force of law, because they are neither regulations nor directives in the sense of Article 249. However, they have served as guidelines for the adoption of legislation and have been cited by the Court of Justice in the interpretation of Treaty-based rights.

The initial purpose of the General Program on establishment, contained in the Selected Documents, was to set a timetable for legislative action before December 31, 1969. The General Program's continuing value lies in its long list of the types of discriminatory national regulations or practices that are deemed to violate Article 43. This serves as the same sort of useful checklist of prohibited rules or practices as Directive 70/50's list of prohibited measures equivalent to quantitative restriction on the free movement of goods, and merits careful reading.

Some notable examples of discriminatory rules or practices are those which require non-nationals to obtain a special authorization or permit, or undergo a period of prior residence and training before qualification to conduct a business or profession, or which impose specific taxation or other financial burdens upon non-nationals. A companion list prohibited the imposition of conditions or limitations upon foreign nationals or enterprises only. These include limitations on the ability of Community nationals to enter into contracts; to obtain licenses or authorizations, or State subsidies; to acquire or use real estate, personal property or intellectual property rights; to enjoy access to loans or credit; or to be a party to litigation or administrative proceedings.

The General Program on services parallels that on establishment, setting out a legislative timetable and providing virtually the same list of discriminatory rules, practices and conditions that were to be eliminated.

The two programs also foresaw an end to restrictions on rights of residence for the self-employed. This was largely achieved by Directive 73/148 of May 21, 1973 on the abolition of restrictions on movement and residence, O.J. L 172/14 (June 28, 1973). The terms of this directive essentially parallel those set down for workers in Directive 68/360, described in Chapter 15B. In addition, Council Directive 75/34, O.J. L 14/10 (Jan. 20, 1975) permits the self-employed and their family members to continue to reside in a host State after the retirement or permanent incapacity of the self-employed person. Also relevant is Council Directive 64/221 on the application of public policy, public security or public health limits on residence rights, described in Chapter 15C. This directive applies to self-employed persons as well as to workers. The Court of Justice's tendency to construe narrowly these limits on residence rights is also manifest in cases involving the self-employed. See Royer, Case 48/75, [1976] ECR 497.

The legislative process to facilitate enjoyment of establishment and service rights, sector by sector, concentrated in the 1960s and 1970s on agriculture, the crafts and general business and commercial fields. Over 50 directives eliminated discriminatory rules, practices and conditions in such diverse fields as agriculture, forestry, fisheries, mining of certain minerals, manufacturing of specific products, the hotel, restaurant and tavern industries, film production and distribution, real estate brokerage, and general wholesale and retail operations. For a description of the most important of these directives, see D. Lasok, The Professions and Services in the European Economic Community (Kluwer 1986). In the context of the SLIM program for the simplification and codification of legislation (see Chapter 14B), a recent directive sets out a general mechanism for the recognition of qualifications in crafts, O.J.L. 201/77 (July 31, 1999), consolidating in one text 35 directives adopted between 1963 and 1982.

Especially important sectors have occasioned a series of directives. The company law harmonization program, described below in section D, began in 1968, and that for securities law harmonization in 1977. Insurance law harmonization started with reinsurance in 1964 and the first banking directive came in 1973, but in both fields progress was initially quite limited.

The 1985 White Paper on Completing the Internal Market expressed dissatisfaction with the level of progress in attaining service and establishment rights and in facilitating Community-wide operations in the financial services, information and audio-visual industries. The White Paper urged a new approach based on mutual recognition, a concept carried over from the free movement of goods. As previously indicated, the internal market program dramatically changed the legislative picture, and harmonization efforts in these fields have largely been crowned with success. We will discuss the Television Without Frontiers Directive in section B. The legislative program in the financial services sector is described in Chapter 32.

3. THE COMMERCIAL AGENTS DIRECTIVE

Analysis of a typical directive helps illustrate how the Community harmonizes State rules to facilitate the right of establishment in a given field. Council Directive 86/653 on self-employed commercial agents, O.J. L 382/17 (Dec. 31, 1986), reproduced in the Selected Documents, has considerable importance in the merchandising sector.

Commercial agents are intermediaries who either sell products, or negotiate contracts of sale to third parties on behalf of principals. (They are to be distinguished from distributors, who buy and sell products for their own account.) The sales contract is entered into directly between the principal and the third party. A commercial agent is remunerated by the principal through a fixed fee or commission or both. Commercial agents often perform other services for the principal, such as providing local advertising and market prospection, handling customs and sales tax, arranging for warehousing and transport of products, and handling after-sales service and repairs.

Prior to 1986, most continental European states had laws that protected commercial agents by granting them rights of notice and indemnities when terminated without cause by the principal. However, these laws varied widely in the scope of the rights and remedies of commercial agents, and the UK, Ireland and some other states did not provide any protection to commercial agents.

According to one of its whereas clauses, the goal of the commercial agent directive is to achieve equal conditions of competition in the common market by fixing uniform rules for commercial agents. The directive guarantees specific rights to commercial agents, notably to receive commissions at the level "customarily allowed" in the trade for all sales to the agent's customers, or for sales achieved through the agent's efforts; if the agent has a specific territory, then commissions are due on all contracts with buyers located within that territory (arts. 6–8). The directive further requires that commercial agents be given from one to three months' notice before termination of an indefinite term contract (art. 15). Agents are also entitled upon termination to indemnities for the value of the on-going customer relations, up to a ceiling of one year's remuneration (art. 17). The parties cannot by contract derogate from these rights (arts. 11, 15 & 19).

Notes and Questions

1. Do you agree that all States should provide this sort of protection to commercial agents in order to "achieve equal conditions of competition in the common market"? Is the goal of a level competitive playing field within the Community important enough to override a State's discretionary policy on whether or not to protect a particular type of commercial intermediary? Whether the need for a level competitive playing field requires all States to have the same substantive law in a given sector is an issue which frequently gives rise to heated debate when draft directives are being considered. In the US, instead of adopting federal legislation in some fields, expert bodies prepare model uniform laws which states freely decide to adopt, modify, or reject. What factors influence the difference in approach between the Community and the US?

2. The policy rationale for protecting commercial agents is that they are usually small enterprises dealing at a disadvantage with economically powerful principals, so that it is appropriate that states should mandate that the agents receive certain economic benefits. (There is a definite analogy to the policy rationale for protection of employees in the event of dismissal. See Chapter 36. Note the text of the directive's fifth whereas clause.) Why should commercial agents be protected, but not distributors or franchisees? Do you think this policy should override the general free market principle of freedom of contract? How might a principal adjust for the economic cost of these benefits to commercial agents? If, in some cases, the consumer must pay a higher price to cover the economic cost of benefits to commercial agents, is that a desirable result?

3. Does the directive strike the proper balance between principal and agent? Is it desirable that the directive regulates matters such as the time of payment of commissions, the minimum level of commissions, and whether the contract must be written or oral, or does this represent unwarranted interference in contractual relations? Is the prescribed indemnity level too high, too low, or about right? What happens if the agent commits a "serious fault" and what should constitute such a fault?

4. In the US, states do not have legislation protecting commercial agents. However, a majority of states have laws protecting franchisees, and some of the laws impose notice and indemnity requirements. The usual rationale given for protecting franchisees through these state laws parallels that given to justify protection of commercial agents in the Community. What factors might account for the fact that the Community protects commercial agents, but not franchisees, while some US states do the reverse?

INGMAR GB v. EATON LEONARD TECHNOLOGIES

Case C–381/98, [2000] ECR ___ (Nov. 9, 2000).

[In 1989, Ingmar was appointed Eaton's commercial agent for the United Kingdom by a contract whose choice of law clause required the application of California law. After the contract was terminated in 1996, Ingmar sued for damages caused by termination pursuant to article 17 of the directive. The Court of Appeal asked the Court of Justice whether the directive's indemnity on termination provisions were mandatory in character, overriding the customary application of a choice of law clause.]

15   The parties to the main proceedings, the United Kingdom and German Governments and the Commission agree that the freedom of contracting parties to choose the system of law by which they wish their contractual relations to be governed is a basic tenet of private international law and that that freedom is removed only by rules that are mandatory.

16   However, their submissions differ as to the conditions which a legal rule must satisfy in order to be classified as a mandatory rule for the purposes of private international law.

* * *

21   The purpose of Articles 17 to 19 of the Directive, in particular, is to protect the commercial agent after termination of the contract. The regime established by the Directive for that purpose is mandatory in nature. Article 17 requires Member States to put in place a mechanism for providing reparation to the commercial agent after termination of the contract. Admittedly, that article allows the Member States to choose between indemnification and compensation for damage. However, Articles 17 and 18 prescribe a precise framework within which the Member States may exercise their discretion as to choice of methods for calculating the indemnity or compensation to be granted.

22   The mandatory nature of those articles is confirmed by the fact that, under Article 19 of the Directive, the parties may not derogate from them to the detriment of the commercial agent before the contract expires.* * *

23   Second, it should be borne in mind that, as is apparent from the second recital in the preamble to the Directive, the harmonizing measures laid down by the Directive are intended, *inter alia*, to eliminate restrictions on the carrying-on of the activities of commercial agents, to make the conditions of competition within the Community uniform and to increase the security of commercial transactions.

24   The purpose of the regime established in Articles 17 to 19 of the Directive is thus to protect, for all commercial agents, freedom of establishment and the operation of undistorted competition in the internal market. Those provisions must therefore be observed throughout the Community if those Treaty objectives are to be attained.

25   [Therefore,] it is essential for the Community legal order that a principal established in a non-member country, whose commercial agent carries on his activity within the Community, cannot evade those provisions by the simple expedient of a choice-of-law clause. The purpose served by the provisions in question requires that they be applied where the situation is closely connected with the Community, in particular where the commercial agent carries on his activity in the territory of a Member State, irrespective of the law by which the parties intended the contract to be governed.

BELLONE v. YOKAHAMA

Case C–215/97, [1998] ECR I–2191.

[An Italian law required commercial agents to be entered on a register of commercial agents. Italian courts treated this obligation as mandatory and invalidated contracts entered into between principals and agents who did not inscribe themselves on the register. When Bellone, a non-registered agent, sought indemnities after her termination as a commercial agent by Yokahama, the trial court asked the Court of Justice whether the mandatory registration obligation was compatible with the directive.]

11   It is common ground that the Directive does not deal with the question of registration of commercial agents. Even though according to the Commission, the general introduction of a register of agents was proposed by the Economic and Social Committee during the preparatory work preceding adoption of the Directive, that proposal was not retained in the final draft of the Directive, for reasons of legal certainty. It is therefore left to the Member States to require entry in the appropriate register if they consider it expedient so to do in order to satisfy certain administrative needs. As the Advocate General pointed out * * *, registration of commercial agents is required by law in a number of Member States.

* * *

13   [I]t should be borne in mind, first, that the Directive is designed to protect commercial agents, within the meaning of the Directive. According to Article 1(2), a commercial agent is 'a self-employed intermediary who has continuing authority to negotiate the sale or the purchase of goods on behalf of another person * * * or to negotiate and conclude such transactions on behalf of and in the name of that principal'. Since entry in a register is not referred to as a condition for protection under the Directive, it follows that protection under the Directive is not conditional upon entry in a register.

14   As regards, next, the form of the agency contract, Article 13(2) of the Directive * * * permits Member States to 'provide that an agency contract shall not be valid unless evidenced in writing'. It follows that the Directive starts from the principle that the contract is not subject to any formal requirement, whilst leaving it open to the Member States to require it to be in writing. [Moreover], as the Commission pointed out and the Advocate General noted * * *, by referring only to the requirement that the contract be in writing in order to be valid, the Community legislature dealt exhaustively with the matter in that provision. Member States may therefore not impose any condition other than requiring that a written document be drawn up.

15   That conclusion is confirmed by the fact that whenever the Directive allows the Member States to derogate from its provisions, express provision is made to that effect [citing examples]. If Article 13(2) of the Directive leaves it open to the Member States to require only that the document be in writing, it therefore follows that other derogations from the principle of freedom of form are contrary to the Directive. The entry of

the agent in a register can therefore not be accepted as a condition for the validity of the contract.

[16] That interpretation of the Directive is borne out by the fact that, as already mentioned, the question of registration of agents had already been addressing during the preparatory work, but was not taken up, since it was not considered necessary for agents to be registered in order to enjoy rights under the Directive.

Notes and Questions

1. Principals in the United States, where indemnities to commercial agents after a contract's termination are essentially unknown, naturally would like to contract out of an obligation to pay such indemnities to commercial agents in the Community. Choice of law clauses usually are accorded great respect by courts. Do you agree with the Court of Justice in *Ingmar* that the directive's indemnity provisions are mandatory, i.e., represent a strong public policy that overrides the choice of California law? Does the "level playing field" motive for the directive provide a justification for the Court's view?

2. Seven Member States required commercial agents to be listed on a register, but Italy was the only one that sanctioned non-registration with the nullity of the contract; the other States imposed fines. Note that the *Bellone* judgement is a rare example of the use of legislative history by the Court in its interpretation of a directive. See Chapter 14C.

B.   CASE LAW ON FREEDOM TO PROVIDE SERVICES

When discussing the subject of free movement of goods, we noted that Community legislation and Court of Justice case law had evolved in tandem, with reciprocal influence on one another. That is likewise the situation with the freedom to provide services.

1.   THE RIGHT TO PROVIDE CROSS–BORDER SERVICES

An issue that was bound to arise was whether Article 49(ex Article 59) could have direct effect. The Commission and legal commentators initially regarded this as not likely, because of the reference in the initial text of Article 59 to the need for progressive abolition of restrictions on the right during the transitional period (now deleted as superfluous in the current Article 49). The Court of Justice took a different view.

VAN BINSBERGEN v. BESTUUR VAN DE BEDRIJFSVERENIGING
Case 33/74, [1974] ECR 1299.

[Kortmann, a Dutch legal representative, was engaged by van Binsbergen to represent him in a Dutch administrative proceeding. The Dutch authorities refused to allow Kortmann to continue to act in the matter after he became a Belgian resident, because Dutch law required legal representatives to reside in the Netherlands. Kortmann appealed this decision. The Supreme Court for Social Security Affairs inquired whether the then Articles 59 and 60 (renumbered as 49 and 50) had direct effect.]

23   Article [49, ex Article 59] * * * expresses the intention to abolish restrictions on freedom to provide services by the end of the transitional period, the latest date for the entry into force of all the rules laid down by the Treaty [i.e., Dec. 31, 1969].

24   The provisions of Article [49], the application of which was to be prepared by directives issued during the transitional period, therefore became unconditional on the expiry of that period.

25   The provisions of that article abolish all discrimination against the person providing the service by reason of his nationality or the fact that he is established in a Member State other than that in which the service is to be provided.

26   Therefore, as regards at least the specific requirement of nationality or of residence, Articles [49] and [50] impose a well-defined obligation, the fulfilment of which by the Member States cannot be delayed or jeopardized by the absence of provisions which were to be adopted in pursuance of powers conferred under Articles [52 and 55, ex Articles 63 and 66].

[The Court also considered whether a State can require residence as a condition to perform the services in question.]

11   [A] requirement that the person providing the service must be habitually resident within the territory of the State where the service is to be provided may * * * have the result of depriving Article [49] of all useful effect, in view of the fact that the precise object of that Article is to abolish restrictions on freedom to provide services imposed on persons who are not established in the State where the service is to be provided.

12   However, * * *, specific requirements imposed on the person providing the service cannot be considered incompatible with the Treaty where they have as their purpose the application of professional rules justified by the general good—in particular rules relating to organization, qualifications, professional ethics, supervision and liability—which are binding upon any person established in the State in which the service is provided, where the person providing the service would escape from the ambit of those rules being established in another Member State.

13   Likewise, a Member State cannot be denied the right to take measures to prevent the exercise by a person providing services whose activity is entirely or principally directed towards its territory of the freedom guaranteed by Article [49] for the purpose of avoiding the professional rules of conduct which would be applicable to him if he were established within that State * * *.

14   In accordance with these principles, the requirement that persons whose functions are to assist the administration of justice must be permanently established for professional purposes within the jurisdiction of certain courts or tribunals cannot be considered incompatible with the provisions of Articles [49] and [50], where such requirement is objectively justified by the need to ensure observance of professional rules of conduct connected, in particular, with the administration of justice and with respect for professional ethics.

15   That cannot, however, be the case when the provision of certain services in a Member State is not subject to any sort of qualification or professional

regulation and when the requirement of habitual residence is fixed by reference to the territory of the State in question.

[16] [In that case], the requirement of residence within that State constitutes a restriction which is incompatible with Articles [49] and [50] of the Treaty if the administration of justice can satisfactorily be ensured by measures which are less restrictive, such as the choosing of an address for service.

Notes and Questions

1. *Van Binsbergen's* conclusion that Articles 49 and 50 [ex Articles 59 and 60] had direct effect followed by a few months the Court's conclusion in *Reyners*, infra page 714, that Article 43 [ex Article 52] on the right of establishment had direct effect. In the next Chapter, we shall see that the Court's judgements in the two cases catalyzed the Council into adopting a series of harmonization directives in the professional services sector. Naturally, the Court's judgements enabled individual persons and enterprises to obtain the recognition of their rights to provide commercial services in a variety of contexts.

2. We have already seen that the Court often treats a State's residency requirement as an indirect mode of discrimination on the basis of nationality in the context of free movement of workers. *Van Binsbergen's* ¶ 11 is, however, the first instance of this analytical approach. *Van Binsbergen's* conclusion in ¶ 12 that States may impose limits on trans-border service providers in order to protect a "general good" interest is also seminal. Do you agree that national professional qualification and ethics rules constitute a "general good" interest? Why is Kortmann nonetheless permitted to provide legal services in the Netherlands?

3. *Van Binsbergen* is also seminal in setting out an exception in ¶ 13. When may a State legitimately restrict or forbid persons from providing trans-border services? A good example is Vereniging Veronica v. Commissariaat voor de Media, Case C–148/91, [1993] ECR I–487, in which a Dutch company was accused of setting up and financing a Luxembourg television station intended to broadcast programs in Dutch by cable into the Netherlands, when the broadcasts would not comply with the Dutch law regulating television broadcasting. The Court first held that State rules requiring broadcasters to follow a pluralist and non-commercial cultural policy could constitute a general good interest. The Court then held that the Netherlands could forbid television broadcasts from Luxembourg into the Netherlands if the television station could be shown to have been established in order to circumvent the Dutch broadcasting rules. A useful casenote is by W. Hins, 31 Common Mkt. L. Rev. 901(1994).

NEW HAMPSHIRE v. PIPER

470 U.S. 274, 105 S.Ct. 1272, 84 L.Ed.2d 205 (1985).

[Piper, a resident of Vermont, passed the New Hampshire bar examination, but was denied admission to the bar because New Hampshire required its lawyers to be residents. Piper lived 400 yards from New Hampshire. She was married and owned a house with her husband in Vermont. When her challenge of the residence requirement reached the Supreme Court, Justice Powell, speaking for eight Justices, held that the residence requirement violated the Privileges and Immunities Clause.]

Derived * * * from the Articles of Confederation, the Privileges and Immunities Clause was intended to create a national economic union. It is therefore not surprising that this Court repeatedly has found that "one of the privileges which the Clause guarantees to citizens of State A is that of doing business in State B on terms of substantial equality with the citizens of that State" [quoting *Toomer* v. *Witsell, infra* note 1].

There is nothing in [our precedents] suggesting that the practice of law should not be viewed as a "privilege" under Art. IV, § 2. Like the occupations considered in our earlier cases, the practice of law is important to the national economy. As the Court noted in *Goldfarb* v. *Virginia State Bar*, 421 U.S. 773, 788, 95 S.Ct. 2004, 2014, 44 L.Ed.2d 572, the "activities of lawyers play an important part in commercial intercourse."

The lawyer's role in the national economy is not the only reason that the opportunity to practice law should be considered a "fundamental right." We believe that the legal profession has a noncommercial role and duty that reinforce the view that the practice of law falls within the ambit of Privileges and Immunities Clause. Out-of-state lawyers may–and often do–represent persons who raise unpopular federal claims. In some cases, representation by nonresident counsel may be the only means available for the vindication of federal rights. The lawyer who champions unpopular causes surely is as important to the "maintenance or well-being of the Union," *Baldwin*, 436 U.S., at 388, 98 S.Ct., at 1863, as was the shrimp fisherman in *Toomer*, or the pipeline worker in *Hicklin* [supra, page 581].

* * *

Because, under *Griffiths* [infra page 735], a lawyer is not an "officer" of the State in any political sense, there is no reason for New Hampshire to exclude from its bar nonresidents. We therefore conclude that the right to practice law is protected by the Privileges and Immunities Clause.

Our holding in this case does not interfere with the ability of the States to regulate their bars. The nonresident who seeks to join a bar, unlike the *pro hac vice* applicant, must have the same professional and personal qualifications required of resident lawyers. Furthermore, the nonresident member of the bar is subject to the full force of New Hampshire's disciplinary rules.

[Justice Powell then rejected New Hampshire's arguments that non-resident lawyers might be less familiar with its rules and procedures, less apt to behave ethically, or less likely to be available for court proceedings.]

[Justice Rehnquist dissented]

The [Court's] decision will be surprising to many, because it so clearly disregards the fact that the practice of law is—almost by definition—fundamentally different from those other occupations that are practiced across state lines without significant deviation from State to State. The fact that each State is free, in a large number of areas, to establish *independently* of the other States its own laws for the governance of its citizens, is a fundamental precept of our Constitution that, I submit, is of equal stature with the need for the States to form a cohesive union. What is at issue here is New Hampshire's rights to decide that those people who in many ways will intimately deal with New Hampshire's self-governance should reside within that State.

* * *

The reason that the practice of law should be treated differently is that law is one occupation that does not readily translate across state lines. Certain aspects of legal practice are distinctly and intentionally *nonnational*; in this regard one might view this country's legal system as the antithesis of the norms embodied in the Art. IV Privileges and Immunities Clause. Put simply, the State has a substantial interest in creating its own set of laws responsive to its own local interests, and it is reasonable for a State to decide that those people who have been trained to analyze law and policy are better equipped to write those state laws and adjudicate cases arising under them.

* * *

A State similarly might determine that because lawyers play an important role in the formulation of state policy through their adversary representation, they would be intimately conversant with the local concerns that should inform such policies. And the State likewise might conclude that those citizens trained in the law are likely to bring their useful expertise to other important functions that benefit from such expertise and are of interest to state governments–such as trusteeships, or directorships of corporations or charitable organizations, or school board positions, or merely the role of the interested citizen at a town meeting.

Notes and Questions

1. Justice Powell in *Piper* declared that the Privileges and Immunities Clause was intended by its draftsman, Charles Pinckney, to express the ideas of the Articles of Confederation, which stated in article four: "the people of each State shall have free ingress and regress to and from any other State, and shall enjoy therein all the privileges of trade and commerce, subject to the same duties, impositions and restrictions as the inhabitants thereof." *Piper* continues a line of cases in which the Privileges and Immunities Clause or the dormant Commerce Clause were used to invalidate state laws charging salesmen or peddlers selling out-of-state goods substantially higher state license fees than persons selling products of the state, e.g., in Ward v. Maryland, 79 (12 Wall.) 418, 20 L.Ed. 449 (1871), and Welton v. Missouri, 91 U.S. (1 Otto) 275, 23 L.Ed. 347 (1875). In a modern analogue, in Toomer v. Witsell, 334 U.S. 385, 68 S.Ct. 1156, 92 L.Ed. 1460 (1948), the Court relied on the Privileges and Immunities Clause to invalidate a South Carolina law imposing a $2,500 license fee on nonresident shrimp fishermen, in contrast to a $25 fee for resident fishermen.

2. In *Piper*, would you agree with Justice Powell or then Justice Rehnquist? Note that both the Court in *Van Binsbergen* and Justice Powell in *Piper* declare that the host State may impose its professional rules on the non-resident lawyer. In the next chapter we will consider whether that approach can produce difficulties, especially when the lawyer only occasionally provides trans-border services.

CRIMINAL PROCEEDINGS AGAINST WEBB

Case 279/80, [1981] ECR 3305.

[Dutch law forbids persons to engage in the supply of personnel for temporary help without a license, which is granted after review of whether the applicant's operations "might harm good relations in the labour market" or insufficiently safeguard the interests of the personnel supplied. A UK company, the International Engineering Services Bureau (IESB), and its manager, Webb, were prosecuted for supplying technical staff on a temporary basis to Dutch firms without a Dutch license. The staff remained employees of IESB. IESB held a license granted by UK authorities for personnel supply services, but never obtained a Dutch license, even though its principal business was in the Netherlands. After conviction, IESB and Webb appealed. The Dutch Supreme Court asked the Court of Justice to rule on whether the supply of personnel constituted a service and, if so, whether the Dutch license requirements complied with Article 50 (ex Article 60), especially since IESB had a UK license.]

16 The principal aim of the third paragraph in Article [50, ex Article 60] is to enable the provider of the service to pursue his activities in the Member State where the service is given without suffering discrimination in favour of the nationals of that State. However, it does not mean that all national legislation applicable to nationals of that State and usually applied to the permanent activities of undertakings established therein may be similarly applied in its entirety to the temporary activities of undertakings which are established in other Member States.

17 * * * [T]he freedom to provide services is one of the fundamental principles of the Treaty and may be restricted only by provisions which are justified by the general good and which are imposed on all persons or undertakings operating in the said State in so far as that interest is not safeguarded by the provisions to which the provider of the service is subject in the Member State of his establishment.

18 [T]he provision of manpower is a particularly sensitive matter from the occupational and social point of view.* * * [P]ursuit of such a business directly affects both relations on the labour market and the lawful interests of the workforce concerned.* * *

19 It follows in particular that it is permissible for Member States, and amounts for them to a legitimate choice of policy pursued in the public interest, to subject the provision of manpower within their borders to a system of licensing in order to be able to refuse licences where there is reason to fear that such activities may harm good relations on the labour market or that the interests of the workforce affected are not adequately safeguarded. * * * [T]he Member State in which the services are to be supplied has unquestionably the right to require possession of a licence issued on the same conditions as in the case of its own nationals.

20 Such a measure would be excessive in relation to the aim pursued, however, if the requirements to which the issue of a licence is subject coincided with the proofs and guarantees required in the State of establishment. In order to maintain the principle of freedom to provide services

the first requirement is that in considering applications for licences and in granting them the Member State in which the service is to be provided may not make any distinction based on the nationality of the provider of the services or the place of his establishment; the second requirement is that it must take into account the evidence and guarantees already furnished by the provider of the services for the pursuit of his activities in the Member State of his establishment.

PROCEEDINGS AGAINST CORSTEN

Case C–58/98, [2000] ECR ___ (Oct. 3, 2000).

[The German Skilled Trades Order requires all independent skilled craftsmen to have passed a master's examination and to be entered on the Skilled Trades Register, with subsequent subscription payments to a trade chamber. In compliance with a 1964 directive on the mutual recognition of craft qualifications, persons from other Member States may provide documentary evidence of their skills instead of taking a German examination. When Corsten, an architect, engaged a Dutch contractor to lay floors in a building in Germany, he was prosecuted for obtaining black market work, because the contractor was not entered on the Skilled Trade Register. Corsten challenged the fine. The trial court asked the Court of Justice whether the German register obligations was compatible with Community law. The Court initially concluded that the 1964 directive did not decide the issue.]

33 It is settled case-law that Article [49, ex 59] of the Treaty requires not only the elimination of all discrimination on the grounds of nationality against providers of services who are established in another Member State but also the abolition of any restriction, even if it applies to national providers of services and to those of other Member States alike, which is liable to prohibit, impede or render less advantageous the activities of a provider of services established in another Member State where he lawfully provides similar services [citing numerous cases].

34 In that respect, the requirement imposed on an undertaking established in one Member State which wishes, as a provider of a service, to carry on a skilled trade activity in another Member State to be entered on the latter's trades register constitutes a restriction within the meaning of Article [49, ex 59] of the Treaty.

35 It is also settled case-law that, even if there is no harmonization in the field, such a restriction on the fundamental principle of freedom to provide services can be based only on rules justified by overriding requirements relating to the public interest and applicable to all persons and undertakings operating in the territory of the State where the service is provided, in so far as that interest is not safeguarded by the rules to which the provider of such a service is subject in the Member State where he is established [citing *Webb* and other cases].

* * *

38 It must be acknowledged, as the Commission pointed out, that the objective of guaranteeing the quality of skilled trade work and of protecting those who have commissioned such work is an overriding requirement

relating to the public interest capable of justifying a restriction on freedom to provide services.

39   However, in accordance with the principle of proportionality, the application of national rules to providers of services established in other Member States must be appropriate for securing attainment of the objective which they pursue and must not go beyond what is necessary in order to attain it.

* * *

42   The reasons for the requirement of entry on the Register being purely of an administrative nature, such considerations cannot justify derogation by a Member State from the rules of Community law, especially where the derogation in question amounts to preventing or restricting the exercise of one of the fundamental freedoms of Community law.

45   Even if the requirement of entry on that Register, entailing compulsory membership of the Chamber of Skilled Trades for the undertakings concerned and therefore payment of the related subscription, could be justified in the case of establishment in the host Member State, which is not the situation in the main proceedings, the same is not true for undertakings which intend to provide services in the host Member State only on an occasional basis, indeed perhaps only once.

46   The latter are liable to be dissuaded from going ahead with their plans if, because of the compulsory requirement that they be entered on the Register, the authorization procedure is made lengthier and more expensive, so that the profit anticipated, at least for small contracts, is no longer economically worthwhile. For those undertakings, therefore, the freedom to provide services, a fundamental principle of the Treaty, [is] liable to become ineffective.

47   In consequence, the authorization procedure instituted by the host Member State should neither delay nor complicate exercise of the right of persons established in another Member State to provide their services [provided that in the home State] examination of the conditions governing access to the activities concerned has been carried out and it has been established that those conditions are satisfied.

48   Moreover, any requirement of entry on the trades register of the host Member State, assuming it was justified, should neither give rise to additional administrative expense nor entail compulsory payment of subscriptions to the chamber of trades.

Notes and Questions

1. The national rules in *Webb* and *Corsten* were applied both to domestic persons and firms and to those providing services from other States. Accordingly, they did not violate the national treatment obligation expressed in Article 50 paragraph 3. Already in 1981 in ¶ 17 of *Webb*, the Court went beyond the obligation not to discriminate on the basis of nationality, and enunciated the doctrine that State rules restricting services are compatible with the Treaty only if they are justified by a general good interest. As we shall see, this doctrine is not only crucial in the area of free movement of services, but has now been carried over to the right of establishment. What was the general good interest that the

Court accepted in *Webb*? What consideration must the Netherlands give to IESB's UK license?

2.   In *Webb* and in *Corsten* the Court applied the mutual recognition principle we previously saw as integral to the *Cassis de Dijon* doctrine in the free movement of goods: the host State should accept the home State's examination of the qualifications of the service provider. In *Corsten* the Court also applies the principle of proportionality to conclude that Germany cannot require foreign craftsmen to be entered on the Skilled Trade Register. Germany has a strong tradition of demanding high quality workmanship in its crafts and undoubtedly felt the Register entry system provided beneficial guarantees to the public. There is a certain analogy between the German policy here and that behind its quality standards in *German beer*, supra page 499.

3.   Contractors who erect buildings and plants or construct bridges, railroads, dams, etc. constitute a major sector in trans-border services. Because contractors frequently bring a large work force from their home States to the construction sites, where the workers stay for long periods of time, host States naturally want to impose their employment rules on the contractors. It is well settled that the host State can require the contractors to pay its minimum wage (a significant point, since minimum wage scales vary radically among the States). In Criminal proceedings against Arblade and Leloup, Cases C–369/96 & C–376/96, [1999] ECR I–8453, the Court held that Belgium could require French contractors who used French workers for months on sites in Belgium to pay the higher Belgium minimum wage and to comply with Belgian worker health and safety standards, but could not require that a variety of documents be kept in Belgium when comparable ones could be made available on need from France. Directive 96/71 on the posting of workers, O.J.L 18/1 (Jan. 21, 1997) now harmonizes many of the national rules in this sector, and requires cooperation among the regulatory authorities.

COMMISSION v. FRANCE

(Tour guides)
Case C–154/89, [1991] ECR I–659.

[A 1975 French law required all tour guides to possess a French license in order to conduct groups of French and foreign tourists in museums and historical monuments and on public transport. The license was accorded after passage of an examination on the history, culture and economy of France, with part of the oral examination conducted in French. The Commission brought an Article 226 (ex 169) proceeding against France, contending that a license requirement for guides who conducted groups from other Member States violated Article 49 (ex 59). The Commission did not contest a license obligation for guides in museums or monuments whose rules of entry required a specialized professional guide.]

[12]   Articles [49 and 50, ex 59 and 60] of the Treaty require not only the abolition of any discrimination against a person providing services on account of his nationality but also the abolition of any restriction on the freedom to provide services imposed on the ground that the person providing a service is established in a Member State other than the one in which the service is provided. In particular, the Member State cannot make the performance of the services in its territory subject to observance of all the conditions required for establishment; were it to do so the

provisions securing freedom to provide services would be deprived of all practical effect.

13   The requirements imposed by the * * * French legislation amount to such a restriction. By making the provision of services by tourist guides accompanying a group of tourists from another Member State subject to possession of a specific qualification, that legislation prevents both tour companies from providing that service with their own staff and self-employed tourist guides from offering their services to those companies for organized tours. It also prevents tourists taking part in such organized tours from availing themselves at will of the services in question.

* * *

15   [T]hose requirements can be regarded as compatible with Articles [49 and 50] of the Treaty only if it is established that with regard to the activity in question there are overriding reasons relating to the public interest which justify restrictions on the freedom to provide services, that the public interest is not already protected by the rules of the State of establishment and that the same result cannot be obtained by less restrictive rules.

16   The French Government contends that the French legislation in question seeks to ensure the protection of general interests relating to the proper appreciation of places and things of historical interest and the widest possible dissemination of knowledge of the artistic and cultural heritage of the country. According to the French Government, those interests are not adequately safeguarded by the rules to which the provider of the services, in this case the tour company, is subject in the Member State in which it is established. Several States require no occupational qualifications for tourist guides or demand no special knowledge of the historical and cultural heritage of other countries.* * *

17   The general interest in the proper appreciation of places and things of historical interest and the widest possible dissemination of knowledge of the artistic and cultural heritage of a country can constitute an overriding reason justifying a restriction on the freedom to provide services. However, the requirement in question contained in the French legislation goes beyond what is necessary to ensure the safeguarding of that interest inasmuch as it makes the activities of a tourist guide accompanying groups of tourists from another Member State subject to possession of a licence.

18   The service of accompanying tourists is performed under quite specific conditions. The independent or employed tourist guide travels with the tourists and accompanies them in a closed group; in that group they move temporarily from the Member State of establishment to the Member State to be visited.

19   In those circumstances a licence requirement imposed by the Member State of destination has the effect of reducing the number of tourist guides qualified to accompany tourists in a closed group, which may lead a tour operator to have recourse instead to local guides employed or established in the Member State in which the service is to be performed. However, that consequence may have the drawback that tourists who are the recipients of the services in question do not have a guide who is familiar with their language, their interests and their specific expectations.

[20] Moreover, the profitable operation of such a group tour depends on the commercial reputation of the operator, who faces competitive pressure from other tour companies; the need to maintain that reputation and the competitive pressure themselves compel companies to be selective in employing tourist guides and exercise some control over the quality of their services. Depending on the specific expectations of the groups of tourists in question, that factor is likely to contribute to the proper appreciation of places and things of historical interest and to the widest possible dissemination of knowledge relating to the artistic and cultural heritage, in the case of conducted tours of places other than museums or historical monuments which may be visited only with a professional guide.

[21] It follows that in view of the scale of the restrictions it imposes, the legislation in issue is disproportionate in relation to the objective pursued, namely to ensure the proper appreciation of places and things of historical interest and the widest dissemination of knowledge of the artistic and cultural heritage of the Member State in which the tour is conducted.

Notes and Questions

1. The Court accepted that France had a genuine public interest concern in an accurate depiction of its culture and history in the *French tour guides* judgement. (The term, 'public interest,' is used synonymously with 'general good.') Why then did the Court refuse to permit France to require a license for tour guides accompanying groups from other States? Do you agree with the Court comment in ¶ 20 that "competitive pressure" will ensure adequately qualified guides? The Commission won parallel cases against Greece and Italy. Advocate General Lenz's analytical opinion notes that for tour groups and their guides, the provider of services and the recipients of services will be physically together in the same State, but enjoy Treaty rights because they are both exercising a right of free movement to a host State.

2. In Commission v. Belgium (Private security firms), Case C–355/98, [2000] ECR __ (Mar. 9, 2000, a Belgian law required all firms providing security services intended to safeguard persons and property to have a place of business within Belgium, and all service firm managers to reside in Belgium. The Commission challenged these rules as covert discrimination based on nationality. Should the Court agree?

3. The Commission Communication on free movement of services, O.J.C 334/3 (Dec. 9, 1993), reproduced in the Selected Documents, is a valuable summary of the applicable rules in a clear fashion, covering the case law up to that point.

2. APPROPRIATE PUBLIC INTEREST LIMITS ON CROSS–BORDER SERVICES

COMMISSION v. GERMANY

(German insurance)
Case 205/84, [1986] ECR 3755.

[The Commission brought an Article 226 proceeding against Germany for violation of Articles 49 and 50 [ex Articles 59 and 60] and for improper implementation of three directives adopted in the 1970s to partially coordinate national rules on the regulation of cross-border insurance services. The proceeding involved many distinct issues, and occasioned a long, complex judgment.

Our concern here is with perhaps the two most important issues: 1) could Germany require Community insurers to obtain an authorization, and 2) could it require a permanent establishment in Germany in order to carry out the cross-border insurance operations permitted by the directives. Germany contended that both constituted appropriate conditions because they permitted the type of supervision of business operations necessary in order to protect adequately the interests of consumers, in this case, the insured persons.]

27　[T]he freedom to provide services, as one of the fundamental principles of the Treaty, may be restricted only by provisions which are justified by the general good and which are applied to all persons or undertakings operating within the territory of the State in which the service is provided in so far as that interest is not safeguarded by the provisions to which the provider of a service is subject in the Member State of his establishment. In addition, such requirements must be objectively justified by the need to ensure that professional rules of conduct are complied with and that the interests which such rules are designed to safeguard are protected.

28　[T]he requirements in question in these proceedings, namely that an insurer who is established in another Member State, authorized by the supervisory authority of that State and subject to the supervision of that authority, must have a permanent establishment within the territory of the State in which the service is provided and that he must obtain a separate authorization from the supervisory authority of that State, constitute restrictions on the freedom to provide services inasmuch as they increase the cost of such services in the State in which they are provided, in particular where the insurer conducts business in that State only occasionally.

29　It follows that those requirements may be regarded as compatible with Articles 49 and 50 [ex Articles 59 and 60] of the EEC Treaty only if it is established that in the field of activity concerned there are imperative reasons relating to the public interest which justify restrictions on the freedom to provide services, that the public interest is not already protected by the rules of the State of establishment and that the same result cannot be obtained by less restrictive rules.

(a) The Existence of an Interest Justifying Certain Restrictions on the Freedom to Provide Insurance Services

30　As the German Government [argued], the insurance sector is a particularly sensitive area from the point of view of the protection of the consumer both as a policy-holder and as an insured person. This is so in particular because of the specific nature of the service provided by the insurer, which is linked to future events, the occurrence of which, or at least the timing of which, is uncertain at the time when the contract is concluded. An insured person who does not obtain payment under a policy following an event giving rise to a claim may find himself in a very precarious position. Similarly, it is as a rule very difficult for a person seeking insurance to judge whether the likely future development of the insurer's financial position and the terms of the contract, usually imposed by the insurer, offer him sufficient guarantees that he will receive payment under the policy if a claimable event occurs.

31 It must also be borne in mind, as the German Government has pointed out, that in certain fields insurance has become a mass phenomenon. Contracts are concluded by such enormous numbers of policy-holders that the protection of the interests of insured persons and injured third parties affects virtually the whole population.

32 Those special characteristics, which are peculiar to the insurance sector, have led all the Member States to introduce legislation making insurance undertakings subject to mandatory rules both as regards their financial position and the conditions of insurance which they apply, and to permanent supervision to ensure that those rules are complied with.

33 It therefore appears that in the field in question there are imperative reasons relating to the public interest which may justify restrictions on the freedom to provide services, provided, however, that the rules of the State of establishment are not adequate in order to achieve the necessary level of protection and that the requirements of the State in which the service is provided do not exceed what is necessary in that respect.

[The Court next considered whether Germany could require an authorization or license in order to protect certain consumer interests in Germany.]

(c) The Necessity of an Authorization Procedure

44 [I]n all the Member States the supervision of insurance undertakings is organized in the form of an authorization procedure * * *. In each of [the insurance] directives Article 6 * * * provides that each Member State must make the taking-up of the business of insurance in its territory subject to an official authorization. An undertaking which sets up branches and agencies in Member States other than that in which its head office is situated must therefore obtain an authorization from the supervisory authority of each of those States.

* * *

46 [T]he German Government's argument to the effect that only the requirement of an authorization can provide an effective means of ensuring the supervision which, having regard to the foregoing considerations, is justified on grounds relating to the protection of the consumer both as a policy-holder and as an insured person, must be accepted. Since a system such as that proposed in the draft for a second [insurance] directive, which entrusts the operation of the authorization procedure to the Member State in which the undertaking is established, working in close cooperation with the State in which the service is provided, can be set up only by legislation, it must also be acknowledged that, in the present state of Community law, it is for the State in which the service is provided to grant and withdraw that authorization.

47 It should however be emphasized that the authorization must be granted on request to any undertaking established in another Member State which meets the conditions laid down by the legislation of the State in which the service is provided, that those conditions may not duplicate equivalent

statutory conditions which have already been satisfied in the State in which the undertaking is established and that the supervisory authority of the State in which the service is provided must take into account supervision and verifications which have already been carried out in the Member State of establishment. * * *

* * *

(d) The Necessity of Establishment

[52] If the requirement of an authorization constitutes a restriction on the freedom to provide services, the requirement of a permanent establishment is the very negation of that freedom. It has the result of depriving Article 59 [now Article 49] of the Treaty of all effectiveness * * *. If such a requirement is to be accepted, it must be shown that it constitutes a condition which is indispensable for attaining the objective pursued.

[53] In that respect, the German Government points out in particular that the requirement of an establishment in the State in which the service is provided makes it possible for the supervisory authority of that State to carry out verifications in *situ* and to monitor continuously the activities carried on by the authorized insurer * * *.

[54] [C]onsiderations of an administrative nature cannot justify derogation by a Member State from the rules of Community law. * * * [I]t is therefore not sufficient that the presence on the undertaking's premises of all the documents needed for supervision by the authorities of the State in which the service is provided may make it easier for those authorities to perform their task. It must also be shown that those authorities cannot, even under an authorization procedure, carry out their supervisory tasks effectively unless the undertaking has in the aforesaid State a permanent establishment at which all the necessary documents are kept.

[55] That has not been shown to be the case. * * * Community law on insurance does not, as it stands at present, prohibit the State in which the service is provided from requiring that the assets representing the technical reserves covering business conducted on its territory be localized in that State. In that case the presence of such assets may be verified in *situ*, even if the undertaking does not have any permanent establishment in the State. As regards the other conditions for the conduct of business which are subject to supervision, it appears to the Court that such supervision may be effected on the basis of copies of balance sheets, accounts and commercial documents, including the conditions of insurance and schemes of operation, sent from the State of establishment and duly certified by the authorities of that Member State. It is possible under an authorization procedure to subject the undertaking to such conditions of supervision by means of a provision in the certificate of authorization and to ensure compliance with those conditions, if necessary by withdrawing that certificate.

[56] It has therefore not been established that the considerations acknowledged above concerning the protection of policy-holders and insured persons make the establishment of the insurer in the territory of the State in which the service is provided an indispensable requirement.

Notes and Questions

1. After *van Binsbergen,* the *German insurance* case is undoubtedly the most influential judgment in the services field. Both in the excerpt and the omitted part of the judgment, the Court provided guidelines which substantially influenced the Commission's drafting of later insurance harmonization directives and the Second Banking Directive. See Chapter 32(3).

2. Observe that the Court of Justice in *German insurance* adopted in ¶ 29 the *Cassis de Dijon* rule of reason approach to Article 28 (see Chapter 13C) as equally applicable to Articles 49 and 50 [ex 59 and 60]. *German insurance* provides more precise guidelines than does the earlier rule in *van Binsbergen.* This is another example of the spread of a helpful Community law doctrine to other areas. The Court's reasoning in striking down Germany's requirement of a permanent establishment echoes that in the *Pharmaceutical representatives* case, supra page 479, involving Article 28.

HER MAJESTY'S CUSTOMS AND EXCISE v. SCHINDLER

Case C–275/92, [1994] ECR I–1039.

[The 1976 United Kingdom Lotteries and Amusements Act prohibits lotteries, but makes an exception for small-scale lotteries for charitable purposes. The Act also forbids the importation of tickets for foreign lotteries, or the transfer abroad of money to acquire foreign lottery tickets. Schindler was an independent agent for the sale of tickets on behalf of the SKL, a public body organizing lotteries for four south German states. After Schindler sent invitations to buy tickets in an SKL lottery from the Netherlands to the UK, he was prosecuted for violation of the Act. When Schindler raised Treaty issues in his defense, the trial court asked the Court of Justice whether lottery tickets constituted goods, or their sale represented a service, and whether the Act could be justified under the Treaty exceptions to free movement of goods or services.

The Court first concluded that the mailing of application forms and tickets was entirely accessory to the participation in a lottery, so that the proper Treaty focus was upon Articles 49 and 50. The Court next found that the sale of lottery tickets constituted a service for remuneration (the price of the ticket) and the trans-border mailing fell under Article 49. The Court then examined whether the UK rules could be considered to be justified.]

42 The Belgian and Luxembourg Governments submit that legislation such as the United Kingdom legislation does not restrict freedom to provide services because it is applicable without distinction.

43 According to the case-law of the Court (see the judgment in Case C–76/90 *Säger v. Dennemeyer* [1991] ECR I–4221), national legislation may fall within the ambit of Article [49, ex 59] of the Treaty, even if it is applicable without distinction, when it is liable to prohibit or otherwise impede the activities of a provider of services established in another Member State where he lawfully provides similar services.

44 [T]his is the case with * * * the United Kingdom legislation on lotteries which wholly precludes lottery operators from other Member States from promoting their lotteries and selling their tickets, whether directly or

through independent agents, in the Member State which enacted that legislation.

* * *

[The Court then considered the crucial issue, whether "concerns of social policy and of the prevention of fraud" would justify the UK restrictions on services.]

[49] The Commission and the defendants * * * argue * * * that legislation such as the United Kingdom lotteries legislation is in fact discriminatory. They submit that, although such legislation prohibits large lotteries in the United Kingdom in an apparently non-discriminatory manner, it permits the simultaneous operation by the same person of several small lotteries, which is equivalent to one large lottery and further the operation of games of chance which are comparable in nature and scale to large lotteries, such as football pools or "bingo".

* * *

[51] However, even though the amounts at stake in the games so permitted in the United Kingdom may be comparable to those in large-scale lotteries and even though those games involve a significant element of chance they differ in their object, rules and methods of organization from * * * large-scale lotteries * * *.

[52] In those circumstances legislation such as the United Kingdom legislation cannot be considered to be discriminatory.

* * *

[56] The defendants * * * argue * * * that the reasons invoked to justify the prohibition at issue cannot constitute overriding considerations of public interest since legislation such as the United Kingdom legislation does not contain an equivalent prohibition of gambling of the same nature as large-scale lotteries.

[57] [T]he United Kingdom legislation, before its amendment by the 1993 Act establishing the national lottery, pursued the following objectives: to prevent crime and to ensure that gamblers would be treated honestly; to avoid stimulating demand in the gambling sector which has damaging social consequences when taken to excess; and to ensure that lotteries could not be operated for personal and commercial profit but solely for charitable, sporting or cultural purposes.

* * *

[60] [I]t is not possible to disregard the moral, religious or cultural aspects of lotteries, like other types of gambling, in all the Member States. The general tendency of the Member States is to restrict, or even prohibit, the practice of gambling and to prevent it from being a source of private profit. Secondly, lotteries involve a high risk of crime or fraud, given the size of the amounts which can be staked and of the winnings which they can hold out to the players, particularly when they are operated on a large scale. Thirdly, they are an incitement to spend which may have damaging individual and social consequences. A final ground which is not without relevance, although it cannot in itself be regarded as an objective justifica-

tion, is that lotteries may make a significant contribution to the financing of benevolent or public interest activities such as social works, charitable works, sport or culture.

61   [Accordingly] national authorities [have] latitude to determine what is required to protect the players and, more generally, in the light of the specific social and cultural features of each Member State, to maintain order in society, as regards the manner in which lotteries are operated, the size of the stakes, and the allocation of the profits they yield. [The Member States may] assess not only whether it is necessary to restrict the activities of lotteries but also whether they should be prohibited, provided that those restrictions are not discriminatory.

62   When a Member State prohibits in its territory the operation of large-scale lotteries and in particular the advertising and distribution of tickets for that type of lottery, the prohibition on the importation of materials intended to enable nationals of that Member State to participate in such lotteries organized in another Member State cannot be regarded as a measure involving an unjustified interference with the freedom to provide services. Such a prohibition on import is a necessary part of the protection which the Member State seeks to secure in its territory in relation to lotteries.

63   Accordingly, the reply to be given to the [final] question must be that the Treaty provisions relating to freedom to provide services do not preclude legislation such as the United Kingdom lotteries legislation, in view of the concerns of social policy and the prevention of fraud which justify it.

Notes and Questions

1.   *Schindler* was decided four months after *Keck*, page 522 supra, which introduced the new doctrine that non-discriminatory rules regulating "selling arrangements" do not violate Article 28. In ¶¶ 43–44, the Court did not follow that approach in applying Article 49. Do you see any reason why the Court might conclude that the *Keck* doctrine should not carry over to the field of services?

2.   The Court's ultimate conclusion is based on a general good or public interest analysis. Certainly the prevention of fraud represents a legitimate consumer interest. But is there really any risk of fraud in the sale of tickets in a German state lottery by an authorized agent? The Commission argued that the UK Act violated the principle of proportionality. How might that principle have been applied here? For useful information on the extent of gambling in the UK, and a critical review of the judgment, see the casenotes by L. Gormley, 19 Eur. L. Rev. 644 (1994), and V. Hatzopoulos, 32 Common Mkt. L. Rev. 841 (1995).

3.   In *Familiapresse*, supra page 529, the Court held that magazine pages which contained crosswords or puzzles, whose correct solution could enable the person solving them to win a prize, constituted games of chance on such a small scale that they could not be equated with a large scale lottery which a State could legitimately forbid on public interest grounds.

4.   The Court in *Schindler* also refers to social and cultural interests as a justification of the Act. What examples were given by the Court? Do you agree that these are important enough to justify the Act? Ironically, as noted in ¶ 31, the UK established a national lottery in 1993. Having created its own national lottery, could the UK today bar the sale of German state lottery tickets? Would that not

represent discriminatory treatment of a foreign provider of services? Note the final clause in ¶ 61.

5. In Laara v. District Prosecutor of Finland, Case C–124/97, [1999] ECR I–6067, Laara, together with a UK company, was prosecuted for operating slot machines in Finland, where a 1965 law grants a monopoly for slot-machine operation to an association licensed by Finland. The net proceeds of the association's slot machine operations are paid over to the Ministry of Social Affairs, which distributes them to social and charitable groups. The Court's reply to questions referred indicated that the operation of slot machines constituted the providing of a service. The Court then quoted ¶ 60 of *Schindler* concerning the public interest justification for state regulation of large scale lotteries, and held that the same public interest justified regulation of slot machine operations. Finally, the Court held that the Finnish approach of granting a licensed monopoly for slot machine operation, rather than forbidding slot machines, was a justifiable and proportionate approach: "Limited authorisation of such games on an exclusive basis, which has the advantage of confining the desire to gamble and the exploitation of gambling within controlled channels, of preventing the risk of fraud or crime in the context of such exploitation, and of using the resulting profits for public interest purposes, likewise falls within the ambit of [public interest] objectives" (¶ 37).

6. In Federacion de Distribuidores Cinematograficos v. Spain, Case C–17/92, [1993] ECR I–2239, a Spanish law obliged distributors of films produced in non–EC states to agree to distribute a film made in Spain in order to get a license to dub the foreign film into one of the recognized Spanish languages. The Court held that the distribution of foreign films, whether in cinemas or on television, constituted a transborder service and that the Spanish law was clearly discriminatory, since it indirectly subsidized films made in Spain as compared with films made elsewhere in the Community. Spain argued that the aid to Spanish production constituted a form of protection of Spanish culture. Would this represent an interest legitimately protected under the general good doctrine? If so, do you think the law really protects an important cultural interest?

3. RIGHT TO RECEIVE SERVICES IN OTHER STATES

Article 49 (ex Article 59) protects the "freedom to provide services" and Article 50 (ex 60) guarantees the right of a person providing a service to reside temporarily in the State where the service is provided. There is no express reference to any right of a person to travel to and stay in another State in order to receive services. Nonetheless, it was soon recognized that the recipients of services ought to have correlative rights.

Accordingly, both Council Directive 64/221 on public policy, public security and public health exceptions (art. 1), and Council Directive 73/148 on rights of movement and residence (art. 1(c)), discussed in section A above, expressly covered recipients as well as providers of services. The Court of Justice first authoritatively interpreted Articles 49 and 50 in that sense in *Luisi and Carbone,* a free movement of capital case discussed at page 1175, stating that a right to travel to other States to receive medical, educational and tourist services was implicit in Article 49.

COWAN v. TRÉSOR PUBLIC

Case 186/87, [1989] ECR 195.

[A French law provides that the state will pay compensation for serious injuries to French nationals who are victims of crimes. The law also grants such compensation to foreign nationals who hold a residence permit. Cowan, a UK national, was assaulted and seriously injured during a robbery at a metro station while on a visit to Paris. When Cowan applied for compensation, the French commission which makes such grants asked the Court of Justice whether the prohibition of discrimination on grounds of nationality contained in Article 12 (ex Article 7) required that compensation be paid to nationals of other Member States when injured during a visit to France.]

10   By prohibiting 'any discrimination on grounds of nationality' Article [12, ex 7] of the Treaty requires that persons in a situation governed by Community law be placed on a completely equal footing with nationals of the Member State. In so far as this principle is applicable it therefore precludes a Member State from making the grant of a right to such a person subject to the condition that he reside on the territory of that State—that condition is not imposed on the State's own nationals.

* * *

15   [I]n its judgment *Luisi and Carbone* [infra, page 1175], the Court held that the freedom to provide services includes the freedom for the recipients of services to go to another Member State in order to receive a service there, without being obstructed by restrictions, and that tourists, among others, must be regarded as recipients of services.

16   [T]he French Government submitted that as Community law now stands a recipient of services may not rely on the prohibition of discrimination to the extent that the national law at issue does not create any barrier to freedom of movement. A provision such as that at issue in the main proceedings, it says, imposes no restrictions in that respect. Furthermore, it concerns a right which is a manifestation of the principle of national solidarity. Such a right presupposes a closer bond with the State than that of a recipient of services, and for that reason it may be restricted to persons who are either nationals of that State or foreign nationals resident on the territory of that State.

17   That reasoning cannot be accepted. When Community law guarantees a natural person the freedom to go to another Member State the protection of that person from harm in the Member State in question, on the same basis as that of nationals and persons residing there, is a corollary of that freedom of movement. It follows that the prohibition of discrimination is applicable to recipients of services within the meaning of the Treaty as regards protection against the risk of assault and the right to obtain financial compensation provided for by national law when that risk materializes. The fact that the compensation at issue is financed by the Public Treasury cannot alter the rules regarding the protection of the rights guaranteed by the Treaty.

* * *

[20] [Accordingly,] the prohibition of discrimination laid down in particular in Article [12, ex 7] of the EEC Treaty must be interpreted as meaning that in respect of persons whose freedom to travel to a Member State, in particular as recipients of services, is guaranteed by Community law that State may not make the award of State compensation for harm caused in that State to the victim of an assault resulting in physical injury subject to the condition that he hold a residence permit * * *.

Notes and Questions

1. *Luisi and Carbone* and *Cowan* exemplify the Court of Justice's philosophy that Treaty articles are to be interpreted expansively in order to further the basic goals of the Treaty. Do you agree with this teleological analysis of Article 49 or do you feel it represents excessive judicial activism? In *Cowan*, the French law was clearly discriminatory, but is there a sufficient nexus to a Treaty-based right? In concluding that tourists have rights under Articles 12 and 49, the Court has gone rather far, but the judgment has generally been approved. See the case notes by Professors Anthony Arnull in 14 Eur.L.Rev. 166 (1989) and Stephen Weatherill in 26 Common Mkt.L.Rev. 563 (1989). The Court has in effect created a right to travel, parallel in some respects to that recognized by the US Supreme Court in an equally broad reading of the US Constitution. (See Chapter 15A.)

2. In *Cowan* the Court neither defined "tourist" nor specifically indicated what sort of services Cowan received that brought Article 49 into play. Advocate General Lenz's opinion provides a highly sophisticated analysis, suggesting that a tourist is anyone who crosses frontiers and receives economic services, such as those provided by hotels, restaurants, theaters or museums. He regarded even the metro, where Cowan was injured, as providing a service to tourists, because it constituted necessary local transportation. Do you agree with the Advocate General or would you limit the concept of tourist to persons who receive some significant minimum level of services specifically designed for travellers from other States?

3. In Commission v. Spain (Museum fees), Case C–45/93, [1994] I–911, the Commission contended that Spain's imposition of fees for admission to its museums upon adult visitors from other Member States, while granting free admission to its nationals and residents, constituted a violation of Articles 12 and 49. How should the Court decide the case? In Ciola v. Land Vorarlberg, Case C–244/97, [1999] ECR I–2517, an Austrian province bordering on Lake Constance limited non-resident boat owners to a quota of 60 out of 200 mooring (dock) sites. Is a quota on non-resident boat owners' ability to moor their boats at a marina an indirect violation of Articles 12 and 49? Would you accept the Austrian alleged justification, which was that otherwise local boat owners would lose sites to non-residents willing to pay higher rental charges?

4. In Kohll v Union des Caisses de Maladie, Case C-158/96, [1998] ECR I–1931, Kohll challenged a Luxembourg law which denied him the reimbursement of the cost of dental treatment provided by an orthodontist in another Member State because he had not obtained a prior authorization for such treatment. The issues and the Court's judgement paralleled those in *Decker*, supra page 502, where Luxembourg's rules requiring prior authorization for the purchase of eyeglasses outside Luxembourg were struck down. In *Kohll*, Luxembourg's alleged public health justification for the prior authorization obligation was not accepted. The Court observed that the quality of dental care throughout the Community must be

considered "equivalent" in view of the professional harmonization directives described in the next chapter (¶¶ 47–48).

SOCIETY FOR THE PROTECTION OF UNBORN CHILDREN IRELAND [SPUC] v. GROGAN

Case C–159/90, [1991] ECR I–4685.

[The SPUC, a private association whose purpose is to protect life from the moment of conception, sought to enjoin Grogan and other student association officers from disseminating, free of charge, information identifying clinics in the UK where abortions were carried out. The Irish Constitution's Article 40(3)(3) declares: "The State acknowledges the right to life of the unborn and, with due regard to the equal right to life of the mother, guarantees in its laws to respect, and, as far as practicable, by its laws defend and vindicate that right." The Irish Supreme Court held in 1988 in an unrelated case that Article 40(3)(3) prohibited providing information to pregnant women to assist them to travel abroad to obtain abortions.

In the present proceeding, the High Court referred to the Court of Justice questions on the application of Article 50 (ex Article 60). On appeal, the Supreme Court ordered that the students be immediately enjoined from disseminating the information, but allowed the High Court's reference to the Court of Justice to go forward. The Irish Supreme Court opinion is excerpted at page 333 supra.]

17   According to [Article 50], services are to be considered to be "services" within the meaning of the Treaty where they are normally provided for remuneration* * *. [T]he second paragraph of Article [50] expressly states that activities of the professions fall within the definition of services.

18   [T]ermination of pregnancy, as lawfully practised in several Member States, is a medical activity which is normally provided for remuneration and may be carried out as part of a professional activity. In any event, the Court has already held in *Luisi and Carbone* that medical activities fall within the scope of Article [50, ex 60] of the Treaty.

19   S.P.U.C., however, maintains that the provision of abortion cannot be regarded as being a service, on the grounds that it is grossly immoral and involves the destruction of the life of a human being, namely the unborn child.

20   Whatever the merits of those arguments on the moral plane, they cannot influence the answer to the national court's first question. It is not for the Court to substitute its assessment for that of the legislature in those Member States where the activities in question are practised legally.

* * *

22   [T]he national court seeks [further] to establish whether it is contrary to Community law for a Member State in which medical termination of pregnancy is forbidden to prohibit students associations from distributing information about the identity and location of clinics in another Member State where voluntary termination of pregnancy is lawfully carried out

and the means of communicating with those clinics, where the clinics in question have no involvement in the distribution of the said information.

* * *

[24] [I]t is apparent from the facts of the case that the link between the activity of the students associations * * * and medical terminations of pregnancies carried out in clinics in another Member State is too tenuous for the prohibition on the distribution of information to be capable of being regarded as a restriction within the meaning of Article [49, ex 59] of the Treaty.

* * *

[26] The information to which the national court's questions refer is not distributed on behalf of an economic operator established in another Member State. On the contrary, the information constitutes a manifestation of freedom of expression and of the freedom to impart and receive information which is independent of the economic activity carried on by clinics established in another Member State.

Notes and Questions

1. Because Article 50 describes services as "provided for remuneration," the Court's conclusion that the students' gratuitous dissemination of information does not raise a question under Article 49 is certainly plausible. However, as we saw in Chapter 9, the Court of Justice usually responds to questions framed by national courts so long as they are relevant. The High Court's questions were stated in general terms, not linked to the students' activities as such. The Court's position permitted it to avoid the important issue, omitted from the excerpt, whether the Irish prohibition on dissemination of information violated freedom of expression, one of the fundamental rights which the Court of Justice has bound itself to observe in the application of Community law. In fact, *Grogan* gave rise to a separate action before the European Court of Human Rights in Strasbourg, based on a claim that the Irish government violated the freedom of expression as guaranteed by Article 10(1) of the European Convention of Human Rights. In *Open Door Counseling* the Strasbourg Court held, 15–8, that the Irish information ban violated the Convention. Eur. Court H.R. 1992, Series A, No.246. See the discussion of further developments, supra page 334, and the thoughtful *Grogan* case notes by D. Curtin, 29 Common Market L.Rev. 585 (1992), and S. O'Leary, 17 Eur.L.Rev. 138 (1992).

2. *Grogan* did not involve a pregnant woman's right to travel to obtain an abortion in a Member State where abortions are legal. May one infer from ¶ ¶ 16–20 in *Grogan* that a pregnant woman has a right to travel to receive abortion services in a State where they are legal? Compare Doe v. Bolton, 410 U.S. 179, 93 S.Ct. 739, 35 L.Ed.2d 201 (1973), in which the Supreme Court, in a 7–2 opinion by Justice Blackmun, held a Georgia statute restricting abortion unconstitutional. Among other things, the statute forbid the providing of abortions to non-residents. The Supreme Court held this "violative of the right to travel" and considered that the Privileges and Immunities Clause protected "persons who enter Georgia seeking the medical services that are available there." Id. at 200, 93 Sup. Ct. at 751.

CRIMINAL PROCEEDINGS AGAINST BICKEL AND FRANZ

[See the excerpt at page 636 supra. The Italian trial court also asked the Court of Justice whether Bickel (the Austrian truck driver) and Franz (the

German tourist) could claim a right to have criminal proceedings conducted against them in German based upon the non-discrimination rights which Article 49 (ex 59) accords to the providers or receivers of services.]

[13] The first point to note is that in the context of a Community based on the principles of freedom of movement for persons and freedom of establishment, the protection of the linguistic rights and privileges of individuals is of particular importance [citing *Mutsch*, supra page 592].

[14] Secondly, by prohibiting 'any discrimination on grounds of nationality', Article [12, ex 7] of the Treaty requires that persons in a situation governed by Community law be placed entirely on an equal footing with nationals of the Member State [citing *Cowan*].

[15] Situations governed by Community law include those covered by the freedom to provide services * * *. The Court has consistently held that this right includes the freedom for the recipients of services to go to another Member State in order to receive a service there (*Cowan*, paragraph 15). Article [49] therefore covers all nationals of Member States who, independently of other freedoms guaranteed by the Treaty, visit another Member State where they intend or are likely to receive services. Such persons-and they include both Mr. Bickel and Mr. Franz—are free to visit and move around within the host State. Furthermore, pursuant to Article [18, ex 8a] of the Treaty, '[e]very citizen of the Union shall have the right to move and reside freely within the territory of the Member States, subject to the limitations and conditions laid down in this Treaty and by the measures adopted to give it effect'.

[16] In that regard, the exercise of the right to move and reside freely in another Member State is enhanced if the citizens of the Union are able to use a given language to communicate with the administrative and judicial authorities of a State on the same footing as its nationals. Consequently, persons such as Mr. Bickel and Mr Franz, in exercising that right in another Member State, are in principle entitled, pursuant to Article [12] of the Treaty, to treatment no less favourable than that accorded to nationals of the host State so far as concerns the use of languages which are spoken there.

[17] Although, generally speaking, criminal legislation and the rules of criminal procedure—such as the national rule in issue, which govern the language of the proceedings—are matters for which the Member States are responsible, the Court has consistently held that Community law sets certain limits to their power in that respect. Such legislative provisions may not discriminate against persons to whom Community law gives the right to equal treatment or restrict the fundamental freedoms guaranteed by Community law.

* * *

[19] Accordingly, the answer to the first part of the question referred for a preliminary ruling must be that the right conferred by national rules to have criminal proceedings conducted in a language other than the principle language of the State concerned falls within the scope of the Treaty and must comply with Article [12] thereof.

Notes and Questions

1.   The policy reason for the Court's conclusion in *Mutsch*, supra page 592, namely, the need to integrate a migrant worker into the host State community, is not applicable in *Bickel and Franz*. Nonetheless, the judgement is not surprising as a sequel to *Cowan*.

2.   In Criminal proceedings against Calfa, Case C–348/96, [1999] ECR I–11, Calfa, an Italian tourist in Crete, was convicted of the possession of prohibited drugs and sentenced to three months imprisonment. Under Greek law, the court was obliged to order her expulsion for life from Greece after conviction on a drug offense. Greek nationals can be forbidden to reside in a particular region, but only if convicted of drug dealing. The trial court asked the Court of Justice whether the expulsion for life was compatible with the Treaty. Recall the Court's views in *Rutili, Bouchereau* and *Adoui* in Chapter 15C. What do you think should be the reply to the Greek court?

4.   CROSS–BORDER SERVICES PROVIDED BY TECHNOLOGICAL MEANS

Some types of services are provided across borders without physical movement by either the provider or the recipient. The best example is radio and television broadcasting, but cross-border services can also be provided by modern telecommunications or computer networks (e.g., transmission of messages or information by telex, fax, or computer software). Does Article 49 cover these technological transmissions?

Already in 1974 the Court held in Sacchi, Case 155/73, [1974] ECR 490, that the broadcasting of television across frontiers fell within the scope of free movement of services. A series of cases in the 1980's dealt with questions raised when national rules restricted trans-border television broadcasting. Thus, in Procureur du Roi v. Debauve, Case 52/79, [1980] ECR 833, the Court held that Belgium, which then prohibited advertising in television broadcasts, could forbid a cable television retransmission of programs from other States that contained advertising. The Court stated that the Belgian law was justified by "grounds of general interest" (¶ 15), without defining the interest. Later, in Bond van Adverteerders v. Netherlands, Case 352/85, [1988] ECR 2085, a Dutch advertising association successfully challenged as discriminatory a Dutch law regulating cable television because it allowed the Dutch national broadcasting system to transmit programs from other States containing commercial advertising, but prohibited private cable television companies from broadcasting commercial advertising contained in foreign programs.

The Court's conclusion that television broadcasting across frontiers constituted a cross-border service prompted the Commission to reflect on the implications of television broadcasting for the common market. In May 1984, the Commission issued the influential Green Paper, "Television Without Frontiers," COM(84) 300. This study document indicated the desirability of achieving a Community-wide television broadcasting area in which harmonized national rules would facilitate cross-border transmissions. In addition to its economic value, the Commission stressed the cultural importance of achieving such an area.

The Green Paper led to Council Directive 89/552 on the coordination of rules concerning television broadcasting activities, O.J. L 298/23 (Oct. 17,

1989), in the Selected Documents. Often called the Television Without Frontiers Directive, this measure sought to create a common television program production and distribution market. The directive requires Member States to ensure freedom of reception and retransmission of television broadcasts from other Member States (art. 2(2)).

The heart of the directive is its regulation of television advertising and sponsorship. Advertising must be readily recognizable; subliminal or surreptitious advertising is forbidden (art. 10). The frequency of advertising breaks and the total advertising share of daily broadcast time is restricted (arts. 11 and 18). Sponsors of programs must be clearly identified and may not influence the "editorial independence" of the broadcaster (art. 17).

Advertising for all tobacco products and for prescription medication is prohibited (arts. 13–14) and advertising for alcoholic beverages is restricted (art. 15). Advertising may not involve discrimination on grounds of race, sex or nationality, be "offensive to religious or political beliefs," or "encourage behavior prejudicial to the protection of the environment" (art. 12). Moreover, the directive permits Member States to have more detailed or stricter rules regulating advertising.

Apart from the regulation of advertising, the directive requires that programs not "seriously impair the physical, mental or moral development of minors, in particular [by display of] pornography or gratuitous violence" (art. 22). Programs which might have this effect are to be broadcast at times when minors would normally not be watching television.

The Green Paper placed great emphasis on the cultural role of television. This led to the directive's most controversial feature, the requirement that a "majority proportion" of broadcast time, apart from news and sports, be devoted "where practicable" to "European works" (art. 4(1)). "European works" were defined to include not only those produced in Member States, but, under certain conditions, those produced in other European states. The "European works" requirement was motivated by concern over the dominance of non-European (usually US) feature films, comedies and serials. Estimates vary, but by 1989 in some States non-European production probably amounted to 70% of total broadcasts. France and some other States wanted 60% of broadcast time to have European content but the Council declined to go that far.

US producers of motion picture films and films made for television vehemently criticized the European content provision in the draft directive and the US Government strongly urged its elimination. The US film industry feared a significant decline in its European revenues, estimated at around one billion dollars in 1989, representing a 500% increase since 1980. A US House of Representatives resolution denounced the directive as "trade restrictive." Despite vigorous efforts, the US was unable to have the 1993 GATT agreement, concluded at the end of the Uruguay Round, forbid national quotas or preferences for feature film or television film distribution. Thus, the US continues to protest the "majority proportion" clause in the television broadcasting directive as a serious instance of trade protection, but without any ability to secure recourse through a WTO panel. See Chapter 29.

In July 1995, the Council adopted the Media II program to provide 265 million ECU in aid for the training of skilled audio-visual professionals and for production and distribution in the industry during 1996–2000. In 2000, its final year, Media II financed 907 audio-visual projects, principally to support pre-production development of films, the distribution of films outside national territory, and film festivals. In December 2000, the Parliament and Council agreed upon a successor, Media Plus, with 400 million Euros to fund programs in 2001–05.

Notes and Questions

1. The Television Without Frontiers Directive not only facilitates cross-border broadcasting, but also sets the basic rules for all broadcasting. It is thus a far-reaching example of harmonization. On the whole, what is your reaction? Are its rules well-founded and fair? Would you like to see some of these rules (apart from European content) adopted in the US? Might First Amendment concerns make it difficult to adopt some rules?

2. Commissioner Bangemann, responsible for the Commission unit that drafted the directive, was quoted in the New York Times (Oct. 4, 1989, at A1, col. 5) as stating that the European works provision was a "political commitment" and "not a legal obligation." Assuming he was correctly quoted, do you agree with that assessment? If the Commission opts not to enforce the clause against a Member State, could Parliament take action against the Commission? If a private party had standing, could it sue a Member State for noncompliance or the Commission for failure to act?

3. Do you think that the Community's concern over protection of European culture is genuine or merely veils economic protectionism? Assuming the concern is genuine, do you think it justifies this type of provision?

4. In May 1995, the Commission proposed to amend the Television without Frontiers Directive by the deletion of the qualification, "where practicable," before the majority content requirement. Although President Chirac of France pressed vigorously for this approach at the June European Council meeting in Cannes, the UK and several other States opposed the deletion. In the fall, the Parliament endorsed the deletion by a majority vote, but not by the absolute majority required to keep the amendment under discussion in the codecision process. The words, "where practicable," accordingly remain as a qualification. However, the Commission in a July 2000 report monitoring the effect of the directive indicated that in 1997–98 almost all States were respecting the majority European works content clause and that the major television channels' broadcasts of European works averaged between 53% and 82% of the total broadcast time.

5. Directive 97/36, O.J.L. 202/60 (July 30, 1997), made a series of clarificatory and substantive amendments to the Television Without Frontiers Directive. The principal modifications make more precise the jurisdiction provisions and enable the directive to cover the field of telemarketing, rapidly growing in Europe as it has in the US. The most heated debate came over a new article 3a, proposed by Parliament, which permits States to designate certain sporting events, and other events of "major importance for society" (e.g., the Olympic games, the Derby or the Tour de France), for which exclusive broadcast rights cannot be granted and access by the general viewing public must be ensured.

The television broadcasting directive has now been interpreted in several leading cases, some of which influenced the clarificatory amendments mentioned above.

KONSUMENTOMBUDSMANNEN v. DE AGOSTINI (SVENKSA) FORLAG

Cases C–34 to 36/95, [1997] ECR I–3843.

[In the first Article 234 reference from Sweden, questions were raised concerning the propriety of the Consumer Ombudsman's efforts to enjoin advertisements initially broadcast by TV3, a UK broadcaster, and retransmitted by satellite for broadcast in Sweden. In two cases, the Ombudsman sought to prevent TV–Shop Europe from making allegedly unsubstantiated health and therapeutic claims and deceptive comparative prices for a skin-care product, and from claiming that a detergent was "environmentally friendly" and "biodegradable" without having proof of these claims.

In a third case, an Italian magazine publisher advertised "Everything about Dinosaurs," a children's magazine series that featured the inclusion of dinosaur model parts that could be assembled by purchase of the entire series. The Ombudsman contended that this violated the Swedish Broadcasting law prohibiting advertising directed at children less than 12 years old. Besides questions on the interpretation of Directive 89/552, the referring court inquired whether the Swedish law might violate Article 49.

The Court began by indicating that Directive 89/552 accorded the home State the responsibility for the supervision of broadcasters on its territory to ensure compliance with the Directive's substantive rules, including those on advertising. However, the Court noted that the Directive's 17th recital stated that its provisions were "without prejudice to existing or future Community acts of harmonization, in particular to satisfy overriding considerations of consumer protection, fair trading and competition." (¶ 28.) The Court continued:]

32 Consequently, it follows that, as regards the activity of broadcasting and distribution of television programmes, the Directive, whilst coordinating provisions laid down by law, regulation or administrative action on television advertising and sponsorship, does so only partially.

* * *

34 Thus the Directive does not in principle preclude application of national rules with the general aim of consumer protection provided that they do not involve secondary control of television broadcasts in addition to the control which the broadcasting Member State must carry out.

35 Consequently, where a Member State's legislation * * *, for the purpose of protecting consumers, provides for a system of prohibitions and restraining orders to be imposed on advertisers, enforceable by financial penalties, application of such legislation to television broadcasts from other Member States cannot be considered to constitute an obstacle prohibited by the Directive.

36 According to De Agostini, TV–Shop and the Commission, the principle that broadcasts are to be controlled by the State having jurisdiction over the broadcaster would be seriously undermined in both its purpose and effect if the Directive were held to be inapplicable to advertisers. They argue

that a restriction relating to advertising has an impact on television broadcasts, even if the restriction concerns only advertising.

37   In response to that objection, it is sufficient to observe that Council Directive 84/450/EEC relating to the approximation of the laws, regulations and administrative provisions of the Member States concerning misleading advertising, which provides in particular in Article 4(1) that Member States are to ensure that adequate and effective means exist for the control of misleading advertising in the interests of consumers as well as competitors and the general public, could be robbed of its substance in the field of television advertising if the receiving Member State were deprived of all possibility of adopting measures against an advertiser and that this would be in contradiction with the express intention of the Community legislature.

38   It follows from the foregoing that the Directive does not preclude a Member State from taking, pursuant to general legislation on protection of consumers against misleading advertising, measures against an advertiser in relation to television advertising broadcast from another Member State, provided that those measures do not prevent the retransmission, as such, in its territory of television broadcasts coming from that other Member State.

* * *

As regards Article [49, ex 59] of the Treaty

50   Provisions such as those in question in the main proceedings, where they restrict the possibility for television broadcasters established in the broadcasting State to broadcast, for advertisers established in the receiving State, television advertising specifically directed at the public in the receiving State, involve a restriction on freedom to provide services.

* * *

53   [A]ccording to settled case-law, fair trading and the protection of consumers in general are overriding requirements of public interest which may justify restrictions on freedom to provide services [citing *Alpine Investments*, infra page 1187].

54   The answer to be given must therefore be that, on a proper construction of Article [49, ex 59] of the Treaty, a Member State is not precluded from taking, on the basis of provisions of its domestic legislation, measures against an advertiser in relation to television advertising. However, it is for the national court to determine whether those provisions are necessary for meeting overriding requirements of general public importance or one of the aims mentioned in Article 56 of the EC Treaty, whether they are proportionate for that purpose and whether those aims or overriding requirements could be met by measures less restrictive of intra-Community trade.

The second question

55   By its second question the [Swedish court] asks the Court for an interpretation of Community law with regard to a provision of a domestic broadcasting law which provides that advertisements broadcast during commer-

cial breaks on television must not be designed to attract the attention of children under 12 years of age.

[56] Application of such a domestic provision to advertising broadcast by a television broadcaster established in the same State cannot be contrary to the Directive since Article 3(1) of that provision does not contain any restriction as regards the interests which the Member States may take into consideration when laying down more strict rules for television broadcasters established in their territory. However, the situation is not the same where television broadcasters established in another Member State are concerned.

[57] In Articles 16 and 22, the Directive contains a set of provisions specifically devoted to the protection of minors in relation to television programmes in general and television advertising in particular.

[58] The broadcasting State must ensure that those provisions are complied with.

[59] This certainly does not have the effect of prohibiting application of legislation of the receiving State designed to protect consumers or minors in general, provided that its application does not prevent retransmission, as such, in its territory of broadcasts from another Member State.

[60] However, the receiving Member State may no longer, under any circumstances, apply provisions specifically designed to control the content of television advertising with regard to minors.

[61] If provisions of the receiving State regulating the content of television broadcasts for reasons relating to the protection of minors against advertising were applied to broadcasts from other Member States, this would add a secondary control to the control which the broadcasting Member State must exercise under the Directive.

[62] It follows that the Directive is to be interpreted as precluding the application to television broadcasts from other Member States of a provision of a domestic broadcasting law which provides that advertisements broadcast in commercial breaks on television must not be designed to attract the attention of children under 12 years of age.

Notes and Questions

1. In the Swedish *Consumer Ombudsman* case, note that in ¶ 36 the Commission supported the defendants' argument that only the State of initial broadcasting should monitor claims of false and misleading advertising. Obviously, there is a clash between the goal of promoting an internal market in TV broadcasting and that of protecting local consumer interests. Do you agree with the Court's resolution of the issue in favor of permitting the supervision of misleading advertising claims by the State receiving the broadcast? The Court's view imposes a substantial cost on the UK advertiser to check for compliance with the consumer protection rules in every State into which the program is broadcast. On the other hand, giving the monitoring role only to the State of initial broadcast may make it both costly and procedurally difficult for consumers in States receiving the broadcast to get adequate recourse against misleading advertising. If TV3 were to broadcast from the UK a program in Swedish for a Swedish audience,

could the UK authorities easily apply UK misleading advertising rules to review the advertising?

2. Since the Court permitted Sweden to apply its misleading advertising rules, why did it prevent Sweden from enforcing its rule against advertising directed at children under 12? The judgement applies the preemption rules described in Chapter 14C. Do you agree? On policy grounds, would you support the amendment of the television broadcasting directive to incorporate the Swedish rule? Would such a rule be desirable, or legally feasible in the US?

3. *Leclerc–Siplec*, a 1995 judgement previously discussed at page 531 supra for its application of the *Keck* doctrine, also dealt with the issue whether the French law which forbid television advertising of distribution was preempted by the Television Without Frontiers Directive, which prohibits advertising for tobacco and prescription medicines and sets limits for the advertising of alcoholic beverages, but does not otherwise limit advertising of products. Advocate General Jacobs remarked that amendments during the legislative process had made the directive's intent in this regard ambiguous. The Court ultimately concluded that the directive's article 3(1) was meant to permit States to set stricter rules in all the areas covered by the directive, and thus implicitly permitted France to forbid television advertising of distribution.

4. In Commission v. Belgium, (Cable TV transmission), Case C–11/95, [1996] ECR I–4115, the Court held that the French and Flemish regional rules requiring a system of prior review for cable broadcasts from other Community States violated the directive's article 2, which gives jurisdiction to the State of initial broadcast to ensure compliance with the directive. Belgium's claim that its review was necessary to protect cultural interests and "pluralism in the audiovisual field" was rejected.

The Court followed this precedent in Criminal Proceedings against Denuit, Case C–14/96, [1997] ECR I–2785, informing the trial court that it should not penalize a Belgian rebroadcaster of the Turner Cartoon Network prosecuted because of an alleged failure to respect the directive's majority European content rules. As the cartoon broadcasts originated in the UK, the Court held that it was the UK's responsibility to monitor compliance with the European content rules, noting that Belgium could bring an Article 227 proceeding against the UK if it considered that the UK was not carrying out its responsibilities.

C. CASE LAW ON THE RIGHT OF ESTABLISHMENT FOR INDIVIDUALS AND COMMERCIAL FIRMS

1. APPLICATION OF NON–DISCRIMINATION RULES

Shortly before *van Binsbergen* was decided, the Court of Justice held that Article 43 (ex Article 52) had direct effect insofar as it prohibited discrimination on the basis of nationality. The judgment, *Reyners v. Belgium,* involved professional establishment and is therefore excerpted in the next chapter. Subsequent judgments have invalidated other forms of discriminatory treatment, even in the absence of directives harmonizing rules in particular commercial or financial sectors.

COMMISSION v. ITALY

(Housing loans)
Case 63/86, [1988] ECR 29.

[Italy permitted only nationals to obtain preferential rate state loans to purchase residential housing and to buy inexpensive housing built or renovated with state funds. When sued in an Article 226 proceeding, Italy contended that "there is no direct link between the pursuit of occupations and the right of access to social housing or a reduced-rate mortgage loan [for] housing." Italy maintained that a requirement of national treatment for the self-employed in respect of housing could only be based on legislation adopted to implement Article 43 (ex 52), much as Regulation 1612/68 implemented the right of free movement of workers.]

13   [Articles 43 and 49] are thus intended to secure the benefit of national treatment for a national of a Member State who wishes to pursue an activity as a self-employed person in another Member State and they prohibit all discrimination on grounds of nationality resulting from national or regional legislation and preventing the taking up or pursuit of such an activity.

14   As is apparent from the general programmes which were adopted by the Council on 18 December 1961 * * * and which * * * provide useful guidance with a view to the implementation of the provisions of the Treaty relating to the right of establishment and the freedom to provide services, the aforesaid prohibition is concerned not solely with the specific rules on the pursuit of occupational activities but also with the rules relating to the various general facilities which are of assistance in the pursuit of those activities. Among the examples mentioned in the two programs are the right to purchase, exploit and transfer real and personal property and the right to obtain loans and in particular to have access to the various forms of credit.

15   For a natural person the pursuit of an occupation does not presuppose solely the possibility of access to premises from which the occupation can be pursued, if necessary by borrowing the amount needed to purchase them, but also the possibility of obtaining housing. It follows that restrictions contained in the housing legislation applicable to the place where the occupation is pursued are liable to constitute an obstacle to that pursuit.

16   If complete equality of competition is to be assured, the national of a Member State who wishes to pursue an activity as a self-employed person in another Member State must therefore be able to obtain housing in conditions equivalent to those enjoyed by those of his competitors who are nationals of the latter State. Accordingly, any restriction placed not only on the right of access to housing but also on the various facilities granted to those nationals in order to alleviate the financial burden must be regarded as an obstacle to the pursuit of the occupation itself.

17   That being so, housing legislation, even where it concerns social housing, must be regarded as part of the legislation that is subject to the principle of national treatment * * *.

[18] It is true, as the Italian Government has contended, that * * * as a rule [the need to find permanent housing] is not felt in the case of the provision of services. * * *

[19] However, it cannot be held to be *a priori* out of the question that a person, whilst retaining his principal place of establishment in one Member State, may be led to pursue his occupational activities in another Member State for such an extended period that he needs to have permanent housing there and that he may satisfy the conditions of a non-discriminatory nature for access to social housing. It follows * * * that providers of services cannot be excluded from the benefit of the fundamental principle of national treatment.

Notes and Questions

1. If Italy had discriminated against other Community nationals in granting state loans to buy or rent business premises, the violation of Article 43 (ex 52) would be evident. See Steinhauser v. City of Biarritz, Case 197/84, [1985] ECR 1819 (requiring national treatment for a German artist seeking access to the rental of city-owned shops to sell craft goods). The link between Article 43 and residential housing is not so apparent. Do you agree with Italy that protection against discrimination in residential housing required Community legislation and could not be achieved through a Court gloss on Article 43? Or do you agree with the Court that such a right flows naturally from Article 43's goal of achieving "complete equality of competition"?

Note also the Court's observation that persons might perform cross-border services for such an extended period as to acquire a right to national treatment in residential housing. Do you agree, or do you think that such reasoning blurs the line between providing services and establishment?

2. In Meeusen v. Hoofdirectie van de Informatie Beheer Groep, Case C–337/97, [1999] ECR I–3289, a Belgian national managed his own firm in the Netherlands while residing in Belgium. His daughter, also a Belgian national and resident, requested Dutch financial aid for studies at a Technical Institute for Chemistry. As we saw in *Di Leo*, page 599, the dependent child of a migrant worker is entitled to non-discriminatory access to financial aid for higher education studies. Should the child of a self-employed business person exercising the right of establishment likewise receive such financial aid?

3. In Commission v. Greece (Music and dancing schools), Case 147/86, [1988] ECR 1637, a Greek law permitted only Greek nationals to set up and run private music and dancing schools. When the Commission brought an Article 226 (ex 169) proceeding to challenge this law as violating Article 43, Greece contended that operating schools constituted the exercise of "official authority" under Article 45, because of the state's deep concern with educational policy. What should the Court decide?

4. Sodemare is a Luxembourg holding company whose Italian subsidiary owns residential homes for elderly persons in the region of Lombardy. A Lombardy regional social welfare law provides subsidies derived from the Italian National Health Fund for health-care services for elderly infirm people in authorized residence facilities for the elderly. Only non-profit enterprises can receive long-term contracts from the Region to carry out the services and hence receive the subsidies. Although Sodemare was authorized by the Province of Brescia to operate an old people's home, its request for a health-care contract and subsidy

was denied because it is a profit-making company. When Sodemare sued to obtain a contract, the administrative court raised questions on Sodemare's rights under Article 43. The Court held that the Lombard Region was justified in limiting its health service contracts for the elderly and its subsidies to non-profit entities. Would you agree? See Sodemare SA v. Regione Lombardia, Case C–70/95, [1997] ECR I–3395.

2. ESTABLISHMENT RIGHTS OF CORPORATIONS AND SHARE-HOLDERS

REGINA v. SECRETARY OF STATE FOR TRANSPORT ex parte FACTORTAME

(Factortame II)

Case C–221/89, [1991] ECR 3905.

[Among its efforts to prevent Spanish fishing interests from taking a part of the UK catch quota under the Common Fisheries Policy, the UK in 1988 amended its regulations for the registration of fishing vessels. The amendments required that: 1) a British fishing vessel be British-owned and be managed and controlled from within the UK; 2) if a British fishing vessel is owned by a company, the company must be a) incorporated and have its principal place of business in the UK; b) have 75% of its shares "legally and beneficially" owned by UK citizens; and c) have 75% of its directors be UK citizens. The plaintiffs, Spanish nationals who together owned 95 UK-registered fishing vessels, sued to enjoin the operation of these amendments as a violation of Articles 12, 43 and 48. The trial court asked the Court of Justice to rule on the compatibility of the UK legislation with Community law. The power of the trial court to restrain enforcement of the 1988 UK law was the subject of the leading supremacy judgment, *Factortame I,* discussed at page 274.]

[20] [T]he concept of establishment within the meaning of art. [43, ex 52] of the Treaty involves the actual pursuit of an economic activity through a fixed establishment in another member state for an indefinite period.

[21] Consequently, the registration of a vessel does not necessarily involve establishment within the meaning of the Treaty, in particular where the vessel is not used to pursue an economic activity or where the application for registration is made by or on behalf of a person who is not established, and has no intention of becoming established, in the state concerned.

[22] However, where the vessel constitutes an instrument for pursuing an economic activity which involves a fixed establishment in the member state concerned, the registration of that vessel cannot be dissociated from the exercise of the freedom of establishment.

[23] It follows that the conditions laid down for the registration of vessels must not form an obstacle to freedom of establishment within the meaning of art. [43, ex 52] of the Treaty.

* * *

[26] The UK, Belgium, Denmark and Greece consider that the Treaty does not preclude a nationality requirement of the type at issue * * *. [They contend that] what is involved is not discriminatory treatment on grounds

of nationality but a condition for the grant of nationality, and the member states are free to determine to whom they will grant or refuse their nationality, in the case of natural persons and ships alike.

27   In that connection, it must be observed that the concept of the "nationality" of ships, which are not persons, is different from that of the "nationality" of natural persons.

28   The prohibition of discrimination on grounds of nationality * * * as regards the right of establishment * * * is concerned with differences of treatment as between natural persons who are nationals of member states and as between companies who are treated in the same way as such parsons by virtue of art. [48, ex 58].

29   Consequently, in exercising its powers for the purposes of defining the conditions for the grant of its "nationality" to a ship, each member state must comply with the prohibition of discrimination against nationals of member states on grounds of their nationality.

30   It follows from the foregoing that a condition of the type at issue in the main proceedings, which stipulates that where a vessel is owned or chartered by natural persons they must be of a particular nationality and where it is owned or chartered by a company the shareholders and directors must be of that nationality, is contrary to art. [43] of the Treaty.

31   Such a condition is also contrary to art. [294, ex 221] of the Treaty, under which member states must accord nationals of the other member states the same treatment as their own nationals as regards participation in the capital of companies or firms within the meaning of art. [43].

32   As for the requirement for the owners, charterers, managers and operators of the vessel and, in the case of a company, the shareholders and directors to be resident and domiciled in the member state in which the vessel is to be registered, it must be held that such a requirement, which is not justified by the rights and obligations created by the grant of a national flag to a vessel, results in discrimination on grounds of nationality. The great majority of nationals of the member state in question are resident and domiciled in that state and therefore meet that requirement automatically, whereas nationals of other member states would, in most cases, have to move their residence and domicile to that state in order to comply with the requirements of its legislation. It follows that such a requirement is contrary to art. [43].

* * *

34   [However,] a requirement for the registration of a vessel to the effect that it must be managed and its operations directed and controlled from within the member state in which it is to be registered essentially coincides with the actual concept of establishment within the meaning of art. [43] et seq. of the Treaty, which implies a fixed establishment. It follows that those articles, which enshrine the very concept of freedom of establishment, cannot be interpreted as precluding such a requirement.

35   Such a requirement, however, would not be compatible with those provisions if it had to be interpreted as precluding registration in the event that a secondary establishment or the centre for directing the operations of the

vessel in the member state in which the vessel was to be registered acted on instructions from a decision-taking centre located in the member state of the principal establishment.

[36] Consequently, the reply to the national court must be that it is not contrary to Community law for a member state to stipulate as a condition for the registration of a fishing vessel in its national register that the vessel in question must be managed and its operations directed and controlled from within that member state.

Notes and Questions

1.   *Factortame II* is part of a series of cases which have enriched Community law in several respects. The judgment in *Factortame II* confirmed the accuracy of the trial court's surmise in *Factortame I,* excerpted at page 274, that the 1988 Merchant Shipping Act amendments violated Community law and should accordingly be enjoined. In Commission v. France (Registration of vessels), Case C–334/94, [1996] I–1307, the Court not only followed *Factortame II* in invalidating French ship registry rules requiring the owners of commercial vessels to be French nationals, or companies owned by French nationals, it also held that nationals of other Member States exercising a right of free movement to become a worker or to be self-employed in France had as a corollary the right to enter their leisure vessels (e.g., yachts or sailboats) on the French registry.

2.   The basic principle that Member States may not discriminate against companies owned or managed by Community nationals follows naturally from the terms of Articles 43 and 294. The difficult issue was whether this principle should apply to companies owning vessels, since States traditionally have discretion to determine the standards for granting vessels their "nationality." Do you agree with the Court's resolution of this issue? Remember that under Article 46 States may limit establishment rights on grounds of public policy or public security. Presumably a State can invoke these considerations to prevent a company owned or managed by non-nationals from engaging in defense contracting. Why couldn't the UK rely on public policy to uphold its law?

3.   The Court's language in ¶¶ 34–36 is worth noting. The Court allowed the UK to require that a vessel be "managed and its operations directed and controlled from within that member state." For all sorts of business reasons, corporations create "paper subsidiaries," which have few or no employees and limited assets, in other States. Does the Court's language create a risk that such entities might be denied a right of establishment and be subject to discrimination? In your view, does the approach of the Court represent sound policy?

4.   In Commission v. Belgium (Registration of aircraft), Case C–203/98 [1999] ECR I–4899, a Belgian law permitted "foreigners" to register airplanes in Belgium and to operate such airplanes from Belgian airfields only if they had been resident or established in Belgium for one year. The Commission challenged the law as a violation of Article 43. Should Article 43 apply to aircraft registration just as it does to the registration of ships? Belgium declared that it had not enforced the law since 1996. Does that make any difference in an Article 226 proceeding? Recall the discussion in Chapter 11.

LEWIS v. BT INVESTMENT MANAGERS

447 U.S. 27, 100 S.Ct. 2009, 64 L.Ed.2d 702 (1980).

[When Bankers Trust, a New York corporation, established a subsidiary in Florida to provide portfolio investment services and advice on industry conditions, the Florida legislature promptly adopted a statute prohibiting an out-of-state bank holding company from providing investment advisory services through a subsidiary or branch. There was evidence that the law was prompted by the local banking community. When Bankers Trust's challenge reached the Supreme Court, Justice Blackman's opinion for a unanimous Court held that the statute violated the Dormant Commerce Clause.]

Over the years, the Court has used a variety of formulations for the Commerce Clause limitation upon the States, but it consistently has distinguished between outright protectionism and more indirect burdens on the free flow of trade. The Court has observed that "where simple economic protectionism is effected by state legislation, a virtually per se rule of invalidity has been erected" [citing *Philadelphia* v. *New Jersey*, infra page 1264].

> We readily accept the submission that, both as a matter of history and as a matter of present commercial reality, banking and related financial activities are of profound local concern. As appellees freely concede, sound financial institutions and honest financial practices are essential to the health of any State's economy and to the well-being of its people. * * *

> Nonetheless, it does not follow that these same activities lack important interstate attributes. An impressive array of federal statutes regulating not only the provision of banking services but also the formation of banking organizations, the rendering of investment advice, and the conduct of national investment markets, is substantial evidence to the contrary. * * * This Court has observed that the same interstate attributes that establish Congress' power to regulate commerce also support constitutional limitations on the powers of the States.

> * * *

> [The Florida statute] prevents competition in local markets by out-of-state firms with the kinds of resources and business interests that make them likely to attempt *de novo* entry. Appellant virtually concedes this effect * * *, and the circumstances of enactment suggest that it was the legislature's principal objective.

> * * *

> We are convinced that the disparate treatment of out-of-state bank holding companies cannot be justified as an incidental burden necessitated by legitimate local concerns.

> * * *

> Appellant has demonstrated no basis for an inference that all out-of-state bank holding companies are likely to possess the evils of monopoly power, that they are more likely to do so than their homegrown counter-

parts, or that they are any more inclined to engage in sharp practices than bank holding companies that are locally based. Nor is there any reason to conclude that outright prohibition of entry, rather than some intermediate form of regulation, is the only effective method of protecting against the presumed evils * * *.

* * *

In almost any Commerce Clause case it would be possible for a State to argue that it has an interest in bolstering local ownership, or wealth, or control of business enterprise. Yet these arguments are at odds with the general principle that the Commerce Clause prohibits a State from using its regulatory power to protect its own citizens from outside competition.

Notes and Questions

1. Only occasionally do dormant Commerce Clause considerations arise in the context of establishment of a subsidiary or branch. *Bankers Trust* demonstrates that clear discrimination against the subsidiaries of out-of-state corporate parents is virtually a per se violation of the dormant Commerce Clause. The Court distinguished Exxon Corp. v. Maryland, 437 U.S. 117, 98 S.Ct. 2207, 57 L.Ed.2d 91 (1978), where the Court accepted Maryland's prohibition of the ownership of retail petroleum dealers within Maryland by out-of-state petroleum producers, holding that Maryland had shown a need to regulate the gasoline retail market in view of serious shortages during the 1973 energy crisis. In view of *Factortame II*, how would the Court of Justice deal with a case parallel to *Bankers Trust?*

CENTROS v. ERHVERVS–OG SELSKABSSTYRELSEN

Case C–212/97, [1999] ECR II–1459.

[Denmark requires 200,000 Danish Kroner (ca. $24,000) to be paid in as capital when a private limited company is formed, while the UK does not require any paid-in capital for such a company. (The Community company law directives do not require any initial paid-in capital for private limited companies-see section D.) Bryde and her husband created Centros, a UK company without paid-in capital, with its registered office at a friend's home, with no intention of doing business in the UK. Bryde, Centros' sole director, applied to the Danish Companies Board to register a Centros branch in Denmark, in order to conduct a wine trading business. The Board rejected the application, deeming the creation of a branch to be an evasion of Danish company capital requirements. On appeal, the Danish court asked the Court of Justice whether the Brydes' right of establishment was violated by the rejection.]

15   [T]he Board does not in any way deny that a joint stock or private limited company with its registered office in another Member State may carry on business in Denmark through a branch.* * * In particular, it has added that, if Centros had conducted any business in England and Wales, the Board would have agreed to' register its branch in Denmark.

17   In this respect, it should be noted that a situation in which a company formed in accordance with the law of a Member State in which it has its registered office desires to set up a branch in another Member State falls within the scope of Community law. In that regard, it is immaterial that

the company was formed in the first Member State only for the purpose of establishing itself in the second, where its main, or indeed entire, business is to be conducted.

19   [The freedom of establishment] conferred by Article [43] of the Treaty on Community nationals, includes the right for them to take up and pursue activities as self-employed persons and to set up and manage undertakings under the same conditions as are laid down by the law of the Member State of establishment for its own nationals. Furthermore, under Article [48] of the Treaty companies or firms formed in accordance with the law of a Member State and having their registered office, central administration or principal place of business within the Community are to be treated in the same way as natural persons who are nationals of Member States.

20   The immediate consequence of this is that those companies are entitled to carry on their business in another Member State through an agency, branch or subsidiary. The location of their registered office, central administration or principal place of business serves as the connecting factor with the legal system of a particular State in the same way as does nationality in the case of natural person.

* * *

23   According to the Danish authorities, however, Mr. and Mrs. Bryde cannot rely on those provisions, since the sole purpose of the company formation which they have in mind is to circumvent the application of the national law governing formation of private limited companies and therefore constitutes abuse of the freedom of establishment.* * *

24   It is true that according to the case-law of the Court a Member State is entitled to take measures designed to prevent certain of its nationals from attempting, under cover of the rights created by the Treaty, improperly to circumvent their national legislation or to prevent individuals from improperly or fraudulently taking advantage of provisions of Community law (see, in particular, regarding freedom to supply services [*Van Binsbergen* and *Veronica*, supra pages 662 and 664].

25   However, although, in such circumstances, the national courts may, case by case, take account—on the basis of objective evidence—of abuse or fraudulent conduct on the part of the persons concerned in order, where appropriate, to deny them the benefit of the provisions of Community law on which they seek to rely, they must nevertheless assess such conduct in the light of the objectives pursued by those provisions.

* * *

27   [T]he fact that a national of a Member State who wishes to set up a company chooses to form it in the Member State whose rules of company law seem to him the least restrictive and to set up branches in other Member States cannot, in itself, constitute an abuse of the right of establishment. The right to form a company in accordance with the law of a Member State and to set up branches in other Member States is inherent in the exercise, in a single market, of the freedom of establishment guaranteed by the Treaty.

* * *

29 In addition, * * * the fact that a company does not conduct any business in the Member State in which it has its registered office and pursues its activities only in the Member State where its branch is established is not sufficient to prove the existence of abuse or fraudulent conduct which would entitle the latter Member State to deny that company the benefit of the provisions of Community law relating to the right of establishment.

* * *

32 [T]he Board argues that the requirement that private limited companies provide for and pay up a minimum share capital [protects] all creditors, whether public or private, by anticipating the risk of fraudulent bankruptcy due to the insolvency of companies whose initial capitalisation was inadequate.

34 * * * [A]ccording to the court's case-law, national measures liable to hinder or make less attractive the exercise of fundamental freedoms guaranteed by the Treaty must fulfil four conditions: they must be applied in a non-discriminatory manner; they must be justified by imperative requirements in the general interest; they must be suitable for securing the attainment of the objective which they pursue; and they must not go beyond what is necessary in order to attain it [citing *Gebhard, infra* page 735].

35 Those conditions are not fulfilled in the case in the main proceedings. First, the practice in question is not such as to attain the objective of protecting creditors which it purports to pursue since, if the company concerned had conducted business in the United Kingdom, its branch would have been registered in Denmark, even though Danish creditors might have been equally exposed to risk.

37 Second, * * * it is possible to adopt measures which are less restrictive, or which interfere less with fundamental freedoms, by, for example, making it possible in law for public creditors to obtain the necessary guarantees.

38 Lastly, the fact that a Member State may not refuse to register a branch of a company formed in accordance with the law of another Member State in which it has its registered office does not preclude that first State from adopting any appropriate measure for preventing or penalizing fraud, either in relation to the company itself, if need be in cooperation with the Member State in which it was formed, or in relation to its members, where it has been established that they are in fact attempting, by means of the formation of the company, to evade their obligations towards private or public creditors established on the territory of a Member State concerned. In any event, combating fraud cannot justify a practice of refusing to register a branch of a company which has its registered office in another Member State.

Notes and Questions

1. That a company incorporated in one Member State need not be doing business in its home State in order to create a branch that does business in another State is not a surprising conclusion, because it is a literal application of the text of Article 43.

The more debatable issue is whether the Danish shareholders may use this device to avoid the Danish paid-in capital requirements. Because the modern American corporate law view is that paid-in capital does not really protect creditors (see the discussion of the Second Company directive in section D infra), to American lawyers the Court's conclusion in *Centros* appears easily justifiable. Continental European corporate lawyers, accustomed to the view that capital somehow does protect creditors, may react critically to the judgement. Does *Centros* suggest the desirability of harmonization of private limited company laws? Or is it preferable to let prospective shareholders opt among different corporate law systems, as is the case in the US?

2.   The Queen v. H.M. Treasury ex parte Daily Mail, Case 81/87, [1988] ECR 5483, attracted great attention among corporate and tax lawyers. Daily Mail, a large UK company, wanted to transfer its registered head office to the Netherlands, while remaining incorporated in the UK, which is possible under both UK and Dutch company law principles. Thereafter, Daily Mail intended to dispose of investment assets worth 300 million pounds without paying a UK capital gains tax. The UK Treasury sought to impose a condition that Daily Mail first sell a significant part of its assets before the head office transfer. Daily Mail then sought a declaratory judgement that it was entitled under Article 43 (ex 52) to make the head office transfer unconditionally.

In a reference proceeding, the Court held that "unlike natural persons, companies are creatures of the law" and subject to varying national legislation (¶ 19). The Court then observed that some States permit the transfer of a head office to other countries, while other States treat it as the liquidation of a company. Absent harmonization of these rules, the Court held that each Member State may set its own rules on the subject of such a head office transfer (¶ 23).

While it is certainly true that France, Germany, and several other civil law States do not permit a company to move its registered head office or central management to another country, treating an attempt to do so as a voluntary corporate liquidation with tax consequences, one may wonder why the Court considered this civil law view relevant when in fact the Netherlands allows companies to have head offices in other States. Why didn't the Court defer to the company law principles of the UK and the Netherlands in this regard, just as it would to their definition of industrial property rights? (See Chapter 19A.) Several commentators have criticized the Court for failing to interpret the right of establishment broadly to permit a transfer of the registered head office to another State when this does not violate company law rules in either State. Others have felt that, in the absence of Community rules on the subject, the Court's view is sound. See W. Ebke & M. Gockel, European Corporate Law—The Daily Mail, 24 Int'l Law. 239 (1990).

3.   The Court of Justice has dealt with numerous cases of direct or indirect discrimination in the taxation of corporations since the early 1990's. An obvious example of discrimination was a French special tax levied in 1996 on companies selling pharmaceuticals, which permitted them to deduct from the tax costs for research carried out in France, but not elsewhere. In Baxter v. Premier Ministre, Case C–254/97, [1999] ECR I–4809, the Court held that Article 43 required that French subsidiaries of pharmaceutical companies whose parents are established in other States must be able to deduct the cost of research carried out elsewhere in the Community. Somewhat comparable is Camps Newfound/Owatonna v. Town of Harrison, 520 U.S. 564, 117 S.Ct. 1590, 137 L.Ed.2d 852 (1997), in which the Supreme Court held that Maine's grant of an exemption from real estate taxes to

charitable institutions serving Maine residents only violated the dormant Commerce Clause, because it unjustifiably discriminated against a Christian Science summer camp in Maine that cared principally for non-resident campers.

D. COMPANY LAW HARMONIZATION

The program to harmonize company laws, pursuant to Article 44(2)(g), began in 1968. It has proved an arduous task, not only because of the great diversity in company law systems, but also because Member States strongly espouse the policies behind their own national provisions, so that a consensus is difficult to attain. Nonetheless, the program has produced several important directives.

Most continental states have created by law two quite different company forms: 1) the public stock corporation (for example, the societe anonyme, or SA, in France, and Aktiengesellschaft, or AG, in Germany), which has a complex shareholding and management structure and is frequently quoted on stock exchanges; and 2) the private limited liability company (for example, the societe a responsibilite limitee, or SARL, in France, and the Gesellschaft mit beschrankter Haftung, or GmbH, in Germany), which has a simple shareholding and management structure, is favored by small business, and is rarely quoted. The UK also has two types of companies, the public company and the private company, which imitate to some degree the two continental forms, but are not so clearly differentiated. Community harmonization efforts have concentrated on the public stock corporation form.

1. PRESENT DIRECTIVES

The three initial directives (reproduced in the Selected Documents) deal with aspects of company structure. The First Directive 68/151, O.J. L 85/1 (Mar. 14, 1968), covers both the public stock corporation and private limited liability company forms. Its principal effect is to require States to maintain a central register or commercial register, open to the public, which keeps of record a file for each company, comprising in particular the instrument of constitution (articles of incorporation and by-laws), a list of the managers and members of the board of directors, a description of the capital, and the annual balance sheet and profit and loss statement. In contrast, US state law usually requires only the articles of incorporation to be filed with a state office. A few states require the annual financial statements to be provided to all shareholders, but not to the public.

The Second Directive 77/91, O.J. L 26/1 (Jan. 31, 1977), which applies only to public stock corporations, requires certain information about the corporate purpose, the nature of share class rights and obligations, the composition and powers of management bodies, and the amount of capital, to be described in the instrument of incorporation. The directive sets out detailed rules on capital, capital increases and reductions, and procedures related to this subject. The directive also forbids companies to acquire their own shares, except on limited conditions (chiefly to facilitate employee stock option plans), and a 1992 amendment forbids a subsidiary from voting any shares it owns in its parent. Finally, the directive requires that all shareholders have preemptive rights, i.e., rights to subscribe to any capital increase in proportion to their existing shareholdings.

Ironically, shortly after this directive's adoption, article 6.21 of the US Model Business Corporation Act (MBCA) was amended to abolish the concept of capital as outmoded, serving no purpose, and potentially misleading to creditors. The MBCA reflects in this regard the views of most US corporate finance experts. Moreover, most US state laws no longer require preemptive rights, but make them optional. See MBCA, article 6.30. In practice, corporations rarely opt for preemptive rights, because they are perceived as an unnecessary complication and expense in issuing shares.

The Third Directive 78/855, O.J. L 295/36 (Oct. 20, 1978, creates for public companies a modern procedure for carrying out mergers, both between unrelated companies and between parents and subsidiaries. Mergers may take place either through the transfer of all assets and liabilities from one company to another surviving entity (the acquisition mode), or through the formation of a new company to which two or more companies transfer all of their assets and liabilities. The directive sets out detailed procedures for the execution of mergers and for the protection of shareholders and bondholders. This directive is undoubtedly one of the most beneficial of all company law directives, because many States had totally outmoded rules on mergers prior to implementing the directive. The Third Directive presents more modern and better structured rules for mergers than those prevailing in the US. Although the MBCA has modern merger provisions, articles 11.01–.04, most US states have older and complicated merger rules, which are to some degree supplemented by case law for the protection of shareholder interests.

Three other important directives deal with accounting. The Fourth Directive 78/660, O.J. L 222/11 (Aug. 14, 1978), as amended, O.J. L 162/65 (June 26, 1999) (reproduced in the Selected Documents), set standards for annual financial statements and reports, while the Seventh Directive 83/349, O.J. L 193/1 (July 181 1983) deals with those for consolidated accounts for groups of companies. An essential accessory is Directive 84/253, O.J. L 126/20 (May 12, 1984), setting minimum standards for the training and certification of auditors. These directives have radically improved the quality of accounting standards and auditors, reports in many States. The directives have thus greatly aided business operations. For example, the ability to rely on the quality of financial statements for companies throughout the Community is indispensable to achieving securities law harmonization. In June 2000, the Commission indicated that it intended to propose amendments to the accounting directives in order to adopt international accounting standards. In this context, in April 2001, the Commission recommended that all company auditors be subject to regular quality reviews, either by peer reviews or periodic monitoring, to ensure more reliable audits, especially of quoted companies and financial institutions. Recommendation 2001/256, O.J. L 91/91 (Mar. 31, 2001).

The Fourth Directive on Accounting covers both public and private companies, whether quoted or not, so long as they attain a minimum level of assets, turnover and employees. The directive fixes in considerable detail the nature and layout of the annual balance sheet and profit and loss statement, and requires that both be audited. (Unfortunately, the directive does not cover the financial statement on cash flow, which in the US is considered to be of equal importance.) Article 2 requires the financial reports to present a "true and fair view." Moreover, article 46 obliges companies to produce an annual report which presents a "fair review of the business, recent important events and likely future developments."

In contrast, US state laws generally contain no direct requirements on the nature of financial statements, although case law on the fiduciary duty of management to shareholders requires that financial reports be reliable and not misleading. Federal securities regulations set precise requirements for the financial statements, auditors' reports and management operating reports of companies that issue shares to the public. It can fairly be said that these requirements are more detailed and more effectively policed in the US than are the accounting rules set by the Community directives.

Finally, related to the company law program is Regulation 2137/85 on the European Economic Interest Grouping (EEIG), O.J. L 199/1 (July 31, 1985) (reproduced in the Selected Documents). Although it is sometimes erroneously classified as a company, an EEIG may best be described as a statutory joint venture or partnership. The EEIG Regulation facilitates cross-border joint ventures by providing a legal structure protecting the interests of venture members and third parties. The EEIG is a flexible device which can be used for a variety of purposes, for example, joint research, production, marketing and advertising for commercial firms, as well as cooperation among law, accounting or other professional firms.

Notes and Questions

1. Although proposals for harmonization of state corporate laws through federal legislation have been advanced since the 1970s, the US continues to allow the states to set their own rules. Moreover, although the Model Business Corporation Act has influenced the corporate law in many states, Delaware, New York, California and other states follow their own policies. What factors have influenced the US and the Community to take different approaches in this sector? For a thoughtful comparative analysis, see the study by Professors R. Buxbaum and K. Hopt Legal Harmonization and the Business Enterprise, Integration Through Law, Vol. 4 (M. Cappelletti, M. Seccombe & J. Weiler eds. De Gruyter 1988).

2. Harmonization is most beneficial when a modern, carefully structured set of Community rules is substituted for older disparate regulation in the Member States. The merger directive is a good example. However, harmonization runs the risk of freezing in place rules which might otherwise evolve into better forms. For example, was it sensible to set complex and inflexible rules concerning capital in the Second Directive? Compare those rules with the abolition of the concept of capital in article 6.21 of the MBCA. Does either the MBCA or the Second Directive represent an erroneous approach? Or do business differences between the Community and the US justify their opposite approaches? If the Second Directive's rules concerning capital should be modified, how easy would it be to amend the directive?

In recent years, the Court has had several occasions to interpret provisions in the First, Second, and Fourth Directives.

DAIHATSU HANDLER v. DAIHATSU DEUTSCHLAND
Case C–97/96, [1997] ECR II–6843.

[Article 6 of the First Company Directive requires Member States to impose "appropriate penalties" for a company's failure to file its annual financial statements on the public Register. A German law provides for periodic penalties, but only shareholders, creditors and the works council (which represents the employees) may request a court to impose such penalties. The Daihatsu retail dealer association applied for the imposition of penalties to the court where Daihatsu Deutschland was entered on the Register, because the company had not filed its annual financial statements on the Register for several years. The trial court essentially asked the Court of Justice whether the German law had properly implemented the directive.]

17   [T]he German Government maintains that the Federal Republic of Germany has correctly transposed Article 6 of the First Directive. In accordance with Article [44(2)(g)] of the EC Treaty, the coordination of national systems of company law is designed to safeguard the interests of members 'and others'. The latter do not comprise all natural and legal persons but only those who have a legal relationship with the company. * * * German academic legal writing [considers] that the term 'others' * * * covers only creditors of the company.

[The Court then presented its conclusion.]

11   Article [44(2)(g)] of the Treaty refers to the need to protect the interests of others, generally, without distinguishing or excluding any categories falling within the ambit of that term.

20   Consequently, the term 'others' * * * cannot be limited merely to creditors of the company.

21   Moreover, the objective of abolishing restrictions on freedom? of establishment [contained in Article 44(1)] cannot be circumscribed by the provisions of Article [44(2)which] merely sets out a non-exhaustive list of measures to be taken in order to attain that objective, as is borne out by the use in that provision of the words 'in particular'.

22   As regards Article 6 of the First Directive, the fourth recital in the preamble shows that disclosure of annual accounts is primarily designed to provide information for third parties who do not know or cannot obtain sufficient knowledge of the company's accounting and financial situation. Article 3 of the First Directive, which provides for the maintenance of a public register in which all documents and particulars to be disclosed must be entered, and pursuant to which copies of the annual accounts must be obtainable by any person upon application, confirms the concern to enable any interested persons to inform themselves of these matters. That concern also finds expression in the recitals in the preamble to the Fourth Directive, which refer to the need to establish in the Community minimum equivalent legal requirements as regards the extent of the financial information that should be made available to the public by companies that are in competition with one another.

23   In view of the foregoing considerations, the answer to this part of the question must be that Article 6 of the First Directive is to be interpreted as precluding the legislation of a Member State from restricting to members or creditors of the company, the central works council or the company's works council the right to apply for imposition of the penalty provided for by the law of that Member State in the event of failure by a company

to fulfil the obligations regarding disclosure of annual accounts laid down by the First Directive.

COMMISSION v. GERMANY

(First Company Directive penalties)
Case C–191/95, [1998] ECR II–5449.

[Contending that 93% of German companies failed to file their annual financial statements with the Register, the Commission brought an Article 226 (ex 169) proceeding against Germany for its failure to impose "appropriate penalties" under the First Company Directive. The Commission argued specifically that "appropriate penalties" were not possible when the court responsible for the Register had no power on its own motion to impose penalties for the company's non-compliance with the disclosure obligation.]

21   On 25 August 1993 the German Government declared itself ready to reinforce the penalties in cases where documents concerning annual accounts had not been disclosed * * * [and proposed] a draft concerning the introduction of reinforced penalties to enter into force, for all companies limited by shares, with progressive effect from 1 January 1999. In that connection, the German Government pointed out that if such provisions were introduced with immediate effect, the [German states], which had competence in such matters, would be unable to ensure immediate compliance, in view of the large number of proceedings that would have to be brought and the sizeable number of civil servants in the former [German states] who had been assigned to the reconstruction of the new [German states] following German reunification.

22   On 3 March 1994, the Commissioner responsible replied that penalties envisaged must be applicable immediately and without distinction to all companies of the types concerned which were not complying with their obligation of disclosure.

* * *

[After the Commission rejected the German proposal, Germany took no action on it, but maintained that its penalty system was not in violation of the directive. The Court summarily held otherwise.]

68   [I]t must be pointed out that the lack of appropriate penalties cannot be justified by the fact that, because of the large numbers involved, application of such penalties to all companies that do not publish their accounts would create considerable difficulties for the German administrative authorities which would be disproportionate to the aim pursued by the Community legislature. The Court has consistently held that a Member State may not plead internal circumstances in order to justify a failure to comply with obligations and time-limits resulting from rules of Community law.

Notes and Questions

1.   Certainly, the reference in Article 44(2) (g) to safeguards to protect "others" besides "members" is inherently ambiguous. In the context of the First Company Directive, "members" obviously means the shareholders, but who are the "others"? Germany's restriction of "others" to shareholders, employees and

creditors, who all have a legal interest in knowing the company's financial health, has a certain plausibility. Do you agree with the Court's view in ¶ 22 of *Daihatsu*, which would permit anyone with any lawful interest (in *Daihatsu*, the company's retailers who were engaged in a dispute with the company) to force the filing of the annual financial statements? Note the sharp contrast with US state corporate law—only California, New York, and a minority of states require that annual financial statements be provided automatically to shareholders, and the laws in other states on shareholder inspection rights require shareholders to have a proper purpose in order to obtain financial statements, which makes such statements often difficult to obtain, and generally unavailable to creditors and competitors. (Publicly quoted companies must, of course, disclose their annual financial statements in accordance with federal securities law.)

2. The First Company Directive's provision that Member States must impose "appropriate penalties" to enforce its obligations is paralleled by similar provisions in banking, securities, environmental protection and other harmonization directives. After the *Marshall II* judgment, supra page 393, held that State action to secure compliance with Community law must have a "real deterrent effect," the Commission has warned several States that their penalties to enforce some directives (e.g., on money laundering) were inadequate. The German First Company Directive penalties case is therefore probably a harbinger of future Article 226 proceedings. Incidentally, the judgement is also of importance because of the Court's analysis of the "principle of collegiality" which requires the entire Commission to take the policy decision to send the reasoned opinion and to bring Germany before the Court.

SIEMENS v. NOLD

Case C–42/95, [1996] ECR I–6017.

[Article 29 of the Second Company Directive requires a shareholder right of preemption, i.e., that a shareholder have the option to subscribe to new shares whenever they are issued for cash, unless the shareholders, meeting restricts or withdraws the right when it authorizes the new share issue. Article 29 does not however refer to any right of preemption when shares are issued for consideration other than cash.

The management board of Siemens, a major corporation with a large number of shareholders, recommended to its shareholders meeting that it should authorize the issue of 300 million DM of shares to use in employee stock option plans and in acquiring holdings in other companies (presumably in a stock-for-stock acquisition or merger). Nold, a shareholder owning 10 shares, sued to enjoin the issue of new shares. Under German Supreme Court precedents, preemption is required when shares are issued for consideration other than cash, unless the shareholders' meeting eliminates or restricts preemption based upon a management report providing serious reasons for so doing, subject to court review. In the present case, the German Supreme Court held that issuing shares to be used in an exchange for "acquisition of holdings in other companies" was not a sufficient reason to eliminate the preemption rights of existing shareholders, but then felt it must raise an Article 234 question to see if this view conformed to a proper interpretation of article 29 of the directive.]

16   The fact that [Article 29] does not refer to increases in capital by consideration in kind does not mean that the conclusion can be drawn that

the Community legislator elected to restrict the shareholders' right of pre-emption to increases in capital by consideration in cash, thereby precluding Member States from extending it also to increases in capital by consideration in kind.

17   Contrary to the arguments put forward by Siemens, neither does that conclusion follow from the fact that Article 27 of the Second Directive, which is among the provisions on increases in capital by consideration other than in cash, does not introduce a right of pre-emption for shareholders.

18   On the contrary, since the Second Directive merely prescribes a right of pre-emption in the event of increases in capital by consideration in cash, whilst refraining from laying down rules on the complex situation—unknown in most Member States—where the right of pre-emption is exercised in the event of increases in capital by consideration in kind, it left Member States at liberty to provide or not to provide for a right of pre-emption in the latter case.

19   [A] national rule extending the principle that shareholders should have a right of pre-emption to increases in capital by consideration in kind, while providing for the possibility of restricting or withdrawing that right in certain circumstances, is consistent with one of the aims of the Second Directive, namely that of ensuring more effective protection for shareholders. Indeed, such a rule enables shareholders to avoid the fraction of the capital represented by their shareholdings from being diluted also in such an event.

20   According to Siemens, however, [the German Supreme Court's] case-law protects the right of pre-emption disproportionately in so far as it makes it possible for minority shareholders to challenge decisions of the general meeting in order to block increases in capital to the detriment of the company and its creditors.

21   It must be held in this regard that a substantive review [by a court of a shareholder meeting's decision to restrict preemption] which ensures a high degree of protection for shareholders, does not run counter to the aims of the Second Directive, even if it might give rise to delays in carrying out increases in capital.

22   [Accordingly,] the Second Directive, in particular Article 29(1) and (4) thereof, does not preclude a Member State's domestic law from granting a right of pre-emption to shareholders in the event of an increase in capital by consideration in kind and from subjecting the legality of a decision withdrawing that right of pre-emption to a substantive review of the kind laid down by the [German Supreme Court].

PAFITIS v. TRAPEZA KENTRIKIS ELLADOS

Case C–441/93, [1996] ECR 1–1347.

[Greek banking law permits the Governor of the Bank of Greece to appoint an administrator for banks in financial difficulties in order to protect the interests of depositors, creditors, and the State, and to prevent adverse repercussions on the financial market. An administrator has the power to order an increase in capital. When such an administrator for the Trapeza Kentrikis Ellados bank ordered a capital increase, Pafitis and other shareholders sued to annul the increase as a violation of the Second Directive's obligation to call a shareholders meeting to carry out a capital increase. The trial court requested the Court of Justice's interpretation of the directive's provisions with reference to their application to banks.]

38   [T]he Second Directive is intended, in accordance with Article [44(2)(g)] of the EC Treaty, to coordinate the safeguards which are required by Member States of companies or firms within the meaning of the second paragraph of Article [48] of the Treaty with a view to making such safeguards equivalent and protecting the interests of members and others. The Second Directive thus seeks to ensure a minimum level of protection for shareholders in all the Member States.

39   That objective would be seriously frustrated if the Member States were entitled to derogate from the provisions of the directive by maintaining in force rules—even rules categorized as special or exceptional—under which it is possible to decide by administrative measure, separately from any decision by the general meeting of shareholders, to effect an increase in the company's capital.

40   For those reasons, the Court has thus already held that Article 25(1) of the Second Directive precludes the application of rules which, being designed to ensure the reorganization and continued trading of undertakings that are of particular importance to the national economy and are in exceptional situation by reason of their burden, allow an increase in capital to be decided upon by administrative measure, without any resolution being passed by the general meeting.

46   The defendants in the main proceedings contend, [however,] that the *lex specialis* status of banking legislation is closely linked to the fact that supervisory rules are provisions dictated by the public interest. The rules on the supervision of credit institutions, they maintain, constitute a closed system of provisions designed, first, to protect the financial structure and preserve public confidence in it, and, secondly, to protect depositors. They consider that measures for the reorganization of credit institutions, which form an integral part of the supervisory rules, pursue the same objectives. Under the Greek legislation in force, those measures include increases in company capital by decision of a temporary administrator.

* * *

49   It is true that considerations concerning the need to protect the interests of savers and, more generally, the equilibrium of the savings system, require strict supervisory rules in order to ensure the continuing stability of the banking system.

50   However, it does not follow that national rules of that kind must necessarily provide for measures which deprive the organs of a credit institution of the powers vested in them, as organs of a public limited liability company, by Article 25 of the Second Directive.

51   The interests at issue can, as the Advocate General has rightly pointed out in his opinion, be given equal and appropriate protection by other means, such as for example the creation of a generalized system to guarantee

deposits, which seek to achieve the same result but do not impede attainment of the objective pursued by the Second Directive of providing a minimum level of protection for shareholders in all the member States.

Notes and Questions

1.   Do you agree with the Court's interpretation of the Second Directive in *Siemens?* If article 29 deliberately did not require preemption when shares are issued for consideration other than cash, and nine States expressly adopt that position, doesn't that suggest that the better corporate policy is against preemption, contrary to the Court's analysis? In terms of sound corporate management policy, should small shareholders be able to delay large corporate share offerings and render the process of carrying out stock-for-stock acquisitions and mergers more expensive and time-consuming? Since the early days of this century, the US corporate law view has been that preemption should not be required when shares are issued to acquire assets or to carry out a merger. For the modern US approach to this effect, see the MBCA article 6.30(3).

2.   In Pafitis, the Court treats the question presented as essentially one of preemption of national rules by overriding Community rules (see Chapter 14C), and holds that the Second Directive provides for no derogations from its capital increase procedures other than those stated expressly in the directive. The hard question, though, is whether the Greek Central Bank rules are not entirely outside company law, governing the quasi-insolvency of banks, based upon a legitimate concern for the integrity of the banking system. Do you agree with the Court's views in ¶¶ 49–51? Even if depositors' interests can be safeguarded, what of the interests of creditors, or the concern for the ripple effect of a bank collapse? Apart from the special situation of banks, the Court had interpreted strictly Article 25's obligations to hold a shareholders meeting before execution of a capital increase in several judgements, notably Syndesmos Melon v. Greece, Case C–381/89, [1992] ECR I–2111, invalidating Greece's rules authorizing a public entity to take over the temporary administration of companies in financial difficulties, with the power to carry out capital increases without a shareholders meeting.

3.   The Fourth Directive's guiding principle that annual financial statements must present a "true and fair view" has been interpreted for the first time in Tomberger v. Gebruder von der Wettern, Case C–234/94, [1996] ECR I–3133, noted by W. Schon, 34 Common Mkt. L. Rev. 681 (1997), where a holding company's annual balance sheet was considered to properly include a subsidiary's profit for the same financial year, provided the subsidiary had declared a dividend of the profit before the parent's results were audited and approved. Other cases requiring the interpretation of the Fourth and related accounting directives are certain to arise.

2.   PROPOSALS FOR COMMUNITY LEGISLATION

There are a number of draft legislative proposals concerning company law, most of them quite controversial. The well-known draft Fifth Directive, initially proposed in 1972, has been amended successively in O.J. C 240/2 (Sept. 9, 1983), O.J. C 7/4 (Nov. 1, 1990) and O.J. C 321/9 (Dec. 12, 1991). The draft Fifth Directive would harmonize aspects of shareholder rights and management structure for public stock corporations. Many of its provisions would be clearly beneficial, including procedures for holding shareholders meetings and for shareholder rights to inspect company documents. The draft

Fifth is controversial because of its proposals to harmonize the management structure and to mandate employee participation in management. The initial version of the draft Fifth Directive would have required stock corporations to adopt the German AG model of split management, with a supervisory board and a management board, and employee participation on each. This met with such strong opposition that the draft has been progressively modified. The current proposal calls for four different management options, but as all would still require some minimal level of employee participation, it is unlikely that the draft Fifth Directive will soon be adopted, if ever.

The Commission has also proposed Regulation 263/07 to create a European company form, O.J. C 263/41 (Oct. 10, 1989), as amended, O.J.C 176/1 (July 8, 1991). This complex document is essentially a corporation code, which would enable business enterprises to operate through a European company rather than through a national one. The text basically follows the approach of the existing harmonization directives and the draft Fifth. Because the draft Regulation raises issues concerning management structure and employee participation in management similar to those raised by the draft Fifth, the legislative process has moved slowly. However, in December 2000, the Council reached a political agreement on some of the key issues. The final text of the company regulation was in the process of adoption in fall 2001.

Another controversial proposal is the draft Thirteenth Directive on take-over bids (tender offers). The initial and rather ambitious 1989 proposal set out the procedure for initial takeover bids, their revision, and competing bids, and prescribed in great detail the information that both the bidder and the company subject to the bid (the target company) must provide to shareholders. The proposal also described the powers of Member State supervisory authorities and required them to ensure that certain principles are followed, notably the equal treatment of shareholders and the obligation of the target board to act "in the interests of all the shareholders." The initial draft also barred the target management from employing several common defensive tactics without the consent of the shareholders, notably the issuance of new securities, the acquisition of the target's own shares, and the acquisition or sale of significant assets. Finally, the initial proposal contained a compulsory buy-out provision to protect minority shareholders: any person who acquired one-third of a company's voting rights had to make a bid to buy the securities of all other shareholders.

Only France and the UK have long-standing regulation of takeover bids and significant experience with hostile bids. Germany, Italy and the Netherlands have a variety of structural and legal defenses which make hostile takeovers virtually impossible. Moreover, the UK's regulation of takeover bids is through a City Code with which all public companies voluntarily comply. The UK believes that recourse to courts to review takeover bids and tactics would cause delays, legal maneuvering and excessive regulation.

As a result of strongly held and differing views in the Council and Parliament, the draft Thirteenth's fate is still uncertain. A substantially revised and shortened text, O.J.C 378/10 (Dec. 13, 1997), continued to set the procedure for an initial tender offer and prescribes minimum disclosures by the bidder, but allows the Member States to decide how to deal with changes in bids and competing tender offers. Under article 5, target companies must give all security holders "equivalent treatment" and "act in all the interests of the company including employment." More important, under Article 8a, the target company may not take "any action which may result in the frustration of the offer" without approval of the shareholders meeting given during the term of the bid. A compulsory purchase of outstanding shareholders (usually a minority) after a bidder takes control is still required, but not if there are "equivalent means" to protect them (article 3). Finally, at the UK's insistence, article 4 states that the supervisory authority may be a private body, and judicial review is not required if "an injured party enjoys appropriate and adequate remedies."

After relatively minor amendments, this 1997 draft appeared close to approval at the end of 2000. Unfortunately, during the codecision procedure, Parliament wanted a specific right for target companies to create anti-takeover defenses in advance of any bid (popularly called "poison pill" defenses), which the Council would not accept. On July 4, 2001, Parliament rejected by a tie vote a Conciliation Committee proposal and thus ended the legislative process. The Commission was greatly disappointed, but has announced that it will soon launch another draft text.

The draft Thirteenth Directive differs considerably from the regulation of tender offers in the US under the Williams Act, § 14D of the Securities Exchange Act of 1934, and the implementing SEC regulations, which govern tender offer procedures and the information to be provided to investors and publicly disclosed. Moreover, US state legislation and case law permit target company management to employ many types of takeover defenses, subject to judicial review under complex standards.

Chapter 18

RIGHTS OF PRACTICE FOR LAWYERS AND OTHER PROFESSIONALS

Achieving for professionals a right of establishment and freedom to provide services represents a significant step toward attaining an integrated internal market. The operations of multinational enterprises are greatly facilitated by multinational professional firms offering accounting, legal, architectural, engineering, public relations and other services. In particular, the need for expert legal assistance provided on a Community-wide basis has steadily grown as the Community wave of legislation advances in such complex fields as banking, insurance, securities, intellectual property, telecommunications, public procurement, environmental protection and employee rights.

Although this chapter provides an overview of the rights of professionals generally, it concentrates on the right of lawyers to practice on a Community-wide basis. Several important Court judgments have dealt with lawyers' rights, providing a useful focus for our analysis. Building upon the Court's doctrines, several directives have substantially liberalized the rights of lawyers to practice throughout the Community, both on a temporary and a permanent basis. We will contrast this liberal regime with the more restrictive state practice rules in the US.

A. TREATY PROVISIONS AND LEGISLATIVE MEASURES

1. INITIAL DEVELOPMENTS

The pertinent Treaty articles are those reviewed in the preceding chapter. Particularly important is Article 47 (ex 57). Access to virtually all professions in the Member States requires a license or authorization, which is usually only granted upon the presentation of educational and/or professional training credentials. At the time the Community was created, persons seeking to obtain a professional license usually encountered great difficulty if they had been educated or professionally trained elsewhere in the Community. The purpose of Article 47 was to promote professional mobility by permitting legislative harmonization of national standards for education and training, and the recognition of diplomas or certificates awarded at their conclusion.

Little progress was made until 1974. Although the Commission proposed numerous draft directives for specific professions under Article 47, their adoption was delayed because the Council could not reach unanimous agreement on them. It was also generally believed that professionals from one Member State could not claim establishment rights in other States in the absence of a directive under Article 47. The situation appeared quite bleak. Fortunately the Court of Justice ended this impasse.

REYNERS v. BELGIUM

Case 2/74, [1974] ECR 631.

[Reyners, a Dutch national, raised and educated in Belgium, had successfully obtained a Belgian law diploma and the other credentials necessary to acquire the status of an *avocat.* Because a Belgian law required Belgian citizenship as a condition for the status of *avocat,* his application was denied. On appeal, the Belgian Supreme Administrative Court asked the Court of Justice for a ruling on whether Article 43 (ex 52) had direct effect. A second question, concerning Article 45, is treated at page ___ below.]

21   [In] the Chapter on the right of establishment the "general programme" and the directives provided for by the Treaty are intended to accomplish two functions, the first being to eliminate obstacles in the way of attaining freedom of establishment during the transitional period, the second being to introduce into the law of Member States a set of provisions intended to facilitate the effective exercise of this freedom for the purpose of assisting economic and social interpenetration within the Community in the sphere of activities as self-employed persons.

* * *

23   The effect of the provisions of Article [43, ex Article 52] must be decided within the framework of this system.

24   The rule on equal treatment with nationals is one of the fundamental legal provisions of the Community.

25   As a reference to a set of legislative provisions effectively applied by the country of establishment to its own nationals, this rule is, by its essence, capable of being directly invoked by nationals of all the other Member States.

26   In laying down that freedom of establishment shall be attained at the end of the transitional period, [i.e., by Dec. 31, 1969], Article [43, ex 52] thus imposes an obligation to attain a precise result, the fulfilment of which had to be made easier by, but not made dependent on, the implementation of a programme of progressive measures.

27   The fact that this progression has not been adhered to leaves the obligation itself intact beyond the end of the period provided for its fulfilment.

* * *

29 It is not possible to invoke against such an effect the fact that the Council has failed to issue the directives provided for by Articles [44] and [47] or the fact that certain of the directives actually issued have not fully attained the objective of non-discrimination required by Article [43].

30 After the expiry of the transitional period the directives provided for by the Chapter on the right of establishment have become superfluous with regard to implementing the rule on nationality, since this is henceforth sanctioned by the Treaty itself with direct effect.

31 These directives have however not lost all interest since they [may] make easier the effective exercise of the right of freedom of establishment.

Notes and Questions

1. Does the language of Article 43 appear to you to be clear, precise and unconditional, the test for direct effect presented in Chapter 7? Why do you think the Court of Justice interpreted Article 43 in an expansive fashion? *Reyners* was decided a few months before *van Binsbergen,* excerpted in the prior chapter, whose analysis closely follows *Reyners. Reyners* was decided only a few months after Application of Griffiths, 413 U.S. 717, 93 S.Ct. 2851, 37 L.Ed.2d 910 (1973), the US Supreme Court opinion which held that Connecticut could not make US citizenship a prerequisite for admission to the bar. See page 735 *infra.* Some observers have speculated that *Griffiths* influenced *Reyners.*

2. In the US, states require licenses for the practice of most professions, usually conditioned on the successful passage of an examination. In Dent v. West Virginia, 129 U.S. 114, 9 S.Ct. 231, 32 L.Ed. 623 (1889), the Supreme Court upheld a state license requirement for doctors against a Due Process Clause challenge as necessary "for the protection of society," but observed that the license must be based upon reasonable educational qualifications and an examination applied in a non-arbitrary manner.

2. LEGISLATIVE ACTION

Reyners and *van Binsbergen* recognized the right of Community professionals to be treated without discrimination by host State authorities. Still, this represented only partial progress. Before claiming either a right to perform services or to practice while residing in a host State, Community professionals had to prove that their other qualifications or credentials were substantially equal to those required for the comparable host State professionals. Obviously, this made the adoption of implementing directives under Articles 44, 47 and 52 crucial. In 1974, the Commission revised its draft directives in the light of *Reyners* and *van Binsbergen,* and the Council began to adopt directives of great importance to specific professions.

The breakthrough for the medical profession came with Council Directive 75/363, O.J. L 167/14 (June 30, 1975), which established minimum standards for medical education and the diplomas granted on the completion of this education, and Council Directive 75/362, O.J. L 167/1 (June 30, 1975), which required mutual recognition of these diplomas. Because the Community had over 500,000 doctors at the time these directives were adopted, they had a major impact. The Council adopted similar directives with regard to nurses, dentists and veterinarians in the late 1970s and pharmacists in 1985. Finally, Council Directive 85/384, O.J. L 223/15 (Aug. 24, 1985), mandated mutual recognition of educational diplomas for architects.

These directives (except that for architects) follow a common approach. First, they harmonize the professional education and training standards throughout the Community, effectively setting a basic floor of qualifications for all members of the profession in question. This makes it relatively easy for these professionals to meet the requirements of practice in different Member States. Second, the medical professions and the architects directives require Member States to accept the diplomas of higher educational institutions in other Member States, thus enabling a foreign-trained professional to obtain fairly readily a host State license to practice. It can be safely assumed that all the medical profession directives are sufficiently clear and unconditional to have direct effect. See Auer v. Ministére Public, Case 271/82, [1983] ECR 2727. Incidentally, although consideration was given to allowing the host State to require proof of fluency in the host language, no provision to this effect was adopted. The directives tacitly assume that the foreign professional will attain sufficient knowledge of the host State language to be able to practice competently.

This initial harmonization approach suffered from two serious defects. First, it required considerable time and effort for the Commission to elaborate a commonly accepted course of studies and training for any particular profession, and then for the Council to reach agreement on the standards. (For pharmacists, this process took fifteen years from the initial Commission draft directive.) Second, for some professions the substantive materials covered in the education and training, as well as the scope of professional activities, vary so widely that it is difficult to develop a common course of studies. This is particularly the case for the legal profession, given the fundamental differences between the common law and the civil law systems, and profound differences in approach even within the civil law world.

Thus by the early 1980s, the pace of progress in attaining the rights of professionals to practice freely throughout the Community was clearly too slow, and a new approach was needed. Accordingly, in the June 1985 White Paper on Completing the Internal Market, the Commission proposed a general approach to cover all professions where the rules had not yet been harmonized. This approach, borrowed from the sphere of the free movement of goods, was to be one of mutual trust and mutual recognition: each Member State would trust the quality of higher education in every other State and recognize the other State's diplomas as being essentially equivalent to its own.

The ultimate result was Council Directive 89/48 of December 21, 1988 on a general system for the recognition of higher-education diplomas, O.J. L 19/16 (Jan. 24, 1989), commonly known as the Diploma Recognition Directive, included in the Selected Documents. The directive's importance can be seen from the long list of professionals covered, including accountants, lawyers, engineers, surveyors, patent agents, insurance agents, bankers, brokers, physicists, chemists, biologists, foresters, and librarians. The medical professions, pharmacists and architects continue to be covered by their specific directives.

The heart of the directive is the obligation placed on Member States to recognize any diploma or certificate awarded by a higher educational institution in any other Member State after a course of at least three years duration (art. 1(a)). Such a diploma must, generally speaking, be recognized as equivalent to a State's own higher-education diplomas when they are required for persons seeking access to a regulated profession (art. 3).

The directive applies to any Member State "national wishing to pursue a regulated profession in a host Member State in a self-employed capacity or as an employed person" (art. 2). Accordingly, a national of a non-Community state cannot benefit from the directive, even if he or she has obtained a diploma from an educational institution within the Community.

Once a foreign applicant fulfills all the conditions for admission to the host State's regulated profession, he or she will be fully integrated into that profession, using the host State professional title (art. 7). In effect, this protects the foreign professional, once admitted in the host State, from the risk of treatment as a "second-class citizen."

The principle of general recognition of diplomas has, however, important exceptions. These exceptions, described in article 4, essentially arise whenever there is a substantial difference in education and/or training between the host State and the home State of an applicant, and whenever there is a significant difference between the scope of practice between the two States involved. In the event that one of these exceptions applies, the host State may require the foreign applicant either to take an "aptitude test" to assess knowledge of certain subjects or to complete an "adaptation period" of practice of up to three years supervised by a host State professional. Accordingly, the directive's success will be determined to some degree by the leniency or rigor with which a host State decides to use aptitude tests and adaptation periods.

The Diploma Recognition Directive probably has its greatest impact on young professionals. Increased opportunities for study in other countries, enhanced language capabilities, and social and marital ties with persons of other nationalities have all contributed to efforts by young professionals to reside and work in other States. The Community's Erasmus program, discussed in Chapter 16C, which facilitates studies in other States, also promotes professional mobility.

A useful supplement, Directive 92/51, O.J. L 209/25 (July 24, 1992), parallels the Diploma Recognition Directive's provisions in requiring the mutual recognition of higher education certificates and diplomas awarded after less than three years. While principally of use for short term vocational training certificates, the new directive may also be used to achieve the mutual recognition of masters' degrees (see *Kraus*, infra).

Finally, the Commission's program of codification and modernization produced Directive 93/16, O.J. L 165/1 (July 7, 1993), which replaced the 1975 and 1976 directives on doctors' education and diplomas. The 1993 directive continued to set minimum education standards (essentially, six years of study and practical training). An important innovation was the directive's express coverage of employed as well as self-employed doctors.

Notes and Questions

1. The Diploma Recognition Directive is founded on mutual trust by Member States of the quality of professional education and training provided in other States. Is this sound policy or does it create unacceptable risks for clients and the general public? Do you think that the aptitude test or adaptation period will suffice to lower the risks to acceptable levels?

2. What specifically is an aptitude test supposed to assess? (See art. 1(g).) Why should a host State be permitted to examine knowledge of its professional rules? How do you anticipate an adaptation period will be carried out? May a host State require both an aptitude test and an adaptation period? (See art. 4.) What are their comparative advantages and drawbacks?

3. The Court of Justice frequently must provide guidance on the interpretation of these directives on the recognition of professional diplomas. Thus, in an early judgment interpreting the doctors' directives, Broekmeulen v. Huisarts Registratie Commissie, Case 246/80, [1981] ECR 2311, the Court established the principle that a national of one State may require his or her own State to recognize a diploma and related qualifications obtained in another State. The Court rejected Netherlands' attempt to claim that Broekmeulen had no treaty-based rights, arguing for use of the internal affairs doctrine, and held that Broekmeulen's reliance on his medical degree from Belgium constituted an application of his right of free movement to study abroad.

4. To what extent can a State define the limits of its professions and the attendant practice monopoly granted to its professionals? In Criminal proceedings against Bouchoucha, Case C–61/89, [1990] ECR 3551, the Court held that France could include osteopathy within the sphere of medical practice, so that a French national could not rely on an osteopathy diploma obtained in the UK to practice osteopathy. The Court held that "the definition of acts restricted to the medical profession is, in principle, a matter for the Member States" (¶ 12).

The Court's views subsequently evolved in MacQuen v. Union Professionnelle Belge des Médecines Specialistes en Ophtalmologie, Case C–108/96, [2001] ECR ____ (Feb. 1, 2001), in which the ophthalmologist profession claimed that various opticians were engaged in the unauthorized practice of medicine when they used modern instruments to conduct eye examinations in order to check eye problems, instead of merely determining the proper corrective lenses for glasses. The Court held that Belgium's power to define the scope of medical activities must be exercised proportionately, and indicated that the Belgian court should consider whether the use by opticians of modern instruments to conduct certain eye examinations genuinely represented any health risk (citing a German Supreme Court judgment that held that opticians could safely execute such examinations) (¶ ¶ 35–37). See also Commission v. Spain (Architects' activities), Case C–421/98, [2000] ECR ____ (Nov. 23, 2000), in which the Court held that Spain could not restrict architects with diplomas from other Community States to the sphere of activities covered by the diplomas in their home State, but must permit them to carry out any activities permitted to the holder of a Spanish architecture diploma.

5. Haim v. Kassenzahrartzliche Vereinigung Nordrhein, Case C–424/97, [2000] ECR ____ (July 4, 2000), involved the rules of Germany's social security system which required a dentist qualified in Belgium to speak German as a condition for practicing as a dentist in Germany. As noted above, the medical and dentist harmonization directives do not contain a requirement of competency in the host language. In agreement with the Advocate General, the Court nonetheless held:

[59] [T]he reliability of a dental practitioner's communication with his patient and with administrative authorities and professional bodies constitutes an over-riding reason of general interest such as to justify making the appointment as a dental practitioner under a social security scheme subject to language requirements. Dialogue with patients, compliance with rules of professional conduct and law specific to dentistry in the Member State of establishment

and performance of administrative tasks require an appropriate knowledge of the language of that State.

60   However, it is important that language requirements designed to ensure that the dental practitioner will be able to communicate effectively with his patients, whose mother tongue is that of the Member State concerned, * * * do not go beyond what is necessary to attain that objective. In this respect, it is in the interest of patients whose mother tongue is not the national language that there exist a certain number of dental practitioners who are also capable of communicating with such persons in their own language.

Do you consider the Court's approach to be the right one? To what degree does ¶ 60 affect the conclusion in ¶ 59?

KRAUS v. LAND BADEN–WÜRTTEMBERG

Case C–19/92, [1993] ECR I–1663.

[Kraus, a German national, obtained an LL.M. in 1988 from the University of Edinburgh after a year's study. A 1939 German law permitted persons to use a Germany university degree title, but required a specific authorization from a German state in order to use the title of a degree given by a foreign university. Before granting such an authorization, the state of Baden–Württemberg required applicants to furnish various documents and pay a 130 DM (ca. $65) fee. Kraus supplied only a copy of his Edinburgh diploma and refused to pay the fee, claiming that the German authorization procedure violated Community law. At this time, Kraus was engaged in the training period required between the first and second state examinations which lead to the attainment of the status of *Rechtsanwalt* (lawyer). However, Kraus had previously worked as a paid assistant to a German university professor, a post which sometimes leads toward the status of professor.

After refusal of the authorization, Kraus sued in an administrative court, which essentially asked the Court of Justice whether an authorization procedure only for foreign postgraduate degrees violated Article 43, when the degree is not required for access to any profession, but could enhance the exercise of a profession. The Court first replied that the internal affairs doctrine does not apply when a Member State national wants to use a diploma based on studies in another State in order to gain access to a profession in his own State (*see Broekmeulen, supra*). The Court then addressed the harder question presented to it.]

18   Although a postgraduate academic title is not usually a prerequisite for access to a profession, either as an employee or on a self-employed basis, the possession of such a title nevertheless constitutes * * * an advantage for the purpose both of gaining entry to such a profession and of prospering in it.

19   Accordingly, in so far as it constitutes proof of possession of an additional professional qualification and thereby confirms its holder's fitness for a particular post, and * * * his command of the language of the country where it was awarded, a university diploma of the kind in point in the main proceedings is by its nature such as to improve its holder's chances of appointment as compared with those of other candidates who are

unable to make use of any qualification supplementary to the basic education and training required for the post in question.

20 In some cases possession of a postgraduate academic title obtained in another State may even be a prerequisite for access to certain professions, where those professions require specific knowledge such as that evidenced by the diploma in question. That may be so in the case of a postgraduate diploma in law required, for example, for access to an academic career in the fields of international or comparative law.

21 Furthermore, the holder of [such] a diploma * * * may find himself in an advantageous position in the pursuit of his professional activity in so far, as through possession of that diploma, he can obtain higher remuneration or more rapid advancement or, in the course of his career, access to certain specific posts reserved to persons with particularly high qualifications.

22 Similarly, the possibility of using academic titles awarded abroad and supplementing national diplomas required for access to a profession greatly facilitates establishment as an independent practitioner and the pursuit of a corresponding professional activity.

23 It follows that the situation of a Community national who holds a postgraduate academic title which, obtained in another Member State, facilitates access to a profession or, at least, the pursuit of an economic activity, is governed by Community law, even as regards the relations between that national and the Member State whose nationality he possesses.

[The Court noted that the Diploma Recognition Directive governed only degrees obtained after three years' study and the supplementary Directive 92/51 was not yet in force. Absent Community harmonization, Member States may regulate the field, provided their rules are justified by important public interest considerations.]

35 The need to protect a public * * * [from] abuse of academic titles which have not been awarded according to the rules laid down in the country in which the holder of the title intends to make use of it constitutes a legitimate interest such as to justify a restriction * * * of the fundamental freedoms guaranteed by the Treaty.

36 It follows that the fact that a Member State establishes a procedure for the issue of administrative authorizations, to be obtained prior to using postgraduate academic titles awarded in another State, and prescribes criminal penalties for non-compliance with that procedure is not, in itself, incompatible with the requirements of Community law.

Notes and Questions

1. Although the preamble to Directive 92/51, which requires recognition of certificates obtained after less than three years' study, refers to mutual recognition of diplomas that lead to access to a profession, *Kraus* suggests that the directive might now be interpreted to encompass post-graduate degrees that only facilitate the exercise of a profession. Do you agree with the Court's conclusion that Article 43 implicitly provides rights to those who obtain Master's degrees in other Member States because they may enhance employment opportunities or professional income?

2. Advocate General van Gerven approached the issue quite differently. He contended that the German law is facially discriminatory, since it purports to protect against abusive reference to foreign degrees, but not German ones. He then reasoned that the law violates the duty of non-discrimination linked to Article 150 (ex 128), since its impact might be to induce students to seek German post-graduate rather than foreign degrees. He concluded that the authorization process itself violates Community law. Do you agree with his view or that of the Court? For contrasting case notes, see W.H. Roth, 30 Common Mkt. L. Rev. 1251 (1993); L. Smith, 19 Eur. L. Rev. 67 (1994).

3. The Court has also given guidance on how Member States should treat persons who have acquired some qualifications in other States, but not a diploma that requires recognition. Prior to the effective date of the Diploma Recognition Directive, in Vlassopoulou v. Ministerium fur Justiz Baden–Wurttemberg, Case C–340/89, [1991] ECR I–2357, the Court held that Germany must examine the educational qualifications and professional experience of a Greek lawyer who applied to become a German lawyer, compare them with those of a German applicant, and give credit to the extent that the Greek lawyer's education and experience are comparable. Bobadilla v. Museo Nacional del Prado, Case C–234/97, [1999] ECR I–4773, followed *Vlassapoulou* in holding that Spain must consider Bobadilla's Bachelor's and Master's degrees in art history from Boston University and Newcastle Polytechnic in assessing her qualifications to become an art restorer.

4. If Spain accepts an Argentine medical diploma as sufficient to enable a Spanish–Argentine dual national to practice medicine in Spain as a specialist in urology, must France permit the individual concerned to practice medicine in France? The Court answered this intriguing question in Hocsman v. Ministre de l'Emploi, Case C–238/98, [2000] ECR ___ (Sept. 14, 2000). Because Hocsman had no medical diploma from Spain, the doctors' diploma directive did not provide him with any rights. Consider, however, whether Article 43 implicitly does so in the light of *Vlassapoulou.*

B. LAWYERS' RIGHT TO PROVIDE SERVICES

Directive 77/249, O.J. L 78/17 (March 26, 1977), commonly called the Lawyers' Services Directive, was adopted to facilitate the effective exercise by lawyers of the freedom to provide services. The text is in the Selected Documents and should be read at this point. Although it does not resolve all the issues, it provides a framework permitting most Member State lawyers to provide occasional cross-border services in other Community States.

Notes and Questions

1. The list of classes of lawyers in article 1(2) of the Lawyers' Services Directive does not include a number of organized legal professions, notably notaries, who in most civil law States have a monopoly over the right to handle decedents' estates and real estate title transfers, and legal advisors (e.g., the *conseil juridique* in France or Belgium and the *Rechtsbeistand* in Germany), who handle commercial and administrative law affairs. Why might these types of legal professionals have been omitted? Is their omission justified? Note that in *van Binsbergen,* excerpted in the previous chapter, the professional granted a right to provide cross-border services was a "legal representative," not a Dutch *advocaat.*

2.   Observe the limitations that article 5 places on cross-border practice in "legal proceedings" (not defined, but presumably meaning civil and criminal litigation). What might they be intended to achieve? Are they justified?

3.   Try to analyze the method for determining applicable rules of professional conduct in article 4. Do you see the influence of *van Binsbergen* on article 4? Why is a distinction made between the services in 4(2) and 4(4)? What might the phrase "without prejudice" mean? Do you think that in the event of conflict between host State and home State rules, one should always prevail? If so, which one in article 4(2)? In article 4(4)?

COMMISSION v. GERMANY

(Lawyers' services)
Case 427/85, [1988] ECR 1123.

[Germany required a foreign lawyer providing services in litigation or in certain administrative proceedings to collaborate with a German lawyer (*Rechtsanwalt*), with the German lawyer assuming the primary role of "authorized representative or defending counsel." Moreover, the local German lawyer had to be present at all times during the court or administrative proceedings or when the foreign lawyer sought to visit a client in jail. The Commission brought an Article 226 proceeding against Germany, which maintained that its approach was justified by article 5 of the 1977 directive, which obliges a foreign lawyer to work "in conjunction with" a host State lawyer.]

12   * * * [T]he freedom to provide services is one of the fundamental principles of the Treaty and may be restricted only by rules which are justified by the general good and are imposed on all persons pursuing activities in the host Member State, in so far as that interest is not safeguarded by the rules to which the provider of the service is subject in the Member State in which he is established.

13   The Directive must be interpreted in the light of those principles. Article 5 of the Directive may not have the effect of imposing upon a lawyer providing services requirements for which there is no equivalent in the professional rules which would apply in the absence of any provision of services within the meaning of the Treaty. It is undisputed that, in proceedings for which German law does not make representation by a lawyer mandatory, the parties may conduct their cases themselves; in such proceedings, German law also allows representation to be entrusted to a person who is neither a lawyer nor a specialist, provided that that person does not act in a professional capacity.

14   In those circumstances, it is apparent that there is no consideration relating to the public interest which, in court proceedings for which representation by a lawyer is not mandatory, can justify the obligation for a lawyer established in another Member State, who is providing his services in a professional capacity, to work in conjunction with a German lawyer.

* * *

[The Court then considered the application of article 5 of the directive in proceedings in which a lawyer's services is mandatory.]

20   According to the German Government, [its] rules are a direct consequence of Article 5 of the Directive, which provides that the German lawyer with whom the work in conjunction is to be carried out must practise before the judicial authority in question and is, "where necessary, answerable to that authority". A German lawyer can only be so answerable if he is familiar with all the steps taken by the lawyer providing services and becomes aware of them at the right time, namely before they have taken effect. For that reason, the German lawyer must be constantly involved in the development of the case; such involvement in the case can be ensured only if * * * the German lawyer is present at the oral stage of the proceedings and if he can claim the status of authorized representative or defending counsel.

21   The German Government also claims that the freedom to provide services should not interfere with the proper administration of justice. Unlimited access by foreign lawyers to proceedings before German courts would be likely to create difficulties arising from insufficient knowledge of the rules of substantive and procedural law applied by those courts. Only the involvement of a local lawyer can ensure that cases are properly presented to the court.

* * *

23   [W]hilst the Directive allows national legislation to require a lawyer providing services to work in conjunction with a local lawyer, it is intended to make it possible for the former to carry out the tasks entrusted to him by his client, whilst at the same time having due regard for the proper administration of justice. Seen from that viewpoint, the obligation imposed upon him to act in conjunction with a local lawyer is intended to provide him with the support necessary to enable him to act within a judicial system different from that to which he is accustomed and to assure the judicial authority concerned that the lawyer providing services actually has that support and is thus in a position fully to comply with the procedural and ethical rules that apply.

24   Accordingly, the lawyer providing services and the local lawyer, both being subject to the ethical rules applicable in the host Member State, must be regarded as being capable, in compliance with those ethical rules and in the exercise of their professional independence, of agreeing upon a form of cooperation appropriate to their client's instructions.

* * *

26   [T]he German Law of 1980 imposes upon the two lawyers who are required to work in conjunction obligations which go further than is necessary for the attainment of those objectives. Neither the presence of the German lawyer throughout the oral proceedings nor the requirement that the German lawyer must himself be the authorized representative or defending counsel nor the detailed provisions concerning proof of work in conjunction are in general necessary or even useful for the provision of the support required by the lawyer providing services.

27   * * * [T]he problem of possibly inadequate knowledge of German law referred to by the German Government to justify the requirements of the Law of 1980 forms part of the responsibility of the lawyer providing

services vis-à-vis his client, who is free to entrust his interests to a lawyer of his choice.

28 [T]he German Government's argument that only the forms of work in conjunction provided for by the German legislation make it possible to ensure that lawyers pursue their activities in such a way as to maintain sufficient contact with their clients and the judicial authorities is untenable. As the Court stated in [*Klopp, infra*], modern methods of transport and telecommunications enable lawyers to ensure the necessary contacts in an appropriate manner.

29 The reasons for considering that the detailed arrangements for work in conjunction laid down by the Law of 1980 are, by reason of their disproportionality, incompatible with the Treaty do not however apply in the same way to the provisions of that law concerning visits to persons held in custody. * * *

30 [I]t must be recognized that there may be cogent reasons, in particular those which relate to public security * * * for a Member State to lay down rules governing contacts between lawyers and persons in custody.

* * *

32 However, in so far as the German law provides that a lawyer providing services may not, as defending counsel, visit a person in custody unless accompanied by the German lawyer with whom he is working in conjunction, and cannot correspond with a person held in custody except through that German lawyer, without any exception being allowed, even with the authorization of the court or of the authority responsible for contacts with persons in custody, the restrictions laid down by that law go further than is necessary to achieve the legitimate objectives which that law pursues.

33 Accordingly, the Commission's complaints concerning the procedures for work in conjunction must be upheld.

GEBHARD v. CONSIGLIO DELL'ORDINE DEGLI AVVOCATI DI MILANO

Case C–55/94, [1995] ECR I–4165.

[A German national, Gebhard, became a Rechtsanwalt in Stuttgart in 1977. From 1978–89, he practiced professionally in Milan as a "collaborator" with a firm of Italian lawyers. Since 1978, Gebhard has resided with his family in Milan, paying income tax only in Italy. In 1989, Gebhard opened his own office in Milan, chiefly representing German and Austrian clients in Italy, with the aid of Italian lawyers. However, around 35% of his practice consists in the representation of Italian clients in German and Austria, and he is a "collaborator" in a Stuttgart law firm.

In 1989, the Milan Bar Association began disciplinary proceedings against Gebhard because of his permanent practice in Italy using the title, "*Avvocato*," without being qualified as an Italian lawyer. In 1991, Gebhard applied to become a member of the Milan bar pursuant to the Diploma Recognition Directive, but no action was taken and no issue concerning this was referred to the Court of Justice. When in 1992 the Milan Bar Council imposed upon him the sanction of a total prohibition of practice for six months, Gebhard appealed to the National Bar Council, claiming in particular that he had a right to practice in Italy under the Lawyers' Services Directive. In its Article 234 reference, the National Bar Council inquired whether a 1982 Italian law had properly implemented the directive, and how to assess the criteria to be used in determining whether a lawyer's practice came under that directive. The Court provided guidelines on how to distinguish between a lawyer's right of establishment and a lawyer's right to provide services.]

22   The provisions of the chapter on services are subordinate to those of the chapter on the right of establishment in so far, first, as the wording of the first paragraph of Article [49, ex 59] assumes that the provider and the recipient of the service concerned are "established" in two different Member States and, second, as the first paragraph of Article [50, ex 60] specifies that the provisions relating to services apply only if those relating to the right of establishment do not apply. It is therefore necessary to consider the scope of the concept of "establishment".

23   The right of establishment, provided for in Articles [43 to 48] of the Treaty, is granted both to legal persons within the meaning of Article [48] and to natural persons who are nationals of a Member State of the Community. Subject to the exceptions and conditions laid down, it allows all types of self-employed activity to be taken up and pursued on the territory of any other Member State * * *.

24   It follows that a person may be established, within the meaning of the Treaty, in more than one Member State, in the case of members of the professions, by establishing a second professional base [citing *Klopp, infra*].

25   The concept of establishment within the meaning of the Treaty is therefore a very broad one, allowing a Community national to participate, on a stable and continuous basis, in the economic life of a Member State other than his State of origin and to profit therefrom, so contributing to economic and social interpenetration within the Community in the sphere of activities as self-employed persons [citing *Reyners*].

26   In contrast, where the provider of services moves to another Member State, the provisions of the chapter on services, in particular the third paragraph of Article [50], envisage that he is to pursue his activity there on a temporary basis.

27   As the Advocate General has pointed out, the temporary nature of the activities in question has to be determined in the light, not only of the duration of the provision of the service, but also of its regularity, periodicity or continuity. The fact that the provision of services is temporary does not mean that the provider of services within the meaning of the Treaty may not equip himself with some form of infrastructure in the host Member State (including an office, chambers or consulting rooms) in so far as such infrastructure is necessary for the purposes of performing the services in question.

28   However, that situation is to be distinguished from that of Mr. Gebhard who, as a national of a Member State, pursues a professional activity on a stable and continuous basis in another Member State where he holds himself out from an established professional base to, amongst others,

nationals of that State. Such a national comes under the provisions of the chapter relating to the right of establishment and not those of the chapter relating to services.

[29]   The Milan Bar Council has argued that a person such as Mr. Gebhard cannot be regarded for the purposes of the Treaty as being 'established' in a Member State—in his case, Italy—unless he belongs to the professional body of that State or, at least, pursues his activity in collaboration or in association with persons belonging to that body.

[30]   That argument cannot be accepted.

[31]   The provisions relating to the right of establishment cover the taking-up and pursuit of activities. Membership of a professional body may be a condition of taking up and pursuit of particular activities. It cannot itself be constitutive of establishment.

Notes and Questions

1.   In the *German Lawyers' services* case, the Court narrowly construed the obligations of article 5 of the directive, applying the principle of *van Binsbergen* that restrictions on the right to provide services must be justified by the "general good." Do you think the Court has struck the proper balance between the right of cross-border legal practice and the protection of clients' interests? Should clients or a State fix the allocation of responsibility between host and home State lawyers in a legal proceeding?

2.   In *Gebhard,* the Court's analysis of the distinction between the right of establishment and the right to provide services is its most precise and detailed one to date and clearly applies to commercial activities as well as to professional ones. What are the critical elements in drawing the distinction set forth in the judgment? How can a trans-border service provider have a permanent office or other infra-structure in a host State, and still be deemed to be only providing services rather than being established? In a financial services context, the Commission has stated its view that a bank may operate a group of automatic cash machines in a host State and still be considered only to be providing services. Do you agree with this basic approach?

3.   When do you suppose a permanent office or infrastructure might prove useful for lawyers providing services in another State? Could administrative, secretarial or accounting personnel be employed permanently by such an office, provided they are not attempting to carry out any law practice? Under the test for temporary services set in ¶ 27 of the *Gebhard* judgment, could a German lawyer come to Paris or London ten times or more a year, totaling five or six months, to engage in international arbitration practice, without being deemed to be established?

4.   In Reiseburo Broede, Case C–3/95, [1996] ECR I–6511, the Court held that German rules restricting to lawyers the collection of debts in court proceedings satisfied the general good interest criterion because they "protect creditors or safeguard the sound administration of justice." (¶ 36.) Accordingly, a French debt-collection enterprise was prevented from carrying out its activities in Germany. Most States do not restrict debt-collection to lawyers and the Commission considered the German rule to be disproportionate. The judgment may be contrasted with Sager v. Dennemeyer, Case C–7/90, [1991] ECR I–4221, where the Court held that a German law restricting patent maintenance and the handling of routine patent renewals to lawyers only was disproportionate, thus permitting a UK

patent agent company to provide these services in Germany. Why do you think the Court reached a different result in *Reiseburo Broede*? On a comparative note, in National Revenue Corp. v. Violet, 807 F.2d 285 (1st Cir.1986), the First Circuit held that Rhode Island's statutory definition of debt collection as part of the practice of law violated the dormant Interstate Commerce Clause, noting that no other state restricted debt collection to attorneys.

BIRBROWER, MONTALBANO, CONDON & FRANK v. SUPERIOR COURT

17 Cal.4th 119, 70 Cal.Rptr.2d 304, 949 P.2d 1 (1998).

[In 1992–93, Birbrower, a New York law firm, performed legal services for a California corporation, ESQ Business Services. This corporation was owned by the Sandhu family who had been Birbrower clients since 1986, largely for New York matters. ESQ had a software development and marketing contract dispute with Tandem, another California corporation. The contract, which apparently had been drafted by Birbrower, was governed by California law. Two Birbrower attorneys traveled several times to California to perform legal services, notably negotiating with Tandem representatives and preparing and filing a complaint for arbitration in San Francisco. After the ESQ–Tandem dispute was settled, Birbrower requested fees in excess of one million dollars based on a fee agreement. ESQ sued to set aside the agreement, claiming that Birbrower had engaged in the unauthorized practice of law. The issue went to the California Supreme Court. Six justices concurred in Justice Chin's opinion.]

[After the State Bar Act comprehensively regulated the practice of law in 1927,] no one but an active member of the State Bar may practice law for another person in California. The prohibition against unauthorized law practice is within the state's police power and is designed to ensure that those performing legal services do so competently.

* * *

No one may recover compensation for services as an attorney at law in this state unless [the person] was at the time the services were performed a member of the State Bar.

* * *

In our view, the practice of law "in California" entails sufficient contact with the California client to render the nature of the legal service a clear legal representation. In addition to a quantitative analysis, we must consider the nature of the unlicensed lawyer's activities in the state. Mere fortuitous or attenuated contacts will not sustain a finding that the unlicensed lawyer practiced law "in California." The primary inquiry is whether the unlicensed lawyer engaged in sufficient activities in the state, or created a continuing relationship with the California client that included legal duties and obligations.

Our definition does not necessarily depend on or require the unlicensed lawyer's physical presence in the state. * * * [O]ne may practice law in the state in violation of [the State Bar Act] although not physically present here by advising a California client on California law in connection with a California legal dispute by telephone, fax, computer, or other modern technological means.

* * *

Birbrower argues that because out-of-state attorneys have been licensed to practice in other jurisdictions, they have already demonstrated sufficient competence to protect California clients. But Birbrower's argument overlooks the obvious fact that other states' laws may differ substantially from California law. Competence in one jurisdiction does not necessarily guarantee competence in another.

* * *

We conclude that Birbrower violated [the State Bar Act] by practicing law in California. To the extent the fee agreement allows payment for those illegal local services, it is void, and Birbrower is not entitled to recover fees under the agreement for those services. The fee agreement is enforceable, however, to the extent it is possible to sever the portions of the consideration attributable to Birbrower's services illegally rendered in California from those attributable to Birbrower's New York services.

[Justice Kennard's dissent argued that services connected with an arbitration should not be considered to be legal services that constituted the unauthorized practice of law. Shortly after *Birbrower* was decided, the California legislature amended its Rules of Court to permit out-of-state lawyers to appear in a private arbitration when authorized by the arbitration tribunal.]

Notes and Questions

1. Because Birbrower involved a large New York law firm acting at its client's request in a significant transaction in California, and because the California Supreme Court's views are often influential, the judgment has attracted widespread attention in US law firms. Several other state and federal courts have reached similar conclusions. Thus, in Spivak v. Sachs, 16 N.Y.2d 163, 263 N.Y.S.2d 953, 211 N.E.2d 329 (N.Y. 1965), the New York Court of Appeals held that a California lawyer could not collect his fees for two weeks of work in New York, counseling a client on her divorce proceedings in Connecticut, even though the client expressly requested the lawyer to come to New York.

2. The recently approved American Law Institute's Restatement (Third) of the Law Governing Lawyers, § 3(3), Comment e (2000), criticizes *Birbrower* and *Spivak* as unduly restrictive, and urges that lawyers qualified in one state should be permitted to carry on temporary transborder legal practice in other states whenever the activities "arise out of or are otherwise reasonably relate[d] to the lawyer's practice" in his or her home state, especially when acting for a regular client of the lawyer, or when the issues mix home and host state law, or relate to federal law. A lawyer's appearance in litigation in other states is regulated by *pro hac vice* rules of the host state, which the Supreme Court held to be within the total discretion of the host state in Leis v. Flynt, 439 U.S. 438, 99 S.Ct. 698, 58 L.Ed.2d 717 (1979). For a comparative description of the EC and US rules on the temporary providing of legal services in other states, see R. Goebel, The Liberalization of Interstate Legal Practice in the European Union: Lessons For the United States? 34 Int'l Lawyer 307 (2000), urging a change in US state policies to follow the liberal approach in the Community. The American Bar Association currently has a study group examining the issues in multi-state legal practice.

NOTE ON THE CCBE CODE OF
CONDUCT FOR LAWYERS

Some professional rules for lawyers attempt to articulate ethical standards; some indicate a responsible mode of assisting courts and other instruments of justice; others attempt to protect client interests; others relate to the organization of the profession and protection of its reputation; and still other rules simply reflect traditional modes of practicing law in a Member State. Moreover, in some States, rules of professional conduct for lawyers were developed years ago and have only recently begun to be seriously reexamined in light of modern practice. Some national rules might be appropriate to certain types of practice but not others. Also, some national rules, while perfectly appropriate for domestic legal practice, may not be sufficiently founded on "general good" considerations to represent justifiable limitations on cross-border legal practice.

Article 4 of the Lawyers' Services Directive does not conclusively determine the set of rules that should prevail in the event of conflict between host and home State rules of professional conduct. There is certainly a significant risk of such conflicts. For example, Member State professional rules for lawyers vary considerably on a wide variety of subjects: the permissibility of contingent fees; the application of fixed fee rates to various services; the right to sue for fees; the handling of client funds; the necessity for professional insurance and its scope; the permissibility of advertising or other public relations; the extent of the attorney-client privilege or professional secrecy; and the nature and extent of conflict of interest rules.

In an effort to reduce the risk of conflicts, the Council of Bars and Law Societies (CCBE) (comprised of all those in Member States and some neighboring ones) adopted on October 28, 1988 a Code of Conduct for Lawyers in the European Community. The Code was rapidly adopted by Member State authorities in all Community States. A slightly amended version of November 1998 is presently in the course of adoption.

The Code of Conduct is intended to set core principles for certain professional and ethical rules in a cross-border practice context, on matters such as confidential communications, conflicts of interest, respect for courts, protection of client funds, and professional insurance. In some instances, the Code may influence national bar associations to introduce similar rules for domestic national practice where they do not already exist. For example, several Community States did not in 1988 have rules requiring the segregation of clients' funds or malpractice insurance.

In some cases, the Code does not try to harmonize concepts, but rather establishes a rule for the resolution of conflicts. Thus, it would require the service-providing lawyer to follow the host State rules on advertising, on contingent fees, and on the incompatibility of a lawyer's functioning in certain roles, such as membership on a corporation's board of directors. Home State rules are to be followed with respect to fee arrangements other than contingent fees.

The Code of Conduct is cast in the form of relatively short and simple principles. This means that the Code is easy to understand, which has obvious merit, but it also means that the Code is only a starting point, because many issues of potential conflict between home and host rules are only partially resolved, or not resolved at all. Nonetheless, the Code of Conduct is quite valuable in promoting the resolution of some significant differences between national rules of professional conduct. For the text of the 1988 Code and an analysis by a CCBE expert, see J. Toulmin, A Worldwide Common Code of Professional Conduct?, 15 Ford. Int'l L.J. 673 (1991–1992).

Notes and Questions

1. How to determine the applicable rule in case of conflict between rules of conduct has also become a difficult issue in the US, because a substantial minority of states declined to adopt the 1983 ABA Model Rules on Professional Conduct and have either continued to adhere to the earlier ABA Code of Professional Responsibility or combined elements of the Rules and Code. This has produced some serious differences, for example, on the extent of protection of client confidences, and on whether there exists a right, and possibly even a duty, to disclose the ongoing illegal or fraudulent conduct of a client. See ABA Committee on Counsel Responsibility, Risks of Violation of Rules of Professional Responsibility by Reason of the Increased Disparity Among the States, 45 Bus.Law. 1229 (1990).

2. In the article cited in the text, John Toulmin suggests that the Code of Conduct might serve as the basis for common rules governing the provision of services by US and Community lawyers in one another's jurisdiction. Does this seem a sensible idea? Even if it should not prove possible to reach agreement on a mutually acceptable text, the process of comparing rules should prove illuminating.

3. In October 1992, Director General Ehlermann of the Directorate General for Competition announced that professional rules would be examined to see if they violated Article 81 (ex 85), particularly rules governing fees or restricting advertising. On February 1, 1995 the Commission required the Spanish association of industrial property agents to revoke rules setting minimum fees for various services. Most Member State rules of conduct for lawyers forbid or narrowly restrict advertising and forbid contingency fees, and some set minimum fees for prescribed services. These rules may now come under examination and perhaps be challenged. However, in Criminal proceedings against Arduino, Case C–35/99, Advocate General Leger provided an opinion on July 10, 2001 to the effect that a professional association of lawyers could set maximum and minimum fees for specified legal services, provided that the state authorities exercised effective control over the fee scales to ensure that they pursue a legitimate public interest. The Court's judgment is bound to prove an important precedent.

4. M. Daly & R. Goebel, eds., Rights, Liability and Ethics in International Legal Practice (Transnational Juris 1995) is a comprehensive comparative study. For a comparison of the CCBE Code of Conduct with US ethical rules, see L. Terry, Introduction to the EC's Legal Ethics Code, 7 Georgetown J. Legal Ethics 1 (1993). See also J. van den Wall Bake & Y. Comtois, Restrictive Publicity Rules for Lawyers: Towards a "Community" Definition of the "Standing of the Profession", 18 Eur. L. Rev. 109 (1993).

C. LAWYERS' RIGHT OF ESTABLISHMENT

1. LIBERAL CASE LAW ON THE APPLICATION OF PRACTICE RIGHTS

REYNERS v. BELGIUM

Case 2/74, [1974] ECR 631.

[When Reyners, a Dutch national, sought to become a Belgian *avocat* in the circumstances described on page 714, the second question referred to the Court of Justice was whether Belgium could restrict the status of *avocat* to its nationals on the grounds that *avocats* exercise "official authority" under Article 45 (ex 55).]

35 The Luxembourg Government and the [Belgian *avocat* association] consider that the whole profession of *avocat* is exonerated from the rules in the Treaty on the right of establishment by the fact that it is connected organically with the functioning of the public service of the administration of justice.

36 This situation (it is argued) results both from the legal organization of the Bar, involving a set of strict conditions for admission and discipline, and from the functions performed by the *avocat* in the context of judicial procedure where his participation is largely obligatory.

37 These activities, which make the advocate an indispensable auxiliary of the administration of justice, form a coherent whole, the parts of which cannot be separated.

38 The plaintiff in the main action, for his part, contends that at most only certain activities of the profession of *avocat* are connected with the exercise of official authority and that they alone therefore come within the exception created by Article [45] to the principle of free establishment.

* * *

43 Having regard to the fundamental character of freedom of establishment and the rule on equal treatment with nationals in the system of the Treaty, the exceptions allowed by the first paragraph of Article [45] cannot be given a scope which would exceed the objective for which this exemption clause was inserted.

* * *

45 This need is fully satisfied when the exclusion of nationals is limited to those activities which, taken on their own, constitute a direct and specific connexion with the exercise of official authority.

46 An extension of the exception allowed by Article [45] to a whole profession would be possible only in cases where such activities were linked with that profession in such a way that freedom of establishment would result in imposing on the Member State concerned the obligation to allow the exercise, even occasionally, by non-nationals of functions appertaining to official authority.

47   This extension is on the other hand not possible when, within the framework of an independent profession, the activities connected with the exercise of official authority are separable from the professional activity in question taken as a whole.

48   In the absence of any directive issued under Article [47, ex 57] for the purpose of harmonizing the national provisions relating * * * to professions such as that of *avocat,* the practice of such professions remains governed by the law of the various Member States.

* * *

50   This consideration must however take into account the Community character of the limits imposed by Article [45] on the exceptions permitted to the principle of freedom of establishment in order to avoid the effectiveness of the Treaty being defeated by unilateral provisions of Member States.

* * *

52   The most typical activities of the profession of *avocat,* in particular, such as consultation and legal assistance and also representation and the defence of parties in court, even when the intervention or assistance of the *avocat* is compulsory or is a legal monopoly, cannot be considered as connected with the exercise of official authority.

53   The exercise of these activities leaves the discretion of judicial authority and the free exercise of judicial power intact.

54   [Therefore,] the exception to freedom of establishment provided for by the first paragraph of Article [45] must be restricted to those of the activities referred to in Article [43, ex 52] which in themselves involve a direct and specific connexion with the exercise of official authority.

THIEFFRY v. CONSEIL DE L'ORDRE DES AVOCATS À LA COUR DE PARIS

Case 71/76, [1977] ECR 765.

[Thieffry, a Belgian *avocat,* practiced in Brussels from 1956–1969, and then moved to Paris. In 1974, the University of Paris recognized Thieffry's Belgian law degree as the equivalent of a French law degree, apparently for the purpose of establishing his capacity to take the French bar examination (the CAPA). He then successfully passed the French bar examination in 1975. Based on the University of Paris recognition of equivalency and his passage of the bar examination, Thieffry applied to the Paris bar council for admission as *avocat.* The council refused, on the ground that he had not received any French law degree, as required by the French law regulating the profession of *avocat.* On appeal, the Paris Court of Appeal asked the Court to rule on whether France could require applicants for the status of *avocat* to possess a French law degree.]

15   [F]reedom of establishment, subject to observance of professional rules justified by the general good, is one of the objectives of the Treaty.

16   In so far as Community law makes no special provision, these objectives may be attained by measures enacted by the Member States, which under

Article [10, ex 5] of the Treaty are bound to take "all appropriate measures, whether general or particular, to ensure fulfilment of the obligations arising out of this Treaty or resulting from action taken by the institutions of the Community", and to abstain "from any measure which could jeopardize the attainment of the objectives of this Treaty."

17   Consequently, if the freedom of establishment provided for by Article [43, ex 52] can be ensured in a Member State either under the provisions of the laws and regulations in force, or by virtue of the practices of the public service or of professional bodies, a person subject to Community law cannot be denied the practical benefit of that freedom solely by virtue of the fact that, for a particular profession, the directives provided for by Article [47, ex 57] of the Treaty have not yet been adopted.

18   [Therefore,]it is incumbent upon the competent public authorities—including legally recognized professional bodies—to ensure that such practice or legislation is applied in accordance with the objective defined by the provisions of the Treaty relating to freedom of establishment.

19   In particular, there is an unjustified restriction on that freedom where * * * admission to a particular profession is refused to a person covered by the Treaty who holds a diploma which has been recognized as an equivalent qualification by the competent authority of the country of establishment and who furthermore has fulfilled the specific conditions regarding professional training in force in that country, solely by reason of the fact that the person concerned does not possess the national diploma * * *.

* * *

27   In these circumstances, * * * the act of demanding the national diploma prescribed by the legislation of the country of establishment constitutes, even in the absence of the directives provided for in Article [47], a restriction incompatible with the freedom of establishment guaranteed by Article [43] of the Treaty.

ORDRE DES AVOCATS AU BARREAU DE PARIS v. KLOPP

Case 107/83, [1984] ECR 2971.

[Klopp, a German *Rechtsanwalt* practicing in Düsseldorf, obtained a doctorate from the University of Paris in 1969. He passed the French bar examination in 1980 and sought to open a second law office in Paris, intending to reside and practice in both Düsseldorf and Paris. Under Paris bar rules established in accordance with French legislation, an *avocat* in Paris may not have an office outside of the territorial jurisdiction of the French court for the Paris region. The issue presented by the French Supreme Court to the Court of Justice was whether this longstanding French rule could prevail over the right of establishment.]

12   The Paris Bar Council and the French Government maintain that Article [43, ex 52] of the Treaty makes access and exercise of freedom of establishment depend on the conditions laid down by the Member State of establishment. [The French rules] are applicable without distinction to

French nationals and those of other Member States. Those provisions provide that an *avocat* may establish chambers in one place only.

* * *

16   The Paris Bar Council and the French Government [argue that the] rule that an *avocat* may have his chambers in one place only is based on the need for *avocats* to genuinely practice before a court in order to ensure their availability to both the court and their clients. It should be respected as being a rule pertaining to the administration of justice and to professional ethics, objectively necessary and consistent with the public interest.

17   It should be emphasized that under the second paragraph of Article [43] freedom of establishment includes access to and the pursuit of the activities of self-employed persons "under the conditions laid down for its own nationals by the law of the country where such establishment is effected." It follows from that provision and its context that in the absence of specific Community rules in the matter each Member State is free to regulate the exercise of the legal profession in its territory.

18   Nevertheless that rule does not mean that the legislation of a Member State may require a lawyer to have only one establishment throughout the Community territory. Such a restrictive interpretation would mean that a lawyer once established in a particular Member State would be able to enjoy the freedom of the Treaty to establish himself in another Member State only at the price of abandoning the establishment he already had.

19   That freedom of establishment is not confined to the right to create a single establishment within the Community is confirmed by the very words of Article [43] of the Treaty, according to which the progressive abolition of the restrictions on freedom of establishment applies to restrictions on the setting up of agencies, branches or subsidiaries by nationals of any Member State established in the territory of another Member State. That rule must be regarded as a specific statement of a general principle, applicable equally to the liberal professions, according to which the right of establishment includes freedom to set up and maintain, subject to observance of the professional rules of conduct, more than one place of work within the Community.

20   In view of the special nature of the legal profession, however, the second Member State must have the right, in the interests of the due administration of justice, to require that lawyers enrolled at a Bar in its territory should practise in such a way as to maintain sufficient contact with their clients and the judicial authorities and abide by the rules of the profession. Nevertheless such requirements must not prevent the nationals of other Member States from exercising properly the right of establishment guaranteed them by the Treaty.

21   In that respect * * * modern methods of transport and telecommunications facilitate proper contact with clients and the judicial authorities. Similarly, the existence of a second set of chambers in another Member State does not prevent the application of the rules of ethics in the host Member State.

22   [Therefore,]even in the absence of any directive coordinating national provisions governing access to the exercise of the legal profession, Article

[43 prevents] a Member State from denying, on the basis of the national legislation and the rules of professional conduct which are in force in that State, to a national of another Member State the right to enter and to exercise the legal profession solely on the ground that he maintains chambers simultaneously in another Member State.

Notes and Questions

1. Although in retrospect the Court of Justice's conclusion in *Reyners* that lawyers do not exercise "official authority" seems fairly evident, it was by no means an obvious result at the time. Incidentally, Advocate General Mayras, who urged that result, considered that judges and lawyers employed by the state could be described as exercising "official authority." Would you agree? In *Reyners'* US parallel, Application of Griffiths, 413 U.S. 717, 93 S.Ct. 2851, 37 L.Ed.2d 910 (1973), the US Supreme Court also rejected an argument that lawyers must be citizens because they serve as "officers of the court." Justice Powell's majority opinion held that "a lawyer is engaged in a private profession," and does not have a role similar to that of a judge, marshall or court clerk. Chief Justice Burger's dissent argued that the "concept of a lawyer as an officer of the court" is a traditional feature of the common law.

2. Both in *Thieffry* and *Klopp,* the Court expanded the scope of the right of establishment by invalidating rules that were not discriminatory in any way. Do you think the Court's use of Article 10 (ex 5) to achieve this result represents sound policy? *Klopp* also states an important principle: a Member State's professional rules will be allowed to limit an establishment right only if they are objectively justified by the "general good." This is the same principle that was applied to services in *van Binsbergen, Webb* and the *German insurance* case in the preceding chapter.

3. *Thieffry* was followed in Patrick v. Ministre des Affaires Culturelles, Case 11/77, [1977] ECR 1199, which required France to allow a British architect to qualify as an architect in France, because a French Culture Ministry decree treated his UK architect certificate as equivalent to one in France.

4. An analysis of the Community rules on lawyers' establishment up to *Klopp* is in R. Goebel, Lawyers in the European Community: Progress Towards Community–Wide Rights of Practice, 15 Fordham Int'l L.J. 556 (1991–92).

GEBHARD v. MILAN BAR COUNCIL

[For the description of facts, see page 724. The Court concluded its judgment by setting forth the rules governing the practice of law by a lawyer qualified in one Member State who has a permanent establishment in another Member State.]

33   Under the terms of the second paragraph of Article [43, ex 52], freedom of establishment is to be exercised under the conditions laid down for its own nationals by the law of the country where establishment is effected.

34   In the event that the specific activities in question are not subject to any rules in the host State, so that a national of that Member State does not have to have any specific qualification in order to pursue them, a national of any other Member State is entitled to establish himself on the territory of the first State and pursue those activities there.

35 However, the taking-up and pursuit of certain self-employed activities may be conditional on complying with certain provisions laid down by law, regulation or administrative action justified by the general good, such as rules relating to organization, qualifications, professional ethics, supervision and liability [citing *Thieffry*]. Such provisions may stipulate in particular that pursuit of a particular activity is restricted to holders of a diploma, certificate or other evidence of formal qualifications, to persons belonging to a professional body or to persons subject to particular rules or supervision, as the case may be. They may also lay down the conditions for the use of professional titles, such as *avvocato*.

36 Where the taking-up or pursuit of a specific activity is subject to such conditions in the host Member State, a national of another Member State intending to pursue that activity must in principle comply with them. It is for this reason that Article [47, ex 57] provides that the Council is to issue directives, such as Directive 89/48, for the mutual recognition of diplomas, certificates and other evidence of formal qualifications * * * .

37 It follows, however, from the Court's case-law that national measures liable to hinder or make less attractive the exercise of fundamental freedoms guaranteed by the Treaty must fulfil four conditions: they must be applied in a non-discriminatory manner; they must be justified by imperative requirements in the general interest; they must be suitable for securing the attainment of the objective which they pursue; and they must not go beyond what is necessary in order to attain it [citing *Kraus,* supra].

38 Likewise, in applying their national provisions, Member States may not ignore the knowledge and qualifications already acquired by the person concerned in another Member State [citing *Vlassopoulou, supra*]. Consequently, they must take account of the equivalence of diplomas and, if necessary, proceed to a comparison of the knowledge and qualifications required by their national rules and those of the person concerned.

Notes and Questions

1. The principal importance of the *Gebhard* judgment lies in ¶ 37's express absorption of the *Cassis de Dijon* rule of reason doctrine into the establishment context. This doctrinal approach was taken with regard to services in the *German insurance* judgment in the preceding chapter, and had been suggested in less clear fashion in the establishment context, notably in *Kraus*. More recent commercial establishment cases cite *Gebhard* and follow the same line—see the *Italian Stockbroker rules* judgment, *infra,* page 1190. How helpful is it to have essentially the same doctrinal standards applied to the free movement of goods, the providing of trans-border services, and the right of establishment?

2. Consider how the Italian National Bar Council should apply the Court's guidelines. May Gebhard be forbidden to use the title "avvocato"? (Could the Paris bar forbid a Belgian avocat established in Paris from using the title, "avocat"?) Does Gebhard have the right to practice law in some fashion permanently in Milan? For example, can he assist Italian clients in operations in Germany and Austria or provide general advice to any clients on German, Community or international law? Can he provide advice on Italian law or draft Italian commercial instruments? Can he, either regularly or occasionally, appear in an Italian court proceeding? After *Gebhard*, the answers were subject to considerable debate, with lawyers from different countries tending to adopt

radically different views. For a helpful appraisal, see the casenote by J. Lonbay, 33 Common Mkt. L. Rev. 1073 (1996).

3. What about Gebhard's application to become an *avvocato* by means of the Diploma Recognition Directive? Should this be fairly easy? What is the relevance of ¶ 38?

2. THE DIRECTIVE ON THE ESTABLISHMENT OF LAWYERS

Although the Court's liberal case law on a lawyer's right of establishment, combined with the practical impact of the Diploma Recognition Directive, greatly facilitated the ability of lawyers, especially young lawyers, to move to other Member States and engage in practice there, significant issues remained open, even after *Gebhard*. Moreover, no Court judgment has expressly addressed the ability of law firms to open branches in other States (although this appears to be possible as an application of *Klopp*).

By the mid–1990's, many law firms in Member States (especially UK solicitor firms) had established branch offices in other States, usually staffed in part by lawyers using their home State titles and in part by host State lawyers. The UK itself has customarily permitted foreign lawyers and law firms (including US lawyers and law firms) to register with the solicitors' society and practice in their home State professional capacity, using their home State title. Germany's 1989 legal profession rules expressly permitted this, although lawyers from other Member States were only permitted to practice their home State law, Community law and international law; and several other Member States permitted or tolerated such practice to some extent. On the other hand, France's 1990 law merging the professions of *avocat* and *conseil juridique* (legal advisor) appeared to forbid lawyers from other Member States to practice unless they become French *avocats*.

Throughout the 1980's, the Council of Bars and Law Societies of the European Community (the CCBE), which had prepared the Code of Conduct discussed above, worked to elaborate a draft directive on the right of establishment for lawyers. See H. Weil, The Proposal for a Directive on the Right of Establishment for Lawyers in the European Community, 15 Ford. Int'l L.J. 699 (1991–1992). The final 1992 version of the CCBE's proposal for a directive resembled in many respects the rules introduced in 1974 by the New York Court of Appeals to enable qualified foreign lawyers to practice in New York as foreign legal consultants. N.Y.Ct.App.R. Part 520.

In December 1994, the Commission proposed a directive to facilitate a lawyer's right of establishment. Although inspired in large measure by the CCBE's final version, the Commission proposal contained many significant differences. In particular, the initial Commission text would have limited a lawyer's right to practice in a host State under the home State title to a period of five years, after which in principle the lawyer would have to be integrated into the host State legal profession, although in an easier fashion than the system provided for in the Diploma Recognition Directive. This approach was sharply criticized by the bar associations of Germany, the UK and a majority of States, while being defended by those of France and Luxembourg. After the Parliament recommended the deletion of the compulsory integration provision and proposed other amendments, the Commission revised its initial text.

In 1998, Directive 98/5 was finally adopted, O.J.L. 77/36 (Mar. 14, 1998) (see the Selected Documents). In its fifth recital the directive notes that a permanent right of establishment not only would benefit lawyers, but also their clients, in view of the increasing volume of trans-border transactions engendered by the internal market. The seventh recital declares that national professional rules need be modified only if necessary to achieve the directive's provisions, not otherwise.

Article 1 states that a lawyer (defined by the same list of professions as that figuring in the Lawyers' Services Directive) shall have the right of permanent practice, either self-employed or as an employee, in a host State. However, article 2 prescribes that the established lawyer must use his or her home State title, and article 4 notes that the host State may require that the home State title be clearly distinguished from the host State title if necessary for consumer protection. Further, article 3 requires that the established lawyer be inscribed on a special list in the host State.

Under article 5, the established lawyer will have broad practice rights, including the capacity to give opinions or provide services concerning the home State laws, Community or international law, and the laws of the host State. However, the host State may limit any court appearance to the same degree as is the case in the Lawyers Services Directive, and the host State may also forbid established lawyers from handling real estate title transfers or carrying out inheritance and estate law practice. Moreover, article 6 submits the established lawyer to the host State professional rules for practice on its territory, and article 7 provides for disciplinary proceedings under the host State rules, although with some cooperation with the home State authorities.

An important further express right in article 11 enables practice in association, by partnership or any other legal form, to the same degree that this is permitted to host State lawyers. Law firms may have branches in host States. Lawyers from any Community State may be associated with those from any other State or States.

Finally, a somewhat complex article 10 enables the established lawyer to become integrated into the host State legal profession in an easier fashion than through the system of the Diploma Recognition Directive, after an "effective and regular" practice of host State law for three years. However, the integrated lawyer may continue to use his or her home State title as well as that of the host State.

The liberal provisions of the directive should facilitate enormously trans-border practice within the Community by individual lawyers and multinational law firms. It may be that a further attempt will be made to facilitate practice by US lawyers in the Community, and by Community lawyers in the US, either by informal bar arrangements (such as presently exist between the Brussels bar and the ABA), or by an accord within the context of the Transatlantic Agenda, discussed in Chapter 29C. US and other non-Community lawyers and law firms have no claim to establishment rights in the Community under Article 43 or the Diploma Recognition Directive (except in the case of dual nationals, who qualify as a lawyer in the Community State whose nationality they possess). Fortunately, at the present time most Member States permit non-Community lawyers to conduct most types of practice in their home State professional capacity, using the home State title, although sometimes only on a basis of reciprocity. The WTO is currently attempting to liberalize national rules governing accountants and has also begun initial consideration of liberalization of legal practice rights.

On a comparative note, in August 1993, the American Bar Association approved Model Rules for Legal Consultants. The following November, the New York Court of Appeals made minor changes in its rules to follow this Model. Over twenty US states and the District of Columbia now have some form of legal consultant rule. An annex to NAFTA calls for Canada, Mexico and the US to facilitate legal practice under legal consultant rules.

LUXEMBOURG v. PARLIAMENT AND COUNCIL
(Lawyers' establishment directive)
Case C–168/98, [2000] ECR ___ (Nov. 7, 2000).

[Luxembourg, which had voted against the Lawyers' Establishment Directive, challenged its validity, claiming that it violated Treaty rights, and harmed the interests of consumers and the sound administration of justice. Luxembourg also contended that the reasons given for the directive were not sufficient under Article 253 (ex Article 190).]

17   The Grand Duchy of Luxembourg argues that * * * the right of establishment may not be granted in breach of overriding principles governing the self-employed professions, common to the laws of the various Member States.

18   [Luxembourg further] claims that, while harmonization may justify dispensing with any assessment of knowledge of international law, Community law and the law of the Member State of origin, no such dispensation can be contemplated as regards the law of the host Member State. The knowledge to be acquired in the field of national law, unlike the knowledge imparted in other training contexts, is not identical or even broadly the same from one Member State to another.

20   In [Luxembourg's view,] by abolishing all requirement of prior training in the law of the host Member State and by permitting migrant lawyers to practice that law, Directive 98/5 unjustifiably discriminates between nationals and migrants * * * contrary to Article [43, ex 52] of the Treaty, which does not authorize the Community legislature to abolish a requirement of prior training in a directive which does not purport to harmonize training conditions.

* * *

22   The Parliament and the Council, supported by [the Netherlands, Spain and the UK] ,deny the existence of any reverse discrimination. They submit that lawyers practicing under their home-country professional title and lawyers practicing under the professional title of the host Member State are in different situations, the first being subject to several restrictions on the pursuit of their activity. In any event, it is no part of the function of Article [43, ex 52] of the Treaty to prescribe limits on the process of liberalizing access to self-employed activity.

[The Court then stated its conclusions.]

23   [T]he prohibition of discrimination laid down in Article [43] of the Treaty is only the specific expression of the general principle of equality which * * * requires that comparable situations should not be treated differently unless such difference in treatment is objectively justified.

24   In this case, the Community legislature has not infringed that principle, since the situation of a migrant lawyer practicing under his home-country title and the situation of a lawyer practicing under the professional title of the host Member State are not comparable.

25   Whereas the latter may undertake all the activities open or reserved to the profession of lawyer by the host Member State, the former may be forbidden to pursue certain activities and, with regard to the representation or defence of clients in legal proceedings, may be subject to certain obligations.

29   The complaint of discrimination against lawyers practicing under the professional title of the host Member State is therefore unfounded.

30   [Luxembourg further challenges] the validity of Directive 98/5 in the interests of consumers and in the interest of the proper administration of justice. * * * By abolishing all requirement of training in the law of the host Member State, Directive 98/5 prejudices the public interest, in particular the protection of consumers, pursued by the various Member States in requiring, for access to and practice of the profession of lawyer, a legally prescribed qualification. In this connection, [Luxembourg] argues that to accept that training may be acquired in practice necessarily implies that practice precedes training. * * *

31   The Parliament and Council * * * submit that Directive 98/5 takes into account overriding public interest grounds, in particular those of consumer protection, in Articles 4, 5, 6 and 7. The Parliament and the United Kingdom point out that, under the rules of professional conduct, lawyers are in any event obliged not to handle cases when they know or ought to know that those cases fall outside their competence and that any breach of that rule constitutes a disciplinary offence.

32   In that regard, the Court observes that * * * the Community legislature is to have regard to the public interest pursued by the various Member States and to adopt a level of protection for that interest which seems acceptable in the Community. It enjoys a measure of discretion for the purposes of its assessment of the acceptable level of protection.

33   In this instance it is clear that several of the provisions of Directive 98/5 lay down rules intended to protect consumers and to ensure the proper administration of justice.

34   Thus, Article 4 provides that a lawyer practicing under his home-country professional title is required to do so under that title, so that consumers are informed that the professional to whom they entrust the defense of their interests has not obtained his qualification in the host Member State and that his initial training did not necessarily cover the host Member State's national law.

35   [Moreover,] Article 5(2) and (3) authorize the host Member State, subject to certain conditions, to forbid migrant lawyers to undertake certain

activities and to impose certain obligations on them in connection with the representation or defense of a client in legal proceedings.

36   Article 6(1) makes a lawyer practicing under his home-country professional title subject not only to the rules of professional conduct applicable in his home Member State but also to the same rules of professional conduct as lawyers practicing under the professional title of the host Member State in respect of all the activities which he pursues in its territory.

42   Furthermore, it should be noted that, quite apart from the applicable rules of professional liability, the rules of professional conduct applicable to lawyers generally entail, like Article 3.1.3 of the Code of Professional Conduct adopted by the Council of the Bars and Law Societies of the European Union (CCBE), an obligation, breach of which may incur disciplinary sanctions, not to handle matters which the professionals concerned know or ought to know they are not competent to handle.

43   It would therefore seem that the Community legislature, with a view to making it easier for a particular class of migrant lawyers to exercise the fundamental freedom of establishment, has chosen * * * a plan of action combining consumer information, restrictions on the extent to which or the detailed rules under which certain activities of the profession may be practiced, a number of applicable rules of professional conduct, compulsory insurance, as well as a system of discipline involving both the competent authorities of the home Member State and the host State. The legislature has not abolished the requirement that the lawyer concerned should know the national law applicable in the cases he handles, but has simply released him from the obligation to prove that knowledge in advance. It has thus allowed, in some circumstances, gradual assimilation of knowledge through practice, that assimilation being made easier by experience of other laws gained in the home Member State. It was also able to take account of the dissuasive effect of the system of discipline and the rules of professional liability.

* * *

[The Court then turned to Luxembourg's contention that the directive did not contain adequate reasons to justify its provisions.]

62   [T]he Court has consistently held that the scope of the obligation to state reasons depends on the nature of the measure in question and that, in the case of measures of general application, the statement of reasons may be confined to indicating the general situation which led to its adoption, on the one hand, and the general objectives which it is intended to achieve, on the other. If the contested measure clearly discloses the essential objective pursued by the institution, it would be excessive to require a specific statement of reasons for the various technical choices made.

63   In the present case, Directive 98/5 contains a coherent and sufficient description of the general situation which led to its adoption:

— the abolition, as between Member States, of obstacles to freedom of movement for persons and services constitutes one of the objectives of the Community, that freedom of movement involving *inter alia* the possibility for nationals of the Member States of practicing a profession, whether in a self-employed or a salaried capacity, in a Member State other than that in which they obtained their professional qualifications (first recital);

* * *

— only a few Member States already permit in their territory the pursuit of activities of lawyers, otherwise than by way of provision of services, by lawyers from other Member States practicing under their home-country professional titles; however, in Member States where this possibility exists, the practical details differ considerably, and such a diversity of situations leading to inequalities and distortions in competition between lawyers from the Member States and constituting an obstacle to freedom of movement (sixth recital).

64   Directive 98/5 also contains a statement of the general objectives which it proposes to attain:

— fully qualified lawyers who do not become quickly integrated into the profession in the host Member State, *inter alia* by passing an aptitude test as provided for in Directive 89/48 [the Diploma Recognition Directive], should be able to achieve such integration after a certain period of professional practice in the host Member State under their home-country professional titles or else continue to practice under their home-country professional titles (third recital);

— action along these lines at Community level is intended, on the one hand, to provide lawyers with an easier means whereby they can integrate into the profession in a host Member State compared with the general recognition system and, on the other, to meet the needs of consumers of legal services carrying out cross-border transactions (fifth recital);

— it also seeks to resolve the problems linked to distortion of competition and obstacles to freedom of movement caused by great differences in the practical details attaching to the practice of the profession under the home-country professional title in the Member States which already permit such practice (sixth recital);

— Directive 98/5 seeks to ensure that consumers are properly informed by providing that lawyers who are not integrated into the profession in the host Member State are required to practice in that State under their home-country professional titles (ninth recital).

65   Thus, it is clear that, in its adoption of a measure of general application, the Community legislature has satisfied the obligation to state reasons laid down in Article [253, ex 190] of the Treaty.

Notes and Questions

1. Luxembourg's principal argument was that the directive does not adequately protect clients against foreign lawyers who are insufficiently trained in host State substantive and procedural law. The Netherlands, Spain and the UK supported the Parliament, Council and Commission in contending that the directive contained adequate safeguards. What forms of protection for clients are contained in the directive? Do you consider them adequate? Overall, do you consider that the directive's goal of achieving a Community-wide integrated legal practice outweighs any risks to consumers? Certainly the branches of multination-

al law firms are apt to be serving only relatively sophisticated clients, but is that also true of individual practitioners?

2.   Luxembourg also argued reverse discrimination, i.e., that its lawyers had to prove their competence in host State law, while lawyers from other Member States could, in effect, learn Luxembourg law in the course of their practice. What was the Court's response? What is your view on the issue?

3.   In the US, lawyers who desire to practice on a permanent basis in a state other than that of their initial qualification must either pass the host state bar examination or be admitted on motion. However, only about half the states (including New York, but not California or Florida) permit admission on motion, and these states usually restrict it: a) to lawyers who have practiced for five years in their home state, and b) to lawyers from states that also admit on motion (i.e., they require reciprocal treatment). The restrictive state rules are usually justified by claims that they are necessary for consumer protection and to ensure that courts will have properly qualified litigating lawyers. However, some leading commentators doubt the validity of these justifications. Professor Wolfram has trenchantly observed that there is a "distinct possibility that [local practice] rules are motivated by the local bar's desire to be protected against out-of-state competition." C. Wolfram, Modern Legal Ethics 865 (1986). Do you think that the Lawyers' Establishment Directive could, or should, serve as a model for liberalization of US state rules?

Chapter 19

INDUSTRIAL AND COMMERCIAL
PROPERTY RIGHTS

The 1985 White Paper on Completing the Internal Market listed the field of industrial and commercial property rights as one of the prime areas for Community legislative efforts. It was evident that the Community needed to achieve both harmonization of national rights and the creation of new types of rights in order to better achieve technological progress and commercial integration in the internal market. Moreover, as noted in Chapter 13A, the Treaty permitted industrial and commercial property rights to be used as an exception to free movement of goods. Without harmonization of national systems of such rights, they might lead to division of certain markets along national lines.

This chapter will first focus on the Court of Justice's doctrines concerning the nature and scope of industrial and commercial property rights, including the important rule that these rights can be "exhausted" when products protected by them are first placed on the market. We will then summarize the many important legislative measures adopted since the late 1980's in this field, concentrating on the harmonization produced by the 1989 Trademark Directive and the Community-wide trademark system achieved by the 1994 Trademark Regulation.

A natural first question is how to define the concept "industrial and commercial property rights." (Modern American authorities tend to prefer the generic title, intellectual property rights, but, for the sake of consistency, we shall use the Treaty terminology.)

The three traditional categories of such rights, recognized by all modern free-enterprise legal systems, are patents, trademarks and copyrights. Patent rights grant exclusive rights to inventors for the exploitation of their inventions for a period of years (usually 20). Trademark rights grant to the originators of marks exclusive rights for the exploitation of words or symbols in conjunction with specified products or services, usually in perpetuity. Copyright rights grant to authors or artists exclusive rights for the representation and reproduction of a written work, a theatrical or cinematographic production, a piece of music, an art object, and, more recently, software programs, for a long term of years (usually 50 or more). In each case, this legal monopoly exploitation right is granted as a reward for the benefit to society generally, and/or to industry and commerce, through the creation of the invention, mark, or written or artistic work.

Not surprisingly, Member States' legal systems initially had different approaches as to the precise definition of the rights, their acquisition, term, scope, administration, etc. Early Community endeavors to eliminate or reduce these differences through harmonization, or through the creation of Community-wide rights, met with little success.

Inevitably, the Court of Justice was called upon to interpret and apply the Treaty rules in this sector. There are several major issues in the interplay between national industrial and commercial property rights and the Community principle of free movement of goods. The first is the determination of those national rights which qualify for recognition under Article 30 (ex Article 36). The second issue is the demarcation of the field of application and level of protection of industrial and commercial property rights. Third is the issue of whether, and when, the exercise of these rights can be said to be "exhausted." A fourth issue is the level of the appropriate exploitation of these rights within the context of Community competition rules, a topic covered in Chapter 22, infra.

Note that the US has national legislation defining the nature and scope of patents, trademarks and copyrights, so that state rules do not, generally speaking, restrict the exploitation of these rights on the national marketplace. Hence there is no precise American analogue to the issues facing the Community.

A. DETERMINATION OF RIGHTS QUALIFYING UNDER ARTICLE 30

The absence of a Treaty definition of industrial and commercial property rights makes it difficult to decide whether a national right should qualify for Article 30 protection, particularly when the right is protected in only one Member State, or a few States, or when national recognition of the right is of recent origin. Confronted with this issue, the Court of Justice might have emphasized the fundamental importance of the principle of free movement of goods and accordingly declined to recognize a particular type of right as one qualifying for Article 30 protection unless the right is recognized in a majority, or at least in a substantial number of Member States. In fact, the Court did not take that approach, but rather has been quite deferential to each State's legal system in this regard.

That patents and trademarks, the quintessential industrial and commercial property rights, should qualify for the Article 30 exception was obvious. Copyright posed more of a problem, since some national systems classified it as an artistic or literary property right, rather than as an industrial or commercial property right. However, music copyright was implicitly recognized as qualifying under Article 30 (ex Article 36) in Deutsche Grammophon v. Metro, Case 78/70, [1971] ECR 487, and expressly recognized as so qualifying in Musik–Vertrieb v. GEMA, Cases 55 & 57/80, [1981] ECR 147. Whether to classify trade design rights as industrial and commercial property rights posed greater difficulty.

KEURKOOP v. NANCY KEAN GIFTS

Case 144/81, [1982] ECR 2853.

[The 1966 Uniform Benelux Law on Designs, in force in the Netherlands since 1975, grants exclusive rights to product designs. The exclusive right is given to the first person who files the design at the design register, rather than the creator of the design. Nancy Kean Gifts filed a design for a handbag. (The creator of the design was a US person not involved in the proceedings.) When Keurkoop imported handbags from Germany (in free circulation after their importation from Taiwan), which allegedly infringed the design right, Nancy Kean obtained an injunction against the marketing of the handbags. An appellate court referred questions under Article 234.]

14 [A]s the Court has already held as regards patent rights, trade marks and copyright, the protection of designs comes under the protection of industrial and commercial property within the meaning of Article [30] inasmuch as its aim is to define exclusive rights which are characteristic of that property.

15 [T]he Uniform Benelux Law [protects] the novel feature of a product serving a utility purpose,[provided that the product] has not been commonly known in the industrial or commercial circles concerned in the Benelux territory during the 50 years prior to the filing of the design. According to Article 3 the exclusive right to a design is acquired by the first person to file it without it being necessary to inquire whether that person is also the author of the design or a person entitled under him. The reason for the rule is to be found in the function of the right to the design in economic life and in a concern for simplicity and efficacy.* * *

16 [Accordingly, the Uniform Benelux Law on Designs] constitutes legislation for the protection of industrial and commercial property for the purposes of Article [30] of the Treaty.

* * *

21 The second question [is whether] the owner of an exclusive right to a design protected by the legislation of a Member State may rely on that legislation in order to oppose the importation of products, whose appearance is identical to the design which has been filed, from [another Member State where it was legally on the market].

22 [I]n principle the protection of industrial and commercial property established by Article [30] would be rendered meaningless if a person other than the owner of the right to the design in a Member State could be allowed to market in that State a product which is identical in appearance to the protected design. That observation loses none of its force in the particular case [where the imported product was legally marketed in another Member State].

CONSORZIO ITALIANO v. REGIE NATIONALE DES USINES RENAULT

Case 53/87, [1988] ECR 6039.

[The French automobile manufacturer, Renault, obtained in Italy design rights for spare parts, allegedly ornamental in character. An Italian trade association of producers of automotive spare parts, the Consorzio Italiano, sued to have Renault's design rights declared void, so that the Italian competing producers could market spare parts for sale in Italy or export sale within the Community. The Italian court referred questions concerning Article 30 and the Community competition rules.]

4   The national court considers that protective rights in respect of an ornamental design for the car bodywork parts are in conformity with Italian law. However, it considers that the exercise of the exclusive rights deriving therefrom appears, in this instance, to be contrary to the provisions of the Treaty.

5   It points out * * * that a return for the proprietor of the rights is already guaranteed by the exclusive rights in respect of the bodywork as a whole and that protection of separate bodywork components is therefore unjustified. It adds that Renault* * * enjoys a monopoly which enables it to eliminate competition from independent manufacturers of spare parts, and at the same time to continue to charge high prices.

6   [T]he national court [considers] that the protective rights vested in Renault may constitute a means of arbitrary discrimination or a disguised restriction on trade between Member States within the meaning of Article [30] of the Treaty, and that the monopoly thus enjoyed by Renault might possibly contravene [the competition provisions] of the Treaty.

* * *

10   [First,] as the Court held in Keurkoop v. Nancy Kean Gifts, with respect to the protection of designs and models, in the present state of Community law and in the absence of Community standardization or harmonization of laws the determination of the conditions and procedures under which such protection is granted is a matter for national rules. It is for the national legislature to determine which products qualify for protection, even if they form part of a unit already protected as such.

11   [T]he authority of a proprietor of a protective right in respect of an ornamental model to oppose the manufacture by third parties, for the purposes of sale on the internal market or export, of products incorporating the design or to prevent the import of such products manufactured without its consent in other Member States constitutes the substance of his exclusive right. To prevent the application of the national legislation in such circumstances would therefore be tantamount to challenging the very existence of that right.

12   [R]estrictions on imports or exports justified on grounds of the protection of industrial and commercial property are permissible provided that they do not constitute a means of arbitrary discrimination or a disguised restriction on trade between the Member States. * * * [I]n the light of the

documents before the Court * * * the exclusive right granted by the national legislation to the proprietors of protective rights in respect of ornamental models for car bodywork components may be enforced, without distinction, both against those persons who manufacture spare parts within national territory and against those who import them from other Member States, and such legislation is not intended to favour national products at the expense of products originating in other Member States.

13 Accordingly, * * * the rules on the free movement of goods do not preclude the application of national legislation under which a car manufacturer who holds protective rights in an ornamental design in respect of spare parts intended for cars of its manufacture is entitled to prohibit third parties from manufacturing parts covered by those rights for the purpose of sale on the domestic market or for exportation or to prevent the importation from other Member States of parts covered by those rights which have been manufactured there without his consent.

Notes and Questions

1. It is perhaps not surprising that the Court of Justice classified trade design rights as within industrial and commercial property, since Denmark, France, Germany, Italy, and the UK all protected trade designs, although some did so as a right analogous to patents, and others as a right analogous to copyright. Note, however, that the Court neither states a reason for its conclusion, nor offers any guidance as to when an alleged right should qualify as an industrial or commercial right under Article 30. Note also that the Benelux law reviewed in *Nancy Kean* does not protect the creator of the trade design, but rather the first person filing the design. Why should the Court of Justice give Community law protection to such a person when only some Member States do so, while others protect only the creator of the design? Do you think a State ought to have unfettered discretion to designate rights as industrial or commercial property rights, and to specify the persons entitled to acquire them, or that there should be some Community law minimum standard for this, just as there is for health and safety protection?

2. A trade design for an automobile spare part may be very valuable indeed, given the large market not only for completed automobiles but also for spare parts for repairs. Consorzio Italiano argued that gross sales of spare parts in the Community in 1984 equaled $30 billion. Since an automobile manufacturer already receives an economic return for the sale of the automobile, the national court in paragraphs 4–6 considered that the Italian law's creation of trade design protection for spare parts constituted a disproportionate use of Article 30. Are you satisfied with the Court of Justice's handling of this issue? Think about this question again after reading the exhaustion of rights cases in section D.

3. After years of debate, Directive 98/71 on the legal protection of designs, O.J. L 289/28 (Oct. 28, 1998), harmonizes national rules on the nature of design rights, their term of protection (from five to twenty-five years) and grounds for invalidity. Design rights are possible for jewelry, cars, furniture, consumer electronics, machinery, tools and many other products. The chief dispute during the drafting of the directive concerned the treatment of automotive spare parts. A Commission proposal to require car manufacturers to grant a compulsory license to spare parts producers for a "fair and reasonable remuneration" failed. The directive in recital 19 indicates that States will retain their present rules governing spare parts, which in many States permit car manufacturers to retain their

design right monopoly over spare parts. Would you have supported the proposal for a compulsory license, which would have enabled competition in the spare parts market, while still granting the car producer a royalty on the parts?

4. Omitted from the excerpt of the *Consorzio* judgment is discussion of an important competition law issue. The monopoly granted by a national industrial or commercial property law to the owner of the right is a classic example of a potential dominant position on a competitive marketplace. Article 82 (ex Article 86) of the Treaty does not forbid a dominant position as such, but it does forbid its abuse. Accordingly, an industrial or commercial property owner's legal monopoly right does not violate Article 82, but the exercise of such a right may be deemed an abuse of the dominant position, especially when the exercise is considered to go beyond the essence of the right. See the discussion of the limits placed by Community competition law on the exercise of industrial and commercial property rights in Chapter 22.

B.   DESIGNATIONS OF ORIGIN AND GENERIC PRODUCT NAMES

1.   DESIGNATIONS OF ORIGIN

Many European states have long protected references to the region in which certain products originate, commonly called designations or appellations of origin (e.g., Champagne or Cognac). These are not trademarks or trade names, because they do not identify a specific product, nor do they represent property rights as such. States protect designations of origin because they are deemed to serve a useful role in identifying products considered to possess special characteristics or higher quality.

Under Community law, the question immediately arises whether designations of origin may nonetheless be evaluated as sufficiently analogous to industrial and commercial product rights to warrant protection under Article 30. The favorable reference to appellations of origin in the Court of Justice's 1975 *Sekt and Weinbrand* judgement, *supra* page 480, suggested that they would so qualify. Only recently, however, has the question been unequivocally resolved.

Within the scope of the Common Agricultural Policy, the Council adopted Regulation 823/87 on quality wines produced in specified regions, O.J. L 84/59 (March 27, 1987), and later Regulation 2081/92 on designations of origin for agricultural products, O.J. L 208/1 (July 24, 1992). Both were intended to promote agricultural products and to provide clear and reliable information to consumers, while ensuring fair competition between producers. Article 2 of the 1992 Regulation limits designations of origin to the name of a region or place when the products concerned have characteristics "essentially or exclusively due to a particular geographical environment with its inherent natural and human factors" and the products are processed or manufactured in that geographic area. The Regulation sets up a system of Community registration (articles 5–7) and forbids the registration of generic names. The quality wine regulation's terms are essentially analogous, although setting more rigorous standards for verification of quality.

The two regulations provide a substantial degree of legal certainty to a field of great practical importance in the European market place. Not surprisingly, the Court of Justice has had occasion to interpret the regulations and fit them into the context of free movement of goods.

BELGIUM v. SPAIN

(Rioja wine)

Case C–388/95, [2000] ECR 23.

[Since 1970, Spain has had rules permitting wine to be granted a "controlled designation of origin," which not only sets the conditions for qualifying wine from a specified region, but also requires that the wine be bottled in wine cellars within that region. Wine from the Rioja region was so qualified in 1991. Spain considers the regional bottling obligation to be justified under the wine quality regulation, which permits States to supplement the regulation's rules by others, "taking into account fair and traditional practices." Belgium used Article 227 (ex Article 170) to sue Spain, contending that the bottling obligation prevented the export of wine in bulk for bottling in Belgium, a violation of Article 29 (ex Article 34). Belgium was supported by four other wine-importing States, while Spain was supported by Italy, Portugal and the Commission. The Court of Justice easily found that the regional bottling requirement represented a restriction on exports and then turned to the question of its justification.]

53   Community legislation displays a general tendency to enhance the quality of products within the framework of the common agricultural policy, in order to promote the reputation of those products, through *inter alia*, the use of designations of origin which enjoy special protection. That general tendency has become apparent in the quality wines sector * * *.

54   Designations of origin fall within the scope of industrial and commercial property rights. The applicable rules protect those entitled to use them against improper use of those designations by third parties seeking to profit from the reputation which they have acquired. They are intended to guarantee that the product bearing them comes from a specified geographical area and displays certain particular characteristics.

55   They may enjoy a high reputation amongst consumers and constitute for producers who fulfil the conditions for using them an essential means of attracting custom.

56   The reputation of designations of origin depends on their image in the minds of consumers. That image in turn depends essentially on particular characteristics and more generally on the quality of the product. It is on the latter, ultimately, that the product's reputation is based.

57   It must be observed that a quality wine is a very specific product, a fact not contested in relation to Rioja wine. Its particular qualities and characteristics, which result from a combination of natural and human factors, are linked to its geographical area of origin * * *.

58   The rules governing the Rioja [controlled designation of origin] are designed to uphold those qualities and characteristics. By ensuring that operators in the wine growing sector of the Rioja region * * * control bottling as well, they pursue the aim of better safeguarding the quality of the product and, consequently, the reputation of the designation * * *.

* * *

60   The Spanish Government, supported by the Commission, submits that * * * [t]ransport and bottling outside the region of production would put the quality of the wine at risk * * *.

61   * * * [I]t is undisputed that the bottling of wine is an important operation which, if not carried out in accordance with strict requirements, may seriously impair the quality of the product. Bottling does not involve merely filling empty containers but normally entails, before filling, a series of complex oenological operations (filtering, clarifying, cooling, and so on) which, if not carried out in accordance with the prescribed rules of the trade, may adversely affect the quality and alter the characteristics of the wine.

62   Nor is it contested that bulk transport of wine may seriously impair its quality if not undertaken under optimum conditions. If the conditions of transport are not perfect, the wine will be exposed to oxidation reduction [and] to the risk of variations in temperature.

63   [Belgium contends nonetheless that] the bulk transport and bottling of wine outside the region may be carried out under conditions such as to safeguard its quality and reputation.

64   On the basis of the information produced to the Court in this case, it must be accepted that, in the best conditions, a wine's characteristics and quality may indeed be maintained when it has been transported in bulk and bottled outside the region of production.

65   However, in the case of bottling, the best conditions are more certain to be assured if bottling is done by undertakings established in the region of those entitled to use the designation and operating under their direct control, since they have specialised experience and thorough knowledge of the specific characteristics of the wine in question * * *.

* * *

74   [Accordingly,] the risk to which the quality of the product finally offered to consumers is exposed is greater where it has been transported and bottled outside the region of production than when those operations have taken place within the region.

76   Finally, it must be recognised that the measure is necessary for attainment of the objective pursued, in that there are no less restrictive alternative measures capable of attaining it.

77   [The controlled designation of origin] would not enjoy comparable protection if operators established outside the region of production were placed under an obligation to inform consumers by means of appropriate labelling that the wine had been bottled outside that region. Any deterioration in the quality of a wine bottled outside the region of production, resulting from materialisation of the risks associated with transport in bulk or subsequent bottling operations, might harm the reputation of all wines marketed under the Rioja [controlled designation of origin] including those bottled in the region of production under the control of the group of producers entitled to use that designation.

Notes and Questions

1.   *Rioja wine* is a rare example of an Article 227 proceeding, a direct dispute between or among Member States. (See Chapter 11D for a discussion of this case in the context of Article 227 proceedings.) Why were so many States concerned by the issue in *Rioja wine*? It is also rare in that the Court effectively overruled a prior judgment, Etablissements Delhaize/Promalvin, Case C–47/90, [1992] ECR I–3669, which had held that regional bottling of Rioja wine was not essential to preserve its characteristics. In ¶ 52, the Court stated that "new information" warranted its change of view. The issue is manifestly a close one—with which side do you agree? The judgment's greatest importance is the unequivocal declaration in ¶ 54 that designations of origin constitute a type of industrial and commercial property rights. American intellectual property experts are unlikely to agree, because in the US unfair competition law principles constitute the legal basis for the protection of designations of origin.

2.   In Pike v. Bruce Church, 397 U.S. 137, 90 S.Ct. 844, 25 L.Ed.2d 174 (1970), the Arizona Fruit and Vegetable Standardization Act required cantaloupes grown in Arizona to be packed there as well in order to identified as of Arizona origin. Arizona contended the rule was needed to prevent deceptive packaging. Although recognizing the validity of the consumer interest, the Supreme Court applied its balancing test, and concluded that Arizona's interest was minimal in comparison to the burden on interstate commerce. The Supreme Court declared that it "viewed with particular suspicion state statutes requiring business operations to be performed in the home State that could more efficiently be elsewhere." How do you think the Supreme Court would decide a case similar to *Rioja wine*, or the Court of Justice an analogue to *Pike*?

3.   In Denmark v. Commission (Feta cheese), Case C–289/96, [1999] ECR I–1541, Denmark, France and Germany challenged a Commission decision that Feta cheese could be registered as a description of origin by Greece under the procedures laid down by Regulation 2081/92. Supporting the Commission's decision were the facts that Feta cheese originated centuries ago in Greece and the southern Balkans, that Greece produced around three-quarters of all Feta cheese, and that 50% of those responding in a 1994 Eurobarometer survey identified it as originating in Greece. In reply, Denmark demonstrated that it has produced Feta cheese since 1963 under the name "Danish feta," that Greece has never blocked imports of Danish feta cheese, and that 47% of the Eurobarometer respondents considered Feta cheese to be a generic name. How would you decide the case? The Court annulled the Commission decision and instructed it in further proceedings to consider "traditional fair practice and . . . the likelihood of confusion," as well as the fact that non-Greek products had been legally marketed under the Feta cheese name throughout the Community prior to the effective date of the Regulation.

4.   Protecting designations of origin is an important Community concern in international trade. Settling a long-standing issue, on March 25, 1994 the EC and the US exchanged letters indicating their agreement that the US would protect "Scotch Whiskey," "Irish Whiskey," "Cognac," "Armangnac" and other names for well-known Community products, while the Community would protect "Tennessee Whiskey," "Bourbon Whiskey" and "Bourbon" for US products. O.J. L 157/36 (June 24, 1994).

2. GENERIC NAMES

In Europe, many traditional generic names are used for products of identifiable character which do not originate in a particular region, because the generic name easily identifies to consumers products with recognizable characteristics.

Thus, "Edam" is a well-known type of cheese, identified as such in the 1951 Stresa Convention on the Use of Designations of Origin and Names for Cheeses, and produced in many Community states. When Deserbais imported from Germany "Edam" cheese with a fat content of 34%, he was prosecuted in France for violation of a law which limited the name "Edam" to cheese with at least 40% fat content. In Ministère Public v. Deserbais, Case 286/86, [1988] ECR 4907, the Court of Justice held that such a generic name could be protected by a Member State law, but the protection must be proportionate in character–a clear label would be sufficient. In accord with *Deserbais* is Criminal proceedings against Miro BV, Case 182/84, [1985] ECR 3731 (the Netherlands may not restrict the name "jenever" to gin with a 35% alcohol content, when "jenever" with a 30% alcohol content has traditionally been produced in Belgium and exported to Holland). A recent case posed similar issues.

CRIMINAL PROCEEDINGS AGAINST GUIMONT

Case C–448/98, [2000] ECR ___ (Dec. 5, 2000).

[Guimont was prosecuted for violating French deceptive labelling rules by selling Emmenthal cheese without a hard rind. Emmenthal is a generic name for a variety of hard cheese with large holes. A 1935 French law on cheeses prescribes that it must have a hard, dry rind. In his defense, Guimont claimed that Emmenthal cheese is produced and sold without a rind in other Member States. The Tribunal asked the Court of Justice how free movement of goods principles should apply to the case.]

26   National legislation which subjects goods from other Member States, where they are lawfully manufactured and marketed, to certain conditions in order to be able to use the generic designation commonly used for that product, and which thus in certain cases requires producers to use designations which are unknown to, or less highly regarded by, consumers, does not, it is true absolutely preclude the importation into the Member State concerned of products originating in other Member States. It is, however, likely to make their marketing more difficult and thus impede trade between Member States.

27   * * * [N]ational rules adopted in the absence of common or harmonised rules and applicable without distinction to national products and to products imported from other Member States may be compatible with the Treaty in so far as they are necessary in order to satisfy overriding requirements relating, *inter alia*, to fair trading and consumer protection [and] they are proportionate to the objective pursued * * *.

* * *

30   [A]ccording to the case-law of the Court, Member States may, for the purpose of ensuring fair trading and the protection of consumers, require the persons concerned to alter the description of a foodstuff where a product offered for sale under a particular name is so different, in terms of its composition or production, from the products generally understood as

falling within that description within the Community that it cannot be regarded as falling within the same category.

31   However, where the difference is of minor importance, appropriate labelling should be sufficient to provide the purchaser or consumer with the necessary information.

32   [A]ccording to the Codex alimentarius [of the UN Food and Agriculture Organisation], a cheese manufactured without rind may be given the name 'Emmenthal' since it is made from ingredients and in accordance with a method of manufacture identical to those used for Emmenthal with rind, save for a difference in treatment at the maturing stage. Moreover, it is undisputed that such an Emmenthal cheese variant is lawfully manufactured and marketed in Member States other than the French Republic.

35   [T]herefore [Article 28] precludes a Member State from applying to products imported from another Member State, where they are lawfully produced and marketed, a national rule prohibiting the marketing of a cheese without rind under the designation 'Emmenthal.'

Notes and Questions

1. In Commission v. France (Foie gras), Case C–184/96, [1998] ECR I–6197, the Commission attacked a French law which set detailed standards for foie gras and preparations made with it, because the law did not permit the sale in France of foie gras made in other Member States which might deviate from the detailed standards. France processes 95% of the world production of foie gras. Advocate General La Pergola considered that the Commission had raised a purely hypothetical issue, since it had not demonstrated that France had blocked any imports of non-conforming foie gras. The Court, however, held that Article 28 applies "not only to the actual effects but also to the potential effects of legislation." (¶ 17.) Recall how the Court of Justice handled Germany's rule restricting the use of the term, "Bier," in *German beer*, supra page 516. How should the Court treat the French rules on foie gras?

C. SCOPE AND PROTECTION OF INDUSTRIAL AND COMMERCIAL PROPERTY RIGHTS

Once an industrial or commercial property right is recognized under Article 30 (ex Article 36), the next question concerns its proper scope and protection.

When a Member State law grants a monopoly of exploitation to the owner of such a right, it follows that the owner may forbid any unauthorized third party, or infringer, from any sale, use or other exploitation within that State. If an industrial or commercial property right has considerable economic significance, the owner in one State usually seeks to obtain parallel protection in all of the other States of the Community. This is not always possible, either because someone else has prior conflicting rights in another State, or because another State does not protect the right, or imposes differing requirements for recognition of the right. That sets the stage for a Community law conflict.

In the leading early judgment, Parke, Davis v. Probel, Case 24/67, [1968] ECR 55, a major US pharmaceutical manufacturer held a Dutch patent for an antibiotic. Under Italian patent law at that time, patents were not available for pharmaceuticals. (Some developing countries even today contend that the social interest in having inexpensive drugs on the market outweighs the claim of a pharmaceutical inventor to a patent reward for its ingenuity and expense.) A Dutch drug wholesaler tried to sell the antibiotic, which had been lawfully produced in Italy by a company unrelated to Parke, Davis. The Court of Justice held that Parke, Davis could properly invoke Article 30 to bar any unauthorized sale of an infringing product in the Netherlands, even when the product was lawfully manufactured and marketed in another State.

Similarly, in EMI Electrola GmbH v. Patricia, Case 341/87, [1989] ECR 79, a British company, EMI Records, owned the reproduction and distribution rights to records made in 1958 by a popular British singer, Cliff Richard. The Danish copyright expired in 1983, after 25 years, but the German copyright continued until 1990. Because the records were in the public domain in Denmark, anyone could freely make and sell them there. A competitor of EMI made re-recordings of Richard's 1958 records in Denmark and tried to sell them in Germany. The Court of Justice held that EMI could rely on the longer German copyright term to bar the imports. Partly to prevent similar controversies, Directive 93/98 was adopted to harmonize the term of copyrights throughout the Community. See section E.

Because *Parke, Davis* and *EMI Electrola* remain good law, they create the risk that the Community market can be effectively divided into national markets whenever unrelated parties have acquired identical or similar patent, trademark or copyright rights in different states. This happens not infrequently with regard to trademarks, when a mark owner in State A commences marketing in State B, where an unrelated party owns the same or a confusingly similar mark. An issue of steadily growing importance is how, under Community law, one should determine whether the two marks are indeed confusingly similar.

TERRAPIN (OVERSEAS) v. TERRANOVA INDUSTRIE

Case 119/75, [1976] ECR 1039.

[Terranova is a German company owning in Germany the registered trademarks "Terra" and "Terranova" for the category of construction materials. Terrapin is a UK company owning in the UK the registered trademark "Terrapin." Terrapin commenced selling prefabricated houses and components for the construction of such houses in Germany, using "Terrapin" as its mark and trade name. Terranova sued to enjoin the use of "Terrapin" either as a trademark or trade name. The German Supreme Court concluded that the two trademarks and trade names were confusingly similar under German law principles, but asked the Court of Justice whether Terrapin might have Treaty-based rights.]

[7]   [I]n the present state of Community law an industrial or commercial property right legally acquired in a Member State may legally be used to prevent under the first sentence of Article [30] of the Treaty the import of products marketed under a name giving rise to confusion where the rights in question have been acquired by different and independent proprietors under different national laws. If in such a case the principle of the free movement of goods were to prevail over the protection given by the

respective national laws, the specific objective of industrial and commercial property rights would be undermined. In the particular situation the requirements of the free movement of goods and the safeguarding of industrial and commercial property rights must be so reconciled that protection is ensured for the legitimate use of the rights conferred by national laws, coming within the prohibitions on imports "justified" within the meaning of Article [30] of the Treaty, but denied on the other hand in respect of any improper exercise of the same rights of such a nature as to maintain or effect artificial partitions within the common market.

Notes and Questions

1. The United Kingdom argued in support of Terrapin that there would have been no confusion of the two marks if UK trademark principles were applied, and that the German standards for confusion were too strict. The UK urged the Court to state that Community law required an examination to ensure that minimum standards for appraising confusion be applied. The Court obviously did not do this. Why not? If the Court can use a principle of proportionality to test whether a Member State has properly claimed health or safety protection under Article 30, why can't it use proportionality to test a State's claims of trademark rights protection? For a criticism of *Terrapin* and *Deutsche Renault, infra,* on this basis, see P. Oliver, Free Movement of Goods in the European Community § 8.137 (3d ed. Sweet & Maxwell 1996). An amusing point is that the German court's finding that "Terrapin" and "Terranova" are similar was in part based on the view that both came from the Latin root "terra," meaning "earth." This is simply wrong, as in fact the word "terrapin" comes from the Algonquin Indian name for a turtle.

2. The Court of Justice continued to defer to national standards for appraising the risk of confusion in Deutsche Renault v. Audi, Case C–317/91, [1993] ECR I–6227 (German trademark confusion rules can properly be used to bar Renault's sale of four-wheel drive vehicles under the mark "Espace Quadra" when Audi has a prior mark, "quattro" for similar vehicles). However, the 1989 Trademark Directive which harmonized national rules contained provisions on trademark confusion. When called upon to interpret these provisions, the Court of Justice developed Community rules governing the concept which now significantly limit State discretion in setting trademark confusion standards. See section E2 infra.

D. EXHAUSTION OF RIGHTS DOCTRINE

The most controversial aspect of Community law on industrial and commercial property rights is the exhaustion of rights doctrine. The essential idea is quite simple. An industrial or commercial property right owner has a monopoly over its economic exploitation. However, Article 30 (ex 36), as an exception to the free movement of goods principle, should be read strictly, and the exercise of industrial or commercial property rights should be narrowly construed so as to be proportionate to the end served. Thus, once the owner has initially exploited its right by obtaining some form of economic reward as to a specific product, the economic monopoly ends: it has been "exhausted." This "exhaustion" concept is applied by many modern national legal systems (including the US) in their internal markets, but not in all, and is, of course, not even hinted at in the Treaty.

The exhaustion of rights doctrine made its first appearance in Deutsche Grammophon GmbH v. Metro, Case 78/70, [1971] ECR 487. The Court of

Justice held that when Deutsche Grammophon, owner of a German music copyright, sold records through its French subsidiary in Alsace, it could not take advantage of Article 30 to bar the re-import and resale of the records in Germany. This doctrine sparked a controversy which erupted in full vigor in the next case, involving the pharmaceutical industry.

CENTRAFARM v. WINTHROP

Case 16/74, [1974] ECR 1183.

[Sterling Drug manufactured and sold in the UK a drug under the trademark, "Negram." Sterling's wholly-owned Dutch subsidiary Winthrop customarily marketed the drug, also under the trademark "Negram," in the Netherlands. A Dutch pharmaceutical wholesaler, Centrafarm, bought the drug in quantity in the UK and resold it in the Netherlands under the mark "Negram." UK law placed strict price controls on pharmaceuticals, which was not the case in the Netherlands. Hence Centrafarm could sell the drug at a substantial profit while still undercutting Winthrop's prices, which were nearly double those in the UK. Winthrop brought an action to enjoin the resale in the Netherlands as a trademark infringement. Centrafarm lost and appealed. The Dutch Supreme Court made an Article 234 reference.]

6 [I]t is clear from * * * [Article 30], in particular its second sentence, ... that whilst the Treaty does not affect the existence of rights recognized by the legislation of a Member State in matters of industrial and commercial property, yet the exercise of these rights may nevertheless * * * be affected by the prohibitions in the Treaty.

7 Inasmuch as it provides an exception to one of the fundamental principles of the Common Market, Article [30] in fact only admits of derogations from the free movement of goods where such derogations are justified for the purpose of safeguarding rights which constitute the specific subject-matter of this property.

8 In relation to trade marks, the specific subject-matter of the industrial property is the guarantee that the owner of the trade mark has the exclusive right to use that trade mark, for the purpose of putting products protected by the trade mark into circulation for the first time, and is therefore intended to protect him against competitors wishing to take advantage of the status and reputation of the trade mark by selling products illegally bearing that trade mark.

9 An obstacle to the free movement of goods may arise out of the existence, within a national legislation concerning industrial and commercial property, of provisions laying down that a trade mark owner's right is not exhausted when the product protected by the trade mark is marketed in another Member State, with the result that the trade mark owner can prevent importation of the product into his own Member State when it has been marketed in another Member State.

10 Such an obstacle is not justified when the product has been put onto the market in a legal manner in the Member State from which it has been imported, by the trade mark owner himself or with his consent, so that there can be no question of abuse or infringement of the trade mark.

[11] In fact, if a trade mark owner could prevent the import of protected products marketed by him or with his consent in another Member State, he would be able to partition off national markets and thereby restrict trade between Member States, in a situation where no such restriction was necessary to guarantee the essence of the exclusive right flowing from the trade mark.

[12] The question referred should therefore be answered to the effect that the exercise, by the owner of a trade mark, of the right which he enjoys under the legislation of a Member State to prohibit the sale, in that State, of a product which has been marketed under the trade mark in another Member State by the trade mark owner or with his consent is incompatible with the rules of the EEC Treaty concerning the free movement of goods within the Common Market.

* * *

[15] [The next] question requires the Court to state, in substance, whether the trade mark owner can, notwithstanding the answer given to the first question, prevent importation of products marketed under the trade mark, given the existence of price differences resulting from governmental measures adopted in the exporting country with a view to controlling prices of those products.

[16] It is part of the Community authorities' task to eliminate factors likely to distort competition between Member States, in particular by the harmonization of national measures for the control of prices and by the prohibition of aids which are incompatible with the Common Market, in addition to the exercise of their powers in the field of competition.

[17] The existence of [price controls in one] Member State, however, cannot justify measures [in a second Member State] which are incompatible with the rules concerning the free movement of goods, in particular in the field of industrial and commercial property.

[18] The question referred should therefore be answered in the negative.

[19] [The final] question requires the Court to state whether the trade mark owner is authorized to exercise the rights conferred on him by the trade mark, notwithstanding Community rules concerning the free movement of goods, for the purpose of controlling the distribution of a pharmaceutical product with a view to protecting the public against the risks arising from defects therein.

[20] The protection of the public against risks arising from defective pharmaceutical products is a matter of legitimate concern, and Article [30] of the Treaty authorizes the Member States to derogate from the rules concerning the free movement of goods on grounds of the protection of health and life of humans and animals.

[21] However, the measures necessary to achieve this must be such as may properly be adopted in the field of health control, and must not constitute a misuse of the rules concerning industrial and commercial property.

Notes and Questions

1. In a parallel proceeding, Sterling Drug, which owned patents for the drug in both the UK and the Netherlands, brought an action against Centrafarm for

patent infringement in the Netherlands. In an Article 234 reference, the Court of Justice held that Sterling Drug could not exercise its Dutch patent rights in such a case. The Court used language virtually identical to that of the *Winthrop* judgment. Centrafarm BV v. Sterling Drug Inc., Case 15/74, [1974] ECR 1147. Thus, the Community exhaustion of rights doctrine has been applied to patents, trademarks and copyright.

2.   Centrafarm did not challenge the validity of Winthrop's trademark, so why isn't this a straightforward case of trademark infringement? Observe the Court's limitation of Article 30, as an exception to the fundamental principle of free movement of goods, to the narrowest exercise of a trademark right possible. The Court's approach in narrowly limiting the exercise of Article 30 interests parallels that taken in limiting the protection of imperative state interests recognized under *Cassis de Dijon* doctrine. This approach is an application of the principle of proportionality, discussed in Chapter 5, requiring that the means be tailored as narrowly as possible to achieve the desired end.

3.   Consider paragraphs 8–11 of the judgment, analyzing the exercise of trademark rights in terms of the exhaustion doctrine. The Court of Justice is imposing an exhaustion of rights doctrine as to imported products legally acquired under the same trademark elsewhere in the Community, on the policy ground that a broader protection of trademark exercise rights would represent a "disguised restriction on trade" forbidden by the final sentence of Article 30. Although the Court in *Winthrop* and later cases speaks in terms of limiting the exercise, but not the existence, of industrial and commercial property rights, some commentators find this language misleading. For an argument that the exhaustion of rights doctrine does affect the nature of the industrial and commercial property rights themselves, see G. Marenco & K. Banks, Intellectual Property and the Community Rules on Free Movement: Discrimination Unearthed, 15 Eur.L.Rev. 224 (1990).

4.   The Court's conclusion reflects a concern that trademark owners might otherwise use the identical trademark in several Member States as a means to "partition off national markets." How does the exhaustion of rights doctrine prevent this from happening? Once again, Community market integration is the key policy principle.

5.   In this case, Winthrop was a wholly-owned subsidiary of Sterling. More often, a patent, trademark or copyright owner will grant licenses to independent third parties in different Community States. If the license is exclusive for an entire State, and the licensee by virtue of a clause in the license agreement attempts to bar imports placed on the market in another State by the licensor or another licensee, then the license agreement will be deemed an agreement to restrict trade between Member States, and held to violate the competition law principles of Article 81 (ex Article 85). This type of illegal license agreement clause (frequently called a "parallel export" or "parallel import" ban) is one of the most common violations of Article 81 and has been the subject of extensive case law ever since the landmark decision of *Consten and Grundig,* excerpted at page 793.

NOTE ON THE CONTROVERSY CONCERNING THE EXHAUSTION OF RIGHTS DOCTRINE

The Court of Justice's enunciation of the exhaustion of rights doctrine as to patents, trademarks and copyrights has great commercial significance. Substantial price differentials on various national markets, partly occasioned by the impact of government price controls in certain fields, existed in the

1970s and still exist today to a significant degree. Product fields marked by such differentials include automobiles, electronic consumer goods, pharmaceuticals, books and records.

This creates a temptation for owners of patent, trademark or copyright rights to try to use them to protect the price levels of their subsidiaries, licensees or distributors on national markets where high prices prevail. By the same token, wholesalers or retailers (such as Centrafarm) have a substantial incentive to seek to procure products in large quantities in Member States where prices are low, in order to resell them at good profits in States where prices are high.

Owners of industrial and commercial property rights complain—and not entirely without justification—that the Court's exhaustion of rights doctrine enables competing distributors to become "free riders," benefiting from the research and development, advertising, marketing, warranty protection and other costs which the owners of the rights incur. (See the discussion of distribution and "free riders" in Chapter 25, infra.) Those firms in product sectors where governmental price controls account for all or part of the price differentials complain that the Community should either eliminate these price controls or else create a Community-wide harmonized system of price controls.

A number of academic specialists in industrial and commercial property contend that the Court of Justice's exhaustion of rights doctrine fails to show proper respect for traditional concepts of these rights. (Note, however, that the Court has otherwise demonstrated great deference to idiosyncratic national law definition of industrial and commercial property rights, as manifested in *Nancy Kean* and *Consorzio*.) Commentators sympathetic to the Court's doctrine (as well as the Commission, which aggressively combats what it perceives to be abuses of industrial and commercial property rights, especially through competition law enforcement) respond that free movement of goods and Community market integration is an overriding goal. Concern for industrial and commercial property rights, just as concern for health, safety and consumer interests, must be tailored so as not excessively to hinder market integration.

Whatever view one may take on this controversy, the application of the exhaustion of rights doctrine has occasioned a complex body of case law.

CENTRAFARM v. AMERICAN HOME PRODUCTS

Case 3/78, [1978] ECR 1823.

[American Home Products (AHP) sold a drug with identical therapeutic qualities under the marks "Serenid D" in the UK and "Seresta" in the Netherlands. Because of the large price differential between the UK and the Netherlands, Centrafarm bought quantities of the drug in the UK and replaced "Serenid D" with "Seresta" before attempting to resell the drug in the Netherlands. In an injunction proceeding, the Dutch court made an Article 234 reference. The Court of Justice first discussed, in language nearly identical to that in *Winthrop,* the status of trademarks under Article 30 as a limited derogation from the free movement of goods. After quoting paragraphs 7–8 of *Winthrop*, the Court then continued its analysis.]

12   [T]he precise scope of that exclusive right granted to the proprietor of the mark [is based upon] the essential function of the trade-mark, which is to guarantee the identity of the origin of the trade-marked product to the consumer or ultimate user.

13   This guarantee of origin means that only the proprietor may confer an identity upon the product by affixing the mark.

14   The guarantee of origin would in fact be jeopardized if it were permissible for a third party to affix the mark to the product, even to an original product.

15   [Therefore,] even where the manufacturer * * * is the proprietor of two different marks for the same product, [national legislation may prevent] an unauthorized third party from usurping the right to affix one or other mark to any part whatsoever of the production or to change the marks affixed by the proprietor to different parts of the production.

* * *

17   The right granted to the proprietor to prohibit any unauthorized affixing of his mark to his product accordingly comes within the specific subject-matter of the trade-mark.

18   The proprietor of a trade-mark which is protected in one Member State is accordingly justified pursuant to the first sentence of Article [30] in preventing a product from being marketed by a third party in that Member State under the mark in question even if previously that product has been lawfully marketed in another Member State under another mark held in the latter State by the same proprietor.

19   Nevertheless it is still necessary to consider whether the exercise of that right may constitute a "disguised restriction on trade between Member States" within the meaning of the second sentence of Article [30].

20   [I]t may be lawful for the manufacturer of a product to use in different Member States different marks for the same product.

21   Nevertheless it is possible for such a practice to be followed by the proprietor of the marks as part of a system of marketing intended to partition the markets artificially.

22   In such a case the prohibition by the proprietor of the unauthorized affixing of the mark by a third party constitutes a disguised restriction on intra-Community trade for the purposes of the above-mentioned provision.

23   It is for the national court to settle in each particular case whether the proprietor has followed the practice of using different marks for the same product for the purpose of partitioning the markets.

Notes and Questions

1.   Note that either party could win in the trial court, because that court has to determine whether AHP's motive in using two different marks for the same product was legitimate or improper. Exploiting the same mark for the entire Community (or indeed the entire world) is usually desirable, because it reduces advertising and marketing costs. That makes AHP's use of slightly different marks in the Netherlands and the UK look suspiciously like an effort to block parallel imports. However, sometimes, because of conflicting prior rights (as in

Terrapin), or because an initial mark has unfortunate connotations in another language, a producer legitimately must use different marks for the same product in different countries. Accordingly, AHP might have had a justification for the use of different marks. In any event, note that *Paranova II*, infra, has further limited the right of a producer to use different marks for the same product in different Member States.

2. In the 1970s, Hoffmann–La Roche (HLR) sold its well-known drug "Valium" in different packages on different national markets. In Germany, HLR marketed packages containing 20 to 50 tablets to consumers. In the UK, the HLR packages contained up to 500 tablets and sold at considerably lower prices. Centrafarm bought the drug in large quantities in the UK, then repackaged it into units with 1000 tablets for resale in Germany. Centrafarm put the "Valium" mark on the larger package, together with a notice that Centrafarm marketed the package. A German court found that the repackaging violated German trademark principles, but then asked the Court of Justice whether Community law would nonetheless permit Centrafarm to repackage the tablets and affix the "Valium" mark. What do you think? See Hoffmann–La Roche AG v. Centrafarm, Case 102/77, [1978] ECR 1139.

BRISTOL-MYERS SQUIBB & ORRS v. PARANOVA

[Paranova I]

Cases C–427/93, C–429/93 & C–436/93, [1996] ECR I–3457.

[Paranova, a parallel importer, developed a substantial business by buying pharmaceuticals cheaply in Greece, Portugal, Spain and the UK (all of which have price regulations), repackaging and relabeling them under the producers' trademarks, and reselling the products in Denmark. Paranova sometimes added information for users in Danish. Despite the costs involved, Paranova could sell more cheaply than the authorized distributors. Bristol–Myers and a German pharmaceutical producer sued for injunctions in Denmark. They relied heavily on the 1989 Trademark Directive's article 7 on exhaustion, which stipulated an exception to the usual exhaustion principle if the parallel importer "changed or impaired" the products. (The Trademark Directive is summarized in section E1 and reproduced in the Selected Documents.) The Court's lengthy judgment began by declaring in ¶ 36 that article 7 was not intended to change the Court's prior doctrine (and indeed could not, because Community legislation cannot deviate from free movement principles).]

40   Article 7 of the directive, like Article [30, ex Article 36] of the Treaty, is intended to reconcile the fundamental interest in protecting trade mark rights with the fundamental interest in the free movement of goods within the common market, so that those two provisions, which pursue the same result, must be interpreted in the same way.

* * *

42   Article [30] allows derogations from the fundamental principle of the free movement of goods within the common market only in so far as such derogations are justified in order to safeguard the rights which constitute the specific subject-matter of the industrial and commercial property in question.

* * *

45 [T]he owner of a trade mark protected by the legislation of a Member State cannot rely on that legislation in order to oppose the importation or marketing of a product which was put on the market in another Member State by him or with his consent [citing *Winthrop*].

46 Trade mark rights are not intended to allow their owners to partition national markets and thus promote the retention of price differences which may exist between Member States. Whilst, in the pharmaceutical market especially, such price differences may result from factors over which trade mark owners have no control, such as divergent rules between the Member States on the fixing of maximum prices, the profit margins of pharmaceutical wholesalers and pharmacies, or the maximum amount of medical expenses which may be reimbursed under sickness insurance schemes, distortions caused by divergent pricing rules in one Member State must be remedied by measures of the Community authorities and not by another Member State introducing measures which are incompatible with the rules on the free movement of goods [citing *Winthrop*].

47 In answering the question whether a trade mark owner's exclusive rights include the power to oppose the use of the trade mark by a third party after the product has been repackaged, account must be taken of the essential function of the trade mark, which is to guarantee to the consumer or end user the identity of the trade-marked product's origin by enabling him to distinguish it without any risk of confusion from products of different origin. That guarantee of origin means that the consumer or end user can be certain that a trade-marked product offered to him has not been subject at a previous stage of marketing to interference by a third person, without the authorization of the trade mark owner, in such a way as to affect the original condition of the product.

* * *

Artificial partitioning of the markets between Member States

52 Reliance on trade mark rights by their owner in order to oppose marketing under that trade mark of products repackaged by a third party would contribute to the partitioning of markets between Member States in particular where the owner has placed an identical pharmaceutical product on the market in several Member States in various forms of packaging * * *.

53 The trade mark owner cannot oppose the repackaging of the product in new external packaging when the size of packet used by the owner in the Member State where the importer purchased the product cannot be marketed in the Member State of importation by reason, in particular, of a rule authorizing packaging only of a certain size * * * or well-established medical prescription practices based, *inter alia*, on standard sizes recommended by professional groups and sickness insurance institutions.

* * *

55 The owner may, on the other hand, oppose the repackaging of the product in new external packaging where the importer is able to achieve packaging which may be marketed in the Member State of importation by, for example, affixing to the original external or inner packaging new labels

* * * or by adding new user instructions or information in the language of the Member State of importation * * * .

56   The power of the owner of trade mark rights protected in a Member State to oppose the marketing of repackaged products under the trade mark should be limited only in so far as the repackaging undertaken by the importer is necessary in order to market the product in the Member State of importation.

57   Finally, contrary to the argument of the plaintiffs in the main actions, the Court's use of the words 'artificial partitioning of the markets' [in *AHP*] does not imply that the importer must demonstrate that, by putting an identical product on the market in varying forms of packaging in different Member States, the trade mark owner deliberately sought to partition the markets between Member States. * * *

Whether the original condition of the product is adversely affected

58   [I]t should be clarified at the outset that the concept of adverse effects on the original condition of the product refers to the condition of the product inside the packaging.

59   The trade mark owner may therefore oppose any repackaging involving a risk of the product inside the package being exposed to tampering or to influences affecting its original condition. * * *

60   As regards pharmaceutical products, * * * repackaging [is] not capable of affecting the original condition of the product where, for example, the trade mark owner has placed the product on the market in double packaging and the repackaging affects only the external layer, leaving the inner packaging intact * * * .

61   [Similarly,] the mere removal of blister packs, flasks, phials, ampoules or inhalers from their original external packaging and their replacement in new external packaging cannot affect the original condition of the product inside the packaging.

* * *

64   As for operations consisting in the fixing of self-stick labels to flasks, phials, ampoules or inhalers, the addition to the packaging of new user instructions or information in the language of the Member State of importation, or the insertion of an extra article, such as a spray, from a source other than the trade mark owner, there is nothing to suggest that the original condition of the product inside the packaging is directly affected thereby.

65   It should be recognized, however, that the original condition of the product inside the packaging might be indirectly affected where, for example:

— the external or inner packaging of the repackaged product, or a new set of user instructions or information, omits certain important information or give inaccurate information concerning the nature, composition, effect, use or storage of the product, or

— an extra article inserted into the packaging by the importer and designed for the ingestion and dosage of the product does not comply with the method of use and the doses envisaged by the manufacturer.

* * *

The other requirements to be met by the parallel importer

67   If the repackaging is carried out in conditions which cannot affect the original condition of the product inside the packaging, the essential function of the trade mark as a guarantee of origin is safeguarded. Thus, the consumer or end user is not misled as to the origin of the products, and does in fact receive products manufactured under the sole supervision of the trade mark owner.

* * *

70   Since it is in the trade mark owner's interest that the consumer or end user should not be led to believe that the owner is responsible for the repackaging, an indication must be given on the packaging of who repackaged the product.

* * *

75   Even if the person who carried out the repackaging is indicated on the packaging of the product, there remains the possibility that the reputation of the trade mark, and thus of its owner, may nevertheless suffer from an inappropriate presentation of the repackaged product.

76   In the case of pharmaceutical products, [for] which the public is particularly demanding as to the quality and integrity of the product, the presentation of the product may indeed be capable of inspiring public confidence in that regard. It follows that defective, poor quality or untidy packaging could damage the trade mark's reputation.

* * *

78   Finally, as the Court pointed out in *Hoffmann-La Roche*, the trade mark owner must be given advance notice of the repackaged product being put on sale. The owner may also require the importer to supply him with a specimen of the repackaged product before it goes on sale, to enable him to check that the repackaging is not carried out in such a way as directly or indirectly to affect the original condition of the product and that the presentation after repackaging is not likely to damage the reputation of the trade mark. Similarly, such a requirement affords the trade mark owner a better possibility of protecting himself against counterfeiting.

PHARMACIA & UPJOHN v. PARANOVA
[Paranova II]

Case C–379/97, [1999] ECR I–6927.

[The Upjohn Group produces and sells an antibiotic in Denmark, Germany and Spain under the mark "Dalacin," but under "Dalacin C" in other Community States. Under a 1968 trademark dispute settlement with a competitor, Upjohn agreed to use "Dalacin C" wherever possible, but the competitor permitted Upjohn to use "Dalacin" in countries where it could not register "Delacin C." Paranova bought the antibiotic under the "Delacin C" mark in Greece and France (where it was exceptionally sold as "Delacine"), and sold it in Denmark after putting the "Delacin" mark on the antibiotic. When Upjohn sued to enjoin this, the trial court requested guidance on how to apply the *AHP* judgment's language concerning the use of different marks to achieve the partitioning of markets. After summarizing its prior case law, notably *Paranova I*, the Court reexamined the issue raised in *AHP* as to whether a parallel importer can legitimately substitute one mark for another, when both are used by a producer for the same product in different States.]

* * *

[33] Upjohn argues that * * * no exceptions should be made to the right of the proprietor to oppose replacement of the trade mark, unless in accordance with the judgment in *American Home Products*, evidence is adduced of a subjective intention on the part of the proprietor to partition the markets. * * *

[34] Paranova argues that the subjective circumstances of the proprietor of a trade mark cannot be decisive where the trade mark has been altered. It takes the view that it is no longer necessary to draw a strict distinction between the case where there is repackaging with reaffixing of the original trade mark and that in which the trade mark is replaced, and that these two situations must be regulated according to the same principles.

* * *

[36] The Commission submits that there is no direct reason for maintaining the subjective condition that there must be an intention on the part of the proprietor of trade marks to partition the markets in the case where one trade mark is replaced by another and not in the case where pharmaceutical products have been repackaged or the labelling has been changed. The determining factor ought to be whether the essential function of the trade mark, which is to guarantee the identity of origin, is jeopardised by the replacement of one trade mark by another.

[37] The view expressed by Paranova * * * and by the Commission, in this respect is correct: there is no objective difference between reaffixing a trade mark after repackaging and replacing the original trade mark by another which is capable of justifying the condition of artificial partitioning being applied differently in each of those cases.

[38] In the first place, the practice of using different packaging and that of using different trade marks for the same product, in contributing similarly to the partitioning of the single market, adversely affect intracommunity trade in the same way; secondly, the reaffixing of the original trade mark on the repackaged product and its replacement by another trade mark both represent a use by the parallel importer of a trade mark which does not belong to him.

[39] Consequently, where the trade-mark rights in the importing Member State allow the proprietor of the trade mark to prevent it being reaffixed after repackaging of the product or being replaced, and where the repackaging with reaffixing or the replacement of the trade mark is necessary to enable the products to be marketed by the parallel importer in the importing Member State, there are obstacles to intracommunity trade giving rise to artificial partitioning of the markets between Member States within the meaning of the case-law cited, whether or not the proprietor intended such partitioning.

* * *

43   * * * [I]t is for the national courts to examine whether the circumstances prevailing at the time of marketing made it objectively necessary to replace the original trade mark by that of the importing Member State in order that the product in question could be placed on the market in that State by the parallel importer. This condition of necessity is satisfied if, in a specific case, the prohibition imposed on the importer against replacing the trade mark hinders effective access to the markets of the importing Member States. That would be the case if the rules or practices in the importing Member State prevent the product in question from being marketed in that State under its trade mark in the exporting Member State. This is so where a rule for the protection of consumers prohibits the use, in the importing Member State, of the trade mark used in the exporting Member State on the ground that it is liable to mislead consumers.

44   In contrast, the condition of necessity will not be satisfied if replacement of the trade mark is explicable solely by the parallel importer's attempt to secure a commercial advantage.

45   It is for the national courts to determine, in each specific case, whether it was objectively necessary for the parallel importer to use the trade mark used in the Member State of import in order to enable the imported products to be marketed.

Notes and Questions

1. In both judgments, the Court was aided by Advocate General Jacobs' analysis of the complex fact patterns and his suggestions on new legal rules. In ¶¶ 73–75 of his opinion in *Paranova I*, Advocate General Jacobs observed that the root of the problem is the wide disparity in pharmaceutical price levels due to the substantially different price restrictions and social security schemes in different States. In this state of affairs, do you think the Court has struck the proper balance between the interest of parallel importers, whose sales arguably promote an integrated European market, and the pharmaceutical producers' concern for the reputation of their trademarks, as well as for a fair return on their capital investment in research and development and on their production costs? Are the producers apt to be successful in lobbying for a Community-wide uniform system of price regulations in the pharmaceutical field?

2. Has the Court in *Paranova II* effectively overruled its judgment in *AHP*? If a manufacturer (not just of pharmaceuticals, but of any products) uses different marks in different States for identical products, does his intent matter any more? After the two *Paranova* judgements, is it fair to say that a parallel importer can almost always repackage a product to meet the market needs in the State of sale, including applying the producer's trademark in that State, or are there still significant limitations upon the parallel importer? Do you agree with these judgments, or do you think they go too far?

3. In Parfums Christian Dior v. Evora, Case C–337/95, [1997] ECR I–6013, Dior sold its prestigious line of perfumes in Europe only through selected retailers who met high quality standards. In the Netherlands, Evora operates a chain of chemists' shops (drug stores). Evora obtained Dior perfumes by parallel imports and depicted Dior bottles of perfume in its advertising leaflets. Dior sued to enjoin this practice as a trademark infringement. In answering questions raised by the Dutch Supreme Court, the Court of Justice held that the exhaustion doctrine

implies that a parallel importer must have the right to refer to a producer's trademark in commercializing the product (¶ 37). Although the reseller must "endeavour to prevent his advertising from * * * detracting from the allure and prestigious image of the goods" (¶ 45), the reseller may use modes of advertising "customary in his trade sector" (¶ 46)—which might well be quite different for a chain of drug stores than for Dior's high quality perfume and cosmetic retailers. Do you agree? Advocate General Jacobs trenchantly remarked that if a parallel importer could not advertize with the producer's mark, "that would drive a coach and horses through the principle of the exhaustion of rights" (¶ 31).

4.   The exhaustion of rights doctrine is limited to the Community market (plus Iceland, Norway and Liechtenstein, pursuant to the European Economic Area Agreement). In Silhouette International Schmied v. Hartlauer, Case C–355/96, [1998] ECR I–4799, Silhouette, an Austrian producer of high quality eyeglasses, sold them in Austria only to opticians. In 1995, Silhouette sold 21,000 out-of-fashion eyeglasses to a Bulgarian company for resale there or in Russia. Hartlauer, an Austrian eyeglass retailer, secured them and offered them for resale in Austria. When Silhouette sought an injunction, the Austrian court dismissed the action. On appeal, the Supreme Court asked the Court of Justice whether Austria could apply the international exhaustion doctrine after it adopted the Trademark Directive. The Court of Justice answered in the negative, reasoning that article 7 of the directive did not expressly permit use of the international exhaustion doctrine and that to permit some States to apply an international exhaustion doctrine while others did not would occasion new barriers to the free movement of goods.

WARNER BROTHERS v. CHRISTIANSEN

Case 158/86, [1988] ECR 2605.

A copyright owner of film rights can produce video-cassettes (videotapes). The owner can market the cassettes, directly or by license, either by selling them, usually at a high price, or by renting them a number of times at a lower price through video rental stores. A Danish law recognizes the rental of video-cassettes as a form of copyright exploitation separate from that of outright sale. UK law draws no such distinction.

Warner Brothers sold cassettes of "Never Say Never Again," a popular James Bond film, in the UK. Christiansen, who operated a video rental business in Copenhagen, bought cassettes of this film in London, imported them to Denmark, and tried to rent them. Warner's Danish licensee for video-cassette rental of the film sued to enjoin Christiansen.

Advocate General Mancini observed that only Denmark and France split the copyright exploitation rights for video-cassettes into separate sale and rental rights. The UK, Germany, the Netherlands and Ireland all treated either a sale or rental as exhausting the economic remuneration right of a copyright owner, while in the remaining States the question was then open.]

10   [T]he commercial distribution of video-cassettes takes the form not only of sales but also, and increasingly, that of hiring-out to individuals who possess video-tape recorders. The right to prohibit such hiring-out in a Member State is therefore liable to influence trade in video-cassettes in that State and hence, indirectly, to affect intra-Community trade in those products. Legislation of the kind which gave rise to the main proceedings

must therefore, be regarded as a measure having an effect equivalent to a quantitative restriction on imports * * *.

11 Consideration should therefore be given to whether such legislation may be considered justified on grounds of the protection of industrial and commercial property within the meaning of Article [30]—a term which was held by the Court, in its judgment in Case 262/81 (Coditel v. Ciné–Vog [1982] ECR 3381), to include literary and artistic property.

12 [T]he Danish legislation applies without distinction to video-cassettes produced *in situ* and video-cassettes imported from another Member State. The determining factor for the purposes of its application is the type of transaction in video-cassettes which is in question, not the origin of those video-cassettes. Such legislation does not therefore, in itself, operate any arbitrary discrimination in trade between Member States.

* * *

14 Lastly, consideration must be given to the emergence, demonstrated by the Commission, of a specific market for the hiring-out of such recordings, as distinct from their sale. The existence of that market was made possible by various factors such as the improvement of manufacturing methods for video-cassettes which increased their strength and life in use, the growing awareness amongst viewers that they watch only occasionally the video-cassettes which they have bought and, lastly, their relatively high purchase price. The market for the hiring-out of video-cassettes reaches a wider public than the market for their sale and, at present, offers great potential as a source of revenue for makers of films.

15 However, it is apparent that, by authorizing the collection of royalties only on sales to private individuals and to persons hiring out video-cassettes, it is impossible to guarantee to makers of films a remuneration which reflects the number of occasions on which the video-cassettes are actually hired out and which secures for them a satisfactory share of the rental market. That explains why * * * certain national laws have recently provided specific protection of the right to hire out video-cassettes.

16 Laws of that kind are therefore clearly justified on grounds of the protection of industrial and commercial property pursuant to Article [30] of the Treaty.

17 However, the defendant * * * contends that the author is at liberty to choose the Member State in which he will market his work. * * * [A] maker of a film who has offered the video-cassette of that film for sale in a Member State whose legislation confers on him no exclusive right of hiring it out (as in the main proceedings) must accept the consequences of his choice and the exhaustion of his right to restrain the hiring-out of that video-cassette in any other Member State.

18 That objection cannot be upheld. * * * [W]here national legislation confers on authors a specific right to hire out video-cassettes, that right would be rendered worthless if its owner were not in a position to authorize the operations for doing so. * * * [T]he marketing by a film-maker of a video-cassette containing one of his works, in a Member State which does not provide specific protection for the right to hire it out, [cannot] have repercussions on the right conferred on that same film-maker by the

legislation of another Member State to restrain, in that State, the hiring-out of that video-cassette.

Notes and Questions

1. How is the factual situation here different from that in *Winthrop?* Observe that the video-cassette bought in London is not being resold in Denmark, but rather exploited in a rental business. If Christiansen had tried to resell the video-cassette in Denmark, even at a substantial profit, he would have been allowed to do so under the exhaustion of rights doctrine. Why does the rental form of exploitation make a difference? Note that the Commission informed the Court that 90% of video-cassettes are exploited through rentals, rather than sales. Incited to some degree by the outcome in *Warner Brothers*, the Council adopted Directive 92/100 on copyright rental and lending rights, creating such rights in those States, like the UK, which did not recognize them. The directive is summarized in Section E infra.

2. Advocate General Mancini thought that the exhaustion of rights doctrine should apply. In his view, once Warner sold the video-cassette in the UK, it lost its ability to control the exploitation of the video-cassette any further, whether in the UK or in Denmark. He felt that if Warner had wanted additional compensation for a buyer's exploitation of a cassette by commercial rental, Warner could have placed a condition to that effect in the contract of sale. Once Warner placed the cassette into the Community stream of commerce, Warner should not be able to take advantage of the Danish law to secure new revenues from rentals. Do you agree with the Court of Justice or with the Advocate General? For an interesting analysis, see R. Hacon's casenote, 13 Eur.L.Rev. 415 (1988).

E. TOWARD COMMUNITY–WIDE INDUSTRIAL AND COMMERCIAL PROPERTY RIGHTS

As indicated at the outset of this chapter, the Commission's 1985 White Paper on Completing the Internal Market proposed new legislative efforts in the field of industrial and commercial property rights. The Single European Act's endorsement of the internal market goal and its modification of the legislative procedure used in harmonization of laws facilitated action in this field as in others.

There are two possible legislative solutions to the problem of diverse national laws. One is to harmonize by a directive the most important features of those laws, while still leaving the rights themselves a matter of national law. The second is to create a Community-wide system for a particular right. As we shall see, both approaches are being used.

1. TRADEMARKS

Legislation on trademarks represents the greatest success of the internal market program in this field. First came the adoption of Directive 89/104 to approximate laws relating to trademarks, O.J. L 140/1 (Feb. 11, 1989). (See the Selected Documents.) A Whereas clause states that the directive is not intended to achieve "full-scale approximation," but only to harmonize those aspects of national law "which most directly affect the functioning of the internal market." The Trademark Directive became effective in 1993.

The directive covers all trademarks registered in any Member State, directly or by virtue of an international registration (art. 1). A trademark is defined as any sign, words, designs, letters, numbers, as well as the "shape of goods or their packaging" used to distinguish goods or services (art. 2). This definition is broader than the former law in some States, which did not recognize service marks, or marks based on the shape or form of packages or containers.

Article 3 harmonizes trademark registration requirements by forbidding registration of certain types of putative marks, including nondistinctive marks, deceptive marks, marks which are only descriptive of characteristics, quality, purpose or geographic origin of goods or services, marks which are contrary to public policy or morality, etc. Article 4 prohibits the registration of identical or similar marks in the same field of goods or services whenever "there exists a likelihood of confusion on the part of the public." The Court of Justice has now authoritatively interpreted this provision on trademark confusion. See sub-section 2, infra.

Article 5 grants the mark owner exclusive rights of exploitation within the national territory. It also entitles the owner to bring infringement actions, though article 7 codifies the Court of Justice's exhaustion of rights doctrine as a limitation on infringement actions. (As noted above, the Court in *Paranova I* interpreted the directive's exhaustion of rights clause to have the same content as its prior doctrine.) Article 8 allows the mark owner to grant exclusive or non-exclusive licenses for all or only part of the field of goods or services, and for all or only part of the territory of the State concerned.

If a mark has not been put "to genuine use" within its registered field of goods or services within five years after registration, Article 10 permits the mark to be totally revoked (art. 12), or revoked as to some goods or services (art. 13), or partially invalidated (art. 11). For several States, these articles represent a significant change in law.

The directive has achieved a substantial degree of harmonization, clarifying trademark rights and eliminating some traditional peculiarities of national law. Nonetheless, the directive leaves trademark law still a matter of national law. Marks remain limited to the territory of each State, occasioning a risk of conflict between similar marks recognized by different States as the marketing under the marks expands within the Community.

Obviously, a preferable approach is that of creating Community trademarks, registered only once, governed by a single set of rules, and valid throughout the entire Community (just as federally–registered trademarks are valid throughout the US). The legislative road to achieve this proved a rocky one. The Commission published a draft Convention in 1973, but abandoned that approach in favor of a draft regulation in 1980. Only after the adoption of the Trademark Directive could serious progress be made on the regulation.

Council Regulation 40/94 on the Community trademark was finally adopted on December 20, 1993. O.J. L 11/1 (Jan. 14, 1994). The Trademark Regulation permits persons to register a mark for the entire Community. Indeed, such a Community trademark cannot be assigned, revoked or prohibited except for the entire Community (art. 1), although it may be licensed either exclusively or non-exclusively for part of the Community (art. 22). The Community trademark is good for ten years, renewable for further ten year periods (art. 46). The detailed provisions of the Regulation are too long for summary here, but they essentially parallel those of the Trademark Directive.

Because the Trademark Office has extensive powers in the registration process, including revocation proceedings, and a specialized trademark bar was expected to develop near the Office, several States wanted the Office site. The European Council allotted the Office to Spain, which chose Alicante, an attractive Mediterranean resort.

The Office for Harmonization in the Internal Market (Trademarks and Designs) opened for business on April 1, 1996, and was promptly flooded with applications for Community trademarks, almost one-third being filed by US owned enterprises. By the end of 2000, several hundred thousand applications had been filed, most accepted, but some refused by the Trademark Office, or the subject of third party challenge.

The Trademark Office has a Board of Appeal, with a further appeal possible to the Court of First Instance (art. 63). Since 1999, the Court of First Instance has reviewed a significant number of appeals from decisions of the Board of Appeal. Space concerns prevent coverage of these rather technical judgements. Just as an illustration, the Court of First Instance held in DVK v. OHIM, Case T–19/99, [2000] ECR __ (Jan. 12, 2000), that 'Companyline' constituted merely the linking of two generic words and could not qualify as a mark in the field of insurance. In contrast, the Court reversed the Board of Appeal to hold that Procter & Gamble could register a distinctive shape of a bar of soap as a mark in Procter & Gamble v. OHIM, Case T–163/98, [2000] ECR __ (Feb. 16, 2000).

In what may prove to be an interesting precedent, the Office uses English, French, German, Italian and Spanish as operational languages, one of which must be chosen by the applicant as a second language in addition to the applicant's own official language (art. 115). The Trademark Regulation's provision that only five State languages would be used for operational purposes was challenged by a Dutch trademark lawyer in Kik v. OHIM, Case T–120/99, [2001] ECR __ (July 12, 2001).

Kik filed a Community trademark application only in Dutch. When the application was rejected because it was not filed in one of the five languages permitted for operational purposes, Kik appealed, claiming that the Trademark Regulation's failure to permit Dutch to be used constituted an indirect discrimination on nationality, prohibited by Article 12 (ex 6) of the Treaty. Greece intervened in support of Kik's contention. The Court of First Instance held that Article 290 (ex 217) authorized the Council, acting unanimously, to set the "rules governing the languages of the institutions," which in turn enabled the Council to set the operational languages of the Trademark Office. The Court considered the Council decision to satisfy the principle of proportionality, because the use for operational purposes of any one of the most widely known languages could be considered justified by considerations of efficiency and transparency. See also page 181 supra on equal treatment aspects of the case.

2. TRADEMARK CONFUSION AFTER THE TRADEMARK DIRECTIVE

Read carefully the Trademark Directive's article 4(1) on "the likelihood of confusion" with an earlier trademark as a bar to the registration of a new one, and article 5(1) on "the likelihood of confusion" with a registered trademark as the basis for an action to bar the use of an infringing mark. In several cases the Court has now set Community-wide standards for the rather elusive concept of confusion through its interpretation of the two parallel articles.

SABEL v. PUMA

Case C–251/95, [1997] ECR I–6191.

[The German company, Puma, had registered a silhouette picture of a puma bounding towards the right as a trademark for leather products, handbags and clothing. When Sabel, a Dutch company, sought to register in Germany a mark composed of a silhouette picture of a cheetah bounding to the right above its name, Sabel, for the same product categories, Puma opposed the registration. On appeal, the Supreme Patent Court considered that there probably would be confusing similarity between the two marks based solely on customary German doctrine, but referred questions to the Court concerning the proper interpretation of article 4(1) of the Trademark Directive. The Court's reply not only provided guidance on the concept of confusion, but suggested that the risk of confusion in this case was minimal.]

22   Article 4(1)(b) of the Directive does not apply where there is no likelihood of confusion on the part of the public. * * * [T]he tenth recital in the preamble to the Directive [indicates] that the appreciation of the likelihood of confusion 'depends on numerous elements and, in particular, on the recognition of the trade mark on the market, of the association which can be made with the used or registered sign, of the degree of similarity between the trade mark and the sign and between the goods or services identified'. The likelihood of confusion must therefore be appreciated globally, taking into account all factors relevant to the circumstances of the case.

23   That global appreciation of the visual, aural or conceptual similarity of the marks in question, must be based on the overall impression given by the marks, bearing in mind, in particular, their distinctive and dominant components. The wording of Article 4(1)(b) of the Directive— '. . . there exists a likelihood of confusion on the part of the public" . . .—shows that the perception of marks in the mind of the average consumer of the type of goods or services in question plays a decisive role in the global appreciation of the likelihood of confusion. The average consumer normally perceives a mark as a whole and does not proceed to analyse its various details.

24   In that perspective, the more distinctive the earlier mark, the greater will be the likelihood of confusion. It is therefore not impossible that the conceptual similarity resulting from the fact that two marks use images with analogous semantic content may give rise to a likelihood of confusion where the earlier mark has a particularly distinctive character, either *per se* or because of the reputation it enjoys with the public.

25   However, in circumstances such as those in point in the main proceedings, where the earlier mark is not especially well known to the public and consists of an image with little imaginative content, the mere fact that the

two marks are conceptually similar is not sufficient to give rise to a likelihood of confusion.

LLOYD SCHUHFABRIK MEYER v. KLIJSEN HANDEL

Case C–342/97, [1999] ECR I–3819.

[Lloyd, a German manufacturer of shoes, has used the trade mark "Lloyd" since 1927. Klijsen, a Dutch manufacturer of shoes, obtained the mark "Loint's" for shoes in 1970 in the Netherlands and 1991 in Germany. When Lloyd sought to enjoin the use of "Loint's" as infringing on its German mark, the trial court referred questions concerning the application of article 5(1) of the Trademark Directive. The trial court noted that a survey indicated that 36% of those responding identified "Lloyd" as a brand of shoes. In its response, the Court provided more sophisticated and detailed criteria for determining whether confusion can occur.]

21 [F]or the purposes of art 5(1)(b) of the directive, there may be a likelihood of confusion, notwithstanding a lesser degree of similarity between the trade marks, where the goods or services covered by them are very similar and the earlier mark is highly distinctive.

22 In determining the distinctive character of a mark and, accordingly, in assessing whether it is highly distinctive, the national court must make an overall assessment of the greater or lesser capacity of the mark to identify the goods or services for which it has been registered as coming from a particular undertaking, and thus to distinguish those goods or services from those of other undertakings.

23 In making that assessment, account should be taken, in particular, of:

● the inherent characteristics of the mark, including the fact that it does or does not contain an element descriptive of the goods or services for which it has been registered;

● the market share held by the mark;

● how intensive, geographically widespread and long-standing use of the mark has been;

● the amount invested by the undertaking in promoting the mark;

● the proportion of the relevant section of the public which, because of the mark, identifies the goods or services as originating from a particular undertaking; and

● statements from chambers of commerce and industry or other trade and professional associations.

24 It follows that it is not possible to state in general terms, for example by referring to given percentages relating to the degree of recognition attained by the mark within the relevant section of the public, when a mark has a strong distinctive character.

25 In addition, the global appreciation of the likelihood of confusion must, as regards the visual, aural or conceptual similarity of the marks in question, be based on the overall impression created by them, bearing in mind, in particular, their distinctive and dominant components. * * * [T]he perception of marks in the mind of the average consumer of the category of goods

or services in question plays a decisive role in the global appreciation of the likelihood of confusion. The average consumer normally perceives a mark as a whole and does not proceed to analyse its various details [citing *Sabel*].

26   For the purposes of that global appreciation, the average consumer of the category of products concerned is deemed to be reasonably well-informed and reasonably observant and circumspect. However, account should be taken of the fact that the average consumer only rarely has the chance to make a direct comparison between the different marks but must place his trust in the imperfect picture of them that he has kept in his mind. It should also be borne in mind that the average consumer's level of attention is likely to vary according to the category of goods or services in question.

27   In order to assess the degree of similarity between the marks concerned, the national court must determine the degree of visual, aural or conceptual similarity between them and, where appropriate, evaluate the importance to be attached to those different elements, taking account of the category of goods or services in question and the circumstances in which they are marketed.

28   In the light of the foregoing, the answer to the questions referred to the court must be that it is possible that mere aural similarity between trade marks may create a likelihood of confusion within the meaning of art. 5(1)(b) of the directive. The more similar the goods or services covered and the more distinctive the earlier mark, the greater will be the likelihood of confusion.

Notes and Questions

1.   Advocate General Jacobs, an acknowledged expert on trademarks, wrote the opinions in these and virtually all other trademark cases in the last decade. His careful reasoning has clearly influenced the Court's views. In ¶ 51 of his opinion in *Sabel*, he contends that in dealing with confusion in article 4(1), the directive is "laying down a common standard" which should not be set at too high a level because it is necessary to avoid "the effect of insulating the national markets". He further argued that "the directive should accordingly not be read as imposing the most restrictive standard found in the laws of member states." In ¶ 55, he contended that there must be "a genuine and properly substantiated likelihood of confusion" to justify any bar to a new mark. Does the Court's judgment follow this approach? Does it represent a better balance between the proper protection of trademarks and free movement of goods than the Court's early judgment in *Terrapin*, supra page 755? How should the German court apply the Court's answer in *Sabel*?

2.   The Court of Justice's more detailed guidance in *Lloyd* on how to interpret the concept of confusion still leaves considerable leeway to trial courts. Note the Court's emphasis on the "reasonably well informed and reasonably observant" consumer standard, which we saw previously applied in the *Irish Hallmarking* and *Estee Lauder* opinions in Chapter 13C. Applying this standard, do you think "Lloyd" can be considered a highly distinctive mark in Germany? Are "Lloyd" and "Loint's" very similar, or only superficially so?

3. COPYRIGHT AND RELATED RIGHTS

In recent years, copyright law has been one of the most active areas of Community harmonization endeavors. The initial impetus came from a major study project, the Commission's 1988 Green Paper on Copyright and the Challenge of Technology, COM (88) 172. (In the 1980s, the Commission adopted the British nomenclature in referring to studies as Green Papers, and programs for action as White Papers.) The Green Paper provoked extensive commentary from both academic and business experts and led to a variety of Commission initiatives. The Commission's 1991 White Paper on Copyright and Neighboring Rights, COM (90) 584 final, set out a number of proposals for immediate or long-term legislative action.

Perhaps the most important new measure is Directive 93/98 harmonizing the term of protection of copyright and certain related fields, O.J. L 290/9 (Nov. 24, 1993). Although most Member States granted copyright protection for the life of the author(s) plus fifty years, several granted a longer term. Indeed, Germany's longer term enjoyed constitutional status.

The Copyright Term Directive chose to harmonize the term at life plus seventy years, the German model, explaining in recital 5 that this was in order to provide rights to two generations of author's descendants. The ironic result is that this harmonization directive creates a longer period in which a division of the market is possible, if different parties own copyrights in different States. Indeed, under article 10, the directive enables the revival of rights already expired in some States, if the term is still running in Germany or another longer term State. The new duration is accorded not only to authors of written material and music, but also to the principal director and other authors of cinematographic and audiovisual works (art. 2). The directive had a direct influence on the recent adoption of longer copyright terms in the US.

Directive 92/100 on rental and lending rights, O.J. L 346/61 (Nov. 27, 1992), is another innovative copyright directive, creating such rights in several States which had not previously recognized them. The directive established a common system for the recognition and protection of rights of authors, performing artists, and the producers of films, records and tapes when their works are the subject of commercial exploitation by rental or lending. This directive may also incite legislative action in the US to recognize such rights.

Another important initiative is Directive 93/83 coordinating copyright applicable to satellite broadcasting, O.J. L 248/15 (Oct. 6, 1993), which significantly facilitates transborder satellite and cable television transmission.

In the neighboring rights field, the most significant breakthrough came with the adoption of Directive 91/250 on the legal protection of computer programs, O.J. L 122/42 (May 17, 1991). The proper mode and level of protection for computer software had long been uncertain. Five Member States had recognized a form of copyright for software, while others had relied on protection through contract and unfair competition principles.

Article 1 of the directive requires all States to give copyright protection to a computer program that is "original in the sense that it is the author's own intellectual creation." However, the ideas and principles which underlie a program, as well as the "interface" between the software and hardware, are not protected. Article 8 sets the term as the life of the author plus 50 years.

Article 4 indicates the scope of protection: the reproduction of the program, its translation, adaptation or alteration, its sale, rental or other form of contractually authorized use. However, article 5 permits persons who have a right of use to make a back-up copy, as well as to study or test the program and to determine its underlying ideas and principles.

The computer software programs directive was adopted after lengthy review by the institutions and by expert advisors from computer software producers and users, and attempts to strike a balance among the interests concerned. By ensuring a clear and definite form of copyright protection for computer programs throughout the Community, the directive has substantially improved the legal climate for the development and use of such programs.

Another important neighboring rights measure is Directive 96/9/EC on the legal protection of databases, O.J. L 77/1 (Mar. 27, 1996). This creates a new *sui generis* exclusive economic right for the contents of a database (e.g., a telephone directory) if it cannot qualify for copyright protection, which is usually the case, thus protecting the investment costs of its maker. On July 19, 1995, the Commission also released for discussion its Green Paper, "Copyright and Related Rights in the Information Society."

4. PATENTS

The European Patent Convention (EPC) of Oct. 5, 1973, TS No. 20 (1978), 13 I.L.M. 270, which came into force in 1977, was not a Community endeavor as such, but strongly promotes the harmonization of patent rules. Most of the Member States and several non-EC states have ratified it, so the EPC is effective throughout most of Western Europe.

The EPC provides that an inventor may apply for a European patent at the European Patent Office in Munich, or its branch in The Hague. After the Office has conducted a priority search and examined the application for the originality and capability of industrial use, it may grant a European patent. In that event, the inventor is deemed to have acquired a patent in each of the ratifying states for 20 years from the date of application. The EPC has also harmonized a number of key substantive patent law concepts in the ratifying states and provides for a central system to review challenges to the application or patent. However, many aspects of the European patent continue to be governed by different national laws.

The then nine Member States signed the Community Patent Convention (CPC), O.J. L 17/1 (Jan. 26, 1976), as modified, O.J. L 401/10 (Dec. 30, 1989), as a supplement to the EPC. Although the Commission was not involved in the drafting of the EPC, it did provide advice on that for the CPC. Unfortunately, the CPC has never come into effect, because Denmark and Ireland have not ratified it.

On June 24,1997, the Commission issued a Green Paper on patents, raising issues for discussion by all interested parties. Subsequently, on Feb. 5, 1999, the Commission adopted a communication of proposed measures, notably a regulation to create a Community patent system instead of the previous convention approach. The concept was endorsed by the Lisbon European

Council in March 2000, and the Commission then issued its draft Community Patent Regulation on Aug. 1, 2000. Com (97) 314.

The draft regulation would enable the European Patent Office to issue a Community patent valid in all Member States, after the process of investigation and opportunity for challenge by third parties. Translation costs, presently quite substantial, would be reduced because the full text would be published only in either English, French, or German, with the claims alone being translated into the other two languages. (As a matter of fact, current practice makes English virtually the universal language for patents.) The draft foresees the creation of a specialized tribunal that would be competent for all issues of interpretation of the Regulation and the application of Community patents, subject to review by the Court of Justice, thus eliminating the risk of divergent interpretation by national courts. The Treaty of Nice, when ratified, will introduce a new Article 225a authorizing the Council to create a specialized judicial panel in this field, and a new Article 229a enabling the Council to provide for appeals to the Court of Justice.

One important measure has already been adopted, Directive 98/44 on the legal protection of biotechnological inventions, O.J. L 213/13 (July 30, 1998). A prior draft version was rejected by Parliament in 1995, a rare instance where the Parliament would not accept a Conciliation Committee report in the codecision legislative process. The Commission began again in 1996, this time with success.

The biotechnological patent directive requires Member States to issue patents for products containing biological material or produced by genetic engineering, provided that they are susceptible of industrial application. At Parliament's insistence, a clause provides that the human body and its elements, including genes, cannot be patented, and another clause states that "processes for cloning human beings" and "uses of human embryos for industrial or commercial purposes" cannot be patented. The Commission's European Group on Ethics in Science and New Technologies shall evaluate "all ethical aspects of biotechnology."

In order to compensate pharmaceutical producers for the lengthy delay in marketing drugs based upon patents due to the careful administrative review process before marketing authorization is granted, the Council adopted Regulation 1768/92 creating a supplementary protection certificate for medicinal products, O.J. L 182/1 (July 2, 1992). The regulation extends "the same rights as conferred by the basic patent" for a period of time that compensates partially for the review procedure delay, up to a maximum possible added period of five years.

The Council used Article 100a (now Article 95) as the legal basis, enabling the adoption of the regulation by a qualified majority vote. Spain's challenge of the regulation occasioned an important judgment on the Community power to legislate, not only to create patent rights, but to create any type of intellectual property right. See Spain v. Council (Medicinal product certificates), excerpted at page 108 as a prime example of implied Community power to legislate to achieve the internal market. The judgement removes any doubt that the Community has the legislative power either to harmonize national intellectual property systems, or to create new Community intellectual property rights.

Further Reading

The annual spring international intellectual property conference held at Fordham Law School results in a volume composed of all the papers presented at the conference. Nine volumes have been published under various titles by Juris Publishers. European Community legislation and case law is always featured in the conferences.

See also the books listed for further reading at the end of Chapter 13.

*

Part IV

COMPETITION POLICY

As we saw in Chapter 1 on the history of the European Community, and again in Part III on the genesis of the four freedoms, Western Europe was balkanized at the end of World War II. Each nation's borders were economic frontiers, and the frontiers were barriers to trade. Political and economic nationalism divided Europe.

The political economy of the nations varied. Some had statist regimes, with a plethora of state-owned enterprises. Most had significant degrees of government regulation. The nations were largely not hospitable to foreign investment, and high trade barriers in the form of quotas and tariffs kept foreign goods from flowing across the borders. The enterprises within each nation were plagued by inefficiencies and stagnation. Thus, European business lagged in a world on the brink of global trade and competition.

We have seen that the EC Treaty was designed to foster hospitable relations and thus peace among the nations and peoples of Europe by breaking down the economic barriers in the internal market and achieving one common market. The four freedoms would eliminate state barriers to trade, investment, and the establishment of business. Competition policy was synergistic. Business actors would not be allowed to erect or re-erect barriers or otherwise impair trade and competition.

With the traditional tariff and nontariff barriers removed, "competition policy" became the governing trade-and-competition policy for the internal market. National antidumping laws were forbidden, after the period of transition. Member State subsidies and other state aids were subjected to rules of transparency and were tightly restricted. Commercial actors, public as well as private, were forbidden to abuse a dominant position or enter agreements with the object or effect of restricting competition. State monopolies were prohibited from discriminating against non-nationals, particularly so as not to impair imports or exports.

From the outset the EC Treaty mandated, as one of the specified activities necessary to carry out the purposes of the Community, "the institution of a system insuring that competition in the common market is not distorted...." Article 3(f) [now 3(1)(g)].

Under the EC Treaty, competition policy is to be carried out by several means. First, free movement—the four freedoms—provides a basic framework. Second, Article 81 (ex 85) prohibits undertakings from making anticompetitive agreements, and Article 82 (ex 86) prohibits dominant undertakings from abusing their dominance. Third, public undertakings and undertakings to which Member States grant special or exclusive rights are, under Article 86 (ex 90), subject to the competition rules except to the extent that application of those rules would obstruct the performance of their public tasks. Fourth, since competition could be distorted not only by enterprises but also by state subsidies and other aids, Articles 87 to 89 (ex 92 to 94) provide for the identification, and justification or elimination, of state aids.

Fifth, recognizing also that state action may unduly obstruct trade and competition, the Treaty imposes obligations on the Member States. We have studied at length how the Treaty prohibits the Member States from adopting or retaining obstructive measures; e.g., Article 28, ex 30, prohibits quantitative restrictions on imports and measures of equivalent effect. Also, the Treaty requires Member States to "progressively adjust any State monopolies of a commercial character" to assure no discrimination in procurement or marketing (Article 31, ex 37), and to "facilitate the achievement of the Community's tasks" and abstain from measures that could jeopardize achievement of the Treaty's objectives (Article 10, ex 5). The objectives include undistorted competition. Accordingly, Member States are restricted in adopting anticompetitive legislation; but this constraint is importantly qualified by states' rights to adopt nondiscriminatory regulation in pursuit of justifiable public ends.

The unitary quality of the European Union's competition policy is greater than that of the United States and of other nations and regions. In the United States, policy regarding public restraints is more sharply separated from policy regarding private restraints, states retain more sovereign power to enact laws that have anticompetitive impacts, and there is no system disciplining state-granted aids.

In Chapter 20 we introduce the Treaty provisions directed towards market actors ("undertakings"); namely, Articles 81 and 82. At the outset we focus on the market-integrating aspects of the Community's competition policy. In Chapter 21 we consider a core anticompetitive restraint—agreements among competitors that have no purpose except to eliminate competition among the competitors; that is, cartels, which most commonly include market-division, price-fixing and bid rigging. In introducing the law against cartels we explain the economics of competition policy; and in connection with transnational cartels, we provide materials on jurisdiction and jurisdictional conflicts.

While Article 81 regulates agreements, Article 82 regulates the conduct firms in a dominant position. This major provision of EC competition law is the subject of Chapter 22. In Chapter 22 we ask: When does a firm have a dominant position, and when does conduct by that firm amount to a prohibited abuse?

We have mentioned cartels, which by definition eliminate competition. Various other cooperative agreements among competitors may improve production, distribution and economic and technological progress. Chapter 23 deals with these agreements, distinguishing permissible collaborations from forbidden ones.

Chapter 24 treats a related problem that arises under Article 81: contracts and combinations that amount to vertical restraints. These are restraints in the course of distribution and licensing, including the licensing of technology. This chapter includes exclusionary and market-blocking restraints, and distribution through selected outlets. Chapter 24 illustrates, also, the administrative system of notification of agreements to the Commission and the Commission's grant or denial of exemptions for individual agreements, and the device of block or group exemptions for specified common forms of transactions. The authorization/exemption procedure is currently under review in connection with a widely discussed proposal for "modernisation," and is likely to be eliminated.

The law of mergers is covered in Chapter 25. This chapter presents the very important Merger Regulation, including merger analysis and notification under the merger control system, and conflict and coordination in world merger review.

Chapter 26 concludes the study of competition law by addressing competition policy as it applies to government action. The law so applies in a number of ways: public enterprises and state granted monopolies are subject to competition principles; Member States are required to facilitate the achievement of the Community's tasks, including undistorted competition; and all state aids must be reported and justified or eliminated. Taken together with the positive freedoms of movement (the four freedoms), the law on government action rounds the circle of competition policy.

Competition is one of the few areas of law for the internal market—along with agriculture, transport and tax—that the EC Treaty treated from the outset as common policy. Why? Could the founders of the Community just as wisely have left competition law to the Member States, and perhaps later sought to harmonize the competition laws of the various Member States? Would harmonization have been a good or poor substitute for common competition policy?

Competition law and its enforcement form the fullest body of administrative law within the European Union. In most other areas the Member States are the principal agents for carrying out Community law, which they are empowered and bound to do, as we saw in cases such as *Factortame*. In competition law, the Commission has been the principal administrator and enforcer of the law. That is why many of the cases already studied, such as those relating to standing and procedural rights of litigants, have been competition cases.

Chapter 20

COMPETITION POLICY AND THE SINGLE MARKET

A. THE OBJECTIVES OF COMMUNITY COMPETITION POLICY

Competition law is a vital part of European Community law. It is informed by many interrelated policies. Every year the Competition Directorate publishes a report on competition policy. From time to time it reexamines the objectives of Community competition policy. Below are excerpts from recent Competition Policy Reports.

XXXth REPORT ON COMPETITION POLICY (2000)
excerpt

[1] Competition Policy is one of the pillars of the European Commission's action in the economic field. This action is founded on the principle, enshrined in the Treaty, of "an open market economy with free competition". It acknowledges the fundamental role of the market and of competition in guaranteeing consumer welfare, in encouraging the optimum allocation of resources and in granting economic agents the appropriate incentives to pursue productive efficiency, quality, and innovation. However, the principle of an open market economy does not imply an attitude of blind faith or, possibly, indifference towards the operation of market mechanisms; on the contrary, it requires constant vigilance aimed at preserving those mechanisms. This is particularly true in the present context of markets evolving at a fast pace and becoming increasingly integrated at global level. . . .

[2] Both technological developments and policy initiatives are reshaping the economic environment. Economies are increasingly based on knowledge, as evidenced by the growth of the service sector. Information systems have forced companies to re-evaluate and adapt their commercial relationships with both customers and suppliers and have enabled them to adopt more tightly managed and efficient business practices. We are now beginning to see the emergence of business-to-business (B2B) exchanges that are in the process of revolutionising the management of supply chains. Institutional changes have been added to technological developments. The single market

programme culminated in the adoption of a single currency, further integrating markets and enhancing competition between firms. The liberalisation of the network industries has opened many crucial sectors previously closed to competition. These developments affect all aspects of competition policy. * * *

4   Enforcement of competition rules reflected the reality of new markets and business practices. The creation of electronic marketplaces and the use by certain industries of voluntary agreements with environmental aims are just two examples of emerging practices [that have] led to Commission decisions. A large part of the Commission's enforcement activity in 2000 was focused on recently liberalised markets, where a competitive environment is not yet fully established.

XXIXth REPORT ON COMPETITION POLICY (1999)
excerpt

2   The first objective of competition policy is the maintenance of competitive markets. Competition policy serves as an instrument to encourage industrial efficiency, the optimal allocation of resources, technical progress and the flexibility to adjust to a changing environment. In order for the Community to be competitive on worldwide markets, it needs a competitive home market. Thus, the Community's competition policy has always taken a very strong line against price-fixing, market-sharing cartels, abuses of dominant positions, and anticompetitive mergers. It has also prohibited unjustified state-granted monopoly rights and state aid measures which do not ensure the long-term viability of firms but distort competition by keeping them artificially in business.

3   The second is the single market objective. An internal market is an essential condition for the development of an efficient and competitive industry. As the Community has progressively broken down government-erected trade barriers between Member States, companies operating in what they had regarded as "their" national markets were and are for the first time exposed to competitors able to compete on a level playing field. There are two possible reactions to this: either to seek to compete on the merits, looking to expand into other territories and benefit from the opportunities offered by a single market, or to erect private barriers to trade—to retrench and act defensively—in the hope of preventing market penetration. The Commission has used its competition policy as an active tool to prevent this, prohibiting, and fining heavily the parties to, two main types of agreement: distribution and licensing agreements that prevent parallel trade between Member States, and agreements between competitors to keep out of one another's "territories". Moreover, the objectives of competition policy have been integrated into the Commission's new strategy for the European single market adopted on 24 November [1999]. The aim is to prevent anticompetitive practices from undermining the single market's achievements.

Three years earlier, the Report on Competition Policy put competition policy into this broader context:

XXVIth REPORT ON COMPETITION POLICY (1996)
excerpt

2   Competition policy is ... both a Commission policy in its own right and an integral part of a large number of European Union policies and with them seeks to achieve the Community objectives set out in Article 2 of the Treaty, including the promotion of harmonious and balanced development of economic activities, sustainable and non-inflationary growth which respects the environment, a high level of employment and of social protection, the raising of the standard of living and quality of life, and economic and social cohesion.

3   In the final analysis, like all other Community policies, competition policy aims to enhance the economic prosperity of the European Union and the well-being of all its people. [T]he Commission forcefully reaffirmed these ideas [in a communication,] stating that, "market forces produce a better allocation of resources and greater effectiveness in the supply of services, the principal beneficiary being the consumer, who gets better quality at a lower price". However, the Commission is also well aware that "these mechanisms sometimes have their limits; as a result the potential benefits might not extend to the entire population and the objective of promoting social and territorial cohesion may not be attained. The public authority must then ensure that the general interest is taken into account".

4   The positive interaction between competition policy and other Community policy areas was particularly evident on the employment front in 1996. In line with the approach pursued through the Single European Act and the "White Paper on growth, competitiveness and employment", the [employment] pact proposes four types of structural action: "to complete the internal market and implement it more effectively; to enhance the overall competitive environment in Europe; to help small and medium-sized enterprises; to open up wider access to the world market", the first three of which are closely linked to competition policy. The first two types of action involve essential competition policy objectives under Articles 85, 86 and 90 [now Articles 81, 82 and 86] of the Treaty and the Merger Regulation. The third was pursued this year in the policy on state aid, with the adoption of a new, simpler and more broadly based *de minimis* rule, the introduction of new guidelines on aid for SMEs and a notice on the monitoring of state aid and reduction of labour costs.

5   If it is to perform its function fully, competition policy as a structural policy must work with and anticipate trends in the economy so as to ensure operation of markets without acting unduly as a brake on their performance. It must in particular:

—take account of globalization;

—help to develop the full potential of the internal market;

—modernize its instruments. * * *

[8] ... [T]he Commission's policy is to promote the competitiveness of European industry as a whole by strict enforcement of the competition rules applicable to Member States and those applicable to undertakings, looking at each market individually and taking account of its size.

Thus, in its policy on liberalization, through gradual and balanced liberalization of the network industries that are crucial to the competitiveness of European industry as a whole, such as telecommunications, energy and transport, the Commission's aim is to overcome the handicap created by the cost of such services for European firms.... Parallel to this, in the policy it pursues on state aid, the Commission may take a positive view of aid that allows the rationalization of production and the restructuring of a firm in order to enhance its competitiveness and in the long term safeguard employment. On the other hand, it takes a negative view of aid which merely bails out a firm without providing any guarantee of its future viability.

In its antitrust and merger control policy, the Commission endeavours to prevent the foreclosure of European markets, and in particular of emerging or recently demonopolized markets, while at the same time fostering the development of a powerful European industry that can meet the challenges of world competition. * * *

Notes and Questions

1. Does the XXVIth Report complement or complicate the statement of goals in the XXIXth and the XXXth Reports?

2. Describe in your own words the goals of the competition policy of the European Union. Which of the following objectives do you think are most basic, and therefore should be preferred in the event of conflict or tension: consumer welfare, strength of European business, help for small and medium sized enterprises, market integration, market access, market liberalization, level playing field, fairness?

3. What is the relationship of competition policy to:

a. the competitiveness of European businesses in world markets

b. the environment

c. employment

d. cohesion (e.g. lifting up the poorest nations)

e. liberalization?

4. In the United States, competition law (antitrust) is not so interrelated with other objectives; at least not explicitly. Since the 1980s it has often been said that US antitrust law and policy has one goal—consumer welfare. Antitrust officials assert that no other goal or value should diffuse this focus. They often claim that antitrust policy should influence other policies (e.g. trade barriers) but that no other policies should influence antitrust.

Compare the US with the EU approach. What are the advantages and disadvantages of each? What political or economic factors might have produced the differences? Would you expect the differences to endure, or the objectives and admissable considerations to converge?

B. INTRODUCTION TO ARTICLES 81 AND 82 AND THE IMPLEMENTING REGULATION

The Treaty specifies rules that regulate agreements and concerted practices, and rules that control dominant firm behavior. (Articles 81 and 82.) Together with the Merger Regulation, adopted in 1989, these provisions form the heart of European competition policy.

After the EC Treaty was adopted in 1957, it was necessary for the Council to adopt legislation to implement the competition articles. The Council adopted the initial implementing measure in 1962. This is Regulation 17 (which is expected to be replaced by modernising legislation).

Article 81(1) declares, in short, that agreements that distort competition are incompatible with the common market; Article 81(2) declares such agreements void; and Article 81(3)allows exemption for such agreements or practices that are economically progressive and benefit consumers. Article 82 prohibits abuse of a dominant position. We set forth the text of Articles 81 and 82 below, and then describe Regulation 17.

Article 81, ex 85

1. The following shall be prohibited as incompatible with the common market: all agreements between undertakings, decisions by associations of undertakings and concerted practices which may affect trade between Member States and which have as their object or effect the prevention, restriction or distortion of competition within the common market, and in particular those which:

(*a*) directly or indirectly fix purchase or selling prices or any other trading conditions;

(*b*) limit or control production, markets, technical development, or investment;

(*c*) share markets or sources of supply;

(*d*) apply dissimilar conditions to equivalent transactions with other trading parties, thereby placing them at a competitive disadvantage;

(*e*) make the conclusion of contracts subject to acceptance by the other parties of supplementary obligations which, by their nature or according to commercial usage, have no connection with the subject of such contracts.

2. Any agreements or decisions prohibited pursuant to this Article shall be automatically void.

3. The provisions of paragraph 1 may, however, be declared inapplicable in the case of:

— any agreement or category of agreements between undertakings;

— any decision or category of decisions by associations of undertakings;

— any concerted practice or category of concerted practices;

which contributes to improving the production or distribution of goods or to promoting technical or economic progress, while allowing consumers a fair share of the resulting benefit, and which does not:

    (*a*) impose on the undertakings concerned restrictions which are not indispensable to the attainment of these objectives;

    (*b*) afford such undertakings the possibility of eliminating competition in respect of a substantial part of the products in question.

Article 82, ex 86

Any abuse by one or more undertakings of a dominant position within the common market or in a substantial part of it shall be prohibited as incompatible with the common market in so far as it may affect trade between Member States. Such abuse may, in particular, consist in:

    (*a*) directly or indirectly imposing unfair purchase or selling prices or other unfair trading conditions;

    (*b*) limiting production, markets or technical development to the prejudice of consumers;

    (*c*) applying dissimilar conditions to equivalent transactions with other trading parties, thereby placing them at a competitive disadvantage;

    (*d*) making the conclusion of contracts subject to acceptance by the other parties of supplementary obligations which, by their nature or according to commercial usage, have no connection with the subject of such contracts.

Note the examples of restrictive agreements or conduct in Article 81(1) and in Article 82. To what extent are they virtually identical? What is the major difference?

Why do you think that restrictive agreements can be authorized but restrictive conduct that amounts to abuse of dominance cannot?

Regulation 17 was adopted by the Council to give the Commission the necessary powers to administer and enforce the Treaty provisions, and to give procedural rights to individuals. Regulation 17 is printed in the Selected Documents as Competition Doc. No. 1. Proposals for a dramatic revamping of Regulation 17 are under consideration.

Regulation 17 states that agreements, decisions and concerted practices within the scope of Article 81(1) must be notified to the Commission; no exemption may be granted until notification has been filed. Parties to agreements and transactions that do not infringe Article 81(1) or Article 82 may obtain a "negative clearance." That is, the Commission may certify that "on the basis of the facts in its possession, there are no grounds under Article [81(1)] or Article [82] of the Treaty for action."

Notified agreements that meet the substantive criteria of Article 81(3) may be exempted. As Article 9 of Regulation 17 states, "the Commission shall have the sole power to declare Article [81(1)] inapplicable pursuant to Article

[81(3)] of the Treaty." Thus, Regulation 17 gave neither national authorities nor national courts the power to grant exemptions.

What are the implications of this allocation of power to the Commission? What considerations, do you think, lay behind the notification/approval system, and the grant of power of exemption solely to the Commission?

Agreements and conduct may be accorded one of two forms of approval in addition to individual exemptions under Article 81(3). One is informal and carries with it no legal protection. This is the "comfort letter." Instead of granting a negative clearance or an exemption, the Commission may send a comfort letter stating that it has no reason to take action and is closing the file. The second is legislative and is called a "block exemption." In certain areas of routine transactions, such as restraints in the course of distributing goods and services (vertical restraints), the Commission has designed block exemptions. If an agreement meets the terms of a block exemption, Article 81(1) is automatically inapplicable. In the relatively few cases in which the Commission has concerns that a particular agreement is anticompetitive even though it complies with the block exemption, the Commission may withdraw the benefits of the block exemption.

Regulation 17 authorizes the Commission to terminate infringements and to impose large fines for violation of Articles 81 and 82. The Commission may impose fines of 1000 to one million Euros or 10% of the undertaking's past-year turnover, whichever is greater. But if an agreement within Article 81(1) has been notified and is later held not to be entitled to an exemption, no fines may be imposed for the period after notification and before the Commission's decision. Under a 1999 amendment, however, preparing the way for further reform, vertical restraint agreements need not be notified prior to the grant of an individual exemption; the Commission may not impose fines until after a declaration of invalidity.

Regulation 17 also authorizes the Commission to undertake investigations. When the Commission is on the trail of a violation and fears that, if it gives notice of its concerns, the evidence will disappear, the Commission may make surprise raids; "dawn raids," as they are called. In this and related contexts, targets of investigation have asserted and won procedural due process rights. These cases have become a part of the basic rights jurisprudence of the European Union.

C. MARKET INTEGRATION AND THE BLOCKAGE OF IMPORTS

1. GENERAL

Business actors may restrain the flow of trade over Member State lines, sometimes undermining market integration, harming competition, and violating Articles 81 and 82.

In this section we telescope three categories of such restraints, and proceed to concentrate on the third: vertical restraints blocking parallel imports.

First, competitors established in different Member States, feeling the heat of cross-border competition, might enter into a truce with their competitors, re-partitioning the common market. ("I take France, you take Germany.") In an economic as well as a Community sense, this is the worst kind of restraint. The competitors' agreement frustrates natural competition and its benefits for consumers and the economy, and it totally undermines the liberalizing effort to tear down barriers at Member State lines. Article 81 is applicable to such market-division cartels, which we treat in Chapter 21.

Second, a dominant firm that has the power to do so might block competitors from entering "its" Member State. This is an equally harmful restraint. It keeps out competitors and makes it possible for the dominant firm to continue to exercise its monopoly power, and in doing so it undermines market integration. Without the help of government, however, a firm, acting alone, does not normally have such power; and when a government has conferred an exclusive right on a chosen entity, often it has done so in response to a considered "public interest," as in the case of the Swedish alcohol monopoly (see Chapter 26). Market blockage by a dominant firm can be a serious abuse of dominance in violation of Article 82 and sometimes the combination of Articles 82 and 86 (ex 86/90). Abuse of dominance is treated in Chapter 22.

Third, a single producer may enlist a distributor for each Member State and may try to empower its distributors to keep out imports of its own product, so that the designated distributor alone can sell the same-brand product in the territory. This is called, variously, a vertical restraint, an intrabrand restraint, and a restraint on parallel imports. We turn now to this latter form of restraint.

2. PARALLEL IMPORTS

a. *Consten and Grundig*

Grundig, a manufacturer of radios, television sets, tape recorders, and dictating machines, appointed Consten to be its exclusive distributor in France. Consten and Grundig wanted Consten to be the only distributor of the Grundig products in France; thus, they wanted Consten to be in the position of excluding from France Grundig products put on the market in other nations. To achieve this result they relied on the French trademark law as well as the distribution contract. Since French case law held that only the owner of a trademark was entitled to enforce the trademark, the parties agreed that Consten should apply for and own the trademark GINT (Grundig International). Consten and Grundig agreed that if Consten should cease to be the distributor for Grundig in France, Consten would assign the mark to Grundig. Grundig made similar exclusive distribution and trademark arrangements with each of its distributors in the other countries.

Recall that, before the EC Treaty was adopted, the Western European nations had high tariffs and low quotas. Quotas would prevent goods from moving across national borders. The EC Treaty required the Member States to remove the quotas (and tariffs) in the internal market. In the spring of 1961 when French quotas ended, the French discounter UNEF began purchasing GINT television sets, tape recorders, dictaphones and other electronic equipment from German wholesalers (who had also accepted export bans) and selling them in competition with Consten's dealers in France. Consten sued

UNEF under French law for unfair competition and trademark infringement, alleging that UNEF knew that the sales to it were in breach of contract and that the sales by UNEF undermined Consten's contract. Thereupon, UNEF petitioned the Commission to declare the agreement between Consten and Grundig void under Article 85(2). Meanwhile, Regulation 17 came into effect, and Grundig filed a notification of its distribution agreement and sought an exemption under Article 85(3). In justification of the territorial division, Grundig argued that German buyers were familiar with its product and French buyers were not, and that the French market demanded a higher level of service and promotion than the German market. Moreover, it noted that Consten was responsible for guarantees, repair, customer service, accepting advance orders, maintaining stocks, and advertising in France. Grundig argued that cheap imports form Germany would undercut Consten's incentives to fulfill these duties, and that Consten's failure to fulfill its duties would undercut the brand's reputation and frustrate sales. Grundig depicted the market for electronics products as highly competitive, with prices dropping steadily even before UNEF's appearance on the French market.

The Commission refused to consider evidence of competition from other producers competitive with Grundig, and denied Grundig's request for an exemption under Article 85(3). It observed that prices for Grundig products in France were substantially higher than prices for Grundig products in Germany. Consten and Grundig sued the Commission, seeking annulment of its decision.

The Advocate General, Karl Roemer, criticized the Commission for considering only competition among distributors of Grundig's products. Advocate General Roemer said:

> [I]t is not proper if the Commission proceeds in such a manner that from the very outset it considers *exclusively* the last-mentioned internal competition [intraband competition] and completely neglects in its considerations the competition with similar products [interbrand competition]. In fact, it is conceivable that the competition between different products or, to be more precise, between different producers is so severe as not to leave any room worth mentioning for what was called internal competition in a product (possibly with regard to price and service). . . . Rightfully, it was . . . therefore incumbent on the Commission to make a survey of the entire competition situation. . . . Such a survey of the effects on the market would possibly have led to a result favorable for the plaintiffs. . . . Such more favorable result might have been possible in view of the relatively small share of Grundig in the French market for tape recorders and dictating machines (roughly 17 percent)—as far as we know, the Commission has not conducted any investigations concerning other products—or in view of the plaintiffs' allegation that the markets for television sets . . . and for transistor sets showed so severe a competition of various, and sometimes very strong producers of the Community and of third countries that it repeatedly became necessary to reduce the prices of Grundig sets considerably.

Because of the Commission's narrow concept of the term "restraint of competition," no such survey was made, and the Court of Justice in its proceeding cannot be obligated to make the survey itself belatedly. The only thing we can do in this situation is to find that the results which the Commission arrived at in the investigation of the criterion "restraint of competition" must be deemed to lack a sufficient foundation and must for that reason be rejected.

The Court of Justice disagreed. Here are excerpts from its judgment.

CONSTEN AND GRUNDIG v. COMMISSION

Cases 56, 58/64, [1966] ECR 299.

... [A]n agreement between producer and distributor which might tend to restore the national divisions in trade between Member States might be such as to frustrate the most fundamental objectives of the Community. The Treaty, whose preamble and content aim at abolishing the barriers between States, and which in several provisions gives evidence of a stern attitude with regard to their reappearance, could not allow undertakings to reconstruct such barriers. Article 85(1) is designed to pursue this aim, even in the case of agreements between undertakings placed at different levels in the economic process.

[The Court found that the agreement affected trade between Member States because it limited the freedom of undertakings to trade across borders. It stated that this conclusion would hold even if the effect of the agreement were to increase the volume of trade between Member States.] ...

The applicants and the German Government maintain that since the Commission restricted its examination solely to Grundig products the decision was based upon a false concept of competition and of the rules on prohibition contained in Article 85(1), since this concept applies particularly to competition between similar products of different makes....

The principle of freedom of competition concerns the various stages and manifestations of competition. Although competition between producers is generally more noticeable than that between distributors of products of the same make, it does not thereby follow that an agreement tending to restrict the latter kind of competition should escape the prohibition of Article 85(1) merely because it might increase the former.

Besides, for the purpose of applying Article 85(1), there is no need to take account of the concrete effects of an agreement once it appears that it has as its object the prevention, restriction or distortion of competition.

Therefore the absence in the contested decision of any analysis of the effects of the agreement on competition between similar products of different makes does not, of itself, constitute a defect in the decision.

It thus remains to consider whether the contested decision was right in founding the prohibition of the disputed agreement under Article 85(1) on the restriction on competition created by the agreement in the sphere of the distribution of Grundig products alone. The infringement which was found to exist by the contested decision results from the absolute territorial protection created [by] the said contract in favour of Consten on the basis of French law. The applicants thus wished to eliminate any possibility of competition at the wholesale level in Grundig products in the territory specified in the contract essentially by two methods.

First, Grundig undertook not to deliver even indirectly to third parties products intended for the area covered by the contract. The restrictive nature of that undertaking is obvious if it is considered in the light of the prohibition on exporting which was imposed not only on Consten but also on all the other sole concessionnaires of Grundig, as well as the German wholesalers. Secondly, the registration in France by Consten of the GINT trade mark, which Grundig affixes to all its products, is intended to increase the protection inherent in the disputed agreement, against the risk of parallel imports into France of Grundig products, by adding the protection deriving from the law on industrial property rights. Thus no third party could import Grundig products from other Member States of the Community for resale in France without running serious risks....

The situation as ascertained above results in the isolation of the French market and makes it possible to charge for the products in question prices which are sheltered from all effective competition. In addition, the more producers succeed in their efforts to render their own makes of product individually distinct in the eyes of the consumer, the more the effectiveness of competition between producers tends to diminish. Because of the considerable impact of distribution costs on the aggregate cost price, it seems important that competition between dealers should also be stimulated. The efforts of the dealer are stimulated by competition between distributors of products of the same make. Since the agreement thus aims at isolating the French market for Grundig products and maintaining artificially, for products of a very well-known brand, separate national markets within the Community, it is therefore such as to distort competition in the Common Market.

It was therefore proper for the contested decision to hold that the agreement constitutes an infringement of Article 85(1). No further considerations, whether of economic data (price differences between France and Germany, representative character of the type of appliance considered, level of overheads borne by Consten) or of the corrections of the criteria upon which the Commission relied in its comparisons between the situations of the French and German markets, and no possible favourable effects of the agreement in other respects, can in any way lead, in the face of abovementioned restrictions, to a different solution under Article 85(1)....

The applicants maintain more particularly that the criticized effect on competition is due not to the agreement but to the registration of the trade-mark in accordance with French law, which gives rise to an original inherent right of the holder of the trade-mark from which the absolute territorial protection derives under national law.

Consten's right under the contract to the exclusive use in France of the GINT trade-mark, which may be used in a similar manner in other countries, is intended to make it possible to keep under surveillance and to place an obstacle in the way of parallel imports. Thus, the agreement by which Grundig, as the holder of the trade-mark by virtue of an international registration, authorized Consten to register it in France in its own name tends to restrict competition....

That agreement therefore is one which may be caught by the prohibition in Article 85(1). The prohibition would be ineffective if Consten could continue to use the trade-mark to achieve the same object as that pursued by the agreement which has been held to be unlawful.

[The Court did not interfere with the Commission's decision to deny an exemption under Article 85(3). It acknowledged that Consten, as Grundig's distributor in France, was required to perform various obligations such as to accept advance orders and to provide warranty and after-sales service. The Court stated that territorial protection would give the parties to the agreement an advantage in *their* production and distribution activities. But, it said, to qualify for exemption the "improvement must in particular show appreciable objective advantages of such a character as to compensate for the disadvantages which they cause in the field of competition," and must be indispensable. The argument that every "improvement as conceived by the parties to the agreement must be maintained intact" ... "not only tends to weaken the requirement of indispensability but also among other consequences to confuse solicitude for the specific interests of the parties with the objective improvements contemplated by the Treaty."]

Notes and Questions

1. Grundig appointed an exclusive distributor for each territory; Grundig agreed that it, itself, would not distribute GINT-brand product in the assigned territory; and each distributor agreed with Grundig to "work" its territory and to stay within its territory. These obligations are of the essence of an exclusive distribution agreement. The producer says to the distributor: I appoint you and you alone to distribute my product in this territory.

The Commission does not regard such an agreement as within Article 81(1). Why?

2. The additional obligations on both Consten and Grundig are the key obligations in the case. What were these additional obligations and why were they of particular concern? Did they lessen competition?

3. How does the rule of *Consten and Grundig* increase market integration? Are you convinced?

4. Why do you suppose that German prices were lower than French prices? Why might you want to know? Is the answer relevant to a) whether the restraint is caught by Article 81(1)? (b) whether the restraint is entitled to an exemption under Article 81(3)?

5. Note the relationship between French trademark law and EC competition law. Which has the upper hand? Is the Court's answer consistent with Article 295 (ex 222)? Is it consistent with the case law you studied in Chapter 19? In your view, did the Court properly resolve the tension?

6. After *Consten and Grundig,* can an agreement that absolutely eliminates parallel imports ever be justified as essential for improvement of production or distribution?

7. The United States once had a legal rule very similar to the rule of *Consten and Grundig.* Under United States v. Arnold, Schwinn & Co., 388 U.S. 365, 87 S.Ct. 1856, 18 L.Ed.2d 1249 (1967) (overruled in 1977), a manufacturer's imposition of absolute territorial restrictions on its distributors was held to be illegal on its face. A manufacturer could not lawfully assign an exclusive territory to a

distributor, require the distributor to stay within the territory, and agree to keep parallel imports out of the territory. The existence of robust interbrand competition was irrelevant. The *Schwinn* decision protected the autonomy of distributors to sell where they wished. Ten years later the US Supreme Court overruled *Schwinn*. Continental T.V., Inc. v. GTE Sylvania Inc., 433 U.S. 36, 97 S.Ct. 2549, 53 L.Ed.2d 568 (1977). In *Sylvania* the Supreme Court observed that non-price restraints imposed by a manufacturer on its own distributors can improve the efficiency and competitiveness of the manufacturer, and it held that improvements in interbrand competition (e.g., competition between Sylvania and Sony TVs) can outweigh any harm from the decrease in intrabrand competition (i.e., competition among Sylvania's own distributors).

Subsequent US cases go farther and maintain that intrabrand restraints have no negative significance in themselves; that competition among producers, where it exists, forces manufacturers to behave competitively and assures that any restraints imposed by manufacturers on their distributors are efficient and procompetitive; the market will pressure the manufacturers to distribute their products as efficiently as possible. Can *Consten and Grundig* be reconciled with this line of reasoning? Is one position right and the other wrong? Or is the difference justified by context?

b. *Development of the Rule Against Market Partitioning*

The rule of *Consten and Grundig* has remained a robust rule in the European Union.

In 1983 the Court of Justice decided SA Musique Diffusion Française v. Commission (*Pioneer*), Cases 100–103/80, [1983] ECR 1825. Pioneer Europe, a subsidiary of Pioneer Tokyo, had facilitated an agreement among the French, German and British distributors of its hi-fidelity sound equipment to stay out of one another's markets; particularly, the agreement aimed to keep low-priced British and German product out of the high-priced French market. At the Court of Justice, Pioneer and its distributors lost all significant arguments, including the claims that there was no agreement, that their agreement, if any, did not affect Member State trade, and that the fines were set at an unprecedented level (2% to 4% of total turnover) and were disproportionate. The Court said, as to effect on trade and proportionality of the fines:

Effect on trade

[82]   MDF and Pioneer GB ... consider that their market shares in 1976 were 3.38% in France and 3.18% in the United Kingdom. They maintain that such market shares are not sufficient for their conduct to be regarded as capable of affecting trade between Member States within the meaning of Article 85(1) of the Treaty. * * *

[86]   ... The studies produced by MDF and Pioneer GB show that the market in hi-fi products in France and the United Kingdom is very large but that it is markedly divided between a very great number of brands, so that the percentages stated by the applicants exceed those of most of their competitors. If regard is had solely to imported brands, it even seems that the two applicants were amongst the largest suppliers of the two markets. In those circumstances, regard being had to their absolute turnover figures, it cannot be denied that conduct by those undertakings seeking to restrain parallel imports and therefore to partition national markets was capable of

exercising an influence on the pattern of trade between Member States in a way capable of hindering the attainment of the objectives of a single market. * * *

Level of fines

[104] According to the Commission, however, such a level is fully justified by the nature of the infringements. After 20 years of Community competition policy an appreciable increase in the level of fines is necessary, in its view, at least for types of infringement which have long been well defined and are known to those concerned, such as prohibitions on exports and imports. In fact those constitute the most serious infringements since they deprive consumers of all the benefits resulting from the elimination of customs duties and quantitative restrictions; they hinder the integration of the economies of the Member States and leave distributors and retailers in a position of subordination towards producers. Heavier fines are particularly necessary where, as in the present case, the principal aim of the infringement is to maintain a higher level of prices for consumers. The Commission states that many undertakings carry on conduct which they know to be contrary to Community law because the profit which they derive from their unlawful conduct exceeds the fines imposed hitherto. Conduct of that kind can only be deterred by fines which are heavier than in the past. * * *

[107] [T]he Commission was right to classify as very serious infringements prohibitions on exports and imports seeking artificially to maintain price differences between the markets of the various Member States. Such prohibitions jeopardize the freedom of intra-Community trade, which is a fundamental principle of the Treaty, and they prevent the attainment of one of its objectives, namely the creation of a single market. * * *

In the 1990s, when the Italian lire was depressed, Volkswagen, maker of Volkswagens and Audis, tried to protect the German and Austrian dealers in its network from a shift of buyers to Italy. It entered into agreements with its subsidiaries and Italian dealers, imposing supply quotas and a bonus system designed to induce the Italian dealers to sell at least 85% of their available vehicles in Italy. The Commission severely fined Volkswagen for partitioning national markets. The Commission describes the case as follows, in the 1998 Competition Policy Report:

Opening-up of markets

[68] The Commission has always kept a close eye on distribution agreements and their restrictive effects in so far as they hindered intra-Community trade. Some exclusive distribution agreements lead to the setting-up of watertight national distribution networks. In particular, clauses which prohibit distributors from supplying customers based outside the contract territory. In this way, national markets are artificially isolated from one another. The Commission considers that measures should be taken to combat this situation, not just in order to re-establish effective competition between economic operators but also in order to promote market integration. In practice, the compartmentalisation of national markets pre-

vents price convergence within the Union and restricts access by consumers to the markets with the lowest prices. With the creation of the single currency, price differentials will be obvious because they will be expressed in euro. They will be increasingly viewed as unjustified by ordinary people, who will want to derive full benefit from economic and monetary union.

[69]   In 1998 the Commission clearly demonstrated its determination to promote the opening-up of markets, a prime example of this being the *Volkswagen* case [O.J. L 124, 23/4/98]. Since 1995 the Commission had received numerous complaints from European consumers, particularly from Germany and Austria, who had been confronted with various difficulties when attempting to buy new Volkswagen and Audi cars in Italy. These consumers wanted to benefit from the price differentials between their Member State and Italy, where prices were particularly advantageous. Following a series of inspections at the offices of Volkswagen AG, Audi AG and Autogerma SpA, which is a subsidiary of Volkswagen and the official importer for both makes in Italy, and at the offices of a number of Italian dealers, the Commission concluded that Europe's largest motor-manufacturing group had been pursuing a market-partitioning policy in the Union for about 10 years. Volkswagen AG had systematically forced its dealers in Italy to refuse to sell Volkswagen and Audi cars to foreign buyers, especially from Germany and Austria. The Commission fined Volkswagen ECU 102 million, the largest fine ever imposed on a single company.

The Court of First Instance confirmed the existence and gravity of the infringements. It reduced the fine to 90 million Euros since the Commission had overstated the time period of the infringement; still the fine set a record. Case T–62/98, Volkswagen AG v. Commission, [2000] ECR II–2707.

In what sense were the quota system and bonuses based on sales in Italy "partitioning markets"? Should Volkswagen have been able to protect its German and Austrian dealers from the siphoning off of sales by a bad exchange rate?

Volkswagen is one of several car brands that continued to be sold at widely varying prices in different Member States even after the introduction of the Euro. Fines were imposed, also, on Opel and DaimlerChrysler for employing distribution systems that, in the view of the Commission, deprived consumers of their single-market right to buy a car wherever the price is lowest. In view of the persistence of the differentials, the Commission adopted a draft motor vehicle block exemption regulation (specifying restrictions permissible and not permissible under the law; see Chapter 24F) intended to come into force on October 1, 2002. The regulation may be accessed at http://europa.eu.int/comm/competition/car_sector/. What restrictions are allowed, under the block exemption? What restrictions are not allowed? How important is the rule that qualified dealers must be permitted to sell via the Internet? Will the motor vehicle block exemption regulation assure a single market in cars?

Note that in 2000, the Commission liberalized its policy on vertical restraints in general, but it nonetheless preserved as a hard-core and non-exemptible clause a restriction that absolutely prevents parallel imports from flowing over Member State lines. See Chapter 24 infra.

References. Among the most useful references on European Competition law are:

Annual Reports on Competition Policy of the European Commission

C. Bellamy & G. Child, rev. ed. by Roth, Child & Bellamy, European Community Law of Competition (Sweet & Maxwell 5th ed. 2001)

J. Faull & A. Nikpay, The EC Law of Competition (Oxford U. Press 1999)

D.G. Goyder, EC Competition Law (Oxford U. Press 3d ed. 1998)

B. Hawk, ed., Fordham Corp. L. Inst., 1982 to date, published annually, Juris Publishing

C. Jones & M. van der Woude, E.C. Competition Law Handbook (10th ed. Sweet & Maxwell 2001/02)

V. Korah, An Introduction to EC Competition Law and Practice (Hart 7th ed. 2000)

R. Whish, Competition Law (Butterworths 4th ed. 2001)

The web site for the Competition Directorate is very useful and may be found at http://europe.eu.int/en/comm/competition/.

Chapter 21

CARTELS

A. INTRODUCTION

Cartels are agreements among competitors to lessen the competition among them. They are the classic example of anticompetitive agreements. As the Commission said in its 1999 Report on Competition Policy:

[44] Of all restrictions of competition, restrictive practices in the form of secret agreements are undoubtedly the most destructive. Very often, these practices involve a substantial number of economic operators in a given area of activity and, as such, they have a very marked impact on the relevant markets. Furthermore, they almost invariably concern prices and thus severely undermine competition. The Commission is committed to an extremely tough stance against cartels, particularly following the adoption of the euro as a common currency. The changeover to the euro in 11 Member States should increase price transparency within the Union and, as a result, intensify competition to the benefit of consumers. This must not be countered by restrictive agreements designed to sidestep market confrontation by artificially fixing prices or other trading conditions, which in the longer term could push up inflation and undermine the foundations of economic and monetary union.

Cartels are usually secret, often carried out through trade associations, and often implemented by mechanisms that may give clues as to their existence. They usually take the form of agreements to fix prices and agreements to divide markets, i.e., to preserve domestic markets for domestic producers. Market division cartels seriously harm the market integration effort. Also, they remove producers' incentives to perform at the highest level possible, thus undermining the goal of producing robust and competitive businesses, and they keep prices higher and performance lower, thus harming buyers.

Cartels may be nation-wide, and therefore of special concern to an individual Member State; but in view of the tearing down of national barriers in Europe, they are more likely to be trans-European; and in view of the lowering of trade barriers in the world, they are more and more commonly world-wide. Lower trade and non-trade barriers tend to beget cartels, because firms that had enjoyed protection from competition by government barriers are suddenly confronted by competitive neighbors and often try to hold them back, and protect their own profit margins, by agreement. World cartels today are often challenged both by the United States Justice Department and the European Commission, and sometimes by the authorities of other countries as well. For example, in the 1990s, Asian and American producers of lysine, an amino acid used in animal foodstuffs for nutrition, fixed prices and sales quotas, and carried on an extensive information exchange to support the price and quota fixing, for sales worldwide including Europe. The cartel members were prosecuted criminally in the United States, resulting in high fines and jail terms. In Europe the Commission brought proceedings (no criminal prosecution is available under EC law) and levied fines against the US, Japanese and Korean conspirators totaling nearly 110 million Euros.

Similarly a worldwide vitamins conspiracy—this time led by the Swiss firm Hoffmann–La Roche—produced US prison terms and US and EU fines.

We begin this section with a short explanation of the economics of competition and of cartels. We then present cartel cases. The cases concern factual as well as legal analysis. The competition authorities must prove the existence of the cartel. We then reach the jurisdictional question: To what extent does the EC Treaty reach foreign firms that cartelize abroad but harm the European market? Finally, we consider cartel defenses; in particular: Is there a crisis cartel defense?

B. CARTELS AND THE ECONOMICS OF COMPETITION

Certain basic economic principles lie behind competition law. Moreover, economics can be applied to help a society achieve any of its goals more directly and at lower cost.

Many analysts assume that a system of free enterprise with competition law exists only to obtain a more efficient allocation of resources or only to prevent price rises to consumers, and that competition law has exactly and only this goal. Of course, as we have seen, that is not the case. Competition law usually has other goals as well. In the European Union, these goals include market integration, openness, control of dominance, fairness, and competitiveness (the growth of efficient, dynamic and responsive firms for the sake of European economic strength in world markets). Pursuit of some of the goals tends to produce allocative efficiency or prevent consumer price-rises; thus the goals may share common ground. But sometimes goals other than efficiency (in its various forms) may be in tension with efficiency goals, and a society may choose them nonetheless. In either event, it is important to understand some basic principles of the economics of competition law in the service of efficiency.

Economics often focuses on monopoly power. It shows how firms with sustained monopoly power normally have the incentive to act inefficiently, both in the sense of letting costs rise and in the sense of using their power to exploit buyers. Also, they may have the incentive to preserve their monopolies by striking down competitors or blocking them from markets. Firms that have grown to monopoly or dominant size under conditions of free enterprise may have achieved their positions by competition on the merits. To preserve incentives to excel as well as to preserve a firm's organic efficiencies, we may wish to control a dominant firm's behavior and to work on other fronts to reduce barriers, rather than to strike down the structure itself. This is the approach of the European Community to dominant firms, as reflected in Article 82, as we will discuss in Chapter 22.

This section deals largely with the less ambiguous economic problem of cartels. In connection with cartels, the efficiency and non-efficiency goals of competition policy tend to converge. A rule against cartels serves goals of efficiency, fairness, and market integration.

Here, then, is a brief introduction to market economics.

In a system of perfect competition, there would be a number of sellers, a number of buyers, and perfect market information available to all. The sellers, competing among themselves for business, would be induced to make and provide what their customers want. To do so they would aspire to be inventive and progressive and to minimize costs. The pressures of competition would keep prices near costs. The producers would make and provide as much product as the buyers wanted and were willing to buy at cost or more. Consumers would be sovereign.

The same responsiveness would be observed even in a market of few sellers if there were no significant barriers to entry into the market and if entry were very quick and easy. In that case, potential competitors would (in theory, for barriers are seldom so inconsequential) provide the same pressures as do actual competitors. Also, in theory, sophisticated and powerful buyers could provide the same pressures on sellers to behave competitively, especially if the buyers were in a position to enter the market themselves or to finance entry by others if they were not satisfied with the performance of the existing sellers. Further, in high technology markets marked by rapid changes in technology (new economy markets), the threat of break-through innovations by potential competitors may provide a pressure inducing responsiveness of even a dominant firm.

If all markets in the world were characterized by effective competition—with efficient and fully responsive sellers—competition itself would allocate resources to the production and distribution of all goods and services in the proportions buyers demand. The fullest possible production would then be squeezed out of the world's scarce resources. Demand would remain a function of the existing distribution of wealth, however, for the distribution of wealth influences what people choose to buy.

Real markets deviate substantially from the ideal. But nonetheless, competition tends to produce an efficient allocation of resources, push cost downwards, and help intermediate buyers and ultimately consumers get what they want, and at a price more or less near cost (including a reasonable return on investment). Competition is one of the most important mechanisms that society relies on to produce efficiency and serve consumers.

Competition also tends to keep markets free and open, and thereby to provide opportunities for entrepreneurs and small and medium-sized firms. Also, competition is a product of freedom of enterprise. It fosters diversity and pluralism, and it provides rewards based on merit. Therefore, competition both reflects and tends to support democratic institutions. Finally, forces of competition know no artificial divisions, such as national borders. If the French as well as the Germans demand sugar produced in Germany, the market will drive sugar across national lines. In that sense, along with the affirmative dismantling of state-imposed barriers, competition is market integrating. Competition policy combined with the free movement principle is to the European Union what the free enterprise ethic combined with the interstate commerce clause of the Constitution is to the United States.

While competition and freedom to compete on the merits serve all of the above objectives, private firms can sometimes restrain competition and thereby undermine the objectives of competition policy. The most obvious way in which firms can restrain competition and harm consumers is by forming a cartel, which is a combination of competitors to eliminate the competition among them. The classic form of cartel is a price-fixing or market division agreement by all significant firms in the market. In theory, parties to a price-fixing agreement could agree to charge a high price and not to compete on price. If buyers have no good substitutes and barriers to entry are high, the conspirators would have the power to raise prices considerably above the competitive price (i.e., considerably higher than the cost of efficient firms including a reasonable return on investment). The cartel members would naturally be able to sell less product at this higher price. They would have to prevent the production and sale of more product, for extra production would drive the price back down. Accordingly, the cartel members would hold back output, and they would exploit the buyers who remain in the market. Essentially, the same thing would happen if the parties agree to divide markets; each would become the monopolist in its market and would raise prices; buyers would demand less of the goods at the supracompetitive price, and the firms would reduce output.

This phenomenon may be depicted graphically as follows:

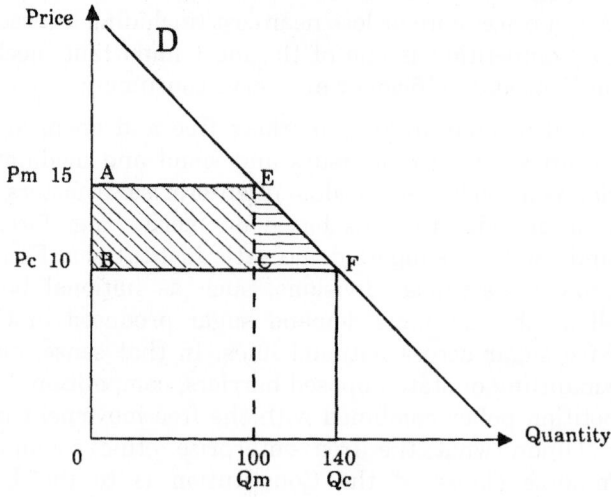

The demand curve (D) slopes downwards. The base line represents the quantity demanded at a given price. The vertical line represents the price. Less is demanded as price rises. Therefore higher price yields lower quantity. If the firms' cost is 10 (the competitive price), and upon forming a cartel their profit-maximizing price is 15 (the monopoly price), given the depicted demand function, the cartel members would reduce production from 140 units to 100 units. They would make more money by producing less because of their ability to exploit the remaining customers. Society loses. Triangle CEF is called the dead weight or welfare loss. People wanted to buy the amount depicted by the triangle, and they were willing to buy it at cost or more, but this amount was never produced. Rectangle ABCE represents the product sold at the extra-high price, and it represents a wealth transfer. Under conditions of competition buyers would have kept the money represented by rectangle ABCE. The cartel empowered the sellers to extract this surplus from the buyers.

As noted, cartelists can use mechanisms other than price fixing to achieve the same ends. They can allocate territories so that each becomes a monopolist in its own territory. They can allocate customers, creating monopoly power over each customer. Or they can parcel out production quotas—one of the devices used by the OPEC (oil) cartel of the oil-producing nations. Setting quotas as a means of limiting output is the other side of the price-fixing coin. By setting a high price, the quantity demanded will fall. By setting quotas, the collaborators create scarcity and the price will rise. Several devices can be used in tandem. Cartelists often fix prices and then set quotas, to avoid squabbling about who gets to enjoy the high price. Moreover, if no member can sell more than a fixed quota, it will not be able to cheat on its co-conspirators (i.e., secretly violate its obligations) by selling more goods at a lower price.

We have spoken above of the static effect of cartels; that is, a cartel will normally cause the price of a known good, produced in known ways, to be higher and output to be lower than under conditions of independent decision-making. Cartels also have a negative dynamic effect. If firms have agreed not to compete and do not anticipate rivalry, they tend to let costs rise and their incentives to innovate to find new and better ways of pleasing their customers are muted. This effect is called x-inefficiency.

The objectives of the cartel can sometimes be achieved through means short of conspiracy. If a market is highly concentrated (i.e., there are few firms) and incumbents are insulated by barriers to entry—especially if the sellers are relatively similar to one another in cost structure and the product is homogeneous—the price and output moves of the incumbents may be relatively transparent to one another. The price that will maximize the profits of each is likely to be approximately the same. No firm would charge a price higher than the common price because it would be outcompeted and it would lose its sales. None would venture to charge a lower price because competition would break out and all producers would be worse off: they would sell approximately the same quantity of goods but at a lower price. As a result, unless legal risks are sufficiently great, the firms may find it both possible and profitable to form a cartel, and they may be able to achieve cartel effects—higher price, lower output, lower dynamism—even without an explicit agreement.

In an oligopolistic market (one comprised of few firms), firms may coordinate their actions by price leadership. Also, they may coordinate by staying within their own traditional territories. A territorial strategy has often been employed by firms in Europe, where national markets were historically isolated by trade barriers. French firms feared that if they began to sell in Germany, German firms, in retaliation, would dump their product on the French market, and vice versa. Patterns of mutual deference or spheres of influence developed, reinforcing oligopoly behavior. The more concentrated the market, the less need there was for an explicit agreement, because the result could be achieved without one.

Since merging is one way to reduce the number of players in the market, and the fewness of players makes coordination easier, mergers that result in high concentration may produce cartel effects; i.e. the firms left in the market may adopt cooperative rather than competitive modes of behavior. Mergers, however, are integrative and may produce synergies and efficiencies, while cartels are virtually always inefficient and are by definition formed to suppress competition. Therefore the law treats cartels much more harshly than it treats mergers.

C. PROOF OF CARTELS

The most powerful and tempting way for firms to control the market is to join with one another, that is, to collaborate rather than to compete. Accordingly, all antitrust or competition laws prohibit certain combinations or concerted practices. In the Treaty of Rome, the prohibition is contained in Article 81 (ex 85). While it is not always clear whether a collaboration is one that harms competition, cartels are by definition agreements that harm competition. Thus, this section begins with the simple cartel.

The cases typically involve both basic and complex questions of fact and law. For example, as to the facts: Did the parties agree not to compete? Can an agreement be inferred from the firms' behavior and from facts about the market? As to the law: May the parties justify their agreement by showing that it did not harm competition; that it had no effect?

Cartel cases involving quinine, dyestuffs, cement and sugar were formative cases in the development of EC competition law. As you will see in the *Quinine* case below, much of the analysis concerns whether the Commission and Court can infer from the facts that the firms cartelized the market or a part of it. Consider also, as you read the *Quinine* case, what the firms did that would help to form a cartel, to make it work and to make it stable. What characteristics about the market and its structure made it more or less likely for a cartel to work?

Quinine is probably the earliest case of trans-Atlantic agency cooperation in prosecuting an international cartel.

1. THE QUININE CASE

ACF CHEMIEFARMA v. COMMISSION

(Quinine)

Case 41/69, [1970] ECR 661.

[Nedchem and five other Dutch firms, and Boehringer and Buchler, both German firms, produced quinine and quinidine, ingredients used to manufacture drugs to treat malaria and heart disease. In 1958 they entered into a series of agreements to reserve their home markets for themselves and to fix prices and quotas for exports to all other countries. After the German Federal Cartel Office discovered the cartel, Nedchem and Boehringer concluded a new agreement that excluded deliveries within the EC from the arrangement. In March 1960 Nedchem, the two German firms, and French and British producers of quinine and quinidine concluded a new export cartel agreement. The new agreement excluded sales into EC Member States, set quotas for exports to non-member nations, and reserved certain markets outside of the common market for specified cartel members. It also provided for equalization of quantities to be sold by members if quotas were exceeded or not reached and provided that no cartel member could cooperate in the production or sale of quinine or quinidine outside of the common market with firms not participating in the agreement. Each party agreed to supply the others with information about where, to whom, and how much they sold, on the basis of which Nedchem would equalize the quantities to be sold by each.

In April 1960, two gentlemen's agreements were drawn up among the parties—though never signed—which extended the provisions of the export agreements to sales within the common market and reserved home markets. The French parties agreed not to manufacture synthetic quinidine, and all parties agreed that noncompliance with the gentlemen's agreement would terminate the written export agreement and vice versa. The agreements were supplemented by a pool agreement for bark to make quinine. The parties would jointly purchase this critical raw material through Nedchem. Nedchem would buy stockpile surpluses of bark from the United States' General Services Administration, allocate the bark among the cartel members, and receive a two percent commission from the members.

In 1962, Regulation 17 went into effect, giving the Commission the powers necessary to enforce Article 85. Also in 1962, a dispute arose regarding the bark pool, and the parties claimed that they abandoned their gentlemen's agreement shortly thereafter.

In 1963–64 the United States, needing quinine to save the lives of sick American soldiers in Viet Nam, became suspicious of the existence of an international quinine cartel as a result of Nedchem's purchases of large quantities of the United States bark stockpile. The Department of Justice conducted extensive investigations (eventually resulting in civil and criminal cases under the US Sherman Act), and in 1967 it shared information with the EC Commission. See 1 W. Fugate, Foreign Commerce and the Antitrust Laws § 4.2 (5th ed. 1996). The Commission and national authorities began investigations into whether and to what extent the gentlemen's agreements were being applied in the common market after 1962. The Commission found that violations continued until February 1965, and imposed fines.]

115 The defendant bases its view that the gentlemen's agreement was continued until February1965 on documents and declarations emanating from the parties to the agreement the tenor of which is indistinct and indeed contradictory so that it is impossible to conclude whether those undertakings intended to terminate the gentlemen's agreement at their meeting on 29 October 1962.

116 The conduct of the undertakings in the Common Market after 29 October 1962 must therefore be considered in relation to the following four points: sharing out of domestic markets, fixing of common prices, determination of sales quotas and prohibition against manufacturing synthetic quinidine.

Protection of the Producers' Domestic Markets

117 The gentlemen's agreement guaranteed protection of each domestic market for the producers in the various Member States.

118 After October 1962 when significant supplies were delivered on one of those markets by producers who were not nationals, as for example in the case of sales of quinine and quinidine in France, there was a substantial alignment of prices conforming to French domestic prices which were higher than the export prices to third countries.

119 It does not appear that there were alterations in the insignificant volume of trade between the other Member States referred to by the clause relating to domestic protection in spite of considerable differences in the prices prevailing in each of those States.

120 The divergences between the domestic legislation of those States cannot by itself explain those differences in price or the substantial absence of trade.

121 Obstacles which might arise in the trade in quinine and quinidine from differences between national legislation governing pharmaceutical products under trademark cannot relevantly be invoked to explain those facts.

122 The correspondence exchanged in October and November 1963 between the parties to the export agreement with regard to the protection of domestic markets merely confirmed the intention of those undertakings to allow this state of affairs to remain unchanged.

[123] This intention was subsequently confirmed by Nedchem during the meeting of the undertakings concerned in Brussels on 14 March 1964.

[124] From those circumstances it is clear that with regard to the restriction on competition arising from the protection of the producers' domestic markets the producers continued after the meeting on 29 October 1962 to abide by the gentlemen's agreement of 1960 and confirmed their common intention to do so.

[125] The applicant maintains that owing in particular to the shortage of raw materials the sharing out of domestic markets, as emerges from the exchange of letters of October and November 1963, had no effect on competition in the Common Market.

[126] Despite the scarcity of raw materials and an increase in the demand for the products in question, as the contested decision finds, a serious threat of shortage nevertheless emerged only in 1964 as a result of the interruption of Nedchem's supplies from the American General Service Administration.

[127] On the other hand such a situation cannot render lawful an agreement the object of which is to restrict competition in the Common Market and which affects trade between the Member States.

[128] The sharing out of domestic markets has as its object the restriction of competition and trade within the Common Market.

[129] The fact that, if there were a threatened shortage of raw materials, such an agreement might in practice have had less influence on competition and on international trade than in a normal period in no way alters the fact that the parties did not terminate their activities.

[130] Furthermore the applicant has furnished no conclusive evidence capable of proving that it had ceased to act in accordance with the agreement before the date of expiry of the export agreement.

[131] Consequently, the submissions concerning that part of the decision relating to the continuation of the agreement on the protection of the producers' domestic markets until the beginning of February 1965 are unfounded.

Joint Fixing of Sales Prices

[132] With regard to the joint fixing of sales prices for the markets which were not shared out, that is to say, the Belgo–Luxembourg Economic Union and Italy, the gentlemen's agreement provided for the application to such sales of the current prices for exports to third countries fixed by mutual agreement, in accordance with the export agreement. * * *

[134] If, as the defendant maintains, the parties to the export agreement continued until February 1965 to apply their current export prices to supplies to the above-mentioned Member States, it would follow that they continued to abide by that part of the gentlemen's agreement relating to the joint fixing of sales prices.

[135] With regard to the period from November 1962 to April 1964, the figures supplied by the defendant show a substantial and constant identity between the current prices fixed for export within the framework of the agreement and the prices maintained by the undertakings concerned,

including the applicant, for their sales in unprotected domestic markets in the Community.

136　Where such prices deviate from the scale of export prices they do so in terms of rebates or increases corresponding generally to those agreed on under the gentlemen's agreement.

137　The applicant had supplied no evidence capable of proving that this argument is unfounded.

138　Moreover the increase in prices of 15%, which was jointly decided upon on 12 March 1964 under the export agreement which led Nedchem to withdraw its opposition, was uniformly applied—although that undertaking would have preferred to continue to fix lower prices—with regard to supplies to Italy, Belgium and Luxembourg also.

139　These circumstances show that with regard to sales prices the parties to the export agreement continued after October 1962 to act in the Common Market as if the gentlemen's agreement of 1960 were still in force. * * *

141　It is clear from the oral procedure, taking into account the information supplied by the parties, that during 1964 and in particular from May onwards, a party to the agreement applied prices which in an increasing number of cases deviated from the current export prices, and that the defendant has been unable to give a convincing explanation as to how this might be reconciled with the continuation in force of the agreement in question.

142　The failure to communicate to the undertakings concerned the results of the investigations carried out in Italy and Belgium, which excluded any possibility of clarification and discussion at the stage of the administrative procedure, may have contributed to leaving unexplained facts which ought to have been clarified.

143　In these circumstances proof has not been sufficiently established in law that the applicant by mutual agreement with the other producers maintained uniform prices for its sales in the Belgo–Luxembourg Economic Union and Italy after May 1964.

144　Consequently the period from May 1964 to February 1965 must be omitted from the infringement. * * *

Restrictions on the Manufacture of Synthetic Quinidine

154　The gentlemen's agreement prohibited the group of French undertakings from manufacturing synthetic quinidine. * * *

156　The fact relied upon that, when the gentlemen's agreement was concluded, the French undertakings were not in a position to manufacture synthetic quinidine does not render lawful such a restriction which entirely precluded them from taking up this activity.

157　That the French undertakings should accede to this restriction of their freedom of action is explicable in terms of their interest—owing to the particularly high prices which they maintained for their products in France—in preserving the territorial protection which they enjoyed on their domestic market.

[158] Taking into account the connexion thus existing between those two restrictions on competition, it may reasonably be concluded that the prohibition on production lasted as long as the territorial protection. * * *

[160] Although it is possible that, owing to the scarcity of raw materials which [w]as established by the contested decision (No 29, last paragraph), in its ultimate period protection of the domestic markets did not have important effects on competition and trade between Member States, this cartel nevertheless lasted until February 1965.

[161] In the absence of any indication to the contrary and having regard to the above-mentioned connexions between the two aspects of the cartel, it must be considered that the agreement restricting the French undertakings' freedom to manufacture was of the same duration.

[162] Consequently the applicant's complaints in this respect are unfounded.

General Appraisal of the Agreement Within the Common Market

[163] It is clear from the foregoing that the applicant participated with other producers of quinine and quinidine in an agreement prohibited by Article 85 of the EEC Treaty.

[164] This agreement continued in most of its forms even after the meeting on 29 October 1962.

[165] Serious doubts as to the continuation of the agreement after 1962 exist only with regard to the application of sales quotas.

[166] Nevertheless, the fact that the undertakings did not continue to apply the system of quotas does not seem perceptibly to have improved the conditions of competition, since they continued jointly to fix prices, to apply uniformly to their deliveries in the Common Market joint price increases arranged in March and October 1964 and decided within the framework of the export agreement and finally to maintain protection of their respective domestic markets and the prohibition on the French undertakings' production of synthetic quinidine.

[167] However, the application of uniform prices for deliveries to Italy, Belgium and Luxembourg has only been proved to exist up to April 1964.

[168] Finally, even if it must be conceded that the export agreement could have operated independently of the agreement relating to the Common Market, it must be found that in fact the members of the cartel attributed great importance to the joint application of both agreements.

[169] Although from October 1963 the export agreement was declared to be "in abeyance", it is clear from the declarations made by the undertakings concerned at their subsequent meetings together with their subsequent conduct as a whole that they continued to have an interest in upholding that agreement, in particular with regard to its possible employment within the Common Market.

* * *

2. THE DYESTUFFS CASE

Enterprises in all six Member States, and ICI in the UK, were charged with fixing the prices of dyestuffs and dividing markets. The Commission brought proceedings in 1972, the year before the United Kingdom joined the European Community. ICI sought dismissal on jurisdictional grounds; but ICI had subsidiaries in the European Community, and the Court of Justice held the parent and subsidiaries to be one economic entity with sufficient presence in Europe. See, for jurisdictional aspects, section E infra.

Ten large producers supplied 80% of the dyestuffs market. There were more than a thousand different dyestuffs, and specialty markets tended to be oligopolistic. The prices on the various national markets differed from country to country.

The basic pattern of behavior was one of price leadership, with one firm announcing its intention to increase prices by a stated percentage, often to take effect at a specified later date. The competitors usually followed suit, often announcing within two or three days their intention to raise prices by the same percentage.

The dyestuff companies argued that the Commission had proved no agreement or concertation; merely, it had shown oligopoly behavior (the tendency of oligopolists to act interdependently because of the structure of the market). The Commission disagreed, and the Court of Justice upheld the Commission's decision. Here is a brief excerpt.

IMPERIAL CHEMICAL INDUSTRIES LTD.
v. COMMISSION (DYESTUFFS)

Cases 48, 49, 51–57/69, [1972] ECR 619.

[66] Although parallel behaviour may not by itself be identified with a concerted practice, it may however amount to strong evidence of such a practice if it leads to conditions of competition which do not correspond to the normal conditions of the market, having regard to the nature of the products, the size and number of the undertakings, and the volume of the said market. * * *

[109] . . . [A]lthough parallel conduct in respect of prices may well have been an attractive and risk-free objective for the undertakings concerned, it is hardly conceivable that the same action could be taken spontaneously at the same time, on the same national markets and for the same range of products.

[110] Nor is it any more plausible that the increases of January 1964, introduced on the Italian market and copied on the Netherlands and Belgo–Luxembourg markets, which have little in common with each other either as regards the level of prices or the pattern of competition, could have been brought into effect within a period of two to three days without prior concertation.

[111] As regards the increases of 1965 and 1967 concertation took place openly, since all the announcements of the intention to increase prices with effect from a certain date and for a certain range of products made it possible for producers to decide on their conduct regarding the special cases of France and Italy.

[112] In proceeding in this way, the undertakings mutually eliminated in advance any uncertainties concerning their reciprocal behaviour on the

different markets and thereby also eliminated a large part of the risk inherent in any independent change of conduct on those markets.

113   The general and uniform increase on those different markets can only be explained by a common intention on the part of those undertakings, first, to adjust the level of prices and the situation resulting from competition in the form of discounts, and secondly, to avoid the risk, which is inherent in any price increase, of changing the conditions of competition.

114   The fact that the price increases announced were not introduced in Italy and that ACNA only partially adopted the 1967 increase in other markets, far from undermining this conclusion, tends to confirm it. * * *

118   Although every producer is free to change his prices, taking into account in so doing the present or foreseeable conduct of his competitors, nevertheless it is contrary to the rules on competition contained in the Treaty for a producer to cooperate with his competitors, in any way whatsoever, in order to determine a coordinated course of action relating to a price increase and to ensure its success by prior elimination of all uncertainty as to each other's conduct regarding the essential elements of that action, such as the amount, subject-matter, date and place of the increases.

119   In these circumstances and taking into account the nature of the market in the products in question, the conduct of the applicant, in conjunction with other undertakings against which proceedings have been taken, was designed to replace the risks of competition and the hazards of competitors' spontaneous reactions by cooperation constituting a concerted practice prohibited by Article 85(1) of the Treaty.

Effect of the Concerted Practice on Trade Between Member States

120   The applicant argues that the uniform price increases were not capable of affecting trade between Member States because notwithstanding the noticeable differences existing between prices charged in the different States consumers have always preferred to make their purchases of dyestuffs in their own country.

121   However, it appears from what has already been said that the concerted practices, by seeking to keep the market in a fragmented state, were liable to affect the circumstances in which trade in the products in question takes place between the Member States. * * *

123   The fact that the increases were uniform and simultaneous has in particular served to maintain the *status quo,* ensuring that the undertakings would not lose custom, and has thus helped to keep the traditional national markets in those goods "cemented" to the detriment of any real freedom of movement of the products in question in the Common Market.

124   Therefore this submission is unfounded.

3. THE SUGAR CARTEL CASE

The *Sugar cartel* case was the last of the formative cartel judgments. Suiker Unie v. Commission (Sugar cartel), Cases 40–48, 50, 54–56, 111, 113–114/73, [1975] ECR 1663. Among other things, various sugar producers from the Netherlands, Belgium and Germany allegedly entered into understandings and practices to coordinate their behavior in order to moderate the impact of overproduction of sugar in Belgium and to restrain the Belgian dealers from exporting large amounts of Belgian sugar to the Netherlands. The firms denied that they had a cartel. Further, they argued that the sugar market was so highly regulated by national quotas and a community-wide intervention purchase price that it was impossible for private parties to distort trade. The Court disagreed on both counts, noting that the government regulation left "a residual field of competition." It found a multitude of serious infringements. The case is well known for its definition of the word "concert":

[172] SU and CSM submit that since the concept of "concerted practices" presupposes a plan and the aim of removing in advance any doubt as to the future conduct of competitors, the reciprocal knowledge which the parties concerned could have of the parallel or complementary nature of their respective decisions cannot in itself be sufficient to establish a concerted practice; otherwise every attempt by an undertaking to react as intelligently as possible to the acts of its competitors would be an offence.

[173] The criteria of coordination and cooperation laid down by the caselaw of the Court, which in no way require the working out of an actual plan, must be understood in the light of the concept inherent in the provisions of the Treaty relating to competition that each economic operator must determine independently the policy which he intends to adopt on the common market including the choice of the persons and undertakings to which he makes offers or sells.

[174] Although it is correct to say that this requirement of independence does not deprive economic operators of the right to adapt themselves intelligently to the existing and anticipated conduct of their competitors, it does however strictly preclude any direct or indirect contact between such operators, the object or effect whereof is either to influence the conduct on the market of an actual or potential competitor or to disclose to such a competitor the course of conduct which they themselves have decided to adopt or contemplate adopting on the market.

Notes and Questions

1. In the *Quinine* case, consider the evidence—which was only circumstantial—from which the Court concluded that the gentlemen's agreements continued after 1962. Did the facts raise an inference that the agreements continued in force? A strong inference? How strong was the alternative inference that, after 1962, the parties had no agreement with respect to sales in the Community; that each one simply chose to follow past patterns of behavior and hoped that its export partners would do so too? Does the latter scenario constitute concerted action under *Quinine*? *Dyestuffs*? *Sugar*?

2. What do *Dyestuffs* and *Sugar* add to your understanding of "concerted" action? Is it enough that the firms acted successively in parallel ways and (1) thereby replaced some of the uncertainties of competition with information about the competitors' intentions to raise prices? and/or (2) the effect was to preserve the status quo: different prices in different Member States? Bear in mind that in the 1970s and 80s the law was still evolving; the issue of proof of concerted action was to come before the Court once again in *Wood pulp*, point 4 below.

3. In an important American case, motion picture distributors changed their pattern of behavior in a sudden, dramatic, uniform, and exploitative way. As the Supreme Court concluded, it would strain credulity to believe that each firm acted

independently. Moreover, the change in behavior was profitable if all firms did the same thing; but if only one of them had raised its prices, it would have priced itself out of the market. The Supreme Court upheld the lower court's finding of conspiracy under Section 1 of the Sherman Antitrust Act.[1] Interstate Circuit, Inc. v. United States, 306 U.S. 208, 59 S.Ct. 467, 83 L.Ed. 610 (1939). But the Supreme Court has also held that mere conscious parallelism is not equivalent to a combination or conspiracy and therefore does not constitute a violation of the Sherman Act. Theatre Enterprises, Inc. v. Paramount Film Distributing Corp., 346 U.S. 537, 74 S.Ct. 257, 98 L.Ed. 273 (1954). The Court has dismissed cases of parallel action that can be just as plausibly explained by independent action. See Matsushita Electrical Industrial Co., Ltd. v. Zenith Radio Corp., 475 U.S. 574, 106 S.Ct. 1348, 89 L.Ed.2d 538 (1986).

4.   In the United States in the 1950s, the steel industry was a tight oligopoly. US Steel was the price leader. When US Steel decided that conditions were favorable, it would announce a future price increase. If the few other steel producers announced the same increase in the same time frame, US Steel would put the price increase into effect. Otherwise it would revoke the announced increase. After severe public criticism in 1962, US Steel retreated to a "new diplomacy" and withdrew from leadership. Bethlehem Steel then emerged as the price leader. See F.M. Scherer & D. Ross, Industrial Market Structure and Economic Performance 252–54 (3rd ed. 1990). These simple facts do not constitute a violation of Section 1 of the Sherman Act.

Did the steel companies engage in a concerted practice within the meaning of the EC Treaty?

5.   Note how the quinine export cartel tended to facilitate a domestic (European) cartel. Note also how the parties used various devices that helped to make the cartel work. For example, by pooling raw material purchases in the early years of the agreement and by designating one of their members—Nedchem—to be their purchasing agent and to allocate the raw material in accordance with assigned quotas, the firms could police their own cartel agreement and be sure that no one cheated by producing too much. Likewise, as a result of sharing extensive information with one another, cheating would become obvious, and cheating was explicitly punishable by expulsion from both cartels. Finally, the agreement not to produce synthetic quinine by the French, who were selling at a particularly high price in France, tended to keep off the market a substitute product that could have undermined the cartel by driving down the cartel price.

6.   After the *Quinine* case, what are firms entitled to prove in the defense of a cartel? Can they defend their conduct on grounds that their agreement had no effect because market forces overwhelmed their attempt to raise prices (i.e., they tried to run a cartel, but they failed)? Can they successfully argue that an aborted cartel had no effect on trade between Member States? Should "no effect" be a defense? Why? See United States v. Socony–Vacuum Oil Co., Inc., 310 U.S. 150, 60 S.Ct. 811, 84 L.Ed. 1129 (1940) (lack of effect is not a defense to a cartel violation under US law). But see United States v. Nippon Paper Indus., 62 F.Supp. 2d 173 (D.Mass.1999)(in suit against foreign defendants conspiring abroad, proof of intended and substantial effects in US market was constituent element of violation).

1.   Section 1 of the Sherman Act (15 U.S.C. § 1) provides in relevant part:

Every contract, combination in the form of trust or otherwise, or conspiracy, in restraint of trade or commerce among the several states, or with foreign nations, is declared to be illegal.

7. Why was the quinine export agreement as such of no interest to the Court? What is the scope of EC law with respect to export cartels selling to destinations outside of the Community? Consult the language of the EC Treaty, Article 81.

Like European Community law, United States antitrust law excludes from its scope export cartels that hurt foreigners only. See the Foreign Trade Antitrust Improvements Act of 1982, codified in the Sherman Antitrust Act as Section 7A (15 U.S.C. § 6a). Is this good policy? Comment from the point of view of world-wide free movement and efficiency, and from the point of view of sovereignty of nations.

Price fixing of exports to the United States may be challenged by the United States—as long as a US court can get personal jurisdiction over the price fixers and has jurisdiction over the subject matter of the case. For treatment of subject matter jurisdiction under EC law, see *Wood pulp* (jurisdiction) at E below. Point 4 directly below concerns proof of agreement.

4. WOOD PULP

United States, Canadian, Finnish, Swedish and Norwegian firms shipped wood pulp to the European Community. The Commission alleged and found that the US, Canadian and Finnish firms concerted on prices, and it imposed large fines. The companies sought annulment of the Commission decision before the Court of Justice. They asserted lack of jurisdiction by reason of extraterritoriality. Also, they claimed that there was not sufficient evidence from which the Commission could find concert of action. The *Sugar* judgment, quoted above, was the common referent for the definition of concertation.

A ÅHLSTRÖM OSAKEYHTIÖ v. COMMISSION

(Wood pulp) (proof of agreement)
Cases C–89, 104, 114, 116–117, 125–129/85 [1993] ECR I–1307.

[The Commission brought proceedings against 40 wood pulp producers from the United States, Canada and Finland and three of their trade associations for concerting on price announcements and on price. The producers made quarterly price announcements sometimes simultaneously and sometimes nearly so. Prices were almost always quoted in dollars, a practice that both increased the transparency of the producers' intentions to one another and assured that shifts in exchange rates in the various Member States would have no impact. Prices and price changes tended to be uniform. The Commission found, for example:

> that the prices announced by the Canadian and US producers were the same from the first quarter of 1975 to the third quarter of 1977 and from the first quarter of 1978 to the third quarter of 1981, that the prices announced by the Swedish and Finnish producers were the same from the first quarter of 1975 to the second quarter of 1977 and from the third quarter of 1978 to the third quarter of 1981 and, finally, that the prices of all the producers were the same from the first quarter of 1976 to the second quarter of 1977 and from the third quarter of 1979 to the third quarter of 1981.

The Commission determined that the pulp producers had engaged in concerted conduct in violation of Article 85.

The Court annulled most of the Commission's decision.]

55   The Finnish, US and Canadian applicants have sought the annulment of art. 1(1) of the decision, according to which they, and other Swedish, US and Norwegian producers, concerted "on prices for bleached sulphate wood pulp announced for deliveries to the European Economic Community" during the whole or part of the period from 1975 to 1981. * * *

A.   *Quarterly price announcements as the infringement*

59   According to the Commission's first hypothesis, it is the system of quarterly price announcements in itself which constitutes the infringement of art. 85 of the Treaty.

60   First, the Commission considers that that system was deliberately introduced by the pulp producers in order to enable them to ascertain the prices that would be charged by their competitors in the following quarters. The disclosure of prices to third parties, especially to the press and agents working for several producers, well before their application at the beginning of a new quarter, gave the other producers sufficient time to announce their own, corresponding, new prices before that quarter and to apply them from the commencement of that quarter.

61   Secondly, the Commission considers that the implementation of that mechanism had the effect of making the market artificially transparent by enabling producers to obtain a rapid and accurate picture of the prices quoted by their competitors. * * *

63   According to the court's judgment in *Suiker Unie* ..., a concerted practice refers to a form of co-ordination between undertakings which, without having been taken to the stage where an agreement properly so-called has been concluded, knowingly substitutes for the risks of competition practical co-operation between them. In the same judgment, the court added that the criteria of co-ordination and co-operation must be understood in the light of the concept inherent in the provisions of the Treaty relating to competition that each economic operator must determine independently the policy which he intends to adopt on the common market.

64   In this case, the communications arise from the price announcements made to users. They constitute in themselves market behaviour which does not lessen each undertaking's uncertainty as to the future attitude of its competitors. At the time when each undertaking engages in such behaviour, it cannot be sure of the future conduct of the others.

65   Accordingly, the system of quarterly price announcements on the pulp market is not to be regarded as constituting in itself an infringement of art. 85(1) of the Treaty.

B.   *Concertation on announced prices as the infringement*

66   In the second hypothesis, the Commission considers that the system of price announcements constitutes evidence of concertation at an earlier stage.... [T]he Commission states that, as proof of such concertation, it relied on the parallel conduct of the pulp producers in the period from 1975 to 1981 and on different kinds of direct or indirect exchange of information. * * *

70   Since the Commission has no documents which directly establish the existence of concertation between the producers concerned, it is necessary to ascertain whether the system of quarterly price announcements, the simultaneity or near-simultaneity of the price announcements and the parallelism of price announcements as found during the period from 1975 to 1981 constitute a firm, precise and consistent body of evidence of prior concertation.

71   In determining the probative value of those different factors, it must be noted that parallel conduct cannot be regarded as furnishing proof of concertation unless concertation constitutes the only plausible explanation for such conduct. It is necessary to bear in mind that, although art. 85 of the Treaty prohibits any form of collusion which distorts competition, it does not deprive economic operators of the right to adapt themselves intelligently to the existing and anticipated conduct of their competitors.

72   Accordingly, it is necessary in this case to ascertain whether the parallel conduct alleged by the Commission cannot, taking account of the nature of the products, the size and the number of the undertakings and the volume of the market in question, be explained otherwise than by concertation.

(a) *System of price announcements* * * *

74   In their pleadings, on the other hand, the applicants maintain that the system is ascribable to the particular commercial requirements of the pulp market. * * *

76   The experts [appointed by the Court] observe first that the system of announcements at issue must be viewed in the context of the long-term relationships which existed between producers and their customers and which were a result both of the method of manufacturing the pulp and of the cyclical nature of the market. In view of the fact that each type of paper was the result of a particular mixture of pulps having their own characteristics and that the mixture was difficult to change, a relationship based on close co-operation was established between the pulp producers and the paper manufacturers. Such relations were all the closer since they also had the advantage of protecting both sides against the uncertainties inherent in the cyclical nature of the market: they guaranteed security of supply to buyers and at the same time security of demand to producers.

77   The experts point out that it is in the context of those long-term relationships that, after the Second World War, purchasers demanded the introduction of that system of announcements. Since pulp accounts for between 50–75 per cent of the cost of paper, those purchasers wished to ascertain as soon as possible the prices which they might be charged in order to estimate their costs and to fix the prices of their own products. However, as those purchasers did not wish to be bound by a high fixed price in the event of the market weakening, the announced price was regarded as a ceiling price below which the transaction price could always be renegotiated.

78   The explanation given for the use of a quarterly cycle is that it is the result of a compromise between the paper manufacturers' desire for a degree of foreseeability as regards the price of pulp and the producers'

desire not to miss any opportunities to make a profit in the event of a strengthening of the market.

79 The US dollar was, according to the experts, introduced on the market by the North American producers during the 1960s. That development was generally welcomed by purchasers who regarded it as a means of ensuring that they did not pay a higher price than their competitors.

(b) Simultaneity or near-simultaneity of announcements

80 ... [T]he Commission claims that the close succession or even simultaneity of price announcements would not have been possible without a constant flow of information between the undertakings concerned.

81 According to the applicants, the simultaneity or near-simultaneity of the announcements—even if it were established—must instead be regarded as a direct result of the very high degree of transparency of the market. Such transparency, far from being artificial, can be explained by the extremely well-developed network of relations which, in view of the nature and the structure of the market, have been established between the various traders.

* * *

83 First, ... a buyer was always in contact with several pulp producers. One reason for that was connected with the paper-making process, but another was that, in order to avoid becoming overdependent on one producer, pulp buyers took the precaution of diversifying their sources of supply. With a view to obtaining the lowest possible prices, they were in the habit, especially in times of falling prices, of disclosing to their suppliers the prices announced by their competitors.

84 Secondly, it should be noted that most of the pulp was sold to a relatively small number of large paper manufacturers. Those few buyers maintained very close links with each other and exchanged information on changes in prices of which they were aware.

85 Thirdly, several producers who made paper themselves purchased pulp from other producers and were thus informed, in times of both rising prices and falling prices, of the prices charged by their competitors. That information was also accessible to producers who did not themselves manufacture paper but were linked to groups that did.

86 Fourthly, that high degree of transparency in the pulp market resulting from the links between traders or groups of traders was further reinforced by the existence of agents established in the Community who worked for several producers and by the existence of a very dynamic trade press. * * *

88 Finally, it is necessary to add that the use of rapid means of communications, such as the telephone and telex, and the very frequent recourse by the paper manufacturers to very well-informed trade buyers meant that, notwithstanding the number of stages involved—producer, agent, buyer, agent, producer—information on the level of the announced prices spreads within a matter of days, if not within a matter of hours on the pulp market. * * *

Conclusions

[126] Following that analysis, it must be stated that, in this case, concertation is not the only plausible explanation for the parallel conduct. To begin with, the system of price announcements may be regarded as constituting a rational response to the fact that the pulp market constituted a long-term market and to the need felt by both buyers and sellers to limit commercial risks. Further, the similarity in the dates of price announcements may be regarded as a direct result of the high degree of market transparency, which does not have to be described as artificial. Finally, the parallelism of prices and the price trends may be satisfactorily explained by the oligopolistic tendencies of the market and by the specific circumstances prevailing in certain periods. Accordingly, the parallel conduct established by the Commission does not constitute evidence of concertation.

Notes and Questions

1. Is the judgment consistent with *Dyestuffs* and *Sugar*? Is it distinguishable? What distinctive characteristic in *Dyestuffs* made the producers' behavior particularly vulnerable to condemnation?

2. In para. 64 the Court says that the system of quarterly price announcements "does not lessen each undertaking's uncertainty as to the future attitude of its competitors." Why not? Argue for the Commission that the system does lessen uncertainty. Would this interpretation change the outcome?

3. In para. 71 the Court declares that parallel conduct cannot furnish proof of concertation "unless concertation constitutes the only plausible explanation for such conduct." Why such a heavy burden? If agreement was the most probable explanation of the parallel price moves, should the Court have drawn an inference of a concerted practice?

4. The buyers desired advance price information. Does that explain the quarterly price announcements? Does it explain the virtual simultaneity of the price announcements? Does it explain the uniform price rises?

5. What was the experts' explanation for parallel prices and price stability? See especially paragraphs 102 to 105. Did the experts provide an account indicating that the behavior was not procompetitive but was nonetheless not conspiratorial?

6. Consider, once again, the definition of "concertation." When you read the excerpts from the *Sugar* case, did you infer that oligopolistic interdependence was to be treated as concertation? What do you now believe is the relationship between oligopolistic interdependence and concertation under EC law?

In the United States, the Supreme Court has similarly moved from a "soft" test for proof of "combination" or "concert" to a demanding standard that puts a significant burden on the plaintiff. Compare *Interstate Circuit* with *Matsushita*, page 814 supra. What are the policy reasons for the current approach?

7. Observe the conundrum of oligopoly behavior. A few firms in a high-barrier market may be able to mimic the effects of a cartel without an explicit agreement or even an understanding. Should this phenomenon be relevant to a judicial construction of the word "concert"?

D. MAY CARTELS BE JUSTIFIED?—CRISIS CARTELS

In some instances an industry is plagued by structural overcapacity. The industry members claim there is a market failure and that an industry combination can solve the problem more efficiently than competition. Should the producers be permitted to form a crisis cartel?

STICHTING BAKSTEEN

(Dutch brick makers)

Commission Decision, Case IV/34.456 O.J. L 131/15 (May 26, 1994).

The agreement, the market

6   On 19 August 1991 the Dutch foundation Stichting Baksteen (which is composed of and represents seven Dutch brick manufacturers) notified the Commission of a series of agreements between Dutch brick manufacturers aimed at rationalizing production with a view to eliminating or preventing overcapacity.

However, after a preliminary examination of the case, the Commission formally opposed the first plan [. The measures] went well beyond what was needed to attain the objective in question. * * *

7   Having taken another thorough look at the situation and trend on the market, the same producers arrived at the conclusion that it was nevertheless essential to implement a coordinated plan to reduce capacity in order to overcome the difficulties which have affected the Dutch brick industry for several years, and which may be summarized as follows:

at the end of 1991 brick stocks in the Netherlands totalled 448 million bricks, equivalent to some 32% of total brick sales by Dutch firms. Although the industry considers that a stockpile representing around 20% of sales is sustainable, existing stocks of 32% easily exceed this critical threshold and the costs of maintaining such unused capacity are very high. The surplus is attributable chiefly to technological developments (introduction of new processes and construction of larger plants to achieve economies of scale) and to falling demand. It should be noted that the drop in demand is structural in nature and the direct result of the steady decline in the consumption of bricks relative to other building materials.... Relative consumption has fallen by 20% in the last five years. The trend is still downward, chiefly because alternative materials are cheaper and give better technical results; this explains the growing tendency to replace bearing walls made with bricks by concrete and steel and to use sheet materials instead of other forms of brickwork.

In those circumstances, and given the pessimistic forecasts for medium-term sales trends, it must be assumed that the stockpile will increase steadily, leading in the short-term to a stockpile/sales ratio that will be difficult to put up with.... * * *

[Capacity utilization had fallen by 10% to 83%; price had fallen 30% since 1980.]

8   In the circumstances, the parties consider that action is essential in order gradually to restore a lasting balance between supply and demand, thereby resolving the crisis in the Dutch brick industry.

On 25 August 1992 another agreement on the restructuring and reorganization of the Dutch brick industry was concluded, this time between 16 firms; it is aimed at a coordinate reduction in brick production capacity of the order of 217 million units, and forms the subject of this Decision.

Agreement

9   ... [T]he parties to the agreement concluded that a capacity cut of 200 million to 220 million bricks was necessary in order to restore the balance between supply and demand in the medium term, whilst at the same time gradually reducing the stockpile.

10   Under the agreement, four Dutch brick producers have undertaken to close down seven production units definitively and irreversibly: this will represent the effective dismantling of surplus production capacity amounting to 217 million bricks. The firms in question have also undertaken:

—   to halt production of ceramic building materials at the seven production sites to be dismantled, for a period of 30 years (this undertaking being automatically transferred to any future purchasers of the units),

—   to refrain from selling any of the dismantled plant to producers who would use it to increase their production capacity within a 500–kilometre radius of the Dutch frontier for a period of 30 years, and to impose this obligation on any future purchasers, even if they are outside the geographical area referred to.

Provision is made for a system of fines in order to prevent any failure to comply with these obligations, and the parties accept the principle of verification of total closure of their units by independent qualified experts.

11   The restructuring operation will be financed by the 16 firms that have signed the agreement. From 1 October 1992 they will contribute over a five-year (or possibly shorter) period to a compensation fund managed by Stichting Baksteen. Each firm will contribute either Fl 20, Fl 15 or Fl 6 per 1000 bricks produced and undertakes to supply all details concerning its annual output to Stichting Baksteen, which is required not to divulge this information to the other parties.

The financial resources thus accruing to Stichting Baksteen will be allocated to those parties that have definitively dismantled capacity, as a contribution to the costs of closure, including the associated social costs. The definitive closure of the capacity will be certified by independent qualified experts.

12   A social plan for the sector has been negotiated with the trade unions, the implementation of which is to be monitored by Stichting Baksteen. The parties will endeavour to ensure that, in carrying out the restructuring operation, employees are redeployed wherever possible and in accordance with the legal and/or contractual obligations in force in the Netherlands.

13   The parties to the agreement are strictly prohibited from bringing on stream new capacity during the financing period and a list has been

drawn up to that end by Stichting Basteen indicating the current production capacity of each part. * * *

Legal assessment—Article 85(1)

15 The notified agreement is an agreement between undertakings which has the object and effect of restricting competition within the common market. * * *

Legal assessment—Article 85(3) * * *

21 In the case in question, the forces present on the market were and still are unable individually to make the necessary capacity cuts to restore and eventually maintain an efficient competitive structure. That is why the firms concerned organized, together and for a limited period, the necessary structural adjustment.

22 Whilst in principle it is for firms to adopt flexible pricing policies in order to influence demand levels, demand for bricks is a derived demand as they represent only 2–3% of the cost of a building. Consequently, there is very little or no elasticity of demand with respect to price levels in the short or medium term. Brick price levels are not likely to affect the rate of construction or, therefore, total demand for building materials.

23 Furthermore, there is very little flexibility in the brick production process, not only as regards changes in capacity utilization—given the very high fixed and semi-fixed costs—but also when it comes to reducing capacity. As half of the parties already have only one kiln, they are technically incapable of making any capacity cuts whatsoever.

24 The other parties, as leading manufacturers, would not have decided individually and independently to reduce capacity had they not been certain that competitors would follow their example or provide financial support, and that no new capacity would be introduced during the period of the agreement. * * *

26 By reducing capacity, firms throw off the financial burden of maintaining unused surplus capacities and, by increasing utilization of the capacity utilization of the capacity retained, do not have to reduce output.

As the capacity closures concern production units that are the least suitable and least efficient because of obsolescence, limited size or outdated technology, production will in future be concentrated in the more modern plants which will then be able to operate at higher capacity and productivity levels; this will lead to a corresponding reduction in the incidence of fixed costs, which form a large proportion of net costs.

As a result, it is possible to predict a future increase in the profitability of the Dutch brick industry and, therefore, a return to normal competitiveness.

27 In addition, because the closures are coordinated, restructuring can be carried out in acceptable social conditions, including the redeployment of employees.

28 It can, therefore, be concluded that the agreement helps to improve production and to promote technical and economic progress.

29   Article 85 (3) provides that an agreement must allow consumers a fair share of the resulting benefit. Consumers in the present case should benefit from the improvement in production because in the long term they will be dealing with a healthy industry offering competitive supplies and, in the short term, they will go on enjoying the advantages of continuing competition between the parties. Thanks to the agreement they can also be sure that structural adjustment keeps competitive firms or capacities on the market whilst eliminating outmoded or obsolescent capacity which might otherwise have affected healthy capacity through lost compensation within a group.

30   There are a sufficient number of producers remaining, whether or not parties to the agreement, to give consumers a choice of supplier and security of supply, while ruling out the risk of over-concentrated supply.

31   A capacity-reduction agreement accompanied by a financing system is, however, liable to lead in the short term to higher prices for consumers. In the present case, however, such risks are largely offset by the fact that the high costs of financing stockpiles will diminish. The special nature of the market for bricks, where unit costs are very sensitive to capacity utilization rates, makes it possible to expect a favourable effect on prices. Consumers also have the option, if the prices charged by the parties to the agreement are unfair, of obtaining supplies from other available sources.

32   Another crucial factor as regards the application of Article 85 (3) is whether the measures aimed at reducing capacity are indispensable to the attainment of that objective.

33   The agreement relates only to the reduction of surplus capacities: to that end, it is necessary for the agreement to contain a detailed and binding closure plan which guarantees, firstly, that surplus capacity will be effectively and permanently dismantled and, secondly, that throughout the period of its application no fresh capacity will be installed apart from the replacement capacity provided for in the restructuring plan. For the rest, the freedom of the parties in matters of production, pricing, conditions of sale, imports and exports, deliveries, mergers and acquisitions is not affected by the agreement. . . .

34   The system of compensatory payments must be regarded as indispensable to the attainment of the objective. Half the firms concerned were unable to reduce their capacity as they had only one kiln; the financing scheme must thus be regarded as an incentive to the others to reduce their structural overcapacity. It provides compensation for firms carrying out closures, and helps them to cover the costs of the operation, especially the social costs incurred. The five-year period (which could be shorter, depending on actual financing) serves to amortize, share out and stagger the financial charges.

35   It was deemed essential to introduce binding guarantees in respect of the definitive closure of the seven production units concerned and the actual dismantling of plant in order to ensure that the capacity cuts were irreversible. As the effectiveness of the agreement depends on compliance with these commitments, provision is made for contractual fines and the transfer of the obligation to any future purchaser not party to the

agreement of the sites or plant to ensure that capacity earmarked for closure is actually dismantled. * * *

[37]   It can therefore be concluded that the restrictions on means of production imposed on the parties are indispensable to the attainment of the objectives in question.

[38]   For the purposes of Article 85 (3), the agreement does not afford the firms the possibility of eliminating competition in respect of a substantial part of the products in question.

[39]   It should first be noted that the firms continue to compete on both prices and, more generally, all those aspects not covered by the agreement. As the coordinated capacity reduction forms only one element of the firms' competitive strategies—albeit an important one—they are not surrendering all freedom to act on the market, which ensures that a certain degree of internal competition is maintained.

[40]   External competition is generally assured through the presence of other producers and importers not parties to the agreement.

[41]   The contract products compete against a wide range of alternative building and finishing materials that are sufficiently substitutable to make them competitors.

[42]   Lastly, because the agreement has from the start been strictly limited in time, the certainty that full competition will soon be restored encourages the firms concerned to bear in mind when taking action under the agreement that, when it expires, they will again be competing fully against each other.

Notes and Questions

1.   Note how the authorized cartel works to compensate those who agreed to take their capacity off the market, and how it works to keep everyone in line. How is the welfare of the workers taken into account?

2.   Are there any findings that you question in the legal assessment under Article 85(3)? What about para. 28? 29? 38? How can it be argued that the cartel does not eliminate competition in respect of a substantial part of the Dutch brick market? Isn't this the point of the agreement?

3.   Why shouldn't the Dutch brick makers have been left to the vagaries of the market? Would the most efficient firms survive? If the Dutch brick makers are entitled to operate as a cartel, why aren't all producers who are faced with sharp winds of competition entitled to operate as a cartel? What makes this case special? Are you convinced that it is?

4.   What is the significance beyond Europe of an Article 81(3) exemption? If there is a market for Dutch bricks in the United States and the collaboration permitted by the Commission's decision results in a price rise in the United States, can US buyers successfully sue the Dutch brick makers under the US antitrust laws? See Section E. below.

5.   The wisdom of allowing judicial or administrative authorization of crisis or restructuring cartels is much debated. United States law makes no allowance for crises, on the theory that market solutions are better than private solutions, and a crisis justification for cartels would weaken the strong, clear rule of law. German law allows authorization of crisis cartels. German Law Against Restraints

of Competition (GWB), §§ 1, 6, 1957 Bundesgesetzblatt (BGB1) I 1081, as amended. For many years the UK allowed cartels if they were in the "public interest." UK Restrictive Trade Practices Act 1976 (replaced by a law in the image of Article 81). Until 1999, Japanese law allowed authorization of depression and rationalization cartels. Antimonopoly Law of Japan, § 24(3), Law No. 54, 1947 (amended). Many less developed countries use state-run cartels to maximize profits from special endowments of resources such as oil. See International Ass'n of Machinists v. OPEC, 649 F.2d 1354 (9th Cir.1981), *cert. denied*, 454 U.S. 1163, 102 S.Ct. 1036, 71 L.Ed.2d 319 (1982) (dismissing suit challenging the OPEC cartel on grounds of Act of State).

What is the best approach? Is your answer for the European Union different from your answer for the United States?

E.　WORLD CARTELS AND OFFSHORE CARTELS— JURISDICTION, COMITY, AND COOPERATION

With increasing frequently, a conspiracy in one country harms consumers in another country.

The United States was the pioneer of the "effects" doctrine, under which US law catches offshore anticompetitive conduct targeted at Americans. This is the holding of United States v. Aluminum Corp. of America (*Alcoa*), 148 F.2d 416 (2d Cir.1945). (See Notes and Questions below.) For many years US trading partners, and particularly the UK, adamantly opposed application of the effects doctrine to their nationals, labeling the doctrine an affront to their sovereignty.

But as years went by, nations other than the United States began to feel the threat of offshore anticompetitive acts targeted at their nationals, and the effects doctrine became necessary self-protection.

The first major European Court case on point was the dyestuffs cartel, Imperial Chemical Industries Ltd. v. Commission, Cases 48, 49, 51–57/69, [1972] ECR 619; see p. 811 supra. ICI, a UK company, was part of the dyestuffs cartel. The UK had not yet joined the European Community. ICI sought dismissal for lack of jurisdiction. The Commission rejected ICI's argument, and applied the effects test. On appeal, the Court of Justice sidestepped the controversy surrounding the effects doctrine. ICI had subsidiaries in the Community, and, the Court said, ICI exercised "decisive influence" over them. Therefore the parent and its subsidiaries were one economic unit. The Court said, in para. 130:

> By making use of its power to control its subsidiaries established in the Community, the applicant was able to ensure that its decision was implemented on that market.

The issue arose in a starker form in *Wood pulp*. Not all of the alleged conspirators had subsidiaries in Europe. Sixteen years had passed since *Dyestuffs*. Globalization had increased nations' vulnerability to offshore cartels.

United States, Finnish, Swedish and Canadian firms exported wood pulp into the common market, themselves or through export associations. To facilitate exports, the United States had enacted the Webb–Pomerene Act, and the US wood pulp firms were members of a Webb–Pomerene Association, which, under the terms of that statute, exempted the exporters and their association from the United States antitrust laws except to the extent that they harmed competition in the United States.

The European Commission charged the firms and two of their export associations with fixing the price of wood pulp that was being sold to buyers in the Community. The Commission found infringements and imposed fines. The undertakings sued for annulment, on grounds that included lack of jurisdiction. The jurisdictional issue reached the Court of Justice before the question of proof of the cartel, treated above; so we assume, for purposes of the jurisdictional judgment, that there was in fact a cartel agreement.

ÅHLSTRÖM OSAKEYHTIÖ v. COMMISSION

(Wood pulp) (jurisdiction)
Cases C–89, 104, 114, 116–117, 125–129/85, [1988] ECR 5193.

3   [T]he Commission set out the grounds which in its view justify the Community's jurisdiction to apply Article 85 of the Treaty to the concertation in question. It stated first that all the addressees of the decision were either exporting directly to purchasers within the Community or were doing business within the Community through branches, subsidiaries, agencies or other establishments in the Community. It further pointed out that the concertation applied to the vast majority of the sales of those undertakings to and in the Community. Finally it stated that two-thirds of total shipments and 60% of consumption of the product in question in the Community had been affected by such concertation. The Commission concluded that: "The effect of the agreements and practices on prices announced and/or charged to customers and on resale of pulp within the EEC was therefore not only substantial but intended, and was the primary and direct result of the agreements and practices." * * *

6   All the applicants which have made submissions regarding jurisdiction maintain first of all that by applying the competition rules of the Treaty to them the Commission has misconstrued the territorial scope of Article 85. They note that in its judgment of 14 July 1972 in Case 48/69 (*ICI v. Commission* [1972] ECR 619) the Court did not adopt the "effects doctrine" but emphasized that the case involved conduct restricting competition within the common market because of the activities of subsidiaries which could be imputed to the parent companies. The applicants add that even if there is a basis in Community law for applying Article 85 to them, the action of applying the rule interpreted in that way would be contrary to public international law which precludes any claim by the Community to regulate conduct restricting competition adopted outside the territory of the Community merely by reason of the economic repercussions which that conduct produces within the Community.

7   The applicants which are members of the KEA [Kraft Export Association] further submit that the application of Community competition rules to them is contrary to public international law in so far as it is in breach of the principle of non-interference. They maintain that in this case the application of Article 85 harmed the interest of the United States in promoting exports by United States undertakings as recognized in the

Webb Pomerene Act of 1918 under which export associations, like the KEA, are exempt from United States anti-trust laws.

8   Certain Canadian applicants also maintain that by imposing fines on them and making reduction of those fines conditional on the producers giving undertakings as to their future conduct the Commission has infringed Canada's sovereignty and thus breached the principle of international comity. * * *

Territorial Scope of Article 85 and Public International Law

(a) The Individual Undertakings

11 In so far as the submission concerning the infringement of Article 85 of the Treaty itself is concerned, it should be recalled that that provision prohibits all agreements between undertakings and concerted practices which may affect trade between Member States and which have as their object or effect the restriction of competition within the common market.

12 It should be noted that the main sources of supply of wood pulp are outside the Community, in Canada, the United States, Sweden and Finland and that the market therefore has global dimensions. Where wood pulp producers established in those countries sell directly to purchasers established in the Community and engage in price competition in order to win orders from those customers, that constitutes competition within the common market.

13 It follows that where those producers concert on the prices to be charged to their customers in the Community and put that concertation into effect by selling at prices which are actually coordinated, they are taking part in concertation which has the object and effect of restricting competition within the common market within the meaning of Article 85 of the Treaty.

14 Accordingly, it must be concluded that by applying the competition rules in the Treaty in the circumstances of this case to undertakings whose registered offices are situated outside the Community, the Commission has not made an incorrect assessment of the territorial scope of Article 85.

15 The applicants have submitted that the decision is incompatible with public international law on the grounds that the application of the competition rules in this case was founded exclusively on the economic repercussions within the common market of conduct restricting competition which was adopted outside the Community.

16 It should be observed that an infringement of Article 85, such as the conclusion of an agreement which has had the effect of restricting competition within the common market, consists of conduct made up of two elements, the formation of the agreement, decision or concerted practice and the implementation thereof. If the applicability of prohibitions laid down under competition law were made to depend on the place where the agreement, decision or concerted practice was formed, the result would obviously be to give undertakings an easy means of evading those prohibitions. The decisive factor is therefore the place where it is implemented.

17 The producers in this case implemented their pricing agreement within the common market. It is immaterial in that respect whether or not they had recourse to subsidiaries, agents, sub-agents, or branches within the

Community in order to make their contacts with purchasers within the Community.

[18] Accordingly the Community's jurisdiction to apply its competition rules to such conduct is covered by the territoriality principle as universally recognized in public international law.

[19] As regards the argument based on the infringement of the principle of non-interference, it should be pointed out that the applicants who are members of KEA have referred to a rule according to which where two States have jurisdiction to lay down and enforce rules and the effect of those rules is that a person finds himself subject to contradictory orders as to the conduct he must adopt, each State is obliged to exercise its jurisdiction with moderation. The applicants have concluded that by disregarding that rule in applying its competition rules the Community has infringed the principle of non-interference.

[20] There is no need to enquire into the existence in international law of such a rule since it suffices to observe that the conditions for its application are in any event not satisfied. There is not, in this case, any contradiction between the conduct required by the United States and that required by the Community since the Webb Pomerene Act merely exempts the conclusion of export cartels from the application of United States anti-trust laws but does not require such cartels to be concluded.

[21] It should further be pointed out that the United States authorities raised no objections regarding any conflict of jurisdiction when consulted by the Commission pursuant to the OECD Council Recommendation of 25 October 1979 concerning cooperation between member countries on restrictive business practices affecting international trade (*Acts of the organization,* Vol. 19, p. 376).

[22] As regards the argument relating to disregard of international comity, it suffices to observe that it amounts to calling in question the Community's jurisdiction to apply its competition rules to conduct such as that found to exist in this case and that, as such, that argument has already been rejected.

[23] Accordingly it must be concluded that the Commission's decision is not contrary to Article 85 of the Treaty or to the rules of public international law relied on by the applicants.

(b) KEA

[24] According to its Articles of Association, KEA is a non-profit-making association whose purpose is the promotion of the commercial interests of its members in the exportation of their products and it serves primarily as a clearing-house for its members for information regarding their export markets. KEA does not itself engage in manufacture, selling or distribution.

[25] It should further be pointed out that within KEA a number of groups have been formed, including the Pulp Group, to cover the different sectors of the pulp and paper industry. Under Article 1 of the by-laws of KEA, undertakings may only join KEA by becoming a member of one of those groups. Article 2 of the by-laws provides that the groups enjoy full independence in the management of their affairs.

26　It should lastly be noted that according to a policy statement adopted by the Pulp Group, referred to in paragraph 32 of the contested decision, the members of the group may conclude price agreements at meetings which they hold from time to time provided that each member is informed in advance that prices will be discussed and that the meeting is quorate. The unanimous agreement of the members present is also binding on members who are absent when the decision is adopted.

27　It is apparent from the foregoing that KEA's price recommendations cannot be distinguished from the pricing agreements concluded by undertakings which are members of the Pulp Group and that KEA has not played a separate role in the implementation of those agreements.

28　In those circumstances the decision should be declared void in so far as it concerns KEA.

Notes and Questions

1.　The United States has a larger, more developed body of case law on subject matter jurisdiction than any other nation or community. Since the 1940s, US courts have had "effects" jurisdiction; that is, if foreigners act, even abroad, with the intent to affect US commerce and they cause a direct effect on US commerce, the United States courts have subject matter jurisdiction and may apply the Sherman Act. United States v. Aluminum Co. of America, 148 F.2d 416 (2d Cir.1945). US courts may not, however, require foreign firms acting in their home territory to do what their home government forbids, or to abstain from doing what their home government requires, for such an order would interfere impermissibly with the sovereignty of the foreign government. See United States v. Watchmakers of Switzerland Info. Center, 1963 (CCH) Trade Cas. ¶ 70,600 (S.D.N.Y.1962); 1965 (CCH) Trade Cas. ¶ 71,352 (S.D.N.Y.1965) (judgment revised to apply only to conduct that operated outside of Switzerland).

In the 1960s and 1970s, applications of the *Alcoa* doctrine were criticized by various nations, especially Great Britain, whose nationals were sued for treble damages in US courts as members of world cartels that had targeted American buyers. Cases against Rio Tinto Zinc and others for allegedly participating in a world-wide uranium cartel targeted at Westinghouse and the United States caused an outcry by the British and it, along with proceedings against a shipping conference, led to Britain's enactment of a blocking and clawback statute, The British Protection of Trading Interests Act, 1980, ch. 11. The blocking provisions block the production, for foreign litigation, of documents located in the UK, and the clawback provisions allow a British firm to recover (to "claw back") in Great Britain penal damages paid pursuant to a foreign judgment; thus, two-thirds of a treble damage award may be retrieved. Various other nations, including France, Germany, Australia and Canada, also adopted blocking statutes or blocking and clawback statutes. See Restatement (Third) of the Foreign Relations Law of the United States § 442, Reporters' Note No. 4 (1987).

Apparently in response to the criticism and to threats of retaliation by trading partners, some United States courts developed balancing principles. They stated that courts should refrain from exercising jurisdiction if foreign nations' and foreign nationals' interests in nonenforcement of US law outbalance the United States' interest in enforcement. Timberlane Lumber Co. v. Bank of America, 549 F.2d 597 (9th Cir.1976); Mannington Mills, Inc. v. Congoleum Corp., 595 F.2d 1287 (3d Cir.1979).

But United States law was not to be so quickly harmonized. At least one other American court observed that a court cannot balance incommensurables (i.e., American interests in antitrust enforcement cannot be balanced against British interests against it), and the court declared that it had concurrent jurisdiction with UK courts over a conspiracy among American, British and other airlines allegedly designed to destroy Freddie Laker's no-frills "sky train" that featured low-cost flights between London and New York. Laker Airways Limited v. Sabena, Belgian World Airlines, 731 F.2d 909 (D.C.Cir.1984).

In 1993 the United States Supreme Court decided its first antitrust extraterritoriality case in a quarter of a century. Lloyds of London reinsurers had allegedly collaborated in London with Americans, and some had collaborated separately in London only among themselves, to cut back the coverage of reinsurance policies that they would offer on the US market. When sued, these British defendants moved to dismiss, asserting that the US court lacked jurisdiction or that comity considerations required dismissal. They claimed that their conduct was lawful where performed (in the UK), and that in view of the UK regulatory policy, which conferred self-regulation on Lloyds of London, a conflict existed that required dismissal by the US courts. The Supreme Court disagreed. It noted that there was no direct conflict, in the sense that UK law did not require (much less encourage) the London firms to boycott Americans. In this context it stated:

> [I]t is well established by now that the Sherman Act applies to foreign conduct that was meant to produce and did in fact produce some substantial effect in the United States.

Hartford Fire Ins. Co. v. California, 509 U.S. 764, 796, 113 S.Ct. 2891, 125 L.Ed.2d 612 (1993).

Is there any difference between the holding of *Hartford* and the holding of *Wood pulp*? Has the European Union adopted the effects test?

Can American brick buyers recover damages from the Dutch brick makers (see D. above) whose authorized crisis cartel raises brick prices in the United States?

2.   Would the outcome of *Wood pulp* be the same if the producers sold FOB New York without knowledge that the wood pulp was being shipped directly into the Community? Should the rules of jurisdiction be the same regardless whether the sale and transfer of title took place in New York or the Netherlands? Is the harm to competition within the Community the same? Are the sovereignty interests of the affected countries the same?

3.   In *Wood pulp*, why did the Court declare the Commission's decision against KEA void? What would the result have been if there were no sector groups within KEA and if KEA's price recommendations were autonomous and distinct from joint actions of its members? Why was the jurisdictional decision regarding KEA harder than the jurisdictional decision regarding the individual producers?

4.   The US Justice Department has announced that it may in a proper case sue American subsidiaries of foreign firms that conspire to exclude American exporters from the foreign market. Is this an appropriate exercise of enforcement power? Would European authorities have power to enforce Article 81 against American cartelists that excluded European firms from the US market? Suppose American farmers organize a boycott against EU agricultural products because they are subsidized. Would the European competition authorities be entitled to bring proceedings under Article 81?

5. As the Court in *Wood pulp* notes, import cartels can be every bit as harmful as domestic cartels. If every exporting nation facilitates outbound cartels to help its own enterprises increase their profits at the expense of the importing nation's consumers, and if every importing nation stays its hand out of respect for the sovereignty of (or in expectation of reciprocity by) the exporting nation, the world will be cartelized. Consider the choice between enforcing domestic law to protect competition and consumers in the nation, and exercising restraint to respect sovereignty of an exporting nation. On which side should a nation err?

6. The international cartel problem is deepened by the international merger problem. Both the EU and the US consider themselves empowered to prohibit offshore mergers that, by their calculus, harm their citizens. See Chapter 25. The European Union, the United States, and other trading partners recognize the need for cooperation and coordination. The European Union has entered several bilateral agreements for cooperation on competition policy, and it advocates the introduction of competition policy in agreements within the framework of the World Trade Organization.

Chapter 22

ABUSE OF A DOMINANT POSITION

A. THE TREATY

Article 82 [ex 86] forbids the abuse of a dominant position. It provides:

Any abuse by one or more undertakings of a dominant position within the Common Market or in a substantial part of it shall be prohibited as incompatible with the Common Market in so far as it may affect trade between Member States. Such abuse may in particular consist in:

(a) directly or indirectly imposing unfair purchase or selling prices or other unfair trading conditions;

(b) limiting production, markets or technical development to the prejudice of consumers;

(c) applying dissimilar conditions to equivalent transactions with other trading parties, thereby placing them at a competitive disadvantage;

(d) making the conclusion of contracts subject to acceptance by the other parties of supplementary obligations which, by their nature or according to commercial usage, have no connection to the subject of such contracts.

The drafters of Article 86 drew upon the law of West Germany and also the law of the United States. German law prohibits market-dominant enterprises from abusing their single-firm or group dominance by hindering competitors or exploiting or discriminating against buyers or sellers. Act Against Restraints of Competition § 19. Section 2 of the United States Sherman Antitrust Act provides that no person shall "monopolize, or attempt to monopolize, or combine or conspire with any other person or persons, to monopolize...." 15 U.S.C. § 2.

United States antitrust law was adopted at the time of the industrial revolution in response to a distrust of bigness and a fear of excessive concentration of private power. See E. Fox, The Modernization of Antitrust: A New Equilibrium, 66 Cornell L.Rev. 1140 (1981). German cartel law was adopted at the end of World War II in connection with American aid under the Marshall Plan. By safeguarding freedom of trade, the German law was designed to diffuse power and to prevent the ascendancy of another Hitler. The law was welcomed by the Freiburg School, which espoused a "social market economy." A. Peacock and H. Willgerodt, eds., German Neo–Liberals and the Social Market Economy (1989); J. Maxeiner, Policy and Methods in German and American Antitrust Law (1986); V. Berghahn, The Americanization of West German Industry, 1945–1973 (1986).

Among the Western European nations, however, fear of big business as such was not the problem. Europe was a continent of many small nations, each isolated by high trade barriers. Private business firms were normally operating below efficient scale. Consolidations, particularly cross-border consolidations, were desired in order to increase efficiency and integrate the Common Market. When adopted in 1957, Article 86 was seen not as a means to check the size of business but as a vehicle for regulating the conduct of firms that had economic power. See R. Joliet, Monopolisation and Abuse of Dominant Position: A Comparative Study of American and European Approaches to the Control of Economic Power 8–13, 131–33 (1970).

Review the four examples of abuses set forth in Article 82. What generalizations can you make about the type of conduct or transactions that the signers of the Treaty wished to prevent? Does Article 82 appear to deal only with conduct, or also with business structure (e.g., mergers)? Does it seem designed to help buyers and consumers? sellers? also competitors? Does it seem designed to achieve only efficiency or also fairness? Which is the most appropriate course for Western Europe?

Compare the substance, form and structure of Article 82 with that of Article 81. What is similar and what is different about the examples of offenses? Why does Article 81 authorize exemptions while Article 82 does not? Would you expect the Article 81(3) justifications to be applicable in some way to the conduct of a dominant firm?

B. DOMINANCE

Article 82 prohibits abuse of a "dominant position." The Court of Justice defined dominant position in *Hoffmann–La Roche v. Commission*, Case 85/76, [1979] ECR 461:

[38] The dominant position ... referred to [in Article 86] relates to a position of economic strength enjoyed by an undertaking which enables it to prevent effective competition being maintained on the relevant market by affording it the power to behave to an appreciable extent independently of its competitors, its customers and ultimately of the consumers.

[39] Such a position does not preclude some competition, which it does where there is a monopoly or a quasi-monopoly, but enables the undertaking which profits by it, if not to determine, at least to have an appreciable influence on the conditions under which that competition will develop, and in any case to act largely in disregard of it so long as such conduct does not operate to its detriment.

A dominant position must also be distinguished from parallel courses of conduct which are peculiar to oligopolies in that in an oligopoly the courses of conduct interact, while in the case of an undertaking occupying a dominant position the conduct of the undertaking which derives profits from that position is to a great extent determined unilaterally.

The existence of a dominant position may derive from several factors which, taken separately, are not necessarily determinative but among these factors a highly important one is the existence of very large market shares.

[40] A substantial market share as evidence of the existence of a dominant position is not a constant factor and its importance varies from market to market according to the structure of these markets, especially as far as production, supply and demand are concerned.

Even though each group of vitamins constitutes a separate market, these different markets, as has emerged from the examination of their structure, nevertheless have a sufficient number of features in common to make it possible for the same criteria to be applied to them as far as concerns the importance of the market shares for the purpose of determining whether there is a dominant position or not.

[41] Furthermore although the importance of the market shares may vary from one market to another the view may legitimately be taken that very large shares are in themselves, and save in exceptional circumstances, evidence of the existence of a dominant position.

An undertaking which has a very large market share and holds it for some time, by means of the volume of production and the scale of the supply which it stands for—without those having much smaller market shares being able to meet rapidly the demand from those who would like to break away from the undertaking which has the largest market share—is by virtue of that share in a position of strength which makes it an unavoidable trading partner and which, already because of this secures for it, at the very least during relatively long periods, that freedom of action which is the special feature of a dominant position. * * *

[48] On the other hand the relationship between the market shares of the undertaking concerned and of its competitors, especially those of the next largest, the technological lead of an undertaking over its competitors, the existence of a highly developed sales network and the absence of potential competition are relevant factors, the first because it enables the competitive strength of the undertaking in question to be assessed, the second and third because they represent in themselves technical and commercial advantages and the fourth because it is the consequence of the existence of obstacles preventing new competitors from having access to the market.

A dominant position connotes economic power in a market, power to impose market terms on competitors, or more generally power to hinder the maintenance of effective competition. For legal purposes, dominance may be inferred from a large market share where the next largest firm is half the size of the largest firm or less. The Court of Justice has stated that market shares of 40% and upwards, combined with entry barriers and a size gap with the next largest firm, presumptively confer dominance. In *Hoffmann-La Roche*, a 47% share of one market (Vitamin A) was enough to confer dominance in view of the structure of the market (the next largest competitors had 27% and 18%), Roche's technological lead over its competitors, the absence of potential competition, and Roche's overcapacity.

Some years later the Court in *AKZO* said, quoting from *Hoffmann-La Roche:* "very large market shares are in themselves, and save in exceptional circumstances, evidence of the existence of a dominant position." The Court in *AKZO* added: "That is the situation where there is a market share of 50% such as that found to exist in this case." *AKZO* Chemie BV v. Commission, Case 62/86, [1991] ECR I–3359, para. 60.

Vertical and other integration combined with a large market share and a strong trade name has also been held to confer dominance. United Brands Co. v. Commission, page 843 infra.

Can a firm be dominant if it does not have the power to raise its prices significantly above its costs (and thus charge supracompetitive prices)? Can a firm be dominant because exogenous factors have produced a temporary shortage of the goods it produces, or because distributors or customers have locked themselves into a position of dependence on the firm? The answer may depend on the Treaty's goals, and whether control of dominance has a fairness dimension as well as an efficiency dimension.

Joint Dominance

Article 82 prohibits abuse of a dominant position by "one or more undertakings." What is "joint dominance" within the meaning of this clause?

Joint dominance is not simply cartel behavior, which is caught, if at all, by Article 81. Società Italiano Vetro SpA v. Commission (Italian flat glass), Case T–68, 77 & 78/89, [1992] ECR II–1403. In *Italian flat glass* the Court of First Instance declared that to establish an infringement of Article 86 "it is not sufficient ... to 'recycle' the facts constituting an infringement of Article 85...." Id., para. 360. But, the Court has said, independent entities can be "united by such economic links that ... together they hold a dominant position vis-à-vis the other operators on the same market." Deutsche Grammophon Gesellschaft GmbH v. Metro–SB–Grossmärkte GmbH & Co. KG, Case 78/70, [1971] ECR 487.

In *Compagnie Maritime Belge*, members of a shipping conference in the liner market betweeen northern Europe and western Africa joined together as "fighting ships" to destroy an independent competitor. Shipping conferences are authorized by regulation to cooperate on rates and allocation of cargo, and they enjoy a limited block exemption from Articles 81 and 82. The liners defended Article 86 (now 82) charges by denying, among other things, that they held a collective dominant position. They asserted that there were no economic links between them apart from the conference agreement, and that the Commission was merely transposing an Article 85 (now 81) complaint. Rejecting these arguments, the Court of Justice declared that links are relevant but not necessary for the existence of a collective dominant position. "[I]t must be ascertained whether economic links exist between the undertakings concerned which enable them to act together independently of their competitors, their customers and consumers." But the critical question is whether "from an economic point of view [the undertakings] present themselves or act together on a particular market as a collective entity." "[A] liner conference [as defined in the block exemption] can be characterised as a collective entity which presents itself as such on the market vis-à-vis both users and competitors." Compagnie Maritime Belge Transports SA v. Commission, Cases C–395/96P and C–396/96P, [2000] ECR I–1365, paras. 42, 36, 48.

Does *Compagnie Maritime Belge* dilute the meaning of "links" in favor of economic reality? Must the "collectively dominant" firms act as if they were one?

US law does not have an identical concept. But compare E.I. du Pont de Nemours & Co. v. FTC, 729 F.2d 128 (2d Cir.1984), which states in dictum that oligopolists' non-collusive adoption of the same oppressive, unjustified anticompetitive business practices could constitute an unfair method of competition within the meaning of Section 5 of the Federal Trade Commission Act. Section 5 of the FTC Act, unlike the Sherman Act, requires neither joint action nor monopolistic power.

C. MARKET DEFINITION

If a firm is dominant, it is dominant within a defined market. Accordingly, market definition—determination of both the product market and the geographic market—must precede a determination of dominance.

A great many competition decisions and judgments involve market definition. In an early case an American company that manufactured containers for meat and fish (Continental Can), acquired a West German and a Dutch company that manufactured containers for meat and fish. The case raised two important questions: (1) What was the relevant market? and (2) Is structural change that increases dominance (as opposed to conduct that does so) caught by Article 82 (ex 86)? The second question involved a major and controversial issue of law. The Commission held that Article 86 (now 82) may cover structural change. This interpretation was upheld by the Court of Justice.

The relevant market question involved both law and fact. The Commission found certain distinct, narrow, and one might say "gerrymandered" markets; e.g., light containers for canned meats, light containers for canned seafood, and metal closures for food containers other than crown corks. This definition brought the market shares of the combining firms to a figure as high as 90%. The Court's analysis on the point is contained in the following excerpt:

EUROPEMBALLAGE CORPORATION v. COMMISSION

(Continental Can)
Case 6/72, [1973] ECR 215.

[31] ... The decision ... excluded the possibility of competition arising from substitute products (glass and plastic containers) relying on reasons which do not stand up to examination. * * *

[33] ... Similarly, nothing is said about how these three markets differ from the general market for light metal containers, namely the market for metal containers for fruit and vegetables, condensed milk, olive oil, fruit juices and chemico-technical products. In order to be regarded as constituting a distinct market, the products in question must be individualized, not only by the mere fact that they are used for packing certain products,

but by particular characteristics of production which make them specifically suitable for this purpose. Consequently, a dominant position on the market for light metal containers for meat and fish cannot be decisive, as long as it has not been proved that competitors from other sectors of the market for light metal containers are not in a position to enter this market, by a simple adaptation, with sufficient strength to create a serious counterweight.

34 Besides, there are in the decision itself indications which make one doubt whether the three markets are to be considered separately from other markets for light metal containers, indications which rather lead one to conclude that they are parts of a larger market. In the first part of the statement of reasons, where, under letter J, it deals with the main competitors of SLW in Germany and of TDV in Benelux, the decision mentions a German undertaking which holds a higher share of production of light metal containers for fruit and vegetables than SLW, and another one which supplies 38 to 40% of the German demand for crown corks: this seems to confirm that the production of metal cans for meat and fish cannot be considered separately from the production of metal cans for other purposes and that, when considering the production of metal closures, crown corks must not be left out. Furthermore, the decision, when examining the possibilities of competition by substitutes, does not ... confine itself to the three relevant "markets", but deals with the market for light metal containers for other purposes as well; in this connection it states that these containers could be replaced by containers made of other material to a limited extent only. The fact that the Commission could not maintain this allegation in view of the facts put forward by the applicants in the course of the proceedings, proves in itself how necessary it is sufficiently to define the market concerned. . . .

35 . . . The argument put forward in ... the statement of reasons that the plants of certain manufacturers in the countries bordering on Germany were located too far away from most German consumers to enable the latter to decide to use them as a permanent source of supply, has not been substantiated. Moreover, this argument is difficult to reconcile with the allegation in No 25(a) that the break-even distances for the transport of empty containers are 150–300 kilometres for the relatively large containers, and 500–1000 kilometres for smaller ones. In addition, it is uncontested that transport costs are of no essential significance in the case of metal closures.

36 Besides, as far as potential competition from large consumers capable of manufacturing their own cans is concerned ... [i]t can be concluded ... that some undertakings which have begun to manufacture their own containers were able to overcome the technological difficulties, yet the decision does not contain any criteria for evaluating the power of competition of these undertakings. . . .

37 All this leads to the conclusion that the decision has not, as a matter of law, sufficiently shown the facts and the assessments on which it is based. It must therefore be annulled. * * *

Why is "metal cans for meat and fish" not a market? Why was it improper to draw the geographic market at the German border? Note how the Court applies the economic concept that good product substitutes, and firms that can quickly and efficiently sell the relevant product to the buyers, must be included in the market. They are a part of the forces of competition operating on the market.

Several years later in *Hugin-Liptons*, the Court faced a different market definition issue: May a single brand constitute a market? Hugin Kassaregister AB v. Commission, Case 22/78, [1979] ECR 1869.

Hugin was a significant but not dominant manufacturer of cash registers. It accounted for approximately 13% of cash registers sold in Great Britain. National Cash Register accounted for 40% of the market, and the second and third ranking firms held, respectively, 18% and 16%. Liptons was in the business of servicing, repairing and reconditioning cash registers. It bought spare parts from an importer of Hugin cash registers in Great Britain, while continuing its service and repair business. In the late 1960s it became necessary to convert all cash registers in the UK to the decimal system, leading to a boom market for new cash registers. In 1969 Hugin appointed Liptons to be its main distributor in Great Britain.

After Liptons had been Hugin's main distributor for a few years, Hugin offered Liptons a new distributorship agreement. Liptons regarded the profit margins as too low, and declined the offer. Thereafter, Hugin refused to supply Liptons with cash registers or spare parts at wholesale. Liptons tried to get the parts elsewhere, but was unable to do so because Hugin sold its spare parts only to its authorized distributors and it prohibited its distributors from selling the parts to others. Liptons complained to the Commission. The Commission determined that Hugin's refusal to supply was an abuse of a dominant position in Hugin spare parts.

In Hugin's suit for annulment, the Court upheld the Commission's finding that Hugin spare parts was a proper market. It reasoned that independent firms specialized in maintenance and repair of cash registers, reconditioning used cash registers, selling used machines, and renting machines. These firms needed spare parts and they needed Hugin spare parts for Hugin machines because non-Hugin spare parts were not interchangeable with them. Consequently, said the Court, "the market thus constituted by Hugin spare parts required by independent undertakings must be regarded as the relevant market...." Thus, Hugin had a dominant position. (The Court dismissed the case, however, because Hugin's conduct did not affect trade between Member States.)

In 1997 the Commission issued a notice on the definition of the relevant market. The Notice should be consulted. It is printed in the Selected Documents as Competition Doc. No. 3. Brief excerpts follow.

> The main purpose of market definition is to identify in a systematic way the competitive constraints that the undertakings involved face. The objective of defining a market in both its product and geographic dimension is to identify those actual competitors of the undertakings involved

that are capable of constraining their behaviour and of preventing them from behaving independently of an effective competitive pressure. It is from this perspective, that the market definition makes it possible, inter alia, to calculate market shares that would convey meaningful information regarding market power for the purposes of assessing dominance or for the purposes of applying Article 85.

* * *

Relevant product markets are defined as follows:

"A relevant product market comprises all those products and/or services which are regarded as interchangeable or substitutable by the consumer, by reason of the products' characteristics, their prices and their intended use."

Relevant geographic markets are defined as follows:

"The relevant geographic market comprises the area in which the undertakings concerned are involved in the supply and demand of products or services, in which the conditions of competition are sufficiently homogeneous and which can be distinguished from neighbouring areas because the conditions of competition are appreciably different in those areas".
* * *

Competitive constraints

Firms are subject to three main sources of competitive constraints: demand substitutability, supply substitutability and potential competition. From an economic point of view, for the definition of the relevant market, demand substitution constitutes the most immediate and effective disciplinary force on the suppliers of a given product, in particular in relation to their pricing decisions. A firm or a group of firms cannot have a significant impact on the prevailing conditions of sale, such as prices, if its customers are in a position to switch easily to available substitute products or to suppliers located elsewhere. Basically, the exercise of market definition consists in identifying the effective alternative sources of supply for the customers of the undertakings involved, both in terms of products/services and geographic location of suppliers. * * *

The assessment of demand substitution entails a determination of the range of products which are viewed as substitutes by the consumer. One way of making this determination can be viewed, as a thought experiment, postulating a hypothetical small, non-transitory change in relative prices and evaluating the likely reactions of customers to that increase. The exercise of market definition focuses on prices for operational and practical purposes, and more precisely on demand substitution arising from small, permanent changes in relative prices. This concept can provide clear indications as to the evidence that is relevant to define markets.

Conceptually, this approach implies that starting from the type of products that the undertakings involved sell and the area in which they sell them, additional products and areas will be included into or excluded from the market definition depending on whether competition from these other products and areas affect or restrain sufficiently the pricing of the parties' products in the short term.

The question to be answered is whether the parties' customers would switch to readily available substitutes or to suppliers located elsewhere in response to an hypothetical small (in the range 5%–10%), permanent relative price increase in the products and areas being considered. If substitution would be enough to make the price increase unprofitable because of the resulting loss of sales, additional substitutes and areas are included in the relevant market. This would be done until the set of products and geographic areas is such that small, permanent increases in relative prices would be profitable. * * *

Generally, and in particular for the analysis of merger cases, the price to take into account will be the prevailing market price. This might not be the case where the prevailing price has been determined in the absence of sufficient competition. In particular for investigation of abuses of dominant positions, the fact that the prevailing price might already have been substantially increased will be taken into account. * * *

Notes and Questions

1. Does the Notice codify the principles of *Continental Can* and *Hugin-Liptons*?

2. To define a market, one must always start with a hypothesis. We aim to define an area wherein, if there were only one firm, it could exploit its customers, raising price and lowering output, without much fear that other suppliers would simply fill the slack. We normally start with the smallest plausible market hypothesis. Thus, if the putative dominant firm is United Brands (see Section D.2. infra), we may start with bananas; we would not start with all fruit. Bananas are a distinctive fruit, and we do not know how many people readily substitute other fruit for bananas. If in all significant geographic areas people switch readily or if people would switch readily if the banana czar raised its prices, a banana producer would not have market power.

As we have seen, a large share of a well defined market is often used as a proxy for, or rebuttable presumption of, market power.

3. The question of single-brand aftermarkets arose also in the United States. Eastman Kodak Co. v. Image Technical Services, Inc., 504 U.S. 451, 112 S.Ct. 2072, 119 L.Ed.2d 265 (1992). Kodak was a producer of reproduction and imaging machinery. The machinery market was competitive and Kodak was not dominant therein. At the time of its entry into the machinery market, Kodak encouraged independent service organizations (ISOs) to establish themselves in business to service and repair the Kodak machines, and it supplied them with the necessary repair parts or advised them of designated manufacturers from whom they could buy the repair parts. After the business of servicing the Kodak machines became quite lucrative, Kodak cut off the ISOs from access to the repair parts and did the servicing business itself. When sued by the ISOs for monopolizing aftermarket service of Kodak machines, Kodak moved for summary judgment, arguing that there could not be a market for service or repair of *Kodak* machines, and that the market for original equipment of all brands—which was competitive—would keep constant pressure on Kodak to provide the best service to the Kodak machine owners.

The US Supreme Court, reversing the district court, ruled that a single brand aftermarket was possible, and its existence was an issue for trial. The ISOs had introduced evidence that Kodak's customers anticipated an open repair market in which competition would set the price of repair services. Further, when they bought the machines, Kodak's customers did not have sufficient information to assess their future costs of repair. Since, after the sale, they were locked in to Kodak equipment, the machine buyers were vulnerable to Kodak's exercise of market power to charge them a supracompetitive price for repair services. How similar is this reasoning to that in *Hugin-Liptons?* Why was the U.S. Supreme Court concerned only about Kodak's customers and not about the foreclosed ISOs?

4.   In the *Italian banana tax* case, a major question was whether untaxed imported bananas would push down the price of Italian table fruit. If so, the Italian tax on bananas was protectionist; it would have removed an important procompetitive force and thus protected Italian fruit growers from the competition of non-Italian fruit growers. *See* Commission v. Italy (Banana tax), page 470 supra. Is it possible for both of the following propositions to be true at the same time: 1) bananas imported into Italy without a tax would cause the price of Italian table fruit to be lower than it otherwise would have been, and 2) a banana monopolist in the EU would have power to sell bananas at a supracompetitive price in one or more Member States despite competition from other table fruit? If so, both markets—Italian table fruit in the tax case, and bananas in the competition case—may properly be identified as relevant product markets. That is, bananas could play a procompetitive role in keeping down the price (and keeping up the quality) of non-banana table fruit, even while Dole-brand bananas could play a more powerful role than apples in keeping down the price (and keeping up the quality) of Chiquita bananas.

5.   As we proceed to examine the offense of abuse we will consider many cases that have a relevant market component. We do not always concentrate on market definition. As you read the cases that follow, apply the principles of this section to the market definitions accepted by the Court, and ask yourself whether you agree with the Court's market definition or whether a different one would have been more plausible.

D.   ABUSIVE CONDUCT

1.   INTRODUCTION

What does it mean to "abuse" a dominant position?

Article 82 lists four particular courses of conduct that may be abusive. The list includes some conduct that is directly associated with the existence of market power and is often referred to as exploitative in that it represents the use of power over price to extract more than "fair" or "competitive" prices from customers. Imposing unfair prices and limiting production fall within this category. Other conduct on the list is coercive, such as requiring a contracting party to accept an obligation that has no relationship to the subject of the contract, or conduct that is otherwise unfair, such as discriminating among customers and thereby placing the disfavored customer at a competitive disadvantage.

In this section we deal with a variety of possible abuses of dominance, including excessive pricing, discriminatory pricing, refusals to deal, requirements and exclusive dealing contracts, tying, loyalty rebates, and price predation.

2. EXCESSIVE AND DISCRIMINATORY PRICES AND UNFAIR TERMS

BRITISH LEYLAND PLC v. COMMISSION

(British Leyland)
Case 226/84, [1986] ECR 3263.

[The United Kingdom gave British Leyland the exclusive right to determine whether imported British Leyland cars conformed to UK national standards, and to issue certificates of conformity. British Leyland arbitrarily refused to grant certain certificates to applicants and it set much higher fees for left-hand-drive than for right-hand-drive cars.]

27   As the Court held in its judgment in *General Motors*, an undertaking abuses its dominant position where it has an administrative monopoly and charges for its services fees which are disproportionate to the economic value of the service provided.

28   It appears from the documents before the Court and the information provided by the parties that, in the case of both right-hand-drive and left-hand-drive vehicles, in order to issue a certificate of conformity it is necessary to determine from the chassis number the date of manufacture of the vehicle. It is then possible to identify the number of the corresponding NTA certificate. It is, therefore, a simple administrative check which cannot entail significant costs. For left-hand-drive vehicles the certificate is in principle issued before conversion, if they are converted to right-hand-drive. The only difference in relation to the issue of a certificate for a right-hand-drive vehicle lies in the need to verify that the four alterations essential for a left-hand-drive vehicle have been made, namely the adjustment of headlights, full beam and dipped, the calibration of the speedometer in miles per hour, the adaptation of the rear fog lamp and the addition of a wing-mirror on the right front door. That verification does not require an inspection of the vehicle. It is effected on the basis of a certificate furnished by a garage and, on the basis of the cost incurred, cannot therefore justify the charging of different fees for the issue of certificates of conformity according to whether the vehicles are right-hand-drive or left-hand-drive. Initially the fee for left-hand-drive vehicles was six times greater than that for right-hand-drive vehicles.

29   Moreover, BL itself admitted at the hearing that the difference which existed at one time according to whether the certificate was requested by a dealer, who was charged UKL 150, or by a private individual, who was charged only UKL 100, was not based on the cost but on the consideration that the trader who was carrying out a transaction for gain could be required to pay a higher fee. The fact that the fee was first reduced to UKL 100 and then UKL 50, whilst for right-hand-drive vehicles it remained at UKL 25, also suggests that it was fixed solely with a view to making the re-importation of left-hand-drive vehicles less attractive.

30 In those circumstances, the Commission was entitled to conclude that the fee was fixed at a level which was clearly disproportionate to the economic value of the service provided and that that practice constituted an abuse by BL of the monopoly it held by virtue of the British rules.* * *

33 Finally, BL's argument that the amount of the fee had no detrimental effect on the volume of the re-importations is, as the Court has already stated above, irrelevant.

34 In conclusion, it must be held that the complaints made by the Commission in the contested decision are established.

British Leyland was a toll-taker, enabled by government license. A more ambiguous case of unfair pricing was pressed against United Brands some years earlier.

UNITED BRANDS CO. v. COMMISSION

(pricing practices)
Case 27/76, [1978] ECR 207.

[United Brands was the biggest banana producer in the world and in the Community. It was a vertically integrated company that grew bananas in South America, bought from other growers half of the bananas it sold, and accounted for some 40% of the sales of bananas in the Community, which was more than twice that of its nearest rival. It owned and promoted the Chiquita brand, the best known and the most heavily advertised brand in the world. Its system of distribution involved sales to ripeners/distributors, who would buy the green bananas, ripen them in special sheds and in specified gases, and resell them. The Commission alleged a series of abuses, including the cut-off of a Danish ripener-distributor, excessive pricing and discriminatory pricing.

United Brands sold all bananas to its distributors free on rail Rotterdam or Bremerhaven. There was a 100% difference between the prices charged to the distributor for Ireland, where Chiquita was an unknown brand and demand was low, and the prices charged to the distributor for Denmark, where the brand was well known and demand was strong. There were also disparities between the price charged to the Danish distributors and to the distributors for the other Member States. United Brands' prices were approximately 7% higher than the prices of its nearest rivals, and they were 30% to 40% higher than unbranded bananas. The Commission found discriminatory and excessive pricing violations and ordered United Brands to reduce its prices to distributors other than the distributors for Ireland by at least 15%.]

1. *Discriminatory prices*

204 All the bananas marketed by UBC under the brand name "Chiquita" on the relevant market have the same geographic origin, belong to the same variety (Cavendish Valery) and are of almost the same quality.

205 They are unloaded in two ports, Rotterdam and Bremerhaven, where unloading costs only differ by a few cents in the dollar per box of 20 kilogrammes, and are resold, except to Scipio and in Ireland, subject to the same conditions of sale and terms of payment after they have been

loaded on the buyers' wagons or lorries, the price of a box amounting on average to between 3 and 4 dollars and going up to 5 dollars in 1974.

206 The costs of carriage from the unloading ports to the ripening installations and the amount of any duty payable under the Common Customs Tariff are borne by the purchaser except in Ireland.

207 This being so all those customers going to Rotterdam and Bremerhaven to obtain their supplies might be expected to find that UBC offers them all the same selling price for "Chiquita" bananas.

208 The Commission blames the applicant for charging each week for the sale of its branded bananas—without objective justification—a selling price which differs appreciably according to the Member State where its customers are established. * * *

212 The price customers in Belgium are asked to pay is on average 80% higher than that paid by customers in Ireland.

213 The greatest difference in price is 138% between the delivered Rotterdam price charged by UBC to its customers in Ireland and the f.o.r. Bremerhaven price charged by UBC to its customers in Denmark, that is to say the price paid by Danish customers is 2.38 times the price paid by Irish customers. * * *

225 In fact the bananas sold by UBC are all freighted in the same ships, are unloaded at the same cost in Rotterdam or Bremerhaven and the price differences relate to substantially similar quantities of bananas of the same variety, which have been brought to the same degree of ripening, are of similar quality and sold under the same "Chiquita" brand name under the same conditions of sale and payment for loading on to the purchaser's own means of transport and the latter have to pay customs duties, taxes and transport costs from these ports. * * *

227 Although the responsibility for establishing the single banana market does not lie with the applicant, it can only endeavour to take "what the market can bear" provided that it complies with the rules for the regulation and coordination of the market laid down by the Treaty.

228 Once it can be grasped that differences in transport costs, taxation, customs duties, the wages of the labour force, the conditions of marketing, the differences in the parity of currencies, the density of competition may eventually culminate in different retail selling price levels according to the Member States, then it follows those differences are factors which UBC only has to take into account to a limited extent since it sells a product which is always the same and at the same place to ripener/distributors who—alone—bear the risks of the consumers' market.

229 The interplay of supply and demand should, owing to its nature, only be applied to each stage where it is really manifest.

230 The mechanisms of the market are adversely affected if the price is calculated by leaving out one stage of the market and taking into account the law of supply and demand as between the vendor and the ultimate consumer and not as between the vendor (UBC) and the purchaser (the ripener/distributors).

231   Thus, by reason of its dominant position UBC, fed with information by its local representatives, was in fact able to impose its selling price on the intermediate purchaser. This price and also the "weekly quota allocated" is only fixed and notified to the customer four days before the vessel carrying the bananas berths.

232   These discriminatory prices, which varied according to the circumstances of the Member States, were just so many obstacles to the free movement of goods and their effect was intensified by the clause forbidding the resale of bananas while still green and by reducing the deliveries of the quantities ordered.

233   A rigid partitioning of national markets was thus created at price levels, which were artificially different, placing certain distributor/ripeners at a competitive disadvantage, since compared with what it should have been competition had thereby been distorted.

234   Consequently the policy of differing prices enabling UBC to apply dissimilar conditions to equivalent transactions with other trading parties, thereby placing them at a competitive disadvantage, was an abuse of a dominant position.

2. *Unfair prices* * * *

252   The questions ... to be determined are whether the difference between the costs actually incurred and the price actually charged is excessive, and, if the answer to this question is in the affirmative, whether a price has been imposed which is either unfair in itself or when compared to competing products.

253   Other ways may be devised—and economic theorists have not failed to think up several—of selecting the rules for determining whether the price of a product is unfair. * * *

258   The Commission bases its view that prices are excessive on an analysis of the differences—in its view excessive—between the prices charged in the different Member States and on the policy of discriminatory prices which has been considered above.

259   The foundation of its argument has been the applicant's letter of 10 December 1974 which acknowledged that the margin allowed by the sale of bananas to Irish ripeners was much smaller than in some other Member States and it concluded from this that the amount by which the actual prices f.o.r. Bremerhaven and Rotterdam exceed the delivered Rotterdam prices for bananas to be sold to Irish customers c.i.f. Dublin must represent a profit of the same order of magnitude.

260   Having found that the prices charged to ripeners of the other Member States were considerably higher, sometimes by as much as 100%, than the prices charged to customers in Ireland it concluded that UBC was making a very substantial profit.

261   Nevertheless the Commission has not taken into account in its reasoning several of UBC's letters in which were enclosed a confidential document retracting what is said in its letter of 10 December 1974 and pointing out that the prices charged in Ireland had produced a loss.

262 The applicant also states that the prices charged on the relevant market did not allow it to make any profits during the last five years, except in 1975. * * *

264 However unreliable the particulars supplied by UBC may be (and in particular the document mentioned previously which works out the "losses" on the Irish market in 1974 without any supporting evidence), the fact remains that it is for the Commission to prove that the applicant charged unfair prices.

265 UBC's retraction, which the Commission has not effectively refuted, establishes beyond doubt that the basis for the calculation adopted by the latter to prove that UBC's prices are excessive is open to criticism and on this particular point there is doubt which must benefit the applicant, especially as for nearly 20 years banana prices, in real terms, have not risen on the relevant market. * * *

267 In these circumstances it appears that the Commission has not adduced adequate legal proof of the facts and evaluations which formed the foundation of its finding that UBC had infringed Article 86 of the Treaty by directly and indirectly imposing unfair selling prices for bananas.

Notes and Questions

1. Why does Article 82 condemn excessive pricing? Who is hurt? How can the Commission correct the harm? In answering this question, consider not only what constitutes prima facie proof of excessive pricing, but what constitutes an acceptable justification for high prices. What relief may the Commission order?

2. What is the relationship between excessive and discriminatory pricing in *United Brands?* Is one offense more central than the other to Community objectives?

3. Is the Court correct that the discriminatory prices "were just so many obstacles to the free movement of goods"? (para. 232) Is price discrimination a barrier to free movement? What were the real barriers to free movement? Why did the Court blame lack of mobility of the bananas on the price discrimination rather than on the green banana clause?

4. Price discrimination can be a way to exploit (to get more money from those who are willing to pay more), and it can be a way to compete (to lower price and make more sales). United Brands was apparently charging high prices where consumers had a strong preference for bananas, and low prices to break into markets where Chiquita was not well known and other fruits were in strong demand. In areas in which demand for Chiquita bananas was strong, was the real question who would get the extra profits, United Brands or its distributor? Would prohibition of price discrimination push prices towards the lower end of United Brands' price range throughout the Community?

5. United States antitrust law does not prohibit excessive pricing. It prohibits price discrimination only if the discriminatory pricing is likely to produce monopoly or hurt disfavored buyers in their competition with favored ones. The US antitrust agencies seldom enforce the US price discrimination law—Robinson–Patman Act—because they fear that most applications of this law are anticompetitive. (Why?) As a result, most Robinson–Patman actions are private actions. Competitors of the price discriminator have been greatly restricted in their ability to sue, however (imagine Standard Fruit suing United Brands for price discrimi-

nation among UB's dealers), because they must prove antitrust injury and antitrust damages, and this requires proof that consumers are harmed. This is hard to prove. See, e.g., Brooke Group Ltd. v. Brown & Williamson Tobacco Corp., 509 U.S. 209, 113 S.Ct. 2578, 125 L.Ed.2d 168 (1993), page 871 infra.

As for excessive pricing, the Court of Appeals for the Second Circuit said in Berkey Photo, Inc. v. Eastman Kodak Co.:

> Excessive prices, maintained through exercise of a monopolist's control of the market, constituted one of the primary evils that the Sherman Act was intended to correct....

> But unless the monopoly has bolstered its power by wrongful actions, it will not be required to pay damages merely because its prices may later be found excessive. Setting a high price may be a use of monopoly power, but it is not in itself anticompetitive. Indeed, although a monopolist may be expect-ed to charge a somewhat higher price than would prevail in a competitive market, there is probably no better way to guarantee that its dominance will be challenged than by greedily extracting the highest price it can.... Judicial oversight of pricing policies would place the courts in a role akin to that of a public regulatory commission.... We would be wise to decline that function unless Congress clearly bestows it upon us.

Berkey Photo, Inc. v. Eastman Kodak Co., 603 F.2d 263, 294 (2d Cir.1979), cert. denied, 444 U.S. 1093, 100 S.Ct. 1061, 62 L.Ed.2d 783 (1980).

Consider the differences between United States and European Community law on excessive pricing. Does one or the other do a better job of achieving the benefits of competitive markets? integrated markets? fairness?

Virtually all of the post-communist, newly free-enterprise economies adopt the EC model, not the US model. Why do you suppose that these countries find a law against unfair prices important? Is there an argument that such a law in a post-communist country is especially important? especially unwise?

6. Despite the well-recognized United States antitrust principle reflected in *Berkey/Kodak,* legislators and enforcement agencies do react when private firms have enormous power and exploit the public. In the wake of the 1990 oil shock, Pennsylvania passed excessive pricing laws; the National Association of [State] Attorneys General developed a plan to support anti-price gouging legislation, and the Department of Justice opened an investigation to determine whether the sudden sharp increases in the price of gasoline were collusive. See 59 BNA Antitrust & Trade Reg. Rep. 267, 301, 340 (Aug. 30, 1990). In the late 1980s when the price of infant milk formula rose high above costs, the Federal Trade Commission began an investigation into causes and cures. K. Day, A New Activism on Antitrust Policy: The FTC Initiates Aggressive Inquiry Into Alleged Price Fixing by Infant Formula Giants, Washington Post, Jan. 13, 1991, at H1. Exorbitant prices of AIDS drugs have led to public uproar, jawboning, and "voluntary" price reductions. See Sheryl Gay Stolberg, Africa's AIDS War, NY Times, March 10, 2001, p. 1. Does the political response to price-gouging belie the sanguine finding of the court in *Berkey/Kodak* that use of the power to exploit is the best way to guarantee its demise?

3. REFUSAL TO DEAL

ISTITUTO CHEMIOTERAPICO ITALIANO SPA v. COMMISSION

(Commercial Solvents)
Cases 6, 7/73, [1974] ECR 223.

[Commercial Solvents Corporation was a manufacturer of raw materials—nitropropane and aminobutanol—which were used to manufacture ethambutol, an antituberculosis drug. Aminobutanol was also used as an emulsifier for paint. Commercial Solvents Corporation acquired 51 percent of the shares of an Italian company, Istituto, which bought the raw materials from its parent, Commercial Solvents, and sold them to another Italian company, Zoja, which used them to manufacture ethambutol-based specialties.

Istituto sought to acquire Zoja, but the negotiations aborted. Istituto then increased the price at which it sold aminobutanol to Zoja. Zoja, however, discovered a cheaper source for aminobutanol—firms that bought the raw material from Commercial Solvents for use in paint. Zoja persuaded Istituto to cancel a large part of Zoja's order. Soon thereafter, Zoja's supply of cheaper aminobutanol dried up, largely because Commercial Solvents forbade its paint-making customers to resell aminobutanol for pharmaceutical use. Commercial Solvents then announced that it was withdrawing from the market for sales of the raw material, and it integrated vertically, using the raw material for its own production. When Zoja tried to reorder aminobutanol from Commercial Solvents, Commercial Solvents refused to accept the order.

The Commission held that Commercial Solvents had a dominant position in the market for the raw material and ordered Commercial Solvents to resume supplying Zoja and to pay a fine for the refusal to sell.]

23   The applicants state that they ought not to be held responsible for stopping supplies of aminobutanol to Zoja for this was due to the fact that in the spring of 1970 Zoja itself informed Istituto that it was cancelling the purchase of large quantities of aminobutanol which had been provided for in a contract then in force between Istituto and Zoja. When at the end of 1970 Zoja again contacted Istituto to obtain this product, the latter was obliged to reply, after consulting CSC, that in the meantime CSC had changed its commercial policy and that the product was no longer available. The change of policy by CSC was, they claim, inspired by a legitimate consideration of the advantage that would accrue to it of expanding its production to include the manufacture of finished products and not limiting itself to that of raw material or intermediate products. In pursuance of this policy it decided to improve its product and no longer to supply aminobutanol save in respect of commitments already entered into by its distributors. * * *

25   However, an undertaking being in a dominant position as regards the production of raw material and therefore able to control the supply to manufacturers of derivatives, cannot, just because it decides to start manufacturing these derivatives (in competition with its former customers) act in such a way as to eliminate their competition which in the case in question would amount to eliminating one of the principal manufactur-

ers of ethambutol in the Common Market. Since such conduct is contrary to the objectives expressed in Article 3(f) of the Treaty and set out in greater detail in Articles 85 and 86, it follows that an undertaking which has a dominant position in the market in raw materials and which, with the object of reserving such raw material for manufacturing its own derivatives, refuses to supply a customer, which is itself a manufacturer of these derivatives, and therefore risks eliminating all competition on the part of this customer, is abusing its dominant position within the meaning of Article 86. In this context it does not matter that the undertaking ceased to supply in the spring of 1970 because of the cancellation of the purchases by Zoja, because it appears from the applicants' own statement that, when the supplies provided for in the contract had been completed, the sale of aminobutanol would have stopped in any case. * * *

28   ... [T]he applicants do not seriously dispute the statement in the Decision in question to the effect that "in view of the production capacity of the CSC plant it can be confirmed that CSC can satisfy Zoja's needs, since Zoja represents a very small percentage (approximately 5–6%) of CSC's global production of nitropropane." It must be concluded that the Commission was justified in considering that such statements could not be taken into account.

UNITED BRANDS CO. v. COMMISSION
(refusal to deal)
Case 27/76, [1978] ECR 207.

[Olesen, a ripener/distributor of bananas in Denmark, was the largest importer in Denmark of United Brand's "Chiquita" bananas. Olesen wanted United Brands to give it preferential treatment over the other United Brands' ripeners in Denmark but United Brands refused to do so. While continuing to order bananas from United Brands, Olesen became the exclusive distributor for Standard Fruit, the producer of the Dole banana. (Standard Fruit was later bought by Castle and Cooke.) United Brands claimed that Olesen had begun to "push" Dole bananas and to neglect Chiquita bananas, and it refused to continue to supply Chiquita bananas to Olesen. Olesen complained to the Commission. (See *United Brands' pricing practices*, p. 843 supra, for additional facts.)]

The Commission's Argument

168   The Commission regards this refusal to continue supplies to Olesen, which cannot be justified objectively, as an arbitrary interference in the management of the Olesen business which has caused it to suffer damage and was designed to dissuade UBC's ripeners from selling bananas bearing competing brand names or at least from advertising them and these are facts which amount to an infringement of Article 86 of the Treaty.

United Brand's Argument

169   The applicant claims that the marketing policy it pursues is more liberal than that of its competitors.

170   Its ripeners are free to sell products bearing competing brand names, to advertise these products, to reduce their orders, to cancel them and to terminate their relations when they think fit.

[171] The Olesen incident must be seen in this setting.

[172] In 1967, since the latter had become the largest importer of "Chiquita" bananas in Denmark, it put pressure on UBC to give it preferential treatment compared with the seven other Danish ripeners duly appointed by the applicant.

[173] When UBC refused to do so, Olesen became in 1969 the exclusive importer/distributor of the Standard Fruit Company.

[174] In 1973 Standard Fruit announced at a press conference that the Dole banana was going to oust the "Chiquita" banana throughout the world.

[175] Olesen then sold less and less Chiquita bananas and deliberately pushed the sale of Dole bananas. It did not take the same amount of trouble when ripening Chiquita bananas as it did when ripening bananas bearing other brand names.

[176] The breach, which was not unexpected and unforeseeable, arose in these circumstances, punctuated by discussions spread over a long period.

[177] This breach was therefore fully justified by the fact that if a firm is directly attacked by its main competitor who has succeeded in making one of that firm's most important long standing customers his exclusive distributor for the whole of the country, that firm in its own interest and that of competition has no option but to fight back or else disappear from this national market.

[178] The applicant goes on to say that this refusal to sell to Olesen, which was justified, was not an abuse, because it did not affect the actual competition on the Danish market which recorded a fall of 40% in two weeks at the end of 1974 in the retail price of Chiquita bananas as a result of the competition between competitors which was generated by these circumstances. * * *

The Court's Analysis

[182] In view of these conflicting arguments it is advisable to assert positively from the outset that an undertaking in a dominant position for the purpose of marketing a product—which cashes in on the reputation of a brand name known to and valued by the consumers—cannot stop supplying a long standing customer who abides by regular commercial practice, if the orders placed by that customer are in no way out of the ordinary.

[183] Such conduct is inconsistent with the objectives laid down in Article 3(f) of the Treaty, which are set out in detail in Article 86, especially in paragraphs (b) and (c), since the refusal to sell would limit markets to the prejudice of consumers and would amount to discrimination which might in the end eliminate a trading party from the relevant market.

[184] It is therefore necessary to ascertain whether the discontinuance of supplies by UBC in October 1973 was justified.

[185] The reason given is in the applicant's letter of 11 October 1973 in which it upbraided Olesen in no uncertain manner for having participated in an advertising campaign for one of its competitors.

186   Later on UBC added to this reason a number of complaints, for example, that Olesen was the exclusive representative of its main competitor on the Danish market.

187   This was not a new situation since it goes back to 1969 and was not in any case inconsistent with fair trade practices.

188   Finally UBC has not put forward any relevant argument to justify the refusal of supplies.

189   Although it is true, as the applicant points out, that the fact that an undertaking is in a dominant position cannot disentitle it from protecting its own commercial interests if they are attacked, and that such an undertaking must be conceded the right to take such reasonable steps as it deems appropriate to protect its said interests, such behaviour cannot be countenanced if its actual purpose is to strengthen this dominant position and abuse it.

190   Even if the possibility of a counter-attack is acceptable that attack must still be proportionate to the threat taking into account the economic strength of the undertakings confronting each other.

191   The sanction consisting of a refusal to supply by an undertaking in a dominant position was in excess of what might, if such a situation were to arise, reasonably be contemplated as a sanction for conduct similar to that for which UBC blamed Olesen.

192   In fact UBC could not be unaware of that fact that by acting in this way it would discourage its other ripener/distributors from supporting the advertising of other brand names and that the deterrent effect of the sanction imposed upon one of them would make its position of strength on the relevant market that much more effective.

193   Such a course of conduct amounts therefore to a serious interference with the independence of small and medium sized firms in their commercial relations with the undertaking in a dominant position and this independence implies the right to give preference to competitors' goods.

194   In this case the adoption of such a course of conduct is designed to have a serious adverse effect on competition on the relevant banana market by only allowing firms dependant upon the dominant undertaking to stay in business.

195   The applicant's argument that in its view the 40% fall in the price of bananas on the Danish market shows that competition has not been affected by the refusal to supply Olesen cannot be upheld.

196   In fact this fall in prices was only due to the very lively competition—called at the time the ''banana war''—in which the two transnational companies UBC and Castle and Cooke engaged.

Notes and Questions

1.   What main principle of law governs these two cases? Cite the key paragraph in each judgment. Is this principle based on: efficiency and consumer interests? fairness and rights of competitors?

2. The dominant firm has the opportunity to provide an objective justification for its conduct. How would you evaluate the justification offered by United Brands? Are you any more sympathetic than the Court?

3. Is there a possible set of facts that would have justified United Brands' conduct? Commercial Solvents' conduct?

4. In *Oscar Bronner*, the Court of Justice rejected the claim of Bronner, owner of a small daily newspaper, that the distribution system of Mediaprint, the near-monopolist publisher and owner of the only nation-wide newspaper distribution system, was an essential facility to which he had a right of access. The Court said that Mediaprint's refusal to distribute Bronner's newspaper would not amount to an abuse of dominance unless it was likely to eliminate all competition in the daily newspaper market, access was indispensable to Bronner's business, and the refusal could not be objectively justified. Bronner had not made this case. Among other things, there were no technical or legal obstacles preventing Bronner, alone or in combination with other small papers, from setting up an alternative distribution system. Oscar Bronner GmbH & Co. KG v. Mediaprint Zeitungs und Zeitschriftenverlag GmbH & Co., Case C–7/97, [1998] ECR I–7791. Can *Oscar Bronner* be distinguished from *Commercial Solvents* and *United Brands*?

5. We have seen that Community law applies a presumption of illegality to dominant firms' refusals to deal with their traditional customers. US law, on the other hand, applies a presumption of freedom of firms to choose to deal or not to deal, regardless of a prior course of dealing. *See* United States v. Colgate & Co., 250 U.S. 300, 39 S.Ct. 465, 63 L.Ed. 992 (1919); Olympia Equipment Leasing Co. v. Western Union Telegraph Co., 797 F.2d 370 (7th Cir.1986), *cert. denied*, 480 U.S. 934, 107 S.Ct. 1574, 94 L.Ed.2d 765 (1987); NYNEX Corp. v. Discon, Inc., 525 U.S. 128, 119 S.Ct. 493, 142 L.Ed.2d 510 (1998). There are two limiting principles to the US rule. A firm that controls an essential facility is required to give access to competitors if it can do so without impairing its own performance. *See* United States v. American Telephone and Telegraph, 524 F.Supp. 1336, 1352 (D.D.C. 1981). Also, if a firm that holds a monopoly or near monopoly refuses to deal as part of a strategy to impose costs on a competitor and the strategy will increase or preserve the firm's power and harm consumers, the refusal is illegal. See Eastman Kodak Co. v. Image Technical Services, Inc., 504 U.S. 451, 112 S.Ct. 2072, 119 L.Ed.2d 265 (1992); Aspen Skiing Co. v. Aspen Highlands Skiing Corp., 472 U.S. 585, 105 S.Ct. 2847, 86 L.Ed.2d 467 (1985); Lorain Journal Co. v. United States, 342 U.S. 143, 72 S.Ct. 181, 96 L.Ed. 162 (1951); United States v. Microsoft Corp., 253 F.3d 34 (D.C.Cir.), cert. denied, ___ U.S. ___, 122 S.Ct. 350, 151 L.Ed.2d 264 (2001). The burden of proof to show market harm remains on the plaintiff.

How would the *Commercial Solvents* and *United Brands* cases be resolved under US law? What, if any, additional facts would you need to know? In *United Brands*, how would the following alternative assumptions affect your analysis under US law: (1) Because of the great demand for Chiquita bananas and the large firm size needed to enjoy economies of scale, all distributor/ripeners needed to carry some Chiquita brand bananas to be efficient. (2) Contrariwise, small distributor/ripeners were able to capture all economies of scale. Why were these questions not important in the *United Brands* case?

IS INTELLECTUAL PROPERTY A SPECIAL CASE?

A firm may own intellectual property rights, which typically grant the exclusive right to practice, use or license a patent, trademark, copyright or design. If the owner of intellectual property has a dominant position and declines to license it, is the duty to deal relaxed on grounds that the intellectual property owner has state-granted exclusive rights? Or is the duty to deal stronger on grounds that the intellectual property right reflects economic power and exclusive privileges and the state-granted rights may be used to obstruct free movement of goods and to partition the common market?

Intellectual property rights are a subject of Article 30 (ex 36) of the Treaty, which provides that Articles 28 and 29, guaranteeing free movement of goods, shall not preclude "restrictions on imports, exports or goods in transit justified on grounds of . . . the protection of industrial and commercial property" as long as such restrictions are not "a means of arbitrary discrimination or a disguised restriction on trade between Member States." (See Chapters 13 and 19 supra.) Does this language imply a hospitable stance towards intellectual property rights? Does it imply that intellectual property rights normally trump free movement rights? As you know from Chapters 13 and 19, it does not.

The Court of Justice held, in Deutsche Grammophon Gesellschaft GmbH v. Metro–SB–Grossmärkte GmbH, Case 78/70, [1971] ECR 487, para. 11:

> Article 36 only admits derogations from [free movement principles] to the extent to which they are justified for the purpose of safeguarding rights which constitute the specific subject-matter of such property.

What does "the specific subject matter of such property" mean? Remember that in *Consten and Grundig,* page 793 supra, with the blessing of Grundig, Consten had tried to use its exclusive rights to the trademark GINT (Grundig International) to keep imported GINT products out of France, because it, Consten, had been appointed the exclusive distributor in France. The Court held that Consten and Grundig's agreement to restrain parallel imports could not be justified as a "mere" exercise of trademark rights.

In 1988 the Court of Justice considered questions posed to it by national courts regarding exclusive design rights in automobile parts of Volvo and Renault. In the *Volvo* judgment the Court said:

> [T]he rights of the proprietor of a protected design to prevent third parties from manufacturing and selling or importing, without its consent, products incorporating the design constitutes the very subject-matter of his exclusive right. It follows . . . that a refusal to grant such a license cannot in itself constitute an abuse of a dominant position.

> [T]he exercise of an exclusive right by the proprietor of a registered design in respect of car body panels may be prohibited by Article 86 if it involves, on the part of an undertaking holding a dominant position, certain abusive conduct such as the arbitrary refusal to supply spare parts to independent repairers, the fixing of prices for spare parts at an unfair level or a decision no longer to produce spare parts for a particular model even though many cars of that model are still in circulation, provided that such conduct is liable to affect trade between Member States.

Volvo AB v. Erik Veng (UK) Ltd., Case 238/87 [1988] ECR 6211, paras. 8–9.

When is such a refusal to supply "arbitrary," and when, on the other hand, does it go to the heart of the industrial property owner's right of exclusivity? Give examples. How would the *Volvo* rule apply to Kodak's withholding its patented repair parts from the independent service operators whom it had been supplying? (See page 840 supra, Note 3.)

The principle of deference to IP holders' essential rights was soon to be tested in a case in which the copyright holders' right not to license conflicted directly with the public's right to competition. (But doesn't it always?) The question arose whether each of the three significant TV broadcasters in Ireland were required to license their TV schedules to a third party who proposed to publish a consolidated TV guide.

RADIO TELEFIS EIREANN v. COMMISSION

(Magill)

Cases C–241/91P and C–242/91P, [1995] ECR I–743.

[Radio Telefis Eireann ("RTE"), BBC, and Independent Television Publications ("ITP") operated TV stations. Each published weekly listings of its programs in Ireland and Northern Ireland, gave newspapers its schedule free on a daily basis, and claimed copyright protection over its program listings. At that, time, no composite TV guide existed. Magill conceived the idea to publish a weekly magazine, the Magill TV Guide, listing all available TV programs in Ireland and Northern Ireland. It sought licenses from RTE, BBC and ITP, but the licenses were denied. Magill nonetheless proceeded with the publication. In a suit by the three copyright owners, the Irish High Court enjoined Magill from using the copyrighted listings of RTE, BBC and ITP. Magill complained to the Commission. The Commission found that each of the three broadcasters had and abused a dominant position. Two of the stations challenged the decision, claiming that they had done nothing more than exercise their rights under the Irish copyright law. The Irish copyright law protected a TV station's schedule of its programs. The Irish law itself was valid under Articles 28/30, ex 30/36, for it conferred intellectual property rights and was not an arbitrary discrimination or disguised restriction on trade between Member States. [Reread Articles 28, 30 and 295.] The TV stations claimed that they had done nothing more than exercise their copyright right to refuse to license. Moreover, each station argued that it was not dominant; it supplied less than a third of the market. The Court of First Instance upheld the Commission, and the stations appealed.]

(a) Existence of a dominant position

46   So far as dominant position is concerned, it is to be remembered at the outset that mere ownership of an intellectual property right cannot confer such a position.

47   However, the basic information as to the channel, day, time and title of programmes is the necessary result of programming by television stations, which are thus the only source of such information for an undertaking, like Magill, which wishes to publish it together with commentaries or pictures. By force of circumstance, RTE and ITP, as the agent of ITV, enjoy, along with the BBC, a *de facto* monopoly over the information used to compile listings for the television programmes received in most households in Ireland and 30% to 40% of households in Northern Ireland. The appellants are thus in a position to prevent effective competition on the market in weekly television magazines. [They therefore] occupied a dominant position. . . .

(b) Existence of abuse

48   With regard to the issue of abuse, the arguments of the appellants and IPO wrongly presuppose that where the conduct of an undertaking in a dominant position consists of the exercise of a right classified by national law as "copyright", such conduct can never be reviewed in relation to Article 86 of the Treaty.

49   Admittedly, in the absence of Community standardization or harmonization of laws, determination of the conditions and procedures for granting protection of an intellectual property right is a matter for national rules. Further, the exclusive right of reproduction forms part of the author's rights, so that refusal to grant a licence, even if it is the act of an undertaking holding a dominant position, cannot in itself constitute abuse of a dominant position.

50   However, it is also clear from that judgment (paragraph 9) that the exercise of an exclusive right by the proprietor may, in exceptional circumstances, involve abusive conduct.

51   In the present case, the conduct objected to is the appellants' reliance on copyright conferred by national legislation so as to prevent Magill—or any other undertaking having the same intention—from publishing on a weekly basis information (channel, day, time and title of programmes) together with commentaries and pictures obtained independently of the appellants.

52   Among the circumstances taken into account by the Court of First Instance in concluding that such conduct was abusive was, first, the fact that there was, according to the findings of the Court of First Instance, no actual or potential substitute for a weekly television guide offering information on the programmes for the week ahead. On this point, the Court of First Instance confirmed the Commission's finding that the complete lists of programmes for a 24-hour period—and for a 48-hour period at weekends and before public holidays—published in certain daily and Sunday newspapers, and the television sections of certain magazines covering, in addition, "highlights" of the week's programmes, were only to a limited extent substitutable for advance information to viewers on all the week's programmes. Only weekly television guides containing comprehensive listings for the week ahead would enable users to decide in advance which programmes they wished to follow and arrange their leisure activities for the week accordingly. The Court of First Instance also established that there was a specific, constant and regular potential demand on the part of consumers. . . .

53   Thus the appellants—who were, by force of circumstance, the only source of the basic information on programme scheduling which is the indispensable raw material for compiling a weekly television guide—gave viewers wishing to obtain information on the choice of programmes for the week ahead no choice but to buy the weekly guides for each station and draw from each of them the information they needed to make comparisons.

54   The appellants' refusal to provide basic information by relying on national copyright provisions thus prevented the appearance of a new product, a comprehensive weekly guide to television programmes, which the appellants did not offer and for which there was a potential consumer demand.

Such refusal constitutes an abuse under heading (b) of the second paragraph of Article 86 of the Treaty.

[55] Second, there was no justification for such refusal either in the activity of television broadcasting or in that of publishing television magazines. . . .

[56] Third, and finally, as the Court of First Instance also held, the appellants, by their conduct, reserved to themselves the secondary market of weekly television guides by excluding all competition on that market since they denied access to the basic information which is the raw material indispensable for the compilation of such a guide.

[57] In the light of all those circumstances, the Court of First Instance did not err in law in holding that the appellants' conduct was an abuse of a dominant position within the meaning of Article 86 of the Treaty. * * *

Notes and Questions

1. How did the Court find dominance? Was each of the three broadcasters dominant?

2. What is the holding of *Magill*? When does a dominant firm's refusal to license intellectual property constitute an abuse? Does *Magill* erode the rule in *Volvo*? What is the significance of the fact that the TV stations "prevented the appearance of a new product"? If the stations had formed a joint venture to produce a TV guide, could they have lawfully refused to grant a license to Magill?

3. Examine the Court's reasoning. Intellectual property embodies the right to refuse to grant a license. The right of exclusivity is the essence of intellectual property rights, even if a holder of the right is dominant. *Magill*, para. 49.

How and when does the right of exclusivity cease to become an essential ingredient of the intellectual property right? Does it lose this character whenever competition and consumer interests would be better served by the grant of a license? If so, doesn't Article 82 eclipse Article 30? How does the Court prevent this eclipse? Is the limiting rule arbitrary, or principled?

4. There is a lurking, unexplored question in *Magill*: Wasn't the Irish copyright law excessive in protecting the mere listing of a TV schedule? Is copyright protection of the schedule even arguably necessary or important to preserve incentives to invent and to be creative? Few other countries protect a mere schedule. For the United States, *see* Feist Publications, Inc. v. Rural Telephone Service Co., Inc., 499 U.S. 340, 111 S.Ct. 1282, 113 L.Ed.2d 358 (1991), which holds that alphabetical listings of names and numbers in telephone book white pages are not protectable by copyright because they are merely lists of non-copyrightable facts. Could the Court have solved the *Magill* problem by declaring that Ireland stepped out of bounds by trying to give copyright protection to TV listings? Could it have solved the problem by declaring that, on the particular facts, the Article 82 interests outweighed the Article 30 interests? What problems are raised by each of these approaches? Alternatively, if the Court felt constrained to defer to the Irish law (see Article 295, ex 222), what would be so bad about annulling the Commission decision and upholding the rights of the applicants? Wouldn't the market soon work to provide a TV guide to TV fans? Even if not, would you be more satisfied with the principle of law?

5. *Magill* has been narrowly construed. See *Oscar Bronner*, described in Question 4, page 852 supra.

6. IMS Health Inc. is a market research company that provides services to the pharmaceutical industry. It devised a "brick structure" in which it divides a country into geographic areas that are used to measure and report sales of individual pharmaceutical products. In Germany its efforts culminated in the development of the 1860 brick structure—a format for categorizing and reporting data that is the central feature of its German regional and wholesaler data-information services. The format is protected by German copyright law.

National Data Corporation entered the German market to provide marketing data to the pharmaceutical industry, in competition with IMS. It asked IMS for a license for the 1860 brick structure format, but IMS refused. It thereupon began selling marketing data to the pharmaceutical industry based on copies of the 1860 brick structure, thereby infringing the German copyright law.

Did IMS (a dominant firm) violate Article 82 by refusing to license the brick structure? Does it matter whether the 1860 brick structure had become the industry standard data format?

Based on *Magill*, paras. 50–56, should the Commission grant an interim order? Would the following order be appropriate:

> IMS Health is hereby required to grant a licence without delay to all undertakings currently present on the market for German regional sales data services for the pharmaceutical industry, on request and on a non-discriminatory basis, for the use of the 1860 brick structure, in order to permit the use of and sales by such undertakings of regional sales data formatted according to this structure.

What are the implications of such an order for intellectual property rights? for competition? for subsidiarity? See NDC Health/IMS Health: Interim measures, Case COMP D3/38.044 Commission decision of July 3, 2001, suspended pending proceedings for interim relief, IMS Health Inc. v. Commission, Case T–184/01 R, [2001] ECR 11–2349, and, further suspending pending final judgment, order of CFI of Oct. 26, 2001.

7. US cases have held that an intellectual property owner has an absolute right to merely refuse to license its intellectual property. See Independent Serv. Organizations Antitrust Litigation (CSU v. Xerox), 203 F.3d 1322 (Fed. Cir. 2000), cert. denied, 531 U.S. 1143, 121 S.Ct. 1077, 148 L.Ed.2d 954 (2001). How would the US courts decide *Magill,* assuming the copyright protection were valid? How would they decide *IMS?*

4. EXCLUSIVE DEALING, TYING AND EXCLUSIONARY REBATES

Abusive conduct may be exploitative or exclusionary. Often the two effects are intertwined. If Commercial Solvents refuses to supply a scarce and needed input to its competitor, Zoja, the refusal is exclusionary as to Zoja, and, by eliminating the competition of the only competitor, it is likely to be price-raising to the end-use customers.

Price discrimination may have both exploitative and exclusionary effects. United Brands surcharged banana distributors who were willing to pay more than other banana distributors (because they could command more from their customers), and charged competitively low, promotional prices to distributors in nations whose people had to be convinced to buy bananas.

Moreover, a firm may use the practice of tying (e.g. "You must buy nails from me if you want to buy my nail gun") in order to identify and surcharge those who put the tying product to heavier use and therefore are able and willing to pay more. By putting a premium on the tied nails, the seller can charge more to heavy users and less to light users. *See* Hilti v. Commission, Case C–53/92P, [1994] ECR I–667.

Was United Brands' low price in Ireland exclusionary with respect to its competitor Standard Fruit? Did it deprive Standard Fruit of the right to compete on the merits and threaten to exclude it from banana sales in Ireland? Did the nail gun maker's tie-in exclude other suppliers of nails from the nail market? Did the conduct, in either case, harm competition in a way that would be harmful to consumers? Do you need more facts? What facts?

Consider how rebates are a form of price discrimination and how rebates that are offered for fidelity to a particular supplier can induce the customer to be "loyal"; i.e. to buy its requirements or most of them from the particular seller. Consider, as you read the following cases: When does a dominant supplier cross the line from price competition to abuse of dominance? And when does an enforcement agency cross the line from protecting competition to harming it?

NOTE ON THE *SUGAR* CASE

In one of the *Sugar* cases (see page 812 supra), Sudzuker–Verkauf (SZV) was charged with abusing its dominant position in southern Germany by granting loyalty rebates to customers who bought their annual requirements exclusively from members of SZV.

Sugar buyers in southern Germany had to buy at least part of their supplies from SZV because the buyers' storage facilities were inadequate, they needed regular supplies, and SZV was the only supplier who could assure regular deliveries. Producers located outside of the territory offered sugar at a much lower price, however, even after adding the high freight rates.

SZV offered rebates in contracts with big buyers. The rebates were calculated to make it more expensive for the customers to buy foreign sugar to satisfy their residual needs than to buy their residual requirements from SZV.

The Commission challenged the rebates as an abuse of dominance. SZV argued that the rebate was a "normal price reduction" and was procompetitive.

The Commission found that the loyalty rebates were price discrimination constituting an abuse of a dominant position. The Court of Justice agreed. This was not a quantity rebate linked to volume, the Court noted, but a rebate linked to loyalty "to prevent customers [from] obtaining their supplies from competing producers." para. 518. The Court said that SZV " 'applied dissimilar conditions to equivalent transactions with other trading parties' within the meaning of Article 86(c) of the Treaty." para. 523. It noted that large industrial buyers from SZV competed with other buyers from it, thereby placing customers that did not qualify for the rebate at a competitive disadvantage with those that did qualify. Further:

[526]   ... [T]he system complained of was likely to limit markets to the prejudice of consumers within the meaning of Article 86(b), because it gave other producers and especially those having their places of business in other Member States no chance or restricted their opportunities of competing with sugar sold by SZV.

[527]   ... The loyalty rebate in question which may further consolidate SZV's dominant position is incompatible with this provision.

Suiker Unie UA v. Commission (Sugar), Cases 40–48, 50, 54–56, 111, 113–114/73, [1975] ECR 1663.

Notes and Questions

1. Was the Court concerned about unfairness to non-qualifying sugar buyers, unfairness to the foreign competitors of SZV, or harm to market integration from partitioning the market?

2. Is it true that the potential competitors could not sell their sugar to the big buyers in southern Germany? Why? What would the competitors have to do to make an offer attractive? Was it all a matter of price? If so, why weren't the rebates just price competition and why wouldn't the market-partitioning argument fail? Or is it invidious for a dominant firm to give loyalty rebates that make it nearly impossible for even an efficient competitor to compete on the merits? Does it/should it matter whether the buyers are aggrieved?

3. Most of the very lengthy *Sugar* case is about a series of cartels. Recalling Chapter 21, do you think that the rebate program was a device to facilitate a cartel?

HOFFMANN–LA ROCHE & CO. AG v. COMMISSION

(Vitamins)

Case 85/76, [1979] ECR 461.

[Hoffmann–La Roche had a dominant position in each of several vitamins. These included vitamin A, of which it held 47%, and vitamin B_6 of which it held more than 80%. Roche had contracted with 22 large purchasers, including Merck and Unilever, for the sale of vitamins to them.

Some purchasers agreed to buy several kinds of vitamins exclusively from Roche. Some contracts were requirements contracts, entered into at the request of purchasers who wanted assurance that their requirements would be filled.

In other cases, buyers agreed to buy most of their needs from Roche, and Roche agreed to give the buyer "fidelity rebates." These discounts became effective as to all past purchases when the buyer passed certain thresholds representing portions of the requirements of the buyer. The rebates applied cumulatively to the purchase of more than one kind of vitamin.

Many of the fidelity rebate contracts contained "English clauses." Under these clauses, if a customer received a better offer from a competitor and Roche refused to lower its price to meet the better offer, the customer was free to obtain supplies from the competitor without losing the benefit of the rebate. To meet the conditions of the escape clause, the better terms had to be offered by another competitor operating in Europe and on the same scale as Roche, and the offer had to be comparable.

Roche also entered into several contracts with large purchasers tailored to the parties' needs. For example, it had a contract with Merck for the sale of vitamin B_6. In the Merck contract, Roche recited that it planned to double its production capacity and would like to cover part of Merck's requirements. Merck agreed to buy from Roche its requirements above its own manufacturing capacity. Roche agreed to give Merck a 20% discount, Merck agreed not to resell the vitamins purchased at this discount, and Roche agreed to buy its requirements of phosphoric ester from Merck under the same conditions.

The Court of Justice held that the exclusive supply and requirements contracts were an abuse of a dominant position, even when entered into at the request of the purchaser. As for the Merck contract, the Court concluded that the purpose was to secure a stable market for Roche's increased production and to protect Roche from "the risks of competition," and that it, too, offended Article 86.

The fidelity rebates were also singled out for condemnation. The rebates were (as in the *Sugar* case) price discrimination based on loyalty, not quantity discounts based on lower costs. Once a purchaser began to buy from Roche, the Court said, the customer had a "powerful incentive" not to buy elsewhere.]

The Court

89 An undertaking which is in a dominant position on a market and ties purchasers—even if it does so at their request—by an obligation or promise on their part to obtain all or most of their requirements exclusively from the said undertaking abuses its dominant position within the meaning of Article 86 of the Treaty, whether the obligation in question is stipulated without further qualification or whether it is undertaken in consideration of the grant of a rebate.

The same applies if the said undertaking, without tying the purchasers by a formal obligation, applies, either under the terms of agreements concluded with these purchasers or unilaterally, a system of fidelity rebates, that is to say discounts conditional on the customer's obtaining all or most of its requirements—whether the quantity of its purchases be large or small—from the undertaking in a dominant position.

90 Obligations of this kind to obtain supplies exclusively from a particular undertaking, whether or not they are in consideration of rebates or of the granting of fidelity rebates intended to give the purchaser an incentive to obtain his supplies exclusively from the undertaking in a dominant position, are incompatible with the objective of undistorted competition within the Common Market, because—unless there are exceptional circumstances which may make an agreement between undertakings in the context of Article 85 and in particular of paragraph (3) of that article, permissible—they are not based on an economic transaction which justifies this burden or benefit but are designed to deprive the purchaser of or restrict his possible choices of sources of supply and to deny other producers access to the market.

The fidelity rebate, unlike quantity rebates exclusively linked with the volume of purchases from the producer concerned, is designed through the grant of a financial advantage to prevent customers from obtaining their supplies from competing producers.

Furthermore the effect of fidelity rebates is to apply dissimilar conditions to equivalent transactions with other trading parties in that two purchasers pay a different price for the same quantity of the same product depending on whether they obtain their supplies exclusively from the undertaking in a dominant position or have several sources of supply.

Finally these practices by an undertaking in a dominant position and especially on an expanding market tend to consolidate this position by means of a form of competition which is not based on the transactions effected and is therefore distorted.

91   For the purpose of rejecting the finding that there has been an abuse of a dominant position the interpretation suggested by the applicant that an abuse implies that the use of the economic power bestowed by a dominant position is the means whereby the abuse has been brought about cannot be accepted.

The concept of abuse is an objective concept relating to the behaviour of an undertaking in a dominant position which is such as to influence the structure of a market where, as a result of the very presence of the undertaking in question, the degree of competition is weakened and which, through recourse to methods different from those which condition normal competition in products or services on the basis of the transactions of commercial operators, has the effect of hindering the maintenance of the degree of competition still existing in the market or the growth of that competition. * * *

Roche had argued that the English clause—where it existed—nullified any negative effect of the fidelity rebates, since either competition would cause Roche to meet the more attractive offer of a competitor or the purchaser could buy from the lower-priced competitor without losing the rebate. The Court disagreed. Although recognizing that the English clause could alleviate the foreclosure effect, the Court affirmatively condemned the clause. Under the English clause, Roche's customers would inform it of more favorable offers by competitors, thus helping Roche to identify competitors who offered to sell at a lower price. This "places at the disposal of [Roche] information about market conditions and also about the alternatives open to, and the actions of, its competitors which is of great value for the carrying out of market strategy." para. 107. The machinery of the English clause gave Roche the ability to decide "whether, by adjusting its prices or not, it will permit competition." Thus, the English clause "is of such a kind as to aggravate the exploitation of the dominant position in an abusive way." Id.

A few years later, the Court summarized the concept of abuse in another exclusive dealing case, *Michelin:*

70   Article 86 covers practices which are likely to affect the structure of a market where, as a direct result of the presence of the undertaking in question, competition has already been weakened and which, through recourse to methods different from those governing normal competition in products or services based on traders' performance, have the effect of hindering the maintenance or development of the level of competition still existing on the market.

NV Nederlandsche Banden–Industrie Michelin v. Commission, Case 322/81, [1983] ECR 3461.

Stressing its concern that fidelity rebates distort competition, the Commission summarized as follows proceedings against British Airways:

> The Commission set out its policy on commissions paid by airlines to travel agents in its decision in the *Virgin/BA* case [decision of 14 July 1999]. Virgin's complaint against BA was the first of a series of complaints received by the Commission alleging abuses of a dominant position by airlines operating loyalty rebate schemes which effectively tie travel agents to a dominant airline. The Commission found that the commissions offered by BA to UK travel agents were equivalent to a 'loyalty discount' i.e. a discount based not on cost savings but on loyalty. Schemes of this type have been consistently condemned as an abuse of a dominant position in other industries in the past. It is well-established Community law that a dominant supplier cannot give incentives to its customers and distributors to be loyal to it, thereby foreclosing market access by the dominant firm's competitors. As a dominant firm, BA should provide supplementary commissions to travel agents only where these reflect extra services provided by the agent or efficiencies realised by BA. The Commission is taking all measures necessary to ensure that the principles in this decision are applied to other EC airlines in equivalent situations. The Commission imposed a fine of EUR 6.8 million on British Airways for a serious abuse of a dominant position over a period of seven years.

XXIXth Report on Competition Policy (1999), para. 60.

Notes and Questions

1. Consider the rebate schemes in *Sugar, Roche* and *British Airways*. Were there any acceptable justifications that might have been offered by SZV? Roche? BA? Were the rebates procompetitive or anticompetitive? Could competitors have beaten the dominant firm at its game by offering a lower, competitive price on all of its sales (rather than lower prices triggered only by incremental sales)?

2. What would you expect to be the effect on business conduct of the *Sugar* judgment? of the *Roche* judgment?

3. Compare the discriminatory low pricing in United Brands, page 843 supra. Did the price discrimination in *United Brands* differ in purpose or effect from that in *Sugar* and *Roche*? How? Which type of price discrimination do you regard as more harmful to competition? to other values of the EU?

4. US law makes the distinction between primary line discrimination and secondary line discrimination. Primary line price discrimination is discrimination that has its direct and immediate impact on the discriminating firm's competitors; thus, the claim is that competition is lessened on the "primary line" (e.g., competition among SZV and its sugar producing competitors) rather than in the market in which the favored and disfavored purchasers compete ("the secondary line"; e.g., competition among SZV's customers). The US Robinson–Patman Act prohibits price discrimination that lessens competition at either level and, that in a secondary line case, harms a disfavored buyer in its competition. 15 U.S.C. §§ 13, 13a, 13b, 21a.

Section 2 of the Sherman Act prohibits "monopolization." Primary line discrimination may be a means to monopolize. That is, the low-price prong of the discrimination may be predatorily low: intended and likely to eliminate competitors and then produce a higher monopoly price. *See* Brooke Group Ltd. v. Brown & Williamson Tobacco Corp., 509 U.S. 209, 113 S.Ct. 2578, 125 L.Ed.2d 168 (1993). See price predation, at Section D.5. *infra.*

US law does not normally condemn rebates or discounts as monopolistic. A US district court said in the *Japanese Electronics* case:

> [I]t is plainly in the interest of a purchaser to obtain a rebate so as to get the lowest possible price. Although plaintiffs decry the activities of Sears in securing rebates from Sanyo and Toshiba, ... it appears to be procompetitive and in Sears' interest for Sears, or any buyer, to get the best price it can.[1]

British Airways' conduct was not condemned under US law. Virgin Atlantic Airways Ltd. v. British Airways PLC, 257 F.3d 256 (2d Cir.2001). Would SZV's pricing practices have offended United States law? Would Roche's?

5. Under United States law, requirements and exclusive dealing contracts are usually lawful. They may be motivated by the purchaser's needs for a sufficient and reliable source of supply, enabling the purchaser to be more efficient and competitive, and by the supplier's needs for an assured outlet or for loyalty in distribution. Both could be illegal if they foreclose so much of the supply or outlet that it is not possible for efficient firms to survive or to wage efficient competition on the merits and (some courts would add) the harm is not outweighed by procompetitive and efficiency benefits. See United States v. Microsoft Corp., 253 F.3d 34 (D.C.Cir.), cert. denied, ___ U.S. ___, 122 S.Ct. 350, 151 L.Ed.2d 264 (2001); Omega Environmental, Inc. v. Gilbarco, Inc., 127 F.3d 1157 (9th Cir.1997); Barry Wright Corp. v. ITT Grinnell Corp., 724 F.2d 227 (1st Cir.1983).

How would Roche's exclusive and requirements contracts fare under United States law?

6. Which set of principles—European or American—does a better job in promoting efficiency? consumer well-being? fairness? equal opportunity to compete on the merits?

TETRA PAK INTERNATIONAL SA v. COMMISSION

(tying)
Case T–83/91, [1994] ECR II–755, aff'd,
Case C–333/94P, [1996] ECR I–5951.

[Tetra Pak was a Swiss-based group that made packaging machines and packaging for liquid and semi-liquid food, especially for milk. It operated in the aseptic sector, especially for UHT milk, and also in the non-aseptic sector. It accounted for 78% of both sectors combined, which was seven times more than its leading competitor. The structure of the market for aseptic packaging systems was quasi-monopolistic, with Tetra Pak holding 90% to 95% of the Community market.

In the non-aseptic sector the market was oligopolistic. Tetra–Pak held 50% to 55%, and the Norwegian group Elopak held 27%, followed by PKL with 11%. Non-aseptic packaging, principally of fresh pasteurized milk, requires less sterility and less sophisticated equipment than aseptic packaging. Tetra Pak's principal non-aseptic carton was the Tetra Rex, which was in direct competition with Elopak's Pure–Pak.

---

1. Zenith Radio Corp. v. Matsushita Elec. Indus. Co., Ltd., 513 F.Supp. 1100, 1251 (E.D.Pa.1981), rev'd on other grounds, 723 F.2d 238 (3d Cir.1983), rev'd, 475 U.S. 574, 106 S.Ct. 1348, 89 L.Ed.2d 538 (1986).

The Commission charged Tetra Pak with tying and predatory pricing. It asserted four separate markets: aseptic cartons, aseptic filling machines, non-aseptic cartons, and non-aseptic filling machines, and it introduced evidence showing Tetra Pak's dominance in the aseptic sector. The Commission found that Tetra Pak had a dominant position on the aseptic markets and abused its dominance by its commercial practices on the non-aseptic markets; namely, requiring buyers of its non-aseptic machines to use Tetra Pak cartons for those machines, and predatorily pricing the non-aseptic cartons in Italy and the non-aseptic machines in the UK. The Court of First Instance upheld the decision ruling:]

126   The applicant submits that the marketing of complete packaging systems was objectively justified by the concern to protect public health and thus its reputation through exclusive control of the entire packaging process. Cartons are much more sophisticated containers than traditional containers such as bottles, and this entails a significant risk of technical errors liable to cause serious problems in vulnerable sectors of the population. For that reason the clauses at issue were justified, even for the non-aseptic machines acquired by Tetra Pak from Nimco and Cherry Purrel, which had to be modified to Tetra Pak's specifications. * * *

135   ... [T]he court considers that the Commission correctly found in the decision that the combined effect of the other 24 contractual clauses at issue ... was an overall strategy aiming to make the customer totally dependent on Tetra Pak for the entire life of the machine once purchased or leased, thereby excluding in particular any possibility of competition at the level both of cartons and of associated products. Their effect on competition must therefore be considered in conjunction with [the exclusivity] clauses ..., referred to above, which were intended to make the market in cartons wholly dependent on that in machines and which reinforced and completed the elimination of that market. Moreover, those other clauses could be considered as abusive in themselves since their object was in particular, depending on the clause, to make the sale of machines and cartons subject to accepting additional services of a different type, such as maintenance and repair and the provision of spare parts; to grant discounts, in particular on the costs of assistance, maintenance and updating the machines, or on part of the rent, depending on the number of cartons from Tetra Pak; and, finally, to give Tetra Pak control over its customers' activities and to retain for it the exclusive ownership of all technical improvements or modifications made to the cartons by their users.

136   Since it has been established that the clauses complained of all contributed to the attainment of the same objective, it must be ascertained whether, as claimed by the applicant, the resulting system of tied sales was objectively justified in the light of commercial usage and the very 'nature' of the products in question within the meaning of art. 86(d) of the treaty.

137   That argument by the applicant cannot be accepted. For the reasons already given by the court ..., the tied sale of filling machines and cartons cannot be considered to be in accordance with commercial usage. Moreover and in any event, even if such a usage were shown to exist, it

would not be sufficient to justify recourse to a system of tied sales by an undertaking in a dominant position. Even a usage which is acceptable in a normal situation, on a competitive market, cannot be accepted in the case of a market where competition is already restricted. The Court of Justice has in particular ruled that, where an undertaking in a dominant position directly or indirectly ties its customers by an exclusive supply obligation, that constitutes an abuse since it deprives the customer of the ability to choose his sources of supply and denies other producers access to the market. . . .

[138] As for the fundamental justification pleaded by Tetra Pak, concerning the integrated and indivisible nature of its packaging systems as a matter of economics, the court has already also found, in the course of reviewing the definition of the relevant markets . . ., that it does not stand up to examination. The technical considerations and those relating to product liability, protection of public health and protection of its reputation put forward by Tetra Pak must be assessed in the light of the principles enshrined in the judgment in *Hilti v EC Commission*, . . . in which the Court of First Instance held that it was: " . . . clearly not the task of an undertaking in a dominant position to take steps on its own initiative to eliminate products which, rightly or wrongly, it regards as dangerous or at least as inferior in quality to its own products."

[139] In this case, reliability of the packaging equipment for dairies and other users and compliance with standards of hygiene in relation to the final consumer could be ensured by disclosing to users of Tetra Pak machines all the technical specifications concerning the cartons to be used on those systems, without the applicant's intellectual property rights being thereby prejudiced. Moreover, the measures imposed on Tetra Pak inform any customers purchasing or leasing a machine of the specifications which packing cartons must meet in order to be used on its machines. Furthermore and in any event, even if using another brand of cartons on Tetra Pak machines involved a risk it was for the applicant to use the possibilities afforded it by the relevant national legislation in the various member states.

[140] In those circumstances, it is clear that the tied-sale clauses and the other clauses referred to in the decision went beyond their ostensible purpose and were intended to strengthen Tetra Pak's dominant position by reinforcing its customers' economic dependence on it. Those clauses were therefore wholly unreasonable in the context of protecting public health, and also went beyond the recognised right of an undertaking in a dominant position to protect its commercial interests. . . . Whether considered in isolation or together, they were unfair.

———————

Tetra Pak argued on appeal that Article 86 was inapplicable because the tie-in neither strengthened its dominant position in the tying market nor threatened to create a new dominant position in the market of the tied product. The Court of Justice rejected Tetra Pak's argument as a matter of law. It referred extensively to the judgment of the Court of First Instance, and said:

27 It is true that application of art. 86 presupposes a link between the dominant position and the alleged abusive conduct, which is normally not present where conduct on a market distinct from the dominated market produces effects on that distinct market. In the case of distinct, but associated, markets, as in the present case, application of art. 86 to conduct found on the associated, non-dominated, market and having effects on that associated market can only be justified by special circumstances.

28 In that regard, the Court of First Instance first considered ... that it was relevant that Tetra Pak held 78 per cent of the overall market in packaging in both aseptic and non-aseptic cartons, that is to say seven times more than its closest competitor.... [I]t stressed Tetra Pak's leading position in the non-aseptic sector. Then ... it found that Tetra Pak's position on the aseptic markets, of which it held nearly a 90 per cent share, was quasi-monopolistic. It noted that that position also made Tetra Pak a favoured supplier of non-aseptic systems. Finally, ... it concluded that, in the circumstances of the case, application of art. 86 was justified by the situation on the different markets and the close associative links between them.

29 The relevance of the associative links which the Court of First Instance thus took into account cannot be denied. The fact that the various materials involved are used for packaging the same basic liquid products shows that Tetra Pak's customers in one sector are also potential customers in the other. That possibility is borne out by statistics showing that in 1987 approximately 35 per cent of Tetra Pak's customers bought both aseptic and non-aseptic systems. It is also relevant to note that Tetra Pak and its most important competitor, PKL, were present on all four markets. Given its almost complete domination of the aseptic markets, Tetra Pak could also count on a favoured status on the non-aseptic markets. Thanks to its position on the former markets, it could concentrate its efforts on the latter by acting independently of the other economic operators.

30 The circumstances thus described, taken together and not separately, justified the Court of First Instance, without any need to show that the undertaking was dominant on the non-aseptic markets, in finding that Tetra Pak enjoyed freedom of conduct compared with the other economic operators on those markets.

31 Accordingly, the Court of First Instance was right to accept the application of art. 86 of the treaty in this case, given that the quasi-monopoly enjoyed by Tetra Pak on the aseptic markets and its leading position on the distinct, though closely associated, non-aseptic markets placed it in a situation comparable to that of holding a dominant position on the markets in question as a whole.

Notes and Questions

1. What was the relationship of Tetra Pak's dominance in the aseptic market to its ability to tie non-aseptic cartons to non-aseptic machines? What was the relationship between Tetra Pak's dominance in the aseptic market and the effect of its conduct on competition in the non-aseptic market? (Does para. 29 help

you answer these questions?) Do you agree that Tetra Pak's tie-in was capable of constituting an abuse of a dominant position?

2. How important was the fact that Tetra Pak had a leading position in the non-aseptic market, and that the non-aseptic market was oligopolistic? If the non-aseptic market had been atomistic and competitive, would the outcome have been different?

3. In the United States, use of market power in one market to get competitive advantages in another market is called leveraging. Tying agreements, a form of leveraging, are illegal under Section 1 of the Sherman Act if used by a firm with power in one market to force the buyer to accept a separate product, and a minimal dollar amount of commerce is affected. See, e.g., Eastman Kodak Co. v. Image Technical Services, 504 U.S. 451, 112 S.Ct. 2072, 119 L.Ed.2d 265 (1992). Justifications such as good will, safety and reputation may possibly be admissible, but they are seldom proved.

This qualified per se rule against tie-ins evolved at a time when US antitrust law embraced open market values as well as consumer welfare goals. The case law at that time declared that competitors have a right not be fenced out of markets. *E.g.,* International Salt Co. v. United States, 332 U.S. 392, 68 S.Ct. 12, 92 L.Ed. 20 (1947). Contemporary US jurists often try to justify the tie-in law in terms of consumer welfare, or back away from the qualified per se rule and require the plaintiff to prove that the tie increased defendant's market power. See concurring opinion of Justice O'Connor in Jefferson Parish Hospital District No. 2 v. Hyde, 466 U.S. 2, 32, 104 S.Ct. 1551, 80 L.Ed.2d 2 (1984). See United States v. Microsoft Corp., 147 F.3d 935 (D.C.Cir.1998) and 253 F.3d 34 (D.C.Cir.), cert. denied, ___ U.S. ___, 122 S.Ct. 350, 151 L.Ed.2d 264 (2001) (bundling of additional functionalities with platform software must be analyzed under the rule of reason).

Apart from tying, most US courts reject the proposition that use of leverage to get market share at the expense of competitors, without proof of harm to consumers, constitutes a Sherman Act violation. Judge Thomas Penfield Jackson rejected a leveraging claim at the outset of the *Microsoft* case. Dismissing the claim that Microsoft used its power in the operating system market to get market share in the browser market at the expense of Netscape, the court said:

> The States bring a separate claim of monopoly "leveraging" under § 2. Under this theory ..., a seller who has a monopoly in one product violates § 2 when it uses a tie-in to obtain a competitive advantage in a second market, *"even if there has not been an attempt to monopolize the second market."* See *id.*

> The continuing viability of the monopoly leveraging theory is in serious doubt....

> The D.C. Circuit has never spoken definitively on the leveraging theory, but has noted "substantial academic criticism cast upon the leveraging concept." ... Assuming that Microsoft has an operating system monopoly and browsers are being sold competitively, Microsoft's incentive is to extract all available monopoly profits from the OS/browser *combination.* Accordingly, it already prices its operating system at the monopoly profit-maximizing price, considering what consumers are willing to pay for the entire package. Even if Microsoft were to obtain a monopoly in the market for browsers, the profit-maximizing price for the combination wouldn't change; Microsoft could not make additional monopoly profits even by monopolizing the browser market as well....

The Court will grant Microsoft's motion for summary judgment on the States' leveraging claim. While the Supreme Court has not considered a leveraging claim *per se*, it has clearly stated that a firm violates § 2 only when it actually monopolizes or dangerously threatens to do so. . . .

United States v. Microsoft Corp., 1998–2 Trade Cas. ¶ 72,261 (D.D.C.1998).

What is the European position on this point?

4. Consider as a whole the European exclusionary practice cases—e.g., *United Brands (Olesen), Commercial Solvents, Hoffmann–La Roche* and *Tetra Pak*. In condemning exclusionary practices, what values does the European law protect? Is it: economic opportunity? fairness? market integration? consumer welfare? efficiency? Is there support for all of these values in Treaty Articles 2 and 3? When does the pursuit of fairness and economic opportunity clash with the pursuit of consumer welfare, efficiency and competitiveness? How should the tension be resolved, in view of the EC Treaty, the TEU, and the Treaty of Amsterdam?

5. What problems are created if the European Commission prohibits Microsoft from bundling functionalities such as instant messaging in Windows XP as a use of leverage that deprives competitors of fair market access and thus harms competition in instant messaging, while US authorities or courts regard the combination as efficient and pro-consumer?

5. PRICE PREDATION

AKZO CHEMIE BV v. COMMISSION
Case C–62/86, [1991] ECR I–3359.

[AKZO, a large Dutch multinational firm, and ECS (Engineering and Chemical Supplies Ltd.), a small UK firm, both manufactured organic peroxides. AKZO had a market share of 50%. Benzoyl peroxide is the most important organic peroxide. Benzoyl peroxide is a bleaching agent for flour and is also used in plastics as an initiator of the polymer production process. ECS was engaged in the flour segment of the market. For a decade, ECS was content with its sales for the flour business, but in 1979 it developed excess capacity and started to sell to plastics makers, soliciting and selling to some of AKZO's customers. An AKZO official told ECS's manager Sullivan "that AKZO would take aggressive commercial action on the milling products unless [Sullivan] refrained from supplying his products to the plastics industry." The AKZO official told Sullivan AKZO would pry away ECS's flour customers at prices far below prevailing prices. When ECS ignored AKZO's threats, AKZO implemented selective, low prices, with the intent to damage the business of ECS.

From the end of 1980 for about four years, AKZO targeted ECS's customers in the flour segment, selling to them at prices that were below its average total cost and that were much lower than the previously prevailing rates. Meanwhile, AKZO charged its own loyal customers (whose business was not at risk) about sixty percent more than the targeted customers of ECS. As part of its strategy, AKZO sold these customers flour milling complements they needed at prices below AKZO's average variable cost, and it sold them some vitamin mixes (which it bought specifically for resale to these customers) below its own purchase price. ECS's business declined by about seventy percent in four years, and its profit margins fell.

The Commission initiated proceedings and obtained an interim order enjoining AKZO's conduct. In its decision on the merits, the Commission noted AKZO's "clear predatory intent" as well as its scheme of price discrimination. However, perhaps because of the interim order, the predatory campaign had little affect on ECS. ECS's share in the flour additive sector went from 35% to 30%, and AKZO's share went from 52% to 55%.

Placing much weight on AKZO's intent to eliminate its competitor, the Commission found an infringement and levied a fine of 10 million ECUs on AKZO.]

A. *Dominant position*

[60] With regard to market shares the Court has held that very large shares are in themselves, and save in exceptional circumstances, evidence of the existence of a dominant position (judgment in Case 85/6 *Hoffmann-La Roche v Commission* [1979] ECR 461, paragraph 41). That is the situation where there is a market share of 50% such as that found to exist in this case.

[61] Moreover, the Commission rightly pointed out that other factors confirmed AKZO's predominance in the market. In addition to the fact that AKZO regards itself as the world leader in the peroxides market, it should be observed that, as AKZO itself admits, it has the most highly developed marketing organization, both commercially and technically, and wider knowledge than that of their competitors with regard to safety and toxicology. . . .

[62] The pleas put forward by AKZO in order to deny that it had a dominant position within the organic peroxides market as a whole must therefore be rejected.

B. *Abuse of a dominant position*

[63] According to the contested decision (point 75) AKZO had abusively exploited its dominant position by endeavouring to eliminate ECS from the organic peroxides market mainly by massive and prolonged price-cutting in the flour additives sector. * * *

[69] It should be observed that . . . the concept of abuse is an objective concept relating to the behaviour of an undertaking in a dominant position which is such as to influence the structure of a market where, as a result of the very presence of the undertaking in question, the degree of competition is weakened and through recourse to methods which, different from those which condition normal competition in products or services on the basis of the transactions of commercial operators, has the effect of hindering the maintenance of the degree of competition still existing in the market or the growth of that competition.

[70] It follows that Article 86 prohibits a dominant undertaking from eliminating a competitor and thereby strengthening its position by using methods other than those which come within the scope of competition on the basis of quality. From that point of view, however, not all competition by means of price can be regarded as legitimate.

[71] Prices below average variable costs (that is to say, those which vary depending on the quantities produced) by means of which a dominant undertaking seeks to eliminate a competitor must be regarded as abusive. A dominant undertaking has no interest in applying such prices except that of eliminating competitors so as to enable it subsequently to raise its prices by taking advantage of its monopolistic position, since each sale generates a loss, namely the total amount of the fixed costs (that is to say, those which remain constant regardless of the quantities produced) and, at least, part of the variable costs relating to the unit produced.

[72] Moreover, prices below average total costs, that is to say, fixed costs plus variable costs, but above average variable costs, must be regarded as abusive if they are determined as part of a plan for eliminating a competitor. Such prices can drive from the market undertakings which are perhaps as efficient as the dominant undertaking but which, because of their smaller financial resources, are incapable of withstanding the competition waged against them.

[73] These are the criteria that must be applied to the situation in the present case. * * *

[114] The prices charged by AKZO to its own customers were above its average total costs, whereas those offered to customers of ECS were below its average total costs.

[115] AKZO is thus able, at least partly, to set off losses resulting from the sales to customers of ECS against profits made on the sales to the 'large independents' which were among its customers. This behaviour shows that AKZO's intention was not to pursue a general policy of favourable prices, but to adopt a strategy that could damage ECS. The complaint is therefore substantiated. * * *

[140] By maintaining prices below its average total costs over a prolonged period, without any objective justification, AKZO was thus able to damage ECS by dissuading it from making inroads into its customers. * * *

[The Court concluded that AKZO, at various times, offered customers of ECS prices lower than AKZO's total or average variable costs, and did so as part of its threat to obtain ECS's withdrawal from the plastics sector.

[162] ... [I]t must be observed that the infringement committed by AKZO is particularly serious, since the behaviour complained of was intended to prevent a competitor from extending its activity into a market in which AKZO held a dominant position.

[The Court reduced the fine to 7.5 million ECUs on grounds that the controlling law had not previously been specified and the infraction did not have a significant effect on market shares.]

Notes and Questions

1. Was AKZO's below-cost pricing a strategy to: 1) drive out the competitors and raise price? 2) compete? 3) divide markets? What is the significance of these different hypotheses?

2. In the United States, a pioneer in low-priced, no-frills, non-branded cigarettes sued a major tobacco company for embarking on a predatory pricing campaign to destroy or contain the new product. This case, *Brooke Group,* was

later to be cited to the Court of Justice by a low-pricing firm that was accused of predatory pricing by the European Commission and that tried to defend its conduct as procompetitive. (See *Tetra Pak*, below.)

BROOKE GROUP LTD. v. BROWN & WILLIAMSON TOBACCO CORP.

509 U.S. 209, 113 S.Ct. 2578, 125 L.Ed.2d 168 (1993).

JUSTICE KENNEDY: [Cigarette manufacturing is a concentrated industry dominated by only six firms, including the two parties here. In 1980, petitioner (hereinafter Liggett) pioneered the economy segment of the market by developing a line of generic cigarettes offered at a list price roughly 30% lower than that of branded cigarettes. By 1984, generics had captured 4% of the market at the expense of branded cigarettes, and respondent Brown & Williamson entered the economy segment, beating Liggett's net price. Liggett responded in kind, precipitating a price war, which ended, according to Liggett, with Brown & Williamson selling its generics at a loss. Liggett filed this suit, alleging, inter alia, that volume rebates by Brown & Williamson to wholesalers amounted to price discrimination that had a reasonable possibility of injuring competition in violation of § 2(a) of the Clayton Act, as amended by the Robinson–Patman Act. Liggett claimed that the rebates were integral to a predatory pricing scheme, in which Brown & Williamson set below-cost prices to pressure Liggett to raise list prices on its generics, thus restraining the economy segment's growth and preserving Brown & Williamson's supracompetitive profits on branded cigarettes. After a jury returned a verdict in favor of Liggett, the District Court held that Brown & Williamson was entitled to judgment as a matter of law. The Court of Appeals affirmed.] * * *

Liggett contends that Brown & Williamson's discriminatory volume rebates to wholesalers threatened substantial competitive injury by furthering a predatory pricing scheme designed to purge competition from the economy segment of the cigarette market. This type of injury, ... [w]hether the claim alleges predatory pricing under § 2 of the Sherman Act or primary-line price discrimination under the Robinson–Patman Act, two prerequisites to recovery remain the same. First, a plaintiff seeking to establish competitive injury resulting from a rival's low price must prove that the prices complained of are below an appropriate measure of its rival's costs.... Although [we have] reserved as a formal matter the question " 'whether recovery should ever be available ... when the pricing in question is above some measure of incremental cost,' " ... the reasoning in [our] opinions suggests that only below-cost prices should suffice, and we have rejected elsewhere the notion that above-cost prices that are below general market levels or the costs of a firm's competitors inflict injury to competition cognizable under the antitrust laws.... As a general rule, the exclusionary effect of prices above a relevant measure of cost either reflects the lower cost structure of the alleged predator, and so represents competition on the merits, or is beyond the practical ability of a judicial tribunal to control without courting intolerable risks of chilling legitimate price-cutting....

Even in an oligopolistic market, when a firm drops its prices to a competitive level to demonstrate to a maverick the unprofitability of straying from the group, it would be illogical to condemn the price cut: The antitrust laws then would be an obstacle to the chain of events most conducive to a breakdown of oligopoly pricing and the onset of competition. Even if the ultimate effect of the cut is to induce or reestablish supracompetitive pricing, discouraging a price cut and forcing firms to maintain supracompetitive prices, thus depriving consumers of the benefits of lower prices in the interim, does not constitute sound antitrust policy....

The second prerequisite to holding a competitor liable under the antitrust laws for charging low prices is a demonstration that the competitor had a reasonable prospect, or, under § 2 of the Sherman Act, a dangerous probability, of recouping its investment in below-cost prices.... "For the investment to be rational, the [predator] must have a reasonable expectation of recovering, in the form of later monopoly profits, more than the losses suffered." ... Recoupment is the ultimate object of an unlawful predatory pricing scheme; it is the means by which a predator profits from predation. Without it, predatory pricing produces lower aggregate prices in the market, and consumer welfare is enhanced. Although unsuccessful predatory pricing may encourage some inefficient substitution toward the product being sold at less than its cost, unsuccessful predation is in general a boon to consumers.

That below-cost pricing may impose painful losses on its target is of no moment to the antitrust laws if competition is not injured: ...

Even an act of pure malice by one business competitor against another does not, without more, state a claim under the federal antitrust laws; those laws do not create a federal law of unfair competition....

For recoupment to occur, below-cost pricing must be capable, as a threshold matter, of producing the intended effects on the firm's rivals, whether driving them from the market, or, as was alleged to be the goal here, causing them to raise their prices to supracompetitive levels within a disciplined oligopoly. This requires an understanding of the extent and duration of the alleged predation, the relative financial strength of the predator and its intended victim, and their respective incentives and will.... The inquiry is whether, given the aggregate losses caused by the below-cost pricing, the intended target would likely succumb.

If circumstances indicate that below-cost pricing could likely produce its intended effect on the target, there is still the further question whether it would likely injure competition in the relevant market. The plaintiff must demonstrate that there is a likelihood that the predatory scheme alleged would cause a rise in prices above a competitive level that would be sufficient to compensate for the amounts expended on the predation, including the time value of the money invested in it. As we have observed on a prior occasion, "[i]n order to recoup their losses, [predators] must obtain enough market power to set higher than competitive prices, and then must sustain those prices long enough to earn in excess profits what they earlier gave up in below-cost prices." *Matsushita*, 475 U.S., at 590–591.

Evidence of below-cost pricing is not alone sufficient to permit an inference of probable recoupment and injury to competition. Determining whether recoupment of predatory losses is likely requires an estimate of the cost of the alleged predation and a close analysis of both the scheme alleged by the plaintiff and the structure and conditions of the relevant market.... If market circumstances or deficiencies in proof would bar a reasonable jury from finding that the scheme alleged would likely result in sustained supra-competitive pricing, the plaintiff's case has failed. . . .

These prerequisites to recovery are not easy to establish, but they are not artificial obstacles to recovery; rather, they are essential components of real market injury. As we have said in the Sherman Act context, "predatory pricing schemes are rarely tried, and even more rarely successful," *Matsushita,* supra, at 589, and the costs of an erroneous finding of liability are high. . . . * * *

. . . While a reasonable jury could conclude that Brown & Williamson's intent was anticompetitive and that the price of its generics was below its costs for 18 months, the evidence was inadequate to show a reasonable prospect of cost recoupment. * * * Affirmed.

The *Brooke Group* standards and assumptions have been questioned. See J. Brodley, P. Bolton and M. Riordan, Predatory Pricing: Strategic Theory and Legal Policy, 88 Georgetown L.J. 2239 (2000), further elaboration at 89 Georgetown L.J. 2495 (2001).

TETRA PAK INTERNATIONAL SA v. COMMISSION

(predatory pricing)
Case T–83/91, [1994] ECR II–755,
aff'd Case C–333/94P, [1996] ECR I–5951
(see tie-in portion of case at page 863 supra).

Arguments of parties

[142]   The applicant maintains that the prices it charged from 1976 to 1982 in Italy for non-aseptic Tetra Rex cartons were not predatory as regards competitors. Those prices were justified by the conditions of competition on the Italian market and in particular by the fierce commercial contest between Tetra Pak and Elopak when Tetra Rex cartons were launched with a view to competing with the Pure–Pak cartons manufactured by Elopak and already well established on the market.

[143]   The applicant denies that setting the price well below not only their cost price but also their average direct variable cost was opposed to any economic rationale other that as part of an eviction strategy. It submits that *AKZO v EC Commission* . . . cannot be interpreted as prohibiting an undertaking in a dominant position from charging prices below average variable cost. It is for the Commission first to prove an eliminatory intent. Secondly, as the applicant stated at the hearing, on the basis of the judgment of the Supreme Court of the US of 21 June 1993, *Brooke Group v Brown & Williamson Tobacco,* sales at a loss are eliminatory only where the undertaking in question has a reasonable prospect of subsequently recouping losses so incurred. * * *

Assessment of the court

[147]   As a preliminary point, although it may be acceptable for an undertaking in a dominant position to sell at a loss in certain circumstances, that would clearly not be the case where such selling was predatory. Although Community competition law recognises that an undertaking in a dominant position has the right to take reasonable steps to protect its commercial interests, it does not countenance acts whose actual purpose

is to strengthen that dominant position and abuse it.... In particular, art. 86 of the treaty prohibits an undertaking in a dominant position from eliminating a competitor by practising competition by means of price which does not come within the scope of competition on the basis of quality (judgment in *AKZO v EC Commission*, para. 70).

148   In the light of those precepts, the existence of gross or semi-gross margins obtained by subtracting from the sale price the variable direct costs or the average variable costs, being the costs relating to the unit produced which are negative suggests that a pricing practice is eliminatory. As the Court of Justice held in *AKZO v EC Commission,* para. 71, an undertaking in a dominant position has no interest in applying prices below average variable costs (that is to say, those which vary depending on the quantities produced) except that of eliminating competitors so as to enable it subsequently to raise its prices by taking advantage of its monopolistic position, since each sale generates a loss equal to the total amount of the fixed costs (that is to say, those which remain constant regardless of the quantities produced) and at least part of the variable costs relating to the unit produced.

149   The Court of Justice also held in *AKZO v EC Commission* that ... if the prices are below average total costs (fixed costs plus variable costs), but above average variable costs, those prices must be regarded as abusive if they are determined as part of a plan for eliminating a competitor. The period during which such prices are applied as part of a plan for damaging a competitor is accordingly a factor to be taken into consideration (para. 72, 140 and 146).

150   ... The sale of Tetra Rex cartons constantly below not only their sale price but also their variable direct cost is sufficient evidence that the applicant pursued a policy of eviction from 1976 to 1981. By their scale and their very nature, the purpose of such losses, which cannot reflect any economic rationale other than ousting Elopak, was unquestionably to strengthen Tetra Pak's position on the markets in non-aseptic cartons where it already had a leading position as has already been found ... , thereby weakening competition on those markets. Contrary to the applicant's allegation, such conduct thus constituted abuse within the meaning of art. 86 of the treaty, in accordance with settled case law ... , and it is not necessary to demonstrate specifically that the undertaking in question had a reasonable prospect of recouping losses so incurred.

151   The same applied to 1982, during which the net margin was -11.4 per cent. A whole series of important and convergent factors provides evidence of the existence of an eliminatory intent. Such intent is apparent in particular from the duration, the continuity and the scale of the sales at a loss made throughout the period from 1976 to 1982. Moreover, the existence of a plan for eliminating Elopak in Italy is demonstrated by the accounting data which show that the applicant, which did not manufacture Tetra Rex cartons in Italy from 1976 to 1980, imported them in order to resell them in that country at prices lower by 10–34 per cent than their purchase price. On that basis, the Commission found in particular, as is shown by certain documents concerning orders, without being contradicted on this point by the applicant, that the latter resold in Italy at prices

lower by 17–29 per cent than their purchase price Rex cartons imported from Sweden. More generally, another point to note is that the prices of Tetra Rex cartons sold in Italy were lower by 20 per cent at least and often by 50 per cent than the prices applied in other member states, which the applicant does not dispute. Furthermore, the presumption of an eliminatory intent is consistent with the reports of Tetra Pak Italiana's board of directors of 1979 and 1980, referring to the need to make major financial sacrifices in the area of prices and supply terms in order to fight competition, in particular from Pure–Pak. * * *

Tetra Pak appealed, urging the Court of Justice to adopt the rule in *Brooke Group*. Advocate General Ruiz–Jarabo Colomer urged the Court to reject *Brooke Group*. The Court agreed with the advocate general. It affirmed the Court of First Instance in all respects. C–333/94P, [1996] ECR I–5951. Responding to Tetra Pak's argument that the sales below cost took place only on the non-aseptic (non-dominated) market and that therefore Tetra Pak had no realistic chance of recouping its losses (competition would prevent it from raising its prices), the Court of Justice confirmed that recoupment is not a constituent element of a price predation case under European law. Thus:

41   In *AKZO* this court did indeed sanction the existence of two different methods of analysis for determining whether an undertaking has practised predatory pricing. First, prices below average variable costs must always be considered abusive. In such a case, there is no conceivable economic purpose other than the elimination of a competitor, since each item produced and sold entails a loss for the undertaking. Secondly, prices below average total costs but above average variable costs are only to be considered abusive if an intention to eliminate can be shown.

42   ... For sales of non-aseptic cartons in Italy between 1976 and 1981, ... prices were considerably lower than average variable costs. Proof of intention to eliminate competitors was therefore not necessary. In 1982, prices for those cartons lay between average variable costs and average total costs. For that reason ... the Court of First Instance was at pains to establish—and the appellant has not criticised it in that regard—that Tetra Pak intended to eliminate a competitor.

43   The Court of First Instance was also right ... to apply exactly the same reasoning to sales of non-aseptic machines in the UK between 1981 and 1984.

44   Furthermore, it would not be appropriate, in the circumstances of the present case, to require in addition proof that Tetra Pak had a realistic chance of recouping its losses. It must be possible to penalise predatory pricing whenever there is a risk that competitors will be eliminated. The Court of First Instance found ... that there was such a risk in this case. The aim pursued, which is to maintain undistorted competition, rules out waiting until such a strategy leads to the actual elimination of competitors.

Notes and Questions

1.   Why would Tetra Pak have charged below its marginal cost if it could not later expect to make up the losses in higher than competitive prices for non-

aseptic cartons? Why would Brown & Williamson have done so if it did not expect to protect its branded cigarette sales from erosion?

2. For predatory pricing, what are the differences in premises and legal rules under the US law and the EC law? Is one approach wiser than the other? To what extent do the differences derive from different objectives of the competition laws? different understandings about economics? different assumptions underlying economic analysis? different judgments about the wisdom and efficacy of government intervention to stop predatory pricing en route to monopolization?

3. Consider, now, the variety of ways in which a dominant firm can abuse its dominance. Recall that Article 86 was initially conceived as a means to regulate the conduct of the dominant firm; to prevent other market actors, including competitors, from being abused by firms with power.

Which practices that you have identified are most harmful to competition? Which practices are more ambiguous, in the sense that they may increase competition? If you were in charge of enforcing Article 82 for the European Union, which practices would be your principal targets?

4. The following articles may be useful:

Per Jebsen and Robert Stevens, Assumptions, Goals and Dominant Undertakings: The Regulation of Competition under Article 86 of the European Union, 64 Antitrust L.J 443 (1996).

T. Kauper, Whither Article 86: Observations on Excessive Prices and Refusals to Deal, Chapter 28 in 1989 Ford. Corp. Law Inst. (B. Hawk, ed., Transnational Juris 1990).

E. Fox, Monopolization and Dominance in the United States and the European Community: Efficiency, Opportunity, and Fairness, 61 Notre Dame L.Rev. 981 (1986).

Chapter 23

HORIZONTAL RESTRAINTS UNDER ARTICLE 81

A. AGREEMENTS AMONG COMPETITORS— GENERAL

In Chapter 21 we dealt with hard core cartels: agreements among competitors specifically designed to lessen the competition among them. There are many other kinds of collaborations among competitors, often designed for legitimate purposes; e.g., sharing risks and creating synergies, getting market information, setting standards to facilitate trade, protecting the environment.

Beginning in the early days of enforcement of EC competition law, the Commission issued various notices and block exemptions supporting or authorizing ventures of small and middle-sized firms and various collaborations that almost always increase competition or innovation. Thus, in 1968, the Commission issued a notice declaring that certain forms of cooperation are not prohibited by Article 85(1) [now 81(1)]; for example agreements designed solely to exchange opinion, carry out comparative studies, cooperate in accounting matters, jointly collect debts, jointly execute research and development, jointly store and transport equipment, and jointly use a common label that is available to all competitors. In 1970 the Commission issued a notice on *de minimis* restraints which (after amendments in 2001) declares that agreements other than hard-core restraints among competitors or potential competitors who together do not occupy more than 10% of the market are in a safeharbor.[1] In 1972 the Commission issued a block exemption on specialisation agreements for small and middle-sized firms and in 1984 it issued a block exemption for certain research and development agreements. In years 2000–01, these block exemption regulations were substantially amended, and the Commission issued guidelines setting out principles for assessment of horizontal cooperation agreements.

For the parties to a business transaction, a great deal turns on whether the transaction falls within Article 81(1) and therefore requires an exemption. If the transaction does not fall within Article 81(1), national courts as well as the Commission can declare the agreement valid, and national courts can

---

1. Separate thresholds are stated for non-competitors (15%), and for markets subject to cumulative foreclosure effect (5%). The Notice is printed in the Selected Documents as Competition Doc. No. 2.

enforce the contract. If the transaction falls within Article 81(1), only the Commission can grant an exemption under current law (although modernisation proposals promise to extend this power to national authorities and courts). The Commission has considerable discretion to grant or withhold an exemption, and may insist on conditions that change the structure of the transaction.

This chapter first presents selected caselaw, so that the student may understand when an agreement is deemed a restriction or distortion of competition within Article 81(1), and when the agreement is deemed to satisfy the four conditions of Article 81(3). We then turn to the block exemptions, which are quite technical, and to the guidelines.

The caselaw is organized according to: joint buying and selling, joint ventures and strategic alliances, data exchanges, and the more specialized areas of innovation, environment, and labor. In connection with all of these areas, there are certain constant principles of economics to bear in mind:

We have spoken before about hard core restraints that are illegal on their face. This implies that there is no need to define the relevant market. In all other cases, it is necessary to define the market, which includes relatively good substitutes to which consumers may turn. In defining the market, once again, the Notice on market definition should be consulted. See Selected Documents Competition Doc. No. 3. Sometimes the market is obvious and other times we have not included the market definition analysis in order to focus on other substantive points.

Within the market, if it is competitive, the competing firms normally put pressure on one another, giving them incentives to respond to buyers. If some firms pair off to cooperate in various ways, e.g., research or production, they may achieve efficiencies and they may still be disciplined by strong competition. But if there are few firms in the market, and if new entry or expansion of small firms is difficult, market pressures may be lacking. If two competitors, or a major competitor and major potential competitor, pair off, even to do a productive task, they may weaken further the competitive dynamic in the market; their arrangement may facilitate lock-step, higher prices. And if firms that together have market power join together as a buying or selling group, they may save costs but they may also exert power against their suppliers or buyers. Moreover, when firms form joint ventures, they often need ancillary restraints to make the deal work, but they may also be able to bargain for excessive restraints that make the deal richer for them. The competition analysis can be very complex, but basically it focuses on a few points:

1. Is the market concentrated or fragmented; are barriers high or low?

2. What are the market shares and market positions of the collaborating firms? What is the structure of the remainder of the market?

3. What are the reasons for the collaboration? Are they good business reasons; e.g. to share risks, to gain efficiencies, to make a better product, to deliver the product better, to compete better?

4. Is the collaboration likely to create market power and raise prices? Is it likely to lower prices? To produce innovations? Is it likely to exclude competitors from important inputs or outlets more than necessary to achieve the efficiencies of the deal? Will the exclusion

deprive consumers from getting what they want? Will it result in market-wide coordinated behavior (oligopoly behavior) and higher prices to consumers?

5.   Do ancillary restraints, such as non-competition clauses, affect market competition, and if so are they necessary and tightly tailored in duration and scope to making the collaboration work?

6.   Do the procompetitive aspects outweigh the anticompetitive aspects, so that consumers get a fair share of the benefits?

We begin with joint buying, and older cases that illustrate some of these points. We advance to modern cases, including *European Night Services* and the Commission's analysis of business-to-business (B2B) internet exchanges.

B.   JOINT BUYING AND SELLING

Competitors sometimes collaborate to gain synergies and to become more competitive; but they sometimes collaborate to eliminate competition and gain market power. The analyst must pursue three lines of inquiry: (1) Is the restraint perceptible and more than de minimis? (2) If so, does the agreement fall within a block exemption? (3) If not, does the restraint meet the four conditions for an individual exemption set forth in Article 81(3)?

(a) Joint Buying

INTERGROUP (SPAR)

Commission Decision 75/482
O.J. L 212/23 (Aug. 9, 1975).

[Some 35,000 small food retailers and 180 small food wholesalers located across Europe formed INTERGROUP to establish the trademark SPAR, to act as intermediary in the purchase and sale of SPAR goods, and to provide legal and technical assistance to customers. INTERGROUP would negotiate purchase prices but would not set sale prices. INTERGROUP's purchases accounted for 2.4% of all purchases of the relevant products and accounted for less than 1% of the turnover of SPAR wholesalers. The INTERGROUP members were free not to use INTERGROUP as their purchasing agent and INTERGROUP was free to trade in any product, even products competing with SPAR.]

3   [T]he object of the agreements is to enable INTERGROUP customers, and particularly the SPAR chains, to carry out joint imports under identical purchasing conditions more favourable than those they would have received had they imported separately. Accordingly, the object of the agreements is to confront suppliers with a combined single order from purchasers, who thereby hold a stronger position resulting, not from their strength as individuals, but from the fact that they are operating together.

4   The SPAR chains are however free not to use INTERGROUP's services when making purchases and, when availing themselves of those services, they, like any other INTERGROUP customer, are in any event free to determine their prices and resale terms without being subject to any form of coordination by INTERGROUP in respect of marketing the goods.

INTERGROUP is free to trade in any product both within and outside the context of the notified agreement, and in the latter case may deal in products competing with those bearing SPAR trademarks.

5 The agreements, furthermore, do not have any substantial effects on competition, since imports effected by the SPAR chains through or after negotiation by INTERGROUP represent only a small part of their total turnover, and because purchases effected or negotiated by INTERGROUP account for a relatively small proportion of the total turnover in the retail food trade in each of the EEC member countries. The freedom of choice in both supply and demand in respect of the products concerned is not therefore affected by the agreements to any appreciable extent.

6 Having regard both to facts currently available and to the way they have been seen to develop in past activities of ISC and can reasonably be expected to develop in the future, neither the volume of these purchases for each product nor the number of products concerned is likely to increase to any appreciable extent in the near future. This is not only because of the marginal scale of the joint imports by wholesalers but also because it has always been found difficult in practice to promote concerted action by wholesalers, since the diversity and abundance of supplies often enable them to obtain better conditions acting individually than those to be obtained by acting together. Moreover, imports from non-member countries to EEC countries have been and remain at an insignificant level as compared with total consumption capacities in each of the Member States. As the goods concerned are very often not produced in the EEC, such purchases seem not likely to increase in scale in the near future since, apart from the coordination difficulties already mentioned, wholesalers in each region are obliged to take account of the very slow development of consumer tastes and of consumers' preference for local products.

7 At present the agreements seem to have no substantial implications for the market position of suppliers of the relevant goods within the EEC. They have neither as their object nor as their effect the prevention, restriction or distortion of competition within the common market. Nor are these agreements likely to have appreciable restrictive effects in the near future.

8 Accordingly, the agreements do not fall within Article 85(1) of the Treaty.... [N]egative clearance can accordingly be given. * * *

Notes and Questions

1. In *National Sulphuric Acid*, almost all of the producers of sulfuric acid in the UK and Ireland formed a pool to purchase crude sulfur, which had to be imported from North America, Poland and France. The supplier market was highly concentrated, with only three major sources, and the crude sulfur was subject to shortages. Sulexco in the United States was the dominant supplier. The buyers wished to offset its power. The members of the pool agreed to obtain all of their requirements from the pool (reduced after Commission intervention to 25% of their requirements), and they agreed to various restrictions on the use and resale of the crude sulfur brought through the pool, such as no sales to non-members. The Commission found Article 85(1) applicable, because the rules of the pool restricted competition among the pool members. It granted an exemption in view of significant advantages in price and security of supply, subject to the elimination of the restrictions on use and resale. Commission Decision 80/917 O.J.

L 260/24 (Oct. 3, 1980), extended for 10 years in 1990. Commission Decision 89/408, O.J. L 190/22 (July 5, 1989).

2. Joint buying groups are generally regarded favorably. Commonly, when competitors join forces to purchase an input, their objective is to achieve efficiencies in buying.

This is not always the case. Recall the *Quinine* case, page 806 supra, in which the bark pool was a device to allocate the scarce bark that was the source of quinine among the cartel members, assuring that each adhered to its sales quota.

3. When are buying groups cartels? Might competitors join together to use buying power in order to transfer profits from their suppliers to themselves? Under United States law, an agreement with the purpose and effect of gaining and using buying power—as opposed to gaining economies of scale—is a buying cartel and is illegal per se. E.g., Mandeville Island Farms, Inc. v. American Crystal Sugar Co., 334 U.S. 219, 68 S.Ct. 996, 92 L.Ed. 1328 (1948).

4. Do you think that the sulphur buying pool was simply an efficient collaboration, or was it a buying cartel? On what basis did the agreement in *National Sulphuric Acid* come within Article 85(1) (now 81(1)) while the agreement in *INTERGROUP* did not?

5. Do you agree with the Commission's analysis regarding the four requirements of Article 85(3) (now 81(3))?

6. In the age of e-commerce, competitors may set up electronic marketplaces for buying and selling (business-to-business, or B2B). Note that this is not necessarily joint buying or selling, but a jointly sponsored e-marketplace. Suppose all of the major car producers in Europe wish to establish a web site for the purchase of inputs by Internet of the products in the automotive supply chain: e.g., engines, tires, fabricated steel parts. What efficiencies might flow from such a venture—for sellers and for buyers? What possible anticompetitive effects (assume there are six European car producers, supply markets vary from fragmented to highly concentrated, and barriers are high)? How would you structure the arrangement to obtain an exemption?

In August 2001, the Commission gave approval to Covisint, a B2B Internet marketplace created by Ford, DaimlerChrysler, General Motors, Renault, Nissan and Peugeot Citroen. The United States and Brazil had previously granted approval.

We revisit B2B marketplaces after "joint selling."

(b) *Joint Selling*

Firms might agree to pool their selling efforts in order to gain efficiencies or in order to eliminate competition. If the firms have market power, the elimination of competition is likely to have a significant anticompetitive effect. Joint selling may have the same effect as price fixing. But if the market is competitive and the firms have no market power, market forces will continue to set the price and the joint sales agency will continue to be a price taker. The purpose of the arrangement, then, would probably be to gain efficiencies and thereby compete more effectively.

The joint selling cases cover the range of possibilities, from inappreciable restraints by small-firm cooperation, to clear exercises of market power, to large firm cooperation with strong efficiency properties.

Joint Selling By Small Firms

In *SAFCO* (Re le Société Anonyme de Fabricants de Conserves Alimentaires, Commission Decision 72/23, O.J. L 13/44 (Jan. 17, 1972)), small French producers of canned food agreed to a joint sales venture for exports to other parts of the Community. The producers sought a negative clearance. The Commission said:

> There is very keen competition, characterised by the sale of numerous national products and imports, similar in quality and at competitive prices, [and] the members of SAFCO are companies of limited size, which are still in competition with one another in their principal market ... and who ... come into contact on all the Community markets with the efficient competition of a large number of companies of greater size and more significance; consequently if the conclusion of this agreement abolished the possibility of export competition between the company members of SAFCO, at the present time that does not constitute an appreciable limitation of competition; * * *

> Whereas otherwise in a competitive situation such as this, the amalgamation of small productive sections of a local market or purely national market might even encourage competition as a result of new activity or increased exportation; in effect, particularly bearing in mind the limited size of the companies concerned, it is only by means of this co-operation that they started and developed an export business, notably in relation to the markets of the E.E.C. countries, as previously none of them exported regularly and in appreciable quantities.

The Commission granted the negative clearance.

Joint Selling by Large Firms

The sole producer of potassium salts in France and the sole producer of potassium salts in Germany agreed to establish a joint agency for their sales in Italy and the Netherlands. They coordinated exports throughout the Community and the world. Ruling on their request for an exemption, the Commission said:

> The appointment in these two cases of the same distributor by two normally competing undertakings of the size of VDK (now Kali and Salz) and SCPA necessarily implies agreement on their part not to compete on the markets in question. This joint appointment must therefore be regarded as the effect of a concerted practice between the two undertakings with a view to preventing or restricting competition between themselves in the Netherlands and in Italy.

The Commission denied the exemption. Société Commerciale des Potasses et de l'Azote, Commission Decision 73/213, O.J. L 217/3 (Aug. 6, 1973).

Then Kali and Salz (K & S) joined another collaboration.

Kali & Salz produced 88.9% of German potash production, and Kali Chemie (KC) produced 11.1%. K & S had a marketing system for distributing a complete range of potash products. KC's mine was nearly worked out and was flooding. Moreover, KC had abandoned its own sales organization and lacked the means to market its straight potash. K & S and KC entered into a ten-year agreement pursuant to which KC would sell to K & S the potash it produced but did not market or use for its own fertilizers. K & S agreed to buy a stated amount of potash from KC, equivalent to KC's anticipated surplus. KC was using an increasing amount of its production in the manufacture of a compound, so that its own potash sales to K & S under the agreement were declining. The Commission found that the agreement infringed Article 85(1) and did not merit an exemption. The Court annulled the Commission decision. The Commission had not made the case that the agreement afforded the undertakings the possibility of eliminating competition in respect of a substantial part of the market. Kali & Salz AG v. Commission, Cases 19, 20/74, [1975] ECR 499.

Notes and Questions

1. Is *SAFCO* consistent with the potassium decision? Is *Kali & Salz* consistent with the potassium decision?

2. Joint selling arrangements can be covers for cartels, but also, they can be vehicles for achieving efficiencies. The World Wide Web increasingly provides opportunities for sellers (as well as buyers) to come together—not necessarily to become joint sellers; they may simply establish an electronic marketplace where buyers can get quick, current, convenient information. B2B marketplaces and B2C (to consumer) marketplaces can entail both benefits and harms to competition. The Commission described possible benefits and harms in the following excerpt from its XXXth Report on competition policy (2000), point 2:

The Commission is increasingly called upon to assess the competitive impact of B2B electronic marketplaces. These are software systems that allow buyers and sellers of similar goods to carry out procurement activities using common computer systems. The Commission has already assessed and cleared a number of such marketplaces in a wide variety of industries. Examples include electronic markets for aircraft components, services to the chemical industry, office equipment, public administration services, foreign currency options, and mutual funds.

There are four general market types, all with numerous variations: buyer-managed exchanges are set up by large buyers, often in conjunction with technology partners. Supplier-managed exchanges are set up by suppliers. Marketmakers are independent exchanges not controlled by buyers or sellers. They tend to be backed by venture capital and were often early innovators. Content aggregators are sites that go beyond setting up a mere exchange. Instead they build and maintain multi-vendor catalogues which allow customers to access the offerings of several suppliers using a common search structure.

B2B electronic markets can have major procompetitive effects. Their main effect will be to increase market transparency. This will not only exert downward pressure on prices, it will also contribute to further integration of separate geographic markets, as the Internet removes the geographic barriers to buyers and sellers efficiently discovering each other. Online exchanges that allow buyers to aggregate their demand may be of particular benefit to small and medium-sized enterprises. In addition, B2B electronic marketplaces are expected to be a source of substantial efficiencies, as they allow transaction costs to be reduced and inventory management to be improved.

These positive effects could, however, in certain cases be offset by possible competition concerns. They are in fact not new; the question is to what extent these concerns stemming from the old economy are valid in the new economy. The following non-exhaustive list of possible competition problems can be drawn up:

(a) *network dominance*: Network effects and potential problems of network dominance are present when the value of a system to the individual user increases with the number of users. They can lead to market 'tipping' and the creation of a dominant position if the network effects are strong enough to induce all market participants to use the same network. This problem could potentially arise in the context of B2B electronic marketplaces as the benefits will often increase with the number of buyers and suppliers linked to the same system.

(b) *exchange of information*: This concern relates to the ability of the buyers or sellers to exchange or discover sensitive information on prices and quantities. It is linked to the design of the system, in particular its openness in terms of individual data originating from other parties.

(c) *joint purchasing/joint selling*: This concern relates to the question whether the participants in an electronic market can effectively bundle purchasing or selling volumes. If this is the case, a competition concern would arise if they were able to coordinate their behaviour as buyers or sellers. This concern can in principle arise equally in "normal" joint purchasing or selling. The discussion of these questions in the new horizontal guidelines would therefore constitute a good starting-point for the assessment.

(d) *discrimination/foreclosure*: This concern relates to the ownership of B2B electronic marketplaces and the rules governing them. These rules could be used, for instance, to exclude certain participants from the most efficient marketplace, thus putting them at a competitive disadvantage. An issue of discrimination could arise if certain market participants (e.g. the founders) received privileged information about transactions in the market. This issue arose in the *Volbroker* case, the first B2B exchange cleared under Article 81. In this case, six major banks set up a joint venture offering an electronic brokerage service for trading foreign currency options. The case raised concerns regarding the access to confidential information by the parent companies. To deal with this concern, the owners of the Volbroker.com exchange gave the Commission the assurance that they would set up "Chinese walls" to impede any information flows between the parent companies and the joint venture.

The competition assessment of B2B exchanges is still evolving. The Commission will need to analyse carefully the workings of any proposed B2B trading system and its effects on the market. In view of the global nature of many exchanges, this will be done in close cooperation with other competition authorities.

       Comment on the benefits and dangers of B2B and B2C selling. If the market is fragmented, would you have any concerns with the creation of a marketplace for information? Does it matter whether entry to other sellers is open or closed? What if the market is highly concentrated and the four leading car companies establish a closed site? Or the four leading sugar or cement firms do so? Why would they want to do so? What are the probable risks and benefits?

C.   JOINT VENTURES AND STRATEGIC ALLIANCES

       Major German, French, Dutch and Finnish electronics/telecommunications firms agreed to form a consortium to develop a pan-European mobile telephone system. More than six other similar consortia were being formed by other firms. The consortium would jointly develop, manufacture and sell a digital cellular mobile system. The only potential buyers were the national network operators. The Commission said that in view of the investment required and the time schedule for bids, the parties acting individually could not have been competitors for the purpose of entry into the field of the joint venture. It granted a negative clearance. Alcatel Espace/ANT Nachrichten- technik (AEG, Alcatel and Oy Nokia), Commission Decision 90/46, O.J. L 32/19 (Feb. 3, 1990).

In another transaction, Elopak and Metal Box, both operating in the packing industry, set up a joint venture, ODIN, to develop and exploit a new carton and the technology for filling it. Their agreement granted non-exclu- sive licenses, restricted use of know-how after termination of the joint venture, and contained various other ancillary restrictions. The Commission determined that the parties could not realistically be regarded as competitors or potential competitors because they were in different areas of the packing industry and were unlikely to undertake the R & D risks alone. The Commis- sion concluded that the joint venture did not distort competition, and that all restrictions were reasonably necessary for an efficient operation. It granted a negative clearance. Elopak/Metal Box–Odin, Commission Decision 90/410, O.J. L 209/15 (Aug. 8, 1990).

Why did the Commission grant negative clearances in *AEG/Alcatel* and *Elopak*, rather than exemptions? What if the partners *could* realistically have entered the market alone, but wished to capture the synergies of a joint venture? Could the Commission have granted a clearance based on the competitive structure of the market?

Joint ventures, alliances, and merger and acquisition agreements fre- quently contain ancillary restrictions on competition. For example, if a seller of assets including good will remained free to compete with the buyer immediately after the sale, the seller would probably reappropriate the good will it sold. Therefore the buyer insists on a non-compete clause. A Commis- sion Notice declares that ancillary restraints "directly related and necessary to the implementation of the concentration" may be cleared along with a concentration under the Merger Regulation, but it there is any dispute as to whether the restrictions are directly related and necessary to the implementa- tion of the concentration, their restrictive effects may be assessed by the Commission under Articles 81 and 82, and by national courts. Noncompetition clauses must be tightly limited in time and geography. Commission Notice on restrictions directly related and necessary to concentrations, O.J. C 188/5 (July 4, 2001).

In Remia BV v. Commission, [1985] ECR 2545, involving a seller's non- compete covenant in connection with the sale of a major sauces business, the Court said: "such clauses [to be valid] must be necessary to the transfer of the undertakings concerned and their duration and scope must be strictly limited to that purpose. The Commission was therefore right in holding that where those conditions are satisfied such clauses are free of the prohibition laid down in Article 85(1)" (para. 20) (granting an exemption limiting the dura- tion of the covenant to four years).

The reach of Article 85(1), now 81(1), was seriously tested when four major railway firms combined to provide night services through the Channel Tunnel.

EUROPEAN NIGHT SERVICES v. COMMISSION
Cases T–374–375, 384 & 388/94
[1998] ECR II–3141.

[Four railway firms—the railway companies of Britain (BR), Germany (DB), the Netherlands (NS), and France (SNCF)—agreed to form a joint venture, European Night Services (ENS), to provide overnight passenger rail services between the UK and the continent by way of the Channel Tunnel. They filed their agreements with the Commission, seeking a negative clearance or an exemption under the regulation applying competition rules to rail transport. The Commission found, as the relevant markets, the market for the transport of business travelers (for whom air travel, among other things, is a substitute) and the market for the transport of leisure travelers (for whom car travel, among other things, is a substitute). It made no reference in its decision to market shares of ENS or any competing operators, but later referred to data in the parties' notification to contend that a conservative estimate of ENS' market share was 7% to 8%. The Commission denied a negative clearance and granted an exemption for a period of eight years on condition that the parent companies supply equivalent services on the same terms to any international grouping of railways and any transport operator wishing to compete with ENS in the Channel Tunnel. The railways appealed, contending that the Commission had not shown grounds for application of Article 85(1), that ENS' market share was less than 5% on most routes and in any case was insignificant, and that in any event the conditions imposed by the Commission were disproportionate and improper and the term of exemption was too short.

The Court of First Instance said:]

As to the appreciable effect of the agreement

102   ... [E]ven if, as noted above, ENS's share of the tourist travel market was in fact likely to exceed 5 per cent on certain routes, attaining 7 per cent on the London–Amsterdam route and 6 per cent on the London–Frankfurt/Dortmund route, it must be borne in mind that, according to the case law, an agreement may fall outside the prohibition in Article 85(1) of the Treaty if it has only an insignificant effect on the market, taking into account the weak position which the parties concerned have on the product or service market in question.... With regard to the quantitative effect on the market, the Commission has argued that, in accordance with its notice on agreements of minor importance, Article 85(1) applies to an agreement when the market share of the parties to the agreement amounts to 5 per cent. However, the mere fact that that threshold may be reached and even exceeded does not make it possible to conclude with certainty that an agreement is caught by Article 85(1) of the Treaty. Point 3 of that notice itself states that "the quantitative definition of 'appreciable' given by the Commission is, however, no absolute yardstick" and that in "individual cases ... agreements between

undertakings which exceed these limits may ... have only a negligible effect on trade between Member States or on competition, and are therefore not caught by Article 85(1)''.... It is noteworthy, moreover, if only as an indication, that that analysis is corroborated by the Commission's 1997 notice on agreements of minor importance ... according to which even agreements which are not of minor importance can escape the prohibition on agreements on account of their exclusively favourable impact on competition.

103   That being so, where, as in the present case, horizontal agreements between undertakings reach or only very slightly exceed the 5 per cent threshold regarded by the Commission itself as critical and such as to justify application of Article 85(1) of the Treaty, the Commission must provide an adequate statement of its reasons for considering such agreements to be caught by the prohibition in Article 85(1) of the Treaty. Its obligation to do so is all the more imperative here, where, as the applicants stated in their notification, ENS has to operate on markets largely dominated by other modes of transport, such as air transport, and where, on the assumption of an increase in demand on the relevant markets and having regard to the limited possibilities for ENS to increase its capacity, its market shares will either fall or remain stable.... * * *

105   It must be concluded from the foregoing that the contested decision does not contain a sufficient statement of reasons to enable the Court to make a ruling on the shares held by ENS on the various relevant markets and, consequently, on whether the ENS agreements have an appreciable effect on trade between Member States, and the decision must therefore be annulled on that ground. * * *

As to the Commission's requirement that the parent railroads supply to competitors of ENS the same necessary services that they supply to ENS

205   According to paragraph 79 of the contested decision, the aim of the [requirement to supply services to competitors] is that of "preventing the restrictions of competition from going beyond what is indispensable". * * *

207   ... [E]ven if the Commission had made an adequate and correct assessment of the restrictions of competition in question, it would be necessary to consider whether it was a proper application of Article 85(3) to impose on the notifying parties the condition that train paths, locomotives and crews must be supplied to third parties on the same terms as to ENS, on the ground that they are necessary or that they constitute essential facilities, as discussed by the parties in their pleadings and at the hearing. * * *

209   ... [W]ith regard to an agreement such as that in the present case, setting up a joint venture, which falls within Article 85(1) of the Treaty, the Court considers that neither the parent undertakings nor the joint venture thus set up may be regarded as being in possession of infrastructure, products or services which are "necessary" or "essential" for entry to the relevant market unless such infrastructure, products or services are not "interchangeable" and unless, by reason of their special characteristics—in particular the prohibitive cost of and/or time reasonably

required for reproducing them—there are no viable alternatives available to potential competitors of the joint venture, which are thereby excluded from the market.

210 The question whether the Commission could validly regard the supply of (a) train paths, (b) locomotives and (c) crews to ENS by its parent undertakings as necessary or essential services which had to be made available to third parties on the same terms as to ENS and whether, in so doing, it provided a valid statement of reasons for its decision must be examined in the light of the above considerations and by analogy with the case law.... Finally, that examination will also serve as the basis for determining whether the Commission made a correct analysis of the alleged restrictions of competition with regard to third parties arising out of the special relationship between the parent undertakings and ENS.

211 With regard, first, to train paths, [the Commission's decision is based on a false premise because it erroneously treated ENS as a transport operator].

212 With regard, second, to the supply of locomotives, as pointed out above, locomotives cannot be regarded as necessary or essential facilities unless they are essential for ENS's competitors, in the sense that without them they would be unable either to penetrate the relevant market or to continue operating on it. However, since the decision defined the relevant market as the market for the transport of business travellers and the market for the transport of leisure travellers, both of which are intermodal, and since ENS's market share does not exceed 7 per cent to 8 per cent according to the Commission, or 5 per cent according to the notification of the parties, on either of those intermodal markets, it cannot be accepted that a possible refusal by the notifying undertakings to supply ENS's competitors with special locomotives for the Channel Tunnel could have the effect of excluding such competitors from the relevant market as thus defined. It has not been demonstrated that an undertaking having such a small market share can be in a position to exert any influence whatever on the functioning or structure of the market in question.

213 Only if the market under consideration were the completely different, intramodal, market for business and leisure travel by rail, on which the railway undertakings currently hold a dominant position, could a refusal to supply locomotives possibly have an effect on competition. However, it was not that intramodal market which was finally considered relevant by the Commission, but the intermodal market.... * * *

215 As the applicants have argued, the contested decision does not contain any analysis demonstrating that the locomotives in question are necessary or essential. More specifically, it is not possible to conclude from reading the contested decision that third parties cannot obtain them either directly from manufacturers or indirectly by renting them from other undertakings. Nor has any correspondence between the Commission and third parties, demonstrating that the locomotives in question cannot be obtained on the market, been produced before the Court. As the applicants have stated, any undertaking wishing to operate the same rail services as ENS through the Channel Tunnel may freely purchase or rent the locomotives in question on the market. ...

216　　... [T]he Commission has ... merely asserted that ... only the notifying undertakings actually possess such locomotives. That argument cannot, however, be accepted. The fact that the notifying undertakings have been the first to acquire the locomotives in question on the market does not mean that they are alone in being able to do so.

217　　Consequently, the Commission's assessment of the necessary or essential nature of the special locomotives designed for the Channel Tunnel and, thus, the obligation imposed on the parent undertakings to supply such locomotives to third parties are vitiated by an absence or, at the very least, an insufficiency of reasoning.

218　　For the same reasons, the obligation imposed on the parent undertakings also to supply train crews for special locomotives for the Channel Tunnel to third parties is similarly vitiated by an absence or an insufficiency of reasoning.

219　　Consequently, the contested decision is vitiated by an absence or, at the very least, an insufficiency of reasoning in so far as it requires the applicants to supply to third parties in competition with ENS the same "necessary services" as it supplies to ENS. * * *

221　　As regards, first, access to infrastructure (train paths), it is true that access for third parties may in principle be hindered when it is controlled by competitors; nevertheless, the obligation of railway undertakings which are also infrastructure managers to grant such access on fair and non-discriminatory terms to international groupings competing with ENS is explicitly provided for and guaranteed by Directive 91/440. The ENS agreements therefore cannot, by definition, impede access to infrastructure by third parties. As regards the supply to ENS of special locomotives and crew for the Channel Tunnel, the mere fact of its benefitting from such a service could impede access by third parties to the downstream market only if such locomotives and crew were to be regarded as essential facilities. Since ... they cannot be categorised as such, the fact that they are to be supplied to ENS under the operating agreements for night rail services cannot be regarded as restricting competition *vis-à-vis* third parties. That aspect of the Commission's analysis of restrictions of competition *vis-à-vis* third parties is therefore also unfounded.

As to duration of the exemption granted

222　　The applicants emphasise that the ENS agreements relate to a major long-term investment and that the return on the project is dependent on the securing of advantageous 20–year financing for the purchase of the specialised rolling stock, so that the limitation of the exemption to eight years is inadequate.... * * *

230　　... [E]ven if it is assumed that the Commission's assessment of the restrictions on competition in the contested decision was adequate and correct, the Court considers that the duration of an exemption granted under Article 85(3) of the Treaty—or, as here, Article 5 of Regulation 1017/68—and Article 53(3) EEA must be sufficient to enable the beneficiaries to achieve the benefits justifying such exemption, namely, in the present case, the contribution to economic progress and the benefits to consumers provided by the introduction of new high-quality transport services.... Since, moreover, such progress and benefits cannot be achieved without considerable investment, the length of time required to ensure a proper return on that investment is necessarily an essential factor to be taken into account when determining the duration of an exemption, particularly in a case such as the present, where it is undisputed that the services in question are completely new, involve major investments and substantial financial risks and require the pooling of know-how by the participating undertakings.

231 The consideration set out in ... the decision, that "the duration of the exemption will therefore depend inter alia on the period for which it can reasonably be supposed that market conditions will remain substantially the same," cannot, therefore, be regarded as decisive, on its own, for determining the duration of the exemption, without also taking account of the length of time necessary to enable the parties to achieve a satisfactory return on their investment.

232 However, the contested decision does not contain any detailed assessment of the length of time required to achieve a return on the investments in question under conditions of legal certainty, in the light, in particular, of the fact that the parties have entered into financial commitments covering a period of 20 years for the purchase of the special rolling stock.... * * *

234 Consequently, the Commission's decision to limit the duration of the exemption granted for the ENS agreements is in any event vitiated by an absence of reasoning. * * *

[T]he contested decision must be annulled.

Notes and Questions

1. After *ENS*, how is the Commission to determine whether an agreement has no more than a negligible effect on trade or competition and therefore is not even caught by Article 81(1)? Is a combined market share below 10% presumptively negligible? How does market definition affect this judgment? Could the Commission have avoided the problem by finding a rail transport submarket?

2. Is the Commission required, or even authorized, to weigh competitive benefits against competitive harms in determining whether an agreement is caught by Article 81(1)?

Note the railroads' and the Commission's different approaches to whether an agreement is caught by Article 81(1):

130 [According to the railroads,] the case law ... establishes that [the Commission] is bound [under 85(1)] to apply a "rule of reason" and to balance the competitive benefits and harms of the agreement. [The Commission disagrees. It says that] such an approach is required in the context of Article 85(3) of the Treaty but not in respect of the appraisal of restrictions of competition under Article 85(1).

Who is right? If any question remained after *ENS*, it was resolved in *Métropole TV*. Six major firms in the French TV sector formed a satellite TV joint venture, TPS, which entered the market dominated by Canal+. The applicants argued that they were entitled to negative clearance, rather than exemption, of a clause providing that certain channels were to be broadcast exclusively on TPS. Their argument depended upon the availability of rule-of-reason analysis under

Article 81(1). The CFI rejected this approach, holding that the clause was caught by Article 81(1) because it restricted competition; the competitors of TPS were denied access to programs considered attractive to numerous French viewers. The positive effects had to be weighed under Article 81(3). Métropole Télévision (M6) v. Commission, Case T–112/99, September 18, 2001 CFI.

3. How does the essential facility obligation of joint venturers compare with the essential facility obligation of dominant firms? If, in *ENS*, the market were rail travel and the joint venturers were the only firms that possessed locomotives fit to travel through the Channel Tunnel, would the Commission's requirement that the joint venturers supply locomotives to third parties on the same terms as they supply *ENS* withstand scrutiny?

4. Is the Court of First Instance concerned that excessive requirements and legal uncertainty will chill procompetitive and efficient joint ventures? How does it express this point? This is a concern often expressed in the United States case law, but one that is much less often observed in EC law.

D. DATA EXCHANGES

Economics teaches that information (knowledge of the market) is good. It helps sellers understand supply and demand; it helps them determine the efficient amount for them to produce, and where, to whom, and how much to sell. Similarly it helps buyers understand the efficient amount to buy and the lowest price at which they can buy. Information helps make markets work.

But in highly concentrated, high-barrier markets where firms have incentives to behave cooperatively, the sharing of market information can have outbalancing negative qualities. Oligopolists' knowledge of the sensitive business details of one another can help them coordinate and stabilize prices upwards. When firms are few, aggregated data can usually be disaggregated. Moreover when the information is obtained as the result of agreement among the firms, the danger signals are compounded: firms are not likely to give their sensitive information (e.g. cost, output, forecasts) to a competitor if they expect the data to be used against them. They are more likely to share the information if they can expect cooperation in lessening competition.

Often, when market conditions point to a negative (price-raising) effect, one suspects that the data sharing agreement is meant to facilitate a cartel; for, as we saw in the cartel chapter, cartelists need to know the most sensitive information about one another to find a jointly profit-maximizing price, and they need to police their cartel agreement. Information sharing supports both tasks.

NOTE ON JOHN DEERE LTD. v. COMMISSION

The Agricultural Engineers Association was a trade association of producers and importers of agricultural tractors in the UK. It had some 200 members, and was open to membership by all other agricultural tractor companies. The market was oligopolistic; the four largest firms accounted for almost 80% of sales. The firms' market shares were stable and entry barriers were high. The product was homogeneous. The association organized an exchange of information among its members (who accounted for 88% of sales) based on the information contained in registration forms that were required to be filed by the UK. The data revealed great detail of sales and market shares, broken down by year, quarter, month and week, and by country, region, county, and dealer territory, and made it possible to identify not only the sales of each producer but also the imports and exports between dealer territories.

The information exchanged did not directly concern prices, and there was no evidence that the information exchange was designed in support of a cartel. Indeed, there was no claim that the *object* of the agreement was to harm trade or competition; and the Commission was unable to establish that the agreement, which was in force for 20 years, produced an actual anticompetitive effect (higher prices).

The Commission found that the information exchange agreement was caught by Article 85(1) and was not entitled to an exemption. The Court of First Instance agreed. It upheld Commission findings that the data exchange (1) disadvantaged non-members, who would forgo the information exchanged; (2) produced *potential* anticompetitive effects among members, by providing a forum for facilitating a high price policy; and (3) made it possible for each participating manufacturer to monitor *its* dealers' sales and thus made "it possible for [manufacturers] to confer absolute territorial protection on each of their dealers." para. 96. Further, the association did not show that the restrictions on competition resulting from the agreement were indispensable, "particularly with regard to the objectives of contributing to economic progress and equitable distribution of the benefits." para. 105. Case T–35/92, [1995] ECR II–957. The Court of Justice affirmed. Case C–7/95 P, [1998] ECR I–3111. It rejected John Deere's arguments, among others, that Article 81(1) does not prohibit purely potential effects on competition, and that the Court of First Instance improperly inferred harm to competition from high concentration without any evidence of higher prices or changes in the pattern of trade.

John Deere was the first prohibition by the Commission and Court of a pure information exchange of non-price information.

Were the Court and Commission correct? How is such an agreement "exclusionary" to non-members? How does the exchange of sales information harm competition among members? Do you suspect that the members shared sales data to compete or to lessen competition? Do you believe that this exchange of information chilled parallel imports; i.e., kept each producer's product within each of its dealer's territories and thus kept the producer's product from competing with itself? Could this have been a device to help the producers cartelize? Which of the possible effects would most concern you if you were a competition authority?

NOTE ON WIRTSCHAFTSVEREINIGUNG STAHL

(from 1997 Report on Competition Policy, p. 127)

On 26 November the Commission adopted a decision under Article 65 of the ECSC Treaty [the counterpart in the Coal and Steel Treaty to former Article 85 of the EC Treaty] prohibiting an information exchange system notified by Wirtschaftsvereinigung Stahl, the German steel industry association. The system, which had not been implemented, provided for the exchange between association members of sensitive, recent and individualised data on supplies of more than 40 steel products in the various Member States, broken down by steel quality. The exchange would also have concerned the breakdown by consumer sector and the market shares of member companies on the German market. The leading German steel producers were to have participated in the system.

After analysing these homogeneous product markets in detail, the Commission drew a distinction between two types of market. It raised no objection to the exchange of sensitive information on dispersed markets. On the other hand, it did prohibit the exchange of data on all markets for flat products and on the markets for beams, sheet piling, permanent way material and wire rod of stainless steel. These are concentrated markets characterized by low import penetration, stable trade flows between Member States and chronic overcapacity.

The notified information exchange agreement would have restricted competition between the parties by increasing market transparency to such a degree that any independent competitive action on the part of one company would have been noticed immediately by its competitor, which would have been able to take suitable retaliatory measures such as systematically canvassing customers or offering temporary or local selective discounts. This increased transparency would thus have been liable to deter companies from trying to increase their market shares, a fundamental competitive activity. In addition, the frequency of the exchange, i.e. monthly, and the freshness of the data exchanged (one month old) would have reduced considerably the time during which a company could have derived any benefit from behaving competitively.

The decision is consistent with the Commission's practice, which has been upheld by the Court of First Instance [citing *John Deere*], of viewing as anticompetitive any systems involving the exchange of sensitive, recent and individualised data on a concentrated market in homogeneous products.

———————

What do you think was the principal harm feared from the steel industry's information exchange?

Are the two cases—tractors and steel—basically the same or basically different? In which case is the economic concern on stronger ground?

E.　INNOVATION AND COMPETITIVENESS

Consider the following two matters, as summarized by the Commission in its 1996 Competition Policy Report, both of which involve strategic alliances—i.e., synergistic joint ventures that enable the partners to enter new markets and expand their capabilities.

Iridium

The Commission, by formal decision, gave the green light to the creation of Iridium, a company led by the US corporation Motorola, which intends to provide from the last quarter of 1998 global digital wireless communications services using a constellation of 66 low earth orbit (LEO) satellites, to be launched and placed in orbit during the next 24 months. Services will include mobile voice telephony, paging and basic data services (such as facsimile) and will be provided via portable hand-held (dual mode or single mode) telephones, vehicle-mounted telephones, pagers and other subscriber equipment.

Apart from Motorola, Iridium is owned by 16 strategic investors including a number of telecommunication services providers and equipment manufacturers from around the world. Two European companies figure among those strategic investors: Stet (Italy; 3.8%) and Vebacom (Germany; 10%). Each of the two has its own gateway service territory covering different parts of Europe and the associated exclusive right to construct and operate a gateway within its respective territory.

In the decision, the creation of Iridium has been concluded to fall outside the scope of both Article 85(1) of the EC Treaty and Article 53(1) of the EEA [European Economic Area] Agreement. In this respect, it was concluded that none of the strategic investors could be reasonably expected to separately assume the very high level of investments required (nearly USD 5 billion) and the very high risk of technical and commercial failure associated with such a new system. In addition, no investor has all the necessary licences to operate such a system.

Satellite systems like Iridium (commonly referred to as S–PCS systems) are expected to complement wireless terrestrial mobile technologies (such as GSM) in areas where those terrestrial technologies have failed to penetrate (i.e. rural parts of the developed world and both urban and rural parts of lower income countries) or where terrestrial roaming is not available because of incompatible technologies. In addition, S–PCS systems are expected to act as a complement and even a substitute for the public switched fixed telephone network, enhancing service coverage in remote areas of low population density and/or where the terrestrial infrastructure is very poor.

The same conclusion as to the inapplicability of the competition rules of both the EC Treaty and the EEA Agreement was reached in respect of several ancillary restraints; namely as regards the distribution of the Iridium services and the pricing policies which Iridium may suggest as guidelines to gateways investor operators.

* * *

Atlas/GlobalOne

On 17 July [1996] the Commission authorized the Atlas project, a joint venture between Deutsche Telekom AG (DT) and France Télécom (FT) aimed at providing telecommunications services to large users in Europe. The services provided by Atlas include network services, outsourcing and very small aperture satellite (VSAT) services. The Commission also authorized the proposed GlobalOne joint venture, an alliance between Atlas and Sprint Corporation (Sprint) for the supply of the above services worldwide. Within GlobalOne, the parties will provide the same services as within Atlas, together with traveller services and telecommunications services to other telecommunications organizations (TOs).

In the relevant markets, the services provided to corporate users raise important issues to do with competition in the EEA. This is the case, for example, with the market for the transmission of data via terrestrial networks. DT and FT have market shares there well in excess of 70% in Germany and France respectively, buttressed by a legal monopoly over the supply of infrastructure. In addition, the Atlas project provided for the elimination of a competitor of DT in Germany, namely FT's local subsidiary, Info AG.

In the course of the proceeding, France and Germany first of all undertook to liberalize the alternative infrastructures by introducing a system under which licences would be granted to any operator meeting certain technical requirements, thereby making competitors less dependent on the networks of FT and DT. The Commission made the Atlas/GlobalOne authorization conditional on the granting of the first two infrastructure licences in France and Germany.

DT and FT have postponed the transfer of their domestic data transmission networks to the joint venture pending full liberalization of infrastructure services in France and Germany. FT has undertaken to sell Info AG. This modified contractual framework, coupled as it is with strict conditions and obligations, will help to ensure that the two projects satisfy an increasingly urgent demand and compete with the few telecommunications services providers existing at world level without, however, resulting in any elimination of competition.

Notes and Questions

1.   Did Iridium restrict or distort competition? Were its members competitors? potential competitors?

2.   How did Atlas and GlobalOne restrict competition? How did the Commission counteract the problems? How did the Commission use the occasion to impose conditions that would increase competition?

3.   What is the Commission's approach towards innovation and competitiveness?

F.   THE ENVIRONMENT AND COMPETITIVENESS

European Union policy supports environmental measures and the integration of environmental concerns into the various Community policies. In its 1998 Competition Policy Report, the Commission summarized as follows its activity regarding competition and the environment:

[129]   At the Cardiff European Summit, the Member States recalled the provisions of the Treaty of Amsterdam [Article 6] stipulating that Community policies should take account of environmental protection with a view to achieving sustainable development, an approach which was endorsed at the Vienna Summit. In its XXVth the Report on Competition Policy, the Commission spelt out its position regarding implementation of the Community competition rules in the environmental field. In particular, it stated: 'When the Commission examines individual cases, it weighs up the restrictions of competition arising out of an agreement against the environmental objectives of the agreement, and applies the principle of proportionality in accordance with Article 85(3). In particular, improving the environment is regarded as a factor which contributes to improving production or distribution or to promoting economic or technical prog-

ress.' In that connection, 1998 was marked by four cases reflecting the Commission's commitment to take a positive approach to environmental issues in its competition analyses.

130   The Commission approved the agreement signed by the European Associ- ation of Consumer Electronics Manufacturers (EACEM) and 16 of its members, all major manufacturers of television sets and video cassette recorders. This agreement is a voluntary commitment to reduce the electricity consumption of this equipment when it is in stand-by mode. The Commission exempted the agreement under Article 81(3) on the ground that the energy-saving and environmental benefits of the scheme clearly represented technical and economic progress and, by their nature, would be passed on to consumers. The energy saving could amount to 3.2 TWh a year from 2005. This reduction in energy consumption will have a significant impact in terms of the management of energy resources, reductions in CO_2 emissions and, accordingly, measures to counter global warming. The Commission also ascertained that the scheme would not eliminate competition in the affected markets and that its restrictive effect was essential to achieving its full benefits.

131   The Association of European Automobile Manufacturers (ACEA) has undertaken, on behalf of its members, to reduce CO_2 emissions from passenger cars. This effort is in line with the Community policy of reducing CO_2 emissions into the atmosphere. ACEA has set a reduction target of 25% by 2008. The Commission and the Member States will monitor the efforts made to achieve that target. The Commission also took the view that this agreement between European automobile manu- facturers did not infringe the competition rules. ACEA determines an average reduction target for all its members, but each of them is free to set its own level, which will encourage them to develop and introduce new CO_2-efficient technologies independently and in competition with one another. Accordingly, ACEA's voluntary agreement does not constitute a restriction of competition and is not caught by Article 81(1).

132   [EUCAR is the European Council for Automotive Research and Develop- ment. It consists of Opel, BMW (including Rover), Mercedes, Fiat, Ford PSA, Porsche, Renault, VW and Volvo.] In the *EUCAR* case, the Commis- sion adopted a favourable stance on a cooperation agreement between Europe's leading motor manufacturers which is designed to boost re- search in the [European] motor industry, particularly on environmental issues. Most of the projects that will be developed involve experimental research on, for example, limiting noise or emission pollution caused by motor vehicles. The products obtained from this research may not be directly usable in a specific type of vehicle. The Commission therefore took the view that the research was at the pre-competitive stage and that the agreements did not infringe Community law.

133   Finally, the Commission approved the membership agreements of Valpak, a non-profit-making, industry-led compliance scheme operating in the United Kingdom which has been set up to discharge the packaging waste recovery and recycling obligations of its members. The legal framework set up in the United Kingdom to implement the [EU] directive [on

packaging waste] provides scope for competition in the market for compliance-scheme services which seek to fulfil recovery and recycling obligations on behalf of a business. While Valpak is currently the largest compliance scheme operating in the United Kingdom, other competing schemes exist and have notified their arrangements to the Commission.

134 Following its examination of Valpak's membership agreements, the Commission concluded that the agreements restricted competition within the meaning of Article 81(1) because they obliged businesses wishing to join the scheme to transfer the totality of their obligations in all packaging materials. This 'all or nothing' approach, which transposes a regulatory provision, restricts the extent to which Valpak and other schemes will be able to compete against one another on a material-specific basis. The Commission went on to consider whether the notified arrangements could benefit from exemption under Article 81(3). In view of the emerging nature of the market and the likelihood that Valpak and other schemes would be obliged to invest in the United Kingdom's collection and/or reprocessing infrastructure in order to meet their members' obligations in the future, the Commission concluded that an 'all or nothing' approach was necessary, at least in the short term, if schemes such as Valpak were to succeed in securing sufficient funding to allow the necessary investment to take place. The Commission informed Valpak at the same time that it reserved the right to reexamine the case after three years.

Notes and Questions

1. Consider, in the case of each agreement, the possible harm to competition. What is the case for harm to competition? Are the agreements caught by Article 81(1)? Do you agree with the Commission's analysis regarding when an exemption is necessary?

2. A Danish recycling law limited bottle types for beer and soft drinks sold in Denmark, creating an obstacle to out-of-state beer and soft drink sellers. See Commission v. Denmark, Case 302/86, [1988] ECR 4607, page 1265 infra. Suppose the restraint was imposed by agreement among the Danish beverage makers and their retailers, rather than by the legislature of Denmark. Analyze the agreement. Does it fall within Article 81(1)? Should it get an exemption? Suppose the Danish beverage makers make a convincing case that the proliferation of un-recyclable bottles will impose serious costs on the environment. How should the Commission make the trade-off between free movement, competition and the environment?

3. May the European beef processors agree not to supply beef to wholesalers or retailers that sell beef injected with hormones?

4. Under US antitrust law, where an agreement has anticompetitive aspects, it can be justified only by outbalancing procompetitive aspects. National Society of Professional Engineers v. United States, 435 U.S. 679, 98 S.Ct. 1355, 55 L.Ed.2d 637 (1978). "Anticompetitive" normally entails a lessening of rivalry that harms the consumer. How would each of the above agreements fare under US law? Which is the better approach—that of the US or of the EU?

CECED

Commission Decision, Case IV F 1/36.718
O.J. L 187/47 (July 26, 2000).

[Almost all producers and importers of washing machines in Europe entered into an agreement designed to reduce energy consumption and thereby to reduce polluting emissions from washing machines. The agreement was notified to the Commission by their trade association, the European Council of Domestic Appliance Manufacturers (CECED). Under the agreement, the producers and importers agreed to stop producing for, and importing into, the EU the least energy efficient washing machines, designated as categories D to G by a Commission Directive. Categories D to G represented 10%–11% of all washing machines sold in the EU, and comprised a significant proportion of the sales of some of the agreeing manufacturers. Energy efficiency was an import focus of advertising and sales. The market was fragmented. The agreeing manufacturers accounted for more than 95% of the market.

The Commission granted a short (less than one-year) exemption, stating, as to the four conditions of Article 81(3):]

— The agreement objectively contributes to technical and economic progress, by focusing production on more efficient machines. Such benefits would be unlikely or would occur less quickly without the agreement.

— Consumers derive benefits at the same time individually and for society as a whole: likely higher purchase costs of more efficient washing machines are quickly compensated by savings in electricity bills; the agreement contributes to EC environmental objectives and the benefits very largely exceed potential cost increases triggered as a result of the agreement. Even if individual purchasers were not to derive the financial benefits that they actually attain, the magnitude of environmental benefits is such that the net contribution to society's economic welfare would still be positive.

— The restrictions of competition are indispensable to attaining those benefits. Consumers do not sufficiently take external costs into account in their purchase decisions. The application of a minimum efficiency ratio mitigates this market failure. Alternatives such as public awareness campaigns or application of ecolables would be complementary, rather than substitutable to the agreement.

— The agreement does not eliminate competition. Various technical means to improve energy efficiency of washing machines are economically available to all manufacturers; competition remains also on important purchase criteria such as prices, technical effectiveness, brand image etc.; finally, 90% of sales of washing machines are not directly concerned.

Notes and Questions

1. Are you confident that consumer benefits outweigh costs? What about the consumers who prefer the low price, or other features of machines that happen to fall within categories D to G, and who prefer not to be altruistic?

2. What is the significance of the fact that some of the collaborating manufacturers made D-to-G machines? Would the agreement be more suspect if none of them did? Even so, can we trust these producers to set the standard in the public interest?

3. Suppose you represent a Canadian manufacturer whose washing machines are low priced, offer features householders love, and fall within category D. Your machines are relatively new, and your European fortunes—and market share—were fast rising. You are suddenly faced with a private European boycott. You and your loyal European consuming public consider a suit to annul the Commission decision granting exemption. Frame your analysis of the anticompetitive effects of the CECED agreement. Review each of the four requirements for exemption. Which are most vulnerable? What are your odds of winning in court?

4. If the European Union wanted energy standards that excluded machines in categories D to G, why did it not adopt legislation setting an energy efficiency floor that excluded those categories?

5. Might the Commission exemption constitute a blockage of market access to exporters from other nations in violation of the General Agreement on Tariffs and Trade (GATT)? Article XI of the GATT prohibits states from imposing quantitative restrictions on imports. Article XX provides a derogation for a state measure necessary for health and safety; this must be backed up by scientific evidence.

G. LABOR

ALBANY INTERNATIONAL BV AND TEXTILE INDUSTRY PENSION FUNDS

Case C–67/96, [1999] ECR I–5751.

[The Netherlands maintains a pension system. A compulsory statutory scheme entitles the whole population to receive a basic pension, calculated by reference to the statutory minimum wage. This amount, however, is quite limited.

Industry sectors are covered by supplementary pensions managed by collective schemes negotiated in the context of collective worker-employer agreements. The law requires employers in the sector to be affiliated with the sectoral fund, subject to satisfying conditions for exemption.

Albany International BV was a textile company. It was not party to the collective agreement. It provided its own supplementary coverage through an insurer of its choice; it sought and was denied an exemption from the statutory scheme, and it refused to pay its mandatory contributions to the statutorily designated fund, the Textile Industry Trade Fund. When sued for arrears, it challenged the Dutch law's requirement of compulsory affiliation and the collective agreement providing for the designated fund, as contrary to Articles 3(g), 5, 85, 86 and 90 (now 3(1)(g), 10, 81, 82 and 86). Questions were referred to the Court of Justice.]

47 Albany contends that the request by management and labour to make affiliation to a sectoral pension fund compulsory constitutes an agreement between the undertakings operating in the sector concerned, contrary to Article 85 (1) of the Treaty.

⁴⁸ Such an agreement, in its view, restricts competition in two ways. First, by entrusting the operation of a compulsory scheme to a single manager, it deprives the undertakings operating in the sector concerned of the possibility of affiliation to another pension scheme managed by other insurers. Second, that agreement excludes the latter insurers from a substantial part of the pension insurance market.

⁴⁹ The effects of such an agreement on competition are 'appreciable' because it affects the entire Netherlands textile sector. They are aggravated by the cumulative effect of making affiliation to pension schemes compulsory in numerous sectors of the economy and for all undertakings in those sectors.

⁵⁰ Moreover, such an agreement affects trade between Member States in so far as it concerns undertakings which engage in cross-frontier business and deprives insurers established in other Member States of the opportunity to offer a full pension scheme in the Netherlands either by virtue of cross-frontier services or through branches or subsidiaries.

⁵¹ Therefore, according to Albany, by creating a legal framework for, and acceding to a request from, the two sides of industry to make affiliation to the sectoral pension fund compulsory, the public authorities favoured or furthered the implementation and operation of agreements between undertakings operating in the sectors concerned which are contrary to Article 85 (1) of the Treaty, thereby infringing Articles 3(g), 5 and 85 of the Treaty.

⁵² It is necessary to consider first whether a decision taken by the organisations representing employers and workers in a given sector, in the context of a collective agreement, to set up in that sector a single pension fund responsible for managing a supplementary pension scheme and to request the public authorities to make affiliation to that fund compulsory for all workers in that sector is contrary to Article 85 of the Treaty. * * *

⁵⁴ ... [I]t is important to bear in mind that, under Article 3 (g) and (i) of the EC Treaty (now Article 3(1)(g) and (j)), the activities of the Community are to include not only a 'system ensuring that competition in the internal market is not distorted' but also 'a policy in the social sphere'. Article 2 of the EC Treaty provides that a particular task of the Community is 'to promote throughout the Community a harmonious and balanced development of economic activities' and 'a high level of employment and of social protection'.

⁵⁵ In that connection, Article 118 of the EC Treaty (Articles 117 to 120 of the EC Treaty hav[ing] been replaced by Articles 136 EC to 143 EC) provides that the Commission is to promote close cooperation between Member States in the social field, particularly in matters relating to the right of association and collective bargaining between employers and workers.

⁵⁶ Article 118b of the EC Treaty (Articles 117 to 120 of the EC Treaty having been replaced by Articles 136 EC to 143 EC) adds that the Commission is to endeavour to develop the dialogue between management and labour at European level which could, if the two sides consider it desirable, lead to relations based on agreement.

⁵⁷ Moreover, Article 1 of the Agreement on social policy (OJ 1992 C 191, p. 91) states that the objectives to be pursued by the Community and the

Member States include improved living and working conditions, proper social protection, dialogue between management and labour, the development of human resources with a view to lasting high employment and the combatting of exclusion.

58   Under Article 4(1) and (2) of the Agreement, the dialogue between management and labour at Community level may lead, if they so desire, to contractual relations, including agreements, which will be implemented either in accordance with the procedures and practices specific to management and labour and the Member States, or, at the joint request of the signatory parties, by a Council decision on a proposal from the Commission.

59   It is beyond question that certain restrictions of competition are inherent in collective agreements between organisations representing employers and workers. However, the social policy objectives pursued by such agreements would be seriously undermined if management and labour were subject to Article 85 (1) of the Treaty when seeking jointly to adopt measures to improve conditions of work and employment.

60   It therefore follows from an interpretation of the provisions of the Treaty as a whole which is both effective and consistent that agreements concluded in the context of collective negotiations between management and labour in pursuit of such objectives must, by virtue of their nature and purpose, be regarded as falling outside the scope of Article 85 (1) of the Treaty.

61   The next question is therefore whether the nature and purpose of the agreement at issue in the main proceedings justify its exclusion from the scope of Article 85 (1) of the Treaty.

62   First, like the category of agreements referred to above which derive from social dialogue, the agreement at issue in the main proceedings was concluded in the form of a collective agreement and is the outcome of collective negotiations between organisations representing employers and workers.

63   Second, as far as its purpose is concerned, that agreement establishes, in a given sector, a supplementary pension scheme managed by a pension fund to which affiliation may be made compulsory. Such a scheme seeks generally to guarantee a certain level of pension for all workers in that sector and therefore contributes directly to improving one of their working conditions, namely their remuneration.

64   Consequently, the agreement at issue in the main proceedings does not, by reason of its nature and purpose, fall within the scope of Article 85 (1) of the Treaty.

Notes and Questions

1.   Albany articulated a number of ways in which the requirement of compulsory affiliation harmed competition: it could not choose its own insurer; it could get a better rate from its own insurer, which was likely to be more efficient than a monopolist fund; insurers—including non-Dutch insurers—would be deprived of access to the market. Indeed the Court, finding the sectoral pension fund to be an undertaking, observed that the fund was engaged in economic activity in competi-

tion with insurance companies, and that its pursuit of a social objective through cross-subsidization of risks ("manifestations of solidarity") could render its services less competitive than comparable services. paras 84–86. See also paras 97–98: competition was restricted; firms might otherwise provide their workers with a superior scheme. Why wouldn't these effects bring the agreement within Article 81(1), leaving the question of overriding social benefits for analysis under 81(3)?

2. Did the Court simply, in effect, grant an exemption to bona fide labor agreements? Was this a good idea?

In the United States, Section 6 of the Clayton Act grants an exemption to agreements among workers (e.g., collaboration under the auspices of labor unions). "The labor of a human being is not a commodity or article of commerce." The courts have expanded the exemption to cover bona fide labor negotiations, including by employers, and the resulting collective bargaining agreements. This is called the non-statutory labor exemption.

3. After *Albany*, and in view of the Court's invocation of the social aspects of the Treaty, how would you expect the Commission and Court to treat agreements other than collective bargaining agreements that allegedly promise benefits to jobs and workers? Can benefits to workers and the economy be balanced against harms to competition as aspects of economic progress under Article 81(3)?

H. BLOCK EXEMPTIONS

We noted at the outset of the chapter the two important block exemptions on horizontal cooperation: research and development, and specialisation. In year 2000, the Commission revised most block exemptions in an attempt to move from a formalistic regulatory approach to a more open economic approach. The Commission recognizes that most R & D cooperation and most specialisation agreements are efficient.

1. RESEARCH AND DEVELOPMENT

Research and development lies at the core of innovation, competition, and competitiveness. The R & D block exemption singles out cooperative research and development for protection. The block exemption is contained in Commission Regulation 2659/2000, O.J. L 304/7, (Dec. 5, 2000), printed in the Selected Documents as Competition Doc. No. 6.

Of course not all R & D agreements fall within Article 81(1). Collaboration of small enterprises are normally not caught. Moreover, collaboration on pure R & D even by large firms generally does not fall within Article 81(1) unless the parties agree not to carry out R & D in the same field. Recital (3).

Article 1 of the regulation declares exempt joint R & D and joint exploitation of its results, and necessary ancillary restraints including agreement not to carry out independently or with third parties R & D in the same or a closely related field, as long as the parties' market share does not exceed 25%[2] and the agreement does not include black-listed clauses. Moreover, to qualify for block exemption: 1) each party must have access to the results in order to further its research, 2) the supplying partner, in the event of specialisation not entailing joint distribution, must fulfill orders for supplies

---

2. Where the parties are not competitors in the market of the improvement, the cap begins to apply seven years from the time the goods are first marketed in the Community.

from other partners, and 3) in the event of joint exploitation, the results must be IP-protected and must be sufficiently important; i.e., they must:

> substantially contribute to technical or economic progress and ... be decisive for the manufacture of the contract products or the application of the contract processes. Art. 3(4).[3]

Contemplate the above qualifying clauses. Are they difficult to fulfill? How difficult is it for parties to assess whether their agreement meets the qualifications? Which requirement is most indeterminate?

Black list. The group exemption does not apply to agreements that have as their object:

1) restriction on the freedom of parties to carry out R & D independently or with third parties in an unconnected field, or, after completion of the subject R & D, any field,

2) agreement not to challenge validity of IP rights,

3) restriction on output or sales,

4) fixing prices of the contract product to third parties,

5) after 7 years of putting the product on the common market, restriction on customers,

6) restricting passive sales in territories reserved for other parties,

7) after 7 years on the common market, restricting active sales in others' territories,

8) absent exploitation by one or more of the parties, prohibition on granting licenses to manufacture or apply,

9) requirement to refuse to meet demand of buyers who would resell in other territories in the common market,

10) requirement to make it difficult for buyers to obtain the product from other resellers in the common market, e.g. by the use of IP rights;

except that joint producers may set production targets, and joint distributors may set sales targets and the price of their product. (Art. 5)

What is the reason for black-listing each practice? Is it sound?

The Commission may withdraw the exemption if it finds that effects incompatible with Article 81(3) may occur; in particular, if it finds that:

1) the agreements substantially restrict third parties' scope for R & D or their access to the contract product,

2) without justification, the parties do not exploit the results,

3) the contract products face no effective competition, or

4) the agreement eliminates effective R & D competition in a market.

Parties to agreements that fall outside of the block exemption (e.g., because their market exceeds 25%), may seek an individual exemption.

In the same year that the Community adopted its first block exemption for joint research and development, the United States Congress enacted the National Cooperative Research Act (NCRA) of 1984, which was amended in

---

3. This is a thumbnail sketch. It generalizes the regulation, which should be consulted.

1993. 15 U.S.C.A. § 4301. Congress feared that the antitrust laws were chilling research and development, especially in view of the fact that successful private plaintiffs are entitled to three times the damage they suffer. The NCRA states that research joint ventures shall be judged under a rule of reason in view of all relevant market facts and shall not be condemned per se. Also, Congress provided a notification procedure. If a transaction is notified and is later found to lessen competition, the parties can be assessed compensatory damages but not treble damages. This protection applies to the production phase of a research joint venture but only if the principal production facilities are in the United States and the controlling persons are American or from a country with equally favorable antitrust treatment. (Is this consistent with GATT obligations of non-discrimination?) A notified transaction may be enjoined if it is found to be anticompetitive.

The NCRA makes no distinction as to firm size. It applies equally to large and small firms.

How significant is the US special treatment for R & D joint ventures? Would you expect the US statute to encourage research and development? Would you expect the European block exemption to encourage research and development?

2. SPECIALISATION

The specialisation block exemption is provided by Commission Regulation 2658/2000, and may be found at O.J. L 304/3 (Dec. 5, 2000). It is printed in the Selected Documents as Competition Doc. No. 5.

At the outset, the Commission contemplated reciprocal specialisation: one firm made product A, the other made complementary product B; they would each agree to supply their specialty product to the other, and they would each agree not to manufacture the product that was the specialty of the other. More recently, firms began to adopt unilateral specialisation: A outsources from B; B agrees to manufacture and supply to A all of its needs of an input. A agrees to cease its production of that input. The block exemption covers reciprocal specialisation and unilateral specialisation between competitors. The regulation recites that specialisation agreements generally contribute to improving production or distribution because they enable firms to concentrate on the manufacture of certain products and thus to operate more efficiently and supply goods more cheaply.

Article 1 of the specialisation exemption declares exempt agreements for specialisation, including ancillary restraints necessary for their implementation, where the combined market shares do not exceed 20%, except for blacklisted provisions. The exemption also applies where the parties agree to exclusive purchase or supply in the context of specialisation or joint production, or the parties do not separately distribute the objects of specialisation but provide for joint distribution or distribution by a non-competitor. (Arts. 3, 4)

Black list. The exemption does not apply to agreements that have as their object:

1) price fixing to third parties,

2) limiting output or sales, or

3) allocating markets or customers;

except that parties may agree on the amount of goods in the context of specialisation, or the production volume of a production joint venture, and on sales targets and on prices and a production joint venture charges its direct customers. (Art. 5)

The exemption may be withdrawn if the Commission finds that the agreement has effects incompatible with Article 81(3); in particular: a) "the agreement is not yielding significant results in terms of rationalisation or consumers are not receiving a fair share of the resulting benefit," or (b) the subject products are not subject to effective competition. (Art. 7 (a)-(b))

Parties that fall outside the block exemption may seek individual exemption.

Why is it necessary for competitors, seeking to achieve the efficiency benefits of specialisation, to promise to stay out of the manufacturing market of the other? In the United States, this aspect of specialisation agreements would normally be regarded as a cartel-like violation of the law, unless the parties could meet a rather high burden to show that the commitment was necessary to make the joint venture work.

On the other hand, if the combined market shares are not in excess of 20%, how could the agreement possibly harm competition? Why is a block exemption necessary at all? Is it because of the breadth of Article 81(1)? Is Article 7(b) surplus?

Why should the Commission be able to withdraw the benefit of the block exemption if the agreement is not yielding significant results in terms of rationalisation? (Art. 7(a)) Does this clause indicate that the Commission believes the agreements are necessarily anticompetitive and are justifiable only if they produce outbalancing efficiencies? Do you agree?

I. GUIDELINES

In 2001 the Commission issued guidelines on the applicability of Article 81 to horizontal cooperation agreements. O.J. C 3/2 (Jan. 6, 2001). The guidelines give long and detailed guidance. Their analytical framework is summarized in the Commission's XXXth Report on Competition Policy (2000) as follows:

[28] The guidelines complement the block exemption regulations. They describe the general approach which should be followed when assessing horizontal cooperation agreements. They are thus applicable to R & D and production agreements not covered by the block exemptions as well as to all other common types of competitor collaboration. The following types are covered: R & D, production, purchasing, marketing, standardisation and environmental agreements. The guidelines describe the general approach which should be followed when assessing horizontal cooperation agreements and set out a common analytical framework. This will help companies to assess with greater certainty whether or not an agreement restricts competition and, if so, whether it would qualify for an exemption.

[29] All types of horizontal cooperation agreement covered are analysed according to a common analytical framework. This framework can be summar-

ised as follows: a horizontal cooperation agreement is only able to restrict competition if it is likely to reduce competition in the market to such an extent that negative market effects as to prices, output, innovation or the variety or quality of goods and services can be expected. To cause a restriction of competition the parties normally need appropriate tools to coordinate their behaviour and a degree of market power. Consequently, cooperation has to be assessed in its economic context taking into account both the nature of the agreement and the parties' combined market power, which determine—together with other structural factors—the capability of the cooperation to reduce overall competition to such a significant extent.

30   These two criteria normally have to be assessed together. There are, however, some instances where the nature of the cooperation indicates from the outset that it is caught by Article 81(1). This concerns primarily agreements that have the object of restricting competition by means of price fixing, output limitation or sharing of markets, customers or sources of supply. These so-called "hardcore" restrictions are considered to be the most harmful, because they directly interfere with the outcome of the competitive process. It can therefore be presumed that these restrictions have negative market effects and do not result in any efficiency gains or benefits to consumers. They are therefore almost always prohibited.

31   On the other hand, there are also some horizontal agreements regarding which it can be said from the outset Article 81(1) does not generally apply. These include agreements between non-competitors, agreements between competing companies that cannot independently carry out the project or activity covered by the cooperation, or cooperation concerning an activity which does not influence the relevant parameters of competition. These cooperation agreements could only come under Article 81(1) if they involve firms with significant market power and are likely to cause foreclosure problems vis-à-vis third parties.

32   All other agreements need to be examined in the light of each of the two criteria (nature of the agreement and market power and market structure) in order to decide whether they fall under Article 81(1).

33   The discussion by category of agreement makes it easier to take account of specific competition problems related to the different forms of cooperation. It also addresses the most common types of combination, e.g. joint R & D with subsequent joint production.

34   In the absence of hardcore restrictions and below a certain level of market power, defined in terms of market share, the guidelines provide so called "safe havens" for purchasing agreements and marketing agreements. Similar to coverage by a block exemption regulation, once inside these safe havens, economic operators do not normally have to assess the impact of their agreements on the market.

35   In the case of purchasing agreements, while recognising that there is no absolute threshold which indicates that buying cooperation creates some degree of market power and thus falls under Article 81(1), the guidelines stress that in most cases it is unlikely that such market power exists if the parties to the agreement have a combined market share of less than 15% on the purchasing market(s) as well as a combined market share of less than 15% on the selling market(s). Where an agreement below these

market share thresholds falls under Article 81(1), the guidelines state that below those levels of market share it is likely to fulfil the conditions of Article 81(3).

[36] In the case of marketing agreements which do not involve the fixing of prices, the guidelines stress that, in most cases, it is unlikely that a sufficient degree of market power exists if the parties to the agreement have a combined market share of less than 15%. Where an agreement below this level of market share falls under Article 81(1), the guidelines state that below this level of market share it is likely to fulfil the conditions of Article 81(3).

Do the block exemptions fit tightly with the scheme of the guidelines?

The United States agencies have also promulgated guidelines on competitor collaboration. They were published in year 2000 and can be found at 4 CCH Trade Reg. Rep. ¶ 13,160.

In both cases the guidelines are very general and it is important to examine the caselaw to understand the application of the rules. A main difference between US and EC law lies in the bifurcated structure of Article 81. Article 81(1) is "wide." It catches many agreements that, in the United States, would not be deemed anticompetitive because they do not create, facilitate or reflect the use of market power and resulting higher prices to consumers. If an agreement is caught by Article 81(1), the parties must justify the agreement under the four factors of Article 81(3). In the EU, proof that the agreement does not create, facilitate or reflect the use of market power is not a defense. Consider the importance of burdens. Can burdens influence outcomes?

It is an expressed hope of some European competition officials that modernisation will make analysis under Article 81(1) and (3) more nearly seamless. If so, will the difference between US and EC analysis tend to fade?

Chapter 24

VERTICAL RESTRAINTS
UNDER ARTICLE 81

A. VERTICAL RESTRAINTS AND THEIR EFFECTS

Vertical restraints are restraints in the course of distributing a product or service, or in the course of bringing technology and its commercial applications to market.

In distribution agreements, a producer might instruct its distributor where or to whom to sell the product, and at what price. Since a producer offers a particular kind or brand of product, the restraints that a producer imposes on its distributors are called intrabrand restraints.

Intrabrand restraints may help a producer get to market more efficiently, e.g., by giving the distributor a stronger incentive to work its territory and by preventing "free riders" (who do not invest in the territory) from "skimming the cream" off the top of the demand primed by the designated distributor's investment. If the restraints are cost-effective and if the brands in the market compete robustly against one another, the interbrand competition will probably ensure that consumers receive the benefits of the restraints.

However, in some circumstances, intrabrand restraints may also help the producer *exploit* the consumer. For example, in a concentrated, high barrier market, the restraints may help the few producers coordinate their prices; or they may help an individual producer with market power extract more money from consumers. For these reasons, resale price fixing agreements that set minimum prices (RPM) are illegal on their face in the EU, in the United States, and in many other jurisdictions (even while economists point out that a firm might in theory use RPM as an efficient business strategy to cause its distributors to provide more service).

We have seen that a principal goal of EC competition law is to integrate the common market. Can intrabrand restraints that prevent parallel imports calcify price differentials among Member States and undermine the market integration goal? But can prohibition of those restraints undermine the efficiency goal? Is there a tension between integration and efficiency?

The first vertical restraint case to reach the Court of Justice under Article 85 (now 81) posed such a challenge.

B. PARALLEL IMPORTS AND EXPORTS

CONSTEN AND GRUNDIG v. COMMISSION

Cases 56, 58/64, [1966] ECR 299
Reread case, at p. 791 *supra*.

NOTE ON DISTILLERS COMPANY LTD. v. COMMISSION

Distillers Company Ltd. (DCL), the world's largest seller of Scotch whiskey, established 38 subsidiaries producing spirits in the United Kingdom. It accounted for approximately 70% of all gin sales in the UK, 30% to 50% of Scotch whiskey in the UK, and lower percentages on the Continent.

DCL imposed the following conditions of sale:

(a) "[T]he various allowances, rebates and discounts are designed to meet the particular requirements of the home trade and customers are only entitled to them when the goods are in fact consumed within the UK."

(b) "Accordingly, if you wish to buy for export to other Common Market countries you must indicate this on your order and purchase must be made at the gross price."

(c) "... If ... a customer obtains or claims any home trade allowances, rebates or discounts in respect of goods which he has bought and any of those goods turn up in any country outside the UK, the right is reserved for all companies in the DCL group to sell thereafter to such customer only at the gross price."

The punitive measures were to be applicable in the following circumstances:

"When a DCL subsidiary has a reasonable belief that any quantity of goods bought by the purchaser from any DCL subsidiary has been or will be consumed outside the United Kingdom;

even when the exports are made by a subsequent purchaser;

regardless of the quantity ordered, until and to the extent that the purchaser produces evidence satisfactory to the selling DCL subsidiary company that the goods will be consumed in the United Kingdom."

When investigated by the Commission, Distillers claimed that its dual pricing was justified by the following facts: In the UK its brands were very well known, prices were depressed by price controls, and Distillers sold directly to very large and powerful brewery groups that had retail outlets and that demanded very low prices. Outside of the UK, the brands were unknown. Moreover, France banned advertisements, and some countries imposed discriminatory taxes. Distillers had to invest significant additional amounts of money for promotion on the Continent if it was to sell there at all.

The Commission declared that Distillers price agreements would not be granted an exemption under Article 85(3) because the dual pricing system interfered with parallel imports and isolated the UK market. Distillers then withdrew Johnnie Walker Red Label and Dimple Haig whiskeys from sale in the UK, stating that it could not make sales at the higher price in the UK and it could not cover promotion costs if it sold at the lower price on the Continent. It announced a new brand to replace Johnnie Walker. Distillers sued for annulment of the Commission's decision. The Court of Justice held, simply, that the legal effect of Distillers' failure to notify the price terms was that the price terms could not be exempted. Case 30/78, [1980] ECR 2229.

We have noted that US law is different from EC law with respect to vertical restraints on parallel imports or exports. In the United States, such restraints, like all vertical restraints other than minimum resale price fixing, are presumptively efficient and procompetitive. Consider the following two US cases.

BUSINESS ELECTRONICS CORP. v. SHARP ELECTRONICS CORP.

485 U.S. 717, 108 S.Ct. 1515, 99 L.Ed.2d 808 (1988).

JUSTICE SCALIA: ... Although vertical agreements on resale prices have been illegal *per se** since Dr. Miles Medical Co. v. John D. Park & Sons Co., 220 U.S. 373 (1911), we have recognized that the scope of *per se* illegality should be narrow in the context of vertical restraints. In Continental T.V., Inc. v. GTE Sylvania Inc. [433 U.S. 36 (1977)], we refused to extend *per se* illegality to vertical nonprice restraints, specifically to a manufacturer's termination of one dealer pursuant to an exclusive territory agreement with another. We noted that especially in the vertical restraint context "departure from the rule-of-reason standard must be based on demonstrable economic effect rather than ... upon formalistic line drawing." *Id.,* at 58–59. We concluded that vertical nonprice restraints had not been shown to have such a " 'pernicious effect on competition' " and to be so " 'lack[ing] [in] ... redeeming value' " as to justify *per se* illegality. Rather, we found, they had real potential to stimulate interbrand competition, "the primary concern of antitrust law," 433 U.S., at 52, n. 19:

> "[N]ew manufacturers and manufacturers entering new markets can use the restrictions in order to induce competent and aggressive retailers to make the kind of investment of capital and labor that is often required in the distribution of products unknown to the consumer. Established manufacturers can use them to induce retailers to engage in promotional activities or to provide service and repair facilities necessary to the efficient marketing of their products. Service and repair are vital for many products.... The availability and quality of such services affect a manufacturer's goodwill and the competitiveness of his product. Because of market imperfections such as the so-called 'free-rider' effect, these services might not be provided by retailers in a purely competitive situation, despite the fact that each retailer's benefit would be greater if all provided the services than if none did." Id., at 55.

Moreover, we observed that a rule of *per se* illegality for vertical nonprice restraints was not needed or effective to protect *intra*brand competition. First,

---

* Editors' note: Illegal per se means illegal on its face without regard to underlying facts that could otherwise be relevant to purpose or effect.

so long as interbrand competition existed, that would provide a "significant check" on any attempt to exploit intrabrand market power. In fact, in order to meet that interbrand competition, a manufacturer's dominant incentive is to lower resale prices. Second, the *per se* illegality of vertical restraints would create a perverse incentive for manufacturers to integrate vertically into distribution, an outcome hardly conducive to fostering the creation and maintenance of small businesses.

Finally, our opinion in *GTE Sylvania* noted a significant distinction between vertical nonprice and vertical price restraints. That is, there was support for the proposition that vertical price restraints reduce *inter*brand price competition because they " 'facilitate cartelizing.' " Id., at 51, n. 18, quoting Posner, Antitrust Policy and the Supreme Court: An Analysis of the Restricted Distribution, Horizontal Merger and Potential Competition Decisions, 75 Colum.L.Rev. 282, 294 (1975). The authorities cited by the Court suggested how vertical price agreements might assist horizontal price fixing at the manufacturer level (by reducing the manufacturer's incentive to cheat on a cartel, since its retailers could not pass on lower prices to consumers) or might be used to organize cartels at the retailer level. Similar support for the cartel-facilitating effect of vertical nonprice restraints was and remains lacking. * * *

———

Therefore, according to the Court, the agreement between the manufacturer and its full-price distributor to cut off the discounter was not suspect and would not be illegal unless the cut-off discounter could show that the cut off would cause prices of business calculators in the market as whole to rise.

———

VALLEY LIQUORS, INC. v. RENFIELD IMPORTERS, LTD.

678 F.2d 742 (7th Cir.1982).

JUDGE POSNER: . . . We reject the equation of intrabrand price competition with interbrand competition. The elimination of a price cutter who is taking a free ride on the promotional efforts of competing distributors will tend to stimulate nonprice competition among the distributors at the same time that it dampens price competition among them, so that the net effect on intrabrand competition need not be negative. In any event, the suggestion that proof of a reduction in intrabrand competition creates a presumption of illegality is inconsistent with the test that the courts apply in restricted distribution cases. . . . The plaintiff in a restricted distribution case must show that the restriction he is complaining of was unreasonable because, weighing effects on both intrabrand and interbrand competition, it made consumers worse off.

Admittedly, this test of illegality is easier to state than to apply, the effects to be weighed being so difficult to measure or even estimate by the methods of litigation. The courts have therefore looked for shortcuts. A popular one is to say that the balance tips in the defendant's favor if the plaintiff fails to show that the defendant has significant market power (that is, power to raise prices significantly above the competitive level without losing all of one's business).

... A firm that has no market power is unlikely to adopt policies that disserve its consumers; it cannot afford to. And if it blunders and does adopt such a policy, market retribution will be swift. Thus its mistakes do not seriously threaten consumer welfare, which is the objective that we are told should guide us in interpreting the Sherman Act....

Since market power can rarely be measured directly by the methods of litigation, it is normally inferred from possession of a substantial percentage of the sales in a market carefully defined in terms of both product and geography. In this case no evidence of market share was presented. In fact, no market was defined, either in product or in geographical terms, so that we do not have even a rough idea whether Renfield [the liquor firm limiting distribution of its product] was a big firm in its market or a small firm. * * *

Notes and Questions

1.　What was the probable purpose and effect of Grundig's parallel restraints and Distillers' dual pricing? How did they isolate the French/UK markets? Whom did they hurt?

2.　Compare Judge Posner's judicial opinion, above, with Advocate General Roemer's opinion in *Consten and Grundig*. Why did the Court reject the Roemer/Posner approach?

3.　Review the free movement/industrial property (exhaustion-of-rights) *Centrafarm* cases, Chapter 19D *supra*. Relate these cases to the parallel import and export competition cases. Consider the strong principles for free movement and market integration and against the partitioning of markets. Are you convinced, in both sets of cases, that the Court's rules of law promote market integration? What is their effect on efficiency and competitiveness?

NOTE ON SA MUSIQUE DIFFUSION FRANÇAISE v. COMMISSION (PIONEER)

A few years after *Distillers* the Court of Justice reaffirmed the egregiousness of restraints on parallel imports and exports. Pioneer produced high fidelity music equipment. Wholesalers of electronic products in France discovered that they could purchase Pioneer hi-fi equipment from the German and the UK exclusive distributors at a price 30% lower than the price charged by Pioneer's French exclusive distributor, MDF. The French wholesalers bought from the UK and German sources, and MDF complained to Pioneer. Pioneer organized a meeting. Immediately thereafter the French wholesalers' cheap, out-of-state supply dried up. According to MDF and Pioneer, Pioneer's share of the hi-fi market was just over 3% in France and in the UK.

The Commission brought proceedings and assessed unusually high fines at 2% and 4% of total turnover, even though only a small part of the companies' turnover related to hi-fi equipment and the fines would nearly bankrupt the German distributor. The Court of Justice rejected all arguments of the applicants. Cases 100–103/80, [1983] ECR 1825. It stated, in connection with the level of fines:

[104] According to the Commission, however, such a level is fully justified by the nature of the infringements. After 20 years of Community competition policy an appreciable increase in the level of fines is necessary, in its view, at least for types of infringement which have long been well defined and are known to those concerned, such as prohibitions on exports and imports. In fact those constitute the most serious infringements since they deprive consumers of all the benefits resulting from the elimination of customs duties and quantitative restrictions; they hinder the integration of the economies of the Member States and leave distributors and retailers in a position of subordination towards producers. Heavier fines are particularly necessary where, as in the present case, the principal aim of the infringement is to maintain a higher level of prices for consumers. The Commission states that many undertakings carry on conduct which they know to be contrary to Community law because the profit which they derive from their unlawful conduct exceeds the fines imposed hitherto. Conduct of that kind can only be deterred by fines which are heavier than in the past. * * *

[107] [T]he Commission was right to classify as very serious infringements prohibitions on exports and imports seeking artificially to maintain price differences between the markets of the various Member States. Such prohibitions jeopardize the freedom of intra-Community trade, which is a fundamental principle of the Treaty, and they prevent the attainment of one of its objectives, namely the creation of a single market.

Notes and Questions

We have seen the seriousness with which the Court treats producers' agreements requiring their distributors to refrain from parallel exports and empowering them to block parallel imports. Can a company achieve the same effect by setting up its own distribution business or by buying its distributors? In *Viho Europe v. Commission*, Case T–102/92, [1995] ECR II–217, affirmed, Case C–73/95P, [1996] ECR I–5457, Viho, a wholesale importer/exporter, complained that Parker Pen imposed export bans on Parker's wholly-owned subsidiaries. The Commission rejected the complaint, and Viho sued for annulment of the Commission's decision to reject the complaint. The Court of First Instance rebuffed Viho. It stated that Parker controlled the behavior of its subsidiaries and therefore Parker and its subsidiaries acted as a single economic unit; therefore the territorial division of responsibilities could not run afoul of Article 85(1).

NOTE ON VOLKSWAGEN AG v. COMMISSION

In the early 1990s when the Italian lire was weak against the Deutsche mark, Volkswagen feared a rush of German and Austrian car buyers to Italy. Through its Italian subsidiary Autogerma, which had agreements with its Italian dealers, it took measures to stem the tide that would undermine the business of its German and Austrian dealers (see Chapter 18): Autogerma limited the supplies of VWs and Audis sold to Italian dealers. It undertook to pay a 3% bonus to its dealers based on vehicles sold in their territory, plus vehicles sold outside of their territory if those sales did not exceed 15% of their sales. It threatened to and did terminate dealers who made "excessive sales" outside of their territory. Autogerma instituted "a systematic policy of surveillance of dealers" to police the sales each dealer made outside of its territory.

Forewarned of the policy, Italian dealers refrained from exporting the vehicles and German dealers ceased importing them. The Commission concluded that the measures were part of the contractual relations under the selective distribution system; that they infringed Article 85(1), now 81(1); and that an individual exemption would not have been forthcoming even if the agreement had been notified because "the barriers to re-exportation are at variance with the objective of consumer protection set out in Article 85(3) of the Treaty." (para. 26) The Court of First Instance affirmed. Case T–62/98, [2000] ECR II–2707.

Notes and Questions

1. In *Volkswagen*, the court did not require the Commission to define the market on grounds that it was obvious that the agreement affected trade between Member States and had as its object or effect the prevention, restriction, or distortion of competition in the common market. In this respect the rule against agreements to prevent parallel imports/exports is equivalent to, in US terminology, a *per se* rule. Indeed, in the 1960s and 1970s (but no longer), US law prohibited *per se* just such agreements as identified in the *VW* case.

Today in the United States, the VW-type restraint would be governed by the analysis in *Business Electronics,* supra page 910, and *Valley Liquors,* supra p. 911. Does this analysis fit the single-market concerns of Europe? Consider the motor vehicle block exemption, http://europa.eu.int/comm/competition/car_sector/ and pages 798–99 supra. Comment on the different approaches of the US and the EU to intrabrand restraints and their regulation.

2. Was VW/Autogerm's action essentially unilateral, or was it essentially concerted (with dealers)? Did the dealers consent? Did they have a choice? Should so much turn on whether the measures are characterized as concerted or unilateral?

3. In *Bayer v. Commission (Adalat)*, Case T–41/96, [2000] ECR II–3383, Bayer, producer of the cardio-vascular-treating drug Adalat, faced several Member States with widely varying price ceilings. The controlled price in France and Spain was 40% lower than in the UK. Bayer took measures to prevent arbitrage by French and Spanish wholesalers from undermining its market. It provided supplies of the drug to the French and Spanish wholesalers at their historic base plus 10% (to reflect expected growth), and placed obligations on the wholesalers to serve their territories. It knew that the wholesalers would make marginal exports whenever they could, and that they did not accept no-export limitations. The Commission found that the conduct was concerted and violated of Article 85(1); it imposed a fine of 3 million ECUs. The Court of First Instance annulled the decision, however, concluding that there was no "common intention" between Bayer and the wholesalers.

Where is the line between *VW* and *Bayer*? Is Bayer's conduct virtually as "bad" as VW's, but just cleverly beyond reach? Or is VW's conduct virtually as good or normal as Bayer's, but VW just crossed a technical line? Was Bayer's fate fortuitous, in the sense that its wholesalers never said (and surely not in writing): "I understand your policy. I know I must please you because I wish to protect my valuable line of supply of Adalat. Therefore I will comply."

VW and *Bayer* find resonances in the history and evolution of US antitrust law. For years, restraints against parallel imports and exports (tight territorial confinement) as well as resale price agreements, were illegal *per se*; and courts were very quick to find agreements. Most of the caselaw on concerted or unilateral action arose in connection with RPM. A simple refusal to sell to (or a cut-off of) dealers that failed to comply with a stated resale price is unilateral and not illegal (the *"Colgate"* doctrine). Concerted action was found, and condemned, however, in United States v. Parke, Davis & Co., 362 U.S. 29, 80 S.Ct. 503, 4 L.Ed.2d 505 (1960), where Parke Davis, a pharmaceutical producer, announced an RPM policy to its wholesalers and retailers, and it policed the policy, bringing discounting drug stores into line. After *Parke Davis*, dictum of the courts warned that there was a thin line between *Colgate* and *Parke Davis*. A refusal to deal with non-compliers could quickly spill over into concertation. As one court said: "The Supreme Court has left a narrow channel through which a manufacturer may pass even though the facts would have to be of such Doric simplicity as to be somewhat rare in this day of complex business enterprise." George W. Warner & Co. v. Black & Decker Mfg. Co., 277 F.2d 787, 790 (2d Cir.1960).

The Federal Trade Commission tested the line in a case against Russell Stover Candies. Stover had a widespread and intricate system for designating resale prices and terminating retailers who sold more cheaply. However, it neither requested nor accepted assurances of compliance from retailers. The Commission found concerted action between Stover and the multitude of retailers who unwillingly complied in order to avoid termination. 100 FTC 1, 45–46 (1982). Stover appealed and won. Unwilling compliance alone, the court said, is neither assent nor sufficient coercion. Russell Stover Candies, Inc. v. FTC, 718 F.2d 256 (8th Cir.1983).

Bayer, like Stover, walked successfully through the channel. But is the channel of the same dimensions in the US and in the EU? Consider the CFI's description in *Bayer*:

[71] Th[e] case law shows that a distinction should be drawn between cases in which an undertaking has adopted a genuinely unilateral measure, and thus without the express or implied participation of another undertaking, and those in which the unilateral character of the measure is merely apparent. Whilst the former do not fall within Article 85(1) of the Treaty, the latter must be regarded as revealing an agreement between undertakings and may therefore fall within the scope of that article. That is the case, in particular, with practices and measures in restraint of competition which, though apparently adopted unilaterally by the manufacturer in the context of its contractual relations with its dealers, nevertheless receive at least the tacit acquiescence of those dealers.

What does the court mean by: "the unilateral character ... is merely apparent"? What is "tacit acquiescence"? Did the intimidated candy stores in *Russell Stover* "acquiesce" in Stover's demands?

Note the essential difference between concert among competitors, and "concert" between a producer and its distributor. In horizontal cases, the effectiveness of the conspiracy depends on concert. Each member of a cartel must pull its oar. Nedchem could not have restrained competition in quinine without the reciprocal undertaking of Boeringer, et al., and vice versa. But in vertical cases where the producer has the power, the distributor must "take it or leave it." Why does "I acquiesce" turn the conduct into an agreement?

4. If goods are put on the market with the consent of the trademark owner in one Member State, a firm may not assert its trademark rights to prevent the import of goods into another Member State. This is the doctrine of exhaustion; see Chapter 19D *supra*. In *Silhouette*, Case C–355/96, [1998] ECR I–4799, the Court of Justice held that there is no international exhaustion; a firm may assert its trademark rights to prevent imports from abroad.

Does *Silhouette* imply that producers' decisions to assign out airtight markets to distributors harm market integration but not necessarily competition? If Consten used its French trademark GINT to bar shipments of Grundig electronic products from America, how would you analyze the restraint under Article 81?

C. EXCLUSIVE PURCHASING, TYING AND RELATED FORECLOSURES

A producer or other seller of a product may wish to obligate its distributor or other buyers to buy the product, or a portion of its needs, only from the seller. For example, in *Hoffmann-La Roche*, page 833 supra, vitamin producer Merck contracted with the dominant vitamin producer Hoffmann–La Roche to buy from Roche its needs of vitamin B_6 in excess of its own manufacturing capacity. And in *Tetra Pak*, page 863 supra, the dominant supplier of aseptic cartons for milk and juice required buyers to buy, also, their needs of non-aseptic cartons. In both cases the Court condemned the requirements as abuses of dominance on grounds that they "deprive[d] the purchaser of or restrict[ed] his possible choices of sources of supply and ... den[ied] other producers access to the market." [quoting from *Hoffmann-La Roche*].

Are exclusive, requirements or tie-in contracts of dominant, and possibly not dominant, firms also caught by Article 81(1)? Under what conditions? Can they be justified under Article 81(3)? Note that the clauses may have efficiency benefits. Their adoption may be responsive to market conditions, such as the need of the buyer for an assured source of supply or, in the case of tying, the interest of the seller in protecting its reputation.

STERGIOS DELIMITIS v. HENNINGER BRÄU AG

Case C–234/89, [1991] ECR I–935.

[Stergios Delimitis rented a pub from Henninger Bräu, agreeing to sell only Henninger Bräu beer in the pub. Asserting that the contract violated Article 85 and was void, Delimitis failed to pay rent, and Henninger deducted the rent from Delimitis' rental deposit. Delimitis sued for return of the rent. Henninger relied on the contract, which presumably was not intended to distort competition but reflected the brewery's desire for an assured outlet for its beer and Delimitis' desire for the premises and an assured supply.

The national court sought a preliminary ruling on whether the contract was caught by Article 85(1) and if so whether it fell within the block exemption on exclusive purchasing (see F. below). The Court of Justice set forth the following framework for determining whether exclusive contracts that are part of a network of similar contracts have the effect, if not the object, of "preventing, restricting or distorting competition":]

15   . . . [I]t is necessary to analyse the effects of a beer supply agreement, taken together with other contracts of the same type, on the opportunities of national competitors or those from other Member States, to gain access to the market for beer consumption or to increase their market share and, accordingly, the effects on the range of products offered to consumers.
* * *

18   [The relevant market is] the national market for beer distribution in premises for the sale and consumption of drinks.

19   In order to assess whether the existence of several beer supply agreements impedes access to the market as so defined, it is further necessary to examine the nature and extent of those agreements in their totality, comprising all similar contracts tying a large number of points of sale to several national producers. The effect of those networks of contracts on access to the market depends specifically on the number of outlets thus tied to national producers in relation to the number of public houses which are not so tied, the duration of the commitments entered into, the quantities of beer to which those commitments relate, and on the proportion between those quantities and the quantities sold by free distributors.

20   The existence of a bundle of similar contracts, even if it has a considerable effect on the opportunities for gaining access to the market, is not, however, sufficient in itself to support a finding that the relevant market is inaccessible, inasmuch as it is only one factor, amongst others, pertaining to the economic and legal context in which an agreement must be appraised. The other factors to be taken into account are, in the first instance, those also relating to opportunities for access.

21   In that connection it is necessary to examine whether there are real concrete possibilities for a new competitor to penetrate the bundle of contracts by acquiring a brewery already established on the market together with its network of sales outlets, or to circumvent the bundle of contracts by opening new public houses. For that purpose it is necessary to have regard to the legal rules and agreements on the acquisition of companies and the establishment of outlets, and to the minimum number of outlets necessary for the economic operation of a distribution system. The presence of beer wholesalers not tied to producers who are active on the market is also a factor capable of facilitating a new producer's access to that market since he can make use of those wholesaler's sales networks to distribute his own beer.

22   Secondly, account must be taken of the conditions under which competitive forces operate on the relevant market. In that connection it is necessary to know not only the number and the size of producers present on the market, but also the degree of saturation of that market and customer fidelity to existing brands, for it is generally more difficult to penetrate a saturated market in which customers are loyal to a small number of large producers than a market in full expansion in which a large number of small producers are operating without any strong brand names. . . .

23   If an examination of all similar contracts entered into on the relevant market and the other factors relevant to the economic and legal context in which the contract must be examined shows that those agreements do not

have the cumulative effect of denying access to that market to new national and foreign competitors, the individual agreements comprising the bundle of agreements cannot be held to restrict competition within the meaning of Article 85(1) of the Treaty. They do not, therefore, fall under the prohibition laid down in that provision.

24 If, on the other hand, such examination reveals that it is difficult to gain access to the relevant market, it is necessary to assess the extent to which the agreements entered into by the brewery in question contribute to the cumulative effect produced in that respect by the totality of the similar contracts found on that market. Under the Community rules on competition, responsibility for such an effect of closing off the market must be attributed to the breweries which make an appreciable contribution thereto. Beer supply agreements entered into by breweries whose contribution to the cumulative effect is insignificant do not therefore fall under the prohibition under Article 85(1). * * *

27 The reply to be given to the first three questions is therefore that a beer supply agreement is prohibited by Article 85(1) of the EEC Treaty, if two cumulative conditions are met. The first is that, having regard to the economic and legal context of the agreement at issue, it is difficult for competitors who could enter the market or increase their market share to gain access to the national market for the distribution of beer in premises for the sale and consumption of drinks. The fact that, in that market, the agreement in issue is one of a number of similar agreements having a cumulative effect on competition constitutes only one factor amongst others in assessing whether access to that market is indeed difficult. The second condition is that the agreement in question must make a significant contribution to the sealing-off effect brought about by the totality of those agreements in their economic and legal context. The extent of the contribution made by the individual agreement depends on the position of the contracting parties in the relevant market and on the duration of the agreement.

Notes and Questions

1. What is the main concern that may lead to a finding of harm to competition?

2. Why is the Court centrally concerned with outsiders' ability to gain access to the market? If many beer producers were already in the market and the competition among them kept prices paid by the pubs close to cost, would that be the end of the matter?

3. Note that duration of exclusive contracts is a factor to be considered, because long duration can contribute to a "sealing off effect." In *Neste Markkinointi Oy*, Neste, the leading petrol supplier in Finland, sued former service station proprietors for abandoning their service stations without giving the contractually required one-year notice. The proprietors defended that the contract was void because it contained an exclusivity clause (for one year), that Neste's network of agreements, or its network combined with those of other suppliers, significantly foreclosed access of new oil companies, and that the network ran afoul of Article 81(1). The national court posed to the Court of Justice the question whether the contracts allowing termination on short notice could be separated from contracts of long duration in considering compatibility of the

plaintiffs' contracts with the Treaty. The Court noted that all gas stations carry only one brand of motor fuels; the supplier must invest in adapting the sales point to the brand image, so that exclusivity as such was not in question; rather "duration is the decisive factor in the market-sealing effect." (para. 32) A one-year period is reasonably necessary to protect the interests of the parties. The one-year contracts in effect at any given time represented a very small portion of the exclusive purchasing agreements of any particular supplier; therefore they made no significant contribution to any cumulative effect; therefore they were not caught by Article 81(1). Case C–214/99, 7 Dec. 2000 CFI. Is the Court correct? Can you understand the full effect of the entire network if you peal away the short-term contracts?

4. Why did the gas station proprietors in *Neste* (who breached their agreement to give proper notice) and the beer house tenant in Delimitis (who owed rent) have standing to claim that their commitment to purchase goods only from their supplier, combined with a network of similar contracts, amounted to an anticompetitive sealing off of the market for those goods, making life difficult for new or aspiring entrants into the goods market?

SCHÖLLER LEBENSMITTEL v. COMMISSION

Case T–9/93, [1995] ECR II–1611.

[Langnese–Iglo, a subsidiary of Unilever, and Schöller Lebensmittel were the leading firms in Germany in the sale of ice cream; particularly impulse-buying ice cream. Each, separately, had a network of agreements with retailers requiring that the retailers purchase ice cream only from it, or supplying freezers "free" and requiring that the retailer use the freezer only for the supplier's ice cream and not for the ice cream of competitors.

Mars, a French manufacturer of ice cream bars, was trying to pierce the German impulse ice cream market. Finding the two firms' supply contracts to be road blocks to market access, Mars complained to the Commission. The Commission brought proceedings against each. The Commission withdrew a comfort letter that it had previously given to Schöller and decided both the question of applicability of Article 85(1) [now 81(1)] and the question of entitlement of the applicants to an individual exemption.

In *Schöller*, the court first examined whether the contested supply agreements had an appreciable effect on competition. It found "that the applicant holds a strong position in the relevant market"; it held "more than 25 per cent" in the traditional trade, and, by its agreements, tied more than 10% of the sales outlets. Combined with Langnese's contracts, the tying-in exceeded 30%.]

83   With respect to [other] factors, the Commission has drawn attention to the existence of additional substantial barriers to access to the market, both in the grocery trade and in the traditional trade.... [A]ccess to the market for new competitors is made more difficult by the existence of a system under which a large number of freezer cabinets are lent by the applicant to retailers both in the grocery trade and in the traditional trade ..., the retailers being obliged to use them exclusively for the applicant's products.

84   The Court considers that the Commission was right to treat that factor as contributing to making access to the market more difficult. The necessary

consequence of that situation is that any new competitor entering the market must either persuade the retailer to exchange the freezer cabinet installed by the applicant for another, which involves giving up the turnover in the products from the previous supplier, or to persuade the retailer to install an additional freezer cabinet, which may prove impossible, particularly because of lack of space in small sales outlets. Moreover, if the new competitor is able to offer only a limited range of products, as in the case of the intervener, it may prove difficult for it to persuade the retailer to terminate its agreement with the previous supplier.

85 It is also apparent from the documents before the Court that, in the traditional trade, there are numerous individual retailers whose average turnover is rather low. The establishment of a profitable distribution system therefore presupposes that a new competitor must have a large number of retailers concentrated within a specified geographical area which can be supplied through regional or central warehouses. The fact that there are no independent intermediaries means that this fragmentation of demand constitutes an additional barrier to access to the market. Finally, the Commission rightly took into account the fact that the applicant's product brands are very well known.

86 In those circumstances, the Court considers that examination of all the similar agreements concluded on the market and of other aspects of the economic and legal context in which they operate, as examined in paragraphs [83] to [85] above, shows that the exclusive purchasing agreements concluded by the applicant are liable appreciably to affect competition within the meaning of Article 85(1) of the Treaty.

87 In view of the strong position occupied by the applicant in the relevant market and, in particular, its market share, the Court considers that the agreements contribute significantly to the closing-off of the market.

88 In view of all the foregoing, the Court considers that the Commission was right to conclude that the contested agreements give rise to an appreciable restriction of competition in the relevant market. * * *

139 In considering whether the Commission was right to refuse to grant an individual exemption, it must first be borne in mind that an individual exemption decision may be granted only if, in particular, the four conditions laid down by Article 85(3) of the Treaty are all met by the agreement in question, with the result that an exemption must be refused if any of the four conditions is not met. * * *

142 As regards the first of the four conditions laid down by Article 85(3) of the Treaty, the Court points out that, according to that provision, the agreements capable of being exempted are those which contribute "to improving the production or distribution of goods or to promoting technical or economic progress". It is settled law that the improvement cannot be identified with all the advantages which the parties obtain from the agreement in their production or distribution activities. The improvement must in particular display appreciable objective advantages of such a character as to compensate for the disadvantages which they cause in the field of competition.

143   ... Although it is apparent from the fifth recital in the preamble to Regulation No. 1984/83 that exclusive purchasing agreements lead in general to an improvement in distribution, in that they enable the supplier to plan the sale of his goods with greater precision and for a longer period and ensure that the reseller's requirements will be met on a regular basis for the duration of the agreement, and even if it is assumed that it would be necessary for the applicant, for reasons of cost, to terminate supplies to certain small sales outlets if it were obliged to give up supplies to them on an exclusive basis, the Commission considers nevertheless that the contested agreements do not give rise to objective and specific advantages for the public interest such as to compensate for the disadvantages which they cause in the field of competition.

144   In support of that argument, the Commission states, first, that, in view of the strong position on the market held by the applicant, the contested agreements do not, contrary to the expectation expressed in the sixth recital in the preamble to Regulation No. 1984/83, have the effect of intensifying competition between different brands of products. The Commission rightly took the view that the network of agreements at issue constitutes a major barrier to access to the market, with the result that competition is restricted.

145   ... [It is clear] that the Commission considered that supplies to any small sales outlets abandoned by the applicant, for reasons of costs, would be taken over either by other suppliers, for example small local producers, or by independent dealers selling several ranges of products. Moreover, the Commission points out that the applicant itself recognised that it continues to supply even very small sales outlets, whose annual turnover hovers around 300 German marks, in those cases where their geographical situation is favourable.

146   Against that background, it must be borne in mind that the intervener, Mars, stated that it is wholly exceptional for impulse products to be distributed using a transport system owned by the producers. The parties agree that it is only in Germany, Denmark and Italy that undertakings in the Unilever group, including Langnese, have concluded exclusive agreements covering sales outlets.

147   Although the applicant claims that it would be obliged, for reasons of cost, to cease supplying a number of small sales outlets if it had to give up its exclusive purchasing agreements, the Court considers that it has not provided any evidence to show that such a situation would be liable to jeopardise regular supplies of impulse ice-cream to the territory as a whole and, in particular, that the small sales outlets concerned would not subsequently be supplied by other suppliers or wholesalers, simply as a consequence of the unrestricted competition which would then prevail. Nor has the applicant produced any convincing evidence of the special conditions in Germany which made it necessary to create an ice-cream distribution system belonging to the producers. The Court therefore considers that the applicant has not shown that the Commission committed a manifest error of assessment in considering that the contested agreements did not fulfil the first condition laid down by Article 85(3) of the Treaty.... * * *

Notes and Questions

1. Did Schöller have market power? Is market power important to the decision? Should it be?

2. What were the effects of the exclusivity and freezer clauses—on competitors? on potential competitors? on partitioning of the market (explain)? on consumers? Which effects are most important?

3. What were the efficiencies of the exclusive supply contracts? of the "free" freezer arrangements? How, in your view, do the efficiencies balance against the anticompetitive aspects of the agreements? What was the court's view?

4. What was the strongest case for granting the exemption? Was the Commission right to deny it?

5. If you were Mars and if (counter-factually) you could not expect the European Commission to grant you relief from your competitors' exclusivity and freezer clauses, what strategies would you adopt?

6. If Schöller and Langnese withdrew the exclusivity obligation and offered retailers the choice of a) freezers for sale at market price, b) freezers for rent at market price, or c) freezers "free" with an obligation to use only the supplier's ice cream in the freezer, would the new arrangement be permissible? What if virtually all of the retailers chose option (c)? See Van den Bergh Foods Ltd. (subsidiary of Unilever), Cases IV/34.073, 34.395, 35.436, Commission Decision 98/531 of 11 March 1998, O.J. L 246/1 (Sept. 4, 1998). Langnese-Iglo GmbH v. Commission, Case T–7/93, the companion case to *Schöller,* is reported at [1995] ECR II–1533, aff'd, [1998] ECR I–5609.

7. United States law is different. Under US law, after defining the market, the court assesses the defendant's market power. If the defendant does not have market power, the case is dismissed. See Jefferson Parish Hospital District No. 2 v. Hyde, 466 U.S. 2, 104 S.Ct. 1551, 80 L.Ed.2d 2 (1984) (less than 30% market share may be considered an insufficient basis to infer market power). If the defendant has market power, the court examines market structure, concentration, degree of competition, market share foreclosed (from its contracts and its competitors' similar contracts), and efficiency properties of the contracts. If foreclosure is small, the case will be dismissed. If foreclosure is significant, a court asks: Was the market nonetheless competitive, and how could and would efficient competitors maneuver around the restraints and fend for themselves? The plaintiff must prove that the restraints give the defendant such power that they harm competition and consumers; e.g., that because of freezer exclusivity clauses, total output/sales of impulse ice cream would decline and prices would rise. If plaintiff proves harm to competition, defendant may prove procompetitive or efficiency justifications, and if it does, plaintiff must prove that the harms to competition outweigh the benefits, all from the viewpoint of consumers. See United States v. Microsoft Corp., 253 F.3d 34 (D.C.Cir.), cert. denied, ___ U.S. ___, 122 S.Ct. 350, 151 L.Ed.2d 264 (2001).

Describe the differences between the EC and US analysis, including who has what burdens. Would the Commission have succeeded if US burdens were imposed? What are the comparative merits of the EC and US law?

8. The Irish court has taken an entirely different view of the freezer arrangement and its effects. Masterfoods (Mars) had been enlisting numerous retailers in Ireland to stock and display Mars bars in their freezers. HB Ice-cream (of the Unilever family) sought to enforce its exclusive contracts with the retailers, and in 1992 it persuaded an Irish court to permanently restrain Masterfoods from

inducing breach of HB's contracts. The Irish court, by Judge Lynch, analyzed the contracts as follows:

> I think that a breach of paragraph (e) [distorting competition by imposing unrelated obligations] does not arise at all in this case. The contracts in question are bailments of freezers whether they be on loan or hire. The terms objected to relate to the very basis of the contract of bailment, namely, the purpose for which the goods (the freezers) are bailed to the bailee (the retailer). The freezers are bailed to the bailees for the purpose of storing, selling and advertising HB ice cream products only. Those terms are not supplementary obligations nor by their nature or according to commercial usage do they not have an essential connection with the contracts of bailment. They do. It would seem that none of the particular breaches set out in paragraphs (a) to (e) of Article 85 (1) apply: certainly, none clearly apply to the facts of Article 85 if it was reasonably clear that there was a contravention of the general intention of the article. Is it reasonably likely that these contracts of bailment of freezers may affect trade between member states of the European Community and may prevent, restrict or distort competition within the common market? I am not satisfied that Mars has made out a sufficient prima facie or serious case to that effect.

H.B. Ice-cream Ltd. v. Masterfoods Ltd. (trading as Mars Ireland), [1990] 2 IR 463.

Masterfoods complained to the European Commission about the exclusivity clauses and the Irish court injunction. The Commission sent, withdrew, and resent a statement of objections to HB, eventually producing a Commission decision holding:

> [T]he exclusivity provision in the freezer-cabinet agreement concluded between HB and retailers in Ireland, for the placement of cabinets in retail outlets which have only one or more freezer cabinets supplied by HB for the stocking of single-wrapped items of impulse ice cream, and not having a freezer cabinet either procured by themselves or provided by another ice-cream manufacturer constitutes an infringement of Article 85(1) of the Treaty. * * *

> HB's inducement to retailers in Ireland to enter into freezer-cabinet agreements subject to a condition of exclusivity by offering to supply them with one or more freezer cabinets for the stocking of single-wrapped items of impulse ice cream and to maintain the cabinets, free of any direct charge, constitutes an infringement of Article 86 of the Treaty.

Van den Bergh Foods Ltd., Cases IV/34.073, IV/34.395 and IV/35.436, Commission Decision 98/531 of 11 March 1998, O.J. L 246/1 (Sept. 4, 1998), Arts. 1, 3.

Van den Bergh, a subsidiary of Unilever, filed an application in the Court of First Instance to annul the Commission's decision.

Meanwhile, the Irish Supreme Court stayed the Irish appeal and asked the European Court of Justice whether its obligation of sincere cooperation (Art. 10) required it to stay the Irish case pending the disposition of Van den Bergh's appeal. The Court of Justice responded in the affirmative, holding that Ireland may not maintain a judgment inconsistent with the Community disposition of the same issue. Masterfoods Ltd. (Mars Ireland), Case C–344/98, 14 Dec. 2000.

D.   SELECTIVE DISTRIBUTION

A producer might wish to distribute its product through a network of selected distributors. The producer would appoint its distributors on the basis of qualifications and willingness to fulfill quality and service standards, such as technically trained staffs, adequate displays, and provision of information and other services.

Between 1970 and 1975, the Commission gave negative clearances for simple selective distribution systems wherein the manufacturer admitted into the system all who met stated qualifications. It exempted others that imposed certain additional obligations. In 1977, the Court of Justice handed down its first judgment on selective distribution.

METRO SB–GROSSMÄRKTE GmbH & CO. v. COMMISSION

(Metro I)
Case 26/76, [1977] ECR 1875.

[SABA was a German consumer electronics company. (See page 143 supra for the standing aspects of the case.) SABA sold 3% of all consumer electronic products in the Community and 11% in West Germany. It maintained a selective distribution system throughout the Community. Metro was a discounting, cash and carry, self-service wholesale/retailer. Metro applied to SABA to be part of SABA's selective distribution system but it was denied admission because it refused to agree to a number of SABA's requirements. Metro complained to the Commission, unsuccessfully, and then sought annulment of the Commission's decision granting an exemption.]

A.   Misuse of Powers

20   The requirement contained in Articles 3 and 85 of the EEC Treaty that competition shall not be distorted implies the existence on the market of workable competition, that is to say the degree of competition necessary to ensure the observance of the basic requirements and the attainment of the objectives of the Treaty, in particular the creation of a single market achieving conditions similar to those of a domestic market.

In accordance with this requirement the nature and intensiveness of competition may vary to an extent dictated by the products or services in question and the economic structure of the relevant market sectors.

In the sector covering the production of high quality and technically advanced consumer durables, where a relatively small number of large- and medium-scale producers offer a varied range of items which, or so consumers may consider, are readily interchangeable, the structure of the market does not preclude the existence of a variety of channels of distribution adapted to the peculiar characteristics of the various producers and to the requirements of the various categories of consumers.

On this view the Commission was justified in recognizing that selective distribution systems constituted, together with others, an aspect of competition which accords with Article 85(1), provided that resellers are chosen on the basis of objective criteria of a qualitative nature relating to the technical qualifications of the reseller and his staff and the suitability of his trading premises and that such conditions are laid down uniformly for all potential resellers and are not applied in a discriminatory fashion.

21   It is true that in such systems of distribution price competition is not generally emphasized either as an exclusive or indeed as a principal factor.

This is particularly so when, as in the present case, access to the distribution network is subject to conditions exceeding the requirements of an appropriate distribution of the products.

However, although price competition is so important that it can never be eliminated it does not constitute the only effective form of competition or that to which absolute priority must in all circumstances be accorded.

The powers conferred upon the Commission under Article 85(3) show that the requirements for the maintenance of workable competition may be reconciled with the safeguarding of objectives of a different nature and that to this end certain restrictions on competition are permissible, provided that they are essential to the attainment of those objectives and that they do not result in the elimination of competition for a substantial part of the Common Market.

For specialist wholesalers and retailers the desire to maintain a certain price level, which corresponds to the desire to preserve, in the interests of consumers, the possibility of the continued existence of this channel of distribution in conjunction with new methods of distribution based on a different type of competition policy, forms one of the objectives which may be pursued without necessarily falling under the prohibition contained in Article 85(1), and, if it does fall thereunder, either wholly or in part, coming within the framework of Article 85(3).

This argument is strengthened if, in addition, such conditions promote improved competition inasmuch as it relates to factors other than prices.

22   Although the figures submitted by both sides concerning the existence of price competition amongst SABA distributors ultimately indicate that the price structure is somewhat rigid, they do not, especially in view of the existence at the same time of competition between products of the same brand (intra-brand competition) and the existence of effective competition between different brands, permit the conclusion that competition has been restricted or eliminated on the market in electronic equipment for leisure purposes.

Nevertheless, the Commission must ensure that this structural rigidity is not reinforced, as might happen if there were an increase in the number of selective distribution networks for marketing the same product.

Since the Commission granted the desired exemption only for a period expiring on 21 July 1980 it retains the possibility of reconsidering within a reasonable time the consequences of this aspect of its decision.

In those circumstances the submission based on the existence of a misuse of powers must be rejected. * * *

⁵⁰ It is clear from the foregoing considerations that the conditions laid down by SABA for appointment as a wholesaler may largely be fulfilled without inconvenience by self-service wholesale undertakings.

Nevertheless, although the supply estimates which wholesalers are obliged to sign under the cooperation agreements in all probability constitute an element foreign to the methods appropriate to that distribution channel, it does not appear that, in weighing up, in the context of the electronic leisure equipment sector, the relative importance of the need for cooperation agreements, giving sufficient coherence to SABA's marketing network, especially with regard to specialist wholesalers, on the one hand, and the surmountable difficulties which that involves for self-service wholesale traders, on the other, and deciding in favour of the former, the Commission exceeded its discretionary power in this sphere.

The outcome could be different if, in particular as the result of an increase in selective distribution networks of a nature similar to SABA's self-service wholesale traders were in fact eliminated as distributors on the market in electronic equipment for leisure purposes. * * *

METRO SB–GROSSMÄRKTE GmbH & CO. v. COMMISSION

(Metro II)

Case 75/84, [1986] ECR 3021.

[After SABA's initial exemption was granted, SABA relaxed its restrictions to allow wholesalers to admit qualifying retailers to the system and to allow SABA wholesalers to supply wholesalers who were not part of the system but who met the requirements. When the exemption was expiring, SABA sought a renewal. Over Metro's objection, the Commission extended SABA's exemption. Metro noted that, since the date on which the first exemption was granted, there had been a significant increase in the adoption of selective distribution systems by major electronics firms.]

⁴⁰ It must be borne in mind that, although the Court has held in previous decisions that "simple" selective distribution systems are capable of constituting an aspect of competition compatible with Article 85(1) of the Treaty, there may nevertheless be a restriction or elimination of competition where the existence of a certain number of such systems does not leave any room for other forms of distribution based on a different type of competition policy or results in a rigidity in price structure which is not counterbalanced by other aspects of competition between products of the same brand and by the existence of effective competition between different brands.

⁴¹ Consequently, the existence of a large number of selective distribution systems for a particular product does not in itself permit the conclusion that competition is restricted or distorted. Nor is the existence of such systems decisive as regards the granting or refusal of an exemption under Article 85(3), since the only factor to be taken into consideration in that regard is the effect which such systems actually have on the competitive situation. Therefore the coverage ratio of selective distribution systems for

colour television sets, to which Metro refers, cannot in itself be regarded as a factor preventing an exemption from being granted. * * *

Conditions of Application of Article 85(3)

[48] The complaints raised by Metro relate to the following points in particular:

(a) The SABA system is not indispensable, in view of the nature of the products in question;

(b) The consumer derives no benefit from the SABA system;

(c) The system provides SABA with an opportunity of eliminating competition for a substantial part of the products in question. * * *

[53] As regards the nature of the products in question, Metro alleges that although some consumers may require information in relation to certain sophisticated products such as hi-fi systems, the opinion of specialists is scarcely needed for the purchase of television sets, in view of their high degree of quality, reliability and standardization. Metro states that television sets represent more than two-thirds of the total production of consumer electronics equipment in the Community. * * *

[61] Metro admits that in theory it could adapt itself to meet the requirements of the selective distribution systems which are operated. However, in its case such adaptation would require it to abandon its commercial strategy and become an entirely different kind of chain store. * * *

[64] It must be stated in the first place that the fact that Metro cannot obtain supplies of SABA products directly does not constitute an elimination of competition within the meaning of Article 85(3), when it is possible for Metro or other self-service wholesalers to market consumer electronics equipment, and colour television sets in particular, obtained from other producers.

[65] As the Court pointed out in its judgment in *Metro I,* the powers conferred upon the Commission under Article 85(3) show that the requirements for the maintenance of workable competition may be reconciled with the safeguarding of objectives of a different nature and that to this end certain restrictions on competition are permissible, provided that they are essential to the attainment of those objectives and that they do not result in the elimination of competition for a substantial part of the common market. Competition could not be eliminated if the channel of distribution in question continues to exist in conjunction with methods of distribution based on a different type of competition policy.

[66] Metro has not, however, proved that other methods of distribution of a different kind, such as the self-service wholesale trade, no longer exist on the relevant market. That being so, the complaint concerning the elimination of competition cannot be upheld. * * *

Notes and Questions

1. What are the necessary conditions for a valid selective distribution system? Why are these necessary conditions? Given SABA's small market share, why was the Court concerned with the balance between letting SABA maintain the

coherence of its network and allowing entrepreneurs (like Metro) to become part of the network? How would the case be treated under the Vertical Guidelines?

2.   What is the relationship between selective distribution, price competition, and consumer welfare? Does the proliferation of selective distribution in a market increase the producer's ability to exploit consumers? Might it enable producers to partition markets? The Commission's concerns are revealed in the motor vehicle block exemption regulation. See http://europa.eu.int/comm/competition/car_sector/ and pages 798–99 supra.

3.   A & B Ltd. sells dinnerware (dishes, cups, saucers, etc.) in the competitive but concentrated dinnerware market in the Community. It accounts for 31% of the market and distributes through selective distribution. A & B requires its approved retailers to sell the A & B brand only with other brands of the same quality and image, it requires them to promote the A & B brand, and it prohibits them from selling to non-approved retailers. You represent A & B. Does the restraint fall within Article 81(1)? Can you expect the Commission to grant an exemption?

4.   Suppose that SABA, faced with significant interbrand competition and worried that its distributors would not maintain the high quality of service it demanded, wishes to institute a system of minimum resale prices. (How will this help SABA?) It asks your advice on whether its contemplated distribution agreement falls within Article 81(1) and if so whether it is likely to be granted an Article 81(3) exemption. What is your opinion? See AEG–Telefunken AG v. Commission, Case 107/82, [1983] ECR 3151.

5.   Consider the different approach of US law: Producers without market power—and even those with market power—may adopt any kind of distribution system they choose. They may decide to admit to or exclude from their distribution system anyone they choose (NYNEX v. Discon, 525 U.S. 128, 119 S.Ct. 493, 142 L.Ed.2d 510 (1998)) subject to the rare case of the monopolist that controls essential facilities needed by its competitors. Which is the better approach?

6.   In *Metro III*, Cartier marketed its products worldwide through a selective distribution system. Cartier had not authorized Metro to carry its products, but Metro nonetheless managed to obtain Cartier's fine watches on a regular basis from dealers outside of the Community and to sell them in the Community at Metro stores. Cartier refused to provide a guarantee free of additional charge for watches purchased outside of its official network.

Metro sued Cartier in a German court alleging that, since the Cartier selective distribution system was not impervious to unauthorized dealers, it was not compatible with Article 85(1), and further, that the restriction of the guarantee to watches bought from authorized dealers breached Article 85(1). How should Cartier argue in defense of its restriction of the guarantee?

The national court posed two questions to the Court of Justice and the Court answered them adversely to Metro: (1) The fact that Cartier was unable to prevent unauthorized dealers from handling its product and that therefore its selective distribution system was not "pure" did not destroy the system's compatibility with Article 85(1). (2) A manufacturer's restriction of its guarantee to products obtained from authorized dealers pursuant to a valid selective distribution system is also valid. Metro SB-Grossmärkte GmbH & Co. v. Cartier SA, Case C–376/92, [1994] ECR I–32 (*Metro III*).

E. FRANCHISING

Franchising provides yet another methodology for distribution, as well as a channel for entrepreneurship. A franchisor—who usually holds intellectual property rights in distinctive goods or in a distinctive way of providing goods or services—grants licenses to franchisees, who participate in the operation of a uniform distribution network. Franchising provides individuals and small businesses with opportunities for market entry at relatively low cost and low risk, while providing franchisors with a means for rapid penetration of markets using little capital. Franchising as a way of doing business rapidly expanded in the United States, and then in Europe, beginning in the 1970s.

Franchising agreements often contain exclusive supply and exclusive distribution clauses. Before the 1980s, a principal question was whether Article 85(1) applied to franchise agreements. If so, did the block exemption for exclusive dealing apply and to what extent were negative clearances and individual exemptions available? The Court of Justice issued its first ruling on franchising in 1986.

PRONUPTIA DE PARIS GmbH
v. PRONUPTIA DE PARIS

Case 161/84, [1986] ECR 353.

[2] [Q]uestions arose in proceedings between Pronuptia de Paris GmbH, Frankfurt am Main (hereinafter referred to as "the franchisor"), a subsidiary of the French company of the same name, and Mrs. Schillgalis, who carries on business in Hamburg under the name Pronuptia de Paris and is referred to hereinafter as "the franchisee", regarding the franchisee's obligation to pay to the franchisor arrears of royalties on her turnover for the years 1978 to 1980. [Mrs. Schillgalis defended that the franchise contract was void.] * * *

[15] In a system of distribution franchises of [the] kind [in point] an undertaking which has established itself as a distributor on a given market and thus developed certain business methods grants independent traders, for a fee, the right to establish themselves in other markets using its business name and the business methods which have made it successful. Rather than a method of distribution, it is a way for an undertaking to derive financial benefit from its expertise without investing its own capital. Moreover, the system gives traders who do not have the necessary experience access to methods which they could not have learned without considerable effort and allows them to benefit from the reputation of the franchisor's business name. Franchise agreements for the distribution of goods differ in that regard from dealerships or contracts which incorporate approved retailers into a selective distribution system, which do not involve the use of a single business name, the application of uniform business methods or the payment of royalties in return for the benefits granted. Such a system, which allows the franchisor to profit from his success, does not in itself interfere with competition. In order for the system to work two conditions must be met.

[16] First, the franchisor must be able to communicate his know-how to the franchisees and provide them with the necessary assistance in order to

enable them to apply his methods, without running the risk that that know-how and assistance might benefit competitors, even indirectly. It follows that provisions which are essential in order to avoid that risk do not constitute restrictions on competition for the purposes of Article 85(1). That is also true of a clause prohibiting the franchisee, during the period of validity of the contract and for a reasonable period after its expiry, from opening a shop of the same or a similar nature in an area where he may compete with a member of the network. The same may be said of the franchisee's obligation not to transfer his shop to another party without the prior approval of the franchisor; that provision is intended to prevent competitors from indirectly benefiting from the know-how and assistance provided.

[17] Secondly, the franchisor must be able to take the measures necessary for maintaining the identity and reputation of the network bearing his business name or symbol. It follows that provisions which establish the means of control necessary for that purpose do not constitute restrictions on competition for the purposes of Article 85(1).

[18] The same is true of the franchisee's obligation to apply the business methods developed by the franchisor and to use the know-how provided.

[19] That is also the case with regard to the franchisee's obligation to sell the goods covered by the contract only in premises laid out and decorated according to the franchisor's instructions, which is intended to ensure uniform presentation in conformity with certain requirements. The same requirements apply to the location of the shop, the choice of which is also likely to affect the network's reputation. It is thus understandable that the franchisee cannot transfer his shop to another location without the franchisor's approval.

[20] The prohibition of the assignment by the franchisee of his rights and obligations under the contract without the franchisor's approval protects the latter's right freely to choose the franchisees, on whose business qualifications the establishment and maintenance of the network's reputation depend.

[21] By means of the control exerted by the franchisor on the selection of goods offered by the franchisee, the public is able to obtain goods of the same quality from each franchisee. It may in certain cases—for instance, the distribution of fashion articles—be impractical to lay down objective quality specifications. Because of the large number of franchisees it may also be too expensive to ensure that such specifications are observed. In such circumstances a provision requiring the franchisee to sell only products supplied by the franchisor or by suppliers selected by him may be considered necessary for the protection of the network's reputation. Such a provision may not however have the effect of preventing the franchisee from obtaining those products from other franchisees.

[22] Finally, since advertising helps to define the image of the network's name or symbol in the eyes of the public, a provision requiring the franchisee to obtain the franchisor's approval for all advertising is also essential for the

maintenance of the network's identity, so long as that provision concerns only the nature of the advertising.

23   It must be emphasized on the other hand that, far from being necessary for the protection of the know-how provided or the maintenance of the network's identity and reputation, certain provisions restrict competition between the members of the network. That is true of provisions which share markets between the franchisor and franchisees or between franchisees or prevent franchisees from engaging in price competition with each other.

24   In that regard, the attention of the national court should be drawn to the provision which obliges the franchisee to sell goods covered by the contract only in the premises specified therein. That provision prohibits the franchisee from opening a second shop. Its real effect becomes clear if it is examined in conjunction with the franchisor's undertaking to ensure that the franchisee has the exclusive use of his business name or symbol in a given territory. In order to comply with that undertaking the franchisor must not only refrain from establishing himself within that territory but also require other franchisees to give an undertaking not to open a second shop outside their own territory. A combination of provisions of that kind results in a sharing of markets between the franchisor and the franchisees or between franchisees and thus restricts competition within the network. As is clear from ... Consten and Grundig v. Commission [1966] ECR 299, a restriction of that kind constitutes a limitation of competition for the purposes of Article 85(1) if it concerns a business name or symbol which is already well-known. It is of course possible that a prospective franchisee would not take the risk of becoming part of the chain, investing his own money, paying a relatively high entry fee and undertaking to pay a substantial annual royalty, unless he could hope, thanks to a degree of protection against competition on the part of the franchisor and other franchisees, that his business would be profitable. That consideration, however, is relevant only to an examination of the agreement in the light of the conditions laid down in Article 85(3).

25   Although provisions which impair the franchisee's freedom to determine his own prices are restrictive of competition, that is not the case where the franchisor simply provides franchisees with price guidelines, so long as there is no concerted practice between the franchisor and the franchisees or between the franchisees themselves for the actual application of such prices. It is for the national court to determine whether that is indeed the case. * * *

[The Court noted several respects in which franchise agreements are essentially different from exclusive dealing agreements and concluded that the then-existing exclusive dealing block exemption was not applicable. Since 1999, the vertical block exemption has covered franchising.]

Notes and Questions

1.   Compare *Pronuptia* with *Metro I* and *II* and *Consten and Grundig*. Was *Pronuptia* a natural next step? Or did the Court in *Pronuptia* strike a different balance between autonomy of the distributor and freedom of the producer/franchi-

sor? In all four cases, what is the role and weight of consumer interests? interbrand competition? market efficiency?

2.   After *Pronuptia,* what obligations may be contained in a franchise agreement without distorting competition within the meaning of Article 81(1)?

Pronuptia gave exclusive licenses to each of its franchisees. In each territory Pronuptia appointed one franchisee alone, specified its locations, and gave it absolute territorial protection from other Pronuptia franchisees. Within its territory, Pronuptia gave each franchisee the exclusive right and the obligation to use the Pronuptia trademark, symbol and designs; required the franchisees to fit out their premises in accordance with specifications, required them to pay specified royalties, and, for a period of one year after the end of the contract, required them to agree not to compete with Pronuptia in the territory in which they had operated. Do these clauses, alone or in a combination, fall within Article 81(1)? If Pronuptia accounted for more than 30% of the wedding dress market and thus was outside of the vertical block exemption (see infra), would the Commission have to conduct a factual inquiry to determine whether Article 81(1) applies?

3.   Pronuptia's franchise territories and contract premises were so located that no two franchisees would be in competition with one another. Pronuptia's CEO convinces you that the territorial protection is strictly necessary to make the franchise system work. You know that the wedding dress market is competitive, especially at the low-price end in which your client does business. If you sign a contract giving absolute territorial protection to your client's franchisees, do you fall clear of Article 81(1)? If not, can you get an exemption? If so, can you square this result with *Consten and Grundig?*

4.   Franchise agreements are not likely to offend the United States antitrust laws unless they contain resale price fixing. Market definition and assessment of market power is an important first inquiry. Having no market power, new entrants have virtually total freedom to decide how to structure their systems in order to be as effective as possible.

US franchisees often complain about tie-ins. Firms with market power cannot lawfully impose tie-ins where a substantial dollar amount of commerce is involved. See Eastman Kodak Co. v. Image Technical Services, Inc., 504 U.S. 451, 112 S.Ct. 2072, 119 L.Ed.2d 265 (1992); Jefferson Parish, Hospital District No. 2 v. Hyde, 466 U.S. 2, 104 S.Ct. 1551, 80 L.Ed.2d 2 (1984); Principe v. McDonald's Corp., 631 F.2d 303 (4th Cir.1980), cert. denied, 451 U.S. 970, 101 S.Ct. 2047, 68 L.Ed.2d 349 (1981). However, the sale or license of a package is not necessarily a tie-in. In *Principe* the court held that, if all parts of a franchise package are "integral components of the business method being franchised" and "the challenged aggregation is an essential ingredient of the franchised system's formula for success, there is but a single product and no tie-in exists as a matter of law." 631 F.2d at 309. Moreover, the market includes all substitutes, and the franchisor may not have power in the broader market. See Queen City Pizza, Inc. v. Domino's Pizza, Inc., 124 F.3d 430 (3d Cir.1997), cert. denied, 523 U.S. 1059, 118 S.Ct. 1385, 140 L.Ed.2d 645 (holding irrelevant the franchisor's power over the franchisee). How similar is the United States law to Community law? How well calibrated are these laws to the goals of: protecting markets (and consumers) from anticompetitive restraints? protecting franchisees (and others) from unfair loss of freedom and access? protecting franchisors' freedom to design and run their systems?

F. BLOCK EXEMPTIONS AND REFORM

(a) History

Consten and Grundig, Pioneer, and the ice cream cases demonstrate the breadth of Article 81(1) in "catching" distribution agreements, which would then need exemptions or be void.

Not surprisingly, as soon as Regulation 17 became effective in 1962, thousands of notifications of distribution agreements began virtually flooding the Competition Directorate, which was obliged to examine each to determine whether an exemption should issue. The Commission responded to the un-manageable work load, as well as the opportunity to give guidance, by issuing its first block exemption, Commission Regulation 67/67, regarding agreements for the exclusive distribution of goods and agreements for the licensing of intellectual property.

The Commission issued a second, superseding set of block exemptions for exclusive agreements in 1983. In 1984 it issued a block exemption for patents; in 1989, for technology transfers (knowhow); in 1995 for motor vehicle distribution, and in 1996, a superseding regulation for patents and knowhow (Regulation 240/96).

The 1983 regulations, which were the most comprehensive, provided separate block exemptions for exclusive distribution (Regulation 1983/83) and for exclusive purchasing (Regulation 1984/83). These regulations, which were in effect until 1999, provided detailed roadmaps of what parties must, could, and must not do in order to have the benefit of exemption without filing a notification and seeking an individual exemption. For example, the Exclusive Distribution Regulation 1983/83, Article 1, exempted from Article 85(1) (now 81(1)) certain agreements between two, and only two, undertakings wherein one agreed to supply only to the other certain goods for resale within the common market or a defined part of it.

The only additional restriction that could be imposed on the supplier was the obligation not to supply the contract goods to users in the contract territory. The exclusive distributor could be obliged not to manufacture or distribute competing goods; to obtain the contract goods only from the other party, and to refrain from establishing a sales depot or from seeking custom-ers outside of the contract territory. Moreover, the exclusive distributor was allowed to agree to buy complete ranges of goods and minimum quantities, to sell the goods under trademarks or present them as specified by the other party, and to employ a trained staff and advertise and promote sales. (Art. 2) Article 3 was the black list. It declared Article 1 inapplicable where:

(a) manufacturers of identical goods or of goods which are considered by users as equivalent in view of their characteristics, price, and intended use enter into reciprocal exclusive distribution agreements between them-selves in respect of such goods;

(b) manufacturers of identical goods or of goods which are considered by users as equivalent in view of their characteristics, price, and intended use enter into a non-reciprocal exclusive distribution agreement between themselves in respect of such goods unless at least one of them has a total annual turnover of no more than 100 million ECU;

(c) users can obtain the contract goods in the contract territory only from the exclusive distributor and have no alternative source of supply outside the contract territory;

(d) one or both of the parties makes it difficult for intermediaries or users to obtain the contract goods from other dealers inside the common market or, in so far as no alternative source of supply is available there, from outside the common market, in particular where one or both of them:

    1. exercises industrial property rights so as to prevent dealers or users from obtaining outside, or from selling in, the contract territory properly marked or otherwise properly marketed contract goods;

    2. exercises other rights or takes other measures so as to prevent dealers or users from obtaining outside, or from selling in, the contract territory contract goods.

The other regulations had their own black and white lists. The Commission always retained the right to withdraw the benefits of the block exemption if it discovered that, under the circumstances, competition was harmed.

(b) Reform

Business firms organized entire distribution systems to conform with the block exemptions. Eventually, the EC system of narrow block exemptions, and different block exemptions for different kinds of distribution, came under severe criticism. They were formalistic. They were not united by economic or other theory.

The Commission set in motion an intensive reexamination of its treatment of vertical restraints and in particular the block exemptions. It issued an influential green paper, EC Competition Policy COM(96) 721 final, [1997] 4 C.M.L.R. 519, *http://europa.eu.int/comm/competition/antitrust/96721en_en.pdf*. The green paper includes economic analysis recognizing the efficiency of most vertical restraints.

At the conclusion of the long process, important changes were made. First, the Council amended Regulation 17 (which is now the subject of a more dramatic revision in light of modernisation) to exempt all vertical agreements from the requirement that they be notified at the time of execution in order to secure an exemption effective from the date of the agreement. Notification of vertical agreements and request for an exemption may now be made at any time, and the Commission can grant an exemption retroactively. Council Regulation 1216/99, O.J. L 148/5 (June 15, 1999). See Selected Documents, Competition Doc. No. 1.

Second, the Council adopted a broader, simpler block exemption, replacing the block exemptions on exclusive distribution, exclusive purchasing, and franchising. Regulation 2790/99, O.J. L 336/21 (Dec. 29, 1999), effective June 1, 2000. See Selected Documents, Competition Doc. No. 4. The block exemption for patent and knowhow licensing is expected to be replaced by a broader block exemption in the style of Regulation 2790/99. The Commission's Evaluation Report on the 1996 technology block exemption, and eventually the new block exemption, may be found at http://europa.eu.int/comm/competition/antitrust/technology_transfer/.

Third, the Commission issued lengthy Guidelines, effective May 24, 2000. The Guidelines, together with Regulation 2790/99, are intended to form the basis of a more economic, less regulatory approach to vertical agreements. The Guidelines may be found at *http://europa.eu.int/comm/competition/antitrust/legislation/*. Click on III. Block exemptions, Vertical agreements.

(c) *Regulation 2790/99 and the Guidelines*

The regulation for vertical restraints became effective in January 2000. It is printed in the Selected Documents as Competition Doc. No. 4. The recitals recognize the efficiency-enhancing effects of most vertical agreements, as follows:

(6) Vertical agreements of the category defined in this Regulation can improve economic efficiency within a chain of production or distribution by facilitating better coordination between the participating undertakings; in particular, they can lead to a reduction in the transaction and distribution costs of the parties and to an optimisation of their sales and investment levels.

(7) The likelihood that such efficiency-enhancing effects will outweigh any anti-competitive effects due to restrictions contained in vertical agreements depends on the degree of market power of the undertakings concerned and, therefore, on the extent to which those undertakings face competition from other suppliers of goods or services regarded by the buyer as interchangeable or substitutable for one another, by reason of the products' characteristics, their prices and their intended use.

(8) It can be presumed that, where the share of the relevant market accounted for by the supplier does not exceed 30%, vertical agreements which do not contain certain types of severely anti-competitive restraints generally lead to an improvement in production or distribution and allow consumers a fair share of the resulting benefits; in the case of vertical agreements containing exclusive supply obligations, it is the market share of the buyer which is relevant in determining the overall effects of such vertical agreements on the market.

The scheme of the regulation is to grant block exemption to all solely vertical agreements (Art. 2) where the supplier does not have more than 30% of the market, or in the case of exclusive supply obligations ("you supply me exclusively and not my competitors") the buyer has no more than 30% of the market (Art. 3); and the agreement does not contain "hard core" restraints, namely: including fixing minimum resale prices, prohibiting distributors from making passive (unsolicited) sales, e.g. outside of a territory, restricting members of a selective distribution system from selling to end-users or to other authorized distributors, and in the case of a producer/fabricator, restricting component suppliers from selling the components to end users or independent repairers. (Art. 4)

A second set of restrictions is not automatically exempt; they may under certain circumstances merit individual exemption. The most important of these is a covenant not to compete that exceeds five years. Also: obliging the buyer, after termination of the agreement, not to make, buy or sell the subject goods or services, and obliging a member of a selective distribution system not to sell the brands of particular competing suppliers. (Art. 5)

Article 6 authorizes the Commission to withdraw the benefit of the Regulation where it finds effects incompatible with Article 81(3), especially where market access is significantly impeded by the cumulative effects of similar networks.

This summary does not contain nuances of the Regulation, which should be consulted in the Selected Documents.

The Guidelines provide, inter alia, a framework of analysis for agreements that fall outside of the block exemption. While the Guidelines are long and detailed, they include this summary:

1.3. General rules for the evaluation of vertical restraints

[119] In evaluating vertical restraints from a competition policy perspective, some general rules can be formulated:

(1) For most vertical restraints competition concerns can only arise if there is insufficient inter-brand competition....

(2) Vertical restraints which reduce inter-brand competition are generally more harmful than vertical restraints that reduce intra-brand competition....

(3) Vertical restraints from the limited distribution group, in the absence of sufficient inter-brand competition, may significantly restrict the choices available to consumers. They are particularly harmful when more efficient distributors or distributors with a different distribution format are foreclosed....

(4) Exclusive dealing arrangements are generally worse for competition than non-exclusive arrangements....

(5) Vertical restraints agreed for non-branded goods and services are in general less harmful than restraints affecting the distribution of branded goods and services. * * *

(6) In general, a combination of vertical restraints aggravates their negative effects. However, certain combinations of vertical restraints are better for competition than their use in isolation from each other. For instance, in an exclusive distribution system, the distributor may be tempted to increase the price of the products as intra-brand competition has been reduced. The use of quantity forcing or the setting of a maximum resale price may limit such price increases.

(7) Possible negative effects of vertical restraints are reinforced when several suppliers and their buyers organise their trade in a similar way. These so-called cumulative effects may be a problem in a number of sectors.

(8) The more the vertical restraint is linked to the transfer of know-how, the more reason there may be to expect efficiencies to arise and the more a vertical restraint may be necessary to protect the know-how transferred or the investment costs incurred.

(9) The more the vertical restraint is linked to investments which are relationship-specific, the more justification there is for certain vertical

restraints. The justified duration will depend on the time necessary to depreciate the investment.

(10) In the case of a new product, or where an existing product is sold for the first time on a different geographic market, it may be difficult for the company to define the market or its market share may be very high. However, this should not be considered a major problem, as vertical restraints linked to opening up new product or geographic markets in general do not restrict competition. . . .

1.4. Methodology of analysis

120   The assessment of a vertical restraint involves in general the following four steps:

(1) First, the undertakings involved need to define the relevant market in order to establish the market share of the supplier or the buyer, depending on the vertical restraint involved.

(2) If the relevant market share does not exceed the 30% threshold, the vertical agreement is covered by the Block Exemption Regulation, subject to the hardcore restrictions and conditions set out in that regulation.

(3) If the relevant market share is above the 30% threshold, it is necessary to assess whether the vertical agreement falls within Article 81(1).

(4) If the vertical agreement falls within Article 81(1), it is necessary to examine whether it fulfils the conditions for exemption under Article 81(3).

1.4.1. Relevant factors for the assessment under Article 81(1)

121   In assessing cases above the market share threshold of 30%, the Commission will make a full competition analysis. The following factors are the most important to establish whether a vertical agreement brings about an appreciable restriction of competition under Article 81(1): (a) market position of the supplier; (b) market position of competitors; (c) market position of the buyer; (d) entry barriers; (e) maturity of the market; (f) level of trade; (g) nature of the product; (h) other factors.

122   The importance of individual factors may vary from case to case and depends on all other factors. For instance, a high market share of the supplier is usually a good indicator of market power, but in the case of low entry barriers it may not indicate market power. It is therefore not possible to provide strict rules on the importance of the individual factors. However the following can be said:

Market position of the supplier

123   The market position of the supplier is established first and foremost by his market share on the relevant product and geographic market. The higher his market share, the greater his market power is likely to be. The market position of the supplier is further strengthened if he has certain cost advantages over his competitors. These competitive advantages may result from a first mover advantage (having the best site, etc.), holding essential patents, having superior technology, being the brand leader or having a superior portfolio.

Market position of competitors

[124] The same indicators, that is market share and possible competitive advantages, are used to describe the market position of competitors. The stronger the established competitors are and the greater their number, the less risk there is that the supplier or buyer in question will be able to foreclose the market individually and the less there is a risk of a reduction of inter-brand competition. However, if the number of competitors becomes rather small and their market position (size, costs, R & D potential, etc.) is rather similar, this market structure may increase the risk of collusion. Fluctuating or rapidly changing market shares are in general an indication of intense competition.

Market position of the buyer

[125] Buying power derives from the market position of the buyer. The first indicator of buying power is the market share of the buyer on the purchase market. This share reflects the importance of his demand for his possible suppliers. Other indicators focus on the market position of the buyer on his resale market including characteristics such as a wide geographic spread of his outlets, own brands of the buyer/distributor and his image amongst final consumers. The effect of buying power on the likelihood of anti-competitive effects is not the same for the different vertical restraints. Buying power may in particular increase the negative effects in case of restraints from the limited distribution and market partitioning groups such as exclusive supply, exclusive distribution and quantitative selective distribution.

Entry barriers

[126] Entry barriers are measured by the extent to which incumbent companies can increase their price above the competitive level, usually above minimum average total cost, and make supra-normal profits without attracting entry. Without any entry barriers, easy and quick entry would eliminate such profits. In as far as effective entry, which would prevent or erode the supra-normal profits, is likely to occur within one or two years, entry barriers can be said to be low.

[127] Entry barriers may result from a wide variety of factors such as economies of scale and scope, government regulations, especially where they establish exclusive rights, state aid, import tariffs, intellectual property rights, ownership of resources where the supply is limited due to for instance natural limitations (30), essential facilities, a first mover advantage and brand loyalty of consumers created by strong advertising. Vertical restraints and vertical integration may also work as an entry barrier by making access more difficult and foreclosing (potential) competitors. Entry barriers may be present at only the supplier or buyer level or at both levels.

[128] The question whether certain of these factors should be described as entry barriers depends on whether they are related to sunk costs. Sunk costs are those costs that have to be incurred to enter or be active on a market but that are lost when the market is exited. . . .

129 In general, entry requires sunk costs, sometimes minor and sometimes major. Therefore, actual competition is in general more effective and will weigh more in the assessment of a case than potential competition.

Maturity of the market

130 A mature market is a market that has existed for some time, where the technology used is well known and widespread and not changing very much, where there are no major brand innovations and in which demand is relatively stable or declining. In such a market negative effects are more likely than in more dynamic markets.

Level of trade

131 The level of trade is linked to the distinction between intermediate and final goods and services. As indicated earlier, negative effects are in general less likely at the level of intermediate goods and services.

Nature of the product

132 The nature of the product plays a role in particular for final products in assessing both the likely negative and the likely positive effects. When assessing the likely negative effects, it is important whether the products on the market are more homogeneous or heterogeneous, whether the product is expensive, taking up a large part of the consumer's budget, or is inexpensive and whether the product is a one-off purchase or repeatedly purchased. In general, when the product is more heterogeneous, less expensive and resembles more a one-off purchase, vertical restraints are more likely to have negative effects.

Other factors

133 In the assessment of particular restraints other factors may have to be taken into account. Among these factors can be the cumulative effect, i.e. the coverage of the market by similar agreements, the duration of the agreements, whether the agreement is "imposed" (mainly one party is subject to the restrictions or obligations) or "agreed" (both parties accept restrictions or obligations), the regulatory environment and behaviour that may indicate or facilitate collusion like price leadership, pre-announced price changes and discussions on the "right" price, price rigidity in response to excess capacity, price discrimination and past collusive behaviour.

1.4.2. Relevant factors for the assessment under Article 81(3)

134 There are four cumulative conditions for the application of Article 81(3):

— the vertical agreement must contribute to improving production or distribution or to promoting technical or economic progress;

— the vertical agreement must allow consumers a fair share of these benefits;

— the vertical agreement must not impose on the undertakings concerned vertical restraints which are not indispensable to the attainment of these benefits;

— the vertical agreement must not afford such undertakings the possibility of eliminating competition in respect of a substantial part of the products in question.

[135] The last criterion of elimination of competition for a substantial part of the products in question is related to the question of dominance. Where an undertaking is dominant or becoming dominant as a consequence of the vertical agreement, a vertical restraint that has appreciable anti-competitive effects can in principle not be exempted. The vertical agreement may however fall outside Article 81(1) if there is an objective justification, for instance if it is necessary for the protection of relationship-specific investments or for the transfer of substantial know-how without which the supply or purchase of certain goods or services would not take place. * * *

Notes and Questions

1.   Note that the benefits of the block exemption, as well as the analysis for individual exemptions, depend heavily on market share and therefore definition of the market. What are the benefits and pitfalls of this approach?

2.   Note the treatment of dominant firms, para. 135. Should dominant firms in principle be denied the right to impose efficient vertical restraints?

3.   Where if at all do you disagree with the Commission's characterization of restraints as anticompetitive?

4.   What is the Commission's attitude toward efficiency?

5.   Applying the modernized analysis to the facts of the following cases, consider whether the restraints fall clear of Article 81(1), if not whether they come within the vertical block exemption, and if not whether they would be entitled to an individual exemption under the framework of the vertical guidelines:

Consten and Grundig

Pioneer

Delimitis

Schöller

Metro/SABA

Pronuptia.

Chapter 25

MERGER CONTROL

A. INTRODUCTION

The EC Treaty of 1957 was not directed against mergers. Facing trade barriers at every frontier, many business enterprises were too small to be efficient. Mergers—especially mergers between firms from different Member States—held the promise of promoting market integration. Moreover, the Member States were not prepared to yield to the Community sovereignty over the structure of their economies, and Community competence over mergers was regarded by many as unreasonably intrusive. Accordingly, the competition provisions of the Treaty did not mention mergers. Article 85 was designed to regulate agreements and ongoing collaborations. If the agreements enhanced production or distribution, they could be granted conditional approval for a term of years, under the surveillance of the Commission. Article 86 was designed to regulate the behavior of dominant firms.

By contrast to the EC Treaty, the European Coal and Steel Treaty—which had been adopted six years earlier—specifically prohibited mergers that created power "to determine prices, to control or restrict production or distribution or to hinder effective competition in a substantial part of the market...." (Art. 66 para. 2) Thus, from the start, the Member States expressly conceded control over coal and steel mergers, underscoring the deliberateness of the omission of merger control in the Rome Treaty.

The merger movement of the 1960s sparked wide debate concerning the Treaty's applicability to mergers. The Commission studied the matter and, through the Memorandum Colonna, determined that Article 85 (now 81) was not applicable to mergers and other concentrations but that Article 86 (now 82) could be applicable in a proper case.[1]

But the matter was not put to rest. When the first merger case came before the Court of Justice, the Court declared Article 86 applicable to mergers. Article 86, the Court held, prohibited mergers that entrench dominance. Europemballage Corp. v. Commission (Continental Can), Case 6/72, [1973] ECR 215. Some years later the Court determined that Article 85 could catch agreements to acquire corporate control. British American Tobacco Co.

---

1. See G. Bernini, Jurisdictional Issues: EEC Merger Regulation, Member State Laws and Articles 85–86, 1990 Fordham Corp.L.Inst. 611, 612 (B. Hawk ed. Transnational Juris 1991).

Ltd. v. Commission (Philip Morris/Rothmans), Cases 142, 156/84, [1987] ECR 4487. Still later the Council promulgated the Merger Regulation, officially providing a merger control system for the Community.

The adoption of European merger control coincided with important economic and political changes in the world. The Berlin wall fell. Nations of the Soviet bloc severed ties to Russia, and nations including Russia moved from communism to democracy and from command-and-control economies to markets protected by competition laws. Most of these nations adopted merger laws. So too did Latin American, African and Asian countries. More than 60 nations now have merger control/notification regimes. Since many of the possibly anticompetitive mergers are between firms that operate in transnational markets, problems of jurisdiction, conflict, and cooperation emerge. We return to these problems and challenges below, after discussing the detail of the Merger Regulation.

B. THE MERGER REGULATION

1. COVERAGE AND PROCEDURES

After 16 years of debate, on December 21, 1989 the Council adopted the Merger Control Regulation, with an effective date of September 21, 1990.[2] The Merger Regulation had three major purposes: (1) to provide specific authority for the Commission to challenge mergers and acquisitions that would harm competition, and thus to put an end to the debate whether the Treaty conferred such authority; (2) to provide a structure for merger control, giving the Commission necessary market information before mergers are consummated and the power to stop anticompetitive mergers before their consummation; and (3) to centralize merger enforcement in the hands of the Community authorities so that enterprises would not be subject to multiple and potentially inconsistent substantive standards, notice requirements and waiting periods.

Specifically, subject to exceptions that we note below, the parties to a concentration with a Community dimension must file premerger notification forms and wait a three-week period, subject to extension. The Commission has exclusive power, vis-à-vis Member State authorities, to allow or disallow these transactions. The Member States have ceded authority to prevent or authorize such transactions, except when legitimate national interests such as security, plurality of media, and prudential concerns are at stake, and except in certain circumstances when a distinct State market is affected.

A concentration has a Community dimension when:

(a) the combined aggregate worldwide turnover of all the undertakings concerned is more than 5 billion ECUs; and

(b) the aggregate Community-wide turnover of each of at least two of the undertakings concerned is more than 250 million ECUs, unless each

2. Council Regulation 4064/89, O.J. L 395/1 (Dec. 30, 1989), corrected version O.J. L 257/14 (Sept. 21, 1990), amended, Council Regulation 1310/97, O.J. L 180/1 (July 9, 1997), corrected version O.J. L 40/17 (Feb. 13, 1998), effective March 1, 1998. The Merger Regulation is printed in the Selected Documents as Competition Doc. No. 7, and may be found on the website of DG Competition at *http://europa.eu.int/ comm/competition/mergers/legislation/*.

of the undertakings concerned achieves more than two-thirds of its aggregate Community-wide turnover within one and the same Member State.

These very high thresholds led to a problem. A number of large transactions fell below the thresholds and, of these, many were subject to notification and clearance in several Member States. In order to secure one-stop shopping for these transactions, too, the Council amended the Merger Regulation to add:

Concentrations also have a Community dimension and thus come within the Merger Regulation if :

(1) The undertakings have combined aggregate world-wide turnover of at least 2.5 billion ECUs,

(2) The undertakings have combined aggregate turnover of at least 100 million ECUs in at least three Member States,

(3) At least two of the undertakings have at least 25 million ECUs turnover in the same three Member States, and

(4) At least two undertakings have at least 100 million ECUs turnover in the Community,

unless each of the undertakings achieves more than two-thirds of its aggregate Community-wide turnover in the same Member State.

Concentrations below the thresholds remain subject to the laws of the Member States.

In some cases a concentration even with a Community dimension threatens competition in a distinct market within one Member State. In such cases the Member State authority may ask the Commission to refer the concentration to it, and the Commission *may* grant the reference; but if the affected territory is not a substantial part of the Common Market, the Commission *must* grant the reference. The applicable clause—Article 9—was called the German clause, since it was proposed by Germany in response to its concerns that Germany would be stripped of its power to prohibit concentrations that uniquely harmed Germany. Another clause, Article 22, previously known as the Dutch clause, allows the Commission to investigate mergers not of Community dimension at the request of one or more Member States.

Joint ventures are "concentrations" if they are created to "perform[] on a lasting basis all the functions of an autonomous economic entity." These joint ventures are called "full-function" joint ventures. Full-function joint ventures get the benefit of the one-stop Merger Regulation if they meet the thresholds. If the joint venture may give rise to coordination of the competitive behavior of firms that remain independent, or if it entails ancillary agreements that are not obviously directly related and necessary to the concentration, the Commission must appraise the potentially cooperative or exclusionary aspects under Article 81 or 82.

Concentrative transactions with a Community dimension must be notified to the Commission not more than one week after the conclusion of the agreement, of a public bid, or of the acquisition of a controlling interest. The Commission must then evaluate the concentration to determine whether it is compatible with the common market. A concentration covered by the regulation may not be put into effect for a period of three weeks after the notification is complete, or a longer period if the Commission finds it necessary to extend the suspension in order to determine whether the concentration is or is not compatible with the common market. If the Commission advances to the stage of opening proceedings, it must do so within one month of the notification, and it must render its decision within four months thereafter.

The Merger Regulation provides that the implementing legislation that empowers Commission enforcement of Articles 81 and 82 does not apply to concentrations, whether they fall above or below the thresholds. Moreover, the Commission has represented that it will not normally apply Articles 81 or 82 to concentrations. Therefore the Merger Regulation has effectively become the only European Community measure for controlling concentrations.

2. THE SUBSTANTIVE STANDARD

The substantive standard is set forth in Article 2 of the Merger Regulation, which provides:

1. Concentrations within the scope of this Regulation shall be appraised in accordance with the following provisions with a view to establishing whether or not they are compatible with the common market.

In making this appraisal, the Commission shall take into account:

(a) the need to maintain and develop effective competition within the common market in view of, among other things, the structure of all the markets concerned and the actual or potential competition from undertakings located either within or without the Community;

(b) the market positions of the undertakings concerned and their economic and financial power, the alternatives available to suppliers and users, their access to supplies or markets, any legal or other barriers to entry, supply and demand trends for relevant goods and services, the interests of the intermediate and ultimate consumers, and the development of technical and economic progress provided that it is to consumers' advantage and does not form an obstacle to competition.

2. A concentration which does not create or strengthen a dominant position as a result of which effective competition would be significantly impeded in the common market or in a substantial part of it shall be declared compatible with the common market.

3. A concentration which creates or strengthens a dominant position as a result of which effective competition would be significantly impeded in the common market or in a substantial part of it shall be declared incompatible with the common market.

The body of the Merger Regulation is preceded by a number of recitals. Recital 13 states that the Community must place its competition appraisal within the framework of the fundamental objectives of the Community referred to in Article 2 of the Treaty, including "strengthening the Community's economic and social cohesion." Recital 15 states:

(15) Whereas concentrations which, by reason of the limited market share of the undertakings concerned, are not liable to impede effective competition may be presumed to be compatible with the common market; whereas, without prejudice to Articles 85 and 86 of the Treaty, an indication to this effect exists, in particular, where the market share of the undertakings concerned does not exceed 25% in either the common market or in a substantial part of it. . . .

Notes and Questions

1. Review the substantive standard for proscribing concentrations under the Merger Regulation. In considering whether the merger is compatible with the common market, is the Commission limited to weighing procompetitive and anticompetitive aspects of the concentration? If the acquisition strengthens a dominant position, is it relevant that the acquisition also saves jobs? that it produces productive efficiencies that help the firm compete in world markets? that it creates a European champion that by some measure might make Europe better off?

2. The United States does not have one-stop shopping. The United States federal merger law may be enforced by the Justice Department or the Federal Trade Commission, by the attorney general of any affected states, and by private parties. See California v. American Stores Co., 495 U.S. 271, 110 S.Ct. 1853, 109 L.Ed.2d 240 (1990). In addition, the states that have antimerger laws may seek to enforce them against mergers that significantly impact intrastate commerce even though interstate commerce is also affected. Well aware that multiplicity of law without agency coordination could have unacceptable costs, the state attorneys general collaborate on the substantive standard for prohibition, and they invite merging parties to make joint filings with all interested states.[3] Moreover, the state enforcers collaborate with the federal enforcers.

State enforcement played a noticeable role in the United States in the 1980s, when the federal government's laissez faire philosophy resulted in an unusually low level of merger challenges. State attorneys general stepped into the breach. While many observers welcomed the state activity as an important safeguard for competition, others decried it as unreasonable proliferation of law, posing additional risks and costs for merging firms.

Should the United States adopt the European Union approach of centralized enforcement? Should the European Union adopt the United States system of multiple enforcement centers? Is there a need for multinational cooperation in merger control, as more and more mega-mergers have impacts around the world?

C. THE ECONOMICS OF MERGER ANALYSIS

1. INTRODUCTION

During all of the years of debate about whether there should be merger control at the European level and what a merger regulation should provide, there was very little discussion of what categories of mergers would be prohibited or how to analyze a merger to determine whether it was likely to

---

3. See National Association of Attorneys General, Voluntary Pre–Merger Disclosure Compact, reprinted at 3 B. Fox and E. Fox, Corporate Acquisitions & Mergers, App. 24 (2002). For state enforcement generally, see 2 B. Fox and E. Fox, Corporate Acquisitions and Mergers, § 7A.04.

cause undesirable effects. As adopted, the Merger Regulation declares incompatible with the common market mergers that "create or strengthen a dominant position as a result of which effective competition would be significantly impeded...." This language seemed to—and in fact has been construed to—import, more or less, common understandings of how mergers may harm competition by creating market power or facilitating its exercise. The language has been construed, also, to incorporate EC principles regarding competitors' rights to market access and to a level playing field.

In this section we review some basic economics that may guide analysis of competitive harms, principally from a consumer or efficiency point of view. First, we analyze the effects of mergers on competition, assuming the relevant market. Second, we return to the question of market definition, which is guided by the Commission's December 1997 Notice on Definition of Relevant Market. See pp. 838–40 supra and Selected Documents, Competition Doc. No. 3.

2. COMPETITION–LESSENING EFFECTS

Mergers may harm competition, causing output to fall and prices to rise, and sometimes chilling innovation, by creating or entrenching market power or facilitating the exercise of market power. It can do this by one of two routes: creating single firm power (dominance), or creating a tight oligopoly (oligopolistic dominance) wherein the few remaining firms in a market are likely to behave like collaborators rather than rivals. Oligopoly behavior is sometimes called cartel-like or cooperative behavior.

The negative effects (higher price and lower output) cannot be expected if barriers to entry are low, strong potential competitors are waiting in the wings, smaller firms can easily and quickly expand without rising costs, or big buyers credibly threaten to integrate backwards if their suppliers do not perform competitively. In such cases the market would regulate itself. The economic forces would put pressure on the existing market actors, causing them to be responsive to buyers' needs.

Of all mergers, mergers of competitors are most likely to harm competition. Also, mergers between a leading firm and a most important potential competitor can have the same cartel or dominance-creating effect. Potential competitors can exert competitive pressure on prices. Incumbents may hold their prices down so as not to attract their entry. If a dominant firm acquires the most or only important potential competitor, the acquisition removes this competitive check. Also, if the potential entrant would have entered the market on its own and added a dynamic force to an oligopolistic or monopolistic market, the merger would prevent this force from materializing.

Mergers between buyers and suppliers ("vertical mergers") can also lessen competition, although in many cases they simply reshuffle buyer and supplier alliances. Vertical mergers may make it more likely that the firms will deal with each other to the exclusion of or in preference to dealing with corporate strangers. Favoring one's own is especially likely in times of short supply or contracted demand.

Most often, a vertical merger is efficient and does not foreclose unintegrated rivals from access to needed supplies or outlets, raising their costs and pushing up price. The rivals may be able to buy from other suppliers or to supply other buyers, or to integrate vertically by contract or acquisition. But if leading firms in their respective fields merge, if barriers to entry are high, if concentration at the relevant market level is high, and if foreclosure of unintegrated rivals from necessary inputs or outlets threatens to squeeze rivals out of the market or incapacitate them, a vertical merger may increase dominance or facilitate oligopoly behavior in the relevant market, raising consumer prices. EC competition law is concerned also with competitors' access to markets, key assets and infrastructure (gateways), and with competitors' rights to compete on the merits free from blockage by a dominant firms' bundling and other strategies. Mergers that give dominant firms preferred access to important inputs, customers, or gateways may be subjected to conditions such as duties to deal.

Mergers that are neither horizontal, potential-horizontal nor vertical are called conglomerate mergers. The label merely signifies an "all other" category. Conglomerate mergers are much less likely than horizontal, potential-horizontal or vertical mergers to lessen competition. In some cases however, merging partners may be able to use leverage to create competition-lessening foreclosures (see vertical effects, above) or to entrench their dominance through acquiring strategic advantages such as access to cheap capital or a family of complementary products that may lead to full line forcing. In the United States today, the law treats anticompetitive effects of conglomerate mergers as negligible and speculative, and conglomerate mergers are substantially discounted as a source of competitive concern. In the EU, enforcers and policymakers are much more likely to entertain arguments that the merger creates anticompetitive "portfolio effects," advantaging a leading full-line firm over single line firms and leading to a deterioration of the competitive structure of the market, and arguments that the merged firm will control the gateway to important inputs or outlets and therefore has the duty to grant nondiscriminatory access to its competitors.

3. OTHER EFFECTS

Mergers may produce efficiencies; they may increase competition; and mergers between firms from different Member States may increase market integration. A merger may create synergies, which vertical mergers are especially likely to do. Also, they may yield economies of scope, as is often the case for mergers between firms that produce products distributed through the same distribution channels. If the market is already competitive, market forces are likely to cause cost savings to be passed on to consumers. If the market is monopolistic or oligopolistic, the merging partners are more likely to retain most of the savings and possibly raise prices as well.

4. COMPETITIVENESS

It is possible for a merger to yield efficiencies and increase the merged firm's competitiveness in world markets and at the same time to lessen competition in the domestic market. Despite world competition, competition may be lessened in the domestic market if it is concentrated and the merged firm has (for example) locational or cultural advantages or the home market maintains barriers to foreign competition. To address the situation in which these two effects (efficiency in global competition and power at home) coexist, the regulating nation must make a policy judgment as to which costs it wishes to avoid and which benefits it wishes to preserve. US law holds that a merger that lessens competition in the United States is illegal regardless of the claim that the merger helps the firm compete in global markets. The claim that a merger that increases market power in the United States may enhance global competitiveness is regarded with skepticism and in fact is rarely substantiated. In contemplating this trade-off for the European Union, policymakers would want to consider the welfare of European consumers versus gains from greater economic strength abroad. Also of relevance is the speed with which remaining internal and European barriers may be dismantled, for without barriers to entry into the Community, European consumers are not likely to be subject to exploitation.

5. MARKETS, CONCENTRATION, BARRIERS, AND EFFICIENCIES

In the paragraphs above we assumed well-defined markets, high concentration therein, and significant barriers to entry. All three of these concepts require detailed, fact-specific evaluation. Market definition is the crucial first step in merger analysis. Earlier we described the methodologies used to define markets, treating a market as an area in which, if there were a single seller, that firm would have market power; it would be able to raise the price of its product substantially and profitably for a significant period of time without fear that too many of its customers would shift to another product. All good substitutes are included in the market. Study, again, the Notice on market definition, summarized in Chapter 22C and printed in the Selected Documents as Competition Doc. No. 3.

Volvo wished to acquire control of Scania. Both firms were important Swedish truck makers. Neither made light trucks, and Scania had only a small position in medium trucks. Both were active in Europe and the world in sales of heavy trucks. In heavy trucks, they were particularly strong in Sweden, and also in Norway, Finland and Ireland. The merged firm would have held 31% of all heavy trucks in the EEA. DaimlerChrysler was the number two firm with about 20%. The merged firm would have held 90% of Swedish sales and 50% of Irish sales. The two merging firms were the closest competitors to one another.

Was there a product market of heavy trucks (more than 16 tons)? Was the geographic market national? European? worldwide?

The Commission found a heavy truck market. Heavy trucks had a distinctive technical configuration. Engines and axels on heavy trucks were more sophisticated and more durable, which are qualities necessary for transporting heavy loads long distances. Heavy trucks are produced from different production lines than lighter trucks, and they appeal to different groups of customers.

Moreover, the Commission found that the geographic markets were national. The Commission observed differences among nations in purchasing habits, technical requirements, price levels, and market shares. For example, prices were 10% to 20% higher in Sweden than in Denmark or Norway, and the price differentials did not lead to significant cross-border trade. Sales normally included a local service package that tended to attract local buyers to local sellers, and purchasing was normally done on a national basis.

Do you agree with the Commission's geographic market definition? Do you need more information? See Volvo/Scania, Comp/M. 1672 (March 15, 2000) (prohibiting the merger).

After defining the relevant market, the analyst normally counts sales or capacity of each firm in the market and assigns a market share to each. There are two accepted frameworks for counting what is in the market. One is the snapshot method—to count what is actually there; i.e., to record who sells how much of the relevant product. The other is the method employed both by the 1997 Commission Notice and by the 1992 United States Federal Agency Merger Guidelines: to incorporate, as if already in the market, the goods that would flow into the market if a hypothetical monopolist should try to raise price. The latter method incorporates the near potential competition. Whether or not near potential competition is incorporated directly into the market, it is a positive force to be taken into account.

Next the analyst measures concentration. There are two recognized ways of stating the measurement of concentration. One is the use of n-firm concentration ratios;[4] e.g., the top two firms account for $x\%$ of the market; the top four firms account for $y\%$ of the market. The second is the use of the Herfindahl–Hirschman Index (HHI). To calculate the HHI, one lists each firm in the market and its market share, squares each market share, and then adds the squares of the shares. The sum of the squares is the HHI index number. Under each methodology, the key figures are those that represent the increase in concentration and the post-merger concentration. As a rule of thumb a market may be considered concentrated when the four leading firms have 75% or more of the market, or when the market has an HHI of 1800 to 2000 or more. The bare figures greatly overgeneralize facts, and the analysis should remain fact-specific.

Barriers and other hurdles to entry and expansion are then assessed. Even if a market is highly concentrated, the threat of entry may keep behavior competitive if entry at an efficient scale can be easily achieved.

Efficiencies may be relevant in two quite different ways. First, if the merger produces economies and saves costs and the market is competitive, cost savings may be passed on to consumers and the cost-saving strategies may be mimicked by competitors. These effects are directly relevant to whether competition is helped or hurt by the merger. Second, in some cases even where a merger lessens competitive rivalry, cost savings may neutralize the price effect on consumers, or in any event the producer's gain may be greater than the consumers' loss. This latter aspect might be called an efficiency *defense*. Community law has not adopted an efficiencies defense. Few jurisdictions have done so where the merger lessens competition and harms consumers.

D. SUBSTANTIVE LAW UNDER THE MERGER REGULATION

1. MERGERS OF COMPETITORS THAT INCREASE DOMINANCE

As of the end of the first year of operation of the Merger Regulation, 48 notifications had been made to the Commission. Some of the transactions

---

4. "N" represents an unspecified number.

notified were mergers of large, leading competitors. Yet, despite some clearances conditioned on spin-offs of overlapping assets, not one merger had been prohibited by the Commission. In the thirteenth month, the Commission examined the acquisition of de Havilland, the second largest commuter aircraft manufacturer in the world, by a joint venture owned by France and Italy that was the largest commuter aircraft manufacturer in the world.

a. De Havilland

AEROSPATIALE–ALENIA/de HAVILLAND

Commission Decision 91/619
O.J. L 334/42 (Dec. 5, 1991).

[The United States aircraft manufacturer, Boeing, agreed to sell its Canadian aircraft subsidiary de Havilland to a joint venture of two European firms, Aerospatiale of France and Alenia e Selenia of Italy. The joint venture, ATR, was the world's leading producer of turboprop or commuter aircraft; de Havilland was the number two producer. British Aerospace and Fokker were the only significant European competitors. Japanese firms were not in the market and not likely to enter "such a low-technology non-strategic market." Other possible potential competitors, notably firms from Indonesia and Eastern Europe, were either in financial difficulties or not capable of producing a product of sufficient quality for the world market.

The acquisition would lead to an increase in market shares for ATR in the world market for commuters between 40 to 59 seats from 46% to 63%. The nearest competitor (Fokker) would have 22%. ATR would increase its share of the overall worldwide commuter market of 20 to 70 seats from 30% to 50%. Saab, the nearest competitor, would have 19%. The new entity would account for half the world market and more than two and a half times the share of its nearest competitor.]

[30] ... The higher market share could give ATR more flexibility to compete on price (including financing) than its smaller competitors. ATR would be able to react with more flexibility to initiatives of competitors in the market place.

Following a concentration between ATR and de Havilland, the competitors would be faced with the combined strength of two large companies. This would mean that where an airline was considering placing a new order, the competitors would be in competition with the combined product range of ATR and de Havilland. The sales strategy of the formerly separate companies would now be concerted. The combination could enable the new entity ATR/de Havilland to be more flexible in setting its price than its competitors where a sale is contestable, because of their absolute size advantage in terms of sales base. Furthermore, unlike the competitors, the combined entity would have all the advantages of a family of commuters to offer. This may give rise to the ability, inter alia, of offering favourable conditions for a specific type of aircraft in mixed deals. It may be conceivable that, for example, where an airline wants to acquire a small commuter of around 30 seats and a commuter of around 60 seats, the ATR/de Havilland could offer special conditions for the ATR 72 when it is ordered with a Dash 8–100 where more competition is likely.

* * *

31   [The Commission found that de Havilland had plans to develop a new aircraft, and its potential competition would be eliminated. Moreover, despite de Havilland's financial difficulties, there was no likelihood that de Havilland would be phased out if the transaction did not proceed.]

32   The new entity ATR/de Havilland would be the only commuter manufacturer present in all the various commuter markets as defined above.

* * *

It appears that, in the sector concerned, having a complete range of products would give ATR/de Havilland a significant advantage in itself. From the demand side, airlines derive cost advantages from buying different types from the same seller.

* * *

According to a study submitted by the parties, it is argued that the inability of a manufacturer to offer a full range of seating capacities under the same umbrella may harm the demand for other existing aircraft of that manufacturer. Thus, a significant regional carrier whose aircraft needs may call for a full complement of aircraft capacities to meet the route needs of that carrier might be dissuaded from purchasing smaller aircraft from a single manufacturer if the needs of the carrier for a large aircraft could not also be met from the same aircraft manufacturer. This logic flows from the fixed costs borne by the carrier for each aircraft manufacturer dealt with by that carrier. These costs include the fixed costs of pilot and mechanic training as well as the costs of maintaining different in-house inventories of parts and the fixed costs of dealing with several manufacturers when ordering parts stocked only by the individual manufacturers themselves.

One of the stated main strategic objectives of the parties in acquiring de Havilland is to obtain coverage of the whole range of commuter aircraft. The competitive advantages which would arise from this would emerge over time.

* * *

In the short term, ATR and de Havilland would establish common marketing and product support which may result in some cost savings for the combined entity. It may be possible later to further rationalize product support by increasing the 30% commonality of spare parts between ATR and de Havilland which already exists. This rationalization would have cost-saving implications also for customers where they acquire aircraft types of both ATR and de Havilland.

* * *

33   ATR would significantly broaden its customer base after the concentration.

* * *

The customer base is an important element of market power for aircraft manufacturers since there is at least to some extent a lock-in effect for customers once their initial choice of aircraft is made.

Once a customer has made a commitment to a particular manufacturer, then there is usually a cost consideration in placing orders with another manufacturer. Customers indicate that there are relatively high costs arising from different technology used leading to training costs for maintenance and for pilots, and to different spare part requirements. The analysis of the fleets of the airlines shows that all airlines have only one type of new generation aircraft within a particular relevant product market. Furthermore, where airlines have aircraft from different relevant product markets, the fleet analysis shows that they always operate aircraft of the same manufacturer across different markets where the manufacturer produces types of the size required. . . .

* * *

51 The combined entity ATR/de Havilland will obtain a very strong position in the world and Community commuter markets of 40 seats and over, and in the overall world and Community commuter markets, as a result of the proposed concentration. The competitors in these markets are relatively weak. The bargaining ability of the customers is limited. The combination of these factors leads to the conclusion that the new entity could act to a significant extent independently of its competitors and customers, and would thus have a dominant position on the commuter markets as defined.

* * *

53 [The position would not be temporary. Entry was unlikely because sunk costs were high, time lag for entry was great, and demand was declining.]

65 The parties argue that one of their objectives in acquiring de Havilland is to reduce costs. The potential cost savings arising from the concentration which have been identified amount to only some ECU 5 million per year. According to the estimates of the parties' economic consultants, these cost savings to the combined entity would arise from rationalizing parts procurement, marketing and product support.

Without prejudice as to whether such considerations are relevant for assessment under Article 2 of the Merger Regulation, such cost savings would have a negligible impact on the overall operation of ATR/de Havilland, amounting to around 0.5% of the combined turnover. The parties have identified (although not quantified) cost savings which could be made by better management of certain aspects of de Havilland's internal operation. These cost savings would not arise as a consequence of the concentration per se, but are cost savings which could be achieved by de Havilland's existing owner or by any other potential acquirer.

66 The parties have not claimed that cost savings will arise from combining the research and development activities of ATR and de Havilland. This is in line with undertakings given to the Canadian authorities to maintain de Havilland as a full-function aircraft manufacturer.

* * *

69 For the above reasons, the Commission does not consider that the proposed concentration would contribute to the development of technical and economic progress within the meaning of Article 2(1)(b) of the Merger Regulation. Even if there was such progress, this would not be to the consumers' advantage.

The consumers will be faced with a dominant position which combines the most popular aircraft families on the market. Choice will be significantly reduced. There is a high risk that in the foreseeable future, the dominant position of ATR/de Havilland would be translated into a monopoly.

Both British Aerospace and Fokker, the two principal competitors in the markets of 40 seats and above, have stated that the concentration would seriously jeopardize the survival of the ATP and Fokker 50 aircraft. These two competitors expect that the proposed concentration would lead to ATR/de Havilland pursuing a strategy of initially lowering prices so as to eliminate the competitors at least in the key markets of 40 seats and above.

Neither Fokker nor British Aerospace consider it possible for them to withstand such a price war. Consequently, both would leave the markets.

In evaluating these statements, it is noted that such conduct could be rational since the proposed concentration would mean that ATR/de Havilland would exceed the threshold of market shares which would make such a pricing policy likely given that it would be the optimal profit-maximizing strategy.

Having established a monopoly, ATR/de Havilland would be able to increase prices without any competitive check.

70   With this perspective, the proposed concentration would become even more harmful to the customers over time as the dominant position translates to a monopoly. Higher prices for commuters have a proportionally large impact on regional airlines since the price of an aircraft accounts for some 30 to 40% of their total operating costs.

* * *

The proposed concentration ... is declared incompatible with the common market.

Notes and Questions

1. How did the Commission assess the efficiency effects of the acquisition? What is the rule of treatment for efficiencies?

2. How did the Commission assess ATR/de Havilland's possible strategies to foreclose and eliminate competition? Do you agree with the Commission's prediction of devastating price wars leading to a more complete monopoly?

3. Consider another scenario: The now strengthened ATR leads its few remaining competitors in a mutual accommodation strategy. ATR is the price leader. The others follow suit, charging marginally less to account for their lack of a full line. If this is the probable effect, would the merger infringe the Merger Regulation? Which was more likely: predation or détente?

4. *De Havilland* was the first merger prohibition under the Merger Regulation. The Governments of France and Italy, owners of the would-be acquirer ATR, were highly critical of the Commission's decision. So, too, was Commissioner Bangemann, Commissioner for the Internal Market, who argued that the acquisition was good for Europe and that the Competition Directorate and the Commission had improperly failed to take account of the interests of Europe—as opposed to merely the interests of competition. They threatened to press for an amendment to the Merger Regulation to assure that the Commission could weigh industrial policy. (Bangemann and French and Italian spokespeople argued also that the merger did not create or increase dominance.)

Look again at the Merger Regulation. Can the Commission take industrial policy into account? On what basis, and if so how and to what extent? Is it good or bad policy to allow an industrial policy counterweight to a dominance-creating merger? If the de Havilland acquisition had produced a European champion in a world market otherwise dominated by a strong American firm and a strong Japanese firm, do you think that the Commission might have decided the case differently?

5.   Meanwhile, Canada, home to de Havilland, had cleared the merger under its merger control procedures. Canada had strongly supported the merger, because de Havilland was in financial difficulties and constantly needed subsidies—which Canada paid, to protect Canadian jobs. The acquisition by ATR had seemed a promising route to turn around the fortunes of de Havilland. When the acquisition was declared incompatible with the common market, Canada sought another suitor for de Havilland. It identified Bombardier, which agreed to acquire de Havilland but which required a continuing and even greater subsidy.

6.   In the years since *de Havilland*, potential for international controversy has become a hallmark of merger control. As globalization has increased, so too have transnational mergers. Both the EU and the US have pre-merger notification and reporting systems that are triggered by relatively minimal sales in the jurisdiction. Some 40 other jurisdictions also have premerger notification laws, 20 more have merger notification systems, and extraterritorial application of the law has become standard practice. By the early 1990s, the EU and the US freely applied their laws to mergers of firms located abroad that had effects within their territories. Conflict was sure to follow.

b.   *Boeing/McDonnell Douglas*

In the same year that *de Havilland* was decided, the EU and the US anticipated the need for greater cooperation, and entered into the Cooperation Agreement of 1991. In this agreement, each party agreed to notify the other upon becoming aware "that their enforcement activities may affect important interests of the other party." "[W]ithin the framework of its own laws and to the extent compatible with its important interests," each agreed "to take into account the important interests of the other Party," and to seek "an appropriate accommodation of the competing interests." The agreement was invoked six years later, in connection with Boeing's plan to acquire McDonnell Douglas.

Boeing was the largest manufacturer of commercial jet aircraft in the world, accounting for about 64% of world market sales. Its only competitors were McDonnell Douglas, with about 5%, and Airbus Industrie, with about 30%. Airbus was a consortium of manufacturers in Britain, France, Germany and Spain. Those countries had helped to finance Airbus.

Boeing and McDonnell Douglas were US companies and had no production assets in Europe, although they regularly made sales there. McDonnell Douglas also produced military jets, and its technology portfolio included patents from research and development undertaken with US government financing. In the commercial jet market, McDonnell Douglas had failed to invest in important new-generation developments and was facing financial and competitive difficulties. Its market share was withering. Boeing, meanwhile, had recently concluded 20–year exclusive supply agreements with three big American airlines—Delta, American, and Continental. The exclusive supply agreements represented about 11% of all world purchases of big commercial jets.

Commercial jet airplanes are very complex and sell in the range of $32 million to $171 million each. An order from an airline is typically worth billions of dollars. In view of the fact that each sale to an airline is so significant, Airbus and Boeing were fierce competitors for sales around the world.

Boeing and McDonnell Douglas filed premerger notifications in the United States and in the European Union. EC Competition Commissioner Karel Van Miert immediately expressed concerns about the merger and the exclusive agreements. On the US side, the Federal Trade Commission opened an investigation. The European Commission and the FTC made notifications to one another under the 1991 agreement, and the European and American officials shared their perspectives. They sharply disagreed on the analysis of anticompetitive effects.

Early on, politicians entered the fray, with Europeans declaring that the merger was blatantly anticompetitive and seriously harmful to competition and to Airbus, and Americans declaring that the merger was good for the American economy. Laura D'Andrea Tyson, former head of the Council of Economic Advisors, was quoted in the Washington Post (May 4, 1997, p. H6) as saying that this merger was good for America "even if consumers of airplane seats are somewhat worse off." Commissioner Van Miert threatened that, if the merger should be consummated without EC approval, the European Commission would impose prohibitive fines on Boeing and might seize Boeing planes flying into the European Union.

On July 1, 1997, the US FTC issued a statement announcing the closing of its investigation.

IN THE MATTER OF THE BOEING COMPANY/McDONNELL DOUGLAS CORPORATION

U.S. Federal Trade Commission, Statement
5 CCH Trade Reg. Rep. ¶ 24,295 (July 1, 1997).

After an extensive and exhaustive investigation, the Federal Trade Commission has decided to close the investigation of The Boeing Company's proposed acquisition of McDonnell Douglas Corporation. For reasons discussed below, we have concluded that the acquisition would not substantially lessen competition or tend to create a monopoly in either defense or commercial aircraft markets.

There has been speculation in the press and elsewhere that the United States antitrust authorities might allow this transaction to go forward—particularly the portion of the transaction dealing with the manufacture of commercial aircraft—because aircraft manufacturing occurs in a global market, and the United States, in order to compete in that market, needs a single powerful firm to serve as its "national champion." A powerful United States firm is all the more important, the argument proceeds, because that firm's success contributes much to improving the United States' balance of trade and to providing jobs for U.S. workers. * * *

We do not have the discretion to authorize anticompetitive but "good" mergers because they may be thought to advance the United States' trade interests. If that were thought to be a wise approach, only Congress could implement it. In any event, the "national champion" argument is almost certainly a delusion. In reality, the best way to boost the United States' exports, address concerns about the balance of trade, and create jobs is to require United States' firms to compete vigorously at home and abroad....

On its face, the proposed merger appears to raise serious antitrust concerns. The transaction involves the acquisition by Boeing, a company that accounts for roughly 60% of the sales of large commercial aircraft, of a non-failing direct competitor in a market in which there is only one other significant rival, Airbus Industrie, and extremely high barriers to entry. The merger would also combine two firms in the U.S. defense industry that develop fighter aircraft and other defense products. Nevertheless, for reasons we will now discuss, we do not find that this merger will substantially lessen competition in any relevant market. * * *

The evidence collected during the staff investigation, including the virtually unanimous testimony of forty airlines that staff interviewed, revealed that McDonnell Douglas's commercial aircraft division, Douglas Aircraft Company, can no longer exert a competitive influence in the worldwide market for commercial aircraft. Over the past several decades, McDonnell Douglas has not invested at nearly the rate of its competitors in new product lines, production facilities, company infrastructure, or research and development. As a result, Douglas Aircraft's product line is not only very limited, but lacks the state of the art technology and performance characteristics that Boeing and Airbus have developed. Moreover, Douglas Aircraft's line of aircraft do not have common features such as cockpit design or engine type, and thus cannot generate valuable efficiencies in interchangeable spare parts and pilot training that an airline may obtain from a family of aircraft, such as Boeing's 737 family or Airbus's A–320 family.

In short, the staff investigation revealed that the failure to improve the technology and efficiency of its commercial aircraft products has lead to a deterioration of Douglas Aircraft's product line to the point that the vast majority of airlines will no longer consider purchasing Douglas aircraft and that the company is no longer in a position to influence significantly the competitive dynamics of the commercial aircraft market. * * *

Procedurally, the closing of the investigation was not a judicial finding that the merger was lawful under US law. Unlike a decision in Europe, an initial US decision not to challenge a merger does not preclude subsequent challenge. It remained theoretically possible for the merger to be tested in the US courts; e.g. in a private action by Airbus or in a suit by a state, if not by the Federal Government. Nonetheless, immediately after the FTC closed its investigation, the Clinton Administration began to take an active political role in defending the merger to Europe. Key White House officials, including the President of the United States, argued to key European officials, including the President of the European Commission, that the merger was not anticompetitive, that it was important to the defense interests of the United States (because the military assets of McDonnell Douglas would be best preserved in the hands of Boeing), and to employment in the United States, and that the United States was "considering how to retaliate against Europe if it makes good on its threat to try and undermine the merger of [the] U.S. aerospace giants...." The Washington Post, July 17, 1997, p. C1. Reportedly, the Administration officials were considering imposing tariffs on European planes, limiting flights between the United States and France (the most adamant objector to the merger), and filing a protest with the World Trade Organization in view of European subsidies to Airbus.

Meanwhile, Boeing was negotiating with the European Commission, and at the eleventh hour it agreed to conditions acceptable to the Commission. The conditions were not acceptable to France, however, which continued to argue that only a prohibition would cure the essential problems. On July 30, 1997, the Commission issued its decision in the matter of Boeing/McDonnell Douglas.

BOEING/McDONNELL DOUGLAS

Commission Decision, Case IV/M877
O.J. L 336/16 (Dec. 8, 1997).

Effects on World Market for Large Commercial Jet Aircraft

I.   *Current structure of the market for large commercial jet aircraft* * * *

Fleet in service

40   Boeing, as the company itself states in its 1995 annual report, has led the world production of commercial aeroplanes for more than three decades and has built more jet aircraft than all the other manufacturers combined. Given the typical long operating life of these products, Boeing has by far the broadest customer base which gives it a significant competitive advantage vis-a-vis its competitors.

41   It is estimated that Boeing has a share of around 60% of the current worldwide fleet in service of western-built, large passenger aircraft. The share of MDC is around 24% and that of Airbus only around 14% even more than 25 years after Airbus began operations. The remaining 2% are related to Lockheed aircraft still in operation; Lockheed has, however, no longer been active in the production of commercial aircraft since 1984. It is true that the existence of a large fleet in service is not a guarantee of the success of a supplier of commercial aircraft, particularly when a supplier offers only a limited range of aircraft types. However, where a large fleet in service is combined with a broad product range, the existing fleet in service can be a key factor which may often determine decisions of airlines on fleet planning or acquisitions. Cost savings arising from commonality benefits, such as engineering spares inventory and flight crew qualifications, are very influential in an airline's decision-making process for aircraft type selections and may frequently lead to the acquisition of a certain type of aircraft even if the price of competing products is lower. The importance of the existing fleet in service for the choice of new aircraft has been underlined by all airlines which replied to the Commission's questions on this point.

42   In this context, it should be noted that Boeing has not only by far the largest fleet in service, but also by far the broadest product range and it offers a family of aircraft which covers all conceivable segments of large commercial aircraft.

Exclusive deals

43   Boeing has recently entered into exclusive arrangements for the supply of large commercial jet aircraft to American Airlines (American), Delta Airlines (Delta), and Continental Airlines (Continental). * * *

45   The fact that three of the biggest airlines in the world have locked themselves into a 20–year supply agreement with a single supplier is already an indication that Boeing enjoys a dominant position in the large commercial aircraft market. Furthermore it is likely that those three deals were facilitated by the proposed merger (as explained below). Although, as indicated, the customers are to receive economic benefits from the deals, these are likely to be more than offset by the rigidity incurred by being locked into a single supplier for so long a period, during which it might prove to be the case that competitors' prices become lower, their technology and related services superior.

46   The existing exclusive deals between Boeing and the three airlines in question will have important foreclosure effects on the worldwide market for large commercial jet aircraft over the next 20 years. It is estimated that 14 400 new aircraft will be delivered worldwide between 1997 and 2016, of which about 2 400 are on firm order with Boeing, MDC or Airbus. There thus remains an open market for about 12 000 aircraft. However, Boeing's exclusive deals including options and purchase rights, account for an estimated 13% of this open market (or over 30% of the US market). * * *

Potential competition

48   In its notification Boeing states that there are potential new entrants to the large commercial jet aircraft market, particularly companies situated in Russia, India and the Far East (China, Japan, South Korea and Indonesia).

49   However, Boeing itself effectively admits that there are massive barriers to entry to this market. Initial development and investment costs are huge (over US $10 billion to develop a new wide-body jet, according to Boeing). The production process itself is characterized by very significant learning curve effects and economies of scale and scope, which must be attained if a new entrant is to compete effectively over time. Very strict safety regulations need to be complied with at US, European and other national levels. * * *

51   It can therefore be excluded that potential competition will have any significant impact on the present competitive situation over the foreseeable future.

Conclusion

52   In view of the various characteristics of the current structure of the markets for large commercial jet aircraft, as described above, in particular the existing market shares of Boeing, the size of its fleet in service, the recent conclusion of long-term exclusive supply deals with major customers, and the lack of potential new entrants, the Commission has reached the conclusion that Boeing already enjoys a dominant position on the overall market for large commercial aircraft as well as on the markets for narrow-body and wide-body aircraft.

II.   Strengthening of Boeing's dominant position

53   The proposed concentration would lead to a strengthening of Boeing's dominant position in large commercial aircraft through:

— the addition of MDC's competitive potential in large commercial aircraft to Boeing's existing position in this market,

— the large increase in Boeing's overall resources and in Boeing's defence and space business which has a significant spill-over effect on Boeing's position in large commercial aircraft and makes this position even less assailable.

Impact of MDC's commercial aircraft business

54   The immediate effect of the proposed concentration would be that:

(a) Boeing would increase its market share in the overall market for large commercial aircraft from 64% to 70%;

(b) by taking over the activities of MDC, Boeing would, in future, be faced with only one competitor in this market;

(c) Boeing would increase its customer base from 60% to 84% of the current fleet in service;

(d) Boeing would increase its capacity in commercial aircraft, particularly in terms of skilled work force;

(e) Boeing would increase its ability to induce airlines to enter into exclusivity deals, thereby further foreclosing the market. * * *

Competitive potential of MDC

(i) The competitive influence of MDC was in the past greater than reflected by its market share

58   Although, as outlined above, the market share of MDC has been continuously declining, it appears that the impact of MDC on the conditions of competition in the market for large commercial aircraft was higher than reflected by its market share in 1996.

The Commission has received replies from 31 airlines which have all purchased new large commercial aircraft over the last five years. Two of them purchased only MDC aircraft. Out of the remaining 29 airlines, 20 stated that in those cases where they had placed orders with Boeing or Airbus, MDC had been in competition for all or a part of the orders. Out of the 20 airlines, 13 stated that competition from MDC had an influence on the outcome of their negotiations with the winner of the bid in terms of a better price or better purchasing conditions. Two airlines stated that this influence was of major importance and three stated that this influence was of minor importance. Seven airlines stated that the influence of MDC's competition was of significant importance.

This is confirmed by a study conducted by Lexecon Ltd. on behalf of Airbus and presented at the Hearing, in which 52 aircraft-supply competitions between 1994 and 1996 were analysed, comparing those in which MDC participated with those in which it did not participate. In this study, it was found that the MDC presence led to a reduction of over 7% in the realized price as compared with the list price as far as orders placed with Airbus were concerned.

(ii) However, today MDC is no longer a real force in the market for the sale of new aircraft on a stand-alone basis

59 The Douglas Aircraft Company (DAC), which operates the commercial aircraft business of MDC, generated in 1996 operating earnings of US $100 million as compared with US $39 million and US $47 million in 1995 and 1994 respectively. Furthermore, DAC has still a firm backlog of US $7 billion. However, it appears that the operating earnings of DAC were essentially related to DAC's spare parts and product support business rather than to the sale of new aircraft. In contrast to the broader and more modern families of aircraft offered by Boeing and Airbus, DAC currently offers only three types of narrow-body and one type of wide-body aircraft which do not provide, according to Boeing, significant commonality benefits and are all themselves derivatives of earlier Douglas models, rather than entirely new designs. It appears that these are the main reasons for the continuous decline of DAC's market shares. Furthermore, the current backlog covers only a limited period of future production. Since the cancellation of the MDXX program in October 1996, DAC has virtually received no new firm orders. This reflects the perception of airlines that MDC is no longer committed to the commercial aircraft business and may leave the market over time. In this context, it is also important that DAC lost over the last nine months its core customers American, Northwest Airlines, Delta and Continental, the four largest operators of DAC aircraft. The loss of these 'mainstream' airline customers, which are points of reference for others and one of which, Delta, was even the launch customer for the MD90, gave a further signal to the market that DAC would have no prospects in the market for large commercial aircraft. In these circumstances, it has to be concluded that DAC is today no longer a real force in the market on a stand-alone basis.

(iii) It is unlikely that a third party would acquire MDC's commercial aircraft business

60 ... DAC's position on the market deteriorated dramatically in 1997. Extensive market enquiries carried out by the Commission made it clear that it is in practice highly unlikely that a third party would acquire DAC. It appears that this is inter alia due to the deterioration of the situation of DAC. Neither Airbus, the only competitor left in the market for large commercial aircraft, nor one of its parent companies showed an interest in the acquisition of DAC. Furthermore, no other potential buyers were interested in entering the market for large commercial aircraft through the acquisition of DAC. It appears, therefore, that, given the current competitive situation of DAC, only Boeing is prepared to take over MDC's commercial aircraft business.

(iv) The competitive potential of MDC's commercial aircraft business can, however, be a significant factor in the market when it is integrated into the Boeing group

61 Boeing has stated that it could decide on the continuation or discontinuation of DAC's product lines only once it has had access to DAC's internal data.... In the event that Boeing continues production of DAC aircraft, the existing negative perception of MDC's prospects could be removed. That could equally remove the reluctance, to a certain extent, on the part

of airlines to buy DAC aircraft stemming from uncertainty about the future of its commercial aircraft business. As a part of the Boeing Group, DAC aircraft could be marketed together with Boeing aircraft and Boeing would be able to decide when to put DAC aircraft into a competition and when not.

If, by contrast, Boeing were to decide to phase out production of all or some DAC aircraft over time, Boeing would be better placed than Airbus to gain the market shares freed by such a decision. Through Boeing's preferential access to the large existing customer base of DAC, as outlined below, Boeing would be in an advantageous position to replace, over time, DAC aircraft which are in service today.

Fleet in service

62   Boeing would increase its share in the existing fleet in service from 60% to 84% (as opposed to only 14% for Airbus) and would, therefore, increase its long-term relationships with customers and its position in customer support. It would also significantly broaden its customer base. It appears that out of the 561 airlines operating Boeing, MDC and Airbus aircraft at the end of 1996, 75 operators use only MDC aircraft and 10 operators use only MDC and Airbus aircraft. In addition to the 316 airlines operating only Boeing aircraft, the 50 airlines operating Boeing and MDC, the 62 airlines operating Boeing and Airbus and the 26 airlines operating Boeing, MDC and Airbus (only 22 airlines operate exclusively Airbus), Boeing would also get access to a further 85 airlines which do not as yet operate Boeing aircraft.

63   The opportunity for closer contacts with those airlines resulting from ongoing support activities could provide opportunities for future sales by allowing Boeing to influence customer needs. However, it has to be recognized that Boeing already has close contacts with a large number of airlines through its own product support activities.

64   In general, the acquisition of MDC's spare-parts and maintenance business may confer on Boeing significant additional leverage over existing MDC aircraft users, whose combined MDC fleets constitute, as already stated, 24% of the total aircraft fleet worldwide.

*Use of MDC's capacity * * ***

67   In the aircraft industry, flexibility of capacity, or the ability to increase and decrease production easily, is an important factor. From the standpoint of the airlines, a manufacturer that can offer the required delivery slots in periods of rapidly increasing demand clearly has an advantage. One crucial element for a rapid increase in capacity is the availability of skilled labour, which would be increased for Boeing through the access to MDC's workforce.

Exclusive deals

68   The proposed merger would significantly enhance Boeing's capacity to enter into agreements such as those concluded with American, Delta and Continental. It should be noted that such airlines are amongst the world's largest and are 'launch customers for new aircraft models, that is to say, they are in effect the only airlines with sufficient resources to commit themselves to entirely new aircraft models or new families of aircraft. In

particular, with respect to those airlines which currently operate both Boeing and MDC aircraft, within the framework of an exclusivity deal, Boeing could also offer the provision of additional MDC aircraft, as well as spare-parts and support services for older MDC aircraft. On the other hand, where airlines which have ordered MDC aircraft want to streamline their fleet, Boeing, being in control of MDC, would simply cancel those MDC orders and the penalties which normally have to be paid by airlines in the event of cancellation of orders would be of no significance. * * *

[70] More generally, Boeing's broader product range after the merger, its financial resources and its higher capacity which enables it to respond to airlines' needs for deliveries on a short lead time would, in combination, significantly increase Boeing's ability to induce airlines to enter into exclusive deals. It should be noted that it would be impossible for Airbus to offer exclusive deals because Airbus is unable to offer a full 'family' of aircraft.

[71] The potential effect of exclusive deals with the world's top ten airlines would be to block over 40% of the worldwide market (based on those airlines' existing fleet in service as a proportion of the worldwide fleet). Such a scenario is quite feasible, since there could be a knock-on effect whereby further large airlines would not want to miss out on the apparent advantages accruing to their competitors who have already entered into exclusive deals. The result could be a split worldwide market, with the biggest airlines with the largest fleets exclusively controlled by Boeing following the merger, leaving competition possible only for the supply of the aircraft requirements of smaller airlines. * * *

Overall effects resulting from the defence and space business of MDC

[72] The overall effects resulting from the take-over of MDC's defence and space business would lead to a strengthening of Boeing's dominant position through:

(a) an increase in Boeing's overall financial resources;

(b) an increase in Boeing's access to publicly funded R & D and intellectual property portfolio;

(c) an increase in Boeing's bargaining power vis-a-vis suppliers;

(d) opportunities for offset and 'bundling deals'. * * *

[109] Offset deals are a mechanism whereby a supplier provides technology or production capacity in the purchasing country in exchange for that country purchasing the supplier's product. Direct offset consists of production or technology related to the product being sold. Indirect offset is unrelated to the product, but typically in a related technology field.

[110] Offsets in commercial aircraft sales are less common than in military aircraft sales where they are the rule. In the commercial aircraft sector, offsets have also, in part, been limited by international agreement. However, it appears that in the commercial aircraft sector offsets do play quite a significant role, particularly in countries with State-owned national carriers. Two recent instances may be cited as examples. In 1996 Malaysian Airlines ordered 25 aeroplanes from Boeing on the basis of an offset programme to help Malaysia develop its avionics and composite

materials industry. According to the press, the Department of Trade and Industry of South Africa has recently imposed a 50% offset requirement on all long-term government purchases. This new offset policy will also apply to South African Airways where attempts to purchase seven new aircraft from Boeing were frozen pending the formalization of new offset rules. Boeing itself has stated that in the past it has entered into a number of commercial offset deals. * * *

[113] For the reasons outlined above, the Commission has reached the conclusion that the proposed concentration would lead to the strengthening of a dominant position through which effective competition would be significantly impeded in the common market within the meaning of Article 2(3) of the Merger Regulation.

Remedies

[Boeing undertook, among other things: not to enforce its exclusivity rights under the agreements with American, Delta and Continental; not to enter into exclusive agreements until 2007; not to "use its privileged access to the existing fleet in service of DAC aircraft in order to leverage its opportunities for persuading current DAC operators to purchase Boeing aircraft"; to license to competitors upon request all US-funded patents usable in the manufacture or sale of commercial jet aircraft; and not to leverage its relationship with suppliers to refuse to deal with Boeing's competitors or to grant preferential treatment to Boeing.]

Notes and Questions

1. Analyze the merger. Apply the *de Havilland* analysis. Does *de Havilland* dictate the result in *Boeing*?

2. How did the merger create or strengthen a dominant position as a result of which effective competition in the common market would be significantly impaired? What is the significance of the fact that Boeing would gain a fuller line of jet planes, and that buyers (the airlines) saved money and time—including pilot training costs and replacement and maintenance costs—by dealing with one producer? What is the significance of the fact that Boeing would have access to technology that was funded by the US Government? (Was this funding a subsidy?)

What is the significance of the facts that: McDonnell Douglas was "no longer a real force in the market for the sale of new aircraft on a stand-alone basis" (para. 58); no one but Boeing wanted to acquire McDonnell Douglas; and, if the merger was prohibited Boeing would probably absorb McDonnell Douglas' share anyway? Why didn't these facts destroy the Commission's case that the *merger* (as opposed to the ultimate demise of McDonnell Douglas) would strengthen a dominant position and impair effective competition?

3. If the merger did strengthen Boeing's dominance, why wasn't France correct that only a prohibition would cure the problem?

4. Comment on the statement by the US Federal Trade Commission. Do you believe that the national champion argument was irrelevant? Should it be relevant?

US law treats merger cases from the point of view of consumer welfare. The inquiry is whether the merger will raise prices or suppress innovation. What was the probable effect of the Boeing merger on price competition or innovation? Do any of the following theories support the prediction of a price rise, as applied to the facts in *Boeing*?

a) Oligopolistic (duopolistic) collaboration:

(i) The hypothesis that Boeing and Airbus would divide markets or reach détente on price or innovation competition.

(ii) The hypothesis that competition was already suppressed and—absent the merger—a new investor from Asia or elsewhere would have bought McDonnell Douglas, infused it with new life, and caused competition to break out.

b) Monopolistic predation: the hypothesis that Boeing would lower its prices (possibly, the price of a bundled portfolio of planes) below its own costs or below the point at which Airbus could afford to sell; squeeze Airbus out of the market; and raise its prices to a monopoly level without attracting new entry.

5. Would European merger law require that one of the above scenarios be probable in order for the merger to be incompatible with the common market? What if the principal effect of the merger was to create competitive advantages for Boeing over Airbus, through exclusive contracts, subsidies, a "foot in the door" to attract McDonnell Douglas' customers, and Boeing's ability to supply a full line of jets; and these advantages allowed Boeing to charge a lower price? Are any of these advantages illegal? unfair?

6. European analysis takes account of competitors' access to markets as well as consumer prices and choice. Also, under EC law, when a firm's market share increases from 60% to 70 or 80%, this presumptively constitutes an increase in dominance. (Why not also under US law?) Moreover, the European Commission saw the exclusive dealing contracts as facilitated by and integral to the merger, while the FTC saw them as independent of the merger. (Which were they? and were they essentially efficient or exclusionary?) Do these points explain the different outcomes reached by the European Commission and by the US FTC? If not, what does?

7. Was *Boeing-McDonnell Douglas* purely a competition case? Who had the stronger side of the argument: the Europeans, most of whom seemed to believe that the US green light was industrial policy to promote Boeing as the US national champion? or the Americans, most of whom seemed to believe that the EU opposition was industrial policy to protect Airbus as the European champion? Might both accusations have been correct?

c.   *The Failing Firm Defense*

FRANCE v. COMMISSION (KALI + SALZ)

Cases C–68/94, C–30/95, [1998] ECR I–1375.

[After the fall of the Berlin wall and in view of the plan and then the reality of German unification, Germany established the Treuhandanstalt ("Treuhand"), a public institution entrusted with the task of restructuring the firms of the former German Democratic Republic. The Treuhand had title to, among others, Mitteldeutsche Kali AG ("MdK"), which held all of the GDR's operations in potash and rock salt. The business had escalating losses and was likely to close down if not taken over by a private firm. The only available, willing purchaser was Kali und Salz AG ("K+S"), a subsidiary of

BASF chemicals group. It was proposed that K+S buy 51% of the stock of MdK, leaving 49% with the Truehand. This would result in K+S's achieving 98% of the German market for potash-salt-based products for agricultural use.

With respect to the German market:]

11 . . . applying the theory of the 'failing company defence', [the Commission] reached the conclusion that the proposed concentration was not the cause of the strengthening of the dominant position of K+S on the German market. . . . [T]he conditions for the 'failing company defence' were met, namely that K+S's dominant position would be reinforced even in the absence of the merger, because MdK would withdraw from the market in the foreseeable future if it was not acquired by another undertaking and its market share would then accrue to K+S; it can be practically ruled out that an undertaking other than K+S would acquire all or a substantial part of MdK'. . . . The Commission further observed in point 95 that, given the severe structural weakness of the regions in East Germany which were affected by the proposed concentration, and the likelihood of serious consequences for them of the closure of MdK, the conclusion it had reached was also in line with the fundamental objective of strengthening the Community's economic and social cohesion, referred to in the 13th recital in the preamble to the Regulation.

[France sought annulment of the Commission's decision to allow the acquisition with respect to the German market without imposing any conditions. The Court of Justice rejected this claim.]

106 The German Government submits that, under Article 2(3) of the Regulation, a concentration may be prohibited only if it will worsen conditions of competition. There is no causal link between the concentration and its effect on competition where the identical worsening of conditions of competition is to be expected even without the concentration. That will be the case when the three conditions applied by the Commission are satisfied.

107 The German Government submits that, contrary to the French Government's contention, the Commission has shown to the necessary legal standard that the conditions it laid down were satisfied. First, MdK is not viable on its own, that is to say, it is not possible to restructure the undertaking while preserving its autonomy in the market. In point 76 of the contested decision, the Commission gave solid reasons for considering that with Treuhand's 100% ownership being maintained MdK was not likely to be rescued in the long term. Second, there is no doubt that MdK's market share would automatically be absorbed by K+S, since K+S would be alone on the relevant market after MdK had been forced out, and that is an essential condition in this context. Third, the German Government submits that the Commission gave exhaustive reasons as to why no alternative means of acquiring MdK was available.

108 As to the approval of the concentration on the German market without conditions or obligations, the German Government observes that in the absence of a causal link between the concentration and the strengthening of a dominant position, one of the conditions for imposing a prohibition

under Article 2(3) of the Regulation was not fulfilled. The concentration therefore had to be authorised without obligations or conditions.

[109] The Court observes at the outset that under Article 2(2) of the Regulation, a 'concentration which does not create or strengthen a dominant position as a result of which effective competition would be significantly impeded in the common market or in a substantial part of it shall be declared compatible with the common market'.

[110] Thus if a concentration is not the cause of the creation or strengthening of a dominant position which has a significant impact on the competitive situation on the relevant market, it must be declared compatible with the common market.

[111] It appears from point 71 of the contested decision that, in the Commission's opinion, a concentration which would normally be considered as leading to the creation or reinforcement of a dominant position on the part of the acquiring undertaking may be regarded as not being the cause of it if, even in the event of the concentration being prohibited, that undertaking would inevitably achieve or reinforce a dominant position. Point 71 goes on to state that, as a general matter, a concentration is not the cause of the deterioration of the competitive structure if it is clear that:

— the acquired undertaking would in the near future be forced out of the market if not taken over by another undertaking,

— the acquiring undertaking would gain the market share of the acquired undertaking if it were forced out of the market,

— there is no less anticompetitive alternative purchase. * * *

[The Commission was entitled to conclude that there was an "absence of a causal link between the concentration and the deterioration of the competitive structure of the German market. . . ." In this case "it is not possible . . . to attach any condition whatever to [the] declaration of the concentration's compatibility." para. 124.]

Notes and Questions

1. A failing firm defense is also found in US caselaw, to which the Court referred. The US and EU defenses are quite similar but not identical. "Causal" link analysis is not specifically contained in US law; but the need for causation is implicit. See Citizen Publishing Co. v. United States, 394 U.S. 131, 89 S.Ct. 927, 22 L.Ed.2d 148 (1969).

2. Note the Commission's industrial policy argument, in paragraph 11: Saving MdK will save jobs in the former East Germany and strengthen economic and social cohesion. Is this argument admissible under the Merger Regulation? Would it have saved the merger if there were a causal link between the concentration and the entrenchment of monopoly power? Should it have?

In the United States, saving jobs and community formed a major part of the reason for creating the failing firm defense. See International Shoe Co. v. FTC, 280 U.S. 291, 302, 50 S.Ct. 89, 74 L.Ed. 431 (1930).

3. Why wasn't the causal link between the concentration and the harm to competition similarly lacking in *Boeing*, *supra*, given the Commission's concessions that: "[I]t has to be concluded that DAC is today no longer a real force in

the market on a stand-alone basis." (para. 59) "[D]ue to the deterioration of the situation of DAC ... , only Boeing is prepared to take over MDC's commercial aircraft business." (para. 60).

2. MERGERS OF COMPETITORS THAT FACILITATE COORDINATED BEHAVIOR (COLLECTIVE DOMINANCE)

The Merger Regulation prohibits *dominance* that may impede effective competition. But the problem of anticompetitive mergers is not limited to the problem of dominance. Duopoly and oligopoly problems are at least as compelling. The Commission was quite aware of this possible gap in the law, and from the early days of the Merger Regulation, it sought a test case.

FRANCE v. COMMISSION (KALI + SALZ)

Cases C–68/94, 30/95, [1998] ECR I–1375
(duopoly aspects; community market outside of Germany).

[As seen above, Kali and Salz (K + S), the largest potash producer in the Community, proposed to acquire Mitteldeutsche Kali AG (MdK), formerly the state-owned potash producer in East Germany. MdK was the second largest potash producer in the Community. As a result of the acquisition, K + S and SCPA would hold 60% of the Community potash market outside of Germany (which was held to be a separate geographic market). The Commission concluded that there would probably be no effective competition remaining on the market because of the weak, fragmented fringe firms, the past behavior of K + S and SCPA, and the long standing and close commercial links between K + S and SCPA, including their participation in an export cartel to third countries, a joint venture in Canada, and a buyer/supplier relationship in France. The Commission allowed the merger subject to conditions that basically would sever the links.

France and SCPA sought annulment of the Commission's decision, arguing, among other things, that the Merger Regulation proscribes only the creation or strengthening of a *dominant* position, not the creation or strengthening of a duopoly (two firms) or oligopoly (few firms)].

152 The French Government and the applicant companies submit that the Regulation does not authorise the Commission to apply it in cases where there is a collective dominant position. On this point, they observe that the wording of the Regulation, in particular Article 2 thereof, unlike Article 86 of the EC Treaty does not expressly refer to collective dominant positions. Whereas Article 86 of the Treaty prohibits abuse by one or more undertakings of a 'dominant position', Article 2 of the Regulation regards as compatible with the common market concentrations which do not create or strengthen an anticompetitive dominant position, and as incompatible those which do. [Nor does the legislative history support the view that the Merger Regulation covers more than single firm dominance; the recitals undercut the position; and the position would expose third parties that participate in the collective dominance to consequences without rights of participation.] * * *

165 The Court finds, first of all, that the applicants' submission, to the effect that the choice of legal bases in itself militates in favour of the argument that the Regulation does not apply to collective dominant positions,

cannot be accepted.... Articles 87 and 235 of the Treaty can in principle be used as the legal bases of a regulation permitting preventive action with respect to concentrations which create or strengthen a collective dominant position liable to have a significant effect on competition.

[166] Second, it cannot be deduced from the wording of Article 2 of the Regulation that only concentrations which create or strengthen an individual dominant position, that is, a dominant position held by the parties to the concentration, come within the scope of the Regulation. Article 2, in referring to a concentration which creates or strengthens a 'dominant position', does not in itself exclude the possibility of applying the Regulation to cases where concentrations lead to the creation or strengthening of a collective dominant position, that is, a dominant position held by the parties to the concentration together with an entity not a party thereto.

[167] Third, with respect to the travaux preparatoires [the claim that the legislative history does not support coverage of collective dominance], it appears from the documents in the case that they cannot be regarded as expressing clearly the intention of the authors of the Regulation as to the scope of the term 'dominant position'. In those circumstances, the travaux preparatoires provide no assistance for the interpretation of the disputed concept.

[168] Since the textual and historical interpretations of the Regulation, and in particular Article 2 thereof, do not permit its precise scope to be assessed as regards the type of dominant position concerned, the provision in question must be interpreted by reference to its purpose and general structure.

[169] As may be seen from the first and second recitals in its preamble, the Regulation is founded on the premise that the objective of instituting a system to ensure that competition in the common market is not distorted is essential for the achievement of the internal market by 1992 and for its future development.

[170] It follows from the sixth, seventh, tenth and eleventh recitals in the preamble that the Regulation, unlike Articles 85 and 86 of the Treaty, is intended to apply to all concentrations with a Community dimension in so far as they are likely, because of their effect on the structure of competition within the Community, to prove incompatible with the system of undistorted competition envisaged by the Treaty.

[171] A concentration which creates or strengthens a dominant position on the part of the parties concerned with an entity not involved in the concentration is liable to prove incompatible with the system of undistorted competition which the Treaty seeks to secure. Consequently, if it were accepted that only concentrations creating or strengthening a dominant position on the part of the parties to the concentration were covered by the Regulation, its purpose as indicated in particular by the abovementioned recitals would be partially frustrated. The Regulation would thus be deprived of a not insignificant aspect of its effectiveness, without that being necessary from the perspective of the general structure of the Community system of control of concentrations. * * *

174   In any event, even on the assumption that a finding by the Commission
       that the proposed concentration creates or strengthens a collective domi-
       nant position involving the undertakings concerned on the one hand and
       a third party on the other may in itself adversely affect that third party, it
       must be borne in mind that observance of the right to be heard is, in all
       proceedings liable to culminate in a measure adversely affecting a particu-
       lar person, a fundamental principle of Community law which must be
       guaranteed even in the absence of any rules governing the procedure.

175   Given the existence of that principle, and the purpose of the Regulation as
       explained above, the fact that the Community legislature did not express-
       ly provide in the Regulation for a procedure safeguarding the right to be
       heard of third party undertakings alleged to hold a collective dominant
       position together with the undertakings involved in the concentration
       cannot be regarded as decisive evidence of the Regulation's inapplicability
       to collective dominant positions.

176   As to the second argument, the presumption that concentrations are
       compatible with the common market if the undertakings concerned have
       a combined market share of less than 25%, as stated in the 15th recital in
       the preamble, is not developed in any way in the operative part of the
       Regulation.

177   The 15th recital in the preamble to the Regulation must, having regard in
       particular to the realities of the market underlying this recital, be
       interpreted as meaning that a concentration which does not give the
       undertakings concerned a combined share of at least 25% of the reference
       market is presumed not to create or strengthen an anticompetitive
       dominant position on the part of those undertakings.

178   It follows from the foregoing that collective dominant positions do not fall
       outside the scope of the Regulation.

* * *

The Court proceeded to examine the Commission's conclusion that the
concentration would give rise to a collective dominant position. According to
the Commission, this conclusion flowed from the degree of concentration, the
market position of the competitors, the inelasticity of demand (potash is an
essential fertilizer for agriculture; it cannot be replaced), homogeneity of the
product and transparency of transactions, the barriers to entry, the existence
of parallel conduct, and the existence of structural links between K+S and
SCPA. The links "were the essential factor relied on by the Commission in
making its own assessment. . . ." (para. 227)

The Court concluded that the structural links were much less substantial
than the Commission had alleged, and that competitive pressure from rivals,
including imports, were much more substantial than the Commission had
alleged. "[I]t is apparent that the Commission has not on any view established
to the necessary legal standard that the concentration would give rise to a
collective dominant position on the part of K+S/MdK and SCPA liable to
impede significantly effective competition on the relevant market." (para.
249)

The Court annulled the entire decision.

Notes and Questions

1. Did the Court do the right thing in construing the Merger Regulation to cover duopoly and oligopoly? Does textual construction lead to this result? Does legislative history?

2. In view of *Kali + Salz*, what is the meaning of collective dominance? What must the Commission show to prove that a merger creates or enhances collective dominance?

3. Recall that under Article 82, leading firms might collectively abuse dominance. Does collective abuse of dominance require that two firms act as if they were one economic actor, consciously coordinating their behavior? Does it require, also, that the firms have "links" between them: e.g., cross shareholding, interlocking directors or officers, possibly membership in the same associations, such as export associations, in which they actively coordinate their behavior? Or does the existence of links simply provide the opportunity and in some circumstances the incentive for the firms to coordinate their behavior on the relevant market? Do *Flat glass* and *Compagnie Maritime Belge* (see pages 835–36 supra) illuminate this problem?

4. In the United States the concept that most nearly corresponds with "collective dominance" is simply oligopoly and its entrenchment. If a merger creates or facilitates the exercise of significant market power, the merger is illegal. There are two types of market structures susceptible to this effect: single firm power (the monopoly, dominance, or unilateral effects model),[2] and joint power (the duopoly or oligopoly model). For a merger to be illegal under the latter structure, the market conditions must make it likely for the few significant firms to behave collaboratively or interdependently and thus to raise price and lower output without a significant prospect that fringe firms would efficiently expand or potential competitors enter, put more goods on the market, and beat back the price increase. See US Department of Justice and Federal Trade Commission Horizontal Merger Guidelines, 1992, amended 1997, 4 CCH Trade Reg. Rep. ¶ 13,104.

Do the facts of *Kali + Salz* suggest a plausible case for violation under the US standard? What factual questions would need to be answered? Is the language of the Merger Regulation elastic enough to adopt the US standard?

The holding of *Kali + Salz* regarding proof of collective dominance and the need for links between collectively dominant firms was to be tested in *Gencor/Lonrho*.

GENCOR LTD. v. COMMISSION

Case T–102/96 [1999] ECR II–753, app. pending.

[Two South African platinum and rhodium mining companies merged, combining Implats, a subsidiary of Gencor, having about 17% of world market sales, and LPD (a subsidiary of the UK firm, Lonrho), having about 15% of sales. The combined firm would have had 32% of sales. The leading firm, Anglo American ("Amplats"), had about 43% of sales. Together the two

---

2. In an oligopoly market, even where a merger does not create an increased risk of cooperative or interdependent behavior, a single merged firm may gain increased pricing power when the two merger partners' products are the best substitutes for one another. This is a unilateral effect.

resulting South African firms would have held about 89% of world reserves. Russia, through its firm Almaz, had a 22% share of sales and 10% of reserves. North American producers accounted for 5% of sales and had 1% reserves; and recycling firms accounted for 6% of sales. Russia was expected to dispose of its stocks in two years.

The Commission found that the concentration would create a dominant duopoly and was therefore incompatible with the common market, and it prohibited the concentration. Gencor contested the decision. The Court of First Instance analyzed as follows the evidence regarding whether the merger did indeed create a market structure in which the resulting two leading firms would gain collective dominance.]

222　... [G]iven the similarity in the market shares, shares of world reserves and cost structures of the undertakings at issue, the Commission was entitled to conclude that, following the concentration, the interests of Amplats and Implats/LPD with regard to the development of the market would have coincided to a higher degree and that this alignment of interests would have increased the likelihood of anti-competitive parallel behaviour, for example restrictions of output. * * *

3.　Characteristics of the market

[The Commission was entitled to find high transparency of price, production, sales, reserves, and new investment; and that given slow growth in demand, new competitors would not be encouraged to enter the market and existing competitors would not be encouraged to adopt aggressive strategies to capture additional demand.]

248　The applicant points out in that regard that the South African Government's letter of 19 April 1996 indicates that world reserves outside South Africa and Zimbabwe could theoretically satisfy world demand for 20 years. * * *

252　As regards the applicant's argument that the 37% of the market accounted for by the marginal sources of supply and other influences would have curbed price increases, the Commission points out that the South African producers alone accounted for 63% of the market in 1995, a figure that was to increase significantly (to a level approaching 80%) when, from 1997, Russia would no longer be selling from its stocks. Furthermore, a significant proportion of the marginal competition was hypothetical and could not in any event have exerted any pressure on the market for some years. * * *

254　The applicant's view has no factual basis. ... * * *

264　The applicant claims that the Commission did not take account of the case-law of the Court of First Instance (*'Flat Glass'* case) which, in the context of Article 86 of the Treaty, requires for findings of collective dominance that there be structural links between the two undertakings, for example through a technological lead by agreements or licences, which give them the power to behave independently of their competitors, of their customers and, ultimately, of consumers. In the instant case, the Commission has failed to demonstrate the existence of structural links or to prove that the merged entity and Amplats intended to behave as if they constituted a single dominant entity. ... * * *

The Court

273 In its judgment in the *Flat Glass* case, the Court referred to links of a structural nature only by way of example and did not lay down that such links must exist in order for a finding of collective dominance to be made.

274 It merely stated that there is nothing, in principle, to prevent two or more independent economic entities from being united by economic links in a specific market and, by virtue of that fact, from together holding a dominant position *vis-à-vis* the other operators on the same market. It added (in the same paragraph) that that could be the case, for example, where two or more independent undertakings jointly had, through agreements or licences, a technological lead affording them the power to behave to an appreciable extent independently of their competitors, their customers and, ultimately, of consumers.

275 Nor can it be deduced from the same judgment that the Court has restricted the notion of economic links to the notion of structural links referred to by the applicant.

276 Furthermore, there is no reason whatsoever in legal or economic terms to exclude from the notion of economic links the relationship of interdependence existing between the parties to a tight oligopoly within which, in a market with the appropriate characteristics, in particular in terms of market concentration, transparency and product homogeneity, those parties are in a position to anticipate one another's behaviour and are therefore strongly encouraged to align their conduct in the market, in particular in such a way as to maximise their joint profits by restricting production with a view to increasing prices. In such a context, each trader is aware that highly competitive action on its part designed to increase its market share (for example a price cut) would provoke identical action by the others, so that it would derive no benefit from its initiative. All the traders would thus be affected by the reduction in price levels.

277 That conclusion is all the more pertinent with regard to the control of concentrations, whose objective is to prevent anti-competitive market structures from arising or being strengthened. Those structures may result from the existence of economic links in the strict sense argued by the applicant or from market structures of an oligopolistic kind where each undertaking may become aware of common interests and, in particular, cause prices to increase without having to enter into an agreement or resort to a concerted practice.

278 In the instant case, therefore, the applicant's ground of challenge alleging that the Commission failed to establish the existence of structural links is misplaced.

279 The Commission was entitled to conclude, relying on the envisaged alteration in the structure of the market and on the similarity of the costs of Amplats and Implats/LPD, that the proposed transaction would create a collective dominant position and lead in actual fact to a duopoly constituted by those two undertakings . * * *

Notes and Questions

1. Gencor argued (and the South African authorities believed) that the combination of Implats and LPD would create a more efficient number two firm

that could and would better compete against the dominant firm, Amplats. How do we know who was correct—Gencor and South Africa, or the European Commission? What are the most important points on each side?

2. Did the Commission have to prove that Amplats and the merged firm would collude, at least tacitly, and thereby behave like *one* dominant firm? Or was it enough for the Commission to prove that the firms would behave interdependently, taking into account the probable strategies of one another and estimating if and when they would be jointly served by higher prices? How should the Court decide? Consider the text and the spirit of the Merger Regulation.

3. Do you think that the Commission made the case that Implats/LPD would collaborate rather than compete, and thereby raise world prices, as a matter of probability? Did the Commission's proof meet a lower threshold, such as: there was a reasonable chance that the merged firm would gain price-raising power after the Russian stocks were depleted? What is the significance of the Russian stocks? Why wouldn't Implats/LPD raise prices immediately and expect Amplats and Almaz to follow or at least not increase their output?

4. South Africa argued that it was not necessary to stop the merger; that if the merger did create conditions that made collaborative behavior more likely, and if the merger did eventually produce such behavior, it would (and authorities should) intervene at that point to stop the collaboration. Was this a better tack?

5. The court states in para. 271 that even if links are required for a Article 82 violations, they are not required for merger violations. State the case for this proposition. Do you agree? What is the significance of "links" after *Gencor*?

6. *Kali + Salz* and *Gencor/Lonrho* were both mergers to duopoly. The cases show the difficulties of proving that even a merger from three to two significant firms will produce collective dominance, in the sense of probable tacit collusion. The theory of collective dominance was tested further in *Airtours/First Choice*, involving a merger from four to three firms in the short haul holiday (air and hotel) package market. The post-merger shares were 32% for Airtours/First Choice, 27% for Thomson, and 20% for Thomas Cook. The Commission found that the market was characterized by stagnant demand, a low level of innovation, low price sensitivity, and similar cost structures of the three market leaders, with commercial links, transparency, and interdependence among them. It found that the merger would have significantly reduced fringe firms' ability to provide charter airline seats, thereby reducing the competitive threat of mavericks. Stating that collective dominance is "not just about tacit collusion," the Commission found that the resulting three leading firms would hold a collective dominant position after the merger, and it prohibited the merger. Case IV/M.1524, Commission decision of Sept. 22, 1999, O.J. L 9/13 (April 13, 2000), appeal pending.

But aren't barriers to entry and expansion in the holiday package-trip market low? And why wouldn't vacationers package their own trips on the Internet if the price of packaged trips was too high?

3. MERGERS THAT CREATE LEVERAGE AND PORTFOLIO EFFECTS

Some mergers combine firms that make complementary products. In some cases buyers need a full range of products and, all other things being equal, would prefer to deal with the full line seller. If a firm with market power acquires a fuller line, does the acquisition give it "portfolio power"—the power to foreclose access to single line firms and extend power from one market to another? Under what circumstances could it do so? What is the role of efficiencies? of buyers' preferences for a one-stop shop? What was the Commission's answer to these questions in *de Havilland*? in *Boeing*?

"Portfolio power" as a term was not used in *de Havilland* or *Boeing*. It came into use in connection with the merger of the spirits subsidiaries of Guinness and Grand Metropolitan. In some product and geographic markets, the firms had direct horizontal overlaps, the effects of which the Commission addressed by conditioning the merger on spin-offs of whiskey brands, termination of a vodka distribution agreement, and appointment of a third-party distributor for gin.

In the Greek market, the problem was different: there was no competitive overlap, but the merged firm would have the advantages conferred by a full portfolio.

GUINNESS/GRAND METROPOLITAN

Commission Decision, Case IV/M.938,
O.J. L 288/24 (Oct. 27, 1998).

* * *

91 Although there is no horizontal aggregation in other categories, the merger will bring together existing high market shares in gin, brandy and rum. Guinness' Gordon's gin accounts for over [75–85%] of the gin market and is complemented by two premium quality brands, that is Tanqueray (Guinness) and Bombay Sapphire (GrandMet). * * *

97 As stated above, whiskey is by far the largest category of spirits sold in Greece. However, the fact that GMG will include brands with very significant market shares in smaller categories is also important. For example, even if gin or rum have lower sales than whiskey, the presence of Gordon's and Bacardi is of crucial importance to a particular outlet, as these brands have been driving their respective categories for a long time and are identified with the category to which they belong. According to Canadean 1996 on Greece, 'gin continues to grow, largely due to a strong performance by Gordon's.' The same industry report refers to the rum market as consisting essentially of Bacardi.

98 It is true that other competitors supply important brands, some of which have achieved high sales volumes. For instance, on the merits of their sales performance, Cutty Sark whisky and Stolichnaya vodka would not face particular problems in access to the trade. However, the potential power of those brands is significantly reduced by the fact that they are spread out among different suppliers. That fragmentation of the market, as contrasted to the combined portfolio of GMG, deprives such brands of their potential portfolio power.

99 More particularly, a deep portfolio of whiskey brands, spread out across the various quality and price segments, confers considerable price flexibility and marketing opportunities. Therefore, the supplier is shielded from market pressures, as he is able to face price competition from other suppliers' brands by positioning and pricing his various brands within the category. For instance, with its secure high market performance of the

best-selling whiskey brands, GMG will be able to devote as many resources as necessary in order to maintain its secondary brands in their position or to reposition the weaker brands upwards by expanding their share at the expense of competing brands, or in order to counter eventual competitive pressure coming from those brands. The parties have argued that such 'pull-through' has not occurred in the past and is accordingly unlikely to occur in the future. However, this argument ignores the substantial increase in the parties' market shares and resources that the merger will create.

100   Moreover, a wide portfolio of categories confers major marketing advantages, giving GMG the possibility of bundling sales or increasing the sales volume of one category by tying it to the sale of another category. Both Guinness and GrandMet have made use of their portfolios of brands in bundling deals. For instance, in 1995, GrandMet rewarded customers who collected and delivered [...]* bottle-caps of Smirnoff, Cuervo and J & B, by offering them a free [...]. For the same number of caps, wholesalers received a credit note of [...]. Moreover, Guinness made joint promotions of different categories and brands, whereby customers purchasing a 12–bottle pack containing Johnnie Walter Red Label (7 bottles), Gordon's gin (2 bottles) and White Horse (3 bottles) obtained a discount of [...]. ...

101   In the on-trade, where spirits producers build a brand's strength and image, GMG, through its broad portfolio of brands, would be able to influence what products are stocked or displayed in the limited space available behind the bar (the so-called back-bar), thus further strengthening its market power. For small outlets which have smaller back-bars, or for Greek night-clubs which concentrate on whiskey, the combined entity would be an attractive solution for one-stop-shopping considerations. In addition, larger modern outlets, which usually stock a much broader variety of brands, may also become a target of the combined entity, should it attempt to gain more back-bar space or use the image of fashionable clubs in order to launch its brands. GMG could afford to make substantial offers, discounts and credits or organise and finance promotional events, that would also accrue to the outlet itself, and use its strength in leading brands, such as Johnnie Walker Red Label, Gordon's gin and Bacardi rum, in order to induce bars to list brands in the same or another category. Given that those premises could not afford not to stock the brands set out above, the negotiating power of GMG would be significantly strengthened. Therefore, it would be much easier for GMG to induce bartenders to adopt GMG brands as pouring brands (that is, the brand offered when a customer fails to specify a brand by name), thus increasing their sales volumes and public awareness.

102   In the off-trade, the elimination of competition between Guinness and Grand Met for in-store promotions will serve to enable GMG to plan jointly the timing of promotions, negotiate jointly the terms of promotions and coordinate any price changes. Moreover, through its variety of

---

* Editors' note: Omissions are in published   tiality.
text. They are intended to preserve confiden-

brands, GMG could also alternate branded products promoted over a period of time, thus occupying long promotion periods and excluding competitors from access to the promotion calendar for long periods.

[103] By comparison, competitors have weaker portfolios and fewer strong brands.... Indeed, in contrast to the complete GMG portfolio, the discontinuity of the competitors' portfolios would deprive them of price flexibility and make them more vulnerable to market pressures. For example, when their brands start losing sales volume, they will have to commit disproportionately stronger resources in order to avoid situations that could in the long run restrict their competitive scope. * * *

Conclusions on Greece

[114] On the basis of the above, GMG will account for [45–55%] of the whiskey market. Coupled with its broad portfolio of whiskey brands, ranging across all the various quality and price sub-segments, that will confer on the combined entity considerable marketing advantages.

[115] Moreover, ... GMG already has dominant positions in gin [80–90%], brandy [70–80%] and rum [75–85%] and a very broad portfolio of brands, including the best-selling brands across all the spirits categories, with the exception of vodka, and will have [35–45%] of overall spirits consumption in Greece.

[116] Furthermore, existing competitors do not have such a portfolio of brands, that they would be able to constrain GMG's market power. In addition, the various trade channels are not able to exercise countervailing buyer power. Finally, barriers to entry are important, preventing thus new entrants from limiting the power of GMG.

[117] Therefore, for all these reasons, the merger will result in the creation of a dominant position in the Greek market for the supply of whiskey.

[118] Finally, through the portfolio effects set out above, the existing dominant positions in gin, rum and brandy will be reinforced.

The Commission accepted conditions to address the portfolio problem, including terminating the distribution agreement for Bacardi rum in Greece.

Concern about bundling and leveraging was to arise again in connection with General Electric's proposed acquisition of Honeywell.

GENERAL ELECTRIC/HONEYWELL
Commission Decision, Case COMP/M.2220, July 3, 2001.

[General Electric Company is the world's largest producer of large and small jet engines for commercial and military aircraft. It and its joint venture account for more than 52% of all engines on large commercial jets still in production. It accounts for 60–70% of engines in large regional aircraft in production; 40–50% of engines in the installed base of large regional aircraft; and 10–20% (in both categories) of engines for corporate jets. The engine market is concentrated, with Pratt & Whitney as number two and Rolls–Royce as number three. GE Commercial Aviation Service (GECAS) is one of the world's largest aircraft leasing companies and one of the largest buyers of planes. It buys about 10% of aircraft, it and a sister corporation GE Capital finance the purchase of airplanes, and it is an important launch customer for airplanes. It provides equity seed financing for smaller planes with GE engines, creating "commonality" considerations that influence the airlines to select similar equipment in the future whether or not those planes are acquired from GECAS. Once an aircraft manufacturer chooses to incorporate a particular supplier's engine and other elements, it tends to continue purchasing the same brand because of significant efficiencies such as acquired knowledge and training and replaceability of parts across a fleet. GE had in the past made known its policy to buy only aircraft that incorporated GE engines.

Honeywell International is a leading firm in the production of aerospace products including navigating equipment, non-avionic products, engines for corporate jets, and engine starters. It accounts for 50–60% of avionic products generally (although this is not a single relevant market). It accounts for 60–70% of engines in medium corporate jets in production. For aerospace equipment other than engines, it is the largest worldwide supplier, with BF Goodrich ranking second, United Technologies Corporation (UTC) third, and Rockwell Collins fourth. Its principal competitor in non-avionic products is UTC. Honeywell is the only equipment manufacturer that offers a complete range of avionics equipment. It is the leading supplier of engine controls to engine manufacturers, particularly engine starters. Pratt & Whitney also makes engine starters, for its own use.

GE and Honeywell agreed to merge, in what would have been the largest industrial merger in history. They filed their merger notifications with the US authorities, who cleared the deal after requiring a spinoff of competitively overlapping engine assets, and they filed with the European Commission, among numerous other jurisdictions.]

4. EFFECTS ON COMPETITION

4.A. INTRODUCTION

341   The proposed merger will bring about anti-competitive effects as a result of horizontal overlaps and the vertical and conglomerate integration of the merging parties activities. GE has dominant positions in the markets for large commercial aircraft engines and large regional jet aircraft engines. The transaction will strengthen GE's position on the markets for large commercial aircraft engines and for large regional jet aircraft engines and will create a dominant position on the markets for corporate jet engines. Honeywell already enjoys significant leading positions on the markets for avionics and non-avionics as well as in engine starters. Following the transaction Honeywell will become dominant in the BFE [buyer-furnished equipment], SFE [supplier-furnished equipment] and SFE-option avionics markets.

4.B. SFE AVIONICS & NON-AVIONICS

4.B.1. CREATION OF A DOMINANT POSITION

(1) FORECLOSURE THROUGH THE VERTICAL INTEGRATION

342 The main effect of the proposed transaction on the markets for SFE avionics and non-avionics products would be the combination of Honeywell's activities with GE's financial strength and vertical integration into financial services, aircraft purchasing and leasing, as well as into after-market services.

343 SFE are products selected on an exclusive basis by the airframe manufacturer and supplied as standard equipment for the life cycle of an aircraft. Consequently, for a supplier of SFE the initial selection of its products on a platform can guarantee a long-term source of revenues. In this sense, SFE products bear a strong similarity with engines supplied on an exclusive basis (such as in the Boeing 737 or 777X). The ability of GE to obtain engine exclusivity on platforms was discussed in the previous paragraphs, where it was seen that in order to benefit from such a long-term revenue stream, GE used its considerable financial resources and vertical integration to induce the relevant airframe manufacturer to grant an engine exclusivity. As a consequence of its financial capabilities and vertical integration into aircraft purchasing, GE has managed to win all the major competitions to obtain engine exclusivity.

344 Following the proposed merger, Honeywell will immediately benefit from GE Capital's ability to secure the exclusive selection of its SFE products on new platforms. By leveraging its financial power and vertical integration on the launch of new platforms (for example, through financing and/or through orders placed by GECAS), the merged entity will be able to promote the selection of Honeywell's SFE products, thereby denying competitors the possibility to place their products on such new platforms. That would delay the cash inception of Honeywell's competitors and deprive them of the necessary return to fund future investments and innovation. Honeywell's products will, in particular, benefit from GECAS's role as a significant purchaser of aircraft. Post-merger, GECAS will extend its GE-only policy to Honeywell products to the detriment of competitors such as Collins, Thales and Hamilton Sundstrand and ultimately of customers. Indeed, given the relative indifference of airlines towards component selection, the benefits of a non-GE offer for airframe manufacturers would become less significant than the benefits they could achieve in the form of additional aircraft purchase[s] by GECAS.

345 Furthermore, owing to GE's strong generation of cash flows resulting from the conglomerate's leading positions on several markets, Honeywell will, following the merger, be in a position to benefit from GE's financing surface and ability to cross-subsidise its different business segments.

346 Accordingly, GE's strategic use of GECAS's market access and GE Capital's financial strength to favour Honeywell's products will position Honeywell as the dominant supplier on the markets for SFE avionics and non-avionics products where it already enjoys leading positions.

347 The effect on rival avionics and non-avionics manufacturers will be to deprive them of the future revenue streams generated by the sales of the original equipment and spare parts. Future revenues are needed to fund development expenditures for future products, foster innovation and allow for a potential leapfrogging effect. By being progressively marginalised as

a result of the integration of Honeywell into GE, Honeywell's competitors will be deprived of a vital source of revenue and see their ability to invest for the future and develop the next generation of aircraft systems eventually eliminated.

348 Indeed, given the fact that Honeywell's avionics and non-avionics competitors are unable to reproduce GE's financial strength and vertical integration to any appreciable degree (see above on the assessment of large commercial aircraft), their limited size and financial strength would probably lead to a reduction of their competitive strength in those markets where the extension of GE's business practices to Honeywell's products would reduce seriously their chances to win future competitions.

(2) FORECLOSURE THROUGH PACKAGED OFFERS

349 As described below, this situation will be compounded by the new entity's ability to offer product packages to the airframe manufacturers. The complementary nature of the GE and Honeywell product offerings coupled with their respective existing market positions will give the merged entity the ability and the economically rational incentive to engage in bundled offers or cross-subsidisation across product sales to both categories of customers (see below on BFE).

4.C. BFE (AND SFE–OPTION) AVIONICS & NON-AVIONICS

4.C.1. CREATION OF A DOMINANT POSITION

(1) FORECLOSURE THROUGH PACKAGED OFFERS

350 In the post-merger market structure, the merged entity will be able to offer a package of products that has never been put together on the market prior to the merger and that cannot be challenged by any other competitor on its own. The effects of the proposed merger on BFE and SFE-option avionics and non-avionics products will thus be felt in terms of the merged entity's ability to sell packages of complementary products, in particular BFE and SFE-option avionics and non-avionics and engines. Sales of BFE and SFE-option products are made to airlines on a regular basis, in particular each time an airline replaces or complements its fleet of aircraft. On each of these occasions, the merged entity may promote the selection of Honeywell's BFE and SFE-option products by selling them as part of a broader package comprising engines and GE's ancillary services such as maintenance, leasing, finance, training, and so forth.

351 The sale of complementary products through packaged deals may take several forms. It may include, for instance, mixed bundling whereby complementary products are sold together at a price which, owing to the discounts that apply across the product range, is lower than the price charged when they are sold separately. It may also take the form of pure bundling whereby the entity sells only the bundle but does not make the individual components available on a stand-alone basis. Pure bundling may also take the form of technical bundling, whereby the individual components only function effectively as part of the bundled system, and cannot be used alongside components from other suppliers, that is to say, they are made incompatible with the latter components.

352 The practice of selling packages of products and services has been confirmed throughout the market investigation. Indeed, the Commission's investigation has shown that such practices have repeatedly occurred in this industry. Moreover, the Commission has evaluated the theoretical premises of mixed bundling as presented to it in the economic analyses submitted by the parties and third parties. The various economic analyses have been subject to theoretical controversy, in particular as far as the economic model of mixed bundling, prepared by one of the third parties, is concerned. However, the Commission does not consider the reliance on one or the other model necessary for the conclusion that the packaged deals that the merged entity will be in a position to offer will foreclose competitors from the engines and avionics/non-avionics markets.

353 As a result of the proposed merger, the merged entity will be able to price its packaged deals in such a way as to induce customers to buy GE engines and Honeywell BFE and SFE-option products over those of competitors, thus increasing the combined share of GE and Honeywell on both markets. This will occur as a result of the financial ability of the merged entity to cross-subsidise discounts across the products composing the packaged deal. The Commission's market investigation has indicated that both airframe manufacturers and airlines are price-sensitive customers.

354 The incentives for the merged entity to sell bundles of products may change over the short to medium term, for instance when new generations of aircraft platforms and aircraft equipment are developed. Instead of proposing, for example, product bundles at a better price than stand-alone products, while leaving the customer the choice to buy individual products among the bundle or to only offer a bundle of products, the merged entity can also be expected to engage in technical bundling—that is, to make its products available only as an integrated system that is incompatible with competing individual components. This can potentially reduce the profitability of competitors to a greater degree than in the case of mixed bundling and thus increase the likelihood of market foreclosure. Competitors will find it more difficult to place their products on the market, since technical bundling restricts the market share available to them. Overall, technical bundling will adversely affect competitors' incentives to compete and under such circumstances, they are not likely to be a constraining factor to the independent behaviour of the merged entity. Indeed, non-integrated competitors are not in a position to duplicate technical bundling. As a result of these commercial practices, the merged entity is expected to gain additional market shares. Competitors are expected to lose market shares and see their profits shrink, in some cases, significantly. In the medium term, competitors will have to take decisions as to whether, in view of their anticipated reduced market share and profitability, they are able and willing to continue competing in the markets where the merged entity is active.

355 The merger will, in the short term, affect suppliers of BFE and SFE-option products. As BFE products are sold and purchased on a regular basis, the merged entity's packaged offers will manifest their effects after the merger goes through. Because of their lack of ability to match the bundle offer, these component suppliers will lose market shares to the

benefit of the merged entity and experience an immediate damaging profit shrinkage. As a result, the merger is likely to lead to market foreclosure on those existing aircraft platforms and subsequently to the elimination of competition in these areas. * * *

(3) Effects of Packaged Deals on Competitors

398 The ability of the merged entity to cross-subsidise its various complementary activities and to engage in profitable forms of packaged sales will have an adverse effect on the profitability of competing producers of avionics and non avionics products, as a result of market share erosion. This is likely to lead to market exit of existing competitors and market foreclosure both over the short term, insofar as price is below average variable cost, and over the longer term, insofar as competitors would be unable to cover their fixed costs if they were to remain active and to proceed with the new investment in R & D so as to compete viably and in the future.

399 While this longer-term foreclosure impact on the profits of competitors would not be linear but instead is expected to occur in a step-by-step fashion, the effect on competitors' ability to invest in R & D and focus on new product developments for future competitions will materialise as soon as the cash flow expected to be generated internally could not support the necessary capital expenditures for product development and innovation.

400 The erosion of the market shares of GE and Honeywell's competitors resulting from the merger will impact the future strategic choices of the latter. Significant reductions in profits will lead to substantial decrease of profitability ratios such as Return on Capital ("ROC"). When compared to the rate of return required by investors (i.e., the financial markets), decreased ROC will result in companies experiencing strong difficulties in attracting new funds and spending on R & D. This will in turn seriously threaten the ability of GE and Honeywell's competitors to invest for the future so as to safeguard their market position and viability.

401 Therefore, due to steep decreases in their ROC, some of the avionics and non-avionics competitors will see their viability threatened over the short-term, whereas some others will gradually lose their ability and incentive to compete vigorously, insofar as the returns they can achieve from a shrunk customer base are severely reduced. * * *

403 Engine and components suppliers compete on innovation for future products on the basis of R & D expenditures that have to be financed by current and expected cash flows. In industries such as that under examination in this case, such expenditures are conditioned by the large sunk costs incurred by firms, the long lead times before investment returns materialise, the high risk as well as the asymmetric information. Since companies are expected, in such circumstances, to use retained earnings, rather than raise or borrow capital, any significant reduction in the current profits will seriously hamper their ability to invest in the future. This in turn will reduce their incentives to invest due to lower than expected future profits. Moreover, those effects would be further exacerbated were the merged entity to engage in pure ("technical") bundling,

which is likely to be the case in relation to future platforms. Pure bundling will further reduce the future market available to competitors and consequently will lower their incentives to strategically invest in this market. Companies' incentives to engage in R & D activities depend on the volume of their output in the market to the extent that R & D costs are largely sunk. Any significant reduction of this output—stemming from a reduction of the market available to competing firms—will reduce expected future profits and therefore current R & D expenditures.

[404] Bundling will result in the foreclosure of suppliers of BFE products since no other supplier or team of suppliers will be able to replicate the bundled offer by the merged entity. As a result, competitors on the markets for BFE avionics and non-avionics products are expected to be affected in their ability and incentive to compete and innovate following likely significant immediate market share and revenue losses. Consequently, in the light of their inability to compete on the merits, exposed competitors will have to reconsider their activities and withdraw from those markets dominated by the Honeywell BFE avionics and non-avionics products, which will ultimately negatively impact competition.

(4) FORECLOSURE THROUGH THE VERTICAL INTEGRATION

[405] In addition to the implementation of bundling on the markets for BFE avionics and non-avionics products, the combination of Honeywell with GE's financial strength and vertical integration in financial services, aircraft purchasing and leasing, as well as in aftermarket services, will contribute to the foreclosure effect already described for SFE avionics and non-avionics.

[406] Following the proposed merger, Honeywell's BFE product range will benefit from GE Capital's ability to secure exclusive positions for its products with airlines (see the Continental Airlines example) and GE-CAS's instrumental leverage ability to foster the placement of GE products through the extension of its GE-only policy to Honeywell products.

[407] Honeywell's BFE products will also benefit from GE's range of products and services to target competitors' components on the occasion of replacements, upgrades and retrofits through GECAS's ability to favour GE products vis-à-vis airlines.

[408] Furthermore, GE will also have the incentive to accelerate the on-going trend of airframe manufacturers to change BFE products into SFE products since it could later target those products and achieve exclusive positions by deploying the set of business practices described in the previous paragraphs.

[409] GE's strategic use of GECAS and GE Capital's financial strength will thus position Honeywell as the dominant supplier of BFE avionics and non-avionics products where it already enjoys leading positions. In the light of their inability to reproduce GE's financial strength and integration to any significant degree, the effect on rival BFE manufacturers will be to lead them to progressively reconsider their strategy and not to compete fiercely in those markets dominated by the merged entity.

[410] The parties have argued that insofar as customers have the ability and the incentive to maintain a competitive supplier base they will not accept at any cost bundling practices or the effects of vertical integration. However, the market investigation has shown, first, that airlines are relatively indifferent as to the choice of SFE avionics and non-avionics. Second, when selecting the SFE equipment that will remain on the aircraft for its lifetime, airframe manufacturers cannot ignore the importance of GECAS as an aircraft buyer since selling one or two additional aircraft is likely to offset all financial incentives that Honeywell's competitors can offer. As far as BFE equipment is concerned, although commonality and customer preferences exist, the airlines are, due to their limited profit margins, not in a position to reject commercial offers that represent short-term cost savings....

[411] It can accordingly be concluded that the proposed transaction will create a dominant position on the markets for SFE and BFE avionics and non-avionics.

[The Commission rejected the firms' claims that they lacked dominance, they would not have power to impose bundling or use leverage, their customers would not accept bundling, there would be no cross-subsidization, and competitors could outcompete the incumbent supplier by offering counterbundles or that they could "leapfrog" GE by introducing technological improvements to their products.]

Notes and Questions

1. Note the symmetry between the EC law on abuse of dominance through leverage under Article 82 and the merger control law that addresses creation or entrenchment of dominance through structural change that produces incentives to use leverage.

Describe the harm to competition in both *Guinness/GrandMet* and *GE/Honeywell*. In each case the merger created advantages for the merged firm over competitors. Are there ways in which both mergers would have given advantages to consumers? Would these have been offset by eventual harm to consumers? Did the Commission condition the Guinness merger and prohibit the GE merger because of the disadvantage to competitors? because of harm to competition? to consumers?

2. The United States authorities, having cleared the GE/Honeywell merger under US law, sharply criticized the Commission decision. Charles James, Assistant Attorney General in Charge of Antitrust, declared that US law protects consumers but the European Commission protects competitors. He said that the Commission prohibited this merger (of US companies) because GE would have become too effective a competitor.

Develop this argument. Consult paras. 344–48, 354, 398, 403–04, 410. What are the merits of the argument? What are its weaknesses? How strong do you think is the inference that, as a result of the merger, competitors would have been marginalized and weakened, and prices would have risen? How strong is the argument, to the contrary, that if bundling and leveraging should occur competitors would be feisty; they would find a way to fight back?

Note that the European Commission sees as its mission preserving the competitive structure of the market, and US authorities see as their mission allowing mergers (which are presumed efficient) unless the enforcer can prove that prices will probably rise. Can this difference translate into different assessments of the same merger?

For international implications of divergences, see E. below.

3. United States, too, was once concerned with mergers that created leverage by a tying or package effect, or by reciprocity power ("If you buy my product, I'll buy yours"), because it can create economic advantages not on the merits and induce customers to switch to the firm with leverage. FTC v. Procter & Gamble, 386 U.S. 568, 87 S.Ct. 1224, 18 L.Ed.2d 303 (1967); FTC v. Texaco Inc., 393 U.S. 223, 89 S.Ct. 429, 21 L.Ed.2d 394 (1968); FTC v. Consolidated Foods Corp., 380 U.S. 592, 85 S.Ct. 1220, 14 L.Ed.2d 95 (1965). US antitrust law has now abandoned this line of authority, on grounds that a fuller line of products normally benefits consumers; that illegal tying can be dealt with on its own terms; that reciprocity effect is not a barrier; the single-line firm need only make a better product or offer it at a better price; and that "foreclosure" is an elusive term invoked by competitors who ought simply to compete harder.

If there is a leveraging violation, should the parties be entitled to justify on grounds that the transaction was a pro-competitive or pro-consumer response to the market?

5. NEW ECONOMY ISSUES: THE GATEKEEPER

Mergers in new economy markets, typically involving computers, telecommunications, TV, and other information or media, may create a dominant firm that controls access to key inputs or key channels of distribution. In some such cases, depending on the extent of alternative sources of supply or distribution for competitors, the merger may harm competition. (In what sense? by raising price? to whom? by chilling incentives to pioneer alternative paths for innovation? by drying up the production of content? by threatening to homogenize content? How can we measure these effects?)

The European Commission has prohibited or imposed conditions (especially requirements of nondiscriminatory access) on a number of new economy mergers. In many cases the new market is emerging; it is not yet formed and its directions are uncertain. A dominant or leading firm is poised to seize advantages in that market. The Commission has tried to anticipate the development of the market.[1]

Competition Commissioner Mario Monti has described the Commission's approach to new economy mergers as follows:[2]

... I see the new economy as a strong potential ally for competition. The Internet and other quickly developing information technologies can bring substantial doses of transparency to the markets, thus making them more efficient. They can also contribute to the integration of markets, by facilitating the contacts between suppliers and customers and, thus, making location of companies a much less relevant factor for competition.

---

1. See Vodafone AirTouch/Mannesmann, COMP/M.1795, Commission decision of Dec. 12, 2000. Vodafone's acquisition of Mannesmann would give it mobile networks throughout Europe, creating the possibility of a seamless, pan-European mobile telecommunications service, which would give it advantages over its competitors. The Commission found Vodafone dominant in this prospective market, and imposed access conditions.

2. Mario Monti, European Competition Policy for the 21st Century, Ford. Corp. L. Inst. (2000).

The constant reallocation of resources from the declining firms or sectors to the emerging and fast growing ones is a corollary of a well functioning market economy. In the realm of the "new economy" this process has become extremely rapid. It is of paramount importance not to hinder this reallocation and to allow transformation and restructuring to take place in a non-traumatic way, through mergers, joint ventures and acquisitions of firms.

This process, however, is not without its dangers. Co-operation between companies could sometimes lead to anti-competitive outcomes. Mergers may result in a market structure, which is too concentrated, with poorer choice for the consumer and greater scope for collusion between a few remaining producers. Our task is to favour the transition towards new and more efficient market equilibrium, while, at the same time, preserving the competitive environment. * * *

Some commentators have argued that in high technology markets there are often no real concerns of long-term dominance, due to quickly eroding entry barriers and that, therefore, competition policy only has a very limited role to play in these markets.

I would caution against such an approach. Even temporary market power can be a serious concern, particularly when it may have a negative impact on the levels of innovation and consumer choice in a given market.

Other commentators consider that the uncertainties surrounding the future developments of new economy markets and the complexities associated to these sectors should discourage competition authorities from even trying to intervene.

I cannot share this approach either. I acknowledge the difficulties linked to the assessment of cases in markets under quick development. But our duty is to foresee the best we can the consequences of a given operation and to react to it if it is likely to create competition concerns. Complexity or uncertainty should not be reasons for us not to act when the interests of the consumers are at stake.

Let me turn now to explain some of our recent cases, which will show the type of concerns for competition that can derive from the developments linked to the new economy. I believe they will also illustrate how the basic principles of competition rules adapt to changing markets and industries.

In new economy sectors, where access to networks is essential to be able to provide a wide range of services, "gate-keeper" effects can become a major concern. I refer, by this term, to these situations where a company is in control of an infrastructure that is essential for other players to develop their business and innovate.

Gate-keeper effects can occur as a result of both horizontal and vertical operations. In the first case, normally the merger between two network operators leads, through the addition of their assets, to the creation of a facility of such a nature that cannot be replicated by competitors.

Let me give you some examples of recent cases of this nature. One concerning a European and another a world-wide market:

- First, the *Vodafone/Mannesmann* transaction raised competition concerns on the emerging market for pan-European seamless mobile telephony services. The merged company, with its extensive network, would be in a unique position vis-à-vis its competitors to roll out such services. In order to remedy these concerns, *Vodafone* accepted to give competitors non-discriminatory access to its integrated network. However, in order to ensure that competitors would not exclusively rely on the merged company, neglecting the development of their own infrastructure, the Commission limited the undertaking to three years. The Commission considered, inter alia, that in this period, UMTS licenses would be awarded in sufficient number to allow competitors to replicate the Vodafone network.

- Second, in June this year, the Commission prohibited the merger between the two US communications companies *MCI WorldCom* and *Sprint*. It found that the combination of the parties' extensive Internet networks and large customer bases would have allowed the merged entity to dictate terms and conditions for access to its Internet networks in a manner that could have had significant anti-competitive effects and hindered innovation. The Commission's investigation, which was carried out in close co-operation with the American antitrust authorities, showed that despite liberalisation, regional and local providers are still dependent on the largest top-level providers to gain full and effective access to the Internet.

I have indicated that gatekeeper effects can also arise as a result of vertical operations, in other words, operations among companies operating in related up stream or down stream markets. In these cases, foreclosure concerns are only likely to arise where one of the merging parties enjoys significant market power. Mergers in the media sector, between content providers and delivery operators, can lead to such concerns.

Let me comment, on this regard, two cases on which the Commission has very recently adopted a decision.

- First, ... on 11 October [2000] the European Commission approved the proposed merger between *America Online Inc* (AOL) and *Time Warner Inc* (TW) after AOL offered to sever all structural links with German media group Bertelsmann AG.

  In this case, the Commission was concerned that AOL, because of the merger with Time Warner, which in turn had planned to merge its music recording and publishing activities with EMI, and because of its European joint ventures with Bertelsmann, would have controlled the leading source of music publishing rights in Europe. In Europe *TW*, *EMI* and *Bertelsmann* together would hold approximately 50% of the music publishing rights. Against this background, AOL could have emerged as the *gatekeeper* in the emerging market for Internet music delivery on-line.

  The proposed undertakings, and the fact that the EMI/TW deal did not take place, will prevent AOL from having access to Europe's leading source of music publishing rights. In view of this, the Commission could approve the operation.

- Secondly, ... (on 13 October [2000]), the European Commission approved the acquisition by French telecommunications and media company *Vivendi* and its subsidiary *Canal+* of Canada's *Seagram*.

  The Commission had been concerned that the deal would have allowed *Vivendi/Canal+* to have preferential or even exclusive access to Universal films rights and, therefore, would have created or strengthened its existing dominant position in pay-television in a substantial number of countries.

The parties offered substantial undertakings to address the competition problems. They agreed not to grant Canal+ first window rights for more than a certain percentage of Universal production. But most notably, they also agree to divest their stake in British pay-TV company BskyB. This will enable BskyB to be an independent competitor to Canal+ and at the same time will sever any links between Universal and Fox Studios, another major film producer that is controlled by the BskyB group.

You can see a certain pattern emerging from all these cases. First, the Commission has taken action each time that it has identified that a gatekeeper concern was likely to arise in the short or the medium term. In most cases, however, the problems could be limited in time or scope and solutions have been found through granting access to competitors. When, however, the problem could not be resolved, like in MCI–Worldcom/Sprint, a prohibition was the only possible outcome.

Notes and Questions

1. Is the Commission wisely proactive or overly aggressive in intervening in new economy mergers?

2. What do you understand by "gatekeeper" effects? Whom does the doctrine help—competitors? consumers/computer users/viewers? Do the conditions or prohibitions have any negative consequences for user/viewers?

3. From the viewpoint of user/viewers, is competitor access more important in some circumstances than others? Are you more concerned that a merger would give a telecom/media company sole rights to Universal films (Universal makes about 8% of theatrical feature films), or that a merger would give a telecom/Internet company sole rights to an extensive cable network needed by telecom and Internet competitors?

E. THE INTERNATIONAL DIMENSION

In 1988 the Court of Justice decided, in *Wood pulp* (see page 826 supra), that EC competition law reprehends off-shore cartels "implemented" in the Community. In 1997, the Commission vetted Boeing's acquisition of McDonnell Douglas (two US firms with no assets in Europe but engaged in a world market). It nearly enjoined the acquisition, which had been cleared by US authorities, but in the end allowed it subject to important conditions. See page 957. (The United States authorities, too, feel free to challenge off-shore mergers.)

In 1999, the Commission enjoined the merger of Gencor and LPD (Lonrho), two South African firms, one of which had a presence in Europe. The Court of First Instance affirmed. (See page 970.) This was the first merger prohibited and aborted on grounds of collective dominance; the *Kali + Salz* prohibition having been annulled. We deal here with the jurisdictional issues raised in *Gencor/Lonrho*.

NOTE ON GENCOR LTD. v. COMMISSION

See facts at page 970 supra.

After the South African platinum mining companies, Gencor and LPD, agreed to merge, the South African Competition Board vetted the merger and found no competition problem. The European Commission vetted the merger and was concerned that, when the Russian stocks were depleted in a couple of years, Gencor/LPD (Lonrho) and Anglo American, the world market leader, would jointly exercise dominant market power (collective dominance). Recall that LPD's parent, Lonrho, was a British firm, and Lonrho maintained its principal sales office in Belgium.

Examining the proposed merger, the Competition Directorate of the European Commission invited comment from the South African authorities. The South African Deputy Minister of Foreign Affairs officially submitted his government's observations to the Commission. He stated in a letter to the European Commission that the South African Government favored the consolidation. As to competitive effects, the Minister noted that the two remaining platinum firms in South Africa were now more equally matched, and he conveyed the South African view that the market would work better with two equally matched competitors than under market domination by Anglo American. The Minister did not contest the intervention of the European Community. However, he wrote: "Having regard to the importance of mineral resources to the South African economy," South Africa favored allowing the consolidation and attacking any collusion between Anglo American and Gencor/LPD if and when it arose. (judgment, para. 3)

The European Commission prohibited the merger. Gencor sought annulment in the Court of First Instance on both jurisdictional and substantive grounds. Gencor argued that the Community had no jurisdiction over this concentration since it involved economic activities conducted within the territory of a non-member country and had been approved by authorities of that country. Gencor contended that the Merger Regulation applies only to concentrations carried out within the Community. It based its construction on the language of the Merger Regulation (especially recitals), the Treaty articles on which the Regulation was based, and the international law principle of territoriality. Gencor distinguished the *Wood pulp* case, wherein the Court of Justice had asserted jurisdiction over an offshore cartel designedly raising prices in Europe, on grounds that the cartel was implemented in Europe. Gencor said, of *Wood pulp*: While the high prices were agreed to offshore, the conspiracy to raise prices was implemented by selling at the conspiratorial prices into the Community. By contrast, the platinum merger was implemented in South Africa and "is thus primarily relevant to the industrial and competition policy of that non-member country." (para. 56)

The Court of First Instance rejected Gencor's construction of the Regulation. Case T–102/96, [1999] ECR II–753 (CFI), app. pending. The Court said:

> According to *Wood pulp*, the criterion as to the implementation of an agreement is satisfied by mere sale within the Community, irrespective of the location of the sources of supply and the production plant. It is not disputed that Gencor and Lonrho carried out sales in the Community

before the concentration and would have continued to do so thereafter. (para. 87)

The CFI proceeded to assess the legitimacy of jurisdiction under international law. Noting that the transaction entailed merger of the firms' marketing operations throughout the world, including the Community, it said:

> Application of the Regulation is justified under public international law when it is foreseeable that a proposed concentration will have an immediate and substantial effect in the Community. (para. 90)

The CFI concluded that the merger's effect in the Community would be immediate, substantial and foreseeable. It construed "immediate" to include "medium term"—after Russian platinum stocks were exhausted and thus after a force that could be disruptive of Anglo and Gencor's duopoly behavior would have been removed. It concluded that an *abuse* (a price rise resulting from collective behavior) need not be immediate; it is enough that a transaction causes a lasting structural alteration, making abusive behavior economically rational.

As to substantiality of the effect, Gencor claimed that the merging parties' sales and market shares in Europe were too small to cause a substantial effect and that the merging parties' greater sales elsewhere—Japan and the United States—undermined "substantiality." The court rejected this claim. It said:

> The fact that, in a world market, other parts of the world are affected by the concentration cannot prevent the Community from exercising its control over a concentration which substantially affects competition within the common market by creating a dominant position.

Likewise, the court rejected the claim that the exercise of jurisdiction violated an international principle of non-interference, if there is such a principle, or the principle of proportionality. The court said that there was no conflict between the laws of the two jurisdictions and therefore no interference because South Africa did not require the firms to do what the European Community required them not to do. Nor was it shown how the completion of the merger would enhance South Africa's vital economic or commercial interests.

Moreover, as the European Commission had argued, the merger was like an export cartel. Only a small amount of platinum was sold in South Africa. South Africa stood to gain more by exploiting the world than it stood to lose by exploiting its own consumers.

Thus, the court held, the court had jurisdiction.

South Africa did not further resist the result of *Gencor/Lonrho*. But when, two years later, the European Commission signaled its serious problems with the GE/Honeywell merger, US senators, cabinet members, and the President declared the European "intrusion" into the "American" merger inappropriate. After the European prohibition, US Assistant Attorney General in charge of Antitrust Charles James issued a statement taking issue with the European analysis, not the jurisdiction. "Antitrust laws protect competition, not competitors," he said. The merger "would have been procompetitive and beneficial to consumers.... [The European Commission] apparently concluded that a more diversified, and thus more competitive GE, could somehow disadvantage other market participants.... This matter points to the continuing need ... to move toward a greater policy convergence."[1]

Notes and Questions

1. In *Gencor/Lonrho*, was the CFI's concept of conflict the same as or different from that of the US Supreme Court in *Hartford* (see page 830 supra)? Was there really no conflict?

2. Does the European Commission have subject matter jurisdiction over offshore mergers? Does *Wood pulp* help you answer the question? The US federal antitrust agencies' International Guidelines declare that the US agencies have jurisdiction to challenge an anticompetitive merger of foreign firms that hurts US consumers; and that they even have jurisdiction to challenge an off-shore merger that merely hurts US exporters. Antitrust Enforcement Guidelines for International Operations (April 1995), 4 CCH Trade Reg. Rep. ¶ 13,107, Illustrative Example H.

Is there anything to be said for a rule of law that would give only the United States the right to enjoin a merger of US firms with substantial sales in the United States, and only the EU the right to prohibit a merger of European firms with substantial sales in EEA? What if the merger harms consumers beyond the borders of the home country? (*Gencor/Lonrho*) What if the merger harms only producer interests (e.g., rights of access to markets) and the foreign law protects these interests? (Compare *Boeing/McDonnell Douglas*.)

3. Do these cases—mergers in global markets having impacts around the world—suggest a need for international law or principles? Philip Condit, then Chairman of Boeing, told the Washington Post [July 24, 1997, E1] at the conclusion of Boeing's negotiations with the EU: "In a global economy, a single set of rules is, in fact, preferable[.] Over time, we have to keep working in that direction."

Comment on Mr. Condit's statement. Is it realistic? How might we reach a single set of merger rules for the world? How—and by whom—might the single set be applied, objectively and without nationalistic bias?

4. The following books might be helpful in the study of European merger law: B. Hawk & H. Huser, European Community Merger Control: a Practitioner's Guide (Kluwer 1996); B. Fox & E. Fox, Corporate Acquisitions and Mergers (Lexis–Matthew Bender, revised ed. 2002).

1. 81 BNA Antitrust & Trade Reg. Rep. 15
(July 6, 2001).

Chapter 26

PUBLIC ENTERPRISES, STATE ACTION AND COMPETITION POLICY

A. INTRODUCTION

Thus far we have focused our attention on harms to competition by business actors; largely, private actors. In this chapter we consider harms to competition by the state itself—by Member States or actors to whom they grant special privileges.

The first part of this chapter puts all of competition policy into perspective, for the decision to adopt competition policy and the task of constructing the particular competition law system involves questions about the role of government in the economy, the balance between freedom of enterprise and public regulation, and, for the EU, the balance between Member States' autonomy to pursue their own political economy preferences and the interests of the Community in integration, competitiveness of business, and the general welfare of the people.

At the outset of the chapter, we treat the compatibility of state monopoly and monopoly privileges with the Treaty. We proceed to ask when anticompetitive state measures violate the competition provisions in combination with other articles, such as Article 10, ex 5: Member States must "facilitate the achievement of the Community's tasks"; and when State measures shield anticompetitive private action that they facilitate. Finally, we turn to the explicit Treaty provisions that control State distortions of competition by grants of aid.

B. STATE MONOPOLIES OF A COMMERCIAL CHARACTER—APPLICATION OF ARTICLES 28 (ex 30) and 31 (ex 37)

Is it permissible for the State to control its economy? Does the very existence of competition policy imply, as you will recall Mr. Costa argued in *Costa v. ENEL* (pages 243, 269 supra),[1] that the Treaty adopts freedom of

---

1. Costa challenged Italy's nationalization of its electricity system. You may recall that the Milan magistrate agreed with Mr. Costa that creating a state monopoly by nationaliza-

enterprise and sets itself against "statism"? We begin with the unanswered question in *Costa*: Is state monopoly consistent with the Treaty?

The principal relevant provision of the Treaty is Article 31, ex 37, which is taken together with other provisions such as Article 28, ex 30. Article 31 provides:

1. Member States shall adjust any State monopolies of a commercial character so as to ensure that no discrimination regarding the conditions under which goods are procured and marketed exists between nationals of Member States.

The provisions of this Article shall apply to any body through which a Member State, in law or in fact, either directly or indirectly supervises, determines or appreciably influences imports or exports between Member States. These provisions shall likewise apply to monopolies delegated by the State to others.

2. Member States shall refrain from introducing any new measure which is contrary to the principles laid down in paragraph 1 or which restricts the scope of the Articles dealing with the prohibition of customs duties and quantitative restrictions between Member States. * * *

To address a serious problem of alcohol abuse, Sweden brought the liquor business under State control. It formed a state-owned company, V & S, with exclusive rights to produce and export spirits and to import beer, wine and spirits. It formed another state-owned company, Systembolaget, and gave it the exclusive right to sell alcoholic beverages at wholesale to restaurants and the exclusive right to sell alcoholic beverages at retail.

To facilitate its accession to the European Union, Sweden abolished the privileges of V & S and the wholesale privileges of Systembolaget and replaced them with a system of licenses, while retaining for Systembolaget its retail monopoly. Licenses for import, export, production, and wholesaling were to be issued at the discretion of the Alcohol Inspectorate upon the making of an application, which required documentation and the payment of a high, non-reimbursable fee. The fees, including annual renewal fees, were much higher per litre for low sales volume than for high sales volume, and thus the fee structure favored the large incumbent supplier, V & S.

Advocate General Elmer, who was the advocate general in a reference involving the criminal prosecution of an unauthorized wine importer, summarized the basis and workings of the Swedish system as follows:

The fundamental aim of Swedish alcohol policy throughout the twentieth century has been to limit the effect of market forces, namely competition and private profits. The reason for this was the conviction that competition and private profits encourage active marketing and active selling, which lead to increased consumption. The greater the number of undertakings having an interest in increased alcohol sales, the better alcoholic beverages will fare in the competition for consumers' money. In the case of a sector which society does not wish to see expand, market mechanisms such as competition and profit are not particularly suitable as means of control.

tion violated Community law, but the case was
ultimately dismissed for lack of standing.

In the Government's view, the principle of limiting private profits in the alcohol trade remains valid and must guide the State when it draws up rules on the marketing of alcoholic beverages and guidelines for retail sales of these beverages. In the sectors in which monopolies in alcohol must be abolished, that is to say, the manufacturing, import and wholesale sectors, the principle takes on a new meaning. Previously, State action was intended to preclude private interests from the alcohol trade. From now on, the guiding principle will be the control of market forces through a system of licences, supervision and sanctions which will be administered by a new alcohol authority [while preserving the retail monopoly of the State]. (*Franzen*, see infra.)

FRANZEN

(Swedish alcohol monopoly)
Case C–189/95, [1997] ECR I–5909.

[Harry Franzen, without a license, imported wine from Denmark and sold it in Sweden. Prosecuted for a criminal violation, he pled that the Swedish law was invalid for violating Articles 30 and 37 (now 28 and 31). The national court referred questions regarding Articles 30 and 37 to the Court of Justice.

Advocate General Elmer agreed with Mr. Franzen that the Swedish alcohol monopoly violated Community law. As to Article (ex) 30 he said: it "is intended to ensure access to the market of products from other Member States" (para. 59) and "to prevent lacunae in the protection of free movement" (para. 65). As to Article (ex) 37:

Advocate General Elmer

68   . . . Article 37 of the Treaty refers to the traders who supply the market in products. That provision therefore differs from Article 30 of the Treaty, first by being limited to discrimination and secondly by not protecting the free movement of goods as such but by protecting the traders of the other Member States who participate in the free movement of goods.

69   That was confirmed in . . . Commission v. Greece [[1990] ECR I–4747], where the Court held that to maintain in force the State's rights with regard to the importation and marketing of petroleum products gave rise to discrimination within the meaning of Article 37(1) against exporters established in other Member States. Presumably, the determining factor in that case was that the State's monopoly was of such a kind as to prevent certain traders, in particular those with whom the Greek State's monopoly did not have commercial relations, from exporting to the Greek market. There was therefore discrimination between nationals of the Member States, as mentioned in Article 37(1).

70   I could also refer to the Manghera judgment [1976 ECR 91]. In that judgment the Court, after stating that the exclusive right to import manufactured tobacco products enjoyed by the monopoly of the Italian State constituted, in respect of Community exports, discrimination prohibited by Article 37(1) of the Treaty, held that that provision must be interpreted "as meaning that . . . every national monopoly of a commercial character must be adjusted so as to eliminate the exclusive right to import from other Member States". That finding is quite general and must be

interpreted as meaning that the Court accepted that national import monopolies in themselves constitute discrimination between nationals of the Member States and that it is therefore unnecessary to ascertain on a case-by-case basis whether such import monopolies actually lead to discrimination between nationals of the Member States. * * *

72 Furthermore, in its decisions the Court has sometimes applied Articles 30 and 37 concurrently to a national monopoly of a commercial character and sometimes applied only Article 30 to exclusive rights conferred on a national monopolistic undertaking. Thus in ... Commission v. Greece, the Court held that the exclusive right to import and market finished petroleum products was contrary to both Article 30 and Article 37(1). In the telecommunications terminals judgment [France v. Commission, [1991] ECR I–1223] the Court held that exclusive rights to import and market terminal equipment constituted a measure having equivalent effect to a quantitative restriction on imports within the meaning of Article 30 of the Treaty.

The advocate general concluded that the Swedish monopoly and regulation necessarily hindered trade in violation of former Article 30; that it had the same effect as an import monopoly and therefore a discriminatory effect in violation of former Article 37; and that the system was not justified under former Article 36 since health and life could be protected by less restrictive means.

The Court

The rules relating to the existence and operation of the monopoly

[The Retail Monopoly]

39 The purpose of Article 37 of the Treaty is to reconcile the possibility for Member States to maintain certain monopolies of a commercial character as instruments for the pursuit of public interest aims with the requirements of the establishment and functioning of the common market. It aims at the elimination of obstacles to the free movement of goods, save, however, for restrictions on trade which are inherent in the existence of the monopolies in question.

40 Thus, Article 37 requires that the organization and operation of the monopoly be arranged so as to exclude any discrimination between nationals of Member States as regards conditions of supply and outlets, so that trade in goods from other Member States is not put at a disadvantage, in law or in fact, in relation to that in domestic goods and that competition between the economies of the Member States is not distorted.

41 In the present case, it is not contested that, in aiming to protect public health against the harm caused by alcohol, a domestic monopoly on the retail of alcoholic beverages, such as that conferred on Systembolaget, pursues a public interest aim.

42 It is therefore necessary to determine whether a monopoly of this kind is arranged in a way which meets the conditions referred to in paragraphs 39 and 40 above. * * *

The monopoly's sales network

53   Mr Franzen contends that the sales network maintained by Systembolaget is restricted and does not offer the full range of beverages available, which restricts even more the possibilities of sale.

54   It is true that a monopoly such as Systembolaget has only a limited number of 'shops'. However, it does not appear from the information provided to the Court that the number of sales outlets are limited to the point of compromising consumers' procurement of supplies of domestic or imported alcoholic beverages.

55   First of all, under the agreement which it has made with the State, Systembolaget must establish or close sales outlets on the basis of management constraints, consumer demand and the necessities of alcohol policy and ensure that each commune which so wishes has a sales outlet and that all points of the territory are served at least by dispatch deliveries.

56   Second, according to the information provided to the Court, alcoholic beverages may be ordered and supplied in the monopoly's 384 'shops', through around 550 sales outlets as well as along 56 bus routes and on 45 rural post rounds. Furthermore, there is at least one 'shop' in 259 of the 288 Swedish communes and Systembolaget is planning for every commune to have at least one 'shop' in 1998.

57   Finally, even if the retail network of Systembolaget is still imperfect, this circumstance does not adversely affect the sale of alcoholic beverages from other Member States more than the sale of alcoholic beverages produced in Sweden.

The promotion of alcoholic beverages

58   Mr Franzen also contends that the system for promoting alcoholic beverages favours the marketing of beverages produced in Sweden. He points out that the promotion of alcoholic beverages is confined to mere provision of information about the products, varying in form depending on whether the products are in the 'basic' assortment or in the 'by order' assortment, that the information is provided by the monopoly alone, without any control by suppliers and, furthermore, that suppliers may not canvas persons in charge of the monopoly's 'shops'.

59   As far as these points are concerned, it must be observed first of all that the restriction of the possibilities for promoting alcoholic beverages to the public is inherent in the situation where there is only one operator on the market for their retail.

60   Second, the monopoly rules do not prohibit producers or importers from promoting their products to the monopoly. . . .

61   It must also be pointed out that the promotion of alcoholic beverages to the public is subject, in the Member State in question, to a general restriction, the validity of which has not been called in question by the national court nor challenged by Mr Franzen. That restriction consists, in particular, of a ban on advertising on radio and television and in all newspapers or other periodicals, that is to say the means traditionally used by producers to promote their products to the public. However, alcoholic beverages selected by Systembolaget may be advertised in written material available at sales outlets. Furthermore, any alcoholic beverage may be mentioned in press articles. * * *

[64] Finally, it must be noted that the method of promotion used by the monopoly applies independently of products' origin and is not in itself apt to put at a disadvantage, in fact or in law, beverages imported from other Member States in relation to those produced on national territory. * * *

[66] So, having regard to the evidence before the Court, it appears that a retail monopoly such as that in question in the main proceedings meets the conditions for being compatible with Article 37 of the Treaty. . . .

Article 30 [now 28] [The Production and Wholesaling Restrictions]

[68] . . . Mr Franzen observes that the monopoly may obtain supplies only from holders of production licences or wholesale licences whose grant is subject to restrictive conditions and that such an obligation necessarily impedes imports of products from other Member States. * * *

[70] In a national system such as that in question in the main proceedings, only holders of production licences or wholesale licences are allowed to import alcoholic beverages, that is to say traders who fulfil the restrictive conditions to which issue of those licences is subject. According to the information provided to the Court during the proceedings, the traders in question must provide sufficient personal and financial guarantees to carry on the activities in question, concerning in particular their professional knowledge, their financial capacity and possession of storage capacity sufficient to meet the needs of their activities. Furthermore, the submission of an application is subject to payment of a high fixed charge . . . , which is not reimbursed if the application is rejected. Finally, in order to keep his licence, a trader must pay an annual supervision fee, which is also high. . . .

[71] The licensing system constitutes an obstacle to the importation of alcoholic beverages from other Member States in that it imposes additional costs on such beverages, such as intermediary costs, payment of charges and fees for the grant of a licence, and costs arising from the obligation to maintain storage capacity in Sweden.

[72] According to the Swedish Government's own evidence, the number of licences issued is low (223 in October 1996) and almost all of these licences have been issued to traders established in Sweden.

[73] Domestic legislation such as that in question in the main proceedings is therefore contrary to Article 30 of the Treaty.

[74] The Swedish Government has, however, invoked Article 36 of the EC Treaty. It maintains that its legislation was justified on grounds relating to the protection of human health.

[75] It is indeed so that measures contrary to Article 30 may be justified on the basis of Article 36 of the Treaty. All the same, according to established case-law (Cassis de Dijon . . .), the domestic provisions in question must be proportionate to the aim pursued and not attainable by measures less restrictive of intra-Community trade.

[76] Although the protection of human health against the harmful effects of alcohol, on which the Swedish Government relies, is indisputably one of the grounds which may justify derogation from Article 30 of the Treaty, the Swedish Government has not established that the licensing system set

up by the Law on Alcohol, in particular as regards the conditions relating to storage capacity and the high fees and charges which licence-holders are required to pay, was proportionate to the public health aim pursued or that this aim could not have been attained by measures less restrictive of intra-Community trade.

[77] It must therefore be held that Articles 30 and 36 of the Treaty preclude domestic provisions allowing only traders holding a production licence or a wholesale licence to import alcoholic beverages on conditions such as those laid down by Swedish legislation.

Notes and Questions

1. What is the practical effect of the judgment? Why can Sweden keep its retail monopoly? Why can't it keep its import and wholesale monopoly?

2. The New York Times assessed the impact of the judgment on Sweden in an article, Europe Making Sweden Ease Alcohol Rules, Mar. 28, 2001, Int'l ed., p. A1:

> ... [P]iece by piece, Sweden is being forced to take apart its anti-alcohol policies because most violate the European Union's rules of fair competition. Some liquor stores are open late and on Saturdays. A few have been remade into cheerfully decorated self-service stores. And wine lovers can delight in a wide selection. * * *

> Experts say that what is happening in Sweden over alcohol policy is in many ways a prime example of the difficulties the European Union faces as it tries to extend its reach and harmonize policies. Stretching from freezing climates to desert regions and incorporating vastly different cultures, the union is seeing that what may be a market commodity in one country is a health issue in another.

> "On this issue, we can't even really understand each other," said Dr. Gunar Agren, the executive manager of Sweden's National Institute of Health. "We just see things very differently and in fact we have different problems with alcohol."

Is the *Franzen* judgment a triumph of free movement and free competition over monopoly? or a triumph of European regulation over national cultural choices?

3. The monopoly cases bring together the trade and the competition concerns that disfavor monopoly. How did the Swedish system harm competition? Who was hurt? Consider all of Mr. Franzen's arguments. Were these harms essentially costs the nation was willing to pay for a national social policy? Or were they harms also to the whole Community? When effects of national, market-restricting policies spill over to other nations, who should decide whether the costs are worth the benefits? How did the Court of Justice deal with this problem in *Cassis de Dijon*, and later in *Keck*? Is the Court's approach consistent with *Keck*? See pages 508, 522 supra.

4. In view of *Franzen*, was Mr. Costa right or wrong?

C. EXCLUSIVE PRIVILEGES—ARTICLE 86 (ex 90)

Article 86 (ex 90) prohibits public undertakings and undertakings to which Member States grant special or exclusive rights from violating the competition provisions insofar as application of those rules does not obstruct the performance of the tasks assigned. Specifically:

Article 86 (ex Article 90)

1.   In the case of public undertakings and undertakings to which Member States grant special or exclusive rights, Member States shall neither enact nor maintain in force any measure contrary to the rules contained in this Treaty, in particular to those rules provided for in Article 12 [non-discrimination] and Articles 81 to 89 [restrictive agreements, abuse of dominance, state aids].

2.   Undertakings entrusted with the operation of services of general economic interest or having the character of a revenue-producing monopoly shall be subject to the rules contained in this Treaty, in particular to the rules on competition, insofar as the application of such rules does not obstruct the performance, in law or in fact, of the particular tasks assigned to them. The development of trade must not be affected to such an extent as would be contrary to the interests of the Community. * * *

The next case asks when enjoyment of a state-granted monopoly right, which is the right to keep out the competition, violates Article 86 (ex 90).

HÖFNER v. MACROTRON GmbH

Case C–41/90, [1991] ECR I–1979.

[German law, intended to achieve a high level of employment and to improve the distribution of jobs, conferred on the Bundesanstalt für Arbeit (Federal Employment Office) the exclusive right of placement; i.e. exclusivity as employment agent. The law required the Office to provide the service free of charge. Placement activities by others were punishable by fine. Messrs. Höfner and Elser contracted with Macrotron to present to Macrotron a suitable candidate for the post of sales manager, for a fee. They presented such a candidate, but Macrotron decided not to employ him and refused to pay the fee stipulated, alleging, inter alia, that the contract was void by reason of the German law. Höfner and Elser rejoined that the German law was void because it unnecessarily restrained their competition in violation of Article 90 (now 86), and exclusion of their competition amounted to abuse of dominance under Article 86 (now 82). The national court referred questions to the Court of Justice.]

16   In its fourth question, the national court asks more specifically whether the monopoly of employment procurement in respect of business executives granted to a public employment agency constitutes an abuse of a dominant position within the meaning of Article 86, having regard to Article 90(2)....

17   According to the appellants in the main proceedings, an agency such as the Bundesanstalt is both a public undertaking within the meaning of Article 90(1) and an undertaking entrusted with the operation of services of general economic interest within the meaning of Article 90(2) of the Treaty. The Bundesanstalt is therefore, they maintain, subject to the competition rules to the extent to which the application thereof does not obstruct the performance of the particular task assigned to it, and it does

not in the present case. The appellants also claim that the action taken by the Bundesanstalt, which extended its statutory monopoly over employment procurement to activities for which the establishment of a monopoly is not in the public interest, constitutes an abuse within the meaning of Article 86 of the Treaty. They also consider that any Member State which makes such an abuse possible is in breach of Article 90(1) and of the general principle whereby the Member States must refrain from taking any measure which could destroy the effectiveness of the Community competition rules.

18   The Commission takes a somewhat different view. The maintenance of a monopoly on executive recruitment constitutes, in its view, an infringement of Article 90(1) read in conjunction with Article 86 of the Treaty where the grantee of the monopoly is not willing or able to carry out that task fully, according to the demand existing on the market, and provided that such conduct is liable to affect trade between Member States. * * *

21   It must be observed, in the context of competition law, first that the concept of an undertaking encompasses every entity engaged in an economic activity, regardless of the legal status of the entity and the way in which it is financed and, secondly, that employment procurement is an economic activity.

22   The fact that employment procurement activities are normally entrusted to public agencies cannot affect the economic nature of such activities. Employment procurement has not always been, and is not necessarily, carried out by public entities. That finding applies in particular to executive recruitment.

23   It follows that an entity such as a public employment agency engaged in the business of employment procurement may be classified as an undertaking for the purpose of applying the Community competition rules.

24   It must be pointed out that a public employment agency which is entrusted, under the legislation of a Member State, with the operation of services of general economic interest ... remains subject to the competition rules pursuant to Article 90(2) of the Treaty unless and to the extent to which it is shown that their application is incompatible with the discharge of its duties.

25   As regards the manner in which a public employment agency enjoying an exclusive right of employment procurement conducts itself in relation to executive recruitment undertaken by private recruitment consultancy companies, it must be stated that the application of Article 86 of the Treaty cannot obstruct the performance of the particular task assigned to that agency in so far as the latter is manifestly not in a position to satisfy demand in that area of the market and in fact allows its exclusive rights to be encroached on by those companies.

26   Whilst it is true that Article 86 concerns undertakings and may be applied within the limits laid down by Article 90(2) to public undertakings or undertakings vested with exclusive rights or specific rights, the fact nevertheless remains that the Treaty requires the Member States not to take or maintain in force measures which could destroy the effectiveness of that provision. . . . * * *

29   ... [T]he simple fact of creating a dominant position of that kind by granting an exclusive right within the meaning of Article 90(1) is not as such incompatible with Article 86 of the Treaty. A Member State is in breach of the prohibition contained in those two provisions only if the undertaking in question, merely by exercising the exclusive right granted to it, cannot avoid abusing its dominant position.

30   Pursuant to Article 86(b), such an abuse may in particular consist in limiting the provision of a service, to the prejudice of those seeking to avail themselves of it.

31   A Member State creates a situation in which the provision of a service is limited when the undertaking to which it grants an exclusive right extending to executive recruitment activities is manifestly not in a position to satisfy the demand prevailing on the market for activities of that kind and when the effective pursuit of such activities by private companies is rendered impossible by the maintenance in force of a statutory provision under which such activities are prohibited and non-observance of that prohibition renders the contracts concerned void. * * *

34   In view of the foregoing considerations, it must be stated in reply to the fourth question that a public employment agency engaged in employment procurement activities is subject to the prohibition contained in Article 86 of the Treaty, so long as the application of that provision does not obstruct the performance of the particular task assigned to it. A Member State which has conferred an exclusive right to carry on that activity upon the public employment agency is in breach of Article 90(1) of the Treaty where it creates a situation in which that agency cannot avoid infringing Article 86 of the Treaty. That is the case, in particular, where the following conditions are satisfied:

— the exclusive right extends to executive recruitment activities

— the public employment agency is manifestly incapable of satisfying demand prevailing on the market for such activities

— the actual pursuit of those activities by private recruitment consultants is rendered impossible by the maintenance in force of a statutory provision under which such activities are prohibited and non-observance of that prohibition renders the contracts concerned void

— the activities in question may extend to the nationals or to the territory of other Member States.

Notes and Questions

1.   What is the standard for running afoul of Article 86 (ex 90)? How difficult will it be for Messrs. Höfner and Elser to win their argument before the national court?

2.   Note the difference between plaintiffs' proposed formulation and the Commission's. Which did the Court accept? Which is the more workable? Which is the better standard, given the Community's dual interests in respecting Member State regulation in the public interest and supporting freedom of competition?

3.   Does the Court in effect require an efficiency audit of the Federal Employment Office to determine whether it can satisfy demand? Isn't the Office's ability to satisfy demand a function of the resources the German government

makes available to it? Why does the Community care whether Germany sufficiently funds its free employment service? Do all dominant firms abuse their dominance by simply not providing enough goods or service (at what price level?), or is it critical that the government-granted exclusive privilege prevents anyone else from serving the market?

4.   Messrs. Höfner and Elser also claimed a violation of Article 59 (now 49) in conjunction with Article 7 (now 12); but since all parties, including the employment candidate, were German, the Court found Article 59 inapplicable. If the candidate or the private employment agency were Belgian, would Article 49, ex 59, protect the private agency's right to its fee?

5.   In Régie des Postes v. Corbeau, Case C–320/91, [1993] ECR I–2533, a Belgian law—enacted before the development of courier service—gave exclusive mail delivery rights to the Belgian Post Office and prohibited private mail delivery. Mr. Corbeau set up a private mail delivery service in Liège. Corbeau collected mail from his clients and guaranteed delivery before noon the following day to all addressees within town limits. He delivered in-town mail and dispatched the out-of-town mail by post. When prosecuted, Corbeau asserted a violation of Article 90 (now 86).

In an Article 177 reference, the Court of Justice advised the Belgian court that an undertaking charged with the provision of universal service may not restrict competition more than necessary to achieve its public mission in view of contemporary market conditions, leaving it to the national court to determine what was more than necessary.

Was Corbeau skimming the cream from the Belgian Post's business? At some point, would cream-skimming compromise the economic stability of the post office and disable it from fulfilling its obligation to provide universal service? How can the national court determine how much competition is too much competition for the Belgian Post to fulfill its public mission?

ALBANY INTERNATIONAL BV AND TEXTILE INDUSTRY PENSION FUNDS

Case C–67/96, [1999] ECR I–5751.

[Albany International, a textile firm that wished to provide pensions for its workers through an insurer of its choice, contended that the Dutch law granting to a specified fund an exclusive right to manage supplementary textile industry pensions violated Articles 86 and 90 (now 82 and 86). (For Article 81 implications, see page 899 supra.) Citing *Höfner*, the Court repeated that mere creation of a dominant position (which the Netherlands conferred on the pension fund) is not incompatible with Article 86. Rather, to run afoul of the law, the Member State must create a situation in which the undertaking cannot avoid abusing its dominance.]

[98] It is therefore necessary to consider whether, as contended by the Fund, the Netherlands Government and the Commission, the exclusive right of the sectoral pension fund to manage supplementary pensions in a given sector and the resultant restriction of competition may be justified under Article 90 (2) of the Treaty as a measure necessary for the performance of a particular social task of general interest with which that fund has been charged. * * *

102 It is important to bear in mind first of all that, under Article 90 (2) of the Treaty, undertakings entrusted with the operation of services of general economic interest are subject to the rules on competition in so far as the application of such rules does not obstruct the performance, in law or in fact, of the particular tasks assigned to them.

103 In allowing, in certain circumstances, derogations from the general rules of the Treaty, Article 90(2) of the Treaty seeks to reconcile the Member States' interest in using certain undertakings, in particular in the public sector, as an instrument of economic or fiscal policy with the Community's interest in ensuring compliance with the rules on competition and preservation of the unity of the common market.

104 In view of the interest of the Member States thus defined they cannot be precluded, when determining what services of general economic interest they entrust to certain undertakings, from taking account of objectives pertaining to their national policy or from endeavouring to attain them by means of obligations and constraints which they impose on such undertakings.

105 The supplementary pension scheme at issue in the main proceedings fulfils an essential social function within the Netherlands pensions system by reason of the limited amount of the statutory pension, which is calculated on the basis of the minimum statutory wage.

106 Moreover, the importance of the social function attributed to supplementary pensions has recently been recognised by the Community legislature's adoption of Council Directive 98/49/EC of 29 June 1998 on safeguarding the supplementary pension rights of employed and self-employed persons moving within the Community.

107 Next, it is not necessary, in order for the conditions for the application of Article 90 (2) of the Treaty to be fulfilled, that the financial balance or economic viability of the undertaking entrusted with the operation of a service of general economic interest should be threatened. It is sufficient that, in the absence of the rights at issue, it would not be possible for the undertaking to perform the particular tasks entrusted to it, defined by reference to the obligations and constraints to which it is subject or that maintenance of those rights is necessary to enable the holder of them to perform tasks of general economic interest which have been assigned to it under economically acceptable conditions.

108 If the exclusive right of the fund to manage the supplementary pension scheme for all workers in a given sector were removed, undertakings with young employees in good health engaged in non-dangerous activities would seek more advantageous insurance terms from private insurers. The progressive departure of 'good' risks would leave the sectoral pension fund with responsibility for an increasing share of 'bad' risks, thereby increasing the cost of pensions for workers, particularly those in small and medium-sized undertakings with older employees engaged in dangerous activities, to which the fund could no longer offer pensions at an acceptable cost.

109 Such a situation would arise particularly in a case where, as in the main proceedings, the supplementary pension scheme managed exclusively by

the Fund displays a high level of solidarity resulting, in particular, from the fact that contributions do not reflect the risk, from the obligation to accept all workers without a prior medical examination, the continuing accrual of pension rights despite exemption from the payment of contributions in the event of incapacity for work, the discharge by the Fund of arrears of contributions due from an employer in the event of insolvency and the indexing of the amount of pensions in order to maintain their value.

110   Such constraints, which render the service provided by the Fund less competitive than a comparable service provided by insurance companies, go towards justifying the exclusive right of the Fund to manage the supplementary pension scheme.

111   It follows that the removal of the exclusive right conferred on the Fund might make it impossible for it to perform the tasks of general economic interest entrusted to it under economically acceptable conditions and threaten its financial equilibrium. * * *

[The Fund has the power to grant exemptions from its own exclusivity. It has the duty to grant such exemptions if specific criteria are met, thus providing a check against discriminatory or arbitrary denials.]

122   Finally, as regards Albany's argument that an adequate level of pension for workers could be assured by laying down minimum requirements to be met by pensions offered by insurance companies, it must be emphasised that, in view of the social function of supplementary pension schemes and the margin of appreciation enjoyed, according to settled case-law, by the Member States in organising their social security systems, it is incumbent on each Member State to consider whether, in view of the particular features of its national pension system, laying down minimum requirements would still enable it to ensure the level of pension which it seeks to guarantee in a sector by compulsory affiliation to a pension fund.

123   The answer to the third question must therefore be that Articles 86 and 90 of the Treaty do not preclude the public authorities from conferring on a pension fund the exclusive right to manage a supplementary pension scheme in a given sector.

Does the Court grant wide berth to the State to carry out its social purpose of solidarity, despite the fact that its chosen solution might not be efficient? Or does the Court imply some level of serious scrutiny? If the Netherlands can assure an adequate level of pensions by laying down minimum requirements, must it abandon its system? See para. 122. Who determines whether adequate pensions can be assured by less restrictive means? Does para. 122 mean that a grant of exclusive rights *can*, in itself, violate the Treaty simply because it restricts competition and the restriction was unnecessary to achieve the public goal?

DEUTSCHE POST AG v. GZS, DEUTSCHE POST AG v. CITICORP

Cases C–147/97, 148/97, 2000 ECR I–825.

[Some Member States, including the Netherlands and Denmark, have lower postal charges than others. Consequently, residents of high-rate States may be induced to go to low-rate States to post their mailings. According to the Universal Postal Convention (UPC) of which Germany is a member, postal services of a contracting state must deliver to addressees items addressed to in-state persons that are passed to them by the postal services of another contracting state. The state of the posting pays specified terminal dues to the state of the addressees; but usually, the dues do not cover the costs. A 1989 amendment to the UPC (Art. 25) allows a state not to deliver in-state mail posted in a foreign country by its residents to profit from the lower charges of the other nation, or items posted in large quantities by its residents in another country (regardless of intent to profit from lower charges); in such cases, the state of the addressees may either return the mail or charge postage at its internal rates.

Citibank Group includes CKG, whose registered office is in Frankfurt. CKG prepares and dispatches statements for Visa card and other cards. It set up a special body to receive the data and dispatch the statements in the Netherlands, where they were posted to addressees in Germany.

GZS is comprised of credit institutions that issue the Eurocard credit card. It is the largest operator for carrying out Eurocard credit transactions in Germany. It transmits the data by electronic transfer to its Danish partner, which draws up the statements and hands them to the Danish post office, which transmits them to the Deutsche Post for delivery in Germany.

In both cases, Deutsche Post demanded internal mailing rates for delivery of the mail in Germany, and the companies refused to pay. Deutsche Post sued in a German court. A German appellate court made references to the Court of Justice asking whether Deutsche Post's demands violated Articles 5, 30, 59, 85, 86 and 90 (now 10, 28, 49, 81, 82 and 86).]

36 ... [T]he national court is to be understood in the first three questions as essentially asking whether it is contrary to Article 90 of the Treaty, read in conjunction with Articles 86 and 59 thereof, for a body such as Deutsche Post to exercise the right provided for by Article 25(3) of the UPC to charge, in the cases referred to in the second sentence of Article 25(1) and Article 25(2), internal postage on items of mail posted in large quantities with the postal services of a Member State other than the Member State to which that body belongs.

37 To reply to that question, as reformulated, it should first be noted that a body such as Deutsche Post, which has been granted exclusive rights as regards the collection, carriage and delivery of mail, must be regarded as an undertaking to which the Member State concerned has granted exclusive rights within the meaning of Article 90(1) of the Treaty. * * *

41 [Article 90(1)] must be read in conjunction with Article 90(2) which provides that undertakings entrusted with the operation of services of

general economic interest are to be subject to the rules contained in the Treaty in so far as the application of such rules does not obstruct the performance, in law or in fact, of the particular tasks assigned to them. * * *

43   [T]he UPC is designed to establish rules ensuring that international items of mail addressed to residents of a Contracting State and passed on by the postal services of other Contracting States are forwarded and delivered. One of the fundamental principles of the UPC ... is the obligation of the postal administration of the Contracting State to which international mail is sent to forward and deliver it to addressees resident in its territory using the most rapid means of its letter post. In that regard, the States which have adopted the Convention of the Universal Postal Union constitute a single postal territory, in which the freedom of transit of reciprocal international mail is in principle guaranteed.

44   For the postal services of the Member States, performance of the obligations flowing from the UPC is thus in itself a service of general economic interest within the meaning of Article 90(2) of the Treaty.

45   In the present case, German legislation assigns the operation of that service to Deutsche Post.

46   ... [P]ostal services initially delivered international mail without being paid for that task. However, when it became apparent that the flows of postal traffic between two Contracting States frequently did not balance out, so that the postal services of the various Contracting States had to process quantities of international mail which differed greatly, specific provisions were laid down in that regard, one of which is Article 25 of the UPC.

47   Under Article 25(3) of the UPC, the postal services of the Contracting States may in particular, in the cases referred to in Article 25(1) and (2), charge postage on items of mail at their internal rates.

48   The grant to a body such as Deutsche Post of the right to treat international items of mail as internal post in such cases creates a situation where that body may be led, to the detriment of users of postal services, to abuse its dominant position resulting from the exclusive right granted to it to forward and deliver those items to the relevant addressees.

49   It is accordingly necessary to examine the extent to which exercise of such a right is necessary to enable a body of that kind to perform its task of general interest pursuant to the obligations flowing from the UPC and, in particular, to operate under economically acceptable conditions.

50   If a body such as Deutsche Post were obliged to forward and deliver to addressees resident in Germany mail posted in large quantities by senders resident in Germany using postal services of other Member States, without any provision allowing it to be financially compensated for all the costs occasioned by that obligation, the performance, in economically balanced conditions, of that task of general interest would be jeopardised.

51   The postal services of a Member State cannot simultaneously bear the costs entailed in the performance of the service of general economic interest of forwarding and delivering international items of mail, which is their responsibility by virtue of the UPC, and the loss of income resulting

from the fact that bulk mailings are no longer posted with the postal services of the Member State in which the addressees are resident but with those of other Member States.

52 In such a case, it must be regarded as justified, for the purposes of the performance, in economically balanced conditions, of the task of general interest entrusted to Deutsche Post by the UPC, to treat cross-border mail as internal mail and, consequently, to charge internal postage. * * *

54 Article 90(2) of the Treaty therefore justifies, in the absence of an agreement between the postal services of the Member States concerned fixing terminal dues in relation to the actual costs of processing and delivering incoming trans-border mail, the grant by a Member State to its postal services of the statutory right to charge internal postage on items of mail where senders resident in that State post items, or cause them to be posted, in large quantities with the postal services of another Member State in order to send them to the first Member State. * * *

56 On the other hand, in so far as part of the forwarding and delivery costs is offset by terminal dues paid by the postal services of other Member States, it is not necessary, in order for a body such as Deutsche Post to fulfil the obligations flowing from the UPC, that postage be charged at the full internal rate on items posted in large quantities with those services. * * *

58 Thus, the exercise by such a body of the right to demand the full amount of the internal postage, where the costs relating to the forwarding and delivery of mail posted in large quantities with the postal services of a Member State other than the State in which both the senders and the addressees of that mail are resident are not offset by the terminal dues paid by those services, may be regarded as an abuse of a dominant position within the meaning of Article 86 of the Treaty.

59 In order to prevent a body such as Deutsche Post from exercising its right, provided for by Article 25(3) of the UPC, to return items of mail to origin, the senders of those items have no choice but to pay the full amount of the internal postage.

60 As the Court has stated in relation to a refusal to sell on the part of an undertaking holding a dominant position within the meaning of Article 86 of the Treaty, such action would be inconsistent with the objective laid down by Article 3(g) of the EC Treaty ..., as explained in Article 86, in particular in subparagraphs (b) and (c) of its second paragraph.

61 It follows from all the foregoing considerations that, in the absence of an agreement between the postal services of the Member States concerned fixing terminal dues in relation to the actual costs of processing and delivering incoming trans-border mail, it is not contrary to Article 90 of the Treaty, read in conjunction with Articles 86 and 59 thereof, for a body such as Deutsche Post to exercise the right provided for by Article 25(3) of the UPC ... to charge ... internal postage on items of mail posted in large quantities with the postal services of a Member State other than the Member State to which that body belongs. On the other hand, the exercise of such a right is contrary to Article 90(1) of the Treaty, read in conjunction with Article 86 thereof, in so far as the result is that such a body may demand the entire internal postage applicable in the Member

State to which it belongs without deducting the terminal dues corresponding to those items of mail paid by the abovementioned postal services.

Notes and Comments

1. Citibank and GZS observed that movement of mail would be freer if Deutsche Post could not impose a "border" charge. Does the charge for internal delivery obstruct free movement in any relevant way? Does the answer depend on whether the charge is necessary to cover in-state delivery costs? Does the Court in *Deutsche Post* rule that Article 49 (ex 59) implies the availability of a justification allowed under 86(2) (ex 90(2)), and that without such a justification Article 49, as well as 82 and 86, would be violated?

2. Is this just another case about possibly excessive prices or insufficient output under Article 82, where the undertaking happens to be a state-owned enterprise entrusted with exclusive privileges? Compare *Corbeau* and *Höfner*. Or is this case about the freedom of firms to move (part of) their business to wherever the cost of inputs is lower?

3. Since the late 1970s, the Commission and Court have taken a number of actions to limit the power of state-owned monopolies and undertakings enjoying exclusive rights. In 1980 the Commission issued a directive under Article 90(3) (now 86(3)) requiring Member States to reveal financial information about their state-owned enterprises. Commission Directive 80/723, O.J. L 195/35 (July 29, 1980), amended by Commission Directive 85/413, O.J. L 229/20 (Aug. 28, 1985). In 1988 the Commission took the dramatic step of requiring Member States to abolish monopoly rights of telecommunications enterprises (most of which were state owned) to supply telephone terminal equipment. Commission Directive 88/301, O.J. L 131/73 (May 27, 1988) (Telecommunications Terminals Directive). France and several other States insisted that the Telecommunications Terminals Directive was a usurpation of power, but the Court of Justice rejected the claim.

In a number of situations the case is a straightforward Article 82 (ex 86) case, and state ownership or state-granted privilege does not provide a shield. In *British Telecom* (Italy v. Commission), the Court held that a state telecommunications monopoly abused its dominance by preventing private message-forwarding agencies from receiving and forwarding international telephone calls. Case 41/83, [1985] ECR 873. In *Telemarketing*, the Court stated that a broadcasting monopoly enterprise would abuse its dominant position by refusing to sell broadcasting time to a telemarketing firm that competed with the monopoly firm's subsidiary. Centre Belge d'Etudes de Marché-Télé-marketing SA v. Compagnie Luxembourgeoise de Télédiffusion SA, Case 311/84, [1985] ECR 3261.

D. STATE MEASURES—ARTICLES 3, 10, 81, 82 (ex 3, 5, 85, 86)

1. STATE RESPONSIBILITY

State legislation is a frequent source of distortion of competition. Distortions may result from national laws on price control, sector regulation (e.g., oil, tobacco, transport), taxation, and various social and national industrial policies.

Treaty Articles 3(1)(g), 10 (ex 5), and the four freedoms, combined with the competition law sections, might have produced a broad preemption by

Community competition policy of anticompetitive state legislation. The Court bowed in this direction in its judgment in NV GB–INNO–BM v. Vereniging van de Kleinhandelaars in Tabak (INNO/ATAB), Case 13/77, [1977] ECR 2115. There the Court said, regarding a Belgian law requiring, for tax collection purposes, that tobacco products be sold at a price affixed to the label by the manufacturer or importer:

> [W]hile it is true that Article 86 [now 82] is directed at undertakings, nonetheless it is also true that the Treaty [Article 5, now 10] imposes a duty on Member States not to adopt or maintain in force any measure which could deprive that provision of its effectiveness. Id., para. 31.

Even so, the Court has been reluctant to condemn Member States' regulatory laws for undermining Articles 81 and 82, especially since the *Keck* revolution in 1993, which signaled greater deference to State autonomy vis-à-vis Article 30, now 28 (see Chapter 13C *supra*). Three competition cases decided at the time of *Keck* reflect the new deference; namely: *Ohra, Meng* and *Reiff*.

Ohra, a Dutch insurance firm that dealt directly with customers rather than through intermediaries, tried to become more competitive by giving credit cards to its customers. Ohra was prosecuted for violating a Dutch law that prohibited insurance companies and their agents from granting rebates or other things of value. Ohra responded that the law was anticompetitive and constituted a violation of Member States' obligations under Articles 3(g) and 5, as linked with 85 and 86.

In *Meng*, in the face of a similar German law, insurance agent Meng rebated his commissions to his clients. When prosecuted, he presented the same defense as Ohra: he was competing; the prohibition was illegal.

Reiff involved a German law that delegated truck tariff-setting to tariff boards whose members were appointed by the Federal Minister upon the recommendation of the truckers themselves. In setting the tariffs, the board members were obliged to take account of the public interest criteria laid down by the public authority, and the Minister of Transport was entitled to participate in the meetings, to reject tariffs that were not in the public interest, and to set tariffs himself. A trucking company charged Reiff, a shipper, a price less than the mandated tariff. The federal office proceeded against Reiff for the difference, and Reiff defended on grounds that the the law was anticompetitive and void. Ohra Schadeverzekeringen NV v. Netherlands (Ohra), Case C–245/91, [1993] ECR I–5872; M. Meng v. Germany (Meng), Case C–2/91, [1993] ECR I–5751; Gebrüder Reiff GmbH & Co. KG v. Bundesanstalt für den Güterfernverkehr (Reiff), Case C–185/91, [1993] ECR I–5801.

The three cases came to the Court of Justice on Article 177 (now 234) references. The Court held: a Member State would infringe (former) Articles 3(g) and 5 if it "requires or favors the adoption of agreements, decisions or concerted practices contrary to Article 85, or reinforces such effects, or deprives its own legislation of its official character by delegating economic responsibility to private traders" (quoting from *INNO/ATAB*). None of the three laws fit the prohibited category.

Do you agree? What are the anticompetitive effects in each case? In which of the cases can you make the best argument that the national measure would tend to reinforce a private cartel or that it delegated economic responsibility for an anticompetitive act to private traders?

2. PRIVATE RESPONSIBILITY

Private actors may disclaim responsibility on grounds that the anticompetitive act was not theirs; it was the act of the State.

COMMISSION AND FRANCE v. LADBROKE RACING LTD.

Cases C–359/95 P and C–379/95 P, [1997] ECR I–6265.

[French law created Pari Mutuel Urbain (PMU) as a joint service of the authorized racing companies to manage their rights in off-track betting, and it granted PMU exclusive rights to run off-track betting on horse races held in France and horse race betting organized in France. French law prohibited anyone other than PMU to place or accept bets on horse races.

Ladbroke Racing Ltd., an operator of off-track betting, lodged with the Commission a complaint against France under Article 90 (now 86), and a complaint against the ten main racing companies in France and PMU under Articles 85 and 86 (now 81 and 82).

Before taking a position on the Article 90 claim, which included allegations of illegal state aid, the Commission rejected the complaint for violation of Articles 85 and 86 on grounds that those articles did not apply.

The Court of First Instance annulled the Commission's decision to reject the complaint, on grounds that a definitive determination could not be made by the Commission before completing its investigation regarding the compatibility of the French law with the competition rules. The Commission and France appealed to the Court of Justice.]

20   ... [T]he Commission submits that it is necessary to distinguish between State measures requiring undertakings to engage in conduct contrary to Articles 85 and 86 and measures that do not require any conduct contrary to those rules but simply create a legal framework that itself restricts competition. In the first case, the Commission considers that Article 85 remains applicable to undertakings' conduct despite the existence of national statutory obligations and irrespective of the possible application of Articles 3(g), 5 and 85 of the Treaty with regard to those State measures. In fact, the Commission argues that an undertaking can and, by virtue of the primacy of Community law and the direct effect of Articles 85(1) and 86 of the Treaty, must refuse to comply with a State measure that requires conduct contrary to those provisions.

21   In the second case, by contrast, Article 85 may in certain circumstances not apply. That is the case here, since the 1974 legislation does not require the conclusion of an agreement between the main racing companies but itself grants the PMU the exclusive right to organize off-course totalizator betting. The restriction of competition thus flowed directly from the national legislation, without any action on the part of undertakings being necessary. * * *

[33] Articles 85 and 86 of the Treaty apply only to anti-competitive conduct engaged in by undertakings on their own initiative. If anti-competitive conduct is required of undertakings by national legislation or if the latter creates a legal framework which itself eliminates any possibility of competitive activity on their part, Articles 85 and 86 do not apply. In such a situation, the restriction of competition is not attributable, as those provisions implicitly require, to the autonomous conduct of the undertakings.

[34] Articles 85 and 86 may apply, however, if it is found that the national legislation does not preclude undertakings from engaging in autonomous conduct which prevents, restricts or distorts competition.

[35] When the Commission is considering the applicability of Articles 85 and 86 of the Treaty to the conduct of undertakings, a prior evaluation of national legislation affecting such conduct should therefore be directed solely to ascertaining whether that legislation prevents undertakings from engaging in autonomous conduct which prevents, restricts or distorts competition.

[The Commission was therefore entitled to find (former) Articles 85 and 86 inapplicable without completing its investigation into the compatibility of the French legislation with the competition law. The Court set aside the judgment of the CFI.]

Notes and Questions

1.   Describe the anticompetitive aspects of the French off-track betting system. Why might France desire such a system nonetheless?

2.   The Commission held that there was no *private* anticompetitive action. Defend the result, including the distinction made by the Commission in paragraphs 20–21.

3.   What do paragraphs 33 and 34 mean?

4.   Were the State measures (apart from state aid) likely to be compatible with Treaty Article 86 (ex 90)? What if the PMU establishments shut their doors at 5:00 p.m. and gamblers claimed they were shut out of betting? (Consider *Höfner*.) Would the outcome of the case have been different if the PMU were an undertaking in the sole control of the ten racing companies?

COMMISSION v. ITALY
(CNSD)
C–35/96, [1998] ECR I–3851.

[Customs agents are professionals who offer services to carry out customs formalities relating to the import, export and transit of goods, and related monetary, fiscal and commercial services. In Italy the Departmental Councils of Customs Agents, whose members are elected by the customs agents, are constituted by Italian law to supervise the activity of the customs agents. Also constituted by Italian law, the Consiglio Nazionale degli Spedizionieri Doganali (National Council of Customs Agents, or CNSD) governs the Departmental Councils. It is legally responsible for setting the tariff for the services provided by customs agents on the basis of proposals from the Departmental Councils. Its members are customs agents elected by the Departmental Councils. Customs agents who deviate from the tariff are subject to discipline, which can include suspension or removal from the register of customs agents.

The Commission brought an action against Italy under Article 169 (now 226) for a declaration that Italy failed to fulfill its obligations under Articles 5 and 85 (now 10 and 81) by requiring the CNSD to adopt a decision by an association of undertakings (a minimum compulsory tariff; i.e. to price fix) contrary to Article 85.

A related action by the Commission for a declaration that Italy's law infringed Articles 9 and 12 (now 23 and 25) failed on grounds that importers did not need to use the services of professional customs agents in all circumstances.

In the Articles 5/85 case, Italy argued that the customs agents were professionals exercising a liberal profession; that their activity was intellectual, and that they and their association CNSD were not "undertakings" subject to Article 85.

The Court held first that CNSD engaged in economic activity on the market and therefore was an association of undertakings.]

43   ... [T]he CNSD is responsible for setting the tariff for the professional services of customs agents on the basis of proposals from the Departmental Councils (Article 14(d) of Law No 1612/1960)....

44   It follows that the members of the CNSD cannot be characterised as independent experts and that they are not required, under the law, to set tariffs taking into account not only the interests of the undertakings or associations of undertakings in the sector which has appointed them but also the general interest and the interests of undertakings in other sectors or users of the services in question.

45   Secondly, it must be held that the decisions by which the CNSD set a uniform, compulsory tariff for all customs agents restrict competition within the meaning of Article 85 of the Treaty and are capable of affecting intra-Community trade.

46   The tariff directly sets the prices for customs agents' services. It provides, for each separate type of operation, the maximum and minimum prices which can be charged to customers. Furthermore, the tariff lays down various scales on the basis of the value or the weight of the goods to be cleared through customs or of the specific type of goods, or type of professional service (Article 1).

47   Lastly, the tariff is mandatory (Article 5), so that a customs agent may not depart from it on his own initiative. Only the CNSD is empowered to provide for derogations (Article 6).

48   As regards the question whether intra-Community trade is affected, it need merely be pointed out that an agreement extending over the whole of the territory of a Member State has, by its very nature, the effect of reinforcing the compartmentalisation of markets on a national basis, thereby holding up the economic interpenetration which the Treaty is designed to bring about.

49   That effect is all the more appreciable in this case because the various types of import or export operations within the Community, as well as transactions between Community traders, require customs formalities to

be carried out and may, in consequence, make it necessary for an independent registered customs agent to be involved.

50 That is true of so-called 'internal transit' operations, covering the dispatching of goods from Italy to a Member State, that is to say from one point in the customs territory of the Community to another, by way of transit through a non-Member country (for example, Switzerland). That type of operation is particularly important for Italy, since a large proportion of goods dispatched from regions in the north-east of the country to Germany and the Netherlands transit through Switzerland.

51 From the foregoing considerations, it follows that, in adopting the tariff, the CNSD infringed Article 85(1) of the Treaty.

52 Thirdly, the question of the extent to which that infringement can be attributed to the Italian Republic must be considered.

53 Although Article 85 of the Treaty is, in itself, concerned solely with the conduct of undertakings and not with measures adopted by Member States by law or regulation, the fact nevertheless remains that Article 85 of the Treaty, in conjunction with Article 5, requires the Member States not to introduce or maintain in force measures, even of a legislative nature, which may render ineffective the competition rules applicable to undertakings (for Article 85 of the Treaty, see *Van Eycke, . . . Reiff . . .*).

54 Such would be the case if a Member State were to require or favour the adoption of agreements, decisions or concerted practices contrary to Article 85 or to reinforce their effects, or to deprive its own rules of the character of legislation by delegating to private economic operators responsibility for taking decisions affecting the economic sphere (see . . . *Van Eycke, Reiff . . .*).

55 By adopting the national legislation in question, the Italian Republic clearly not only required the conclusion of an agreement contrary to Article 85 of the Treaty and declined to influence its terms, but also assists in ensuring compliance with that agreement.

56 First, Article 14(d) of Law No 1612/1960 requires the CNSD to compile a compulsory, uniform tariff for the services of customs agents.

57 Secondly, as is clear from paragraphs 41 to 44 of this judgment, the national legislation in question wholly relinquished to private economic operators the powers of the public authorities as regards the setting of tariffs.

58 Thirdly, the Italian legislation expressly prohibits registered customs agents from derogating from the tariff on pain of exclusion, suspension or removal from the register.

59 Fourthly, although no provision laid down by law or regulation confers on the Minister for Finance the power to approve the tariff, it remains the case that the Decree of the Minister for Finance of 6 July 1988 bestowed upon it the appearance of a public regulation. First, publication in the 'General Series' of the *Gazzetta Ufficiale della Repubblica Italiana* gave rise to a presumption of knowledge of the tariff on the part of third parties, to which the CNSD's decision could never have laid claim. Second, the official character thus conferred on the tariff facilitates the application

by customs agents of the prices that it sets. Lastly, its nature is such as to deter customers who might wish to contest the prices demanded by customs agents.

60   In the light of the foregoing considerations, it must be held that, by adopting and maintaining in force a law which, in granting the relative decision-making power, requires the CNSD to adopt a decision by an association of undertakings contrary to Article 85 of the EC Treaty, consisting of setting a compulsory tariff for all customs agents, the Italian Republic has failed to fulfil its obligations under Articles 5 and 85 of the Treaty.

Notes and Questions

1.   Was the Court in the related proceeding correct in rejecting the action for violation of Articles 9 and 12 (now 23 and 25)?

2.   In the aftermath of *CNSD*, can the Italian government take back its decision-making prerogative and set the tariff itself? If so, is the probable effect of the Court's judgment merely to cause the government to take on this tariff-setting task? (Are there public benefits to requiring the government, as opposed to private economic actors, to do so?) Or is the government likely to rethink whether the public interest requires price-setting?

3.   Is the judgment unfair to CNSD, which was held to have acted pursuant to the command of its government? Note the Court's choices. It could have regarded CNSD as protected from an Article 85 violation by state command. But if it had recognized CNSD's state action defense, could it have held Italy in violation of Articles 5/85? Reread paragraphs 53–55.

4.   Is *CNSD* consistent with *Ladbroke*? Where is the private autonomous action in *CNSD*?

5.   US law is nearly identical in result. A person or firm that merely follows an anticompetitive command of the state (e.g. not to advertise) is protected from antitrust liability by the state action defense; but a state of the United States may not delegate to private parties the power (and duty) to fix prices and shield them from federal liability for price fixing. California Retail Liquor Dealers Ass'n v. Midcal Aluminum, Inc., 445 U.S. 97, 100 S.Ct. 937, 63 L.Ed.2d 233 (1980); Schwegmann Bros. v. Calvert Distillers Corp., 341 U.S. 384, 71 S.Ct. 745, 95 L.Ed. 1035 (1951).

In other respects, also, United States law is similar to European Community law on state action, supremacy and preemption, even though the Community institutions have far broader power than United States courts to override anti-competitive state legislation. When Congress passed the US antitrust laws, it could have chosen to preempt anticompetitive state law that affected interstate commerce, but it did not. Accordingly, subject to the constraint of the commerce clause in the US Constitution, states of the United States may adopt and enforce regulatory statutes that have significant anticompetitive effects. See, e.g., Exxon Corp. v. Governor of Maryland, 437 U.S. 117, 98 S.Ct. 2207, 57 L.Ed.2d 91 (1978) (prohibiting oil producers/refiners from operating retail service stations in the state for fear that they would favor their own stations). Unlike EC law, state antitrust law—even law that is more prohibitory than federal antitrust law—is normally valid, and it functions in tandem with federal law. California v. ARC America Corp., 490 U.S. 93, 109 S.Ct. 1661, 104 L.Ed.2d 86 (1989) (allowing California to authorize indirect purchaser lawsuits even though federal law disallows them). Private parties acting under a lawful but anticompetitive state regime are protected from federal antitrust enforcement as long as the state has clearly articulated its policy that displaces competition with regulation and supervises the private action. Southern Motor Carriers Rate Conference, Inc. v. United States, 471 U.S. 48, 105 S.Ct. 1721, 85 L.Ed.2d 36 (1985).

A state may not impose an unreasonable burden on interstate commerce (e.g., discrimination against imports); but seldom is such a burden found when the law applies equally to residents and outsiders. Compare Exxon Corp. v. Governor of Maryland, supra, with West Lynn Creamery v. Healy, 512 U.S. 186, 114 S.Ct. 2205, 129 L.Ed.2d 157 (1994).

E. STATE AIDS

1. INTRODUCTION

Nations may be tempted to grant money and other benefits to support local business firms and to attract other business. Frequently, they are asked to favor one competitor, sector or region over another, often on grounds of impending business failure and loss of jobs if aid is not forthcoming. At mid-twentieth century, extensive state support of industry was the norm in Europe, and if trade barriers were to be removed but state aids were to flourish, Europe would fall short of its goal of one common market.

Thus, in order to contain state aids and provide transparency for permissible aid, the Treaty includes Articles 87–89 (ex 92 to 94).

State aid is "any aid granted by a Member State or through state resources in any form whatsoever...." Direct subsidy is the most common form of aid, but state aid also includes exemptions from fiscal or social charges, credit guarantees, credit at low interest, credit or equity investments that would not be available in the market, payment by the state of a higher price to domestic suppliers, sale by the state below the market price to domestic buyers, assumption by the state of part of an undertaking's risk, tax concessions (e.g., to encourage the takeover of an ailing firm), and virtually any other benefit conferred by the state on terms that would not be acceptable to a private investor.

Article 87(1) declares that any state aid that "distorts or threatens to distort competition by favouring certain undertakings or the production of certain goods shall, insofar as it affects trade between Member States, be incompatible with the common market." Paragraphs (2) and (3) are derogations from this general prohibition.

Paragraph (2) lists forms of aid that "shall be compatible" with the common market. Aid that shall be compatible under paragraph (2) is:

(a) aid of a social character granted to individual consumers without discrimination as to origin of products,

(b) damage relief in natural disasters or exceptional occurrences, and

(c) aid to the economy of certain areas of the Federal Republic of Germany affected by the division of Germany insofar as it is required to compensate for economic disadvantages caused by that division.

Paragraph (3) specifies aid that the Commission *may* declare compatible with the common market. Frequently invoked by Member States, this section empowers the Commission to declare compatible aid in the following five categories:

(a) "aid to promote the economic development of areas where the standard of living is abnormally low or where there is serious underemployment";

(b) "aid to promote the execution of an important project of common European interest or to remedy a serious disturbance in the economy of a Member State";

(c) "aid to facilitate the development of certain economic activities or of certain economic areas, where such aid does not adversely affect trading conditions to an extent contrary to the common interest";

(d) "aid to promote cultural and heritage conservation where such aid does not affect trading conditions and competition in the Community to an extent that is contrary to the common interest"; and

(e) other categories added by decision of the Council.

Article 88 sets forth a notification, waiting and adjudication procedure for state aids. Member States must notify to the Commission all proposed measures of state aid that may affect Member State commerce. The proposed measures must not be put into effect until clearance. The Commission may authorize the aid without conditions, authorize the aid after agreed modifications, or open formal proceedings. The Commission must give notice to concerned parties to submit their comments. If the Commission finds that the proposed aid is not compatible with the common market or that aid is being misused, it must direct the state to abolish or alter the aid within a specified time period. If the Member State fails to comply, the Commission or an interested Member State may refer the matter to the Court of Justice. If a Member State grants illegal aid, it must recover it from the recipient.

Regulations create exemptions for aid to small and medium-sized enterprises, for training, and for *de minimis* aid. Guidelines clarify limits of aid for environmental protection, research and development, employment and training, rescue and restructuring, and regional aid.

2. STATE AID POLICY

State aid control is a major facet of Community policy. It accounts for half of the enforcement activity of the Competition Directorate. Director General for Competition Alexander Schaub has described the system as follows:

General developments in State aid control

> ... [T]he maintenance of a system of free and undistorted competition is one of the cornerstones of the European Union. It is undisputed that competition may be distorted by advantages given by public authorities to certain companies which compete with other companies in the Union. All efforts under the anti-trust rules to ensure that companies do not distort competition and trade within the Union would be to no avail if Member States were allowed to seek to outbid each other in offering subsidies to save firms in economic difficulties or to attract investment.

> Today, this applies more than ever. There are three major reasons for the increasing importance of State aid control:

— First, as the Internal Market becomes a reality, the elimination of a vast number of trade barriers between Member States also progresses. This means that the more classical forms of distortion of competition by Member States have disappeared. If not properly controlled, state aid may be used to replace the barriers to trade that have already been dismantled.

— Second, the single market in Europe and increased world-wide competition have led to widespread liberalisation of sectors where competition was or is still restricted or even excluded, such as telecommunications, postal services and energy. The consequence of this trend is obvious: introducing competition necessarily means enlarging the scope of State aid control to these sectors.

— There is a third reason for the increasing importance of State aid control: in periods of serious economic difficulties with politically unsustainable levels of unemployment, Governments—not only in the EU, but also in other regions of the world—are tempted to use aid as an instrument to combat unemployment, often merely shifting the problem to another factory, another sector, another area, another country.

The characteristics of State aid control in the EU

One might, of course, at least in theory, advocate the simple ban of State aid to achieve free and undistorted competition throughout the European Union. However, experience has shown that in some cases there are valid reasons to grant aid.

Properly controlled, the granting of aid may contribute to the development of the Community as a whole, whilst potentially harmful or protectionist effects can be eliminated.

But who would be able to carry out this task in a neutral and well-balanced way? The Treaty of Rome solved this question by entrusting the Commission with the task of ensuring a level playing field of competition throughout Europe.

This is indeed the very centre-piece of State aid control in the European Union: the Treaty of Rome not only obliges the Member States to inform the Commission of subsidies granted to enterprises. The obligation goes an important step further and makes the award of aid subject to prior approval by the Commission.

The obligation of notification prior to implementation and, more than that, the fact that the implementation of a plan to grant or alter aid is subject to approval by an independent authority, is one of three key elements which make the control of State aid in the European Union unique both in international and national law. Only the Commission may find aid compatible by applying one of the exemption clauses provided for in the Treaty. Implementing new aid without having obtained the Commission's approval is illegal.

The second element characterizing the State aid control system established by the European Union follows from the first: there are remedies against State aid decisions. Also private operators, in particular aid recipients and competitors, may seek judicial review before the European Courts.

Third, the Commission is not only entrusted with the day-to-day application of the State aid rules, but is also empowered to develop the Community's State aid control policy. Within the wide margin of discretion entrusted to it, the Commission has gradually developed policy through cases and through a variety of policy frameworks, communications and notices. Furthermore, we have established a strict and consistent policy on recovery of incompatible aid in cases where a Member State has not fulfilled its obligation to await the Commission's decision before awarding aid.

To sum up: what we have achieved during the past years is an increased notification discipline and a very high public awareness of the distortive effects of aid. In many sectors, industry is the Commission's best ally in combatting unlawfully granted aid—through complaints to the Commission and through an increasing number of cases brought to national Courts. I take this as an encouraging sign that industry widely supports a strict state aid discipline. . . .

Alexander Schaub, remarks to CIRFS General Assembly, European Competition Policy—in particular developments in policy on State aid control, Brussels, May 14, 1997.

The following case illustrates both the notion of "distorted competition" and the difficulties of justification.

GERMANY v. COMMISSION

(State aids for small business)
Case C–156/98, [2000] ECR I–6857.

[After unification of Germany, the promoters of small and medium-sized companies in the new Länder were unable to find sufficient capital for their formation. Germany responded by enacting a law (the EStG) giving tax benefits to investors in the new Länder that had no more than 250 employees. Challenged by the Commission, Germany responded that the benefits did not affect Member State trade, did not distort competition, and were exempted under Article 87(2)(c).]

29   . . . [S]o far as concerns the risk of distortion of competition, it must be stated that the German Government has not demonstrated that the Commission erred in its determination that Paragraph 52(8) of the EStG had the effect of reducing the costs of certain financing charges for the undertakings in question.

30   In principle, operating aid, that is to say aid which, like that provided for by Paragraph 52(8) of the EStG, is intended to release an undertaking from costs which it would normally have had to bear in its day-to-day management or normal activities, distorts the conditions of competition.

31   The Commission therefore rightly considered that the aid provided for by the measure at issue threatened to distort competition.

32   As regards the effects of the provision in question on trade between Member States, the Court has consistently held that the relatively small amount of aid or the relatively small size of the undertaking which receives it does not as such exclude the possibility that intra-Community trade might be affected.

[33] When aid granted by the State or through State resources strengthens the position of an undertaking compared with other undertakings competing in intra-Community trade the latter must be regarded as affected by that aid.

[34] That is the case in this instance, since any undertaking other than those to which the measure in issue applies can increase its own resources only on less advantageous terms, whether it is established in Germany or in another Member State.

[35] It follows that the Commission rightly considered that the aid introduced by the measure at issue affected trade between Member States. * * *

[101] With regard to the Commission's assessment of the effects of the aid introduced by the contested decision on competition and intra-Community trade, it would appear that the contested decision deduces logically from the characteristics of that measure, the purpose of which is to improve the contractual conditions under which holdings may be taken up in certain undertakings, that the application of this measure is liable to distort competition, since it makes other undertakings less attractive on the capital market, and to affect the intra-Community trade in which Community undertakings participate. . . .

The Court held that the aid did not fall within Article 87(2)(c) (exempting aid necessary to compensate for the economic disadvantages caused by the division of Germany) because the economic disadvantages in the East were not directly caused by the geographic division of Germany but by the different politico-economic systems in the East and the West. (paras. 52–55). Therefore the aid was held impermissible.

European state aid policy helps Member States resist protectionist pleas from their businesses. Also, by disallowing subsidies, the policy encourages liberalization through privatization. Since States can no longer privilege their state-owned enterprises, they are less inclined to foster state-owned enterprises.

At times, however, the Commission has found it hard to resist the pressures of Member States. Famously, in 1994, Italy prevailed upon the Commission to authorize, under the Coal and Steel Treaty, a grant of huge subsidies for the closing of 68 steel mills. See Brussels U-turn Revives Strategy for Steel Rescue, Financial Times, June 16, 1994, p. 1. In recent years, however, the Competition Directorate and the Commission have worked hard to rationalize state aid policy by providing broader block exemptions for trivial aid and more rigorous conditions for allowable aid.

Notes and Questions

1. What does Article 87 mean by "distort[ing] competition"? Give regard both to the text of the Treaty and to the language of the Court of Justice in *Germany v. Commission*. Does the phrase mean the same thing in Article 87(1) as in Article 81(1)?

2. Do you agree that state aid normally "distorts competition"? In what sense? Does it harm competition from the viewpoint of consumers? from the viewpoint of competitors? from the vantage of protecting the competition process and the equal right to compete on the merits? Did the tax benefit in *Germany v.*

Commission hurt consumers efficiency? Can state aid intensify competition? How can or should the Commission and Court deal with procompetitive effects (lower prices, more business formation) of state aids?

3. The United States, in contrast with the EU, has no national subsidy control, except as required by the GATT/WTO, and except for prohibition of discriminatory subsidies that impose a burden on interstate commerce. See West Lynn Creamery v. Healy, 512 U.S. 186, 114 S.Ct. 2205, 129 L.Ed.2d 157 (1994), excerpted supra at page 462. US law reflects the belief that freedom of state and local governments to grant subsidies or other benefits, whether to compete for business establishment or to prop up business in financial difficulty, is a healthy form of autonomy. See Camps Newfound/Owatonna, Inc. v. Town of Harrison, 520 U.S. 564, 589, 117 S.Ct. 1590, 137 L.Ed.2d 852 (1997); and see Scalia, J., dissenting, at 605–08.

4. Firms frequently challenge a grant of state aid to their rivals, and typically they are accorded standing to do so. (See Chapter 5A1–2 for standing and ripeness issues.) Thus, when Ford and Volkswagen set up a joint venture in Portugal to make multi-purpose vehicles—a new endeavor for both joint venture partners—Matra, the dominant maker of MPVs, complained that Portugal's grant of infrastructure aid to the new entrant violated Article 92 (now 87), and that the joint venture agreement itself violated Articles 85 and 86 (now 81 and 82) in part because the aid distorted competition. (How would it argue this point?) Matra lost on the merits; both the aid and the joint venture were allowed. See Matra Hachette SA v. Commission, Case T–17/93, [1994] ECR II–0595.

Why would a firm challenge a grant of aid to its rival? Why, in particular, would a dominant firm challenge a grant of aid to a new entrant? Is it likely to be complaining about harm to competition, about unfair advantages, or about competition itself? Would buyers of the products produced by a subsidized firm ever have an interest in challenging a state aid? Would it be accurate to view rivals' complaints about grants of state aid as complaints about *unfair* competition?

CONCLUSION

In this chapter we have examined state interventions, considered how state actions may harm trade and competition, and observed how the Treaty limits anticompetitive state actions. It is often said that, for harms to competition, the state is the biggest culprit, because it can, if undisciplined, erect impenetrable barriers and thus privilege itself and its businesses, as no private actor can do. The state can be a powerful source of restraint, but of course it is also a guardian of the public good. Through Articles 3, 10, 28, 31, 86 (in tandem with 81 and 82), and 87–89, the Treaty attempts to do the job of limiting the trade-restraining, anticompetitive excesses of the state, particularly when they undermine the coherence of one internal market. Thus, in matters of discipline on state action, competition and single-market policy converge.

Part V

EXTERNAL RELATIONS AND COMMERCIAL POLICY

From the very outset, the nature of the European Community has required it to have extensive dealings with nonmember countries. Article 23 (ex 9) specifies that "[t]he Community shall be based on a customs union." As a customs union, one of the principal activities of the Community is the operation of a common commercial policy, which includes its common customs tariff. EC Treaty Art. 3(b). In today's world, tariffs and other international trade policies are negotiated bilaterally and multilaterally. Consequently, the Community has extensive dealings with the rest of the world, through a vast network of multilateral and bilateral agreements.

The Community's relationships with third countries are not limited to implementation of the common customs tariff and the common commercial policy. The creation of the internal market has led to Community involvement in almost all areas of economic activity, many of which also have an external aspect. For example, the EC Treaty calls for the Community to adopt a common transport policy. If that policy is to be complete, it must deal with transportation into and out of the Community, and that requires dealing with third countries. To take another example, the Community is charged with the creation of a common fisheries policy, which has inevitably led to a series of fisheries agreements with third countries.

Over time, as the Community has taken steps toward closer political union, the Member States have cooperated in foreign affairs, first under European Political Cooperation and now as part of the EU's Common Foreign and Security Policy.

This Part of the casebook examines the external relations power and the common commercial policy of the European Community. Chapter 27 commences with an examination of the scope of the EC's external relations policy under the EC Treaty, focusing on the applicable provisions of the Treaty and several important decisions by the Court of Justice. In particular, we consider the breadth of the concept of the common commercial policy and the extent to which the Court of Justice has implied external powers in Treaty provisions that make no explicit reference to such powers. The precise scope of the Community's powers is important because the Member States will be prohibited from acting where the Community's powers are deemed exclusive. We also consider in Chapter 27 the extent to which the Community's international agreements can be invoked by private parties in the courts and the development of the EU's Common Foreign and Security Policy.

The remainder of Part V deals with the common commercial policy and the Community's relations generally with the rest of the world. We start in Chapter 28 with an overview of the Community's preferential trading relationships with third countries. These relationships are most developed with the nonmember countries in Europe and with the former colonies of Member States. In Chapter 29, we examine in some depth the Community's participation in the World Trade Organization, which is the basis for its commercial relationships with its most important trading partner, the United States.

Chapters 30 and 31 examine the Community Customs Code and the Community's rules against unfairly traded goods, such as those that are dumped, subsidized or traded in violation of WTO rules. A significant amount of the work of lawyers specializing in Community law involves these trade rules.

Chapter 27

THE EXTERNAL RELATIONS POWERS OF THE EUROPEAN COMMUNITY

The EC Treaty essentially provides that the foreign commercial and trade policies of the EC are to be conducted by the Community itself, not by Member States acting individually. This general approach raises a number of difficult legal issues. First, there is a question of authority. On what basis does the Community exercise its external relations activities? Second, there is the question of exclusivity. To what extent can the Member States act independently of, or participate jointly with, the Community in an area where the Community has competence under the Treaty? Third, it is necessary to consider how the Community's external relations powers are divided among the Community's institutions. May the Commission act independently of the Council? What is the European Parliament's role? We examine these questions in this chapter, and also consider the extent that litigants may invoke the Community's international agreements in the EC and Member State courts. We conclude with a brief look at the EU's Common Foreign and Security Policy.

A. THE EC TREATY PROVISIONS ON EXTERNAL RELATIONS

The EC Treaty does not outline in detail the external relations powers of the European Community. Consequently, the Court of Justice has played a critical role in defining the scope of the Community's foreign affairs powers. It has done so through several sweeping opinions. However, the EC Treaty does contain provisions on the Community's powers in external relations in certain specific contexts, and we shall first review those express grants of power and then consider the role of the European Parliament in external relations.

1. EXPRESS GRANTS OF EXTERNAL RELATIONS POWERS

The most comprehensive treatment in the Treaty of the external relations powers of the Community is found in the Treaty's provisions on the establishment of the common commercial policy. The Treaty provides in Article 133(3)(ex 113(3)):

Where agreements with one or more States or international organisations need to be negotiated, the Commission shall make recommendations to the Council, which shall authorize the Commission to open the necessary negotiations. *The Council and the Commission shall be responsible for ensuring that the agreements negotiated are compatible with internal Community policies and rules.*

The Commission shall conduct these negotiations in consultation with a special committee appointed by the Council to assist the Commission in this task and within the framework of such directives as the Council may issue to it. *The Commission shall report regularly to the special committee on the progress of negotiations.*

The relevant provisions of Article 300 shall apply.[1]

As we will see, Article 133 has been interpreted expansively, and the Community has entered into many agreements pursuant to it. The scope of Article 133 will be expanded significantly when the Treaty of Nice enters into force. Those changes are discussed in Chapter 29(B)(2).

Although Article 133 charges the Commission with conducting negotiations, the Council has a very significant role. To begin with, it must authorize the negotiations and give the Commission its negotiating instructions. Thereafter, it keeps a close watch on the negotiations through the so-called Article 133 Committee, on which all Member States are represented and which monitors the Commission's activities in negotiations and implementation of the Common Commercial Policy. Finally, the Council must decide whether to accept the results of the negotiations. As noted below, there is no general Treaty requirement that Parliament approve Article 133 agreements.

Article 310 (ex 238) of the Treaty provides that the Community may conclude agreements "establishing an association involving reciprocal rights and obligations, common action and special procedure[s]" with other countries or international organizations. Article 310 was apparently initially intended to permit the Community to enter into agreements establishing a Europe-wide free trade area, but it has been used by the Community to enter into a wide variety of agreements with many countries. Some of these association agreements are described further in Chapter 28 infra.

Article 310 could serve as a basis for attributing a general foreign affairs power to the Community, but as we will see from the cases in this chapter, the Court of Justice has tended to base its expansive decisions in the external relations area on other grounds and Treaty provisions. As noted in the next section, since the ratification of the Single European Act in 1987, association agreements must be approved by an absolute majority of the members of the European Parliament.

The power of the Community in external relations was addressed in two amendments introduced by the Single European Act. Article 170 authorizes the Community to enter into agreements providing for third-country cooperation in Community research and development programs, such agreements to be negotiated and concluded pursuant to Article 300. A similar provision in respect of the environment is contained in Article 174(4). In 1993, the Maastricht Treaty added provisions on international agreements in the con-

---

1. The italicized text would be added by the Treaty of Nice.

text of monetary union, Article 111, and of development cooperation, Article 181. The Nice Treaty will add Article 181a, which authorizes economic, financial and technical cooperation measures with third countries. In four cases, these provisions state that they are without prejudice to Member State rights to negotiate and conclude international agreements. Articles 111, 174(4), 181, 181a. The tenth declaration to the Maastricht Final Act notes that these provisions do not affect the principles resulting from the *ERTA* case, which is excerpted in the next section.

The Treaty also provides that the Commission shall maintain relations with United Nations and other international organizations (Article 302). Articles 303 and 304 provide for cooperation between the EC and the Council of Europe and the OECD. Although the Treaty contains no specific provisions on diplomatic relations, in 2001 the Commission maintained over 100 delegations in foreign countries and at various international organizations (for example, it has observer status at the United Nations), and there were diplomatic missions from numerous third countries accredited to the EC.

Finally, Article 182 provides for the association with the Community of the non-European territories of the Member States. When the Treaty initially came into force in 1958, there were many such territories. Over time, almost all of them have become independent and their relations with the Community are no longer dealt with in Articles 182–188, but rather through such arrangements as the Lomé and Cotonou Conventions, discussed in Chapter 28 infra.

2. APPROVAL OF INTERNATIONAL AGREEMENTS AND THE ROLE OF THE EUROPEAN PARLIAMENT

Article 300 (ex 228) deals generally with the roles of the various Community institutions in the approval of international agreements. It specifies that where the EC Treaty provides for the conclusion of international agreements by the Community, the agreements shall be negotiated by the Commission and concluded by the Council. Under Article 300(2), the Council is authorized to act by qualified majority on a Commission proposal, except that unanimity is required for Article 310 association agreements and agreements covering a field for which unanimity would be required for the adoption of internal rules.

The extent to which the European Parliament must assent to or be consulted in respect of international agreements has expanded over time. Article 300 originally required consultation only in respect of Article 310 association agreements. In the case of agreements reached under Article 133, no parliamentary consultation was required. However, under the Luns–Westerterp procedures, the Council voluntarily committed itself to inform Parliament prior to commencing negotiations and prior to signing and formally concluding association agreements (1964) and commercial agreements (1973).[2] In addition, the Stuttgart European Council concluded in 1983 that, as a matter of policy, Parliament should be consulted prior to the conclusion of all significant international agreements.[3]

---

2. Bull. EC 1973–10, p. 90. See generally J.-V. Louis & P. Brückner, Relations Extérieures 42–44, in 12 J. Megret et al., eds., Le Droit de la Communauté Économique Européenne (Editions de l'Université de Bruxelles 1980).

3. Solemn Declaration on European Union, para. 2.3.7., in Bull. EC 1983–6, pp. 26–27.

As a result of the Maastricht Treaty, since 1993 Article 300(3) requires generally that Parliament must be consulted prior to conclusion of all agreements, except those concluded under Article 133(3). In addition, Article 300(3) now establishes that the assent of Parliament is required for Article 310 association agreements,[4] agreements establishing a specific institutional framework by organizing cooperation procedures, agreements having important budgetary implications for the Community and agreements entailing amendment of an act adopted under the Article 251 co-decision procedures (described in Chapter 3 supra). The assent requirement means that an absolute majority of Parliament must approve the agreement. Parliament has no power to amend agreements.

Article 300 has two other important features. First, it provides that agreements concluded in accordance with its provisions shall be binding on the Community and the Member States. Second, it establishes a reference procedure that allows the Parliament, the Commission, the Council or a Member State to obtain an opinion of the Court of Justice as to whether an envisaged agreement is compatible with the Treaty.

One interesting question presented by the foregoing provisions is how to determine precisely when parliamentary assent is required. In particular, what exactly is "an agreement establishing a specific institutional framework by organizing cooperation procedures"? What would constitute "important budgetary implications"? The Court of Justice considered the latter question in the following case.

PARLIAMENT v. COUNCIL

(EC/Mauritania fisheries agreement)
Case C–189/97, [1999] ECR I–4741.

[In 1996, the EC and Mauritania entered into a fisheries agreement that provided for five annual payments to Mauritania of approximately 50 million ECU. The Commission proposed a regulation to conclude the agreement that provided for the assent of Parliament to be obtained. The Council, however, decided to adopt a regulation on the conclusion of the agreement based on Article 37, which deals with the common agricultural policy, in conjunction with Article 300(2) and the first sub-paragraph of Article 300(3). In its regulation, the Council simply referred to Parliament's "opinion". In its consideration of the agreement, Parliament had substituted the second sub-paragraph of Article 300(3) for the legal basis cited by the Council and assented to the adoption of the regulation. Parliament then sued the Council, claiming that its prerogatives had been infringed.

Parliament argued that "in determining whether an agreement has important budgetary implications, the criteria to be taken into account should include the fact that expenditure under the agreement is spread over several years, the relative share of such expenditure in relation to the expenditures of the same kind under the budget heading concerned, and the rate of increase in expenditure under the agreement in question in relation to the financial section of the previous agreement" (para. 20). In that regard, it noted that the payments represented "more than 20% of the appropriations entered under

---

4. This requirement was added by the Single European Act.

the budget heading concerned (heading B7–8000, international fisheries agreements) [and that] the outlay in favor of [Mauritania had] increased more than fivefold in relation to the previous agreement" (para. 21).

The Council maintained that "in order to assess whether an agreement has important budgetary implications, it is necessary to refer to the overall budget of the Community, and that it did not act in a manifestly erroneous and arbitrary manner in seeking merely an opinion of the Parliament for a fisheries agreement under which the annual expenditure amounted to 0.07% of that budget" (para. 24).

The Court rejected the Council's argument, noting "that appropriations allocated to the external operations of the Community traditionally account for a marginal fraction of the Community budget. Thus, in 1996 and 1997, those appropriations, grouped under subsection B7, external operations, barely exceeded 5% of the overall budget. In those circumstances, a comparison between the annual financial cost of an agreement and the overall Community budget scarcely appears significant, and to apply such a criteria might render the relevant wording of the second sub-paragraph of Article [300(3)] of the Treaty wholly ineffective" (para. 26). As to Parliament's criteria, the Court ruled:]

29   As regards the three criteria proposed by Parliament, the Court finds that the first of them may indeed contribute towards characterizing an agreement as having important budgetary implications. Relatively modest annual expenditures may, over a number of years, represent a significant budgetary outlay.

30   The second and third criteria put forward by Parliament do not, however, appear to be relevant. In the first place, budget headings, which can be moreover be altered, vary substantially in importance, so that the relative share of the expenditure under the agreement may be large in relation to the appropriations of the same kind entered under the budget heading concerned, even though the expenditure in question is small. Moreover, the rate of increase in expenditure under the agreement may be high in comparison with that arising from the previous agreement, whilst the amounts involved may still be small.

31   As has been pointed out in paragraph 26 of this judgment, a comparison between the annual financial cost of an international agreement and the overall budget scarcely appears significant. However, comparison of the expenditure under an agreement with the amount of the appropriations designed to finance the Community's external operations * * * enables that agreement to be set in context of the budgetary outlay approved by the Community for its external policy. That comparison thus offers a more appropriate means of assessing the financial importance which the agreement actually has for the Community.

32   Where, as in this case, a sectoral agreement is involved, the above analysis may, in appropriate cases, and without excluding the possibility of taking other factors into account, be complemented by a comparison between the expenditures entailed by the agreement and the whole of the budgetary appropriations for the sector in question, taking the internal and external aspects together. Such a comparison makes it possible to determine, from another angle and in an equally consistent context, the financial outlay

approved by the Community in entering into that agreement. However, since the sectors vary substantially in terms of their budgetary importance, that examination cannot result in the financial implications of an agreement being found to be important where they do not represent a significant share of the appropriations designed to finance the Community's external operations.

[33] In this case, the fisheries agreement with Mauritania was concluded for five years, which is not a particularly lengthy period. Moreover, the financial compensation for which it makes provision is split into annual tranches the amounts of which vary between ECU 51,560,000 and ECU 55,160,000. In respect of the previous budgetary years, those amounts, whilst exceeding 5% of expenditures on fisheries, represent barely more than 1% of the whole of the payment appropriations allocated for external operations of the Community, a proportion which, whilst far from negligible, can scarcely be described as important. In those circumstances, if the Council had taken that comparison into account, it would also have been entitled to take the view that the fisheries agreement with Mauritania did not have important budgetary implications for Community within the meaning of the second sub-paragraph of Article [300(3)] of the Treaty.

Notes and Questions

1. Do you agree with the Court's analysis? Does it potentially allow too many agreements to escape the scrutiny of the parliamentary assent requirement?

2. As to the level of spending that would have important budgetary implications, it is especially noteworthy that the Council conceded that the budgetary implications of the fisheries agreement with Morocco, which apparently involved a little more than twice the outlay of the Mauritania agreement, were important (Judgment, para. 27).

3. To what extent might agreements concluded under Article 133(3) be subject to the assent requirement?

B.   THE COURT OF JUSTICE AND THE COMMUNITY'S POWERS IN EXTERNAL RELATIONS

1.   IMPLIED POWERS: THE ERTA CASE

The first major case in which the Court of Justice discussed the external relations power of the EC was the so-called *ERTA* case, which involved a dispute between the Commission and the Council over whether the Commission or the Member States had the right to negotiate the European Road Transport Agreement (ERTA, or AETR in French) with non Member States.

COMMISSION v. COUNCIL
(ERTA)
Case 22/70, [1971] ECR 263.

1.   THE INITIAL QUESTION

[6] The Commission takes the view that Article 75 [now 71] of the Treaty, which conferred on the Community powers defined in wide terms with a

view to implementing the common transport policy, must apply to external relations just as much as to domestic measures in the sphere envisaged.

[7] It believes that the full effect of this provision would be jeopardized if the powers which it confers, particularly that of laying down "any appropriate provisions", within the meaning of subparagraph (1)(c) of the article cited, did not extend to the conclusion of agreements with third countries.

[8] Even if, it is argued, this power did not originally embrace the whole sphere of transport, it would tend to become general and exclusive as and where the common policy in this field came to be implemented.

[9] The Council, on the other hand, contends that since the Community only has such powers as have been conferred on it, authority to enter into agreements with third countries cannot be assumed in the absence of an express provision in the Treaty.

[10] More particularly, Article 75 relates only to measures internal to the Community, and cannot be interpreted as authorizing the conclusion of international agreements.

[11] Even if it were otherwise, such authority could not be general and exclusive, but at the most concurrent with that of the Member States.

[12] In the absence of specific provisions of the Treaty relating to the negotiation and conclusion of international agreements in the sphere of transport policy—a category into which, essentially, the AETR falls—one must turn to the general system of Community law in the sphere of relations with third countries.

[13] Article 210 [now 281] provides that "The Community shall have legal personality".

[14] This provision, placed at the head of Part Six of the Treaty, devoted to "General and Final Provisions", means that in its external relations the Community enjoys the capacity to establish contractual links with third countries over the whole field of objectives defined in Part One of the Treaty, which Part Six supplements.

[15] To determine in a particular case the Community's authority to enter into international agreements, regard must be had to the whole scheme of the Treaty no less than to its substantive provisions.

[16] Such authority arises not only from an express conferment by the Treaty—as is the case with Articles 113 [now 133] and 114 [now deleted] for tariff and trade agreements and with Article 238 [now 310] for association agreements—but may equally flow from other provisions of the Treaty and from measures adopted, within the framework of those provisions, by the Community institutions.

[17] In particular, each time the Community, with a view to implementing a common policy envisaged by the Treaty, adopts provisions laying down common rules, whatever form these may take, the Member States no longer have the right, acting individually or even collectively, to undertake obligations with third countries which affect those rules.

[18] As and when such common rules come into being, the Community alone is in a position to assume and carry out contractual obligations towards third

countries affecting the whole sphere of application of the Community legal system.

19   With regard to the implementation of the provisions of the Treaty the system of internal Community measures may not therefore be separated from that of external relations.

20   Under Article 3(e) [now 3(f)], the adoption of a common policy in the sphere of transport is specially mentioned amongst the objectives of the Community.

21   Under Article 5 [now 10], the Member States are required on the one hand to take all appropriate measures to ensure fulfillment of the obligations arising out of the Treaty or resulting from action taken by the institutions and, on the other, hand, to abstain from any measure which might jeopardize the attainment of the objectives of the Treaty.

22   If these two provisions are read in conjunction, it follows that to the extent to which Community rules are promulgated for the attainment of the objectives of the Treaty, the Member States cannot, outside the framework of the Community institutions, assume obligations which might affect those rules or alter their scope.

23   According to Article 74 [now 70], the objectives of the Treaty in matters of transport are to be pursued within the framework of a common policy.

24   With this in view, Article 75(1) [now 71(1)] directs the Council to lay down common rules and, in addition, "any other appropriate provisions".

25   By the terms of subparagraph (a) of the same provision, those common rules are applicable "to international transport to or from the territory of a Member State or passing across the territory of one or more Member States".

26   This provision is equally concerned with transport from or to third countries, as regards that part of the journey which takes place on Community territory.

27   It thus assumes that the powers of the Community extend to relationships arising from international law, and hence involve the need in the sphere in question for agreements with the third countries concerned.

28   Although it is true that Articles 74 and 75 do not expressly confer on the Community authority to enter into international agreements, nevertheless the bringing into force, on 25 March 1969, of Regulation No 543/69 of the Council on the harmonization of certain social legislation relating to road transport necessarily vested in the Community power to enter into any agreements with third countries relating to the subject-matter governed by that regulation.

29   This grant of power is moreover expressly recognized by Article 3 of the said regulation which prescribes that: "The Community shall enter into any negotiations with third countries which may prove necessary for the purpose of implementing this regulation".

30   Since the subject-matter of the AETR falls within the scope of Regulation No 543/69, the Community has been empowered to negotiate and conclude the agreement in question since the entry into force of the said regulation.

³¹　These Community powers exclude the possibility of concurrent powers on the part of Member States, since any steps taken outside the framework of the Community institutions would be incompatible with the unity of the Common Market and the uniform application of Community law.

³²　This is the legal position in the light of which the question of admissibility has to be resolved.

[The Court found the Commission's application to be admissible, as noted in Chapter 3(A).]

3.　SUBSTANCE

⁶⁸　Essentially, the Commission disputes the validity of the proceedings of 20 March 1970 on the ground that they involved infringements of provisions of the Treaty, more particularly of Articles 75, 228 and 235 [now 71, 300 and 308] concerning the distribution of powers between the Council and the Commission, and consequently the rights which it was the Commission's duty to exercise in the negotiations on the AETR.

* * *

⁷⁷　If these various provisions are read in conjunction, it is clear that wherever a matter forms the subject of a common policy, the Member States are bound in every case to act jointly in defence of the interests of the Community.

⁷⁸　This requirement of joint action was in fact respected by the proceedings of 20 March 1970, which cannot give rise to any criticism in this respect.

⁷⁹　Moreover, it follows from these provisions taken as a whole, and particularly from Article 228(1), that the right to conclude the agreement was vested in the Council.

⁸⁰　The Commission for its part was required to act in two ways, first by exercising its right to make proposals, which arises from Article 75(1) and the first paragraph of Article 116 [now deleted], and, secondly, in its capacity as negotiator by the terms of the first subparagraph of Article 228(1).

[The Court then noted that an earlier version of the AETR had been drawn up in 1962, at a time when power to conclude the agreement was still vested in the Member States. The negotiations involved in the case were not aimed at working out a new agreement, but simply at introducing into the version drawn up in 1962 such modifications as were necessary to enable all the contracting parties to ratify it.]

⁸⁵　It appears therefore that on 20 March 1970 the Council acted in a situation where it no longer enjoyed complete freedom of action in its relations with the third countries taking part in the same negotiations.

⁸⁶　At that stage of the negotiations, to have suggested to the third countries concerned that there was now a new distribution of powers within the Community might well have jeopardized the successful outcome of the negotiations, as was indeed recognized by the Commission's representative in the course of the Council's deliberations.

87   In such a situation it was for the two institutions whose powers were directly concerned, namely, the Council and the Commission, to reach agreement, in accordance with Article 15 of the Treaty of April 1965 establishing a Single Council and a Single Commission of the European Communities, on the appropriate methods of cooperation with a view to ensuring most effectively the defence of the interests of the Community.

88   It is clear from the minutes of the meeting of 20 March 1970 that the Commission made no formal use of the right to submit proposals open to it under Articles 75 and 116.

89   Nor did it demand the simple application of Article 228(1) in regard to its right of negotiation.

90   It may therefore be accepted that, in carrying on the negotiations and concluding the agreement simultaneously in the manner decided on by the Council, the Member States acted, and continue to act, in the interest and on behalf of the Community in accordance with their obligations under Article 5 of the Treaty.

91   Hence, in deciding in these circumstances on joint action by the Member States, the Council has not failed in its obligations arising from Articles 75 and 228.

92   For these reasons, the submission must be rejected.

* * *

Opinion of Advocate–General Dutheillet De Lamothe Delivered on 10 March 1971

* * *

It should be emphasized from the outset that Title IV [now V] of Part Two of the Treaty, the only title devoted to transport, has no express provision relating to the Community's "treaty-making power", to use an expression employed by Anglo–Saxon lawyers.

To vest authority or power in the Community to negotiate and conclude agreements with third countries relating to transport, it is thus necessary:

— either to declare applicable to this matter the provisions appearing in the parts of the Treaty devoted to matters other than transport;

— or to interpret certain of the general provisions of the Treaty as also applying to transport.

For my part I consider that both these solutions would involve the Court in a discretionary construction of the law, or, in other words, a judicial interpretation far exceeding the bounds which the Court has hitherto set regarding its power to interpret the Treaty.

* * *

No matter what legal basis the Court finds for it, recognition of the Community's authority in external matters for negotiating and concluding the AETR concedes by implication that the Community authorities exercise, in addition to the powers expressly conferred upon them by the Treaty, those implied powers whereby the Supreme Court of the United States supplements the powers of the federal bodies in relation to those of the confederated States.

I for my part consider that Community powers should be regarded as those termed in European law "conferred powers" (in French, "compétences d'attribution").

Such conferred powers may indeed be very widely construed when they are only the direct and necessary extension of powers relating to *intra-Community* questions, as the Court has already ruled with regard to the ECSC.

But can the Community's authority to conclude agreements with third countries in the sphere of transport be so widely construed?

This is not in fact as necessary as has recently been asserted before the Court. Even without according it "implied powers", with regard to transport the Community is not in a state of "permanent weakness", to borrow the expression recently employed by the Commission's agent. Article 235 [now 308] exists precisely to vest in the Community whatever powers it may need.

On the other hand, this is extremely difficult from the legal point of view, on the basis of the provisions at present in force.

It appears clear from the general scheme of the Treaty of Rome that its authors intended strictly to limit the Community's authority in external matters to the cases which they expressly laid down.

In this connexion a comparison between the ECSC Treaty and the Treaty of Rome is instructive. Whereas in the ECSC Treaty the negotiators of 1951 laid down that (Article 6): "In international relations, the Community shall enjoy the legal capacity it requires to perform its functions and attain its objectives", the negotiators of the Treaty of Rome in 1957 merely provided that the Community shall have legal personality (Article 210 [now 281]), although, with regard to external relations, they expressly laid down in Article 228 [now 300] that the Community's authority in external matters may only be exercised "where this Treaty [so] provides".

Is it not the case that to recognize that the Community has implied powers with regard to negotiations with third countries would far exceed the intentions of the authors of the Treaty and of the States which signed and accepted it?

This is my view, and it is the principle reason which brings me to propose to the Court a relatively strict interpretation of the Treaty in this sphere.

Notes and Questions

1. Do you find the reasoning of the Court or of the Advocate–General to be more persuasive? Why? Suppose the Court had adopted the position espoused by the Advocate–General. What sort of problems would such a decision have created for the Community?

2. The Court of Justice elaborated on the scope of the *ERTA* case in its 1994 opinion on EC adherence to the Agreement Establishing the World Trade Organization. We will postpone consideration of that case until Chapter 29, where that agreement is described in some detail.

3. The Advocate–General notes his opposition to the US Supreme Court cases that give "implied" powers to the federal government. As you read the rest of the cases in this section, you might consider how much the US federal government and in particular the President have relied on implied powers in the field of foreign affairs. For example in Missouri v. Holland, 252 U.S. 416, 40 S.Ct. 382, 64 L.Ed. 641 (1920), the Supreme Court held that a valid treaty (with Canada relating to migratory birds) must prevail over state law, even if a United States federal statute on the subject might be considered an unconstitutional interference with state power in the absence of a treaty. Justice Holmes said in this case (252 U.S. at 433):

> * * * Acts of Congress are the supreme law of the land only when made in pursuance of the Constitution, while treaties are declared to be so when made under the authority of the United States. It is open to question whether the authority of the United States means more than the formal acts prescribed to make the convention. We do not mean to imply that there are no qualifications to the treaty-making power; but they must be ascertained in a different way. It is obvious that there may be matters of the sharpest exigency for the national well-being that an act of Congress could not deal with but that a treaty followed by such an act could, and it is not lightly to be assumed that, in matters requiring national action, "a power which must belong to and somewhere reside in every civilized government" is not to be found.

Subsequent cases suggest some limitations on the treaty-making power, such as constitutional civil liberties limitations (see Reid v. Covert, 354 U.S. 1, 77 S.Ct. 1222, 1 L.Ed.2d 1148 (1957), holding that United States civilian dependents of armed forces members overseas could not constitutionally be tried by a court martial, even though an executive agreement or treaty would so provide).

The Supreme Court has found that the US President has certain powers in foreign affairs. Consider United States v. Curtiss–Wright Export Corp., 299 U.S. 304, 57 S.Ct. 216, 81 L.Ed. 255 (1936) (expansive view of President's "inherent" foreign affairs powers); Dames & Moore v. Regan, 453 U.S. 654, 101 S.Ct. 2972, 69 L.Ed.2d 918 (1981) (President held to have authority to terminate claims against Iran in US courts as part of hostage settlement). Does the Commission have such powers? In France v. Commission (Antitrust agreement with US), Case C–327/91, [1994] ECR I–3641, the Court of Justice held that the Commission did not have the power to conclude an agreement on application of competition laws with the US. The agreement provided for various forms of cooperation in the field of competition law (e.g., notifications, exchange of information, consultations). While the parties recognized certain Commission powers with respect to concluding administrative or working agreements with other international organizations, the Court relied on the explicit grant of the power to the Council to conclude agreements under Article 300 as the basis for its decision.

4. As to the question of the Community's legal capacity to enter into international agreements, where does the *ERTA* Court find that capacity in the EEC Treaty?

5. If the Community enters into an international agreement in respect of a particular subject, does its action preempt action by the Member States? In other words, is the Community's power to make international agreements an exclusive one? In Local Cost Standard, Opinion 1/75, [1975] ECR 1355, the Court of Justice was asked whether the Community had exclusive power to enter into an understanding with the other parties to the Organization for Economic Cooperation and

Development (OECD) concerning conditions for granting export credits. The Court responded ([1975] ECR at 1363–64):

> * * * [T]he subject-matter of the standard, and therefore of the Understanding, is one of those measures belonging to the common commercial policy prescribed by Article 113 [now 133] of the Treaty.
>
> Such a policy is conceived in that article in the context of the operation of the Common Market, for the defence of the common interests of the Community, within which the particular interests of the Member States must endeavour to adapt to each other.
>
> Quite clearly, however, this conception is incompatible with the freedom to which the Member States could lay claim by invoking a concurrent power, so as to ensure that their own interests were separately satisfied in external relations, at the risk of compromising the effective defence of the common interests of the Community.
>
> In fact any unilateral action on the part of the Member States would lead to disparities in the conditions for the grant of export credits, calculated to distort competition between undertakings of the various Member States in external markets. Such distortion can be eliminated only by means of a strict uniformity of credit conditions granted to undertakings in the Community, whatever their nationality.
>
> It cannot therefore be accepted that, in a field such as that governed by the Understanding in question, which is covered by export policy and more generally by the common commercial policy, the Member States should exercise a power concurrent to that of the Community, in the Community sphere and in the international sphere. The provisions of Articles 113 and 114 concerning the conditions under which, according to the Treaty, agreements on commercial policy must be concluded show clearly that the exercise of concurrent powers by the Member States and the Community in this matter is impossible.
>
> To accept that the contrary were true would amount to recognizing that, in relations with third countries, Member States may adopt positions which differ from those which the Community intends to adopt, and would thereby distort the institutional framework, call into question the mutual trust within the Community and prevent the latter from fulfilling its task in the defence of the common interest.
>
> It is of little importance that the obligations and financial burdens inherent in the execution of the agreement envisaged are borne directly by the Member States. The "internal" and "external" measures adopted by the Community within the framework of the common commercial policy do not necessarily involve, in order to ensure their compatibility with the Treaty, a transfer to the institutions of the Community of the obligations and financial burdens which they may involve: such measures are solely concerned to substitute for the unilateral action of the Member States, in the field under consideration, a common action based upon uniform principles on behalf of the whole of the Community.

6. Somewhat in contrast, in an opinion on the power of the EC to conclude an International Labor Organization (ILO) convention on safety in the use of chemicals at work, Opinion 2/91, [1993] ECR I–1061, the Court ruled that the EC's competence in this field was not exclusive. It noted that Member States were also free to act in certain respects in this field since Article 118a(3) [now 137(5)] of

the EC Treaty allowed them to impose stricter rules than specified by the Community in respect of worker safety and that rules stricter than those mandated by the ILO convention were permitted by that convention. The Court noted that there were some areas covered by the convention where the EC harmonization rules were widespread and related to the removal of trade barriers and that as to those areas Member States could not undertake commitments outside the framework of Community institutions. Thus, it ruled that there was joint competence to conclude the ILO convention. How does the this opinion relate generally to the issue of subsidiarity (discussed in Chapter 4(D) supra)?

7. *ERTA* and *Local Cost Standard* involved subject areas where the Treaty calls for common policies. Do you think that the Court would view the Community's powers as broadly in other subject areas?

8. What constitutes an agreement for purposes of Article 133 or Article 300? The Court dealt with that issue in the *Local Cost Standard* case (see Note 5 supra). In that case, what was at issue was an understanding concerning export credits, which was to be adopted in the form of a resolution by the Council of the Organization for Economic Cooperation and Development (OECD). The Court concluded that the concept of an agreement extended to "any undertaking entered into by entities subject to international law which has binding force, whatever its formal designation." [1975] ECR at 1360.

9. Review Article 308. Would it have been appropriate for the *ERTA* Court to suggest the use of this article if there was no explicit authority in the Treaty to enter into an international agreement? How would such a decision, as compared to the Court's actual decision, affect the powers of the Community institutions in the international arena? In particular, what are the voting rules in the Council and the powers of Parliament in respect of an agreement negotiated under Article 133, Article 308, Article 310? See Commission v. Council (Generalized tariff preferences I), Case 45/86, [1987] ECR 1493, which is excerpted in Chapter 4(A) supra.

2. THE SCOPE OF EXPLICIT POWERS: THE *RUBBER AGREEMENT* OPINION

The *Rubber Agreement* opinion involved an agreement negotiated as part of an Integrated Program for Commodities developed by UNCTAD, the United Nations Conference on Trade and Development. UNCTAD was created in part to give developing countries a greater say in international trade negotiations than they felt that they had in GATT. It did not supplant GATT (nor the WTO) as the principal forum for international trade negotiations, however, except in the case of some commodities.

Under its commodities program, UNCTAD hoped to promote agreements between the producers and users of specific commodities: bananas, cocoa, coffee, sugar, meat, tea, vegetable oils, cotton, hard fibers, jute, natural rubber, timber, bauxite, copper, iron ore, manganese, phosphate and tin. In the case of natural rubber, the agreement established an organization to hold a "buffer stock" of rubber, which would be increased through market purchases of rubber when the price of rubber was low and reduced when the price of rubber was high. The basic aim of the program was to smooth out fluctuations in the price of rubber, so as to provide increased and stable export earnings for the developing countries exporting rubber. In addition, the agreement provided for development aid to those countries.

INTERNATIONAL AGREEMENT ON NATURAL RUBBER

Opinion 1/78, [1979] ECR 2871.

[The Commission asked the Court to give its opinion under Article 300 on whether the Community was competent to conclude the International Agreement on Natural Rubber.]

IV.   THE SUBJECT-MATTER AND OBJECTIVES OF THE AGREEMENT ENVISAGED

* * *

37   The central question raised by the Commission's request is whether the international agreement on rubber comes as a whole or at least in essentials within the sphere of the "common commercial policy" referred to in Article 113 [now 133] of the Treaty. It is common ground that the agreement envisaged is closely connected with commercial policy. The difference of views relates to the extent of the sphere of application of Article 113 so that it remains uncertain whether that provision entirely covers the subject-matter of the agreement in question.

* * *

(a) Consideration of the Agreement's Links With Commercial Policy and Development Problems

41   By its special machinery as much as by certain aspects of its legal structure, the International Agreement on Natural Rubber which it is proposed to conclude stands apart from ordinary commercial and tariff agreements which are based primarily on the operation of customs duties and quantitative restrictions. The agreement in question is a more structured instrument in the form of an organization of the market on a world scale and in this way it is distinguished from classical commercial agreements. * * *

42   [UNCTAD's] Nairobi Resolution, which is the basis of the negotiations in progress on natural rubber, shows that commodity agreements have complex objectives. * * * As regards, more particularly, the interests of the developing countries, it is true that commodity agreements may involve the granting of advantages which are characteristic of development aid; it must however be acknowledged also that for those countries such agreements respond more fundamentally to the preoccupation of bringing about an improvement in the "terms of trade" and thus of increasing their export earnings. This characteristic is particularly brought out in the agreement in question, which seeks to establish a fair balance between the interests of the producer countries and those of the consumer countries. * * *

43   The link between the various agreements on commodities which were emphasized by the Nairobi Resolution must also be taken into account. As an increasing number of products which are particularly important from the economic point of view are concerned, it is clear that a coherent commercial policy would no longer be practicable if the Community were not in a position to exercise its powers also in connexion with a category of

agreements which are becoming, alongside traditional commercial agreements, one of the major factors in the regulation of international trade.

44   * * * It is therefore not possible to lay down, for Article 113 [now 133] of the EEC Treaty, an interpretation the effect of which would be to restrict the common commercial policy to the use of instruments intended to have an effect only on the traditional aspects of external trade to the exclusion of more highly developed mechanisms such as appear in the agreement envisaged. A "commercial policy" understood in that sense would be destined to become nugatory in the course of time. Although it may be thought that at the time when the Treaty was drafted liberalization of trade was the dominant idea, the Treaty nevertheless does not form a barrier to the possibility of the Community's developing a commercial policy aiming at a regulation of the world market for certain products rather than at a mere liberalization of trade.

45   Article 113 [now 133] empowers the Community to formulate a commercial "policy", based on "uniform principles" thus showing that the question of external trade must be governed from a wide point of view and not only having regard to the administration of precise systems such as customs and quantitative restrictions. The same conclusion may be deduced from the fact that the enumeration in Article 113 of the subjects covered by commercial policy (changes in tariff rates, the conclusion of tariff and trade agreements, the achievement of uniformity in measures of liberalization, export policy and measures to protect trade) is conceived as a non-exhaustive enumeration which must not, as such, close the door to the application in a Community context of any other process intended to regulate external trade. A restrictive interpretation of the concept of common commercial policy would risk causing disturbances in intra-Community trade by reason of the disparities which would then exist in certain sectors of economic relations with non-member countries.

46   Moreover, when the whole canvas of existing and planned agreements is considered it appears that as far as the Community is concerned a wide range of interests is involved in the negotiation of those agreements and that there are connexions with the most varied spheres in which the Community has undertaken responsibilities. Thus, * * * there are other agreements, for example those concerning products such as wheat, oils and fats and sugar, in which the Community is interested also as a producer and by which its export policy, expressly mentioned in Article 113 [now 133] as being amongst the objectives of the common commercial policy, is affected. * * * Several of the agreements belonging to this category are furthermore directly related to the execution of the common agricultural policy.

(b) The Agreement's Links With General Economic Policy

47   In its arguments the Council has raised the problem of the interrelation within the structure of the Treaty of the concepts of "economic policy" and "commercial policy". In certain provisions economic policy is indeed considered primarily as a question of national interest; such is the meaning of that concept in Articles 6 [now deleted] and 145 [now 202] which, for that reason, prescribe for the Member States nothing more than a duty

to ensure co-ordination. In other provisions economic policy is envisaged as being a matter of common interest as is the case with Articles 103 to 116, which are grouped together in a title devoted to the "economic policy" of the Community [now Title VII, Chapter 1, Articles 98–104, with the provisions on the "common commercial policy" in Title IX, Articles 131–134]. * * *

48 The considerations set out above already form to some extent an answer to the arguments relating to the distinction to be drawn between the spheres of general economic policy and those of the common commercial policy since international co-operation, inasmuch as it does not belong to commercial policy, would be confused with the domain of general economic policy. If it appears that it comes, at least in part, under the common commercial policy, as has been indicated above, it follows clearly that it could not, under the name of general economic policy, be withdrawn from the competence of the Community.

49 * * * [W]here the organization of the Community's economic links with non-member countries may have repercussions on certain sectors of economic policy such as the supply of raw materials to the Community or price policy, as is precisely the case with the regulation of international trade in commodities, that consideration does not constitute a reason for excluding such objectives from the field of application of the rules relating to the common commercial policy. Similarly, the fact that a product may have a political importance by reason of the building up of security stocks is not a reason for excluding that product from the domain of the common commercial policy.

* * *

V. PROBLEMS RAISED BY THE FINANCING OF THE AGREEMENT AND BY OTHER SPECIFIC PROVISIONS

52 Consideration must still be given, having regard to what has been stated above as regards correspondence between the objective and purposes of the agreement envisaged and the concept of common commercial policy, whether the detailed arrangements for financing the buffer stock, or certain specific clauses of the agreement, concerning technological assistance, research programmes, the maintenance of fair conditions of labour in the rubber industry and consultations relating to national tax policies which may have an effect on the price of rubber lead to a negation of the Community's exclusive competence.

* * *

56 The Court takes the view that the fact that the agreement may cover subjects such as technological assistance, research programmes, labour conditions in the industry concerned or consultations relating to national tax policies which may have an effect on the price of rubber cannot modify the description of the agreement which must be assessed having regard to its essential objective rather than in terms of individual clauses of an altogether subsidiary or ancillary nature. * * * The negotiation and execu-

tion of these clauses must therefore follow the system applicable to the agreement considered as a whole.

* * *

58   [With regard to the system of financing,] the Court feels bound to have regard to two possible situations: one in which the financial burdens envisaged by the agreement would be entered in the Community budget and one in which the burdens would be directly charged to the budgets of the Member States. * * *

59   In the first case no problem would arise as regards the exclusive powers of the Community to conclude the agreement in question. * * *

60   * * * If on the other hand the financing is to be by the Member States that will imply the participation of those States in the decision-making machinery or, at least, their agreement with regard to the arrangements for financing envisaged and consequently their participation in the agreement together with the Community. The exclusive competence of the Community could not be envisaged in such a case, [which was in fact the situation in the *Rubber Agreement* case.]

Notes and Questions

1.   Who really won the *Rubber Agreement* case—the Commission or the Council and the Member States? What difference does it make if the Member States are or are not involved in the negotiations? How might their individual interests diverge from the Community's interests? How might their participation affect the results of the negotiations?

2.   The Court affirmed its broad reading of Article 133 in Commission v. Council (Generalized tariff preferences I), Case 45/86, [1987] ECR 1493. See Chapter 4(A) supra. The Court elaborated on the scope of Article 133 in its 1994 opinion on EC adherence to the Agreement Establishing the World Trade Organization. We will postpone consideration of that case until Chapter 29, where that agreement is described in some detail. Article 133 would be significantly expanded in scope by the Nice Treaty, the relevant provision of which is described in notes to Chapter 29(B)(1) infra.

3.   Is the basis of the *Rubber Agreement* decision different from that of the *ERTA* decision? Is the Court concerned with implied or explicit powers in the *Rubber Agreement* case? Do you agree with the Court's expansive reading of Article 133?

4.   The opinion in the *Rubber Agreement* case deals with the problems of so-called mixed agreements, international agreements in which both the Community and the Member States participate because neither has exclusive competence over the matters dealt with in the agreements. For example, many trade and association agreements require direct financial help from Member States and therefore must be signed by them in addition to the Community. Examples of mixed multilateral agreements would include commodities agreements, the Ozone Layer Convention and the Law of the Sea Convention. The latter involves fishing, an exclusive concern of the EC, but also deep sea mining and the peaceful passage of warships, concerns of the Member States (see Note 6 below).

5.   If both the Community and the Member States have some competence in respect of the subject matter of an international agreement, what sort of obli-

gations do they have to cooperate with each other in the negotiations? This issue is addressed in the *WTO* opinion excerpted in Chapter 29(B)(1) infra.

6.   If the subject matter of an international agreement is exclusively within the competence of the Community, is a mixed agreement appropriate? How does uncertainty about the respective roles of the Community and its Member States in external affairs affect third parties? If you were representing the United States in negotiations with the EC, what might you do to reduce such uncertainty?

In this regard, the Law of the Sea Convention, which the Community ratified in 1998, requires that "[a]t the time of signature an international organization [defined to include the EC] shall make a declaration specifying the matters governed by this Convention in respect of which competence has been transferred to that organization by its member states which are signatories, and the nature and extent of that competence." (Annex IX, art. 2) In its declaration the Community noted that the division of competence between it and its Member States was subject to change over time ("continuous development") and it stated that it would amend its declaration as necessary.[5]

C. INTERNATIONAL AGREEMENTS IN COMMUNITY LAW

One interesting issue that arises in respect of international agreements entered into by the Community is their position in Community law. Article 300(7) provides that agreements concluded under Article 300 "shall be binding on the institutions of the Community and on Member States." This raises the question of whether such agreements can be invoked by litigants in EC and Member State courts.

OPEL AUSTRIA GMBH v. COUNCIL
Case T–115/94, [1997] ECR II–39.

[On December 20, 1993, the Council adopted a regulation imposing a duty of 4.9% on F–15 car gearboxes produced by General Motors Austria and originating in Austria. It did so to offset certain state aids extended by Austria to General Motors. The regulation was adopted on the basis of Article 133 of the EC Treaty and a 1972 Council regulation on imposition of safeguards provided for in the Austria–EC Free Trade Agreement ("FTA"). That agreement was superceded by the European Economic Area ("EEA") Agreement, which entered into force on January 1, 1994 and which is described in Chapter 28. The following decision of the Court of First Instance was not appealed.]

[89]   The applicant * * * claims that the EEA Agreement was part of the factual and legal situation existing at the time when the contested regulation was adopted on 20 December 1993 and that, by adopting that regulation a few days before the EEA Agreement entered into force, the Council infringed the principle of public international law ("the principle of good faith") according to which, pending the entry into force of an

5. United Nations, Multilateral Treaties Deposited with the Secretary General, Status as of 31 December 1989, XXI.6, 785–786 (1990); Council Decision of March 23, 1998, Annex II, O.J. L179/129–130 (June 23, 1998).

international agreement, the signatories to an international agreement may not adopt measures which would defeat its object and purpose.

90 The Court holds in this connection, first, that the principle of good faith is a rule of customary international law whose existence is recognized by the International Court of Justice and is therefore binding on the Community.

91 That principle has been codified by Article 18 of the first Vienna Convention, which provides as follows:

"A State is obliged to refrain from acts which would defeat the object and purpose of a treaty when:

(a) it has signed the treaty or has exchanged instruments constituting the treaty subject to ratification, acceptance or approval, until it shall have made its intention clear not to become a party to the treaty or

(b) it has expressed its consent to be bound by the treaty, pending the entry into force of the treaty and provided that such entry into force is not unduly delayed."

92 In this case, the Council adopted the contested regulation on 20 December 1993, that is to say, seven days after the Communities, as the last Contracting Parties, had approved the EEA Agreement * * *. Accordingly, as from 13 December 1993 the Communities were aware [that the EEA Agreement was to enter into force on January 1, 1994].

93 Secondly, the principle of good faith is the corollary in public international law of the principle of protection of legitimate expectations which, according to the case-law, forms part of the Community legal order. Any economic operator to whom an institution has given justified hopes may rely on the principle of protection of legitimate expectations.

94 In a situation where the Communities have deposited their instruments of approval of an international agreement and the date of entry into force of that agreement is known, traders may rely on the principle of protection of legitimate expectations in order to challenge the adoption by the institutions, during the period preceding the entry into force of that agreement, of any measure contrary to the provisions of that agreement which will have direct effect on them after it has entered into force.

[The Court first determined that the relevant provisions of the EEA Agreement took the place of the provisions of the FTA and that the EEA Agreement was applicable to the products at issue in this case.]

100 Secondly, it is necessary to consider whether Article 10 of the EEA Agreement is capable of having direct effect following the entry into force of that agreement.

101 As appears from Article 228(7) [now 300(7)] of the EC Treaty, international agreements concluded by the Community in conformity with the Treaty are binding on the institutions and the Member States. It is settled case-law that the provisions of such an agreement form an integral part of the Community legal order once the agreement has entered into force. It is also settled case-law that the provisions of such an agreement may have direct effect if they are unconditional and sufficiently precise.

102 In that regard, the Court observes that nothing in the case-file suggests that the EEA Agreement, which was concluded by the Community on the

basis of Article 238 [now 310] of the EC Treaty, was not concluded in conformity with the Treaty. It follows that since the Agreement entered into force on 1 January 1994 the provisions of the Agreement form an integral part of the Community legal order. It should also be borne in mind that the first sentence of Article 10 of the EEA Agreement provides that customs duties on imports and exports and any charges having equivalent effect are prohibited between the Contracting Parties. The second sentence of that article provides that, without prejudice to the arrangements set out in Protocol 5, customs duties of a fiscal nature are likewise prohibited. Article 10 thus lays down an unconditional and precise rule, subject to a single exception which is itself unconditional and precise. It follows that ever since the EEA Agreement entered into force Article 10 has had direct effect.

103   Thirdly, it is necessary to decide whether, by reintroducing a duty of 4.9%, the contested regulation infringed Article 10 of the EEA Agreement.

104   Article 6 of the EEA Agreement provides:

"Without prejudice to future developments of case-law, the provisions of this Agreement, in so far as they are identical in substance to correspond-ing rules of the Treaty establishing the European Economic Community and the Treaty establishing the European Coal and Steel Community and to acts adopted in application of these two Treaties, shall, in their implementation and application, be interpreted in conformity with the relevant rulings of the Court of Justice of the European Communities given prior to the date of signature of this Agreement."

105   The Council contends that, notwithstanding that provision, Article 10 of the EEA Agreement should not be interpreted in the same way as the corresponding provisions of the EC Treaty, because there are major differences between the EC Treaty and the EEA Agreement.

106   That argument cannot be accepted. It is clear from the case-law that in order to determine whether the interpretation of a provision contained in the EC Treaty must be extended to an identical provision contained in an agreement such as the EEA Agreement, that provision should be analysed in the light of both the purpose and the objective of the Agreement and in its context. According to Article 1(1) of the EEA Agreement, the aim of that agreement is to promote a continuous and balanced strengthening of trade and economic relations between the Contracting Parties with equal conditions of competition, and the respect of the same rules, with a view to creating a homogeneous European Economic Area. To that end, the Contracting Parties decided to eliminate virtually all trade barriers, in conformity with the provisions of the GATT on the establishment of free-trade areas.

107   In that context, the EEA Agreement involves a high degree of integration, with objectives which exceed those of a mere free-trade agreement. Thus, as is clear from Article 1(2), the EEA involves, inter alia, the free movement of goods, persons, services and capital and the setting up of a system ensuring that competition is not distorted and that the rules relating thereto are equally respected. The rules applicable to relations between the Contracting Parties in the fields covered by the Agreement

essentially correspond to the parallel provisions of the EC and ECSC Treaties and the measures adopted in pursuance of those treaties. * * *

* * *

110 It follows from those findings that Article 6 of the EEA Agreement must be interpreted as meaning that where a provision of the EEA Agreement is identical in substance to corresponding rules of the EC and ECSC Treaties and to the acts adopted in application of those two treaties it must be interpreted in conformity with the relevant rulings of the Court of Justice and of the Court of First Instance given prior to the date of signature of the EEA Agreement.

111 The Court further finds that Article 10 of the EEA Agreement is identical in substance to Articles 12 [now Article 25], 13, 16 and 17 [all deleted] of the EC Treaty which, with effect from the end of the transitional period, prohibit customs duties on imports or exports and any charges having equivalent effect between the Member States. Consequently, by virtue of Article 6 of the EEA Agreement, Article 10 must be interpreted in conformity with the relevant rulings of the Court of Justice and the Court of First Instance prior to the date of signature of the Agreement.

* * *

119 In view of all these factors, it is accordingly necessary to consider whether, following the entry into force of the EEA Agreement, the contested regulation is contrary to Article 10 of that agreement when interpreted, pursuant to Article 6, in conformity with the relevant rulings of the Court of Justice and the Court of First Instance prior to the date of signature of the EEA Agreement.

* * *

121 [I]t is settled case-law that "any pecuniary charge, however small and whatever its designation and mode of application, which is imposed unilaterally on domestic or foreign goods by reason of the fact that they cross a frontier, and which is not a customs duty in the strict sense, constitutes a charge having equivalent effect within the meaning of Articles 9 and 12 [now Articles 23 and 25] of the Treaty, even if it is not imposed for the benefit of the State, is not discriminatory or protective in effect or if the product on which the charge is imposed is not in competition with any domestic product" (Sociaal Fonds voor de Diamantarbeiders v Brachfeld, paragraph 15/18, [excerpted in Chapter 12]).

122 The measure introduced by the contested regulation constitutes a pecuniary charge imposed unilaterally by the Community on F–15 gearboxes by reason of the fact that they cross a frontier. Consequently, it must be held that the measure constitutes, at the very least, a charge having equivalent effect within the meaning of Article 10 of the EEA Agreement and it is unnecessary to determine whether it must be regarded as a customs duty on imports in the strict sense. It is therefore clear that, following the entry into force of the EEA Agreement, the contested regulation was contrary to that article.

123 It follows that, by adopting the contested regulation in the period preceding the entry into force of the EEA Agreement after the Communities had

deposited their instruments of approval, the Council infringed the applicant's legitimate expectations.

Notes and Questions

1. The position of international law in the Community was underscored in Commission v. Germany (International Dairy Arrangement), Case C–61/94, [1994] ECR I–3989, where the Court permitted the Commission to initiate an Article 226 action against Germany for failing to comply with an international agreement that had been ratified by the Community in a Council decision. The Court noted that under Article 211 (ex 155), "the Commission is responsible for ensuring application of the Treaty, and, accordingly, compliance with international agreements concluded by the Community which, pursuant to Article 228 [now 300], are binding both on the Community institutions and the Member States" (para. 15).

2. In Hauptzollamt Mainz v. C.A. Kupferberg & Cie., Case 104/81, [1982] ECR 3641, the Court of Justice examined the EC–Portuguese Free Trade Agreement, which was in force prior to Portugal's accession to the Community. The case involved Article 21 of the Agreement, which provided that the parties would not implement tax measures that resulted, directly or indirectly, in discrimination between the domestic and imported products. The company involved claimed that Germany had engaged in such discrimination and that Article 21 was directly applicable. The Court concluded (at 3665):

23   * * * In order to reply to the question on the direct effect of the first paragraph of Article 21 of the Agreement between the Community and Portugal it is necessary to analyse the provision in the light of both the object and purpose of the Agreement and of its context.

24   The purpose of the Agreement is to create a system of free trade in which rules restricting commerce are eliminated in respect of virtually all trade in products originating in the territory of the parties, in particular by abolishing customs duties and charges having equivalent effect and eliminating quantitative restrictions and measures having equivalent effect.

25   Seen in that context the first paragraph of Article 21 of the Agreement seeks to prevent the liberalization of the trade in goods through the abolition of customs duties and charges having equivalent effect and quantitative restrictions and measures having equivalent effect from being rendered nugatory by fiscal practices of the Contracting Parties. That would be so if the product imported of one party were taxed more heavily than the similar domestic products which it encounters on the market of the other party.

26   It appears from the foregoing that the first paragraph of Article 21 of the Agreement imposes on the Contracting Parties an unconditional rule against discrimination in matters of taxation, which is dependent only on a finding that the products affected by a particular system of taxation are of like nature, and the limits of which are the direct consequence of the purpose of the Agreement. As such this provision may be applied by a court and thus produce direct effects throughout the Community.

The Court in *Kupferberg* ultimately concluded that the German law did not violate the EC–Portuguese Agreement.

3. Should the fact that the other party to an international agreement might not allow litigants to invoke the agreement in its domestic courts cause the Court of Justice to adopt a similar policy for itself and Member State courts? In *Kupferberg* the Court rejected such an argument.

4.   In Polydor Ltd. v. Harlequin Record Shops Ltd., Case 270/80, [1982] ECR 329, which also involved the interpretation of the EC–Portuguese Free Trade Agreement, the Court was faced with a case involving records lawfully made and marketed in Portugal by the Portuguese copyright holder and then exported to the United Kingdom, where another party held the copyright. As explained in Chapter 19(D) supra, under the Court's interpretation of Articles 28 and 30 of the EC Treaty, a product marketed by the copyright holder in Member State A can often be lawfully exported to Member State B, even if another party holds the copyright in Member State B. The question in this case was whether Articles 14(2) and 23 of the Agreement, which were almost identical to Articles 28 and 30 of the EC Treaty, should be interpreted in the same way. The Court concluded at 348–349:

14   The provisions of the Agreement on the elimination of restrictions on trade between the Community and Portugal are expressed in terms which in several respects are similar to those of the EEC Treaty on the abolition of restrictions on intra-Community trade. Harlequin and Simons pointed out in particular the similarity between the terms of Articles 14(2) and 23 of the Agreement on the one hand and those of Articles 30 and 36 [now 28 and 30] of the EEC Treaty on the other.

15   However, such similarity of terms is not a sufficient reason for transposing to the provisions of the Agreement the above-mentioned case-law, which determines in the context of the Community the relationship between the protection of industrial and commercial property rights and the rules on the free movement of goods.

16   The scope of that case-law must indeed be determined in the light of the Community's objectives and activities as defined by Articles 2 and 3 of the EEC Treaty. As the Court has had occasion to emphasize in various contexts, the Treaty, by establishing a common market and progressively approximating the economic policies of the Member States, seeks to unite national markets into a single market having the characteristics of a domestic market.

17   Having regard to those objectives, the Court, *inter alia,* in Terrapin (Overseas) Ltd. v. Terranova Industrie [see Chapter 19(C) supra], interpreted Articles 30 and 36 [now 28 and 30] of the Treaty as meaning that the territorial protection afforded by national laws to industrial and commercial property may not have the effect of legitimizing the insulation of national markets and of leading to an artificial partitioning of the markets and that consequently the proprietor of an industrial or commercial property right protected by the law of a Member State cannot rely on that law to prevent the importation of a product which has lawfully been marketed in another Member State by the proprietor himself or with his consent.

18   The considerations which led to that interpretation of Articles 30 and 36 of the Treaty do not apply in the context of the relations between the Community and Portugal as defined by the Agreement. It is apparent from an examination of the Agreement that although it makes provision for the unconditional abolition of certain restrictions on trade between the Community and Portugal, such as quantitative restrictions and measures having equivalent effect, it does not have the same purpose as the EEC Treaty, inasmuch as the latter, as has been stated above, seeks to create a single market reproducing as closely as possible the conditions of a domestic market.

19   It follows that in the context of the Agreement restrictions on trade in goods may be considered to be justified on the ground of the protection of industrial

and commercial property in a situation in which their justification would not be possible within the Community.

[20] In the present case such a distinction is all the more necessary inasmuch as the instruments which the Community has at its disposal in order to achieve the uniform application of Community law and the progressive abolition of legislative disparities within the common market have no equivalent in the context of the relations between the Community and Portugal.

[21] It follows from the foregoing that a prohibition on the importation into the Community of a product originating in Portugal based on the protection of copyright is justified in the framework of the free-trade arrangements established by the Agreement by virtue of the first sentence of Article 23. The findings of the national court do not disclose any factor which would permit the conclusion that the enforcement of copyright in a case such as the present constitutes a means of arbitrary discrimination or a disguised restriction on trade within the meaning of the second sentence of that article.

Do you agree with the Court's distinction in para. 18? Isn't the goal of both the EC Treaty and the Agreement liberalization of trade and market integration?

5.   The Court on several occasions has ruled that workers (or their families) may rely on the provisions of EC-third country association/cooperation agreements to challenge discrimination against them in respect of certain unemployment or disability benefits. See, e.g., Yousfi v. Belgium, Case C–58/93, [1994] ECR I–1353; Office National de l'Emploi v. Kziber, Case C–18/90, [1991] ECR I–119. The two cited cases involved Articles 40 and 41 of the EC–Morocco Cooperation Agreement, which require Member States to treat Moroccan workers employed in their territory non-discriminatorily in terms of working conditions and remuneration and to treat family members living with them non-discriminatorily in respect of social security. See also Eroglu v. Land Baden–Württemberg, Case C–355/93, [1994] ECR I–5113 (Association Agreement with Turkey).

Article 6(1) of Decision 1/80 of the EC–Turkey Association Council (established under the EC–Turkey Association Agreement) provides that the EC and Turkey will be "guided by Articles 48, 49 and 50 of the [EC Treaty] for the purposes of progressively securing freedom of movement for workers between them." In Recep Tetik v. Land Berlin, Case C–171/95, [1997] ECR I–329, the Court ruled that since Article 6 of Decision 1/80 has direct effect and may be relied upon by Turkish nationals in Member State courts, a Turkish worker who had been legally employed for more than four years in a Member State, who had voluntarily left his employment in order to seek new work in the same Member State and who was unable immediately to enter into a new employment relation, had a right of residence for a reasonable period of time for the purpose of seeking new employment. The Court noted that it was for the Member State concerned (or in the absence of legislation, the Member State's courts) to fix such reasonable period. See also Eyüp v. Landesgeshäftsstelle des Arbeitsmarktservice Vorarlberg, Case C–65/98, [2000] ECR I—(June 22, 2000)("family member" for purposes of five-year lawful residence requirement for employment rights under Decision 1/80 includes person who was married to worker for two years, divorced but cohabited with worker for ten years and then remarried to worker for four years).

6.   The Court of Justice has not been receptive to arguments that GATT or WTO provisions should be given direct effect. See Chapter 29(B)(2) infra. After reading that material, do think the cases discussed here and the *Portuguese Republic* case in Chapter 29 are consistent?

7. If an international agreement concluded by the EC is found to be directly applicable, would such an agreement prevail over (a) the EC Treaty? (b) Community acts adopted subsequently to its conclusion? (c) Community acts adopted prior to conclusion of the agreement? (d) the constitution of a Member State? (e) Member State legislation adopted after its conclusion? (f) such legislation adopted prior to conclusion of the agreement?

8. Under US law, an international agreement is not self-executing "(a) if the agreement manifests an intention that it shall not become effective as domestic law without the enactment of implementing legislation, (b) if the Senate in giving consent to a treaty, or Congress by resolution, requires implementing legislation, or (c) if implementing legislation is constitutionally required." Restatement of the Law: The Foreign Relations Law of the United States (Third) sec. 111(4) (1987).

D. EUROPEAN POLITICAL COOPERATION AND THE COMMON FOREIGN AND SECURITY POLICY

Ever since the early days of the Community there have been proposals that the Member States coordinate their foreign policies, from both those who wanted to see Europe progress beyond economic union toward political union and those who viewed common efforts in foreign relations as a practical means to increase the influence of the Member States in world affairs.

The basis for Member State cooperation in foreign policy, which initially was known as European Political Cooperation (EPC), grew out of a decision at the 1969 Hague summit of the heads of state and government to have the EC foreign ministers study ways of achieving progress toward political unification. Successive summit meetings of Community leaders at Copenhagen in 1973, London in 1981 and Stuttgart in 1983 substantially reinforced EPC, but EPC was not given a treaty basis until its inclusion in title III of the Single European Act, which came into effect in 1987. This foundation was significantly expanded by title V of the Treaty on European Union, which provides for a Common Foreign and Security Policy (CFSP). The TEU's provisions on the CFSP were modified in the Amsterdam and Nice Treaties and are now contained in TEU Articles 11–28.

The Court of Justice has no jurisdiction in respect of TEU Title V (TEU art. 46), although actions taken under the EC Treaty to implement foreign policy decisions may be reviewed by the Court. In this section, we will outline briefly the operation of the Common Foreign Policy and the nascent Common Security Policy and then consider a case where an EPC policy resulted in trade sanctions that were challenged in the Court of Justice.

1. THE COMMON FOREIGN POLICY

The Treaty on European Union provides that "[t]he Union shall define and implement a common foreign and security policy covering all areas of foreign and security policy" (TEU, art. 11(1)). The specific objectives of the policy are listed in TEU Article 11(1). As to the Member States, they "shall support the Union's external and security policy actively and unreservedly in a spirit of loyalty and mutual solidarity. * * * They shall refrain from any action which is contrary to the interests of the Union or likely to impair its effectiveness as a cohesive force in international relations." TEU, art. 11(2).

Under TEU Article 12, the European Council is responsible for defining the principles and general guidelines of the CFSP and deciding on common strategies. The Council is charged with implementing the CFSP and the common strategies through joint actions and common decisions.

The decision-making procedures are set out in TEU Article 23. As a general principle, decisions under the CFSC are taken by the Council acting unanimously, although abstentions do not prevent the adoption of decisions. When abstaining, a Member State may qualify its abstention by making a formal declaration. In that case, it is not obligated to apply the decision, but must accept that the decision commits the Union. The Member State concerned, in the spirit of mutual solidarity, is expected to refrain from any action likely to conflict with or impede Union action based on that decision. If the Member States qualifying their abstentions in this way represent more than one-third of the votes weighted in accordance with Article 205(2) of the EC Treaty, the decision would not be adopted.

In a significant derogation from the foregoing general unanimity principle, joint actions, common positions or decisions taken on the basis of a common strategy, and decisions to implement a joint action or common position (except those having military or defense implications) may be adopted by the Council acting by a qualified majority. For adoption, such decisions require at least 62 votes in favor, cast by at least 10 Member States. However, if a Member State declares formally that, for important and stated reasons of national policy, it intends to oppose the adoption of a decision by qualified majority, a vote on the decision is not be taken. In such a case, the Council, acting by a qualified majority, may refer the matter to the European Council, for decision by unanimity.

The Amsterdam Treaty provided that the Presidency of the Council would represent the Union in matters coming within the CFSC, with the assistance of the Secretary–General of the Council, who would exercise the function of High Representative for the Common Foreign and Security Policy. The hope is that the High Representative will provide a sense of permanence to the CFSP, which some believe has suffered because of the twice-annual changes in the Presidency of the Council. The first High Representative is Javier Solana, who was appointed to a five-year term staring in October 1999. He had previously been Secretary–General of NATO (1995–1999) and Foreign Affairs Minister of Spain (1992–1995). The High Representative is assisted within the Council secretariat by a policy planning unit.

The implementation of the CFSP takes place through the European Council (which meets at least twice annually and which as of 2001 had adopted common strategies for Russia, Ukraine and the Mediterranean Region), the General Affairs Council (which meets at least monthly and decides on external relations issues), Coreper (which meets weekly to prepare Council meetings), the Political Committee (consisting of Member State Political Directors and the Commission, which meets twice a month), European Correspondents (who coordinate daily CFSP matters and prepare meetings of the Political Directors, General Affairs Council and European Council on CFSP matters), as well as working groups on specific issues. All of this activity produces numerous EU statements on foreign policy issues. The Council section of the EU website is an excellent, up-to-date source of Union pronouncements on foreign affairs.

The TEU provides that the Commission is to be "fully associated" with the work on the CFSP (TEU, art. 27), and as noted above, it participates in the Political Committee. The Presidency of the Council is obligated to consult the European Parliament on the main aspects of the CFSP and "shall ensure that the views of the European Parliament are duly taken into consideration." TEU, art. 21.

It is probably too early to evaluate the effectiveness of the recent changes in the operation of the CFSP, as the new structures and the High Representative have been in place for only about two years. For materials evaluating the EPC and CFSP, see John Peterson & Helen Sjursen, eds., A Common Foreign Policy for Europe: Competing Visions of the CFSP (1998); Jan Zielonka, ed., Paradoxes of European Foreign Policy (1998); Alan Cafruny & Patrick Peters, eds., The Union and the World (1998); A. Pijpers, E. Regelsberger & W. Wessels, eds., European Political Cooperation in the 1980s: A Common Foreign Policy for Western Europe? (1988).

2. THE COMMON SECURITY POLICY

The TEU provides that the CFSP "shall include all questions relating to the security of the Union, including the progressive framing of a common defense policy, which might lead to a common defense, should the European Council so decide." TEU, art. 17(1). The TEU specifies that the EU Security Policy shall not prejudice the specific character of the security and defense policy of certain Member States and shall respect the obligations of certain Member States, which see their common defense realized in the North Atlantic Treaty Organization (NATO) and shall be compatible with the common security and defense policy established within that framework. TEU, art. 17(1).

Initially, the TEU provided that the EU would rely on the Western European Union, which then consisted of nine Member States, to elaborate and implement decisions and actions of the EU which had defense implications. However, the Nice Treaty will remove from the TEU those references to the WEU. Separately, in November 2000, the WEU decided to transfer its principal activities to the EU.

The transfer of functions from the WEU to the EU is a clear indication of the extent to which the European Security Policy is rapidly being put into place. The Helsinki European Council in December 1999 set as a target that (i) that by 2003 Member States must be able to deploy for EU-led operations, within 60 days and sustain for one year, a military force of 50,000–60,000 persons capable of performing humanitarian and rescue tasks, and peacekeeping and certain peacemaking tasks and (ii) the EU must have appropriate structures in place to direct such operations. In March 2000, interim structures were put in place, and at the December 2000 Nice European Council, it was agreed to establish a standing Political and Security Committee, a Military Committee and a Military Staff.

Probably the most interesting issue in respect of the common security policy in the near term (2001–2005) is how its relationship with NATO evolves and whether the policy leads to tensions with the US.

3. TRADE SANCTIONS FOR POLITICAL PURPOSES

Article 301 (ex 228a) of the EC Treaty provides that if a common position or joint action adopted pursuant to the CFSP calls for the Community to interrupt economic relations with a third country, the Council may take urgent measures, by qualified majority, acting on a proposal from the Commission. This provision was added by the 1993 Maastricht Treaty and clarified the legal basis for imposing trade sanctions for political purposes. While actions taken under the TEU in connection with the CFSP are not reviewable in the EC courts, the EC measures imposing trade sanctions are reviewable and such sanctions have led to a number of cases in the Court of Justice.

BOSPHORUS HAVA YOLLARI TURIZM VE TICARET AS v. MINISTER FOR TRANSPORT, ENERGY & COMMUNICATION

Case C–84/95, [1996] ECR I–3953.

[Bosphorus Hava Yollari Turizm ve Ticaret AS ("Bosphorus Airways") is a Turkish company which operated principally as an air charterer and travel organizer. In April 1992, it leased two aircraft owned by the Yugoslav national airline JAT. The lease covered only the aircraft. Bosphorus Airways provided its own crews and had complete control of the day-to-day management of the aircraft. JAT remained the owner of the aircraft. It appeared that the lease was entered into in complete good faith and was not intended to circumvent the sanctions against the Yugoslavia which had been decided by United Nations resolutions and implemented in the Community by Regulation 990/93. Under the sanctions, the rent due under the lease was paid into blocked accounts, not to JAT. The aircraft were used exclusively by Bosphorus Airways for flights between Turkey on the one hand and several Member States and Switzerland on the other.

One of the aircraft was later seized by Irish authorities under Article 8 of Regulation 990/93, which provided that all aircraft "in which a majority or controlling interest is held by a person or undertaking in or operating from the Federal Republic of Yugoslavia (Serbia and Montenegro) shall be impounded by the competent authorities of the Member States". The Supreme Court of Ireland stayed the proceedings and asked for a preliminary ruling from the Court of Justice on whether Article 8 applied to an aircraft leased under the above-described conditions.]

[9] In support of its argument, Bosphorus Airways submits that the aim of the regulation in question is to penalize the Federal Republic of Yugoslavia and its nationals as well as to apply sanctions against them, but is certainly not to extend those sanctions unnecessarily to wholly innocent parties pursuing their activities from a neighboring State, with which, moreover, the Community has friendly relations.

[10] That argument cannot be accepted.

11   As the Court has stated in its case-law, in interpreting a provision of Community law it is necessary to consider its wording, its context and its aims.

12   Nothing in the wording of [Article 8] suggests that it is based on a distinction between ownership of an aircraft on the one hand and its day-to-day operation and control on the other. Nor is it anywhere stated in that provision that it is not applicable to an aircraft owned by a person or undertaking based in or operating from the Federal Republic of Yugoslavia if that person or undertaking does not have day-to-day operation and control of the aircraft.

13   As to context and aims, it should be noted that by Regulation No 990/93 the Council gave effect to the decision of the Community and its Member States, meeting within the framework of political cooperation, to have recourse to a Community instrument to implement in the Community certain aspects of the sanctions taken against the Federal Republic of Yugoslavia by the Security Council of the United Nations * * *.

14   To determine the scope of the first paragraph of Article 8 of Regulation No 990/93, account must therefore also be taken of the text and the aim of those [UN] resolutions, [one of] which provides that "all States shall impound all vessels, freight vehicles, rolling stock and aircraft in their territories in which a majority or controlling interest is held by a person or undertaking in or operating from the Federal Republic of Yugoslavia (Serbia and Montenegro)".

15   Thus the wording of [the UN Resolution] confirms that [Article 8] is to apply to any aircraft which is the property of a person or undertaking based in or operating from the Federal Republic of Yugoslavia, and that it is not necessary for that person or undertaking also to have actual control of the aircraft. The word "interest" in [the UN resolution] cannot, on any view, exclude ownership as a determining criterion for impounding. Moreover, that word is used in that paragraph in conjunction with the word "majority", which clearly implies the concept of ownership.

16   That conclusion is borne out by the fact that most of the language versions of [Article 8] use terms with explicit connotations of ownership. * * *

17   Furthermore, the impounding of any aircraft owned by a person or undertaking based in or operating from the Federal Republic of Yugoslavia, even if an undertaking such as Bosphorus Airways has taken over its day-to-day operation and control, contributes to restricting the exercise by the Federal Republic of Yugoslavia and its nationals of their property rights and is thus consistent with the aim of the sanctions, namely to put pressure on that republic.

18   By contrast, the use of day-to-day operation and control, rather than ownership, as the decisive criterion for applying the measures prescribed by [Article 8] would jeopardize the effectiveness of the strengthening of the sanctions, which consist in impounding all means of transport of the Federal Republic of Yugoslavia and its nationals, including aircraft, in order further to increase the pressure on that republic. The mere transfer of day-to-day operation and control of means of transport, by a lease or

other method, without transferring ownership would allow that republic or its nationals to evade application of those sanctions.

Fundamental rights and the principle of proportionality

19   Bosphorus Airways submits, in the second place, that to interpret [Article 8] as meaning that an aircraft whose day-to-day operation and control are carried out under a lease by a person or undertaking not based in or operating from the Federal Republic of Yugoslavia must nevertheless be impounded because it belongs to an undertaking based in that republic, would infringe Bosphorus's fundamental rights, in particular its right to peaceful enjoyment of its property and its freedom to pursue a commercial activity, in that it would have the effect of destroying and obliterating its air charter and travel organization business.

20   That interpretation, according to Bosphorus Airways, would also infringe the principle of proportionality, since the owner of the aircraft in question has already been penalized by the rent being held in blocked accounts and the impounding of the aircraft was therefore a manifestly unnecessary penalty, disproportionate with respect to a wholly innocent party.

21   It is settled case-law that the fundamental rights invoked by Bosphorus Airways are not absolute and their exercise may be subject to restrictions justified by objectives of general interest pursued by the Community.

22   Any measure imposing sanctions has, by definition, consequences which affect the right to property and the freedom to pursue a trade or business, thereby causing harm to persons who are in no way responsible for the situation which led to the adoption of the sanctions.

23   Moreover, the importance of the aims pursued by the regulation at issue is such as to justify negative consequences, even of a substantial nature, for some operators.

24   The provisions of Regulation No 990/93 contribute in particular to the implementation at Community level of the sanctions against the Federal Republic of Yugoslavia adopted, and later strengthened, by several resolutions of the Security Council of the United Nations. The third recital in the preamble to Regulation No 990/93 states that "the prolonged direct and indirect activities of the Federal Republic of Yugoslavia (Serbia and Montenegro) in, and with regard to, the Republic of Bosnia–Herzegovina are the main cause for the dramatic developments in the Republic of Bosnia–Herzegovina"; the fourth recital states that "a continuation of these activities will lead to further unacceptable loss of human life and material damage and to a further breach of international peace and security in the region"; and the seventh recital states that "the Bosnian Serb party has hitherto not accepted, in full, the peace plan of the International Conference on the Former Yugoslavia in spite of appeals thereto by the Security Council".

25   It is in the light of those circumstances that the aim pursued by the sanctions assumes especial importance, which is, in particular, in terms of Regulation No 990/93 and more especially the eighth recital in the preamble thereto, to dissuade the Federal Republic of Yugoslavia from "further violating the integrity and security of the Republic of Bosnia–Herzegovina

and to induce the Bosnian Serb party to cooperate in the restoration of peace in this Republic''.

[26] As compared with an objective of general interest so fundamental for the international community, which consists in putting an end to the state of war in the region and to the massive violations of human rights and humanitarian international law in the Republic of Bosnia–Herzegovina, the impounding of the aircraft in question, which is owned by an undertaking based in or operating from the Federal Republic of Yugoslavia, cannot be regarded as inappropriate or disproportionate.

Notes and Questions

1. While the decision of the Court is not surprising, do you think that Bosphorus Airways was treated fairly? Even if justified, was the decision proportional? Could some use be found for the payments due, such as redirection to programs for the benefit of refugees?

2. Two other EC Treaty provisions are relevant to sanctions. Article 60 authorizes restrictions on movements of capital and payments in cases envisaged by Article 301. In the absence of Community action, Article 60 permits Member States to take such actions unilaterally for serious political reasons on grounds of urgency, subject to a decision to the contrary by the Council. More generally, Article 297 requires Member States to consult on the need to take actions together so as to prevent the functioning of the common market being affected by measures that an individual Member State may be called upon to take in the event of serious internal disturbances, war or serious international tension constituting a threat of war.

3. The Community has only occasionally imposed trade sanctions for political reasons. For example, it imposed sanctions on Rhodesia (now Zimbabwe) in the 1960s and 1970s, in accordance with a UN Security Council resolution, in an effort to pressure the white minority government in that country to permit black majority rule. In 1980, the Member States in consultation with the Community took certain measures against Iran in an effort to get Iran to release the hostages taken at the US embassy in Teheran. Community measures were taken against Soviet Union to protest its invasion of Afghanistan and its intervention in Poland in 1981–1982, and imports from Argentina were suspended during the Falklands Islands crisis of 1982. In 1990, in accordance with UN Security Council resolutions, the Community prohibited all trade between the Community and Iraq, except for certain foodstuffs and medicines, in an effort to get Iraq to withdraw from Kuwait. More recently, as exemplified by the instant case, it has applied trade sanctions in an attempt to force negotiated settlements to the various conflicts in the former Yugoslavia.

Some of these actions have been controversial politically. For example, despite the adoption of binding Community measures suspending imports from Argentina, Italy and Ireland refused to implement the suspension in part. At times, there was considerable disagreement over the legal basis for implementing trade sanctions, and, in particular, over whether Article 133 with its qualified majority voting rules was sufficient. As noted above, this legal basis issue has now been clarified.

Chapter 28

THE COMMON COMMERCIAL POLICY: PREFERENTIAL ARRANGEMENTS AND ACCESSION NEGOTIATIONS

Companies in the EC trade all over the world and the EC imports a significant amount of goods and services form the rest of the world. Indeed, imports into the EC from the rest of the world constituted 12.4% of the Community's gross national product in 1999. While individual transactions in international trade are largely conducted pursuant to private contracts, the general framework in which such trade occurs is usually established by international agreements, such as the WTO Agreement and any number of multilateral, regional and bilateral agreements.

As we saw in Chapter 27, the Community is responsible for negotiating and applying such agreements since they are part of its common commercial policy. Before we examine the key components of that policy—its customs law and its rules on unfair trade practices in Chapters 30 and 31, it is useful to consider in overview the general framework of the Community's commercial relations with the rest of the world. In this chapter, we examine the Community's relations with other countries in Europe and the Mediterranean region, as well as its relations with the third world, much of which was governed by Europe in the recent past. In Chapter 29, we examine the World Trade Organization and the Community's position therein, paying particular attention to its trading relationship with the United States, which is largely WTO-based. Many of the Community agreements regulating trade with third countries deal with other issues as well, particularly development assistance and cooperative arrangements in a wide range of fields.

A. THE EC AND EUROPE

The EC's commercial relations with Europe can be divided usefully into three parts: first, its relations with the other industrialized countries of Western Europe, notably the EFTA countries; second, its relations with the countries of Central and Eastern Europe; and finally, its relations with the Mediterranean countries, some of which, of course, are not in Europe.

1. THE EFTA COUNTRIES

a. *The History of EC–Western European Relations*

After the European Economic Community was founded in 1957, seven European countries, led by the United Kingdom, negotiated a free trade agreement in 1960, known as the European Free Trade Association (EFTA) or the Stockholm Convention.[1] Generally speaking, the EFTA countries wanted to liberalize trade between themselves but also wanted a looser form of confederation than the EEC Treaty established. The current members of EFTA are Iceland, Liechtenstein, Norway and Switzerland. Austria, Denmark, Finland, Portugal, Sweden and the United Kingdom were once members of EFTA but subsequently joined the EC.

EFTA is a free trade area, rather than a customs union like the EC. The basic feature of a free trade area is the elimination of trade barriers between its members. In the case of EFTA, customs duties and import quotas on trade in industrial products between EFTA members were eliminated by 1966. Agricultural and fisheries products are excluded from EFTA's free trade provisions, although EFTA does promote trade within EFTA of those products. EFTA differs from a customs union in that it does not have a common commercial policy toward third countries. Such a policy is required for customs unions under WTO rules.

EFTA contains provisions designed to ensure that fair competition prevails in trade between EFTA countries. It thus bans certain state aids and restrictive business practices, such as agreements between companies that prevent, restrict or distort competition and actions that take unfair advantage of a dominant position. EFTA also attempts to reduce technical barriers to trade among its member states. The new EFTA Convention, the Vaduz Convention of June 21, 2001, will cover free movement of persons, intellectual property rights, investment, services and government procurement.

From the foregoing, it is clear that EFTA bears some similarity to the EC in terms of its trade-related provisions. Nonetheless, it is a fundamentally different organization. The EFTA secretariat does not resemble the EC Commission at all; it has relatively few permanent employees. There is no court with jurisdiction comparable to the Court of Justice, nor is there an independent parliament. EFTA affairs are overseen by the EFTA Council, which normally consists of the heads of the member state delegations to EFTA, but which twice a year meets at the ministerial level. The Council has the power to take certain decisions that are binding on the member states, but generally the Council acts only by unanimous vote. Thus, EFTA does not have the lawmaking and law administering bodies found in the EC. As noted by the Court of Justice in its *EEA* opinion (set out below), the EC involves the transfer of sovereign powers from the Member States to the Community institutions, but EFTA does not.

It was inevitable that the EC and EFTA would have close economic ties. In connection with the 1973 accession to the EC of Denmark and the United Kingdom (both EFTA members), the EC negotiated virtually identical free

---

1. Additional information on EFTA, including legal texts, is available at www.efta.int. An updated EFTA convention (the Vaduz Convention) was signed on June 21, 2001.

trade agreements with each of the EFTA members. Under these agreements, trade in industrial products between the EC and the EFTA countries has been free of duties and quotas since 1984. Many barriers to trade in agricultural products remain, however. The EC–EFTA agreements provide that certain state aids and restrictions on competition are incompatible with the proper functioning of the agreements. They also contain provisions designed to prevent discrimination in internal taxation. As we saw in Chapter 27(C) supra, in the *Polydor* and *Kupferberg* cases, these agreements may be invoked by individuals in some circumstances in EC and Member State courts.

The achievement in 1984 of the elimination of duties and quotas on EC–EFTA trade in industrial products raised the question of how the EC–EFTA relationship would evolve thereafter. This issue was addressed at the first formal ministerial level meeting between the EC, its Member States and the members of EFTA, which occurred in Luxembourg in 1984. That meeting produced the so-called Luxembourg Declaration, which called for increased cooperation in many fields between the EC and EFTA, "with the aim of creating a dynamic European economic space."[2]

b. *The European Economic Area*

The implementation by the EC of its single market program raised the question of how completion of the internal market would affect the EFTA countries. The continuation of the existing free trade arrangements was never in question. What was uncertain was the degree to which a closer relationship between the EC and the EFTA countries would develop. Generally, the EFTA countries pressed for a closer relationship, in part to obtain the benefits of participating in a larger market, in part out of fear of EC protectionism—the possibility that a "Fortress Europe" would result from the 1992 single market program. The EC was receptive to expanding its relationship with the EFTA countries, and the result was an agreement, signed in May 1992, on a European Economic Area (EEA). The agreement came into force on January 1, 1994, as noted in the *Opel Austria* case in Chapter 27(C) supra.

The EEA agreement provides for very close economic ties between the Community and the EFTA countries (save for Switzerland, which has not joined the EEA). For the three EFTA countries that joined the EC in 1995 (Austria, Finland and Sweden), the agreement eased their accession since they were required under the EEA to adopt many EC measures. For the remaining EFTA countries in the EEA (Iceland, Liechtenstein and Norway), the agreement ensures that they will have a privileged position among the Community's trading partners.

The EEA agreement is divided into six substantive parts, dealing with free movement of goods, free movement of persons, services and capital, competition and other common rules, miscellaneous provisions relevant to the four freedoms, cooperation outside the four freedoms and institutional provisions. Although it is very broad, the agreement does not create a customs union, the EFTA states remain free to follow their own commercial policies toward the rest of the world.

---

2. Declaration issued following Ministerial meeting between the European Community and its Member States and the States of the European Free Trade Association (Luxembourg, April 9, 1984), reproduced in Bull. EC 1984–4, p. 9.

In respect of free movement of goods, the agreement prohibits customs duties and charges having equivalent effect, internal taxation that discriminates against imports, as well as import and export quotas, subject to exceptions of the sort permitted by Article 30 of the EC Treaty. In addition, the agreement provides that antidumping measures, countervailing duties and measures against illicit commercial practices (see Chapter 31 infra) shall not be applied to trade between the parties. There are, however, special rules for agricultural and maritime products, coal, steel and energy. Indeed, fishing rights were one of the most controversial issues at the conclusion of the negotiations.

The agreement provides for free movement of workers among the EC Member States and the other EEA countries. It specifically requires the abolition of any discrimination based on nationality as regards employment, remuneration and other conditions of work and employment. The agreement also contains provisions on coordination of social security rules and for the mutual recognition of diplomas.

Freedom of establishment is instituted under terms similar to the EC Treaty, as is the freedom to provide services. There are special provisions applicable to transport services, where the issue of transalpine trucking rights proved to be very controversial. The agreement also provides for the free movement of capital, subject to various derogations and safeguard measures.

The agreement's rules on competition are similar to those in the EC Treaty. Application of the rules is complicated, however, by a division of enforcement responsibility between the Commission and the so-called EFTA Surveillance Authority, a body established by the EFTA states. The Surveillance Authority essentially has jurisdiction of Article 81–type cases (i) when only trade between EFTA states is involved, (ii) when only trade between one EC member state and EFTA states is involved and 33% or more of the turnover in the EEA of the involved undertakings is in the EFTA states, and (iii) when the effects on trade between EC Member States are negligible. Article 82–type cases are handled depending on where the dominant position exists. Where it exists in both the EC and an EFTA jurisdiction(s), the rules for Article 81–type cases are applied. Mergers subject to control under the EC merger regulation are to be handled in accordance with that regulation, with the EFTA Surveillance Authority handling other mergers subject to the agreement (without prejudice to the rights of EC Member States to deal with such mergers). The authority is based in Brussels, is headed by a three-person body appointed for four-year terms and is assisted by a staff, which numbered about 50 in 2001.

In the case of state aids, the agreement contains a provision similar to Article 87 of the EC Treaty. It also provides for the review of all existing systems of aid, by the EC in the case of EC Member States and by the EFTA Surveillance Authority in case of the EFTA countries.

The EEA agreement contains provisions on social policy, consumer protection, environment and company law. The approach taken in this part of the EEA agreement is to set out a general statement in which the parties recognize the importance of the subject and then to provide that the EC measures listed in various annexes will be adopted by the other EEA countries. The chapter on the environment specifically provides that parties may maintain or introduce more stringent protective measures so long as they are compatible with the EEA agreement.

Finally, the EEA agreement provides for cooperation between the EC and the other EEA states in a number of subject areas, including research and technical development; information services; the environment; education, training and youth; social policy; consumer protection; small and medium-sized enterprises; tourism; the audiovisual sector; and civil protection. The EEA countries also agreed to contribute to a "cohesion fund" for the benefit of the EC's poorer Member States.

From this outline of the substantive provisions of the EEA agreement, it should be clear that the obligations of the EEA states are similar in many respects to the obligations of EC Member States under the EC Treaty. This is underscored by the fact that the many annexes to the agreement list approximately 1500 EC legislative measures that they agree to observe. In the first seven years of the EEA that list grew to 3800.

The institutional provisions of the EEA are complex. While the EEA states do not have the right to participate directly in EC decision-making, when the EC decides to adopt or amend legislation covered by the agreement, it informs them and consults with them. When such new EC legislation is adopted, the EEA Joint Committee (composed of representatives of the EC and the other EEA states, with each side having one vote) normally includes the legislation in the coverage of the EEA agreement. If the Joint Committee is unable to agree to apply the new measure, it considers whether there are acceptable alternatives. If none can be found, the EEA states are not bound by the new measure.

In addition, the Joint Committee is charged with promoting the uniform interpretation of the provisions of the EEA agreement and Community law and is empowered to settle any dispute over interpretation of the EEA agreement. Its activities in this regard do not affect the case law of the Court of Justice. However, as part of this function, it is authorized to ask the Court of Justice to give a ruling on the interpretation of the relevant provisions. The Court of Justice is of the opinion that its rulings in such cases would be binding on all parties. European Economic Area, Opinion 1/92, [1992] ECR I–2821.

The agreement also establishes an EEA Council, to which problems under the agreement may be referred. It consists of representatives of the EC Council and Commission and of the other EEA states. Council decisions are to be made by agreement between the EC and EEA representatives.

Also, an EFTA Court has been created to hear appeals from the EFTA Surveillance Authority and disputes between EFTA states. It also gives advisory opinions to courts in EFTA states on interpretation of EEA rules. The EFTA Court has jurisdiction only within the framework of EFTA and has no personnel or functional links to the Court of Justice. The EFTA Court is based in Luxembourg and consists of three judges (one from each EFTA State) assisted by a dozen staff members. It hears only a handful of cases per year.

Finally, the EEA agreement provides that courts in an EEA state can request the Court of Justice to decide on the interpretation of a provision of the EEA agreement which is identical in substance to a provision of Community law. The Court of Justice views that its decision in such a case would be binding.

Notes and Questions

1. The EEA structure is quite elaborate given that only Iceland, Liechtenstein and Norway participate. Initially, some thought that the EEA could be used more broadly as a stage in the accession process (e.g., for Eastern Europe), but that has not happened. For the moment, it does not seem likely that Iceland or Norway will soon join the EU. Norwegian voters have twice rejected accession after the Norwegian government had negotiated it (1972 and 1994), although as the EU expands to the East, Norway may conclude that accession is needed to avoid marginalization in European affairs. In any event, Iceland seems unlikely to subject its prized fishing industry to the common fisheries policy.

2. Despite the rejection by Swiss voters of EEA membership (and the resultant cessation of accession negotiations), the EC and Switzerland continue to work toward closer economic integration. In 1999, the EC and Switzerland reached agreements dealing with free movement of persons, air and land transport, agriculture, public procurement, research and mutual recognition. Switzerland ratified the agreements in October 2000, following a 67% approval vote in a referendum. The European Parliament has approved the agreements, but not yet all of the Member States. While the Swiss government continues to plan for eventual accession despite voter turndown of the EEA, it opposed a 2001 referendum calling for the immediate opening of accession negotiations. The referendum lost by a wide margin, although a significant part of the opposition (including the government's) was based on a belief that such negotiations would be premature, not that they would be ultimately undesirable. Nonetheless, it is not clear that Switzerland will soon be ready for accession.

3. One of the difficult issues in the EEA negotiations was the question of precisely how EFTA or the EFTA countries could be given some role in EC decisions that affect the EEA and what effect such a role would have on the EC decision-making process. For example, would it make the process more cumbersome and slower? How would votes be weighted? How was this issue resolved? How much influence will the EFTA countries have in your view? Do you think that countries that do not undertake the full burdens of EC membership should have any special input into EC decision-making?

4. The EEA agreement gave rise to the following important Court of Justice opinion on the institutional structure of the EC and the position of the Court of Justice in that structure.

EUROPEAN ECONOMIC AREA

Opinion 1/91, [1991] ECR I–6084.

[As initially agreed upon, the EEA agreement established an EEA Court, to consist of five judges from the Court of Justice and three chosen by the EFTA states. The EEA Court would have heard, inter alia, disputes concerning the application of the EEA agreement referred to it by the Joint Committee or a party to the EEA. In considering the agreement's consistency with the EC Treaty, the Court of Justice first noted the fundamental differences between the EC and the EEA.]

13   Before considering the questions raised by the Commission's request for an opinion, it is appropriate to compare the aims and context of the agreement, on the one hand, with those of the Community, on the other.

14   The fact that the provisions of the agreement and the corresponding Community provisions are identically worded does not mean that they must be interpreted identically. An international agreement is to be interpreted not only on the basis of its wording, but also in light of its objectives.

[The Court then contrasted the objectives of the EEA, which it noted "concerned * * * free trade and competition * * * between the Contracting Parties" (para. 15) with the objectives of the Community, where the EEC Treaty "aims to achieve economic integration" and the Single European Act made it clear that "the objective of all of the Community treaties is to contribute together to making concrete progress towards European unity" (para. 17). In then examined the context in which the EEA and the Community agreements were situated.]

20   The EEA is to be established on the basis of an international treaty which, essentially, merely creates rights and obligations as between the Contracting Parties and provides for no transfer of sovereign rights to the intergovernmental institutions which it sets up.

21   In contrast, the EEC Treaty, albeit concluded in the form of an international agreement, none the less constitutes the constitutional charter of a Community based on the rule of law. As the Court of Justice has consistently held, the Community treaties established a new legal order for the benefit of which the States have limited their sovereign rights, in ever wider fields, and the subjects of which comprise not only Member States but also their nationals (citing *Van Gend & Loos*). The essential characteristics of the Community legal order which has thus been established are in particular its primacy over the law of the Member States and the direct effect of a whole series of provisions which are applicable to their nationals and to the Member States themselves.

[The Court accordingly concluded that these divergences stood in the way of achieving the objective of homogeneity in the interpretation and application of the two treaties. It then switched to an examination of whether the proposed system of courts might undermine the autonomy of the Community legal order in pursuing its own particular objectives.]

33   The expression "Contracting Parties" is defined in Article 2(c) of the agreement. As far as the Community and its Member States are concerned, it covers the Community and the Member States, or the Community, or the Member States, depending on the case. Which of the three possibilities is to be chosen is to be deduced in each case from the relevant provisions of the agreement and from the respective competences of the Community and the Member States as they follow from the EEC Treaty and the ECSC Treaty.

34   This means that, when a dispute relating to the interpretation or application of one or more provisions of the agreement is brought before it, the EEA Court may be called upon to interpret the expression "Contracting Party", within the meaning of Article 2(c) of the agreement, in order to

determine whether, for the purposes of the provision at issue, the expression "Contracting Party" means the Community, the Community and the Member States, or simply the Member States. Consequently, the EEA Court will have to rule on the respective competences of the Community and the Member States as regards the matters governed by the provisions of the agreement.

35   It follows that the jurisdiction conferred on the EEA Court under Article 2(c), Article 96(1)(a) and Article 117(1) of the agreement is likely adversely to affect the allocation of responsibilities defined in the Treaties and, hence, the autonomy of the Community legal order, respect for which must be assured by the Court of Justice pursuant to Article 164 [now 220] of the EEC Treaty. This exclusive jurisdiction of the Court of Justice is confirmed by Article 219 [now 292] of the EEC Treaty, under which Member States undertake not to submit a dispute concerning the interpretation or application of that treaty to any method of settlement other than those provided for in the Treaty. Article 87 of the ECSC Treaty embodies a provision to the same effect.

* * *

40   An international agreement providing for [its own] system of courts is in principle compatible with Community law. The Community's competence in the field of international relations and its capacity to conclude international agreements necessarily entails the power to submit to the decisions of a court which is created or designated by such an agreement as regards the interpretation and application of its provisions. [The Court then noted the difference here, where there was overlap between the agreements and their provisions.]

* * *

47   The threat posed by the court system set up by the agreement to the autonomy of the Community legal order is not reduced by the fact that Articles 95 and 101 of the agreement seek to create organic links between the EEA Court and the Court of Justice by providing that judges from the Court of Justice are to sit on the EEA Court and in its chambers. * * *

48   On the contrary, it is to be feared that the application of those provisions will accentuate the general problems arising from the court system to be set up by the agreement.

49   In this connection, it should be borne in mind that the EEA Court is to ensure the sound operation of rules on free trade and competition under an international treaty which creates obligations only between the Contracting Parties.

50   In contrast, the Court of Justice has to secure observance of a particular legal order and to foster its development with a view to achieving the objectives set out in particular in Articles 2, 8a and 102a [now 2, 18 and 98] of the EEC Treaty and to attaining a European Union among the Member States, as is stated in the Solemn Declaration of Stuttgart of 19 June 1983 (section 2.5) referred to in the first recital in the preamble to the Single European Act. In that context, free trade and competition are merely means of achieving those objectives.

[51] Consequently, depending on whether they are sitting on the Court of Justice or on the EEA Court, the judges of the Court of Justice who are members of the EEA Court will have to apply and interpret the same provisions but using different approaches, methods and concepts in order to take account of the nature of each treaty and of its particular objectives.

[52] In those circumstances, it will be very difficult, if not impossible, for those judges, when sitting in the Court of Justice, to tackle questions with completely open minds where they have taken part in determining those questions as members of the EEA Court.

[53] However, since the judicial system set up by the agreement is in any event incompatible with the EEC Treaty it is unnecessary to give fuller consideration to this question or to the question whether the system is not liable to raise serious doubts as to the confidence which individuals are entitled to have in the ability of the Court of Justice to carry out its functions in complete independence.

* * *

[69] In its last question, the Commission asks whether Article 238 [now 310] of the EEC Treaty, which deals with the conclusion by the Community of association agreements with a third State, a union of States or an international organization, authorizes the establishment of a system of courts as provided for in this agreement. The Commission stated in this connection that, in the event that the Court were to answer this question in the negative, Article 238 could be amended so as to permit such a system to be set up.

[70] As already pointed out in paragraph 40, an international agreement providing for a system of courts, including a court with jurisdiction to interpret its provisions, is not in principle incompatible with Community law and may therefore have Article 238 of the EEC Treaty as its legal basis.

[71] However, Article 238 [now 310] of the EEC Treaty does not provide any basis for setting up a system of courts which conflicts with Article 164 [now 220] of the EEC Treaty and, more generally, with the very foundations of the Community.

[72] For the same reasons, an amendment of Article 238 in the way indicated by the Commission could not cure the incompatibility with Community law of the system of courts to be set up by the agreement.

Notes and Questions

1. This is an important "constitutional" case that expresses important principles in respect of the organization of the Community and the role and powers of its institutions.

2. The Commission had suggested that Article 310 could be amended to permit association agreements to contain the sort of judicial arrangements proposed for the EEA. In paragraphs 71 and 72 of its opinion, is the Court suggesting that certain basic principles of the Community (such as the court system) cannot be altered, even by amendment; or only that an amendment of Article 310 cannot alter the basic principles of the Community's judicial system? What is the authority for either position?

2. CENTRAL AND EASTERN EUROPE

a. *History of EC–Eastern European Relations*

Prior to the Second World War there was extensive trade between the countries of Eastern and Western Europe. In 1938 some 70% of Eastern European trade was with Western European countries. Thirty years later that figure had shrunk to 20%. Eastern European trade has long been a much less important component of overall Western European trade. It amounted to some 9–10% of such trade before the war, but only one-half that in the early 1970s. These changes were due in large part to the postwar division of Europe into opposing political camps.

As the Cold War in Europe ended at the outset of the 1990s, and the East European countries became more democratic and market-oriented, commercial relations between the Community and the countries of Eastern Europe grew much closer. Indeed, the great economic success of the Community compared to Eastern Europe was an important factor in spurring the recent political and economic changes in that region. It is, however, useful to trace the evolution of EC–East European relations over time, so as to put the recent developments in context.

The formation of the EC was not welcomed by the Soviet Union and its East European allies. It was initially denounced as a capitalist tool doomed to fail. The Soviet bloc did, however, respond to the creation of the Community and in 1962 the Council for Mutual Economic Assistance (the CMEA or COMECON) became more active as a rival multilateral trade organization. Its initial members were the Soviet Union and its East European allies. Although sometimes compared to the EC, COMECON was a very different organization. It served mainly as a coordinating body through which long term trade agreements were concluded between its constituent members. These agreements often involved so-called countertrade, i.e. the barter of one product for another, rather than the exchange of goods and services for money.

During the 1970s and the early 1980s, the trading relationships between the Community and the individual East European countries did not develop significantly. In 1974, when the EC took over management of Member State trade relationships with the countries of Eastern Europe, it did not adopt a comprehensive policy towards them because they refused to negotiate commercial agreements with the EC. Instead it largely continued the prior policies of the individual Member States under the auspices of the Community. The result was that much of the trade between the EC and the countries of Eastern Europe was subject to individual Member States quotas. While the Community set and adjusted the quotas, this was done in large part in accordance with the wishes of the affected Member States.

Although the EC and COMECON commenced negotiations in 1977, little progress was made until the issuance of a joint declaration in 1988 in which the two sides established official relations with each other and agreed to develop cooperation in areas within their respective spheres of competence.[3] This essentially meant that the Community was free to negotiate trade

---

3. Joint Declaration on the Establishment of Official Relations Between the European Economic Community and the Council for Mu- tual Economic Assistance, O.J. L 157/35 (June 24, 1988).

agreements directly with the various East European countries, which it began to do. Its relationship with COMECON was short-lived, however, because by 1991 COMECON was defunct.

After the joint declaration with COMECON in 1988, Community relations with the East began to improve and developments in EC–East European trading relationships further accelerated as the Communist regimes in Eastern Europe fell one after the other. In the course of the 1990s, the Community entered into association agreements, known as "Europe Agreements," with the countries of Eastern Europe. These agreements are much more comprehensive than past EC association agreements. Most significantly, the agreements explicitly provided for the possibility that the countries could accede to the EU in the future.

The Europe Agreements are open-ended, with a general ten-year transitional period. In addition to trade-related provisions, the agreements contain provisions on political dialogue (aimed at coordinating foreign policy positions) and on broad-based cooperation in the economic, financial and cultural spheres. They are aimed at establishing free trade arrangements between the Community and the countries of Bulgaria, the Czech Republic, Estonia, Hungary, Latvia, Lithuania, Poland, Romania, Slovenia and the Slovak Republic.

The agreements do not provide for free movement of workers, but contain provisions aimed at improving the situation of workers legally established in the EC. With regard to the right of establishment, the agreements call for national treatment to be afforded for the establishment of companies and professions. There are also rules that require liberalization of financial transfers related to the free movement of goods, services or persons and direct investment.

In addition, the ten countries agree to adopt rules on competition based on the Community's rules. Indeed, in general, the countries are to adapt much of their legislation to EC legislation, which is one of the prerequisites for their successful economic integration into the Community.

b. The Accession of the Countries of Central and Eastern Europe

Since the establishment of democratic governments in Central and Eastern Europe in the 1989–1991 period, the countries of that region have sought ultimately to join the European Union. As noted above, the Europe Agreements with the ten countries of the region explicitly foresee the possibility of accession. Cyprus, Malta and Turkey have the same aspiration. Consequently, all 13 countries have applied for membership in the EU.

Article 49 of the Treaty on European Union provides that any European State that respects the principles of Article 6(1) of the Treaty (liberty, democracy, respect for human rights and fundamental freedoms, and the rule of law) may apply to the Council for membership. Ultimately, the Council must act unanimously on applications, after consulting the Commission and receiving the assent of the Parliament. The conditions of accession and any adjustments to the existing treaties are set out in an agreement between the applicant and the other Member States.

The basic criteria that countries must meet to join the EU were elaborated at the 1993 Copenhagen European Council as follows:

— the stability of institutions guaranteeing democracy, the rule of law, human rights and respect for and protections of minorities (the so-called political criterion);

— the existence of a functioning market economy as well as the capacity to cope with competitive pressure and market forces within the EU (the economic criterion); and

— the ability to take on the obligations of membership including adherence to the aims of political, economic and monetary union (the *acquis communitaire* criterion).

Following the applications of the 13 countries mentioned above, the Commission evaluated the political, economic and administrative conditions of the applicants and issued opinions in respect thereof. As a result of those evaluations, in 1998, the EU opened negotiations with six candidate countries: Cyprus, the Czech Republic, Estonia, Hungary, Poland and Slovenia. Subsequently, in 2000, negotiations were opened with Bulgaria, Latvia, Lithuania, Malta, Romania and the Slovak Republic. As described in the notes following this section, negotiations have not been opened with Turkey.

In considering the actual process of accession negotiations for the various applicants, it is useful to examine each of the above-mentioned three criteria.

First, in respect of the political criterion, there have been some concerns raised simply because the ten former Communist countries have only a decade's worth of experience as democracies, with modern judicial systems based upon the rule of law. Moreover, there have been specific concerns regarding human rights (e.g., the rights of Russian residents in the Baltic states; the rights of gypsies in central Europe) and the rule of law (e.g., existence of organized crime and government corruption). In the accession process, the EU puts considerable pressure on candidate countries to demonstrate that they are effectively dealing with issues such as these. It also funds programs designed to promote respect for human rights and the rule of law, including through education programs for national judges in EC legal principles.

Second, in respect of the economic criterion, the focus is on whether the candidates have viable market economies. In particular, the issue is whether their economic institutions and firms can cope with the competitive and market forces that will ensue when they enter the Union. This is a serious concern since most of the applicant countries had state-controlled economies until recently. The experience of integrating the economies of the two parts of Germany following reunification has demonstrated that even with very substantial government assistance for infrastructure projects and other reforms, the task is a formidable one. Similar problems may well arise in integrating the candidate countries into the EU. In this regard, it should be mentioned that part of the accession process involves substantial Community financial assistance to help address potential problem areas.

Third, and of fundamental importance, is the *acquis communitaire* criterion.[4] New members must take on all obligations contained in the treaties, as well as subscribe to the broad statements of objectives for the future such as are contained in Article 2 of the TEU. In that sense, the negotiations on the *acquis* would seem to be straightforward. The candidate countries must accept the *acquis*. Thus, the end-point of the negotiating process is clear; and the only issues are in respect of transitions—both for the candidates and the Member States. In practical terms, the negotiations are organized around 31 chapters covering all aspects of the *acquis*. In the negotiations on each chapter, the EU indicates what is required to implement the acquis, the parties evaluate what has been (and is planned to be) done in respect of such implementation, consider whether transitional provisions will be needed and discuss ways in which the EU can facilitate implementation. In particular, it is likely that compliance with EC environmental rules will be exceedingly expensive for the candidates and will take some time to accomplish.

In respect of the first group of candidates, preliminary discussions had been held on all 31 chapters as of July 2001, with negotiations on 29 chapters having been formally opened (all but the chapters on institutions and "other"). Negotiations had been preliminarily closed on two-thirds to three-quarters of the chapters (there being considerable variation across the candidates as to which chapters were closed). In general, however, the open chapters involved the more difficult topics—free movement of workers, agriculture, competition, transport, taxation, regional matters, justice and home affairs, and financial matters. In the case of free movement of workers, it is likely that there will be some transition period before all the Member States must recognize this right, Germany and Austria having expressed particular concerns on this issue. At the same time, some of the candidate countries are concerned with opening land ownership to non-citizens.

The Commission reports regularly and in detail on the state of the negotiations, discussing the extent to which the three basic criteria have been met. In the case of the *acquis*, the Commission reports, which are available at the Commission website, contain a very detailed discussion of the state of implementation. An accession agreement will be finalized only when the EU is satisfied that the candidate is ready for and able to undertake EU membership.

At the same time, the existing Member States must decide on how they are willing to accommodate themselves to new members. One of the more difficult issues in the current accession process was the institutional question of how many votes the candidate countries would have under the qualified majority voting rules. This issue was resolved, along with some other institutional issues, in the Nice Treaty's Protocol on the Enlargement of the European Union and related declarations. There remain financial issues, however. Exactly how much support for agriculture, regional development and so forth will the EU be able to afford to provide to the new members, who are generally much less well off than most Member States? Will the pace of accession have to be slowed so that the new member states can be accommodated financially? The rejection of the Nice Treaty by Irish voters in a 2001

---

4. The meaning of this term has been elaborated upon by Professor Goebel in Roger J. Goebel, The European Union Grows: The Constitutional Impact of the Accession of Austria, Finland and Sweden, 18 Fordham J. Intl. L. 1092, 1140–1157 (1995).

referendum seemed to be based in part on an unwillingness to agree to future reductions in EU regional assistance to Ireland.

At the Nice and Göteborg European Councils (December 2000/June 2001), it was agreed that negotiations with the best prepared candidates should be concluded before the end of 2002 so that they would be able to participate in the 2004 elections for the European Parliament. Speculation on whether this target date will be met is probably unwise. An up-to-date view can be obtained from the Commission's website (Enlargement Directorate), including the most recent Commission report on each candidate.

Notes and Questions

1. The accession of Cyprus raises the question of whether the EU should admit only the Greek half of the island or whether a settlement of the long-running dispute between the Greek and Turkish halves should be required. The Helsinki European Council (December 1999) stressed that a settlement would facilitate accession, but was not a prerequisite.

2. The situation of Turkey has presented delicate problems for the EU. Turkey is a long-standing member of NATO and an important strategic ally of the EU. At the same time, Greece (a Member State since 1981) and Turkey have had stormy relations at times, including in the recent past. Moreover, while part of Turkey is in Europe, the vast majority of the country is in Asia and it is overwhelming Muslim, unlike Europe. However, the 1963 association agreement with Turkey foresaw possible accession (as did the 1961 agreement with Greece) and that association agreement has led to the formation of the EC–Turkey customs union. Moreover, the Luxembourg (December 1997) and Helsinki (December 1999) European Councils confirmed Turkey's eligibility for EU membership.

Negotiations have not yet been opened with Turkey, although in March 2001, the Council decided on an accession partnership program with Turkey. In its November 2000 report on Turkey, the Commission concluded that Turkey does not meet the political criteria for entering into accession negotiations. In particular, there are concerns over human rights, i.e. treatment of the Kurdish population, and the need for institutional reforms to guarantee democracy and the rule of law. The Commission recognized progress in the other areas, but noted that much remained to be done there as well.

3. In respect of the Balkans, in April 2001, the EU signed a stabilization and association agreement with Macedonia. Albania and the other components of former Yugoslavia (except of course for Slovenia, which is on the fast track to accession) are likely to negotiate such agreements over the next few years. These countries would all seem to be future candidates for accession, but perhaps not for some time.

4. The EC has negotiated partnership and cooperation agreements with the twelve non-Baltic former Soviet republics. The agreement with Russia came into force in 1997, that with Ukraine in 1998 and the others (except for Belarus and Turkmenistan) in 1999. These agreements generally provide for WTO (most-favored-nation), not preferential, treatment for trade in goods. Unlike the Europe Agreements, there is no mention of possible EU membership for Russia or the other non-Baltic former Soviet republics in their partnership agreements.

3. EC MEDITERRANEAN AND OTHER ASSOCIATION AGREE-MENTS

Article 310 (ex 238) of the EC Treaty provides that the Community and other countries may enter into association agreements establishing reciprocal rights and obligations, common action and special procedures. The Community has relied on this provision to enter into a number of different kinds of agreements. In particular, these agreements have been used in respect of countries bordering the Mediterranean Sea.

Typically, the initial series of agreements with the Mediterranean countries provided for duty-and quota-free imports of industrial goods and reduced duties for some agricultural products. In addition, they provided for economic and technical assistance to these countries in the form of grants and loans. The agreements also required the parties to promote private investment and cooperate in a wide range of activities, such as science, technology, environmental protection and fisheries. In addition, there were provisions on migrant labor, which provided that the workers of one party working in the other party were to be free from any discrimination based on nationality as regards such issues as working conditions, remuneration and social security benefits. As noted in Chapter 27(C) supra, some of these provisions have been found to have direct effect. Each agreement also established procedures for high-level meetings to coordinate implementation and resolve any disputes between the EC and the country involved.

The initial association agreement was with Greece in 1961, followed by an association agreement with Turkey in 1963. Although these agreements contemplated the possibility of future EC membership for Greece and Turkey, only Greece has become a Member State. As noted above, Turkey is now considered a potential future candidate country for accession. The Community subsequently entered into association agreements with Malta (1971) and Cyprus (1973), both of which are now negotiating EU membership. In addition, in the course of the 1970s, as a part of the Community's Mediterranean program, the Community entered into broad-based cooperation agreements with Israel, the Maghreb countries (Algeria, Morocco and Tunisia), the Mashreq countries (Egypt, Jordan, Lebanon and Syria) and Yugoslavia (1980).[5] The net effect of these various agreements was to provide the Mediterranean countries with a relatively favorable status among the trading partners of the Community.

For the future, the Barcelona Partnership Declaration of November 1995 sets the rather ambitious target of a free trade zone by 2010 between the EC and Algeria, Morocco, Tunisia, Egypt, Israel, Jordan, Lebanon, the Palestinian autonomous territories, Syria, Turkey, Cyprus and Malta. To implement the Barcelona Declaration, the EC is in the process of negotiating so-called Euro–Med agreements with most Mediterranean countries. These agreements will cover more than trade in goods. They have political aspects, calling for respect of human rights and democratic principles. Trade in agricultural products and services are to be gradually liberalized. They also provide for harmonization of rules in such areas as intellectual property, procurement and competition rules. Finally, they contain provisions on cooperation on various issues. In

---

5. The agreement with Yugoslavia was de-nounced in late 1991, although its benefits were effectively maintained for parts of Yugoslavia.

that regard, the EC has committed significant funding to promote economic development. The agreements do not have accession clauses (as did the Europe Agreements). As of the end of 2000, new agreements were in force with Israel, Morocco and Tunisia, and an interim agreement was in effect with the Palestinian Authority. Negotiations had been completed with Egypt and Jordan and were ongoing with Algeria, Lebanon and Syria. Cyprus and Malta are now in accession negotiations, and Turkey entered into a customs union with the EC in 1996.

B.   THE EC AND THE DEVELOPING WORLD

The original members of the European Economic Community had extensive colonial holdings in 1957, and the United Kingdom, which joined the Community in 1973, headed a commonwealth organization made up of former British colonies. Thus, from the outset, the EC has had to deal with trade relations between the Member States and their colonies, most of which soon became independent countries. In addition, it had to develop a commercial policy toward developing countries that had no special ties with the various Member States. In this section, we examine briefly how it has dealt with these countries.

1.   THE LOMÉ CONVENTIONS AND THE COTONOU AGREEMENT

The first association agreement involving the EC and the developing world was the Yaoundé Convention of 1963 between the Community and 18 former French and Belgian African colonies. Six years later the second Yaoundé Convention was concluded for the period 1969–1975 and the Community entered into the Arusha Agreement with Kenya, Tanzania and Uganda. These agreements dealt with trade issues and also provided for financial and technical aid. With the accession of the United Kingdom in 1973, it became necessary to consider how to establish analogous relations with Commonwealth countries. The result was the first Lomé Convention, signed in 1975 between the Community and its Member States and 46 countries in Africa, the Caribbean and the Pacific (often called the "ACP countries"). Lomé I was followed by Lomé II (signed in 1979), Lomé III (signed in 1984) and Lomé IV (signed in 1989). The first three Lomé agreements had terms of 5 years; Lomé IV was concluded for a ten year period ending March 1, 2000.[6] At present, the 70 ACP countries include all African states (except those bordering the Mediterranean), Belize, Guyana, Surinam and over 25 island countries in the Caribbean Sea, the Indian Ocean and the South Pacific.

The Lomé conventions emphasize cooperation between the ACP countries and the Community. That cooperation takes several forms, including preferential trade treatment and financial and technical assistance. First, as to trade, the conventions have provided duty-free and quota-free access to EC markets. Only some agricultural products are excepted, and the ACP countries generally receive preferential treatment as to those products as well. The ACP countries in return pledge to the Community most favored nation treatment in respect of EC products and any investment protection agreements negotiated under the convention.

---

6.   The text of Lomé IV is found in O.J. L 229/3 (August 17, 1991). It came into effect on Sept. 1, 1991.

Second, Lomé I established the so-called Stabex system to stabilize the earnings of the ACP countries on exports to the EC. The export earnings of many of those countries have traditionally depended on agricultural commodities (foodstuffs and other raw materials) and have been subject to significant fluctuations as the prices of those commodities are often subject to wide swings on world markets. As modified in Lomé IV, the Stabex system applies if a country's export earnings from one of 49 designated agricultural commodities exceed five percent of its total export earnings (one percent in the case of the least developed, landlocked and island countries). Essentially, the Stabex system compensates a country to the extent that its export earnings from a covered commodity fall below a reference level based on the six prior years. The country is responsible for a portion of the shortfall, but not more than 4.5% (one percent in the case of the least developed developing countries) of the reference level. Thus, if a country is particularly dependent on export earnings from one or more of the covered commodities and world prices or demand falls, much of the decline in export earnings will be covered by the Community.

In addition to Stabex, the Community has participated in a number of commodities agreements negotiated under the auspices of UNCTAD and others, such as the natural rubber agreement discussed in Chapter 27(B)(2) supra. These agreements are also aimed at stabilizing prices and providing assistance to developing countries.

Third, Lomé II established the Sysmin system, which is designed to help ACP countries that are heavily dependent on the export of mining products. It applies where a country derives 15% of its export earnings from one of the covered minerals or 20% of such earnings from all mining products (excluding precious metals other than gold, gas and oil).

Fourth, Lomé IV provides for financial and technical cooperation. The areas of cooperation are wide-ranging: the environment, agriculture and rural development, fisheries, commodities, industrial and enterprise development, mining, energy, development of services (including tourism and modern telecommunications) and trade and cultural and regional cooperation. In its provisions on environmental cooperation, Lomé IV requires the EC to prohibit the export of toxic waste to the ACP countries.

Lomé IV is to be replaced by the Cotonou Agreement, which was signed by 77 ACP countries in June 2000 and will last for 20 years. From the EC perspective, there are five pillars of the Cotonou Agreement. First, it has a comprehensive political dimension in which respect for human rights, democratic principles and the rules of law is stressed. Second, the agreement promotes a participatory approach that promotes the involvement of civil society. Third, as for development, the key objective is poverty reduction. As to trade, the agreement continues the provisions of Lomé IV through 2008, by which time it is expected that there will be a new economic partnership (free-trade area) in place, to be implemented by 2020. Finally, the agreement provides for expanded EC financial contributions (E20 billion over 5–7 years).

2. ASIAN AND LATIN AMERICAN COUNTRIES

Most of the developing countries of Latin America and Asia are not in ACP group. The EC has, however, been pursuing increasingly closer relations with many of these countries. For example, since 1971 it has extended preferential tariff treatment to them as part of its generalized system of preferences (GSP). This system provides duty free treatment for industrial products and reduced duties on agricultural products. The benefits provided under the EC's GSP scheme are not as favorable as those provided under the Lomé Convention or the various Mediterranean agreements, in particular because for some sensitive products there are quantitative limits on the preferences granted. In the 1980s, the EC embarked on a program of negotiating cooperation agreements with individual countries (such as Argentina, Brazil, Mexico and Uruguay in Latin America and Bangladesh, India, Pakistan and Sri Lanka in Asia) and regional groupings (such as the Andean Pact, the Association of South–East Asian Nations (ASEAN) and the Gulf Cooperation Council). Generally these agreements are framework agreements that cover trade, economic cooperation and development cooperation.

More recently, the EC has signed a free-trade agreement with Mexico and is negotiating free-trade agreements with Chile and Mercosur. The new agreement with Mexico was inspired in large part to counter the effects of the North American Free Trade Agreement (NAFTA)—a free trade agreement among Canada, Mexico and the United States. Under NAFTA, Canadian and US products enter Mexico at reduced (soon to be zero) rates. The EU–Mexico Free Trade Agreement, the trade provisions of which entered into force on July 1, 2000, will liberalize over 96% of EC–Mexico trade by 2007. By 2003, when industrialized products will be fully liberalized under NAFTA, all Mexican exports will enter the EC duty free and EC exports will be subject to maximum duty of 5% in Mexico. There will also be improved market access for specific agricultural products of interest to both parties. The agreement also contains provisions on government procurement, investment, services and intellectual property rights.

It will be interesting to see if the EC aggressively pursues additional free trade arrangements in the Western Hemisphere.

Notes and Questions

1.   From the perspective of developing countries, the value of preferential tariff treatment has been declining as tariff rates generally decline. The difference between a 30% tariff and tariff free treatment is significant; the difference between a 4% tariff (which is about the average tariff in the EC, Japan and the US) and a 0% tariff may not be. Should anything be done about this? What?

2.   Do you think that in the long run programs such as Stabex and Sysmin will have a tendency to reduce or to increase developing country reliance on commodity exports? Or is the degree of such reliance a product of other factors? The United States does not have any program analogous to Stabex or Sysmin, in part because of a belief in the beneficial effect of free-market forces. Would you agree with US or EC policy in this area?

3.   In recent years, the developing countries have pressed in GATT, the WTO and elsewhere for differential and more favorable treatment in many contexts. There is controversy over whether it has benefited from this approach. Some believe that developing countries would have been better off if they had not asked for special treatment, but rather had opened their economies to imports and promoted foreign investment, which would probably have resulted in expanded exports. Some of these issues are treated in R. Hudec, Developing Countries in the GATT Legal System (Gower 1987).

Chapter 29

THE COMMON COMMERCIAL POLICY: THE EC IN THE WTO

An introduction to the World Trade Organization (WTO)[1] is essential to an understanding of the EC's common commercial policy. The most important Court of Justice case on the scope of the EC's external powers concerns the EC's accession to the WTO. The WTO dispute settlement system is now the arena in which major trade disputes between the EC and other industrialized countries are resolved. The WTO is also the forum where the Community negotiates generally on international trade issues. In the GATT Uruguay Round negotiations (1986–1994), which led to the creation of the WTO, agricultural trade and subsidies were a major issue, directly impacting the EC common agricultural policy (CAP), which accounts for a majority of the Community's budgetary outlays. Indeed, much of the impetus in recent years to reform the CAP in recent years has come from the need for the Community to be in a position to negotiate in the WTO.

The Commission has a particularly important role in respect of international trade negotiations in light of the provisions on the common commercial policy in Article 133 (ex 113). Since the 1960's, it has been accepted as the Community spokesperson, first in GATT and now in the WTO. Indeed, except on budgetary and personnel issues, the Member State representatives typically do not utter a word at formal WTO meetings.

In this chapter, we describe the WTO, its basic principles and rules, and its dispute settlement system, highlighting those aspects of particular concern to the EC. We then examine two important Court of Justice decisions relating to the WTO. We conclude with an examination of EC–US relations.

A. THE WORLD TRADE ORGANIZATION

The Marrakesh Agreement Establishing the World Trade Organization assigns three important functions to the WTO. First, the WTO oversees the operation of the WTO agreements on international trade. These include (i) the General Agreement on Tariffs and Trade (GATT) and 12 related agree-

---

1. Extensive information on the WTO is available at www.wto.org.

ments on trade in goods dealing with agriculture, sanitary measures, textiles, technical barriers to trade, dumping, subsidies, safeguards, trade-related investment measures, customs valuation, import licensing, pre-shipment inspection and rules of origin; (ii) the General Agreement on Trade in Services (GATS); and (iii) the Agreement on Trade–Related Aspects of Intellectual Property (TRIPS Agreement). Second, the WTO serves as a forum for trade negotiations. Third, the WTO administers a dispute settlement system, described below, which has come to play a very significant role in EC–US relations.

The WTO Agreement does not contain a specific list of basic principles, but there are four that can be gleaned from its preamble and the rules of the various agreements: trade liberalization; nondiscrimination in international trade; fair trade; and transparency.

1. TRADE LIBERALIZATION

The preamble to the WTO Agreement calls for expansion of trade in goods and services so as to raise standards of living. This is to be accomplished through reciprocal arrangements to reduce substantially tariffs and other barriers to trade. The preamble also provides that this should be accomplished while allowing optimal use of the world's resources in accordance with the objective of sustainable development, so as to protect and preserve the environment. In addition, it recognizes the need for positive efforts to ensure that developing countries secure a share in the growth of international trade.

The WTO agreements implement the preamble's direction to reduce barriers to international trade by defining the types of barriers that are generally permitted and by limiting their use through negotiations. For example, in the area of trade in goods, the two principal instruments used by nations to keep out imports are tariffs and quotas. Under WTO rules, the use of quotas and other non-tariff barriers is severely restricted, and while tariffs are permitted, members are encouraged over time to reduce them. The WTO's ambitions in this are similar to those of Articles 23–31 of the EC Treaty, albeit more limited in scope and effect.

GATT Article II obligates WTO members not to charge tariffs in excess of maximum levels that they have negotiated for specific products. In GATT jargon, countries "bind" their tariffs on specific products. Beginning in 1947, GATT sponsored eight "rounds" of tariff negotiations, and as a result average tariff rates for the major industrialized countries have fallen from around 40% to less than 5%. Tariff negotiations are based upon the idea of reciprocity: each member offers tariff reductions so as to achieve a mutually acceptable balance. However, it is for each member to assess for itself whether it is satisfied with the outcome of a negotiation. Since different members make tariff concessions on different products, there is no GATT-wide rate for a specific product. Rather, the applicable bound tariff rates on a specific product vary from country to country.

The trade-increasing effects of an agreement to lower tariffs can be offset indirectly by any number of actions by the importing country. To counter this possibility, GATT contains provisions designed to protect the integrity of tariff bindings. For example, there is a separate agreement to standardize the valuation of goods for tariff assessment purposes and there are rules limiting the use of fees for customs inspections or other services.

GATT Article XI prohibits the use of quotas and other restrictions on imports besides duties. While it has not been interpreted as expansively as Article 28 of the EC Treaty, Article XI has been interpreted broadly. However, for most of GATT's history, trade in agricultural and textile products was largely conducted outside of GATT rules, and quotas and similar restrictions were common. With the advent of the WTO, these two sectors have been brought back under GATT disciplines.

In the case of agriculture, in the Agreement on Agriculture, WTO members agreed to convert their non-tariff import restrictions on agricultural products to tariffs and generally not to use such restrictions in the future. The initial tariffs were set at very high levels, but it is expected that they will be reduced over time. In addition, certain minimum market access is to be provided. As to domestic farm subsidies, developed WTO members agreed to cut specified domestic subsidies. The aim is to encourage the use of subsidies, such as direct income supports, that do not promote production or distort trade flows. In respect of export subsidies, the agreement requires that they be reduced over time.

The negotiation of the Agreement on Agriculture was quite difficult for the EC. The common agricultural policy (CAP), which came into existence in the 1960's was based on a number of basic principles, including a preference for Community production and a desire to attain self-sufficiency in basic agricultural products. The implementation of that policy resulted in high target prices being set for basic commodities produced in the Community, with the Community being the buyer of last resort. Over time, the CAP resulted in significant surpluses in some products where the Community had been a net importer (e.g., cereals and sugar). Since the Community was often the buyer of last resort, the CAP was a very expensive program but reform seemed almost impossible. The Community's use of export subsidies to reduce its costs by enabling Community surpluses to be marketed overseas caused tensions both with the United States, which countered with its own export promotion schemes, and with other agricultural exporters, who were unable to counter-subsidize and thus felt victimized by both the EC and the US.

To implement the Community preference, the EC kept out certain foreign agricultural products through the use of variable levies, which were charges on imports adjusted as frequently as necessary to make exporting to the Community unprofitable whatever the level of prevailing world prices. While never the subject of GATT dispute settlement, some argued that the levies were GATT-inconsistent. As the foregoing description of the WTO Agriculture Agreement indicates, the EC has had to change the CAP so as to convert its levies to tariffs and to allow some, albeit limited, access to EC markets. It has also had to limit its use of agricultural export subsidies.

In the case of textiles, starting in 1974, international trade between the developed and developing countries was conducted under the so-called Multi–Fibre Arrangement (MFA). Under the MFA, the EC and other developed countries negotiated specific quotas for the textile and apparel products. To meet concerns of developing countries, the WTO Agreement on Textiles and Clothing generally requires that MFA quotas be phased out in four stages, ending in 2005. Consequently, the EC is now phasing out its clothing and textile quotas.

Unlike GATT which dealt with services trade only incidentally, the WTO Agreement includes a General Agreement on Trade in Services (GATS). GATS defines trade in services as the supply of a service (i) from the territory of one member to another, (ii) in the territory of one member to a consumer of another member, and (iii) by a service supplier of one member through commercial presence or (iv) the presence of natural persons in the territory of another. This categorization resembles in part the way in which the EC has treated services (see Chapter 17 supra).

The basic obligation of GATS is to provide most-favored-nation treatment in respect of services and service suppliers, with the possibility of members listing specific exceptions, which are for at most 10 years and subject to negotiation in future liberalizing rounds. Insofar as market access is concerned, WTO members have made market opening commitments in specific service sectors. It is up to each member, in negotiations with others, to determine sectors in which its market access commitments are made. Those commitments may be made subject to qualifications. GATS contains a national treatment obligation, but it only applies in service sectors where market access commitments have been made and, moreover, may be made subject to qualifications. A new round of negotiations in the services area started in 2000. A major issue for the Community has been to avoid making commitments in the audio-visual sector. The sensitivity of this sector, particularly to the French, has led to special treatment of the sector (along with cultural, educational, social and health services) in Article 133 (discussed in section B below).

2. NONDISCRIMINATION

The second general principle and rule by which the WTO attempts to achieve its objective of increasing international trade and economic well being is to eliminate discrimination in international trade. GATT does this through two provisions: Article I—the most-favored-nation clause—which prohibits discrimination among foreign countries in certain trade matters and Article III—the national treatment clause—which prohibits discrimination between national and foreign products in certain trade matters.

GATT Article I—the so-called MFN clause—essentially bans discrimination based on the source of goods with respect to customs matters, internal taxes and internal sales regulations. If an advantage of any kind in respect of those subjects is extended to the products of one country it must immediately and unconditionally be extended to the like products coming from all WTO members. Thus, if a tariff of 5% is assessed on goods of one country, a higher tariff must not be assessed on like goods coming from WTO members. The most-favored-nation concept is very basic to GATT and many other GATT provisions contain MFN or similar nondiscrimination rules.

There are two major exceptions to the MFN obligation. First, it does not apply in the case of free trade areas and customs unions qualifying under GATT Article XXIV. The EC is, of course, the prime example of a customs union, and as noted in the preceding chapter, it has a network of free trade agreements with other countries. The second exception to the MFN requirement is that it does not preclude granting differential and more favorable treatment to developing countries, which the EC does in a number of ways, as discussed in the Chapter 28.

The national treatment clause of GATT Article III establishes the general principle that WTO members should not distinguish between products of domestic origin and those of foreign origin with respect to (i) internal taxes and charges, (ii) laws, regulations and requirements affecting the internal sale, offering for sale, purchase, transportation, distribution or use of products or (iii) internal quantitative regulations requiring the mixture, processing or use of products in specific amounts or proportions. The basic idea underlying Article III and the national treatment clause is that once goods have cleared border controls (tariffs paid, other entry conditions satisfied), they should be treated no differently than domestically produced goods. In the words of Article III:1, tax and regulatory measures "should not be applied to imported or domestic products so as to afford protection to domestic production." This has been interpreted to mean that a regulation must not adversely modify the conditions of competition between domestic and imported products. In the words of one panel report, Article III:4 requires effective equality of opportunities for imported products in so far as the application of internal sales regulations is concerned.

There have been several WTO/GATT cases in the sector of alcoholic beverages involving Article III:2's ban on discriminatory internal taxes. Although the cases have generally dealt only with distilled liquors and thus do not go as far as the EC cases under Article 90 (recall the cases in Chapter 12(B)), they obviously raise similar issues.

There are two important exceptions in the national treatment clause. These exceptions permit discrimination against imported goods in the case of government procurement policies and permit the payment of subsidies exclusively to domestic producers. As to government procurement, it should be noted that most industrialized WTO members, including the EC, are parties to an agreement on government procurement that requires national treatment in respect of procurement contracts entered into by certain government agencies where the contracts exceed certain threshold amounts. In the case of domestic subsidies, there are rules relating to their use in the WTO agreements on subsidies and agriculture.

3. PROMOTING FAIR INTERNATIONAL TRADE

The WTO agreements contain several provisions that can be characterized as fair trade provisions. Indeed, the whole of the TRIPS Agreement may be viewed in that light. In addition, GATT contains provisions dealing with the practice of dumping and the export of subsidized products, which are elaborated upon in separate agreements on dumping and subsidies.

GATT Article VI condemns, but does not prohibit, dumping, which is effectively defined as the sale of a product for export at a price below that charged in the home market or below that necessary to recover the cost of producing the product. It authorizes antidumping duties to be imposed to offset dumping if a country's domestic industry is materially injured. The EC's rules on imposition of antidumping duties, which are based on the WTO rules, are explored in Chapter 31.

Under the WTO Agreement on Subsidies and Countervailing Measures, a subsidy is defined as a financial contribution by a government or public body that confers a benefit. Under the agreement, export subsidies and subsidies contingent upon the use of domestic over imported goods are prohibited (except as allowed by the Agreement on Agriculture). The agreement contains an illustrative list of export subsidies. In addition, the agreement provides that no member should cause, through the use of any specific (i.e., not generally available), nonagricultural subsidy, adverse effects to the interests of other members. Three types of adverse interests are listed: injury to the domestic industry of another member; nullification or impairment of benefits accruing to other members under GATT rules (e.g., tariff bindings); and serious prejudice to the interests of another member. Finally, the agreement authorizes the use of countervailing duties if a specific subsidy causes material injury to a member's domestic industry. The EC rules on countervailing duties are discussed in Chapter 31.

The Agreement on Trade–Related Aspects of Intellectual Property Rights (TRIPS Agreement) is quite broad in scope. In general terms, it is designed to provide minimum levels of intellectual property protection, without creating new barriers to trade, and to provide a framework for dealing with international trade in counterfeit goods. The latter issue is of particular interest of the EC because of its production of luxury goods (e.g., perfumes). The TRIPS agreement's substantive obligations can be divided into three types. First, there is a series of basic principles, such as general MFN and national treatment obligations. Second, there are specified minimum standards of protection for copyrights, trademarks, geographical indications, industrial designs, patents, integrated circuits and trade secrets. This has resulted in some harmonization of intellectual property rights legislation in the EC, a subject of Chapter 19. Third, there are minimum standards required for the enforcement of intellectual property rights. For example, national judicial authorities must have the power to order provisional measures and to enjoin violations and award damages in appropriate cases.

4. TRANSPARENCY OF INTERNATIONAL TRADE REGULATIONS

One of the most useful underlying principles of the WTO Agreement promotes the transparency of international trade regulations. One major hindrance to international trade is the difficulty of finding out the rules that are applicable in faraway markets. The WTO's rules on transparency are designed to address this issue. There are three kinds of transparency provisions. First, GATT Article X requires the publication of laws, regulations, judicial decisions and administrative rulings pertaining to a wide range of trade matters. It also requires mechanisms to review decisions of lower level officials. Second, most WTO agreements require notification to the WTO of various laws and regulations affecting trade, in some cases in advance so that affected parties may comment. In addition, they often require WTO members to establish enquiry points where further information can be obtained about such laws and regulations. The WTO maintains these notifications in a central registry. Third, there are regular procedures for reviews of members' trade policies. The most far-reaching review is thorough the Trade Policy Review Mechanism, pursuant to which the trade policies of WTO members are reviewed by the WTO Secretariat and other members on a regular basis.

5.　THE MAJOR EXCEPTIONS TO THE BASIC RULES

There are four major exceptions to WTO rules. They deal with quite different issues—national security, balance of payments, safeguards and public policy, but they are usefully treated together to facilitate comparisons of the different extent to which they may be invoked and to which they are subject to multilateral control.

GATT Article XXI—the so-called national security exception—provides that GATT does not prevent any member from taking any action which it considers necessary for the protection of its essential security interests (i) relating to fissionable materials, (ii) relating to arms traffic and traffic in goods carried on for the purpose of military supply and (iii) taken in time of war or other emergency in international relations. GATS and the TRIPS Agreement have similar provisions.

A WTO member experiencing balance-of-payments problems may impose trade restrictive measures under GATT Articles XII and XVIII:B (applicable to developing countries) and GATS Article XII. There is a WTO Committee on Balance-of-Payments Restrictions that monitors the use of trade measures taken because of such problems.

The most important exception to the bound tariff levels and the ban on quotas is the so-called Escape Clause of GATT Article XIX. It is a basic GATT tenet that expanded international trade is desirable. It has long been recognized, however, that international trade, even if beneficial overall, produces winners and losers within a national economy. As lower-priced or higher-quality imports gain market share, consumers obviously benefit, but the domestic producer of competing products loses market share and may have to lay off workers or even close down. Recognizing this reality, GATT Article XIX provides that if a product is being imported in such increased quantities as to cause or threaten serious injury to domestic producers of like or directly competing products, a WTO member may impose import restrictions.

The use of the Article XIX exception is governed by the WTO Agreement on Safeguards. The agreement requires that investigations be held to determine whether the conditions of Article XIX have been met. Any safeguard measures that are imposed are not to extend for more than four years (subject to extension for up to four more years) and are to be progressively liberalized over their effective period. They may be imposed selectively (i.e. on a non-MFN basis) only in limited circumstances. In some circumstances the member imposing a safeguard measure may have to provide compensation to adversely affected WTO members, but normally not during the first three years of a safeguard measure. The EC rules on safeguards are described in Chapter 30. As of April 2001, the EC had not imposed any safeguards under WTO rules, although it had challenged successfully in WTO dispute settlement proceedings safeguards imposed by Argentina, Korea and the United States.

GATT Article XX provides a general exception to GATT provisions for measures that are (i) not applied in an arbitrary or unjustifiably discriminatory manner between members, (ii) not a disguised restriction on international trade and (iii), inter alia, necessary to protect public morals or health or to secure compliance with GATT consistent regulations or related to the conservation of exhaustible natural resources. GATS Article XIV is similar. In WTO dispute settlement, the meaning of Article XX has been evolving. There are two important WTO agreements related to Article XX—the Agreement on Sanitary and Phytosanitary Measures (the SPS Agreement) and the Agreement on Technical Barriers to Trade (the TBT Agreement).

GATT Article XX(b) allows for measures necessary to protect health. This provision is effectively interpreted in the SPS Agreement, which covers measures applied to protect humans, animals and plants from the diseases and pests. Under the SPS Agreement, SPS measures must be necessary and based on science. In particular, they are to be based on a risk assessment, which evaluates the likelihood of the occurrence of the negative consequences aimed at by the SPS measure. Any measure must be rationally related to the risk assessment. Second, measures are not to discriminate arbitrarily or unjustifiably between members where identical or similar conditions prevail, nor in a manner that would constitute a disguised restriction on trade, not be unnecessarily trade restrictive. Third, the agreement promotes the use of international standards, although it clearly gives each WTO member the right to set its own level of protection. In addition, the agreement has a number of transparency provisions. One of the more controversial recent trade disputes between the EC and the US concerns the EC ban on beef from cattle treated with growth hormones. This dispute is described Section C below.

The WTO Agreement on Technical Barriers to Trade (the TBT Agreement) applies to technical regulations (excluding SPS measures) and standards. Its basic obligation is a commitment to provide MFN and national treatment and to ensure that technical regulations on products are not applied with a view to or with the effect of creating unnecessary obstacles to international trade. The agreement accordingly provides that such regulations shall not be more trade restrictive than necessary to fulfil a legitimate objective, such as the protection of human health or safety. The agreement also establishes similar rules with respect to standards and conformity assessment procedures. One of the principles of the agreement is transparency, and it has detailed rules calling for publication of proposed technical regulations for comment prior to their implementation. The agreement promotes the use of international instead of national standards, the use of performance rather than design criteria and the recognition of testing in foreign laboratories. The approach of the agreement is not so dissimilar to EC activities in the technical harmonization area described in Chapter 14.

6. THE WTO DISPUTE SETTLEMENT MECHANISM

The WTO agreements provide extensive rights and impose many duties on WTO members and their conduct of international trade. Obviously, a mechanism is needed to resolve disputes over what these rules mean and whether they have been broken in a specific case. Without such a mechanism, the elaborate structure of rights and duties would mean little. In the WTO, the rules for dispute resolution are contained in the WTO Dispute Settlement Understanding (DSU). The DSU grew out of GATT practice dating back to the 1950s, whereby disputes were referred to panels of individuals for resolution, with the panel reports being subject to adoption by the GATT parties, who acted by consensus.

Although the GATT system was quite successful, the requirement that a panel report be adopted by a consensus (which included the losing party) sometimes resulted in stalemate. As explained below, a major innovation of the DSU is that reports are adopted unless there is a consensus *not to adopt the report*. This fundamental change in approach was accepted by the EC and Japan, who generally had preferred a less adjudicative approach to GATT dispute settlement, in exchange for (i) the creation of an appeals process and (ii) a commitment by the US to bring all WTO disputes to the WTO and not to act unilaterally under Section 301 of its 1974 Trade Act.

Among the general provisions of the DSU are (i) a commitment on the part of WTO Members to submit all WTO-related disputes to the WTO system and not to take unilateral action; (ii) a statement that the aim of dispute settlement is to secure a positive solution to a dispute and that a solution that is acceptable to the parties and consistent with the WTO agreements is preferred; and (iii) a statement that the dispute settlement system serves to preserve the rights and obligations of members and to clarify the existing provisions of WTO agreements in accordance with the customary rules of interpretation of public international law, but must not add to or diminish the rights and obligations provided in the agreements. The DSU attempts to ensure prompt resolution of disputes by establishing rather tight timeframes for each phase of the four phases of the process: consultations, panel proceedings, appellate review and surveillance of implementation.

A WTO member may ask for consultations with another member if the complaining member believes that the other member has violated a WTO agreement or otherwise nullified or impaired benefits accruing to it. The goal of the consultation stage is to enable the disputing parties to understand better the factual situation and the legal claims in respect of the dispute and to resolve the matter without further proceedings.

If consultations fail to resolve the dispute within 60 days of the request for consultations, the complaining WTO member may demand the establishment of a panel of three independent experts to rule on the dispute. The vast majority of panelists are current or former government officials and come from a wide range of WTO members. The DSU provides that panelists serve in their individual capacities and there are rules of conduct to ensure their impartiality. DSU article 11 provides that a panel shall make an objective assessment of the matter before it, including an objective assessment of the facts of the case and the applicability of and conformity with the relevant WTO agreements.

There are normally two meetings between the panel and the parties to discuss the substantive issues in the case. Each meeting is preceded by the filing of written submissions. After the hearings with the parties are concluded, the panel submits an interim report to the parties for comment. Thereafter, a final report is issued. After its circulation to WTO members, the final report is referred for formal adoption to the WTO Dispute Settlement Body, which oversees the operation of the dispute settlement system. Adoption is automatic unless there is a consensus not to adopt the report or an appeal of the report to the WTO Appellate Body. The panel process is supposed to be completed in nine months, although many cases take somewhat longer to complete, particularly where a panel feels the need to consult experts.

The possibility of an appeal is a new feature of the WTO dispute settlement system. The Appellate Body consists of seven individuals, appointed by the DSB for four-year terms, renewable once. The Appellate Body hears appeals of panel reports in divisions of three, although its rules provide for the division hearing a case to exchange views with the other four Appellate Body members before the division finalizes its report. The members of the division that hears a particular appeal are selected by a secret procedure that is based on randomness, unpredictability and the opportunity for all members to serve without regard to national origin. The Appellate Body's report is to be issued within 90 days of the appeal and is adopted automatically by the DSB, absent consensus to the contrary.

The final phase of the WTO dispute settlement process is the surveillance stage. This is designed to ensure that the results contained in adopted panel/Appellate Body reports are implemented. If a violation is found, the report typically recommends that the member concerned bring the offending measure into conformity with its WTO obligations. While the report may suggest ways of implementation, it is ultimately left to the member to determine how it will implement the report. Under the surveillance function, the offending member is required to state its intentions with respect to implementation within 30 days of the adoption of the applicable report by the DSB. If immediate implementation is impractical, it is to be afforded a reasonable period of time for implementation. Absent agreement, that period of time may be set by arbitration. The DSU provides that, as a guideline for the arbitrator, the period should not exceed 15 months. If a party fails to implement the report within the reasonable period of time, the prevailing party may request compensation. If that is not forthcoming, it may request the DSB to authorize it to suspend concessions owed to the non-implementing party (i.e., take retaliatory action). DSB authorization is automatic, absent consensus to the contrary, subject to arbitration of the level of suspension if requested by the non-implementing member. If there is a dispute over whether implementation has taken place, the matter is referred back to the original panel for an expedited decision.

The WTO dispute settlement system has been quite active since the founding of the WTO on January 1, 1995. As of September 1, 2001, there had been more than 237 consultation requests. It appears that roughly one-half of these cases were resolved by the parties without the need for recourse to the panel process. Panel/Appellate Body reports had been adopted in 52 cases and another dozen or so cases were pending. In addition, there had been six compliance/suspension reports adopted. The record of implementation of reports has been reasonably good. So far, there have been essentially three major non-implementation problems, two of which involved the EC. The EC did not implement the results of the *Bananas* and *Hormones* (described below) in a timely matter, although it announced in April 2001 that it had reached a settlement with the US (and later Ecuador) in the *Bananas* dispute.

Notwithstanding its problems with adverse decisions in the *Bananas* and *Hormones* cases, the EC has been a major user of the WTO dispute settlement system. Of the 52 cases where reports had been adopted as of September 2001, approximately one-third—16—involved successful complaints by the EC against eight other WTO members: three cases involved discriminatory alcohol taxation by Japan, Korea, and Chile; three cases concerned safeguards imposed by Argentina, Korea and the US; three cases were brought under the TRIPS Agreement against Canada, India and the US; two cases involved discriminatory treatment of auto imports by Canada and Indonesia; one case concerned export restrictions maintained by Argentina and four additional cases were brought against the US (involving prohibited export subsides under the US Foreign Sales Corporation Act; certain "premature" retaliatory measures taken by the US in the *Bananas* case; US countervailing duties on British steel exports and the 1916 US Antidumping Act). In addition, the EC successfully defended itself in two cases: one brought by the US in respect of the tariff classification of LAN equipment; the other brought by Canada against French asbestos regulations. On the other side of the ledger, the EC was an unsuccessful complainant in one case against the US (a challenge of US Section 301 (see Chapter 30) and an unsuccessful respondent in two cases in addition to *Bananas* and *Hormones*. One case involved a challenge by Brazil to EC rules affecting poultry imports (in fact the EC prevailed on most issues) and the other a challenge by India to EC antidumping duties on bed linen.

These statistics demonstrate the very important role that WTO dispute settlement plays in EC relations with its major trading partners. In fact, the statistics do not tell the whole story because the EC has been involved in many other cases that have settled or where it was an interested third party. Moreover, because of its role as a forum for negotiations, many other aspects of the EC's common commercial policy are dealt with in the WTO.

7. FUTURE WTO NEGOTIATIONS

An attempt to launch a new round of WTO negotiations at a WTO ministerial meeting in Seattle in 1999 was unsuccessful and occasioned violent protests against such negotiations. For the most part, the same issues were considered in November 2001 at a WTO ministerial meeting in Doha, Qatar, where it was agreed to launch negotiations on a broad range of topics. Those topics include (i) the trade and environment interface; (ii) competition and (iii) investment, which were strongly pushed by the EC (for the latter two subjects, the negotiations will only start in 2004 following an agreement on modalities of negotiation in late 2003). The EC was unsuccessful in avoiding the adoption of a negotiating goal calling for the phasing out of agricultural export subsidies, but succeeded in avoiding any target date for such phase–out. There will also be negotiations on services, specific intellectual property issues (e.g., geographical indications), tariff levels and WTO rules on dumping and subsidies.

B. THE COURT OF JUSTICE AND THE WTO AGREEMENT

The Court of Justice has considered the WTO Agreement in two major contexts—in defining the scope of the Community's implied and explicit powers in respect of the common commercial policy and in decisions on its possible direct effect. We consider both issues in this section.

1. THE SCOPE OF THE COMMON COMMERCIAL POLICY

The negotiations that led to the creation of the WTO dealt with trade in services and certain aspects of intellectual property. During the negotiations, the Commission had acted as the sole negotiator on behalf of the EC and the Member States, but it had been agreed that its role was without prejudice to the issue of competence under the EC Treaty. When the negotiations were successfully completed and the agreement signed in April 1994, the question was thus presented: Who had the power to conclude the WTO agreements and, in particular, the General Agreement on Trade in Services (GATS) and the Agreement on Trade–Related Aspects of Intellectual Property Rights (TRIPs)? Were they within the exclusive purview of the Community? Only within the competence of the Member States? Within the joint competence of the EC and the Member States? In addition, there was the issue of representation of the EC in the WTO. The EC had exclusively represented the Member States in GATT, but did the addition of these new subject matters—services and intellectual property—mean that the Member States would now have an independent role in the WTO? In an opinion of major importance the Court of Justice addressed these issues in November 1994. The Court acted quickly— only seven months elapsed between the request and the opinion—and it heard all six Advocates–General (although their opinions were not published).

OPINION 1/94

[1994]   ECR I–5267
(World Trade Organization—WTO).

VII.   ARTICLE 113 [NOW 133] OF THE EC TREATY, GATS AND TRIPS

35   The Commission's main contention is that the conclusion of both GATS and TRIPs falls within the exclusive competence conferred on the Community in commercial policy matters by Article 113 [now 133] of the EC Treaty. That point of view has been vigorously disputed * * * by the Council, by the Member States * * * and by the European Parliament. * * *

A.   GATS

* * *

38   As regards [services other than transport], it should be recalled at the outset that in Opinion 1/75 [Local Cost Standard, see Chapter 27(B)(1), Note 5] the Court, which had been asked to rule on the scope of Community competence as to the arrangements relating to a local cost standard, held that "the field of common commercial policy, and more particularly that of export policy, necessarily covers systems of aid for exports and more particularly measures concerning credits for the financing of local costs linked to export operations." The local costs in question concerned expenses incurred for the supply of both goods and services. Nevertheless, the Court recognized the exclusive competence of the Community, without drawing a distinction between goods and services.

39   In its Opinion 1/78 [Rubber Agreement, see Chapter 27(B)(2)], the Court rejected an interpretation of Article 113 [now 133] "the effect of which would be to restrict the common commercial policy to the use of instruments intended to have an effect only on the traditional aspects of external trade." On the contrary, it considered that "the question of external trade must be governed from a wide point of view," as is

confirmed by "the fact that the enumeration in Article 113 of the subjects covered by commercial policy . . . is conceived as a non-exhaustive enumeration."

[40] The Commission points out in its request for an opinion that in certain developed countries the services sector has become the dominant sector of the economy and that the global economy has been undergoing fundamental structural changes. The trend is for basic industry to be transferred to developing countries, whilst the developed economies have tended to become, in the main, exporters of services and of goods with a high value-added content. The Court notes that this trend is borne out by the WTO Agreement and its annexes, which were the subject of a single process of negotiation covering both goods and services.

[41] Having regard to this trend in international trade, it follows from the open nature of the common commercial policy, within the meaning of the Treaty, that trade in services cannot immediately, and as a matter of principle, be excluded from the scope of Article 113 [now 133], as some of the Governments which have submitted observations contend.

[42] In order to make that conclusion more specific, however, one must take into account the definition of trade in services given in GATS in order to see whether the overall scheme of the Treaty is not such as to limit the extent to which trade in services can be included within Article 113 [now 133].

[43] Under Article I(2) of GATS trade in services is defined, for the purposes of that agreement, as comprising four modes of supply of services: (1) cross-frontier supplies not involving any movement of persons; (2) consumption abroad, which entails the movement of the consumer into the territory of the WTO member country in which the supplier is established; (3) commercial presence, i.e. the presence of a subsidiary or branch in the territory of the WTO member country in which the service is to be rendered; (4) the presence of natural persons from a WTO member country, enabling a supplier from one member country to supply services within the territory of any other member country.

[44] As regards cross-frontier supplies, the service is rendered by a supplier established in one country to a consumer residing in another. The supplier does not move to the consumer's country; nor, conversely, does the consumer move to the supplier's country. That situation is, therefore, not unlike trade in goods, which is unquestionably covered by the common commercial policy within the meaning of the Treaty. There is thus no particular reason why such a supply should not fall within the concept of the common commercial policy.

[45] The same cannot be said of the other three modes of supply of services covered by GATS, namely, consumption abroad, commercial presence and the presence of natural persons.

[46] As regards natural persons, it is clear from Article 3 of the Treaty, which distinguishes between "a common commercial policy" in paragraph (b) and "measures concerning the entry and movement of persons" in paragraph (d), that the treatment of nationals of non-member countries on crossing the external frontiers of Member States cannot be regarded as

falling within the common commercial policy. More generally, the existence in the Treaty of specific chapters on the free movement of natural and legal persons shows that those matters do not fall within the common commercial policy.

47 It follows that the modes of supply of services referred to by GATS as "consumption abroad," "commercial presence" and the "presence of natural persons" are not covered by the common commercial policy.

* * *

B.   TRIPs

54 The Commission's argument in support of its contention that the Community has exclusive competence under Article 113 [now 133] is essentially that the rules concerning intellectual property rights are closely linked to trade in the products and services to which they apply.

55 It should be noted, first that Section 4 of Part III of TRIPs, which concerns the means of enforcement of intellectual property rights, contains specific rules as to measures to be applied at border crossing points. As the United Kingdom has pointed out, that section has its counterpart in the provisions of Council Regulation 3842/86 of 1 December 1986 laying down measures to prohibit the release for free circulation of counterfeit goods. Inasmuch as that regulation concerns the prohibition of the release into free circulation of counterfeit goods, it was rightly based on Article 113 [now 133] of the Treaty: it relates to measures to be taken by the customs authorities at the external frontiers of the Community. Since measures of that type can be adopted autonomously by the Community institutions on the basis of Article 113 of the EC Treaty, it is for the Community alone to conclude international agreements on such matters.

56 However, as regards matters other than the provisions of TRIPs on the release into free circulation of counterfeit goods, the Commission's arguments cannot be accepted.

[Although the Court conceded that there is a connection between intellectual property rights and trade in goods, it noted that is not enough to bring such rights them within the scope of Article 133, especially since they affect internal trade just as much as, if not more than, international trade. Moreover, the Court noted that while Articles 94, 95 and 308 provide a basis for harmonizing national laws on intellectual property, the decision-making rules under those articles differ from those applicable under Article 133.]

60 If the Community were to be recognized as having exclusive competence to enter into agreements with non-member countries to harmonize the protection of intellectual property and, at the same time, to achieve harmonization at Community level, the Community institutions would be able to escape the internal constraints to which they are subject in relation to procedures and to rules as to voting.

* * *

71 In the light of the foregoing, it must be held that, apart from those of its provisions which concern the prohibition of the release into free circula-

tion of counterfeit goods, TRIPs does not fall within the scope of the common commercial policy.

VIII.   The Community's Implied External Powers, GATS and TRIPs

72   In the event of the Court rejecting its main contention that the Community has exclusive competence pursuant to Article 113 [now 133], the Commission maintains in the alternative that the Community's exclusive competence to conclude GATS and TRIPs flows implicitly from the provisions of the Treaty establishing its internal competence, or from the existence of legislative acts of the institutions giving effect to that internal competence, or else from the need to enter into international commitments with a view to achieving an internal Community objective. The Commission also argues that, even if the Community does not have adequate powers on the basis of specific provisions of the Treaty or legislative acts of the institutions, it has exclusive competence by virtue of Articles 100a and 235 [now 95 and 308] of the Treaty. The Council and the Member States which have submitted observations acknowledge that the Community has certain powers, but deny that they are exclusive.

A.   GATS

73   With particular regard to GATS, the Commission cites three possible sources for exclusive external competence on the part of the Community: the powers conferred on the Community institutions by the Treaty at internal level, the need to conclude the agreement in order to achieve a Community objective, and, lastly, Articles 100a and 235 [now 95 and 308].

74   The Commission argues, first, that there is no area or specific provision in GATS in respect of which the Community does not have corresponding powers to adopt measures at internal level. According to the Commission, those powers are set out in the chapters on the right of establishment, freedom to provide services and transport. Exclusive external competence flows from those internal powers.

75   That argument must be rejected.

76   It was on the basis of Article 75(1)(a) [now 71(1)(a)] which, as regards that part of a journey which takes place on Community territory, also concerns transport from or to non-member countries, that the Court held in *ERTA* that the "powers of the Community extend to relationships arising from international law, and hence involve the need in the sphere in question for agreements with the third countries concerned."

77   However, even in the field of transport, the Community's exclusive external competence does not automatically flow from its power to lay down rules at internal level. As the Court pointed out in *ERTA*, the Member States, whether acting individually or collectively, only lose their right to assume obligations with non-member countries as and when common rules which could be affected by those obligations come into being. Only in so far as common rules have been established at internal level does the external competence of the Community become exclusive. However, not all transport matters are already covered by common rules.

78   The Commission asserted at the hearing that the Member States' continuing freedom to conduct an external policy based on bilateral agreements

with nonmember countries will inevitably lead to distortions in the flow of services and will progressively undermine the internal market. * * *

[79] In reply to that argument, suffice it to say that there is nothing in the Treaty which prevents the institutions from arranging, in the common rules laid down by them, concerted action in relation to non-member countries or from prescribing the approach to be taken by the Member States in their external dealings. * * *

* * *

[81] Unlike the chapter on transport, the chapters on the right of establishment and on freedom to provide services do not contain any provision expressly extending the competence of the Community to "relationships arising from international law." As has rightly been observed by the Council and most of the Member States which have submitted observations, the sole objective of those chapters is to secure the right of establishment and freedom to provide services for nationals of Member States. They contain no provisions on the problem of the first establishment of nationals of non-member countries and the rules governing their access to self-employed activities. One cannot therefore infer from those chapters that the Community has exclusive competence to conclude an agreement with non-member countries to liberalize first establishment and access to service markets, other than those which are the subject of cross-border supplies within the meaning of GATS, which are covered by Article 113 [now 133] (see paragraph 42 above).

* * *

[87] Third, the Commission refers to Articles 100a and 235 [now 95 and 308] of the Treaty as the basis of exclusive external competence.

[88] As regards Article 100a [now 95], it is undeniable that, where harmonizing powers have been exercised, the harmonization measures thus adopted may limit, or even remove, the freedom of the Member States to negotiate with non-member countries. However, an internal power to harmonize which has not been exercised in a specific field cannot confer exclusive external competence in that field on the Community.

[89] Article 235 [now 308], which enables the Community to cope with any insufficiency in the powers conferred on it, expressly or by implication, for the achievement of its objectives, cannot in itself vest exclusive competence in the Community at international level. Save where internal powers can only be effectively exercised at the same time as external powers (see paragraph 85 above), internal competence can give rise to exclusive external competence only if it is exercised. This applies a fortiori to Article 235.

[90] Although the only objective expressly mentioned in the chapters on the right of establishment and on freedom to provide services is the attainment of those freedoms for nationals of the Member States of the Community, it does not follow that the Community institutions are prohibited from using the powers conferred on them in that field in order to specify the treatment which is to be accorded to nationals of non-member countries. Numerous acts adopted by the Council on the basis of Articles 54

and 57(2) [now 44 and 47] of the Treaty—but not mentioned by it—contain provisions in that regard. The Commission has listed them in response to a question from the Court.

91   It is evident from an examination of those acts that very different objectives may be pursued by incorporation of external provisions.

92   The directives on coordination of disclosure requirements and company accounts applied only to companies as such and not to their branches. That gave rise to some disparity, as regards the protection of members and third parties, between companies operating in other Member States by setting up branches and companies operating there by setting up subsidiaries. Consequently, Council Directive 89/666/EEC, which is based on Article 54 [now 44] of the Treaty, was introduced to regulate the disclosure requirements applying to such branches. In order to avoid any discrimination based on a company's country of origin, that directive also had to cover branches established by companies governed by the laws of non-member countries.

93   Moreover, the Second [Banking] Directive, which is based on Article 57(2) [now 47] of the Treaty, contains a Title III "on relations with third countries." That directive established a system of uniform authorization and requires the mutual recognition of controls.

94   Once it is authorized in one Member State, a credit institution may pursue its activities in another Member State (for example, by setting up a branch there) without having to seek fresh authorization from that State. In those circumstances, it was enough for a credit institution having its seat in a nonmember country to establish a subsidiary in a Member State or to acquire control of an establishment having its seat there to enable it to set up branches in all the Member States of the Community without having to seek further authorizations. For that reason, Title III of that directive provides for a series of measures, including negotiation procedures, with a view to obtaining comparable competitive opportunities for Community credit institutions in nonmember countries. Similar provisions have been adopted in the field of insurance and in the field of finance.

95   Whenever the Community has included in its internal legislative acts provisions relating to the treatment of nationals of non-member countries or expressly conferred on its institutions powers to negotiate with non-member countries, it acquires exclusive external competence in the spheres covered by those acts.

96   The same applies in any event, even in the absence of any express provision authorizing its institutions to negotiate with non-member countries, where the Community has achieved complete harmonization of the rules governing access to a self-employed activity, because the common rules thus adopted could be affected within the meaning of *ERTA* if the Member States retained freedom to negotiate with non-member countries.

97   That is not the case in all service sectors, however, as the Commission has itself acknowledged.

98   It follows that competence to conclude GATS is shared between the Community and the Member States.

B. TRIPs

[The Commission raised arguments similar to the foregoing in respect of the TRIPS Agreement. The Court rejected them for the same reasons set out above in respect of GATS. Although the Court rejected Member State arguments that suggested that the Community lacked powers in respect of some matters covered by the TRIPS Agreement (e.g., the requirement for effective protection of intellectual property rights through judicial remedies), the lack of harmonization in many of the areas covered by the TRIPS Agreement led it to conclude that the Community and the Member States were jointly competent to conclude the TRIPS Agreement.]

IX. THE DUTY OF COOPERATION BETWEEN THE MEMBER
STATES AND THE COMMUNITY INSTITUTIONS

106 At the hearing, the Commission drew the Court's attention to the problems which would arise, as regards the administration of the agreements, if the Community and the Member States were recognized as sharing competence to participate in the conclusion of the GATS and TRIPs agreements. While it is true that, in the negotiation of the agreements, the procedure under Article 113 [now 133] of the Treaty prevailed subject to certain very minor adjustments, the Member States will, in the context of the WTO, undoubtedly seek to express their views individually on matters falling within their competence whenever no consensus has been found. Furthermore, interminable discussions will ensue to determine whether a given matter falls within the competence of the Community, so that the Community mechanisms laid down by the relevant provisions of the Treaty will apply, or whether it is within the competence of the Member States, in which case the consensus rule will operate. The Community's unity of action *vis-à-vis* the rest of the world will thus be undermined and its negotiating power greatly weakened.

107 In response to that concern, which is quite legitimate, it must be stressed, first, that any problems which may arise in implementation of the WTO Agreement and its annexes as regards the coordination necessary to ensure unity of action where the Community and the Member States participate jointly cannot modify the answer to the question of competence, that being a prior issue. As the Council has pointed out, resolution of the issue of the allocation of competence cannot depend on problems which may possibly arise in administration of the agreements.

108 Next, where it is apparent that the subject-matter of an agreement or convention falls in part within the competence of the Community and in part within that of the Member States, it is essential to ensure close cooperation between the Member States and the Community institutions, both in the process of negotiation and conclusion and in the fulfilment of the commitments entered into. That obligation to cooperate flows from the requirement of unity in the international representation of the Community.

109 The duty to cooperate is all the more imperative in the case of agreements such as those annexed to the WTO Agreement, which are inextricably interlinked, and in view of the cross-retaliation measures established by the [WTO] Dispute Settlement Understanding. Thus, in the absence of

close cooperation, where a Member State, duly authorized within its sphere of competence to take cross-retaliation measures, considered that they would be ineffective if taken in the fields covered by GATS or TRIPs, it would not, under Community law, be empowered to retaliate in the area of trade in goods, since that is an area which on any view falls within the exclusive competence of the Community under Article 113 [now 133] of the Treaty. Conversely, if the Community were given the right to retaliate in the sector of goods but found itself incapable of exercising that right, it would, in the absence of close cooperation, find itself unable, in law, to retaliate in the areas covered by GATS or TRIPs, those being within the competence of the Member States.

Notes and Questions

1. The Court also ruled that the EC had the exclusive power to conclude the GATT-related agreements on trade in goods, including products subject to the ECSC and Euratom Treaties, and that Article 133 was a sufficient basis for such action, even in respect of the agreements on agriculture and sanitary and phytosanitary measures. In this regard, the Court stated:

29 * * * "The objective of the [WTO] Agreement on Agriculture is to establish, on a worldwide basis, a fair and market-oriented agricultural trading system" (see the preamble to that Agreement). The fact that commitments entered into under that Agreement require internal measures to be adopted on the basis of Article 43 [now 37] of the Treaty does not prevent the international commitments themselves from being entered into pursuant to Article 113 [now 133] alone.

The Court also rejected the argument that because the Member States would contribute to the operating budget of the WTO, there was joint competence (*cf. Rubber Agreement*). The Court drew a distinction between an operating budget and a "financial policy instrument," such as was involved in the *Rubber Agreement* case.

2. Would you say that the Court's opinion on the WTO Agreements represents an advance on, retreat from, or a simple application of, the principles adopted in the *ERTA* and the *Rubber Agreement* cases discussed in Chapter 27? Why?

3. The Court took the position that since title V covers international agreements on transport, Article 133 does not. See Opinion, para. 48. What implications could this have for the scope of Article 133? Is it consistent with the Court's position that the WTO Agreement on Agriculture falls under Article 133? See Note 1 above. What difference does it make in a procedural sense (approvals, etc.)?

4. In its argument, the Commission cited various Community instruments and agreements that in the past had been adopted solely under Article 133 and that contained provisions on services or intellectual property rights in general. The Court dismissed the examples without much discussion. Does that mean that those instruments and agreements were invalid? Is such past practice relevant in EC Treaty interpretation?

5. In respect of areas of joint competence in the WTO, do you think that the duty of cooperation discussed by the Court at the end of its opinion will adequately solve the problems raised by the Commission? These will be significantly reduced in the future as the Nice Treaty revised Article 133 to provide that

the general rules on the common commercial policy shall apply to agreements relating to trade in services and the commercial aspects of intellectual property, subject to certain exceptions.[2] EC Treaty, art. 133(5). The exceptions include a requirement for unanimous decision-making where that would be required for internal rules and where the Community has not yet exercised its powers by adopting internal rules. Moreover, certain services (cultural and audiovisual, educational, social and health) are declared to be shared competences with the Member States and international agreements on transport continue to be governed by Title V and Article 300. Art. 133(6). There is also a provision allowing the Council, acting unanimously, to extend the regular common commercial policy rules to international agreements on non-commercial aspects of intellectual property.

6.   At the WTO, the Commission normally speaks for the EC and its Member States (except on budgetary matters, since the Member States pay their own dues). The WTO Agreement provides that the EC and its Member States cannot cast more than 15 votes, even though the EC itself and all 15 Member States are WTO members. Since WTO decisions are virtually always taken by consensus, this has not been an issue.

2.   DIRECT EFFECT OF THE WTO AGREEMENT

The Court of Justice held on several occasions that the General Agreement on Tariffs and Trade did not have direct effect. See, e.g., International Fruit Co. v. Produktschap, Cases 21–24/72, [1972] ECR 1219; Germany v. Council (Bananas), Case C–280/93, [1994] ECR I–4973. In *International Fruit*, the Court described GATT as "characterized by the great flexibility of its provisions," in particular those related to safeguards and dispute settlement (para. 21). Given the changes introduced by the WTO Agreement, particularly in respect of more detailed rules and the strengthened dispute settlement system, the question naturally arose whether the Court would find that the WTO Agreement could have such effect.

PORTUGUESE REPUBLIC v. COUNCIL
Case C–149/96
[1998] ECR I–7379.

[In 1994, the Community negotiated agreements related to textile products with India and Pakistan. The agreements were approved in a decision adopted by qualified majority, over the objections of Greece, Spain and Portugal. Portugal subsequently challenged the decision on grounds that it violated WTO rules, as well as certain rules and principles of Community law. The Court addressed the WTO issue as follows:]

35   It should also be remembered that according to the general rules of international law there must be *bona fide* performance of every agreement. Although each contracting party is responsible for executing fully the commitments which it has undertaken it is nevertheless free to determine the legal means appropriate for attaining that end in its legal system, unless the agreement, interpreted in the light of its subject-matter and purpose, itself specifies those means.

---

2.   Under the Amsterdam Treaty, the Council was given the power to extend Article 133 to cover services and intellectual property, but unanimity was required and no such action has been taken.

36   While it is true that the WTO agreements, as the Portuguese Government observes, differ significantly from the provisions of GATT 1947, in particular by reason of the strengthening of the system of safeguards and the mechanism for resolving disputes, the system resulting from those agreements nevertheless accords considerable importance to negotiation between the parties.

37   Although the main purpose of the mechanism for resolving disputes is in principle, according to Article 3(7) of the Understanding on Rules and Procedures Governing the Settlement of Disputes (Annex 2 to the WTO), to secure the withdrawal of the measures in question if they are found to be inconsistent with the WTO rules, that understanding provides that where the immediate withdrawal of the measures is impracticable compensation may be granted on an interim basis pending the withdrawal of the inconsistent measure.

38   According to Article 22(1) of that Understanding, compensation is a temporary measure available in the event that the recommendations and rulings of the dispute settlement body provided for in Article 2(1) of that Understanding are not implemented within a reasonable period of time, and Article 22(1) shows a preference for full implementation of a recommendation to bring a measure into conformity with the WTO agreements in question.

39   However, Article 22(2) provides that if the member concerned fails to fulfil its obligation to implement the said recommendations and rulings within a reasonable period of time, it is, if so requested, and on the expiry of a reasonable period at the latest, to enter into negotiations with any party having invoked the dispute settlement procedures, with a view to finding mutually acceptable compensation.

40   Consequently, to require the judicial organs to refrain from applying the rules of domestic law which are inconsistent with the WTO agreements would have the consequence of depriving the legislative or executive organs of the contracting parties of the possibility afforded by Article 22 of that memorandum of entering into negotiated arrangements even on a temporary basis.

41   It follows that the WTO agreements, interpreted in the light of their subject-matter and purpose, do not determine the appropriate legal means of ensuring that they are applied in good faith in the legal order of the contracting parties.

42   As regards, more particularly, the application of the WTO agreements in the Community legal order, it must be noted that, according to its preamble, the agreement establishing the WTO, including the annexes, is still founded, like GATT 1947, on the principle of negotiations with a view to "entering into reciprocal and mutually advantageous arrangements" and is thus distinguished, from the viewpoint of the Community, from the agreements concluded between the Community and non-member countries which introduce a certain asymmetry of obligations, or create special relations of integration with the Community, such as the agreement which the Court was required to interpret in *Kupferberg*.

43   It is common ground, moreover, that some of the contracting parties, which are among the most important commercial partners of the Community, have concluded from the subject-matter and purpose of the WTO agreements that they are not among the rules applicable by their judicial organs when reviewing the legality of their rules of domestic law.

44   Admittedly, the fact that the courts of one of the parties consider that some of the provisions of the agreement concluded by the Community are of direct application whereas the courts of the other party do not recognize such direct application is not in itself such as to constitute a lack of reciprocity in the implementation of the agreement.

45   However, the lack of reciprocity in that regard on the part of the Community's trading partners, in relation to the WTO agreements which are based on reciprocal and mutually advantageous arrangements and which must *ipso facto* be distinguished from agreements concluded by the Community, referred to in paragraph 42 of the present judgment, may lead to disuniform application of the WTO rules.

46   To accept that the role of ensuring that those rules comply with Community law devolves directly on the Community judicature would deprive the legislative or executive organs of the Community of the scope for maneuver enjoyed by their counterparts in the Community's trading partners.

47   It follows from all those considerations that, having regard to their nature and structure, the WTO agreements are not in principle among the rules in the light of which the Court is to review the legality of measures adopted by the Community institutions.

48   That interpretation corresponds, moreover, to what is stated in the final recital in the preamble to Decision 94/800 [approving WTO Agreement], according to which "by its nature, the Agreement establishing the World Trade Organization, including the Annexes thereto, is not susceptible to being directly invoked in Community or Member State courts".

49   It is only where the Community intended to implement a particular obligation assumed in the context of the WTO, or where the Community measure refers expressly to the precise provisions of the WTO agreements, that it is for the Court to review the legality of the Community measure in question in the light of the WTO rules.

50   It is therefore necessary to examine whether, as the Portuguese Government claims, that is so in the present case.

51   The answer must be in the negative. The contested decision is not designed to ensure the implementation in the Community legal order of a particular obligation assumed in the context of the WTO, nor does it make express reference to any specific provisions of the WTO agreements. Its purpose is merely to approve the Memoranda of Understanding negotiated by the Community with Pakistan and India.

52   It follows from all the foregoing that the claim of the Portuguese Republic that the contested decision was adopted in breach of certain rules and fundamental principles of the WTO is unfounded.

Notes and Questions

1. Is the Court's reasoning in this case consistent with its reasoning in the cases we examined in Chapter 27(C) supra? Are you persuaded by the Court's argument that direct effect should not be recognized because it would take away the Community's "right" to delay implementation? Is that a "right" or simply a provision of a detailed dispute settlement system that has provisions dealing with non-compliance? Does the existence of the reasoned opinion procedure of Article 226 and the possibility of fines under Article 228 suggest that Member States also have a right to delay implementation of Community legislation and choose those alternatives?

2. For examples of para. 49, see Nakajima v. Council, [1991] ECR I–2069; Schieving–Nijstadt v. Groeneweld, Case 89/99, [2001] ECR I–___.

3. The Court refers to a Council Decision in paragraph 48. Should this sort of statement by the Council affect the Court's analysis of the issue in this case? In cases involving other Community legislation?

C. THE EC AND THE US

In this section we consider the EC's view of its trading relationship with the US and then in the notes consider the US view, as well as some of the main disputes pending between them as of early 2001. EC–US trade is quite substantial. According to US statistics, in 2000, the US exported $165 billion in goods and $85 billion in services to the EC, and it imported $220 billion in goods and $63 billion in services from the EC. The stock of US investment in the EC was $512 billion.

EUROPEAN COMMISSION, 2000 REPORT ON UNITED STATES BARRIERS TO TRADE AND INVESTMENT

[This report] is the sixteenth such annual report. [It] needs to be placed in the context of a transatlantic economic relationship which has grown particularly strongly over the years, to the benefit of both economies, and which is underpinned by the most extensive trade and investment links in the world.

EU–US relations are currently conducted within the framework of the New Transatlantic Agenda (NTA) and accompanying EU–US Joint Action Plan adopted at the EU–US Summit of December 1995. Efforts under the NTA to intensify and extend multilateral and bilateral co-operation in the field of trade and investment led to the adoption, at the EU/US Summit in London in May 1998, of a joint statement on the Transatlantic Economic Partnership (TEP) and the subsequent TEP Action Plan, endorsed at the December 1998 EU/US Summit in Washington. Under the Action Plan, we are giving particular priority this year to specific initiatives in the fields of technical barriers to trade and regulatory cooperation, extended Mutual Recognition Agreements in the goods sector, to expand MRAs to certain services sectors and to specific joint projects on biotechnology.

Furthermore, the EU–US Summit in Bonn on 21 June 1999 approved a set of "early warning" principles, that aim at identifying and preventing potential bilateral problems at an early stage, in order to prevent conflicts and facilitate problem resolution before they risk undermining the much broader

EU–US relationship. We are now in the process of finding ways to making these principles function in practice.

This Report must therefore be seen against the background of the joint commitment of the EU and the US, in the NTA and in the TEP, to strengthen and consolidate the multilateral trading system, and to progressively reduce or eliminate barriers that hinder the flow of goods, services and capital between the EU and the US.

The fact remains that a considerable number of impediments, ranging from more traditional tariff and non-tariff barriers, to differences in the legal and regulatory systems, or due to the absence or limitation of internationally agreed rules and disciplines, still need to be tackled. * * *

Summary

Extraterritoriality. The EU strongly opposes the extra-territorial provisions of certain US legislation, which hamper international trade and investment by seeking to regulate EU trade with third countries conducted by companies outside the US. Of particular concern at the present time are the Helms–Burton Act and the Iran Libya Sanctions Act. Important headway towards a lasting solution to this dispute was made at the 18 May 1998 EU/US Summit in London. However, implementation of the Understanding reached at that occasion continues to depend on US Congress legislative action.

Unilateralism. Unilateralism in US trade legislation also remains a matter of concern. Whilst the US has in practice made extensive use of the WTO dispute settlement system, it retains the opportunity to take unilateral trade measures. Recently the EU has won two dispute settlement cases before the WTO, one against the suspension of customs liquidation in the banana dispute, and one against Sections 301 to 310 of the US 1974 Trade Act. The EU has also initiated dispute settlement proceedings against the "carousel" legislation signed into law on 18 May 2000 (section 470 of the Trade and Development Act of 2000).

Tariff barriers. Tariffs have been substantially reduced in successive GATT rounds. As a result, the EU's concern is now focused on a relatively limited number of US "peaks" and other significant tariffs where less progress has been made.

Other customs barriers. EU exports also face a number of additional customs impediments, such as the customs user fees and the excessive invoicing requirements on importers, which add to costs in a similar way to tariffs. The US also changed in 1996 its origin rules giving rise to specific problems for various EU textile and clothing products that are no longer able to claim their national origin, but this problem is almost resolved as a result of the imminent adoption of new rules of origin. The EU is also very concerned about the discriminatory nature of the US Harbor Maintenance Tax, levied on waterborne imports in all US ports. In March 1998 the EU requested WTO dispute settlement consultations and is not satisfied with alternative legislation introduced in the US Congress.

Trade defense instruments. A WTO panel established in January 1999 after an investigation under the Trade Barrier Regulation has ruled that the

1916 US Antidumping Act is in contradiction with the WTO Anti-dumping Agreement and GATT 1994. The WTO Appellate Body has also condemned on 10 May 2000 the countervailing duties maintained after the arm's length privatization of the British Steel company, thereby rejecting the methodology followed by the US Department of Commerce. The EU has also been active against the abusive recourse by the US to the safeguard instrument, in particular in the wheat gluten case. Regulations restricting exports, perceived as hindering trade for third parties, are also a matter of concern.

Technical barriers to trade. EU exporters continue to face a number of behind-the-border impediments. The proliferation of regulation at State level presents particular problems for companies without offices in the US. In addition, some federal standards differ from international norms meaning that manufacturers cannot directly export to the US products made to EU standards (normally based on international standards). Other related difficulties concern labeling requirements and excessive reliance on third-party certification. The FDA drug approval procedures continue to give non-US based firms difficulties. In the agricultural area, a number of sanitary and phytosanitary issues remain a significant source of difficulty for the EU, although some of these may be solved by the Veterinary Equivalence Agreement, signed on 20 July 1999.

Government procurement. Even before the Uruguay Round was ratified, the EU and US had concluded negotiations on a further bilateral procurement agreement that improves on the provisions of the WTO Government Procurement Agreement. These two agreements increased substantially the bidding opportunities for the two sides. However, the EU remains concerned about the wide variety of Buy America provisions that persist, and to which are being added others for federally funded infrastructure programs. Small business set-aside schemes also limit bidding opportunities for EU contractors in a substantial manner. The EU also opposes sub-federal selective purchasing legislation, restricting the ability of EU and other companies doing business with specific countries to bid for contracts in various States and cities. Apart from other actions, the EU considers that an increase in the coverage of the US GPA offer (and in particular the elimination of the existing exceptions) would contribute to an improvement of this situation.

Aeronautics industry. Despite the existence of the 1992 EC–US Large Civil Aircraft agreement the EU remains concerned about the level of indirect support to US aircraft manufacturers. This is also an area for multilateral action, and progress needs to be made on the Civil Aircraft Agreement that remains stalled in the WTO.

Shipbuilding. The 1994 OECD Shipbuilding Agreement which aims at regulating unfair practices, measures of support and injurious pricing still cannot enter into force due to the absence of the US ratification of the Agreement. The maintenance of a number of US subsidies, protective legislation and tax policies, remain a matter of concern.

National security restrictions. Although the principle of national security has a long tradition in trade policy, the EU has repeatedly expressed concern about its excessive use by the US as a disguised form of protectionism, particularly in relation to the application of import, procurement and investment restrictions, as well as the extraterritorial application of export restrictions. In particular, the 1988 Exon–Florio amendment and following legislation to restrain foreign investment in, or ownership of, businesses relating to national security has proved to be problematic. However, the absence of a clear definition of "national security" has led to an overly wide interpretation of the term.

Conditional national treatment. Furthermore, the provision of conditional national treatment in various US laws, and notably in the area of science and technology research remains troublesome.

Tax measures. Concerns about federal tax measures focus on the nature of reporting requirements and the specific manner for calculating what is due. The EU deems State "world-wide" unitary taxes as inconsistent with US obligations under its tax treaties with third countries. Foreign Sales Corporations (FSC) legislation remains a matter of major concern, and the WTO Appellate Body recently affirmed in a report of 24 February 2000 that the FSC is incompatible with the WTO Subsidies Agreement and the Agreement on Agriculture. The EU is closely monitoring the evolution of this case and in particular how the US will implement the WTO ruling by 1 October 2000.

Intellectual property. Despite a number of positive changes in US legislation following Uruguay Round commitments, problems remain due to discrepancies between US legislation and other international commitments. In addition, the issue of informing right-holders of government use of patents as well as various others related to appellations of origin, geographical indications, copyright, trademarks and patent protection have not been resolved. The Community and its Member States recently won a WTO Dispute Settlement case regarding obstacles to the licensing of music works in the US (section 110(5) of the US Copyright Act), but it remains to be seen how the US will implement the panel's recommendations. The protection of trademarks in the US, notably those stemming from Cuban origin, also raises concerns in respect of the compatibility with the TRIPs Agreement. Moreover, the co-existence of fundamentally different patent systems (US first-to-invent system versus first-to-file system followed in the rest of the world) continues to create considerable interface problems for EU companies.

[The report also raises issues in respect of communications, air transport, maritime and professional services.]

Notes and Questions

1. The Commission's report on US trade barriers appears annually and is a response to an annual US report that lists trade barriers of US trading partners. As usual, the US 2001 National Trade Estimate Report on Foreign Trade Barriers contains a long list of EU barriers (pp. 104–139). In a separate report on its activities in 2000, the US Trade Representative listed nine major trade and investment issues involving the EU: technical standards, telecommunications, Airbus subsidies, US tax rules on foreign sales corporations, the EU banana regime, hormone-treated beef, EU approval of biotech products, veterinary equivalence and wine trade.

2. In many respects, the controversial issues between the EU and the US remain largely the same over time. In particular, the EU has long been particularly critical of what it views as extra-territorial US legislation (e.g., the Helms–Burton Act) and US unilateralism (Section 301 of the 1974 Trade Act). In

agriculture, the US has long criticized EU subsidies, while the EU has been reluctant to accept imports of hormone treated beef and, more recently, biotech products generally. In aircraft, the US claims that EU Member States subsidize Airbus, while the EU argues that Boeing is subsidized indirectly through military and space contracts.

3. Five particularly controversial disputes between the EU and the US have come to the WTO dispute settlement system: Bananas, Hormones, Helms–Burton, Section 301 and Foreign Sales Corporations. Since they will probably remain controversial for the next few years, the underlying facts of each is detailed below.

Bananas. In 1993, the Council created a common market organization for bananas. The regulation provided for subsidies to EU banana production up to certain levels (mainly in the Canary Islands and the French West Indies), tariff-free treatment for bananas from ACP countries within certain limits (see Chapter 28) and a tariff quota for bananas from other third countries. Additional imports were possible only after payment of very high duties. Licenses to use the third-country tariff quota, which were quite valuable, were split between those who had traditionally dealt in third-country bananas and those who had traditionally dealt in ACP bananas.

Several GATT parties in the third-country category successfully challenged the rules in a GATT panel proceeding in 1994. Although the EU did not permit the panel report to be adopted, it reached a settlement with some of the parties that gave them specific shares of the third-country quota. After formation of the WTO, a new challenge was brought by one of the GATT complainants that had not settled (Guatemala), two new members (Ecuador and Honduras), Mexico and the US. The result was that the banana regime was found to be discriminatory under both GATT and GATS because of discrimination in allocating licenses for third-country bananas to EU and ACP operators, as well as in respect of quota shares given to the countries that had settled.

The EU adopted a new banana import regime as of the beginning of 1999, which was immediately challenged in the WTO, and again a violation of WTO rules was found, and the US and later Ecuador were authorized to take retaliatory action. In the case of the US, it imposed 100% tariffs on $191 million of EU products. As of April 2001, the EU and the US announced a settlement of the matter. The long-term intention of the EU is to move to a tariff-only regime, which should be WTO-consistent.

Hormones. In a challenge by the US and Canada to the EU's ban on imports of meat and meat products from cattle treated with growth promoting hormones, the WTO dispute settlement system ruled that the EU ban was not based on a risk assessment, as required by the WTO's SPS Agreement. Although given 15 months to implement the result, the EU admitted that the various studies it had commissioned of the safety of the six hormones at issue had not been completed, and the US and Canada were authorized to take retaliatory action in mid–1999. As of mid–2001, the EU position is that the studies have shown that one of the hormones at issue is carcinogenic and should be banned, while there is insufficient evidence to conclude that the other five are safe, such that they should be provisionally banned. It has not yet enacted new legislation on the subject, however. It should be noted that the SPS Agreement contains a provision that allows provisional action to be taken where relevant scientific evidence is insufficient. The EU declined to invoke that provision in the dispute settlement proceeding, but apparently will invoke it in its implementation actions.

Although not related to the *Hormones* case, another similar, potential dispute between the EU and the US involves the EU hesitancy to approve the use of genetically modified organisms (GMOs). A high percentage of certain US crops (corn, cotton and soybeans) are grown from genetically modified seeds. As of mid 2001, the US had not pursued this dispute in the WTO.

Helms-Burton. A major controversy in EU–US relations in 1996 concerned the so-called Helms–Burton Act, the popular name of the "Cuban Liberty and Democratic Solidarity Act of 1996". Among other things, this Act reaffirms the long-standing US economic embargo of Cuba. It also provides for the establishment of a civil cause of action against persons who "traffic" in (e.g., own, lease, use, manage or derive commercial benefit from) property confiscated by the Cuban government after Fidel Castro came to power in 1959. A successful plaintiff would be entitled to recover treble the value of the property, plus attorneys fees and costs. The US President has the power to postpone indefinitely (but only for six months at a time) the creation of this civil cause of action, and President Clintons and Bush have so far acted to do so. In addition, the Act provides for the exclusion from entry into the United States of persons involved with trafficking in such property, such as officials (and their families) of companies who traffic in such property. These exclusion rules are in effect and several European business persons have been denied entry into the US.

The EU strongly protested this legislation as extraterritorial and brought a complaint against the US in the WTO. It also enacted legislation designed to counteract the effects of the Helms–Burton Act. Council Regulation 2271/96, O.J. L 309/1 (Nov. 29, 1996). The Regulation specifically forbids compliance with the Helms Burton Act (and the Iran/Libya Sanctions Act) by any EU natural or legal person; declares invalid and unenforceable any US judgment or order issued pursuant to the legislation; and, through a so-called "clawback" provision, permits EU persons to sue in the EU to recover any damages paid to a successful US plaintiff under the legislation. In addition, the Regulation provides for (i) the possible imposition of visa and immigration restrictions on US interests, (ii) a requirement that all EU nationals notify the Commission of any adverse economic effects suffered as a result of the legislation and (iii) the compilation of a "watch list" of US companies invoking the legislation.

As a result of an indication by President Clinton that he would continue to postpone the effectiveness of the civil liability provisions of the Act and apparent non-vigorous enforcement of the visa provisions, the WTO proceeding was abandoned. As long as the law remains on the books, however, the dispute may reignite.

Section 301. As explained in Chapter 31(C), Section 301 of the US Trade Act of 1974 establishes a procedure under which the US government may initiate investigations of other countries' trade practices, at the request of a private party or on its own initiative, and take action against them if they are found to be in violation of an international agreement or if they are unjustifiable, unreasonable or discriminatory in a way that burdens US commerce. This provision is quite controversial in the world at large because of its invocation by the US government to take various unilateral actions to protest other countries' trade, intellectual property or investment policies. In 1999, the EU challenged Section 301 in the WTO. According to the EU, Section 301 violated the WTO Dispute Settlement Understanding (DSU) because it required the US Trade Representative to make determinations of WTO-inconsistency prior to the completion of the relevant WTO dispute settlement proceedings. The WTO panel found that while the US statute appeared on its face to violate the DSU, it was not inconsistent with the DSU given certain formal US undertakings to act under Section 301 consistently with the rules of the DSU. Both the EU and the US claimed victory and neither appealed. From the standpoint of the EU, it would be difficult in the future for the US to act inconsistently with the undertakings relied upon by the panel and thus difficult for the US to act unilaterally.

US Foreign Sales Corporations. In February 2000, the EU successfully established in WTO dispute settlement that the tax treatment given by the US to so-called foreign sales corporations was a prohibited export subsidy. The US subsequently changed the law in question in November 2000, but the EU maintained that the new legislation still provides an export subsidy and the matter has been referred back to WTO dispute settlement where a decision in favor of the EU was adopted early in 2002. The EU claims that the amount of trade affected (and the appropriate measure of any retaliatory measures) is $4 billion, which far exceeds the amount of the retaliatory measures taken against the EU by the US in *Bananas* and *Hormones*. An EU request for authorization to retaliate against the US is pending at the WTO, but will not be acted upon until the level of retaliation is set by arbitration.

Chapter 30

THE COMMUNITY CUSTOMS CODE

The European Community is a customs union (EC Treaty Art. 23). Under the GATT rule permitting customs unions, the constituent members must establish substantially the same duties and commercial restrictions toward nonmembers (GATT art. XXIV). Thus, the EC Treaty provides for the creation of a common customs tariff applicable to goods imported from abroad (Arts. 23–27) and a common commercial policy for dealing with third countries (Arts. 131–134). In this chapter, we will examine the Community Customs Code, as well as the Community's general rules for imports and exports. In the following chapter, we will consider one very important aspect of the common commercial policy—the EC rules designed to combat unfairly traded and injurious imports.

A. INTRODUCTION

The Common Customs Tariff (CCT) was established pursuant to Articles 18–29 of the EEC Treaty. The basic rule for establishing the common duties included in the CCT was to set those duties at the arithmetical average of the duties charged by the four relevant Member State jurisdictions (West Germany, France, Italy and the Benelux countries, who had already formed a customs union among themselves). There were, of course, many exceptions to the general rule—some were spelled out in the Treaty, others relating to particularly sensitive products were left to later negotiations between the Member States. The CCT came into force on July 1, 1968. The rates established in the CCT have been reduced over time as a result of the Community's participation in GATT and WTO tariff-cutting negotiations.

When a new state accedes to the EC, there is a phase-in period during which its tariffs are progressively aligned with the EC tariffs. If the new Member State has previously agreed to limit its tariffs in the WTO and the alignment process leads to an increase in its tariffs for a particular product, the Community may have to compensate other WTO members for such increase by lowering the Community tariff on other products.

As of January 1, 1988, the CCT was replaced by a new common tariff called the Combined Nomenclature (CN). The CN is based on an international agreement known as the Harmonized Commodity Description and Coding

System, which has also been used by the EC's major trading partners and which was drafted under the auspices of the Customs Cooperation Council, an international organization based in Brussels that deals with customs matters and that is now known as the World Customs Organization (WCO). The CN is supplemented by the Taric, the integrated Community tariff, which is used for statistical reporting purposes and which incorporates information on import rules not included in the CN, such as indications of tariff quotas, suspensions and preferences, and antidumping duties.

It is important to remember as we discuss customs issues that, although the Community establishes the detailed rules, the Community does not have a customs service. Thus, it is left to the Member States and their respective customs services to apply the rules. The Community does, however, keep the revenues collected (minus an administrative charge) as part of its own resources. This arrangement explains why customs law cases usually come to the Court of Justice as Article 234 references from national courts.

The operation of a comprehensive customs system is very complex. Every good that might be traded must be categorized and a decision made on what the applicable tariff rate will be. Since tariffs are usually ad valorem (i.e., set at a fixed percentage of a product's value), it is also necessary to have a system of valuing products at the time of import. To further complicate matters, a product may be subject to different tariff rates depending on where it comes from. It is therefore necessary for a customs system to have rules for deciding the origin of products. Accordingly, customs rules have to be very detailed, but clear and simple enough so that they can be readily and consistently applied by thousands of customs inspectors in the multitude of transactions that occur each day. Needless to say, despite the best efforts of customs officials, ambiguities inevitably arise, and many customs questions ultimately end up in the courts.

The rules for making these customs determinations are contained in the Community Customs Code, which came into force on January 1, 1994, parts of which are excerpted in the Selected Documents.[1] The Code gathers in one place the Community's basic rules on customs matters. Article 247 of the Code establishes a Customs Code committee, composed of Member State representatives and chaired by the Commission, which may examine any question concerning customs legislation. In this chapter, we will examine the basic issues that arise in the administration of tariffs–classification of goods, valuation and origin, as well as a number of other general matters involving the regulation of imports and exports.

B. CLASSIFICATION OF GOODS

Any attempt to compile a comprehensive list of products that might be traded internationally is a formidable task, especially if the end result is to be easily usable by millions of businesses and customs officials. The Combined Nomenclature categorizes products into 99 main chapters, with thousands of

1. Council Regulation 2913/92 of October 12, 1992, establishing the Community Customs Code, O.J. L 302/1 (Oct. 19, 1992). There is also a detailed Commission regulation implementing the Code. Commission Regulation 2454/93 of July 2, 1993 laying down provisions for the implementation of Council Regulation 2913/92 establishing the Community Customs Code, O.J. L 253/1 (Oct. 11, 1993).

headings and subheadings, using an eight digit code. It is probably inevitable that there will be products that arguably fit in more than one place in the list. In some cases, rules of the sort set out below may be used to choose between competing categories, but not infrequently resort to the Court of Justice is necessary.

COUNCIL REGULATION 2658/87 OF JULY 23, 1987

O.J. L 256/1, 15–16 (Sept. 7, 1987), as amended for 2001, O.J. L 264 (Oct. 18, 2000).

ANNEX I. COMBINED NOMENCLATURE

Part I. Preliminary Provisions

Section I

GENERAL RULES

A.   GENERAL RULES FOR THE INTERPRETATION OF THE COMBINED NOMENCLATURE

Classification of goods in the Combined Nomenclature shall be governed by the following principles:

1.   The titles of sections, chapters and sub-chapters are provided for ease of reference only; for legal purposes, classification shall be determined according to the terms of the headings and any relative section or chapter notes and, provided such headings or notes do not otherwise require, according to the following provisions:

2.   (a) Any reference in a heading to an article shall be taken to include a reference to that article incomplete or unfinished, provided that, as presented, the incomplete or unfinished article has the essential character of the complete or finished article. It shall also be taken to include a reference to that article complete or finished (or failing to be classified as complete or finished by virtue of this rule), presented unassembled or disassembled.

(b) Any reference in a heading to a material or substance shall be taken to include a reference to mixtures or combinations of that material or substance with other materials or substances. Any reference to goods of a given material or substance shall be taken to include a reference to goods consisting wholly or partly of such material or substance. The classification of goods consisting of more than one material or substance shall be according to the principles of rule 3.

3.   When by application of rule 2(b) or for any other reason, goods are *prima facie* classifiable under two or more headings, classification shall be effected as follows:

(a) the heading which provides the most specific description shall be preferred to headings providing a more general description. However, when two or more headings each refer to part only of the materials or substances contained in mixed or composite goods or to part only of the items in a set put up for retail sale, those headings are to be regarded as equally specific in relation to those goods, even if one of them gives a more complete or precise description of the goods.

(b) mixtures, composite goods consisting of different materials or made up of different components, and goods put up in sets for retail sale, which cannot be classified by reference to 3(a), shall be classified as if they consisted of the material or component which gives them their essential character in so far as this criterion is applicable.

(c) when goods cannot be classified by reference to 3(a) or (b), they shall be classified under the heading which occurs last in numerical order among those which equally merit consideration.

4.   Goods which cannot be classified in accordance with the above rules shall be classified under the heading appropriate to the goods to which they are most akin.

* * *

Notes and Questions

1.   There are more specific interpretative rules established for each section and chapter of the CN.

2.   Which general rule would you rely on to classify:

(a) a box containing several major elements of a tape recorder and the necessary parts to assemble it? What if the elements were imported separately?

(b) a first aid kit in which there are several distinct items classifiable under the CN?

E.I. DU PONT DE NEMOURS INC. v. COMMISSIONERS OF CUSTOMS & EXCISE

Case 234/81, [1982] ECR 3515.

[This case, which was referred to the Court of Justice by a UK court, involves a dispute over how the Du Pont product "Corian" should be classified under the Common Customs Tariff (CCT). Corian resembles marble, but consists by weight of about two-thirds aluminium hydroxide obtained from bauxite ore and one-third polymethyl methacrylate, an artificial plastic material, plus a very small amount of catalytic and other curing agents.

Du Pont maintained that Corian should be classified under CCT heading 68.11 (artificial stone). The UK authorities argued that it should be classified under subheading 39.02 C XII (methacrylic polymers), if imported in sheets, or 39.07 B V (d) (articles of materials covered by headings 39.01 to 39.06), if imported in other forms.]

[4]   In order to determine the correct tariff classification of Corian regard must be had, first, to Rule 2(b) of the Rules for the Interpretation of the Nomenclature of the Common Customs Tariff, which provides that: "Any reference in a heading to a material or substance shall be taken to include a reference to mixtures or combinations of that material or substance with other materials or substances. Any reference to goods of a given material or substance shall be taken to include a reference to goods consisting wholly or partly of such material or substance. The classification of goods consisting of more than one material or substance shall be according to the principles of Rule 3."

5   Inasmuch as Corian contains a material, namely polymethyl methacrylate, which comes under subheadings 39.02 C XII and 39.07 B V (d), it is *prima facie* classifiable under those subheadings pursuant to Rule 2(b).

6   By contrast, the presence of the other component, aluminium hydroxide, is not a reason for considering heading 26.01, which covers metallic ores, even if that substance is regarded as gibbsite, and therefore an ore. That is because, according to Note 2 to Chapter 26, that heading includes only metallic ores which have not been "submitted to processes not normal to the metallurgical industry", which is manifestly not true of the gibbsite present in Corian since it is in fact obtained by means of a chemical process. Heading 28.20, which covers *inter alia* aluminium oxide and aluminium hydroxide, must likewise be rejected on the basis of Note 1 to Chapter 28, according to which the chapter covers only "separate chemical elements and separate chemically defined compounds", a description not satisfied by the aluminium hydroxide present in Corian.

7   The other tariff heading which might be considered for the classification of Corian is heading 68.11, provided, however, that that product may be regarded, as Du Pont and Dewfield maintain, as "artificial stone".

8   There is no universally accepted interpretation of that concept in either trade or scientific circles, although the prevailing view is that "artificial stone contains natural stone". That approach was adopted in the Explanatory Notes of the Customs Cooperation Council, to which reference may be made in order to interpret headings in the Common Customs Tariff. According to those Notes, "artificial stone is an imitation of natural stone usually obtained by agglomerating pieces of natural stone, crushed or powdered natural stone (limestone, marble, granite, porphyry, serpentine, etc.) with lime or cement or other binders (e.g., artificial plastic material)".

9   It was submitted by Du Pont and Dewfield that the word "usually" ("en particulier" in the French version), which was used in the Notes, implies that there may be exceptions and thus allows even products which do not contain natural stone to be regarded as "artificial stone". That argument cannot be accepted, however, for the position of the word "usually", which precedes the words "by agglomerating" and not the words "powdered natural stone", indicates in fact that an exception might be made at most to allow for the possibility of using a manufacturing process other than the agglomeration of binders with powdered natural stone, but not for the case where no natural stone is used.

10   It follows that the only headings of the Common Customs Tariff which may be considered for the classification of Corian are subheadings 39.02 C XII and 39.07 B V (d).

11   The result would in any case be the same, even if it were accepted, for the sake of argument, that Corian may also be classified, *prima facie,* under heading 68.11 of the Common Customs Tariff.

12   If that were so Rule 3 of the General Rules would apply, paragraph (a) of which states that "the heading which provides the most specific description shall be preferred to headings providing a more general description". But heading 68.11, which, according to Du Pont and Dewfield, includes "any material with the characteristics of an imitation of natural stone", is

plainly far more general in scope, if thus construed, than subheadings 39.02 C XII and 39.07 B V (d).

13   The reply to be given to the national court must therefore be that the provisions of the Common Customs Tariff are to be construed as meaning that the product known as Corian, which consists by weight of approximately 66% aluminium hydroxide, approximately 33% polymethyl methacrylate and a very small percentage of catalytic and other curing agents, falls under subheading 39.02 C XII of the Common Customs Tariff when it is imported in the form of slabs, and under subheading 39.07 B V (d) when it is imported in the form of articles made of that material, and is not classifiable under any other heading of the Common Customs Tariff.

PEACOCK AG v. HAUPTZOLLAMT PADERBORN

Case C–339/98, [2000] ECR I-___ (Oct. 19, 2000).

[This Article 234 reference concerns the classification of network cards imported by Peacock that were designed to be installed in personal computers to enable them to exchange information or data with other computers via a local area network to which they are all connected. The cards were initially classified under subheading 8473 30 as parts and accessories of automatic data-processing machines of heading No 8471. The Hauptzollamt Paderborn later determined that the cards should be classified under heading No 8517 as electrical apparatus for line telephony or line telegraphy.]

5   Peacock challenged [that determination] on the ground that network cards are * * * computer parts whose function is to control the flow of data between computers connected via the network and that heading No 8517 of the Combined Nomenclature is not apt because network cards do not operate according to telephony or telegraphy techniques.

6   Note 5(B) to Chapter 84 of the Combined Nomenclature is worded as follows:

> "Automatic data-processing machines may be in the form of systems consisting of a variable number of separately housed units. A unit is to be regarded as being a part of the complete system if it meets all the following conditions:
>
> (a) it is connectable to the central processing unit either directly or through one or more other units;
>
> (b) it is specifically designed as part of such a system (it must, in particular, unless it is a power supply unit, be able to accept or deliver data in a form (code or signals) which can be used by the system).
>
> Such units presented separately are also to be classified within heading No 8471.
>
> Heading No 8471 does not cover machines incorporating or working in conjunction with an automatic data-processing machine and performing a specific function. Such machines are classified in the headings appropriate to their respective functions or, failing that, in residual headings."

* * *

9   As the Court has repeatedly held, the decisive criterion for the customs classification of goods must be sought generally in their objective characteristics and qualities, as defined in the relevant heading of the Common Customs Tariff and in the notes to the sections or chapters.

10 Both the notes which head the chapters of the Common Customs Tariff and the Explanatory Notes to the Nomenclature of the [World Customs Organisation] are important means of ensuring the uniform application of the Tariff and as such may be regarded as useful aids to its interpretation.

11 At the material time, heading Nos 8471, 8473 and 8517 of the Combined Nomenclature and the World Customs Organisation (WCO) harmonised system were worded as follows:

> —"8471 Automatic data-processing machines and units thereof; magnetic or optical readers, machines for transcribing data onto data media in coded form and machines for processing such data, not elsewhere specified or included",

> —"8473 Parts and accessories (other than covers, carrying cases and the like) suitable for use solely or principally with machines of headings 8469 to 8472",

> —"8517 Electrical apparatus for line telephony or line telegraphy, including such apparatus for carrier-current line systems."

12 Although network cards are designed solely to be installed in automatic data-processing machines, the Commission states that they fulfill a specific function other than data-processing and that, having regard to Note 5(B) to Chapter 84 of the Combined Nomenclature, they are therefore excluded from heading No 8471. According to the Commission, the function of network cards is to transmit data. Since the transmission techniques used are telecommunications techniques, the cards should therefore be classified under heading No 8517.

13 Since a network card is not a "machine incorporating" an automatic data-processing machine within the meaning of Note 5(B) to Chapter 84 of the Combined Nomenclature, it is necessary to consider whether it is nonetheless a machine working in conjunction with a machine of that type and performing a specific function. Those conditions must both be satisfied.

14 In that regard, the Commission submits that network cards perform a specific function distinct from information processing, namely the transmission of information.

15 It should be noted that such an assessment is based not on the objective characteristics and properties of a network card but on the functions which it allows an automatic information processing machine, as a whole, to perform.

16 As the national court has observed, network cards are designed solely for automatic information processing machines, they are directly connected to those machines and their function is to supply and accept data in a form which those machines can use. Network cards are thus comparable with any other medium whereby an automatic information processing machine accepts or delivers data in the sense that they have no function which they would be capable of performing without the assistance of such a machine.

17   It is therefore unnecessary to consider whether network cards could be classified as machines within the meaning of Note 5(B) to Chapter 84 of the Combined Nomenclature, since they cannot in any event be regarded as performing "a specific function".

18   Consequently, Note 5(B) to the Combined Nomenclature does not preclude network cards from being classified under heading No 8471.

19   It is also necessary to consider whether network cards are to be classified in the Combined Nomenclature under heading No 8471 as "units of automatic data-processing machines" or under heading No 8473 as "parts or accessories" of machines of that type.

20   In that regard, network cards satisfy the conditions relating to "units" set out in Note 5(B) to Chapter 84 of the Combined Nomenclature, since they can be connected to the central unit and are specifically designed as parts of an automatic data-processing system.

21   The word "part", on the other hand, implies a whole for the operation of which the part is essential and this is not so in the case of network cards. In that respect, it appears from the documents before the Court that network cards, which come in the form of slot-in cards, may also take other forms, in particular that of a stand alone unit.

22   The explanatory notes to the WCO harmonised system take as an example of "accessories" diskettes for cleaning disk drives in computer equipment. Network cards are clearly different in nature, and belong rather to the examples relating to "units" given in the explanatory notes to the WCO harmonised system. Thus explanatory note (I)(D) concerning heading No 8471 of the Combined Nomenclature refers to control and adaptor units interconnecting the central unit to other automatic data processing units and to signal converting units which, at input, enable an external signal to be understood by the machine or which, at output, convert the processed signals into signals which can be used externally.

23   It follows from all the foregoing considerations that network cards must be classified under heading No 8471 of the Combined Nomenclature as "units" of automatic data processing machines.

Notes and Questions

1.   The problem of classification would be eliminated if a single tariff rate were used for all goods of the same origin. There are a number of reasons why this is not done. While tariffs do have a revenue raising function, they largely serve to protect domestic industry from import competition. If a product is not produced locally, a tariff would only raise its cost to consumers. While that may be deemed desirable in the case of luxury imports, if the product is a raw material for a domestic processing industry, a tariff would make that industry less competitive. Thus, there will be pressures for zero or low tariffs on goods not produced domestically. As to other goods, the extent to which an industry needs (or is able to obtain) protection from import competition will differ and tariff rates may vary as a consequence.

2.   The *Corian* case is a good example of how classification problems must be approached. In that case there were a number of possible classifications. The first step is to see if there are any applicable general or specific rules that will eliminate some of the possibilities. Then it is necessary to examine the exact

wording of the remaining possible classifications. When the relevant terms are defined, the answer usually is revealed.

3.   The *Peacock* case involved another significant classification problem: How does one classify new products? Interestingly, a related issue was considered in the WTO in a dispute between the US and the EC in which the US alleged that the EC had violated WTO rules by changing the way in which adapter cards and similar equipment were classified so as to defeat US expectations as to the tariff concessions it had negotiated with the EC. The WTO ruled that the US had failed to establish its claim,[2] although a WTO-related agreement on the tariff treatment of information technology products has since resulted in zero tariffs on most such products.

4.   There are a number of amusing classification cases involving dolls and toys. For example, in Bienengraber & Co. v. Hauptzollamt Hamburg–Jonas, Case 38/85, [1986] ECR 811, the Court of Justice was faced with the question of how to classify "Kikis," which were "half human in appearance, in so far as their hands, feet, the shape of their eyes, cheeks and mouth are concerned, and half animal, with regard in particular to their nose and tail and to the fur which covers their torso and limbs." (para. 3). The importer claimed that the Kikis were dolls. However, the notes to the CCT provided that "only * * * such articles as are representations of human beings (including those of a caricature type)" were to be regarded as dolls. (para. 11). The German customs authorities rejected the importer's claim on the basis of (i) an opinion poll in which 71% of the mothers interviewed thought that the Kikis represented an animal rather than a human being and (ii) an expert opinion from a customs training college that they represented animals. The Court concluded (paras. 12–13):

> Inasmuch as the representation of a human being may, according to the wording of those Explanatory Notes, be deformed or even stylized, it may also include certain characteristics borrowed from the animal kingdom. Such animal characteristics must, however, remain minor and secondary and must not put in question the general appearance of the figure which must essentially correspond to that of a human being.

> The answer to the questions referred by the Bundesfinanzhof must therefore be that Note 3 to Chapter 97 of the Common Customs Tariff is to be interpreted as meaning that a figure may be regarded as a doll within the meaning of subheading 97.02 A of the Common Customs Tariff only if any animal features which it may have are minor and secondary and the figure's general appearance is essentially that of a human being.

Who won? The case highlights an important aspect of customs law. There is always an attempt made, in light of the relevant notes, to give the normal meaning to words used in a classification description.

5.   How would you classify a stereo component system including the following five components, with their respective values indicated separately in deutsche marks:

compact disc player (DM 164)

amplifier (DM 173.50)

tuner (DM 124)

double cassette recorder (DM 179)

---

2. European Communities–Customs Classification of Certain Computer Equipment, WT/ DS62/AB/R, WTO Appellate Body Report adopted on June 22, 1998.

record player (DM 55)

Assume your choices are:

(1) 8519 9910—other sound-producing apparatus with laser optical reading systems (based on the CD player)

(2) 8527—radio reception apparatus (based on tuner)

(3) 8519 3900—record player, or

(4) 8520 3190—double cassette player.

What result under Rule 3 of the general rules for interpretation of the CN? The German Federal Supreme Finance Court concluded that Rules 3a and 3b were not helpful, leaving Rule 3c as determinative. In re Import of a Compact Disc Player, [1993] 1 CMLR 780 (Case VII K 2/91, Bundesfinanzhof, June 2, 1992).

6. As of 1987, imports of original engravings, prints and lithographs (heading 99.02) were exempt from duties, while photographs (heading 49.11) from the United States were subject to a 5.8% duty. How should 36 photographs by artist Robert Mapplethorpe, worth DM 66,783 (approximately $36,000), be classified? In Rabb v. Hauptzollamt Berlin–Packhof, Case C–1/89, [1989] ECR 4432, which was referred to the Court of Justice, the importer of the photographs claimed that

> the photographs in question, of which only a limited number of copies were made from artistically prepared original plates and the value of which was far higher than the value of the materials used, should be regarded as works of art within the meaning of Chapter 99 of the Common Customs Tariff [Works of art, collectors' pieces and antiques] and classified under Heading 99.02 because they were related to the field of the graphic arts.

[1989] ECR at 4434. Do you agree? Or should the existence of a specific heading for photographs preclude such classification? What is the relevance of the broad wording of the heading to Chapter 99, quoted above in brackets? See General Rule 1 at the beginning of this section. Would there be any administrative problems in distinguishing between artistic photographs and other photographs?

Note 2 to Chapter 99 states that for the purposes of heading 99.02, the expression "original engravings, prints and lithographs" means "impressions produced directly, in black or white or in colour, of one or several plates wholly executed by hand by the artist, irrespective of the process or of the material employed by him, but not including any mechanical or photomechanical process." How would this note affect your answer?

7. In order to enhance predictability, the Community Customs Code provides a mechanism whereby an importer may obtain a ruling from the customs authorities in advance on the classification of a particular product through obtaining so-called "binding tariff information". This procedure is quite popular and tens of thousands of requests have been acted upon. See Article 12 of the CCC.

8. Article 7 of Regulation 2658/87 establishes a Nomenclature Committee, consisting of representatives from each of the Member States and chaired by the Commission, to help the Commission administer the CN. Among other things, the committee makes classification rulings. The WCO, which sponsored the Harmonized Convention that is the basis of the CN, also issues classification opinions from time to time.

9. For a general discussion of EC classification rules, see Stefano Inama & Edwin Vermulst, Customs and Trade Laws of the European Community 136–166

(1999). For materials on US tariff classification issues, see J. Jackson, W. Davey & A. Sykes, Legal Problems of International Economic Relations ch. 8 (West 4th ed. 2002).

C. VALUATION OF GOODS

The second issue that arises in implementing the CN is valuation. Since most duties are ad valorem, it is necessary to determine the value on which the percentage duty rate will be applied. The Community rules on valuation, which are found in articles 28–36 of the Community Customs Code (excerpted in the Selected Documents), are based on the WTO Customs Valuation Agreement, which was based on the 1979 GATT Customs Valuation Code. The essential feature of the WTO agreement is the requirement that normally the "transaction value," i.e. the price actually paid by the buyer of the good, should be the basis for valuing a good for customs purposes. Prior to the adoption of the code, the major trading nations used many different methods to value goods for customs purposes. For example, in the EC, "normal value" was used, which meant that the customs value of a good might be more than the price actually paid for it if the customs authorities thought that it was usually sold in arms' length transactions for a higher price. The change to the use of transaction value generally favors importers and reduces considerably the discretion formerly exercised by customs officials in valuation matters.

HANS SOMMER GmbH & CO. KG v. HAUPTZOLLAMT BREMEN

Case C–15/99, [2000] ECR I–___ (Oct. 19, 2000).

[This preliminary reference concerns the valuation of honey from the former USSR that Hans Sommer GmbH & Co. (Sommer) had bought from Kessler before the honey had been cleared through customs. The goods, delivered pursuant to contracts of sale c.i.f. Hamburg, were also the subject of supplementary agreements stipulating "costs" of completing the transaction, calculated at a flat rate per ton of honey. Those costs, invoiced separately by Kessler, included the expenses of unloading, taking possession of the goods until storage, removal from the warehouse by lorry, FOT costs, the costs of taking and analyzing samples, and warehousing charges. In its declarations of value for customs purposes, Sommer declared only the prices which had been agreed with Kessler in the contracts of sale c.i.f. Hamburg.]

[3] Article 3 of Regulation No 1224/80 [now Article 29 of the Community Customs Code] provides:

> "(1) The customs value of imported goods * * * shall be the transaction value, that is, the price actually paid or payable for the goods when sold for export to the customs territory of the Community [adjusted in accordance with Articles 32 and 33 of the Code] ..."
>
> . . .
>
> "(3)(a) The price actually paid or payable is the total payment made or to be made by the buyer to or for the benefit of the seller for the imported goods and includes all payments made or to be made as a condition of sale of the imported goods by the buyer to the seller or

by the buyer to a third party to satisfy an obligation of the seller . . . ."

* * *

19 [The first question asked by Finanzgericht Bremen is] whether the costs of analyses designed to establish the conformity of the imported goods with the national legislation of the importing Member State, which the importer invoices to the buyer in addition to the price of goods, must be regarded as an integral part of their "transaction value" within the meaning of Article 3(1) of Regulation No 1224/80.

20 Sommer submits that the question should be answered in the negative. It argues that those costs are in respect of services supplied in the Community by undertakings established there and relate to goods which have already been sold for export to the Community customs territory. It is therefore necessary to apply the case-law of the Court to the effect that, subject to the adjustments provided for in Article 8 of Regulation No 1224/80 [Articles 32 and 33 of the Code], payment for services provided to the buyer on the purchase of imported goods is not included in the customs value of the goods.

21 The national court and the Commission observe that the seller undertook to deliver honey of a quality specified in the contract of sale by reference to a "detailed analysis" made by the seller in accordance with the applicable German legislation. The analysis costs should therefore be regarded as pertaining to a "condition of sale of the imported goods" and, accordingly, are part of the customs value of those goods in accordance with Article 3(3)(a) of Regulation No 1224/80.

22 In answering the first question, it should be borne in mind that under the system established by Regulation No 1224/80 the concept of "transaction value", that is to say, as a general rule, the price actually paid or payable for the goods, forms the basis for calculating the customs value. That calculation must therefore be made on the basis of the conditions on which the individual sale was made.

23 It is apparent from the national court's findings that in the contracts of sale Kessler undertook to deliver to Sommer honey satisfying the quality requirements laid down by German legislation. It follows that the analyses performed after importation in order to establish the quality of the honey were necessary in order for the goods to be delivered in accordance with the provisions of the contracts.

24 The costs pertaining to those analyses must therefore be regarded as part of the "payments made or to be made as a condition of sale of the imported goods by the buyer to the seller . . . to satisfy an obligation of the seller" within the meaning of Article 3(3)(a) of Regulation No 1224/80 and, accordingly, as an integral part of the customs value.

25 That interpretation is in conformity with the objective of the Community legislation on customs valuation, which, as may be seen from the sixth recital in the preamble to Regulation No 1224/80, is to introduce a fair, uniform and neutral system excluding the use of arbitrary or fictitious customs values.

[26] As the Advocate General points out in paragraph 42 of his Opinion, goods whose quality is certified by the seller have a greater economic value than goods for which there is no such certificate. When calculating the customs value, it is therefore justified to take into account the costs of paying to obtain that certification.

Notes and Questions

1. In Ospig Textilgesellschaft KG W. Alhers v. Hauptzollamt Bremen–Ost, Case 7/83, [1984] ECR 609, the Court considered whether quota charges should be included in the value of the goods for Community customs purposes. The quota charges at issue were amounts paid to obtain a Hong Kong export permit, which was required by EC rules to be presented on importation into the Community of certain Hong Kong products. The permit was part of the mechanism by which the EC enforced certain quantitative restrictions on imports of textiles and apparel from Hong Kong. In light of the *Sommers* case, should the amount be included? Should it matter whether the Hong Kong exporter purchases the export permit or the Community importer purchases it and gives it to the exporter?

The Court of Justice noted that the Community valuation rules did not deal explicitly with quota charges and ruled that the charges should not be included. The Court seemed to be concerned that to include the charges would mean that identical goods sold for the same basic price might have different values on entering the EC, depending on whether and to whom the importer paid a quota fee. Do you agree with the result? Why isn't the cost of obtaining necessary import documentation like the cost of transporting the goods to the Community frontier? On the other hand, is there any specific relationship between the value of the goods and the amount of the quota charge? Isn't it possible that identical goods might enter under quotas costing significantly different amounts? Should it matter that the quota charges may not inure to the benefit of the seller of the goods, but to some third party who happened to possess quota rights? In Klaus Thierschmidt GmbH v. Hauptzollamt Essen, Case C–340/93, [1994] ECR I–3905, the Court ruled that quota charges paid by a buyer to a seller who had obtained the necessary quotas free of charge were to be included in the customs value of the goods at issue. The Court seemed to view its ruling as consistent with *Ospig*. Why? Do you agree? Compare Generra Sportswear Co. v. United States, 905 F.2d 377 (Fed.Cir.1990) (quota charges paid by buyer are dutiable).

2. Suppose that the contract between the exporter and the importer provided that the total purchase price for the goods was based on their net delivered weight. If the importer pays for weighing the cargo, is the amount of the weighing fee to be included in the customs value? Since the exporter was obligated to deliver the goods to the importer, isn't determining the weight of the goods part of that obligation? Would it matter that it was customary for sellers to bear weighing costs under this type of contract? In Hauptzollamt Hamburg–Ericus v. Van Houten International GmbH, Case 65/85, [1986] ECR 447, the Court of Justice ruled that it was necessary to look at the individual transaction in question, not at trade practice. Since the weighing costs were in fact paid for by the buyer and since there are no specific provisions in the regulation dealing with weighing costs, it concluded that they were not to be included in the customs value of the goods. In light of articles 29, 32 and 33 of the Community Customs Code, do you agree with the Court?

3. As noted above, the EC rules aim to use the actual price paid as the basis for valuation, subject to certain adjustments specified in the regulation. Suppose,

however, that the transaction is between related parties, such as a parent company and one of its subsidiaries. (In fact, much of international trade takes place under these circumstances.) In such a situation, must the customs authorities accept the price paid by the related party for valuation purposes? See Community Customs Code, art. 29(1)(d), (2). If the transaction value is not used, how is the customs value determined? See art. 29(2). Essentially, the Regulation provides that recourse should first be had to the transaction value in identical transactions (art. 29(2)(a)) and then to the transaction value in similar transactions (art. 29(2)(b)). If these alternatives are also unsuitable or unavailable, it permits, at the option of the importer, the use of (i) the value at which the imported goods are sold in the greatest aggregate quantity to persons unrelated to the seller (art. 29(2)(c)), or (ii) constructed value, which is established by adding up all of the costs involved in producing the product and transporting it to the Community (art. 29(2)(d)). Some of these issues are treated in S.A. Caterpillar Overseas v. Belgium, Case 111/79, [1980] ECR 773, which interprets a predecessor regulation.

4. How does the Code treat (a) royalties and (b) "assists"? See art. 32(1)(b)-(c). How does this treatment comport with the philosophy of the Code as expressed in the *Sommers* case?

5. For a general discussion of EC valuation rules, see Stefano Inama & Edwin Vermulst, Customs and Trade Laws of the European Community 166–174 (1999). For materials on US customs valuation issues, see J. Jackson, W. Davey & A. Sykes, Legal Problems of International Economic Relations ch. 8 (West 4th ed. 2002).

D. ORIGIN OF GOODS

Even if an import has been properly classified and valued, it still may not be possible to assess the duty because different duty rates are applicable to the same product depending on the product's origin. For example, many goods from many countries may enter the Community duty free, either because they originate in countries with whom the EC has a free trade area (such as the EFTA countries) or in developing countries to which the EC grants tariff preferences. Rules to determine the origin of goods are obviously necessary. The EC's general origin rules are contained in the Community Customs Code, articles 22–27, which are excerpted in the Selected Documents. The heart of the rules is article 24, the predecessor of which is interpreted in the following two cases.

GESELLSCHAFT FÜR ÜBERSEEHANDEL MBH v. HANDELSKAMMER HAMBURG

Case 49/76, [1977] ECR 41.

[The plaintiff in this case operated a factory in Germany in which raw casein from a nonEC country was cleaned, ground to various degrees of fineness, graded and then appropriately packaged. The case arose when the Hamburg chamber of commerce refused to certify that the casein produced by the plaintiff originated in Germany. The case turned on the interpretation of what is now article 24 of the Code, in respect of which the German court referred questions to the Court of Justice.]

[3]   Article 5 of Regulation No 802/68 provides:

> "A product in the production of which two or more countries were concerned shall be regarded as originating in the country in which the last substantial process or operation that is economically justified was performed, having been carried out in an undertaking equipped for the purpose, and resulting in the manufacture of a new product or representing an important stage of manufacture."[3]

It appears from the order for reference that it is not denied that, in accordance with the said provision, the process or operation to which the raw casein is subjected in this case constitutes an activity "carried out in an undertaking equipped for the purpose", and that it is "economically justified" because it is necessary for the industrial use of the product.

Thus, the dispute is concerned in essence with the question whether the said activity constitutes a "substantial" process or operation for the purposes of Article 5 of Regulation No 802/68, resulting in "the manufacture of a new product" or representing "an important stage of manufacture".

It is therefore in respect of this question that an answer should be given to the national court.

* * *

[5]   According to the last recital in the preamble to Regulation No 802/68 and to Article 1 of that regulation, a common definition of the concept of the origin of goods constitutes an indispensable means of ensuring the uniform application of the Common Customs Tariff, of quantitative restrictions and of all other measures adopted, in relation to the importation or exportation of goods, by the Community or by the Member States.

> For those purposes, Articles 4[4] and 5 of the regulation base such a definition on objective criteria, making it possible to ensure the uniform application in all the Member States of the concept of the origin of goods and thus to avoid deflections of trade and abuses.

In particular, there can be seen in Article 6[5] of the regulation the intention to prevent the origin of goods in the production of which two or more countries are concerned from being determined by way of a non-substantial process or operation in such a manner as to defeat the purposes of Article 1 or to circumvent the measures adopted by the Member States in relation to importation or exportation.

In these circumstances, it would not seem sufficient to seek criteria defining the origin of goods in the tariff classification of the processed products, for the Common Customs Tariff has been conceived to fulfil special purposes and not in relation to the determination of the origin of products.

---

3. Article 24 of the Code is worded somewhat differently, although it is in substance virtually the same: "Goods whose production involved more than one country shall be deemed to originate in the country where they underwent their last, substantial, economically justified processing or working in an undertaking equipped for that purpose and resulting in the manufacture of a new product or representing an important stage of manufacture."

4. Code, art. 23.

5. Code, art. 25.

On the contrary, in order to meet the purposes and requirements of Regulation No 802/68, the determination of the origin of goods must be based on a real and objective distinction between raw material and processed product, depending fundamentally on the specific material qualities of each of those products.

6 Therefore, the last process or operation referred to in Article 5 of the regulation is only "substantial" for the purposes of that provision if the product resulting therefrom has its own properties and a composition of its own, which it did not possess before that process or operation.

In providing that the said process or operation must, in order to confer a particular origin, result in the manufacture of a new product or represent an important stage of manufacture, the abovementioned Article 5 shows in fact that activities affecting the presentation of the product for the purposes of its use, but which do not bring about a significant qualitative change in its properties, are not of such a nature as to determine the origin of the said product.

7 The grinding of a raw material such as raw casein to various degrees of fineness cannot be considered as a process or operation for the purposes of Article 5 of Regulation No 802/68, because the only effect of doing so is to change the consistency of the product and its presentation for the purposes of its later use; it does not bring about a significant qualitative change in the raw material.

Furthermore, the quality control by grading to which the ground product is subjected and the manner in which it is packaged relate only to the requirements for marketing the product and do not affect its substantial properties.

8 [T]he Committee on Origin set up under Article 12 of Regulation No 802/68 has found that the grinding to different degrees of fineness, the sorting and packaging of casein do not constitute activities involving a process or operation conferring on the product resulting from those activities a particular origin for the purposes of the said regulation.

Although opinions expressed by the Committee are not binding, except in so far as the Commission has adopted implementing provisions in application of Article 14(3)(a) of Regulation No 802/68, nevertheless, until such time as the Commission adopts contrary provisions under subparagraphs (b) and (c) of the said Article 14(3), they constitute an important criterion for interpreting Article 5 of the said regulation, the scope of which they define in respect of specific cases.

9 It is therefore to be concluded that the cleaning and grinding of a raw material, such as raw casein imported from a third country into a Member State, together with the grading and packaging of the product obtained, do not constitute a substantial process or operation for the purposes of Article 5 of Regulation No 802/68, and do not confer a Community origin on the said product, according to that regulation.

BROTHER INT'L v. HAUPTZOLLAMT GEISSEN

Case 26/88, [1989] ECR 4253.

[In 1984 and 1985 Brother imported electronic typewriters from Taiwan into Germany and declared them to originate in Taiwan, where it had assembled the typewriters out of parts, some of which came from Japan. After an investigation, German customs authorities ruled that the typewriters actually originated in Japan and were therefore subject to the antidumping duties that had been imposed by the EC on Japanese typewriters. Brother contested this decision in German court, which referred questions to the Court of Justice.]

The Interpretation of Article 5 of Regulation (EEC) No 802/68[6]

11   In its first question the national court is essentially asking under what conditions the mere assembly of previously manufactured parts originating in a country other than that of assembly suffices to confer on the resulting product the origin of the country where the assembly took place.

* * *

13   Brother considers that the conditions set out in Article 5 are of a technical nature and that an assembly constitutes a classic processing operation for the purposes of that provision in so far as it consists, as in the present case, of assembling a large number of parts to form a new coherent whole. An implementing regulation adopted under Article 14 of Regulation No 802/68 laying down the conditions for conferring origin might define the economic criteria of an assembly but not criteria in relation to its intellectual content.

14   The Commission considers on the other hand that the mere assembly of previously manufactured parts should not be regarded as a substantial process or operation within the meaning of Article 5 of the regulation where, in view of the work involved and the expenditure on materials on the one hand and the value added on the other, the operation is clearly less important than other processes or operations carried out in another country or countries.

15   It is clear from Article 5 as interpreted in previous judgments of the Court that the decisive criterion is that of the last substantial process or operation. That view is moreover confirmed by Rule 3 of Annex D.1 to the International Convention on the simplification and harmonization of customs procedures (the Kyoto Convention), which was accepted on behalf of the Community by Council Decision 77/415/EEC of 3 June 1977. Rule 3 reads "Where two or more countries have taken part in the production of the goods, the origin of the goods shall be determined according to the substantial transformation criterion".

16   Article 5 of Regulation No 802/68 does not specify to what extent assembly operations may be regarded as a substantial process or operation. Rule 6 of the Kyoto Convention states that

---

6. Code, art. 24 (see note 3 supra).

"operations which do not contribute or which contribute to only a small extent to the essential characteristics or properties of the goods, and in particular operations confined to one or more of those listed below, shall not be regarded as constituting substantial manufacturing or processing:

* * *

(c) simple assembly operations;

* * * ".

17 "Simple assembly operations" means operations which do not require staff with special qualifications for the work in question or sophisticated tools or specially equipped factories for the purposes of assembly. Such operations cannot be held to be such as to contribute to the essential characteristics or properties of the goods in question.

18 The Kyoto Convention confines itself to excluding from the concept of substantial process or operation simple assembly operations without specifying the conditions under which other types of assembly may constitute a substantial process or operation. For such other types of assembly it is necessary to determine in each case and on the basis of objective criteria whether or not they represent a substantial process or operation.

19 An assembly operation may be regarded as conferring origin where it represents from a technical point of view and having regard to the definition of the goods in question the decisive production stage during which the use to which the component parts are to be put becomes definite and the goods in question are given their specific qualities.

20 In view however of the variety of operations which may be described as assembly there are situations where consideration on the basis of technical criteria may not be decisive in determining the origin of goods. In such cases it is necessary to take account of the value added by the assembly as an ancillary criterion.

21 The relevance of that criterion is moreover confirmed by the Kyoto Convention, the notes of which in relation to Rule 3 of Annex D.1 state that in practice the substantial transformation criterion can be expressed by the *ad valorem* percentage rule, where either the percentage value of the materials utilized or the percentage of the value added reaches a specified level.

22 As regards the application of that criterion and in particular the question of the amount of value added which is necessary to determine the origin of the goods in question, the basis should be that the assembly operations as a whole must involve an appreciable increase in the commercial value of the finished product at the ex-factory stage. In that respect it is necessary to consider in each particular case whether the amount of the value added in the country of assembly in comparison with the value added in other countries justifies conferring the origin of the country of assembly.

23 Where only two countries are concerned in the production of goods and examination of technical criteria proves insufficient to determine the origin, the mere assembly of those goods in one country from previously manufactured parts originating in the other is not sufficient to confer on the resulting product the origin of the country of assembly if the value

added there is appreciably less than the value imparted in the other country. It should be stated that in such a situation value added of less than 10%, which corresponds to the estimate put forward by the Commission in its observations, cannot in any event be regarded as sufficient to confer on the finished product the origin of the country of assembly.

24   The origin of goods which have been the subject of assembly operations must be determined on the basis of the abovementioned criteria without it being necessary to determine whether the assembly involves any intellectual contribution, that criterion not being envisaged in Article 5.

25   In view of the foregoing, the answer to the first question must be that the mere assembly of previously manufactured parts originating in a country different from that in which they were assembled is sufficient to confer on the resulting product the origin of the country in which assembly took place, provided that from a technical point of view and having regard to the definition of the goods in question such assembly represents the decisive production stage during which the use to which the component parts are to be put becomes definite and the goods in question are given their specific qualities; if the application of that criterion is not conclusive, it is necessary to examine whether all the assembly operations in question result in an appreciable increase in the commercial, ex-factory value of the finished product.

The Interpretation of Article 6 of Regulation (EEC) No 802/68[7]

26   In its second question the national court is asking whether the transfer of the assembly from the country of manufacture of the component parts to a country where use is made of already existing factories in itself justifies the presumption that the sole object of the transfer was to circumvent the applicable provisions, and in particular the application of anti-dumping duties, within the meaning of Article 6 of the Regulation.

27   Article 6 provides that

"any process or work in respect of which it is established, or in respect of which the facts as ascertained justify the presumption, that its *sole* object was to circumvent the provisions applicable in the Community or the Member States to goods from specific countries shall in no case be considered, under Article 5, as conferring on the goods thus produced the origin of the country where it is carried out".

28   The transfer of the assembly from the country where the parts are manufactured to another country where use is made of factories already in existence is no ground in itself for such a presumption. There may be other reasons to justify such a transfer. Where however the transfer of the assembly coincides with the entry into force of the relevant rules, the trader concerned must prove that there were reasonable grounds, other than avoiding the consequences of the provisions in question, for carrying

---

7. The analogous Code provision is article 25, which is worded similarly: "Any processing or working in respect of which it is established, or in respect of which the facts as ascertained justify the presumption, that its sole object was to circumvent the provisions applicable in the Community to goods from specific countries shall under no circumstances be deemed to confer on the goods thus produced the origin of the country where it is carried out with the meaning of Article 24."

out the assembly operations in the country from which the goods were exported.

29   The answer to the second question put by the national court must therefore be that the transfer of assembly from the country in which the parts were manufactured to another country in which use is made of existing factories does not in itself justify the presumption that the sole object of the transfer was to circumvent the applicable provisions unless the transfer of assembly coincides with the entry into force of the relevant regulations. In that case, the manufacturer concerned must prove that there were reasonable grounds, other than avoiding the consequences of the provisions in question, for carrying out the assembly operations in the country from which the goods were exported.

Notes and Questions

1.   Do you agree with the Court's approach in the *Brother* case? Has the Court shifted the analysis of whether a process is substantial from an evaluation of the process to a value added test? Is that justified under what is now article 24 of the Code? Do you agree with the Court's analysis of what is now article 25 of the Code? With its assignment of the burden of proof?

2.   In addition to the rules discussed in the *Brother* case, the EC has adopted special origin rules for products subject to antidumping duties, which are discussed in the next chapter.

3.   Besides the general rules on origin contained in Community Customs Code, the EC has adopted special, usually more restrictive, origin rules in respect of a number of products. In some cases, these special rules of origin have been criticized as having been motivated by general trade policy considerations and not by technical issues arguably more appropriate for deciding origin questions. Indeed, since origin rules can spur investment in more complex manufacturing operations in particular locations, they can obviously be used to promote investment in the EC. For example, an EC origin rule that grants origin to products only if they have undergone a complex assembly operation may cause companies to invest in such assembly operations in the EC. Should origin rules be used for such purposes?

4.   Since the benefits of preferential tariff treatment should presumably be limited to the countries to which it was granted, special rules of origin often govern cases of preferential customs treatment. These rules are more difficult to meet than those for regular treatment, and can in fact be quite complicated. See generally I. Forrester, EEC Customs Law: Rules of Origin and Preferential Duty Treatment—Parts I & II, 5 Eur.L.Rev. 167 & 257 (1980).

Preferential rules of origin typically require either that the product be wholly obtained in a country or that a specified amount of processing have taken place in the country. Rather than speak in general terms of undergoing a substantial process, rules of preferential origin may specify value added tests that must be met for origin, indicate precisely the activities that must be performed to establish origin or establish other tests designed to ensure that substantial processing has occurred (such as a requirement that the imported components and the final product fall under different tariff headings). For example, in the recently negotiated Cotonou Agreement (see Chapter 28), special origin rules fill more than 40 pages of small type.

Every product has a nonpreferential origin. In particular, given the restrictiveness of preferential origin rules compared to the regular origin rules, it is not unusual for a product that fails the preferential origin tests applicable to country X to be considered as having originated in country X for regular origin purposes. The effect will be that the product is subject to the regular duty rate instead of duty-free treatment.

In today's global economy, it is not unusual for components of a product to have originated in several countries or for a product to have been transported in unfinished states for processing in several countries. This may make it difficult to meet preferential origin requirements. However, if the countries involved in the processing are EC countries and one beneficiary country, or are beneficiary countries benefiting from the same or related preferential agreements with the EC, it is sometimes possible to cumulate activities undertaken in one beneficiary country with those taken in the EC or, in some cases, in another beneficiary country. Needless to say, this can make application of the origin rules even more complex than suggested above. See id. at 266–281.

5. For a general discussion of EC origin rules, see Stefano Inama & Edwin Vermulst, Customs and Trade Laws of the European Community 93–135, 174–190 (1999). For a discussion of US origin rules, see J. Jackson, W. Davey & A. Sykes, Legal Problems of International Economic Relations ch. 8 (West 4th ed. 2002).

E.   IMPORT MEASURES

In addition to tariffs, the EC imposes other measures that restrict imports into the Community. This section examines the general Community rules on safeguards, which are actions taken to protect a Community industry that is suffering or threatened with serious injury; the possibility of intra-Community safeguards; and miscellaneous import restrictions imposed by the Community.

1. FORMAL SAFEGUARD MEASURES

As described in Chapter 29, WTO rules generally prohibit the imposition of quantitative and other nontariff restrictions on imports. Article XIX of GATT 1994 and the WTO Agreement on Safeguards, however, allow a WTO Member to impose such restrictions if its domestic injury has been "seriously injured" or is threatened with serious injury by imports. The EC recognizes these WTO rules in its common rules for imports, established by Regulation 3285/94,[8] and applicable to products other than certain textile products and products from certain former state trading countries.

Generally, the common rules for imports provide that imports into the Community shall be free of quantitative restrictions. Regulation 3285/94, art. 1. There are, however, two important exceptions as the rules provide for the use of surveillance and safeguard measures. Imports may be subjected to Community surveillance, normally by Commission action, if they threaten to cause injury to Community producers of like or directly competing products. Regulation 3285/94, art. 11. Under the surveillance procedures, imports may be put into free circulation in the Community only on production of an import document issued or endorsed by a Member State. The import document is to

---

8. Council Regulation 3285/94 of Dec. 22, 1994, O.J. L 349/53 (Dec. 31, 1994).

be issued free of charge, for any quantity requested and within five days. Regulation 3285/94, art. 12.

The object of the surveillance procedure is to collect detailed, up-to-date information on the volume of imports so that protective measures may be introduced promptly if necessary. Although in practice there may be some disruptive effect on trade, products subject to surveillance can enter the Community in unlimited quantities. Surveillance measures have been imposed by the Community, but relatively sparingly.

Community safeguard measures, such as quotas, may be imposed by the Commission, if a product is imported into the Community in such greatly increased quantities and/or on such terms and conditions as to cause, or threaten to cause, serious injury to Community producers of like or directly competing products. Serious injury is defined as "a significant overall impairment in the position of Community producers." Regulation 3285/94, art. 5(3)(a), 16. Regulation 3285/94 imposes a number of procedural rules for safeguard investigations, which are designed to ensure that Community practices conform to the requirements of the WTO Agreement on Safeguards. For example, although only the Commission and Member States are involved in the initiation of a safeguards investigation, interested parties may submit relevant information to the Commission and are entitled to a hearing. If quotas are imposed, the Regulation requires that account be taken, inter alia, of traditional trade flows and existing contracts and exempts goods in transit to the Community at the time the quotas are imposed. Regulation 3285/94, art. 16(3),(5). Formal safeguard measures have seldom imposed by the Community. For materials on the WTO Agreement on Safeguards, GATT Article XIX and the US rules based on it, see J. Jackson, W. Davey & A. Sykes, Legal Problems of International Economic Relations, ch. 15 (West 4th ed. 2002).

As noted at the outset of this section, Regulation 3285/94 does not apply to imports from state trading countries or to certain textile imports. The Community traditionally subjected certain imports from state trading countries to quotas. Under Regulation 519/94,[9] imports from those countries are, with some exceptions, generally to be free of quantitative restrictions. The Regulation contains provisions on surveillance and safeguards similar to those in Regulation 3285/94, although without all of the procedural safeguards and rules found in the latter. Many textile and apparel imports into the EC have historically been subject to quantitative restrictions, imposed autonomously by the EC or pursuant to agreements, particularly the Multifiber Arrangement (MFA) between developing country textile exporters and several importing developed countries. Those quotas are required to be phased out by January 1, 2005, pursuant to the WTO Agreement on Textiles and Clothing.

2. INFORMAL SAFEGUARD ARRANGEMENTS

Prior to the entry into force of the WTO Agreement on Safeguards on January 1, 1995, the Community had often used informal arrangements to stem the flow of imports into the EC from other countries. These arrangements were referred to as voluntary export restraints (VERs) or voluntary

---

9. Council Regulation 519/94 on common rules for imports from certain third countries, O.J. L 67/89 (Mar. 10, 1994).

restraint agreements (VRAs). Among the Community imports that were subject to VRAs were a number of Japanese products (e.g., semiconductors, videorecorders, color TV tubes and sets, cars, motorcycles, machine tools, light commercial vehicles, quartz watches, forklift trucks and hi-fi equipment), as well as a smaller group of similar South Korean products. Such informal arrangements are now prohibited by the WTO Agreement on Safeguards (art. 11).

3. INTRA-COMMUNITY SAFEGUARD ARRANGEMENTS (ARTICLE 134)

Article 79 of the Community Customs Code provides that release for free circulation (i.e. customs clearance in one Member State) confers on non-Community goods the customs status of Community goods, which means that they may circulate freely within the Community. See EC Treaty, art. 24; KappAhl Oy, Case C–233/97, [1998] ECR I–8069 (Finland's transitional right to impose additional duties on goods from certain non-Member countries does not apply to such goods when they enter Finland through another Member State). However, Article 134 (ex 115) of the EC Treaty permits the Commission, under certain circumstances, to impose restrictions on intra-Community trade of goods originating in third countries in order to prevent circumvention of national trade measures. With the completion of the internal market and the full implementation of the common commercial policy, Article 134 would not seem to have any current relevance since there should no longer be any such national trade measures. The provision has not been deleted from the Treaty, however, although the Commission has not reported using it since 1992. In the main Court of Justice case dealing with Article 134, the Court indicated that it had to be strictly construed and suggested that its relevance was limited to situations where the common commercial policy had not been completely implemented. Donckerwolcke v. Procureur, Case 41/76, [1976] ECR 1921. Compare Tezi Textile BV v. Commission, Case 59/84, [1986] ECR 887.

4. OTHER IMPORT RESTRICTIONS

In addition to the foregoing general rules on imports, in some cases the Community bans imports of specific products in light of other Community policies. Thus, there are restrictions imposed on imports for health or environmental considerations, or for political reasons.

F. EXPORT ARRANGEMENTS

The common commercial policy extends to exports as well as imports. The common rules for exports, which are contained in Regulation 2603/69,[10] establish the basic principle that the export of products from the Community to third countries shall be free of quantitative restrictions. Regulation 2603/69, art. 1. A number of products are exempted from this free export principle, particularly oil products and products subject to restriction pursuant to a decision under the common foreign and security policy (see Chapter 27). The rules provide for the possibility of Community protective measures

---

10. Council Regulation 2603/69 of Dec. 20, 1969, O.J. L 324/25 (Dec. 12, 1969).

limiting exports of specific products in order to prevent a critical situation arising from shortages of essential products or to allow fulfillment of international undertakings. Regulation 2603/69, arts. 6–9. Until 1990, the Community from time to time limited the export of certain nonferrous metal scrap and waste; otherwise, protective measures have generally not been imposed under the common rules. In addition, the Community has limited certain exports for environmental or security reasons outside of the framework of the common rules.

G. OTHER CUSTOMS RULES

In addition to basic rules on classification, valuation and origin, the EC has numerous other customs rules that space limits preclude examining here. The Community Customs Code includes provisions on (i) rules on customs warehouses where goods can be stored in the EC without having yet cleared customs, (ii) rules on inward processing, which allows the duty-free import of goods that are going to be re-exported after processing in the EC, (iii) rules on outward processing, which allows the EC origin component of goods processed abroad to enter the Community duty free and (iv) rules on free zones where goods imported into the EC are not subject to EC duties and commercial policy measures. The Code also contains provisions on how duties are to be paid, on the use of bonds and on appeal procedures. The latter ensure that someone aggrieved by a customs decision can ultimately have that appeal considered by a court able to refer questions to the Court of Justice.

Chapter 31

EC REMEDIES FOR UNFAIR INTERNATIONAL TRADE PRACTICES

In this chapter, we explore the remedies that are available under EC rules for EC industries that have been injured by unfair international trade practices. The first such practice that we examine is dumping—the export of goods to the EC at a price below the exporter's home market price or below their cost of production. We then consider a second unfair trade practice—direct and indirect government subsidization of exports. Finally, the third section of the chapter deals with the EC's Trade Barriers Regulation, which establishes a procedure under which the Community may initiate challenges to trade barriers of other countries in the World Trade Organization. We will concentrate our attention on the antidumping actions because they are the most utilized of the three remedies for alleged unfair trade practices under EC rules.

At the outset you will properly ask: What does "unfair" mean? Why and to whom is the practice unfair? Having studied the competition chapters, you know that less efficient competitors virtually always see competition as unfair, yet competition is normally treated as being in the public interest because it promotes a progressive, vibrant economy, and it benefits consumers. Indeed, as we saw in Part IV, the EC Treaty generally fosters competition by regulating anticompetitive behavior. When you examine the EC rules against unfair international trade practices, you should consider whether they are designed to promote competition or simply to protect EC-based competitors.

In analyzing the unfair international trade practices treated in this Chapter, you should also consider how these practices would be dealt with in the internal EC market. For example, how do the rules on dumping compare to those on predatory pricing discussed in Chapter 22(D)(5) supra? How different is the treatment of foreign subsidies and EC domestic subsidies (see Chapter 26 supra)? Should similar foreign and domestic activities be treated the same? If not, why not?

In the concluding note to section (A) of this Chapter, the utility of antidumping laws is considered from a general economic point of view. As you read these materials, try to formulate economic arguments on both sides of the question of whether antidumping laws are economically desirable.

A. REGULATION OF DUMPED IMPORTS

First, a bit of history. Canada adopted an antidumping law in 1904. It was soon followed by New Zealand (1905), Australia (1906), and later by such countries as the United Kingdom (1921) and the United States (1921). These laws are permitted by WTO/GATT rules, which condemn injurious dumping and authorize WTO members to impose antidumping duties to offset dumping that causes material injury to a domestic industry. The imposition of anti-dumping duties is regulated by the WTO Antidumping Agreement (see Chapter 29(A) supra), which defines the basic substantive requirements for establishing dumping, material injury and the required causal link between them and which specifies minimum procedural standards for antidumping investigations.

Despite their long history, antidumping laws were not utilized frequently until the 1970s. Through the 1980s they were used extensively by only four jurisdictions: the Community, the United States, Australia and Canada. In recent years, however, many developing countries have adopted antidumping laws and are now actively using them. For example, as of June 30, 1999, the WTO reported that the number of individual national antidumping measures in force was as follows: US (336), EC (183), Mexico (88), South Africa (86), Canada (77), India (73), Australia (48), Argentina (42), Brazil (35) and Turkey (34).[1] The main initiators of antidumping investigations in the first half of 1999 were India (40), EC (32), US (20), Argentina (11), Australia (10) and Canada (10). The main targets during that period were the EC (20), Korea (18), China (16), Japan (11), Russia (10) and Thailand (10).[2] The spread of antidumping laws and their increased use has led a number of countries, particularly the exporting nations of the Pacific Rim and some other developing countries, to propose that WTO rules more strictly limit the use of such laws, as they believe antidumping laws are now sometimes applied simply for protectionist purposes. The US (and to a lesser degree, the EC) generally oppose such changes.

The Community adopted its first antidumping regulation in 1968. The current version, Regulation 384/96, is set out in the Selected Documents.[3] The Commission reports annually on its administration of the EC's antidumping rules, as well as the other regulations governing unfair trade practices discussed in this chapter.[4]

The process by which dumped imports may be made subject to antidumping duties under Community law is quite complex and provides much work for a small group of specialized lawyers in Brussels. In this section, we will first lay out the basic terms of the Community antidumping regulation and the procedures followed by the Commission in antidumping investigations. We will note when they differ significantly from US practice. We will then

---

1. WTO Annual Report 2000, p. 47.

2. Id. at p. 48.

3. Council Regulation 384/96 of Dec. 22, 1995, O.J. L 56/1 (Mar. 6, 1996), as amended.

4. The 18th Annual Report on activities in 1999 was issued in July 2000 (COM(2000)440 final, July 11, 2000).

consider a recent EC decision that discusses typical issues in such investigations. Finally, we will look at the role of the EC courts in reviewing decisions in these cases.

1. SUBSTANTIVE ASPECTS OF THE EC ANTIDUMPING REGULATION

The EC antidumping regulation establishes three prerequisites for imposing antidumping duties: the product must have been dumped, a Community industry must have been materially injured as a result and the imposition of an antidumping duty must be in the interest of the Community. Because of the complexity of these issues, we will describe the regulation's provisions on each of them before turning to an examination of a typical case.

(a) Dumping

The regulation provides that "[a] product shall be considered to have been dumped if its export price to the Community is less than the normal value of the like product" (art. 2(2)). The essential questions raised by that test are: What is normal value? What is the export price? How are they compared?

Normal Value. "[N]ormal value shall normally be based on the prices paid or payable, in the ordinary course of trade, by independent customers in the exporting country." Art. 2(1). On the basis of this definition, dumping is often described as international price discrimination, i.e., exporting at a price below one's home market price, and, in fact, higher average sales prices in the home country are often the basis on which the existence of dumping is established. In many cases, however, normal value is established by other methods. In particular, there are special rules for cases (i) where there have been few or no sales in the home market, (ii) where home-market sales have been made at a loss, (iii) where the goods have originated in a non-market economy and (iv) where the home-market sales have otherwise not been made in the ordinary course of trade (e.g., between related companies).

The absence of adequate home-market sales (usually defined as sales equal to less than 5% of exports to the EC) is not unusual. Because of global sourcing of components, nations' promotion of their export sectors and the tailoring of product characteristics to special needs in different national markets, many companies produce certain products or product models mainly for export. If there are inadequate home-market sales, the EC authorities may use as normal value either (a) the constructed value of the product or (b) the price of the product when exported to any other country (art. 2(3)). The constructed value is calculated by aggregating all of the production costs of a product and then adding a reasonable margin for selling costs, overhead and profit (art. 2(5)-(6)).

The second situation in which some or all home-market prices of a product are not used to determine normal value is when the Commission has reasonable grounds to believe that home-market sales are being made at below-cost prices. If a sufficiently large percentage of home-market sales are made at a loss, normal value is based on constructed value (art. 2(4)).

The third situation in which normal value is not based on home-market prices is when the goods originate in a non-market economy.[5] In these cases, normal value may be based on the price or constructed value in a market-economy third country, or on prices from such a country to other countries (including the EC), or, if these are not possible, on any other reasonable basis. Art. 2(7). The most important determination in a dumping case involving a non-market economy is the selection of the comparable market-economy country. Non-market economies tend to be compared with economically more advanced countries, and, not surprisingly, the dumping margins found are often quite high. Since 1998, it has been possible for a producer in certain non-market economies[6] to establish that market-economy conditions prevail for that producer in respect of the manufacture and sale of its product, in which case the normal antidumping rules apply.

It should be emphasized that the price discrimination or below-cost sales necessary to establish the existence of dumping need not reach the level of "predatory" pricing, the competition law concept for a strategy of low pricing with the intent and prospect of eliminating all significant competitors, monopolizing the market and charging monopoly prices for a sustained period of time. See Chapter 22(D)(5) supra. In order for antidumping duties to be imposed, it is not necessary to show that the dumping company has market power or that there is a threat of monopoly.

The harm protected against by the dumping laws is harm to domestic competitors, not harm to competition generally. However, there is no private right of action against dumping, and dumping is not unlawful. The relief is not in the form of compensation paid to domestic industry or fines imposed on dumpers, but rather the elimination of the dumping (or the injury caused thereby) through imposition of customs duties to reduce imports.

Export Price. The export price, against which the normal value is to be compared, is defined as "the price actually paid or payable for the product sold from the exporting country to the Community" (art. 2(8)). In certain cases, and in particular when the exporter and importer are related (which is often the case), the export price may be constructed on the basis of the price at which the exported product is first sold to an independent buyer. If there is no resale to an independent buyer or when the product is not sold in the condition imported, the export price may be constructed on any reasonable basis.

Comparison of Export Price With Normal Value. The normal value and export price of a product usually need to be adjusted so that they can be fairly compared. Article 2(10) provides that a "fair comparison * * * shall be made at the same level of trade and in respect of sales made at as nearly as possible the same time." It provides for adjustments to account for factors that affect price comparability such as differences in respect of physical characteristics; import charges and indirect taxes; discounts and rebates (including for quantities); level of trade (where shown by consistent and distinct differences in functions and prices of the seller for the different levels of trade, adjust-

---

5. As of 1995, the non-market economy rules were applied to the non-Baltic republics of the former Soviet Union, Albania, China, Mongolia, North Korea and Vietnam.

6. This rule has applied to China and Russia since July 1, 1998. In October 2000, it was extended to Kazahkstan, Ukraine, Vietnam and those nations listed in footnote 5 who are WTO members.

ment to be based on the market value of the difference); transport, insurance, handling, loading and ancillary costs; packing; credit; after-sales cost (e.g., warranties); commissions and currency conversions. Adjustments are always necessary and many of the contested issues in a case involve the appropriateness and amount of the adjustments. The goal of the adjustment process is to arrive at a comparable "ex-factory" normal value and export price.

Once normal value and export prices have been adjusted so that they are comparable, they are compared and a dumping margin is calculated. Article 2(11) now requires that the comparison be of average normal values and average export prices or on an individual-normal-value to individual-export-price basis, subject to an exception "if there is a pattern of export prices which differ significantly among different purchasers, regions or time periods and [the average-to-average or individual-to-individual comparisons] would not reflect the full degree of dumping." There are specific provisions authorizing the use of sampling techniques where large numbers of participants or transactions are involved. Art. 17.

Two points should be obvious from the foregoing material. First, the volume of data required for calculating normal value and export prices may be enormous. In some cases, thousands of invoices, shipping documents, and the like may have to be examined. Second, the Commission has wide discretion in appraising both the calculation methods employed and the quality of the data supplied. This means that there is considerable room for criticism by EC industries who may feel that the Commission is not sufficiently forceful in protecting their interests and even more by third country exporters who feel that the Commission is unfairly evaluating data to produce a protectionist result.

(b) Material Injury

An antidumping duty may not be imposed unless it is determined that a Community industry has been injured by the dumping. Injury is defined as "material injury to the Community industry, threat of material injury to the Community industry or material retardation of the establishment of such an industry" (art. 3(1)). Dumped imports from several countries may be cumulated in assessing injury.

The regulation treats at length the criteria pursuant to which injury is to be determined (art. 3(2)-(8)). The specific factors that must be examined in the injury investigation are: (a) the volume of dumped imports (and, in particular, whether there has been a significant increase in absolute or percentage terms relative to Community production or consumption); (b) the effect of dumped imports on prices in the Community market (and, in particular, whether there has been significant price undercutting); and (c) the "consequent" impact on Community industry, as indicated by whether it is still recovering from the effects of past dumping or subsidization; the magnitude of the dumping margin; actual or potential declines in sales, profits, output, market share, productivity, return on investments, capacity utilization; and actual and potential negative effects on cash flow, inventories, employment, wages, growth, and ability to raise capital. The list is not exhaustive and no one factor is decisive. Art. 3(5).

The causal connection that must be found is stated as follows: "It must be demonstrated * * * that dumped imports are causing injury * * *. Specifically, this shall entail a demonstration that the volume and/or price levels identified [in Article 3(3)] are responsible for an impact on the Community industry as provided for in [Article 3(5)], and that this impact exists to a degree which enables it to be classified as material." Art. 3(6).

If dumping is found, injury is likely to be found as well. The existence of dumping implies that imports are selling at a price below that at which they otherwise should have been sold. These lower prices may well result in the Community industry losing some sales, which will have a negative impact on its production, capacity utilization, market share and profits. But that is not always the case, and noninjury findings do occur. Community industry may be able to undersell the dumped imports at a reasonable profit, or its injury may be due to factors other than dumping, such as low-priced, undumped goods from other sources within or without the Community.

The regulation also contains provisions that define de minimis situations where no antidumping duties are to be imposed. Imports from an investigated country are deemed de minimis if they are less than one percent of all imports, unless imports from such countries collectively exceed three percent of all imports. Arts. 5(7), 9(3). Dumping margins of less than two percent are considered de minimis, although in the case where some exporters from a country do not have de minimis margins, the proceeding is not terminated in respect of any individual exporters, which means that they may be subject to future investigations if there is a review of the dumping margins. Art. 9(3).

(c) Community Interest

In addition to findings of dumping and material injury caused thereby, the regulation requires that imposition of a duty be in the Community's interest (arts. 7(1), 9(4)). This differs from the situation in the United States, where duties are imposed automatically if dumping and injury are established.

Community interest is defined in detail in Article 21. It provides that the interests of users and consumers shall be considered, although "the need to eliminate the trade distorting effects of injurious dumping and to restore effective competition shall be given special consideration." Art. 21(1). Representative users and consumer organizations, as well as Community industry and importers, are authorized to provide and receive information and are entitled to a hearing (if they set out particular reasons why they should be heard). Art. 21(2)-(3).

Since the imposition of an antidumping duty will normally raise the cost of a product to its purchasers, the argument is often raised by such purchasers or the exporters that it is not in the Community's interest to impose such a duty. That argument is usually rejected on the grounds that it is in the Community's interest to afford relief to Community industry, particularly where that industry is technologically important or represents significant capital investment and employment. Of course, if the EC purchasers belong to a technologically important EC industry, the Commission may be more sympathetic to their arguments. A rare instance in which the Commission accepted consumer interest over industry interest involved certain photo albums that were not produced in adequate volume by Community industry with the result that the Commission felt that there might be shortages if protective measures were taken. Commission Decision of May 22 1990, O.J. L 138/48 (May 31, 1990) (photo albums from South Korea and Hong Kong).

2.   PROCEDURAL ASPECTS OF THE EC ANTIDUMPING REGULATION

An antidumping investigation is normally commenced in response to the filing of a complaint by a Community industry trade association alleging that the industry has been injured or is threatened with injury by dumped products. The Commission makes an effort to verify the principal allegations in the complaint before actually opening an investigation. The Commission is required to decide whether or not to initiate an investigation within 45 days of receiving a complaint. Art. 5(9). Provisional measures, if any, are to be imposed within nine months of initiation (but not within 60 days thereof). Art. 7(1). Finally, investigations are normally to be concluded within one year, or at most, 15 months. Art. 6(9).

If, following consultation with its Advisory Committee of Member State representatives, the Commission decides to initiate an investigation, the Commission publishes a notice in the Official Journal. This notice specifies the product subject to investigation, the time period covered, the exporting countries and the known producers, exporters and importers. The Commission sends a copy of the notice and a questionnaire to those importers, exporters and producers known to be involved. The questionnaire requests data on all export sales to the Community and in the home market during the investigation period, which is normally the six to twelve months immediately preceding the opening of the investigation. The exporter may be asked to complete a section of the questionnaire on its production costs. The questionnaire also inquires into the existence of factors typically justifying adjustments to the normal value or export price. The Commission simultaneously secures information from all EC producers in order to determine whether a Community industry has been materially injured by dumping.

Only a brief period, less than two months, including normal extensions, is allowed for the response to the questionnaire. This places the respondents under great time pressure to locate, organize and provide data that in many cases do not exist in the precise form desired by the questionnaire and therefore have to be assembled especially for this purpose.

After the Commission has received responses to its questionnaires, it typically proceeds to verify the accuracy of the responses. This normally means that the Commission officials assigned to the case will travel to visit the parties responding to the questionnaire to check their original invoices and other records to see that the answers in the questionnaire are accurate. For companies located outside the EC, there is no obligation to cooperate with a Commission investigation. However, in the case of noncooperation, the Commission is authorized to base its findings on available facts, which may be the allegations of the complaining industry or information supplied by competitors (art. 7(7)(b)). Thus, while cooperation is not required, it may be the only practical response to an investigation.

Once an investigation is initiated, essentially three results are possible: termination, "settlement" or imposition of antidumping duties.

Termination. After consulting with its advisory committee of Member State representatives, the Commission may conclude that the investigation should be terminated, either because there is no evidence of dumping or no evidence of injury (art. 9).

Settlement. The Commission, after consulting with the advisory committee, may "settle" the investigation by adopting a formal decision to accept an undertaking from the exporters concerned to raise their prices or take other action so that the dumping margin or the injurious effects thereof are eliminated (art. 8). Contrary to US practice where settlements are quite rare, the settlement of antidumping cases by acceptance of undertakings is a common resolution of EC antidumping cases.

The terms of an undertaking are the subject of negotiation and vary from case to case. Typically, the Commission aims to require the exporters to agree to procedures to ensure that no dumping will occur in the future (e.g., reporting requirements). An exporter generally prefers an undertaking to a duty because it would rather keep the extra profit from the required price increase than pay a tax to the Community in the form of higher duties. In addition, the exporter has the possibility at any time to ask the Commission to modify the undertaking in light of changed circumstances, a request to which the Commission can respond promptly, whereas an exporter that is subject to a duty may find it much more difficult to have the duty modified in light of changed circumstances since the investigation will normally have to be reopened, which can be a lengthy process.

Why do you think that the United States is skeptical of using undertakings? Consider how undertakings resemble cartels. See Chapter 21 supra. Are undertakings particularly anticompetitive? Do the terms of the typical undertaking, as outlined above, resemble procedures used by cartels to prevent cheating? To the extent that they are procured by domestic industry, do they resemble crisis cartels? See Chapter 21(D) supra.

The process through which price undertakings are offered and accepted can raise competition law problems, since undertakings involve low-priced competitors fixing price levels in response to complaints by a combination of high-priced competitors, albeit with the intervention of a government agency. See generally J. Temple Lang, Reconciling European Community Antitrust and Antidumping, Transport and Trade Safeguard Policies—Practical Problems, in B. Hawk, ed., 1988 Fordham Corp.L.Inst. ch. 7 (Matthew Bender 1989). But cf. T. Calvani & R. Tritell, Invocation of United States Import Relief Laws as an Antitrust Violation, 31 Antitrust Bull. 2 (Summer 1986).

Antidumping duties. The Commission may impose provisional duties, normally after consulting with the advisory committee. Its decision may be overruled by a qualified majority of the Council. Art. 7(4), (6). Provisional duties may be imposed for six months without consent of the exporters, and for a total of nine months with their consent. Art. 7(7). It is not necessary to pay the provisional duty, but security for payment thereof must be posted when goods under investigation are imported. Thereafter (assuming no undertaking is accepted), on the basis of a Commission proposal in light of the facts as finally established, the Council may adopt a definitive antidumping duty by a simple majority. The simple majority requirement (introduced in the mid–1990s) makes it more difficult than in the past for the less protectionist

Member States to block imposition of antidumping duties or to moderate their levels.

Duties are usually ad valorem and are set at different rates for different companies, depending on the margins of dumping established for each company. Unlike the United States, where the antidumping duty reflects the full amount of the dumping margin, the EC imposes a duty in an amount less than the full margin of dumping if it determines that the lesser duty will eliminate the injury to EC industry (art. 9(4)). Antidumping duties expire after five years unless they are extended following a review that examines whether their expiration would result in renewed injury to Community industry (art. 11(2)).

The regulation provides that an investigation should normally be concluded, either by termination or definitive action, within one year of its initiation (art. 6(9)).

3. THE STEEL WIRE ROPE CASE

The key questions that arise in an antidumping case are (i) how is the normal value of the product in the exporting country established, (ii) how are the export prices calculated, (iii) what adjustments are necessary to make the normal value and export prices comparable, (iv) how are injury and causation established and (v) whether a duty is in the Community interest. The following case is a straightforward one, but a number of interesting issues are presented. Note that the case is a Commission decision imposing a provisional duty; only the Council can impose a definitive duty. Provisional decisions, however, often provide a fuller discussion of the basic issues in a case, with the final decision only discussing findings in the provisional decision that are contested.

COMMISSION REGULATION NO 230/2001 OF 2 FEBRUARY 2001 IMPOSING A PROVISIONAL ANTI–DUMPING DUTY ON CERTAIN IRON OR STEEL ROPES AND CABLES ORIGINATING IN THE CZECH REPUBLIC, RUSSIA, THAILAND AND TURKEY AND ACCEPTING UNDERTAKINGS OFFERED BY CERTAIN EXPORTERS IN THE CZECH REPUBLIC AND TURKEY

O.J. L34/4 (Feb. 3, 2001).

A. PROCEDURE

1. *Initiation*

[1] On 5 May 2000, the Commission announced by a notice (hereinafter referred to as "notice of initiation") published in the Official Journal of the European Communities the initiation of an anti-dumping proceeding with regard to imports into the Community of certain iron or steel ropes and cables originating in the Czech Republic, the Republic of Korea (hereinafter referred to as "Korea"), Malaysia, Russia, Thailand and Turkey.

[2] The proceeding was initiated as a result of a complaint lodged in March 2000 by the Liaison Committee of European Union Wire Rope Industries

(EWRIS) (hereinafter referred to as the "complainant") on behalf of producers representing a major proportion, i.e. 76% of the Community production of the product concerned. The complaint contained evidence of dumping of the said product and of material injury resulting therefrom, which was considered sufficient to justify the initiation of a proceeding.

3 The Commission officially advised the exporting producers, exporters and importers known to be concerned as well as their associations, the representatives of the exporting countries concerned, the EU–Czech Republic and EC–Turkey Association Councils, the complainant and all known Community producers, raw material suppliers and users, about the initiation of the proceeding. Interested parties were given the opportunity to make their views known in writing and to request a hearing within the time limit set in the notice of initiation.

4 A number of exporting producers in the countries concerned, as well as Community producers and importers made their views known in writing. All parties who so requested within the above time limit and who demonstrated that there were particular reasons why they should be heard were granted the opportunity to be heard.

5 The Commission sent questionnaires to all parties known to be concerned and to all other companies which made themselves known within the deadlines set out in the notice of initiation. Replies were received from 19 Community producers, 11 exporting producers in the countries concerned, as well as from their related importers in the Community, from one unrelated importer in the Community and one raw material supplier. No user responded to the questionnaire.

6 In order to allow exporting producers from Russia to submit a claim for market economy status (MES) or individual treatment if they so wished, the Commission sent to Russian companies known to be concerned a market economy status and an individual treatment claim form. * * *

7 The Commission sought and verified all the information it deemed necessary for the purpose of a preliminary determination of dumping, injury and Community interest. * * *

8 The investigation of dumping and injury covered the period from 1 April 1999 to 31 March 2000 (hereinafter referred to as "investigation period" or "IP"). The examination of trends relevant for the assessment of injury covered the period from 1 January 1997 up to the end of the IP (hereinafter referred to as "period considered").

2. *Product concerned and like product*

(a) Product concerned

9 The product concerned is ropes and cables, including locked coil ropes, of iron or steel but not stainless steel, with a maximum cross-sectional dimension exceeding 3 mm, with attached fittings or not. These products are often referred to by the industry as "steel wire ropes" (SWR). * * *

* * *

13 The investigation revealed that SWR are produced in a wide range of different types with a certain degree of physical and technical differences

and that various types of SWR can be classified into a number of product groups reflecting their physical and technical characteristics. However, it was also found that all of them have the same basic physical characteristics and the same technical characteristics and while products in the bottom end and in the top end of the range are not interchangeable, products in adjoining groups are. It was therefore concluded that a certain degree of overlapping and competition existed between SWR in different groups. Moreover, products in the same group may have different applications. In the absence of a clear dividing line in the range of SWR and given that all of them have the same basic physical and technical characteristics, all SWR are considered as one product.

(b) Like product

[14] Certain interested parties argued that the product under consideration [the allegedly dumped product] and that manufactured and sold by the Community industry on the Community market are different given that the former consists mostly of general purpose SWR whereas the latter include mostly high performance ropes. In view of the reasons given in recital 13, this argument could not be accepted.

* * *

B.   DUMPING

1.   General methodology

[17] The general methodology set out hereinafter has been applied for all exporting countries concerned. The presentation of the findings on dumping for each of the six countries concerned therefore only describes what is specific for each exporting country.

(a) Normal value

[18] As far as the determination of normal value is concerned, the Commission first established, for each exporting producer, whether its total domestic sales of SWR were representative in comparison with its total export sales to the Community. In accordance with Article 2(2) of the basic Regulation, domestic sales were considered representative when the total domestic sales volume of each exporting producer was at least 5% of its total export sales volume to the Community.

[19] The Commission subsequently identified, for the companies having representative domestic sales, those types of SWR sold domestically that were identical or directly comparable to the types sold for export to the Community. * * *

[20] For each of the types sold by the exporting producers on their domestic markets and found to be directly comparable to types sold for export to the Community, it was established whether domestic sales were sufficiently representative for the purposes of Article 2(2) of the basic Regulation. Domestic sales of a particular type were considered sufficiently representative when the total domestic sales volume of SWR of that type during the IP represented 5% or more of the total sales volume of SWR of the comparable type exported to the Community.

21   An examination was also made as to whether the domestic sales of each type could be regarded as having been made in the ordinary course of trade, by establishing the proportion of profitable sales to independent customers of the product type in question. In cases where the sales volume sold at a net sales price equal to or above the calculated cost of production (also referred to as "profitable sales") represented 80% or more of the total sales volume and where the weighted average price of that type was equal to or above cost of production, normal value was based on the weighted average of the prices of all domestic sales made during the IP, irrespective of whether all these sales were profitable or not. In cases where the volume of profitable sales represented less than 80% but 10% or more of the total sales volume, normal value was based on the weighted average price of profitable sales only.

22   In cases where the volume of profitable sales of any type of SWR represented less than 10% of the total sales volume, it was considered that this particular type was sold in insufficient quantities for the domestic price to provide an appropriate basis for the establishment of the normal value.

23   Wherever domestic prices of a particular type sold by an exporting producer could not be used, normal value was based on the weighted average of the prices charged by other producers in the country concerned for representative domestic sales of the corresponding product type made in the ordinary course of trade in accordance with Article 2(1) of the basic Regulation, whenever such data were available.

24   Where, per product type, there were insufficient sales or no such representative domestic sales by other producers in the country concerned, normal value was constructed, in accordance with Article 2(3) of the basic Regulation, by adding to the manufacturing costs of the exported types, adjusted where necessary, a reasonable percentage for selling, general and administrative expenses (SG & A) and a reasonable margin of profit. To this end, the Commission examined whether the SG & A incurred and the profit realized by each of the exporting producers concerned on the domestic market constituted reliable data.

25   Actual domestic SG & A expenses were considered reliable when the domestic sales volume of the like product by the company concerned could be regarded as representative. The domestic profit margin was determined on the basis of domestic sales of the product concerned made in the ordinary course of trade as defined in recital 21.

(b) Export price

26   In all cases where SWR were exported to independent customers in the Community, the export price was established in accordance with Article 2(8) of the basic Regulation, namely on the basis of prices actually paid or payable.

27   Where the export sale was made to a related importer, the export price was constructed pursuant to Article 2(9) of the basic Regulation, namely on the basis of the price at which the imported products were first resold to an independent buyer. In such cases, adjustments were made for all costs incurred between importation and resale and for profits accruing, in order to establish a reliable export price. * * *

(c) Comparison

28   For the purpose of ensuring a fair comparison between the normal value and the export price, due allowance in the form of adjustments was made for differences affecting price comparability in accordance with Article 2(10) of the basic Regulation.

(d) Dumping margin for the companies investigated

29   According to Article 2(11) of the basic Regulation, the dumping margins were established on the basis of a comparison between the weighted average normal value per product type and the weighted average export price at ex-factory level and at the same level of trade. When there was a pattern of export prices differing among purchasers, regions or time periods and the method previously described did not reflect the full degree of dumping, normal value established on a weighted average basis was compared to prices of all individual export transactions to the Community.

(e) Residual dumping margin

30   For those exporting producers which neither replied to the questionnaire nor otherwise made themselves known, the dumping margin was established on the basis of the facts available, in accordance with Article 18(1) of the basic Regulation.

[Czech Republic, Korea, Malaysia, Thailand omitted]

6.   Turkey

77   Two companies replied to the questionnaire for exporting producers.

(a) Normal value

78   In line with the general methodology, it was possible, for some of the product types, to establish normal value on the basis of the domestic price of comparable types in accordance with Article 2(1) of the basic Regulation. Representativeness and ordinary course of trade tests for the domestic sales of comparable types were carried out on a monthly basis given the high inflation in Turkey during the IP.

79   For all other types of the product concerned sold for export to the Community by the cooperating companies, normal value was constructed in accordance with Article 2(3) of the basic Regulation. The companies' own domestic SG & A expenses and the profit margin realized on the domestic market in the ordinary course of trade were added to the manufacturing cost. To account for the high inflation, constructed normal values were calculated for each month of the IP.

(b) Export price

80   All sales of the product concerned made by the cooperating companies on the Community market were to independent customers in the Community. Consequently, the export price was established on the basis of the prices actually paid or payable as provided for in Article 2(8) of the basic Regulation.

(c) Comparison

81   Allowances for differences in import charges and indirect taxes, discounts, rebates and quantities, transport, insurance, handling, loading and ancillary costs, credit, technical assistance, commissions have been made where applicable and justified.

* * *

83   One exporting producer claimed an adjustment to the domestic prices for differences in levels of trade pursuant to Article 2(10)(d)(i) of the basic Regulation on the ground that all exports to the Community were to retailers whereas domestic sales were to retailers and to end-users. This adjustment was not granted since the company was unable to demonstrate that there were consistent and distinct differences in prices and functions on the domestic market for the alleged different levels of trade. The other exporting producer described its distribution channels in the Community and on the domestic market and submitted a claim for an allowance without any explanation on how this affected price comparability. Moreover, explanations received on the spot established that its distribution channel in the Community could not be described as claimed. Accordingly, no adjustment was made at this stage of the investigation.

* * *

(d) Dumping margin

89   Pursuant to Article 2(11) of the basic Regulation, the weighted average normal value of each type of the product concerned exported to the Community was compared to the weighted average export price of each corresponding type of the product concerned. Indeed, although both exporting producers declared that there was a different pattern of prices between customers, regions and time periods, this method reflected the full degree of dumping being practiced.

90   This comparison shows the existence of dumping for the cooperating companies. The provisional dumping margins expressed as a percentage of the cif import price at the Community frontier duty unpaid are for:

— Celik Halat ve Tel Sanayii A.S: 58.1%

— Has Celik ve Halat San Tic A.S: 19.2%

* * *

7. Russia

(a) General aspects

(i) Analysis of market economy status

[Two Russian companies requested market economy status (MES), pursuant to Article 2(7)(b) of the basic Regulation, although only one submitted the necessary information.]

94   It was established that this company did not meet several of the criteria laid down in Article 2(7)(c) of the basic Regulation, notably that it had several contradicting and irreconcilable sets of basic accounting records,

some costs did not substantially reflect market values and some payments were made via compensation of debts.

95   Consequently, after consultation of the Advisory Committee, both companies were informed that their MES applications could not be granted.

(ii) Choice of analogue country

96   In the absence of any companies fulfilling the requirements of MES, it was necessary to compare the export prices of the Russian exporting producers with a normal value established in an appropriate market economy country, pursuant to Article 2(7)(a) of the basic Regulation.

97   The Czech Republic was suggested by the complainant. The Commission envisaged in the notice of initiation the Czech Republic or Brazil. Within the required time limit, two Russian exporting producers provisionally expressed their agreement with the countries envisaged and indicated that they could also accept the choice of South Korea as a possible analogue country. The complainant expressed some concerns about the choice of Brazil in particular given the high level of custom duties. The complainant confirmed that the Czech Republic was an appropriate choice in its opinion and also suggested Canada as an alternative.

98   None of the contacted Brazilian producers replied to the request for cooperation. The Commission also tried without success to obtain cooperation from Canadian producers. Other known producing countries were not envisaged as either imports of the product concerned originating in these countries were currently under anti-dumping measures or the previous investigation established they were not an appropriate choice on grounds which had remained unchanged (i.e. limited competition in Norway, non-cooperation in the USA).

99   The cooperating exporting producer in the Czech Republic sold on the domestic market mostly types of the product concerned different from those exported by the Russian producers to the Community.

100   Under these circumstances, the Commission have investigated the appropriateness to use one of the other countries involved in the proceeding. The Republic of Korea was considered the most appropriate analogue country in accordance with Article 2(7)(a) of the basic Regulation. First, the South Korean domestic market is the largest in size, characterized by a significant number of competing local producers; second, South Korean domestic sales of the product concerned are the most representative in terms of types and volume when compared with Russian exports to the Community. Interested parties were informed, pursuant to Article 2(7)(a) of the basic Regulation, that the Republic of Korea was envisaged as analogue country and no objections were received.

* * *

(e) Dumping margin

110   As provided by Article 2(11) of the basic Regulation, the weighted average normal values of each type of the product concerned exported to the Community were compared to the weighted average export price of each corresponding type of the product concerned.

111   The provisional dumping margin expressed as a percentage of the cif import price at the Community frontier duty unpaid has been established for the company granted individual treatment as follows:

— Cherepovetsky Staleprokatny Zavod: 35.8%

112   Since a known exporting producer did deliberately not cooperate, the methodology followed to determine a provisional residual dumping margin for Russia was the one explained in recital 33 [omitted] for countries where the level of cooperation was low. On this basis, the residual dumping margin is 50.7%.

8.   Conclusion on dumping

113   The Commission established substantial dumping margins for all cooperating companies in the Czech Republic, Russia, Thailand and Turkey. In the case of the Republic of Korea and Malaysia the dumping margins found were de minimis.

* * *

D.   INJURY

1.   Preliminary remarks

121   Since the margins of dumping found for Korea and Malaysia are de minimis, the analysis of injury and causality refers to the remaining countries under investigation, i.e. the Czech Republic, Russia, Thailand and Turkey (hereinafter referred to as the "countries concerned").

122   The analysis of injury should be seen in the light of the anti-dumping measures imposed on the product concerned by Council Regulation (EC) No. 1796/1999. The latter imposed a definitive anti-dumping duty on imports of the product concerned originating in the People's Republic of China, Hungary, India, Mexico, Poland, South Africa and Ukraine.

* * *

2.   Collection of injury data

123   The Commission requested information from the whole Community industry relating to the product concerned with respect to production, capacity, capacity utilization, sales, stocks and employment. * * *

[The Commission based its analysis on the cumulative effects of the dumped imports. Article 3(4). Among other factors, it noted that the prices of the imports had decreased 16% between 1997 and 1998 and thereafter stabilized. It calculated that the margin of price undercutting ranged from 16.4% to 51.4%. The market share of Community industry was largely unchanged (as imports from countries subject to the earlier anti-dumping duties decreased). Employment was down 8%.]

(k)   Conclusion on injury

158   During the period considered, the volume of dumped imports from the countries concerned increased by 215% and their market share went from 3.3% to 10.8%.

159   Following the imposition of anti-dumping measures in 1999, the situation of the Community industry stabilized in the IP but was still weak: production remained largely stable, capacity utilization was kept at the same level and stocks decreased slightly from 30,050 to 29,660 tonnes. Although sales increased modestly from 66,331 in 1999 to 67,671 tonnes in the IP, the Community industry's market share did not increase despite the restored, effective competition from the countries subject to anti-dumping measures.

160   Regarding the profitability of the Community industry, although it improved slightly from –1.4% to 0% over the period considered, it still remained at a level which is insufficient for the long-term viability of the Community industry. Furthermore, in the IP, the Community industry's prices did not increase as expected following the anti-dumping measures imposed in 1999. Therefore the Community industry could hardly benefit from the imposition of anti-dumping measures in 1999 due to the increase in the volume of imports from the countries concerned at prices which significantly undercut those of the Community industry.

161   In view of the above, it has been provisionally concluded that the Community industry has suffered material injury within the meaning of Article 3(2) of the basic Regulation.

E.   CAUSATION

1.   Preliminary remarks

162   In order to reach its provisional conclusion as to whether there is a causal link between the dumped imports and the injury suffered by the Community industry, the Commission examined the impact of the dumped imports from the countries concerned on the situation in that industry.

163   Pursuant to Article 3(7) of the basic Regulation, other known factors, such as the development of consumption, the situation of other Community producers, the export performance of the Community industry, the evolution and impact of imports from third countries and the effect of changes in the cost of raw materials are analyzed below in order to examine whether any causal link between the dumped imports and the injury suffered by the Community industry could have been broken by factors other than the dumped imports.

* * *

4.   Conclusion

183   In the light of the above, it is concluded that, although other factors, namely the imports from Korea and Malaysia [whose combined market share went from 2.4% in 1997 to 10% in the IP, compared to the share of the countries concerned, which went from 3.3% to 10.8%], may have had a negative impact on the situation of the Community industry in the IP, this impact is not such as to break the causal link between the dumped imports and the situation of the Community industry. Therefore, the imports from the countries concerned taken in isolation have been found to cause material injury to the Community industry.

F. COMMUNITY INTEREST

* * *

7. Conclusion on Community interest

212 The investigation has shown that the imposition of measures can be expected to allow the Community industry to increase prices and volumes and therefore to improve profitability, with consequent beneficial effects on the competitive conditions on the Community market. The imposition of anti-dumping duties is also expected to benefit raw material suppliers.

213 Whilst any negative effects are likely to result for the importers in price increases, the extent of these may be reduced by decreasing margins or by increasing the prices charged to the user industry.

214 The user industry, in turn, is unlikely to suffer serious consequences from such an increase given the low incidence of SWR on their final products.

215 In the light of the above, the Commission considers that no compelling reasons exist for not imposing measures and that the application of anti-dumping duties would be in the interests of the Community.

G. PROVISIONAL ANTI–DUMPING MEASURES

1. Injury elimination level

216 Having established that the dumped imports under consideration caused material injury to the Community industry and that there are no compelling reasons not to take action, the measures envisaged should be imposed at a level sufficient to eliminate the injury caused by these imports without exceeding the dumping margins found.

217 When calculating the amount of duty necessary to remove the effects of the injurious dumping, it was considered that any measures should allow the Community industry to cover its costs and obtain overall a profit before tax that could be reasonably achieved under normal conditions of competition, i.e. in the absence of dumped imports, on the sales of the like product in the Community.

218 On the basis of the information provided by interested parties, it was preliminarily found that a profit margin of 5% of turnover could be regarded as an appropriate minimum which the Community industry could be expected to obtain in the absence of injurious dumping. It is also considered that this profit margin would allow the Community industry to make the necessary investments.

219 On this basis, the weighted average export prices of SWR, adjusted according to the methodology described in recitals 138 and 139 [omitted], were compared with the selling prices charged by the Community industry, adjusted to reflect a reasonable profit margin of 5%. The result was then expressed as a percentage of the exporting producers' export prices on a cif Community frontier level, i.e. the injury margin.

2. Provisional anti-dumping measures

220 In the light of the foregoing, it is considered that a provisional anti-dumping duty should be imposed at the level of the dumping margins

found, except for a company in Turkey for which the duty should be imposed at the level of the injury margin which is lower, in accordance with Article 7(2) of the basic Regulation.

221 The individual company anti-dumping duty rates specified in this Regulation were established on the basis of the findings of the present investigation. Therefore, they reflect the situation found during that investigation with respect to these companies. These duty rates (as opposed to the residual duty applicable to "all other companies") are thus exclusively applicable to imports of products originating in the country concerned and produced by the companies and thus by the specific legal entities mentioned. Imported products produced by any other company not specifically mentioned in the operative part of this Regulation with its name and address, including entities related to those specifically mentioned, cannot benefit from these rates and shall be subject to the duty rate applicable to "all other companies".

222 Any claim requesting the application of these individual company anti-dumping duty rates (e.g. following a change in the name of the entity or following the setting up of new production or sales entities) should be addressed to the Commission forthwith with all relevant information, in particular any modification in the company's activities linked to production, domestic and export sales associated with, for example that name change or that change in the production and sales entities. The Commission, if appropriate, will, after consultation of the Advisory Committee, amend the Regulation accordingly by updating the list of companies benefiting from individual duty rates.

3. Non-imposition of provisional measures in respect of Korea and Malaysia

223 In view of the results of the investigation concerning Korea and Malaysia, and considering that the dumping margin found in the case of these two countries is below the 2% threshold set in Article 9(3) of the basic Regulation, no provisional measures should be imposed in respect of Korea and Malaysia. The Commission will continue to investigate and consider any further evidence submitted. Should the provisional findings be confirmed at the definitive stage, the proceeding would be terminated as regards these imports.

4. Undertakings

224 The exporting producers in the Czech Republic and Turkey have offered price undertakings in accordance with Article 8(1) of the basic Regulation. By doing so, they have agreed to sell the product concerned at or above price levels which eliminate the injurious effects of dumping. The companies will also provide the Commission with regular and detailed information concerning their exports to the Community, meaning that the undertakings can be monitored effectively by the Commission. In addition, the nature of the product, the structure of the companies and their sales patterns is such that the risk of circumvention of the undertakings is also minimized.

225   In view of this, the offers of undertakings are therefore considered acceptable and the companies concerned have been informed of the essential facts, considerations and obligations upon which acceptance is based.

226   To further enable the Commission to effectively monitor the compliance of the companies with their undertakings, when the request for release for free circulation is presented to the relevant customs authority, exemption from the anti-dumping duty shall be conditional on the presentation of a commercial invoice containing at least the elements listed in the Annex. This level of information is also necessary to enable customs authorities to ascertain with sufficient precision that shipments correspond to the commercial documents. Where no such invoice is presented, or when it does not correspond to the product presented to customs, the appropriate rate of anti-dumping duty will instead be payable.

227   It should be noted that in the event of a breach or withdrawal of the undertaking or a suspected breach, an anti-dumping duty may be imposed, pursuant to Article 8(9) and (10) of the basic Regulation.

Notes and Questions

1.   Suppose that X Corp. sells goods for export to the EC at a price of $136/unit, delivered dockside at Rotterdam. In its home country, the United States, X Corp. sells similar goods for $125/unit, delivered at the factory gate. Suppose further that X Corp. spends $8/unit for shipping and $2/unit for insuring the goods on their way to Rotterdam. Moreover, although X Corp. does not advertise in the EC, it spends an average of $0.25/unit on advertising in the US. It requires its overseas customers to pay by letter of credit at the time of shipment; its US customers are invoiced and are expected to pay in 30 days. The difference in credit costs to X Corp. is $1.00/unit. Given this information, is X Corp. dumping? What is the margin of dumping or "safety"? Suppose the EC purchaser is a subsidiary of X Corp. How might that change your answer?

2.   The use of constructed values is sometimes controversial. The Commission normally relies upon the producer's cost allocations, but it is not bound to accept them and may decide to allocate additional costs to the product under investigation, which results in an increased dumping margin. The problem of cost allocation is particularly serious in industries where there are significant research and development costs or startup costs. The shorter the period over which such costs must be amortized, the more likely that a dumping margin will be found.

3.   Assuming that all appropriate adjustments have been made to make the prices comparable, suppose ABC, a US company, sells a product in the US for $9, $10 and $11 respectively on each of three different dates and the same product in the EC at the same prices on the same dates. Is there dumping? Although your first reaction might be no, that has not always been clear. The Commission formerly considered normal value to be the *average* home market price and calculated the dumping margin by comparing that average price to each export price. Here the normal value—the average home market price—is $10. When the export prices are compared to the normal value, there is dumping of $1 in respect of one of the export transactions and no dumping in respect of the other two. It was also the view of the Commission that negative dumping margins (such as results from comparing the $11 export price with the normal value of $10) do not offset positive ones (known as "zeroing" because negative margins were counted

as zero). Thus, the weighted average dumping margin given these facts would be $0.33 (overall dumping of $1.00 spread over three equivalent transactions). As a result of the Uruguay Round negotiations, EC rules now provide for the use of average-to-average price comparison, except in certain cases. As indicated in paragraph 29 of the *SWR* case, however, the Commission still uses average to individual comparisons in some cases. In 2001, India successfully challenged the EC's use of zeroing in a WTO dispute settlement proceeding.[7]

4.   Much of the information relevant to the calculation of dumping margins and to the establishment of injury is commercially sensitive as it concerns company-specific cost and price data. As noted above, although exporters cannot be forced to cooperate in the investigation, they may be subject to higher duties if they do not. The Commission treats price and cost data as confidential. As a lawyer representing exporters or Community industry, how can be sure that the Commission appropriately assesses data? In the US, lawyers are permitted to examine such data, on the understanding that they will not reveal it to their clients. Should the Community adopt such a policy?

5.   It is necessary to compare normal value and export prices in the same currency even though the actual transactions may have been denominated in different currencies. This means that nondumping prices may become dumping prices if exchange rates change. What would be an example of this?

6.   Were you convinced in the *SWR* case that Community industry was materially injured? Was the industry profitable? Was its market share declining significantly? Did the Commission correctly analyze the presence and growth in the Community market of low-priced, but undumped imports from Korea and Malaysia? Was the injury in the *SWR* case due to an unfair trade practice or competition itself? Should there have been a discussion of market structure and the possible achievement of market power? Would that be necessary in a competition case? Is it required by the antidumping regulation? If there any justification for the difference in approach? Can the difference be explained by private interest lobbying? Would you expect domestic industry to be better able to lobby for protection from foreign competitors than from other domestic competitors? For a proposal to base the injury analysis in trade cases on competition law principles, see D. Wood, "Unfair" Trade Injury: A Competition–Based Approach, 41 Stanford L.Rev. 1153 (1989).

7.   Were you convinced that it was in the Community's interest in the *SWR* case to impose antidumping duties? Is it ever in a nation's interest to exclude low-priced imports when the exporters have no chance of gaining market power in that nation's market and there is no barrier to entry by equally efficient domestic competitors who are willing to accept an equally low profit margin? How did the treatment of consumer interests in the *SWR* case compare with the treatment that consumer interests receive under competition law? See Chapter 23 supra. If you were going to attack the Council's conclusions on Community interest in the Court of Justice, what arguments would you make?

The relatively weak standing accorded to consumer interests in EC antidumping proceedings was underscored in Bureau Européen des Unions de Consommateurs v. Commission, Case C–170/89, [1991] ECR I–5709, where the Court of Justice held that an association of European consumers unions had no right to inspect even the *non*confidential Commission files in an antidumping case, that right being reserved under the regulation to the parties in interest (complainants,

---

7. EC–Anti-dumping Duties on Imports of Cotton–Type Bed Linen from India, WT/   DS141/AB/R, WTO Appellate Body Report adopted March 12, 2001.

exporters, importers, governments). The Court rejected an argument that such access should be accorded under general principles of law, even if not explicitly provided for in the regulation. In light of the Community's concern about consumer interests in other areas (especially in consumer protection, see Chapter 35 infra), is the status given to consumers in this decision sound? Currently, consumer organizations have a right to present information and argument and to review information and arguments presented by other participants in antidumping proceedings. They are still not entitled to review confidential information. In the United States, public and consumer interests receive no consideration in antidumping proceedings. The law requires that if dumping and injury are found, then antidumping duties in the amount of the dumping margin must be imposed.

8.   The EC imposes antidumping duties on a prospective basis, i.e. all future imports are assessed the antidumping duty. This raises the question of whether an exporter can stop dumping and avoid the duties. The EC regulation allows an exporter to have the duty rate reviewed after one year and provides a refund mechanism applicable where no dumping has occurred in specific transactions. The provisions on reviews and refunds are in article 11. There are specific provisions for:

—a so-called "sunset" review after five years if requested by Community industry (absent such a review, the duties expire automatically), art. 11(2);

— interim reviews (after one year), art. 11(3);

— reviews to set rates for new exporters, art. 11(4); and

— refunds, art. 11(8).

Some practitioners of EC antidumping laws complain that the review and refund procedures are ineffective. The desire to avoid prospective duties is believed to be a major factor in causing exporters to "settle" antidumping cases by entering into undertakings with the Commission.

In contrast, antidumping duties in the US are applied retrospectively. Each year (in theory), the US authorities review the past year's exports to the United States and assess antidumping duties. Importers are required to deposit estimated duties in cash on the basis of the rate established in the initial investigation or most recent review. Undertakings are possible under US law, but relatively rare.

9.   Can retroactive antidumping duties be imposed? See art. 10.

10.   The effect of antidumping duties can be effectively countered if they are absorbed by the exporter, so that prices of the product in the Community do not rise following imposition of the duty. While the exporter may find this expensive, it may decide that it is worth the expense to retain its EC market share. In 1988, the EC added a new provision to its antidumping regulation to prevent this behavior. As now formulated, it essentially requires a new investigation and recalculation of antidumping duties when it is invoked. Art. 12. As a consequence, it largely duplicates the interim review procedure of article 11(2).

11.   One controversial issue in antidumping law is how to deal with attempts to circumvent antidumping duties. Antidumping duties are normally imposed on a specific product coming from a specific country, usually on a company-by-company basis. From our discussion of customs law in the previous chapter, several possible circumvention strategies should be evident. First, the product exported to the EC could be modified so that it would fall under a different tariff classification and thus not be subject to the antidumping duties. Second, the product could be manufactured in a way that would give it a different origin. For example, if an

assembly plant were established in a third country, the finished product would arguably originate in that country and not be subject to antidumping duties. In Chapter 30(D) supra, in the *Brother* case, the Court of Justice dealt with a case involving this strategy. Third, if an assembly plant were established in the EC, components not subject to the dumping order could be imported into the EC for assembly and antidumping duties thereby avoided. There was no agreement reached on what would constitute acceptable anti-circumvention procedures in the Uruguay Round. For the moment, the Community's anti-circumvention rules are contained in article 13 of the regulation. How do they deal with the three strategies mentioned above?

12.   The requirement that the Commission consult at major stages in an investigation with an advisory committee of Member State representatives is significant. It means that the Member States play an indirect role in determining the outcome of antidumping cases, which in turn means that participants in these cases may try to lobby Member State officials for a particular outcome that they cannot obtain from the Commission.

13.   Finally, it should be noted that antidumping laws are quite controversial for a number of reasons. See W. Davey, Antidumping Laws: A Time for Restriction, in B. Hawk, ed., 1988 Fordham Corp.L.Inst. ch. 8 (Matthew Bender 1989).

First, critics of antidumping laws argue that they have a questionable economic basis. Generally, an importing country will benefit from low-priced imports unless the importer is engaging in predatory behavior and attempting to drive out competition so that it can later charge excessive prices. Antidumping laws, of course, do not require proof of predatory behavior as a prerequisite to the imposition of antidumping duties, and many economists believe that predatory behavior, defined as pricing below marginal or average variable cost, seldom occurs since the firm would usually have to lose substantial amounts of money on each unit of output and, unless there were high barriers to entry, would not be able to recoup its losses before new entrants would be attracted to the industry by the high prices. See Chapter 22(D)(5) supra. See also Matsushita Electric Industrial Co., Ltd. v. Zenith Radio Corp., 475 U.S. 574, 106 S.Ct. 1348, 89 L.Ed.2d 538 (1986), where in authorizing dismissal of a case alleging a low price conspiracy by Japanese television exporters, the Court noted that such a conspiracy did not make economic sense because barriers to entry were low, there were many Japanese competitors, and the Japanese exporters would never be able to raise their prices to supra-competitive levels to recoup losses from a period of below-cost pricing. See F. Easterbrook, The Limits of Antitrust, 63 Texas L.Rev. 1 (1989).

It is true, of course, that low-priced imports displace domestic products, but that is the result of all international trade and in the long run the resources and people employed in that industry should and will shift to more productive activities and the domestic economy will be better off as a result. Moreover, to the extent that dumping laws penalize all sales below total cost, they are discouraging rational conduct. Sales below total cost are still profit-maximizing for a time as long as marginal revenue exceeds marginal costs, even if total costs are not recovered. Such sales are common in recessions.

Second, critics argue that antidumping laws have anticompetitive effects. They prevent buyers from getting the benefit of low prices. They eliminate a procompetitive dynamic pressure on less efficient or responsive firms. They tend to be used most often by concentrated industries to protect their domestic markets from competition. Third, antidumping laws are arguably unfair to exporters because they penalize conduct that would not be actionable in the domestic context. For example, below-cost sales by a domestic company usually do not violate any laws so long as they are not predatory. Similarly, while there are anti price discrimination laws applicable in the domestic setting (e.g., the Robinson–Patman Act in the US), the coverage of those laws is much narrower than the antidumping laws.

As globalization of industry proceeds apace, antidumping laws sometimes seem anachronistic. In 1991, a Japanese-based typewriter maker (Brother) filed a US antidumping complaint against Smith–Corona, a US-based company, alleging that dumped typewriters from Smith Corona's Singapore plant were injuring US industry, specifically Brother's Tennessee typewriter plant. In years past, Smith Corona had successfully brought actions against the dumping of typewriters from Japan by Brother. While this complaint was settled, it does foreshadow future difficulties in determining who represents domestic industry in an age of global manufacturing, as well as the susceptibility of the antidumping laws to being used in strategic anticompetitive behavior. Indeed, as trade relations between countries become closer, antidumping laws tend to be eliminated or more tightly controlled. For example, no antidumping laws apply to trade between the Member States of the EC (except during transitional periods) or to trade in industrial products within the European Economic Area.

Despite these criticisms, antidumping laws are not likely to disappear in the near future as they have strong supporters. In its Eleventh Annual Report on its antidumping activities in 1993, the Commission noted that dumping effectively requires that the exporting market be segregated and the importing market be open. If not, arbitrage would likely result and largely eliminate any dumping. There is an advantage operating from a segregated market that is not based on economic efficiency and hence can be considered unfair. In the Commission's view:

"There are three types of dumping which are particularly damaging:

— state trade dumping from economies whose main aim may not be efficiency but to earn hard currency at any price. In these cases the margins by which the prices of the Community producers are undercut may be unusually high. Because the exporters in question often do not follow normal business behavior, this type of dumping in unpredictable in view of its occurrence, volume, price and duration;

— "cyclical" dumping occurs in industries subject to periodic excess supply and capacity in which there is an incentive to export during the period of shrinking domestic demand to dump excess production at prices below full cost, thus exporting unemployment. Cyclical dumping can be expected in industries with high investment and consequently high fixed costs, like the steel or chemical industry, and has the effect of exacerbating the difficulties facing an industrial sector in the importing country which is already affected by economic recession;

— strategic dumping aimed at achieving, through an aggressive export strategy, a strong position on important export markets. The long-term character of such dumping usually stems from the fact that the dumper operates from a home market base where foreign competition is weak or nonexistent. This strategy has as its main aim the expansion of production to benefit from scale and learning economies for products such as in the electronic sector."

In light of the foregoing, how would you assess the appropriateness of antidumping laws?

14. For more materials on the WTO and US antidumping rules, see J. Jackson, W. Davey & A. Sykes, Legal Problems of International Economic Relations, chs. 16 & 17 (West 4th ed. 2002). On EC rules, see E. Vermulst & P. Waer, E.C. Anti-dumping Law and Practice (1996); S. Inama & E. Vermulst, Customs and Trade Laws of the European Community 211–89 (1999).

4. THE COURT OF JUSTICE AND ANTIDUMPING

Decisions by the Court of Justice and the Court of the First Instance in antidumping cases have played a significant role in expanding the opportunities for judicial review and protecting procedural rights under Community law. It is less clear that the courts have had much impact on the development of the substantive aspects of Community antidumping law, however, because they tend to accord considerable deference to decisions of the Commission and the Council in what are viewed as matters of economic assessment.

(a) Reviewability

The threshold question in judicial review is who has the right to challenge actions taken or not taken in antidumping proceedings. Antidumping duties have always been levied by regulation. As we saw in Chapter 5 supra, regulations cannot usually be challenged by individuals under Article 230. Nonetheless, the Court of Justice, in a striking series of cases, granted judicial review to most parties concerned by antidumping procedures.

The Court of Justice first treated the reviewability question in its 1979 *Ballbearings* decision, NTN Toyo Bearing Co. v. Council, Cases 113, 118–121/77, [1979] ECR 1185. In that case, a Council regulation provided for the collection of provisional antidumping duties deposited in respect of products of four named Japanese companies. It did so even though (1) the relevant proceeding had been settled by undertakings, (2) no definitive duties were imposed and (3) the basic Community regulation on antidumping procedures did *not* authorize the collection of provisional duties in such a case. The Court of Justice concluded that the regulation constituted a collective decision and was therefore reviewable under Article 230. Its judgment was narrowly drawn and did not suggest that any group generally had standing to appeal the results of antidumping proceedings.

In Alusuisse Italia SpA v. Council, Case 307/81, [1982] ECR 3463, an Italian importer of orthoxylene sought to challenge under Article 230 a regulation imposing an antidumping duty on US-origin orthoxylene. The Italian importer was not legally related to the US exporters. The Court held that the antidumping regulation in question, with respect to importers, was a measure having general application and therefore not reviewable under Article 230. Interestingly, the Court drew a distinction between "independent importers who, in contrast to exporters, are not expressly named in the regulations." This distinction proved critical in Allied Corp. v. Commission, Cases 239 & 275/82, [1984] ECR 1005. In addressing whether a challenge to an antidumping regulation should be permitted, the Court noted that

[11] [a]lthough it is true that, in the light of the criteria set out in the second paragraph of Article 173 [now 230], such measures are, in fact, as regards their nature and their scope, of a legislative character, inasmuch as they apply to all the traders concerned, taken as a whole, the provisions may none the less be of direct and individual concern to those producers and

exporters who are charged with practicing dumping. It is clear from [the basic antidumping regulation] that anti-dumping duties may be imposed only on the basis of the findings resulting from investigations concerning the production prices and export prices of undertakings which have been individually identified.

[12] It is thus clear that measures imposing anti-dumping duties are liable to be of direct and individual concern to those producers and exporters who are able to establish that they were identified in the measures adopted by the Commission or the Council or were concerned by the preliminary investigations.

Notes and Questions

1. Since regulations imposing antidumping duties virtually always name the producers or exporters involved in the case, they now effectively have the right to contest such regulations in an Article 230 proceeding. What avenues of judicial review would exporters have if the Court had ruled that they did not have standing?

2. An importer is clearly affected by an antidumping regulation since it is the importer that has to pay increased duties. While the importer may be able to challenge the duties before the Court of Justice through an Article 234 reference, is that as satisfactory as having a right of direct appeal? Does it make sense to distinguish importers and exporters in respect of direct appeals to the Court? Moreover, doesn't the independent importer best represent one of the two conflicting prongs of the Community interest at stake (the other being represented by the domestic producers)? The Court has modified its decision in *Alusuisse* in respect of appeals by certain categories of importers, such as one who has imported large quantities of specially ordered material (as in Nashua Corporation v. Commission, Cases 133 & 150/87, [1990] ECR I–719), or who is the largest EC importer and a competitor of the major EC producer (as in Extramet Industrie SA v. Council, Case C–358/89, [1991] ECR I–2501).

3. What about complainants—the Community producers who allege dumping? Can they challenge the adequacy of the relief accorded by the Commission when it does impose antidumping or countervailing duties? When it does not impose duties? See Timex Corp. v. Council & Commission, Case 264/82, [1985] ECR 849 (contested regulation was of direct and individual concern to Timex, the largest Community producer of the goods at issue, who had originated the complaint and participated in the investigation and in light of whose injury the duty was assessed).

4. In 2000, the Court of First Instance summarized the rules as follows:

"The Community judicature has held that, generally speaking, in the case of producers and exporters who are alleged to be involved in dumping, particular provisions of regulations imposing antidumping duties may be considered to be of direct and individual concern to them on the basis of data concerning their commercial activities. This is particularly so where producers or exporters are able to demonstrate that they were identified in the measures adopted by the Commission or the Council, or were concerned by the preliminary investigations. * * * As a general rule, certain provisions of regulations imposing anti-dumping duties are also of direct and individual concern to importers whose resale prices were taken into account for the construction of export prices. Finally, the Court of Justice has also recognized the admissibility of an action contesting such a regulation where it was brought by an independent importer in exceptional circumstances, in particular, when the regulation seriously affected its business activities (citing *Extramet*)."

Euromin v. Council, Case T–597/97, [2000] ECR II–___ (June 20, 2000) (rejecting claim of special circumstances).

(b) Procedural Rights in Antidumping Proceedings

The Advocate General in the 1979 *Ballbearings* case was quite critical of the procedural aspects of the then existing EC antidumping rules, and procedural protections for all parties were expanded when the EC adopted a revised antidumping regulation in 1979. The scope of procedural rights is dealt with in the following two cases.

EEC SEED CRUSHERS' & OIL PROCESSORS' FED'N (FEDIOL) v. COMMISSION

Case 191/82, [1983] ECR 2913.

[In 1980, FEDIOL asked the Commission to initiate an antisubsidy investigation of Brazilian soya-bean oil-cake. The Commission declined to do so and informed FEDIOL of its decision. FEDIOL then challenged the Commission's action in the Court of Justice.

The Commission conceded that the applicable regulation, which governs both antidumping and antisubsidy proceedings, gave the appellant the right to lodge a complaint, but argued that it did not give the applicant a right to compel the initiation of a proceeding in light of the wide discretion reserved to the Commission under the regulation. In particular, the Commission noted that the purpose of the regulation is not only to protect Community industry but also to safeguard the general interests of the Community, including its economic and political interests. Accordingly, the Commission argued that its decision not to open a proceeding did not constitute a measure open to challenge under Article 230.

The appellant argued that once it had submitted sufficient evidence to show the existence of a subsidy and injury, the Commission was obligated to initiate an official investigation.

The Court decided that it had to assess the appellant's claim in light of "the whole scheme of investigation and protection created by [the regulation.]" It concluded:]

25   It appears from a comparison of the provisions governing the successive procedural stages described above that the regulation recognizes the existence of a legitimate interest on the part of Community producers in the adoption of anti-subsidy measures and that it defines certain specific rights in their favour, namely the right to submit to the Commission all evidence which they consider appropriate, the right to see all information obtained by the Commission subject to certain exceptions, the right to be heard at their request and to have the opportunity of meeting the other parties concerned in the same proceeding, and finally the right to be informed if the Commission decides not to pursue a complaint. In the case of the proceedings being terminated on the completion of the stage of preliminary investigation provided for in Article 5 that information must

comprise at least a statement of the Commission's basic conclusions and a summary of the reasons therefor as is required by Article 9 in the event of the termination of formal investigations.

26   Whilst it is true that the Commission, when exercising the powers assigned to it in [the Regulation], is under a duty to establish objectively the facts concerning the existence of subsidization practices and of injury caused thereby to Community undertakings, it is no less true that it has a very wide discretion to decide, in terms of the interests of the Community, any measures needed to deal with the situation which it has established.

27   It is in the light of those considerations, originating in the scheme of [the Regulation] that it is necessary to decide whether complainants have the right to bring an action.

28   It seems clear, first, in that respect—and the point is not disputed by the Commission—that complainants must be acknowledged to have a right to bring an action where it is alleged that the Community authorities have disregarded rights which have been recognized specifically in the regulation, namely the right to lodge a complaint, the right, which is inherent in the aforementioned right, to have that complaint considered by the Commission with proper care and according to the procedure provided for, the right to receive information within the limits set by the regulation and finally, if the Commission decides not to proceed with the complaint, the right to receive information comprising at the least the explanations guaranteed by Article 9(2) of the regulation.

29   Furthermore it must be acknowledged that, in the spirit of the principles which lie behind Articles 164 [now 220] and 173 [now 230] of the Treaty, complainants have the right to avail themselves, with regard both to the assessment of the facts and to the adoption of the protective measures provided for by the regulation, of a review by the Court appropriate to the nature of the powers reserved to the Community institutions on the subject.

30   It follows that complainants may not be refused the right to put before the Court any matters which would facilitate a review as to whether the Commission has observed the procedural guarantees granted to complainants by [the Regulation] and whether or not it has committed manifest errors in its assessment of the facts, has omitted to take into consideration any essential matters of such a nature as to give rise to a belief in the existence of subsidization or has based the reasons for its decision on considerations amounting to a misuse of powers. In that respect, the Court is required to exercise its normal powers of review over a discretion granted to a public authority, even though it has no jurisdiction to intervene in the exercise of the discretion reserved to the Community authorities by the aforementioned regulation.

31   It follows from the foregoing that the attitude adopted by the Commission is excessive inasmuch as it considers that any action brought by the complainants described in Article 5 of the regulation is, in principle, inadmissible. As has been shown above, the regulation acknowledges that undertakings and associations of undertakings injured by subsidization practices on the part of non-member countries have a legitimate interest in the initiation of protective action by the Community; it must therefore

be acknowledged that they have a right of action within the framework of the legal status which the regulation confers upon them.

[32] It is therefore for the applicant to put forward its submissions in the course of the subsequent proceedings and to show that they fall within the limits of the legal protection given to it by [the Regulation] and by the general principles of the Treaty.

AL-JUBAIL FERTILIZER CO. v. COUNCIL

Case C–49/88, [1991] ECR I–3187.

[In 1987, the Council imposed an antidumping duty on urea from Saudi Arabia. This case was an appeal by two Saudi urea producers. They claimed, inter alia, that they were denied their right to have a fair hearing.]

[8] In support of this submission, the applicants claim that they were not informed in advance of the reasons why the Council [rejected] their request for an allowance to take account of difference in levels of trade and in quantities sold in Saudi Arabia * * *. They also claim that they were not warned in advance in the change in the type of anti-dumping imposed [from a provisional floor price duty of 133 ECU to an ad valorem duty allegedly imposing a much heavier charge], that they received no answer to the questions which they had raised regarding the determination of the injury threshold and that the allowance granted by the Commission in respect of warehousing was insufficient.

* * *

[14] It should be recalled at the outset that under Article 7(4)(a) and (b) of the basic regulation[8]

"(a) The complainant and the importers and exporters known to be concerned * * * may inspect all information made available to the Commission * * *, provided that it is relevant to the defence of their interests and not confidential within the meaning of Article 8 and that it is used by the Commission in the investigation * * *

"(b) Exporters and importers of the product subject to investigation * * * may request to be informed of the essential facts and considerations on the basis of which it is intended to recommend the imposition of definitive duties * * * ".

[15] Secondly, according to the well-established case-law of the Court, fundamental rights form an integral part of the general principles of law, whose observance is ensured by the Court. Consequently, it is necessary when interpreting Article 7(4) of the basic regulation to take account in particular of the requirements stemming from the right to a fair hearing, a principle whose fundamental character has been stressed on numerous occasions in the case-law of the Court. Those requirements must be observed not only in the course of proceedings which may result in the imposition of penalties, but also in investigative proceedings prior to the adoption of anti-dumping regulations which, despite their general scope,

---

8. For the current rules, see articles 6(7) and 20 of the Regulation.

may directly and individually affect the undertakings concerned and entail adverse consequences for them.

16   It should be added that, with regard to the right to a fair hearing, any action taken by the Community institutions must be all the more scrupulous in view of the fact that, as they stand at present, the rules in question do not provide all the procedural guarantees for the protection of the individual which may exist in certain national legal systems.

17   Consequently, in performing their duty to provide information, the Community institutions must act with all due diligence by seeking, as the Court stated in Timex v. Council, [1985] ECR 849, to provide the undertakings concerned, as far as is compatible with the obligation not to disclose business secrets, with information relevant to the defence of their interests, choosing, if necessary on their own initiative, the appropriate means of providing such information. In any event, the undertakings concerned should have been placed in a position during the administrative procedure in which they could effectively make known their views on the correctness and relevance of the facts and circumstances alleged and on the evidence presented by the Commission in support of its allegation concerning the existence of dumping and the resultant injury.

18   There is nothing in the documents before the Court to show that the Community institutions discharged their duty to place at the applicants' disposal all the information which would have enabled them effectively to defend their interests.

19   With regard to the allowances requested in order to take account of the differences in quantities and levels of trade, the defendant, in support of its contentions, relies solely on an internal mission report drawn up by Commission officials following checks carried out in Saudi Arabia, and on the minutes of two meetings held in Brussels on 22 May and 5 October 1987 with the representatives of the parties in question. Given that the documents before the Court show that the information contained in such internal documents was not brought by other means to the attention of the applicants, there is all the less reason for such documents to be accorded probative value.

20   Although the information requested may, under Article 7(4)(c)(ii) of the basic regulation, be supplied in a purely oral manner, that possibility cannot release the Community authorities from their obligation to ensure that they have evidence enabling them, if necessary, to prove that such information was actually communicated. Since the Council has failed to adduce any evidence in support of its contentions, it must be concluded that the applicants' first two arguments are well founded.

21   The same holds true with regard to the arguments based on the irregularities committed by the Commission in determining the injury threshold and calculating the allowance for warehousing.

22   The defendant constantly referred in this regard to a letter of 8 September 1988 which the applicants claim never to have received. For the reasons already outlined, that letter, which was not sent by registered post and the reception of which by the addressee could consequently not be established with absolute certainty, cannot be regarded as a diligent method of

discharging the obligation to provide information laid down in the basic regulation. For that reason, these two complaints must also be upheld.

[23]   With regard finally to the failure to provide information relating to the change in the method of calculating the definitive duty, it is necessary first of all to point out that, while it is true that the amount of the definitive duty constitutes essential information, such is not the case with regard to the type of duty ultimately adopted by the Council and the method of calculating that duty.

[24]   In view of the fact that the choice between the various types of anti-dumping duties has in principle no effect on the final amount of that duty and that the *ad valorem* duty is by far the most common type of duty in cases of dumping, the information concerning the method of calculating the anti-dumping duty cannot be regarded as essential, nor consequently can the absence of such information be treated as infringing the right to a fair hearing. That argument must therefore be rejected.

[25]   It follows from the foregoing, however, that the submission based on the infringement of the right to a fair hearing must be accepted. As a result, Article 1 of Regulation No 3339/87 must be declared void in so far as it imposes an anti-dumping duty on the applicants, without its being necessary to examine the applicants' remaining submissions on which they have relied.

Notes and Questions

1.   How do the Court's decisions on procedural rights in antidumping cases compare to its analogous decisions in competition cases?

2.   Why is the issue of judicial review under Article 230 for the complaining industry in *FEDIOL* an easy one compared to the issues raised in *Alusuisse* and *Allied?* Note the reference to Article 164 [now 220]. Why is it relevant? Note also the reference to the specific procedural points upon which challenges can be raised. Similar procedural rights are accorded to producers and exporters as well.

3.   Is there any harm in giving all persons affected by a decision the standing to challenge it? Do complainants' interests conflict with a public interest of the Community? How? Consider what the Commission meant by "the general interests of the Community in all their complexity" (para. 11). In the United States, any "interested party" who is a party to the proceeding can appeal an administrative decision in an antidumping matter. See 19 U.S.C.A. sec. 1516a. The statute defines interested parties as including foreign manufacturers and exporters of the merchandise under investigation, US importers, manufacturers and wholesalers thereof (and their trade associations), US unions representative of a US industry producing such merchandise and foreign governments of countries in which such merchandise is manufactured. 19 U.S.C.A. sec. 1677(9).

(c) *Substantive Review of Antidumping Cases*

The expanded availability of judicial review in antidumping cases has led to many appeals in recent years. Appellants have challenged virtually every aspect of the Commission's findings on dumping and injury. As shown in the following material, the EC courts have thus far usually deferred to the decisions reached by the Commission and Council. Accordingly, the Commission's considerable discretion in these matters is not closely controlled. In the United States, judicial review of antidumping orders has been more intrusive.

An example of judicial deference is seen in NTN Toyo Bearing Co. v. Council, Case 240/84, [1987] ECR 1809, which was an appeal of a regulation imposing antidumping duties on Japanese ballbearings. The issue in the case arose from the manner in which the Commission had compared average normal value with individual export prices and had not considered "negative" dumping margins as offsetting positive ones (see note 3 to the *SWR* case). In the view of the Court of Justice:

[19] [T]he choice between the different methods of calculation [of antidumping margins specified the Regulation] requires an appraisal of complex economic situations. The Court must therefore limit its review of such an appraisal to verifying whether the relevant procedural rules have been complied with, whether the facts on which the choice is based have been accurately stated and whether there has been a manifest error of appraisal or a misuse of powers.

[20] The line of argument put forward by the applicant is tantamount to alleging that the institutions made a manifestly incorrect appraisal of the facts in adopting a method of assessing the dumping margin which does not take account of export prices above the normal value and thus gives rise to an inequitable result.

[21] Such a line of argument cannot be accepted. It must be stated firstly that, contrary to what the applicant maintains, the transaction-by-transaction method does not exclude from the calculation of the dumping margin transactions at prices above the normal value. It merely artificially reduces such prices to the level of the normal value but includes them in the calculation of the weighted average of all the prices charged on the export market.

[22] Secondly, it should be stressed that the freedom to choose one of the methods specified in Article 2(13)(b) of Regulation No 3017/79 is specifically intended to ensure the application of the method most appropriate to the purpose of the anti-dumping proceeding. Articles 2(1) and 4(1) of that regulation provide that the purpose of such a proceeding is to eliminate the injury or threat of injury caused by dumping to an established Community industry.

[23] The transaction-by-transaction method is the only method capable of dealing with certain manoeuvres in which dumping is disguised by charging different prices, some above the normal value and some below it. The application of the weighted average method in such a situation would not meet the purpose of the anti-dumping proceeding, since that method would in essence mask sales at dumping prices by those at what are known as "negative" dumping prices, and would thus in no way eliminate the injury suffered by the Community industry concerned.

[24] It must therefore be accepted that the Commission did not in this case commit any manifest error in its appraisal of the facts by applying the transaction-by-transaction method in order to calculate the dumping margin; this submission must therefore be rejected.

Notes and Questions

1.   French administrative courts traditionally did not review the application of law to facts by government agencies. The "manifest error" standard used by the Court of Justice (see para. 19) was apparently developed by the French courts to give them some limited control of administration discretion. "The doctrine of *erreur manifeste* seems to have given the courts a means of ensuring that the government's application of the law to the facts in discretionary and technical matters is always reasonable, even if not always right." G. Bermann, The Scope of Judicial Review in French Administrative Law, 16 Colum.J.Transnat'l L. 195, 243 (1977). In the words of one French court official, "*Erreur manifeste* is a palpable error that is raised by the parties, recognized by the judge, and about which no enlightened person can have doubt." Id. at 244. How does this standard compare to that used by U.S. courts? Which seems to be more deferential? Do you think that the Court loses sight of what is "fair" in favor of a technical reading of the regulation?

2.   In 1992, the Court of Justice proposed, with Commission support, that the Court of First Instance be vested with jurisdiction over appeals from, inter alia, antidumping and antisubsidy cases. The Court of First Instance was given jurisdiction over appeals of Community actions in antidumping cases as of March 15, 1994. Although there is a perception that the Court of First Instance examines antidumping cases more thoroughly than did the Court of Justice, it has tended to uphold the Community authorities in challenges to antidumping measures. But it has not always done so. See, e.g., Commission v. Koyo Seiko Co. Ltd., Case C–245/95, [1998] ECR I–403, upholding NTN Corporation v. Council, Cases T–163 & 165/94, [1995] ECR II–1381 (CFI ruled that article 4 of the then effective antidumping regulation, which defined material injury, applied in the context of a review procedure. Since the Commission had evaluated injury using a factor not permitted by article 4, the CFI annulled the Commission decision.) It may be expected that the prospect of more demanding judicial review will cause Community authorities to pay greater attention to ensuring that Community actions in this area are in strict compliance with the relevant EC rules, even if they are confident that their substantive decision will usually be upheld.

3.   In an interesting case involving anti-dumping and countervailing duties on salmon from Norway, a Norwegian exporter made an undertaking to respect certain minimum prices, which was accepted by the Commission. Pursuant to the undertaking, on October 22, 1997, the exporter submitted certain data to the Commission covering its exports of salmon to the EC during the third quarter of 1997. The data showed that the exporter had complied with the terms of its undertaking. As of December 18, 1997, the Commission imposed provisional duties on the exporter's salmon exports to the EC and removed its name from the list of companies from which the Commission had accepted undertakings. The Commission did so because it had concluded, after making certain adjustments to the exporter's third-quarter report, that the exporter had not complied with the undertaking. The exporter immediately ceased exports to the EC and complained to the Commission that it had made incorrect adjustments. On January 30, 1998, the Commission informed the exporter that it agreed that the undertaking had been respected, although it did not repeal the provisional duty until March 25, 1998. In a case for damages brought under Article 288, the Court of First Instance ruled that the facts of this case simply involved the Commission's administration of an undertaking, as opposed to its exercise of legislative discretion in matters of economic policy. As such, the court concluded that liability would be found if the exporter could show that the Commission "committed an error which an adminis-

trative authority exercising ordinary care and diligence would not have committed in the same circumstances." (para. 62) The court found that the Commission could not simply change the exporter's report "without explaining to it the reasons prompting it to ignore [certain] entries and without checking with it whether the changes so made affected the reliability of the information provided." (para. 76) By doing so, the court concluded the Commission had not met the standard set out above. While the court found the exporter was not blameless, it ordered the Commission to pay damages to the exporter in an amount of 431,000 Norwegian krone (roughly $50,000). Fresh Marine Co. v. Commission, Case T–178/98, [2000] ECR II–3331.

B.   REGULATION OF SUBSIDIZED IMPORTS

WTO rules permit a WTO member to impose countervailing duties to offset the effect of subsidized imports if those imports cause material injury to its domestic industry. As in the case of dumping, there is a WTO agreement— the Agreement on Subsidies and Countervailing Measures (the SCM Agreement)—that governs the use of countervailing duties. It establishes procedural requirements similar to those established for dumping investigations.

The SCM Agreement defines a subsidy as a financial contribution by a government or a public body that confers a benefit. It prohibits the use of nonagricultural export subsidies and subsidies contingent on the use of domestic instead of imported products. (A separate agreement deals with agricultural subsidies.) The SCM Agreement also provides that WTO members should not cause adverse effects to the interests of other members through the use of specific, nonagricultural subsidies. A specific subsidy is one that is limited to an enterprise or industry or group of enterprises or industries. A nonspecific subsidy would be one that is available automatically to any entity that meets general eligibility criteria. The agreement's limitations only apply to specific subsidies.

In light of the detailed provisions of the SCM Agreement, the EC adopted Council Regulation 2026/97 on protection against subsidized imports, which is excerpted in the Selected Documents.[9] The regulation restates the SCM Agreement's definition of subsidy and its specificity requirement. Arts. 2–3. It contains specific rules for calculating the amount of the countervailing duties, which are based on a calculation of the benefit of the subsidy to the recipient (as opposed to the cost to the government, which was formerly the Community standard and which is considered to be narrower). Art. 5. The regulation's provisions on injury and procedures are generally similar to those in the antidumping regulation, although the details of the two regulations differ in some respects (provisional duties are limited to four months; the de minimis thresholds are different; there is more involvement of the subsidizing government in a subsidies/countervailing duty investigation).

Until the late 1990s, the EC had not often initiated countervailing duty actions. In the 19–year period from 1977 to 1995, it brought only 12 such actions. In the following four years—1996–1999—it initiated 26.[10] While the duties imposed have usually not been significant, the decisions on the type of

---

9. Council Regulation 2026/97 of Oct. 6, 1997, on protection against subsidized imports from countries not members of the European Community, O.J. L 288/1 (Oct. 21, 1997).

10. Edwin Vermulst, EC Countervailing Duty Practice After the Uruguay Round Revisited, 27 Legal Issues of Economic Integration 217 (2000).

subsidies that are countervailable have been broad, such that the groundwork seems to have been laid for possible future more extensive use of the regulation.

When the EC initiates countervailing duty investigations, there are three issues that must be resolved: to what extent have imports been subsidized? has a Community industry suffered or is it threatened with material injury? and would imposition of countervailing duties be in the interest of the Community? The last two issues are essentially treated in the same manner as if they arose in an antidumping case and will not be separately treated here. The first issue involves determinations of whether a government benefit is a subsidy, as defined by the Regulation, and whether it is "specific" in nature, so as to be countervailable. If a subsidy is countervailable, then it must be valued overall and on a unit basis so that duties may be imposed. The following decision deals with these questions.

COMMISSION REGULATION 1741/2000 OF 3 AUGUST 2000 IMPOSING A PROVISIONAL COUNTERVAILING DUTY ON IMPORTS OF POLYETHYLENE TEREPHTHALATE (PET) ORIGINATING IN INDIA, MALAYSIA, TAIWAN AND THAILAND

O.J. L 199/6 (August 5, 2000).

[This investigation involved PET originating in India, Indonesia, Malaysia, Korea, Taiwan and Thailand. In this regulation, the Commission imposes a provisional countervailing duty on imports from four of the six countries investigated. The following excerpts explain how the Commission evaluates whether a subsidy is countervailable under EC rules.]

IV.   MALAYSIA

1.   *Introduction*

[80] On the basis of the information contained in the complaint and in the replies to the Commission's questionnaire, the Commission services investigated the following alleged subsidy schemes: * * *

2.   *Pioneer status*

(a) *Legal basis*

[81] The legal basis for a company to obtain pioneer status is the Promotion of Investments Act of 1986. This Act also contains the list of promoted activities and promoted products. The list of promoted areas is listed in the Promotion of Investments (promoted areas) Order of 1994. The Promotion of Investments Order of 1995 contains special rules for promoted products for high technology companies.

(b) *Eligibility*

[82] Pioneer status may be granted to all companies intending to produce a "promoted" product (manufacturing sector) or a "promoted" activity (service sector) including a product/activity which is of national and strategic importance to Malaysia. Promoted products are products which are listed in the schedule to the Promotion of Investments Act.

[83] Pursuant to section 4 of the Act, the Minister of International Trade and Industry "shall from time to time determine such activities or products as he may deem fit to be promoted activities or promoted products". According to the Act, in order to promote a certain product, the Minister may take into consideration the following criteria:

— activity to be carried out or the product to be produced in Malaysia on a commercial scale which is suitable to the economic requirements or development of Malaysia,

— favorable prospects for further development of the activity or product,

— national and strategic requirements of Malaysia.

[84] The promoted areas are the eastern corridor of the Malaysian peninsular, Sabah, Sarawak and the federal territory of Labuan. An additional list of promoted products was drafted for companies located in promoted areas. These areas are considered to be lesser-developed areas of Malaysia. Neither company concerned is located in the promoted areas.

[85] Pioneer status can only be granted if the promoted activity or promoted product is new for the company and it cannot be cumulated for the same tax year with investment tax allowance or reinvestment allowance.

(c) Amount of benefit

[86] Any company which is granted pioneer status enjoys a tax exemption on 70% of its statutory income (= gross income less allowable expenses and incentives for double deductions on certain expenses) from the "production day".

[87] Companies with pioneer status and which are located in a promoted area obtain a tax exemption on 85% of their income. The "production day" is fixed by the Minister of International Trade and Industry by means of the pioneer certificate; it determines the commencement of the pioneer period for implementation of the tax benefit with the Inland Revenue Board. The tax exemptions granted are limited to a five-year period. In principle, no extensions for the benefits are given except where the Minister decides that the activity is of national and strategic importance to Malaysia. Finally, companies which produce promoted products for high technology will obtain a 100% tax exemption for a period of 10 years.

(d) Practical implementation

[88] In order to obtain the pioneer status, a company makes an application to the Malaysian Industrial Development Authority (MIDA), a statutory body reporting directly to the Minister of International Trade and Industry.

[89] It is verified whether the future production falls within the list of promoted products and whether at least two out of the four following conditions are met by the company:

— value added,

— local content,

— industrial linkage, and

— technology measures by way of an increase in the number of managerial, supervising and technical employees in the company.

90   If the above requirements are fulfilled, the Action Committee on Industries, a committee composed of representatives of MITI and the Department of Treasury will recommend the Ministers of International Trade
and of Finance to approve the granting of pioneer status to that company.

91   If a company is granted pioneer status, it submits a claim to the Inland
Revenue Board together with the annual tax return containing the calculation of the claim for the tax incentive.

92   The company can claim the first tax exemption in the tax year following
the year of first production.

(e) Countervailability

93   The tax exemptions under the Promotion of Investments Act constitute
countervailable subsidies in the sense of Article 3(2)(a) of the basic
Regulation. The GOM [Government of Malaysia] has limited the access to
the subsidy to enterprises that manufacture a promoted product. Since the
GOM has made the incentive available for the production of a limited
number of products, it automatically limits the access to these enterprises
producing the products as defined in the Act. The product under investigation in this proceeding is listed as a promoted product.

94   Furthermore, the GOM has wide discretion in the designation of promoted
products. The criteria, i.e. the suitability to the economic development of
Malaysia, favorable prospects for further development and the national
and strategic requirements of Malaysia, under which a product can be
classified as a promoted product are vague and cannot be considered as
objective criteria. It was established that there is no further definition of
these criteria. Furthermore, the GOM has provided for differentiated rates
of tax exemption depending on the type of promoted product and the
location in a promoted area. As a consequence, the GOM favors certain
enterprises over other enterprises whether it is because of the production
of a "more" promoted product or the location in a certain geographical
area. Finally, since local content is one of the criteria which in practice is
taken into account, this program aims to promote the use of domestic over
imported goods.

95   The scheme constitutes a subsidy, as the financial contribution by the
GOM in the form of tax exemption confers a benefit. It is a subsidy that is
specific to certain enterprises in Malaysia pursuant to Article 3(2)(a) of the
basic Regulation.

(f) Calculation of the benefit

96   The benefit to the exporting producers should be calculated on the basis of
the corporate income tax exemption and the resulting tax saving that was
effectively granted to the exporting producers during the investigation
period. The amount of benefit should be allocated over the total turnover
during the investigation period.

97   One company benefited from this scheme and obtained a subsidy of 4%.

* * *

4.　Double deduction of insurance premiums for importers

(a) Legal Basis

[99]　This program is regulated by subsection 154 of the Income Tax Act of 1967 and the Income Tax Rules of 1982.

(b) Eligibility

[100]　The double deduction is available for manufacturing or agricultural companies in respect of premiums payable for insurance of cargo imported by that person or company, provided that the insurer is a company incorporated in Malaysia. All importers are eligible to apply for this double deduction regardless of whether the imported products are to be consumed domestically or subsequently re-exported.

(c) Countervailability

[101]　The double deduction of insurance premiums for importers constitutes a subsidy as there is a financial contribution by the GOM in the form of double deduction of expenses (i.e. a reduced tax liability) which confers a benefit.

[102]　However, this double deduction of insurance premium for importers does not constitute a countervailable subsidy in the sense of the basic Regulation because it is not specific. The GOM has not limited the access to the subsidy to certain enterprises and applies objective criteria in the granting of the subsidy.

* * *

6.　Import duty exemption and sales tax exemption
"Licensed manufacturing warehouse" (LMW)

(a) Legal basis

[106]　Pursuant to Item 88 of the Customs Duties (Exemption) Order 1988, which is part of the Customs Act 1967, imported raw materials, machinery and equipment of a "Licensed manufacturing warehouse" (LMW) are exempted from import duties. The sales tax exemption for LMW companies is regulated by Item 83 Schedule B of the Sales Tax (Exemption) Order 1980.

[107]　One co-operating producer/exporter is identified as a LMW.

(b) Eligibility

[108]　LMW companies are manufacturing companies which are export oriented, i.e. companies having in 1998 an obligation to export a minimum 80% of their production; this rate has become 50 since 1 January 1999.

[109]　In order to qualify for the import duty exemption and the sales tax exemption on raw materials, machinery and equipment (including accessories and spare parts), an LMW company has to use those directly in the manufacturing process of an approved finished product which is, at least for a major part, exported to a third market and the equipment is to be used for environmental control, recycling, maintenance and quality control. The manufacturing process starts from the initial stage of manufac-

turing until the finished product is finally packed ready for export; this includes packaging materials and casings.

(c) Practical implementation

[110] As regards the imported raw materials, it was found that the main raw materials for the manufacturing of the product concerned, imported by the cooperating company, were subject to "nil" import duty rate and sales tax rate.

[111] For the imported machinery and equipment (including accessories and spare parts), the procedure is as follows:

[112] The company, prior to importation, files an application to the State Director of Customs which verifies whether the input can be directly used in the manufacturing process of the finished product

[113] After approval, the imports made under this scheme are declared through import declaration form 1 to the customs authorities. The imports are registered and examined by customs to verify if they are in compliance with the declaration approved by the State Director of Customs.

[114] Exemptions (import duty and sales tax) are consequently granted by the customs authorities by means of a "stamp" on the import declaration form.

(d) Countervailability

[115] This scheme constitutes a subsidy under Article 2 of the basic Regulation since it consists of a financial contribution by the GOM in the form of import duties and sales taxes foregone that are otherwise due and it confers a benefit to the recipient.

[116] Since, for LMW, it is limited to companies located in certain areas and furthermore it is contingent upon export performance, it is deemed to be specific within the meaning of Article 3(2)(a) and 3(4)(a) of the basic Regulation.

(e) Calculation of the benefit

[117] The amount of subsidy is the difference between the amount of import duties and sales tax actually paid on machinery/equipment and the amount of import duties and sales tax which would normally be payable without the benefit of the exemption.

[118] The benefit should be allocated over the normal lifetime of the machinery which is on average 10 years in Malaysia. The amount pertaining to the investigation period should be allocated over the total export turnover during the period of investigation for LMW companies. One company benefited from this scheme and obtained subsidies of 0.21%.

"Principal customs area" (PCA)

(a) Legal basis

[119] Section 14(2) of the Customs Act 1967 provides for customs duties exemption on imported raw materials, machinery and equipment for all companies not considered as LMW companies nor as "free zone" companies which can then only be companies located in a "Principal customs

area" (PCA). The legal basis for the sales tax exemption on imported raw materials, machinery and equipment is section 10 of the sales Tax Act. One co-operating producer/exporter is located in a "principal customs area".

(b) Eligibility

120　With regard to PCA companies, the import duty exemption and sales tax exemption on raw materials, machinery and equipment (also including accessories and spare parts) is granted by the Minister for Finance only to manufacturing companies fulfilling the conditions he may deem fit to impose.

121　These conditions include, amongst others, the requirement that the machinery and equipment concerned should be used directly in the manufacturing process of the finished goods.

(c) Practical implementation

122　As regards the imported raw materials, it was found that the main raw materials used in the manufacturing process of the product concerned, imported by the cooperating company, were subject to "nil" import duty-rate and sales tax rate.

123　The raw materials concerned are consequently not subject to an import duty and sales tax exemption.

124　For the imported machinery and equipment (including accessories and spare parts) the practical procedure is as follows:

125　The company, prior to importation, files an application to the Malaysian Industrial Development Authority (MIDA), a government body, which verifies whether the equipment can be directly used in the manufacturing process of the finished product. After approval, MIDA proposes to the Minister for Finance to grant import duty and sales tax exemptions to the applicant company for the specified machinery/equipment. The Minister for Finance issues an exemption letter listing all machinery/equipment approved to be imported without paying the normal duties (import and sales tax). The approval to import the listed equipment is valid for one year. When the machinery is imported, the company completes and files the Import declaration form 1 with the customs authorities. The imports are registered and examined by customs to verify if they are in compliance with the authorization granted by the Minister for Finance. Exemptions (import duty and sales tax) are consequently granted by the customs authorities by means of a "stamp" on the import declaration form.

(d) Countervailability

126　This scheme constitutes a subsidy under Article 2 of the basic Regulation since it consists of a financial contribution by the GOM in the form of import duties and sales taxes foregone that are otherwise due and it confers a benefit to the recipient.

127　For PCA companies, the import duty exemptions and sales tax exemptions are only available to manufacturing companies which import specific equipment under conditions set by the GOM "which it may deem fit to impose". These conditions are not considered to be objective since they are not neutral and economic in nature and horizontal in application. These criteria are furthermore not clearly set out by law. Since the eligibility is expressly limited to certain enterprises and not based on neutral criteria within the meaning of Article 3(2)(b) of the basic Regulation, the scheme is considered specific in accordance with Article 3(2)(a) of the basic Regulation.

(e) Calculation of the benefit

128   The amount of subsidy is the difference between the amount of import duties and sales tax actually paid on machinery and the amount of import duties and sales tax which would normally be payable without the benefit of the exemption.

129   The benefit should be allocated over the normal lifetime of the machinery which is on average 10 years in Malaysia. The amount pertaining to the investigation period should be allocated over the total turnover during the period of investigation for PCA companies.

130   One company benefited from this scheme and obtained subsidies of 0.91%.

* * *

8.   Amount of countervailable subsidies

132   The level of cooperation for Malaysia was very high (above 90%). The two companies producing PET in Malaysia did cooperate. The country wide weighted average subsidy margin is 4.2% which is above the applicable de minimis level of 2%.

133   In view of the high level of cooperation, the residual rate for non-cooperating companies was determined as the rate of the cooperating company with the highest subsidy margin i.e. 4.2%

V.   TAIWAN

1.   Introduction

134   On the basis of the information contained in the complaint and the replies to the Commission's questionnaire, the Commission services investigated the following alleged subsidy schemes:

* * *

3.   Import duty exemption

3.1.   Import duty exemption for machinery

(a) Legal basis

159   Chapters 84, 85 and 90 of the Customs import tariff and classification of import and export commodities of the Republic of China (hereinafter "the Customs Code").

(b) Eligibility

160   Pursuant to the abovementioned provisions of the Customs Code, a manufacturing company which imports machinery for the development of

new products, quality upgrading, increase of production, achievement of energy conservation, promotion of recycling or improvement of production techniques, which is not yet being manufactured locally, is exempt from import duties.

(c) Practical implementation

161   A company which intends to import machinery or equipment makes an application to IDB prior to the importation of the machinery. If IDB is satisfied that the machinery is not produced in Taiwan, it will issue a certificate which is sent to the applicant and the customs department. The customs services will verify whether the imported machinery is identical to the machinery described in the IDB certificate. This verification is undertaken on a random basis.

(d) Amount of duty exemption

162   The amount of subsidy is the amount of import duties which would normally be payable without the benefit of the exemption. The normal duty rate for machinery lies between 2% and 20%.

(e) Countervailability

163   The import duty exemption pursuant to the Customs Code constitutes a countervailable subsidy. Due to the nature of the subsidy, the program will automatically be disproportionately used by certain industry sectors. The industry sectors whose machinery is produced in Taiwan will not be eligible to use this program. Consequently, eligibility for the import duty exemption is limited to industries who are obliged to import machinery since the machinery is not available on the local market. Industries which import machinery which is also produced in Taiwan cannot obtain the benefit.

164   Therefore, it is considered that the import duty exemption on machinery constitutes a countervailable subsidy in the sense of Article 3(2)(a) of the basic Regulation.

(f) Calculation of the benefit

165   The benefit to the exporters should be calculated as the amount of import duties payable without the benefit of the exemption under this scheme. This amount should be allocated over the normal service life of the machinery in this industry, i.e. seven years.

166   All companies made use of this program and obtained benefits of 0.07% to 1.92%.

* * *

4. Loans at preferential interest rates

172   It was alleged that there are several programs regarding preferential loans available to the companies under investigation. The Commission established that only loans for automation and loans for anti-pollution incentives were used by the producers of the product concerned.

(a) Eligibility

[173] These schemes are covered by Article 21, paragraph 1, item 3 of the [statute for upgrading industries]. The GOT [Government of Taiwan] has established a development fund and makes use of such a development fund for providing loans in line with the government industrial policy for assisting the sound development of industries.

(b) Practical implementation

[174] A company has to file an application to the Chiao Tung Bank (which is partly State owned), or to certain other designated banks. The bank will verify whether the application falls within the criteria. Based on the financial situation of the applicant, the Chiao Tung Bank will decide on the amount of the loan.

(c) Countervailability

[175] The Commission established that there is a financial contribution by the GOT since the executive Yuan of the Development Fund, which is responsible for drafting and amending the rules relating to these types of loans is State controlled. Furthermore, the Chiao Tung Bank, which is also State-controlled, channels the loans to the companies. In addition, a benefit is conferred on the recipient of the loan since the interest rates of these loans are generally lower than comparable commercial loans. Low-interest loans are only available to companies which purchase specific equipment under specific conditions set by the executive Yuan of the Development Fund. Since the eligibility is expressly limited to certain enterprises and not based on neutral criteria within the meaning of Article 3(2)(b) of the basic anti-subsidy-Regulation, the scheme is considered specific in accordance with Article 3(2)(a) of the basic Regulation.

(d) Calculation of the subsidy amount

[176] The subsidy is the difference between the amount of interest paid on the loan during the investigation period and the interest normally payable on a comparable commercial loan during the investigation period. The comparable loan should be a loan of a similar amount with a similar repayment period actually obtained by the recipient from a representative private bank operating on the domestic market. In this investigation there were no such comparable commercial loans granted to the respective companies. Therefore the Commission considered that the appropriate benchmark would be the average commercial interest rate during the investigation period (9%). All companies availed themselves of this scheme and obtained a benefit of 0.02% to 0.09%.

Notes and Questions

1. Compare the Commission's position in the *PET* case with the Community's stance toward subsidies in the internal market under Article 87. See Chapter 26 supra. Are the Community's internal and external policies inconsistent? If not, should they be harmonized? If a foreign subsidy is of a type that would be found to be compatible with the common market under the terms of Article 87, should it ever be countervailed against?

2. In light of the *PET* case, what factors would you say are important in determining whether a subsidy is specific? In particular, note the treatment of export subsidies and subsidies promoting the use of local goods and the importance of government discretion.

3. How are subsidies valued and allocated over time? For example, how is the benefit of a subsidized interest rate calculated?

4. Many of the countervailing duty cases brought by the EC in the late 1990s were linked to antidumping investigations. While antidumping and countervailing duties may both be imposed, "double-counting" must be avoided.

5. For materials on WTO and US rules on subsidies and countervailing duties, see J. Jackson, W. Davey & A. Sykes, Legal Problems of International Economic Relations ch. 18 (West 4th ed. 2002).

C. THE TRADE BARRIERS REGULATION

The Trade Barriers Regulation (TBR)[11] provides a mechanism by which (i) a Community industry may complain to the Commission that it has suffered injury as a result of obstacles to trade that have an effect on the Community market and (ii) Community enterprises may complain to the Commission that they have suffered adverse effects as a result of obstacles to trade that have an effect on a third-country market. TBR, arts. 3–4. An "obstacle to trade" is defined principally as a trade practice of a third country that international trade rules prohibit. TBR, art. 2(1). Thus, the TBR can be invoked with the aim of obtaining access to third-country markets when such access is being denied contrary to the WTO agreements. In essence, the conditions for invoking the TBR are that (i) a trade barrier exists in a third country that violates an international agreement; (ii) the barrier adversely affects the trade of the Community petitioner and (iii) it is in the Community's interest to take action against the third country. The TBR, which was adopted in 1994, replaces the so-called new commercial policy instrument of 1984.

When a complaint against a trade barrier is filed with the Commission, it normally decides within 45 days whether to open an investigation. If it does so, it gathers information from the Community complainant and the country involved, as well as from other interested parties. The Commission's investigation is to be completed within five to seven months, at the end of which the Commission is to report to an Advisory Committee. If the Commission concludes that a trade barrier exists, the Commission will attempt to arrange for the removal of barrier. If the third country involved declines to take appropriate action, then the Commission may pursue international dispute settlement possibilities (most likely at the WTO). If the Community prevails in dispute settlement and the third country fails to bring its measure into compliance with its international obligations, the Council may adopt "retaliatory" measures within 30 days on the basis of a Commission proposal. From 1995 through September 2000, the Commission initiated 17 TBR investigations, four of which resulted in WTO dispute settlement proceedings.

The TBR (and its predecessor) were in large part designed to counter a similar procedure that exists under US law: Section 301 of the Trade Act of

---

11. Regulation 3286/94, O.J. L349/71 (Dec. 22, 1994).

1974. This provision allows US entities to as the US Trade Representative to take action against a foreign country on the grounds that it has violated an agreement with the US or has engaged in unjustifiable, unfair or discriminatory practices that burden US commerce. The EC unsuccessfully challenged the WTO-consistency of Section 301 in WTO dispute settlement. See Chapter 29 infra. For more materials on Section 301, see J. Jackson, W. Davey & A. Sykes, International Economic Relations, ch. 7 (West 4th ed. 2002).

Part VI

FREE MOVEMENT OF CAPITAL AND ECONOMIC AND MONETARY UNION

Free movement of capital is an essential prerequisite for achieving the internal market and a necessary precondition for Economic and Monetary Union (EMU). Although free movement of capital was one of the four freedoms in the initial EEC Treaty, progress towards its attainment was limited until 1988. Chapter 32 describes the initial developments, the 1988 liberalization directive, the Maastricht Treaty provisions that firmly established free movement of capital, and recent Court case law.

Linked to free movement of capital is the goal of an integrated financial market. Chapter 32 also describes the essential legal principles of Community law in this sector, together with a survey of the legislation and case law intended to achieve banking and securities law harmonization.

In the last decade, no political and legal development in the European Union has been more important than the creation of the Economic and Monetary Union. Building upon plans initially adopted in 1970, the Treaty of Maastricht introduced Monetary Union as a primary treaty goal in 1993. Within a remarkably short period of time, twelve Member States achieved the economic and monetary criteria set to enable the commencement of centralized monetary coordination under the European Central Bank (ECB) in 1999. Chapter 33 describes the planning for Monetary Union and the economic criteria necessary for States to join in it, as well as the structure, role and policy goals of the ECB. The chapter concludes by describing the legislative and other measures necessary for centralized monetary control and for the launch of the Euro as a single European currency in 2002.

Chapter 32

FREE MOVEMENT OF CAPITAL AND THE INTEGRATED FINANCIAL MARKET

Free movement of capital is a vital accessory to the other three basic freedoms. Free movement of goods is impeded if payment for the goods is restricted. Free movement of workers is limited if workers cannot bring funds from the home State or if their income and savings cannot be freely transferred back to the home State. The right of establishment for commercial and financial enterprises and the right to provide cross-border services are substantially frustrated by significant restrictions on capital movements. Moreover, free movement of capital is essential to achieve an integrated financial market in which banking, securities, insurance, and other financial enterprises can operate without hindrance throughout the Community. Likewise, free movement of capital is an indispensable precondition for Monetary Union, because centralized monetary controls by the European Central Bank would be ineffectual if Member States could control capital movements.

This chapter will first describe the limited progress toward free movement of capital until the end of the 1980's, and then the Maastricht Treaty provisions mandating free movement, with limited exceptions. The chapter next presents the current Court case law reviewing State rules purporting to be justified exceptions to free movement, and rules that are indirect limitations on free movement of capital. We will then describe the Community goal of an integrated financial market, surveying the key legislation and Court judgements in two sectors, banking and securities law. The next chapter, devoted to Economic and Monetary Union, will describe the link between free movement of capital and EMU.

A. INITIAL DEVELOPMENTS

1. EEC TREATY PROVISIONS AND LEGISLATION

In post-World War II Europe, states followed radically different policies on the restriction of capital movements. Germany, the Netherlands and the Scandinavian states generally followed a philosophy of monetary liberalism, allowing capital to flow freely across their frontiers. France, Greece, Italy,

Portugal and Spain imposed restrictive regulations on many types of capital movements. Other states, like the UK, used regulations to restrict capital movements only in times of monetary crisis.

Restrictions on capital movements are commonly called exchange and investment controls. They serve several distinct functions, among them, restriction on capital outflows (especially in a monetary crisis), limitation on the import or export of certain goods or services in accordance with foreign trade policy, and restriction on all or certain types of foreign investment in pursuit of national economic, security, or industrial development policies. Depending on the policy goal, exchange controls restrict a variety of transactions, for example, the transfer of currency (especially in large amounts), payment for certain types of imports or exports, foreign-source borrowing or lending, the purchase or sale of realty, the purchase or sale of securities, the transfer abroad of royalties on intellectual property rights, and the inward or outward flow of investment capital and repatriation of the proceeds of investment.

In view of its importance, the initial EEC Treaty devoted a chapter to the progressive liberalization of capital movements. The core provision was Article 67(1) (now deleted):

> During the transitional period [i.e., before Dec. 31, 1969] and to the extent necessary to ensure the proper functioning of the common market, Member States shall progressively abolish between themselves all restrictions on the movement of capital belonging to persons resident in Member States and any discrimination based on the nationality or on the place of residence of the parties or on the place where such capital is invested.

The initial Article 69 (now deleted) authorized the Council to issue directives to implement Article 67 by a qualified majority vote. Parliament was not involved in the legislative process, not even after the Single European Act.

Article 73 (now deleted), which permitted "protective measures in the field of capital movements," constituted an important limitation on Article 67. The Commission was given the power to authorize a State to take protective measures at a time of "disturbances in the functioning of the capital market." The Council subsequently could confirm, amend or revoke the measures. In case of urgency, a Member State could act itself, subject to review by the Commission.

An initial Treaty Article 106 (now deleted) required Member States to authorize payments connected to movements of goods, services and capital. Such current payments represent a form of capital movement, but are usually treated differently than long-term capital movements. The obligation to allow such current payments was designed to proceed in tandem with the underlying liberalization of the movement of goods, services, persons and capital as each would be achieved pursuant to the Treaty.

The Community made substantial progress toward free movement of capital in its initial years. Indeed, this was one of the most significant achievements of the early common market. To implement Article 67, the Council adopted the First Directive 921/60, O.J. English Spec.Ed.1960, at 49, which was amended to achieve a greater degree of liberalization by the Second Directive 63/21, O.J. English Spec.Ed. 1963–64, at 5.

The First and Second Directives freed most common commercial and private movements of capital from any form of exchange control. Among the movements thus freed were most direct investments or disinvestments of a commercial character; investments in real estate; personal capital movements, such as gifts, transfers on inheritance or transfers when a person changes residence from one Member State to another; the transfer of insurance premiums and payments; short and medium term loans related to commercial transactions or services; and the purchase or sale of securities on stock exchanges anywhere in the Community. However, States were not required to liberalize many important types of capital movements, notably most common banking or finance transactions, such as the placing of funds in current or long-term deposit accounts, and non-commercial loans and credits.

Unfortunately, the initial progress was not maintained. Many Member States entered a period of monetary instability in the 1970s, which was exacerbated by the energy recession. In addition, Greece, Portugal and Spain had exchange control regulations which the respective treaties of accession allowed them to maintain. France, Italy and other States took advantage of the safeguard measures allowed by Article 73 and the Commission almost routinely authorized the measures until the late 1980s. Thus, national exchange control systems represented a far more serious barrier to the free movement of capital in the 1970s and 80s than they did in the 1960s.

Notes and Questions

1. Why do some states rely upon exchange controls as a means to achieve monetary stability while others do not? Is the difference chiefly a reflection of varying levels of economic strength? Or is it primarily based on different policy views as to the degree to which governments should intervene in monetary affairs? Do you think exchange controls are ever economically justified?

2. Many states use direct investment controls as a means to prevent or restrict foreign investment in agriculture or industry. Do you think that investment controls represent sound policy when applied to sensitive industries, such as defense procurement, utilities and transport? When applied to high technology industries? When applied to any other form of industry or agriculture? Or do you regard investment controls as merely a protectionist device? (Note that since the Exon–Florio amendment to the 1988 omnibus trade act, 50 U.S.C.A. § 2170, the US also restricts foreign investment in sensitive industries.)

2. CASE LAW OF THE COURT OF JUSTICE

In view of the circumstances described above, it is not surprising that private parties sought to obtain rulings from the Court of Justice favorable to the free movement of capital. In particular, after the Court had held that so many other Treaty articles had direct effect, it was inevitable that this issue would be raised concerning Article 67.

In Criminal proceedings against Casati, Case 203/80, [1981] ECR 2595, Casati, an Italian national resident in Germany, was prosecuted for violation of Italian exchange controls when he attempted to take out of Italy large sums of Lira, the Italian currency. The Italian exchange control regulations set substantial fines and possible jail sentences as penalties for any violations. In addition to a defense that he acted in good faith, Casati claimed that the then Article 67 should have direct effect, negating the Italian exchange controls.

In its judgement, the Court declined to give Article 67 direct effect, concluding that the clause, "to the extent necessary to ensure the proper functioning of the Common Market," conditioned the goal of free movement of capital, and necessarily implied that Council legislation was necessary in order to achieve free movement. The Court emphasized the economic sensitivity of regulations of capital movements, stating that "[a]t present, * * * free movement of capital may undermine the economic policy of one of the Member States." (¶ 9.)

Subsequently, in Luisi and Carbone v. Ministero del Tresoro, Cases 286/82 & 26/83, [1984] ECR 377, the Court did strike down one feature of Italian exchange control regulations. Since 1967, an Italian decree forbid Italian residents to take out of Italy more than small stated amounts of Lira. When prosecuted for violating the decree, Luisi claimed that he intended to pay for medical treatment in Germany with the currency that he had attempted to take across the border. Carbone contended that he wanted to take enough Lira with him to cover his expenses during three months of tourism in Germany. As noted at page 679 supra, the Court's judgement is most important for its conclusion that Community nationals have a right to receive services in other States, as well as to perform them there.

With regard to capital movements, the Court observed that the export of currency to pay for medical or touristic services represented a current payment, covered by the then Article 106, rather than a long-term capital transfer covered by the then Article 67. The Court concluded that free movement of currency for current payments for services had to be permitted, because free movement of services under Article 49 (ex 59) was guaranteed with direct effect after 1970. However, the Court noted that Italy retained a right to verify whether its currency was taken out of its borders genuinely for use to pay for services, or constituted a disguised transfer of capital. Although *Luisi and Carbone* had only a limited impact, the judgement was certainly popular with business travelers, students and tourists who had previously been restricted in the duration and nature of their travel due to the limits set by Italian, French, and other exchange controls on the maximum amount of the currency they were permitted to take abroad.

B.   SUCCESS IN ACHIEVING FREE MOVEMENT OF CAPITAL

1.   THE 1988 DIRECTIVE: LEGISLATIVE LIBERALIZATION

The Commission's 1985 White Paper on Completing the Internal Market, described in Chapter 14B, urged greater liberalization of capital movements for three reasons: first, to enable "access to efficient financial services" within the context of an integrated financial market; second, as a part of the efforts to achieve monetary stability, and third, to promote the "optimum allocation of European savings". The White Paper did not call for the removal of all exchange controls. As the internal market program moved forward, however, the Commission concluded that the time was ripe to propose an end to exchange controls.

The adoption of Directive 88/361 to implement Article 67, reproduced in the Selected Documents, testifies to the strength of the Member States' commitment to the internal market goal. The adoption of such a far-reaching measure became possible only because the States viewed it as indispensable to an integrated financial market.

The 1988 directive mandated the abolition of virtually all restrictions on capital movements by July 1, 1990. Under article 4, Member States were allowed to verify the nature of capital movements for statistical purposes and to adopt measures to prevent violations of their taxation laws or rules applicable in the supervision of financial institutions. Although some consideration had been given to eliminating any possibility of safeguard measures, article 3 continued to permit the States to adopt them, but under more stringent conditions than in the past.

France, Italy and Spain rapidly implemented the directive and ended their exchange control systems. This was a dramatic development, since their systems dated to the 1950s. Greece, Ireland and Portugal ended their restrictions on capital movements in the early 1990s. Austria, Finland and Sweden did not receive any derogations concerning capital restrictions when they became Member States on January 1, 1995. Thus, free movement of capital has now essentially been achieved throughout the European Union.

The 1988 directive was crucial to the success of an integrated financial market because it permitted the free transfer of capital for any purpose. In particular, it permitted cross-border banking and other credit operations, which were not liberalized by the First and Second Directives. The 1988 directive was also crucial to the attainment of the Economic and European Monetary Union. Indeed, July 1, 1990, the directive's implementation date, was used to mark the start of the first stage in the development of the EMU. See the next chapter. Finally, the 1988 directive contributed strongly to the sense of Community citizenship, because individuals and enterprises could transfer their funds freely throughout the Community.

The implications of free movement of capital for the banking industry were rapidly made evident in a 1995 Court of Justice judgement.

SVENSSON v. MINISTRE DU LOGEMENT

Case C–484/93, [1995] ECR I–3955.

[A married Swedish couple, residing in Luxembourg, borrowed from a Belgian bank in order to finance the construction of their house in Luxembourg. When they applied in 1991 for an interest rate subsidy from the Luxembourg authorities, they were turned down, because the subsidy was only provided for housing loans made by Luxembourg credit institutions. When they sued to demand the subsidy, the Luxembourg court asked whether the Luxembourg rule violated the then Article 67. At the time of the refusal of the subsidy, Directive 88/361 had become effective. The Court of Justice initially cited *Casati*'s holding that Article 67 does not have direct effect, but then noted that Directive 88/361 clearly prohibited State restrictions on financial loans and credits.]

[10]   Provisions implying that a bank must be established in a Member State in order for recipients of loans residing in its territory to obtain an interest

rate subsidy from the State out of public funds are liable to dissuade those concerned from approaching banks established in another Member State and therefore constitute an obstacle to movements of capital such as bank loans.

11   It should also be noted that by virtue of Article [51(2)] of the Treaty "the liberalization of banking and insurance services connected with movements of capital shall be effected in step with the progressive liberalization of movement of capital". Since transactions such as building loans provided by banks constitute services within the meaning of Article [49] of the Treaty, it is also necessary to ascertain whether the rule referred to by the national court is compatible with the Treaty provisions on freedom to provide services.

12   [F]irst, a rule which makes the grant of interest rate subsidies subject to the requirement that the loans have been obtained from an establishment approved in the Member State in question constitutes discrimination against credit institutions established in other Member States, which is prohibited by the first paragraph of Article [49] of the Treaty.

13   Secondly, it is necessary to consider whether Treaty provisions may justify such a rule. In that context the Luxembourg Government observes that the requirement constitutes part of a social policy which has considerable financial and economic repercussions. Solely for 1994 the figure entered in the national budget for the subsidies was * * * nearly 1% of the total budget. However, a large portion—approximately one half—of the interest rate subsidies paid out are recovered by the Grand Duchy of Luxembourg by means of the profit tax on financial establishments, which enables it to pursue a social policy favourable to housing and to place large sums in a special housing fund. In the absence of the contested rule, therefore, the housing policy would be a failure, or at least could not be as generous as it is at present * * *.

14   That argument cannot be accepted.

15   [D]iscrimination based on the place of establishment * * * can only be justified on the general interest grounds referred to in Article [46, applicable to services by Article 56] and which do not include economic aims.

16   Admittedly, the Court [has held] that rules liable to restrict both free movement of workers and freedom to provide services could be justified by the need to maintain the integrity of the fiscal regime.

17   That is not the case here, however.

18   In those cases there was a direct link between the deductibility of the contributions and the tax on the sums payable by the insurers under death and old-age insurance policies, a link which had to be preserved in order to preserve the integrity of the relevant fiscal regime, whereas there is no direct link whatsoever in this case between the grant of the interest rate subsidy to borrowers on the one hand and its financing by means of the profit tax on financial establishments on the other.

19   The reply to be given to the national court should therefore be that it is not compatible with Articles [49] and 67 of the Treaty for a Member State to make the grant of a housing benefit, in particular an interest rate subsidy, subject to the requirement that the loans intended to finance the

construction, acquisition or improvement of the housing which is to benefit from the subsidy have been obtained from a credit institution approved in that Member State, which implies that it must be established there.

Notes and Questions

1.   The Court had no difficulty in concluding in ¶ 10 that denial of an interest rate subsidy to persons securing mortgage loans outside of Luxembourg constituted an indirect restriction upon free movement of capital. In the remainder of the judgement, the Court's analyzed Luxembourg's attempt to justify its violation of the plaintiff's rights to receive trans-border financial services. *Svensson* is an important precedent with regard to the conduct of any type of trans-border financial services, not just banking. *Svensson* makes obvious that trans-border financial services can no longer be limited by any form of capital restriction, except to prevent violations of national tax and prudential supervision rules, and that trans-border financial service restrictions must be reviewed under the "general good" or "public interest" doctrines described in Chapter 17B. National preference rules in the financial services sector have traditionally been common, and the Commission has now requested the Member States to review their rules and to eliminate discriminatory ones. For a useful discussion of *Svensson*'s implications, see the casenote by V. Hatzopoulos, 33 Common Mkt. L. Rev. 569 (1996).

2.   THE MAASTRICHT TREATY MANDATES FREE MOVEMENT OF CAPITAL

The Maastricht Treaty deleted the entire initial Treaty chapter on capital and replaced it with an express ban on restrictions upon capital movements, effective on Jan. 1, 1994, with very limited exceptions. The new text was intended to provide a Treaty-based assurance that free movement of capital would be ensured in the progressive evolution of EMU.

The new Article 56 (ex 73b) prohibits "all restrictions on the movement of capital," as well as all restrictions on current payments, not only between Member States, but also between States and third countries. However, Article 57(ex 73c) grants an exception for pre–1994 restrictions, under either national or Community law, upon capital coming from third states for use in direct investment and in the sectors of real estate, financial services, and securities markets. The same article authorizes the Council, acting by qualified majority upon a Commission proposal (but without any reference to the Parliament), to liberalize restrictions on capital movements to or from third countries (or, acting unanimously, to further restrict them).

Probably more important is Article 58 (ex 73d), which permits Member States to take measures that restrict capital or payment movements for the purpose of preventing "infringements of national law," especially in the sensitive sectors of taxation and supervision of financial institutions. The article also permits measures based upon public policy or public security (presumably to control terrorism, drug traffic or other serious crimes).

Notes and Questions

1.   Recall that article 3 of the 1988 directive permitted Member States to adopt emergency safeguard restrictions on capital movements. Is this directive

provision still valid after 1994, when Article 56 became effective? On November 24, 1992, the Commission informed the Council of its view that the safeguard provisions of article 3 of the 1988 directive would become redundant after Article 56 became effective, but that no amendment need be undertaken. In view of the tendency of certain Member States to use emergency safeguards in the past, is it advisable to leave article 3 in the directive?

2. Article 57 permits the Community or Member States to retain pre–1994 measures restricting direct investment from third countries. Such restrictions are common for certain sensitive industries, such as defense contracting or the media. Some States have also occasionally restricted direct investment from abroad in high technology industries. Article 57 is the sort of Treaty provision which raises concern about "fortress Europe." Do you think such concerns are justified? Remember that the US has analogous restrictions on foreign investment.

Do Articles 56 and 58 have direct effect? How broad or narrow are the Article 58 exceptions for Member State measures to prevent infringements of national law? When do State measures indirectly restrict capital movements? The Court has recently had to address each of these issues.

CRIMINAL PROCEEDINGS AGAINST SANZ DE LERA
Cases C–163/94, 165/94 and 250/94, [1995] ECR I–4821.

[Several Spanish and Turkish defendants were prosecuted for attempting to take over 5 million Pesetas each (ca. 35,000 dollars) to Switzerland and Turkey, respectively, without the prior authorization required for the export of banknotes under a 1991 Spanish decree. Using Article 234, the Spanish court sought guidance on whether either a prior authorization or a prior declaration before the export of banknotes to a non-Community state was consonant with the new Maastricht Treaty capital provisions. Although the defendant's conduct occurred in 1993 before the entry into force of the Maastricht Treaty, Spanish penal procedure permits a retroactive application of more favorable rules applicable to allegedly criminal conduct. The Court began by analyzing Article 56 and 58 (ex 73b and d).]

22 [T]he measures which are necessary to prevent the commission of certain infringements and are permitted by Article 4(1) of [Directive 88/361], in particular those designed to ensure effective fiscal supervision and to prevent illegal activities such as tax evasion, money laundering, drug trafficking or terrorism, are also covered by Article [58(1)].

23 It is therefore necessary to consider whether the requirement of an authorization or a prior declaration for the export of coins, banknotes or bearer cheques is necessary in order to uphold the objectives pursued and whether those objectives might be attained by measures less restrictive of the free movement of capital.

24 [A]uthorization has the effect of suspending currency exports and makes them conditional in each case upon the consent of the administrative authorities, which must be sought by means of a special application.

25 The effect of such a requirement is to cause the exercise of the free movement of capital to be subject to the discretion of the administrative authorities and thus be such as to render that freedom illusory [citing *Luisi and Carbone*, supra].

[26] However, the restriction on the free movement of capital resulting from that requirement could be eliminated without thereby detracting from the effective pursuit of the aims of those rules.

[27] As the Commission has rightly pointed out, it would be sufficient to set up an adequate system of declarations indicating the nature of the planned operation and the identity of the declarant, which would require the competent authorities to proceed with a rapid examination of the declaration and enable them, if necessary, to carry out in due time the investigations found to be necessary to determine whether capital was being unlawfully transferred and to impose the requisite penalties if national legislation was being contravened.

[28] Thus, unlike prior authorization, such a system of declarations would not suspend the operation concerned but would nevertheless enable the national authorities to carry out, in order to uphold public policy, effective supervision to prevent infringements of national law and regulations.

[29] As regards the Spanish Government's argument that only a system of authorization makes it possible to establish that a criminal offence has been committed and impose penalties under criminal law, such considerations cannot justify the maintenance of measures which are incompatible with Community law.

[30] It follows that Articles [56(1) and 58(1)] of the Treaty preclude rules which make the export of coins, banknotes or bearer cheques conditional on prior authorization but do not by contrast preclude a transaction of that nature being made conditional on a prior declaration.

[The Court then held, not surprisingly, that Articles 56(1) and 58(1)(b) had direct effect.]

Notes and Questions

1. What is the significance of the Court's conclusion that the principal substantive provisions of articles 56 and 58 have direct effect? Does Directive 88/361 serve any useful purpose after the Court's ruling?

2. The principal importance of *Sanz de Lera* lies in the Court's broad reading of Article 56 and its unwillingness to allow Spain to require any form of prior authorization system before the export of banknotes. Obviously, this is a sensitive sector, since unregulated export of banknotes can exacerbate the already serious problem of money-laundering for terrorism, drug traffic, etc. Do you agree with the Court that a prior declaration system will serve just as well? For a useful review, see the casenote by F. Castillo de la Torre, 33 Common Mkt. L. Rev. 1065 (1996).

ASSOCIATION EGLISE DE SCIENTOLOGIE DE PARIS v. THE PRIME MINISTER
Case C–54/99, [2000] ECR ___ (Mar. 14, 2000).

[A 1989 French decree forbids all foreigners from making certain direct investments unless the Minister for the Economy has granted a prior authorization. A 1996 law stipulates that foreign investments which "represent a threat to public policy, public health or public security," or which are made in the research, production or trade in arms or munitions, require such a prior authorization. The Paris Church of Scientology sued to set aside these rules as violations of the free movement of capital. In an Article 234 proceeding, the French Supreme Administrative Court inquired whether the French rules were permitted by the exceptions in Article 58 (ex 73d).]

17   [W]hile Member States are still, in principle, free to determine the requirements of public policy and public security in the light of their national needs, those grounds must, in the Community context and as derogations from the fundamental principle of free movement of capital, be interpreted strictly, so that their scope cannot be determined unilaterally by each Member State without any control by the Community institutions. Thus, public policy and public security may be relied on only if there is a genuine and sufficiently serious threat to a fundamental interest of society [citing *Rutili* ¶ 28, supra page 603]. Moreover, those derogations must not be misapplied so as, in fact, to serve purely economic ends (to this effect, see *Rutili*, ¶ 30). Further, any person affected by a restrictive measure based on such a derogation must have access to legal redress.

18   Second, measures which restrict the free movement of capital may be justified on public-policy and public-security grounds only if they are necessary for the protection of the interests which they are intended to guarantee and only in so far as those objectives cannot be attained by less restrictive measures (see, to this effect *Sanz de Lera*).

19   However, although the Court has held * * * that systems of prior authorisation were not, in the circumstances particular to [the export of currency in Sanz de *Lera*, supra], necessary in order to enable the national authorities to carry out checks designed to prevent infringements of their laws and regulations and that such systems consequently constituted restrictions contrary to Article [56] of the Treaty, it has not held that a system of prior authorisation can never be justified, particularly where such authorisation is in fact necessary for the protection of public policy or public security [citing *Konle*, infra].

20   In the case of direct foreign investments, the difficulty in identifying and blocking capital once it has entered a Member State may make it necessary to prevent, at the outset, transactions which would adversely affect public policy or public security. It follows that, in the case of direct foreign investments which constitute a genuine and sufficiently serious threat to public policy and public security, a system of prior declaration may prove to be inadequate to counter such a threat.

21   In the present case, however, * * * prior authorisation is required for every direct foreign investment which is 'such as to represent a threat to public policy [and] public security,' without any more detailed definition. Thus, the investors concerned are given no indication whatever as to the specific circumstances in which prior authorisation is required.

22   Such lack of precision does not enable individuals to be appraised of the extent of their rights and obligations deriving from Article [56] of the Treaty. That being so, the system established is contrary to the principle of legal certainty.

23   The answer to the question submitted must therefore be that Article [58(1)(b)] of the Treaty must be interpreted as precluding a system of

prior authorisation for direct foreign investments which confines itself to defining in general terms the affected investments as being investments that are such as to represent a threat to public policy and public security, with the result that the persons concerned are unable to ascertain the specific circumstances in which prior authorisation is required.

IN RE ALBORE

Case C–423/98, [2000] ECR ___ (July 13, 2000).

[Albore, an Italian notary, sued to compel the Naples Property Registry to record the sale to a German national of real property situated on the island of Ischia. A 1976 Italian law forbids the sale of real property to non-nationals when located in zones "designated as being of military importance by decree of the Minister for Defence." Ischia is such a zone. The Naples Court of Appeal asked the Court of Justice whether the Italian law qualified as an Article 58 exception.]

18   Although no justification is mentioned in the order for reference * * *, it is clear from the objective of the legislation at issue that the contested measure may be regarded as having been adopted in relation to public security, a concept which, within the meaning of the Treaty, includes the external security of a Member State [citing *Richardt*, supra page 508].

19   However, the requirements of public security cannot justify derogations from the Treaty rules such as the freedom of capital movements unless the principle of proportionality is observed, which means that any derogation must remain within the limits of what is appropriate and necessary for achieving the aim in view.

20   Furthermore, under Article 73d(3) of the EC Treaty (now Article 58(3) EC), such requirements may not be relied on to justify measures constituting a means of arbitrary discrimination or a disguised restriction on the free movement of capital.

21   In that regard, a mere reference to the requirements of defense of the national territory * * * cannot suffice to justify discrimination on grounds of nationality against nationals of other Member States regarding access to immovable property on all or part of the national territory of the first State.

22   The position would be different only if it were demonstrated, for each area to which the restriction applies, that non-discriminatory treatment of the nationals of all the Member States would expose the military interests of the Member State concerned to real, specific and serious risks which could not be countered by less restrictive procedures.

23   In the absence of any evidence enabling the Court to examine whether the existence of such circumstances might be demonstrated in relation to the island of Ischia, it is for the national court to decide, in the case before it, whether or not there is sufficient justification within the meaning of the foregoing paragraph.

Notes and Questions

1. As noted previously, many (perhaps all) Member States continue to restrict or totally forbid foreign capital investments in sectors considered to affect

public security, especially defense, as well as other sensitive sectors which are deemed vital for public policy reasons, such as the media or energy. In *Paris Church of Scientology*, the French rules were obviously intended to give the government a wide power of discretion in identifying and restricting sensitive foreign investments. (Note that the US Department of Commerce regulations on foreign direct investment are equally vague in specifying the sectors involved.) Do you agree with the Court conclusion that the French restrictions are simply too indefinite? How easy will it be for the government to be more precise and detailed, and what risks would that involve? Do you think the French requirement of authorization before investment in the arms and munition field is definite enough to qualify for the Article 58 exception? Note finally how the Court has brought to its interpretation of Article 58 the doctrine limiting the concepts of public policy and public security first enunciated in *Rutili* with regard to the same exceptions to free movement of workers. Is that sensible?

2.   Although Ischia, like its more famous neighbor, Capri, is renowned as a holiday resort, Italy presumably felt that its coastal islands have a strategic national defense importance. In view of the Court's "real, specific and serious risks" standard in evaluating whether public security rules may appropriately limit capital investment in real estate, do you think the Naples court in *Albore* will now register, or not, the sale of realty to a German buyer? Could the Italian law be properly invoked to forbid the sale of realty immediately adjacent to a military airfield? A civil airfield? Realty located 30 miles from an airfield?

3.   The Italian law dates to 1976, and the French 1996 law essentially replicated prior rules. Presumably Article 57 grants them a derogation, so that they could be applied to limit foreign investments coming from the US, or any other third country. Do you think negotiations should be undertaken between the US and the Community to reduce the scope of such restrictions? Note that the Community also has concerns about US restrictions on foreign direct investment under the 1988 Exon–Florio trade law. For example, in the mid–1990s, Thomson–Brandt, majority owned by the French government, protested the US government's refusal to let it buy a US aerospace defense contractor.

4.   Article 58 (ex 73d) also permits States to limit capital movements in order to prevent violations of their tax regulations. Austria imposes a 0.8% stamp tax on the face value of loans evidenced by loan documents. In Sandoz v. Finanzlandesdirektion fur Wien, Case C–439/97, [1999] ECR 7041, Austria demanded that an Austrian company, Sandoz, pay the stamp tax on a loan that it received, denominated in Austrian schillings, from Sandoz Management Services in Belgium. (Presumably both companies are affiliates within the Sandoz pharmaceutical group.) There was no formal loan contract, but the Austrian company recorded the loan on its books. When questions were referred by the Austrian tax court to the Court of Justice, the Court held that imposition of the Austrian stamp tax on loans received from lenders in other States constituted an indirect restriction on capital, because it tended to discourage foreign borrowing (citing *Svensson*, supra). The Court then held the imposition of the tax upon a foreign loan not evidenced by a contract was discriminatory, because the tax would not be imposed in Austria unless the domestic loan was in fact evidenced by a document. The Court finally rejected the Austrian argument that imposition of the stamp tax upon a foreign loan which is not evidenced by a formal contract is necessary to avoid tax fraud under Article 58.

IN RE TRUMMER AND MAYER

Case C–222/97, [1999] ECR I–1661.

[Under an Austrian law dating to 1871, mortgages on real estate can be recorded on the Land Register only if denominated in Schillings. When in 1995, Mayer, a German owner of real estate in Austria, sold it to Trummer, an Austrian buyer, the parties agreed that Trummer could pay the purchase price in German Marks over a period of time. Trummer's ownership interest was to be subject to a mortgage in favor of Mayer. When the Land Register refused to record a mortgage denominated in Marks, the parties sued to compel this. The Austrian Supreme Court asked the Court of Justice whether the law violated Article 56 (ex 73b). The Court initially observed that an annex to the 1988 capital movement directive indicated that transfers of funds to pay mortgages or pledges were to be considered as capital movements, and held that the directive provision accurately classified such transfers.]

16   It should be stressed at the outset, first, that the national legislation at issue in the main proceedings precludes neither the denomination of a debt in a foreign currency nor the possibility of securing such a debt by means of guarantee, even in the form of a mortgage. It prohibits only the registration in a foreign currency of the mortgage securing a debt.

* * *

24   A mortgage of the kind at issue in the main proceedings is inextricably linked to a capital movement—in the present case, the liquidation of an investment in a real property. In addition, it is included within point IX of the nomenclature of capital movements annexed to Directive 88/361. Consequently, it is covered by Article [56] of the Treaty.

25   Second, it is necessary to consider whether the rule prohibiting registration of the mortgage in the currency of another Member State constitutes a restriction on the movement of capital.

26   The effect of national rules such as those at issue in the main proceedings is to weaken the link between the debt to be secured, payable in the currency of another Member State, and the mortgage, whose value may, as a result of the subsequent currency exchange fluctuations, come to be lower than that of the debt to be secured. This can only reduce the effectiveness of such a security, and thus its attractiveness. Consequently, those rules are liable to dissuade the parties concerned from denominating a debt in the currency of another Member State, and may thus deprive them of a right which constitutes a component element of the free movement of capital and payments.

27   Furthermore, the rules at issue may well cause the contracting parties to incur additional costs, by requiring them, purely for the purposes of registering the mortgage, to value the debt in the national currency and, as the case may be, formally to record that currency conversion.

28   In those circumstances, an obligation to have recourse to the national currency for the purposes of creating a mortgage must be regarded, in

principle, as a restriction on the movement of capital within the meaning of Article [56] of the Treaty.

29   The Finnish Government submits, however, that the free movement of capital is not an absolute principle and the national rules at issue in the main proceedings are designed to ensure the foreseeability and transparency of the mortgage system, which constitutes an overriding factor serving the public interest, and is such as to justify the rules in question.

30   It should be noted that a Member State is entitled to take the necessary measures to ensure that the mortgage system clearly and transparently prescribes the respective rights of mortgagees *inter se,* as well as the rights of mortgagees as a whole *vis-a-vis* other creditors. Since the mortgage system is governed by the law of the State in which the mortgaged property is located, it is the law of that State which determines the means by which the attainment of that objective is to be ensured.

31   Neither the Austrian Government nor the parties to the main proceedings have submitted observations to the Court. But even assuming that rules such as those in issue are in fact designed to attain that objective, it appears that those rules enable lower-ranking creditors to establish the precise amount of prior-ranking debts, and thus to assess the value of the security offered to them, only at the price of a lack of security for creditors whose debts are denominated in foreign currencies.

32   In the light of the foregoing considerations, the answer to be given to the national court must be that Article [56] of the Treaty precludes the application of national rules such as those at issue in the main proceedings, requiring a mortgage securing a debt payable in the currency of another Member State to be registered in the national currency.

Notes and Questions

1.   In *Trummer and Mayer*, Austrian law did not forbid either foreign currency loans or mortgages stipulated in foreign currency, so that there was no direct limit on free movement of capital. Do you agree with the Court view that failure to register a mortgage denominated in Marks constitutes an indirect substantive restriction on capital movements?

2.   Several European countries seek to limit or prohibit the ownership of secondary residences (e.g., holiday or part time retirement homes) by non-resident foreign nationals. Denmark obtained a Protocol to the Treaty of Maastricht enabling it to retain its restrictions of that sort. Austria obtained a five year derogation (1995–99) in its Accession Treaty for its restrictions. Why do you think this is a concern for these States?

In Konle v. Austria, Case C–302/97, [1999] ECR I–3099, the Court of Justice held that Austria's 1996 law on secondary residences was significantly different from its 1993 law (struck down by the Austrian Supreme Court as an unjustified limit on the right to property), and therefore was not protected by the derogation stipulated in the Accession Treaty. The 1996 law requires a prior authorization before the purchase of land in Tyrol and generally forbids a purchase for use as a secondary residence. The Court held:

38   [A]lthough the system of property ownership continues to be a matter for each Member State under Article 295 EC, that provision does not have the effect of exempting such a system from the fundamental rules of the Treaty.

[39] Accordingly, a procedure of prior authorisation, such as that under the 1996 [Austrian law], which entails, by its very purpose, a restriction on the free movement of capital, can be regarded as compatible with Article 56 EC only on certain conditions.

[40] In that regard, to the extent that a Member State can justify its requirement of prior authorisation by relying on a town and country planning objective such as maintaining, in the general interest, a permanent population and an economic activity independent of the tourist sector in certain regions, the restrictive measure inherent in such a requirement can be accepted [but] only if it is not applied in a discriminatory manner and if the same result cannot be achieved by other less restrictive procedures.

The Court then concluded that the Austrian authorization procedure in practice give too great a discretionary latitude to the officials, which in practice had a discriminatory impact on non-nationals, and hence constituted an indirect limit on free movement of capital in violation of Article 56.

C. THE INTEGRATED FINANCIAL MARKET

1. BASIC PRINCIPLES

One of the key aspects of the internal market is the integrated financial services market. The Commission stressed this in the White Paper, urging the use of the *Cassis de Dijon* approach of mutual trust and mutual recognition to facilitate cross-border provision of financial services. The Commission further urged that future harmonization be carried out on the basis of "home country control," i.e., "attributing the primary task of supervising the financial institution to the competent authorities of its Member State of origin." This would be facilitated by a "minimum harmonisation of surveillance standards," so that all State authorities would be following a comparable approach in supervision.

One of the great achievements of the White Paper program was the adoption of key harmonization directives in the banking, securities and insurance industries. Space considerations prevent coverage of insurance, but we will describe below harmonization directives in the banking and securities fields. Having largely harmonized and liberalized the rules governing its own financial sector, the Community has become the most vigorous advocate for international liberalization of financial services in the GATS negotiations within the WTO. See Chapter 29A.

Building upon the basic legislative harmonization program, in October 1998 the Commission proposed a Framework for Action in the financial services sector, followed by an action plan of May 11, 1999 containing specific proposals for policies and measures, both refinements in existing directives and totally new initiatives. One of the greatest challenges is to adapt the Member State rules governing private company and industry-wide occupational pension plans to the needs of the internal market. In October 2000, the Commission proposed a directive to harmonize and improve prudential supervision rules for occupational pensions, O.J. C 96/136 (Mar. 27, 2001). The Commission intends to address later the issues of taxation of pension contributions and benefits and of the measures needed to facilitate labor mobility between States by ensuring continuing rights under such pension schemes.

Directive 2000/31 on information society services and electronic commerce, O.J.L. 178/1 (July 17, 2000), should significantly reduce barriers to modern Community-wide financial and commercial operations. The general provisions on information service providers enable them to operate throughout the Community without prior authorization in a host State. With regard to electronic commerce, the directive provides that commercial communications and promotional offers must be clearly identifiable and unambiguous. Most types of contracts can be created by electronic means, but must comply with the usual national legal requirements.

Naturally, the doctrines of the Court of Justice have contributed substantially to efforts to achieve an integrated financial marketplace. In Chapter 17B, we observed how the 1986 *German insurance* judgement set out the general good or public interest principle as the standard for evaluating whether national rules in the insurance sector (and, analogously, for all the financial fields) could be permitted even though they limit the free providing of services. That judgement also recognized consumer protection as an important public interest justifying such State regulation. Subsequently the Court has recognized another important public interest that justifies certain types of State financial regulations. The Court has also emphasized that public interest considerations cannot justify a State rule requiring stockbrokers to operate in a corporate form.

ALPINE INVESTMENTS v. MINISTER VAN FINANCIEN

Case C–384/93, [1995] ECR I–1141.

[As part of its overall securities regulations, the Netherlands adopted in 1991 a rule totally forbidding the solicitation by telephone of brokerage transactions for commodities futures, or the actual sales by telephone of commodities futures, when the customers have not previously authorized the telephone contact. This form of telephone marketing is commonly referred to as "cold calling." The Ministry of Finance acted after numerous complaints from investors concerning "cold calling" for commodities futures trading. The ban applied both to telephone marketing within and outside the Netherlands.

Alpine Investments, a commodities broker which had engaged in "cold calling" only in order to offer prospective customers commodities sales information or to invite them to seminars where its brokerage services were described (allegedly with no customer complaints), challenged the ban under Articles 49 and 50 (ex 59 and 60).

The Court readily found that restrictions on trans-border marketing by telephone could violate Article 49 even though the service provider does not physically move from its State of establishment (¶¶ 20–22), and even though the marketing restrictions are imposed by the State where the telephone calls originated, rather than by the State of residence of the consumer. (¶ 30.) The Court turned then to the more difficult issues.]

40 The national court's third question asks whether imperative reasons of public interest justify the prohibition of cold calling and whether that prohibition must be considered to be objectively necessary and proportionate to the objective pursued.

41   The Netherlands Government argues that the prohibition of cold calling in off-market commodities futures trading seeks both to safeguard the reputation of the Netherlands financial markets and to protect the investing public.

42   Financial markets play an important role in the financing of economic operators and, given the speculative nature and the complexity of commodities futures contracts, the smooth operation of financial markets is largely contingent on the confidence they inspire in investors. That confidence depends in particular on the existence of professional regulations serving to ensure the competence and trustworthiness of the financial intermediaries on whom investors are particularly reliant.

43   Although the protection of consumers in the other Member States is not, as such, a matter for the Netherlands authorities, the nature and extent of that protection does none the less have a direct effect on the good reputation of Netherlands financial services.

44   Maintaining the good reputation of the national financial sector may therefore constitute an imperative reason of public interest capable of justifying restrictions on the freedom to provide financial services.

45   As for the proportionality of the restriction at issue, it is settled case-law that requirements imposed on the providers of services must be appropriate to ensure achievement of the intended aim and must not go beyond that which is necessary in order to achieve that objective.

46   As the Netherlands Government has justifiably submitted, in the case of cold calling the individual, generally caught unawares, is in a position neither to ascertain the risks inherent in the type of transactions offered to him nor to compare the quality and price of the caller's services with competitors' offers. Since the commodities futures market is highly speculative and barely comprehensible for non-expert investors, it was necessary to protect them from the most aggressive selling techniques.

47   Alpine Investments argues however that the Netherlands Government's prohibition of cold calling is not necessary because the Member State of the provider of services should rely on the controls imposed by the Member State of the recipient.

48   That argument must be rejected. The Member State from which the telephone call is made is best placed to regulate cold calling. Even if the receiving State wishes to prohibit cold calling or to make it subject to certain conditions, it is not in a position to prevent or control telephone calls from another Member State without the cooperation of the competent authorities of that State.

49   Consequently, the prohibition of cold calling by the Member State from which the telephone call is made, with a view to protecting investor confidence in the financial markets of that State, cannot be considered to be inappropriate to achieve the objective of securing the integrity of those markets.

50   Alpine Investments also argues that a general prohibition of telephone canvassing of potential clients is not necessary for the achievement of the objectives pursued by the Netherlands authorities. Requiring broking (sic) firms to tape-record unsolicited telephone calls made by them would

suffice to protect consumers effectively. Such rules have moreover been adopted in the United Kingdom by the Securities and Futures Authority.

51   That point of view cannot be accepted. As the Advocate General correctly states, * * * the fact that one Member State imposes less strict rules than another Member State does not mean that the latter's rules are disproportionate and hence incompatible with Community law.

52   Alpine Investments argues finally that, since it is of a general nature, the prohibition of cold calling does not take into account the conduct of individual undertakings and accordingly imposes an unnecessary burden on undertakings which have never been the subject of complaints by consumers.

53   That argument must also be rejected. Limiting the prohibition of cold calling to certain undertakings because of their past conduct might not be sufficient to achieve the objective of restoring and maintaining investor confidence in the national securities markets in general.

54   In any event, the rules at issue are limited in scope. First, they prohibit only the contacting of potential clients by telephone or in person without their prior agreement in writing, while other techniques for making contact are still permitted. Next, the measure affects relations with potential clients but not with existing clients who may still give their written agreement to further calls. Finally, the prohibition of unsolicited telephone calls is limited to the sector in which abuses have been found, namely the commodities futures market.

55   In the light of the above, the prohibition of cold calling does not appear disproportionate to the objective which it pursues.

56   The answer to the third question is therefore that Article [49] does not preclude national rules which, in order to protect investor confidence in national financial markets, prohibit the practice of making unsolicited telephone calls to potential clients resident in other Member States to offer them services linked to investment in commodities futures.

Notes and Questions

1.   The Court has accepted a new "imperative reason of public interest," namely the protection of a financial market's reputation for integrity. Do you agree that this represents a sufficiently important interest to limit financial service-providing, or do you think the trans-border financial market should largely be self-regulating? The Court's view can be read as an endorsement of the general policy approach in the recent Community legislation in banking, securities and insurance which reserves the chief supervisory role to the home State authorities (the State where the financial enterprise's center is located), rather than those of the host State (the State where the consumers of the trans-border transaction are located). For valuable appraisals of the judgment, see the casenotes by V. Hatzopoulos, 32 Common Mkt. L. Rev. 1427 (1995), and P. Knobl, 2 Maastricht J. Eur. & Comp. L. 306 (1995).

2.   Perhaps Alpine Investment's best argument was that a total ban was too severe and disproportionate. Do you agree? If the UK, which has a far more important financial market than that in the Netherlands, can safely permit "cold calling," subject to verification of tape-recordings of actual calls, why should the Dutch have to impose a total ban? Note also that Alpine did not actually execute

sales in an initial "cold call," but only provided information on its brokerage services. The Court's acceptance of the Dutch ban is reminiscent of its acceptance of the total French marketing ban on language instruction courses in *Buet*, supra page 562, in both instances respecting the regulatory authority's discretion in responding to numerous consumer complaints.

COMMISSION v. ITALY

(Stockbroker rules)
Case C–101/94, [1996] ECR I–2691.

[In 1991, Italy modernized its securities market rules, regulating with greater precision the activities of stockbrokers. In particular, the law required dealers in "transferable securities," either as brokers, managers of share assets, or financial advisors on the securities market, to be licensed by the National Commission for Companies and the Stock Exchange (Consob). To be licensed, a broker had to be constituted as an Italian stock corporation. A number of brokers that had previously operated as Italian branches of foreign firms were now required to incorporate in order to comply with the law, so they complained to the Commission, which brought an Article 226 proceeding.]

9 Under the second paragraph of Article [43, ex Article 52] of the Treaty, freedom of establishment is to be exercised under the conditions laid down by the law of the country of establishment for its own nationals.

10 Access to and the exercise of certain self-employed activities may thus be conditional on compliance with provisions laid down by law, regulation or administrative action justified by the general interest, such as rules relating to organization, qualifications, professional ethics, supervision and liability [citing *Gebhard,* supra page 735]. Those provisions may stipulate in particular that the exercise of a specific activity is restricted to persons presenting certain guarantees and subject to particular rules or supervision.

11 Where access to or the exercise of a specific activity is subject to such conditions in the host Member State, a national of another Member State who wishes to exercise that activity must in principle comply with them (*Gebhard,* ¶ 36).

12 However, as the Court has already held, Article [43, ex 52] of the Treaty, which embodies one of the fundamental principles of the Community, is intended *inter alia* to ensure, with respect to establishment, that all nationals of Member States who wish to establish themselves in another Member State, even if that establishment is only secondary, for the purpose of pursuing activities there as self-employed persons receive the same treatment as nationals of that State.

* * *

14 The Italian Government does not deny that its legislation prevents dealers from other Member States from using certain forms of secondary establishment or that it causes them to incur additional costs which Italian dealers do not have to bear. It simply argues that that difference in treatment is objectively justified.

[15] The Italian Government considers that it is not possible to compare the conditions laid down by the Italian legislation with those laid down by the other Member States, as the Commission suggests. It submits that that is the case in particular with guarantees regarding companies' own funds, which are determined by a method different from that used in the other Member States.

* * *

[17] [However], according to the Commission, which was not contradicted on this point, the different methods used by Member States to determine own funds requirements ensure equivalent protection overall, even if one method may prove more protective, case by case, than another.

[18] The argument that it is not possible to compare the rules on access to the profession of securities dealer in the various Member States, in particular with regard to companies' own funds, must therefore be rejected.

[19] The Italian Government also considers that dealers cannot be supervised and effectively sanctioned unless they have their principal establishment in Italy. It considers that only if the principal establishment, and in particular the registered office, is located on the national territory is it possible to have all the information available which is necessary for supervision and all the factors which ensure that sanctions are effective.

[20] Such an argument cannot be accepted either. * * *

[21] While the obligation to have the registered office in Italy facilitates the supervision and control of the operators in the market, such an obligation is not the only means of making sure that they comply with the rules for pursuing the activity of dealer in transferable securities laid down by the Italian legislature and of imposing effective sanctions on dealers who breach those rules.

[22] As the Commission observes, it is possible to require dealers who wish to operate in Italy to agree to be subject to checks or to supply the Italian authorities with the necessary documents and information to ensure that they satisfy the conditions imposed by Italian law. In particular, they could be required to supply information and documents relating specifically to the activities of their secondary establishments in Italy.

[23] With respect to the solvency of operators, activity in Italy can be made subject to the provision of financial guarantees on Italian territory to cover the operations carried out on that territory.

[24] Furthermore, the Italian authorities might conclude cooperation agreements regarding supervision of markets and agents [with other State supervisory authorities].

[25] The Italian Government cannot rely on Article [46, ex 56] of the EC Treaty, either, to argue that its legislation is consistent with Community law.

[26] Even if the aims pursued by the Italian legislation may be regarded as aims of 'public policy' within the meaning of those provisions, it follows *a fortiori* from what has been said above that the obligations at issue are not indispensable for achieving those aims and thus cannot be regarded as justified from the point of view of those provisions.

Notes and Questions

1. In what respects does this judgment go further than the *German insurance* and *Factortame II* cases? Italy clearly believed that it had a strong investor protection policy behind its modern regulation. Do you agree with the Court that, even in the absence of a harmonized system, Italy has no discretion to protect investors in this way? Can Italy require the foreign broker to deposit assets in Italy as a reserve protection for its customers?

2. Directive 93/22 on investment services in the securities field, described below, now covers the regulation of trans-border services throughout the Community by stock brokers and financial advisors established in any Member State. However, the Commission began its Article 226 proceeding against Italy before the Council finally adopted the directive, and Italy was one of the States that opposed some of the draft directive's provisions. Although the directive grants clear rights to branches to conduct brokerage operations, host States may impose "rules of conduct" on the branches, a provision that Italy strongly advocated.

2. SECURITIES LAW HARMONIZATION

The process of harmonization of securities law began in the late 1970s as an outgrowth of company law harmonization. The First Directive 79/279, O.J. L 66/21 (Mar. 16, 1979), lays down the conditions for quotation of securities on a stock exchange. These conditions cover in great detail the share and capital structure and the management of the issuing company, as well as the nature and rights of the quoted securities. The 1979 directive establishes the principle that a company that satisfies these conditions may be quoted on any official stock exchange in the Community.

The Second Directive 80/390, O.J. L 100/1, (Apr. 17, 1980), standardizes the "listing particulars" or the public information required for quoted shares (equivalent to a registration statement in the US), describing the essential financial information for the listed company and the rights of the quoted securities. This promotes investor confidence in dealing with stock or other securities quoted on exchanges outside of the country of residence of the investor. Moreover, this 1980 directive was significantly amended in 1987, O.J. L 185/81 (July 4, 1987), to establish the principle of reciprocal recognition, which means that if a security is listed on an exchange in its home country and is simultaneously or very soon thereafter to be quoted on a stock exchange in another Member State, then the second stock exchange must accept as fully adequate the listing particulars that were accepted by the first exchange. This obviously facilitates the quotation of securities on two or more exchanges in different parts of the Community.

Directive 94/18, O.J. L 135/1 (May 31, 1994), amending the Second Directive 80/390 on listing particulars, is also intended to promote cross-border securities dealing. The amendment authorizes States to permit "companies of high quality and international standing," which have been listed for over three years on another State's regulated exchange, to become listed on their exchange(s) by publishing certain minimum information and providing the latest annual financial statements.

The Third Directive 82/121, O.J. L 48/26 (Feb. 20, 1982), requires the regular publication of information by quoted companies in annual and semi-annual reports. The reports must describe the financial statements and operating information in considerable detail, and include the auditor's certification. Both annual and semi-annual reports must be published and made available to the public, which again promotes investor confidence in companies quoted on different exchanges within the Community.

Directive 85/611, O.J. L 375/3 (Dec. 31, 1985), sets standards for undertakings for collective investment in transferable securities (known by the acronym, "UCITS"). Such an undertaking can take the form of a mutual fund, a management company for a security investment fund, a unit trust, or an investment company, depending on the legal framework in each Member State. The UCITS directive was intended to help small investors by fostering Community-wide trading in mutual funds. An authorized UCITS can freely buy and sell securities quoted on any Community exchange, and can itself freely sell or repurchase its own investment interests to and from investors throughout the Community. In 1998, the Commission proposed an amendment to the directive, both to enable UCITS to offer a wider variety of investments (including money market investments, options and futures), and to require minimum prudential supervision standards. The amended draft is published in O.J. C 339/1 (Nov. 29, 2000).

Following the White Paper on Completing the Internal Market, the Council adopted several "second generation" securities directives. Directive 89/228 on requirements for a prospectus, O.J. L 124/8 (May 5, 1989), regulates the minimum content of information to be provided to investors in a public offering of securities that are not quoted on an exchange. The prospectus directive principally covers Eurobond offerings. The draft was long delayed by UK opposition, but the new climate of compromise induced by the internal market program facilitated its adoption.

Until the mid–1980s, only France and the United Kingdom prohibited insider trading. Prompted to some degree by the international insider trading scandals of the late 1980s, the Council adopted Directive 89/592 on insider dealing, O.J. L 334/30 (Nov. 18, 1989). The directive defines inside information and insider dealing, and forbids persons who have acquired inside information from trading in quoted securities, or providing tips to others who trade in such securities. The directive's definitions and prohibitions are more precise and detailed than the famous US securities Rule 10b 5, but there is concern that some Member States have not been very active in enforcing the directive. In May 2001, the Commission announced its intention to propose amendments to the directive in order to add a prohibition of securities market manipulation and to prescribe more effective enforcement duties.

Directive 88/627, O.J. L 348/62 (Dec. 17, 1988), requires the disclosure of major shareholdings in a quoted company. Shareholders who acquire amounts of voting stock which reach certain thresholds (10%, 20%, ⅓, 50%, ⅔, or 90%), or dispose of voting stock to go below these thresholds, are obliged to disclose this to the company involved within seven calendar days. The quoted company must in turn disclose to the general public the identity of the shareholder and the stock amount involved within nine calendar days. The directive's provisions parallel to some degree the requirements of § 13D of the 1934 Securities Exchange Act, but, unlike § 13D, the directive does not require the shareholder to disclose its intent vis-à-vis the quoted company (e.g., to attempt to take control of the company involved, or modify its structure or management, or to remain a passive investor).

After four years of difficult debate, in 1993 the Council adopted Directive 93/22 on investment services in the securities field, O.J. L 141/27 (June 11, 1993), regulating the status and activities of stockbrokers and financial advisors in the securities sector. Although initially modeled on the Second Banking Directive, Directive 93/22 has some quite distinctive provisions. To some extent, these represent compromises between the view of the more liberal northern States and that of the Mediterranean States which preferred stricter regulation. The basic principle remains that of a "single license" enabling brokerage firms, underwriters and financial advisors established in any State to operate throughout the Community, with the home State responsible for authorization and ongoing prudential supervision. However, under article 11, the host State may adopt compulsory "rules of conduct" for the protection of "clients and the integrity of the market," and under article 21 the host State must require daily and hourly disclosure of minimum information on financial market transactions.

Viewed as an ensemble, the securities directives represent a remarkable body of sophisticated regulation of stock exchanges and companies issuing shares, both in terms of investor protection and adoption of modern forms of raising capital. While they may have only moderately improved the regulation of issuers of securities and of trading on certain stock exchanges, such as that in London, the directives have transformed and modernized the regulation of the securities markets in many States. The stock exchanges in London, Frankfurt, Amsterdam and Paris have flourished, adding many new quoted companies and expanding enormously in market volume and technical trading sophistication, while smaller exchanges in Brussels, Madrid, Milan and elsewhere now also offer modern securities trading with investor safety. Currently, several exchanges are negotiating to create or improve cooperative trading links or even to merge their operations.

This development is situated in a wider context, that of an evolving international securities market. The US Securities and Exchange Commission and the Directorate–General on Financial Institutions have regular contacts to exchange information and ideas. Discussions have commenced on the reciprocal recognition of prospectuses and filing documentation, but substantial differences between the US and Community regulations make these discussions difficult and quite uncertain of ultimate success.

3. BASIC BANKING LAW HARMONIZATION

Efforts to harmonize national banking laws initially lagged behind harmonization in the insurance and securities sectors. However, the White Paper on Completing the Internal Market gave banking law harmonization a strong impetus, producing a series of important directives starting in 1989.

The First Directive 77/780 on credit institutions, O.J. L 322/30 (Dec. 17, 1977), represented the first step in harmonization efforts. In article 1, the directive defined a "credit institution" as an entity which receives deposits from the public and grants "credits for its own account." (Such an entity is usually called a bank.) The directive then required Member States to set up a system for the authorization and regulation of all credit institutions. Such institutions could be authorized only if they satisfied certain minimum criteria concerning their funds and management (art. 3), a provision now superseded by the Second Directive.

Interstate banking by means of branches was covered in article 4, which required host States to authorize all branches on the same basis as domestic banks. This had the effect of obliging branches to maintain minimum funds in the host State and of confining them to the financial activities permitted for host State banks. Finally, the First Directive required cooperation between home and host State authorities and created an Advisory Committee, representing the appropriate authorities in all Member States, that would assist the Commission in the banking sector.

As noted above, the White Paper called for a new approach in the financial services industry: home State control and mutual recognition. The momentum of the White Paper program enabled the adoption of the Second Directive 89/646 on credit institutions, O.J. L 386/1 (Dec. 30, 1989), commonly called the Second Banking Directive, considered by many to be the greatest achievement in the financial services field. The Second Banking Directive, contained in the Documents Supplement, is long and complicated. We present here only a brief sketch.

The Second Directive covers only credit institutions as defined in the First Directive. The Commission had proposed covering also financial lending institutions, such as those engaged in financing home mortgages or car purchases, or providing consumer credit, but the Council declined to go that far.

Following the approach of the White Paper, the Second Directive enunciates three key policies: home State control of branches in other states, minimum harmonization of essential standards, and universal banking activities.

The shift from host State supervision of branches to the supervision of branches by the authorities of the State of the head office, or home State, commonly called the "single license" approach, reflects the acceptance of the mutual trust principle. Each State trusts the quality of banking supervision by the others. Article 19 details the review of a branch that home State authorities are supposed to carry out, including examinations of the adequacy of the branch's administrative structure and its financial situation. Article 6 bars the host State from obliging a branch of a Community-based bank to obtain an authorization and from requiring any local "endowment capital." However, the host State may monitor a branch's compliance with that State's own liquidity and monetary policy measures (art. 14).

The Second Banking Directive harmonizes several substantive requirements for credit institutions. Each must have a minimum capital of 5 million Euro (formerly ECU) (arts. 4 and 10) and must be managed by shareholders whose identity and background is disclosed to the authorities (arts. 5 and 11). The home State authorities must carry out "prudential supervision" and ensure that credit institutions possess "sound administrative and accounting procedures and adequate internal control mechanisms" (art. 13). Finally, a credit institution may not have excessively large shareholdings in non-financial enterprises: no more than 60% of its "own funds" (a defined technical term) may be invested in such enterprises, or more than 15% in any one entity.

The Second Banking Directive's third important feature is its authorization of "universal banking." Article 18 states that a branch may carry on in a host State any of the activities that the head office may engage in under the home State's regulations, so long as the activities are listed in the Annex to the directive. This Annex lists some activities generally recognized throughout the Community as appropriate for banks, such as the acceptance of deposits, making of loans, factoring, and issuance of letters of credit, travellers' checks and credit cards. However, the Annex also lists finance leasing and dealing in securities, including the handling of customers' securities accounts, trading as a broker or for the bank's own account, and participation in the issuance of shares. Previously, banks in Germany and the Netherlands were permitted to engage in the securities business, but banks in most Community States were not.

Although Article 19 does not oblige host States to modify their rules to permit domestic banks to engage in underwriting or trading in securities, or any other activities that they are at present forbidden to perform, it is generally believed that competitive market pressures will lead to this result. Over time, universal banking will probably spread throughout the Community.

If a bank from a third country should establish or acquire a credit institution as a subsidiary in a Community State, that entity would have to comply with all the rules of the State of establishment, but could then operate through branches anywhere in the Community on the same basis as a Community bank. The initial Commission proposal for the Second Banking Directive would have granted rights to banks from third states only on the basis of reciprocity. US banks and the US Government vigorously protested the reciprocity provision and the text was modified to read in its present more moderate form. Article 9 only requires that Community credit institutions receive in a third state "national treatment" and "effective market access," both terms having a recognized meaning within GATT. If Community banks complain about their treatment in a third state, and a Commission investigation substantiates the complaint, the principal recourse stated in Article 9 is the commencement of negotiations with the third state. It is worth noting that neither the US nor the Community has complained about discriminatory or restrictive treatment of its banks since the Second Banking Directive entered into force.

Although Community credit institutions tend to carry on business in other Member States through branches, they may also do so through subsidiaries. The Second Banking Directive does not cover subsidiaries. The consolidated supervision of a parent and its subsidiaries is achieved by Directive 83/350, O.J. L 193/18 (July 18, 1983), which makes the authorities of a parent institution's State responsible for supervising all subsidiaries (defined as entities majority-owned or controlled)—again, home State rather than host State control. If a credit institution has a shareholding of 50% or less in an entity in another State, then the home and host State authorities together decide which is to supervise the subsidiary. Incited to some degree by the BCCI scandal, the Council substantially revised the consolidated supervision directive, O.J. L 110/52 (Apr. 28, 1992), in order to prescribe more precisely the responsibilities of the supervisory authority.

In Chapter 14B, we noted that the SLIM program endeavored to codify legislation in particular fields. In March 2000, the First and Second Banking Directives, together with the consolidated supervision and several supplementary directives, were all codified in Directive 2000/12, O.J. L 126/1 (May 26, 2000).

Notes and Questions

1.   What interests are promoted by the Second Banking Directive's designation of the home State authorities as responsible for supervision of branches throughout the Community? In the *German insurance* case, supra page 672, the Court of Justice stated that consumer interests might limit the right to provide financial services. Do you think that home State supervision protects sufficiently host State consumers (e.g., depositors, borrowers, clients of securities brokerage operations)? How does the directive allocate the power to investigate and penalize possible misconduct by a branch? In general, do you agree with the policy decision to give the home State authorities the responsibility for supervising host State branches?

2.   Some banks in Germany and the Netherlands act as insurance agents and brokers. May they do so through branches in other States? Why do you think insurance brokerage is not on the Annex, even though the Annex lists aspects of the securities business? Do you think that the decision to allow host State branches to engage in the securities business if their home office can do so represents sound policy?

3.   Banks in Germany and some other States have traditionally owned large shareholdings in commercial and industrial companies and significantly influenced their management, while certain other States forbid banks to own shares of non-financial entities. Does article 12 of the Second Banking Directive represent a reasonable compromise or does it go too far in one direction or the other? The percentage limits set in article 12 for investment in non-financial entities are intended to reduce the "contagion risk" for the bank if a non-financial entity in which it has a large investment should develop serious financial problems or become insolvent. Do you think the percentages are reasonably calculated to meet that risk?

4.   The *German insurance* judgment influenced the language in article 19(4) of the Second Banking Directive. What sort of limits might a host State impose on a branch to serve an "interest of the general good"? Might a host State successfully invoke article 19(4) to prevent a branch from dealing in securities?

5.   If a US bank operates in the Community through a branch in one State, may it rely on the Directive in order to open branches elsewhere in the Community? The 19th Whereas clause in the Second Banking Directive provides the answer (demonstrating the need to read Whereas clauses as well as the substantive articles).

The Court has now had occasion to interpret both the First and Second Banking Directives, together with free movement of capital and free movement of services principles.

SOCIETE CIVILE IMMOBILIERE PARODI
v. BANQUE H. ALBERT DE BARY

Case C–222/95,[1997] ECR I–3899.

[In 1984, Banque de Bary, a Dutch bank, lent Parodi, a French real estate company, a mortgage loan of 930,000 German Marks. De Bary never obtained an authorization from the French authorities to conduct business as a bank in France. The 1984 French law on the supervision of credit institutions was intended to implement the First Banking Directive. In 1990, Parodi sued to contest the validity of the interest upon de Bary's loan. (Apparently Parodi did not challenge its obligation to repay the loan principal.) Parodi appealed an adverse judgment to the French Supreme Court, which asked the Court of Justice whether de Bary had a right to provide a mortgage loan in France under the First Banking Directive and Article 49 on the right to provide services. The Court of Justice initially noted that the French exchange controls on capital movements only restricted bank loans in excess of 50 million Francs (far above the mortgage loan amount).]

19   Even if a national rule such as the 1984 Law is not discriminatory and applies without distinction to national providers of services and to those of other Member States, it none the less makes it more difficult for a credit institution established in another Member State and authorized by the supervisory authority of that Member State to grant a mortgage loan in France in so far as it requires that institution to obtain a fresh authorization from the supervisory authority of the State of destination. Such a national rule thus creates a restriction on the freedom to provide services.

* * *

21   [A]s a fundamental principle of the Treaty, the freedom to provide services may be limited only by rules which are justified by imperative reasons relating to the public interest and which apply to all persons or undertakings pursuing an activity in the State of destination, in so far as that interest is not protected by the rules which the person providing the services is subject in the Member State in which he is established. In particular, those requirements must be objectively necessary in order to ensure compliance with professional rules and to guarantee the protection of the recipient of services and they must not exceed what is necessary to attain those objectives [citing *Webb* and *German insurance*, supra].

* * *

25   The first banking directive confined itself to imposing a number of minimum conditions on Member States. Member States were, however, obliged under Article 3 thereof to require authorization on the part of all credit institutions wishing to commence banking activity within their territory of origin. * * *

26   It must therefore be accepted that, as Community law stood at the time of the facts in the main proceedings, there were within the banking sector imperative reasons relating to the public interest capable of justifying the imposition by the Member State of destination of conditions regarding access to the activity of credit institutions and their supervision which

could go beyond the minimum conditions required by the first banking directive * * *.

27　It is for the national court to determine whether the French legislation contains conditions of this kind * * * and whether such conditions are in accordance with the criteria established by the case-law cited in paragraph 21 of this judgement.

28　As the Advocate General rightly notes * * *, the Court does not have information as to the exact purpose served by the authorization required by the national legislation or as to the competent authorities' practice in regard to banks established in other Member States. However, the national provisions applicable in the main proceedings do not appear to be specifically designed to protect borrowers but rather to give effect to prudential rules intended to guarantee that the banks are solvent in regard to savers.

29　Furthermore, a distinction must be drawn according to the nature of the banking activity in question and of the risk incurred by the person for whom the service is intended. Thus, the conclusion of a contract for a mortgage loan presents the consumer with risks that differ from those associated with the lodging of funds with a credit institution. In this regard, the need to protect the borrower will vary according to the nature of the mortgage loans, and there may be cases where, precisely because of the nature of the loan granted and the status of the borrower, there is no need to protect the latter by the application of the mandatory rules of his national law [citing ¶ 49 of the *German insurance* opinion, supra page 672].

30　Finally, the de Bary Bank and the Belgian Government submit that the authorization required by the French legislation was coupled with a condition of establishment, thereby making it impossible to carry out banking activities in France by way of the free provision of services. That is denied by the French Government.

31　Subject to the national court's determination of this issue, it must be noted that, as the Court has already pointed out, if the requirement of an authorization constitutes a restriction on the freedom to provide services, the requirement of a permanent establishment is the very negation of that freedom. It has the result of depriving Article [49] of the Treaty of all effectiveness [citing ¶ 52 of the *German insurance* opinion].

32　The reply to the question submitted must therefore be that, with regard to the period preceding the entry into force of the second banking directive, Article [49] of the Treaty must be construed as precluding a Member State from requiring a credit institution already authorized in another Member State to obtain an authorization in order to be able to grant a mortgage loan to a person resident within its territory, unless that authorization is required of every person or company pursuing such an activity within the territory of the Member State of destination; is justified on grounds of public interest, such as consumer protection; and is objectively necessary to ensure compliance with the rules applicable in the sector under consideration and to protect the interests which those rules are intended to safeguard, and the same result cannot be achieved by less restrictive rules.

CRIMINAL PROCEEDINGS AGAINST AMBRY

Case C–410/96, [1998] ECR I–7875.

[The French law governing travel agents and group tour or group holiday operators, adopted to implement Directive 90/314 on package travel and tours, requires them to have a French license. One of the license conditions is that the travel agent or tour operator provide evidence of a financial guarantee sufficient to repay the cost of repatriation of travelers, in particular in the case of bankruptcy. The guarantee must be supplied by a French bank or insurance company, or, if supplied by one in another Member State, a French bank or insurance company must agree with the guarantor in order to provide immediate payment to the customers concerned. Ambry, a French tour group manager, was prosecuted for handling travel arrangements with a guaranty supplied by an Italian finance company, without a French bank or insurance company being involved. The trial court asked the Court of Justice whether the French rules were permissible under the Second Banking Directive and Article 49.]

26   Under the contested legislation the obligation to conclude an agreement with an institution situated in France applies to credit institutions and insurance companies situated in other Member States where a travel agent situated in France arranges the provision of security with such an establishment. It was stated by the French Government at the hearing that this agreement is in addition to the initial security provided by the credit institution or the insurance company to the travel operator. The agreement must be concluded between the initial guarantor and a credit institution or insurance company situated in the Member State of the travel agent, and that body must undertake in turn to guarantee that the funds will be available for immediate payment.

27   Thus, where the security required by Article 7 of Directive 90/314 is arranged with a financial institution situated in France, only one contract is required, whereas, if it is arranged with a financial institution situated in another Member State, it must be backed by a supplementary agreement in the form of a further guarantee provided by a financial institution situated in France.

28   That requirement has the effect, first and foremost, of restricting and discouraging financial institutions established in other Member States, inasmuch as it prevents them from offering the security required directly to the travel organiser on the same basis as a guarantor situated in France.

29   It is also likely to discourage the travel operator from approaching a financial institution situated in another Member State, since the fact that such an institution must enter into a further guarantee agreement is liable to give rise to additional costs which would normally be passed on to the travel operator.

30   Consequently, rules such as those in issue in the main proceedings, which require financial institutions situated in another Member State to conclude an additional agreement, must be held to constitute a restriction on

the freedom to provide services laid down by Article [49] of the Treaty and by [the Second Banking Directive].

31   It must, however, be considered whether such a restriction can be justified as being necessary for the protection of consumers.

32   The French Government submits that the practical difficulties involved in making funds immediately available where a financial institution is established in another Member State justify the requirement of an additional agreement for such institutions. In particular, it is made necessary by the length of time required for cross-border transfers of funds and by the fact that it is difficult or even impossible, in the event of a dispute or of the guarantor's reluctance to release funds, to make use of certain administrative procedures or seek interim injunctions in other Member States.

* * *

36   As to the part of the security intended to guarantee the repatriation of the traveller, in respect of which the requirement that funds must be available for immediate payment is justified, it should be noted that at the hearing Mr. Ambry argued that transfers of funds between European banks could be made very quickly—within 24 to 48 hours by the international transfer system—which the French Government accepted, although it added that the time taken was variable and could be considerably longer.

37   It appears that the requirement that funds must be available for immediate payment can normally be met adequately even where the guarantor is established in another Member State. In any event, the contested rules do not even offer a travel agent the opportunity to prove that he can make the funds covered by the security as rapidly available as those rules require.

38   Finally, as regards the argument that it is impossible to ensure, in the other Member States, the same degree of effectiveness as is provided by certain administrative measures or judicial decisions within France, it must be borne in mind that, even if some administrative measures cannot be enforced in the same way against undertakings situated in other Member States, it is always possible to make use of the urgent legal procedures which exist in all the Member States of the Community. The effectiveness of the decisions taken on such procedures will depend on the substance of the guarantee agreement concluded between the financial institution situated in another Member State and the travel agent.

39   It must therefore be concluded that it is contrary to Article [49] of the Treaty and to [the Second Banking and Third Insurance directives] for national rules such as those in issue in the main proceedings to require, with a view to implementing Article 7 of Directive 90/314, that, where financial security is provided by a credit institution or insurance company situated in another Member State, the guarantor must conclude an agreement with a credit institution or insurance company situated in France.

Notes and Questions

1.   States often treat the sector of real estate housing mortgage loans as one involving serious consumer and bank solvency interests and regulate it carefully.

The facts in *Banque de Bary* occurred when only the First Banking Directive was in effect. Did its provisions help the Court to decide the case? What principles applicable to mortgage loan regulation did the Court derive from its prior case law on the freedom to provide financial services? Do you think the trial court is apt to permit France to exclude the Dutch bank from financing commercial mortgages in France? What about housing mortgages? Does the Second Banking Directive give the Dutch bank a stronger basis for claiming the right to provide either commercial or residential mortgages in France?

2. In *Ambry*, the French rules were presumably intended to ensure that travellers should immediately receive funds to enable them to return to their starting point, should any default in their return transport occur—a laudable consumer protection goal. Do you agree with the Court's view that a tour operator's reliance on a guaranty from a bank in another State, even if it does not provide funds to travellers as rapidly, must be permitted in order to achieve free movement of financial services? Does article 18 of the Second Banking Directive influence the outcome of *Ambry*?

3. In Criminal Proceedings against Romanelli, Case C–366/97, [1999] ECR I–855, the Court had to interpret the definition of a credit institution in Article 1 of the First Banking Directive (not changed in the Second Banking Directive). Relying upon recitals that indicated "the protection of savers" is one of the objectives of the two directives, the Court held that trust securities issued by an Italian financial institution constituted "repayable funds" analogous to bank deposits, because the contract for the trust securities guaranteed the repayment of the face amount plus interest. The Court's interpretation presumably led to the consequence that the Italian financial institution could be penalized for operating as a bank without being authorized to do so.

4. SUPPLEMENTAL BANKING LEGISLATION

The minimum harmonization of the Second Banking Directive is supplemented by several other technical directives of considerable importance. Directive 89/299, O.J. L 124/16 (May 5, 1989), which sets the rules for a credit institution's "own funds," Directive 89/647, O.J. L 386/14 (Dec. 30, 1989), which indicates the requisite solvency ratio for banks, and Directive 93/6 on capital adequacy for banks and for investment service institutions, O.J. L 141/1 (June 11, 1993), were all rapidly adopted. The three directives have now been included in the codified bank directive text mentioned above.

The important directive on prudential supervision (sometimes known as the post-BCCI directive) was finally adopted, after a difficult dialogue between the Council and the Parliament, in June 1995. O.J. L 168/7 (July 18, 1995). It obligates the independent auditors of banks to notify the public authorities of any material breach of law by a bank being audited, and prescribes duties of enhanced cooperation between bank supervisory authorities.

Directive 91/308, O.J. L 166/77 (June 28, 1991), on the prevention of money laundering, has steadily increased in importance. Inspired by the UN's 1988 Vienna Convention on illicit traffic in narcotic substances, the directive only forbids money laundering of the proceeds of drug dealing (although a recital urges States to apply the directive's rules and procedures to other types of money laundering). Banks and financial institutions are obligated to verify the identity of their customers and to examine any transaction likely to constitute money laundering, reporting on their own initiative any suspicious transactions to the authorities. They are specifically required in article 11 to set up "adequate procedures of internal control" and to carry out training programs for employees to combat money laundering. The directive did not expressly require States to make money laundering a criminal offense because of doubts that the EC Treaty grants any implicit legislative power to do that, but article 14 obligates States to "take appropriate measures to ensure full application" of the directive. A 1998 Commission report indicated that all States had made money laundering of the proceeds from illicit drug traffic a criminal offense.

In June 2000, the Commission proposed to amend the money laundering directive so that it covers the laundering of the proceeds of any form of organized crime. O.J. C 177/1 (June 26, 2000). The proposal would significantly expand the scope of the directive, requiring lawyers, notaries, accountants, tax advisors, real estate agents, dealers in high-value goods and casinos to examine transactions that appear to constitute money laundering and report them to the public authorities. For lawyers, a derogation is proposed if the lawyer learns of the money laundering through confidential information from a client being represented in a legal proceeding.

Directive 94/19 on deposit-guarantee schemes, O.J. L 135/5 (May 31, 1994), is not only an important "flanking" directive, but also interesting because it was the first directive adopted under the co-decision procedure after the Council and Parliament accepted a conciliation committee report. The directive requires all States to have some form of guarantee ensuring that each depositor will receive up to 20,000 Euros if the deposits are unavailable for 21 days. A State may set a higher guarantee level for its banks and branches of banks from other States. However, a branch in a host State cannot offer its depositors a higher guarantee level than that set in the host State, even if its home office must provide a higher level to home State depositors because of the home State rules.

Germany, which voted against the directive, unsuccessfully challenged it in an Article 230 proceeding, based in part on the directive's alleged violation of the principle of subsidiarity. This aspect of the judgment is excerpted at page 123, supra. Germany also argued that the directive did not adequately protect consumer interests, an aspect dealt with at page 1272 infra.

Among the many substantive issues raised by Germany, perhaps the most important dealt with the directive's requirement in article 4(2) that branches would have to join a supplemental guarantee scheme in host Member States when the host State scheme provides greater protection than that offered by the home State. Germany argued that this violated the principle of home State control of branches in other States laid down in the Second Banking Directive. The Court held that the principle of home State supervision of banks did not require "systematically subordinating all other rules in [the banking] sphere to that principle" (¶ 64). Advocate General Leger noted that article 4(2) is only intended to be a transitional measure.

After three years of studies showed that customers faced high fees, delays and inadequate information in cross-border funds transfers, the Commission proposed in 1994 a directive to regulate such transfers. Directive 97/5 on cross-border credit transfers, O.J. L 43/25 (Feb. 14, 1997), sets out minimum standards for the information to be provided on credit transfer conditions, the maximum permissible time period for the execution of the transfer, and the identification of the person (sender or beneficiary) who bears the administrative charge for the transfer.

The above summary of the harmonization of Member State banking rules makes it quite clear that in a remarkably short period of time—approximately ten years-the structure has been set in place to enable Community-wide banking operations. Not only does this manifestly promote greatly the attainment of the internal market, it is also apt to promote greater competition among banks and more efficient and less costly banking services, all without sacrificing consumer protection of depositors and borrowers. In recent years, bank mergers and acquisitions, both within States and across their borders, have increased in number and size. The largest European banks are now active competitors with the largest US, Japanese and Hong–Kong banks on the international financial marketplace.

Further Reading

Books

P. Kapteyn & P. Verloren Van Themaat, Introduction to the Law of the European Communities (L. Gormley ed.)(3d ed. Kluwer 1998)

D. Lasok, The Professions and Services in the European Economic Community (Kluwer 1986)

J. Stuyck, ed., Financial and Monetary Integration in the EEC (Kluwer 1993)

M. van Empel & R. Smits, eds., Banking and EC Law Commentary (Kluwer 1993)

M. van Empel & R. Smits, eds., Financial Services and EC Law Commentary (Kluwer 1993)

D. Wyatt & A. Dashwood, The Substantive Law of the EEC (3d ed. Sweet & Maxwell 1992)

Chapter 33

ECONOMIC AND MONETARY UNION

No more important political, economic or legal development occurred in the European Union in the 1990s than the creation of the Economic and Monetary Union (EMU). The European Council and the Commission, during the successive presidencies of Jacques Delors, viewed EMU as complementing the internal market program, providing four substantial benefits: a centralized and stable monetary system, a single Europan currency, a significant reduction in cross-border financial and commercial transaction costs, and a better integrated competitive marketplace for producers and consumers.

At the present time, as the single currency, the Euro, is being launched, it is not yet certain how successful the Monetary Union will prove to be, but it has already radically changed the economic landscape of the Community. The constitutional and political implications of EMU are also dramatic: a further substantial transfer of sovereignty to a central structure, notably the European Central Bank (ECB) and the Economic and Finance (Ecofin) Council, together with the role of the Euro as a powerful symbol of European integration.

This Chapter will first set out the goals of EMU and the early stages of economic and monetary cooperation. Following this comes a review of the preparations for the final stage of EMU. The structure of the European Central Bank is then analyzed, with special emphasis upon the principle of independence and the treaty-mandated goal of price stability. We will then describe the commencement of the ECB's operations in the control of monetary policy. Finally we will review the regulatory framework and the practical preparation for the launch of the Euro as a single currency.

R. Goebel, European Economic and Monetary Union: Will the EMU Ever Fly?, 4 Colum. J. Eur. L. 249 (1998), provides a comprehensive coverage of this topic prior to the final third stage of EMU. Rene Smits, The European Central Bank (Kluwer 1997), is an authoritative review of the EMU Treaty provisions and the developments before 1997.

A. THE GOALS AND BENEFITS OF ECONOMIC AND MONETARY UNION

The attainment of an Economic and Monetary Union will transform the European Union in a more fundamental manner than any development since the substantial achievement of the internal market program. Indeed, the 1995 Green Paper on the Introduction of the Single Currency depicted EMU as the "logical and essential complement" to the common market. The rapid preparation and attainment of the Monetary Union undoubtedly stemmed in large measure from the generally satisfactory progress in attaining a single market.

EMU's principal components are: (1) an integrated Community monetary system; (2) an institutional structure, with a European Central Bank at its center; (3) a single currency, the Euro, replacing present national currencies in all the participating Member States. Each will be described in greater detail later, but some preliminary notes should be made.

An integrated Community monetary system with a European Central Bank at its core is seen as essential to achieve greater monetary stability. The necessity to meet rather high economic and monetary standards in order to participate in the Monetary Union compelled virtually all the Member States to adopt much stricter monetary policies, in effect, putting their financial households in order. Because the European Central Bank has the power to adopt stable monetary policy programs and the power to implement them, with a minimum of political interference from Member State governments and Community institutions, the prospect is one of a more solid monetary structure for all the participating States.

Since Member States participating in the Monetary Union may no longer resort easily to deficit financing, their rate of economic growth is apt to be steadier, and they will be more likely to attract international and domestic investment. A reduction in deficit spending and a lowering of long-term debt brings the corollary of less frequent need to float state loans and the obtention of lower rates for state debt. The private sector likewise benefits because financial and commercial enterprises are then able to float bonds and borrow long-term funds in a more liquid market, again at lower rates.

With regard to the adoption of the single currency, the Euro, the Commission estimates that use of a single currency will save the Community annually around 20–25 billion ECU, or approximately 0.3–0.4% of GDP, through the elimination of currency-related transaction costs (i.e., the expense of changes in currency when transacting commercial and personal affairs across frontiers within the Community). After the elimination of different national currencies, financial and commercial enterprises need no longer use currency options, futures or insurance to hedge against shifts in national currency value when transacting trans-border financial and commercial affairs within the Community.

But there is a further and more important economic benefit flowing from a single currency, namely, the achievement of far greater price and cost transparency in all trans-border financial, commercial and private transactions. Thus, purchasers of raw materials and supplies, intermediate distributors of products, persons providing services, and consumers of goods, services or credit will all be able easily and quickly to compare prices or expenses when dealing with domestic and foreign parties.

Prospects of greater market integration, especially in the financial services sector, are bound to lead to enhanced merger and acquisition activity, resulting in the disappearance of many smaller or less efficient enterprises. The Commission estimates that several Member States are "over-banked," possessing too many banks or other financial institutions in proportion to their general population and overall level of commercial activity. The wave of trans-border and domestic financial sector mergers and acquisitions that increased sharply in 1996–2001 may be expected to continue. Manifestly leading to a more efficient financial sector, this process will also produce far more powerful market players,more capable of competing internationally.

On the global monetary stage, a successful EMU will also play a leading role. Use of the Euro for international trade and investment will be far more substantial than is the present use of individual national currencies, even the German Mark. Moreover, the existence of a European Central Bank with a mandate for price stability and a strong currency is quite apt to promote the desirability of the use of the Euro in international trade and investment. Over the long term, the Euro may become a serious competitor for the US dollar in global transactions, especially in trans-border credit and financial operations.

Finally, a successful EMU is bound to have a great impact on the political aspect of the European Community. One of the most essential types of sovereign power, namely the control over monetary policy, is being transferred to a Community institution. It is true that, as we shall see later, the institution, the European Central Bank, will be independent of the traditional Community political institutions, namely the Commission, Council and Parliament. Nevertheless, power over monetary policy will rest with a *Community* entity. Such a transfer of vital power necessarily diminishes the role of national governments to a significant degree.

The transfer of monetary power to the European Central Bank and the creation of a single common currency are bound also to produce significant psychological consequences. Citizens of the Member States will perceive more readily the extent, importance and hopefully the value of European integration. Replacement of national currency and coins by the Euro represents a far more meaningful symbol of Union integration than the current European passport or the Union flag can ever be. Migrant workers and professionals in particular will see tangible benefits from the use of the Euro, since they will more readily be able to compare income levels and the cost of living in different Member States, as well as to transfer funds to a new place of residence or back to their home or family.

The role of the European Council in deciding upon the key aspects of the proposed structure of EMU, and in promoting its steady evolution toward reality, has been an unusually marked one. As we shall see later, successive meetings of the European Council have resulted in crucial policy decisions, or achieved critical compromise breakthroughs on intransigent issues, in shaping the progress toward EMU. Moreover, the Treaty itself specifies that the decision upon the designation of the Member States that qualify to join in its final stage is to be taken by the Council meeting in the unusual composition of the Heads of State and Government, instead of its more customary composition of finance ministers or foreign affairs ministers.

Finally, in the creation of a Monetary Union, not only should great tribute be paid to the vision of Commission President Jacques Delors, but also to the vision and political will of Chancellor Kohl of Germany and President Mitterand of France, who together provided the principal leadership in the planning. Also playing important roles in the political process were Prime Ministers Dehaene of Belgium, Lubbers of the Netherlands and Gonzalez of Spain. Tribute should also be paid to the less prominent but quite crucial role of the central bank governors, such as Pohl of the Bundesbank (the German Central Bank), and Duisenberg of the Dutch Central Bank, who, together with their staffs, provided much of the expertise necessary in the drafting of the various treaty provisions.

B. THE INITIAL STAGES

1. THE EEC TREATY: ECONOMIC COORDINATION

At the time of the EEC Treaty in 1958, the global monetary system governed by the Bretton Woods accords and supervised by the International Monetary Fund (IMF) provided a substantial degree of international monetary stability. In the halcyon days of the 1950s and 1960s, the currency exchange rates of different countries were fixed in relation to one another, and the US dollar, backed by substantial gold reserves, provided substantial stability to the fixed exchange rate system. Accordingly, the authors of the EEC Treaty presumably saw no need for far-reaching initiatives in the monetary sector. Articles 104 and 105 in Title II on Economic Policy merely required Member States to pursue stable economic policies, and to coordinate economic and monetary policies.

The Community first felt a need to create its own monetary structure at the end of the 1960s, when the world monetary system currency governing exchange rates under the Bretton Woods accords started to break down. As world trade and investment expanded enormously in the 1960s, nations became much more interdependent, both in economic and monetary terms. Then, as the economies of some states developed far more rapidly than others, and as certain states suffered serious bouts of inflation, balance of payments difficulties became inevitable. France, Italy, and the UK were compelled to devalue their currencies in successive monetary crises, while Germany, the Netherlands and Switzerland were obliged to revalue them.

The most serious international monetary crisis arose when the dollar came under severe pressure in 1971. President Nixon decided to end the gold standard on August 15, 1971, allowing the dollar to float against other currencies. The Smithsonian Accord of December 18, 1971 institutionalized the system of such floating rates. However, because floating exchange rates create uncertainty and instability in both medium and long-term financial and commercial transactions, ever since 1971 governments have sought to find a way to return to some form of fixed, or at least relatively stable, rates.

Making use of then Treaty Article 105, the Commission and Council began a series of attempts to alleviate monetary crises in particular Member States and to coordinate economic and monetary policy in order to achieve greater stability within the Community. A stage-by-stage plan for attaining economic and monetary union was presented to the Council of Ministers in March 1971 in the form of the Werner Report, named after the Prime Minister of Luxembourg. Bull. EC 1970–II Supplement. A later Council decision urged Member States to align their economic policies with guidelines to be issued periodically by the Council, and called on the central banks to coordinate their monetary policies. Council Decision 74/120, O.J. L 63/1 (Mar. 5, 1974). Unfortunately, the energy recession of the mid–1970s and further monetary crises in certain Member States prevented these Community measures from becoming truly effective. Coordination efforts were reduced, rather than enhanced, in the late 1970s. The goal of a union receded farther into the distance.

2.　THE EUROPEAN MONETARY SYSTEM

In the late 1970s, the leadership of President Giscard d'Estaing of France, Chancellor Helmut Schmidt of Germany, both former finance ministers, and Commission President Roy Jenkins, previously the UK Chancellor of the Exchequer, caused new attention to be focused on monetary coordination and stabilization. The European Council Meeting at Bremen in August 1978 officially endorsed the concept of a European Monetary System (EMS), which came into force in March 1979. Bull. EC 1978–6, at 5.

Membership in the EMS was voluntary only, and therefore produced a sort of "two-tier" Europe. The UK initially joined, but withdrew after a two-month run on its currency reserves, and only joined again in October 1990. By 1992, all the other States except Greece had become members.

The European Monetary System had three basic components: an artificial currency, the ECU; exchange rates which were permitted to fluctuate only in a narrow band; and a system of credit and loan reserves to stabilize Member State currencies in times of crisis. We will briefly describe all three.

First, the EMS created an artificial European monetary unit, the European Currency Unit, or ECU, which replaced the prior artificial unit known as the European Unit of Account (EUA). The value of the ECU was fixed as a composite of a "basket" of Member State currencies with weighted values one to another. A macroeconomic calculation of the proportionate strength of the national economy underlying each State's currency was used in allocating weights to the different currencies. Thus, in the calculation of the composite ECU value in 1989, the German Mark represented 30% of the total "basket," the French Franc 19%, the UK Pound 13%, the Italian Lira 10%, etc. The weighted value was revised every five years, for the final time in 1989.

The European Community used the ECU for its own budget. All revenues and all expenditures were calculated in the form of ECUs. This enabled a standard base to be used in the calculation of budget items from year to year. The European Investment Fund and other financial organs of the Community on occasion floated loans on international markets denominated in ECUs. For that matter, private financial institutions also on occasion floated loans denominated in ECUs. The ECU was quoted on monetary exchanges and floated against the dollar and other currencies. For example, in June 1992, one ECU equaled $1.35. The ECU was, of course, not an actual currency:

there were no bills or coins denominated in ECU, nor was the ECU used as legal tender for everyday private commercial transactions.

The second component of the European Monetary System was the stabilization of the exchange rates of the currencies of the Member States participating in the EMS. This was called the Exchange Rate Mechanism (ERM). The exchange rates were fixed in 1979 and were changed during the 1980s only at relatively infrequent intervals. A very moderate degree of floating was allowed between currencies, within a band with a maximum range of 2.25% above or below the exchange rate. This band was increased to 6% for certain States during periods of monetary stress or weakness. Thus, Italy was allowed to use the 6% margin until 1989, and Portugal and Spain entered the ERM with the same 6% margin.

The functional merit of this limited rate of fluctuation around pegged rates set for long periods of time was that it served as a reasonably close approximation of the fixed rates of the Bretton Woods system. This meant that financial institutions, commercial enterprises, and private investors could enter into medium and long-term transactions with a reasonable assurance that neither an unexpectedly large exchange rate gain nor loss would occur at the end of the transaction.

The third component of the European Monetary System was a credit mechanism by which short and medium support could be given to Member States encountering serious monetary troubles. A reserve fund of 25 billion ECU was created, composed of the equivalent of 20% of the gold and 20% of the dollars held by each participating central bank.

The operational success of EMS in the 1980s created a climate of confidence. The Commission under President Delors and the political leadership in most Member States believed that the monetary stability provided by the EMS enabled the Community to commence plans for a Monetary Union. These plans reached fruition in the EMU provisions of the Treaty of Maastricht at the end of 1991, as we shall see below.

Unfortunately, confidence in the exchange rate mechanism of the EMS was badly shaken in September 1992. Stimulated by concern that France might not ratify the Maastricht Treaty in its September referendum, substantial speculation developed on the currency markets, directed in favor of the German Mark. Investors perceived the German Mark as the safest long-term currency, because the German central bank persisted in keeping interest rates at very high levels in order to prevent inflation from being spurred by large government expenditures to meet the cost of German unification. Major financial interests, such as multinational corporations and pension funds, decided that it was more prudent to shift large volumes of capital from other currencies to the German Mark.

Despite massive intervention efforts by central banks to support currencies under attack, the pressure increased. Several States nearly exhausted their currency reserves in a fruitless effort to stabilize their currency. Italy and the United Kingdom concluded that they must withdraw from the ERM and float their currencies, which then dropped sharply in an effective devaluation, and Ireland and Spain instituted emergency exchange controls followed by devaluation of their currencies. Financial observers noted that currency market activity had increased enormously since the 1970s, which made it very difficult for governments and central banks to cope with speculative attacks on currencies.

The ERM, already shaken in September 1992, was again seriously undermined in 1993. Despite France's relatively healthy economic condition, the French Franc became the subject of such a severe speculative attack in August 1993 that even massive intervention by the German and French central banks was not sufficient to support it. The Community finance ministers and central bank governors were compelled to enlarge radically the fluctuation bands of the ERM from 2.25% to 15% above or below the central standard rate. Although the exchange markets then quieted without a devaluation of the franc, the ERM never formally returned to a narrower band. Indeed, at the end of 1993, some media commentators questioned whether it was still possible to proceed with the plans for EMU.

Fortunately, after 1995 the currency markets in the Community calmed down and exchange rate shifts were minor. By the end of 1996, the currencies of almost all the States operating within the Exchange Rate Mechanism were well within the 2.25% fluctuation band that had prevailed in the 1980s.

Notes and Questions

1. Why are relatively stable exchange rates still considered desirable, even though sophisticated methods of protection against exchange rate changes through "hedging," insurance or the purchase of currency futures on commodities exchanges, have developed over the years?

2. What is the link between a state's economic policies and its exchange rates? Specifically, how do economic conditions such as a serious inflation or recession, or monetary policy decisions, such as high deficit financing or high interest rates, affect exchange rates? Why is it often difficult for a state to take measures to stabilize its exchange rates? What is the effect on trade and investment when a state is obliged to devalue or revalue its currency substantially?

3. PLANNING FOR ECONOMIC AND MONETARY UNION

In January 1985, when a new Commission took office under the Presidency of Jacques Delors, its initial agenda included efforts to attain EMU as well as to complete the internal market. Accordingly, in the late 1980s as the Community progressed toward achievement of the internal market program, proposals for EMU moved to center stage. At its June 1988 Hanover meeting, the European Council "confirmed the objective of progressive realization of economic and monetary union." Bull. EC 1988–6, at 20. It created a special committee, chaired by Jacques Delors, President of the Commission, to study and propose "concrete stages" toward this goal. The committee consisted of all the central bank governors and several economic and banking experts.

The Delors Committee Report of April 17, 1989 provided a thorough review of the essential character of an Economic and Monetary Union, together with a pragmatic presentation of three proposed stages in its development. Bull. EC 1989–4, at 8. Due partly to the practical nature of the committee's proposals, and partly to respect for the high qualifications of the committee itself, this report not only formed the basis for all subsequent discussions, but largely shaped the agenda of the 1990–91 Intergovernmental Conference which produced the Treaty of Maastricht.

The Delors Report defined the EMU's goal as the common management of monetary and economic policies to attain common macroeconomic goals. The report also endorsed the ultimate creation of a single European currency. The report proposed a treaty amendment to create a major new institution, the European System of Central Banks (ESCB). The ESCB's ultimate role would be to formulate and implement monetary policy for the Community, assist Member States to attain price stability and curb budgetary deficits. (The German Bundesbank and the US Federal Reserve System were obviously the two models for the ESCB structure.)

The Delors Committee Report further laid out three proposed stages toward achieving the EMU. Each stage would require the attainment of certain goals, both at the Community and Member State level. The final stage would give the ESCB responsibility for monetary policy, and lead to the creation of a common Community currency. Because so many of the report's proposals were adopted in the Treaty of Maastricht, we need not go into detail at this point. The report is analyzed by Professor Jean–Victor Louis, General Counsel to the Bank of Belgium, in A Monetary Union for Tomorrow, 26 Common Mkt.L.Rev. 301 (1989).

The Delors Report initiated a widespread and probing debate on the necessity for, and the goals of, an EMU, both at the Community level and in the private sector, and the topic received great attention in the media. It quickly became the most fascinating single idea for the further political and economic development of the European Community since the June 1985 White Paper on Completing the Internal Market. Although most commentary on the Delors Report was favorable, John Major, then UK Chancellor of the Exchequer, issued on November 2, 1989 a policy statement for the United Kingdom advocating national control over monetary policy and criticizing any transfer of power to a centralized bureaucracy, specifically repudiating the idea of a single European currency.

At this point, the reaction of the European Council to the Delors Report became critical. At its December 1989 meeting in Strasbourg, the European Council approved the main themes of the Delors Report, and decided, despite the opposition of the United Kingdom, to call an intergovernmental conference for the purpose of adopting an Economic and Monetary Union. The European Council also decided that the first stage set out in the Delors Report should commence as of July 1, 1990, the date of entry into effect of the 1988 directive described in the preceding chapter which essentially required total freedom for capital movements throughout the Community.

The Intergovernmental Conference worked earnestly for nearly a year on the EMU proposal. Most of the text was prepared by technical experts representing Germany and the Netherlands, both States with powerful central banks and a tradition of strict monetary policy and hard currencies. Reaching a consensus proved extremely difficult, due not only to UK opposition, but also to hesitations on the part of other States. Ultimately, several issues were left to the European Council meeting at Maastricht in December 1991, which, after intensive debate, arrived at essential compromises. The most decisive compromise was to permit the UK and Denmark to opt out of EMU, while ensuring that the other States could go forward.

4. THE EMU PROVISIONS OF THE TREATY OF MAASTRICHT

No aspect of the Maastricht Treaty is of greater importance than the provisions on EMU. Article 2(ex B) of the TEU lists an economic and monetary union and a single currency as among the principal objectives of European Union. A new Article 4 (ex 3a) of the EC Treaty declares that Community activities shall include, i.a. "the close coordination of Member States' economic policies," "the definition and conduct of a single monetary policy," and "the introduction of a single currency."

The EC Treaty provisions on EMU are extremely complicated. We will sketch only the key features of EMU and the progressive steps in its creation. At the outset, it should be emphasized that the Monetary Union is an integral part of the European Community, and does not represent a separate intergovernmental "pillar," as is the case for the Common Foreign and Security Policy and Cooperation in Justice and Home Affairs. Although it has many distinctive features, Monetary Union is woven into the institutional framework of the Community.

As noted above, on June 1, 1990, the Community began the first stage of progress toward the EMU. The first stage had three different components: 1) free movement of capital, already achieved by the 1988 directive mentioned above, 2) adherence of all Member States to the Exchange Rate Mechanism of the EMS; and 3) an increased level of monetary coordination, both by governmental action and through coordination among the central banks. Somewhat curiously, the Maastricht Treaty never refers to the first stage.

In Article 116 (ex 109e), the Treaty set Jan. 1, 1994 as the starting date for the second stage. During this stage, Member States were to begin coordinating their economic policies and become subject to guidelines issued by the Ecofin Council. During the second stage, Member States were to be obligated to conduct strict economic and monetary policies in order to achieve several convergence criteria set out in the Treaty. Only upon satisfactory attainment of these criteria could States become eligible to join in the third stage of Monetary Union.

In Article 121 (ex 109j), the Treaty set Jan. 1, 1999 as the latest possible date for the commencement of the third and final stage for those States which had satisfied the convergence criteria. The Council, meeting in an extraordinary composition of Heads of State or Government, was to determine which States so qualified. The States joining in the third stage would yield control of their monetary policy to the European System of Central Banks. Subsequently, the States in the third stage would have their national currencies replaced by a single currency.

As noted above, one of the essential compromises at the Maastricht European Council meeting was the agreement upon two Protocols to the Treaty which provided the United Kingdom and Denmark with the right to opt out of participation in the third stage, either temporarily or permanently.

For a detailed analysis of the Treaty provisions, see J. Pipkorn, Legal Arrangements in the Treaty of Maastricht for the Effectiveness of the EMU, 31 Common Mkt. L. Rev. 263(1994).

Not surprisingly, the Maastricht Treaty's provisions on EMU proved to be highly controversial during the debates over its ratification in many States.

Some political parties, prominent politicians and media leaders opposed a Community-wide centralized monetary structure and feared the loss of sovereignty necessarily involved. Not only did many citizens of some States share these concerns, but they particularly opposed the loss of their currencies, which always are a strong symbol of nationality. This was undoubtedly a factor in the rejection of the Treaty in the first Danish referendum in 1992, and the Danish government's exercise of its opt-out presumably contributed to the ultimate vote in favor of ratification in the second Danish referendum in May 1993. Opposition to EMU within the Conservative Party resulted in Prime Minister Major's extremely narrow one-vote margin in favor of ratification in the UK Parliament's vote in July 1993. Eventually, however, all the Member States ratified the Treaty of Maastricht, which entered into effect on Nov. 1, 1993, enabling the formal start of the second stage on Jan. 1, 1994.

C. THE SECOND STAGE: 1994–98

1. THE EUROPEAN MONETARY INSTITUTE

On Jan. 1, 1994, the start of the second stage, the European Monetary Institute (EMI) commenced operations. As described in Treaty Article 117 (ex 109f), the EMI was composed of a President, named by the Council, and one governor from each national central bank. The EMI was sited in Frankfurt in accord with a European Council decision reached with some difficulty (the UK sought the seat for London, and the Netherlands for Amsterdam). The European Central Bank, as the successor to the EMI, likewise has its seat in Frankfurt.

The first President of the EMI was a highly respected banking expert, Alexandre Lamfalussy, formerly head of the Bank of International Settlements in Basel. Wim Duisenberg, its second president, who took office on July 1, 1997, was the former president of the Netherlands Central Bank, well-known as an advocate of a strong central bank and strict monetary policy.

In 1994, the EMI started the task of advising Member States on their monetary policies. The EMI issued an annual report on monetary policy each April, and regularly prepared studies and recommendations on aspects of monetary policy, banking and finance. Together with the Commission, the EMI provided the recommendations for legislation and policy in preparing the transition to the third stage of monetary union. In particular, the EMI commenced the technical preparation for the bank notes that would be used as the single currency-an essential step because of the substantial lead-time necessary before billions of notes could be printed and issued. See section F2 below.

2. ECONOMIC COORDINATION

The Maastricht Treaty introduced Article 99 (ex 103), which bound Member States to "regard their economic policies as a matter of common concern" and to coordinate them in accordance with guidelines set by the Council, acting by qualified majority. An unusual feature of this coordination is that the Ecofin Council must submit its draft guidelines to the European Council for its "conclusion" on them. This is one of the rare instances in which the EC Treaty post-Maastricht recognizes a specific role for the

European Council, presumably both because setting these guidelines constitutes a politically sensitive matter and because the European Council's "conclusion" adds political weight to the Ecofin Council's guidelines. As is typical in EMU decision-making, the Parliament is only to be kept informed and has no role in the shaping of the guidelines.

Promptly in 1994, the Community began the coordination of national economic policies. The Treaty ban in Article 104 (ex 104c) on direct financing of government deficits by central banks (popularly referred to as "no more bail-outs") came into effect on January 1, 1994. On November 7, 1994 the Council for the first time issued guidelines to specific Member States for modification of their economic policies.

Since 1994, the guidelines for economic coordination have become more detailed and precise. The procedure begins each spring, when all Member States prepare draft budgets and economic forecasts for the following year and present them to the Commission for review. The Commission carefully reviews each draft budget and forecast, both in the light of each State's economy and that of the Community as a whole, and makes recommendations for each State. Making use of the Commission analysis, the Ecofin Council in June establishes draft guidelines for each State, often suggesting significant budget modifications or other economic actions. The June European Council meeting then states its "conclusions," and the Ecofin Council formally provides its guidelines to each Member State.

In the summer and early fall, each State reacts to the guidelines, usually in accord with them, although occasionally disagreeing with them. In late fall, the Commission reviews again each State's final budget and economic forecasts. The process ends with a final Ecofin Council review of the status of each State's budget and forecast, sometimes with further recommendations. Treaty Article 99(4) provides that if a State's economic policies are not "consistent with the broad guidelines" provided previously by the Council, the Council may make public its further recommendations (which is presumably intended to exert a degree of public pressure on the State concerned).

Commentators have stressed that the economic coordination established by the Maastricht Treaty is purely inter-governmental in character, in contrast to the Community's centralized monetary control by the ESCB for States in the third stage. Although this is certainly true, there are valid reasons for the difference in approach. It is obvious that a monetary union cannot function well without coordination of economic policies, because of the substantial spill-over effect of governmental economic policy decisions upon monetary conditions. However, centralized Community economic policy-making would require an enormous cession of national sovereignty, because of the close link between economic policy and fiscal policy, tax collection, social security and social welfare systems, and so on. It may be that a successful EMU will lead to greater Community harmonization of Member State tax and social security systems, but for the present the EC Treaty only requires coordination of national economic policies.

In any event, in recent years the economic coordination process has exerted a strong influence on the economic policy of the States and is steadily promoting a more Community-wide approach to economic policies.

Notes and Questions

1. May any Member State opt out of the economic coordination process? Because of its role in this process, the Ecofin Council has grown greatly in importance. How significant do you think are the respective roles of the Commission and the European Council in the coordination process? The Parliament plays no role formally-do you consider this exclusion justified, or is it another example of a "democratic deficit"?

2. Although the drafters of the Maastricht Treaty decided that centralized monetary control was possible and essential,they did not believe that centralized economic control was either feasible or desirable. Would you agree? What sensitive governmental policy areas are affected by national economic policy? Do you think that a centralized Economic Union could ever prove possible?

3. THE CONVERGENCE CRITERIA

A key feature of the plan for EMU was the idea that Member States must prove their economic and monetary capability to comply with the obligations of central monetary control. Germany and the Netherlands in particular were concerned that their steady economic growth and monetary stability should not be jeopardized by the inclusion of States in the final stage of EMU if they might thereafter promote inflation or loose money policies. High standards for economic and monetary performance were accordingly inserted into the Treaty.

Article 116 (ex 109e) on the second stage prescribes that Member States shall adopt "multiannual programmes intended to ensure the lasting convergence necessary for the achievement of economic and monetary union, in particular with regard to price stability and sound public finances," and adds that the Member States "shall endeavor to avoid excessive government deficits." Articles 104 (ex 104c) and 121 (ex 109j), supplemented by the Treaty Protocols on the Excessive Deficit Procedure and on the Convergence Criteria, set in more specific terms the economic and monetary conditions Member States must meet for eligibility to participate in the third and final stage of monetary union.

Three of these conditions proved surprisingly attainable. The first is "a high degree of price stability," measured by the attainment of an inflation rate close to that of the three best performing Member States in terms of price stability. Article 1 of the Protocol on Convergence Criteria specifies that "close" shall mean that the target inflation rate should be one not in excess of 1.5% above the inflation rate of the three best performing States, using the "consumer price index on a comparable basis" to gauge the inflation rate.

In the period 1994–1997, the Member States made highly satisfactory progress in lowering their inflation rates, in some cases to one half or one third of their prior level. This taming of prior high inflation rates certainly represents one of the most obvious benefits achieved in the process of achieving the Monetary Union. By the end of 1997, the Commission estimated the average inflation rate of all Member States to be at around 2.1%. The average inflation rate for the three best performing member States was around 1.5%.

Closely connected to the inflation rate criterion is the second one, requiring Member States' long term interest rates to attain a level not exceeding by more than 2% the level of the three best performing States. Long term interest rates tend to move in tandem with inflation rates (although not invariably), and these rates fell throughout the Community in 1994–1997. By the end of 1997, only Greece had long term interest rates exceeding by 2% the average level (slightly above 6%) of the three best performing States.

The third criterion is that a Member State's currency must remain within "the normal fluctuation margins provided for by the exchange rate mechanism of the European Monetary System without severe tensions for at least the last two years before the examination". As noted above, fortunately the foreign exchange markets entered a period of relative calm in late 1995. All of the States that wanted to enter the third stage (again, with the exception of Greece) were able to keep their currencies either within the desired 2.25% fluctuation band of the ERM, or only marginally outside, during 1996 and 1997.

The fourth and by far the most difficult criterion is that Member States must not have an excessive deficit. Under Article 104 and the Protocol on the Excessive Deficit Procedure, this criterion has two aspects: (1) the current annual government deficit should not exceed 3% of the national gross domestic product (GDP) at market prices; and (2) the accumulated total government debt should not exceed 60% of the annual GDP.

The target figures of 3% and 60% of annual national GDP respectively were set late in the Intergovernmental Conference, based upon a study made by the Monetary Committee. In view of the traditional use of deficit financing by many Member States to meet current social and economic needs, and the enormous accumulated government debt loads of several States, satisfying the excessive deficit criterion was always recognized as the "make or break" factor in qualification for the final stage.

Although almost all Member States made remarkable progress in 1995–1997 toward reducing their annual deficit and lowering their accumulated total debt, nonetheless, many would have been unable to meet the Protocol criteria if these were to be applied strictly. This is especially true for the total government debt criterion. Thus, at the end of 1997, Belgium, Greece and Italy had total accumulated governmental debt levels well in excess of 100% of their annual GDP, and the Netherlands and Sweden had debt levels in excess of 70% of their annual GDP.

Fortunately, the drafters of the relevant Treaty provisions foresaw the need for a certain degree of flexibility. Article 121 (ex 109(j)) stipulates that Member States must not have an excessive deficit, but that provision cross-references to Article 104(6) (ex 104c(6)), which gives the Council the responsibility for deciding "after an overall assessment whether an excessive deficit exists." The Council in turn works on the basis of a Commission report which need only find, according to Article 104(2), that the current annual deficit "has declined substantially and continuously" and is "close to the reference level," and that the total accumulated government debt "is sufficiently diminishing and approaching the reference value at a satisfactory pace."

For a critical review of the convergence criteria and the degree to which some Member States had only marginally satisfied them, see P. Beaumont & N. Walker, The Euro and European Legal Order 169, in P. Beaumont & N. Walker, Legal Framework of the Single European Currency (Hart 1999). For an appraisal of the convergence criteria by a leading Princeton economist, see P. Kenen, The Transition to EMU: Issues and Implications, 4 Colum. J. Eur. L. 359 (1998).

In addition to the convergence criteria, the Maastricht Treaty stated one political condition for entry into the third stage. Article 116(5) (ex 109c(5)) required that all States must make their central banks independent during the second stage. Traditionally only the German and Dutch central banks had enjoyed virtual independence from the political authorities. In 1994, France and Spain enacted legislation making their central banks independent of their governments. In a somewhat surprising decision, immediately after Prime Minister Blair took office in the UK in June 1997, his Labor government made the Bank of England independent. By 1998, only Sweden had failed to grant independence to its central bank.

3. PREPARATIONS FOR THE THIRD STAGE

The Madrid European Council session in December 1995 set a "scenario" or time-table for the transition period, requiring all essential legislation to be drafted, reviewed and approved in 1996–98. The Madrid European Council fixed 1998 as the year in which the designs for Euro bank notes and coins should be set and their production started, 1999–2001 as the period in which the Community and participating Member States would use the Euro as the currency unit for their budget and official accounts, and January 1, 2002 for the launch of Euro banknotes and coins into circulation as legal tender.

Regulation 2494/95 on harmonized indices of consumer prices, O.J. L 257/1 (Oct. 27, 1995), established for the first time Community-wide standards for this vitally important index, essential to ensure the accuracy of inflation statistics. More accurate Member State and Community-wide consumer inflation statistics, based upon the directive's standards, accordingly became available in 1996 and 1997 for use in assessing satisfaction of the inflation convergence criterion.

A major debate in 1996 concerned the Commission's proposed "stability and growth pact," intended to ensure that Member States would continue strict monetary policies and budgetary discipline after they entered the final stage of EMU. Obviously, European Central Bank standards for centralized monetary policy could be undermined if some States could "backpedal" to their former easy money and excessive deficit policies without any effective sanction. Germany fought vigorously for strict standards, while most other States wanted more lenient ones. The December 1996 Dublin European Council adopted a compromise position, which was implemented in legislation adopted in 1997.

The pact is now embodied in two Council Regulations. Regulation 1466/97, O.J. L 209/1 (August 2, 1997), sets out the system for on-going surveillance by the Commission and the Council of each State's annual budget and its overall economic performance. Each State participating in the third stage is obligated each spring to prepare an annual "stability program," showing a budget in surplus or close to balance, indicating key economic developments in GDP, employment and inflation, and outlining economic policy measures. These are to be made public, which ensures that opposition party leaders, financial and business experts and the media can all review and debate the reliability of the government's program.

Both the Commission and the Ecofin Council then provide evaluations of the economic realism of the State's program, and can issue recommendations, which can represent an "early warning" to a State that its budget may produce an excessive deficit. The Regulation's prescribed system of surveillance of Euro-zone States' stability programs has now been grafted upon the economic coordination described in section C1.

Regulation 1467/97, O.J. L 209/6 (August 2, 1997), prescribes the mode by which the Council can determine that a State has developed an excessive annual deficit and sets penalties for a State's failure to take adequate corrective action when it has an excessive annual deficit. The basic penalty imposed is the obligation on the deficient State to provide to the Community a non-interest bearing deposit equal at least to 0.2% of its GDP-obviously a very large amount. Failure of a State to correct its deficit status within two years could lead to a Council decision to convert the deposit into a fine. This potential fine is so large as to make it unlikely that a State will not take the necessary corrective action. Indeed, the excessive deficit regulation is presumably intended never to be applied in practice, but to serve as a deterrent threat.

D.　COMMENCING THE FINAL STAGE OF EMU

1.　THE DECISION TO LAUNCH THE THIRD STAGE

In the Spring of 1998, the time came to assess the efforts of the Member States that wanted to join in the third and final stage of EMU. The Mediterranean States in particular made remarkable progress in 1996–97, due in large measure to the determination of their governments (notably Prime Minister Prodi, who pledged to resign if Italy did not make it), and strong support by the media and business leaders. On the other hand, France and Germany encountered severe last minute difficulties in 1997—France, because of the expensive measures taken by the newly-elected Socialist Government to combat high unemployment, and Germany due to the continued high cost of integrating an economically-weak East Germany.

On March 24–25, 1998, the European Monetary Institute and the Commission issued their reports on the degree to which each Member State had satisfied by December 31, 1997 the convergence criteria for entry into the third and final stage. The reports concluded that every State but Greece had attained the Treaty standard for inflation and the long term interest rate—indeed, the entire Community enjoyed an average annual inflation rate of 2.1%, the lowest in decades. All the States likewise had stable exchange rates within or close to the bands prescribed in the Exchange Rate Mechanism (although Sweden and the UK remained outside the ERM).

Finally, all the States but Greece were deemed to have attained the current annual deficit target of 3% of Gross Domestic Product (GDP), and to be making satisfactory progress toward the total government debt target of 60% of GDP. This was a decidedly liberal decision, since Belgium and Italy continued to have a total government debt level of around 120% of GDP, and France, Germany and Italy narrowly managed to hit the current deficit target of 3% of GDP only by extraordinary and somewhat controversial revenue and tax measures.

Accordingly, on May 3, 1998, the Council, in its extraordinary composition of Heads of State or Government,decided that eleven Member States (Austria, Belgium, Finland, France, Germany, Ireland, Italy, Luxembourg, the Netherlands, Portugal and Spain) qualified for entry into the third stage on January 1, 1999. This group of Member States that have entered the third stage are often said to comprise the Euro-zone, or the Euro-area. Denmark and the United Kingdom remained outside the third stage, in virtue of their Maastricht Treaty Protocols.

Greece could not meet the convergence criteria standards, but the Simitis government pledged to attain them soon. Its progress in 1999 was sufficiently satisfactory that in June 2000 the Council, in its extraordinary composition of Heads of State or Government, endorsed Greece's entry into the third stage on Jan. 1, 2001.

Sweden is a somewhat curious case, because it did not negotiate for an opt-out Protocol at the time of its accession to the EU in 1995, but nonetheless failed to meet the EC Treaty condition that it make its central bank independent. Despite this failure, no one expects the Commission to bring an infringement action against Sweden to compel it to make its central bank independent—essentially, Sweden is being permitted to opt out of the third stage without a Treaty Protocol to that effect.

Immediately after deciding upon the eleven States which would enter the third stage on January 1, 1999, the Heads of State and Government designated Wim Duisenberg (President of the EMI since July 1, 1998) as the first European Central Bank President. They also named the other five Executive Board members, choosing prominent economists and national central bank members, for staggered terms of four to eight years.

The European Central Bank commenced operations on July 1, 1998, working intensively to take basic policy decisions (see section E4 below), recruit and structure its staff, set its internal procedures and otherwise prepare to undertake its responsibilities. Its actual control of monetary policy started on January 1, 1999.

Notes and Questions

1. Since Belgium, Greece and Italy have total government debt figures well in excess of 100% of GDP, was it sensible to decide that they were approaching in a satisfactory manner the 60% of GDP target for total government debt? (Reliable estimates indicate that it is apt to take 20 years for the three States to reduce their accumulated debt to 60% of GDP.)

2. THE "INS" AND THE "OUTS"

Although the political leadership of the Community could take great satisfaction in the decision that eleven (and, in 2000, twelve) Member States joined in the third and final stage of EMU—a higher figure than even optimists had hoped for when the Maastricht Treaty was drafted—nonetheless there was a fly in the ointment. The Community is now divided into a "two-tier" structure, certainly for some years, perhaps even permanently.

Accordingly, at the present time the UK, Denmark and Sweden continue to have complete autonomy in the control of their monetary policy, which is set by their central banks independently of the ECB and the ESCB. The three countries likewise retain their own currencies, while the Euro-zone States have now introduced the Euro as a single currency.

The EC Treaty regulates to some degree the status of the three countries, which are called "Member States with a derogation" by Article 122 (1) (ex 109k (1). Not surprisingly, Denmark, Sweden and the UK do not share in the decision-making procedures to launch and to carry on the third stage. Under Article 128 (ex 109 l), they are not involved in the selection of the members of the Executive Board of the ECB nor in the adoption of measures taken to introduce the Euro. Naturally, their central bank governors are not members of the ECB.

On the other hand, so long as the three States remain outside the Euro-zone, the Protocol on the Statute of the ECB provides that there shall be a General Council, composed of the President and Vice–President of the ECB together with the governors of all fifteen Member State national central banks. This General Council replaces the EMI in the role of coordinating monetary policy between the Euro-zone and the three States with a derogation, as well as in monitoring the monetary condition of the three States. Moreover, the economic coordination procedures described in section C2 above continue to fully apply to them.

The Luxembourg European Council in December 1997 dealt with relations between the Member States participating in the third stage and those remaining outside (the "ins and the outs"), deciding that the participating States may meet informally in the Ecofin Council to discuss policy issues concerning the Euro and monetary matters, but that the entire Ecofin Council must vote to take legally binding measures in accordance with the Maastricht Treaty's provisions in this regard. This policy decision is of considerable importance, because some States participating in the third stage had wanted a Council consisting only of the participating States to meet and vote separately-an approach that the UK vehemently opposed.

The "two-tier" division of the Community into the "ins and the outs," the Euro-zone States and the three nations remaining outside, is bound to have significant adverse consequences if it lasts for any appreciable period of time. From a political point of view, there is a definite risk that the Euro-zone States will increasingly share common views and interests, perhaps arising out of their discussions in the so-called Euro–12 Council which meets periodically. The UK's Blair government has on several occasions warned against this risk of a "core" group developing within the Community.

Fortunately, the current governments of Denmark, Sweden and the UK have all indicated their willingness to join in the final stage of EMU at what they consider to be the right time. The Danish government held a referendum on September 28, 2000 on whether or not to join the Euro-zone, but despite the government's vigorous support for a decision in favor, the Danish people voted by a narrow 53% majority against the joining. The Danish media and opinion polls indicated that the negative majority were concerned by fears that the Danish economy would be neglected in Community-wide monetary control, by a distaste for replacing the Kroner by the Euro, and by a general distrust of the "Euro-bureaucracy" of Brussels. It seems unlikely that Denmark will hold another referendum in the near future.

The Swedish government has gradually moved to an endorsement of a decision to join the Euro-zone, after the Socialist and other parties have shifted their position to one of support. The adverse Danish referendum has, however, delayed any action in Sweden.

By far the most important question is whether the UK will join the Euro-zone, not only because the UK is the third-largest national economy in the Community, but also because of the traditional importance of the City of London as the leading financial center of Europe. Both the Conservative Thatcher and Major governments vigorously opposed the UK's entry into the third stage and insisted upon the UK Protocol. The Labor government under Tony Blair changed this policy course as soon as it was elected in May 1997, and the current Labor government, reelected in 2001, has maintained this position. The Blair government's policy position is that the UK should join the final stage of EMU and adopt the Euro as its currency when it is clear that this is in its national economic interest.

The Blair government has set out several economic criteria which should be met before a decision to join would be appropriate. The most important is that the UK and the Euro-zone States should be in the same economic cycle stage (i.e., both enjoying a comparable period of GNP growth, low inflation and moderate unemployment). When the government believes that these criteria are met, a referendum will be held on the issue, perhaps in 2003. All of the opinion polls for the last several years have indicated that a majority of the population opposes joining, strongly influenced by a generally conservative-dominated media. It is clear that the Labor government will have to wage a very energetic campaign in order to achieve a favorable decision when (or if) it chooses to hold a referendum.

Finally, what will happen when some, or most, of the 12 applicant countries from Central Europe and the Mediterranean join the EU in 2004 (the current target date)? President Duisenberg in an October 1999 speech on EU enlargement indicated the likely scenario. None of the applicant nations will be permitted to opt out of joining EMU (in fact, most appear quite eager to join). The EU regards participating in EMU as a part of the *acquis communautaire,* or basic Community policies and programs which all applicant states must accept. Economic and monetary conditions analagous to the convergence criteria will undoubtedly be set in the treaties of accession. Only after an applicant nation satisfies these criteria will it participate in the final stage of EMU, which may accordingly occur several years after it joins the EU.

Notes and Questions

1. The Monetary Union's final stage presently includes twelve Member States—the UK and Denmark have exercised their options to remain outside, and Sweden has taken a political decision to remain outside. What are the advantages and/or risks in this "two-tier" Community structure? Should all of the applicant Central European and Mediterranean countries be required by their treaties of accession to satisfy convergence criteria and join the Monetary Union's final stage?

E. THE EUROPEAN CENTRAL BANK

The heart of the Delors Plan was the creation of a powerful body for the control of monetary policy throughout the Community. This is the European Central Bank, functioning at the core of the European System of Central Banks which operates in the Member States through each one's national central bank.

The essential role of the ECB, working through the ESCB, is to set the monetary policy of the States participating in the third stage (the Euro-zone or Euro-area), determining the goals of that policy in accord with the objectives set in the Treaty (see sub-section 3), and adopting the rules and regulations to execute it.

Although the ECB is not formally one of the institutions of Community, its functional importance is second only to them. This makes its structure and its relations with the Community institutions of great political and practical importance. The ECB's decisions and operations are closely watched by business and financial institutions and the media. Indeed, its current President, Wim Duisenberg, is probably second in popular recognition only to Commission President Prodi.

1. STRUCTURE, POWERS AND JUDICIAL REVIEW

Article 107 (ex 106) declares that the ESCB is composed of the ECB and the participating national central banks (NCBs). The "decision-making bodies" of the ECB are its Executive Board and the Governing Council. The Protocol on the Statute of the ESCB and the ECB specifies that the Executive Board is composed of the President, the Vice–President and four members, all named for eight years by common accord of the Euro-zone States, without any possibility of reappointment.

The Protocol further provides that the ECB's Governing Council is composed of the Executive Board and the Governors of the participating NCBs (currently the Governing Council has a total of eighteen members). The Governing Council has the primary power to set policy guidelines and take decisions on "monetary objectives, key interest rates and the supply of reserves," while the Executive Board implements these policies and decisions in conjunction with the NCBs (Protocol art. 12). The Governing Council meets at least ten times a year and can act by simple majority vote (but President Duisenberg has publicly declared that the Governing Council strives for a consensus, if possible).

Apart from its control of monetary policy (discussed below), the ECB has control of the emission and supply of the Euro as legal currency. Treaty Article 106 (ex 105a) gives the ECB the exclusive power to issue banknotes, operating through the NCBs. Although the same article authorizes the Council to determine the denomination and design of coins, and the Euro-zone States to issue them, the ECB must approve the volume of coins issued, as part of its control of the supply of money.

The European Central Bank has been granted a substantial degree of regulatory power. Pursuant to Article 110(ex 108a), the ECB may issue regulations to implement its monetary policy, to govern the minimum reserves which it requires banking institutions to keep on deposit with the ECB and national central banks, to regulate bank clearing and payment systems, and to carry out prudential supervision of financial institutions (to the extent authorized by the Council). The ECB may also take binding decisions or issue recommendations or opinions.

Further, under a rather extraordinary provision, Article 110(3), the ECB may impose "fines or periodic penalty payments on undertakings for failure to comply with its regulations or decisions." The Ecofin Council adopted Regulation 2531/98, O.J.L 318/4 (Nov. 27, 1998), to provide a more detailed authorization for such ECB fines and penalties.

In view of the scope of the European Central Bank's role and tasks, and the dimension of its regulatory powers, it is important that the EC Treaty clearly delineates the principle of judicial review. The Maastricht Treaty amended Article 230 (ex 173) to grant the Court of Justice jurisdiction over actions brought by Member States, the Council, the Commission or private parties against the ECB to review the legality of its acts, and for actions brought by the ECB against the Community political institutions in order to protect its "prerogatives." Similarly, the ECB has the power to sue the Council, Commission and the Parliament under Article 232 (ex 175) for their failure to fulfill a duty to act in areas "falling within [the ECB's] field of competence," and the ECB can itself be sued for a failure to act to fulfill its duties by those institutions, Member States or private parties.

Article 234 (ex 177) was amended to include the acts of the ECB among those which may be the subject of questions referred to the Court of Justice by national courts. Finally, the Court of Justice was given the power under Article 237(d) to review the compliance of national central banks with their obligations in the ESCB and to compel their compliance if necessary.

It is likely that recourse to a legal challenge of an ECB decision would rarely occur, and the Court is certain to give a broad field of discretion to the ECB's monetary measures. Nonetheless, the possibility of review by the Court of Justice should serve as a restraint against arbitrary, poorly reasoned or inadequately justified rules or decisions, in line with well-established Court precedents on the need for a reasoned basis for Council, Commission and Parliamentary acts. For an appraisal of judicial review, see the excellent study by Prof. Paul Craig of Oxford, EMU, the ECB and Judicial Review, in P. Beaumont & N. Walker, The Legal Framework of the Single European Currency (Hart 1999).

2. THE PRINCIPLE OF INDEPENDENCE

EC Treaty Article 108 (ex 107) states the important principle that the ECB and the ESCB shall have total independence in their decision making. They are categorically forbidden to take instructions either from Community institutions or from Member States. This provision represents a major policy decision, because most central banks were not independent of their governments, and because some Member States were reluctant to allow the ECB and ESCB to enjoy total independence from the Council. The principle of independence was strongly advocated by Germany, whose Bundesbank enjoys such independence from its government, as critical in order to ensure that the ECB and the ESCB would have the freedom to follow strict, and hence often unpopular, monetary policies.

Accessory to the principle of independence of the ECB is that of the independence of the national central banks and their members, because the national central banks represent the usual operational arm of the ESCB. Article 116(5) required Member States to take action to ensure the independence of their central banks during the second stage. As previously noted, all the Member States except Sweden took the necessary action to make their central banks independent by the end of 1997.

A legitimate question may be raised as to the wisdom of incorporating the principle of independence into the EC Treaty as a constitutional principle. As some commentators have observed, this gives the ECB greater independence than the US Federal Reserve Board and virtually all central banks prior to EMU. On a comparative note, the US Federal Reserve Board does not enjoy constitutional status and, although it enjoys great independence by custom, nothing prevents the Congress from adopting legislation mandating certain goals or policies, a power that the Congress has on rare occasion exercised.

Perhaps the best academic commentaries on the subject of the strict independence accorded by the Treaty to the ECB, the ESCB and the national central banks are by Prof. Rosa Lastra, EMU and Central Bank Independence (arguing that a high level of independence promotes price stability, but that independence must be balanced by democratic accountability), and by Professors Jakob de Haan and Laurence Gormley, Independence and Accountability of the ECB (arguing for functional autonomy rather than strict independence and urging greater accountability for the ECB), both contained in M. Andemas, ed., European Economic and Monetary Union (Kluwer 1997).

Although there is no evidence that the independence of the ECB or the ESCB has been disregarded in practice since 1999, a disquieting note was struck at the time of the European Council's choice of Wim Duisenberg in May 1998 as the first President of the ECB. President Chirac of France proposed instead Jean–Claude Trichet, the Governor of the Bank of France, and attempted to block the otherwise unanimous preference for Duisenberg. A compromise was stuck: Duisenberg declared that he "would not want to serve the full term" of eight years at some point after he reached 68, i.e. around 2003. The European Council then informally agreed that Trichet would ultimately serve the remainder of the term. The general reaction of the media and subsequent academic commentators has been that this sort of compromise was not only unseemly, but jeopardized the independence of the ECB, whose first President would either feel obliged to resign regardless of circumstances in 2003, or else seek to obtain the favor of the European Council leadership at that time in order to continue in office.

Notes and Questions

1. Considering the powers which the Treaty grants to the ECB and the ESCB, how important do you think is the transfer of sovereignty made by the States participating in the third stage? Is the structure of the ECB and the ESCB a sound and balanced one, conducive to the effective exercise of their powers? Do you think the ECB should usually strive for a consensus, or operate often on a

simple majority basis? Consider this question again after reading the text below on the ECB's objectives.

2. Do you think the principle of strict independence for the ECB and NCBs represents sound policy or a potentially risky one? Do you consider it possible that some governments might try to influence improperly their central banks, going beyond the proper indication of governmental views essential to the democratic surveillance of monetary policy described below? Do you think that the European Council debate over the designation of President Duisenberg and its controversial resolution suggests a future risk that undue influence could be exerted upon the members of the Executive Board, or not?

3. PRICE STABILITY AND SECONDARY OBJECTIVES OF THE ECB AND THE ESCB

EC Treaty Article 105(1) set "price stability" as the "primary objective" of the ESCB, thus accepting the German argument that the success of the Bundesbank's monetary policy was due in large measure to its principal emphasis on price stability. Price stability is equated with a low inflation rate for consumer products and services. The Treaty fixes no specific target for price stability. This leaves the ECB with considerable discretion in fixing some appropriate target rate for low inflation for the Euro-zone(see sub-section 4 below).

As a secondary duty, the ESCB is required by Article 105 to "support the general economic policies in the Community." The ESCB is also to "act in accordance with the principle of an open market economy with free competition," a major innovation in the Maastricht Treaty urged by Germany as a "ground rule" for ESCB action. In the initial EC Treaty section on basic principles, Article 4(3) lists some other guiding principles for the Community and the Member States, which presumably the ESCB should also respect: "sound public finances and monetary conditions and a sustainable balance of payments." But although the ESCB will certainly often develop rules and shape decisions to achieve one or another of these secondary objectives, Article 105(1)declares these to be "without prejudice to the objective of price stability," which is thus categorically given the primary emphasis.

This Treaty emphasis upon price stability was demanded by Germany, whose fear of inflation is understandable, given its catastrophic inflation during the 1920s. Germany's enviable post World War II record of low inflation was due in large measure to the Bundesbank's strict monetary policies. A low inflation rate encourages long-term investment and promotes confidence in long-term supply contracts, market stability, greater certainty in budgetary planning and tax collection, stable securities markets, insurance for long-term savings, social protection for pensioners, and so on.

But giving primary policy emphasis upon achieving and keeping a low inflation rate may handicap Member State action to combat economic and monetary crises and, in particular, efforts to reduce high unemployment and concomitant social distress. European and American economists are, not surprisingly, divided upon their assessment of the degree of social and economic harm produced by high inflation versus that produced by high unemployment, and upon the precise nature of the link between inflation rates and unemployment rates.

On a comparative note, in the United States the Federal Reserve places a high premium on maintaining price stability, but that is not its only concern. The statutory goal set for the Board of Governors of the Federal Reserve system is to "promote effectively the goals of maximum employment, stable prices, and moderate long-term interest rates." It is noteworthy that for the Federal Reserve price stability is not given special priority and that "maximum employment" is a specific goal, indeed the first mentioned. The Full Employment and Balanced Growth Act of 1978 required the Federal Reserve to provide detailed bi-annual economic reports to Congress, including specifically "past and prospective developments in employment, unemployment, production, investment, real income, productivity, international trade and payments, and prices."

In view of this more balanced presentation of the Federal Reserve's various goals in developing monetary policy, some commentators have questioned whether "price stability" ought to have been stated to be the primary goal of the ECB in the Maastricht Treaty. This is particularly true in view of the grave problem of high unemployment levels in many Member States.

The 1991–1994 recession in the Community was quite severe and produced historically high unemployment virtually everywhere. Some Member States were especially hard hit—Finland, Portugal and Spain had unemployment at or approaching 20%. Although unemployment declined in many States during the 1994–1996 recovery, it still averaged over 10% at the end of 1996.

The Treaty of Amsterdam, effective May 1, 1999, highlighted the importance of Community activity to promote employment by amending TEU Article 2(ex B) to insert "a high level of employment" as a Treaty goal. Similarly, Article 2 of the EC Treaty now includes among the Community's tasks "a high level of employment and social protection," immediately before "sustainable and non-inflationary growth." The Amsterdam Treaty's emphasis on the promotion of high employment naturally has lent vigor to the arguments of those political leaders and media and academic commentators who have urged the ECB to give greater weight to this goal in developing its monetary policies.

4. ECB POLICY 1999–2001

Even before the ECB assumed its control of monetary policy on Jan. 1, 1999, it set the most important elements of its "monetary policy strategy" on Oct. 13, 1998. The ECB then adopted the following standard: "Price stability shall be defined as a year-on-year increase in the Harmonized Index of Consumer Prices (HICP) for the Euro area of below 2%."

Since 1996 a regulation has set common standards for each State's calculation of its consumer price increases, so that the HICP can be considered a reliable measuring indicator for the entire Community. Also, the EMI had previously considered a 2% annual increase in inflation as the appropriate ceiling for price stability, so that the ECB's decision to use 2% as the maximum acceptable level for consumer price inflation was not surprising.

In a press release, the ECB noted several implications that can be drawn from its standard for price stability. The reference to the Euro area as a whole meant that the ECB would "not react to specific regional or national developments." Price stability would be measured "over the medium term" (presumably meaning annually, as a rule), so that the ECB would not seek to control "short term volatility in prices." Also implicit in the definition is that the ECB would act against any deflation in consumer prices that might occur in a serious recession.

Immediately after the ECB assumed its powers in 1999, the debate began over the extent to which it should be concerned with unemployment. In 1999 the Community still averaged over 9% unemployment, even in such relatively stable economies as France and Germany. In early 1999, the then German Socialist Economics Minister La Fontaine sharply criticized the ECB for its failure to take efforts to reduce unemployment into consideration in determining its monetary policies. President Duisenberg's pungent response was that it is "normal for the political side to give suggestions or opinions, but it would be abnormal if these suggestions were listened to."

Throughout 1999–2001, the ECB view, articulated by President Duisenberg and other ECB members, has consistently been that the ECB only has the capacity to work for price stability and would be ineffective in trying to achieve other goals. The ECB considers that unemployment levels can only be reduced by structural measures, such as governmental action to reduce labor rigidity and the level of social welfare benefits and to encourage capital investment.

In response, particularly in 2001 as Germany and other Euro-zone States experienced serious economic downturns and even a recession, some government spokesmen (especially in France and Germany) and many media commentators have criticized the ECB attitude as inflexible and excessively concerned with curbing inflation. They have urged the ECB to take action, notably by reducing target interest rates, to try to stimulate economic growth. Indeed, in 2001 as the US economy slowed and the Federal Reserve lowered target interest rates on eleven occasions to try to stimulate the weakening US economy, US Treasury spokesmen, the IMF, and other commentators urged the ECB to take action to stimulate growth in order to provide some degree of global balance to the US economic weakness.

On a comparative note, as previously observed, the Federal Reserve does take employment levels into consideration in determining its monetary policies. This was strikingly the case in the 1996–99 period when the Federal Reserve, under the leadership of Chairman Greenspan, declined to raise interest rates to cut off incipient inflation that was widely predicted to develop inevitably when unemployment dropped below 6% (in application of an economic theory, the well-known Phillips curve). During those years, the national unemployment rate declined steadily past 5% and down to around 4%, without a sharp increase in inflation. The Federal Reserve also rejects the idea of a specific inflation target level. In October 2001, Chairman Greenspan declared that "a specific numerical inflation target would represent an unhelpful and false precision."

In an overview of the key economic statistics in the Community, the Commission's Annual General Report for the 2000 report showed "a strong and robust" economic picture, with a 3.4% increase in annual GDP and a substantial decline in unemployment to an 8% level. However, not surprisingly, inflation rose to 2.1%, in part due to higher energy costs. The ECB accordingly raised target interest rates several times in 2000 (largely in parallel to similar interest rate raises by the Federal Reserve Board).

Although final statistics are not presently available, the economic situation sharply changed by mid–2001. In early 2001, growth generally continued (except in Germany), but inflation in the Euro-zone increased to between 2.5 and 3.0%, hitting its high point at 3.4% in May. In late 2001, prompted partly by the recession in the US and even more by a recession in Germany and a decided economic downturn in France and Italy, GDP growth in the Community declined to 1.4% in the third quarter and probably lower in the fourth quarter, while unemployment has risen sharply in Germany and France. However, because the consumer inflation rate continued to be above 2% (probably around 2.4%) in the latter part of 2001, the ECB has declined to respond to calls to reduce significantly its target interest rate, and has only cut it twice by minor amounts. This is in sharp contrast to the Federal Reserve, which cut target rates throughout 2001, reducing them to a 40–year low of 1.75%, to try to counter the effects of the US downturn and eventual recession, even though inflation rates remained above 2%. The Federal Reserve appears presently to be quite concerned about the national unemployment rate, which rose from 4% at the end of 2000 to 5.8% in December 2001.

For a legal and political critique of the Treaty emphasis on price stability, see the views of Prof. Matthias Herdegen of Bonn, Price Stability and Budgetary Restraints in the EMU: The Law as Guardian of Economic Wisdom, 35 Common Mkt. L. Rev. 9 (1988). Ottmar Issing, an ECB Executive Board member, defends the ECB position in The ECB's Monetary Policy Experience After the First Year, 22 J. Policy Modeling 325 (2000). A critical view is presented by the well-known US economist Martin Feldstein, The ECB and The Euro: The First Year, 22 J. Policy Modeling 325 (2000).

Notes and Questions

1. Apart from Germany, no other Member State had price stability as the primary objective of its central bank. Do you agree that price stability should be the sole objective of the ECB? Do you think that the Treaty should state the ECB's primary objective, or that this should be left to secondary legislation, which could conceivably be amended from time to time?

2. If the Federal Reserve can take into account the level of unemployment in setting target interest rates, do you think the ECB could likewise do so? Or do you believe that the European high unemployment levels are due to structural factors beyond the influence of the ECB?

4. DEMOCRATIC ACCOUNTABILITY AND TRANSPARENCY

As we have already briefly indicated, the European Parliament was given only a modest role in the developmental stages of EMU, and in its operational structure in the final stage. Parliament need only be consulted in the Council's crucial decision on which Member States qualify for entry into the third stage, and in the designation of the members of the ECB's Executive Board.

In several resolutions during and after the 1990–91 IGC, Parliament requested at least some share in the decision-making process in the creation of the Monetary Union and in operations thereafter. Both the Parliament and a significant number of academic commentators regard its absence from this process as one of the most important and regrettable illustrations of the "democratic deficit."

Some commentators have wondered why the Parliament does not have the right to assent to the determination of the States that qualify for the final stage of EMU, arguing that a decision of such capital political importance ought to have the strongest democratic support. Parliament played no significant role in the May 1999 decision to permit eleven States to qualify for the final stage of EMU, or the June 2000 decision to allow Greece to do so. The issue is not moot, because at some point decisions will have to be taken upon the entry into EMU of the Central European and Mediterranean applicant states, and perhaps upon the entry of Denmark, Sweden or the UK.

Parliament has also complained that it lacked any formal voice in the designation of Executive Board members, despite its request to be involved in this process. On a comparative note, in the US the President's nominees for the Federal Reserve Board are subject to confirmation hearings and must be approved by the Senate. Some commentators support the Parliament's position, considering that not only is democratic legitimacy better respected by a system of formal hearings and approval by the Parliament, but the process enables a careful and public review of a nominee's credentials and policy views.

Fortunately, in 1998 President Duisenberg and the other Executive Board nominees did appear voluntarily before Parliament in what were popularly called confirmation hearings, and Parliament endorsed all the nominees. In an April 1998 resolution, Parliament called upon the Member States not to designate any nominee whom it did not endorse. It is generally believed that the practice of holding such a parliamentary review of future nominees will continue but, of course, it is by no means certain that the Member States would withdraw a nominee's designation if the Parliament should ever criticize the choice.

Now that the ECB and the ESCB are fully operational, the Parliament's role remains decidedly modest. Parliament must give its assent to any Council legislation granting the ECB powers of prudential supervision over credit institutions and other financial institutions, or in any change in significant provisions of the Statute of the ESCB, but such legislation is not very likely, at least in the near future. Otherwise the drafters of the EMU Treaty articles considered that the principle of independence dictated that Parliament should be given no role of legislative supervision over the ESCB's monetary policy decisions and regulations.

Some commentators argue that this total insulation of monetary decision making from democratic control is a highly debatable proposition. Making it hard for Parliament to interfere with the ECB's control of monetary policy is one thing, making it impossible (by the Treaty itself) is quite another. The strongest critique has been offered by Professors L. Gormley & J.de Haan in their article, "The Democratic Deficit of the European Central Bank," 21 European L. Rev. 95, (1996), which concludes that "monetary policy ultimately must be controlled by democratically elected politician." Id. At 112.

Obviously, the drafters of the Treaty believed that it was the better policy to give Parliament no direct role in the shaping of monetary policy, which would be left exclusively to the technical expertise of the ECB and the national central banks.

Although the ECB thus has an extraordinary level of autonomy in its control of monetary policy, it is by no means exempt from democratic accountability—the obligation to explain and perhaps defend its actions and views to the political institutions, namely the Commission, the Ecofin Council and particularly the Parliament. Article 113 requires the ECB to provide an annual report to the Parliament, the Council, the Commission and the European Council. The same article permits Parliament committees to hold sessions to hear the views of the ECB President and other Executive Board members.

On April 2, 1998, Parliament adopted a prominent resolution on the democratic accountability of the ECB. Parliament stressed that such accountability was essential to balance the independence of the ECB, which goes further than that of any prior central bank. Parliament requested that the ECB President or other Executive Board members meet quarterly with its economic committee to assess monetary and economic developments.

Fortunately, the ECB's reaction has been favorable. President Duisenberg and other ECB members have consistently stressed the ECB's desire to be highly transparent, equal to or better than any other central bank in that regard. Although the ECB's meetings and deliberations are strictly secret and its internal votes confidential (unlike the Federal Reserve and the Bank of England, which each provide minutes of their meetings and a summary of votes several weeks after each meeting),the ECB provides a report after each monthly or special meeting and President Duisenberg customarily holds a news conference at that time. The ECB also sends President Duisenberg or another representative to quarterly meetings with the Parliament to explain current ECB policy and its views on economic developments, and to answer questions.

Moreover, in addition to its annual report, which provides each spring an extensive survey of economic and monetary conditions in the preceding year, the ECB publishes a monthly bulletin, which provides interim economic information and an analysis of ECB monetary decisions. The ECB also publishes a plethora of studies and reports on monetary and economic topics, most of them posted on its active website.

For an assessment of the democratic accountability of the ECB and the transparency of its operations, see a trio of contrasting articles: Professor William Buiter's initial strong critique, Alice in Euroland, 37 J. Common Mkt Studies 181 (1999); ECB Executive Board member Ottmar Issing's vigorous defense, The Eurosystem: Transparent and Accountable, or 'Willem in Euroland,' 37 J. Common Mkt. Studies 503 (1999), and a more neutral appraisal by Professors Jakob de Haan & Sylvester Eijffinger, The Democratic Accountability of the ECB: A Comment on Two Fairy Tales, 38 J. Common Mkt. Studies 393 (2000).

Notes and Questions

1. Do you think that there exists a "democratic deficit" in the creation and operation of EMU, or do you think that the decision-making process should be essentially left to monetary experts and insulated from parliamentary interven-

tion? Specifically, should the Parliament be empowered to approve the nominations to the ECB Executive Board, just as it approves the proposed candidates for a new Commission? Should the Parliament in the future exercise a right of assent, or veto, when new States (whether Denmark, the UK or Sweden, or applicant countries from Central Europe and the Mediterranean) seek to join the Euro-zone?

2. How important is the principle of the democratic accountability of the ECB? Should any political body—the European Council, the Ecofin Council, or Parliament—have the power to provide general or long-term policy guidelines to the ECB (as the Congress can to the Federal Reserve)?

3. What importance does the ECB seem to be giving to the transparency of its decision-making and policies? How useful do its reports to Parliament seem to be? Do you think that increased transparency is still necessary?

F.   THE COMING OF THE EURO

From the outset of planning for EMU, the introduction of a new single currency for the Euro-zone States was seen as not only integral to the success of EMU, but providing perhaps its greatest benefits. At the very least, the adoption of a simple currency eliminates transaction costs accompanying the transfer of products and services across frontiers. The Commission estimates the elimination of transaction costs represents a saving of O.3–0.5% in annual GDP, a very substantial sum (ca. $30–40 billion dollars).

The greatest economic benefits provided by a single currency are the creation of immediate price transparency for consumers in the choice of products and services throughout the Euro-zone (notably for tourists and persons residing in frontier zones, or for those purchasing cars, computers or other higher-priced items), and the promotion of greater market integration and inter-state competition, especially in the financial sector, but also for many commercial and professional products and services. These two benefits should in theory lead to two others—a reduction in the inflation rate for widely-distributed consumer products and an increase in competitiveness for Euro-zone enterprises, especially in the financial sector.

Finally, and of great importance to the Community political leadership, is the symbolic value represented by the adoption of a single currency. The use of the Euro by all residents in the Euro-zone inevitably brings home to them on a daily basis a realization of their status as citizens of the European Union.

1. POLICY DECISIONS AND LEGISLATION

The Madrid European Council in December 1995 took the most important policy decisions concerning the Euro as a currency. This meeting endorsed the "scenario for the changeover to the single currency," largely as proposed by the Commission and the EMI. Bull. EU 12/95, at 24–28. The European Council also adopted the name, "Euro," for the banknotes and largest denomination coins for the new single currency, considering the name to be "simple" and to "symbolize Europe" while being easy to use in all languages.

The scenario, or timetable, called for the preparation and approval of all essential legislation concerning the introduction of the Euro by 1997–1998.

During 1999–2001, the Euro would be used for Community and participating Member State accounts, loans and inter-state financial transactions. A Council regulation should provide a "legal framework" for the use of the Euro by private parties beginning in 1999. Banks, financial institutions and commercial enterprises might use the Euro in their transactions starting in 1999, but would not be required to do so (the principle commonly known as "no prohibition, no compulsion"). Euro banknotes and coins should be introduced and become legal tender on January 1, 2002, and national currency should cease to be legal tender no later than June 30, 2002.

The December 1995 Madrid European Council scenario was of capital importance in the evolution toward EMU. It marked the end of any hesitation produced by the prior recession and turmoil in the currency exchange markets during 1991–1994. The approach adopted in the scenario was pragmatic, clear-cut and established a definite agenda for specific actions.

Two key regulations set out the legal terms upon which the Euro should be introduced and operate as the sole currency for the Euro-zone States. The first is Council Regulation 974/98 on the introduction of the Euro, O.J. L 139/1 (May 11, 1998), formally adopted on May 3, 1998 immediately after the Council decision which determined the identity of the States that would participate in the final stage of EMU, and after the designation of the Executive Board members of the ECB.

The regulation on the introduction of the Euro essentially gave legal force to the policy decisions reached by the Madrid European Council in December 1995. Article 2 adopts the name, Euro, for the single currency, and divides one Euro into one hundred cents. Article 3 prescribes that the Euro is to be substituted for national currency units at the irrevocable fixed rates set by the Council pursuant to Article 123(4). The Euro is then to be the unit of account for the ECB and all participating national central banks.

Articles 10–11 of the regulation mandate the ECB to put Euro banknotes into circulation on Jan. 1, 2002 and the Member States to issue Euro and cent coins at the same date, both assuming the status of legal tender. Under Article 15, national currency banknotes and coins may remain legal tender for no longer than six months thereafter. Article 12 requires participating states to "ensure adequate sanctions against counterfeiting" of Euros.

The transition period, 1999–2001, is covered in Articles 6–9 of the regulation, which provide essentially that all legal instruments (laws, regulatory or administrative acts, judicial decisions, contracts, instruments of payment, etc.) may be set either in Euros or in a national currency.

Of equal importance is Council Regulation EC 1103/97 on certain provisions relating to the introduction of the Euro, O.J.L 162/1 (June 19, 1997). This is commonly known as the "continuity of contracts regulation," because that is its principal subject. Although a Recital to the Regulation notes that "it is a generally accepted principle of law that the continuity of contracts and other legal instruments is not affected by the "introduction of a new currency," nonetheless the Regulation was adopted "in order to reinforce legal certainty and clarity."

The key provision is Article 3, which states:

"The introduction of the Euro shall not have the effect of altering any term of a legal instrument or of discharging or excusing performance under any legal instrument, nor give a party the right unilaterally to alter or terminate such an instrument. This provision is subject to anything which parties may have agreed."

This legally binding rule of continuity of contracts is meant to bar completely any claim for recission, cancellation or non-performance under national law based on statutory or case law rules on frustration, impossibility, material alteration of terms, inequity, and so forth. Note however that the principle of party autonomy is respected: the parties may agree to the contrary. Thus, the Regulation provides clear guidance to business operators and avoids unnecessary litigation.

Article 2 of the Regulation further specifies that any reference in a legal instrument to an ECU should be replaced by one to a Euro, on a one ECU to one Euro basis.

In a recital, the Regulation expressed the hope that third countries will respect the principle of continuity of contracts. This found a definite resonance in New York. On July 29, 1997, the New York legislature adopted a statute on Continuity of Contract which provides that in all contracts subject to New York law which refer to a European national currency, or to the ECU, as a subject or medium of payment, the reference should be replaced by a reference to the Euro, if the Member State of the currency is replacing its currency with the Euro. Similar legislation has been adopted in California, Illinois, and several other US states, as well as in Hong Kong. The value of such legislation lies in the legal certainty thus provided to the principle of continuity of contracts in the jurisdiction adopting it; but there is a potential adverse effect if courts in other jurisdictions without such legislation are led to doubt the principle of continuity of contracts in the absence of a specific statute.

For expert analyses of the two regulations, see J. Meyers & D. Levie, The Introduction of the Euro: Overview of the Legal Framework, 4 Colum. J. Eur. L. 321 (1998); W.Van Lembergen & M. Wachenfeld, EMU: Legal Implications of the Arrival of the Single Currency, 22 Fordham Int'l.L.J. (1998)and Prof. John Usher, Legal Background of the Euro, in P. Beaumont & N. Walker, Legal Framework of the Single Currency (Hart 1999). A careful analysis of the continuity of contracts issue in the US is presented in M. Gruson, The Introduction of the Euro and its Implications for Obligations in Currencies Replaced by the Euro, 21 Fordham Int'l. L.J. 65 (1997).

The final crucial decision enabling the use of the Euro as a "virtual currency" during the 1999–2001 transition period was the adoption of irrevocable conversion rates between the Euro and each participating State's national currency (which accordingly irrevocably locked the exchange rates of participating States' currency in relation to each other). This was achieved by Council Regulation 2866/98 on the conversion rates between the Euro and the currencies of the Member States adopting the Euro, O.J.L 359/1 (Dec. 31, 1998). The rates were fixed in accord with the market rates prevailing on Dec. 31, 1998. Thus, during the transition period, one Euro equalled approximately 1.96 German Marks, 6.6 French Francs, 166.4 Spanish Pesetas, 1940 Italian Lira, etc.

Technically speaking, with the adoption of the irrevocable conversion rates, the Euro became the legal currency of the States in the Euro-zone, even though only a "virtual currency" without any banknotes. Each of the national currencies in the Euro-zone became technically only expressions of value of the Euro. Accordingly, not only the Community in its budget and finances, but also all participating States in the Euro-zone in their budget and finances, operated in Euros from 1999–2001.

Notes and Questions

1. The Euro became the currency of eleven Member States in the Euro-zone on Jan. 1, 1999, even though the Euro banknotes and coins were only introduced in 2002. How did this happen? What are "irrevocable" conversion rates from national currencies to the Euro? What has happened to government or private sector bond issues denominated in ECU that were outstanding on Jan. 1, 1999?

2. What does the principle of continuity of contracts mean? What does Regulation 1103/97 say as to the degree to which it applies in the Euro-zone after Jan. 1, 1999? Do you think this represents a sound policy approach? May a party to a contract containing a force majeure clause invoke that clause to invalidate or modify a contract requiring payment in a national currency that will disappear in 2002? Are there benefits or risks to consumers? Is it fair to persons liable under long-term fixed rate housing mortgages or installment payment car purchases?

3. Regulation 1103/97 contains a recital stating that the principle of continuity of contracts should also apply in third states. Do you think that this is apt to be true in US courts? Do you think that the 1997 New York law represents sound policy, or is inadvisable? Should other states follow the New York precedent, or not?

2. PRACTICAL PREPARATIONS FOR THE INTRODUCTION OF THE EURO

Two important Commission studies, a 1994 Commission Communication, "Practical problems involved in introducing the ecu as the European Union's single currency," and a 1995 Green Paper on the Introduction of the Single Currency described the principal technical problems that had to be faced and some of the practical measures necessary in moving toward the introduction of the Euro.

The studies indicated that the banking industry and the financial sector would require massive revision of denominations of loans, deposits, security instruments and operating procedures, and that automatic teller machines had to be modified, computer software programs revised, and so on. Public administrators, especially the tax, social security and budgetary authorities, would likewise have to restructure their accounts and their receipts and payment systems, while in the private sector the retail industry would need to revise its accounting and payment system.

Beginning in 1995, the Commission, together with the European Monetary Institute, encouraged studies and conferences to involve as many interested parties as possible in the process of planning and concrete preparation. To advance planning in the capital markets, the Commission issued in July 1997 the Giovanni Report, prepared by financial sector experts. The report noted that all enterprises organized in corporate form must redenominate their capital, securities and debt in Euros no later than June 30, 2002.

In the three-year period from 1999 to 2001, the Member States in the Euro-zone used the Euro for all national budgetary and accounting purposes, floated any new national debt issues only in Euros, and used Euros for their inter-state monetary movements. During the 1999–2001 period, financial institutions had to record their accounts and make their monetary transfers in Euros in their dealings with central banks and on an inter-bank basis. Commercial enterprises were encouraged to use the Euro as much as possible in their internal accounts and external transactions, but were not required to do so—as noted above the principle, adopted by the December 1995 Madrid European Council, was one of "no prohibition, no compulsion." Many large multi-national groups did indeed set up their internal accounts on a dual basis, keeping them both in Euros and in their national currency, and invoiced and accepted payment in Euros as well as in national currency. Many banks handled client deposit and loan accounts on a dual Euro/national-currency basis, which obviously helped in the process of familiarizing the general public with the new currency. London and other financial centers began to trade some securities denominated in Euros.

Because it took several years to print and safely store the enormous number of new Euro banknotes to issue as legal tender on January 1, 2002, the EMI moved rapidly to fulfill its role of setting the technical specifications for the banknotes. An April 1995 EMI report set the denominations at 5, 10, 20, 50, 100 and 500. After detailed studies and a competition in mid–1996 to select the design for each face of the banknotes, the EMI decided to use non-existent monuments and bridges with a European cultural flair on the banknote faces, together with the European flag and a map depicting Western Europe. Each denomination has a different size and a different color and possesses tactile qualities intended to help the visually impaired to differentiate them. At the start of 1997, the Commission introduced the symbol of the Euro, inspired by the Greek letter epsilon—a written capital E with a small second bar through the middle.

Article 106 (ex 105a) of the EC Treaty gives the Council the power to determine the nature of Euro coins. Council Regulation 975/98 on the denominations and technical specifications of Euro coins, O.J. L 139/6 (May 11, 1998)(which, incidentally, was reviewed by the Parliament under the cooperation procedure), set the standards for and characteristics of the coins. This text required one and two Euro coins, and 1, 2, 5, 10, 20 and 50 cent coins. The text set their shape, size, color and edges, and observes that the vending machine association representatives and the European Blind Union were duly consulted to ensure that the coins would be as suitable as possible for convenient and safe use.

The Commission's most noteworthy contribution to the process of preparing for the Euro came in the form of two Recommendations issued on Apr. 15, 1998. Presumably the Commission did not feel it advisable to propose legislation in view of the diversity of approaches apt to occur in the private sector.

The Commission Recommendation concerning banking charges for conversion to the Euro, O.J.L 130/22 (May 1, 1998), comes closest to soft law in the financial sector. The Recommendation declares that the Commission considers that banks are not legally justified in imposing any charge for the conversion of money received in Euros to the national currency or vice-versa, or for the conversion of accounts stipulated in the national currency to accounts denominated in Euros at the end of the transition period. Significantly, the Commission also recommended that banks convert national currency to Euros "without charge to their customers" when Euro bank notes and coins became available in January 2002, provided the currency involved represented no more than a "household amount."

The Commission Recommendation concerning dual display of prices, O.J. L 130/26 (May 1, 1998), urged retailers and others to employ such dual displays of prices and other relevant information in Euros and the national currency in order to familiarize consumers with the exchange rates. The dual displays should be "unambiguous, easily identifiable and clearly legible." The Commission also urged banks and utilities to display statements and bills on a dual basis.

The process of preparing the bank notes and coins themselves, as well as the mode of launching them as legal tender, received heightened attention in 2000–01. The Commission and the ECB estimated that around 15 billion bank notes and 55 billion coins had to be printed and minted before Jan. 1, 2002. This herculean task required not only intensive speed, but also careful security precautions, especially in the storage and transport of the currency and coins.

Throughout 2001, the Commission and the ECB carried out a "Euro 2002 campaign" aimed at making the financial and retail industries and the general public familiar with the denominations, designs and security features of the Euro notes and coins. Particular attention was given to efforts to inform the visually impaired (estimated to constitute about 2% of the population).

Starting in September 2001, the ECB began the transfer of bank notes and coins to banks in the "frontloading process", so that they would have adequate stocks of currency on hand before Jan. 1, 2002. In December, 2001, the ECB authorized the release by banks to their customers of 300 million "starter kits," each containing an aggregate of coins worth 10 Euros, in order to familiarize the public with coin denominations and appearance. (Reportedly, starter kits became highly popular holiday gifts.) Substantial amounts of Euro bank notes were stocked by banks in December and retailers were permitted to stock them as well.

By all media reports, the initial launch of the Euro as legal tender in January 2002 proved successful. Although some banks and many retail enterprises, especially small ones, did not have adequate supplies of currency and coins, in the main the changeover went smoothly. The ECB estimates that 95% of all cash transactions were in Euros within the Euro-zone by the end of the third week in January. Consumers and other members of the general public naturally will require time for adjustment and many calculation errors in conversion are inevitable in the short term, but the media reported that the public was enthusiastic in its acceptance of the Euro. The concern that merchants would seize the conversion period as an occasion to round up prices sharply does not seem to have been justified, although only time will indicate for certain whether consumer inflation increased in the short term due to the introduction of the Euro.

Notes and Questions

1. The December 1995 Madrid European Council set the transition period of 1999–2001 upon the joint recommendation of the Commission and the EMI. Do you think that a three year transition period was about the right length, or too long or short?

2. What policy decisions were taken to make Euro banknotes and coins convenient to use and appealing to the general public? What particular issues affected the decisions on the size and shape of coins? May Euro-zone States freely decide on the amount of coins they will produce?

3. What are some of the important measures Euro-zone States, and their regional and city governments, have had to take to prepare for the launch of the Euro? What risks arise if their preparation proves to be not fully adequate?

4. What measures did banks, securities brokers, and insurance companies take during the 1999–2001 transition period? To what extent could they immediately convert to Euros for inter-bank or other financial transactions? How helpful to the general public was the use by banks of dual display of Euro values along with national currency amounts? To what extent was the Commission's Recommendation helpful in preventing banks from levying high charges on procedural steps taken in the launch of the Euro?

5. What measures did the Commission recommend commercial firms, especially retail firms, to take to prepare during the final phase of the transition period? Are there risks for consumers at the time of the actual introduction of the Euro as legal tender?

Further Reading

M. Andemas, ed., European Economic and Monetary Union (Kluwer 1997)

P. Beaumont & N. Walker, ed., The Legal Framework of The Single European Currency (Hart 1999)

C. Crouch, ed., After the Euro (Oxford, 2000)

K. Dyson, Elusive Union: The Process of Economic and Monetary Union in Europe (Longman 1994)

L. Bini Smaghi & D. Gros, Open Issues in European Central Banking (St. Martin's, 2000)

K. Gretschmann, ed., Economics and Monetary Union: Implications for National Policy Makers (1993)

R. Smits, The European Central Bank (Kluwer 1997)

J. Usher, The Law of Money and Financial Services in the EC, chs. 7–8 (Clarendon 1994)

P. Welfens, ed., European Monetary Integration (Springer 2d ed. 1994)

Part VII

SPECIFIC COMMUNITY POLICIES

The first six parts of this casebook examined the institutions of the Community, the establishment of the internal market through the free movement of goods, workers, services and capital, the Community's competition rules and its common commercial policy and external relations; as well as monetary union. A quick perusal of the EC Treaty and the TEU reveals that there are many other important aspects of the Community and Union that we have yet to consider. There are, for example, treaty provisions on agriculture, transport, taxation, social policy, education, culture, health, consumer protection, the environment, justice, and research and development, to name only some.

The vast scope of these topics precludes a detailed examination in this casebook. In this Part VII, however, we will treat a number of the more important and interesting topics. Our choice is arbitrary, and we admittedly exclude some very important topics. In particular, we will not examine the common agricultural policy (CAP), even though it involves the most complex scheme of Community regulation and consumes most of the Community's budget. The topic is too complex and in many case too arcane for classroom discussion. We have, of course, considered the CAP indirectly, as many of the cases in the Court of Justice that have challenged Community regulations have involved aspects of the CAP and much of the Court's jurisprudence on proportionality and similar issues arose initially in connection with cases attacking aspects of the CAP.

In this part, we have chosen five topics. We first turn to environmental protection, a field in which the Community has long been active. Chapter 34 describes in general terms the scope of the Community's harmonization efforts and examines the difficult problem of ensuring enforcement of Community norms. We also consider the extent to which independent Member State regulation of the environment is permitted.

Chapter 35 deals with the subject of consumer protection. After a review of the evolution of Community policies in this field, we examine three specific areas where the Community has been active in adopting harmonization directives—misleading advertising, unfair contract terms and products liability.

Since the 1970s, social policy, and particularly the protection of employee rights, has been an important field of Community action. In Chapter 36, we describe the major employee protection directives and their interpretation by the Court of Justice, and examine Community social policy generally.

1239

Because equal treatment of women and men has become such an active aspect of Community social policy, we devote Chapter 37 to this topic. Our initial focus is the equal pay mandate of Article 141 and its interpretation by the Court of Justice. We also analyze the directives intended to achieve equal treatment between women and men in the workplace, including the topic of positive action or reverse discrimination. The chapter concludes with a quick look at discrimination on grounds other than gender and with the topic of social security, pension and pensionable age.

Finally, Chapter 38 examines the Community activities related to cooperation in the area of civil justice, focusing initially on the Brussels Convention on Jurisdiction and the Recognition and Enforcement of Judgments in Civil and Commercial Matters (and the related Lugano Convention) and then on the recent Community regulation on that topic. The chapter examines the main provisions of these instruments in detail, referring in many places to the rich Court of Justice caselaw related to them.

Chapter 34

ENVIRONMENTAL PROTECTION

In this chapter, we examine an issue that has become much more important in recent years than it was at the time the EEC Treaty was signed in 1957—the protection of the environment. In 1987, its importance to the Community was explicitly recognized in the Single European Act, which added provisions on the environment to the EC Treaty (Articles 174–176, ex 130r–130t) and required that Commission proposals concerning environmental and consumer protection under Article 95 (ex 100a) (completion of the internal market) take as a base a high level of protection (para. 3). Modifications or elaborations of these provisions have been included in the Maastricht, Amsterdam and Nice Treaties. As a result, today one of the tasks of the Community is to "promote * * * a high level of protection and improvement of the quality of the environment" (Art. 2) and the activities of the Community are to include "a policy in the sphere of the environment" (Art. 3(l)). The following materials explore the legal basis for Community action on the environment, trace the development of Community legislation and activity in these fields and consider two particular problems: the failure of Member States to implement Community environmental rules and the extent to which Member States may legislate independently on the environment.

A. THE ENVIRONMENT IN THE EC TREATY

1. THE LEGAL BASIS FOR COMMUNITY ACTIVITIES

Even in the absence of express Treaty provisions dealing directly with the environment, the Community has had an active environmental policy since the 1970s. Indeed, the Community's active role in environmental matters is an excellent example of how the EC has grown to encompass areas not originally contemplated and how that growth has been supported by the Court of Justice.

In 1972, a summit of Community leaders in Paris laid down a series of basic environmental principles. This was followed by the adoption of the Community's first environmental action program, covering the five-year period 1972–1976. Three subsequent five-year programs followed: 1977–1981, 1982–1986 and 1987–1992. The fifth and sixth programs are described below. Also as a result of the Paris summit, a separate service was created in the

Commission to deal with environmental and consumer issues. Today, there is a separate Environment Directorate–General.

The motivation behind Community activity in the environmental area is multiple. First, the economic recovery of the Member States after World War II and the resulting dramatic rise in living standards made many Europeans sensitive to new aspects of the quality of their lives. Development and growth at any cost were no longer acceptable. Thus, a significant political constituency to protect and improve the environment appeared. Second, pollution does not respect borders and therefore by its very nature is an international problem. This is particularly true in the EC where a single river may flow through several countries and where airborne pollution quickly moves from its source to neighboring countries.

In addition, uncoordinated efforts by the Member States to deal with environmental issues plainly could cause a fragmentation of the internal market. A Community policy accordingly seemed imperative, though there was bound to be a lingering question over the precise extent to which a Member State may take action that goes beyond standards set by the Community.

Through 1986, the Community's specific environmental initiatives were generally based on Articles 94 (ex 100) or 308 (ex 235). Article 94, discussed in more detail in Chapter 14(A) supra, provides for the harmonization of Member State laws that "directly affect the establishment or functioning of the common market." Article 308 is, of course, the implied powers provision treated in Chapter 4(A). Because both of these provisions require unanimity, the pace of environmental regulation at the Community level was slowed. The unanimity requirement also raised the risk that the Community standard adopted would be that of the Member State having or supporting the lowest standard, thereby weakening any Community legislation.

The Single European Act added a new title on the environment to the Treaty in 1987. This title, which has since been amended in respect of some details, contains three articles. The first—Article 174 (ex 130r)—lays down the objectives of Community environmental action, identifies basic Community principles in this area and lists particular factors for the Community to take into account in preparing its environmental initiatives.

Article 174(1) provides that the Community policy on the environment shall contribute to the pursuit of the following objectives:

— preserving, protecting and improving the quality of the environment

— protecting human health

— prudent and rational utilization of natural resources

— promoting measures at the international level to deal with regional or worldwide environmental problems

Article 174(2) specifies that in achieving these objectives Community policy on the environment shall aim at a high level of protection and shall be based on the precautionary principle and on the principles that preventive action should be taken, environmental damage should be rectified at the source of the problem and the polluter should pay.

Despite its recognition of the EC's environmental competence, the SEA did not change the ground rules for adopting EC environmental rules. Article 175 (ex 130s) required unanimous Council approval for the adoption of environmental measures as such, although it authorized the Council by unanimous action, to "define those matters on which decisions are to be taken by a qualified majority." Some Member States feared that the continued unanimity requirement would prevent adequate environmental actions from being taken, and insisted on the inclusion of Article 176 (ex 130t). That article provides that Community measures adopted under Article 175 shall not prevent any Member State from maintaining or introducing more stringent protective measures compatible with the Treaty.

The Maastricht Treaty amended Article 175 to provide that environmental measures may be adopted under Article 252 (ex 189c), i.e., by a qualified majority of the Council in cooperation with Parliament, except in respect of (i) provisions of a fiscal nature, (ii) measures concerning town and country planning, land use and management of water resources and (iii) measures significantly affecting a Member State's choice between different energy sources and the general structure of its energy supply. The Amsterdam Treaty replaced the Parliamentary cooperation procedure with the co-decision procedure of Article 251, thus allowing adoption of environmental measures by qualified majority (subject to the exceptions listed).

The Amsterdam Treaty also added Article 6 (ex 3c), which provides that "Environmental protection requirements must be integrated into the definition and implementation of the Community's policies and activities referred to in Article 3, in particular with a view toward sustainable development." (A similar requirement, but without the reference to sustainable development, was contained in the changes introduced by the SEA.)

Notes and Questions

1. At the same time that it maintained a unanimity requirement for environmental measures, the SEA introduced through Article 95 (ex 100a) the possibility of qualified majority adoption of measures to achieve the 1992 internal market program. This raised the prospect that an environmental measure might be approved under Article 95 with less than unanimity, and therefore the question arose whether the specific requirements of Article 175 should override the more general provisions of Article 95. The Court of Justice faced this question in 1991 in Commission v. Council (Titanium dioxide), Case C–300/89, [1991] ECR I–2867. In this case, which involved a directive aimed at harmonizing Member State programs for reducing and eventually eliminating pollution caused by waste from the titanium dioxide industry and which is set out in Chapter 3(B) supra, the Court ruled that Article 95 was the proper basis for Community action to achieve the internal market even though the directive involved the environment.

2. Article 174(3) lists a number of factors of which "the Community shall take account" in preparing Community environmental actions. Included are (i) available scientific and technical data, (ii) environmental conditions in the various regions of the Community, (iii) the potential costs and benefits of an action or lack of action and (iv) the economic and social development of the Community as a whole and the balanced development of its regions. May a failure to meet these requirements be invoked in the Court of Justice as a basis for overturning Community environmental activities? See generally D. Vandermeersch, The Single

European Act and the Environmental Policy of the European Economic Community, 12 Eur.L.Rev. 407 (1987).

For example, suppose there is little or no scientific basis for a Community environmental directive? May the directive be voided on that ground? The Court rejected an analogous attack in The Queen v. Minister of Agriculture, Fisheries & Food: ex parte FEDESA, Case C–331/88, [1990] ECR I–4023, which involved a ban on the use of certain growth hormones in beef production adopted under Article 37 (ex 43) as part of the common agricultural policy. Is that case distinguishable on the ground that Article 37 does not contain a "scientific basis" requirement? The Maastricht Treaty added the requirement that Community policy be based on the precautionary principle. How would that affect a challenge to Community environmental legislation on the grounds that it lacked an adequate scientific basis?

The requirement in Article 174(3) that costs and benefits be considered is similar to the general Community legal requirement that measures be proportional. Do you think that the inclusion of this specific provision might cause the Court of Justice to examine Community environmental legislation more carefully than it otherwise would when such legislation is attacked on proportionality grounds?

Article 174(3) further requires that consideration be given to the levels of development in various regions of the Community. A similar requirement is found in Article 15 (ex 8c (and 7c)) on the internal market in general. May a less developed Member State insist legally on less strict controls or demand a derogation for less developed regions? In this respect, it should be noted that the Maastricht Treaty added a fifth paragraph to Article 175, to the effect that if a measure involves costs deemed disproportionate for the public authorities of a Member State, the Council shall lay down appropriate provisions in the form of temporary derogations and/or financial support from the cohesion fund.

Although the Court of Justice might conceivably invoke these factors as a reason for invalidating Community legislation, the Court's tendency to defer to the judgment of the Commission and Council would seem to make that unlikely. If that is the case, did the listing of these factors serve any useful purpose? Does a more detailed specification of the Community's role in environmental regulation help legitimate Community action in this arena? Does it increase the likelihood of Community action? Does it make stricter rules more likely?

3. Community action in the environmental area usually takes the form of directives. This, of course, was necessary when Article 94 (ex 100) was used as a basis for action. Is there such a limitation under Articles 95 (ex 100a) or 175?

4. The use of directives in the environmental area leaves some discretion to the Member States on how to implement Community rules and considerable discretion in respect of their enforcement. Do you think that it would be desirable to reduce that discretion, for example through the use of regulations or a Community enforcement agency? Assuming that the result was more effective enforcement of Community rules, would such an approach be consistent with the principle of subsidiarity? Would such an approach have any impact on the strictness of Community rules?

5. To the extent that environmental policy is implemented by directive, how can an affected individual challenge Community environmental rules in the Court of Justice? Review the materials in Chapter 5 supra.

6. One of the principles of Community environmental policy is that the polluter should pay. See Article 174(2). May a Member State, consistent with this

principle, subsidize some or all of the cost of installing pollution control equipment? The Community has rather strict rules limiting state aids for environmental purposes. See Commission Guidelines on States Aids for Environmental Protection, O.J. C 37/3 (Feb. 3, 2001).

2. THE COURT OF JUSTICE AND EC ENVIRONMENTAL LEGISLATION

Early on, the Court of Justice had to consider the extent to which the Community has the power to carry out an environmental program at all and the relationship between environmental rules and such fundamental Treaty principles as the free movement of goods. More recently, the Court has had to decide how narrowly or expansively to interpret environmental directives. The following cases consider these issues.

COMMISSION v. ITALY

(Sulphur Content of Fuels)
Case 92/79, [1980] ECR 1115.

[The Commission brought an Article 226 (ex 169) action against Italy for its failure to implement Directive 75/716 relating to the sulphur content of certain liquid fuels.]

4   [The Italian Government argues] that the subject-matter of the directive lies "at the fringe" of Community powers and that it is actually a convention drawn up in the form of a directive.

* * *

7   As regards the Italian Government's argument that the directive is actually a convention drawn up in this special form, it need only be recalled that the Court has already said in Case 38/79, *Commission v. Italy* [1970] ECR 47, that a measure which has the features of a decision when viewed in the light of its objective and the institutional framework within which it has been drawn up, cannot be described as an "international agreement". The same considerations apply where a Council directive is concerned.

8   As regards the observations of the Italian Government concerning the powers of the Community in the matter, it should be observed that the directive has been adopted not only within the Programme of Action of the Communities on the Environment; it also comes under the General Programme for the elimination of technical barriers to trade which result from disparities between the provisions laid down by law, regulation or administrative action in Member States, adopted by the Council on 28 May 1969. In this sense it is validly founded upon Article 100 [now 94]. Furthermore it is by no means ruled out that provisions on the environment may be based upon Article 100 of the Treaty. Provisions which are made necessary by considerations relating to the environment and health may be a burden upon the undertakings to which they apply and if there is no harmonization of national provisions on the matter, competition may be appreciably distorted.

* * *

PROCUREUR DE LA RÉPUBLIQUE v. ASSOCIATION DE DÉFENSE DES BRÛLEURS D'HUILES USAGÉES (ADBHU)

Case 240/83, [1985] ECR 531.

[Articles 2–4 of Directive 75/439 on the disposal of waste oils required Member States to take the measures necessary to ensure the safe collection and disposal of waste oils, preferably by recycling. Article 5 provided that if the aims of those articles could not be met, then "Member States shall take the necessary measures to ensure that one or more undertakings carry out the collection and/or disposal of the products offered to them by the holders, where appropriate in the zone assigned to them by the appropriate authorities." Article 6 provided that "any undertaking which disposes of waste oils must obtain a permit." The French decree that implemented Directive 75/439 divided France into zones and authorized waste oil collectors and disposers to operate on a zone-by-zone basis.]

9   The national court asks whether the system of permits is compatible with the principles of free trade, free movement of goods and freedom of competition, but does not elaborate further. In that connection it should be borne in mind that the principles of free movement of goods and freedom of competition, together with freedom of trade as a fundamental right, are general principles of Community law of which the Court ensures observance. The above-mentioned provisions of the directive should therefore be reviewed in the light of those principles.

* * *

12   In the first place it should be observed that the principle of freedom of trade is not to be viewed in absolute terms but is subject to certain limits justified by the objectives of general interest pursued by the Community provided that the rights in question are not substantively impaired.

13   There is no reason to conclude that the directive has exceeded those limits. The directive must be seen in the perspective of environmental protection, which is one of the Community's essential objectives. It is evident, particularly from the third and seventh recitals in the preamble to the directive, that any legislation dealing with the disposal of waste oils must be designed to protect the environment from the harmful effects caused by the discharge, deposit or treatment of such products. It is also evident from the provisions of the directive as a whole that care has been taken to ensure that the principles of proportionality and non-discrimination will be observed if certain restrictions should prove necessary. In particular, Article 5 of the directive permits the creation of a system of zoning "where the aims defined in Articles 2, 3 and 4 cannot otherwise be achieved".

14   In the second place, as far as the free movement of goods is concerned, it should be stressed that the directive must be construed in the light of the seventh recital in the preamble thereto, which states that the treatment of waste oils must not create barriers to intra-Community trade. As the Court has already ruled * * *, an exclusive right of that kind does not automatically authorize the Governments of the Member States to estab-

lish barriers to exports. Indeed, such a partitioning of the markets is not provided for in the Council Directive and would be contrary to the objectives laid down therein.

15   It follows from the foregoing that the measures prescribed by the directive do not create barriers to intra-Community trade, and that in so far as such measures, in particular the requirement that permits must be obtained in advance, have a restrictive effect on the freedom of trade and of competition, they must nevertheless neither be discriminatory nor go beyond the inevitable restrictions which are justified by the pursuit of the objective of environmental protection, which is in the general interest. That being so, Articles 5 and 6 cannot be regarded as incompatible with the fundamental principles of Community law mentioned above.

Notes and Questions

1. In *Commission v. Italy,* Italy questioned the Community's powers in the area of the environment. How did the Court respond? How did the Court respond to a similar challenge in the *ADBHU* case? What was the basis of the *ADBHU* Court's characterization in 1985 of environmental protection as one of the "essential objectives" of the Community?

2. In light of the Court's decisions in *Commission v. Italy* and *ADBHU,* was the new section on the environment in the Single European Act necessary? How much did it add to the Community's powers? In considering your answer, recall the issues raised in the notes at the end of section (A)(1) of this chapter.

3. After *ADBHU,* to what extent will environmental considerations justify Community imposed limitations on the free movement of goods?

WORLD WILDLIFE FUND v. AUTONOME PROVINZ BOZEN

Case C–435/97, [1999] ECR I–5613.

[The Administrative Court, Province of Bolzano requested a preliminary ruling on the interpretation of Council Directive 85/337 on the assessment of the effects of certain public and private projects on the environment ("the Directive", which is set out in the Selected Documents). The questions arose in proceedings seeking to overturn certain governmental decisions concerning the expansion of Bolzano–St Jacob Airport. In connection with the expansion, the runway was to be extended to 1400 meters, which meant that the project fell within Annex II of the Directive. See Annex I(7)(a); Annex II(10)(d). As such, the project was subject to Article 4(2) of the Directive. It appeared that the purpose of the project was to transform an airfield, which had formerly been used largely for non-commercial purposes into an airport with regular scheduled flights, as well as charter and cargo flights. The expansion was provided for in the regional development plan, adopted by law, which required that an environmental impact study be carried out. Such a study was undertaken, although it was accepted that it did not meet the requirements of the Directive.

The proceedings were brought by persons living near the airport and two environmental associations.]

34   By its first and second questions, which should be considered together, the national court essentially raises two issues.

35   The first is whether Articles 4(2) and 2(1) of the Directive are to be interpreted as conferring on a Member State the power to exclude, from the outset and in their entirety, from the environmental impact assessment procedure established by the Directive certain classes of projects falling within Annex II to the Directive, including modifications to those projects, * * * even if they have significant effects on the environment.

36   In that regard, the second subparagraph of Article 4(2) of the Directive confers on Member States a measure of discretion to specify certain types of projects which will be subject to an assessment or to establish the criteria or thresholds applicable. However, the limits of that discretion are to be found in the obligation set out in Article 2(1) that projects likely, by virtue inter alia of their nature, size or location, to have significant effects on the environment are to be subject to an impact assessment.

37   Thus, ruling on legislation of a Member State under which certain entire classes of projects listed in Annex II to the Directive were excluded from the assessment obligation, the Court [has] held that the criteria and/or thresholds mentioned in Article 4(2) of the Directive are designed to facilitate examination of the actual characteristics of any given project in order to determine whether it is subject to the requirement to carry out an assessment, and not to exempt in advance from that obligation certain whole classes of projects listed in Annex II which may be envisaged on the territory of a Member State.

38   The Court [has] also held that a Member State which established criteria or thresholds at a level such that, in practice, an entire class of projects would be exempted in advance from the requirement of an impact assessment would exceed the limits of its discretion under Articles 2(1) and 4(2) of the Directive unless all projects excluded could, when viewed as a whole, be regarded as not being likely to have significant effects on the environment.

39   As regards modifications to such projects, the Court [has] found that the mere fact that the Directive did not expressly refer to modifications to projects included in Annex II, as opposed to modifications to projects included in Annex I, did not justify the conclusion that they were not covered by the Directive.

40   Thus, observing that the scope of the Directive was wide and its purpose very broad, the Court [has] held that the Directive covered "modifications to development projects" even in relation to projects falling within Annex II, on the ground that its purpose would be undermined if "modifications to development projects" were so construed as to enable certain works to escape the requirement of an impact assessment when, by reason of their nature, size or location, they were likely to have significant effects on the environment.

41   The second issue raised by the national court is whether, taking into account the fact that an airport is the only airport in the region in which it is located that can be restructured, Articles 4(2) and 2(1) of the Directive nevertheless confer on a Member State the power to exclude from the assessment procedure established by the Directive a specific project such as that in issue in the main proceedings as not being likely to have

significant effects on the environment, either under national legislation * * * or on the basis of an individual examination of the project.

42 The second subparagraph of Article 4(2) * * * mentions, by way of indication, methods to which the Member States may have recourse when determining which of the projects falling within Annex II are to be subject to an assessment within the meaning of the Directive.

43 Consequently, the Directive confers a measure of discretion on the Member States and does not therefore prevent them from using other methods to specify the projects requiring an environmental impact assessment under the Directive. So the Directive in no way excludes the method consisting in the designation, on the basis of an individual examination of each project concerned or pursuant to national legislation, of a particular project falling within Annex II to the Directive as not being subject to the procedure for assessing its environmental effects.

44 However, the fact that the Member State has the discretion referred to in the previous paragraph is not in itself sufficient to exclude a given project from the assessment procedure under the Directive. If that were not the case, the discretion accorded to the Member States by Article 4(2) of the Directive could be used by them to take a particular project outside the assessment obligation when, by virtue of its nature, size or location, it could have significant environmental effects.

45 Consequently, whatever the method adopted by a Member State to determine whether or not a specific project needs to be assessed, be it by legislative designation or following an individual examination of the project, the method adopted must not undermine the objective of the Directive, which is that no project likely to have significant effects on the environment, within the meaning of the Directive, should be exempt from assessment, unless the specific project excluded could, on the basis of a comprehensive assessment, be regarded as not being likely to have such effects.

46 It should be added, with regard to the exclusion of the project at issue * * * from the assessment procedure * * *, that, even if that project concerns the only airport in the province which can be restructured and it has actually been specified by the legislature, the latter cannot in any event exempt the project from the assessment obligation unless, on the date [on which it adopted the relevant legislation, the legislature] was able to assess precisely the overall environmental impact which all the works entailed by the project were likely to have.

47 As for the exclusion of the project on the basis of an individual examination carried out by the national authorities, the file shows that the contested measures were preceded by an environmental impact study carried out by a team of experts, that information was communicated to the municipalities concerned and that the public was informed by press notices. In addition, the environmental agency [was] consulted.

48 It is for the national court to review whether, on the basis of the individual examination carried out by the competent authorities which resulted in the exclusion of the specific project at issue in the main proceedings from the assessment procedure established by the Directive,

those authorities correctly assessed, in accordance with the Directive, the significance of the effects of that project on the environment.

49   In view of the foregoing considerations, the answer to the first and second questions must be that Articles 4(2) and 2(1) of the Directive are to be interpreted as not conferring on a Member State the power either to exclude, from the outset and in their entirety, from the environmental impact assessment procedure established by the Directive certain classes of projects falling within Annex II to the Directive, including modifications to those projects, or to exempt from such a procedure a specific project, * * * either under national legislation or on the basis of an individual examination of that project, unless those classes of projects in their entirety or the specific project could be regarded, on the basis of a comprehensive assessment, as not being likely to have significant effects on the environment. It is for the national court to review whether, on the basis of the individual examination carried out by the national authorities which resulted in the exclusion of the specific project at issue from the assessment procedure established by the Directive, those authorities correctly assessed, in accordance with the Directive, the significance of the effects of that project on the environment.

50   By its third question, the national court asks essentially whether, in the case of a project requiring assessment under the Directive, Article 2(1) and (2) thereof are to be interpreted as allowing a Member State to use an assessment procedure other than the procedure introduced by the Directive and whether, where that alternative procedure is incorporated in a national procedure which exists or is to be established within the meaning of Article 2(2), it must satisfy the requirements of Articles 3 and 5 to 10 of the Directive, including public participation as provided for in Article 6.

51   In its order for reference the national court explains that it has doubts as to whether the consent procedure laid down in [the local law] is appropriate for fully identifying the effects of the project on the environment. It states that neither noise nor the effects on the atmosphere were investigated, as Article 3 of the Directive requires, and that the public did not participate in that procedure, contrary to Article 6 of the Directive.

52   In that regard, Article 2(2) of the Directive provides: "The environmental impact assessment may be integrated into the existing procedures for consent to projects in the Member States, or, failing this, into other procedures or into procedures to be established to comply with the aims of [the] Directive." It is therefore clear from that provision that the Directive does not prevent the assessment procedure which it introduces from being incorporated in a national procedure which exists or is to be established, provided that the aims of the Directive are met.

53   However, where a project requires assessment within the meaning of the Directive, a Member State cannot, without undermining the Directive's objective, use an alternative procedure, even one incorporated in a national procedure which exists or is to be established, to exempt that project from the requirements laid down in Articles 3 and 5 to 10 of the Directive.

* * *

55   By its fourth question, the national court asks essentially whether Article 1(5) of the Directive is to be interpreted as also applying to a project, such as that at issue in the main proceedings, which, while provided for by a legislative provision setting out a programme, has received development consent under a separate administrative procedure and, if so, what requirements such a provision and the process under which it has been adopted must satisfy in order that the objectives of the Directive, including that of supplying information, can be regarded as achieved.

56   Article 1(5) provides that the Directive is not to apply "to projects the details of which are adopted by a specific act of national legislation, since the objectives of [the] Directive, including that of supplying information, are achieved through the legislative process".

57   That provision accordingly exempts projects envisaged by the Directive from the assessment procedure subject to two conditions. The first requires the details of the project to be adopted by a specific legislative act; under the second, the objectives of the Directive, including that of supplying information, must be achieved through the legislative process.

* * *

60   * * * If the specific legislative act by which a particular project is adopted, and therefore authorised, does not include the elements of the specific project which may be relevant to the assessment of its impact on the environment, the objectives of the Directive would be undermined, because a project could be granted consent without prior assessment of its environmental effects even though they might be significant.

61   That interpretation is borne out by the sixth recital in the preamble to the Directive, which states that development consent for public and private projects which are likely to have significant effects on the environment should be granted only after prior assessment of the likely significant environmental effects of those projects, and that this assessment must be conducted on the basis of the appropriate information supplied by the developer, which may be supplemented by the authorities and by the people who may be concerned by the project.

62   It follows that the details of a project cannot be considered to be adopted by a Law, for the purposes of Article 1(5) of the Directive, if the Law does not include the elements necessary to assess the environmental impact of the project but, on the contrary, requires a study to be carried out for that purpose, which must be drawn up subsequently, and if the adoption of other measures are needed in order for the developer to be entitled to proceed with the project.

* * *

68   By its sixth question, the national court is essentially asking whether Articles 4(2) and 2(1) of the Directive are to be interpreted as meaning that, where the discretion conferred by those provisions has been exceeded by the legislative or administrative authorities of a Member State, individuals may rely on those provisions before a court of that Member State against the national authorities and thus obtain from the latter the setting aside of the national rules or measures incompatible with those provisions.

In such a case, the national court is asking whether it is for the authorities of the Member State to take, according to their relevant powers, all the general or particular measures necessary to ensure that projects are examined in order to determine whether they are likely to have significant effects on the environment and, if so, to ensure that they are subject to an impact assessment.

[69] As regards the right of individuals to rely on a directive and of the national court to take it into consideration, the Court has already held that it would be incompatible with the binding effect conferred on directives by Article 189 of the EC Treaty (now Article 249 EC) for the possibility for those concerned to rely on the obligation which directives impose to be excluded in principle. Particularly where the Community authorities have, by directive, imposed on Member States the obligation to pursue a particular course of conduct, the effectiveness of such an act would be diminished if individuals were prevented from relying on it in legal proceedings and if national courts were prevented from taking it into consideration as a matter of Community law in determining whether the national legislature, in exercising its choice as to the form and methods for implementing the directive, had kept within the limits of its discretion set out in the directive.

[70] Consequently, if that discretion has been exceeded and the national provisions must therefore be set aside on that account, it is for the authorities of the Member State, according to their relevant powers, to take all the general or particular measures necessary to ensure that projects are examined in order to determine whether they are likely to have significant effects on the environment and, if so, to ensure that they are subject to an impact.

Notes and Questions

1. Do you agree with the Court's interpretation of the Directive? Has it effectively removed discretion that the Member States probably thought they had retained for themselves on adoption of the Directive? In particular, consider the two conditions imposed by the Court for the application of article 1(5)?

2. Does the Court give the Directive direct effect? What precise rights are given to individuals to invoke the Directive?

3. A further directive in this area is Directive 2001/42 on the Assessment of the Effects or Certain Plans and Programmes on the Environment, O.J. L 197/30 (July 21, 2001)(implementation deadline: July 21, 2004).

B. COMMUNITY ENVIRONMENTAL LEGISLATION AND ACTIVITIES

The Community's environmental activities range over a wide field. The following materials consist of a short summary of Community action in the environmental field, followed by descriptions of the fifth action program (1992–2000) and the new sixth action program (2001–2010).

EUROPEAN COMMISSION, ENVIRONMENT: CURRENT SITUATION & OUTLOOK

Commission Website, August 2001.[1]

Damage to the environment has been growing steadily worse in recent decades. Every year, some 2 billion tons of waste are produced in the Member States, while CO_2 emissions from our homes and vehicles are increasing, as is our consumption of "dirty" energy. The quality of life for people living in Europe, especially in urban areas, has declined considerably because of pollution, noise and vandalism.

Protection of the environment is therefore one of the major challenges facing Europe. The European Community has been strongly criticized for putting trade and economic development before environmental considerations. It is now recognized that the European model of development cannot be based on the depletion of natural resources and the deterioration of our environment.

Environmental action by the Community began in 1972 with four successive action programs, based on a vertical and sectoral approach to ecological problems. During this period, the Community adopted some 200 pieces of legislation, chiefly concerned with limiting pollution by introducing minimum standards, notably for waste management, water pollution and air pollution.

The introduction of this legislative framework, however, could not of itself prevent deterioration of the environment, and with the growth in public awareness of the risks posed by global environmental problems it has become clear that concerted action at European and international levels is absolutely essential.

Community action developed over the years until the [Maastricht] Treaty conferred on it the status of a policy. A further step was taken with the Treaty of Amsterdam, which enshrines the principle of sustainable development as one of the EC's aims.

To set about achieving this as effectively as possible, the Fifth Community Action Program on the Environment "Towards Sustainability" established the principles of a European strategy of voluntary action for the period 1992–2000 and marked the beginning of a "horizontal" Community approach which would take account of all the causes of pollution (industry, energy, tourism, transport, agriculture, etc.).

This across-the-board approach to environmental policy was confirmed by the Commission in the wake of its 1998 Communication on integrating the environment into EU policies and by the European Council in Vienna (1998). The Community institutions are now obliged to take account of environmental considerations in all their other policies.

Instruments. The range of environmental instruments has expanded as environmental policy has developed. Not only has the Community adopted framework legislation providing for a high level of environmental protection

---

1. http://www.europa.eu.int/scadplus/leg/ en/lvb/128066.htm, visited August 27, 2001.

while guaranteeing the operation of the internal market but it has introduced a financial instrument (the LIFE program) and technical instruments (eco-labeling, the Community system of environmental management and auditing, system for assessment of the effects of public and private projects on the environment).

The European Environment Agency [based in Copenhagen] has come to play an increasingly important role in recent years. It was set up to gather and disseminate comparable environmental data. Its role is purely advisory but its work has become more and more crucial for the adoption of new measures for assessing the impact of decisions already adopted (http://www.eea.eu.int/).

At present, emphasis is being placed on diversifying environmental instruments and, in particular, on introducing environmental taxes (the "polluter pays" principle), environmental accounting and voluntary agreements. No progress can be made unless environmental legislation is actually implemented, and effective implementation involves introducing incentives for economic operators (businesses and consumers).

Waste management. Community policy on waste management involves three complementary strategies: eliminating waste at source by improving product design; encouraging the recycling and re-use of waste; and reducing pollution caused by waste incineration. The Community's approach has been to assign more responsibility to the producer. For example, the 1997 draft directive on end-of-life vehicles provides for the introduction of a system of collecting such vehicles at the manufacturer's expense.

At the international level, this approach was also adopted at the first Conference of the Parties to the OSPAR Convention for the Protection of the Marine Environment of the North–East Atlantic. * * * The Parties * * * adopted the position supported by the European Commission that the dumping of such installations at sea should be banned and that the costs of dismantling and disposing of such installations should be borne by their owners.

The Community is a Party to the Convention on the Control of Transboundary Movements of hazardous Wastes and their Disposal (the Basle Convention), which has been signed by more than 100 countries. The Community has already ratified the amendment to this Convention, banning exports of hazardous wastes from OECD countries, the Community and Lichtenstein to non-OECD countries, regardless of whether such waste is for disposal, recycling or use.

Noise Pollution. The main thrust of Community strategy has long been to adopt maximum permissible levels for noise from certain types of machine (lawnmowers, motorcycles or, more recently, aircraft and equipment used on the outside of buildings). In its 1996 Green Paper, the Commission proposed extending this strategy by reducing noise emissions at source, developing exchanges of information and giving greater force and consistency to Community programs to combat noise.

Water Pollution. A number of directives have been adopted * * * to introduce water quality standards (drinking water, bathing water) and to monitor emissions of pollutants. The Community is a Party to various international conventions aimed at protecting the marine environment * * * and watercourses * * *. The current proposals for directives are aimed at further improving the ecological quality of surface water, at introducing Community action on fresh water and surface water, and at protecting Community estuaries, coastal waters and groundwater.

Air Pollution. Improving air quality is a world priority. To achieve a significant reduction in air pollution, which is the main cause of global warming, national and international efforts must be combined to reduce emissions of the gases responsible. To this end the United National Framework Convention (1992) and the Kyoto Protocol (1997) were adopted. The Parties have undertaken to reduce their emissions of greenhouse gases by at least 5% of their 1990 levels during the period 2008–2012. To achieve this, the Commission's strategy is to take action in all economic sectors which produce polluting gases, chiefly transport, energy, industry and agriculture. * * *

The Community is also a Party to the Geneva Convention on Long–Range Transboundary Air Pollution and to some of its Protocols. Community legislation is this field is principally aimed at cutting emissions from industrial activities and road vehicles. Where transport is concerned, the strategy is to reduce polluting emissions (catalytic converter, roadworthiness test); to reduce fuel consumption of private cars (in collaboration with car manufacturers); [and] to promote clean vehicles (tax incentives).

Nature Conservation. In Europe, some 1000 plant species and more than 150 species of birds are severely threatened or on the brink of extinction. To combat this situation, Community legislation has introduced a number of measures to conserve wildlife (protection of certain species such as birds and seals) and natural habitats (protection of woodlands and watercourses). The Community is a Party to a number of conventions, including the Bern Convention on the Conservation of European Wildlife and Natural Habitats and the Bonn Convention on Conservation of Migratory Species.

Natural and Technological Hazards. Modern societies are increasingly exposed to all kinds of hazards, whether natural, technological or environmental. To help prevent these risks and be prepared to handle emergency situations arising from them, the Community has adopted an action program on civil protection and a directive on the prevention of major industrial accidents. Where nuclear safety is concerned, the Commission has adopted a series of measures including directives on protection against radiation and an action plan for the management of radioactive waste. Technical cooperation to ensure safety of nuclear facilities has also been introduced.

* * *

International Cooperation. According to Article 174 (ex 130r) of the Treaty, one of the objectives of Community policy on the environment is to promote measures at the international level to deal with regional or worldwide environmental problems. Accordingly, under the Treaty, the Community may cooperate with third countries and the competent international organizations. Although this recognition dates back only to the [Maastricht] Treaty, the Community has been a Party to international conventions since the 1970s. At present the Community is a Party to more than 30 conventions and agreements on the environment and takes an active part in the negotiations leading to the adoption of these instruments, within the framework of its competence. * * *

Outlook. In its work program for 1999, the Commission identified environmental protection as one of the fundamental challenges facing the EU. It stated that growing industrialization, food hazards and the rapid degradation of the natural environment require a strategy of sustainable development, involving balanced resource management. As stressed by the European Council in Vienna, the only way that such a strategy can succeed is to make environment and sustainable development an integral part of all Community policies, as provided for by the Amsterdam Treaty. The European Council therefore called on the Council to finalize strategies to take fuller account of the environment in transport, energy and agriculture policy, to develop this side of its development, industrial and internal market policies and to put emphasis on cross-sectoral issues such as climate change and the environmental dimension of employment and enlargement.

National authorities and the general public have understood the importance of integrating the environment into all policies. The concept of sustainable development, originally perceived as a purely environmental matter, is now seen as the only viable social and economic model. Technological progress has enabled the development of new and better ways of protecting the environment which are not only economically viable and give added value to products but also help create jobs.

* * *

EUROPEAN COMMISSION, GLOBAL ASSESSMENT: EUROPE'S ENVIRONMENT: WHAT DIRECTIONS FOR THE FUTURE 9, 7 (2000)

The fifth environmental action program was prepared in parallel to the 1992 Rio Conference and the launch of Agenda 21. It constituted the Community's first commitment to sustainable development. It can be seen in terms of five objectives:

(1) strategies for seven environmental priority issues (climate change, acidification, biodiversity, water, urban environment, coastal zones and waste) and for the management of risks and accidents;

(2) target sectors into which environmental concerns should be integrated (industry, energy, transport, agriculture and tourism);

(3) broadening the range of new instruments;

(4) information, transparency of approach and development of the concept of shared responsibility;

(5) the international dimension reflecting global issues and the Rio Conference.

Some environmental targets were set, but in general there was a lack of quantifiable targets and monitoring mechanisms. The Commission, in the review of the plan in 1996, confirmed these priorities and proposed a new priority on implementation of existing measures.

* * *

This global assessment shows that the Community has made progress in putting into place new and improved instruments to protect the environment and ensure the safety and quality of life of European citizens. This includes better targeting of measures through scientific and economic studies and stakeholder dialogue as well as new market-based and financial instruments. Community policies have brought about, for example, a reduction in trans-boundary air pollution, a better water quality and the phase-out of ozone-depleting substances, and will lead to further improvements over the next few years. At the same time, the implementation of EC environmental law in the Member States is not as good as it should be and the Commission will have to continue exercising its powers in this respect.

Despite some improvements, however, the state of the environment overall remains a cause for concern and pressures on the environment are predicted to grow even further in some areas. * * *

* * * The outlook is that new environmental standards will not keep pace with the growing demand, for example, for transport, consumer goods or tourism. The perspectives are particularly bleak for climate change if trends in the main energy-consuming sectors cannot be reversed. At the same time, it is increasingly clear that damages to the environment have costs to society as a whole, and conversely that environmental action can generate benefits in the form of economic growth, employment and competitiveness.

* * *

The future of environmental policy has to be seen in this wider context, where environmental, social and economic objectives are pursued in a coordinated and mutually compatible way. * * *

However, without a reinforced integration of environmental concerns into economic sectors to address the origins of environmental problems and without a stronger involvement and commitment by citizens and stakeholders, our development will remain environmentally unsustainable overall despite new environmental measures. The current momentum for integration * * * needs to be maintained and translated into concrete decisions and new instruments to promote integration should be put in place. Better information and citizens' involvement in environmental decisions as well as more accountability for action which might harm the environment should be pursued as other priority objectives. The effective application of the "polluter pays" principle and the full internalization of environmental costs onto polluters remain a critical process. * * *

ENVIRONMENT 2010: OUR FUTURE, OUR CHOICE: THE SIXTH ENVIRONMENTAL ACTION PROGRAM OF THE EUROPEAN COMMUNITY 2001–2010

Commission Website, August 2001.[2]

[The Commissioner for the Environment, Margot Wallstrom, presented the Commission's proposed program for 2001–2010 in the following terms:]

The new Environment Action Program entitled *Environment 2010: Our Future, Our Choice* takes a wide-ranging approach to these challenges and gives a strategic direction to the Commission's environmental policy over the next decades, as the Community prepares to expand its boundaries.

The new program identifies four priority areas: climate change, nature and biodiversity, environment and health, and natural resources and waste.

To achieve improvements in these areas, the new Program sets out five approaches. These emphasize the need for more effective implementation and more innovative solutions. The Commission recognizes that a wider constituency must be addressed, including business who can only gain from a successful environmental policy. The Program seeks new and innovative instruments for meeting complex environmental challenges. Legislation is not abandoned, but a more effective use of legislation is sought together with a more participatory approach to policy making.

The five key approaches are to ensure the implementation of existing environmental legislation; integrate environmental concerns into all relevant policy areas; work closely with business and consumers to identify solutions; ensure better and more accessible information on the environment for citizens; and develop a more environmentally conscious attitude toward land use.

The new Program provides the environmental component of the Community's forthcoming strategy for sustainable development. It continues to pursue some of the targets from the Fifth Environment Action Program, which came to an end in 2000. But the new Sixth Environment Action Program * * * goes further, adopting a more strategic approach. It calls for the active involvement and accountability of all sections of society in the search for innovative, workable and sustainable solutions to the environmental problems we face.

Notes and Questions

1. The foregoing is a capsule overview of current and planned EC environmental legislation and activities. How would you characterize and explain the changes in priorities and approaches between the fifth and sixth action programs?

2. How would you compare Community activities in the environmental area with those of the US? While such a comparison is obviously difficult, in 1990 some differences were highlighted in D. Hackett & E. Lewis, European Economic Community Environmental Requirements, in P. Thieffry & G. Whitehead, eds., The European Economic Community: Products Liability Rules and Environmental

---

2. http://www.europa.eu.int/comm/environment/newprg/index.htm, visited August 27, 2001.

Policy 253–283 (Practicing L.Inst.1990). At the time, the authors noted that the EC has tended to follow US regulatory patterns, although as a general rule it appeared that there is less effective enforcement of environmental regulations in the EC than in the United States. This problem, which is due in part to the failure of Member States to implement directives in a timely manner and to lax enforcement activity by some Member States after implementation occurs, is well recognized in the EC and is discussed in the next section.

As to specific subjects, Hackett and Lewis concluded that the EC has regulated air pollution less comprehensively than the US Clean Air Act. On the other hand, they found that the EC's regulation of water generally paralleled the US Clean Water Act. With respect to hazardous waste, they found that the EC placed a much greater emphasis on waste prevention and reduction than did the United States. They also found that the control of waste disposal varied considerably by Member State, with Denmark, Germany and the Netherlands having the most comprehensive regulatory schemes.

It is interesting to speculate on causes of the differences in approach between the EC and the United States. For example, the emphasis on waste prevention may reflect the relative lack of disposal sites in Europe. What might explain other differences?

More recently, the EC has presented itself as much more environmentally concerned than the US, particularly in respect of control of genetically modified organisms and the international efforts to reduce greenhouse gas emissions pursuant to the Kyoto Protocol to the UN Framework Convention on Climate Change. As to the latter, after the US effectively declared the Kyoto Protocol to be unacceptable, the EC was instrumental at the Bonn Conference, July 16–27, 2001, in brokering a compromise among other participants that makes it more likely that the protocol will ultimately come into force.

3.   As noted above, one area in which the Community has been much more active than the US is in the area of waste management, particularly in requiring that packaging materials be recovered and recycled to a significant degree (European Parliament and Council Directive 94/62 of Dec. 20, 1994, on packaging and packaging waste, O.J. L 365/10 (Dec. 31, 1994)) and in requiring recycling of products at the end of their useful lives. The prime example of the latter is European Parliament and Council Directive 2000/53 of 18 September 2000 on end-of-life vehicles, O.J. L 269 (Oct. 21, 2000), which requires vehicle manufacturers to reduce the use of hazardous substances when designing vehicles; design and produce vehicles which facilitate recovery and recycling at the end of their lives; and increase the use of recycled materials in vehicle manufacture. Member States must set up collection systems for end-of-life vehicles and the last holder of an end-of-life vehicle will be able to dispose of it free of charge.

Another area of activity not common to the US is the Community's promotion of eco-labeling. See European Parliament and Council Regulation 1980/2000 of July 17, 2000 on a revised Community eco-label award scheme, O.J. L 237/1 (Sept. 21, 2000).

C.   MEMBER STATE REGULATION
OF THE ENVIRONMENT

A diversity of opinion among the Member States as to whether particular environmental measures are necessary is probably inevitable. This presents two problems. First, those that think the measures are too strict may fail to implement them in a timely matter. Second, those that believe that they are not strict enough may want to take action on their own in the environmental area.

1. MEMBER STATE IMPLEMENTATION OF COMMUNITY LEGIS-LATION

The problem of non-implementation of Community legislation by Member States is not unique to the environmental area. However, it has been a particular problem in that area. Many Member States do not have good records in faithfully implementing Community environmental legislation. This problem has led the Commission to consider how implementation might better be achieved. The problem of ensuring implementation of Community environmental rules was highlighted in a Commission communication to the Council and Parliament of October 22, 1996:

IMPLEMENTING COMMUNITY ENVIRONMENTAL LAW

PART I: INTRODUCTION

3.   Achieving the goal of a high level of environmental protection is only possible if our legal framework is being properly implemented. If the strong *acquis communautaire* on the environment is not properly complied with and equally enforced in all Member States, the Community's future environmental policies cannot be effective and its Treaty objectives cannot be fully and constantly met. The environment will either remain unprotected or the level of protection in different Member States and regions of the Community will be uneven and might, *inter alia*, lead to distortions of competition.

* * *

5.   Within this context, there are weaknesses in the current state of implementation of Community environmental law in most parts of the Community, and more action is needed in order to improve the situation. The Commission's own statistics on implementation show the following: In 1995, Member States had notified implementing measures for only 91% of the Community's environmental directives, leaving as many as 20 or 22 directives not transposed in some Member States. In the same year the Commission registered a total of 265 suspected breaches of Community environmental law, based on complaints from the public, Parliamentary questions and petitions and cases detected by the Commission: this is over 20% of all the infringements registered by the Commission in that year. In October 1996 over 600 environmental complaints and infringement cases were outstanding against Member States, with eighty five of the latter awaiting determination by the Court of Justice.

6.   The Commission's infringement procedures demonstrate the ways in which problems of implementation arise within the Community. Some legislation causes similar difficulties in most Member States: the Commission has had to begin "horizontal" actions against most Member States in relation to the notification of habitat sites under Directive 92/43/EEC and in relation to Directive 91/676/EEC on agricultural nitrates in water. Other infraction procedures show the variety of environmental problems within the Community: although waste disposal is a major concern to European Union citizens and

leads to many complaints to the Commission, in some Member States the main concern is illegal waste dumps while in others it is emissions from waste incinerators. Infraction proceedings also show the intractable nature of some environmental problems: many current cases relate to directives adopted in the 1970s: Directive 76/160/EEC on bathing water and Directive 76/464/EEC on dangerous substances in surface water are two examples where there are continuing problems of compliance in some Member States. * * *

* * *

10. The Commission, as guardian of the European Community Treaty, has the responsibility of ensuring that Community legislation is applied. It exercises this responsibility mainly through exercising the power to bring infringement proceedings against Member States under Article 169 [now 226] of the Treaty. This power is a very important and necessary tool for the Commission with respect to enforcement, as shown by the statistics on infringements given above. The Commission intends to continue to make full use of its enforcement powers based on Article 169.

* * *

12. However, it must be recognized that the procedure under Article 169 may be both lengthy and formal, and was not particularly designed with environmental law cases in mind. Because it operates on decisions and actions after they have been taken, even if Community law is applied as a result, it is not always the best way to prevent degradation or damage to the environment from taking place.

13. There are further fundamental problems with the use of Article 169 [now 226] and Article 171 [now 228] as the sole means of enforcing Community environmental law apart from the limitations mentioned above. Many environmental regulations and directives have to be applied on a daily basis by large numbers of people throughout the Member States. It would be neither possible nor practical for all the legal actions which could arise from these cases to be channeled through one enforcing authority, the Commission, and one court of law, the Court of Justice. In addition, Article 169 creates a Community "enforcement mechanism" which is directed only against the central governments of the Member States: the Commission is unable to oversee, on the ground, the application of individual decisions (either voluntary or binding) necessary to comply with Community legislation.

14. Nor is it possible for a single, Community wide, judicial enforcement system to take into account the legal and administrative structures at national, regional and local levels within the Member States through which Community environmental measures are applied. The use of such structures is essential to the incorporation of Community environmental law into national systems and to their practical application. Consequently, alternative methods of enforcement which can give full effect to these national and local conditions, which are vital to the proper protection of the environment, are required. * * *

15. Finally, there is a wide disparity in environmental inspection mechanisms among the Member States. Although the Commission, as the guardian of the Treaty, has the role of ensuring that Member States comply with Community environmental laws, there are no generally applicable Community

level mechanisms for the monitoring of the practical application of those laws within the Member States. Thus the Commission has only limited powers to monitor the correct application of Community environmental law. It is almost entirely dependent on information supplied to it on an ad hoc basis by complaints, by petitions to and written and oral questions from the European Parliament, by non-governmental organizations, by the media and by the Member States themselves. Although this information is very valuable to the Commission at the current stage, sole reliance on such ad hoc and unverifiable reporting systems and sources of information could have severely detrimental consequences for the environment in the longer term.

* * *

PART II: NEW AREAS FOR ACTION

* * *

25.   The Commission under Article 155 [now 211] has the duty to ensure timely and correct transposition by the Member States, by using political pressures and, if necessary, court action under Articles 169 and 171 [now 226 and 228] of the Treaty. It may also need to generally keep under review the practical application of the legislation and its enforcement in order to ensure that they are carried out in a satisfactory manner. However, this is a Community enforcement mechanism directed only towards Member State central governments. The Commission simply cannot monitor the thousands of individual decisions taken each year in accordance with the transposed or directly applicable environmental legislation, in the different parts and levels of authority within the Member States. The daily application and enforcement of those laws in specific cases must be fully ensured by the authorities in the Member States through mechanisms which will strengthen enforcement and, at the same time, ease the control of Member States by the Commission.

Member State inspection tasks

26.   Article 5 [now 10] of the Treaty, as interpreted by the Court of Justice * * *, binds Member States to make whatever provision for enforcement is effective, proportionate, and equivalent to that for Member State's national laws. This general principle of Community law, although fundamental, has resulted in a wide disparity in enforcement agencies or mechanisms among the Member States, with some putting considerable resources into well-supported inspectorates or other agencies which monitor the practical application of Community environmental law and other making lesser provision or none at all. Moreover, where provision is made, it is varied: inspection competencies are not always exercised by a single national body, but are often decentralized or shared among several layers of authority (local, regional, national, etc.). In a number of cases, environmental inspections form only a part of the responsibilities of the relevant competent authorities. In some Member States, such as Denmark or the UK, the competent authority, in addition to inspecting for compliance, also makes decisions on the grant of permits or bringing of court actions for enforcement, while in other Member States (such as the Netherlands) these tasks are separated.

27. This wide disparity cannot be considered as satisfactory with reference to the objective of correct and level enforcement at the Community level. The need exists to ensure that minimum inspections tasks are carried out, such as the process of monitoring whether the requirements of Community environmental laws, in particular those relating to industrial emissions and environmental quality standards, are in practice being applied. The need exists also to ensure that this is the case in all Member States.

* * *

Member State environmental complaints and investigation procedure

31. Court action to enforce Community environmental law within the Member States also has a number of disadvantages which prevent its being used effectively to protect the environment in such cases. Some of these problems arise in relation to issues of access to justice which are discussed in the next section. However, even apart from questions of access, there are inherent problems within legal systems, including e.g. costs and delays, which can make it unhelpful as a means for individuals to enforce Community environmental law: litigation should be the solution of last resort. A non-judicial complaint investigation procedure could have the advantage of avoiding these inherent problems: it could contribute to a quick and low cost settlement of an issue more accessible to the citizen without any need for legal assistance.

32. The advantages of considering environmental concerns at a local rather than Community level, coupled with the characteristics of speed, low cost and ease of use by citizens and environmental organizations, if applied across the Community, could lead to significant improvements in ensuring the proper implementation of Community environmental law. The Commission will therefore consider whether there is a need to establish minimum criteria for a procedural mechanism for handling environmental complaints and carrying out of investigations (a function which could also be similar to the functions of an ombudsman) in cases where problems arise in relation to the practical application and enforcement of Community environmental legislation by public authorities. These tasks could be carried out either within Member State's existing structures, or by the setting up of ad-hoc bodies.

* * *

Access to Justice

36. Judicial litigation is a last resort to solve problems. However, a Community based on the rule of law has to ensure that laws are respected and if necessary enforced. The role of the courts is crucial in that respect, especially for environmental matters where the source of a problem or damage is geographically confined but the effects may be widespread. Access to justice is, in general, sufficiently ensured if economic interests are at stake. Enforcement of legislation designed to create the framework for prosperous business, for instance in the industrial, commercial or agricultural sector, is likely to be encouraged by economic operators with sufficient resources to fight for enforcement. This is not necessarily the case for ecological interests. Economic operators do not perceive their role as being one of supervising other business' compliance with environmental legislation.

37.   Enforcement of environmental law, in contrast to other areas of Community law such as the internal market and competition, therefore mainly rests with public authorities, and is dependent on their powers, resources and goodwill. Their ability to take into account the need to protect the environment may be limited by any of these factors. It is therefore important that supplementary avenues for improving enforcement of Community environmental law are available. In particular, actions by non-governmental organizations and/or citizens in relation to the application and enforcement of environmental laws (in administrative, civil or criminal courts, as appropriate to the structures of the Member State concerned) would assist in the protection of the environment.

* * *

40.   Better access to courts for non-governmental organizations and individuals would have a number of helpful effects in relation to the implementation of Community environmental law. First, it will make it more likely that, where necessary, individual cases concerning problems of implementation of Community law are resolved in accordance with the requirements of Community law. Second, and probably more important, it will have a general effect of improving practical application and enforcement of Community environmental law, since potentially liable actors will tend to comply with its requirements in order to avoid the greater likelihood of litigation.

41.   Finally, access to Member States' courts would have the desirable effect of channeling litigation on the enforcement of Community environmental law to the most appropriate level, i.e. regional and national. * * *

42.   Restrictions on access to the courts arise in two main ways. Firstly, because legal procedures in the Member States create obstacles to the bringing of enforcement actions in relation to environmental law. For example, a special interest may have to be proven in order to bring a case. For reasons of legal history, such special interests are usually of a type which is easy for a property owner or economic operator to satisfy but less easy for environmental interest groups to satisfy. A further example is that appropriate court procedures may not exist to enable environmental interests to be protected: court procedures which are mainly designed to protect economic interests may not provide appropriate forms of action and remedies for environmental problems. Secondly, the cost of bringing enforcement actions in relation to environmental interests may be prohibitive.

* * *

Notes and Questions

1.   The problem of non-implementation is a particularly serious one in the environmental area, but it obviously arises in other areas as well. As a result, the Commission's thinking on this issue in the context of the environment may have broader general implications as well. We have studied a number of Court of Justice decisions that address in one way or another the problem of non-implementation and attempt to provide rules that mitigate the effects on citizens of non-implementation. The decisions include those on direct effect, damages for non-implementation (*Frankovich*), and judicial interpretation (*Marleasing*) that were examined in Part II. How would you assess the effectiveness of those decisions in promoting implementation of environmental directives?

2. How would you evaluate the effectiveness of the Commission's specific proposals in the foregoing excerpt? What other alternatives might be tried? In particular, would it be possible to include provisions in directives for pollution control that could effectively allow the Court to find private rights of action as it did in the *WWF* case?

3. In its 2000 annual report on application and monitoring of Community Environmental Law (SEC 2000 1219 (final) of July 13, 2000), the Commission noted that it had (i) presented a proposal for a Council Recommendation providing for minimum inspection criteria, (ii) completed a study on Member State approaches to extra-judicial mechanisms for settling disputes and on access to justice and (iii) promoted knowledge of Community environmental law, for example, by creating "green chairs" at European universities. In April 2001, Parliament and the Council adopted the recommendation of minimum inspection criteria. O.J. L 118/41 (Apr. 27, 2001).

4. In 1998, the Commission proposed (COM(98) 344 final) that the EC sign the so-called Aarhus Convention on Access to Information, Public Participation in Decision-making and Access to Justice in Environmental Matters. All of the Member States have signed the Convention, although as of mid–2001, only Denmark and Italy had ratified it. The Convention addresses some of the issues raised by the Commission in its report on implementation. In essence, it would require measures that would promote public participation in the making and enforcement of environmental laws. The text of the Convention is available at http://www.unece.org/env/pp/treatytext.htm.

2. MEMBER STATE ENVIRONMENTAL MEASURES

A second issue that arises in respect of Member States and the environment is the extent to which Member States may adopt their own environmental rules. As noted earlier, some provisions of the EC Treaty (e.g., Arts. 95, 176) allow Member States in certain circumstances to adopt stricter rules than contained in a Community directive. Beyond that, there is the question of how Member State legislation in the environmental area should be analyzed under general Community rules. In that regard the following two well-known cases are of particular importance.

COMMISSION v. DENMARK

(Beverage containers)
Case 302/86, [1988] ECR 4607.

[1] [T]he Commission of the European Communities brought an action under Article 169 [now 226] of the EEC Treaty for a declaration that by introducing and applying by Order No. 397 of 2 July 1981 a system under which all containers for beer and soft drinks must be returnable, the Kingdom of Denmark had failed to fulfil its obligations under Article 30 [now 28] of the EEC Treaty.

[2] The main feature of the system which the Commission challenges as incompatible with Community law is that manufacturers must market beer and soft drinks only in re-usable containers. The containers must be approved by the National Agency for the Protection of the Environment, which may refuse approval of new kinds of container, especially if it considers that a container is not technically suitable for a system for

returning containers or that the return system envisaged does not ensure that a sufficient proportion of containers are actually re-used or if a container of equal capacity, which is both available and suitable for the same use, has already been approved.

3   Order No. 95 of 16 March 1984 amended the aforementioned rules in such a way that, provided that a deposit-and-return system is established, non-approved containers, except for any form of metal container, may be used for quantities not exceeding 3000 hectolitres a year per producer and for drinks which are sold by foreign producers in order to test the market.

* * *

6   The first point which must be made in resolving this dispute is that, according to an established body of case-law of the Court, in the absence of common rules relating to the marketing of the products in question, obstacles to free movement within the Community resulting from disparities between the national laws must be accepted in so far as such rules, applicable to domestic and imported products without distinction, may be recognized as being necessary in order to satisfy mandatory requirements recognized by Community law. Such rules must also be proportionate to the aim in view. If a Member State has a choice between various measures for achieving the same aim, it should choose the means which least restricts the free movement of goods.

7   In the present case the Danish Government contends that the mandatory collection system for containers of beer and soft drinks applied in Denmark is justified by a mandatory requirement related to the protection of the environment.

8   The Court has already held in the *ADBHU* case that the protection of the environment is "one of the Community's essential objectives", which may as such justify certain limitations of the principle of the free movement of goods. That view is moreover confirmed by the Single European Act.

9   In view of the foregoing, it must therefore be stated that the protection of the environment is a mandatory requirement which may limit the application of Article 30 of the Treaty.

10   The Commission submits that the Danish rules are contrary to the principle of proportionality in so far as the aim of the protection of the environment may be achieved by means less restrictive of intra-Community trade.

11   In that regard, it must be pointed out that in [*ADBHU*] the Court stated that measures adopted to protect the environment must not "go beyond the inevitable restrictions which are justified by the pursuit of the objective of environmental protection".

12   It is therefore necessary to examine whether all the restrictions which the contested rules impose on the free movement of goods are necessary to achieve the objectives pursued by those rules.

13   First of all, as regards the obligation to establish a deposit-and-return system for empty containers, it must be observed that this requirement is an indispensable element of a system intended to ensure the re-use of containers and therefore appears necessary to achieve the aims pursued by

the contested rules. That being so, the restrictions which it imposes on the free movement of goods cannot be regarded as disproportionate.

14　Next, it is necessary to consider the requirement that producers and importers must use only containers approved by the National Agency for the Protection of the Environment.

15　The Danish Government stated in the proceedings before the Court that the present deposit-and-return system would not work if the number of approved containers were to exceed 30 or so, since the retailers taking part in the system would not be prepared to accept too many types of bottles owing to the higher handling costs and the need for more storage space. For that reason the Agency has hitherto followed the practice of ensuring that fresh approvals are normally accompanied by the withdrawal of existing approvals.

16　Even though there is some force in that argument, it must nevertheless be observed that under the system at present in force in Denmark the Danish authorities may refuse approval to a foreign producer even if he is prepared to ensure that returned containers are re-used.

17　In those circumstances, a foreign producer who still wished to sell his products in Denmark would be obliged to manufacture or purchase containers of a type already approved, which would involve substantial additional costs for that producer and therefore make the importation of his products into Denmark very difficult.

18　To overcome that obstacle the Danish Government altered its rules by the aforementioned Order No. 95 of 16 March 1984, which allows a producer to market up to 3000 hectolitres of beer and soft drinks a year in non-approved containers, provided that a deposit-and-return system is established.

19　The provision in Order No. 95 restricting the quantity of beer and soft drinks which may be marketed by a producer in non-approved containers to 3000 hectolitres a year is challenged by the Commission on the ground that it is unnecessary to achieve the objectives pursued by the system.

20　It is undoubtedly true that the existing system for returning approved containers ensures a maximum rate of re-use and therefore a very considerable degree of protection of the environment since empty containers can be returned to any retailer of beverages. Non-approved containers, on the other hand, can be returned only to the retailer who sold the beverages, since it is impossible to set up such a comprehensive system for those containers as well.

21　Nevertheless, the system for returning non-approved containers is capable of protecting the environment and, as far as imports are concerned, affects only limited quantities of beverages compared with the quantity of beverages consumed in Denmark owing to the restrictive effect which the requirement that containers should be returnable has on imports. In those circumstances, a restriction of the quantity of products which may be marketed by importers is disproportionate to the objective pursued.

22　It must therefore be held that by restricting, by Order No. 95 of 16 March 1984, the quantity of beer and soft drinks which may be marketed by a single producer in non-approved containers to 3000 hectolitres a year, the

Kingdom of Denmark has failed, as regards imports of those products from other Member States, to fulfil its obligations under Article 30 [now 28] of the EEC Treaty.

Notes and Questions

1. The extent to which Member States may justify measures restricting the free movement of goods on grounds of so-called "mandatory requirements" is dealt with more generally in Chapter 13(C) supra in such cases as *Cassis de Dijon*.

2. As noted earlier, the EC Treaty contains a number of provisions recognizing the right of a Member State to take unilateral action. See, e.g., Articles 95, 176. Does the Court's decision in *Beverage containers* suggest limits on the Member States' right to invoke these provisions? To what extent does Article 28, in particular, limit that right?

3. Article 174(4), as added by the Single European Act, essentially provided that the so-called principle of subsidiarity (see Chapter 4(D) supra) applied to the environmental area. This means that the Community should leave environmental issues to the Member States when they are better equipped to handle such matters at the national level than the Community is at the Community level. This principle was applied generally to Community legislation by the Maastricht Treaty (EC Treaty Art. 5 (ex 3b)). To what extent would application of this principle actually restrict Community competence in environmental matters? Do you think that a Member State would be able successfully to challenge Community action in the Court of Justice by claiming a breach of this principle?

4. Are you satisfied with thoroughness of the Court's analysis of the facts? How does it compare in your view to the approach that a US court would take? As to the substance, how would a law similar to the Danish bottle law be analyzed in the United States? In particular, could an argument be made that it violated the commerce clause? In Minnesota v. Clover Leaf Creamery Co., 449 U.S. 456, 101 S.Ct. 715, 66 L.Ed.2d 659 (1981), the US Supreme Court was faced with a Minnesota statute banning the retail sale of milk in plastic nonreturnable, nonrefillable containers, but permitting such sale in other nonreturnable, nonrefillable containers, such as paperboard milk cartons. The Court upheld the statute against challenges on equal protection and commerce clause grounds. In doing so it noted (449 U.S. at 471, 101 S.Ct. at 727):

> When legislating in areas of legitimate local concern, such as environmental protection and resource conservation, States are nonetheless limited by the Commerce Clause. If a state law purporting to promote environmental purposes is in reality "simple economic protectionism," we have applied a "virtually *per se* rule of invalidity." Philadelphia v. New Jersey, 437 U.S. 617, 624, 98 S.Ct. 2531, 2535, 57 L.Ed.2d 475 (1978). Even if a statute regulates "evenhandedly," and imposes only "incidental" burdens on interstate commerce, the courts must nevertheless strike it down if "the burden imposed on such commerce is clearly excessive in relation to the putative local benefits." Pike v. Bruce Church, Inc., 397 U.S. 137, 142, 90 S.Ct. 844, 847, 25 L.Ed.2d 174 (1970).

The Court concluded that the Minnesota statute was evenhanded and did not effect simple protectionism, even though the trial court had found that the "actual basis [for the statute] was to promote the economic interests of certain segments of the local dairy and pulpwood industries at the expense of the economic interest of other segments of the dairy industry and the plastics industry." 449 U.S. at 475, 101 S.Ct. at 729. In the Court's view, the burden on interstate commerce was "relatively minor" (449 U.S. at 472, 101 S.Ct. at 728) and the relatively greater burden on the out-of-state plastics industry compared to the Minnesota pulpwood industry was not "clearly excessive" (449 U.S. at 473, 101 S.Ct. at 729). How does this result compare with that in the *Beverage containers* case?

5. Automobile emission controls are one subject on which the Council has been particularly divided at times and action on this subject accordingly has sometimes been taken only after very lengthy debates. While debate continues, may a Member State adopt a tax incentive program encouraging the purchase of automobiles that meet a standard in excess of the existing Community standard? May it exempt such automobiles from driving bans during smog emergencies? Would such measures violate Article 28? See Written Question No 255/91, O.J. C 261/5 (Oct. 7, 1991).

COMMISSION v. BELGIUM

(Walloon waste)
Case C–2/90, [1992] ECR I–4431.

[At issue in the case was a Walloon Region regulation that prohibited the deposit in Wallonia of waste produced elsewhere. As to hazardous waste, the Court found that the regulation was inconsistent with a Community directive applicable to hazardous waste. As to nonhazardous waste, which was not subject to comprehensive Community regulation, the Court concluded that a ban on importation of such waste would violate Article 28 (ex 30), since it viewed waste as a product the movement of which could not be impeded under that Article. The Court noted, however, that since the accumulation of waste threatens the environment, measures that control it typically can be justified by public-interest objectives (referred to as "mandatory" or "imperative" requirements prior to *Keck*), such as environmental protection. While normally the excuse of a public-interest objective can be relied upon only where there is not discrimination between national and imported products, the Court viewed waste as a special case:]

30　With respect to the environment, it is important to note that waste is matter of a special kind. Accumulation of waste, even before it becomes a health hazard, constitutes a danger to the environment, regard being had in particular to the limited capacity of each region or locality for waste reception.

31　In the instant case the Belgian Government argued, without being contradicted by the Commission, that in view of the abnormal large-scale inflow of waste from other regions for tipping in Wallonia, there was a real danger to the environment, having regard to the limited capacity of that region.

32　It follows that the argument that the contested measures were justified by imperative requirements of environmental protection must be considered to be well founded.

33　The Commission argues, however, that those imperative requirements cannot be relied upon in the present case, given that the measures in question discriminate against waste originating in other Member States, which is no more harmful than waste produced in Wallonia.

[34]   Imperative requirements can indeed be taken into account only in the case of measures which apply without distinction to both domestic and imported products. However, in assessing whether or not the barrier in question is discriminatory, account must be taken of the particular nature of waste. The principle that environmental damage should as a matter of priority be remedied at source, laid down by Article 130r(2) [now 174(2)] of the Treaty as a basis for action by the Community relating to the environment, entails that it is for each region, municipality or other local authority to take appropriate steps to ensure that its own waste is collected, treated and disposed of; it must accordingly be disposed of as close as possible to the place where it is produced, in order to limit as far as possible the transport of waste.

[35]   Moreover, that principle is consistent with the principles of self-sufficiency and proximity set out in the Basel Convention of 22 March 1989 on the control of transboundary movements of hazardous wastes and their disposal, to which the Community is a signatory.

[36]   It follows that having regard to the differences between waste produced in different places and to the connection of the waste with its place of production, the contested measures cannot be regarded as discriminatory.

Notes and Questions

1. Do you accept the Court's conclusion that waste can be categorized by place of origin and that a ban on non-local waste is not discriminatory because such waste is a different good than local waste? Could such reasoning be expanded to find other differences in what appear to be like products in a way that would undermine Article 28?

2. It is interesting to compare this result with US cases. In Fort Gratiot Sanitary Landfill, Inc. v. Michigan Dept. of Natural Resources, 504 U.S. 353, 112 S.Ct. 2019, 119 L.Ed.2d 139 (1992); Chemical Waste Mgt., Inc. v. Hunt, 504 U.S. 334, 112 S.Ct. 2009, 119 L.Ed.2d 121 (1992) the US Supreme Court concluded that a ban or discrimination against out-of-state waste violated the Commerce Clause of the US Constitution. What fundamental difference is there between the EC Treaty and the US Constitution that helps explain why the US Supreme Court has reached a different result in these similar cases? Does the US Constitution need an environmental clause?

Chapter 35

CONSUMER PROTECTION

The impetus for a Community consumer protection policy, like that for the environment, came from the Paris summit of Community leaders in 1972. In 1975, the Council adopted a preliminary program for consumer protection. Since that time multi-year programs have been regularly adopted, most recently a Community Policy Action Plan for 1999–2001. In this chapter, we first review the evolution of the legal basis for Community action on consumer protection and then overview the Community's activities in this field. Thereafter, we examine three areas of Community activity: consumer advertising, unfair contract terms and products liability.

A. THE LEGAL BASIS FOR COMMUNITY CONSUMER PROTECTION ACTIVITIES

The EEC Treaty directed the Community to take the interests of consumers into account in certain aspects of the common agricultural policy (Article 33(1)(e), ex 39(1)(e)) and competition rules (Article 81(3), ex 85(3)). It did not initially contain any general provisions on consumers, with the result that Community consumer protection legislation was based on Article 94 (ex 100) on harmonization or Article 308 (ex 235) on general powers. Unlike the case of the environment, the Single European Act did not add a title on consumer protection. However, it added Article 95 (ex 100a) on completing the internal market, which offered an additional legal basis for consumer protection legislation, and more notably one governed by qualified majority voting. At the same time, paragraph 3 of that article required the Commission to take as a base "a high level of protection" in formulating proposals for completion of the internal market that deal with consumer protection.

The Maastricht Treaty added Article 3(t) (ex 3(s)), which formally made "the strengthening of consumer protection" a Community activity. Moreover, it inserted a new provision, what is now Article 153 of the EC Treaty. Article 153(1) initially set as a goal "a high level of consumer protection." In addition to measures adopted under Article 95 to achieve the internal market, it authorized the adoption of "specific action" in the field of consumer protection. It also provided that consumer protection measures taken in connection with the completion of the internal market under Article 95 were to be adopted pursuant to the parliamentary co-decision procedure. Article 153(3) was essentially identical to Article 176 on the environment in allowing Member States to take more stringent actions in the consumer protection field than taken by the Community. Thus, although many consumer interest measures had been adopted since the recognition of the importance of consumer protection in the early 1970s, the Maastricht Treaty amendments formally authorized legislative action and highlighted its importance.

The 1998 Amsterdam Treaty amended Article 153 to insert a new paragraph (1) that makes the goal of the article more precise and detailed: "protecting the health, safety and economic interests of consumers, as well as promoting their right to information, education and to organize themselves in order to safeguard their interests." The amendment also inserted a new second paragraph: "2. Consumer protection requirements shall be taken into account in defining and implementing other Community policies and activities." Thus, consumer protection, like environmental protection, is increasingly being given a privileged position in Community legislative and administrative action.

However, consumer protection does not necessarily always triumph over internal market considerations. In Germany v. Parliament and Council, Case C–233/94, [1997] ECR I–2405, one of the grounds for Germany's challenge to the Bank Deposit Guarantee Directive was that the directive's provisions constituted a compromise average level of consumer protection, rather than the high level sought by Article 153. In para. 48, the Court rejected this, declaring that:

> "although consumer protection is one of the objectives of the Community, it is clearly not the sole objective.* * * [T]he Directive aims to promote the right of establishment and the freedom to provide services in the banking sector. Admittedly, there must be a high level of consumer protection concomitantly with those freedoms; however, no provision of the Treaty obliges the Community legislature to adopt the highest level of protection which can be found in a particular Member State. The reduction in the level of protection which may thereby result in certain cases * * * does not call into question the general result which the Directive seeks to achieve, namely a considerable improvement in the protection of depositors within the Community."

In another case, the Court held that Article 153 did not justify changing the Court's general view that directives do not have the horizontal direct effect. El Corte Ingles, Case C–192/94, [1996] ECR I–1281.

B. OVERVIEW OF COMMUNITY CONSUMER PROTECTION ACTIVITIES

Against this background detailing the legal basis on which the Community is authorized to act to protect consumers, we now take a brief overview of Community activities in this field. We begin with an excerpt from the first basic statement of Community policy in this area, and then consider a concise, but comprehensive survey of Community consumer protection activity through the 1999–2001 action program.

PRELIMINARY PROGRAM OF THE EUROPEAN ECONOMIC COMMUNITY FOR A CONSUMER PROTECTION AND INFORMATION POLICY

O.J. C 92/2 (Apr. 25, 1975).

II.   OBJECTIVES OF COMMUNITY POLICY TOWARDS CONSUMERS

14.   Given the tasks assigned to the Community, it follows that all action taken has repercussions on the consumer. One of the Community's prime objectives, in general terms, is therefore to take full account of consumer interests in the various sectors of Community activity, and to satisfy their collective and individual needs. Thus there would seem to be a need to formulate a specific Community consumer information and protection policy. In relation to the other common policies, such a policy would take the form of a general guideline aimed at improving the position of consumers whatever the production, distribution or service sector in question. The aims of such a policy are to secure:

A.   effective protection against hazards to consumer health and safety,

B.   effective protection against damage to consumers' economic interests,

C.   adequate facilities for advice, help and redress,

D.   consumer information and education,

E.   consultation with and representation of consumers in the framing of decisions affecting their interests.

A.   *Protection of Consumer Health and Safety*

15.   Measures for achieving this objective should be based on the following principles:

(a)(i) Goods and services offered to consumers must be such that, under normal or foreseeable conditions of use, they present no risk to the health or safety of consumers. There should be quick and simple procedures for withdrawing them from the market in the event of their presenting such risks.

In general, consumers should be informed in an appropriate manner of any risk liable to result from a foreseeable use of goods and services, taking account of the nature of the goods and services and of the persons for whom they are intended.

(ii) The consumer must be protected against the consequences of physical injury caused by defective products and services supplied by manufacturers of goods and providers of services.

(iii) Substances or preparations which may form part of or be added to foodstuffs should be defined and their use regulated, for example by endeavoring to draw up in Community rules, clear and precise positive lists. Any processing which foodstuffs may undergo should also be defined and their use regulated where this is required to protect the consumer.

Foodstuffs should not be adulterated or contaminated by packaging or other materials with which they come into contact, by their environment, by the conditions in which they are transported or stored or by persons coming into contact with them, in such a way that they affect the health or safety of consumers or otherwise become unfit for consumption.

(iv) Machines, appliances and electrical and electronic equipment and any other category of goods which may prejudicially affect the health and safety of consumers either in themselves or by their use, should be covered by special rules and be subject to a procedure recognized or approved by the public authorities (such as type approval or declaration of conformity with harmonized standards or rules) to ensure that they are safe for use.

(v) Certain categories of new products which may prejudicially affect the health or safety of consumers should be made subject to special authorization procedures harmonized throughout the Community.

* * *

B. Protection of the Economic Interests of the Consumers

18. This kind of protection should be ensured by laws and regulations which are either harmonized at Community level or adopted directly at that level and are based on the principles set out below.

19. (a)(i) Purchasers of goods or services should be protected against the abuse of power by the seller, in particular against one-sided standard contracts, the unfair exclusion of essential rights in contracts, harsh conditions of credit, demands for payment for unsolicited goods and against high-pressure selling methods.

(ii) The consumer should be protected against damage to his economic interests caused by defective products or unsatisfactory services.

(iii) The presentation and promotion of goods and services, including financial services, should not be designed to mislead, either directly or indirectly, the person to whom they are offered or by whom they have been requested.

(iv) No form of advertising—visual or aural—should mislead the potential buyer of the product or service. An advertiser in any medium should be able to justify, by appropriate means, the validity of any claims he makes.

(v) All information provided on labels at the point of sale or in advertisements must be accurate.

(vi) The consumer is entitled to reliable after-sales service for consumer durables including the provision of spare parts required to carry out repairs.

(vii) The range of goods available to consumers should be such that as far as possible consumers are offered an adequate choice.

EUROPEAN COMMISSION, CONSUMERS:
INTRODUCTION

Commission Website August 2001.[1]

There are 370 million consumers in the EU today. The Member States have adopted policies designed to protect the specific interests of consumers, who play a key economic and political role in society. Investing them with a certain number of fundamental rights, the Member States have put in place policies designed to reduce inequalities, abolish unfair practices, promote safety and health, and improve living standards.

The methods used to guarantee these rights reflect the differences in legal systems, socio-cultural traditions, and institutional and political settings. Certain Member States have opted for a regulation-oriented approach and have created a full fledged administrative structure to address consumer problems. Others have chosen a more pragmatic approach, and allow markets and individual sectors a certain degree of self-regulation. Finally, while certain governments attach priority to food law, others have put the emphasis on trade designations or the supply of goods and services.

The diversity of rules and structures was the rationale underlying the development of a Community-level policy designed to ensure that consumers are confident enough to play an active role in the single market, while enjoying a high level of protection.

Consumer policy first emerged in the mid–1970s. The Treaty of Rome did not provide for such a policy and it was not until the Paris Summit in 1972 that the Heads of state and government first called for political action in this area. Shortly afterwards the Commission presented the first action program on consumer policy. This reference text cites five categories of fundamental rights which are the basis for Community legislation in this area, viz:

— the right to protection of health and safety;

— the right to protection of economic interests;

— the right to damages;

— the right to information and education;

— the right to representation.

This preliminary program stresses the transversal aspect of consumer policy, the objectives mentioned being integrated into specific Community policies, such as economic policy, the Community Agricultural Policy, environment, transport and energy policies, all of which affect consumers one way or the other. Other action programs followed and enshrined a certain number of fundamental rights and principles. Initially the Community legislated in the field of cosmetics safety, food labeling, misleading advertising and doorstep selling, but it was not until the Single European Act and the attendant perspective of the large market that consumer policy really took off.

* * *

1. (http://www.europa.eu.int/scadplus/leg/ en/lvb/132000.htm (visited August 8, 2001).

[As a result of the Single European Act], consumer policy became part and parcel of a more general policy of completing the Single Market—a perspective which has given it a new impetus. The abolition of frontiers and the completion of the Single Market on January 1, 1993 highlighted the existence of a market of more than 340 million consumers and the need for flanking rules. Moreover, consumer confidence was shown to be indispensable for the market to work properly.

The new action programs prioritized:

— consumer representation (the Consumers' Consultative Committee was adapted so as to make it more representative);

— consumer information;

— product safety;

— transactions.

During this period measures were taken in the following areas: toy safety and general product safety, cross-border payments, unfair contract terms, distance selling, and timeshares. Considerable progress was made during these years—with the result that we now have a genuine corpus of Community consumer protection law.

These positive trends were confirmed by the Maastricht Treaty, which enshrined consumer protection as a fully fledged Community policy. While the Treaty's general principles state that the Community must contribute to the "strengthening of consumer protection", Article 153 is the indispensable legal framework for consumer policy. Its adoption led to a new momentum as reflected in several Green Papers (financial services, consumer access to justice, food law, sale of consumer goods and associated guarantees) and legislative initiatives concerning injunctions, contracts negotiated at a distance, comparative advertising and cross-border transfers.

With a view to meeting the new challenges arising from globalization, the restructuring of public services, the emerging information society and developments in biotechnology, the Commission's priorities for 1996–1998 focused on three elements:

— financial services, essential public utility services and food products (measures have already been taken in respect of consumer credit, means of payment, foodstuffs legislation and consumer health);

— consumer education, aimed mainly at encouraging sustainable consumption behavior and facilitating access to the information society;

— assistance for the countries of Eastern Europe and developing countries in order to help them develop their own consumer-oriented policy.

However, owing to the BSE [Mad Cow] crisis, particular emphasis has been placed on health and food safety. The Commission has reorganized the departments concerned with consumer health and food safety * * *.

* * * These developments, designed to boost consumer confidence, were endorsed by the Luxembourg European Council (December 1997), which stressed that the production and supply of safe food must be one of the EU's policy priorities.

Without altering this approach, the Treaty of Amsterdam gives fresh impetus to consumer policy. * * *

This is the background against which the 1999–2001 action plan has been adopted, with three major fields of activity:

— consumer representation and education, entailing more systematic consultation, more effective dialogue between consumer associations and between consumers and business, appropriate information campaigns, expansion of the "Euroguichets" information and advice centers, and greater cooperation with the Member States as regards consumer education;

— consumer health and safety, based on the best possible scientific advice and on consistent analysis of risks, with legislation being adapted in such a way as to guarantee safer products and services and more effective response to emergencies;

— the economic interests of consumers, with steps being taken to ensure that the existing legislation is properly applied and is in tune with developments in products and services, with particular reference to financial services, and with consumers' economic interests being taken into account in other Community policies such as telecommunications, transport and the reform of the Common Agricultural Policy.

Notes and Questions

1. In light of the foregoing description of Community legislation, how successful would you say the Community has been in adopting legislation to achieve its objectives in respect of consumer protection, as excerpted above? How have the foci of its policies changed in recent years?

2. How can the Community be sure that its consumer protection program achieves the optimal level of protection? Suppose, for example, that you are a producer whose business is restricted by a directive, the scientific basis of which you believe is questionable, or a consumer who wants access to risky but useful products that are banned, or a consumer who would prefer to pay a lower price and accept an obligation (such as taking responsibility for use of a lost credit card). How can you challenge the Community action to which you object? Are you likely to succeed?

C. COMMUNITY CONSUMER ADVERTISING RULES

Regulation of advertising to protect a variety of consumer interests is manifestly one of the Community's major concerns. The keystone is Directive 84/450 on misleading advertising, which was amended in 1997 to cover comparative advertising as well.[2] The directive is found in the Selected Documents. Article 2(2) of the directive defines "misleading advertising" as "any advertising which in any way, including its presentation, deceives or is likely to deceive the persons to whom it is addressed or whom it reaches and which, by reason of its deceptive nature, is likely to affect their economic

---

2. Council Directive of 10 September 1994 concerning misleading and comparative adver-   tising, O.J. L 250/17 (Sept. 19, 1984), as amended, O.J. L 290 (Oct. 23, 1997).

behavior or which, for those reasons, injures or is likely to injure a competitor." The directive requires Member States to ensure that adequate and effective means exist for the control of misleading advertising, such as by empowering courts to order the cessation of misleading advertising. Courts must also be authorized to require in appropriate cases that an advertiser furnish evidence as to the accuracy of factual claims in its advertising.

"Comparative advertising" is defined as any advertising which explicitly or by implication identifies a competitor or goods or services offered by a competitor. The directive requires that comparative advertising be permitted if, inter alia, it is not misleading, objectively compares one or more material, relevant, verifiable and representative features of those goods or services (including price), does not create confusion between the advertiser and a competitor and does not discredit or denigrate the trade marks, trade names or other distinguishing signs of a competitor.

Two recent cases applying the Directive 84/450 provide an interesting contrast in approach.

COMPLAINT AGAINST X

Case C–373/90, [1992] ECR I–131.

[Richard–Nissan, the exclusive French distributor for Nissan vehicles, sued to enjoin press advertisements placed by X, a local car dealer in Bergerac, offering to sell Nissan cars originally bought in Belgium. The advertisements stated: "Buy your new vehicle cheaper" and indicated that the cars had a "One year manufacturer's guarantee." Richard–Nissan claimed that the advertisements were false and misleading, in violation of the French law intended to implement Directive 84/450.

Richard–Nissan argued that the imported cars had been registered in Belgium, so that, although never driven, they were not "new," that they could be sold below Nissan dealer prices only because the Belgian models had fewer accessories than those sold in France, and that X had no authorization to provide a manufacturer's warranty. The Court began by noting the importance of parallel importers:]

12 [T]hese aspects of the advertising are of great practical importance for the business of parallel car importers, and, as the Advocate General has pointed out, parallel imports enjoy a certain amount of protection in Community law because they encourage trade and help reinforce competition.

13 On the first point, concerning the claim that the cars in question are new, it should be noted that such advertising cannot be considered misleading within the meaning of Article 2 just because the cars were registered before importation.

14 It is when a car is first driven on the public highway, and not when it is registered, that it loses its character as a new car. Moreover, as the Commission has pointed out, registration before importation makes parallel import operations considerably easier.

15 It is for the national court, however, to ascertain in the circumstances of the particular case and bearing in mind the consumers to which the

advertising is addressed, whether the latter could be misleading in so far as, on the one hand, it seeks to conceal the fact that the cars advertised as new were registered before importation and, on the other hand, that fact would have deterred a significant number of consumers from making a purchase, had they known it.

16   On the second point, concerning the claim that the cars are cheaper, such a claim can only be held misleading if it is established that the decision to buy on the part of a significant number of consumers to whom the advertising in question is addressed was made in ignorance of the fact that the lower price of the vehicles was matched by a smaller number of accessories on the cars sold by the parallel importer.

17   Thirdly and finally, regarding the claim about the manufacturer's guarantee, it should be pointed out that such information cannot be regarded as misleading advertising if it is true.

18   It should be remembered in this respect that in Case 31/85 *ETA v DK Investment* [1985] ECR 3933 the Court held that a guarantee scheme under which a supplier of goods restricts the guarantee to customers of his exclusive distributor places the latter and the retailers to whom he sells in a privileged position as against parallel importers and distributors and must therefore be regarded as having the object or effect of restricting competition within the meaning of Article 85(1) of the Treaty (paragraph 14).

19   [T]herefore * * * Council Directive 84/450 of 10 September 1984 must be interpreted as meaning that it does not preclude vehicles from being advertised as new, less expensive and guaranteed by the manufacturer when the vehicles concerned are registered solely for the purpose of importation, have never been on the road, and are sold in a Member State at a price lower than that charged by dealers established in that Member State because they are equipped with fewer accessories.

KONSUMENTOMBUDSMANNEN v. DE AGOSTINI (SVENKSA) FORLAG

Cases C–34 to 36/95, [1997] ECR I–3843.

[Review case, which is set out in Chapter 17(B)(4) supra].

Notes and Questions

1.   Which two groups are intended to be protected by Directive 84/450? Do you agree that they both need protection? What sort of relief is required to be provided by Directive 84/450? Is it of more interest to consumers or competitors or both?

2.   In *X*, the trial court must still determine whether "a significant number of consumers" might be deceived by the advertisements in paras. 15–16. Do you think in fact that some consumers might consider it deceptive to call the imports cheaper if the lower price is due only to the absence of customary accessories? The thrust of the Court's judgment in *X* is certainly to apply leniently the directive to the advertisements of a parallel importer. Do you recall why parallel importers are favorably regarded from the prior coverage of the exhaustion doctrine in intellec-

tual property rights and the application of Article 81 to vertical distribution? Do you agree with the application of this policy in *X*?

3. We have already examined a number of advertising cases. How would you compare the result in the Swedish *Consumer Ombudsman* case that permitted Sweden to apply Directive 84/450's misleading advertising rules to television advertising rebroadcast from the UK, with the results finding advertising not to be misleading in *Clinique* and *Mars*, Chapter 13(C)(4) supra and in *Adolf Darbo*, Chapter 14(C)(1) supra? Should the Court in the Swedish case have noted a *caveat* that what is deemed "misleading" should not be too strictly defined under purely local rules, but must have a Community content to prevent undue interference with the internal market goal? For other judgments attempting to balance the internal market goal underlying harmonization directives on the labeling of foodstuffs and crystal glass with that of the legitimate protection of consumer interests, see *Meyhui* and *Piageme II*, Chapter 14(C)(2) supra.

4. Prior to a 1997 amendment to Directive 84/450, a number of Member States prohibited comparative advertising (advertising which explicitly or by implication identifies a competitor or goods or services offered by a competitor). To what extent does Directive 84/450 now require that comparative advertising be permitted? What are the limits on its use? Do those limits strike a fair balance between the interests of consumers and competitors?

5. Some laws, ostensibly for consumer protection, may not be in the consumer's economic interest. Certain advertising restrictions may prevent deception, but they may also make it difficult for new suppliers to break into a market, thereby stifling potential competition that might lead to lower prices. This side effect raises the question of whether Member State advertising rules might violate Article 28.

For example, at one time Luxembourg prohibited advertisements of temporary price reductions that (i) cited the difference between the old and temporary new prices or (ii) indicated that the new prices would be in effect for only a limited time. How could these rules be justified as consumer protection measures? Could they be challenged under Article 28? In GB–INNO–BM v. Confederation du Commerce Luxembourgeois, Case C–362/88, [1990] ECR I–683, the Court of Justice ruled that they were incompatible with Article 28:

[18] [U]nder Community law concerning consumer protection the provision of information to the consumer is considered one of the principal requirements. Thus Article 30 [now 28] cannot be interpreted as meaning that national legislation which denies the consumer access to certain kinds of information may be justified by mandatory requirements concerning consumer protection.

[19] In consequence, obstacles to intra-Community trade resulting from national rules of the type at issue in the main proceedings may not be justified by reasons relating to consumer protection. They thus fall under the prohibition laid down in Article 30 of the Treaty.

For further materials on the relationship of Article 28 and Member State consumer protection laws, see Chapter 13(C)(2) and the *Buet* case in Chapter 14(C)(4) supra. To what extent does the *Keck* case affect the continuing validity of these cases?

6. The Community has also been active in regulating advertising for public health purposes. See, e.g., Directive 89/622, mandating warning labels on tobacco products, O.J. L 359/1 (Dec. 8, 1989); Directive 92/28 on the advertising of

medicinal products, O.J. L 113/13 (Apr. 30, 1992). A directive that banned print and radio advertisements for tobacco products was annulled by the Court of Justice, see Chapter 5(D)(1) supra, but a replacement was proposed by the Commission in May 2001. COM (2001) 283 final (May 30, 2001).

7. The basic US federal law on misleading advertising is Section 43(a) of the Lanham Act, codified at 15 U.S.C.A. sec. 1125, which provides in relevant part:

Any person who * * * in commercial advertising or promotion, misrepresents the nature, characteristics, quality, or geographic origin of his or another person's goods, services, or commercial activities, shall be liable in a civil action by any person who believes that he or she is likely to be damaged by such act.

In Pizza Hut, Inc. v. Papa John's Intern., Inc., 227 F.3d 489 (5th Cir. 2000), the court noted that a prima facie case of false advertising under section 43(a) requires the plaintiff to establish: A false or misleading statement of fact about a product; such statement either deceived, or had the capacity to deceive a substantial segment of potential consumers; the deception is material, in that it is likely to influence the consumer's purchasing decision; and the plaintiff has been or is likely to be injured as a result of the statement at issue.

The Papa John's case involved (i) Papa John's four-word slogan "Better Ingredients. Better Pizza;" a series of ads touting taste test results comparing Papa John's and Pizza Hut's pizzas, based on which Papa John's claimed that it "won big time;" and a series of ads comparing specific ingredients used in its pizzas with those used by its "competitors" in which Papa John's touted the superiority of its sauce and its dough. Pizza Hut did not contest the truthfulness of the underlying factual assertions made by Papa John's, but argued that differences cited made no difference in pizza dough.

A jury found that the slogan and the "sauce and dough" claims were false or misleading and deceptive or likely to deceive consumers. The jury also determined that Papa John's "taste test" ads were not deceptive or likely to deceive consumers, and that Papa John's "ingredients claims" were not false or misleading. The District Court thereupon concluded:

When the "Better Ingredients. Better Pizza." slogan is considered in light of the entirety of Papa John's post-May 1997 advertising which violated provisions of the Lanham Act and in the context in which it was juxtaposed with the false and misleading statements contained in Papa John's print and broadcast media advertising, the slogan itself became tainted to the extent that its continued use should be enjoined.

The Court of Appeals reversed on the grounds that

(1) the slogan, standing alone, is not an objectifiable statement of fact upon which consumers would be justified in relying, and thus not actionable under section 43(a); and (2) while the slogan, when utilized in connection with some of the post-May 1997 comparative advertising—specifically, the sauce and dough campaigns—conveyed objectifiable and misleading facts, Pizza Hut has failed to adduce any evidence demonstrating that the facts conveyed by the slogan were material to the purchasing decisions of the consumers to which the slogan was directed.

Among the points made by the Court of Appeals were the following:

Under section 43(a) a plaintiff must demonstrate that the commercial advertisement or promotion is either literally false, or that [if the advertisement is not literally false,] it is likely to mislead and confuse consumers. If the statement is shown to be misleading, the plaintiff must also introduce evidence of the statement's impact on consumers, referred to as materiality.

Essential to any claim under section 43(a) is a determination of whether the challenged statement is one of fact—actionable under section 43(a)—or one of general opinion—not actionable under section 43(a). Bald assertions of superiority or general statements of opinion cannot form the basis of Lanham Act liability. Rather the statements at issue must be a specific and measurable claim, capable of being proved false or of being reasonably interpreted as a statement of objective fact.

One form of non-actionable statements of general opinion under section 43(a) has been referred to as "puffery." * * * A leading authority on unfair competition has defined "puffery" as an "exaggerated advertising, blustering, and boasting upon which no reasonable buyer would rely," or "a general claim of superiority over a comparative product that is so vague, it would be understood as a mere expression of opinion." 4 J. Thomas McCarthy, McCarthy on Trademark and Unfair Competition § 27.38 (4th ed.1996).

As noted, in the view of the Court of Appeals the slogan standing alone was a statement of non-actionable opinion. Nonetheless, when the slogan was viewed in the context of the misleading comparative "sauce and dough" ads, the court found:

> A reasonable consumer would understand the slogan, *when considered in the context of the comparison ads,* as conveying the following message: Papa John's uses "better ingredients," which produces a "better pizza" because Papa John's uses "fresh-pack" tomatoes, fresh dough, and filtered water. In short, Papa John's has given definition to the word "better." Thus, when the slogan is used in this context, it is no longer mere opinion, but rather takes on the characteristics of a statement of fact. When used in the context of the sauce and dough ads, the slogan is misleading for the same reasons we have earlier discussed in connection with the sauce and dough ads.

However, in the court's view, Pizza Hut had failed to adduce evidence establishing that the misleading statement of fact conveyed by the ads and the slogan was material to the consumers to which the slogan was directed. Since evidence of materiality is necessary to establish liability under the Lanham Act, the court found for Papa John's and reversed the district court.

Same result under the EC Directive?

D. PROTECTION OF ECONOMIC INTERESTS: UNFAIR CONTRACT TERMS

Undoubtedly the most important recent measure intended to protect the legal and economic interests of consumers is Directive 93/13, O.J. L 95/29 (Apr. 21, 1993), on Unfair Terms in Consumer Contracts, which is contained in the Selected Documents. This type of legislation began in Scandinavia in the 1960s and spread to most Member States, but varied considerably in scope. The directive covers only contracts between sellers or suppliers and consumers, not contracts between businessmen or professionals *inter se.*

The following recent cases shed light on the Court of Justice's approach to the interpretation of this directive and of consumer protection rules in general. We consider the specific provisions of the directive in the notes following the cases.

OCEANO GRUPO EDITORIAL SA
v. MURCIANO QUINTERO

Case C–240/98, [2000] ECR I—(June 27, 2000).

15 Between 4 May 1995 and 16 October 1996, each of the defendants in the main proceedings, all of whom are resident in Spain, entered into a contract for the purchase by installments of an encyclopedia for personal use. The plaintiffs in the main proceedings are the sellers of the encyclopedias.

16 The contracts contained a term conferring jurisdiction on the courts in Barcelona (Spain), a city in which none of the defendants in the main proceedings is domiciled but where the plaintiffs in those proceedings have their principal place of business.

17 The purchasers of the encyclopedias did not pay the sums due on the agreed dates, and, between 25 July and 19 December 1997, the sellers brought [summary procedures available only for actions involving limited amounts of money] in the Juzgado de Primera Instancia No 35 de Barcelona to obtain an order that the defendants in the main proceedings should pay the sums due.

18 Notice of the claims was not served on the defendants since the national court had doubts as to whether it had jurisdiction over the actions in question. The national court points out that on several occasions the Tribunal Supremo (Supreme Court) has held jurisdiction clauses of the kind at issue in these proceedings to be unfair. However, according to the court making the reference, the decisions of the national courts are inconsistent on the question of whether the court may, in proceedings concerning consumer protection, determine of its own motion whether an unfair term is void.

19 In those circumstances the Juzgado de Primera Instancia No 35 de Barcelona took the view that an interpretation of the Directive was necessary to enable it to reach a decision in the proceedings before it. It decided to stay the proceedings and to refer to the Court of Justice for a preliminary ruling the following question * * * :

> "Is the scope of the consumer protection provided by [the 'unfair contracts' directive] such that the national court may determine of its own motion whether a term of a contract is unfair when making its preliminary assessment as to whether a claim should be allowed to proceed before the ordinary courts?"

* * *

21 First, it should be noted that, where a term of the kind at issue in the main proceedings has been included in a contract concluded between a consumer and a seller or supplier within the meaning of the Directive without being individually negotiated, it satisfies all the criteria enabling it to be classed as unfair for the purposes of the Directive.

22   A term of this kind, the purpose of which is to confer jurisdiction in respect of all disputes arising under the contract on the court in the territorial jurisdiction of which the seller or supplier has his principal place of business, obliges the consumer to submit to the exclusive jurisdiction of a court which may be a long way from his domicile. This may make it difficult for him to enter an appearance. In the case of disputes concerning limited amounts of money, the costs relating to the consumer's entering an appearance could be a deterrent and cause him to forgo any legal remedy or defense. Such a term thus falls within the category of terms which have the object or effect of excluding or hindering the consumer's right to take legal action, a category referred to in subparagraph (q) of paragraph 1 of the Annex to the Directive.

23   By contrast, the term enables the seller or supplier to deal with all the litigation relating to his trade, business or profession in the court in the jurisdiction of which he has his principal place of business. This makes it easier for the seller or supplier to arrange to enter an appearance and makes it less onerous for him to do so.

24   It follows that where a jurisdiction clause is included, without being individually negotiated, in a contract between a consumer and a seller or supplier within the meaning of the Directive and where it confers exclusive jurisdiction on a court in the territorial jurisdiction of which the seller or supplier has his principal place of business, it must be regarded as unfair within the meaning of Article 3 of the Directive in so far as it causes, contrary to the requirement of good faith, a significant imbalance in the parties' rights and obligations arising under the contract, to the detriment of the consumer.

25   As to the question of whether a court seised of a dispute concerning a contract between a seller or supplier and a consumer may determine of its own motion whether a term of the contract is unfair, it should be noted that the system of protection introduced by the Directive is based on the idea that the consumer is in a weak position vis-a-vis the seller or supplier, as regards both his bargaining power and his level of knowledge. This leads to the consumer agreeing to terms drawn up in advance by the seller or supplier without being able to influence the content of the terms.

26   The aim of Article 6 of the Directive, which requires Member States to lay down that unfair terms are not binding on the consumer, would not be achieved if the consumer were himself obliged to raise the unfair nature of such terms. In disputes where the amounts involved are often limited, the lawyers' fees may be higher than the amount at stake, which may deter the consumer from contesting the application of an unfair term. While it is the case that, in a number of Member States, procedural rules enable individuals to defend themselves in such proceedings, there is a real risk that the consumer, particularly because of ignorance of the law, will not challenge the term pleaded against him on the grounds that it is unfair. It follows that effective protection of the consumer may be attained only if the national court acknowledges that it has power to evaluate terms of this kind of its own motion.

27   Moreover, as the Advocate General pointed out in paragraph 24 of his Opinion, the system of protection laid down by the Directive is based on

the notion that the imbalance between the consumer and the seller or supplier may only be corrected by positive action unconnected with the actual parties to the contract. That is why Article 7 of the Directive, paragraph 1 of which requires Member States to implement adequate and effective means to prevent the continued use of unfair terms, specifies in paragraph 2 that those means are to include allowing authorized consumer associations to take action in order to obtain a decision as to whether contractual terms drawn up for general use are unfair and, if need be, to have them prohibited, even if they have not been used in specific contracts.

[28] As the French Government has pointed out, it is hardly conceivable that, in a system requiring the implementation of specific group actions of a preventive nature intended to put a stop to unfair terms detrimental to consumers' interests, a court hearing a dispute on a specific contract containing an unfair term should not be able to set aside application of the relevant term solely because the consumer has not raised the fact that it is unfair. On the contrary, the court's power to determine of its own motion whether a term is unfair must be regarded as constituting a proper means both of achieving the result sought by Article 6 of the Directive, namely, preventing an individual consumer from being bound by an unfair term, and of contributing to achieving the aim of Article 7, since if the court undertakes such an examination, that may act as a deterrent and contribute to preventing unfair terms in contracts concluded between consumers and sellers or suppliers.

[29] It follows from the above that the protection provided for consumers by the Directive entails the national court being able to determine of its own motion whether a term of a contract before it is unfair when making its preliminary assessment as to whether a claim should be allowed to proceed before the national courts.

[30] As regards the position where a directive has not been transposed, it must be noted that it is settled case-law [citing Marleasing and Faccini Dori, see Chapter 7 supra] that, when applying national law, whether adopted before or after the directive, the national court called upon to interpret that law must do so, as far as possible, in the light of the wording and purpose of the directive so as to achieve the result pursued by the directive and thereby comply with the third paragraph of Article 189 of the EC Treaty (now the third paragraph of Article 249 EC).

[31] Since the court making the reference is seised of a case falling within the scope of the Directive and the facts giving rise to the case postdate the expiry of the period allowed for transposing the Directive, it therefore falls to that court, when it applies the provisions of national law * * *, to interpret them, as far as possible, in accordance with the Directive and in such a way that they are applied of the court's own motion.

[32] It is apparent from the above considerations that the national court is obliged, when it applies national law provisions predating or postdating the said Directive, to interpret those provisions, so far as possible, in the light of the wording and purpose of the Directive. The requirement for an interpretation in conformity with the Directive requires the national court,

in particular, to favor the interpretation that would allow it to decline of its own motion the jurisdiction conferred on it by virtue of an unfair term.

COMMISSION v. NETHERLANDS

Case C–144/99, 2001 ECR I—(May 10, 2001).

[In a response to an Article 226 action brought by the Commission against it for failure to implement the "unfair terms" directive, the Netherlands argued that Article 249 leaves the Member States entirely free to choose the form and methods necessary to transpose a directive into national law. In its view, specific implementing measures are not indispensable if the national legal system already secures the aims pursued by the directive. The Court of Justice responded:]

17   It should be borne in mind, in that connection, that, according to settled case-law, whilst legislative action on the part of each Member State is not necessarily required in order to implement a directive, it is essential for national law to guarantee that the national authorities will effectively apply the directive in full, that the legal position under national law should be sufficiently precise and clear and that individuals are made fully aware of their rights and, where appropriate, may rely on them before the national courts.

18   As the Court has already made clear, the last-mentioned condition is of particular importance where the directive in question is intended to accord rights to nationals of other Member States. That is the position in the present case, it being one of the aims of the Directive, according to the sixth recital in its preamble, "to safeguard the citizen in his role as consumer when acquiring goods and services under contracts which are governed by the laws of Member States other than his own."

19   However, for the reasons given by the Advocate General in points 25 and 26 of his Opinion, it appears that the Kingdom of the Netherlands has been unable to show that its legal system contains provisions equivalent to Articles 4(2) and 5 of the Directive.

20   Given that the Netherlands Government has stated that the aims sought by the Directive could be attained through a schematic interpretation of the provisions of Netherlands law, it is enough to point out that, for the reasons set out by the Advocate General in points 26 to 31 of his Opinion, the results intended by the Directive cannot be attained by applying Netherlands law as it stands at present.

21   As regards the argument advanced by the Netherlands Government that, if the Netherlands legislation were interpreted in such a way as to ensure conformity with the Directive—a principle endorsed by the Hoge Raad der Nederlanden—it would be possible in any event to remedy any disparity between the provisions of Netherlands legislation and those of the Directive, suffice it to note that * * * even where the settled case-law of a Member State interprets the provisions of national law in a manner deemed to satisfy the requirements of a directive, that cannot achieve the clarity and precision needed to meet the requirement of legal certainty. That, moreover, is particularly true in the field of consumer protection.

Notes and Questions

1. In US law, probably the most important provision on unfair consumer terms is section 2–302 of the Uniform Commercial Code, which provides:

> "If the court as a matter of law finds the contract or any clause of the contract to have been unconscionable at the time it was made the court may refuse to enforce the contract, or it may enforce the remainder of the contract without the unconscionable clause, or it may limit the application of any unconscionable clause as to avoid any unconscionable result."

The Code does not define "unconscionable", rather it is left to the court (not a jury). The comments to Section 2–302 state that "the basic test is whether, in light of the general commercial background and the commercial needs of the particular trade or case, the clauses involved are so one-sided as to be unconscionable under the circumstances existing at the time of the making of the contract."

A leading treatise on contracts notes that courts have tended to focus on the absence of meaningful choice (procedural unconscionability, which may include questionable bargaining practices and difficult-to-understand or -read language) and unreasonably favorable terms (substantive unconscionability). E. Allan Farnsworth, Contracts 311 (3rd ed.1999). According to Farnsworth, judges have been "cautious" in finding unconscionability. Id. at 312.

2. Directive 93/13 is contained in the Selected Documents and merits close reading. How is it similar in approach to Section 2–302? How does it differ? Which is the better approach? Which is more likely to lead to a voiding of a contract term?

3. To the extent that the provisions of Directive 93/13 go beyond the usual consumer protection afforded by the UCC and case law interpreting "contracts of adhesion" in the US, can the directive's terms be avoided by subjecting a contract with an EC consumer to the law of a US state?

4. Article 3 defines an unfair contract term as one creating "a significant imbalance in the parties' rights and obligations ... to the detriment of the consumer," if contained in a "pre-formulated standard contract" or one otherwise not "individually negotiated." Is that definition sufficiently precise? Consider the Annex's "non-exhaustive" list of unfair terms. Are some fairly common in US standard form contracts? What about (e), (f), (n) and (q)? Do you think the directive represents a policy approach that is desirable, or does it interfere too much with the marketplace? Article 5 also requires that consumer contracts be "drafted in plain, intelligible language," with any ambiguity construed in favor of the consumer.

5. Under article 6, unfair contract terms are not binding, but the contract itself may survive, if appropriate after the severance of the illegal terms. How would that decision be made?

6. Could a corporation rely on Directive 93/13? In Cape Snc v. Idealservice Srl, Case C–541/99, [2001] ECR I-—(Nov. 22, 2001), the Court concluded that "consumer" as used in the directive refers solely to natural persons.

7. In 2000, the Commission issued a report on the implementation of the unfair terms directive (COM (2000) 248 final, April 27, 2000). It has useful information on the experience to date in the Member States in respect of the operation of the directive.

8. Another important recent directive protecting consumer economic interests is that on distance sales, O.J. L 144/19 (June 4, 1997), which governs all

product or service sales by mail, telephone, television, computer, fax, etc., with the exception of financial services. The directive requires precise indication of the contract terms and a right of withdrawal without penalty within seven working days after the contract is entered into. (Note that the Dutch rules protecting purchasers of commodities in "cold calling" telephone sales are analyzed in *Alpine Investments*, Chapter 32(C)(1) infra.)

9. Directive 94/47 on rights to use immovable properties on a time-share basis, O.J. L 280/83 (Oct. 29, 1994), protects persons who buy long-term interests enabling the use of realty for stated periods each year, an arrangement particularly popular in the resorts in the Mediterranean States. After the Commission pledged itself in 1992 to a review of draft directives in order to apply the principle of subsidiarity, the Commission proposed to withdraw this draft. However, objections from Parliament saved the time-share proposal, and the draft received rather expeditious treatment in the Council, where the UK strongly supported it.

10. Directive 99/44 on sale of consumer goods and associated guarantees, O.J. L 171/12 (July 7, 1999), would harmonize Member State rules on those subjects. The basic obligation to be imposed is that the seller must deliver goods conforming to the contract of sale. In the event of nonconformity being discovered within two years, the consumer would be entitled, subject to certain limits, to have the goods brought into conformity free-of-charge through repair or replacement, or to have an appropriate price adjustment, or to have the contract rescinded.

11. Dillenkofer v. Germany, Cases 178/94 et seq., [1996] ECR I–4845, involved the interpretation of Directive 90/314 on package travel, package holiday and package tours, O.J. L 158/59 (June 23, 1990). Article 7 of the directive requires the organizer of such package holiday arrangements to "provide sufficient evidence of security for the refund of money paid over and for the repatriation of the consumer in the event of insolvency." Germany, the Netherlands and the UK argued that this article's purpose was to create a level competitive playing field for package holiday providers, in view of the directive's use of Article 100a as its legal basis. The Court rejected this view, concluding that recitals to the directive demonstrated that it was also intended to protect consumer interests, while article 7 was clearly intended to provide a financial security to consumers in the event of the insolvency of the organizer. This conclusion was essential in order to enable the trial court to find Germany liable in damages to the consumers injured by Germany's failure to implement Directive 90/314 in time.

12. At issue in Faccini Dori v. Recreb Srl, Case C–91/92, [1994] ECR I–3325, was Directive 85/577 concerning protection of consumers in respect of contracts negotiated away from business premises, which was to have been implemented by December 27, 1987. Italy did not implement the directive until 1992. Among other provisions, the directive specified that consumers must be given a notice of their right to cancel such a contract for a period of seven days after receiving the notice. In this case, which is noted in Chapter 10(B) supra, the Court, without being asked, noted that Member State courts have an obligation to achieve the results envisaged by a directive as far as possible through their interpretation of Member State law and that if the result prescribed by a directive can not be achieved by interpretation, it should be borne in mind that *Francovich* (see Chapter 10(B) supra) requires Member States to make good damage caused to individuals through failure to transpose a directive, provided that certain conditions are fulfilled. It went on to suggest that the conditions may have been fulfilled in this case. How does the Court's opinion affect the likelihood that Italy will escape

liability? that consumer protection directives will be more conscientiously implemented by Member States? See generally W. Robinson, Casenote, 32 Common Mkt. L. Rev. 629 (1995).

13. Directive 98/27 on injunctions to protect consumers' interests, O.J. L 166/51 (June 11, 1998), as amended, requires Member States to ensure that injunctive relief is available expeditiously in the enforcement of rules implementing eleven named consumer rights directives. Public and private bodies organized to protect consumer interests, when authorized by States, would have the power to seek such injunctions. The eleven directives include those mentioned earlier in this chapter dealing with misleading advertising, medicinal products advertising, unfair contract terms, timeshares, distance sales, package travel, guarantees and off-premises contracts.

E. THE PRODUCTS LIABILITY DIRECTIVE

The Community first considered the need for a directive on products liability in the 1970s, but because of the disagreement over what it should provide, final agreement on a text could not be reached until 1985.[3] The directive is reproduced in the Selected Documents and should be read at this point.

The directive's basic provision is article 1, which states: "the producer [which is defined to include an importer] shall be liable for damage caused by a defect in his product." However, "the injured person shall be required to prove the damage, the defect and the causal relationship between the defect and the damage" (art. 4).

The directive provides in article 6 that a product is defective when it does not provide the safety that a person is entitled to expect, taking all circumstances into account, including the use to which the product could reasonably be expected to be put. The producer's defenses are listed in article 7. The main defenses are that the defect did not exist when the product was put into circulation or that the state of scientific and technical knowledge at the time when the product was put into circulation was not such as to enable the existence of the defect to be discovered (the "state of the art" or "developmental risk" defense). Whether or not to grant this last defense was one of the most controversial issues in the formulation of the directive. Article 15 provides that a Member State can choose to eliminate this defense and requires the Commission to report in 1995 on the effect of the defense and the Council to consider whether to repeal it.

The directive also allows a Member State to put a cap on damages of not less than 70 million ECU for a producer's liability caused by identical items with the same defect (art. 16).

The scope of the directive was expanded in 1999 to primary agricultural products and game products.

According to a 1999 Commission Green Paper on Liability for defective products (COM (1999) 396 final, July 28, 1999), all the Member States except Finland and Luxembourg retained the developmental risk defense option

3. Council Directive 85/374 of July 25, 1985 on the approximation of the laws, regulations and administrative provisions of the Member States concerning liability for defective products, O.J. L 210/29 (Aug. 7, 1985).

(with an exception for food and medicinal products in Spain and products derived from the human body in France). Damage caps have been set only by Germany, Portugal and Spain.

COMMISSION v. UNITED KINGDOM

(Product liability directive)
Case C–300/95, [1997] ECR I–2649.

[The UK Consumer Protection Act 1987 provides in section 4 that a producer can avoid liability if he establishes

> that the state of scientific and technical knowledge at the relevant time was not such that a producer of products of the same description as the product in question might be expected to have discovered the defect if it had existed in his products while they were under his control.

The Commission contended that this provision deviated significantly from article 7(e) of the Product Liability Directive by substituting "a subjective assessment based on the behavior of a reasonable producer" for the "objective" test of article 7(e). The UK replied that its version was intended also to be objective, and that in any event section 1 of the 1987 Act required it to be construed in accord with the directive.]

24   In order for a producer to incur liability for defective products under Article 4 of the Directive, the victim must prove the damage, the defect and the causal relationship between defect and damage, but not that the producer was at fault. However, in accordance with the principle of fair apportionment of risk between the injured person and the producer set forth in the seventh recital in the preamble to the Directive, Article 7 provides that the producer has a defense if he can prove certain facts exonerating him from liability, including "that the state of scientific and technical knowledge at the time when he put the product into circulation was not such as to enable the existence of the defect to be discovered" (Article 7(e)).

25   Certain general observations can be made as to the wording of Article 7(e) of the Directive.

26   First, as the Advocate General rightly observes in paragraph 20 of his Opinion, since that provision refers to "scientific and technical knowledge at the time when [the producer] put the product into circulation", Article 7(e) is not specifically directed at the practices and safety standards in use in the industrial sector in which the producer is operating, but, unreservedly, at the state of scientific and technical knowledge, including the most advanced level of such knowledge, at the time when the product in question was put into circulation.

27   Second, the clause providing for the defense in question does not contemplate the state of knowledge of which the producer in question actually or subjectively was or could have been apprised, but the objective state of scientific and technical knowledge of which the producer is presumed to have been informed.

28   However, it is implicit in the wording of Article 7(e) that the relevant scientific and technical knowledge must have been accessible at the time when the product in question was put into circulation.

29   It follows that, in order to have a defense under Article 7(e) of the Directive, the producer of a defective product must prove that the objective state of scientific and technical knowledge, including the most advanced level of such knowledge, at the time when the product in question was put into circulation was not such as to enable the existence of the defect to be discovered. Further, in order for the relevant scientific and technical knowledge to be successfully pleaded against the producer, that knowledge must have been accessible at the time when the product in question was put into circulation. On this last point, contrary to what the Commission seems to consider, Article 7(e) of the Directive raises difficulties of interpretation which, in the event of litigation, the national courts will have to resolve having recourse, if necessary, to Article 177 of the EC Treaty.

* * *

37   [Finally,] the Court has consistently held that the scope of national laws, regulations or administrative provisions must be assessed in the light of the interpretation given to them by national courts (see, in particular, Case C–382/92 *Commission v. United Kingdom* [1994] ECR I–2435, paragraph 36). Yet in this case the Commission has not referred in support of its application to any national judicial decision which, in its view, interprets the domestic provision at issue inconsistently with the Directive.

38   Lastly, there is nothing in the material produced to the Court to suggest that the courts in the United Kingdom, if called upon to interpret section 4(1)(e), would not do so in the light of the wording and the purpose of the Directive so as to achieve the result which it has in view and thereby comply with the third paragraph of Article 189 of the Treaty (see, in particular, Case C–91/92 *Faccini Dori v. Recreb* [1994] ECR I–3325, paragraph 26). Moreover, section 1(1) of the Act expressly imposes such an obligation on the national courts.

39   It follows that the Commission has failed to make out its allegation that, having regard to its general legal context and especially section 1(1) of the Act, section 4(1)(e) clearly conflicts with Article 7(e) of the Directive. As a result, the application must be dismissed.

Notes and Questions

1. A number of questions can be raised about the directive. In answering them, the student should consider how the same question would be answered in the United States?

   (a) Does the plaintiff have to prove the producer was at fault?

   (b) How does the plaintiff establish that a product was defective? Is the test objective or subjective?

   (c) What if the plaintiff has used a product in an unexpected way?

   (d) What kind of damages may be recovered? May the plaintiff recover for pain and suffering?

   (e) May a producer avoid liability by including an exculpatory clause in its sales contract?

   (f) What is the statute of limitations under the directive?

For reference, in 1997, the Restatement of the Law Third: Torts–Products Liability was adopted by the American Law Institute. Among its key provisions are[4]

Sec. 1–One engaged in the business of selling or otherwise distributing products who sells or distributes a defective product is subject to liability for harm to persons or property caused by the defect.

Sec. 2–A product is defective when, at the time of sale or distribution, it contains a manufacturing defect, is defective in design, or is defective because of inadequate instructions or warnings. A product:

(a) contains a manufacturing defect when the product departs from its intended design even though all possible care was exercised in the preparation and marketing of the product;

(b) is defective by design when the foreseeable risks of harm posed by the product could have been reduced or avoided by the adoption of a reasonable alternative design by the seller or other distributor, or a predecessor in the commercial chain of distribution, and the omission of the alternative design renders the product not reasonably safe;

(c) is defective because of inadequate instructions or warnings when the foreseeable risks of harm posed by the product could have been reduced or avoided by the provision of reasonable instructions by the seller or other distributor, or a predecessor in the commercial chain of distribution, and the omission of the instructions or warnings renders the product not reasonably safe.

Sec. 15–Whether a product defect caused harm to persons or property is determined by the prevailing rules and principles governing causation in tort.

Sec. 21–For purposes of this Restatement, harm to persons or property includes economic loss if caused by harm to:

(a) the plaintiff's person; or

(b) the person of another when harm to the other interferes with an interest of the plaintiff person protected by tort law; or

(c) the plaintiff's property other than the defective product.

2. To what extent might differences among the Member States' implementing legislation (e.g., different defenses, different damage caps, different rules on recoverable damages) impair the directive's harmonizing effect? To what extent might they create a problem of forum shopping?

3. Can the prospect of liability for defective products justify behavior that would otherwise violate Community law? For example, could a maker of nail guns justify certain anticompetitive actions on the grounds that its competitors' nails were not compatible with its nail guns and inferior to its own nails, such that it had to discourage their use to avoid potential liability for defective products? See Hilti AG v. Commission, Case T–30/89, [1991] ECR II–1439.

4. Despite the adoption and implementation of the products liability directive by the Member States, products liability litigation remained relatively uncommon in Europe as of the beginning of the 1990s. Among the reasons cited for the directive's limited effect were "[t]he absence in Europe of an entrepreneu-

rial plaintiff's bar, the presence of substantial court user fees and cost-shifting rules, the unavailability of juries and general limits on damages." R. Weber, E.C. Directive Follows U.S. No–Fault Approach, But Litigation is Rare, Nat'l L.J., Dec. 23, 1991, at 30–31.

After gathering information pursuant to its above-mentioned 1999 Green Paper, the Commission concluded in 2001 that the impact of the directive has continued to be limited. Among the reasons it cited were belated implementation by Member States and the possibility given to Member States to apply national law. Given the lack of adequate data, the Commission decided not to propose any amendments to the directive, although it is planning to gather additional information in the future. See Report from the Commission of 31 January 2001 on the application of Directive 85/374 on liability for defective products, COM (2000) 893 final.

In 2000, the Commission brought Article 226 actions for failure to implement the directive in certain respects against France (Case C–52/00) and Greece (Case 154/00). The cases were still pending before the Court of Justice as of August 2001.

5. The Commission once issued a proposal for a directive imposing liability on suppliers of services.[5] However, it withdrew its proposal, both because of objections to the text from several States on grounds of subsidiarity, and because of vehement opposition from organized commercial, financial and professional groups.

6. In 1992, the Council adopted a directive on product safety that covers products not covered by specific directives.[6] The general rule is that suppliers may place only safe products on the market (art. 3(1)), a safe product being defined as one that during its normal or reasonably foreseeable conditions of use does not present any risk, or only minimal risks considered to be acceptable and consistent with a high standard of protection for the safety and health of persons. In assessing the acceptability of risk, consideration is to be given to the product's intended or reasonably foreseeable use, in light of the labeling, instructions, etc. provided (art. 2(b)). If a product is not risk free, the supplier must give the user sufficient information to assess the risks and to monitor the safety of the product.

Under the directive, which applies only when there is no specific Community rules governing the safety of a product, suppliers are deemed to meet the general safety requirement if they meet specific Member State safety requirements (art. 4(1)). In the absence of a more specific rule, safety is to be assessed by reference to voluntary standards and good practice codes, the state of the art and technology, as well as to the safety that users or consumers may reasonably expect (art. 4(2)).

The directive requires Member States to establish authorities to monitor compliance with safety standards. These authorities would also be responsible for collecting information and investigating complaints about the safety of products. The directive also requires that they have the power to impose sanctions for violations, including the power to ban products from the market, but it does not require that consumers be given a damage remedy for unsafe products.

How does the product safety directive, as described here, compare with the products liability directive. Is the coverage of the two directives—unsafe products vs. defective products—the same? How does it differ? How do the remedies for an

---

5. O.J. C 12/8 (Jan. 18, 1991).   **6.** Council Directive 92/59, O.J. L 228/24 (Aug. 11, 1992).

injured consumer compare? How would you expect laws based on the two directives to be coordinated?

In 1993, the Council adopted a decision requiring the Member States to set up mechanisms for the exchange of information concerning product safety. Council Decision of Oct. 25, 1993, O.J. L 278/64 (Nov. 11, 1993).

In 2000, the Commission proposed a revision of the product safety directive so as to clarify its coverage, require market surveillance by national authorities to be more active and effective and simplify rules for removing dangerous products from the market. The proposal would also prohibit the export to third countries of products banned in the EC. COM (2000) 139 final/2 (June 15, 2000). As of July 2001, the proposal had not been adopted, although the Commission had amended the proposal once and had expressed views on changes proposed by Parliament.

7. Article 9 of the product safety directive authorizes the Commission in certain circumstances to require Member States to take temporary action in respect of a product if the product raises a serious and immediate risk to health and safety. A German challenge to the legal basis of this provision is noted and briefly excerpted at Chapters 3(B) and 5(D)(3)(a) supra. Germany v. Council, Case C–359/92, [1994] ECR I–3681.

Chapter 36

SOCIAL POLICY

Social policy ranks among the most important fields of action of the Community. Since the Social Action Program of 1974, the political institutions of the Community have adopted numerous and far-reaching legislative measures, which have in many instances been broadened in impact by liberal interpretation by the Court of Justice. In general, this legislation is intended to secure for employees various rights and benefits, but some of the provisions have an impact on other aspects of society. Although much of the legislation and case law merely follows prevailing national views on the continent, some of it represents dramatic innovations in employee rights protection. There is no doubt that social policy is, as the Court of Justice has said, one of the fundamental aspects of the Community.

The over-all picture is one of sharp contrast with prevailing legislation and practices in the US, which in many spheres are far less protective of employee interests. This chapter accordingly yields two benefits: it surveys a major field of regulation of concern to lawyers representing clients in the Community, and it provides the basis for a valuable exercise in comparative law and policy.

This chapter first presents a review of the evolution in Treaty provisions and social action, including policies intended to promote employment. The text then analyzes two important measures providing economic rights to employees, the Collective Redundancy Directive and the Transfer of Undertakings Directive, both the subject of numerous Court judgments. Next, the chapter describes Community action to achieve worker health and safety, notably the directives on Working Time and the Protection of Pregnant Workers. The conclusion surveys other recent legislation, notably the directives on worker information and consultation and parental leave.

A. TREATY PROVISIONS, THE SOCIAL CHARTER AND SOCIAL ACTION PROGRAMS

1. THE EEC TREATY AND THE 1974 SOCIAL ACTION PROGRAM

The initial Treaty of Rome devoted two chapters to social policy. "Social progress" and "the constant improvement of ... working conditions" were included in the goals in the Preamble to the Treaty.

The key provision, the initial Article 117, stated:

> Member States agree upon the need to promote improved working conditions and an improved standard of living for workers....

> They believe that such a development will ensue not only from the functioning of the common market, which will favour the harmonization of social systems, but also from ... the approximation of provisions laid down by law, regulation or administrative action.

The text reflects a certain ambivalence. Apparently some Member States thought that the achievement of the common market would inevitably improve the conditions of workers, while others felt that the Community would have to harmonize national laws for this purpose. In any event, Article 117 did not expressly grant any legislative power, so that social policy measures had to be adopted under Article 100 (now 94), the initial provision authorizing harmonization of rules to achieve the common market. (See Chapter 14A.) That in turn meant that the Council of Ministers had to act by a unanimous vote and the Parliament only had to be consulted.

The Single European Act did not change this situation when it became effective on July 1, 1987. Although the SEA introduced Article 100a (now 95), which authorized the Council to adopt most harmonization measures by qualified majority voting, Article 100a(2) created an exception for measures "relating to the rights and interests of employed persons". (See Chapter 14B.) This was inserted at the UK's insistence to ensure that most social policy legislation would continue to require unanimous Council voting.

Another important social policy provision was the initial Article 118, which assigned the Commission the "task of promoting close cooperation between Member States in the social field" through studies and consultations with regard, for example, to employment, labor law and working conditions, social security, the right of association and collective bargaining. Article 118 did not, however, grant the Commission any legislative power. In Germany v. Commission (Immigration of non-Community workers), Case 281/85, [1987] ECR 3203, the Court held that Article 118 could not be construed to give the Commission implied power to take decisions binding the Member States.

Article 119, establishing the principle of equal pay for men and women, rapidly acquired such importance that we will cover it in depth in the next chapter.

The early social policy chapters did provide for substantial Community social assistance programs. Articles 146–48 (ex 123 to 127) created the European Social Fund, a vehicle for making substantial funds available for "the task of rendering the employment of workers easier and of increasing their geographical and occupational mobility within the Community" (Article 146). The Fund's resources have been used principally for vocational training and resettlement allowances for workers in depressed industries.

The Single European Act added Article 118a (now absorbed into Article 137). This set the specific goal of improving "the health and safety of workers." Equally important, it authorized the Council to adopt directives by qualified majority vote, acting "in cooperation" with the Parliament. As we shall see in section C, Article 118a was used to adopt a considerable body of legislation.

Social policy first became an important field of Community legislation in the 1970s. At their Paris meeting in October 1972, the Heads of State urged that action be undertaken in the social field, which incited the Council of Ministers to adopt a Social Action Program, O.J. C 13/1 (Feb. 12, 1974). An initial wave of social harmonization legislation followed in the late 1970s, due largely to the keen interest manifested by the Socialist governments in Germany under Chancellors Brandt and Schmidt, Labor governments in the UK under Prime Ministers Wilson and Callaghan, and the progressive government in France under President Giscard d'Estaing.

The Social Action Program made efforts to achieve full and better employment a priority, particularly because the energy recession of the mid–1970s caused high levels of unemployment throughout the Community. As part of the Social Action Program, the Council adopted several directives intended to protect the economic interests of employees affected by lay-offs, acquisitions and mergers, and by bankruptcies, described in section B. The Council also adopted the initial measures to promote equal employment rights between women and men, described in the next chapter.

2. THE SOCIAL CHARTER AND THE 1989 SOCIAL ACTION PROGRAM

The climate for social policy legislation changed significantly in the early 1980s. In large measure, this was the result of political change: Margaret Thatcher, an implacable foe of new social legislation, had become the UK Prime Minister and the Christian Democrats under Chancellor Kohl replaced the Socialist government in Germany. Accordingly, no new measures for the protection of any economic interests of employees were passed. When the Commission issued the White Paper of June 1985 on Completing the Internal Market, its legislative program did not include social policy measures, although the White Paper predicted that the internal market program would "stimulate" social policy.

This state of affairs pleased neither the Parliament nor the organized labor movement and both urged that further social legislation be made a component of the internal market program. With impetus from Jacques Delors, President of the Commission and himself a leading French Socialist, the Commission proposed a Community Charter of the Fundamental Social Rights of Workers, which was reviewed and debated throughout 1989. At the Strasbourg European Council Meeting in December 1989, all the Member States but the UK endorsed the Social Charter of 1989, as it is popularly known. (Read carefully its text in the Selected Documents.)

The Preamble to the Social Charter adopts as its basic premise that "in the context of the establishment of the single European market, the same importance must be attached to the social aspects as to the economic aspects." The Preamble further sees a link between social policy and the achievement of the internal market, because "the social consensus contributes to the strengthening of the competitiveness of undertakings and of the economy as a whole."

On the other hand, the Preamble contains a very important reservation in the form of the "principle of subsidiarity," which places responsibility for action in some fields of social policy with "Member States or their constituent parts," rather than Community-wide legislation. The idea behind subsidiarity is that Community action should not be taken when the States can more appropriately act. It is worth noting that the Social Charter's inclusion of the principle of subsidiarity preceded the Maastricht Treaty's enunciation of the principle generally in Article 5 (ex 3b). See page 120.

Although the Social Charter is a highly important statement of policy, much of the text does not represent any new or revolutionary thinking. Many of the sections state employee rights and interests which had already been attained, or were the subject of an on-going program, for example, the sections proclaiming the right to free movement of workers, adequate social security protection, safer work site conditions, access to vocational training and equal rights for women.

In contrast, several sections of the Social Charter that state employee rights or interests were more novel. Thus, a section entitled "Improvement of Living and Working Conditions" referred to a "right to a weekly rest period and to annual paid leave, the duration of which must be harmonized;" and another section dealt with "Information, Consultation and Participation for Workers." Both have influenced subsequent legislation.

There is also a section called "Freedom of Association and Collective Bargaining" which refers to a "dialogue between the two sides of industry at the European level." In this connection, the Commission has sponsored, since 1985, annual meetings of the Union of Industries of the EC (UNICE) and the European Trade Union Confederation (ETUC) in order to forward social dialogue at the European level.

For a detailed analysis of the terms of the Social Charter, see R. Goebel, Employee Rights in the European Community: A Panorama from the 1974 Social Action Program to the Social Charter of 1989, 17 Hastings Int'l & Comp. L. Rev. 1 (1993).

At the end of 1989, the Commission issued a new social action program intended to implement many of the provisions of the Social Charter. In the early 1990s, the Commission proposed over 20 draft directives and released a number of recommendations or policy initiatives. Almost all of the draft directives have now been adopted and are described in sections C and D below. The Commission did not, however, propose any measures concerning minimum wages, rights of association in unions, or retirement benefits, because these are subjects considered to be appropriate only for Member State action in accordance with the principle of subsidiarity.

After the Labor party took over the UK government following the May 1997 election, Prime Minister Blair naturally permitted the Social Charter to become a unanimous Member State declaration of the rights of workers. Not surprisingly, the Treaty of Amsterdam then amended the Preamble to the TEU to state the Union's "attachment to fundamental social rights" as defined in the 1989 Social Charter. This reference may in turn encourage the Court of Justice to cite the Charter as a source of fundamental rights.

3. THE MAASTRICHT TREATY'S SOCIAL PROTOCOL

The December 1989 Strassbourg European Council not only proclaimed the Social Charter, but also endorsed the holding of an Intergovernmental

Conference in 1990–91 (in each case over the opposition of the UK). In order to facilitate an active legislative program in social policy, the IGC proposed a new Treaty social chapter, but the UK, then led by Prime Minister Major, adamantly opposed it. One of the key compromises of the December 1991 European Council meeting at Maastricht was the decision to remove this proposed chapter and to place it in a Social Agreement annexed to a Social Protocol.

The Social Protocol, effective on November 1, 1993 with the Maastricht Treaty itself, lasted until the Treaty of Amsterdam came into effect on May 1, 1999. The Social Protocol effectively created a "two-tier" Community in the sphere of employee rights. The Social Protocol enabled all the Member States but the UK to "have recourse to the institutions, procedures and mechanisms of the Treaty" in order to adopt most social policy measures by a qualified majority vote, instead of unanimity (but the qualified majority was specially calculated without including the UK). Any legislative or other measures adopted in this manner would be binding on the entire Community, except for the UK. When Austria, Finland and Sweden entered the Community in 1995, they adhered to the Social Protocol.

An Agreement on Social Policy, annexed to the Social Protocol, set out the topics within the social policy sector in which legislative or other measures could be adopted by the special qualified majority vote. Parliament received a significant role in the legislative process, which required the use of the cooperation procedure (but not codecision). The Agreement listed several fields in which unanimous Council votes were still required, and even three in which no action could be taken at all. (The current Article 137 essentially replicates the Social Agreement provision on legislative actions–see below.) For an analysis of the Social Protocol and Agreement, see E. Whiteford, Social Policy after Maastricht, 18 Eur. L. Rev. 202 (1993).

Several legislative measures, including the well-known parental leave and European works council consultation directives described in section D, were adopted in 1994–96 through the procedures authorized by the Social Protocol. Not surprisingly, the UK government under Prime Minister Blair agreed in December 1997 to have these directives made applicable to the UK as well.

4. THE SOCIAL CHAPTER OF THE TREATY OF AMSTERDAM

Because the UK elected a Labor government a few weeks before the conclusion of the 1996–97 Intergovernmental Conference, that IGC was able to provide a new social chapter in the Treaty of Amsterdam, largely incorporating the provisions of the Social Agreement. This new social chapter is one of the most important substantive changes made by the Amsterdam Treaty to the EC Treaty.

The social goals of the Community are now set out in Article 136 (replacing Article 117), which refers to the 1989 Social Charter and the earlier 1961 Turin European Social Charter, and then lists "the promotion of employment, improved living and working conditions, ... proper social protection, dialogue between management and labour, the development of human resources with a view to lasting high employment and the combating of exclusion" as the social action goals.

Unlike the initial EEC Treaty, there is now an express grant of legislative power made in Article 137, which authorizes measures concerning worker health and safety, work conditions, information and consultation of workers, and equality between men and women. Legislation can usually be adopted by qualified majority vote in the Council and the parliamentary codecision procedure. However, Article 137(4) grants no legislative power concerning "pay, the right of association, the right to strike or the right to impose lock-outs" (presumably in application of the principle of subsidiarity). Also, Article 137(3) requires a unanimous vote in the Council, after consulting the Parliament, for measures in several fields, notably social security, co-determination, "protection of workers where their employment contract is terminated," and "conditions of employment for third-country nationals legally residing in Community territory."

The social chapter also includes Articles 138 and 139, largely taken over from the Social Agreement, which enable another mode of creating Community rules. The Commission can propose measures to be examined in a dialogue between representative bodies for management and labor at the Community level. These bodies may reach framework agreements, which the Council can then give binding effect by action taken in a manner parallel to its legislative competence under Article 137 (but without any parliamentary action).

The Commission role of encouraging cooperation among Member States through studies and consultation, originally stated in EEC Treaty Article 118, survives in Article 140.

5. EMPLOYMENT POLICY ACTION AND THE TREATY OF AMSTERDAM

In the mid–1990s, Member State leaders and the Commission became extremely concerned over the persistent high rate of unemployment, which rose to twelve percent in the 1991–93 recession, with some countries experiencing over 20% unemployment. At the request of the European Council, the Commission produced in late 1993 the White Paper on Growth, Competitiveness and Employment, COM (93) 700. The White Paper analyzed the serious problems caused by permanent structural and technological unemployment, together with the challenges posed by international competition from high technology nations on the one hand, and mass-production low-labor cost nations on the other. The Commission urged a greater emphasis on education and skills training, aid to new technology and trans-European infra-structure, and greater labor flexibility and mobility.

In successive meetings in Brussels, Corfu, Madrid, Florence, Essen and Dublin in the 1990s, the European Council urged Commission and Council action to implement some of the key proposals of the White Paper. Thus, when Padraig Flynn, the social affairs commissioner, issued in July 1994 a White Paper on European Social Policy, COM (94) 333, the emphasis was placed on combating unemployment and improving the quality of the workforce. (It is worth noting that Commissioner Flynn proposed that the 1996 Intergovernmental Conference should consider a Treaty amendment to authorize Community legislation against discrimination on grounds of race, religion, age and disability, a suggestion that bore fruit—see the next chapter.)

In view of this ongoing concern, it is not surprising that the Treaty of Amsterdam contains a new Title VIII on Employment. Indeed, the importance of Community activity to promote employment is highlighted through the amendment of TEU Article 2 and EC Treaty Article 2 to insert "a high level of employment" as a Treaty goal.

Article 125 requires the Community to develop "a coordinated strategy for employment and particularly for promoting a skilled, trained and adaptable workforce and labour markets responsive to economic change." To this Article 127(2) notably adds: "the objective of a high level of employment shall be taken into consideration in the formulation and implementation of Community policies and activities." Article 128 requires the Council and Commission to make a joint annual report on employment to the European Council, which shall then adopt conclusions on the basis of which the Council, by qualified majority vote, shall draw up guidelines for Member States. The approach is analogous to that used in the economic coordination provisions of the EMU, discussed in Chapter 33C. By Article 129, the Council and the Parliament are authorized to adopt "incentive measures."

Building upon the Treaty of Amsterdam's new emphasis on employment policies, a special European Council session at Luxembourg in November 1997 urged a more systematic and coordinated Community policy to support efforts to increase employment levels. The December 1999 Helsinki European Council noted the successful implementation of the Amsterdam Treaty's procedure for guidelines for employment policies in each Member State. The December 2000 Nice European Council approved a new European Social Agenda, emphasizing the development of a cutting-edge information-based economy, greater labor mobility, improvement in job education and training, and protection against social exclusion.

The Commission's social action program for 1998–2002 centers on proposals for improved labor mobility, modernizing work organization and promoting social protection and inclusion. The Commission's annual general reports since 1998 have noted a gradual reduction in average unemployment levels from 10% to 9%, but unfortunately the recession in Germany in 2001 has increased unemployment there back to 10%.

B.   THE 1974 SOCIAL ACTION PROGRAM: LEGISLATION AND CASE LAW

The initial 1974 Social Action Program yielded three important directives intended to achieve economic protection for employees in the context of layoffs, acquisitions and corporate restructuring and bankruptcies. Not only has this legislation had a substantial impact, but it has given rise to a constant stream of Court judgments which have, in general, broadened the scope of the legislation and enhanced the employee rights stated therein. This provides the basis for a valuable comparison with American law.

1.   THE 1975 DIRECTIVE ON COLLECTIVE REDUNDANCIES

Protection from mass lay-offs (or what the British would call collective redundancies) was a natural candidate for Community action, both because many States had some form of protection and because unions strongly supported a Community measure. Accordingly, Directive 75/129 on collective redundancies, O.J. L 48/29 (Feb. 22, 1975), was the first major social policy measure of the 1970s. (Read carefully the current text in the Selected Documents.)

This directive protects employees in any business entity employing more than 20 workers, when a given number are dismissed or laid off within a 30–day period for general business or economic reasons, rather than any work-related deficiencies of the workers. The usual "trigger" number of dismissals is 10 when the business employs less than 100 workers, 10% or more when 100 to 300 workers are employed, and 30 or more if 300 or more workers are employed (art. 1). The protective rules of the directive expressly do not apply to employees of public authorities or to employees hired for limited periods of time.

The Collective Redundancy Directive protects employees in two ways. The first element of protection is that the employer must give advance notice, 30 days minimum, to the employee representatives in the business entity and also to the public labor authorities (arts. 3, 4). The employer must provide both the employee representatives and the authorities with "all relevant information" as to the dismissals, especially the number of workers to be dismissed, the period of time involved, the criteria used in selecting redundant workers, and the nature of any redundancy benefits, if provided (arts. 2, 3).

The directive obligates the employer to carry out "consultations" with the employee representatives on the proposed dismissals in order to try to reach agreement on ways of "avoiding collective redundancies or reducing the number of workers affected, and of mitigating the consequences" (art. 2(2)). Further, the public authorities may "seek solutions to the problems raised by the projected collective redundancies" (art. 4(2)). In some States, as a matter of practice the employer has little choice but to accept such government-proposed "solutions," even though the directive makes no reference to their legal effect.

Moreover, the directive allows the Member States to adopt rules even more favorable to workers (art. 5), and some States do that. German law, for example, requires binding arbitration when the employer and the employee representatives cannot reach agreement, and French and Dutch rules give the labor inspectors effective veto power over proposed dismissals.

Directive 92/56, O.J. L 245/3 (Aug. 26, 1992), amended the initial text in order to create consultation rights when the decision to dismiss is not taken by the employer, but rather by the management of a parent which controls the employer, but is located in a different Member State. Further, a new article 6 requires Member States to ensure that the employees or their representatives will have administrative and/or judicial recourse to enforce the directive's obligations. The current text, Directive 98/59, O.J. L 225/16 (Aug. 12, 1998), adds some minor amendments to improve the procedure.

In several noteworthy judgments, the Court has liberally interpreted the scope of the information and consultation rights enunciated in the directive.

DANSK METALARBEJDERFORBUND
v. H. NIELSEN & SON

Case 284/83, [1985] ECR 553.

[Nielsen & Son notified its employee representatives of its serious financial difficulties. The representatives asked Nielsen to provide a bank guarantee for the future payment of wages. When Nielsen failed to do so, the employees stopped work. The following week, Nielsen obtained a judicial declaration of insolvency. The employees sued for wages corresponding to the 30–day mandatory notice period set by the directive on collective redundancies. The Danish court asked the Court of Justice to rule on whether the employees could be treated as having been dismissed.]

7 The purpose of the first question is to ascertain whether * * * termination of a contract of employment by the employees in such circumstances may be treated as dismissal by the employer and as such falling under the directive.

8 The answer to that question must first of all be sought in the wording of the directive. * * * Article 1(1)(a) of the directive states " 'collective redundancies' means dismissal effected by an employer". No other provision of the directive supports an extension of its scope to termination of employment by the employees.

9 [The employee representatives argue that] the objective of the directive, which is to strengthen the protection of workers in the event of collective dismissal, implies that the termination by the workers of their employment on the ground that payment of their wages is no longer guaranteed should be treated as dismissal effected by the employer.

10 That argument cannot be accepted. The directive does not affect the employer's freedom to effect or refrain from effecting collective dismissals. Its sole object is to provide for consultation with the trade unions and for notification of the competent public authority prior to such dismissals. * * * [T]o treat termination of their employment by the workers in the manner advocated by [the employee representatives] would give the workers the possibility of bringing about dismissals against the will of the employer and without his being in a position to discharge his obligations under Articles 2 and 3 of the directive. It would lead to a result precisely contrary to that sought by the directive, namely to avoid or reduce collective redundancies.

11 [Accordingly,] the termination by workers of their contract of employment following an announcement by the employer that he is suspending payment of his debts cannot be treated as dismissal by the employer * * *.

12 By the second question the national court asks whether the directive applies where, because of the financial state of the undertaking, the employer ought to have contemplated collective redundancies but did not do so.

* * *

14 [The employee representatives contend] that the effectiveness of the directive would be impaired if the employer were not obliged, by implica-

tion, to foresee collective redundancies as soon as he encounters serious financial difficulties.

[15] As the Guarantee Fund and the Commission rightly state, there is no implied obligation under the directive to foresee collective redundancies. It does not stipulate the circumstances in which the employer must contemplate collective redundancies and in no way affects his freedom to decide whether and when he must formulate plans for collective dismissals.

Notes and Questions

1. It is hard to disagree with the Court's conclusion that employees who voluntarily stop work cannot claim the protection granted by the directive. The second question is more difficult. Do you agree that an employer has no obligation reasonably to foresee an insolvency and the consequent lay-off of employees? Note, however, that under the 1980 insolvency directive discussed below, employees of an insolvent enterprise will at least be guaranteed back pay.

2. In Rockfon A/S v. Specialarbejderforbundet i Danmark, Case C–449/93, [1995] ECR I–4291, a group of four production companies employed altogether 1085 workers in a Danish town. A parent management decision required all four companies to have a joint personnel department. In 1989, Rockfon, one of the four companies, followed the instructions of the personnel department in dismissing 24 of its 162 employees without following the notification and consultation procedures of the Collective Redundancy Directive. In a suit by dismissed employees, the Danish Labour Council found the directive inapplicable, because it treated the dismissal as one executed by the larger group, in which the "trigger" number of 30 dismissed workers was not attained. An appellate court asked the Court of Justice whether Rockfon should be considered the dismissing "establishment" within the terms of article 1(1)a of the directive, or whether the group should be deemed to be the "establishment." How would you reply?

COMMISSION v. UNITED KINGDOM

(Collective redundancies).
Case C–383/92, [1994] ECR I–2479.

[The Commission sued the United Kingdom for defective implementation of the collective redundancies directive. The UK law only obliged employers who had voluntarily accepted trade unions (a minority of all employers) to deal with union representatives in the event of a collective redundancy. Whether the UK ought to have imposed this obligation upon all employers was the principal question. Other issues concerned the meaning of "redundancy" and "consultation," and whether the UK had to provide adequate sanctions to enforce the rules.]

[14] The United Kingdom acknowledges that representation of workers in undertakings * * * has traditionally been based on voluntary recognition of trade unions by employers and for that reason an employer who does not recognize a trade union is not subject to the obligations laid down in the directive. However, it contends that the directive was not intended to amend national rules or practices concerning the designation of workers' representatives. It points out that according to Article 1(1)(b) of the directive, the term "workers' representatives" is to be understood as meaning the workers' representatives "provided for by the laws or prac-

tices of the Member States". It also argues that the directive is limited to a partial harmonization of the rules for the protection of workers in the event of collective redundancies and that it does not require Member States to provide for specific representation of workers in order to comply with the obligations which it lays down.

15   The United Kingdom's point of view cannot be accepted.

16   By harmonizing the rules applicable to collective redundancies, the Community legislature intended both to ensure comparable protection for workers' rights in the different Member States and to harmonize the costs which such protective rules entail for Community undertakings.

* * *

17   Contrary to the United Kingdom's contention, * * * Article 1(1)(b) is not simply a renvoi to the rules in force in the Member States on the designation of workers' representatives. It leaves to Member States only the task of determining the arrangements for designating the workers' representatives who, depending on the circumstances, must or may intervene in the collective redundancy procedure under Articles 2 and 3(2).

20   The interpretation proposed by the United Kingdom would allow Member States to determine the cases in which workers' representatives may be informed and consulted and may intervene, since they can be informed and consulted and can intervene with public authorities only in undertakings where national law provides for the designation of workers' representatives. Such an interpretation would thus permit Member States to deprive Articles 2 and 3(2) of the directive of their full effect.

* * *

27   In those circumstances, United Kingdom law, which allows an employer to frustrate the protection provided for workers by Articles 2 and 3 of the directive, must be regarded as contrary to those articles.

[The Commission also contended that the UK rule interpreted "redundancy" to mean only "a cessation or reduction of the business of an undertaking or a decline in demand" while the directive was intended to cover any discharge not related to the individual workers concerned.]

32   The concept of "redundancy" [in the United Kingdom legislation] does not cover all the cases of "collective redundancy" covered by the directive. In particular, as the Commission points out, it does not cover cases where workers have been dismissed as a result of new working arrangements within an undertaking unconnected with its volume of business.

[The Commission found a further deficiency in the UK wording which only obliged employers to "consider" the views of the workers' representatives, rather than to engage in the consultations specified by the directive.]

36   [Moreover, the UK rules] do not require an employer to consult workers' representatives "with a view to reaching an agreement", as required by Article 2(1) of the directive, nor do they specify that such consultations must, at least, "cover ways and means of avoiding collective redundancies or reducing the number of workers affected, and mitigating the consequences", as required by Article 2(2).

[37] The Commission's third complaint must therefore be upheld.

[Finally, the Commission claimed that the UK had not created adequate sanctions.]

[40] Where a Community directive does not specifically provide any penalty for an infringement or refers for that purpose to national laws, regulations and administrative provisions, Article [10, ex 5] of the Treaty requires the Member States to take all measures necessary to guarantee the application and effectiveness of Community law. For that purpose, while the choice of penalties remains within their discretion, they must ensure in particular that infringements of Community law are penalized under conditions, both procedural and substantive, which are analogous to those applicable to infringements of national law of a similar nature and importance and which, in any event make the penalty effective, proportionate and dissuasive [citing *Vandevenne, supra* page 393].

[41] [Under the UK law,] a "protective award" which an employer may be ordered to make to a dismissed employee if he has failed to comply with the obligation to consult and inform the workers' representatives * * * may be set off against any amounts which he may otherwise be required to pay to that employee under the latter's contract of employment or in respect of breach of that contract * * *.

[42] [Consequently,] the United Kingdom legislation largely deprives [the "protective award"] sanction of its practical effect and its deterrent value. Moreover, an employer will not be penalized even moderately or lightly by the sanction except and only to the extent to which the amount of the "protective award" which he is ordered to make exceeds the sums which he is otherwise required to pay to the person concerned.

[43] The Commission's fourth complaint must therefore be upheld.

Notes and Questions

1. Under the Conservative governments of Prime Ministers Thatcher and Major, the United Kingdom adamantly opposed Community legislation creating a mandatory system of worker consultation, such as exists in one form or another on the continent. See section D3, *infra*. At ¶ 9 in his opinion, Advocate General van Gerven refers to the "politically sensitive nature" of the issue, and agrees with the UK that the directive was never intended to create a general system of workers' representatives. Nonetheless he concludes that the directive's objective would be frustrated if a State does not oblige employers to deal with worker representatives before a collective redundancy, at least on an *ad hoc* basis. However, the UK partial harmonization argument is certainly plausible. Do you agree with the UK, or with the Court and the Advocate General? Does the outcome of this case put the camel's nose under the tent? See the case note by G. More, 19 Eur. L. Rev. 660 (1994), which concludes that the UK's "opt-out" from the Maastricht Treaty's Social Protocol "came too late to prevent the infiltration of Community labour law into United Kingdom labour law." *Id*. at 668.

2. Note that the UK conceded the other defects in its legislation, and had indeed partly remedied them in 1993. The Commission asked the Court not to treat the issues as moot and the Court agreed. How important is the Court's interpretation of the directive in ¶ ¶ 32–37? Is consultation now tantamount to good faith bargaining?

3. Some internal market directives (e.g., those regulating insider trading or money laundering) expressly require States to impose adequate sanctions. Not only does the Collective Redundancy Directive not expressly require sanctions, but it was the 1992 amendment discussed above that introduced article 6, which requires States to "ensure that judicial and/or administrative procedures for the enforcement of obligations under this directive are available to the workers' representatives and/or workers." In ¶ 40, the Court nonetheless concluded that Treaty Article 10 imposed an automatic duty upon States to create "effective, proportionate and dissuasive" sanctions. Do you agree, or do you think sanctions should be obligatory only if expressly required by the directive? Would UK employers be apt to obey this directive if only trivial penalties were imposed for violations? For further discussion of appropriate sanctions to enforce Community rules, see page 387 supra.

NOTE ON WARN

The Collective Redundancies Directive has an American analogue, the Worker Adjustment and Retraining Notification Act of 1988, 29 U.S.C.A. §§ 2101–2109, popularly called WARN, which was adopted after some 15 years of legislative debate. The EC directive apparently influenced the earliest bills. For a review of WARN's background and scope, see C. Yost, The Worker Adjustment and Retraining Notification Act of 1988, 38 Cath.U.L.Rev. 675 (1989).

WARN covers not only the usual form of collective dismissal, a "mass layoff", but also the special case of a dismissal caused by a "plant closing." Every enterprise employing more than 100 employees is subject to WARN. A layoff of 50 or more employees at one job site within 30 days triggers the protective rules for a "plant closing." The dismissal of at least 50 workers, provided that constitutes at least one-third of the work-force, or the dismissal of 500 or more workers, even if that is less than one-third of the work-force, triggers the rules governing a "mass layoff."

If WARN applies, the employer must give 60 days advance notice to union or other employee representatives, to the appropriate state labor authority and to the chief elected official of the local government. Failure to give notice gives rise to economic sanctions: payment of usual salary or other remuneration to each dismissed worker for the missed notice period, and damages of $500 per day of missed notice payable to the local government. In United Food and Commercial Workers Union Local 751 v. Brown Group, Inc., 517 U.S. 544, 116 S. Ct. 1529, 134 L.Ed. 2d 758 (1996), the Supreme Court held that unions had the right to sue to enforce WARN'S procedures, notably to recover damages on behalf of individual employees. WARN does not, however, mandate any form of consultation with either the employee representatives or the local government, and is therefore not as far-reaching as the Collective Redundancy Directive.

Notes and Questions

1. What is your impression of the value of the consultation provisions of the Collective Redundancy Directive? For example, what steps might the employee representatives suggest in order to reduce the size of proposed lay-offs or to mitigate their effect? Do you think employers would be apt to accept such suggestions or ignore them? Is it desirable or generally a waste of time to involve

public authorities? Do you think that the employer's obligation to consult with the employees and the public authorities will have beneficial social and perhaps even economic effects? Was it sensible or unfortunate that WARN does not contain such a provision?

2. Do you think laws like the Collective Redundancies Directive and WARN are helpful because they contribute to social dialogue and help alleviate genuine social distress in a lay-off, or that they are harmful because they slow the process of making businesses more efficient and competitive? If both these views are correct to some extent, where should the balance be struck? Would it be helpful to have empirical studies on the effect of the directive and of WARN? Can empirical studies measure social benefits or only economic factors?

3. Does the passage of WARN suggest that our employee rights rules are apt to be influenced in other ways by the more far-reaching ones in the Community, or are the US and the EC just too different?

2. THE 1977 TRANSFER OF UNDERTAKINGS DIRECTIVE

When all or part of an enterprise is transferred from one owner to another in an acquisition, merger or restructuring, it frequently occurs that some employees have their employment status modified, or are even dismissed, either before the transfer or shortly after it occurs. The new owner usually views such reassignments or dismissals as essential to efficient restructuring, but the employees naturally would like some form of protection. The desire to achieve such protection in a reasonable form inspired the second major employee rights measure, Directive 77/187 on the safeguarding of employees' rights in the event of transfers of undertakings, businesses, or parts of businesses, O.J. L 61/26 (Mar. 5, 1977), often called the "acquired rights" directive. (Read carefully the text in the Selected Documents.) Incidentally, the words "firm," "entity" or "enterprise" are useful synonyms for "undertaking."

The Transfer of Undertakings Directive basically aims to protect certain so-called "acquired rights" of employees when all or part of the entity by which they are employed is transferred to a new owner. The directive declares that the employees are entitled to keep the employee relationship, as well as any specific contractual rights (art. 3(1)). Moreover, any collective bargaining agreement which bound the old employer continues to bind the new employer (art. 3(2)). The concept of a transfer of a business is a broad one, covering not only an acquisition or merger, but, as we shall see from the case law, other legal transactions as well.

The directive also significantly limits a new employer's ability to use the transfer of the business as an occasion for reducing or dismissing the entire work force (art. 4). (For that matter, if the former employer, at the request of the new one, were to reduce the work force prior to the transfer, the dismissal of a sufficiently large number would trigger the procedures required by the Collective Redundancy Directive.) A new employer can reduce the work force only if justified for "economic, technical, or organizational reasons" (art. 4(1)). Moreover, any "substantial change in working conditions to the detriment of the employee" is considered as a constructive dismissal (art. 4(2)).

The directive guarantees employees certain information and consultation rights which largely parallel those provided by the Collective Redundancy

Directive. Both the old and new employer must inform employee representatives of "the legal, economic and social implications" of the transfer and any "measures envisaged in relation to the employees" (art. 6(1)). The new employer must consult with the employees' representatives on any measures affecting employees (such as dismissals or reallocation of employees) "with a view to seeking agreement" on the application of the measures (art. 6(2)).

As in the case of the Collective Redundancies Directive, this directive does not totally preempt Member State law, but rather allows States to have supplementary rules more favorable to employees (art. 7).

The directive was amended by Directive 98/50, O.J. L 201/88 (June 29, 1998), notably to add an article enabling judicial appeals, but also to insert language intended to conform to interpretation by the Court of Justice. A consolidated text appears in Directive 2001/23, O.J. L 82/16 (Mar. 22, 2001).

Overall, the "acquired rights" directive makes it more difficult to carry through an acquisition or a merger in the Community, because besides negotiating the acquisition or merger itself, prospective buyers must also consult with employee representatives if they contemplate reducing the work force or rationalizing the operations in any manner that would affect employees.

The US does not have any comparable federal legislation, but a rather complex case law governs the subject of corporate successor liability. If a corporation disappears in a merger, the surviving entity constitutes a legal successor bound by the collective bargaining agreements and the employee relations of the former entity, because there exists a "substantial continuity of identity in the business enterprise." John Wiley & Sons, Inc. v. Livingston, 376 U.S. 543, 551, 84 S.Ct. 909, 915, 11 L.Ed.2d 898, 905 (1964).

An asset acquisition sometimes also creates successorship rights, even though the former entity's employee relations and collective bargaining agreement are not automatically transferred. In Fall River Dyeing & Finishing Corp. v. NLRB, 482 U.S. 27, 107 S.Ct. 2225, 96 L.Ed.2d 22 (1987), defendant purchased the realty and operating assets of a liquidated entity. Defendant then used the assets to carry on the same business in the same premises with about half the liquidated entity's customers. Since over half of defendant's workforce had been employed by the liquidated entity, and these workers had essentially the same job classifications, the defendant was held to be a corporate successor bound to bargain with the liquidated entity's union. In contrast is Howard Johnson Co. v. Detroit Local Joint Executive Bd., 417 U.S. 249, 94 S.Ct. 2236, 41 L.Ed.2d 46 (1974), where defendant leased motel premises, bought from the landlord most operating assets, and continued the motel business. However, defendant hired only a few of the landlord's employees, and these were only a minority of defendant's employees. The Supreme Court did not consider that this amounted to a corporate succession and collective bargaining rights were not continued. See D. Oesterle, The Law of Mergers and Acquisitions (West 1999); see also Silver, Reflections on the Obligations of a Successor Employer, 2 Cardozo L.Rev. 545 (1981).

Since the mid–1980s, the Court has frequently had occasion to interpret the scope of application of the directive and the nature of the rights that it grants. This body of case law is now quite complex, although the Court's general approach clearly tends to protect employee rights.

SPIJKERS v. BENEDIK ABATTOIR

Case 24/85, [1986] ECR 1119.

[When a company operating a slaughterhouse became insolvent, Benedik bought the assets: "the entire slaughterhouse, with various rooms and offices, the land and certain specified goods." Benedik did not take over the "goodwill" of the insolvent firm, i.e., Benedik did not take over the prior customers. Benedik hired all of the former firm's employees, except for the plaintiff, Spijkers, and one other. Spijkers sued to maintain his employee status. The Dutch Supreme Court asked the Court of Justice whether a transfer of assets to a purchaser who does not take the "goodwill" falls under the "acquired rights" directive.]

8   Mr. Spijkers maintains that there is a transfer of an undertaking within the meaning of Article 1(1) where the undertaking's assets and business are transferred as a unit from one employer to another; it is immaterial whether at the time of the transfer the business activities of the transferor have ceased and the goodwill has already disappeared.

                                          * * *

10   The United Kingdom Government and the Commission suggest that the essential criterion is whether the transferee is put in possession of a going concern and is able to continue its activities or at least activities of the same kind. The Netherlands Government emphasizes that, having regard to the social objective of the directive, it is clear that the term "transfer" implies that the transferee actually carries on the activities of the transferor as part of the same business.

11   That view must be accepted. It is clear from the scheme of Directive No 77/187 and from the terms of Article 1 (1) thereof that the directive is intended to ensure the continuity of employment relationships existing within a business, irrespective of any change of ownership. It follows that the decisive criterion for establishing whether there is a transfer for the purposes of the directive is whether the business in question retains its identity.

12   Consequently, a transfer of an undertaking, business or part of a business does not occur merely because its assets are disposed of. Instead it is necessary to consider, in a case such as the present, whether the business was disposed of as a going concern, as would be indicated, *inter alia,* by the fact that its operation was actually continued or resumed by the new employer, with the same or similar activities.

13   In order to determine whether those conditions are met, it is necessary to consider all the facts characterizing the transaction in question, including the type of undertaking or business, whether or not the business's tangible assets, such as buildings and movable property, are transferred, the value of its intangible assets at the time of the transfer, whether or not the majority of its employees are taken over by the new employer, whether or not its customers are transferred and the degree of similarity between the activities carried on before and after the transfer and the period, if any, for which those activities were suspended. It should be noted, however, that

all those circumstances are merely single factors in the overall assessment which must be made and cannot therefore be considered in isolation.

[14] It is for the national court to make the necessary factual appraisal, in the light of the criteria for interpretation set out above, in order to establish whether or not there is a transfer in the sense indicated above.

BOTZEN v. ROTTERDAMSCHE DROOGDOK MAATSCHAPPIJ

Case 186/83, [1985] ECR 519.

[A company, referred to as the "old RDM," was declared insolvent on Apr. 6, 1983 in a judicial proceeding. A new company, the "new RDM" was incorporated on March 30, 1983 in order to retain some of the business operations of "old RDM." Some of the dismissed "old RDM" employees sued to retain their positions.]

[4] [Under an agreement dated 7 April 1983], the new RDM took over certain departments of the old RDM and all the staff assigned thereto, and in addition took over a number of employees of the [general and administrative] departments not transferred to it. However, the other workers, including the plaintiffs in the main proceedings, were dismissed by the liquidators of the old RDM.

[5] Considering their dismissal to be invalid on the ground that they had *ipso jure* entered the service of the new RDM on the date of the transfer, the plaintiffs in the main proceedings brought an action against the new RDM * * *, seeking payment of the salary due from 7 April 1983 until such time as their employment relationship might be terminated. They also requested, as an interim measure, that the new RDM should be ordered to pay them * * * a monthly amount equivalent to their salary and to allow them to carry out their usual work.

* * *

[14] [T]he Commission considers that the only decisive criterion regarding the transfer of employees' rights and obligations is whether or not a transfer takes place of the department to which they were assigned and which formed the organizational framework within which their employment relationship took effect.

[15] The Commission's view must be upheld. An employment relationship is essentially characterized by the link existing between the employee and the part of the undertaking or business to which he is assigned to carry out his duties. In order to decide whether the rights and obligations under an employment relationship are transferred under Directive No 77/187 by reason of a transfer within the meaning of Article 1(1) thereof, it is therefore sufficient to establish to which part of the undertaking or business the employee was assigned.

[16] [Accordingly,] Article 3(1) of Directive No 77/187 must be interpreted as not covering the transferor's rights and obligations arising from a contract of employment or an employment relationship existing on the date of the transfer and entered into with employees who, although not employed in the transferred part of the undertaking, performed certain duties which

involved the use of assets assigned to the part transferred or who, whilst being employed in an administrative department of the undertaking which has not itself been transferred, carried out certain duties for the benefit of the part transferred.

Notes and Questions

1. Most transfers of a business occur through the acquisition of a business entity (purchase of the shares of a corporation or the partnership interests in a partnership) or through the merger of one business entity with another. In both cases, the Transfer of Undertakings Directive clearly applies. The same result would presumably occur in the US by operation of the corporate successor doctrine.

2. An acquisition of assets of an enterprise poses a much more difficult issue. In *Spijkers,* the Fifth Chamber of the Court of Justice did not provide a simple guideline. The fact that the new firm did not take over the old firm's "goodwill" or customers is neither irrelevant, as the plaintiff urged, nor decisive against the plaintiff, as the defendant urged. The Court provides in ¶ 13 what American corporate lawyers would call a "going concern" test, in which the trial court is to weigh all of the relevant factors. If you were the trial court, which way would you decide this case?

US case law on the application of the corporate successor doctrine in an asset purchase of a business is also not very clear. The *Fall River Dyeing* and *Howard Johnson* cases discussed above would seem to indicate that, even though employee relationships are not transferred with the assets, an obligation to bargain with the former entity's union is imposed when a) substantial business continuity is demonstrated and b) it is shown that a majority of the new firm's employees were also employees of the former firm.

3. *Botzen* poses the issue of a transfer of part of a business, i.e., some assets with some employees. Do you agree that an employment relationship can usually be "linked" to a business department? Obviously not all firms are structured that way, but many are. Could a department, e.g., bookkeeping, consist of just one employee?

4. In Allen v. Amalgamated Construction, Case C–234/98, [1999] ECR I–8643, 24 mineworkers were dismissed by one wholly-owned subsidiary of the AMCO group and immediately hired by another wholly-owned subsidiary to perform mining operations. Under Community competition law doctrine, contractual arrangements between wholly-owned subsidiaries of the same group are ignored, being treated essentially as though they were management decisions within a single enterprise. See *Viho,* supra page 913. The Court declined to apply a similar approach in this context, holding that a transfer of employees between companies in the same group could fall within the terms of the Transfer of Undertakings Directive.

5. In Abels v. Administrative Board, Case 135/83, [1985] ECR 469, the Court held that a "legal transfer" does not include a transfer of all or part of a business during judicial insolvency proceedings. The Court held that application of the directive was not required by its express terms and might interfere with the operations of national insolvency laws. The Court also doubted that bringing insolvency proceedings within the directive's ambit would really further the social policy goals of the directive. The Court may have thought that judicial administrators should be allowed discretion to try to salvage as much of the business and keep jobs for as many of the employees as possible. In contrast, the Court held in

Europieces v. Sanders, Case C–399/96, [1998] ECR I–6965, that when a company voluntarily liquidates by action of its shareholders and management, the Transfer of Undertakings Directive applies whenever part of the business is transferred to a new entity.

FORENINGEN AF ARBEJDSLEDERE
v. DADDY'S DANCE HALL

Case 324/86, [1988] ECR 739.

[A Danish court referred two questions to the Court of Justice, one as to whether the transfer of leased business premises was covered by the 1977 directive, and the second as to whether the parties to an employment contract may modify or waive rights granted by the directive.]

3   Mr. Tellerup was employed as a restaurant manager by Irma Catering A/S, which had taken a non-transferable lease of restaurants and bars belonging to A/S Palads Teatret. The lease was subsequently terminated, and on 28 January 1983 Irma Catering dismissed its staff, including Mr. Tellerup, with the statutory notice, which in the case of Mr. Tellerup expired on 30 April 1983. Irma Catering continued to run the businesses in question with the same staff until 25 February 1983.

4   With effect from that date a new lease was concluded between A/S Palads Teatret and Daddy's Dance Hall A/S. Daddy's Dance Hall immediately re-employed the employees of the former lessee, including Mr. Tellerup, to do the same jobs as before. The new management contract concluded with Mr. Tellerup stipulated, however, that his remuneration, which had previously been in the form of commission, would henceforth take the form of a fixed salary. Furthermore, at Mr. Tellerup's request the parties agreed on a trial period of three months during which either side could give 14 days' notice. On that basis Mr. Tellerup was dismissed on 26 April 1983 with 14 days' notice. The main proceedings concern in essence the period of notice to which the plaintiff was entitled.

* * *

7   In the first question the national court seeks in substance to determine whether Article 1(1) of Council Directive 77/187 * * * must be interpreted as meaning that the directive applies where, upon the termination of a non-transferable lease, the owner of an undertaking leases it to a new lessee who carries on the business without interruption with the same staff, who had been given notice on the expiry of the initial lease.

* * *

9   [T]he purpose of Directive 77/187/EEC is to ensure, so far as possible, that the rights of employees are safeguarded in the event of a change of employer by allowing them to remain in employment with the new employer on the terms and conditions agreed with the transferor. The directive is therefore applicable where, following a legal transfer or merger, there is a change in the natural or legal person who is responsible for carrying on the business and who by virtue of that fact incurs the obligations of an employer *vis-à-vis* employees of the undertaking, regardless of whether or not ownership of the undertaking is transferred.

10   It follows that where, upon the expiry of the lease, the lessee ceases to be the employer and a third party becomes the employer under a new lease concluded with the owner the resulting operation can fall within the scope of the directive as defined in Article 1(1). The fact that in such a case the transfer is effected in two stages, in that the undertaking is first retransferred from the original lessee to the owner and the latter then transfers it to the new lessee, does not prevent the directive from applying, provided that the economic unit in question retains its identity; that is so in particular when, as in this case, the business is carried on without interruption by the new lessee with the same staff as were employed in the business before the transfer.

* * *

12   In its second question the national court seeks in substance to determine whether an employee may waive rights conferred on him by Directive 77/187/EEC if the disadvantages resulting from his waiver are offset by such benefits that, taking the matter as a whole, he is not placed in a worse position.

* * *

14   As was stressed above, the purpose of Directive 77/187/EEC is to ensure that the rights resulting from a contract of employment or employment relationship of employees affected by the transfer of an undertaking are safeguarded. Since this protection is a matter of public policy, and therefore independent of the will of the parties to the contract of employment, the rules of the directive, in particular those concerning the protection of workers against dismissal by reason of the transfer, must be considered to be mandatory, so that it is not possible to derogate from them in a manner unfavourable to employees.

15   It follows that employees are not entitled to waive the rights conferred on them by the directive and that those rights cannot be restricted even with their consent. This interpretation is not affected by the fact that, as in this case, the employee obtains new benefits in compensation for the disadvantages resulting from an amendment to his contract of employment so that, taking the matter as a whole, he is not placed in a worse position than before.

16   However, * * * Directive 77/187/EEC is intended to achieve only partial harmonization * * *. It is not intended to establish a uniform level of protection throughout the Community on the basis of common criteria. Thus the directive can be relied on only to ensure that the employee is protected in his relations with the transferee to the same extent as he was in his relations with the transferor under the legal rules of the Member State concerned.

17   Consequently, in so far as national law allows the employment relationship to be altered in a manner unfavourable to employees in situations other than the transfer of an undertaking, in particular as regards their protection against dismissal, such an alternative is not precluded merely because the undertaking has been transferred in the meantime and the agreement has therefore been made with the new employer. Since by virtue of Article 3(1) of the directive the transferee is subrogated to the

transferor's rights and obligations under the employment relationship, that relationship may be altered with regard to the transferee to the same extent as it could have been with regard to the transferor, provided that the transfer of the undertaking itself may never constitute the reason for that amendment.

[18] For the above reasons the answer to the second question must be that an employee cannot waive the rights conferred on him by the mandatory provisions of Directive 77/187/EEC even if the disadvantages resulting from his waiver are offset by such benefits that, taking the matter as a whole, he is not placed in a worse position. Nevertheless, the directive does not preclude an agreement with the new employer to alter the employment relationship, in so far as such an alteration is permitted by the applicable national law in situations other than the transfer of an undertaking.

Notes and Questions

1. In *Daddy's Dance Hall,* a new business operator conducted the same type of business on the same premises and hired the same employees. However, the old and new employer had no contractual relationship whatsoever. The lease was not transferred; indeed, it was non-transferable. Do you agree with the Third Chamber of the Court that this situation nonetheless amounts to transfer of a business, or do you think this goes too far? What is the likely motivation for the Court's approach?

2. Suppose that a landlord rescinds the lease of premises used as a restaurant and then continues the operation of the restaurant. Is such a case easier to decide than Daddy's Dance Hall? Suppose further that the restaurant was only operated in the summer, and the landlord rescinded the lease in January, without employing any staff until the reopening in April. Do you think the directive should still require the landlord to observe the terms of a collective bargaining agreement entered into by the former lessee with representatives of its employees? See Landesorganizationen v. Ny Molle Kro, Case 287/86, [1987] ECR 5465.

SUZEN v. ZEHNACKER GEBAUDEREINIGUNG
Case C–13/95, [1997] ECR I–1259.

[A German school terminated a cleaning contract with Zehnacker and entered into a new cleaning contract with Lefarth. Zehnacker dismissed all of its seven employees who had cleaned the school. One of them, Suzen, sued to compel Lefarth to take over her employment. The Court began by re-examining the scope of the directive.]

[10] The aim of the directive is to ensure continuity of employment relationships within an economic entity, irrespective of any change of ownership. The decisive criterion for establishing the existence of a transfer within the meaning of the directive is whether the entity in question retains its identity, as indicated *inter alia* by the fact that its operation is actually continued or resumed [citing *Spijkers, supra*].

[11] Whilst the lack of any contractual link between the transferor and the transferee or, as in this case, between the two undertakings successively entrusted with the cleaning of a school, may point to the absence of a transfer within the meaning of the directive, it is certainly not conclusive.

[12] [T]he directive is applicable wherever, in the context of contractual relations, there is a change in the natural or legal person who is responsible for carrying on the business and who incurs the obligations of an employer towards employees of the undertaking. Thus, there is no need, in order for the directive to be applicable, for there to be any direct contractual relationship between the transferor and the transferee: the transfer may also take place in two stages, through the intermediary of a third party such as the owner or the person putting up the capital.

* * *

[14] In order to determine whether the conditions for the transfer of an entity are met, it is necessary to consider all the facts characterizing the transaction in question, including in particular the type of undertaking or business, whether or not its tangible assets, such as buildings and movable property, are transferred, the value of its intangible assets at the time of the transfer, whether or not the majority of its employees are taken over by the new employer, whether or not its customers are transferred, the degree of similarity between the activities carried on before and after the transfer, and the period, if any, for which those activities were suspended. However, all those circumstances are merely single factors in the overall assessment which must be made and cannot therefore be considered in isolation [Citing *Spijkers, supra*].

[15] [T]he mere fact that the service provided by the old and the new awardees of a contract is similar does not therefore support the conclusion that an economic entity has been transferred. An entity cannot be reduced to the activity entrusted to it. Its identity also emerges from other factors, such as its workforce, its management staff, the way in which its work is organized, its operating methods or indeed, where appropriate, the operational resources available to it.

[16] The mere loss of a service contract to a competitor cannot therefore by itself indicate the existence of a transfer within the meaning of the directive. In those circumstances, the service undertaking previously entrusted with the contract does not, on losing a customer, thereby cease fully to exist, and a business or part of a business belonging to it cannot be considered to have been transferred to the new awardee of the contract.

[17] It must also be noted that, although the transfer of assets is one of the criteria to be taken into account by the national court in deciding whether an undertaking has in fact been transferred, the absence of such assets does not necessarily preclude the existence of such a transfer.

* * *

[19] The United Kingdom Government and the Commission have argued that, for the entity previously entrusted with a service contract to have been the subject of a transfer within the meaning of the directive, it may be sufficient in certain circumstances for the new awardee of the contract to have voluntarily taken over the majority of the employees specially assigned by his predecessor to the performance of the contract.

[20] In that regard, the factual circumstances to be taken into account in determining whether the conditions for a transfer are met include in

21   particular, in addition to the degree of similarity of the activity carried on before and after the transfer and the type of undertaking or business concerned, the question whether or not the majority of the employees were taken over by the new employer (*Spijkers,* cited above, paragraph 13).

21   Since in certain labour-intensive sectors a group of workers engaged in a joint activity on a permanent basis may constitute an economic entity, it must be recognized that such an entity is capable of maintaining its identity after it has been transferred where the new employer does not merely pursue the activity in question but also takes over a major part, in terms of their numbers and skills, of the employees specially assigned by his predecessor to that task. In those circumstances, the new employer takes over a body of assets enabling him to carry on the activities or certain activities of the transferor undertaking on a regular basis.

22   It is for the national court to establish, in the light of the foregoing interpretative guidance, whether a transfer has occurred in this case.

23   The answer to the questions from the national court must therefore be that Article 1(1) of the directive is to be interpreted as meaning that the directive does not apply to a situation in which a person who had entrusted the cleaning of his premises to a first undertaking terminates his contract with the latter and, for the performance of similar work, enters into a new contract with a second undertaking, if there is no concomitant transfer from one undertaking to the other of significant tangible or intangible assets or taking over by the new employer of a major part of the workforce, in terms of their numbers and skills, assigned by his predecessor to the performance of the contract.

Notes and Questions

1.   Advocate General La Pergola's opinion noted his "misgivings" with the application of some prior precedents, notably *Daddy's Dance Hall,* to the present facts. He perceived this contract transfer "in competitive circumstances" to be quite different from the transfers reviewed in prior caselaw and would have flatly concluded that the present case did not fall under Directive 77/187. The Court's views, though more nuanced, certainly were influenced by his analysis.

2.   Can you distinguish this case from *Daddy's Dance Hall,* or not? Does the Court's judgment represent a policy shift, or merely the application of the same policy to different facts? In your view, would it make a difference if Lefarth, the new cleaner, had an adequate staff to clean the school before getting the contract, or if, in contrast, Lefarth needed to hire three or four of the Zehnacker cleaning staff, but didn't hire Suzen? In later cases, the Court applied the *Suzen* criteria to hold that "in certain sectors, such as cleaning ... the activity is essentially based on manpower. Thus, an organized grouping of wage earners who are specifically and permanently assigned to a common task may ... amount to an economic entity." Vidal v. Perez, Cases C–127/96, C–229/96 and C–74/97, [1998] ECR I–8179, at 8231. In consequence, if the new employer "takes over a major part, in terms of their numbers and skills, of the employees specifically assigned by his predecessor to that task," id. at 8233, the provisions of the Transfer of Undertakings Directive should apply. Accord, with regard to the transfer of mine workers, engaged essentially in the same mining activity, from one group company to another, Allen v. Amalgamated Construction, *supra* page 1312.

3. Ford's Belgian sales company was the controlling shareholder in a Brussels dealer, Anfo Motors. In 1987, Ford decided to liquidate Anfo and to give its former territory to an adjacent independent dealer, Novarobel, in an arrangement which purported to transfer 14 of Anfo's employees to Novarobel. Although assured that he would have the same duties, status and seniority, a salesman, Merckx, refused to accept the transfer, claiming that the change in work site and the risk of loss of clientele upon which his income would depend represented a constructive dismissal. Anfo sold no assets to Novarobel and did not turn over its customer list. Does the transfer of a car dealer franchise fall under the Transfer of Undertakings Directive? If so, does Novarobel's refusal to guarantee Merckx that his income, based on sales commissions, would remain at the level he had under Anfo, constitute a constructive dismissal under article 4(2) of the directive? See Merckx v. Ford Motors Company Belgium SA, Cases C–171 & 172/94, [1996] ECR I–1253.

COMMISSION v. UNITED KINGDOM

(Transfer of undertakings).
Case C–382/92, [1994] ECR I–2435.

[In a parallel proceeding to its attack on the United Kingdom law implementing the Collective Redundancy Directive, supra, the Commission also challenged the UK's 1981 Regulation intended to implement the Transfer of Undertakings Directive. The two principal issues concerned the Regulation's application only to employers who voluntarily recognized trade union representatives, and the Regulation's low level of sanctions. In both instances, the Court concluded that the UK had inadequately implemented the directive, ruling in language virtually identical to that used in the *UK collective redundancy* case. However, the Court also had to deal with two other issues.]

32 In its second complaint, the Commission argues that the UK Regulations, as interpreted by courts and tribunals in the United Kingdom, do not apply to transfers which do not involve the transfer of the property of an undertaking, contrary to Article 1(1) of the directive, as interpreted by the Court in *Ny Molle Kro* and *Daddy's Dance Hall*.* * *

36 [T]he scope of national laws, regulations or administrative provisions must be assessed in the light of the interpretation given to them by national courts.

37 The decisions of United Kingdom courts and tribunals relied on by the Commission * * * predate the judgment of the House of Lords cited by the United Kingdom * * * which, as the Commission concedes, holds that the UK Regulations must, as far as possible, be interpreted in accordance with the wording and objectives of the directive and with the court's interpretation thereof.* * *

38 In those circumstances, the Commission has failed to establish that [the UK regulation] had the scope attributed to it by the Commission.

40 The Commission argues in its third complaint that the UK Regulations * * * do not apply to non-profit-making undertakings, contrary to Article 1(1) of the directive, as interpreted by the Court [citing *Dr. Sophie Redmond Stichting v. Bartol, infra*].

[41]   [The UK] regulation 2(1) defines an "undertaking" as including "any trade or business" but expressly excludes "any undertaking or part of an undertaking which is not in the nature of a commercial venture". * * *

[42]   The United Kingdom submits that the directive cannot apply, as the Commission claims, to transfers of non-profit-making undertakings on the ground that such undertakings, which are not engaged in "economic activities" within the meaning of the Treaty, do not come within its scope.

[43]   That argument must be rejected.

[44]   The Court has already accepted, at least implicitly, in [*Redmond Stichting*], that a body might be engaged in economic activities and be regarded as an "undertaking" for the purposes of Community law even though it did not operate with a view to profit.

[45]   [T]he fact that an undertaking is engaged in non-profit-making activities is not in itself sufficient to deprive such activities of their economic character or to remove the undertaking from the scope of the directive.

Notes and Questions

1.   The excerpt's initial issue raises some tantalizing questions. Suppose that the House of Lords judgment which essentially overruled the lower courts' erroneous approach had not been handed down prior to the Court of Justice's response in this proceeding. Do you agree that the UK should be made responsible in an Article 226 proceeding for the erroneous views of lower courts? Suppose the House of Lords had fallen into the error of the lower courts. What could the UK government do if it lost an Article 226 proceeding based on the erroneous views of its highest court? See the discussion at page 441 n.4.

2.   In ruling that the transfer of undertakings directive covers non-profit entities, such as associations and foundations, as well as commercial and professional enterprises, the Court expanded on its conclusion in Dr. Sophie Redmond Stichting v. Bartol, Case C–29/91, [1992] ECR I–3189. A Dutch city ended its subsidy to a foundation providing treatment and other aid to drug addicts. Having no other income, the foundation sought to dismiss its staff. The staff, however, claimed that a transfer of undertakings had occurred because the Dutch city had simultaneously started paying the same subsidy to another foundation, Sigma, to provide similar types of aid to drug addicts. Making a detailed study, Advocate General van Gerven had urged that the directive should cover such foundations. Without any specific analysis, the Court agreed.

3.   In Henke v. Gemeinde Schierke, Case C–298/94, [1996] ECR I–4989, the Court declined to extend the protection afforded by the Transfer of Undertakings Directive to an employee of a municipality when all of the municipality's administrative functions were taken over by the administrative office of a group of municipalities. Although Advocate General Lenz argued that the plaintiff's position as the head of an industrial development and tourism unit did not represent a public function, the Court held that the municipality was not an "undertaking" covered by the directive, because it exercised "public authority." (¶¶ 14–17.)

In contrast, when Italy privatized its state-owned telecommunications company, transferring all of its assets and rights and most of its employees to Telecom Italia, employees who claimed that their retirement benefits had been adversely affected by the transfer were held to be protected by the terms of the directive in Collino v. Telecom Italia, Case C–343/98, [2000] ECR ___ (Sept. 14, 2000). The

Court considered that telecommunications operations constituted an economic service, not one "involving the exercise of public authority."

3. EMPLOYEE PROTECTION IN EMPLOYER INSOLVENCIES

Because the Collective Redundancies Directive did not cover employees who lose their jobs when the employer becomes insolvent, it was obvious that specific legislation was necessary. Directive 80/987 on the protection of employees in the event of insolvency of their employer, O.J. L 283/23 (Oct. 28, 1980), requires Member States to ensure that "guarantee institutions" provide guarantees for payment of any outstanding employee claims for pay or benefits prior to the onset of insolvency (art. 3). The guarantee institutions must have assets "independent of the employers' operating capital and be inaccessible to proceedings for insolvency," with the assets coming from employers' contributions or from a state agency (art. 5). The directive enables much more rapid and certain payment of amounts due to unpaid employees, and avoids the risk that they would receive only limited recourse as unsecured creditors in an insolvency proceeding.

Italy's failure to implement this directive on time gave rise to the landmark judgment on Member State liability in damages, *Francovich*, excerpted at page 407. In Miret v. Fondo de Garantia Salarial, Case C–334/92, [1993] ECR I–6911, the issue was whether the Spanish guaranty fund ought to have covered the director-general of a Spanish company (a post equivalent to that of president). When it joined the Community, Spain had negotiated an exception for household personnel from the directive's scope, but had not mentioned senior management. The Court held that the directive was intended to protect all "salaried employees," which would also include senior management.

Somewhat surprisingly, the 1980 directive does not specify which national guaranty fund is liable for the back pay of employees of a branch in one Member State when the company itself, established in another Member State, becomes insolvent. In Everson & Anor v. Secretary of State for Trade, Case C–198/98, [1999] ECR I–8903, the Court concluded that the UK guaranty fund was liable for the back pay and benefits of 200 employees of a UK branch of an insolvent Irish shipping company. The Court noted that the employees paid taxes and social security contributions to the UK.

C.   WORKER HEALTH AND SAFETY LEGISLATION

1. GENERIC HEALTH AND SAFETY MEASURES

Adoption of worker health and safety legislation began in the late 1970s and accelerated with the entry into force of Article 118a in 1987. An early example is Directive 77/576, O.J. L 229/12 (Sept. 7, 1977), amended in O.J. L 245/23 (Aug. 26, 1992),which set minimum standards for safety signs at plants and construction sites and required the use of standard symbols that would be easily recognized even by migrant workers who cannot speak the local language. Directive 80/1107 on the protection of workers from risks related to exposure to chemical, physical and biological agents at work, O.J. L 327/8 (Dec. 3, 1980), initiated a procedure for classifying dangerous risk factors, set rules on maximum exposure and monitoring of health, and established a system of emergency health measures. Immediate standards were set for a certain number of dangerous substances, such as arsenic, cadmium, lead and mercury. The directive has been periodically amended to add additional dangerous substances and refine standards as further risks are identified. Other significant directives required operational safety standards and prescribed measures for warning the public in the event of serious accidents in industrial operations, O.J. L 230/1 (Aug. 5, 1982) (prompted by the well-known chemical plant explosion in Seveso, Italy), and set standards for exposure to noise at work, O.J. L 137/28 (May 24, 1986).

In Chapter 14D, we learned that the new approach to technical harmonization called for the adoption of "framework" directives to establish general principles, with detailed regulation or specific standards to be provided in later directives for specific fields, or through the action of Community standardization bodies. A leading example is the "framework" Directive 89/391 on measures to encourage improvements in the safety and health of workers at work, O.J. L 183/1 (June 29, 1989). This directive sets certain generic rules for protection of workers at their principal place of employment, requiring, for example, first aid centers, information and training for workers as to common health or safety risks, and consultation with employee representatives on ways to avoid such hazards.

Also noteworthy is Regulation 2062/94 creating a European Agency for Safety and Health at Work, O.J. L 216/1 (Aug. 20, 1994). This agency, sited at Bilbao, Spain, serves as a center for study and exchange of information.

2. THE PREGNANT AND ADOLESCENT WORKERS DIRECTIVES

Influenced by text in the Social Charter, the Commission proposed directives to protect pregnant workers and working mothers, as well as to protect working adolescents and children. Because both directives focused primarily on the need to protect the health of the workers concerned, they were ultimately adopted through use of Article 118a.

Directive 92/85 on improvements in the safety and health at work of pregnant workers and workers who have recently given birth or are breast feeding, O.J. L 348/1 (Nov. 28, 1992), is one of the best-known recent social action measures. (See the Selected Documents.) The particular health risks of such workers, both from exposure to chemical, physical and biological agents and from mental and physical fatigue, are to be assessed by the employers, as well as by the Commission on a Community-wide basis. Employers are obligated to reduce the worker's exposure to risks, if necessary re-assigning the worker to other tasks, or placing the worker on leave (art. 5). Pregnant workers and mothers of newborns are entitled to a minimum of 14 weeks' maternity leave before and/or after confinement, with two of the weeks being compulsory (art. 8). Pregnant workers cannot be dismissed, except for reasons manifestly not connected with their condition (art. 10). During any leave period, the workers are entitled to remuneration calculated to be at least at the level of sick pay required by national law (art. 11).

The UK opposed several aspects of the directive proposal, notably the maternity leave and economic benefits provisions, claiming that they might cost UK employers 100 million pounds annually. After the UK succeeded in having the leave remuneration reduced from full pay to the sick pay level, it abstained when the directive was adopted.

We need only briefly to mention Directive 94/33 on the protection of young people at work, O.J. L 216/12 (Aug. 20, 1994), which was not particularly controversial. This generally forbids employment for children under fourteen, permits young people between fourteen and eighteen to work, but only twelve hours per week during school terms, forbids night work by adolescents, etc. Virtually all the States had to change some aspect of their prior protective legislation for young people.

3. THE WORKING TIME DIRECTIVE

Directive 93/104 on the organization of working time, O.J. L 307/1 (Dec. 13, 1993) (see the Selected Documents), is undoubtedly the best known and also the most controversial legislation adopted through use of Article 118a. Proposed by the Commission in 1990 to embody rights enunciated in the Social Charter, the draft was warmly supported by France and other liberal governments on the continent, but bitterly opposed by Prime Ministers Thatcher and Major of the UK. The text was finally adopted only with UK-inspired compromise language intended to reduce the scope of some provisions and delay the implementation of others. The UK government contended that it was only trying to protect the interests of millions of UK workers who wanted to work more than 48 hours a week and had no desire to take long holidays.

The principal purpose of the Working Time Directive is to set minimum standards for daily and weekly rest periods and for annual leave. Recitals not only quote the Social Charter's description of these as rights, but declare that these "periods of rest" are essential for worker safety and health, which "should not be subordinated to purely economic considerations." In the substantive provisions, article 3 requires "a minimum daily rest period of 11 consecutive hours per 24–hour period," to which article 4 adds a "rest break" if a work day exceeds 6 hours. Article 6 sets a maximum of 48 hours of work, including overtime, in each weekly period, to which article 5 adds a requirement of a 24 hour uninterrupted period of rest every week (which rest period should "in principle include Sunday"). With regard to annual leave, article 7 requires "paid annual leave of at least four weeks," and forbids substituting added remuneration for the annual leave.

The directive also provides particular protections in the special circumstances of night work and work in shifts. Article 8 sets an 8 hour maximum for night work. Article 9 provides that night workers should receive free health assessments at regular intervals, and states that workers with health problems occasioned by night work have a right to transfer to suitable day work, whenever possible. Article 13 deals with work in shifts or "according to a certain pattern," and requires efforts to alleviate "monotonous work and work at a predetermined work rate."

Article 15 authorizes States to have rules more favorable to workers, or to permit labor-management collective agreements more favorable to workers. This is common in continental States, which often set 38 or 40 hour maximum work weeks–indeed, the Jospin government in France reduced the maximum to 35 hours in an apparently successful effort to reduce unemployment. Also, labor-management agreements often add a fifth week of paid vacation.

Many of the compromise provisions in the directive relate to exceptions and derogations. Article 1 provides a blanket exception for air, rail, road and sea transport, sea fishing, and "the activities of doctors in training." A 1997 Commission White Paper estimated that about 5.6 million workers, 4% of the total work force, was thus excluded, and proposed supplemental legislation. Accordingly, Directive 2000/34, O.J. L 195/41 (Aug. 1, 2000), amended the Working Time Directive to apply it to all the excepted fields, but with additional derogations specific to each field.

The Working Time Directive became effective on Nov. 23, 1996, but in article 18 the UK obtained a three year extension for a three week paid annual leave instead of article 7's four weeks of leave. The UK also insisted that article 18b provide for a seven year suspension of the maximum 48 hour work week, subject to an employer's obtaining the consent of each worker concerned to work for longer periods. In addition, article 17 provides a long list of derogations from the usual rules, principally "on account of the specific characteristics of the activity," e.g., in health care in hospitals or custodial care in prisons and residential institutions, for ambulance, fire and civil protection, for the media and telecommunications, for energy provision and pollution control, and for periodic surges in essential work in agriculture and tourism. A derogation is also granted for managerial personnel. (Note that there is no specific derogation for lawyers, accountants, engineers or other professionals, although there is for persons engaged in research and development.)

Over all, the directive provisions stand in sharp contrast to the US, where there is no comparable federal legislation and where collective bargaining agreements customarily provide for rest and vacation periods (e.g., the common 40 hour work week and two weeks' paid vacation), but permit substantial overtime. In September 2001, an International Labor Organization study indicated that in the 1990s Americans increased their average annual working time to 1979 hours, 15% more than the UK average and 33% more than the German average. Although the US naturally leads the world in productivity per worker, France and Belgium lead in productivity per work hour.

The UK promptly attacked the Working Time Directive in an Article 230 (ex 173) appeal, contending principally that the directive was not properly adopted by use of Article 118a and that its provisions violated proportionality and the principle of subsidiarity. Moreover, the directive's provisions have now been interpreted in two significant recent cases.

UNITED KINGDOM v. COUNCIL
(Working time directive).

[For the excerpted Court judgment, see pages 92, 124 and 175 *supra*.]

Notes and Questions

1. In ¶ 15, the Court defines broadly the worker health and safety which Article 118a can be used to protect. Do you agree? Specifically, is the Court interpretation permitting measures intended only to promote well-being, as opposed to the removal of health and safety risks, a justified approach?

2. Certainly limits on consecutive hours of work in a day, or upon night work, can be justified on health and safety grounds, but are the 48 hour work week and four weeks paid vacation provisions genuinely intended for health and safety or only for a desirable quality of life? Do you agree with the Court view that the Council did not need to have scientific evidence for its precise rules, but could make a general assessment of health benefits?

3. It is noteworthy that the Court struck down the directive language making Sunday "in principle" a part of the compulsory weekly rest period, because this provision did not benefit worker health. Do you think such a provision could be adopted under the new post-Amsterdam legislative power in Article 137?

4. The UK may have lost in advance its argument that the directive violated the principles of proportionality and subsidiarity when it obtained derogations and exceptions in the text, notably the delay in phasing in four weeks of vacation and the 48 hour work week. In that connection, do you consider that workers should be able to agree with employers that they will work on average more than 48 hours, or do you think that governments should not permit this? Also, do you agree with the directive's prohibition of remuneration instead of the four weeks paid leave?

5. Comparable legislation in the US is probably inconceivable, but as a matter of policy, do you think the US would benefit if legislation restricted the length of the work week or set a minimum paid vacation? On the other hand, do you agree with many American economists and European business leaders who believe that the directive will reduce Community industry's ability to compete in the global marketplace? Or do you agree with those Europeans who believe that the directive provides health and safety and quality of life benefits that outweigh economic considerations?

QUEEN v. SECRETARY OF STATE FOR TRADE EX PARTE BECTU

Case C–173/99, [2001] ECR ___ (June 26, 2001).

[When the UK Labor government adopted a regulation in 1998 to implement the Working Time Directive, it provided that employees did not obtain any right to annual paid leave until after being "continuously employed for 13 weeks." The Broadcasting, Entertainment, Cinematographic and Theater Union (BECTU) challenged this provision on behalf of its 30,000 members, contending that it deprived many of its members of any form of annual leave because they were customarily employed on short term fixed contracts for less than 13 weeks. The High Court referred questions on the proper interpretation of the Directive. The Court of Justice initially noted that the directive was inspired by the Social Charter clause on annual leave.]

40 [T]he directive makes it clear in Article 17, that only certain of its provisions, which are exhaustively listed, may be the subject of derogations introduced by the Member States or the two sides of industry. Moreover, the implementation of such derogations is subject to the condition that the general principles of protection of the health and safety of workers are complied with or that the workers concerned are afforded equivalent periods of compensatory rest or else appropriate protection.

41 Now it is clear that Article 7 [on annual leave] is not one of the provisions from which Directive 93/104 expressly allows derogations.

* * *

43 [T]he entitlement of every worker to paid annual leave must be regarded as a particularly important principle of Community social law from which there can be no derogations and whose implementation by the competent national authorities must be confined within the limits expressly laid down by Directive 93/104.

44 It is significant in that connection that the directive also embodies the rule that a worker must normally be entitled to actual rest, with a view to ensuring effective protection of his health and safety, since it is only where the employment relationship is terminated that Article 7(2) allows an allowance to be paid in lieu of paid annual leave.

* * *

46 Furthermore, Directive 93/104 draws no distinction between workers employed under a contract of indefinite duration and those employed under a fixed-term contract. On the contrary, * * * the provisions concerning minimum rest periods * * * refer in most cases to 'every worker', as indeed does Article 7(1) in relation to entitlement to paid annual leave.

* * *

49 [Under the UK regulation,] workers whose employment relationship comes to an end before completion of the minimum period of 13 weeks' uninterrupted work for the same employer are deprived of any entitlement to paid annual leave and likewise receive no allowance in lieu even though they have in fact worked for a certain period and, under Directive 93/104, minimum rest periods are essential for the protection of their health and safety.

50 National rules of that kind are manifestly incompatible with the scheme of Directive 93/104 which, in contrast to its treatment of other matters, makes no provision for any possible derogation regarding entitlement to paid annual leave and therefore, *a fortiori*, prevents a Member State from unilaterally restricting that entitlement which is conferred on all workers by that directive.

51 Furthermore, rules of the kind at issue in the main proceedings are liable to give rise to abuse because employers might be tempted to evade the obligation to grant the paid annual leave to which every worker is entitled by more frequent resort to short-term employment relationships.

52 Consequently, Directive 93/104 must be interpreted as precluding Member States from unilaterally limiting the entitlement to paid annual leave conferred on all workers by applying a precondition for such entitlement which has the effect of preventing certain workers from benefitting from it.

* * *

57 The United Kingdom Government contends * * * that the condition for entitlement to paid annual leave laid down in its regulations strikes a fair

balance between the objective of [protecting] the health and safety of workers, and the need to avoid imposing excessive constraints on small and medium-sized undertakings, in accordance with the second paragraph of Article 118a(2) of the Treaty, which constitutes the legal basis of that directive. Apart from the cost of the leave itself, the administrative costs of organizing annual leave for staff engaged for short periods would be particularly high and would weigh more heavily on small and medium-sized undertakings.

[58] On that point, first, the regulations at issue in the main proceedings are of general application since the rule that entitlement to paid annual leave is conditional upon completion of a minimum uninterrupted period of 13 weeks' employment with the same employer applies to all workers and does not vary according to the category of undertaking in which they are employed.

[59] Second, it is clear from the fifth recital in the preamble to Directive 93/104 that 'the improvement of workers' safety, hygiene and health at work is an objective which should not be subordinated to purely economic considerations.' However, the United Kingdom's argument is incontestably based on such a consideration.

Notes and Questions

1. The Labor government was presumably in good faith in adopting the contested provision, because it generally endorses Community social policy measures. It is certainly plausible to require a minimum period of employment before any right to a proportionate share of an annual paid leave should accrue. The UK noted that other States had similar provisions. Do you agree with the Court's interpretation? As a matter of policy, do you consider that the directive would have been better drafted if it required a minimum period of employment? Do you agree with the Court that the UK's desire to reduce the administrative burden of smaller enterprises constituted only an "economic" justification?

2. In Sindicato de Medicos v. Conselleria de Sanidad de la Generalidad Valenciana, Case C–303/98, [2000] ECR ___ (Oct. 3, 2000), the Court held that the directive contained no express derogation for rules governing medical doctors, as opposed to doctors in training. Accordingly, the Spanish rules on providing primary medical care in rural regions will have to be revised, because they permitted doctors to be on call in residence at facilities for excessively long periods of time (the plaintiff association of doctors claimed that doctors could be on call for 31 hours without rest). How to balance the rest requirements for doctors, nurses and other health care providers with the social need for continuous medical care is obviously a difficult issue in many countries (including the US). As a policy matter, do you think the directive should have contained special rules for the medical care sector?

D. SOCIAL ACTION LEGISLATION IN THE 1990s

As indicated above, the 1989 Social Action Program produced a series of measures in the 1990s that have significantly enhanced employee rights and affected other aspects of society. Due to the opposition of the Conservative government in the UK until 1997, only a couple of measures were adopted for the entire Community, except for those described in section C that were adopted through use of Article 118a. The rest were adopted by use of the Social Protocol. After the election of the Blair government in 1997, the UK has accepted all of the legislation produced through the Social Protocol. New initiatives are now being considered for adoption under Article 137, since it became effective on May 1, 1999.

Space concerns prevent a complete coverage of this active social legislative program. We will only review four measures which have had a major impact on social life in the Community and provide valuable comparisons with US rules and policies.

1. THE EMPLOYMENT TERMS AND POSTING OF WORKERS DIRECTIVES

The first significant measure adopted in the 1989 Social Action Program was Directive 91/533 on form of proof of an employment relationship, O.J. L 288/32 (Nov. 18, 1991) (see the Selected Documents), which requires employers to keep on record and provide to employees the written terms of their employment. The terms must specify the job description, the usual daily and weekly period of employment, paid leave, remuneration and social benefits and any applicable collective agreements. As many employers previously did not utilize written agreements, this directive has had a considerable impact. Incidentally, even though its legal basis was Article 100 (now 94), the directive could be adopted because the UK chose to abstain rather than vote against it.

The directive does not expressly cover the subject of overtime work. In Lange v. Georg Schunemann, Case C–350/99, [2001] ECR ___ (Feb. 8, 2001), an employee sued for relief after his dismissal for a refusal to work overtime when the subject of overtime was not mentioned in his contract. The Court held that the directive article requiring identification of the usual length of the "normal working day or week" did not implicitly require coverage of overtime, but then went on to conclude that an obligation upon an employee to work overtime whenever the employer requests (as opposed, presumably, to overtime mutually agreed upon) constituted an essential aspect of the employment relationship that ought to have been specified in the terms of employment. The Court then noted that article 8 of the directive requires States to provide an employee with judicial recourse, but leaves the States free to set an appropriate penalty for the employer's omission of an essential term from the agreement.

Although adopted on the basis of Article 57 (now 47), another measure of great importance to workers is Directive 96/71 on the posting of workers during the providing of trans-frontier services, O.J. L 18/1 (Jan. 21, 1997). Especially in the construction industry, enterprises providing services in another State have been using labor brought in from the home State of the enterprise, often for substantial periods of time, benefiting from the lower pay and benefit scales of the home State. For years, contractors in States like Germany, with high salaries and benefits, have complained that enterprises from States like the UK, with low salaries and benefits, have in effect been engaging in unfair competition.

The posting of workers directive was intended to rectify this situation and was accordingly initially opposed by the Major government, which contended that the UK firms' practice represented fair rather than unfair competition. Various compromises enabled the directive's adoption. With certain exceptions for workers employed in a host State for less than a month, Directive 96/71 requires the employers to abide by host State rules concerning minimum pay, mandatory benefits (other than retirement pensions), maximum work periods, minimum paid holidays, and health and safety at work. Do you think the directive represents sound social and competition policy, or an unfortunate interference with free market competition? For the applicable Court doctrine prior to the directive, see *Arblade & Leloup, supra* page 670.

2. THE PARENTAL LEAVE DIRECTIVE

Directive 96/34 on the framework agreement on parental leave is probably the most innovative social measure of the 1990s. Most States already had legislation protecting pregnant workers and the mothers of newborns before the directive on that subject, but relatively few had legislation granting any form of parental leave rights. The Commission first proposed such a directive in 1983, but it received little support in the Council. The adoption of the current measure is undoubtedly due to a gradual shift in social attitudes concerning the desirability of parental leave.

The Parental Leave Directive is one of those adopted by the unusual procedure of negotiations on a Framework Agreement text between Community-level representative bodies of management and labor, which was then endorsed by the Council under the Social Agreement as a directive effective in 1998. The UK was accordingly not initially bound by the directive, but, as noted above, the Labor government agreed to accept its terms in a supplemental directive in December 1997.

The Preamble to the Framework Agreement refers to the Social Charter's statement that "measures should be developed to enable men and women to reconcile their occupational and family obligations." The Preamble further declares that "measures to reconcile work and family life should encourage the introduction of new flexible ways of organizing work and time which are better suited to the changing needs of society." Although the Preamble also refers to the need to take into consideration "the competitiveness of the Community economy," it is quite apparent that the Parental Leave Directive is principally intended to achieve a broad social policy goal.

The directive grants men and women workers a right to parental leave for at least three months to take care of a child, including an adopted child, until a given age up to 8 years, with the age to be chosen by the State and/or its management and labor bodies. There is no requirement that the leave be paid, but at the end of the leave the worker has the right to return to the same job, if possible, or to similar work. Member States may opt to make the parental leave subject to the employee having worked for at least one year for the employer, and to a suitable notice period. The State and/or its management and bodies may also opt to protect employers' interests and postpone leave for justifiable reasons, e.g., when a replacement cannot be found within the notice period, or when "a specific function is of strategic importance." The directive also declares that "special arrangements to meet the operational and organizational requirements of small undertakings" can be made.

Apart from parental leave, the directive also requires States to adopt measures to permit leave "on grounds of force majeure," which is specified as meaning "for urgent family reasons in case of sickness or accident." No minimum leave time or conditions are set. Presumably this text grants a right to leave for a reasonable period of time to a worker who needs to care for a spouse, child or other close relative.

An interesting comparison can be drawn between the directive and the US Family and Medical Leave Act, Pub. L. No. 103–03 (1993), the first major legislation in the Clinton administration. The Act grants up to twelve weeks of unpaid leave per year, requiring most employers to grant such leave to employees who desire to meet a variety of family obligations in addition to pregnancy or childbirth.

A Community-wide association representing small and medium-sized enterprises challenged the Parental Leave Directive in Union Europeenne de l'Artisanat et des Petites et Moyennes Enterprises v. Council, Case T–135/96, [1998] ECR II–2335. The association felt that the interests of small enterprises were not adequately protected by the directive's terms and sought to annul the directive under Article 230 (ex 173) for failure to comply with the appropriate procedure for its adoption. The association essentially claimed that it should not only have been consulted (as it was), but should also have been included with the three Community-wide representative bodies of management and labor when they drafted the terms of the Framework Agreement.

The Court of First Instance dismissed the association's complaint on the grounds that it lacked standing to challenge a directive, a legislative act. However, the court reviewed with great care the procedure followed before concluding that the management bodies engaged in the drafting adequately represented the interests of small enterprises, and that both the Commission and the Council had appropriately determined the representative character of the management bodies.

The CFI observed that the Social Agreement procedure enabled the Council to adopt the Framework Agreement as a directive without any legislative participation of the Parliament. The CFI notably held that "the principle of democracy on which the Union is founded requires–in the absence of the participation of the European Parliament in the legislative process–that the participation of the people be otherwise assured, in this instance through the parties representative of management and labour." (¶ 89.)

Notes and Questions

1. Do you agree with the basic policy behind the Parental Leave Directive, namely that States must compel employers to accept short term leave periods for child care by both parents? Would you prefer encouragement of such leaves by subsidies to employers, rather than by binding rules? Overall, do you think the benefit to society from such leaves outweighs the manifest operational inefficiency they represent for employers?

2. The Commission is supposed to review the directive's impact after several years. Would you like to see aspects of the directive's rules strengthened at that time, e.g., to permit leave for child care at any time until a child reaches maturity,

or to permit longer periods of leave? Do you think other examples of force majeure might be indicated?

3.   The procedural mode of permitting Community-wide management and labor associations to negotiate and draft texts of laws is certainly surprising, from an American viewpoint. The procedure has been taken over from the Social Agreement and is now outlined in Articles 138 and 139. Some critics have contended that the failure to include parliamentary co-decision in the approval by the Council represents another example of a "democratic deficit." Would you agree?

3.   WORKER INFORMATION AND CONSULTATION DIRECTIVES

No proposal in the social action field has engendered greater controversy over the years than that to adopt Community measures to harmonize rules on structures to provide operational information from management to workers and to require management-employee consultation on certain issues. Although such rules have long been common in continental States, they varied considerably in scope and operational features. Of course, the whole approach is alien to traditional management-labor relations in the UK and Ireland (and the US). Incidentally, these consultation rules should not be confused with the corporate structure of employee co-determination in management, which requires that corporate supervisory and management boards (corresponding to American corporate boards of directors) must include a certain number of employee members. A variety of corporate co-determination rules are mandatory for companies employing large numbers of workers in Germany, Denmark, Luxembourg and the Netherlands. See Chapter 17D.

All the continental States of the Community have long had some form of system for employee representatives in enterprise or work councils in large and medium-sized firms. Thus, in France, every firm employing more than fifty persons must have a works council consisting of two or more representatives elected by all employees (not selected by unions, although union leaders may be elected as employee representatives on the works council). A works council deals with management on all employee concerns, including the discharge of employees, labor grievances, workers' health, and work conditions. The works council has the right to inspect the annual financial statements and to receive certain relevant operational information.

Since the 1970s, European unions have urged the creation of similar bodies to represent all the employees of a multinational corporation with subsidiaries or branches in several States. The Commission endorsed the idea, proposing in 1980 a draft directive on procedures for informing and consulting employees, which was reissued in amended form in 1983, O.J. C 217/3 (Aug. 12, 1983) (popularly known as the "Vredeling" proposal after a prominent Commission for social affairs). The principal forces in opposition predictably included the UK Government, the European Confederation of Industries, and the subsidiaries of US companies. A Council resolution of June 21, 1986 tabled the proposal.

The 1989 Social Charter contained a section on "Information, Consultation and Participation for Workers," which called for measures to achieve this goal. With the principle thus endorsed by the European Council (except for the UK), the Commission launched a new proposal in 1991. Due to adamant opposition from the UK under Prime Minister Major, the draft was shifted to the procedures set out in Social Protocol, and was adopted as Directive 94/45 on the establishment of a European Works Council, O.J. L 254/64 (Sept. 30, 1994). As noted above, the Labor government elected in 1997 accepted a supplemental Directive 97/74, O.J. L 10/22 (Jan. 16, 1998), which slightly amended the directive to enable its extension to the UK.

The European Works Council (EWC) Directive is intended to ensure that employees of "Community-scale undertakings and Community-scale groups" shall be represented in an EWC with the right to obtain significant operational information and to consult systematically with the "central management." (Note that the EWC directive does not require States to have a general system for works councils for smaller enterprises, nor even for larger enterprises with few or no employees outside of one State.)

To be a "Community-scale undertaking" or "group," the enterprise or group must employ a least 1000 employees (including part-time employees) on average for two years, with bodies of at least 150 employees in two Member States. Obviously, not only large but many medium-sized enterprises will meet these thresholds. Note also that there is no reference to corporate form– limited liability companies and partnerships are encompassed. The concept of a group obviously includes any controlled subsidiary, whether control is exercised by "ownership, financial participation, or the rules which govern it" (art. 3).

Central management and a "special negotiating body" chosen to represent all employees must negotiate an agreement which defines the composition and membership of the EWC, "the functions and the procedure for information and consultation," "the venue, frequency and duration of meetings," and the financial resources for the EWC (which, incidentally, are provided by the central management) (art. 6). EWC members, employee representatives and experts assisting them (e.g., economists, accountants, lawyers) are naturally bound by a duty to keep information confidential (art. 8).

An annex details the scope of the information and consultation rights. Central management must meet annually with the EWC (more often, if "exceptional circumstances," such as the closure of establishments or collective redundancies, are envisaged). The scope of the information and consultation is quite broad:

> "The meeting shall relate in particular to the structure, economic and financial situation, the probable development of the business and of production and sales, the situation and probable trend of employment, investments, and substantial changes concerning organization, introduction of new working methods or production processes, transfers of production, mergers, cut-backs or closures of undertakings, establishments or important parts thereof, and collective redundancies."

However, under Article 8, management need not provide information that "according to objective criteria, would seriously harm the functioning of the undertakings concerned or would be prejudicial to them."

A European Trade Confederation study in 1995 estimated that 1144 multinational companies would have to create EWCs, including 186 groups controlled by US and 106 by UK parents. Despite criticism of the directive by multinational companies or groups (including US companies), EWCs are now operational and have apparently not thus far generated any serious structural problems for management.

Before closing, we should note that a general framework directive intended to require States to have a system for works councils in smaller enterprises is under active consideration and close to approval. The Commission proposed a draft in 1999, O.J. C 2/3 (Jan. 5, 1999), which reached the stage of a Council Common Position, O.J. C 307/16 (Oct. 31, 2001), and was being negotiated in a conciliation procedure with Parliament at the end of 2001. The text currently would require any enterprise employing at least 50 employees (or even 20, at a State's option) to have a works council, and would require that the works council receive information and be able to consult with management concerning the enterprise's activities, economic situation and work force.

Notes and Questions

1. In several well-publicized cases in the 1980s, a European group in one State closed plants or establishments in other States with little or no warning to the workers laid off and without significant efforts to alleviate the social distress thus occasioned. This partially motivated the efforts to adopt an EWC directive. Do you think that when a group has an EWC, it will promote more balanced treatment of the interests of employees in different States, or not?

2. Consider the various types of information that central management must provide an EWC. Do you think that all the types represent information that employee representatives genuinely need to receive to protect employee interests? Do you think that some EWC members might violate their duty of confidentiality, e.g., by transmitting to union leaders sensitive economic data when contract negotiations are imminent (one of the arguments frequently raised by business leaders in opposing the directive)? Is management's right to withhold sensitive data in article 8 adequate?

3. It is difficult for an American to evaluate objectively the merits or risks of EWCs (or, for that matter, works councils for smaller enterprises), because the approach is so different from our traditional management-labor policies. Many American economists contend that worker information and consultation rights make European industry less competitive on a global scale, because they occasion ongoing employment costs and delays, and tend to reduce restructuring and rationalization for greater market efficiency. Europeans often respond that these rights facilitate labor peace, reduce the risk of serious management-labor conflicts and strikes, and promote higher worker productivity. What is your view? In any event, do the rights promote the quality of life for employees?

Chapter 37

EQUAL RIGHTS

A. TREATY ARTICLES AND BASIC CONCEPTS

From the start, the Treaty has protected equal rights for women. The Treaty as first adopted did so in Article 119, which required that Member States ensure application of the principle of equal pay for equal work. Directives expanded the original obligation, assuring equal treatment more broadly. Eventually, Member State initiatives forced Community institutions to focus on hard questions of affirmative action and reverse discrimination, resulting in a subject area that might now be called: equal rights for women and men. Moreover, concern for equal treatment of human beings inevitably led to protections against discrimination based on race, sexual orientation, ethnic origin, and the like.

This chapter principally concerns equal rights for women and men, but it describes also the Community's initiatives beyond gender discrimination.

The principal Treaty provision is Article 141, which is a revision of former Article 119. In its first two paragraphs, it provides.

Article 141

1. Each Member State shall ensure that the application of the principle of equal pay for male and female workers for equal work or work of equal value is applied.

2. For the purpose of this Article, "pay" means the ordinary basic or minimum wage or salary and any other consideration, whether in cash or in kind, which the worker receives, directly or indirectly, in respect of his employment from his employer.

Equal pay without discrimination based on sex means:

(a) that pay for the same work at piece rates shall be calculated on the basis of the same unit of measurement;

(b) that pay for work at time rates shall be the same for the same job. * * *

The language of Article 119 was exactly the same as the first two paragraphs of Article 141 (which now contains two more paragraphs) except for the first sentence, which read:

Each Member State shall during the first stage ensure and subsequently maintain the application of the principle that men and women should receive equal pay for equal work.

Why do we find equal rights for women enshrined in the basic document constituting the European Economic Community, whose immediate objective was to tear down barriers between Member States and form one common market? The article was proposed by France. The French Constitution required French businesses to grant equal pay to women for equal work. If other Member States could exploit women by paying them less than men and, since the barriers to trade were removed, could compete full force with French firms in France, French firms would face an unlevel playing field; the competition would be unfair competition. Once in the Treaty, however, Article 119 achieved a human rights aura more than a commercial fair trade character.

The Treaty of Amsterdam took significant steps to elevate the importance of equal rights. It amended Article 2 of the EC Treaty so that it now includes among the Community's tasks the promotion of "equality between men and women." Also it amended Article 3(2), which now requires that, in pursuing its activities, the Community "shall aim to eliminate inequalities, and to promote equality, between men and women."

It added the following two paragraphs to Article 119 (now 141):

3. The Council, acting in accordance with the procedure referred to in Article 251, and after consulting the Economic and Social Committee, shall adopt measures to ensure the application of the principle of equal opportunities and equal treatment of men and women in matters of employment and occupation, including the principle of equal pay for equal work or work of equal value.

4. With a view to ensuring full equality in practice between men and women in working life, the principle of equal treatment shall not prevent any Member State from maintaining or adopting measures providing for specific advantages in order to make it easier for the underrepresented sex to pursue a vocational activity or to prevent or compensate for disadvantages in professional careers.

Article 141 is complemented by Article 137, which provides:

With a view to achieving the objectives of [the Community's Social Policy] the Community shall support and complement the activities of the Member States in the following fields: . . .

— equality between men and women with regard to labour market opportunities and treatment at work.

Moreover, the Amsterdam Treaty introduced Article 13, which reads:

Without prejudice to the other provisions of this Treaty and within the limits of the powers conferred by it upon the Community, the Council, acting unanimously on a proposal from the Commission and after consulting the European Parliament, may take appropriate action to combat discrimination based on sex, racial or ethnic origin, religion or belief, disability, age or sexual orientation.

In the mid–1970s the Council took advantage of the favorable climate for social legislation to adopt important directives expanding women's rights to equal pay and equal treatment. In 2000 the Council made use of its new powers under Article 13 by introducing two far-reaching directives to combat discrimination based on racial or ethnic origin, religion or belief, disability, age or sexual orientation.

Before discussing the directives, we reconsider a landmark Court judgment that significantly shaped Community law on equal rights for women.

DEFRENNE v. SABENA

Case 43/75 [1976] 1 ECR 455.

Read excerpt at page 248 *supra*.

Notes and Questions

1. *Defrenne* held that Article 119 (now, as amended, 141) has direct effect in cases of "direct and overt discrimination." What sort of discrimination is "direct and overt"? See paragraphs 22–23 of the judgment. Note that paragraph 39 forbids discrimination in pay by private sector employers (as well as by the state as an employer), even in the absence of implementing legislation. *Defrenne* is one of the rare instances in which the Court interpreted an article to have horizontal direct effect.

2. The Court refused to apply the equal pay obligation from the date the Treaty provision acquired its force—in this case, December 31, 1961. It acceded to the warnings of the UK and Ireland that private employers' liability for claims of pay discrimination since 1961 might drive some of them into bankruptcy. Do employers' treasuries override women's Treaty rights to non-discrimination? Or was the ambiguity regarding horizontal direct effect (and thus direct applicability of the Treaty standard) a compelling equity?

3. The US Constitution does not contain any express provision on equality between men and women. The proposed Equal Rights Amendment was intended to achieve this purpose but was not adopted by a sufficient number of states. However, nine states (including Pennsylvania and Texas) have amended their constitutions to provide for equal rights for men and women. Moreover, on a federal level, the Equal Pay Act of 1963, 29 U.S.C.A. § 206(d)(1), forbids sex-based discrimination as to pay, and Title VII of the Civil Rights Act of 1964, 42 U.S.C.A. § 2000e, includes sex-based discrimination as a type of employment discrimination. A large body of caselaw interprets the EPA and Title VII. Specialized statutes address other forms of discrimination, such as discrimination based on age and physical disability.

B. EQUAL PAY FOR WOMEN AND MEN

1. THE EQUAL PAY DIRECTIVE

The Council's first equal rights measure was Directive 75/117 of February 10, 1975 on equal pay for men and women, O.J. L 45/19 (Feb. 19, 1975). This directive is printed in the Selected Documents as ER (Equal Rights) Doc. No. 1. Because the directive was adopted before the Court's judgment in *Defrenne,* when it was generally believed that Article 119 did not have direct effect, the directive was viewed as necessary to implement Article 119. Even after *Defrenne,* the directive remains important because it defines "equal work" and because it creates procedures for enforcing rights. Read the directive.

Article 1 of the 1975 directive expanded Article 119's reference to "equal work" by adding "work to which equal value is attributed." This is the "comparable worth" standard. (How can "mere" legislation so alter the Treaty? This language was subsequently incorporated into the Treaty.) Article 1 of the 1975 directive also requires that any "job classification system" be non-discriminatory in character.

Equally important, the directive requires Member States to undertake vigorous enforcement of the right to equal pay. Thus, article 3 mandates that States should review their laws, regulations and practices to eliminate any discriminatory provisions. Article 4 obligates Member States to ensure that both collective bargaining agreements applicable to an industry and private employment contracts abide by the equal pay principle. Article 6 requires that States generally "ensure that the principle of equal pay is applied" and article 2 reinforces this obligation by mandating judicial procedures to enable enforcement of rights. Article 7 requires States to inform employees of their rights "at their place of employment." This a powerful package of procedural measures to enforce the right of equal pay.

By way of comparison, the Equal Pay Act of 1963 (EPA), 29 U.S.C.A. § 206(d)(1), forbids any sex-based discrimination as to pay within the same establishment "for equal work on jobs the performance of which requires equal skill, effort and responsibility, and which are performed under similar working conditions." The EPA permits exceptions based on seniority, merit, or objective factors other than sex.

Article 141 (ex Article 119) and the 1975 directive have given rise to a growing body of caselaw. Most of the cases generated by Article 177 (now 234) referrals have come from Denmark, Germany, the Netherlands and the UK. This statistic does not imply that discrimination is more rampant in those States, but may reflect the States' more effective procedures for challenging discrimination and a more organized women's rights movement.

Despite the above measures and efforts to enforce them, statistics for the year 2000 show that most women in the European Union work in lower-paid services (domestic and health services and teaching) than men and that almost seven times as many women as men work part-time. EC Bull 12/93, at 38. In 1999, women accounted for 77% of low-income employees in the European Union. *Equal Opportunities for Women and Men in the European Union, 2000 Annual Report*, published by the European Commission: COM(2001)179 final.

2. DEFINING THE CONCEPT OF "PAY"

What is "pay"? Look again at the definition in Article 119, now 141. Does it include payment in kind? Must it be bargained for? How would you treat annual bonuses? Commissions based on sales? Paid leave to care for a sick child? Christmas or holiday gifts?

Does it include indirect forms of remuneration? In *Garland v. British Rail Engineering Ltd.*, Case 12/81, [1982] ECR 359, the Court held that free or reduced fares given to retired male employees of a railroad constituted a form of pay. The Court defined "pay" as "consideration, whether cash or in kind, whether immediate or future, provided that the worker receives it, albeit indirectly, in respect of his employment from his employer." Id. at 369.

The fact that the employer gratuitously provided the lower rail fares did not remove the benefit from the category of pay.

More important is the Court's decision in *Bilka–Kaufhaus GmbH v. von Hartz*, excerpted below, that an employer's private pension plan (as opposed to state social security) constitutes pay. Such an "occupational pension scheme" was an "integral part of the contracts of employment" and had been in part agreed upon in negotiations with employee representatives.

3. INDIRECT DISCRIMINATION

How does the law deal with indirect discrimination? Recall that *Defrenne* limited Article 119's direct effect to cases of "direct and overt discrimination." We will observe in later cases an evolution in the Court's view of the Treaty provision, as well as the effect of the 1975 Equal Pay Directive and later directives.

In many business sectors, most part-time workers are women. Part-time workers are frequently paid less, proportionately, than full-time employees. Does lower pay for part-time workers constitute indirect discrimination against female employees? Are part-time workers less valuable to the employer? More exploitable? If there is a salary differential for part-time workers, is it likely to reflect an employer's bias against women, or more bargaining power to exploit those individuals (men and women) who are less flexible in their work hours? Does this difference matter?

JENKINS v. KINGSGATE (CLOTHING PRODUCTIONS) LTD.

Case 96/80, [1981] ECR 911.

[Kingsgate employs 35 men and 54 women full-time (40 hours per week), and five women and one man part-time. Full-time employees are paid an equal hourly rate. Part-time workers receive 90% of the full-time rate. Ms. Jenkins, who worked 30 hours per week, sued for equal pay with full-time employees, claiming sex discrimination. Kingsgate argued that the differential was justified by its desire to discourage absenteeism, to ensure greater productivity, and to ensure maximum operating time for the expensive machinery. The Industrial Tribunal held that working 75% of full-time constituted a material difference which justified the lower pay. On appeal, the appellate court requested the Court of Justice to rule on the application of Article 119 to a pay differential for part-time workers.]

9   [T]he national court is principally concerned to know whether a difference in the level of pay for work carried out part-time and the same work carried out full-time may amount to discrimination of a kind prohibited by Article 119 of the Treaty when the category of part-time workers is exclusively or predominantly comprised of women.

10 [T]he purpose of Article 119 is to ensure the application of the principle of equal pay for men and women for the same work. The differences in pay prohibited by that provision are therefore exclusively those based on the difference of the sex of the workers. Consequently the fact that part-time work is paid at an hourly rate lower than pay for full-time work does not amount *per se* to discrimination prohibited by Article 119 provided that

the hourly rates are applied to workers belonging to either category without distinction based on sex.

[11] If there is no such distinction, therefore, the fact that work paid at time rates is remunerated at an hourly rate which varies according to the number of hours worked per week does not offend against the principle of equal pay laid down in Article 119 of the Treaty in so far as the difference in pay between part-time work and full-time work is attributable to factors which are objectively justified and are in no way related to any discrimination based on sex.

[12] Such may be the case, in particular, when by giving hourly rates of pay which are lower for part-time work than those for full-time work the employer is endeavouring, on economic grounds which may be objectively justified, to encourage full-time work irrespective of the sex of the worker.

[13] By contrast, if it is established that a considerably smaller percentage of women than of men perform the minimum number of weekly working hours required in order to be able to claim the full-time hourly rate of pay, the inequality in pay will be contrary to Article 119 of the Treaty where, regard being had to the difficulties encountered by women in arranging to work that minimum number of hours per week, the pay policy of the undertaking in question cannot be explained by factors other than discrimination based on sex.

[14] Where the hourly rate of pay differs according to whether the work is part-time or full-time it is for the national courts to decide in each individual case whether, regard being had to the facts of the case, its history and the employer's intention, a pay policy such as that which is at issue in the main proceedings although represented as a difference based on weekly working hours is or is not in reality discrimination based on the sex of the worker.

[15] The reply to the ... questions must therefore be that a difference in pay between full-time workers and part-time workers does not amount to discrimination prohibited by Article 119 of the Treaty unless it is in reality merely an indirect way of reducing the level of pay of part-time workers on the ground that that group of workers is composed exclusively or predominantly of women.

BILKA–KAUFHAUS GmbH v. VON HARTZ

Case 170/84, [1986] ECR 1607.

[The Bilka department store chain provided an occupational (employer's private) pension plan to its full-time employees. Part-time employees were allowed to benefit from the plan only if they had at some point worked full-time for 15 years. Ms. von Hartz, a part-time employee, sued for a pension, claiming the plan terms constituted sex discrimination because most part-time employees were women. The case came before the German Supreme Labor Court, which made an Article 177 (now 234) reference.]

[29] If ... it should be found that a much lower proportion of women than of men work full-time, the exclusion of part-time workers from the occupational pension scheme would be contrary to Article 119 of the Treaty

where, taking into account the difficulties encountered by women workers in working full-time, that measure could not be explained by factors which exclude any discrimination on grounds of sex.

[30] However, if the undertaking is able to show that its pay practice may be explained by objectively justified factors unrelated to any discrimination on grounds of sex there is no breach of Article 119. * * *

[33] Bilka argues that the exclusion of part-time workers from the occupational pension scheme is intended solely to discourage part-time work, since in general part-time workers refuse to work in the late afternoon and on Saturdays. In order to ensure the presence of an adequate workforce during those periods it was therefore necessary to make full-time work more attractive than part-time work, by making the occupational pension scheme open only to full-time workers. Bilka concludes that on the basis of the judgment of 31 March 1981 it cannot be accused of having infringed Article 119. * * *

[35] ... If the national court finds that the measures chosen by Bilka correspond to a real need on the part of the undertaking, are appropriate with a view to achieving the objectives pursued and are necessary to that end, the fact that the measures affect a far greater number of women than men is not sufficient to show that they constitute an infringement of Article 119.

Notes and Questions

1. *Jenkins* holds that lower part-time than full-time pay does not constitute sex discrimination *per se* even when the majority of part-time workers are women. Why? (Is it relevant that the majority of full-time workers were also women?) The Court observes that the pay gap might be objectively justified. What would be a good objective justification? Were the employer's justifications convincing? Note the Court's reference in paragraph 14 to the history of the case as a factor to be considered. Prior to 1975, Kingsgate paid full-time women workers less than men. When full-time women workers were raised to parity in wages with men, the 90% pay level for part-time workers was introduced. Is this history relevant?

2. In *Bilka,* the Court shifted the burden of proof: it is the employer who must show "objectively justified economic grounds" to warrant the poorer treatment of part-time employees when a majority are women. In practice, how significant is such a shift?

3. Note Bilka's arguments to justify the higher pay to full-time workers. Bilka also observed that women received 81% of all pensions, even though only 72% of employees were women. The German Supreme Labor Court expressed the view that "in the department store sector there are no reasons of commercial expediency" to necessitate inferior treatment of part-time workers. How would you decide the case on the merits?

4. Compare *Corning Glass Works v. Brennan,* 417 U.S. 188, 94 S.Ct. 2223, 41 L.Ed.2d 1 (1974), in which the Department of Labor sued Corning because it paid night shift product inspectors more than day shift product inspectors. All day shift inspectors were women, while most night shift inspectors were men. Although the EPA was silent as to burden of proof, the Supreme Court held that the employer had the burden of showing objective factors that would justify a pay differential. Since Corning could not show that night work was more difficult or hazardous, the female day inspectors had to be paid the same wages as the night inspectors.

5. A German law requires employers to pay sick pay to employees temporarily unable to work, but states that sick pay is not required for those who do not work 10 hours per week. The majority of German part-time workers are women. Is the German law compatible with Article 119, now 141? See Rinner–Kühn v. FWW S–G GmbH, Case 171/88, [1989] ECR 2743.

UNION OF COMMERCIAL AND CLERICAL EMPLOYEES v. DANISH EMPLOYERS' ASSOCIATION EX PARTE DANFOSS

Case 109/88, [1989] ECR 3199.

[Pursuant to a collective bargaining agreement, Danfoss paid salary supplements to base pay, calculated on factors such as mobility, special training and length of service. The average wage paid to men was 6.85% higher than that paid to women. When the union claimed sex discrimination, the Danish Industrial Arbitration Board asked the Court of Justice whether the use of such criteria in calculating pay violated Article 119 or the Equal Pay Directive.

Danfoss made the strained argument that "mobility" really meant overall quality. The Court first held that, where a pay system results in a male/female differential and the reasons for the difference are not transparent, the employer has the burden to prove that the system is not discriminatory. It then said:]

19   ... [A] distinction must be made according to whether the criterion of mobility is employed to reward the quality of work done by the employee or is used to reward the employee's adaptability to variable hours and varying places of work.

20   In the first case the criterion of mobility is undoubtedly wholly neutral from the point of view of sex. Where it systematically works to the disadvantage of women that can only be because the employer has misapplied it. It is inconceivable that the quality of work done by women should generally be less good. The employer cannot therefore justify applying the criterion of mobility, so understood, where its application proves to work systematically to the disadvantage of women.

21   The position is different in the second case. If it is understood as covering the employee's adaptability to variable hours and varying places of work, the criterion of mobility may also work to the disadvantage of female employees, who, because of household and family duties for which they are frequently responsible, are not as able as men to organize their working time flexibly.

22   ... The employer may ... justify the remuneration of such adaptability by showing it is of importance for the performance of specific tasks entrusted to the employee.

23   In the second place, as regards the criterion of training, it is not to be excluded that it may work to the disadvantage of women in so far as they have had less opportunity than men for training or have taken less advantage of such opportunity. Nevertheless, in view of the considerations set out in the aforementioned judgment of 13 May 1986 the employer may

justify remuneration of special training by showing that it is of importance for the performance of specific tasks entrusted to the employee.

[24] In the third place, as regards the criterion of length of service, it is also not to be excluded, as with training, that it may involve less advantageous treatment of women than of men in so far as women have entered the labour market more recently than men or more frequently suffer an interruption of their career. Nevertheless, since length of service goes hand in hand with experience and since experience generally enables the employee to perform his duties better, the employer is free to reward it without having to establish the importance it has in the performance of specific tasks entrusted to the employee.

Notes and Questions

1.   If the factor of mobility connotes an employee's ability and willingness to work overtime or to travel, may an employer reward male employees for this characteristic when female employees may be hampered by family obligations? Contrast *Shultz v. Wheaton Glass Co.*, 421 F.2d 259 (3d Cir.1970), where the court refused to accept an employer's claim that male workers could be paid more on a factor of "flexibility" when male workers could occasionally work as handymen, while female workers did not do so.

2.   Do you agree with the Court's conclusion that supplemental pay for special training can be objectively justified, and that credit for length of service is automatically justified? Note that the US EPA allows higher pay for employees with greater seniority.

3.   The Court's decision in *Danfoss* on burden of proof has been formalized in the Burden of Proof Directive. Council Directive 97/80/EC of 15 December 1997 on the burden of proof in cases of discrimination based on sex. See Selected Documents, ER Doc. No. 4.

4.   A definition of "indirect discrimination" was introduced by the 1997 directive: indirect discrimination occurs "where an apparently neutral provision, criterion or practice disadvantages a substantially higher proportion of the members of one sex unless that provision, criterion or practice is appropriate and necessary and can be justified by objective factors unrelated to sex." Does the directive impose a stricter test than that developed by the Court of Justice? Contrast the approach of the 1997 directive with the definition of "indirect discrimination" contained in the more recent Race and Framework Employment directives, discussed in Section D below.

5.   Statistics can provide some evidence of discrimination. When comparing statistics regarding one sex with statistics regarding the other in any given employment scenario, what difference in ratio constitutes a "much lower proportion" [*Bilka*] or a "substantially higher proportion"? See the 1997 directive. See *R v. Secretary of State, ex parte Seymour Smith and Perez*, Case C–167/97 [1999] ECR I–623. Current Community policy appears not to require a plaintiff to introduce elaborate statistical evidence in order to succeed in a claim of indirect discrimination. See the definition of indirect discrimination contained in the Race Directive and the Framework Employment Directive in Section D.

6.   In the United States, employment practices that have a statistically disparate impact in depriving minorities or women of employment opportunities violate the Civil Rights Act unless the employer shows that "they are demonstrably a reasonable measure of job performance." Griggs v. Duke Power Co., 401 U.S. 424, 436, 91 S.Ct. 849, 28 L.Ed.2d 158 (1971).

4.   DETERMINING WORK OF "EQUAL VALUE"

MURPHY v. BORD TELECOM EIREANN

Case 157/86, [1988] ECR 673.

[Twenty-nine women employed as factory workers, engaged in dismantling, cleaning, oiling and reassembling telephones, claimed a right to be paid at the same higher level as a male worker employed in collecting and delivering equipment. The Irish Equality Officer who reviewed the facts concluded that the plaintiffs' work was of a higher value than that of the male worker and hence did not constitute "like work" within the meaning of the Irish law implementing the 1975 directive. The plaintiffs therefore lost. On appeal, the High Court made an Article 177 (now 234) reference.]

[8]   Bord Telecom Eireann contends that the [equal pay] principle does not apply in the situation where a lower wage is paid for work of higher value. In support of its view it maintains that the term "equal work" in Article 119 of the EEC Treaty cannot be understood as embracing unequal work and that the effect of a contrary interpretation would be that equal pay would have to be paid for work of different value.

[9]   It is true that Article 119 expressly requires the application of the principle of equal pay for men and women solely in the case of equal work or, according to a consistent line of decisions of the Court, in the case of work of equal value, and not in the case of work of unequal value. Nevertheless, if that principle forbids workers of one sex engaged in work of equal value to that of workers of the opposite sex to be paid a lower wage than the latter on grounds of sex, it *a fortiori* prohibits such a difference in pay where the lower-paid category of workers is engaged in work of higher value.

[10]   To adopt a contrary interpretation would be tantamount to rendering the principle of equal pay ineffective and nugatory. As the Irish Government rightly emphasized, in that case an employer would easily be able to circumvent the principle by assigning additional or more onerous duties to workers of a particular sex, who could then be paid a lower wage.

[11]   In so far as it is established that the difference in wage levels in question is based on discrimination on grounds of sex, Article 119 of the EEC Treaty is directly applicable in the sense that the workers concerned may rely on it in legal proceedings in order to obtain equal pay within the meaning of the provision and in the sense that national courts or tribunals must take it into account as a constituent part of Community law. It is for the national court, within the limits of its discretion under national law, when interpreting and applying domestic law, to give to it, where possible, an interpretation which accords with the requirements of the applicable Community law and, to the extent that this is not possible, to hold such domestic law inapplicable.

Notes and Questions

1.   A judgment for the Telecom Board would surely have been a triumph of technicality over substance, spirit and policy. But does Article 119 or the Equal

Pay Directive give the women in *Murphy* a right to higher pay than the male workers performing less valuable work?

2.   The Court decided *Murphy* on the basis of Article 119 and not article 1 of the 1975 directive. After *Murphy*, and since Article 119 has been amended explicitly to cover "work of equal value" (see Article 141), what importance does the Equal Pay Directive have?

3.   In *Commission v. United Kingdom* (Equal pay), Case 61/81, [1982] ECR 2601, the Commission brought an Article 169 (now 226) proceeding for deficiencies in the UK's implementation of the 1975 directive. The UK law allowed employees to claim equal pay only for "work to which equal value is attributed" if the employer had a job classification system which permitted comparisons by the nature of the work. The UK maintained that a job classification was a prerequisite to any resolution of disputes and that "the criterion of work of equal value is too abstract to be applied by the courts." The Court of Justice held:

> The Court cannot endorse that view. The implementation of the directive implies that the assessment of the "equal value" to be "attributed" to particular work, may be effected notwithstanding the employer's wishes, if necessary in the context of adversary proceedings. The Member States must endow an authority with the requisite jurisdiction to decide whether work has the same value as other work, after obtaining such information as may be required. Id. at 2617.

4.   In *Rummler v. Dato–Druck GmbH*, Case 237/85, [1986] ECR 2101, the Court of Justice was asked to appraise a job classification system in the printing industry which permitted higher pay for jobs involving more muscular effort (usually performed by men). The Court held that article 1 of the 1975 directive required that a job classification system "must not be organized, as a whole, in such a manner that it has the practical effect of discriminating generally against workers of one sex." Id. at 2114. Hence, if muscular capacity is considered, then the classification must also consider "other criteria in relation to which women workers may have a particular aptitude." Id. at 2115. What are examples of such "other criteria"?

5.   In *County of Washington v. Gunther*, 452 U.S. 161, 101 S.Ct. 2242, 68 L.Ed.2d 751 (1981), female jail guards sued because they were paid 70% of the male jail guards' salary. The Supreme Court held that, even though there were objective differences in the work performed by male and female guards, the county could not pay the female guards less than what the county itself estimated their work was objectively worth. (Plaintiffs claimed the county had estimated their worth at 95% of the male guards' worth.) Several circuit courts have held that the Equal Pay Act and Title VII of the Civil Rights Act do not require employers to make a "comparable worth" evaluation of different job categories, and correspondingly raise the pay of job categories in which women predominate. Employers can justify lower pay to certain job categories by citing to prevailing external job market pay scales. Spaulding v. University of Washington, 740 F.2d 686 (9th Cir.1984) (female nursing faculty need not be compared with male architecture or pharmacy faculty); Christensen v. State of Iowa, 563 F.2d 353 (8th Cir.1977) (female secretaries need not be compared with male physical plant employees). Contrast Article 141, *Murphy, Commission v. UK* and *Rummler* with the US caselaw. Which system protects more aggressively the right to equal pay for work of equal value?

ENDERBY v. FRENCHAY HEALTH AUTHORITY

Case C–127/92, [1993] ECR I–5535.

[In 1986, Enderby, a speech therapist, sued her employer, a unit within the United Kingdom National Health Service, claiming pay discrimination based on sex. She submitted evidence that senior level pharmacists were paid approximately 40% more than senior level speech therapists, and that the former profession was composed predominantly of men at the senior level, while speech therapists were overwhelmingly women. Before assessing the qualifications required in the two professions, the UK Court of Appeal asked the Court of Justice: 1) who should bear the burden of proof when the plaintiff claims that two different job categories constitute work of "equal value;" ... 2) whether the use of collective bargaining to set the pay scales for different job categories serves as an objective justification for any difference in pay level; and 3) whether job market factors may justify, in whole or in part, pay scale differences between job categories found to have "equal value."]

13   It is normally for the person alleging facts in support of a claim to adduce proof of such facts. Thus, in principle, the burden of proving the existence of sex discrimination as to pay lies with the worker who, believing himself to be the victim of such discrimination, brings legal proceedings against his employer with a view to removing the discrimination.

14   However, ... the onus may shift when that is necessary to avoid depriving workers who appear to be the victims of discrimination of any effective means of enforcing the principle of equal pay.

15   In this case, ... it is not a question of *de facto* discrimination ... such as may apply ... in the case of part-time workers. Secondly, there can be no complaint that the employer has applied a system of pay wholly lacking in transparency since the rates of pay of NHS speech therapists and pharmacists are decided by regular collective bargaining processes in which there is no evidence of discrimination as regards either of those two professions.

16   However, if the pay of speech therapists is significantly lower than that of pharmacists and if the former are almost exclusively women while the latter are predominantly men, there is a *prima facie* case of sex discrimination, at least where the two jobs in question are of equal value and the statistics describing that situation are valid.

17   It is for the national court to assess whether it may take into account those statistics, that is to say, whether they cover enough individuals, whether they illustrate purely fortuitous or short-term phenomena, and whether, in general, they appear to be significant.

18   Where there is a *prima facie* case of discrimination, it is for the employer to show that there are objective reasons for the difference in pay. Workers would be unable to enforce the principle of equal pay before national courts if evidence of a *prima facie* case of discrimination did not shift to the employer the onus of showing that the pay differential is not in fact discriminatory (see, by analogy, *Danfoss*).

19   [Therefore,] where significant statistics disclose an appreciable difference in pay between two jobs of equal value, one of which is carried out almost

exclusively by women and the other predominantly by men, Art. 119 of the treaty requires the employer to show that the difference is based on objectively justified factors unrelated to any discrimination on grounds of sex.

20 In its second question, the Court of Appeal wishes to know whether the employer can rely, as sufficient justification for the difference in pay, upon the fact that the rates of pay of the jobs in question were decided by collective bargaining processes which, ... considered separately, have no discriminatory effect.

21 As is clear from art. 4 of Council Directive 75/117, collective agreements, like laws, regulations or administrative provisions, must observe the principle enshrined in art. 119 of the treaty.

22 The fact that the rates of pay at issue are decided by collective bargaining processes conducted separately for each of the two professional groups concerned, without any discriminatory effect within each group, does not preclude a finding of *prima facie* discrimination where the results of those processes show that two groups with the same employer and the same trade union are treated differently. If the employer could rely on the absence of discrimination within each of the collective bargaining processes taken separately as sufficient justification for the difference in pay, he could, as the German Government pointed out, easily circumvent the principle of equal pay by using separate bargaining processes. * * *

24 In its third question, the Court of Appeal wishes to know to what extent— wholly, in part or not at all—the fact that part of the difference in pay is attributable to a shortage of candidates for one job and to the need to attract them by higher salaries can objectively justify that pay differential.

25 The Court has consistently held that it is for the national court, which has sole jurisdiction to make findings of fact, to determine whether and to what extent the grounds put forward by an employer to explain the adoption of a pay practice which applies independently of a worker's sex but in fact affects more women than men, may be regarded as objectively justified economic grounds (*Bilka-Kaufhaus*). Those grounds may include, if they can be attributed to the needs and objectives of the undertaking, different criteria such as the worker's flexibility or adaptability to hours and places of work, his training or his length of service (*Danfoss*).

26 The state of the employment market, which may lead an employer to increase the pay of a particular job in order to attract candidates, may constitute an objectively justified economic ground within the meaning of the case law cited above. How it is to be applied in the circumstances of each case depends on the facts and so falls within the jurisdiction of the national court.

27 If ... the national court has been able to determine precisely what proportion of the increase in pay is attributable to market forces, it must necessarily accept that the pay differential is objectively justified to the extent of that proportion. When national authorities have to apply Community law, they must apply the principle of proportionality.

Notes and Questions

1. From what does the Court conclude that pharmacy and speech therapy are comparable occupations? See para. 16. Are you convinced?

2. Why isn't the setting of pay scales for different job categories by collective bargaining a solid defense for the employer? To what extent should market factors justify an employer's setting of different pay scales in different job categories?

3. Does *Enderby* open floodgates, or can the employer almost always show non-comparability or "the market made me do it"?

C. EQUAL TREATMENT FOR WOMEN AND MEN

1. THE 1976 AND 1986 EQUAL TREATMENT DIRECTIVES

Defrenne sued Sabena for damages for discriminatory dismissal. Sabena's policy was to require flight hostesses to retire at age 40, while allowing flight stewards to work beyond that age. Belgian labor courts held that she had no claim under Belgian law. On appeal, the Belgian Supreme Court asked the Court of Justice whether Defrenne might have a remedy under Article 119 (now, after amendment, Article 141). Unfortunately for Defrenne, the Court replied that Article 119 covered only discrimination as to pay, not discrimination as to other types of employment discrimination, even when they might have pecuniary consequences. Defrenne v. Sabena, Case 149/77, [1978] ECR 1365.

If Defrenne had been dismissed in 1979, she would have obtained relief, because by that time Member States should have implemented the second major equal rights measure, Directive 76/207 of February 9, 1976 on equal treatment for men and women, O.J. L 39/40 (Feb. 14, 1976). See Selected Documents, ER Doc. No. 2. Because this directive goes beyond the scope of Article 119, the Council used Article 235 (now 308), the "elastic clause" grant of legislative power, to adopt it. Read the directive.

Article 1 of the 1976 directive establishes the principle of equal treatment in hiring, promotion, all working conditions, and vocational training. Article 2(1) prohibits not only direct discrimination on the basis of sex, but also indirect discrimination by reference to "marital or family status."

Article 2 makes an exception for three types of discrimination. Two are for the benefit of women: article 2(3) permits protective treatment "as regards pregnancy and maternity"; and 2(4) permits "measures to promote equal opportunity . . . by removing existing inequalities" (i.e., remedial affirmative action policies). Article 2(2) allows Member States to permit discrimination in "occupational activities" for which workers of only one sex are appropriate. The rest of the equal treatment directive's provisions replicate those of the equal pay directive: Member States are to review and reform their own laws and practices, police collective bargaining agreements and individual employment contracts, and introduce systems of judicial recourse (arts. 3–7).

The 1976 directive was supplemented by Directive 86/613 O.J. L 359/56 (Dec. 19, 1986), extending the principle of equal treatment to those self-employed, notably those engaged in business, farming and the professions. Thus, for example, women partners in a commercial, accounting or law partnership are guaranteed rights of equal treatment.

A Commission recommendation of November 27, 1991 for the protection of the dignity of women and men at work, O.J. C 27/4 (Feb. 4, 1992), endorsed by the Council in O.J. C 27/1 (Feb. 4, 1992), urges Member States to take action against sexual harassment and intimidating, hostile or humiliating work environments.

The US analogue to the 1976 Equal Treatment Directive is Title VII of the Civil Rights Act 1964, which covers not only discrimination in compensation but also in hiring, dismissal and the "terms, conditions or privileges of employment." Title VII prohibits discriminatory conduct only by employers. It does not parallel the 1986 directive on equal treatment for the self-employed.

Notes and Questions

1. In *Commission v. United Kingdom* (Equal treatment), Case 165/82, [1983] ECR 3431, the Court held that the UK improperly implemented the 1976 Equal Treatment Directive because it did not forbid discriminatory provisions in collective bargaining agreements and because it created an exception for businesses employing less than five persons, and for private households. As it noted, private households can take advantage of the "occupational activity" exception. (Can employers require butlers to be men or women's handmaids to be women?) Contrast this judgment with Title VII § 701(6), which excludes employers with fewer than 15 employees from the requirements of Title VII. Has the EU gone too far in trying to regulate conduct in small businesses, or has the United States not gone far enough?

2. The Equal Treatment Directive, like the Equal Pay Directive, requires Member States to ensure effective judicial recourse for persons injured by sex discrimination but does not provide for any specific sanctions. The *Von Colson and Kamann* judgment, discussed at page 390 *supra*, is a leading precedent requiring State sanctions to "guarantee real and effective judicial protection" of the right to equal treatment. [1984] ECR 1891, 1910. What measure of damages do you think would be appropriate to achieve such protection? Should a system of fines be required?

3. Does the Equal Treatment Directive have vertical direct effect against a state body? The Court held that it does in the *Marshall* case, excerpted at page 188 *supra*.

What is a state body on which a vertically effective directive is binding? In *Foster v. British Gas PLC*, Case C–188/89, [1990] ECR I–3313, 3348–49, the Court held:

> [A] body, whatever its legal form, which has been made responsible, pursuant to a measure adopted by the state, for providing a public service under the control of the state and has for that purpose special powers beyond those which result from the normal rules applicable in relations between individuals is included in any event among the bodies against which the provisions of a directive capable of having direct effect may be relied upon.

Is the directive binding on state-owned steel, chemical or automobile manufacturers? What about electrical, water or telephone utilities, or railroads or airlines, which in most Member States are traditionally state-owned but in some are private? Do such state-owned entities perform a "public service"? Contrast *Foster* with the caselaw in Chapter 15C on the narrow construction of the Article 39(4) (ex Article 48(4)) "public service" exception to free movement of workers. In applying the Equal Treatment Directive, is there any reason why the Court might construe Article 48(4) narrowly while construing broadly the concept of a state body providing a public service?

4. Indirect discrimination, discussed in the context of equal pay, also raises difficult questions in the field of equal treatment. For example, does Community law prohibit a national provision under which, where the number of qualified applicants for a practical course for trainee lawyers exceeds the number of places available, priority is given to individuals who meet certain "hardship criteria," one of which—that of having completed military service—can in fact be fulfilled only by men? See *Schnorbus v. Land Hessen*, Case C–79/99 (Court of Justice, Dec. 7, 2000), approving the measure as compatible with Article 119 and the directives.

2. SCOPE OF THE EQUAL TREATMENT DIRECTIVES

One question left unresolved by the wording of Article 119 (now 141) and the Equal Treatment Directive was whether the prohibition of discrimination on grounds of sex was wide enough to encompass practices which discriminated against transsexuals and homosexuals.

P v. S

Case C–13/94, [1996] ECR I–2143.

[P, a manager in an educational establishment of the Cornwall County Council, underwent surgery to achieve a gender reassignment. Following the operation, P "dressed and behaved as a woman." S, the general manager, dismissed P on this ground only. P sued, claiming a violation of the UK Sex Discrimination Act, intended to implement the 1976 Equal Treatment Directive. The Industrial Tribunal, noting that the UK civil register does not permit a change of a person's gender identification, believed that English law would provide no recourse to P, but referred questions to the Court as to the possible application of the Equal Treatment Directive. The Commission supported the UK view that the dismissal did not constitute sex discrimination under the directive. The Court began by citing the European Court of Human Rights' description of transsexuals.]

16   The European Court of Human Rights has held that 'the term "transsexual" is usually applied to those who, whilst belonging physically to one sex, feel convinced that they belong to the other; they often seek to achieve a more integrated, unambiguous identity by undergoing medical treatment and surgical operations to adapt their physical characteristics to their psychological nature. Transsexuals who have been operated upon thus form a fairly well-defined and identifiable group'.

17   The principle of equal treatment 'for men and women' to which the directive refers in its title, preamble and provisions means, as Articles 2(1) and 3(1) in particular indicate, that there should be 'no discrimination whatsoever on grounds of sex'.

18   Thus, the directive is simply the expression, in the relevant field, of the principle of equality, which is one of the fundamental principles of Community law.

19   Moreover, as the Court has repeatedly held, the right not to be discriminated against on grounds of sex is one of the fundamental human rights whose observance the Court has a duty to ensure.

20   Accordingly, the scope of the directive cannot be confined simply to discrimination based on the fact that a person is of one or other sex. In view of its purpose and the nature of the rights which it seeks to safeguard, the scope of the directive is also such as to apply to discrimination arising, as in this case, from the gender reassignment of the person concerned.

21   Such discrimination is based, essentially if not exclusively, on the sex of the person concerned. Where a person is dismissed on the ground that he or she intends to undergo, or has undergone, gender reassignment, he or she is treated unfavourably by comparison with persons of the sex to which he or she was deemed to belong before undergoing gender reassignment.

22   To tolerate such discrimination would be tantamount, as regards such a person, to a failure to respect the dignity and freedom to which he or she is entitled, and which the Court has a duty to safeguard.

23   Dismissal of such a person must therefore be regarded as contrary to Article 5(1) of the directive, unless the dismissal could be justified under Article 2(2). There is, however, no material before the Court to suggest that this was so here.

24   It follows from the foregoing that the reply to the questions referred by the Industrial Tribunal must be that, in view of the objective pursued by the directive, Article 5(1) of the directive precludes dismissal of a transsexual for a reason related to a gender reassignment.

Notes and Questions

1.   The Court was undoubtedly influenced by the carefully reasoned advocacy of this result in Advocate General Tesauro's opinion. He relied upon evolving social views in the treatment of transsexuals in most Member States, citing especially the statutory permission in Germany, the Netherlands and Sweden for a change in the civil register to accord with the new sexual identity. He also discussed the caselaw of the European Court of Human Rights, notably the 1992 judgment, *B v. France*, in which France was required to change the civil status of a transsexual. Advocate General Tesauro urged the Court to take a "courageous decision"; one in accord with "social justice."

2.   *P* v. *S* has attracted wide, and decidedly mixed, media attention. A useful casenote is L. Flynn, P v. S, 34 Common Mkt. L. Rev. 367 (1997). The chief point of speculation was whether the Court's language was broad enough to cover discrimination against homosexuals generally, and not only the much smaller group of transsexuals. This issue had already been presented to the Court in *Grant v. South–West Trains*.

GRANT v. SOUTH–WEST TRAINS LTD.

Case C–249/96 [1998] ECR I–621.

[Grant, a lesbian employed by a UK state railway, claimed sex discrimination under Article 119 and the Equal Pay Directive, for refusal to provide fringe benefits for her woman partner when such benefits were accorded to spouses and to persons of the opposite sex with whom an employee had a stable relationship outside of marriage.]

24 [T]he first question to answer is whether a condition in the regulations of an undertaking such as that in issue in the main proceedings constitutes discrimination based directly on the sex of the worker. If it does not, the next point to examine will be whether Community law requires that stable relationships between two persons of the same sex should be regarded by all employers as equivalent to marriages or stable relationships outside marriage between two persons of opposite sex. Finally, it will have to be considered whether discrimination based on sexual orientation constitutes discrimination based on the sex of the worker. * * *

27 [The] condition, the effect of which is that the worker must live in a stable relationship with a person of the opposite sex in order to benefit from the travel concessions, is, like the other alternative conditions prescribed in the undertaking's regulations, applied regardless of the sex of the worker concerned. Thus travel concessions are refused to a male worker if he is living with a person of the same sex, just as they are to a female worker if she is living with a person of the same sex.

28 Since the condition imposed by the undertaking's regulations applies in the same way to female and male workers, it cannot be regarded as constituting discrimination directly based on sex.

29 Second, the Court must consider whether, with respect to the application of a condition such as that in issue in the main proceedings, persons who have a stable relationship with a partner of the same sex are in the same situation as those who are married or have a stable relationship outside marriage with a partner of the opposite sex. * * *

35 ... [I]n the present state of the law within the Community, stable relationships between two persons of the same sex are not regarded as equivalent to marriages or stable relationships outside marriage between persons of opposite sex. Consequently, an employer is not required by Community law to treat the situation of a person who has a stable relationship with a partner of the same sex as equivalent to that of a person who is married to or has a stable relationship outside marriage with a partner of the opposite sex.

36 In those circumstances, it is for the legislature alone to adopt, if appropriate, measures which may affect that position.

37 Finally, Ms Grant submits that it follows from *P* v *S* that differences of treatment based on sexual orientation are included in the 'discrimination based on sex' prohibited by Article 119 of the Treaty.

38 In *P* v *S* the Court was asked whether a dismissal based on the change of sex of the worker concerned was to be regarded as 'discrimination on grounds of sex' within the meaning of Directive 76/207. * * *

42 The Court considered that such discrimination was in fact based, essentially if not exclusively, on the sex of the person concerned. That reasoning, which leads to the conclusion that such discrimination is to be prohibited just as is discrimination based on the fact that a person belongs to a particular sex, is limited to the case of a worker's gender reassignment and does not therefore apply to differences of treatment based on a person's sexual orientation.

[43] Ms Grant submits, however, that, like certain provisions of national law or of international conventions, the Community provisions on equal treatment of men and women should be interpreted as covering discrimination based on sexual orientation. She refers in particular to the International Covenant on Civil and Political Rights of 19 December 1966 (*United Nations Treaty Series*, Vol. 999, p. 171), in which, in the view of the Human Rights Committee established under Article 28 of the Covenant, the term 'sex' is to be taken as including sexual orientation (Communication No 488/1992, *Toonen* v *Australia*, views adopted on 31 March 1994, 50th session, point 8.7).

[44] The Covenant is one of the international instruments relating to the protection of human rights of which the Court takes account in applying the fundamental principles of Community law.

[45] However, although respect for the fundamental rights which form an integral part of those general principles of law is a condition of the legality of Community acts, those rights cannot in themselves have the effect of extending the scope of the Treaty provisions beyond the competences of the Community. * * *

[47] Such an observation, which does not in any event appear to reflect the interpretation so far generally accepted of the concept of discrimination based on sex which appears in various international instruments concerning the protection of fundamental rights, cannot in any case constitute a basis for the Court to extend the scope of Article 119 of the Treaty. That being so, the scope of that article, as of any provision of Community law, is to be determined only by having regard to its wording and purpose, its place in the scheme of the Treaty and its legal context. It follows from the considerations set out above that Community law as it stands at present does not cover discrimination based on sexual orientation, such as that in issue in the main proceedings.

[48] It should be observed, however, that the Treaty of Amsterdam amending the Treaty on European Union, the Treaties establishing the European Communities and certain related acts, signed on 2 October 1997, provides for the insertion in the Treaty of an Article 6a which, once the Treaty of Amsterdam has entered into force, will allow the Council under certain conditions (a unanimous vote on a proposal from the Commission after consulting the European Parliament) to take appropriate action to eliminate various forms of discrimination, in the way that Article 6 does with regard to non-discrimination including discrimination based on sexual orientation. * * *

Notes and Questions

1. Is the Court's decision consistent with its judgment in *P v. S*? Do you think the Court was influenced by the legislative agenda identified in paragraph 48 of its judgment? By concern for the limits of its powers? What is the significance of leaving problems of discrimination on grounds of sexual orientation to Article 6a (now 13), rather than including them within the scope of Article 119 (now, after amendment, Article 141)? Might the Treaty changes influence the Court to take further "courageous judgments," even though Article 6a does not, as such, enunciate a binding Treaty principle of non-discrimination?

2. Directive 2000/78/EC establishing a general framework for equal treatment in employment and occupation of 2 December 2000 covers discrimination based on Parliament Resolution on sexual discrimination in the workplace, O.J. C 104/46 (Apr. 16, 1984), urges the Commission to propose measures to end employment discrimination against homosexuals and urges Member States to end discrimination against homosexuals in a variety of legal circumstances. See, also, Section D below.

3. "OCCUPATIONAL ACTIVITIES" SUITABLE FOR ONLY ONE SEX

Article 2(2) of the 1976 Equal Treatment Directive permits an exception for "occupational activities ... for which, by reason of their nature or the context in which they are carried out, the sex of the worker constitutes a determining factor." Parallel to this in US law is the exception in Title VII § 703(e)(1) for a "bona fide occupational qualification reasonably necessary to the normal operation of that particular business."

It is common sense to exclude one or the other sex from a few occupational activities. Actors and actresses are not usually interchangeable. Even in the 1982 film "Tootsie," only a man would do for a female pretender's role. Men usually sell men's suits and women usually sell women's clothes when physical contact is required. Valets are men and nursemaids are women. Women can be police officers, fire fighters, coal miners and construction workers. Do employers tend to exaggerate real difficulties and create imaginary ones in trying to justify single-sex occupations?

JOHNSTON v. CHIEF CONSTABLE OF THE ROYAL ULSTER CONSTABULARY

Case 222/84, [1986] ECR 1651.

[In view of violent civil disorder in Northern Ireland, male police officers of the Royal Ulster Constabulary (RUC) were required to carry arms. Fifty-nine police officers died as assassination targets in the 1970s. In 1980, the RUC concluded that women police officers should not bear arms for various reasons, including a concern that they might then become assassination targets. The number of policewomen was reduced because they were restricted to certain tasks only, such as family welfare work. Although Mrs. Johnston had served satisfactorily as a police officer for six years, her contract was not renewed because of the new RUC policy. Mrs. Johnston sued to require renewal of her contract. The Industrial Tribunal asked the Court of Justice to interpret articles 2(2) and 2(3) of the Equal Treatment Directive, and also queried whether public safety concerns could justify the RUC policy.]

Applicability of Directive to Measures Taken to Protect Public Safety

22 It is necessary to examine next the Industrial Tribunal's first question by which it seeks to ascertain whether, having regard to the fact that Directive No 76/207 contains no express provision concerning measures taken for the purpose of safeguarding national security or of protecting public order, and more particularly public safety, the directive is applicable to such measures. * * *

26 It must be observed in this regard that the only articles in which the Treaty provides for derogations applicable in situations which may involve

public safety are Articles 36, 48, 56, 223 and 224 which deal with exceptional and clearly defined cases. Because of their limited character those articles do not lend themselves to a wide interpretation and it is not possible to infer from them that there is inherent in the Treaty a general proviso covering all measures taken for reasons of public safety. If every provision of Community law were held to be subject to a general proviso, regardless of the specific requirements laid down by the provisions of the Treaty, this might impair the binding nature of Community law and its uniform application.

27   It follows that the application of the principle of equal treatment for men and women is not subject to any general reservation as regards measures taken on grounds of the protection of public safety.... The facts which induced the competent authority to invoke the need to protect public safety must therefore if necessary be taken into consideration ... in the context of the application of the specific provisions of the directive.

28   The answer to the first question must therefore be that acts of sex discrimination done for reasons related to the protection of public safety must be examined in the light of the exceptions to the principle of equal treatment for men and women laid down in Directive No 76/207.

Article 2(2): Occupational Context

29   The Industrial Tribunal's second and third questions are concerned with the interpretation of the derogation, provided for in Article 2(2) of the directive, from the principle of equal treatment and are designed to enable the Tribunal to decide whether a difference in treatment, such as that in question, is covered by that derogation. It asks to be informed of the criteria and principles to be applied for determining whether an activity such as that in question in the present case is one of the activities for which "by reason of their nature or the context in which they are carried out, the sex of the worker constitutes a determining factor". * * *

34   [F]irst of all ..., in so far as the competent police authorities in Northern Ireland have decided, because of the requirements of public safety, to depart from the principle, generally applied in other parts of the United Kingdom, of not arming the police in the ordinary course of their duties, that decision does not in itself involve any discrimination between men and women and is therefore outside the scope of the principle of equal treatment. It is only in so far as the Chief Constable decided that women would not be armed or trained in the use of fire-arms, that general policing duties would in future be carried out only by armed male officers and that contracts of women in the RUC full-time Reserve who, like Mrs. Johnston, had previously been entrusted with general policing duties, would not be renewed, that an appraisal of those measures in the light of the provisions of the directive is relevant. ...

35   As is clear from the Industrial Tribunal's decision, the policy towards women in the RUC full-time Reserve was adopted by the Chief Constable because he considered that if women were armed they might become a more frequent target for assassination and their fire-arms could fall into the hands of their assailants, that the public would not welcome the carrying of fire-arms by women, which would conflict too much with the

ideal of an unarmed police force, and that armed policewomen would be less effective in police work in the social field with families and children in which the services of policewomen are particularly appreciated. The reasons which the Chief Constable thus gave for his policy were related to the special conditions in which the police must work in the situation existing in Northern Ireland, having regard to the requirements of the protection of public safety in a context of serious internal disturbances.

[36] As regards the question whether such reasons may be covered by Article 2(2) of the directive, it should first be observed that that provision, being a derogation from an individual right laid down in the directive, must be interpreted strictly. However, it must be recognized that the context in which the occupational activity of members of an armed police force are carried out is determined by the environment in which that activity is carried out. In this regard, the possibility cannot be excluded that in a situation characterized by serious internal disturbances the carrying of fire-arms by policewomen might create additional risks of their being assassinated and might therefore be contrary to the requirements of public safety.

[37] In such circumstances, the context of certain policing activities may be such that the sex of police officers constitutes a determining factor for carrying them out. If that is so, a Member State may therefore restrict such tasks, and the training leading thereto, to men. In such a case, as is clear from Article 9(2) of the directive, the Member States have a duty to assess periodically the activities concerned in order to decide whether, in the light of social developments, the derogation from the general scheme of the directive may still be maintained.

[38] It must also be borne in mind that, in determining the scope of any derogation from an individual right such as the equal treatment of men and women provided for by the directive, the principle of proportionality, one of the general principles of law underlying the Community legal order, must be observed. That principle requires that derogations remain within the limits of what is appropriate and necessary for achieving the aim in view and requires the principle of equal treatment to be reconciled as far as possible with the requirements of public safety which constitute the decisive factor as regards the context of the activity in question.

[39] By reason of the division of jurisdiction provided for in Article 177 of the EEC Treaty, it is for the national court to say whether the reasons on which the Chief Constable based his decision are in fact well founded and justify the specific measure taken in Mrs. Johnston's case. It is also for the national court to ensure that the principle of proportionality is observed and to determine whether the refusal to renew Mrs. Johnston's contract could not be avoided by allocating to women duties which, without jeopardizing the aims pursued, can be performed without fire-arms. * * *

Article 2(3): Protection of Women

[41] In its fourth and fifth question the Industrial Tribunal then asks the Court for an interpretation of the expressions "protection of women" in Article 2(3) of the directive and "concern for protection" in Article 3(2)(c), which inspired certain provisions of national law, so that it can decide whether the difference in treatment in question may fall within the scope

of the derogations from the principle of equal treatment laid down for those purposes. * * *

[44] It must be observed in this regard that, like Article 2(2) of the directive, Article 2(3), which also determines the scope of Article 3(2)(c), must be interpreted strictly. It is clear from the express reference to pregnancy and maternity that the directive is intended to protect a woman's biological condition and the special relationship which exists between a woman and her child. That provision of the directive does not therefore allow women to be excluded from a certain type of employment on the ground that public opinion demands that women be given greater protection than men against risks which affect men and women in the same way and which are distinct from women's specific needs of protection, such as those expressly mentioned.

[45] It does not appear that the risks and dangers to which women are exposed when performing their duties in the police force in a situation such as exists in Northern Ireland are different from those to which any man is also exposed when performing the same duties. A total exclusion of women from such an occupational activity which, owing to a general risk not specific to women, is imposed for reasons of public safety is not one of the differences in treatment that Article 2(3) of the directive allows out of a concern to protect women.

Notes and Questions

1. Why did the Court refuse to consider public safety as a generic derogation to the directive but admit public safety as a factor relevant to the scope of the "occupational activity" exception of article 2(2)?

2. In paragraph 35, the Court cites a number of reasons given by the RUC to justify its decision. Did the Court accept these reasons, or was it solely concerned with the risk that armed police women might be assassinated? In its analysis of article 2(3), the Court rules out protection of women as a rationale for discrimination. Why does this reasoning not apply to article 2(2)?

3. Suppose the Court had found public safety not admissible under article 2(2) to justify exclusion of women from police work in the social field. What would have been Ireland's response? Might the Court have been influenced by a concern about Ireland's response to a judgment disallowing the RUC's action?

4. What issues were left to the national court? How would you expect it to rule?

SIRDAR v. THE ARMY BOARD AND SECRETARY OF STATE FOR DEFENCE

Case C–273/97 [1999] ECR I–7403.

[Mrs. Sirdar, who had been employed as a chef in the British Army and in a commando regiment of the Royal Artillery, was refused employment as chef in the Royal Marines on grounds that the Royal Marines did not admit women. She instituted proceedings claiming discrimination on grounds of sex. After affirming its ruling in *Johnston* that the principle of equal treatment was not subject to any general reservation on grounds of public security, the Court said:]

[7] According to the decision referring the case, the responsible authorities in the Royal Marines have a policy of excluding women from service on the ground that their presence is incompatible with the requirement of 'interoperability', that is to say, the need for every Marine, irrespective of his specialisation, to be capable of fighting in a commando unit. This policy was set out in a report of 10 June 1994 entitled 'Revised Employment Policy for Women in the Army—Effect on the Royal Marines'. Paragraph 2(b) of that report, which is cited in paragraph 42 of the referring decision, states in particular that: 'In a small corps, in times of crisis and manpower shortage, all Royal Marines must be capable at any time of serving at their rank and skill level in a commando unit.... Employment of women in the Royal Marines will not allow for interoperability.' * * *

[21] ... [T]he national tribunal asks whether, and if so under what conditions, the exclusion of women from service in combat units such as the Royal Marines may be justified under Article 2(2) of the Directive. * * *

[23] Under Article 2(2) of the Directive, Member States have the option of excluding from the scope of that directive occupational activities for which, by reason of their nature or the context in which they are carried out, sex constitutes a determining factor; it must be noted, however, that, as a derogation from an individual right laid down in the Directive, that provision must be interpreted strictly (*Johnston*, paragraph 36).

[24] The Court has thus recognised, for example, that sex may be a determining factor for posts such as those of prison wardens and head prison wardens (Case 318/86 *Commission* v *France* [1988] ECR 3559, paragraphs 11 to 18), or for certain activities such as policing activities where there are serious internal disturbances (*Johnston*, paragraph 37). * * *

[30] It is clear from the documents in the case that, according to the findings already made by the national court, the organisation of the Royal Marines differs fundamentally from that of other units in the British armed forces, of which they are the 'point of the arrow head'. They are a small force and are intended to be the first line of attack. It has been established that, within this corps, chefs are indeed also required to serve as front-line commandos, that all members of the corps are engaged and trained for that purpose, and that there are no exceptions to this rule at the time of recruitment.

[31] In such circumstances, the competent authorities were entitled, in the exercise of their discretion as to whether to maintain the exclusion in question in the light of social developments, and without abusing the principle of proportionality, to come to the view that the specific conditions for deployment of the assault units of which the Royal Marines are composed, and in particular the rule of interoperability to which they are subject, justified their composition remaining exclusively male.

[32] The answer to the fifth and sixth questions must therefore be that the exclusion of women from service in special combat units such as the Royal Marines may be justified under Article 2(2) of the Directive by reason of the nature of the activities in question and the context in which they are carried out.

KREIL v. FEDERAL REPUBLIC OF GERMANY

Case C–285/98 [2000] ECR I–69.

[Ms. Kreil, who was trained in electronics, applied for a position in the weapons electronics maintenance arm of the Federal German Army (Bundeswehr). Her application was rejected on grounds that the German Constitution prohibited women from holding any military post involving the use of arms. Pursuant to this constitutional provision, secondary legislation in Germany limited women's involvement in the military to medical and military-music services. Kreil brought proceedings in the German Administrative Court claiming that the rejection of her application on grounds based solely on sex was contrary to the 1976 Equal Treatment Directive.]

26 ... [T]he refusal to engage the applicant in the main proceedings in the service of the Bundeswehr in which she wished to be employed was based on provisions of German law which bar women outright from military posts involving the use of arms and which allow women access only to the medical and military-music services.

27 In view of its scope, such an exclusion, which applies to almost all military posts in the Bundeswehr, cannot be regarded as a derogating measure justified by the specific nature of the posts in question or by the particular context in which the activities in question are carried out. However, the derogations provided for in Article 2(2) of the Directive can apply only to specific activities.

28 Moreover, having regard to the very nature of armed forces, the fact that persons serving in those forces may be called on to use arms cannot in itself justify the exclusion of women from access to military posts. As the German Government explained, in the services of the Bundeswehr that are accessible to women, basic training in the use of arms, to enable personnel in those services to defend themselves and to assist others, is provided.

29 In those circumstances, even taking account of the discretion which they have as regards the possibility of maintaining the exclusion in question, the national authorities could not, without contravening the principle of proportionality, adopt the general position that the composition of all armed units in the Bundeswehr had to remain exclusively male.

30 Finally, as regards the possible application of Article 2(3) of the Directive, upon which the German Government also relies, this provision ... is intended to protect a woman's biological condition and the special relationship which exists between a woman and her child. It does not therefore allow women to be excluded from a certain type of employment on the ground that they should be given greater protection than men against risks which are distinct from women's specific needs of protection, such as those expressly mentioned.

31 It follows that the total exclusion of women from all military posts involving the use of arms is not one of the differences of treatment allowed by Article 2(3) of the Directive out of concern to protect women.

32 The answer to be given to the question must therefore be that the Directive precludes the application of national provisions, such as those of

German law, which impose a general exclusion of women from military posts involving the use of arms and which allow them access only to the medical and military-music services.

Notes and Questions

1.   Where does the Court draw the line between permissible and impermissible derogations from equal treatment? *Kreil* is a striking illustration of how the supremacy of Community law can be a hard pill to swallow for a Member State. Germany is still grappling with how to deal with the principle, enshrined in its Constitution, excluding women from posts involving use of arms.

2.   A subsequent case examined whether men can be excluded from the practice of midwifery. The Court of Justice said yes, citing "personal sensitivities" of patients. Commission v. United Kingdom (Equal treatment), Case 165/82, [1983] ECR 3431. Do you agree? What standard should the Court use to decide when personal sensitivities justify exclusion of one sex from an occupation and when they merely reflect a sexual stereotype?

3.   A US case examined the issue whether states must allow women to serve as prison guards in an all-male prison. In *Dothard v. Rawlinson*, 433 U.S. 321, 97 S.Ct. 2720, 53 L.Ed.2d 786 (1977), the Supreme Court held that Alabama could exclude women from serving as guards in male prisons because of the risk of sexual assault from aggressive prisoners and a general concern for prison security. The Court so concluded even though, as it held, the bona fide occupational qualification defense was meant to be a very narrow exception to the general anti-discrimination rule.

In *United States v. Virginia*, 518 U.S. 515, 116 S.Ct. 2264, 135 L.Ed.2d 735 (1996), however, the US Supreme Court held that Virginia's categorical exclusion of women from the Virginia Military Institute denied equal protection to women. A state defending gender-based action must demonstrate an "exceedingly persuasive justification." It must show that the classification serves important governmental objectives and that the means employed are substantially related to those objectives. Does the United States follow the *Johnston/Sirdar/Kreil* divide?

4.   *Johnston* is frequently cited, also, as a major precedent protecting the basic right of judicial review. A Northern Ireland order had purported to give conclusive effect to a certificate of the Secretary of State finding that sex discrimination was necessary to protect public safety. The Court of Justice held that such a provision is "contrary to the principle of effective judicial control laid down in Article 6 of the directive." para. 20.

4.   PROTECTION OF WOMEN, POSITIVE ACTION AND REVERSE DISCRIMINATION

To what extent can women be favored or protected in employment, either as a class, or when pregnant or caring for young children?

a.   The Scope for Positive Action

As in the United States, the scope for positive action (affirmative action) in the name of gender equality has proven controversial. At what point does positive action become impermissible discrimination against a member of the majority group? The issue here is how to interpret articles 2(3) and article 2(4) of the 1976 Equal Treatment Directive and Article 141(4) of the Treaty (an amendment inserted in 1999 by the Treaty of Amsterdam).

Article 141(4) of the Treaty provides:

> With a view to ensuring full equality in practice between men and women in working life, the principle of equal treatment shall not prevent any Member State from maintaining or adopting measures providing for specific advantages in order to make it easier for the under-represented sex to pursue a vocational activity or to prevent or compensate for disadvantages in professional careers.

Because Article 141(4) is of recent origin, most of the caselaw has arisen under article 2(4) of the Equal Treatment Directive, which states:

> [T]his Directive shall be without prejudice to measures to promote equal opportunity for men and women, in particular by removing existing inequalities which affect women's opportunities . . . .

KALANKE v. FREIE HANSESTADT BREMEN

Case C–450/93, [1995] ECR I–3051.

[In 1990, the German state of Bremen adopted a regulation governing appointments or promotions to public administrative posts in any sector where women are under-represented, which is presumed to be the case if women do not make up at least half of the staff. The regulation provided that "women who have the same qualifications as men applying for the same post are to given priority" in the appointment or promotion involved. Kalanke, a male candidate for promotion to the post of manager in the Parks Department, sued to challenge the choice of an allegedly equally qualified female candidate for the post.

On appeal from the dismissal of his application, the German Supreme Labor Court asked the Court of Justice under Article 177, now 234, whether the priority thus given to women was in accord with article 2(4) of the Equal Treatment Directive. The German court noted its view that the Bremen rule was in accord with the German constitutional guarantee of equal treatment of the sexes because it did not constitute a strict quota of posts for women regardless of their qualifications. The Court of Justice easily concluded that the Bremen system represented "discrimination on grounds of sex" (paragraph 16), and then turned to the harder question of its possible justification under article 2(4).]

[18] That provision is specifically and exclusively designed to allow measures which, although discriminatory in appearance, are in fact intended to eliminate or reduce actual instances of inequality which may exist in the reality of social life.

[19] It thus permits national measures relating to access to employment, including promotion, which give a specific advantage to women with a view to improving their ability to compete on the labour market and to pursue a career on an equal footing with men.

[20] As the Council considered in the third recital in the preamble to Recommendation 84/635/EEC of 13 December 1984 on the promotion of positive action for women (OJ 1984 L 331, p. 34), 'existing legal provisions on equal treatment, which are designed to afford rights to individuals, are inadequate for the elimination of all existing inequalities unless parallel

action is taken by governments, both sides of industry and other bodies concerned, to counteract the prejudicial effects on women in employment which arise from social attitudes, behaviour and structures'.

[21] Nevertheless, as a derogation from an individual right laid down in the Directive Article 2(4) must be interpreted strictly.

[22] National rules which guarantee women absolute and unconditional priority for appointment or promotion go beyond promoting equal opportunities and overstep the limits of the exception in Article 2(4) of the Directive.

[23] Furthermore, in so far as it seeks to achieve equal representation of men and women in all grades and levels within a department, such a system substitutes for equality of opportunity as envisaged in Article 2(4) the result which is only to be arrived at by providing such equality of opportunity.

[24] The answer to the national court's questions must therefore be that Article 2(1) and (4) of the Directive precludes national rules such as those in the present case which, where candidates of different sexes shortlisted for promotion are equally qualified, automatically give priority to women in sectors where they are under-represented, under-representation being deemed to exist when women do not make up at least half of the staff in the individual pay brackets in the relevant personnel group or in the function levels provided for in the organization chart.

Thereafter, the Court treated as consistent with article 2(4) a German measure that, where fewer women than men were employed in a particular higher grade civil service bracket, women got job priority over men of equal suitability, competence and professional performance unless criteria specific to an individual male candidate "tilted the balance"; the measure required an objective assessment of all criteria. Marschall v. Land Nordrhein Westfalen, Case C–409/97, [1997] ECR I–6363. Also, the Court allowed a German law in the region of Hesse that guaranteed half the places in training courses to women, and half the interview slots to women, for jobs for which women were underrepresented. Badeck v. Hessischer Ministerpräsident, Case C–158/97, [2000] ECR I–1875. (Does *Badeck* fall easily within the rubric of eliminating barriers to women?)

Then the Court heard the complaint of Mr. Anderson, who, in the competition for a professorial post in Sweden, lost out to the less qualified Ms. Fogelqvist. The Swedish measure, unlike the German ones, authorized positive action on behalf of the *underrepresented sex* (now a requirement of Article 141(4)), rather than only on behalf of women. But this did not save the measure.

ABRAHAMSSON and ANDERSON v. FOGELQVIST
Case 407/98 [2000] ECR I–5539.

[In a drive to boost the number of female professors in certain universities, Sweden enacted a law providing that, when filling 30 particular posts during 1995–1996, "[a] candidate belonging to an under-represented sex who possesses sufficient qualifications ... must be granted preference over a candidate of the opposite sex who would otherwise have been chosen (positive discrimination) where it proves necessary to do so in order for a candidate of the under-represented sex to be appointed. Positive discrimination must, however, not be applied where the difference between the candidates' qualifications is so great that such application would give rise to a breach of the requirement of objectivity in making appointments." One such university post was offered to Ms. Fogelqvist, even though the selectors agreed that the plaintiff, Mr. Anderson, was more highly qualified.]

45   In contrast to the national legislation on positive discrimination examined by the Court in its *Kalanke, Marschall* and *Badeck* judgments, the national legislation at issue in the main proceedings enables preference to be given to a candidate of the under-represented sex who, although sufficiently qualified, does not possess qualifications equal to those of other candidates of the opposite sex. * * *

52   It follows that the legislation at issue in the main proceedings automatically grants preference to candidates belonging to the under-represented sex, provided that they are sufficiently qualified, subject only to the proviso that the difference between the merits of the candidates of each sex is not so great as to result in a breach of the requirement of objectivity in making appointments.

53   The scope and effect of that condition cannot be precisely determined, with the result that the selection of a candidate from among those who are sufficiently qualified is ultimately based on the mere fact of belonging to the under-represented sex, and that this is so even if the merits of the candidate so selected are inferior to those of a candidate of the opposite sex. Moreover, candidatures are not subjected to an objective assessment taking account of the specific personal situations of all the candidates. It follows that such a method of selection is not such as to be permitted by Article 2(4) of the Directive.

54   In those circumstances, it is necessary to determine whether legislation such as that at issue in the main proceedings is justified by Article 141(4) EC.

55   In that connection, it is enough to point out that, even though Article 141(4) EC allows the Member States to maintain or adopt measures providing for special advantages intended to prevent or compensate for disadvantages in professional careers in order to ensure full equality between men and women in professional life, it cannot be inferred from this that it allows a selection method of the kind at issue in the main proceedings which appears, on any view, to be disproportionate to the aim pursued.

56   The answer to the first question must therefore be that Article 2(1) and (4) of the Directive and Article 141(4) EC preclude national legislation under which a candidate for a public post who belongs to the under-represented sex and possesses sufficient qualifications for that post must be chosen in preference to a candidate of the opposite sex who would otherwise have been appointed, where this is necessary to secure the appointment of a candidate of the under-represented sex and the difference between the respective merits of the candidates is not so great as to give rise to a breach of the requirement of objectivity in making appointments.

Notes and Questions

1. In *Kalanke*, Advocate General Tesauro had discussed in detail various systems of affirmative action and even cited the leading US cases. He contended that a State may appropriately adopt rules that favor women by eliminating customary barriers to their integration in their workforce, especially the difficulties confronted by working mothers, but concluded that the Bremen rule simply gave priority to women without removing any barriers and therefore could not fall under article 2(4). He noted that his view would be unpopular in some circles, even perhaps in the Parliament.

Indeed, the *Kalanke* judgment provoked a strong adverse reaction in Germany and got quite mixed media commentary elsewhere. See L. Senden, Positive Action in the EU Put to the Test, 3 Maastricht J. Eur. L. 1466 (1996), and the thoughtful casenote by S. Prechal, 33 Common Mkt. L. Rev. 1245 (1996).

2. Why does the Bremen measure fail the test of "removing existing inequalities which affect women's opportunities"? If the Bremen rule fails the test, how can the measure in *Marschall* meet it? Does *Abrahamsson* undermine *Marschall*?

3. How would you revise the Bremen measure to meet the requirements of *Abrahamsson*?

4. Proposals to amend the Equal Treatment Directive would delete article 2(4), leaving Treaty Article 141(4) as the test.

5. *Abrahamsson* presented the Court with its first opportunity to interpret Article 141(4). Consider the following academic commentary:

> [In *Abrahamsson*] the Court declined an opportunity to make a fresh start on positive action in Community law, but rather has woven Article 141(4)EC into the principles already established through its existing case law.

Lisa Waddington and Mark Bell, More Equal than Others: Distinguishing European Union Equality Directives, 38 Common Mkt.L.Rev. 587, 602 (2001).

Comment on this point. How might the Court have made a progressive "fresh start"?

6. The issue is similarly perplexing in the United States. The scope for affirmative action by government is limited; it may violate the Equal Protection Clause of the Constitution. In *Wygant v. Jackson Board of Education*, 476 U.S. 267, 106 S.Ct. 1842, 90 L.Ed.2d 260 (1986), a plurality of the Supreme Court declared that the school board could not constitutionally lay off white teachers with more seniority than minority teachers in order to retain a preexisting percentage of minority teachers, all in an attempt to correct for lack of cultural diversity, to remedy general societal discrimination, and to provide role models for minority school children. Rather, the employer must prove a specific link such as prior discrimination by the government unit involved, and the program must be narrowly tailored to serve the compelling government interest. This analytical model is called "strict scrutiny." The tension between the individual rights conception of the Equal Protection Clause and the disadvantaged group-rights conception is still playing itself out in cases that poignantly raise the moral and legal problems of affirmative action. See Adarand Constructors, Inc. v. Slater, 228 F.3d 1147 (10th Cir. 2000) (disadvantaged business set-aside program), cert. dismissed, 534 U.S. 103, S.Ct. 511, 151 L.Ed.2d 489 (2001). Hopwood v. State of Texas, 236 F.3d 256 (5th Cir. 2000) (college admissions), cert. denied, ___ U.S. ___, 121 S.Ct. 2550, 150 L.Ed.2d 717 (2001); Taxman v. Board of Education of Township of Piscataway, 91 F.3d 1547 (3d Cir. 1996) (teacher lay-offs).

b. *Measures to Protect Workers during Pregnancy and Maternity*

The 1976 Equal Treatment Directive acknowledged that affording special protection to women during periods of pregnancy and maternity could be consistent with the principle of equal treatment. Indeed, only by such protection could genuine equality be achieved. Article 2(3) of the directive makes clear that its equality provisions are "without prejudice to provisions concerning the protection of women, particularly as regards pregnancy and maternity."

In 1992 the Community supplemented the protection afforded to pregnant women under the national laws of the Member States by adopting the Pregnant Workers Directive. Council Directive 92/85/EEC of 19 October 1992 on the introduction of measures to encourage improvements in the safety and health at work of pregnant workers and workers who have recently given birth or are breastfeeding. This directive, which was adopted pursuant to the health and safety clause of the EC Treaty (now Article 138), gave a wide range of new protections to women who are pregnant, have recently given birth, or are breastfeeding.

Even prior to adoption of the Pregnant Workers Directive, the Court had been faced with the task of defining the precise limits of the derogation provided in article 2(3) of the Equal Treatment Directive. To what extent, if any, could special protection afforded to mothers constitute discrimination against fathers or other male workers?

HOFMANN v. BARMER ERSATZKASSE

Case 184/83, [1984] ECR 3047.

[German law grants working mothers eight weeks' paid leave after childbirth, followed by a further four months of unpaid maternity leave. During the unpaid leave, the mother is paid a daily allowance from a state fund. Mr. Hofmann, father of a newborn, obtained six months unpaid leave from his employer, while the mother resumed work as a teacher. Hofmann sued for the daily allowance grant, claiming that the unpaid leave and corresponding grant was made to a mother for child care and was not connected with maternity. In support of his view, he noted that the unpaid leave and allowance would be cancelled should the infant die. The German Social Court asked the Court of Justice whether limiting the unpaid leave and daily allowance to mothers was justified under article 2(3) of the Equal Treatment Directive.]

[11] According to the plaintiff, the protection of the mother against the multiplicity of burdens imposed by motherhood and her employment could be achieved by non-discriminatory measures, such as enabling the father to enjoy the leave or creating a period of parental leave, so as to release the mother from the responsibility of caring for the child and thereby allow her to resume employment as soon as the statutory protective period had expired. The plaintiff further claims that the choice between the options thereby created should, in conformity with the principle on non-discrimination between the sexes, be left completely at the discretion of the parents of the child. * * *

24   It is apparent ... that the directive is not designed to settle questions concerned with the organization of the family, or to alter the division of responsibility between parents.

25   It should further be added, with particular reference to paragraph (3), that, by reserving to Member States the right to retain, or introduce provisions which are intended to protect women in connection with "pregnancy and maternity", the directive recognizes the legitimacy, in terms of the principle of equal treatment, of protecting a woman's needs in two respects. First, it is legitimate to ensure the protection of a woman's biological condition during pregnancy and thereafter until such time as her physiological and mental functions have returned to normal after childbirth; secondly, it is legitimate to protect the special relationship between a woman and her child over the period which follows pregnancy and childbirth, by preventing that relationship from being disturbed by the multiple burdens which would result from the simultaneous pursuit of employment.

26   In principle, therefore, a measure such as maternity leave granted to a woman on expiry of the statutory protective period falls within the scope of Article 2(3) of Directive 76/207, inasmuch as it seeks to protect a woman in connection with the effects of pregnancy and motherhood. That being so, such leave may legitimately be reserved to the mother to the exclusion of any other person, in view of the fact that it is only the mother who may find herself subject to undesirable pressures to return to work prematurely.

27   Furthermore, it should be pointed out that the directive leaves Member States with a discretion as to the social measures which they adopt in order to guarantee, within the framework laid down by the directive, the protection of women in connection with pregnancy and maternity and to offset the disadvantages which women, by comparison with men, suffer with regard to the retention of employment. Such measures are, as the Government of the United Kingdom has rightly observed, closely linked to the general system of social protection in the various Member States. It must therefore be concluded that the Member States enjoy a reasonable margin of discretion as regards both the nature of the protective measures and the detailed arrangements for their implementation.

28   It follows from the foregoing that the reply to be given to the question submitted by the [Social Court] is that Articles 1, 2 and 5(1) of Council Directive 76/207 must be interpreted as meaning that a Member State may, after the statutory protective period has expired, grant to mothers a period of maternity leave which the State encourages them to take by the payment of an allowance. The directive does not impose on Member States a requirement that they shall, as an alternative, allow such leave to be granted to fathers, even where the parents so decide.

Notes and Questions

1. Not long after the judgment in *Hoffman*, the Commission challenged France's implementation of the 1976 directive because France specifically allowed collective bargaining agreements and individual enterprise rules and contracts to contain provisions benefitting only women. Commission v. France (Equal treat-

ment), Case 312/86, [1988] ECR 6315. The Commission cited as examples a Mother's Day holiday, shorter work hours for women over 59, leave days for female employees when a child is ill or at the beginning of the school year, allowances to mothers to pay for nurseries or child attendants, and daily breaks for women telephone operators or typists.

The Court held that none of these protective measures was justified by article 2(4). Equally important, it construed article 2(3)'s protection of pregnancy and maternity to end within a reasonable period following childbirth, and held that article 2(3) should not be read expansively to cover child care because that is a responsibility of both parents. It would thus appear that if an employer is willing (or obliged by a collective agreement) to grant time off to care for a sick or injured child, or to pay an allowance for nursery or child care, either parent should have a right to claim the benefit.

2. Why shouldn't the parents be allowed to decide who should care for the infant and who should work? How can this be treated as a maternity benefit if it is cancelled when the infant dies? Is the Court's later judgment in *Commission v. France (Equal treatment)* inconsistent with *Hofmann,* or is there a valid distinction between the care of young infants and that of older children? If you agree with *Hofmann,* do you think *Commission v. France* is wrong in forbidding child care leave days or allowances given only to working mothers? Do fathers often stay home from work to take care of ill children? Should a State discourage them from doing so? Contrast *Weinberger v. Wiesenfeld,* 420 U.S. 636, 95 S.Ct. 1225, 43 L.Ed.2d 514 (1975), which held that social security benefits paid to widows who cease working to care for minor children must also be paid to widowers who do the same thing.

3. Since the adoption in 1996 of the Parental Leave Directive 96/34, both male and female workers enjoy the benefit of certain rights "to reconcile their work and family responsibilities," including a right "to take parental leave on the ground of the birth or adoption of a child to enable them to take care of that child, for at least three months, until a given age up to eight years to be defined by Member States and/or management and labour." This directive was the first to be negotiated by the social partners under the Social Policy Agreement annexed to the Treaty of Maastricht.

4. In *Handels-og Kontorfunktionaerernes Forbund v. Dansk Arbejdsgiverforening,* Case C–179/88, [1990] ECR I–3979, Mrs. Hertz, a part-time cashier, was fired after being sick for 100 days. Her illness was due to complications arising from a pregnancy the year before. The Court of Justice held that article 2(3) prevented dismissal of a worker because of pregnancy, as well as dismissal during maternity leave, but did not forbid dismissal for inability to work due to an illness, even if the illness had been originally caused by complications arising from pregnancy. Equal treatment merely required that a woman not be fired for prolonged inability to work due to illness if a man would not be fired in a similar case, whatever his illness might be. Do you agree?

5. May an employer hire a woman who is not pregnant rather than a better qualified pregnant woman in order to avoid the costs of the social benefits provided to pregnant women? Would this violate article 2 or 3 of the Equal Treatment Directive? See Dekker v. Stichting Vormingscentrum VJV, Case C–177/88, [1990] ECR I–3941.

HABERMANN–BELTERMANN v.
ARBEITERWOHLFAHRT

Case C–421/92, [1994] ECR I–1657.

[The German Law for the Protection of Mothers forbids night-time work for pregnant women. When on March 23, 1992, Habermann, a nurse, was hired by a retirement home to perform night-time duties, she had just become pregnant but was not aware of her pregnancy. After she informed her employer in May, the employer attempted to rescind the employment contract on the ground of mutual mistake of fact concerning an essential condition. The trial court asked whether such a rescission, normally appropriate under German law, would violate articles 3 and 5 of the Equal Treatment Directive.]

14 The first question which arises is whether the annulment or avoidance (*Anfechtung*) of an employment contract in a case such as this constitutes direct discrimination on grounds of sex for the purposes of the directive. To that end, it must be established whether the fundamental reason for the annulment or avoidance of the contract applies without distinction to workers of both sexes or . . . to one sex only.

15 It is clear that the termination of an employment contract on account of the employee's pregnancy, whether by annulment or avoidance, concerns women alone and constitutes, therefore, direct discrimination on grounds of sex, as the Court has held in cases where a pregnant woman was denied employment or dismissed (see *Dekker* and *Hertz*).

16 However, the unequal treatment in a case such as this, unlike the *Dekker* case . . . is not based directly on the woman's pregnancy but is the result of the statutory prohibition on night-time work during pregnancy. * * *

18 The question, therefore, is whether the directive precludes compliance with the prohibition on night-time work by pregnant women, which is unquestionably compatible with Article 2(3) [of the Equal Treatment Directive], from rendering an employment contract invalid or allowing it to be avoided on the ground that the prohibition prevents the employee from doing the night-time work for which she was engaged.

19 According to the Arbeiterwohlfahrt, the Member States possess a wide and independent discretion in appraising the interests of workers, both male and female, and of employers and society. Excessive protection of mothers might lead to abuse by women and also to discrimination against men who do not have the same opportunity of being paid without having to work in return.

20 That argument must be rejected.

22 As the Court has held (see *Hofmann*), the directive leaves Member States with a discretion as to the social measures which must be adopted in order to guarantee, within the framework laid down by the directive, the protection of women in connection with pregnancy and maternity and to offset the disadvantages which women, by comparison with men, suffer with regard to the retention of employment.

23 In this case, the questions submitted for a ruling relate to a contract for an indefinite period and the prohibition on night-time work by pregnant

women therefore takes effect only for a limited period in relation to the total length of the contract.

24 In the circumstances, to acknowledge that the contract may be held to be invalid or may be avoided because of the temporary inability of the pregnant employee to perform the night-time work for which she has been engaged would be contrary to the objective of protecting such persons pursued by Article 2(3) of the directive, and would deprive that provision of its effectiveness.

25 Accordingly, termination of a contract for an indefinite period on grounds of the woman's pregnancy, whether by annulment or avoidance, cannot be justified by the fact that she is temporarily prevented, by a statutory prohibition imposed because of pregnancy, from performing night-time work.

Notes and Questions

1. If the Pregnant Workers Directive had come into effect prior to these proceedings, the issue would have been easily resolved: Article 5 of the directive now requires employers to provide pregnant workers with alternative employment instead of night work or, if that is not possible, to place them on unpaid leave. Absent such legislation, do you agree with the Court that the principle of non-discrimination prevents the normal application of the civil code doctrine of mutual mistake of fact?

2. Since this was a private contract dispute, and directives do not have horizontal direct effect, how is the Equal Treatment Directive relevant at all? In paragraphs 9–10, the Court dealt with this issue by applying the *Marleasing* doctrine, *supra* at 262, which requires national courts to interpret national law rules insofar as reasonably possible in accordance with the principles of directives, in this case, the principle of non-discrimination.

3. In *Mahlburg v. Land Mecklenburg–Vorpommern*, Case C–207/98, [2000] ECR I–549, the Court of Justice ruled that the 1976 Equal Treatment Directive precluded a refusal to appoint a pregnant woman to a permanent nursing position, on the grounds that German law (Mutterschutzgesetz) prohibited employers from employing pregnant women in areas in which they would be exposed to the harmful effects of dangerous substances. The plaintiff was employed as an operating-theater nurse on a fixed term contract in a German heart surgery clinic. When she applied for a permanent position in the clinic, she was pregnant. Her employer decided not to appoint her to the permanent post on the basis that German law prohibited employers from placing pregnant women in any position involving exposure to harmful substances. The Court held that the provisions of the 1976 directive concerning the protection of pregnant women could not result in unfavorable treatment regarding their access to employment. Consequently, it was not permissible for an employer to refuse to appoint a pregnant woman to a post of unlimited duration, in circumstances where a prohibition on employment arising as a result of her pregnancy would prevent her being employed from the outset and for the duration of her pregnancy.

4. Compare the US decision, *Automobile Workers v. Johnson Controls, Inc.,* 499 U.S. 187, 111 S.Ct. 1196, 113 L.Ed.2d 158 (1991), holding impermissible under Title VII as amended by the Pregnancy Discrimination Act a battery manufacturer's rule barring all women, except those whose infertility was medically documented, from jobs involving certain levels of lead exposure.

c. Framework Strategy on Gender Equality

In 2000, the Commission published a *Community Framework Strategy on Gender Equality* (2001–2005) COM(2000)335. The document outlines an approach called "gender mainstreaming," which aspires to close the equality gap between men and women. It states in part:

> [C]onsiderable progress has been made regarding the situation of women in the Member States, but gender equality in day-to-day life is still being undermined by the fact that women and men do not enjoy equal rights in practice.
>
> This situation can be tackled effectively by integrating the gender equality objective into the policies that have a direct or indirect impact on the lives of women and men. Women's concerns, needs and aspirations should be taken into account and assume the same importance as men's concerns in the design and implementation of policies. This is the *gender mainstreaming* approach. . . .
>
> In parallel to gender mainstreaming, persistent inequalities continue to require the implementation of specific actions in favour of women. The proposed framework strategy is based on this dual-track approach.

d. Proposed Amendments to the 1976 Equal Treatment Directive

At the time of writing, proposals to amend the 1976 Equal Treatment Directive are at an advanced stage. Proposed amendments would include the following:

1. The gender mainstreaming approach (outlined above) would be mandated. All Member States would be required to introduce such measures as are necessary to eliminate inequalities, and actively and visibly promote the objective of equality between men and women by incorporation of the approach into national law and policy.

2. Sexual harassment in the workplace, as defined in the proposals, would be deemed to constitute discrimination on the grounds of sex for the purposes of the 1976 Equal Treatment Directive.

3. Article 2(4) of the Equal Treatment Directive, which allows Member States to adopt policies of positive action, would be deleted. Instead, all such policies would be based directly on Article 141(4) of the Treaty, as inserted by the Treaty of Amsterdam.

4. New definitions of direct and indirect discrimination would be introduced to bring the Equal Treatment Directive into conformity with the corresponding provisions of the Race and Framework Employment directives (see Section D below). Direct discrimination would be defined as "the situation where a person is treated less favourably than another is, has been, or would be treated in a similar situation, on grounds of sex." Indirect discrimination would describe "the situation where an apparently neutral provision, criterion or practice puts persons of one sex at a particular disadvantage compared with persons of the other sex, unless

that provision, criterion or practice is objectively justified by a legitimate and proportionate aim, and the means of achieving that aim are appropriate and necessary."

5. An amendment would tighten the derogation on grounds of occupational requirements, permitted to Member States by article 2(2) of the Equal Treatment Directive, following the Court's decisions in *Johnston, Sirdar* and *Kreil*. In order to invoke the derogation successfully, Member States would be required to identify a "precise and definite occupational requirement" and to show that such a requirement is a "proportionate" response to a "legitimate" policy objective.

6. Finally, the proposals would make explicit the principle that a woman who has given birth is entitled, after the end of her maternity leave period (or after absence directly related to or as a consequence of pregnancy and/or confinement) to return to her job or to an equivalent job on terms and conditions which are not less favourable to her, and to benefit from any improvement in working conditions to which she would have been entitled during her absence.

For the full text of these proposals, see: Proposal for a Directive of the European Parliament and of the Council amending Council Directive 76/207/ EEC on the implementation of the principle of equal treatment for men and women as regards access to employment, vocational training and promotion, and working conditions, of June 7, 2000 COM(2000) 334 final, and the amendments to this Proposal presented by the Commission on June 7, 2001 COM(2001) 321 final.

D.   DISCRIMINATION ON GROUNDS OTHER THAN GENDER

Article 13, inserted in 1999 by the Treaty of Amsterdam, significantly expanded the scope for Community action in the area of non-gender discrimination. Armed with this new legislative competence, the Commission wasted little time in proposing two new directives designed to widen the reach of Community non-discrimination law: (i) a draft Framework Employment Directive addressing discrimination in employment on the grounds of religion or belief, disability, age or sexual orientation; and (ii) a draft Race Directive concerning the specific problem of racial/ethnic discrimination, not only in employment but also in other areas such as social security and education.

Amid growing concerns over the incidence of racism and xenophobia in certain parts of the Community, the Race Directive was adopted by the Council without delay and came into force on July 19, 2000. Directive 2000/43/EC implementing the principle of equal treatment between persons irrespective of racial or ethnic origin, O.J. 200 L 180/22, printed in Selected Documents as ER Doc. 5. Later that year, the Council also adopted the Framework Employment Directive, addressing discrimination on the grounds of religion or belief, disability, age or sexual orientation. Directive 2000/78/EC establishing a general framework for equal treatment in employment and occupation, O.J. 2000 L 303/16, printed in Selected Documents as ER Doc. 6.

The main provisions of the two directives are as follows:

Framework Employment Directive

The Framework Employment Directive outlaws direct and indirect discrimination on the grounds of religion or belief, disability, age or sexual orientation. Indirect discrimination is defined as occurring "where an apparently neutral provision, criterion or practice would put persons having a particular religion or belief, a particular disability, a particular age, or a particular sexual orientation at a particular disadvantage compared with other persons unless that provision, criterion or practice is objectively justified by a legitimate aim and the means of achieving that aim are appropriate and necessary."

The Directive covers not only employment and working conditions, including dismissals and pay, but also extends to access to employment, recruitment, promotion and vocational training.

In keeping with the policy established by the 1997 Burden of Proof Directive, where a complainant has established "facts from which it may be presumed that there has been direct or indirect discrimination," the respondent must prove that there has been no discrimination.

For the first time in Community equal treatment law, harassment is expressly forbidden. Harassment relating to age, religion or belief, disability or sexual orientation will constitute discrimination if it has the purpose or effect of creating "an intimidating, hostile, degrading humiliating or offensive environment." The proposals to amend the 1976 Equal Treatment Directive, discussed above, would incorporate this approach into the 1976 directive.

In order to guarantee compliance with the principle of equal treatment for persons with disabilities, employers are required to provide "reasonable accommodation," if needed in a particular case, to enable disabled employees "to have access to, participate in, or advance in employment, or to undergo training, unless such measures would impose a disproportionate burden on the employer."

The Directive also contains an "occupational requirement" provision, as found in article 2(2) of the 1976 Equal Treatment Directive. The wording is, however, more restrictive than that contained in the original 1976 directive; it requires Member States to show that any difference in treatment is the result of a "genuine and determining occupational requirement" made pursuant to a legitimate policy objective and proportionate to that objective.

In contrast to the strict wording of this provision, other parts of the directive give Member States some discretion in specific areas, including differences of treatment based on age and employment in churches or other organizations the ethos of which is based on religion or belief.

The exceptions to the directive are equally important. The legislation is expressed to be without prejudice to national provisions laying down retirement ages, or national laws on marital status and benefits dependant thereon. Armed forces are excluded from the directive's terms, insofar as they relate to age or disability. However, the provisions banning discrimination on grounds of sexual orientation, religion or belief apply to employment in the armed forces.

Finally, because the directive lays down only minimum requirements, Member States remain free to introduce or maintain provisions, including position action measures, which are more favorable to equal treatment than those contained in the directive. Member States are required to implement the provisions concerning sexual orientation and religion or belief on or before December 2, 2003. The deadline for implementation of the age and disability provisions is December 2, 2006.

The Race Directive

The Race Directive prohibits direct or indirect discrimination on the grounds of racial or ethnic origin. In many aspects, the approach taken in the Race Directive is identical to that set out in the Framework Employment Directive. In particular, the Race Directive imports the same concept of indirect discrimination; includes harassment within the concept of discrimination; has a similar derogation for "genuine and determining" occupational requirements; follows the same rule in respect of the burden of proof; and allows Member States to introduce or maintain more favorable measures, including positive action, at national level.

The two directives differ significantly in their material scope. In addition to the grounds covered by the Framework Employment Directive, the Race Directive also extends to social protection, including social security and healthcare; social advantages; education; and access to and supply of goods and services available to the public, including housing. The Race Directive requires Member States to adopt implementing measures by July 19, 2003.

E. SOCIAL SECURITY, PENSIONS AND PENSIONABLE AGE

1. SOCIAL SECURITY DIRECTIVES

Neither Article 119 nor the 1976 Equal Treatment Directive required equal treatment of men and women in state social security plans (see the first *Defrenne* case and the discussion of the 1976 directive above). To fill the gap, the Council adopted Directive 79/7, O.J. L 6/24 (Jan. 10, 1979), which is printed in the Selected Documents as ER Doc. No 7. Article 235, now 308, served as the legal basis for this directive.

The State Social Security Directive covers all statutory social security benefit plans, including those for sickness, old age, accidents at work, and unemployment (art. 3). The directive mandates equal treatment as to a) the scope of the plans and conditions for coverage; b) the obligation to contribute and the calculation of contributions; and c) the calculation of benefits and their duration (art. 4). As in the Equal Pay and Equal Treatment Directives, Member States are required to modify their legislation and practices to comply with the directive, and to create a system of judicial recourse (arts. 5 and 6).

The directive contains a number of exceptions to the principle of equal treatment, such as survivor's benefits and special treatment for women on the grounds of maternity. Most importantly, pursuant to article 7, Member States are not obliged to fix the same age for eligibility for old-age pensions for men and women or grant them the same derived rights. The reason is that several States allow women to receive old-age pensions at an earlier age than men. To raise the lower eligibility age for women would be quite unpopular, while to lower the eligibility age for men would be extremely costly.

The State Social Security Directive was supplemented by Directive 86/378 O.J. L 225/40 (Aug. 12, 1986), adopted also on the basis of Article 235. This directive requires equal treatment for men and women in occupational social security schemes (i.e., employer or private sector social benefit plans).

The 1986 Employer Social Benefit Directive's coverage of types of benefits and the scope of equal treatment parallels most of the provisions of the 1979 State Social Security Directive. The Employer Social Benefit Directive forbids different treatment for men and women as to the age at which an employee qualifies to receive benefits and as to the minimum retirement age (art. 6). However, by a special derogation the directive permits Member States to allow employer plans to parallel different ages of eligibility for pensions set for men and women by the state retirement pension plan (art. 9). In 1996, the Council adopted Directive 96/97 O.J. L 151/39 (Dec. 20, 1996), amending the 1986 directive. It made equal treatment in pensions apply to all employees after May 17, 1990, including retrospectively to that date and, for those who filed their claims earlier, even before that date.

Notes and Questions

1. Several Member States that allow women to retire earlier than men are reluctant to introduce the same "pensionable age" for men and women. Why?

2. The United Kingdom social security system permits women to retire at 60 while men retire at 65. As a corollary, the plan requires men to continue to make contributions when working while aged 60–64. On average, men pay into the state plan for a longer period and receive benefits for a shorter period. In *The Queen v. Secretary of State for Social Security*, Case C–9/91, [1992] ECR I–4297, the Equal Opportunities Commission claimed that this financial discrimination did not fall under the derogation for different old-age pension eligibility stated in article 7 of the State Social Security Directive. The Court disagreed. It concluded that the derogation for a different pensionable age for men and women was "intended to allow Member States to maintain temporarily the advantage accorded to women with respect to retirement in order to enable them progressively to adapt their pension systems in this respect without disrupting the complex financial equilibrium of those systems, the importance of which could not be ignored." A contrary decision would have created a serious financial and political problem.

The UK retirement age will be equalized at 65 over a period of ten years starting April 2010 (Pension Act 1995, §§ 118–1220). Other countries, including Austria, Germany, Italy and Portugal, also plan to introduce a uniform retirement age, to be set at 65.

2. SOCIAL SECURITY AND PENSIONS CASELAW

REGINA VIRGINIA HEPPLE v. ADJUDICATION OFFICER; ADJUDICATION OFFICER v. ANNA STEC
Case C–196, ECR [2000] I–3701.

[Under UK law, an employer was required to pay a weekly cash benefit to employees and former employees who had suffered a reduction in earnings following an accident at work. This reduced earnings allowance (REA) was further reduced to 25% when recipients reached retirement age, which was 65 for men and 60 for women. Ms. Hepple qualified for the REA but objected to the further reduction at the women's retirement age. The Court found that the REA falls within the scope of the 1979 directive and may be classified as a benefit for which the determination of retirement age might have repercussions. The Court proceeded to consider whether Member States that have different retirement ages for men and women could introduce further discriminatory measures.]

25   According to settled case-law, where, pursuant to Article 7(1)(a) of the Directive, a Member State prescribes different pensionable ages for men and women for the purposes of granting old-age and retirement pensions, the scope of the permitted derogation, defined by the words 'possible consequences thereof for other benefits', contained in Article 7(1)(a), is limited to the forms of discrimination existing under other benefit schemes which are necessarily and objectively linked to the difference in pensionable age.

26   That will be the position where such forms of discrimination are objectively necessary in order to avoid disturbing the financial equilibrium of the social-security system or to ensure coherence between the retirement-pension scheme and other benefit schemes.

27   As regards, first, the requirement of preserving financial equilibrium of the social-security system, it must be borne in mind that the Court has already held that the grant of benefits under non-contributory schemes to persons in respect of whom certain risks have materialised, regardless of the entitlement of such persons to an old-age pension by virtue of contribution periods completed by them, has no direct influence on the financial equilibrium of contributory pension schemes.

28   It must also be noted that in none of the observations submitted to the Court has it been argued that considerations of financial equilibrium might be applicable to non-contributory benefits, such as those at issue in this case, and the United Kingdom has even expressly excluded that possibility.

29   In those circumstances, it must be held that removal of the discrimination at issue in the main proceedings would have no effect on the financial equilibrium of the social-security system of the United Kingdom as a whole.

30   As regards, second, coherence between the retirement-pension scheme and other benefit schemes, it must be considered whether it is objectively necessary for different age conditions based on sex to apply to the benefit at issue in this case.

31   In that respect, the principal aim of the successive legislative amendments ... was to discontinue payment of REA—an allowance designed to compensate for an impairment of earning capacity following an accident at work or occupational disease—to persons no longer of working age by imposing conditions based on the statutory retirement age.

32   Thus, as a result of those legislative amendments, there is coherence between REA, which is designed to compensate for a decrease in earnings, and the old-age pension scheme. It follows that maintenance of the rules

at issue in the main proceedings is objectively necessary to preserve such coherence. * * *

[34] It follows that discrimination of the kind at issue in the main proceedings is objectively and necessarily linked to the difference between the retirement age for men and that for women, so that it is covered by the derogation for which Article 7(1)(a) of the Directive provides.

Notes and Questions

1. Do you agree? Would the UK have disturbed the financial equilibrium of its social security system by foregoing the 75% reduction until the beneficiary—man or woman—was 65?

2. A number of other challenges have been launched against the remnants of discrimination arguably allowed by the 1979 directive's derogation clause. Most have failed, just like *Hepple* above.

3. AGE OF QUALIFICATION FOR RETIREMENT PENSIONS

As noted above, the 1978 State Social Security Directive permits Member States to set different pensionable ages for men and women. Private employer pension plans frequently also fix different pensionable ages for men and women. Several important cases have raised the issue whether such private plan discrimination violates Community law.

The first, *Burton v. British Railways Board*, Case 19/81, [1982] ECR 555, involved voluntary redundancy (dismissal) benefits paid by British Railways to employees taking early retirement. The benefits paid to Mr. Burton were lower than those paid to a woman of the same age, due to the fact that British Railways' private pension plan allowed women to retire at 55 while men could do so only at 60. Burton sued to challenge this discrimination. The Court of Justice first held that the voluntary redundancy plan constituted a work condition and therefore the 1976 Equal Treatment Directive was applicable. The Court then held that when a private employer benefit plan parallels the different pensionable ages for men and women set by the state social security system, the private plan does not violate equal treatment. After *Burton* came *Marshall*, which, you will recall, also concerned the direct effect of the directive).

MARSHALL v. SOUTHAMPTON & SOUTH–WEST HAMPSHIRE AREA HEALTH AUTHORITY

Case 152/84, [1986] ECR 723.

[The UK state social security system granted pensions to men at 65 and women at 60. The Health Authority, a state agency, normally required men to retire at 65 and women at 60. The Health Authority initially granted Ms. Marshall, a dietician, a two-year extension, but then forced her to retire at age 62. She sued for damages for discriminatory dismissal. The Industrial Tribunal decided in her favor on the basis of the 1976 Equal Treatment Directive. On appeal, the Court of Appeal asked the Court of Justice whether the earlier retirement age for women violated the Equal Treatment Directive.

[21] By the first question the Court of Appeal seeks to ascertain whether or not Article 5(1) of Directive No 76/207 must be interpreted as meaning that a

general policy concerning dismissal, followed by a State authority, involving the dismissal of a woman solely because she has attained or passed the qualifying age for a State pension, which age is different under national legislation for men and for women, constitutes discrimination on grounds of sex, contrary to that directive. * * *

[32] The Court observes in the first place that the question of interpretation which has been referred to it does not concern access to a statutory or occupational retirement scheme, that is to say the conditions for payment of an old-age or retirement pension, but the fixing of an age limit with regard to the termination of employment pursuant to a general policy concerning dismissal. The question therefore relates to the conditions governing dismissal and falls to be considered under Directive No 76/207.

[33] Article 5(1) of Directive No 76/207 provides that application of the principle of equal treatment with regard to working conditions, including the conditions governing dismissal, means that men and women are to be guaranteed the same conditions without discrimination on grounds of sex.

[34] In its judgment in the *Burton* case the Court has already stated that the term "dismissal" contained in that provision must be given a wide meaning. Consequently, an age limit for the compulsory dismissal of workers pursuant to an employer's general policy concerning retirement falls within the term "dismissal" construed in that manner, even if the dismissal involves the grant of a retirement pension.

[35] As the Court emphasized in its judgment in the *Burton* case, Article 7 of Directive No 79/7 expressly provides that the directive does not prejudice the right of Member States to exclude from its scope the determination of pensionable age for the purposes of granting old-age and retirement pensions and the possible consequences thereof for other benefits falling within the statutory social security schemes. The Court thus acknowledged that benefits tied to a national scheme which lays down a different minimum pensionable age for men and women may lie outside the ambit of the aforementioned obligation.

[36] However, in view of the fundamental importance of the principle of equality of treatment, which the Court has reaffirmed on numerous occasions, Article 1(2) of Directive No 76/207, which excludes social security matters from the scope of that directive, must be interpreted strictly. Consequently, the exception to the prohibition of discrimination on grounds of sex provided for in Article 7(1)(a) of Directive No 79/7 applies only to the determination of pensionable age for the purposes of granting old-age and retirement pensions and the possible consequences thereof for other benefits.

[37] In that respect it must be emphasized that, whereas the exception contained in Article 7 of Directive No 79/7 concerns the consequences which pensionable age has for social security benefits, this case is concerned with dismissal within the meaning of Article 5 of Directive No 76/207.

[38] Consequently, the answer to the first question referred to the Court by the Court of Appeal must be that Article 5(1) of Directive No 76/207 must be interpreted as meaning that a general policy concerning dismissal involving the dismissal of a woman solely because she has attained the qualify-

ing age for a State pension, which age is different under national legislation for men and for women, constitutes discrimination on grounds of sex, contrary to that directive.

BARBER v. GUARDIAN ROYAL EXCHANGE ASSUR. GROUP

Case 262/88, [1990] ECR I–1889.

[Guardian Royal granted early retirement pensions to employees dismissed in a collective redundancy (mass lay-off). Its normal pensionable age was 62 for men and 57 for women, three years less than the state social security pension ages of 65 for men and 60 for women. Guardian Royal followed this model in offering early retirement pensions to the dismissed employees at the age of 55 for men and 50 for women. Mr. Barber, dismissed at 52, was therefore not offered an early retirement pension, although women his age were offered one. He sued to claim equal treatment. The Court of Appeal referred questions to the Court of Justice.]

[10] In its first question the Court of Appeal seeks to ascertain, in substance, whether the benefits paid by an employer to a worker in connection with the latter's compulsory redundancy fall within the scope of Article 119 of the Treaty and the directive on equal pay or within the scope of the directive on equal treatment. * * *

[12] As the Court has held, the concept of pay, within the meaning of the second paragraph of Article 119, comprises any other consideration, whether in cash or in kind, whether immediate or future, provided that the worker receives it, albeit indirectly, in respect of his employment from his employer (see, in particular, *Garland v. British Rail Engineering* [1982] ECR 359, paragraph 5). Accordingly, the fact that certain benefits are paid after the termination of the employment relationship does not prevent them from being in the nature of pay, within the meaning of Article 119 of the Treaty. * * *

[14] It follows that compensation granted to a worker in connection with his redundancy falls in principle within the concept of pay for the purposes of Article 119 of the Treaty.

[15] At the hearing, the United Kingdom argued that the statutory redundancy payment fell outside the scope of Article 119 of the Treaty because it constituted a social security benefit and not a form of pay.

[16] In that regard it must be pointed out that a redundancy payment made by the employer, such as that which is at issue, cannot cease to constitute a form of pay on the sole ground that, rather than deriving from the contract of employment, it is a statutory or *ex gratia* payment.

[17] In the case of statutory redundancy payments it must be borne in mind that ... Article 119 of the Treaty also applies to discrimination arising directly from legislative provisions. This means that benefits provided for by law may come within the concept of pay for the purposes of that provision.

[18] Although it is true that many advantages granted by an employer also reflect considerations of social policy, the fact that a benefit is in the

nature of pay cannot be called in question where the worker is entitled to receive the benefit in question from his employer by reason of the existence of the employment relationship.

19   In the case of *ex gratia* payments by the employer, it is clear from *Garland,* cited above, paragraph 10, that Article 119 also applies to advantages which an employer grants to workers although he is not required to do so by contract.

20   Accordingly, without there being any need to discuss whether or not the directive on equal treatment is applicable, the answer to the first question must be that the benefits paid by an employer to a worker in connection with the latter's compulsory redundancy fall within the scope of the second paragraph of Article 119, whether they are paid under a contract of employment, by virtue of legislative provisions or on a voluntary basis.

21   [T]he second question must be understood as seeking in substance to ascertain whether a retirement pension paid under a contracted-out private occupational scheme falls within the scope of Article 119 of the Treaty, in particular where that pension is awarded in connection with compulsory redundancy. * * *

25   [T]he schemes in question are the result either of an agreement between workers and employers or of a unilateral decision taken by the employer. They are wholly financed by the employer or by both the employer and the workers without any contribution being made by the public authorities in any circumstances. Accordingly, such schemes form part of the consideration offered to workers by the employer.

26   Secondly, such schemes are not compulsorily applicable to general categories of workers. On the contrary, they apply only to workers employed by certain undertakings, with the result that affiliation to those schemes derives of necessity from the employment relationship with a given employer. Furthermore, even if the schemes in question are established in conformity with national legislation and consequently satisfy the conditions laid down by it for recognition as contracted-out schemes, they are governed by their own rules.

27   Thirdly, it must be pointed out that, even if the contributions paid to those schemes and the benefits which they provide are in part a substitute for those of the general statutory scheme, that fact cannot preclude the application of Article 119. It is apparent from the documents before the Court that occupational schemes such as that referred to in this case may grant to their members benefits greater than those which would be paid by the statutory scheme, with the result that their economic function is similar to that of the supplementary schemes which exist in certain Member States, where affiliation and contribution to the statutory scheme is compulsory and no derogation is allowed. In [*Bilka, supra* at 1338], the Court held that the benefits awarded under a supplementary pension scheme fell within the concept of pay, within the meaning of Article 119.

28   It must therefore be concluded that, unlike the benefits awarded by national statutory social security schemes, a pension paid under a contracted-out scheme constitutes consideration paid by the employer to the

worker in respect of his employment and consequently falls within the scope of Article 119 of the Treaty.

29   [In the third question,] the Court of Appeal seeks in substance to ascertain, in the first place, whether it is contrary to Article 119 of the Treaty for a man made compulsorily redundant to be entitled only to a deferred pension payable at the normal pensionable age when a woman in the same position receives an immediate retirement pension as a result of the application of an age condition that varies according to sex in the same way as is provided for by the national statutory pension scheme....

30   [I]t is sufficient to point out that Article 119 prohibits any discrimination with regard to pay as between men and women, whatever the system which gives rise to such inequality. Accordingly, it is contrary to Article 119 to impose an age condition which differs according to sex in respect of pensions paid under a contracted-out scheme, even if the difference between the pensionable age for men and that for women is based on the one provided for by the national statutory scheme.

Notes and Questions

1. Has *Marshall* tacitly overruled *Burton*? Has the Court effectively required the Health Authority to raise its normal retirement age for women to 65, or can the Authority continue to set its normal retirement age for women at 60 while allowing women to elect to work until 65? If the Health Authority continues to allow women to retire earlier than men, can a man claim violation of the equal treatment principle?

2. Note that the Court treated the issue in *Barber* as one of equal pay and then resolved it by an expansive interpretation of Article 119. Mr. Barber's claim was not that he should not have been dismissed at all (which was what Ms. Marshall argued), but rather that he was entitled to the same level of severance benefits as women employees of the same age. Do you agree with the outcome?

3. *Barber* created an uproar in the UK, because many companies had private plans granting women early retirement benefits or allowing them to retire at an earlier age. It has been estimated that the Court judgment will cost British employers millions of pounds, since they must now treat men employees as favorably as women. Perhaps predictably, the effect of requiring equal treatment has been not to reduce the normal pensionable age of men to the lower one for women but to raise the lower one for women.

4. Article 9 of the 1986 directive on occupational social security schemes allowed States to permit private employers to set different pensionable ages for men and women corresponding to those set in the State social security plan. The Commission concluded that *Barber* had effectively nullified article 9 and accordingly proposed an amendment to bring the directive into accord with *Barber*. The proposal was adopted in Directive 96/97, O.J. L 46/20 (Feb. 17, 1997).

5. The Court in *Barber* declared that Article 119's direct effect could not be relied upon in order to "claim entitlement to a pension, with effect from a date prior to that of this judgment" (which was May 17, 1990). To further clarify the matter, a Protocol to the Maastricht Treaty provides that "benefits under occupational social security schemes shall not be considered as remuneration if and so far as they are attributable to periods of employment prior to 17 May 1990, except in the case of workers or those claiming under them who have initiated legal proceedings or introduced an equivalent claim under the applicable national law."

6. The "hundred million pound question" as to how the non-retroactive language of *Barber* would be applied was answered in Case C–109/91, *Ten Oever v. Stichting Bedrijfspensioen fonds*, [1993] ECR I–4879. When a widower claimed a surviving spouse benefit from a Dutch occupational pension fund whose rules give such a benefit only to widows, the Court first held that a survivor's benefit constituted pay, even though not paid to the employee, because it came from the employer by virtue of an employment relation. However, the Court then explained that its language in *Barber* meant that the amount of the benefit in question could be limited to that "payable in respect of periods of employment subsequent to 17 May 1990." Since Mr. Ten Oever's spouse died in 1988, prior to May 17, 1990, presumably he could not claim a survivor's benefit, but someone whose deceased spouse was employed after that date could claim a benefit calculated with respect to the post-May 17, 1990 employment period.

Ten Oever was greeted with relief in the United Kingdom and other affected States.

7. *Barber* triggered a series of applications from various Member States asking for clarification. The Court consolidated several of the cases and delivered contemporaneous judgments in *Coloroll*, Case C–200/91, [1994] ECR I–4389; *van den Akker*, Case C–28/93 [1994] ECR I–4527; *Vroege*, Case C–57/93, [1994] ECR I–4541; *Smith v. Avdel Systems*, Case C–408/92, [1994] ECR I–4435; *Fisscher*, Case C–128/93, [1994] ECR I–4583, *Beune*, Case C–7/93, [1994] ECR I–4471, and *Moroni*, Case C–110/91, [1993] ECR I–6591, together referred as *The Equality Cases*. In these cases the Court confirmed the non-retroactivity principle of *Barber*, made clear that equal treatment applies to all contributory and non-contributory schemes except for voluntary employee contributions, and referred questions of implementation of the principle of equal treatment to local courts. Indeed, as to the latter, the Court pleaded strongly for an end to preliminary references on details of application of the directive regarding pension matters.

———————

European Union law proscribing discrimination based on personal characteristics has thus evolved from the Treaty right of equal pay for women to a broad and still evolving body of Treaty law, legislation, and caselaw spanning the full range of discriminations against individuals.

Chapter 38

JURISDICTION AND JUDGMENTS IN CIVIL AND COMMERCIAL LITIGATION

Cooperation in civil justice has lately become a highly active arena of Community lawmaking. This is due chiefly to treaty changes brought about by the Treaties of Maastricht and Amsterdam. Until that time, it was assumed that cooperation in this field would be accomplished, if at all, through the conclusion of separate conventions by the Member States. At the present time, the subject matter of this chapter is fully a "pillar one"—i.e., Community law—affair. The important developments charted in this chapter thus reflect both a heightening of normative activity and a "mainstreaming" of civil justice into European law.

At the outset, the EC Treaty implied that legal unification on matters such as jurisdiction and judgments in civil and commercial litigation was a subject for international agreement among the Member States rather than for Community legislation as such. Notwithstanding the evident link between Member States practices on jurisdiction and judgments, on the one hand, and the free movement of goods, persons, services and capital, on the other, Article 293(4) (ex 220(4)) of the Treaty specifically mandated that the Member States enter into negotiations for the conclusion of agreements on certain matters, among them "the simplification of formalities governing the reciprocal recognition and enforcement of judgments of courts or tribunals and of arbitration awards." On the basis of this language, the Member States entered into what would become by far the most prominent convention predicated on Article 293(4): the 1968 Brussels Convention on Jurisdiction and the Recognition and Enforcement of Judgments in Civil and Commercial Matters,[1] commonly known simply as the Brussels Convention. It took over thirty years—until 2000—for Treaty amendments and newer conceptions of the scope of Community law to render cooperation in civil justice a genuine Community law matter marked by directly applicable and effective Community legislation.

A. THE BRUSSELS CONVENTION: AN OVERVIEW

1. Consolidated version, O.J. C 27/1 (Jan. 26, 1998).

The Brussels Convention, which was signed on September 27, 1968 by the then six Member States, essentially (1) harmonized the bases on which the courts of the Member States could assert personal jurisdiction over domiciliaries of another Member State, and (2) obligated Member State courts to recognize and enforce covered judgments rendered by the courts of other Member States, provided those judgments (a) respected the limitations on the exercise of personal jurisdiction laid down in the Convention and (b) comported with certain additional requirements for recognition and enforcement exclusively laid down by the Convention. Because the Brussels Convention consciously "linked" recognition and enforcement, on the one hand, with the exercise of personal jurisdiction, on the other, it was said to exemplify a "double" as opposed to a "single" convention (the latter denoting an agreement that harmonizes *either* personal jurisdiction *or* recognition and enforcement, without connecting the two). By its terms (art. 66), the Brussels Convention was to remain in force for an unlimited period of time.

To begin with jurisdiction, the Brussels Convention basically enumerates "permissible" jurisdictional grounds, i.e. those that the courts of one Contracting State may assert as against another Contracting State's domiciliaries. The Convention excludes in such circumstances the use of any other jurisdictional basis, even one that the law of the forum ordinarily regards as permissible (and that may continue to be applied in that forum against domiciliaries of third States). The Convention also specifically declares certain jurisdictional bases customarily used in Contracting States to be impermissible as against domiciliaries of other Contracting States. Such excluded bases of jurisdiction are commonly referred to as "exorbitant." Besides identifying permissible and impermissible jurisdictional bases in actions against domiciliaries of other Member States, the Brussels Convention also lays down rules on other important jurisdiction-related issues, such as the validity of forum selection clauses, *lis pendens*, and the availability of provisional relief in aid of litigation in another Contracting State. We briefly look at these harmonized rules as well.

Turning to recognition and enforcement, the Brussels Convention obligates the courts of all Contracting States to recognize and enforce fully the final judgments rendered by courts of other Contracting States in civil and commercial matters. This obligation, however, is conditional on a judgment's satisfying certain minimum criteria laid down in the Convention. Not surprisingly, a judgment may not be denied recognition or enforcement on grounds of lack of personal jurisdiction where the rendering court relied upon a jurisdictional ground that the Convention specifically declares to be permissible. This, after all, is what makes the Brussels Convention a "double" convention. As we shall see below, despite this seemingly simple schema, disputes have commonly arisen over the recognizability and enforceability of Member State judgments in the courts of other Member States.

Though broad in scope, the Brussels Convention has its limitations. As its name suggests, it is confined to jurisdiction and judgments in civil and commercial matters. (To reinforce this limitation, the Convention expressly provides in Article 1 that it shall not apply to revenue, customs or administrative matters.) But the Convention is subject to specific exclusions even within the fields of civil and commercial law, namely the status or legal capacity of natural persons, rights in property arising out of matrimonial relationships, wills and successions, and bankruptcy and insolvency.[2] Certain of these gaps— such as matrimonial matters—would eventually be filled by additional, more specialized, agreements among the Member States on jurisdiction and judgments.

Articles 55 through 59 of the Brussels Convention address the Convention's relationship to other international agreements. Article 55 lists a large number of bilateral and multilateral conventions that are superseded, albeit (according to Article 56) only to the extent that they cover matters addressed by the Convention.[3] The very fact of this list suggests the inconsistencies among Member State laws that the Convention was seeking to overcome.

More importantly, Article 59 reserves in general terms the right of a Contracting State, through a convention entered into with a third State, to agree not to recognize or enforce judgments given in other Contracting States against defendants domiciled or habitually resident in the third State, where the only possible jurisdictional basis for the judgment is one that the Convention regards as "exorbitant."

As already noted, the Brussels Convention, though plainly linked to Community objectives, was assumed not to represent Community law as such. It was neither a treaty that "constituted" the Community legal order (such as the EC Treaty itself), nor a legislative act taken by the institutions of the Community (such as a regulation, directive or decision). Though foreseen in general terms by the EC Treaty, the Brussels Convention remained an agreement entered into by and among the Member States in their separate sovereign capacities.

Still, the Brussels Convention was not to remain an ordinary international agreement. First, as already noted, the EC Treaty had in a sense mandated it. Second, Article 63 of the Convention provides that any State seeking membership in the European Community is required to accept the Convention as a requirement of membership. Historically, accession negotiations with every new Member State resulted in an obligation to join the Brussels Convention "system," and with each accession the Convention has been appropriately amended.

Finally, as early as 1971, the states signatory to the Brussels Convention entered into a Protocol vesting in the Court of Justice jurisdiction to render preliminary rulings on the interpretation of the Convention at the request of signatory state courts. Protocol 75/464, O.J. 204/28 (Aug. 2, 1975), republished as amended at O.J. C 27/28 (Jan. 26, 1998). Such rulings are understood to be no less binding on national courts, or authoritative, than preliminary rulings by the Court of Justice on the interpretation or validity of EC law rendered under the then Article 177 (now 234) of the EC Treaty. By centralizing judicial interpretation of the Brussels Convention in the Court of Justice, the signatory states sought to ensure not only a uniform meaning and application of the Convention among the courts of the Member States, but also a meaning that would be consistent with both the Convention's and the Community's

---

2. Social security matters and arbitration are also expressly excluded from the Convention's coverage (art. 1).

3. On the other hand, Article 57 allows a limited category of jurisdictional conventions on particular to remain in effect.

underlying purposes. (Interestingly, however, the Protocol restricts access to the Court's preliminary reference jurisdiction. According to the Protocol's Article 2, only courts of last resort, or other courts when sitting on appeal, may request preliminary rulings in cases arising under the Convention.)

Since it was signed in 1968, the Brussels Convention has undergone only relatively minor changes, some of them, of course, the result of new accessions. The Convention in its latest consolidated version, is reproduced at O.J. C 27 (Jan. 26, 1998), and it is that version to which reference is made in this chapter. Both the Brussels Convention in that form and the Special Protocol on the Court of Justice may be found in the Selected Documents, Part VII.

As the EC developed closer ties with the EFTA States (some of which were likely accession candidates and others of which would soon join the EC Member States in forming the European Economic Area), it seemed desirable and appropriate for non-EC States to be permitted to join the Brussels Convention system. Accordingly, on September 16, 1988, a separate Lugano Convention was signed, extending the Convention system to Austria, Finland, Iceland, Norway, Sweden, and Switzerland. (Austria, Finland and Sweden would, of course, upon their 1995 accession to the EU, become parties to the Brussels Convention, leaving Iceland, Norway and Switzerland as the only strictly "Lugano Convention" states.) In declarations annexed to the Lugano Convention, the EC Member States called upon the Court of Justice, when interpreting the Brussels Convention, to "pay due account" to rulings under the Lugano Convention; conversely, the EFTA States called upon their courts to show like respect to rulings by the Court of Justice and the courts of the Member States. The Lugano Convention's Protocol on the Uniform Interpretation of the Convention strengthens this requirement by providing for a centralized system of exchange of information on court judgments interpreting the Convention. (The Lugano Convention may be found at O.J. L 319/9 (Nov. 25, 1988)).

B. FROM CONVENTION TO REGULATION

Although the Brussels Convention took the form of a Member State convention contemplated by Article 293 (ex 220), the Community institutions arguably had from the start the authority under the EC Treaty to adopt legislation harmonizing jurisdictional and recognition/enforcement standards among the Member States. Such harmonization could conceivably promote the free movement of goods, persons, services and capital among the Member States, and thus constitute a proper exercise of legislative harmonization under Article 95 of the EC Treaty. Free movement of the factors of production could also be counted on to generate disputes of various kinds, with the resulting prospect of civil and commercial disputes. It is not implausible that agreement on the bases upon which Member State courts might be able to assert jurisdiction over nationals of other Member States in civil and commercial litigation would facilitate the decision by producers and consumers to participate in the movement of persons, goods, services and capital across Member State borders. The "harmonization" case for recognition and enforcement of "sister-state" judgments is even stronger. A system of mutual recognition and enforcement of judgments offers an important measure of security to those who engage in cross-border activity, since economic actors may be encouraged to buy and sell, work and hire, render and purchase services, and invest across borders, if they know that they may rely on other Member States' courts to recognize and enforce judgements rendered in their favor at home. (Of course, agreements on jurisdiction and on the mutual recognition and enforcement of judgments may also strengthen the accountability of these same actors, where the asserted cross-border liability is theirs.)

With the Maastricht Treaty, the European Union acquired a more solid (albeit non-Community law) basis for the Brussels Convention and like agreements, for they exemplify precisely the sort of intergovernmental cooperation that lay at the core of the TEU's "pillar three" on cooperation in Justice and Home Affairs. (As we shall see, when the Council in 1998 drafted a matrimonial jurisdiction and judgments convention and recommended it for adoption by the States, it did so on this "pillar three" basis.)

The Amsterdam Treaty, it will be recalled, went further, shifting cooperation in civil justice from pillar three to pillar one decision-making—as an aspect of the EC Treaty's new chapter establishing "an area of freedom, justice and security." Thus was the way cleared both for converting the 1968 Brussels Convention (and indeed also the 1998 matrimonial jurisdiction and judgments convention) into directly applicable Community legislation and for enacting fresh legislation on other civil justice matters.

The relevant EC Treaty basis is accordingly now Article 65 (ex 73m):

Measures in the field of judicial cooperation in civil matters having cross-border implications . . . insofar as necessary for the proper functioning of the internal market, shall include:

(a) improving and simplifying . . . the recognition and enforcement of decisions in civil and commercial cases . . . [and] promoting the compatibility of the rules applicable in the Member States concerning the conflict of laws and of jurisdiction . . .

By way of procedure, Article 65 calls for the application of Article 67 (ex 73o), according to which, during a transitional period of five years from the Amsterdam Treaty's entry into force (i.e. until 2004), measures are to be adopted by the Council acting unanimously on a proposal from the Commission or on the initiative of a Member State and after consulting the European Parliament. After that period, the Council may decide unanimously to make the adoption of any such measures subject to the parliamentary codecision procedure (art. 251), which of course entails qualified majority voting and parliamentary assent.

In December 2000, the Council, acting unanimously under Article 65, adopted Regulation 44/2001 on Jurisdiction and the Recognition and Enforcement of Judgments in Civil and Commercial Matters, O.J. L 12/1 (Jan. 16, 2001). (The Regulation is found in Part VII of the Selected Documents.) The Commission's hope in proposing the measure had been to replace the Brussels Convention in its entirety with directly applicable and directly effective legislation. Matters were not to be that simple, however, due to the fact that Denmark, Ireland and the UK did not participate fully in the EC Treaty's chapter on "an area of freedom, justice and security" to which Article 65 belongs. Eventually, the UK and Ireland endorsed the proposed regulation, but Denmark did not. As a result, the 1968 Brussels Convention, as amended, continues in effect, remaining applicable insofar as Denmark is concerned.[4]

Article 66 provides that Regulation 44/2001 shall apply to legal proceedings instituted and to documents formally drawn up or registered as authentic instruments after the entry into force of the Regulation (which, according to Article 76, is March 1, 2002). Under stated circumstances, judgments rendered after March 1, 2002 are also to be recognized and enforced under the rules laid down in the Regulation, even though the underlying proceedings were begun prior to that date. Article 67 provides that the Regulation shall not prejudice existing Community law instruments governing jurisdiction and the recognition and enforcement of judgments in specific matters, or national legislation harmonized pursuant to any such instruments. On the other hand, the Regulation, according to Article 68, supersedes the Brussels Convention, except as regards the former colonial territories of the Member States. After entry into force of the Regulation 44/2001, any reference to the Brussels Convention is deemed to be a reference to the Regulation.[5]

Note that the Regulation does not fully maintain the article numbering of the Brussels Convention. In this chapter, article numbers refer, except where otherwise indicated, to the relevant provisions of the Brussels Convention rather than the Regulation.

C. JURISDICTION UNDER THE BRUSSELS CONVENTION

The 1968 Brussels Convention is generally regarded as a well-conceived and well-drafted instrument. In the pages that follow, we explore the main features of the Convention as a framework for both the exercise of jurisdiction and the recognition and enforcement of judgments. Nevertheless, the drafters of the Protocol on the Court of Justice correctly foresaw that important questions of interpretation of the Convention would inevitably arise as to which it would be desirable to furnish a common answer. Preliminary rulings by the Court of Justice thus figure importantly in this chapter as well. Regulation 44/2001 and the related new regulations will undoubtedly continue to generate preliminary references and rulings.

National courts in applying Regulation 44/2001, like the Court of Justice in interpreting it, will almost certainly be guided by the understandings that have arisen surrounding the parallel provisions of the 1968 Convention as well as by the case law produced by the Court of Justice. Given this fact, and the fact of Regulation 44/2001's recent vintage, these understandings and this

---

4. Due to Denmark's refusal to participate, Article 1 of Regulation 44/2001 specifically excludes Denmark from the definition of "Member States."

5. Like the Brussels Convention, Regulation 44/2001 (art. 70) lists those bilateral and multilateral conventions on jurisdiction and judgments that are superseded to the extent that they cover the same ground as the Convention. Certain other Member State agreements that relate to jurisdiction or judgments are unaffected (art. 71). Article 72 of Regulation 44/2001 maintains in effect such third party conventions as were entered into prior to the Regulation's entry into force, and which (under Article 59 of the Convention) required Contracting States to withhold recognition of judgments of other Contracting States against defendants domiciled in third countries where those judgments are based on excluded "exorbitant" jurisdictional grounds.

case law under the Convention necessarily predominate in the pages that follow.

1. THE BRUSSELS CONVENTION'S SPHERE OF APPLICATION

For some time, exactly which State was to determine whether a particular judgment is a "civil or commercial matter" remained a point of confusion under the Convention, especially given the absence of any definition of these terms in the Convention itself. The Court addressed this question in the *Eurocontrol* case, *infra*, which held that for purposes of the Convention's application, reference should be made not to the law of one or more of the States concerned but, first and foremost, to the objectives and scheme of the Convention itself.

LTU LUFTTRANSPORTUNTERNEHMEN GMBH & CO. KG v. EUROCONTROL

Case C–29/76, [1976] ECR 1541.

[In an action to enforce a Belgian monetary judgment, a German appeals court asked the Court of Justice whether, for purposes of interpreting the term "civil or commercial matters," reference should be made to the law of the state where the judgment was rendered or to the law of the state where enforcement is sought. The underlying action was a suit by a public aviation safety authority (Eurocontrol) to recover charges payable to it by a private firm for the use of equipment and services.]

* * *

3 ... [I]t is necessary, in order to ensure, as far as possible, that the rights and obligations which derive from [the Convention] for the contracting states and the persons to whom it applies are equal and uniform, that the terms of that provision should not be interpreted as a mere reference to the internal law of one or other of the states concerned.

... [T]he concept "civil and commercial matters" cannot [accordingly] be interpreted solely in the light of the division of jurisdiction between the various types of courts existing in certain states.

The concept in question must ... be regarded as independent and must be interpreted by reference, first, to the objectives and scheme of the convention and, secondly, to the general principles which stem from the corpus of the national legal systems.

4 ... [C]ertain types of judicial decision must be regarded as excluded from the area of application of the convention, either by reason of the legal relationships between the parties to the action or of the subject-matter of the action.

Although certain judgments given in actions between a public authority and a person governed by private law may fall within the area of application of the convention, this is not so where the public authority acts in the exercise of its powers.

Such is the case in a dispute which, like that between the parties to the main action, concerns the recovery of charges payable by a person governed by private law to a national or international body governed by public law for the use of equipment and services provided by such body, in particular where such use is obligatory and exclusive.

This applies in particular where the rate of charges, the methods of calculation and the procedures for collection are fixed unilaterally in relation to the users, as is the position in the present case. . . .

⁵ . . . On the basis of these criteria, a judgment given in an action between a public authority and a person governed by private law, in which a public authority has acted in the exercise of its powers, is excluded from the area of application of the convention.

Notes and Questions

1. Is the Court correct in insisting on a definition of "civil or commercial" that transcends the legal usage in a particular Member State? But then what is meant by "the general principles which stem from the corpus of the national legal systems," referred to in paragraph 3 of the judgment?

2. The Court of Justice has held that a claim for civil damages entertained by a criminal court in conjunction with a related criminal prosecution falls within the scope of the term "civil matters" within the meaning of the Convention. Sonntag v. Waidmann, Case C–172/91, [1993] ECR I–1963. (The case involved a schoolteacher who was prosecuted for criminal negligence for failure properly to supervise students during a school trip, resulting in the death of a student. In a joined proceeding in the criminal court the teacher was also sued in damages by the student's parents.)

2. GENERAL JURISDICTION

The Brussels Convention adopts domicile as the fundamental basis of "general" jurisdiction. According to Article 2, unless otherwise provided, "persons domiciled in a Contracting State shall, whatever their nationality, be sued in the courts of that State." A person domiciled in a Contracting State is therefore subject to the jurisdiction of the courts of that State in matters falling within the Convention's scope, whatever links the parties or cause of action may have to some other State.⁶ (Article 2 goes on to declare that domiciliaries of Contracting States may be sued in the courts of another Contracting State only in the circumstances specifically prescribed by the Convention. These are the cases of "special" jurisdiction dealt with below.)

How is a party's domicile, for purposes of the Convention, to be determined? Notwithstanding the reasoning of the *Eurocontrol* case, Article 52 of the Brussels Convention provides for a Contracting State to apply its own internal law to determine whether or not a particular party is domiciled in that State. Once having found that the party is not a domiciliary of that State, the court is then to decide whether the party is a domiciliary of another

---

6. This is subject to an exception for cases of "exclusive jurisdiction" (treated in Article 16 of the Convention) under which a cause of action may only be brought in the designated forum to the exclusion of all other fora, including the defendant's domicile. A valid forum selection clause, under Article 17 (see section 8 *infra*), if construed to constitute the exclusive forum for the resolution of disputes between the parties, presumably also "ousts" the jurisdiction of the defendant's domicile.

Contracting State by applying the law of that other State. The situation is somewhat different as regards the domicile of a company, trust or other legal person or association. Article 53 declares that the place where the entity's seat is located shall be treated as its domicile, and that in identifying that place, the court seised of the dispute should apply its own conflict of law rules.

Regulation 44/2001 changes the manner of determining a company or other legal person's domicile in favor of more uniform results. Article 60 defines that the legal person's domicile as the place where it has its: a) statutory seat, b) central administration, or c) principal place of business.[7] Article 60 thus plainly contemplates the possibility of multiple domiciles. Might this complicate operation of the Convention?

In an effort to fortify the Convention's general preference for the defendant's domicile as jurisdictional basis, Article 20 requires that, where a defendant who is domiciled in one Contracting State fails to enter an appearance in a court of another Contracting State, the court "shall declare of its own motion that it has no jurisdiction unless its jurisdiction is derived from [other] provisions of the Convention."[8] Thus, for example, a domiciliary of a Contracting State is not required to appear in the court of another Contracting State in order to contest the latter's jurisdiction under the Convention. He or she may default and assume that the forum will "enforce" the Convention's rules on his or her behalf. Is there not a risk in that strategy, however? In considering the risk, bear in mind that, as we shall see (section 3 *infra*), the Convention also recognizes, for certain causes of action, "special" jurisdictions in addition to the place of defendant's domicile where the defendant may be sued.

To further underscore that domicile is the Convention's presumptively exclusive basis of general jurisdiction assertable against EU domiciliaries, Article 3 explicitly precludes Contracting State courts from using against such domiciliaries certain other bases of jurisdiction traditionally considered to give rise to general jurisdiction under domestic law. These are the so-called "exorbitant bases" referred to earlier. Article 3 lists for 14 of the 15 Member States (all but Spain) jurisdictional bases deemed to be exorbitant for these purposes. The designated bases include, for example Articles 14 and 15 of the French Civil Code (making the plaintiff's nationality a sufficient basis of jurisdiction over a non-national and permitting a French defendant to be sued abroad only by virtue of a forum selection agreement), Section 23 of the German Civil Procedure Code (making the defendant's ownership of property in the jurisdiction a sufficient basis for full *in personam* jurisdiction, even unrelated to the property), and Articles 126(3) and 127 of the Dutch Civil Procedure Code (similar to the French provisions, but making the plaintiff's domicile rather than nationality decisive for jurisdiction over non-Dutch domiciliaries or residents), as well as (for Ireland and the UK) "transient jurisdiction" and (for the UK) the presence or seizure by plaintiff of property

---

7. Article 60 goes on to define "statutory seat," for purposes of the UK and Ireland, as the registered office and, failing a registered office, then the place of incorporation, and failing both a registered office and place of incorporation, then the place of contract formation.

8. In default situations, Article 20 further directs the court to stay proceedings until it is satisfied that the defendant received notice of the action in sufficient time to enable him or her to prepare a defense.

belonging to the defendant. EU domiciliaries are thus specifically protected from the assertion of general jurisdiction on any of these grounds.

Non–EU domiciliaries enjoy no such protection. Where the defendant is a domiciliary of a non-Contracting State, Article 4 permits Contracting States to apply their own domestic rules of jurisdiction (including exorbitant ones). Plaintiffs who are domiciled in a Contracting State may, whatever their nationality, resort to these exorbitant bases against non-EU domiciliaries as fully as may plaintiffs who are nationals of that State.

While, as noted above, a defaulting defendant may be protected by the forum's obligation (under Article 20) to verify its own jurisdiction, the situation is quite different where the defendant makes a voluntary appearance. "[A] court of a Contracting State before whom a defendant enters an appearance shall have jurisdiction," subject only to two exceptions: (1) where appearance was entered solely to contest jurisdiction and (2) where another court has exclusive jurisdiction over the dispute according to Article 16 (discussed in section 7 *infra*).

Note that the Brussels Convention provisions on general jurisdiction apply according to the domicile *of the defendant*. Does the plaintiff's domicile (or nationality) have any bearing? In Group Josi Reinsurance Company S.A. v. Universal General Insurance Co. (UGIC), Case C–412/98, [2000] ECR I–5925, a Canadian insurance company (UGIC) which was in liquidation brought suit against a Belgian reinsurance company (Group Josi) for money claimed under a reinsurance contract between them. Group Josi refused to pay on the ground that it had been induced to enter into the reinsurance contract through false representations. When Universal sued Group Josi in the Commercial Court of Nanterre, France, Group Josi argued that it could be sued only in the Commercial Court of Brussels where it had its registered office. The Nanterre court upheld its own jurisdiction on the ground that Universal, being a Canadian corporation and having no place of business in the Community, could not invoke the Convention. On appeal, the Cour d'Appel of Versailles made a preliminary reference on the question whether a plaintiff in national court needs a European domicile in order to invoke the Convention.

The Court observed that in certain special cases ("special jurisdiction"), the Convention treats the plaintiff's domicile as an adequate jurisdictional basis. For example, with the aim of protecting the weaker party, Article 14 allows holders of insurance policies and consumers to bring proceedings against the other party to their contract in the courts of the Contracting State in which they are domiciled. Otherwise, however, the Convention attaches no significance to the plaintiff's domicile:

[50] ... [T]he Convention appears clearly hostile towards the attribution of jurisdiction to the courts of the plaintiff's domicile. It follows that the Convention must not be interpreted as meaning that, otherwise than in the cases expressly provided for, it recognises the jurisdiction of the courts of the plaintiff's domicile and therefore enables a plaintiff to determine the court with jurisdiction by his choice of domicile.

3. SPECIAL JURISDICTION

As already mentioned, in addition to establishing general jurisdiction based on the defendant's domicile, the Convention permits plaintiffs—at their option—also to bring certain specified categories of disputes in designated fora. Thus, persons domiciled in a Contracting State may also, by way of exception in stated circumstances, be sued in the courts of a Contracting State other than their State of domicile. These rules of "special jurisdiction" are laid down limitatively in Articles 5 to 12a of the Convention.

Article 5 recognizes seven "long-arm"-like special jurisdictions. These relate to the following actions: contracts (art. 5(1)); maintenance (art. 5(2)); tort, delict and quasi-delict (art. 5(3)); claims for civil damages or restitution based on a criminal act (art. 5(4)); disputes arising out of the operations of a branch, agency or other establishment (art. 5(5)); disputes relating to a settlor, trustee or beneficiary of a trust (art. 5(6)); and claims for remuneration in respect of salvage of cargo or freight (art. 5(7)). In these cases, an EU domiciliary need not necessarily be sued in his or her State of domicile, but may also be sued in one of the other stated fora. In this section, we focus on the contract and tort provisions.

(a) Place of Performance in Contract

According to Article 5(1):

A person domiciled in a Contracting State may, in another Contracting State be sued ... (1) in matters relating to a contract, in the courts for the place of performance of the obligation in question; in matters relating to individual contracts of employment, this place is that where the employee habitually carries out his work, or if the employee does not habitually carry out his work in any one country, the employer may also be sued in the courts for the place where the business which engaged the employee was or is now situated....

In Industrie Tessili Italiana Como v. Dunlop AG, Case 12/76, [1976] ECR 1473, the Court was called upon to clarify the meaning of "place of performance of the obligation in question," within the meaning of Article 5(1). The Court confirmed that, as a general matter, the terms in which the rules of special jurisdiction are couched required an "autonomous" meaning, that is to say, a meaning disengaged from the special understandings that might be associated with those terms in particular Member States. But the Court continued:

13 [In] the case of an action relating to contractual obligations article 5(1) allows a plaintiff to bring the matter before the court for the place "of performance" of the obligation in question. It is for the court before which the matter is brought to establish under the convention whether the place of performance is situate within its territorial jurisdiction. For this purpose it must determine in accordance with its own rules of conflict of laws what is the law applicable to the legal relationship in question and define in accordance with that law the place of performance of the contractual obligation in question.

14 Having regard to the differences obtaining between national laws of contract and to the absence at this stage of legal development of any unification in the substantive law applicable, it does not appear possible to give any more substantial guide to the interpretation of the reference made by article 5(1) to the "place of performance" of contractual obligations. This is all the more true since the determination of the place of

performance of obligations depends on the contractual context to which these obligations belong.

[15] In these circumstances the reference in the Convention to the place of performance of contractual obligations cannot be understood otherwise than by reference to the substantive law applicable under the rules of conflict of laws of the court before which the matter is brought.

Though roundly criticized by legal scholars, the *Industrie Tessili* decision has been repeatedly reaffirmed. Consider Custom Made Commercial Ltd. v. Stawa Metallbau GmbH, Case C–288/92, [1994] ECR I–2913, a case complicated by the fact that the domestic conflict of law rule pointed to application of a Uniform Law, namely the Uniform Law on the International Sale of Goods, which was annexed to the Hague Convention of July 1, 1964. The Court defended its approach:

[16] It has been submitted, certainly, that the criterion of the place of performance of the obligation ... may in certain cases have the effect of conferring jurisdiction on a court which has no connection with the dispute....

* * *

[18] [However, t]he use of criteria other than that of the place of performance, where that confers jurisdiction on a court which has no connection with the case, might jeopardize the possibility of foreseeing which court will have jurisdiction and for that reason be incompatible with the aim of the Convention.

[19] [Otherwise,] the court before which the dispute is brought [would be obliged] to consider other factors, in particular the pleas relied on by the defendant, in order to determine whether [it has jurisdiction, which] would thus render Article 5(1) nugatory.

[20] Such an examination would also be contrary to the purposes and spirit of the Convention, which requires an interpretation of Article 5 enabling the national court to rule on its own jurisdiction without being compelled to consider the substance of the case.

[21] It follows that under Article 5(1), in matters relating to a contract, a defendant may be sued in the courts for the place of performance of the obligation in question, even where the court thus designated is not that which has the closest connection with the dispute.

[The Court restated the rule laid down in *Industrie Tessili, supra.*]

[27] That interpretation must also be accepted in the case where the conflicts rules of the court seised refer to the application to contractual relations of a "uniform law" such as that in issue in the main proceedings.

In contrast to the approach in *Industrie Tessili*, the Court of Justice held in Mulox IBC Ltd. v. Hendrick Geels, Case C–125/92, [1993] ECR I–4075, that in the case of employment contracts, the place of performance of an obligation is to be determined not by reference to the applicable national law designated by the conflict rules of the forum, but rather to uniform criteria established by the Court of Justice on the basis of the scheme and objectives of the Convention. The Court proceeded to rule that the place of performance in employment contracts is the place where the employee actually carries out the work covered by the contract, and that where the employee performs his or her work in more than one contracting state, the place of performance shall be the place where or from which the employee principally discharges his or her employment obligations.

Consider also Ivenel v. Schwab, Case C–133/81, [1982] ECR 1891, a case involving a commercial agency contract. A commercial agent based in Strasbourg sued a Bavarian machine parts manufacturer for payment of commissions and a claim for compensation for breach of contract. The question was whether the place of performance of the obligation, within the meaning of Article 5(1) of the Convention, was the place of performance of the work of representation (viz. collation and execution of orders in Strasbourg) or the payment of commissions and compensation, payable at the manufacturer's place of business in Bavaria. The Court held that, in such a contract, which entails different claims arising from different obligations, the obligation to be considered in localizing performance is the one which "characterizes" the contract. The Court found the characteristic obligation to be the obligation to carry out the "work" of the contract. In opting for a single place of performance, the Court emphasized the need to interpret the Convention in such a way as to avoid the result that a national court has jurisdiction to adjudicate certain claims under a given contract, but not others.

Why should employment contracts and commercial agency contracts (unlike the contract in *Industrie Tessili*) necessarily be subject to a uniform Convention rule on place of performance? Is it because there is greater consensus among the Member State legal systems about the place of performance in such contracts? Doesn't efficiency argue equally for a uniform rule in all these cases? Or is the difference due to the fact that the Court was seeking to establish a particular place of performance rule that would tend to favor the weaker party to employment and commercial agency contract relationships?

In any event, the place of performance test may not be as simple to apply as it appears.

LEATHERTEX v. BODETEX

Case C–420/97, [1999] ECR I–6747.

[Bodetex, a Belgian company, acted as commercial agent for Leathertex, an Italian manufacturer in the Belgian and Dutch markets, under a long-term arrangement by which it received 5% commission on sales. When in 1987 Leathertex declined to pay Bodetex commissions that Bodetex claimed it was owed, Bodetex announced that it regarded the commercial agency agreement as having thereby been terminated and sought payment of arrears of commission. Eventually Bodetex brought suit in the Rechtbank van Koophandel (Commercial Court) of Courtrai, Belgium.

In a 1991 judgment, the Rechtbank van Koophandel found that the action was based on two separate obligations: (1) the obligation to give a reasonable period of notice prior to termination of a commercial agency agreement (or, failing that, the obligation to compensate for the failure) and (2) the obligation to pay commissions. The Court found that the first obligation was to be performed in Belgium, while the second was to be performed in Italy (under the principle that debts are payable where the debtor is resident). However, finding that it had jurisdiction in respect of the obligation to give notice, the Belgian court assumed jurisdiction over the whole proceedings due to the close connection between the two obligations. On the merits, the court ordered Leathertex to pay Bodetex both compensation in lieu of notice and arrears of commission. The ruling was affirmed in all respects by the Court of Appeal of Ghent.

On appeal by Leathertex, the Belgian Supreme Court asked the Court of Justice to assume that the two obligations sued upon were in fact co-equal. The United Kingdom argued in the case that Belgian precedent allowed a court to decide the entire case only if the obligation whose performance founded the court's jurisdiction was the defendant's principal obligation (the *maxim accessorium sequitur* principle), and that under that approach the Belgian court lacked jurisdiction over the whole case because the obligation to pay commissions had to be regarded as the principal obligation.]

21   [I]n view of the allocation of jurisdiction under the preliminary ruling procedure . . . , it is for the national court to assess the relative importance of the contractual obligations at issue in the main proceedings and for the Court of Justice to interpret the Convention in the light of the findings made by the national court.

[The Court accordingly bypassed the UK's objection and shared the Belgian court's supposition that the two obligations sued upon were co-equal.]

29   [T]he Commission submits that, where a plaintiff brings two claims based on two obligations of equal rank, a court which has jurisdiction to hear one of the claims under Article 5(1) of the Convention also has jurisdiction to hear the other claim if there is such a close relationship between the claims that it is advantageous to hear and decide them at the same time in order to avoid the possibility of irreconcilable decisions if the cases were decided separately.

30   According to the Commission, such a solution . . . is called for by Article 22 of the Convention [according to which where "related" actions are brought in the courts of different Contracting States, any court other than the first one seised may stay proceedings]. In a dispute such as that before the national court, if the plaintiff decided, in accordance with Article 5(1) of the Convention, to bring the action for payment of compensation in one Contracting State and that for payment of the arrears of commission in another Contracting State, Article 22 of the Convention would apply because of the relation between the two actions. Article 5(1) of the Convention should therefore be interpreted in such a way as to avoid in advance situations to which Article 22 of the Convention would be applicable.

[The Court observed that the contract at issue did not constitute a contract of employment.]

* * *

38   [T]he court which has jurisdiction to hear the claim for payment of compensation in lieu of notice [cannot] found its jurisdiction in respect of the claim for payment of commission on any relation between those two claims. As the Court has made clear, Article 22 of the Convention is

intended to establish how related actions which have been brought before courts of different Contracting States are to be dealt with. It does not confer jurisdiction. In particular, it does not accord jurisdiction to a court of a Contracting State to try an action which is related to another action of which that court is seised pursuant to the rules of the Convention.

[39] [W]hen a dispute relates to a number of obligations of equal rank arising from the same contract, the court before which the matter is brought cannot, when determining whether it has jurisdiction, be guided by the *maxim accessorium sequitur* principle. . . .

[40] The same court does not therefore have jurisdiction to hear the whole of an action founded on two obligations of equal rank arising from the same contract when, according to the conflict rules of the State where that court is situated, one of those obligations is to be performed in that State and the other in another Contracting State.

[41] It should be remembered that, while there are disadvantages in having different courts ruling on different aspects of the same dispute, the plaintiff always has the option, under Article 2 of the Convention, of bringing his entire claim before the courts for the place where the defendant is domiciled.

Notes and Questions

1. Note that *Leathertex*, like the *Ivenel* case, *supra* page 1392, involved a commercial agency. Are the Court's analyses of place of performance consistent?

2. Why did the position advanced by the Commission, on the basis of Article 22 of the Convention, not prevail? (Article 22 is treated in section 9 *infra.*)

3. Regulation 44/2001 (art. 5(1)) modifies the Brussels Convention solution by defining "place of performance of the obligation in question," unless otherwise agreed, as "in the case of the sale of goods, the place in a Member State where, under the contract, the goods were delivered or should have been delivered" and "in the case of the provision of services, the place in a Member State where, under the contract, the services were provided or should have been provided."

(b) Place of Tort

Article 5(3), the fundamental provision on special jurisdiction in tort, delict or quasi-delict, provides as follows:

A person domiciled in a Contracting State may, in another Contracting state be sued . . . (3) in matters relating to tort, delict or quasi-delict, in the courts for the place where the harmful event occurred.

Regulation 44/2001 adds to the end of Article 5(3) the language "or may occur."

HANDELSKWEKERIJ G.J. BIER BV v. MINES DE POTASSE D'ALSACE SA.
Case 21/76, [1976], ECR 1735.

[A Rotterdam trial court declined jurisdiction over a suit that a Dutch horticulturalist and a Dutch public interest group had brought against a company, Mines de Potasse d'Alsace, based in Mulhouse (France), for allegedly polluting the waters of the Rhine River through the discharge of saline waste into the river. (The plaintiffs alleged that the high salt content of river water caused damage to plantings and required expensive damage control measures.) The Rotterdam trial court believed that only the courts of France, the place where the discharge at issue took place, had jurisdiction under the Convention. A Dutch appeals court referred a question to the Court of Justice on the meaning of Article 5(3).]

13   In the context of the Convention, the meaning of [the] expression ["the place where the harmful event occurred"] is unclear when the place of the event which is at the origin of the damage is situated in a state other than the one in which the place where the damage occurred is situated, as is the case ... with atmospheric or water pollution beyond the frontiers of a state.

14   The form of words "place where the harmful event occurred," used in all the language versions of the Convention, leaves open the question whether, in the situation described, it is necessary, in determining jurisdiction, to choose as the connecting factor the place of the event giving rise to the damage, or the place where the damage occurred, or to accept that the plaintiff has an option between the one and the other of those two connecting factors.

* * *

17   Taking into account the close connexion between the component parts of every sort of liability, it does not appear appropriate to opt for one of the two connecting factors mentioned to the exclusion of the other, since each of them can, depending on the circumstances, be particularly helpful from the point of view of the evidence and of the conduct of the proceedings.

* * *

19   Thus the meaning of the expression "place where the harmful event occurred" in article 5(3) must be established in such a way as to acknowledge that the plaintiff has an option to commence proceedings either at the place where the damage occurred or the place of the event giving rise to it.

* * *

22   [I]t appears from a comparison of the national legislative provisions and national case-law on the distribution of jurisdiction—both as regards internal relationships, as between courts for different areas, and in international relationships—that, albeit by differing legal techniques, a place is found for both of the connecting factors here considered and that in several states they are accepted concurrently.

23   In these circumstances, the interpretation stated above has the advantage of avoiding any upheaval in the solutions worked out in the various national systems of law, since it looks to unification, in conformity with article 5(3) of the Convention, by way of a systematization of solutions which, as to their principle, have already been established in most of the states concerned.

[24] Thus it should be answered that where the place of the happening of the event which may give rise to liability in tort, delict or quasi-delict and the place where that event results in damage are not identical, the expression "place where the harmful event occurred," in article 5(3) of the convention, must be understood as being intended to cover both the place where the damage occurred and the place of the event giving rise to it.

DUMEZ FRANCE SA AND TACOBA SARL
v. HESSISCHE LANDESBANK

Case C–220/88, [1990], ECR I–49.

[Dumez France and Oth, as assignees of two French companies (Scepoer and Tracoba), brought a tort action in France against a number of German banks for the damage caused to Scepoer and Tracoba on account of the insolvency of Scepoer and Tracoba's German subsidiaries. (This insolvency was allegedly caused in turn by the banks having suspended financing of a property development project on which Scepoer and Tracoba's German subsidiaries were subcontractors.)

Dumez France and Oth failed to convince the lower French courts that the latter had jurisdiction over the German banks. Dumez France and Oth appealed to the Cour de Cassation, invoking *Mines de potasse d'Alsace*.]

[12] [T]he judgment in *Mines de potasse d'Alsace* related to a situation in which the damage—to crops in the Netherlands—occurred at some distance from the event giving rise to the damage—the discharge of saline waste into the Rhine by an undertaking established in France—but by the direct effect of the causal agent, namely the saline waste which had moved physically from one place to another.

[13] By contrast, in the present case, the damage allegedly suffered by Dumez and Oth through cancellation, by the German banks, of the loans granted for financing the works originated and produced its direct consequences in the same Member State, namely the one in which the lending banks, the prime contractor and the subsidiaries of Dumez and Oth, which were responsible for the building work, were all established. The harm alleged by the parent companies, Dumez and Oth, is merely the indirect consequence of the financial losses initially suffered by their subsidiaries following cancellation of the loans and the subsequent suspension of the works.

[14] It follows that, in a case such as this, the damage alleged is no more than the indirect consequence of the harm initially suffered by other legal persons who were the direct victims of damage which occurred at a place different from that where the indirect victim subsequently suffered harm.

[15] It is therefore necessary to consider whether the expression "place where the damage occurred" as used in the judgment in *Mines de potasse d'Alsace* may be interpreted as referring to the place where the indirect victims of the damage ascertain the repercussions on their own assets.

[The Court recalled the Convention's "hostility ... towards the attribution of jurisdiction to the courts of the plaintiff's domicile," citing Article 3(2).]

[17] It is only by way of exception to the general rule [attributing] jurisdiction ... to the courts of the defendant's domicile that [the Convention]

attributes special jurisdiction in certain cases, including the case envisaged by Article 5(3).... As the Court has already held [in *Mines de potasse d'Alsace*], those cases of special jurisdiction, the choice of which is a matter for the plaintiff, are based on the existence of a particularly close connecting factor between the dispute and courts other than those of the defendant's domicile, which justifies the attribution of jurisdiction to those courts for reasons relating to the sound administration of justice and the efficacious conduct of proceedings.

[18]   In order to meet that objective, which is of fundamental importance in a convention which has essentially to promote the recognition and enforcement of judgments in States other than those in which they were delivered, it is necessary to avoid the multiplication of courts of competent jurisdiction which would heighten the risk of irreconcilable decisions, this being the reason for which recognition or an order for enforcement is withheld by virtue of Article 27(3) of the Convention.

[19]   Furthermore, that objective militates against any interpretation of the Convention which, otherwise than in the cases expressly provided for, might lead to recognition of the jurisdiction of the courts of the plaintiff's domicile and would enable a plaintiff to determine the competent court by his choice of domicile.

[20]   It follows from the foregoing considerations that although, by virtue of ... *Mines de potasse d'Alsace*, the expression "place where the harmful event occurred" contained in Article 5(3) of the Convention may refer to the place where the damage occurred, the latter concept can be understood only as indicating the place where the event giving rise to the damage, and entailing tortious, delictual or quasi-delictual liability, directly produced its harmful effects upon the person who is the immediate victim of that event.

Notes and Questions

1.   The Court of Justice has consistently maintained the rule that the term "place where the harmful event occurred" may not be construed so extensively as to encompass any place where the adverse consequences can be felt of an event which has already caused damage actually arising elsewhere. See, for example, Marinari v. Lloyd's Bank plc and Zubaidi Trading Company, Case C–364/93, [1995] ECR I–2719.

2.   In Shevill v. Presse Alliance SA, Case C–68/93, [1995] ECR I–415, the Court held that the victim of a libel by a newspaper article distributed in several Contracting States could bring an action for damages against the publisher either before the courts of the Contracting State of the place where the publisher of the defamatory publication is established (which have jurisdiction to award damages for all the harm caused by the defamation), or before the courts of each Contracting State in which the publication was distributed and where the victim claims to have suffered injury to his reputation (each of which, however, has jurisdiction to rule solely in respect of the harm caused in the State of the court seized). The Court held that the criteria for assessing whether the event in question is harmful and for assessing the evidence required of the existence and extent of the harm alleged by the plaintiff are not governed by the Convention, but rather by the substantive law designated by the national conflict of laws rules of the court seised on the basis of the Convention. In view of that, it made no difference that under

UK law damage is presumed in libel actions. The action as to UK-based harm could still be maintained there.

3. The Court has defined the category of actions sounding in tort, delict or quasi-delict very broadly, holding in Kalfelis v Schröder, Case C–189/87, [1988] ECR 5565, that it "cover[s] all actions which seek to establish the liability of a defendant and which are not related to a 'contract' within the meaning of Article 5(1)."

Consider in this regard the case of Réunion Européenne SA v. Spliethoff's Bevrachtingskantoor BV, Case C–51/97, [1998] ECR I–6511. There, it was held that, while a French insurance company as subrogee could not invoke the Convention's special jurisdiction in contract to sue the Dutch shipper and the Dutch vessel for transporting damaged fruit to the insured French fruit dealer (because the latter's contract was not with the shipper or vessel but with the fruit sellers and because the bill of lading is not a contract as such), the insurance company could sue the shipper and vessel in tort in light of Article 5(3)'s broad scope.

Even so, the tort claim could not be pursued in France due to the "indirect damage rule." The consignee of damaged goods may invoke the Convention's "special jurisdiction" rule for tort to sue the carrier only by proceeding in the place where the damage occurred or the place of the events that gave rise to it, not the place of delivery or the place where the damage was otherwise ascertained.

Did the Court properly apply the "indirect damage rule" to this case? Was the Court unduly influenced by a desire not to privilege the place of plaintiff's (as opposed to defendant's) domicile in tort cases?

4. JURISDICTION BASED ON MULTI–PARTY STATUS

Article 6 of the Brussels Convention opens up the prospect of still further additional fora, this time, however, based on certain specified linkages between the defendant and other parties and other claims. It reads:

A person domiciled in a Contracting State may also be sued:

1. where he is one of a number of defendants, in the courts for the place where any one of them is domiciled;

2. as a third party in an action on a warranty or guarantee or in any other third party proceedings, in the court seised of the original proceedings, unless these were instituted solely with the object of removing him from the jurisdiction of the court would be competent in his case:

3. on a counter-claim arising from the same contract or facts on which the original claim was based, in the court in which the original claim is pending;

4. in matters relating to a contract, if the action may be combined with an action against the same defendant in matters relating to rights in rem in immovable property, in the court of the Contracting State in which the property is situated.

Of the additional bases of jurisdiction set out above, the first has proved by far the most controversial, particularly because it permits the exercise of jurisdiction over a party in a state to which that party might have no relationship whatsoever; the mere fact that a co-defendant properly fell within the court's jurisdiction was considered to suffice. Regulation 44/2001 takes due account of the criticism leveled at co-defendant-based jurisdiction. Under Article 6 of the Regulation, a person domiciled in a Member State is now amenable to suit in another contracting state by virtue of a co-defendant's domicile in the latter jurisdiction only if the claims are "so closely connected that it is expedient to hear and determine them together to avoid the risk of irreconcilable judgments resulting from separate proceedings."

5.　INSURANCE AND CONSUMER CONTRACTS

Articles 7 through 25 of the Convention lay down mandatory jurisdictional rules for contracts of insurance and consumer contracts, except where the parties have otherwise agreed and could, by virtue of the Convention, validly do so.

(a)　Insurance Contracts

Article 8 states the basic Convention rule on actions against insurance companies. It permits an insurer domiciled in a Contracting State to be sued either (1) in the courts of the State where it is domiciled, (2) in the courts of the Contracting State in which the policyholder is domiciled, or (3), if it is a co-insurer, in the courts of a Contracting State in which proceedings are brought against the lead insurer. Moreover, an insurer which is not domiciled in a Contracting State but which has a branch, agency or other establishment in one of the Contracting States is deemed, for disputes arising out of the operations of the branch, agency or establishment, to be domiciled in that State.[9] Lastly, Article 10 permits the insurer to be joined, if the law of the court permits it, to proceedings that the injured party has already instituted against the insured.[10]

Jurisdiction over suits brought by the insurer against the policyholder, the insured or a beneficiary is a much simpler matter. Under Article 11, suit may be brought only in the courts of the Contracting State where the defendant is domiciled (subject, however, to the insurer's right to bring a counterclaim in the court in which a claim has been brought against it).

That leaves only the possibility of party agreements on jurisdiction. According to Article 12 of the Convention, such agreements may validly depart from the ordinary jurisdictional rules in insurance actions as just described, but only (1) where the agreement is subsequent to the dispute, (2) where the agreement allows the policyholder, insured or beneficiary to bring suit in another State, or (3) in other stated circumstances.[11] Article 12, finally, permits party agreements relating to certain stated "risks,"[12] a category that

9.　Article 9 of the Convention, dealing specifically with insurance of immovable property, permits an insurer also to be sued in the courts where the harmful event occurred.

10.　Article 10 further states that the provisions of Articles, 7, 8 and 9 shall apply to direct actions by the injured party against the insurer where such direct actions are permitted, and if the law governing such direct actions provides that the policyholder or the insured may be joined as a party to that action, the same court shall have jurisdiction over them.

11.　The other stated circumstances are (3) where the policyholder and the insurer are domiciled in the same Contracting State and the agreement confers jurisdiction on the courts of that State, even though the harmful event occurred elsewhere, and (4) where the agreement is concluded with a policyholder not domiciled in a Contracting State (unless the insurance is compulsory or relates to immovable property in a Contracting State).

12.　These "risks" (largely relating to loss of or damage to ships, aircraft, goods in transit by ship or aircraft, and certain liabilities arising from the operations of ships or aircraft) are set out in Article 12a.

Regulation 44/2001 enlarges somewhat.[13]

Regulation 44/2001 brings a significant change to the jurisdictional rules in insurance matters. Article 9(1) of the Regulation alters Article 12 by providing that not only the policyholder (as before), but also the insured and the beneficiary may sue the insurer in the courts of the plaintiff's domicile. Under the same article, however, the insurer may still (subject to the right to bring a counterclaim in the court where the original claim is pending) only bring suit against the policyholder, insured or beneficiary in the latter's place of domicile.

(b) Consumer Contracts

The Brussels Convention provisions relating to consumer contracts (Articles 13–15) were introduced in the Convention upon accession to the Community of the UK, Ireland and Denmark, replacing the original provisions dealing with installment sales and loans. The Convention, viewing the non-merchant consumer as generally the weaker party in a consumer transaction, essentially widens the consumer's choice of fora for suit against the other party.

Article 14 provides that a consumer may be sued by the other party only in the courts of the Contracting State in which the consumer is domiciled.[14] However, the consumer may bring proceedings against the other party in the courts of the Contracting State in which either party is domiciled. In this regard, Article 13 contains a special rule of domicile for the situation where a consumer contracts with a party which is not domiciled in a Contracting State but which has a branch, agency or other establishment in a Contracting States; insofar as disputes with the consumer arise out of the operations of that branch, agency or establishment, the party is deemed to be a domiciliary of that State.

A "consumer" is defined in Article 13 as a person who enters into a contract "for a purpose which can be regarded as being outside his trade or profession." Article 13 and 14 provide that their jurisdictional rules shall apply to the question of jurisdiction over both parties, but only as to certain categories of consumer contracts. Those categories of contracts include not only (1) contracts for the sale of goods on installment credit terms and (2) contracts for a loan repayable by installments, or for any other form of credit, made to finance the sale of goods, but (3) any other contract for the supply of goods or a contract for the supply of services, provided (a) conclusion of the contract in the State of the consumer's domicile was preceded by a specific solicitation or by advertising, and (b) the consumer took in that same State the steps necessary to conclude the contract.[15] Regulation 44/2001 (art. 15(1)(c)) replaces the third-mentioned category with a more broadly formulat-

---

13. Article 14 of Regulation 44/2001 allows forum selection agreements as to all so-called "large risks," as defined in Council Directive 73/239/EEC, as amended by Council Directives 88/357/EEC and 90/618/EEC.

14. Article 14, however, leaves unaffected the right to bring a counter-claim in the court in which an original claim is pending.

15. Contracts of transport are specifically excluded. Brussels Convention, art. 13. The Regulation changes Article 13(3) of the Convention to distinguish between contracts of transport, on the one hand, and contracts that involve a combination of travel and accommodation, on the other. Article 15(3) of the Regulation confines the section's application to a contract of transport "which, for an inclusive price, provides for a combination of travel and accommodation."

ed one: any contract concluded with a person who "pursues commercial or professional activities in the Member State of the consumer's domicile or, by any means, directs such activities to that Member State," so long as the contract falls within the scope of those activities.

Article 15 (like Article 12 respecting insurance contracts) identifies the circumstances in which parties to consumer contracts will be permitted to enter into jurisdiction agreements that deviate from the basic rules. These include agreements (1) which are entered into after a dispute has arisen, (2) which allow the consumer to bring suit other than in the forum designated by the Convention, or (3) which vest jurisdiction in the Contracting State in which both parties to the contract were domiciled or habitually resident at the time of contract.

The notion of consumer has predictably given rise to Court of Justice case law. In Shearson Lehman Hutton Inc. v. TVB Treuhandgesellschaft für Vermögensverwaltung und Beteiligungen mbH, Case C–89/91, [1993] ECR I–139, the Court held that the assignee of the claim of an individual investor against Shearson was not a consumer since it, as assignee, was engaged in trade and professional activities (even though the original investor/assignor was not). According to the Court, only "private final" consumers, not engaged in trade or professional activities, may avail themselves of the advantages of the Convention's special rules for consumer contracts.

Is the result in *TVB Treuhandgesellschaft* consistent with the notion of assignment? The Court buttressed its position with the customary argument that jurisdictional bases designating the plaintiff's domicile as the competent forum should be strictly construed, and in any event applied only insofar as they actually the serve to protect the weaker party. "The protective role fulfilled by those provisions implies that the application of the rules of special jurisdiction laid down to that end by the Convention should not be extended to persons for whom that protection is not justified" (para. 19). Is this a sound approach?[16]

6. INDIVIDUAL CONTRACTS OF EMPLOYMENT

The Brussels and Lugano Conventions did not contain special provisions for employment contracts (although, as noted, Court of Justice case law treated such contracts differently from others in certain respects). However, Regulation 44/2001 (arts. 18–21) introduces a regime that liberalizes jurisdiction in favor of employees in contracts of this sort.

First, the Regulation redefines the employer's domicile in the case of an individual contract of employment, while at the same time making it no longer the only place where the employer may be sued. Thus, Article 18 provides that where an employee enters into an individual contract of employment with an employer which is not domiciled in a Member State, but which has a branch, agency or other establishment in any Member State, the employer shall be deemed to be domiciled in the State of that branch, agency

16. See also Benincasa v. Dentalkit SA, Case C–269/95, [1997] ECR I–3767, where the Court held that the consumer contract rules apply only to contracts concluded outside and independently of any trade or professional ac- tivity or purpose, *whether present or future.* Thus, a party that concludes a contract with a view to future pursuit of a trade or profession may not be regarded as a consumer.

or establishment for purposes of jurisdiction over disputes arising out of the operations of that branch, agency or establishment. Article 19 then enlarges the available fora for actions against an employer domiciled in a Member State. Suit may be brought not only in the place of the employer's domicile, but also in another Member State, namely (1) the place where the employee habitually carries out his work (or in the last place where he did so), or (2) if the employee does not or did not habitually carry out his work in any one country, then in the place where the business which engaged the employee is or was situated.[17]

Finally, Article 21 makes the Regulation's jurisdictional protections of the employee in principle waivable by an otherwise valid forum selection clause, provided it is entered into after the dispute has arisen. Pre-dispute jurisdiction agreements over are also valid to the extent that they allow the employee to bring proceedings in courts other than those provided for by the Regulation.

7. RULES ON EXCLUSIVE JURISDICTION

Notwithstanding the Convention's embrace of defendant's domicile as place of general jurisdiction (and its recognition of certain cases of special jurisdiction), Article 16 exceptionally subjects certain categories of disputes for exclusive jurisdiction in a designated forum. Such jurisdiction is even exclusive of the courts of the defendant's domicile and presumably also of the courts designated by a forum selection clause (see section 8 *infra*). Article 16 is reinforced by Article 19, which provides that "where a court of a Contracting State is seised of a claim which is principally concerned with a matter over which the courts of another Contracting State have exclusive jurisdiction by virtue of Article 16, it shall declare of its own motion that it has no jurisdiction."

Within important stated limits, Article 16 provides for exclusive jurisdiction (regardless of domicile) as follows:

1) suits regarding rights *in rem* in immovable property or tenancies of immovable property are to be brought exclusively in the place where immovable property is situated,[18]

2) suits concerning the validity of the constitution, the nullity or dissolution of companies or other legal persons or associations of natural or legal persons, or the decisions of their organs are to be brought exclusively in the place where the company, legal person or association has its seat,

3) proceedings concerning the validity of entries in public registers are to be brought exclusively in the place where such registers are kept,

17. Article 20 underscores that the Regulation favors only the employee, and not the employer. The employer (subject to the possibility of bringing a counter-claim) may sue the employee only in the place of the latter's domicile.

18. There is an exception for proceedings dealing with tenancies of immovable property

concluded for temporary private use for a maximum period of six consecutive months, in which case the courts of the Contracting State in which the defendant is domiciled also has jurisdiction, provided both landlord and tenant are natural persons and domiciled in the same Contracting State.

4) proceedings relating to the validity of patents, trade marks, designs, or other similar rights are to be brought exclusively in the place in which the deposit or registration of such patents or other rights has been applied for, has taken place, or is deemed to have taken place under the terms of an international convention, and

5) proceedings concerning the enforcement of a judgment are to be brought exclusively in the place in which the judgment has been or is to be enforced.

Regulation 44/2001 makes only minor changes to the Convention's provisions on exclusive jurisdiction. Article 22(2) instructs a court sitting in proceedings on the validity of the constitution, the nullity or the dissolution of companies or associations to apply its own conflict of law rules to determine in which Member State the company's seat is located. As for proceedings concerning the registration or validity of patents, trade marks, designs, or similar rights required to be deposited or registered, Article 22(4) specifies that, in the case of European patents, the courts of each Member State shall have exclusive jurisdiction in actions concerning the registration or validity of a European patent granted for that State.

In Dansommer A/S v. Götz, Case C–8/98, [2000] ECR I–393, a German court asked whether the rule conferring exclusive jurisdiction in proceedings concerning tenancies of immovable property applies to an action for damages to premises which a private individual had rented for a few weeks' holidays, where the action was brought not by the owner of the property, but by a professional tour operator from whom the person in question had rented the premises. The Court began by observing that the Convention provisions establishing exclusive jurisdiction have to be construed narrowly, "since the article deprives the parties of the choice of forum which would otherwise be theirs and, in certain cases, results in their being brought before a court which is not that of the domicile of any of them" (para. 21). Nevertheless, the Court considered the damage action to be "directly linked to a leasing contract concerning immovable property and consequently to a tenancy of immovable property within the meaning of Article 16(1)(a) of the Convention," this being the only interpretation which would ensure that disputes arising out of tenancies of immovable property are heard in the place best situated to conduct the necessary investigation and to identify the relevant local standards and practices. The Court was uninfluenced by the fact that the suit against the tenant had been brought not by the owner of the immovable property, but rather by Dansommer, the tour operator. Due to subrogation, Dansommer was acting not in its capacity as tour operator but as if it were the owner of the property in question.[19]

---

19. The Court distinguished the case of Hacker v. Euro–Relais GmbH, Case C–280/90, [1992] ECR I–1111, in which it had previously ruled that the relationship established by a contract between a professional travel organizer and a customer did not constitute a tenancy of immovable property, within the meaning of Article 16(1). According to the Court, that contract, which admittedly provided for the use of short-term holiday accommodation, also included a range of other services, including travel information and advice, reservation of seats in connection with travel, reception at the destination, and the purchase of travel cancellation insurance. By contrast, the contract at issue in *Dansommer* concerned exclusively the lease of immovable property.

Is the Court's attitude toward subrogation consistent with its apparent attitude toward assignments, as evidenced by the *TVB Treuhandgesellschaft* case, *supra* page 1401?

8. FORUM SELECTION CLAUSES

Subject to a limited exception for individual contracts of employment,[20] Article 17 of the Brussels Convention broadly accommodated party autonomy in forum selection. A dispute subject to the Convention could by party agreement be made subject to the exclusive jurisdiction of a court or the courts of any Contracting State, provided at least one of the parties to the agreement was domiciled in a Contracting State.[21] Such an agreement could apply both to disputes that have arisen and those that may later arise in connection with a particular legal relationship. As far as form is concerned, the agreement could either take written form[22] or simply accord with past practices between the parties or with usage in international trade or commerce.[23]

Forum selection clauses have generated considerable litigation under the Convention. In Powell Duffryn plc v. Petereit, Case C–214/89, [1992] ECR I–1745, a UK company (Powell Duffryn) had subscribed for shares in IBH, a German holding company, upon an increase in the latter's capital. At a general shareholders meeting, the shareholders agreed by a show of hands to include in the company's the following clause: "By subscribing for or acquiring shares or interim certificates the shareholder submits, with regard to all disputes between himself and the company or its organs, to the jurisdiction of the courts ordinarily competent to entertain suits concerning the company." Thereafter, on the occasion of successive increases in the capital of IBH, Powell Duffryn subscribed for further shares and received corresponding dividends. Eventually, IBH went into liquidation. The liquidator (Petereit) sued Powell Duffryn, claiming that the latter had not made the cash payments due in respect of the increases in capital and seeking to recover dividends wrongly paid to Powell Duffryn.

Powell Duffryn unsuccessfully contested jurisdiction and appealed, maintaining that a clause conferring jurisdiction which is contained in the statutes of a company cannot constitute an agreement because the statutes are

20. Under the Convention (art. 17), forum selection agreements concerning individual contracts of employment had legal force only if entered into after a dispute had arisen or if the employee invokes it in order to bring suit other than in the place of the defendant's domicile or in the place of special jurisdiction for contract cases designated by article 5(1). This specific provision is not carried over into Regulation 44/2001, inasmuch as the Regulation deals with individual contracts of employment in a whole separate article (15).

Article 17 contains special rules on the application and validity of forum selections contained in trust agreements.

21. Article 17 also gives limited recognition to forum selection agreements entered into by parties neither of whom is domiciled in a Contracting State. In that case, the courts of the other Contracting State are without jurisdiction over the dispute, unless and until the chosen court has actually declined jurisdiction.

22. Regulation 44/2001 contains a new provision (art. 23(2)), induced by the emergence of new forms electronic commerce, to the effect that, "[a]ny communication by electronic means which provides a durable record of the agreement shall be equivalent to a 'writing.' "

23. Article 17 provides that, where it can be ascertained that a jurisdictional agreement was concluded for the benefit of only one of the parties (a "one-sided agreement"), that party (and that party alone) retains the right to bring proceedings in any other court which would otherwise enjoy jurisdiction under the Convention. This provision is not carried over into the new Regulation 44/2001.

"normative" by nature and non-negotiable. Petereit and the Commission argued that German law (in particular the provisions of the German company law statute (Aktiengesetz) deemed the by-laws to be contractual by nature, thus enabling the clause to constitute an agreement within the meaning of Article 17 of the Convention.

Not surprisingly, the Court on preliminary reference insisted that, notwithstanding different national attitudes toward the relationship between companies and shareholders, the notion of "agreement conferring jurisdiction" in Article 17 of the Brussels Convention had to be given an independent interpretation. The Court adopted the following reasoning and reached the stated result:

16 [T]he links between the shareholders of a company are comparable to those between the parties to a contract. The setting up of a company is the expression of the existence of a community of interests between the shareholders in the pursuit of a common objective . . . . . It follows that, for the purposes of the application of the Brussels Convention, the company's statutes must be regarded as a contract covering both the relations between the shareholders and also the relations between them and the company they set up.

17 [A] clause conferring jurisdiction in the statutes of a company limited by shares is [therefore to be regarded as] an agreement, within the meaning of Article 17 of the Brussels Convention, which is binding on all the shareholders.

The Court considered it "immaterial" that the shareholder resisting the jurisdiction agreement voted in opposition to the agreement or became a shareholder after the clause's adoption. "Any other interpretation of Article 17 . . . would lead to a multiplication of the heads of jurisdiction for disputes arising from the same legal and factual relationship between the company and its shareholders and would run counter to the principle of legal certainty."[24]

The Court of Justice continues to evidence a fairly liberal understanding of what constitutes a party agreement on jurisdiction within the meaning of the Convention. In Coreck Maritime GmbH v. Handelsveem BV, Case C–387/98, [2000] ECR I–9337, the Court was faced with a jurisdiction clause contained in a bill of lading. The Court decided that the meaning of such a clause need not be ascertainable by its wording alone, provided its meaning is understood by the parties. "It is sufficient that the clause state the objective

---

24. The national court also sought to know what was meant by Article 17's requirement that the forum agreement relate to disputes "in connection with a particular legal relationship." The Court of Justice replied:

31 [The purpose of the requirement] is to avoid a party being taken by surprise by the assignment of jurisdiction to a given forum as regards all disputes which may arise out of its relationship with the other party to the contract and stem from a relationship other than that in connection with which the agreement conferring jurisdiction was made.

32 In that regard, a clause conferring jurisdiction contained in a company's statutes

satisfies that requirement if it relates to disputes which have arisen or which may arise in connection with the relationship between the company and its shareholders as such.

However, the Court did not itself decide whether the forum selection clause in the dispute at hand did in fact relate to disputes "which have arisen or which may arise in connection with the relationship between the company and its shareholders as such." It also considered the question whether the clause, as drafted, covered the dispute at to be a question of contract interpretation and therefore properly for the national court to decide.

factors on the basis of which the parties have agreed to choose a court or the courts to which they wish to submit disputes which have arisen or which may arise between them. Those factors ... must be sufficiently precise to enable the court seized to ascertain whether it has jurisdiction ...'' Moreover, such a clause, once agreed to by a carrier and a shipper, and appearing in a bill of lading, is enforceable against a third party bearer of the bill of lading who is deemed under the applicable national law to have succeeded to the rights and obligations of the shipper.

9. PROCEDURAL MATTERS

Though concerned primarily with jurisdiction and judgments, and not with civil procedure as such, the Brussels Convention takes up selected procedural matters that bear especially closely on jurisdiction, recognition and enforcement. Among these are *lis pendens* and provisional relief.

(a) Lis pendens

The Convention provisions on *lis pendens* (Articles 21 though 23) come into play when duplicative and/or related causes of action between the same parties are filed in the courts of different Contracting states. According to Article 21, where a second suit is brought on the "same" cause of action, any court other then the court first seized must, of its own motion, stay proceedings until such time as the jurisdiction of the court first seized is established. Once the jurisdiction of the court first seized is established, all other courts must decline jurisdiction in favor of that court. (Article 23 addresses the possibility that the courts of more than one State might assert exclusive jurisdiction over a dispute, pursuant to Article 16. Even there, "any court other than the court first seised shall decline jurisdiction in favour of that court."[25])

The rule is somewhat different as concerns merely "related" causes of action filed in the courts of different Contracting States.[26] Under Article 22, any court other than the court first seized may stay its proceedings. It may also, on application of one of the parties, decline jurisdiction if the law of that court permits related actions to be consolidated and the court first seised has jurisdiction over both actions.

Article 28 of Regulation 44/2001 leaves the Convention's *lis pendens* policies essentially unchanged. However, the Regulation, in Article 30, now defines when a court is "seised" of an action.[27]

25. An exception is made for provisional measures. Article 24 provides allows a court of a Contracting State to order protective measures pursuant to its own law in a case over which the courts of another Contracting State have jurisdiction, and even exclusive jurisdiction, as to the merits.

26. For purposes of Article 22, actions are deemed to be "related" where they are so closely connected that it is expedient to hear and determine them together to avoid the risk of irreconcilable judgments resulting from separate proceedings.

27. A court is "seised":

1. at the time when the document instituting the proceedings or an equivalent document is lodged with the court, provided that the plaintiff has not subsequently failed to take the steps he was required to take to have service effected on the defendant, or

2. if the document has to be served before being lodged with the court, at the time when it is received by the authority responsible for service, provided that the plaintiff has not subsequently failed to take the steps he was required to take to have the document lodged with the court.

The Court of Justice stated in Tatry v. Maciej Rataj, Case C–406/92, [1994] ECR I–5439, that the *lis pendens* principle is meant "in the interests of the proper administration of justice within the Community, to prevent parallel proceedings before the courts of different Contracting States and to avoid conflicts between decisions which might result therefrom." Rules for the avoidance of inconsistent judgments are all the more important in the Convention context since Article 27(3) of the Convention states as a ground for non-recognition and non-enforcement of a judgment the latter's inconsistency with a judgment in a dispute between the same parties in the State where recognition or enforcement is sought.

Since application of *lis pendens* presupposes an identity between the parties and the sameness (or relatedness) of the causes of action, the Court of Justice finds itself drawn into questions of this sort. This is because, as the Court insisted in the case of Tatry v. Maciej Rataj, referred to above, the terms "same cause of action" and "between the same parties" have to be given a meaning independent of the specific features of the law in force in each Contracting State.

Thus, in the *Tatry* case, the *lis pendens* doctrine was applied only in part, due to the fact that the parties were only partially overlapping. But the question also arose as to what constitutes the same cause of action. The Court ruled that a suit by the plaintiff seeking to have the defendant held liable for causing loss and ordered to pay damages presents the same cause of action and the same object as an earlier proceeding brought by that defendant seeking a declaration that he is not liable for that loss—and this, even though one action was *in personam* and the other *in rem*.

The Court has held that an insurer and its insured must be considered to be one and the same party for the purposes of Article 21, where there is such a degree of identity between their interests that a judgment delivered against one would have the force of *res judicata* as against the other. On the other hand, Article 21 can not be applied so as to preclude the insurer and insured, where their interests diverge, from asserting their respective interests before the courts as against the other parties concerned. Thus, in Drouot assurances SA v. Consolidated metallurgical industries, Case C–351/96, [1998] ECR I–3075, the Court held that Article 21 did not apply in the case of two actions brought in the wake of the foundering of a vessel. One action was brought by the insurer of the vessel against the owner and insurer of the cargo being carried at the time of the disaster; the other action was brought by the owner and the insurer of the cargo against the owner and the charterer of the vessel. *Lis pendens* did not apply, unless it could be established that the interests of the vessel's insurer were identical to and inseparable from those of the vessel's insured, the vessel's owner, and the vessel's charterer.

(b) Provisional relief

The Brussels Convention invites certain difficulties by attempting to establish clear and limited (and in some cases exclusive) grounds of jurisdiction, while at the same time allowing the grant of transnational provisional relief (i.e. provisional relief ordered by a court other than the court hearing the main action). Article 24 addresses the question by expressly permitting application to the courts of a Contracting State for provisional or protective measures even if, under the Convention, the courts of another Contracting State have jurisdiction over the merits.

In its judgment in van Uden Maritime BV v. Kommanditgesellschaften in Firma Deco–Line, Case C–391/95, [1998] ECR I–7091, the Court ruled that provisional or protective measures may be ordered on the basis of Article 24 only if there exists "a real connecting link between the subject-matter of the measures sought and the territorial jurisdiction of the Contracting State of the court before which those measures are sought."

Consider the case of Mietz v. Intership Yachting Sneek BV, Case C–99/96, [1999] ECR I–2277. Mietz entered into a contract with Intership for the purchase of a customized recreational vessel for the sum of DM 250,000, payable in five instalments. When Mietz failed to meet his payment obligation in full, Intership sued in the Netherlands, winning a judgment. A German court thereafter declared the Dutch judgment enforceable and issued an order for its enforcement. Mietz appealed to the German appellate court and to the German Supreme Court, arguing that the parties had in fact agreed on all details of the sale at a boat show in Düsseldorf, Germany, and that the signing in the Netherlands was a pure formality, so that Germany (Mietz's domicile) had exclusive jurisdiction.

The question then arose whether, assuming the German courts did indeed have exclusive jurisdiction, the Dutch judgment could be regarded as provisional relief and thus justified as an exercise of authority under Article 24. The Court felt obliged to place limits on the issuance of provisional relief by courts that lack jurisdiction to rule on the merits.

42　　[I]n the case of a judgment delivered solely by virtue of the jurisdiction provided for under Article 24 ... and ordering interim payment of a contractual consideration, the Court ruled in [citing *Van Uden v. Deco–Line, supra*] that such a judgment does not constitute a provisional measure within the meaning of Article 24 unless, first, repayment to the defendant of the sum awarded is guaranteed if the plaintiff is unsuccessful as regards the substance of his claim and [unless], second, the measure ordered relates only to specific assets of the defendant located or to be located within the confines of the territorial jurisdiction of the court to which application is made.

The Court further observed that, while the Convention generally requires Contracting States to recognize and enforce judgments entered by other Contracting States, the obligation to recognize and enforce does not extend to "provisional or protective measures [which are] allegedly founded on ... Article 24 of the Convention, but which go beyond the limits of that jurisdiction" (para. 47). The Court turned to the characteristics of the Dutch judgment at hand, noting specifically that (1) it was issued following summary proceedings for the grant of interim measures, (2) the defendant was not domiciled in the Netherlands, and the Dutch court did not otherwise have jurisdiction under the Convention as to the merits, and (3) the judgment ordered payment of a contractual sum of money without either (a) guaranteeing repayment to the defendant if the plaintiff proves to be unsuccessful on the merits or (b) limiting the measure to specific assets of the defendant located within the Netherlands (para. 53). The Court of Justice concluded that, under these circumstances, the German court should find that the Dutch judgment is not a genuine Article 24 provisional measure and therefore not enforceable under the Convention.

In Denilauler SNC v. Couchet Frères, Case 125/79, [1980] ECR 1553, the Court ruled that provisional measures, by their very nature, must be permissible under Article 24, even if ordered without the opposing party being heard. However, those measures are not necessarily entitled to benefit from the Convention's simplified recognition and enforcement procedures because fundamental procedural fairness to the opposing party requires a right to be heard at some stage to help ensure that the measures are subject to appropriate conditions (e.g. time limits, requirement of a repayment guarantee in the event the applicant for provisional relief ultimately loses on the merits). Is this a sound compromise, and is it consistent with the Convention's logic?

D. RECOGNITION AND ENFORCEMENT OF JUDGMENTS

The drafters of the Brussels Convention hoped that, having established a uniform framework for the exercise of jurisdiction in civil and commercial matters, they had facilitated the recognition and enforcement of Convention judgments throughout the Community by removing personal jurisdiction as a litigable issue at that stage. Title III of the Convention (arts. 25 through 49) deals directly with recognition and enforcement.

The basic rule is stated in Article 26 which requires the mutual recognition of Contracting State judgments in the other Contracting States "without any special procedure being required."[28] This rule is, however, subject to specified exceptions under Article 27. Judgments falling within the Convention's scope shall not be recognized (1) if contrary to the public policy of the state of recognition, (2) if there was a default judgment and a defect in service, (3) if the judgment is irreconcilable with a judgment given in a dispute between the same parties in the State in which recognition is sought, (4) if the judgment conflicts with local laws of private international law regarding the law of persons or property rights arising out of matrimonial relationships, wills or successions; or (5) if the judgment is irreconcilable with an earlier judgment given in a non-Contracting State involving the same cause of action and between the same parties, provided that this latter judgment fulfils the conditions necessary for its recognition in the State addressed. (Regulation 44/2001 (art. 34) eliminates the fourth-mentioned defense to recognition and enforcement listed above.)

Note that, under Article 30, the fact that a judgment is on appeal, or is still subject to appeal, where rendered is not a ground for denying recognition or enforcement. Article 30, however, permits the court in which recognition of a judgment is sought to stay proceedings if an ordinary appeal against the judgment has been lodged.

Article 28 separately addresses the prospect of denying recognition or enforcement to a Convention judgment on grounds of lack of personal jurisdiction. It specifically provides that where a judgment conflicts with the

---

28. Article 25 defines "judgment" as "any judgment given by a court or tribunal of a Contracting State, whatever the judgment may be called, including a decree, order, decision or writ of execution, as well as the determination of costs or expenses by an officer of the court."

provisions of the Convention relating to insurance, consumer contracts, exclusive jurisdiction or with a Contracting State's treaty obligations with a third party state, that judgment shall not be recognized. In this regard, Article 28 goes on to specify that "the court or authority applied to shall be bound by the findings of fact on which the court of the State of origin based its jurisdiction"—a formulation which suggests that the recognizing or enforcing court is not, however, bound by the legal characterization that the rendering court gave to those findings of fact. As to other cases in which an alleged jurisdictional defect is raised, Article 28 is clear and categorical: "[T]he jurisdiction of the court of the State of origin may not be reviewed." (For good measure, Article 28 also precludes a State from applying the "public policy" defense in such a way as to review the jurisdiction of the court of the rendering court.) Thus, in the great majority of cases, the court where recognition or enforcement is sought is fully bound on the jurisdictional question—not only as to the findings of fact on which the court of the State of origin based its jurisdiction, but also as to the legal characterization to be given to those findings.

Clearly, the Brussels Convention relies heavily in the recognition and enforcement process on the Convention's own personal jurisdiction provisions. Not only does the Convention strictly limit the permissible exercise of personal jurisdiction, but in most cases it effectively makes both the findings of fact and legal characterizations on the basis of which a court determines that it has personal jurisdiction in a given case fully binding, as to the jurisdictional question, on any contracting State court called upon to recognize or enforce the resulting judgment. Needless to say, the Convention absolutely prohibits review of the foreign judgment on the merits. (According to Article 29, "[u]nder no circumstances may a foreign judgment be reviewed as to its substance.")

Is the policy of "full faith and credit" to the jurisdictional assertions of Contracting States a sound one or does it go too far? Suppose a court does not merely err in its interpretation or application of a permissible jurisdictional basis, but instead avowedly employs a forbidden one?

As for actual enforcement, Article 31 renders a judgment given in a Contracting State and enforceable in that State enforceable in another Contracting State when, on the application of any interested party, it is declared enforceable there.[29] There follow more or less technical provisions on such matters as venue and procedures for filing applications for enforcement (arts. 32–33), the issuance of enforcement decisions and notice thereof (arts. 34–35), and appeals (arts. 36–40).[30] These procedures have only been slightly modified by Regulation 44/2001. The Regulation (art. 42(2)) requires that the declaration of enforceability be served on the party against whom enforcement is sought, accompanied by the judgment, if not already served on the party. Moreover, while the Brussels Convention (art. 36) gave only the party against

---

29. Article 31 continues: "However, in the United Kingdom, such a judgment shall be enforced in England and Wales, in Scotland, or in Northern Ireland when, on application of any interested party, it has been registered for enforcement in that part of the United Kingdom."

30. Article 39 prohibits execution of decisions of enforcement during the time in which an appeal is pending, except for the execution of protective measures taken against the property of the party against whom enforcement is sought.

whom enforcement is sought the right to appeal the decision declaring a judgment enforceable, Article 43 of the Regulation entitles either party to appeal.[31]

KROMBACH v. BAMBERSKI

Case C–7/98, [2000] ECR I–1935.

[Krombach was the subject of a preliminary investigation following the death in Germany of a 14–year-old girl of French nationality. That preliminary investigation was subsequently discontinued. Subsequently, Bamberski, the father of the young girl, caused a preliminary investigation to be opened in France, the French courts basing their jurisdiction on the fact that the victim was a French national. Following the investigation, Krombach was, by judgment of the chambre d'accusation (chamber for indictments) of the Cour d'Appel de Paris, committed for trial before the Cour d'Assises. As is permitted under French procedure, Bamberski introduced a civil claim in damages in connection with the criminal proceeding, as a so-called *partie civile*.

Although Krombach was duly notified of the joined criminal and civil actions, he did not attend the hearing. Thereupon, the court set in motion the contempt procedure provided for by Article 627 et seq. of the French Criminal Procedure Code. Article 630 of the Code does not permit the person charged with contempt to be represented by counsel. In the end, the Cour d'Assises found Krombach guilty of involuntary manslaughter, sentencing him to 15 years. Ruling on the civil claim, it ordered him to pay damages to Bamberski in the amount of 350,000 francs.

Upon application by Bamberski, the German court trial court declared the French civil judgment to be enforceable in Germany. Following an unsuccessful appeal, Krombach sought relief in the German Federal Supreme Court, arguing that he had been unable effectively to defend himself against the judgment against him entered by the French court.]

19   The Convention is intended to facilitate, to the greatest possible extent, the free movement of judgments by providing for a simple and rapid enforcement procedure.

* * *

21   So far as Article 27 of the Convention is concerned, the Court has held that this provision must be interpreted strictly inasmuch as it constitutes an obstacle to the attainment of one of the fundamental objectives of the Convention.

22   It follows that, while the Contracting States in principle remain free . . . to determine, according to their own conceptions, what public policy requires, the limits of that concept are a matter for interpretation of the Convention.

---

31. In a move to further liberalize the movement of judgments across borders, Regulation 44/2001 (art. 52) provides that in proceedings for a declaration of enforceability, no charge, duty or fee calculated by reference to the value of the matter at issue may be levied by the State where enforcement is sought. Article 54 introduces a new standardized certificate of the judgment (see Annex V to the Regulation).

23   Consequently, while it is not for the Court to define the content of the public policy of a Contracting State, it is none the less required to review the limits within which the courts of a Contracting State may have recourse to that concept for the purpose of refusing recognition to a judgment emanating from a court in another Contracting State.

24   It should be noted in this regard that, since the Convention was concluded on the basis of Article 220 [now 293] of the Treaty and within the framework which it defines, its provisions are linked to the Treaty [citing Mund & Fester v Hatrex Internationaal Transport, Case C–398/92, [1994] ECR I–467, para. 12].

25   The Court has consistently held that fundamental rights form an integral part of the general principles of law whose observance the Court ensures. For that purpose, the Court draws inspiration from the constitutional traditions common to the Member States and from the guidelines supplied by international treaties for the protection of human rights on which the Member States have collaborated or of which they are signatories. In that regard, the European Convention for the Protection of Human Rights and Fundamental Freedoms (hereinafter 'the ECHR') has particular significance.

26   The Court has thus expressly recognised the general principle of Community law that everyone is entitled to fair legal process, which is inspired by those fundamental rights.

[The Court also cited TEU Article 6(2) (ex F(2)) which consolidated that case-law.]

29   [The first question asked is] whether, regard being had to the public-policy clause ... of the Convention, the court of the State in which enforcement is sought can, with respect to a defendant domiciled in that State, take into account the fact that the court of the State of origin based its jurisdiction on the nationality of the victim of an offence.

* * *

31   Under the system of the Convention, with the exception of certain cases exhaustively listed in the first paragraph of Article 28, none of which corresponds to the facts of the case in the main proceedings, the court before which enforcement is sought cannot review the jurisdiction of the court of the State of origin. This fundamental principle, which is set out in the first phrase of the third paragraph of Article 28 of the Convention, is reinforced by the specific statement, in the second phrase of the same paragraph, that "the test of public policy referred to in point 1 of Article 27 may not be applied to the rules relating to jurisdiction."

32   It follows that the public policy of the State in which enforcement is sought cannot be raised as a bar to recognition or enforcement of a judgment given in another Contracting State solely on the ground that the court of origin failed to comply with the rules of the Convention which relate to jurisdiction.

* * *

35   By [its second] question, the national court is essentially asking whether, in relation to the public-policy clause in Article 27, point 1, of the

Convention, the court of the State in which enforcement is sought can, with respect to a defendant domiciled in its territory and charged with an intentional offence, take into account the fact that the court of the State of origin refused to allow that defendant to have his defence presented unless he appeared in person.

36   By disallowing any review of a foreign judgment as to its substance, Article 29 and the third paragraph of Article 34 of the Convention prohibit the court of the State in which enforcement is sought from refusing to recognise or enforce that judgment solely on the ground that there is a discrepancy between the legal rule applied by the court of the State of origin and that which would have been applied by the court of the State in which enforcement is sought had it been seised of the dispute. Similarly, the court of the State in which enforcement is sought cannot review the accuracy of the findings of law or fact made by the court of the State of origin.

37   Recourse to the public-policy clause in Article 27, point 1, of the Convention can be envisaged only where recognition or enforcement of the judgment delivered in another Contracting State would be at variance to an unacceptable degree with the legal order of the State in which enforcement is sought inasmuch as it infringes a fundamental principle. In order for the prohibition of any review of the foreign judgment as to its substance to be observed, the infringement would have to constitute a manifest breach of a rule of law regarded as essential in the legal order of the State in which enforcement is sought or of a right recognised as being fundamental within that legal order.

38   With regard to the right to be defended ... this occupies a prominent position in the organisation and conduct of a fair trial and is one of the fundamental rights deriving from the constitutional traditions common to the Member States.

39   More specifically still, the European Court of Human Rights has on several occasions ruled in cases relating to criminal proceedings that, although not absolute, the right of every person charged with an offence to be effectively defended by a lawyer, if need be one appointed by the court, is one of the fundamental elements in a fair trial and an accused person does not forfeit entitlement to such a right simply because he is not present at the hearing [citing several ECHR judgments].

40   It follows from that case-law that a national court of a Member State is entitled to hold that a refusal to hear the defence of an accused person who is not present at the hearing constitutes a manifest breach of a fundamental right.

* * *

43   ... [E]ven though the Convention is intended to secure the simplification of formalities governing the reciprocal recognition and enforcement of judgments of courts or tribunals, it is not permissible to achieve that aim by undermining the right to a fair hearing.

44   It follows ... that recourse to the public-policy clause must be regarded as being possible in exceptional cases where the guarantees laid down in the legislation of the State of origin and in the Convention itself have been

insufficient to protect the defendant from a manifest breach of his right to defend himself before the court of origin, as recognised by the ECHR. Consequently, Article II of the Protocol cannot be construed as precluding the court of the State in which enforcement is sought from being entitled to take account, in relation to public policy, as referred to in Article 27, point 1, of the Convention, of the fact that, in an action for damages based on an offence, the court of the State of origin refused to hear the defence of the accused person, who was being prosecuted for an intentional offence, solely on the ground that that person was not present at the hearing.

Notes and Questions

1. Should there be any question that the Convention applies to decisions rendered in a civil matter by a criminal court? Re-read Article 1, paragraph 1 of the Convention, and see Sonntag v Waidmann, Case C–172/91, [1993] ECR I–1963, cited at page 1387 *supra*.

2. Article 61 of Regulation 44/2001 contains a special provision for persons domiciled in one Member State who are prosecuted in the criminal courts of another Member State of which they are not nationals for an offense not intentionally committed. Such a person may be defended by persons qualified to do so, even if they do not appear in person. The court seised of the matter may nevertheless order the personal appearance of the defendant, but if the latter fails to appear, the resulting judgment in a joined civil action need not be recognized or enforced in the other Members States. How is the inclusion of such a provision in the Regulation to be explained?

3. Boch, an Italian distributor of agricultural machinery produced by the German company, Solo Kleinmotoren, sued Solo in a Milan civil court, winning a judgment of 48 million lire for wrongful termination. A German court issued an order of enforcement of the judgment and Solo appealed to a Stuttgart appeals court, at which point the parties reached a monetary settlement, coupled with a written understanding that "[a]ll the parties' claims against one another arising from their business relationship are hereby resolved." Boch thereafter instituted suit against Solo in a Bologna civil court for infringement of the trade name "Solo" and for unfair competition, and Boch was eventually held liable to pay LIT 180,000,000. The Bologna court ruled that the settlement reached in the German court could not be relied on to preclude the second action, both because the settlement had not been declared enforceable in Italy and because the subject matter of the Bologna action did not fall within the scope of the settlement agreement.

Boch won an order of enforcement of the Bologna judgment in the Stuttgart courts and Solo appealed to the German Supreme Court, which made a preliminary reference to the Court of Justice on whether the prior settlement precluded enforcement under Article 27(3) of the Convention.

The Court denied preclusion, citing Article 25's definition of "judgment" as "any judgment given by a court or tribunal of a Contracting State, whatever the judgment may be called, including a decree, order, decision or writ of execution . . ." According to the Court, this wording limits judgments, for these purposes, to decisions that "emanate from a judicial body of a Contracting State deciding on its own authority on the issues between the parties" (para. 17). "That condition is not fulfilled in the case of a settlement, even if [the settlement] was reached in a court of a Contracting State and brings legal proceedings to an end. Settlements in court are essentially contractual in that their terms depend first and foremost on the parties' intention...." (para. 18). Solo Kleinmotoren GmbH v. Boch, Case C–414/92, [1994] ECR I–2237.

Do you agree with the Court's characterization? Is it sound in terms of fulfilling the Convention's objectives? (On the latter point, the Court remarked: "Article 27 constitutes an obstacle to the achievement of one of the fundamental objectives of the Convention, which is to facilitate, to the greatest extent possible, the free movement of judgments by providing for a simple and rapid enforcement procedure. Article 27 must therefore be interpreted strictly...." (para. 20)). Note that Article 51 of the Brussels Convention (in language largely carried over in Regulation 44/2001, art. 58) provided that "[a] settlement which has been approved by a court in the course of proceedings and is enforceable in the State in which it was concluded shall be enforceable in the State in which enforcement is sought...." Shouldn't that language have dictated a different outcome in the *Solo Kleinmotoren* case?

4. The case of Minalmet GmbH v. Brandeis Ltd., Case C–123/91, [1992] ECR I–5661, raised the question whether Article 27(2), which ordinarily precludes recognition of a default judgment entered upon allegedly defective service, applies even if the defaulting defendant had become aware of the judgment and failed to exhaust the remedies then still available to him in the courts of the state of origin. The Court refused to engraft a limitation on the exception based on waiver of available national remedies. Is this consistent with the Court's policy of narrow construction of exceptions to recognition and enforcement?

E. THE MATRIMONIAL JURISDICTION AND JUDGMENTS CONVENTION

It will be recalled that the Brussels Convention by its terms did not apply to matrimonial matters. The reason offered at the time was that Member State laws on these matters were simply too divergent, and that the Member States were not prepared to subject them (particularly laws on such matters as divorce) to the Brussels Convention's very limited review of foreign judgments upon the occasion of their recognition and enforcement. In 1998, however, the Member States entered into a separate convention on Jurisdiction, Recognition and the Enforcement of Judgments in Matrimonial Matters, O.J. C 221 (July 16, 1998). According to the Explanatory Report on the 1998 Matrimonial Jurisdiction and Judgments Convention:[32]

> European integration was mainly an economic affair to begin with and for that reason the legal instruments established were designed to serve an economic purpose. However, the situation has changed fundamentally in recent times so that integration is now no longer purely economic and is coming to have an increasingly profound effect on the life of the European citizen, who finds it hard to understand that he encounters problems in matters of family law while so much progress has been made in property law. The issue of family law therefore has to be faced as part of the phenomenon of European integration. We only need to look at the questions put in the European Parliament not only on dissolution of marriages but also on more general aspects of family law (marriage contracts, paternity, child abduction, adoption, etc.). This Convention is a

---

32. O.J. C 221/27–64 (July 16, 1998).

first step, and a positive and decisive one, along this new road and it may open the way to other texts on matters of family law and succession.

Although the 1998 Convention could have been based on EC Treaty Article 293 (ex 220), as the 1968 Brussels Convention had been, it was in fact based on the then TEU Article K.3 (introduced by the Maastricht Treaty), which invited the Council to draw up conventions to be recommended for adoption by the Member States on any of the matters set down in the then TEU Art. K.1, including "judicial cooperation in civil matters." The Convention was accordingly a "pillar three" instrument. To distinguish the 1998 Matrimonial Convention, which likewise was signed in Brussels, from the 1968 Brussels Convention, it came to be known simply as *Brussels II,* and the original Brussels Convention thereafter as *Brussels I.*

The Preamble to *Brussels II* identified as among the Convention's main purposes "to introduce uniform modern standards for jurisdiction on annulment, divorce and separation and to facilitate the rapid and automatic recognition among Member States of judgments on such matters given in the Member States." The Preamble also highlights "[t]he importance of laying down rules of jurisdiction concerning parental responsibility over the children of both spouses on the occasion of such proceedings and therefore simplifying the formalities governing the rapid and automatic recognition and enforcement of the relevant judgments." Like *Brussels I, Brussels II* is a "double convention" in that it contains rules of direct jurisdiction linked to rules on the recognition and enforcement of foreign judgments.

Title I of the Convention describes the scope of *Brussels II* as covering proceedings for divorce, legal separation or marriage annulment and proceedings relating to parental responsibility for the children of both spouses on the occasion of an application for divorce, separation or annulment. Title II contains rules of direct international jurisdiction, rules which the court of origin must respect prior to assuming jurisdiction to conduct matrimonial proceedings. Title II of *Brussels II,* like *Brussels I,* also deals with *lis pendens* and dependent actions, as well as with provisional and protective measures. Finally, Title III of the Convention guarantees the recognition and enforcement of judgments in matrimonial matter, subject to the usual conditions.

The Convention on Jurisdiction, Recognition and Enforcement in Matrimonial Matters (*Brussels II*) has likewise subsequently been transposed into a Regulation. Regulation 1347/2000 on Jurisdiction, Recognition and the Enforcement of Judgments in Matrimonial Matters and Matters of Parental Responsibility for Children of Both Spouses, O.J. L 160/19 (June 30, 2000), adopted May 29, 2000. The content of the Regulation is essentially unchanged as compared to *Brussels II.* As with Regulation 44/2001, Denmark has elected not to participate.

F. THE INSOLVENCY PROCEEDINGS REGULATION

While in the process of transforming *Brussels I* and *II* into Community law proper, the Council took other action under Article 65 relating to jurisdiction and judgments. Thus, the Council adopted Regulation 1346/2000 on insolvency proceedings, O.J. L 160/1 (June 30, 2000). It will be recalled that bankruptcy proceedings, proceedings relating to the winding-up of insolvent companies or other legal persons, judicial arrangements, compositions and analogous proceedings were specifically excluded from the scope of *Brussels I.* Although a separate draft Bankruptcy Convention had been proposed as early as 1980, agreement on a text was long in coming and in fact no text was ever opened for ratification. The fact remains, however, that when an undertaking with transnational obligations and creditors becomes insolvent, the proper functioning of the internal market can be significantly affected. More particularly, there was a perceived need to coordinate measures taken in regard to an insolvent debtor's assets. Finally, it was thought desirable to remove incentives for parties to a transaction to transfer assets from one Member State to another in anticipation of bankruptcy proceedings, or to engage in forum shopping so as to obtain relief from liability as a debtor or more favorable rank as a creditor.

Regulation 1346/2000 applies to insolvency proceedings, whether the debtor is a natural person or a legal person, or a trader or private party. However, insolvency proceedings of insurance undertakings, credit institutions, investment undertakings holding funds or securities for third parties and collective investment undertakings are excluded from its scope, presumably because they are deemed adequately covered by preexisting special arrangements.

The Regulation (art. 3) contemplates that main insolvency proceedings will be opened in the Member State where the debtor has its "center of main interests." These proceedings may accordingly encompass all of the debtor's assets. However, the Regulation also permits secondary proceedings to be opened and to run in parallel with the main proceeding in the Member State where the debtor has an establishment, on condition that the effects of such secondary proceedings are limited to the assets located in that State. To help ensure coherence and consistency, the Regulation imposes on secondary proceedings mandatory rules of coordination with the main proceedings.[33]

Except where otherwise provided, the substantive law of the Member State of the opening of the proceedings (*lex concursus*)—be they main or secondary—is applicable (arts. 4, 28). It governs all the conditions for the opening, conduct and closure of insolvency proceedings, as well as the effects of such proceedings, both procedural and substantive, on the persons and legal relations concerned.[34]

Regulation 1346/2000 seeks to enable every creditor, including tax authorities and social insurance institutions (art. 39), having habitual residence, domicile or a registered office within the Community to lodge claims in each of the insolvency proceedings pending in the Community which relate to the debtor's assets. The point is to ensure coordination in the distribution of

---

33. Under Article 3, prior to the opening of the main insolvency proceedings in the appropriate State, any proceeding opened in another Member State where the debtor has an establishment must be limited to local creditors and creditors of the local establishment or to the situation in which main proceedings cannot be opened under the law of the Member State where the debtor has its center of main interest. Article 31 mandates cooperation between liquidators in the main and secondary proceedings.

34. Regulation 1346/2000 contains special provisions for rights *in rem* (art. 5), set-offs (art. 6), and payment systems and financial markets (art. 9). At the same time, it seeks to limit the effects of insolvency proceedings on the continuation or termination or employment (art. 10).

proceeds and thereby equal treatment of creditors. The transparency and publicity of the proceedings is an evident preoccupation of the Regulation.

The Regulation provides for immediate recognition of all judgments concerning the opening, conduct and closure of insolvency proceedings falling within its scope, as well as all judgments rendered in direct connection with such proceedings (arts. 16 and 17). Article 18 provides that the powers of the liquidator are to be governed by the law of the State of the opening of procedures; it also entitles the liquidator to take certain action on the territory and before the courts of the other Member States. As might be expected, available grounds for non-recognition of judgments are drastically curtailed (art. 25).

G. NEW LEGAL INSTRUMENTS ON COOPERATION IN CIVIL JUSTICE

Using its authority under Articles 61 and 65 of the EC Treaty, the Council has lately adopted still other regulations in the area of judicial cooperation in civil matters. In May 2000, the Council adopted Regulation 1348/2000 on the Service of Judicial and Extra Judicial Documents in Civil or Commercial Matters, O.J. L160/37 (June 30, 2000), a measure which establishes speedy, reliable and agreed upon means of transmitting between Member States documents pertaining to civil and commercial litigation in a Member State court. The measure basically obligates Member State courts to effectuate service of such documents provided the request meets the conditions and requirements laid down in the Regulation.

A year later, the Council adopted Regulation 1206/2001 on Cooperation between the Courts of the Member States in the Taking of Evidence in Civil or Commercial Matters, O.J. L 174 (June 27, 2001). Similarly, this Regulation establishes standardized means of requesting forms of cooperation in the taking of evidence on the territory of one State for use in civil or commercial litigation pending or contemplated in the courts of another. Provided the requirements of a valid request, as laid down in the Regulation, have been satisfied, the Member States are obligated to provide the assistance requested and to do so expeditiously. Courts are required to comply unless doing so "is incompatible with the law of the Member State of the requested court or by reason of major practical difficulties," and they must make available the same coercive measures applicable in analogous domestic litigation circumstances. The Regulation provides certain procedural protections, in the form both of the right of the parties to be present and participate in the taking of evidence and the availability of certain testimonial and documentary privileges.

Besides providing for the taking of evidence by the requested court, Regulation 1206/2001 also contemplates the direct taking of evidence by the requesting court in the territory of the other State. Only designated personnel of the requesting State may engage in the direct taking of evidence, and use of this means is limited to situations in which evidence-taking sought can be performed on a voluntary basis, and thus without need for coercive measures. Requests of this type may be refused only if they fall outside the scope of the

Regulation, are formally or technically deficient, or are "contrary to fundamental principles of law in [the requested] Member State."

Both of these Regulations, while clearly inspired by two multilateral Hague Conventions—the 1965 Convention on Service of Documents and the 1970 Convention on Taking of Evidence, respectively—expressly declare that, within their sphere of application, they take precedence over those instruments (and indeed over other international agreements on the same subjects to which a Member State may be a party). While Ireland and the UK once again agreed to participate in both measures, Denmark did not, and is accordingly not subject to them.

Articles 61 and 65 of the EC Treaty have furnished the basis of still more far-ranging initiatives. Council Regulation 290/2001, O.J. L 43 (Feb. 14, 2001), establishes a legislative basis for continuation of the so-called "Grotius" program of incentives and exchanges for legal practitioners in the area of civil law, entailing training, exchange, work-experience programs, meetings, studies, research and information. More recently, Council Decision 2001/470, O.J. L 174 (June 27, 2001), established a so-called "European Judicial Network in Civil and Commercial Matters" The Network has the general task of facilitating judicial cooperation between the Member States in civil and commercial matters both in areas where existing legal instruments exist (such as the Regulations discussed in this chapter) and in areas where they do not. The Decision contemplates as means to this end the maintenance of information systems and the promotion of contacts between relevant Member State authorities, including periodic direct meetings. (Denmark participates in neither of these initiatives.)

To date, the Council has not adopted any general legislative measures under Article 65 harmonizing choice of law rules in Member State courts, though such measures would surely be authorized under that treaty article. As of the present writing, the 1980 Rome Convention on the Law Applicable to Contractual Obligations remains a purely international convention and one that, due to an insufficient number of ratifications, is still not in force. Nevertheless, a 1998 Protocol confers on the Court of Justice powers to interpret the Convention's provisions. O.J. C 27 (Jan. 26, 1998).

Given the rapidity with which the developments charted in this chapter followed the Amsterdam Treaty's transfer of civil justice cooperation from pillar three to pillar one, it seems reasonable to anticipate extensive further use of this new authority to enact Community legislation in the field of judicial cooperation in civil matters.

NOTE ON THE PROPOSED INTERNATIONAL JURISDICTION AND JUDGMENTS CONVENTION

Cooperation in civil and commercial litigation—and, more specifically, in jurisdiction and judgments in civil and commercial matters—is not confined to the legislative arenas of the EU. The EU Member States have also been active in the workings of the Hague Conference on Private International Law, under the auspices of which numerous multilateral agreements on such subjects have been adopted. Two of the most salient agreements—on the service of documents and on the taking of evidence in civil and commercial matters—have already been mentioned. Both are longstanding and much in use.

At present, the Hague Conference is pursuing an ambitious international convention on the very subject of the Brussels Convention and Regulation 44/2001, namely jurisdiction and recognition of judgments in civil and commercial matters. Like these instruments, it adopts the "double convention" approach referred to earlier. As of this writing, progress has foundered, not because of differences of agreement among the participating European States (which, after all, have now enacted a directly binding regulation for themselves on the subject), but rather because of the strong divide that still separates the United States and the their negotiating partners on issues ranging from the acceptability of broad "doing business" jurisdiction, to the use of *forum non conveniens* to decline jurisdiction, to the exercise of "universal jurisdiction" over human rights violations, to various issues of e-commerce and jurisdiction in intellectual property suits.

Index

References are to Pages
